October 24–28, 2011
Glasgow, Scotland, UK

Association for Computing Machinery

Advancing Computing as a Science & Profession

CIKM 2011 GLASGOW

CIKM'11

Proceedings of the 2011 ACM International

Conference on Information and Knowledge Management

Sponsored by:

ACM SIGIR & ACM SIGWEB

Association for
Computing Machinery

Advancing Computing as a Science & Profession

The Association for Computing Machinery
2 Penn Plaza, Suite 701
New York, New York 10121-0701

ISBN: 978-1-4503-0717-8 (Digital)

ISBN: 978-1-4503-1353-7 (Print)

Additional copies may be ordered prepaid from:

ACM Order Department
PO Box 30777
New York, NY 10087-0777, USA

Phone: 1-800-342-6626 (USA and Canada)
+1-212-626-0500 (Global)
Fax: +1-212-944-1318
E-mail: acmhelp@acm.org
Hours of Operation: 8:30 am – 4:30 pm ET

ACM Order Number: 605110

Printed in the USA

CIKM 2011 Chairs' Welcome

On behalf of the organizing committee, it is our great pleasure to welcome you to the *20th ACM Conference on Information and Knowledge Management* in Glasgow!

Since its inception, the CIKM conference has provided a unique international forum for the presentation, discussion and dissemination of research findings in data management, information retrieval and knowledge management. The purpose of the conference is to identify challenging problems facing the development of future knowledge and information systems and to shape future research directions through the publication of high quality, applied and theoretical research findings. The conference has been a leading forum in which experts from academic, industry and the public sector gather to exchange ideas, research achievements and technical developments in multidisciplinary research areas.

CIKM is one of the world's most recognized conferences in the field. This year CIKM received 918 full paper submissions, 220 poster submissions, and 56 demonstration submissions. This is a great demonstration of the lively research areas that contribute to the CIKM area. In addition, CIKM 2011 will host 10 tutorials from leading researchers, 15 workshops on cutting-edge areas of research, a panel session on Social and Collaborative Search and a dedicated Industry Day featuring leading industrial practitioners. We are grateful to all authors who chose to submit their research to CIKM 2011 and are very excited by the final program.

CIKM values interdisciplinary research and we are proud to present three keynote speakers, Professor Justin Zobel, Professor Maurizio Lenzerini and Professor David Karger, all of whom will give presentations that cross discipline boundaries.

The program of CIKM 2011 represents a huge amount of effort on behalf of many people. The contributions to the technical program were selected by a large program committee headed by our three program chairs, Arjen de Vries, Bettina Berendt and Wenfei Fan. We are grateful to them for all their hard work in managing such a complex reviewing task and to their senior program committee members, program committee members and additional reviewers who freely gave their time, effort and intelligence to the difficult task of selecting which contributions would form the program. We are also very grateful to Fidel Cacheda, Matt Lease and Sara Hawkins, who monitored and managed the process of editing the proceedings to meet very tight production schedules.

We are also grateful to Gianni Amati who ran CIKM's first dedicated poster submission route; Omar Alonso who managed the demonstrations track and introduced demo boaster sessions into the program; Craig Macdonald who handled the very difficult job of organizing the workshop program; Jaap Kamps and Fabrizio Silvestri who solicited a great range of tutorials; Donald Metzler who was a great publicity chair; Leif Azzopardi for handling the student award scheme and student volunteers; Ryen White and Marius Pasca who were very active sponsorship chairs and whose hard work allowed us to award grants to several student attendees; Daniel Tunkelang and Tony Russell-Rose for organizing such an interesting Industry program; Jeremy Pickens for organizing an exciting panel session; David Carmel for organizing the Best Paper Awards committee. The local arrangements team has been superbly managed by Jon Richie, our local arrangements chair who has made a huge effort into every aspect of the conference. Finally, we value the efforts of Richard McCreadie (invitation letters) and Rodrygo Santos (website & social media).

We would like to express our appreciation to all our sponsors: EMC^2, Microsoft Research, Google, Yahoo! Research, SAP, Yandex, IBM Research, eBay Research Labs, Cambridge University Press, Springer, Taylor & Francis and CrossRef. Google generously provided travel support for East European attendees and Springer kindly sponsored the Best Paper Awards. All their generous sponsorship and support made this conference successful and possible. We would also like to thank the sponsoring SIGs, SIGIR and SIGWEB, and their respective chairs, James Allan (SIGIR), Ethan Munson and Simon Harper (SIGWEB) for their advice and support.

It is a great pleasure to be able to welcome you to CIKM 2011 in Glasgow. We hope that attendees find the technical program of CIKM 2011 to be interesting and productive and you enjoy CIKM 2011 and your stay in Glasgow.

Iadh Ounis
CIKM 2011 General Co-Chair
University of Glasgow

Ian Ruthven
CIKM 2011 General Co-Chair
University of Strathclyde

Message from the Program Committee Chairs

Welcome to the 20th ACM Conference on Information and Knowledge Management. Since 1992, CIKM has been successfully bringing together leading researchers from the database, information retrieval, and knowledge management communities. The purpose of the conference is to identify challenging problems facing the development of future knowledge and information systems, and to shape future research directions through the publication of high-quality research findings, both theoretical and applied. In CIKM 2011, we continued the tradition of promoting collaboration among the general areas of databases, information retrieval, and knowledge management. This year's call for papers attracted 918 submissions from Africa, the Americas, Asia, Australia, Europe, and the Middle East. The program committee accepted 134 submissions as full papers for oral presentation (15%), an additional 93 as short papers for oral presentation and 98 as poster presentations (a cumulative acceptance rate of 35%). We also accepted 21 demonstrations, 10 tutorials and 15 workshops. CIKM 2011 also organized the first direct call for poster submissions, resulting in 220 submissions and 66 poster acceptances.

We'd like to acknowledge everyone who made this technical program possible. First, we would like to thank the authors for providing the contents of the program: the conference would not be possible without your contributions. Our gratitude goes out to the program committee and external reviewers, who worked extremely hard in providing feedback on the submissions. The senior program committees deserve much recognition for shepherding the review process and for helping along the way. A very big "thank you" goes out to all the countless others who have contributed to making CIKM 2011 a success. Finally, we would like to thank all our corporate sponsors for their generous support.

We hope that you will find this program interesting and thought-provoking. Please enjoy the conference and the opportunity to network with friends and colleagues from around the world.

Bettina Berendt
CIKM 2011 KM Chair
Katholieke Universiteit Leuven, Belgium

Arjen de Vries
CIKM 2011 IR Chair
Centrum Wiskunde & Informatica, The Netherlands

Wenfei Fan
CIKM 2011 DB Chair
University of Edinburgh, UK

Table of Contents

Session 5: Type and Structure

Session Chair: Leif Azzopardi *(University of Glasgow)*

Session 6: Machine Learning for Information Retrieval

Session Chair: Stephen Robertson *(Microsoft Research Cambridge)*

Session 7: Information Retrieval Implementation Techniques

Session Chair: Justin Zobel *(The University of Melbourne)*

Session 8: Language Technology and Information Retrieval
Session Chair: Jussi Karlgen *(Swedish Institute of Computer Science)*

Session 9: Results in Context
Session Chair: Noriko Kando *(NII)*

Session 10: Algorithms
Session Chair: Felix Naumann *(Hasso-Plattner-Institute)*

Session 11: Image Retrieval
Session Chair: Yi Chang *(Yahoo! Labs)*

Session 12: Social Media

Session Chair: Jun Wang *(University College London)*

Session 13: Personalization and Advertising

Session Chair: Emine Yilmaz *(Microsoft Research Cambridge)*

Session 14: Evaluation and Analysis

Session Chair: Jaap Kamps *(University of Amsterdam)*

Session 15: Classification and Evaluation

Session Chair: Nicolas Garcia Pedrajas *(University of Córdoba)*

Session 16: Information Filtering

Session Chair: Yan Zhang *(Vermont Information Processing)*

Session 17: Topics and Events

Session Chair: Ram Akella *(Stanford University & University of California)*

Session 18: Temporal, Stream and Spatial Information

Session Chair: Massimo Ruffolo *(ICAR-CNR)*

Session 19: Text Mining

Session Chair: Yunyao Li *(IBM Research)*

Session 20: Privacy

Session Chair: Gene Golovchinsky *(FX Palo Alto Research Lab)*

VOLUME 2

Session 21: Unsupervised and Semi-supervised Learning

Session Chair: Shin Ando *(Gunma University)*

Session 22: Social Networks and Communities

Session Chair: Fosca Giannotti *(ISTI-CNR)*

Session 23: Sentiments and Other Perspectives

Session Chair: James Caverlee *(Texas A&M University)*

Session 24: Classification and Clustering: Large-scale Statistical Techniques

Session Chair: Alfredo Cuzzocrea *(University of Calabria)*

Session 25: Link Prediction

Session Chair: B. Barla Cambazoglu *(Yahoo! Research)*

Session 26: Link, Graph and Relation Mining

Session Chair: Roi Blanco *(Yahoo! Research)*

Session 27: Science, the Past, and the Future

Session Chair: Giorgio Orsi *(University of Oxford)*

Session 28: Information Extraction and Entities

Session Chair: Xiaofeng Yu *(The Chinese University of Hong Kong)*

Session 29: Queries, Questions and Tags Mining

Session Chair: Jian-Tao Sun *(Microsoft Research Asia)*

Session 30: Preparing, Mining and Evaluating with and for Different Views

Session Chair: Hwanjo Yu *(POSTECH)*

Session 34: Semantic Web and Information Retrieval

Session Chair: Alfredo Cuzzocrea *(University of Calabria)*

Session 35: Query Answering and Social Search

Session Chair: Yuqing Wu *(Indiana University)*

Session 36: Distributed Data Management and Data Integration

Session Chair: Philip Bohannon *(Yahoo! Research)*

Session 37: Keyword Search and Ranked Queries

Session Chair: Seung-won Hwang *(POSTECH)*

Session 38: Data Cleaning and Analysis

Session Chair: Riccardo Torlone *(Universitá Roma Tre)*

Session 39: Graph Management and Queries

Session Chair: Hongzhi Wang *(Harbin Institute of Technology)*

Session 40: Social, Search, and Other Behaviour

Session Chair: David Carmel *(IBM Research)*

Session 41: Applications in Different Areas

Session Chair: David Hawking *(Funnelback Pty Ltd and Australian National University)*

VOLUME 3

Poster Session: Information Retrieval

Poster Session: Knowledge Management

Poster Session: Databases

Demonstration Session 1

Demonstration Session 2

Demonstration Session 3

Co-located Tutorial Summaries

Co-located Workshop Summaries

Panel

CIKM 2011 Conference Organization

General Conference Chairs:	Iadh Ounis *(University of Glasgow, UK)* Ian Ruthven *(University of Strathclyde, UK)*
Chair-at-Large:	Craig Macdonald *(University of Glasgow, UK)*
DB Track Program Chair:	Wenfei Fan *(University of Edinburgh, UK)*
IR Track Program Chair:	Arjen de Vries *(Centrum Wiskunde & Informatica, The Netherlands)*
KM Track Program Chair:	Bettina Berendt *(Katholieke Universiteit Leuven, Belgium)*
Workshops Chair:	Craig Macdonald *(University of Glasgow, UK)*
Posters Chair:	Gianni Amati *(FUB, Italy)*
Tutorials Chairs:	Jaap Kamps *(University of Amsterdam, The Netherlands)* Fabrizio Silvestri *(ISTI-CNR, Italy)*
Industry Event Chairs:	Daniel Tunkelang *(LinkedIn, US)* Tony Russell-Rose *(UXLabs and City University London, UK)*
Demonstrations Chair:	Omar Alonso *(Microsoft, US)*
Panel Chair:	Jeremy Pickens *(Catalyst Repository Systems, US)*
Proceedings Chairs:	Fidel Cacheda *(University of A Coruña, Spain)* Matt Lease *(University of Texas at Austin, US)*
Local Arrangements Chair:	Jon Ritchie *(University of Glasgow, UK)*
Travel Award Chair:	Leif Azzopardi *(University of Glasgow, UK)*
Publicity Chair:	Donald Metzler *(University of Southern California ,US)*
Sponsorship Chairs:	Marius Pasca *(Google, US)* Ryen White *(Microsoft Research, US)*
Awards Chair:	David Carmel *(IBM Research Lab, Israel)*
Registration Chair:	Richard McCreadie *(University of Glasgow, UK)*,
Steering Committee Chair:	E.K. Park *(City University of New York, US)*

CIKM 2011 DB Track Program Committees

Senior Program Committee:

Marcelo Arenas (*Pontificia Universidad Católica de Chile, Chile)*
Pablo Barcelo (*Universidad de Chile, Chile)*
Philip Bohannon (*Yahoo! Research, US)*
Diego Calvanese (*Free University of Bozen-Bolzano, Italy)*
Chee-Yong Chan (*National University of Singapore, Singapore)*
Lei Chen (*Hong Kong University of Science and Technology, Hong Kong)*
Giuseppe De Giacomo (*University of Rome La Sapienza, Italy)*
Xin (Luna) Dong (*ATT Labs-Research, US)*
Alan Fekete (*University of Sydney, Australia)*
Floris Geerts (*University of Edinburgh, UK)*
Torsten Grust (*Universität Tübingen, Germany)*
Anastasios Kementsietsidis (*IBM T.J. Watson Research Center, US)*
Frank McSherry (*Microsoft Research Silicon Valley, US)*
Divesh Srivastava (*AT&T Labs, US)*
Yufei Tao (*Chinese University of Hong Kong, Hong Kong)*
Jeffrey Yu (*Chinese University of Hong Kong, Hong Kong)*

Program Committee:

Ashraf Aboulnaga (*University of Waterloo, Canada)*
Yanif Ahmad (*Johns Hopkins University, US)*
Denilson Barbosa (*University of Alberta, Canada)*
Zohra Bellahsene (*Université Montpellier, France)*
Michael Benedikt (*Oxford University, UK)*
Leopoldo Bertossi (*Carleton University, Canada)*
Mikolaj Bojanczyk (*Warsaw University, Poland)*
Angela Bonifati (*CNR, Italy)*
Michael Cafarella (*University of Michigan, US)*
Zhipeng Cai (*Mississippi State University, US)*
Kevin C. Chang (*University of Illinois, US)*
Haiming Chen (*Chinese Academy of Sciences, China)*
Wenguang Chen (*Peking University, China)*
Rada Chirkova (*North Carolina State University, US)*
Gao Cong (*NTU, Singapore)*
Richard Connor (*University of Strathclyde, UK)*
Alfredo Cuzzocrea (*University of Calabria, Italy)*
Anish Das Sarma (*Google Research, US)*
Ting Deng (*Beihang University, China)*
Jens Dittrich (*Saarland University, Germany)*
Guozhu Dong (*Wright State University, US)*
Songyun Duan (*IBM T.J. Watson Research Center, US)*
Irini Fundulaki (*Foundation for Research and Technology - Hellas, Greece)*
Avigdor Gal (*Technion - Israel Institute of Technology, Israel)*

Program Committee (continued):

Minos Garofalakis (*Technical University of Crete, Greece)*
Tingjian Ge (*University of Kentucky, US)*
Lukasz Golab (*AT&T Labs Research, US)*
Wook-Shin Han (*Kyungpook National University, Korea)*
Sven Helmer (*Birkbeck, University of London, UK)*
Kien Hua (*University of Central Florida, US)*
Ela Hunt (*ETH Zurich, Switzerland)*
Seung-won Hwang (*POSTECH, Korea)*
Zack Ives (*University of Pennsylvania, US)*
Gao Jun (*Peking University, China)*
Jaewoo Kang (*Korea University, Korea)*
Carl-Christian Kanne (*IBM Almaden Research Center, US)*
Raghav Kaushik (*Microsoft Research, US)*
Eamonn Keogh (*University of California Riverside, US)*
Benny Kimelfeld (*IBM, US)*
Masaru Kitsuregawa (*University of Tokyo, Japan)*
Solmaz Kolahi (*University of British Columbia, Canada)*
Hank Korth (*Lehigh University, Bethlehem, US)*
Maurizio Lenzerini (*Università di Roma La Sapienza, Italy)*
Feifei Li (*Florida State University, US)*
Yingshu Li (*Georgia State University, US)*
Jianzhong Li (*Harbin Institute of Technology, China)*
Xiang Lian (*HKUST, Hong Kong)*
Xuemin Lin (*University of New South Wales, Australia)*
Shuai Ma (*Beihang University, China)*
Jayant Madhavan (*Google, US)*
Ioana Manolescu (*INRIA, France)*
Wim Martens (*Technische Universität Dortmund, Germany)*
Maarten Marx (*University of Amsterdam, The Netherlands)*
Weiyi Meng (*SUNY Binghamton, US)*
Bongki Moon (*University of Arizona, US)*
Filip Murlak (*University of Warsaw, Poland)*
Muthu Muthukrishnan (*Rutgers University, US)*
Rimma Nehme (*Microsoft, US)*
Wolfgang Nejdl (*University of Hannover, Germany)*
Joachim Niehren (*INRIA Lille, France)*
Werner Nutt (*Free University of Bozen-Bolzano, Italy)*
Dan Olteanu (*Oxford University, UK)*
Dimitris Papadias (*HKUST, Hong Kong)*
Mary-Angela Papalaskari (*Villanova University, US)*
Alexandra Poulovassilis (*Birkbeck, University of London, UK)*
Sunil Prabhakar (*Purdue University, US)*
Lu Qin (*CUHK, China)*
Christopher Re (*University of Wisconsin-Madison, US)*
Dimitris Sacharidis (*IMIS "Athena" Research Centre , Greece)*
Arnaud Sahuguet (*Google, US)*
Marc H Scholl (*Universitaet Konstanz, Germany)*
Thomas Schwentick (*TU Dortmund, Germany)*
Jianhua Shao (*Cardiff University, UK)*
Mohamed Sharaf (*University of Queensland, Australia)*
Kian Lee Tan (*National University of Singapore, Singapore)*
Nan Tang (*University of Edinburgh, UK)*
Val Tannen (*University of Pennsylvania, US)*
Evimaria Terzi (*Boston University, US)*
Jens Teubner (*ETH Zurich, Switzerland)*

Program Committee (continued):

Alex Thomo (*University of Victoria, Canada)*
Marcos Vaz Salles (*Cornell University, US)*
Dirk Van Gucht (*Indiana University, US)*
Millist Vincent (*University of South Australia, Australia)*
Wei Wang (*University of North Carolina, US)*
Hongzhi Wang (*Harbin Institute of Technology, China)*
Jianmin Wang (*Tsinghua University, China)*
Junhu Wang (*Griffith University, Australia)*
Wei Wang (*Fudan University, China)*
Haixun Wang (*Microsoft Research Asia, China)*
Jianyong Wang (*Tsinghua University, China)*
Jef Wijsen (*University of Mons, Belgium)*
Ouri E. Wolfson (*University of Illinois at Chicago, US)*
Limsoon Wong (*National University of Singapore, Singapore)*
Peter Wood (*Birkbeck, University of London, UK)*
Yuqing Wu (*Indiana University, US)*
Ming Xiong (*Google, US)*
Fei Xu (*Microsoft, US)*
Ke Yi (*Hong Kong University of Science and Technology, Hong Kong)*
Ken Yocum (*UC San Diego, US)*
Clement Yu (*University of Illinois at Chicago, US)*
Xiaohui Yu (*York University, Canada)*

CIKM 2011 IR Track Program Committees

Senior Program Committee:

James Allan (*University of Massachusetts Amherst, US)*
Javed Aslam (*Northeastern University, US)*
Leif Azzopardi (*University of Glasgow, UK)*
Nicholas Belkin (*Rutgers University, US)*
Paul Bennett (*Microsoft Research, US)*
Wray Buntine (*National ICT Australia Limited, NICTA), Australia)*
Yi Chang (*Yahoo! Labs, US)*
Paul Clough (*University of Sheffield, UK)*
Fabio Crestani (*University of Lugano, Switzerland)*
Maarten de Rijke (*University of Amsterdam, The Netherlands)*
Patrick Gallinari (*University Pierre & Marie Curie, France)*
Bin Gao (*Microsoft Research Asia, China)*
Cathal Gurrin (*Dublin City University, Ireland)*
Djoerd Hiemstra (*University of Twente, The Netherlands)*
Winston Hsu (*National Taiwan University, Taiwan)*
Panos Ipeirotis (*New York University, US)*
Gareth Jones (*Dublin City University, Ireland)*
Jaap Kamps (*University of Amsterdam, The Netherlands)*
Noriko Kando (*NII, Japan)*
Jaana Kekäläinen (*University of Tampere, Finland)*
Oren Kurland (*Technion, Israel)*
Elizabeth Liddy (*Syracuse University, US)*
Mounia Lalmas (*Yahoo! Research, Spain)*
Paul McNamee (*Johns Hopkins University, US)*
Peter Mika (*Yahoo! Research Barcelona, Spain)*
Wolfgang Nejdl (*L3S Research Center, Germany)*
Omar Alonso (*Microsoft Research, US)*
Tetsuya Sakai (*Microsoft Research Asia, China)*
Fabrizio Silvestri (*ISTI - CNR, Italy)*
Torsten Suel (*NYU Poly, US)*
Andrew Trotman (*University of Otago, New Zealand)*
Ellen Voorhees (*National Institute of Standards and Technology, US)*
Jun Wang (*University College London, UK)*
Ji-Rong Wen (*Microsoft Research Asia, China)*
Ryen White (*Microsoft Research, US)*
Emine Yilmaz (*Microsoft Research Cambridge, UK)*
ChengXiang Zhai (*University of Illinois at Urbana-Champaign, US)*
Min Zhang (*Tsinghua University, China)*

Program Committee:

Maristella Agosti (*University of Padua, Italy)*
Robin Aly (*University of Twente, The Netherlands)*
Giambattista Amati (*Fondazione Ugo Bordoni, Italy)*
Marcos Andre Goncalves (*Universidade Federal de Minas Gerais, Brazil)*
Avi Arampatzis (*Democritus University of Thrace, Greece)*
Jaime Arguello (*Carnegie Mellon University, US)*
Hany Azzam (*Queen Mary, University of London, UK)*
Jing Bai (*Microsoft Corporation, US)*
Niranjan Balasubramanian (*University of Massachusetts Amherst, US)*
Krisztian Balog (*Norwegian University of Science and Technolog, Norway)*
Alejandro Bellogín Kouki (*Universidad Autónoma de Madrid, Spain)*
Michael Bendersky (*University of Massachusetts, Amherst, US)*
Paul Bennett (*Microsoft Research, US)*
Pushpak Bhattacharyya (*IIT Bombay, India)*
Jiang Bian (*Yahoo! Labs, US)*
Cui Bin (*Beijing University, China)*
Roi Blanco (*Yahoo! Research Barcelona, Spain)*
Toine Bogers (*RSLIS, Denmark)*
Gloria Bordogna (*CNR IDPA, Italy)*
Corrado Boscarino (*Centrum Wiskunde & Informatica, The Netherlands)*
Mohand Boughanem (*Universite Paul Sabatier, France)*
Sam Brody (*Rutgers, US)*
Wray Buntine (*National ICT Australia Limited, Australia)*
Fidel Cacheda (*University of Coruña, Spain)*
Pavel Calado (*Technical Univ. of Lisbon, Portugal)*
Gilberto Camara (*INPE - National Institute for Space Research, Brazil)*
Guihong Cao (*Microsoft, US)*
Ben Carterette (*University of Delaware, US)*
Marc-Allen Cartright (*University of Massachusetts Amherst, US)*
Pablo Castells (*Universidad Autonoma de Madrid, Spain)*
Carlos Castillo (*Yahoo! Research, Spain)*
Zheng Chen (*Microsoft Research Asia, China)*
Xueqi Cheng (*Institute of Computing Technology, CAS, China)*
Gordon Cormack (*University of Waterloo, Canada)*
Ricardo da Silva Torres (*University of Campinas, Brazil)*
Franciska de Jong (*University of Twente, The Netherlands)*
Gianluca Demartini (*Université de Fribourg, Switzerland)*
Ludovic Denoyer (*LIP6, France)*
Giorgio Maria Di Nunzio (*University of Padova, Italy)*
Fernando Diaz (*Yahoo! Research, US)*
Lan Du (*ANU & NICTA, Australia)*
Carsten Eickhoff (*Delft University of Technology, The Netherlands)*
Li Fan (*Yahoo, US)*
Hui Fang (*University of Delaware, US)*
Ayman Farahat (*Yahoo, US)*
Henry Feild (*University of Massachusetts Amherst, US)*
Juanma Fernández-Luna (*University of Granada, Spain)*
Nicola Ferro (*University of Padova, Italy)*

Program Committee (continued):

Dennis Fetterly (*Microsoft Research, US)*
Boudin Florian (*Université d'Avignon, France)*
Colum Foley (*Dublin City University, Ireland)*
Ingo Frommholz (*University of Bedfordshire, UK)*
Susan Gauch (*University of Arkansas, US)*
Eric Gaussier (*Laboratoire d'Informatique de Grenoble, France)*
Shlomo Geva (*Queensland University of Technology, Australia)*
Fredric Gey (*University of California, Berkeley, US)*
Ayse Goker (*City University London, UK)*
Gregory Grefenstette (*EXALEAD, France)*
Nils Grimsmo (*NTNU, Norway)*
Maxim Gurevich (*Yahoo! Research, US)*
Karl Gyllstrom (*Katholieke Universiteit Leuven, Belgium)*
Harry Halpin (*University of Edinburgh, UK)*
Claudia Hauff (*Delft University of Technology, The Netherlands)*
David Hawking (*Funnelback Ltd and Australian National University, Australia)*
Daqing He (*University of Pittsburgh, US)*
Jiyin He (*Centrum Wiskunde & Informatica, The Netherlands)*
Ben He (*Graduate University of CAS, China)*
Andreas Henrich (*University of Bamberg, Germany)*
Eduard Hoenkamp (*Queensland University of Technology, Australia)*
Katja Hofmann (*University of Amsterdam, The Netherlands)*
Laura Hollink (*Delft University of Technology, The Netherlands)*
Vera Hollink (*Centrum Wiskunde & Informatica, The Netherlands)*
Vivian Hu (*York University, Canada)*
Xuanjing Huang (*Fudan University, China), China)*
Gilles Hubert (*IRIT, University of Toulouse, France)*
Tereza Iofciu (*L3S Research Center, Germany)*
Daxin Jiang (*Microsoft Research Asia, China)*
Hideo Joho (*University of Tsukuba, Japan)*
Joemon Jose (*University of Glasgow, UK)*
Vanja Josifovski (*Yahoo! Research, US)*
Marko Junkkari (*University of Tampere, FI)*
Changsung Kang (*Yahoo! Labs, US)*
Gabriella Kazai (*Microsoft Research, UK)*
Heikki Keskustalo (*University of Tampere, FI)*
Jinyoung Kim (*University of Massachusetts, Amherst, US)*
Sang-Wook Kim (*Hanyang University, Korea)*
Irwin King (*The Chinese University Hong Kong, Hong Kong)*
Marijn Koolen (*University of Amsterdam, The Netherlands)*
Veit Koeppen (*Otto-von-Guericke-Universität Magdeburg, Germany)*
Donald Kraft (*Colorado Technical University, US)*
Raghu Krishnapuram (*IBM India Research Lab, India)*
Jérôme Kunegis (*University of Koblenz-Landau, Germany)*
Monica Landoni (*University of Lugano, Switzerland)*
Birger Larsen (*Royal School of LIS, Denmark)*
Martha Larson (*Delft University of Technology, The Netherlands)*
Hady Lauw (*Institute for Infocomm Research, Singapore)*
Victor Lavrenko (*University of Edinburgh, UK)*
Fotis Lazarinis (*University of Teesside, UK)*
Ronny Lempel (*Yahoo! Labs, Israel)*
Johannes Leveling (*CNGL, Dublin City University, Ireland)*

Program Committee (continued):

Qing Li (*City University of Hong Kong, Hong Kong*)
Huajing Li (*Facebook, US*)
Wen Li (*Delft University of Technology, The Netherlands*)
Xiaoming Li (*Peking University, China*)
Zhoujun Li (*Beihang University, China*)
Xia Lin (*Drexel University, US*)
Chin-Yew Lin (*Microsoft Research Asia, China*)
Hongfei Lin (*Dalian University of Technology, China*)
Yang Liu (*Shandong University, China*)
Alexander Löser (*TU Berlin, Germany*)
Claudio Lucchese (*ISTI-CNR Pisa, Italy*)
Yuanhua Lv (*University of Illinois Urbana-Champaign, US*)
Craig Macdonald (*University of Glasgow, UK*)
Walid Magdy (*Dublin City University, Ireland*)
Marco Maggini (*University of Siena, Italy*)
Yosi Mass (*IBM Research Lab at Haifa, Israel*)
James Mayfield (*Johns Hopkins University, US*)
Richard Mccreadie (*University of Glasgow, UK*)
Edgar Meij (*University of Amsterdam, The Netherlands*)
Dalila Mekhaldi (*University of Wolverhampton, UK*)
Donald Metzler (*University of Southern California, US*)
Jun Miao (*York University, Canada*)
Natasa Milic-Frayling (*Microsoft Research, UK*)
Vibhu Mittal (*Root-1, US*)
Dunja Mladenic (*Jozef Stefan Institute, Slovenia*)
Marie-Francine Moens (*Katholieke Universiteit Leuven, Belgium*)
Josiane Mothe (*Université de Toulouse, France*)
Vanessa Murdock (*Yahoo! Research, Spain*)
Arlindo L. Oliveira (*Instituto Superior Tecnico / INESC-ID, Portugal*)
Sandeep Pandey (*Yahoo Research, US*)
Gabriella Pasi (*Università degli Studi di Milano Bicocca, Italy*)
Raffaele Perego (*ISTI-CNR, Italy*)
Nils Pharo (*Oslo University College, Norway*)
Karen Pinel-Sauvagnat (*IRIT, University of Toulouse, France*)
Benjamin Piwowarski (*University of Glasgow, UK*)
Vassilis Plachouras (*Presans, France*)
Barbara Poblete (*Yahoo! Research, CL*)
Tamara Polajnar (*University of Glasgow, UK*)
Jeffrey Pound (*University of Waterloo, Canada*)
Kunal Punera (*Yahoo! Research, US*)
Tao Qin (*Microsoft Research Asia, China*)
Novi Quadrianto (*ANU & NICTA, Australia*)
Filip Radlinski (*Microsoft, Canada*)
Davood Rafiei (*University of Alberta, Canada*)
Georgina Ramirez (*Universitat Pompeu Fabra, Spain*)
Jan Ramon (*Katholieke Universiteit Leuven, Belgium*)
Edie Rasmussen (*University of British Columbia, Canada*)
Andreas Rauber (*Vienna University of Technology, Austria*)
Stephen Robertson (*Microsoft Research Cambridge, UK*)
Monica Rogati (*LinkedIn, US*)
Stevan Rudinac (*Delft University of Technology, The Netherlands*)
Scott Sanner (*NICTA & ANU, Australia*)

Program Committee (continued):

Rodrygo Santos (*University of Glasgow, UK)*
Ralf Schenkel (*Max-Planck-Institut Informatik, Germany, Germany)*
Falk Scholer (*RMIT University, Australia)*
Pavel Serdyukov (*Yandex, RU)*
James G Shanahan (*Church and Duncan Group, US)*
Milad Shokouhi (*Microsoft Research, UK)*
Wolf Siberski (*L3S Research Center, University of Hannover, Germany)*
Mark Smucker (*University of Waterloo, Canada)*
Cees Snoek (*University of Amsterdam, The Netherlands)*
Dawei Song (*Robert Gordon University, UK)*
Benno Stein (*Bauhaus-Universität Weimar, Germany)*
Venkata Subramaniam (*IBM Research India, India)*
Krysta M. Svore (*Microsoft Research, US)*
Lynda Tamine (*IRIT- Paul Sabatier University, France)*
Paul Thompson (*Dartmouth Medical School, US)*
Nicola Tonellotto (*CNR, Italy)*
Thanh D. Tran (*Institute AIFB, KIT, Germany)*
Dolf Trieschnigg (*University of Twente, The Netherlands)*
Ming-Feng Tsai (*National Chengchi University, Taiwan)*
Theodora Tsikrika (*University of Applied Sciences Western Switzerland, Switzerland)*
David Vallet (*Universidad Autonoma de Madrid, Spain)*
Arthur van Bunningen (*Teezir, The Netherlands)*
Theo P. van der Weide (*Radboud University, The Netherlands)*
Olga Vechtomova (*University of Waterloo, Canada)*
Suzan Verberne (*Radboud University Nijmegen, The Netherlands)*
Jesus Vilares (*University of A Coruña, Spain)*
Robert Villa (*University of Sheffield, UK)*
Vishwa Vinay (*Microsoft Research, UK)*
Stefanos Vrochidis (*CERTH-ITI, Greece)*
Xiaojun Wan (*Peking University, China)*
Bin Wang (*Institute of Computing Technology, CAS, China)*
Christian Wartena (*Novay, The Netherlands)*
Takashi Washio (*ISIR - Osaka University, Japan)*
William Webber (*University of Melbourne, Australia)*
Wouter Weerkamp (*University of Amsterdam, The Netherlands)*
Thijs Westerveld (*Teezir, The Netherlands)*
Yuchen Wu (*Google, US)*
Wensi Xi (*Google, US)*
Christopher C. Yang (*Drexel University, US)*
Shuang-Hong Yang (*Georgia Institute of Technology, US)*
Zheng Ye (*York University, Canada)*
Wai Gen Yee (*Orbitz, LLC, US)*
Xing Yi (*University of Massachusetts, Amherst, US)*
Hwan-Seung Yong (*Ewha Womans University, KR)*
Shichao Zhang (*Guangxi Normal University, China)*
Jun Zhao (*National Laboratory of Pattern Recognition, China)*
Zhaohui Zheng (*Yahoo! Inc, US)*
Ding Zhou (*Facebook, US)*
Nivio Ziviani (*UFMG, Brazil)*

CIKM 2011 KM Track Program Committees

Senior Program Committee:

Sarabjot Anand (*University of Warwick, UK)*
Francesco Bonchi (*Yahoo! Research, Spain)*
Ulrik Brandes (*University of Konstanz, Germany)*
Ronen Feldman (*Hebrew University of Jerusalem, Israel)*
Fosca Giannotti (*CNR, Italy)*
Dunja Mladenic (*Jozef Stefan Institute, Slovenia)*
Bamshad Mobasher (*DePaul University, US)*
Siegfried Nijssen (*Katholieke Universiteit Leuven*, Belgium)
Sanjay Ranka (*University of Florida, US)*
Yucel Saygin (*Sabanci University, Turkey)*
Myra Spiliopoulou (*University of Magdeburg, Germany)*
Xindong Wu (*University of Vermont, US)*
Qiang Yang (*Hong Kong University of Science and Technology, Hong Kong)*
Xingquan Zhu (*University of Technology Sydney, Australia)*

Program Committee (continued):

Tim Furche (*Oxford University, UK*)
Jose Gamez (*University of Castilla-La Mancha, Spain*)
Matjaz Gams (*Jozef Stefan Institute, Slovenia*)
Nicolas Garcia-Pedrajas (*University of Córdoba, Spain*)
Minos Garofalakis (*Technical University of Crete, Greece*)
Bugra Gedik (*IBM Research, US*)
Michael Gertz (*University of Heidelberg, Germany*)
Rayid Ghani (*Accenture Technology Labs, US*)
S.K. Ghosh (*Indian Institute of Technology, Kharagpur, IN*)
Bart Goethals (*University of Antwerp, Belgium*)
Jesus Gonzalez (*National Institute Astrophysics, Optics and Electronics, Mexico*)
Sergio Greco (*University of Calabria, Italy*)
Le Gruenwald (*University of Oklahoma, US*)
Christian Gütl (*Curtin University of Technology, Austria*)
Ido Guy (*IBM Research Haifa, Israel*)
Peng Han (*Chongqing Academy of Science & Technology, China*)
Dan He (*University of California, Los Angeles, US*)
Andreas Hotho (*University of Würzburg, Germany*)
Vagelis Hristidis (*Florida International University, US*)
Kien Hua (*University of Central Florida, US*)
Luke Huan (*University of Kansas, US*)
Jimmy Huang (*York University, Canada*)
Eyke Huellermeier (*Marburg University, Germany*)
Jing Jiang (*Singapore Management University, Singapore*)
Wei Jiang (*Missouri University of Science and Technology, US*)
Ruoming Jin (*Kent state University, US*)
Zhi Jin (*Peking University, China*)
Murat Kantarcioglu (*University of Texas at Dallas, US*)
Hung-Yu Kao (*National Cheng Kung University, Taiwan*)
Shiva Kasiviswanathan (*IBM T.J. Watson Research Center, US*)
Chan Keith (*Hong Kong Polytechnic University, Hong Kong*)
Eamonn Keogh (*University of California Riverside, US*)
Vlado Keselj (*Dalhousie University, Canada*)
Latifur Khan (*University of Texas at Dallas, US*)
Deepak Khemani (*IIT Madras, India*)
Hyerin Kim (*Korea Advanced Institute of Technology, Korea*)
Frank Klawonn (*Ostfalia University of Applied Sciences, Germany*)
Alek Kolcz (*Microsoft Live Labs, US*)
Patty Kostkova (*City eHealth Research Centre, UK*)
Wai Lam (*Chinese University of Hong Kong, Hong Kong*)
Won Suk Lee (*Yonsei University Korea, Korea*)
Young-Koo Lee (*Kyung Hee University, Korea*)
Carson K. Leung (*University of Manitoba, Canada*)
Bin Li (*University of Technology, Sydney, Australia*)

Program Committee (continued):

Jianzhong Li (*Harbin Institute of Technology, China)*
Tao Li (*Florida International University, US)*
Althea Liang (*HP Cloud and Security Lab, Singapore)*
Giuseppe Liotta (*Università di Perugia, Italy)*
Huan Liu (*Arizona State University, US)*
Nathan Liu (*Hong Kong University of Science and Technology, Hong Kong)*
Yan Liu (*IBM Research, US)*
Yang Liu (*Shandong University, China)*
Ying Liu (*KAIST, South Korea)*
Dmitri Loguinov (*Texas A&M University, US)*
Chang-Tien Lu (*Virginia Tech, US)*
Ping Luo (*Hewlett Packard Labs China, China)*
Mondher Maddouri (*URPAH, Tunisia)*
Hiroshi Mamitsuka (*Kyoto University, Japan)*
Bruno Martins (*Instituto Superior Técnico / INESC-ID, Portugal)*
Sergio Mascetti (*Università degli Studi di Milano, Italy)*
Stan Matwin (*University of Ottawa, Canada)*
Guy Melancon (*Université Bordeaux I, France)*
Gabor Melli (*PredictionWorks Inc., Canada)*
Ernestina Menasalvas (*Universidad Politecnica de Madrid, Spain)*
Ralf Moeller (*Hamburg University of Technology, Germany)*
Yang-Sae Moon (*Kangwon National University, Korea)*
Roser Morante (*University of Antwerp, Belgium)*
Ion Muslea (*Language Weaver, US)*
Mirco Nanni (*CNR, Italy)*
Olfa Nasraoui (*University of Louisville, US)*
Roberto Navigli (*Sapienza University of Rome, Italy)*
Tim Oates (*University of Maryland Baltimore County, US)*
Daniel O'Leary (*University of Southern California, US)*
Jonice Oliveira (*Federal University of Rio de Janeiro, Brazil)*
Weike Pan (*HKUST, China)*
Youngja Park (*IBM Research, US)*
Nikos Pelekis (*University of Piraeus, Greece)*
Kumaraguru Ponnurangam (*Indraprastha Institute of Information Technology, India)*
Vikram Pudi (*IIIT Hyderabad, India)*
Naren Ramakrishnan (*Virginia Tech, US)*
Vikas Raykar (*Siemens Healthcare, US)*
Daniele Riboni (*Universita degli Studi di Milano, Italy)*
Rong Pan (*Sun Yat-sen University, China)*
Massimo Ruffolo (*ICAR-CNR, Italy)*
Giovanni Maria Sacco (*Universita di Torino, Italy)*
Kazuhiro Seki (*Kobe University, Japan)*
Yi-dong Shen (*Chinese Academy of Science, China)*
Kyuseok Shim (*Seoul National University, Korea)*
Andrzej Skowron (*University of Warsaw, Poland)*
Dominik Slezak (*University of Warsaw, Poland)*

CIKM 2011 Industry Track, Workshop, Tutorial and Demonstration Committees

Industry Track Program Committee:

Steve Beitzel (*Telcordia Technologies, US)*
Jidong Chen (*EMC Research China, China)*
Nikesh Garera (*Kosmix, US)*
David Grossman (*Illinois Institute of Technology, US)*
Yoshinori Hara (*Kyoto University, Japan)*
Arvind Hulgeri (*Persistent Systems, India)*
Mizuho Iwaihara (*Waseda University, Japan)*
Giridhar Kumaran (*Microsoft Corporation, US)*
Ni Lao (*Carnegie Mellon University, US)*
Jonathan Ledlie (*Nokia Research, US)*
Wookey Lee (*Inha University, Korea)*
Wen-Syan Li (*Directorial MTS, China)*
Einat Minkov (*University of Haifa, Israel)*
Fuchun Peng (*Microsoft, US)*
Diego Puppin (*Google, US)*
Prasan Roy (*IBM Research, India)*
Robert Warren (*University of Waterloo, Canada)*

Tutorial Program Committee:

Daniel J. Abadi (*Yale University, US)*
Philip A. Bernstein (*Microsoft, US)*
Albert Bifet (*University of Waikato, New Zealand)*
Francesco Bonchi (*Yahoo!, Spain)*
Gianluca Demartini (*University of Fribourg, Switzerland)*
Thore Graepel (*Microsoft, UK)*
Antonio Gulli (*Microsoft, UK)*
Djoerd Hiemstra (*University of Twente, The Netherlands)*
Rosie Jones (*Akamai, US)*
Jaap Kamps (*University of Amsterdam, The Netherlands)*
Ray R. Larson (*UC Berkeley, US)*
Leonid Libkin (*University of Edinburgh, UK)*
Claudio Lucchese (*ISTI-CNR, Italy)*
Paul Ogilvie (*LinkedIn, US)*
Fabrizio Silvestri (*ISTI-CNR, Italy)*
Trevor Strohman (*Google, US)*
Daniel Tunkelang (*LinkedIn, US)*
Arjen P. de Vries (*CWI & Technical University of Delft, The Netherlands)*
Daniel J. Abadi (*Yale University, US)*
Philip A. Bernstein (*Microsoft, US)*

Demonstration Program Committee:

Enrique Alfonseca (*Google, Switzerland)*
Klaus Berberich (*Max-Planck Institute, Germany)*
Joaquin Delgado (*Yahoo, US)*
Alex Dow (*Microsoft, US)*
Conny Junghans (*University of Heidelberg, Germany)*
Vasilis Kandylas (*Microsoft, US)*
Jussi Karlgren (*SICS, Sweden)*
Dmitry Lenkov (*Oracle, US)*
David Losada (*University of Santiago de Compostela, Spain)*
Bertram Ludaescher (*University of California, Davis, US)*
Gerard de Melo (*Max-Planck Institute, Germany)*
Ullas Nambiar (*IBM Research, India)*
Alexandros Ntoulas (*Zynga, US)*
Ximena Olivares (*eBay, US)*
Cristobal Pedregal-Martin (*Oracle, US)*
Alvaro Pereira (*Federal University of Ouro Preto, Brazil)*
Igor Perisic (*LinkedIn, US)*
Jorge Quiane-Ruiz (*Saarland University, Germany)*
Mandar Rahurkar (*Yahoo!, US)*
Martin Theobald (*Max-Planck, Germany)*

Workshop Program Committee:

Karl Aberer (*EPFL, Switzerland)*
James Allan (*University of Massachusetts, Amherst, US)*
Roi Blanco (*Yahoo! Research, Spain)*
Pia Borlund (*Royal School of Library and Information Science, Denmark)*
Wray Buntine (*NICTA, Australia)*
Marcos Goncalves (*Universidade Federal de Minas Gerais, Brazil)*
Alasdair Gray (*University of Manchester, UK)*
Donna Harman (*NIST, US)*
Bill Hersh (*Oregon Health & Science University, US)*
Noriko Kando (*National Institute of Informatics, Japan)*
Anastasios Kementsietsidis (*IBM Research, US)*
Elizabeth Liddy (*Syracuse University, US)*
Hervé Martin (*Joseph Fourier University (France)*
Mirjam Minor (*University Trier, Germany)*
Pavel Serdyukov (*Yandex LLC, Russia)*
Nicola Tonellotto (*CNR, Italy)*
Rosina Weber (*Drexel University, US)*
Emine Yilmaz (*Microsoft, UK)*
Shichao Zhang (*University of Technology Sydney, Australia)*

Poster Program Committee (continued):

Bill Eberle (*Tennessee Tech University, US)*
Hui Fang (*University of Delaware, US)*
Nicola Ferro (*University of Padova, Italy)*
Boudin Florian (*Université d'Avignon, France)*
Giorgio Gambosi (*University of Rome "Tor Vergata", Italy)*
Giorgos Giannopoulos (*NTU Athens, Greece)*
Jesus Gonzalez (*National Institute of Astrophysics, Optics and Electronics, Mexico)*
Sergio Greco (*University of Calabria, Italy)*
Gregory Grefenstette (*EXALEAD, France)*
Cathal Gurrin (*Dublin City University, Ireland)*
Ido Guy (*IBM Research Haifa, Israel)*
Claudia Hauff (*Delft University of Technology, Netherlands)*
Ben He (*Graduate University of Chinese Academy of Sciences, China)*
Andreas Henrich (*University of Bamberg, Germany)*
Vivian Hu (*York University, Canada)*
Qiang Huang (*University of East Anglia, UK)*
Rong Huang (*NC State University, US)*
Xiaojiang Huang (*Peking University, China)*
Gilles Hubert (*IRIT, University of Toulouse, France)*
Kai Hui (*Graduate University of Chinese Academy of Sciences, China)*
Arvind Hulgeri (*Persistent Systems, India)*
Ela Hunt (*ETH Zurich, Switzerland)*
Seung-won Hwang (*POSTECH, Korea)*
Giacomo Inches (*University of Lugano, Switzerland)*
Jing Jiang (*Singapore Management University, Singapore)*
Hideo Joho (*University of Tsukuba, Japan)*
Gao Jun (*Peking University, China)*
Mouna Kacimi (*Free University of Bozen-Bolzano, Italy)*
Toshihiro Kamishima (*AIST, Japan)*
Jaewoo Kang (*Korea University, Korea)*
Abhijith Kashyap (*Florida International University, US)*
Gabriella Kazai (*Microsoft Research, UK)*
Chan Keith (*The Hong Kong Polytechnic University, Hong Kong)*
Anastasios Kementsietsidis (*IBM T.J. Watson Research Center, US)*
Eamonn Keogh (*University of California Riverside, US)*
Sang-Wook Kim (*Hanyang University, Korea)*
Benny Kimelfeld (*IBM, US)*
Iraklis Klampanos (*University of Glasgow, UK)*
Solmaz Kolahi (*University of British Columbia, Canada)*
Donald Kraft (*Colorado Technical University, US)*
Giridhar Kumaran (*Microsoft Corporation, US)*
Wai Lam (*The Chinese University of Hong Kong, Hong Kong)*
Monica Landoni (*University of Lugano, Switzerland)*
Ni Lao (*Carnegie Mellon University, US)*
Birger Larsen (*Royal School of LIS, Denmark)*
Martha Larson (*Delft University of Technology, Netherlands)*
Hady Lauw (*Institute for Infocomm Research, Singapore)*
Won Suk Lee (*Yonsei University Korea, Korea)*
Maurizio Lenzerini (*Università di Roma La Sapienza, Italy)*
Johannes Leveling (*CNGL, Dublin City University, Ireland)*
Bin Li (*University of Technology, Sydney, Australia)*

Poster Program Committee (continued):

Zheng Ye (*York University, Canada*)
Wai Gen Yee (*Orbitz Worldwide, US*)
Jeonghee Yi (*Yahoo! Inc, US*)
Emine Yilmaz (*Microsoft Research Cambridge, UK*)
Ken Yocum (*University of California, San Diego, US*)
Xiaohui Yu (*York University, Canada*)
Markus Zanker (*Alpen-Adria-Universitaet Klagenfurt, Austria*)
Yi Zeng (*Beijing University Of Technology, China*)
Yan Zhang (*Vermont Information Processing, US*)
Peng Zhang (*The Robert Gordon University, UK*)
Peng Zhang (*Texas State University - San Marcos, US*)
Wei Zhang (*Amazon.com Inc., US*)
Jessie Zhao (*York University, Canada*)
Zhi-Hua Zhou (*Nanjing University, China*)
Dong Zhou (*Trinity College Dublin, Ireland*)
Jianhan Zhu (*University College London, UK*)
Xingquan Zhu (*University of Technology, Australia*)
Guido Zuccon (*University of Glasgow, UK*)

CIKM 2011 Additional Reviewers

Additional reviewers:

Jaafar Ben Abdallah
Joel Barajas
Letizia Bertolaja
Romaric Besançon
Karla Caballero
Weiwei Cheng
Krzysztof Dembczynski
Nurcan Durak
Liyue Fan
Stefan Gindl
Jonatan Gomez
Slawomir Goryczka
Basheer Hawwash
Christian Kop
Elizabeth Leon
Thomas Lukasiewicz
Ana Cristina Mendes
Roberto Mirizzi
Thomas Peetz
Arthur Pitman
Esin Saka
Sofiane Sellah
Christian Sengstock
Jannik Strötgen
Ilija Subasic
Abhradeep Guha Thakurata
Jasna Tusek
Mathias Verbeke
Carmen Ruiz Vicente
Willem Waegeman
Chunye Wang
Xufei Wang
Albert Weichselbraun
Evan Wei Xiang
Yonghui Xiao
Lili Zhao
Erheng Zhong

CIKM 2011 Sponsors & Supporters

Sponsors: SIGIR Special Interest Group on Information Retrieval; sig web

Platinum Supporter: EMC²

Gold Supporters: Google™; Microsoft Research

Silver Supporter: SAP®

Bronze Supporters: ebY® Research Labs; YAHOO! LABS; Yandex

Supporters: crossref; IBM Research

Exhibitors: Cambridge University Press; Springer the language of science; Taylor & Francis Group an informa business

Organisations: Glasgow: Scotland with style; University of Glasgow; University of Strathclyde Glasgow

Can Irrelevant Data Help Semi-supervised Learning, Why and How?

Haiqin Yang[1], Shenghuo Zhu[2], Irwin King[1,3], Michael R. Lyu[1]

[1]Computer Sciences and Engineering
The Chinese University of Hong Kong
Shatin, N.T., Hong Kong
{hqyang, king, lyu}@cse.cuhk.edu.hk

[2]NEC Laboratories America
10080 N. Wolfe Rd, SW3-350
Cupertino, CA 95014, USA
zsh@sv.nec-labs.com

[3]AT&T Labs Research
201 Mission Street
San Francisco, CA, USA
irwin@research.att.com

ABSTRACT

Previous semi-supervised learning (SSL) techniques usually assume unlabeled data are relevant to the target task. That is, they follow the same distribution as the targeted labeled data. In this paper, we address a different and very difficult scenario in SSL, where the unlabeled data may be a mixture of data relevant or irrelevant to the target binary classification task. In our framework, we do not require explicitly prior knowledge on the relatedness of the unlabeled data to the target data. In order to alleviate the effect of the irrelevant unlabeled data and utilize the implicit knowledge among all available data, we develop a novel maximum margin classifier, named the *tri-class support vector machine* (3C-SVM), to seek an inductive rule to separate the target binary classification task well while finding out the irrelevant data by-product. To attain this goal, we introduce a new min loss function, which can relieve the impact of the irrelevant data while relying more on the labeled data and the relevant unlabeled data. This loss function can therefore achieve the maximum entropy principle. The 3C-SVM can then generalize standard SVMs, Semi-supervised SVMs, and SVMs learned from the universum as its special cases. We further analyze the property of 3C-SVM on why the irrelevant data can help to improve the model performance. For implementation, we make relaxation and approximate the objective by the convex-concave procedure, which turns the original optimization from integral programming problem to a problem by just solving a finite number of quadratic programming problems. Empirical results are reported to demonstrate the advantages of our 3C-SVM model.

Categories and Subject Descriptors

I.2.6 [**Learning**]: Induction; G.1.6 [**Optimization**]: Integer programming, Quadratic programming methods

General Terms

Algorithms, Experimentation, Performance

Keywords

Semi-supervised learning, Concave-convex procedure

1. INTRODUCTION

Traditional supervised learning usually needs a large number of labeled training samples to learn the inductive rule. However, labeling data is usually expansive and time consuming since it needs experts' knowledge. Due to the limited amount of labeled training samples, researchers have proposed various methods, such as active learning [20], transfer learning [17], and semi-supervised learning (SSL) [33], to resolve this problem. Active learning requires users' additional interaction to label the data during the training procedure. Transfer learning transfers the knowledge learned from related tasks to the target task, where the related tasks may need sufficient labeled data. On the contrary, semi-supervised learning needs the least labeled data. It automatically learns a model based on both labeled and unlabeled data. Currently, a variety of SSL methods, including EM with generative mixture models, co-training, Transductive/Semi-Supervised Support Vector Machines, and graph-based, have been proposed in the literature [5, 13, 31, 32, 35].

Previously proposed semi-supervised learning models usually assume unlabeled data are relevant to the target task, i.e., they follow the same distribution as the target labeled data [1, 2]. This assumption implicitly indicates that the unlabeled data are well prepared [5, 33]. That is, the unlabeled data has excluded all irrelevant data, which follow distributions different from the target labeled data. However, in real world applications, without carefully preprocessing, irrelevant data are easy to be included as unlabeled data. For example, when crawling web pages as unlabeled data to help classifying corresponding categories, it is very easy to collect some irrelevant web pages for them. Similarly, as illustrated in Fig. 1(a) and Fig. 1(b), when we classify the digits "5" and "8" with the help of unlabeled digits. It is possible to include other digits into unlabeled data. In these cases, learning from the labeled and the mixed unlabeled data indeed do harm to the previously proposed semi-supervised learning models [15, 21].

Hence, it is important to resolve the effect of the irrelevant data in the mixed unlabeled data. To achieve this goal and to utilize the irrelevant data, in this paper, we propose a novel maximal margin semi-supervised classifier, named the *tri-class support vector machine* (3C-SVM). The 3C-SVM can find the inductive rule to separate the targeted binary data well while determining the irrelevant data as the 0-class. More specifically, we introduce a novel min loss function to measure the empirical risk on the unlabeled data. This loss function can take advantages of the symmetrical

(a) USPS (b) MNIST (c) Classifiers illustration

Figure 1: Illustration of two benchmark handwritten digit datasets and classifiers trained by different models on a mixed unlabeled synthetic dataset. In Fig. 1(a) and Fig. 1(b), block digits are labeled data on the target task, while black digits are unlabeled data mixed with other digits. The irrelevant digits affect the model in seeking optimal decision. Figure (c) illustrates that 3C-SVM (the thin solid line) attains the best result, which is closest to the Bayesian optimal classifier (the thick solid line), among all SVM-related classifiers and automatically distinguishes the irrelevant unlabeled data (black dots with red circles) well.

hinge loss function and the ε-insensitive loss function. More importantly, our model can achieve the maximum entropy principle, i.e., the decision function can rely more on the labeled data and the relevant data, while maximally ignore the irrelevant data.

We highlight the main contributions of our work as follows:

- First, our 3C-SVM generalizes several popular maximum margin classifiers, including standard SVMs, Semi-supervised SVMs (S^3VMs), and SVMs learned from universum data ($\mathcal{U}$-SVMs).
- Second, we provide theoretical analysis on 3C-SVM to indicate why the irrelevant data can help the SSL, i.e., the irrelevant data play the role of seeking a good subspace of the decision boundary.
- Third, the original formulation of 3C-SVM is an integer programming problem. We relax the objective and solve it by the concave-convex procedure (CCCP) [29]. This finally transforms it by solving a finite number of quadratic programming (QP) problems, which yields the same worst case time complexity as that of S^3VMs [6].
- Fourth, we conduct a series of empirical evaluation to demonstrate the advantages of the 3C-SVM.

The rest of the paper is organized as follows: In Section 2, we review the related work on learning from both labeled and universum data. In Section 3, the proposed 3C-SVM with its properties is presented. In section 4, we detail how to solve 3C-SVM algorithm through CCCP. We report the experimental comparison and results in section 5 and conclude the paper in section 6.

2. RELATED WORK

In literature, many models have been proposed to learning a binary classifier with the help from other auxiliary data. These models usually only work when the auxiliary data are "clean" and satisfy the models' assumption [5, 25].

A typical kind of methods is semi-supervised learning [5, 34], including generative methods for SSL [12, 16], graph-based SSL methods [2, 35], maximum margin classifiers [5, 6, 11], etc. These methods utilize the labeled data and the unlabeled data to improve model performance. Usually, they assume that the given auxiliary data follow the same distribution as the labeled data [5, 35]. However, when unlabeled data are mixed with irrelevant data, they will hurt the SSL models [21]. An illustration is shown as the dash line in Figure 1(c).

Another line of work is the $\mathcal{U}$-SVMs [27], which learns from labeled data and the universum data, a third kind of data whose distribution is different from neither of the positive class nor the negative class. The universum can play the role of seeking the subspace for the decision function [22], but they have to be specified explicitly and chosen carefully before the training. Hence, without prior knowledge on the label of the given auxiliary data, e.g., data may be mixed with universum data and relevant data, the relevant data will also disturb the $\mathcal{U}$-SVM eventually; see e.g., the dash-dot line in Figure 1(c).

The third line of work is similar to what we consider in this paper, where the unlabeled data is noisy. In [30], a graph-based semi-supervised learning model is proposed to learn from both labeled and unlabeled data, where the unlabeled data is assumed following the same distribution of the targeted binary classification task and the labeled data contain the universum data. This model needs to explicitly indicate the label of the universum data. In [10], a semi-supervised support vector machine is extended to learn from both labeled and mixed unlabeled data. The proposed model is solved by a Semi-Definite Programming (SDP) problem, whose time complexity scales to $\mathcal{O}((L+U^2)^2(L+U)^{2.5})$ (L and U denote the number of labeled and unlabeled data, respectively.), the same as that of the relaxed transductive SVM by SDP [4]. In [14], the safe semi-supervised support vector machine method is proposed to alleviate the effect of the noise in the unlabeled data. The proposed method consists of two steps: 1) to train a SVM and a S^3VM simultaneously; 2) to determine the label of a data point by the confidence of the SVM or the S^3VM. This method needs a postprocess on the results and do not consider the case of mixture unlabeled data.

In summary, previously proposed methods contain insufficiency in solving the problem of semi-supervised learning with mixed unlabeled data. Hence, in this paper, we try to alleviate the effect of those unspecified irrelevant data and utilize them in determining the decision function.

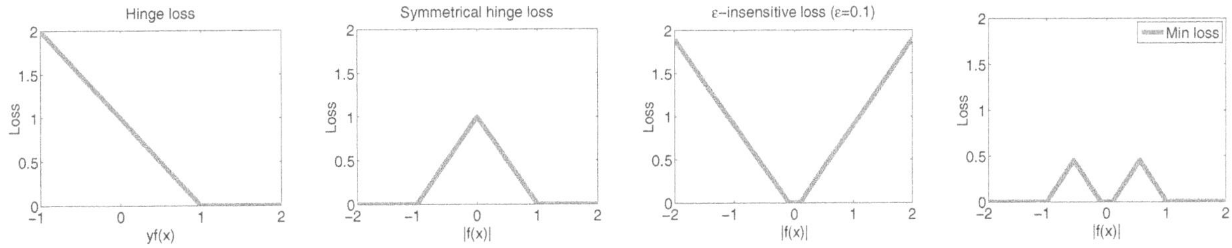

(a) Hinge loss (b) Symmetric hinge loss (c) ε-insensitive loss (d) Min loss

Figure 2: Illustration of different loss functions, including hinge loss, symmetrical hinge loss, ε-insensitive loss, and our proposed min **loss.**

3. LEARNING WITH IRRELEVANT DATA

In this section, we first define the problem setup of learning with irrelevant data. Next, we formulate the problem and propose the tri-class support vector machine, namely 3C-SVM. After that, we study the properties of 3C-SVM.

3.1 Problem Statement and Formulation

Suppose we are given two sets of data, labeled data $\mathcal{L}$ and unlabeled data $\mathcal{U}$, where the set of labeled data consists of L labeled samples, $\mathcal{L} = \{(\mathbf{x}_i, y_i)\}_{i=1}^{L}$, and the set of unlabeled data consists of U unlabeled samples, $\mathcal{U} = \{\mathbf{x}_i\}_{i=L+1}^{L+U}$. Here, $\mathbf{x}_i \in \mathcal{X} \subseteq \mathbb{R}^d$, and the label is triple, i.e., $y_i \in \{-1, 0, 1\}$. Hence, the labeled data consist of two sets of data, $\mathcal{L}_{\pm 1}$ and $\mathcal{L}_0$, where data in $\mathcal{L}_{\pm 1}$ follows the same distribution in the target task and they are labeled by -1 or $+1$; while data in $\mathcal{L}_0$ are irrelevant to the target task. That is, data with distributions different from the labeled target data are all cast into 0-class to construct the $\mathcal{L}_0$ dataset. Similarly, unlabeled data are a mixture of these data. We denote them as $\mathcal{U} = \mathcal{U}_{\mathcal{L}} \cup \mathcal{U}_0$, where data in $\mathcal{U}_{\mathcal{L}}$ follow the same distribution of ± 1 data, and data in $\mathcal{U}_0$ follow distributions different from the ± 1 data. Normally, the number of unlabeled data is much larger than the number of the labeled target data, i.e., $|\mathcal{L}_{\pm 1}| \ll U$, and given an unlabeled data point, one does not know whether it comes from $\mathcal{U}_{\mathcal{L}}$ or from $\mathcal{U}_0$.

Here, the goal is to seek a decision boundary, $f_{\boldsymbol{\vartheta}}(\mathbf{x}) = \mathbf{w}^\top \phi(\mathbf{x}) + b$, to classify the ± 1 data well with the help of given labeled and mixed unlabeled data, where $\boldsymbol{\vartheta} = (\mathbf{w}, b)$ and $\phi : \mathbb{R}^d \to \mathbb{R}^f$, is a feature mapping function often implicitly defined by a Mercer kernel [19, 24]. Hence, we formulate the objective as follows:

$$\min_{\boldsymbol{\vartheta}} \frac{\lambda}{2}\|\mathbf{w}\|^2 + \sum_{\mathbf{x}_i \in \mathcal{L}} r_i \ell_L(f_{\boldsymbol{\vartheta}}(\mathbf{x}_i), y_i) + \sum_{\mathbf{x}_i \in \mathcal{U}} r_i \ell_U(f_{\boldsymbol{\vartheta}}(\mathbf{x}_i)), \quad (1)$$

where minimizing $\|\mathbf{w}\|^2$ corresponds to maximizing the margin width [24] and avoids the overfitting. The parameter λ is a trade-off constant for the regularization term. $\ell_L(\cdot, \cdot)$ is a loss function to measure the empirical risk of the labeled data and $\ell_U(\cdot)$ is a loss function to measure the empirical risk of the unlabeled data. $r_i, i = 1, \ldots, L+U$, is a ratio penalty to balance the loss on the point $\mathbf{x}_i$ and the regularization term.

Typically, one may choose different loss functions to measure the empirical risk on the given data. These loss functions include

- **Hinge loss:** $H_1(u) = \max\{0, 1-u\}$, a loss function has been used to measure the empirical risk of labeled data in standard SVMs [24]; see Figure 2(a).
- **Symmetric hinge loss:** $H_1(|\cdot|)$, a loss function has been applied to measure the empirical risk on unlabeled data for S^3VMs [6]; see Figure 2(b).
- **ε-insensitive loss:** $I_\varepsilon(u) = \max\{0, |u| - \varepsilon\}$, a loss function has been adopted to measure the empirical risk in Support Vector Regression [24] and the Universum data in $\mathcal{U}$-SVMs [27]; see Figure 2(c).

In our problem setup, the unlabeled data may be a mixture of data relevant or irrelevant to the target task. Actually, this assumption matches natural to normal scenarios when the unlabeled data do not well prepared. However, without prior knowledge, how to distinguish the relevant and irrelevant data correctly is a very difficult task.

Here, in order to relieve the effect of irrelevant unlabeled data, we try to utilize them based on the following two principles. First, from *logistic regression* perspective [9, 18], when a data point lies farther away from the decision boundary, the data is more likely to be classified as data from ± 1-class; while data points lie near the decision boundary, they are less confident to be classified correctly. Hence, ideally, data from ± 1-class should lie on or outside of the margin gap; while other irrelevant data are close to the decision boundary. Second, the *maximum entropy principle* indicates that a classifier should rely more on the labeled and relevant data, while maximally ignore the irrelevant data. These two principles indicate that irrelevant data should lie around the sought decision boundary.

In order to fulfill the above principles, we adopt a min loss function to measure the risk of unlabeled data, so as to separate the unlabeled data into relevant and irrelevant data. This loss function determines and measures the error of an unlabeled data point by the min value of the symmetric hinge loss and the ε-insensitive loss (see Figure 2(d)):

$$\ell_{\min}(\mathbf{x}) = \min\{H_1(|f_{\boldsymbol{\vartheta}}(\mathbf{x}_i)|), I_\varepsilon(|f_{\boldsymbol{\vartheta}}(\mathbf{x}_i)|)\}. \quad (2)$$

Hence, for an unlabeled data point, when the error measured by the ε-insensitive loss is smaller than the error measured by the symmetric hinge loss, we can deem it as irrelevant data; otherwise, we set it as relevant data.

With this loss function, we can develop a novel maximum margin classifier, named the *tri-class support vector machine* (3C-SVM), as follows:

$$\min_{\boldsymbol{\vartheta}} \frac{\lambda}{2}\|\mathbf{w}\|^2 + \sum_{\mathbf{x}_i \in \mathcal{L}_{\pm 1}} r_i H_1(y_i f_{\boldsymbol{\vartheta}}(\mathbf{x}_i)) + \sum_{\mathbf{x}_i \in \mathcal{L}_0} r_i I_\varepsilon(f_{\boldsymbol{\vartheta}}(\mathbf{x}_i))$$
$$+ \sum_{\mathbf{x}_i \in \mathcal{U}} r_i \min\{H_1(|f_{\boldsymbol{\vartheta}}(\mathbf{x}_i)|), I_\varepsilon(|f_{\boldsymbol{\vartheta}}(\mathbf{x}_i)|)\}. \quad (3)$$

In the above, the first two terms correspond to the formulation of a standard SVM [24]. The third term measures the empirical risk of $\mathcal{L}_0$ data, the same in $\mathcal{U}$-SVMs [27]. The last term measures the loss of unlabeled data. Hence, we can determine the class of a data

Table 1: Relation between different models and the training data.

	3C-SVM			SVM			S^3VM			$\mathcal{U}$-SVM		
$\mathcal{L}$	−1	0	1	−1		1	−1		1	−1	0	1
$\mathcal{U}$	−1	0	1				−1		1			

point $\mathbf{x}$ by the following criterion:

$$c(\mathbf{x}) = \begin{cases} +1 & \text{if } f_{\vartheta}(\mathbf{x}) > \frac{1+\varepsilon}{2} \\ -1 & \text{if } f_{\vartheta}(\mathbf{x}) < -\frac{1+\varepsilon}{2} \\ 0 & \text{otherwise} \end{cases}. \tag{4}$$

The above criterion separate the data into three classes. The 0-class data corresponds to the irrelevant data.

3.2 Properties of 3C-SVMs

We first list the generalization property of our 3C-SVM, then outline the intuition behind 3C-SVMs through a specific case with $r_i = \infty$ for unlabeled data and $\varepsilon = 0$.

Our 3C-SVM provides a framework for the following popular maximum margin classifiers:

1. A standard SVM formulation [24] is a special case of the 3C-SVM. This can be attained by setting r_i to zero for the third and fourth terms in (3). When only labeled data are given in the training set, we can adopt this formulation.

2. An S^3VM formulation [5] is a special case of the 3C-SVM. This can be achieved by setting r_i to zero in the third term and using only symmetrical hinge loss to measure the empirical risk of unlabeled data in the fourth term in (3). When only labeled data and relevant unlabeled data are given, we can use this formulation.

3. The 3C-SVM also includes a $\mathcal{U}$-SVM [27]. It can be easily obtained by setting r_i to zero in the fourth term of (3). This formulation works when only labeled data and universum data are given.

Hence, our 3C-SVM, a general maximum margin semi-supervised learning formulation, includes standard SVMs, S^3VMs, and $\mathcal{U}$-SVMs as its special cases. A summarization is shown in Table 1.

Intuitively, our 3C-SVM may not work for all the cases since it seems that it requires the irrelevant data falls close to the decision function. However, we claim that we can tackle this problem by mapping the original data to a suitable space through the kernel trick. We then study why the 3C-SVM possibly works and give an insight of the model in the following theorem:

THEOREM 1. *A 3C-SVM with $r_i = \infty$ for unlabeled data and $\varepsilon = 0$ is equivalent to one of the following two cases: 1) training a general S^3VM to keep the unlabeled data falling on or out of the margin gap with only one or non of the unlabeled data in the decision boundary; or 2) separating the unlabeled data into two sets, $\mathcal{U}_{\mathcal{L}}$ and $\mathcal{U}_0$ with $|\mathcal{U}_0| \geq 2$, and training a general S^3VM on the training data projected onto the orthogonal complement of span $\{\phi(\mathbf{x}_j) - \phi(\mathbf{x}_0),\ \mathbf{x}_j \in \mathcal{U}_0\}$, where $\mathbf{x}_0$ is an arbitrary data point from $\mathcal{U}_0$, while keeping the unlabeled data in the set of $\mathcal{U}_{\mathcal{L}}$ falling on or out of the margin gap.*

Proof: $r_i = \infty$ for $\mathcal{U}$ data and $\varepsilon = 0$ imply that the min term in the fourth term of (3) vanish and the optimal solution of $\mathbf{w}$ and b in (3) is attained when one of the following conditions is fulfilled: (a) $|\mathbf{w}^\top \phi(\mathbf{x}_j) + b| \geq 1$, or (b) $\mathbf{w}^\top \phi(\mathbf{x}_j) + b = 0$. Hence, the above conditions set up the criterion of separating the unlabeled data into two sets, $\mathcal{U}_{\mathcal{L}}$ and $\mathcal{U}_0$, where data in $\mathcal{U}_{\mathcal{L}}$ satisfy the condition of (a) and data in $\mathcal{U}_0$ satisfy the condition of (b).

First, if $|\mathcal{U}_0| = 0$, or 1, it leads to the result of case 1) in the above theorem. Here, a general S^3VM means that it is a generalization of the S^3VM and the $\mathcal{U}$-SVM.

Next, if $\mathcal{U}_0$ contains at least two samples. For the data $\mathbf{x}_j$ from $\mathcal{U}_0$, we have $\mathbf{w}^\top \phi(\mathbf{x}_j) + b = 0$. Hence, picking arbitrary data $\mathbf{x}_0$ from $\mathcal{U}_0$, we obtain $\mathbf{w}^\top(\phi(\mathbf{x}_j) - \phi(\mathbf{x}_0)) = 0$. That is, $\mathbf{w}$ is orthogonal to span $\{\phi(\mathbf{x}_j) - \phi(\mathbf{x}_0),\ \mathbf{x}_j \in \mathcal{U}_0\}$. Now, let $P_{\mathcal{U}_0^\perp}$ denote an orthogonal project on the orthogonal complement of the mapped set $\mathcal{U}_0$, we have $\mathbf{w} = P_{\mathcal{U}_0^\perp}\mathbf{w}$, $\mathbf{w}^\top\mathbf{w} = \mathbf{w}^\top P_{\mathcal{U}_0^\perp}^\top P_{\mathcal{U}_0^\perp}\mathbf{w} = \mathbf{w}^\top\mathbf{w}$, and $\mathbf{w}^\top\mathbf{x}_i = \mathbf{w}^\top P_{\mathcal{U}_0^\perp}^\top \mathbf{x}_i = \mathbf{w}^\top P_{\mathcal{U}_0^\perp}\mathbf{x}_i$. This means that the optimal $\mathbf{w}$ is sought by training a general S^3VM on the projected labeled data and $\mathcal{U}_{\mathcal{L}}$ data with projection by $P_{\mathcal{U}_0^\perp}$ while keeping the condition (a) valid, or other unlabeled data falling on or out the margin gap. ■

Theorem 1 clearly shows that the optimization of our proposed model eventually is to find the most suitable subspace in which the margin is maximized while the overall empirical risk is minimized. The irrelevant data play the role of finding the subspace.

4. SOLUTION AND COMPUTATION

Due to the non-convexity of the min loss function, the formulation of the 3C-SVM in (3) is non-convex in general. Moreover, there are two difficulties to be solved in the formulation, the min term and the *absolute operation* on the unlabeled data. In the following, we show how to solve these two difficult problems.

4.1 Elimination of Min Terms and Absolute Values

First, we introduce decision variables, $d_k \in \{0, 1\}$, to remove the min term. This trick is similar to the L_1-norm S^3VM in [3]. We then transform the optimization into a mixed integer programming problem as follows:

$$\begin{aligned} \min_{\vartheta,\mathbf{d}} \ & \frac{\lambda}{2}\|\mathbf{w}\|^2 + \sum_{\mathbf{x}_i \in \mathcal{L}_{\pm 1}} r_i H_1(y_i f_{\vartheta}(\mathbf{x}_i)) + \sum_{\mathbf{x}_i \in \mathcal{L}_0} r_i I_{\varepsilon}(f_{\vartheta}(\mathbf{x}_i)) \\ & + \sum_{\mathbf{x}_{kL} \in \mathcal{U}} r_{kL} \underbrace{H_1(|f_{\vartheta}(\mathbf{x}_{kL})| + D(1 - d_k))}_{Q_1} \\ & + \sum_{\mathbf{x}_{kL} \in \mathcal{U}} r_{kL} \underbrace{I_{\varepsilon}(|f_{\vartheta}(\mathbf{x}_{kL})| - Dd_k)}_{Q_2}, \end{aligned} \tag{5}$$

where $kL = k + L$, $D > 0$ is a suitable constant making $Q_1 = 0$ when $d_k = 0$ and $Q_2 = 0$ when $d_k = 1$. That means, when $d_k = 0$, the error is counted from Q_2 and the unlabeled data are classified as 0-class and its error is measured by the ε-insensitive loss function; when $d_k = 1$, the error is incurred by Q_1 and the unlabeled data are classified as one of the ± 1-class, where its error is measured by the symmetrical hinge loss function.

Next, we deal with the absolute terms in the loss function by considering the properties of the loss functions. The shifted symmetrical hinge loss function in Q_1 can be abstracted as $H_1(|u| + a)$, or $H_1(|u| + a) = \max\{0, 1 - |u| - a\} = H_{1-a}(|u|)$. It can be approximated by a symmetrical loss, which is similar to the ramp loss used in [6, 26], as follows:

$$H_1(|u|+a) \approx H_{1-a}(u) - H_\kappa(u) + H_{1-a}(-u) - H_\kappa(-u).$$

The shifted ε-insensitive loss function in Q_2 can be transformed to another symmetrical loss as follows:

$$I_\varepsilon(|u|-a) = H_{-\varepsilon-a}(-u) + H_{-\varepsilon-a}(u).$$

Due to the symmetry of both loss functions, we introduce new pair-data for the unlabeled data to simplify the expression as [6]. The new pair-data are

$$\begin{aligned} \mathbf{x}_{kL} &= \mathbf{x}_{k+L}, \quad y_{kL} = 1, \\ \mathbf{x}_{kLU} &= \mathbf{x}_{k+L}, \quad y_{kLU} = -1, \quad k = 1, \ldots, U, \end{aligned}$$

where kL means $k+L$ and kLU means $k+L+U$.

4.2 Concave-Convex Procedure (CCCP)

Hence, we can transform the problem in (5) into $Q^\kappa(\boldsymbol{\vartheta}, \mathbf{d})$, which is the summation of two terms, $Q_{vex}(\boldsymbol{\vartheta}, \mathbf{d})$ and $Q^\kappa_{cav}(\boldsymbol{\vartheta})$. They are defined as follows

$$\begin{aligned} & Q_{vex}(\boldsymbol{\vartheta}, \mathbf{d}) \\ &= \frac{\lambda}{2}\|\mathbf{w}\|^2 + \sum_{\mathbf{x}_i \in \mathcal{L}_{\pm 1}} r_i H_1(y_i f_{\boldsymbol{\vartheta}}(\mathbf{x}_i)) + \sum_{\mathbf{x}_i \in \mathcal{L}_0} r_i I_\varepsilon(f_{\boldsymbol{\vartheta}}(\mathbf{x}_i)) \\ &+ \sum_{k=1}^{U} r_{kL} H_{\tilde{1}}(y_{kL} f_{\boldsymbol{\vartheta}}(\mathbf{x}_{kL})) + \sum_{k=1}^{U} r_{kL} H_{\tilde{1}}(y_{kLU} f_{\boldsymbol{\vartheta}}(\mathbf{x}_{kLU})) \\ &+ \sum_{k=1}^{U} r_{kL} H_{\tilde{\varepsilon}}(y_{kL} f_{\boldsymbol{\vartheta}}(\mathbf{x}_{kL})) + \sum_{k=1}^{U} r_{kL} H_{\tilde{\varepsilon}}(y_{kLU} f_{\boldsymbol{\vartheta}}(\mathbf{x}_{kLU}))), \\ & Q^\kappa_{cav}(\boldsymbol{\vartheta}) = -\sum_{j=L+1}^{L+2U} r_j H_\kappa(y_j f_{\boldsymbol{\vartheta}}(\mathbf{x}_j)). \end{aligned}$$

where $\tilde{1} = 1 - D(1-d_k)$ and $\tilde{\varepsilon} = -\varepsilon - Dd_k$.

Note that the above concave term, Q^κ_{cav}, keeps the non-convexity of the model following from the ramp loss in approximating the Q_1. The optimization in $Q^\kappa(\boldsymbol{\vartheta}, \mathbf{d})$ is a summation of a convex term and a concave term, or difference of convex programming. Hence, it can be solved by the concave-convex procedure (CCCP) [29], a technique has been adopted in large scale transductive SVMs [6] and SVMs on data with missing values [23].

In the CCCP, we need to use the first order Taylor expansion to approximate the concave term of Q^κ_{cav}. Since the variable $\mathbf{d}$ does not appear in the concave term, we only need to apply the first order Taylor expansion of Q^κ_{cav} at $\boldsymbol{\vartheta}^t$. Hence, we can seek the optimal variables by solving a sequence of the following optimization problem:

$$\min_{\boldsymbol{\vartheta}, \mathbf{d}} \left(Q_{vex}(\boldsymbol{\vartheta}, \mathbf{d}) + \frac{\partial Q^\kappa_{cav}(\boldsymbol{\vartheta}^t)}{\partial \boldsymbol{\vartheta}} \cdot \boldsymbol{\vartheta} \right), \tag{6}$$

The above optimization is a mixed integer optimization problem since $\mathbf{d}$ is an integer vector. Here, we adopt a standard routine to solve the integer programming problem [28]: 1) relaxing the integer variable to a real variable, then solve the whole optimization together; 2) rounding the corresponding variable to get its integer solution.

For 3C-SVM in (6), we relax the decision variable d_k from $\{0, 1\}$ to $[0, 1]$ and solve the optimization problem in (6) first. We then determine the value of d_k by its definition, the error incurred is less when the data is assigned to the associated class, as follows

$$d_k = \begin{cases} 1 & \text{if } \ \xi_k \le \xi_k^* \\ 0 & \text{otherwise} \end{cases}, \tag{7}$$

where $\xi_k = H_1(|f_{\boldsymbol{\vartheta}}(\mathbf{x}_{kL})|)$ and $\xi_k^* = I_\varepsilon(|f_{\boldsymbol{\vartheta}}(\mathbf{x}_{kL})|)$, $k = 1, \ldots, U$.

To simplify the first order approximation of the concave term in (6), we define

$$\mu_{k+\mathfrak{s}} = y_{k+\mathfrak{s}} \frac{\partial Q^\kappa_{cav}(\boldsymbol{\vartheta})}{\partial f_{\boldsymbol{\vartheta}}(\mathbf{x}_{k+\mathfrak{s}})} = \begin{cases} r_{k+\mathfrak{s}} & \text{if } y_{k+\mathfrak{s}} f_{\boldsymbol{\vartheta}}(\mathbf{x}_{k+\mathfrak{s}}) < \kappa \\ 0 & \text{otherwise} \end{cases}, \tag{8}$$

for those unlabeled samples $\mathbf{x}_{k+\mathfrak{s}}$ with $d_k = 1$, where $k = 1, \ldots, U$, and $\mathfrak{s}$ is L or $L+U$. Hence, the first order Taylor expansion of the concave term is then expressed as

$$\frac{\partial Q^\kappa_{cav}(\boldsymbol{\vartheta}^t)}{\partial \boldsymbol{\vartheta}} \cdot \boldsymbol{\vartheta} = \sum_{j=L+1}^{L+2U} \mu_j y_j f_{\boldsymbol{\vartheta}}(\mathbf{x}_j).$$

Now we turn to solve the relaxed optimization in (6) and summarize the result in the following theorem:

THEOREM 2. *The dual problem of the relaxed optimization in (6) is a Quadratic Programming (QP) problem as follows:*

$$\begin{aligned} \max_{\boldsymbol{\alpha}, \boldsymbol{\alpha}^*} \quad & -\frac{1}{2\lambda}[\boldsymbol{\alpha}; \boldsymbol{\alpha}^*]^\top \boldsymbol{\Omega} [\boldsymbol{\alpha}; \boldsymbol{\alpha}^*] + \boldsymbol{\varrho}^\top [\boldsymbol{\alpha}; \boldsymbol{\alpha}^*] \\ s.t. \quad & \mathbf{0} \le \boldsymbol{\alpha}, \boldsymbol{\alpha}^* \le \mathbf{r}, \\ & \mathbf{A}_e [\boldsymbol{\alpha}; \boldsymbol{\alpha}^*] = \boldsymbol{\mu}^\top \mathbf{Y}_{\bullet 2U}, \\ & \mathbf{A}[\boldsymbol{\alpha}; \boldsymbol{\alpha}^*] \le \mathbf{0}, \end{aligned} \tag{9}$$

where the Lagrangian multipliers $[\boldsymbol{\alpha}; \boldsymbol{\alpha}^*]$ *consists of an* $|\mathcal{L}_0| + L + 4U$*-dimensional vector. The matrix* $\boldsymbol{\Omega}$ *on the quadratic term is defined as* $\boldsymbol{\Omega} = \begin{bmatrix} Q_{|\mathcal{L}_0|+L+2U, |\mathcal{L}_0|+L+2U} & Q_{|\mathcal{L}_0|+L+2U, 2U} \\ Q_{2U, |\mathcal{L}_0|+L+2U} & Q_{2U,2U} \end{bmatrix}$, *and the coefficient for the linear term is*

$$\boldsymbol{\varrho} = \frac{1}{\lambda} \begin{bmatrix} Q_{2U, |\mathcal{L}_0|+L+2U} \\ Q_{2U,2U} \end{bmatrix} \boldsymbol{\mu} + \begin{bmatrix} -\varepsilon \mathbf{1}_{2|\mathcal{L}_0|} \\ \mathbf{1}_{L-|\mathcal{L}_0|} \\ (1-D)\mathbf{1}_{2U} \\ -\varepsilon \mathbf{1}_{2U} \end{bmatrix},$$

$\mathbf{A}_e = [\mathbf{Y}; \mathbf{Y}_{\bullet 2U}]$ *and* $\mathbf{A} = [\mathbf{0}_{U,L}, -\mathbf{I}_U, -\mathbf{I}_U, \mathbf{I}_U, \mathbf{I}_U]$, $\mathbf{Y}$ *is a vector containing the label value of all training data including the expanding auxiliary labels, and* $\mathbf{Y}_{\bullet 2U}$ *denotes the last* $2U$*-element in* $\mathbf{Y}$.

The above theorem can be derived based on the standard Lagrangian multiplier method, where Eq. (9) corresponds to the dual form of the optimization on (6).

After solving the QP problem in (9), we obtain $\mathbf{w}$ as a linear combination of the dual variables, $\boldsymbol{\alpha}$ and $\boldsymbol{\alpha}^*$,

$$\mathbf{w} = \frac{1}{\lambda} \left(\sum_{i=-|\mathcal{L}_0|, i \ne 0}^{L+2U} \alpha_i y_i \phi(\mathbf{x}_i) + \sum_{i=L+1}^{L+2U} (\alpha_i^* - \mu_i) y_i \phi(\mathbf{x}_i) \right), \tag{10}$$

and the variable b corresponds to the dual variable of the equality constraint. The form of the weight we obtained is similar to that in [2]. We can also define the corresponding *support vectors*. They are those labeled data $\mathbf{x}_i$'s with non-zero α_i values and unlabeled data $\mathbf{x}_j$'s with non-zero $(\alpha_j + \alpha_j^* - \mu_j)$ values.

Hence, we obtain Algorithm 1 to solve the 3C-SVM algorithm. Recalling Theorem 1, we can know that, intuitively, the Algorithm 1 works in the following way: 1) first finding out those unlabeled data which are certainly outside the margin gap, removing them from the training set; 2) then training a $\mathcal{U}$-SVM model on the labeled data with the rest unlabeled data.

Moreover, the convergence of Algorithm 1 is guaranteed by the following theorem:

THEOREM 3. *The algorithm 1 converges in a finite number of iterations.*

Proof: First, we prove that the objective Q^κ decreases in each iteration. From the CCCP, we have

$$Q_{vex}(\boldsymbol{\vartheta}^{t+1}, \mathbf{d}) + \partial Q^\kappa_{cav}(\boldsymbol{\vartheta}^t) \cdot \boldsymbol{\vartheta}^{t+1} \leq Q_{vex}(\boldsymbol{\vartheta}^t, \mathbf{d}) + \partial Q^\kappa_{cav}(\boldsymbol{\vartheta}^t) \cdot \boldsymbol{\vartheta}^t \quad (11)$$

$$Q^\kappa_{cav}(\boldsymbol{\vartheta}^{t+1}) \leq Q^\kappa_{cav}(\boldsymbol{\vartheta}^t) + \partial Q^\kappa_{cav}(\boldsymbol{\vartheta}^t) \cdot (\boldsymbol{\vartheta}^{t+1} - \boldsymbol{\vartheta}^t), \quad (12)$$

where ∂Q^κ_{cav} defines the partial derivative of Q^κ_{cav} with respect to $\boldsymbol{\vartheta}$. Hence, summing (11) and (12) together, we get $Q^\kappa(\boldsymbol{\vartheta}^{t+1}, \mathbf{d}) \leq Q^\kappa(\boldsymbol{\vartheta}^t, \mathbf{d})$ for the same $\mathbf{d}$.

After rounding, the objective value Q^κ is $Q^\kappa(\boldsymbol{\vartheta}^{t+1}, \mathbf{d}^{t+1})$. It may be greater than $Q^\kappa(\boldsymbol{\vartheta}^t, \mathbf{d}^t)$. In order to avoid this case, we restore $\mathbf{d}^{t+1}$ to $\mathbf{d}^t$ and seek $\boldsymbol{\vartheta}^{t+1}$ again by minimizing Q^κ with fixed $\mathbf{d}$. This additional step guarantees to decrease the objective of Q^κ at each step.

Second, the variable $\boldsymbol{\mu}$ can only take a finite number of distinct values. The algorithm converges in several steps since Q^κ decreases in each iteration and the inequality (12) is strict unless $\boldsymbol{\mu}$ remains unchanged. ■

Algorithm 1 CCCP for 3C-SVMs

Initialization:
$t = 0$
Calculate $\boldsymbol{\vartheta}^0 = (\mathbf{w}^0, b^0)$ from a $\mathcal{U}$-SVM solution on the labeled/unlabeled data
Compute
$$\mu_i^0 = \begin{cases} r_i & \text{if } y_i f_{\boldsymbol{\vartheta}^0}(\mathbf{x}_i) < \kappa \text{ and } i \geq L+1 \\ 0 & \text{otherwise} \end{cases}$$
repeat
  $t \leftarrow t + 1$
  Solve the optimization in (9) to obtain $\boldsymbol{\vartheta}^t$
  Update $\mathbf{d}^t$ from (7)
  Update $\boldsymbol{\mu}^t$ from (8)
  while $Q^\kappa(\boldsymbol{\vartheta}^t, \mathbf{d}^t) > Q^\kappa(\boldsymbol{\vartheta}^{t-1}, \mathbf{d}^{t-1})$ **do**
    Restore $\mathbf{d}^t$ to $\mathbf{d}^{t-1}$
    Update $\boldsymbol{\mu}^{t-1}$ from (8) with $\boldsymbol{\vartheta}^t$
    Solve the optimization in (9) to obtain $\boldsymbol{\vartheta}^t$
    Update $\mathbf{d}^t$ from (7)
    Update $\boldsymbol{\mu}^t$ from (8)
  end while
until $|\boldsymbol{\mu}^{t+1} - \boldsymbol{\mu}^t| \leq \epsilon$

Remark Note that the local optimal issue of the 3C-SVM has been alleviated by its initialization and the additional step to avoid increasing the rounded objective function is not needed usually. Our observation from the experimental results shows that our 3C-SVM works well using current initialization and the rounded objective function, $Q^\kappa(\boldsymbol{\vartheta}^t, \mathbf{d}^t)$, actually decreases in each step; see empirical study in Section 5.

Complexity Analysis Algorithm 1 has to solve a sequence of QPs in (9). In practice, we find that the number of iteration steps is a constant, usually less than 10; see Figure 4. Thus, training a 3C-SVM is equivalent to solving a constant number of QP problems with $|\mathcal{L}_0| + L + 4U$ variables. Therefore, the 3C-SVM algorithm has a worst case complexity of $\mathcal{O}((|\mathcal{L}_0| + L + 4U)^3)$ [8, 19]. Possible tricks may be applied to speed up the 3C-SVM algorithm in a quadratic scale [6, 19]. Furthermore, by exploring the sparsity structure among the dual variables, we can reduce the number of variables to the number of non-zero variables. This can reduce the computation cost of 3C-SVM largely.

4.3 Balance Constraint

In the formulation of (3), we do not consider the balance constraint for the unlabeled data. Actually, balance constraint can be easily incorporated in our formulation.

There are two observations: 1) Data from $\mathcal{U}_\mathcal{L}$ need the balance constraint [25]; 2) Data from $\mathcal{U}_{\mathcal{L}_0}$ do not need the balance constraint. By Theorem 1, ideally, the decision values of $\mathcal{U}_{\mathcal{L}_0}$ data approach to zero. Hence, summarizing the decision values of all unlabeled data, we can obtain the same balance constraint as that used in [7],

$$\frac{1}{U}\sum_{t=L+1}^{L+U} f_{\boldsymbol{\vartheta}}(\mathbf{x}_t) = \frac{1}{L}\sum_{i=1}^{L} y_i. \quad (13)$$

This constraint can be easily included in the optimization of (6) and rewrite into kernel form in (9) similar to the trick in [7].

It is noted that the balance constraint in (13) is affected by the summation of y_i. A possible better setting for the balance constraint is $\frac{1}{U}\sum_{t=L+1}^{L+U} f_{\boldsymbol{\vartheta}}(\mathbf{x}_t) = c$, where c is a user-specified constant related to the portion of the number of the unlabeled data assigning to the positive class [5]. However, it again introduces another hyperparameter. Actually, our empirical evaluation finds that balance constraint is insensitive to the model performance. One reason may be that the $\mathcal{U}_0$ data has played the role of balance constrant in the model.

5. EXPERIMENTS

In this section, we evaluate our proposed 3C-SVM algorithm on both synthetic and real-world datasets and compare it with SVM, S^{3}VM [6], and $\mathcal{U}$-SVM [27]. Our 3C-SVM algorithm is implemented in Matlab 7.3 and the QP problem is solved by a general optimization toolbox, MOSEK[1]. In the experiments, we try to investigate the following questions: (1) What is the performance of 3C-SVM comparing with other three maximum-margin based algorithms? (2) What is the trade-off on the parameters D and ε on 3C-SVM? (3) What is the convergence of 3C-SVM?

Table 2: Description of data

Dataset	d	L	U	$\mathcal{U}_0$
Synthetic	50	20, 50 200, 500	500	Two designed cases
USPS	256	10	100, 1000	Except "5" and "8"
MNIST	784	10	100, 1000	Except "5" and "8"

5.1 Synthetic Datasets

The synthetic data is a 50-dimensional dataset. The ± 1-class are generated following the scheme of [22], where the means are $c_i^\pm = \pm 0.3$ for $i = 1, \ldots, 50$ and variance values are $\sigma^2_{1,2} = 0.08$ and $\sigma^2_{3,\ldots,50} = 10$. In this setting, we can generate two Gaussians with the Bayes risk being approximately 5%. Two kinds of $\mathcal{U}_0$ data similar to those in [22] are generated:

- For the first kind, it is a zero mean with $\sigma^2_{1,2} = 0.1$ and $\sigma^2_{3,\ldots,50} = 10$. It contains a zero mean, where the optimal Bayesian decision boundary passes through it, but it contains larger variances on the first two dimensions of the data than those of the ± 1-class data.

[1] http://www.mosek.com

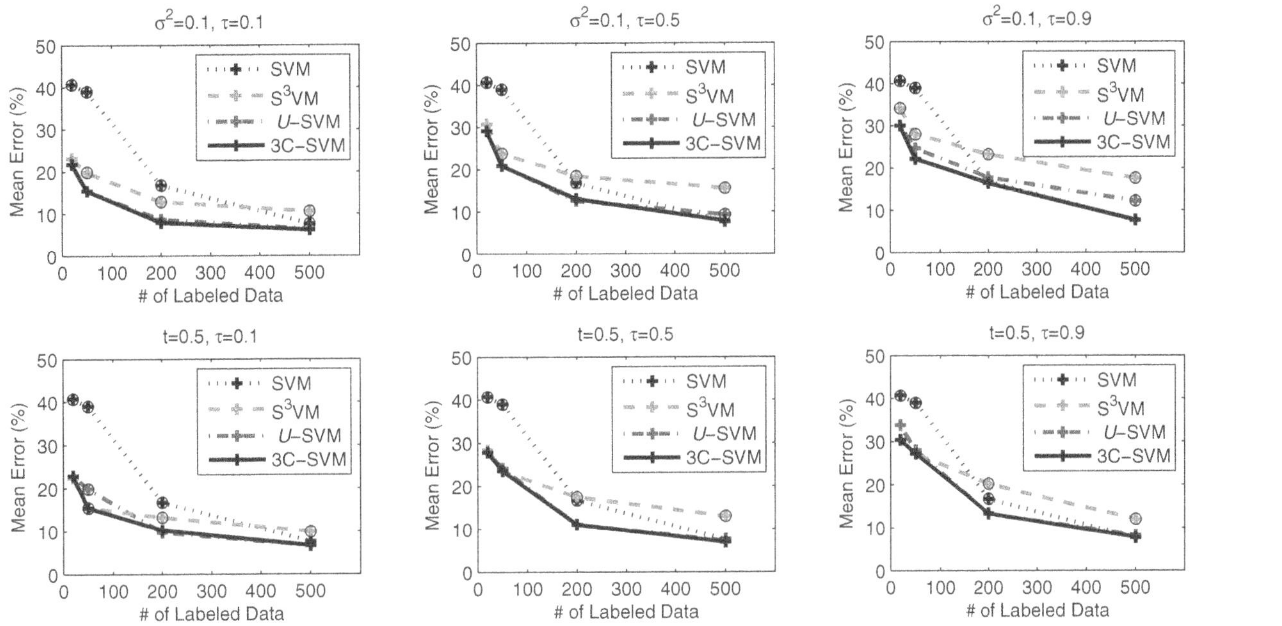

Figure 3: The performance of four algorithms on toy datasets with different combinations of mixed unlabeled data. The results of 3C-SVMs outperform the corresponding models with 95% significant level on paired t-test are marked by circles.

- For the second kind, the variance values are the same as the ± 1-class data, but the mean is $\frac{t}{2} \cdot (\mathbf{c}^+ - \mathbf{c}^-)$ $(t = 0.5)$, shifted a little bit from the origin, where the optimal Bayesian classifier passes through.

It is noted that the optimal decision boundary is a linear classifier for the synthetic datasets. Hence, we employ the linear kernel in fitting the data.

As reported in Table 2, we test the number of labeled data from $\{20, 50, 200, 500\}$ and vary the proportion of the mixed unlabeled data by $(\tau U, (1-\tau)U)$, where τU data are randomly chosen from ± 1-class and $(1-\tau)U$ data are randomly chosen from $\mathcal{U}_0$ data. τ is tested in $\{0.1, 0.5, 0.9\}$. We then evaluate the performance of the model on a separated test data with 500 data samples.

In the comparison, there are different parameters for different models need to be tuned. They include:

- the soft-margin hyperparameter C for SVM [24];
- the soft-margin hyperparameter, C, the trade-off constant for the loss of unlabeled data, $C_{\mathcal{U}}$, and the parameter for the ε-insensitive loss function, ε, in $\mathcal{U}$-SVM [22, 27];
- the soft-margin hyperparameter, C, the trade-off constant for the loss of unlabeled data $C_{\mathcal{U}}$, and the approximate parameter for ramp loss, κ, in S^{3}VM.

A problem of 3C-SVM is that its parameters are large and they will affect the model performance. These parameters in 3C-SVM not only include C in SVM, $C_{\mathcal{U}}$ in $\mathcal{U}$-SVM and S^{3}VM, ε in $\mathcal{U}$-SVM and κ in S^{3}VM, but also include the parameter D. It is terrible to tune all the parameters, e.g., by cross validation, together. To resolve this problem, we adopt a simple way to tune them. More specifically, we first tune the parameters in SVM, $\mathcal{U}$-SVM, and S^{3}VM on the test set, individually. Next, we set the parameters of our 3C-SVM based on the obtained optimal parameters from other models. That is, λ is set to $\frac{1}{C}$, $r_i = 1$ for labeled data and $r_i = \frac{C_{\mathcal{U}}}{C}$ for unlabeled data, where C and $C_{\mathcal{U}}$ are the optimal one corresponds to $\mathcal{U}$-SVM since this set of parameters obtains better performance than that of S^{3}VM. The parameters ε and κ are set the same as the optimal value from the $\mathcal{U}$-SVM and S^{3}VM, respectively. D is set to 2 for simplicity since the results have shown that our 3C-SVM can achieve very good performance.

Figure 3 reports the average performance (10 runs) of all four algorithms in the above all cases. It is shown that 3C-SVMs consistently attain the best results. $\mathcal{U}$-SVM achieves similar performance as 3C-SVM when the number of $\mathcal{U}_0$ data is large. However, its performance decreases when the number of $\mathcal{U}_0$ data decreases and cannot beat SVM when the size of the labeled training data is 500. Similar trend is obtained for S^{3}VM. On the contrary, our 3C-SVMs keep nearly the same accuracies and outperform $\mathcal{U}$-SVM and S^{3}VM when the number of labeled training data is large.

Convergence Study. We also study the convergence of 3C-SVM on the synthetic dataset with different settings ($L = 20/200$, $U = 500$). Figure 4 shows the one trial result on the objective function value and test errors at each CCCP iteration. The figures show that the 3C-SVM algorithm decreases the objective function value and the test error rates decrease correspondingly at each iteration. At the same time, 3C-SVM tends to converge in only a few iterations, less than 10.

5.2 Results on Real-World Handwritten Digit Datasets

The USPS dataset and the MNIST dataset are two popular benchmark handwritten digit datasets which have been used in literature to validate the corresponding classification models [6, 19]. As reported in Table 2, each image in USPS was normalized and centered with the size of 16×16, which forms 256-dimensional data (see examples in Figure 1(a)). This dataset contains 9,298 grayscale handwritten digit images, 7,291 of which are used as the training set, while the remaining 2,007 are used as the test set. The MNIST dataset consists of a training set of 60,000 digits and a test

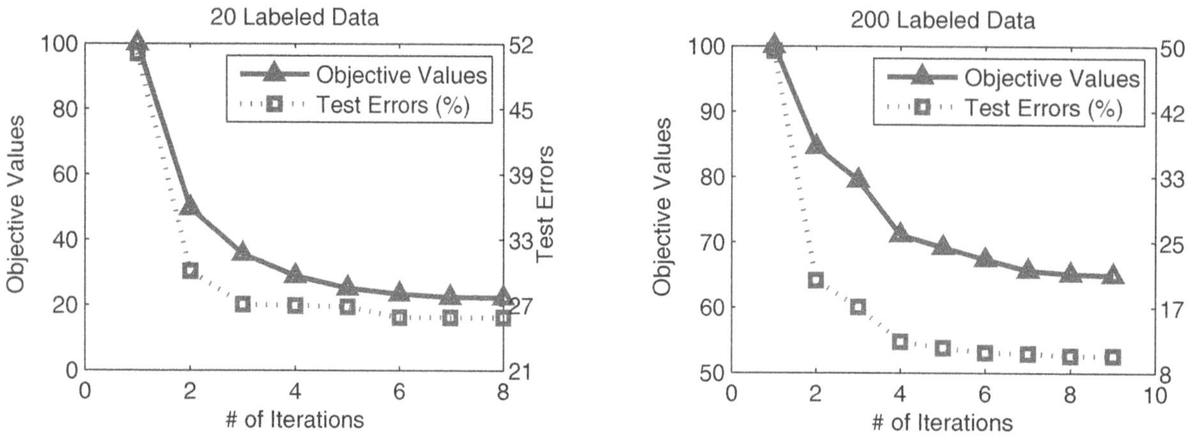

Figure 4: One trial result on the value of the objective function and test error during the CCCP iterations of training 3C-SVM on synthetic dataset with different number of labeled data. 3C-SVM converges only by a few iterations, less than 10.

set of 10,000 digits (see examples in Figure 1(b)). The digits are grayscale handwritten images normalized and centered in 28×28, which forms 784-dimensional data. We have normalized each pixel value in an image to the range of -1 and 1.

Similar to the setup in [22, 27], we employ digits "5" and "8" to construct the ± 1-class data, but differently, we utilize all other digits as 0-class. In the evaluation, we test the number of labeled data in 10 and the number of unlabeled data is 100 and 1000, while the proportion of the mixed unlabeled data is set as $(\tau U, (1-\tau)U)$, where where τU data are randomly chosen from digits "5" and "8" and $(1-\tau)U$ data are randomly chosen from other digits. τ is tested in $\{0.1, 0.5, 0.9\}$. The performance of the models is evaluated on the test set of digits "5" and "8".

Here, since the data are linearly nonseparable in the original feature space [19], we employ the RBF kernel on all the models. That is, $K(\mathbf{x}, \mathbf{y}) = \exp(-\gamma\|\mathbf{x} - \mathbf{y}\|^2)$, is adopted as the kernel, where γ is the width of the RBF kernel. Since we also need to tune an additional parameter, this makes it more difficult in tuning the parameters for 3C-SVM, and for other three models. Similar to the procedure in [5], we seek the optimal parameters on a separate validation set by maximizing the performance on the test set. More specifically, the parameters are sought as follows:

- For SVM, C is selected from $\{10^{-1}, 1, 10, 10^2, 10^3\}$. The width of the RBF kernel is set to $\gamma = \delta \times \frac{1}{d}$ as [19], where d is the number of data dimension, i.e., 256 for USPS and 784 for MNIST. δ is selected from $\{\frac{1}{32}, \frac{1}{16}, \frac{1}{8}, \frac{1}{4}, \frac{1}{2}, 1, 2, 4, 8\}$.
- For $\mathcal{U}$-SVM, C is tested in the same range of SVM and $C_{\mathcal{U}}$ is tested from $\{10^{-1}, 1, 10, 10^2\}$, where we find that when $C_{\mathcal{U}}$ is greater than 100, the model performance cannot be increased. The kernel parameter, γ, is tested as the same cases of SVM. ε is test in $\{0.01, 0.1, 0.2, 0.5, 0.8, 1\}$.
- For S^3VM, C, $C_{\mathcal{U}}$, and γ are tested the same as $\mathcal{U}$-SVM. κ is tested in $\{0.01, 0.1, 0.2, 0.5\}$.
- For 3C-SVM, we first fix ε as the optimal one obtained from $\mathcal{U}$-SVM and κ as the optimal one obtained from S^3VM. We then set $D = 2$ and test 3C-SVM by the optimal parameters from $\mathcal{U}$-SVM and by those from S^3VM. Our objective is to see which set of parameters can attain better performance. The empirical study indicates that adopting the parameters C, $C_{\mathcal{U}}$, and γ from $\mathcal{U}$-SVM, our 3C-SVM can achieve better results. Hence, we employ C, $C_{\mathcal{U}}$, and γ, which corresponds to the optimal ones from $\mathcal{U}$-SVM, in the experiment. In addition, we find that κ does not affect the result too much when it is around 0.1. So we do not specifically tune it in the experiment. After that, we tune ε in the same cases of $\mathcal{U}$-SVM and D in $\{1, 2, 10\}$ simultaneously.

Table 3 reports the average (10 runs) accuracies of four algorithms on the two handwritten digit datasets. 3C-SVM consistently attains better results in all cases. By examining the details of the results, we have the following observations:

- For SVM, since the model is optimized on the test datasets, it achieves satisfactory results. In practical, when we has limited number of labeled data, it is usually difficult to obtain good performance without the help of unlabeled data.
- For S^3VM, it is interesting to find that it is less sensitive to the proportion of the $\mathcal{U}_{\mathcal{L}}$ data and $\mathcal{U}_0$ data. For USPS, the performance of S^3VM does not change when the number of unlabeled data increases from 100 to 1000; while for MNIST, the performance of S^3VM is even worse in the case of $U = 1000$ than the case of $U = 100$. This indicates that the mixed unlabeled data actually hurts S^3VM.
- For $\mathcal{U}$-SVM, the performance decreases slightly as the number of $\mathcal{U}_0$ data decreases. This indicates that the $\mathcal{U}_0$ data actually plays the effect on helping $\mathcal{U}$-SVM. Similar to S^3VM on MNIST, $\mathcal{U}$-SVM also achieves worst performance when the number of unlabeled data increases in the USPS dataset. The decay may be due to the effect of the $\mathcal{U}_{\mathcal{L}}$ data.
- For 3C-SVM, it attains the best results and outperforms SVM for all cases, S^3VM for five cases on USPS and two cases on MNIST, and totally seven cases on $\mathcal{U}$-SVM for both datasets. It is observed that the performance of 3C-SVM also decreases slightly as the number of $\mathcal{U}_0$ data decreases. The reason lies that we employ the same regularization parameters of $\mathcal{U}$-SVM in the experiment.

5.3 Sensitivity Analysis

In the experiment, we also conduct sensitivity analysis on two parameters, ε and D, in 3C-SVM. The analysis of the hyperparameter, e.g., C, $C_{\mathcal{U}}$, γ, can be referred to [6, 19]. For κ, since it is insensitive when it is about 0.1, we do not study its effect in this section.

In the test, we change ε in $\{0, 0.01, 0.1, 0.2, 0.5, 0.8, 1.0\}$ and D in $\{1, 2, 10\}$ and test on the case of balance mixed unlabeled

Table 3: The average (10 runs) accuracies (%) of SVMs, S^{3}VMs, $\mathcal{U}$-SVMs, and 3C-SVMs on the USPS and the MNIST ("5" vs "8") datasets for different combinations of mixed unlabeled data. The p-values of paired t-test on 3C-SVMs against other algorithms are given in brackets. Significant improvement with 95% confidence level and the best accuracy are in bold.

Dataset	Setting	Algorithm	$\tau = 0.1$	$\tau = 0.5$	$\tau = 0.9$
USPS	$L = 10$ $U = 100$	SVM	87.1±1.7 (**0.5**)	87.1±1.7 (**1.2**)	87.1±1.7 (**0.8**)
		S^{3}VM	87.6±4.2 (**4.4**)	87.6±4.2 (5.1)	87.6±4.2 (**5.0**)
		$\mathcal{U}$-SVM	88.9±3.1 (17.1)	**88.8**±3.1 (25.1)	88.6±3.1 (10.2)
		3C-SVM	**89.2**±2.6	**88.8**±3.1	**88.8**±3.2
USPS	$L = 10$ $U = 1000$	SVM	87.1±1.7 (**0.4**)	87.1±1.7 (**0.9**)	87.1±1.7 (**0.9**)
		S^{3}VM	87.6±4.2 (**4.8**)	87.6±4.2 (**4.2**)	87.6±4.2 (**4.1**)
		$\mathcal{U}$-SVM	88.9±2.7 (6.7)	88.0±3.2 (**4.9**)	87.2±3.3 (**3.2**)
		3C-SVM	**89.3**±2.7	**89.1**±2.9	**89.1**±3.0
MNIST	$L = 10$ $U = 100$	SVM	71.0±9.3 (**0.5**)	71.0±9.3 (**0.8**)	71.0±9.3 (**0.9**)
		S^{3}VM	76.3±8.0 (17.8)	76.3±8.0 (22.1)	76.3±8.0 (30.2)
		$\mathcal{U}$-SVM	74.0±8.6 (**3.7**)	73.4±8.2 (**2.9**)	73.2±8.2 (**2.2**)
		3C-SVM	**76.8**±8.4	**76.7**±8.0	**76.3**±7.6
MNIST	$L = 10$ $U = 1000$	SVM	71.0±9.3 (**0.1**)	71.0±9.3 (**0.2**)	71.0±9.3 (**0.6**)
		S^{3}VM	75.9±7.9 (**4.8**)	75.9±7.9 (7.8)	75.9±7.9 (**0.6**)
		$\mathcal{U}$-SVM	74.0±8.4 (**1.7**)	73.9±8.1 (**1.5**)	73.3±7.9 (9.2)
		3C-SVM	**77.0**±7.4	**76.9**±7.9	**76.5**±8.0

data (i.e., $\tau = 0.5$). Figure 5 shows the changing trend with ε and D, respectively. It should be noted that the best results in Figure 5 also refer to the results in fifth column in Table 3. By examining these results, we have the following observations:

- 3C-SVM achieves the best performance on USPS when $\varepsilon = 1.0$, $D = 2$ and on MNIST when $\varepsilon = 0.5$, $D = 2$, respectively.
- For USPS dataset, when ε increases, the performance of 3C-SVM increases gradually and it achieves the best result when $\varepsilon = 1.0$, i.e., taking all unlabeled data as irrelevant data. For MNIST data, the performance increases gradually until $\varepsilon = 0.5$, then it decreases gradually.
- In terms of the effect of D, for both datasets, the performance of 3C-SVM increases gradually as D increases and decreases dramatically when $D = 10$. The best results are obtained when $D = 2$ for both datasets.

6. CONCLUSION

In this paper, we have proposed a novel maximum margin semi-supervised classifier, named the *tri-class support vector machine*, to learn from mixed unlabeled data. More specifically, we introduce a new min loss function to distinguish the mixed unlabeled data into relevant and irrelevant data based on which error occurred is smaller when assigning the data to the associated class. The min loss function can therefore achieve the maximum entropy principle and force the irrelevant data close to the decision boundary. In generalization, 3C-SVM includes several popular maximum margin classifiers, such as SVMs, S^{3}VMs, and $\mathcal{U}$-SVMs, as its special cases. Furthermore, we provide detailed theoretical analysis to show the role of irrelevant data and why the model works. Moreover, in implementation, we transform 3C-SVM from an integer programming problem to a sequence of QP problems. The approximation by the concave-convex procedure has speeded up the model largely and finally yielded the same worst case time complexity as that of S^{3}VMs.

This work opens several interesting research issues. One worthy direction is to further speed up the model by warm-starting or by exploiting the sparsity structure of the solution. The other direction is to design an efficient way to tune the model parameters or to design a scheme to automatically learn the model parameters. We will also consider to extend the model to solve multi-class classification tasks and verify its performance.

Acknowledgment

This work is supported by two grants from the Research Grants Council of the Hong Kong SAR, China (Project No. CUHK 413210 and Project No. CUHK 415410) and a grant supported by a research funding from Google Focused Grant Project "Mobile 2014".

7. REFERENCES

[1] R. K. Ando and T. Zhang. A framework for learning predictive structures from multiple tasks and unlabeled data. *Journal of Machine Learning Research*, 6:1817–1853, 2005.

[2] M. Belkin, P. Niyogi, and V. Sindhwani. Manifold regularization: A geometric framework for learning from labeled and unlabeled examples. *Journal of Machine Learning Research*, 7:2399–2434, 2006.

[3] K. P. Bennett and A. Demiriz. Semi-supervised support vector machines. In *Advances in Neural Information Processing Systems (NIPS)*, pages 1831–1850, 1998.

[4] T. D. Bie and N. Cristianini. Convex methods for transduction. In *Advances in Neural Information Processing Systems 16*, pages 73–80. MIT Press, 2003.

[5] O. Chapelle, B. Schölkopf, and A. Zien, editors. *Semi-Supervised Learning*. MIT Press, Cambridge, MA, 2006.

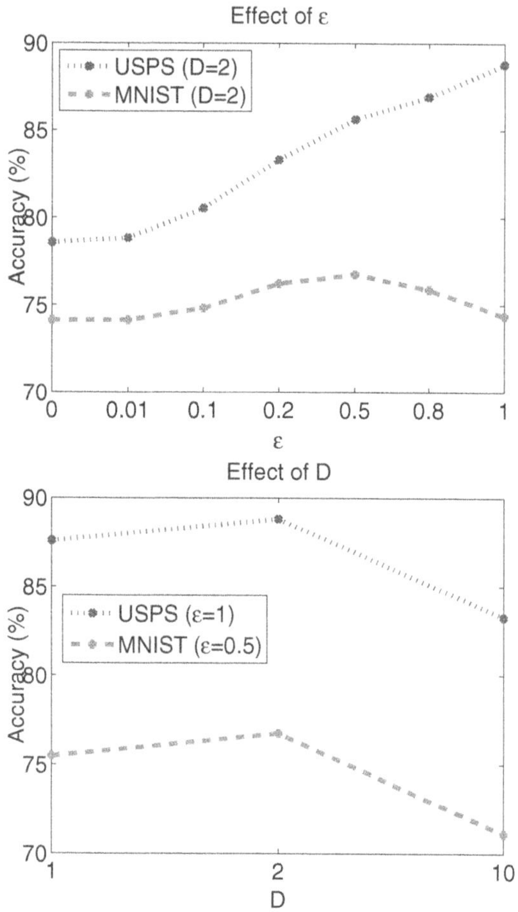

Figure 5: Effect on ε and D for two handwritten digit datasets. The best results of 3C-SVM are obtained when $\varepsilon = 1.0$, $D = 2$ for USPS and when $\varepsilon = 0.5$, $D = 2$ for MNIST, respectively.

[6] R. Collobert, F. H. Sinz, J. Weston, and L. Bottou. Large scale transductive svms. *Journal of Machine Learning Research*, 7:1687–1712, 2006.

[7] R. Collobert, F. H. Sinz, J. Weston, and L. Bottou. Trading convexity for scalability. In *ICML*, pages 201–208, 2006.

[8] D. Goldfarb and S. Liu. An $o(n^3 l)$ primal interior point algorithm for convex quadratic programming. *Math. Program.*, 49(3):325–340, 1991.

[9] D. W. Hosmer and S. Lemeshow. *Applied logistic regression*. Wiley-Interscience Publication, 2nd edition, 2000.

[10] K. Huang, Z. Xu, I. King, and M. R. Lyu. Semi-supervised learning from general unlabeled data. In *the IEEE International Conference on Data Mining, ICDM 2008*, pages 273–282, 2008.

[11] T. Joachims. Transductive inference for text classification using support vector machines. In *International Conference on Machine Learning (ICML)*, pages 200–209, Bled, Slowenien, 1999.

[12] N. D. Lawrence and M. I. Jordan. Semi-supervised learning via gaussian processes. In L. K. Saul, Y. Weiss, and L. Bottou, editors, *Advances in Neural Information Processing Systems 17*, pages 753–760, Cambridge, MA, 2005. MIT Press.

[13] Y.-F. Li, J. T. Kwok, and Z.-H. Zhou. Cost-sensitive semi-supervised support vector machine. In *AAAI*, pages 500–505, 2010.

[14] Y.-F. Li and Z.-H. Zhou. S4vm: Safe semi-supervised support vector machine, 2010. arXiv:1005.1545.

[15] M. Mojdeh and G. V. Cormack. Semi-supervised spam filtering: does it work? In *SIGIR*, pages 745–746, 2008.

[16] K. Nigam, A. McCallum, S. Thrun, and T. M. Mitchell. Text classification from labeled and unlabeled documents using em. *Machine Learning*, 39(2/3):103–134, 2000.

[17] S. J. Pan and Q. Yang. A survey on transfer learning. *IEEE Trans. Knowl. Data Eng.*, 22(10):1345–1359, 2010.

[18] J. C. Platt. Probabilistic outputs for support vector machines and comparisons to regularized likelihood methods. In *Advances in Large Margin Classifiers*, pages 61–74. MIT Press, 1999.

[19] B. Schölkopf and A. Smola. *Learning with Kernels*. MIT Press, Cambridge, MA, 2002.

[20] B. Settles. Active learning literature survey. Technical Report 1648, Computer Sciences, University of Wisconsin-Madison, 2010.

[21] A. Singh, R. D. Nowak, and X. Zhu. Unlabeled data: Now it helps, now it doesn't. In *NIPS*, pages 1513–1520, 2008.

[22] F. H. Sinz, O. Chapelle, A. Agarwal, and B. Schölkopf. An analysis of inference with the universum. In *NIPS*, pages 1369–1376, 2008.

[23] A. J. Smola, S. V. N. Vishwanathan, and T. Hofmann. Kernel methods for missing variables. In *Proceedings of the tenth International Workshop on Artificial Intelligence and Statistics*, 2005.

[24] V. Vapnik. *The Nature of Statistical Learning Theory*. Springer, New York, 2nd edition, 1999.

[25] V. Vapnik and S. Kotz. *Estimation of Dependences Based on Empirical Data: Empirical Inference Science (Information Science and Statistics)*. Springer-Verlag New York, Inc., Secaucus, NJ, USA, 2nd edition, 2006.

[26] J. Wang, X. Shen, and W. Pan. On efficient large margin semisupervised learning: Method and theory. *Journal of the Royal Statistical Society, Series B*, 10(Mar):719–742, 2009.

[27] J. Weston, R. Collobert, F. H. Sinz, L. Bottou, and V. Vapnik. Inference with the universum. In *ICML*, pages 1009–1016, 2006.

[28] L. A. Wolsey. *Integer programming*. Wiley-Interscience, 1 edition, September 1998.

[29] A. L. Yuille and A. Rangarajan. The concave-convex procedure. *Neural Computation*, 15(4):915–936, 2003.

[30] D. Zhang, J. Wang, F. Wang, and C. Zhang. Semi-supervised classification with universum. In *SDM*, pages 323–333, 2008.

[31] Z.-H. Zhou and M. Li. Semi-supervised learning by disagreement. *Knowl. Inf. Syst.*, 24(3):415–439, 2010.

[32] Z.-H. Zhou, D.-C. Zhan, and Q. Yang. Semi-supervised learning with very few labeled training examples. In *AAAI*, pages 675–680, 2007.

[33] X. Zhu. Semi-supervised learning literature survey. Technical Report 1530, Department of Computer Sciences, University of Wisconsin, Madison, 2005.

[34] X. Zhu, Z. Ghahramani, and J. D. Lafferty. Semi-supervised learning using gaussian fields and harmonic functions. In *ICML*, pages 912–919, 2003.

[35] X. Zhu and A. B. Goldberg. *Introduction to Semi-Supervised Learning*. Morgan & Claypool, 2009.

Toward Interactive Training and Evaluation

Gregory Druck
University of Massachusetts Amherst
gdruck@cs.umass.edu

Andrew McCallum
University of Massachusetts Amherst
mccallum@cs.umass.edu

ABSTRACT

Machine learning often relies on costly labeled data, and this impedes its application to new classification and information extraction problems. This has motivated the development of methods for leveraging abundant prior knowledge about these problems, including methods for lightly supervised learning using model expectation constraints. Building on this work, we envision an interactive training paradigm in which practitioners perform evaluation, analyze errors, and provide and refine expectation constraints in a closed loop. In this paper, we focus on several key subproblems in this paradigm that can be cast as selecting a representative sample of the unlabeled data for the practitioner to inspect. To address these problems, we propose stratified sampling methods that use model expectations as a proxy for latent output variables. In classification and sequence labeling experiments, these sampling strategies reduce accuracy evaluation effort by as much as 53%, provide more reliable estimates of F_1 for rare labels, and aid in the specification and refinement of constraints.

Categories and Subject Descriptors

I.2.6 [**Artificial Intelligence**]: Learning

General Terms

Algorithm, Experimentation, Measurement, Performance

Keywords

interactive training, stratified sampling, evaluation, lightly supervised learning

1. INTRODUCTION

Machine learning often relies on costly labeled data, and this impedes its application to new classification and information extraction problems. However, even in the absence of labeled data we typically have a wealth of prior knowledge about these problems. For example, when extracting information from research papers, we know that the word *ACM* should usually be part of a *journal* or a *conference*. Though this knowledge does not yield labeled data, it does provide a desirable aggregate property of predictions for unlabeled data. Several methods incorporate such properties into learning by encoding them as constraints on the expectations of a probabilistic model [6, 9, 15, 16].

Building on this work, we envision an interactive training paradigm in which users perform evaluation, analyze errors, and specify and refine supervision in a closed loop. In contrast to active learning [21], in this paradigm the system aids the user in understanding what the model is predicting, and the user leverages this insight to direct the learning process. There are at least two benefits to building this paradigm around methods for learning with expectation constraints. First, expectation constraints provide a flexible and powerful language for users to give feedback to the system. Second, interactive analysis may enable users to specify more accurate and useful constraints than would be possible otherwise.

In this paper, we focus on several key subproblems in our interactive training paradigm that can be cast as selecting a representative sample of the unlabeled data for the user to inspect. Specifically, we develop methods to assist the user in performing evaluation at multiple levels of granularity, and in specifying and refining constraints. Random sampling can be applied to these problems, but the resulting sample may not be representative. Instead, we develop sampling strategies based on stratified sampling [24], a method that has a long history in statistics [17]. In stratified sampling, points are grouped into strata, and random sampling is performed within each stratum. If the statistic of interest varies across the strata, then stratified sampling yields a lower variance estimator than random sampling. To perform stratification, we use model expectations as a proxy for latent output variables. In classification and sequence labeling experiments, these sampling strategies reduce accuracy evaluation effort by as much as 53%, provide more reliable estimates of F_1 for rare labels, and aid in the specification and refinement of constraints.

2. RELATED WORK

In contrast to active learning [21], in which the system queries the user, our interactive training paradigm allows the user to provide supervision based on error analysis, which may enable more efficient training. Our interactive paradigm and active learning with expectation constraints [7, 15] could also be combined, allowing a mixture of user-initiated and system-initiated interactions.

CIKM'11, October 24–28, 2011, Glasgow, Scotland, UK.

There is growing interest in interaction in machine learning, including some work in interactive training and model selection. Huang and Mitchell [10] develop methods for interactive clustering, including allowing the user to provide features that indicate cluster membership, assign instances to clusters, or delete clusters. Roth and Small [18] develop *interactive feature space construction*, in which an annotator uses domain knowledge to iteratively modify model features. Culotta et al. [3] develop a method for interactively correcting errors of Conditional Random Fields (CRFs) [13] using constrained inference. Settles [22] develops an interface for interactive training in which users can label both instances and features. Kumar et al. [12] argue for an interactive classification framework in which annotation cost and both current and future utility are jointly optimized. In contrast, the proposed paradigm is based on learning with expectation constraints[1], and assists the user in evaluation, analysis, and the specification and refinement of constraints.

Note that interactive machine learning often refers to learning directly from interactions with the world, for example based on rewards received for taking context-dependent actions [14]. Though we are interested in exploring this direction in future work, in this paper learning is user-directed.

This paper focuses on developing sampling methods for various subproblems in interactive training. These methods are based on stratified sampling, discussed in Section 4.1, and use model expectations as a proxy for latent output variables. Stratified sampling using model predictions has also been applied to address specific evaluation problems in information retrieval [25]. More closely related, Bennett and Carvalho [1] develop a confidence-based stratified sampling method for estimating classifier accuracy. In contrast, we apply stratified sampling to rapid evaluation of classifiers and structured models trained using expectation constraints. We propose an extension to the method of Bennett and Carvalho [1] that reduces error in this setting in Section 5.1. Additionally, we propose a general approach that is also applicable to other problems in interactive training. Alternatives to stratified sampling include methods based on importance sampling [19, 20]. We plan to consider these approaches in future work.

3. BACKGROUND

In this paper we train discriminative probabilistic models of output variables $\mathbf{y}$ conditioned on observed input variables $\mathbf{x}$. For classification tasks we use logistic regression models, also known as maximum entropy classifiers

$$p(y|\mathbf{x};\boldsymbol{\theta}) = \frac{1}{Z(\mathbf{x};\boldsymbol{\theta})} \exp\left(\boldsymbol{\theta}\cdot\mathbf{f}(\mathbf{x},y)\right),$$

where $\boldsymbol{\theta}$ are parameters, $\mathbf{f}$ are model feature functions, and $Z(\mathbf{x};\boldsymbol{\theta}) = \sum_y \exp\left(\boldsymbol{\theta}\cdot\mathbf{f}(\mathbf{x},y)\right)$ is the partition function, which ensures that $\sum_y p(y|\mathbf{x};\boldsymbol{\theta}) = 1$.

For sequence labeling tasks, we use first-order linear chain Conditional Random Fields (CRFs) [13]

$$p(\mathbf{y}|\mathbf{x};\boldsymbol{\theta}) = \frac{1}{Z(\mathbf{x};\boldsymbol{\theta})} \exp\Big(\sum_{t=1}^{T}\boldsymbol{\theta}\cdot\mathbf{f}(\mathbf{x},y_{t-1},y_t)\Big),$$

where $Z(\mathbf{x};\boldsymbol{\theta}) = \sum_{\mathbf{y}} \exp\left(\sum_{t=1}^{T}\boldsymbol{\theta}\cdot\mathbf{f}(\mathbf{x},y_{t-1},y_t)\right)$ is the partition function and T is the sequence length. Inference is performed using the Viterbi and Forward-Backward algorithms. For more detail the reader is referred to [23].

Parameters $\boldsymbol{\theta}$ can be estimated to maximize likelihood if labeled data is available. However, we typically have an abundance of knowledge about the tasks we would like to solve that does not come in the form of labeled instances. For example, when extracting information from research papers, we know that the word *ACM* should usually be part of a *journal* or a *conference*. Recently methods have been developed for estimating parameters with such knowledge and unlabeled data [6, 9, 15, 16]. Formally, these methods encode knowledge as preferences about the values of model expectations of constraint features $\boldsymbol{\phi}(\mathbf{x},\mathbf{y})$. Given unlabeled data $\mathcal{D} = \{\mathbf{x}^1,\ldots,\mathbf{x}^N\}$, the model expectation of $\boldsymbol{\phi}$ is

$$\sum_{j=1}^{N} \mathrm{E}_{p(\mathbf{y}|\mathbf{x}^j;\theta)}[\boldsymbol{\phi}(\mathbf{x}^j,\mathbf{y})] = \sum_{j=1}^{N}\sum_{\mathbf{y}} p(\mathbf{y}|\mathbf{x}^j;\theta)\boldsymbol{\phi}(\mathbf{x}^j,\mathbf{y}).$$

In this paper we use the Generalized Expectation (GE) framework, though the methods we develop are also applicable to other frameworks such as Posterior Regularization [9]. GE expresses preferences with a score function S that evaluates model expectations of constraint features. A higher score signifies that the model complies with our preferences more closely. To estimate parameters, we solve

$$\hat{\boldsymbol{\theta}} = \operatorname*{argmax}_{\boldsymbol{\theta}}\ \mathrm{S}\Big(\sum_{j=1}^{N} \mathrm{E}_{p(\mathbf{y}|\mathbf{x}^j;\theta)}[\boldsymbol{\phi}(\mathbf{x}^j,\mathbf{y})]\Big) + \log p(\boldsymbol{\theta}).$$

GE has been applied to both logistic regression models [6] and linear chain CRFs [7, 16][2]. GE provides a flexible and powerful framework for users to give feedback to the system during interactive training. Understanding the details of GE is not critical to understanding this paper, so for additional detail the reader is referred to the aforementioned papers.

As in previous work [6, 7, 16], in this paper we predominantly use *input feature label distribution* constraints. For text classification tasks, these constraints specify a target distribution over labels for documents that contain a particular word. For sequence labeling tasks, these constraints specify a target distribution over labels for tokens for which a particular input feature fires. The constraint features $\boldsymbol{\phi}$ are designed so that their expectations are probability distributions, and we use the negative KL divergence from some target distribution $\tilde{\boldsymbol{\phi}}$ as the score function S. These constraints can be obtained by having the user "label" input features, and converting these labels to target distributions using simple heuristics [6, 7, 16]. For example, a user could label *puck* as *hockey*, or *ACM* as *journal* and *conference*.

3.1 Tasks and Data Sets

We conduct text classification and sequence labeling experiments. For classification, the data sets are binary subsets of the *20 Newsgroups* data set used in a previous application of GE to logistic regression [6]. The model features $\mathbf{f}(\mathbf{x},y)$ are word counts, after removing stopwords. To make the experiments in this paper more realistic, we use the input feature label distribution constraints that users provided in the experiments in [6]. We use models trained with these

[1]Settles [22] uses a naive Bayes based method rather than GE (Section 3), but we hypothesize that GE will provide higher accuracy for complex, structured problems, and in settings where constraints have precise target expectations.

[2]Note that an $O(|\mathcal{Y}|^2)$ (rather than $O(|\mathcal{Y}|^3)$ [16]) algorithm has been developed for GE training of linear chain CRFs [5].

constraints as starting points for performing interactive evaluation, error analysis, and refinement. This simulates a scenario in which a user specifies constraints to train an initial model, and then improves the model interactively.

We also conduct experiments with the *Cora* citation extraction data set. The task is to extract 13 BibTex-like fields such as *title* and *journal* from research paper citations. We use a standard set of word, lexicon, and regular expression features, as well as context features in a window of ±3 tokens [7]. We again use input feature label distribution constraints that were provided by users in previous work [7].

4. SELECTING REPRESENTATIVE SAMPLES

In this paper we aim to develop methods to assist the user in evaluation, error analysis, and the specification and refinement of constraints. We cast these problems as instances of the following more general problem: selecting a sample of the data for the user to inspect. In this section we summarize our *stratified sampling* approach to this problem.

4.1 Stratified Sampling

We first review *stratified sampling* [24], a sampling method we use pervasively in this paper. We assume an iid unlabeled dataset $\mathcal{D} = \{\mathbf{x}^1, \ldots, \mathbf{x}^N\}$. We aim to compute the mean of a per-instance function $r(\mathbf{x}^j, \mathbf{y}^j)$ that considers both the input variables and the true values of the latent output variables. To simplify notation in this section we define $r^j = r(\mathbf{x}^j, \mathbf{y}^j)$. The true mean is $\bar{r}^* = \frac{1}{N}\sum_{j=1}^N r^j$. Because the output variables $\mathbf{y}^j$ are latent, evaluating r is costly. Rather than evaluating r for each instance, we choose a sample S of size n and use it to estimate the mean of r.

The most basic strategy is *random sampling*, in which n instances are selected uniformly at random from $\mathcal{D}$. The estimate of the population mean is the sample mean $\hat{\bar{r}}_{rs} = \frac{1}{n}\sum_{j=1}^n r^j$. This estimator is unbiased, meaning that the expected value of $\hat{\bar{r}}_{rs}$ over all possible samples of size n is $\bar{r}^*$. However, when the sample size n is small, $\hat{\bar{r}}_{rs}$ has high variance. With replacement[3], the estimated variance of $\hat{\bar{r}}_{rs}$ is $\hat{V}ar(\hat{\bar{r}}_{rs}) = \frac{S^2}{n}$, where S^2 is the sample variance.

Stratified sampling has a long history in statistics [17]. In stratified sampling, instances are partitioned into m strata $\{\mathcal{D}_{s1}, \ldots, \mathcal{D}_{sm}\}$, where each $x^j \in \mathcal{D}$ appears in exactly one stratum. To obtain a complete sample of size n, for each stratum i, n_i instances are randomly sampled ($n = \sum_{i=1}^m n_i$). An estimate of the mean of r can be obtained using

$$\hat{\bar{r}}_{ss} = \sum_{i=1}^m \frac{N_i}{N}\frac{1}{n_i}\sum_{j=1}^{n_i} r_i^j = \sum_{i=1}^m W_i \hat{\bar{r}}_i,$$

where r_i^j is r for the jth instance in the ith stratum, $W_i = N_i/N$ is the *weight* of the ith stratum, and $\hat{\bar{r}}_i = \frac{1}{n_i}\sum_{j=1}^{n_i} r_i^j$ is the mean estimate for the ith stratum. This estimator is also unbiased. The estimated variance of $\hat{\bar{r}}_{ss}$ is

$$\hat{V}ar(\hat{\bar{r}}_{ss}) = \sum_{i=1}^m W_i^2 \hat{V}ar(\hat{\bar{r}}_i),$$

where $\hat{V}ar(\hat{\bar{r}}_i) = S_i^2/n_i$ is the estimated variance of $\hat{\bar{r}}_i$. A $1-\alpha$ confidence interval for $\hat{\bar{r}}_{ss}$ is $\hat{\bar{r}}_{ss} \pm z_{\alpha/2}\sqrt{\hat{V}ar(\hat{\bar{r}}_{ss})}$.

[3]Without replacement $\hat{V}ar(\hat{\bar{r}}_{rs}) = (1 - \frac{n}{N})\frac{S^2}{n}$.

For a given sample size n, we consider two methods for choosing the number of samples from each stratum. With *proportional allocation*, the sampling proportions are equal to the weights, $n_i/n = W_i$. It can be shown that the true variance of the proportional allocation estimator is lower than the true variance of the random sampling estimator: $Var(\hat{\bar{r}}_{ss}) \leq Var(\hat{\bar{r}}_{rs})$. The difference of the variances is

$$Var(\hat{\bar{r}}_{rs}) - Var(\hat{\bar{r}}_{ss}) = \frac{1}{n}\sum_{i=1}^m W_i(\bar{r}_i^* - \bar{r}^*)^2. \qquad (1)$$

Equation 1 has implications in stratification, as it shows that the variance reduction is larger when strata means $\bar{r}_i^*$ have high variance, or are very different from each other.

The second sample allocation method is *optimal allocation*. In optimal allocation, per-stratum sample sizes n_i are not proportional to the size of the stratum. Instead, the idea is to use more samples in strata where r has higher variance. Formally, suppose that the true standard deviations σ_i for each stratum are known. Optimal allocation assigns samples to each stratum using the following equation

$$n_i = n \times \frac{N_i \sigma_i}{\sum_{i'=1}^m N_{i'}\sigma_{i'}}.$$

Optimal allocation can outperform proportional allocation when the variance of r varies across different strata.

Because the r^j are latent, we must select proxy variables to stand in for them to perform stratified sampling. These proxy variables can be used for both stratification and estimating strata variances for optimal allocation.

4.2 Estimating Vector-Valued and Non-Linear Functions

In many applications of interest we need to estimate the means of several functions simultaneously, which we view as estimating the mean of a vector-valued function $\mathbf{r}$ instead of a scalar function r. Often a vector-valued function $\mathbf{r}$ is required because we are interested in estimating a *non-linear* function with the sample. A non-linear function is one that cannot be computed as the mean of a function on individual instances in the sample. For example, accuracy is the mean of a function that evaluates correctness on each instance, but F_1 is non-linear, as computing it requires the number of correct, predicted, and true instances in the entire sample. Vector-valued and non-linear functions have implications in stratification, sample allocation, and estimation.

Stratification & Sample Allocation: As described in Section 4.1, for scalar r strata should be selected so that stratum means $\bar{r}_i^*$ are much different than the population mean $\bar{r}^*$. In the vector-valued $\mathbf{r}$ case, stratification is less straightforward. Intuitively, the stratification should be helpful for estimating all elements of $\mathbf{r}$, but note that for some non-linear functions certain estimates r_i may be more important than others. We simply stratify so that a composite variable, correlated with $\mathbf{r}$, varies across strata. Alternative methods for future study include multi-way [2] and clustering-based stratification. We also perform optimal allocation using the estimated standard deviation of a composite variable.

Estimation: A natural estimator of a non-linear function ω is $\hat{\omega} = \omega(\hat{\bar{\mathbf{r}}})$ [11]. Note that although $\hat{\bar{\mathbf{r}}}$ is an unbiased estimate of $\bar{\mathbf{r}}^*$, $\hat{\omega}$ is not necessarily an unbiased estimate of $\omega(\bar{\mathbf{r}}^*)$. Computing the variance of $\hat{\omega}$ is not straightforward, as we only obtain one value of ω from the sample. A general approach is to use re-sampling methods such as jackknifing, in which each instance is held out of the sample in turn, providing n different function values that can be used to estimate variance [8]. Jackknife estimates for stratified sampling have also been developed [11].

4.3 General Stratified Sampling Approach

For each stratified sampling method we propose throughout this paper, we describe four components: the *target function*, the *stratification function*, the *stratification scheme*, and the *sample allocation scheme*. We next describe these components and our general approach to designing them.

As described in the previous section, in some cases we are not interested in the mean estimates $\hat{\mathbf{r}}$, but rather some non-linear function of the estimates $\omega(\hat{\mathbf{r}})$. We refer to the non-linear function ω as the *target function*. The target function varies in different applications. In the linear case the target function is the identity function.

The *stratification function* s computes a proxy value for each instance that can be used for stratification and sample allocation. Though the output variables $\mathbf{y}$ are latent, if we have a trained model we do have some information about the values of these variables. Our general approach is to use current model predictions as a proxy for latent output variables $\mathbf{y}$. Specifically, a method we use pervasively is to stratify according to the *expectation* of some function of interest r' (often $r' = r$)

$$s(\mathbf{x}^j) = \mathrm{E}_{p(\mathbf{y}|\mathbf{x}^j;\boldsymbol{\theta})}[r'(\mathbf{x}^j, \mathbf{y})] = \sum_{\mathbf{y}} p(\mathbf{y}|\mathbf{x}^j;\boldsymbol{\theta}) r'(\mathbf{x}^j, \mathbf{y}).$$

This approach makes the reasonable assumption that model predictions are correlated with the true output variables. This implies that the improvement provided by stratified sampling is bounded by accuracy of the current model.

When estimating a vector of means $\hat{\mathbf{r}}$, we take a simple approach and continue to use a scalar stratification function $s(\mathbf{x})$, essentially defining a composite variable. One simple strategy is to use the expectation of a single element of the vector: $r' = r_i$, $s(\mathbf{x}) = \mathrm{E}_{p(\mathbf{y}|\mathbf{x}^j;\boldsymbol{\theta})}[r_i(\mathbf{x}^j, \mathbf{y})]$.

The *stratification scheme* takes as input the values computed by the stratification function and defines the strata. We use two methods for defining strata, which we discuss in detail in the following sections.

Finally, the *sample allocation scheme* defines how samples are allocated to strata. If optimal allocation is used, rather than proportional allocation, then a *stratum variance estimator* that defines a procedure for estimating the variance of strata must also be defined. We estimate within-stratum variances by using the sample estimates (for instances that have already been inspected), using model probabilities as a proxy for the latent output variables, or a combination. To use model probabilities, we advocate a simple strategy in which values for the latent output variables are sampled according to the model, r is computed, and the resulting sample variance estimates of r stand-in for true variances.

Note that, in general, inspecting individual instances to estimate a statistic could also yield labeled instances as a by-product. In future work we could perform training using both constraints and labeled instances.

5. OVERALL EVALUATION

Suppose we have an initial model for the task we would like to solve. Our goal is to interactively improve this model. A natural first step is to come to an understanding of what the model is predicting and how accurate it is, in order to decide where to focus analysis and provide supervision. Importantly, we want to do this with minimal effort. In this section we apply stratified sampling to choose sets of instances (with model predictions) for manual inspection. For concreteness and to allow thorough validation, we focus on the task of using the sample to estimate a performance metric such as accuracy. However, we also suggest that with appropriate adjustments to the sampling scheme, viewing a sample of instances selected by this method would provide accurate representations of other properties of interest.

Note that the methods described here, though motivated by interactive training, could also be used in a non-interactive setting to evaluate lightly supervised learning. This is an important problem on its own, as in a lightly supervised setting there is typically no data available for evaluation.

5.1 Evaluating Classification Accuracy

We first estimate classification accuracy. Formally, we aim to estimate the mean of the correctness indicator function

$$r_c(\mathbf{x}, y) = 1_{\{\hat{y}=y\}},$$

where $\hat{y}$ is the predicted label, $\hat{y} = \mathrm{argmax}_y\, p(y|\mathbf{x};\boldsymbol{\theta})$, and $1_{\{p\}}$ returns 1 if the predicate p is true, and 0 otherwise. When computed with the true label, r_c returns 1 if the model is correct, and 0 otherwise. We next devise several stratified sampling schemes for estimating $\hat{\bar{r}}_c$.

Target Function: Classification accuracy is a linear function, as $\hat{\bar{r}}_c$ is an estimate of accuracy. Consequently the target function ω is simply the identity function $\omega(\hat{\bar{r}}_c) = \hat{\bar{r}}_c$.

Stratification Function: Equation 1 suggests that strata should be defined to maximize the variance in individual stratum accuracies. Because the stratum accuracies are unavailable, we instead stratify using the expectation of r_c.

$$\begin{aligned} s_c(\mathbf{x}^j) &= \mathrm{E}_{p(y|\mathbf{x}^j;\boldsymbol{\theta})}[r_c(\mathbf{x}^j, y)] \\ &= \sum_y p(y|\mathbf{x}^j;\boldsymbol{\theta}) 1_{\{\hat{y}=y\}} = p(\hat{y}|\mathbf{x}^j;\boldsymbol{\theta}) \end{aligned} \qquad (2)$$

Equation 2 shows that the model expectation of r_c is the probability of the best label, or the model's *confidence* in its prediction. Note that, using our general approach, we recover the stratification function of Bennett and Carvalho [1]. When applied to other tasks in interactive training our approach yields different stratification functions.

Stratification Scheme: We use a *uniform size stratification scheme*. First, we sort unlabeled instances according to $s_c(\mathbf{x}^j)$. Then, we define strata by splitting the sorted list into m pieces, each containing the same number of instances.

Sample Allocation: Finally, we must allocate samples to the strata. With a uniform size stratification scheme, *proportional allocation* allocates n/m samples to each stratum. We additionally use *optimal allocation*, where the challenge is estimating the standard deviations in each stratum $\hat{\sigma}_i$.

Bennett and Carvalho [1] propose *online stratified sampling*, in which the $\hat{\sigma}_i$ are re-estimated using the observed values r_i^j after each sample. As the number of samples increases, the estimates become more accurate, and savings increase. However, a potential disadvantage of this approach is that many samples may be required to obtain estimates that are accurate enough to be beneficial. Because we are especially interested in evaluation with minimal effort, we propose two additional methods for estimating $\hat{\sigma}_i$ that leverage model predictions.

We can model each unobserved r_i^j in stratum i as a Bernoulli random variable c_i^j with $p_i^j = p(\hat{y}|\mathbf{x}^j;\boldsymbol{\theta})$. Summing all c_i^j for stratum i yields an expected accuracy random variable with a *Poisson Binomial* distribution[4]. We can use the variance of this distribution as an estimate of the stratum variance $\hat{\sigma}_i^2 = \sum_j p_i^j(1-p_i^j)$. This method prioritizes strata where there are expected to be a mix of correct and incorrect predictions over strata with expected accuracy near 0 or 1.

As n increases, we expect *online stratified sampling* to eventually provide better estimates than the above method. Consequently, we propose a novel compromise. In each iteration, we sample a correctness value for each unlabeled instance $c_i^j \sim p(\mathbf{y}^j|\mathbf{x}^j;\boldsymbol{\theta})$, and treat these values as pseudo-observations of r_i^j that are down-weighted by parameter α. We then estimate $\hat{\sigma}_i$ as in *online stratified sampling*, combining the true and pseudo-observations.

5.2 Classification Experiments

We compare approaches for evaluating the accuracy of document classifiers for binary subsets of *20 Newsgroups* (see Section 3.1). The classifiers are trained with GE using constraints provided by users in previous work [6].

We compare random sampling (*random*) and stratified sampling approaches that use confidence stratification with $m = 5$ strata and different sample allocation methods: proportional allocation (*pro conf*), optimal allocation using online variance estimation (*opt online*) [1], and optimal allocation using the combined confidence and online variance estimation method (*opt conf online*). We also conduct but do not display experiments with confidence-based optimal allocation. In general, *opt conf online* outperforms this method more as n increases. We begin stratified sampling by allocating two samples to each stratum. For the optimal allocation methods, we reestimate $\hat{\sigma}_i$ after each sample, and smooth the estimates with 10 pseudo-observations[5]; for *opt online* these pseudo-observations are uniform, while for *opt conf online* the pseudo-observations are sampled correctness values (i.e. $\alpha = 10/N_i$). To compute estimates of $\hat{\bar{r}}$, we reveal the true labels for instances in the sample. We run 1000 trials, and report the mean absolute accuracy estimation error.

Figure 1 displays error vs. n. First, note that the stratified sampling approaches provide lower mean absolute error than random sampling. We assess significance with a Mann-Whitney U test, the non-parametric counterpart of an unpaired t-test. Of the 216 possible comparisons between random sampling and a stratified sampling method (9 tasks × 8 different sample sizes × 3 stratified sampling methods), stratified sampling provides significantly lower error (significance level $\alpha = 0.05$) in 209 cases. Random sampling never significantly outperforms stratified sampling. Attaining the same mean absolute error with random sampling would often require significantly more effort. For example, in the *med-space* task with *User 1*'s constraints, a sample of size $n = 20$ using *opt conf online* gives error of 0.0406. *Random* attains comparable performance with 30 samples, giving an error of 0.0418. This is a 33% reduction in evaluation effort.

[4]The sum is a Binomial random variable if p is the same for each instance.

[5]We initially smoothed with $1/\sqrt{n_i}$ pseudo-observations as in [1], but this significantly increased error for *opt online*.

We conclude that the accuracy of classifiers trained with GE can be estimated more efficiently using stratified sampling.

Opt conf online provides lower mean absolute error than any other method in 54 of the 72 cases (9 tasks × 8 sample sizes). Of the 162 reductions in these 54 cases, 133 are significant. *Opt conf online* significantly outperforms *opt online* 43 times, and is significantly outperformed by *opt online* only once. Error analysis reveals that *opt online* tends to overestimate the differences in variance between strata. Additional smoothing reduces error with large n, but increases error with small n, as *opt online* approaches *pro conf* as the amount of smoothing increases. We conclude that *opt conf online* is preferable for minimal effort evaluation.

5.3 Estimating Token Accuracy

We next propose stratified sampling methods for evaluating token accuracy for sequence labeling models. We estimate the mean of the vector-valued function $\mathbf{r}_{sc}$ defined

$$r_{sc0}(\mathbf{x},\mathbf{y}) = \sum_{t=1}^{T} 1_{\{\hat{y}_t = y_t\}}$$
$$r_{sc1}(\mathbf{x},\mathbf{y}) = T,$$

where T is the length of the sequence and t indexes positions in the sequence. The function $\mathbf{r}_{sc}$ returns the number of correctly predicted labels in the first position, and the length in the second. We describe the components of several stratified sampling schemes.

Target Function: While instance accuracy and average token accuracy are linear, token accuracy is non-linear. Token accuracy is defined $\omega_{ta}(\hat{\bar{\mathbf{r}}}_{sc}) = \hat{\bar{r}}_{sc0}/\hat{\bar{r}}_{sc1}$[6].

Stratification Functions: We propose two stratification functions. The first is the expectation of r_{sc0}.

$$s_{exc}(\mathbf{x}^j) = \mathrm{E}_{p(\mathbf{y}|\mathbf{x}^j;\boldsymbol{\theta})}[r_{sc0}(\mathbf{x}^j,\mathbf{y})] = \sum_{t=1}^{T} p(\hat{y}_t|\mathbf{x}^j;\boldsymbol{\theta})$$

This can be interpreted as the expected number of correct tokens, where $p(\hat{y}_t|\mathbf{x}^j;\boldsymbol{\theta})$ is the marginal probability of the predicted label at position t. The stratification function s_{conf} is the expectation of a function that returns 1 only if the labeling of the entire sequence is correct.

$$s_{conf}(\mathbf{x}^j) = \mathrm{E}_{p(\mathbf{y}|\mathbf{x}^j;\boldsymbol{\theta})}[1_{\{\hat{\mathbf{y}}=\mathbf{y}\}}] = p(\hat{\mathbf{y}}|\mathbf{x}^j;\boldsymbol{\theta}).$$

The expectation is the probability of the predicted label sequence. This can be interpreted as model confidence.

Stratification Scheme: We use the *uniform size stratification scheme*, described in Section 5.1, for this task.

Sample Allocation: We use both proportional and optimal allocation. In optimal allocation, we allocate samples using estimates of the standard deviation of $r_{sc0}(\mathbf{x}^j,\mathbf{y})$. This is preferable to using the standard deviation of $1_{\{\hat{\mathbf{y}}=\mathbf{y}\}}$ in the applications we explore here, as complete instance accuracy is low. As in Section 5.1, we use both online estimation of the variance with the samples, and a combined method. In the combined method, pseudo-observations of token correctness are sampled according to the marginal

[6]We could use the population mean length in place of $\hat{\bar{r}}_{sc1}$. Stratified sampling provides even larger improvements with this estimator, but the estimates have higher error due to discrepancies between the population mean length and $\hat{\bar{r}}_{sc1}$. This may result in accuracy >1, for example. Therefore, in this paper we estimate all arguments to ω from S.

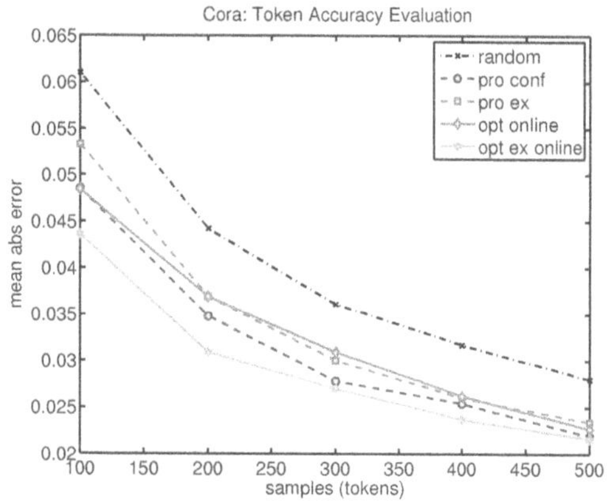

Figure 2: Stratified sampling methods significantly outperform random sampling for evaluating token accuracy on the *Cora* data set.

probabilities of the predicted labels $p(\hat{y}_t|\mathbf{x}^j;\boldsymbol{\theta})$, and these pseudo-observations are combined with the labeled sample estimates, as described in Section 5.1.

5.4 Sequence Labeling Experiments

This experiment uses the *Cora* data set as described in Section 3.1. The model is trained with the constraints provided by User 3 in [7], and an additional constraint with weight 10 that specifies that 80% of transitions between labels should be self-transitions. In this task each sequence is a complete citation. To enable precise sampling, we split citations into smaller subsequences. However, using very short subsequences would obscure helpful context, making the user's task more difficult. Consequently, we split citations into subsequences of maximum length 10.

The sampling strategies for this experiment are *random*, s_{conf} stratification with proportional allocation (*pro conf*), s_{exc} stratification with proportional allocation (*pro ex*), s_{conf} stratification with online optimal allocation (*opt online*), and s_{conf} stratification with combined optimal allocation (*opt ex online*). We do not report results with s_{exc} stratification and optimal allocation. The results are similar to *opt ex online*, but with higher error. For *opt online*, we used the same smoothing strategy as [1], which performed better than a fixed value of 10 for this task (the opposite was true in Section 5.2). We did not tune α for *opt ex online*, keeping $\alpha = 10/N_i$, giving an advantage to *opt online*. We use $m = 5$ strata, and conduct 1000 trials. To simulate rapid evaluation, we use 100-500 tokens (~10-50 subsequences).

Figure 2 displays the results. The x-axis is the total number of tokens evaluated. All stratified sampling methods significantly outperform random sampling (Mann Whitney U test with significance level $\alpha = 0.05$). *Opt ex online* outperforms all methods significantly at each point on the graph except for *pro conf* at 300, and *pro conf* and *opt online* at 500. At 200 tokens, the mean absolute error with *opt ex online* is 0.0309. *Random* sampling does not attain a comparable error of 0.0311 until $n = 425$. This is a savings of 225 tokens, or 53% of total evaluation effort.

In this experiment *pro conf* outperforms *pro ex*. Note that $s_{exc} \leq T$. Error analysis shows that s_{exc} yields strata that are more correlated with T than s_{conf}.

6. FINE-GRAINED EVALUATION

In Section 5, we found that stratified sampling methods can provide significantly more accurate estimates of overall performance than random sampling. One possible next step in interactive training is to drill down and perform fine-grained evaluation, with the goal of using this information to refine or provide new supervision. In this section, we propose a stratified sampling approach to fine-grained evaluation and error analysis. As an example error analysis task, we consider computing token F_1 for a particular label of interest ℓ for sequence labeling tasks. This is an important problem because in a particular application some labels may be more important than others. Additionally, awareness of low F_1 for ℓ provides a path for improving the model.

The function of interest, $\mathbf{r}_{f\ell}$, is defined as

$$r_{f\ell 0}(\mathbf{x},\mathbf{y}) = \sum_{t=1}^{T} 1_{\{y_t=\ell \,\wedge\, \hat{y}_t=\ell\}}$$
$$r_{f\ell 1}(\mathbf{x},\mathbf{y}) = \sum_{t=1}^{T} 1_{\{\hat{y}_t=\ell\}}$$
$$r_{f\ell 2}(\mathbf{x},\mathbf{y}) = \sum_{t=1}^{T} 1_{\{y_t=\ell\}}.$$

In words, the first element is the number of correctly predicted labels whose value is ℓ, the second element is the number of predictions of ℓ, and the third element is the number of true labels whose value is ℓ.

Target Function: The F_1 target function for label ℓ is

$$\omega_{F_1}(\hat{\bar{\mathbf{r}}}_{f\ell}) = \frac{2 \times \hat{\bar{r}}_{f\ell 0}/\hat{\bar{r}}_{f\ell 1} \times \hat{\bar{r}}_{f\ell 0}/\hat{\bar{r}}_{f\ell 2}}{\hat{\bar{r}}_{f\ell 0}/\hat{\bar{r}}_{f\ell 1} + \hat{\bar{r}}_{f\ell 0}/\hat{\bar{r}}_{f\ell 2}}.$$

Stratification Function: The stratification function is the expectation of $r_{f\ell 2}$

$$s_{f\ell 2}(\mathbf{x}^j) = \mathrm{E}_{p(\mathbf{y}|\mathbf{x}^j;\boldsymbol{\theta})}[r_{f\ell 2}(\mathbf{x}^j,\mathbf{y})] = \sum_{t=1}^{T} p(y_t=\ell|\mathbf{x}^j;\boldsymbol{\theta}).$$

This can be interpreted as the expected number of ℓ tokens.

Stratification Scheme: We again use the *uniform size stratification scheme*. However, we find that the density of $r_{f\ell 2}$ is less uniform than the density of the stratification functions used for overall evaluation. There are often a few $\mathbf{x}^j$ for which $s_{f\ell 2}$ is large, and many $\mathbf{x}^j$ for which $s_{f\ell 2}$ is very small. This occurs when ℓ is infrequent, for example.

Consequently, we also experiment with non-uniform size stratification. A standard method for determining stratum boundaries is the *cum* $\sqrt{F}$ *rule* [4], which aims to minimize within-stratum variance. Performing stratification according to the cum $\sqrt{F}$ rule first involves splitting the instances into k initial sorted classes, where C_i denotes the ith class. Next, the cumulative function c of the square root of the class frequencies is computed.

$$c(j) = \sum_{i=1}^{j} \sqrt{|C_i|}$$

The *stratum width* w is then computed as $w = c(k)/m$. Finally, the initial classes are grouped into strata of equal width w using the cum $\sqrt{F}$ values, $c(j)$.

Sample Allocation: We allocate two initial samples to each stratum (to enable computing $\hat{Var}(\hat{r}_{ss})$ if needed), and allocate the remaining samples proportionally. When $n = 2m$, this can be viewed as optimal allocation with $\hat{\sigma}_i$ that are inversely proportional to the stratum sizes, $\hat{\sigma}_i = 1/N_i$. This scheme is appropriate because in this setting large strata are likely to have small $s_{f\ell 2}$ values, and consequently we expect few occurrences of ℓ in those strata.

6.1 Experiments

We use the same data set and initial model as in Section 5.4. Citations are again split into subsequences of maximum length 10. To simulate obtaining a rapid estimate of token F_1 for ℓ, we evaluate using $n = 10$ subsequences.

We compare *random* sampling, sampling proportionally from equal-sized strata using $s_{f\ell 2}$ (*ex uniform*), and sampling proportionally from strata determined by the cum $\sqrt{F}$ rule using $s_{f\ell 2}$ (*ex cum*$\sqrt{F}$). We use $m = 5$ strata. For the *cum* $\sqrt{F}$ rule, we use $k = 20$ initial classes that each cover a fixed-width segment of the range of $s_{f\ell 2}$ (i.e. one class is all $\mathbf{x}$ with $s_{f\ell 2}(\mathbf{x}) \in [0, 0.5]$). In some cases with $k = 20$ initial classes less than m of them contain instances — empirical evidence of the statement above that the density of $s_{f\ell 2}$ can be highly non-uniform. In this case we multiply k by 10 iteratively until we have at least $m + 1$ non-empty classes.

Table 1 reports the results. We evaluate both the mean absolute error in the F_1 estimate (F_1 *err*) and the percentage of wasted trials (*waste*). A wasted trial occurs when none of the 10 subsequences contain a true occurrence of the label of interest. In this case it is not possible to obtain a meaningful recall estimate[7]. Bold denotes that a method gives the lowest F_1 *err* or *waste*. A * in the F_1 *err* column denotes statistical significance (Mann Whitney U test with significance level $\alpha = 0.05$).

The *ex cum*$\sqrt{F}$ method performs as well as or better than the other methods. In terms of F_1, it always significantly outperforms *random*, and significantly outperforms *ex uniform* in all cases except *title* and *date*. The *ex cum*$\sqrt{F}$ method also avoids a wasted sample in 1000 trials in all cases except for *note*. Using non-uniform strata with $s_{f\ell 2}$ typically results in a small stratum with instances that are very likely to contain ℓ. This greatly reduces waste. However, stratified sampling also samples other instances, ensuring that we obtain an unbiased estimate of $\bar{\mathbf{r}}^*$ even if model predictions are poorly correlated with the true labels. This illustrates the utility of stratified sampling for targeted evaluation.

	random		ex uniform		ex cum$\sqrt{F}$	
	F_1 err	waste	F_1 err	waste	F_1 err	waste
author	0.073	0.004	0.051	**0.000**	**0.041***	**0.000**
journal	0.273	0.069	0.221	0.006	**0.143***	**0.000**
note	0.843	0.843	0.822	0.822	**0.274***	**0.274**
booktitle	0.183	0.017	0.139	**0.000**	**0.105***	**0.000**
tech	0.392	0.501	0.363	0.364	**0.129***	**0.000**
volume	0.293	0.084	0.239	0.004	**0.091***	**0.000**
location	0.286	0.286	0.262	0.145	**0.093***	**0.000**
editor	0.510	0.605	0.468	0.488	**0.172***	**0.000**
institut.	0.351	0.427	0.339	0.257	**0.136***	**0.000**
title	0.079	**0.000**	0.056	**0.000**	**0.051**	**0.000**
date	0.123	0.006	0.080	**0.000**	**0.077**	**0.000**
pages	0.183	0.052	0.133	**0.000**	**0.081***	**0.000**
publisher	0.392	0.149	0.356	0.071	**0.157***	**0.000**

Table 1: Using $n = 10$ subsequences to evaluate token label F_1 for each *Cora* label. Stratified sampling provides more accurate F_1 estimates and avoids wasted samples.

7. SPECIFYING NEW CONSTRAINTS

Thus far we have focused on evaluation and analysis. We now shift our focus to improving the model. Users could specify new constraints manually, or select from candidate constraints [6, 7]. In this section we propose a new paradigm in which the user specifies constraints while inspecting data. For example, after inspecting [*journal*: Transactions] [*title*: on Pattern Analysis] ..., the user may choose to add new constraints that specify that *Transactions* should almost always be labeled *journal*, and that transitions from *journal* to *title* are extremely unlikely. This paradigm can help the user specify more accurate constraints, find constraints that are particularly useful, and may suggest constraints to the user that they may not have considered otherwise. Note that constraints apply to the entire data set, and hence provide more supervision than labeling data [6, 7]. However, in future work we plan to allow both types of supervision. We focus on *targeted improvement* of the model. In this section we aim to improve token F_1 for a particular label ℓ.

We can view this as an estimation problem as follows. Based on their prior knowledge, the user has some set of candidate constraints that they are capable of specifying. For each instance, the function $\mathbf{r}$ simply returns the number of times each candidate constraint is applicable with respect to the targeted improvement task. Note that computing $\mathbf{r}$ is expensive, since the user must manually inspect instances. The user decides which constraints to add based on the mean candidate constraint estimate $\hat{\bar{\mathbf{r}}}$. When applying stratified sampling to improve label ℓ, we use the same sample allocation and cum $\sqrt{F}$ stratification method as in Section 6.

7.1 Experiments

We use the same data set and constraints as in Section 5.4. Initial models are trained with either the *full* set of 108 constraints or a random subsample of 52 constraints (*small*).

We simulate the specification of new constraints so that we can conduct a large number of trials. To simulate user prior knowledge, we use labeled data to define constraints as in previous work [6, 7, 15]. Candidate constraints include input feature label distribution constraints of the form used in [7] for input features that occur at least 10 times and have label distribution entropy ≤ 0.7. In addition, there are candidate constraints that discourage unlikely label transitions[8]. In this experiment unlikely transitions are those that do not occur in the labeled data. Candidate constraints are applicable if they apply to a token with true or predicted label ℓ. Any constraint i with $\hat{\bar{r}}_i \geq 0$ is then added. For input feature label distributions, the target distribution is assigned using the "labeling" method used in [7].

We evaluate the targeted improvement of three moderately infrequent labels in the *Cora* data set: *institution*, *journal*, and *location*. We use $n = 10$ sub-sequences of length at most 10 to find constraints, and subsequently retrain the model with the augmented set of constraints. Results com-

[7]Following standard conventions, recall is 1 if there are no true occurrences of ℓ in the sample, and precision is 1 if there are no predicted occurrences of ℓ in the sample.

[8]The probability of taking any transition in the unlikely set is encouraged to be close to 0 using KL divergence. To balance this constraint with the others, its weight is set to the number of labeled feature constraints.

constraints	label	initial	random	stratified
small	institution	0.178	0.271	**0.448***
	journal	0.341	0.473	**0.634***
	location	0.466	0.580	**0.684***
full	institution	0.661	0.682	**0.717***
	journal	0.635	0.593	**0.671***
	location	0.655	0.685	**0.727***

Table 2: Using stratified sampling to find new constraints improves token F_1 for a label of interest.

paring *random* and *stratified* sampling with 100 trials are presented in Table 2. In all cases, stratified sampling yields significantly higher token F_1 for ℓ. The improvement is the result of finding additional applicable constraints. While specifying these constraints takes additional time, when ℓ is infrequent, we expect finding appropriate constraints to dominate the time required to specify them. As in Section 6, this method encourages the sample to contain a mix of correct predictions of ℓ, false positives, and false negatives. Other sampling strategies do not provide this coverage. For example, uncertainty sampling may miss true occurrences of ℓ, and certainty sampling method may miss false negatives.

8. ESTIMATING TARGET EXPECTATIONS

Input feature label distribution constraints typically use target distributions over labels that are set with simple heuristics [6, 7, 16]. It is known that as these target distributions become more precise, the resulting model becomes more accurate [16]. Additionally, users occasionally make mistakes when specifying constraints. For example, in the *baseball-hockey* task, User 1 mistakenly provided the constraint that *Devils* $\mapsto$ *baseball*. The user was likely thinking of the Tampa Bay Devil Rays, rather than the New Jersey *Devils* (a hockey team). Such incorrect constraints can be detrimental to GE.

Incorrect constraints can be corrected and imprecise constraints can be refined by having the user view a few occurrences of the constraint feature ϕ in context. Mann and McCallum [16] found that this target estimation method gave higher accuracy than traditional sequence labeling with the same number of labels. In this section we use stratified sampling to ensure that the small number of occurrences considered by the user are representative. Note that these ideas could be applied to other expectation estimation problems.

The specific task we consider is estimating a distribution over labels for a particular input feature q. The function of interest returns a vector with the count of q with each label. For a classification task, the function $\mathbf{r}_q$ is

$$r_{q\ell}(\mathbf{x}, y) = 1_{\{y=\ell\}} q(\mathbf{x})$$

For a sequence labeling task, the function $\mathbf{r}_q$ is

$$r_{q\ell}(\mathbf{x}, \mathbf{y}) = \sum_{t=1}^{T} 1_{\{y_t=\ell\}} q(\mathbf{x}, t)$$

Target Function: We aim to estimate the distribution over labels for each input feature. Consequently $\omega_{ex}(\hat{\bar{\mathbf{r}}}_q)$ simply returns $\hat{\bar{\mathbf{r}}}_q$ normalized to sum to 1.

Stratification Functions: We need only consider $\mathbf{x}^j$ where $q(\mathbf{x}^j)=1$, or $q(\mathbf{x}^j, t)=1$ for some t. For binary classification tasks, the stratification function is the expectation of r_{q0}, where 0 refers to one of the labels.

$$s_{q0}(\mathbf{x}^j) = \mathrm{E}_{p(y|\mathbf{x}^j;\boldsymbol{\theta})}[r_{q0}(\mathbf{x}^j, y)] = p(y=0|\mathbf{x}^j;\boldsymbol{\theta}),$$

<table>
<tr><th rowspan="2">constraint and data sets</th><th colspan="2">random</th><th colspan="2">stratified</th></tr>
<tr><th>err</th><th>rt acc</th><th>err</th><th>rt acc</th></tr>
<tr><td>(1) baseball-hockey</td><td>0.178</td><td>0.932</td><td>0.113*</td><td>0.948*</td></tr>
<tr><td>(1) ibm-mac</td><td>0.274</td><td>0.784</td><td>0.244*</td><td>0.790*</td></tr>
<tr><td>(1) med-space</td><td>0.139</td><td>0.921</td><td>0.108*</td><td>0.931*</td></tr>
<tr><td>(2) baseball-hockey</td><td>0.234</td><td>0.912</td><td>0.163*</td><td>0.932*</td></tr>
<tr><td>(2) ibm-mac</td><td>0.310</td><td>0.782</td><td>0.303*</td><td>0.782</td></tr>
<tr><td>(2) med-space</td><td>0.205</td><td>0.912</td><td>0.175*</td><td>0.919*</td></tr>
<tr><td>(3) baseball-hockey</td><td>0.178</td><td>0.923</td><td>0.119*</td><td>0.942*</td></tr>
<tr><td>(3) ibm-mac</td><td>0.250</td><td>0.809</td><td>0.226*</td><td>0.816*</td></tr>
<tr><td>(3) med-space</td><td>0.112</td><td>0.922</td><td>0.094*</td><td>0.928*</td></tr>
</table>

Table 3: Stratified sampling provides lower error target expectation estimates, and higher accuracy when the classifier is retrained with the refined targets.

where again we only consider $\mathbf{x}^j$ with $q(\mathbf{x}^j)=1$.

For a non-binary task we stratify according to the index of the most frequently predicted label ℓ_{max}.

$$s_{\ell_{max}}(\mathbf{x}^j) = \mathrm{E}_{p(\mathbf{y}|\mathbf{x}^j;\boldsymbol{\theta})}[r_{q\ell_{max}}(\mathbf{x}^j, \mathbf{y})] = \sum_{t=1}^{T} p(y_t = \ell_{max}|\mathbf{x}^j;\boldsymbol{\theta}) q(\mathbf{x}^j, t).$$

In ongoing work we are developing improved, clustering-based methods for stratification for expectation estimation.

Stratification Scheme and Sample Allocation: We use the *cum* $\sqrt{F}$ *rule*, described in Section 6, for stratification, and the same sample allocation scheme.

8.1 Classification Experiment

For this experiment we use the same data sets and constraints as the experiments in Section 5.2. We use $m = 2$ strata, 4 samples per constraint, and repeat the experiment 1000 times with different random seeds. We evaluate using the mean absolute expectation estimation error (*err*), and the accuracy of the logistic regression model after re-training with the refined constraints (*rt acc*). Table 3 displays results comparing *random* sampling and stratified sampling with cum $\sqrt{F}$ rule stratification using s_{q0} (*stratified*). Stratified sampling always provides more accurate expectation estimates, and provides higher accuracy when the model is retrained with the refined constraints in all cases except one. Cases in which stratified sampling significantly outperforms random sampling are indicated with a *.

8.2 Sequence Labeling Experiment

Finally, we refine User 3's constraints for *Cora* with $n=4$ and $n=10$ samples of the constraint occurring in context. We use $m=2$ strata for $n=4$, $m=5$ strata for $n=10$, and conduct 100 trials. We use the same initial model as in Section 5.4, which has accuracy of 82.8%. Note that here strata with low $s_{\ell_{max}}$ values do not necessarily have low variance. Therefore, in this experiment we avoid over-stratifying, allowing $< m$ strata if there are fewer non-empty initial classes.

Using random sampling gives mean absolute expectation estimation error of 0.259 with $n=4$ and error of 0.171 with $n=10$. Using proportional allocation with s_{qmax} and cum $\sqrt{F}$ stratification gives error of 0.215 with $n=4$, a 17% error reduction, and error of 0.136 with $n=10$, a 20% error reduction. Retraining the model with the refined constraints obtained using *random* sampling gives accuracy of 82.5% with $n=4$ and accuracy of 86.3% with $n=10$, while retraining the model with refined constraints using stratified sampling gives statistically significantly higher accuracy of 84.0% with $n=4$ and accuracy of 87.2% with $n=10$. Random sampling requires $n=16$ samples per constraint to match the accuracy of stratified sampling with $n=10$, a 37.5% reduction.

The user may instead use the sample to specify their own target expectation. In this case, we want the sample to include as many labels as possible, to remind the user of the input feature's uses. Random sampling with $n=4$ finds 61.1% of the labels input features occur with, whereas stratified sampling finds 70.4%. With $n=10$, random sampling finds 69.5%, whereas stratified sampling finds 82.9%.

We also conjecture that in applications where the target label distributions have higher entropy, reductions in target estimation error will yield larger accuracy improvements.

9. FUTURE WORK

In this paper we addressed subproblems in interactive training that can be cast as selecting a representative sample for the user to review. In this section we discuss future opportunities in interactive training. In addition to the directions below, we are interested in stratification schemes that additionally consider the input variables, and in developing a complete interactive training system.

Model Prediction Rationales: In addition to helping the user understand what the model is predicting, it may be beneficial to help the user understand why the model is making a prediction. For example, knowing why the model is making a mistake could help a user add the necessary constraints to fix it. We conjecture that a user could understand a model prediction by inspecting similar contexts and studying the way the prediction changes with the input.

Summarizing Differences between Models: We are interested in developing sampling methods for summarizing the similarities and differences between two models. This could help the user understand how the model is changing with the addition of new constraints.

Detecting Incorrect Constraints: In some cases we suspect that incorrect constraints could be automatically detected, as we have observed that constraints whose targets are poorly matched during training are often incorrect. This method could assist the user in prioritizing refinement.

10. ACKNOWLEDGEMENTS

This work was supported in part by the Center for Intelligent Information Retrieval, and the University of Massachusetts gratefully acknowledges the support of the Defense Advanced Research Projects Agency (DARPA) Machine Reading Program under Air Force Research Laboratory (AFRL) prime contract no. FA8750-09-C-0181. Any opinions, findings, conclusions, or recommendations expressed are those of the authors and do not necessarily reflect the view of DARPA, AFRL, or the US government.

11. REFERENCES

[1] P. N. Bennett and V. R. Carvalho. Online stratified sampling: evaluating classifiers at web-scale. In *CIKM*, pages 1581–1584, 2010.

[2] D. J. H. C. J. Skinner and D. Holt. Multiple frame sampling for multivariate stratification. *International Statistical Review*, 62(3):333–347, 1994.

[3] A. Culotta, T. Kristjansson, A. McCallum, and P. Viola. Corrective feedback and persistent learning for information extraction. *Artificial Intelligence*, 170(14):1101–1122, 2006.

[4] T. Dalenius and J. Hodges. Minimum variance stratification. *J. Amer. Statist. Ass.*, 30(219-229), 1959.

[5] G. Druck. *Generalized Expectation Criteria for Lightly Supervised Learning*. PhD thesis, University of Massachusetts Amherst, 2011.

[6] G. Druck, G. Mann, and A. McCallum. Learning from labeled features using generalized expectation criteria. In *SIGIR*, 2008.

[7] G. Druck, B. Settles, and A. McCallum. Active learning by labeling features. In *Proceedings of Conference on Empirical Methods in Natural Language Processing (EMNLP 2009)*, pages 81—90, 2009.

[8] B. Efron. *The Jackknife, the Bootstrap, and Other Resampling Plans*. CBMS-NSF Regional Conference Series in Applied Mathematics. Society for Industrial Mathematics, 1987.

[9] K. Ganchev, J. Graça, J. Gillenwater, and B. Taskar. Posterior regularization for structured latent variable models. *Journal of Machine Learning Research*, 11:2001–2049, July 2010.

[10] Y. Huang and T. M. Mitchell. Text clustering with extended user feedback. In *SIGIR*, pages 413–420, 2006.

[11] D. Krewski and J. N. K. Rao. Inference from stratified samples: Properties of the linearization, jackknife and balanced repeated replication methods. *The Annals of Statistics*, 9(5):1010–1019, 1981.

[12] M. Kumar, R. Ghani, M. Shah, J. G. Carbonell, and A. I. Rudnicky. Framework for interactive classification problems. In *ICML Workshop on Combining Learning Strategies to Reduce Label Cost*, 2011.

[13] J. Lafferty, A. McCallum, and F. Pereira. Conditional random fields: Probabilistic models for segmenting and labeling sequence data. In *Proc. Int'l. Conf. on Machine Learning*, pages 282–289, 2001.

[14] J. Langford and T. Zhang. The epoch-greedy algorithm for multi-armed bandits with side information. In *NIPS*, 2007.

[15] P. Liang, M. I. Jordan, and D. Klein. Learning from measurements in exponential families. In *Proc. Int'l. Conf. on Machine Learning*, pages 641–648, 2009.

[16] G. Mann and A. McCallum. Generalized expectation criteria for semi-supervised learning of conditional random fields. In *Proc. of Meeting of Assoc. for Computational Linguistics*, pages 870–878, 2008.

[17] J. Neyman. On the two different aspects of the representative method: The method of stratified sampling and the method of purposive selection. *Journal of the Royal Statistical Society*, 97(4):558–625, 1934.

[18] D. Roth and K. Small. Interactive feature space construction using semantic information. In *CoNLL*, 2009.

[19] C. Sawade, N. Landwehr, S. Bickel, and T. Scheffer. Active risk estimation. In *Proceedings of the International Conference on Machine Learning*, 2010.

[20] C. Sawade, N. Landwehr, and T. Scheffer. Active evaluation of f-measures. In *Advances in Neural Information Processing Systems*. 2010.

[21] B. Settles. Active learning literature survey. Technical Report 1648, University of Wisconsin - Madison, 2009.

[22] B. Settles. Closing the loop: Fast, interactive semi-supervised annotation with queries on features and instances. In *Proceedings of the 2011 Conference on Empirical Methods in Natural Language Processing*, pages 1467–1478, 2011.

[23] C. Sutton and A. Mccallum. An introduction to conditional random fields for relational learning. In L. Getoor and B. Taskar, editors, *Introduction to Statistical Relational Learning*. MIT Press, 2006.

[24] S. K. Thompson. *Sampling*. Wiley-Interscience, 2002.

[25] E. Yilmaz, E. Kanoulas, and J. A. Aslam. A simple and efficient sampling method for estimating AP and NDCG. In *Proceedings of the ACM SIGIR Conference on Research and Development in Information Retrieval (SIGIR)*, pages 603–610, 2008.

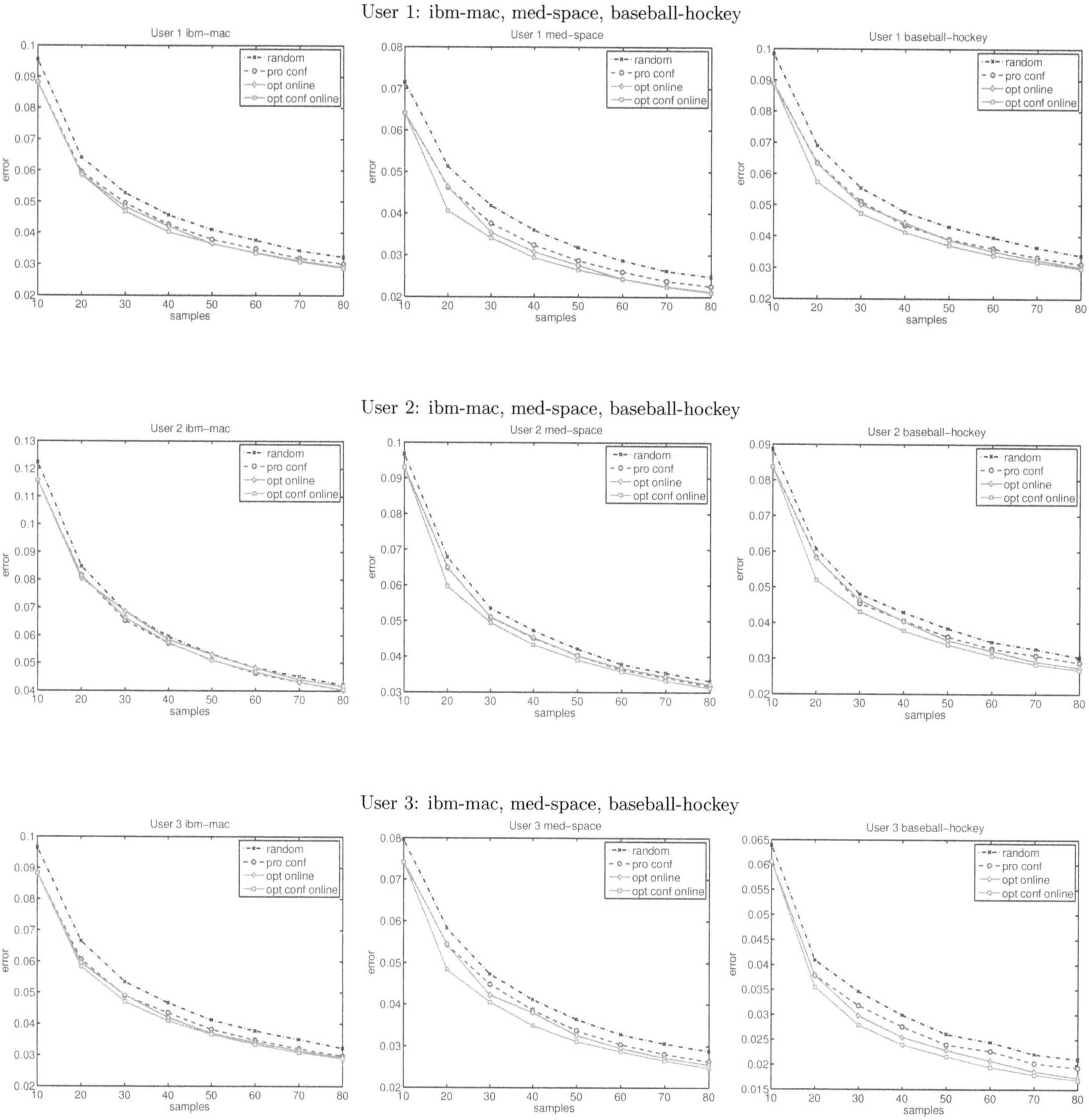

Figure 1: Stratified sampling methods provide classification accuracy estimates with lower error. ***Opt conf online*** **typically outperforms all other methods.**

Semi-supervised Multi-task Learning of Structured Prediction Models for Web Information Extraction

Paramveer S. Dhillon
University of Pennsylvania
Philadelphia PA
U.S.A
dhillon@cis.upenn.edu

Sundararajan Sellamanickam
Yahoo! Labs
Bangalore, India
ssrajan@yahoo-inc.com

Sathiya Keerthi Selvaraj
Yahoo! Labs
Santa Clara, CA
U.S.A
selvarak@yahoo-inc.com

ABSTRACT

Extracting information from web pages is an important problem; it has several applications such as providing improved search results and construction of databases to serve user queries. In this paper we propose a novel structured prediction method to address two important aspects of the extraction problem: (1) labeled data is available only for a small number of sites and (2) a machine learned global model does not generalize adequately well across many websites. For this purpose, we propose a weight space based graph regularization method. This method has several advantages. First, it can use unlabeled data to address the limited labeled data problem and falls in the class of graph regularization based semi-supervised learning approaches. Second, to address the generalization inadequacy of a global model, this method builds a local model for each website. Viewing the problem of building a local model for each website as a task, we learn the models for a collection of sites jointly; thus our method can also be seen as a graph regularization based multi-task learning approach. Learning the models jointly with the proposed method is very useful in two ways: (1) learning a local model for a website can be effectively influenced by labeled and unlabeled data from other websites; and (2) even for a website with only unlabeled examples it is possible to learn a decent local model. We demonstrate the efficacy of our method on several real-life data; experimental results show that significant performance improvement can be obtained by combining semi-supervised and multi-task learning in a single framework.

Categories and Subject Descriptors: H.3.m [Information Storage and Retrieval] Miscellaneous - Information Extraction, Web

General Terms: Algorithms, Experimentation

Keywords: Information Extraction, Semi-supervised learning, Multi-task learning, Structured Predictions

CIKM'11, October 24–28, 2011, Glasgow, Scotland, UK.

1. INTRODUCTION

Extracting information from web pages is an important problem. It has several web applications such as providing improved search results, serving user queries related to reviews, pricing information of products, etc., using databases constructed from information extraction. We consider the problem of *domain-centric extraction* where a schema corresponding to a domain of interest is given. The goal is to extract attributes specified by the schema from a collection of pages. Examples of a *domain* include Books, Restaurant, Publications etc. The schema for the Books domain will have attributes such as Title, Author, Publisher and Price. The pages for this domain are obtained from a collection of websites like `www.amazon.com`, `www.booksamillion.com`, etc. Similarly, a schema for the Publications domain will have attributes such as Author, Title, Conference, Pages etc., and these can be extracted from home pages of faculty members of different universities.

In all these examples, the attributes of interest are often organized either as *records* in a list page or as a single record in a detail page. Each record is a set of attribute values of one entity, e.g., a Book or a Publication. Unsupervised methods [11, 39, 3, 25] are very successful in *extracting records* from list pages using structural patterns present in one or more web pages. In the case of a detail page, the informative region of the web page plays the role of a record and it can be obtained using methods such as the ones proposed in [38]. Therefore, throughout this paper *we will assume that records are given and focus on the finer and challenging problem of extracting attributes from records*. It is worth noting that the unsupervised methods mentioned above are inadequate for solving this attribute extraction problem. The problem is challenging due to the following reasons: (1) there are wide variations in presentation style of information *across* the websites. For example, *attribute ordering, font size, font type* (e.g., italic, capital), html tag structures, etc., are often different, (2) the number of websites is large, and (3) some of the attributes are *optional* (may not be present in all the records) and some of the attributes are *missing* (in all the records from a website). These reasons also make it hard *to build a global model that generalizes well across the websites.*

Other challenges arise from the approach taken to address the extraction problem. For example, the wrapper induction [19, 27] method requires supervision; it utilizes labeled data to learn extraction rules on the HTML tag structure of pages. The need to have labeled data for *each website* and the presence of noisy structures within a website makes this method impractical for scaling to a large number of websites.

In recent years there has been a significant amount of research work done in building machine learned models for web information extraction. [5, 1, 29, 30, 41] apply sequential models like Hidden Markov Models (HMM), Conditional Random Fields (CRF) and Markov Logic Networks (MLN) to segment instances such as citations and addresses. All these methods focus on building a global model. Global models do not generalize well across websites whenever there are wide variations in structure and formatting across the websites (as frequently observed in domain-centric extraction problem). We demonstrate this issue using CRF models on the attribute extraction problem from records. This issue is expected to arise even when sophisticated models like hierarchical CRFs (HCRF) [41] and MLNs [30] are used. The key reason for this is that important features (e.g., attribute ordering, font type) that are discriminative *within a site* tend to become less effective whenever these features vary widely in the training examples from different websites. This problem can be alleviated by building local models where these discriminative features can be effectively made use of. Note that although we use a simple CRF model in our attribute extraction problem to demonstrate the usefulness of local models, our approach is quite generic and can be extended with HCRFs and MLNs. Therefore, our intention in this paper is not to demonstrate superiority over any of the existing information extraction methods using HCRF or MLN models; hence, we do not make any such comparisons. Our focus is on demonstrating the usefulness of building machine-learned local models and how these models can be effectively learned *jointly* when the labeled examples are scarcely available.

Building machine-learned models in supervised and semi-supervised settings require labeled data. In our problem context, getting labeled data from each website is extremely difficult as the number of websites is large. Furthermore, it is expensive to get a large amount of labeled data even for a few websites, particularly for *structured data* (such as a *sequence* or a tree) where the number of *nodes* and attributes is large.

The aim of the paper is to address two important aspects of the domain-centric extraction problem: (1) limited labeled data is available only for a small number of websites but plenty of unlabeled data is available from all the websites in a collection, and (2) a machine-learned global model does not generalize adequately well across many websites.

Our approach is based on connecting examples from different websites through a graph and learning local models for the websites *jointly* via *graph regularization* (Section 4). It exploits the fact that although there are variations in the presentation styles across the websites, there is useful common information that exists across the websites. For example, attributes such as Author, Title, Conference, Pages have (similar) content features that are common across the websites; our approach makes good use of such information.

1.1 Our Contributions

We propose a weight space based graph regularization method. Our method has several advantages. First, it can use unlabeled data to address the limited labeled data problem and falls in the class of graph regularization based semi-supervised learning (SSL) approaches. In this aspect, our work is related to [20, 2]. But, our formulation is much simpler and a lot easier to implement with publicly available software packages for structured predictions; unlike [20, 2] we directly work in the *weight space* formulation instead of the *dual* formulation.

Next, to address the generalization inadequacy of a global model, we propose to build a local model for each website. Furthermore, we suggest to learn the local models jointly to address the limited labeled data aspect; again, the weight space based graph regularization method can be used for joint learning. Viewing the problem of building a local model for each website as a task, our method can also be seen as a graph regularization based multi-task learning (MTL) approach. Learning the models jointly via the proposed method is useful in two ways: (1) learning a local model for a website can be effectively influenced by labeled and unlabeled data from other websites to get improved performance; and (2) even for a website with only unlabeled examples it is possible to learn a decent local model for it (which is not possible even for wrapper learning approaches). Thus, our method addresses the limited labeled data aspect via a unified framework for semi-supervised and multi-task learning. From a multi-task learning viewpoint, our work is related to [13]. However, our formulation goes beyond binary/multi-class problems, applies to structured prediction models, and is suitable for web information extraction. We are not aware of any work on multi-task learning that addresses the problem of learning local structured prediction models for totally unlabeled websites.

We conduct experiments on several real world datasets constructed from web pages of domains such as Books, CS-Faculty, Seminars and MLConfs. The experimental results demonstrate the effectiveness of the proposed method for SEMI-SUPERVISED, MULTI-TASK and SEMI-SUPERVISED MULTI-TASK (combined semi-supervised and multi-task) learning scenarios. The results also show that the performance of local models built for totally unlabeled websites is better than that of the global model.

2. PROBLEM FORMULATION

Consider the problem of extracting attributes from a given set of records. Let $\mathbf{x}$ and $\mathbf{y}$ denote the input and output representation of a record. We choose a suitable tokenization and view each record as a sequence of nodes; $\mathbf{x}$ is a sequence of feature vectors that are functions of the textual content and/or certain structural properties of these nodes; $\mathbf{y}$ is a sequence of labels assigned to these nodes where each label belongs to a label space $\mathcal{Y}$. For example, the label space of a publication record could be {Author, Title, Date, Conference, Pages, Others}. We use the terms *record*, *example* and *sequence* interchangeably in this paper.

Data: Assume that we have a set of labeled and unlabeled examples. These examples come from a collection of websites: $\mathcal{S} = \{S_1, S_2, \ldots, S_M\}$. Let $\mathcal{S}_L$ denote the set of websites which contain at least one labeled example. Websites in $\mathcal{S}_L$ can also have unlabeled examples. Let $\mathcal{S}_U$ denote the set of websites in which we have *only* unlabeled examples; $|\mathcal{S}_U|$ and $|\mathcal{S}_L|$ denote the cardinalities of $\mathcal{S}_U$ and $\mathcal{S}_L$. Let $(\mathbf{x}_i^{(m)}, \mathbf{y}_i^{(m)})$ denote the i-th example in S_m and let $T_m = \{(\mathbf{x}_i^{(m)}, \mathbf{y}_i^{(m)}) : i = 1, \ldots n_m\}$ denote the training set in S_m. Let L_m and U_m denote the set of indices of the labeled and unlabeled sequences from S_m. Thus, a label $\mathbf{y}_i^{(m)}$ is available only if $S_m \in \mathcal{S}_L$ and $i \in L_m$. Finally, let $T_{\mathcal{M}} = \cup_{m=1}^{M} T_m$ where $\mathcal{M} = \{1, \ldots, M\}$.

Problem Formulation (Local Models): We are interested in building a local probabilistic model $p(\mathbf{y}|\mathbf{x};\mathbf{W}_m)$ for each website S_m to extract the attributes from the sequences. $\mathbf{W}_m$ denotes the local model weight vector of S_m. Thus, given a set of labeled and unlabeled examples from $\mathcal{S}$, the goal is to learn the local model weights $\mathcal{W} = \{\mathbf{W}_m : m = 1, 2, \ldots, M\}$.

When we have *only* labeled examples, we can build the local models by optimizing the objective function $\mathcal{L}(\mathcal{T}_\mathcal{M}, \mathcal{W})$ defined as:

$$\frac{\lambda}{2}\sum_{m:S_m\in\mathcal{S}_L}||\mathbf{W}_m||^2 - \frac{1}{|L_m|}\sum_{i\in L_m}\log p(\mathbf{y}_i^{(m)}|\mathbf{x}_i^{(m)};\mathbf{W}_m) \quad (1)$$

where $\lambda > 0$ is a regularization constant. Note that in the absence of connections between the learning *tasks* of the websites, (1) becomes separable. For such a case, the local model for each website is built separately using only the labeled examples from that website. We will refer to the models built in this scenario simply as the Local models.

Problem Formulation (Global Model): Traditional extraction models learn a global weight vector $\mathbf{W}$ that is same for all websites. When we have *only* labeled examples, the global model is built by optimizing the objective function $\mathcal{L}(\mathcal{T}_\mathcal{M}, \mathbf{W})$ defined as:

$$\frac{|\mathcal{S}_L|\lambda}{2}||\mathbf{W}||^2 - \sum_{m:S_m\in\mathcal{S}_L}\frac{1}{|L_m|}\sum_{i\in L_m}\log p(\mathbf{y}_i^{(m)}|\mathbf{x}_i^{(m)};\mathbf{W}). \quad (2)$$

We will refer to the model thus built as the Global model.

Recall the two main goals of this paper: (1) to address the limited labeled data problem and (2) to overcome the generalization inadequacy of a global model. We address these problems through a graph regularization based semi-supervised multi-task learning method. The use of unlabeled examples results in SEMI-SUPERVISED learning. The problem of building a local model for each website can be viewed as one task; and, learning the models *jointly* results in MULTI-TASK learning. Now, the objective functions (1) and (2) are not adequate for semi-supervised learning (SSL) as there are no terms that involve unlabeled examples. It is also not adequate for multi-task learning (MTL) because there are no terms that connect the multiple tasks. Thus, to facilitate SSL and MTL we propose *to add a weight space based graph regularization term $\mathcal{G}(\mathcal{W})$ to the objective functions (1) and (2).* Before we present our approach, we give details of the probabilistic model for sequences that we use in this paper.

3. CRF MODEL

We now make precise, the probabilistic model $p(\mathbf{y}|\mathbf{x};\mathbf{W})$ for sequences used in the previous section. Given a record, we pose the problem of extracting attributes as a *sequence labeling* problem. For this purpose, we use the conditional random field (CRF) model [21]. CRF is a Markov random field that defines a conditional distribution of the labels $\mathbf{y}$ of a sequence conditioned on the input $\mathbf{x}$ in the following form: $p(\mathbf{y}|\mathbf{x};\mathbf{W}) = \frac{1}{Z_\mathbf{x}}\prod_{c\in\mathcal{C}}\psi(\mathbf{x}_c,\mathbf{y}_c)$ where: $\mathbf{W}$ denotes the model weights; $\mathcal{C}$ is the set of cliques present in the sequence; $\mathbf{y}_c$ denotes the components of $\mathbf{y}$ present in a clique c; $\psi(\cdot)$ is a potential function that takes non-negative values; and, $Z_\mathbf{x}$ is the partition function defined as $Z_\mathbf{x} = \sum_\mathbf{y}\prod_{c\in\mathcal{C}}\psi(\mathbf{x}_c,\mathbf{y}_c)$. The potential functions are expressed as: $\psi(\mathbf{x}_c,\mathbf{y}_c) = \exp(\sum_k w_k f_k(\mathbf{x}_c,\mathbf{y}_c))$ where the $f_k(\mathbf{x}_c,\mathbf{y}_c)$s are feature functions. Then, we have:

$$p(\mathbf{y}|\mathbf{x};\mathbf{W}) = \frac{1}{Z_\mathbf{x}}\exp(\sum_{c\in\mathcal{C}}\sum_k w_k f_k(\mathbf{x}_c,\mathbf{y}_c)). \quad (3)$$

In linear chain sequence labeling problems [21], common feature functions are represented as $f_k(\mathbf{x}_c,\mathbf{y}_c)$ where c is either a node clique c with $\mathbf{y}_c \in \mathcal{Y}$ or an edge clique c connecting two adjacent nodes in a sequence, with $\mathbf{y}_c \in \mathcal{Y}^2$. Thus, we have two types of feature functions, namely, *node* and *edge* feature functions. In general the individual feature functions take real values; in many cases they are boolean. For example, a node feature function $f_k(\mathbf{x}_c,\mathbf{y}_c) = \mathcal{I}(\mathbf{x}_c \in \mathsf{AddressDictionary}) \wedge (\mathbf{y}_c = \mathsf{Address})$ is TRUE when the textual content of $\mathbf{x}_c$ is in the address dictionary and assigned label Address. Here, $\mathcal{I}(\cdot)$ is the indicator function taking value 1 when the argument is TRUE and 0 otherwise.

In supervised learning, the CRF model weights $\mathbf{W}$ are learned using a set of labeled training examples, $T = \{(\mathbf{x}_i,\mathbf{y}_i) : i = 1,\ldots,n\}$ by minimizing a regularized negative log likelihood function: $\mathcal{L}(T,\mathbf{W}) = \frac{\lambda}{2}||\mathbf{W}||^2 - \frac{1}{n}\sum_{i=1}^n\log p(\mathbf{y}_i|\mathbf{x}_i;\mathbf{W})$. Thus, the function in (1) is $\mathcal{L}(\mathcal{T}_\mathcal{M},\mathcal{W}) = \sum_{m=1}^M\mathcal{L}(T_m,\mathbf{W}_m)$. The objective functions (such as $\mathcal{L}(T,\mathbf{W})$) considered in this paper do not have closed form solutions to their minimizers; so, the optimal solutions are obtained by using optimization techniques like L-BFGS. Finally, using the learned weights, the optimal labeling of a new sequence (referred as inference) is defined as: $\hat{\mathbf{y}} = argmax_\mathbf{y} p(\mathbf{y}|\mathbf{x};\mathbf{W})$, and is obtained using the Viterbi algorithm.

4. OUR APPROACH

In this section we present our weight space based graph regularization method. This method can be used in one of the following three modes: (1) semi-supervised learning using labeled and unlabeled examples; (2) multi-task learning of local models; and (3) combined semi-supervised and multi-task learning of local models. The third combined setting is especially powerful since local models can be learned *even for websites with only unlabeled examples.*

Our approach is to construct a graph that connects sequences from same or different websites. The basic idea is to make use of common information that exist across the sequences in influencing the node labels of the sequences. That is, *if two nodes belonging to two different records have nearly the same features firing then these nodes are highly likely to have the same label.* We illustrate this idea through some examples.

Consider two publication records, one each from two different conference websites. Such records consist of nodes with labels such as Author, Title, Affiliation. For example, suppose we have node j and the node features are: $\mathcal{I}(\mathsf{FirstLetterCapital}(\mathbf{x}_j))$, $\mathcal{I}(\mathbf{x}_j \in \mathsf{AuthorDictionary})$, $\mathcal{I}(\mathbf{x}_j \in \mathsf{TechTermDictionary})$ and $\mathcal{I}(\mathsf{ContainsPunctuation}(\mathbf{x}_{j+1}))$. Let us say node j has label Author. The contents of this node may be such that the three features other than $\mathcal{I}(\mathbf{x}_j \in \mathsf{TechTermDictionary})$ fire. Suppose there is another node j' with content such that the same set of features fire. It is very likely that the node j' also has the label Author. For some other node j'' let us say the feature $\mathcal{I}(\mathbf{x}_j \in \mathsf{AuthorDictionary})$ also does not fire. It is likely that j'' also has Author as the label, but to a lesser extent than j'. Thus, it is reasonable to capture our *belief* that two nodes have the same label by using a *similarity score* computed from their feature vectors (e.g., the number of features that are commonly fired)[1].

We can extend this idea to connect an edge (i.e., a pair of adjacent nodes) in one record to an edge in another record. In this case, for computing similarity we concatenate the feature vectors of the two nodes that constitute the edge. If two edges have similar concatenated feature vectors then it is very likely that both have the same label pairs. Connecting such edges (i.e., putting pressure to make them have the same label pairs) is certainly very useful for improving a local model since the same label ordering is expected in all records of one website. Even in the case of edge connections going across websites with different attribute ordering, the edge connections are useful in handling self transitions such as (Title,Title) and (Author,Author).

Which features should we use for determining similarity? Clearly, using global features that are useful both within and across websites is a good idea. Within a local model, it is also helpful to use *local* features. For example, XPath features (i.e., html tag structure with some DOM node properties) are very useful for structured pages, where DOM nodes with the same XPath are expected to have the same label. Similarly, we may expect an attribute to have the same formatting properties, e.g., FontSize, FontType (i.e., bold, italic), etc. Due to the *local* nature of such features, we can connect nodes using these features *only* within each website and not *across* websites.

To encode our expectation that *similar* nodes (or edges) have *same label (label pair)*, we enforce their class *marginal probabilities* to be *close*, through regularization. Note that *marginal probability* computation takes the entire sequence into account. Below, we formalize the above idea, and facilitate SSL and MTL by adding a graph regularization term $\mathcal{G}(\mathcal{W})$ to the objective functions (1) and (2).

Graph Regularization: The graph regularization term is a function defined on a graph $\mathcal{G}$. The graph $\mathcal{G}$ consists of a set of vertices ($\mathcal{V}$) and connections ($\mathcal{O}$). To avoid confusion, we use the terminologies (*node,edge*) for the CRF cliques in the input sequences, and (*vertex,connection*) for the graph $\mathcal{G}$. Each vertex has a *score vector* and each connection has a *weight*. A *connection weight* is a similarity score computed using features of the vertices involved in the connection. The vertices correspond to the nodes and edges of the sequences. Then, the graph regularization term is defined using the connection weights and vertex scores. As we show below, the vertex scores are dependent on the *model weights*. Thus, the method derives the name *weight space* based graph regularization. The basic idea is to regularize the model weights by constraining the scores of a pair of vertices to be close when their connection weight is large. Before we define the graph regularization term, we first explain how: (1) vertices are formed and connected, (2) connection weights are computed and (3) vertex scores are assigned.

Vertices and Connecting Sequences: The role of $\mathcal{G}$ is to connect the sequences using some similarity measure. From section 3, we know that a sequence is characterized by a set of node and edge cliques, where an edge connects two adjacent nodes. We connect two sequences by connecting the *cliques* of the sequences. Thus, *each clique* forms a *vertex* in $\mathcal{G}$. With this definition, a vertex v is indexed by a 3-tuple (m, i, c) where c is a clique in the i-th sequence from the m-th website. Let $\mathcal{N}$ and $\mathcal{E}$ denote the sets of node and edge cliques in the collection of sequences. We have $\mathcal{V} = \mathcal{N} \cup \mathcal{E}$ and $|\mathcal{V}| = |\mathcal{N}| + |\mathcal{E}|$. *Two cliques (vertices) are connected only if they are of the same type.* In other words, a *node (edge) clique* is connected only to other *node (edge) cliques.*

Graph Structure: $\mathcal{G}$ is constructed by connecting cliques of labeled and unlabeled sequences obeying the above *type* constraint. Thus, $\mathcal{G}$ has two *separate* components which we refer to as *node graph* $\mathcal{G}_{\mathcal{N}}$ and *edge graph* $\mathcal{G}_{\mathcal{E}}$.

Connection Weights Computation: We now give details on finding the connection weight $\phi_{v,v'}$ for each connection $(v, v') \in \mathcal{G}$. From Section 3 we know that the feature functions $f_k(\mathbf{x}_c, \mathbf{y}_c)$ are dependent on different features illustrated above. There will be many such features for a clique c and we collect these features into a feature vector $\mathbf{F}_v$. Note that for an edge clique we collect feature vectors of *both* the nodes into a single feature vector. Using feature vectors of the vertices in a connection, we set the connection weight as: $\phi_{v,v'} = D(\mathbf{F}_v, \mathbf{F}_{v'}) \geq 0$, a similarity score between the feature vectors. An example of a similarity score is the inner product of the two feature vectors. Thus, when the feature vectors of the two vertices (v, v') are similar, $\phi_{v,v'} \to 1$ and when they are dissimilar $\phi_{v,v'} \to 0$.

The connection weights of $\mathcal{G}_{\mathcal{N}}$ and $\mathcal{G}_{\mathcal{E}}$ can be collected into two *separate* matrices, $\Phi_{\mathcal{N}}$ and $\Phi_{\mathcal{E}}$. Note that $\Phi_{\mathcal{N}}$ is of size $|\mathcal{N}| \times |\mathcal{N}|$ and $\Phi_{\mathcal{E}}$ is of size $|\mathcal{E}| \times |\mathcal{E}|$. When the number of examples (particularly, with the unlabeled examples) is large these matrices can be huge. Therefore, it is useful from storage and computational viewpoints to construct sparse matrices by connecting each vertex to only its k nearest neighbors. In our information extraction application, the number of features is small; therefore, defining a distance metric and finding nearest neighbors are not difficult.

Vertex Scores Computation: To encode our expectation that vertices having similar feature vectors have the same label, we assign the class marginal probability distribution as the score vector for each vertex. Note that for each clique c, the marginal probability distribution is defined over *all possible* label assignments of $\mathbf{y}_c$. Thus, the score vector is of size $|\mathcal{Y}|$ for a node clique, and is of size $|\mathcal{Y}|^2$ for an edge clique. Let us call this score vector of a vertex v as $(\mathbf{g}_v)$. For notational simplicity we have suppressed the dependence of $\mathbf{g}_v$ on the weights and the nodes associated with the clique.

Graph Regularization Term $\mathcal{G}(\mathcal{W})$: Given $\mathcal{G}$, vertex scores, $\mathbf{g}_v, \forall v \in \mathcal{V}$ and connection weights, $\phi_{v,v'}, \forall(v, v') \in \mathcal{O}$, we define $\mathcal{G}(\mathcal{W})$ as:

$$\frac{\mu_N}{Z_N} \sum_{v,v' \in \mathcal{N}} \phi_{v,v'} \mathcal{D}(\mathbf{g}_v, \mathbf{g}_{v'}) + \frac{\mu_E}{Z_E} \sum_{v,v' \in \mathcal{E}} \phi_{v,v'} \mathcal{D}(\mathbf{g}_v, \mathbf{g}_{v'}) \quad (4)$$

where μ_N and μ_E are regularization constants; $\mathcal{D}(\cdot)$ is a divergence measure such as Kullback-Leibler or squared error loss; Z_N and Z_E are graph normalization[2] terms defined

[1]Relational information has been used for collective classification of web documents; see for example, [23, 17, 33]. However, our work is different as we work with structured prediction models in the information extraction context; furthermore, we build local models.

[2]Other graph normalization schemes such as normalizing the connection weights by the degree of a vertex are also possible. For example, use $\tilde{\phi}_{v,v'} = \frac{\phi_{v,v'}}{\sum_{v' \in \mathcal{G}_{\mathcal{N}}} \phi_{v,v'}}, \forall v \in \mathcal{G}_{\mathcal{N}}$ and

as $Z_N = \sum_{v,v' \in \mathcal{N}} \phi_{v,v'}$ and $Z_E = \sum_{v,v' \in \mathcal{E}} \phi_{v,v'}$. Other graph normalization schemes can also be used. Thus, the graph regularization term connects the sequences by connecting their cliques. The first and second terms represent contributions from the node graph $\mathcal{G}_{\mathcal{N}}$ and the edge graph $\mathcal{G}_{\mathcal{E}}$ respectively. The model weights are regularized by constraining the scores of the cliques to be close whenever the similarity score between the cliques is large.

With the introduction of (4) the objective functions associated with the Local and Global models in (1) and (2) get modified to $\mathcal{L}(\mathcal{T}_{\mathcal{M}}, \mathcal{W}) + \frac{\lambda}{2} \sum_{m:S_m \in \mathcal{S}_U} ||\mathbf{W}_m||^2 + \mathcal{G}(\mathcal{W})$ and $\mathcal{L}(\mathcal{T}_{\mathcal{M}}, \mathbf{W}) + \frac{|\mathcal{S}_U|\lambda}{2}||\mathbf{W}||^2 + \mathcal{G}(\mathbf{W})$ respectively. Note that weight regularization corresponding to $\mathcal{S}_U$ is also added.

The complexity of function and gradient computations of $\mathbf{g}_v$ is $O(|F|V)$ where $|F|$ and V are the feature size and sequence length respectively; this causes the optimization of the above mentioned objective functions to be expensive for large datasets. Therefore, to reduce the computational cost, we use an *alternate* score vector. From (3), we see that the score of a sequence $(\mathbf{x}, \mathbf{y})$ can be defined as: $H(\mathbf{x}, \mathbf{y}) = \sum_{c \in \mathcal{C}} h_c(\mathbf{x}_c, \mathbf{y}_c; \mathbf{W})$ where $h_c(\mathbf{x}_c, \mathbf{y}_c; \mathbf{W}) = \sum_k w_k f_k(\mathbf{x}_c, \mathbf{y}_c)$ is the score contribution from clique c and is dependent on $\mathbf{y}_c$. Thus, for each clique c, we compute $\mathbf{g}_v$ comprising of the scores corresponding to *all possible* label assignments of $\mathbf{y}_c$. Note that $\mathbf{g}_v$ is linear in the model weights; therefore, the function and gradient computations are cheap.

There is an additional advantage associated with using the alternate score vector. Since $\mathbf{g}_v$ is linear in the model weights and $\phi_{v,v'} \geq 0, \forall v, v' \in \mathcal{V}$, each of the sub-terms in (4) is quadratic in the model weights, and is convex. Note that (2) and (1) are also convex. Therefore, adding (4) to (2) or (1) results in a convex optimization problem with a unique solution. This solution is easily and dependably obtained by using optimization techniques like L-BFGS. The alternate score is not just cheaper; our experimental results (see the next section) show that very good generalization performance is achieved with it. Finally, with learned $\mathbf{W}$, the Viterbi algorithm is used to make predictions.

Learning Scenarios: Let us revisit the three modes of using $\mathcal{G}$ mentioned at the beginning of this section. We make use of $\mathcal{G}$ for two purposes. It is used to connect the examples (labeled and unlabeled), and it is also used to connect multiple tasks by connecting the examples of two different tasks. We show below how different learning scenarios can be created by setting up the graph in different ways. In each scenario the solution is obtained by using optimization techniques like L-BFGS (as in supervised learning).

(1) SEMI-SUPERVISED LEARNING: In the Global model scenario, $\mathcal{G}$ connects the examples (labeled and unlabeled) across all the websites ($\mathcal{S}$). In the Local models scenario, $\mathcal{G}$ connects the examples (labeled and unlabeled) only *within* each website. In this scenario, the examples from $\mathcal{S}_U$ are not used, and the local models can be learned *independently* as there are no connections between the examples from different sites. In these scenarios, the unlabeled examples are also used to learn the models. We refer the models built in these scenarios as SSL-Global and SSL-Local model(s) respectively.

(2) MULTI-TASK LEARNING: This is applicable only in the Local models scenario and assume that there are *only* labeled examples (i.e.,$\mathcal{S}_U$ is empty and all the unlabeled sets U_m in $\mathcal{S}_L$ are empty). The graph *connects the labeled examples* of any two different tasks. We refer the model built in this scenario as MTL models and all the models are learned *jointly*. Thus, the local model of a website is influenced by the labeled examples from other websites. This is useful when the number of labeled examples in each website is small.

(3) SEMI-SUPERVISED MULTI-TASK LEARNING: In this scenario, the graph connects labeled and unlabeled examples of any two tasks. Furthermore, all the models are learned *jointly*. We can *also* have only unlabeled examples from a website.[3] Thus, unlike the above mentioned SSL and MTL learning scenarios, *we can learn a local model for such a totally unlabeled website* as well. The models built in this scenario are referred as SSL-MTL models.

set $Z_N = \frac{1}{|\mathcal{N}|}$. Similar normalization can be done for all the vertices in $\mathcal{G}_{\mathcal{E}}$ and set $Z_E = \frac{1}{|\mathcal{G}_E|}$.

5. EXPERIMENTS

In this section, we report experimental results with real life datasets which demonstrate the effectiveness of our graph based regularization method in SEMI-SUPERVISED, MULTI-TASK and SEMI-SUPERVISED MULTI-TASK learning scenarios.

5.1 Experimental Setup

Learning Scenarios: As explained in Sections 2 and 4, we consider various learning scenarios and they are summarized in Table 1. These scenarios arise due to the following variations: (1) the composition of dataset (labeled examples (*Lab.*), unlabeled examples (*UnLab.*) and a combination), (2) model learning (*independent* (abbreviated as *indep.*) and *joint*); also, we have SL: SUPERVISED, : SSL: SEMI-SUPERVISED and MTL: MULTI-TASK learning, (3) connection (*within* sites and *across* sites) and (4) number of models ($|\mathcal{S}_L|$ and $|\mathcal{S}_U|$ denote the number of labeled and unlabeled websites).

Datasets: We constructed four datasets Books,Seminars, CS-Faculty and ML-Confs. Each dataset consists of a collection of list pages and each list page has multiple records. The list pages were collected from different websites and grouped per website to facilitate *local model* learning. The Books dataset has pages from eight *business* websites like www.amazon.com with one page per site. In most pages, the number of records per page varies from 15 to 100. Each record represents attributes (given below) of a book. The Seminars dataset has pages from five university websites and there were $2 - 4$ pages per website. The number of records per website is around 50. Each record represents attributes of seminar announcement. The CS-Faculty dataset has pages from five university websites with one page per website. The number of records per page is around 40. Each record represents attributes of a faculty in a university. The ML-Confs dataset has 5 websites with one page per site and each page has around 50 records representing paper details (from ICML and KDD conferences).

Attributes: The *attributes* for each dataset are given as:
Books: Title, Author, Publisher, Price, ISBN
Seminars: Title, Speaker, Date, Affiliation, Host

[3]The local model weights for a completely unlabeled website is derived using only the weight and graph regularization terms. Therefore, closed form expression can be obtained in the case when the squared error graph regularization term defined in (4) is used.

Model	*Lab.*	*UnLab.*	$\mathcal{G}(\mathcal{W})$	Learning	# Models	Obj. Function
Local	Yes	No	No	independent (SL)	$\lvert\mathcal{S}_L\rvert$	$\sum_{m:S_m \in \mathcal{S}_L} \mathcal{L}(T_m, \mathbf{W}_m)$ (equation (1))
Global	Yes	No	No	(SL)	1	$\sum_{m:S_m \in \mathcal{S}_L} \mathcal{L}(T_m, \mathbf{W})$ (equation (2))
MTL	Yes	No	*across*	joint (SL-MTL)	$\lvert\mathcal{S}_L\rvert$	$\sum_{m:S_m \in \mathcal{S}_L} \mathcal{L}(T_m, \mathbf{W}_m) + \mathcal{G}(\mathcal{W}_{\mathcal{S}_L})$
SSL-Local	Yes	Yes	*within*	independent (SSL)	$\lvert\mathcal{S}_L\rvert$	$\sum_{m:S_m \in \mathcal{S}_L} \mathcal{L}(T_m, \mathbf{W}_m) + \mathcal{G}(\mathcal{W}_{\mathcal{S}_L})$
SSL-Global	Yes	Yes	*across*	(SSL)	1	$\sum_{m:S_m \in \mathcal{S}_L} \mathcal{L}(T_m, \mathbf{W}) + \frac{\lvert\mathcal{S}_U\rvert\lambda}{2}\lvert\lvert\mathbf{W}\rvert\rvert^2 + \mathcal{G}(\mathbf{W})$
SSL-MTL	Yes	Yes	*across*	joint (SSL-MTL)	$\lvert\mathcal{S}_L \cup \mathcal{S}_U\rvert$	$\sum_{m:S_m \in \mathcal{S}_L} \mathcal{L}(T_m, \mathbf{W}_m) + \sum_{m \in \mathcal{S}_U} \frac{\lambda}{2}\lvert\lvert\mathbf{W}_m\rvert\rvert^2 + \mathcal{G}(\mathcal{W})$

Table 1: Learning Scenarios (see sections 4 and 5.1 for more details). Notations: $\mathcal{S}_L$ and $\mathcal{S}_U$ are labeled and unlabeled websites. $\mathcal{W}_{\mathcal{S}_L} = \{\mathbf{W}_m \mid m : S_m \in \mathcal{S}_L\}$ and $\mathcal{W} = \mathcal{W}_{\mathcal{S}_L \cup \mathcal{S}_U}$.

CS-Faculty: Title, Name, Position, Education, Research Interests, Phone, e-mail
ML-Confs: Title, Author, Affiliation, PaperID
In each dataset, there is also an attribute Others which captures any text that does not fall under the above categories. We manually labeled all the attributes in each record for all the datasets.

Features: We used only *global* features in all our experiments.[4] The records were tokenized at word level. Of course, one could use simple segmentation models and this would help in improving the performance further. The content features were defined at a higher level of abstraction. Thus, the number of features was small. For numeric attributes like Date, Price, Phone, ISBN, PaperID, we used features such as ContainsNumber, ContainsPriceSymbol, Has3Digits, Has10Digits, HasMonth, ContainsAMPM, etc. We used a dictionary of person names for attributes such as Author, Speaker, Host and had a feature InPersonNameDictionary. We also had dictionaries for other attributes Title, Research Interests, Position etc, and these dictionaries were constructed from the dataset. These types of content features were used to generate the *node* and *edge* features of the CRF model.

Train-Test Split: We used 70% of the total dataset for training and 30% for testing. Note that the split happens for each website so that we can evaluate the performance for the local models at the site level. The training set was split into two sets: (1) labeled examples and (2) unlabeled examples. We varied the percentage of labeled examples from 5-40% and evaluated the performance. Note that in many cases, the number of labeled records per site is 1 when the percentage of labeled examples is small. Finally, note that as we increase the percentage of labeled examples, the size of the unlabeled examples reduces. This is because the training set size is fixed.

Evaluation Metric: We evaluated the F-score performance for each attribute on the test data. Due to space constraint, we present only average F1-score performance computed using all the tokens (attributes). In the experiments that involve *partial labeled websites* (that is, $S_m \in \mathcal{S}_L$) and *totally unlabeled websites* ($S_m \in \mathcal{S}_U$) we also report the performance on the test sets of partially labeled websites and totally unlabeled websites *separately*.

Graph Construction and Parameter Settings: To construct $\mathcal{G}$ we used inner product of the feature vectors of the cliques to compute similarity scores. To restrict the graph size, we used k-nearest neighbors and set $k = 20$. We ensure that an unlabeled example is connected to a labeled example *within one hop*. This helps in getting improved performance. For graph normalization, we used $Z_{\mathcal{N}} = Z_{\mathcal{E}} = \sum_{(v,v') \in \mathcal{G}} \phi_{v,v'}$ and set $\mu_{\mathcal{N}} = \mu_{\mathcal{E}} = 200$. For weight regularization, we set $\lambda = 0.01$. Due to computational reasons, we did not use cross-validation (CV) to set these parameters. Using CV would help in getting improved performance.

5.2 Experimental Results

We conducted several experiments with each experiment focusing on a different learning scenario. In all the experiments we used 3 partially labeled websites (PLS) (i.e.,$\lvert\mathcal{S}_L\rvert = 3$). We indicate explicitly whenever totally unlabeled websites were included; we experimented with $\lvert\mathcal{S}_U\rvert = 1$ and 2. We evaluated the performance on varying combinations of the websites in $\mathcal{S}_L$ and $\mathcal{S}_U$. Due to space constraint, we present only some of the results.

1. Local versus Global:
We used three websites as the dataset and varied the percentage of labeled examples. The results are shown in the top row of Figure 1. Two key observations can be made. (1) As the number of labeled examples per website increases, the performance of the Local models is significantly better than the Global model; this emphasizes the need for Local models. (2) When the number of labeled examples per website is insufficient, node features from other websites help; as a result the Global model is better (except the case of Books dataset). In the Books dataset we had at least 8% more records per site on average than the other datasets; therefore, Local models were able to learn better even with 5% labeled data per site.

2. Local versus MTL:
The dataset is same as the one used in the Local models scenario. The results are given in the bottom row of Figure 1. It is clearly seen that the MTL local models learned *jointly* using graph regularization outperform the Local models learned independently. On comparing the two rows in Figure 1, we also see that the performance of the MTL model outperforms the Global model. It is seen that our weight space based graph regularization with MTL helps in making use of labeled examples from other websites constructively (even in the presence of variations across the websites); and, the improvement is significant (3% – 8%) when very few labeled examples are available. Thus, the proposed method addresses both the limited labeled data and generalization inadequacy problems.

3. Global versus SSL-Global:
We expand the dataset used in the experiment to build the Global model by including unlabeled examples. Figure 2 shows the performance comparison of the Global and SSL-Global models. When the number of labeled examples is not very small, SSL-Global model outperforms the Global

[4]This is done to show a proof of concept of our approach. Inclusion of local features can boost the performance of our method significantly.

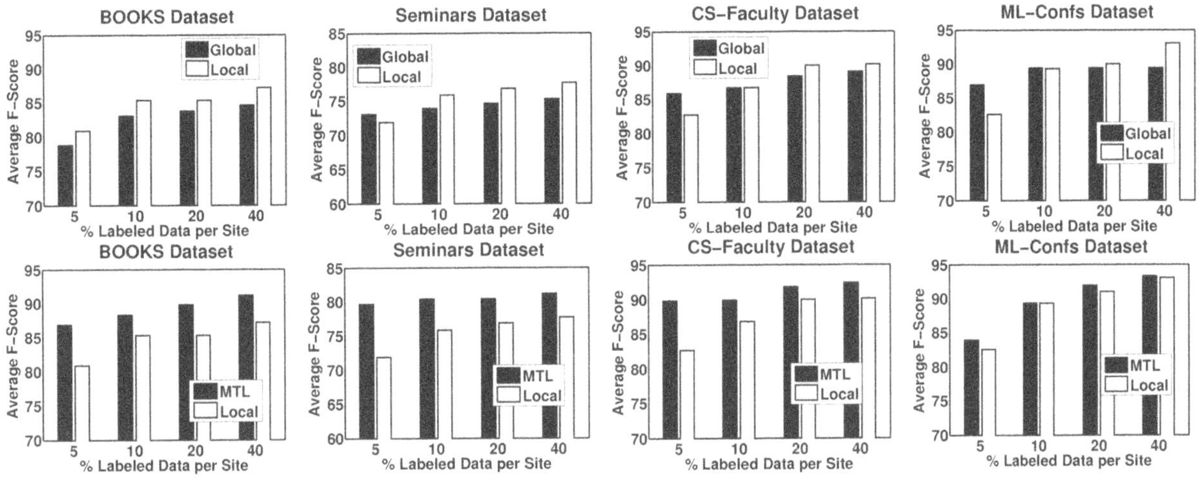

Figure 1: Supervised and Multi-task Learning - **Average F1-score performance. Top Row:** Local **Models versus** Global **Model. Bottom Row:** Local **versus** MTL **Models.** $|\mathcal{S}_L| = 3$ **and** $|\mathcal{S}_U| = 0$.

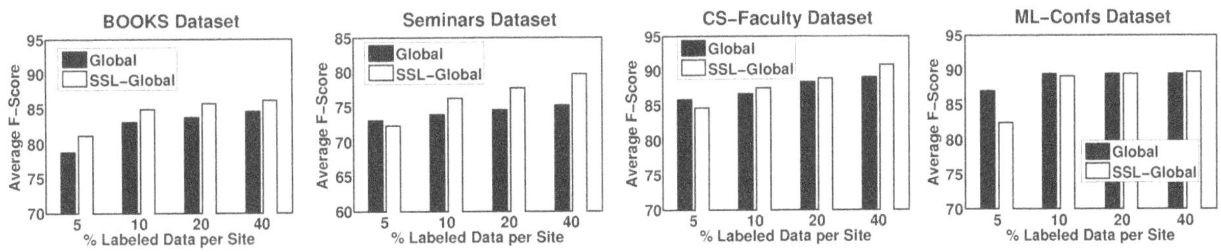

Figure 2: Supervised and Semi-supervised Learning - **Average F1-score performance** - Global versus SSL-Global. $|\mathcal{S}_L| = 3$ **and** $|\mathcal{S}_U| = 0$.

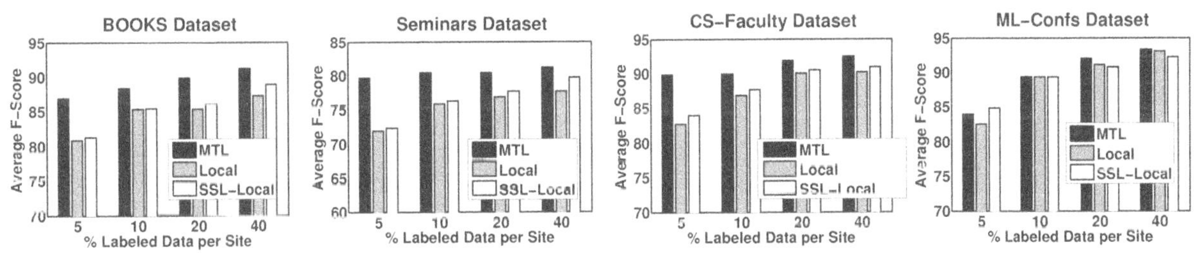

Figure 3: Supervised, Semi-supervised and Multi-task Learning - **Average F1-score performance** - Local, SSL-Local **and** MTL **models.** $|\mathcal{S}_L| = 3$ **and** $|\mathcal{S}_U| = 0$.

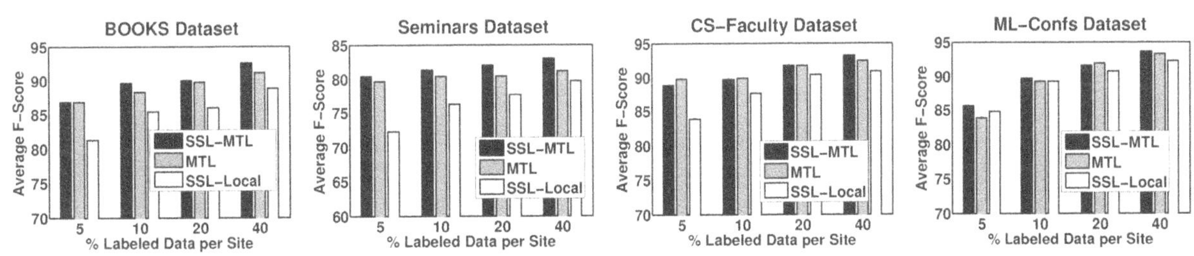

Figure 4: Semi-supervised, Multi-task and Semi-supervised Multi-task Learning - **Average F1-score performance** - SSL-Local, MTL **and** SSL-MTL **models.** $|\mathcal{S}_L| = 3$ **and** $|\mathcal{S}_U| = 0$.

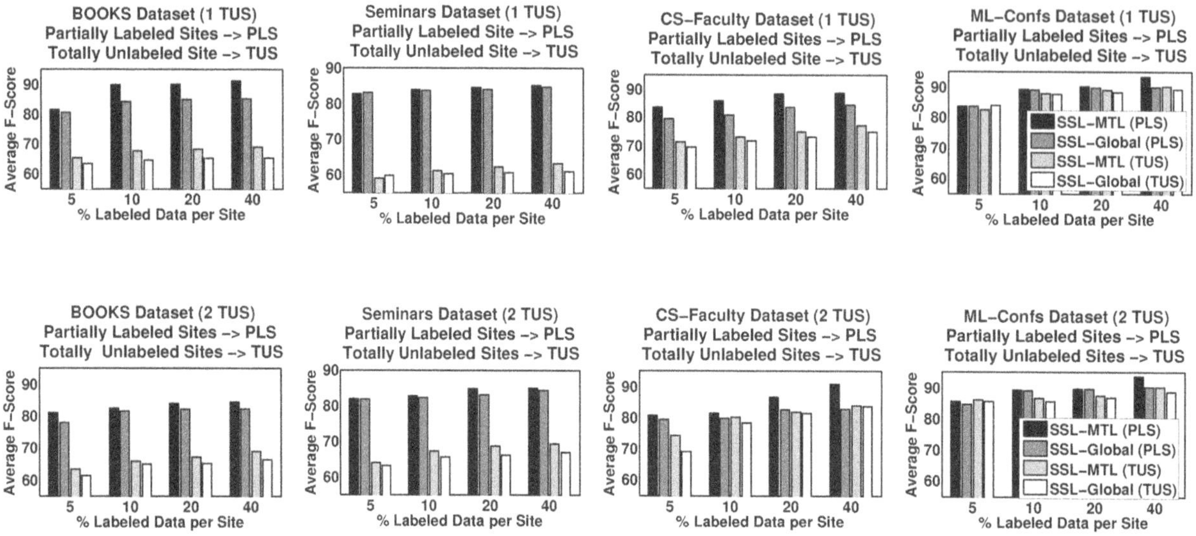

Figure 5: Totally Unlabeled Sites (TUS) **Scenario: Average F1-score performance of the SSL-MTL and Global-SSL models on test sequences of partially labeled sites (PLS - $|\mathcal{S}_L| = 3$) and TUS on various datasets. Top Row: 1 TUS and Bottom Row: 2 TUS. Legends in the right most plots applies to all the plots.**

model on Books, Seminars and CS-Faculty datasets. In the ML-Confs dataset, the graph is not that good (compared to other datasets), possibly due to weaker features for the attribute Title, resulting in no improvement; this is also observed in SSL-Local and SSL-MTL models discussed below.

4. Local versus SSL-Local:

From Figure 3 we see that the performance of SSL-Local is better than Local in most cases and it is significant in some cases. The performance is slightly inferior only in one case, on the MLConfs dataset (when the number of labeled examples is high).

5. SSL-Local versus MTL:

We also compare the performance of Local models with Semi-supervised (SSL-Local) and Multi-task (MTL) learning. Figure 3 shows that the performance improvement obtained using MULTI-TASK learning is significantly higher. Note that in the MTL scenario, the connections are between the labeled examples across the sites. Thus, the weights are adjusted more appropriately by trading-off between the *likelihood* term and graph regularization term. In semi-supervised learning, there are also connections between unlabeled examples. Therefore, there is more freedom. Recall the *within one hop* condition used in our graph construction. Thus, the scores of the connections having only unlabeled examples are regularized only indirectly through the score propagation between the labeled and unlabeled examples, resulting in lesser gain.

6. SSL-MTL:

Recall from Table 1 that SSL-MTL *combines* semi-supervised and multi-task learning. Figure 4 depicts the performance comparison of various local model learning scenarios. We have already seen that MTL models outperform Local models. Here, we see that combined SEMI-SUPERVISED MULTI-TASK learning provides significant additional gain in several cases (see for instance, Books and Seminars datasets). Thus, the proposed method is effective in combining SEMI-SUPERVISED and MULTI-TASK learning in a single framework.

7. Totally Unlabeled Websites:

The aim of this experiment is to demonstrate that good local models can be built even for websites with totally unlabeled examples. We evaluate the performance on the *partially labeled sites* (PLS) and *totally unlabeled sites* (TUS). From Figure 5 (one and two totally unlabeled sites), the following observations can be made. (1) In the case of PLS, SSL-MTL models perform better than the SSL-Global model on Books and CS-Faculty datasets; on the remaining datasets, they are comparable. (2) In the case of TUS, SSL-MTL models perform better in many cases, viz., Books, Seminars and CS-Faculty datasets; it is comparable to SSL-Global on ML-Confs dataset. These results clearly demonstrate that decent local models can be built for websites with completely unlabeled examples using our method, though the accuracy is affected by the degree of similarity between the different sites.

8. Varying Unlabeled Website:

In practice we can at most have a few websites with labeled examples. These partially labeled sites are used to build the local models for totally unlabeled websites. One practical scenario is to build a local model for *one* TUS *at a time*. The aim of this experiment is to evaluate the proposed method in this scenario. Figure 6 shows the results obtained on the Books dataset, where we built SSL-MTL models with 3 fixed PLS and varied 1 TUS. The results show that the performance on PLS is almost same. As one would expect some variations in the performance are seen across the totally unlabeled websites. This is because the difficulty of a website varies in terms of several optional and missing attributes in the sequences. However, we get decent performance on all TUS.

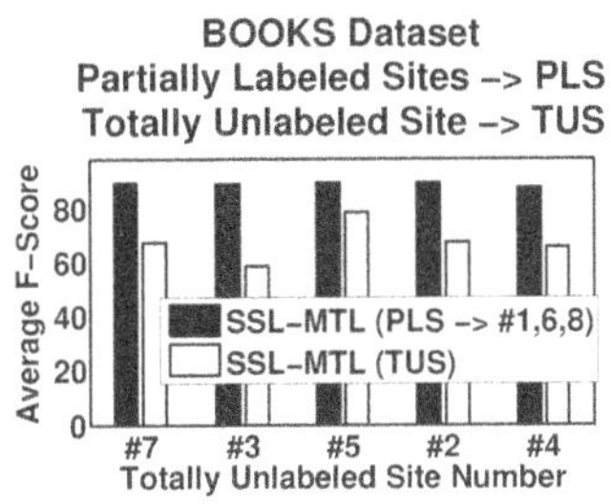

Figure 6: VARYING UNLABELED SITE SCENARIO - **Average F1-score performance of** SSL-MTL **models on the** Books **Dataset. The website numbers used as PLS ($|\mathcal{S}_L| = 3$) and TUS ($|\mathcal{S}_U| = 1$) in a set of 8 websites are indicated.**

6. RELATED WORK

[7, 31] present comprehensive surveys on existing techniques of web information extraction.

As we indicated in section 1, unsupervised learning techniques such as RoadRunner [11], DEPTA [39], and clustering based techniques [3, 25] are useful for extracting records from list pages via repetitive patterns in the HTML tags of one or more pages. They are ineffective for the finer problem of attribute segmentation.

There exist several methods for attribute extraction from many websites using minimal/weak supervision [1, 26, 40, 28, 24, 10, 9, 34, 15]. Let us look at some representative ones. To learn wrappers for new websites, Chuang et al. [9] propose a method for synchronized data extraction using contextual information from reference websites. In contrast, our solution is based on machine-learned discriminative models. Senellart et al. [34] trained CRF models using high precision annotated records which are obtained using domain knowledge. Gupta et al. [15] address the problem of constructing a table for *n-tuple* record type queries. After collecting a set of list pages from the web using the queries, they build independent local CRF models using annotated records obtained from an existing database and extract attributes of interest. The extracted records are then added to the database. This is a pipelined approach that works only when there are matching records across the websites; our method does not require that assumption. Unlike [34, 15] we build the models jointly and make use of unlabeled examples.

Among the SSL approaches for sequence learning [20, 2, 36, 37, 18, 35], our method is closely related to [2, 35]. As in our method, [2] connects cliques of the sequences. While our method is weight space based and simple, [2] optimizes in dual space which requires computationally intensive matrix inversion (cubic in graph size). [35] proposes a graph regularization based SSL approach for a POS tagging domain adaptation problem; unlike our method, their method alternates between model parameter learning and marginal probability smoothing using graph regularization. None of the above mentioned approaches build local models jointly and they do not learn local models for new websites.

There has been a significant amount of work on multi-task learning [6, 14, 13, 4, 22, 16]. Of these only [13] builds local models using a graph that connects multiple tasks; even this work does not build a model for a task with totally unlabeled examples. Also, the main focus of these papers is not on the structured outputs problem for information extraction.

In other related work on domain adaptation [32, 12, 8], the approach of Duan et al. [12] is more close to our approach. However, our graph construction procedure is different; also, like [8] it only addresses a multi-class classification problem and not the structured output problem. Furthermore, unlike our approach none of the above mentioned works learn the models jointly.

7. FUTURE WORK

In this section, we discuss several extensions that are possible in this framework. The graph regularization term that we used in this paper is based on squared error loss. An alternative way is to regularize using Kullback-Leibler (KL) divergence computed using probability scores of cliques. This can be done by defining the probability score for a label assignment y as $\mathbf{p}_v(y) = \frac{1}{Z_v}\exp(\mathbf{g}_v(y)), \forall y \in \mathcal{Y}$ (or $\mathcal{Y}^2$ for an edge clique) where Z_v is a normalizing constant. Next, the graph $\mathcal{G}$ plays a very important role in getting improved performance. Using different similarity measures and graph normalization schemes can also be useful. Another possibility is to group the content features into various sub-groups and construct a graph for each sub-group. From *local* modeling viewpoint, *local features* like XPATH based features are very useful. Therefore, adding local features into the model and constructing a graph based on these local features will help in boosting the performance significantly on the totally unlabeled websites. Use of entropy regularization [18] for semi-supervised learning has been explored. Extending this to SEMI-SUPERVISED MULTI-TASK LEARNING is another interesting direction. Finally, note that although we only experimented with sequences, the framework is general and is applicable to more complex structured outputs such as trees, graphs, etc. Also, it can be used to build structured support vector machine (SVMStruct) models.

8. CONCLUSION

In this paper we proposed a weight space based graph regularization method for SEMI-SUPERVISED, MULTI-TASK and SEMI-SUPERVISED MULTI-TASK learning. We demonstrated its effectiveness in the three learning scenarios for web information extraction. The results clearly demonstrate that the method is useful in addressing the issues of limited labeled data and inadequacy of a global model in generalizing well across websites. An added advantage is that we can learn decent local models for websites without any labeled data also, which is not possible even for wrapper learning approaches. Our method is scalable since we can learn the local models for unlabeled websites in parallel using a fixed set of partially labeled websites. Furthermore, the newly labeled websites obtained through learning can be used to learn subsequent unlabeled websites (by updating the existing list of labeled websites).

Acknowledgments: The authors are thankful to the anonymous reviewers for their helpful comments.

9. REFERENCES

[1] E. Agichtein and V. Ganti. Mining reference tables for automatic text segmentation. In *ACM SIGKDD*, 2004.

[2] Y. Altun, D. McAllester, and M. Belkin. Maximum margin semi-supervised learning for structured variables. In *NIPS*, 2005.

[3] M. Alvarez, A. Pan, J. Raposo, F. Bellas, and F. Cacheda. Using clustering and edit distance techniques for automatic web data extraction. In *WISE*, 2007.

[4] R. K. Ando and T. Zhang. A framework for learning predictive structures from multiple tasks and unlabeled data. In *JMLR*, volume 6, pages 1817–1853, 2005.

[5] V. Borkar, K. Deshmukh, and S. Sarawagi. Automatic segmentation of text into structured records. In *ACM SIGMOD*, 2001.

[6] R. Caruana. Multi-task learning. In *Machine Learning*, volume 28, pages 41–75, 1997.

[7] C.-H. Chang, M. Kayed, M. R. Girgis, and K. Shaalan. A survey of web information extraction systems. *IEEE transactions on knowledge and data engineering*, 18:1411–1428, 2006.

[8] B. Chen, W. Lam, I. Tsang, and T.-L. Wong. Extracting discriminative concepts for domain adaptation in text mining. In *KDD*, 2009.

[9] S.-L. Chuang, K. C.-C. Chang, and C. Zhai. Context-aware wrapping: synchronized data extraction. In *Proceedings of the 33rd international conference on Very large data bases*, VLDB '07, pages 699–710. VLDB Endowment, 2007.

[10] E. Cortez, A. S. da Silva, M. A. Gonçalves, and E. S. de Moura. Ondux: on-demand unsupervised learning for information extraction. In *SIGMOD Conference*, pages 807–818, 2010.

[11] V. Crescenzi, G. Mecca, and P. Merialdo. Roadrunner: Towards automatic data extraction from large web sites. In *VLDB*, 2001.

[12] L. Duan, I. W. Tsang, D. Xu, and T.-S. Chua. Domain adaptation from multiple sources via auxiliary classifiers. In *ICML*, 2009.

[13] T. Evgeniou, C. A. Michelli, and M. Pontil. Learning multiple tasks with kernel methods. In *JMLR*, volume 6, pages 615–637, 2005.

[14] T. Evgeniou and M. Pontil. Regularized multi-task learning. In *KDD*, 2004.

[15] R. Gupta and S. Sarawagi. Answering table augmentation queries from unstrcutured lists on the web. In *VLDB*, 2009.

[16] J. Honorio and D. Samaras. Multi-task learning of Gaussian graphical models. In *ICML*, 2010.

[17] D. Jensen, J. Neville, and B. Gallagher. Why collective inference improves relational classification. In *ACM SIGKDD*, pages 593–598, 2004.

[18] F. Jiao, S. Wang, C.-H. Lee, R. Greiner, and D. Schuurmans. Semi-supervised conditional random fields for improved segmentation and labeling. In *ACL*, 2006.

[19] N. Kushmerick, D. S. Weld, and R. Doorenbos. Wrapper induction for information extraction. In *IJCAI*, 1997.

[20] J. Lafferty, Y. Liu, and X. Zhu. Kernel conditional random fields. In *ICML*, 2004.

[21] J. Lafferty, A. McCallum, and F. Pereira. Conditional random fields: Probabilistic models for segmenting and labeling sequence data. In *ICML*, 2001.

[22] Q. Liu, X. Liao, and L. Carin. Semi-supervised multitask learning. In *NIPS*, 2007.

[23] Q. Lu and L. Getoor. Link based classification. In *ICML*, pages 496–503, 2003.

[24] I. R. Mansuri and S. Sarawagi. Integrating unstructured data into relational databases. In *ICDE*, page 29, 2006.

[25] G. Miao, J. Tatemura, W. Hsiung, A. Sawires, and L. Moser. Extracting data records from the web using tag path clustering. In *WWW*, 2009.

[26] M. Michelson and C. A. Knoblock. Unsupervised information extraction from unstructured, ungrammatical data sources on the world wide web. *IJDAR*, 10(3-4):211–226, 2007.

[27] I. Muslea, S. Minton, and C. Knoblock. Hierarchical wrapper induction for semistructured information sources. *Autonomous Agents and Multi-Agent Systems*, 1(2), 2001.

[28] P. Papotti, V. Crescenzi, P. Merialdo, M. Bronzi, and L. Blanco. Redundancy-driven web data extraction and integration. In *WebDB*, 2010.

[29] F. Peng and A. McCallum. Accurate information extraction from research papers using conditional random fields. In *HLT-NAACL04*, 2004.

[30] H. Poon and P. Domingos. Joint inference in information extraction. In *22nd AAAI*, 2007.

[31] S. Sarawagi. Information extraction. *Foundations and trends in databases*, 1(3):261–377, 2008.

[32] S. Satpal and S. Sarawagi. Domain adaptation of conditional probability models via feature subsetting. In *ECML-PKDD*, 2007.

[33] P. Sen, G. M. Namata, M. Bilgic, L. Getoor, B. Gallagher, and T. Eliassi-Rad. Collective classification in network data. Technical Report CS-TR-4905, University of Maryland, 2008.

[34] P. Senellart, A. Mittal, D. Muschick, R. Gilleron, and M. Tommasi. Automatic wrapper induction from hidden-web sources with domain knowledge. In *WIDM*, 2008.

[35] A. Subramanya, S. Petrov, and F. Pereira. Efficient graph-based semi-supervised learning of structured tagging models. In *EMNLP*, pages 167–176, 2010.

[36] J. Suzuki and H. Isozaki. Semi-supervised sequential labeling and segmentation using giga-word scale unlabeled data. In *ACL*, 2008.

[37] Y. Wang, G. Haffari, S. Wang, and G. Mori. A rate distortion approach for semi-supervised conditional random fields. In *NIPS*, 2009.

[38] T. Weninger, W. H. Hsu, and J. Han. CETR - content extraction via tag ratios. In *WWW*, 2010.

[39] Y. Zhai and B. Liu. Web data extraction based on partial tree assignment. In *WWW*, 2005.

[40] C. Zhao, J. Mahmud, and I. V. Ramakrishnan. Exploiting structured reference data for unsupervised text segmentation with conditional random fields. In *SDM*, pages 420–431, 2008.

[41] J. Zhu, Z. Nie, J. Wen, B. Zhang, and W. Ma. Simultaneous record detection and attribute labeling in web data extraction. In *ACM SIGKDD*, 2006.

Memory-less Unsupervised Clustering for Data Streaming by Versatile Ellipsoidal Function

Niwan Wattanakitrungroj
AVIC Research Center, Department of Mathematics and Computer Science, Faculty of Science, Chulalongkorn University
Bangkok, Thailand
w_niwan_50@hotmail.com

Chidchanok Lursinsap
AVIC Research Center, Department of Mathematics and Computer Science, Faculty of Science, Chulalongkorn University
Bangkok, Thailand
lchidcha@gmail.com

ABSTRACT

The challenge of clustering on data stream is the ability to deal with the continuous incoming data which are unlimited and unable to store all of them. To manage the storage crisis, the data must be processed in a single pass or only once after the arrival and are thrown away outer. All previously clustered data must be mathematically captured in terms of group features since those data are already non-existent.

The proposed data stream clustering algorithm is divided into two main phases, namely on-line and off-line. In the on-line phase, new micro-cluster features are proposed. Our micro-cluster features better represent the arriving data than the traditional micro-cluster features. In the off-line phase, the prepared micro-clusters are categorized by their densities. The proposed method can generate the final clusters with different shapes and densities. Based on entropy, purity, Jaccard coefficient, and Rand statistic measures, our algorithm being applied on synthetic and real data outperforms the other previous data stream clustering algorithms.

Categories and Subject Descriptors

H.3.3 [**Information Storage and Retrieval**]: Information Search and Retrieval—*Clustering*; F.1.2 [**Computation by Abstract Devices**]: Modes of Computation—*Online computation*

General Terms

Theory, Algorithms, Experimentation

Keywords

Data Stream Clustering, Micro-cluster, Online Incrementally

1. INTRODUCTION

In recent applications, the data set are accumulated at a rapidly rate referred to as data stream, i.e., a continuous stream of new data points that be processed as it is produced. The traditional clustering approaches are not sufficiently flexible to deal with data stream that continuously evolves over time. Most of the existing algorithms for clustering data stream consists of two phases, on-line and off-line processes [1, 3, 5–11]. In the on-line phase, all data points cannot be stored but they are summarized in a set of features. When a clustering request arrives, the set of features is processed in an off-line way. This paper proposes the algorithm of data stream clustering, namely *CompactStream*, which consists of on-line and off-line phases. The on-line arriving data are summarized in the new proposed micro-cluster features, *Emc*(Elliptical micro-cluster), which is a hyper-elliptical shape representation. Note that the representing of data in the form of the hyper-elliptical shape is obviously more compact than the hyper-spherical shape. Fig. 1 shows the representation of the micro-cluster in our proposed algorithm and two previous algorithms, i.e., CluSteram and DenStream. All micro-clusters from the on-line phase are used to discover clusters with different shapes, sizes and densities in the off-line phase.

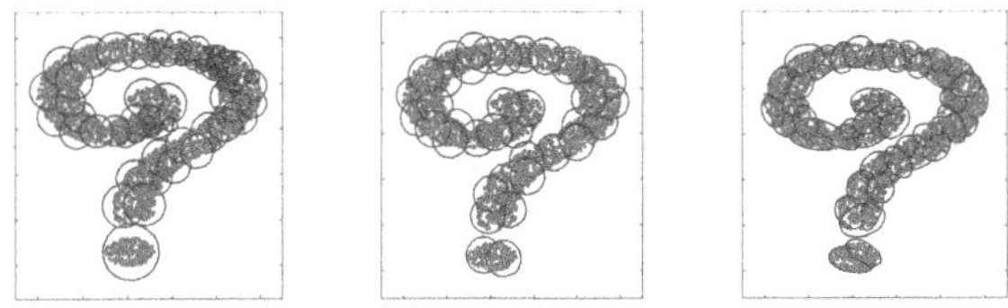

(a) *CluStream* (b) *DenStream* (c) *CompactStream*

Figure 1: Micro-clusters representations from different methods.

The rest of this paper is organized as follows. In section 2, the related works are discussed. The definition and fundamental concepts are introduced in Section 3. Our proposed algorithm is described in Section 4. The performance study on real and synthetic data sets is reported in Section 5. Finally, we conclude the paper in Section 6.

2. RELATED WORKS

In many existing algorithms, the on-line arriving data are summarized in a set of micro-cluster features which are represented as a hyper-spherical shape [1–3, 8, 10, 11]. However, the criteria for maintaining the micro-clusters and discovering the final clusters in each existing algorithms are different.

In CluStream [1], the micro-clusters features are different in sizes of spherical shape representation. It is needed to

CIKM'11, October 24–28, 2011, Glasgow, Scotland, UK.

create a set of initial micro-clusters on a set of initial points using a standard K-means clustering algorithm. It is difficult for CluStream to discover clusters with arbitrary shapes and unable to deal with noise. Moreover, the number K of clusters must be known a priori.

In DenStream [3], a micro-clusters is represented in the form of a spherical shape of the same size. The main different from CluStream is the criteria for the off-line clustering which discover the clusters with an arbitrary shape instead of a spherical shape. They also first need to create the initial micro-clusters on the initial points using the DBSCAN clustering algorithm [4].

Other data stream clustering algorithms [2,8,10,11] based on micro-cluster have been proposed and compared with CluStream and DenStream methods. These algorithms tried to improve the methods in the off-line clustering phase.

In this paper, we introduced the new micro-cluster features which represent the members in the micro-cluster in the form of a hyper-elliptical shape. The performance of our algorithm is compared to two main existing algorithms, CluStream and DenStream. Our proposed ideas and fundamental concepts are presented in the next section.

3. DEFINITIONS AND PROPOSED CONCEPT

In our approach, a micro-cluster is represented in the form of an ellipsoidal shape in arbitrary direction. To explain our concept, only a 2-dimensional ellipsoid function and its feasibility are discussed first. Fig. 2 shows the conceptual micro-cluster boundary which is an ellipsoid with principal directions $\mathbf{q}_1$ and $\mathbf{q}_2$. These principal directions can be defined by the eigenvectors of covariance matrix of the data in micro-cluster. Let $\mathbf{x}=[x_1\ x_2]^T$ be a data point which can be transformed into $\mathbf{y} = [y_1\ y_2]^T$ and $y_i = \mathbf{q}_i^T\mathbf{x}$, $i = 1, 2$. We assume that the length along with these directions are l_1 and l_2, respectively. With respect to $\mathbf{q}_1$ and $\mathbf{q}_2$ directions, the equation of an ellipsoid can be written as follows:

$$\frac{y_1^2}{l_1^2} + \frac{y_2^2}{l_2^2} = 1 \tag{1}$$

Since the eigenvalues represent the variances of the data projected on the corresponding eigenvector, the lengths l_1 and l_2 can be determined by $k\sqrt{\lambda_1}$ and $k\sqrt{\lambda_2}$ where λ_1 and λ_2 are the eigenvalues that correspond to the eigenvectors $\mathbf{q}_1$ and $\mathbf{q}_2$, respectively. Hence, equation (1) can be transformed into the following form: $\frac{y_1^2}{k^2\lambda_1} + \frac{y_2^2}{k^2\lambda_2} = 1$ or $\frac{y_1^2}{\lambda_1} + \frac{y_2^2}{\lambda_2} = k^2$. Similarly, the d-dimensional ellipsoid equation can be written as the following:

$$\frac{y_1^2}{\lambda_1} + ... + \frac{y_j^2}{\lambda_j} + ... + \frac{y_d^2}{\lambda_d} = k^2 \tag{2}$$

where $\lambda_1, ..., \lambda_j, ...\lambda_d$ are the eigenvalues corresponding to the eigenvectors $\mathbf{q}_1, ..., \mathbf{q}_j, ..., \mathbf{q}_d$, respectively.

Generally, let $\mathbf{x} = [x_1...x_d]^T$ be a d-dimensional data vector. The covariance matrix of the set of data vectors is a d-by-d matrix $\mathbf{R}$ as shown by

$$\mathbf{R} = \mathbf{E}[(\mathbf{x} - \mathbf{E}[\mathbf{x}])(\mathbf{x} - \mathbf{E}[\mathbf{x}])^T] \tag{3}$$

where $\mathbf{E}[.]$ represents the expected value or mean value.

Let the eigenvalues of the d-by-d matrix $\mathbf{R}$ be denoted by $\mathbf{\Lambda} = \text{diag}[\lambda_1, ..., \lambda_j, ..., \lambda_d]$, and the associated eigenvectors be denoted by $\mathbf{Q} = [\mathbf{q}_1, ..., \mathbf{q}_j, ..., \mathbf{q}_d]$, respectively. It is necessary and sufficient to have $\mathbf{RQ} = \mathbf{Q\Lambda}$ or

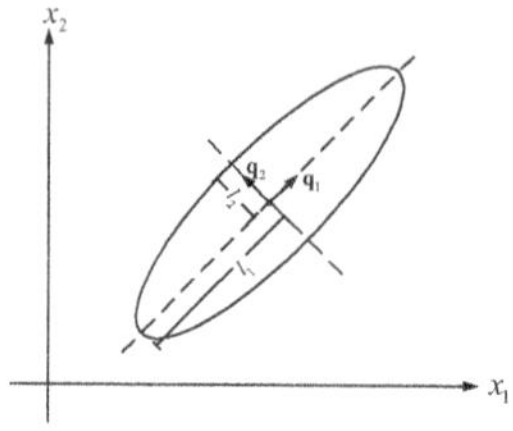

Figure 2: 2D-elliptical micro-cluster boundary.

$$\mathbf{R} = \mathbf{Q\Lambda Q}^{-1}. \tag{4}$$

There are d possible projections of the d-dimensional data points $\mathbf{x}$ to be considered:

$$y_j = \mathbf{q}_j^T\mathbf{x} = \mathbf{x}^T\mathbf{q}_j, j = 1, ..., d. \tag{5}$$

We combine the set of projections into a single vector, as shown by

$$\mathbf{y} = [y_1, ..., y_j, ..., y_d]^T = [\mathbf{q}_1^T\mathbf{x}, ..., \mathbf{q}_j^T\mathbf{x}, ..., \mathbf{q}_d^T\mathbf{x}]^T = \mathbf{Q}^T\mathbf{x} \tag{6}$$

Eq. (2) can be rewritten as:

$$\mathbf{y}^T(\text{diag}[1/\lambda_1, ..., 1/\lambda_j, ..., 1/\lambda_d])\mathbf{y} = \mathbf{y}^T\mathbf{\Lambda}^{-1}\mathbf{y} = k^2 \tag{7}$$

Substitute eq. (6) into eq. (7):

$$(\mathbf{Q}^T\mathbf{x})^T\mathbf{\Lambda}^{-1}(\mathbf{Q}^T\mathbf{x}) = k^2 \tag{8}$$

Substitute $(\mathbf{Q}^T\mathbf{x})^T = \mathbf{x}^T\mathbf{Q}$ into eq. (12):

$$\mathbf{x}^T\mathbf{Q\Lambda}^{-1}(\mathbf{Q}^T\mathbf{x}) = k^2 \tag{9}$$

Since eigenvectors are orthogonal, $\mathbf{Q}^T = \mathbf{Q}^{-1}$, we have

$$\begin{aligned}\mathbf{x}^T\mathbf{Q\Lambda}^{-1}\mathbf{Q}^{-1}\mathbf{x} &= \mathbf{x}^T\mathbf{Q}(\mathbf{Q\Lambda})^{-1}\mathbf{x} = \mathbf{x}^T(\mathbf{Q\Lambda Q}^{-1})^{-1}\mathbf{x} \\ &= \mathbf{x}^T\mathbf{R}^{-1}\mathbf{x} = k^2\end{aligned} \tag{10}$$

Eq. (10) determines the boundary of elliptical shaped micro-clusters. The shape depends on the value of the covariance matrix $\mathbf{R}$ and the constant k. The features of micro-cluster with arbitrary direction elliptical shape, namely *elliptical micro-cluster*, is defined in Definition 1.

Definition 1. The features of the ith elliptical micro-cluster for a set of d-dimensional points $\mathbf{x} = \{\mathbf{x}_{i_1}, ..., \mathbf{x}_{i_n}\}$ with time stamp $t_{i_1}, ..., t_{i_n}$ consist of (1) the covariance matrix of $\mathbf{x}_{i_1}, ..., \mathbf{x}_{i_n}$ denoted by $\mathbf{R}_i = \mathbf{E}[(\mathbf{x} - \mathbf{E}[\mathbf{x}])(\mathbf{x} - \mathbf{E}[\mathbf{x}])^T]$; (2) the center vector $\mathbf{c}_i = \frac{1}{n}\sum_{j=1}^{n}\mathbf{x}_{i_j}$; and (3) the number of data vectors $n_i \geq n_\xi$ in the elliptical micro-cluster. These three features are written as $Emc_i(\mathbf{R}_i, \mathbf{c}_i, n_i)$.

Note that if the micro-cluster is too sparse, $n < n_\xi$, the covariance matrix is not meaningful. These micro-clusters are separately defined as *sparse micro-clusters*. The sparse micro-cluster shape is not elliptical but spherical. The features of the sparse micro-cluster are defined in Definition 2.

Definition 2. The features of the ith sparse micro-cluster for a set of d-dimensional points $\mathbf{x} = \{\mathbf{x}_{i_1}, ..., \mathbf{x}_{i_n}\}$ with time stamp $t_{i_1}, ..., t_{i_n}$ consist of (1) the center vector $\mathbf{c}_i = \frac{1}{n}\sum_{j=1}^{n}\mathbf{x}_{i_j}$ and (2) the number of data vectors $n_i < n_\xi$ in the sparse micro-cluster. These two features are written as $Smc_i(\mathbf{c}_i, n_i)$.

In streaming or on-line environment, the data impose a one-pass constraint. The summary information are represented by the features of micro-cluster as defined in Definition 1 and Definition 2. These information must be stored and updated during the learning process. To update the value of $\mathbf{R}_i$, $\mathbf{c}_i$, and n_i based on only the new incoming data, these features must be written in the forms of the following recursive functions.

For any arbitrary cluster i (both elliptical micro-cluster or sparse micro-cluster), let $n_i^{(old)}$, $\mathbf{c}_i^{(old)}$ and $\mathbf{R}_i^{(old)}$ be the old features of cluster i before being updated and $n_i^{(new)}$, $\mathbf{c}_i^{(new)}$ and $\mathbf{R}_i^{(new)}$ be the new features after being updated. When an incoming data vector $\mathbf{x}_{arr}$ is deterministically assigned to a cluster, the new features of the cluster can be incrementally adjusted as follows:

$$n_i^{(new)} = n_i^{(old)} + 1 \tag{11}$$

$$\mathbf{c}_i^{(new)} = \frac{n_i^{(old)} \times \mathbf{c}_i^{(old)} + \mathbf{x}_{arr}}{n_i^{(new)}} \tag{12}$$

$$\mathbf{R}_i^{(new)} = \frac{n_i^{(old)}(\mathbf{R}_i^{(old)} + \mathbf{c}_i^{(new)}\mathbf{c}_i^{(new)T}) + \mathbf{x}_{arr}\mathbf{x}_{arr}^T}{n_i^{(new)}} - \mathbf{c}_i^{(new)}\mathbf{c}_i^{(new)T} \tag{13}$$

The boundary and size of a cluster is determined by the value of k in equation (10). The greater k leads to the larger boundary. The boundary of a micro-cluster with an arbitrary center is defined in Definition 3.

Definition 3. The boundary of an elliptical micro-cluster i is a set of vectors $\mathbf{x}$ defined by the following equation:

$$\mathbf{B}(\mathbf{R}_i, \mathbf{c}_i, k_\xi) = \{\mathbf{x} | (\mathbf{x} - \mathbf{c}_i)^T \mathbf{R}_i^{-1} (\mathbf{x} - \mathbf{c}_i) = k_\xi^2\} \tag{14}$$

where k_ξ is a positive real number.

Since the direction of each elliptical micro-cluster may be different, the Euclidean distance is not the real distance. In this paper, we proposed another distance measure between two elliptical micro-clusters as the distance between the boundaries of both micro-clusters. Let $Emc_1(\mathbf{R}_1, \mathbf{c}_1, n_1)$ and $Emc_2(\mathbf{R}_2, \mathbf{c}_2, n_2)$ be the features of these two elliptical micro-clusters. The boundary of each micro-cluster determined by a constant $k_\xi = k$ as shown in Fig. 3 is found by the two following equations:

$$\mathbf{B}(\mathbf{R}_1, \mathbf{c}_1, k) = \{\mathbf{x} | (\mathbf{x} - \mathbf{c}_1)^T \mathbf{R}_1^{-1} (\mathbf{x} - \mathbf{c}_1) = k^2\} \tag{15}$$

$$\mathbf{B}(\mathbf{R}_2, \mathbf{c}_2, k) = \{\mathbf{x} | (\mathbf{x} - \mathbf{c}_2)^T \mathbf{R}_2^{-1} (\mathbf{x} - \mathbf{c}_2) = k^2\} \tag{16}$$

Suppose $\mathbf{b}_1$ is a point on the boundary of the first elliptical micro-cluster. The direction from $\mathbf{c}_1$ to $\mathbf{b}_1$ is the same as the direction from $\mathbf{c}_1$ to $\mathbf{c}_2$. Similarly, $\mathbf{b}_2$ is a point on the boundary of the second elliptical micro-cluster. The direction from $\mathbf{c}_2$ to $\mathbf{b}_2$ is the same as the direction from $\mathbf{c}_1$ to $\mathbf{c}_2$. Notice that $\mathbf{c}_1$,$\mathbf{c}_2$,$\mathbf{b}_1$ and $\mathbf{b}_2$ lie on the same straight line. In order to find the distance between both boundaries, let

$$L = ||\mathbf{c}_1 - \mathbf{c}_2||; \; l_1 = ||\mathbf{c}_1 - \mathbf{b}_1||; \; l_2 = ||\mathbf{c}_2 - \mathbf{b}_2|| \tag{17}$$

where $||.||$ represents Euclidean norm. If the values of L, l_1 and l_2 are known, then the distance between the boundaries can be simply determined by

$$d = L - (l_1 + l_2). \tag{18}$$

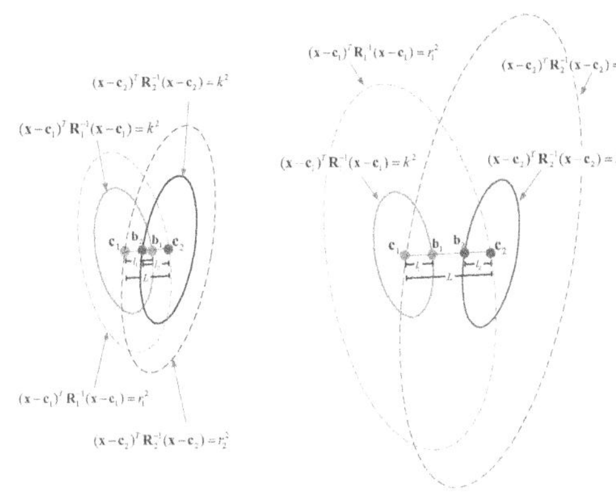

(a) Negative distance (b) Positive distance

Figure 3: The elliptical micro-clusters distance.

However, l_1 and l_2 are indeterminate since $\mathbf{b}_1$ and $\mathbf{b}_2$ are unknown. Then, another boundary of the first elliptical micro-cluster passing the center of the second elliptical micro-cluster $\mathbf{c}_2$ must be defined. Assume that this boundary corresponds to the constant $k_\xi = r_1$. We have

$$\mathbf{B}(\mathbf{R}_1, \mathbf{c}_1, r_1) = \{\mathbf{x} | (\mathbf{x} - \mathbf{c}_1)^T \mathbf{R}_1^{-1} (\mathbf{x} - \mathbf{c}_1) = r_1^2\} \tag{19}$$

and since $\mathbf{c}_2 \in \mathbf{B}(\mathbf{R}_1, \mathbf{c}_1, r_1)$, hence

$$(\mathbf{c}_2 - \mathbf{c}_1)^T \mathbf{R}_1^{-1} (\mathbf{c}_2 - \mathbf{c}_1) = r_1^2. \tag{20}$$

Similarly, the boundary of the second elliptical micro-cluster defined by a constant $k_\xi = r_2$ can be determined by this equation.

$$\mathbf{B}(\mathbf{R}_2, \mathbf{c}_2, r_2) = \{\mathbf{x} | (\mathbf{x} - \mathbf{c}_2)^T \mathbf{R}_2^{-1} (\mathbf{x} - \mathbf{c}_2) = r_2^2\}. \tag{21}$$

Since $\mathbf{c}_1 \in \mathbf{B}(\mathbf{R}_2, \mathbf{c}_2, r_2)$, thus

$$(\mathbf{c}_1 - \mathbf{c}_2)^T \mathbf{R}_2^{-1} (\mathbf{c}_1 - \mathbf{c}_2) = r_2^2. \tag{22}$$

Note that the boundaries in eq. (19) and (21) are shown in Fig. 4 by the dash lines. In order to get the values of l_1 and l_2, we multiply both sides of eq. (20) and (22) by $\frac{k^2}{r_1^2}$ and $\frac{k^2}{r_2^2}$, respectively. We get the following equations:

$$\left(\frac{k}{r_1}(\mathbf{c}_2 - \mathbf{c}_1)\right)^T \mathbf{R}_1^{-1} \left(\frac{k}{r_1}(\mathbf{c}_2 - \mathbf{c}_1)\right) = k^2 \tag{23}$$

$$\left(\frac{k}{r_2}(\mathbf{c}_1 - \mathbf{c}_2)\right)^T \mathbf{R}_2^{-1} \left(\frac{k}{r_2}(\mathbf{c}_1 - \mathbf{c}_2)\right) = k^2. \tag{24}$$

Since $\mathbf{b}_1 \in \mathbf{B}(\mathbf{R}_1, \mathbf{c}_1, k)$ and $\mathbf{b}_2 \in \mathbf{B}(\mathbf{R}_2, \mathbf{c}_2, k)$, we get

$$(\mathbf{b}_1 - \mathbf{c}_1)^T \mathbf{R}_1^{-1} (\mathbf{b}_1 - \mathbf{c}_1) = k^2 \tag{25}$$

$$(\mathbf{b}_2 - \mathbf{c}_2)^T \mathbf{R}_2^{-1} (\mathbf{b}_2 - \mathbf{c}_2) = k^2. \tag{26}$$

From equations (23) and (25), we have

$$\mathbf{b}_1 - \mathbf{c}_1 = \frac{k}{r_1}(\mathbf{c}_2 - \mathbf{c}_1). \tag{27}$$

From equations (24) and (26), we have

$$\mathbf{b}_2 - \mathbf{c}_2 = \frac{k}{r_2}(\mathbf{c}_1 - \mathbf{c}_2). \tag{28}$$

Thus, l_1 and l_2 can be computed as follows:

$$l_1 = \|\mathbf{c}_1 - \mathbf{b}_1\| = \|\mathbf{b}_1 - \mathbf{c}_1\| = \frac{k}{r_1} \|(\mathbf{c}_1 - \mathbf{c}_2)\|, \tag{29}$$

$$l_2 = \|\mathbf{c}_2 - \mathbf{b}_2\| = \|\mathbf{b}_2 - \mathbf{c}_2\| = \frac{k}{r_2}\|(\mathbf{c}_2 - \mathbf{c}_1)\|. \quad (30)$$

Therefore, the distance between the boundaries of two elliptical micro-clusters can be computed by:

$$d = \|\mathbf{c}_1 - \mathbf{c}_2\|\left[1 - k\left(\frac{1}{r_1} + \frac{1}{r_2}\right)\right] \quad (31)$$

where $r_1 = ((\mathbf{c}_1 - \mathbf{c}_2)^T\mathbf{R}_1^{-1}(\mathbf{c}_1 - \mathbf{c}_2))^{\frac{1}{2}}$ and $r_2 = ((\mathbf{c}_2 - \mathbf{c}_1)^T\mathbf{R}_2^{-1}(\mathbf{c}_2 - \mathbf{c}_1))^{\frac{1}{2}}$.

Note that the distance d between two elliptical micro-clusters can be any real number. If $d < 0$, both elliptical micro-clusters are intersecting as shown in Fig 3(a). In Fig 3(b), both elliptical micro-clusters are separate since $d > 0$.

The described concept and definitions will be used in the proposed algorithm of the next section.

4. ALGORITHM DESCRIPTION

The proposed algorithm for data steam clustering is divided into two processes, on-line process and off-line process.

4.1 On-line Process

In this process, the features of an elliptical micro-cluster and a spares micro-cluster are defined in Definition 1 and Definition 2, respectively. When the data arrive, there are four possible situations: (1) the features of an elliptical micro-cluster are updated; (2) the features of a sparse micro-cluster are updated; (3) a new elliptical micro-cluster is created and a sparse micro-cluster is deleted; or (4) a new sparse micro-cluster is created.

If the arriving data point falls within the boundary of an elliptical micro-cluster. The boundary of the elliptical-micro-cluster is defined in Definition 3. The scale of the boundary depends on the constant k_ξ. In our proposed algorithm, the arriving data point will be assigned to the elliptical micro-cluster having highest density area.

If the arriving data point does not fall within the boundary of the elliptical micro-cluster but within the boundary of the sparse micro-cluster, the features of this sparse micro-cluster are updated instead. Whenever the features of the sparse micro-cluster are updated, a new elliptical micro-cluster will be created by this sparse micro-cluster if the number of members is enough ($n \geq n_\xi$). In such case, the shape of the newly initiated elliptical micro-cluster is the same as the sparse micro-cluster. The features $\mathbf{c}$ and n of the newly created elliptical micro-cluster are initiated in the same way as those of the sparse micro-cluster and its covariance matrix is initiated as $\mathbf{R} = \text{diag}\left[r_\xi^2/k_\xi^2, ..., r_\xi^2/k_\xi^2\right]$.

Note that after the new elliptical micro-cluster is created by the sparse micro-cluster, this sparse-micro-cluster is deleted. However, if the arriving data point does not fall within any elliptical micro-cluster and sparse micro-cluster, then the new sparse micro-cluster is created by this arriving data point. Let N_{Emc} and N_{Smc} be the total numbers of elliptical micro-clusters and sparse micro-clusters, respectively. The summary of the on-line process is shown in Algorithm 1.

Algorithm 1: On-line Process ($\mathbf{p}$)

Get the arriving data point $\mathbf{p}$
$i^* = \underset{i=1,...,N_{Emc}}{\text{argmin}} \left\{(\mathbf{p} - \mathbf{c}_i)^T\mathbf{R}_i^{-1}(\mathbf{p} - \mathbf{c}_i)\right\}$,
where $\mathbf{c}_i$ and $\mathbf{R}_i$ are the center vector and covariance matrix of the i-th elliptical micro-cluster, respectively.
if $(\mathbf{p} - \mathbf{c}_{i*})^T\mathbf{R}_{i*}^{-1}(\mathbf{p} - \mathbf{c}_{i*}) \leq k_\xi$ **then**
  Update $Emc_{i*}(\mathbf{R}_{i*}, \mathbf{c}_{i*}, n_{i*})$, as the eq. (17), (18), (19).
else
  $j^* = \underset{i=1,...,N_{Smc}}{\text{argmin}} \{||\mathbf{p} - \mathbf{c}_j||\}$,
  where $\mathbf{c}_j$ is the center vector of the j-th spare micro-cluster.
  if $||\mathbf{p} - \mathbf{c}_{j*}|| \leq r_\xi$ **then**
    Update $Smc_{j*}(\mathbf{c}_{j*}, n_{j*})$, as the eq. (17),(18).
    if $n_{j*} \geq n_\xi$ **then**
      Create a new elliptical micro-cluster by the j^*-th sparse micro-cluster.
    end
  else
    Create new sparse-micro-cluster by the arriving data point $\mathbf{p}$.
  end
end

4.2 Off-line Process

When a clustering request arrives, the micro-clusters are treated as the arbitrary elliptical objects. Note that a micro-cluster is firstly created as the spherical shape which is not compact for the members in the micro-cluster. Once the number of members of micro-cluster is large enough, the micro-cluster shape is transformed to the elliptical shape which is more compact. Thus, in the off-line clustering process, we categorize the micro-cluster into two natures, i.e., compact (if $n \geq 2n_\xi$) and non-compact (if $n < 2n_\xi$) shapes. Let EMC and SMC be the sets of elliptical micro-clusters and sparse micro-clusters, respectively.

Initially, all elliptical micro-clusters and sparse micro-clusters are not labelled. Each cluster is created by expanding the compact elliptical micro-cluster which is not labelled. If a non-labelled elliptical micro-cluster connects to the labelled

Algorithm 2: Off-line Process (EMC, SMC, n_ξ)

Label all $Emc_i \in EMC$, as NON-LABELLED
Initial $ClsId = 0$
for *each NON-LABELLED* $Emc_i \in EMC$ **do**
  if $Emc_i(n) \geq 2n_\xi$ **then**
    Increment $ClsId$ by 1
    Label Emc_i as $ClsId$
    ExpandCls ($ClsId$,Emc_i,$2n_\xi$)
  end
end
for *each NON-LABELLED* $Emc_i \in EMC$ **do**
  Increment $ClsId$ by 1
  Label Emc_i as $ClsId$
  ExpandCls ($ClsId$,Emc_i,n_ξ)
end
Label all $Smc_i \in \mathbf{SMC}$, as NON-LABELLED
for *each NON-LABELLED* $Smc_i \in SMC$ **do**
  $j^* = \underset{j=1,...,|\mathbf{EMC}|}{\text{arg}} \; dist(Smc_i, Emc_j) \leq 0$
  if $j^* \neq \emptyset$ **then**
    Label Smc_i is the same as Emc_{j*}
  end
end

Function: ***ExpandCls***($ClsId$,Emc_{curr},n_δ)

for *each NON-LABELLED* $Emc_j \in EMC$ **do**
  if $dist(Emc_{curr}, Emc_j) \leq 0$ **then**
    Label Emc_j as $ClsId$
    if $Emc_j(n) \geq n_\delta$ **then**
      ExpandCls ($ClsId$,Emc_j,n_δ)
    end
  end
end

compact elliptical micro-cluster then it will be labelled as the same cluster. Moreover, if it is also compact then it can expand to other elliptical micro-clusters.

After that, the other new clusters are created by expanding the rest non-labelled elliptical micro-clusters. The non-labelled elliptical micro-cluster which connect to the last labelled micro-cluster will be labelled as the same cluster and expanded to other non-labelled elliptical micro-clusters.

Lastly, if the sparse micro-clusters connects to an elliptical micro-cluster, then mark it as the same cluster label, otherwise mark it as noise. The description of the off-line clustering process is shown in Algorithm 2.

5. EXPERIMENTAL EVALUATION

In our experiment, the proposed algorithm is compared with CluStream and DenStream. In each algorithm, we tried to set fairly parameters summarized in Table 1.

5.1 Experiments on synthetic datasets

The experimental results showed that our proposed algorithm outperformed the existing algorithms for dealing with noise as shown in Fig 4-6. The blue dot (.) symbols represent the points which are contained in one of all micro-clusters. The red plus (+) symbols represent the data points which are treated as outliers. The circular and elliptical lines represent the micro-clusters boundaries. The stream speed was set as 100 points per time stamp.

A set of initial points was unnecessary in our approach. In contrast, the initial 500 points were needed to create a set of initial micro-clusters in *CluStream* and *DenStream* as shown in Fig 4(a) and Fig 5(a), respectively. After 3150 points arrived, the micro-clusters for three algorithms were represented in Fig 4(b), Fig 5(b) and Fig 6(b). *CluStream* created too many micro-clusters which were not compact for representing the members in the micro-cluster. In *DenStream*, the mistake was occurred because the micro-cluster radius was barely changed by the arriving data point, specifically, in the micro-cluster with a large number of points. Thus, a large amount of points were contained in the micro-cluster even if they were outside the boundary. Evidently, the proposed elliptical micro-clusters were more compact than both two previous methods.

Table 1: The used parameters for three algorithms.

Parameters	Descriptions
CluStream:	
$InitN$	The initial number of points at the beginning
$InitK$	The initial number of micro-clusters at the beginning
t_{RMS}	The factor of the RMS deviation of the data points in the micro-cluster from the centroid
K	The number of higher level clusters for generate the final cluster result
DenStream:	
$InitN$	The initial number of points at the beginning
ϵ	The threshold radius of micro-cluster
ξ	The threshold weight or number of points the in the micro-cluster for determine whether micro-cluster is the core micro-cluster
β	The outlier threshold for determine whether micro-cluster is the outlier micro-cluster
CompactStream:(Proposed Alg.)	
r_ξ	The threshold radius of sparse micro-cluster
n_ξ	The threshold weight or number of points the in the micro-cluster for determining whether micro-cluster is the elliptical micro-cluster
k_ξ	The scale of the boundary of the elliptical micro-cluster

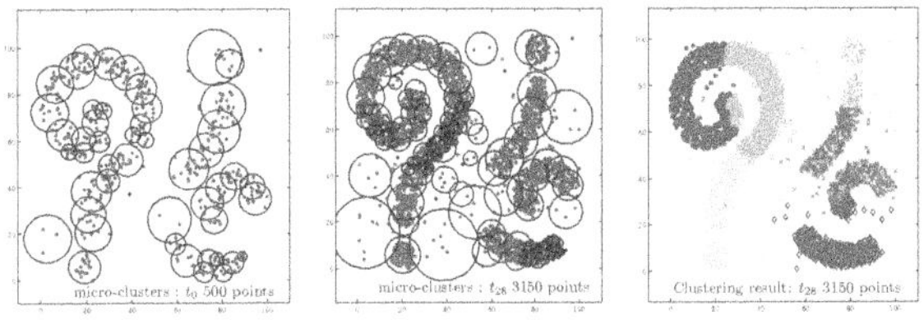

(a) (b) (c)

Figure 4: Experiment on CluStream with $InitN = 500$, $InitK = 50$, $t_{RMS} = 2$ and $K = 6$.

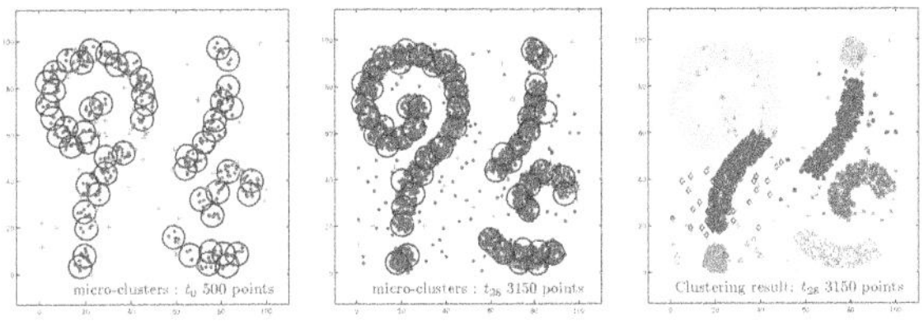

(a) (b) (c)

Figure 5: Experiment on DenStream with $InitN = 500$, $\epsilon = 5$, $\xi = 3$ and $\beta = 0.2$.

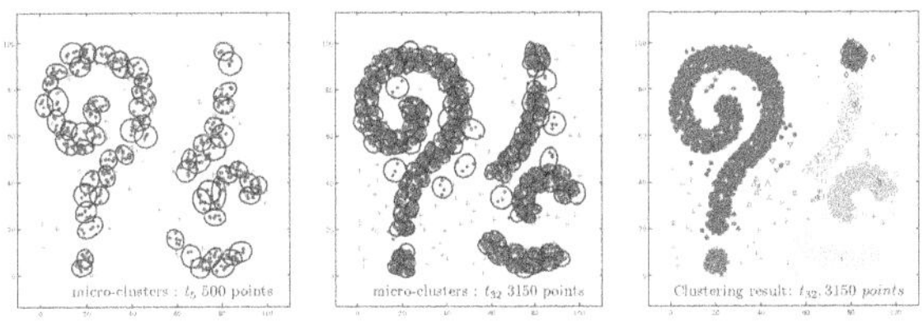

(a) (b) (c)

Figure 6: Experiment on the CompactStream (proposed algorithm) with $r_\xi = 5$, $n_\xi = 3$ and $k_\xi = 2$.

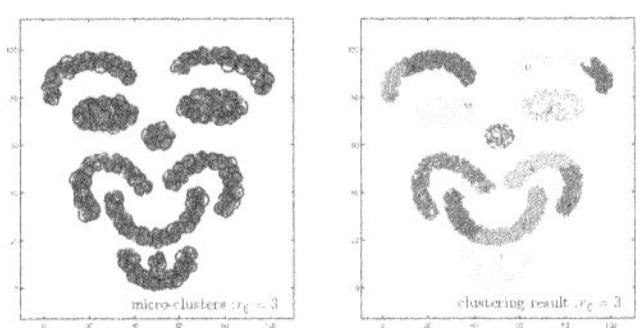

(a) (b)

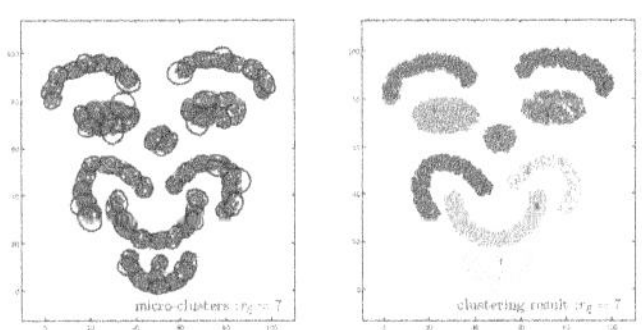

(c) (d)

Figure 7: Effect of r_ξ

The clustering results for three algorithms were shown in Fig 4(c), Fig 5(c) and Fig 6(c). *CluStream*, generated the clustering result by applying K-means which produced the incorrect groups. In *DenStream*, the clustering result was incorrect even if it was derived by applying DBSCAN [4] which can deal with arbitrary shapes in the static data set. Because the micro-cluster boundary (w.r.t. radius) was not compact for representing the points in the micro-clusters. The clustering result in Fig 6(c) claimed that the proposed algorithm is more efficient than CluStream and DenStream when the clusters are the different sizes, shapes and densities in noisy.

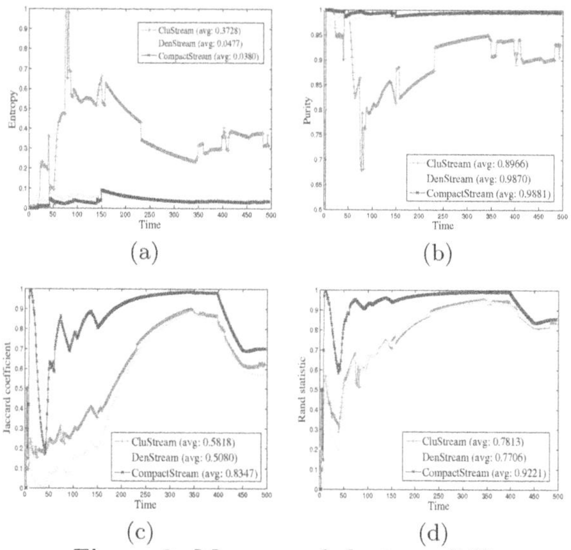

Figure 8: Measure of cluster validity.

The importance parameter setting in our algorithm was the initial radius (r_ξ) when the new sparse micro-cluster was created. Figures 7 showed the results with the different threshold radii. The larger radius provided the lower number of micro-clusters as in Fig 7(a) and (c). If the threshold radius was too small, the clusters were possibly separated by the tiny distance between micro-clusters as shown in Fig 7(b).

Although the threshold radius was chosen in advance, it just affected the earliest stage where an elliptical micro-clusters was created. When the number of data points in the elliptical micro-cluster increased, its shape was converted to the compact elliptical shape ($n \geq 2n_\xi$) which was efficient for representing the members in the micro-cluster without effecting of the chosen threshold radius.

5.2 Experiments on real datasets

In our experiment, the used real data set is KDD-CUP'99 Network Intrusion Detection stream dataset [13] which has been widely used to evaluate accuracy in the existing data stream clustering algorithms. The used data set contains 494020 connections which are the sequences of TPC packets including the total 42 available attributes (all 34 continuous attributes are used). Each connection was labelled as one of 23 attack-types.

The parameters in three algorithms were carefully chosen as follows: CluStream: $InitN$=1000, $InitK$=500, t_{RMS}=2 and K=23. DenStream: $InitN$=1000, ϵ=16, ξ=10. Proposed algorithm: r_ξ=16, n_ξ=10, k_ξ=2. Three algorithms were compared by four measures of cluster validity [12], i.e., entropy, purity, rand statistic and jaccard coefficient.

Entropy and purity are cluster validities based on classification oriented measures. The entropy was used to measure class distribution of data in each cluster, i.e. the lower entropy is better. Fig 8(a) showed that the entropy in the proposed algorithm was always less than the entropy in CluStream at any times and was less than the entropy in DenStream in most of the times.

The purity was used to measure that a cluster contains objects of a single class, i.e. the higher purity is better. Fig 8(b) showed that the purity in the proposed algorithm was often higher than the purity in CluStream and DenStream, specifically in a long period time. Rand statistic and Jaccard coefficient are cluster validities based on similarity oriented measures that any two objects that are in the same cluster should be in the same class and vice versa. Fig 8(c) and Fig 8(d) showed that both Rand statistic and Jaccard coefficient in the proposed algorithm were obvious higher than CluStream and DenSteam.

6. CONCLUSIONS

This paper introduced the new micro-cluster features with versatile elliptic function which is more compact than spherical. These features lead to the efficient clustering result when compared with the other existing techniques based on entropy, purity, Jaccard coefficients, and Rand statistic.

7. REFERENCES

[1] C. C. Aggarwal, J. Han, J. Wang, and P. S. Yu. A framework for clustering evolving data streams. In *Proc. of VLDB*, 2003.

[2] C. C. Aggarwal, J. Han, J. Wang, and P. S. Yu. A framework for projected clustering of high dimensional data streams. In *Proc. of VLDB*, 2004.

[3] F. Cao, M. Ester, W. Qian, and A. Zhou. Density-based clustering over an evolving data stream with noise. In *Proc. of SIAM on Data Mining*, 2006.

[4] M. Ester, H.-P. Kriegel, J. Sander, and X. Xu. A density-based algorithm for discovering clusters in large spatial databases with noise. In *Proc. of KDD*, 1996.

[5] A. Forestiero, C. Pizzuti, and G. Spezzano. Flockstream: a bio-inspired algorithm for clustering evolving data streams. In *IEEE Conf. on Tools with Artificial Intelligence*, 2009.

[6] J. Gao, J. Li, Z. Zhang, and P.-N. Tan. An incremental data stream clustering algorithm based on dense units detection. In *Pacific-Asia Conf. on Knowledge Discovery and Data Mining*, 2005.

[7] C. Jia, C. Tan, and A. Yong. A grid and density-based clustering algorithm for processing data stream. In *Proc. of Conf. on Genetic and Evolutionary Computing*, 2008.

[8] P. Kranen, I. Assent, C. Baldauf, and T. Seidl. The clustree: indexing micro-clusters for anytime stream mining. *Knowledge and Information Systems*, 2010.

[9] S. LÃijhr and M. Lazarescu. Incremental clustering of dynamic data streams using connectivity based representative points. *Data and Knowledge Engineering*, 68(1):1–27, January 2009.

[10] L. Li-xiong, H. Hai, G. Yun-fei, and C. Fu-cai. rdenstream, a clustering algorithm over an evolving data stream. In *IEEE Conf. on Information Engineering and Computer Science(ICIECS)*, 2009.

[11] C. Ruiz, E. Menasalvas, and M. Spiliopoulou. C-denstream: Using domain knowledge on a data stream. In *Proc. of Conf. on Discovery Science(DS)*, 2009.

[12] P.-N. Tan, M. Steinbach, and V. Kumar. *Introduction to Data Mining*. Pearson Addison Wesley, Boston, 2006.

[13] UCI KDD Archive. KDD-CUP'99 Dataset. http://kdd.ics.uci.edu/databases/kddcup99/kddcup99.html. [Online;accessed 23-May-2011].

Coupled Nominal Similarity in Unsupervised Learning

Can Wang*, Longbing Cao,
Jinjiu Li, Wei Wei, Yuming Ou
Centre for Quantum Computation and Intelligent Systems
Advanced Analytics Institute
University of Technology, Sydney, Australia
Can.Wang@student.uts.edu.au

Mingchun Wang†
School of Science
Tianjin University of Technology and Education
Tianjin, China
mchwang123@163.com

ABSTRACT

The similarity between nominal objects is not straightforward, especially in unsupervised learning. This paper proposes coupled similarity metrics for nominal objects, which consider not only intra-coupled similarity within an attribute (i.e., value frequency distribution) but also inter-coupled similarity between attributes (i.e. feature dependency aggregation). Four metrics are designed to calculate the inter-coupled similarity between two categorical values by considering their relationships with other attributes. The theoretical analysis reveals their equivalent accuracy and superior efficiency based on intersection against others, in particular for large-scale data. Substantial experiments on extensive UCI data sets verify the theoretical conclusions. In addition, experiments of clustering based on the derived dissimilarity metrics show a significant performance improvement.

Categories and Subject Descriptors: H.2.8 [**Database Management**]: Database Applications–*data mining*

General Terms: Algorithms, Measurement, Performance

Keywords: Similarity measure, Complexity, Accuracy

1. INTRODUCTION

Similarity analysis has been a problem of great practical importance in several domains, including data mining, for decades [8]. By defining certain similarity measures between attribute values, it gauges the strength of the relationship between two data objects: the more two objects resemble each other, the larger the similarity is [7].

When objects are described by numerical features, their similarity measures geometric analogies which reflect the relationship of data values. For instance, the values $10m$ and $12m$ are more similar than $10m$ and $2m$. A variety of similarity metrics have been developed for numerical data, such as Euclidean and Minkowski distances [7]. By contrast, the similarity analysis between records described by nominal variables has received much less attention. Heterogeneous Distances [10] and Modified Value Distance Matrix (*MVDM*) [5], for example, depict the similarity between categorical values in supervised learning. For unlabeled data, only a few works [7], including Simple Matching Similarity (*SMS*, which only uses 0s and 1s to distinguish similarities between distinct and identical categorical values) and Occurrence Frequency [2], discuss the similarity between nominal values. We illustrate the problem with these works and the challenge of analyzing similarity for categorical data below.

*The first author of this paper for correspondence.

†The third author of this paper.

CIKM'11, October 24–28, 2011, Glasgow, Scotland, UK.

Table 1: An Instance of the Movie Database

Movie	Director	Actor	Genre	Class
Godfather II	Scorsese	De Niro	Crime	G_1
Good Fellas	Coppola	De Niro	Crime	G_1
Vertigo	Hitchcock	Stewart	Thriller	G_2
N by NW	Hitchcock	Grant	Thriller	G_2
Bishop's Wife	Koster	Grant	Comedy	G_2
Harvey	Koster	Stewart	Comedy	G_2

Taking the Movie data (Table 1) as an example, six movie objects are divided into two classes with three nominal features: director, actor and genre. The *SMS* measure between directors "*Scorsese*" and "*Coppola*" is 0, but "*Scorsese*" and "*Coppola*" are very similar directors[1]. Another observation by following *SMS* is that the similarity between "*Koster*" and "*Hitchcock*" is equal to that between "*Koster*" and "*Coppola*"; however, the similarity of the former pair should be greater since it belongs to the same class G_2.

Both instances show that it is much more complex to analyze similarity between nominal variables than continuous data, and *SMS* and its variants fail to capture the genuine relationship between nominal values. With the increase of categorical data such as that derived from social networks, it is important to develop effective and efficient measures for capturing similarity between nominal variables.

Thus, we discuss the similarity for categorical values by considering data characteristics. Two attribute values are similar if they present analogous frequency distributions for one attribute [2]; this reflects the intra-coupled similarity within a feature. For example, two directors are very similar if they appear with almost the same frequency, such as "*Scorsese*" with "*Coppola*" and "*Koster*" with "*Hitchcock*". However, the reality is that the former director pair is more

[1]A conclusion drawn from a well-informed cinematic source.

similar than the latter. To improve the accuracy of intra-coupled similarity, it is believed that the object co-occurrence probabilities of attribute values induced on other features are comparable [1]. To this end, the similarity between directors should also cater for the dependencies on other features such as "actor" and "genre" over all the movie objects, namely, the inter-coupled similarity between attributes. The coupling relationships between values and between attributes contribute to a more comprehensive understanding of object similarity [4]. No work that systematically considers both intra-coupled and inter-coupled similarities has been reported in the literature. This fact leads to the incomplete description of categorical value similarities, and apart from this, the similarity analysis on dependency aggregation is usually very costly.

In this paper, we propose a Coupled Object Similarity (COS) measure by considering both Intra-coupled and Inter-coupled Attribute Value Similarities ($IaAVS$ and $IeAVS$), which capture the attribute value frequency distribution and feature dependency aggregation with a high learning accuracy and relatively low complexity, respectively. We compare accuracies and efficiencies among the four proposed metrics for $IeAVS$, and come up with an optimal one from both theoretical and experimental aspects; we then evaluate our proposed measure with an existing metric on a variety of benchmark categorical data sets in terms of clustering qualities; and we develop a method to define dissimilarity metrics flexibly with our fundamental similarity building blocks according to specific requirements..

The paper is organized as follows. In Section 2, we briefly review the related work. Preliminary definitions are specified in Section 3. Section 4 proposes the coupled similarities, and the theoretical analysis is given in Section 5. We demonstrate the efficiency and effectiveness of COS in Section 6 with experiments. Finally, we end this paper in Section 7.

2. RELATED WORK

There are some surveys [2, 7] that discuss the similarity between categorical attributes. Cost and Salzberg [5] proposed $MVDM$ based on labels, while Wilson and Martinez [10] studied heterogeneous distances for instance based learning. Unlike our focus here, the measures in their study are only designed for supervised approaches.

For unsupervised learning, there exist some data mining techniques for nominal data [1, 2]. The most famous are the SMS measure and its diverse variants such as Jaccard coefficients [7], which are all intuitively based on the principle that the similarity measure is 1 with identical values and is otherwise 0. More recently, attribute value frequency distribution has been considered for similarity measures [2]; neighborhood-based similarities [8] are explored to describe the object neighborhood by using an overlap measure. They are different from our proposed method, which directly reveals the similarity between a pair of objects.

Recently, increasing numbers of researchers have argued that the attribute value similarities are also dependent on their coupling relations [2, 4]. Das and Mannila presented the Iterated Contextual Distances algorithm, believing that the feature and object similarities are inter-dependent [6]. Ahmad and Dey [1] proposed computing the dissimilarity by considering the co-occurrence. While the dissimilarity metric of the latter leads to high accuracy, the computation is usually very costly, which limits its application in large-scale problems.

Table 2: An Example of Information Table

U \ A	a_1	a_2	a_3
u_1	A_1	B_1	C_1
u_2	A_2	B_1	C_1
u_3	A_2	B_2	C_2
u_4	A_3	B_3	C_2
u_5	A_4	B_3	C_3
u_6	A_4	B_2	C_3

3. PROBLEM STATEMENT

A large number of data objects with the same features can be organized by an information table $S =< U, A, V, f >$, where $U = \{u_1, \cdots, u_m\}$ is composed of a nonempty finite set of data objects; $A = \{a_1, \cdots, a_n\}$ is a finite set of features; $V = \bigcup_{j=1}^{n} V_j$ is a set of all attribute values, in which V_j is the set of attribute values of feature $a_j (1 \le j \le m)$; and $f = \wedge_{j=1}^{n} f_j$ $(f_j : U \to V_j)$ is an information function which assigns a particular value of each feature to every object. For instance, Table 2 consists of six objects and three features, with $f_2(u_1) = B_1$ and $V_2 = \{B_1, B_2, B_3\}$.

Generally speaking, the similarity between two objects $u_{i_1}, u_{i_2} \in U$ is built on top of the similarities within their values $x, y \in V_j$ for all the features a_j. The basic concepts below are defined to facilitate the formulation for attribute value similarities, where $|H|$ is the number of elements in H.

DEFINITION 3.1. *Given an information table S, three* ***Set Information Functions (SIFs)*** *are defined as $f_j^* : 2^U \to 2^{V_j}$, $g_j : V_j \to 2^U$, and $g_j^* : 2^{V_j} \to 2^U$. Specifically:*

$$f_j^*(\{u_{k_1}, \cdots, u_{k_t}\}) = \{f_j(u_{k_1}), \cdots, f_j(u_{k_t})\}, \quad (3.1)$$

$$g_j(x) = \{u_i | f_j(u_i) = x, 1 \le j \le n, 1 \le i \le m\}, \quad (3.2)$$

$$g_j^*(W) = \{u_i | f_j(u_i) \in W, 1 \le j \le n, 1 \le i \le m\}, \quad (3.3)$$

where $u_i, u_{k_1}, \cdots, u_{k_t} \in U$, and $W \subseteq V_j$.

These SIFs describe the relationships between objects and attribute values from different levels. For example, $f_2^*(\{u_1, u_2, u_3\}) = \{B_1, B_2\}$, $g_2(B_1) = \{u_1, u_2\}$ for value B_1, while $g_2^*(\{B_1, B_2\}) = \{u_1, u_2, u_3, u_6\}$ if given $W = \{B_1, B_2\}$.

DEFINITION 3.2. *Given an information table S, its* ***Inter-information Function (IIF)*** *$\varphi_{j \to k} : V_j \to 2^{V_k}$ is defined:*

$$\varphi_{j \to k}(x) = f_k^*(g_j(x)). \quad (3.4)$$

This IIF $\varphi_{j \to k}$ is the composition of f_k^* and g_j. It obtains the kth attribute value subset for the corresponding objects, which are derived from the jth attribute value x. For example, $\varphi_{2 \to 1}(B_1) = \{A_1, A_2\}$.

DEFINITION 3.3. *Given an information table S, the kth attribute value subset $W \subseteq V_k$, and the jth attribute value $x \in V_j$, the* ***Information Conditional Probability (ICP)*** *of W with respect to x is $P_{k|j}(W|x)$:*

$$P_{k|j}(W|x) = \frac{|g_k^*(W) \bigcap g_j(x)|}{|g_j(x)|}. \quad (3.5)$$

Intuitively, when given all the objects with the jth attribute value x, *ICP* is the percentage of the common objects whose kth attribute values fall in subset W and jth attribute value is exactly x as well. For example, $P_{1|2}(\{A_1\}|B_1) = 0.5$.

All these concepts and functions are composed to formalize the so-called coupled interactions between categorical attribute values, as presented below.

4. COUPLED SIMILARITIES

In this section, ***Coupled Attribute Value Similarity (CAVS)*** is proposed in terms of both intra-coupled and inter-coupled value similarities. When we consider the similarity between attribute values, "intra-coupled" indicates the involvement of attribute value occurrence frequencies within one feature, while the "inter-coupled" means the interaction of other features with this attribute. For example, the coupled value similarity between B_1 and B_2 concerns both the intra-coupled relationship specified by the repeated times of values B_1 and B_2: 2 and 2, and the inter-coupled interaction triggered by the other two features (a_1 and a_3).

Suppose we have the ***Intra-coupled Attribute Value Similarity (IaAVS)*** measure $\delta_j^{Ia}(x, y)$ and ***Inter-coupled Attribute Value Similarity (IeAVS)*** measure $\delta_j^{Ie}(x, y)$ for feature a_j and $x, y \in V_j$, then *CAVS* $\delta_j^A(x, y)$ is naturally derived by simultaneously considering both of them.

DEFINITION 4.1. *Given an information table S, the **Coupled Attribute Value Similarity (CAVS)** between attribute values x and y of feature a_j is:*

$$\delta_j^A(x, y) = \delta_j^{Ia}(x, y) \cdot \delta_j^{Ie}(x, y) \tag{4.1}$$

where δ_j^{Ia} and δ_j^{Ie} are IaAVS and IeAVS, respectively.

4.1 Intra-coupled Interaction

According to [7], it is a fact that the discrepancy of attribute value occurrence times reflects the value similarity in terms of frequency distribution. Thus, when calculating attribute value similarity, we consider the relationship between attribute value frequencies on one feature, proposed as intra-coupled similarity in the following.

DEFINITION 4.2. *Given an information table S, the **Intra-coupled Attribute Value Similarity (IaAVS)** between attribute values x and y of feature a_j is:*

$$\delta_j^{Ia}(x, y) = \frac{|g_j(x)| \cdot |g_j(y)|}{|g_j(x)| + |g_j(y)| + |g_j(x)| \cdot |g_j(y)|}. \tag{4.2}$$

In this way, different occurrence frequencies indicate distinct levels of attribute value significance. Gan et al. [7] reveal that greater similarity is assigned to the attribute value pair which owns approximately equal frequencies. The higher these frequencies are, the closer such two values are. Thus, function (4.2) is designed to satisfy these two principles. Besides, since $1 \le |g_j(x)|, |g_j(y)| \le m$, then $\delta_j^{Ia} \in [1/3, m/(m+2)]$. For example, in Table 2, both values B_1 and B_2 are observed twice, so $\delta_2^{Ia}(B_1, B_2) = 0.5$.

Hence, by taking into account the frequencies of categories, an effective measure (*IaAVS*) has been captured to characterize the value similarity in terms of occurrence times.

4.2 Inter-coupled Interaction

In terms of *IaAVS*, we have considered the intra-coupled similarity, i.e., the interaction of attribute values within one feature a_j. This does not, however, involve the couplings between other features $a_k (k \ne j)$ and feature a_j when calculating attribute value similarity. Accordingly, we discuss this dependency aggregation, i.e., inter-coupled interaction.

In 1993, Cost and Salzberg [5] proposed a powerful method, *MVDM*, for measuring the dissimilarity between categorical values. *MVDM* considers the overall similarities of classification of all objects on each possible value of each feature. The idea is that attribute values are identified as being similar if they occur with the same relative frequency for all classifications. In the absence of labels, the above measure is adapted to satisfy our target problem by replacing the class label with some other feature to enable unsupervised learning. We regard this interaction between features as inter-coupled similarity in terms of the co-occurrence comparisons of *ICP*. The most intuitive variant is *IRSP*:

DEFINITION 4.3. *Given an information table S, the **Inter-coupled Relative Similarity based on Power Set (IRSP)** between attribute values x and y of feature a_j based on another feature a_k is:*

$$\delta_{j|k}^P(x, y) = \min_{W \subseteq V_k} \{2 - P_{k|j}(W|x) - P_{k|j}(\overline{W}|y)\}, \tag{4.3}$$

where $\overline{W} = V_k \backslash W$ is the complementary set of a set W under the complete set V_k.

In fact, two attribute values are closer to each other if they have more similar probabilities with other attribute value subsets in terms of co-occurrence object frequencies. In Table 2, by employing (4.3), we want to get $\delta_{2|1}^P(B_1, B_2)$, i.e. the similarity between two attribute values B_1, B_2 of feature a_2 regarding feature a_1. Since the set of all attribute values of feature a_1 is $V_1 = \{A_1, A_2, A_3, A_4\}$, the number of all power sets within V_1 is 2^4, i.e., the number of the combinations consisting of $W \subseteq V_1$ and $\overline{W} \subseteq V_1$ is 2^4. The minimal value among them is 0.5, which indicates that similarity $\delta_{2|1}^P(B_1, B_2) = 0.5$.

This process shows the combinational explosion brought about by the power set needs to be considered when calculating attribute value similarity by *IRSP*. We therefore try to define three more similarities based on *IRSP* as follows.

DEFINITION 4.4. *Given an information table S, the **Inter-coupled Relative Similarity based on Universal Set (IRSU), Join Set (IRSJ), and Intersection Set (IRSI)** between attribute values x and y of feature a_j based on another feature a_k are the following formulae respectively:*

$$\delta_{j|k}^U(x, y) = 2 - \sum_{w \in V_k} \max\{P_{k|j}(\{w\}|x), P_{k|j}(\{w\}|y)\}, \tag{4.4}$$

$$\delta_{j|k}^J(x, y) = 2 - \sum_{w \in \bigcup} \max\{P_{k|j}(\{w\}|x), P_{k|j}(\{w\}|y)\}, \tag{4.5}$$

$$\delta_{j|k}^I(x, y) = \sum_{w \in \bigcap} \min\{P_{k|j}(\{w\}|x), P_{k|j}(\{w\}|y)\}, \tag{4.6}$$

where $w \in \bigcup$ and $w \in \bigcap$ denote $w \in \varphi_{j \to k}(x) \bigcup \varphi_{j \to k}(y)$ and $w \in \varphi_{j \to k}(x) \bigcap \varphi_{j \to k}(y)$, respectively.

Each kth attribute value $w \in V_k$, rather than its value subset $W \subseteq V_k$, is considered to reduce computational complexity. In this way, *IRSU* is applied to compute similarity

$\delta^U_{2|1}(B_1, B_2)$, and we get $\delta^U_{2|1}(B_1, B_2) = 0.5$. Since *IRSU* only concerns all the single attribute values rather than exploring the whole power set, it has solved the combinational explosion issue to a great extent. In *IRSU*, *ICP* is merely calculated 8 times compared with 32 times by *IRSP*, which leads to a substantial improvement in efficiency. Then with (4.5), the calculation of $\delta^J_{2|1}(B_1, B_2)$ is further simplified since $A_3 \notin \varphi_{2\to1}(B_1) \bigcup \varphi_{2\to1}(B_2)$. Thus, we obtain $\delta^J_{2|1}(B_1, B_2) = 0.5$, which reveals the fact that it is enough to compute *ICP* with $w \in V_1$ that belongs to $\varphi_{2\to1}(B_1) \bigcup \varphi_{2\to1}(B_2)$ instead of all the elements in V_1. From this perspective, *IRSJ* reduces the complexity further when compared with *IRSU*. Based on *IRSU*, an alternative *IRSI* is considered. For example, with (4.6), the calculation of $\delta^I_{2|1}(B_1, B_2)$ is once again simplified since only $A_2 \in \varphi_{2\to1}(B_1) \bigcap \varphi_{2\to1}(B_2)$. Then, we easily get $\delta^I_{2|1}(B_1, B_2) = 0.5$. In this case, it is sufficient to compute *ICP* with $w \in V_1$ which only belongs to $\varphi_{2\to1}(B_1) \bigcap \varphi_{2\to1}(B_2)$. It is trivial that the cardinality of intersection $\bigcap$ is no larger than that of join set $\bigcup$. Thus, *IRSI* is further more efficient than *IRSU* due to the reduction of intra-coupled relative similarity complexity.

Intuitively speaking, it is a fact that *IRSI* is the most efficient of all the proposed inter-coupled relative similarity measures: *IRSP*, *IRSU*, *IRSJ*, *IRSI*. In addition, all four measures lead to the same similarity result, such as 0.5.

According to the above discussion, we can naturally define the similarity between the jth attribute value pair (x, y) on top of these four optional measures by aggregating all the relative similarities on features other than attribute a_j.

DEFINITION 4.5. *Given an information table S, the* ***Inter-coupled Attribute Value Similarity (IeAVS)*** *between attribute values x and y of feature a_j is:*

$$\delta^{Ie}_j(x, y) = \sum_{k=1, k\neq j}^{n} \alpha_k \delta_{j|k}(x, y), \tag{4.7}$$

where α_k is the weight parameter for feature a_k, $\sum_{k=1}^{n} \alpha_k = 1$, $\alpha_k \in [0, 1]$, and $\delta_{j|k}(x, y)$ is one of the inter-coupled relative similarity candidates.

Accordingly, we have $\delta^{Ie}_j \in [0, 1]$, then $\delta^A_j = \delta^{Ia}_j \cdot \delta^{Ie}_j \in [0, m/(m+2)]$ since $\delta^{Ia}_j \in [1/3, m/(m+2)]$. In Table 2, for example, $\delta^{Ie}_2(B_1, B_2) = 0.5 \cdot \delta_{2|1}(B_1, B_2) + 0.5 \cdot \delta_{2|3}(B_1, B_2) = (0.5 + 0)/2 = 0.25$ if $\alpha_1 = \alpha_3 = 0.5$ is taken with equal weight. Furthermore, coupled attribute value similarity (4.1) is obtained as $\delta^A_2(B_1, B_2) = \delta^{Ia}_2(B_1, B_2) \cdot \delta^{Ie}_2(B_1, B_2) = 0.5 \times 0.25 = 0.125$. For the Movie data set in Section 1, then $\delta^A_{Director}(Scorsese, Coppola) = \delta^A_{Director}(Coppola, Coppola) = 0.33$, and $\delta^A_{Director}$ (*Koster*, *Coppola*) $= 0$ while $\delta^A_{Director}$ $(Koster, Hitchcock) = 0.25$. They correspond to the fact that "*Scorsese*" and "*Coppola*" are very similar directors just as "*Coppola*" is to himself, and the similarity between "*Koster*" and "*Hitchcock*" is larger than that between "*Koster*" and "*Coppola*", as clarified in Section 1.

After specifying *IaAVS* and *IeAVS*, a coupled similarity between objects is built based on *CAVS*. Then, we consider the sum of all these *CAVS*s analogous to the construction of Manhattan dissimilarity [7]. Formally, we have:

DEFINITION 4.6. *Given an information table S, the* ***Coupled Object Similarity (COS)*** *between objects u_{i_1} and u_{i_2}:*

$$COS(u_{i_1}, u_{i_2}) = \sum_{j=1}^{n} \delta^A_j(x_{i_1 j}, x_{i_2 j}), \tag{4.8}$$

where δ^A_j is the CAVS *measure defined in (4.1), $x_{i_1 j}$ and $x_{i_2 j}$ are the attribute values of feature a_j for objects u_{i_1} and u_{i_2} respectively, and $1 \le i_1, i_2 \le m$, $1 \le j \le n$.*

Table 3: Computational Complexity for *CAVS*

Metric	Calculation Steps	Flops per Step	Complexity
IRSP	$nR(R-1)/2$	$2(n-1)2^R$	$O(n^2R^22^R)$
IRSU	$nR(R-1)/2$	$2(n-1)R$	$O(n^2R^2R)$
IRSJ	$nR(R-1)/2$	$2(n-1)P$	$O(n^2R^2R)$
IRSI	$nR(R-1)/2$	$2(n-1)Q$	$O(n^2R^2R)$

For *COS*, all the *CAVS*s with each feature are summed up for two objects. For example (Table 2), $COS(u_2, u_3) = \sum_{j=1}^{3} \delta_j(x_{2j}, x_{3j}) = 0.5 + 0.125 + 0.125 = 0.75$.

5. THEORETICAL ANALYSIS

This section compares four proposed inter-coupled relative similarity measures (*IRSP*, *IRSU*, *IRSJ* and *IRSI*) in terms of their computational accuracies and complexities.

1) Computational Accuracy Equivalence

From the aspect of set theory, these four measures are equivalent to one another in calculating value similarity.

THEOREM 5.1. *IRSP, IRSU, IRSJ and IRSI are all equivalent to one another.*[2]

The above theorem also explains the similarity result in Section 4.2. Thus, these measures induce exactly the same computational accuracy in machine learning tasks.

2) Computational Complexity Comparison

Suppose we have an information table S with m objects and n features, the maximal number of attribute values for all the features is R. In total, the number of attribute value pairs for all the features is at most $n \cdot R(R-1)/2$, which is also the number of calculation steps. For each inter-coupled relative similarity, we calculate *ICP* for $|ICP^{(M)}_{j|k}|$ times by a measure *IRSM*. As we have n attributes, the total *ICP* time costs for *CAVS* is $2|ICP^{(M)}_{j|k}| \cdot (n-1)$ flops per step. Since we have four options for M, the computational complexities for calculating all the *CAVS*s are shown in Table 3.

As indicated in Table 3, all the measures have the same calculation steps, while their flops per step are sorted in descending order since $2^R > R \ge P \ge Q$, in which P and Q are the join and intersection sets of the corresponding *IIF*s, respectively. This evidences that the computational complexity essentially depends on the time costs of *ICP* linearly with given data. Specifically, *IRSP* has the largest complexity $O(n^2R^22^R)$, compared to the smaller equal ones $O(n^2R^3)$ presented by the other three measures (*IRSU*, *IRSJ*, and *IRSI*). Of the latter three candidates, though they have the same computational complexity, *IRSI* is the most efficient due to $Q \le P \le R$. In fact, the dissimilarity that Ahmad and Dey [1] have used for mixed data clustering corresponds to the worst measure *IRSP* discussed here.

Considering both the accuracy analysis and complexity comparison, we conclude that *IRSI* is the best performing because it indicates the least complexity but still maintains an equal accuracy to present coupling.

[2]All detailed proofs of Theorem 5.1 are available on request.

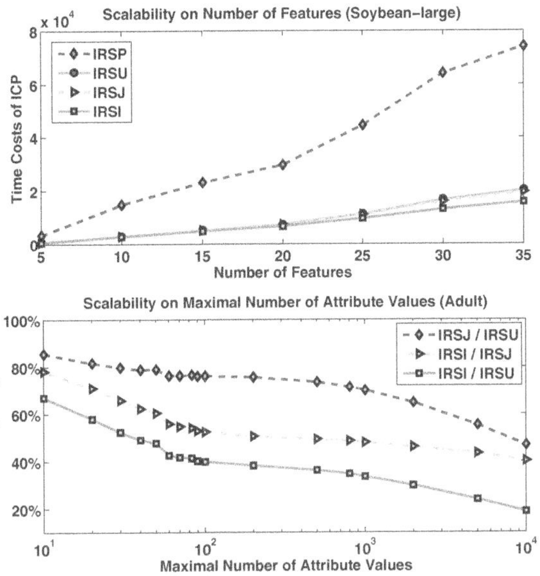

Figure 1: Scalability on $|A|$ and R respectively.

6. EXPERIMENT AND EVALUATION

In this section, several experiments are performed on extensive UCI data sets to show the effectiveness and efficiency of our proposed coupled similarities. The experiments are divided into two categories: coupled similarity comparison and *COS* application. For simplicity, we just assign the weight vector $\alpha = (\alpha_k)_{1\times n}$ with values $\alpha(k) = 1/n$ in (4.7).

6.1 Coupled Similarity Comparison

To compare efficiencies, we conduct extensive experiments on the inter-coupled relative similarity metrics: *IRSP*, *IRSU*, *IRSJ*, and *IRSI*. The goal in this set of experiments is to show the obvious superiority of *IRSI*, compared with the most time-consuming measure *IRSP*. As discussed in Section 5, the computational complexity linearly depends on the time costs of *ICP* with given data. Thus, we consider a comparison of complexities represented by the time costs of *ICP*. Also explained in Section 5, the complexity for *IRSP* is $O(n^2R^22^R)$, while the other three have equal smaller complexity $O(n^2R^3)$. Here, scalability analysis is explored in terms of these two factors separately: the number of features $|A|$ and the maximal number of attribute values R.

From the perspective of $|A|$, Soybean-large data set is considered with 307 objects and 35 features. Here, we fix R to be 7, and focus on $|A|$ ranging from 5 to 35 with step 5. In terms of the total time costs of *ICP*, the computational complexity comparisons among four measures (*IRSP*, *IRSU*, *IRSJ*, and *IRSI*) are depicted in Figure 1($|A|$). The result indicates that the complexities of all these measures keep increasing when $|A|$ becomes larger. The acceleration of *IRSP* (from 3328 to 74128) is the greatest compared with the slightest acceleration of *IRSI* (from 632 to 15704). Apart from these two, the scalability curves are almost the same for *IRSU* and *IRSI*, though the complexity of *IRSU* is slightly higher than that of *IRSJ* with varied $|A|$. Therefore, *IRSI* is the most stable and efficient measure to calculate the intra-coupled relative similarity in terms of $|A|$.

From the perspective of R, the variation of R is considered when $|A|$ is confirmed. Here, we take advantage of the Adult data set with 30718 objects and 13 features chosen. Specifically, the integer feature "fnlwgt" is discretized into different intervals (from 10 to 10000) to form distinct R ranging from 16 to 10000, since one of the existing categorial attributes "education" already has 16 values. The outcomes are shown in Figure 1(R), in which the horizontal axis refers to R, and the vertical axis indicates the relative complexity ratios in terms of $\xi(J/U)$, $\xi(I/J)$, and $\xi(I/U)$. From this figure, we observe all the ratios between 10% and 100%, which again verifies the complexity order for these four measures indicated in Section 5. Another issue is that all three curves decrease as R grows, which means the efficiency advantages of *IRSJ* upon *IRSU* (from 85.5% to 46.8%), *IRSI* upon *IRSJ* (from 78.2% to 40.2%), and *IRSI* upon *IRSU* (from 66.9% to 18.8%) all become more and more obvious with the increasing of R. The general trend of these ratios always falling comes from the fact that there is a higher probability of getting a join set smaller than the whole set, and an intersection set smaller than the join set, with larger R. The same conclusion also holds for the ratio $\xi(U/P)$, but this is due to the fact that $q^{-1}(x) = x/2^x$ is a strictly monotonously decreasing function when $x > 1$. We omit this ratio in Figure 1(R) since the denominator $|ICP^{(P)}|$ becomes exponentially large when R grows, e.g., it equals to 5.12×10^{83} when $R = 500$. Hence, *IRSI* is the least time-consuming intra-coupled similarity with regard to R.

In summary, all the above experiment results clearly show that *IRSI* outperforms *IRSP*, *IRSU*, and *IRSJ* in terms of the computational complexity. In particular, with the increasing numbers of either features or attribute values, *IRSI* demonstrates superior efficiency compared to the others. *IRSJ* and *IRSU* follow, with *IRSP* being the most time-consuming, especially for the large-scale data set.

6.2 Application

In this part of our experiments, we focus on the computational accuracy comparison. In the following, we evaluate the *COD* which is derived from (4.8):

$$COD(u_{i_1}, u_{i_2}) = \sum_{j=1}^{n} h_1(\delta_j^{Ia}(x_{i_1j}, x_{i_2j})) \cdot h_2(\delta_j^{Ie}(x_{i_1j}, x_{i_2j})), \tag{6.1}$$

where $h_1(t)$ and $h_2(t)$ are decreasing functions. Based on intra-coupled and inter-coupled similarities, $h_1(t)$ and $h_2(t)$ can be flexibly chosen to build dissimilarity measures according to specific requirements. Here, we consider $h_1(t) = 1/t - 1$ and $h_2(t) = 1 - t$ to reflect the complementarity of similarity and dissimilarity measures. In terms of the capability on revealing the relationship between data, the better the dissimilarity induced, the better is its similarity.

To demonstrate the effectiveness of our proposed *COD* in application, we compare two clustering methods based on two dissimilarity metrics on six data sets. Here, *COD* is used with the outperforming measure *IRSI*.

One of the clustering approaches is the k-modes (*KM*) algorithm [7], designed to cluster categorical data sets. The main idea of *KM* is to specify the number of clusters k and then to select k initial modes, followed by allocating every object to the nearest mode. The other is a branch of graph-based clustering, i.e., spectral clustering (*SC*) [9], which makes use of the Laplacian Eigenmaps on dissimilarity matrix to perform dimensionality reduction for clustering prior to the k-means algorithm. In respect of feature dependency aggregations, however, Ahmad and Dey [1] evidenced that

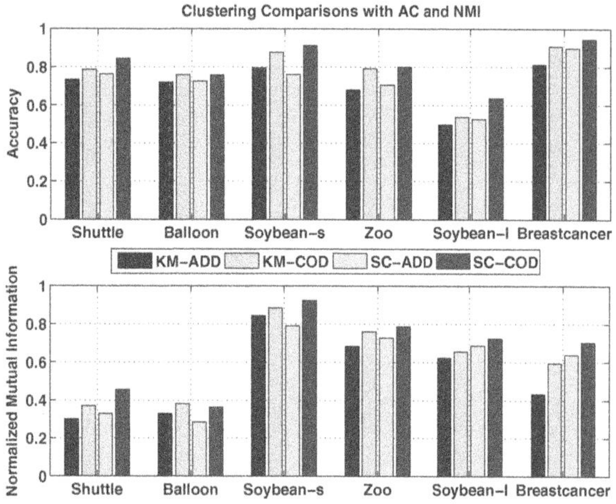

Figure 2: Clustering evaluation on six data sets

their proposed metric ADD outperforms SMD in terms of KM clustering. Thus, we aim to compare the performances of ADD [1] and COD (6.1) for further clustering evaluations.

We conduct four groups of experiments on the same data sets: KM with ADD, KM withCOD, SC with ADD, and SC withCOD. The clustering performance is evaluated by comparing the obtained cluster of each object with that provided by the data label in terms of accuracy (AC) and normalized mutual information (NMI) [3]. $AC\in[0,1]$ is a degree of closeness between the obtained clusters and its actual data labels, while $NMI\in[0,1]$ is a quantity that measures the mutual dependence of two variables: clusters and labels. $AC=1$ or $NMI=1$ if the clusters and labels are identical, and $AC=0$ or $NMI=0$ if the two sets are independent. In fact, the larger AC or NMI is, the better the clustering is, and the better the corresponding dissimilarity metric is.

Figure 2 reports the results on six data sets with different $|U|$, ranging from 15 to 699 in increasing order. In terms of AC and NMI, the evaluations are conducted with KM-ADD, KM-COD, SC-ADD, and SC-COD individually. Followed by Laplacian Eigenmaps, the subspace dimensions are determined by the number of labels in SC. For each data set, the average performance is computed over 100 tests for KM and k-means in SC with distinct start points.

As can be clearly seen from Figure 2, the clustering methods with COD, whether KM or SC, outperform those with ADD in terms of both AC and NMI measures. That is to say, dissimilarity metric COD is better than ADD on clustering qualities. Specifically for KM, the AC improving rate ranges from 5.56% (Balloon) to 16.50% (Zoo), while the NMI improving rate falls within 4.76% (Soybean-s) and 37.38% (Breastcancer). With regard to SC, the former rate takes the minimal and maximal ratios as 4.21% (Balloon) and 20.84% (Soybean-l), respectively; however, the latter rate belongs to [5.45% (Soybean-l), 38.12% (Shuttle)]. Since AC and NMI evaluate clustering quality from different aspects, they generally take minimal and maximal ratios on distinct data sets. Another significant observation is that SC mostly outperforms KM a little whenever it has the same dissimilarity metric; in fact, Luxburg [9] has indicated that SC very often outperforms k-means for numerical data.

We draw the following two conclusions: 1) intra-coupled relative similarity $IRSI$ is the most efficient one when compared with $IRSP$, $IRSU$ and $IRSJ$, especially for large-scale data; 2) our proposed object dissimilarity metric COD is better than others, such as dependency aggregation only ADD, for categorical data in terms of clustering qualities.

7. CONCLUSION

We have proposed COS, a novel coupled object similarity metric which involves both attribute value frequency distribution (intra-coupling) and feature dependency aggregation (inter-coupling) in measuring attribute value similarity for unsupervised learning of nominal data. Theoretical analysis and substantial experiments have shown that inter-coupled relative similarity measure $IRSI$ significantly outperforms the others ($IRSP$, $IRSU$, $IRSJ$) in terms of efficiency, in particular on large-scale data, while maintaining equal accuracy. Moreover, our derived dissimilarity metric is more comprehensive and accurate in capturing the clustering qualities in accordance with substantial empirical results.

We are currently applying the COS measure with $IRSI$ to feature discretization, clustering ensemble, and other data mining tasks. We are also considering extending the notion of "coupling" for the similarity of numerical data. Moreover, the proposed concepts *Inter-information Function* and *Information Conditional Probability* for the information table have potential for other applications.

8. ACKNOWLEDGMENT

This work is sponsored by Australian Research Council Grants (DP1096218, DP0988016, LP100200774, LP0989721), Tianjin Research Project (10JCYBJC07500), and QCIS (Center for Quantum Computation and Intelligent Systems).

9. REFERENCES

[1] A. Ahmad and L. Dey. A k-mean clustering algorithm for mixed numeric and categorical data. *Data and Knowledge Engineering*, 63:503–527, 2007.

[2] S. Boriah, V. Chandola, and V. Kumar. Similarity measures for categorical data: a comparative evaluation. In *SDM 2008*, pages 243–254, 2008.

[3] D. Cai, X. He, and J. Han. Document clustering using locality preserving indexing. *IEEE TKDE*, 17(12):1624–1637, 2005.

[4] L. Cao, Y. Ou, and P. Yu. Coupled behavior analysis with applications. *IEEE Transactions on Knowledge and Data Engineering*, 2011.

[5] S. Cost and S. Salzberg. A weighted nearest neighbor algorithm for learning with symbolic features. *Machine Learning*, 10(1):57–78, 1993.

[6] G. Das and H. Mannila. Context-based similarity measures for categorical databases. In *PKDD 2000*, pages 201–210, 2000.

[7] G. Gan, C. Ma, and J. Wu. *Data clustering: theory, algorithms, and applications*. ASA-SIAM Series on Statistics and Applied Probability, VA, 2007.

[8] M. Houle, V. Oria, and U. Qasim. Active caching for similarity queries based on shared-neighbor information. In *CIKM 2010*, pages 669–678, 2010.

[9] U. Luxburg. A tutorial on spectral clustering. *Statistics and Computing*, 17(4):1–32, 2007.

[10] D. Wilson and T. Martinez. Improved heterogeneous distance functions. *Journal of Artificial Intelligence Research*, 6:1–34, 1997.

Feature Selection using Hierarchical Feature Clustering

Huawen Liu
Zhejiang Normal University &
Key Laboratory of SCKE
688 Yingbin Avenue
Jinhua, P.R.China
huaw.liu@gmail.com

Xindong Wu
University of Vermont
33 Colchester Avenue
Burlington, Vermont,USA
xwu@cs.uvm.edu

Shichao Zhang
University of Technology,
Sydney
Broadway NSW 2007
Sydney, Australia
zhangsc@it.uts.edu.au

ABSTRACT

One of the challenges in data mining is the dimensionality of data, which is often very high and prevalent in many domains, such as text categorization and bio-informatics. The high-dimensionality of data may bring many adverse situations to traditional learning algorithms. To cope with this issue, feature selection has been put forward. Currently, many efforts have been attempted in this field and lots of feature selection algorithms have been developed. In this paper we propose a new selection method to pick discriminative features by using information measurement. The main characteristic of our selection method is that the selection procedure works like feature clustering in a hierarchically agglomerative way, where each feature is considered as a cluster and the between-cluster and within-cluster distances are measured by mutual information and the coefficient of relevancy respectively. Consequently, the final aggregated cluster is the selection result, which has the minimal redundancy among its members and the maximal relevancy with the class labels. The simulation experiments on seven datasets show that the proposed method outperforms other popular feature selection algorithms in classification performance.

Categories and Subject Descriptors

I.5.2 [**Pattern Recognition**]: Design Methodology-Feature evaluation and selection; H.2.8 [**Database Management**]: Database Applications-Data mining

General Terms

Algorithms

Keywords

Feature selection, Mutual Information, Classification, Feature Clustering, Learning

1. INTRODUCTION

Pattern classification, whose purpose is to induce hypotheses and identify useful patterns from known data, is an essential task in data mining [8]. In a classification model, features play an important role as they provide a discriminative capability to distinguish one class from the others. Generally speaking, a classifier involving more features should have more discriminative power.

In many application fields, such as text categorization and bio-informatics, the dimensionality of data is getting higher and higher. The high-dimensionality of data brings both advantages and challenges to a learning algorithm. On one hand, many features are available to construct a classification model. On the other hand, not all features can contribute to the discriminative power in practice, because most of them are often correlated or redundant to each other [8]. The correlated features may bring many adverse situations to traditional learning algorithms, such as over-fitting, low efficiency and poor performance, and even give rise to the problem of "the curse of dimensionality". Thus, it is necessary to reduce the high-dimensionality of data for practical reasons.

Feature selection aims at selecting discriminative features for classification and eliminating redundant ones [22]. Since it can bring lots of advantages to learning algorithms, such as better performance, easier comprehensibility and more robustness to noise [11], feature selection has gained much attention in data mining and many selection algorithms have been developed [11, 22, 26].

Roughly speaking, feature selection methods can be divided into three categories, i.e., embedded, filter and wrapper models, depending on their evaluation manner [11, 22, 26]. The wrapper and embedded models are tightly coupled with in-built classifiers. Thus, they have a relatively better performance, but less generality, and require much more time during the training process. Contrastively, the filter method evaluates the interestingness of features by intrinsic properties of data [22]. It is more competitive in computational expense and more robust than the others. In the filter method, the evaluation criterion of interestingness plays a vital role. Among the proposed evaluation measurements, the information criterion is widely studied and used in reality because of its capability in quantifying the uncertainties of features. Several extensive experiments have also demonstrated that the information metrics work well in many cases [21].

In this paper we propose a new filter feature selection algorithm using information metrics. The center idea of the

CIKM'11, October 24–28, 2011, Glasgow, Scotland, UK.

proposed method is data clustering and its selection procedure which works like clustering in a hierarchical way. The difference between them is that cluster points in our method are features rather than instances. More specifically, each feature is initially taken as an individual cluster point, and all features are divided into three disjoint parts: a selected cluster, candidate clusters and a class cluster. They are represented as selected features, candidate features and the class labels respectively. Under this context, the 'clustering' process of our method is to identify the selected cluster with the minimal intra-distance and the maximal inter-distance with the class cluster. Moreover, we adopt two information criteria, i.e., mutual information and the coefficient of relevancy, to measure the inter- and intra-distances between clusters respectively. Unlike traditional methods of feature clustering, which group features into different clusters by virtue of the similarity of features [16, 20, 27], the 'clustering' process in our method mainly serves the purpose of selecting informative features for classification. That is to say, the selected feature at each step contributes the least redundancy to the selected subset (i.e., intra-distance) and the most relevancy (i.e., inter-distance) to the classes.

The rest of the paper is organized as follows. Section 2 briefly recalls previous related work about feature selection methods. Section 3 presents some basic concepts about information theory. In Section 4, the distance measurements based on the information entropy are discussed, and then a new feature selection algorithm based on feature clustering is provided. Section 5 shows experimental results conducted to evaluate the usefulness and effectiveness of the proposed approach. Finally, conclusions and future work are given in the end.

2. RELATED WORK

By now, many feature selection algorithms have been witnessed. In this section, only the latest selection methods will be discussed briefly. Interested readers can refer to good survey literatures (see, e.g. [11, 22, 26]) to get more details.

Depending on specific criteria or applications, feature selection algorithms can be organized into different categories. For example, according to the evaluation manner of features, feature selection methods have three categories: embedded, filter and wrapper. The wrappers take the classification performance of features as the evaluation criterion, whereas the embedded and filter models evaluate features by virtue of their relevancy with the classes [22]. Recently, hybrid or sophisticated techniques have also been introduced. As a typical example, Bacauskiene et al. [3] firstly percolated insignificant features by comparing with a noise one, and then evaluated the rest features by the genetic algorithm (GA). Saeys et al. [25] provided an ensemble classifier by combining multiple classifiers built with different selection methods.

As mentioned above, currently many evaluation criteria, such as distance, information, dependency and consistency measurements [1], have been proposed. For instance, Relief [17] and FCBF [29] evaluate the relevancy between features by using Euclidean distance and symmetric uncertainty respectively. Among these criteria, the information one seems to be the most comprehensively studied one and this kind of feature selection algorithm is called MIFSA.

The most naive MIFSA is BIF, whose evaluation criterion is mutual information [15]. Since BIF does not involve the redundancy between features, many works have been done on maximizing the relevancy with the classes and minimizing the redundancy of the selected subset (see, e.g., MIFS [4], MIFS-U [18], mMIFS-U [23] and mRMR [24]). Meanwhile, the criterion of mutual information is incline to the features with more values. Thus, it is often normalized in several MIFSAs. For instance, NMIFS [9] is a representative example of this kind. FCBF [29] measures the relevancy between features by Symmetrical uncertainty (SU) and discards irrelevant features by using the approximate Markov blanket. CFS [12] also takes SU to measure the correlation between discrete features. In addition, conditional mutual information has also been adopted in some MIFSAs [16, 27], e.g., CMIM [10].

It is noticeable that in high dimensional space the estimation of mutual information is imprecise because of the finite training data. Hence, several MIFSAs estimate mutual information by approximate methods, such as nearest neighbors, entropy graph, minimal spanning tree [6], Gaussian kernel function and Renyi entropy [8]. As an illustration, Hild et al. [13] estimated the Renyi's quadratic entropy with Parzen windows and Gaussian kernels to reduce the computational complexity. Levi and Ullman [19] replaced the selected subset with a single selected feature in estimating the joint mutual information. For the selection methods using mutual information (MIFSAs), Liu et al. [21] presented an unified framework and discussed their relationship in details.

Here we bring the advantages of filter, heuristic search and information criterion together and propose a new feature selection algorithm called FSFC. The center idea of FSFC comes from feature clustering, where the feature with maximal relevancy and minimal redundancy will be chosen at each time. As a result, it lessens the computational and unfaithful problems in estimating the information criterion.

3. PRELIMINARIES

Let X be a discrete random variable and $p(x)$ be its probability density function (pdf) for all possible events $x \in dom(X)$. The uncertainty of X measured by the Shannon's information entropy $H(X)$ is defined as [7]

$$H(X) = -\sum_{x \in dom(X)} p(x) \log p(x). \quad (1)$$

$H(X)$ represents as the information amount of the random variable X. From this definition, one may observe that $H(x)$ does not depend on the actual values of a variable. If X is a continuous one, its entropy $H(X)$ is taken as the integral form, i.e., $H(X) = -\int_x p(x) \log p(x) dx$. For the sake of simplification, hereafter the subscript $dom(X)$ will be ignored if the context is unambiguous, and only random variables with finite discrete values will be discussed.

Assume that X and Y are two random variables, their joint entropy $H(X, Y)$ is

$$H(X, Y) = -\sum \sum p(x, y) \log p(x, y). \quad (2)$$

Conditional entropy is used to measure the remaining uncertainty of one variable when another is known. Specifically, given the observing values of Y, the conditional entropy $H(X|Y)$ of X with respect to Y is

$$H(X|Y) = -\sum \sum p(x, y) \log p(x|y). \quad (3)$$

If X is fully dependent on Y, $H(X|Y)$ is zero. This means that no more information is required to describe X when

Y is known. Otherwise, $H(X|Y) = H(X)$ if they are independent with each other. In this case, knowing Y will do nothing to observe X.

Given two variables X and Y with joint pdf $p(x, y)$, and marginal pdfs $p(x)$ and $p(y)$, respectively, their mutual information (MI) $I(X; Y)$, which is mainly used to quantify how much information is shared between them, is

$$I(X;Y) = \sum \sum p(x, y) \log \frac{p(x, y)}{p(x)p(y)}. \quad (4)$$

MI can be interpreted as the quantity of information one variable can predict about the other. The more relevant two variables are, the higher their MI is, and $I(X;Y)$=0 means that these two variables are totally irrelevant to each other. Since MI is calculated over joint and marginal pdfs of the variables and does not utilize statistics of any grade or order, it is capable of measuring any kind of relationship between variables. According to its definition, MI can be rewritten as $I(X;Y) = H(X) - H(X|Y) = H(X) + H(Y) - H(X, Y)$.

Assume that $\mathcal{T}$=$(\mathcal{D}, \mathcal{F}, \mathcal{C})$ is a dataset, where $\mathcal{D} = \{o_1, .., o_n\}$, $\mathcal{F} = \{f_1, .., f_m\}$ and $\mathcal{C} = \{l_1, .., l_k\}$ are instances, features and class labels respectively. Usually, each instance o_i is represented as a form of value vector of $\mathcal{F}$ and $\mathcal{C}$. The purpose of learning algorithms is to map the input feature space $\mathcal{F}$ onto the class space $\mathcal{C}$ according to the instances in $\mathcal{D}$. That is to say, the input features are relevant to the output classes and each mapped input feature should encapsulate information, which can contribute to the distribution of classes.

As mentioned above, feature selection aims at choosing a subset $S \subset \mathcal{F}$, which can preserve most of information contained in the original space. Without loss of generality, let $J(S)$ be the evaluation function to measure the relevant degree between the feature subset S and the classes C. Since mutual information $I(S;C)$ is good at representing the relevancy between S and C, many selection methods take it as the evaluation criterion. However, due to the high dimensionality of data, it is prohibitive to calculate the criterion $J(S) = I(S;C)$. The common strategy for most MIFSAs adopts the monotonic property of subset during the selection process, that is, increasing the number of features will improve the performance of learning algorithms [22]. Under this context, the problem is immigrated into evaluating individual feature $J(f)$.

4. FEATURE SELECTION USING FEATURE CLUSTERING

4.1 Feature clustering

The common assumption behind feature selection algorithms is that a good feature subset contains features highly relevant to the class labels, while its elements are uncorrelated with each other. This, however, is similar to the notion of data clustering, which partitions data into different clusters (or groups) so that the members of a cluster are more similar to each other than to members in other clusters [8].

Let $\mathcal{D}$ be a data set consisting of n instances. Data clustering groups these n instances into k different clusters, where data instances that belong to the same group are as near (or similar) to each other as possible, while far (i.e., dissimilar) from others in different groups. To achieve a good result, within-cluster distance S_w and between-cluster distance S_b should be taken into consideration.

Recently the idea of clustering has also been used to serve the purpose of feature selection [16, 20, 27]. This kind of selection methods is called feature clustering, where features firstly are grouped into different clusters in terms of similarity criteria (e.g., correlation coefficient [14], MI [20] and conditional MI [16, 27]). After the procedure of feature clustering, a feature subset is formed by picking a representative feature out from each cluster. This selection framework, however, is a unsupervised one and has not exploited the label information.

Here we also take the characteristics of data clustering to achieve the goal of feature selection. Unlike feature clustering in literatures, whose aim is to group features into several clusters in terms of similarity [16, 27], our clustering method works like a supervised one, where the class labels are treated as a special cluster C_k and used to guide the process of clustering. In our method, features are grouped into two kinds of clusters: a selected cluster S and several candidate clusters. Each point(i.e., feature) in S has already been selected to separate the classes $\mathcal{C}$. Each candidate cluster consists of only one candidate feature f, which has still not been selected. Under this context, the candidate cluster (feature), which has minimal within-cluster dispersion S_w (redundancy) with the selected cluster (selected feature subset) S and maximal between-cluster dispersion S_b (relevancy) with the class cluster C_k, will be aggregated with the selected cluster. Eventually, the selected cluster S is the final selected subset.

4.2 Clustering distances

As we know, the final result of clustering heavily relies on different aspects, especially on the choice of distance function. Euclidean distance perhaps is the most widely used one in reality application. As mentioned above, MI $I(X;Y)$ can also be used to measure the relevancy between the features f and the class labels C, for it is non-parameteric one and represents the amount of information reduction of X when Y is known. Indeed, the higher $I(S;C)$ is, the more the prediction error of a classifier approaches the Bayes error.

Based on this principle, the between-cluster distance $S_b(C, S)$ of the selected cluster S and the class cluster C in our method is defined as

$$S_b(C, S) = \sum_{s \in S} I(s; C). \quad (5)$$

To estimate the redundancy in S, both the total amount and its incremental ratio of redundancy are needed to considered, for we always expect the selected feature has lower incremental ratio. Therefore, coefficient of relevance [7] (also termed as variable relevance [5]) is introduced. Given two features s and f, their coefficient of relevance is defined as the relative reduction of uncertainty of s when f is known, i.e., $CR(s, f) = \frac{I(s;f)}{H(s)}$. If s is fully dependent on f, then $CR(s, f)$=1. On the other hand, $CR(s, f)$=0 means that s and f are independent with each other.

In our method, the distance between the candidate cluster f and the selected cluster S is defined as the sum of distance $CR(s, f)$ between f and all feature points s in S, i.e.,

$$S(f) = \sum_{s \in S} CR(s; f). \quad (6)$$

This is our within-cluster distance $S_w(S)$ of the selected cluster S, and it can be obtained accumulatively. Initially,

$S_w(S)$ is zero and then plus $S(f)$ at a time when the candidate cluster f has been merged with the selected one S, i.e.,

$$S_w(S \cup f) = S_w(S) + S(f). \quad (7)$$

Based on above analysis, for the candidate feature f, our evaluation function is

$$J(f) = \frac{S_b(C, S) + I(f; C)}{|S| + S_w(S \cup f)}, \quad (8)$$

where $|S|$ is the number of elements in S. This evaluation criterion means that the candidate cluster with the remotest distance from the class cluster C will be aggregated with the selected cluster S with high priority, if it will not increase greatly the redundancy with S at the same time. As a result, the margin of clusters will not be degraded greatly.

4.3 Our selection algorithm

On the basis of the evaluation function $J(f)$, we propose a new feature selection method using feature clustering called FSFC. Without loss of generality, the search strategy adopted in our method is the sequential forward selection. At the beginning, the initiation step is required, where each feature f in $\mathcal{F}$ is initialized as a candidate cluster and the class labels $\mathcal{C}$ is taken as the class cluster C. Then for each f, its between-cluster distance $S_b(C, f)$ with C will be calculated. The candidate cluster f with the largest value of MI will be assigned to the selected cluster S. After these procedures, the hierarchical clustering iteration is launched, in which the candidate cluster f with the largest $J(f)$ will be aggregated together with S. The clustering procedure will not be terminated unless the number of features in S is larger than a pre-specified threshold. the specific implementation of FSFC is shown as follows:

Input: A training data set $\mathcal{T} = (\mathcal{D}, \mathcal{F}, \mathcal{C})$.
Output: The selected feature subset S.
  Initialize parameters: $F = \mathcal{F}; S = \emptyset; C_k = \mathcal{C}$;
  Calculate the distance $S_b(C_k, f)$ for each f;
  $F = F - \{f\}; S = \{f\}; S_w = 0$;
  While $|S| < \delta$ **do**
    For each candidate cluster $f \in F$ **do**
      Calculate $J(f)$ according to Eq.(8);
    Choose f with the largest $J(f)$;
    Clustering S with f;
    UpdateS_w and S_b of S;
  End
  Return S as the final selection result.

Assume that there are n instances and m features in $\mathcal{T}$. The time complexity of FSFC is $O(knm^2)$, where k is the selected number of features. For the value of k, it may be adaptively determined by cross-validate or data consistency. Usually, as the information amount of S approximately equals to those of the original space F, the process of feature selection stops and k is determined. In our later experiments, the value of k is determined by FCBF.

5. PERFORMANCE EVALUATION

To demonstrate the effectiveness of our method, simulation experiments have been carried out on UCI datasets. During our experiments, four popular feature selectors, i.e., Relief [17], CFS [12], FCBF [29] and mMIFS-U [23] were used to compare with FSFC. These feature selectors stand for different types of selection algorithms.

5.1 Experimental Settings

To compare performance roundly, seven UCI benchmark datasets with different types and sizes are chosen in our experiments. They can be downloaded from the UCI Machine Learning Repository [2]. These datasets are often used to evaluate the performance of learning and selection algorithms in data mining community. Table 1 summarizes their brief descriptions. For the sake of fair comparison and computational cost, missing values were replaced with the most frequent values (or means) for nominal (or numeric) features, and continuous features were discretized into nominal ones by the minimum description length method in our experiments.

Table 1: The descriptions of datasets in our experiments

No	Datasets	#instances	#features	#classes
1	Ionosphere	355	34	2
2	Mfeat-factors	2000	216	10
3	Optdigits	5620	64	10
4	Splice	3190	60	3
5	Sponge	76	44	3
6	Colon	62	2000	2
7	Prostate	102	12600	2

Each feature selector chose the same quantity of features for the purpose of achieving impartial results. For the convenience of simplification, the number of selected features was determined by FCBF, which can obtain a feature subset without pre-defined parameters. Additionally, two classical and representative classifiers, i.e., Naive Bayes(NB) and 1-Nearest Neighbor(1-NN), were chosen to evaluate the performance of the selected results. The experimental platform was Weka toolkit [28], and the relative parameters of the classifiers adopted were assigned to default values in the experiments. To roundly verify performance, three times of 10-fold cross validation had been adopted in experiments, and the average values were the desirable results. Moreover, statistical t-test was used to analyze the means and standard deviations between the final results at the significance level of 0.05.

5.2 Results and Discussion

Table 2 shows classification performance of the NB classifier with the five feature selection algorithms on the benchmark datasets. In this table, *Total* column denotes the performance of the NB classifier over the original datasets with the whole feature space. The last row represents the mean values of accurate ratios. Meanwhile, bold value refers to the largest one among the five feature selectors, and notation 'v' (or '$*$') is used to guide that the performance of the classifier with the corresponding feature selector is significantly better (or worse) than that without performing feature selection (i.e., the *Total* column) at the level of 0.05 in statistics.

From the results in Table 2, one may observe that the proposed method can effectively improve the classification performance of the Naive Bayes classifier on most of the benchmark datasets, except the *Optdigits* database (i.e., Line 3).

Nonetheless, the classification performance was not deteriorated significantly by our method on this situation. Indeed, it was the highest one than those of other four selectors. Meanwhile, there were four cases where the classification performance had been strengthened significantly by the FSFC selector.

Table 2: A comparison of accuracies (%) of the Naive Bayes classifier using feature selectors

Total	FSFC	CFS	FCBF	mMIFS-U	Relief
90.60	**92.38** v	91.52	**92.38** v	92.00	90.76
93.65	**96.15**	96.11	95.33	95.38	88.56
92.31	**91.73**	91.57	91.46	91.41	85.15 *
95.36	**96.21** v	96.08 v	96.13 v	95.96	95.57
92.50	94.76	**94.82**	**94.82**	94.76	90.54
69.52	**91.90** v	84.76 v	89.68 v	89.76 v	79.76 v
61.00	**97.09** v	96.12 v	97.06 v	94.12 v	92.79 v
84.99	**94.32**	93.00	93.84	93.34	89.02

It is noticeable that in the Naive Bayes classifier, FSFC is superior to others at several aspects. For example, the average performance of our method, which was 94.32%, was the largest one among the feature selectors; There were six over seven datasets, on which the performance of FSFC was the best and far more than those of the rest feature selectors. In addition, the number of datasets whose performance had been upgraded by other four selection methods was no more than four. Meanwhile, for the FSFC selector, there was none dataset whose correct rate was the lowest one in comparing with CFS, FCBF, mMIFS-U and Relief. Further, only one over seven databases where the classification errors induced by FSFC were higher than the corresponding ones by FCBF, CFS or mMIFS-U, and there was none situation whose performance had been significantly deteriorated by our selection method.

In order to demonstrate that our proposed method surpasses others roundly, we also assessed its performance with 1-NN. The experimental results are given in Table 3. In the 1-NN classifier (Table 3), the classification accuracies using FSFC were significantly better than those without using feature selectors on three databases, i.e., *Splice*, *Colon* and *Prostate*, notwithstanding there were two cases on which the performance induced by FSFC were relatively poor than the original one. This, however, results from the characteristic of the 1-NN classifier, that is, the more features contained, the higher classification performance of 1-NN. As a matter of fact, the classification capability of the 1-NN classifier was also degraded by other feature selection algorithms on most cases. There were only one over seven situations, where the performance using FSFC was inferior to other selectors. Additionally, the mean value of FSFC was higher than that of the unselected one, and still distinctly better than those of other selection algorithms. All of these signifies a fact that FSFC performs better than other four feature selectors in the 1-NN classifier.

Besides, we also averaged the classification performance of these two classifiers on each dataset to make a comparison on the overall aspect. The specific results of absolute difference of performance between FSFC and the rest four feature selectors are presented as a bar graph (Figure 5.2), where the baseline is FSFC. In this illustration, a bar above (or below) the zero line denotes that the performance induced by the corresponding selector is better (or worse) than the one of FSFC. For instance, the value of the first blue bar is -2.57, and this value implies that the mean performance of CFS was worse than that of FSFC on the *Ionosphere* dataset. From this figure, we can observe that the mean performance of FSFC was better than others on most databases.

Table 3: A comparison of accuracies (%) of the 1-NN classifier using feature selectors

Total	FSFC	CFS	FCBF	mMIFS-U	Relief
93.17	**91.14**	86.86 *	88.10	88.10	84.48 *
95.55	**95.60**	95.51	95.23	95.05	89.24 *
93.77	**91.24**	90.59	90.69	91.21	87.25 *
75.92	**82.48** v	82.03 v	81.77 v	81.64 v	80.49 v
92.14	**93.51**	89.40	89.40	**93.51**	88.69
69.29	**85.79** v	77.70 v	83.73 v	78.17 v	83.02 v
78.36	**97.03** v	95.76 v	96.09 v	93.45 v	92.09 v
85.46	**90.97**	88.26	89.29	88.73	86.47

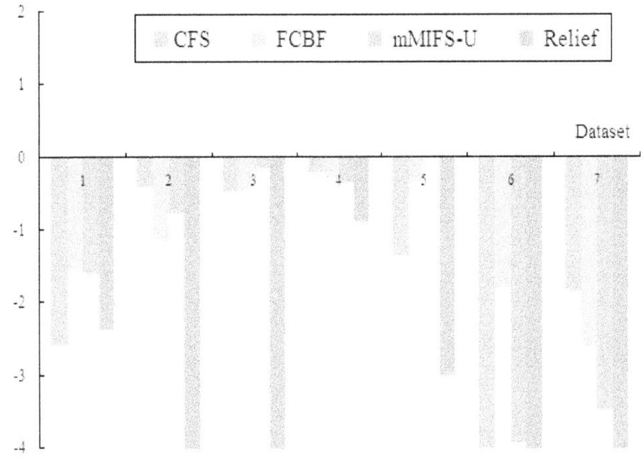

Figure 1: Absolute difference of performance between FSFC and other feature selectors.

6. CONCLUSIONS

The high-dimensionality of data may pose great challenges to traditional learning algorithms, such as over-fitting, poor performance and low efficiency. Thus, effective techniques are required to cut down the dimensionality of data. In this paper, we proposed a new feature selection method using the information criterion. The primary characteristic of the proposed method is that it works like hierarchical clustering. Compared to traditional data clustering, an individual cluster in our method corresponds to a feature, not an instance. Unlike feature clustering in the literature, which groups features into different clusters by virtue of the similarity of the features, our clustering method is a supervised one, and serves the purpose of selecting informative features for classification. The advantage is that the selected feature at each step contributes the least redundancy to the selected subset and the most relevancy to the classes. The simulation experiments conducted on UCI datasets showed that FSFC is superior to other popular feature selection algorithms.

In our experiments, we found the efficiency of FSFC is

relatively lower in comparison to FCBF, though it is better than others. Thus, we will take this aspect into consideration in our future work.

Acknowledgements

The authors are grateful to the anonymous referees for their valuable and constructive comments and suggestions. This work is supported by the U.S. NSF (CCF-0905337), the Australian Research Council (ARC) (DP0985456), the NSF of China (90718020), the Open Funds of the Key Discipline of Computer Software and Theories of Zhejiang Province at ZJNU (ZSDZZZZXK05), the Open Funds of the Key Laboratory of Symbol Computation and Knowledge Engineering of the Ministry of Education (93K-17-2010-K02), and the Fundamental Research Funds for the Central Universities of China (2011HGZY0003).

7. REFERENCES

[1] A Arauzo-Azofra, JM Benitez, JL Castro, Consistency measures for feature selection. Journal of Intelligence Information System 30: 273-292, 2008.

[2] A Asuncion, DJ Newman, UCI Machine Learning Repository. Available from http://wwwicsuciedu/~mlearn/MLRepositoryhtml, Department of Information and Computer Science, University of California Irvine, 2007.

[3] M Bacauskiene, A Verikas, A Gelzinis, D Valincius, A feature selection technique for generation of classification committees and its application to categorization of laryngeal images. Pattern Recognition 42(5): 645-654, 2009.

[4] R Battiti, Using Mutual Information for Selecting Features in Supervised Neural Net Learning. IEEE Transactions on Neural Networks 5(4): 537-550, 1994.

[5] DA Bell, H Wang, A Formalism for Relevance and Its Application in Feature Subset Selection. Machine Learning 41: 175-195, 2000.

[6] B Bonev, F Escolano, M Cazorla, Feature selection mutual information and the classification of high-dimensional patterns. Pattern Analysis and Application 11: 309-319, 2008.

[7] TM Cover, JA Thomas, Elements of Information Theory. New York Wiley, 1991.

[8] RO Duda, PE Hart, DG Stork, Pattern Classification. New York:John Wiley Sons Inc, 2001.

[9] PA Estévez, M Tesmer, CA Perez, JM Zurada, Normalized Mutual Information Feature Selection, IEEE Transactions on Neural Networks 20(2): 189-201, 2009.

[10] F Fleuret, Fast Binary Feature Selection with Conditional Mutual Information. Journal of Machine Learning Research 5: 1531-1555, 2004.

[11] I Guyon, A Elisseeff, An Introduction to Variable and Feature Selection. Journal of Machine Learning Research 3: 1157-1182, 2003.

[12] MA Hall, Correlation-based Feature Subset Selection for Machine Learning. PhD Thesis, Department of Computer Science University of Waikato, Hamilton, NewZealand, 1999.

[13] KE Hild, D Erdogmus, K Torkkola, JC Principe, Feature extraction using information theoretic learning, IEEE Trans. Pattern Anal. Mach. Intell. 28(9): 1385-1392, 2006.

[14] HH Hsu, CW Hsieh, Feature Selection via Correlation Coefficient Clustering, Journal of Software 5(12): 1371-1377, 2010.

[15] AK Jain, RPW Duin, J Mao, Statistical Pattern Recognition: A Review. IEEE Transactions on Pattern Analysis and Machine Intelligence 22(1): 4-37, 2000.

[16] CS Jung, H Seo, HG Kang, Estimating redundancy information of selected features in multi-dimensional pattern. Pattern Recognition Letters 32: 590-596, 2011.

[17] K Kira, L Rendell, A practical approach to feature selection. In: Proceedings of the 9th International Conference on Machine Learning, Morgan Kaufmann, pp 249-256, 1992.

[18] N Kwak, CH Choi, Input feature selection by mutual information based on Parzen window. IEEE Transactions on Pattern Analysis and Machine Intelligence 24(12): 1667-1671, 2002.

[19] D Levi, S Ullman, Learning to classify by ongoing feature selection. Image and Vision Computing 28(4): 715-723, 2010.

[20] H Liu, L Liu, H Zhang, Ensemble gene selection for cancer classification. Pattern Recognition 43(8): 2763-2772, 2010.

[21] H Liu, J Sun, L Liu, H Zhang, Feature selection with dynamic mutual information. Pattern Recognition 42: 1330-1339, 2009.

[22] H Liu, L Yu, Toward Integrating Feature Selection Algorithms for Classification and Clustering. IEEE Transactions on Knowledge and Data Engineering 17(4): 491-502, 2005.

[23] J Novovičová, P Somol, M Haindl, P Pudil, Conditional Mutual Information Based Feature Selection for Classification Task. In: Proceedings of the 12th Iberoamericann Congress on Pattern Recognition Valparaiso, Chile, pp 417-426, 2007.

[24] H Peng, F Long, C Ding, Feature Selection Based on Mutual Information: Criteria of Max-Dependency Max-Relevanceand Min-Redundancy. IEEE Transactions on Pattern Analysis and Machine Intelligence 27(8): 1226-1238, 2005.

[25] Y Saeys, T Abeel, YV de Peer, Robust Feature Selection Using Ensemble Feature Selection Techniques. In: Proceedings of ECML/PKDD 2008, LNAI 5212, Springer, pp 313-325, 2008.

[26] Y Saeys, I Inza, L Larrañaga, A review of feature selection techniques in bioinformatics. Bioinformatics 23(19): 2507-2517, 2007.

[27] JM Sotoca, F Pla, Supervised feature selection by clustering using conditional mutual information-based distances, Pattern Recognition 43: 2068-2081, 2010.

[28] IH Witten, E Frank, Data Mining - Pracitcal Machine Learning Tools and Techniques with JAVA Implementations, 2nd eds, Morgan Kaufmann Publishers, 2005.

[29] L Yu, H Liu, Efficient Feature Selection via Analysis of Relevance and Redundancy. Journal of Machine Learning Research 5: 1205-1224, 2004.

Discovering Top-k Teams of Experts with/without a Leader in Social Networks

Mehdi Kargar and Aijun An
Department of Computer Science and Engineering
York University, Toronto, Canada
{kargar,aan}@cse.yorku.ca

ABSTRACT

We study the problem of discovering a team of experts from a social network. Given a project whose completion requires a set of skills, our goal is to find a set of experts that together have all of the required skills and also have the minimal communication cost among them. We propose two communication cost functions designed for two types of communication structures. We show that the problem of finding the team of experts that minimizes one of the proposed cost functions is NP-hard. Thus, an approximation algorithm with an approximation ratio of two is designed. We introduce the problem of finding a team of experts with a leader. The leader is responsible for monitoring and coordinating the project, and thus a different communication cost function is used in this problem. To solve this problem, an exact polynomial algorithm is proposed. We show that the total number of teams may be exponential with respect to the number of required skills. Thus, two procedures that produce top-k teams of experts with or without a leader in polynomial delay are proposed. Extensive experiments on real datasets demonstrate the effectiveness and scalability of the proposed methods.

Categories and Subject Descriptors

H.2.8 [**Database Management**]: Database Applications-Data Mining

General Terms

Algorithms, Experimentation, Theory

Keywords

Team Formation, Approximation Algorithms, Social Networks

1. INTRODUCTION

A project cannot be successfully completed without effective communications and collaborations among its team members. Given a project whose completion requires a set of skills, we tackle the problem of finding from a social network a team of individuals that not only cover all the required skills but can also communicate and collaborate effectively. The social network is modeled as a graph whose nodes represent experts, each with one or more skills, and whose edge between two nodes is weighted by the communication cost between the two corresponding experts.

This problem has been introduced in the data mining community by Lappas et al. [10]. They defined two functions for estimating the communication cost of a team. The first function uses the diameter of the subgraph formed by the team to measure the team communication cost, which is the largest shortest path between any two nodes in the subgraph. The second function uses the cost of the minimum spanning tree (MST) on the subgraph. However, such functions may not measure the communication cost well, especially when the project requires that the holders of each pair of the required skills communicate with each other to perform the corresponding tasks in the project. The diameter function only measures the communication cost between the two experts that are furthest away from each other, and the MST function does not measure the cost of all the required communication either. Another disadvantage of these functions is their instability: a slight change in the graph may result in a radical change in the solution. At the same time, the diameter and MST based functions may be insensitive to adding or deleting a connection in the graph since they only measure part of the communication cost.

In this paper, we introduce two new cost functions. We consider two types of communication structures within a team. Assume that each required skill corresponds to a task in the project. In the first communication structure, the experts for each pair of required skills need to communicate to each other to complete the corresponding tasks. For such a structure, we define a cost function, called *Sum of Distances*, to measure the communication cost of a team using the sum of the shortest distances between the experts for each pair of skills. In the second type of communication structure, a leader needs to communicate with each team member to monitor and coordinate the project. For such a structure we define a cost function, named *Leader Distance*, that computes the sum of shortest distances between the leader and each skill holder in the team.

Based on these two new cost functions, we define two problems of team formation from a social network. One is to find a team of experts without a leader which covers the required skills and minimizes the *Sum of Distances* function.

CIKM 11, October 24–28, 2011, Glasgow, Scotland, UK.

The other is to find a team of experts with a leader which covers the required skills but minimizes the *Leader Distance* function. We propose algorithms for solving both problems. In many situations, the user is not satisfied with only one answer. Instead, he/she is interested in exploring top-k answers. Previous work in this area only found one single best answer [10]. We present two procedures that enumerate top-k teams of experts with or without a leader in polynomial delay. The contributions of this paper are summarized below:

1. We propose two new functions for measuring the communication cost of a team of experts in social networks. The *Sum of Distances* function considers communication costs between each pair of skill holders. The *Leader Distance* function considers the costs between a leader and each of the skill holders in the team.

2. We prove that the problem of finding a team of experts that minimizes the *Sum of Distances* function is NP-hard, and propose an approximation algorithm with approximation ratio of two to solve the problem.

3. We introduce the problem of finding a team of experts with a leader that minimizes the *Leader Distance* function. An exact polynomial algorithm for finding the best team with a leader is proposed.

4. To generate more answers, we design two procedures that enumerate top-k teams of experts with or without a leader in polynomial delay.

5. We conduct extensive experimental evaluations on real data sets that show the effectiveness of our methods.

The paper is organized as follows. Problem statements and definitions are given in section 2. The algorithms for finding the best team of experts with/without a leader are presented in sections 3 and 4. Procedures for enumerating top-k teams of experts are presented in section 5. The experimental results are illustrated in section 6. Related work is presented in section 7 and section 8 concludes the paper.

2. PROBLEM STATEMENTS

Let $C = \{c_1, c_2, \ldots, c_n\}$ denote a set of n experts, and $S = \{s_1, s_2, \ldots, s_m\}$ denote a set of m skills. Each expert c_i has a set of skills, denoted as $Q(c_i)$, and $Q(c_i) \subseteq S$. If $s_j \in Q(c_i)$, expert c_i has skill s_j. In addition, a subset of experts $C' \subseteq C$ have skill s_j if at least one of them has s_j. For each skill s_j, the set of all experts having skill s_j is denoted as $C(s_j) = \{c_i | s_j \in Q(c_i)\}$. A project $P \subseteq S$ is defined as a set of skills required to complete the project. A subset of experts $C' \subseteq C$ is said to *cover* a project P if $\forall s_j \in P \; \exists \; c_i \in C', s_j \in Q(c_i)$.

The experts in C are connected together in a social network, which is modeled as an undirected and weighted graph G. Each node in G represents an expert in C. In the following, terms *expert* and *node* are used interchangeably. Two nodes in G are connected by an edge if the experts have collaborated or communicated before. The weight of an edge represents the communication cost between two experts. The lower the weight of the edge between two nodes, the more easily the two experts can collaborate or communicate, and the lower the communication cost between them.

The **distance** between two nodes c_i and c_j, denoted as $d(c_i, c_j)$, is the sum of the weights on the shortest path between them in G. It should be noted that the shortest distance function is a metric and satisfies the triangle inequality. If c_i and c_j are not connected in G (directly or indirectly), the distance between them is set to a large value, bigger than the sum of all the pairwise shortest distances between two connected nodes in G [10]. In addition, the **distance** between a node c_i and a subset of nodes C' is defined as $d(c_i, C') = \min d(c_i, c_j) \; \forall \; c_j \in C'$. The node that has the closest distance to c_i among the nodes in C' is defined as $N(c_i, C') = c_x \mid \forall \; c_j \in C' \; d(c_i, c_x) \leq d(c_i, c_j)$. If $C' = \emptyset$, we define $d(c_i, C') = \infty$, and $N(c_i, C') = \emptyset$. Now, we are ready to formally define a team of experts and the problems we tackle.

2.1 Team Formation without a Leader

DEFINITION 1. ***(Team of Experts)*** *Given a set of experts C and a project P that requires a set of skills $\{s_1, s_2, \ldots, s_p$* a team of experts *for P is a set of p skill-expert pairs: $\{\langle s_1, c_{s_1}\rangle, \langle s_2, c_{s_2}\rangle, \ldots, \langle s_p, c_{s_p}\rangle\}$, where c_{s_j} is an expert in C having skill s_j for $j = 1, \ldots, p$. A skill-expert pair $\langle s_i, c_{s_i}\rangle$ means that expert c_{s_i} is responsible for skill s_i in the project.*

According to this definition, for each skill s_j in project P, there is one and only one skill-expert pair in the team that contains s_j. In other words, each skill is coupled with exactly one expert, but an expert may be assigned to more than one skill in the project. Clearly, the number of possible teams is $O(|C_{max}|^p)$, where $|C_{max}| = \max |C(s_i)| \; 1 \leq i \leq p$ and $|C(s_i)|$ denotes the cardinality of set $C(s_i)$. This value is exponential with respect to the number of required skills, i.e. p. Thus, it is not feasible to produce all the teams and rank them according to the cost function.

DEFINITION 2. ***(Sum of Distances)*** *Given a team T of experts for a project: $\{\langle s_1, c_{s_1}\rangle, \langle s_2, c_{s_2}\rangle, \ldots, \langle s_p, c_{s_p}\rangle\}$, the* sum of distances *of T is defined as*

$$sumDistance = \sum_{i=1}^{p} \sum_{j=i+1}^{p} d(c_{s_i}, c_{s_j})$$

In other words, the sum of distances of a team of experts is the sum of the shortest distances between the experts responsible for each pair of skills. It measures the communication cost of the team, assuming that the experts with each pair of required skills need to communicate in order to coordinate on the two corresponding tasks in the project.

PROBLEM 1. ***(Team Formation without a Leader)*** *Given a project P and a graph G representing the social network of a set of experts C, the problem of team formation without a leader is to find a team of experts T for P from G so that the communication cost of T, defined as the sum of distances of T, is minimized.*

Below we compare the sum of distances with two other functions defined in [10]. Suppose the two subgraphs G_1 and G_2 in Figure 1 represent two teams of experts for a project that requires skills a, b, c and d. Experts P and T are responsible for skills a and b in the two teams, respectively. The other experts are each responsible for only one

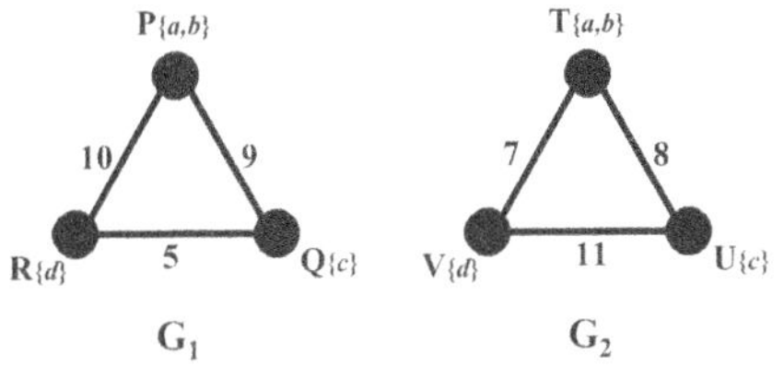

Figure 1: Two teams for project $\{a, b, c, d\}$.

skill (c or d). Suppose the weight on each edge is the shortest distance between the two nodes. The diameter of G_1 is 10, while the diameter of G_2 is 11. The MST cost of G_1 and G_2 is 5+9=14 and 7+8=15 respectively. Thus, the algorithm that minimizes the diameter or MST considers G_1 as the better team. Let d_{i-j} denote the shortest distance between the experts for skills i and j in a team. The *sum of distances* of G_1 is equal to $d_{a-b} + d_{a-c} + d_{a-d} + d_{b-c} + d_{b-d} + d_{c-d} = 0 + 9 + 10 + 9 + 10 + 5 = 43$. Using the same method, the *sum of distances* of G_2 is 41. Thus, with the *sum of distances* function, G_2 is chosen as the better team. As can be seen, the diameter and MST cost functions take into account only part of the communication cost in a team, while the sum of distances adds up the costs between experts for each pair of required skills. Also, our cost function is different from a function that would add up the shortest distances between each pair of experts in the team. Such a function would give G_1 a value of $10 + 9 + 5 = 24$ and G_2 a value of $7 + 8 + 11 = 26$, which results in the selection of G_1. The sum of distances function considers each pair of skills in its computation. We argue that this is more reasonable because for each pair of tasks (i.e., skills) the experts responsible for them need to communicate to coordinate on the tasks. For example, expert T in G_2 needs to communicate with expert V twice, one to coordinate between a and d and the other between b and d. Thus, the contribution of an expert to the total communication cost of the team is proportional to the number of tasks he/she performs in the project.

THEOREM 1. *Solving Problem 1 with the* sum of distances *communication cost function introduced in Definition 2 is an NP-hard problem.*

PROOF. We prove that the decision version of the problem is NP-hard. Thus, as a direct result, Problem 1 is NP-hard too. The decision problem asks whether there exists a team C' which covers a project P with the communication cost **at most** w ($w > 0$), for some constant w. The communication cost of C' is defined in Definition 2.

The problem is obviously in NP. We prove the theorem by a reduction from 3-satisfiability (3-SAT)[1]. First, consider a set of m clauses $D_k = x_k \vee y_k \vee z_k$ ($k = 1, \ldots, m$) and $\{x_k, y_k, z_k\} \subset \{u_1, \overline{u}_1, \ldots, u_n, \overline{u}_n\}$. We define an instance of the above problem as follows. For each pair of variables u_i and $\overline{u}_i$, two experts are created. Thus, we have $2 \times n$ experts. For each pair of variables u_i and $\overline{u}_i$, we create one skill s_i ($i = 1, \ldots, n$). Thus, u_i and $\overline{u}_i$ have skill s_i and the only holders of s_i are u_i and $\overline{u}_i$. In addition, for every clause D_k, we create one skill s_{n+k} ($k = 1, \ldots, m$) such that the holders of skill s_{n+k} consists of the triplet of experts associated with those of x_k, y_k and z_k. Therefore, the number of required skills is $n + m$. We set the distance between each variable and its negation (i.e. u_i and $\overline{u}_i$) to $2 \times w$. The distance between other variables is set to $\frac{w}{\binom{n+m}{2}}$. The distance of each node to itself is set to zero.

A feasible solution to the above problem with $sumDistance$ at most w is any set of experts such that from each pair of experts corresponding to u_i and $\overline{u}_i$, exactly one is selected and from each triplet of experts corresponding to x_k, y_k and z_k, one is selected. Thus, if there exists a subset of $sumDistance$ at most w, then there exists a satisfying assignment for $D_1 \wedge D_2 \wedge \cdots \wedge D_m$. On the other hand, a satisfying assignment apparently determines a feasible set of experts with $sumDistance$ at most w. Therefore, the proof is complete.

□

[1]Note that the same approach is used in [2] and [9] for proving the NP-hardness of the *multiple choice cover* problem and a graph keyword search problem, respectively.

2.2 Team Formation with a Leader

A project team often has a leader who is responsible for monitoring and coordinating the project. In such a case, each expert in the team needs to communicate with the leader to report the progress and discuss issues related to the project. Thus, the communication cost of the team heavily depends on the distance between the leader and each of the project members. We define the *leader distance* to measure such a communication cost.

DEFINITION 3. ***(Leader Distance)*** *Given a project $P = \{s_1, s_2, \ldots, s_p\}$, a team T of experts selected from graph G for P is $\{\langle s_1, c_{s_1}\rangle, \langle s_2, c_{s_2}\rangle, \ldots, \langle s_p, c_{s_p}\rangle\}$. Assume that team T has a leader L, where L is an expert in graph G, which may or may not belong to $\{c_{s_1}, c_{s_2}, \ldots, c_{s_p}\}$. The* leader distance *of T with leader L is defined as*

$$leaderDistance = \sum_{i=1}^{p} d(c_{s_i}, L)$$

In other words, the *leader distance* of a team of experts is the sum of the shortest distances between its leader and the expert for each required skill. We consider each skill (instead of each expert) when computing the leader distance because for each task an expert performs, communication with the leader is often needed. Thus, the more skills an expert is responsible for in the team, the more important his/her cost of communication with the leader is to the total communication cost of the team.

PROBLEM 2. ***(Team Formation with a Leader)*** *Given a project P and a graph G representing the social network of a set of experts C, the problem of* team formation with a leader *is to find a team of experts T for P and an expert L from C as the leader of the team so that the communication cost, defined as the leader distance of T with leader L, is minimized.*

Note that leader L is chosen from C, meaning that it is not necessary for L to have a skill required by project P. Our priority here is to minimize the leadership communication cost, i.e. the leader distance. A leader that can communicate the most effectively with all the other members of the team is most preferable, no matter whether the leader possesses any of the required skills. The number of possible teams of experts with a leader is $O(|C_{max}|^p \times n)$, where p is the number of required skills in the project, n is the number of experts in G and $|C_{max}| = \max |C(s_i)|\ 1 \leq i \leq p$.

It can be proved that $leaderDistance \geq \frac{sumDistance}{p-1}$, where $sumDistance$ is the sum of distances defined in Definition 2 and p is the number of required skills in the project[2]. Thus, minimizing the leader distance is equivalent to minimizing an upper bound of $sumDistance$. A practical benefit of finding a team with the least leader distance is that polynomial algorithms can be designed to find teams that minimize the leader distance. We propose such an algorithm in Section 4 and demonstrate in Section 6.4 that such an exact algorithm outperforms the approximation algorithm for minimizing the diameter, MST or the sum of distances when using the diameter, MST and the sum of distances as performance measures.

3. FINDING BEST TEAM OF EXPERTS WITHOUT A LEADER

Since Problem 1 is an NP-hard problem, we hereby propose an approximation algorithm that finds the best team with 2-approximation. The pseudo code of this algorithm is presented in Algorithm 1. It takes as input a graph G (i.e., the social network) and a project $P = \{s_1, s_2, \ldots, s_p\}$ representing the required skills. In addition, for each skill s_i, the set of experts in G having s_i (i.e., $C(s_i)$) can be obtained by the algorithm through a pre-built inverted index. The algorithm returns a team, denoted as $bestTeam$, whose communication cost is at most twice that of the optimal team. It also returns the communication cost of $bestTeam$.

The algorithm works as follows. It first initializes $bestTeam$ to $\emptyset$ and its communication cost, $leastSumDistance$, to ∞. Then, for each required skill s_i ($i = 1, \ldots, p$), the following steps are performed. For each expert, $candidate$, having skill s_i, a team is initialized to have $\langle s_i, candidate\rangle$ and its $sumDistance$ is initialized to 0 (lines 5-6). Then, in lines 7-11, for each of the other required skills, s_j, the algorithm finds the expert with s_j that is closest to $candidate$ and adds it (coupled with s_j) to the team. The $sumDistance$ of the team is updated by adding the shortest distance between $candidate$ and the selected expert. After the team has all the required skills (if none of the $C(s_i)$s is empty), if its $sumDistance$ is smaller than that of the current $bestTeam$, it replaces the $bestTeam$ (lines 12-14).

As defined in Section 2, $d(candidate, C(s_j))$ is the shortest distance between $candidate$ and the set of experts $C(s_j)$, which is the shortest distance between $candidate$ and its nearest neighbor in $C(s_j)$. $N(candidate, C(s_j))$ denotes this nearest neighbor. To efficiently find the shortest distance between an expert and a set of experts, the shortest distance between each pair of experts in G, i.e., $d(c_i, c_j)$, has been pre-computed and a hash table is used to store the shortest distances of all pairs for quick access by this algorithm[3]. Thus, the run time of functions $d(candidate, N(s_j))$ and $N(candidate, C(s_j))$ is $O(|C_{max}|)$, where $|C_{max}| = \max |C(s_i)|$ $1 \leq i \leq p$. The **time complexity** of Algorithm 1 is $O(p^2 \times |C_{max}|^2)$, where p is the number of required skills. In the worst case, $|C_{max}| = O(n)$ and the run time of the algorithm is $O(p^2 \times n^2)$, where n is the number of nodes in G. However, in real data sets, $|C_{max}|$ is smaller than n by orders of magnitude [10]. Below we prove that the algorithm finds the best answer with the approximation ratio of two.

Algorithm 1 Finding Best Team without a Leader

Input: graph G, project $P = \{s_1, s_2, \ldots, s_p\}$ and the set of experts with skill s_i, $C(s_i)$, for $i = 1, \ldots, p$.
Output: the best team and its cost

```
1: leastSumDistance ← +∞
2: bestTeam ← ∅
3: for i ← 1 to p do
4:   for every candidate ∈ C(s_i) do
5:     sumDistance ← 0
6:     team ← {⟨s_i, candidate⟩}
7:     for j ← 1 to p and j ≠ i do
8:       distance ← d(candidate, C(s_j))
9:       selectedExpert ← N(candidate, C(s_j))
10:      sumDistance ← sumDistance + distance
11:      team.add(⟨s_j, selectedExpert⟩)
12:    if sumDistance < leastSumDistance then
13:      leastSumDistance ← sumDistance
14:      bestTeam ← team
15: return bestTeam, leastSumDistance
```

THEOREM 2. *Algorithm 1 finds the team of experts that minimizes the sum of distances defined in Definition 2 with 2-approximation.*

PROOF. Consider two teams, one *optimal team* and the team produced by Algorithm 1, denoted here as *best team*[4]. Assume that the number of required skills is p. We denote a node in the *best team* that has the smallest sum of the shortest distances to the other nodes in the team as *candidate node*. Without loss of generality, assume that the *candidate node* is the node related to the first required skill, i.e. s_1. Let's call the shortest distance from the *candidate node* to each of the other nodes in the team $d_{12}, d_{13}, \ldots, d_{1p}$. Thus, the sum of shortest distances from this candidate to all the other nodes in the team is $\sum_{i=2}^{p} d_{1i}$. Let's call this distance the sum of the nearest neighbor distances of the candidate. Based on Algorithm 1, the candidate node has the smallest sum of the nearest neighbor distances among all the nodes in the team and also among all the nodes of all the possible teams including the *optimal team* because Algorithm 1 minimizes such a sum of distances. Let's consider the node with skill s_j in the *optimal team*. Its shortest distance to the node with each of other skills in the *optimal team* is denoted as $o_{1j}, o_{2j}, \ldots, o_{(j-1)j}, o_{j(j+1)}, \ldots, o_{jp}$, respectively. Based on Algorithm 1, the following holds for each j (where $j = 1, \ldots, p$):

$$\sum_{i=1}^{j-1} o_{ij} + \sum_{i=j+1}^{p} o_{ji} \geq \sum_{i=2}^{p} d_{1i} \quad (1)$$

[2] This is due to the triangle inequality: $d(c_i, L) + d(c_j, L) \geq d(c_i, c_j)$, where c_i and c_j are two team members and L is the leader. The proof is omitted due to the space limit.

[3] Note that the pre-computation of the shortest distances was done in [10] as well. If the hash table cannot reside in memory, other indexing techniques such as the one introduced in [6] can be used.

[4] A similar proof is given for the third theorem in our paper [9] for a graph keyword search algorithm.

If we write the above equation for all the p nodes of the *optimal team* and sum up both sides of the inequalities, we have the following equation:

$$2 \times \sum_{i=1}^{p} \sum_{j=i+1}^{p} o_{ij} \geq p \times \sum_{i=2}^{p} d_{1i} \tag{2}$$

The left side of the above equation is twice the communication cost of the *optimal team*. Thus, we have:

$$2 \times (optimal\ cost) \geq p \times \sum_{i=2}^{p} d_{1i} \tag{3}$$

The communication cost of the *best team* is:

$$best\ cost = \sum_{i=1}^{p} \sum_{j=i+1}^{p} d_{ij} = \sum_{i=2}^{p} d_{1i} + \sum_{i=2}^{p} \sum_{j=i+1}^{p} d_{ij} \tag{4}$$

Since the shortest distances satisfy triangle inequality (i.e., $d_{ij} \leq d_{1i} + d_{1j}, i \neq j \neq 1$), the following holds:

$$\sum_{i=2}^{p} d_{1i} + \sum_{i=2}^{p} \sum_{j=i+1}^{p} d_{ij} \leq \sum_{i=2}^{p} d_{1i} + \sum_{i=2}^{p} \sum_{j=i+1}^{p} (d_{1i} + d_{1j}) \tag{5}$$

In the right side of the above equation, each distance d_{1i} appears exactly $p-1$ times. Thus, we have:

$$\sum_{i=2}^{p} d_{1i} + \sum_{i=2}^{p} \sum_{j=i+1}^{p} (d_{1i} + d_{1j}) = (p-1) \times \sum_{i=2}^{p} d_{1i} \tag{6}$$

As a result, we have:

$$best\ cost \leq (p-1) \times \sum_{i=2}^{p} d_{1i} \tag{7}$$

Based on equations 3 and 7, we have:

$$\frac{2 \times (p-1)}{p} \times (optimal\ cost) \geq best\ cost \tag{8}$$

It proves that the sum of the distances of the *best team* is at most twice that of the *optimal team*.

□

4. FINDING BEST TEAM OF EXPERTS WITH A LEADER

To solve Problem 2, we propose the following exact polynomial algorithm. The pseudo code of the algorithm is shown in Algorithm 2. The input of the algorithm is the same as the one for Algorithm 1. The output is the best team of experts with the lowest leader distance (*bestTeam*), its cost (*leastLeaderDistance*) and leader (*bestLeader*). The algorithm works as follows. Each expert in G is a candidate for the leadership. For each node (expert) in graph G, denoted as *leader*, a *team* and its *leaderDistance* are initialized in lines 5 and 6. Then, for each of the skills $s_i, 1 \leq i \leq p$, the closest expert to *leader* with skill s_i and its distance to the *leader* are identified in lines 8 and 9. The identified expert is added to the team coupled with skill s_i and the *leaderDistance* is updated accordingly in lines 10-11. After the team has all the required skills, if its *leaderDistance* is smaller than *leastLeaderDistance*, the value of *leastLeaderDistance*, *bestTeam* and *bestLeader* are updated in lines 13-15. The *bestTeam*, *leastLeaderDistance* and *bestLeader* are returned in line 16. In summary, the algorithm selects a leader from all the nodes in G that has the smallest sum of the distances to all sets $C(s_i)$ $(1 \leq i \leq p)$, and forms the team using the expert in each $C(s_i)$ that is closest to the leader.

Since the run time of functions $d(leader, C(s_j))$ and $N(leader, C(s_j))$ is $O(|C_{max}|)$, the **time complexity** of Algorithm 2 is $O(p \times |C_{max}| \times n)$, where p is the number of required skills, $|C_{max}| = \max |C(s_i)|$ $1 \leq i \leq p$ and n is the total number of nodes (experts) in G. One way to reduce the time complexity is to choose the leader from $\bigcup_{i=1}^{p} C(s_i)$. That is, the algorithm does not check all of the nodes in G but only the ones with the required skills. This can be done by adopting Algorithm 1 that finds the team of experts without a leader and returning the *candidate* node in the best team as the leader of the team. However, the team of experts generated in this way may not be an optimal team with respect to the leader distance because it does not check all the possible leaders in G. Similar to the proof of Theorem 2, it can be proved that the approximation ratio of the revised algorithm is two. Due to the space limit, we omit the proof. In the experiments, we use the exact algorithm, i.e., Algorithm 2, for finding the best team of experts with a leader.

Algorithm 2 Finding Best Team with a Leader

Input: graph G, project $P = \{s_1, s_2, \ldots, s_p\}$ and the set of experts with skill s_i, $C(s_i)$, for $i = 1, \ldots, p$.
Output: the best team, its cost and leader

1: $leastLeaderDistance \leftarrow +\infty$
2: $bestTeam \leftarrow \emptyset$
3: $bestLeader \leftarrow \emptyset$
4: **for** every $leader \in G$ **do**
5:   $leaderDistance \leftarrow 0$
6:   $team \leftarrow \emptyset$
7:   **for** $i \leftarrow 1$ **to** p **do**
8:     $distance \leftarrow d(leader, C(s_i))$
9:     $selectedExpert \leftarrow N(leader, C(s_i))$
10:     $team$.add($\langle s_i, selectedExpert \rangle$)
11:     $leaderDistance \leftarrow leaderDistance + distance$
12:   **if** $leaderDistance < leastLeaderDistance$ **then**
13:     $leastLeaderDistance \leftarrow leaderDistance$
14:     $bestTeam \leftarrow team$
15:     $bestLeader \leftarrow leader$
16: **return** $bestTeam, leastLeaderDistance, bestLeader$

5. ENUMERATING TOP-K TEAMS OF EXPERTS IN POLYNOMIAL DELAY

Sometimes people are interested in finding more than one team with lowest communication costs to form up alternative teams. Since it is infeasible to produce all the teams because the number of possible teams is exponential in the number of required skills, we propose a procedure for producing top-k teams of experts in polynomial delay. Our algorithm for producing a ranked list of results is an adaption of Lawler's procedure [11] for calculating the top-k answers to discrete optimization problems. In Lawler's procedure, the

Table 1: Dividing the search space into disjoint subspaces for finding the teams of experts without a leader.

Subspace	Representative set
SB_0	$\{c_{s_1}\} \times \{c_{s_2}\} \times \{c_{s_3}\} \times \{c_{s_4}\}$
SB_1	$[C(s_1) - \{c_{s_1}\}] \times C(s_2) \times C(s_3) \times C(s_4)$
SB_2	$\{c_{s_1}\} \times [C(s_2) - \{c_{s_2}\}] \times C(s_3) \times C(s_4)$
SB_3	$\{c_{s_1}\} \times \{c_{s_2}\} \times [C(s_3) - \{c_{s_3}\}] \times C(s_4)$
SB_4	$\{c_{s_1}\} \times \{c_{s_2}\} \times \{c_{s_3}\} \times [C(s_4) - \{c_{s_4}\}]$

Algorithm 3 Algorithm for Generating Top-k Teams with a Leader in Polynomial Delay

Input: graph G; project $P = \{s_1, s_2, \ldots, s_p\}$; number of required teams k and the sets of experts each with a required skill $W = \{C(s_1), C(s_2), \ldots, C(s_p)\}$
Output: the set of top-k ordered teams of experts printed with polynomial delay

```
1: Queue ← an empty priority queue
2: ⟨A, cost⟩ ← FindBestTeam(G, T, W)
3: if A ≠ ∅ then
4:    Queue.insert(⟨A, cost, W⟩)
5: while Queue ≠ ∅ do
6:    ⟨A, V⟩ ← Queue.removeTop()
7:    print(A)
8:    k ← k − 1
9:    if k = 0 then
10:      return
11:   ⟨SV_1, SV_2, ..., SV_p⟩ ← ProduceSubSpaces(A, V)
12:   for i ← 1 to p do
13:      ⟨A_i, cost_i⟩ ← FindBestTeam(G, T, SV_i)
14:      if A_i ≠ ∅ then
15:         Queue.insert(⟨A_i, cost_i, SV_i⟩)
```

search space is first divided into disjoint sub-spaces; then the best answer in each subspace is found and used to produce the current global best answer. The sub-space that produces the best global answer is further divided into sub-subspaces and the best answer among its sub-subspaces is used to compete with the best answers in other sub-spaces in the previous level to find the next best global answer. Two main issues in this procedure are how to divide a space into disjoint subspaces and how to find the best answer within a (sub)space. Lawler proved that if these two issues are solved in polynomial time, the procedure generates ranked list of answers in polynomial delay [11].

5.1 Finding Top-k Teams without a Leader

We first informally describe the idea for dividing the search space into disjoint subsets using an example[5]. Suppose that the project consists of four skills, i.e., $\{s_1, s_2, s_3, s_4\}$, and we want to find the top-k teams of experts without a leader. Let $C(s_i)$ be the set of experts in graph G that have skill s_i. Thus, the search space that contains the best answer can be represented as $C(s_1) \times C(s_2) \times C(s_3) \times C(s_4)$. From this space, we can use Algorithm 1 for finding the best (approximate) team in polynomial time. Assume that the best answer is $(c_{s_1}, c_{s_2}, c_{s_3}, c_{s_4})$, where c_{s_i} is a node (expert) in graph G which has skill s_i. Based on this best answer, the search space is divided into 5 subspaces SB_0, SB_1, SB_2, SB_3 and SB_4 as shown in Table 1, where SB_0 contains only the best answer. It should be noted that the subspaces are **disjoint** and their union covers the whole search space.

After finding the best answer and dividing the search space into disjoint subsets, the best answer in each subspace except SB_0 is found using Algorithm 1. These best answers are inserted into a priority queue, where the answers are ranked in ascending order according to their communication cost. Obviously, the second best answer is the one at the top of the priority queue. Then, the top answer is returned and removed from the queue, its corresponding space is divided into subspaces and the best answer (if any) in each new subspace is added to the priority queue. This procedure continues until the priority queue becomes empty or the required number of teams, i.e. k, is returned by the algorithm.

The pseudo code of algorithm that generates top-k teams without a leader is presented in Algorithm 3. The main body of the algorithm is similar to other polynomial delay algorithms discussed in [7, 13]. It is modified to perform in the setting of producing ranked teams of experts from a graph. In line 2, procedure $FindBestTeam$ is called to find the best answer in space W in polynomial time. This procedure can be Algorithm 1 or one of the two algorithms introduced in [10], all having polynomial time complexity. It should be noted that W is the whole search space that contains all of the experts with their skills. Thus, the first best answer should be found in this space. If the best answer exists (i.e., A is not empty), A, together with its cost and related space W, is inserted into $Queue$ in line 4. The $Queue$ is maintained in the way that its elements are ordered in ascending order according to their communication costs. The while loop starting at line 5 is executed until the $Queue$ becomes empty or k answers have been outputted. In line 6, the top of the $Queue$ is removed, which contains the best answer in the $Queue$ and the space that this answer is produced from. We assign this space to V and the best answer to A. The answer in A is outputted in line 7. If the number of answers has reached k, the algorithm terminates in line 10. In line 11, procedure $ProduceSubSpaces$ produces p new subspaces based on the current answer A and current search space V. These subspaces are shown by SV_i. In lines 12-15, for each of these new subspaces, the best answer is found and inserted into the $Queue$ with its cost and related subspace. As stated before, procedure $FindBestTeam$ terminates in polynomial time. Thus, if procedure $ProduceSubSpaces$ terminates in polynomial time, then Algorithm 3 produces answers in polynomial delay. The pseudo code of procedure $ProduceSubSpaces$ is presented in Algorithm 4. It takes the best answer of the previous step, i.e. A, and the search space of previous step, i.e. V, as input. It produces p disjoint subspaces, $\langle SV_1, \ldots, SV_p \rangle$, as output. In this procedure, SV_i^j specifies the j-th element of SV_i. It is a polynomial procedure and runs in $O(p^2)$.

[5]Our approach for dividing a search space is similar to the idea used in [13].

5.2 Finding Top-k Teams with a Leader

The procedure for finding the top-k teams with a leader is similar to Algorithm 3. But since the search space for the best team is $C(s_1) \times C(s_2) \cdots \times C(s_p) \times C$, where C is the set of experts in G from which the leader is chosen, the search space is divided into $p + 2$ subspaces after the best answer is found (instead of $p + 1$ subspaces as in Algorithm 3). Table 2 illustrates the subspaces divided from the search

Table 2: Dividing the search space into disjoint subspaces for finding the teams of experts with a leader. C is the set of experts in G. The leader of the best answer $(c_{s_1}, c_{s_2}, c_{s_3}, c_{s_4})$ is L_1.

Subspace	Representative set
SB_0	$\{c_{s_1}\} \times \{c_{s_2}\} \times \{c_{s_3}\} \times \{c_{s_4}\} \times \{L_1\}$
SB_1	$[C(s_1) - \{c_{s_1}\}] \times C(s_2) \times C(s_3) \times C(s_4) \times C$
SB_2	$\{c_{s_1}\} \times [C(s_2) - \{c_{s_2}\}] \times C(s_3) \times C(s_4) \times C$
SB_3	$\{c_{s_1}\} \times \{c_{s_2}\} \times [C(s_3) - \{c_{s_3}\}] \times C(s_4) \times C$
SB_4	$\{c_{s_1}\} \times \{c_{s_2}\} \times \{c_{s_3}\} \times [C(s_4) - \{c_{s_4}\}] \times C$
SB_5	$C(s_1) \times C(s_2) \times C(s_3) \times C(s_4) \times [C - \{L_1\}]$

space after the first best team with a leader is found for the same example in Table 1. Both Algorithms 3 and 4 are changed to reflect the extension of the search space and difference in partitioning the search space. For example. *ProduceSubSpaces* takes also the leader of the best team and the previous search space for the leader as input. It produces $p+1$ (instead of p as in Algorithm 4) subspaces. The *FindBestTeam* procedure should be Algorithm 2 and returns a leader in addition to the best team and its cost. Due to the space limit, we omit further details.

Algorithm 4 Algorithm for Producing Sub Spaces

Input: the best answer of previous step $A = \langle c_1, c_2, \ldots c_p\rangle$ and set of experts which have the required skills $V = \{C(s_1), C(s_2), \ldots, C(s_p)\}$
Output: p new subspaces $\langle SV_1, \ldots, SV_p\rangle$

```
1: for i ← 1 to p do
2:   for j ← 1 to i − 1 do
3:     SV_i^j ← {c_j}
4:   SV_i^i ← V_i − {c_i}
5:   for j ← i + 1 to p do
6:     SV_i^j ← V_j
7: return ⟨SV_1, ..., SV_p⟩, where SV_i = SV_i^1 × ··· × SV_i^p
```

6. EMPIRICAL EVALUATION

In this section, we refer to the approximation Algorithm 1 as BEST-SUMDISTANCE and Algorithm 2 as BEST-LEADER. For the purpose of comparison, we implemented two algorithms introduced in [10]. The first algorithm that minimizes the diameter of the team is referred to as RAREST-FIRST and the second one that minimizes the weight of the MST of the team is referred to as ENHANCED-STEINER [10]. All the algorithms are implemented in Java. The experiments are conducted on an Intel(R) Core(TM) i7 2.80GHz computer with 4GB of RAM.

6.1 The Datasets

The DBLP and IMDb data sets are used in our experiments. The DBLP graph is produced from the DBLP XML data[6] taken on June 24, 2010. The dataset contains information about a collection of papers and their authors. The set of experts and skills are generated in the same way as in [10] as follows. We only keep the papers of some major conferences in computer science: Data Base = {SIGMOD, VLDB, ICDE, ICDT, EDBT, PODS}, Data Mining = {KDD, WWW , SDM, PKDD, ICDM}, Artificial Intelligence = {ICML, ECML, COLT, UAI} and Theory = {SODA, FOCS, STOC, STACS}. The set of experts consists of authors that have at least three papers in the DBLP. The skills of each expert is the set of terms that appear in the titles of at least two publications of the expert. Two experts are connected together if they have at least two papers together. The weight of the edge between two nodes n_i and n_j is equal to $1 - |\frac{p_{n_i} \cap p_{n_j}}{p_{n_i} \cup p_{n_j}}|$ where p_{n_i} is the set of papers of author (node) n_i. The final graph has 5,658 nodes (experts) and 8,588 edges.

The part of the IMDb dataset used in our experiments contains information about the actors and the list of movies that each actor played in[7]. The titles of the movies and the names of the actors are specified in the dataset. We consider as experts the actors who have played at least eight movies from 2000 to 2002. The skills of each actor is the set of terms that appear in the title of a movie of the actor. Two actors are connected together if they played in at least four movies together. The weight of an edge is determined in the same way as for DBLP. The final graph has 6,784 nodes and 35,875 edges. Clearly, the graph of IMDb is denser than that of DBLP. We do not use movie genres as skills because the number of genres in IMDb is only 20 and many actors have played in a great portion of genres, which leads to generation of top-100 teams each with only one member since many actors have played in all the required genres. Although using terms in movie titles as skills may not be meaningful, the data set is still good to use for the purpose of comparing the algorithms in some performance measures.

6.2 Experimental Setup

The *projects* used in the experiments are generated as follows. Each project is specified by a set of skills. We allow the number of skills in a project, i.e., p, to vary from 4 to 10. For each value of p, we randomly generate 100 projects and compute the average result obtained by each algorithm. Skills have different frequencies. The frequency of a skill is the percentage of experts in the social network that possess the skill. The frequency of the skills in our experiments varies from 0.5 to 5.0 percent. Other values of skill frequency lead to similar conclusions. We run the top-k procedures proposed in Section 5 using 4 different algorithms as the *FindBestTeam* procedure (i.e., BEST-SUMDISTANCE, BEST-LEADER, RAREST-FIRST, or ENHANCED-STEINER). We experimented with different values of k from 1 to 100. When it is not varied, the value of k is set to 50 by default. Also, the same as in [10], if, for a project, the team produced by at least one of the algorithms does not lead to a connected graph, the result of this project is ignored.

6.3 Performance Measures

We use two sets of performance measures to evaluate the quality of the teams produced by different algorithms. The first set contains three communication cost measures: (1) the diameter of the team, which is the largest shortest distance between any two nodes in the team, (2) the cost of the minimum spanning tree (MST) on the subgraph of the team and (3) the sum of distances measure defined in this paper. Recall that RAREST-FIRST is a greedy algorithm that aims at minimizing the diameter of the team, ENHANCED-STEINER is an approximation algorithm that tries to minimize MST, and BEST-SUMDISTANCE is an approximation

[6]http://dblp.uni-trier.de/xml/

[7]http://www.imdb.com/interfaces

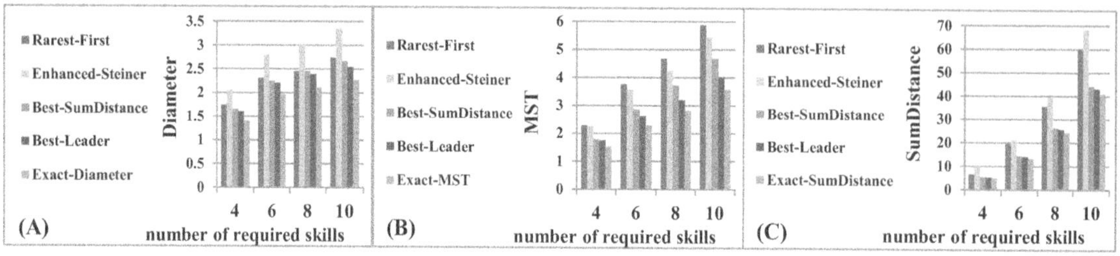

Figure 2: Results on the DBLP graph Using the First Set of Performance Measures.

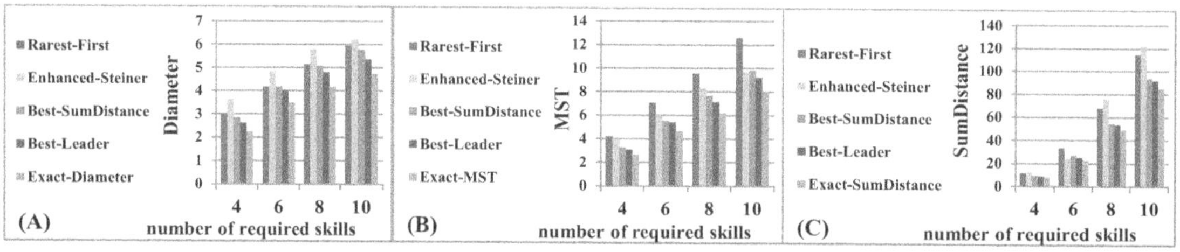

Figure 3: Results on the IMDb graph Using the First Set of Performance Measures.

algorithm for minimizing the sum of distances. The purpose of using these performance measures is to see how well each algorithm minimizes each of these cost measures in comparison to other algorithms.

The second set of performance measures is for evaluating the team quality on the DBLP data set. It contains three metrics. The first one is the cardinality of the team. To reduce the communication cost of a project, we usually prefer teams with smaller cardinality [10]. The second metric is the number of common publications shared by at least two experts in the team, which is the number of the papers in DBLP co-authored by at least two experts in the team. The more common publications the experts have, the higher chance that they can communicate well with each other. The third metric is the skill count, defined as the average number of times that a skill appears in the list of papers of an expert in the team, averaged over all the skills required in the project and over all the experts in the team. The higher the skill count, the more expertise the team has with respect to the set of skills in the project. The purpose of using these performance measures is to look at the quality of resulting teams from aspects different than communication costs.

6.4 Results on the First Set of Performance Measures

Figures 2 and 3 show the results of the four algorithms in terms of the diameter, MST, and sum of distances costs of the top ranking teams on the DBLP and IMDb datasets respectively. Each bar represents the average cost of the top-50 answers from an algorithm over 100 randomly generated projects for a specific number of required skills. In each subgraph, we also include the results of an exact algorithm that minimizes the cost metric used as the performance measure. For example, the results of the exact algorithm that minimizes the diameter of the team on the DBLP data set is shown in Figure 2 (A) and is named as EXACT-DIAMETER. Note that finding a team of experts that minimizes the diameter or MST is an NP-hard problem [10]. We proved that finding teams of experts which minimizes the sum of the distances is also NP-hard. Thus, it is not possible to find the best team of experts that minimizes any of these measures in polynomial time. The exact algorithms use exhaustive search to find all the possible teams for each project, rank the teams based on their respective cost measure, and output the top ranking teams. The purpose of showing the exact algorithm results is to provide the ground truth for each measure and see how close each approximation algorithm performs to the ground truth.

As shown in the results, in almost all of the experiments, algorithms BEST-SUMDISTANCE and BEST-LEADER outperforms RAREST-FIRST and ENHANCED-STEINER on all of the three cost measures. Their results are very close to the optimal answers produced by the exact algorithms whose performance is the best in each subgraph as expected. Note that although BEST-SUMDISTANCE and BEST-LEADER do not minimize the diameter or the MST cost of the teams, they produce better teams with lower diameter and MST costs than RAREST-FIRST and ENHANCED-STEINER. This is due to the search strategy used in the RAREST-FIRST and ENHANCED-STEINER approximation algorithms: RAREST-FIRST only checks the nodes having the skill with the lowest cardinality support [10], and ENHANCED-STEINER starts with a random node from the set of skill holders [10]. Both algorithms might miss some good teams.

Between BEST-LEADER and BEST-SUMDISTANCE, the results of BEST-LEADER are a bit better. This is because BEST-LEADER evaluates all nodes in the graph for finding the best leader. Comparing the results of BEST-SUMDISTANCE to those of EXACT-SUMDISTANCE in subgraph (C) of Figure 2 or 3, we observe that although in theory the sum of distances of an answer from BEST-SUMDISTANCE can be twice that of the corresponding optimal answer, the difference is small in practice (less than 10% in the worst case). This indicates that the quality of the proposed approximation algorithm is high.

6.5 Results on the Second Set of Performance Measures

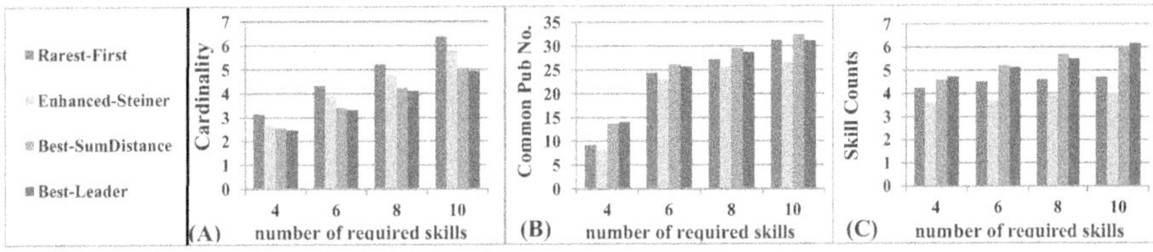

Figure 4: Results of Four Algorithms on DBLP Using the Second Set of Performance Metrics

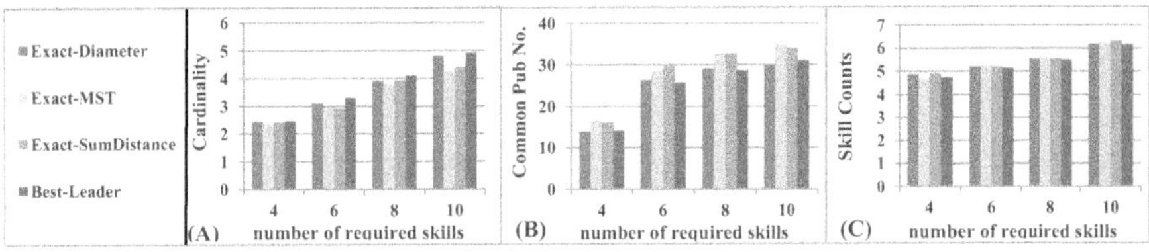

Figure 5: Comparison of Exact Algorithms on DBLP Using the Second Set of Performance Metrics.

Figure 4 compares the four algorithms in terms of the cardinality, the number of common publications and the skill count of the team. The results show that Best-SumDistance and Best-Leader outperforms Rarest-First and Enhanced-Steiner on all these metrics, that is, they produce smaller teams with higher number of shared publications and more expertise in the required skills. The results of Best-SumDistance and Best-Leader are very close to each other. Although our proposed algorithms do not explicitly optimize these metrics, they generate teams with higher quality than two other algorithms with respect to these metrics.

In order to see which cost function (diameter, MST, sum of distances and leader distance) is the best to optimize regardless of the search strategies (i.e., the approximation algorithms designed for them), we present in Figure 5 the results of the four **exact** algorithms in terms of the team cardinality, common publication number and skill count. Note that the Best-Leader algorithm is an exact algorithm for minimizing the leader distance of a team. The results show that the MST and sum of distances functions have very similar performance in all the three metrics. Both of them are better than the diameter and leader distance functions in terms of team cardinality and common publication numbers. The four functions perform almost the same on the skill count. The reason why the leader distance leads to a bit larger team and fewer common publications than the sum of distances and MST is that the selected leader may be an "extra" member without a required skill.

Since it is not possible to have polynomial exact algorithms that minimize diameter, MST or sum of distances, how to design the approximation algorithm is important. The results in Figures 2, 3 and 4 indicate that our proposed polynomial algorithms (i.e., Best-SumDistance and Best-Leader) for finding teams of experts with or without a leader outperform the existing **approximation** algorithms that minimize the diameter or MST function.

6.6 Scalability

To test the scalability of the proposed algorithms, we generate DBLP graphs of different sizes by using different thresholds for the number of papers an expert has authored to determine whether a node (i.e., expert) should be included in the graph. The threshold is set to 6, 5, 4 and 3 to generate graphs of 4 different sizes ranging from 2.2k to 5.6k nodes. Figure 6 (A) illustrates how the average run time of algorithm Best-SumDistance for producing one team changes with the number of nodes in the DBLP graph for different numbers of required skills. Although in the worst case (when all the experts in the graph possess a required skill), the run time is quadratic with respect to the number of nodes (as discussed in Section 3), in practice this rarely happens and we observe that the run time increases (almost) linearly when the number of nodes increases. Figure 6 (B) shows how the average time for producing one team (which is the total run time divided by k) changes with k, i.e., the number of top teams produced. Obviously, the time does not change with the value of k, which indicates that the total run time of our top-k algorithm grows linearly when k increases. This indicates that Best-SumDistance and our top-k procedure scale well with the number of nodes and k values. Due to the space limit, the results of Best-Leader are not presented. But they showed similar trends.

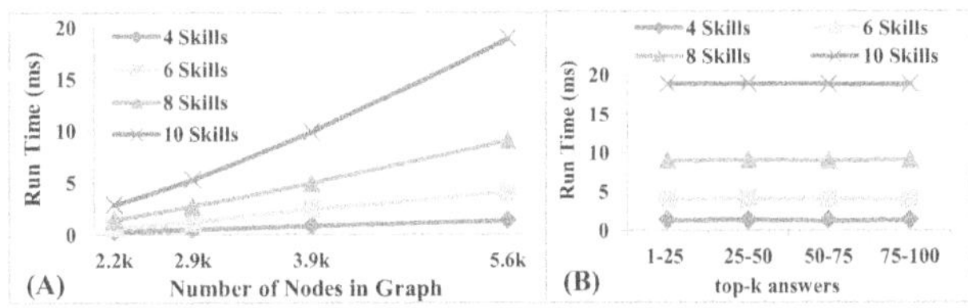

Figure 6: Scalability of Best-SumDistance on DBLP.

6.7 A Sample Result

We compare the algorithms through an example. We form a project by randomly selecting 4 keywords as the required skills from the paper titles listed on the "Awards" page of the CIKM 2010 web site[8]. The keywords are *multilingual, interface, ranking* and *constraints*. The best team formed by each algorithm is shown in Table 3. The common publication number (denoted as *Pub. No*) of both Best-SumDistance

[8]http://www.yorku.ca/cikm10/awards.php

Table 3: **Best teams for project requiring "skills": *multilingual, interface, ranking* and *constraints***

Algorithm	*Multilingual*	*Interface*	*Ranking*	*Constraints*	Leader	Pub. No.	*Diameter*	*MST*	*SumDis*
Rarest-First	*A. Kumaran*	*H. Jagadish*	*M. Ramanath*	*W. Fan*	–	0	3.6	5.4	14.6
Enhanced-Steiner	*A. Kumaran*	*H. Jagadish*	*M. Ramanath*	*W. Fan*	–	0	3.6	5.4	14.6
Best-SumDistance	*A. Kumaran*	*R. Agrawal*	*R. Agrawal*	*K. Shim*	–	3	3.6	4.5	12.9
Best-Leader	*A. Kumaran*	*R. Agrawal*	*R. Agrawal*	*K. Shim*	R. Agrawal	3	3.6	4.5	12.9

and Best-Leader is 3 while it is 0 for Rarest-First and Enhanced-Steiner. Also, Best-SumDistance and Best-Leader produce teams with less MST and sum of distances costs than Rarest-First and Enhanced-Steiner. All the teams have the same diameter in this example.

7. RELATED WORK

Discovering a team of experts from a social network has been introduced in [10]. Authors of [12] generalize this problem by associating each required skill with a specific number of experts. However, they do not provide an approximation ratio for their heuristic algorithms. Authors of [1] proposed methods for finding teams of experts in which the load of the experts are balanced in the presence of several tasks. They do not consider finding teams with low communication cost. In this work, we extend the work of [10] in several directions as follows. Two new communication cost functions are proposed. An approximation algorithm which find the best team of experts is proposed. The problem of finding a team of experts with a leader is defined. A procedure for producing top-k teams of experts is also designed.

The team formation problem has been studied in the operation research community. The authors use branch and bound, genetic algorithms and simulated annealing to solve the problem [4, 14, 5]. The authors of [3] study the dynamics of group formation procedures and how they affect on the formation of groups in the network. In a later work, authors discuss this problem from a game-theoretic point of view [8]. The basic difference between our work and the works in operation research is that they do not assume the existing of a social network behind the experts.

The problem of keyword search in graphs takes a considerable amount of attention in the database community in recent years [7, 13, 9]. Each node in the graph consists of some keywords. The purpose is to find a subgraph that covers the input keywords and whose nodes are close to each other, which is similar to the objective of team formation in social networks that minimizes the team communication cost. The *leader distance* function defined in this paper has not been used in either team formation or keyword search. Also, in algorithms for keyword search over graphs, a threshold is usually set for the maximum distance between two nodes in a final answer [13], but it is not used here.

8. CONCLUSION

We studied the problem of discovering a team of experts from a social network that minimizes the communication cost among team members. We defined two communication cost functions and proposed an approximation algorithm for finding the best team of experts without a leader that minimizes the sum of distance function. We proved that the approximation ratio of the algorithm is 2. We also defined the problem of finding a team of experts with a leader and proposed an exact polynomial algorithm to solve this problem. In addition, we proposed procedures for producing top-k teams of experts with or without an expert in polynomial delay. Our experiments on two real data sets showed that the proposed algorithms produce teams with lower communication costs than two existing approximation algorithms. We also showed that our algorithms produce smaller teams with more common publications and more expertise in the required skills than the two existing approximation algorithms on the DBLP dataset. In the future, we will explore how to incorporate constraints in team formation in social networks.

9. REFERENCES

[1] A. Anagnostopoulos, L. Becchetti, C. Castillo, A. Gionis, and S. Leonardi. Power in unity: Forming teams in large-scale community systems. In *Proc. of CIKM'10*, 2010.

[2] E. M. Arkin and R. Hassin. Minimum-diameter covering problems. *Networks*, 36, 2000.

[3] L. Backstrom, D. Huttenlocher, J. Kleinberg, and X. Lan. Group formation in large social networks: membership, growth, and evolution. In *Proc. of KDD'06*, 2006.

[4] A. Baykasoglu, T. Dereli, and S. Das. Project team selection using fuzzy optimization approach. *Cybern. Syst.*, 38(2):155–185, 2007.

[5] E. Fitzpatrick and R. Askin. Forming effective worker teams with multi functional skill requirements. *Comput. Ind. Eng.*, 48(3):593–608, 2005.

[6] R. Goldman, N. Shivakumar, S. Venkatasubramanian, and H. Garcia-Molina. Proximity search in databases. In *Proc. of VLDB'98*, 1998.

[7] K. Golenberg, B. Kimelfeld, and Y. Sagiv. Keyword proximity search in complex data graphs. In *Proc. of SIGMOD'08*, 2008.

[8] M. Jackson. *Network formation.* The New Palgrave Dictionary of Economics and the Law, 2008.

[9] M. Kargar and A. An. Keyword search in graphs: Finding r-cliques. In *Proc. of VLDB'11*, 2011.

[10] T. Lappas, L. Liu, and E. Terzi. Finding a team of experts in social networks. In *Proc. of KDD'09*, 2009.

[11] E. Lawler. A procedure for computing the k best solutions to discrete optimization problems and its application to the shortest path problem. *Management Science*, 18, 1972.

[12] C. Li and M. Shan. Team formation for generalized tasks in expertise social networks. In *Proc. of IEEE International Conference on Social Computing*, 2010.

[13] L. Qin, J. Yu, L. Chang, and Y. Tao. Querying communities in relational databases. In *Proc. of ICDE'09*, 2009.

[14] H. Wi, S. Oh, J. Mun, and M. Jung. A team formation model based on knowledge and collaboration. *Expert Syst. Appl.*, 36(5):9121–9134, 2009.

Content based Social Behavior Prediction: A Multi-task Learning Approach

Hongliang Fei, Ruoyi Jiang, Yuhao Yang, Bo Luo, Jun Huan
Department of EECS, University of Kansas
Lawrence, KS 66047-7621, USA
{hfei, jiangruoyi, yyang, bluo, jhuan}@ittc.ku.edu

ABSTRACT

The study of information flow analyzes the principles and mechanisms of social information distribution. It is becoming an extremely important research topic in social network research. Traditional approaches are primarily based on the social network graph topology. However, topology itself can not accurately reflect user interests or behavior. In this paper, we adopt a "microeconomics" approach to study social information diffusion. In particular, we aim to answer the question that how social information flow and socialization behaviors are related to content similarities and user interests. We study content-based social activity prediction, i.e., to predict a user's response (e.g. comment or like) to their friends' postings (e.g. blogs) w.r.t. message content. In our solution, we cast the social behavior prediction problem as a multi-task learning problem, in which each task corresponds to a user. We have designed a novel multi-task learning algorithm for predicting information flow in social networks. In our model, we apply l_1 and Tikhonov regularization to obtain a sparse and smooth model in a linear multi-task learning framework. With comprehensive experiments, we have demonstrated the effectiveness of the proposed learning method.

Categories and Subject Descriptors

H.2.8 [**Database Management**]: Database Applications-Data Mining

General Terms

Algorithms, Experimentation

Keywords

Multi-task Learning, Social Networks, Heterogenous Structured Tasks, Regularization

1. INTRODUCTION

The study of information flow is to analyze the principles and mechanisms of social information distribution, which is an essential research topic in social networks [14, 26]. Full understanding and control of information flow in social networks is essential for a number of tasks, including efficient emergency notifications (e.g. [30]), personalized advertising/recommnadation and stopping rumor dissemination.

Most of the existing approaches on network information flow are based on the social network graph topology [16, 24]. For instance, maximum flow and betweenness centrality are the basic measurements employed to assess overall information flow and nodes' specific contributions to it [28]. However, topology itself can not accurately reflect the user interests or activities. It has been widely observed that it is more likely for a message to propagate between users that are mutually interested in the message.

Recently [22] performs a large scale trace on information diffusion in Twitter, and discovers that there are fundamental differences of diffusion behaviors across different topics. The phenomena discovered in [22] further confirms that information content plays a major role in social information flow. However, [22] did not provide a solution of how to quantitatively model or predict social information diffusion process with regard to information content.

In this paper, we adopt a "microeconomics" approach to study social information diffusion and aim to answer the question that how social information flow and socialization behaviors are related to content similarity and user interests. In particular, we study content-based social activity prediction, i.e., to predict a user's response (e.g., comment or like) to their friends' postings (e.g., blogs, tweets). In our solution, we cast the social behavior prediction problem as a multi-task learning problem, in which each task corresponds to a user. Similar to traditional supervised learning algorithm, the information content (i.e. sample) is represented as a high dimensional feature vector and its labels indicate the users' responses towards the information. We choose multi-task learning as the starting point of our investigation since MTL boosts the generalization performance by learning several related tasks simultaneously [3, 10, 15, 23].

Our contributions in this paper are multifaced. At the conceptual level, we take the first step to model social network information flow w.r.t. information content in social networks. For modeling algorithms, we formalize the related modeling problem as a multi-task learning problem and provide a novel algorithm specifically designed for learning with information flow in social networks. To our best knowledge, we present the first case of developing and applying multi-task learning to the social behavior prediction. Finally we

CIKM'11, October 24–28, 2011, Glasgow, Scotland, UK.

have derived a practical solution based on an advanced optimization technique. Experiment results show that our approach significantly improves prediction accuracy using real world data sets.

The rest of the paper is organized as following: we first introduce related works in Section 2. We formalize the problem, and describe the details of our model in Section 3. We present the experimental results in Section 4, and finally conclude the paper.

2. RELATED WORK

There are tremendous studies on how information is distributed in social networks through user socialization activities [1, 16, 17, 24, 31]. In particular, [16] provides an algorithm to select a subset of nodes whose information adoption activities can trigger a large cascade of information flow. [17] studies Internet chain-letter data, and finds that the letters spread in a "narrow but very deep tree-like pattern", instead of spreading widely. [24] models social information flow with a diffusion-rate based model and continuous-time Markov chain. While most existing approaches model information diffusion using graph topology (i.e. information follows the links to propagate from nodes to neighbors), [31] takes a different route that models information flow based on observed infection history. Last but not least, from the social science perspective, different types of social relationships (e.g. strong ties vs. weak ties) [13] have been used to study information flow.

On the other hand, *multi-task learning* (MTL) has been widely investigated from different researchers and aspects, hence it is impossible to cover all the related works in depth and we only discuss these works that are related to our method. Multi-task feature learning [2, 18, 19] assumes all the tasks are uniformly related, and aim to learn a common low dimensional representation without actually learning the task relationships. MTL with known task relationships [10, 15] utilizes the prior knowledge on task relationships to learn model parameters so that similar tasks share similar parameters. They use all the features to build MTL model, hence they are not suitable for high dimensional data. Besides, the task relationship is homogenous.

Though information flow analysis and MTL have been studied for a long time, none of the existing method considers formalizing the content based information flow analysis as MTL problem while considering the heterogenous social relationships. The objective of this paper is to incorporate the heterogenous relationships on tasks into MTL and build a more accurate and interpretable prediction model.

3. METHODOLOGY

We formalize the user behavior prediction problem with the following model. Considering a social network with millions of users, we focus on one user, i.e. the "seed" user. We represent each article published by the seed user using a bag-of-words model, where features are terms extracted from all the articles the seed has published and the value of a feature is the TF-IDF weight. There are a group of users who actively receive articles published by the seed (i.e. the "followers" of the seed). We treat each follower as a learning task. If the follower performed an action on an article (e.g. writing comments about the article), we record the user response as positive (1). Otherwise, the user response is negative (-1). Figure 1 illustrate this data representation approach.

3.1 Learning Challenges

In adopting MTL for social behavior prediction, the major challenge is to group tasks (followers) with similar characteristics. We have three possible strategies: (1) group all tasks in a single group and totally ignore the possible difference of tasks [7, 9, 18]; (2) use social network topology to model tasks relationships; (3) use previous history of tasks to estimate the possible structure of tasks.

In our experimental study, we have implemented all three strategies and done a case study as shown in Table 2. Our results show that the third strategy is the best over all, which demonstrates that the social network topology itself cannot accurately reflect user interests or behavior. For example, in Figure 1, we show three users. Clearly F_1 and F_2 are somehow related since they are follower of each other. After a careful investigation, we conclude that F_1 and F_2 are following each other is due to the fact that both of the users are active in reading and posting entertainment related articles. Following this observation in our multitask learning practice, if our objective is to model the information flow for entertainment related articles, F_1 and F_2 should be group together due to the common interest. However, if our objective is to model the information flow for technology related articles, F_1 and F_2 have quite different interest. Learning F_1 and F_2 together will confuse any learning algorithm.

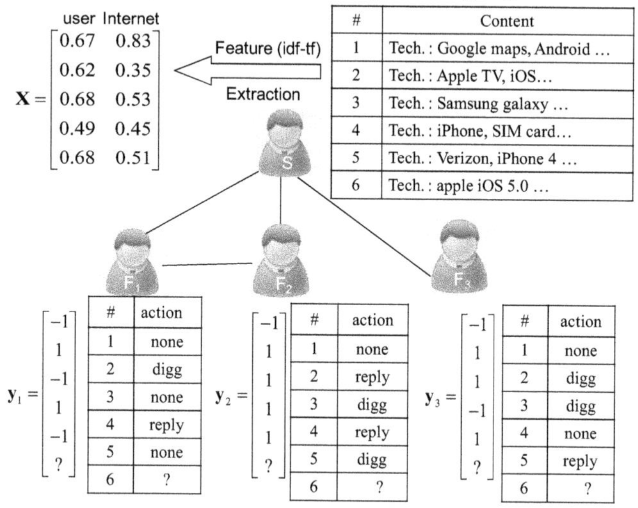

Figure 1: Data Representation of the frmaework. Five articles with actions of three followers and two words with tf-idf are shown for demonstration only. X: object-feature matrix with each row representing an article and each column representing a feature.

In summary, we observe that the relationship between tasks in social networks is multilayered in the sense that the relationship may change based on the information content. Based on the observation, we have designed a multigraph representation of task relationship. With the multigraph representation, we have modified an existing MTL algorithm by incorporating additional constraint based on the multigraph representation of task relationships and investigated the related optimization techniques. In the following subsections we elaborate the description by focusing on four important problems: (i) content based task similarity definition, (ii) multigraph representation of task similarity, (iii) MTL with multigraph constraints, and (iv) efficient optimization. Before we present our model, we list

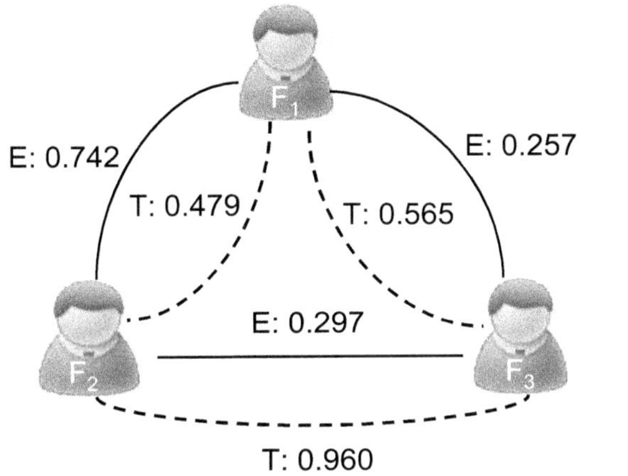

Figure 2: Heterogenous social relationships between F_1, F_2 and F_3 for category T: technology and E: entertainment. Dashed line represents the technology connection and solid line represents the entertainment connection.

notations in this paper. We use lowercase letters to represent scalar values, lower-case bold letters to represent vectors (e.g. $\mathbf{a}$), uppercase bold letters to represent matrices (e.g. $\mathbf{A}$), Greek letters $\{\lambda, \lambda_1, \cdots\}$ to represent Lagrange multipliers, and uppercase calligraphic letters to represent sets. We use $\|\mathbf{A}\|_1 = \sum_{i,j}^p |a_{ij}|$ to denote the l_1 norm of $\mathbf{A}$, $<\mathbf{A}, \mathbf{B}>= tr(\mathbf{A}^T\mathbf{B})$ to represent the inner product between two matrices where $tr(.)$ is the trace of matrix. Furthermore, given matrix $A \in \mathbb{R}^{p\times k}$, $\mathbf{A}_{i,:}$ is the ith row and $\mathbf{A}_{:,j}$ is the jth column. Unless state otherwise, all vectors in this paper are column vectors.

3.2 Problem Statement

Formally, suppose we are given k users (tasks) $\{T_i\}_{i=1}^k$. For the ith user T_i, the training set $\mathcal{D}_i$ consists of n articles (samples) $(\mathbf{x}_j^i, y_j^i)$, $j = 1, \cdots, n_i$, where $\mathbf{x}_j^i \in \mathcal{R}^p$. We collect $y_j^i \in \{-1, 1\}$ for the user's response T_i on article $\mathbf{x}_j^i$. For simplicity, we assume all the tasks have the same number of training samples. The goal of the modeling practice is to learn a function $f_i(\mathbf{x})$ to map the content of the article to the user response, where $f_i(\mathbf{x}) = \mathbf{w}_i^T\mathbf{x}$. The learning task is to seek $\mathbf{W} = [\mathbf{w}_1, \mathbf{w}_2, \cdots, \mathbf{w}_k]$ with $\mathbf{w}_i$ corresponding to the ith user by solving $\min_{\mathbf{W}} \sum_{i=1}^k \sum_{j=1}^n \ell(y_j^i, f_i(\mathbf{x}_j^i))$. In this paper, we use linear regression with least square loss function $\ell(y_j^i, f_i(\mathbf{x}_j^i)) = 1/2(y_j^i - f_i(\mathbf{x}_j^i))^2$ to perform classification, which is equivalent to a linear discriminant analysis (LDA) for binary classification [12]. Such a procedure is also widely used in other MTL algorithms for classification [6, 18, 32].

The above objective is ill-posed for high dimension low sample size problems. To remedy the problem, we add l_1 regularization [25] on $\mathbf{W}$ to stabilize it and obtain a sparse solution. However, the resulting model neglects the heterogenous structural relationship among tasks, which we will address in the following sections.

3.3 Content Based User Similarity

With the heterogeneity of social networks, we cannot rely on network topology as we discussed in the introduction section, but have to consider the information content. Additionally, in order to build a more interpretable model, we expect the users that share the same interest will have similar prediction models when seeing the articles from their favorite information categories.

We collect followers' actions to quantify the similarity between two users. More specifically, for each follower, we build an activity profile for each content category and calculate pair-wise user similarity as:

DEFINITION 3.1. *Suppose that the data set contains k users and covers t categories with q possible actions in the social network (excluding no action), the* user profile $\mathbf{P}^{(l)}$ *for the lth user is a $q \times t$ matrix with entries $p_{ij}^{(l)}$ representing the number of action i on category j, where $1 \le k \le n$, $1 \le i \le q$ and $1 \le j \le t$. Furthermore, the similarity $a_{ij}^{(l)}$ between user i and j for the lth category is the cosine value between vector $\mathbf{P}_{:,l}^{(i)}$ and $\mathbf{P}_{:,l}^{(j)}$:*

$$a_{ij}^{(l)} = \frac{<\mathbf{P}_{:,l}^{(i)}, \mathbf{P}_{:,l}^{(j)}>}{\|\mathbf{P}_{:,l}^{(i)}\|\|\mathbf{P}_{:,l}^{(j)}\|} \tag{1}$$

where $<.,.>$ denotes the inner product, $\|.\|$ represents the vector l_2 norm and $\mathbf{P}_{:,l}^{(i)}$ is the lth column of profile matrix of user i.

Let $\mathbf{A}^{(l)} = \{a_{ij}^{(l)}\}_{i,j=1}^n$, we can view $\mathbf{A}^{(l)}$ as an adjacency matrix for a weighted graph $G^{(l)}$ capturing the structure of users for category l. Since the categories are often diverse in social network, the relationship among users is heterogenous. In the following section, we detail how to incorporate the heterogenous relationship into learning framework.

3.4 Heterogenous Task Relationship Incorporation

We capture the structure relationships among tasks for t categories as an undirected multi-graph $G = \{G^{(l)}\}_{l=1}^t$, whose nodes correspond to the set of k tasks. Edges in the graph G are multi-edges and weighted, with $\mathbf{a}_{ij} \in \mathcal{R}^t$ defined in Equation (1) representing the similarity vector between user i and j. In Figure 2, we have shown a multi-graph with two categories on three users.

Given n articles (training samples) and the multi graph collected from the whole social network for k users, we further assume all the tasks share the same training data since our goal is to predict the user activities towards these n samples. We incorporate the heterogenous structure information by adding a Tikhonov regularization factor $\sum_{l=1}^n \sum_{i,j=1}^k \mathbf{I}_{:,l}^T \mathbf{a}_{ij}\|\mathbf{w}_i - \mathbf{w}_j\|_2^2$ to enforce that the task parameters vary smoothly for neighboring users, where $\mathbf{I}_{t\times n}$ is the indicator matrix with $I_{jk} = 1$ if the kth article belongs to the jth category and 0 otherwise.

The Tikhonov regularization factor can be conveniently written in matrix format in terms of graph Laplacian matrix for individual graph $G^{(l)}$, $(1 \le l \le t)$ defined on each category of information content $\sum_{i=1}^t r_i tr(\mathbf{W}\mathbf{L}_i\mathbf{W}^T)$, where $r_i = \sum_j I_{ij}$, $(1 \le i \le t)$ is the sum of the ith row in matrix $\mathbf{I}$ to summarize the number of posts belonging to the ith category. Note that we also allow overlapping categories, which means that each column of $\mathbf{I}$ may have multiple 1s.

Combining with l_1 penalty, the composite regularization function is:

$$R(\mathbf{W}) = \lambda_1\|\mathbf{W}\|_1 + \frac{\lambda_2}{2}\sum_{i=1}^t r_i tr(\mathbf{W}\mathbf{L}^{(i)}\mathbf{W}^T) \tag{2}$$

where $\lambda_1 > 0$, $\lambda_2 > 0$ are the regularization parameters, $\mathbf{L}^{(i)}$ is the Laplacian matrix of $G^{(i)}$ given by $\mathbf{L}^{(i)} = \mathbf{D}^{(i)} - \mathbf{A}^{(i)}$. $\mathbf{A}^{(i)}$ is the k by k adjacency matrix for category i and $\mathbf{D}^{(i)}$ is the density matrix of $\mathbf{A}^{(i)}$, defined as $\mathbf{D}^{(i)} = (d_{j,l}^{(i)})_{j,l=1}^{k}$ where $d_{j,l}^{(i)} = \begin{cases} \sum_{p=1}^{k} A_{j,p}^{(i)} & \text{if } j = l \\ 0 & \text{otherwise} \end{cases}$. To avoid any user (task) or category dominate (2), we use normalized graph laplacian defined in [8] and normalized category vector $\mathbf{r} = [r_1, \cdots, r_t]^T$ by dividing $max\{r_i | 1 \leq i \leq t\}$.

3.5 MTL with Heterogenous Task Relationships

By combining (2) with loss function, we have the following objective: $\min_{\mathbf{W}} \sum_{i=1}^{k} \sum_{j=1}^{n} \ell(y_j^i, f_i(\mathbf{x}_j)) + R(\mathbf{W})$. Since all tasks share the same design matrix, it can be further simplified as:

$$\min_{\mathbf{W}} \frac{1}{2} \|\mathbf{Y} - \mathbf{X}\mathbf{W}\|_F^2 + R(\mathbf{W}) \tag{3}$$

where $\mathcal{Y}_{n \times k} = [\mathbf{y}_1, \cdots, \mathbf{y}_k]$ is the response matrix with ith column $\mathbf{y}_i \in \mathcal{R}^n$, $\mathcal{X}_{n \times p} = [\tilde{\mathbf{x}}_1, \cdots, \tilde{\mathbf{x}}_n]^T$ is the data matrix with the ith row $\tilde{\mathbf{x}}_i \in \mathcal{R}^p$.

Equation (3) treats all samples equally, which is only suitable for balanced data sets. Due to the unbalanced class ratio (a user only responses to a limited number of messages), we introduce a weighting scheme based on positive and negative sample ratio for each task to guarantee that the misclassification cost is more on rare samples. Consider the following optimization problem:

$$\min_{\mathbf{W}} \frac{1}{2} \|\mathbf{B} \circ (\mathbf{Y} - \mathbf{X}\mathbf{W})\|_F^2 + \lambda_1 \|\mathbf{W}\|_1 + \frac{\lambda_2}{2} \sum_{i=1}^{t} r_i tr(\mathbf{W}\mathbf{L}^{(i)}\mathbf{W}^T) \tag{4}$$

where $\circ$ is the element-wise product and $\mathbf{B}_{n \times k}$ is the weight matrix. For the ith task, let $\mathcal{P} = \{j | y_j^i = 1\}$ denotes the indices of positive samples, then the weights for positive samples in ith task are given by $B_{\mathcal{P},i} = 1 - |\mathcal{P}|/n$ and negative sample weights are $B_{[1,k] \setminus \mathcal{P},i} = |\mathcal{P}|/n$, where $|\mathcal{P}|$ is the cardinality of the set $\mathcal{P}$.

3.6 Optimization

The major challenge in fitting the model described in Equation (4) to data is to estimate the parameters $\mathbf{W}$ efficiently and accurately. We propose an efficient algorithm to solve (4) based on accelerated gradient decent [21] and projected gradient [4]. The convergence rate of ordinary first order gradient method is $O(1/\epsilon)$ [21] for smooth problems, where ϵ is the desired accuracy. To have a better convergence rate, we use Nestrerov accelerated gradient descent method [21] with $O(1/\sqrt{\epsilon})$ convergence rate, and solve the *generalized gradient update step* for each gradient update step. Due to the space constrain, we do not show detailed algorithm. Refer to the longer version of this paper at `http://people.eecs.ku.edu/~hfei/cikm2011longer.pdf`.

4. EXPERIMENT

We have conducted experiments with four real world data sets crawled from digg.com. To evaluate the performance of our MTL algorithm (MTLTLap), we compared our method with: (1) single task learning algorithm linear kernel SVM [27] with feature selection method SVMRFE [11]; (2) Multi-task feature learning with l_1/l_2 regularization (MTLF) [19] without considering task relationship; and (3) MTL with homogenous networked task relationship (MTLALap) [15]. We have carefully implemented our method MTLTLap, MTLALap and used LIBSVM [5] integrated with spider toolbox [29] for SVM and SLEP package [20] for MTLF.

4.1 Data sets

We have crawled four data sets from digg.com, in which there are 10 categories of articles. Due to the tremendous number of users in digg.com, it is impossible to perform analysis for every user. Instead we randomly select four users as "seeds" and collect their article contents as well as their followers' activities towards these articles. The activities are comment, digg, comment & digg and no action. For a seed user, we treat each article as a sample with bag-of-words representation, where the words (features) are extracted from all the articles the seed user submitted. We remove stop words, normalize words and calculate their TF-IDF values with porter stemmer available at `http://sourceforge.net/projects/wvtool/`. Each follower corresponds to a task, where the action of comment or digg are treated as 1 and no action as -1. We eliminate these followers whose total number of comments and diggs on the seed is less than 5.

Table 1: Data set: the symbol of the data set. $\#T$: total number of tasks (followers), $\#S$: total number of samples (stories), $\#F$: total number of features, $\#C$: total number of categories

Seed	username	$\#T$	$\#S$	$\#F$	$\#C$
S_1	nichewp	11	71	942	3
S_2	buhlerchelsey	15	61	3217	5
S_3	GIVINGAWAY	12	57	1167	2
S_4	arjunchauhan24	10	41	1416	5

To build the multigraph for capturing the heterogenous relationships among the followers, we also collect the number of submissions, diggs and comments of these followers on each category. Each follower has a 3 by 10 user profile matrix. In Table 1, we summarize the characteristics of the five data sets.

4.2 Evaluation Criteria

Model Construction: We partition each data set into 5 folds to perform 5-fold cross-validation (CV). For MTL methods, we use another 5-fold CV on the training data set to select the regularization parameters λ_1 and/or λ_2 with a simple grid search in the range of $[2^{10}, 2^9, \cdots, 2^{-10}]$. For SVM, we first use 5-fold CV to select the number features in the rage of $\{25, 50, 75, \cdots, 300\}$, then another 5-fold CV to select parameter C in the range of $[2^{10}, 2^9, \cdots, 2^{-10}]$.

Model Evaluation: We collect the following metrics:

$$\begin{aligned} precision &= TP/(TP + FP) \\ recall &= TP/(TP + FN) \\ F_1 &= 2 * precision * recall/(precision + recall) \end{aligned}$$

where TP stands for true positive, FP stands for false positive, TN stands for true negative, FN stands for false negative. All the values reported are collected from the testing data set only and are averaged across 5-fold CV with 6 replicates. Note that since there is even no positive samples available in testing data during cross validation due to the imbalanced class ratio, we skip such folds when averaging the final F_1 score.

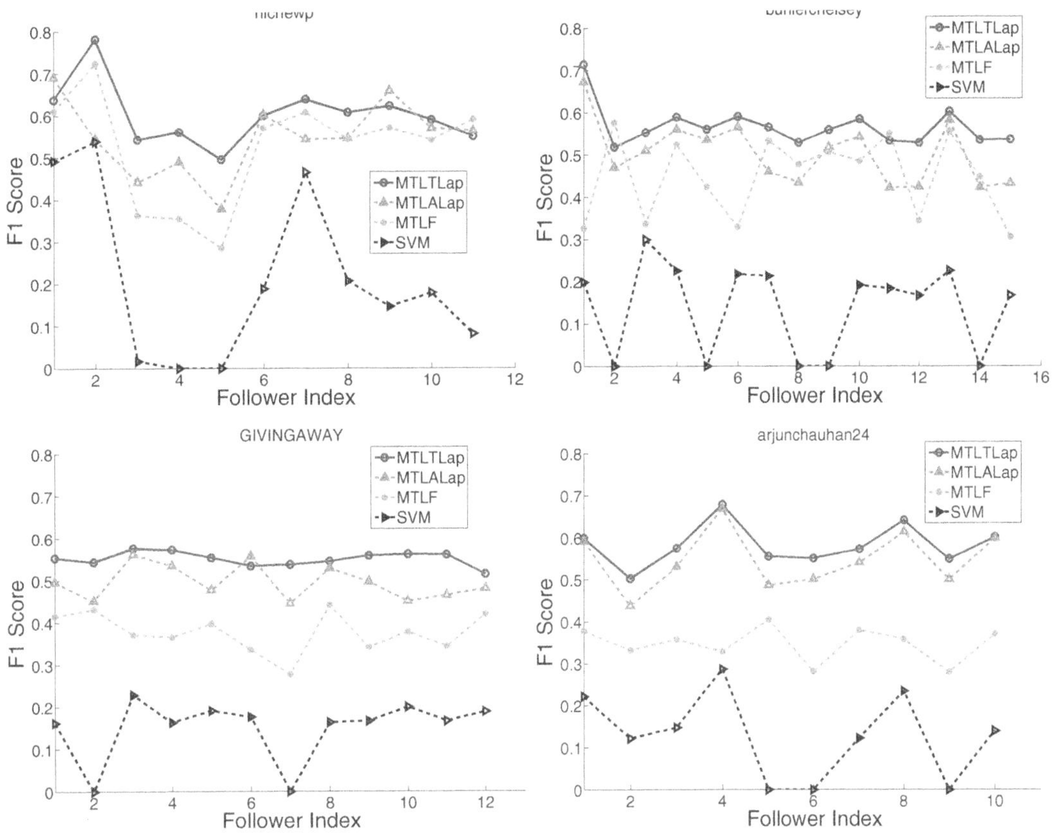

Figure 3: Average F_1 score for 4 seed users. Each figure's title corresponds to a username.

4.3 Experiment Performance

We compare our method with SVM, MTLF and MTLALap in terms of the average F_1 score for four different data sets in Figure 3. The standard deviation for each task is around 8%-15% for all the methods and we do not report them for simplicity. From Figure 3, we observe that the performance of single task SVM is very unstable compared with MTL approaches. For example, the average F_1 score is 0 for the 5th task of nichewp (S_1) because SVM predicts all the samples as negative (no comment or digg action) when the class ratio is unbalanced. However for the 2nd task, the performance is comparable to MTLF because the class ratio is balanced. Such an observation demonstrates the advantages of MTL vs STL for improving the generalization performance especially when training samples are limited and imbalanced.

Among the MTL methods, MTLALap and our method MTLTLap outperform MTLF for most tasks for four data sets, which confirms that considering the relationship among tasks will boost the learning performance. Finally, compared with MTLALap without differentiating the heterogenous social connections, our approach MTLTLap performs better, although the difference is subtle for some tasks. The reason is that when the training samples are dominated by only one or two categories (i.e. S_2), our method may not perform very well compared with MTLALap especially when the true topology actually reflects the user interests.

To further explore why our approach provides a reasonable performance compared with the other methods, we select three followers 2, 4 and 10 from S_2, which corresponds to the example shown in Figure 1. The data set of S_2 covers 5 categories dominated by technology and game and the result is shown in Table 2. We see that MTLTLap and MTLALap outperforms MTLF for two out of three tasks, which confirms the importance of task relationship incorporation. Meanwhile, the F_1 score and recall of the third strategy MTLTLap is consistently better than MTLALap, which demonstrates that our approach can more effectively identify positive samples in an unbalanced classification task.

To explain this phenomenon, we recall the similarities of the three followers as shown in Figure 2. F_1, F_2 and F_3 all like technology but with different levels; Meanwhile, F_1 and F_2 share interests in entertainment. Disregarding the information content category in the training data, the heterogenous relationship among followers will be either mixed (i.e. MTLALap) or ignored (i.e. MTLF). However in our approach, by introducing heterogenous task relationship induced by different categories and the weight of each category in the training data, we enforce similar tasks to have similar parameters based on the categories specified in the training data. Hence our prediction result is more stable and the resulting model is more interpretable.

5. CONCLUSIONS

In this paper, we tackle the problem of predicting user behavior to friends' postings in social networks. We argue that social information flow and socialization behaviors are not only related to social relationships (i.e. graph topology), but also information contents and user interests. Therefore, we should integrate all these factors to construct a better model. Towards that end, we presented a multi-task learn-

Table 2: Average F_1 score, Precision and Recall of three MTL methods on 3 tasks of seed S_2. black fonts denote the highest values among all competing methods for a task.

	T_2			T_4			T_{10}		
Method	F_1	Precision	Recall	F_1	Precision	Recall	F_1	Precision	Recall
MTLTLap	0.519	0.402	**0.733**	**0.590**	0.485	**0.751**	**0.585**	**0.446**	**0.850**
MTLALap	0.470	0.363	0.667	0.561	0.461	0.714	0.542	0.413	0.789
MTLF	**0.577**	**0.573**	0.581	0.525	**0.517**	0.533	0.485	0.419	0.576

ing algorithm with heterogenous task relationships, in which we capture the heterogenous relationships induced by different information categories among users as an undirected multigraph and incorporate such information by introducing a trace norm regularized graph Laplacian to standard MTL formalization. Using a comprehensive experimental study with social network data collected from digg.com and comparing with current state-of-the-art, we demonstrate that the new algorithm achieves better prediction performance.

Acknowledgments

The work is partially supported by the NSF award IIS (0845951) and University of Kansas General Research Fund (GRF: 2301420).

6. REFERENCES

[1] M. A. Ahmad and A. Teredesai. Modeling spread of ideas in online social networks. In *Proceedings of the fifth Australasian conference on Data mining and analystics - Volume 61*, AusDM '06, pages 185–190, Darlinghurst, Australia, Australia, 2006. Australian Computer Society, Inc.

[2] A. Argyriou, T. Evgeniou, and M. Pontil. Multi-task feature learning. In *NIPS*, 2006.

[3] B. Bakker and T. Heskes. Task clustering and gating for bayesian multitask learning. *Journal of Machine Learning Research*, 4:2003, 2003.

[4] S. Boyd and L. Vandenberghe. *Convex Optimization*. Cambridge University Press, 2004.

[5] C. Chang and C. Lin. Libsvm: a library for support vector machines, 2001. Software available at `http://www.csie.ntu.edu.tw/~cjlin/libsvm`.

[6] J. Chen, J. Liu, and J. Ye. Learning incoherent sparse and low-rank patterns from multiple tasks. In *The Sixteenth ACM SIGKDD International Conference On Knowledge Discovery and Data Mining (SIGKDD 2010)*, 2010.

[7] X. Chen, W. Pan, J. T. Kwok, and J. G. Carbonell. Accelerated gradient method for multi-task sparse learning problem. *IEEE International Conference on Data Mining (ICDM09)*, 0:746–751, 2009.

[8] F. Chung. Spectral graph theory. *CBMS Reginal Conferences Series*, 92, 1997.

[9] J. Duchi and Y. Singer. Boosting with structural sparsity. In *ICML '09: Proceedings of the 26th Annual International Conference on Machine Learning*, pages 297–304, 2009.

[10] T. Evgeniou, C. A. Micchelli, and M. Pontil. Learning multiple tasks with kernel methods. *Journal of Machine Learning Research*, 2005.

[11] I. Guyon, J. Weston, S. Barnhill, and V. Vapnik. Gene selection for cancer classification using support vector machines. *Machine Learning*, 46:389–422, 2002 January.

[12] T. Hastie, R. Tibshirani, and J. Friedman. *The Elements of Statistical Learning*. Springer-Verlag, 2009.

[13] C. Haythornthwaite. Social network analysis: An approach and technique for the study of information exchange. *Library and Information Science Research*, 18:323–342, 1996.

[14] R. Huckfeldt and J. Sprangue. Networks in context: The social flow of political information. *The Academy of Management Review*, 81(4):1179–1216, 1979.

[15] T. Kato, H. Kashima, and K. A. Masashi Sugiyama. Multi-task learning via conic programming. In *NIPS*, 2007.

[16] D. Kempe, J. Kleinberg, and E. Tardos. Maximizing the spread of influence through a social network. In *Proceedings of the ninth ACM SIGKDD international conference on Knowledge discovery and data mining*, KDD '03, pages 137–146, New York, NY, USA, 2003. ACM.

[17] D. Liben-Nowell and J. Kleinberg. Tracing information flow on a global scale using internet chain-letter data. *PNAS*, 105(12):4633–4638, 2008.

[18] H. Liu, M. Palatucci, and J. Zhang. Blockwise coordinate descent procedures for the multi-task lasso, with applications to neural semantic basis discovery. In *In proceedings of The 26th International Conference on Machine Learning (ICML 2009)*, 2009.

[19] J. Liu, S. Ji, and J. Ye. Multi-task feature learning via efficient $\ell_{2,1}$-norm minimization. In *Uncertainty in Artificial Intelligence*, 2009.

[20] J. Liu, S. Ji, and J. Ye. *SLEP: Sparse Learning with Efficient Projections*. Arizona State University, 2009.

[21] Y. Nesterov. Introductory lectures on convex optimization: A basic course. 2003.

[22] D. M. Romero, B. Meeder, and J. M. Kleinberg. Differences in the mechanics of information diffusion across topics: idioms, political hashtags, and complex contagion on twitter. In *WWW*, pages 695–704, 2011.

[23] A. Schwaighofer, V. Tresp, and K. Yu. Learning gaussian process kernels via hierarchical bayes. In *In Advances in Neural Information Processing Systems (NIPS*, pages 1209–1216. MIT Press, 2004.

[24] X. Song, Y. Chi, K. Hino, and B. L. Tseng. Information flow modeling based on diffusion rate for prediction and ranking. In *Proceedings of the 16th international conference on World Wide Web*, WWW '07, pages 191–200, New York, NY, USA, 2007. ACM.

[25] R. Tibshirani. Regression shrinkage and selection via the lasso. *Journal of the Royal Statistical Society B*, 58:267–288, 1996.

[26] N. Tichy, M. Tushman, and C. Fombrun. Social network analysis for organizations. *The American Political Science Review*, 4(4):507–519, 1979.

[27] V. N. Vapnik. The nature of statistical learning theory. *Springer-Verlag*, 1995.

[28] S. Wasserman and K. Faust. *Social Network Analysis: Methods and Applications*. New York: Cambridge University Press, 1994.

[29] J. Weston, A. Elisseeff, G. BakIr, and F. Sinz. Spider: General purpose machine learning toolbox in matlab, 2007. Software available at `www.kyb.mpg.de/bs/people/spider/`.

[30] C. White, L. Plotnick, J. Kushma, S. R. Hiltz, and M. Turoff. An online social network for emergency management. *International Journal of Emergency Management*, 6(3-4):369–382, 2009.

[31] J. Yang and J. Leskovec. Modeling information diffusion in implicit networks. *Data Mining, IEEE International Conference on*, 0:599–608, 2010.

[32] Y. Zhang and D.-Y. Yeung. A convex formulation for learning task relationships in multi-task learning. In *In Proceedings of the 26th Conference on Uncertainty in Artificial Intelligence (UAI 2010)*, pages 733–742, 2010.

Improving User Interest Inference from Social Neighbors

Zhen Wen
IBM T.J. Watson Research Center
19 Skyline Drive
Hawthorne, NY 10532 USA
zhenwen@us.ibm.com

Ching-Yung Lin
IBM T.J. Watson Research Center
19 Skyline Drive
Hawthorne, NY 10532 USA
chingyung@us.ibm.com

ABSTRACT

Prior research has provided some evidence of social correlation (*i.e.*, "you are who you know"), which makes it possible to infer one's interests from his or her social neighbors. However, it is also shown to be challenging to consistently obtain high quality inference. This challenge can be partially attributed to the fact that people usually maintain diverse social relationships, in order to tap into diverse information and knowledge. It is unlikely that a person would possess all interests of his/her social neighbors. Instead, s/he may selectively acquire just a subset of them. This paper intends to improve inferring interests from neighbors given this observation. We conduct this study by implementing a privacy-preserving large distributed social sensor system in a large global IT company to capture the multifaceted activities (*e.g.*, emails, instant messaging, social bookmarking, *etc.*) of 25K+ people. These activities occupy the majority of employees' time, and thus, provide a higher quality view of the diverse aspects of their professional interests compared to the friending activity on online social networking sites. In this paper, we propose a technique that exploits the correlation among the attributes that a person possesses to improve social-correlation-based inference quality. Our technique offers two unique contributions. First, we demonstrate that the proposed technique can significantly improve inference quality by as much as 76.1%. Second, we study the interaction between the two factors: social correlation and attribute correlation under different situations. The results can inform practical applications how the inference quality would change in various scenarios.

Categories and Subject Descriptors

J.4 [**Computer Applications**]: Social and Behavioral Sciences—*Sociology*

General Terms

Algorithms, Experimentation, Human Factors

Keywords

User interest modeling, Social correlation, Attribute correlation, Inference

1. INTRODUCTION

Research has shown that a user's interests and attributes may be inferred from his or her social neighbors [14, 15]. Such inferred interests can enable applications to provide personalized results to meet an individual user's needs, even when the user is new to the applications. In addition, such inference may reveal attributes that a user intends to keep private. We can keep the user aware of the attributes that may be accurately inferred from his/her social neighbors, such that the user can mark related social relationships as private to improve privacy control.

It is, however, challenging to obtain consistently high quality results in inferring user interests from social neighbors [15]. The quality can vary significantly due to several factors. First, users may not use social applications intensively to leave enough traces to reveal about their social interactions. Second, certain user attributes can be difficult to infer from social neighbors. For example, the social correlation of a group of college students' hometowns can be much lower than the correlation of their ages [14]. As a result, high quality inference results may be only achieved for a small subset of users.

One particular challenge is that a user usually maintains many different types of diverse social relationships. For example, a social software researcher, whom we call Alice, interacts with different social neighbors for different purposes. Alice may share a few interests with many of her social neighbors, such as "social network" and "web technologies". However, Alice is not likely to be interested in everything her neighbors are interested, such as her personal friends' "VLSI" job. Even in one type of social relationships such as "personal friends", Alice's interests may still significantly vary from her friends, except for a few common hobbies.

To address the challenge, this paper focuses on improving the quality of inferring user interests from social neighbors. Specifically, we propose a novel method that exploits the correlation among multiple attributes of a user, in addition to the social correlation of an attribute among a group of users. It first uses social correlation to obtain initial inference from neighbors. Then, it refines the inference using attribute correlation to remove less likely attribute combinations (*e.g.* "social software" and "VLSI"). In this study, we do not consider the friending activity on online social networking sites. Instead, we implemented a privacy-preserving large distributed social sensor system [12] in a large global IT company to capture the multifaceted information of 25K+ people, including profiles with 1000+ attributes, 20+ million records of communications (*e.g.*, emails, instant messaging, *etc.*) and Web 2.0 activities (*e.g.*, social bookmarking, blogging, *etc.*). Such data enable us to examine attribute correlation in large attribute sets. With attribute sets of different sizes, we may understand thoroughly how attribute correlation would be complementary to social correlation for inferring user interests. To the best of our knowledge, we propose the first optimization-based method combining social correlation and attributes correlation to improve user interest inference from social neighbors. We demonstrate that it can improve inference quality significantly. For instance, for the two datasets tested, the average inference quality is improved from 45.1% to 60.3%, and from 30.1% to 53%, respectively. We also show how the correlation among a set of attributes would impact inference quality in different situations. For example, the usefulness of attribute correlation depends on its value distribution in different datasets.

2. RELATED WORK

Social influence and correlation among people's behavior have been extensively studied by social network researchers [11]. Lately, researchers have explored data mining techniques to model various aspects of social influence in online social networks [3, 7]. Based on social correlation, various approaches have been developed for inferring patterns and making prediction. Jensen *et al.* [10], among others, propose a relational knowledge discovery scheme called collective classification (*a.k.a.*, collective intelligence) that utilizes the relationship between individual entities. Getoor and Diehl present a survey of collective classification research in [9]. In contrast to previous work, we exploit the correlation of attributes possessed by an individual to improve the inference quality.

In addition, a large number of researches have been done to discover patterns from the correlation of attributes in large datasets. Association rule mining [1] is one of the most popular approaches. A few researches on social network analysis have recognized the benefits of combining social and attribute correlation. Lindamood *et al.* [13] obtain 1% improvement in attribute predictions by averaging results based on links and content. To achieve more significant improvement, our work further explores optimization-based approaches to combine social and attribute correlation. Other researches [2, 5, 6] have also jointly modeled social links and topic information to better identify communities. While they are good at providing holistic views of overall social-topic distributions, our work focuses on utilizing the distributions to optimize predicting individual people's attributes.

3. IMPROVING USER INTEREST INFERENCE FROM NEIGHBORS

Users usually maintain social relationship with a diverse set of social neighbors. Different aspects of their behavior and interests may be influenced by different social neighbors. Therefore, a user may not have all of his or her neighbors' interests. In this section, we present an approach to improving user interest inference by exploiting attribute correlation to remove less likely combinations of interests/attributes. First, we briefly overview social-correlation-based user interest inference, proposed in [15]. Then, we describe how to improve it by incorporating attribute correlation.

In this study, we adopt user interest models in [15], and communication data collected by a privacy-preserving large distributed social sensor system [12]. In particular, we focus on improving the precision, because inference based on social correlation tends to achieve high recall and low precision [15]. Nevertheless, the precision is usually more important for practical applications to provide personalized services.

3.1 Inferring Interests by Social Correlation

To infer users' interests, we let variable $\mathbf{Z}$ denote the degree users are interested in a set of attributes, where z_{ij} is the i-th user's interest in the j-th attribute. The attribute can be a topic in the implicit user interests expressed in their conversations, or a term in the explicit user interests specified in their profiles. Our baseline approach in [15] utilize a network autocorrelation model to infer user interests from social neighbors.

The quality of inference is not reliable using only the social correlation model. For example, the mean quality of the inferred implicit interests is 45.1%, and the variance is as large as 21.7% [15]. One solution that has been proposed in [15] is to use a inference quality predictor, which predicts how good the inference will be based on social network features. Then, the interests of a user is inferred only when the predictor gives good estimates. The results showed that this technique improves the mean quality of inferred implicit interests to 64.4%, but only for about 5% of the users (see Figure 5(b)). Therefore, further improvement is needed.

3.2 Incorporating Attribute Correlation

Users typically interact with different sets of people for different purposes. In other words, they can participate in a diverse set of communities where interests/attributes in each community may be quite different. In this situation, the interests of a particular user may not be the union of the interests from all his or her communities. Instead, his or her interests are likely to be a subset of the union. Previous data mining researches on association rules have shown that interesting correlation can be discovered among attributes in large datasets. We therefore exploit such attribute correlation to refine inferred attributes obtained by social correlation.

We compute the correlation between the j-th attribute and the k-th attribute as the Pearson correlation coefficient:

$$r_{jk} = \frac{U\sum_i z_{ij}z_{ik} - \sum_i z_{ij}\sum_i z_{ik}}{\sqrt{U\sum_i z_{ij}^2 - (\sum_i z_{ij})^2}\sqrt{U\sum_i z_{ik}^2 - (\sum_i z_{ik})^2}}$$

where z_{ij} is the j-th attribute of user i.

Then, given an initial set of attributes $\mathbf{A}_0$ inferred based on social correlation for user i, we try to find the optimal subset $\mathbf{A} =< a_1, .., a_n >$ by balancing three constraints. First, the total degree of interests on attributes in $\mathbf{A}$ (*i.e.*, $\sum_{k=1}^{n} z_{i,a_k}$) should be maximized. Next, the overall pairwise attribute correlation in $\mathbf{A}$ (*i.e.*, $\sum_{k\neq j}\sum_{j=1}^{n} r_{jk}$) should be maximized. Finally, smaller size of $\mathbf{A}$ (*i.e.*, $len(\mathbf{A})$) should be favored, if everything else equals (*i.e.*, Occam's razor principle). This optimization can be formulated as a generalized assignment problem, which is NP-hard [8]. Thus, we use a greedy approach to approximating the optimization.

```
Procedure OptimizeInterests(A_0)
A ← A_0
minReward ← min_{j∈A}[reward(j, A)]
minJ ← argmin_{j∈A}[reward(j, A)]
while minReward < 0
    delete minJ from A
    minReward ← min_{j∈A}[reward(j, A)]
    minJ ← argmin_{j∈A}[reward(j, A)]
return A
```

Figure 1: A greedy algorithm for improving inferred interests based on attribute correlation.

3.2.1 Greedy Algorithm

Figure 1 gives an outline of the algorithm. We define a reward function to measure the desirability of keeping an attribute in the target optimal attribute set **A**. For the i-th user's attribute j in **A**, the reward function is:

$$reward(j, \mathbf{A}) = o_1 \cdot z_{ij} + o_2 \cdot AttrCorr(j, \mathbf{A}) - o_3 \cdot len(\mathbf{A}) \quad (1)$$

where $AttrCorr(j, \mathbf{A})$ measures the attribute-correlation-based desirability of attribute j given **A**, and o_1, o_2 and o_3 are weights controlling the relative importance of the three factors. $AttrCorr(j, \mathbf{A})$ is defined as:

$$AttrCorr(j, \mathbf{A}) = \frac{1}{len(\mathbf{A})} \sum_{a \in \mathbf{A}, a \neq j} r_{ja}$$

The intuition of $AttrCorr(j, \mathbf{A})$ is that a good candidate for the optimal attribute set is an attribute with the high correlation with all the other attributes.

For weights o_1, o_2 and o_3, we have $o_1 + o_2 + o_3 = 1$. In our study, we set $o_3 = 0.05$ to favor result sets with size less than 20, since many practical search and recommender applications focus on users' top interests (*e.g.*, top 20). Next, we experiment with two weighting strategies for o_1, which are described in details in Section 3.2.2. Finally, o_2 can be computed as $1 - o_3 - o_1$.

3.2.2 Weighting Schemes

In our approach, we investigate two different weighting schemes to control the relative importance of the social and attribute correlation.

Fixed weights

A simple scheme is to use fixed values for o_1 and o_2 during the optimization process. In our experiment, we evaluate the quality of inference using different values of the weights. In Section 4, we show that even this simple scheme would yield good improvement over previous approaches.

Dynamic weights

We hypothesize that social correlation is more important at the initial stage of the inference, since no attributes are known for a user. However, as more attributes are inferred for the user, attribute correlation may provide more cues than social correlation. Therefore, a dynamic weighting scheme for o_1 may work better than fixed weights. To this end, we propose o_1 as an exponential decay function of set **A**'s size. Moreover, the decay needs to depend on the usefulness of the attribute correlation to inference. A possible usefulness indicator can be the distribution of attribute correlation values Pr. For example, a distribution with more non-zero values may provide more useful inputs to the attribute-correlation-based inference, and thus the weight of social correlation o_1 should be smaller. We define o_1 as

$$o_1 = exp(-f(Pr) \cdot len(\mathbf{A})) \quad (2)$$

where $f(Pr)$ is a usefulness indicator computed from the attribute correlation distribution Pr. In our work, we fit Pr to an exponential distribution with exponent b ($b < 0$). A smaller $|b|$ value means a heavier tail and thus more non-zero attribute correlation values can be used as cues for our inference algorithm. Therefore, we set $f(Pr) = \frac{c}{|b|}$, where b is the exponential distribution exponent and c is a positive constant factor to be determined in experiments.

In addition, we hypothesize that the weights may be affected by the diversity of a person's network. For example, if s/he has very diverse social neighbors, his/her attributes inferred based on social correlation can be very diverse too. For such users, the attribute correlation can be more important in identifying likely combinations of attributes. We use a network diversity metric [15] to measure the degree to which nodes have diverse social neighbors in a network. For an individual i, the network diversity of i is defined as $d(i) = 1 - \sum_l (\rho_{il} + \sum_{m \neq i,l} \rho_{im} \cdot \rho_{ml})^2$, where ρ_{il} is the proportion of node i's network efforts invested in communicating with node l. Small values of $d(i)$ indicate that the neighbors of node i are considered concentrated instead of diverse. Then, Equation 2 can be augmented as:

$$o_1 = exp(-d(i) \cdot f(Pr) \cdot len(\mathbf{A})) \quad (3)$$

3.3 Incorporating Quality Predictor

The improved user interest inference algorithm can also be used together with a inference quality predictor such as the one proposed in [15]. Such predictor estimates inference quality based on easily observed social network features (*e.g.*, network in-degree, out-degree, betweenness centrality and *etc.*), in order to allow search and recommendation applications make informed decisions on when to utilize inferred user interests. In [15], it is shown that significantly higher inference quality can be achieved for users identified by the predictor. It is natural to assume that using the inference quality predictor will further improve the performance of our approach, since the two are complementary: the quality predictor leverages social network properties, and our approach exploits attribute correlation. However, the users identified by the predictor are the ones for whom we can observe strong social correlation. Therefore, the contribution of attribution correlation may be relatively small, in terms of improving inferring user interests. In Section 4.4, we validate our hypothesis that this combination can yield further improvement in performance.

4. EVALUATION

In our experiment, we evaluate the performance of our approach under various conditions.

4.1 Fixed Weighting Scheme

First, we examine the inference quality of the proposed approach, when using fixed weights in the reward function (Equation 1). We compare it to a baseline approach using

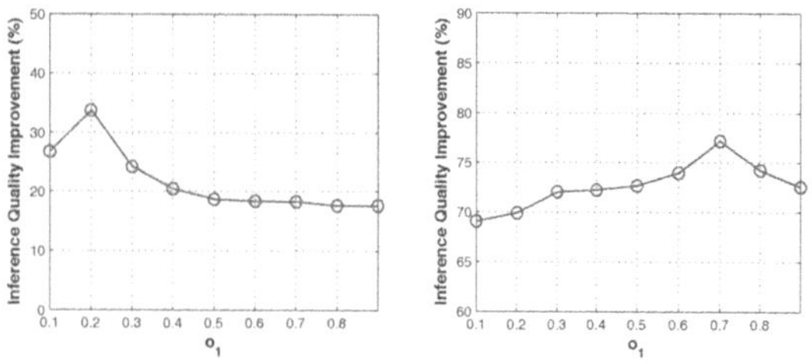

(a) (b)

Figure 2: The performance improvement of mean inference quality in inferring user interests for different fixed social correlation weight o_1: (a) the implicit interests; (b) the explicit interests.

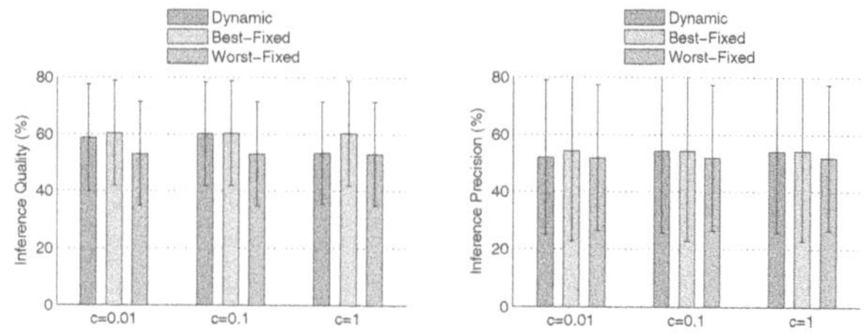

(a) (b)

Figure 3: The performance of inferring user interests using dynamic social correlation weight o_1: (a) the implicit interests; (b) the explicit interests. Best-Fixed and Worst-Fixed refer to the best and worst performance for various fixed o_1 values.

only social correlation [15]. For inferring implicit interests on the same data sets, the baseline approach achieved a mean inference quality of 45.1%, with a standard deviation of 21.7%. We experiment with different values for o_1. The improvement over the baseline approach is shown in Figure 2(a). Our approach can achieve inference quality up to 60.3%, an improvement of 33.8%. Moreover, we observe that different weights yield significantly different improvements. The best improvement (33.8%) is achieved when $o_1 = 0.2$, which means social correlation plays a less important role than the attribute correlation among the implicit interests.

We also investigate the performance improvement for inferring explicit user interests. The baseline method has a mean inference precision of 30.1% and a standard deviation of 26.9%. In Figure 2(b), we see that our method can achieve a mean inference precision of 53.0%, an improvement of 76.1% over the baseline method. In addition, the standard deviation is roughly at the same level. In contrast to the implicit interest inference (Figure 2(a)), the best improvement for explicit interest inference (76.1%) is obtained at $o_1 = 0.7$. This larger optimal o_1 value suggests that social correlation is more important here. Since users' social relationships are the same for both cases, we attribute the difference to the different correlation among different sets of attributes.

4.2 Dynamic Weighting Scheme

To address the deficiency of the fixed weight scheme, we design a dynamic weight scheme where the social correlation weight o_1 exponentially decays based on the properties of the attribute correlation distribution (Section 3.2.2).

We first examine the distribution of attribute correlation by fitting it to an exponential curve. For both types of interests, we obtain R-square statistics larger than 0.97 and $p < 0.01$, suggesting good fits to the exponential distribution. Specifically, the exponent b for the implicit interests is -1.39, and the exponent b for the explicit interests is -12.95. That means the attribute correlation values of the explicit interests decrease much faster than those of the implicit interests do. Therefore, there are more non-zero correlation values for the implicit user interests. That is, the attribute correlation can be more important for the implicit interest inference than the explicit interest inference. It helps to explain why the optimal social correlation weight o_1 in the fixed weighting scheme (Section 4.1) is smaller for the implicit interests than the explicit interests.

We then evaluate how the dynamic weighting scheme in Equation 2 can improve the inference quality for both types of interests. For the usefulness indicator $f(Pr)$ in Equation 2, we also vary its constant c to examine its impact. In our experiment, we see that the dynamic weight scheme with $c = 0.1$ can achieve performance very close to the optimal performance in the fixed weighting scheme (Section 4.1), for both types of interests (Figure 3). Hence, compared to the fixed weighting scheme, the dynamic weighting scheme can be more easily generalized to different datasets since it incorporates the datasets' attribute correlation properties.

Next, we examine the performance of the dynamic weighting scheme that incorporates network diversity metric (Equation 3). The improvements over the results in Figure 3 are less than 1% and statistically not significant. One possible explanation for this insignificant difference is that a person with diverse networks may also have higher capacities in processing information in social interactions, and thus can have more diverse interests.

4.3 Number of Attributes

In addition to the distribution of attribute correlation, we hypothesize that the number of attributes also influences our approach's performance. Intuitively, the more attributes there are, the more likely an attribute is correlated with other attributes. Thus, our approach may better exploit attribute correlation to improve inference as the number of attributes increases. To validate this hypothesis, we perform random sampling to obtain data with attribute sets of different sizes, for both the implicit and the explicit interests. For each attribute set size, we obtain 20 datasets through sampling to ensure statistical significance. Figure 4 shows how the improvements vary as the number of attributes changes. The dashed lines show the 25% and 75% quantiles. For both of the implicit and the explicit interests, we can observe a trend matching our hypothesis: the more attributes we have, the more we can improve inferring interests. Specifically, if there are just a small number of attributes (*e.g.*, < 100), we may not get a significant improvement by exploiting attribute correlation.

4.4 Inference Quality Predictor

To make inferred user interests useful for applications, a previous approach [15] proposed a technique to predict inference quality based on network characteristics. The technique then only infers interests for users with predicted qual-

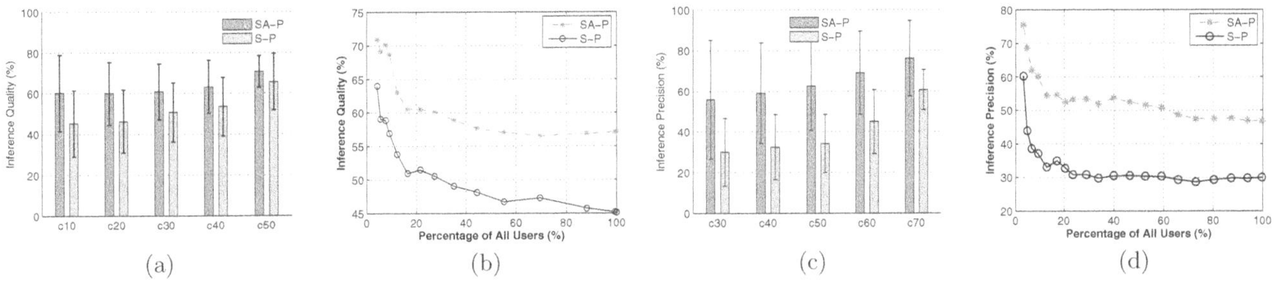

Figure 5: Compare the quality improvements of our approach and the baseline approach [15] when using the inference quality predictor: (a) the implicit user interests using different criteria of the predictor; (b) the implicit user interests for different percentage of users; (c) the explicit user interests using different criteria of the predictor; (d) the explicit user interests for different percentage of users.

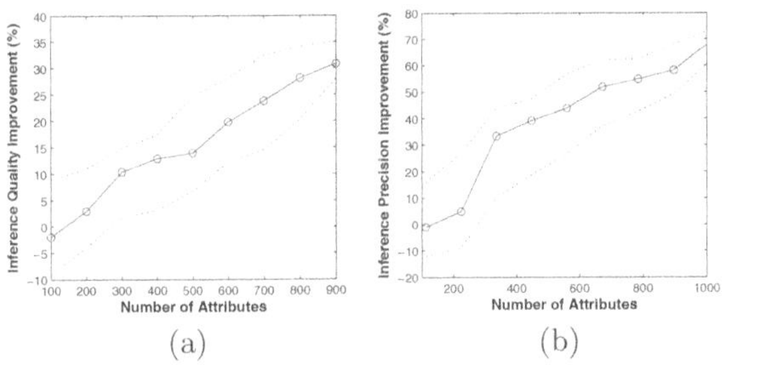

Figure 4: The quality improvements of user interest inference for different number of attributes: (a) the implicit user interest; (b) the explicit user interest.

ity higher than a predefined criterion. For example, a predictor with the criterion $c50$, or $quality > 50\%$, means that the predictor only outputs users for whom the predicted quality is larger than 50%. On the same dataset, it achieved a quality up to 64.4% for the implicit interests, and a precision up to 60.5% for the explicit interests. However, such performance is only for a small subset of the users, *i.e.*, less than 5%. In our experiment, we compare the performance of our approach and the baseline approach in [15], when using the inference quality predictor. Let **S-P** denote the baseline approach that uses only **S**ocial correlation with the **P**redictor, and **SA-P** denote our approach that uses **S**ocial and **A**ttribute correlation with the **P**redictor. The comparisons are shown in Figure 5.

In Figure 5(a) and 5(c), we can see that exploiting attribute correlation gives significant improvement for the quality predictors with different criteria, for both the implicit and the explicit interests. Specifically, such improvement is the largest for predictors with the lowest criterion (*e.g.*, $c10$), and then gradually decreases as higher criteria are used (*e.g.*, $c50$). The trend can be attributed to the fact that a predictor with higher criteria (*e.g.*, $c50$) is likely to identify users with stronger social correlation. Therefore, the benefit of exploiting attribute correlation can be reduced for this set of users. Then, we examine the relationship between inference quality and the percentage of users that are identified by the predictor. We vary the criteria of the predictor, and obtain the corresponding inference quality and the percentage of users identified. The results are illustrated in Figure 5(b) and 5(d). In both types of interests, our approach offers consistent improvements. Overall, for the majority of the users, our approach improves inference quality in a range of 10% to 15% for the implicit interests (Figure 5(b)), and 18% to 25% for the explicit interests (Figure 5(d)). When the predictor uses higher criteria to select a small percentage of users (*e.g.*, < 20%), the inference quality of the baseline method quickly improves for identified users. Yet our approach still significantly outperforms by 5% to 15%.

4.5 Comparing to Joint Social-Attribute Clustering Techniques

In this section, we compare the performance of our approach with clustering techniques that jointly model social-attribute correlation. In particular, we compare with an implementation [4] of mixed membership stochastic blockmodels (MMSB) [2]. MMSB can associate a node in a network with multiple clusters, based on network connections as well as the node attributes. For our dataset, this method can find the probabilities the i-th person belongs to M latent "communities" $< \mathfrak{p}_{i1}, \mathfrak{p}_{i2}, ..., \mathfrak{p}_{iM} >$. Then, the person's interests in the j-th attribute can be inferred as $z_{ij} = \sum_{k=1}^{M} \mathfrak{p}_{ik} \cdot \mathfrak{A}_{kj}$, where $\mathfrak{A}_{kj}$ is the strength of the j-th attributes in the k-th community. It is computed by averaging people's interests in attribute j within the community.

We can use a threshold to filter the inferred set of attributes, and then measure the corresponding precision and recall defined in [15]. By varying the threshold, we obtain a precision-recall curve for MMSB. Figure 6 shows such a curve derived for explicit user interests and $M = 50$. In our experiment, we tested M values ranging from 20 to 100, and the curves are similar. For our proposed approach, we use the dynamic weighting scheme in Section 4.2 and vary the scaling factor c of $f(Pr)$ to get a precision-recall curve. The figure shows that both approaches perform better than the baseline method [15] that only utilizes social correlation. In addition, we can see that our approach provides significant advantage over MMSB. The advantage may be explained by that people can still have quite diverse attributes even in the same community identified by MMSB. This has been observed in other community-based approaches (*e.g.*, [14]) as well, especially in weak communities. Therefore, optimizing inference for each individual may still improve performance. We also experimented with inferring implicit user interests, as well as incorporating inference quality predictor as in Section 4.4. Similar trends of improvement can be observed so that they are omitted here due to space limit.

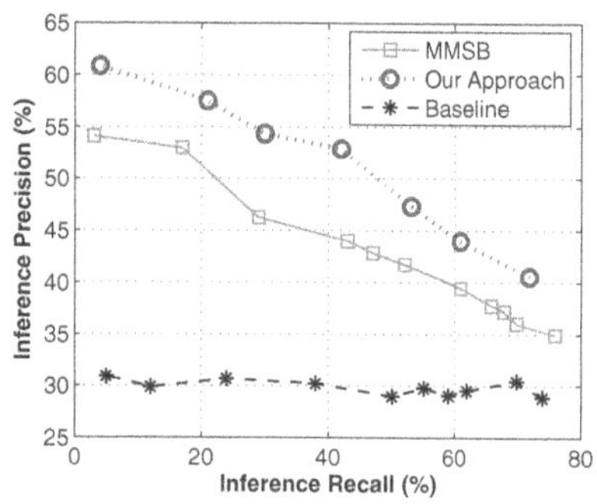

Figure 6: The performance comparison of our approach with MMSB [2] and the baseline method [15] in inferring explicit user interests.

5. DISCUSSION

Our results can help to improve personalized services. In addition, they may help to improve privacy control in social networks. Users usually want to control what information to share about themselves. However, it becomes challenging as our and other researches have shown that such information may be inferred from their social neighbors.

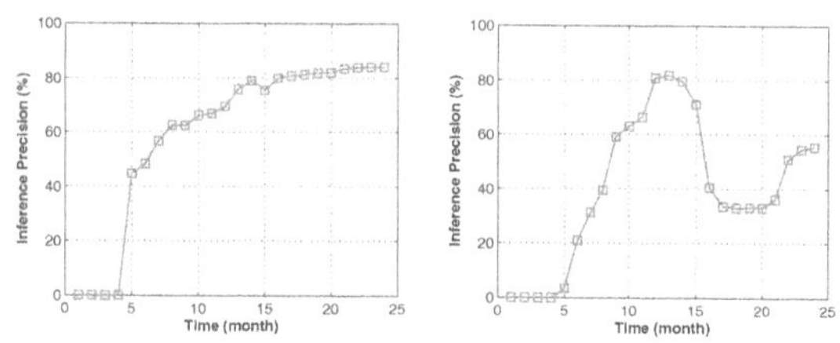

Figure 7: The inference quality change over a 24-month period for two attributes of a user: (a) attribute j_1; (b) attribute j_2.

To assist users to achieve better privacy control in such complex situations, our technique can be used to show users how well their attributes can be inferred. For example, Figure 7 illustrates that a user in our system can keep track of how likely two of his/her attributes will "leak" out via the social neighbors. Comparing the two attributes, attribute j_1 (in Figure 7(a)) is an attribute shared by relatively more people (*e.g.*, being interested in knowledge management). Thus, a growing network will mostly make it easier to infer it. In contrast, attribute j_2 in Figure 7(b) is shared by less people (*e.g.*, being interested in a small company). Therefore, the ability of inferring this attribute from social neighbors is more sensitive to changes in networks. If the user wants to prevent others to infer an attribute (*e.g.*, j_1), our technique can recommend him/her to mark private the social relationships where the neighbors have attributes highly correlated with j_1. During this process, our technique keeps updating the display of the inference quality to help the user make sure that his/her goals are achieved. For example, to make attribute j_1 private (*e.g.*, inference precision $< 3\%$), the user needs to hide 13% of his/her social neighbors. In contrast, only 4% of relationship needs to be hidden to protect attribute j_2.

6. CONCLUSION

We propose a technique combining social and attribute correlation to improve inferring user interests from social neighbors. Using data in one of the largest global organizations, we demonstrate that our technique significantly improve inference quality by as much as 76.1% over existing approaches. To help practical applications better utilize this technique in different situations, we further investigate the interaction between the two factors in our technique: social and attribute correlation. Specifically, we show how they would impact the inference quality under different conditions. For example, as the number of observable attributes grows, the inference quality can be significantly improved, even for users with weak observed social correlation. Our findings can be useful for social applications that aim to provide personalized services but have to infer many new users' interests from friends because of widely varied participation rate. In addition, our results can be exploited to design better privacy control tools in social applications.

7. ACKNOWLEDGEMENT

This research is continuing through participation in the Network Science Collaborative Technology Alliance sponsored by the U.S. Army Research Laboratory under Agreement Number W911NF-09-2-0053. The views and conclusions contained in this document are those of the authors and should not be interpreted as representing the official policies, either expressed or implied, of the Army Research Laboratory or the U.S. Government. The U.S. Government is authorized to reproduce and distribute reprints for Government purposes notwithstanding any copyright notation here on.

8. REFERENCES

[1] R. Agrawal, T. Imielinski, and A. Swami. Mining association rules between sets of items in large databases. In *Proc. of SIGMOD*, pages 207–216, 1993.

[2] E. Airoldi, D. Blei, S. Fienberg, and E. Xing. Mixed membership stochastic blockmodels. *Journal of Machine Learning Research*, 9:1981–2014, 2008.

[3] A. Anagnostopoulos, R. Kumar, and M. Mahdian. Influence and correlation in social networks. In *KDD*, pages 7–15, 2008.

[4] J. Chang. lda: Collapsed gibbs sampling methods for topic models. http://cran.r-project.org/web/packages/lda/.

[5] J. Chang and D. Blei. Relational topic models for document networks. *Artificial Intelligence and Statistics*, pages 81–88, 2009.

[6] J. Chang, J. Boyd-Graber, and D. Blei. Connections between the lines: Augmenting social networks with text. In *Proc. of KDD*, pages 169–178, 2009.

[7] D. J. Crandall, D. Cosley, D. P. Huttenlocher, J. M. Kleinberg, and S. Suri. Feedback effects between similarity and social influence in online communities. In *KDD*, pages 160–168, 2008.

[8] L. Fleischer, M. Goemans, V. Mirrokni, and M. Sviridenko. Tight approximation algorithms for maximum general assignment problems. In *Proc. of SODA*, pages 611–620, 2006.

[9] L. Getoor and C. Diehl. Link mining: a survey. *SIGKDD Explor. Newsl.*, 7:3–12, December 2005.

[10] D. Jensen, J. Neville, and B. Gallagher. Why collective inference improves relational classification. In *Proc. of KDD*, pages 593–598, 2004.

[11] R. T. Leenders. Modeling social influence through network autocorrelation: constructing the weight matrix. *Social Networks*, 24:21–47, 2002.

[12] C. Lin, K. Ehrlich, V. Griffiths-Fisher, and C. Desforges. Smallblue: People mining for expertise search,. *IEEE Multimedia Magazine*, 15(1):78–84, 2008.

[13] J. Lindamood, R. Heatherly, M. Kantarcioglu, and B. Thuraisingham. Inferring private information using social network data. In *Proc. of WWW*, pages 1145–1146, 2009.

[14] A. Mislove, B. Viswanath, P. Gummadi, and P. Druschel. You are who you know: inferring user profiles in online social networks. In *WSDM*, pages 251–260, 2010.

[15] Z. Wen and C.-Y. Lin. On the quality of inferring interests from social neighbors. In *KDD*, pages 373–382, 2010.

CASINO: Towards Conformity-aware Social Influence Analysis in Online Social Networks

Hui Li
herolee@pmail.ntu.edu.sg

Sourav S Bhowmick
assourav@ntu.edu.sg

Aixin Sun
axsun@ntu.edu.sg

School of Computer Engineering
Nanyang Technological University, Singapore, 639798

ABSTRACT

Social influence analysis in online social networks is the study of people's influence by analyzing the social interactions between individuals. There have been increasing research efforts to understand the influence propagation phenomenon due to its importance to information dissemination among others. Despite the progress achieved by state-of-the-art social influence analysis techniques, a key limitation of these techniques is that they *only* utilize *positive* interactions (*e.g.*, agreement, trust) between individuals, ignoring two equally important factors, namely, *negative* relationships (*e.g.*, distrust, disagreement) between individuals and *conformity* of people, which refers to a person's inclination to be influenced.

In this paper, we propose a novel algorithm CASINO (**C**onformity-**A**ware **S**ocial **IN**fluence c**O**mputation) to study the interplay between *influence* and *conformity* of each individual. Given a social network, CASINO first extracts a set of *topic-based subgraphs* where each subgraph depicts the social interactions associated with a specific topic. Then it optionally labels the edges (relationships) between individuals with positive or negative signs. Finally, it computes the *influence* and *conformity indices* of each individual in each *signed* topic-based subgraph. Our empirical study with several real-world social networks demonstrates superior effectiveness and accuracy of CASINO compared to state-of-the-art methods. Furthermore, we revealed several interesting characteristics of "influentials" and "conformers" in these networks.

Categories and Subject Descriptors

H.3.3 [**Information Storage and Retrieval**]: Information Search and Retrieval—*Information Filtering*; J.4 [**Computer Applications**]: Social and Behavior Sciences

General Terms

Algorithms, Experimentation

Keywords

Social networks, Influence, Conformity, topic-based subgraphs, Signed edge, Twitter

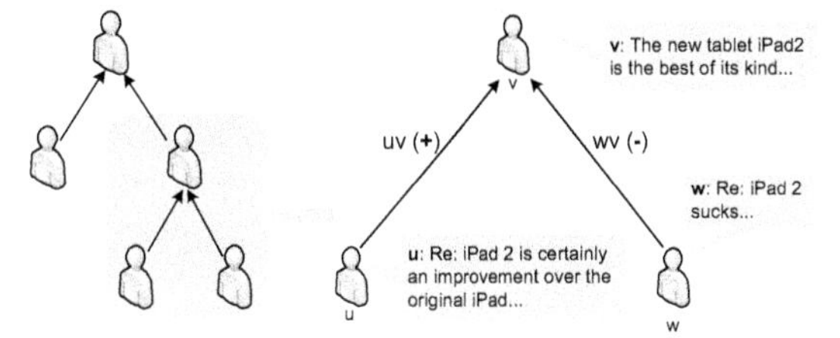

Figure 1: Social influence propagation scenario.

1. INTRODUCTION

Though the field of social network analysis (SNA) has developed over many years, it is with the recent emergence of large-scale online social networking applications that techniques from this area have received a great deal of attention. We are now faced with the opportunity to analyze social network data at unprecedented levels of scale and temporal resolution. In this paper, we present our work towards addressing one of the challenges, namely the *social influence analysis* problem.

The goal of social influence analysis is to study individuals' influence by analyzing the social interactions. By identifying the "influentials" in a social network, users may be able to maximize the influence of a piece of information [6]. Informally, influentials are those individuals whose opinions or advices are often accepted and supported by others. For instance, Kempe et al. [6] proposed a greedy algorithm which aimed to find a limited number of influentials from whom the information diffusion can be maximized.

Recently, social networks are viewed as *signed* networks [7], where social interactions involve both positive and negative relationships. Consider the signed network in Figure 1 depicting interactions between a set of individuals. An edge pointing from u to v denotes that person u trust/agree (*resp.*, distrust/disagree) person v. An edge representing trust relationship is labeled as positive (*e.g.*, $\overrightarrow{uv}$), otherwise negative (*e.g.*, $\overrightarrow{wv}$). Note that social influence flows in the opposite direction of the edges (*i.e.*, v influenced u and w).

A closer analysis of social influence phenomenon in signed networks reveals that there are three important factors. Firstly, an individual's ability to influence others (*e.g.*, v). Secondly, the nature of social interactions (positive/negative) between individuals (*e.g.*, $\overrightarrow{uv}$, $\overrightarrow{wv}$). Lastly, *conformity* of an individual, which is a person's inclination to be influenced by others [2]. Note that an individual's ability to influence or conform is *context-sensitive*. For example, in Figure 1 u conforms to v's opinion on `iPad 2`. However, it does not necessarily mean that u will always conform to v on *any* topic. For instance, u may not agree with v on conversation related to `salsa dancing` as u may believe that she is a better dancer than v.

Despite the benefits of the state-of-the-art social influence analysis techniques, a key limitation is their inability to systematically

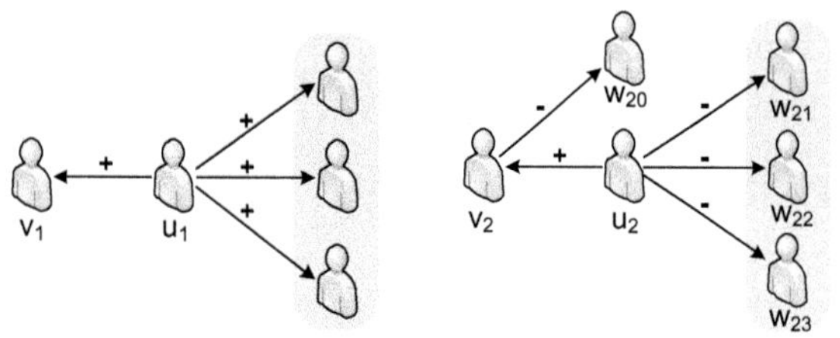

Figure 2: Conformity and negative edge effect.

exploit the aforementioned second and third factors for superior analysis. Consider the two signed networks in Figure 2 where an edge $\overrightarrow{uv}$ with positive (*resp.,* negative) sign indicates u trust (*resp.,* distrust) v. The shadowed part depicts the conformity of individuals u_1 and u_2. Specifically, u_1 is easily convinced by others whereas u_2 is not. Thus, it is easier for v_1 to influence u_1 than v_2 to influence u_2. However, state-of-the-art approaches have ignored this issue and failed to differentiate between these two cases. Thus, they may compute the same *influence score* for v_1 and v_2. However, an individual's influence should be increased if a larger number of users conform to her (positive interactions) but decreased if she is distrusted by many individuals (negative interactions).

We propose a novel algorithm called CASINO (**C**onformity-**A**ware **S**ocial **IN**fluence c**O**mputation) that somewhat departs from existing influence analysis techniques in the following way: CASINO focuses on integrating the interplay of influence and conformity of individuals for social influence analysis by exploiting the positive and negative signs of edges. *To the best of our knowledge, we are the first to study the interplay of influentials and conformers with the goal of social influence analysis.* Additionally, CASINO is *context-aware,* allowing the same individual to exhibit different influence and conformity over different topics of social interactions.

Given a social network, if it is a *context-aware* one, then CASINO first extracts a set of *topic-based subgraphs.* Each subgraph depicts the social interactions between individuals associated with a specific topic. Since the edges of a social network may not be always explicitly labeled with positive or negative signs, CASINO exploits an existing sentiment analysis technique to label the edges in each topic-based subgraph. Finally, given a set of signed topic-based subgraphs, the algorithm iteratively computes the *influence* and *conformity indices* of each individual in each subgraph. By applying CASINO to real-world online social media sites (*Slashdot* (`slashdot.org`), *Epinions* (`www.epinions.com`), and *Twitter*), we strongly demonstrate the effectiveness and superiority of CASINO compared to state-of-the-art approaches and at the same time reveal several interesting characteristics of influentials and conformers in these sites.

2. RELATED WORK

Leskovec et al. [7] used logistic regression to predict the signs of edges in signed networks by exploiting 7-dimensional degree features and 16-dimensional triad features. Cai et al. [3] proposed another feature (*i.e.,* influence) aside from the 7-dimensional degree features in [7]. A PageRank-like algorithm was developed to compute the influence of individual users and then use it as another feature in an SVM classifier to predict the signs of edges. In contrast, we not only study the influence of u on the sign of edge $\overrightarrow{uv}$ but also investigate the conformity of v and its effect on u's influence. Moreover, we also enable the same individual to exhibit different influence and conformity in different topics.

The notion of *conformity* originated in social psychology and is defined as yielding to perceived group pressure by copying the behavior and beliefs of others [2]. We are inspired by the conformity study in social psychology and utilize it to enhance social influence analysis in online social networks. We take into account the conformity in social influence and propose a model to evaluate the conformity in a social group.

3. INFLUENCE AND CONFORMITY

In this section, we formally introduce the notion of *influence* and *conformity* in the context of signed social networks.

Social interactions in online social networks can be either positive (*i.e.,* friendship) or negative (*i.e.,* distrust and opposition). For instance in *Epinions*, people can give both positive and negative ratings to other users. In online discussion sites such as *Slashdot*, users can tag other users as "friends" (positive) and "foes" (negative). In *Twitter*, the retweet can be a positive or a negative one. In the following discussion, we treat such social interaction as signed directed graph.

In a *signed* social network $G(V,E)$, each edge has a positive or negative sign depending on whether it expresses a positive or negative attitude from the generator of the edge to the recipient [7]. A positive sign indicates that the recipient supports the opinion of the generator whereas the negative sign represents otherwise. For example, Figure 2(b) depicts a signed social network. The positive edge $E^+ = \{\overrightarrow{u_2v_2}\}$ represents trust relationship while the negative ones ($E^- = \{\overrightarrow{w_{20}v_2}, \overrightarrow{u_2w_{21}}, \overrightarrow{u_2w_{22}}, \overrightarrow{u_2w_{23}}\}$) represent distrust relationships. Note that the signs on the edges are not always available explicitly. In networks such as *Epinions* and *Slashdot*, the sign of each edge is explicitly provided. However, in other networks such as blogosphere and *Twitter* the sign of each edge is not explicitly available. In this case, we need to preprocess the network using text mining methods to discover signs associated with the links (detailed in Section 4). Consequently, a social network $G(V,E)$ containing both positive and negative edges can be represented using a pair of graphs $G^+(V,E^+)$ and $G^-(V,E^-)$ denoting the induced graph of positive edges E^+ (trust/agreement) and negative edges E^- (distrust/disagreement), respectively.

In our approach, each individual (vertex) in a signed network is associated with a pair of *influence index* and *conformity index* to describe the power of influence and conformity. Reconsider the signed network in Figure 2(b). Intuitively, the influence of v_2 should increase as aggregated conformity of those who trust v_2 (*i.e.,* u_2) increases. On the other hand, the influence of v_2 should decrease if the aggregated conformity of those who distrust v_2 (*i.e.,* w_{20}) increases. Thus, the *influence index* of an individual should capture this interplay of influence and conformity and penalize her whenever necessary.

DEFINITION 1. ***[Influence Index]*** *Let $G^+(V,E^+)$ and $G^-(V,E^-)$ be the induced graphs of the signed social network $G(V,E)$. The influence index of vertex $v \in V$, denoted as $\Phi(v)$, is defined as follows.*

$$\Phi(v) = \sum_{\overrightarrow{uv} \in E^+} \Omega(u) - \sum_{\overrightarrow{uv} \in E^-} \Omega(u)$$

where $\Omega(u)$ represents the conformity index of vertex $u \in V$. ∎

Similarly, the *conformity index* of u_2 in Figure 2(b) depends on the influences of vertices which are trusted or distrusted by u_2. Intuitively, as the aggregated influence of those vertices which u_2 trust (*e.g.,* v_2) increases, u_2 is more inclined to conform to others. On the other hand, when the aggregated influence of vertices which u_2 distrust (*e.g.,,* w_{21}, w_{22}, w_{23}) increases, u_2 is less inclined to conform to others. This intuition is captured by *conformity index* which is defined as follows.

Algorithm 1: The CASINO algorithm.

Input: Social network $G(V,E)$
Output: the influence index $\mathbb{I}_A = (\Phi_A(u_1), \Phi_A(u_2), \ldots, \Phi_A(u_\ell))$ and conformity index $\mathbb{C}_A = (\Omega_A(u_1), \Omega_A(u_2), \ldots, \Omega_A(u_\ell))$ for $V = \{u_1, u_2, \ldots, u_\ell\}$ and for each topic A

1 **begin**
2   **if** *G is context-aware* **then**
3     $\mathcal{G} \leftarrow$ **extractSubgraph**(G);
4   **else**
5     $\mathcal{G} = \{G\}$;
6   **foreach** $G_A \in \mathcal{G}$ **do**
7   **if** *G_A is not a signed network* **then**
8       $(G_A^+(V_A, E_A^+), G_A^-(V_A, E_A^-)) \leftarrow$ **edgeLabel**(G_A);
9     $(\mathbb{I}_A, \mathbb{C}_A) \leftarrow$ **indicesCompute**($G_A^+(V_A, E_A^+), G_A^-(V_A, E_A^-)$);
10 **end**

Algorithm 2: The *edgeLabel* procedure.

Input: Topic-based subgraph $G_A(V_A, E_A)$ induced by topic A,
Output: $G_A^+(V_A, E_A^+)$ and $G_A^-(V_A, E_A^-)$ such that: $E_A^+ \cup E_A^- = E_A$ and $E_A^+ \cap E_A^- = \emptyset$

1 **begin**
2   $E_A^+ = E_A^- = \emptyset$;
3   **foreach** $\overrightarrow{uAv} \in E_A$ **do**
4     $u.sentiment \leftarrow LingPipe.$**sentExtr**($u$);
5     $v.sentiment \leftarrow LingPipe.$**sentExtr**($v$);
6   **if** $|u.sentiment - v.sentiment| < \varepsilon$ **then**
7       $E_A^+ = E_A^+ \cup \{\overrightarrow{uAv}\}$
8   **else**
9       $E_A^- = E_A^- \cup \{\overrightarrow{uAv}\}$
10 **end**

DEFINITION 2. ***[Conformity Index]*** *Let $G^+(V, E^+)$ and $G^-(V, E^-)$ be the induced graphs of the signed social network $G(V,E)$. The conformity index of vertex $u \in V$, denoted as $\Omega(u)$, is defined as follows.*

$$\Omega(u) = \sum_{\overrightarrow{uv} \in E^+} \Phi(v) - \sum_{\overrightarrow{uv} \in E^-} \Phi(v)$$

where $\Phi(v)$ is the influence index of vertex $v \in V$. ∎

Thus, according to the above definition the influence index of v_2 in Figure 2(b) can be computed as $\Phi(v_2) = \Omega(u_2) - \Omega(w_{20})$. The conformity index of u_2 is computed as $\Omega(u_2) = \Phi(v_2) - \Phi(w_{21}) - \Phi(w_{22}) - \Phi(w_{23})$. Observe that the aforementioned definitions of influence and conformity are mutually dependent on each other. Consequently, a recursive computation framework is necessary to compute these two indices.

4. THE CASINO ALGORITHM

In this section, we formally describe the algorithm CASINO for computing conformity and influence indices of individuals in a social network containing positive and negative edges. Online social networks can be classified into *context-aware* and *context-free* networks. The former represent networks where the edges are associated with topics (context) as social interactions may often involve conversations on specific topics. For example, each conversation in *Twitter* is based on a specific topic. On the other hand, interactions in context-free networks do not involve specific topics. For example, in *Epinions* and *Slashdot* individuals trust (distrust) each other regardless of any specific topic. The leftmost social network in Figure 3 is an example of context-aware social network where an edge labeled as A_1, A_2 indicates that the pair of individuals communicate with each other on topics A_1 and A_2.

The CASINO algorithm is outlined in Algorithm 1 and consists of three phases, namely the *topic-based subgraph extraction* phase (Line 3), the *edge labeling* phase (Line 8), and the *indices computation* phase (Line 9).

Figure 3 depicts an overview of CASINO algorithm. Given a social network $G(V,E)$, if it is context-aware then the *topic-based subgraph extraction* phase extracts a set of subgraphs $\mathcal{G}$ where each subgraph $G_A(V_A, E_A) \in \mathcal{G}$ contains all the vertices and edges in G associated with a specific topic A. Each subgraph G_A represents positive or negative attitudes of individuals toward opinions of others in G with respect to the topic A. For instance, in Figure 3, this phase generates three topic-based subgraphs, namely, G_{A_1}, G_{A_2}, and G_{A_3}, for topics A_1, A_2, and A_3, respectively. Recall that edges of a social network may not be explicitly labeled with positive or negative signs. This is especially true for context-aware networks (*e.g., Twitter*). On the other hand, links in many context-free networks (*e.g., Slashdot* and *Epinions*) are explicitly labeled with signs. Hence, it is important to label the edges in each topic-based subgraph G_A. The objective of the *edge labeling* phase is to assign sign to each edge by analyzing the sentiment expressed by the edge. Figure 3 depicts the labeling of G_{A_1}. Finally, given a set of signed topic-based subgraphs $\mathcal{G}$, the goal of the *indices computation* phase is to iteratively compute the influence and conformity indices of each individual in each $G_A \in \mathcal{G}$. Observe that a vertex v in G may have multiple pairs of indices if v is involved in more than one topic-based subgraph. Since the first phase is straightforward, we now elaborate on the remaining two phases in turn.

The edge labeling phase. The edge labeling method varies with dataset. In this paper, we adopt the method described in Algorithm 2. For each edge $\overrightarrow{uAv}$ (the edge pointing from u to v on context topic A) in G_A, we identify 5-level sentiment (*i.e.,* like, somewhat like, neutral, somewhat dislike, dislike) expressed at both ends using *LingPipe* [1] which is a popular sentiment mining package adopted in several recent research [4] (Lines 4-5). If the sentiments at both ends are similar (*sentiment similarity threshold* is less than ε), we denote the edge as positive (Lines 6-7). Otherwise, we denote it as negative (Lines 8-9).

Indices computation phase. Given a topic A and topic-based subgraph G_A, the preceding phase generates G_A^+ and G_A^-. Without loss of generality, assume that there are $|\mathcal{G}|$ different topics. Then, we are able to compute an individual's influence and conformity indices for each topic (*i.e.,* $\Phi_A(u)$ and $\Omega_A(u)$). Algorithm 3 outlines the strategy for computing a pair of influence and conformity indices ($\Phi(u)$, $\Omega(u)$) for each vertex u. It first initializes the influence index and conformity index of all vertices to be 1 (Lines 1-4). Subsequently, in each iteration it computes them for each vertex by using the values of the indices in previous iteration (Lines 6-8) and normalizing these values using the square root of the summation of all vertices' index values (Lines 9-13). The algorithm terminates when both indices converge. In [8], we have proved that CASINO is guaranteed to converge after a fixed number of iterations n. Observe that the technique can easily be extended to compute the aggregated indices of an individual by taking into account the entire social network G over all topics $A = 1, \ldots, |\mathcal{G}|$. In this case, E^+ and E^- in Definitions 1 and 2 are replaced by $\bigcup_{A=1}^{|\mathcal{G}|} E_A^+$ and $\bigcup_{A=1}^{|\mathcal{G}|} E_A^-$, respectively.

5. EXPERIMENTAL STUDY

In this section, we present the experiments conducted to evaluate the performance of CASINO and report some of the results obtained. A more detailed results is available in [8]. To this end, we borrow

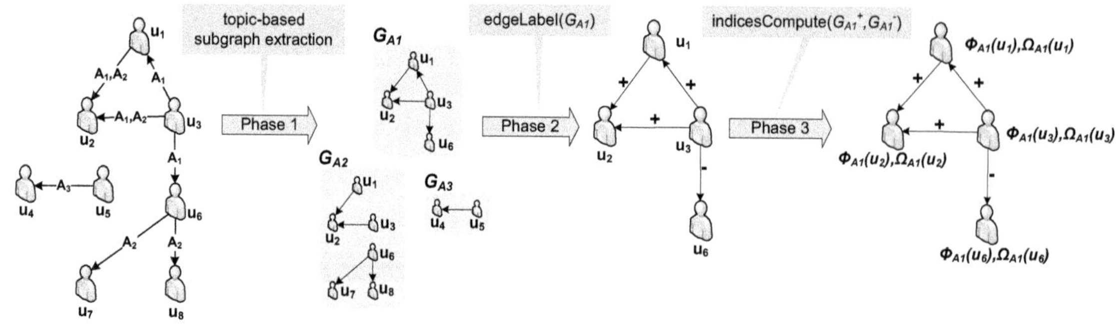

Figure 3: Overview of CASINO.

Algorithm 3: The *indicesCompute* procedure.

Input: $G(V,E) = G^+(V,E^+) \cup G^-(V,E^-)$
Output: the influence index $\mathbb{I} = (\Phi(u_1), \Phi(u_2), \ldots, \Phi(u_\ell))$ and conformity index $\mathbb{C} = (\Omega(u_1), \Omega(u_2), \ldots, \Omega(u_\ell))$ for $V = \{u_1, u_2, \ldots, u_\ell\}$

begin
  $k = 1$ /*initialize iteration counter*/ ;
  foreach $u \in V$ **do**
    $\Phi^k(u) = \Omega^k(u) = 1$
  while $\mathbb{I}$ *or* $\mathbb{C}$ *not converged* **do**
    foreach $u \in V$ **do**
      $\Phi_0^{k+1}(u) = \sum_{\vec{vu} \in E^+} \Omega^k(v) - \sum_{\vec{vu} \in E^-} \Omega(v);$
      $\Omega_0^{k+1}(u) = \sum_{\vec{uv} \in E^+} \Phi^k(v) - \sum_{\vec{uv} \in E^-} \Phi(v);$
    foreach $u \in V$ **do**
      $\Phi^{k+1}(u) = \frac{\Phi_0^{k+1}(u)}{\sqrt{\sum_{v \in V} \Phi_0^{k+1}(v)^2}};$
      $\Omega^{k+1}(u) = \frac{\Omega_0^{k+1}(u)}{\sqrt{\sum_{v \in V} \Omega_0^{k+1}(v)^2}};$
    $\mathbb{I}^{k+1} = (\Phi^{k+1}(u_1), \Phi^{k+1}(u_2), \ldots, \Phi^{k+1}(u_l));$
    $\mathbb{C}^{k+1} = (\Omega^{k+1}(u_1), \Omega^{k+1}(u_2), \ldots, \Omega^{k+1}(u_l));$
    $k = k + 1;$
end

Table 1: Statistics of datasets.

Dataset	*#nodes*	*#edges*	*#positive edges*	*#negative edges*
Slashdot	77,357	516,575	396,378	120,197
Epinions	131,828	841,372	717,667	123,705
Twitter	576,894	1,230,748	1,015,492	195,256

the experimental framework articulated by Leskovec et al. [7], in which machine-learning based approach is used for discovering the presence of unknown edges and edge sign prediction by exploiting various edge features. By considering conformity and influence indices as new features for classification, it is expected that these additional features will provide more concrete evidence for edge prediction compared to state-of-the-art strategies.

We consider the following context-free and context-aware networks where each link is explicitly or implicitly labeled as positive or negative. (a) **Context-free network data:** In order to compare the performance of CASINO with state-of-the-art efforts on influence evaluation in signed networks [3, 7], we adopt the same datasets that have been used in these work: *Slashdot* and *Epinions* [1] (Table 1). Recall that these network data are context-free and contain explicit signs of edges to indicate the attitudes of individuals towards one another. (b) **Context-aware network data:** We use the *Twitter* dataset to investigate the performance on a context-aware network. The dataset was crawled using the *Twitter* API [2] during Dec 2010 to Feb 2011 (Table 1). We extracted top 20 trends keywords at hourly duration and retrieved up to 1500 tweets for each trend. Then we identified the relationships between all the tweets in the dataset. The reader may refer to [8] for details related to statistics of the dataset and construction of context-aware interaction graphs from it.

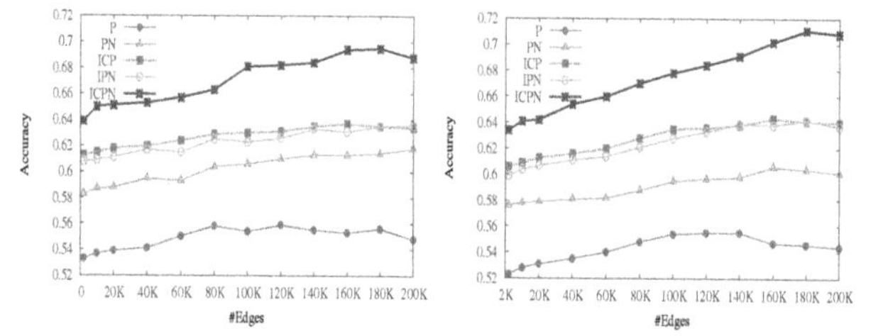

(a) Epinions (b) Slashdot

Figure 4: Positive edge presence prediction.

5.1 Experimental Setup

We have implemented CASINO in Java and run all the experiments on a 1.86GHz Intel 6300 machine with 4GB RAM with Windows XP. The algorithm converges after average 30 iterations. We set the *sentiment similarity threshold* ε (Algorithm 2) to 1.

Similar to [3, 7], in our experiments, the task of edge sign prediction is considered as a binary classification problem. We adopted SVM^{light} classifier [5] and classification *accuracy* is taken as the main measure for evaluation. The reason for adopting accuracy as evaluation measure over precision and recall is that the former is suitable for quantifying the prediction performances of both positive and negative samples. This is crucial in our framework as in most experiments both positive and negative edges are being predicted. In order to avoid biased classification, we adopt the same strategy used in [3, 7]. Specifically, we create a balanced dataset with same number of positive and negative edges for training and testing. Based on the learned model (discussed below), we predict a label 1 or -1 for each target edge indicating its possibility to be positive or negative, respectively.

In order to compare the prediction accuracy of the proposed approach with state-of-the-art efforts, a baseline classifier is constructed by referring to the structural features discussed in [7]. Specifically, given an edge from vertex u to v, a 7-dimensional feature vector $\{d^+_{in}(v), d^-_{in}(v), d^+_{out}(u), d^-_{out}(u), d_{in}(v), d_{out}(u), C(u,v)\}$ is constructed, where features $d^+_{in}(v)$ and $d^-_{in}(v)$ denote the number of positive and negative incoming edges to v, features $d^+_{out}(u)$ and $d^-_{out}(u)$ represent the number of positive and negative outgo-

[1] `http://snap.stanford.edu/data/`

[2] `http://dev.twitter.com/doc`

Table 2: Features involved in different approaches. (P: positive, N: negative, I: influence, C: conformity, A: topic)

Features \ Approaches	P	PN	IPN	ICP	ICPN	ICAPN
$d_{in}^{+}(v)$	✓	✓	✓	✓	✓	✓
$d_{in}^{-}(v)$	-	✓	✓	-	✓	✓
$d_{out}^{+}(u)$	✓	✓	✓	✓	✓	✓
$d_{out}^{-}(u)$	-	✓	✓	-	✓	✓
$d_{in}(v)$	-	✓	✓	-	✓	✓
$d_{out}(u)$	-	✓	✓	-	✓	✓
$C(u,v)$	✓	✓	✓	✓	✓	✓
$\Phi(u)$	-	-	✓	-	-	-
$\Phi(v)$	-	-	✓	✓	✓	✓
$\Omega(u)$	-	-	-	✓	✓	✓
context A	-	-	-	-	-	✓
$\Phi_A(v)$	-	-	-	-	-	✓
$\Omega_A(u)$	-	-	-	-	-	✓

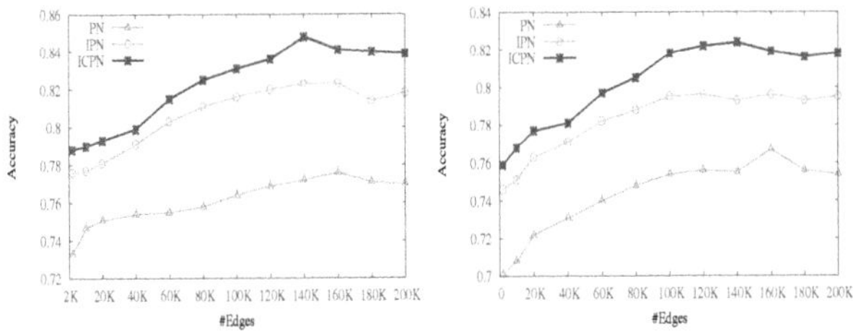

(a) Epinions (b) Slashdot

Figure 5: Signed edge prediction.

ing edges from u, features $d_{in}(v)$ and $d_{out}(u)$ denote the number of in-degree and out-degree of v and u, and $C(u,v)$ denotes the total number of common neighbors of u and v without considering the edge direction. Then, we create variants of this baseline classifier by adding influence index and conformity index as new features. Table 2 describes the features involved in the feature vector for each edge $\overrightarrow{uv}$ for different variations of the baseline classifier.

5.2 Experimental Results

Positive edge presence prediction. We first conduct a series of experiments to predict the presence of positive edges. In order to test the effect of negative edges in predicting the presence of positive edges, we adopted a regression function of SVM^{light} where presence of positive edges are labeled as 1 and negative edges are labeled as -1. Figure 4 shows the average accuracy for the benchmark datasets, where the results are compared between different classifiers for different size of training and testing data. We can make the following observations. First, for each dataset PN performs better than P indicating that information related to negative edges enhance the quality of edge presence prediction. Second, the prediction accuracy is further improved when we incorporate the influence index or conformity index as a feature (ICP and IPN). Note that ICP performs slightly better than IPN but the improvement is not significant. When the training set is large both approaches exhibit similar performance. Third, ICPN consistently reports the best prediction performance. That is, edge presence prediction is enhanced when we consider the interplay between influentials and conformers.

Signed edge prediction. Next, we undertake a series of experiments to predict the signs of edges. Our goal is to predict the signs of edges which maybe either positive or negative. Figure 5 reports the prediction accuracies of the classifiers. Observe that among the three approaches involving both positive and negative edges (PN, IPN, and ICPN), ICPN performs the best, followed by IPN and PN, respectively. Thus, by taking into account the influence and conformity of vertices, the accuracy of sign prediction task can improve significantly.

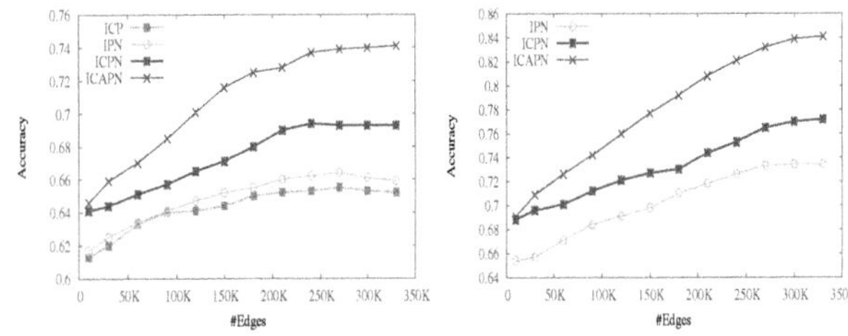

(a) Positive edge presence (b) Edge sign prediction

Figure 6: Context-aware prediction accuracy.

Edge presence and signed edge prediction in context-aware networks. We now report the performance of our model on a context-aware network (*Twitter*). In this experiment we adopt the classifier ICAPN which takes into account the topic information associated with each edge. Figure 6 plots the prediction accuracies of the relevant classifiers. Observe that in both figures ICAPN outperforms the rest. Note that the performances of ICAPN and ICPN are similar when the training set is very small. This is because there may not be enough training edges in each topic-based subgraphs G_A when the training set is very small. Consequently, not enough information is available to accurately compute $\Phi_A(v)$ and $\Omega_A(u)$. All these evidences demonstrate that by leveraging on the influence and conformity indices in topic-based subgraphs, the proposed model leads to superior prediction performance for both positive edge presence and edge sign prediction tasks.

Influentials and conformers. We analyze the list of influentials and conformers detected by the CASINO algorithm. Figure 7 depicts the distribution heatmaps of influence index versus conformity index for each benchmark dataset. For each individual u in a network we compute $\Phi(u)$ and $\Omega(u)$ and represent it as a point in the influence-conformity 2-D plane. Then we separate the plane into grids of size 0.005×0.005 and count the number of points in each grid. The color shade of a grid denotes the number of points residing in it. Note that both influence index and conformity index are normalized into the range of $[0,1)$. For each figure, we explicitly draw a boundary line along which the vertices exhibit identical influence index and conformity index. Observe that the line separates the influence-conformity plane into two areas. In the sequel, we refer to the top area as '*Area I*' and the down one as '*Area II*'. The points belonging to '*Area I*' exhibit higher influence index compared to conformity index, indicating that individuals in this area are more prone to influence others than being influenced. We refer to them as *influence-biased*. On the other hand, '*Area II*' represent individuals who are more prone to be influenced than influencing others. We refer to these individuals as *conformity-biased*.

We first analyze the context-free networks (Figures 7(a)(b)). Consider Figure 7(a) related to *Epinions* dataset. Observe that 31% of all individuals belong to '*Area I*'. Consequently, fewer number of individuals in this network are influence-biased. That is, majority of individuals in *Epinions* are often conforming to the others. Similar phenomenon also exists in the *Slashdot* dataset. Observe that those vertices in *Epinions* which exhibit very high conformity index values also have high influence index values. On the other hand, vertices with highest influence index values have a wider range of conformity indices (*i.e.*, from 0 to 0.11). Such phenomenon indicates that in *Epinions* most influence-biased individuals may also conform to others whereas the most conformity-biased individuals are always influencing others. Interestingly, the phenomenon is different in *Slashdot* dataset (Figure 7(b)). Specifically, individuals who are associated with highest influence index values have very

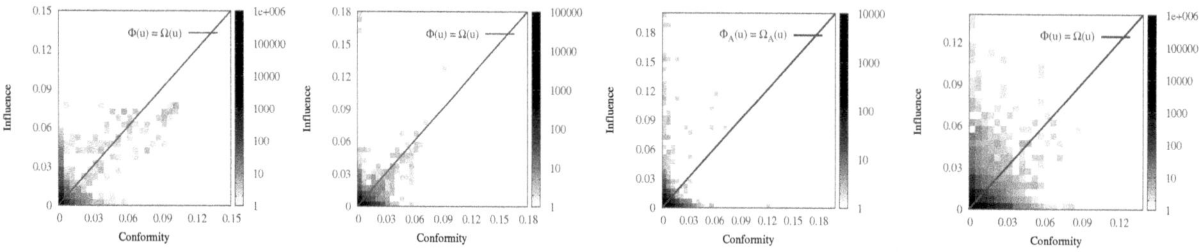

(a) Epinions (b) Slashdot (c) Twitter (Top-1) (d) Twitter (All)

Figure 7: Influence vs. conformity distribution heatmap.

Table 3: Top 10 authors with the highest influence index and conformity index.

Rank	Influential twitter (#positive in-links/#in-links)			Conformer twitter (#positive out-links/#out-links)		
	All	*Top-1*	*Top-2*	*All*	*Top-1*	*Top-2*
1	142987924 (66/73)	3453454 (13/13)	950596 (31/34)	51389816 (35/37)	121836131 (14/16)	49276778 (101/144)
2	49276778 (61/82)	56068621 (11/11)	190108655 (11/11)	172039151 (31/34)	105332925 (13/14)	202346609 (45/61)
3	119394881 (60/77)	3984874 (10/10)	3498571 (8/9)	177173204 (30/35)	177255919 (11/12)	197538544 (26/30)
4	231134989 (55/71)	133282617 (11/11)	147327886 (5/5)	143062806 (27/34)	193206052 (11/12)	184930795 (22/26)
5	2109823 (56/72)	199855121 (7/7)	49126931 (5/5)	128118710 (25/33)	36525648 (9/10)	148335502 (21/23)
6	92503401 (55/78)	8234375 (5/5)	121158546 (5/5)	130414633 (30/41)	90723076 (7/8)	171387567 (17/20)
7	206661373 (51/66)	1465130 (3/3)	129009252 (5/5)	4782790 (23/30)	123606641 (6/8)	126407259 (18/22)
8	220490093 (46/60)	2894822 (3/3)	79897503 (4/4)	125551983 (22/34)	51513825 (6/6)	114455733 (14/20)
9	168175236 (40/51)	21755211 (2/2)	83629945 (4/4)	91930055 (21/28)	203774695 (5/6)	217826740 (15/20)
10	171287044 (41/62)	4051581 (2/2)	166830172 (4/4)	145339829 (22/31)	203780314 (4/4)	159724683 (12/17)

small conformity index (*i.e.,* less than 0.02). But individuals with highest conformity index may not exhibit small influence index values. In fact, the conformity index values of these conformity-biased individuals are distributed along the boundary line ($\Phi(u) = \Omega(u)$). Thus, we can make the following observations regarding *Slashdot*. Firstly, there are a few influence-biased individuals who exhibit very high influence but are not easily influenced by others. Secondly, there do not exist conformity-biased individuals who are not influencing others at all.

Next, we analyze the context-aware network (Figures 7(c)(d)). Figures 7(c) show the distributions of influence and conformity indices for the top-1 topic (`Mumford & Sons`) with the most number of tweets (4390). Observe that 40% of all the individuals fall in '*Area I*' for Figure 7(c). Notably, it exhibits *certain* influence-biased characteristics similar to *Slashdot*. That is, there are a few influence-biased individuals who exhibit very high influence but are not easily influenced by others. This similarity may be due to the fact that both *Slashdot* and *Twitter* are driven by user conversations where majority individuals are commenting or following a few individuals who started the conversations. Figure 7(d) plots the distribution of indices computed over *all* topics. In this case, 41% of all individuals belong to '*Area I*'.

Table 3 shows IDs of top-10 authors who exhibit the highest influence index and conformity index for top-1, top-2 and all topics. Consider the top two twitters for all topics. The author `'142987924'` who has the highest influence index receives 66 conforming edges out of 73 in-links over 22 topics. On the other hand, the author `'51389816'` who exhibits the highest conformity index initiates 35 conforming edges out of 37 out-links over 37 topics indicating that she has high chance to conform to others' opinions in almost all the topics she is involved in. We can make the following observations. Firstly, none of the top-10 authors occupies a position in *both* indices. Secondly, the top-10 individuals having highest influence and conformity indices are different for different topics. This confirms our hypothesis that social influence phenomenon is context-sensitive as same individual may exhibit different influence and conformity over different topics of social interactions.

6. CONCLUSIONS

The social influence analysis for online social networks is an important problem with applications to viral marketing and information dissemination among others. State-of-the-art social influence analysis techniques ignore two equally important factors, namely, negative relationships and conformity of people. In this paper, we propose a novel algorithm for social influence analysis called CASINO, which quantifies the influence and conformity of each individual in a network by utilizing the positive and negative relationships between individuals. Our exhaustive experimental study using several online social media sites demonstrates the effectiveness and superior accuracy of CASINO compared to state-of-the-art methods. Specifically, our investigation revealed that the knowledge of conformity of individuals enhance the accuracy of social influence analysis. We also observed several interesting characteristics of influentials and conformers in *Slashdot*, *Epinions*, and *Twitter*.

Acknowledgement: The work of the third author is supported by MOE AcRF Tier-1 Grant RG13/10, Singapore.

7. REFERENCES

[1] A-lias. Lingpipe 4.0.1. http://alias-i.com/lingpipe, 2008.
[2] E. Aronson, T. D. Wilson, and R. M. Akert. *Social Psychology*. Prentice Hall, fifth edition, Feb. 2004.
[3] K. Cai, S. Bao, Z. Yang, et al. Oolam: an opinion oriented link analysis model for influence persona discovery. In *WSDM*, 2011.
[4] Y. Jo and A. H. Oh. Aspect and sentiment unification model for online review analysis. In *WSDM*, 2011.
[5] T. Joachims. Making large-scale SVM learning practical. In B. Schölkopf, C. Burges, and A. Smola, editors, *Advances in Kernel Methods - Support Vector Learning*. MIT Press, USA, 1999.
[6] D. Kempe, J. M. Kleinberg, and É. Tardos. Maximizing the spread of influence through a social network. In *KDD*, 2003.
[7] J. Leskovec, D. P. Huttenlocher, and J. M. Kleinberg. Predicting positive and negative links in online social networks. In *WWW*, 2010.
[8] H. Li, S. S. Bhowmick, and A. Sun. CASINO: Towards conformity-aware social influence analysis in online social networks. Technical report, Available at `http://www.cais.ntu.edu.sg/~assourav/TechReports/CASINO-TR.pdf`, July 2011.

Mining Direct Antagonistic Communities in Explicit Trust Networks

David Lo, Didi Surian, Kuan Zhang*, and Ee-Peng Lim
School of Information Systems, Singapore Management University
Singapore
{davidlo,didisurian,eplim}@smu.edu.sg, zkspirit2@gmail.com

ABSTRACT

There has been a recent increase of interest in analyzing trust and friendship networks to gain insights about relationship dynamics among users. Many sites such as Epinions, Facebook, and other social networking sites allow users to declare trusts or friendships between different members of the community. In this work, we are interested in extracting direct antagonistic communities (DACs) within a rich trust network involving trusts and distrusts. Each DAC is formed by two sub-communities with trust relationships among members of each sub-community but distrust relationships across the sub-communities. We develop an efficient algorithm that could analyze large trust networks leveraging the unique property of direct antagonistic community. We have experimented with synthetic and real datasets (myGamma and Epinions) to demonstrate the scalability of our proposed solution.

Categories and Subject Descriptors

H.2.8 [**Database Management**]: Database Applications—*Data Mining*; J.4 [**Computer Applications**]: Social and Behavioral Sciences—*Sociology*

General Terms

Algorithms, Experimentation

Keywords

Direct antagonistic community, Mining maximal bi-cliques, Signed social network

1. INTRODUCTION

Each of us forms trust and distrust relationships with others. With these relationships, communities are formed. At times, due to the nature of human interactions, some communities exhibit antagonistic behaviors among their members. Examples of such communities are many including social groups that hold differing opinions on topics such as industrialism vs. conservation, and formal organizations that are direct competitors in a market.

Several researchers have studied the nature of antagonistic communities [6, 5, 7]. It is well known that individual level antagonism exists in any social network. However, the existence of well "organized" form of antagonism between sub-groups should be detected in an early stage because they are potentially detrimental to the productivity and harmony of the community. Moreover, identification of antagonistic communities in the social networks could potentially open a path to further study about the structure of the community, the evolution of the community, etc.

Antagonistic communities on the other hand are not always bad. In some cases, they are actually welcomed. In massively multiple player online games, gamers are expected to form groups to fight with gamers that do not belong to the same groups. Here, a game's success depends very much on antagonistic behaviors among different gamer groups. The more antagonistic, the more challenging is the game.

In this study, our goal is to discover antagonistic communities automatically from their explicit trust and distrust relationships. We design a new graph mining algorithm to mine antagonistic communities by leveraging past work on computation of strongest connected components and bi-cliques. We take as an input a large graph of trusts and distrusts. From this graph, we would like to extract all pairs of user groups where within each pair, each group forms a connected trust network within themselves but distrusts members of the other group.

The contributions of this work are as follows:

1 We propose a new problem of mining antagonistic communities based on their explicit trust and distrust links.
2 We build a novel algorithm by using existing building blocks that have been shown to scale to large dataset hence enabling our approach to scale too.
3 We experiment our approach to extract antagonistic communities from real social networks, including a trust-distrust network and a friend-foe network.

The structure of this paper is as follows. Section 2 describes related work. Section 3 describes some preliminary definitions. Section 4 describes our approach. Experiments are presented in Section 5. We conclude and discuss future work in Section 6.

*The work was done while the author was with School of Information Systems, Singapore Management University

CIKM'11, October 24–28, 2011, Glasgow, Scotland, UK.

2. RELATED WORK

Vuong *et al.* [13] investigated content deletion between any two Wikipedia users as a form of disputes between them, and developed models to determine the degrees of controversy of users and articles using the dispute information. Different from Vuong *et al.*'s work, we mine direct antagonistic communities from networks with trust-distrust/friend-foe links.

Social network researchers have conducted a number of studies in signed networks (i.e., networks with both positive and negative relationships) in order to give more understanding about interaction between people in a community. The social balance theory developed for signed networks identifies triads with all positive relationships and triads with only one positive and two negative relationships as the balanced structure constructs [9]. Triads of other forms are known to be unbalanced. Dorean [8] studied how to partition signed social network. Yang *et al.* [14] mined communities in signed network using a heuristic clustering approach. In this work, we capture a set of people that are linked together by trust relationships and they also consistently oppose a common set of "enemies" in online social networks.

There are also several researchers who have studied intergroup antagonism concept [6, 7]. This body of work however has not been widely validated on large online social networks.

The enumeration of bi-cliques from graph data has been studied before. Including in this body of work are the work by Makino and Uno in [11] and Li *et al.* in [10]. The work by Li *et al.* in [10], to the best of our knowledge, is the latest in the series. They proposed a mapping between maximal bi-clique mining to frequent itemset mining problem [4]. We make use of their translation and extend their technique to mine for Direct Antagonistic Communities (DACs). A DAC is not a bi-clique, but some constraints within a DAC, in particular distrust relationships could be mapped to the problem of finding bi-cliques within a dataset. We use specific nature of DACs to prune additional nodes. The resultant technique scales well to mine from large real networks at low minimum size threshold within 15 minutes.

The closest to our work is the very recent work by Zhang *et al.* in [15]. Zhang *et al.* proposed an approach to mine for antagonistic communities based on rating data. Different from Zhang *et al.*'s work, in this work we mine for antagonistic communities based on *explicit* trust relationships. We believe *explicit* trust relationships are more reliable than common or differing ratings. A user could trust another user although they might have different "taste" on some common items of interest. Also, due to the different nature of the problem, there is a need to develop a new algorithm to mine for *direct* antagonistic communities from *explicit* trust networks.

3. PRELIMINARIES & PROBLEM DEFN.

In this section, we first describe preliminary concepts and definitions on graphs and frequent pattern mining. We then formalize some new definitions and our problem statement.

3.1 Preliminaries

Some standard definitions of graph, strongly connected subgraphs, strongly connected components, and bi-cliques are given in Definitions 1, 2, 3, 4 respectively.

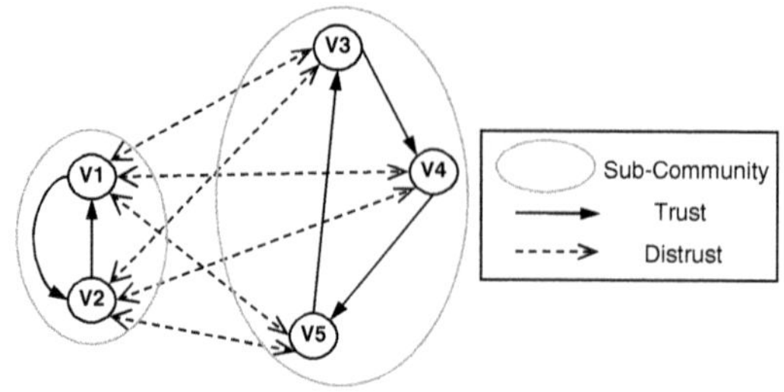

Figure 1: A Direct Antagonistic Community.

Definition 1 **(Graph).** *A graph is composed of a set of nodes and edges and is denoted as G=(N,E). An edge is a mapping from one node to another node.*

Definition 2 **(Strongly Connected Subgraphs).** *A strongly connected subgraph (SCS) is a sub-graph G' in a larger graph G where: For each node n' in G', there exists a series of edges in G' connecting n' to every other node in G'.*

Definition 3 **(Strongly Connected Component).** *A strongly connected component (SCC) is a strongly connected sub-graph that is maximal in size.*

Definition 4 **(Bi-Cliques).** *A bi-clique is a graph whose nodes could be decomposed of two sets of nodes where:*

1. *There are no edges among the nodes in each set*
2. *Each node is connected to every node in the other set.*

We denote a bi-clique as (L,R), where L and R are the two sets of nodes having the characteristics described above.

Next, we describe some preliminary definitions of transaction database, mapping function, itemsets, frequent itemsets and closed patterns in Definitions 5, 6, 7, 8 respectively. These terms are commonly used in frequent itemset mining first proposed in [4].

Definition 5 **(Transaction DB & Mapping Func.).** *A transaction is a set of items from a domain D. A transaction database DB consists of a bag of transactions. Let map(S) be a mapping between a set of items S to the identifiers of the transactions in the DB containing S.*

Definition 6 **(Itemset Patterns).** *An itemset pattern is a set of items. Consider a transaction database DB, the support of a itemset pattern P, is the number of transactions in DB that are super-sets of P. The support of P is denoted as sup(P).*

Definition 7 **(Frequent Itemsets).** *An itemset P is a frequent itemset with respect to a transaction database DB and a minimum support threshold min_sup if* $sup(P) > min\_sup$.

Definition 8 **(Closed Patterns).** *An itemset P is a closed pattern, if P is frequent and there is no P' where* $P' \supseteq P$ *and* $sup(P') = sup(P)$.

3.2 Definitions & Problem Statement

We take as input a network of users expressing trusts/friendships and distrusts/foe relationships among themselves. We refer to this network as a trust-distrust (T-D) network defined in Definition 9.

Definition 9 (**Trust-Distrust Network**). *A trust-distrust (T-D) network is a graph whose nodes represent individuals and edges represent trust relationships among them. The edges are directed and are labeled with either: trust (T) or distrust (D). The nodes are labeled with the identifiers of respective individuals. A trust-distrust network could then be denoted as* $G=(N,E,N_L,E_L)$ *where* N, E, N_L, *and* E_L *correspond to the nodes, edges, a mapping from nodes to labels, and a mapping from edges to labels respectively.*

Our goal is to mine a set of communities of antagonistic groups expressing explicit trust among themselves and distrust with members of the opposing group/sub-community. We refer to these communities as direct antagonistic communities defined in Definition 10.

Definition 10 (**Direct Antagonistic Community**). *A Direct Antagonistic Community (DAC) is composed of two sub-communities L and R. L and R are both SCSs with respect to the directed trust edges. Furthermore L and R form a bi-clique considering bidirectional distrust edges.*

An example of such Direct Antagonistic Community (DAC) is shown in Figure 1.

We are interested in DAC obeying a minimum size requirement, i.e., $|L| \geq min\_size$ and $|R| \geq min\_size$. We refer to such DACs as *significant* DACs. In Figure 1, the DAC example is significant if the minimum size threshold is set at 2; it would not be significant if the minimum size threshold is set at 3.

We next introduce the concept of *redundant* DACs, but first we need to describe *sub-bi-clique* operation. This is defined in Definition 11.

Definition 11 (**Sub-Bi-Clique**). *Consider a bi-clique* $C = (L,R)$. *We define a sub-bi-clique of C, as a bi-clique* $C' = (L',R')$ *where either* $L' \subseteq L$ *and* $R' \subset R$, *or* $L' \subset L$ *and* $R' \subseteq R$. *A sub-bi-clique of a bi-clique is a bi-clique.*

All sub-bi-cliques of a significant DAC are potentially significant DACs. Thus to prevent an explosion on the number of DACs, we mine only a compact representation of DACs. Given a set of mined DACs, we define redundant ones based on Definition 12. Only non-redundant DACs would be mined.

Definition 12 (**Redundant DAC**). *Consider a set of DACs ASET. One DAC a in ASET is deemed as* redundant *iff there exists another DAC a', where considering the bidirectional distrust edges, a is a sub-bi-clique of a'.*

With the above concepts and definitions, our problem definition is as follows:

Problem Definition. Given a trust-distrust network and a minimum size threshold *min_size*, find all significant non-redundant DACs.

4. MINING ANTAGONISTIC COMMUNITIES

In this section, we describe some properties of direct antagonistic communities and present our algorithm to mine them.

4.1 Properties

We use three properties in our mining algorithm outlined below. First, Property 1 describes a rule governing a node's membership to a significant DAC.

Property 1 (**Membership**). *Consider a node n in graph G, if n is not a part of any SCSs of size min_size, n could not be a part of any significant DACs.*

Proof. *From Definition 10, each sub-community in the DAC must be a SCS of size at least min_size. Hence, such a node n could not be a part of any DACs.* □

Next, Property 2 describes the relationship between a strongly connected subgraph and a strongly connected component in a trust-distrust network.

Property 2 (**SCS and SCC**). *Every Strongly Connected Subgraph (SCS) must be a part of a Strongly Connected Component (SCC).*

Proof. *From Definitions 2 & 3, a SCS could either be a SCC, or there is a super-graph of SCS which is a SCC.* □

We now define a new operation to convert a graph to a transaction database.

Definition 13 (**Graph to Transaction DB**). *The GTD operation converts a graph G to a transaction database DB by creating a new set of transactions* $t = \{g' | (g,g') \in G.Edges\}$ *for each node g in G and affixing the identifiers of g and g' to t. The resultant set of transactions is the result of the operation GTD(G).*

Figure 2 illustrates the GTD operation to derive a transaction database. With this operation, the duality between bi-cliques and closed patterns is established by Property 3.

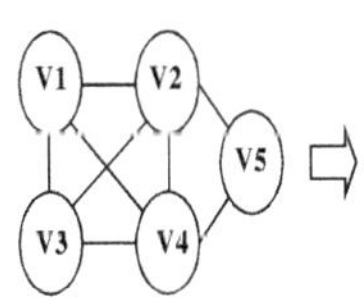

Adjacency Matrix

	V1	V2	V3	V4	V5
V1	0	1	1	1	0
V2	1	0	1	1	1
V3	1	1	0	1	0
V4	1	1	1	0	1
V5	0	1	0	1	0

id	itemsets
V1	V2, V3, V4
V2	V1, V3, V4, V5
V3	V1, V2, V4
V4	V1, V2, V3
V5	V2, V4

Figure 2: Graph to Transaction DB Operation

Property 3 (**Bi-cliques and Patterns: Duality**). *Consider a graph G and a transaction database GTD(G). The set of all bi-cliques correspond to the set* $\{(c,map(c)) | c \in CLS\}$ *where CLS is the set of all closed patterns in GTD(G).*

Proof. *The above property has been proven in [10].* □

4.2 Proposed Algorithm

A Direct Antagonistic Community (DAC) has two basic requirements based on the trust and distrust relationships. On one hand, each community must form trust network in the form of strongly connected component. On the other hand, members of one community must form distrust relationships with all members of the other community. To mine for DACs, we perform the following steps:

1. Project input trust-distrust network g, to a graph g_t keeping only trust edges in graph g.

2. Extract SCCs from g_t of size more than the minimum support size *min_size*. These are candidate communities of DACs. Nodes that are not part of SCCs of size at least *min_size* could not be part of any DACs (see Properties 1 & 2). We keep the set of nodes $N_+ = \{n|n \text{ is a node in the identified SCCs}\}$.

3. Project the input trust-distrust network g, to a graph g_d keeping only nodes in N_+ and bidirectional distrust edges.

4. Identify the set of maximal bi-cliques BCQ from g_d using Property 3.

5. For each bi-clique in BCQ with set of nodes n_b, project the input trust-distrust network g, to a graph g_{n_b} keeping only nodes in n_b and their trust edges. Find SCCs from the projected network g_{n_b}. Each SCC satisfying *min_size* is a part of a DAC.

6. Eliminate redundant DACs. There could still be redundant DACs at the end of step 5. This is the case even after we mine for maximal bi-cliques of distrust at step 4, the DACs are sub-bi-cliques of the maximal one. We iterate through the set of DACs generated at step 5 and remove redundant ones based on Definition 12.

As a running example, we consider the graph shown in Figure 3 (Left). The graph contains trust edges (denoted as solid arrows) and bi-directional distrust edges (denoted as dashed bi-directional arrows).

Pruning by Trust: Steps 1 & 2. First, we prune candidate nodes based on trust relationships. Distrust edges are removed from the projected graph. Based on this trust graph, our goal is to throw away nodes which are not part of any large enough trust networks. Due to the nature of the trust network, the number of links of the nodes in the network follows power law, i.e., most nodes are not connected to any other nodes. Hence, a large number of nodes could be removed from the consideration.

To realize this goal, we employ Tarjan's algorithm [12], that could compute maximal SCCs by a single depth-first search pass on the trust network. Hence, it is very scalable as the runtime cost is linear to the size of the graph. We extract nodes that are part of a maximal SCC with size $\geq$ *min_size*.

Example.Consider *min_size* threshold being set to 2. From the example T-D network described in Figure 3 (Left), there are two SCCs. The first SCC consists of the set {V1,V2}. The second consists of the set {V4,V5,V6,V7}. The two SCCs are drawn in Figure 3 (Right). Hence we only retain nodes in the set {V1,V2,V4,V5,V6,V7} to be considered in the next step.

Pruning by Distrust: Steps 3 & 4. At these steps, we focus on the *strong* (i.e., bi-directional) distrust relationships. We project the input trust network, by removing trust edges and non bi-directional distrust edges. Two sub-communities in a direct antagonistic community must form a bi-clique with respect to the bi-directional distrust edges.

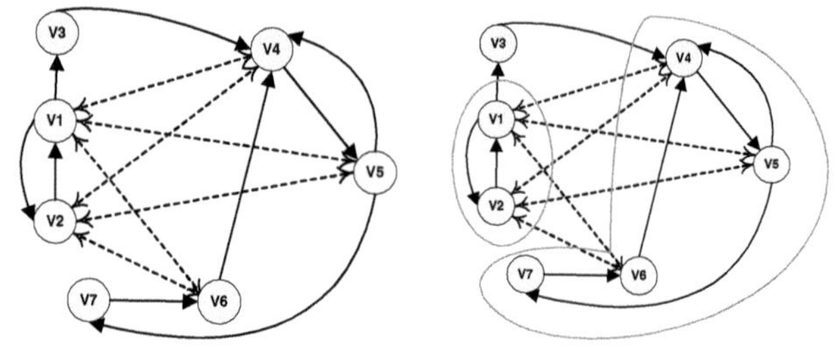

(a) (b)

Figure 3: Running Ex.: T-D Network (Left) & Two SCCs (Right)

TID	Itemset
V1	{V4,V5,V6}
V2	{V4,V5,V6}
V4	{V1,V2}
V5	{V1,V2}
V6	{V1,V2}
V7	{}

Table 1: Running Ex.: Transaction DB

To realize the goal, we adapt a recent algorithm in [10] that extracts maximal bi-cliques from a graph following Property 3. The algorithm would return all maximal bi-cliques from the input bi-directional distrust network.

Example. Consider the distrust network projection on nodes {V4,V5,V6,V7} we come the network shown in Figure 4 (Left). This network is then converted to a transaction database shown in Table 1. Mining for closed patterns from this transaction database would result in the set of patterns: {{V1,V2}, {V4,V5,V6}}. This would correspond to one maximal bi-clique with L = {V1,V2} and R = {V4,V5,V6}.

Formation of DACs : Step 5. Each maximal bi-clique mined at step 4 is not necessarily a DAC as each of the two sets in the bi-clique is not necessarily a connected trust community. A bi-clique could map to 0 or more DACs.

Following Definition 11, every sub-biclique of a bi-clique is a bi-clique and hence satisfies the distrust requirement. Hence, we could extract sub-bi-cliques SBQ from each bi-clique in which each of the two sets of nodes forms a SCS of size larger than *min_size*.

To realize this, we process each bi-clique BCQ identified in step 4. For each of the two sets of nodes in BCQ, i.e., BCQ.L and BCQ.R, we find SCSs on the projected trust network containing nodes in BCQ.L/BCQ.R. These operations would result in two sets of SCSs. Pairing one SCS from one set with another from another set, would form a DAC which could then be included in the final result.

Example. Considering the maximal bi-clique with L = {V1, V2} and R = {V4,V5,V6}, the projection over the trust-distrust network is shown in Figure 4 (Right). From this projection, we could identify a DAC consisting of nodes {V1,V2} which is opposing nodes {V4,V5}. This DAC is shown by the red circles in the figure.

Removal of Redundant DACs : Step 6. Usually, there are no or few redundant DACs left at the end of step 5. The running example is one of such cases. However, there exist corner cases where redundant DACs are present. This is the case as mined DACs are sub-bi-cliques of the maximal bi-cliques mined at steps 3 & 4. We remove redundant DACs

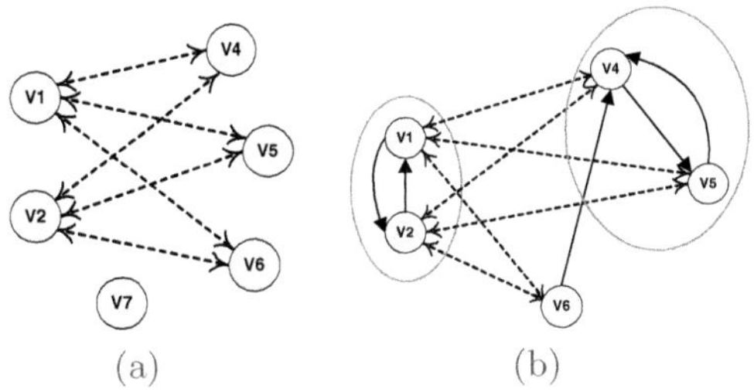

Figure 4: Running Ex.: Distrust Projected Network (Left) & Resultant Projected Network and The Mined DAC (Circled in Red) (Right)

by analyzing the list of DACs mined at step 5 and detect for redundancies based on Definition 12. We do this by comparing each DAC with every other larger DAC mined at step 5; each of these comparisons simply involves checking for subset relations among sub-communities of two DACs which is sufficient to decide whether one is a sub-bi-clique of the other.

We invite interested readers to [1] to investigate a corner case for T-D network where redundant DACs still exist after step 5 of the algorithm.

Pseudocode. Our algorithm's pseudocode is shown in Figure 5. At line 1, we perform graph projection and extract only the trust network from the input T-D network. At lines 2-3, we perform SCC computation and extract nodes that participate in an SCC of size at least *min_size*. At lines 4, we extract bi-directional distrust network from the input T-D network. This network is then converted to a special transaction database, and bi-cliques are identified via a closed itemset mining algorithm (lines 5-6). At lines 7-16, we check each bi-clique if it corresponds to zero, one, or more direct antagonistic communities of size at least *min_size*. At lines 10-11, we construct SCCs from the left and right set of nodes of each bi-cliques considering only trust links. We remove SCCs with size less than *min_size* at line 12. These SCCs are then composed to form direct antagonistic communities (lines 13-15). A non-redundancy check is performed at line 16.

4.3 Baseline Algorithm

The search space of all possible DACs is the set of all possible combinations of members in the T-D Network. As a baseline algorithm we perform a standard depth-first search traversal of this search space. We start with sets of users with one member and then grow each of these sets by adding additional members one by one. At each step of the process, we check if the set is a DAC. Due to space limitation, we present our baseline algorithm in [1].

5. EXPERIMENTS & ANALYSIS

To evaluate the scalability and efficacy of our approach, we experiment with both synthetic and real datasets. We build our own synthetic trust network generator that generates networks of different sizes for scalability test. We also consider two real datasets, a trust/distrust network from Epinions [3] and a friend/foe network from myGamma mobile social network site [2]. All these networks include both positive and negative edges.

The Epinions and myGamma datasets have 56,371 and 629,086 user nodes respectively, and about 250K and 8.1M

```
Procedure Mine Direct Antagonistic Communities
Inputs:  G: Trust-Distrust Network;
         min_size: Minimum size threshold;
Outputs: Direct antagonistic communities with each opposing
         sub-community's size ≥ min_size;
Method:
1:  Let G_t = Project trust network from G;
2:  Let SCCList = Get maximal SCCs from the graph G_t
        by running [12];
3:  Let N_+ = {n | n∈s1 ∧ s1∈SCCList ∧ |s1| ≥ min_size};
4:  Let G_d = Project bi-directional distrust network in G
        for nodes in N_+;
5:  Let T_Dis = GTD(G_Dis);
6:  Let CP = Mine for closed itemsets from T_Dis with
        minimum support = min_size;
7:  For each p in CP
8:    If |p| ≥ min_size
9:      Let BC = Form bi-clique (p,map(p));
10:     Let LT = Construct trust SCCs from nodes in BC.L;
11:     Let RT = Construct trust SCCs from nodes in BC.R;
12:     Remove SCCs from LT and RT with size < min_size;
13:     For each pair l ∈ LT and r ∈ RT
14:       Create a new DAC adc from l and r;
15:       Add adc to Result;
16: Remove redundant DACs from Result;
17: Output Result;
```

Figure 5: Mine Direct Antagonistic Communities

Network	# Nodes	# +ve Links	# −ve Links
Epinions	47,910	208,531 (∼ 99.49%)	1,071 (∼ 0.51%)
myGamma	611,211	7,563,927 (∼ 92.99%)	570,066 (∼ 7.01%)

Table 2: Real Datasets: Statistics

links. As not all users have links, we remove those without trust/friendship or distrust/foe links and obtain the numbers of nodes as shown in Table 2. Both real datasets have more than 90% positive links. myGamma is has roughly 12.7 times more nodes and 38.8 times more links compared with Epinions.

We run our algorithm on an Intel(R) Core(TM) 2 2.13GHz PC with 2 GB of RAM running 32-bit Windows XP, Service Pack 3. The algorithm is written in Visual C#.Net.

We describe our scalability experiments in the following subsections. We have also performed an efficacy study; however, due to space limitation, we move its description to a technical report [1].

5.1 Scalability Experiment using Synthetic Datasets

We develop a synthetic trust network generator that uses three input parameters, i.e., $|N|$ (i.e., the number of nodes in the graph), $|E|$ (i.e., the number of edges in the graph), and τ (proportion of distrust links). By varying the three parameters, networks of different sizes (i.e., $|N|$ and $|E|$) and composition of trust and distrust links (τ) can be generated. We present detail steps of our synthetic network generation process in [1].

Five synthetic trust networks have been created with: (a) $|N|$=100, $|E|$=6,000, τ=0.4; (b) $|N|$=150, $|E|$=13,500, τ=0.4; (c) $|N|$=500,000, $|E|$=15,000,000, τ=0.1; (d) $|N|$=800, 000, $|E|$=38, 400,000, τ=0.1; (e) $|N|$=1,000,000, $|E|$=6,000, 000, τ=0.1. We mine DACs from these synthetic T-D networks with *min_size* set to 2 using our proposed algorithm

Dataset	Proposed Algorithm	Baseline Algorithm
(a)	0.297 s	372.930 s
(b)	0.937 s	2,985.169 s
(c)	127.333 s	>24 hours
(d)	360.771 s	>24 hours
(e)	812.989 s	>24 hours

Table 3: Running Time for Synthetic Network

	Epinions		myGamma	
min_size	Time (s)	$\|DACs\|$	Time (s)	$\|DACs\|$
1	3.875	562	844.727	50455
2	1.703	21	82.958	50
3	1.641	7	78.397	4
4	1.641	1	76.95	0
5	1.609	0	81.164	0

Table 4: Time & $|DACs|$: Epinions and myGamma

and our baseline algorithm (with maximum DAC size threshold set at 5[1]). We show the running time for each synthetic trust network using our proposed algorithm and our baseline algorithm in Table 3.

From Table 3, we show that our approach is able to efficiently process a large network of 1 million nodes using a low *min_size* threshold within 14 minutes. We also observe that the running time increases with the network size. This is particularly due to the computational overhead of mining bicliques in the algorithm. We also notice that our proposed approach is more than 1,000 times faster than the baseline approach. The baseline approach is not able to complete within one day for the larger T-D networks (i.e., network (c)-(e)). This result shows the power of our proposed pruning strategies.

5.2 Scalability Experiments using Real Datasets

The running times for mining DACs on Epinions and myGamma datasets at various minimum size thresholds using our proposed approach are shown in Table 4. Our baseline approach is not able to complete for these datasets. We show the number of direct antagonistic communities mined along with the time needed to mine them.

As shown in Table 4, our algorithm completes extracting all DACs from the Epinions dataset within 3.875 seconds. We do not find any large DACs with sub-community size ≥ 5, as there are zero antagonistic communities when the size threshold is set to be 5. On the myGamma dataset, the running time ranges from 81.164 seconds (for *min_size*=5) to 844.727 seconds (for *min_size*= 1). The running time required is larger than that for Epinions data due to larger data size. We also notice that there are more DACs mined from myGamma. However, interestingly, proportion-wise, Epinions dataset has DACs of slightly larger sizes. myGamma does not have any DACs of size 4 and above.

6. CONCLUSION AND FUTURE WORK

In this study, we analyze large graphs of trust and distrust to extract direct antagonistic communities (DACs). Within a DAC there are two opposing sub-communities. We propose a new framework to extract DACs efficiently from large networks. Our approach consists of several steps including: pruning of nodes not involved in any trust network, detection of bi-directional distrust bi-cliques among two sets of users, formation of DACs from distrust bi-cliques, and detection of redundant DACs. Experiments have been conducted on both synthetic and real datasets. On the synthetic dataset our approach is able to scale to 1,000,000 nodes and 6,000,000 edges. Our approach could also run on two medium-large real datasets from Epinions and myGamma within a reasonable time. Our approach uses less than 5 seconds to extract DACs from Epinions dataset that has more than 250,000 links among more than 560,000 members. Moreover, our approach needs less than 15 minutes to deal with myGamma dataset that has more than 8 millions links among more than 600,000 members.

As future work, we plan to investigate the evolution of DACs as a social network changes over time. Also, we plan to investigate factors leading to the creation of antagonistic communities.

Acknowledgement. We would like to thank Paolo Massa for sharing his Epinions dataset. We also would like to thank myGamma for sharing their dataset with us, and National Research Foundation (NRF) (NRF2008IDM-IDM004-036) for funding the work.

7. REFERENCES

[1] http://www.mysmu.edu/faculty/davidlo/papers/LoSurianZhangLimTR.pdf.

[2] "Buzzcity - myGamma - the world's leading wireless community," http://www.buzzcity.com/f/mygamma.

[3] "Reviews from Epinions." http://www.epinions.com/.

[4] R. Agrawal and R. Srikant, "Fast algorithms for mining association rules," in *VLDB*, 1994.

[5] I. Dasgupta, "'living' wage, class conflict and ethnic strife," *Journal of Economic Behavior & Organization*, 2009, in press.

[6] I. Dasgupta and R. Kanbur, "Community and class antagonism," *Journal of Public Economics*, vol. 91, no. 9, pp. 1816–1842, Sep 2007.

[7] J. Denrell, "Why most people disapprove of me: Experience sampling in impression formation," *Psychological Review*, vol. 112, no. 4, pp. 951–978, 2005.

[8] P. Doreian and A. Mrvar, "Partitioning Signed Social Networks," *Social Networks*, vol. 31, pp. 1–11, 2009.

[9] D. Easley and J. Kleinberg, "Positive and negative relationships," in *Networks, Crowds, and Markets: Reasoning about a Highly Connected World*. Cambridge University Press, 2010, pp. 119–152.

[10] J. Li, G. Liu, H.Li, and L. Wong, "Maximal biclique subgraphs and closed pattern pairs of the adjacency matrix: A one-to-one correspondence and mining algorithms." *TKDE*, vol. 19, no. 12, pp. 1625–1637, Dec 2007.

[11] K. Makino and T. Uno, "New algorithms for enumerating all maximal cliques," in *Proceedings of the 9th Scandinavian Workshop on Algorithm Theory*, 2004.

[12] R. Tarjan, "Depth-first search and linear graph algorithms," *SIAM Journal on Computing*, vol. 1, no. 2, pp. 146–160, 1972.

[13] B.-Q. Vuong, E.-P. Lim, A. Sun, M.-T. Le, H. Lauw, and K. Chang, "On ranking controversies in wikipedia: Models and evaluation." in *WSDM*, 2008.

[14] B. Yang and D.-Y. Liu, "A Heuristic Clustering Algorithm for Mining Communities in Signed Networks," *Journal of Computer Science and Technology*, vol. 22, pp. 320–328, 2007.

[15] K. Zhang, D. Lo, and E.-P. Lim, "Mining antagonistic communities from social networks," in *PAKDD*, 2010.

[1]The largest size of maximal DACs reported by our approach in dataset (a) is 5 which we use to set this threshold.

Connecting Users with Similar Interests via Tag Network Inference

Xufei Wang and Huan Liu
Computer Science and Engineering
Arizona State University
Tempe, AZ 85281
{xufei.wang, huan.liu}@asu.edu

Wei Fan
IBM T.J. Watson Research Center
19 Skyline Drive
Hawthorne, NY 10532
weifan@us.ibm.com

ABSTRACT

The popularity of social networking greatly increases interaction among people. However, one major challenge remains — how to connect people who share similar interests. In a social network, the majority of people who share similar interests with given a user are in the long tail that accounts for 80% of total population. Searching for similar users by following links in social network has two limitations: it is inefficient and incomplete. Thus, it is desirable to design new methods to find like-minded people. In this paper, we propose to use collective wisdom from the crowd or tag networks to solve the problem. In a tag network, each node represents a tag as described by some words, and the weight of an undirected edge represents the co-occurrence of two tags. As such, the tag network describes the semantic relationships among tags. In order to connect to other users of similar interests via a tag network, we use diffusion kernels on the tag network to measure the similarity between pairs of tags. The similarity of people's interests are measured on the basis of similar tags they share. To recommend people who are alike, we retrieve top k people sharing the most similar tags. Compared to two baseline methods triadic closure and LSI, the proposed tag network approach achieves 108% and 27% relative improvements on the BlogCatalog dataset, respectively.

Categories and Subject Descriptors

J.4 [**Social and Behavioral Sciences**]: Sociology; I.5 [**Pattern Recognition**]: Applications

General Terms

Algorithms,Experimentation

Keywords

Tag Network, Diffusion Kernel, Like-Minded Users

CIKM'11, October 24–28, 2011, Glasgow, Scotland, UK.

1. INTRODUCTION

Social networking is increasingly becoming an integral part of social life in which friend recommendation is an important feature. However, friend recommendation merely based on connectivity has two main limitations: it is inefficient and incomplete. For instance, the space complexity of an exhaustive search is exponential; an incomplete search risks of not being able to find anybody. Reaching the long tail users who accounts for 80% of the populatioin in a social network is not trivial, and in certain scenarios, some long tail users are not reachable at all. Thus search methods based on links could fail.

Nonetheless, recommending people of similar interests is an important task. Connecting to "people like you" also has a psychological component [6]: a sense of self-worth and fulfillment, being reassured of their worth and value, a sense of belonging to a community, the need to both seek help from and provide help to others, etc. Instead of recommending people of similar interests, following links alone can mostly recommend people you may (already) know. Thus, the proposed work of connecting like-minded people beyond using links is of practical significance.

- Connecting to people who are alike could accelerate information sharing and problem solving. For instance, we may want to find other people who have prior experience in using a system or a tool for advice when we have difficulty using them. We may want to find the right people for advice before we buy a product. We may want to find collaborators in a research field, etc.

- Connecting like-minded people in a social network is rewarding from the perspective of service providers who may be more interested in the behavior of groups of people than of individuals. For example, they may design more effective services, or place more relevant advertisements by understanding the common interests of a particular group.

- Connecting a small amount of people who are alike in the long tail is a challenging task which is not suitable for traditional data mining approaches. Searching for a few long tail users who are far apart from each other by leveraging connectivity between users is ineffective and inefficient.

The challenges of connecting like-minded users are summarized below. First, people only have an egocentric view of the social network, i.e., users only see their immediate

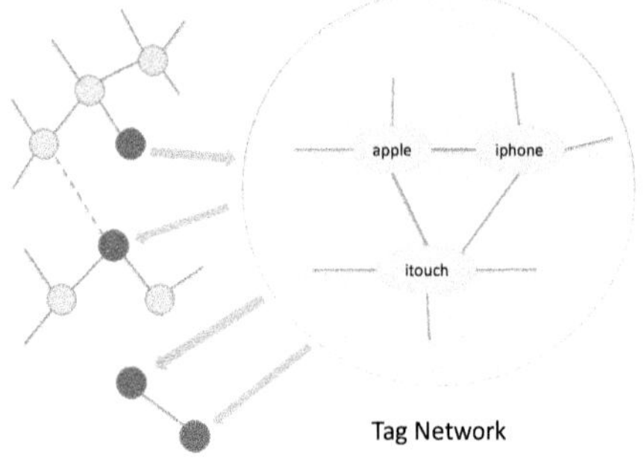

Figure 1: Connecting Like-Minded Users in a Tag Network Approach. The blue nodes represent Apple fans. The dashed line represents users who are connected via some intermediates. Given a seed user on the top left, the toy example demonstrates returning other Apple fans within the network.

Figure 2: A Snapshot of a Blog Description. Six semantically relevant tags are used to describe the purpose of the website: *apple*, *ipod*, *iphone*, *mac*, *apple iphone*, *iphone apps*. Mobile Tech and Gadgets are the two categories the blog is listed under.

contacts. Second, the scale of a social network website like Facebook, Twitter, or LinkedIn makes manual search unrealistic. Thus, more effective and efficient tools are necessary. Third, as shown earlier, recommendation based on links have limitations due to the long tail distribution.

1.1 Recommend via Tag Network Inference

We propose to connect like-minded users via tag network inference. The basic idea is illustrated in Figure 1. Nodes with different colors represent users in a social network. Some users are in the largest component of the network, whereas other users are disconnected, thus either isolated or in small groups. The four nodes highlighted in blue (dark) are fans of Apple products such as iPhone, iTouch, etc. Thus, the four users are deemed "like-minded" (A formal definition will be given in Section 3). The right part of the figure represents a tag network in which each node represents a tag, and the weight between two tags corresponds to users who use the two tags simultaneously.

Providing "wisdom of the crowd", the tag network describes the semantic relationships among tags. The similarity in the use of tags provides a way of measuring how similar two users are. For example, assume we want to connect other Apple fans to the upper left user in blue (dark). Instead of traversing links, we use the tag network, and return the other three Apple fans in the lower left.

The proposed approach requires no parameter tuning, thus is easy to use in practice. It is also efficient since the time complexity for recommendation is linear in the number of users and tags in a social network.

1.2 Summary

Connecting people of similar interests is not a link prediction problem [8]. The key difference between these two concepts is their objectives. The former attempts to find "familiar strangers" who have similar experiences, opinions, interests, etc but who do not know each other, whereas link prediction attempts to recommend people you may already know. There is no causal relationship between similarity and friendship. For instance, people who have similar interests may not be friends, and vice versa.

- We propose to use a tag network to represent the semantic relevance between tags, and show that the tag network is more powerful in capturing the semantic relevance than latent semantic indexing (LSI).
- We propose to connect like-minded users via tag network inference by leveraging the collective wisdom from the crowd. The tag network approach is effective compared to baseline methods.

2. TAG NETWORK CONSTRUCTION

Tagging is an activity for organizing various objects like bookmarks and blogs for future browsing, management, and sharing using informal vocabularies. Tags can be words or phrases, and *informal* means they may not be found in any dictionary. Figure 2 is a snapshot of a description for a blog on BlogCatalog including tags[1]. As shown in the figure, the blog, which is a news and review website on iPhone and iPhone applications, was added on September 2008. It has a major category *Mobile Tech* and a sub-category *Gadgets*. Categories imply the owner's interests. Six tags that are semantically relevant are specified by the owner such that other readers can easily discover the topics of the blog without browsing hundreds of articles within it.

Tagging is a knowledge that reflects thoughts on various web resources [4]. Collective wisdom emerges by combining many people's tagging knowledge together. The hypothesis of the work is that collective tagging naturally brings semantically relevant tags closer. For example, if two tags (e.g., iPhone and Apple iPhone) are used simultaneously by many people, there could be a semantic relevance between them. We represent the connectivity of tags in a network format: *Tag Network*.

We illustrate the steps to construct a tag network on the BlogCatalog dataset (more about the data in Section 6).

- For each object (e.g. blog) and its descriptive tags, we connect the tags as a clique as shown in Figure 3 (a);
- For each person, we combine all cliques corresponding to the objects she owns and form one or more **unweighted** tag networks, since her tags may or may not be connected in a tag network;

[1] http://www.blogcatalog.com/blogs/apple-iphone-news-and-app-reviews-ifonescom#

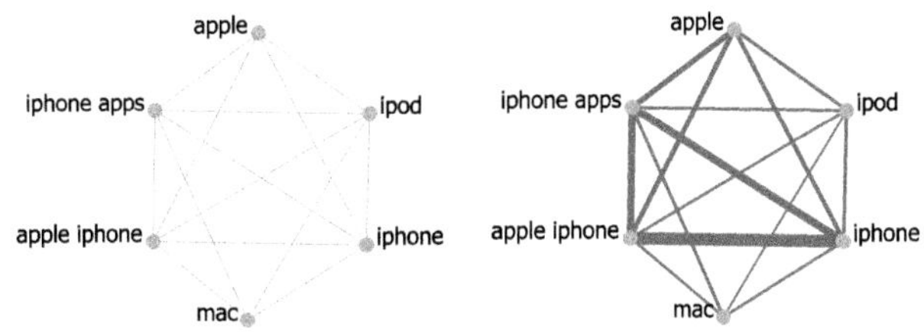

(a) Tag Network of a Blog (b) Tag Network of a Site

Figure 3: Examples of Tag Networks: (a) an unweighted tag network corresponds to the blog shown in Figure 2, and (b) a snapshot of the tag network constructed on BlogCatalog (other tags not shown). The weight of a link represents the number of users who use the two tags simultaneously.

- We construct a **weighted** tag network by aggregating all tag networks belonging to each person. In the weighted tag network, tags correspond to the union of all users' vocabularies, and the weight of each link represents the number of users who use both tags simultaneously.

A snapshot of the weighted tag network is demonstrated in Figure 3 (b). Note that other tags and the corresponding links are not shown. We count *the number of users* instead of *the number of times* two tags are used simultaneously as the weight of each link to avoid bias from spam users, i.e., those who may use automated tools to assign the same group of tags many times. However, it could be interesting to consider user influence in assigning link weights as future work. Tags are available in most social networking sites in different forms such as user interests, bookmarks, labels, etc. Thus, the construction process can be easily adapted.

3. PROBLEM STATEMENT

A social network $\mathcal{G} = (\mathcal{U}, \mathcal{E})$ is represented as an undirected graph, in which $\mathcal{U} = \{u_1, u_2, \ldots, u_n\}$ represents a set of n users and $\mathcal{E} = \{e_1, e_2, \ldots, e_\ell\}$ represents ℓ connections amongst the set of users. Each user subscribes to a certain number of tags. We denote the tag subscription relationship as a matrix $U \in R^{t \times n}$, in which each entry represents the number of times a tag is used by a given user. Let the number of unique tags associated to u_i be $\|u_i\|$. Denote $u_i^{interest}$ as a set of interests (e.g., categories specified by users on BlogCatalog) explicitly declared by the i-th user. Two users are said to be like-minded if they share some interests, e.g., both of them are fans of Apple iPhone.

$$u_i^{interest} \cap u_j^{interest} \neq \emptyset, 1 \leq i, j \leq n \tag{1}$$

However, two Apple fans may not necessarily use the same tags, e.g., one person likes to use *iPhone* as tags, the other person prefers to use *apple iPhone*.

A tag network $W \in R^{t \times t}$ is a symmetric graph in which each node represents a tag that could be a word or a phrase, a non-zero entry w_{ij} in W represents the number of users who use the two corresponding tags simultaneously. A diffusion kernel K_β defined on a tag network is utilized to measure the tag similarities, where β is the parameter which controls the speed of diffusion. Table 1 summarizes the notations. The problem is then defined as follows:

Table 1: Notations

Notations	Description
$\mathcal{G}$	Social Network
U	User Tag matrix
W	Tag Network
u_i	The i-th user in $\mathcal{U}$
$u_i^{interest}$	Interests of the u_i
$\|u_i\|$	Number of unique tags of u_i
S_i	The set of top k most similar users of u_i
k	Number of users to be selected
K_β	Diffusion kernel with parameter β
MSI_j	Mean Shared Interests between u_i and the j-th user in S_i averaged on all u_is in $\mathcal{G}$

- **Input:** Given a social network $\mathcal{G}$, a user u_i ($1 \leq i \leq n$), a tag network $W \in R^{t \times t}$, and a scalar k.
- **Output:** top k most similar users from $\mathcal{G}$.

4. DIFFUSION ON TAG NETWORK

The tag network enables us to measure the similarities between any pair of tags within it. The simplest measure of similarity between two tags is the shortest path distance. However, the shortest path distance is susceptible to change in graph structure, i.e., newly added or removed tags and links might dramatically affect the distance between two nodes. Therefore, we prefer to average all path distances between two given tags for a more robust similarity measure, which leads to the idea of random walk with varying steps, equivalent to a diffusion kernel on a network [7, 9]. The concept of diffusion kernels is well established, thus readers who are familiar with it can simply skip.

Given a tag network $W \in R^{t \times t}$, where t represents the number of unique tags in a social network, we define a matrix L, whose negation is called Laplacian matrix, as follows,

$$L = W - D, \tag{2}$$

where D is a diagonal matrix in which the i-th diagonal entry corresponds to the summation of the entries in i-th column of matrix W. The diffusion kernel K_β of a tag network is defined as follows,

$$e^{\beta L} = \lim_{s \to \infty} (I + \frac{\beta L}{s})^s, \tag{3}$$

where $\beta \geq 0$ is a user specified parameter which controls the speed of diffusion. A larger β value means a faster information diffusion speed on the network; and there is no diffusion when β is set to 0. The diffusion kernel is positive semi-definite, thus is a valid kernel for measuring similarity between any pair of two tags [9].

The computation of a diffusion kernel requires an eigen-decomposition of L such that $L = V \Sigma V^\top$,

$$\begin{aligned} K_\beta &= e^{\beta L} \\ &= I + \beta L + \frac{(\beta L)^2}{2!} + \frac{(\beta L)^3}{3!} + \ldots \\ &= V\big(I + \beta\Sigma + \frac{\beta^2}{2!}\Sigma^2 + \frac{\beta^3}{3!}\Sigma^3 + \ldots\big)V^\top \\ &= V e^{\beta\Sigma} V^\top \end{aligned} \tag{4}$$

where the columns of V are the eigenvectors, Σ is a diagonal matrix whose diagonal entries are eigenvalues, and $(e^{\beta\Sigma})_{ii} = e^{\beta\Sigma_{ii}}$, other non-diagonal elements are all zeros.

5. RECOMMEND LIKE-MINDED USERS

Let u_i be a seed user, K_β be the kernel, the goal is to select the top k most relevant users in terms of similarity from the social network. The similarity between two users is aggregated on the pair-wise tag similarity given below,

$$sim(u_i, u_j) = \sum_{t \in u_i, t' \in u_j} \frac{u_i(t)}{\sqrt{\|u_i\|}} \cdot K_\beta(t, t') \cdot \frac{u_j(t')}{\sqrt{\|u_j\|}}, \quad (5)$$

where $u_i(t)$ represents the number of times the tag t is used by the i-th user and two normalization terms $\sqrt{\|u_i\|}$ and $\sqrt{\|u_j\|}$ are applied to the two users, respectively. The normalization is necessary because it prevents selecting spammers who use a large number of tags. But users who share more semantically relevant tags are credited thus we use the square root for both normalization terms. The intuition of Equation (5) is that two users are more *like-minded* if they share more semantically relevant tags.

Denote Z as a diagonal matrix whose diagonal entries are $Z_{ii} = \frac{1}{\sqrt{\|u_i\|}}$. We rewrite the similarity between u_i to other users in the social network as follows,

$$sim(u_i, \cdot) = u_i^\top \cdot K_\beta \cdot U \cdot Z \quad (6)$$

We discard the normalization term $\|u_i\|$ since it does not affect the final ranking. Without prior knowledge, determining parameter β is difficult in practice. However, tag network does provide heuristics for β selection. Tags that are frequently used simultaneously are semantically relevant, which is also the basic idea behind Latent Semantic Indexing (LSI) which leverages term co-occurrence in articles [2]. In a tag network, many semantically relevant tags are close or even immediate neighbors, thus it is desirable to select *small* values of βs.

6. DATASET AND EXPERIMENTAL SETUP

BlogCatalog[2] is an online blog service which enables bloggers to register, manage, share, and connect blogs. A blog in BlogCatalog is associated with various pieces of information such as the categories that the blog is listed under, blog level tags, blog statistics such as the average rating and recent viewers, posts within the blog, and reviews from peer bloggers. A blogger also connects to other bloggers to form her social circle on BlogCatalog. A blogger's interests could be gauged by the categories (e.g. arts, business, education, etc) she publishes her blogs in. We obtained in total 60 categories in the processed BlogCatalog dataset. We notice that a blogger can specify more than one category for each blog. On average each blogger lists their blog under 1.69 categories. In the rest of the paper, categories are treated as bloggers' interests. Bloggers in this social network form the largest component, thus any blogger can be connected to any other blogger through some intermediate bloggers. The social network is undirected. After post processing, we obtain a dataset with 88,784 bloggers, 5,713 unique tags[3], and 60 categories. The BlogCatalog dataset is published at Social Computing Data Repository at Arizona State University[4].

[2]www.blogcatalog.com
[3]Tags that are used by less than 10 users are removed. This process helps to reduce noisy tags or typos in tags.
[4]http://socialcomputing.asu.edu/

Table 2: Statistics on BlogCatalog

Measure	BlogCatalog
Nodes	88,784
Edges	1,409,112
Average Contacts	49
Unique Tags	5,713
Average Tags	4.0

We first introduce baseline approaches and evaluation metrics for verification in the BlogCatalog social network. Then, we present and discuss detailed experimental results.

6.1 Baseline Methods

Practical friend recommendation systems are often application-oriented and domain-dependent, and it is very challenging to implement such systems for experimental evaluation. Thus, we illustrate two baseline methods that are generally applicable to any friend recommendation task.

Triadic Closure (Transitivity Principle) seeks to find similar users in terms of the number of mutual friends, and is solely based on links. This approach returns the top k people who are two hops away (friends of friends) in a social network. Note that it may return potential friends, but not necessarily return the most similar users.

Latent Semantic Indexing (LSI) is used to capture semantic correlation by applying Singular Value Decomposition (SVD). This approach computes the cosine similarity between an arbitrary pair of users in the latent space and can connect like-minded users who are far apart in a social network.

6.2 Evaluation Metrics

The quality is evaluated by the number of shared interests between the seed user and the selected users. More specifically, if the users selected by approach A share more interests with the seed user than those by approach B, intuitively, we say approach A is better.

On BlogCatalog dataset, each individual has explicit categories (or interests) which serve as the ground truth for evaluation purposes. The metric, Mean Shared Interests (MSI), is formally defined in Equation (7),

$$MSI(j) = \frac{1}{n} \sum_{i=1}^{n} \|u_i^{interest} \cap S_i(j)^{interest}\|, \ 1 \le j \le k, \quad (7)$$

where u_i represents the seed user, $S_i(j)$ $(1 \le j \le k)$ represents the j-th recommended user for u_i, noting each user set S_i (ranked in descending order) depends on u_i. We average the shared interests over all users in a social network.

7. EMPIRICAL FINDINGS

In this section, we first demonstrate the effectiveness of the tag network approach with properly selected parameters. Then we show the advantages of the proposed approach compared with other baseline methods. We also study the top k selected users in depth.

7.1 Comparative Study

The diffusion parameter β is sensitive to the outcomes. In Section 2, we suggest small values of β be selected. Figure 4 shows the MSI values with respect to different β values range from 10^{-1} to 10^{-5}. The performance stabilizes when

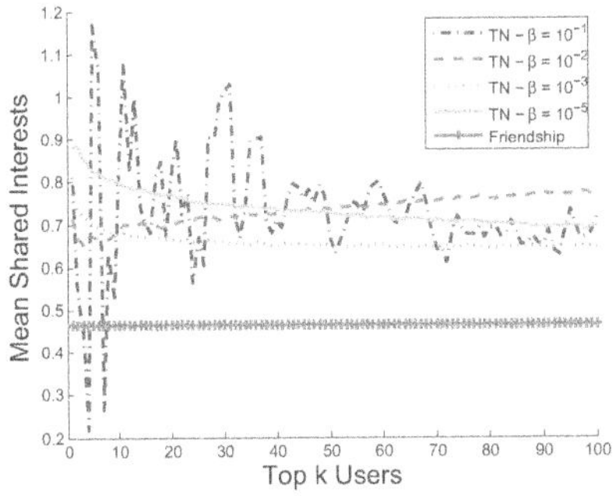

Figure 4: The Shared Interests Correspond to Different Selection of β: Large value of β yields large variation on the user's shared interests. Users selected by tag network approaches share more interests with the seed user than her immediate friends in the social network.

βs are set to smaller than or equal to 10^{-5}. The x-axis represents the top 100 users sorted in descending order in terms of similarity with the seed user. The y-axis denotes the MSI values between the j-th selected user (excluding the seed user's immediate contacts) with the seed user. The plots suggest that the best performance is achieved when β is set to 10^{-5}, since we often recommend few users as candidates, e.g., 10 or 15. We also notice that large β values cause large variations. For instance, when β is set to 0.1, the performance is not stable. As a baseline measure, we compute the average shared interests between the user and her immediate neighbors, denoted by the lower solid line in Figure 4. The higher MSI values of the proposed approach suggest that more like-minded users could be returned.

Theoretically, in a connected network, there is a path from any user to any other user. Thus, it is possible to connect all like-minded users by following links. However, exhaustive search is expensive and inefficient for a contemporary social network which can have hundreds of millions of nodes. As an alternative, applying triadic closure only searches for candidates up to two hops away. Therefore, the search by triadic closure principle is incomplete.

For comparison, we include all three approaches: triadic closure, LSI, and tag network with a specified parameter. The results are plotted in Figure 5. The LSI approach does provide improvement to some extent compared to the baseline measure as indicated by Friendship. It should be noted that the best performance for LSI is obtained when the latent dimension is set to 200 for the studied dataset. The proposed method outperforms the LSI approach significantly under t-test ($p < 0.001$). In computing the MSI values for above two approaches, the seed user's immediate contacts are excluded. The approach based on triadic closure is not as effective as the other two approaches, as indicated by the bottom curve in Figure 5. Comparing to the baseline methods (or measures), on average, the relative improvements of the tag network approach are 27%, 60%, and 108% for LSI, Friendship, and Triadic Closure, respectively.

Further Discussions Tag network and Latent Semantic Indexing are both capable of capturing the semantic correlation between tags, but diffusion on tag network appears to be more capable than LSI. The probable reasons for this are (1) the collective wisdom from the crowd brings the semantically relevant tags close to each other in terms of the number of hops; (2) although LSI also leverages the tag co-occurrence for dimension reduction, the diffusion kernel is more capable of measuring the similarity between any pair of two tags. We interpret the difference between LSI and diffusion on tag networks: LSI uses one path (i.e. the co-occurrence of two tags), whereas diffusion kernel combines all paths between any two tags (i.e. random walks with different number of steps on the tag network).

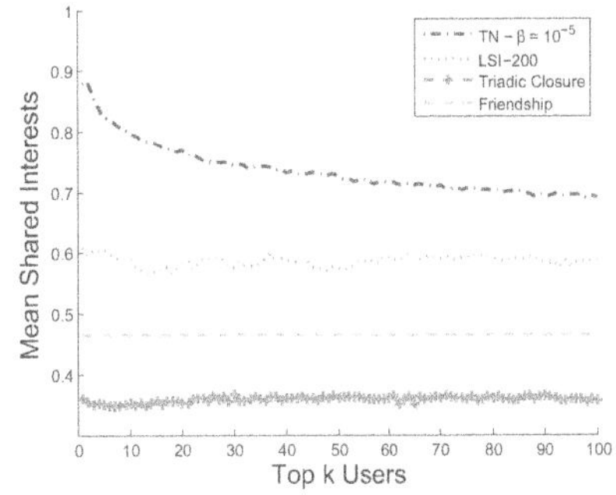

Figure 5: The Shared Interests w.r.t Different Approaches: the tag network approach outperforms the other approaches.

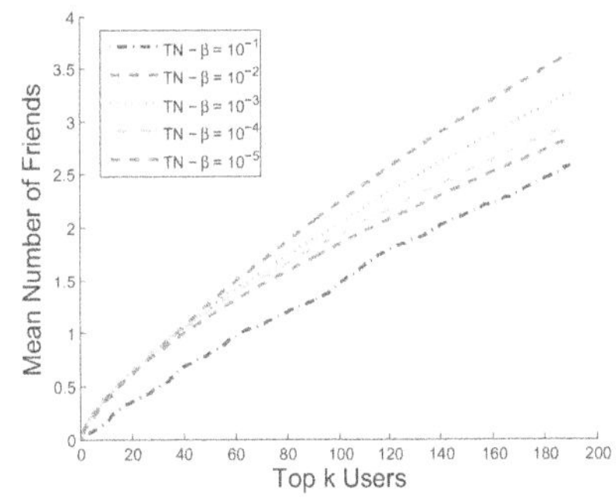

Figure 6: The Number of Friends in the Top k Most Similar Users: immediate friends account for around 2% of the people who are deemed as like-minded.

7.2 Correlation Analysis

In this section, we demonstrate the overlap between the true friends of the seed user and the top k most similar users. We find that a small set of selected users are actually the user's friends. The correlation between the friends and the returned top k users are presented in Figure 6. The x-axis represents top k most similar users sorted in descending order; y-axis represents the number of users who are actually friends, noting that y-axis values are averaged over all users in the social network. Consistent with the conclusion we draw in Section 7.1, most similar users (around 98%), thoese who share interests with the seed users, are not her immediate friends. We evalute different kernels but they all show very similar performance.

7.3 Hop Distance from the Seed Users

We observe on the BlogCatalog dataset that users that are multiple hops away could be like-minded. Thus, we compute the number of hops between the seed users and their top k

Table 3: Distance Distribution of Top k Candidates

# of Hops	1	2	3	4	5	6
Top 10(%)	1.555	20.197	**55.825**	12.160	0.263	0.002
Top 50(%)	1.062	29.035	**57.406**	12.229	0.264	0.003
Top 100(%)	0.875	28.528	**58.072**	12.260	0.261	0.003

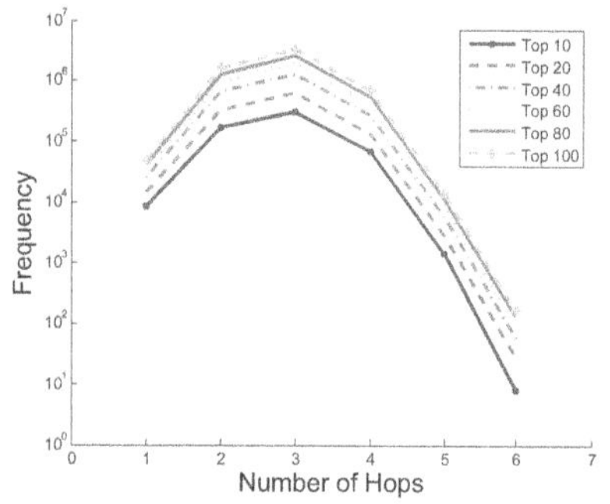

Figure 7: Hop Distance Distribution of the Top k Selected Users from Corresponding Seed Users: the majority of returned users are not immediate friends; small number of long-distanced users are also returned by the proposed approach.

most similar users. The computation is done by a breadth first search starting from a seed user, then each of the top k users is assigned the number of hops from the corresponding seed user. Finally we aggregate the number of users by hop distance from their corresponding seed users.

The distance distribution is presented in Figure 7, in which the curves from bottom to top represent top k ($k = 10, 20, \ldots, 100$) users who are considered. As shown in this figure, statistically, the majority of the most similar users are 2, 3, and 4 hops away. A small number of users who are 5 or 6 hops away from the seed users, (the diameter of the BlogCatalog social network is only 7) are also suggested as like-minded. The percentages of users with different hops from the seed users are summarized in Table 3. The immediate friends who are 1-hop away from a seed user account for less than 2%. The above results demonstrate that the tag network approach is capable of returning distant like-minded people for future interactions.

8. RELATED WORK

Recommendation Systems are growing in popularity in social media. Recommending items such as products, movies, services, or information entails trying to predict a user's preferences on things that may be attractive in the future. Collaborative Filtering (CF) is widely used in many applications. The key idea of collaborative filtering is that people who agreed in the past tend to agree in the future. Thus the collaborative filtering algorithm is to find the set of people of similar tastes and recommend items. A second type of recommendation system tries to recommend people instead of items. The Facebook recommendation system *People You May Know*[5] recommends potential friends by mutual friends or the triadic closure principle [10]: if two people have strong connections with a third person, it is more likely there is a strong or weak tie between them [11].

Link prediction is the task to infer future interactions between users in a social network with the knowledge at current time stamp. The key idea of this line of work is to recommend potential friends in terms of proximity with the seed user [8]. Many extensions have been studied recently by leveraging the user profile, activities and interactions, user-generated content [1, 5], network structure [11], etc.

[5]http://blog.facebook.com/blog.php?post=15610312130

9. CONCLUSION AND FUTURE WORK

In this paper, we propose to connect like-minded users via tag network inference. A tag network represents collective knowledge. We demonstrate that the tag network approach outperforms the two baseline methods based on triadic closure and latent semantic indexing. Experimental results also show the proposed approach is capable of recommending users with similar interests who are far apart when using links as the distance metric. The tag network approach can be used for on-line recommendation since the time complexity of recommending top k most alike users for a seed user is linear with respect to the number of users and the number of tags in a social network.

There are several topics that are worth further exploration. One direction is to apply the knowledge of tag networks to other applications such as tag recommendation, query expansion, etc. Another line of work would be integrating the link information and tag network for improved friend recommendation. Another possible area is to study tag selection in tag network construction.

Acknowledgements This work was supported, in part, by the Office of Naval Research (ONR) under the research grant N000141010091.

10. REFERENCES

[1] J. Chen, W. Geyer, C. Dugan, M. Muller, and I. Guy. "make new friends, but keep the old" — recommending people on social networking sites. In CHI'09.

[2] S. T. Dumais. Enhancing performance in latent semantic indexing (lsi) retrieval. Unpublished manuscript, September 1992.

[3] D. Easley and J. Kleinberg. *Networks, Crowds, and Markets: Reasoning about a Highly Connected World.* Cambridge University Press, 2010.

[4] P. Heymann, A. Paepcke, and H. Garcia-Molina. Tagging human knowledge. In WSDM'10.

[5] D. Horowitz and S. D. Kamvar. The anatomy of a large-scale social search engine. In WWW'10.

[6] M. Joel. *Six Pixels of Separation.* Business Plus, 2009.

[7] R. I. Kondor and J. Lafferty. Diffusion kernels on graphs and other discrete structures. In ICML'02.

[8] D. Liben-Nowell and J. Kleinberg. The link prediction problem for social networks. In CIKM'03.

[9] B. Schölkopf, K. Tsuda, and J.-P. Vert, editors. *Kernel Methods in Computational Biology,* chapter Diffusion Kernels, pages 171 – 192. The MIT Press, 2004.

[10] S. Wasserman and K. Faust. *Social Network Analysis: Methods and Applications.* Cambridge University Press, 1994.

[11] D. Easley and J. Kleinberg. *Networks, Crowds, and Markets: Reasoning about a Highly Connected World.* Cambridge University Press, 2010.

Do All Birds Tweet the Same? Characterizing Twitter Around the World

Barbara Poblete[1,2] Ruth Garcia[3,4]
Marcelo Mendoza[5,2] Alejandro Jaimes[3]

{bpoblete,ruthgavi,mendozam,ajaimes}@yahoo-inc.com
[1]Department of Computer Science, University of Chile, Chile
[2]Yahoo! Research Latin-America, Chile
[3]Yahoo! Research Barcelona, Spain
[4]Universitat Pompeu Fabra, Spain
[5]Universidad Técnica Federico Santa María, Chile

ABSTRACT

Social media services have spread throughout the world in just a few years. They have become not only a new source of information, but also new mechanisms for societies world-wide to organize themselves and communicate. Therefore, social media has a very strong impact in many aspects – at personal level, in business, and in politics, among many others. In spite of its fast adoption, little is known about social media usage in different countries, and whether patterns of behavior remain the same or not. To provide deep understanding of differences between countries can be useful in many ways, e.g.: to improve the design of social media systems (which features work best for which country?), and influence marketing and political campaigns. Moreover, this type of analysis can provide relevant insight into how societies might differ. In this paper we present a summary of a large-scale analysis of Twitter for an extended period of time. We analyze in detail various aspects of social media for the ten countries we identified as most active. We collected one year's worth of data and report differences and similarities in terms of activity, sentiment, use of languages, and network structure. To the best of our knowledge, this is the first on-line social network study of such characteristics.

Categories and Subject Descriptors

H.3.1 [**Information Storage and Retrieval**]: Content Analysis and Indexing

General Terms

Measurement

Keywords

Social Media Analytics, Social Networks, Twitter

1. INTRODUCTION

The use of social media has grown tremendously all over the world in recent years, and the impact of such growth has expanded in unexpected ways. Twitter, in particular, has become the most widely used microblogging service, and messages posted on it, in many ways, reflected real life events– from the revolutions in Tunisia and Egypt, to natural disasters such as the Chilean and Japanese earthquakes. Twitter users, however, post and share all kinds of information, ranging from personal opinions on important political issues, to mundane statements that may have little interest to most, except for their closest friends.

The range and scope of the service, and the fact that most user profiles and tweets are public, creates a huge opportunity for researchers. Using Twitter data, they can gain insights not just into how that particular service is used, but also into questions that are relevant in a social system for a particular point in time. This includes how news propagates, how people communicate, and maybe how they influence each other. Given this context, two key questions in the study of social media are how its use differs across cultures and countries, and whether any patterns revealed reflect behavioral differences and similarities between different groups. In spite of a long tradition and a lot of research in cultural anthropology, sociology, and other fields that address cultural differences, very little work has been carried out which takes into account large data sets that specifically examine differences across countries[1].

In this paper we present a summary of some of our findings when analyzing a large data set from Twitter. We perform this analysis in order to examine possible differences and similarities in several aspects of the use of the service. In particular, we focus on examining a year's worth of Twitter data for a large number of "active" users in the ten countries which tweet the most. We report on differences in terms of level of activity (number of tweets per user), languages used per country, the happiness levels of tweets, the content of tweets in terms of re-tweets, mentions, URLs, and the use of hashtags. Additionally, we report differences and similarities in terms of the network structure. Our main contribution is to provide a series of insights on how tweeting behavior varies across countries, and on possible explanations for such differences. To the best of our knowledge, this is the largest study done to date

[1]It is out of the scope of this paper to provide an in-depth review, but here we refer specifically to analyzing differences in social media *across different countries*, as there has been of course a lot of work on social network analysis of large data sets.

on microblogging data, and the first one that specifically examines differences across different countries.

The rest of the paper is organized as follows. In Section 2 we give a brief overview of related work and in Section 3 we describe our data set. In Section 4 we describe the distribution of languages used in each of the ten most active countries in our data set, and the main findings of our analysis on the level of happiness in each country. Section 5 focuses on the content of the tweets and network structure, and we conclude by summarizing our main findings in sections 6 and 7.

2. RELATED WORK

The structure of social networks has been studied extensively because structure is strongly related to the detection of communities and to how information propagates. Mislove et al. [10], for example, studied basic characteristics of the structure of Flickr, Orkut, LiveJournal, and YouTube, and found Power-law, small-world, and scale free properties. The authors argue that the findings are useful in informing the design of social network-based systems. Kwak et al. [9], examined the Twitter network aiming to determine it's basic characteristics. One of their main findings is that Twitter does not properly exhibit a "traditional" social network structure since it lacks reciprocity (only 22% of all connections on Twitter were found to be reciprocal), so it behaves more like news media, facilitating quick propagation of news. Java et al. [8], on the other hand, studied the topological and geographical properties of Twitter's social network and observed that there is high reciprocity and the tendency for users to participate in communities of common interest, and to share personal information. Onnela et al. [11], present a study on a large-scale network of mobile calls and text messages. They found no relationship between topological centrality and physical centrality of nodes in the network, and examined differences among big and small communities.

One of the key questions relating to communities and network structure is influence. De Choudhury et al. [4] examine Twitter data and study how different sampling methods can influence the level of diffusion of information. They found that sampling techniques incorporating context (activity or location) and topology have better diffusion than if only context or topology are considered. They also observed the presence of homophily, showing that users get together with "similar" users, but that the diffusion of tweets also depends on topics. Cha et al. [3] studied the in-degree and out-degree of the Twitter network and observed that influence is in fact not related to the number of followers, but that having active followers who retweet or mention the user is more important.

3. DATASET DESCRIPTION

Twitter is a platform which allows users to choose between keeping their profiles and activity (*tweets*) public or private. Users with private profiles make their information available only to a selected group of friends. For obvious reasons, we limit our research only to information provided by users with public profiles[2].

The focus of our research is mostly on characterizing large online social networks, based on user geographical location, for which Twitter provides limited information. Therefore, we perform an initial filter of users based on activity and profile information. First, we choose users which we determine to be *active*. For this we examine a 10-day continuous time window of user activity, selecting day-1 randomly from the year 2010. Then, we consider *only* as active, users which generated tweets during this time frame. Secondly, we filtered the resulting users to keep only active users which had also entered a *valid location* into their profiles during this same time period. We considered as a valid location any text which could be parsed correctly into latitude and longitude (using the Yahoo! public PlaceMaker API[3]). It should be noted, that we performed basically a static analysis, so we did not consider user mobility during this period. We did not process location information which was automatically generated for the user with a GPS device on their client application, based on the fact that location changes continuously with the user. Since in this work we are interested more in characterizing geographical communities of users, we decided to use the location which reflects more accurately the user's *home country*.

Using this criteria, we obtained a set of $6,263,457$ active users with valid location information, which were divided into 246 different countries. For the rest of our analysis, we selected the Top-10 countries with more activity and gathered all of the tweets generated by these users for the entire duration of 2010. In total our working dataset consisted of $4,736,629$ users (76% of the initial 10-day user sample), and $5,270,609,213$ tweets. Figure 1 shows the distribution of the users in our dataset into the top-10 countries, and the activity that they generated for 2010. Note that the amount of activity registered for each country is not necessarily proportional to the number of users. This is explicitly shown in Figure 2, which displays the tweet/user ratio for each country. This ratio is independent of the number of users in each local network.

4. LANGUAGES AND SENTIMENT

Languages. To analyze the language in which tweets are written, we classify each tweet using proprietary software. As a result, 99.05% of the tweets were classified into 69 languages. The 10 most popular languages are shown in Figure 3. English is the most popular language, and it corresponds to nearly 53% of the tweets. Additionally, Figure 4 shows the three most common languages for each of the top-10 countries, as well as the percentage of tweets which correspond to these languages. It is worth noting that English is one of the three most frequently used languages for these countries, and for the Netherlands, Indonesia, and Mexico more than 10% of tweets are in English, while for Brazil it is 9%. Additionally, a special consideration should be taken for the languages of Italian and Catalan, which appear in Figure 3 and Figure 4. This is strange finding given the fact that Italy is not considered in the top-10 countries of our study and the number of people who speak Catalan world-wide is very small. By sampling the tweets for Catalan and Italian we find that many of them correspond to false positives given by our classifier, since they actually correspond to Portuguese and Spanish. The high resemblance of these languages, in addition to the common use of slang, along with misspellings, makes automatic language identification particularly challenging.

Sentiment Analysis. We also analyzed the sentiment component of tweets, for this we use the measure of *happiness* as coined by Dodds et al. [5], which is also more commonly referred to as *valence*. This value represents the psychological reaction which humans have to a specific word, according to a scale which ranges from "happy" to "unhappy". In particular, we analyze the happiness levels for each of the top-10 countries, considering only tweets classified as English and Spanish. To achieve this, we used the 1999 Affective Norms for English Words (ANEW) list by Bradley and Lang [1] for English tweets, and for Spanish, we used its adaptation by Redondo et al. [12]. The ANEW list contains 1,034 words

[2]All processing was anonymous and aggregated. No personal user information was used

[3]http://developer.yahoo.com/geo/placemaker/

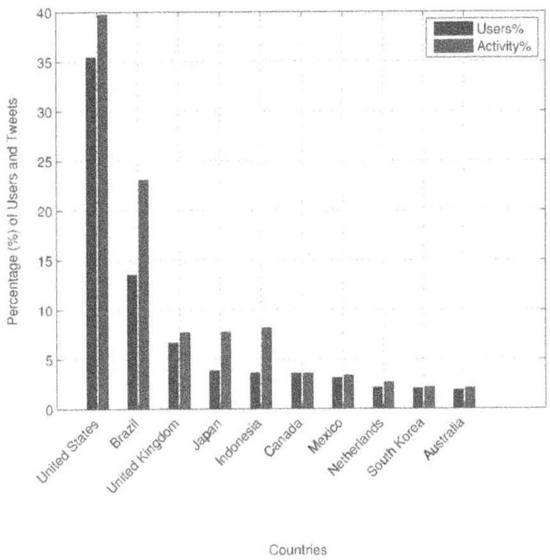

Figure 1: Distribution of users (%) in the dataset for each Top-10 country and their activity (%).

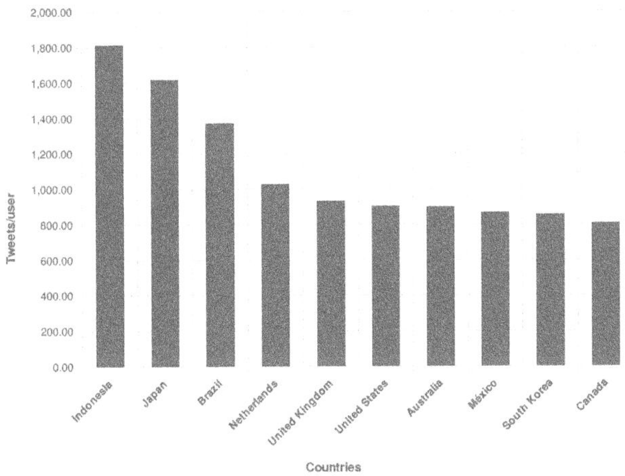

Figure 2: tweet/user ratio for each Top-10 country.

and each word has a score in a 1 to 9 range, which indicates its level of happiness. We computed the "weighted average happiness level", based on the algorithms of Dodds et al. [5], as follows:

$$happiness(C_l) = \frac{\sum_{i=1}^{N_l} w_i f_{i,C_l}}{\sum_{i=1}^{N_l} f_{i,C_l}} = \sum_{i=1}^{N_l} w_i p_{i,C_l} \qquad (1)$$

where $happiness(C_l)$ represents the weighted average happiness level for a country C, based on all of its tweets in language l (English or Spanish), during 2010. Therefore C_l represents all of the tweets registered for the country C which are expressed in the language l. Additionally, N_l represents the number of words in the ANEW list for the language l, while w_i is the score for the i-th word in the ANEW list for l, and f_{i,C_l} corresponds to the frequency of this word in the collection C_l. Finally, we denote p_{i,C_l} as the normalized frequency of each sentiment scored word in C_l.

The results of this sentiment analysis for (a) English and (b) Spanish, are shown in Figure 5. These results agree with those reported by Dodds et al. [5]: the values are between 5 and 7 for both languages and there is also a general increase in happiness towards the end of the year. It is interesting to note that Brazil has the highest values almost every month, even though we are not particularly considering Portuguese. Nevertheless, after August happiness

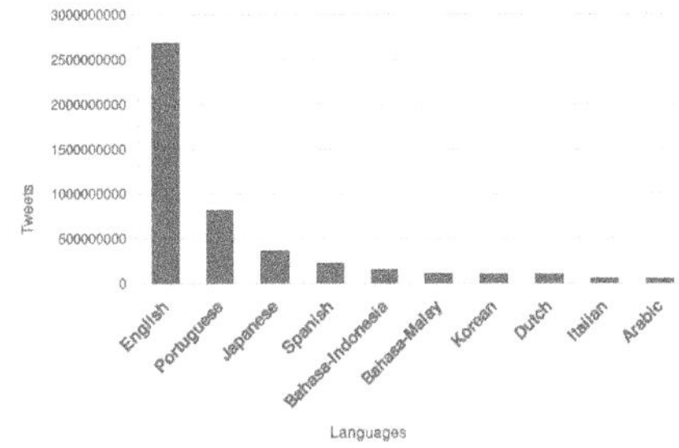

Figure 3: Most commonly used languages in each top-10 country.

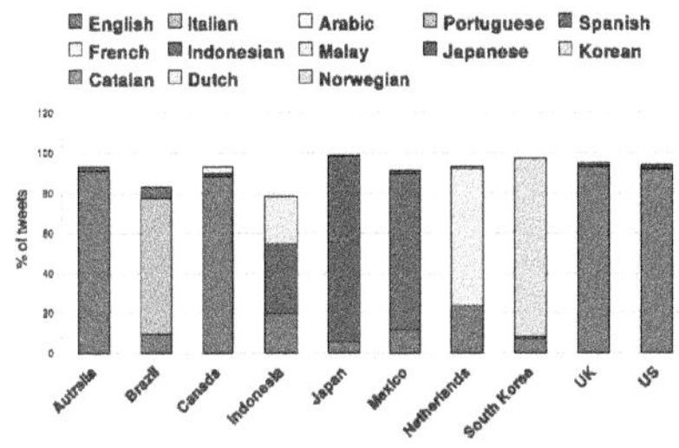

Figure 4: Three most popular languages for tweets in each top-10 country.

levels in Brazil decreases until November. Also, in December all countries show an increase in their happiness level.

Some differences can be appreciated in the results for Spanish tweets, Figure 5.b. The number of tweets in Spanish is disproportional as 7 countries account for less than 1% of the tweets, while Mexico, USA and Brazil together account for almost 98% of the total. Nevertheless, USA and Mexico have happiness patterns that are similar to most countries. Only Brazil and Indonesia results which differ from the rest: there is a strong increase in happiness from June to July for Brazil and Indonesia. Interesting drops in levels happen in Indonesia during the months of May and August. Brazil has clearly the highest values for all months, but it also presents higher ups and downs.

5. CONTENT AND NETWORK STRUCTURE

Tweet Contents. In this part of our study, we analyze briefly certain tweet features for each top-10 country. These features have also been used in prior work, such as [2]:

- *#*: indicates if a tweet contains a "#" symbol, which denotes a tweet with a particular topic.
- *RT*: indicates if a tweet has a "RT", which indicates a *re-tweet* or re-post of a message of another user.
- *@*: indicates whether a tweet contains an "@" symbol, used preceding a user name and which indicates a user mention.
- *URL*: Denotes whether a tweet contains a URL or not.

We computed the average per user for each country as follows:

$$AVG(symbol) = \frac{\sum_{i=1}^{N} \frac{T(symbol)_{u_i}}{T_{U_i}}}{\sum_{i=1}^{N} U_i} \qquad (2)$$

Where $AVG(symbol)$ is the average number of tweets per user of a particular country containing a feature denoted by *symbol* (e.g. #, RT, URL, @). Also, N is the total number of users for a particular country and $T(symbol)_{U_i}$ is the total number of tweets containing that feature for user U_i

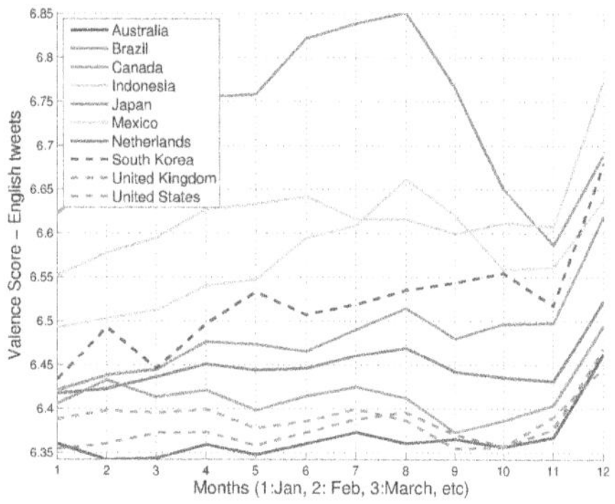

(a)

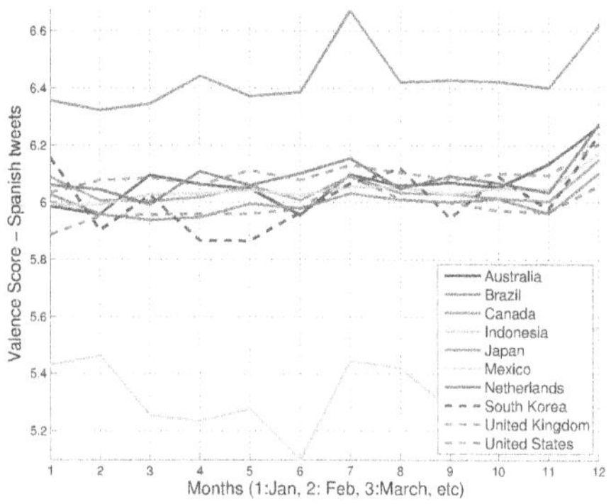

(b)

Figure 5: Average *happiness* level (a) English and (b) Spanish.

Country	$\frac{Tweets}{Users}$	$(URL)\%$	$(\#)\%$	$(@)\%$	$(RT)\%$
Indonesia	1813.53	14.95	7.63	58.24	9.71
Japan	1617.35	16.30	6.81	39.14	5.65
Brazil	1370.27	19.23	13.41	45.57	12.80
Netherlands	1026.44	24.40	18.24	42.33	9.12
UK	930.58	27.11	13.03	45.61	11.65
US	900.79	32.64	14.32	40.03	11.78
Australia	897.41	31.37	14.89	43.27	11.73
Mexico	865.7	17.49	12.38	49.79	12.61
S. Korea	853.92	19.67	5.83	58.02	9.02
Canada	806	31.09	14.68	42.50	12.50

Table 1: Average usage of features per user for each country

Table 1 shows the average per country as well as the ratio $\frac{tweets}{user}$. Countries are ordered according to the ratio $\frac{Tweets}{User}$. Results show that Indonesia ranks first in tweets per user, followed by Japan and Brazil. It is interesting also to see that Indonesia and South Korea have the highest percentage of mentions in contrast to Japan that has the lowest, and it seems also to be the country with the fewest re-tweets in our data set. This indicates a higher use of Twitter for conversation than in other countries. The Netherlands is the country with most hashtags per user, while the US seems to be the country with most mentions of URLs per user. At first glance, this could indicate that the US uses Twitter more for formal news dissemination, citing constantly external sources.

Network. Twitter also provides a social network structure for its users. This is, users connect to each other through directed links, therefore relationships are not necessarily reciprocal, as in Facebook[4]. Users can choose to *follow* other users, by subscribing to their updates. These connections between users can be viewed as a large directed graph.

[4] `http://www.facebook.com`

Country	Users	Cov.(%)	Links	Cov.(%)	Recip.(%)
US	1,616,702	12.47	11,310,538	12.46	18.91
Brazil	688,427	5.31	4,248,259	4.68	13.49
UK	286,520	2.21	1,370,699	1.51	17.22
Japan	133,536	1.03	408,486	0.45	**32.01**
Canada	132,240	1.02	553,726	0.61	**26.11**
Indonesia	130,943	1.01	199,704	0.22	**26.97**
Mexico	112,793	0.87	399,409	0.44	17.27
Netherlands	86,863	0.67	354,021	0.39	22.11
South Korea	80,381	0.62	499,261	0.55	**28.14**
Australia	67,416	0.52	299,556	0.33	23.51

Table 2: General summary of network statistics per country.

Country	Avg. δ	Density	Avg. Clus. Coef.	Strongly CC
US	8.95	0.56 E-04	0.0645	9,667
Brazil	7.55	1.09 E-04	0.0711	4,813
Indonesia	2.12	1.62 E-04	0.0618	7,942
United Kingdom	6.05	2.11 E-04	0.0933	14,818
Japan	4.36	3.26 E-04	0.0603	6,052
Mexico	4.44	3.91 E-04	0.0826	6,885
Canada	5.73	4.33 E-04	0.1001	6,630
South Korea	8.61	10.67 E-04	0.0879	3,864
Netherlands	5.39	6.16 E-04	0.1017	4,626
Australia	5.83	8.52 E-04	0.0959	3,423

Table 3: Summary of network density statistics per country.

In this section we focus on the analysis of the Twitter social network graph for each top-10 country and its active users (as defined in Section 3). In order to obtain this graph, we extracted user relationships using the public Twitter API (4J), collecting the list of followers/followees for each user. In this particular graph, connections between users are highly dynamic, so we worked with a snapshot of the graph, which was crawled between November 25 to December 2, 2010. This crawl resulted in $12,964,735$ users and $90,774,786$ edges. We cleaned this dataset to keep only edges and users which corresponded to our *active user set*. Prior work [10] has shown that analysis of partial crawls of social networks can underestimate certain measures, such as degree distribution, but continue to preserve accuracy for other metrics, such as density, reciprocity and connectivity. Therefore, by preserving the active component of the graph we are analyzing the most relevant part of the social structure.

Table 2 shows a summary of each countries' statistics. For each local network analysis, we consider only connections between users in the same country. The second and third columns in Table 2 show the node and edge coverage of each country in relation to the complete graph. We also show the percent of reciprocity, which is the fraction of ties between users which are symmetric. Overall, the top-10 most active countries cover 25.73% of the total of active users in the social graph. Additionally, these countries cover 21.64% of the total number of edges in the global network. Table 2 shows that for some countries reciprocity is very significant in particular for Japan, South Korea, Indonesia and Canada. The symmetric nature of social ties affects network structure, increasing connectivity and reducing the diameter, as we show in the remaining of this work.

Table 3 shows a summary of graph density statistics, such as average degree (δ), density and average clustering coefficient. The US and South Korea are the countries with the highest averaged degree per node, meaning that users tend to concentrate more followers and followees than in other countries. Indonesia, on the other hand, presents a very low degree (only 2.12 edges per node on average)

Country	Modularity	Number of communities
US	0.418	2,954
Brazil	0.462	2,896
Indonesia	0.537	3,358
United Kingdom	0.397	2,486
Japan	0.458	1,998
Mexico	0.358	1,406
Canada	0.568	1,269
South Korea	0.312	756
Netherlands	0.412	936
Australia	0.452	634

Table 4: Summary of graph modularity statistics per country

Country	Diameter	Avg. Path length	Shortest paths
US	18	6.49	5,746,903,535
Brazil	16	6.37	2,147,483,647
Indonesia	35	9.69	33,940,227
United Kingdom	15	5.19	402,698,573
Japan	18	5.26	86,348,633
Mexico	16	5.27	50,512,898
Canada	16	4.71	77,645,673
South Korea	11	4.02	33,517,802
Netherlands	17	4.81	33,628,133
Australia	14	4.52	22,271,542

Table 5: Summary of graph distance measures per country

in spite of being a very active community. The second column in Table 3 shows each local network's density values. Density is computed as $\frac{m}{n(n-1)}$, where n is the number of nodes and m is the number of edges. The density is 0 for a graph without edges and 1 for a fully connected graph. In our study, South Korea displays the highest density of all countries. Additionally, density increases as the network becomes smaller, i.e. the US has the lowest density, and the highest values correspond to South Korea, Netherlands and Australia. Therefore, smaller communities are in general more well connected, within their own country.

The third column in Table 3 shows the average clustering coefficient. We can observe that communities with high clustering coefficient and less reciprocity may indicate more hierarchical-type relationships between users (i.e., two users who share a reciprocal tie follow a same third user who does not reciprocate). The fourth column of Table 3 shows the number of strongly connected components that exist in each country.

Table 4 shows the the modularity of each social network graph, we use this coefficient as defined by Girvan and Newman [6], which evaluates how well a graph can be partitioned. A value of 0.4 or greater is generally considered meaningful. In our analysis we can appreciate that Indonesia and Canada display high modularity, which indicates that the communities found in these countries are more compact and closed than in other countries. On the other hand, Mexico, South Korea and United Kingdom indicate less separation between their communities. In addition, in Table 5 we summarize some general network distance measures per country. Table 5 shows that Indonesia presents the highest diameter, indicating that this network is very partitioned, which agrees with its high modularity coefficient. Several countries register diameter values in the range of 16-18. The lowest diameter is found South Korea. We can also see that average path lengths are proportional to diameter values. In general, the number of shortest paths is proportional to the number of edges in the graph. Notice that, for example, the three graphs with the highest edge coverage values (US, Brazil and United Kingdom) are also the three countries with the highest shortest path values (see Table 2).

We analyze the existence of a direct relationship between average path length and diameter with reciprocity. Intuitively, we would expect that shorter paths and diameters would result from networks with high reciprocity. Nevertheless, experimentally, we do not observe any apparent relationship. On the contrary, several countries show significant reciprocity and at the same time large diameters. The most noticeable case is Indonesia, which shows the largest diameter and also high reciprocity. This suggests that graph structure strongly influences the relationship between reciprocity and diameter. Given our previous observation, which was that Indonesia had high modularity (see Table 4), this supports the idea that this country has very compact and isolated communities of users. On the other hand, Canada also shows a very significant modularity value but its diameter and average path length values are very similar to countries that do not show a community structure. The main difference between Indonesia and Canada from our observation is that the first has a much lower clustering coefficient and density than the second. This might indicate that Indonesia has more users than Canada which do not participate in large communities.

We also examine the graph structure of each network by considering node degree distribution. Degree distributions of many social networks have been shown power laws behaviors. This kind of networks are networks where the probability that a node has degree k is proportional to k^{γ}, where γ is known as the power law coefficient. Table 6 shows a summary of the graph degrees and assortativity coefficient.

Country	In-degree Power Law	Out-degree Power Law	Assortativity
US	9.51	13.62	-0.19
Brazil	7.56	12.42	-0.17
Indonesia	6.21	9.48	-0.06
United Kingdom	7.31	10.89	-0.18
Japan	7.48	9.68	-0.07
Mexico	5.91	9.26	-0.21
Canada	8.31	9.30	-0.11
South Korea	6.36	8.21	-0.27
Netherlands	6.67	8.64	-0.17
Australia	7.72	8.12	-0.11

Table 6: Summary of graph degrees and assortativity statistics per country

Finally, we analyze the number of in-links and out-links from one community to another. These results are shown in Figure 6. In this illustration it is interesting to observe that all countries di rect the majority of their external out-links to the US. Nevertheless, several countries concentrate their most significant amount of links towards themselves, with the exceptions of Canada, Australia and UK, which connect to the US almost as much as to themselves.

6. SUMMARY AND DISCUSSION

Network reciprocity tells us about the degree of cohesion, trust and social capital in sociology [7]. In this context, the equilibrium tendency in some human societies is to have reciprocal connections. Nevertheless, Twitter networks seem to work towards an equilibrium which is not reciprocal and more hierarchical. Therefore, it tends more to follow a model in which we have authorities which receive many ties but do not reciprocate.

On the other hand, we observe that countries which have high reciprocity tend to have a higher tweets/user ratio. Additionally, smaller networks also have a tendency to have higher reciprocity. Indicating more local communities. Additionally, we see that communities which tend to be less hierarchical and more reciprocal,

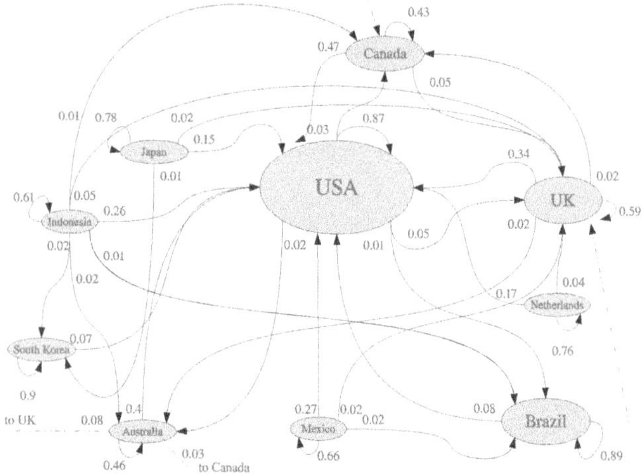

Figure 6: Ties between countries, sizes are proportional the size of the community. Weights represent fraction of ties estimated over the total number of ties of a given country.

also displays *happier* language in their content updates. In this sense countries with high conversation levels (@), shown in Table 1, display higher levels of *happiness* too. This is reasonable, if we think that higher conversational levels can imply that users privilege more informal communication, as opposed to formal news dissemination. Following this reasoning, we can hypothesize that these users, use Twitter more as a conversation channel than formal information source. Therefore, their interaction is highly conversational with friends, as opposed to being more formal. which is the case of the US. High reciprocity does not imply that these countries are more well connected overall, in cases such as Indonesia, reciprocity is contained within very compact and closed groups. This increases the overall diameter of the network, as seen in Table 4.

By analyzing Table 3, we can observe that smaller communities, tend to present more reciprocal ties between users in general, along with high density and average clustering coefficient (not always, but this is the tendency). Pointing towards more reciprocal relationships. Additionally, high reciprocity creates high activity in communities such as Indonesia and Japan. On the other hand, we can see in Table 3 that countries with high density and high clustering coefficient, such as South Korea, Netherlands and Australia, contain users which participate in small and compact communities. Other countries, such as the US, have low clustering coefficient and density, which indicates that many users do not participate in a small compact community.

7. CONCLUSIONS

We have presented a broad study of the Twitter on-line social network. We have segmented our analysis into the top-10 countries with most activity and collected data from a representative sample of users for one year. We analyze several aspects, such as language, sentiment, content and network properties.

In particular some countries standout, based on their peculiar characteristics. Some smaller networks display high reciprocity and more conversation. This indicates a high conversational use within compact communities, as opposed to broad dissemination of news information. In this sense, there also seems to be a correlation between reciprocity and levels of happiness detected in language, examples are Indonesia and Brazil. On the other hand, users in the US give Twitter a more informative purpose, which is reflected in more globalized communities, which are more hierarchical.

In future work we expect to explore more formally correlations between network structure measurements, hierarchy and happiness levels. Also we would like to compare our findings with similar research in other social networks, such as sociological studies.

Acknowledgments. This research was partially supported by European Community's Seventh Framework Programme FP7/2007-2013 under the ARCOMEM project and by the Spanish Centre for the Development of Industrial Technology under the CENIT program, project CEN-20101037 (www.cenitsocialmedia.es), "Social Media". Additionally, this work has also been partially supported by FONDEF-CONICYT project D09I1185.

8. REFERENCES

[1] M. M. Bradley and P. J. Lang. Affective norms for english words (ANEW): Stimuli, instruction manual, and affective ratings. In *In Technical Report C-1, The Center for Research in Psychophysiology*, Gainesville, Florida, 1999.

[2] C. Castillo, M. Mendoza, and B. Poblete. Information credibility on twitter. In *Proceedings of the 20th international conference on World wide web*, WWW '11, pages 675–684, New York, NY, USA, 2011. ACM.

[3] M. Cha, H. Haddadi, F. Benevenuto, and K. P. Gummadi. Measuring User Influence in Twitter: The Million Follower Fallacy. In *In Proceedings of the 4th International AAAI Conference on Weblogs and Social Media (ICWSM)*.

[4] M. D. Choudhury, Y.-R. Lin, H. Sundaram, K. S. Cnadan, L. Xie, and A. Kelliher. How does the data sampling strategy impact the discovery of information difussion in social media? Many May, 2010.

[5] P. S. Dodds, K. D. Harris, I. M. Kloumann, C. A. Bliss, and C. M. Danforth. Temporal patterns of happiness and information in a global social network: Hedonometrics and Twitter. *Computing Research Repository abs/1101.5120v3[physics.soc-ph]*, Feb. 2011.

[6] M. Girvan and M. E. J. Newman. Community structure in social and biological networks. *Proceedings of the National Academy of Sciences*, 99(12):7821–7826, 2002.

[7] R. Hanneman and M. Riddle. *Introduction to social network methods*. University of California Riverside, CA, 2005.

[8] A. Java, X. Song, T. Finin, and B. Tseng. Why we twitter: understanding microblogging usage and communities. In *Proceedings of the 9th WebKDD and 1st SNA-KDD 2007 workshop on Web mining and social network analysis*, WebKDD/SNA-KDD '07, pages 56–65, New York, NY, USA, 2007. ACM.

[9] H. Kwak, C. Lee, H. Park, and S. Moon. What is twitter, a social network or a news media? In *Proceedings of the 19th international conference on World wide web*, WWW '10, pages 591–600, New York, NY, USA, 2010. ACM.

[10] A. Mislove, M. Marcon, P. K. Gummadi, P. Druschel, and B. Bhattacharjee. Measurement and analysis of online social networks. In *Internet Measurement Comference*, pages 29–42, 2007.

[11] J.-P. Onnela, S. Arbesman, A.-L. Barabási, and N. A. Christakis. Geographic constraints on social network groups. Nov. 2010.

[12] J. Redondo, I. Fraga, I. Padrn, and M. Comesaa. The spanish adaptation of anew (affective norms for english words). In *Volumne 39*, number 3, pages 600–605. Psychonomic Society Publications, 2007.

Topic Sentiment Analysis in Twitter: A Graph-based Hashtag Sentiment Classification Approach

Xiaolong Wang [†*], Furu Wei [‡], Xiaohua Liu [‡], Ming Zhou [‡], Ming Zhang [†]
[†] School of EECS, Peking University, Beijing, China
[‡] Microsoft Research Asia, Beijing, China
[†] xwang95@illinois.edu, mzhang@net.pku.edu.cn
[‡] {fuwei, xiaoliu, mingzhou}@microsoft.com

ABSTRACT

Twitter is one of the biggest platforms where massive instant messages (i.e. tweets) are published every day. Users tend to express their real feelings freely in Twitter, which makes it an ideal source for capturing the opinions towards various interesting topics, such as brands, products or celebrities, etc. Naturally, people may anticipate an approach to receiving the common sentiment tendency towards these topics directly rather than through reading the huge amount of tweets about them. On the other side, Hashtags, starting with a symbol "#" ahead of keywords or phrases, are widely used in tweets as coarse-grained topics. In this paper, instead of presenting the sentiment polarity of each tweet relevant to the topic, we focus our study on hashtag-level sentiment classification. This task aims to automatically generate the overall sentiment polarity for a given hashtag in a certain time period, which markedly differs from the conventional sentence-level and document-level sentiment analysis. Our investigation illustrates that three types of information is useful to address the task, including (1) sentiment polarity of tweets containing the hashtag; (2) hashtags co-occurrence relationship and (3) the literal meaning of hashtags. Consequently, in order to incorporate the first two types of information into a classification framework where hashtags can be classified collectively, we propose a novel graph model and investigate three approximate collective classification algorithms for inference. Going one step further, we show that the performance can be remarkably improved using an enhanced boosting classification setting in which we employ the literal meaning of hashtags as semi-supervised information. Experimental results on a real-life data set consisting of 29,195 tweets and 2,181 hashtags show the effectiveness of the proposed model and algorithms.

Categories and Subject Descriptors

I.2.7 [**ARTIFICIAL INTELLIGENCE**]: Natural Language Processing—*Text analysis*

*This work has been done when the author was visiting Microsoft Research Asia.

CIKM'11, October 24–28, 2011, Glasgow, Scotland, UK.

General Terms

Algorithms, Experimentation

Keywords

Sentiment Analysis, Hashtag, Twitter, Graph-based Classification

1. INTRODUCTION

Twitter [1] is popular for its massive spreading of instant messages (i.e. tweets) and the nature of freedom. Bursts of world news, entertainment gossips about celebrities, and discussions over the recently released products are all collected in Twitter vividly. Beyond merely displaying news and reports, the Twitter itself is also a large platform where different opinions are presented and exchanged. No matter where people come from, what religious belief they hold, rich or poor, civilized or uneducated, they comment, discuss, compliment, argue and complain over topics they are interested in, sharing their own feelings freely. It has been well recognized that these user-generated content with rich sentiment information should be utilized for many applications such as search engines and other information systems.

While tweet level sentiment analysis results indeed provide very useful information, the overall or general sentiment tendency towards topics are more appealing in some scenarios. For example, people are curious about how others feel about Apple's new product "iPhone4" and it will offer great convenience for them if major opinions are collected from massive tweets. Fans of Lady Gaga are fascinated about what is going on with their superstar and the reaction from other people. While reading news about political elections, it is expected to get an overview about the support and opposition for presidential candidates in Twitter at the same time. In all these scenarios, a comprehensive sentiment tendency analysis towards the topic during a time period is in need. In this paper, to address this demand, we utilize the unique characteristic of *hashtag* in Twitter.

In twitter, hashtags are a community-driven convention for adding additional context and metadata to tweets. They are created organically by Twitter users as a way to categorize messages and to highlight topics, which is done by simply prefixing a word or a phrase with a hash symbol, such as "#hashtag". The extensive use of hashtags makes Twitter more expressive and welcomed by people. We measured on a dataset with around 0.6 million randomly selected tweets and found that around 14.6% of them have at least one hashtags in each. When only considering the subjective

[1] http://twitter.com/

tweets (tweets with positive/negative sentiment expressions), this number increases to 27.5%. The statistics shows a great potential for sentiment analysis with hashtags in Twitter. Another aspect of analysis illustrates the close connection among the topic, sentiment and hashtags in Twitter. To be precise, hashtags can be categorized into three types. Most hashtags (*topic hashtags*) serve as user-annotated coarse topics, like in tweet "*yesterday I watched ur movie again, and this time I cried. love u so much! #Justin_Bieber*". In other cases, hashtags (*sentiment hashtags*) could be an easy way to highlight the sentiment information. This category of hashtags are composed of sentiment words only, such as "#love", "#sucks", etc. Besides, the third kind of hashtags (*sentiment-topic* hashtags) are those in which the topical word and the sentiment words appear together without separating blanks. For example, "#iloveobama" (I love Obama) directly expresses positive opinion towards President Obama. Hence, hashtags falling in this category are even more informative since they explicitly indicate the sentiment target and its expression at the same time. Based on these observations, we believe the hashtag-level sentiment analysis will bring about much understanding about topics in Twitter.

One intuitive idea about the hashtag-level sentiment classification is to aggregate the sentiment polarity with the classification results for each corresponding tweet containing the hashtag. However, this straightforward method does not perform well in our experiments. One major reason contributing to the poor performance is that even for the state-of-the-art sentiment classification algorithm, the accuracy for tweet-level sentiment classification is usually not as high as expected, making the hashtag-level classification task even more challenging and intractable. We do not focus on the tweet-level sentiment analysis. Instead, we aim to seek other characteristics of hashtags to produce robust and reliable hashtag-level sentiment classification results. Specifically, besides the tweet-level sentiment analysis results, we have identified other two types of information which is powerful for determining the sentiment polarity of hashtags. First, the co-occurrence relationship among hashtags is important. In our Twitter dataset, we observe that for any two co-occurring hashtags, the probability to share the same sentiment polarity is over 0.8055. However, when they are randomly chosen, the value drops to 0.5324. This comparison implies the possibility to employ this pair-wise information to boost the classification performance. Second, the hashtag literal meaning is another useful feature. For the sentiment hashtags (e.g. "#love", "#sucks"), we find they often appear together with topic hashtags (e.g. "#iPad", "#Obama") to form tweets, conveying the sentiment tendency towards the topics clearly; For the sentiment-topic hashtags like "#iloveobama", they are sufficiently self-explainable to indicate the sentiment polarity and the targets explicitly. Accordingly, we are motivated to incorporate the co-occurrence relationsip and the literal information of hashtags into the classification framework, leading us to the the hashtag graph model as presented in this paper.

Particularly, we propose a novel graph model, which incorporates the co-occurrence information of hashtags, to tackle the problem and adopted three popular inference algorithms for the graph-based classification (Loopy belief propagation (LBP) [18], Relaxation labeling (RL) [19] and Iterative classification algorithms (ICA) [15]). Furthermore, we utilized the literal meaning of hashtags as semi-supervision information in our enhanced boosting setting. We compare the results with the SVM-voting baseline, which employs a two-stage support vector machine (SVM) [4, 2] to generate the tweets' sentiment polarity probability distribution and then votes for hashtag classification. Experiment results on a real-life tweet corpus demonstrates the effectiveness of the proposed model and algorithms.

Paper Organization The rest of this paper is organized as follows. We present our graph model and three classification algorithms in section 3 after a brief review of the related work in Section 2. Then, we present the experiments in Section 4 and conclude the paper in Section 5 with some future work.

2. RELATED WORK

The task of sentiment analysis (SA), a.k.a. opinion mining, has been a hot topic in the research community for years. Previous research on sentiment analysis [8, 30] mainly focuses on product or movie reviews, which are experimentally convenient and easy for evaluation. For other document types including webpages and news, efforts are also made to explore the same task [28]. While the bulk of such work has focused on the document level, some others [27, 23, 22] address the sentiment analysis in the phrase and sentence level which regards sentences (phrases) as classification samples. The objective of above works is to obtain the sentiment polarity for given text (snippets, sentences, or documents). As compared to this thoroughly studied problem, the sentiment analysis for topics is rarely investigated. Though some work attempt to incorporate the sentiment factor into topic models like probabilistic latent semantic indexing (PLSI) or latent Dirichlet allocation (LDA) to give the description about opinion generation [12, 10], it is still hard to reach an agreement for the definitions about topics and how to explain the meaning of sentiment classification (positive/negative) for them. The problem lies in that the definition for topic/entity sentiment polarity using only one-bit representation (positive or negative) is not well-posed. In our work, we try to avoid this critical question but instead aim to provide a sentiment-based snapshot for topics in one period through analyzing corresponding tweets and investigating other features. This task is more clarified and clearer because the opinion tendency for a given topic in a certain time interval is usually associated with some burst events and hence the sentiment classification for topics makes sense.

In terms of methodology, natural language processing techniques and machine learning approaches are two major popular methods for sentiment analysis. Many research followed the natural language processing way to tackle the problem. Nasukawa and Yi [14] proposed an approach to identify the semantic relationship between the target and expression with a syntactic parser and sentiment lexicon. In addition, Ding and Liu [7] used linguistic rules to detect the sentiment orientations in product reviews. Although rule-based methods for identifying the sentiment polarity and targets are effective, the major drawbacks are that it cannot be extended without expert knowledge and the coverage of rules is not satisfactory. While on the other hand, Pang et al. [17] investigated three machine learning methods to produce automated classifiers to generate the class labels for movie reviews. They tested on Naïve Bayes, Maximum Entropy and Support Vector Machine, and evaluated the contribution of different features including unigrams, bigrams, adjectives and POS-tags. Their experimental results found that the SVM classifier with unigram presence features outperformed other competitors. In [16], they tried to separate the subjective portions from the objective ones through finding minimum cuts in graphs to achieve better sentiment analysis performance. Generally, the machine learning based approaches usually have higher recall than rule-based methods because of the strong generalization ability of classifiers. However, the performance of classifiers is extremely sensitive to the quality of training data [13, 3, 29], making the text-level sentiment analysis using machine learning techniques rather unreliable. As a result, in this paper, we not only leverage the sentiment classification for each tweet but also incorporate the link information among hashtags and the literal meaning of them to solve the hashtag sentiment classification problem, which is expected to be more robust and reliable.

Recently, the opinion mining research has begun to pay more and more attention to social networks such as Twitter because they give rise to the massive user-generated publishing activities. In Twitter, a huge amount of tweets contain sentiment information. Barbosa and Feng [2] first investigat a two-stage SVM (subjectivity and polarity) classifier which seems to be more robust regarding biased and noisy data. In this paper, we adopt this two-stage classification framework to build our tweet-level classifier. In Twitter, some unique characteristics can also be utilized for sentiment classification. Davidov et al. [5] employ hashtags and smileys as sentiment labels for classification to allow diverse sentiment types for short texts. In their another paper [6], they analyze the use of "#sarcasm" hashtags and addressed the problem of sarcastic tweets recognition. Jiang et al. [9] propose to take the target of sentiment into consideration in Twitter sentiment analysis, where the hashtags were also utilized as unigram features. Although the hashtag has become a key feature in many micro-blog services, to our best knowledge, our paper is the first to address the task of hashtag-level sentiment classification.

3. HASHTAG-LEVEL SENTIMENT CLASSIFICATION

We start this section with a formal definition for the task of hashtag-level sentiment classification [2]. Given a set of hashtags $\mathcal{H} = \{h_1, h_2, \ldots, h_m\}$ where each hashtag h_i is associated with a set of tweets $\mathcal{T}_i = \{\tau_{i1}, \tau_{i2}, \ldots, \tau_{in}\}$, we aim to collectively infer the sentiment polarities, $\mathbf{y} = \{y_1, y_2, \ldots, y_m\}$ where $y_i \in \{pos, neg\}$ [3], for $\mathcal{H}$. We assume the hashtags in $\mathcal{H}$ are *with* sentiments. The reason lies in that we are particularly interested in the hot hashtags (i.e. topics) which are usually accompanied with sentiment since people tend to express rich sentiment information in their tweets towards these hot topics. The hashtag-level sentiment classification inherently bases upon the tweet-level sentiment analysis results. Let $\mathcal{C}_\mathcal{T}$ be a tweet-level classifier where each tweet τ can be assigned with positive or negative probability $\Pr_{pos}(\tau)$ and $\Pr_{neg}(\tau)$, ensuring that $\Pr_{pos}(\tau)+\Pr_{neg}(\tau) = 1$ to form a binary probability distribution. Here, neutral tweets are ignored since they are not useful for the polarity prediction of hashtags. We develop $\mathcal{C}_\mathcal{T}$ using the state-of-the-art sentiment analysis method, which is presented in details in Section. 4.2.

We can obviously induce the sentiment polarity y_i for the hashtag h_i through aggregating the results from $\mathcal{C}_\mathcal{T}$ by a simple voting strategy. This approach, as stated in Section. 4.3, takes the classification for each hashtag independently. As seen in our experiments, the result is not promising. We have shown that hashtags co-occurring in tweets have much higher probability to share the same sentiment polarity than that if they are randomly selected. This observation clearly motivates us to conduct the hashtag-level sentiment classification collectively, which has been proven to be effective in link-based text classification [24, 20]. In the rest of this section, we will first introduce the hashtag graph model and then present the classification framework and the approximate algorithms for inference.

[2]For the sake of simplicity, we restrict our scenario within the context of Twitter, although applying this framework to other microblogs where hashtags also exist is straightforward.

[3]Hereafter, we use *pos* and *neg* to represent positive and negative label, respectively.

3.1 The Hashtag Graph Model

We define a hashtag graph $\mathbf{HG} = \{\mathcal{H}, \mathcal{E}\}$, in which the edge set $\mathcal{E}$ consists of links between hashtags and each edge e_{ij} represents an undirected link between hashtags h_i and h_j, which co-occur in at least one tweet. Figure. 1 illustrates an example of the hashtag graph, in which hashtags are linked if and only if they co-occur at least once in tweets. Here we take the hastag "#obama" as an example. The surrounding hashtags are generally of three categories: (1) topics which is closely connected to Obama (e.g. "#president" and "#healthcare", etc.); (2) sentiment hashtags which expresses subjective opinions towards Obama, like "#ideal", "#leader" and (3) sentiment-topic hashtags which indicate the target and the sentiment polarity simultaneously, such as "#iloveobama". From this figure, as we can see, the neighbor hashtags more or less lend some sentiment tendency to "#obama". Consequently, It would be unwise if we independently determine the sentiment polarity of each hashtag. Our graph model is aimed at incorporating the co-occurrence relationship and deciding sentiment polarity collectively.

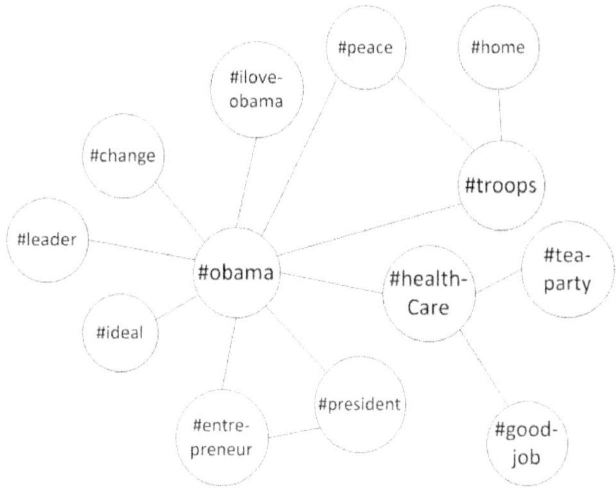

Figure 1: An example of a Hashtag Graph Model

Given the hashtag graph, our ultimate goal is to assign each hashtag h_i with a proper sentiment label $y_i \in \{pos, neg\}$. We make the Markov assumption that the determination of sentiment polarity y_i can only be influenced by either the content of corresponding tweets $\tau \in \mathcal{T}_i$ or sentiment assignments of neighbor hashtag h_j $s.t.(h_i, h_j) \in \mathcal{E}$, which results in our HG a *pairwise Markov Network* [21]. This leads us to the following factorized distribution:

$$\log\left(\Pr\left(\mathbf{y}|\mathbf{HG}\right)\right) = \sum_{h_i \in \mathcal{H}} \log\left(\phi_i(y_i|h_i)\right) + \sum_{(h_j,h_k)\in\mathcal{E}} \log\left(\psi_{j,k}(y_j, y_k|h_j, h_k)\right) - \log Z \quad (1)$$

where the first and second sums correspond to the potential functions of a tweet-based factor and a hashtag-hashtag factor. Z is the regularization factor. The potential function of tweet-based factor can be directly obtained through calculation of the polarity probability for each corresponding tweet; while the hashtag-hashtag factor potential function should incorporate the link information to allow the neighbor hashtags to influence the classification result. The potential functions will be explained together with the inference algorithms in the subsequent section. Given this formula, our objective is to maximize the following function with appropriate sentiment labels:

$$\hat{\mathbf{y}} = \arg\max_{\mathbf{y}} \log\left(\Pr\left(\mathbf{y}|\mathbf{HG}\right)\right) \tag{2}$$

3.2 Approximate Collective Classification Algorithms

As for solving the assignment inference problem given the graph model, many efforts are made and some good inference algorithms are proposed as well. In [11], a structured logistic regression based algorithm is investigated as inference method in a link-based text classification framework. Angelova and Weikum [1] combine Relaxation Labeling [19] inference algorithm and Naïve Bayes to form a context-aware approach for hyperlinked text classification. In this paper, we investigate LBP, RL and ICA as inference approaches to solve the hashtag-level sentiment classification problem.

With graph **HG** containing cycles and no apparent structure, it becomes infeasible to apply exact inference to the optimization function (Equation. 2). Instead, we present three approximate collective classification algorithms (ACCAs): Loopy Belief Propagation (LBP), Relaxation Labeling (RL) and Iterative Classification Algorithm (ICA) to infer the probable sentiment assignment to each hashtag.

3.2.1 *Loopy Belief Propagation (LBP)*

As an iterative algorithm, LBP tries to classify each node in a graph through belief message passing. It is originally proposed to work for tree-like networks as a Bayes likelihood-ration updating rule [18]. Although not guaranteed to converge to a fixed point after any number of iterations, LBP shows surprisingly good performance in practice, as discovered by [25]. In fact, the propagation process tries to reach the stationary points of the Bethe approximation free energy for a factor graph [26].

We define the potential functions as follows:

$$\phi_i(y_i|h_i) = \sum_{\tau\in\mathcal{T}_i} \Pr_{y_i}(\tau) \tag{3}$$

$$\psi_{j,k}(y_j, y_k|h_j, h_k) = \frac{\#(h_j, h_k)}{\#(h_j) + \#(h_k)} \cdot \mathrm{I}_{y_j=y_k} \tag{4}$$

where $\mathrm{I}_{y_j=y_k}$ is the identity function with value 1 when $y_j = y_k$ and 0 otherwise. $\#(h_j, h_k)$ denotes the number of co-occurrence for hashtag h_j and h_k and $\#(h_j)$ is the number of occurrence that h_j appears in tweets. Through this setting, the co-occurrence relationship and the label information of the hashtags are taken into account in the hashtag-hashtag factor potential function.

To obtain the result, we compute in an iterative fashion. The Algorithm. 1 is described in pseudo code. In the algorithm, α is a provisional computed normalized factor which keeps that $m_{i\to j}(pos) + m_{i\to j}(neg) = 1$. The sum of polarity probability of corresponding tweets was used as tweet-based factor potential function. The tweet-level classifier is used as a weak classifier to generate the initial classification probability for hashtags. Propagation procedure can be viewed as a boosting process which relabels the hashtags after iteration terminates. During the loops, the positive (or negative) messages conveyed from hashtag h_i to h_j, as denoted by $m_{i\to j}(pos)$ (or $m_{i\to j}(neg)$), are continuously updated until convergence is reached, as shown in the innermost loop of the iterative procedure. These converged message values are then used to compute the final class labels at last.

Algorithm 1: Loopy Belief Propagation

Input: Hashtag Graph **HG**
Output: Sentiment label for each hashtag h
begin
  foreach $(h_i, h_j) \in \mathcal{E}$ **do**
    foreach $y \in \{pos, neg\}$ **do**
      $m_{i\to j}(y) \leftarrow 1$
      $m_{j\to i}(y) \leftarrow 1$
  repeat
    foreach $h_i \in \mathcal{H}$ **do**
      foreach $h_j \in \mathrm{N}(h_i)$ **do**
        foreach $y_j \in \{pos, neg\}$ **do**
          $m_{i\to j}(y_j) \leftarrow$
          $\alpha \sum_{y_i} \psi_{i,j}(y_i, y_j)\phi_i(y_i) \prod_{h_k\in N(h_i)\backslash h_j} m_{k\to i}(y_i)$
  until *all* $m_{i\to j}(y_j)$ *stop changing*;
  foreach $h_i \in \mathcal{H}$ **do**
    $\hat{y_i} \leftarrow \arg\max_{y\in\{pos,neg\}} \alpha\phi_i(y) \prod_{h_j\in N(h_i)} m_{j\to i}(y)$
  return $\{\hat{y_i}\}$

3.2.2 *Relaxation Labeling (RL)*

Relaxation Labeling is an alternative inference algorithm for graph-based classification models. Rosenfeld et al. [19] first investigate the RL algorithm in the vision community. Later, it was applied as a general rational classification algorithm. In [1], the algorithm was adopted for text categorization. Unlike LBP, which explicitly defines the potential functions for tweet-based factor and hashtag-hashtag factor, RL assumes that $d_{i,j}$ denotes the "improtance" of node j to its neighbor i and $r(y_i, y_j)$ to be the "compatibility" between labels y_i and y_j, and hence updates the polarity probability of hashtags accordingly at each iteration.

Here, we use $b_i(y_i)$ to denote the possibility that hashtag h_i is labeled with assignment y_i. To measure the compatibility of two sentiment labels, we compute the correlation of any two label (positive or negative) types, as suggested in the nonlinear probabilistic case by [19]. To be precise, at the initialization stage of the algorithm, we aggregate the averaged polarity probability of corresponding tweets as the sentiment probability distribution for hashtags, and then assign the label with the max probability to hashtags. Then, the marginal probability of a label and joint probability of any two labels (*pos-pos*, *neg-neg* and *pos-neg*) can be directly estimated from the assignments. The correlation function is defined as:

$$\mathrm{r}(y_i, y_j) = \frac{\mathrm{p}(y_i, y_j) - \mathrm{p}(y_i)\mathrm{p}(y_j)}{(\mathrm{p}(y_i) - \mathrm{p}(y_i)^2)^2(\mathrm{p}(y_j) - \mathrm{p}(y_j)^2)^2} \tag{5}$$

Naturally, it is expected that the hashtags that are more likely to co-occur in tweets to have more mutual influence. We hereby have:

$$d_{i,j} = \frac{\#(h_i, h_j)}{\#(h_i)} \tag{6}$$

The procedure is presented in Algorithm. 2

3.2.3 *Iterative Classification Algorithm (ICA)*

In [15], the iterative classification algorithm is presented to explore the relational data. Algorithm. 3 begins by classifying each hashtag using its tweet-based factor potential function. Each iteration recomputes the hashtag's polarity distribution conditioned on

Algorithm 2: Relaxation Labeling

Input: Hashtag Graph **HG**
Output: Sentiment label for each hashtag h
begin
  foreach $h_i \in \mathcal{H}$ **do**
    foreach $y_i \in \{pos, neg\}$ **do**
      $b_i(y_i) \leftarrow \frac{\sum_{\tau \in T_i} \Pr_{y_i}(\tau)}{\sum_{\tau \in T_i} \sum_{y} \Pr_y(\tau)}$
  repeat
    foreach $h_i \in \mathcal{H}$ **do**
      foreach $y_i \in \{pos, neg\}$ **do**
        $q_i(y_i) \leftarrow \sum_{h_j \in N(h_i)} d_{i,j} \left[\sum_{y_j} r(y_i, y_j) b_j(y_j)\right]$
        $\alpha_i \leftarrow \sum_{y} b_i(y) \left[1 + q_i(y)\right]$
        $b_i(y_i) \leftarrow \frac{1}{\alpha_i} b_i(y_i) \left[1 + q_i(y_i)\right]$
  until *all* $b_i(y_i)$ *stabilize*;
  foreach $h_i \in \mathcal{H}$ **do**
    $\hat{y_i} \leftarrow \arg\max_{y \in \{pos, neg\}} b_i(y)$
  return $\{\hat{y_i}\}$

the current neighborhood polarity probabilities. At the end of each iteration, it relabels the top-k confident hashtags, where k is a value linearly increasing with the number of iterations. And the last iteration will update polarity assignments for all hashtags.

In our experiment, we have:

$$p_i(y_i|\mathbf{HG}, \mathbf{y}) \propto \exp\ \Big(\sum_{h_j \in N(h_i)} d_{i,j} \cdot p_j(y_i) \cdot \phi_i(y_i|h_i)\Big) \quad (7)$$

We describe the algorithm below in Algorithm. 3

Algorithm 3: Iterative Classification Algorithm

Input: Hashtag Graph **HG**
Output: Sentiment label for each hashtag h
begin
  foreach $h_i \in \mathcal{H}$ **do**
    $y_i \leftarrow \arg\max_{y \in \{pos, neg\}} \phi(y|h_i)$
  for $t = 1$ to M **do**
    foreach $h_i \in \mathcal{H}$ **do**
      compute $p_i(y_i|\mathbf{HG}, \mathbf{y})$
      Store $p_i \leftarrow \max_{y} p_i(y|\mathbf{HG}, \mathbf{y})$
      Store $y_i \leftarrow \arg\max_{y} p_i(y|\mathbf{HG}, \mathbf{y})$
    $k \leftarrow |\mathcal{H}| \frac{t}{M}$
    Update the hashtag labels with top-k p_i
  return $\{y_i\}$

3.3 Enhanced Boosting Classification

The three approaches mentioned above use the sentiment labels of corresponding tweets obtained from the tweet-level classifier to initialize the sentiment polarity distribution for every hashtag. Through taking the co-occurrence relationship among hashtags into consideration, the graph-based model, however, boosts the classification result.

Based on previous observations, the sentiment hashtag and sentiment-topic hashtags can indicate the opinion tendency from its literal information. Examples like "#iloveobama", "#sucks", "#awesome", "#horrible", are all self-explainable to infer the sentiment information merely from the hashtag itself explicitly. An interesting observation is that these two kinds of hashtags are usually accompanied with topical hashtags. One simple example tweet is: *"Restoring my #Ipod yet again. #Apple software is such crap that I have to do this routinely. #Apple, fix your software for #Ipod. It #sucks!"*. The topical hashtags "#Apple", "#Ipod" show up together with hashtag "#sucks". This pattern strongly conveys negative opinion from "#sucks" to "#Apple" and "#Ipod".

We expect to further enhance the classification algorithms through introducing a semi-supervised adaptive iteration manner which also take advantage of the literal meaning of hashtags. In our work, we first construct a strong sentiment lexicon, specified with labels $\{pos, neg\}$. We assume that hashtags containing these words have the same polarity as the sentiment lexicon. In the three graph-based algorithms, provided the semi-supervision information, we do not use the tweet-level classifier to initialize its sentiment distribution of these self-explainable hashtags. Instead, we fix their sentiment polarity probability from the beginning. In other words, these label-fixed hashtags are not involved in polarity distribution updating, but only offer sentiment influence to others. Experimental results show that this semi-supervised manner of enhanced boosting classification significantly improves the performance.

Because the enhanced boosting settings for three inference algorithms are similar, due to the page length constraint, we only present the major difference of the boosted LBP algorithm as compared with the original version.

For hashtag set $\tilde{\mathcal{H}} \subseteq \mathcal{H}$, each hashtag h_i in $\tilde{\mathcal{H}}$ contains strong sentiment lexicon which is sufficient to indicate the sentiment polarity $y^*_{h_i}$. Unlike the original initialization stage, for $h_i \in \mathcal{H}$:

$$\phi_i(y_i|h_i) \quad = \quad \sum_{\tau \in T_i} \mathrm{I}_{y^*_{h_i} = y_i} \quad (8)$$

$$\psi_{i,j}(y_i, y_j|h_i, h_j) \quad = \quad \frac{\#(h_i, h_j)}{\#(h_i) + \#(h_j)} \cdot \mathrm{I}_{y_i = y_j \wedge y^*_{h_i} = y_i} \quad (9)$$

Thus the formulas ensure the sentiment assignment for hashtags in $\tilde{\mathcal{H}}$ to be the same as its contained sentiment words. The main difference with the unboost version lies in the iteration procedure, we show the different part in Algorithm. 4:

Algorithm 4: Enhanced Boosting Loopy Belief Propagation

Input: Hashtag Graph **HG**
Output: Sentiment label for each hashtag h
begin
  ...
  repeat
    foreach $h_i \in \mathcal{H}$ **do**
      foreach $h_j \in \mathrm{N}(h_i)$ **do**
        if $h_j \in \tilde{\mathcal{H}}$ **then**
          continue;
        else
          foreach $y_j \in \{pos, neg\}$ **do**
            $m_{i \to j}(y_j) \leftarrow \alpha \sum_{y_i} \psi_{i,j}(y_i, y_j) \phi_i(y_i) \prod_{h_k \in N(h_i) \backslash h_j} m_{k \to i}(y_i)$
  until *all* $m_{i \to j}(y_j)$ *stop changing*;
  ...

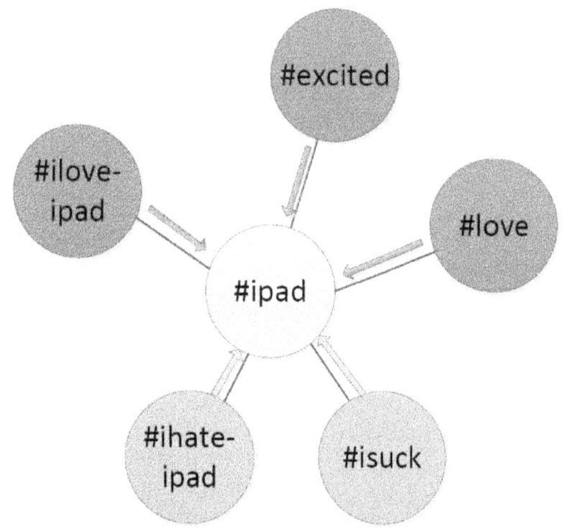

Figure 2: An example of the enhanced boosting classification setting in which strong sentiment hashtags only provide polarity influence to neighbors. Hashtags in red are positive label-fixed nodes and green are negative.

To illustrate this better, we present an example in Figure. 2, where the hashtag "#ipad" has several strong sentiment neighbors such as "#love" and "#isuck". In our enhanced boosting setting, these colored neighbors will not get involved in dynamic updating themselves but only send polarity influence to surrounding neighbors. The propagation from "#ipad" to these colored neighbors will be neglected and blocked.

4. EXPERIMENTAL STUDY

4.1 Data Collection and Evaluation

The evaluation of the hashtag-level sentiment classification is challenging because it is difficult to collect the "golden standard" data set. Although human annotation is possible, we maintain that the workload is rather demanding for large scale evaluation data. What makes it more unreliable is that the satisfactory inter-annotator agreement cannot be achieved, with two contributing factors being that hashtags are often used in tweets with different sentiments, and the sentiment polarity of tweets cannot always be determined with confidence. Instead, in our experiments, to evaluate the performance of the hashtag sentiment classification and to collect the training data for enhanced boosting classification, we use a self-annotation manner to label the dataset.

The data collection process is described as follows. We first ran a coarse-grained selection to find hashtags that we are interested in. We picked 10 topics including "Obama", "Bush", "Lady Gaga", "Justin Bieber", "Islam", "Lakers", "Youtube", "iPad", "Android" and "Microsoft". Then we searched from the tweets pool for hashtags containing the topic words as our seeds. This seed set was hence expanded into our hashtag set $\mathcal{H}$ by retrieving all hashtags that has co-occurred with at least one of the seed hashtags. Finally, for the selected hashtags in $\mathcal{H}$, we labeled hashtags containing sentiment words[4] with appropriate sentiment polarity labels (*pos*, *neg*). This subset of $\mathcal{H}$, denoted by $\tilde{\mathcal{H}}$, is used as our label-fixed set for enhanced boosting classification and test set for evaluation to measure the accuracy, precision, recall and F1 metrics. In addition, we conduct a case study to illustrate some interesting results in Section. 4.6.

In our experiments, our tweets pool has about 0.6 million tweets which were collected in one week period from Twitter. After the seeds selection and data enrichment process, we obtain $\mathcal{H}$ consisting of 2,181 hashtags which occur in 29,195 tweets. The size of edge set $\mathcal{E}$ is 27,430. Selecting hashtags containing strong sentiment words results in a subset $\tilde{\mathcal{H}}$ containing 947 examples, which has 595 positive samples and 352 negative samples. The remaining hashtags in $\mathcal{H}$ do not have a automatic annotated groundtruth, but the classification of them can be evaluated through the case study. This dataset is used for measuring the performance of hashtag sentiment classification algorithms. For enhanced boosting classification approaches, this dataset will be spilled into the training set and test set to evaluate the classification result with cross validation.

4.2 Tweet Level Sentiment Classifier

In this paper, we build the hashtag-level sentiment classification on top of the tweet-level sentiment analysis results. Basically, we adopted the state-of-the-art tweet-level sentiment classification approach [2], which uses a two-stage SVM classifier to determine the sentiment polarity of a tweet. The first (i.e. subjectivity) classifier determines whether a tweet is neutral or subjective while the second one (i.e. polarity classifier) assigns a subjective tweet with positive or negative polarity. The SVM^{light} package [5] is used in our experiments. The two SVM classifiers take the same features as input, which are divided into two categories:

- Content features: including unigram words, punctuation and emoticons. We treat the presence of a token (unigram word, punctuation, or emoticon) as a binary feature which is 1 if the corresponding token occurs in tweet and 0 otherwise.
- Sentiment lexicon features: we employ the lexicon from the General Inquirer [6] and count the number of positive or negative words in tweets as features. There are two dimensions in the feature vector which denote the number of positive and negative words in the tweet.

Classifier	Accuracy	Precision	Recall	F1
subjectivity(1)	83.13%	59.45%	36.59%	45.27%
polarity(2)	88.96%	90.49%	94.82%	92.60%
(1)+(2)	84.13%	/	/	/

Table 1: Performance of the tweet-level classifier

We use the subjectivity classifier to filter out the neutral tweets. The output of the polarity classifier for a subjective tweet is a real value score s which is positive when predicting the tweet t as positive and negative when predicting as negative. Since we need to convert this value into the polarity probability, we use an empirical threshold $\xi = 2$ and the following formula is adopted, which is similar to the manner introduced in [16] :

$$\Pr_{pos}(t) = \begin{cases} 1 & s >= \xi \\ 0.5 + s/(2\xi) & s \in (-\xi, \xi) \\ 0 & s <= -\xi \end{cases} \quad (10)$$

$$\Pr_{neg}(t) = 1 - \Pr_{pos}(t) \quad (11)$$

[4]In our experiments, we selected 50 strong positive and 50 strong negative words as our sentiment lexicon

[5]http://svmlight.joachims.org/

[6]http://www.wjh.harvard.edu/ inquirer/

Setup	Accuracy(%)	Pos-Precision(%)	Pos-Recall(%)	Pos-F1(%)	Neg-Precision(%)	Neg-Recall(%)	Neg-F1(%)
SVM-voting	55.96	64.03	**68.23**	66.06	39.61	35.22	37.29
LBP	56.28	73.26	47.89	57.92	44.44	70.45	54.50
RL	58.07	71.90	54.62	62.08	45.45	63.92	53.12
ICA	59.23	71.81	57.81	64.05	46.36	61.64	52.92
LBP-Boost	**77.72**	97.30	66.69	**79.14**	62.91	95.88	75.97
RL-Boost	72.97	**98.33**	57.80	72.81	57.99	**98.33**	72.95
ICA-Boost	77.40	95.57	67.05	78.88	**63.02**	96.04	**76.11**

Table 2: Performance of the hashtag-level classifiers.

We manually annotated around 15,000 tweets which are randomly selected from the 0.6 million tweets. The tweets are labeled with positive, negative or neutral. Table. 1 shows results of the two-stage SVM tweet-level classifier with 5-fold cross validation. For the two binary classifiers, i.e. subjectivity SVM and polarity SVM, we report the accuracy, precision, recall and F1 values for subjective and positive classes respectively. We also give the overall accuracy for the tweet-level sentiment classifier.

It should be noted that while the accuracy gives an overall evaluation of the classification performance, the precision, recall and F1 values are equally important. These metrics reveal much more information about the classification property, especially when the data is imbalanced. In real-life tweets data, the subjective class is only a minority part: merely 23.8% tweets are subjective in our 15,000 tweets dataset. It is worthy observing that the subjectivity classifier, though have a high accuracy (83.13%), shows extremely low precision (59.45%) and recall (36.59%) for the subjective class, which points out the low ability for discriminating subjective tweets. However, the error analysis and the improving for the tweet-level sentiment classifier is out of the scope of this paper.

4.3 The SVM-Voting Baseline

Intuitively, we can aggregate the hashtag-level sentiment polarity from the results of the tweets containing the hashtag through simple voting methods. We build the SVM-voting baseline approach on the tweet-level classifier. To estimate the positive/negative probability for one hashtag, we use the average polarity distribution of tweets containing hashtag h:

$$\Pr(y_i|h_i) = \frac{\sum_{\tau\in\mathcal{T}_i} \Pr_{y_i}(\tau)}{\sum_{\tau\in\mathcal{T}_i} \Pr_{pos}(\tau) + \sum_{\tau\in\mathcal{T}_i} \Pr_{neg}(\tau)} \quad (12)$$

$$y = \arg\max_{y_i\in\{pos,neg\}} \Pr(y_i|h_i) \quad (13)$$

The results of the SVM-Voting method is presented in Table. 2, which is not promising. The reason lies in that the tweet-level sentiment analysis results are not reliable. We maintain that the low discriminating ability for subjective class is the major cause of this low accuracy (55.96%). This observation motivates us to exploit other available information for this task, as detailed in Section 4.4.

4.4 Evaluation of Graph-based Hashtag-level Sentiment Classification

We compare the three approximate collective classification algorithms with the SVM-voting baseline in this section. The aim is to examine the effectiveness of employing the hashtag co-occurrence information and enhanced boosting techniques in the context of hashtag-level sentiment classification.

Table. 2 shows the comparison results. The iteration number for ICA is set to $M = 10$ in our experiments. As shown, linked-based algorithms (i.e. LBP, RL and ICA) achieve encouraging results compared to the baseline approach, which clearly demonstrates the effectiveness of the hashtag co-occurrence information in the proposed graph-based model for hashtag-level sentiment classification. The improvement mainly comes from the identifying of negative class, the F1 score of which has a remarkable increase from 37.29% to 54.50% (for LBP). Since the number of negative hashtags (352 out of 947) is much less than that of the positive ones, this benefit from link-based algorithms is not very significant. Another major reason for this result, as we found in the experiments, is that the hashtag Graph **HG** suffers the problem of sparseness. The graph density $\mathcal{D}$ [7] is as low as 0.011, which indicates **HG** is very sparse. Therefore, many hashtags receive little sentiment propagation from their few neighbors and the final classification result is biased by the SVM-voting outcome.

We further add the enhanced boosting versions of the graph-based algorithms into our performance comparison. In this boosting setting, we run each experiment with 10-fold cross validation, separating the hashtags containing strong sentiment words $\tilde{\mathcal{H}}$ (947 samples) into a training set and a test set (the proportion of the training set to $\tilde{\mathcal{H}}$ is 0.9). The polarity distribution of the labeled set is fixed during iterations. These label-fixed hashtags only play the role of sentiment propagation. Their impact to neighbors is strengthened and results in a notable performance gain, which can be shown from the comparison. In Table. 2, we observe that the most significant improvement is from the boosting loopy belief propagation, with the high classification accuracy up to 77.72%. The other two boosting ACCAs also increase the performance considerably, as compared with the corresponding un-boosting versions. As for the precision of positive (up to 98.33%) and negative class (up to 63.02%), significant progress is also witnessed. Taking these factors into consideration, we conclude that the literal information of hashtags and the semi-supervised boosting classification approaches are able to greatly enhance the discriminating ability for hashtag-level sentiment classification.

4.5 Effects of the Amount of Supervision

In our enhanced boosting setting, we utilized the literal meaning of hashtags as semi-supervision information. Specifically, we separate the hashtag set $\tilde{\mathcal{H}}$ into a label-fixed training set and an test set for performance evaluation. The training set provides sentiment influence to other hashtags in iterations but blocks the propagation back from them. We vary the size of label-fixed set used in each algorithm by randomly selecting a certain number of labeled hashtags. The size of training set is measured by the proportion to the

[7]To measure the density of a graph, we use the metric "Graph Density", which is defined as: $\mathcal{D} = \frac{2|\mathcal{E}|}{|\mathcal{H}|(|\mathcal{H}|-1)}$.

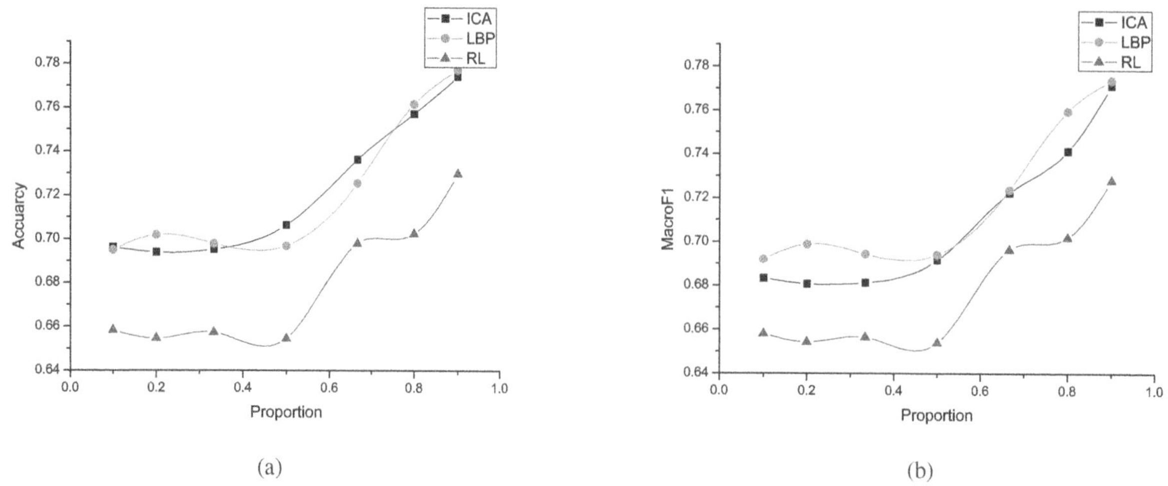

Figure 3: Accuracy and MacroF1 with different training set. The X-axis value denotes the proportion of labeled-fixed training set to all strong sentiment hashtags $\tilde{\mathcal{H}}$ (947 hashtags). The remaining hashtags in $\mathcal{H}$ are unlabeled.

Hashtag	SVM	HG	Neighbors offering correct impacts	Example tweets
#ipad	neg	pos	#love, #free #iloveApple	Games for Cats on #iPad #jaja #ILoveApple http://youtu.be/vaif2uq_0Vc
#youtube	neg	pos	#fun, #video, #twitter	#youtube channel: :D more views, more comments. MORE #FUN! :D #pdkgaming
#obama	neg	pos	#iloveobama, #change, #peace, #ideal, #freedom	#Hope #Change #Peace #Freedom #Dignity #Nonviolence #Beliving #ideal, #peace & #stability #Obama,am i watching mr #LarryKing or it's all about #UsA interests
#islam	pos	neg	#jihad, #terror, #igiveup	*PLS RT*: The Documentary Tehran Doesn't Want u 2 See http://v.gd/OePtiI #islam #terror #jihad #tcot #tlot #a4a #jcot #sgp #ocra #hhrs #gop
#gaga	pos	neg	#hate, #gay	Say I worship #Gaga... Ok... does that mean I am #gay?
#bush	pos	neg	#kill, #iraq, #fail	MitchDaniels was #Bush's budget director. #FAIL Rs goin2Radical...

Table 3: Case study: examples of hashtags classified correctly only in our proposed graph model.

total labeled 947 hashtags $\tilde{\mathcal{H}}$. Meanwhile, we should keep it in mind that there are altogether 2181 hashtags in **HG**, the remaining of which are not included in the performance test for calculation of precision, recall, F1 and accuracy metrics, but will be used for case study in the following section.

Figure. 3 presents the values of macro F1 and accuracy against varying amount of label-fixed hashtags. The reported values are calculated with 10-fold cross validation. It reflects a strong consistence of the changing tendency for the two metrics. We observe that when little labeled data is provided (0.1 to 0.4), the performance for the three algorithms is stable. The values for macro F1 and accuracy has a notable increase when more labeled hashtags are added, strongly indicating that increasing the amount of training set will effectively improve the overall performance for our graph models. Besides, we can see the performance for ICA and LBP are very close with each other. While on the other hand, we argue that the performance of RL is below the other two algorithms all along. This is because that the correlation between two labels is calculated with the initial probability distribution and will not be updated afterwards in RL.

4.6 Case Study

We investigate the result of hashtag-level sentiment classification by looking at some specific examples. We list some interesting hashtags that can be classified correctly only by our proposed graph model in Table. 3. Since we do not intend to highlight the performance of any specific ACCA, we present the result obtained from LBP only. We list the hashtags together with their neighbors that offer impacts to change their polarity assignments into correct labels[8] and corresponding tweets.

In this list, topic hashtags like "#obama" were classified as negative by SVM-voting at first. This is not true since through our analysis, we found that "#iloveobama", "#change", and "#ideal", and other positive hashtags are often show up together with "#obama", and these neighbor hashtags are created by users to highlight their sentiment tendency towards "#obama", as shown in the following tweets in Table. 3. The collective classification for hashtags can be extremely effective especially when the tweets are not straightforward enough for sentiment classification with the two-stage SVM. The example tweets for "#ipad": "Games for Cats on #iPad #jaja #ILoveIPad http://youtu.be/vaif2uq_0Vc", fails to be predicted correctly with the tweet-level classifier since it cannot capture the positive sentiment from "#ILoveApple" at all. Another tweet talking about Lady Gaga "Say I worship #Gaga... Ok... does that mean I am #gay?" implicitly conveys the negative sentiment which is far too difficult for the tweet-level sentiment classification.

There are three reasons for the low performance of the SVM-voting baseline: (1) Tweets are short and it is hard to infer the sentiment polarity only with the unigram and sentiment lexicon features; (2) tweets contain links directing (or redirecting, such as "http://bit.ly/eZJDoJ") to videos or news that reflect the author's underlying sentiment towards the topics cannot be analyzed successfully. (3) Tweets contain both positive and negative sentiment expression towards topics, like "*iTunes is good software but it fails as usually as you use :) #fail #itunes #apple*". These factors make the tweet-level classifier and our baseline rather sensitive to noisy

[8]After reprocessing, hashtags are case-insensitive.

data, leading to an poor hashtag-level sentiment analysis performance.

Incorporating the neighbor hashtag sentiment information gives us a chance to relabel hashtag polarity collectively. This method improves the performance since it tolerates the error introduced by the tweet-level classification and allow the mutual sentiment influence among hashtags.

5. CONCLUSION REMARK AND FUTURE WORK

In this paper, we investigate a novel task, i.e. sentiment classification of hashtags in Twitter. We believe this is important for sentiment analysis of topics since hashtags can be approximately viewed as user-annotated topics. We develop the baseline approach on sentiment analysis results of the tweets containing the hashtag through simple voting strategy. The performance of this intuitive approach is not encouraging as we expected. In order to improve the hashtag-level sentiment classification, we propose a graph model to boost the results from the voting baseline, which effectively incorporates the tweets sentiment information and hashtags co-occurrence relationship. The preliminary results demonstrate that our graph model is able to give competitive performance as compared with the baseline. Going one step further, by extracting the literal sentiment hint from hashtags, we construct the enhanced boosting hashtag classification framework, in which self-explainable hashstags are label-fixed and not updated for polarity, but only offering sentiment influence to neighbor hashtags. Experiment results show significant improvements are achieved in this boosting settings.

There exists some possible extensions to our work. It would be interesting if we can produce a short summary for hashtags based on the sentiment classification. For example, for a new product it is expected to present a list of related features together with typical sentiment expressions, beyond the one-bit snapshot (positive or negative). In addition, we envision to employ the classification of hashtags to enhance the tweet-level sentiment categorization in return.

6. ACKNOWLEDGMENTS

This study is partially supported by the HGJ Grant (No. 2011ZX 01042-001-001) as well as The Specialized Research Fund for the Doctoral Program of Higher Education of China under Grant ("FSSP" Grant No.20100001110203).

7. REFERENCES

[1] R. Angelova and G. Weikum. Graph-based text classification: learn from your neighbors. In *Proceedings of the 29th Annual International ACM SIGIR Conference on Research and Development in Information Retrieval*, SIGIR '06, pages 485–492, 2006.

[2] L. Barbosa and J. Feng. Robust sentiment detection on twitter from biased and noisy data. In *Proceedings of the 23rd International Conference on Computational Linguistics: Posters*, COLING '10, pages 36–44, Stroudsburg, PA, USA, 2010. Association for Computational Linguistics.

[3] D. Blaheta. Handling noisy training and testing data. In *Proceedings of the ACL-02 conference on Empirical methods in natural language processing-Volume 10*, pages 111–116. Association for Computational Linguistics, 2002.

[4] C. Cortes and V. Vapnik. Support-vector networks. *Machine Learning*, 20:273–297, 1995.

[5] D. Davidov, O. Tsur, and A. Rappoport. Enhanced sentiment learning using twitter hashtags and smileys. In *Proceedings of the 23rd International Conference on Computational Linguistics: Posters*, COLING '10, pages 241–249, Stroudsburg, PA, USA, 2010. Association for Computational Linguistics.

[6] D. Davidov, O. Tsur, and A. Rappoport. Semi-supervised recognition of sarcastic sentences in twitter and amazon. In *Proceedings of the Fourteenth Conference on Computational Natural Language Learning*, CoNLL '10, pages 107–116, Stroudsburg, PA, USA, 2010. Association for Computational Linguistics.

[7] X. Ding and B. Liu. The utility of linguistic rules in opinion mining. In *Proceedings of the 30th annual international ACM SIGIR conference on Research and development in information retrieval*, SIGIR '07, pages 811–812, New York, NY, USA, 2007. ACM.

[8] M. Hu and B. Liu. Mining and summarizing customer reviews. In *Proceedings of the tenth ACM SIGKDD international conference on Knowledge discovery and data mining*, KDD '04, pages 168–177, New York, NY, USA, 2004. ACM.

[9] L. Jiang, M. Yu, M. Zhou, X. Liu, and T. Zhao. Target-dependent twitter sentiment classification. In *Proceedings of the 49th Annual Meeting of the Association for Computational Linguistics: Human Language Technologies*, pages 151–160, Portland, Oregon, USA, June 2011. Association for Computational Linguistics.

[10] C. Lin and Y. He. Joint sentiment/topic model for sentiment analysis. In *Proceeding of the 18th ACM conference on Information and knowledge management*, CIKM '09, pages 375–384, New York, NY, USA, 2009. ACM.

[11] Q. Lu and L. Getoor. Link-based classification. In *Machine Learning, Proceedings of the Twentieth International Conference*, ICML '03, pages 496–503. AAAI Press, 2003.

[12] Q. Mei, X. Ling, M. Wondra, H. Su, and C. Zhai. Topic sentiment mixture: modeling facets and opinions in weblogs. In *Proceedings of the 16th international conference on World Wide Web*, WWW '07, pages 171–180, New York, NY, USA, 2007. ACM.

[13] P. Melville, N. Shah, L. Mihalkova, and R. Mooney. Experiments on ensembles with missing and noisy data. *Multiple Classifier Systems*, pages 293 302, 2004.

[14] T. Nasukawa and J. Yi. Sentiment analysis: capturing favorability using natural language processing. In *Proceedings of the 2nd International Conference on Knowledge Capture*, K-CAP '03, pages 70–77, 2003.

[15] J. Neville and D. Jensen. Iterative classification in relational data. In *Proceedings of the AAAI 2000 Workshop Learning Statistical Models from Relational Data*, AAAI '00, pages 42–49. AAAI Press, 2000.

[16] B. Pang and L. Lee. A sentimental education: Sentiment analysis using subjectivity summarization based on minimum cuts. In *Proceedings of the 42nd Annual Meeting of the Association for Computational Linguistics*, ACL '04, pages 271–278, Stroudsburg, PA, USA, 2004. Association for Computational Linguistics.

[17] B. Pang, L. Lee, and S. Vaithyanathan. Thumbs up? sentiment classification using machine learning techniques. In *Proceedings of the Conference on Empirical Methods in Natural Language Processing*, EMNLP '02, 2002.

[18] J. Pearl. Reverend bayes on inference engines: A distributed

hierarchical approach. In *Proceedings of the National Conference on Artificial Intelligence*, AAAI '82, pages 133–136, 1982.

[19] A. Rosenfeld, R. A. Hummel, and S. W. Zucker. Scene labeling by relaxation operations. *IEEE Transactions on Systems, Man, and Cybernetics*, SMC-6(6):420–433, 1976.

[20] P. Sen and L. Getoor. Link-based classification. In *Technical Report*, 2007.

[21] B. Taskar, P. Abbeel, and D. Koller. Discriminative probabilistic models for relational data. In *Proceedings of the 18th Conference in Uncertainty in Artificial Intelligence*, UAI '02, pages 485–492. Morgan Kaufmann, 2002.

[22] T. Wilson, J. Wiebe, and P. Hoffmann. Recognizing contextual polarity in phrase-level sentiment analysis. In *Proceedings of the conference on Human Language Technology and Empirical Methods in Natural Language Processing*, pages 347–354. Association for Computational Linguistics, 2005.

[23] T. Wilson, J. Wiebe, and P. Hoffmann. Recognizing contextual polarity: an exploration of features for phrase-level sentiment analysis. *Computational Linguistics*, 35(3):399–433, 2009.

[24] Y. Yang, S. Slattery, and R. Ghani. A study of approaches to hypertext categorization. *J. Intell. Inf. Syst.*, 18:219–241, March 2002.

[25] J. S. Yedidia, W. T. Freeman, and Y. Weiss. Generalized belief propagation. In *Advances in Neural Information Processing Systems 13, Papers from Neural Information Processing Systems*, NIPS '00, pages 689–695. MIT Press, 2000.

[26] J. S. Yedidia, W. T. Freeman, and Y. Weiss. Constructing free-energy approximations and generalized belief propagation algorithms. *IEEE Transactions on Information Theory*, 51(7):2282–2312, 2005.

[27] H. Yu and V. Hatzivassiloglou. Towards answering opinion questions: Separating facts from opinions and identifying the polarity of opinion sentences. In *Proceedings of the 2003 conference on Empirical methods in natural language processing-Volume 10*, pages 129–136. Association for Computational Linguistics, 2003.

[28] W. Zhang, C. Yu, and W. Meng. Opinion retrieval from blogs. In *Proceedings of the sixteenth ACM conference on Conference on information and knowledge management*, CIKM '07, pages 831–840, New York, NY, USA, 2007. ACM.

[29] X. Zhu, X. Wu, and Y. Yang. Effective classification of noisy data streams with attribute-oriented dynamic classifier selection. *Knowledge and Information Systems*, 9(3):339–363, 2006.

[30] L. Zhuang, F. Jing, and X. Y. Zhu. Movie review mining and summarization. In *Proceedings of the 15th ACM international conference on Information and knowledge management*, CIKM '06, pages 43–50, New York, NY, USA, 2006. ACM.

Language-independent Sentiment Classification Using Three Common Words

Zheng Lin
Institute of Computing Technology,
Chinese Academy of Sciences
Beijing, China 100080
+86-13718850926
linzheng@ict.ac.cn

Songbo Tan
Institute of Computing Technology,
Chinese Academy of Sciences
Beijing, China 100080
+86-13426133070
tansongbo@software.ict.ac.cn

Xueqi Cheng
Institute of Computing Technology,
Chinese Academy of Sciences
Beijing, China 100080
+86-13910791815
cxq@ict.ac.cn

ABSTRACT
Many methods for cross-lingual processing tasks are resource-dependent, which will not work without machine translation system or bilingual lexicon. In this paper, we propose a novel approach for multilingual sentiment classification just by few seed words. For a given language, the proposed approach learns a sentiment classifier from the initial seed words instead of any labeled data. We employ our method both in supervised learning and unsupervised learning. Experimental results demonstrate that our method relies less on external resource but performs as well as or better than the baseline.

Categories and Subject Descriptors
I.2.7 [**Artificial Intelligence**]: Natural Language Processing

General Terms
Algorithms, Experimentation, Performance

Keywords
multilingual sentiment classification, opinion words, clustering, machine translation

1. INTRODUCTION
With the rapid development of Internet and globalization, many multilingual websites are built. For a non-native reader, it is hard to acquire useful information from cross-lingual customer reviews, thus cross-lingual sentiment analysis has received more attention recently.

To cope with the problem of cross language, a variety of translation-based methods have been developed. Through translation, the training data and testing data belong to the same language, so that monolingual sentiment classification algorithms can be conducted. However, it is expensive and challenging to build the translation system or bilingual lexicon for the languages that are lack of adequate parallel corpora. Even if there are already translation tools, the translation-based methods suffer from two major drawbacks. On one hand, machine translation system usually generates only one best translation result, so the loss of translation accuracy may deteriorate the sentiment classification accuracy. On the other, the source language and target language may follow different distributions, so the cross-lingual classifier may not perform as well as the monolingual classifier.

In this paper, we propose a novel approach for multilingual sentiment classification just by few seed words. For a given language, the proposed approach learns a sentiment classifier from the initial seed words instead of any labeled data. Our work can be described into three steps: The first step is to extract the candidate opinion words by an adverb. The second step is using two adjectives to cluster the opinion words and unlabeled data into two categories (positive or negative) simultaneously. In opinion words and samples clustering, we propose an iterative KL-divergence method to enhance the performance. The third step is to learn a classifier by semi-supervised learning.

Unlike previous work, our method relies less on external resource but performs as well as or better than the machine translation method. The improvements achieved are mainly because it overcomes the drawbacks of machine translation method. However, our approach is language independent because we don't require any labeled data in either source language or target language. Instead, all we need are few seed words and an amount of unlabeled data in the target language.

2. Related Word

2.1 Monolingual Sentiment Classification
Sentiment analysis has recently received a lot of attention in the Natural Language Processing community (Tang and Tan,2009). A key problem of sentiment analysis is to determine the polarity of a review is positive (thumbs up) or negative (thumbs down). Pang et al.(2002) compared multiple supervised machine learning algorithms (Naive Bayes, Maximum Entropy, Support Vector Machines) for the task of sentiment classification. This dependency on annotated training data is one major shortcoming of all supervised methods.

Turney (2002) describes a method of unsupervised sentiment classification using two human-selected seed words (the words "poor" and "excellent") in conjunction with a very large text corpus; the semantic orientation of phrases is computed as their association with the seed words. The sentiment of a sample is calculated as the average semantic orientation of all such phrases.

CIKM'11, October 24–28, 2011, Glasgow, Scotland, UK.

2.2 Cross-lingual Sentiment Classification

Cross-lingual text categorization was first studied by Bel, Koster, et al. (2003). Mihalcea et al. (2007) discussed different shortcomings of lexicon-based translation scheme and proposed to use a parallel-corpus to train a new classifier with sentences in the target language corresponding to source language.

With the boom of statistical machine translations, methods based on machine translation have been prevailed. Fortuna and Shawe-Taylor (2005) studies the use of machine translation tools for the purpose of cross-lingual text classification and mining. Wan (2009) applies a co-training method to leverage resources from both a source and a target language. Shi et al. (2010) transfers the classification knowledge by translating the model features and by using an Expectation Maximization algorithm.

A series of adaptation methods (Tan, 2007; Tan, 2009) have been applied to cross-lingual sentiment analysis recently. Blitzer et al. (2006) propose an effective algorithm for unsupervised domain adaptation, called structural correspondence learning. Prettenhofer and Stein (2010) propose a cross-lingual text classification approach that builds on SCL. The approach uses unlabeled samples, along with a simple word translation oracle, in order to induce task-specific, cross-lingual word correspondences.

3. Multilingual Sentiment Classification

3.1 Problem

Many methods for cross-lingual sentiment analysis are resource-dependent, which will not work without machine translation system or bilingual lexicon. Futhermore, methods based on machine translation rely on the machine translation tool while machine translation itself is a hard problem. Methods based on SCL need a word translation oracle and several human-selected pivot features. However, it is expensive and challenging to build the translation system or bilingual lexicon for the languages that are lack of adequate parallel corpora.

Besides, those methods learn knowledge for classification from the labeled source language. When confronted with a target language without any annotated source language data, traditional methods don't work.

We aim to solve such problems and propose a language-independent method for multilingual sentiment classification.

3.2 Opinion words Extraction

In customer reviews, opinion words are used to express opinion, sentiment or attitude of reviewers. The intuition of opinion words extraction is to find out words with strong emotion, for these words are informative and discriminative when predicting the polarity of a sample.

Our approach is on the assumption that there is an adverb of degree in every language. For example, "very" is often used to give emphasis to adjectives or adverbs in English. Therefore, we first use "very" as heuristic information to extract the candidate opinion words by Pattern "*very* w_i", and then remove stop words from candidate opinion words, such as "of", "the". Here, stop words are generated by words with high frequency for individual language. For every extracted opinion word w_i, its weight is assigned by Equation 1:

$$\alpha(w_i) = \frac{f(very, w_i)}{\sum_{i=1}^{n} f(very, w_i)} \qquad (1)$$

The algorithm of opinion word extraction is described as Algorithm 1.

Algorithm 1 Opinion Word Extraction

Input: Unlabeled data, a seed word

Output: Stop word list and opinion word list

Procedure:

1. Extract all w_i according to pattern "w_i BEHIND *very*" to get the candidate opinion word set C
2. Generate stop words list automatically

   Statistic the frequency of every word in unlabeled data

   Put the word with frequency over threshold into stop word list
3. Remove stop word from C to get opinion word List S
4. for every word in S

   Statistic the co-occurrence frequency of "*very* w_i" and assign the weight of w_i by Equation 1

3.3 Opinion words Clustering

After opinion word extraction, we already have opinion word list but we don't know the polarity of each word, so we hope to classify the opinion words into two categories. For a given language, there're at least two adjectives representing the positive polarity and the negative polarity, such as "good", "bad" in English and "好", "坏" in Chinese. These adjectives can be regarded as seed words to cluster the opinion words. In this paper, we propose an iterative KL divergence method to cluster the opinion words and samples simultaneously. Our method can be described as three steps:

The first step is using two polar seed words to label samples and opinion words roughly. More specifically, a sample containing word "good/bad" is regarded as positive/negative and the opinion words in that sample are labeled as positive/negative too.

The second step is to assign an exclusive polarity to each opinion word. A opinion word may occur in both positive and negative samples, so its polarity is ambiguous. We introduce KL-divergence to do the disambiguation work. First, let's explain the basic idea of KL divergence. KL-divergence is a non-symmetric measure of the difference between two probability distributions P and Q. If KL-divergence is applied to single sample, it is called pointwise KL-divergence:

$$\delta(w; P \| Q) = P(w) \log \frac{P(w)}{Q(w)} \qquad (2)$$

If a word appears in P distribution frequently and seldom appears in Q distribution, junction between this word and P distribution is tight, and vice versa. In our work, P represents the positive samples and Q represents the negative samples. The polarity of each ambiguous opinion word is assigned by comparing its *δ(w; pos||neg)* and *δ(w; neg|| pos)*, and the function is defined as:

$$polarity(w)=\begin{cases} pos & \delta(w;pos\,||\,neg)\geq\delta(w;neg\,||\,pos)\\ neg & \delta(w;pos\,||\,neg)<\delta(w;neg\,||\,pos)\end{cases} \quad (3)$$

The third step is to cluster the opinion words and samples iteratively. After step 1 and step 2, more polar opinion words are acquired and they provide more heuristic information that can be utilized to re-label the samples. According to the re-labeled samples, we can obtain more accurate polar words and then apply Equation 3 to refine the polarity labeling. Here, the sample is re-labeled by the up-to-date polar opinion word and the opinion word score of a sample *d* is calculated as:

$$score(d)=\frac{\sum_{i=1}^{m}\alpha(w_i\in pos)}{len(d)}-\frac{\sum_{i=1}^{n}\alpha(w_i\in neg)}{len(d)} \quad (4)$$

where *len(d)* represents the length of *d*, *m* represents the number of positive opinion words, *n* represents the number of negative words in *d*, $\alpha(w_i)$ represents the weight of opinion word w_i.

The algorithm of opinion words clustering is described as Algorithm 2.

Algorithm 2 Opinion word Clustering

Input: Unlabeled data, unlabeled opinion words, two seed words

Output: Labeled opinion words and labeled data

Procedure:

1. Labeled all samples and opinion words by two polar words

Loop for *I* iterations

2. Select *n* positive and *n* negative the most confidently predicted samples as seed samples
3. Label the opinion words according to selected seed samples
   Rectify the label of opinion words by Equation 3
4. Re-label all samples according to the up-to-date labeled opinion words by Equation 4

If the accuracy of labeled samples is improved, the accuracy of labeled opinion words can be improved too, and vice versa. Therefore, we employ an iterative strategy to make labeled samples and labeled opinion words boost each other.

3.4 Semi-supervised Learning

Translation-based methods can be categorized into two types: corpus translation and features translation. In corpus translation, either the training data is translated into target language or the testing data is translated into source language, so that monolingual sentiment classification algorithms can be applied. In features translation, classifier training on source language is transferred by translating the features into target language. Above two methods both suffers from the errors caused by translation and the discrepancy of culture and expression between two different languages. Instead, our method is self-learning and perform as well as or better than the translation-based method.

After opinion words clustering, all samples are labeled. Firstly, we choose a small number of the most confidently labeled samples as initial training data. Secondly, a classifier is trained on the initial training data. Finally, the most confidently predicted samples are added to training data to retrain the classifier in each iteration. It is well known that the performance of semi-supervised learning depends on the initial samples chosen and criterion for samples selected during iteration. In order to improve the accuracy of initial training data, we sort all the samples by opinion word score (Equation 4) and pick out the highest ranked samples. Moreover, bias is unavoidable in self-learning, for this reason we propose a new criterion for sample selection. The new criterion combines the posterior probability generated by classification model and the opinion word we have already acquired. For a sample, its final score is calculated as the posterior probability plus the opinion word score under the corresponding category.

Algorithm 3 Semi-supervised Learning

Input: Initial training data, unlabeled data, labeled opinion words

Output: Sentiment Classifier

Procedure:

1. Train a base classifier on initial training data

Loop for *I* iterations

2. for each sample
   Generate the posterior probability *p* for each category
   Calculate the opinion word score *s* for each category
3. Rank all samples according to (*p*+*s*) for each category
4. Select *n* positive and *n* negative samples with the highest (*p*+*s*)
5. Add the chosen samples to existing training data and retrain the classifier

---

4. Experiments

4.1 Experimental Setup

To testify the effectiveness of the proposed method, we conduct experiments on multilingual hotel reviews (French, German, Spanish, Dutch). These multilingual samples are collected from a multilingual hotel website http://www.booking.com/. Each set of the four languages contains 2000 positive and 2000 negative reviews.

In comparison experiment of cross-lingual sentiment classification, we choose English as source language for the reason that many annotated corpora for English sentiment classification are freely available on the Web. In the experiments of translation-based sentiment classification, we choose 50% labeled data of source language for training and 50% labeled data of target language for testing. In semi-supervised learning, we choose 10% the most confidently predicted samples as seed, 50% labeled data as testing set and 40% data as unlabeled set.

In multilingual sentiment classification, we choose three seed words as heuristic information. One of the three seed words is used to opinion word extraction and the other two are used to opinion word clustering. For English, we choose the mostly common used three words "very", "good" and "bad". For the other languages, the seed words are translated by Google translation system from "very", "good" and "bad" directly. Table 1 shows the seed words we used in our experiments.

Table 1: Three heuristic words for each language

Language	Adverb of Degree	Positive	Negative
French	très	bonne	mauvaise
German	sehr	gut	schlecht
Spanish	muy	bueno	malo
Dutch	zeer	goede	slecht

In the experiments, we choose Naïve Bayesian (George and Pat, 1995) as base classifier and all words in the corpus as features without reduction and selection. In the contrast test, our approach is compared with two baseline methods:

(1) Baseline 1 (translation-based method): First, we train a sentiment classifier on the labeled data of source language and then translate the testing data of target language into source language by Google translation system. Finally, we apply the sentiment classifier trained on source language to the translated testing data.

(2) Baseline 2 (lexicon-based method): First, we translate the sentiment-lexicon of source language into target language. Then, we classify the reviews by translated sentiment-lexicon instead of the classifier trained on labeled data.

4.2 Experimental Results

To evaluate the effectiveness of iterative KL-divergence method that we proposed, we conduct several experiments on multilingual hotel reviews. Table 2 contrasts the accuracy of the first 10% confidently predicted samples before and after applying the iterative KL-divergence method. Seen from table 2, after KL iteration, the average accuracy of the first 10% selected samples exceeds the baseline method with a performance improvement of 6.54%. The comparison results demonstrate that using iterative KL-divergence method can improve the performance of initial training data selection.

Table2: Accuracy of the first 10% confidently predicted samples

Language	Before_KL	After_KL
French	0.9298	0.9667
German	0.9455	0.9706
Spanish	0.7813	0.9565
Dutch	0.9	0.9247
Average	0.8892	0.9546

In cross-lingual sentiment classification task, we compare our multilingual sentiment classification approach in supervised learning and unsupervised learning respectively. In supervised learning, testing data of target language is translated into English. In unsupervised learning, the English sentiment-lexicon is translated into target language. From Table 3, we can see that our approach outperforms the baseline1 and baseline2 with a performance improvement of 7.23% and 2.01% on average respectively after semi-supervised learning.

Table 3 Comparison of machine translation method and sentiment lexicon method with our language-independent method

Language	Baseline 1	Baseline 2	Semi-supervised (Initially)	Semi-supervised (Finally)
English->French	0.7041	0.7700	0.7770	0.8037
English->German	0.7402	0.7779	0.7245	0.7913
English->Spanish	0.7483	0.7895	0.7935	0.8005
English->Dutch	0.7270	0.7910	0.7945	0.8133
Average	0.7299	0.7821	0.7724	0.8022

Seen from table 3, baseline1 method performs the worst, which proves that machine-translation-based method is better than sentiment-lexicon-based method in cross-lingual sentiment classification. Our multilingual sentiment classification approach outperforms machine-translation-based method because our approach overcomes the drawbacks of machine translation method. For one reason, machine translation system usually generates only one best translation result, and errors caused by translation may deteriorate the sentiment classification accuracy. For the other, the source language and target language follow different distributions, so the cross-lingual classifier may not perform as well as the monolingual classifier. However, our method learns the sentiment classifier on target language directly and its performance just depends on the quality and characteristics of target language.

5. Conclusions

In this paper, we propose a novel approach for multilingual sentiment classification by the least resource. Moreover, our approach is language-independent because we don't require any labeled data in either source language or target language. All we need are few seed words and an amount of unlabeled data in the target language. Our work can be described into three steps: The first step is to extract the candidate opinion words by one seed word. The second step is using two seed words to cluster the opinion words and unlabeled data into two categories (positive or negative) simultaneously. In opinion words and samples clustering, we propose an iterative KL-divergence method to enhance the performance. The third step is to learn a classifier by semi-supervised learning. In order to avoid bias, we combine the posterior probability of classifier and opinion word score together to select samples in each iteration.

6. ACKNOWLEDGMENTS

This work was mainly supported by two funds, i.e., the National Natural Science Foundation of China (60933005 & 60803085).

7. REFERENCES

[1] Blaž Fortuna and John Shawe-Taylor. 2005. The use of machine translation tools for cross-lingual text mining. In Proceedings of the ICML Workshop on Learning with Multiple Views.

[2] Bo Pang, Lillian Lee, and Shivakumar Vaithyanathan. 2002. Thumbs up? Sentiment Classification using Machine Learning Techniques. In Proceedings of EMNLP-2002.

[3] John Blitzer, Ryan McDonald, and Fernando Pereira.2006. Domain adaptation with structural correspondence learning. In Proceedings of EMNLP-06, pages 120–128, Sydney.

[4] John Blitzer, Mark Dredze, and Fernando Pereira. 2007. Biographies, bollywood, boom-boxes and blenders: Domain adaptation for sentiment classification. In Proceedings of ACL-07, pages 440–447, Prague.

[5] John George and Langley Pat. 1995. Estimating Continuous Distributions in Bayesian Classifiers. In Proceedings of the Eleventh Conference on Uncertainty in Artificial Intelligence. pages 338-345. Morgan Kaufmann, San Mateo.

[6] Lei Shi, Rada Mihalcea et al.2010. Cross-lingual Text Classification by Model Translation and Semi-Supervised Learning. In Proceedings of EMNLP-10, pages 1057-1067.

[7] Nuria Bel, Cornelis H. A. Koster, and Marta Villegas. 2003. Cross-lingual text categorization. In Proceedings of ECDL-03, pages 126–139, Trondheim.

[8] Peter Prettenhofer and Benno Stein. 2010. Cross-lingual Text Classification using Structural Correspondence Learning. In Proceedings of ACL-10, pages 1118–1127.

[9] Peter Turney. 2002. Thumbs up or thumbs down? Semantic orientation applied to unsupervised classification of reviews. In Proceedings of ACL-2002.

[10] Rada Mihalcea and Carmen Banea. 2007. Learning multilingual subjective language via cross-lingual projections. In Proceedings of the Association for Computational Linguistics, Prague, Czech Republic.

[11] Xiaojun Wan. 2009. Co-training for crosslingual sentiment classification. In Proceedings of ACL/AFNLP-09, pages 235–243, Singapore.

[12] H. Tang, S. Tan and X. Cheng. A Survey on Sentiment Detection of Reviews. Expert Systems with Applications. 2009.

[13] S. Tan, G. Wu, H. Tang and X. Cheng. A novel scheme for domain-transfer problem in the context of sentiment analysis. CIKM 2007.

[14] S. Tan, X. Cheng, Y. Wang, H. Xu. Adapting Naive Bayes to Domain Adaptation for Sentiment Analysis. ECIR 2009.

A Cross-domain Adaptation Method for Sentiment Classification Using Probabilistic Latent Analysis

Sheng Gao
Institute for Infocomm Research (I2R), A*STAR
1 Fusionopolis Way, Connexis (South Tower),
Singapore, 138632
gaosheng@i2r.a-star.edu.sg

Haizhou Li
Institute for Infocomm Research (I2R), A*STAR
1 Fusionopolis Way, Connexis (South Tower),
Singapore, 138632
hli@i2r.a-star.edu.sg

ABSTRACT
Sentiment classification is becoming attractive in recent years because of its potential commercial applications. It exploits supervised learning methods to learn the classifiers from the annotated training documents. The challenge in sentiment classification is in that the sentiment domains are diverse, heterogeneous and fast-growing. The classifiers trained on one domain (source domain) could not classify a document from another domain (target domain). Moreover, it is impractical to prepare training samples for the coming domain. To make use of unlabeled samples in the target domain and labeled ones in the source domain, domain adaptation is a suitable technology. This paper will present a cross-domain topic indexing (CDTI) method so that a common semantic space is found from the prior between-domain term correspondences and the term co-occurrences in the cross-domain documents. These observations are characterized with the mixture model in CDTI, each component being a possible topic and being shared by the source and target domains. Thus the common topics are found to index the cross-domain content. Our contributions include 1) a probabilistic framework is presented to model the between-domain statistics; 2) EM based algorithm is presented to learn the topic model; and 3) the inference algorithm is presented to obtain the topic distribution for a specific (source or target) document. Our evaluation on the multi-domain sentiment classification shows that CDTI outperforms the state-of-art domain adaptation method, i.e. spectral feature alignment (SFA), and the traditional latent semantic indexing method.

Categories and Subject Descriptors
H.3.3 [**Information Search and Retrieval**]: Clustering; I.2.6 [**Learning**]: Concept learning, I.2.7 [**Natural Language Processing**]: Text analysis

General Terms
Algorithms, Experimentation

Keywords
Domain adaptation, Latent topic analysis, Sentiment classification, Opinion mining

1. INTRODUCTION
In the virtual world of the web, we are seeing that growing people utilize the platform to freely express their feelings or write their opinions on anything that happens. This results in a huge volume of user generated content (UGC) such as blogs, user reviews, etc. In the paper, we are interesting in the UGC which carries the user's sentiment such as positive or negative opinion on the object. The sentiment UGC is widely scattered in the webs. For example, the Amazon web site [1] hosts a lot of user reviews on the products. The reviews may express the user experiences on a product, the facets which the users like or dislike, and have a scale to measure the overall user likeness while in the IMDB site[2], the users post their comments on the movies. Most of the reviews are long and contain the detailed expressiveness. In contrary, the user's comments in the twitter [3] are often short but are instant and dynamic. In a word, UGC data are diverse, heterogeneous and fast-growing.

The UGC data are informative and useful in improving the business decision. They provide large-scale instant and up-to-date user's experiences on the products. However, it seems impossible to let the human reading and digesting the opinions because of their dynamic and huge size. We need a tool to digest the user opinions through automatically analyzing the reviews. Classifying a review as positive or negative is just a binary classification problem. However, the unique challenges are faced in UGC data.

In recent years, sentiment classification is becoming attractive. Many researchers, who are from the different areas such as natural language processing, data mining and information retrieval, work together to address the issues in sentiment analysis, classification and summary [3, 4, 8, 9, 14]. One of challenges is how to learn a good classifier for the target domain in case of only unlabelled documents available. If the source domain is similar to the target domain, i.e. the term usages in two domains are similar, the classifier in the source domain (source classifier) may work well in the target domain (target classifier). However, in most scenarios, the target domain is quite different from the source domain in many facets. Firstly, the topic in two domains may be different, e.g. one about the new launching iPad and another about a book. Secondly, the written languages may be different, one written in Chinese and another in English. Finally, the term usages are different. As an example, we select the two domains *book* and *dvd* from the multi-domain dataset used in our experiment [4] for explanation. The reviews in the former frequently use the term *book, reading, author, chapter*, etc., while the latter frequently use the terms *dvd, watch, film, scenes*, etc.

Although the differences exist in the cross-domain, there are still a few cross-domain relations to be exploited to bridge them together. In the above mentioned domains, i.e. *book* and *dvd*, some terms are

CIKM'11, October 24–28, 2011, Glasgow, Scotland, UK.

[1] http://www.amazon.com/
[2] http://www.imdb.com/
[3] http://twitter.com/
[4] Data from http://www.cs.jhu.edu/~mdredze/datasets/sentiment/

observed in both domains, e.g. *action, American, about*, etc. These terms, which are named as *pivot features* in [6, 8], are the clues which can be used to link the two domains. In cases of documents in the domains written in different languages, the pivot features will be extracted from the translation dictionary [20]. The pivot features are the prior knowledge of the between-domain correspondence.

The pivot features divide the terms in each domain into two sets, i.e. one set including domain-independent terms (i.e. pivot features) and the other including domain-specific terms. In order to extract the cross-domain common feature space, we need to extract the cross-domain pair-wise term occurrences from the source and target domains. However, the cross-domain evidences are not obvious like the term occurrences in a single document because the documents in the source and target domain are collected independently and it lacks the pair-wise relation between a source document and a target document. One possible way is to propagate the relation through the pivot features such as in [8]. For example, if a source domain-specific term w_s co-occurs with a pivot feature w_l, which further co-occurs with a target domain-specific term w_t, thus there will be a relation between the two domain-specific terms w_s and w_t.

From the cross-domain document pair, i.e. a pair of source document and target document, the co-occurrence of a pair of the source-domain term and the target-domain term could be extracted with the help of pivot features. In the recent state-of-art methods on domain adaptation, the observed evidences are often modeled using the bipartite graph and the common space is solved using spectral clustering algorithm [8, 13, 17]. For example, in the recent work of spectral feature alignment (SFA) [8], the bipartite term graph is built from the pair-wise term co-occurrences (i.e. the pair of domain-independent term and domain-specific term). Then the spectral clustering algorithm [18] is exploited to extract the low-dimensional eigen-space. Thus the source-domain document will be represented in the eigen-space. So does the target-domain document. However, if we need to analyze the latent topics in the cross-domain, the clustering algorithms (e.g. K-means) must be run on the documents in both domains, which are represented in the eigen-space. In order to get the topics, two steps are needed. More importantly, when building the bipartite graph, the term co-occurrence is counted at the corpus level without considering the document identities. Therefore, it has no capability to explain how the topics are distributed in a specific document.

In the paper, we will present a cross-domain topic indexing (CDTI) method so that the topics are the natural output of learning stage and the topic distribution in a specific document from the source or target domain can be inferred. Rather than modeling corpus-level co-occurrence of the term pair, CDTI uses the mixture model to characterize the source-target pair-wise term occurrences from the specific source-target document pair. The component in the model, i.e. topic model, explains the source-target term pair distribution in a topic, $P(w_s, w_t|z)$. The topic models are latent in CDTI. In order to estimate them, the EM algorithm is presented. As the topic models are known, the topic distribution for a new document can be inferred whether it is from the source domain or the target domain. The detailed algorithms for learning and inference will be discussed in Section 2. The topic distribution will be used as indexing the document content. Because the source domain and target domain are represented in the same topic space, we expect the source classifier could work better compared with the source classifier trained in the original document feature space. It will be elaborated in the experiments reported in Section 4.

CDTI is a novel probabilistic model for estimating latent topics from the cross-domain. It works on the cross-domain rather than single domain such as traditional probabilistic latent semantic analysis (PLSA) [15] and latent Dirichlet allocation (LDA) [5]. It characterizes the source-target pair-wise term statistics rather than the term statistics. In particular, its inference algorithm is quite unique in that it needs to integrate out the source term variables when estimating the document topic distribution for the target domain and vice versa when estimating the topic for the source domain.

Our contributions include:

- Presenting a generative framework to model the cross-domain pair-wise term co-occurrence;
- Presenting the EM based algorithm to learn the topic models from the source and target domain corpus;
- Presenting the novel inference algorithm to extract the topic distribution for any specific (source or target) document.

In the next section, we will introduce the problem of cross-domain topic analysis and present the CDTI models. In Section 3, a short discussion is introduced for cross-domain sentiment classification. We report our experiments on the multi-domain sentiment corpus in Section 4. Finally, we will summarize our findings.

2. CROSS-DOMAIN TOPIC INDEXING

In cross-domain topic analysis, we need to model the co-occurrence among the source domain term, the target domain term, the source domain document identity, and the target domain document identity. The relation among four variables, i.e. *4-VAR*, is more complex than the single domain topic analysis, where there are only two variables, i.e. term and document identity.

In the section, we will discuss all issues faced in CDTI. Firstly, we will formulate the CDTI problem. Then we will elaborate the training and inference algorithms for CDTI. Finally, we will discuss some practical methods to extract 4-VAR co-occurrences.

2.1 Problem Definition

Assume we have two domains, saying source domain C_s and target domain C_t. The corresponding term and dictionary are denoted as w_s, w_t and V_s, V_t, respectively. Given the source-target document pair (d_s, d_t), we have a set of pair-wise term observations (w_s, w_t) from the document pair. The 4-VAR co-occurrence is denoted as $o(w_s, w_t, d_s, d_t)$, or being abbreviated as $o(.)$. So the CDTI will solve the following two problems:

A) *Learning latent topic model*: Given the corpus C_s and C_t and the collection O of 4-VAR observations, $o(.)$, learn a set of latent topic (or cluster), z, which is characterized by $P(w_s, w_t|z)$, i.e cross-domain pair-wise term distribution conditioned on the topic, and the topic distribution in the cross-domain corpus, $P(z)$.

B) *Inferring a topic distribution to represent the document content*: Given the set of topic models, $P(w_s, w_t|z)$, and $P(z)$, find a topic distribution, $P(z|d)$for a document d.

2.2 Learning Latent Topic Model

The cross-domain term occurrence o is modeled as,

$$P(w_s, w_t) = \sum_{z=0}^{K-1} \mathrm{P(z)P}(w_s, w_t|\mathrm{z}) \quad (1)$$

K is the number of topics and each component $\mathrm{P}(w_s, w_t|\mathrm{z})$ is a possible topic model. Obviously Eq.(1) is a generative model.

Thus the likelihood function on the observation collection O is formulated as,

$$L = \sum_{d_s,d_t}\sum_{w_s,w_t} o(.)logP(w_s,w_t,d_s,d_t) \\ = \sum_{d_s,d_t}\sum_{w_s,w_t} o(.)log\sum_{z=0}^{K-1} P(w_s,w_t|z)P(d_s,d_t|z)P(z) \quad (2)$$

Here $o(.)$ is the known 4-VAR observation. $P(w_s,w_t|z)$ and $P(z)$ are the unknown model parameters. $P(d_s,d_t|z)$ is the unknown component relating to the topic for a source-target document pair.

The unknown parameters can be solved through maximizing the likelihood function in Eq. (2). In practice, it is not so easily solved because of the sum operation in the log-function. Of course, we could use the gradient method to find the solution. But it is impractical and inefficient considering the sizes of the corpus and dictionary.

Here we exploit the variational approach [10] to find the solution. We introduce an auxiliary component, $Q(z|w_s,w_t,d_s,d_t)$ (Abbreviation is $Q(.)$ without confusion) to approximate the topic distribution conditioned on the source-target term pair (w_s,w_t) and the source-target document pair (d_s,d_t). After applying the Jensen's inequality and replacing the auxiliary function into Eq. (2), the following function is obtained,

$$L \geq \sum_{d_s,d_t}\sum_{w_s,w_t} o(.)\sum_{z=0}^{K-1}\begin{bmatrix}Q(.)logP(w_s,w_t|z)P(d_s,d_t|z)P(z) \\ -Q(.)logQ(.)\end{bmatrix} \quad (3)$$

We thus get the objective function, F, for estimating CDTI model.

$$F = \sum_{d_s,d_t}\sum_{w_s,w_t} o(.)\sum_{z=0}^{K-1}\begin{bmatrix}Q(.)logP(w_s,w_t|z)P(d_s,d_t|z)P(z) \\ -Q(.)logQ(.)\end{bmatrix}. \quad (4)$$

Obviously, the upper bound in Eq. (4) is equal to the likelihood function Eq. (2). In order to estimate all unknown parameters, we develop an EM algorithm to iteratively update the model parameters and auxiliary parameters by maximizing Eq. (4).

E-step:

$Q(.)$ is estimated while fixing $P(w_s,w_t|z)$, $P(d_s,d_t|z)$, and $P(z)$. Eq. (4) is thus a function of $Q(.)$. Using the Lagrange multiplier method, we add the constraints on $Q(.)$ (See Eq. (5)) into Eq. (4). It thus results in the function F^Q (See Eq. (6)).

$$\sum_{z=1}^{K-1} Q(z|w_s,w_t,d_s,d_t) = 1, w_s \in V_s, w_t \in V_t, d_s \in C_s, d_t \in C_t. \quad (5)$$

$$F^Q = F - \sum_{w_s,w_t,d_s,d_t}\lambda(w_s,w_t,d_s,d_t)(\sum_{z=1}^{K-1} Q(.) - 1). \quad (6)$$

$\lambda(w_s,w_t,d_s,d_t)$ is the Lagrange multiplier.

The derivative of F^Q regarding to $Q(z|w_s,w_t,d_s,d_t)$ is equal to,

$$\frac{\partial F^Q}{\partial Q(.)} = o(.)(logP(w_s,w_t|z)P(d_s,d_t|z)P(z) - logQ(.) - 1) - \lambda \quad (7)$$

Letting Eq.(7) equal to zero, we can obtain $Q(.)$ as,

$$Q(.) = C \cdot e^{P(w_s,w_t|z)P(d_s,d_t|z)P(z)} \quad . (8)$$

$$C = \sum_{z=1}^{K-1} e^{P(w_s,w_t|z)P(d_s,d_t|z)P(z)} \quad . \quad (9)$$

M-step:

Fixing $Q(.)$ estimated in E-step, we then estimate $P(w_s,w_t|z)$, $P(d_s,d_t|z)$ and $P(z)$. Now we have constraints as,

$$\begin{cases}\sum_{w_s,w_t} P(w_s,w_t|z) = 1 \; for \; any \; given \; z \\ \sum_{d_s,d_t} P(d_s,d_t|z) = 1 \; for \; any \; given \; z \\ \sum_z P(z) = 1\end{cases} \quad (10)$$

Using the similar method as E-step, we get the parameters as,

$$P(w_s,w_t|z) \propto C_w \cdot \sum_{d_s d_t} o(w_s,w_t,d_s,d_t)Q(z|w_s,w_t,d_s,d_t) \quad (11)$$

$$P(d_s,d_t|z) \propto C_d \cdot \sum_{w_s w_t} o(w_s,w_t,d_s,d_t)Q(z|w_s,w_t,d_s,d_t) \quad (12)$$

$$P(z) \propto C_z \cdot \sum_{d_s d_t}\sum_{w_s w_t} o(w_s,w_t,d_s,d_t)Q(z|w_s,w_t,d_s,d_t) \quad (13)$$

C_w, C_d and C_z are the normalization constants. Figure 1 summarizes the above training procedure.

Input: source domain documents, C_s, target domain document, C_t, the collection of cross-domain observation, O, stop criterion, the number of topics.
Output: model parameters $P(w_s,w_t|z)$, $P(z)$
Procedure of learning CDPLA:
1. Initialize model parameters, $P(w_s,w_t|z)$, $P(d_s,d_t|z)$, $P(z)$.
2. E-step: update $Q(.)$ using Eqs. (8-9).
3. M-step: update model parameters using Eqs. (11-13)
4. Check whether the stop criterion is satisfied. If no, go to step 2. Otherwise, stop the iteration.

Figure 1. CDPLA latent topic learning algorithm

If we only look the above equations and learning procedure, CDTI looks similar to PLSA. But their differences are obvious. PLSA only models term-document pair in single domain. In contrary, CDTI operates on the cross-domain and models 4-VAR observation. Because there are more dependencies introduced in CDTI, we will see more flexibility in implementing CDTI. For example, we can relax some dependency to get a simpler model. In sub-section 2.4, some possible implementations are discussed. More interestingly, although the topic model in CDTI represents the source-target term pair distribution, we could infer the topic distribution for a document coming from single domain by integrating out some parameters (See section 2.3)).

2.3 Inferring Document Topic Distribution

The inference problem in cross-domain topic analysis is defined as,

Given any target document (or source document) d_u (The term in the document is w_u), the topic models, $P(w_s,w_t|z)$ and $P(z)$, and source domain training documents C_s (or target domain training documents C_t), infer a topic distribution, $P(z|d_u)$.

From the definition, the inference in CDTI is quite different from the traditional latent topic analysis such as PLSA. In CDTI, we need to re-use the training documents. The reason is in that CDTI needs 4-VAR co-occurrence in inference. For example, when inferring a topic distribution for a target domain document, the source domain training documents are needed to extract the 4-VAR co-occurrences. In contrary, the target domain training documents are needed when inferring a topic distribution for a source domain document.

As an example, we begin to discuss the inference algorithm for a document coming from the target domain. Clearly, the proposed algorithm is also suitable for the source domain documents. The objective function in inference is defined in Eq. (14),

$$F^I = \sum_{d_s}\sum_{w_s,w_u} o(.)\sum_{z=0}^{K-1}\begin{bmatrix}Q(.)logP(w_s,w_u|z)P(z,d_s,d_u) \\ -Q(.)logQ(.)\end{bmatrix} \quad (14)$$

Its difference from Eq. (4) is in that the model parameters $P(w_s,w_u|z)$ are fixed in inference. In Eq. (14), the interesting term is $P(z,d_s,d_u)$, which can be learned using the algorithm illustrated in Figure 1. Then the topic distribution is obtained through summing out the uninteresting variable d_s, i.e.,

$$P(z|d_u) = \sum_{d_s} P(z,d_s,d_u)/P(d_u) \quad (15)$$

Eq.(15) is just the topic distribution for the target document. Likewise, the topic distribution for the source document is,

$$P(z|d_u) = \sum_{d_t} P(z, d_t, d_u)/P(d_u) \quad (16)$$

The embedding relation in the above inference discriminates CDTI from the existing latent topic analysis methods.

2.4 Various Implementation of CDTI

In the above discussions, all possible dependencies are considered. It thus results in the high cost of computation and storage and the risk of over-training. Now 4 versions are discussed by relaxing some conditions.

Version A: Dependent CDTI (Dep_CDTI)

In the version, the source and target terms are dependent. So do the source and target documents. It is discussed in the above.

Version B: Term independent CDTI (Tind_ CDTI)

In the version, the source and target terms are independent, but the source and target documents are dependent, i.e.

$$P(w_s, w_t|z) = P(w_s|z)(w_t|z). \quad (17)$$

Version C: Document independent CDTI (Dind_ CDTI)

In the version, the source and target documents are independent. But the source and target term are dependent, i.e.,

$$P(d_s, d_t|z) = P(d_s|z)(d_t|z). \quad (18)$$

Version D: Both term and document independent CDTI (TDind_ CDTI)

In the version, the source and target terms are independent. So do the source document and target document. In the version, both Eq.(17) and Eq.(18) are satisfied.

2.5 Cross-domain Co-occurrence Extraction

In the section, we discuss a practical way to extract the 4-VAR features from the cross-domain documents. The first step is to link the source domain documents with their paired target domain documents. In the scenario of the paper, we study the text sentiment classification written in the same language. The dictionary in the source domain should have some words which also occur in the target domain. These words are our *pivot features* [6, 8]. The pivot features are used to bridge the two domains. Excluding the pivot features, each domain also has a set of domain-specific words. The pivot features, the source domain specific features and the target domain specific features are denoted as V_{DI}, V_{SDS} and V_{TDS} respectively.

For a pair-wise source domain document d_s with its term w_s and target domain document d_t with its term w_t, the 4-VAR observation $o(w_s, w_t, d_s, d_t)$ is defined as,

$$o(w_s, w_t, d_s, d_t) = g(w_s, w_t) f(d_s, d_t) \quad (19)$$

where $g(.)$ measures the association degree between the source domain term and the target domain term and $f(.)$ measures the relevance degree between two documents. The definition is flexible and the particular formulation will be based on the prior knowledge and preliminary experiments. One possible way adopted in our experiments is given in Eqs. (20-21).

$$g(w_s, w_t) = \begin{cases} 1 & \begin{array}{l} if\ w_s \in V_{DI}\ and\ w_t \in V_{TDS} \\ or\ w_s \in V_{SDS}\ and\ w_t \in V_{DI} \end{array} \\ 0 & Otherwise \end{cases} \quad (20)$$

$$f(d_s, d_t) = \begin{cases} 1 & \begin{array}{l} if\ d_s\ and\ d_t\ have\ common \\ pivot\ features \end{array} \\ 0 & Oherwise \end{cases} \quad (21)$$

3. SENTIMENT CLASSIFICATION

In our experiments, we evaluate the indexing power of CDTI for cross-domain sentiment classification. Thus we give a short introduction on sentiment classification. It is a task of predicting the polarity (positive or negative) of a text document, a binary classification problem. There are a lot of papers in the topic. A good literature on the task can be found in [3]. The training set is needed, where a text document is tagged with the positive or negative label. After that, the classifiers such as SVM[5] are trained from the training documents. Finally, the learned classifier is used on a document to predict whether it is positive or negative.

In the paper, we are interesting in domain adaptation, a problem of predicting the positive or negative opinion for a target document using the classifier trained on the source domain documents. Due to the domain mismatch, the source classifier will work worse in the target domain. Many techniques are proposed to adapt the source domain classifier into the target domain. For example, SFA [8] is a method to map the source domain document and target domain document in a shared low-dimensional feature space. Then the source linear SVM is trained on the space, which is used to classify the target document.

4. EXPERIMENTS

In the section, we will evaluate the proposed CDTI method in the task of sentiment classification.

4.1 Multi-domain Sentiment Dataset

The corpus is the multi-domain sentiment data set, which is used in [6] for studying domain adaptation. Recently it is used by many researchers to evaluate domain adaptation algorithms such as in [8]. The data set contains the product reviews in the Amazon site. Each product is treated as one domain. There are 25 domains in the set, of which four domains, i.e. *books (B), dvds (D), electronics (E), and kitchen appliances (K)*, are often used [6, 8]. Following the previous work, the four domains are also chosen in the paper. Thus 12 cross-domain sentiment classification tasks are built, denoted as, *B->D, B->E, B->K, D->B, D-> E, D->K, E->B, E->D, E->K, K->B, K->D, K->E*. In the above denotation, the first letter means the source domain and the second letter means the target domain. We randomly select 100 documents in each domain in our evaluation. The 100 documents are then randomly split into two parts: the training set and testing set. The training set is used to learn CDTI model and to train the classifier. The testing set is used to evaluate the performance.

4.2 Classifier

The prior work in other researchers proved that linear SVM achieved competitive performance in a lot of classification task. It is thus used here[5]. To avoid tuning the SVM configurations, we train a set of SVM classifiers using the costs selected in the range [0.00001, 1000000][6] and evaluate the classification accuracy in the test set for each trained model. Then the best accuracy that can be achieved is reported. So the reported classification accuracy is the upper bound of accuracy that can be obtained by the linear SVM.

---

[5] We use LIBSVM, http://www.csie.ntu.edu.tw/~cjlin/libsvm

[6] The accurate cost in each SVM training is calculated as: $cost = 0.00001 \cdot 10^{n}, n \geq 0$

4.3 CDTI based Domain Adaptation

The training samples in CDTI include: 1) a labeled training set in the source domain and 2) an unlabeled training set in the target domain (See sub-section 4.1 for data detail). Based on the training documents, the cross-domain latent topic models are learned. Then the topic distributions are inferred for the labeled training set in the source domain and the testing set in the target domain. The SVM, being trained on the source domain training set, is used to predict the polarity of the documents in the target domain testing set.

In the paper, we will study the relation between the classification accuracy and the following factors: 1) the implementation versions of CDTI and 2) the size of topics. Then we will evaluate the indexing capability of CDTI. As the comparison, we will build two baseline systems. The first is PLSA based system and the second is spectral feature alignment (SFA) based system [8]. In addition, we train a gold baseline for each domain, where the classifier is trained on the labeled training set of the target domain.

4.3.1 Performance vs. different implementations

In section 2, 4 implementations are discussed. Now we study how the implementation affects on the classification accuracy. The size of topics is 2. The maximal number of cycles is 40. The training set has 30 randomly selected documents from 100 documents and the testing documents are the left 70 ones. The classification accuracy is shown in Table 1. We observe that the TDind_CDTI achieves the average classification accuracy, 55.23%. It performs best among the four. However, the difference is not significant in terms of t-test at the 95% confidence level. Compared with the others, TDind_CDTI needs less computation. So we will use TDind_CDTI to study the property of CDTI hereafter.

Table 1. Classification accuracy (%) on 12 tasks for 4 versions of CDTI (TDind is abbreviation of TDind_ CDTI. Similarly for others, Tind, Dind, Dep)

	TDind	Tind	Dind	Dep
B->D	65.71	61.43	65.71	51.43
B->E	65.71	65.71	47.14	61.43
B->K	62.86	57.14	65.71	55.71
D->B	48.57	61.43	48.57	48.57
D->E	58.57	61.43	58.57	62.86
D->K	64.29	44.29	58.57	45.71
E->B	48.57	48.57	50.00	50.00
E->D	58.57	58.57	65.71	58.57
E->K	48.57	44.28	44.29	44.29
K->B	55.71	57.14	51.43	51.43
K->D	44.29	51.43	41.43	52.86
K->E	41.43	42.86	50.00	41.43
Average	**55.23**	**54.52**	**53.92**	**52.02**

4.3.2 Performance vs. topic size

Now we study the relation between the topic size and the accuracy based on TDind_CDTI. We split 100 documents in each domain into 50 documents in training set and the left 50 document in the testing set. The topic size is varied from 2 to 8 with a step 2. The average accuracies on 12 tasks are reported in Figure 2. They clearly show that the accuracy is increasing significantly with the increasing size of topics. For example, the accuracy is 57% in case of 2 topics. However, at the 8 topics, it reaches 62.17%.

4.3.3 Comparison with the baselines

Now we compare the CDTI based system with 2 baselines: one PLSA based system [15] and the other SFA based system [8]. The PLSA is the representative of traditional latent topic analysis in one domain. With comparing with PLSA, we can see how much benefit is achieved by modeling cross-domain relation in CDTI. SFA is the up-to-date feature space based domain adaptation method. It is closer to our method. As a fair comparison, the topic sizes for TDind_CDTI, PLSA and SFA are set to 8. We do not try to optimize it. But based on our preliminary experiments, we find that 8 topics are suitable for our small training documents. For PLSA, we observe the accuracy is becoming worse when the topic size is larger than 8.

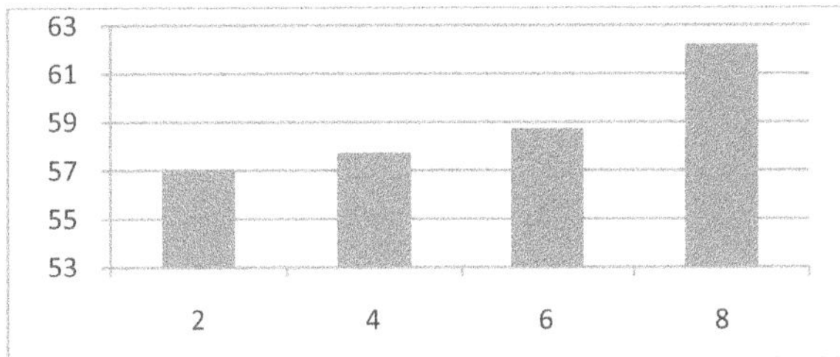

Figure 2. Average accuracy (%) over 12 tasks in selected topic size for TDind_CDTI (X-axis: topic size. Y-axis: accuracy)

A) TDind_CDTI vs. PLSA baseline

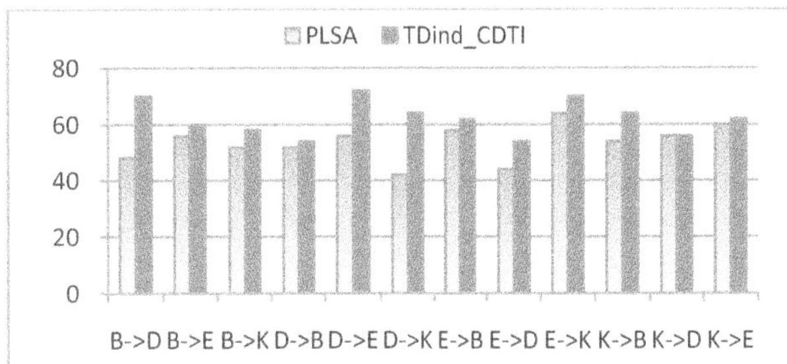

Figure 3. Comparison of accuracy (%) on each task for TDind_CDTI and PLSA (X-axis: the task. Y-axis: accuracy)

The accuracies on 12 tasks for PLSA and TDind_CDTI are illustrated in Figure 3. We find that TDind_CDTI significantly outperforms the PLSA method in all tasks except one task *K→D* (In the task, PSAL and CDTI have equal accuracy.). TDind_CDTI achieves the average classification accuracy 62.16%. In comparison, the PLSA system only gets 53.50% accuracy. The improvement is significant in term of t-test at the 95% confidence level. For a few domain adaptation tasks, the improvement is significant. For example, in the task B->D, the TDind_CDTI increases the accuracy from 48% to 70%, which obtains the 46% relative improvement. The results indicate that although both methods use the same data in learning latent topic model, TDind_CDTI can learn a much better topic space than PLSA from the cross-domain. This proves that incorporating cross-domain correspondence into topic learning can efficiently learn the topic space, in which the discrimination between the source domain document and the target domain document is reduced. It thus makes the source classifier work better in the target domain.

B) TDind_CDTI vs. SFA baseline

The success of SFA on domain adaptation is proved in [8]. It shares some common properties with CDTI, such as modeling the pair-wise term co-occurrence between the pivot feature and the domain-specific feature and mapping the original feature into the low-level semantic space. However, the difference is prominent. CDTI models the document level co-occurrence rather than the corpus level. Thus, the document relation is embedded in the model. It is ignored in SFA. More importantly, CDTI generates a probability model and has a clear explanation for the words distribution in a topic. The SFA method achieves the average accuracy 60.16%. As a comparison, TDind_CDTI achieves the higher accuracy 62.16%, which are comparative. The accuracies on 12 tasks are shown in Figure 4. It is observed that TDind_CDTI performs better than SFA in 7 out of 12 tasks. In some tasks, CDTI significantly outperforms the SFA method. For example, in the task K->B, the CDTI has accuracy 62% compared to 42% in SFA method. Overall we see that CDTI provide a robust performance.

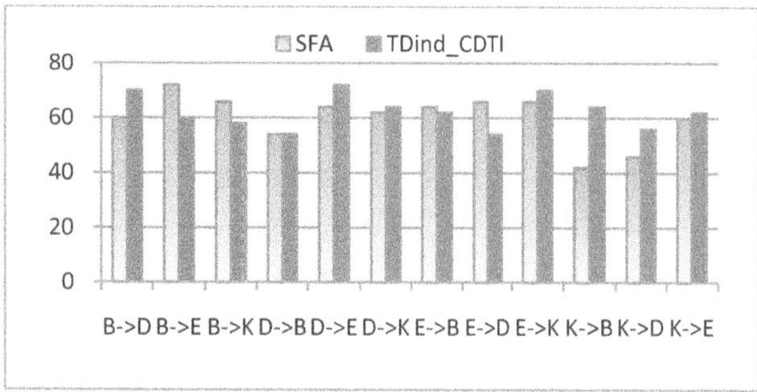

Figure 4. Comparison of classification accuracy (%) on each task between TDind_CDTI and SFA (X-axis: the cross-domain adaptation task. Y-axis: classification accuracy)

C) TDind_CDTI vs. gold baseline

The accuracies on 12 tasks are shown in Figure 5 for CDTI and the gold baseline. The gold baseline has the average accuracy 66%, which is better than 62.16% for TDind_CDTI. In some tasks, our TDind_CDTI system is even better than the gold baseline. For example, in the task B->D, TDind_CDTI has the accuracy 70% verse 64% for the gold baseline. Among 12 tasks, we still observe that TDind_CDTI works better in 4 tasks (B->D, D->E, D->K, E->K). Our further significant test shows that their performance difference is not significant.

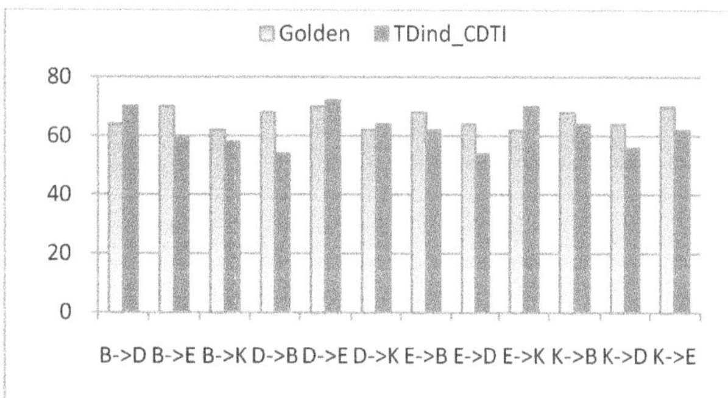

Figure 5. Comparison of accuracy (%) on each task for TDind_CDTI and gold baseline (X-axis: the task. Y-axis: accuracy)

5. CONCLUSION

In the paper, we have proposed cross-domain topic indexing (CDTI) method in order to find the common topic space to facilitate knowledge transfer. We have elaborated the learning algorithm and inference algorithm so that the topic model can be learned from the training documents and the new document can be analyzed to obtain the topic distribution. We have evaluated the proposed models on the multi-domain sentiment dataset and demonstrated its capability to index cross-domain document content. Our experimental results on cross-domain sentiment classification prove that the proposed CDTI outperforms PLSA in terms of index power in cross-domain and is competitive to the state-of-art feature space based adaptation method.

6. REFERENCES

[1] A. Argyriou, T. Evgenio and M. Pontil, Multi-task feature learning. In *Proceedings of NIPS'06*.

[2] B. Chen, W. Lam, I. W. Tsang and T.-L. Wong. Extracting discriminative concepts for domain adaptation in text mining. In *Proceedings of SIGKDD'09*.

[3] B. Pang and L. Lee. Opinion mining and sentiment analysis. *Foundations and Trends in Information Retrieval*, 2008.

[4] B. Pang, L. Lee and S. Vaithyanathan. Thumbs up? Sentiment classification using machine learning techniques. In *Proceedings of EMNLP'02*.

[5] D. M. Blei, A.Y. Ng and M. I. Jordan. Latent Dirichlet allocation. *Journal of Machine Learning Research* 3(Jan):993-1022, 2003.

[6] J. Blitzer, R. McDonald and F. Pereira. Domain adaptation with structural correspondence learning. In *Proceedings of EMNLP'06*.

[7] J. Jiang and C. X. Zhai. Instance weighting for domain adaptation in NLP. *In Proceedings of ACL'07*.

[8] J.L. Pan, X.C. Ni, J.T. Sun, Q. Yang and Z. Chen. Cross-domain sentiment classification via spectral feature alignment. In *Proceedings of WWW'10*.

[9] M. Hu and B. Liu. Mining and summarizing customer review. In *Proceedings of SIGKDD'04*.

[10] M.J. Beal. Variational algorithms for approximate Bayesian inference. In *PhD. Thesis, University College London*, 2003.

[11] R. K. Ando and T. Zhang. A Framework for learning predictive structure from multiple tasks and unlabeled data. *Journal of Machine Learning Research, 6:1817-1853, 2005.*

[12] S. J. Pan and Q. Yang. A survey on transfer learning. *IEEE Trans. On Knowledge and Data Engineering*, 2009.

[13] S. Xie, W. Fan, J. Peng, O. Verscheure and J. Ren. Latent space domain transfer between high dimensional overlapping distributions. In *Proceedings of WWW'09*.

[14] T. Li, V. Sindhwani, C. Ding and Y. Zhang. Knowledge transformation for cross-domain sentiment classification. In *Proceedings of SIGIR'09*.

[15] Thomas Hofmann. Probabilistic Latent Semantic Indexing. In *Proceedings of SIGIR'99*.

[16] W. Dai, G. R. Xue, Q. Yang and Y. Yu. Co-clustering based classification for out-of-domain documents. *In Proceedings of SIGKDD'07*.

[17] W. Dai, O. Jin, G. R. Xue, Q. Yang and Y. Yu. Eigentransfer: a unified framework for transfer learning. In *Proceedings of ICML'09*.

[18] H. Y. Zha, Chris Ding, M. Gu, X. F. He and H. Simon. Spectral Relaxation for K-means Clustering. In *Proceedings of NIPS'01*.

[19] Chih-Chung Chang and Chih-Jen Lin, LIBSVM : a library for support vector machines, 2001.

[20] J. C. Platt, K. Toutanova, W.T. Yih. Translingual Document Representations from Discriminative Projections. In *Proceedings of EMNLP'10*

Using Games with a Purpose and Bootstrapping to Create Domain-Specific Sentiment Lexicons

Albert Weichselbraun
University of Applied Sciences
HTW Chur
Ringstraße 34
7000 Chur, Switzerland
albert.weichsel-braun@htwchur.ch

Stefan Gindl
MODUL University Vienna
Department of New Media Technology
Am Kahlenberg 1
1190 Vienna, Austria
stefan.gindl@modul.ac.at

Arno Scharl
MODUL University Vienna
Department of New Media Technology
Am Kahlenberg 1
1190 Vienna, Austria
arno.scharl@modul.ac.at

ABSTRACT

Sentiment detection analyzes the positive or negative polarity of text. The field has received considerable attention in recent years, since it plays an important role in providing means to assess user opinions regarding an organization's products, services, or actions.

Approaches towards sentiment detection include machine learning techniques as well as computationally less expensive methods. Both approaches rely on the use of language-specific sentiment lexicons, which are lists of sentiment terms with their corresponding sentiment value. The effort involved in creating, customizing, and extending sentiment lexicons is considerable, particularly if less common languages and domains are targeted without access to appropriate language resources.

This paper proposes a semi-automatic approach for the creation of sentiment lexicons which assigns sentiment values to sentiment terms via crowd-sourcing. Furthermore, it introduces a bootstrapping process operating on unlabeled domain documents to extend the created lexicons, and to customize them according to the particular use case. This process considers sentiment terms as well as sentiment indicators occurring in the discourse surrounding a particular topic. Such indicators are associated with a positive or negative context in a particular domain, but might have a neutral connotation in other domains.

A formal evaluation shows that bootstrapping considerably improves the method's recall. Automatically created lexicons yield a performance comparable to professionally created language resources such as the General Inquirer.

Categories and Subject Descriptors

H.3.1 [**Information Storage and Retrieval**]: Content Analysis and Indexing - Linguistic Processing;
H.5.3 [**Group and Organization Interfaces**]: Collaborative Computing

General Terms

Algorithms, Languages, Performance

Keywords

Sentiment Detection, Bootstrapping, Language Resources, Sentiment Lexicon, Crowd-Sourcing

1. INTRODUCTION

Sentiment detection has attracted a lot of research interest in recent years. With the emergence of freely available opinions on the Web the need for efficient methods to interpret these opinions has arisen. Automated sentiment detection is capable of accomplishing this task. It facilitates means of large-scale investigation previously unmanageable for humans, such as tracking political campaigns on the Web or market research in forums or blogs. Reliable sentiment detection is heavily dependent on the comprehensiveness and accuracy of the underlying a-priory knowledge, in most cases a so-called sentiment lexicon. This lexicon contains opinionated terms and is usually manually compiled. The occurrence of these terms in a document serves as indicator for "positiveness" or "negativeness" of a document. Manually compiling sentiment lexicons can be cumbersome and such lexicons may lack comprehensiveness, especially in the case of less-spoken languages. The presented method combines a crowd-sourcing technique, which is used for creating an initial sentiment lexicon, with a bootstrapping approach that automatically expands sentiment lexicons with additional terms. As input serves an unlabeled text corpus, from which a labeled corpus is iteratively extracted. Based on this labeled corpus, previously unknown sentiment terms are extracted and added to the initial lexicon.

The remainder of this paper is structured as follows: Section 2 gives an overview of related work, followed by a description of the proposed method in Section 3. Section 4 performs a comprehensive evaluation of our approach, comparing the semi-automatically created lexicons to lexicons assembled by language experts. Section 5 concludes the paper and outlines future work.

2. RELATED WORK

This paper introduces an approach to combine games with a purpose and a lexicon-based sentiment detection method to create domain-specific sentiment lexicons. The following two subsections discuss related work in the field of sentiment detection, and provide background material on the use of crowd-sourcing applications in the tradition of games with a purpose.

2.1 Sentiment Detection

Sentiment detection heavily relies on so-called sentiment lexicons, i.e. collections of terms and an a-priori assessment of their polarity. Well-known English resources are the General Inquirer [19], the Subjectivity Lexicon [29] and the Subjectivity Sense Annotations [27, 8]. GermanPolarityClues [26] or the lexicon presented by Clematide and Klenner [3] are good examples of equivalent German resources.

Sentiment lexicons are valuable resources, and much work focuses on the creation of such lexicons. This task usually involves a lot of handicraft, making it time-consuming and resource-intensive. This explains the strong interest in reliable automatic approaches.

In an early approach, Hatzivassiloglou and McKeown [9] used syntactical relations to identify new sentiment terms. Turney and Littman [23] use Pointwise Mutual Information (PMI) and Latent Semantic Analysis (LSA) to identify sentiment terms in a large Web corpus. Terms with sufficient co-occurrence frequency with one of 14 paradigm terms (i.e., a gold standard list of seven positive and negative terms) are assigned the same sentiment value as the respective paradigm term. Evaluated on the General Inquirer [19], PMI shows results comparable with the algorithm of Hatzivassiloglou and McKeown [9]. Using three different extraction corpora, Turney and Littman show that PMI does not outperform Hatzivassiloglou's and McKeown's algorithm but is more scalable [24]. LSA provided better results, but was not as scalable as PMI. Turney [22] uses the same techniques to identify new sentiment terms from a paradigm list of only two terms (*excellent* and *poor*). This procedure performed well on the review corpus. Beineke et al. re-interpret the previously discussed mutual association as a Naïve Bayes approach [2]; they also expand this unsupervised approach and create a supervised approach using labeled data.

In Esuli et al. [5] a semi-supervised approach creates *SentiWordNet*, a sentiment resource based on the well-known linguistics resource WordNet [6]. They first manually label all synsets containing 14 seed terms, which results in an amount of 47 synsets with positive label and 58 with negative. All synsets obtained from certain relations (e.g. *direct antonymy*, *similarity* and *derived-from*) with these seed synsets are labeled accordingly. Synsets without connection to the seed sets are classified as objective, as long as they do not have a different sentiment value in the General Inquirer. The so gathered data is used to train eight ternary classifiers, which classify the rest of WordNet. Kim and Hove [10] specify subjects by means of a Named Entity Recognition and assign them the overall sentiment value of the sentence. A list of 44 verbs and 34 adjectives expanded by WordNet synonyms and antonyms serves as sentiment lexicon. A straightforward solution to accomplish sentiment detection in a language without existing sentiment lexicon is to use translation software. Denecke [4] applies a machine learning approach to multi-lingual sentiment detection using movie reviews from six different languages. Google Translate (www.google.com/language_tools) converts foreign-language documents into English. The feature selection procedure extracts a total of 77 features out of four super classes [4]: (i) the frequency of word classes (i.e. the number of verbs, nouns, etc.); (ii) polarity scores for the 20 most frequent words and the averages scores for all verbs, nouns and adjectives are based on SentiWordNet [5]; (iii) the frequency of positive and negative words according to the General Inquirer; and (iv) textual features such as the number of question marks.

The a priori polarity of sentiment terms might change in different contexts. This problem is tackled by Gindl et al. [7], proposing an approach that dynamically refines the polarity by invocation of context. The first step is the identification of ambiguous terms in a sentiment lexicon. For each of these ambiguous terms, probabilities for their occurrence in positive and negative contexts are calculated by analyzing their occurrence in a corpus of positive and negative reviews. Based on this information, the a priori polarity of an ambiguous term is modified by analyzing terms co-occurring with the term in an unknown lexicon. Wilson et al. [29] examine 28 syntactical and linguistic features in a machine learning approach. Several of those features are context-based, e.g. invoking the sentence preceding or succeeding the current one or the document topic. The features are tested using BoosTexter's AdaBoost.MH algorithm [15] on the Multi-perspective Question Answering Opinion Corpus [28]. The approach has two steps: the first step filters subjective sentences from objective ones, and the second assigns sentiment values to the subjective sentences. In their successive work [30] Wilson et al. use four different machine learning algorithms to test their feature selection and also use a larger version of the corpus. Agarwal et al. [1] use the corpus to test n-grams and provide syntactical label for relations as context characteristics. Polanyi and Zaenen propose context handling strategies from a linguistic perspective [12]. They distinguish two main groups of context modifiers: *Sentence Based Contextual Valence Shifters* and *Discourse Based Contextual Valence Shifters.*

Please refer to the surveys by Liu [11] and Tang et al. [21] for a more exhaustive overview of sentiment detection.

2.2 Games with a Purpose

Human language technologies such as information extraction and sentiment detection depend on appropriate language resources. Such resources can be acquired through Games with a purpose [25, 14], a crowd-sourcing mechanism and a special type of serious games that invites communities of users with different levels of expertise to participate in value-adding processes. Games with a purpose leverage collective intelligence, which is described as combining "behavior, preferences, or ideas of a group of people to create novel insights" [17]. Collective intelligence from groups of people often produces better results than individual domain experts [20].

Games with a purpose have been used successfully to solve problems that computers cannot yet solve, such as tagging images [25] and annotating content [18]. The main challenges of game design are motivating users to play the game while generating useful data, and ensuring that the process yields unbiased results. Given appropriate design and authentication mechanisms, such games can capture individual knowledge according to the scientific criteria of objectivity, reliability, validity and representativeness. In the context of this paper, we harness the wisdom of the crowds through games with a purpose to be delivered via large-scale social networking platforms such as Facebook for compiling multilingual sentiment lexicons. Advantages of this approach include a large number of possible players, intrinsic motivation within a social context, and more effective mechanisms to detect and combat attempts of manipulating results. When adopting an approach based on filtering and cross-validation, the intrinsic motivation of users participating in games with a purpose promises superior results compared to crowd-sourcing marketplaces such as Amazon Mechanical Turk (www.mturk.com). Merging several types of games (e.g. sentiment lexicon creation, translation, conflict resolution) further increases the game's attractiveness, reduces the risk of cheating, allocates collective intelligence more efficiently by prioritizing tasks across game types, and helps avoid the situation that dedicated players run out of new challenges.

3. METHOD

Sentiment detection techniques use text features such as sentiment terms and sentiment indicators to assess the polarity (positive, negative) of text fragments. *Sentiment terms* have a distinct polarity and are usually domain-independent. In contrast, *sentiment indicators* occur within the discussion of *topics* which are often used in a positive or negative context (e.g. democracy, public debt, etc.). Therefore, these terms do not contain a polarity by themselves but rather *indicate* that the topic is likely to contain a certain sentiment. This is particularly useful in situations where only rudimentary sentiment lexicons are available (e.g. for less spoken languages or unusual application domains), since sentiment indicators have the potential to considerably improve the accuracy of sentiment detection in such settings (Section 4). Nevertheless, since topics are usually domain-specific, sentiment indicators still have the limitation of being specific to a particular domain and, therefore, cannot be used across domains.

The proposed method introduces an approach which automatically extracts *sentiment terms* and *sentiment indicators* by applying a bootstrapping process to domain-specific documents. The retrieved indicators then complement sentiment dictionaries and increase the sentiment detection's recall.

The sentiment values of *domain-specific sentiment terms* are usually limited to a particular domain. *Sentiment indicators* such as "democracy" or "tax raise" do not contain a sentiment value per se but are associated with a certain sentiment in the given domain. Therefore, they provide a good indication of how an article is going to be perceived by its readers.

One objective of our approach is to improve the recall of sentiment detection for languages where sentiment resources are limited or still under development.

The presented approach starts with the creation of an initial sentiment lexicon as described in Subsection 3.1. Based on this lexicon a bootstrapping algorithm (see Subsection 3.2) extracts further sentiment terms and indicators used to expand the initial lexicon.

3.1 Initial Sentiment Lexicon

This paper builds upon the lessons learnt from the Sentiment Quiz (Figure 2), a Web-based social verification game for sentiment detection. It was developed as part of the US Election 2008 Web Monitor (www.ecoresearch.net/election2008), a project to investigate information diffusion via interactive online media, and the interdependence of news media coverage and public opinion [16].

The game is available in seven different languages and presents the player with potential sentiment terms. The player's task is to evaluate these terms on a five-point scale (very positive, positive, neutral, negative, very negative) and he receives points based on how well his answer corresponds to the other player's assessment of a particular term. If no prior evaluations are available for a term, the game assigns the player a score which is based on his average game performance. The sentiment quiz attracted more than 4 300 players who have created a sentiment lexicon comprising 1 000 high quality terms as a by-product of their activities.

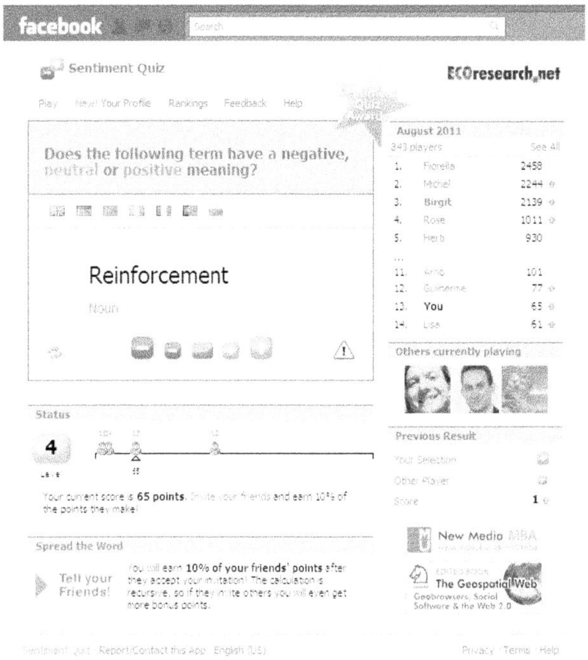

Figure 2: The Sentiment Quiz, a word polarity game (www.modul.ac.at/nmt/sentiment-quiz)

A crucial task when applying such games with a purpose is to make sure that the games yield unbiased results and that users are prevented from raising their score by cheating. On a social networking site, users can identify other players and might collaborate to manipulate the game; e.g. by agreeing in advance on the answers to a limited set of questions. A number of simple measures can be taken to ensure output of high quality: (i) hide the identity of the other player; (ii) analyze the temporal distribution of answers; (iii) assign trust values to each player, which in turn determine the impact of their answers – e.g. insert questions with known answers into the exercise queue and identify users who tend to score low on these questions; (iv) avoid exploitable patterns in the sequence of answers, since users who identify the pattern could quickly earn credits without actually solving the puzzle. We also only consider terms which have received at least seven assessments to ensure a good quality of the initial sentiment lexicon used for the bootstrapping process.

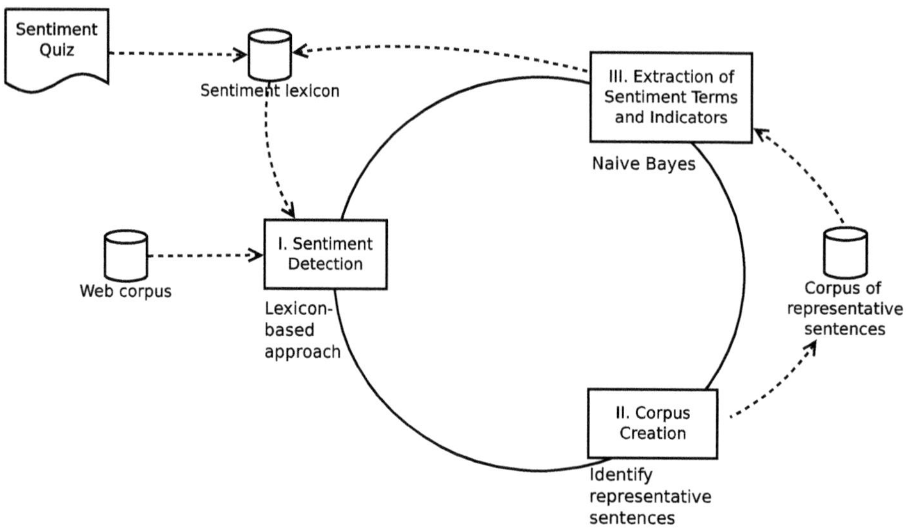

Figure 1: The three-step bootstrapping process

3.2 Bootstrapping Algorithm

We apply a bootstrapping algorithm to extract potential sentiment terms and sentiment indicators for the given domain. An unlabeled corpus of TripAdvisor reviews serves as input for this step.

Figure 1 proves an overview of the three-step bootstrapping process. Initially we apply sentiment detection to determine the sentiment of unlabeled Web reviews (Section 3.2.1) based on an initial sentiment lexicon, which was created by crowd-sourcing the task of annotating vocabulary with sentiment values to a Facebook game with a purpose (Section 3.1). We then identify representative examples of reviews with a positive and negative sentiment and use them to create a corpus of such reviews (Section 3.2.2). Finally, we extract sentiment indicators and terms from this corpus (Section 3.2.3), merge these terms into the sentiment dictionary, and repeat the process as required.

3.2.1 *Sentiment Detection*

Applying a simple lexicon-based sentiment detection approach estimates the sentiment (σ) of the extracted reviews:

$$\sigma(doc_i) = \sum_{t_j \in doc_i} n(t_{j-1})\sigma(t_j), \text{ with} \quad (1)$$

$$n(t_{i-j}) = \begin{cases} -1.0 & \text{if } t_{j-1} \text{is a negation trigger} \\ +1.0 & \text{otherwise} \end{cases} \quad (2)$$

The algorithm uses a bag of words approach and considers negation by scanning for negation triggers such as 'not" and "without" which invert the sentiment value of the following term. We applied a simple lexicon-based approach, which only considers simple grammatical constructs such as negation, for detecting the sentiment of unlabeled documents. For the evaluation we complemented this approach with a Naïve Bayes classifier and Support Vector Machines.

3.2.2 *Corpus Creation*

The next step creates and expands a corpus of positive and negative reviews to be used for the extraction of sentiment terms and indicators. The output of the sentiment detection component helps to identify the k strongest positive and negative reviews (doc_i) and the corresponding sentiment thresholds (σ_k^+ and σ_k^-). Due to the strength of their sentiment values we consider these reviews as *representative examples* of positive and negative discussions and therefore assemble corresponding learning corpora containing positive C^+ and C^- negative examples:

$$C^+ = \{doc_i | \sigma(doc_i) > \sigma_k^+\} \quad (3)$$

$$C^- = \{doc_i | \sigma(doc_i) < \sigma_k^-\} \quad (4)$$

The input corpus is a collection of 1 600 unlabeled holiday reviews downloaded from the website www.tripadvisor.com. The corpus is balanced, containing an equal number of positive and negative reviews. We assign a positive polarity when a review has more than three stars, and a negative if it has less than three stars.

3.2.3 *Extraction of Sentiment Terms and Indicators*

The extraction of new sentiment terms follows each expansion of the corpora (C^+ and C^-). For each term in the knowledge base the system calculates its probability of occurring in positive and negative sentences based on the Naive Bayes algorithm.

$$n(t_j) = n(t_j|C^+) + n(t_j|C^-) \quad (5)$$

$$P(\sigma(t_j)|C^+) = \frac{n(t_j|C^+)}{n(t_j)} \quad (6)$$

$$P(\sigma(t_j)|C^-) = \frac{n(t_j|C^-)}{n(t_j)} \quad (7)$$

Subsequently, the m terms with the highest absolute probability values and the corresponding sentiment thresholds P^+ and P^-, i.e. the strongest m positive and negative terms, are added to the sentiment lexicon. Terms already included in the lexicon are disregarded. We also ignore terms which occur less then n_{min} times in the corpus.

$$\sigma(t_j) := 1 \quad \text{if } P(\sigma(t_j)|C^+) > P^+ \wedge \quad (8)$$
$$n(t_j) \geq n_{min}$$
$$\sigma(t_j) := -1 \quad \text{if } P(\sigma(t_j)|C^-) > P^- \wedge \quad (9)$$
$$n(t_j) \geq n_{min}$$

Our current approach applies this bootstrapping process multiple times and divides the number of representative sentences to include in the corpus creation step (k) by half after every run. The terms yielded by this process include relevant sentiment indicators and sentiment terms which considerably improve the performance of subsequent sentiment detection steps (Section 4).

4. EVALUATION

Figure 3 visualizes the described evaluation process. The evaluation design focuses on the following research questions: (1) is the quality of the bootstrapped and newly included sentiment terms high enough to improve the overall quality of the system, and (2) how well does this lexicon compare to a manually compiled lexicon which was assembled by language experts.

To answer these two questions we performed a 10-fold cross-validation of the following three lexicons based on three different sentiment detection algorithms:

- **The Facebook lexicon:** This lexicon is the result of the Sentiment Quiz described in Section 3.1. It includes 500 positive and 500 negative terms. The game delivered more terms, but we excluded unreliable terms, i.e. we only took those 500 positive and negative terms with the smallest standard deviation from the average assessment of the players
- **The expanded lexicon:** This lexicon is an expansion of the Facebook lexicon. It contains additional terms identified with the bootstrapping algorithm described in Section 3. The system included 127 new terms on average (to accomplish a 10-fold cross validation we had to create an expanded lexicon for each run of the validation to avoid pollution of training data with test data).
- **The General Inquirer lexicon:** This lexicon builds upon the sentiment information contained in the General Inquirer (see Stone [19]). It contains 3 625 sentiment terms in total, 2 006 are negative and 1 619 positive terms.

The corpus used for cross-validation is a collection of 1 600 reviews downloaded from the TripAdvisor website (www.tripadvisor.com). For each run of the cross-validation the system creates an expanded lexicon from the training data. The presented lexicons are used by three different algorithms:

- **Lexical approach:** This algorithm uses a bag of words approach and simple grammar rules (Equation 1 and Equation 2) to determine text sentiment.
- **Naïve Bayes:** The terms in the lexicons serve as features for the Naïve Bayes classifier.
- **Support Vector Machine (SVM):** The lexicon terms also serve as features for the SVM classifier, which uses a linear kernel.

We chose Naïve Bayes and SVM as classifiers since they are standard algorithms and especially SVMs are known to deliver excellent results on high-dimensional data such as textual data. The WEKA tool serves as framework for the evaluation with the Naïve Bayes and the SVM algorithm. For this purpose we first converted the textual reviews into ARFF files, the common file format for WEKA. The lexical algorithm processes the reviews in plain text format. In order to ensure equivalence of the training and test data for both the WEKA environment and the lexical approach we did not use WEKA's built-in 10-fold cross-validation mode but created the corresponding files ourselves.

Tables 1 and 2 contain the results of our evaluation. Table 1 compares the Facebook lexicon with the expanded lexicon. The table can be read as follows: each triple contains the average of either recall, precision, or F-measure achieved with one of the three algorithms using either the Facebook or the expanded lexicon. $\mathbf{R_f}$ refers to the average recall achieved with the Facebook lexicon (f), $\mathbf{R_e}$ refers to recall obtained with the expanded lexicon (e). The column **Sig** has a check mark (✓) when the difference is statistically significant and a dot (·) when it is not. In case the expanded lexicon delivers significantly worse results the column contains a dashed circle (⊖). The R implementation of Wilcoxon's rank sum test serves for calculation of significance values [13]. We regard significance values below 5 % (i.e. $p < 0.05$) as significant.

Table 1: Results of the 10-fold cross-validation with the WEKA LibSVM classifier

Polarity	R_f	R_e	Sig	P_f	P_e	Sig	F_f	F_e	Sig
Lexical									
Positive	77	90	✓	62	69	✓	68	78	✓
Negative	29	43	✓	85	92	✓	43	58	✓
Naïve Bayes									
Positive	63	76	✓	75	79	✓	68	77	✓
Negative	79	79	·	68	76	✓	73	78	✓
SVM									
Positive	73	80	✓	75	79	✓	74	79	✓
Negative	75	78	·	74	80	✓	74	79	✓

Table 2: Comparison of the expanded lexicons with the General Inquirer

Polarity	R_e	R_{gi}	Sig	P_e	P_{gi}	Sig	F_e	F_{gi}	Sig
Lexical									
Positive	90	95	·	69	65	✓	78	77	·
Negative	43	36	✓	92	93	·	58	52	·
Naïve Bayes									
Positive	76	85	⊖	79	82	⊖	77	83	⊖
Negative	79	81	·	76	85	⊖	78	82	⊖
SVM									
Positive	80	86	·	79	82	·	79	84	·
Negative	78	81	·	80	85	·	79	83	·

Table 2 contains a comparison of results achieved with both the expanded lexicon and the General Inquirer lexicon. The results show, that although the semi-automatically

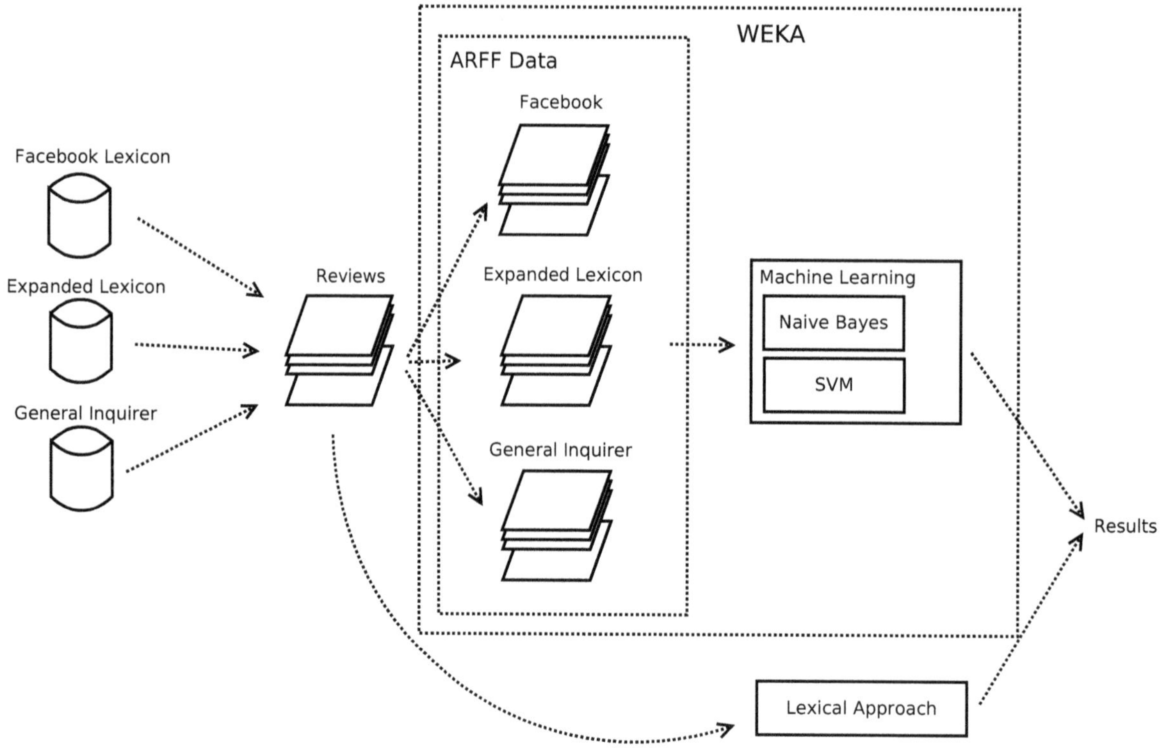

Figure 3: Overview of the evaluation process

compiled sentiment lexicon has less than half the number of sentiment terms, it sill performs similarly to the expert lexicon for two of the three evaluated sentiment detection approaches. The General Inquirer lexicon is only significantly better for results achieved with the Naïve Bayes classifier. We did not observe significant differences for the SVM classifiers, yet the different values still indicate better results of the General Inquirer lexicon. For the lexical approach the expanded lexicon was even able to significantly outperform the General Inquirer lexicon in two cases (precision for positive reviews and recall for negative reviews).

The lexical approach profited the most from the bootstrapping process. We obtained significant improvements for recall, precision, and F-measure. The improvements achieved with the Naïve Bayes and SVM classifiers were all significant except for recall of negative reviews.

Table 3 shows three terms which were incorporated into the sentiment lexicon during the bootstrapping process and lists sentences that illustrate how these terms improve the method's accuracy. Interestingly, the intuitively negative term *stops* was identified as a positive sentiment term. After the lookup of sentences in the databases that contained this sentence, the reason became apparent. The term *stops* referred to bus or subway stations. In general, it is desirable to live close to a bus stop, and the system also identified it correctly. Therefore, *stops* can be considered as one of the afore-mentioned sentiment indicators. Only in the domain of holiday reviews it gets an obvious positive connotation (although it might also be used positively in domains completely different to holiday reviews). The two other examples, *dingy* and *stained* are sentiment terms - one can easily imagine them to be used negatively in a different domain. The significant improvement achieved with the bootstrapped lexicon shows that the proposed method is a valuable tool under circumstances where sentiment resources are sparse.

5. CONCLUSION

This paper proposed a semi-automated process which combines Games with a purpose and a bootstrapping approach to create sentiment lexicons and customize them to a particular domain. Complementing crowd-sourcing with bootstrapping yields an extended sentiment lexicon (containing sentiment terms *and* sentiment indicators), which considerably outperforms the accuracy of the initial dictionary.

The main contributions of this paper are (i) the introduction of the concept of sentiment indicators, which supports sentiment detection by complementing known sentiment terms with domain knowledge, (ii) applying Games with a Purpose to the task of generating language resources which are essential for many natural language detection and knowledge management tasks, (iii) introducing a bootstrapping process which automatically extends these resources by adding sentiment indicators and sentiment terms based on unlabeled domain documents, and (iv) performing a comprehensive evaluation which shows that bootstrapping considerably improves the performance of the created sentiment lexicon, and that the lexicon yielded from the semi-automatic process performs - depending on the used sentiment detection method - about as good or only slightly worse than widely used language resources such as the General Inquirer, which have been compiled by language experts.

Table 3: Examples of terms added after bootstrapping

Term	Sentence
stops (pos)	Also lovely that the tram *stops* were literally outside our front door as it was very snowy a day or two during our week.
	It's just about 5 minutes from Stephansplatz, the U-Bahn and various tram *stops*.
	The hotel is off a quiet street, but easily reached from the airport by the 'CAT' train and then a few *stops* on the U3 underground and then a short stroll from here.
dingy (neg)	The hotel itself was shabby, *dingy* and very dirty looking.
	The lobby is reached through a dark, *dingy* restaurant and one had to walk past the largest smelliest dog I had ever seen.
	Sadly, it was in the rafters, dark and *dingy* seeming.
stained (neg)	The walls of the room were also very scuffed and *stained*.
	Our "Executive Room" featured dirty, *stained* old chairs and a coffee tablet that would have looked more at home in a rubbish skip.
	Stained bedspreads, soiled carpeting, broken telephone, and terribly noisy.

This result is remarkable for a semi-automatically created resource, especially when considering that the main benefit of the introduced method is its applicability to languages and domains for which such high quality resources are not yet available. In such cases the effort required to create language resources is reduced significantly.

The evaluation also demonstrates that the introduced bootstrapping process is very efficient in learning sentiment terms and indicators. Nevertheless, it currently has the disadvantage of not being able to distinguish between domain-independent sentiment terms and topic-related sentiment indicators. This is not a problem for domain-specific sentiment detection as such, but is highly relevant for the ability of reusing sentiment lexicons across domain. Future research will address this shortcoming by applying corpus-based methods such as the one introduced in Gindl et al. [7] for identifying domain-specific sentiment indicators.

We will also explore the applicability of Games with a Purpose to the creation of other language resources such as test collections and text annotations.

6. REFERENCES

[1] Apoorv Agarwal, Fadi Biadsy, and Kathleen R. McKeown. Contextual Phrase-level Polarity Analysis using Lexical Affect Scoring and Syntactic N-grams. In *12th Conference of the European Chapter of the Association for Computational Linguistics on (EACL 2009)*, pages 24–32, Athens, Greece, 2009. ACL.

[2] Philip Beineke, Trevor Hastie, and Christopher Manning. Exploring Sentiment Summarization. In *AAAI Spring Symposium on Exploring Attitude and Affect in Text*, pages 12–15, 2004.

[3] Simon Clematide and Manfred Klenner. Evaluation and Extension of a Polarity Lexicon for German. In *1st Workshop on Computational Approaches to Subjectivity and Sentiment Analysis (WASSA 2010)*, pages 7–13, Lisbon, Portugal, 2010.

[4] Kerstin Denecke. How to Assess Customer Opinions Beyond Language Barriers? In *3rd International Conference on Digital Information Management (ICDIM 2008)*, pages 430–435, London, UK, November 2008. IEEE.

[5] Andrea Esuli, Fabrizio Sebastiani, and Via Giuseppe Moruzzi. SENTIWORDNET: A Publicly Available Lexical Resource for Opinion Mining. In *5th Conference on Language Resources and Evaluation (LREC 2006)*, pages 417–422, Genoa, Italy, 2006.

[6] Christiane Fellbaum. WordNet - An Electronic Lexical Database. *Computational Linguistics*, 25(2):292–296, 1998.

[7] Stefan Gindl, Albert Weichselbraun, and Arno Scharl. Cross-Domain Contextualisation of Sentiment Lexicons. In *19th European Conference on Artificial Intelligence (ECAI 2010)*, pages 771–776, Lisbon, Portugal, August 2010. IOS Press.

[8] Yaw Gyamfi, Janyce Wiebe, Rada Mihalcea, and Cem Akkaya. Integrating Knowledge for Subjectivity Sense Labeling. In *Human Language Technologies: The Annual Conference of the North American Chapter of the Association for Computational Linguistics on (NAACL 2009)*, pages 10–18, Boulder, CO, USA, 2009. ACL.

[9] Vasileios Hatzivassiloglou and Kathleen R McKeown. Predicting the Semantic Orientation of Adjectives. In *8th Conference on the European Chapter of the Association for Computational Linguistics (EACL 1997)*, pages 174–181, Madrid, Spain, 1997. ACL.

[10] Soo-Min Kim and Eduard Hovy. Determining the Sentiment of Opinions. In *20th International Conference on Computational Linguistics (COLING 2004)*, Geneva, Switzerland, 2004. ACL.

[11] Bing Liu. Sentiment analysis and subjectivity. In Nitin Indurkhya and Fred J. Damerau, editors, *Handbook of Natural Language Processing, Second Edition*. CRC Press, Taylor and Francis Group, Boca Raton, FL, 2010.

[12] Livia Polanyi and Annie Zaenen. *Computing Attitude and Affect in Text: Theory and Applications*, chapter Contextual. Springer, Netherlands, 2006.

[13] R Development Core Team. *R: A Language and Environment for Statistical Computing*. R Foundation for Statistical Computing, Vienna, Austria, 2011.

[14] Walter Rafelsberger and Arno Scharl. Games with a Purpose for Social Networking Platforms. In *20th ACM conference on Hypertext and Hypermedia (HT 2009)*, pages 193–198, New York, NY, USA, 2009. ACM.

[15] Robert E. Schapire and Yoram Singer. BoosTexter: A Boosting-based System for Text Categorization. *Machine Learning*, 39(2):135–168, 2000.

[16] Arno Scharl and Albert Weichselbraun. An Automated Approach to Investigating the Online Media Coverage of US Presidential Elections. *Journal of Information Technology & Politics*, 5(1):121–132, 2008.

[17] Toby Segaran. *Collective Intelligence - Building Smart Web 2.0 Applications*. O'Reilly, 2007.

[18] K. Siorpaes and M. Hepp. Games with a Purpose for the Semantic Web. *IEEE Intelligent Systems*, 23:50–60, 2008.

[19] Philip J. Stone. *The General Inquirer: A Computer Approach to Content Analysis*. M.I.T. Press, Cambridge, Massachusetts, U.S.A., 1966.

[20] J. Surowiecki. *The Wisdom of Crowds: Why the Many Are Smarter Than the Few and How Collective Wisdom Shapes Business, Economies, Societies and Nations*. Little, Brown, London, 2004.

[21] Huifeng Tang, Songbo Tan, and Xueqi Cheng. A Survey on Sentiment Detection of Reviews. *Expert Systems with Applications*, 36(7):10760–10773, 2009.

[22] Peter D. Turney. Thumbs Up or Thumbs Down? Semantic Orientation Applied to Unsupervised Classification of Reviews. In *40th Meeting of the Association for Computational Linguistics (ACL 2002)*, pages 417–424, Philadelphia, PA, USA, 2002.

[23] Peter D. Turney and Michael L. Littman. Unsupervised Learning of Semantic Orientation from a Hundred-Billion-Word Corpus. Technical report, National Research Council, Canada, Institute for Information Technology, 2002.

[24] Peter D. Turney and Michael L. Littman. Measuring Praise and Criticism: Inference of Semantic Orientation from Association. *ACM Transactions on Information Systems*, 21(4):315–346, 2003.

[25] L. Von Ahn. Games with a Purpose. *Computer*, 39(6):92–94, 2006.

[26] Ulli Waltinger. GERMANPOLARITYCLUES: A Lexical Resource for German Sentiment Analysis. In *7th International Conference on Language Resources and Evaluation (LREC 2010)*, pages 1638–1642, Valletta, Malta, 2010.

[27] Janyce Wiebe and Rada Mihalcea. Word Sense and Subjectivity. In *Joint Conference of the International Committee on Computational Linguistics and the Association for Computational Linguistics (COLING-ACL 2006)*, pages 1065–1072, Sydney, Australia, 2006. ACL.

[28] Janyce Wiebe, Theresa Wilson, and Claire Cardie. Annotating Expressions of Opinions and Emotions in Language. *Language Resources and Evaluation*, 39(2-3):165–210, 2006.

[29] Theresa Wilson, Janyce Wiebe, and Paul Hoffmann. Recognizing Contextual Polarity in Phrase-Level Sentiment Analysis. In *Conference on Human Language Technology and Empirical Methods in Natural Language Processing (HLT-EMNLP 2005)*, pages 347–354, Vancouver, B.C., Canada, 2005. ACL.

[30] Theresa Wilson, Janyce Wiebe, and Paul Hoffmann. Recognizing Contextual Polarity: An Exploration of Features for Phrase-Level Sentiment Analysis. *Computational Linguistics*, 35(3):399–433, 2009.

Polarity Analysis of Texts using Discourse Structure

Bas Heerschop[1] basheerschop@gmail.com
Frank Goossen[1] frank.goossen@xs4all.nl
Alexander Hogenboom[1] hogenboom@ese.eur.nl
Flavius Frasincar[1] frasincar@ese.eur.nl
Uzay Kaymak[1,2] u.kaymak@ieee.org
Franciska de Jong[1,3] f.m.g.dejong@utwente.nl

[1]Erasmus University Rotterdam, P.O. Box 1738, 3000 DR Rotterdam, the Netherlands
[2]Eindhoven University of Technology, P.O. Box 513, 5600 MB Eindhoven, the Netherlands
[3]Universiteit Twente, P.O. Box 217, 7500 AE Enschede, the Netherlands

ABSTRACT

Sentiment analysis has applications in many areas and the exploration of its potential has only just begun. We propose Pathos, a framework which performs document sentiment analysis (partly) based on a document's discourse structure. We hypothesize that by splitting a text into important and less important text spans, and by subsequently making use of this information by weighting the sentiment conveyed by distinct text spans in accordance with their importance, we can improve the performance of a sentiment classifier. A document's discourse structure is obtained by applying Rhetorical Structure Theory on sentence level. When controlling for each considered method's structural bias towards positive classifications, weights optimized by a genetic algorithm yield an improvement in sentiment classification accuracy and macro-level F_1 score on documents of 4.5% and 4.7%, respectively, in comparison to a baseline not taking into account discourse structure.

Categories and Subject Descriptors

H.3.1 [**Information Storage and Retrieval**]: Content Analysis and Indexing—*Linguistic processing*; I.2.7 [**Artificial Intelligence**]: Natural Language Processing—*Discourse*

General Terms

Algorithms, Experimentation, Performance

Keywords

Discourse Structure, Linguistics, Polarity, Sentiment, RST

1. INTRODUCTION

Sentiment analysis is a rather young research area focusing on how to determine the attitude or subjectivity of a text. It has many applications, such as mining social media like Facebook and Twitter for consumer opinions about products and brands. For companies, sentiment analysis on data obtained from stakeholders can provide highly valuable information. The importance of sentiment analysis in specific areas has been indicated in [1, 5, 15, 16, 18], for financial markets, politics, organizations, brand management, and economic systems, respectively.

The goal of sentiment analysis is typically to determine the polarity of a piece of natural language text. Sentiment analysis methods are mainly rooted in, among others, natural language processing, computational linguistics, and text mining. Several research directions are explored in recent literature, including word sentiment scoring (i.e., learning sentiment scores of single words), subject/aspect relevance filtering (i.e., determining the relevant subject and/or aspect for a sentiment-carrying word), sentiment negation and amplification, and subjectivity analysis (i.e., determining whether sentences are subjective or objective) [12].

A typical approach to sentiment analysis is to use frequencies of positive and negative words in order to determine whether a document is predominantly positive or negative [26, 31]. Such an approach ignores structural aspects of a document, whereas these aspects may contain valuable information [14, 26, 30]. Yet, using knowledge obtained from structural elements in texts is a relatively unexplored direction in sentiment analysis. When capturing a text's discourse structure, this knowledge could be used to improve sentiment analysis (e.g., by assigning different weights to conclusions and footnotes, as conclusions may be more important for the overall sentiment of a text than footnotes).

A popular model for analyzing a text's discourse structure is the Rhetorical Structure Theory (RST) [19]. RST describes how to split a text into spans, each representing a meaningful part of the text. These spans can be either a nucleus or a satellite. A nucleus is considered to be the span with the highest degree of importance with respect to its related spans. Satellites support the nuclei and can therefore be seen as less important spans. By splitting a text into important and less important parts, we can treat these parts differently from each other when determining the overall sentiment. We hypothesize that by weighting text spans in accordance with their importance for the overall document sentiment, the detected document sentiment can be more reliable. We aim to investigate whether the use of discourse structure in sentiment analysis has a significant added value. For this purpose, we propose Pathos, a sentiment analysis framework that can interpret a text using RST, and use this information to classify the text's polarity.

The paper is structured as follows. Section 2 presents the related work. Subsequently, Section 3 elaborates on our proposed sentiment analysis framework, after which we present the results of our evaluation in Section 4. In Section 5, we draw conclusions and propose directions for future work.

2. RELATED WORK

In a recent literature survey on sentiment analysis, Pang and Lee [25] attribute the recent surge of research interest in systems that deal with opinions and sentiment to the fact that, despite today's users' hunger for and reliance upon online advice and recommendations, explicit information on user opinions is often hard to find, confusing, or overwhelming. As sentiment analysis tools may be particularly useful in analyzing, e.g., reviews, a widely used corpus for assessing sentiment analysis approaches is a collection of 2,000 English movie reviews, annotated for sentiment [23].

2.1 State of the Art

In many existing sentiment analysis approaches, a document is represented as a bag of words, i.e., an unordered collection of the words occurring in a document. Such an approach allows for vector representations of documents, enabling the use of machine learning techniques like Support Vector Machines for classifying documents. Features in such representations may be for instance words or parts of words. A binary representation of documents, indicating the presence or absence of specific words, has proven to be an effective approach, yielding an accuracy of 87.2% on the movie review data set [23]. Later research has focused on adding other features to the vector representations of documents. For instance, Whitelaw et al. [32] added features representing semantic distinctions between words based on the Appraisal Theory [20], thus yielding an accuracy of 90.2% on the movie review data set. Paltoglou and Thelwall [22] report a leave-one-out accuracy of 96.9% on this data set, obtained by using *tf-idf*-based weights for word features rather than using a binary representation of documents.

However, even though classifiers like the ones mentioned above may perform very well in the domain that they have been trained on, their performance drops tremendously when they are used in a different domain. In this light, lexicon-based methods, operating at a deeper level of analysis by incorporating the semantic orientation of individual words, can be used as an alternative [29]. A sentiment lexicon typically contains words and their associated sentiment, possibly differentiated by Part-of-Speech (POS) and/or meaning. A relatively straightforward lexicon-based sentiment analysis framework has been shown to have an accuracy up to 59.5% on the full movie review data set [11]. A more sophisticated lexicon-based sentiment analysis approach has been shown to have an accuracy of 59.6% to 76.4% on 1,900 documents from the movie review data set, depending on the sentiment lexicon used [29]. The latter lexicon-based approach is presented as a well-performing method, which is robust across domains and texts. Approaches like the one proposed by Taboada et al. [29] enable a more thorough linguistic analysis to be incorporated in the process of analyzing sentiment in natural language text. Yet, rather than just looking at semantic orientation of individual words or groups of words, one may also consider analyzing the role these textual elements play in conveying the overall sentiment by applying discourse analysis.

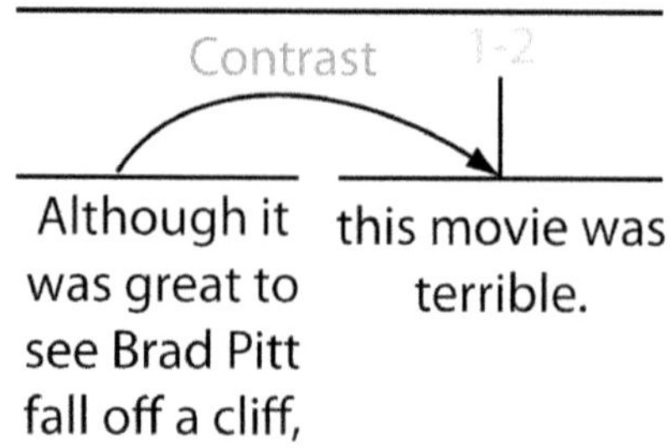

Figure 1: Example of an RST-structured sentence.

2.2 Rhetorical Structure Theory

According to UsingEnglish (`http://www.usingenglish.com`), discourse analysis can be defined as 'the area of linguistics that is concerned with how we build up meaning in the larger communicative rather than grammatical units; meaning in a text, paragraph, conversation, etc., rather than in a single sentence'. In our current endeavors, we apply discourse analysis in order to determine the parts of the text that are most relevant to the overall document sentiment. Intuitively, by splitting the text into parts with different levels of importance, sentiment analysis can be more reliable when weighting sentiment of parts of a text in accordance with their associated impact on a document's sentiment.

One of the leading discourse theories is RST [19], which can be used to split a text into spans which are rhetorically related to each other. There are two forms of relations: hypotactic and paratactic relations. In a hypotactic relation, one span is classified as nucleus, whereas the other spans are classified as satellite. RST claims nuclei to be more significant than satellites with respect to understanding and interpreting a text. In a paratactic relation, spans are equally significant, thus resulting in all spans to be classified as nuclei. RST identifies the smallest text spans that can hold rhetorical relations as Elementary Discourse Units (EDUs). Together, multiple EDUs can form a new text span, which again holds a rhetorical relation to another text span, thus yielding in a hierarchical structure of the text. RST also distinguishes several types of relations (e.g., elaboration, attribution, contrast, etc.). The authoritative paper on RST [19] defines 23 types of relations. In our framework, we differentiate among relation types by assigning them weights according to their importance, which we hypothesize to have a significant influence on the polarity of a document.

Figure 1 shows an example of an RST-structured sentence, where the text 'Although it was great to see Brad Pitt fall off a cliff, the movie was terrible.' is split into two segments. The first span is classified as a satellite and is related to the other span, the nucleus. The relation type is 'contrast', which indicates that the satellite segment of the sentence provides a contrast with the nucleus segment.

A human would typically interpret the specific sentence of Figure 1 as a negative review for the movie, as he would see the second span (the nucleus) as the most important span. However, in a classical (word-counting) sentiment analysis approach, all words would contribute equally to the total sentiment. Accordingly, a computer would count 'great' as very positive, and 'terrible' as very negative, which summed up makes a neutral review. When we exploit the information contained in the RST structure, the nucleus can be given a higher weight than the satellite, thus shifting focus to the nucleus segment. In this case, a higher weight for the nucleus and a lower weight for the satellite would probably lead to a negative sentiment score for this sentence. By using the knowledge obtained from the RST structure, we can thus get a more reliable sentiment score.

2.3 Parsing Structure from Documents

In order to exploit a document's discourse structure and in an analysis of the sentiment conveyed by the text, one needs to first identify the discourse structure. Manual annotation of discourse structure is typically cumbersome, time-consuming, and not easily scalable, thus rendering automatic discourse parsing an attractive alternative. There are several discourse parsers publicly available which can parse an RST structure from a document. One of them is Sentence-level PArsing of DiscoursE (SPADE) [28], which creates RST trees for every sentence in a document. SPADE has been trained and tested on the train and test set of the RST Discourse Treebank (RST-DT) [7], where an F_1 score of 83.1% is reached on identifying the right rhetorical relations and their right arguments [28].

Another publicly available discourse parser is the HIgh-Level Discourse Analyzer [13] (HILDA), which applies statistical machine-learning techniques [8] to parse discourse structures from documents using the Rhetorical Structure Theory. In contrast with SPADE's sentence-level parsing, HILDA offers document-level parsing. HILDA has also been trained and tested on RST-DT, and achieved an F_1 score of 94.1% on identifying relations [13].

2.4 Rhetorical Structure Theory in Sentiment Analysis

Taboada et al. present an RST-based sentiment analysis approach with the Sentiment Orientation CALculator (SO-CAL) [30]. The assumption is that certain parts of a text are more relevant than others with respect to the overall sentiment expressed. Two methods are proposed to extract the relevant sentences: (1) extract nuclei within sentences using the SPADE discourse parser, and (2) extract sentences that are considered on-topic using a decision tree based on the ID3 algorithm [27]. Both approaches have proven to contribute to SO-CAL's performance in classifying sentiment.

However, SO-CAL merely differentiates between core elements of a text (nuclei) on the one hand, and any type of less important (satellite) element on the other hand. Yet, we hypothesize that the contribution of text elements to the overall sentiment of a document depends on their respective positions within the overall discourse structure and hence their relation to other elements. For instance, a contrasting text span may play a different role in conveying the overall sentiment than an elaboration on information in nuclei does. Therefore, we propose a more elaborate approach to utilizing RST in sentiment analysis by taking into account hypotactic relations between nuclei and satellites.

3. PATHOS

We present Pathos, a sentiment analysis framework that is able to interpret a text in terms of its discourse structure, and use this information to classify the text's polarity. First, we provide an overview of all components used in our framework. Then, we discuss the design of our sentiment classifier. Finally, we discuss the approaches to discourse parsing supported by this classifier.

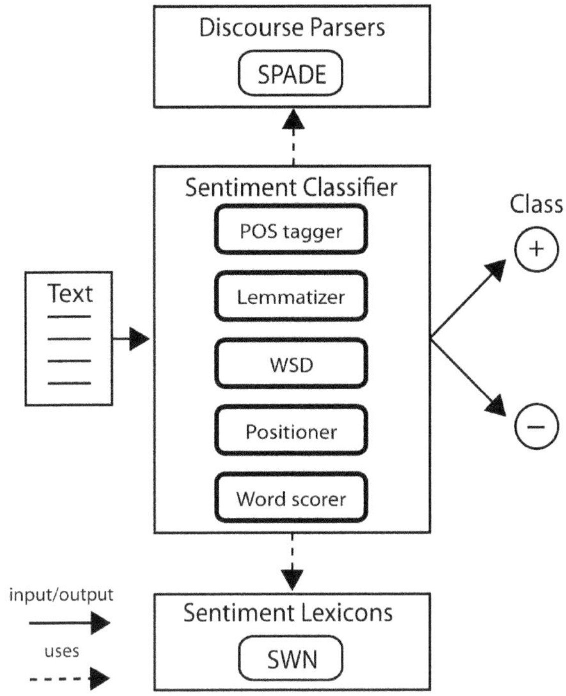

Figure 2: Overview of the Pathos framework.

3.1 Overview

The proposed framework consists of three parts, depicted in Figure 2. The central part is the sentiment classifier which classifies documents as either positive or negative. In order to do this, our framework first identifies the POS and the lemmas of all words and performs Word Sense Disambiguation (WSD). The positioner can employ a discourse parser (SPADE) to transform the input text into EDUs which are used to assign a weight to each individual word. The overall sentiment of a document is then computed as a weighted average of individual word scores, retrieved from a sentiment lexicon which differentiates on POS and word sense – SentiWordNet 3.0 [3, 9] (SWN), which has proven to be very useful for this purpose [11]. Such a lexicon-based sentiment scoring approach is in accordance with the work by Taboada et al. [30].

3.2 Sentiment Classifier

To investigate the merits of taking into account structural aspects of content in sentiment analysis, we propose a lexicon-based sentiment analysis approach, taking into account adjectives, adverbs, verbs, and nouns. Scoring a document for sentiment involves aggregating word-level sentiment scores, retrieved from a sentiment lexicon, after having initially determined each word's POS and lemma. A sentiment lexicon can contain entries for different senses for an arbitrary POS of an arbitrary word. In order to determine the appropriate sense of a word in a particular sentence, we use a similarity function proposed by Baazaoui Zghal et al. [2] and inspired by the Lesk algorithm [17]. We apply this algorithm because it is an unsupervised algorithm, able to compute adequate senses in a relatively small amount of time. Other unsupervised algorithms as SSI [21] and Lesk [17] require more computations which make the WSD a slow process.

Algorithm 1: Word Sense Disambiguation.

```
input  : The word w to be disambiguated, its part-of-speech
         pos, and the sentence s that contains the word
output: The sense i of w with the highest semantic
         similarity to the words in the context
I = All words in s; // The context
senses = retrieveSenses(w, pos);
// All unique senses of w
mostSimilarS_i = 0;
// Most similar set of related synonyms
mostSimilarSynset = ∅;
// The synset with the best similarity to w
if |senses| <= 1 then
    return |senses|;
else
    foreach i in senses do
        containingSynsets =
        retrieveSynsetsContainingSense(i, pos);
        foreach synset in containingSynsets do
            S_i = ∅;
            foreach synonym in synset.Synonyms do
                S_i = {S_i, synonym};
            end
            foreach relation in synset.Relations do
                foreach synonym in relation.Synonyms do
                    S_i = {S_i, synonym};
                end
            end
            if |S_i ∩ I| > |mostSimilarS_i ∩ I| then
                mostSimilarS_i = S_i;
                mostSimilarSynset = synset;
            end
            else if |S_i ∩ I| = |mostSimilarS_i ∩ I| then
                if |S_i| > |mostSimilarS_i| then
                    mostSimilarS_i = S_i;
                    mostSimilarSynset = synset;
                end
            end
        end
        return i;
    end
end
```

In our applied WSD algorithm (described in Algorithm 1), the word sense with the highest semantic similarity to the word's context is selected. Here, the similarity $\mathrm{sim}(S_i, I)$ of a set S_i, denoting the semantic neighborhood of sense i of the word to be disambiguated, with the word's context I (i.e., the set denoting the sentence lexical neighborhood of the word to be disambiguated) can be defined as:

$$\mathrm{sim}(S_i, I) = |S_i \cap I|. \tag{1}$$

S_i contains the word to be disambiguated and all the synonyms, hyponyms, hypernyms, and gloss words of the WordNet synset. Furthermore, I contains all the words in the sentence without the word to be disambiguated. The set which has the highest similarity to I is then selected, and gives the most similar sense i. If there are more sets with the same similarity, the set S_i which has the maximum number of elements is chosen.

When having determined each word's POS, lemma, and its associated word sense, the score $\mathrm{eval}(d)$ of a document d can be computed as the sum of the scores of the individual sentences:

$$\mathrm{eval}(d) = \sum_{s_i \in d} \mathrm{score}(s_i), \tag{2}$$

Algorithm 2: Scoring a document.

```
input  : A document d
output: A floating point number representing the sentiment
         score of document d
docScore = 0;
docScoreSentenceCount = 0;
foreach s in d.Sentences do
    sentenceScore = 0;
    foreach w in s.Words do
        pos = getPOS(w, s);
        lemma = getLemma(w, pos);
        sense = getWordSense(w, s, pos);
        score = getWordScore(lemma, sense, pos);
        weight = getWeight(w, s, document);
        sentenceScore = sentenceScore + (weight × score);
    end
    docScore = docScore + sentenceScore;
end
return docScore;
```

where $\mathrm{score}(s_i)$ is the score of the ith sentence s_i in d. The score of sentence s_i is computed by aggregating all sentiment scores $\mathrm{score}(w_j)$ of all words $w_j \in s_i$, multiplied with their respective weights $\mathrm{weight}(w_j)$:

$$\mathrm{score}(s_i) = \sum_{w_j \in s_i} \mathrm{score}(w_j) \times \mathrm{weight}(w_j), \tag{3}$$

where the weights are computed differently for our three positioners in accordance with the methods explained in Section 3.3. Here, word-level sentiment scores $\mathrm{score}(w_j)$ are assumed to be in the range $[-1, 1]$ (anywhere in between negative and positive, respectively).

Using (2), the classification $\mathrm{class}(d)$ of a document d can finally be determined as follows:

$$\mathrm{class}(d) = \begin{cases} 1 & \text{if } \mathrm{eval}(d) - \mathrm{offset} \geq 0, \\ -1 & \text{if } \mathrm{eval}(d) - \mathrm{offset} < 0, \end{cases} \tag{4}$$

where 1 denotes a positive document, and -1 denotes a negative document. The offset corrects a possible bias in the sentiment scores caused by people's tendency to write negative reviews with rather positive words, which can lead to a small negative sentiment score or sometimes even a positive score for a negative document, whereas a positive document usually gets a high positive sentiment score [30]. The offset can be calculated by taking the average sentiment scores of both positive and negative documents in the training set and subsequently computing the equidistant point of these scores.

Algorithm 2 is used to score a document. Each sentence is scored separately and its score is added to the overall document sentiment score. Sentence scores are essentially weighted averages of the sentiment scores of their individual words. The calculation for each word in a sentence (only non-stopwords) consists of five steps: (1) determining the POS, (2) retrieving the lemma of the word based on its POS-type, (3) determining which meaning of a word to use (using the WSD process described in Algorithm 1), (4) retrieving the score of the word from the sentiment lexicon, and (5) assigning a weight in accordance with the word's position in the document's discourse structure. Pathos supports several methods for parsing a document's discourse structure and assigning corresponding weights to individual words, as further detailed in Section 3.3.

Algorithm 3: Simple positioner.

```
input  : A document d
output: A weighted document d
wordCount = getNumberOfwords(d);
coefficient = 1/wordCount;
weight = 0;
foreach s in d.Sentences do
    foreach w in s.Words do
        w.setWeight(weight);
        weight = weight + coefficient;
    end
end
return d;
```

3.3 Discourse Parsing

Existing work suggests that sentiment analysis may benefit from a better understanding of discourse in texts [14, 26, 30]. Hence, we propose a discourse parsing module that first retrieves the discourse structure of a document and subsequently assigns discourse-based weights to sentiment-carrying words using a so-called positioner. Our framework supports three ways of accounting for discourse structure when determining a document's polarity.

A simple example of a discourse structure found in most sentiment-carrying documents (e.g., movie reviews) is the distinction of 'introduction', 'arguments', and 'conclusions'. Intuitively, one would think that an author typically puts his final and most important opinion towards the end of the text. To test this intuition, Pathos is able to assign weights to each word of a document, based on their respective position. The words are weighted uniformly in the range $[0, 1]$, where the first word is assigned a weight of 0, and the last word is assigned a weight of 1. This Simple positioner approach is described in Algorithm 3.

In order to obtain a more advanced discourse structure, Pathos uses SPADE [28] to extract sentence-level RST structures from texts. Subsequently, Pathos is able to assign a weight to each word based on its position in an RST structure. Table 1 shows all RST relation types handled by Pathos. These relations are a subset of the 23 standard relations defined in [19], encompassing only the relation types occurring in at least 10% of our considered set of reviews (see Section 4 for more details on our corpus).

Taboada et al. [30] hypothesize that adjectives found in nuclei of a document are more important for the overall sentiment, while adjectives found in satellites potentially interfere with the overall sentiment – the latter adjectives may be tangential or even irrelevant for a document's overall sentiment. Pathos can handle the notion of discourse structure thus introduced to the sentiment mining process by means of the SPADE positioner algorithm (Algorithm 4), which tags the words in the top-level nuclei of each sentence as nuclei, and the words in all other top-level elements as satellites. If a sentence only consists of a single text span, all words in that span are tagged as nuclei. Each word can be given a weight based on the RST element in which it resides. Following Taboada et al. [30], we consider two sets of weights for nuclei and satellites: (1) 1 and 0, and (2) 1.5 and 0.5, respectively. Yet, rather than only analyzing adjectives, we additionally handle adverbs, verbs, and nouns.

Algorithm 4: SPADE positioner.

```
input  : A document d
output: A weighted document d
foreach s in d.Sentences do
    foreach w in s.Words do
        rstElement = getRSTElement(w);
        weight = getWeight(rstElement);
        w.setWeight(weight);
    end
end
return d;
```

Building on the idea that some text spans can be more important for the overall sentiment of a document than other text spans, we propose a third approach which further explores satellites and their relation to the nuclei. We hypothesize that a hierarchy exists between the satellite relation types – some satellite relation types may contribute differently to the overall sentiment than others. By employing the SPADE Extended algorithm, shown in Algorithm 5, Pathos can give specific weights to the words in satellite elements based on their RST relation type. In addition to the positive weights considered by Taboada et al. [30] for their RST elements, we consider negative weights, as some text spans (e.g., contrasting text spans) may contribute negatively to the overall sentiment of a document. In order to be able to additionally intensify sentiment in certain text spans, we assume the weights to be in the range $[-2, 2]$. These weights can be optimized by means of a Genetic Algorithm (GA).

To this end, the sum of sentiment scores in the span of each RST relation type in a document (e.g., 'nucleus' in the case of a nucleus span, or 'attribution', 'elaboration', etc. in case of satellites) is first calculated. Subsequently, a set of potential solutions – chromosomes – can be generated, where each chromosome represents a set of weights for all considered RST relation types. These chromosomes are then subject to a process of simulated biological evolution according to the principle of survival of the fittest.

Table 1: Relation types handled by Pathos.

Relation	Description
Attribution	Clauses containing reporting verbs or cognitive predicates related to reported messages presented in nuclei.
Background	Information helping a reader to sufficiently comprehend matters presented in nuclei.
Cause	Information on the effects of causes presented in nuclei.
Condition	Hypothetical, future, or otherwise unrealized situations, the realization of which influences the realization of nucleus matters.
Contrast	Situations juxtaposed to situations in nuclei, where juxtaposed situations are considered as the same in many respects, yet differing in a few respects, and compared with respect to one or more differences.
Elaboration	Rhetorical elements containing additional detail about matters presented in nuclei.
Enablement	Rhetorical elements containing information increasing a reader's potential ability of performing actions presented in nuclei.
Explanation	Justifications or reasons for situations presented in nuclei.

Algorithm 5: SPADE Extended positioner.

```
input  : A document d
output: A weighted document d
foreach s in d.Sentences do
    foreach w in s.Words do
        rstElement = getRSTElement(w);
        if rstElement == 'Satellite' then
            relationType = getRelationType(w);
            weight = getWeight(relationType);
        else
            weight = getWeight(rstElement);
        end
        w.setWeight(weight);
    end
end
return d;
```

To optimize the weights, the GA applies tournament selection, one-point crossover, and two mutation functions, i.e., changing the sign for a random weight in the chromosome and switching weights in the chromosome.

The fitness of a chromosome is computed in terms of its performance in classifying document polarity, which is assessed as follows. For both the positive documents and the negative documents in our data set, we first compute precision, recall, and the F_1 measure. Precision is the proportion of the positively (negatively) classified documents which have an actual classification of positive (negative). Recall is the proportion of the actual positive (negative) documents which are also classified as such. The F_1 measure is the harmonic mean of precision and recall, i.e.,

$$F_1 = \frac{2 \times \text{precision} \times \text{recall}}{\text{precision} + \text{recall}}. \tag{5}$$

The performance of a chromosome on the full corpus can then be assessed by means of the macro-level F_1 measure, which is the average of the F_1 scores of the positive and negative documents.

4. EVALUATION

In this section, we evaluate our different approaches to determine the polarity of texts. Evaluation is done by assessing the processing times, accuracy, precision, recall, and F_1 score of the different positioners for the sentiment analysis framework. We have evaluated our framework on a data set provided by Pang and Lee [24], which was introduced in [23]. The set is a collection of 1,000 positive and 1,000 negative movie reviews, which have been extracted from movie review websites. From the original set, we have extracted a subset of 500 positive and 500 negative reviews, because SPADE was not able to process all reviews due to problems with syntax in over 800 documents.

We have randomly split the dataset into a training and test set, consisting of 60% and 40% of the documents, respectively, with both sets encompassing a proportional number of occurrences of each considered relation type. Thus, our training set contains 300 positive reviews and 300 negative reviews, whereas the test set contains 200 positive reviews and 200 negative reviews. The training set is used to train the GA for the SPADE Extended positioner, as well as to compute an offset value for each individual positioner. The test set is used to measure and compare the performances of all approaches.

For running our experiments, we have built a Graphical User Interface (GUI), enabling us to select different options for an experiment as well as to select the directories containing positive and negative documents. This GUI also displays the results of an experiment, as demonstrated in Figure 3.

To evaluate Pathos' processing performance of a single document, we have created another GUI, which is depicted in Figure 4. The GUI offers the possibility to evaluate all positioners which have been implemented in Pathos. Additionally, this GUI provides insight into the sentiment analysis process. For example, in Figure 4, a document processed by the SPADE Extended positioner is shown. In our GUI, words are colored depending on their sentiment score (a positive word is colored green, and a negative word is colored red), and the underlying information about a word (lemma, score, weight, POS, RST relation) can be requested by selecting the word.

4.1 Experimental Setup

To test the performance of the considered positioners, we have evaluated them in our sentiment analysis framework, the core of which acts as a document processing pipeline (see Section 3.1). In this pipeline, we first determine the POS of words by using the OpenNLP [4] POS tagger, which has an accuracy of 98.7% [6]. We then determine the lemmas of words by means of a third party lemmatizer, based on WordNet using the Java WordNet Library (JWNL) API. Its estimated prediction accuracy is about 98%.

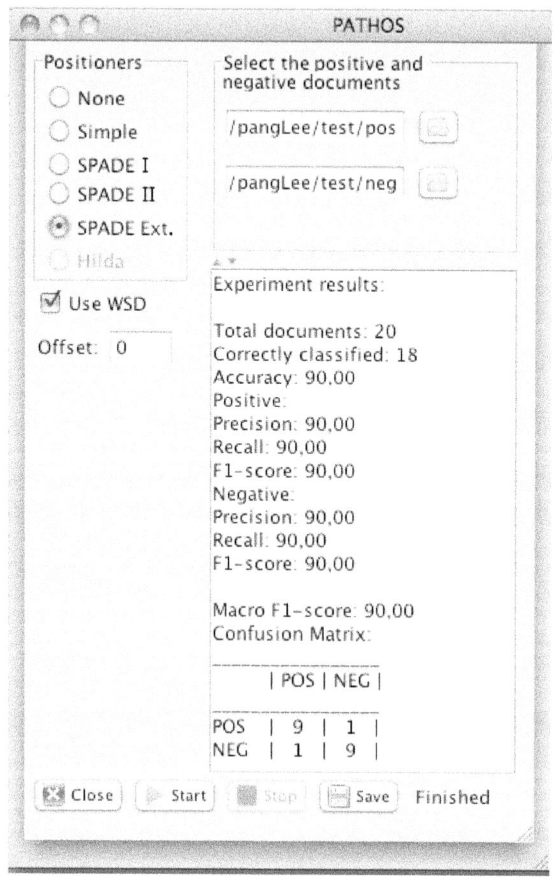

Figure 3: Experiment GUI.

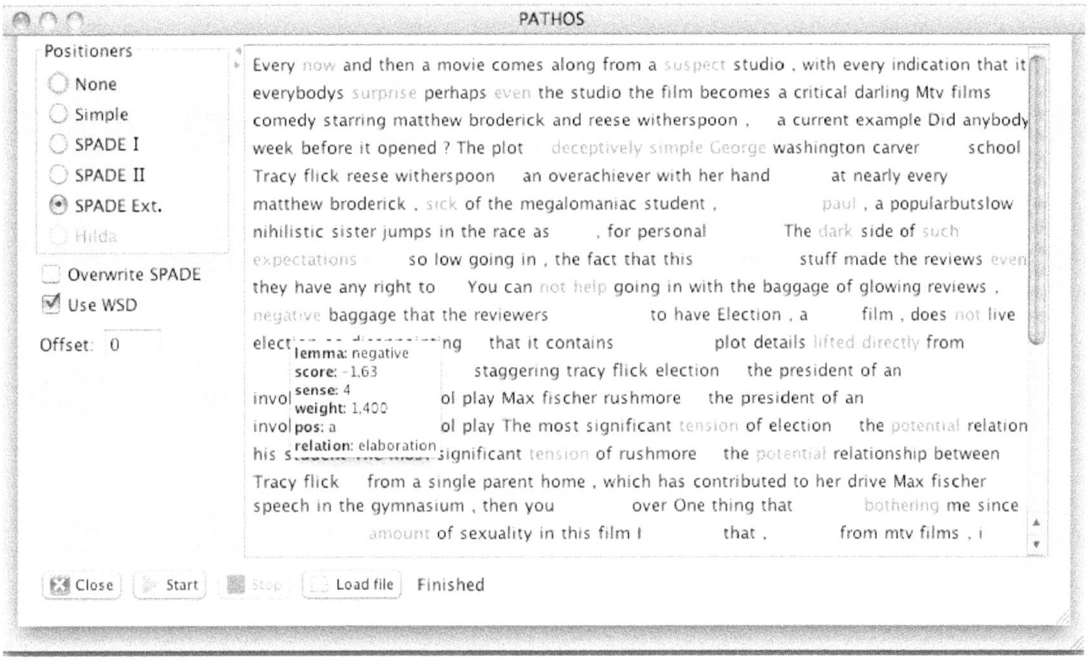

Figure 4: Document test GUI.

In order to subsequently determine which sentiment score of a word to select from our sentiment lexicon, we additionally employ a WSD algorithm (see Algorithm 1). A baseline for this would be always selecting the first sense from WordNet (which is the most common sense) for each word. We have evaluated our WSD algorithm on a test set of 100 sentences extracted from our corpus. The senses of the words in these sentences have been manually evaluated and annotated by three experts until they reached agreement. Our algorithm obtains an accuracy of 68% on this test set, whereas taking the first sense from WordNet yields an accuracy of 44%.

For each non-stopword, the POS, lemma, and sense thus determined are used for retrieving the associated sentiment score from the SentiWordNet 3.0 [3, 9] sentiment lexicon. SentiWordNet is based on WordNet [10], which is a (semantic) lexical resource, organized into sets of synonyms – synsets – which can be differentiated based on their POS type. Each synset expresses a distinct concept and is linked to other synsets through different kinds of relations (e.g., synonymy, antonymy, hyponymy, or meronymy). In SentiWordNet, each WordNet synset σ has been assigned scores in the range $[0, 1]$ on objectivity $Obj(\sigma)$, positivity $Pos(\sigma)$, and negativity $Neg(\sigma)$, the sum of which always equals 1. In our framework, we use SentiWordNet to compute the word sentiment score as a single number computed by subtracting $Neg(\sigma)$ from $Pos(\sigma)$, which results in a real number in the interval $[-1, 1]$, representing sentiment scores in the range from negative to positive, respectively.

The key of our framework is in weighting the retrieved word-level sentiment scores in accordance with the place of these words in the discourse structure of a document. As a baseline, we first assess the performance of our framework on our test set without any positioner (i.e., all words in the document are considered to equally contribute to the overall sentiment). An additional baseline is the Simple positioner, which weights the sentiment of words in accordance with their respective positions in the text. Then, we introduce two additional baselines derived from existing work [30] by evaluating the SPADE positioner with different weights for nucleus and satellite, i.e., 1 and 0 (SPADE I), and 1.5 and 0.5 (SPADE II), respectively. Finally, we assess the use of weights for distinct RST relation types, optimized by a GA, and compare the performance of this positioner (SPADE Extended) with the other considered approaches in an attempt to assess how information conveyed by rhetorical structure can be utilized in sentiment analysis of natural language texts.

4.2 Experimental Results

The optimal set of weights for the different RST elements in our training set is presented in Table 2. With an associated weight of 0.771, 'Nucleus' elements appear to contribute relatively much to the overall document sentiment in our training set. Yet, some satellite elements turn out to play an important role in conveying the overall document sentiment as well.

Table 2: Frequencies in training set of and optimized weights for relation types handled by Pathos.

Relation	Frequency	Weight
Nucleus	600	0.771
Attribution	461	0.451
Background	362	0.017
Cause	89	−0.271
Condition	176	0.304
Contrast	243	−0.660
Elaboration	531	1.400
Enablement	266	0.956
Explanation	134	−0.099

For instance, 'Elaboration' elements receive an even higher weight of 1.400, thus indicating that – in our training set – writers of reviews typically tend to express their sentiment in a more apparent fashion in elaborations on their core message. To a lesser extent, this also holds for rhetorical elements with a purpose of increasing a reader's potential ability of performing actions presented in the core of a review, as 'Enablement' elements are associated with a weight of 0.956. The information presented in 'Attribution', 'Condition', and especially 'Background' elements is clearly less relevant for the overall sentiment in reviews, as these elements receive weights of 0.451, 0.304, and 0.017, respectively.

Conversely, the sentiment conveyed by elements presenting matters contrasting with the information presented in the core of a review is typically inverted with a weight of -0.660. The sentiment conveyed by 'Cause' and 'Explanation' elements is slightly inverted as well, as these elements receive respective weights of -0.271 and -0.099. These minor inversions may however be artifacts of the relatively low frequencies of these elements in our training set, as they occur in only 89 and 134 out of 600 documents, respectively.

Tables 3 and 4 present the results for all considered approaches, respectively without and with offset, on our test set of 400 documents. Table 3 shows that the baseline approach has an overall accuracy of 0.585 and a macro-level F_1 of 0.569. The Simple positioner exhibits the largest improvement with respect to these measures, i.e., 3.9% and 4.8%, respectively. Two out of three considered SPADE positioners show an improvement in terms of these measures as well, albeit to a lesser extent. With respect to the baseline, SPADE I exhibits no change in overall accuracy and a 1.2% decrease in macro-level F_1. Conversely, applying discourse parsing by means of the SPADE II positioner yields a 2.1% increase in both accuracy and macro-level F_1. Yet, the best performing SPADE positioner is the SPADE Extended positioner using the weights presented in Table 2. This positioner exhibits an increase in overall accuracy and macro-level F_1 of 2.6% and 2.1%, respectively.

Yet, Table 3 clearly shows that all considered positioners exhibit a structural bias towards positive classifications. When controlling for each positioner's structural bias, the respective positioners exhibit a less biased performance, as detailed in Table 4. The baseline approach now yields an overall accuracy of 0.688 and a macro-level F_1 of 0.687. Compensation for the structural bias causes the Simple positioner, the SPADE I positioner, as well as the SPADE II positioner to perform below baseline. With respect to the baseline, overall accuracy and macro-level F_1 decrease with 5.8% and 5.5% for the Simple positioner, 1.9% and 1.8% for the SPADE I positioner, and 0.4% and 0.4% for the SPADE II positioner, respectively. Conversely, the SPADE Extended positioner exhibits a 4.5% increase in overall accuracy and a 4.7% increase in macro-level F_1 with respect to the baseline when controlling for each positioner's structural bias.

These results indicate that information contained in discourse structure of documents can improve the classification of sentiment conveyed by these documents. Additionally, the use of offsets improves the overall performance of each considered method, thus confirming the hypothesis of Taboada et al. [30] that a possible structural bias caused by negative documents carrying much positive sentiment can be corrected by applying an offset in the calculation of sentiment scores for documents. Moreover, we improve on existing work due to our more elaborate, optimized weighting scheme, which assigns distinct rhetorical elements different roles in conveying a document's overall sentiment. Our results indicate that both nuclei and satellites play an important role in conveying sentiment, whereas satellites have until now been deemed predominantly irrelevant.

However, these observed performance improvements come at a cost of increased processing time. On a standard 2,400 GHz Intel Core 2 Duo system with 2,048 MB physical memory, the average processing time for the baseline approach is approximately 2,786 milliseconds per document in our test set, with a standard deviation of approximately 1,176 milliseconds. Our Simple positioner has a similar performance, as it takes on average approximately 2,585 milliseconds to process a single document, with a standard deviation of about 1,121 milliseconds. Conversely, the SPADE positioners inspired by existing work [30], i.e., SPADE I and SPADE II, need on average about 45,862 milliseconds to process a document, with a standard deviation of 22,457 milliseconds. As the SPADE Extended positioner ignores less frequently occurring RST elements, it needs slightly less time than the SPADE I and SPADE II positioners for processing a document. On average, the SPADE Extended positioner processes a document in approximately 37,943 milliseconds, with a standard deviation of about 16,556 milliseconds.

The SPADE positioners spend a considerable amount of their processing time on a computationally intensive process of document parsing by means of the freely available SPADE discourse parser [28]. When considering only the time spent on activities other than using the SPADE discourse parser, the SPADE I and SPADE II positioners show an average document processing time of approximately 2,559 milliseconds, with a standard deviation of 1,062 milliseconds, whereas the SPADE Extended positioner needs on average about 2,571 milliseconds to process a document, with a standard deviation of 1,066 milliseconds. These results indicate that a major challenge lies in finding principal ways of efficiently and effectively extracting discourse structure from natural language texts.

5. CONCLUSIONS

While most research in sentiment analysis focuses on the main components of a sentiment classifier (e.g., word sentiment scoring, topic classification, negation, and intensifiers), little research has been done on analyzing the discourse structure of texts in order to identify text spans that are more important for the overall sentiment in a document. We compare three methods for dividing texts into important and less important parts. One method is based on the position of a word in a text. The other two methods exploit discourse structure in natural language text, either by distinguishing between (sentence-level) nuclei and satellites, or by identifying and exploiting (sentence-level) RST relation types. The objective of this paper is to give insights into how information can be harvested from structural aspects of content in order to improve the state-of-the art in sentiment analysis. Our results show that our method exploiting sentence-level RST relation types is the best performing approach, outperforming the baseline with a sentiment classification accuracy increased with 4.5% and a macro-level F_1 score increased with 4.7%, when controlling for each method's structural bias towards positive classifications.

Table 3: Experimental results for all positioners without offset.

		Positive			Negative			Overall	
Positioner	Offset	Precision	Recall	F_1	Precision	Recall	F_1	Accuracy	Macro F_1
Baseline	0.000	0.562	0.775	0.651	0.637	0.395	0.488	0.585	0.569
Simple	0.000	**0.581**	0.770	0.662	0.659	**0.445**	**0.531**	**0.608**	**0.597**
SPADE I (1, 0)	0.000	0.559	**0.810**	0.661	0.655	0.360	0.465	0.585	0.563
SPADE II (1.5, 0.5)	0.000	0.570	0.795	0.664	0.661	0.400	0.498	0.598	0.581
SPADE Extended	0.000	0.570	**0.810**	**0.669**	**0.672**	0.390	0.494	0.600	0.582

Table 4: Experimental results for all positioners with offset.

		Positive			Negative			Overall	
Positioner	Offset	Precision	Recall	F_1	Precision	Recall	F_1	Accuracy	Macro F_1
Baseline	2.016	0.687	0.690	0.688	0.688	0.685	0.687	0.688	0.687
Simple	1.290	0.647	0.660	0.654	0.653	0.640	0.647	0.650	0.650
SPADE I (1, 0)	1.560	0.668	**0.695**	0.681	0.682	0.655	0.668	0.675	0.675
SPADE II (1.5, 0.5)	2.796	0.683	0.690	0.687	0.687	0.680	0.683	0.685	0.685
SPADE Extended	2.562	**0.732**	**0.695**	**0.713**	**0.710**	**0.745**	**0.727**	**0.720**	**0.720**

A major bottleneck when accounting for discourse structure is the processing time required for identifying discourse structure in natural language text. Therefore, as future work, we aim to further explore other, scalable methods of identifying the discourse structure of texts. In addition, we would like to explore the applicability of our results in other types of sentiment mining approaches, e.g., methods making use of Support Vector Machines rather than sentiment lexicons. Furthermore, our currently used discourse parser SPADE only retrieves the RST structure on a sentence level, so it would be interesting to investigate the performance of a document level RST structure. Additionally, we aim to evaluate the performance of our methods on different corpora, which may contain other relation types or exhibit a different relation of discourse structure to the overall sentiment. Another interesting direction for future work would be to summarize a text and evaluate this summary using our sentiment classifier. Last, we would like to investigate how to best present a sentiment analysis system's results in order to suit a typical user's needs.

6. REFERENCES

[1] I. Arnold and E. Vrugt. Fundamental Uncertainty and Stock Market Volatility. *Applied Financial Economics*, 18(17):1425–1440, 2008.

[2] H. Baazaoui Zghal, M. Aufaure, and N. Ben Mustapha. A Model-Driven Approach of Ontological Components for On-line Semantic Web Information Retrieval. *Journal of Web Engineering*, 6(4):309–336, 2007.

[3] S. Baccianella, A. Esuli, and F. Sebastiani. SentiWordNet 3.0: An Enhanced Lexical Resource for Sentiment Analysis and Opinion Mining. In *7th Conference on International Language Resources and Evaluation (LREC 2010)*, pages 2200–2204. European Language Resources Association, 2010.

[4] J. Baldridge and T. Morton. OpenNLP, 2004. Available online, `http://opennlp.sourceforge.net/`.

[5] D. Baron. Competing for the Public through the News Media. *Journal of Economics and Management Strategy*, 14(2):339–376, 2005.

[6] E. Buyko, J. Wermter, M. Poprat, and U. Hahn. Automatically Adapting an NLP Core Engine to the Biology Domain. In *Joint Linking Literature, Information and Knowledge for Biology and the 9th Bio-Ontologies SIG Meeting (ISMB 2006)*, pages 65–68. Oxford University Press, 2006.

[7] L. Carlson, D. Marcu, and M. Okurowski. Building a Discourse-Tagged Corpus in the Framework of Rhetorical Structure Theory. In *Current Directions in Discourse and Dialogue*, pages 85–112. Kluwer Academic Publishers, 2003.

[8] D. duVerle and H. Prendinger. A Novel Discourse Parser Based on Support Vector Machine Classification. In *47th Annual Meeting of the Association for Computational Linguistics and the 4th International Joint Conference on Natural Language Processing of the Asian Federation of Natural Language Processing (ACL/AFNLP 2009)*, pages 665–673. Association for Computational Linguistics, 2009.

[9] A. Esuli and F. Sebastiani. SentiWordNet: A Publicly Available Lexical Resource for Opinion Mining. In *5th Conference on Language Resources and Evaluation (LREC 2006)*, pages 417–422. European Language Resources Association, 2006.

[10] C. Fellbaum. *WordNet: An Electronic Lexical Database*. MIT Press, 1998.

[11] B. Heerschop, A. Hogenboom, and F. Frasincar. Sentiment Lexicon Creation from Lexical Resources. In *14th International Conference on Business Information Systems (BIS 2011)*, volume 87 of *Lecture Notes in Business Information Processing*, pages 185–196. Springer, 2011.

[12] B. Heerschop, P. van Iterson, A. Hogenboom, F. Frasincar, and U. Kaymak. Analyzing Sentiment in a Large Set of Web Data while Accounting for Negation. In *7th Atlantic Web Intelligence Conference (AWIC 2011)*, pages 195–205. Springer, 2011.

[13] H. Hernault, H. Prendinger, D. duVerle, and M. Ishizuka. HILDA: A Discourse Parser Using Support Vector Machine Classification. *Dialogue and Discourse*, 1(3):1–33, 2010.

[14] A. Hogenboom, F. Hogenboom, U. Kaymak, P. Wouters, and F. de Jong. Mining Economic Sentiment using Argumentation Structures. In *7th International Workshop on Web Information Systems Modeling (WISM 2010) at 29th International Conference on Conceptual Modeling (ER 2010)*, volume 6413 of *Lecture Notes in Computer Science*, pages 200–209. Springer, 2010.

[15] C. Holton. Identifying Disgruntled Employee Systems Fraud Risk Through Text Mining: A Simple Solution for a Multi-Billion Dollar Problem. *Decision Support Systems*, 46(4):853–846, 2009.

[16] B. Jansen, M. Zhang, K. Sobel, and A. Chowdury. Twitter Power: Tweets as Electronic Word of Mouth. *Journal of the American Society for Information Science and Technology*, 60(11):2169–2188, 2009.

[17] M. Lesk. Automatic Sense Disambiguation Using Machine Readable Dictionaries: How To Tell a Pine Cone from an Ice Cream Cone. In *5th Annual International Conference on Systems Documentation (SIGDOC 1986)*, pages 24–26. Association for Computing Machinery, 1986.

[18] S. Ludvigson. Consumer Confidence and Consumer Spending. *The Journal of Economic Perspectives*, 18(2):29–50, 2004.

[19] W. Mann and S. Thompson. Rhetorical Structure Theory: Toward a Functional Theory of Text Organization. *Text*, 8(3):243–281, 1988.

[20] J. Martin and P. White. *The Language of Evaluation: Appraisal in English*. Palgrave Macmillan, 2005.

[21] R. Navigli and P. Velardi. Structural Semantic Interconnections: A Knowledge-Based Approach to Word Sense Disambiguation. *IEEE Transactions on Pattern Analysis and Machine Intelligence*, 27(7):671–674, 2005.

[22] G. Paltoglou and M. Thelwall. A study of Information Retrieval weighting schemes for sentiment analysis. In *48th Annual Meeting of the Association for Computational Linguistics (ACL 2010)*, pages 1386–1395. Association for Computational Linguistics, 2010.

[23] B. Pang and L. Lee. A Sentimental Education: Sentiment Analysis using Subjectivity Summarization based on Minimum Cuts. In *42nd Annual Meeting of the Association for Computational Linguistics (ACL 2004)*, pages 271–280. Association for Computational Linguistics, 2004.

[24] B. Pang and L. Lee. Polarity dataset v2.0, 2004. Available online, `http://www.cs.cornell.edu/People/pabo/movie-review-data/`.

[25] B. Pang and L. Lee. Opinion Mining and Sentiment Analysis. *Foundations and Trends in Information Retrieval*, 2(1):1–135, 2008.

[26] B. Pang, L. Lee, and S. Vaithyanathan. Thumbs up? Sentiment Classification using Machine Learning Techniques. In *Empirical Methods in Natural Language Processing (EMNLP 2002)*. Association for Computational Linguistics, 2002.

[27] J. Quinlan. Induction of Decision Trees. *Machine Learning*, 5(1):71–100, 1986.

[28] R. Soricut and D. Marcu. Sentence Level Discourse Parsing using Syntactic and Lexical Information. In *Human Language Technology and North American Association for Computational Linguistics Conference (HLT/NAACL 2003)*, pages 149–156. Association for Computational Linguistics, 2003.

[29] M. Taboada, J. Brooke, M. Tofiloski, K. Voll, and M. Stede. Lexicon-Based Methods for Sentiment Analysis. *Computational Linguistics*, 37(2):267–307, 2011.

[30] M. Taboada, K. Voll, and J. Brooke. Extracting Sentiment as a Function of Discourse Structure and Topicality. Technical Report 20, Simon Fraser University, 2008. Available online, `http://www.cs.sfu.ca/research/publications/techreports/#2008`.

[31] P. Turney. Thumbs Up or Thumbs Down?: Semantic Orientation Applied to Unsupervised Classification of Reviews. In *40th Annual Meeting on Association for Computational Linguistics (ACL 2002)*, pages 417–424. Association for Computational Linguistics, 2002.

[32] C. Whitelaw, N. Garg, and S. Argamon. Using Appraisal Groups for Sentiment Analysis. In *14th ACM International Conference on Information and Knowledge Management (CIKM 2005)*, pages 625–631. Association for Computing Machinery, 2005.

A Query-Based Multi-document Sentiment Summarizer*

Maria Soledad Pera
Computer Science Dept.
Brigham Young University
Provo, Utah 84602, U.S.A.
soledadpera@gmail.com

Rani Qumsiyeh
Computer Science Dept.
Brigham Young University
Provo, Utah 84602, U.S.A.
rani_qumsiyeh@yahoo.com

Yiu-Kai Ng
Computer Science Dept.
Brigham Young University
Provo, Utah 84602, U.S.A.
ng@compsci.byu.edu

ABSTRACT

Review websites, such as Epinions.com, which offer users a platform to share their opinions on diverse products and services, provide a valuable source of opinion-rich information. Browsing through archived reviews to locate different opinions on a product or service, however, is a time-consuming and tedious task, and in most cases, the large amount of available information is difficult for users to absorb. To facilitate the process of synthesizing opinions expressed in reviews on a product or service P specified in a user query/question Q, we introduce $QMSS$, a query-based multi-document sentiment summarizer. $QMSS$ creates a summary for Q, which either reflects the *general* opinions on P or is *tailored* to specific facets (i.e., features) and/or sentiment of P as specified in Q. $QMSS$ (i) identifies the facets addressed in reviews retrieved for Q, (ii) employs a sentence-based, sentiment classifier to determine the polarity of each sentence in each review, and (iii) clusters sentences in reviews according to the *facets* captured in the sentences, which are identified using a keyword-label extraction algorithm. This process dictates which sentences in the reviews should be included in the summary for Q. Empirical studies have verified that $QMSS$ is highly effective in generating summaries that satisfy users' information needs and ranks on top among the state-of-the-art query-based multi-document sentiment summarizers.

Categories and Subject Descriptors

H.3.5 [**Information Storage and Retrieval**]: Online Information Services—*Web-based Services*

General Terms

Design, Experimentation, Algorithms, Performance

1. INTRODUCTION

Websites established exclusively to archive reviews, such as Consumerreports.org and Epinions.com, provide users a forum to express their opinions on various products, i.e., anything that is visible, living, or nonliving, such as a person, a movie, or a book[1]. These websites archive abundant opinions that are valuable for web users who seek feedback on a product. Searching and browsing through large collections of reviews with different opinions, however, is undesirable, since it is a time-consuming and tedious task.

To facilitate the task of synthesizing opinions expressed in various reviews on a particular product P specified in a user query/question Q, we introduce $QMSS$, a query-based, multi-document sentiment summarizer. Given Q and a set of reviews R on P extracted in response to Q from well-known review websites, $QMSS$ creates an extractive summary for Q, which is tailored towards the information needs expressed in Q. A summary for Q is (i) *general* if Q inquires common feedback on P, (ii) *sentiment-specific* if Q asks for positive (negative, respectively) information about P, (iii) *facet-specific* if Q queries specific facets of P (such as the battery life of a camera), and (iv) *facet-sentiment-specific* if Q looks for positive (negative, respectively) information on specific facets of P. Since $QMSS$ considers the *sentiment* expressed in Q to create its summary, it is different from other query-based multi-document summarizers that do not capture sentiment in reviews.

$QMSS$ generates summaries that are (i) *non-redundant*, (ii) *cohesive*, and (iii) *diverse* (in terms of the variety of facets inquired). In addition, $QMSS$ summaries achieve high *coverage* (in terms of information covered in the summaries) and include meaningful and relevant sentences. It (i) does not depend on *pre-defined* knowledge, (ii) is highly *accurate* in capturing useful information presented in a set of reviews, and (iii) summarizes multiple reviews in response to *general*, as well as *specific*, users' information needs. $QMSS$ is *domain-independent* and thus can generate summaries of reviews with different contents and structures, such as blog posts and movie reviews. By developing $QMSS$, we minimize the time and efforts imposed on web users to browse through reviews retrieved by search engines. $QMSS$ advances the technologies that support the development of systems which facilitate information access on reviews and their representation on the web.

2. $QMSS$, A SENTIMENT SUMMARIZER

In this section, we detail the design of $QMSS$ in creating a summary of multiple reviews retrieved in response to a query. Each component of $QMSS$ addresses a particular research problem on its own: (i) identifying products, facets, and sentiment keywords in a user's question using a multi-class SVM based on a number of novel features, (ii) finding opinions on various facets of P using a novel sentence clustering algorithm based on word correlation factors, (iii) condensing each review by excluding sentences

*The full version of this paper can be downloaded from http://faculty.cs.byu.edu/~dennis/papers.html

[1]To simplify the discussion, from now on whenever we refer to the term "product", we mean "product" or "service".

CIKM'11, October 24–28, 2011, Glasgow, Scotland, UK.

in the review that are redundant, relatively uninformative, or lack of opinions, and (iv) ensuring that each $QMSS$-generated multi-document summary is coherent and concise by employing a simple, yet highly effective, sentence selection algorithm.

2.1 Identifying the User's Information Needs

$QMSS$ adopts a one-against-all implementation of a multi-class SVM to identify information needs expressed in a query. To train a multi-class SVM, each training instance is an input vector which captures the SVM-features of a non-numerical keyword K in a training query Q as a succession of '1' ('0', respectively). Each binary value in a vector represents the presence (absence, respectively) of an SVM-feature F (defined by us below) if F applies (does not apply, respectively) to K.

- **Is-Singular** is set (to '1') if K is in a singular form. *Products*, *sentiment keywords*, and *non-essential terms* tend to be expressed in singular form.
- **Is-Capitalized** is set if the first letter of K is capitalized. The first character of a *product* is often capitalized.
- **Is-Adjective** is set if K is given an *adjective* part-of-speech (POS) tag. $QMSS$ employs the Stanford POS tagger (nlp.stanford.edu/software/tagger.shtml), denoted *Stanford-POS*, for assigning POS tags, such as noun or adjective, to keywords in Q. *Sentiment keywords* specified in Q are often adjectives that describe various aspects of the product in Q.
- **Is-Sentiment** is set if K is a *sentiment keyword*, which is determined by using a list of more than 4,000 sentiment keywords provided by the General Inquirer (wjh.harvard.edu/~inquirer/homecat.htm).
- **Is-After-Preposition** is set if K appears immediately after a preposition, which is identified using *Stanford-POS*. Both *products* and *facets* tend to occur after a preposition in Q.
- **Is-After-Apostrophe** is set if K appears immediately after a term in a Saxon genitive form, i.e., a traditional term for the apostrophe-s. *Facets* often appear after an apostrophe-s in Q.
- **Is-Before-Sentiment** is set if K appears immediately before a sentiment keyword in Q. Both *products* and *facets* are often followed by a sentiment keyword in Q.
- **Is-Stopword** is set if K is a stopword[2], which is a *non-essential* term. We compiled our own list of 531 stopwords using multiple stopword lists posted online for this feature.
- **Is-5W1H** is set if K is one of the keywords frequently used in formulating questions, i.e., "what", "when", "where", "who", "why", and "how". 5W1H terms are treated as *non-essential* terms, since "when", "where", "who", and "why" do not appear often in sentiment questions, whereas "how" and "what", which appear more often, do not have a direct impact on the information needs specified in questions.

To verify each SVM-feature accurately identifying its corresponding keywords (in queries) that are either *Products*, *Facets*, *Sentiment Keywords*, or *Non-Essential Terms*, we conducted an empirical study using a dataset, denoted *Property-DS*, which does not overlap with the dataset introduced in Section 3.3 for analyzing the performance of $QMSS$'s multi-class SVM. *Property-DS* consists of 3,000 opinion questions randomly extracted from Yahoo! Answers (answers.yahoo.com) and WikiAnswers (wiki.answers.com). Keywords in each of the questions in *Property-DS* were identified as either products, facets, sentiment keywords, or non-essential terms by independent assessors prior to conducting the evaluation. The study shows that on the average 91% of keywords in *Property-DS* questions of different types are correctly identified by the SVM-features, with the lowest in the 80% and highest 100%.

In identifying the user's information needs in Q, $QMSS$ represents each keyword K in Q using the SVM-features and relies on the trained SVM to determine whether K is a product, facet, sentiment keyword, or non-essential term. $QMSS$ also detects *negation* terms (or their stemmed versions) in Q, such as "not", "no", "without", "except", "excluding", "remove", "nothing", and "leave out", so that the polarity of a *sentiment keyword* in Q is *reversed* if it is *preceded* by a *negation* term.

2.2 Retrieving Relevant Reviews

Having identified the product P specified in a query Q, $QMSS$ queries Epinions.com, Consumersearch.com, and Consumerreports.org, three well-known websites dedicated exclusively for archiving reviews, to retrieve reviews on P for creating the summary for Q. Since search engines at these websites simply process exact keyword searches without accurately relating the sentiment applied to P in Q, $QMSS$ extracts reviews from these websites using a simplified query Q' which includes solely P specified in Q. $QMSS$ gathers the top-33 reviews extracted from each of the three review repositories[3] in response to Q', which yields the set of reviews R for creating a summary (of R) in response to Q.

2.3 Condensing Individual Reviews

Since each review W in R may contain sentences that do not reflect an opinion on P, it is imperative to eliminate non-sentiment information presented in W while preserve the opinions expressed in W. (Eliminating non-sentiment information can significantly shorten the processing time of creating a summary of R as a side effect.) To accomplish this task, $QMSS$ retains sentences in W with the highest *combined sentence scores*, which are rich in opinions, to be included in the condensed version of W. The scores include (i) *sentence similarity*, which determines the similarity between a sentence S and other sentences in W, (ii) *significance factor*, which indicates the significance of each word in S in capturing the content of W, and (iii) *sentiment score* of S, which is computed by using the linguistic type (such as adjective, adverb, or noun) and the SentiWordNet (sentiwordnet.isti.cnr.it/search.php) score, a numerical value describing the neutral, positive, or negative orientation, of each word in S (see Sections 2.4.4 and 2.5.4 for details). In addition, $QMSS$ pre-processes W using *anaphora resolution*, which identifies successive references of the same discourse entity in W. We denote the set of condensed reviews *Cond-Reviews*.

2.4 Sentence Clustering in Condensed Reviews

Since a review in *Cond-Reviews* may address various facets of the same product specified in Q, prior to creating a summary for Q using *Cond-Reviews*, $QMSS$ clusters sentences in *Cond-Reviews* according to the facets they address, if there are any. In doing so, $QMSS$ (i) generates a set of cluster *labels*, which are facets chosen from *Cond-Reviews*, (ii) ranks the generated cluster labels, and (iii) assigns each sentence S in *Cond-Reviews* to a cluster C based on the similarity between the label of C and S. $QMSS$

[2] *Stopwords* are commonly-occurred words, such as articles, prepositions, and conjunctions, which carry little meaning.

[3] $QMSS$ retrieves the first 33 reviews from each repository, if they exist, since a collection of a hundred documents was found to be an ideal set for generating good, informative summaries [1].

clusters sentences to facilitate the process of creating summaries for queries that are *General* or *Facet-Specific* (*Sentiment-Specific* or *Facet-Sentiment-Specific*, respectively), *avoid redundancy*, and achieve *high coverage* (by including significant information in reviews) on the product being processed.

2.4.1 Creating Labels

$QMSS$ creates concise and accurate (keyword) labels that reflect the *facets* addressed in *Cond-Reviews* using a suffix array algorithm, which has been proved to be *efficient* and *effective* in discovering key phrases in large text collections. The suffix array algorithm generates a list of candidate cluster labels which are the suffixes in *Cond-Reviews* sorted alphabetically. Since not all the candidate cluster labels represent facets describing the product P in *Cond-Reviews*, $QMSS$ removes labels that (i) are *numerical* keywords, (ii) cross sentence *boundaries*, since sentence markers indicate a topical shift, (iii) are *incomplete*, i.e., included as substrings in other labels, (iv) end in the *Saxon genitive form*, or (v) are *sentiment* keywords, i.e., terms that express a positive/negative polarity (that are considered only in sentiment summarization). Moreover, candidate cluster labels that reference *web addresses* are discarded and *stopwords* at the *beginning* or *end* of a label are removed, since stripping heading/trailing stopwords increases readability.

The selected cluster labels identify the facets to facilitate the task of grouping sentences in the condensed reviews according to the facets they describe.

2.4.2 Ranking Cluster Labels

To capture the content-significance of the selected cluster labels, $QMSS$ proceeds to rank the labels using various widely-adopted measures, which have been proved to be effective in identifying representative cluster labels and are defined as follows:

- The **frequency** of a label L, denoted $Freq(L)$, reflects the *frequency of occurrence* of L in *Cond-Reviews*. The higher $Freq(L)$ is, the higher the ranking position of L among the cluster labels.

- The **stability** of a label, denoted $Stability(L)$, measures the *mutual information* (dependence[4]) of L. Let L = "$c_1 \ldots c_n$", where c_i ($1 \leq i \leq n$) is a keyword in L, $Stability(L) = \frac{f(L)}{f(L_L)+f(L_R)-f(L)}$, where L_L = "$c_1 \ldots c_{n-1}$", L_R = "$c_2 \ldots c_n$", and $f(L)$, $f(L_L)$, and $f(L_R)$ are the *frequencies of occurrence* of L, L_L, and L_R, respectively in *Cond-Reviews*.

- The **significance** of a label L, denoted $Sig\_L(L)$ and defined as $Freq(L) \times g(|L|)$, is a function that assigns *more* weight to *longer* cluster labels, since longer labels are more meaningful, i.e., descriptive, where $|L|$ is the number of keywords in L, and $g(x)$ is a function such that $g(1) = 0$, $g(x) = log_2\ x$, when $2 \leq x \leq 8$, and $g(x) = 3$, when $x > 8$.

$QMSS$ computes a *ranking score* for each cluster label L, denoted $LRank(L)$, which reflects the significance of L in capturing the content of *Cond-Reviews*, by combining *Freq*, *Stability*, and Sig_L[5] of L using the *Stanford Certainty Factor*.

$$LRank(L) = \frac{Freq(L) + Stability(L) + Sig\_L(L)}{1 - Min\{Freq(L), Stability(L), Sig\_L(L)\}} \quad (1)$$

[4] *Dependence* identifies labels that characterize the contents of sentences in one cluster in contrast to others. The higher the *mutual* information of L is, the more *dependent* L is as a cluster label.

[5] Since *Freq*, *Stability*, and Sig_L are in different numerical scales, $QMSS$ normalizes the values using a logarithmic equation so that they are in the same range.

2.4.3 Assigning Sentences to Clusters

To cluster sentences that address (similar) facets of a product P in *Cond-Reviews*, we develop a simple, effective clustering method.

Given the set of selected cluster labels CL (created in Section 2.4.1), $QMSS$ computes the *degree of similarity* between each sentence S in *Cond-Reviews* and each label L in CL, denoted $LS\_Sim(L, S) = \frac{\sum_{i=1}^{|S|}\sum_{j=1}^{|L|} wcf(w_i, w_j)}{|S|}$, where $|S|$ ($|L|$, respectively) is the number of non-stopwords in S (L, respectively), w_i (w_j, respectively) is a non-stopword in S (L, respectively), and $wcf(w_i, w_j)$ is the *word-correlation factor* [2] of w_i and w_j. The *word-correlation factors* were generated using a set of approximately 880,000 Wikipedia documents, and the correlation factor of any two non-stopwords is computed using their (i) *frequency of co-occurrence* and (ii) *relative distances* in each Wikipedia document. As the length of S can potentially affect $LS\_Sim(L, S)$, since the longer S is, the higher $LS\_Sim(L, S)$ is, $QMSS$ normalizes $LS\_Sim(L, S)$ by dividing the correlation factors of non-stopwords in S and L by the number of non-stopwords in S.

Having computed $LS\_Sim(L, S)$ for each sentence S in *Cond-Reviews* with respect to each label L in CL, S is assigned to the cluster C with label L_C such that the $LS\_Sim(L_C, S)$ score is *higher* than all the LS_Sim scores of S and other labels.

2.4.4 Ranking Sentences in Clusters

After generating clusters of sentences based on the *facets* of a product P, $QMSS$ assigns a *ranking score* to each sentence S in each cluster C which indicates the *relative degree of significance* of S in capturing the content of C using the following measures:

- **Sentence Significance**: $QMSS$ computes the *sentence significance factor* (SSF) of S, $SSF(S) = \frac{|signi\_words|^2}{|S|}$, with respect to the content of C based on *significant words* in S, where $|signi\_words|$ is the number of significant words in S and $|S|$ is the number of non-stopwords in S. A non-stopword w in C is *significant* in C if

$$f_{C,w} \geq \begin{cases} 7 - 0.1 \times (25 - Z) & \text{if } Z < 25 \\ 7 & \text{if } 25 \leq Z \leq 40 \\ 7 + 0.1 \times (Z - 40) & \text{otherwise} \end{cases} \quad (2)$$

where $f_{C,w}$ is the *frequency of occurrence* of w in C, Z is the number of sentences in C, and 25 and 40 are the pre-defined low- and high-frequency cutoff values, respectively.

- **Sentence Similarity**: A representative sentence in C should capture the content of (most of) the remaining sentences in C to a certain degree. $QMSS$ considers the *sentence similarity* of S_i in C, denoted $Sent\_Sim(S_i)$, which indicates the relative degree of S_i in reflecting the contents of other sentences in C. $Sent\_Sim(S_i)$, which is computed using (i) the *word-correlation factors* (wcf) of each non-stop, stemmed word in S_i and non-stop, stemmed words in each remaining sentence S_j in C and (ii) the *Odds ratio* = $\frac{p}{1-p}$, is defined as $Sent\_Sim(S_i) = \frac{\sum_{j=1,i\neq j}^{|C|}\sum_{k=1}^{n}\sum_{l=1}^{m} wcf(w_k, w_l)}{1-\sum_{j=1,i\neq j}^{|C|}\sum_{k=1}^{n}\sum_{l=1}^{m} wcf(w_k, w_l)}$, where $|C|$ is the number of sentences in C, n (m, respectively) is the number of distinct non-stop, stemmed words in S_i (S_j, respectively), w_k (w_l, respectively) is a non-stop, stemmed word in S_i (S_j, respectively).

- **Label-Sentence Similarity**: Since a cluster label captures a facet of P addressed in the sentences in its cluster C, $QMSS$ computes LS_Sim that measures the *degree of resemblance* between the label L_C of C and sentence S in C using word-correlation factors among the non-stopwords in S and L_C.

- **Named-Entity Frequency**: As claimed in [5], sentences that include name entities tend to discuss important information. $QMSS$ computes the *name entity score* of sentence S in its cluster C, denoted $NE(S) = \frac{\sum_{i=1}^{|E|} f(E_{i,s})}{f(E)}$, where $|E|$ is the number of distinct name entities in C, E_i is a name entity in C, $f(E_{i,s})$ is the *frequency of occurrence* of E_i in S, and $f(E)$ denotes the sum of the frequency of occurrence of all the name entities in C.
- **Sentence Length**: As stated in [4], *short* sentences often require some introduction or reference resolution, or some kind of interjection, whereas *long* sentences cover multiple concepts often covered elsewhere in a document, i.e., a cluster in our case. $QMSS$ ranks a sentence S using the *length score* of S, denoted $SL(S) = \begin{cases} -1 & \text{if } |S| < 15 \text{ or } |S| > 30 \\ 0 & \text{otherwise} \end{cases}$, where $|S|$ is the total number of words in S, which penalizes short (with $<$ 15 words) and long (with $>$ 30 words) sentences [4].

$QMSS$ computes a *ranking score* for S, denoted $CRank(S)$, which reflects the *relative degree of significance* of S in C in capturing the content of C and is defined using the *Stanford Certainty Factor* of various measures applied to S. The *ranking score* is formally defined as $CRank(S) = (SSF(S) + Sent\_Sim(S) + LS\_Sim(L_C, S) + NE(S) + SL(S))\ /\ (1 - Min\{SSF(S), Sent\_Sim(S), LS\_Sim(L_C, S), NE(S), SL(S)\})$[6].

Sentences in each cluster with the highest $CRank$ scores are potential sentences to be included in the summary of *Cond-Reviews*, the set of condensed reviews, in response to Q.

2.5 Generating Summaries

$QMSS$ creates a single summary in response to the information need specified in a user query Q. A summary is (i) *General*, if Q inquires on common feedback of a particular product P, (ii) *Sentiment-Specific*, if Q asks for positive or negative information about P, (iii) *Facet-Specific*, if Q queries on specific facets of P, or (iv) *Facet-Sentiment-Specific*, if Q looks for sentiment information on specific facets of P.

2.5.1 The Size of $QMSS$ Summaries

We adopt the length of (approximately) 250 words as the size of each $QMSS$-generated summary according to the guidelines defined for (some of) the datasets archived by the Text Analysis Conference (TAC) (nist.gov/tac/data/forms/index.html), which provides benchmark datasets for assessing the performance of a query-based multi-document summarizer. Since $QMSS$ is a sentence-based, extractive summarizer, $QMSS$ includes in a summary as many sentences as possible up till the size limit so that the total number of words in the summary being constructed after including the second to the last chosen sentence is less than 250.

2.5.2 Selecting Sentences to be Included in a Summary

In creating a summary, $QMSS$ includes some sentences in clusters created in Section 2.4.3. To determine which sentences are to be extracted from which cluster and included in the summary, $QMSS$ relies on the ranked cluster labels, as introduced in Section 2.4.2. Using the ranked labels, $QMSS$ includes in the summary of Q one sentence from a cluster at a time, starting from the cluster with the *highest-ranked label* (based on its $LRank$ score defined in Equation 1), up till the limit of the summary size is reached. If the number of sentences that should be included in a summary *exceeds* the number of generated clusters after selecting the highest-ranked sentence in each cluster, then in the subsequent iterations $QMSS$ selects the next highest-ranked sentence S' in cluster C with the *lowest similarity score*, denoted LSS, with respect to the sentence(s) S in C that has (have) already been included in the summary for Q. The LSS score of S' is computed as the *sum* of the word-correlation factors [2] between each non-stop, stemmed word in S' and S. By considering the LSS score of a sentence S' in a cluster with respect to S in the summary being constructed for Q, $QMSS$ ensures that S and S' are *distinct* in contents, which *avoids redundancy* and maximizes *coverage* in terms of information included in the summary, a novelty of $QMSS$. Furthermore, if a facet F is preceded by a negation term in Q, any cluster label that includes F is excluded from the sentence selection process.

2.5.3 General Summaries

The *General* summary for Q addresses different facets and sentiments of a product being reviewed. It consists of the highest-ranked sentences (regardless of their polarity), along with probably the ones with the lowest LSS scores, in (highly ranked) clusters created in Section 2.4.3, which are chosen by following the procedure established in Section 2.5.2 to be included in the summary.

2.5.4 Sentiment-Specific Summaries

The *Sentiment-Specific* summary for Q is created in the same manner as a *General* summary, except that only the highly-ranked sentences (along with probably the ones with the lowest LSS score) in clusters which satisfy the *sentiment* (i.e., positive or negative) specified in Q (identified using the keyword tagger introduced in Section 2.1) are included in the summary for Q. To determine the positive or negative polarity of a sentence S in a cluster, $QMSS$ calculates the overall sentiment score of S by *subtracting* the sum of its *negative* word SentiWordNet scores from the sum of its *positive* word SentiWordNet scores that reflects the (degree of) sentiment of S such that if its sentiment score is positive (negative, respectively), then S is labeled as positive (negative, respectively). Employing this sentence-based, sentiment approach, $QMSS$ includes in its *Sentiment-Specific* (*Facet-Sentiment-Specific*, respectively as introduced in Section 2.5.6) summaries sentences reflecting the sentiment specified in the corresponding query.

2.5.5 Facet-Specific Summaries

To create the *Facet-Specific* summary for Q, $QMSS$ first identifies the labels (from the set of labels created in Section 2.4.1) that are highly similar to each of the facets F (determined using the keyword tagger in Section 2.1) specified in Q. To identify cluster labels *highly similar* to F, $QMSS$ employs a reduced version of the word-similarity matrix which contains 13% of the most frequently-occurring words (based on their *frequencies of occurrence* in the Wikipedia documents), and for the remaining 87% of the less-frequently-occurring words, only exact-matched correlation factors, i.e., correlation factors of values 1.0, are used. A label L (and its cluster) is considered highly similar to F only if the word-correlation factor of (w_1, w_2) between the non-stop, stemmed word w_1 in L and w_2 in F exists in the *reduced* matrix, which

[6]Since SSF, $Sent\_Sim$, LS_Sim, NE, and SL are in different numerical scales, $QMSS$ normalizes the scores using a logarithmic scale so that they are in the same range.

significantly minimizes the processing time to identify the desired labels without affecting the quality of the created summaries.

In creating the *Facet-Specific* summary, $QMSS$ follows the same procedure as detailed in Section 2.5.2 for selecting sentences, regardless of their polarity, to be included in the summary. Instead of considering ranked labels, $QMSS$ relies on the *ranking* of the *highly similar* labels with respect to F computed using word-correlation factors. Moreover, the content of the *Facet-Specific* summary of Q is uniformly divided among each of the facets specified in Q, i.e., the number of sentences to be included in the summary is uniformly extracted from the clusters with labels highly-similar to or the same as each facet specified in Q.

2.5.6 Facet-Sentiment-Specific Summaries

The *Facet-Sentiment-Specific* summary is created in response to Q by including solely the sentences in clusters which (i) reflect the polarity specified in Q (as detailed in Section 2.5.4) and (ii) belong to the clusters with labels highly similar to or the same as a facet in Q (as in a *Facet-Specific* summary presented in Section 2.5.5).

3. EXPERIMENTAL RESULTS

In this section, we introduce the dataset and metrics used for assessing the performance of $QMSS$ and detail the evaluation of the effectiveness of $QMSS$ in generating sentiment summaries that satisfy the information needs specified in users' queries.

3.1 Dataset

We rely on the benchmark dataset set up for the Opinion Summarization Pilot task of the 2008 Text Analysis Conference, denoted TAC-08, which includes a set of 87 (squishy-list) questions, to assess the effectiveness of $QMSS$. The assessment includes (i) identifying the information need specified in a user's query Q, (ii) creating summaries that satisfy the information inquired in Q, and (iii) generating a high-quality summary of multiple documents on a topic. For each question Q, which is treated as a query, provided by TAC-08, there is (i) a set of documents D (extracted from the TREC Blog06 collection[7]) that serves as the source for creating a summary (of D) and (ii) a list of *expert-created* sentences/phrases that are expected to be included in a summary (of D) with respect to Q. Since the goal of the Opinion Summarization task is to evaluate multi-document sentiment summaries created in response to a query, TAC-08 is ideal for evaluating the effectiveness of $QMSS$.

3.2 Performance Evaluation

3.2.1 Accuracy on Keyword Tagging

To assess the performance of the multi-class SVM adopted by $QMSS$ for *identifying* the information needs expressed in users' queries, we compute the *accuracy* ratio, which is defined as the proportion of the number of keywords *correctly identified* by the multi-class SVM as *products, facets, sentiment keywords, or non-essential terms* over the total number of keywords in the 87 queries.

3.2.2 Nugget Pyramid Score

To verify whether $QMSS$-generated summaries *satisfy the information needs specified in users' queries*, we rely on the *Nugget-Pyramid* score [3]. Consider a test query Q in TAC-08, "What is positive about Carmax?". A *human assessor* creates a list of relevant "*nuggets*," which are expert-created phrases/sentences, e.g., "Carmax prices are firm," that address different aspects of Q. It is expected that a "good" summary includes (the majority of the) nuggets in the corresponding list of *relevant nuggets*. We evaluate a $QMSS$-generated summary S created in response to Q by verifying the (non-)existence of a *conceptual match* between each provided nugget and S, which is a match independent of the distinct wording used in S and the nugget.

3.2.3 Quality Evaluation

To evaluate the quality of the multi-document summaries created by $QMSS$, we apply the *quality measures* defined by TAC-08 that assess the performance of the summarizers participated at the 2008 Text Analysis Conference (nist.gov/tac/data/past-blog06/2008/Op SummQA08.html#OpSumm). Quality measures, which are in the range of 1 to 10 (with 1 being the worse and 10 the best), reflect the overall quality of a generated summary in terms of its *grammaticality, non-redundancy, structure and coherency, responsiveness*, and *readability*. Each measure is computed for each $QMSS$-created multi-document summary to be evaluated.

3.3 Query Keyword Tagging

To train the multi-class SVM (introduced in Section 2.1) for identifying products, facets, sentiment keywords, and non-essential terms in users' queries, we constructed a dataset, denoted $Train\text{-}SVM$, which consists of approximately 32,000 keywords extracted from 5,000 (opinion) queries retrieved from WikiAnswers and Yahoo! Answers. To validate the effectiveness of the multi-class SVM on $Train\text{-}SVM$[8], we adopted the ten-fold cross-validation approach so that in each of the 10 repetitions, 90% of the instances in *Train-SVM* were used for training and the remaining 10% for validation purpose.

The *accuracy* of $QMSS$ in identifying the information needs specified in users' queries was computed using the trained multi-class SVM on each keyword in each of the 87 queries in TAC-08. The overall accuracy of the trained multi-class SVM on identifying the 452 keywords in TAC-08 queries is 96% as shown in Figure 1, along with the accuracy ratios achieved by $QMSS$ on detecting products, facets, sentiment keywords, and non-essential terms.

Note that only 27 of the 452 keywords in TAC-08 questions were *facets*, out of which 4 were misclassified as *products*. The low number of facets in TAC-08, when compared with products, sentiment keywords, and non-essential terms, causes the accuracy ratio for identifying facets to be the lowest (in the mid-80%).

3.4 Assessing Summaries of Input Queries

We have validated $QMSS$ in creating summaries that satisfy the information needs expressed in users' queries using the Nugget-Pyramid score. The *minimum, maximum, median*, and *average* Nugget-Pyramid scores of $QMSS$ based on TAC-08 are 0, 0.31, 0.2, and 0.183, respectively. In comparing the (average) Nugget-Pyramid scores achieved by nineteen[9] query-based multi-document summarizers using TAC-08, $QMSS$ ranks *third*. Note that thirty-six multi-document summarizers originally took part at the 2008 TAC. However, seventeen of the summarizers relied on *snippets*, which are answers to queries in TAC-08 provided by TAC, in creating the summaries. To perform unbiased comparisons, we only considered the nineteen summarizers that operate in a manner similar to $QMSS$, i.e., they do not rely on external information, such

[7]TREC Blog06 is a collection of blog posts downloaded from the web between December 2005 and February 2006.

[8]Keywords in *Train-SVM* and TAC-08 questions were previously labeled by independent assessors as *Products, Facets, Sentiment Keywords*, or *Non-Essential Terms*.

[9]The Nugget-Pyramid and quality scores introduced in Section 3.2 for the nineteen summarizers are available at nist.gov/tac/ protected/past-blog06/2008/QA2008_runs.tar.gz.

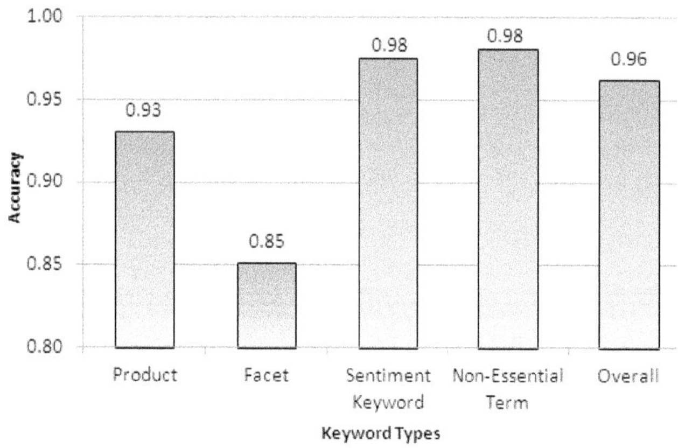

Figure 1: Accuracy of the multi-class SVM of $QMSS$ in identifying users' information needs specified in TAC-08 queries

as snippets, in creating a summary. In addition, we have evaluated 22 summaries, as opposed to the 87 summaries created using the questions and documents in TAC-08. The choice follows the evaluation premises defined by TAC, which provides assessment, using the computed Nugget-Pyramid scores, for only 22 summaries generated by each of the 19 automatic multi-document summarizers. The two summarizers that are ranked higher than $QMSS$ have achieved a Nugget-Pyramid score of 0.251 and 0.223, respectively, which are close to the average score, 0.183, of $QMSS$ and verify the effectiveness of $QMSS$ in generating summaries that satisfy users' information needs.

3.5 Evaluating the Quality of Summaries

We assess the quality of $QMSS$-generated summaries using each of the five quality measures introduced in Section 3.2.3. Following the evaluation methodology established by TAC, we relied on independent appraisers, who manually evaluated the *grammaticality*, *non-redundancy*, *structure and coherency*, *responsiveness*, and *readability* of the summaries created by $QMSS$ using TAC-08 (as introduced in Section 3.1). The quality scores of $QMSS$-generated summaries are shown in Table 1.

To establish a baseline measure on the quality scores achieved by $QMSS$-created summaries, we compare the performance, based on quality scores, of the nineteen automatic multi-document summarizers (mentioned in Section 3.4) with $QMSS$ based on 22 summaries created using TAC-08 (as discussed in Section 3.4). As shown in Table 1, $QMSS$ is significantly outperformed (with 95% confidence) by at most six (out of nineteen) summarizers in terms of creating summaries that are either higher in grammaticality, non-redundancy, structure and coherence, responsiveness, or readability. In fact, there is *not* a single system examined that achieves higher scores than $QMSS$ in all of the quality measures. $QMSS$ achieves the highest *responsiveness* score among all the nineteen summarizers and is only outperformed by one of the nineteen summarizers in creating summaries that are *non-redundant*.

The summarization systems that outperform $QMSS$ on either the *grammar*, *readability*, or *structure* and *coherence* quality measures employ natural language processing techniques to touch up the summaries shown to users as the final products. The summarization approach of $QMSS$, on the other hand, is purely extractive, i.e., it solely extracts sentences in the original document(s) without refinement to create a summary. The summarizer which achieves a better *non-redundancy* quality measure than $QMSS$ uses textual graphs to model opinions in a review and relies on word

$QMSS$	Qual. Score	Significantly Out-Performed by	Sign. Out-perform
Grammaticality	5.73	4 (16, 21, 31, 36)	14
Non-redundancy	7.12	1 (36)	17
Str. & Coherence	2.82	6 (17, 18, 30, 31, 34, 36)	8
Responsiveness	3.59	0	18
Readability	4.12	3 (14, 25, 35)	8

Table 1: Comparisons between $QMSS$ and 19 summarizers participated at TAC-08 where numbers in parentheses are IDs

order to determine redundant sentences, which is not employed by $QMSS$ for simplicity.

Among the 19 summarizers $QMSS$ compared with, CLASSY and PolyU (with System ID 36 and 31, respectively) stand out, since they outperform $QMSS$ on two or more measures. CLASSY generates a summary for a query by (i) *splitting* and *trimming* sentences in a set of documents using pre-defined rules, (ii) extracting *query terms* from a previously constructed list of (un)important keywords, (iii) *scoring* and *selecting* sentences using the conditional probability, and (iv) *removing redundant* sentences with less than 8 distinct terms. CLASSY's algorithm, keyword lists, and sentence trimming are based on observations on the dataset provided by TAC, whereas $QMSS$ requires no accommodations on any dataset. PolyU, on the other hand, measures the informative richness of a sentence using a set of facets and the opinions expressed in sentences, and removes paragraphs in a document without informative sentences to increase the grammar and structure and coherence scores, but decreases the nugget pyramid score.

4. CONCLUSIONS

We have introduced $QMSS$, a query-based, extractive, multi-document sentiment summarizer, which summarizes reviews retrieved from opinion-rich repositories in response to a query Q posted by a web user who is interested in feedback compiled by other users on a product P. $QMSS$ creates a (i) *general* summary for Q that addresses the various facets (and sentiments) of P specified in Q, or (ii) *specific* summary that includes particular *facets* and/or *sentiment* of P. $QMSS$ uses a new label extraction approach to identify facets of P and a novel *clustering* algorithm based on word correlation factors to group sentences in reviews based on the facets of P addressed in the sentences. We have assessed $QMSS$ using TAC-08, a well-known benchmark dataset, that was created for evaluating query-based multi-document sentiment summarizers. Empirical studies show that $QMSS$ ranks at the top among the state-of-the-art approaches in generating query-based, high-quality summaries.

5. REFERENCES

[1] D. Dunlavy, D. O'Leary, J. Conroy, and J. Schlesinger. QCS: A system for querying, clustering and summarizing documents. *IPM*, 43(6):1588–1605, 2007.

[2] J. Koberstein and Y.-K. Ng. Using word clusters to detect similar web documents. In *KSEM*, pages 215–228, 2006.

[3] J. Lin and D. Demner-Fushman. Will pyramids built of nuggets topple over? In *HLT/NAACL*, pages 383–390, 2006.

[4] B. Schiffman, A. Nenkova, and K. McKeown. Experiments in multi-document summarization. In *HLT*, pages 52–58, 2002.

[5] L. Zhang, Y. Pan, and T. Zhang. Focused named entity recognition using machine learning. In *ACM SIGIR*, pages 281–288, 2004.

Scalable Density-Based Subspace Clustering

Emmanuel Müller ○ Ira Assent ◇ Stephan Günnemann • Thomas Seidl •

○Karlsruhe Institute of Technology, Germany
emmanuel.mueller@kit.edu

◇Aarhus University, Denmark
ira@cs.au.dk

•RWTH Aachen University, Germany
{guennemann, seidl}@cs.rwth-aachen.de

ABSTRACT

For knowledge discovery in high dimensional databases, subspace clustering detects clusters in arbitrary subspace projections. Scalability is a crucial issue, as the number of possible projections is exponential in the number of dimensions. We propose a scalable density-based subspace clustering method that *steers* mining to few selected subspace clusters. Our novel steering technique reduces subspace processing by identifying and clustering promising subspaces and their combinations directly. Thereby, it narrows down the search space while maintaining accuracy. Thorough experiments on real and synthetic databases show that steering is efficient and scalable, with high quality results. For future work, our steering paradigm for density-based subspace clustering opens research potential for speeding up other subspace clustering approaches as well.

Categories and Subject Descriptors: H.2.8 Database management: Database applications [Data mining]

General Terms: Algorithms, Performance, Experimentation

Keywords: data mining, high dimensional data, scalability, density-based clustering, subspace clustering

1. INTRODUCTION

Clustering is an established technique for knowledge discovery in databases. Objects are grouped into clusters based on mutual similarity. In high dimensional databases, however, traditional clustering methods fail to identify meaningful groups in all attributes due to the "curse of dimensionality" [9]. In many applications, such as gene expression analysis, environmental surveillance or customer segmentation, one measures for each object a huge variety of attributes. Unfortunately, due to the scattered high dimensional data spaces clusters can not be detected using all available attributes. Groups of objects are hidden in subsets of the attributes, e.g. genes (objects) forming functional groups w.r.t. a specific set of medications (attributes). These application demands have led to research on subspace and projected clustering for more than a decade. Clusters are mined in subspaces of the high dimensional space. Unlike dimensionality reduction methods, subspace clustering determines relevant subspace projections per cluster [27, 25, 19].

As major drawback of existing subspace clustering algorithms, we observe their poor scalability w.r.t. increasing dimensionality. To search for clusters in any combination of the attributes, most subspace clustering algorithms borrow the apriori principle from association rule mining [4], as suggested in the first subspace clustering algorithm CLIQUE [3]. Using a monotonicity property, these approaches proceed in a step-by-step scheme from x-dimensional to $x+1$-dimensional subspaces and prune the search space.

This approach is commonly used in many subspace clustering algorithms [3, 29, 14, 22, 21, 7]. While this step-by-step processing avoids naive search of all possible subspaces, it has to generate exponentially many lower dimensional projections of each high dimensional subspace cluster. For a d-dimensional database, the search space can only be reduced from 2^d (naive search) to 2^k (apriori step-by-step search) where k is the maximal dimensionality of any hidden cluster. As a consequence, scalability with dimensionality is poor. This is also observed in our evaluation study [25], which shows that none of these algorithms scales.

Especially, for the density-based clustering paradigm, e.g., known from DBSCAN [11], and extended to subspace clustering e.g. in [14, 5], runtime performance is not acceptable for high dimensional data. Density-based approaches compute the neighborhood around each object in each subspace under study. Thus, the excessive database access results in poor scalability w.r.t. both dimensionality and database size. For example, runtimes of 7 days have been reported for 50-dimensional databases, and exponential increase w.r.t. maximal cluster dimensionality [14].

Furthermore, it has been shown that the exponential number of lower dimensional projections does not only hinder scalable processing, but also results in a tremendous amount of redundant subspace clusters that overwhelm the user. Recent models have been proposed to select subspace clusters that provide non-redundant result sets [5, 21, 7, 23]. However, it has been proven that selecting an optimal set of subspace clusters is an NP-hard problem [23]. Clearly, generation of all redundant clusters before optimizing the result set is an infeasible processing.

In this work, we take a novel approach to enhance the search space processing. We steer our subspace clustering directly to interesting subspace clusters, and exclude exces-

CIKM'11, October 24–28, 2011, Glasgow, Scotland, UK.

sive processing of many redundant cluster candidates. Thus, our novel processing scheme is scalable to high dimensional data. We reduce the computational overhead by excluding the vast majority of subspaces. We make use of the very effect crippling previous approaches: Any high dimensional subspace cluster shows up in many low dimensional projections. By mining only some of them, we gather enough information to "jump" directly to the more interesting high dimensional subspace clusters without processing the subspaces in-between.

A core contribution of our work is that we actively *steer* the algorithm to find the most interesting subspace clusters. Our steering includes efficient information gathering for the density-based paradigm, but more importantly, we propose a novel processing scheme that requires databases access only in very few subspace regions. It combines intermediate results to progressively identify new regions for subspace clustering in a best-first manner. This means that database scans for density computations are avoided entirely for very many subspace projections. Overall, we thus realize a scalable density-based subspace clustering processing.

Our contributions include:

- General processing scheme for subspace clustering that is scalable with increasing number of dimensions
- Our novel *steering* technique that allows best-first style selection of subspace clusters
- An instantiation of our steering for density-based clustering, extendible to other clustering paradigms

Additionally, we show empirically that our best-first selection of subspace clusters enables a scalable but also high quality subspace clustering. Based on recent subspace clustering models [5, 23], it ensure high quality results. Overall, our novel processing scheme results in enhanced runtime behavior and high quality subspace clustering.

This paper is structured as follows: we review related work in the following section (Section 2). We begin our discussion in Section 3 by providing some preliminaries and reviewing the scalability challenges faced in subspace clustering. We introduce our novel steering technique in Section 4, where we discuss information gathering (Section 4.1) and selective clustering of interesting subspace regions (Section 4.2), before analyzing the runtime complexity (Section 4.3). We demonstrate superior runtime and quality in the experiments (Section 5), before concluding.

2. RELATED WORK

Subspace clustering approaches are summarized in two surveys [27, 19]. Apriori based algorithms going through the search space step-by-step are the most commonly used ones. Both breadth-first [3, 26, 14, 22] and depth-first [29, 7] exhaustive processing of subspace dimensions do not scale w.r.t. the dimensionality and the result becomes overwhelmingly large as confirmed by our comparison study [25]. Similar scalability drawbacks of apriori processing have been observed also in related areas such as frequent itemset mining [4, 32]. However, for subspace clustering apriori based algorithms are still state-of-the-art.

Projected clustering iteratively partitions the database into clusters in subspace projections [1, 2, 30]. This process can be accelerated using randomization [28], or specialized data structures [31]. As opposed to subspace clustering, however, these partitioning approaches only determine a single projection for each object. Hence, they are unable to detect overlapping subspace clusters [19, 25].

Heuristics for selecting subspaces prior to clustering have been proposed [10, 15]. However, these heuristics are limited due to the fact that clusters usually only exist in some regions of a subspace, which are hidden by noise in the remaining regions. Other approaches use density estimation of regions in subspaces [18, 24]. While this improves efficiency, due to the limited information on just one or two dimensions, quality is relatively poor.

Indexing approaches for subspace clustering face the challenge that data needs to be searched w.r.t. arbitrary subsets of the attributes. Consequently, only inverted lists for single dimensions [14], or grid cell count structures for depth-first mining [6, 7] have been proposed for subspace clustering. In general, subspace clustering could benefit from novel index structure development [17, 20]. However, the exponential search space would still be the main problem. Thus, we focus on reducing the search space as the major challenge to be solved for scalable subspace clustering.

3. PRELIMINARIES AND SCALABILITY CHALLENGES

We begin by introducing notations and basic definitions. Given a database DB of objects $o = (o_1, \dots o_d) \in DB$ with d dimensions, traditional clustering aims at detecting groups of objects in all dimensions DIM. Subspace clustering searches for clusters in arbitrary subspace projections $S \subseteq DIM$. In general, a subspace cluster is described by a tuple $C = (O, S)$ with $O \subseteq DB$ being the clustered objects in a subspace S. For density-based subspace clustering, a cluster (O, S) is defined by a set of dense objects in subspace S [14, 5].

DEFINITION 1. ***Density-Based Subspace Cluster***
A subspace cluster $C = (O, S)$ is a set of objects $O \subseteq DB$ which form a dense region in a subspace $S \subseteq DIM$, i.e.:

(1) $\forall o \in O : density_S(o) \geq MinPts$
$density_S(o) = |N_\varepsilon(o)| = |\{p \in DB \mid dist_S(o,p) \leq \varepsilon\}|$

(2) $\forall o, p \in O : \exists q_1 \dots q_n : \; o = q_1 \wedge p = q_n$
$\wedge \forall i : q_{i-1} \in N_\varepsilon(q_i) \wedge q_i$ *fulfills* (1)

(3) $\forall o, p \in DB$ *fulfilling* $(1) \wedge (2) : o \in O \Leftrightarrow p \in O$

Density is assessed by counting the objects in the ε-neighborhood w.r.t. the distance in the subspace projection only, i.e. for the Euclidean Distance in subspace S one uses the distande $dist_S(o,p) = \sqrt{\sum_{i \in S}(o_i - p_i)^2}$. According to the density-based paradigm [11], (1) the objects O form a dense region, (2) they are density-connected and (3) O is a maximal set of objects. As distances are measured in a subspace S, each object is part of at most one cluster in one subspace, but it may be part of multiple clusters in different subspaces.

In a naive computation, one would run density-based clustering on each of the 2^d possible subspaces. This does not scale, and thus, subspace clustering algorithms focus on pruning the exponential search space. Existing work using apriori density-based subspace clustering [3, 26, 29, 14, 7] relies on a density monotonicity property:

DEFINITION 2. ***Density Monotonicity***
If (O, S) is a dense subspace cluster, then for all $S' \subseteq S$ the projection (O, S') is dense as well.

This property has been proven for the density-based paradigm [14]. It is used for pruning by negation: if the lower dimensional projection is not a subspace cluster, then the higher dimensional projection is discarded. This excludes several of the sparse high dimensional subspaces, however, the majority of low dimensional subspaces has to be processed. For a density-based cluster in a k-dimensional subspace, existing techniques have to perform costly database scans in 2^k subspaces. This fact is at the core of the scalability issues faced by these approaches: each subspace cluster is processed redundantly in all its lower dimensional projections, creating a tremendous amount of redundant clusters. This results in exponential runtime w.r.t. number of dimensions.

A second scalability issue arises from density assessment for all objects in each clustered subspace. Naively, checking their ε-neighborhoods has quadratic complexity in the number of objects $O(|DB|^2)$. For a single (full) space, index structures may be used to reduce the complexity to $O(|DB| \log |DB|)$ as in [11]. However, in subspace clustering, one would need index support for any subspace projection. Few index structures have been proposed for subspace projections [17, 20], and only one-dimensional index structures with intersection operations (inverted lists) are used for subspace clustering [14]. Thus, subspace clustering could benefit from novel index structure development, which could be used to support our steering approach as well.

Obviously, state-of-the-art apriori approaches are not scalable neither with the number of objects in the database nor with the number of dimensions. It is our main goal to reduce the number of processed subspaces, and thus, the costly database access.

4. SCALABLE SUBSPACE CLUSTERING

In our work, we tackle the scalability challenges described above. We exploit the monotonicity property of density-based subspace clusters to exclude redundant low dimensional projection. We base on our non-redundant subspace clustering model [23]. It selects only the most interesting subspace clusters $R = \{C_1, \ldots C_n\} \subseteq ALL$ where ALL is the set of all valid density-based subspace clusters according to Def. 1. The goal is to cluster as many objects as possible with only few high dimensional subspace clusters.

In contrast to previous approaches, we directly *steer* to high dimensional subspace clusters. The core idea is that we do not need to search all low dimensional subspaces in order to work our way up to the high dimensional subspaces. Instead, we use the monotonicity property that any high dimensional subspace cluster is reflected in many low dimensional projections (cf. Def. 2). While this redundancy is the drawback for apriori-based approaches that process all of these 2^k subspaces, we use this effect to combine low dimensional information for direct "jumps" to high dimensional subspaces. In Figure 1 this general principle is illustrated: We start with some initial information about the subspace clusters in the data. This initial information (*jump sources*) comprises low dimensional subspace regions which might be projections of the same high dimensional clusters. Their combination leads us directly to higher dimensional subspaces (*jump targets*, green regions in Fig. 1). Substantial runtime improvements are realized since subspaces besides the jump sources and the jump targets do not need to be analyzed. Furthermore, our steering requires only a single database scan for initialization and additional database access for the density-based refinement of each resulting subspace cluster. Overall, this enables the scalability of our processing in both the size and the dimensionality of the database.

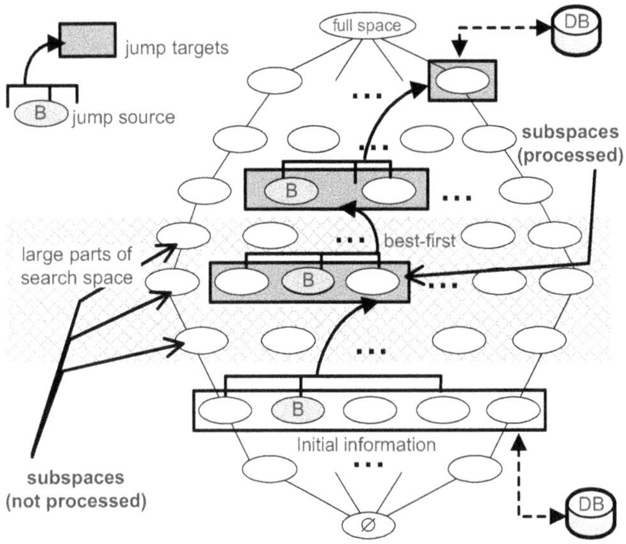

Figure 1: Multiple steered jumps

To reach high dimensional subspaces via jumps, information from the very low dimensional spaces, however, might not be sufficiently accurate. For example, 2-dimensional regions typically do not provide enough insight to jump directly to 20-dimensional regions. Thus, we introduce *multiple jumps* with successive information gathering. As illustrated in Figure 1, our technique jumps based on the initial information to some promising targets; these targets provide us with novel information that can be used for further and higher dimensional jumps in later steps. Thus, the jump targets from previous steps serve as jump sources in later steps. Using this intermediate information leads to better steering of our approach, enhanced jumps, and thus, to better clustering quality. Let us note that we still only use a few jump sources and never generate the full set of potential subspace regions in all the intermediate subspace projections. Thus, we avoid many subspaces altogether, i.e. multiple jumps tackle the exponential search space problem. Our main contribution for scalability and high quality jumps is the choice of the jump targets (cf. Sec. 4.2). However, let us discuss the underlying information gathering first.

4.1 Information Gathering for Steering

Steering requires information about the most promising subspace regions. This information is gathered during multiple jumps and is used to choose the next jump targets. Let us first describe the instantiation of information gathering for the density-based clustering paradigm before we discuss its general properties, which might be of interest for extensions to other paradigms as well.

Density-Based Instantiation. For density-based clustering it is essential to provide an information gathering that ensures scalability w.r.t. the number of objects in the database. Thus, we try to use as few database scans as possible to gather information on promising dense regions. We base on our previous approaches using hyperrectangle approximation of density-based subspace clusters and density estimation techniques [6, 24]. In a nutshell, these techniques do not compute the actual density by costly database scans but they base on object counts in hyperrectangles.

Hyperrectangles are obtained through discretization of the search space. Discretization is a well-known method for speeding up subspace clustering within a given subspace [3, 26, 29, 6]. We define hyperrectangles as follows:

DEFINITION 3. ***Hyperrectangle***
A hyperrectangle H in subspace $S = \{d_1, \ldots, d_s\}$ is defined as a tuple $[(d_1, low_1 - up_1), \ldots, (d_s, low_s - up_s)]$ of lower and upper bound interval identifiers $low_i - up_i$ in dimension d_i.

We write e.g. $H = [(1, 4), (2, 3 - 5), (3, 6)]$ if upper and lower bounds in a dimension are identical, i.e., short for $H = [(1, 4 - 4), (2, 3 - 5), (3, 6 - 6)]$, a hyperrectangle in interval four in dimension one, intervals three to five in dimension two, and interval six in dimension three.

So far, hyperrectangles have been used only in apriori-based processing schemes to process subspace regions from low dimensional to high dimensional subspaces. As all potentially dense regions are processed, these techniques are not able to tackle the exponential search space. We use hyperrectangles as an information source for steering to the most promising subspaces instead.

General Information Gathering. In general, any clustering model could benefit from our steering. The only required property is the underlying monotonicity of interesting regions, i.e., high dimensional subspace clusters are reflected in low dimensions. We gather this low dimensional information, which allows us to steer our processing to the desired high dimensional subspace clusters.

Our main contribution is to change the essential part of subspace clustering algorithms, the processing scheme. In contrast to previous methods we do not process subspaces step-by-step in breadth-first or depth-first order through all lower dimensional projections. Instead, we gather information about processed hyperrectangles in a priority queue and use this as jump information to go directly to the most promising subspaces. The priority queue simply stores the gathered information about dense subspace regions. In our case, it is a sorted list of dense hyperrectangle. The important part is the sorting function in the priority queue, and the selection of the most interesting subspace region as a jump target. Each jump provides a higher dimensional hyperrectangle to be stored in the priority queue. We discuss the jump in the following section.

The general idea of information gathering in our priority queue is based on simple object counts using hyperrectangles as in all of the traditional grid-based subspace clustering definitions [3, 26, 29] or efficiency improvements for density-based subspace clustering [6, 24]. The significant improvement is the novel processing of these hypercubes by a steered best-first search. All other methods use the density monotonicity property (cf. Def. 2) for step-by-step processing in breadth-first or depth-first order. Our algorithm uses these ideas for the efficient information gathering, but the scalability w.r.t. increasing number of dimensions is achieved by the steered jumps. This novel processing is the essential step in our algorithm.

Algorithm 1 Scalable Subspace Cluster Search

```
R = ∅
pqueue = DB.initializeEstimation()
while ∃ candidate (O, S) with uncovered objects do
    candidate = pqueue.getFirst()
    if candidate not yet processed then
        targets = steeredJumps(pqueue)
        pqueue.addAll(targets)
    else
        R = R ∪ {DB.refine(candidate)}
        pqueue.resort(R)
```

A generalized overview of our approach is given in Algorithm 1. First, we initialize our information in the priority queue by density estimation. This gives us the basis for selecting the best candidate from the priority queue. If a candidate is selected for the first time, it is used for steered jumps (cf. Sec. 4.2). We perform multiple jumps to higher dimensional subspaces and add these to our information basis. Else, if the candidate has already been used as jump source before, it is refined (additional database access). We insert it into the result set R and resort the queue according to our sorting function, which depends on the current result set R. The algorithm continues until the database is represented (covered) entirely, except for possible noise.

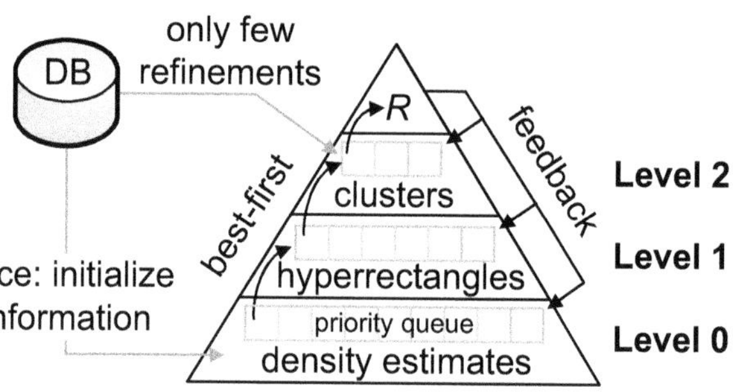

Figure 2: Priority queues for steering

The general processing scheme using our novel steering procedure (cf. Algorithm 1) is instantiated for density-based subspace clustering as follows. We split up the priority queue into three levels for multiple density granularities. Thus, while steering through subspaces, we are able to gather information about density estimates (Level 0), hyperrectangles (Level 1) up to density-based clusters (Level 2) in specific subspace regions.

Figure 2 illustrates the priority queue at three levels: Level 0 at the bottom consists of rough density estimates of subspace regions. For efficient but accurate density estimation, we use density estimation based on 2-dimensional histograms [24]. While the density estimates are very efficiently computable, they give only a rough approximation of potential subspace cluster regions. In order to steer our algorithm effectively through the search space, we use a much tighter approximation of subspace clusters through hyperrectangles on the next level (Level 1). With our novel steering we do best-first refinement of cluster candidates on each level, the most promising dense regions move up to the next levels. At the top, on Level 2 density-based subspace clusters are selected for the final result.

4.2 Steering: Jumping to Promising Subspaces

In this section, we describe how we steer search to the most promising subspace regions. We give details on the steered jumps based on the gathered hyperrectangles and define a preference function for the best-first search. We note the following jump terminologies (cf. Fig. 1):

- The *jump source* is a hyperrectangle B; this candidate is the basis / starting point of a jump and the most promising hyperrectangle detected so far.
- The *jump information* is a set $\mathcal{I}$ of already generated cluster candidates / hyperrectangles; it helps to steer the jump to promising regions and consists of the remaining entries in the priority queue.
- A *jump target* T is a hyperrectangle selected for a jump; it is an extension of the jump source B to new hyperrectangles in higher dimensionalities. We discuss selection below.

In a running example for this section, assume a jump source $B = [(\mathbf{1},\mathbf{2}),(\mathbf{2},\mathbf{2}),(\mathbf{4},\mathbf{2})]$ that consists of the second discretized interval in dimensions one, two and four. With the jump information, assume we identified dimensions and intervals $H = [(\mathbf{5},\mathbf{2}),(\mathbf{7},\mathbf{2}),(\mathbf{6},\mathbf{2}),(\mathbf{11},\mathbf{2})]$ as a meaningful extension for B. The hyperrectangles B and H are combined to jump target T to form a new candidate in a higher dimensional subspace, i.e. the jump target covers all dimensions and intervals of both B and H. Formally, we get the new higher dimensional hyperrectangle T with $Dim(T) = Dim(B) \uplus Dim(H)$, $\forall d_i \in Dim(B) : Int(B, d_i) = Int(T, d_i)$ and $\forall d_i \in Dim(H) : Int(H, d_i) = Int(T, d_i)$. With $Dim(H)$ being the dimensions contained in H, and $Int(H, d_i)$ as the corresponding intervals. In our example, the jump source could be extended using the jump information by simply forming the union of the two:
$B \uplus H = [(\mathbf{1},\mathbf{2}),(\mathbf{2},\mathbf{2}),(\mathbf{4},\mathbf{2}),(\mathbf{5},\mathbf{2}),(\mathbf{7},\mathbf{2}),(\mathbf{6},\mathbf{2}),(\mathbf{11},\mathbf{2})]$. Our goal, of course, is the combination of the jump source with the best hyperrectangles in the jump information, in the sense that most promising jump targets are identified. In the following we discuss the actual selection of jump targets.

Determining jump targets. To find jump targets, i.e., promising high dimensional regions, we need to identify dimensions and intervals from the currently available jump information, for possible combination with the jump source. Obviously, dimensions already included in the jump source do not lead to new jump targets, and neither do combinations of different intervals in the same subspace. Such combinations are therefore not valid for the purpose of steering to promising regions.

We refer to valid combinations of hyperrectangles in the jump information as *jump indicators*. A jump indicator can be imagined as a derived hyperrectangle that does not share any dimension with the jump source. Also, several jump indicators can be combined with the jump source to obtain the jump target of a certain dimensionality. Formally, jump indicators are:

DEFINITION 4. ***Jump indicator***
A jump indicator P of length k is a hyperrectangle, which does not share any common dimensions with the jump source B such that $(Dim(P) \cap Dim(B) = \emptyset)$ and $|Dim(P)| = k$.

In our example, the jump target is derived out of a ranking of indicators $(\mathbf{5},\mathbf{2}),(\mathbf{7},\mathbf{2}),(\mathbf{6},\mathbf{2}),(\mathbf{11},\mathbf{2}),\ldots$ in combination with the jump source. In general, we rank jump indicators by their potential impact, i.e. how "helpful" they are in leading to subspace clusters for our result set. Deriving the impact is discussed later on.

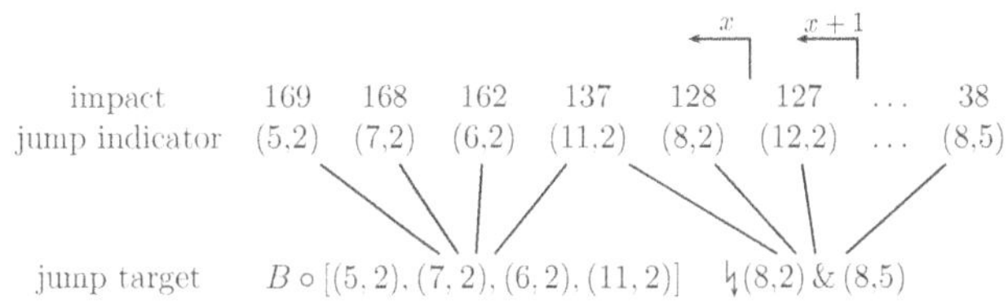

Figure 3: Generating jump targets

In the final step, we combine these ranked jump indicators with the jump source to jump targets. In the following, we illustrate this process assuming $k = 1$ (one-dimensional indicator) for simplicity of presentation. In Figure 3, we give an example ranked list of possible jump indicators (dimension and interval tuples in the center row of the figure) and their impact values (top row of the figure). The combination of four one-dimensional jump indicators with our jump source yields a jump target with the dimensionality of $B = [(1,2),(2,2),(4,2)]$ plus four: $[(5,2),(7,2),(6,2),(11,2)]$. Please note, that some combinations are not valid, since they would result in disjoint intervals in the same dimension. For example, in the lower right in the figure, intervals $(8,2)$ and $(8,5)$ cannot be combined with the source at the same time. By construction of the hyperrectangles, there cannot be a subspace cluster in dimension eight existing in both interval two and interval five.

Thus, we construct jump targets by combining smaller k-dimensional indicators. These potential jump targets are ranked, such that we always process the most promising combinations first. We include jump indicators up to a position x in the ranking (cf. top right in Fig. 3). Jump targets are constructed only from these jump indicators. Once those jump targets have been generated, the position of x is incremented by one, and new jump targets are generated up to the new value of x (arrow for $x + 1$ in the figure).

In order to limit the number of cluster candidates that are processed, we generate only a fixed number of jump targets. Parameter $generatedClusters$ sets the number of subspace clusters that are generated from a given jump source. To show that only few cluster candidates have to be generated, we study this parameter experimentally in Section 5.

Impact of jump indicators. Obviously, the crucial part in determining jump targets lies in the ranking of the jump indicators based on their impact. As mentioned above, we know that any high dimensional subspace cluster is likely to be reflected in many different low dimensional projections. We use this observation to calculate the impact. If a jump indicator P is part of several currently known subspace regions, this suggests that it is a projection of a higher dimensional cluster. The first aspect to calculate the impact is based on the similarities of the jump source B and any hyperrectangle H_i in the jump information. If the cluster similarity $cs(B, H_i)$ (introduced below and formalized in Definition 6) is high and P is included in H_i, the impact should also be high.

As a second aspect, we want to steer the search to novel dense regions that are not yet represented to avoid generating redundant results. Thus, we propose a function cp (cluster preference) to measure representation of new information. Cluster preference is the basis for our best-first search, and provides flexible means to be instantiated also by other user specific interestingness measures. In this work, we restrict ourself to pure coverage of objects as basic measure. Subspace clusters which contain objects which are already represented (covered) by the result set contribute little or no new knowledge to the result. By prioritizing hyperrectangles that are not yet covered, we favor those jump targets which are likely to lead to the desired subspace clusters.

Overall, we define the impact of a jump indicator as the product of the cluster similarity (cf. Def. 6) and the cluster preference (cf. Def. 7) values. Thus, the impact takes the similarity between the jump source and the hyperrectangles into account to identify promising higher dimensional regions, while giving preference to those that contain not yet covered objects. We present the two functions cs and cp in more detail later on.

DEFINITION 5. ***Impact of jump indicators***
Let P be a jump indicator, B the jump source and $\mathcal{I}$ the jump information. The impact of P is the cluster similarity and preference of all hyperrectangles $H_i \in \mathcal{I}$ in which P is contained.

$$\sum_{H_i \in \mathcal{I},\ P \text{ in } H_i} cs(B, H_i) \cdot cp(H_i)$$

An obvious question to ask is how to efficiently obtain the jump indicators and their impact. We propose an efficient way of generating all possible jump indicators along with their impact. We transform the problem of combining hyperrectangles (given by their intervals in the respective dimensions) into a problem of (weighted) itemset mining [12, 13]. A k-dimensional jump indicator can be mapped to a k-itemset, i.e. a set of k items that occur in a transaction. The (weighted) support, i.e. the number of occurrences of this itemset, corresponds to the impact. In itemset mining, efficient algorithms exist [13], which we use to compute the interestingness, and the top-m-ranked results.

An example is given in Fig. 4: at the top, the jump source is given as a set of tuples of dimensions and interval identifiers. To determine the desired jump indicators, the source can be combined with the remaining hyperrectangles in the first column. The second column notes dimensions and intervals which could be used to extend the source. To compute the impact w.r.t. a jump indicator, e.g. [(5, 2)], we sum up the products $cs \cdot cp$ as the (weighted) support of all transactions that contain the jump indicator. So, the first transaction contributes to the support, but not the second, etc. Note that this procedure can easily be extended to ranges of intervals, e.g. an entry $(1, 3-5)$ would be mapped to items $(1, 3), (1, 4), (1, 5)$.

Cluster similarity and cluster preference. Calculation of similarities between subspace clusters is an important aspect for the impact of jump indicators. The higher the similarity $cs(B, H_i)$ of a hyperrectangle H_i, the more interesting this hyperrectangle is with respect to the jump source B. A high similarity indicates that both hyperrectangles might be a projection of the same high dimensional subspace cluster. Thus, this jump indicator should be prioritized. The goal in determining the cluster similarity cs is that the more dimensions are shared by the jump source and another hyperrectangle, the more similar they should be. Also, we need to take into account in which intervals they overlap. Clearly, if the intervals are disjoint, the two hyperrectangles do not represent the same higher dimensional subspace cluster.

jump source: $[(\mathbf{1},\mathbf{2}),(\mathbf{2},\mathbf{2}),(\mathbf{4},\mathbf{2})]$, jump indicator $[(5,2)]$

jump information (hyperrectangle H_i)	transactions (potential extension)	$cs \cdot cp$ w.r.t. H_i	support for $[(5,2)]$
$[(\mathbf{1},\mathbf{2}),(\mathbf{2},\mathbf{2}),(5,2)]$	$\{(5,2)\}$	**2**	+2
$[(\mathbf{2},\mathbf{2}),(\mathbf{4},\mathbf{2}),(7,2)]$	$\{(7,2)\}$	**2**	
$[(\mathbf{1},\mathbf{2}),(5,2),(6,2)]$	$\{(5,2),(6,2)\}$	**1**	+1
$[(\mathbf{1},\mathbf{2}),(5,2),(7,2)]$	$\{(5,2),(7,2)\}$	**1**	+1
⋮	⋮	⋮	⋮

Figure 4: Impact of jump indicators

Thus, only overlapping hyperrectangles have positive similarity values. We define the number of overlapping intervals of two hyperrectangles H_1 and H_2 in dimension d as

$$Overlap(H_1, H_2, d) = \begin{cases} |Int(H_1, d) \cap Int(H_2, d)| & (*) \\ 0 & \text{else} \end{cases}$$

$$(*)\ d \in Dim(H_1) \cap Dim(H_2)$$

Beside just determining the cardinality of the intersection of the dimensions, e.g. $|Dim(B) \cap Dim(H_i)|$, our overall definition of the cluster similarity takes also the portion of overlap into account:

DEFINITION 6. ***Cluster Similarity***
For a given jump source B, and the hyperrectangles H_i available as jump information, let $|Dim(B) \cap Dim(H_i)| = k$. We define the cluster similarity cs as follows:

$$cs(B, H_i) = \begin{cases} k \cdot \sqrt[k]{\prod_{d \in Dim(B) \cap Dim(H_i)} \frac{Overlap(B, H_i, d)}{|Int(B, d)|}} & k > 0 \\ 0 & else \end{cases}$$

Thus, similarity is the average overlap between the jump source and the jump information and therefore it reflects the degree to which promising new hyperrectangles can be generated through their combination.

In the following we give an extended example on the calculation of our cluster similarity function cs. First of all, we require for two similar hyperrectangles that their corresponding intervals overlap. In Figure 5, two hyperrectangles are depicted in their two-dimensional projections. Both of them contain dimensions 1 and 2, but since they do not share intervals in dimension 2, they do not cover the same area in the search space. Thus, they do not represent the same high dimensional cluster, and we cannot infer meaningful jump indicators based on these two hyperrectangles. Consequently, the similarity denotes a value of 0 (cf. Def. 6).

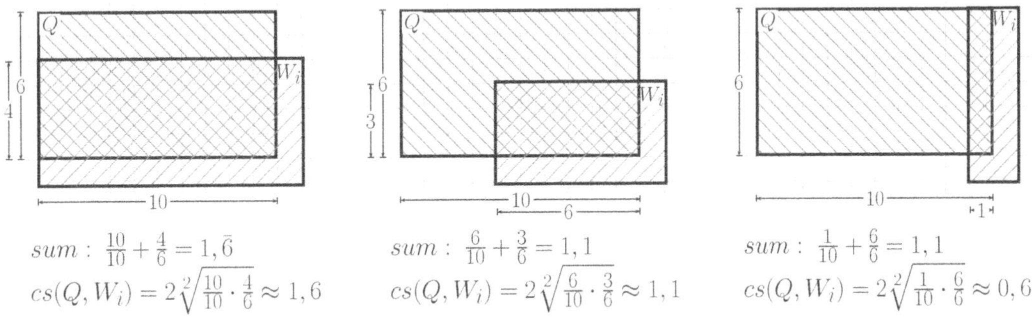

Figure 6: Similarity computation

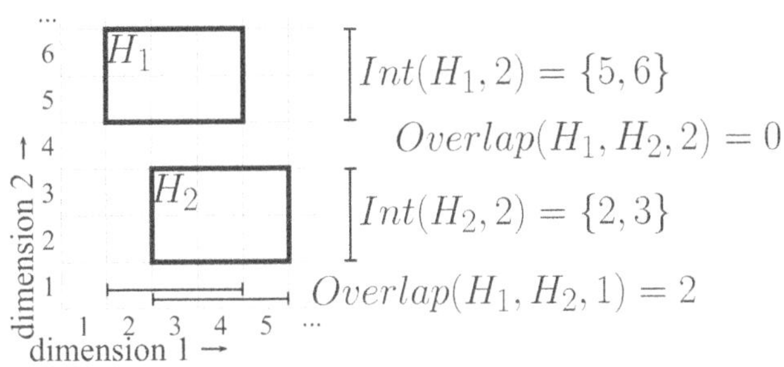

Figure 5: Hyperrectangles in the same subspace with no overlap (disjoint intervals in dimension 2)

As a second aspect, the extent of overlap between two hyperrectangles has to be considered. Hyperrectangles which overlap more (e.g. Fig. 6 (a) more than (b)), are much more likely to be reflections of the same higher dimensional subspace cluster, so they should be considered more similar with respect to the function cs. Consequently, the impact of the corresponding jump indicators is also higher.

To incorporate also the extent we do not simply determine the number of shared dimensions between hyperrectangles, but we consider the overlap with respect to the intervals in the jump source $Overlap(B, H_i, d)/|Int(B, d)|$. Thereby, we much better reflect the degree to which the two hyperrectangles are thought to reflect the same higher dimensional subspace cluster. The sum over these overlaps

$$\sum_{d \in Dim(B) \cap Dim(H_i)} (Overlap(B, H_i, d)/|Int(B, d)|)$$

, however, conceals small overlaps in one dimension if there is a larger overlap in another. We therefore propose using a product of the overlaps. Consider the example in Figure 6: taking the sum of overlaps yields $6/10 + 3/6 = 1.1$ in (b) and also $1/10 + 6/6 = 1.1$ in (c), even though the overlap is considerably larger in (b). Taking the product of the overlapping intervals is e.g. in (c) $1/10 \cdot 6/6 = 1/10$, and in (b) a higher value of $6/10 \cdot 3/6 = 3/10$.

The number of dimensions, however, is underrated: e.g. an overlap of 8/10 per dimension yields $(8/10)^2$ for two dimensions, yet$(8/10)^3$ for three dimensions. To make sure that we still favor those situations where more dimensions overlap, we introduce a normalization factor which intuitively gives us the "average" overlap per dimension. Considering the product, e.g. $1/10 \cdot 6/6 = 1/10$, as a volume in the k-dimensional space, we determine the side length of a hypercube of the same volume, i.e. we compute the kth root of the volume. In the example in (c), this hypercube has a side length of $\sqrt[2]{1/10} \approx 0,32$, whereas (b) has a value of 0,55. Multiplying this value with the number of overlapping dimensions k is our Definition 6 of the cluster similarity.

For the second aspect, the cluster preference function cp should steer the jump to regions not yet covered by other clusters. Thus, w.r.t. the currently known subspace clusters available, R and its covered objects $Cov(R)$, we denote the objects in H that are already contained in R as $|Obj(H) \cap Cov(R)|$ and the number of objects in the hyperrectangle itself as $|Obj(H)|$. We define the preference function such that those hyperrectangles are preferred which contain many objects that are not yet included in other subspace clusters:

DEFINITION 7. ***Cluster preference***
Let R be the current set of already detected clusters. Then we define the cluster preference function cp for a hyperrectangle H as the number of objects in H that are not yet covered:

$$cp(H) = |Obj(H)| - |Obj(H) \cap Cov(R)|$$

Both cluster preference and cluster similarity are combined to steer our best-first search according to Def. 5.

4.3 Complexity Analysis

Our novel jump technique using intermediate jump sources is the key for scalable processing. Let us discuss best and worst case scenarios for the computational complexity of this approach compared with the exponential complexity of traditional step-by-step algorithms. Their best case is our worst case: The multi-jump processing degenerates to a step-by-step processing if we perform jumps with only a single dimension increment. Even approximated density regions cannot reduce expensive database scans in this scenario as all subspaces regions are investigated. Thus, our worst case scenario is computationally equivalent to the best case processing for traditional apriori based methods with a complexity of

$$O(2^k \cdot |DB|^2)$$

where k is the maximal subspace cluster dimensionality, and $|DB|$ denotes the size of the database.

However, in general we do not perform step-by-step processing. Our steering excludes large parts of the search space, and thus, significantly reduces the complexity. In

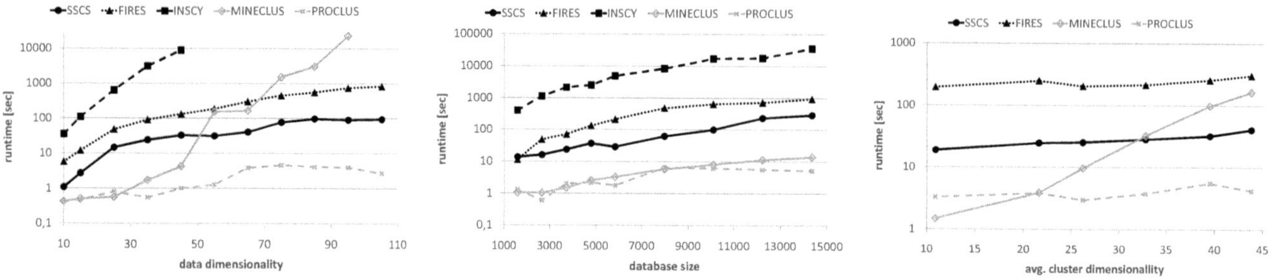

(a) data dimensionality (b) size of the database (c) avg. cluster dimensionality

Figure 7: Scalability w.r.t. dimensionality and size of the database

the best case, our multi-jump technique only investigates the high dimensional density-based clusters that are output as the result R. In addition to a single database scan for initialization, our method directly jumps to the clustered subspace regions and has a best case complexity of:

$$O((1 + |R|) \cdot |DB|^2)$$

i.e. the complexity is independent of the dimensionality, and depends only on the output size. Even though the complexity of our approach remains quadratic in the size of the database, using density estimation and discretization greatly reduces the overall computational cost as intermediate jumps are performed without additional database access. This is confirmed in the experiments (cf. Sec. 5).

The steering based on these intermediate jumps is an important aspect for high quality results. A single jump from low dimensional to high dimensional subspaces is likely to miss parts of the result R due to limited information in the initial jump source. Using multiple jumps, our steering with intermediate jump sources achieves high clustering quality (as validated in the experiments in Sec. 5 as well). Considering the complexity, the intermediate jumps increase the computational cost by processing a few extra subspace regions. They greatly boost quality as they choose promising jump targets.

As we will show in the following section, our subspace processing based on this jump selection efficiently detects high quality clusters and is scalable to large and high dimensional databases.

5. EXPERIMENTS

We compare our scalable subspace cluster search (SSCS) with recent density-based (INSCY [7] and FIRES [18]) and projected clustering (PROCLUS [1] and MINECLUS [31]) algorithms. As measures for clustering quality we use F1 and accuracy [25]. We use synthetic data for scalability evaluation as in [25], as well as benchmark data from the UCI archive [8]. Besides 16-dim. pendigits data, we use 32 and 48-dim. variants by interpolation of polylines. Furthermore, we use 50-dim. Face and 50-dim. Swedish Leafs data sets [16]. All experiments were run on the same machine with Intel Quad Core Opteron 2.3 GHz CPUs. Furthermore, we ensure comparability and repeatability of our experiments by running all experiments in our open-source framework. Supplementary material for evaluation is provided on our project website[1].

[1]http://dme.rwth-aachen.de/OpenSubspace/SSCS

5.1 Scalability on Synthetic Data

We begin with scalability analysis on synthetic data, increasing the number of dimensions, the most important parameter for performance of subspace clustering algorithms.

Data Dimensionality. As depicted in Fig. 7(a), apriori-based approaches do not scale with increasing dimensionality. For example, the step-by-step method INSCY shows exponential runtimes. As analyzed in [25], subspace clustering approaches such as CLIQUE [3] and SUBCLU [14] show even worse performance than INSCY. However, already INSCY did not finish for the 55-dimensional data within 48 hours. In contrast, approximative solutions like FIRES [18] scale slightly better, but provide only poor clustering quality (cf. Fig. 8). They miss relevant subspace clusters due to their rough approximation of subspace clusters. Without any steering logic, clustering amounts to a heuristic guess. In contrast, our approach steers in a principled fashion directly to subspace clusters, which provide best quality.

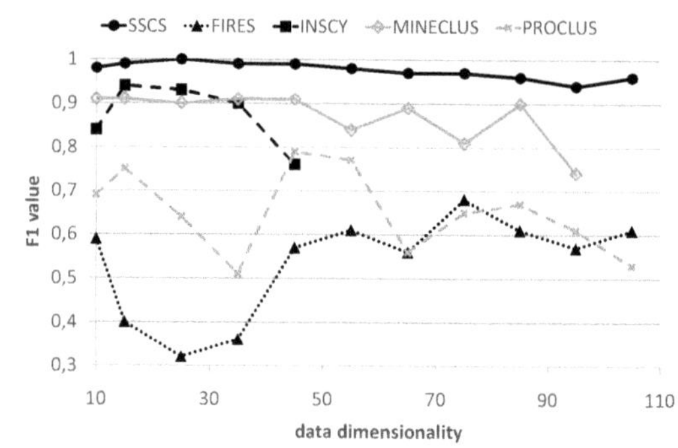

Figure 8: Quality on scalability experiment

As comparison baseline, we depict also projected clustering approaches, which are known to be scalable to high dimensional data [25]. In terms of runtime, approaches like MINECLUS [31] achieve good results for low dimensional data due to their randomization of the search (Fig. 7(a)). However, they show poor scalability. Only the simpler PROCLUS approach scales with almost linear increase of runtime, but shows poorer clustering quality (Fig. 8). Compared to PROCLUS, our approach achieves similar scalability of runtimes while SSCS provides constantly better quality results, not reached by any other subspace clustering algorithm.

Database Size. Figure 7(b) shows runtime of the algorithms with respect to increasing database size. We use

	SSCS			FIRES			INSCY		
	runtime	F1 value	accuracy	runtime	F1 value	accuracy	runtime	F1 value	accuracy
Pendigits16	118	0,63	0,87	150	0,30	0,43	3937	0,51	0,57
Pendigits32	565	0,62	0,86	433	0,23	0,40	X	X	X
Pendigits48	1571	0,60	0,85	6562	0,27	0,50	X	X	X
Face50	982	0,21	0,59	2924	0,17	0,32	X	X	X
Leaf50	934	0,24	0,55	31	0,12	0,32	X	X	X

Table 1: Summary of real world data experiments

20-dimensional databases for comparison with all density-based approaches, as INSCY does not run on most of our higher dimensional databases. For these data we observe best runtimes for the less effective projected clustering approaches as in the previous experiment. Our approach scales well with similar slope in runtime for increasing number of objects. Overall, the results show that subspace clustering is more affected by dimensionality than by database size. Nevertheless, due to our efficient steering to higher dimensional jump targets we achieve far better runtimes than density-based competitors.

Cluster Dimensionality. Figure 7(c) shows the effect of increasing cluster dimensionality. INSCY is not depicted, as for this experiment we have used a high dimensional dataset with 65 dimensions. PROCLUS shows best runtimes due to its simple clustering model. For density-based approaches, our approach clearly outperforms the approximative FIRES, but we also outperform the projected MINECLUS approach that is heavily affected by the increasing cluster dimensionality. Our algorithm scales much better to higher dimensional clusters.

Overall, Figures 7 and 8 show that our approach scales very well in terms of runtime with best clustering quality.

5.2 Evaluation on real world data

In the following experiments, we evaluate real world data. As projected clustering approaches cannot detect overlapping clusters and require the (unknown) number of hidden clusters, PROCLUS and MINECLUS are not comparable (cf. Sec. 2). Table 1 summmarizes runtime (in seconds) and cluster quality via F1 value and accuracy. In addition to the databases Pendigits16, Face50 and Leaf50, we vary the dimensionality of the pendigits data from 16 to 48. For these three datasets we observe similar scalability results as on the synthetic data. INSCY does not scale to more than the 16 dimensional pendigits dataset while the approximative FIRES approach has in most cases higher runtimes than our approach. We have highlighted in gray the lowest runtimes and highest cluster quality for each database. Our approach clearly outperforms existing density-based subspace clustering. Although FIRES achieved lower runtime in two cases, it shows significantly lower quality on all databases. Overall, we efficiently achieve high quality for real world data as well.

5.3 Jump Parameterization

Our multi-jump approach uses gathered information based on low dimensional subspace cluster candidates to determine jumps (cf. Fig. 1). We evaluate the amount of knowledge to extract for multi-jumps. The generated jump targets for each jump ensure a high quality clustering result. We varied the number of generated candidates from 1 to 200 and observe a drop of quality for very low numbers (Fig. 9). However, by generating at least 30 candidates our approach reliably shows high clustering quality. Overall, our steering requires only very few cluster candidates. In contrast to previous approaches, it overcomes the exhaustive generation of cluster candidates by intelligent jumps.

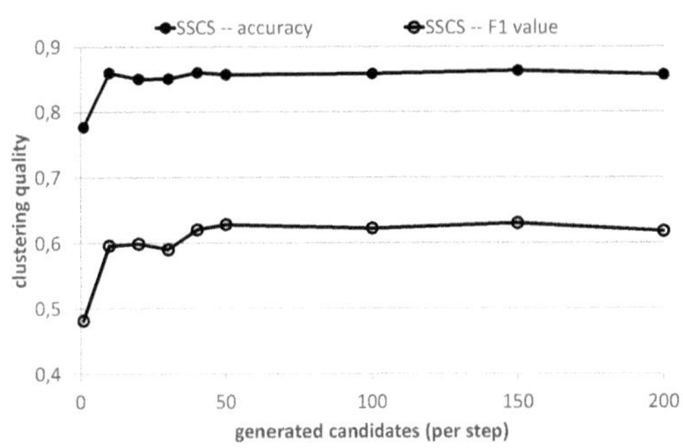

Figure 9: Amount of extracted knowledge

6. CONCLUSION

We introduce a scalable density-based subspace clustering technique. Our main contribution for scalability and high quality is a principled steering of the algorithm in a best-first manner. Information is gathered on promising subspace regions and progressively obtained results are used for multiple jumps that efficiently lead to good subspace clustering results. Our method thereby solves issues faced by apriori-based subspace clustering because of the exponential search space problem and repeated database scans. Overall, our general steering proposes a novel processing scheme for subspace clustering. It ensures scalability w.r.t. increasing number of dimensions, and thus, shows significant runtime improvements compared to the currently used apriori processing scheme.

We propose an instantiation of our steering scheme to the density-based clustering paradigm. It has shown to be a challenging subspace clustering paradigm as it requires quadratic runtime for each of the exponential many subspace projection considered by step-by-step processing schemes. Our steering enables the first density-based subspace clustering technique, which scales to high dimensional data. In our experiments, we demonstrate that our technique is efficient, scales better than existing subspace and projected clustering algorithms, and provides high quality results.

7. FUTURE WORK

For future work, our general steering scheme opens research potential for speeding up other subspace clustering approaches as well. Let us sketch the basic properties for such an instantiation: Steering requires the traditional monotonicity property, as proven for most subspace clustering approaches. This is the only assumption made for the steered jumps in our work. Thus, it is widely applicable with only two hot spots that have to be instantiated in our general processing scheme.

First, information gathering has to be instantiated according to the underlying cluster definition. This can be done similarly to apriori-based techniques. It has to ensure efficient access to required cluster properties without expensive database access, and a sorted list of cluster candidates.

Second, combination of these candidates to higher dimensional clusters is the main idea of steering. As general properties, we proposed cluster preference and cluster similarity functions for this steered jumps. Both should be adapted to the underlying objective function. Given instantiations for these two functions, our steering chooses the best-first order for processing novel subspace clusters.

Acknowledgment

This work has been supported in part by the UMIC Research Centre, RWTH Aachen University, Germany; and by the Danish Council for Strategic Research, grant 10-092316.

8. REFERENCES

[1] C. Aggarwal, J. Wolf, P. Yu, C. Procopiuc, and J. Park. Fast algorithms for projected clustering. In *SIGMOD*, pages 61–72, 1999.

[2] C. Aggarwal and P. Yu. Finding generalized projected clusters in high dimensional spaces. In *SIGMOD*, pages 70–81, 2000.

[3] R. Agrawal, J. Gehrke, D. Gunopulos, and P. Raghavan. Automatic subspace clustering of high dimensional data for data mining applications. In *SIGMOD*, pages 94–105, 1998.

[4] R. Agrawal and R. Srikant. Fast algorithms for mining association rules. In *VLDB*, pages 487–499, 1994.

[5] I. Assent, R. Krieger, E. Müller, and T. Seidl. DUSC: Dimensionality unbiased subspace clustering. In *ICDM*, pages 409–414, 2007.

[6] I. Assent, R. Krieger, E. Müller, and T. Seidl. EDSC: Efficient density-based subspace clustering. In *CIKM*, pages 1093–1102, 2008.

[7] I. Assent, R. Krieger, E. Müller, and T. Seidl. INSCY: Indexing subspace clusters with in-process-removal of redundancy. In *ICDM*, pages 719–724, 2008.

[8] A. Asuncion and D. Newman. UCI machine learning repository: http://www.ics.uci.edu/~mlearn/mlrepository.html, 2007.

[9] K. Beyer, J. Goldstein, R. Ramakrishnan, and U. Shaft. When is nearest neighbors meaningful. In *IDBT*, pages 217–235, 1999.

[10] C.-H. Cheng, A. W. Fu, and Y. Zhang. Entropy-based subspace clustering for mining numerical data. In *KDD*, pages 84–93, 1999.

[11] M. Ester, H.-P. Kriegel, J. Sander, and X. Xu. A density-based algorithm for discovering clusters in large spatial databases. In *KDD*, pages 226–231, 1996.

[12] J. Han and M. Kamber. *Data Mining: Concepts and Techniques*. Morgan Kaufmann, 2001.

[13] J. Han, J. Pei, and Y. Yin. Mining frequent patterns without candidate generation. In *SIGMOD*, pages 1–12, 2000.

[14] K. Kailing, H.-P. Kriegel, and P. Kröger. Density-connected subspace clustering for high-dimensional data. In *SDM*, pages 246–257, 2004.

[15] K. Kailing, H.-P. Kriegel, P. Kröger, and S. Wanka. Ranking interesting subspaces for clustering high dimensional data. In *PKDD*, pages 241–252, 2003.

[16] E. Keogh, X. Xi, L. Wei, and C. A. Ratanamahatana. The ucr time series classification/clustering homepage, 2006.

[17] H. Kriegel, P. Kroger, M. Schubert, and Z. Zhu. Efficient query processing in arbitrary subspaces using vector approximations. In *SSDBM*, pages 184–190, 2006.

[18] H.-P. Kriegel, P. Kröger, M. Renz, and S. Wurst. A generic framework for efficient subspace clustering of high-dimensional data. In *ICDM*, pages 250–257, 2005.

[19] H.-P. Kriegel, P. Kröger, and A. Zimek. Clustering high-dimensional data: A survey on subspace clustering, pattern-based clustering, and correlation clustering. *TKDD*, 3(1), 2009.

[20] X. Lian and L. Chen. Similarity Search in Arbitrary Subspaces Under Lp-Norm. In *ICDE*, pages 317–326. IEEE Computer Society, 2008.

[21] G. Moise and J. Sander. Finding non-redundant, statistically significant regions in high dimensional data: a novel approach to projected and subspace clustering. In *KDD*, pages 533–541, 2008.

[22] G. Moise, J. Sander, and M. Ester. P3C: A robust projected clustering algorithm. In *ICDM*, pages 414–425, 2006.

[23] E. Müller, I. Assent, S. Günnemann, R. Krieger, and T. Seidl. Relevant subspace clustering: Mining the most interesting non-redundant concepts in high dimensional data. In *ICDM*, pages 377–386, 2009.

[24] E. Müller, I. Assent, R. Krieger, S. Günnemann, and T. Seidl. DensEst: Density estimation for data mining in high dimensional spaces. In *SDM*, pages 173–184, 2009.

[25] E. Müller, S. Günnemann, I. Assent, and T. Seidl. Evaluating clustering in subspace projections of high dimensional data. *PVLDB*, 2(1):1270–1281, 2009.

[26] H. Nagesh, S. Goil, and A. Choudhary. Adaptive grids for clustering massive data sets. In *SDM*, 2001.

[27] L. Parsons, E. Haque, and H. Liu. Subspace clustering for high dimensional data: a review. *SIGKDD Explorations*, 6(1):90–105, 2004.

[28] C. Procopiuc, M. Jones, P. Agarwal, and T. Murali. A monte carlo algorithm for fast projective clustering. In *SIGMOD*, pages 418–427, 2002.

[29] K. Sequeira and M. Zaki. SCHISM: A new approach for interesting subspace mining. In *ICDM*, pages 186–193, 2004.

[30] D. Witten and R. Tibshirani. A framework for feature selection in clustering. *Journal of the American Statistical Association*, 105(490):713–726, 2010.

[31] M. L. Yiu and N. Mamoulis. Frequent-pattern based iterative projected clustering. In *ICDM*, pages 689–692, 2003.

[32] F. Zhu, X. Yan, J. Han, P. Yu, and H. Cheng. Mining Colossal Frequent Patterns by Core Pattern Fusion. In *ICDE*, pages 706–715, 2007.

Correlated Multi-Label Feature Selection

Quanquan Gu
Dept. of Computer Science
University of Illinois at Urbana-Champaign
IL, 61801, USA
qgu3@illinois.edu

Zhenhui Li
Dept. of Computer Science
University of Illinois at Urbana-Champaign
IL, 61801, USA
zli28@uiuc.edu

Jiawei Han
Dept. of Computer Science
University of Illinois at Urbana-Champaign
IL, 61801, USA
hanj@cs.uiuc.edu

ABSTRACT

Multi-label learning studies the problem where each instance is associated with a set of labels. There are two challenges in multi-label learning: (1) the labels are interdependent and correlated, and (2) the data are of high dimensionality. In this paper, we aim to tackle these challenges in one shot. In particular, we propose to learn the label correlation and do feature selection simultaneously. We introduce a matrix-variate Normal prior distribution on the weight vectors of the classifier to model the label correlation. Our goal is to find a subset of features, based on which the label correlation regularized loss of label ranking is minimized. The resulting multi-label feature selection problem is a mixed integer programming, which is reformulated as quadratically constrained linear programming (QCLP). It can be solved by cutting plane algorithm, in each iteration of which a minimax optimization problem is solved by dual coordinate descent and projected sub-gradient descent alternatively. Experiments on benchmark data sets illustrate that the proposed methods outperform single-label feature selection method and many other state-of-the-art multi-label learning methods.

Categories and Subject Descriptors

I.2.6 [**Artificial Intelligence**]: Learning; I.5.1 [**Pattern Recognition**]: Models

General Terms

Algorithms, Experimentation

Keywords

Feature Selection, Label Correlation, Multi-Label Learning, Dual Coordinate Descent, Cutting Plane

1. INTRODUCTION

Multi-label learning [7, 30, 35, 39, 13, 27, 4, 11, 31, 36] is a very important topic in data mining and information retrieval. It studies the problem where each instance is associated with a set of labels. This is not uncommon in many important applications, such as protein function classification [7], text categorization [19], and semantic scene classification [1]. For example, one gene can be associated with several functions, one image may have several tags, and one document can cover several topics.

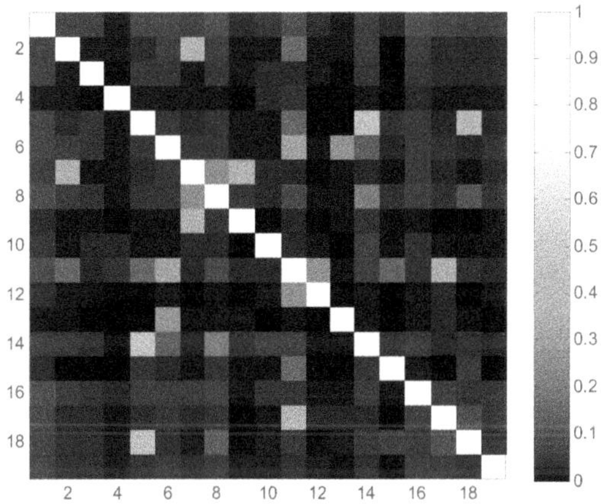

Figure 1: The label correlation computed from the labels of all the data points in the Yahoo/Arts data set

There are mainly two challenges in multi-label learning. First, different from traditional single-label learning where the classes are mutually exclusive, the classes in multi-label learning are typically interdependent and correlated, which poses more difficulties to predict all the relevant labels for a given instance. For example, in image annotation, "sea" and "ship" tend to appear in the same image, while "car" typically does not appear together with "ship". Figure 1 illustrates the label correlation which is computed from the labels of all the data points in the Yahoo/Arts data set. The higher the value between two labels is (lighter color), the more correlated these two labels are. It can be seen that the 5th label is highly correlated with the 14th and 18th labels, while it is not correlated with the 12th label. On the other hand, the label correlation offers a possibility to infer the unknown label of an instance from the known label. In order to utilize the relation between labels, [7, 6] proposed to learn the ranks of labels for each instance, which is basically first-order information. However, the correlation among labels is second-order information [36]. And we will show that it is essential for better performance in our experiments.

The second challenge is that multi-labeled data usually have thousands or even tens of thousands of features. This is especially true for documents and news articles. For example, the news articles in the Yahoo data set used in our experiments are of about 20K features. As we know, high dimensional data may cause the *curse of dimensionality*, which increases the computational burden and deteriorate the generalization ability of the classifier. To overcome this problem, many dimensionality reduction based multi-label learning approaches [35, 39, 13, 31] have been proposed. Although these methods perform good for high dimensional data, they still fail to explicitly model the label correlation, which is crucial for better performance.

In this paper, based on the above motivation, we aim to solve the two challenges in one shot. We built up our model on the label rank support vector machine (LaRank SVM) [7][1], which is among state-of-the-art multi-label learning methods [7, 13]. We introduce a matrix-variate Normal prior distribution [10] on the weight vectors of LaRank SVM. Since the column covariance matrix of matrix-variate Normal distribution characterizes the correlation among the weight vectors, each of which associates with one label, the label correlation is modeled explicitly. To avoid the curse of dimensionality, we incorporate feature selection into LaRank SVM. Our goal is to find a subset of features, based on which the label correlation regularized loss of label ranking [7] is minimized. The resulting multi-label feature selection is a mixed integer programming problem, which is difficult to solve. Fortunately, it can be reformulated as Quadratically Constrained Linear Programming (QCLP) [2]. It is solved by cutting plane algorithm [17], in each iteration of which a minimax optimization problem is solved by dual coordinate descent [12] and projected sub-gradient descent [22] alternatively. As a by-product, we also propose a correlated label rank support vector machine (CLaRank SVM), which is an extension of LaRank SVM [7]. It is worth noting that, the proposed approach is able to not only learn the label correlation automatically, but also reduce the dimensionality of the original data. Experiments on benchmark data sets indicate that the proposed methods outperform single-label feature selection and many other state-of-the-art methods.

The remainder of this paper is organized as follows. In Section 2, we discuss several related works on multi-label learning. In Section 3 we present correlated multi-label feature selection. The experiments on real world data sets are demonstrated in Section 4. Finally, we draw a conclusion and point out the future work in Section 5.

1.1 Notation

In multi-label learning with c labels, each data point $\mathbf{x}_i \in \mathbb{R}^d, i = 1, \ldots, n$ can be associated with a set of labels, i.e., $y_i \subseteq \{1, 2, \ldots, c\}$. We denote the complementary set of y_i by $\bar{y}_i$, and the cardinality of y_i by $|y_i|$. For example, suppose there are totally 6 labels, and $\mathbf{x}_i$ is labeled by the 2nd and 3rd labels, then $y_i = \{2, 3\}$, $\bar{y}_i = \{1, 4, 5, 6\}$ and $|y_i| = 2$. $\mathbf{X} = [\mathbf{x}_1, \mathbf{x}_2, \ldots, \mathbf{x}_n] \in \mathbb{R}^{d \times n}$ represents the data matrix. $\mathbf{x}^j$ denotes the jth row of $\mathbf{X}$. $\mathbf{e}_i$ is a unit vector of all zeros except the ith element equal to 1. $\mathbf{1}$ is a vector of all ones. $\mathbf{0}$ is a vector of all zeros. Given a matrix $\mathbf{R}$, we denote its (k, l)th entry by R_{kl}, and its inverse matrix by $\mathbf{R}^{-1}$. R^{-1}_{kl} is the (k, l)th entry of $\mathbf{R}^{-1}$.

[1]Note that in the original paper, the authors called this model as Rank SVM. To distinguish this model from another well-known Rank SVM proposed in [14] for information retrieval, we call this model as Label Rank SVM or simply LaRank SVM because it ranks the labels rather than data points.

2. RELATED WORK

In this section, we give a brief review of multi-label classification methods which are related to ours. Existing multi-label learning methods can be cast into different families.

The first family of multi-label learning method is to divide multi-label learning into a set of one-against-all binary classification problems [23]. However, since each label is treated independently, it fails to consider the correlation among different labels, which is essential in multi-label learning. It is desirable for a multi-label learning method to make use of label correlation for better performance. Moreover, this approach suffers from imbalanced data when constructing binary classifiers to distinguish each class from the remaining classes. This problem becomes more severe when the number of classes is large.

The second category of multi-label learning approaches are based on *Label Ranking* [7, 6, 4], where ranking-based strategy is taken to learn a ranking function of labels from the labeled instances and apply it to obtain a real-valued score for each instance-label pair, then classify each instance by choosing all the labels whose scores are above the given threshold. They achieve state-of-the-art results and are scalable to large-scale data with the recent progress in support vector machine optimization [15, 25, 12, 16]. However, these methods do not explicitly exploit the label correlation, and are suffering from curse of dimensionality. This motivates us to propose a model built up on LaRank SVM [7], while it is able to overcome the limitations.

Another family of multi-label learning methods are based on dimensionality reduction, which assume that all the labels share a common subspace. For example, [35] extended unsupervised latent sematic indexing to make use of multi-label information. [39] proposed Multi-label Dimensionality reduction via Dependence Maximization (MDDM) method to identify a lower-dimensional subspace by maximizing the dependence between the original features and associated class labels. [31] proposed Multi-Label Linear Discriminant Analysis (MLDA) which is an extension of linear discriminant analysis. [27] proposed to construct a hyper-graph on both the data points and labels, and find a subspace to preserve the information of the hyper-graph for classification. [13] proposed Multi-Label Least Square (MLLS) method to extract a common subspace shared among multiple labels. These methods have been proved very effective for multi-label learning. They are also able to deal with the curse of dimensionality. Subspace based methods utilize the correlation between data and labels. However, they do not consider the correlation among labels, which is not uncommon in multi-label data as shown before. In this paper, rather than subspace learning, we propose to do feature selection for multi-label learning, which can be integrated into LaRank SVM [7] coherently. We assume that all the labels share a common subset of features. Due to the close relationship between subspace learning and feature selection, feature selection plays a similar role as subspace learning. Moreover, to capture the correlation among labels, we propose to learn the label correlation at the same time as feature selection.

3. THE PROPOSED METHOD

Since the proposed method is built upon LaRank SVM [7], we first briefly review the formulation of LaRank SVM. It borrowed the large margin idea to multi-label learning and modified SVM to a ranking system of labels. The basic idea is, for each instance, the ranking scores of the labels assigned to the instance should be higher than the ranking scores of the labels not assigned to it. The resulting maximum margin multi-label ranking system is

$$\begin{aligned} \min_{\mathbf{w},\boldsymbol{\xi}} \quad & \frac{1}{2}\sum_{k=1}^{c}||\mathbf{w}_k||^2 + C\sum_{i=1}^{n}\frac{1}{|y_i||\bar{y}_i|}\sum_{(k,l)\in y_i\times\bar{y}_i}\xi_{ikl} \\ s.t. \quad & \langle \mathbf{w}_k^T - \mathbf{w}_l^T, \mathbf{x}_i\rangle \geq 1 - \xi_{ikl}, (k,l)\in y_i\times\bar{y}_i \\ & \xi_{ikl}\geq 0, i = 1,\ldots,n, \end{aligned} \tag{1}$$

where $C > 0$ is a regularization parameter. Note that a bias term can be incorporated into the form by expanding the weight vector and input feature vector as $\mathbf{w}_k \leftarrow [\mathbf{w}_k^T, b_k]^T$ and $\mathbf{x} \leftarrow [\mathbf{x}^T, 1]^T$. It has been shown that LaRank SVM performs better than SVM [7, 27]. LaRank SVM considers the ordinal relation among labels, which is first-order information. However, LaRank SVM does not consider the label correlation, which is a kind of second-order information among labels. Moreover, when the dimensionality of the data is very high, LaRank SVM does not perform as good as some dimensionality reduction based methods [27, 13]. This motivates us to consider the label correlation and do feature selection (dimensionality reduction) simultaneously in this paper.

3.1 Incorporating Label Correlation

To capture the correlation between labels, we place a matrix-variate Normal distribution prior [10] on the weight vectors of LaRank SVM, i.e., $\mathbf{W} = [\mathbf{w}_1, \ldots, \mathbf{w}_c]$,

$$p(\mathbf{W}|\mathbf{D}) = \mathcal{MN}(\mathbf{0}_{d\times c}, \mathbf{I}_d\otimes\mathbf{D}), \tag{2}$$

where $\mathbf{0}_{d\times c}$ denotes a $d\times c$ zero matrix, $\mathbf{I}_d$ is a $d\times d$ identity matrix, and $\mathcal{MN}(\mathbf{X}|\mathbf{M}, \mathbf{A}\otimes\mathbf{B})$ denotes a matrix-variate normal distribution with mean $\mathbf{M}\in\mathbb{R}^{a\times b}$, row covariance matrix $\mathbf{A}\in\mathbb{R}^{a\times a}$, and column covariance matrix $\mathbf{B}\in\mathbb{R}^{b\times b}$. The probability density function of the matrix-variate normal distribution is defined as

$$\begin{aligned} & p(\mathbf{X}|\mathbf{M}, \mathbf{A}, \mathbf{B}) \\ = & \frac{\exp\left\{-\frac{1}{2}\mathrm{tr}(\mathbf{A}^{-1}(\mathbf{X}-\mathbf{M})\mathbf{B}^{-1}(\mathbf{X}-\mathbf{M})^T)\right\}}{(2\pi)^{ab/2}|\mathbf{A}|^{b/2}|\mathbf{B}|^{a/2}}. \end{aligned} \tag{3}$$

Note that similar prior has been used for multi-task learning [37] and transfer distance metric learning [38]. Plug Eq.(3) into Eq.(2), it can be simplified as

$$p(\mathbf{W}|\mathbf{D}) = \frac{\exp\left\{-\frac{1}{2}\mathrm{tr}(\mathbf{W}\mathbf{D}^{-1}\mathbf{W}^T)\right\}}{(2\pi)^{dc/2}|\mathbf{D}|^{d/2}}. \tag{4}$$

Since the column covariance matrix $\mathbf{D}$ models the correlation between any two $\mathbf{w}_k$, it is able to capture the correlation of different labels.

3.2 Multi-Label Feature Selection

As to feature selection, we introduce a binary variable $p_j\in\{0,1\}, j = 1,\ldots,d$ for each feature, such that if $p_j = 1$, then the jth feature is selected. Otherwise, it is discarded. Our goal is to find a subset of features, such that the the label correlation regularized loss of the LaRank SVM in Eq.(1) is minimized,

$$\begin{aligned} \min_{\mathbf{w},\mathbf{D},\boldsymbol{\xi},\mathbf{p}} \quad & \frac{1}{2}\sum_{k=1}^{c}||\mathbf{w}_k||_2^2 + C\sum_{i=1}^{n}\frac{1}{|y_i||\bar{y}_i|}\sum_{(k,l)\in y_i\times\bar{y}_i}\xi_{ikl} \\ & -\frac{\mu}{2}\log p(\mathbf{W}|\mathbf{D}), \\ s.t. \quad & \langle \mathbf{w}_k^T - \mathbf{w}_l^T, \mathbf{p}\circ\mathbf{x}_i\rangle \geq 1 - \xi_{ikl}, (k,l)\in y_i\times\bar{y}_i \\ & \xi_{ikl}\geq 0, i = 1,\ldots,n, \\ & \mathbf{p}\in\{0,1\}^d, \mathbf{p}^T\mathbf{1} = m, \end{aligned} \tag{5}$$

where $\mathbf{p}\circ\mathbf{x}_i$ is element-wise Hadamard product which performs feature selection. Note that the first two terms in the objective function can be seen as the negative log likelihood of some kind of distribution on $\mathbf{w}_k$, and the third term is the negative logarithm of a prior on $\mathbf{w}_k$. Hence the whole objective function can be seen as a negative logarithm of the posterior on $\mathbf{w}_k$. This is in spirit the same as maximum a posterior principle. Unfortunately, the term $-\frac{\mu}{2}\log p(\mathbf{W}|\mathbf{D}) \propto \frac{1}{2}\mathrm{tr}(\mathbf{W}\mathbf{D}^{-1}\mathbf{W}^T) - \frac{d}{2}\log|\mathbf{D}| - \frac{dc}{2}\log(2\pi)$ is not easy to optimize since it is non-convex. In this paper, we turn to solve the following similar problem,

$$\begin{aligned} \min_{\mathbf{w},\mathbf{D},\boldsymbol{\xi},\mathbf{p}} \quad & \frac{1}{2}\sum_{k=1}^{c}||\mathbf{w}_k||_2^2 + C\sum_{i=1}^{n}\frac{1}{|y_i||\bar{y}_i|}\sum_{(k,l)\in y_i\times\bar{y}_i}\xi_{ikl} \\ & +\frac{\mu}{2}\mathrm{tr}(\mathbf{W}\mathbf{D}^{-1}\mathbf{W}^T), \\ s.t. \quad & \langle \mathbf{w}_k^T - \mathbf{w}_l^T, \mathbf{p}\circ\mathbf{x}_i\rangle \geq 1 - \xi_{ikl}, (k,l)\in y_i\times\bar{y}_i \\ & \xi_{ikl}\geq 0, i = 1,\ldots,n, \\ & \mathbf{p}\in\{0,1\}^d, \mathbf{p}^T\mathbf{1} = m, \\ & \mathbf{D}\succeq 0, \mathrm{tr}(\mathbf{D}) = 1, \end{aligned} \tag{6}$$

We call Eq.(6) as *Correlated Multi-Label Feature Selection* (CMLFS).

Both Eq. (5) and Eq.(6) are mixed integer programming [2]. Compared with Eq.(5), although Eq.(6) sacrifices the sound probabilistic interpretation to some extent, it has a more desirable optimization property, which is stated in the following theorems.

Theorem 3.1 *Given* $\mathbf{p}$, *the optimization problem in Eq.(6) is jointly convex in* $\mathbf{w}_k$ *and* $\mathbf{D}$.

PROOF. Please refer to [37]. □

It is worth noting that there are two special instances of the proposed model in Eq.(6). First, if we set $\mu = 0$, then the model in Eq.(6) reduces to multi-label feature selection without learning the label correlation. In the rest of this paper, we refer to this special model as *Multi-Label Feature Selection* (MLFS). Second, if we fix $\mathbf{p} = \mathbf{1}$, then the model in Eq.(6) can be seen as an extension of label rank SVM, which is not only learning to rank the labels, but also learning the correlation among labels. This special model is referred to as *Correlated Label Rank SVM* (CLaRank SVM). It is obvious that if we set $\mu = 0$ and fix $\mathbf{p} = \mathbf{1}$ simultaneously, then Eq.(6) exactly reduces to original label rank SVM in Eq.(1). In the sequel, we will present the optimization algorithm to solve Eq. (6).

3.3 The Dual Problem

Instead of directly optimizing the problem in Eq. (6), we choose to optimize its dual problem [2].

Theorem 3.2 *The dual of the problem in Eq. (6) is*

$$\min_{\mathbf{D},\mathbf{p}} \max_{\alpha} \quad \sum_{i=1}^{n} \sum_{(k,l)\in y_i\times\bar{y}_i} \alpha_{ikl}$$
$$-\frac{1}{2}\sum_{k,l=1}^{c} R_{kl}^{-1} \sum_{i,j=1}^{n} \beta_{ik}\beta_{jl}(\mathbf{p}\circ\mathbf{x}_i)^T(\mathbf{p}\circ\mathbf{x}_j),$$
$$s.t. \quad 0 \le \alpha_{ikl} \le \frac{C}{|y_i||\bar{y}_i|}$$
$$\mathbf{p}\in\{0,1\}^d, \mathbf{p}^T\mathbf{1} = m$$
$$\mathbf{D}\succeq 0, tr(\mathbf{D}) = 1, \tag{7}$$

where $\mathbf{R} = \mathbf{I} + \mu\mathbf{D}^{-1}$, $\mathbf{R}^{-1}$ *is the inverse matrix of* $\mathbf{R}$, *and* R_{kl}^{-1} *is the* (k,l)*th entry of* $\mathbf{R}^{-1}$, β_{ik} *is defined as*

$$\beta_{ik} = \sum_{(p,q)\in y_i\times\bar{y}_i} \gamma_{ipq}^{k}\alpha_{ipq}, \tag{8}$$

and γ_{ipq}^{k} *is defined as,*

$$\gamma_{ipq}^{k} = \begin{cases} 1, & if\ p = k \\ -1, & if\ q = k \\ 0, & if\ p \ne k\ and\ q \ne k \end{cases}. \tag{9}$$

Moreover, we have

$$\sum_{l=1}^{c} R_{kl}\mathbf{w}_l = \sum_{i=1}^{n} \beta_{ik}\mathbf{p}\circ\mathbf{x}_i. \tag{10}$$

For the sake of notional simplicity, we denote the objective function of Eq.(7) by $f(\boldsymbol{\alpha}, \mathbf{D}, \mathbf{p})$, and define

$$\begin{aligned} \mathcal{D} &= \{\mathbf{D}\succeq 0, \mathrm{tr}(\mathbf{D}) = 1\}, \\ \mathcal{P} &= \left\{\mathbf{p}\in\{0,1\}^d, \mathbf{p}^T\mathbf{1} = m\right\}, \\ \mathcal{A} &= \left\{\boldsymbol{\alpha}|0 \le \alpha_{ikl} \le \frac{C}{|y_i||\bar{y}_i|}, k = 1,\dots,c\right\}. \end{aligned} \tag{11}$$

Then the optimization problem in Eq.(7) can be rewritten as

$$\min_{\mathbf{D}\in\mathcal{D},\mathbf{p}\in\mathcal{P}} \max_{\boldsymbol{\alpha}\in\mathcal{A}} f(\boldsymbol{\alpha}, \mathbf{D}, \mathbf{p}). \tag{12}$$

By interchanging the order of $\min_{\mathbf{D}\in\mathcal{D},\mathbf{p}\in\mathcal{P}}$ and $\max_{\boldsymbol{\alpha}_k\in\mathcal{A}_k}$ in Eq. (12), we obtain

$$\max_{\boldsymbol{\alpha}\in\mathcal{A}} \min_{\mathbf{D}\in\mathcal{D},\mathbf{p}\in\mathcal{P}} f(\boldsymbol{\alpha}, \mathbf{D}, \mathbf{p}). \tag{13}$$

According to the minimax theorem [18], the optimal objective value of Eq.(7) is an upper bound of that of Eq.(13).

The problem in Eq. (13) is indeed a convex-concave optimization problem, and therefore its optimal solution is a saddle point for the function $f(\boldsymbol{\alpha}, \mathbf{D}, \mathbf{p})$ subject to the constraints in Eq. (11). Let $(\boldsymbol{\alpha}^*, \mathbf{D}^*, \mathbf{p}^*)$ be optimal to Eq. (13). For any feasible $\boldsymbol{\alpha}$ and $\mathbf{p}$, we have

$$f(\boldsymbol{\alpha}, \mathbf{D}^*, \mathbf{p}^*) \le f(\boldsymbol{\alpha}^*, \mathbf{D}^*, \mathbf{p}^*) \le f(\boldsymbol{\alpha}^*, \mathbf{D}, \mathbf{p}). \tag{14}$$

Borrowing the idea used in [5] [20] [28], we add an additional variable $\theta\in\mathbb{R}$, then the problem in Eq. (13) can be reformulated equivalently as follows

$$\max_{\boldsymbol{\alpha}\in\mathcal{A}} \min_{\mathbf{D}\in\mathcal{D}} \max_{\theta} -\theta$$
$$\mathrm{s.t.}\ \theta \ge -f(\boldsymbol{\alpha}, \mathbf{D}, \mathbf{p}^t), \mathbf{p}^t\in\mathcal{P}. \tag{15}$$

Note that each $\mathbf{p}^t\in\mathcal{P}$ corresponds to one constraint, so the above optimization problem has $\binom{d}{m}$ constraints. The optimization problem in Eq.(15) is called Quadratically Constrained Linear Programming (QCLP) [2].

We introduce a set of Lagrange multipliers $\lambda_t \ge 0$, each of which corresponds to an inequality constraint $\theta \ge -f(\boldsymbol{\alpha}, \mathbf{D}, \mathbf{p}^t)$. Then the Lagrange function of Eq.(6) is given by

$$\mathcal{L}(\theta) = -\theta + \sum_{t=1}^{|\mathcal{P}|} \lambda_t(\theta + f(\boldsymbol{\alpha}, \mathbf{D}, \mathbf{p}^t)). \tag{16}$$

Taking the partial derivative of $\mathcal{L}$ with respect θ and setting it to zero, we obtain

$$\frac{\partial\mathcal{L}}{\partial\theta} = -1 + \sum_{t=1}^{|\mathcal{P}|} \lambda_t = 0. \tag{17}$$

Plugging Eq.(17) back into Eq.(15), we get the dual problem of the inner maximization problem in Eq(15), we obtain the following problem,

$$\begin{aligned} &\max_{\boldsymbol{\alpha}\in\mathcal{A}} \min_{\mathbf{D}\in\mathcal{D},\lambda_t\in\Lambda} \sum_{t=1}^{|\mathcal{P}|} \lambda_t f(\boldsymbol{\alpha}, \mathbf{D}, \mathbf{p}^t) \\ = &\min_{\mathbf{D}\in\mathcal{D},\lambda_t\in\Lambda} \max_{\boldsymbol{\alpha}\in\mathcal{A}} \sum_{t=1}^{|\mathcal{P}|} \lambda_t f(\boldsymbol{\alpha}, \mathbf{D}, \mathbf{p}^t), \end{aligned} \tag{18}$$

where $\Lambda = \{\lambda_t | \sum_{t=1}^{|\mathcal{P}|} \lambda_t = 1, \lambda_t \ge 0\}$. The equality holds due to the fact that the objective function is concave in $\boldsymbol{\alpha}$ and convex in $\mathbf{D}$ and $\boldsymbol{\lambda}$.

3.4 Alternating Optimization

Actually, Eq. (18) can be seen as a multiple kernel learning problem [22], where the base kernels and kernel weights are the same for all the labels. It is worth noting that [29] proposed a multiple kernel learning with multiple labels. Their method is different from ours. In their method, the kernel weights are different for each label. Moreover, they did not consider the label correlation. As a result, their algorithm cannot be adapted to our problem.

Following the technique used in the state-of-the-art single-label multiple kernel learning [22], we optimize Eq. (18) in an alternative way. In particular, we alternatively solve one variable such as $\boldsymbol{\alpha}$ given the other variables such as $\mathbf{D}$ and $\boldsymbol{\lambda}$ fixed.

3.4.1 *Compute $\boldsymbol{\alpha}$ when $\boldsymbol{\lambda}$ and $\mathbf{D}$ are fixed*

Fixing $\mathbf{D}$ and $\boldsymbol{\lambda}$, the optimization problem in Eq.(18) reduces to

$$\min_{\boldsymbol{\alpha}} \quad g(\boldsymbol{\alpha})$$
$$\mathrm{s.t.} \quad 0 \le \alpha_{ikl} \le \frac{C}{|y_i||\bar{y}_i|}, \tag{19}$$

where $g(\boldsymbol{\alpha})$ is defined as

$$\begin{aligned} g(\boldsymbol{\alpha}) &= \frac{1}{2}\sum_{k,l=1}^{c} R_{kl}^{-1} \sum_{i,j=1}^{n} \beta_{ik}\beta_{jl}(\bar{\mathbf{p}}\circ\bar{\mathbf{x}}_i)^T(\bar{\mathbf{p}}\circ\bar{\mathbf{x}}_j) \\ &- \sum_{i=1}^{n} \sum_{(k,l)\in y_i\times\bar{y}_i} \alpha_{ikl}, \end{aligned} \tag{20}$$

where $\bar{\mathbf{p}} = [\mathbf{p}_1^T, \dots, \mathbf{p}_{|\mathcal{P}|}^T]^T$ and $\bar{\mathbf{x}}_i = [\lambda_1\mathbf{x}_i, \dots, \lambda_{|\mathcal{P}|}\mathbf{x}_i^T]^T$.

The above optimization problem can be efficiently solved by dual coordinate descent method [12]. It updates one variable at a time by minimizing a single variable subproblem. In particular, it picks one variable α_{ikl} at a time and solves the following single variable subproblem while keeping all the other variables fixed,

$$\begin{aligned} \min_{\alpha} \quad & g(\boldsymbol{\alpha} + d\mathbf{e}_{ikl}), \\ \text{s.t.} \quad & 0 \leq \alpha_{ikl} \leq \frac{C}{|y_i||\bar{y}_i|}, \end{aligned} \tag{21}$$

where $\mathbf{e}_{ikl} = (0, \ldots, 0, 1, 0, \ldots, 0)^T$. The objective function of Eq.(21) is a simple quadratic function of d,

$$\begin{aligned} g(\boldsymbol{\alpha} + d\mathbf{e}_{ikl}) &= \frac{S_{kl}}{2}(\bar{\mathbf{p}} \circ \bar{\mathbf{x}}_i)^T(\bar{\mathbf{p}} \circ \bar{\mathbf{x}}_i)d^2 \\ &+ \nabla_{ikl}g(\boldsymbol{\alpha})d + \text{const}, \end{aligned} \tag{22}$$

where $S_{kl} = R_{kk}^{-1} + R_{ll}^{-1} - 2R_{kl}^{-1}$, const is a constant which is independent on d, and $\nabla_{ikl}g(\boldsymbol{\alpha})$ can be computed as

$$\begin{aligned} & \nabla_{ikl}g(\boldsymbol{\alpha}) \\ = & \sum_{q=1}^{c}(R_{kq}^{-1} - R_{lq}^{-1})\sum_{j=1}^{n}\beta_{jq}(\bar{\mathbf{p}} \circ \bar{\mathbf{x}}_j)^T(\bar{\mathbf{p}} \circ \bar{\mathbf{x}}_i) - 1 \\ = & \sum_{q=1}^{c}(R_{kq}^{-1} - R_{lq}^{-1})(\sum_{l=1}^{c}R_{ql}\mathbf{w}_l)^T(\bar{\mathbf{p}} \circ \bar{\mathbf{x}}_i) - 1 \\ = & \sum_{q=1}^{c}(R_{kq}^{-1} - R_{lq}^{-1})\mathbf{u}_q^T(\bar{\mathbf{p}} \circ \bar{\mathbf{x}}_i) - 1 \\ = & (\mathbf{w}_k - \mathbf{w}_l)^T(\bar{\mathbf{p}} \circ \bar{\mathbf{x}}_i) - 1, \end{aligned} \tag{23}$$

where $\mathbf{u}_k = \sum_{l=1}^{c} R_{kl}\mathbf{w}_l$. It can be easily seen that Eq.(21) has an optimum at $d = 0$ if and only if

$$\nabla_{ikl}^{P}g(\boldsymbol{\alpha}) = 0, \tag{24}$$

where $\frac{\partial g(\boldsymbol{\alpha})}{\partial \alpha_{ikl}}$ is the projected gradient

$$\nabla_{ikl}^{P}g(\boldsymbol{\alpha}) = \begin{cases} \nabla_{ikl}g(\boldsymbol{\alpha}), & \text{if } 0 < \alpha_{ikl} < \frac{C}{|y_i||\bar{y}_i|} \\ \min(0, \nabla_{ikl}g(\boldsymbol{\alpha})), & \text{if } \alpha_{ikl} = 0 \\ \max(0, \nabla_{ikl}g(\boldsymbol{\alpha})), & \text{if } \alpha_{ikl} = \frac{C}{|y_i||\bar{y}_i|} \end{cases}. \tag{25}$$

If Eq.(25) holds, we do not need to update α_{ikl} and directly move to the next variable. Otherwise, the optimal solution of Eq.(21) is

$$\alpha_{ikl}^{*} = \min(\max(\alpha_{ikl} - \frac{\nabla_{ikl}^{P}g(\boldsymbol{\alpha})}{S_{kl}(\bar{\mathbf{p}} \circ \bar{\mathbf{x}}_i)^T(\bar{\mathbf{p}} \circ \bar{\mathbf{x}}_i)}, 0), \frac{C}{|y_i||\bar{y}_i|}). \tag{26}$$

This means the subproblem can be solved analytically that ensures the efficiency of the coordinate descent method. Here, we need to calculate $(\bar{\mathbf{p}} \circ \bar{\mathbf{x}}_i)^T(\bar{\mathbf{p}} \circ \bar{\mathbf{x}}_i)$ and $\nabla_{ikl}^{P}g(\boldsymbol{\alpha})$. First, $(\bar{\mathbf{p}} \circ \bar{\mathbf{x}}_i)^T(\bar{\mathbf{p}} \circ \bar{\mathbf{x}}_i)$ can be pre-computed and stored in the memory. Second, to evaluate $\nabla_{ikl}^{P}g(\boldsymbol{\alpha})$ using Eq.(23), we only need to maintain $\mathbf{u}_k$ by

$$\begin{aligned} \mathbf{u}_k &= \mathbf{u}_k + (\alpha_{ikl}^{*} - \alpha_{ikl})\bar{\mathbf{p}} \circ \bar{\mathbf{x}}_i \\ \mathbf{u}_l &= \mathbf{u}_l - (\alpha_{ikl}^{*} - \alpha_{ikl})\bar{\mathbf{p}} \circ \bar{\mathbf{x}}_i. \end{aligned} \tag{27}$$

The dual coordinate descent method for optimizing $\boldsymbol{\alpha}$ is summarized in Algorithm 1.

Theorem 3.3 *The $\boldsymbol{\alpha}$ calculated by Algorithm 1 globally converges to an optimal solution $\boldsymbol{\alpha}^*$. The convergence rate is at least linear. In other words, there is $0 < \tau < 1$ and an iteration t_0, such that*

$$g(\boldsymbol{\alpha}^{t+1}) - g(\boldsymbol{\alpha}^*) \leq \tau(g(\boldsymbol{\alpha}^t) - g(\boldsymbol{\alpha}^*)). \tag{28}$$

PROOF. Please refer to [12]. □

Algorithm 1 Dual Coordinate Descent for Optimizing $\boldsymbol{\alpha}$

Input: C and m;
Output: $\boldsymbol{\alpha}$;
Initialize $\boldsymbol{\alpha} = 0$ and $\mathbf{w}_k = 0, k = 1, \ldots, c$;
repeat
  for $i = 1, \ldots, n$ and $(k, l) \in y_i \times \bar{y}_i$ **do**
    Calculate $G = R_{kl}^{-1}(\mathbf{u}_k - \mathbf{u}_l)^T\mathbf{x}_i - 1$;
    Calculate $PG = \begin{cases} G, & \text{if } 0 < \alpha_{ikl} < \frac{C}{|y_i||\bar{y}_i|} \\ \min(0, G), & \text{if } \alpha_{ikl} = 0 \\ \max(0, G), & \text{if } \alpha_{ikl} = \frac{C}{|y_i||\bar{y}_i|} \end{cases}$.
    if $|PG| \neq 0$ **then**
      $\alpha_{ikl}^* = \min(\max(\alpha_{ikl} - \frac{PG}{S_{kl}(\bar{\mathbf{p}} \circ \bar{\mathbf{x}}_i)^T(\bar{\mathbf{p}} \circ \bar{\mathbf{x}}_i)}, 0), \frac{C}{|y_i||\bar{y}_i|})$
      Calculate $\mathbf{u}_k = \mathbf{u}_k + (\alpha_{ikl}^* - \alpha_{ikl})\bar{\mathbf{p}} \circ \bar{\mathbf{x}}_i$
      Calculate $\mathbf{u}_l = \mathbf{u}_l - (\alpha_{ikl}^* - \alpha_{ikl})\bar{\mathbf{p}} \circ \bar{\mathbf{x}}_i$
    end if
  end for
until converge

The linear convergence result is remarkable, that means Algorithm can achieves an ϵ-accurate solution $\boldsymbol{\alpha}$ in $O(\log(\frac{1}{\epsilon}))$ iterations.

3.4.2 Compute D when α and λ are fixed

Given $\boldsymbol{\alpha}$ and $\boldsymbol{\lambda}$, the optimization problem in Eq.(6) boils down to

$$\begin{aligned} \min_{\mathbf{D}} \quad & \text{tr}(\mathbf{W}\mathbf{D}^{-1}\mathbf{W}^T), \\ s.t. \quad & \mathbf{D} \succeq 0, \text{tr}(\mathbf{D}) = 1, \end{aligned} \tag{29}$$

which is a semi-definite programming (SDP) [2]. Fortunately, it can be solved by spectral method as stated in the following theorem.

Theorem 3.4 *Let $\mathbf{C} = \mathbf{W}^T\mathbf{W}$, the optimal solution of Eq.(29) is*

$$\mathbf{D} = \frac{\mathbf{C}^{\frac{1}{2}}}{tr(\mathbf{C}^{\frac{1}{2}})}, \tag{30}$$

and the optimal value equals to $(tr(\mathbf{C}^{\frac{1}{2}}))^2$

PROOF. The proof is similar to Theorem 4.6 in [9]. Let $\mathbf{D} = \mathbf{A}\text{diag}(\boldsymbol{\lambda})\mathbf{A}^T$ where $\boldsymbol{\lambda} = [\lambda_1, \ldots, \lambda_c] \in \mathbb{R}^d$, then

$$\begin{aligned} & \sum_{j=1}^{d}\mathbf{w}^j\mathbf{D}^{-1}(\mathbf{w}^j)^T = \text{tr}(\mathbf{W}\mathbf{D}^{-1}\mathbf{W}^T) \\ = & \text{tr}(\mathbf{W}\mathbf{A}\text{diag}(\boldsymbol{\lambda})^{-1}\mathbf{A}^T\mathbf{W}^T) \\ = & \text{tr}(\text{diag}(\lambda)^{-1}\mathbf{A}^T\mathbf{W}^T\mathbf{W}\mathbf{A}) \\ = & \sum_{k=1}^{c}\frac{\mathbf{a}_k^T\mathbf{W}^T\mathbf{W}\mathbf{a}_k}{\lambda_k} \geq (\sum_{k=1}^{c}||\mathbf{W}\mathbf{a}_k||_2)^2 \end{aligned}$$

Next, we have

$$\begin{aligned} &||\mathbf{W}\mathbf{a}_k||_2^2 = \mathbf{a}_k^T\mathbf{W}^T\mathbf{W}\mathbf{a}_k \\ =\ & \mathbf{a}_k^T\mathbf{C}\mathbf{a}_k = (\mathbf{a}_k^T\mathbf{C}\mathbf{a}_k)(\mathbf{a}_k^T\mathbf{a}_k) \\ =\ & \text{tr}(\mathbf{C}^{\frac{1}{2}}\mathbf{a}_k\mathbf{a}_k^T\mathbf{C}^{\frac{1}{2}})\text{tr}(\mathbf{a}_k\mathbf{a}_k^T) \\ \geq\ & \text{tr}(\mathbf{C}^{\frac{1}{2}}\mathbf{a}_k\mathbf{a}_k^T\mathbf{C}^{\frac{1}{2}}\mathbf{a}_k\mathbf{a}_k^T) \\ =\ & \text{tr}(\mathbf{a}_k^T\mathbf{C}^{\frac{1}{2}}\mathbf{a}_k\mathbf{a}_k^T\mathbf{C}^{\frac{1}{2}}\mathbf{a}_k) = (\mathbf{a}_k^T\mathbf{C}^{\frac{1}{2}}\mathbf{a}_k)^2 \end{aligned}$$

since $\text{tr}(\mathbf{A})\text{tr}(\mathbf{B}) \geq \text{tr}(\mathbf{AB})$ if $\mathbf{A}$ and $\mathbf{B}$ are positive semi-definite. The equality holds if and only if $\mathbf{C}^{\frac{1}{2}}\mathbf{a}_k\mathbf{a}_k^T = \mu\mathbf{a}_k\mathbf{a}_k^T$ which implies that $\mathbf{C}^{\frac{1}{2}}\mathbf{a}_k = \mu\mathbf{a}_k$, that is, $\mathbf{a}_k$ is an eigenvector of $\mathbf{C}^{\frac{1}{2}}$. The optimal μ is $\text{tr}(C^{\frac{1}{2}})$. Hence we obtain

$$\begin{aligned} &\sum_{j=1}^{d}\mathbf{w}^j\mathbf{D}^{-1}(\mathbf{w}^j)^T \geq (\sum_{k=1}^{c}\mathbf{a}_k^T\mathbf{C}^{\frac{1}{2}}\mathbf{a}_k)^2 \\ =\ & (\text{tr}(\mathbf{A}^T\mathbf{C}^{\frac{1}{2}}\mathbf{A}))^2 = (\text{tr}(\mathbf{C}^{\frac{1}{2}}))^2 \end{aligned}$$

Consequently, the optimal $\mathbf{D} = \frac{\mathbf{C}^{\frac{1}{2}}}{\text{tr}(\mathbf{C}^{\frac{1}{2}})}$. This completes the proof. □

3.4.3 Compute $\boldsymbol{\lambda}$ when $\boldsymbol{\alpha}$ and $\mathbf{D}$ are fixed

Let $h(\boldsymbol{\lambda}) = \sum_t \lambda_t f(\boldsymbol{\alpha}, \mathbf{D}, \mathbf{p}^t)$, we denote the sub-gradient of $h(\boldsymbol{\lambda})$ with respect to λ_t by $\nabla_{\lambda_t}h(\boldsymbol{\lambda})$, which is calculated as

$$\nabla_{\lambda_t}h(\boldsymbol{\lambda}) = -\frac{1}{2}\sum_{k,l=1}^{c}R_{kl}^{-1}\sum_{i,j=1}^{n}\beta_{ik}\beta_{jl}(\mathbf{p}^t\circ\mathbf{x}_i)^T(\mathbf{p}^t\circ\mathbf{x}_j). \quad (31)$$

Following [22], we use projected gradient descent to update the kernel weights λ_t. Note that other techniques such as semi-infinite linear programming [26] and extended level method [32] can also be adopted.

3.5 Cutting Plane Acceleration

Up to now, we have presented the algorithm for optimizing Eq.(18). However, given $\mathcal{P}$, the problem has optimization variables $(\boldsymbol{\alpha}, \mathbf{D}, \boldsymbol{\lambda})$ with $\binom{d}{m}$ constraints, which is impractical to solve. Fortunately, cutting plane technique [17] enables us to deal with this problem, which keeps a polynomial sized subset Ω of working constraints and computes the optimal solution to Eq. (18) subject to the constraints in Ω. In detail, the algorithm adds the most violated constraint in Eq. (15) into Ω in each iteration. In this way, a successively strengthening approximation of the original problem is solved. And the algorithm terminates when no constraints in Eq. (15) is violated.

The remaining thing is how to find the most violated constraint in each iteration. Since the feasibility of a constraint is measured by the corresponding value of θ, the most violated constraint is the one which owns the largest θ. Hence, it could be calculated as follows

$$\begin{aligned} &\arg\max_{\mathbf{p}\in\mathcal{P}} -f(\boldsymbol{\alpha}, \mathbf{D}, \mathbf{p}) \\ =\ & \arg\max_{\mathbf{p}\in\mathcal{P}}\sum_{k,l=1}^{c}R_{kl}\sum_{i,j=1}^{n}\beta_{ik}\beta_{jl}(\mathbf{p}\circ\mathbf{x}_i)^T(\mathbf{p}\circ\mathbf{x}_j) \\ =\ & \arg\max_{\mathbf{p}\in\mathcal{P}}\sum_{j=1}^{d}s_j p_j, \end{aligned} \quad (32)$$

where $s_j = \sum_{k,l=1}^{c}R_{kl}\boldsymbol{\beta}_k^T(\mathbf{x}^j)^T\mathbf{x}^j\boldsymbol{\beta}_l$ and $\boldsymbol{\beta}_k = [\beta_{1k}, \ldots, \beta_{nk}]^T$. According to [28], its optimal solution can be obtained without any numeric optimization solver. Instead, it can be solved by first sorting s_j and then setting the first m numbers corresponding to d_j to 1 and the rests to 0.

We summarize the algorithm to solve the problem in Eq. (18) in Algorithm 2. Note that the final selected features are the union set of the features corresponding to each constraint $\mathbf{p}^t \in \Omega_T$.

Algorithm 2 Correlated Multi-Label Feature Selection

```
Input: C and m;
Output: α and Ω;
Initialize α = 0 and t = 1;
Find the most violated constraint p^1, and set Ω_1 = {p^1};
repeat
  Initialize λ = (1/t)1;
  repeat
    Solve for α using Algorithm 1;
    Solve for D using Eq.(30);
    Solve for λ using sub-gradient descent as in Eq. (31);
  until converge
  Find the most violated constraint p^{t+1} and set Ω_{t+1} =
  Ω_t ∪ p^{t+1};
  t = t + 1;
until converge
```

3.6 Convergence Analysis

We analyze the convergence property of Algorithm 2.

Theorem 3.5 *Let $(\alpha^*, \mathbf{D}^*, \theta^*)$ be the global optimal solution of Eq. (15), $l_t = \max_{1\leq j\leq t}\min_{\boldsymbol{\alpha}\in\mathcal{A},\mathbf{D}\in\mathcal{D}}, -f(\boldsymbol{\alpha}, \mathbf{D}, \mathbf{p}^j)$ and $u_t = \min_{1\leq j\leq t}\max_{\mathbf{p}\in\mathcal{P}} -f(\boldsymbol{\alpha}^j, \mathbf{D}^j, \mathbf{p})$, then*

$$l_t \leq \theta^* \leq u_t. \quad (33)$$

With the number of iteration t increasing, the sequence $\{l_t\}$ is monotonically increasing and the sequence $\{u_t\}$ is monotonically decreasing.

Proof. Please refer to [28]. □

Since the number of constraints in $\mathcal{P}$ is finite, i.e., $\binom{d}{m}$, based on Theorem 3.5, the algorithm will converge within finite number of iterations. Moreover, we can use the gap between l_t and u_t to trace the convergence of Algorithm 2. When the gap is smaller than a predefined tolerance ϵ, we stop the algorithm. Empirical study shows that the algorithm converges within 10 outer-iterations in our experiments.

3.7 Time Complexity Analysis

In each outer iteration of Algorithm 2, it needs to find the most violated $\mathbf{p}$. It can be obtained exactly by finding the m largest ones from d coefficients s_j, which takes only $O(m\log d)$ time. In the inner iteration of Algorithm 2, it solves a minimax problem by alternating optimization. Its complexity is proportional to the sum of the complexity of dual coordinate descent and the complexity of calculating $\mathbf{D}$. The complexity of dual coordinate descent is $O(c^2ns)$, where s is the average number of nonzero features among all the training samples. The complexity of calculating $\mathbf{D}$ is $O(dc)$. Hence the total time complexity of the proposed method is $O(T(c^2ns+dc+m\log d))$, where T is the number of iterations needed to converge, Thus, the proposed method is computationally efficient for large-scale, high dimensional data.

3.8 Set Size Prediction

So far we have only developed a ranking system. To obtain the final labels of each instance, we need to design a label set size predictor $s(\mathbf{x})$. Following [7], we turn to learn a threshold function $t(\mathbf{x})$, which differentiates labels in the target set from others. Given the threshold function, the predictor of the set size is quite straightforward: $s(\mathbf{x}) = |\{k|\mathbf{w}_k^T\mathbf{x} > t(\mathbf{x})\}|$. The remaining problem is how to learn $t(\mathbf{x})$. We formulate it as a regression problem. In detail, given a training instance $\mathbf{x}_i$, its label ranking scores are $\mathbf{w}_1^T\mathbf{x}, \ldots, \mathbf{w}_c^T\mathbf{x}$, we define the corresponding threshold $t_i = t(\mathbf{x}_i)$ by

$$t(\mathbf{x}_i) = \frac{1}{2}(\min_{k\in y_i} \mathbf{w}_k^T\mathbf{x}_i + \max_{l\in \bar{y}_i} \mathbf{w}_l^T\mathbf{x}_i) \qquad (34)$$

Once we generate the thresholds $\{t_i = t(\mathbf{x}_i)\}_{i=1}^n$ for the training set, we can estimate the threshold function $t(\mathbf{x})$ by any regression model. In this paper, we simply use linear regression to estimate $t(\mathbf{x})$.

4. EXPERIMENTS

In this section, we empirically evaluate the effectiveness of the proposed methods. All experiments are performed on a PC with Intel Core i5 3.20G CPU and 4GB RAM and all algorithms in our experiments are implemented in Matlab and C++.

4.1 Data Sets

We carry our experiments on various sets of data, including data sets from LibSVM website[2] and Yahoo[3]. In LibSVM data sets, we choose scene data set [1] and yeast data set [7]. For Yahoo data set [30], we use four categories: Arts, Business, Education, and Health as four data sets. In each category, the sub-categories are the labels for each document. We pre-processed the data sets by removing sub-categories with less than 100 documents and documents with no sub-category. Table 1 summarizes the characteristics of these data sets.

Table 1: Description of the data sets

Datasets	#training	#features	#classes
Scene	2407	294	6
Yeast	2417	103	14
Arts	7441	17973	19
Business	9968	16621	17
Education	11817	20782	14
Health	9109	18430	14

4.2 Evaluation Metrics

To evaluate the performance of different algorithms for multi-label learning, we use three measures: the Area Under the Receiver Operating Characteristic (ROC) Curve (AUC), Micro F1 and Macro F1. For AUC, we first compute the AUC for each class, and then compute the averaged AUC over all the classes. For more details about the measures, please refer to [33].

[2]http://www.csie.ntu.edu.tw/~cjlin/libsvmtools/datasets/multilabel.html
[3]http://www.kecl.ntt.co.jp/as/members/ueda/yahoo.tar.gz

4.3 Parameter Settings

We compare the proposed methods with the related multi-label learning methods and a single-label feature selection method. We choose Fisher score [21] as the representative of single-label feature selection methods. The reason is that our empirical study [8] found that Fisher score is comparable to or even better than the other feature selection methods [34, 24] on the data sets used in our experiments. We will not report the results of MDDM [39] and MLDA [31] because they are not better than MLLS [13]. All the methods and their parameter settings are summarized as follows. By default, the regularization parameter C of SVM type models in all the methods is tune by 5-fold cross validation on the training set via searching the grid $\{10^{-3}, 10^{-2}, \ldots, 10^3\}$.

SVM: linear SVM is used for one-against-all classification individually.

LaRank SVM [7]: The threshold function is learned by linear regression as stated in Section 3.8.

CCA+SVM: Canonical Correlation Analysis is used for dimensionality reduction before SVM. The dimensionality of the subspace is set to $c-1$ where c is the number of classes. The regularization parameter for CCA is tuned by 5-fold cross validation on the training set via searching the grid $\{10^{-5}, 10^{-4}, \ldots, 10^{-1}\}$.

MLLS[4] [13]: The dimensionality of the subspace is set to $c-1$. The two regularization parameters for MLLS is tuned by 5-fold cross validation on the training set by searching the grid $\{10^{-5}, 10^{-4}, \ldots, 10^{-1}\}$.

FS+SVM [21]: Fisher score (FS) is used for each one-against-all binary classification individually, followed with linear SVM. The number of selected features m is tuned by 5-fold cross validation via searching the grid $\{10, 20, \ldots, \lfloor \frac{n}{10} \rfloor \times 10\}$ on Scene and Yeast data sets, and via the grid $\{1000, 2000, \ldots, \lfloor \frac{n}{1000} \rfloor \times 1000\}$ on the Yahoo data sets.

CLaRank SVM: The regularization parameter μ is tuned by 5-fold cross validation on the training set by searching the grid $\{10^{-2}, 10^{-1}, \ldots, 10^2\}$.

MLFS: The m which controls the number of features is also tuned by 5-fold cross validation on the training set over the grid $\{10, 11, \ldots, 20\}$ on scene and yeast data sets, and over the grid $\{1000, 2000, \ldots, 10000\}$ on Yahoo data sets.

CMLFS: The m is tuned the same as above. The regularization parameter μ is tuned the same as CLaRank SVM.

Since learning with small number of labelled data is much more challenging than learning with large number of labelled data, we randomly sample 1000 data points from each data set for training, and the rest for testing. Note that each label is guaranteed to appear in at least one data point of the training set and in at least one data point of the testing set. The process was repeated 10 times and the mean along with standard deviation of measures are reported.

4.4 Classification Results

The classification results of all the methods are shown in Table 2. CMLFS, MLFS and CLaRank SVM are the three methods proposed by us. As is pointed out before, MLFS and CLaRank SVM are two special instances of CMLFS.

[4]http://www.public.asu.edu/šji03/multilabel/

Compared with other methods, these three methods show the best performance. Specifically, CLaRank SVM achieves better results because it considers label correlation. And the good performance of MLFS takes advantage of feature selection. Among these three, CMLFS performs the best. This demonstrates that it is very necessary to combine label correlation and feature selection into classification model simultaneously.

Two state-of-the-art methods, LaRank SVM and MLLS, perform worse than our methods but still are better than the others. LaRank SVM classifies (ranks) all the labels simultaneously. It considers the ordinal (first-order) information between labels, which is beneficial for multi-label learning. MLLS is based on subspace learning, it is able to learn a discriminative subspace for multi-label classification. That is why MLLS generally shows better results than LaRank SVM on Yahoo data sets, which are of high dimensionality.

Let us take a closer look at LaRank SVM in comparison with the proposed methods. CLaRank SVM improves LaRank SVM consistently on all the data sets. The improvement is a result of using the correlation (second-order) information among labels. As we mentioned above, LaRank SVM only considers the first-order information. On the other hand, MLFS performs better than LaRank SVM. The reason is that the feature selection in MLFS helps it avoid the curse of dimensionality.

Comparing MLLS with MLFS, the major problem of MLLS is that it fails to consider the label correlation. Though both MLLS and MLFS involve dimensionality reduction, MLFS is superior to MLLS at most cases because it considers the label rank (first-order information).

CCA+SVM and FS+SVM fail to perform well because both of them are in the fashion of two-stage approach. For CCA+SVM, it first carries out subspace learning and then learns a classification model. FS+SVM does feature selection followed by learning the classifier. Both methods try to deal with high dimensional data but fail to integrate dimensionality reduction and classifier learning into a unified framework. Besides, Fisher score is used in each one-against-all binary classification independently, so the selected features are generally different from each other for each binary classification problem.

4.5 AUC v.s. Number of Features

In this subsection, we study the performance of multi-label learning with respect to the number of selected features. We compare CMLFS and MLFS with the single-label feature selection method, i.e., Fisher score. Since the number of selected features for the CMLFS and MLFS is determined implicitly by m, we increase m gradually and obtain a increasing number of features. Figure 2 depicts the AUC with respect to the increasing number of selected features.

We can see that with a very small number of features, MLFS and CMLFS can achieve very good performance. In contrast, the performance of Fisher score is pretty bad. In fact, the satisfying classification results of Fisher score shown in Table 2 are achieved by selecting almost all the features. This again strengthens the superiorness of the proposed multi-label feature selection methods over single-label feature selection method.

5. CONCLUSION AND FUTURE WORK

In this paper, we present a multi-label feature selection method based on LaRank SVM. It is formulated as quadratically constrained linear programming and solved by cutting plane algorithm, in each iteration of which a minimax optimization problem is solved by dual coordinate descent and stochastic sub-gradient descent alternatively. Its training time is linear in the number of training samples, which enables it applicable to large scale multi-label data.

In our future work, we will study how to solve the feature selection problem in the primal [15, 25]. Moreover, we also plan to study semi-supervised multi-label learning [3].

Acknowledgements

The work was supported in part by NSF IIS-09-05215, U.S. Air Force Office of Scientific Research MURI award FA9550-08-1-0265, and the U.S. Army Research Laboratory under Cooperative Agreement Number W911NF-09-2-0053 (NS-CTA). The views and conclusions contained in this document are those of the authors and should not be interpreted as representing the official policies, either expressed or implied, of the Army Research Laboratory or the U.S. Government. The U.S. Government is authorized to reproduce and distribute reprints for Government purposes notwithstanding any copyright notation here on. We thank the anonymous reviewers for their helpful comments.

6. REFERENCES

[1] M. R. Boutell, J. Luo, X. Shen, and C. M. Brown. Learning multi-label scene classification. *Pattern Recognition*, 37(9):1757–1771, 2004.

[2] S. Boyd and L. Vandenberghe. *Convex optimization.* Cambridge University Press, Cambridge, 2004.

[3] G. Chen, Y. Song, F. Wang, and C. Zhang. Semi-supervised multi-label learning by solving a sylvester equation. In *SDM*, pages 410–419, 2008.

[4] G. Chen, J. Zhang, F. Wang, C. Zhang, and Y. Gao. Efficient multi-label classification with hypergraph regularization. In *CVPR*, pages 1658–1665, 2009.

[5] J. Chen and J. Ye. Training svm with indefinite kernels. In *ICML*, pages 136–143, 2008.

[6] O. Dekel, C. D. Manning, and Y. Singer. Log-linear models for label ranking. In *NIPS*, 2003.

[7] A. Elisseeff and J. Weston. A kernel method for multi-labelled classification. In *NIPS*, pages 681–687, 2001.

[8] Q. Gu, Z. Li, and J. Han. Generalized fisher score for feature selection. In *Proceedings of the International Conference on Uncertainty in Artificial Intelligence*, 2011.

[9] Q. Gu and J. Zhou. Subspace maximum margin clustering. In *CIKM*, pages 1337–1346, 2009.

[10] A. K. Gupta and D. K. Nagar. *Matrix Variate Distributions*, volume 104 of *Monographs and Surveys in Pure and Applied Mathematics.* Chapman Hall/CRC, Florida, 2000.

[11] B. Hariharan, L. Zelnik-Manor, S. V. N. Vishwanathan, and M. Varma. Large scale max-margin multi-label classification with priors. In *ICML*, pages 423–430, 2010.

[12] C.-J. Hsieh, K.-W. Chang, C.-J. Lin, S. S. Keerthi, and S. Sundararajan. A dual coordinate descent method for large-scale linear svm. In *ICML*, pages 408–415, 2008.

Table 2: **The classification results (AUC, Micro F1 and Macro F1) on the six data sets. The higher the measures are, the better the performance is.**

Method	Measure	Scene	Yeast	Arts	Business	Education	Health
SVM	AUC	91.60±0.20	65.63±0.89	73.31±0.38	81.31±1.12	75.15±0.63	82.97±0.33
	Micro F1	68.45±0.84	60.52±0.52	45.47±0.90	76.62±0.46	48.32±1.11	64.89±0.64
	Macro F1	69.78±0.91	46.32±0.64	33.64±0.90	40.37±2.74	38.47±0.92	51.31±1.21
LaRank SVM	AUC	91.85±0.47	66.35±0.58	75.94±0.47	81.38±0.94	77.37±0.72	85.25±0.33
	Micro F1	68.67±1.00	61.55±0.71	46.61±1.28	76.76±1.67	49.68±1.53	67.33±1.23
	Macro F1	69.04±0.87	47.14±0.44	33.67±0.85	40.45±2.29	38.50±2.11	59.51±1.36
CCA+SVM	AUC	85.41±0.49	64.40±1.04	72.18±0.27	80.46±0.98	73.61±0.65	83.02±0.48
	Micro F1	58.06±0.69	59.80±0.98	40.01±1.86	70.77±5.58	42.74±3.17	62.76±1.39
	Macro F1	60.24±0.82	45.28±0.84	28.72±0.95	35.92±2.70	34.10±1.62	53.52±2.07
MLLS	AUC	91.67±0.23	67.82±0.63	77.15±0.39	83.53±0.69	78.09±0.61	86.37±0.29
	Micro F1	68.93±0.97	**62.60±0.26**	46.70±0.71	76.52±0.59	49.42±0.78	68.53±0.48
	Macro F1	70.09±0.90	46.60±0.68	34.61±0.91	41.09±2.12	39.39±1.50	60.07±0.98
FS+SVM	AUC	91.59±0.20	65.92±0.75	73.45±0.45	81.31±1.12	75.15±0.63	84.57±0.45
	Micro F1	68.48±1.07	60.50±0.75	43.70±1.10	76.62±0.46	48.32±1.11	67.49±0.72
	Macro F1	69.72±1.07	46.41±0.72	31.25±0.92	40.37±2.74	38.47±0.92	58.99±1.01
CLaRank SVM	AUC	92.06±0.20	67.39±0.62	76.16±0.47	82.39±0.71	78.52±0.73	86.43±0.49
	Micro F1	69.10±0.50	61.52±0.73	46.89±1.32	76.84±1.12	49.37±1.16	67.79±1.34
	Macro F1	**71.51±0.58**	47.27±0.36	34.50±0.40	40.50±2.09	39.75±1.17	60.93±2.17
MLFS	AUC	91.80±0.24	67.25±0.94	78.69±0.24	84.70±0.64	76.44±0.50	88.20±0.33
	Micro F1	68.39±1.80	60.14±1.11	47.24±0.95	77.54±1.27	48.76±1.31	69.34±1.26
	Macro F1	69.91±0.85	47.21±0.71	34.64±0.72	40.94±1.81	38.43±1.06	61.16±1.87
CMLFS	AUC	**93.11±0.41**	**68.68±1.07**	**79.88±0.23**	**85.81±0.64**	**80.52±0.52**	**89.28±0.33**
	Micro F1	**69.80±1.82**	62.55±0.88	**47.83±1.25**	**77.04±1.17**	**50.04±1.62**	**69.39±1.49**
	Macro F1	70.43±0.57	**47.30±0.77**	**35.42±0.67**	**41.65±1.61**	**40.85±0.96**	**62.10±1.47**

[13] S. Ji, L. Tang, S. Yu, and J. Ye. Extracting shared subspace for multi-label classification. In *KDD*, pages 381–389, 2008.

[14] T. Joachims. Optimizing search engines using clickthrough data. In *KDD*, pages 133–142, 2002.

[15] T. Joachims. Training linear svms in linear time. In *KDD*, pages 217–226, 2006.

[16] T. Joachims, T. Finley, and C.-N. J. Yu. Cutting-plane training of structural svms. *Machine Learning*, 77(1):27–59, 2009.

[17] J. E. Kelley. The cutting plane method for solving convex programs. *Journal of the SIAM*, 8:703–712, 1960.

[18] S.-J. Kim and S. Boyd. A minimax theorem with applications to machine learning, signal processing, and finance. *SIAM J. on Optimization*, 19:1344–1367, November 2008.

[19] D. D. Lewis, Y. Yang, T. G. Rose, and F. Li. Rcv1: A new benchmark collection for text categorization research. *Journal of Machine Learning Research*, 5:361–397, 2004.

[20] Y. Li, I. Tsang, J. Kwok, and Z. Zhou. Tighter and convex maximum margin clusteringe. In *AISTATS*, 2009.

[21] P. E. H. R. O. Duda and D. G. Stork. *Pattern Classification*. Wiley-Interscience Publication, 2001.

[22] A. Rakotomamonjy, F. Bach, S. Canu, and Y. Grandvalet. More efficiency in multiple kernel learning. In *ICML*, pages 775–782, 2007.

[23] R. M. Rifkin and A. Klautau. In defense of one-vs-all classification. *Journal of Machine Learning Research*, 5:101–141, 2004.

[24] M. Rogati and Y. Yang. High-performing feature selection for text classification. In *CIKM*, pages 659–661, 2002.

[25] S. Shalev-Shwartz, Y. Singer, and N. Srebro. Pegasos: Primal estimated sub-gradient solver for svm. In *ICML*, pages 807–814, 2007.

[26] S. Sonnenburg, G. Rätsch, C. Schäfer, and B. Schölkopf. Large scale multiple kernel learning. *Journal of Machine Learning Research*, 7:1531–1565, 2006.

[27] L. Sun, S. Ji, and J. Ye. Hypergraph spectral learning for multi-label classification. In *KDD*, pages 668–676, 2008.

[28] M. Tan, L. Wang, and I. W. Tsang. Learning sparse svm for feature selection on very high dimensional datasets. In *ICML*, pages 1047–1054, 2010.

[29] L. Tang, J. Chen, and J. Ye. On multiple kernel learning with multiple labels. In *IJCAI*, pages 1255–1260, 2009.

[30] N. Ueda and K. Saito. Parametric mixture models for multi-labeled text. In *NIPS*, pages 721–728, 2002.

[31] H. Wang, C. H. Q. Ding, and H. Huang. Multi-label linear discriminant analysis. In *ECCV (6)*, pages 126–139, 2010.

[32] Z. Xu, R. Jin, I. King, and M. R. Lyu. An extended level method for efficient multiple kernel learning. In *NIPS*, pages 1825–1832, 2008.

[33] Y. Yang. An evaluation of statistical approaches to text categorization. *Inf. Retr.*, 1(1-2):69–90, 1999.

[34] Y. Yang and J. O. Pedersen. A comparative study on feature selection in text categorization. In *ICML*, pages 412–420, 1997.

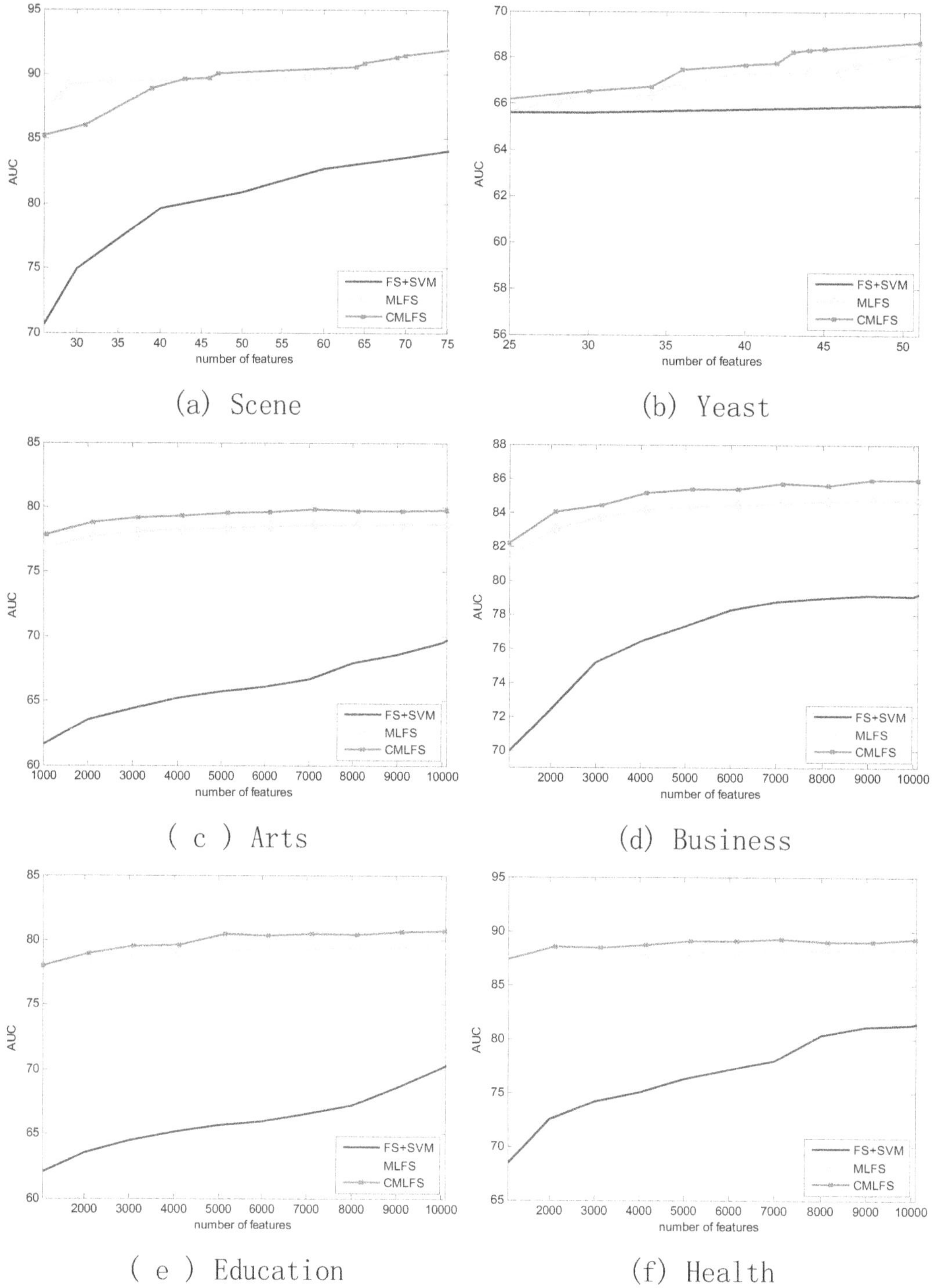

Figure 2: AUC of FS+SVM, MLFS and CMLFS with respect to the number of features on the six data sets

[35] K. Yu, S. Yu, and V. Tresp. Multi-label informed latent semantic indexing. In *SIGIR*, pages 258–265, 2005.

[36] M.-L. Zhang and K. Zhang. Multi-label learning by exploiting label dependency. In *KDD*, pages 999–1008, 2010.

[37] Y. Zhang and D. yan Yeung. A convex formulation for learning task relationships in multi-task learning. In *Proceedings of the Twenty-Sixth Conference on Uncertainty in Artificial Intelligence (UAI)*, 2010.

[38] Y. Zhang and D.-Y. Yeung. Transfer metric learning by learning task relationships. In *KDD*, pages 1199–1208, 2010.

[39] Y. Zhang and Z.-H. Zhou. Multi-label dimensionality reduction via dependence maximization. In *AAAI*, pages 1503–1505, 2008.

Pattern Change Discovery between High Dimensional Data Sets

Yi Xu, Zhongfei Zhang
Computer Science Department
Binghamton University
{yxu,zhongfei}@cs.binghamton.edu

Bo Long
Yahoo! Inc.
bolong@yahoo-inc.com

Philip S. Yu
Computer Science Department
University of Illinois at Chicago
psyu@cs.uic.edu

ABSTRACT

This paper investigates the general problem of pattern change discovery between high-dimensional data sets. Current methods either mainly focus on magnitude change detection of low-dimensional data sets or are under supervised frameworks. In this paper, the notion of the principal angles between the subspaces is introduced to measure the subspace difference between two high-dimensional data sets. Principal angles bear a property to isolate subspace change from the magnitude change. To address the challenge of directly computing the principal angles, we elect to use matrix factorization to serve as a statistical framework and develop the principle of the dominant subspace mapping to transfer the principal angle based detection to a matrix factorization problem. We show how matrix factorization can be naturally embedded into the likelihood ratio test based on the linear models. The proposed method is of an unsupervised nature and addresses the statistical significance of the pattern changes between high-dimensional data sets. We have showcased the different applications of this solution in several specific real-world applications to demonstrate the power and effectiveness of this method.

Categories and Subject Descriptors

H.3.3 [**Information Storage and Retrieval**]: Information Search and Retrieval

General Terms

Algorithms, Experimentation, Measurements

Keywords

Unsupervised Learning, Pattern Change Detection, Principal Angles, Principle of Dominant Subspace Mapping, Matrix Factorization

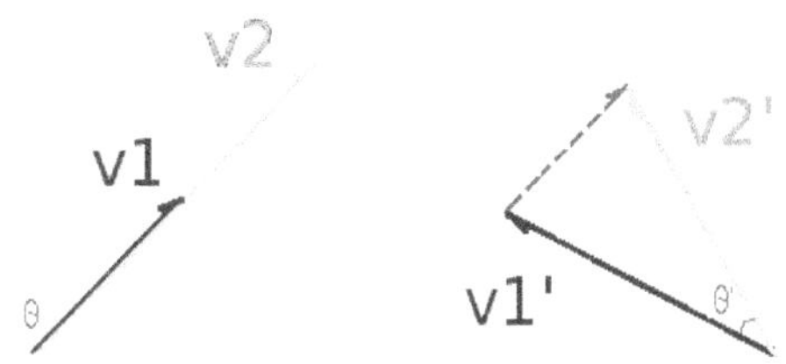

Figure 1: The Euclidean metric fails to differentiate the length difference from the direction difference

1. INTRODUCTION

High dimensional data exist everywhere in our life and in all the sectors of our society in every modality of the data we live with today, including text, imagery, audio, video, and graphics. Pattern change discovery from high dimensional data sets is a general problem that arises in almost every application in the real-world; examples of such applications include concept drift mining in text data, event discovery in surveillance video data, event discovery in news data, hot topic discovery in the literature, image pattern change detection, as well as genome sequence change detection in bioinformatics, to just name a few.

In each of the above applications, we formulate the problem as follows. Given two typically high-dimensional data sets, we intend to determine whether there is a significant pattern change between the two data sets. In different applications, the physical interpretation of the two data sets may be different. For example, in detecting any topic change between two text documents, the two high-dimensional data sets may be the two text documents; in detecting any concept drift among a text stream, any pair of two neighboring snapshots of the text collections in the timeline may be considered as the two high-dimensional data sets; in detecting any pattern change between two images or two collections of images, the two high dimensional data sets may be the two corresponding images or the two collections of the images; in detecting any event occurred in a surveillance video camera, the two high-dimensional data sets may be any pair of two neighboring video frames or groups of video frames in the video stream; in detecting any hot topics in a news data stream, the two high-dimensional data sets may be two neighboring sample windows of the news text data within the stream.

One may wonder what makes high-dimensional data different when it comes to change detection. For almost all the magnitude change detection methods, an invisible pitfall arises with the increase of data's dimensionality. The tricky conflict between Euclidean distance and dimensionality is illustrated in Fig 1. Here we use Euclidean distance because it is the most intuitive and popular metric. Moreover, many commonly used metrics, such as L-norms, K-L divergence, or more generally, Bregman divergence, are defined based on the Euclidean distance. Fig 1 gives two pairs of vectors (v_1, v_2) and (v'_1, v'_2), and the angles, θ, θ' between each pair, respectively. Under Euclidean distance, $\|v_1 - v_2\|$, and $\|v'_1 - v'_2\|$ are the same. In other words, Euclidean distance fails to detect $\theta \neq \theta'$, and therefore, is unable to differentiate the length difference from the direction difference introduced by the dimensionality.

In fact in quite a few real-world applications, high dimensional data per se do not contribute to the data vectors' magnitude change, but to a new combination of a certain subset of the features. For example, we do not intend to conclude that the difference between a human baby and an adult is the same as that between the baby and a little monkey; a banker is not interested in the volume of the financial news but the newly emerged key words; to examine the mutation of a DNA sequence, a biologist needs to find the new combination of Adenine and Guanine instead of the DNA data size change. In these cases, the change of feature subspace should not be confused with the change of data's magnitude. One may argue that we still could round up all the vectors into the same length and then apply the Euclidean distance to avoid the confusion with the magnitude. Such a manipulation theoretically works only when the subspace dimension spanned by data is one (to compare only two vectors). Moreover, the round-up errors and the change of the original data structure may lead to unmanageable consequences.

Based on the above fact, our first motivation is to find a metric that is invariant under data's magnitude change and only characterize the subspace change introduced by dimensionality. Further, we require that such a metric is in a form suitable for computation and manipulation. We would like to clarify that, it is not our intention to underestimate the significance of detecting data's magnitude change. Our standpoint is that to detect the subspace change between high-dimensional data sets through a magnitude-based metric is inaccurate and conceptually confusing. In the rest of the paper, when we say pattern change between high-dimensional data sets, we refer to the subspace change, not the magnitude change.

In order to identify the appropriate subspace for discovering the pattern change between the data sets, we introduce the concept of dominant subspace based on the principal angles [7]. The notion of principal angels between two subspace has a nice property of invariant under an isomorphism, thus is independent of data's magnitude change. The challenge then is to compute the principal angles. To address this challenge, we elect to use matrix factorization to serve as a statistical framework for computing the principal angles. We develop the principle of dominant subspace mapping and show how matrix factorization can be naturally embedded into the likelihood ratio test based on the principle. The proposed method is of an unsupervised nature and addresses the statistical significance of the pattern changes between high-dimensional data sets.

The contribution of this work is highlighted as follows. First, we have studied the very general problem of pattern change discovery among different high dimensional data sets. Second, we have introduced the notion of principal angles between subspaces as a metric for pattern change. Third, we have introduced the principle of the dominant subspace mapping to transfer the principal angle based detection to a matrix factorization problem. Fourth, we have showcased the different applications of this solution in several specific real-world applications to demonstrate the power and effectiveness of this method.

2. RELATED WORK

The classic paradigm for magnitude-based change detection between two data sets is through parameter estimations based on established distribution models. More recent work in this direction [25, 12, 27] attempts to avoid the parametric dependency and to define alternative distance measures between the two distributions. In [25], Song et al. developed a Monte-Carlo framework to detect distribution changes for low dimensional data. In [12], Kifer et al. defined the A-distance to measure the non-parametric distribution change. In [27], Leeuwen and Siebes described the data distributions using their compressed code table and defined the Code-Table-Difference to capture the distribution difference between data sets. The limitation of the low-dimensional distribution models, as Vapnik pointed out at the beginning of his book [28], is that they do not reflect the singularities of the high-dimensional cases, and consequently cannot grasp the change of the subspace.

Based on Vapnik's statistic supervised learning theory, the pattern change detection problem, also called *concept drift* in several specific applications, has been attracted great effort [26, 31, 30, 29, 21]. Classifiers are trained to capture the subspace structures of the high-dimensional data sets via support vectors. The pattern changes can be indirectly reflected through evaluating the classification errors on the data sets. We refer to the survey by Tsymbal [26] for an overview of the important literature on this topic. The main categories of the methods to address the concept drift analysis problem include the instance selection and weighting [13, 11], the ensemble learning [30, 31, 2], and the two-samples hypothesis test [5, 10, 21]. Although supervised learning techniques have the capacity to detect structural changes between high-dimensional data sets, they require labels to train and validate the classifiers. Most of the real-world data sets, however, typically lack sufficient labels that can be used to train the classifiers. In [5], Dries and Rückert proposed a trade-off strategy. Without using real labels, they constructed two virtual classifiers by giving two different types of the labels to the two data sets, respectively, and then proposed three two-sample test methods based on the quality of the classifiers; a good quality indicates a concept drift between the two data sets. Using one classifier to describe the whole dataset, however, oversimplifies the mixture structures of the data sets, and the detection performance is expected to be impaired (see Sec. 5).

As an unsupervised paradigm, matrix factorization is recently considered for subspace analysis of high-dimensional data sets. The theory and applications of matrix factorization have been intensively developed during the last decade. In [16], Lee and Seung developed the breakthrough of the multiplicative updating rules for solving matrix factorization, extending the classical vector quantization and principal components analysis to a new horizon. In [8], Gordon unified the matrix factorization literature with the generalized linear models, strengthening the statistical foundation for matrix factorization. As for the applications, Ding et al. [4] applied non-negative matrix factorization to spectral clustering, graph matching, and clique finding. Long et al. [19, 18] used matrix factorization for relational clustering. Miettinen [20] developed factorization algorithms for binary data sets. In this paper, we use matrix factorization and the notion of the principal angles between subspaces to capture the structural difference between the high-dimensional data sets. We address the statistical significance of the difference through a likelihood hypothesis test based on the linear model. To the best of our knowledge, this is the first time when matrix factorization is used to develop a statistical framework for the pattern change detection.

Other recent efforts on the magnitude-based change detection for specific applications include the event detection from time series data [15, 22] focusing on discovering a significant magnitude change and its duration on a particular feature, word bursts tracking[6, 9], and trend analysis in blogosphere by tracking singular values [3].

3. PRELIMINARIES

3.1 Notations

In this paper, a matrix is denoted as a capital letter in boldface such as $\mathbf{X}$. $\mathbf{X}_{ij}$ is the entry in the ith row and the jth column. $\mathbf{X}_{i\cdot}$ stands for the ith row of $\mathbf{X}$ and $\mathbf{X}_{\cdot j}$ stands for the jth column of $\mathbf{X}$. A vector is a lowercase letter in boldface such as $\mathbf{x}$. A scalar variable is denoted as a lowercase letter such as x. $\mathbf{U}^T$ stands for the transpose of the matrix $\mathbf{U}$. $\mathbf{X}_{m\times n}$ stands for a matrix $\mathbf{X} \in \mathbb{R}^{m\times n}$. $span(\mathbf{A})$ stands for the subspace spanned by the column vectors of the matrix $\mathbf{A}$. $\|\cdot\|$ by default is the Frobenius norm for a matrix; $\|\cdot\|_2$ is the 2-norm [7] for a matrix. $diag(\{x_i\})$ stands for a diagonal matrix with x_i as its ith diagonal entry.

3.2 Principal Angles and Dominant Subspace

In this section, we introduce the *principal angels* between subspaces to measure the subspace difference between data sets of high dimensions. We have already addressed the pitfall of the popular distance metrics and now we explain why the principal angles can avoid it. We start with the same example in Fig 1. We have already shown that Euclidean distance fails to detect $\theta \neq \theta'$, and therefore, is unable to differentiate the length difference from the direction difference introduced by the dimensionality. On the other hand, in this specific example, the principal angle between $span(v_1)$ and $span(v_2)$ is actually θ, and that between $span(v_1')$ and $span(v_2')$ is θ'. One may notice that we here use $span(v)$ instead of just v. This indicates that θ and θ' are invariant under the length shrinking or stretching for the corresponding vectors. Now one can reasonably understand the notion of principal angles between two subspaces as a generalization of an angle between two vectors as the dimensionality goes from one (as for $span(v_1)$) to n where $n \geq 1$. The principal angles have a very important property that all the Euclidean-based metrics do not have – Invariant under an isomorphism and thus independent of the magnitude change (e.g., invariant under scalar multiplication when the dimensionality is one).

Without loss of generality, assume two vector sets $\{\mathbf{x}_i\}_{i=1}^m$ and $\{\mathbf{y}_i\}_{i=1}^l$, $\mathbf{x}_i, \mathbf{y}_i \in \mathbb{R}^n$. Golub and Loan proposed in [7] the definition of principal angles as to measure the structural difference between the two subspaces $S_1 = span(\{\mathbf{x}_i\}_{i=1}^m)$ and $S_2 = span(\{\mathbf{y}_i\}_{i=1}^l)$: An increasing sequence of principal angles $\{\theta_k\}_{k=1}^q$ is defined between two arbitrary subspaces S_1 and S_2 using their orthonormal basis: ([7] Page 602):

DEFINITION 1. *Let S_1 and S_2 be subspaces in $\mathbb{R}^n$ whose dimensions satisfy*

$$p = dim(S_1) \geq dim(S_2) = q \geq 1$$

The principal angles $\theta_k \in [0, \pi/2]$, $k = 1, \ldots, q$, *between S_1 and S_2 are defined recursively as*

$$\cos(\theta_k) = \max_{\mathbf{u}\in S_1, \mathbf{v}\in S_2} \mathbf{u}^T\mathbf{v} = \mathbf{u}_k^T\mathbf{v}_k$$

when $k = 1$, $\|\mathbf{u}_1\| = \|\mathbf{v}_1\| = 1$; *when* $k \geq 2$, $\|\mathbf{u}_k\| = \|\mathbf{v}_k\| = 1$; $\mathbf{u}_k^T\mathbf{u}_i = 0$; $\mathbf{v}_k^T\mathbf{v}_i = 0$ *where* $i = 1, \ldots, k-1$.

In this definition, vectors $\{\mathbf{u}_k\}_{k=1}^q$ and $\{\mathbf{v}_k\}_{k=1}^q$ are actually part of the orthonormal basis for S_1 and S_2; the inner products of each pair $\mathbf{u}_k$ and $\mathbf{v}_k$ form a unique increasing sequence of angles. These angles explicitly give the difference of the subspace structure between S_1 and S_2. The algorithm given in [7] to compute the principal angles takes $\mathcal{O}(4n(q^2 + 2p^2) + 2pq(n + q) + 12q^3)$ in time complexity.

The leading largest principal angles depict the most noticeable structural difference between S_1 and S_2. The corresponding dimensions responsible for the largest principal angles are of great interest as they reflect the major pattern change. We call the subspace formed by these dimensions the *dominant subspace*. Now in order to measure the structural difference between $\{\mathbf{x}_i\}_{i=1}^m$ and $\{\mathbf{y}_i\}_{i=1}^l$, one may resort to directly computing the principal angles between S_1 and S_2, and then obtain the dominant subspace based on the largest principal angles. In practice, however, this is not an optimal solution. First, the values of n, p, and q in Definition 1 can be very large in real-world data sets, resulting in a high complexity to compute the principal angles. Second, since the real-world data sets typically contain noise and outliers, the principal angles directly computed from the raw data may not reflect the true situation. Third, in many applications, given a large amount of samples, one is only interested in the most frequent pattern changes in the majority of the data set and does not care of the principal angles for all the samples. All these issues require to developing an alternative solution to directly computing the principal angles. On the other hand, matrix factorization [16, 1, 4, 24] has been used extensively for reducing dimensionality and extracting collective patterns from noisy data in a form of a linear model. In the next section, we develop the principle of dominant subspace mapping through matrix factorization as the alternative to obtain the dominant subspace.

4. MODEL FORMULATION

Given two data sets $\mathbf{X}' = \{\mathbf{x}_i'\}_{i=1}^{n'}$ and $\mathbf{X} = \{\mathbf{x}_i\}_{i=1}^n$, we present a model to detect the pattern changes between $\mathbf{X}'$ and $\mathbf{X}$. Instead of computing the principal angles directly, we provide a more practical strategy involving three steps: To establish a null-hypothesis on pattern change, to extract a set of basis vectors from $span(\{\mathbf{x}_i\}_{i=1}^n)$ under a null and its alternative hypothesis, and a statistical test to confirm these changes. We will show how principal angles, matrix factorization and linear models work together to serve the purpose.

4.1 Matrix Factorization

Learning mixture patterns from data can be formulated as *generalized² linear² models* [8, 24] using the following matrix factorization term:

$$\mathbf{X} \approx \mathbf{P}\mathbf{S}^T \tag{1}$$

where the matrix $\mathbf{X}_{m\times n} = [\mathbf{x}_1, \mathbf{x}_2 \cdots \mathbf{x}_n], \mathbf{x} \in \mathbb{R}^m$, consist of n data samples represented as the n column vectors. Matrices $\mathbf{P}_{m\times k}$ and $\mathbf{S}_{n\times k}, k \ll \min(m,n)$, are two lower-dimension factors whose product approximates the original data set $\mathbf{X}$. The k column vectors of $\mathbf{P}$ are prototype patterns learned from $\mathbf{X}$; the ith row of $\mathbf{S}$ is a soft indicator using k prototypes to restore the ith sample. Thus, the columns of $\mathbf{P}$ can also be considered as an approximate generating set for the subspace containing samples $\{\mathbf{x}_i\}_{i=1}^n$. In this modeling, we concentrate on $\mathbf{P}$, the prototype patterns, and its changing behavior. $\mathbf{S}$ describes how the k prototypes are distributed among the n samples and may also contains useful information to characterize the dataset; yet in this paper we do not discuss its behavior and leave it as an open question.

Another advantage for matrix factorization is its form as a linear model under which a hypothesis test can be developed. More specifically, given a linear model with additive Gaussian noise $G : \mathbf{X} = \mathbf{PS}^T + \varepsilon$, where $\varepsilon_{\cdot j} \sim N_{m\times 1}(\mathbf{0}, \sigma^2\mathbf{I}_{m\times m})$, our strategy is to check the pattern change in $\mathbf{P}$ by properly constructing a hypothesis on $\mathbf{P}$ and then applying the standard likelihood ratio test.

4.2 Principle of Dominant Subspace Mapping

In order to extract the plausible pattern changes, instead of directly computing the principal angles we develop the principle of dominant subspace mapping through constructing a hypothesis testing as follows. We first establish a hypothesis on the pattern matrix $\mathbf{P}$. Assuming $\mathbf{P}'$ and $\mathbf{P}$ from the two data sets $\mathbf{X}'$ and $\mathbf{X}$, since the principal angles $\{\theta_i\}_{i=1}^k$ between $span(\mathbf{P}')$ and $span(\mathbf{P})$ indicate the scale of pattern changes, it is straightforward to set up the hypothesis on the principal angles to begin with. Now we have two options for the null-hypothesis: To assume no pattern change or to assume an obvious pattern change. If we choose the former, there are two concerns. First, the possibility that two data sets obtained from different times or locations share the same subspace is almost zero, resulting in a hypothesis on an almost impossible event. Second, as shown in definition 1, the principal angles are computed via *cos*; the null-hypothesis of no pattern change gives $H_o : \|diag(\{\cos\theta_i\}_{i=1}^k)\| = k$, indicating that every principal angle is zero; such a setting is vulnerable due to different k value in different applications and we have no prior knowledge about the specific value of k. On the other hand, if we set the hypothesis as an obvious pattern change, it serves both purposes of detecting pattern change and a convenient form of $H_o : \|diag(\{\cos\theta_i\}_{i=1}^k)\| = 0$. If the hypothesis is true, the values of $\{\theta_i\}_{i=1}^k$ are large, indicating the large pattern change between $span(\mathbf{P}) \subseteq \{\mathbf{x}_i\}_{i=1}^n$ and $span(\mathbf{P}') \subseteq \{\mathbf{x}'_i\}_{i=1}^{n'}$. More importantly, this hypothesis is independent of the value k, making the detection more robust despite the possible information loss caused by matrix factorization.

While the hypothesis $H_o : \|diag(\{\cos\theta_i\}_{i=1}^k)\| = 0$ is straightforward, in order to construct a simple statistic test, we elect to use a hypothesis cast directly on $\mathbf{P}$ and $\mathbf{P}'$. For this purpose, we first introduce the following lemma:

LEMMA 1. *Given that $\mathbf{P}' \in \mathbb{R}^{m\times p}$ and $\mathbf{P} \in \mathbb{R}^{m\times q}$, each with linearly independent columns, and that each column is normalized into the same 2-norm length L, and further given the QR factorizations $\mathbf{P} = \mathbf{QR}$ and $\mathbf{P}' = \mathbf{Q}'\mathbf{R}'$, the principal angles $\{\cos\theta_i\}_{i=1}^k$ between $span(\mathbf{P})$ and $span(\mathbf{P}')$ satisfy inequality:*

$$\frac{1}{pqL^2}\|\mathbf{P}'^T\mathbf{P}\| \le \|diag(\{\cos\theta_i\}_{i=1}^k)\| \le \frac{a}{|\sigma_1\sigma_2|}\|\mathbf{P}'^T\mathbf{P}\| \tag{2}$$

where $a \le pq$ is a constant, and σ_1 and σ_2 are the smallest eigenvalues of $\mathbf{R}'$ and $\mathbf{R}$, respectively.

The proof of Lemma 1 is in Appendix A. Lemma 1 gives the upper and lower bounds of $\|diag(\{\cos\theta_i\}_{i=1}^k)\|$ in terms of $\|\mathbf{P}'^T\mathbf{P}\|$. More importantly, due to the Sandwich Theorem, $\|\mathbf{P}'^T\mathbf{P}\|$ and $\|diag(\{\cos\theta_i\}_{i=1}^k)\|$ are asymptotically equivalent as $\|diag(\{\cos\theta_i\}_{i=1}^k)\|$ is close to zero. Therefore, we establish a hypothesis using $\mathbf{P}$ and $\mathbf{P}'$directly, as shown in the following corollary:

COROLLARY 1. *The null-hypothesis*

$$H_o : \|diag(\{\cos\theta_i\}_{i=1}^k)\| = 0$$

has its equivalent form of

$$H_o : \mathbf{P}'^T\mathbf{P} = \mathbf{0} \tag{3}$$

PROOF. It is a direct result due to Lemma 1 and the Sandwich Theorem. □

4.3 Likelihood Ratio Test

Given the simple form of null-hypothesis $H_o : \mathbf{P}'^T\mathbf{P} = \mathbf{0}$ on linear model $G : \mathbf{X} = \mathbf{PS}^T + \varepsilon$, where $\varepsilon_{\cdot j} \sim N_{m\times 1}(\mathbf{0}, \sigma^2\mathbf{I}_{m\times m})$, one can use the standard likelihood ratio test for verification ([23] Page 98): First, estimate $\mathbf{P}$ only based on linear model G. Second, estimate $\mathbf{P}$ under constraint H_o. Finally, compute the likelihood ratio between the two cases.

To estimate $\mathbf{P}$ only based on the given linear model G : $\mathbf{X} = \mathbf{PS}^T + \varepsilon$, where $\varepsilon_{\cdot j} \sim N_{m\times 1}(\mathbf{0}, \sigma^2\mathbf{I}_{m\times m})$, the likelihood function for G is [23]

$$L(\mathbf{P}, \mathbf{S}) = (2\pi\sigma^2)^{-mn} exp[-\frac{1}{2\sigma^2}\|\mathbf{X} - \mathbf{PS}^T\|^2]. \tag{4}$$

Maximizing the likelihood function (4) is equivalent to estimating the factors $\mathbf{P}$ and $\mathbf{S}$ that minimize $\|\mathbf{X} - \mathbf{PS}^T\|^2$. This normal-distribution-based matrix factorization can be efficiently solved via the multiplicative iteration algorithm proposed by Lee and Seung in [16, 17]:

$$\mathbf{P}_{ij}^{update} = \mathbf{P}_{ij}\frac{(\mathbf{P}^T\mathbf{X})_{ij}}{(\mathbf{PS}^T\mathbf{S})_{ij}};$$
$$\mathbf{S}_{ij}^{update} = \mathbf{S}_{ij}\frac{(\mathbf{X}^T\mathbf{P})_{ij}}{(\mathbf{SP}^T\mathbf{P})_{ij}} \tag{5}$$

The proof of the convergence of the updating rule can be found in [17]. This updating rule generates the estimation $\hat{\mathbf{P}}$ and $\hat{\mathbf{S}}$.

Algorithm 1 LRatio

Input: data sets $\mathbf{X}, \mathbf{X}'$, , and threshold h.
Output: Feature basis $\mathbf{P}_H$, indicator matrix $\mathbf{S}_H$, the likelihood ratio test statistic Λ, and the testing result.
Method:

1: Initialize $\mathbf{P}', \mathbf{S}', \hat{\mathbf{P}}, \hat{\mathbf{S}}, \hat{\mathbf{P}}_H$ and $\hat{\mathbf{S}}_H$, and λ randomly.
2: Iteratively update $\mathbf{P}'$ and $\mathbf{S}'$ using (5) until convergence
3: Iteratively update $\hat{\mathbf{P}}$ and $\hat{\mathbf{S}}$ using (5) until convergence
4: Iteratively update $\hat{\mathbf{P}}_H$ and $\hat{\mathbf{S}}_H$ using (7) until convergence
5: Compute Λ using (8)
6: Reject H_o if Λ is smaller than h.

Finding the maximum likelihood estimates subject to the constraint (3) gives the following log likelihood function ([23] Page 98):

$$\mathcal{L}(\mathbf{P}, \mathbf{S}) = -\log L(\mathbf{P}, \mathbf{S}) + \lambda \|\mathbf{P}^T \mathbf{P}'\|^2$$
$$= constant + \frac{np}{2} + \frac{1}{2\sigma^2}\|\mathbf{X} - \mathbf{P}\mathbf{S}^T\|^2 + \lambda\|\mathbf{P}^T\mathbf{P}'\|^2$$

which is equivalent to minimizing:

$$\mathcal{L}(\mathbf{P}, \mathbf{S}) = \|\mathbf{X} - \mathbf{P}\mathbf{S}^T\|^2 + \lambda\|\mathbf{P}^T\mathbf{P}'\|^2 \quad (6)$$

where $\lambda > 0$ is the Lagrange multiplier. To solve this constrained optimization problem, we give the non-increasing updating rule through the following Lemma:

LEMMA 2. *The loss function* (6) *is non-increasing under the updating rule:*

$$\mathbf{P}_{ij}^{update} = \mathbf{P}_{ij} \frac{(\mathbf{X}\mathbf{S})_{ij}}{(\mathbf{P}\mathbf{S}^T\mathbf{S} + \lambda \mathbf{P}'\mathbf{P}'^T\mathbf{P})_{ij}}$$
$$\mathbf{S}_{ij}^{update} = \mathbf{S}_{ij} \frac{(\mathbf{X}^T\mathbf{P})_{ij}}{(\mathbf{S}\mathbf{P}^T\mathbf{P})_{ij}}$$
$$\lambda^{update} = \frac{1}{mk}\sum_{ij}\frac{(\mathbf{X}\mathbf{S} - \mathbf{P}\mathbf{S}^T\mathbf{S})_{ij}}{(\mathbf{P}'\mathbf{P}'^T\mathbf{P})_{ij}} \quad (7)$$

The loss function (6) *is invariant under this rule if and only if* $\mathbf{P}$ *and* $\mathbf{S}$ *are at a stationary point of the loss function.*

The proof of the lemma is in Appendix B. Using updating rule (7), we obtain estimation $\hat{\mathbf{P}}_H$ and $\hat{\mathbf{S}}_H$ under the null-hypothesis. The time complexity of the updating rule (7) for each iteration is $\mathcal{O}(mnk + k^2m)$, where m, n, and k are defined at the beginning of Section 4.1.

After we obtain the estimation of $\hat{\mathbf{P}}$, $\hat{\mathbf{S}}$ and $\hat{\mathbf{P}}_H$, $\hat{\mathbf{S}}_H$, the likelihood ratio statistic is given by ([23] Page 99):

$$\Lambda = \frac{\|\mathbf{X} - \hat{\mathbf{P}}\hat{\mathbf{S}}^T\|^2}{\|\mathbf{X} - \hat{\mathbf{P}}_H\hat{\mathbf{S}}_H^T\|^2} \quad (8)$$

According to the likelihood principle, a small Λ indicates a bad estimation of $\hat{\mathbf{P}}_H$ and $\hat{\mathbf{S}}_H$, and we then reject H_o. On the other hand, a large value of Λ suggests a pattern change detected in $\hat{\mathbf{P}}_H$. The algorithm, called LRatio, is summarized in Algorithm 1.

The time complexity of the updating rule (5) is $\mathcal{O}(mnk)$ in each iteration, and that of (7) is $\mathcal{O}(mnk + k^2m)$ in each iteration; the complexity to compute Λ is $\mathcal{O}(mnk)$, where m, n, and k are defined in Section 4.1. Thus, the total time complexity is $\mathcal{O}(mnk + k^2m)$ for each iteration, which is much lower than that of directly computing the principal angles between $\mathbf{X}$ and $\mathbf{X}'$.

Name	Part 1	Part 2	Sample no.	Dim.
sys	comp.sys.ibm.pc	comp.sys.mac	400 × 2	1558
ossys	comp.os.ms-windows.misc, comp.sys.ibm.pc	comp.sys.mac comp.windows.x	200 × 4	2261
computer	comp.graphics, comp.os.ms-windows.misc, comp.sys.ibm.pc	comp.sys.ibm.pc, comp.sys.mac, sci.electronics	100 × 6	1606
socialtalk	talk.politics.guns, talk.politics.mideast, talk.politics.misc, talk.religion.misc	alt.atheism, soc.religion.christian, talk.politics.misc, talk.religion.misc,	100 × 8	3312
sci	sci.crypt	sci.med	400 × 2	2870
rec-sci	rec.sport.baseball, rec.sport.hockey	sci.electronics, sci.space	200 × 4	2800
comp-sci	comp.graphics, comp.os.ms-windows.misc, comp.sys.ibm.pc	sci.electronics, sci.med, sci.space	100 × 6	1864
rec-talk	rec.autos, rec.motorcycles, rec.sport.baseball, rec.sport.hockey	talk.politics.guns, talk.politics.mideast, talk.politics.misc, talk.religion.misc	100 × 8	2992

Table 1: Configuration of the pattern change data sets.

5. EXPERIMENTS

In order to demonstrate the power and promise of LRatio as well as its superiority to the existing literature in discovering significant pattern changes in different applications in the real-world, we have applied LRatio to several different real-world problems in comparison with the existing methods in the related literature in these different applications.

5.1 Topic Change Detection among Documents

The goal of the first application is to verify the performance of LRatio test using collections of text documents. In this application, we use the standard 20-newsgroup data sets [14], the dimension scale of which is of thousands. As listed in Table 1, we construct eight scenarios using different topic combinations. For each scenario, two parts are set up (Part 1 and Part 2). Each part contains articles evenly mixed from one or more topics. Under each scenario, if the two data sets are sampled from the same part, they should bear similar subspace structure; while if the two data sets are from different parts, their subspace structures are different and LRatio test should be able to reflect this difference through the testing statistic. These eight scenarios are constructed to showcase data sets with different structural complexities and/or pattern change strengths. The first four scenarios intend to imitate moderate pattern change by electing similar topics between the two parts. The next four scenarios imitate strong pattern change by setting different topics between the two parts. We compare the performance of LRatio with the following methods.

Baseline. We apply the standard K-means to each of the two data sets to obtain the data matrices composed of the K centroids, respectively, and then compute the subspaces distance between the pair of the K centroids based on Definition (1). Intuitively, a pattern change shall results in a large distance. We use this distance as a statistic to indicate the pattern change, and compare its sensitivity with LRatio test. For the reference purpose, we call this baseline method as KM.

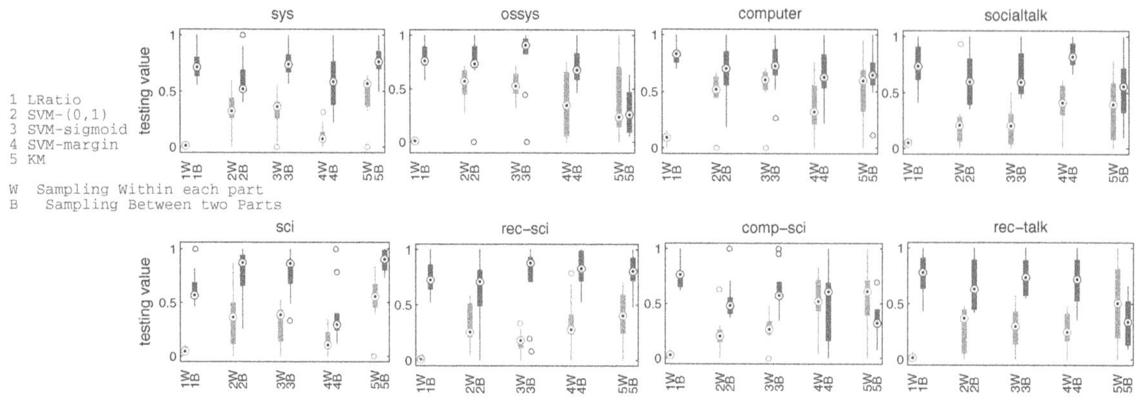

Figure 2: The detection performance of LRatio and 4 comparison methods. For each pair of W and B, a smaller overlap between W and B indicates a better performance.

Peers. We elect to use three different concept drift detection methods in the recent literature [5] by Dries and Rückert for a peer comparison. They are PCA-Bayesian Margin Test and two other error rate based test methods. For the reference purpose, we call them SVM-margin, SVM-sigmoid, and SVM-(0,1), respectively. The reasons why we select these comparing methods are the following. First, under the framework of support vector machine (SVM), their methods are suitable for high-dimensional data sets. Second, although based on supervised techniques, the model does not require real labels and therefore can be used in unsupervised applications. Third, these methods are in a similar two-sample statistical test framework to that of LRatio, resulting in a fair comparison environment.

In order to verify the detection sensitivity, we compare the testing statistics of the data set pair having no pattern change in between with the testing statistics of the data set pair involving a pattern change in between. The evaluation protocol is defined as follows.

For each scenario,

1. Obtain testing statistic from data set pair with no pattern change in between:

i). Constructing two data sets by randomly sampling 200 articles, each dataset with 100 samples, only from Part 1 (or Part 2).

ii). Applying LRatio and the four comparison methods on the two data sets.

iii). Repeating i) and ii) 20 times.

2. Obtain testing statistic from data set pair with pattern changes in between:

i). Constructing the first data set by randomly sampling 100 articles form Part 1; constructing the second data set by randomly sampling 100 articles from Part 2.

ii). Applying LRatio and the four comparison methods on the two data sets.

iii). Repeating i) and ii) 20 times.

3. For each method, normalize the 40 testing statistics to the range of [0, 1] for easy comparison.

Ideally, there should be a big gap between the first 20 testing statistics and the last 20 testing statistics, because the first 20 tests are from the dataset pair that has no pattern change, and the last 20 tests are from the data set pair with pattern changes. Fig. 2 documents all the results of this experiment, where a boxplot is used to represent the numerical distribution of the statistics obtained from the sampling within each part (red boxplots) and sampling between two parts (blue boxplots). In each boxplot, the median(in ⊙), the 25th percentile(in bars), the 75th percentiles(in whiskers) and the outliers(in ∘) of the distribution are drawn. Consequently, for each method and for each of the eight collections, there is a corresponding pair of boxplots representing the statistic distributions for sampling within each part (red boxplot labeled with letter W) and for sampling between two parts (blue boxplot labeled with letter B), respectively. Clearly, more overlap between the pair of boxplots indicates the worse performance in discovering the pattern change for the method. From the figure, all the four comparing methods have the overlaps in the majority of the eight collections; in comparison, LRatio is the only method that has no overlap at all for all the eight collections; further, for the first four scenarios where there expects to be only moderate topic changes between the two parts, LRatio still clearly stands out with no overlap at all between the two boxplots. This demonstrates that LRatio is not only powerful in discovering pattern changes, but also very sensitive to the pattern changes.

5.2 Event Detection from News Streams

While the 20 newsgroups data experiment is for systematic evaluations of the pattern change discovery capabilities and sensitivities, the next experiment is an application scenario of event detection in a news stream data set. We have manually collected Google news data everyday from 23. Oct. to 22. Nov. for the year of 2008 for four specific tracks: political news, financial news, sports news, and entertainment news. To form the news stream data for each of the four tracks, we group the news documents and time-stamp these documents in a unit of every three neighboring days. Since all the five methods we used in the previous experiments are for pattern change discovery between two data sets, we apply each of them to each pair of the neighboring units of the news stream in each track to obtain the statistic value. Consequently, for the whole month news data in each track, each method generates a statistic sequence, which is called the test sequence for the track of the news for the corresponding method.

Fig. 3 documents the political news test sequences within the window between October 23, 2008, and November 22, 2008 for LRatio, KM, and SVM-margin. Since the three methods from [5] are very close in performance, for the clarity purpose in the figure, we only show the test sequence of SVM-margin in this figure. Presumably in the figure for each method a significant peak in the test sequence means a significant pattern change, indicating that significant news events are detected by this method on that day. We manually examined everyday's news data within this whole month to provide the ground truth regarding whether there are any significant news events on everyday of the month, and annotated the specific events.

Since both LRatio and KM conduct the pattern change discovery through the clustering manner, they are both further able to detect the specific events through key words in each cluster, and are able to rank the "significance" of each detected event based on the number of samples in each cluster. Fig. 4 documents the top five detected significant events on Nov. 7, Nov. 13, and Nov. 19 for both methods, respectively, where each event is represented using a bar with the length proportional to the significance of the event, and the same event is ground-truthed with the same color. From the figure, there are three observations. First, for each of the three days, all the five detected events by LRatio are unique and distinct, while there are many duplications of the five top events detected by KM when compared with the ground truth; this is particularly true for Nov. 7 where all the five top events detected by KM are about the *Election Campaign*. Second, as is also observed in Fig. 3, for many events KM is unable to detect them "in time" but rather with a delay; in other words, for many of the news events KM detected are actually old news events. For example, the event that Obama was elected as the US President occurred on Nov. 7 (which LRatio corrected detected in time) is declared as the number one detected event for KM both on Nov. 13 and on Nov. 19, but not on Nov. 7. In fact, for all the three days' top five events detected by KM, only the event *Senator Clinton Became Secretary of State* on Nov. 13 and the event *North Korea Nuclear Crisis* on Nov. 19 are caught by KM in time, whereas all others are actually old news events. Third, the specific event data reported in Fig. 4 coincide with the holistic event detection results reported in Fig. 3 very well. Of all the three days, KM essentially only detected old news events, and that is why in Fig. 3 on these three days there is no peak in the KM test sequence curve, indicating KM fails to detect any significant events for these three days. While SVM-margin does not have the capability to do the clustering analysis to report the specific events detected on each day as LRatio and KM do, it detects the events based on a holistic analysis reported in the test sequence shown in Fig. 3, from which it is clear that SVM-margin still fails to detect any significant events on Nov. 13 and Nov. 19 with an exception on Nov. 7 because the event *Obama Became US President* was such an obvious significant event that SVM-margin did not miss.

The difference in performance between LRatio and the comparing methods is obvious. LRatio aims at discovering pattern changes regardless of whether the pattern changes come from a completely new topic or a new direction of an existing topic. KM, on the other hand, aims at discovering major clusters from the data; thus, new topics need time to "accumulate" to form clusters in order to become significant topics, while new directions of an existing topic are likely to be absorbed into the clusters and would never show up until they eventually dominate the clusters. That is why KM always misses many significant events and often detects an event with a delay in time. For SVM-margin, SVM-(0,1), and SVM-(sigmoid), although they also aim at discovering pattern changes, they work well only when the data have a simple structure and the majority of the samples bear a similar pattern change, which also explains why they only provide a holistic statistic on event detection with no capability for the specific pattern changes.

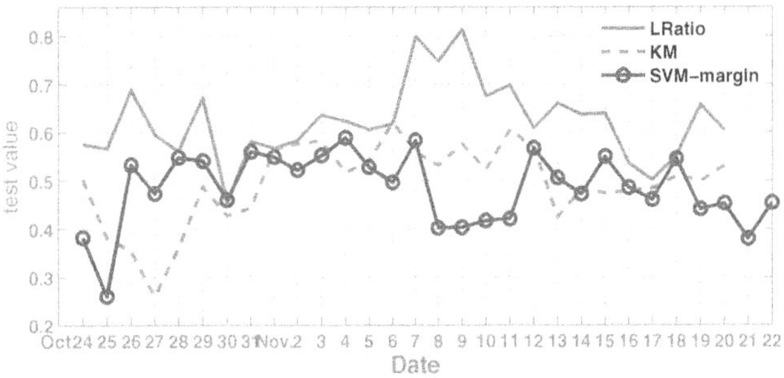

Figure 3: Test sequences for Google political news stream

5.3 Event Detection in Surveillance Video

Finally, we also showcase the application of LRatio to the surveillance video stream data to detect events. In this context, each frame of the video stream is considered as a sample vector. Like the news data stream in the previous experiment, here again we apply LRatio to each pair of neighboring video segments (each segment has 100 frames) to see whether there is any event occurred. To demonstrate the power of the surveillance event detection capability, we apply LRatio to several different video surveillance data sets collected at different specific surveillance applications. Figs. 5 to 7 showcase three different tests of using LRatio for surveillance event detection, where in each of the figures the left panel is a snapshot of the surveillance video stream and the right panel indicates the test sequence of LRatio along the timeline.

6. CONCLUSION

We have studied the very general problem of pattern change discovery among different high dimensional data sets which exist everywhere in almost every application in the real-world, and have identified an approach based on the principal angles to discover the pattern change. We have introduced the principle of the dominant subspace mapping to transfer the principal angle based detection to a matrix factorization problem through a hypothesis testing. Finally, we have showcased the different applications of this solution in several specific real-world applications to demonstrate the power and effectiveness of this method.

Acknowledgments

This work is supported in part by NSF through grants IIS-0503162, IIS-0812114, IIS-0905215, and CCF-1017828. Bryan Bernard, Kevin Hannon, Daniel McFadden, and Greg Stod-

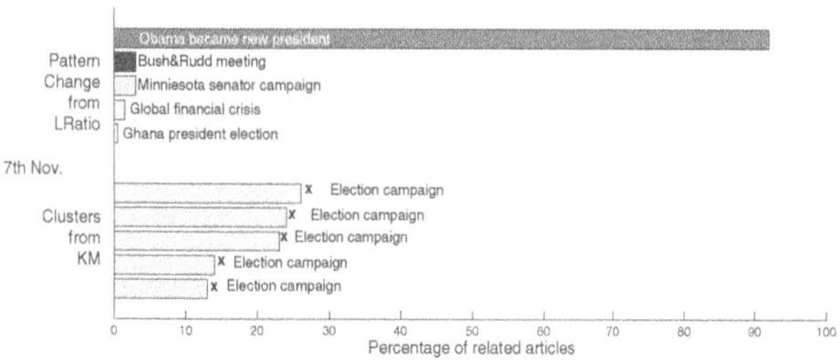

(a) 7th Nov.

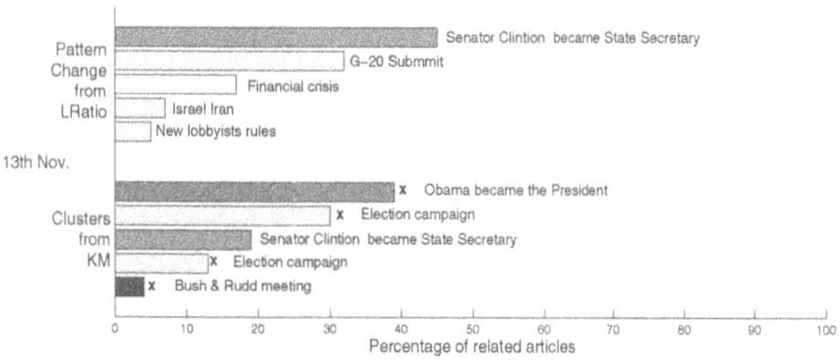

(b) 13th Nov.

(c) 19th Nov.

Figure 4: Pattern changes detected by LRatio v.s. Clusters found by KM. '×' marks the old news topics that have been detected in the previous days. Boxes with the same colors are related to the same news topics

(a)

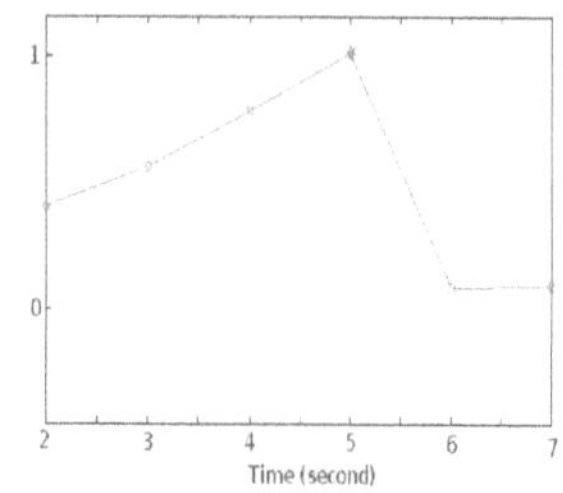

(b)

Figure 5: detection result for video 1; (a) rank 1 event: a man is running towards a cart; (b) the test sequence; the star marks the time when this man begins running.

(a)

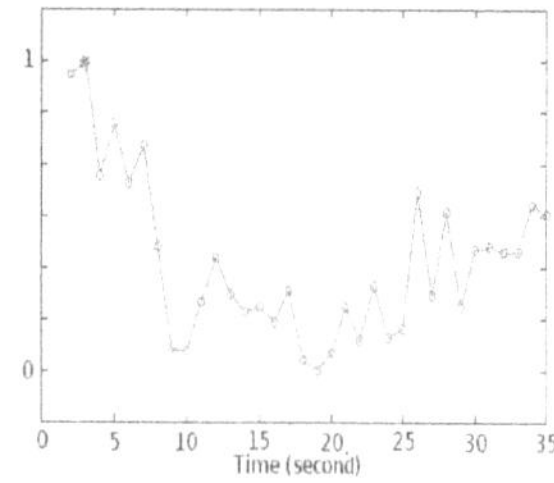

(b)

Figure 6: detection result for video 2; (a) rank 1 event: an earthquake occurs and people are running out; (b) the test sequence; the star marks the time when the earthquake occurs.

dard helped in data collection in this work under an NSF REU grant.

7. REFERENCES

[1] A. Banerjee, S. Merugu, I.S.Dhillon, and J.Ghosh. Clustering with Bregman divergence. *Journal of Machine Learning Research*, 6:1705–1749, 2005.

[2] A. Bifet, G. Holmes, B. Pfahringer, R. Kirkby, and R. Gavaldà. New ensemble methods for evolving data streams. In *KDD '09*, pages 139–148, 2009.

[3] Y. Chi, B. Tseng, and J. Tatemura. Eigen-trend: trend analysis in the blogosphere based on singular value decomposition. In *CIKM*, pages 68–77, 2006.

[4] C. Ding, T. Li, and M. Jordan. Nonnegative matrix factorization for combinatorial optimization: Spectral clustering, graph matching, and clique finding. In *ICDM*, pages 183–192, 2008.

[5] A. Dries and U. Rückert. Adaptive concept drift detection. *Statistical Analysis and Data Mining*, 2(5-6):311–327, 2009.

[6] R. Ge, M. Ester, B. Gao, Z. Hu, B. Bhattacharya, and B. Ben-Moshe. Joint cluster analysis of attribute data and relationship data: The connected k-center problem algorithms and applications. *Trans. on Knowledge discovery from Data*, 2:1–35, 2008.

[7] G. H. Golub and C. F. V. Loan. *Matrix computation.* The Johns Hopkins University Press, Baltimore and London, 1996.

[8] G. Gordon. Generalized^2 linear^2 models. In *NIPS*, 2002.

[9] D. He and D.Parker. Topic dynamics: An alternative model of 'bursts' in streams of topics. In *KDD*, pages 443–452, 2010.

[10] S. Hido, T. Ide, H. Kashima, H. Kubo, and H. Matsuzawa. Unsupervised change analysis using supervised learning. In *Advances in Knowledge Discovery and Data Mining*, pages 148–159. Springer Berlin / Heidelberg, 2008.

[11] G. Hulten, L. Spencer, and P. Domingos. Mining time-changing data streams. In *KDD*, pages 97–106, 2001.

[12] D. Kifer, S. Ben-David, and J. Gehrke. Detecting change in data streams. In *VLDB*, pages 180–191, 2004.

[13] R. Klinkenberg. Learning drifting concepts: Example selection vs. example weighting. *Intelligent Data Analysis*, 8(3):697–717, 2004.

[14] K. Lang. http://people.csail.mit.edu/jrennie/20newsgroups/.

[15] L.Chen and A.Roy. Event detection from flickr data through wavelet-based spatial analysis. In *CIKM*, pages 523–532, 2009.

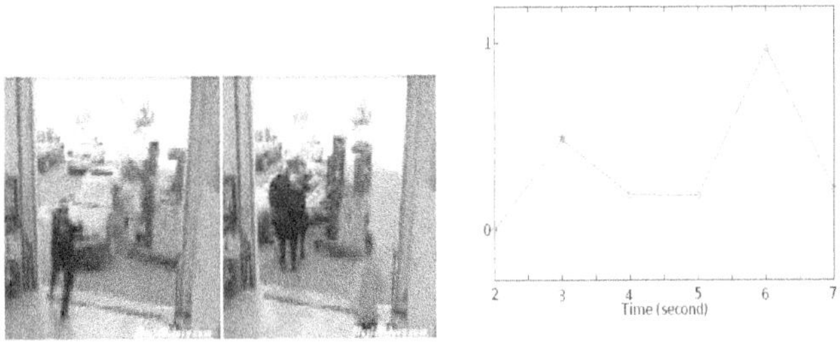

(a) (b) (c)

Figure 7: detection result for video 3; (a) rank 2 event: the car collision occurs;(b) rank 1 event: a man is running towards the accident scene (c) the test sequence; the star marks the time of the collision.

[16] D. Lee and H. Seung. Learning the parts of objects by non-negative matrix factorization. *Nature*, 401:788–791, 1999.

[17] D. Lee and H. Seung. Algorithms for non-negative matrix factorization. In *NIPS*, pages 556–562, 2000.

[18] B. Long, Z. Zhang, and P. Yu. Co-clustering by block value decomposition. In *KDD*, 2005.

[19] B. Long, Z. Zhang, and P. Yu. Unsupervised learning on k-partite graphs. In *KDD*, pages 317–326, 2006.

[20] P. Miettinen. *Matrix Decomposition Methods for Data Mining: Computational Complexity and Algorithms.* Helsinki University Print, 2009.

[21] K. Nishida and K. Yamauchi. Detecting concept drift using statistical testing. In *Proceedings of the 10th international conference on Discovery science*, DS'07, pages 264–269, Berlin, Heidelberg, 2007. Springer-Verlag.

[22] D. Preston, P. Protopapas, and C. Brodley. Event discovery in time series. In *SDM*, pages 61–72, 2009.

[23] G. Seber and A. Lee. *Linear Regression Analysis* Wiley, 2003.

[24] A. P. Singh and G. Gordon. A unified view of matrix factorization models. In *ECML PKDD*, 2008.

[25] X. Song, M. Wu, C. Jermaine, and S. Ranka. Statistical change detection for multi-dimensional data. In *KDD*, 2007.

[26] A. Tsymbal. The problem of concept drift: Definitions and related work. Technical report, 2004.

[27] M. van Leeuwen and A. Siebes. Streamkrimp: Detecting change in data streams. In *ECML*, 2008.

[28] V. N. Vapnik. *Statistical Learning Theory.* John Wiley & sons, 1998.

[29] J. Vreeken, M. Leeuwen, and A. Siebes. Characterising the difference. In *KDD '07*, pages 226–235, 2007.

[30] H. Wang, W. Fan, P. Yu, and J. Han. Mining concept-drifting data streams using ensemble classifiers. In *KDD '03*, pages 226–235, 2003.

[31] P. Zhang, X. Zhu, and Y. Shi. Categorizing and mining concept drifting data streams. In *KDD '08*, pages 812–820, 2008.

Appendix

Poof of Lemma 1

The proof of Lemma 1 uses the method in [7] for computing the principal angles. We first give this method as follows.

Given $\mathbf{A} \in \mathbb{R}^{m\times p}$ and $\mathbf{B} \in \mathbb{R}^{m\times q}$ $(p \geq q)$, each with linearly independent columns, the principal angles between subspaces $span(\mathbf{A})$ and $span(\mathbf{B})$ can be computed as follows . First, compute the QR factorizations for $\mathbf{A}$ and $\mathbf{B}$, respectively

$$\mathbf{A} = \mathbf{Q_A R_A} \qquad \mathbf{Q_A}^T\mathbf{Q_A} = \mathbf{I}_p, \qquad \mathbf{R_A} \in \mathbb{R}^{p\times p}$$
$$\mathbf{B} = \mathbf{Q_B R_B} \qquad \mathbf{Q_B}^T\mathbf{Q_B} = \mathbf{I}_q, \qquad \mathbf{R_B} \in \mathbb{R}^{q\times q}$$

Then, let $\mathbf{C} = \mathbf{Q_A}^T\mathbf{Q_B}$ and compute the SVD (singular value decomposition) of $\mathbf{C}$ such that $\mathbf{Y}^T\mathbf{C}\mathbf{Z} = diag(\cos\boldsymbol{\theta})$, where $diag(\cos\boldsymbol{\theta})$ is short for the diagonal matrix with the cosines of the principal angles $\{\cos\theta_1, \cos\theta_2 \ldots \cos\theta_q\}$ as the diagonal elements.

Proof. Since

$$\|diag(\cos\boldsymbol{\theta})\|^2 = \|\mathbf{Y}(\mathbf{Q}^T\mathbf{Q}')\mathbf{Z}\|^2 = \|\mathbf{Q}^T\mathbf{Q}'\|^2$$

where $diag(\cos\boldsymbol{\theta}) = \mathbf{Y}(\mathbf{Q}^T\mathbf{Q}')\mathbf{Z}$ is the SVD of $\mathbf{Q}^T\mathbf{Q}'$. The inequality we are to prove can now be re-written as:

$$\frac{1}{pqL^2}\|\mathbf{P}'^T\mathbf{P}\| \leq \|\mathbf{Q}^T\mathbf{Q}'\|^2 \leq \frac{a}{|\sigma_1\sigma_2|}\|\mathbf{P}'^T\mathbf{P}\| \tag{9}$$

For the left hand side inequality, since $\|\mathbf{P}\| = \|\mathbf{QR}\| = \|\mathbf{R}\| = pL$ and similarly $\|\mathbf{P}'\| = \|\mathbf{R}'\| = qL$, we have

$$\begin{aligned}\|\mathbf{P}^T\mathbf{P}'\| &= \|\mathbf{R}^T\mathbf{Q}^T\mathbf{Q}'\mathbf{R}'\| \\ &\leq \|\mathbf{R}\|\|\mathbf{Q}^T\mathbf{Q}'\|\|\mathbf{R}'\| = pqL^2\|\mathbf{Q}^T\mathbf{Q}'\|\end{aligned}$$

For the right hand side inequality,

$$\begin{aligned}\|\mathbf{Q}^T\mathbf{Q}'\| &= \|(\mathbf{R}\mathbf{R}^{-1})\mathbf{Q}^T\mathbf{Q}'(\mathbf{R}'\mathbf{R}'^{-1})\| \\ &= \|\mathbf{R}^{-1}\mathbf{P}^T\mathbf{P}'\mathbf{R}'^{-1}\| \\ &\leq \|\mathbf{R}^{-1}\|\|\mathbf{P}^T\mathbf{P}'\|\|\mathbf{R}'^{-1}\|\end{aligned} \tag{10}$$

Since $\mathbf{R}$ and $\mathbf{R}'$ are upper triangular, the inverses $\mathbf{R}^{-1}$ and $\mathbf{R}'^{-1}$ are also upper triangular. Therefore, the eigenvalues of $\mathbf{R}$ are $\{(\mathbf{R})_{ii}|i = 1, \ldots, p\}$, the diagonal entries of $\mathbf{R}$. Hence, the eigenvalues of $\mathbf{R}^{-1}$ are $\{\frac{1}{(\mathbf{R})_{ii}}\}$, the inverse of the diagonal entries of $\mathbf{R}$. The same conclusion also holds true for $\mathbf{R}'^{-1}$. Thus, we have

$$\begin{aligned}\|\mathbf{R}^{-1}\| &\leq \|diag((\mathbf{R})_{ii}^{-1})\| \leq \frac{p}{|\sigma|} \\ \|\mathbf{R}'^{-1}\| &\leq \|diag((\mathbf{R}')_{ii}^{-1})\| \leq \frac{q}{|\sigma'|}\end{aligned} \tag{11}$$

Combining (10) and (11) we obtain

$$\|\mathbf{Q}^T\mathbf{Q}'\| \leq \frac{a}{|\sigma\sigma'|}\|\mathbf{P}^T\mathbf{P}'\|$$

where $a \leq pq$.

This completes the proof of the Lemma. □

Proof of Lemma 2

We first prove the convergence of the updating rules for $\mathbf{P}$ and $\mathbf{S}$, then determin the value of λ.To prove the updating rules for $\mathbf{P}$ and $\mathbf{S}$, we make use of an auxiliary function similar to that used in the Expectation-Maximization algorithm [17].

DEFINITION 2. *$G(u,u')$ is an auxiliary function for $F(u)$ if the conditions*

$$G(u,u') \geq F(u), G(u,u) = F(u) \tag{12}$$

are satisfied.

The auxiliary function is a useful concept due to the following lemma:

LEMMA 3. *If G is an auxiliary function, then F is non-increasing under the update:*

$$u^{t+1} = \arg\min_u G(u, u^t) \tag{13}$$

PROOF. $F(u^{t+1}) \leq G(u^{t+1}, u^t) \leq G(u^t, u^t) = F(u^t)$ □

We show that by defining the appropriate auxiliary function $G(u, u^t)$ for (6), the update rule in Lemma 2 easily follows from (13). Now let $u = \mathbf{P}_{i\cdot}^T$, $u' = \mathbf{P}_{i\cdot}'^T$.

LEMMA 4. *Function*

$$\begin{aligned} G(u,u^t) &= F(u^t) + (u-u^t)^T \nabla F(u^t) \\ &+ \frac{1}{2}(u-u^t)^T K(u^T)(u-u^t) \end{aligned} \tag{14}$$

is an auxiliary function for

$$F(u) = \frac{1}{2}\sum_i (x_i - \sum_a \mathbf{S}_{ia} u_a)^2 + \frac{1}{2}\sum_a (u'_a u_a)^2 \tag{15}$$

where $K(u^t)$ is a diagonal matrix defined as

$$K_{ab}(u^t) = \delta_{ab}(\mathbf{S}^T\mathbf{S}u + \lambda u'^T u' \mathbf{I}u)_a / u_a^t \tag{16}$$

PROOF. Since $G(u,u) = F(u)$ is obvious, we only need to show that $G(u, u^t) \geq F(u)$. To do this, we compare

$$\begin{aligned} F(u) &= F(u^t) + (u-u^t)^T \nabla F(u^t) \\ &+ \frac{1}{2}(u-u^t)^T (\mathbf{S}^T\mathbf{S} + \lambda u'^T u' \mathbf{I})(u-u^t) \end{aligned} \tag{17}$$

with (14) to find that $G(u, u^t) \geq F(u)$ is equivalent to

$$0 \leq (u-u^t)^T [K(u^t) - (\mathbf{S}^T\mathbf{S} + \lambda u'^T u' \mathbf{I})](u-u^t) \tag{18}$$

To prove the positive semidefiniteness, consider the matrix

$$M_{ab}(u^t) = u_a^t (K(u^t) - (\mathbf{S}^T\mathbf{S} + \lambda u'^T u' \mathbf{I}))_{ab} u_b^t \tag{19}$$

which is a rescaling of the components of $K(u^t) - (\mathbf{S}^T\mathbf{S} + \lambda u'^T u' \mathbf{I})$. Then, $K(u^t) - (\mathbf{S}^T\mathbf{S} + \lambda u'^T u' \mathbf{I})$ is positive semidefinite if and only if M is, and

$$\begin{aligned} v^T M v &= \sum_{ab} v_a M_{ab} v_b \\ &= \sum_{ab} u_a^t (\mathbf{S}^T\mathbf{S} + \lambda u'^T u' \mathbf{I})_{ab} u_b^t v_a^2 \\ &- v_a u_a^t (\mathbf{S}^T\mathbf{S} + \lambda u'^T u' \mathbf{I})_{ab} u_b^t v_b \\ &= \frac{1}{2}\sum_{ab} (\mathbf{S}^T\mathbf{S} + \lambda u'^T u' \mathbf{I})_{ab} u_a^t u_b^t [v_a^2 + v_b^2 - 2v_a v_b] \\ &= \frac{1}{2}\sum_{ab} (\mathbf{S}^T\mathbf{S} + \lambda u'^T u' \mathbf{I})_{ab} u_a^t u_b^t (v_a - v_b)^2 \\ &\geq 0 \end{aligned} \tag{20}$$

□

Now we are ready for the proof of the updating rule for $\mathbf{P}$ in Lemma 2.

PROOF. Applying update rule (13) to the auxiliary function (14) results in:

$$u^{t+1} = u^t - K(u^t)^{-1} \nabla F(u^t) \tag{21}$$

Lemma 3 guarantees that F is non-increasing under this update rule. Writing the component of this equation explicitly, we obtain

$$\mathbf{P}_{ij}^{t+1} = \mathbf{P}_{ij}^t \frac{(\mathbf{XS})_{ij}}{(\mathbf{PS}^T\mathbf{S} + \lambda \mathbf{P}'\mathbf{P}'^T\mathbf{P})_{ij}} \tag{22}$$

The proof of update rule for $\mathbf{S}$ is the same as that in [17]. □

The approach to determine λ is more straightforward. Since λ only controls the convergence rate of $\mathbf{P}$ and $\mathbf{S}$, theoretically its value does not influence the final convergence of $\mathbf{P}$ and $\mathbf{S}$. We set the course to regularize λ by using standard Lagrange multiplier procedure. Let

$$\frac{\partial \mathcal{L}(\mathbf{P}, \mathbf{S})}{\partial \mathbf{P}} = \mathbf{PS}^T\mathbf{S} - \mathbf{XS} + \lambda \mathbf{P}'\mathbf{P}'^T\mathbf{P} = 0$$

We then get $\lambda = \frac{(\mathbf{XS} - \mathbf{PS}^T\mathbf{S})_{ij}}{(\mathbf{P}'\mathbf{P}'^T\mathbf{P})_{ij}}$. During the update, each entry of $\mathbf{P}$ and $\mathbf{S}$ may have different gradient speed, we therefore set λ to be the average

$$\lambda = \frac{1}{mk}\sum_{ij} \frac{(\mathbf{XS} - \mathbf{PS}^T\mathbf{S})_{ij}}{(\mathbf{P}'\mathbf{P}'^T\mathbf{P})_{ij}}$$

as given in Lemma 2

MTopS: Scalable Processing of Continuous Top-K Multi-Query Workloads

Avani Shastri, Di Yang, Elke A. Rundensteiner and Matthew O. Ward
Dept. of Computer Science, WPI
Worcester, MA, USA
avanishastri, diyang, rundenst, matt@cs.wpi.edu

ABSTRACT

A continuous top-k query retrieves the k most preferred objects in a data stream according to a given preference function. These queries are important for a broad spectrum of applications ranging from web-based advertising to financial analysis. In various streaming applications, a large number of such continuous top-k queries need to be executed simultaneously against a common popular input stream. To efficiently handle such top-k query workload, we present a comprehensive framework, called MTopS. Within this MTopS framework, several computational components work collaboratively to first analyze the commonalities across the workload; organize the workload for maximized sharing opportunities; execute the workload queries simultaneously in a shared manner; and output query results whenever any input query requires. In particular, MTopS supports two proposed algorithms, MTopBand and MTopList, which both incrementally maintain the top-k objects over time for multiple queries. As the foundation, we first identify the minimal object set from the data stream that is both necessary and sufficient for accurately answering all top-k queries in the workload. Then, the MTopBand algorithm is presented to incrementally maintain such minimum object set and eliminate the need for any recomputation from scratch. To further optimize MTopBand, we design the second algorithm, MTopList which organizes the progressive top-k results of workload queries in a compact structure. MTopList is shown to be memory optimal and also more efficient in terms of CPU time usage than MTopBand. Our experimental study, using real data streams from domains of stock trades and moving object monitoring, demonstrates that both the efficiency and scalability of our proposed techniques are clearly superior to the state-of-the-art solutions.

Categories and Subject Descriptors

H.4 [**Information Systems Applications**]: Miscellaneous

General Terms

Algorithms, Management, Performance

Keywords

Topk Queries, Stream, Multi-Query Optimization

1. INTRODUCTION

Motivation. Continuous top-k queries over streaming windows has been studied by several previous works [14, 15, 16, 17]. Such query semantics, which require continuous reporting of the k most preferred objects from the most recent portion of the stream, has been shown to be able to serve a broad range of real-time applications. For example, a web-site manager may want to continuously monitor the most "clicked" products within the last 1 hour on their web-site, and thus learn the trend of customers' interest. Also, financial analysts may want to continuously monitor the largest transactions in NYSE within the last 10 minutes, as those transactions may have significant impact on the future market change.

However, existing methods mainly focused on designing an efficient execution strategy for a single continuous top-k query. Little effort has been made to solve the problem of simultaneous execution of a large number of top-k queries submitted to the same input stream. In real-world applications, the need for handling a workload composed of multiple continuous top-k queries is clear for the following reasons: 1) Continuous top-k queries are parameterized, namely, when specifying such a query, an analyst needs to provide parameters, including the number of top preferred objects k, the window size and the refresh rate. 2) Thus, multiple analysts monitoring the same input stream may submit multiple continuous top-k queries yet using different parameter settings. For example, the stock transaction stream from NYSE is constantly monitored by thousands of financial analysts. Although many of them may be interested in monitoring the top-k largest transactions that happened most recently, They may submit top-k queries with different parameter settings due to their different analytical tasks. Some of them may want a relatively large k setting, say top 100 or 200, to capture many high volume transactions, while others may be interested in fewer top objects, say top 5 or 10. Also, some of them may specify a high refresh rate, say every 5 or 10 seconds, as they need to conduct frequent trades that need the most updated query results as their decision making support. Others, of course, may be satisfied with a moderate refresh rate, say every 5 or 10 minutes, as their applications require less frequent updates. 3) In fact, even a single analyst may submit multiple queries with different parameter settings with the intent to further analyze retrieved result sets so as to derive a well supported conclusion. For example, the web-site manager mentioned in the above example may want to know the most clicked products within last 3 hours vs. those within last 10 minutes, which may together better reveal the customers' interest changes. Therefore, a stream processing system should be able to accommodate a workload of large number of top-k queries.

Challenges. However, handling a large number of continuous top-k queries in a single system under high input rate is a challenging problem. The naive method of executing each of the queries independently for a huge workload has prohibitively high demands on both computational and memory resources. The state-of-the-art single continuous top-k query processing method [16] may take 10s to update the query result for a window containing 1M tuples tuples. If one simply uses this method to independently execute 100 continuous top-k queries in single system, the response time of each query suddenly increases to around 1000s, which is definitely unaccpetable for streaming applications. Thus, given the real time responsiveness requirement, we need to design efficiently shared execution strategies, which are able to effectively share the both the memory and CPU utilization among multiple queries.

Proposed Solution. To solve this problem, We present a comprehensive framework, called MTopS for **M**ulti **T**op-k **O**ptimized **P**rocessing **S**ystem. Within this framework, we introduce several innovations for optimizing multiple top-k query processing by effectively sharing the available CPU and memory resources.

1) First, a Meta Query Analyzer (MQA) is proposed in MTopS to analyze the workload at the compilation stage. It generates a single meta query to represent the query logic for all workload queries, and thus succeeds to remodel the problem of executing multiple top-k queries into the execution of a single query meta query for our system. Technical details of MQA algorithms are discussed in Section 4.

2) A Runtime Infrastructure (RINF) is designed in MTopS to physically store the progressive top-k results for the meta query (generated by MQA) in highly compact formats. Our RINF designs guarantee that it only holds the minimum necessary set for multiple top-k query execution, and thus achieve optimal memory usage. Infrastructures' design is discussed in Section 5 and 6.

3) A Runtime Multiple Query Scheduler (RMQS) in MTopS manages the timing for updating the progressive top-k results in RINF and generating query results for individual queries.

4) Novel execution strategies are provided in a Meta Query Executor (MQE) to efficiently update the progressive top-k results in RINF over time. MQE algorithms are also discussed in Section 5 and 6.

5) Finally, a Query Result Extractor (QRE) extracts top-k results for individual queries from RINF whenever needed.

Our experimental studies using real streaming data from moving object monitoring and stock trades domains show that our system uses at least 271 times less CPU processing time and 175.4 folds less memory space as compared to the State-of-the-art independent execution solution[16] for handling 1000 queries. In fact, our MTopS system comfortably handles a workload in the order of 1000 queries with the average processing time ranging between 4-30 ms/object depending on the query parameter settings, which satisfies the needs for most real-time applications.

2. PROBLEM DEFINITION

Top-k Queries in Sliding Windows. In a sliding window scenario, the continuous top-k query Q (S,*win*,*slide*,*k*) returns top-k objects within each query window W_i on the data stream S. We use the term 'object' to denote a multi-dimensional tuple in the input data stream. The objects that participate in the top-k results of a given window are referred to as the 'top-k elements' of that window. A query window is a sub stream of objects from stream S that can be either count-based or time-based. The window *win* periodically slides after a fixed amount of objects have arrived (count-based) or a fixed time has passed (time-based) to include new objects from S and to remove expired objects from the previous window W_{i-1}. The top-k results are always generated based on the objects that are alive in the current window W_i.

Multiple Top-k Queries. Given a query workload *WL* with n top-k queries $Q_1(S, win_1, slide_1, k_1)$, $Q_2(S, win_2, slide_2, k_2), \ldots,$ $Q_n(S, win_n, slide_n, k_n)$ querying the same input data stream S while all the other query parameters, i.e, *win*, *slide*, *k* may differ.

We focus on executing all the registered queries simultaneously such that each query is answered accurately at their respective output moments. More specifically, we continuously output the required top-k results for each query at their corresponding slide sizes. Our goal is to minimize both the average processing time for each object and the peak memory space needed by the system.

3. MTOPS FRAMEWORK

We now introduce the architecture of the MTopS framework shown in Figure 1, while details of the techniques used in each block are discussed in the subsequent sections 4 to 8.

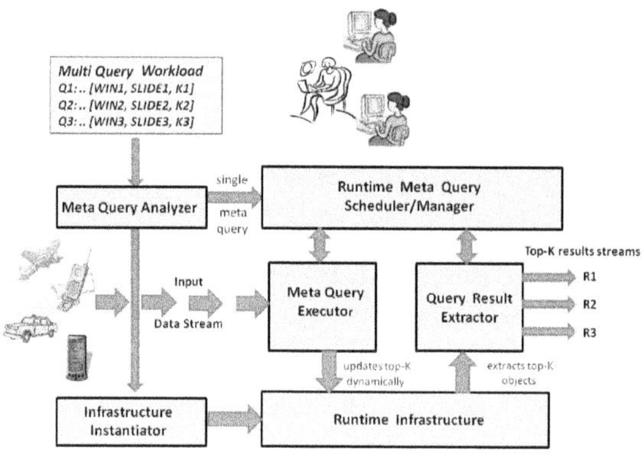

Figure 1: MTopS System Architecture

Multi Query Analyzer (MQA). The functionality of MQA is to analyze the similarity among the member queries in the workload, and thus organize them at the compilation stage with the goal of maximizing the resource-sharing for the later runtime execution. In particular, we propose to use a "meta query strategy", which builds a single meta query Q_{meta} to integrate all the member queries in the given workload. Namely, the input of MQA is a workload of top-k queries with arbitrary parameter settings, and the output of MQA is single meta query.

The meta query Q_{meta} has the following key characteristics. 1)The query window of Q_{meta} always covers all objects in the stream that are necessary to answer every member query. 2) The slide size of Q_{meta} is no longer fixed but rather adaptive during the execution, depending on the nearest time point that any member query needs to output or to conduct a new window addition or expired window removal. The specific algorithm of building such a meta query is discussed in Section V.

Runtime Infrastructure (RINF) and Its Instantiator (IINS). To execute the meta query generated by MQA, we need an infrastructure to physically hold the meta data, namely the top-k candidates, during the meta query execution.

In this work, we propose two runtime infrastructure designs, which not simply collect the top-k candidates, but also encode them into efficiently updatable formats. These two designs are the MTop-Band and MTopList structures. We prove that by using those carefully designed structures, we maintain the minimum object set that is necessary and sufficient for answering all member queries, while any unnecessary object can be discarded immediately when it arrives at the system.

RINF is instantiated by its Instantiator (IINS) at the compilation stage.

Runtime Meta Query Scheduler (RMQS). As we discussed earlier in Multi-Query Analyzer, Q_{meta} needs to adapt its slide size to meet the time points for output, to build new windows or delete expired windows, for member queries.

RMQS sends instructions to MQE and QRE at scheduled window-addition/deletion time points or output time points, and thus tells them to conduct the corresponding operations at proper time. Such instructions guarantee that the RINF is properly updated and the top-k results of all member queries are output as the queries demand.

Meta Query Executor (MQE). MQE is the key online computation module which executes the meta query Q_{meta} by incrementally updating the top-k candidates held in RINF as the input stream passing by. Such update process include two aspects, namely handling the newly arrived objects and purging the expired objects.

When handling newly arrived objects, for each new object o_{new}, MQE first evaluates whether it has the potential to appear in the output of Q_{meta}. o_{new} is inserted only if it is eligible to participate as top-k result, otherwise discarded immediately to avoid unnecessary computation and storage.

When purging expired objects, MQE checks which objects are "completely expired" for the meta query, meaning that they are no longer in the query window of any workload queries. Such objects are physically removed from RINF immediately, while those expired for only some of the queries will still be kept in RINF. In this case MQE updates the properties of RINF.

Query Result Extractor (QRE). The functionality of QRE is to extract the top-k results from RINF for each member query at the moment when the output of this particular query is needed. This result extraction process is non-trivial, because the top-k candidates for all member queries are encoded in a single data structure in RINF.

4. ANALYZING THE MULTI TOP-K QUERY WORKLOAD

We now discuss our queries' parameters analysis that transforms the workload of many queries into single meta query.

Notion of Predicted Views. It is well recognized that in the sliding window scenario, query windows tend to partially overlap ($Q_{meta}.slide < Q_{meta}.win$). Therefore, if an object participates in the top-k result of window W_i, it may also participate in the top-k results of some of the future windows W_{i+1}, W_{i+2}, , W_{i+n} until the end of its life span. Thus based on our knowledge at time W_i, and the slide size *slide*, we can exactly ŞpredictŤ the specific subset of the objects in the current window that will participate in each of the future windows. We call these predicted subsets of future windows as "predicted views".

With this knowledge, we can predetermine (partial) top-k results for each of these future windows based on the objects in the current window after considering the object expiration. We call these partial results as "predicted top-k results". Thus, these predicted top-k results need to be updated only if a new object that arrives to the system is eligible to participate as a top-k result. Otherwise, these predicted top-k result sets will be the actual result sets for future windows. Figure 2 (left) shows the current window W_0 and pre-

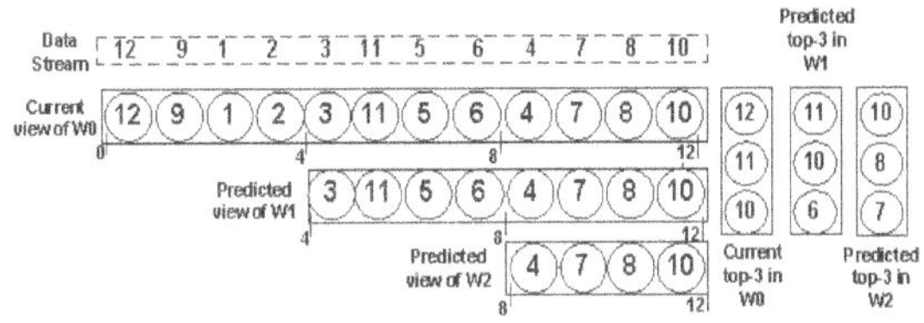

Figure 2: Predicted views of three consecutive windows at W_0

dicted views of two future windows W_1 and W_2 with window size *win* = 12 and the slide size *slide* = 4. The predicted view W_1 contains those objects from W_0 those are still alive after the window W_0 slides. Likewise, predicted view of W_2 contains all objects that are still alie after window W_1 slides. In Figure 2 (left), the numbers shown in the white circles represent the objects' scores. Figure 2 (right) shows the corresponding current and predicted top-k result sets for windows W_0, W_1, and W_2 respectively. Evidently, each of these result sets contain k objects, with highest preference scores, that are still alive.

We exploit this "predictability property" of sliding windows to analyze the parameters of all the workload queries and finally integrate them. Next, we handle the cases where only one of the parameters among all the queries is varying. Later, we discuss more general cases, where two or more query parameters are varying.

4.1 Varying Top-k Parameters - k

Consider the window parameters, i.e., *win* and *slide* are same for all queries in the input workload WL, while the top-k parameter k is different. This implies that all queries share windows and require output at the same time, while the number of objects to be output by each query differs.

Lemma 4.1. *Given a workload WL with all member queries having same slide size - slide and same window size - win but arbitrary top-k parameters k, $Q_i.k$ maintained in each of the predicted view will be sufficient to answer each query such that $Q_i.k$ is the query with largest top-k parameter among WL.*

Proof. Lemma 4.1 holds because the predicted views built for the different queries in the workload are overlapped as the win and $slide$ values are same for all the queries. This means that the life time of an object and the output schedules for all queries are same.

Thus if objects equivalent to the largest top-k parameter are maintained in a predicted view , it is sufficient to answer the queries with smaller top-k parameter as well.

Thus, the number of predicted views that need to be built for processing full workload which might include thousands of input queries is equal to predicted views needed to be built for processing any one query in WL. Clearly, full sharing is achieved.

4.2 Varying Slide Sizes - *slide*.

Consider *win* and k for all queries in the workload WL are same, while their slide sizes - *slide* may differ. For ease of explanation, let us assume that all the queries start simultaneously. Since their window sizes are equal , at any given time they are querying the same portion of the input data stream. The only difference then is each query needs to generate output at different moments.

Example 4.1. *Given three queries Q_1, Q_2, Q_3 such that $Q_1.win = Q_2.win = Q_3.win = 8s$; $Q_1.slide = 6s$, $Q_2.slide = 2s$, and $Q_3.slide = 3s$; and $Q_1.k = Q_2.k = Q_3.k = 3$. Thus, each query requires its output, i.e., top-k result set at every 6, 2, and 3 seconds respectively.*

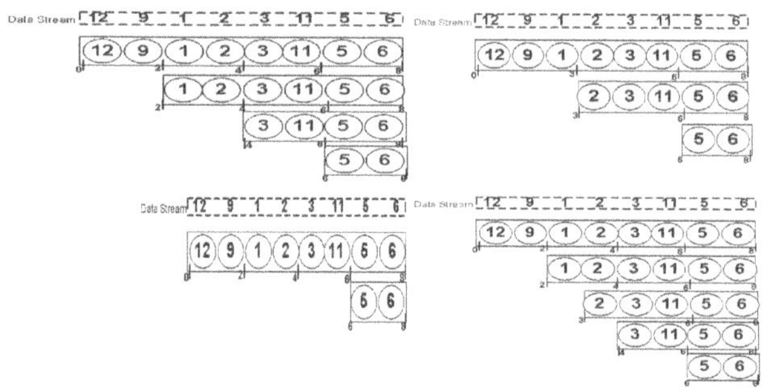

Figure 3: Predicted views needed for processing query Q_1 (top left), Q_2 (top right), Q_3 (bottom left) independently and combined view for meta query Q_{meta} (bottom right)

As consequence, each of these queries may need to maintain different predicted views so as to generate output at their respective slides. Instead, MQA builds a single meta query Q_{meta} that integrates all member queries in workload *WL* to avoid maintaining separate set of predicted views for each query. Figure 3. shows the predicted views that need to be maintained for each of these three queries independently, versus those by the meta query at wall clock time 00:00:08. Q_{meta} has the same window size as all the member queries in *WL* while its slide size is no longer fixed but rather adaptive during the execution. The slide size of Q_{meta} at a particular moment is the nearest moment at which at least one of the queries need to be answered.

For three member queries, MQA builds a meta query Q_{meta} with *WIN* = 8s. At wall clock time 00:00:08, the slide size of Q_{meta} will be 2s as 00:00:10 will be the nearest time at which the member query Q_2 is to be answered. At 00:00:10, its slide sizes are adapted to 1s, 1s and 2s so to output at 00:00:11 (Q_3), at 00:00:12 (Q_2), and at 00:00:14 (Q_1 and Q_2) respectively. Thus, we can now build up all predicted views at 00:00:08 with distinct output points as determined by the meta query. That is we build 6 predicted views starting at 00:00:02,:03,:04,:06, :08 respectively, most of which sere multiple queries.

4.3 Varying Window Sizes - *win*

Consider the slide sizes - *slide* and the top-k parameter - k of all queries are same, while their window sizes *win* differs. Here, we first use the simplifying assumption that all the window sizes of the member queries are multiples of their common slide size. We now observe an important characteristic as below.

Lemma 4.2. *Given a workload WL with queries having the same slide but arbitrary win (multiples of slides), the predicted views maintained for Q_i with $Q_i.win$ the largest window size among WL will be sufficient to answer all input queries in WL.*

This is because the predicted views maintained for Q_i will cover all the predicted windows that need to be maintained for all the other queries.

Discussion. If the window sizes of the queries are not in multiples of their common slide size, the predicted views maintained for Q_i will still cover all the other queries. For example, if the slide sizes of each of the queries are the same as above (2s) while the window sizes are $Q_1.win$ = 6s, $Q_2.win$ = 7s, and $Q_3.win$ = 8s. The predicted views built at moment 00:00:08 will be sufficient to answer all these queries. These windows will start from 00:00:00 (serving Q_3), 00:00:01 (serving Q_2), 00:00:02 (serving Q_1 and Q_3), 00:00:03 (serving Q_2), and 00:00:04 (serving Q_1 and Q_3) and so on.

4.4 Varying Window sizes-win and Varying Slide Sizes-$slide$

Next we consider, when both the window sizes *win* and the slide sizes *slide* of all the member queries are arbitrary. Here, we utilize a combination of previously introduced techniques and show that a single meta query with window size equal to the largest window size amongst all the member queries and adaptive slide sizes is sufficient to answer all such queries.

Example 4.2. *Consider, $Q_1.win = 8s$, $Q_2.win = 6s$ and $Q_3.win = 4$ s; $Q_1.slide$=4s, $Q_2.slide$=3s, $Q_3.slide$ = 2s; and $Q_1.k = Q_3.k = Q_3.k = 2$. Assuming that all the predicted views for the queries end at the largest window size, we build a meta query Q_{meta} such that $Q_{meta}.WIN$ = 8 and $Q_{meta}.SLIDE$ = ADAPTIVE, $Q_{meta}.K$= 2 (same for all queries).*

Thus, in this meta query setup, the window size and top-k parameter are now fixed while the slide size of the meta query is adaptively adjusted. At wall clock time 00:00:08, 5 predicted views are created, starting from 00:00:00 (serving Q_1), 00:00:02 (serving Q_2), 00:00:04 (serving both Q_1 and Q_3), 00:00:05 (serving query Q_2), and 00:00:06 (serving query Q_3). Clearly, only 5 windows (current and predicted) need to be maintained instead of the 9 windows that would here been needed if each query were to be executed independently.

4.5 The Most General Case

Finally, we consider the general case with all queries with arbitrary parameter settings. In this case, we build a meta query with window size $Q_{meta}.WIN$= $Q_i.win$, the largest window size among WL; $Q_{meta}.SLIDE$ = *ADAPTIVE*, as explained in the previous subsection. Lastly, $Q_{meta}.K$ = *ADAPTIVE* as explained below.

We now introduce an adaptive k strategy to achieve memory efficient processing. To be more precise, in a particular window we maintain the top-k objects such that k is equal to $Q_i.k$ where Q_i is the query served by that window. In case one window serves more than one query then k for that window is equivalent to the largest top-k parameter among the queries served by his window.

5. THE MTOPBAND STRUCTURE

Once the single meta-query Q_{meta}, has been designed that logically encapsulates a full workload of queries, we instantiate a runtime infrastructure for managing the meta data needed for execution of Q_{meta}. We call this infrastructure the MTopBand.

5.1 MTopBand Design

The MTopBand data structure stores only the top-k objects for the current and those for each of the predicted views, as generated by the meta query Q_{meta}. These predicted views, as discussed in the Section III, are generated based on the meta query logic and thus represent all the member queries in the workload WL.

For each predicted view only a list of top-k objects is maintained, while all other objects that have no chance of participating in the top-k results of current or any of the future views are discarded immediately. We recall that top-k parameter $Q_{meta}.K$ is adaptive based on the query/queries that require output at the moment when a particular window ends. Thus, for each window we maintain only those top-k tuples eligible to be the output for one or more queries at the time point when the window slides. This means, each window may have different number of tuples as the top-k result sets, depending on the the query in the workload that outputs when the window slides. Each of these result sets are sorted based on the object scores F_{scores}.

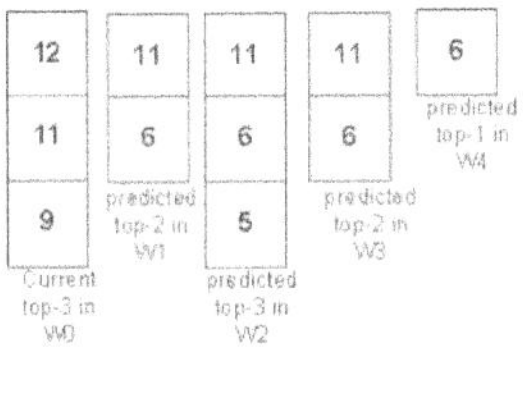

Figure 4: Physical view of MTopBand structure

Figure 4. shows the MTopBand structure based on the workload WL of three queries Q_1, Q_2, and Q_3 introduced in Example 4.2.

Theorem 5.1. *At any time, the top-k result set maintained in the MTopBand structure constitute the minimal object set that is necessary and sufficient for accurate top-k monitoring.*

Proof. We first prove the sufficiency of the objects in the predicted top-k result sets for monitoring the real time top-k results for each of the queries in the workload WL. For each of the future windows W_i (the ones that the life span of any object in the current window can reach), the predicted top-k results maintain $Q_{meta}.W_i.K$ objects with the highest F_{scores} for each W_i based on the objects that are in the current window and are known to participate in W_i. This indicates that any other object in the current window can never become a part of the top-k results in W_i, as there are already at least $W_i.K$ objects with larger F scores than it in W_i. So, they donŠt need to be kept. Then, even if no new object comes into W_i in the future or all newly arriving objects have a lower F score, the predicted top-k results would still have sufficient ($Q_{meta}.W_i.K$) objects to answer the query Q_i for W_i. This proves the sufficiency of the predicted top-k results.

Next we prove that any object maintained in the predicted top-k results are necessary for accurate top-k monitoring. This would imply that this object set is the minimal set that any algorithm needs to maintain for correctly answering all the top-k queries in the given workload WL. Any object in the predicted top-k result for a window W_i may eventually be a part of its actual top-k results for one of the queries if no new object comes into W_i or all new objects have a lower F_{score}. Thus discarding any of them may cause a wrong result to be generated for a future window. This proves the necessity of keeping each of these objects. Based on the sufficiency and necessity we have just proved, the objects in the predicted top-k results constitute namely the minimal object set that is necessary and sufficient for accurate top-k monitoring of all queries in the workload WL.

5.2 MTopBand Maintenance.

The dynamic maintenance of the MTopBand structure requires updating the top-k results for each of the current and predicted views, that include all the queries in the WL, in two scenarios. First, when a new object arriving at the system is eligible to participate in the top-k result sets for one or more queries being served by one or more windows W_i . Secondly, when a window slides some of the objects in the existing top-k result sets may expire and thus require updating the MTopBand data structure. Next, we discuss the proposed algorithms to update the MTopBand structure in the above two scenarios. If a window slides, we update the MTopBand top-k

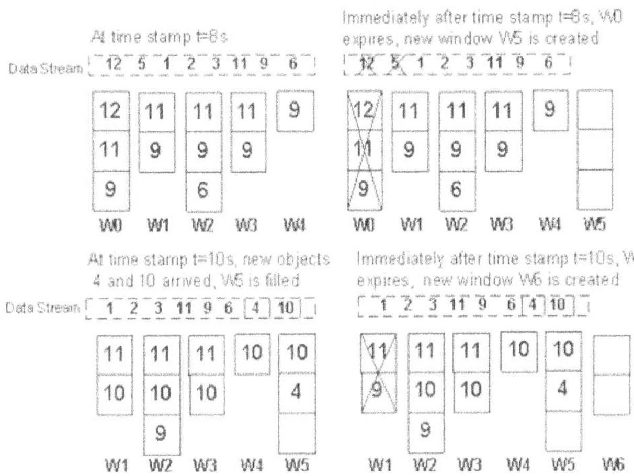

Figure 5: Updating the multi top-k results in MTopBand

result sets in the following two steps.

At step 1, we remove the top-k result set corresponding to the expired window. For example, Figure 5. depicts the MTopBand structure maintenance based on our running Example 4.2. After time t = 8s, when current window W_0 expires, top-k results of W_0 are purged, and W_1 is the new current window. It is easy to see that the effect of window expiration was already taken into account while building the predicted views/ predicted future windows.

At step 2, we create a new empty MTopBand top-k result set corresponding to the newest predicted view (W_5 in figure 5. (top right)) for the next future window to cover the whole life span of the incoming objects.

After the window slide is taken care of, we attempt to insert the newly arrived object O_{new} in each of the current and future win dow. The F_{score} of each O_{new} is compared with the object with minimum F_{score}, called as O_{min} henceforth, in each of the current and predicted top-k result set. If the F_{score} of O_{new} is larger than O_{min} of any of the current and future windows, this object is inserted as one of the top-k results of that particular window. Before inserting the O_{new} into any of these result sets, we must find the correct position of this new object, as each top-k result sets/lists are sorted by F_{scores} in the MTopBand structure. This is a simple operation, we continue comparing the F_{score} of O_{new} with each of the top-k results within a particular list till we find an object with F_{score} larger than F_{score} of O_{new}. O_{new} is inserted just below this object in the top-k result list. Now, the O_{min} is deleted from this particular list as O_{min} is no more a part of top-k results for this window. The object immediately above the O_{min} in the result set/ list becomes the new O_{min}. Any new object arriving at the system will now be compared with this new O_{min}. Every arriving object, regardless of its F_{score}, is inserted in the newly created window W_i until the window has not reached the size of $Q_{meta}.W_i.K$.

5.3 Complexity Analysis.

Memory Costs. The memory costs of MTopBand structure depend mainly on two factors, the number of top-k result sets/lists which depends on the number of active predicted views at a given moment and the size of each result set/list. Complexity wise, the memory requirement of the MTopBand structure is in

O(N_{act}*$Q_{meta}.W_i.K$), where N_{act} is the number of active windows at a given time and $Q_{meta}.W_i.K$ is the adaptive K for a given window in the query workload.

Lemma 5.1. *MTopBand maintains expected O($Q_{meta}.W_i.K$*N_{act})objects.*

Since an object may participate as a top-k result for its complete life time, it usually participates in multiple subsequent active windows. we maintain only one physical copy and multiple references of any objects which participates in multiple windows. As proved in Theorem 5.1, we maintain minimal set in the MTopBand structure.

Computational Costs. Computationally, there are two major actions that contribute to the cost of updating top-k results in the MTopBand structure. We recall that, we first search if the newly arrived object belongs to any of the top-k result sets. This a constant cost operation, that is a total of N_{act} comparisons in the worst case. Second, the cost for positioning new object in the top-k result set, if it makes into this result set, is O(log(k)) in the best case. The cost of inserting this object into top-k result set and deleting the smallest score object from the existing top-k result set is in O(log(k)) again.

Thus, the overall processing costs for handling all new objects for each window slide is O(N_{new} * N_{act_new} * $log(k)$), with N_{new} the number of new objects coming to the system at this slide, and N_{act_new} is the number of windows each object is predicted to make top-k when it arrives at the system. As the object expiration process is trivial, this constitutes the total cost for updating the top-k result at each window slide.

Conclusion. As discussed above, MTopBand structure maintains a minimal object set and also achieves absolute incremental computation. Evidently, we do not need to hold the number of tuples equivalent to the complete window size at any stage for computing the top-k results, rather all the computation is done incrementally. This is a clear win over the existing methods for top-k query computation that need to recompute top-k results from scratch periodically [15, 17].

However, we observe that the resource requirements of MTopBand structure grows with N_{act}, the number of predicted views to be maintained. More specifically, since M-MTopBand stores top-k result sets for each of the predicted views independently/individually, its memory and CPU consumption grows with the number of predicted top-k result sets to be maintained.

We confirm this inefficiency of MTopBand structure when the number of predicted views grow large in the experimental study discussed in Section 7. Next, we discuss various properties of the MTopBand structure and utilizing these observations, we further design the optimized integrated compact structure MTopList structure. We then discuss the maintenance and cost analysis of our proposed structure MTopList.

6. OPTIMIZED TOP-K RESULT-SETS INFRASTRUCTURE: MTOPLIST

To tackle these shortcomings, we now analyze the properties of MTopBand to further design a data structure with resource requirements independent of not only the size of the workload WL and the window size of the meta query Q_{meta}, but also the number of future windows. Next, we discuss various properties of the MTopBand structure and utilizing these observations, we further design the optimized integrated compact structure MTopList structure. We then discuss the maintenance and cost analysis of our proposed structure MTopList.

Observation 1. The MTopBand's top-k results in adjacent predicted views tend to partially overlap, or even be completely identical.

Explanation. Top-k results for the current window are computed based on the scores of the objects within the complete window. Yet, the top-k results of the first predicted view are computed based on exactly the same set of objects except for those few objects that will expire with the first slide. This means that the subsequent predicted views inherit subsets of top-k results from their previous windows.

The top-k result sets of the adjacent predicted views will be identical when 1. the objects that expired after the slide were never a part of the top-k result set, $O_{exp}.F_{score}$ < $O_{curr}.F_{score}$; 2. All the newly arriving object in the current window have an object score smaller than objects that are alive from previous window, $O_{exp}.F_{score}$ < $O_{curr}.F_{score}$.

Observation 2. An object may disappear first and then may reappear later in the top-k result sets of subsequent predicted views in its life time.

Explanation. By Theorem 5.1, top-k results for multiple queries are maintained concomitantly in the MTopBand structure, such that only the minimal object sets that may participate as top-k results for one or more queries are kept. We also recall that the predicted views in the MTopBand structure are built such that each view ends at an output moment of one or more top-k queries.(Section 5)

Observation 3. If object o_i and o_j both participate in the predicted top-k result sets of more than one windows, then the relative positions between o_i and o_j remains the same in each of the predicted top-k result set .

Explanation. First, the F_{score} for any object is fixed. Second, the top-k objects in any predicted view are sorted by their F_{scores}. Thus, o_i will always have a higher rank than o_j in any window in which they both participate, if $F(o_i) > F(o_j)$.

6.1 Integrated Infrastructure: MTopList

Given these properties, we now develop an integrated data structure to represent MTopBand top-k result sets for all predicted views. Our goal is to share the (1.) memory space among views by maintaining by maintaining only distinct objects each of which may participate in the predicted top-k results of possibly many queries; (2.) computation of positioning each new object into the predicted top-k results of all predicted views. This sharing leads us to remarkable savings in CPU and memory resources as discussed below.

To achieve this goal, instead of maintaining N_{act} independent predicted top-k result sets, namely one for each window, we propose to use a single integrated structure to represent the predicted top-k result sets for all windows. We call this structure MTopList.

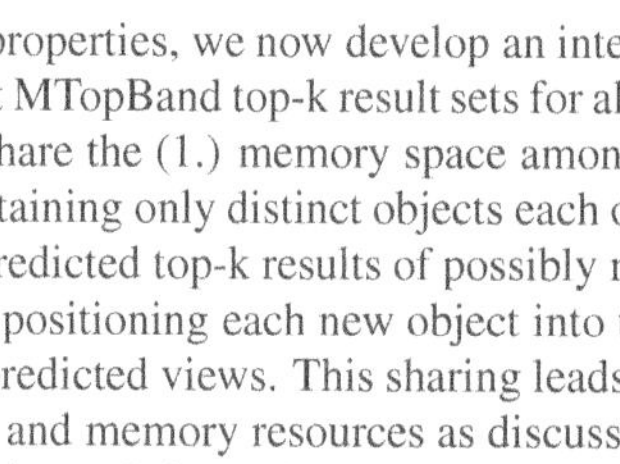

Figure 6: Physical view of MTopList

MTopList is sorted by F_{scores} of these distinct objects. Figure

6. shows the MTopList structure based on the workload WL of the three queries Q1, Q2, and Q3 introduced in Example 4.2. Note that Figure 4 depicts the MTopBand structure for the same example.

MTopList shown in Figure 6 includes all the predicted top-k results in the MTopBand structure. At time stamp t = 8s, a list of only 5 distinct objects with F_{scores} 12, 11, 9 and 6, and 5 are maintained instead of 5 independent top-k result sets for each of the current and future windows with redundant objects between the windows as maintained by MTopBand structure (Figure 4).

Clearly, in the MTopList structure an object may participate in more than one window, and it is usually a part of the top-k results for more than one query. Next, we tackle the problem of how to distinguish among and maintain top-k results for multiple windows and multiple queries in this integrated MTopList structure.

Lemma 6.1. *If top-k parameter k for all queries in WL is equal, then at the output time of the window W_i, the object with the smallest F_{score}, say O_{min_topk} of the predicted top-k results in any future window $W_{i+n}(n > 0)$ has a smaller than or equal F_{score} to that of any window $W_{i+m}(0 \leq m < n)$, i.e. $O_{min\_topk} \leq W_{i+m}.O_{min\_topk}$.*

Proof. When the top-k parameter for all queries is same, the number of predicted top-k results maintained in each current and future window is exactly same. After a window slides, some of the objects from the top-k result set in the current window may expire. The objects in the current window W_i that also participate in W_{i+n}, D_{W_i+n}, is a subset of those will participate in W_{i+m}, D_{Wi+m} (m < n). Thus, the minimal F score of the top-k objects selected from the object set D_{W_i+m} in W_{i+n} cannot be larger than the minimal F score of the top-k objects selected from a super set of $D_W i + n$, namely the object set $D_W i + m$ in W_{i+m}.

Based on Lemma 6.1, we now introduce the first step to distinguish between the objects participating in different windows and in the top-k results of different queries. We call this as *window mark representation.* More specifically, we represent two window marks (window id) for each object in the MTopList, namely the start window mark and the end window mark, which respectively represent the windows in which an object makes its first and its last occurrence to be predicted as the part of top-k result respectively.

Lemma 6.2. *For given windows W_{i+m} serving a query Q_m with top-k parameter $Q_m.k = X$, W_{i+n} with $Q_n.k = Y$, and W_{i+p} with $Q_p.k = X$ such that $0 < m < n < p$ and $X > Y > 0$; top-k elements participating in W_{i+m} with rank greater that Y (based on F_{score}) will not participate in W_{i+n} if the objects from rank 1 through Y in W_{i+m} are still alive at the time of window W_{i+n}. The objects with rank greater than Y will again participate in W_{i+p} if they are all still alive.*

Based on the Lemma 6.2, it can be seen that an object during its life time may participate as part of predicted top-k results in windows $Q_n.k = X$ and disappear for windows with top-k parameter $Q_n.k = Y$ then reappear for the windows with parameter $Q_n.k = X$, such that $Q_n.k = Y < Q_n.k = X$.

Thus, we observe that for all top-k results with rank greater than the top-k parameter $Q_i.k$ such that $Q_i.k$ is the smallest k parameter among all queries in the workload, there is a possibility of discontinuity in their participation as top-k results in the subsequent windows.

Hence, simply maintaining the first occurrence (start window mark) and the last occurrence (end window mark) would be insufficient to track in which windows among that range, a particular object actually participates. To tackle this, we maintain a separate pointer for each window at the lowest top-k object in the top-k result set so as to identify the actual top-k results in any particular window. We now introduce a minimum F_{score} pointer, FP_{min} for each window in the MTopList. The FP_{min} mark points to the object with smallest F_{score} in a particular window. Thus the number of FP_{min} marks maintained within MTopList is equal to N_{act}, namely one for each active window. We further utilize this pointer for updating the MTopList with each newly arriving object in the data stream as discussed in the next subsection.

Lemma 6.3. *At any given time, utilizing the start window mark and the end window mark of an object in the MTopList structure along with the FP_{min} mark for each window is sufficient to generate the top-k result for any query Q_i in the workload WL.*

6.2 The MTopList Maintenance

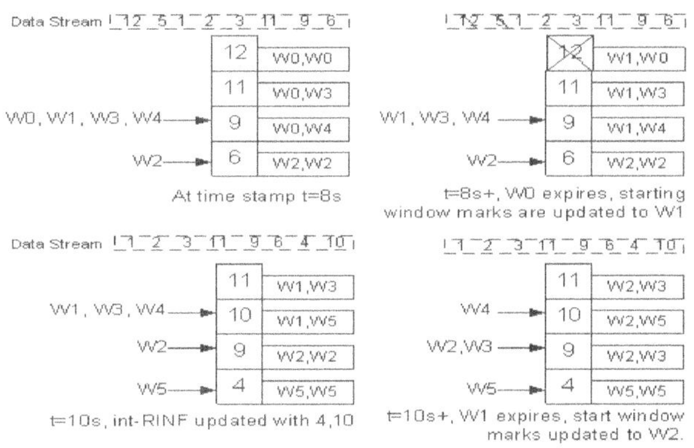

Figure 7: Updating the multi top-k results in integrated structure MTopList

Updating MTopList after expiration of existing objects. A careful mechanism is needed for updating MTopList every time a window slides. As discussed before, each object in the integrated structure may participate as a top-k result in more than one active window. So, if the oldest window W_0 expires the corresponding objects in W_0 cannot simply be deleted from the list. We develop a strategy that uses the starting and ending window marks to decide if an object needs to be physically removed from the MTopList altogether after the window slides.

We observe that, the top-k objects of the current-to-be expired window are the first $Q_{meta}.K$ objects in the MTopList. We recall(Section 4) that $Q_{meta}.K$ is equivalent to $Q_i.k$ where Q_i is the query that needs output when the current window expires. If the window serves more than one member query then $Q_{meta}.K$ is the maximum top-k-parameter of all the queries served by any window. The MTopList is sorted by objects' F_{score}. So, the current-to-expired window being the oldest window will contain $Q_{meta}.K$ objects with highest F_{score} as compared to the other objects in the list.

After the window expires, we increment the starting window mark of all objects in that window by 1. This indicates that window has expired as none of the objects in the list participate in that particular window. After incrementing the starting window marks if any of the objects in the list has a starting window mark larger than the ending window mark then we physically delete this object from the list because this object was participating only in the window that already expired and thus is not needed any more.

Updating MTopList after inserting newly arriving objects. Every time a new object, namely o_{new} is eligible to participate as a top-k result(decided based on o_{new}'s F_{score}) we take the following steps to update MTopList. At step 1, we find the correct position of o_{new} in MTopList. At step 2, we update o_{new}'s starting and ending window mark. Finally, we remove the object with the smallest F_{score} from the windows that the new object is predicted to be part of their top-k results.

For positioning each object into the MTopList, if the predicted top-k result set of any future window represented by the MTopList has not reached the size of k yet, or if its F score is larger than that of any object in the MTopList, we insert it into the MTopList. Otherwise it will be discarded immediately.

The position of O_{new} is easy to find utilizing the min_{FP} marks. $O_{new}.F_{score}$ (F_{score} of the new object O_{new}) is compared each of the min_{FP} starting from the lowest until an object with F_{score} greater than O_{new} is found.

If O_{new} is inserted at its correct position in the MTopList, it is in the predicted top-k results of at least the one window in its life span, its ending window mark is set to be the newest window Id the MTopList such that $O_i.min_{FP}.F_{score} < O_{new}.\ F_{score}$, where $O_i.min_{FP}.F_{score}$ is the F_{score} of the object marked by min_{FP}. The starting window mark of a new object is simply the oldest window on the MTopList, $O_i.min_{FP}.F_{score} < O_{new}\ F_{score}$.

Once we have O_{new}'s updated the starting window mark and ending window mark, we remove the objects pointed by min_{FP} marks from all those windows in which O_{new} is predicted to participate. We note that, here is that O_{new} may not participate as a top-k result in all windows from starting window mark to ending window mark(Observation 2). Thus, only those objects are removed whose $O_i.min_{FP}.F_{score}$ is smaller than $O_{new}\ F_{score}$; $O_i.start_{mark}$ is greater than or equal to $O_{new}.start_{mark}$ and $O_i.start_{mark}$ is smaller than or equal to $O_{new}.end_{mark}$.

7. EXPERIMENTAL STUDY

Our experiments are conducted on a Sony VIAO laptop with Intel Centrino Duo 2.6GHz processor and 1GB memory, running Windows Vista. All the algorithms are implemented in Eclipse IDE using C++.

Real Datasets. We used two real streaming data sets. The first data set, GMTI (Ground Moving Target Indicator) data [18], records the real-time information of moving objects gathered by 24 different data ground stations or aircrafts in 6 hours from Joint STARS. It has around 100,000 records regarding the information of vehicles and helicopters (speed ranging from 0-200 mph) moving in a certain geographic region. The second dataset is the Stock Trading Traces data (STT) from [19], which has one million transaction records throughout the trading hours of a day.

Alternative Algorithms. We compare our proposed algorithm MTopLists performance with two alternative methods, namely, 1. state-of-the-art single top-k query solution MinTopK [16] that processes each query independently in the workload WL. 2. MTopBand, the basic algorithm we first presented in this work (Section 5.).

Experimental Methodologies. We measure two common metrics for stream processing algorithms, namely average processing time for each tuple (CPU time) and memory footprint.

We perform the scalability tests to verify the performance of the proposed algorithms with the increasing number of queries in the input workload. We first evaluate at a time two test cases, each varying on only one of the three query parameters. Then, we test the more general cases of varying two parameters, and finally all three query parameters are set to be arbitrary. For each experiment, we vary *win* in the range of 100K to 1 M, *slide* between 10K to 100K, and *k* in the range of 10-1000.

7.1 Scalability Evaluation

Scalability tests with one arbitrary parameter. For each test case, we prepare three workloads with 10, 100, and 1000 queries respectively by randomly generating one input parameter (in a certain range) for each member query, while using common parameter settings for the other two query parameters.

Fixed win, Fixed $slide$, and Arbitrary k. In this experiment, we evaluate performance of our proposed algorithms as compared to the state-of-art algorithm [16]. We use fixed *win* = 1M and *slide* = 100K, while varying *k* from 10 to 1000. We randomly generate *k* between the range 10 - 1000 for each query.

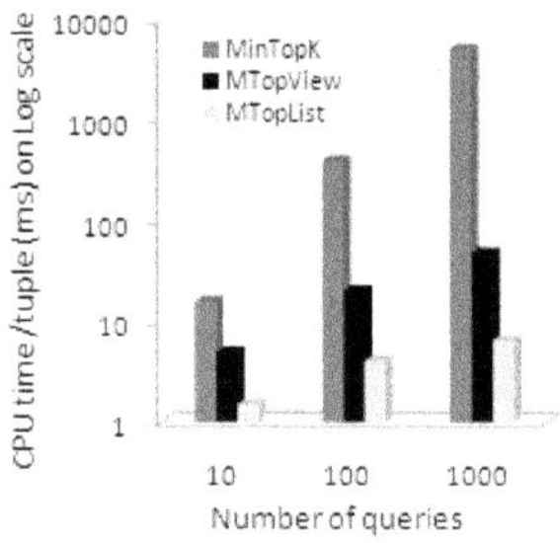

Figure 8: CPU time used by three algorithms with different k values

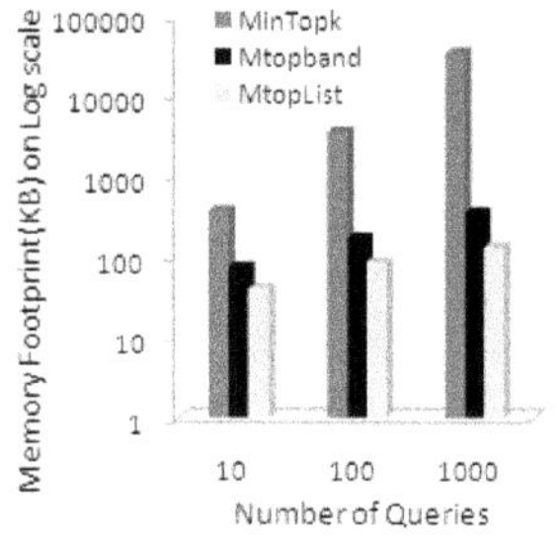

Figure 9: Memory space used by three algorithms with different k values

Figures 8 and 9 show the CPU time and memory space, on logarithmic scale, used by the three algorithms. Clearly, performance of our proposed methods is in order of magnitude better than MinTopK algorithm. Amongst all three compared algorithms , MinTopK's [16] CPU time increases as a direct multiple of the size of workload. The increase in the CPU time is around 100 times when the number of queries increases from 10 to 1000. Put differently, it does not scale well with the cardinality of the workload.

For the memory space used, MTopList has even better performance as its utilization of memory space only increases 2.5 times when the number of queries increases from 10 to 1000, while such increase for MTopBand and MinTopK are 6 times and 99 times respectively.

We note that in this case only top-k parameter *k* is arbitrary. Thus, this is the best possible case for our proposed algorithm as maximum sharing is achieved here. Next, we discuss the experimental evaluation for the cases when *k* is fixed, while other query parameters, *win* or *slide* are varying.

Varying *slide sizes*. In this experiment, we use *win* = 1M and *k* = 1000 , while we randomly generate *slide* values between the range 100K - 1M.

As shown in Figures 10 and 11, both the CPU and memory usage of MTopList is still significantly less than those utilized by the state-of-the-art algorithm MinTopK [16]. In particular, for processing 100 queries , MTopList only takes 0.0066 s to process each object on average, while MinTopK needs 0.712 s for each object. This is as expected and can be explained by the same reasons as in the previous test cases.

However, an important observation made from this experiment is that the performance of of our basic algorithm MTopBand can be affected by the $win/slide$ ratio. We recall that MTopBand maintains the predicted top-k results for each future window indepen-

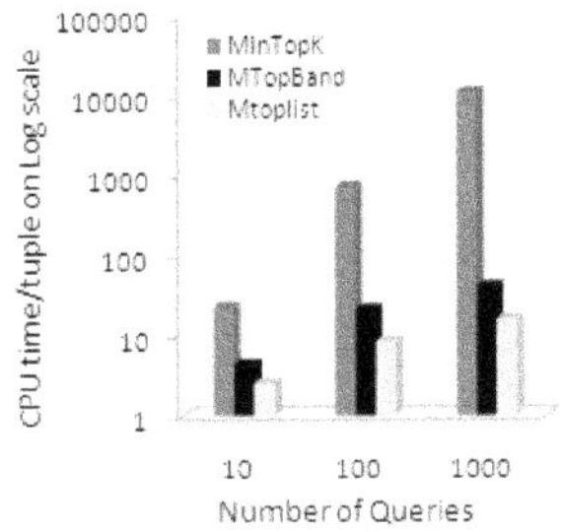

Figure 10: CPU time used by three algorithms with different *slide* values

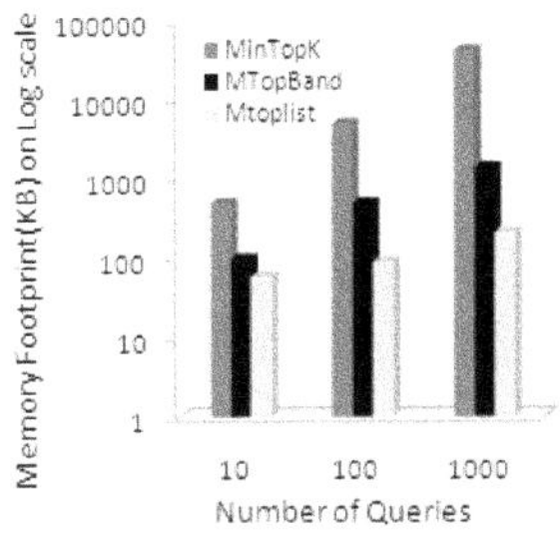

Figure 11: Memory space used by three algorithms with different *slide* values

dently, thus its resource utilization is expected to increase with the number of future windows maintained, which is equal to *win*/*slide*.

In this experiment, *win* is fixed to 1M while *slide* is randomly picked, resulting in a large value of *win*/*slide* ratio for some of the queries in the workload. On the other hand, the performance of MTopList remains unaffected with increase in the *win*/*slide* ratio. This is because MTopList only maintains distinct top-k objects which are not dependent on number of predicted views maintained at a given time.

Scalability tests with more than one arbitrary query parameters For each test case, we prepare three workloads with 10, 100, and 1000 queries respectively by first randomly generating two input parameters (in a certain range) for each member query, while using common parameter settings for just one query parameters. Finally, we evaluate the most general case by randomly generating all three query parameters.

Arbitrary *win*, Arbitrary *slide*, and fixed *k*.

In this case, we use $k = 100$, while varying *win* from 100K to 1M and *slide* from 10K to 100K.

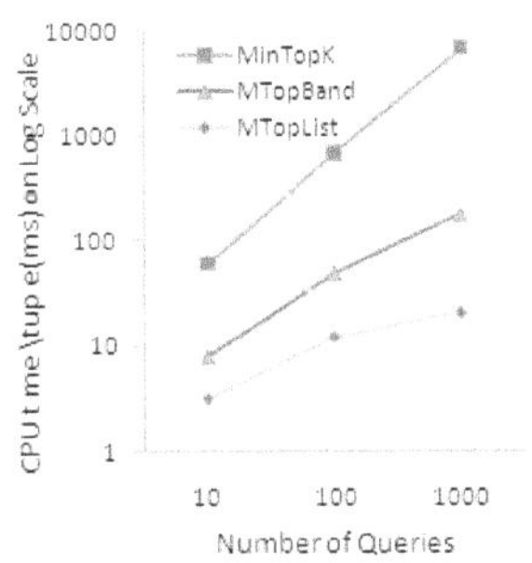

Figure 12: CPU time used by three algorithms with different *win* and *slide* values

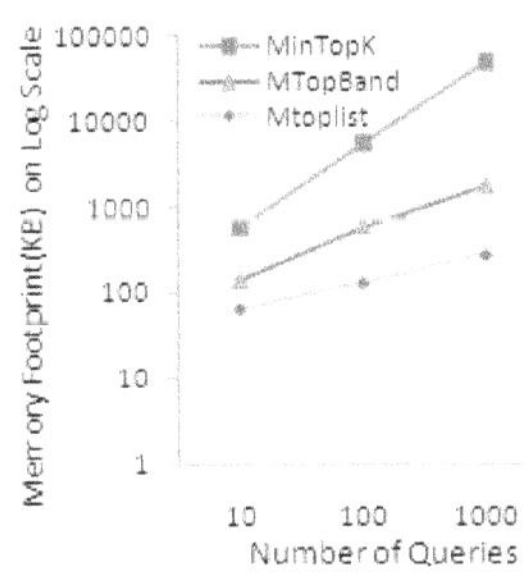

Figure 13: Memory space consumed by three algorithms with different *win* and *slide* values

As shown in Figures 12 and 13, the CPU time consumed by MTopList per tuple increases 4.1 times, when the number of queries increase from 10 to 100 and it further increases around 2.3 times when number of queries increase from 100 to 1000. Whereas for the basic proposed algorithm MTopBand, the CPU time increases around 7 times from 10 to 100 queries and around 4.5 times from 100 to 1000 queries. MinTopK utilizes 99 and 91 times more CPU and memory respectiely when number of queries are increase from 10 to 1000. Clearly, this increase in CPU consumption time of the proposed algorithm with increase in the number of queries is modest as compared to the alternative algorithms.

The ratio of increased CPU consumption time is 1.5 times more as compared to the previous only one arbitrary parameter case. This is because two arbitrary query parameters lead to decrease in the sharing amongst different queries, and thus increases the maintenance costs of both MTopList and MTopBand.

General case: All Arbitrary Parameters. Finally, we evaluate the general case with all three parameters *win*, *slide*, and *k* being varied arbitrarily.

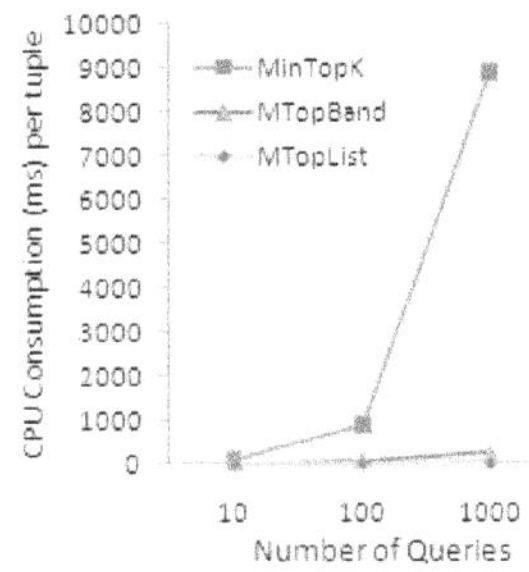

Figure 14: CPU time used by three algorithms with arbitrary *win* and *slide* parameters

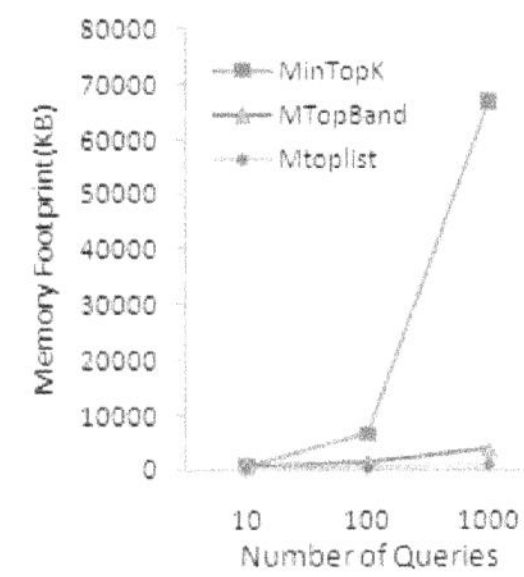

Figure 15: Memory space consumed by three algorithms with arbitrary *win* an

Figures 14 and 15 show the performance of the three algorithms in terms of CPU and memory utilization. Clearly, MTopList wins over the other two algorithms for both CPU and memory utilization in this case too. MTopList takes around 30-40 times less CPU time to process 1000 queries as compared to MTopBand. Also, MTopList takes around 330 times less CPU time as compared to the state-of-art algorithm MinTopK. This saving is less as compared to the previous cases where only one or at the most two parameters are arbitrary. This is caused by too large variations on the parameter settings. The important observation here is MTopList never performs worse than MTopBand for any workload.

8. RELATED WORK

Top-k queries on a static data set have been well studied in the literature. The top-k algorithms, *Onion* [2] and *Prefer* [8], based on preprocessing techniques, require the complete data set to be available in memory for computing the top-k objects.

[10] presents algorithms that reduce the storage and maintenance costs of materialized top-k views in the presence of deletions and updates. Other works in relational databases like [11,12] focus on multidimensional histograms and sampling-based technique to map top-k queries into traditional ranges. [3,4,5] study top-k queries in distributed data repositories. In general, they minimize the communication cost for retrieving the top-k objects from distributed data repositories.

Fagin et al. [13] introduce two methods for processing ranked queries. The TA algorithm is optimal for repositories that support random access, while the NRA algorithm assumes that only sorted access is available. Chang and Hwang [7] introduce MPro, a general algorithm that optimizes the execution of expensive predicates for a variety of top-k queries.

All the above methods are based on the assumption that the relevant data set is available at the compilation stage of query execution either locally or in distributed servers. Also they are designed to report the top-k results only once. Thus these techniques are not suitable for streaming environments where the data are not known in advance, rather they keep changing as new tuples arrive and old ones expire.

More recently researchers have started to look at the problem of top-k queries in streaming environments. Most of this work is focused on single top-k query processing where the assumption is that at a time only one top-k query is registered in the system [6,14,16] . Among these works, [16] presents an optimal technique for top-k query processing both computationally and memory wise. Although optimal for single top-k query processing, this technique does not handle multiple queries simultaneously registered in the system. Our experiments show that our proposed sharing strategy by many orders of magnitude outperforms the solution of executing top-k queries independently for multiple queries.

To the best of our knowledge, [15] and [17] are the only two works that handle simultaneously registered multiple top-k queries in streaming scenario. [15] tackles the problem of exact continuous multiple top-k queries monitoring over a single stream. The proposed techniques share only the indices among different registered queries by maintaining index and bookkeeping structures. They introduce two algorithms. First, the TMA algorithm computes the new answer for a query whenever some of the current top-k points expire. Second, the SMA algorithm maintains a Şsky-band structure" that aims to contain sufficient number of objects so that it need not go back to the full data stream window.

However, unfortunately, neither of these two algorithms eliminates the recomputation bottleneck from the top-k monitoring process. Thus, they both require full storage of all objects in the query window. Furthermore, they both need to conduct expensive top-k recomputation from scratch in certain cases, though SMA conducts recomputation less frequently than TMA. While our proposed algorithm eliminates the recomputation bottleneck altogether thus realize complete incremental computation and minimal memory usage.

Experiments conducted by the optimal technique for top-k query processing [16] shows a significant CPU and memory resource saving over [15]. Our experimental results confirm the improvements by many orders of magnitude achieved by our proposed algorithm over [16] for any workload with a size of 2 queries and greater. Thus, our proposed algorithm achieves a clear win over each the state-of-art techniques.

[17] handles multiple top-k queries, but based on the probabilistic top-k model in data streams. While we work with a complete and non-probabilistic model. Also their focus is to achieve sharing among the queries on the preference function while we focus on other important parameters of a continuous top-k query, namely window size, slide size and K. In short, they in large target different problems from ours. In particular, the key fact affecting the top-k monitoring algorithm design is the meta information maintained for real-time top-k ranking and the corresponding update methods , which vary fundamentally by these respective top-k models.

9. CONCLUSION AND FUTURE WORK

In this work, we present the MTopS framework for efficient shared processing of a large number of top-k queries over streaming windows. MTopS achieves significant resource sharing at the query level by analyzing the parameter settings. MTopS further optimizes the shared processing by identifying and maintaining only the minimal object set from the data stream that is both necessary and sufficient for top-k monitoring of all queries in the workload. Our experimental studies based on both real and synthetic streaming data confirm the clear superiority of MTopS to the state-of-the-art solution. We confirm that MTopS exhibits excellent scalability in terms of being able to handle thousands of queries under high speed input streams in our experiments. As future work, this framework can be used to scale-up considering multiple machines and grouping of workloads into sub-workloads to be assigned to different machines.

10. REFERENCES

[1] A. Arasu, S Babu, and J. Widom. The cql continuous query language; semantic foundation and query execution. *VLDB J.*, 15(2):121-142, 2006.

[2] Y.C. Chang, L.D. Bergman, V. Castelli, C.S. Li, M.L. Lo, and J.R. Smith. The onion technique: Indexing for linear optimization queries. In *SIGMOD*, pp 391-402, 2000.

[3] B. Babcock and C. Olston. Distributed top-k monitoring. In *SIGMOD*, pp 28-39, 2003.

[4] K. C.-C. Chang and S. Won Hwang. Minimal probing: supportive expensive probing: supporting expensive predicates for top-k queries. In *SIGMOD*, pp 391-402, 2000.

[5] S. Chaudhuri, L.Gravano, and A. Marian. Optimizing top-k selection queries over multimedia repositories. $IEEETrans./-Knowl.DataEng.$, 16(8):992-1009,2004.

[6] P. Haghani, S. Michel, and K. Aberer. Evaluating top-k queries over incomplete data streams. In CIKM, pp 877-886, 2009.

[7] K. C.-C. Chang and S. won Hwang. Minimal probing: supporting expensive predicates for top-k queries. In *SIGMOD*, pp 346-357, 2002.

[8] V. Hristidis and Y. Papakonstantinou. Algorithms and applications for answering ranked queries using ranked views. VLDB J. 13(1): 49-70, 2004.

[9] S.Nepal, M.V. Ramakrishnan: Query processing issues in image(multimedia) databases. In *ICDE* (1999).

[10] K. Yi, H. Yu, J. Yang, G. Xia, and Y. Chen. Efficient maintenance of materialized top-k views. In ICDE, pp 189-200, 2003.

[11] N. Bruno, S. Chaudhuri, and L. Gravano. Top-k selection queries over relational databases: Mapping strategies and performance evaluation. TODS,27(2):153-187, 2002.

[12] C.-M. Chen and Y. Ling. A sampling-based estimator for top-k query. In ICDE, pp 617-627, 2002.

[13] R. Fagin, A. Lotem, and M. Naor. Optimal aggregation algorithms for middleware. In *PODS*, 2001.

[14] G. Das,D. Gunopulos, N. Koudas, and N. Sarkas. Adhoc Topk Query Answering for Data Streams. In *VLDB*, 2007, pp 23-28.

[15] K. Mouratidis, S. Bakiras, and D. Papadias. Continuous monitoring of top-k queries over sliding windows. In *SIGMOD*, pp 635-646, 2006.

[16] D. Yang, A. Shastri, E.A. Rundensteiner, and M. O. Ward. An Optimal Strategy for Monitoring Top-k Queries in Streaming Windows. In *EDBT*, pp 138-152, 2011.

[17] C. Jin, K. Yi, L. Chen, J. X. Yu, and X. Lin. Sliding-window top-k queries on uncertain streams. PVLDB, 1(1):301Ű312, 2008.

[18] J. N. Entzminger, C. A. Fowler, and W. J. Kenneally. Jointstars and gmti: Past, present and future. IEEE Transactions on Aerospace and Electronic Systems, 35(2):748-762, april 1999.

[19] I. INETATS. Stock trade traces. http://www.inetats.com/.

[20] K. Yi, H. Yu, J. Y. 0001, G. Xia, and Y. Chen. Efficient maintenance of materialized top-k views. In ICDE, pp 189-200, 2003.

11. ACKNOWLEDGEMENT

This work is supported under NSF grants CCF-0811510, IIS-0119276 and IIS-00414380. We thank our collaborators at MITRE, J. Casper and P. Leveille, for providing us the GMTI data stream.

Probabilistic Near-Duplicate Detection Using Simhash

Sadhan Sood
Texas A&M University
College Station, TX 77843
sadhan@cs.tamu.edu

Dmitri Loguinov*
Texas A&M University
College Station, TX 77843
dmitri@cs.tamu.edu

ABSTRACT

This paper offers a novel look at using a dimensionality-reduction technique called `simhash` [8] to detect similar document pairs in large-scale collections. We show that this algorithm produces interesting intermediate data, which is normally discarded, that can be used to predict which of the bits in the final hash are more susceptible to being flipped in similar documents. This paves the way for a probabilistic search technique in the Hamming space of `simhashes` that can be significantly faster and more space-efficient than the existing `simhash` approaches. We show that with 95% recall compared to deterministic search of prior work [16], our method exhibits 4-14 times faster lookup and requires 2-10 times less RAM on our collection of 70M web pages.

Categories and Subject Descriptors

H.3.3 [**Information Search and Retrieval**]: Clustering

General Terms

Algorithms

Keywords

Hamming distance, similarity, simhash, clustering

1. INTRODUCTION

Many clustering problems in data mining involve *similarity matching*, which is a process of finding pairs of documents in collection $\mathcal{D}$ that are similar (in some sense) to each other. To decouple similarity from page semantics and ultimately human judgement, it is common to preprocess the data by extracting d-dimensional *feature vectors* (i.e., syntactic elements perceived to be important) from each page and solving the matching problem on them.

When the number of dimensions d is large, many traditional clustering approaches [4], [12] are a $\Theta(n^2)$ endeavor, where $n = |\mathcal{D}|$, that requires an all-to-all comparison across the entire dataset. Since this is infeasible for collections larger than a few thousand pages, another approach [6], [8], [14] is to devise *approximate* algorithms that can compute similarity using much smaller data structures and sub-quadratic overhead. One promising technique in this category, called `simhash` [8], [13], [16], relies on replacing feature vectors with b-bit fingerprints that preserve cosine similarity of the vector space.

The main challenge with `simhash` is to quickly find all pairs of fingerprints within a certain Hamming distance h of each other. For large collections (i.e., billions of pages), the currently fastest and most space-efficient solution [16], which we call *Block-Permuted Hamming Search* (BPHS), relies on permuting chunks of each hash and performing lookups in multiple similarly-permuted copies of the dataset. However, since $\mathcal{D}$ must be replicated at least four times in RAM, BPHS may be unsuitable for certain memory-constrained systems. Even if enough RAM exists to hold $4n$ items, unless the number of copies is scaled with dataset size, the search complexity of this method is still quadratic in n.

Noticing that `simhash` is already probabilistic in nature and does not guarantee 100% recall on vector pairs, it makes sense to ask whether by sacrificing a small additional percentage of recall one can reduce RAM consumption of BPHS, speed up the search, and improve scalability as $n \to \infty$. We investigate this question next.

1.1 Our Contributions

We first analyze the construction process of `simhash` and observe that certain bits are much more *volatile* (i.e., likely to be flipped by modification of features) than others. This leads to a conjecture that the Hamming-distance problem on `simhash` can be solved efficiently by an iterative process that intelligently searches to distance h within the volatile bits and performs lookups in a *single* copy of the dataset, keeping RAM overhead at the theoretical minimum.

Thus, the main question with using this approach is how to design an efficient algorithm that decides which bits to flip, in what order, and when to stop (if less than 100% recall is desired). For a given page u, let $p_i(u)$ be the probability that bit i of u's hash is different from that in other pages of the collection and $\mathcal{S} \subseteq \{1, 2, \ldots, b\}$ be some subset of hash bits. Then, the probability that there exists another `simhash` that differs from u only in bits contained in $\mathcal{S}$ can be estimated as:

$$p(u, \mathcal{S}) = \prod_{i \in \mathcal{S}} p_i(u) \prod_{j \notin \mathcal{S}} (1 - p_j(u)), \quad (1)$$

where independence between the bits is assumed from the `simhash` algorithm [8].

*Supported by NSF grants CNS-0720571 and CNS-1017766.

To maximize useful work and allow the search to stop after $k \ll \binom{b}{h}$ attempts, one requires a method for obtaining the top-k subsets $\mathcal{S}$ ($1 \le |\mathcal{S}| \le h$) in decreasing order of their probability $p(\mathcal{S})$, but with much lower complexity than exponential needed to compute all possible values (1) and sort them. To solve this problem, we offer a novel algorithm we call *Volatility Ordered Set Heap* (VOSH), which performs the job in the optimal $\Theta(k \log k)$ time and $\Theta(k)$ space. For the common setting $h = 3$ and $b = 64$ suggested for large datasets [16], we compare VOSH with a matching algorithm that flips bits in random order without repetition. Our results show that for 100% recall, the former requires 61 times fewer attempts than the latter; for 80% recall, 151 times fewer; and for 50% recall, 347 times fewer.

We incorporate VOSH in a system we call *Probabilistic Simhash Matching* (PSM) for finding similar documents in large collections $\mathcal{D}$ under two modes of operation – *online* and *batch*. The former case, assuming that $\mathcal{D}$ fits in RAM, aims to minimize the latency of answering queries about incoming pages u. The latter case, assuming that $\mathcal{D}$ is kept on disk, aims to maximize the query throughput rate. We compare our method against BPHS [16] in terms query speed and RAM usage using a web collection with 70M documents. For 95% recall, our results show that PSM requires $2-10$ times less RAM, while being $5-14$ times faster than BPHS. We also model both approaches and show that with a fixed number of copies of the dataset in RAM, PSM scales as $O(n \log^h(n) \log\log n)$ as opposed to BPHS's $\Theta(n^2)$.

2. RELATED WORK

The first approach to matching similar documents is to convert them to some canonical form in which they become exact duplicates. By removing certain tokens perceived dispensable (e.g., high/low IDF words [9]) and hashing the resulting page to a single fingerprint, similar documents can be found in $\Theta(n \log n)$ time using sorting.

Detecting similar pages over a general space of d-dimensional feature vectors is a more challenging task, especially at non-trivial scale. In the small number of dimensions $d \ll \log_2 n$, special data structures (e.g., R-tree [12], Kd-tree [4]) can find near neighbors in $\Theta(n \log n)$ time; however, their performance deteriorates to that of an exhaustive search (or worse) as d increases. Since web-scale collections usually exhibit dictionaries with millions of unique words, each typically mapping to a feature, this approach is generally inapplicable to such cases.

A more viable solution for large d and n involves approximate algorithms that sacrifice some precision and recall in favor of manageable speed. These include *Locality-Sensitive Hashing* (LSH) [14], *Min-Wise Independent Permutations* [7], `simhash` [8], and many variations [2], [3], [6], [5], [10], [13], [16], [18]. This is the direction we pursue below.

3. FUNDAMENTALS

We start by motivating the usage of fingerprints, analyze the brute-force approach to finding near duplicates, and formulate the problem we aim to solve.

3.1 Framework and Motivation

Since our focus is on large web crawls (i.e., billions of pages), `simhash`'s low space and time complexity [16], as well as high precision [13] compared to other hashing techniques [7], are quite appealing. With this in mind, we next set up the terminology and notation that will be needed later.

n	Cosine $s(u,v)$		Hamming $H(x,y)$	
	Time	RAM	Time	RAM
1M	91 days	1.1 GB	34 min	8 MB
64M	1,020 years	70 GB	97 days	512 MB
8B	261K years	9 TB	68 years	64 GB

Table 1: Extrapolated delay to compute cosine similarity and Hamming distance on all pairs (one core of AMD Phenom II 2.8 GHz).

Let $\mathcal{F} = \{1, 2, \ldots, d\}$ be the set of all unique features across the entire collection and $\mathcal{F}(u) \subseteq \mathcal{F}$ be the set of features present on page $u \in \mathcal{D}$. The number of features $f(u) = |\mathcal{F}(u)|$ can vary from a few hundred to a few thousand depending on which features are selected and the specific dataset. Each feature $i \in \mathcal{F}(u)$ is described by a certain real weight $w_i(u) \in \mathbb{R}$, which measures the importance and contribution of i to u. A combination of $\mathcal{F}(u)$ and weights $\{w_i(u)\}_{i \in \mathcal{F}(u)}$ represents the *feature vector* of page u.

Define $\mathcal{V}$ to be the set of all feature vectors produced by $\mathcal{D}$ and assume some similarity measure $s : \mathcal{V}^2 \to [0, 1]$ that maps pairs of vectors to real numbers (i.e., values close to 0 indicate dissimilar documents and those close to 1 indicate similar ones). In the context of shingles and min-wise hashing [7], $s(u, v)$ is usually Jaccard's coefficient; however, for `simhash` and non-integer weights it is more common to utilize cosine similarity [8], which we also do below whenever comparison in the vector space is needed.

To understand the scale at which similarity can be sought in an all-to-all search among feature vectors, we have the following analysis. Each pair of vectors (u, v) requires $f(u) + f(v)$ operations, some of which can be quite expensive (e.g., multiplication for cosine similarity), for a total overhead of $E[f(u)]n^2$. Assuming ζ bytes are needed to store each feature index and its weight, the expected space requirement of $\mathcal{D}$ is $nE[f(u)]\zeta$. Using our dataset of webpages with $E[f(u)] = 141$ and $\zeta = 8$, the left side of Table 1 shows the amount of time and RAM needed to find all duplicate vectors under cosine $s(u, v)$. Notice in the table that both space and time are prohibitive, even for relatively small datasets.

To make storage and computation more reasonable, a second level of approximation (i.e., `simhash`) is a one-way mapping $\mathcal{V} \to \{0, 1\}^b$ that converts feature vectors to b-bit binary strings. Assuming $\mathcal{H}$ is the collection of hashes produced by $\mathcal{V}$, the main similarity metric on $\mathcal{H}$ is Hamming distance $H(x, y)$ whose benefit over $s(u, v)$ lies in the fact that it can be computed with a handful of CPU instructions [20].

Replacing each feature vector with its 64-bit `simhash`, the right side of Table 1 shows an improvement in computational speed by a factor of 3800 (i.e., from 70K pairs/sec to 268M pairs/sec) and a reduction in space by a factor of 141, both of which are substantial. While this solves the problem for n up to a few million pages, the 3 months for medium-sized collections and the 68 years for large datasets shown in the table are still undesirable in practice. This explains our interest in sub-quadratic techniques for computing Hamming distances over large document sets.

3.2 Problem Formulation

There are two classes of matching problems we consider in this paper. In the first class (e.g., clustering [11]), the

Algorithm 1 Simhash (u)

```
W ← array of b zeros
for i ∈ F(u) do                          ▷ Examine each feature
    φ_i ← UniformHash(i)                 ▷ Compute b-bit hash
    for j = 1 to b do                    ▷ Iterate through each bit
        if φ_ij = 1 then                 ▷ j-th bit of φ_i
            W[j] ← W[j] + w_i            ▷ Add feature weight
        else
            W[j] ← W[j] − w_i            ▷ Subtract feature weight
        end if
    end for
end for
for j = 1 to b do                        ▷ Revisit all bits
    if W[j] ≥ 0 then
        B[j] ← 1                         ▷ Positive weight, set bit to 1
    else
        B[j] ← 0                         ▷ Negative weight, set bit to 0
    end if
end for
return array B[1...b]                    ▷ simhash
```

goal is to find *all* matches for a given page. Knowing pairwise similarity among pages, one can use separate clustering algorithms, which we do not consider here, to combine the various documents into groups.

OBJECTIVE 1. *Given x, find all $y \in \mathcal{H}$ s.t. $H(x, y) \leq h$.*

In the second class (e.g., duplicate elimination [13], plagiarism detection [19]), the goal is to determine if there exists *at least one* similar page in the dataset, without finding all matching documents, which often can save significant processing overhead and increase performance.

OBJECTIVE 2. *Given x, find any $y \in \mathcal{H}$ s.t. $H(x, y) \leq h$.*

It should be noted that these goals are not specific to what features are being used (e.g., individual words, shingles, HTML tags, anchor text, URLs), their weights (e.g., frequency, TF-IDF, HTML highlight), dimensionality of the vectors, or classification purpose.

4. UNDERSTANDING SIMHASH

We next explain the `simhash` construction algorithm and dissect the properties of its hashes.

4.1 Algorithm

Recall that `simhash` is a feature fingerprinting technique that uses random projections to generate compact representation of high-dimensional vectors. Its main characteristic is that the Hamming distance between two document fingerprints is positively correlated with cosine similarity between the corresponding feature vectors.

Using the notation of the previous section, Algorithm 1 explains the `simhash` process of [13], [16], which we discuss in more detail next. Denote by W a vector of temporary weights that the `simhash` function generates. As we will see later, these weights are important elements of the proposed framework. For each feature i in the current document u, Algorithm 1 first computes its uniformly random hash ϕ_i and then decides to either add or subtract the feature's weight w_i to/from W_j based on whether the j-th bit ϕ_{ij} of the uniform hash is zero or one. After all features have been processed, bits of `simhash` with non-negative W_j are set to 1 and the remaining bits are set to 0.

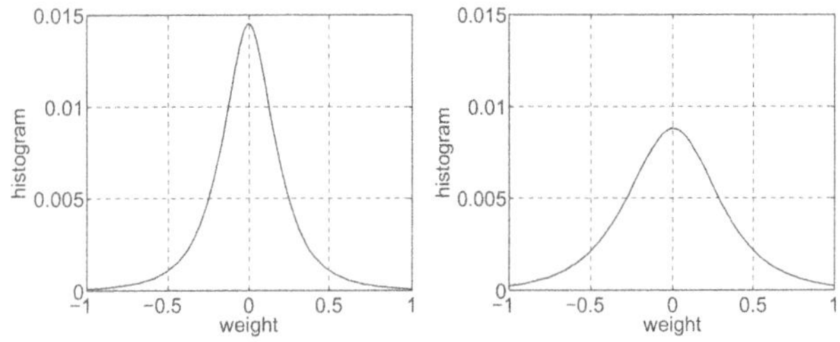

(a) weight $W_1(u)$ (b) re-write weight Y_1

Figure 1: Histograms of simhash weights (bin size 1/150, collection of 70M documents).

4.2 Weights and Hamming Distance

We are now ready to examine the distribution of weights $\{W_j\}$ and lay the foundation for understanding which bits are more likely to be different between similar documents.

Personalizing each variable in the algorithm with its page u, it is not difficult to notice that `simhash` computes a dot-product between a global vector of iid random variables and a vector of u's specific feature weights:

$$W_j(u) = \sum_{i \in \mathcal{F}(u)} (2\phi_{ij} - 1) w_i(u), \tag{2}$$

where $\{\phi_{ij}\}_{ij}$ are iid Bernoulli variables with $E[\phi_{ij}] = 1/2$. This makes each weight $W_j(u)$ zero-mean:

$$E[W_j(u)] = \sum_{i \in \mathcal{F}(u)} E[2\phi_{ij} - 1] E[w_i(u)] = 0. \tag{3}$$

Using normalized TF-IDF weights $w_i(u)$, Figure 1(a) shows the distribution of $W_1(u)$ from (2) using our collection of 70M documents. We focus only on the first bit since the others produce identical results. While the Central Limit Theorem suggests that constant feature weights (e.g., used in [13]) are expected to converge $W_j(u)$ to a Gaussian distribution, TF-IDF weights interestingly lead to a Laplace-like distribution (log-linear plots of tails are omitted for brevity).

To control the variance and distribution of resulting sums, one can generalize (2) to non-Bernoulli cases. Assume $\nu_i = (\nu_{i1}, \ldots, \nu_{ib})$ is a vector permanently associated with feature $i \in \mathcal{F}$ whose elements are drawn from a zero-mean symmetric distribution. Then, (2) becomes:

$$W_j(u) = \sum_{i \in \mathcal{F}(u)} \nu_{ij} w_i(u), \tag{4}$$

while the rest of the algorithm remains the same. Assuming $\theta \in [0, \pi]$ is the angle between two d-dimensional vectors, [8] shows that if ν_{ij} are zero-mean Gaussian variables, the probability that the corresponding fingerprints collide on a given bit is $q = 1 - \theta/\pi \approx (\cos\theta + 1)/2$. While no similar closed-form result is available for (2), intuition suggests that a correlation between $\cos\theta$ and q still exists.

Since $w_i(u)$'s positive contribution to bit j_1 has no bearing on whether its contribution to another bit j_2 will be positive or negative, it follows that bits in the final `simhash` are *pairwise independent*, which implies that $H(x, y)$ is a binomial random variable with parameters b and $1 - q$. While a-priori this tells us nothing about which bits are likely to differ in a random pair (x, y), we next show that utilizing the knowledge of x's **simhash** weights $\{W_j\}$ allows an informed decision.

4.3 Why Bits Flip

Suppose page u undergoes a re-write, which includes deletion of α existing features and addition of β new features. This modifies each **simhash** weight j to:

$$W'_j(u) = W_j(u) - X_j^\alpha + X_j^\beta, \quad (5)$$

where X_j^α and X_j^β are summations in the form of (2) that correspond to the deleted/added features. Define $Y_j = X_j^\alpha - X_j^\beta$ to be the random weight change that occurs in response to these modifications. Since we are interested in changes to u that exist in our collection $\mathcal{D}$ (as opposed to an infinite number of hypothetical modifications), Y_j can be viewed as a random variable with the same distribution as $\{W_j(u) - W_j(v)\}_{u,v\in\mathcal{D}}$, which is shown in Figure 1(b). The main difference from part (a) is the doubled variance (i.e., $Var[Y_j] = Var[W_j(u)] + Var[W_j(v)] = 2Var[W_j(u)]$) and a slightly more Gaussian shape; however, the log-scale shows that both tails remain exponential rather than Gaussian.

Conditioned on $W_j(u) = c$, it follows that $W'_j(u) = c - Y_j$, which suggests that the difficulty of flipping bit j is directly related to the magnitude of c. Indeed, first notice that Y_j is zero-mean since $E[X_j^\alpha] = E[X_j^\beta] = 0$, which follows from (3). Second, averaged over all possible pairs (α, β), the distribution of Y_j is symmetric around 0 since X_α and X_β are iid. We can make this argument due to the non-adversarial nature of changes applied to the page. As a result, we have $P(Y_j > |c|) = P(Y_j < -|c|)$. Finally, in order to flip bit j, one must encounter a modification that satisfies both a) $|Y_j| > |c|$ and b) $\text{sign}(Y_j) = \text{sign}(c)$. The probability of this happening is $P(Y_j > |c|) = 1 - F_j(|c|)$, where $F_j(x)$ is the CDF of Y_j. Due to the monotonicity of CDFs, this probability monotonically decays with $|c|$.

This brings us to our main result of the section. Observe that each **simhash** contains certain bits that are much more volatile than others. Assume page v is similar to u according to cosine similarity at some threshold (e.g., 0.9). Then, if v manages to flip some bits in u's **simhash**, the likely order of these flips follows from the smallest $|W_j(u)|$ to the largest. For example, consider **simhash** weights $(1.9, 0.01, -0.5)$ for the first three bits and the distribution of Y_j from Figure 1(b). If anything at all is flipped by small changes, it will most likely be a single bit 2. Much more effort is needed to flip bit 3, while bit 1 requires massive summations of added/deleted features in (2) to overpower its weight 1.9.

While it is straightforward to generate lookups for Hamming distance $h = 1$ (i.e., by sorting all bits in the increasing order of $|W_j(u)|$), multi-bit flips are more difficult. For example, is the two-bit combination with weights $(1.9, 0.01)$ more likely than a single-bit combination with weight -0.5? We study this question next.

5. BIT ORDER

This section develops an efficient technique for deciding the order in which bits should be attempted during similarity search on $\mathcal{H}$.

5.1 Model

Define $p_j(u) = P(Y_j > |W_j(u)|)$ to be the probability of that another page in $\mathcal{D}$ has flipped bit j in the **simhash** of a given page u. While obtaining a closed-form model for $p_j(u)$ might be possible in future work, an empirical distribution of Y_j sampled from pages in $\mathcal{D}$, e.g., as in Figure 1(b), is sufficient for estimating $p_j(u)$ in practice.

Let $\mathcal{S} \subseteq \{1, 2, \dots, b\}$ be a non-empty subset of hash bits. Then, the probability that there exists a page in $\mathcal{D}$ that differs from u only in the bits contained in $\mathcal{S}$ is:

$$p(u, \mathcal{S}) = \prod_{i\in\mathcal{S}} p_i(u) \prod_{j\notin\mathcal{S}} (1 - p_j(u)). \quad (6)$$

To limit the Hamming search to the most likely subsets, one requires an ordering of $\{\mathcal{S}\}$ according to (6). The brute-force approach would be to generate all possible subsets $\mathcal{S}$, sort them in the decreasing order of $p(u, \mathcal{S})$, and then select the top-k elements, where k controls the tradeoff between overhead and recall. The main problem with this method is that it requires $\Theta(l \log l)$ operations and $\Theta(l)$ space, where $l = \sum_{i=1}^{h} \binom{b}{i}$ is often quite large. We next offer a better algorithm that solves this problem in optimal space and time.

5.2 Volatility Heap

We start by considering the problem at fixed Hamming distance h. We later generalize the solution to all distances up to h. Throughout this section, it is convenient to refer to bits in decreasing order of their probability $p_j(u)$ rather than their physical position in the hash (i.e., bit 1 is the most volatile and bit b is the least). Similarly, each set $\mathcal{S}$ is assumed to be sorted in decreasing volatility of its bits (e.g., $\mathcal{S} = (1, 3, 7)$ refers to the first, third, and seventh most volatile bits of the hash).

Define $\prec$ to be a lexicographical comparison operator on $\{\mathcal{S}\}$. If $\mathcal{S}_1 \prec \mathcal{S}_2$, then there exists an index $i < h$ such that the two sets share the leading i elements, but $\mathcal{S}_2$ is larger in the $(i+1)$-st element. For example, $(1, 3, 7, 15) \prec (1, 3, 9, 10)$. Then, we have the following important result.

LEMMA 1. *If two sets $\mathcal{S}_1, \mathcal{S}_2$ of the same size h differ in exactly 1 bit and $\mathcal{S}_1 \prec \mathcal{S}_2$, then $\forall u : p(u, \mathcal{S}_1) \geq p(u, \mathcal{S}_2)$.*

PROOF. Suppose the bits that differ are i in $\mathcal{S}_1$ and j in $\mathcal{S}_2$. Since (6) has $h - 1$ terms in each product that are common between $p(u, \mathcal{S}_1)$ and $p(u, \mathcal{S}_2)$, we get:

$$\frac{p(u, \mathcal{S}_1)}{p(u, \mathcal{S}_2)} = \frac{p_i(1 - p_j)}{p_j(1 - p_i)} = \frac{p_i - p_i p_j}{p_j - p_i p_j}. \quad (7)$$

Recalling that $\mathcal{S}_1 \prec \mathcal{S}_2$, notice that $i < j$ and $p_i \geq p_j$, which immediately shows that (7) is lower-bounded by 1. □

This result paves the way for an algorithm that sorts bit combinations using a structure we call *Volatility Ordered Set Heap* (VOSH). It starts with the optimal set $\mathcal{S}_0 = (1, 2, \dots, h)$ in the root and iteratively generates for each existing node $\mathcal{S}_i$ two children, each of whom succeeds $\mathcal{S}_i$ according to $\prec$ and differ from the parent in exactly one bit. From Lemma 1, observe that each child's $p(u, \mathcal{S})$ is always no larger than the parent's. Using transitivity of $\prec$ and $\geq$, we obtain that each $\mathcal{S}_i$ contains bits whose combination is at least as likely as that of any node in its entire subtree.

We next describe how the tree is constructed using Algorithm 2. Given node $\mathcal{S}$ with h bits, VOSH attempts to generate two children. The left child always increments the last bit of the parent as long as the result does not exceed b (if it does, the left branch stops). The right child scans the parent's bits from right to left until it finds the first gap

Algorithm 2 ProduceChildren($\mathcal{S}$)

```
if S[h] ≤ b − 1 then                          ▷ Attempt left child
    S_L ← S;   S_L[h] ← S_L[h] + 1              ▷ Add 1 to last bit
else
    S_L ← ∅                                     ▷ Left child is empty
end if
for j = h − 1 downto 1 do                     ▷ Attempt right child
    gap = S[j + 1] − S[j]
    if gap = 2 then                           ▷ Should increment bit j?
        S_R ← S;   S_L[j] ← S_L[j] + 1
    else if gap > 2 then
        S_R ← ∅;   break                        ▷ Right child is empty
    end if
end for
return (S_L, S_R)                             ▷ Produce both children
```

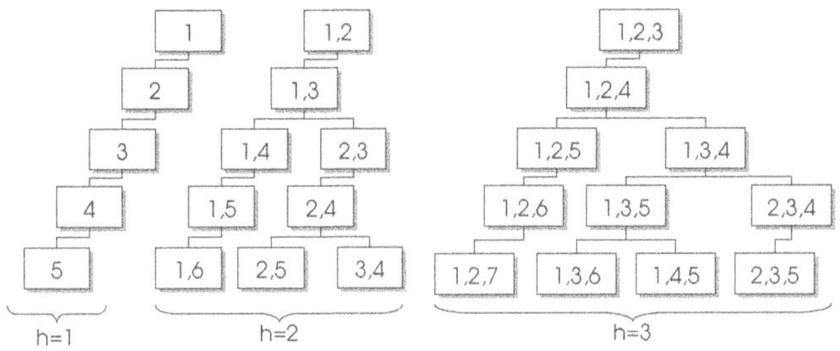

Figure 2: Top five levels of three volatility heaps.

in bit numbers of size at least 2. If the gap is exactly 2, the bit on the left of the gap is incremented. Otherwise, the right child is omitted. The last nuance is necessary to prevent generation of duplicate nodes along different branches of the tree. Figure 2 shows the top five levels of three VOSH heaps that correspond to $h = 1, 2, 3$.

Upper-bounding each heap size by k, space and time complexity of constructing all VOSH trees to depth h is $\Theta(k)$. We next explain how to use them during Hamming search to decide the order of bit flips.

6. PROBABILISTIC SEARCH

In this section, we present our algorithm for near-duplicate search in the `simhash` space. We start with the bit-generation process, verify its effectiveness, and then discuss online/batch-mode operation on large datasets.

6.1 Bit Selection

While VOSH ensures that each subtree should not be traversed before its root, it does not (and cannot) decide which of the two siblings at each level is more optimal. As explained next, we make this decision during run-time using an additional max-heap M that operates on `(key, value)` pairs, where the key is $p(u, \mathcal{S})$ and the value is set $\mathcal{S}$.

Given a page u, we first compute its weights $\{W_j(u)\}$ and the corresponding $\{p_j(u)\}$. We then populate M with tuples $(p(u, \mathcal{S}), \mathcal{S})$ generated by h root nodes of VOSH trees, each corresponding to a different number of bits. At each bit-flip, we extract from M the node with the largest $p(u, \mathcal{S})$, obtain its children from the corresponding VOSH tree, compute their probabilities $p(u, \mathcal{S})$, and insert their tuples into M. This guarantees traversal of bit combinations in the decreasing order of $p(u, \mathcal{S})$ and keeps the total complexity of k flips at the optimal $\Theta(k \log k)$.

In [16], $b = 64$ and $h = 3$ were tested in an 8B-page collection and found to work well. We later verify that these numbers are also quite appropriate for our dataset; in the meantime, use them as our target combination for all experiments and analysis. To understand the performance of VOSH combined with M, we extract from our dataset 8M random pairs of `simhashes` at Hamming distance $h = 1, 2, 3$. We then compare our VOSH-driven approach to random flipping of bits, where the latter considers all possible combinations of exactly h bits, ensuring there is no repetition.

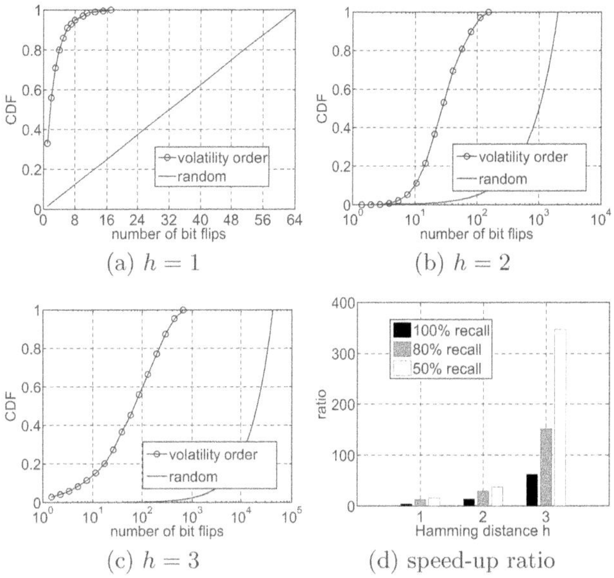

(a) $h = 1$ (b) $h = 2$ (c) $h = 3$ (d) speed-up ratio

Figure 3: Bit flips needed in VOSH compared to random (64-bit hashes).

Figure 3(a) shows the CDF of the number of bit attempts needed to find each of the matches at distance $h = 1$. Observe in the figure that the first VOSH flip finds the matching pair in over 30% of the cases and four flips accomplish the same 80% of the time. All pairs at Hamming distance 1 are discovered in 17 or fewer attempts, while the random approach requires 64 flips to achieve the same 100% recall. For the exact distances $h = 2$ and $h = 3$ (drawn on a log-linear scale), VOSH finds all pairs in 152 and 675 flips, respectively. This compares favorably to 2,016 and 41,664 attempts needed by the random approach.

The difference between VOSH and random flipping becomes more pronounced as h increases and recall decreases. This is illustrated in Figure 3(d), which plots the ratio of the number of attempts needed between the two methods for 50%, 80%, and 100% recall. At $h = 1$, VOSH is 3.7 times faster than random at 100% recall and 16 times faster at 50%. These numbers increase to 13 and 37 respectively for $h = 2$, eventually becoming 61 and 347 for $h = 3$.

With these encouraging results in mind, we next describe how VOSH can be applied to large-scale datasets in a framework we call *Probabilistic Simhash Matching* (PSM).

6.2 Online Queries

In online mode, the existing fingerprints $\mathcal{H}$ are stored in memory to support similarity queries about arriving pages. The main performance metric in this setup is delay τ needed to compare a new document against a set $\mathcal{H}$ of n `simhashes`.

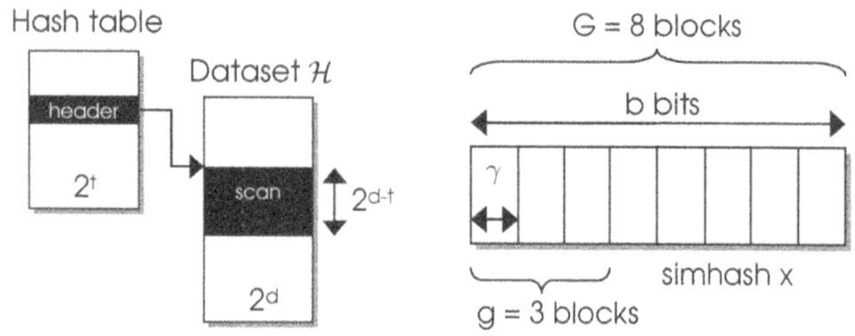

(a) PSM (b) BPHS

Figure 4: Lookup in PSM and BPHS.

To support efficient lookups, assume $\mathcal{H}$ is sorted before the algorithm starts and let $n = 2^d$ be a power of 2. Using VOSH across all b bits is extremely wasteful as it produces a large number of hashes that do not exist in the collection, which is especially noticeable when $n \ll 2^b$. Given $b = 64$, most datasets $\mathcal{D}$ fall into this category. It thus makes sense to limit the random lookups to some small range of $t \leq d$ uppermost bits, which we call the *header*, and perform a linear scan to match the remaining bits.

The matching process may perform a d-step binary search on $\mathcal{H}$ or utilize a hash table of size 2^t for efficient header lookups. We use the latter approach in the paper and illustrate the resulting system in Figure 4(a). Given a query page u with `simhash` x, the first lookup is x itself at Hamming distance 0. We then use VOSH to generate k new queries $x_1, \ldots, x_k$ by working with t most-significant bits of x. In each lookup, if i bits are flipped in the header, the linear scan flags all pages whose Hamming distance to x in the remaining $b - t$ bits is no more than $h - i$.

If only a single-match is desired, the linear scan stops as soon as it identifies the first similar page; otherwise, it continues until a header mismatch. To differentiate these cases, we use PSM$_F$ (first) and PSM$_A$ (all), respectively.

6.3 Batch Queries

In batch mode, the existing collection $\mathcal{H}$ is stored on disk. New fingerprints are accumulated in set $\mathcal{Q}$ until it reaches size m. After $\mathcal{Q}$ becomes full, PSM scans file $\mathcal{H}$ by reading it in chunks of m fingerprints and matching each $x \in \mathcal{Q}$ against the loaded chunk using the online method described above. After $\mathcal{Q}$ is processed to completion, it is sorted and appended to the existing file. This removes the need to sort chunks again when they are loaded in RAM.

It should be noted that PSM$_F$ can stop reading the file as soon as finds at least one near-duplicate for each fingerprint in $\mathcal{Q}$, which in certain cases can save significant amounts of overhead. In the worst case, however, both PSM$_F$ and PSM$_A$ read the entire file for each $\mathcal{Q}$. In a multi-core system, the lookups can be easily parallelized by splitting $\mathcal{Q}$ across threads. It also makes sense to pre-process $\mathcal{Q}$ by identifying the volatile bits in each hash and retaining probabilistic information only related to them. This not only saves memory, but also saves time in identifying top bit-combinations every time a new chunk is loaded into memory.

7. PERFORMANCE MODELING

This section models the currently fastest and most space-efficient `simhash` matching approach [16] and compares its overhead to that of PSM.

7.1 Online BPHS

Efficient search in the Hamming space is an old problem [17] that has remained difficult to solve at large scale. For small h, [16] offers an algorithm, which we call *Block-Permuted Hamming Search* (BPHS), for dealing with large collections $\mathcal{D}$. Suppose we are interested in finding all hashes $y \in \mathcal{H}$ within Hamming distance $h \geq 1$ of x. BPHS first splits the b-bit hash x into $G \geq h+1$ non-overlapping blocks of $\gamma = b/G$ consecutive bits. It then selects an integer g between 1 and $G - h$. If $H(x, y) \leq h$, then block-by-block comparison between x and y is guaranteed to have at least g exact matches. The goal of BPHS is to group all possible combinations of g blocks at the front of the hash and perform the search only on them. This is shown in Figure 4(b) for $G = 8$ and $g = 3$, which is a combination that can support all $h \leq 5$.

Similar to PSM, define the leading g blocks of the hash as its *header*. Then, there are $T = \binom{G}{g}$ ways of selecting the g blocks for the header. Call each of these selections a *block permutation* $\pi_i(x)$ of the original hash. Since the order of blocks neither in the header nor in the rest of the hash matters, there are exactly T unique permutations, which applied to $\mathcal{H}$ produce T copies of the dataset $\mathcal{H}_1, \ldots, \mathcal{H}_T$.

After sorting the copies (which are called *tables* in [16]), the lookup proceeds in T iterations. For the i-th step, BPHS uses a binary search to find the numerically smallest hash in $\mathcal{H}_i$ whose header matches that of $\pi_i(x)$. Starting with that hash, it scans $\mathcal{H}_i$ linearly until the first header mismatch. During this scan, it computes the Hamming distance in the lower $b - (g\gamma)$ bits between each target hash and x, with the rest of the algorithm being similar to PSM. We consider two versions: BPHS$_F$ stops after finding the first match, while BPHS$_A$ always checks every eligible hash.

For the analysis, we assume a sufficiently large b to ignore round-off effects during division and model only the overhead of BPHS$_A$. Define δ_R to be the RAM latency during random access, δ_P to be the delay needed to permute the blocks of x, and δ_L to be the per-hash delay needed to perform Hamming-distance calculations during linear scan. Then, define the number of bits that are matched during binary search as:

$$t = \min(g\gamma, d) = \min\Big(\frac{gb}{G}, d\Big), \tag{8}$$

which has a similar meaning to t in PSM. Note that the min function is necessary since the binary search exhausts the entire dataset in d steps. Then, the total the lookup latency of BPHS in T tables is:

$$\tau = \binom{G}{g}\left(\delta_P + t\delta_R + 2^{d-t}\delta_L\right). \tag{9}$$

The storage overhead (in bytes) of BPHS is simply:

$$\Omega = \binom{G}{g}\frac{nb}{8}. \tag{10}$$

We next analyze the issue of optimally selecting G. For a fixed g and assuming $g\gamma \leq d$, (9) breaks into two terms:

$$\tau = \frac{(G-1)!b}{(G-g)!(g-1)!}\delta_R + \binom{G}{g}\left(\delta_P + 2^{d-gb/G}\delta_L\right), \tag{11}$$

both of which monotonically increase in G. For $g\gamma > d$, we have an even simpler situation:

$$\tau = \binom{G}{g}(\delta_P + d\delta_R + \delta_L), \tag{12}$$

which also shows that choosing the smallest possible G leads to best performance. From (10), we can make the same observation about RAM overhead. Since both space and time decrease with G, it follows that its optimal value is its lower bound $g + h$. Re-writing (9), we have:

$$\tau = \binom{g+h}{g}\left(\delta_P + t\delta_R + 2^{d-t}\delta_L\right). \tag{13}$$

Next, notice that increasing $g\gamma$ beyond d hurts performance in (13) as it keeps $t = d$ constant, but increases the leading binomial coefficient, which makes the final model:

$$\tau(d) = \binom{g+h}{g}\left(\delta_P + \frac{gb}{g+h}\delta_R + 2^{d-gb/(g+h)}\delta_L\right), \tag{14}$$

where

$$g \le \frac{dh}{b-d}. \tag{15}$$

Determination of optimal g is impossible without knowing the relationship between δ_R and δ_L, as well as the value of b in comparison to d. Assuming 8 GB RAM and the absolute minimum number of tables $T = 4$ for $h = 3$ (i.e., $G = 4, g = 1, \gamma = 16$ bits), BPHS admits datasets up to $n = 2^{28}$ with an expected length of linear scans $2^{28-16} = 2^{12}$.

For a RAM-restricted system that cannot grow T to infinity, notice that $\tau(d)$ scales exponentially with d, or in other words, linearly with set size n. Thus, in such cases, similarity search for all document pairs in $\mathcal{H}$ requires complexity $\Theta(n^2)$. We verify this finding in the next section.

7.2 Batch BPHS

Batch mode in BPHS is similar to that in PSM, with two exceptions explained in [16]. First, matching in BPHS proceeds by checking each fingerprint y from the loaded chunk against T tables built around `simhashes` in $\mathcal{Q}$. This is necessary to prevent repeated construction of T permuted copies of each loaded chunk. One peculiar side-effect of this optimization is that BPHS cannot stop when it finds the first match for y since there might be fingerprints $x \in \mathcal{Q}$ that still do not have any matches. Thus, in batch mode, BPHS_F is identical to BPHS_A. The second difference from PSM is that batches $\mathcal{Q}$ do not have to be sorted before being appended to the file since the search runs against $\mathcal{Q}$ rather than $\mathcal{H}$.

To process a batch of $m = |\mathcal{Q}|$ hashes, the I/O delay is the time needed to read the entire file:

$$\tau_{disk} = \frac{nb}{8D}, \tag{16}$$

where D is the read speed of the hard drive. For high-performance RAID-based configurations and overlapped I/O, computation can be executed while the next chunk is being read. In such cases, the bottleneck is in the CPU portion of the overhead, which consists of the time to permute the m incoming hashes T times, sort the corresponding tables, and perform n lookups in them:

$$\tau_{CPU} = Tm(\delta_P + \log_2 m) + n\tau(\log m), \tag{17}$$

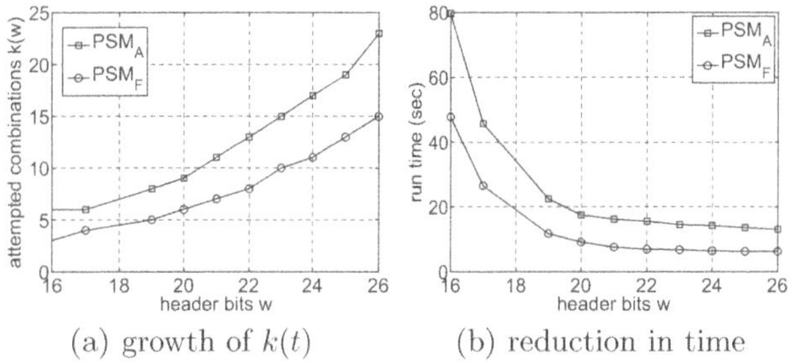

Figure 5: Optimal selection of t in PSM.

where $\tau(.)$ is given by the online model (14). Finally, the throughput of this system in hashes per second is:

$$r = \frac{m}{\max(\tau_{disk}, \tau_{CPU})}. \tag{18}$$

In the experiments below, $\tau_{CPU} \approx 20\tau_{disk}$ dominates and rate r is determined solely by the performance of the studied algorithms rather than the disk speed.

7.3 Online PSM

Recall that VOSH flips k combinations in the upper t bits of each fingerprint x. PSM then searches for these combinations in a single copy of the dataset $\mathcal{H}$ in RAM. The latency of each lookup consists of the VOSH overhead δ_V per examined element in the heap (which hash depth $\log_2 k$), a single visit to the header hash table, and the linear scan:

$$\tau'(d) = k(t)(\delta_V \log_2 k(t) + \delta_R + 2^{\max(d-t,0)}\delta_L), \tag{19}$$

where we make k explicitly depend on t. Since increasing t increases $k(t)$, the following simple analysis helps choose the optimal t. Recall that each VOSH combination is limited to h bits out of t possible, which means that $k(t)$ is upper-bounded by:

$$k(t) \le \sum_{i=1}^{h}\binom{t}{i} = \Theta(t^h). \tag{20}$$

Therefore, ignoring the small terms $\delta_V(k)$ and δ_R in (21) and only considering $t \le d$, the dominating term of the delay is $\Theta(t^h 2^{-t})$, which is minimized when t is maximized. This shows that the optimal choice is $t = d$ and:

$$\tau'(d) = k(d)(\delta_V \log_2 k(d) + \delta_R + \delta_L). \tag{21}$$

To understand the growth of $k(t)$ with t, we partition our 70M-page web collection into two parts – 10M random pages are selected to arrive in online mode and the remaining 60M are chosen for the main dataset $\mathcal{H}$. We first pass each online page through BPHS to find all matches in $\mathcal{H}$ within Hamming distance $h = 3$. We then select for each t such $k(t)$ that achieve 95% recall in PSM compared to BPHS.

The result is plotted in Figure 5(a). As t grows from 16 bits to 26, the number of combinations required by PSM_A increases from 6 to 23 and that for PSM_F from 3 to 15. The exact growth rate cannot be readily ascertained over this small range, but it is visibly super-linear. The total run time to verify 10M hashes in online mode is shown in Figure 5(b). As predicted, the delay is minimized when t is at its maximum (i.e., d), in which case the processing speed reaches 1.6M arriving hashes/sec for PSM_F and 765K/sec for PSM_A.

Since PSM maintains a hash table with 2^t entries and a single copy of $\mathcal{H}$, it storage requirement for $t = d$ is:

$$\Omega' = (2^t + 2^d)\frac{b}{8} = \frac{2nb}{8}, \quad (22)$$

which is equivalent to 2 permuted tables in BPHS. For $h = 3$ and the minimum four tables in BPHS, our approach is at least twice as efficient. Furthermore, for a fixed number of additional tables (i.e., just one), PSM's latency (21) scales as $\Theta(k(d) \log k(d))$, where $d = \log_2 n$. Since $k(d)$ is $O(d^h)$, we obtain that its overall complexity for processing all hashes in $\mathcal{H}$ is $O(n \log^h(n) \log \log n)$. This compares favorably to $\Theta(n^2)$ of BPHS.

7.4 Batch PSM

Given a batch $\mathcal{Q}$ of new pages, PSM loads chunks of $m = |\mathcal{Q}|$ fingerprints from the file, sets up a hash table for each element of the chunk, and performs lookups for all $x \in \mathcal{Q}$. Note that after the first match, PSM_F removes x from $\mathcal{Q}$, which prevents its being checked against subsequent chunks. This allows PSM_F to become much faster as it progresses through the file.

In the worst case, PSM's I/O delay is the same as (16), which in our tests is again much smaller than the CPU latency, where the latter can be broken down into three parts – producing the permutations for m hashes, performing m lookups in each of n/m chunks, and finally sorting the hashes in $\mathcal{Q}$ before writing them to disk:

$$\tau'_{CPU} = m\delta_V \log_2 k + n\tau'(\log m) + m\delta_S \log_2 m, \quad (23)$$

where δ_S is the mean latency of moving hashes while sorting.

As important result of this analysis is how batch size m affects rate r in (18). For a fixed number of tables T, BPHS's τ_{CPU} scales as $\Theta(m)$ and keeps r virtually unchanged. On the other hand, ignoring the VOSH and sorting overhead, PSM's τ'_{CPU} scales as $\Theta(\log^h(m) \log \log m)$. This increases the overall rate r slightly slower than linear, i.e., as $\Theta(m/\log^h(m) \log \log m)$, but nevertheless significantly faster than in BPHS. We re-examine this issue and confirm this result in the next section.

8. EXPERIMENTS

We next describe our dataset $\mathcal{D}$, examine whether `simhash` indeed approximates cosine similarity on $\mathcal{D}$, select the optimal h, and evaluate PSM in comparison to BPHS.

8.1 Dataset

All our experiments involve a set of 100M web pages crawled by IRLbot [15] in April 2008. We process the collection by removing pages that have size less than 5 KB, contain no URLs, have an exact duplicate (identified using a standard hash function), or consist of non-English words, all of which shrinks $\mathcal{D}$ to a total of 70M pages.

We parse each remaining page, removing stop-words and stemming all text outside of HTML tags. We then create feature vectors with weights $t_i(u)$ being the normalize TF-IDF score of each word i on page u. For calculating `simhash` fingerprints, we use the 64-bit MurmurHash function [1].

8.2 Usability of Simhash

While [16] has shown in small-scale manual verification that $h = 3$ and $b = 64$ produce good results on Google's dataset with 8B pages, we aim to verify that the same parameters work well for our $\mathcal{D}$, but using the similarity measure of the feature-vector space and at a much larger scale. To our knowledge this has not been done before.

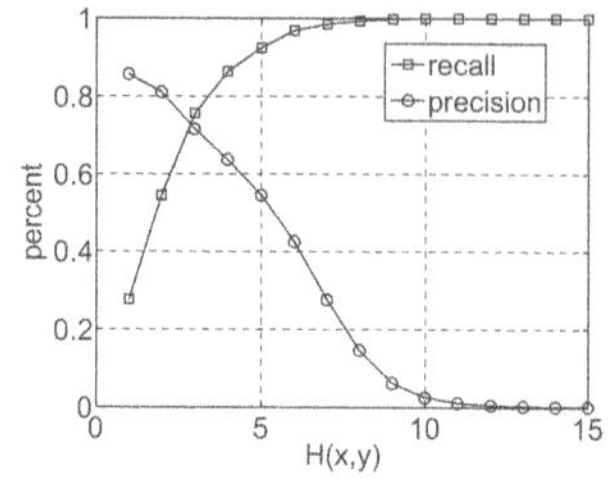

(a) precision/recall

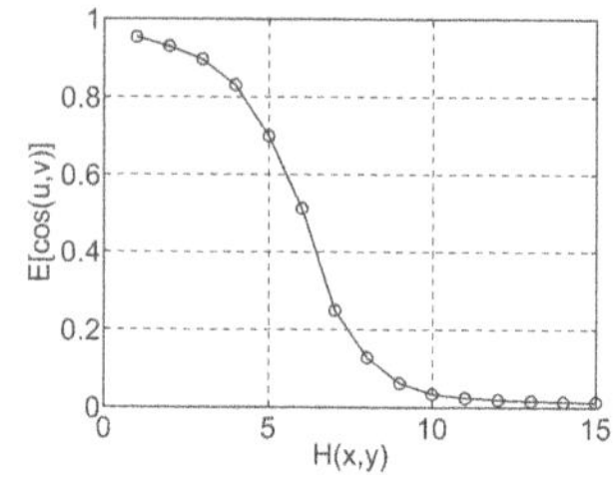

(b) expected cosine

Figure 6: Comparison of simhash against cosine similarity at different Hamming distances.

We randomly sample 100M document pairs (out of a total of 4.9 quadrillion) and place them into set Υ. We then define set $N_{\cos}$ to contain all pairs whose cosine similarity is above threshold $\theta = 0.9$, i.e., $N_{\cos} = \{(u, v) \in \Upsilon : \cos(u, v) \geq \theta\}$. We also define sets N_h (for $h = 1, 2, \ldots, 64$) to contain all sampled pairs of documents within Hamming distance h of each other, i.e., $N_h = \{(x, y) \in \Upsilon : H(x, y) \leq h\}$.

Then, *precision* at distance h is defined as the fraction of pages in N_h that belong to $N_{\cos}$:

$$P(h) = \frac{|N_h \cap N_{\cos}|}{|N_h|} \quad (24)$$

and *recall* at distance h is the fraction of pages in $N_{\cos}$ that belong to N_h:

$$R(h) = \frac{|N_h \cap N_{\cos}|}{|N_{\cos}|} \quad (25)$$

Figure 6(a) plots both metrics as a function of h. Observe that small h produces a high rate of false-negatives, but keeps the false positive rate low. Large values of h offer the opposite condition – many false positives, but few false negatives. Taking the point where both curves intersect, we arrive at $h = 3$ as a sensible balance for this tradeoff.

Figure 6(b) shows the expected cosine $E[\cos(u, v)]$ between document pairs at different Hamming distances. The correlation between the two is very clear, with $H(x, y) \in [1, 3]$ producing $E[\cos(u, v)]$ that ranges from 0.95 down to 0.89, which confirms the applicability of `simhash` as a substitute for $s(u, v)$ on this dataset.

8.3 Implementation Details

We implemented both PSM and BPHS [16] in Visual Studio C++, using similar optimizations and running them on the same hardware, which consisted of a desktop machine with the AMD Phenom II X6 CPU (2.8 GHz), 16 MB of RAM, 5 TB of disk space, and Windows Server 2008 R2.

Since PSM is an approximation to an exact `simhash` search, its *relative recall* R' is computed against the matches found by BPHS. Thus, PSM's *total recall* against cosine similarity is $R(h)R'$, where $R(h)$ is given in (25) and plotted in Figure 6(a). It should be noted that PSM's relative precision is 100% against BPHS and is not a factor in our comparison.

Relative recall R' for our experiments is defined slightly differently for PSM_A and PSM_F. In the former case, we take the number of matching pairs found by PSM_A and normalize

Method	Tables	Time (sec)	Queries/sec
$BPHS_A$	4	65	154K
	10	53	189K
PSM_A	1.06	15.5	645K
	1.125	14.4	694K
	1.25	14.4	694K
	1.5	13.5	741K
	2	13.1	765K
$BPHS_F$	4	54	185K
	10	26	385K
PSM_F	1.06	6.9	1.4M
	1.125	6.7	1.5K
	1.25	6.4	1.56M
	1.5	6.26	1.6M
	2	6.25	1.6M

Table 2: Comparison of PSM to BPHS (online mode, 10M queries, 60M existing hashes).

it by that found by $BPHS_A$. In the latter case, we record the number of `simhashes` for which PSM_F found at least one similar pair and divide it by the same number in $BPHS_F$.

All our experiments use $k(t)$ such that R' achieves recall 95%, unless otherwise specified. As discussed earlier, we divide the full dataset of 70M fingerprints by random sampling into two parts: 10M hashes are used as queries and the remaining 60M are used as the existing collection $\mathcal{H}$.

We experimented with replacing the binary search in BPHS with extrapolation search suggested in [16]. For $d = 26$, this reduced the number of RAM lookups from 26 to 11, but the overall runtime of the algorithm increased due to the larger number of multiplications/divisions needed to compute each jump. We thus do not include it in our comparison.

8.4 Online Mode

In our experiments, we use two most space-efficient BPHS designs suggested in [16], i.e., $T = 4$ and $T = 10$ tables. To make comparison easier to follow, we convert our RAM overhead to the same notation by dividing Ω' by the size of $\mathcal{H}$, i.e., $nb/8$. Thus, PSM's number of tables becomes:

$$T' = 1 + \frac{1}{2^{d-t}}. \quad (26)$$

By varying t, we can achieve any overhead $T' \in [1, 2]$. We study how this selection impacts the result using the total run-time of each algorithm over the entire set of 10M queries. Table 2 shows our results. The top half of the table focuses on finding *all* matches, where PSM_A is $3.4 - 5$ times faster than $BPHS_A$, while reducing its RAM consumption by a factor of 2-10 depending on the choice of t. In the lower half, PSM_F is even better (i.e., $3.7 - 8.7$ times faster than $BPHS_F$) with the same savings in RAM.

Another interesting observation in the table is that PSM is relatively insensitive to RAM usage. After dropping T' from 2 to 1.06, PSM_A loses only 15% in speed and PSM_F only about 9%. Focusing on the ratio of speed (in thousands of queries/sec) to the number of tables used, PSM_A peaks at 617 with $T' = 1.125$ and PSM_F at 1367 with $T' = 1.06$. The best numbers from BPHS are 38 and 46, respectively.

We next focus on the scalability of each method. In the modeling section, we showed that with a fixed number of tables, BPHS's lookup delay for each query scaled linearly with set size n, which is equivalent to an exponential increase when plotted against $d = \log_2 n$. At the same time, we

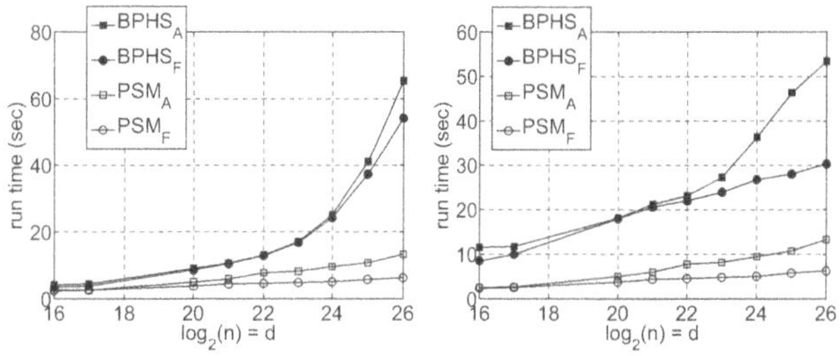

(a) $T = 4$ (b) $T = 10$

Figure 7: Scalability with dataset size (online mode, 10M queries, 60M existing hashes).

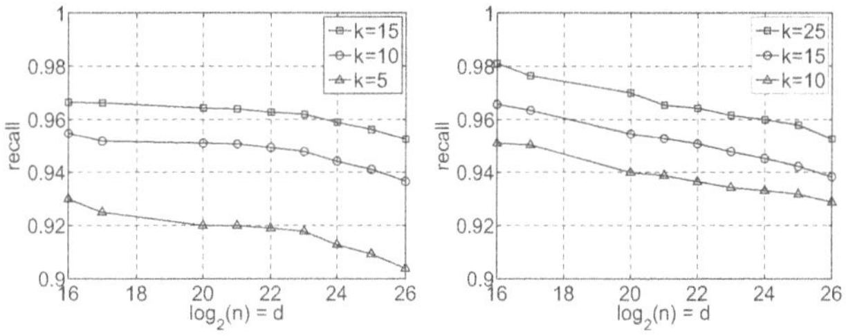

(a) PSM_F (b) PSM_A

Figure 8: Relative recall in PSM with a fixed number of bit flips (online mode, 10M queries, 60M existing hashes).

showed that PSM's CPU overhead could be crudely upper-bounded by $O(d^h)$, which at least in theory should be significantly better.

Figure 7 confirms this result in our implementation. Specifically, in part (a) of the figure, we fix $T = 4$ tables for [16] and keep $T' = 2$ in our method. Notice the aggressive increase in delay for both versions of BPHS and an almost linear increase for PSM. In part (b), the BPHS design calls for $g = 2$ and $G = 5$, which means that the exponential term in (14) does not become active until d exceeds $gb/(b+h) = 25.6$. Thus, most of the visible increase in Figure 7(b) is due to the binary search; however, once the dataset becomes substantially larger, these curves will become exponential in d. Note that in part (a) of the figure, the situation was dramatically different because g was 1 and $gb/(b + h)$ was 16.

We finish this section by keeping the number of attempted combinations $k(t)$ constant and examining how recall R' changes with dataset size d. This demonstrates the decay rate of recall as a function of $|\mathcal{H}|$, which might be interesting to applications that intend to keep per-query CPU overhead constant as $n \to \infty$. In these experiments, we scale the number of header bits as $t = d$ and plot the result in Figure 8. First, notice that recall of PSM_F decreases slightly slower than that of PSM_A. Second, observe that with just $k = 5$ combinations of bit-flips, the former method achieves 90% recall for all datasets up to 60M pages. The latter technique can maintain 93% recall with just $k = 10$ flips, which implies that by lowering the target R' to 90%, our method can become $2.5 - 3$ times faster than already demonstrated.

In real-time systems with hard memory and performance constraints that are ready to sacrifice a small percentage of recall, these results show that PSM offers a significantly

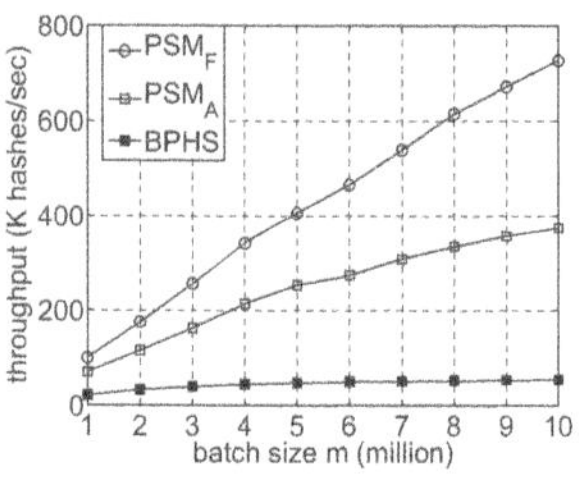

(a) speed vs m

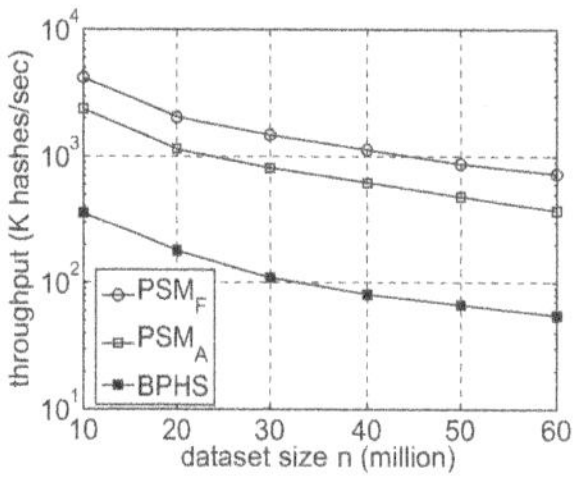

(b) speed vs n

Figure 9: Throughput in batch mode.

faster and more space-efficient solution than currently available in the literature.

8.5 Batch Mode

In these experiments, the existing dataset of 60M fingerprints is read from disk and matched against a query batch with $m = |\mathcal{Q}| = 10$M fingerprints stored in memory. Since in our system τ_{disk} is at least 20 times smaller than τ_{CPU}, the overall performance is dominated by the throughput of the studied algorithms. While we are not concerned with RAM as much as before, simple calculations show that PSM still uses less RAM than BPHS.

Figure 9(a) shows the effect of batch size m on the processing speed. As discussed earlier, BPHS_A and BPHS_F are the same method in batch mode, which we plot as a single curve in the figure. We use the 4-table design for BPHS since it proved faster than the 10-table version for dataset sizes below 2^{25} (see Figure 7). We now come back to the prediction in the modeling section that BPHS's speed should saturate and remain constant with m, while that of PSM should increase sublinearly, but no worse than $m/\log_2^h(m) \log\log m$.

Figure 9(a) confirms both findings, showing that the processing rate of BPHS stabilizes at 55K/sec, while our technique scales from 99K/sec to 727K/sec for PSM_F and from 70K/sec to 373K/sec for PSM_A. At the final batch size (i.e., $m = 10$M), PSM outperforms BPHS by a factor of $7.7 - 14$, which is expected to continue increasing as $m \to \infty$.

It should be noted that even for the largest batch $m = 10$M, both methods in Figure 9(a) are still 50-70% slower than in online mode. For BPHS, this can be explained by the much larger number of binary searches it performs compared to the online version. For PSM, the model predicts that splitting the dataset into small chunks reduces performance since each new hash must be looked up in n/m hash tables.

We finish the paper by examining how both methods behave when n increases, but m stays fixed. The model shows that the run-time of both techniques should be linear in n, which means that their throughput should be $\Theta(1/n)$. Figure 9(b) confirms this fact and shows that the ratio between the PSM and BPHS curves remains constant at approximately 7 for PSM_A and 14 for PSM_F. Combining the various observations, we can conclude that as $n \to \infty$, batch-mode PSM will be able to use larger m and its performance gains over fixed-table BPHS will grow even further.

9. CONCLUSIONS AND FUTURE WORK

In this paper, we presented a novel way of utilizing `simhash` to find near-duplicates in large collections of documents. We showed that by sacrificing a small percentage of recall the proposed approach consistently outperformed [16] in terms of query speed and space consumption, which it was able to simultaneously lower by a factor that ranged from 2 to 14 in various configurations.

Future work involves analysis of feature-selection techniques for better clustering, improvement of `simhash` recall against cosine similarity, and further overhead reduction in our bit-flipping algorithm.

10. REFERENCES

[1] A. Appleby, "MurmurHash." [Online]. Available: http://sites.google.com/site/murmurhash/.

[2] S. Baluja and M. Covell, "Learning 'Forgiving' Hash Functions: Algorithms and Large Scale Tests," in *Proc. IJCAI*, Jan. 2007, pp. 2663–2669.

[3] M. Bawa, T. Condie, and P. Ganesan, "LSH Forest: SelfTuning Indexes for Similarity Search," in *Proc. WWW*, May 2005, pp. 651–660.

[4] J. L. Bentley, "K-D Trees For Semi-Dynamic Point Sets," in *Proc. ACM Symposium on Computational Geometry (SCG)*, Jun. 1990, pp. 187–197.

[5] A. Broder, "Identifying and Filtering Near-Duplicate Documents," in *Proc. CPM*, Jun. 2000, pp. 1–10.

[6] A. Z. Broder, M. Charikar, A. M. Frieze, and M. Mitzenmacher, "Min-Wise Independent Permutations," in *Proc. ACM STOC*, May 1998, pp. 327–336.

[7] A. Z. Broder, S. C. Glassman, M. S. Manasse, and G. Zweig, "Syntactic Clustering of the Web," *Computer Networks and ISDN Systems*, vol. 29, no. 8–13, pp. 1157–1166, Sep. 1997.

[8] M. S. Charikar, "Similarity Estimation Techniques from Rounding Algorithms," in *Proc. ACM STOC*, May 2002, pp. 380–388.

[9] A. Chowdhury, O. Frieder, D. Grossman, and M. C. McCabe, "Collection Statistics for Fast Duplicate Document Detection," *ACM Trans. Inf. Syst.*, vol. 20, no. 2, Apr. 2002.

[10] E. Cohen, M. Datar, S. Fujiwara, A. Gionis, P. Indyk, R. Motwani, J. D. Ullman, and C. Yang, "Finding Interesting Associations without Support Pruning," in *Proc. IEEE ICDE*, Feb. 2000, pp. 489–500.

[11] M. Ester, H.-P. Kriegel, J. Sander, M. Wimmer, and X. Xu, "Incremental Clustering for Mining in a Data Warehousing Environment," in *Proc. VLDB*, Aug. 1998, pp. 323–333.

[12] A. Guttman, "R-Trees: A Dynamic Index Structure for Spatial Searching," in *Proc. ACM SIGMOD*, Jun. 1984, pp. 47–57.

[13] M. R. Henzinger, "Finding Near-Duplicate Web Pages: A Large-Scale Evaluation of Algorithms," in *Proc. ACM SIGIR*, Aug. 2006, pp. 284–291.

[14] P. Indyk and R. Motwani, "Approximate Nearest Neighbors: Towards Removing the Curse of Dimensionality," in *Proc. ACM STOC*, May 1998, pp. 604–613.

[15] H.-T. Lee, D. Leonard, X. Wang, and D. Loguinov, "IRLbot: Scaling to 6 Billion Pages and Beyond," in *Proc. WWW*, Apr. 2008, pp. 427–436.

[16] G. S. Manku, A. Jain, and A. D. Sarma, "Detecting Near Duplicates for Web Crawling," in *Proc. WWW*, May 2007, pp. 141–149.

[17] M. Minsky and S. Papert, *Perceptrons.* MIT Press, 1969.

[18] R. Salakhutdinov and G. Hinton, "Semantic Hashing," *International Journal of Approximate Reasoning*, vol. 50, no. 7, pp. 969–978, July 2009.

[19] B. Stein, S. M. zu Eissen, and M. Potthast, "Strategies for Retrieving Plagiarized Documents," in *Proc. ACM SIGIR*, Jul. 2007, pp. 825–826.

[20] P. Wegner, "A Technique for Counting Ones in a Binary Computer," *Commun. ACM*, vol. 3, no. 5, p. 322, May 1960.

Collective Prediction with Latent Graphs

Xiaoxiao Shi
Department of Computer Science
University of Illinois at Chicago
xiaoxiao@cs.uic.edu

Yao Li
Department of Electrical and Computer Engineering
University of Illinois at Chicago
yli70@uic.edu

Philip S. Yu
Department of Computer Science
University of Illinois at Chicago
psyu@cs.uic.edu

ABSTRACT

Collective classification in relational data has become an important and active research topic in the last decade. It exploits the dependencies of instances in a network to improve predictions. Related applications include hyperlinked document classification, social network analysis and collaboration network analysis. Most of the traditional collective classification models mainly study the scenario that there exists a large amount of labeled examples (labeled nodes). However, in many real-world applications, labeled data are extremely difficult to obtain. For example, in network intrusion detection, there may be only a limited number of identified intrusions whereas there are a huge set of unlabeled nodes. In this situation, most of the data have no connection to labeled nodes; hence, no supervision knowledge can be obtained from the local connections. In this paper, we propose to explore various latent linkages among the nodes and judiciously integrate the linkages to generate a latent graph. This is achieved by finding a graph that maximizes the linkages among the training data with the same label, and maximizes the separation among the data with different labels. The objective is further cast into an optimization problem and is solved with quadratic programming. Finally, we apply label propagation on the latent graph to make prediction. Experiments show that the proposed model LNP (**L**atent **N**etwork **P**ropagation) can improve the learning accuracy significantly. For instance, when there are only 10% of labeled examples, the accuracies of all the comparison models are less than 63%, while that of the proposed model is 74%.

Categories and Subject Descriptors

H.2.8 [**Database Management**]: Database applications—*Data mining*

General Terms

Algorithms

CIKM'11, October 24–28, 2011, Glasgow, Scotland, UK.

1. INTRODUCTION

In relational datasets and information networks, instances are not independent nor identically distributed. Instead, they are correlated with complex dependencies. For example, in collaboration networks, the researchers who collaborate with each other are more likely to share similar research topics than those researchers without any collaboration. To exploit these data dependencies and improve predictions, collective classification (*e.g.*, [12, 6, 13]) is proposed and it receives considerable attentions in the last decade. One of the key ideas of collective classification is to construct new feature vectors by appending a new set of attributes that summarizes the relational information (*e.g.*, [6, 13, 15, 9, 12]). For instance, [12] is among the first works that summarize the labels of neighboring nodes and treat the summary as new features. The approach is illustrated in Fig. 1(a), where node "A" has three positive neighboring nodes and one negative neighboring node. As a result, "<3, 1>" is appended onto the original feature vector as new features as in Fig. 1(a). Note that most of the traditional collective classification models mainly study the scenario where there are a lot of labeled nodes. In this scenario, the supervision knowledge can be effectively propagated in the network and improve the learning accuracy. However, in many applications, the number of training data is actually very limited. The following provides some examples:

- Social targeting (*e.g.*, [8]): social targeting aims at mining the user behaviors in a social network and perform applications such as recommendation. It contains huge amount of unlabeled data and relatively small number of labeled examples (*e.g.*, customers who do buy products after the recommendation).
- Hyperlinked document classification: in nowadays, the number of webpages increases explosively, but the number of labeled webpages is still limited.
- Anomaly detection: for instance, in network intrusion detection, the number of identified intrusions is very limited as compared with the trillions of unlabeled nodes.
- Time evolving social network applications: social network will evolve over time. There are usually a limited number of up-to-date labeled examples.

We illustrate in Fig. 1(b) to show the drawback of traditional collective classification when there are a limited number of training examples. Note that traditional models will first

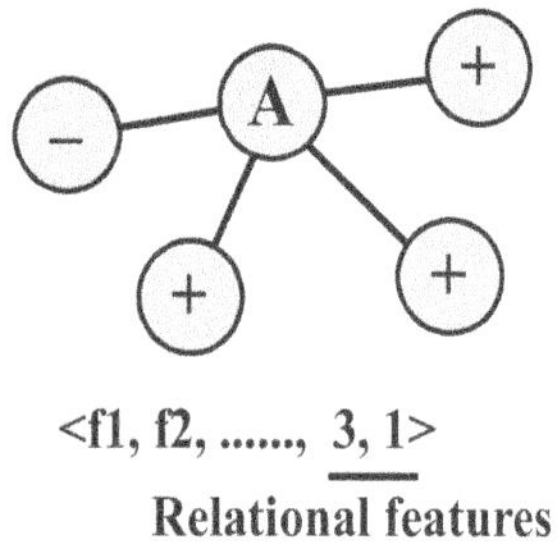

(a) Example of traditional collective classification, $f1, f2, \cdots$ are the original features.

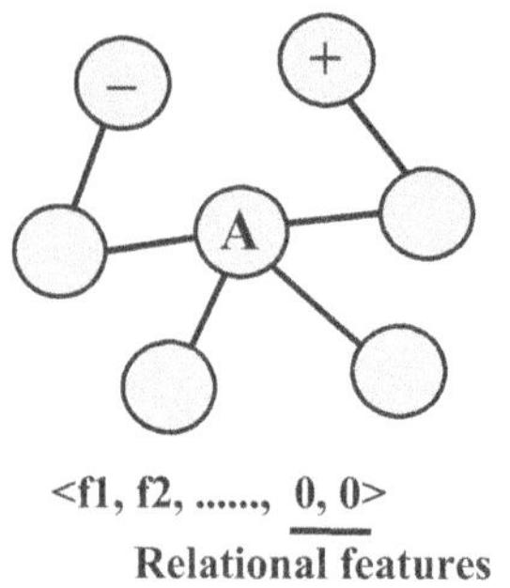

(b) Without sufficient labeled examples, relational summary is all zeros.

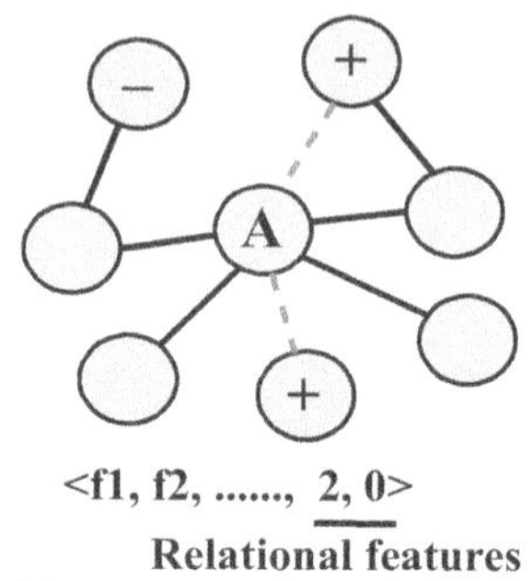

(c) Explore latent linkages to make good use of the limited training examples. Latent linkages are explored from the original dataset and no additional information is used.

Figure 1: Collective classification with limited training data

train a classifier based on the new feature vectors such as the one in Fig. 1(a). However, since there are only a limited number of training data, most of the nodes may not directly link to the labeled nodes, such as node A in Fig. 1(b). In this situation, the relational summary will become all 0's; thus, no local supervision knowledge can be used. As a result, the prediction accuracy drops significantly (more empirical results are studied in Section 4).

To tackle the label deficiency problem, we propose to explore the latent linkages among the nodes, and judiciously integrate them to construct a latent graph. For example, in a citation network, in addition to the citation relations, those papers with similar keywords or concepts may also be similarly. This kind of latent analysis can be obtained through the node attributes, *e.g.*, paper title. If more information, such as abstract or the paper, is available, one can also derive some other latent relations such as semantic similarity. We call such indirect linkages *latent linkages*. Note that these latent linkages are already embedded in the dataset but may need some efforts to dig them out. By adding the latent linkages, the supervision knowledge may be able to propagate more effectively as illustrated in Fig. 1(c). In this paper, we give five examples of latent linkages, and propose a general framework to construct the latent graph by integrating the latent linkages. The objective is to find a graph where the data with the same class label are linked together and those with different class labels are disconnected. It is further formulated as an optimization problem and is solved with quadratic programming. With the optimal latent graph, label propagation is applied to pass the supervision information throughout the network and make predictions. Experiments include three real-world graph datasets, and the proposed model can improve the accuracy by as much as 15% as compared with the traditional collective classifiers.

Contributions

The most important contributions of the proposed approach can be summarized as follows:

- It studies the label deficiency problem where many real world applications may encounter, but traditional collective classifier does not perform well.
- It uses latent linkages to improve the prediction. It is important to emphasize that all the latent information is explored from the original dataset; no additional information from other sources is used.
- Multiple types of latent linkages are integrated judiciously as the latent graph; the optimal solution is found by quadratic programming.

The rest of the paper is organized as follows. We start by a formal description of collective classification. The proposed latent network propagation model (abbreviated as "LNP") is described in Section 3, followed by the experiment in Section 4. A brief introduction of the related work is given in Section 5. In Section 6, we conclude the paper.

2. PROBLEM FORMULATION OF LNP

In this section, we formulate the problem of collective classification, and discuss the reason why it may induce poor performance with insufficient training examples. We first introduce the notations (Table 1) that will be used throughout this paper. Suppose we are given a relational dataset represented as a graph $G(\mathcal{V}, \mathbf{E}, \mathbf{X}, \mathcal{Y})$ where $\mathcal{V} = \{v_1, \cdots, v_n\}$ is a set of nodes, and $\mathbf{E} \in \mathbb{R}^{n \times n}$ is the adjacency matrix where $\mathbf{E}(i,j)$ is the weight of the edge between node v_i and v_j. For each node $v_i \in \mathcal{V}$, it has a class label $y_i \in \{c_1, \cdots, c_k\}$ drawn from the k labels $c_1, \cdots, c_k$, and a vector of attributes $\mathbf{x}_i \in \mathbb{R}^d$ in the d-dimensional input space. Let $\mathbf{X} = \{\mathbf{x}_1, \cdots, \mathbf{x}_n\}$ and $\mathcal{Y} = \{y_1, \cdots, y_n\}$. Further denote $\mathcal{L} \in \mathcal{V}$ as the set of labeled examples and $\mathcal{U} = \mathcal{V} - \mathcal{L}$ as the set of unlabeled data. Our objective is to give predictions on the unlabeled nodes $\mathcal{V}_\mathcal{U}$ by making use of both the attribute vectors $\mathbf{X}$ as well as the network $\mathbf{E}$.

Collective Classification with Limited Labeled Examples

The key idea of collective classification is to generate a new feature vector $\mathbf{f}_i^*$ for each data v_i

$$\mathbf{f}_i^* =< f_1, f_2, \cdots, f_d, c_1, c_2, \cdots, c_k >$$

where $\mathbf{x}_i =< f_1, f_2, \cdots, f_d >$ is the original feature vector and $c_1, c_2, \cdots, c_k$ are the summary of neighboring node class labels. For example, in a binary classification problem, suppose v_i is linked to 4 labeled examples where 3 are positive

Table 1: Notation Descriptions

Notations	Descriptions
G	The relational dataset $G(\mathcal{V}, \mathbf{E}, \mathbf{X}, \mathcal{Y})$.
$\mathcal{V}$	The set of vertices $\mathcal{V} = \{v_1, \cdots, v_n\}$.
$\mathbf{E}$	Adjacency matrix of the weighted directed graph.
$\mathbf{X}$	Feature vectors $\mathbf{X} = \{\mathbf{x}_1, \cdots, \mathbf{x}_n\}$ where $\mathbf{x}_i \in \mathbb{R}^d$.
$\mathcal{Y}$	Class labels $\mathcal{Y} = \{y_1, \cdots, y_n\}$.
	where $y_i \in \{c_1, \cdots, c_k\}$ is the class label of v_i, and k is the number of class labels.
$\hat{\mathbf{E}}$	The adjacency matrix of the optimal latent graph constructed from the latent linkages (Eq. 10).
$\mathcal{L}$	The set of labeled vertices.
$\mathcal{U}$	The set of unlabeled vertices.
	The following notations are used in Section 3.2 and 3.3, which are the examples of latent linkages.
$\mathbf{E}_{\text{K\_STEP}}$	The adjacency matrix of the K-step graph.
$\mathbf{E}_{\text{LABEL}}$	The adjacency matrix of the label graph.
$\mathbf{E}_{\text{ATT}}$	The adjacency matrix of the attribute similarity graph.
$\mathbf{E}_{\text{CON}}$	The adjacency matrix of the prediction confidence similarity graph.
$\mathbf{E}_{\text{STR}}$	The adjacency matrix of the structure similarity graph.
ω	The combination weights of the similarity matrices.
$\mathbf{Y}$	Class label matrix.

and 1 is negative. Then $\mathbf{f}_i^* =< f_1, \cdots, f_d, 3, 1 >$, which is illustrated in Fig. 1(a). In other words, the new feature vector can be generated by appending the class label summary to the original feature vector. With the new feature vectors, many traditional classification models [12, 6, 13] can be applied to give prediction. However, the above schema may not work well when there are a limited number of labeled data. This is because if $|\mathcal{L}| \ll |\mathcal{V}|$, most of the nodes may not connect to labeled examples as illustrated in Fig. 1(b). As such, the class summary part of the new feature vector will be all 0's:

$$\mathbf{f}_i^* =< f_1, f_2, \cdots, f_d, 0, 0, \cdots, 0 >$$

Hence, the relational models degenerates to the unrelational classifiers which only use the original feature vector $\mathbf{f}_i^* =< f_1, f_2, \cdots, f_d >$. Thus the graph information does not contribute to the modeling, and the accuracy may drop. To tackle the label deficient problem, we propose LNP to generate a latent graph by exploring various latent linkages among the nodes. The objective is as follows:

Proposition 1 *It is our objective to find a transformation $G(\mathcal{V}, \mathbf{E}, \mathbf{X}, \mathcal{Y}) \rightarrow G^*(\mathcal{V}, \hat{\mathbf{E}}, \mathbf{X}, \mathcal{Y})$ where $\hat{\mathbf{E}} \in \mathbb{R}^{n \times n}$ is the adjacency matrix of the latent graph (weighted directed graph). And it is desirable that the latent graph has the following properties:*

- *if v_i and v_j have the same class label, $\hat{\mathbf{E}}(i, j)$ is large.*
- *if v_i and v_j have different class labels, $\hat{\mathbf{E}}(i, j) = 0$.*

With the latent graph, we can use various algorithms to give prediction. In this paper, we take label propagation as an example.

3. LATENT GRAPH GENERATION

In this section, a general LNP framework is first proposed to judiciously integrate different kinds of latent linkages to generate a latent graph. We then explore various kinds of latent linkages that can be directly obtained from the relational dataset. The challenge is how to combine the different latent linkages, and we tackle the problem by solving an optimization problem and solve it with quadratic programming. The optimization can automatically determine the optimal weights to combine the latent linkages.

3.1 A General LNP Framework for Latent Linkages Integration

In collective classification and other graph applications, there may exist various informative latent relations among the nodes as discussed in the introduction section. More formally, denote the set of latent relations as $\mathcal{S} = \{\mathbf{E}_1, \mathbf{E}_2, \cdots, \mathbf{E}_m\}$ where $\mathbf{E}_i \in \mathbb{R}^{n \times n}$ is the adjacency matrix of the i-th latent graph. For example, $\mathbf{E}_1$ may describe the links of documents with similar topics and $\mathbf{E}_2$ may describe the links of papers with similar semantic meanings. We will introduce in the next section how to find the latent linkages based on the given dataset, but at the moment, we focus on how to use the latent linkages. Recall that we aim at finding a transformation $G(\mathcal{V}, \mathbf{E}, \mathbf{X}, \mathcal{Y}) \rightarrow G^*(\mathcal{V}, \hat{\mathbf{E}}, \mathbf{X}, \mathcal{Y})$ where $\hat{\mathbf{E}}$ is the adjacency matrix of the target latent graph constructed from the set of latent linkages $\mathcal{S} = \{\mathbf{E}_1, \mathbf{E}_2, \cdots, \mathbf{E}_m\}$

$$\hat{\mathbf{E}} = \sum_{t=1}^{m} (\omega_t \mathbf{E}_t) \quad \text{s.t.} \sum_{t=1}^{m} \omega_t = 1, \ \omega_i \geq 0 \tag{1}$$

In other words, the similarity matrix of the target latent graph $\hat{\mathbf{E}}$ is a linear combination of all the latent relations. The key is how to find the optimal combination weights ω_t in order to construct a latent graph with good properties as described in Proposition 1. We present in Section 3.3 about how to solve the above objective. At this moment, we assume that the latent network $G^*(\mathcal{V}, \hat{\mathbf{E}}, \mathbf{X}, \mathcal{Y})$ is already found, and we apply label propagation to make prediction.

Inference via Label Propagation The basic intuition of label propagation is to perform random walk on the network when time goes to infinity. As a result, each node will gain a vector of probabilities indicating how likely the labeled examples will visit the node. At last, each node is assigned to the label that are most likely to be visited from. More formally, it contains the following steps [23]:

1. Let $\mathbf{D}$ be the diagonal matrix where $\mathbf{D}(i, i) = \sum_{j=1}^{n} \hat{\mathbf{E}}(i, j)$.
2. Calculate $\mathbf{F} = (\mathbf{D} - \alpha\hat{\mathbf{E}})^{-1}\mathbf{Y}$ where α is a parameter less than 1 to ensure $(\mathbf{D} - \alpha\hat{\mathbf{E}})$ is non-singular, and $\mathbf{Y}$

is the label matrix such that $\mathbf{Y}(i,j) = 1$ iff the i-th data is with the j-th class label.

3. Assign v_i to a label $y_i = \arg\max_j \mathbf{F}(i,j)$.

Unlike previous label propagation methods, we do not construct the similarity matrix solely from the attribute vectors. Instead, the relational network as well as various kinds of latent linkages are also considered.

3.2 Latent Graph Exploration

For LNP, we present five examples of latent linkages which can be easily obtained from the original dataset.

3.2.1 K-step Graph

The first latent graph is called K-step graph. It generates links between the nodes that can be reached within k steps. An example of 2-step graph around the center node is given in Fig. 2(b) where the latent linkages are highlighted with dotted red lines. It is formally defined as follows:

Definition 1 **(K-step Graph)** *Given node v_i and v_j, the adjacency matrix of the K-step graph is defined as follows*

$$\mathbf{E}_{\mathbf{K\_STEP}}(i,j) = \begin{cases} 1 & \text{if there is a path from } v_i \\ & \text{to } v_j \text{ with length less than or equal to } k. \\ 0 & \text{Otherwise} \end{cases} \tag{2}$$

In other words, K-step graph increases the connectivity of the original graph by linking the indirect neighbors. And k is set to be 3 in the experiment. We further denote $\mathbf{E}^{(\mathcal{L})}_{\mathbf{K\_STEP}}$ as the K-step graph especially for the training data $\mathcal{L}$. It will be used in Section 3.3 to train the weights of the latent linkages.

3.2.2 Label Similarity Graph

Given the original graph as in Fig. 2(a), we further extend the connectivity of the graph by adding links to the data with the same class label. An example is presented in Fig. 2(c) and it is defined as follows:

Definition 2 **(Label Graph)** *Given node v_i and v_j, the adjacency matrix of the label graph is defined as follows*

$$\mathbf{E}_{\mathbf{LABEL}}(i,j) = \begin{cases} 1 & \text{if } v_i \text{ and } v_j \text{ have the same label} \\ & \text{and they are connected in } \mathbf{E}. \\ 0 & \text{Otherwise} \end{cases} \tag{3}$$

As before, we denote $\mathbf{E}^{(\mathcal{L})}_{\mathbf{LABEL}}$ as the label graph of the training data.

3.2.3 Attribute Similarity Graph

Another straightforward type of latent linkages is the attribute similarity. In other words, we can generate the adjacency matrix by evaluating the pairwise similarity among the nodes. For example, in a citation network, we can apply cosine similarity between each pair of documents to generate the matrix. Hence, similar documents are assigned higher weights. An example is illustrated in Fig. 2(d) and the formal definition is as follows:

Definition 3 **(Attribute Similarity Graph)** *For node v_i and v_j, the attribute similarity is the cosine similarity:*

$$\mathbf{E}_{\mathbf{ATT}}(i,j) = cosine(\mathbf{x}_i, \mathbf{x}_j) = \frac{< \mathbf{x}_i \cdot \mathbf{x}_j >}{\|\mathbf{x}_i\| \|\mathbf{x}_j\|} \tag{4}$$

where $\mathbf{x}_i$ and $\mathbf{x}_j$ are the attribute vectors of v_i and v_j correspondingly, $< * \cdot * >$ is the dot product and $\| * \|$ is the Euclidean norm. Note that we denote $\mathbf{E}^{(\mathcal{L})}_{\mathbf{ATT}}$ as the attribute similarity graph especially for training data. More details can be found in the next section.

3.2.4 Prediction Confidence Graph

Recall that we have a set of labeled examples. Then we can build a classifier with the labeled data, and give prediction to all the data. Hence each node v can be represented as a classification confidence vector $\mathbf{p} = \{p_1, p_2, \cdots, p_k\}$ where $p_i = p(c_i|v)$ is the classification confidence that v belongs to class c_i. As such, the data with similar confidence vectors are considered to be similar. An example can be found in Fig. 2(e). More formally, it can be defined as follows

Definition 4 **(Prediction Confidence Graph)** *Given node v_i and v_j and their corresponding classification confidence vectors $\mathbf{p}_i$ and $\mathbf{p}_j$ defined above, their similarity is defined as*

$$\mathbf{E}_{\mathbf{CON}}(i,j) = cosine(\mathbf{p}_i, \mathbf{p}_j) \tag{5}$$

The similarity matrix on the labeled data is $\mathbf{E}^{(\mathcal{L})}_{\mathbf{CON}}(i,j)$.

3.2.5 Structure Similarity Graph

In this paper, we also consider the original network structure. This is because the original graph will more or less reflect the similarity of the connected nodes. Hence, we define the structure similarity matrix as follows

$$\mathbf{E}_{\mathbf{STR}} = \mathbf{E} \tag{6}$$

However, it is difficult to capture the structure similarity among the labeled examples by the above definition. This is because there may be no connection among the few and randomly distributed labeled examples. To tackle this problem, we use random walk similarity to approximate the structure similarity among the labeled examples:

Definition 5 **(Structure Similarity on Labeled Data)** *Given node $v_i \in \mathcal{V}_{\mathcal{L}}$ and $v_j \in \mathcal{V}_{\mathcal{L}}$, their structure similarity is defined as*

$$\mathbf{E}^{(\mathcal{L})}_{\mathbf{STR}}(i,j) = \mathbf{R}(i,j) \tag{7}$$

where $\mathbf{R} = \sum_{\gamma=1}^{l} c(1-c)^{\gamma}\mathbf{P}^{\gamma}$ is the random walk probability matrix after l step, and $\mathbf{P}$ is the transition probability matrix constructed from the adjacency matrix $\mathbf{E}$.

As in [22], we set $c = 0.2$ and $l = 10$. Hence, even if v_i and v_j has no direct connection, we can still obtain their similarity from the random walk probability matrix.

It is important to note that the above five kinds of latent graphs are just a subset of potential latent linkages. They can be easily obtained from the original dataset. We show in the experiment section that even by using such straightforward latent graphs in the proposed framework, one can improve the prediction accuracy significantly. We next introduce how to judiciously integrate these different latent linkages to find the optimal latent graph.

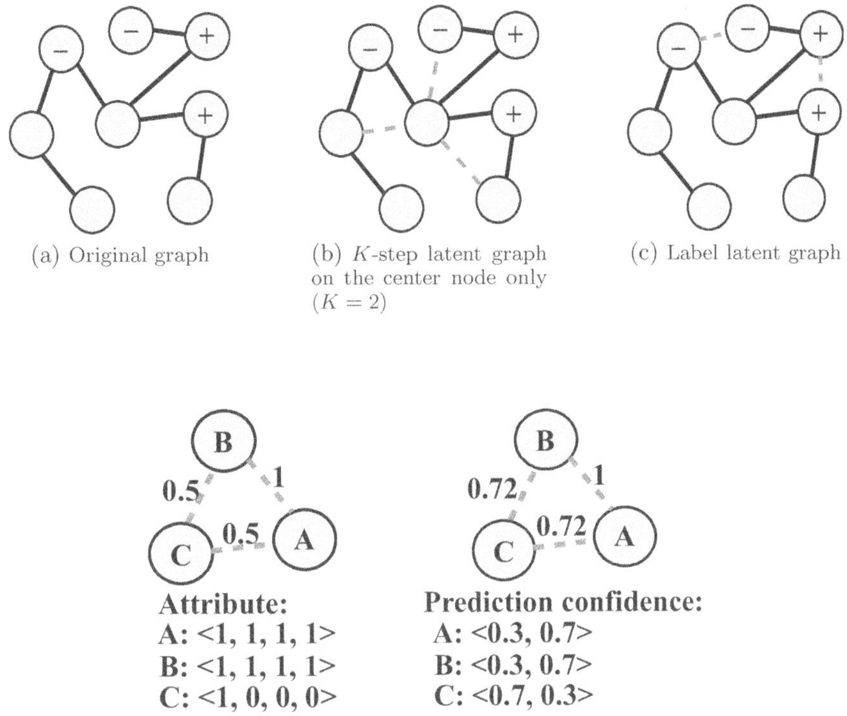

(a) Original graph

(b) K-step latent graph on the center node only ($K = 2$)

(c) Label latent graph

(d) Attribute latent graph

(e) Prediction confidence latent graph

Figure 2: Examples of latent graphs

Input:
Relational Graph $G(\mathcal{V}, \mathbf{E}, \mathbf{X}, \mathcal{Y})$ where $\mathcal{V}_{\mathcal{L}} \subset \mathcal{V}$ is the labeled nodes and $\mathcal{V}_{\mathcal{U}} = \mathcal{V} - \mathcal{V}_{\mathcal{L}}$ is the unlabeled ones.
Output:
The class labels for $\mathcal{V}_{\mathcal{U}}$

1 Generate the latent graphs as in Eq. 2 to 7.
2 Solve the optimization problem in Eq. 10;
3 Generate the latent graph with the learnt weights $\hat{\mathbf{E}} = \sum_{t=1}^{m}(\omega_t \mathbf{E}_t)$;
4 Perform label propagation on the latent graph $\hat{\mathbf{E}}$ to give predictions of the unlabeled nodes $\mathcal{V}_{\mathcal{U}}$.

Algorithm 1: LNP: Latent Network Propagation

3.3 Weight Optimization for LNP

In this section, we introduce how to find the best strategy to integrate the latent linkages to infer the best graph as described in Eq. 1. The key idea is to learn the best weights from the training examples (only) such that the data with the same label are linked together and those with different labels are disconnected. Hence, during the optimization, we only consider the latent linkages among the labeled examples and try the learn the weights from it. Denote a $t \times k$ matrix $\mathbf{Y}$ as the label matrix:

$$\mathbf{Y}(i,j) = \begin{cases} 1 & \text{if the node } v_i \text{ belongs to the } j\text{-th class} \\ 0 & \text{Otherwise} \end{cases} \tag{8}$$

where t is the number of labeled examples and k is the number of class labels. Hence the optimal similarity matrix for the labeled examples should be $\mathbf{M} = \mathbf{Y}\mathbf{Y}^T$ where $\mathbf{M}$ is a $k \times k$ matrix and $\mathbf{M}(i,j) = 1$ iff v_i and v_j have the same class label. Hence, we want to find a linear combination of the latent linkages so that the combining matrix approaches to the optimal matrix $\mathbf{M}$. The objective function in Eq. 1 can thus be written as

$$\begin{aligned} & \min_{\omega} \| \sum_{i=1}^{m} \omega_i \mathbf{E}_i^{(\mathcal{L})} - \mathbf{Y}\mathbf{Y}^T \|_F^2 + \lambda \|\omega\|^2 \\ \text{s.t. } & \sum_{i=1}^{m} \omega_i = 1 \\ & \omega_i \geq 0 \text{ for } i = 1, \cdots, m \end{aligned} \tag{9}$$

where $\mathbf{E}_i^{(\mathcal{L})}$ is the i-th type of latent linkages of the labeled examples $\mathcal{L}$ discussed in the last section, and $\omega = < \omega_1, \omega_2, \cdots, \omega_m >^T$ and λ is a smoothing parameter with default value 0.01. It can also be learnt from the training data with cross-validation.

Theorem 6 *The optimization in Eq. 9 is equivalent to the following quadratic programming problem:*

$$\begin{aligned} & \min_{\omega} \omega^T (\mathbf{K} + \lambda \mathbb{I}) \omega - 2\mathbf{u}^T \omega \\ s.t. \; & \sum_{i=1}^{m} \omega_i = 1 \\ & \omega_i \geq 0 \; for \; i = 1, \cdots, m \end{aligned} \tag{10}$$

where $\mathbb{I}$ is the identity matrix and $\mathbf{K}$ is a $m \times m$ matrix and

u *is a* $m \times 1$ *vector such that*

$$\mathbf{K}(i,j) = tr\Big((\mathbf{E}_i^{(\mathcal{L})})^T \mathbf{E}_j^{(\mathcal{L})}\Big)$$

$$\mathbf{u}(i) = tr(\mathbf{Y}\mathbf{Y}^T \mathbf{E}_i^{(\mathcal{L})})$$

PROOF. The optimization function in Eq. 9 can be written as

$$\begin{aligned}
&\| \sum_i^m \omega_i \mathbf{E}_i^{(\mathcal{L})} - \mathbf{Y}\mathbf{Y}^T \|_F^2 + \lambda \|\omega\|^2 \\
=&tr\Big((\sum_{i=1}^m \omega_i \mathbf{E}_i^{(\mathcal{L})})^T (\sum_{i=1}^m \omega_i \mathbf{E}_i^{(\mathcal{L})}) \\
&- 2\mathbf{Y}\mathbf{Y}^T (\sum_{i=1}^m \omega_i \mathbf{E}_i^{(\mathcal{L})}) + \mathbf{Y}\mathbf{Y}^T\mathbf{Y}\mathbf{Y}^T \Big) + \lambda tr(\omega^T \omega) \\
=&\omega^T(\mathbf{K} + \lambda \mathbb{I})\omega - 2\mathbf{u}^T\omega + tr(\mathbf{Y}\mathbf{Y}^T\mathbf{Y}\mathbf{Y}^T)
\end{aligned}$$

Note that $tr(\mathbf{Y}\mathbf{Y}^T\mathbf{Y}\mathbf{Y}^T)$ is a constant. Hence, the optimization in Eq. 9 is equivalent to that Eq. 10. □

It is important to note that the optimization in Eq. 10 is a quadric programming problem with conventional format and can be solved efficiently with general solver such as [1]. In our algorithm, since we have only five unknown ω's (corresponding to the five latent similarity matrices), the optimal solution can be obtained in constant time. After obtaining the best weights, we can perform label propagation on the latent network to make prediction. The algorithm is described in Algorithm 1. Step 1 is to generate the five latent graphs and Step 2 solves the optimization problem to obtain the optimal weights. Step 3 is to construct the target latent graph , and in Step 4, label propagation is applied to give prediction. It is important to emphasize again that since the optimization takes constant time, the complexity of the whole algorithm is the same as the traditional label propagation. The most expensive step is to calculate the inverse of the matrix, which is $O(n^{2.4})$ [2].

4. EXPERIMENTS

In this section, the proposed model LNP is evaluated on three real world network datasets. The descriptions of the datasets are summarized in Table 2. As it can be observed, all three datasets have multiple classes with two types of features. One is the conventional vector-based feature and the other is the relational feature (network). Hence, a well developed relational model is supposed to make good use of both of the attributes and the networks to give accurate predictions.

Comparison Methods

Three algorithms are compared with LNP:

- The first is the traditional label propagation algorithm [23] (LPP). It is considered as the most comparable method since LNP also adopts the idea but with a new concept called latent graph.
- The second one is a state-of-the-art collective classification algorithm called **I**terative **C**lassification **A**lgorithm (ICA) proposed in [12]. ICA can iteratively adjust the predicted labels of the graphs until convergence, and it is reported in [4] as one of the collective classifiers with the best performances.

Table 2: Description of the data sets

Data set	#Instances	#Features	#Edges	#Classes
Cora	2708	1433	5429	7
Citeseer	3312	3703	4832	6
Gene	672	461	910	15

- The third comparison algorithm is devised by directly combining the latent graphs without weighting. In other words, it is different from the proposed model only in that the different latent graphs are of equal weight and the adjacency matrix of the final graph is: $\hat{\mathbf{E}} = \sum_{t=1}^m(\mathbf{E}_t)$. We call it **E**qual-weight **LNP** (ELNP). This comparison algorithm is to evaluate the weight learning algorithm discussed in Section 3.3.

Note that these are some of the most obvious choices of comparison methods, commonly adopted in the research community. In the discussion section, we also study some modifications of the above models, in order to analyze their behaviors with limited number of training data.

Experiment Setup and Evaluation

In the experiment, all results are summarized on 10 runs. In each run, we apply the snowball sampling technique [12] to select certain proportion of data as the training examples. This sampling technique isolates the effect of class bias and make the evaluation focus more on a "fair" scenario with balanced classes. Another important thing is that the experiment will focus more on the situation when the proportion of training examples is not significantly large. As described in the introduction section, there are many applications that are in such situation, and it is interesting to observe how the collective classifiers work. For evaluation, we use accuracy as a criterion:

$$\text{Accuracy} = \frac{\#\text{Test data that are labeled correctly}}{\text{Total number of test data}} \quad (11)$$

4.1 Experiment Results

In this section, we present the experiment results on three real world datasets: Citeseer, Cora and Gene.

Citeseer Dataset

The Citeseer dataset is a publication dataset[1] and we use a processed version presented in [14]. It is a collection of research publications draw from Citeseer, divided into one of the 6 classes: AI, Agents, DB, HCI, IR and ML. There are 3312 instances and 4832 citation links in the dataset. Each instance is described with the "bag of words" representation. More specifically, the features are binary vectors, which indicate whether the instance (paper) contains the word or not. The vocabulary size here is 3703. It is important to mention that the direction of the citation links are ignored as in [12] to simplify the problem. And we also delete the isolated nodes which do not have connection to any other nodes since the isolated nodes have no contribution to the relational network.

The experiment results summarized on 10 runs are presented in Fig. 3. It can be observed that the comparison

[1] http://www.cs.umd.edu/projects/linqs/projects/lbc

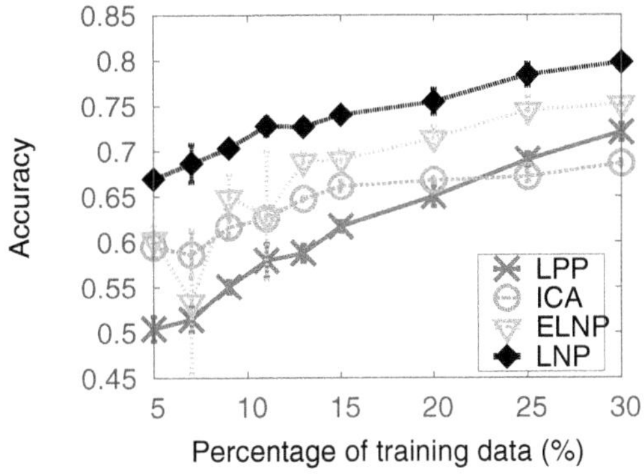

Figure 3: Citeseer dataset

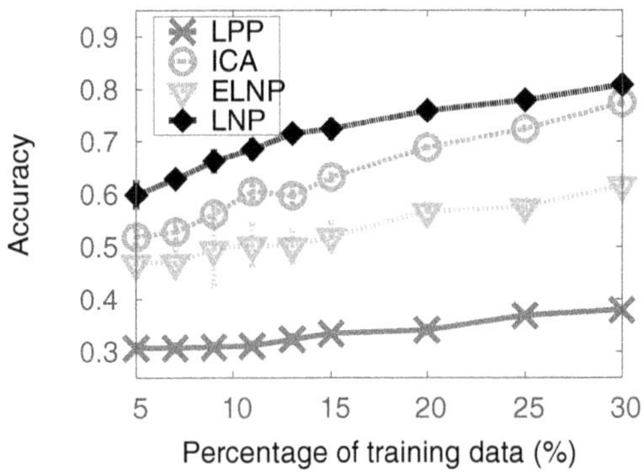

Figure 4: Cora dataset

models do not perform well. This is because most of the instances do not have edge connecting to the limited number of labeled data; hence the label information cannot be propagated through the network effectively. This phenomena is also studied in the introduction and Section 2. It is also important to note that the proposed model substantially outperforms the comparison models by propagating supervision knowledge through the latent linkages. For example, when there are only 10% of training examples, the proposed LNP model can obtain an accuracy of 74% whereas the accuracies of all the comparison models are less than 64%; the improvement is above 15%. This shows the effectiveness and necessity of exploring latent linkages to tackle the label deficiency problem. Another interesting observation is that the equal weight LNP (ELNP) performs a lot worse than LNP. This is because LNP assigns higher weights to the informative latent linkages to find a better latent graph.

Cora Dataset

The Cora dataset is also a publication dataset used in [14], which is a collection of machine learning publications categorized into one of the seven classes: Case Based, Genetic Algorithms, Neural Networks, Probabilistic Methods, Reinforcement Learning, Rule Learning and Theory. It contains 2708 instances and 5429 undirected citation links in total. Each instance is also represented as "bag of words" and is described as a 0/1 feature vector. The vocabulary size is 1433.

We present the results in Fig. 4. In this experiment, it can also be observed that traditional collective classifiers ICA, LPP, and the equal weight LNP (ELNP) do not perform well. The proposed model LNP, instead, outperforms all the comparison models substantially and clearly. For instance, when there are 15% of labeled data, the accuracy of LNP is above 70%, while all the others are below 60%. It is also important to note that in this dataset, the advantage of LNP over the comparison model ICA diminishes as the number of training examples increases. This is because if there are sufficient labeled data, ICA can also propagate the supervision knowledge effectively. But it is usually difficult to estimate how many training data are needed for ICA to get a good result. For example, in the Citeseer dataset and the next dataset Gene, ICA does not perform better even if there are 30% of training examples. This also shows the necessity of LNP to handle label deficiency.

Gene Dataset

The Gene dataset is a gene network of the yeast genome, which is downloaded from the KDD cup 2001[2]. We use the training set provided by the web as the whole network dataset. After pruning those isolated genes that do not have connection to other genes, we get 672 genes and 910 interaction links in total. As the previous two datasets, we ignore the directions of the links. The 15 classes represent the possible localizations of the genome: cytoplasm, cytoskeleton, ER, golgi, mitochondria, nucleus, peroxisome, plasma membrane, transport vesicles and vacuole.

The experiment results are summarized in Fig. 5. Note that this dataset contains 15 class labels, which is essentially a difficult multi-class classification problem. We note that in this situation traditional approach like LPP does very poorly. This is because the traditional collective classifiers require a lot of labeled examples to handle the complicated multi-class classification problem. However, the proposed LNP model beats the comparison models consistently. It is also important to note that the performance differences of LNP, ICA and ELNP are not very significant when there are only 5% of training examples. The reason is that all the approaches cannot obtain enough supervision knowledge from the labeled data to tackle the essentially complicated multi-class classification problem. But with a bit more labeled examples, the accuracy of LNP increases faster and it stays above the accuracies of all the other approaches. Another observation is that LNP beats the equal weight strategy (ELNP) substantially. It reveals the necessity of training unequal weights to emphasize the informative latent linkages and deemphasize those noisy ones.

4.2 Discussion

In this section, we aim at studying the following questions:

- Can the different types of latent linkages work separately? Or in other words, why do we need to integrate different latent linkages?
- Why is it necessary to devise a new model to solve the label deficiency problem? Can traditional collective classifiers solve the problem by just a little modification?
- Why do we use label propagation on the latent graph?

[2] www.cs.wisc.edu/?dpage/kddcip2001

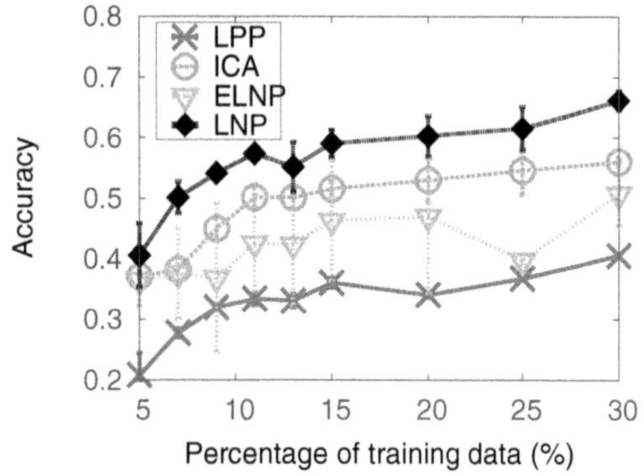

Figure 5: Gene dataset

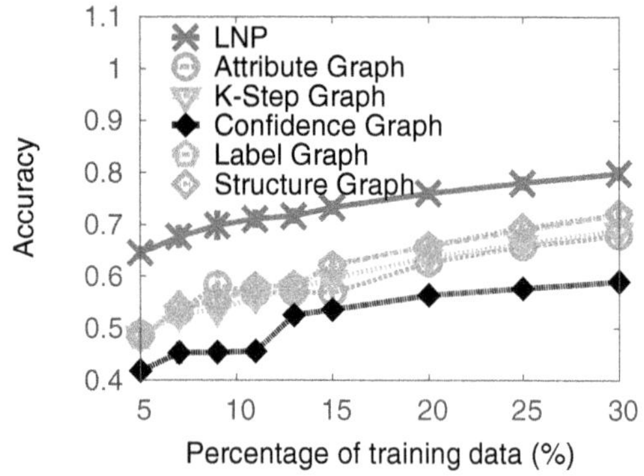

Figure 6: Why we need to integrate latent linkages?

Why do we need to integrate different latent linkages?

In Section 3.2, five different types of latent linkages are introduced. It is thus interesting to study how these different latent linkages contribute to the model and why we need to integrate them. We study the problem on the citeseer dataset where we use the five kinds of latent linkages individually to generate five different latent graphs. They are

1. K-step graph: the graph links nodes together if they are connected with length less than k.

2. Label graph: the graph links nodes together if they are training data and have the same label.

3. Structure similarity graph: the network generated from the original network structure;

4. Attribute similarity graph: the network generated from the cosine similarity of the instances;

5. Prediction similarity graph: the network links the data with similar distributions of the prediction confidence. More details are described in Section 3.2.

We compare the inference performances of the five independent graphs with LNP. The results are presented in Fig. 6. It can be observed that the performances of the five kinds of latent linkages are similar. However, when we apply the proposed LNP model to integrate the five, the accuracy increases by as much as 40%. This is because each type of the latent linkages only provides the node relations from a specific aspect, but the combination of them can lead to a more comprehensive relation network.

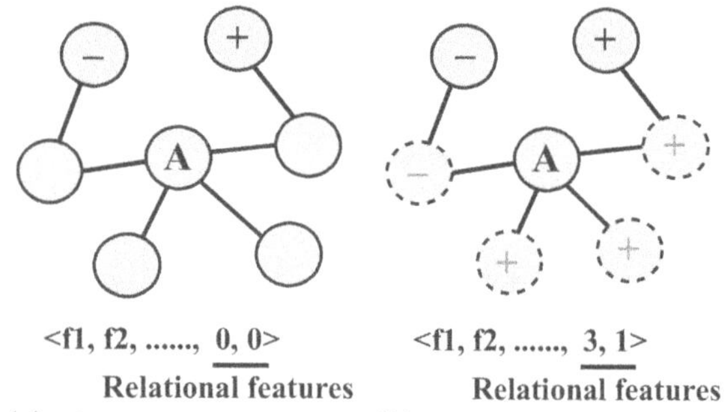

(a) Traditional collective classifiers

(b) Semi-supervised collective classifiers. The nodes with pseudo labels are highlighted with dotted lines.

Figure 7: A straightforward modification of traditional collective classifiers into semi-supervised version

Can semi-supervised ICA work?

Note that traditional collective classifiers such as ICA only train on the labeled examples. Hence, if there are only a limited number of training data, the label information cannot be propagated through the network effectively. In this experiment, we make a little modification on ICA to make use of the unlabeled nodes. To do so, we first use a traditional non-relational classifier, such as logistic regression, to train a model based on the attribute vector only. All nodes are assigned pseudo class labels by the non-relational classifier as in Fig. 7(b). In the second step, we apply ICA to train the model with both attribute vectors and the network summary of the pseudo labels obtained in the last step. It is important to note that in this modification, the whole graph can be viewed as a fully labeled graph with both true labels and pseudo labels. As such, ICA can collect more information from the network summary as illustrated in Fig. 7.

In this experiment, we compare the proposed model with the semi-supervised collective classifier described above. The experiment result on the citeseer dataset is presented in Fig. 8. It is interesting to see that the semi-supervised modification cannot improve the accuracy of ICA too much. This is because when there are a limited number of training examples, the first step of the semi-supervised ICA may generate a lot of incorrect pseudo labels. As such, the performance cannot be improved too much. Hence, it is not trivial to devise a new mechanism to tackle the label deficiency problem. From Fig. 8, it can also be observed that the proposed LNP model outperforms both methods significantly. For instance, when the accuracies of both comparison methods are around 70%, the proposed model can achieve an accuracy of 80%.

Why label propagation on the latent network?

The above question includes two sub-issues: (1) why is label propagation necessary? (2) why is the latent network important? We design four models to answer the above question:

1. Label propagation (abbreviated as LPP in Fig. 9) on the original network ;

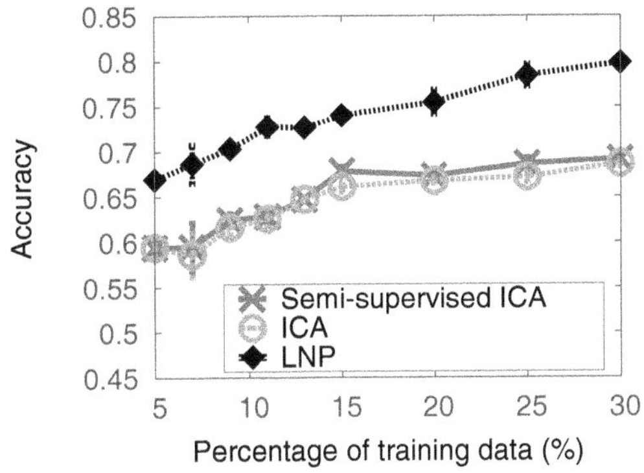

Figure 8: Can semi-supervised ICA work?

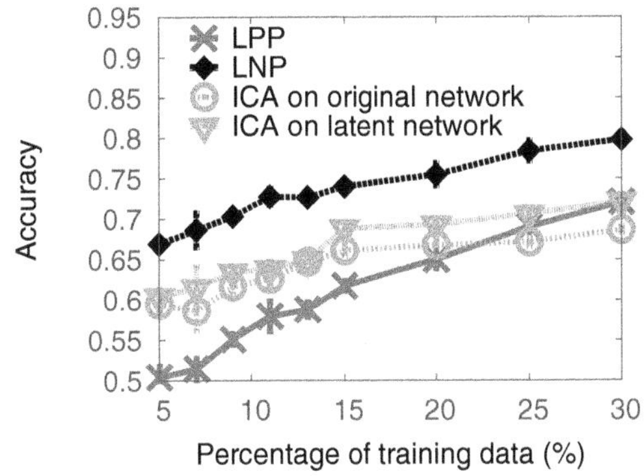

Figure 9: The importance of the latent network and label propagation

2. Label propagation on the latent network (the proposed LNP model);
3. ICA on the original network;
4. ICA on the latent network.

The experiment result on the citeseer dataset is presented in Fig. 9. There are two things that can be observed. First, traditional label propagation LPP does not perform well on the original network. It has the worst result among the four approaches. The reason is that with a limited number of training examples, the original network is not effective enough to propagate the supervision knowledge. Another reason is that traditional label propagation or other graphical inferences models (*e.g.*, [5, 11, 15]) do not take the attribute vector into consideration. They only depend on the given network to give prediction. Without the ability of using vector-based features, the performance of label propagation is even worse than that of ICA as in Fig. 9. However, when we apply label propagation on the latent network (LNP), it obtains the best accuracy among the four models. This shows the importance of the latent network to make good use of the vector-based feature (through Attribute similarity graph) and integrate different supervision knowledge to improve the accuracy. The second observation is that ICA does not perform well on the latent network. It has a similar result with that on the original network. This is because the latent network is generated from both the original network and the node attributes. But ICA already has the same information, and thus the latent network essentially does not provide any additional supervision knowledge to ICA. In summary, first, label propagation does not perform well on the original network because it cannot propagate the label information effectively and cannot use the attribute vector; second, although traditional collective classifiers such as ICA consider both the network and the attributes, they are not very effective when there are a limited number of training data. As such, the proposed LNP model can be viewed as a bridge of collective classification (such as ICA) and traditional graphical inference (such as label propagation) by introducing the latent network.

5. RELATED WORK

With the explosive development of social network, graph based approaches attract intensive attentions in recent years. Several approaches have been proposed to perform inference on a given network (*e.g.*, [24, 18, 19, 21, 10, 20]). For instance, [23] proposes to propagate the labels through the network, and assigns each node with the label that is most likely to be visited from the node. However, this category of algorithms only considers the graph structure or only consider the feature vectors, and it cannot handle the case directly when there is feature vector in a graph. For example, in a citation network, each node is a paper and the links represent a citation relationship. In addition to the linkage information among the nodes, we also have the "bag of words" feature vector for each node. Traditional graph based models cannot directly handle this kind of network data with feature vectors.

Collective classification is then proposed to solve the problem. Its key idea is to combine the supervision knowledge from the traditional tuple-based feature vectors, as well as the linkage information from the network. It has been applied to various applications such as part-of-speech tagging [7], classification of hypertext documents using hyperlinks [15, 3], link prediction in friend-of-a-friend networks [17], predicting disulphide bonds in protein molecules [16], *etc.*.

Iterative Classification Algorithm (ICA [12]) is among the first works proposed to tackle collective classification. The key step is to transform the network summary into feature vectors and treat the network as ordinary features. It is reported in [4] that ICA is a fairly accurate method with robust performance to different strategies of updating the labels. Moreover, Gibbs sampling [6] is further integrated into the ICA framework to enrich the statistical foundation of the algorithm. This is the major reason that we choose ICA and Gibbs sampling as the major collective classifiers to be compared with. In recent years, there are several works proposed to use a similar schema as ICA but with different basic classifiers or in different scenarios [6, 13, 15, 9]. In [9], it is reported that Logistic Regression works the best among these different interpretations. Hence, we set the basic classifier of all the comparison methods as Logistic Regression in the experiment.

It is important to note that most of the above works are mainly studied in the scenario where there are a lot of labeled examples in the network. For example, the models in [15, 9, 12] are all studied and evaluated with k-fold cross-validation where over half of the data are training examples. Although it has been shown that traditional collective classifiers work well in this situation, it is not sure how they behave when the number of training examples is limited. In this paper, we study their behaviors in this situation and analyze the reason why they do not perform well. Furthermore, a general model is proposed to judiciously integrate different latent linkages to generate a latent network to make good use of the limited training examples.

6. CONCLUSION

In many social graph applications, training examples are time-consuming and expensive to obtain. Without sufficient labeled data, traditional collective classifiers and their semi-supervised modifications do not perform well. In this paper, we first explore various kinds of latent linkages from the existing dataset without using the information from other sources. Then, the latent linkages are judiciously integrated to change the network structure in order to allow for effective supervision propagation. The aim is to find a latent graph that can link the data together if they have the same class label and disjoin those with different class labels. The objective is formulated as an optimization problem and is solved via quadratic programming. We perform experiments on three sets of graph datasets. The performances of the proposed model and those of the comparison methods are studied with different sample rates. In most cases, the proposed model can outperform the comparison algorithms substantially. For example, when there are only 15% of training examples in the cora dataset, the accuracies of the comparison methods are below 60% whereas the proposed model achieves an accuracy above 70%.

7. ACKNOWLEDGEMENTS

This work is supported in part by NSF through grants IIS 0905215, DBI-0960443, OISE-0968341 and OIA-0963278.

8. REFERENCES

[1] T. F. Coleman and Y. Li. A reflective newton method for minimizing a quadratic function subject to bounds on some of the variables. *SIAM Journal on Optimization*, 6(4):1040–1058, 1996.

[2] J. Demmel, I. Dumitriu, O. Holtz, and R. Kleinberg. Fast matrix multiplication is stable. *CoRR*, abs/math/0603207, 2006.

[3] B. Gallagher and T. Eliassi-Rad. Leveraging network structure to infer missing values in relational data. Technical Report UCRL-TR-231993.

[4] L. Getoor. *Advanced Methods for Knowledge Discovery from Complex Data*. Springer.

[5] W. R. Grilks, S. Richardson, and D. J. Spiegelhalter. Markov chain monte carlo in practice. *Interdisciplinary Statistics. Chapman and Hall/CRC*, 1996.

[6] D. Jensen, J. Neville, and B. Gallagher. Why collective inference improves relational classification. In *Proceedings of the International Conference on Knowledge Discovery and Data Mining*, 2004.

[7] J. D. Lafferty, A. McCallum, and F. C. N. Pereira. Conditional random fields: Probabilistic models for segmenting and labeling sequence data. In *Proceedings of the International Conference on Machine Learning*, 2001.

[8] J. Leskovec, L. A. Adamic, and B. A. Huberman. The dynamics of viral marketing. *ACM Transactions on the Web (TWEB)*, 1:1559–1131, 2007.

[9] Q. Lu and L. Getoor. Link-based classification. In *Proceedings of the Twentieth International Conference on Machine Learning*, 2003.

[10] S. A. Macskassy and F. Provost. A simple relational classifier. In *Proceedings of the Multi-Relational Data MiningWorkshop at the Ninth ACM SIGKDD International Conference on Knowledge Discovery and Data Mining*, 2003.

[11] A. McCallum, K. Nigam, J. Rennie, and K. Seymore. Automating the construction of internet portals with maching learning. *Information Retrieval*, 2(3):127–163, 2000.

[12] J. Neville and D. Jensen. Iterative classification in relational data. In *Proceeding of the Workshop on Statistical Relational Learning of the National Conference on Artificial Intelligence*, 2000.

[13] J. Neville and D. Jensen. Collective classification with relational dependency networks. In *Proceedings of the 2nd Multi-Relational Data Mining Workshop, ACM SIGKDD International Conference on Knowledge Discovery and Data Mining*, 2003.

[14] P. Sen, G. M. Namata, M. Bilgic, L. Getoor, B. Gallagher, and T. Eliassi-Rad. Collective classification in network data. *AI Magazine*, 29(3):93–106, 2008.

[15] B. Taskar, P. Abbeel, and D. Koller. Discriminative probabilistic models for relational data. In *Proceedings of the Annual Conference on Uncertainty in Artificial Intelligence*, 2002.

[16] B. Taskar, V. Chatalbashev, D. Koller, and C. Guestrin. Learning structured prediction models: A large margin approach. In *Proceedings of the International Conference on Machine Learning*, 2005.

[17] B. Taskar, M. F. Wong, P. Abbeel, and D. Koller. Link prediction in relational data. In *Neural Information Processing Systems*, 2003.

[18] Y. Weiss. *Advanced Mean Field Methods*. MIT Press.

[19] Jonathan S. Yedidia, William T. Freeman, and Yair Weiss. Constructing free energy approximations and generalized belief propagation algorithms. *IEEE Transactions on Information Theory*, 51:2282–2312, 2004.

[20] D. Zhou, O. Bousquet, T. N. Lal, J. Weston, and B. Schaolkopf. Learning with local and global consistency. In *Neural Information Processing Systems*, 2004.

[21] D. Zhou and B. Scholkopf. Learning from labeled and unlabeled data using random walks. In *Proceedings of the DAGM Symposium*, 2004.

[22] Y. Zhou, H. Cheng, and J. X. Yu. Graph clustering based on structural/attribute similarities. In *Proceedings of the Very Large Data Base*, 2009.

[23] X. Zhu. Semi-supervised learning with graphs. Technical report, Carnegie Mellon University, 2005.

[24] X. Zhu, Z. Ghahramani, and J. Lafferty. Semi-supervised learning using gaussian fields and harmonic functions. In *Proceedings of the International Conference on Machine Learning*, 2003.

Who Will Follow You Back? Reciprocal Relationship Prediction*

John Hopcroft
Department of Computer Science
Cornell University
Ithaca NY 14853
jeh@cs.cornell.edu

Tiancheng Lou
Institute for Interdisciplinary Information Sciences
Tsinghua University
Beijing 100084, China
ltc08@tsinghua.edu.cn

Jie Tang
Department of Computer Science
Tsinghua University
Beijing 100084, China
jietang@tsinghua.edu.cn

ABSTRACT

We study the extent to which the formation of a two-way relationship can be predicted in a dynamic social network. A two-way (called reciprocal) relationship, usually developed from a one-way (parasocial) relationship, represents a more trustful relationship between people. Understanding the formation of two-way relationships can provide us insights into the micro-level dynamics of the social network, such as what is the underlying community structure and how users influence each other.

Employing Twitter as a source for our experimental data, we propose a learning framework to formulate the problem of reciprocal relationship prediction into a graphical model. The framework incorporates social theories into a machine learning model. We demonstrate that it is possible to accurately infer 90% of reciprocal relationships in a dynamic network. Our study provides strong evidence of the existence of the structural balance among reciprocal relationships. In addition, we have some interesting findings, e.g., the likelihood of two "elite" users creating a reciprocal relationships is nearly 8 times higher than the likelihood of two ordinary users. More importantly, our findings have potential implications such as how social structures can be inferred from individuals' behaviors.

Categories and Subject Descriptors

H.2.8 [**Database Management**]: Data Mining; J.4 [**Social and Behavioral Sciences**]: Miscellaneous; H.4.m [**Information Systems**]: Miscellaneous

General Terms

Algorithms, Experimentation

Keywords

social network, reciprocal relationship, social influence, predictive model, link prediction, Twitter

*Authors are in alphabetic order. The work were done when the last two authors were visiting Cornell University.

1. INTRODUCTION

Online social networks (e.g., Twitter, Facebook, Myspace) significantly enlarge our social circles. One can follow any elites (celebrities), e.g., politicians, models, actors, and athletes, or close friends in her physical social network. An interesting question here is: when you follow a number of users, who will follow you back? A more specific question is: if you follow those celebrities (elite users) on Twitter, do you think they will follow you back? The answer is often No, but also Yes sometimes. There are a number of top users with tens of thousands of followers, who will follow everyone back. Some even use tools to do follow-back automatically, while others go through the following list and add their new followers manually.[1] Awareness of how these relationships are created can benefit many applications such as friend suggestion, community detection, and "word-of-mouth" product promotion.

In social science, relationships between individuals are classified into two categories: one-way (called parasocial) relationships and two-way (called reciprocal) relationships [9]. The most common form of the former are one-way relationships between celebrities and audience or fans, while the most common form of the latter are two-way relationships between close friends. Twitter and Facebook are respectively typical examples of the two types of social relationships. Social relationships form the basis of the social structure. Indeed, social relationships are always the basic object of analysis for social scientists, for instance, in Max Weber's theory of social action [29]. Understanding the formation of social relationships can give us insights into the micro-level dynamics of the social network, such as how an individual user influences her/his friends through different types of social relationships [26], and how the underlying social structure changes with the dynamics of relationship formation [23].

Employing Twitter as the basis of our analysis, we study how a two-way (reciprocal) relationship has been developed from a one-way (parasocial) relationship. Specifically, we try to answer: "when you follow a particular user (either an elite user or an ordinary user), how likely will she/he follow you back?". This problem also implicitly exists in other social networks such as Facebook and LinkedIn: when you send a friend request to somebody, how likely will she/he confirm your request?

Previous research on social relationships can be classified into three categories: link prediction [2, 16, 17, 23], relationship type inferring [4, 5, 27], and social behavior prediction [1, 25, 33]. Backstrom and Leskovec [2] proposed an approach called supervised random walks to predict and recommend links in social networks. Crandall et al. [4] investigated the problem of inferring social ties between people from co-occurrence in time and space.

[1] http://socialnewswatch.com/top-twitter-users/

Wang et al. [27] proposed an unsupervised algorithm to infer advisor-advisee relationships from a publication network. However, little research systematically studies how two-way relationships can be developed from one-way relationships. More fundamentally, what are the underlying factors that essentially influence the formation of two-way relationships? and how existing social theories (e.g., structural balance theory and homophily) can be connected to the formation process?

In this paper, we try to conduct a systematic investigation on the problem of two-way (reciprocal) relationship prediction. We precisely define the problem and propose a Triad Factor Graph (TriFG) model. The TriFG model incorporates social theories into a semi-supervised learning model, where we have some labeled training data (two-way relationships) but with low reciprocity [13]. Given a historic log of users' following actions from time 0 to t, we try to learn a predictive model to infer whether user A will add a follow-back link to user B at time $(t+1)$ if user B creates a new follow link to user A at time t. We evaluate the proposed model on a Twitter data consisting of 13,442,659 users and their profiles, tweets, following behaviors (new following or follow-back links) for nearly two months.

Results We show that incorporating social theories into the proposed factor graph model can significantly improve the performance (+22%-+27% by F1-Measure) of two-way (reciprocal) relationship prediction compared with several alternative methods. Our study also reveals several interesting phenomena:

1. Elite users tend to follow each other. The likelihood of an elite user following back another elite user is nearly 8 times higher than that of two ordinary users and 30 times that of an elite user and an ordinary user.
2. Two-way relationships on Twitter are balanced, but one-way relationships are not. More than 88% of social triads (groups of three people) with two-way relationships satisfy the social balance theory, while one-way relationships are unbalanced (merely 25% of them satisfy the balance theory).
3. Social networks are going global, but also stay local. No matter how far a user is from you, the likelihood that she/he follows you back is almost the same. While, on the other hand, the number of two-way relationships between users within the same time zone is 20 times higher than the number of users from different time zones.

Organization Section 2 formulates the problem. Section 3 introduces the data set and our analyses on the data set. Section 4 explains the proposed model and describes the algorithm for learning the model. Section 5 presents experimental results that validate the effectiveness of our methodology. Finally, Section 6 reviews the related work and Section 7 concludes this work.

2. PROBLEM DEFINITION

In this section, after presenting several definitions, we formally define the targeted problem in this work. We formulate the problem in the context of Twitter to keep things concrete, though adaptation of this framework to other social-network settings is straightforward.

The Twitter network can be modeled as a directed graph $G = \{V, E\}$, where $V = \{v_1, v_2, \ldots, v_n\}$ is the set of users, and $E \subseteq V \times V$ is the set of directed links between users. Each directed link $e_{ij} = (v_i, v_j) \in E$ indicates that user v_i follows user v_j.

The Twitter network is dynamic in nature, with links added and removed from over time. However, our preliminary statistics on a large Twitter data set show that users tend to add new links much more frequently than to remove existing links (e.g., 97% of changes to links are adding new links). Therefore, adding new links forms the structure of the Twitter network. A new link results when a user performs a behavior of following another user (back) in Twitter. Particularly, we define two types of the link behavior:

Definition 1. **New-follow and Follow-back:** Suppose at time t, user v_i creates a link to v_j, who has no previous link to v_i, then we say v_i performs a new-follow behavior on v_j. When user v_i creates a link to v_j at time t, who already has a link to v_i before time t, we say v_i performs a follow-back behavior on v_j.

The new-follow and follow-back behaviors respectively correspond to the one-way (parasocial) relationship and the two-way (reciprocal) relationship in sociology. In this work, we focus on investigating the formation of follow-back behaviors. For simplicity, let $y_{ij}^t = 1$ denote that user v_i follows back v_j at time t and $y_{ij}^t = 0$ denote user v_i does not follow back. We are concerned with the following prediction problem:

Problem 1. **Follow-back prediction.** Let $< 1, \ldots, t >$ be a sequence of time stamps with a particular time granularity (e.g., day, week etc.). Given Twitter networks from time 1 to t, $\{G^t = (V^t, E^t, Y^t)\}$, where Y^t is the set of follow-back behaviors at time t, the task is to find a predictive function:

$$f : (\{G^1, \cdots, G^t\}) \to Y^{(t+1)},$$

such that we can infer the follow-back behaviors at time $(t + 1)$.

It bears pointing out that our problem is very different from existing link prediction [2, 17, 23] and social action prediction problems [25, 33]. First, as the twitter network is evolving over time, it is infeasible to collect a complete network at time t. Thus it is important to design a method that could take into consideration the unlabeled data as well. Second, it is unclear what are the fundamental factors that cause the formation of follow-back relationships. Finally, one needs to incorporate the different factors (e.g., social theories, statistics, and our intuitions) into a unified model to better predict the follow-back relationship.

3. DATA AND OBSERVATIONS

3.1 Data Collection

We aim to find a large set of users and a continuously updated network among these users, so that we can use the data set as the gold-standard to evaluate different approaches for our prediction. To begin the collection process, we selected the most popular user on Twitter, i.e., "Lady Gaga", and randomly collected 10,000 of her followers. We took these users as seed users and used a crawler to collect all followers of these users by traversing following edges. We continue the traversing process, which produced in total 13,442,659 users and 56,893,234 following links, with an average of 728,509 new links per day. The crawler monitored the change of the network structure from 10/12/2010 to 12/23/2010. We also extracted all tweets posted by these users and in total there are 35,746,366 tweets.

In our analysis, we also consider the geographic location of each user. Specifically, we first extracted the location from the profile of each user[2], and then fed the location information to the Google Map API to fetch its corresponding longitude and latitude values. In this

[2]For example, Lady Gaga's location information is: "Location: New York, NY".

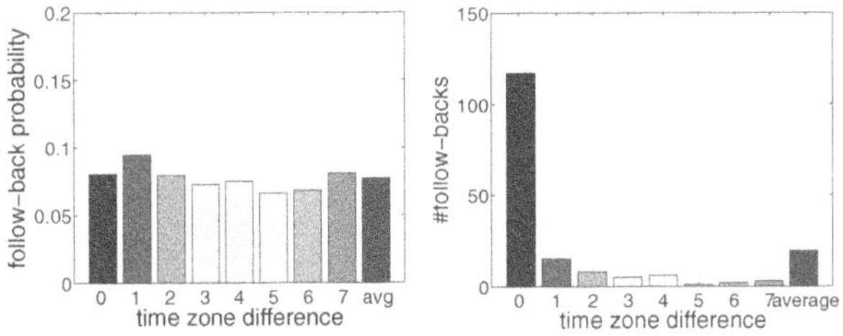

(a) Global (b) Local

Figure 1: Geographic distance correlation. X-axis: time zone difference (0 indicates that users are located in the same time zone); Y-axis: (a) probability that one user follows back another user, conditioned on the time zone difference of the two users. (b) number of two-way relationships among users from the same time zone or different time zones.

way, we obtained the longitude and latitude of about 59% of users in our data set. More detailed analysis and an online demonstration is publicly available. http://arnetminer.org/reciprocal/

3.2 Observations

We first engage in some high-level investigation of how different factors influence the formation of follow-back (reciprocal) relationships, since a major motivation of our work is to find the underlying factors and their influence to this task. In particular, we study the interplay of the following factors with the formation of follow-backs: (1) *Geographic distance:* Do users have a higher probability to follow each other when they are located in the same region? (2) *Homophily:* Do similar users tend to follow each other? (3) *Implicit network:* How does the following network on Twitter correlate with other implicit networks, e.g., retweet and reply network? and (4) *Social balance:* Does the two-way relationship network on Twitter satisfy the social balance theory [6]? To which extent?

Geographic distance Figure 1 shows the correlation between geographic distance and the probability that two users create a two-way relationship (i.e., follow back each other). Interestingly, it seems that online social networks indeed go global: Figure 1(b) shows the likelihood of a user following another user back when they are from the same time zone or from different time zones. Clearly, the geographic distance is already not a factor to stop users from developing a trustful (reciprocal) relationship. Figure 1(a) shows another statistic which indicates a different perspective that the Twitter network (in some sense) still stays local: the average number of two-way (reciprocal) relationships between users from the same time zone is about 50 times higher than the number between users with a distance of three time zones.

Homophily The principle of homophily [15] suggests that users with similar characteristics (e.g., social status, age) tend to associate with each other. In particular, we study two kinds of homophilies on the Twitter network: link homophily and status homophily. For the link homophily, we test whether users who share common links (followers or followees) will have a tendency to associate with each other. Figure 2 clearly shows that the probability of two users following back each other when they share common neighbors is much higher than usual. When the number of common neighbors with two way relationships increases to 3, the likelihood of two users following back each other also triples. The effect is more pronounced when the number increases to 10. But it is worth noting that this only works for two-way (reciprocal) relationships and does not hold for the one-way (parasocial) relationship (as indicated in Figure 2).

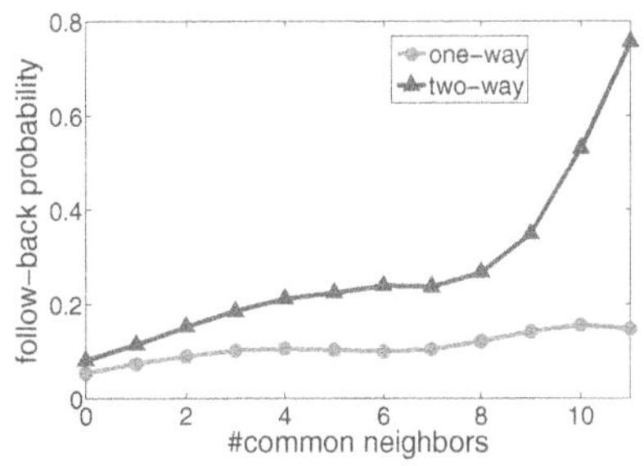

Figure 2: Link homophily. Y-axis: probability that two users follow back each other, conditioned on the number of common neighbors of two-way relationships (or one-way relationships).

For the status homophily, we test whether two users with similar social status are more likely to associate with each other. We categorize users into two groups (elite users and ordinary users) by three different algorithms: PageRank [22][3], #degree, and (α, β) algorithm [8][4]. Specifically, with PageRank, we estimate the importance of each user according to the network structure, and then select as elite users with the top 1% users[5] who have the highest PageRank scores and the rest as ordinary users; while with #degree, we select top 1% users with the highest number of indegree as elite users and the rest as ordinary users. For (α, β), we input the size of the core community as 200, and after running the algorithm, we use users selected in the core community as elite users and the rest as ordinary users. Then, we examine the difference of follow back behaviors among the two groups of users. Figure 3 clearly shows that, though the three algorithms present different statistics, "elite" users have a much stronger tendency to follow each other: the likelihood of two elite users following back each other is nearly 8 times higher than that of ordinary users (by the (α, β) algorithm). The (α, β) algorithm seems able to better distinguish elite users from ordinary users in our problem setting. This is because besides the global network structure, the (α, β) algorithm also considers the community structure among elite users.

Implicit structure On Twitter, besides the explicit network with following links, there are also some implicit network structure that can be induced from the textural information. For example, user A may mention user B in her tweet, i.e. "@B", which is called a reply link; user A may forward user B's tweet, which results in a retweet link. We study how the implicit links correlate with the formation of the follow-back relationship on Twitter. Figure 4 clearly shows that when users A and B retweet or reply each other's tweet, the likelihood of their following back each other is higher (3 times than chance). Another interesting phenomenon is that compared with replying someone's tweet, retweeting (forwarding) her tweet seems to be more helpful (15% vs. 9%) to win her follow-back.

Structural balance Now, we connect our work to a basic social psychological theory: structural balance theory [6]. Let us first explain the structural balance property. For every group of three users

[3]PageRank is an algorithm to estimate the importance of each node in a network.

[4](α, β) algorithm is designed to find core members (elite users) in a social network.

[5]Statistics have shown that less than 1% of the Twitter users produce 50% of its content [31].

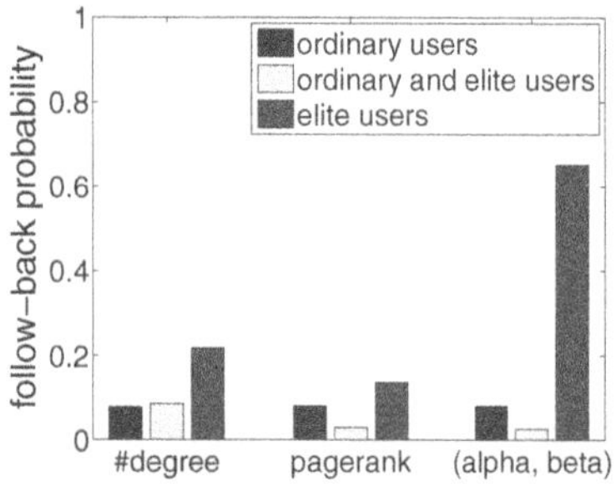

Figure 3: Status homophily by different algorithms. Y-axis: probability that two users follow back each other, conditioned on whether the two users are from the same group of elite/ordinary users or from different groups. #Degree, PageRank, and (α, β) are three algorithms to distinguish elite users from ordinary users.

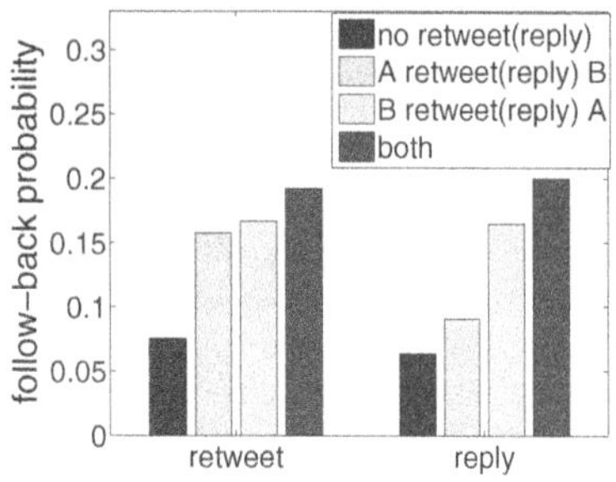

Figure 4: Implicit network correlation. Y-axis: probability that user B follows user A back, conditioned on one user (A or B) retweets or replies the other user's tweet.

(called triad), the balance property implies that either all three of these users are friends or only one pair of them are friends. Figure 5 shows such an example. To adapt the theory to our problem, we can map either the two-way relationship or the one-way relationship on the friendship. Then we examine how the Twitter network with (only two-way relationships or one-way relationships) satisfy the structural balance property. More precisely, we compare the probabilities of the resultant triads that satisfy the balance theory based on two-way relationships and one-way relationships on Twitter. Figure 6 clearly shows that it is much more likely (88%) for users to be connected with a balanced structure of two-way relationships. While with one-way relationships, the resultant structure is very unbalanced. This is because two users are very likely to follow a same movie star, but they do not know each other, which results in a unbalanced triad (Figure 5 (C)).

In summary, according to the statistics above, we have the following observations:

1. Geographic distance has a pronounced effect on the number of two-way relationships created between users, but little effect on the likelihood of users following back each other.
2. Users with common friends of two-way relationships have a tendency (link homophily) to follow each other.
3. Elite users have a much stronger tendency (status homophily) to follow each other than ordinary users.
4. The implicit networks of retweet or reply links have a strong correlation with the formation of two-way (reciprocal) relationships.

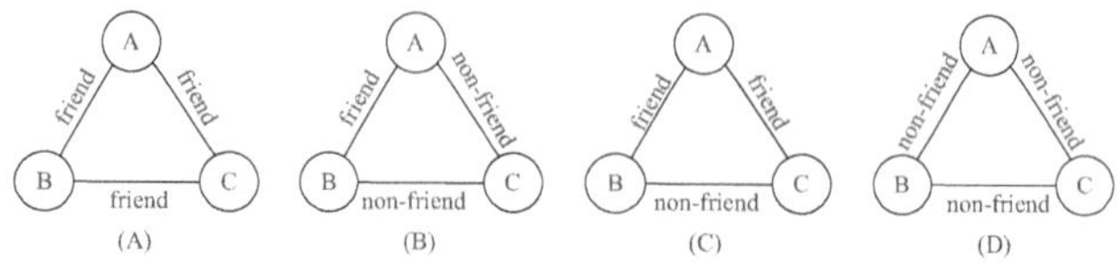

Figure 5: Illustration of structural balance theory. (A) and (B) are balanced, while (C) and (D) are not balanced.

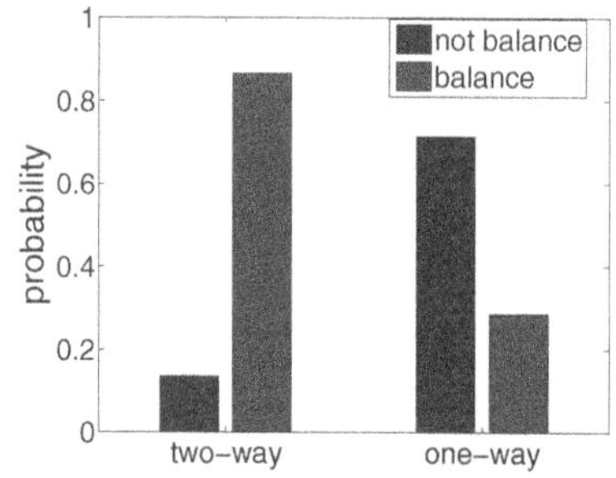

Figure 6: Structural balance correlation. Y-axis: probability that a triad creates two-way (reciprocal) relationships, conditioned on whether the resultant structure is balanced or not.

5. The network of two-way relationships on Twitter is balanced (88% of triads satisfying the structural balance property), while the network of one-way relationships is unbalanced (71% are unbalanced).

4. MODEL FRAMEWORK

In this section, we propose a novel Triad Factor Graph (TriFG) model to incorporate all the information within a single entity for better modeling and predicting the formation of two-way (follow-back) relationships.

For an edge $e_{ij} \in E$, if user v_j follows v_i at time t, our task is to predict whether user v_i will follow v_j back, i.e. $y_{ij} = 1$ or 0. For easy explanation, We introduce a slight change of notation. We write each edge as e_i with its two end users as v_i^s and v_i^u. For the follow-back prediction task, we assume that v_i^s follows v_i^u at time t, and our task is to predict whether v_i^u will follow v_i^s back at time $(t+1)$. Based on the observations in §3, we define a number of attributes for each edge, denoted as $\mathbf{x}_i$. The $|E| \times d$ attribute matrix $\mathbf{X}$ describes edge-specific characteristics, where d is the number of attributes. For example, on Twitter, an attribute can be defined as whether two end users are from the same time zone. An element x_{ij} in the matrix $\mathbf{X}$ indicates the jth attribute value of edge e_i.

4.1 The Proposed Model

We propose a Triad Factor Graph (TriFG) model. The name is derived from the idea that we incorporate social theories (structural balance and homophily) over triads into the factor graph model.

Figure 7 shows the graphical structure of the TriFG model. The left figure shows the following network of six users at time t. Blue arrows indicate new follow actions, black arrows indicate follow actions performed before time t, and blue $\nrightarrow$ indicates user v_i^u does not follow user v_i^s back at time t. The right figure is the factor graph model derived from the left input network. Each gray eclipse indicates an relationship (v_i^u, v_i^s) between users and each white circle indicates the hidden variable y_i, with $y_i = 1$ representing v_i^u performs a follow-back action, $y_i = 0$ not, and $y_i = ?$ unknown, which actually is the variable we need to predict. Factor $h(.)$ represents

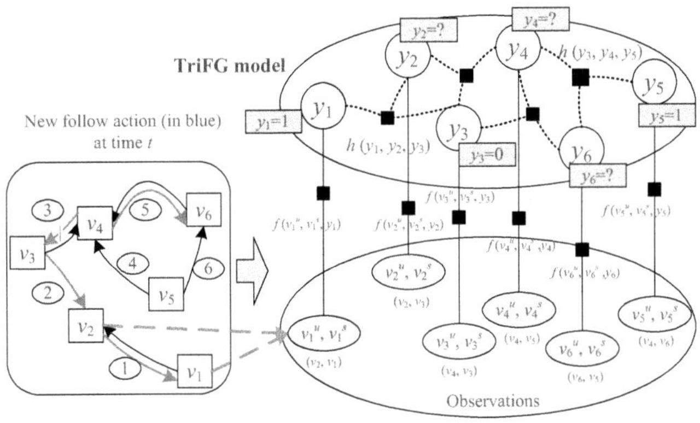

Figure 7: Graphical representation of the TriFG model. The left figure shows the follow network at time t. Blue arrows indicate new follow actions, black arrows indicate previously existing follow links, and blue $\nrightarrow$ indicates user v_i^u does not follow user v_i^s back. The right figure is the TriFG model derived from the following graph. Each gray eclipse indicates an relationship (v_i^u, v_i^s) between users and each white circle indicates the hidden variable y_i. $f(v_i^s, v_i^u, y_i)$ represents an attribute factor function and $h(.)$ represents a triad factor function.

a balance factor function defined on a triad; and $f(v_i^s, v_i^u, y_i)$ (or $f(\mathbf{x}_i, y_i)$) represents a factor to capture the information associated with edge e_i.

Given a network at time t, i.e., $G^t = (V^t, E^t, X^t)$ with some known variables $y = 1$ or 0 and some unknown variables $y =?$, our goal is to infer values of those unknown variables. For simplicity, we remove the superscript t for all variables if there is no ambiguity. We begin with the posterior probability of $P(Y|\mathbf{X}, G)$, according to the Bayes' theorem, we have

$$P(Y|\mathbf{X}, G) = \frac{P(\mathbf{X}, G|Y)P(Y)}{P(\mathbf{X}, G)} \propto P(\mathbf{X}|Y) \cdot P(Y|G) \quad (1)$$

where $P(Y|G)$ denotes the probability of labels given the structure of the network and $P(\mathbf{X}|Y)$ denotes the probability of generating the attributes $\mathbf{X}$ associated with each edge given their label Y. Assuming that the generative probability of attributes given the label of each edge is conditionally independent, we get

$$P(Y|\mathbf{X}, G) \propto P(Y|G) \prod_i P(\mathbf{x}_i|y_i) \quad (2)$$

where $P(\mathbf{x}_i|y_i)$ is the probability of generating attributes $\mathbf{x}_i$ given the label y_i. Now, the problem is how to instantiate the probabilities $P(Y|G)$ and $P(\mathbf{x}_i|y_i)$. In principle, they can be instantiated in different ways. In this work, we model them in a Markov random field, and thus by the Hammersley-Clifford theorem [7], the two probabilities can be instantiated as:

$$P(\mathbf{x}_i|y_i) = \frac{1}{Z_1} \exp\{\sum_{j=1}^{d} \alpha_j f_j(x_{ij}, y_i)\} \quad (3)$$

$$P(Y|G) = \frac{1}{Z_2} \exp\{\sum_c \sum_k \mu_k h_k(Y_c)\} \quad (4)$$

where Z_1 and Z_2 are normalization factors. Eq. 3 indicates that we define a feature function $f_j(x_{ij}, y_i)$ for each attribute x_{ij} associated with edge e_i and α_j is the weight of the jth attribute; while Eq. 4 represents that we define a set of correlation feature functions

Input: network G^t, learning rate η
Output: estimated parameters θ

Initialize $\theta \leftarrow 0$;
repeat
Perform LBP to calculate marginal distribution of unknown variables $P(y_i|x_i, G)$;
Perform LBP to calculate the marginal distribution of triad c, i.e., $P(y_c|\mathbf{X}_c, G)$;
Calculate the gradient of μ_k according to Eq. 7 (for α_j with a similar formula):

$$\frac{\mathcal{O}(\theta)}{\mu_k} = \mathbb{E}[h_k(Y_c)] - \mathbb{E}_{P_{\mu_k}(Y_c|\mathbf{X},G)}[h_k(Y_c)]$$

Update parameter θ with the learning rate η:

$$\theta_{\text{new}} = \theta_{\text{old}} + \eta \cdot \frac{\mathcal{O}(\theta)}{\theta}$$

until *Convergence*;

Algorithm 1: Learning algorithm for the TriFG model.

$\{h_k(Y_c)\}_k$ over each triad Y_c in the network. Here μ_k is the weight of the kth correlation feature function.

Based on Eqs. 2-4, we define the following log-likelihood objective function $\mathcal{O}(\theta) = \log P_\theta(Y|\mathbf{X}, G)$:

$$\mathcal{O}(\theta) = \sum_{i=1}^{|E|} \sum_{j=1}^{d} \alpha_j f_j(x_{ij}, y_i) + \sum_c \sum_k \mu_k h_k(Y_c) - \log Z \quad (5)$$

where Y_c is a triad derived from the input network, $Z = Z_1 Z_2$ is a normalization factor and $\theta = (\{\alpha\}, \{\mu\})$ indicates a parameter configuration. One example of factor decomposition is shown in Figure 7. There are six edges, three with known variables (two $y = 1$ and one $y = 0$) and three with unknown values ($y =?$). We have four triads (e.g., $Y_c = (y_1, y_2, y_3)$) based on the structure of the input network. For each edge, we define a set of factor functions $f(v_i^s, v_i^u, y_i)$ (also written as $f(\mathbf{x}_i, y_i)$).

We now briefly introduce possible ways to define the factor functions $f_j(x_{ij}, y_i)$ and $h_k(Y_c)$. $f_j(x_{ij}, y_i)$ is an attribute factor function. It can be defined as either a binary function or a real-valued function. For example, for the implicit network feature, we simply define it as a binary feature, that is if user v_i^s forwarded (retweeted) v_i^u's tweet before time t and user v_i^u follows user v_i^s back, then a feature $f_j(x_{ij} = 1, y_i = 1)$ is defined and its value is 1; otherwise 0. (Such a feature definition is often used in graphical models such as Conditional Random Fields [14]. For the triad factor function $h(Y_c)$, we define four features, two balanced and two unbalanced factor functions, as depicted in Figure 5. The triad function is defined as a binary function, that is, if a triad satisfies the structural balance property, then the value of a corresponding triad factor function is 1, otherwise 0. More details of the factor function definition are given in Appendix.

4.2 Model Learning and Prediction

We now address the problem of estimating the free parameters and inferring users' follow-back behaviors. Learning the TriFG model is to estimate a parameter configuration $\theta = (\{\alpha\}, \{\mu\})$ to maximize the log-likelihood objective function $\mathcal{O}(\theta) = \log P_\theta(Y|\mathbf{X}, G)$, i.e.,

$$\theta^\star = \arg\max \mathcal{O}(\theta) \quad (6)$$

To solve the objective function, we adopt a gradient decent method (or a Newton-Raphson method). We use μ as the example to explain how we learn the parameters. Specifically, we first write the gradient of each μ_k with regard to the objective function (Eq. 5):

$$\frac{\mathcal{O}(\theta)}{\mu_k} = \mathbb{E}[h_k(Y_c)] - \mathbb{E}_{P_{\mu_k}(Y_c|\mathbf{X},G)}[h_k(Y_c)] \quad (7)$$

where $\mathbb{E}[h_k(Y_c)]$ is the expectation of factor function $h_k(Y_c)$ given the data distribution (essentially it can be considered as the average value of the factor function $h_k(Y_c)$ over all triads in the training data); and $\mathbb{E}_{P_{\mu_k}(Y_c|\mathbf{X},G)}[h_k(Y_c)]$ is the expectation of factor function $h_k(Y_c)$ under the distribution $P_{\mu_k}(Y_c|\mathbf{X}, G)$ given by the estimated model. A similar gradient can be derived for parameter α_j.

One challenge here is that the graphical structure in the TriFG model can be arbitrary and may contain cycles, which makes it intractable to directly calculate the marginal distribution $P_{\mu_k}(Y_c|\mathbf{X}, G)$. A number of approximate algorithms can be considered, such as Loopy Belief Propagation (LBP) [20] and Mean-field [32]. We chose Loopy Belief Propagation due to its ease of implementation and effectiveness. Specifically, we approximate the marginal distribution $P_{\mu_k}(Y_c|\mathbf{X}, G)$ using LBP. With the marginal probabilities, the gradient can be obtained by summing over all triads. It is worth noting that we need to perform the LBP process twice in each iteration, one time for estimating the marginal distribution of unknown variables $y_i =?$ and the other time for marginal distribution over all triads. Finally with the gradient, we update each parameter with a learning rate η. The learning algorithm is summarized in Algorithm 1.

Predicting Follow-back With the estimated parameters θ, we can predict the label of unknown variables $\{y_i =?\}$ by finding a label configuration which maximizes the objective function, i.e., $Y^* = \text{argmax}\mathcal{O}(Y|\mathbf{X}, G, \theta)$. It is still intractable to obtain the exact solution. Again, we utilize the loopy belief propagation to approximate the solution, i.e., to calculate the marginal distribution of each relationship with unknown variable $P(y_i|\mathbf{x}_i, G)$ and finally assign each relationship with label of the maximal probability.

5. EXPERIMENTS

In this section, we first describe our experimental setup. We then present the performance results for different approaches in different settings. Next, we present several analyses and discussions. Finally, we use a case study further to demonstrate the advantage of the proposed model.

5.1 Experimental Setup

Prediction Setting We use the data set described in §3 in our experiments. To quantitatively evaluate the effectiveness of the proposed model and compare with other alternative methods, we carefully select a sub network from the data set, which has a completely historic log of link formation among all users, i.e., each user is associated with a complete list of followers and users they are following at each time stamp. The sub network is comprised of 112,044 users, 468,238 following links among them, and 2,409,768 tweets. Averagely there are 3,337 new follow-back links per day. We divide the sub network into 13 time stamps by viewing every four days as a time stamp.

Our general task is to predict whether a user will follow another user back at the next time stamp when she received a new following link from the other user. By a more careful study however, we

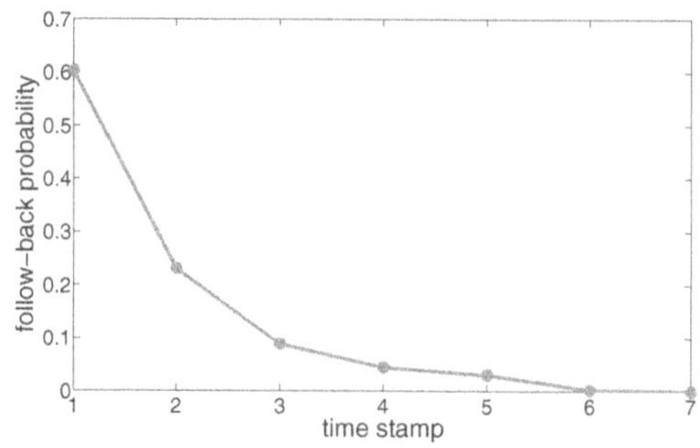

Figure 8: Follow-back probability for different time stamps.

found that it is very challenging if we restrict the prediction just for the next time stamp. Figure 8 shows the distribution of time span in which a user performs the follow-back action, which indicates that 60% of follow-backs are performed in the next time stamp though, 37% of the follow-backs would be still performed in the following three time stamps. A further data analysis, shows that active users often either perform an immediate follow-back (at the next time stamp) or reject to follow-back; while some other (inactive) users may not frequently login into Twitter, thus the time span of follow-backs varies a lot. According to this observation, in our first experiment, we use a network of the first 8 time stamps for training and predicate follow-back actions in the following 4 (9th-12th) time stamps (Test Case 1). Then we incrementally add the network of the 9th time stamp into the training data and again use the following 4 (10th-13th) time stamps for prediction (Test Case 2). We respectively report the prediction performance of different approaches for the two test cases.

Comparison Methods We compare the proposed TriFG model with the following methods:

SVM: it uses the same attributes associated with each edge as features to train a classification model and then employs the classification model to predict edges' label in the test data. For SVM, we employ SVM-light.

LRC: it uses the same attributes associated with each edge as features to train to train a logistic regression classification model [16] and then predict edges' label in the test data.

CRF-balance: it trains a Conditional Random Field [14] model with attributes associated with each edge. The difference of this method from our model is that it does not consider structural balance factors.

CRF: it trains a Conditional Random Field model all factors (including attributes and structural balance factors) and predicts edges' label in the test data.

TriFG: the proposed model, which trains a factor graph model with unlabeled data and all factors we defined in §4.

Weak TriFG (wTriFG): the difference of wTriFG from TriFG is that we do not consider status homophily and structural balance here. We use this method to evaluate how social theories can help this task.

In the five methods, SVM and CRF-balance only considers attribute factors; wTriFG further considers unlabeled data. CRF considers all factors we defined, but does not consider unlabeled data. Our proposed TriFG model considers all factors as well as the unlabeled data.

Evaluation Measures We evaluate the performance of different approaches in terms of Precision (Prec.), Recall (Rec.), F1-Measure (F1), and Accuracy (Accu.).

Table 1: **Follow-back prediction performance of different methods in the two test cases. Test Case 1: predicting follow-back actions in the 9th-12th time stamps; and Test Case 2 for the 10th-13th time stamps.**

Data	Algorithm	Prec.	Rec.	F1	Accu.
Test Case 1	SVM	0.6908	0.6129	0.6495	0.9590
	LRC	0.6957	0.2581	0.3765	0.9510
	CRF-balance	0.9968	0.5161	0.6801	0.9670
	CRF	**1.0000**	0.6290	0.7723	0.9770
	wTriFG	0.9691	0.5483	0.7004	0.9430
	TriFG	**1.0000**	**0.8548**	**0.9217**	**0.9910**
Test Case 2	SVM	0.7323	0.6212	0.6722	0.9534
	LRC	0.8333	0.3030	0.4444	0.9417
	CRF-balance	0.9444	0.5151	0.6667	0.9114
	CRF	**1.0000**	0.6333	0.7755	0.9717
	wTriFG	0.9697	0.5697	0.7177	0.9389
	TriFG	**1.0000**	**0.8788**	**0.9355**	**0.9907**

Table 2: Follow-back prediction performance of TriFG with three different algorithms (#degree, PageRank and (α, β)) for finding elite users from ordinary users.

Data	Algorithm	Prec.	Rec.	F1	Accu.
Test Case 1	(α, β)	**1.0000**	**0.8548**	**0.9217**	**0.9910**
	#degree	**1.0000**	0.7903	0.8829	0.9870
	pagerank	**1.0000**	0.7581	0.8624	0.9850
Test Case 2	(α, β)	**1.0000**	**0.8788**	**0.9355**	**0.9907**
	#degree	**1.0000**	0.8363	0.9109	0.9874
	pagerank	**1.0000**	0.8181	0.9000	0.9860

All algorithms are implemented in C++, and all experiments are performed on a PC running Windows 7 with Intel(R) Core(TM) 2 CPU 6600 (2.4GHz and 2.39GHz) and 4GB memory. All algorithms have a good efficiency performance: the CPU time needed for training and prediction by all methods on the Twitter network ranges from 2 to 5 minutes.

5.2 Prediction Performance

We now describe the performance results for the different methods we considered. Table 1 show the results in the two test cases (prediction performance for the 9th-12th time stamps and that for the 10th-13th time stamps).

It can be clearly seen that our proposed TriFG model significantly outperforms the four comparison methods. In terms of F1-Measure, TriFG achieves a +27% improvement compared with the (SVM). Comparing with the other three graph-based methods, TriFG also results in an improvement of 22-25%. The advantage of TriFG mainly comes from the improvement on recall. One important reason here is that TriFG can detect some difficult cases by leveraging the structural balance correlation and homophily correlation. For example, without considering the two kinds of social correlations, the performance of wTriFG decreases to 70-72% in terms of F1-Measure in the two test cases. Another advantage of TriFG is that it makes use of the unlabeled data. Essentially, it further considers some latent correlation in the data set, which cannot be leveraged with only the labeled training data.

5.3 Analysis and Discussions

Now, we perform several analyses to examine the following aspects of the TriFG model: (1) contribution of different factors in the TriFG model; (2) convergence property of the learning algorithm; (3) Effect of different settings for the time span; and (4) Effect of different algorithms for elite user finding.

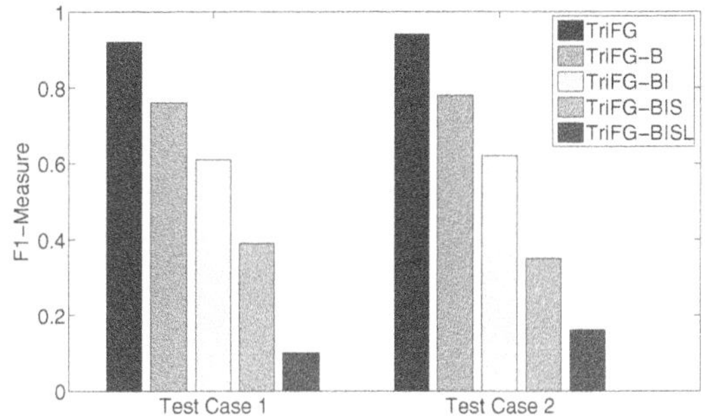

Figure 9: Factor contribution analysis. TriFG-B stands for ignoring structural balance correlation. TriFG-BI stands for ignoring both structural balance correlation and implicit network correlation. TriFG-BIS stands for further ignoring status homophily and TriFG-BISL stands for further ignoring link homophily.

Factor Contribution Analysis In TriFG, we consider five different factor functions: Geographic distance (G), Link homophily (L), Status homophily (S), Implicit network correlation (I), and structural Balance correlation (B). Here we examine the contribution of the different factors defined in our model. We first rank the individual factors by their predictive power[6], then remove them one by one in reversing order of their prediction power. In particular, we first remove structural balance correlation denoted as TriFG-B, followed by further removing the implicit network correlation denoted as TriFG-BI, status homophily denoted as TriFG-BIS, and finally removing link homophily denoted as TriFG-BISL. We train and evaluate the prediction performance of the different versions of TriFG. Figure shows the average F1-Measure score of the different versions of the TriFG model. We can observe clear drop on the performance when ignoring each of the factors. This indicates that our method works well by combining the different factor functions and each factor in our method contributes improvement in the performance.

Convergence Property We conduct an experiment to see the effect of the number of the loopy belief propagation iterations. Figure 10 illustrates the convergence analysis results of the learning algorithm. We see on both test cases, the BLP-based learning algorithm can converges in less than 10 iterations. After only seven learning iterations, the prediction performance of TriFG on both test cases becomes stable. This suggests that learning algorithm is very efficient and has a good convergence property.

Effect of Time Span Figure 8 already shows the distribution of follow-backs in different time stamps. Now, we quantitatively examine how different settings for the time span will affect the prediction performance. Figure 11 lists the average prediction performance of TriFG in the two test cases with different settings of the time span. It shows that when setting the time span as two or less time stamps, the prediction performance of TriFG drops sharply;

[6]We did this by respectively removing each particular factor from our model and evaluated the decrease of the prediction performance by the TriFG model. A larger decrease means a higher predictive power.

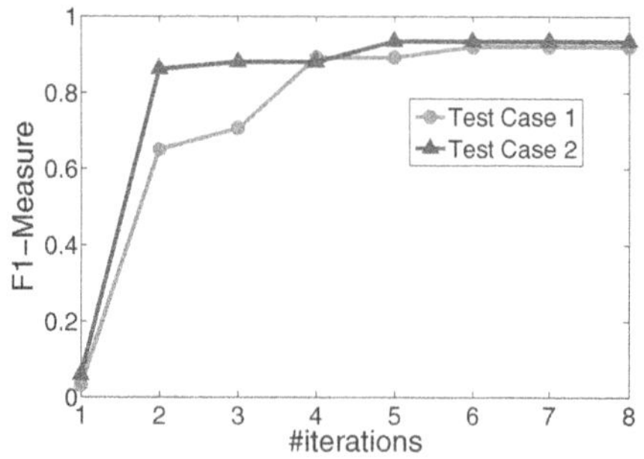

Figure 10: Convergence analysis of the learning algorithm.

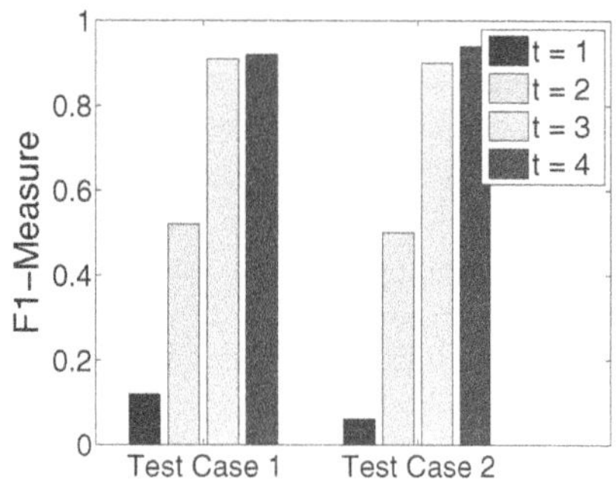

Figure 11: Follow-back prediction for different time stamps.

while when setting it as three time stamps, the performance is acceptable. The results are consistent with the statistics in Figure 8: more than 90% of follow-back actions are performed in the first three time stamps, and only about 80% of the follow-back actions are in the first two time stamps.

Effect of different algorithms for elite user finding The status homophily factor depends on results of elite user finding. We use three different algorithms, i.e., PageRank, #degree, and (α, β) algorithm, to find elite users. Now we examine how the different algorithms would affect the prediction performance. Table 2 shows the prediction performance of TriFG with different elite user finding algorithms in the two test cases. Interestingly, though TriFG with the (α, β) algorithm achieves the best performance, the difference of performance among the three algorithms, especially in the second test case is not that pronounced (with a difference of 1%-4% in terms of F1-measure score). This confirms the effectiveness and generalization of incorporating the status homophily factor into our TriFG model.

5.4 Qualitative Case Study

Now we present a case study to demonstrate the effectiveness of the proposed model. Figure 12 shows an example generated from our experiments. It represents a portion of the Twitter network from the 10th-13th time stamps. Black arrows indicate following links created 4 time stamps (we use 4 time stamps as the time span for prediction) before. Blue arrows indicate new following link in the past 4 time stamps. Dash arrows indicate follow-back links in our data set (a), predicted by SVM (b), and predicted by our model TriFG (c), with green color denoting a correct one and red color denoting a mistake one. Red colored $\nrightarrow$ indicates there should be a follow-back link, which the approach did not detect.

We look at specific examples to study why the proposed model can outperform the comparison methods. "A", "B", and "C" are three elite users identified using the (α, β) algorithm [8]. SVM correctly predicts that there is a follow-back link from "C" to "B", but misses predicting the follow-back link from "C" to "A". Our model TriFG correctly predicted both the follow-back links. This is because TriFG leverages the structural balance factor. The resulting structure among the three users by SVM is unbalanced. TriFG leverages the structural balance factor and tends to result in a balanced structure.

It is also worth looking at the situation of user 9 and 10. TriFG made a mistake here: it does not predict the follow-back link, while the link was correctly predicted by SVM. User 9 and user 10 have a similar social status (similar indegree) and also they are from the same time zone, thus SVM successfully predicted the follow-back link. However, as the resulting structure is unbalanced, TriFG made a compromise and finally resulted in a mistaken prediction.

6. RELATED WORKS

In this section, we review related work on link prediction and Twitter study in social networks.

Our work is related with link prediction, which is one of the core tasks in social networks. Existing work on link prediction can be broadly grouped into two categories based on the learning methods employed: unsupervised link prediction and supervised link prediction. Unsupervised link predictions usually assign scores to potential links based on the intuition - the more similar the pair of users are, the more likely they are linked. Various similarity measures of users are considered, such as the *preferential attachment* [21], and the Katz measure [12]. A survey of unsupervised link prediction can be found in [17]. Recently, [18] designs a flow based method for link prediction.

There are also a number of works which employ supervised approaches to predict links in social networks, such as [28, 18, 2, 16]. Backstrom et al. [2] propose a supervised random walk algorithm to estimate the strength of social links. Leskovec et al. [16] employ a logistic regression model to predict positive and negative links in online social networks. The main differences between existing work on link prediction and our work are about two aspects. First, existing work handles undirected social networks, while we address the directed nature of the Twitter network and predict a directed link between a pair of users given an existing link in the another direction. Secondly, most existing models for link prediction are static. In contrast, our model is dynamic and learned from the evolution of the Twitter network. Moreover, we combine social theories (such as homophily and structural balance theory) into a semi-supervised learning model.

Another type of related work is social behavior analysis. Tang et al. [26] study the difference of the social influence on different topics and propose Topical Affinity Propagation (TAP) to model the topic-level social influence in social networks and develop a parallel model learning algorithm based on the map-reduce programming model. Tan et al. [25] investigate how social actions evolve in a dynamic social network and propose a time-varying factor graph model for modeling and predicting users' social behaviors. The proposed methods in these work can be utilized in the problem defined in this work, but the problem is fundamentally different.

There is little doubt that Twitter has intrigued worldwide netizens, and the research communities alike. Existing Twitter study is mainly centered around the following three aspects: 1) *the Twitter network*. Java et al. [11] study the topological and geographical properties of the Twitter network. Their findings verify the *homophily* phenomenon that users with similar intentions connect with each other. Kwak et al. [13] conduct a similar study on the entire Twittersphere and they observe some notable properties of Twitter, such as a non-power-law follower distribution, a short ef-

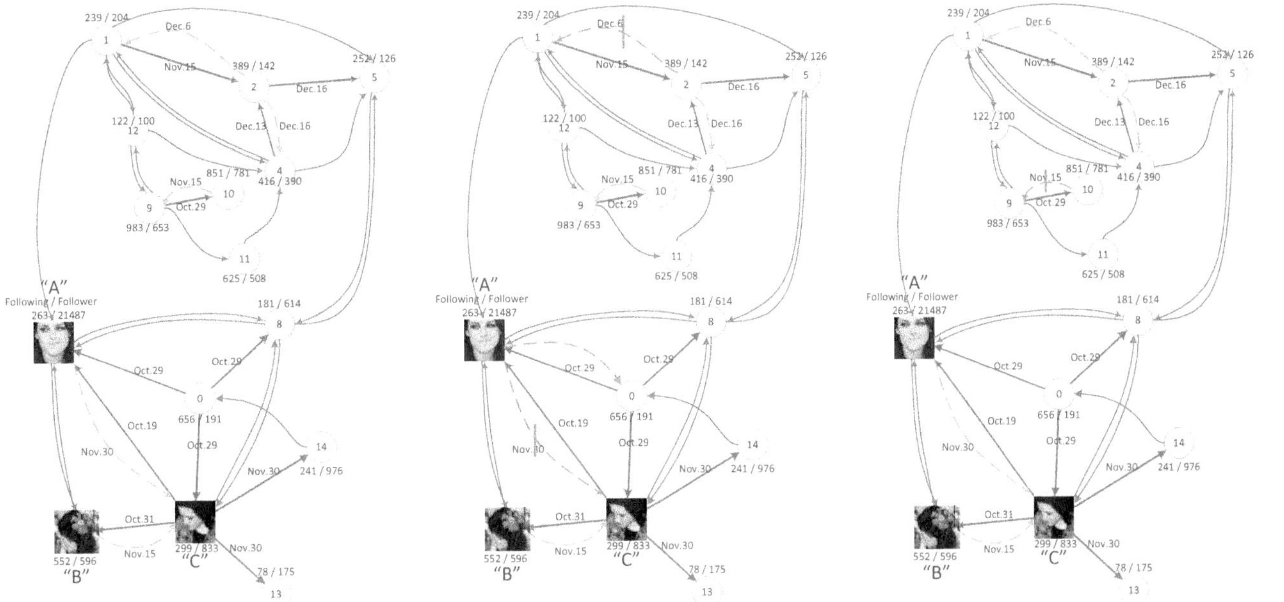

(a) Ground Truth (b) SVM (c) Our approach (TriFG)

Figure 12: Case study. Portion of the Twitter network during the 10th-13th time stamps. The two numbers associated with each user are respectively the number of followees and that of followers. Black arrows indicate following links created 4 time stamps (we use 4 time stamps as the time span for prediction) before. Blue arrows indicate new following link in the past 4 time stamps. Dash arrows indicate follow-back links in our data set (a), predicted by SVM (b), and predicted by our model TriFG (c), with green color denoting a correct one and red color denoting a mistake one. Red colored ↛ indicates there should be a follow-back link, which the approach did not predict.

fective diameter, and low reciprocity, marking a deviation from known characteristics of human social networks. 2) *the Twitter users*. Work of this category mainly focus on identifying influential users in Twitter [30, 3, 13] or examining and predicting tweeting behaviors of users [10, 25]. 3) *the Tweets*. Sakaki et al. [24] propose to utilize the real-time nature of Twitter to detect a target event; while Mathioudakis and Koudas [19] present a system, TwitterMonitor, to detect emerging topics from the Twitter content.

7. CONCLUSION

In this paper, we study the novel problem of two-way relationship prediction in social networks. We formally define the problem and propose a Triad Factor Graph (TriFG) model, which incorporates social theories into a semi-supervised learning model. We evaluate the proposed model on a large Twitter network. We show the proposed factor graph model can significantly improve the performance (+22%-+27% by F1-Measure) for two-way relationship prediction comparing with several alternative methods. Our study also reveals several interesting phenomena.

The general problem of reciprocal relationship prediction represents a new and interesting research direction in social network analysis. There are many potential future directions of this work. First, some other social theories can be further explored and validated for reciprocal relationship prediction. Looking farther ahead, it is also interesting to develop a real friend suggestion system based on the proposed method. We can validate the proposed method based on user feedbacks. We can also further study theoretical methodologies for improving the predictive performance by incorporating user interactions. Finally, building a theory of why and how users create relationships with each other in different kinds of networks is an intriguing direction for further research.

Acknowledgements John Hopcroft was partially supported by the U.S. Air Force Office of Scientific Research under Grant FA9550-09-1-0675. Jie Tang is supported by the Natural Science Foundation of China (No. 61073073) and Chinese National Key Foundation Research (No. 60933013, No.61035004). Tiancheng Lou is supported in part by the National Basic Research Program of China Grant 2007CB807900, 2007CB807901, the National Natural Science Foundation of China Grant 61033001, 61061130540, 61073174.

8. REFERENCES

[1] L. Backstrom, R. Kumar, C. Marlow, J. Novak, and A. Tomkins. Preferential behavior in online groups. In *WSDM'08*, pages 117–128, 2008.

[2] L. Backstrom and J. Leskovec. Supervised random walks: predicting and recommending links in social networks. In *WSDM'11*, pages 635–644, 2011.

[3] M. Cha, H. Haddadi, F. Benevenuto, and P. K. Gummadi. Measuring user influence in twitter: The million follower fallacy. In *ICWSM'10*, 2010.

[4] D. J. Crandall, L. Backstrom, D. Cosley, S. Suri, D. Huttenlocher, and J. Kleinberg. Inferring social ties from geographic coincidences. *PNAS*, 107:22436–22441, Dec. 2010.

[5] N. Eagle, A. S. Pentland, and D. Lazer. Inferring social network structure using mobile phone data. *PNAS*, 106(36), 2009.

[6] D. Easley and J. Kleinberg. *Networks, Crowds, and Markets: Reasoning about a Highly Connected World*. Cambridge University Press, 2010.

[7] J. M. Hammersley and P. Clifford. Markov field on finite graphs and lattices. *Unpublished manuscript*, 1971.

[8] J. He, J. E. Hopcroft, H. Liang, S. Suwajanakorn, and L. Wang. Detecting the structure of social networks using (α, β)-communities. In *WAW'11*, 2011.

[9] D. Horton and R. R. Wohl. Mass communication and para-social interaction: Observations on intimacy at a distance. *Psychiatry*, pages 215–229, 1956.

[10] B. Huberman, D. M. Romero, and F. Wu. Social networks that matter: Twitter under microscope. In *First Monday*, volume 14, pages 118–138, 2009.

[11] A. Java, X. Song, T. Finin, and B. L. Tseng. Why we twitter: An analysis of a microblogging community. In *WebKDD/SNA-KDD*, pages 118–138, 2007.

[12] L. Katz. A new status index derived from sociometric analysis. *Psychometrika*, 18(1):39–43, 1953.

[13] H. Kwak, C. Lee, H. Park, and S. B. Moon. What is twitter, a social network or a news media? In *WWW'10*, pages 591–600, 2010.

[14] J. D. Lafferty, A. McCallum, and F. C. N. Pereira. Conditional random fields: Probabilistic models for segmenting and labeling sequence data. In *ICML'01*, pages 282–289, 2001.

[15] P. F. Lazarsfeld and R. K. Merton. Friendship as a social process: A substantive and methodological analysis. *M. Berger, T. Abel, and C. H. Page, editors, Freedom and control in modern society, New York: Van Nostrand*, pages 8–66, 1954.

[16] J. Leskovec, D. Huttenlocher, and J. Kleinberg. Predicting positive and negative links in online social networks. In *WWW'10*, pages 641–650, 2010.

[17] D. Liben-Nowell and J. M. Kleinberg. The link-prediction problem for social networks. *JASIST*, 58(7):1019–1031, 2007.

[18] R. Lichtenwalter, J. T. Lussier, and N. V. Chawla. New perspectives and methods in link prediction. In *KDD'10*, pages 243–252, 2010.

[19] M. Mathioudakis and N. Koudas. Twittermonitor: trend detection over the twitter stream. In *SIGMOD'10*, pages 1155–1158, 2010.

[20] K. P. Murphy, Y. Weiss, and M. I. Jordan. Loopy belief propagation for approximate inference: An empirical study. In *UAI'99*, pages 467–475, 1999.

[21] M. E. J. Newman. Clustering and preferential attachment in growing networks. *Phys. Rev. E*, 64(2):025102, 2001.

[22] L. Page, S. Brin, R. Motwani, and T. Winograd. The pagerank citation ranking: Bringing order to the web. Technical Report SIDL-WP-1999-0120, Stanford University, 1999.

[23] D. M. Romero and J. M. Kleinberg. The directed closure process in hybrid social-information networks, with an analysis of link formation on twitter. In *ICWSM'10*, 2010.

[24] T. Sakaki, M. Okazaki, and Y. Matsuo. Earthquake shakes twitter users: real-time event detection by social sensors. In *WWW'10*, pages 851–860, 2010.

[25] C. Tan, J. Tang, J. Sun, Q. Lin, and F. Wang. Social action tracking via noise tolerant time-varying factor graphs. In *KDD'10*, pages 1049–1058, 2010.

[26] J. Tang, J. Sun, C. Wang, and Z. Yang. Social influence analysis in large-scale networks. In *KDD'09*, pages 807–816, 2009.

[27] C. Wang, J. Han, Y. Jia, J. Tang, D. Zhang, Y. Yu, and J. Guo. Mining advisor-advisee relationships from research publication networks. In *KDD'10*, pages 203–212, 2010.

[28] C. Wang, V. Satuluri, and S. Parthasarathy. Local probabilistic models for link prediction. In *ICDM'07*, pages 322–331, 2007.

[29] M. Weber. *The Nature of Social Action in Runciman, W.G. 'Weber: Selections in Translation'*. Cambridge University Press, 1991.

[30] J. Weng, E.-P. Lim, J. Jiang, and Q. He. Twitterrank: finding topic-sensitive influential twitterers. In *WSDM'10*, pages 261–270, 2010.

[31] S. Wu, J. M. Hofman, W. A. Mason, and D. J. Watts. Who says what to whom on twitter. In *WWW'11*, pages 705–714, 2011.

[32] E. P. Xing, M. I. Jordan, and S. Russell. A generalized mean field algorithm for variational inference in exponential families. In *UAI'03*, pages 583–591, 2003.

[33] Z. Yang, J. Guo, K. Cai, J. Tang, J. Li, L. Zhang, and Z. Su. Understanding retweeting behaviors in social networks. In *CIKM'10*, pages 1633–1636, 2010.

Appendix: Factor function definition

This section depicts how we define the factor functions in our experiments. In total, we define 25 features of five categories: Geographic distance, Link homophily, Status homophily, Structural balance, and Implicit network correlation.

Geographic distance We use Google Map API to get the exact locations (longitude and latitude) of some users. Based on the two values, we define the following three features : the absolute distance and the time zone difference between two users, and whether or not the two users are from the same country.

Link homophily First, we treat each link as undirected link, and define the following four features : the number of common neighbors, percentage of common neighbors of the two users(respectively) and the average percentage.

Then we consider directed links and define another three features : the number of common two-way links, number of common followers and number of common followees.

Status homophily We also test whether two users have similar social status, and define the following three features : whether or not the two users are both elite users, an ordinary and an elite, and both ordinary users.

Implicit network correlation We consider the interaction between user A and user B, and define the following four features respectively represent the number of retweets(replies) from A to B and from B to A.

Structural balance Based on the structural balance theory, as in Figure 5, we define eight features capturing all situations of structural balance theory for each triad.

Link Prediction: the Power of Maximal Entropy Random Walk

Rong-Hua Li
Chinese Univ. of Hong Kong
rhli@se.cuhk.edu.hk

Jeffrey Xu Yu
Chinese Univ. of Hong Kong
yu@se.cuhk.edu.hk

Jianquan Liu
University of Tsukuba
ljq@dblab.is.tsukuba.ac.jp

ABSTRACT

Link prediction is a fundamental problem in social network analysis. The key technique in unsupervised link prediction is to find an appropriate similarity measure between nodes of a network. A class of wildly used similarity measures are based on random walk on graph. The traditional random walk (TRW) considers the link structures by treating all nodes in a network equivalently, and ignores the centrality of nodes of a network. However, in many real networks, nodes of a network not only prefer to link to the similar node, but also prefer to link to the central nodes of the network. To address this issue, we use maximal entropy random walk (MERW) for link prediction, which incorporates the centrality of nodes of the network. First, we study certain important properties of MERW on graph G by constructing an eigen-weighted graph $\mathcal{G}$. We show that the transition matrix and stationary distribution of MERW on G are identical to the ones of TRW on $\mathcal{G}$. Based on $\mathcal{G}$, we further give the maximal entropy graph Laplacians, and show how to fast compute the hitting time and commute time of MERW. Second, we propose four new graph kernels and two similarity measures based on MERW for link prediction. Finally, to exhibit the power of MERW in link prediction, we compare 27 various link prediction methods over 3 synthetic and 8 real networks. The results show that our newly proposed MERW based methods outperform the state-of-the-art method on most datasets.

Categories and Subject Descriptors

H.2.8 [**Database management**]: Database applications—*Data mining*; G.2.2 [**Discrete mathematics**]: Graph theory—*Graph algorithms*

General Terms

Algorithm, Theory, Experimentation

Keywords

Maximal entropy random walk, graph kernels, similarity measures, link prediction

CIKM'11, October 24–28, 2011, Glasgow, Scotland, UK.

1. INTRODUCTION

Link prediction has been recognized as a fundamental problem in social network analysis that aims to infer which unobserved links will appear in the near future by a given snapshot of a network [24]. Many problems in social computing and data mining can be modeled as a link prediction problem, such as the friends suggestion problem [32] in social network and the product recommendation problem [22] in online shopping system.

Due to the broad applications, the link prediction problem has been attracted much attention in research communities [24, 11, 25]. The key challenges of the link prediction problem are owing to the sparsity and huge size of the networks. Recently, a large number of approaches have been proposed to address this issue. The methods can be classified into two categories: supervised methods and unsupervised methods. The supervised method for link prediction is identified as the state-of-the-art method, which predict the unobserved links by a binary classifier. However, the supervised methods, such as the method proposed in [25], typically suffer from the so-called class imbalance and feature selection problem [2]. Moreover, most classifiers are based on the class distribution of the training data, thus they could perform poorly in some datasets that do not meet the prior assumptions. Instead, the unsupervised methods work in an agnostic way, thus they can naturally avoid this problem. In addition, unsupervised methods do not need to decide which node features and edge features to use for link prediction, thus they also avoid the feature selection problem. In this paper, we focus on unsupervised methods for link prediction.

The key point of the unsupervised methods for link prediction is to find an appropriate similarity measure between nodes of a graph. The widely applied methods to measure similarities between nodes of a graph are based on random walk on graph. We call this random walk the traditional random walk (TRW) in this paper. In TRW, the transition probabilities from a start node to any of its neighbors are equivalent, i.e., the reciprocal of the out-degree of the start node. TRW considers the link structures by treating all nodes of a graph as equivalent entities. In other words, TRW ignores the centrality of nodes of a graph. However, in the context of link prediction, we argue that the centrality of the nodes play an important role. The reason is because the nodes in a network not only prefer to link to the similar nodes, but also prefer to link to the central nodes of the network. Consequently, it is highly desirable to take the centrality of nodes into consideration in the random walk for link prediction task.

To address the issue of node centrality, we resort to maximal entropy random walk (MERW), which incorporates the centrality of nodes of a graph. This is because the transition probabilities of MERW are proportional to the eigenvector centrality of the nodes [5], which is wildly applied to measure the importance of the nodes over a graph. Unlike other centrality measures based on degree, betweenness, and closeness [30], the eigenvector centrality measure is based on the idea that the important of a node in a graph is larger if it has many important neighbors. In other words, the eigenvector centrality measure captures the structural context of a node. In addition to capture the centrality of the nodes, MERW has two nice properties. First, the same length paths between two given nodes have the same probabilities. Second, the longer path between two given nodes has lower probability, which consists with the intuition for measuring the similarity between nodes. As a result, we believe MERW can probably perform much better than TRW in link prediction.

MERW has been studied recently. Burda et al. study the MERW design [6]. Sinatra et al. present the evidence of constructing approximate MERW to make it more practical [34]. Devenne and Libert propose centrality measures for complex networks based on MERW, but they do not systematically analyze the properties of MERW [9]. To the best of our knowledge, we are the first group to investigate a series of important properties of MERW in depth, and systematically design a set of similarity measures based on MERW for link prediction task. Our extensive experiments exhibit the power of MERW in link prediction.

The main contributions of this paper are summarized as follows.

- We propose a set of unsupervised MERW based methods for link prediction. In particular, we propose four new graph kernels and two new similarity measures based on MERW on graph. The new graph kernels and similarity measures capture the centrality of nodes, which is important in link prediction as the nodes in real networks prefer to link to the central nodes.
- We establish a foundation to study MERW over an unweighted and undirected graph by constructing an eigen-weighted graph, whose edges are weighted by the dominant eigenvalue and eigenvector of the adjacency matrix of the graph. Based on the construction of eigen-weighted graph, we study certain important properties of MERW. We define three new graph Laplacians based on MERW, and derive new formula to compute hitting time and commute time of MERW by utilizing pseudo-inverse of the combinatorial graph Laplacian based on MERW. We show that the hitting and commute time of MERW can be deemed as two new dissimilarity measures between nodes of a graph.
- Extensive experiments confirm the power of MERW in link prediction. Specifically, we compare 27 diverse link prediction methods over 11 real and synthetic datasets. Our newly proposed MERW based approach (NMEDK) outperforms the state-of-the-art link prediction algorithm on most datasets.

The rest of the paper is organized as follows. We introduce maximal entropy random walk (MERW) in comparison with traditional random walk (TRW) in Section 2. We give a new construction of eigen-weighted graph as basis to study the important properties of MERW in Section 3. And then we propose new graph kernels and similarity measures based on MERW for link prediction in Section 4. We show the extensive performance results on link prediction in Section 5, and discuss related work in Section 6. Finally, We conclude this work in Section 7.

2. MAXIMAL ENTROPY RANDOM WALK

In this section, we introduce traditional random walk followed by discussions on maximal entropy random walk on graphs. As mentioned in [9], maximal entropy random walk cannot be applied to weighted graphs. We concentrate ourselves on unweighted and undirected graphs in this paper.

Consider an unweighted and undirected graph $G(V, E)$, with a set of nodes V and a set of edges E, where the size of nodes is $n = |V|$. Below, we use V_i to denote a node in a graph and v to denote a vector representation. The graph G can be represented as a symmetric adjacency matrix, $\mathbf{A}$, where $A_{ij} = 1$ if nodes $(V_i, V_j) \in E$ otherwise $A_{ij} = 0$.

The degree of a node $V_i \in G$ is denoted as $d_i = \sum_{j=1}^{n} A_{ij}$. Let $\mathbf{D} = diag(d_1, d_2, \cdots, d_n)$ be a diagonal matrix of node degrees, a random walk on G can be defined using a transition matrix $\mathbf{P} = \mathbf{D}^{-1}\mathbf{A}$, with entries $p_{ij} = \frac{A_{ij}}{d_i}$. We call it traditional random walk (TRW) in order to distinguish from the maximal entropy random walk discussed below. It is well known that TRW on an undirected graph forms a reversible Markov chain and reaches a unique stationary distribution π [26]. The stationary distribution π satisfies the so-called detailed balance equation $\pi_i p_{ij} = \pi_j p_{ji}$, where $\pi_i = \frac{d_i}{\sum_{k=1}^{n} d_k}$, for $1 \leq i \leq n$.

Maximal entropy random walk: We review the maximal entropy random walk (MERW) on graphs [6, 31, 33]. First, we introduce the entropy rate of random walk on graph which is well known in information theory [8]. Consider a path τ_{ij}^t generated by the random walk with length t from V_i to V_j. Suppose the path τ_{ij}^t passes through the nodes $V_i, V_{i_1}, \cdots, V_{i_{t-1}}, V_j$, then the probability $p(\tau_{ij}^t)$ of the path τ_{ij}^t is defined as $p(\tau_{ij}^t) = p_{ii_1}p_{i_1i_2}\cdots p_{i_{t-2}i_{t-1}}p_{i_{t-1}j}$ The Shannon entropy [8] of all paths with length t generated by the walker is $E_t = -\sum_{\forall \tau_{ij}^t} p(\tau_{ij}^t) \ln p(\tau_{ij}^t)$ and the entropy rate of random walk is defined as $\eta = \lim_{t\to\infty} E_t/t$.

A well known result in information theory [8] indicates that the maximal entropy rate of random walk on a graph can be computed from the transition matrix $\mathbf{P}$ and the stationary distribution π as follows.

$$\eta = -\sum_i \pi_i \sum_j p_{ij} \ln p_{ij} \tag{1}$$

On the other hand, the maximal entropy rate of random walk on a graph is bounded by $\ln \lambda$ [31] (In [9, 33], this quantity is called *topological entropy* of a graph.), where λ is the largest eigenvalue (or called dominant eigenvalue) of the adjacency matrix $\mathbf{A}$. As shown in [6], this quantity can be obtained by the following asymptotic value.

$$\eta_{\max} = \lim_{t\to\infty} \frac{\ln \sum_{i,j} (A^t)_{ij}}{t} = \ln \lambda \tag{2}$$

Unlike TRW, MERW aims to maximize the entropy rate of a walk by carefully constructing a probabilistic transition matrix as follows. Let $v = (v_1, v_2, \cdots, v_n)$ be the normalized eigenvector ($\sum_{i=1}^{n} v_i^2 = 1$) with respect to the largest eigenvalue λ of the adjacency matrix $\mathbf{A}$. Obviously, v_i is positive as guaranteed by Forbenius-Perron theorem [20]. Then, the transition probability of MERW becomes

$$p_{ij} = \frac{A_{ij}v_j}{\lambda v_i} \tag{3}$$

We can reformulate it into a matrix form as follows.

$$\mathbf{P_v} = \frac{\mathbf{D_v}^{-1}\mathbf{A}\mathbf{D_v}}{\lambda} \tag{4}$$

where $\mathbf{D_v} = diag(v_1, v_2, \cdots, v_n)$ denotes the diagonal matrix with respect to v. The stationary distribution of MERW becomes $\pi^* = (v_1^2, v_2^2, \cdots, v_n^2)$ [6]. Together with π^* and p_{ij}, it can be easily confirmed that MERW maximizes the entropy rate. In addition, all paths τ_{ij}^t with length t between nodes V_i and V_j have the same probability $p(\tau_{ij}^t) = \frac{v_j}{\lambda^t v_i}$, which is independent of the intermediate nodes in the path. Obviously, the longer path has the smaller probability.

3. IMPORTANT PROPERTIES OF MERW

In this section, we identify certain useful properties of MERW which are crucial to construct MERW based similarity measures on graph. First, we propose an eigen-weighted graph as a basic tool for studying important properties of MERW. Then, we define three new graph Laplacians based on MERW, and show that the hitting time and commute time of MERW can be efficiently computed by the new graph Laplacian.

3.1 Eigen(vector)-weighted graph

TRW has been well studied, but MERW is not yet. In order to investigate the properties of MERW, we propose a new method to construct a family of eigenvector-weighted graphs $\mathbb{G}$ from the original unweighted and undirected graph G. With this construction, we show that the transition matrix and stationary distribution of MERW on G are identical to those of TRW on $\mathbb{G}$, respectively. We further define a special eigenvector-weighted graph, called an eigen-weighted graph $\mathcal{G}$. Based on the special graph, we simplify our investigation of MERW on G by analyzing and deriving from TRW on $\mathcal{G}$.

Definition 3.1: **(Eigenvector-weighted graph)** Given an unweighted and undirected graph $G(V, E)$, its adjacency matrix $\mathbf{A}$, the largest eigenvalue λ of $\mathbf{A}$, and the normalized eigenvector $v = (v_1, v_2, \cdots, v_n)$ w.r.t. λ, an eigenvector-weighted graph is $\mathbb{G}(V, E, \mathbb{W})$, where $\mathbb{W}$ is an *eigenvector-weighting* set, and is constructed by $\mathbb{W}_{ij} = \gamma v_i v_j$, if edge $(V_i, V_j) \in E$, where γ is a real parameter. □

We give two theorems regarding relationships between MERW on G and TRW on $\mathbb{G}$.

Theorem 3.1: *The transition matrix of MERW on graph G is identical to the transition matrix of TRW on the eigenvector-weighted graph $\mathbb{G}$.* □

Proof Sketch: Consider TRW on eigenvector-weighted graph $\mathbb{G}$. Deriving from the transition probability on an edge (V_i, V_j), we have

$$p_{ij} = \frac{A_{ij}\gamma v_i v_j}{\sum_j A_{ij}\gamma v_i v_j} = \frac{A_{ij}v_j}{\sum_j A_{ij}v_j} = \frac{A_{ij}v_j}{\lambda v_i},$$

that is identical to Eq. (3). Hence, the transition matrix of MERW on G is the same as that of TRW on $\mathbb{G}$. □

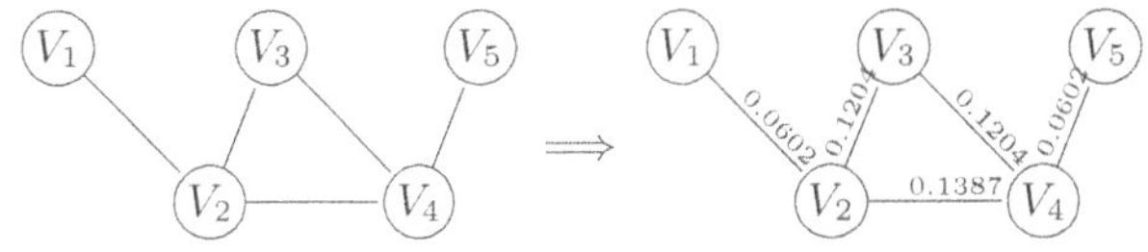

Figure 1: An Example: G (left) and $\mathcal{G}$ (right)

Theorem 3.2: *The stationary distribution of MERW on graph G is identical to the stationary distribution of TRW on the eigenvetor-weighted graph $\mathbb{G}$.* □

Proof Sketch: Consider TRW on a n-node eigenvetor-weighted graph $\mathbb{G}$. Let the stationary distribution of TRW be $\pi = (\pi_1, \pi_2, \cdots, \pi_n)$, we have

$$\pi_i = \frac{\sum_j W_{ij}}{\sum_{i,j} W_{ij}} = \frac{\sum_j A_{ij}\gamma v_i v_j}{\sum_{i,j} A_{ij}\gamma v_i v_j} = \frac{v_i^2}{\sum_i v_i^2} = v_i^2$$

where $i = 1, 2, \cdots, n$. That is identical to the stationary distribution of MERW on graph G. □

In order to define maximal entropy graph Laplacians and to deduce important properties of MERW, we define an eigen-weighted graph which uses the dominant eigenvalue and eigenvector as the weighting set, by letting $\gamma = 1/\lambda$.

Definition 3.2: **(Eigen-weighted graph)** Given an unweighted and undirected graph $G(V, E)$, its adjacency matrix $\mathbf{A}$, the largest eigenvalue λ of $\mathbf{A}$, and the normalized eigenvector $v = (v_1, v_2, \cdots, v_n)$ w.r.t. λ, an eigen-weighted graph is defined as $\mathcal{G}(V, E, W)$, where W is an *eigen-weighting* set, and is constructed by $W_{ij} = \frac{v_i v_j}{\lambda}$, if edge $(V_i, V_j) \in E$. □

It is worth noting that for any connected, non-bipartite, undirected and unweighted graph G, there exists only one eigen-weighted graph $\mathcal{G}$ corresponding to G, based on the uniqueness properties of the dominant eigenvalue and eigenvector of the adjacency matrix of G. On the other hand, TRW on a general weighted graph typically cannot be converted to MERW on the corresponding unweighted graph. This is because it is almost impossible to decompose the weight of a given edge of the weighted graph into the product form of two corresponding elements of the dominant eigenvector. Note that both Theorem 3.1 and Theorem 3.2 hold for eigen-weighted graphs, because the eigen-weighted graph is a special eigenvector-weighted graph.

Fig. 1 shows an example. For the given original graph G (left), the largest value (λ) of $\mathbf{A}$ and the normalized eigenvector v w.r.t. λ can be obtained using the power iteration algorithm. Here, $\lambda = 2.3028$, and $v = (0.2454, 0.5651, 0.4908, 0.5651, 0.2454)$. The resulting eigen-weighted graph $\mathcal{G}$ is shown on the right.

3.2 Graph Laplacians

Graph Laplacian in spectral graph theory [7] is widely used to analyze important parameters of random walk on graph. Here we first study the graph Laplacians on the eigen-weighted graph, and then we propose three new graph Laplacians on the original un-weighted and undirected graph based on MERW.

Laplacian of eigen(vector)-weighted graph: We introduce two graph Laplacians. The first graph Laplacian, which we call general graph Laplacian, is characterized by the transition matrix and stationary distribution of the walk [7, 4]. Let π be the stationary distribution of the walk, $\mathbf{P}$ be the transition matrix, and $\mathbf{\Pi} = \mathbf{diag}(\pi)$, the general graph Laplacian $\mathbb{L}$ can be defined as

$$\mathbb{L} = \mathbf{\Pi}(\mathbf{I} - \mathbf{P}) \tag{5}$$

where $\mathbf{I}$ is an identity matrix. In eigenvector-weighted graph, we have

$$\mathbb{L} = \mathbf{D_v}^2 - \frac{\mathbf{D_v A D_v}}{\lambda} \tag{6}$$

where $\mathbf{D_v} = diag(v_1, v_2, \cdots, v_n)$ and $\mathbf{A}$ is the adjacency matrix of G. Together with Theorem 3.1 and Theorem 3.2, we can conclude that the Laplacian matrix $\mathbb{L}$ defined on the eigenvector-weighted graph $\mathbb{G}$ is identical to the general graph Laplacian defined on the original G based on MERW. The second is the combinatorial graph Laplacian [7]. For any weighted graph, the combinatorial graph Laplacian $\mathcal{L}$ is defined by

$$\mathcal{L} = \mathbf{D} - \mathbf{W}$$

where $\mathbf{W}$ is the adjacency matrix of the weighted graph and $\mathbf{D}$ is a diagonal matrix of row sums of $\mathbf{W}$.

It is easy to verify that, for eigen-weighted graphs, the combinatorial graph Laplacian $\mathcal{L}$ is identical to the general graph Laplacian $\mathbb{L}$. In effect, the eigen-weighted graph is only the case that satisfies $\mathcal{L} = \mathbb{L}$.

Maximal entropy graph Laplacians: Based on the general graph Laplacian (Eq. (6)) and the combinatorial graph Laplacian on the eigen-weighted graph, we introduce three new graph Laplacians based on MERW.

Given an unweighted and undirected graph G, its adjacency matrix $\mathbf{A}$, the largest eigenvalue λ, and the normalized eigenvector $v = (v_1, v_2, \cdots, v_n)$ w.r.t λ. Let $\mathbf{D_v} = diag(v_1, v_2, \cdots, v_n)$. The maximal entropy combinatorial Laplacian (MECL) of G is defined as follows.

$$\mathbf{L} = \mathbf{D_v}^2 - \frac{\mathbf{D_v A D_v}}{\lambda} \tag{7}$$

$\mathbf{L}$ is equal to the combinatorial graph Laplacian defined on the eigen-weighted graph, thus we refer $\mathbf{L}$ to maximal entropy combinatorial Laplacian (MECL). Similar to the normalized Laplacians based on TRW, we can define the normalized maximal entropy Laplacians based on MERW, namely, the symmetric normalized maximal entropy Laplacian $\mathbf{L}_{sym}$, and the asymmetric normalized maximal entropy Laplacian $\mathbf{L}_{rw}$ as follows.

$$\begin{aligned} \mathbf{L}_{sym} &= \mathbf{D_v}^{-1}\mathbf{L}\mathbf{D_v}^{-1} = \mathbf{I} - \mathbf{A}/\lambda & (8)\\ \mathbf{L}_{rw} &= \mathbf{D_v}^{-2}\mathbf{L} = \mathbf{I} - \mathbf{D_v}^{-1}\mathbf{A}\mathbf{D_v}/\lambda & (9) \end{aligned}$$

3.3 Hitting time and commute time of MERW

Hitting time and commute time are two important parameters of TRW. The hitting time $h(i,j)$ defines the average number of steps that start from node V_i and first arrive at node V_j in TRW [26]. It can be computed in an iterative fashion as follows [10, 26].

$$h(i,j) = \begin{cases} 1 + \sum_{k=1}^{n} p_{ik} h(k,j), & if\ i \neq j \\ 0, & otherwise \end{cases} \tag{10}$$

The commute time $c(i,j)$ is defined as the average number of steps that the walker starts at node V_i, reaching node $V_j (i \neq j)$ for the first time, and then goes back to node V_i such that $c(i,j) = h(i,j) + h(j,i)$. As shown in [10, 16], the commute time of TRW on an undirected graph can be used as a distance measure.

It is well known that the hitting time and commute time of TRW can be computed by the pseudo-inverse of the graph Laplacian. We show that the hitting and commute time of MERW can also be computed by the pseudo-inverse of the MECL. Assume the Moore-Penrose pseudo-inverse [10] of MECL is denoted by $\mathbf{L}^+$, with entries L^+_{ij}. We have Theorem 3.3.

Theorem 3.3:

$$\begin{aligned} h(i,j) &= \sum_{k=1}^{n} (L^+_{ik} - L^+_{ij} - L^+_{jk} + L^+_{jj}) v_k^2 & (11)\\ c(i,j) &= L^+_{ii} + L^+_{jj} - 2L^+_{ij} & (12) \end{aligned}$$

□

We give the proof in Appendix A. It is not hard to verify that the hitting and commute time of MERW on an unweighted and undirected graph is equal to that of TRW on the corresponding eigen-weighted graph. Based on the construction of eigen-weighted graph, the commute time of MERW on graph G is also a distance measure.

4. NEW KERNELS AND SIMILARITY MEASURES

The key technique in unsupervised link prediction is to define a similarity measure between nodes of a graph. In this section, we give a class of new graph kernels and similarity measures based on MERW for link prediction.

4.1 Maximal entropy graph kernels

In TRW on graph, the pseudo-inverse of the Laplacian matrix is called commute time kernel [10]. We showed that the commute time of MERW can be computed by the pseudo-inverse of the MECL. Likewise, we can define a new maximal entropy commute time kernel based on MERW. The maximal entropy commute time kernel (CK) and its normalized kernel (CK_N) are given below.

$$\begin{aligned} CK &= \mathbf{L}^+ & (13)\\ CK_N &= \mathbf{L}^+_{sym} & (14) \end{aligned}$$

Since the pseudo-inverse of $\mathbf{L}$ (Eq. (7)) and $\mathbf{L}_{sym}$ (Eq. (8)) are positive semidefinite, CK and CK_N are valid kernels.

As shown in [17], the heat diffusion kernel is closely related to TRW on graph. The heat diffusion kernel is constructed based on heat equation and can be defined as matrix exponentiation. Motivated by this, we define new maximal entropy heat diffusion kernels. The maximal entropy heat diffusion kernel DK and the normalized maximal entropy heat diffusion kernel DK_N are given below.

$$\begin{aligned} DK &= \exp(-\alpha\mathbf{L}) & (15)\\ DK_N &= \exp(-\alpha\mathbf{L}_{sym}) & (16) \end{aligned}$$

where α is a positive real parameter.

The regularized Laplacian kernel of TRW on graph was first presented in [35] based on the regularization operators. By regularization on MECL, we define new maximal entropy regularized Laplacian kernels of MERW on graph. The maximal entropy regularized Laplacian kernel RK and the normalized counterpart RK_N are given below.

$$RK = (\mathbf{I} + \alpha\mathbf{L})^{-1} \quad (17)$$
$$RK_N = (\mathbf{I} + \alpha\mathbf{L}_{sym})^{-1} \quad (18)$$

where α is a positive real parameter, and $\mathbf{I}$ is an identity matrix.

With the help of the eigen-weighted graph, we can also define new maximal entropy Neumann kernels on the eigen-weighted graph $\mathcal{G}$. Firstly, we give a theorem.

Theorem 4.1: *Given a graph G, and its adjacency matrix $\mathbf{A}$, let $\mathbf{D_v}$ be a diagonal matrix defined in Eq. (7), then the matrix $\mathbf{I} - \alpha\mathbf{D_v}\mathbf{A}\mathbf{D_v}/\lambda$ is a positive definite matrix, for $\alpha \in (0,1)$.* □

Proof Sketch: Obviously, the matrix $\mathbf{I} - \alpha\mathbf{D_v}\mathbf{A}\mathbf{D_v}/\lambda$ is symmetric. Let ρ be the spectral radius of matrix $\mathbf{D_v}\mathbf{A}\mathbf{D_v}/\lambda$, then we have

$$\rho \leq ||\frac{\mathbf{D_v}\mathbf{A}\mathbf{D_v}}{\lambda}||_\infty = \max_i\{\sum_j A_{ij}v_i v_j/\lambda\} = \max_i\{v_i^2\} \leq 1$$

First, because v is a normalized vector, the last inequality holds. Second, because $\alpha \in (0,1)$, all eigenvalues of matrix $\mathbf{I} - \alpha\mathbf{D_v}\mathbf{A}\mathbf{D_v}/\lambda$ is positive. This completes the proof. □

Based on the theorem, a maximal entropy Neumann kernel NK and the corresponding normalized version NK_N can be defined as follows.

$$NK = (\mathbf{I} - \alpha\mathbf{D_v}\mathbf{A}\mathbf{D_v}/\lambda)^{-1} \quad (19)$$
$$NK_N = (\mathbf{I} - \alpha\mathbf{A}/\lambda)^{-1} \quad (20)$$

where $\alpha \in (0,1)$ is a real parameter.

The normalized maximal entropy Neumann kernel NK_N is closely related to the Katz index when it is applied for link prediction [15]. In addition, it is not hard to show that the normalized maximal entropy regularized Laplacian kernel is equivalent to the maximal entropy Neumann kernel with a different real parameter, i.e., $RK_N = (1-\beta)(\mathbf{I} - \beta\mathbf{A}/\lambda)^{-1}$, where $\beta = \alpha/(1+\alpha)$.

4.2 Maximal entropy inverse P-distance

In [12], inverse P-distance (P_D) is defined to compute the proximity between nodes, V_i and V_j, on a graph.

$$P_D(i,j) = \sum_{\tau_{ij}:V_i \rightsquigarrow V_j} p(\tau_{ij})\alpha^{l(\tau_{ij})} \quad (21)$$

Here, the summation is taken over all paths τ_{ij} that start at node V_i and ends at node V_j, where $l(\tau_{ij})$ denotes the length of path τ_{ij}. $P_D(i,j)$ measures distances inversely: it is larger for nodes V_i "closer" to V_j. In MERW, all paths with equal length have the same probabilities. The maximal entropy inverse P-distance can be written in a more compact form.

$$P_D(i,j) = \sum_{l=1}^{\infty} (\frac{\alpha}{\lambda})^l \frac{v_j}{v_i}(A^l)_{ij} \quad (22)$$

Here, Eq. (22) can be put in a matrix form as follows.

$$\mathbf{P_D} = \frac{\alpha\mathbf{A}}{\lambda}\mathbf{D_v}^{-1}(\mathbf{I} - \frac{\alpha\mathbf{A}}{\lambda})^{-1}\mathbf{D_v} \quad (23)$$

By replacing α^l by $\frac{\alpha^l}{l!}$ in Eq. (22), we have a matrix exponentiation, denoted as $\mathbf{P_D}'$ as follows.

$$\mathbf{P_D}' = \frac{\alpha\mathbf{A}}{\lambda}\mathbf{D_v}^{-1}\exp(\frac{\alpha\mathbf{A}}{\lambda})\mathbf{D_v} \quad (24)$$

4.3 Maximal entropy SimRank

The original SimRank is based on the idea that two nodes are similar if they are joined to similar neighbors [13]. The SimRank is closely related to the random walk on a product graph. Motivated by this, we propose a new SimRank based maximal entropy random walk on graph, denoted as $S(x,y)$ for two nodes V_x and V_y in Eq. (25).

$$S(x,y) = \begin{cases} \alpha\lambda^{-2}v_x v_y \sum_{a\in N(x)} \sum_{b \in N(y)} \frac{S(a,b)}{v_a v_b}, & if\ x \neq y \\ 1, \quad if\ x = y \end{cases} \quad (25)$$

where $\alpha \in (0,1)$ and $N(x)$ denotes to the neighbor node set of node V_x. We call Eq. (25) the maximal entropy SimRank equation. The existence and uniqueness of the solution to the maximal entropy SimRank equation is guaranteed by the following theorem.

Theorem 4.2: *The maximal entropy SimRank equation defined in Eq. (25) has a unique solution.* □

Proof Sketch: This can be proved in the similar as to prove the original SimRank equation in [13]. □

The maximal entropy SimRank can be computed in an iterative fashion as follows.

$$R_{k+1}(x,y) = \alpha\lambda^{-2}v_x v_y \sum_{a\in N(x)} \sum_{b\in N(y)} \frac{R_k(a,b)}{v_a v_b} \quad (26)$$

where the initial point is defined as $R_0(x,y) = 0$ if $x \neq y$, otherwise $R_0(x,y) = 1$. Since the maximal entropy SimRank equation has an unique solution, Eq. (26) has the same form as Eq. (25), the iterative computation can be reached by a fixed-point. More formally, $S(x,y) = \lim_{k\to\infty} R_k(x,y)$.

Note that SimRank can be computed by the so-called "expected-f meeting distance" of two surfers in a random surfer-pairs model [13]. The random surfer pairs model is identical to a random surfer on a so-called product graph induced by the original graph. Each node in the product graph is a node pair of the original graph. Thus, two random surfers starting at nodes V_x and V_y, respectively, meeting at V_u, is equal to the random surfer starting from node (V_x, V_y) and ending at node (V_u, V_u) in the product graph. The maximal entropy SimRank can also be modeled by a maximal entropy random surfer-pairs model. Below, we first give a maximal entropy expected-f meeting distance and then establish the equivalent relationship between it and maximal entropy SimRank. The maximal entropy expected-f meeting distance $dist(x,y)$ between two nodes V_x and V_y is defined as

$$dist(x,y) = \sum_{\tau:(x,y)\rightsquigarrow(u,u)} p(\tau)\alpha^{l(\tau)} \quad (27)$$

where τ denotes a path generated by the maximal entropy random surfer starting at node (x,y) and ending at node (u,u) in the product graph. $p(\tau)$ denotes the probability of path τ, and $l(\tau)$ is the length of the τ. Based on Eq. (27), we have the following theorem.

Theorem 4.3: *The maximal entropy SimRank between a node pair (x,y) is their maximal entropy expected-f meeting distance traveling back-edges.* □

Proof Sketch: We prove it by splitting the path τ into two parts: the first step $(a,b) \rightsquigarrow (x,y)$, where $a \in N(x), b \in$

$N(y)$; and the remaining path τ'.

$$\begin{aligned} dist(x,y) &= \sum_{\tau:(u,u)\rightsquigarrow(x,y)} p(\tau)\alpha^{l(\tau)} \\ &= \sum_{a\in N(x)}\sum_{b\in N(y)}\sum_{\tau':(u,u)\rightsquigarrow(a,b)} \frac{v_x v_y}{\lambda^2 v_a v_b} p(\tau')\alpha^{l(\tau')+1} \\ &= \frac{\alpha v_x v_y}{\lambda^2} \sum_{a\in N(x)}\sum_{b\in N(y)}\sum_{\tau':(u,u)\rightsquigarrow(a,b)} \frac{p(\tau')\alpha^{l(\tau')+1}}{v_a v_b} \\ &= \frac{\alpha v_x v_y}{\lambda^2} \sum_{a\in N(x)}\sum_{b\in N(y)} \frac{dist(a,b)}{v_a v_b} \end{aligned} \quad (28)$$

Note that $l(\tau) = l(\tau') + 1$ and $p(\tau) = \frac{v_x v_y}{\lambda^2 v_a v_b} p(\tau')$. Since $dist(x, y)$ is equal to the maximal entropy SimRank (Eq. (25)), the maximal entropy expected-f meeting distance between two nodes is equivalent to their maximal entropy SimRank. □

5. EXPERIMENTS

In this section, we evaluate the effectiveness of MERW based similarity measures for link prediction. In the following, we first introduce the experimental setup, and then report our results.

5.1 Experimental setup

Datasets: We conduct our experiments on 3 synthetic and 8 real networks. Specifically, for synthetic networks, we generate three networks with 1,000 nodes using three classic random graph generators: **ER** (Erods-Renyi random graph [30]), **BA** (Barabasi-Albert random graph (scale free graph) [3]), and **SW** (small word random graph [30]). For real networks, we test the proposed methods on 8 representative datasets, which are widely used for link prediction both in computer science community and physics community. Specifically, the first five are **USAir** (network of US air transportation system), **C.elegans** (neural network of the nematode worm [36]), **Yeast** (protein-protein interaction network [14]), **Power** (network of power grid of the western US [36]), and **NetScience** (collaboration network of researchers [29], who work on complex network theory). The second three are collaboration networks collected form Arxiv e-print archive [21], including three different areas of physics. In particular, they are **Gr-Qc** (General Relativity and Quantum Cosmology), **Hep-ph** (High Energy Physics-Phenomenology), and **Hep-Th** (High Energy Physics-Theory). Table 1 shows the numbers of nodes and edges of the networks as well as the numbers of nodes and edges of the giant components (GC) of the networks.

Networks	Nodes	Edges	Nodes of GC	Edges of GC
ER	1000	9997	1000	9997
BA	1000	11964	1000	11964
SW	1000	1995	1000	1995
USAir	332	2126	332	2126
C.elegans	453	2298	453	2298
Yeast	1870	4480	1458	1993
Power	4941	6594	4941	6594
NetScience	1461	2742	397	914
Gr-Qc	5242	14490	4158	13428
Hep-ph	12008	118505	11204	117649
Hep-Th	9877	25748	8638	24806

Table 1: Datasets statistics

Evaluation metrics: We employ two widely used metrics to evaluate the link prediction methods: the Area under the ROC curve (AUC)[25, 27] and precision [27, 2]. The first metric evaluates the overall ranking yielded by the algorithms, while the second metric focuses on top-K predictive results. In our experiments, the AUC is computed by a standard method described in [27]. A larger AUC value indicates a better link prediction performance. The precision is defined as the ratio of relevant number of items over all selected items using $\frac{k}{K}$. Here, we set $K = 30$, and k is the number of links that successfully predicted by the algorithms. Obviously, the larger precision means the higher predictive accuracy.

Baselines: We compare 27 various link prediction algorithms involving 11 MERW based methods, 10 TRW based methods, common neighbor, Adamic/Ada [1], supervised link prediction method [25], and supervised random walk [2]. In particular, the similarity measures we tested include: Commute time of TRW (CTT), Commute time of MERW (CTME), Commute time kernel (CK), Maximal entropy commute time kernel (MECK), Normalized commute time kernel (NCK), Normalized maximal entropy commute time kernel (NMECK), Heat diffusion kernel (DK), Maximal entropy heat diffusion kernel (MEDK), Normalized heat diffusion kernel (NDK), Normalized maximal entropy heat diffusion kernel (NMEDK), Regularized Laplacian kernel (RK), Maximal entropy regularized Laplacian kernel (MERK), Normalized regularized Laplacian kernel (NRK), Normalized maximal entropy regularized Laplacian kernel (NMERK), Neumann kernel (NK), Maximal entropy Neumann kernel (MENK), Normalized Neumann kernel (NNK), Normalized maximal entropy Neumann kernel (NMENK), Inverse P-distance (PD), Maximal entropy inverse P-distance (MEPD), Inverse P-distance with matrix exponentiation (PDM), Maximal entropy inverse P-distance with matrix exponentiation (MEPDM), SimRank (SR), Maximal entropy SimRank (MESR), and Common Neighbor (CN), Adamic/Adar (AA), supervised link prediction method (HPLP+), and supervised random walk (SRW).

Link prediction methodology: For each dataset given in Table 1, first, we extract the giant component of the graph, and randomly split the edges into a training set and a test set. The test set contains 10% of all edges in the giant component. In particular, we conduct 10 times random partitions of training and test sets on the datasets, and the link prediction results are the average over this partitions. Second, we perform the link prediction algorithms on the datasets. Specifically, we consider two cases: the unsupervised methods and supervised methods. For the unsupervised algorithms, which involve MERW and TRW based method, CN, and AA, we compute the similarity matrix on the training set using the similarity measures described in the previous sections. Then, we use the similarity matrix to calculate the predictions for the edges in the test set. For the supervised algorithms, including HPLP+ and SRW, we perform the corresponding learning algorithms on the training set, and then compute predictions on the test set. It is worth mentioning that we implement a naive Bayes classifer using the full feature set (HPLP+) defined in [25] for supervised link prediction, as it obtains the best performance in [25]. Finally, we compare the link prediction performance using the evaluation metrics described above.

Parameter settings: In MERW or TRW based similarity measures, there is only one parameter: the damping factor

α. We set $\alpha = 0.5$, as it is not very sensitive in our experiments. In addition, we set all parameters of other baselines as the same as their original papers respectively.

Experimental environment: All experiments are conducted on the Linux workstation with 2xQuad-Core Intel Xeon 3.06 GHz CPU, 48 Gb memory, and running CentOS 5.5. All the algorithms are implemented by MATLAB 2009 and Visual C++ 6.0.

5.2 Experimental results

Table 2 and Table 3 show the results of 27 various link prediction algorithms on 11 datasets under AUC and precision metric respectively. We can clearly see that the MERW based link prediction methods achieve better predictions than all other unsupervised methods under both AUC and precision metric. Moreover, on most datsets, the MERW based methods perform better than supervised methods. Generally, the normalized maximal entropy graph kernels outperform the non-normalized ones. And the normalized maximal entropy diffusion kernel achieves the best performance among all the MERW based methods. We show the detail analysis as follows.

Commute time kernels: By comparing commute time of TRW (CTT), commute time of MERW (CTME, Eq. (12)), commute time kernel (CK), maximal entropy commute time kernel (MECK, Eq. (13)) and their corresponding normalized kernels (Eq. (14)), we observe that the normalized maximal entropy commute time kernel outperforms the others on most datasets. We also see that both CTT and CTME perform poorly. This consists with a recent result reported in [28], in which the authors claim that the commute time distance converges to a meaningless distance measure, thus it results in poor precision for link prediction.

Heat diffusion/regularized Laplacian kernels/Neumann kernels: Comparing among heat diffusion kernel (DK), maximal entropy heat diffusion kernel (MEDK, Eq. (15)), and their normalized counterparts (NMEDK, Eq. (16)), the results show that NMEDK achieves significant improvement over DK, MEDK, and NDK. For instance, in Yeast dataset (column 7, row 8-11), NMEDK achieves near-optimal AUC, and obtain 67.6%, 517.4%, and 135.9% relative improvement on DK, MEDK, and NDK in terms of precision metric, respectively. The similar comparisons can also be observed between the regularized Laplacian kernels and maximal entropy regularized Laplacian kernels (Eq. (17) and Eq. (18)), and also between the Neumann kernels and maximal entropy Neumann kernels. In addition, it is worth mentioning that the normalized maximal entropy heat diffusion, normalized maximal entropy regularized Laplacian kernel, and the normalized maximal entropy Neumann kernel get the similar performance on most datasets, and they outperform the corresponding non-normalized kernels. The AUC of the maximal entropy graph kernels achieve near-optimal value on most datasets. Moreover, the precision of these graph kernels is close to 1 on USAir, C.elegances, Yeast, and NetScience, as well as the three synthetic graphs. This results indicate that the MERW based similarity measures can probably capture the nature of link formation process of these networks, thus the link predictive precision is close to 1.

Inverse P-distance and SimRank: Among inverse P-distance (PD), inverse P-distance with matrix exponentiation (PDM), SimRank (SR), and their maximal entropy counterparts (Eq. (23), Eq. (24), and Eq. (25)), the maximal entropy P-distances with matrix exponentiation (MEPDM) outperforms others in terms of both AUC and precision. Over all the datasets, the maximal entropy P-distances with matrix exponentiation (MEPDM) improves AUC over PD, MEPD, and PDM by 11.8%, 1%, 16.6% on average, respectively. And also it boosts precision on PD, MEPD, and PDM by 52.8%, 0.7%, 362.6% on average respectively. SimRank measures perform poorly than the graph kernels. More worse, the time complexity of SimRank measures is $O(n^4)$, thus we cannot obtain all the experimental results.

Comparison with supervised methods: Here we compare the MEPDM with supervised link prediction (HPLP+), and supervised random walk (SRW), as MEPDM achieves the best performance over the unsupervised methods in our experiments. We can clearly see that the performance of MEPDM is better than supervised methods (HPLP+ and SRW) over USAir, C.ele, Yeast, NetScience, GrQc, HepTh, and three synthetic networks under both AUC and precision metric. Moreover, on the rest datasets, MEPDM achieves competitive performance with supervised methods. It is worth mentioning that the SRW slightly outperforms HPLP+ under both AUC and precision metric on most datasets. The AUC of MEPDM, HPLP+, and SRW falls into the range (0.72, 0.99), and the precision of this algorithms is roughly between (0.12, 0.96). This results suggest that the MEPDM, as supervised methods do, exhibits very good performance in link prediction.

To summarize, the experimental results highlight the power of MERW in link prediction. Also, the results empirically confirm that the centrality of nodes is very important in link prediction. Since the MERW based methods inherently capture the centrality of nodes, they can yield much better performance than those methods that do not consider the centrality of nodes in link prediction. Indeed, as observed in many real networks [3, 30], the link formation typically consists with a preferential attachment process. That is to say, the nodes in the network tend to link to the central nodes, which results in a so-called "rich-get-richer" phenomenon. In effect, the MERW implicitly incorporates this phenomenon into the random walk process. This is because the transition probability in each step of MERW refers to the eigenvector centrality of the nodes, thus it makes the walk greedily moves to the important nodes. Besides, as opposed to the supervised methods, the MERW based methods work in a agnostic manner, thus they can naturally avoid the class distribution and feature selection problem [2].

6. RELATED WORK

Link prediction and similarity measure on graph: After the seminal work by Liben-Nowell and Kleinberg [24], the link prediction problem has attracted considerable attention in recent years both from computer science and physics community [27, 11, 19, 25, 18, 2]. The existing link prediction approaches can be classified into two categories: unsupervised and supervised methods. Most unsupervised link prediction algorithms are based on the similarity measure between the nodes of a graph. A recent survey can be found in [27]. Below, we focus on the random walk based similarity measures. In [13], SimRank is proposed, based on the idea that two nodes are similar if they are joined to similar neighbor nodes. The complexity of this algorithm is

SM	ER	BA	SW	USAir	C.ele	Yeast	Power	NetSci	GrQc	HepPh	HepTh
CTT	0.710	0.750	0.791	0.847	0.784	0.709	0.713	0.917	0.520	0.523	0.525
CTME	0.720	0.746	0.745	0.855	0.798	0.501	0.501	0.866	0.556	0.645	0.534
CK	0.805	0.883	0.804	0.856	0.809	0.715	0.501	0.799	0.513	0.501	0.513
MECK	0.940	0.981	0.845	0.936	0.856	0.757	0.501	0.975	0.517	0.501	0.503
NCK	0.502	0.501	0.501	0.708	0.706	0.501	0.501	0.501	0.503	0.508	0.501
NMECK	0.903	0.983	0.982	0.931	0.969	0.710	0.501	0.971	0.623	0.750	0.675
DK	0.835	0.813	0.983	0.836	0.838	0.829	0.764	0.965	0.501	0.605	0.593
MEDK	0.999	0.983	0.998	0.991	0.971	0.749	0.812	0.963	0.739	0.735	0.746
NDK	0.786	0.711	0.956	0.920	0.778	0.731	0.857	0.908	0.531	0.530	0.530
NMEDK	**0.999**	**0.983**	**0.998**	**0.997**	**0.978**	**0.970**	0.857	**0.996**	**0.739**	0.755	**0.758**
RK	0.851	0.907	0.973	0.898	0.887	0.803	0.864	0.624	0.632	0.608	0.561
MERK	0.999	0.983	0.998	0.981	0.949	0.812	0.812	0.963	0.618	0.745	0.735
NRK	0.504	0.501	0.501	0.719	0.501	0.703	0.806	0.501	0.501	0.508	0.504
NMERK	0.999	0.983	0.998	0.983	0.975	0.968	0.857	0.986	0.739	0.755	0.756
MENK	0.999	0.983	0.998	0.936	0.975	0.799	0.812	0.963	0.618	0.730	0.746
NNK	0.503	0.501	0.501	0.819	0.501	0.705	0.806	0.501	0.501	0.508	0.504
NMENK	0.999	0.983	0.998	0.983	0.965	0.965	0.857	0.996	0.739	0.755	0.752
PD	0.926	0.974	0.953	0.971	0.866	0.887	0.857	0.722	0.666	0.618	0.628
MEPD	0.999	0.976	0.998	0.993	0.964	0.968	0.857	0.913	0.739	0.755	0.758
PDM	0.805	0.764	0.957	0.972	0.798	0.886	0.857	0.874	0.616	0.660	0.530
MEPDM	0.999	0.983	0.998	0.990	0.976	0.970	0.857	0.996	0.739	0.755	0.758
SR	–	–	–	0.905	0.860	–	–	0.955	–	–	–
MESR	–	–	–	0.960	0.876	–	–	0.963	–	–	–
CN	0.884	0.782	0.501	0.386	0.971	0.752	0.802	0.961	0.617	0.623	0.635
AA	0.886	0.781	0.501	0.409	0.975	0.793	0.806	0.969	0.623	0.630	0.638
HPLP+	0.983	0.971	0.978	0.979	0.974	0.965	**0.886**	0.984	0.725	0.753	0.732
SRW	0.991	0.977	0.989	0.983	0.972	0.967	0.863	0.983	0.731	**0.760**	0.754

Table 2: Comparison of AUC value among 27 various algorithms.

$O(n^4)$. Pei, et al. [23] propose an efficient single-pair SimRank algorithm. In [38], a family of dissimilarity measures are developed based on a biased random walk on graph, which generalize both the commute-time and the shortest-path distances. In [12], a unified distance function, namely inverse P-distance, is proposed. There exists a strong connection between the personalized pagerank and the inverse P-distance. In [11], it uses graph kernels for link prediction task. In [19], a learning framework is proposed for link prediction, which generalizes several graph kernels based methods. Later, in [18], the same authors proposes a spectral evolution model and develops a spectral extrapolation algorithm for link prediction, which is based on the observation that the large networks change over time result in a change of a the graph's spectrum and keeping the eigenvectors unchanged. More recently, the supervised link prediction has attracted much attention [25, 2]. For instance, in [25], the authors propose a supervised method using classic classifier such as naive Bayes, decision tree, and bagging for link prediction. In [2], a supervised random walk is designed for link prediction, which performs random walk on a weighted graph with the weights learned by a supervised learning algorithms. The supervised methods typically suffer from the class imbalance and feature selection problems. However, our MERW based methods are unsupervised approaches, thus they can naturally avoid the feature selection problem.

Maximal entropy random walk on graph: The maximal entropy random walk was first proposed by Ruelle and Bowens in [33] and it was also called Ruelle-Bowens random walk [9]. This random walk on an unweighted graph chooses the transition probabilities proportional to the importance of the nodes measured by its eigenvector centrality, which is a well known centrality measure in sociology [5]. As shown in [31, 6, 9, 34], this process makes all paths between two given nodes with same length have the same probabilities. That is to say, the transition probabilities of this random walk are chosen to maximize the entropy rate of the walk.

In [6], a maximal entropy random walk is designed on an unweighted and undirected graph according to the dominant eigenvector of the adjacency matrix. In [31], it shows that there is one and only one random walk that can achieve the maximal entropy rate. The main problem of designing maximal entropy random walk is that it requires to know the dominant eigenvector of the adjacency matrix, which means one should have global knowledge of the graph. However, such global knowledge is unavailable. To make MERW more practical, [34] shows that one can construct approximate maximal entropy random walk with the degree of the nodes on graph. The most related to our work is [9], where a centrality measure, namely entropy rank, is proposed based on the maximal entropy random walk on an unweighted and directed graph. The entropy rank uses the stationary distribution of the maximal entropy random walk on an unweighted and directed graph as the measure of centrality. As shown in [9], the stationary distribution of MERW on a directed graph is identical to the element-wise product of the dominant left and right singular vector of the adjacency matrix. The major drawback of this measure is that it can make the centrality of the nodes with zero in-degree or out-degree equal to zero. In this work, we explore the power of MERW on undirected graphs in the context of link prediction.

Graph kernel: Graph kernel is a powerful tool. We focus on graph kernels defined as a similarity measure between nodes of a given graph. Kondor and Lafferty [17] first propose to construct kernel on graph. They propose an exponential kernel, namely diffusion kernel, based on the heat equation. This kernel can be naturally constructed by matrix exponentiation. Smola and Kondor extend it based on the regularization operators, which produce several regularized graph kernels [35]. Recently, Fouss, et al. [10] show

SM	ER	BA	SW	USAir	C.ele	Yeast	Power	NetSci	GrQc	HepPh	HepTh
CTT	0.01	0.05	0.21	0.35	0.14	0.11	0.08	0.44	0.02	0.02	0.02
CTME	0.02	0.05	0.05	0.36	0.14	≈0	≈0	0.06	0.11	0.15	0.03
CK	0.71	0.74	0.58	0.06	0.20	0.02	≈0	0.10	0.01	≈0	0.01
MECK	0.74	0.95	0.44	0.60	0.69	0.06	≈0	0.02	0.02	≈0	0.03
NCK	≈0	≈0	≈0	0.01	0.01	≈0	≈0	≈0	≈0	0.01	≈0
NMECK	0.70	0.95	0.79	0.53	0.90	0.01	≈0	0.13	0.12	0.15	0.18
DK	0.22	0.21	0.94	0.14	0.24	0.55	0.1	0.53	≈0	0.11	0.09
MEDK	0.96	0.95	0.95	0.95	0.92	0.15	0.01	0.26	0.16	0.14	0.16
NDK	0.09	0.03	0.86	0.32	0.08	0.39	0.12	0.02	0.03	0.03	0.03
NMEDK	**0.96**	**0.95**	**0.95**	**0.96**	**0.93**	**0.92**	0.12	**0.94**	**0.21**	0.22	**0.24**
RK	0.82	0.79	0.89	0.20	0.39	0.60	0.11	0.62	0.03	0.10	0.06
MERK	0.96	0.95	0.95	0.90	0.85	0.20	0.01	0.26	0.12	0.20	0.20
NRK	≈0	≈0	≈0	0.02	≈0	0.01	0.01	≈0	≈0	0.01	0.004
NMERK	0.96	0.95	0.95	0.92	0.91	0.91	0.12	0.92	0.21	0.22	0.21
MENK	0.96	0.95	0.95	0.94	0.91	0.10	0.01	0.26	0.12	0.21	0.20
NNK	≈0	≈0	≈0	0.02	≈0	0.01	0.01	≈0	≈0	0.01	≈0
NMENK	0.96	0.95	0.95	0.95	0.91	0.91	0.12	0.94	0.21	0.22	0.21
PD	0.93	0.82	0.84	0.58	0.52	0.66	0.12	0.72	0.10	0.09	0.13
MEPD	0.96	0.94	0.95	0.95	0.89	0.91	0.12	0.91	0.21	0.22	0.24
PDM	0.10	0.06	0.85	0.37	0.20	0.58	0.12	0.27	0.12	0.16	0.03
MEPDM	0.96	0.95	0.95	0.94	0.92	0.92	0.12	0.94	0.21	0.22	0.24
SR	–	–	–	0.21	0.14	–	–	0.26	–	–	–
MESR	–	–	–	0.48	0.28	–	–	0.50	–	–	–
CN	0.24	0.04	≈0	0.39	0.16	0.10	0.01	0.36	0.12	0.12	0.14
AA	0.25	0.04	≈0	0.41	0.21	0.09	0.01	0.61	0.12	0.13	0.14
HPLP+	0.92	0.86	0.88	0.81	0.71	0.81	**0.21**	0.73	0.18	0.22	0.20
SRW	0.95	0.87	0.87	0.82	0.70	0.83	0.20	0.75	0.18	**0.24**	0.21

Table 3: Comparison of link predictive precision among 27 various algorithms.

that the Moore-Penrose pseudo-inverse of the graph Laplacian is a kernel, also called commute time kernel. This kernel is wildly used as a similarities measure between nodes of a graph [10, 37]. However, very recently, Luxburg, et al. [28] show that the commute time distance does not consider the structure of the graph and it will converge to a meaningless distance measure on a graph. This results indicate that the commute time kernel is not very well for measure the similarity between nodes of a graph. The other graph kernel is Neumann kernel [11], which can be expressed as infinite series of matrix powers. The Neumann kernel is closely related to the random walk with restart, which is well known for measure the importance of nodes on a graph. It is important to note that all the graph kernels mentioned above are closely related to the transitional random walk on graph. We study new graph kernels based on MERW.

7. CONCLUSION

In this paper, we propose a set of unsupervised link prediction methods that incorporate the centrality of nodes of the graph based on MERW. We first study certain important properties of MERW by constructing a new eigen-weighted graph. Specifically, based on the eigen-weighted graph, we give a class of new graph Laplacians, namely maximal entropy graph Laplacians, and show that the hitting and commute time of MERW can be computed using the pseudo-inverse of the maximal entropy combinatorial Laplacian. Then, we define four types of graph kernels and two similarity measures on graph based on MERW for link prediction. Finally, we compare 27 various link prediction algorithms over 11 diverse datasets, and show our newly proposed MERW based method (NMEDK) outperforms all the other unsupervised approaches as well as the supervised methods on most datasets. Future work includes generalizing the MERW based methods to directed graphs and exploring MERW for other data mining and machine learning applications.

Appendix A

We claim some properties of pseudo-inverse of MECL as follows: (1) $\mathbf{L}^+$ is a positive semidefinite matrix. (2)$\mathbf{L}^+$ has rank $n-1$. (3)$\mathbf{L}^+$ is doubly centered. Since MECL is equal to the graph Laplacian of the corresponding eigen-weighted graph, MECL shares the properties of the ordinary weighted graph Laplacian. Hence, the claims hold. In addition, we give a lemma [20] in order to prove the Theorem 3.3.

Lemma 7.1: *For any irreducible matrix* $\mathbf{A} \in R^{n\times n}$ *with spectral radius* $\rho(\mathbf{A}) = r$, *if* $\mathbf{A}_\mathrm{i}$ *is a principal submatrix of* $\mathbf{A}$ *obtained by removing the i-th row and column of blocks, then matrix* $r\mathbf{I} - \mathbf{A}_\mathrm{i}$ *is nonsingular.* □

With the properties and Lemma 7.1, we can prove Theorem 3.3. First, we reformulate Eq. (10) into a vector form as $h = e + \mathbf{P}h$, where e is a vector with elements all one, h is the hitting time vector, and $\mathbf{P}$ is the transition matrix. Without loss of generality, we remove the n-th row of vector h and e, and remove the n-th row and n-th column of matrix $\mathbf{A}$, and denote them by $\tilde{h}$, $\tilde{e}$, and $\tilde{\mathbf{A}}$ respectively. We can obtain $\tilde{h} = \tilde{e} + \tilde{\mathbf{P}}\tilde{h}$, where $\tilde{\mathbf{P}} = \tilde{\mathbf{D}}_\mathrm{v}^{-1}\tilde{\mathbf{A}}\tilde{\mathbf{D}}_\mathrm{v}/\lambda$. Furthermore, let $\tilde{\mathbf{L}} = \tilde{\mathbf{D}}_\mathrm{v}^2 - \tilde{\mathbf{D}}_\mathrm{v}\tilde{\mathbf{A}}\tilde{\mathbf{D}}_\mathrm{v}/\lambda$, we have $\tilde{\mathbf{L}}\tilde{h} = \tilde{\mathbf{D}}_\mathrm{v}^2\tilde{e}$. According to Lemma 7.1, $\tilde{\mathbf{L}}$ is nonsingular. We thus get $\tilde{h} = \tilde{\mathbf{L}}^+\tilde{\mathbf{D}}_\mathrm{v}^2\tilde{e} = \tilde{\mathbf{L}}^{-1}\tilde{\mathbf{D}}_\mathrm{v}^2\tilde{e}$. With the same techniques used in [10], we can efficiently solve the pseudo-inverse of $\tilde{\mathbf{L}}$ ($\tilde{\mathbf{L}}^+$) by computing the pseudo-inverse of $\mathbf{L}$ ($\mathbf{L}^+$). We have

$$h(i,n) = \sum_{j=1}^{n} (L^+_{ij} - L^+_{in} - L^+_{nj} + L^+_{nn})v_j^2$$

More generally, we have

$$h(i,k) = \sum_{j=1}^{n} (L^+_{ij} - L^+_{ik} - L^+_{kj} + L^+_{kk})v_j^2$$

We can further compute the commute time as follows:

$$c(i,k) = h(i,k) + h(k,i) = (L_{ii}^{+} + L_{kk}^{+} - 2L_{ik}^{+}) \sum_{j=1}^{n} v_j^2$$
$$= (L_{ii}^{+} + L_{kk}^{+} - 2L_{ik}^{+})$$

Since we normalize the dominate eigenvector v, the last equality holds.

Acknowledgments

The work was supported by grants of the Research Grants Council of the Hong Kong SAR, China No. 419008 and 419109.

8. REFERENCES

[1] L. A. Adamic and E. Adar. Friends and neighbors on the web. *Social Networks*, 25(3), 2003.
[2] L. Backstrom and J. Leskovec. Supervised random walks: Predicting and recommending links in social networks. In *WSDM' 11.*
[3] A.-L. Barabasi and R. Albert. Emergence of scaling in random networks. *Science*, 286:509–512, 1999.
[4] D. Boley, G. Ranjan, and Z.-L. Zhang. Commute times for a directed graph using an asymmetric laplacian. Technical report, Computer Science and Engineering, University of Minnesota, 2010.
[5] P. Bonacich. Power and centrality: A family of measures. *The American Journal of Sociology*, 92(5):1170–1182, 1987.
[6] Z. Burda, J. Duda, J. M. Luck, and B. Waclaw. Localization of the maximal entropy randomwalk. *Physical Review Letters*, 102(16), 2009.
[7] F. R. K. Chuang. *Spectral Graph Theory.* Regional Conference Series in mathematics. American Mathematical Society, 1997.
[8] T. M. Cover and J. A. Thomas. *Elements of Information Theory 2nd Edition.* Wiley-Interscience, 2006.
[9] J.-C. Delvenne and A.-S. Libert. Centrality measures and thermodynamic formalism for complex networks. 2010.
[10] F. Fouss, A. Pirotte, J.-M. Renders, and M. Saerens. Random-walk computation of similarities between nodes of a graph with application to collaborative recommendation. *TKDE*, 19(3), 2007.
[11] T. Ito, M. Shimbo, T. Kudo, and Y. Matsumoto. Application of kernels to link analysis. In *KDD' 05.*
[12] G. Jeh and J. Widom. Scaling personalized web search. In *WWW' 03.*
[13] G. Jeh and J. Widom. Simrank: a measure of structural-context similarity. In *KDD' 02.*
[14] H. Jeong, S. P. Mason, A.-L. Barabĺćsi1, and Z. N. Oltvai. Lethality and centrality in protein networks. *Nature*, 411, 2001.
[15] L. Katz. A new status index derived from sociometric analysis. *Psychometrika*, 1953.
[16] D. J. Klein and M. Randic. Resistance distance. *Journal of Mathematical Chemistry*, 12(1):81–95, 1993.
[17] R. I. Kondor and J. Lafferty. Diffusion kernels on graphs and other discrete structures. In *ICML' 02.*
[18] J. Kunegis, D. Fay, and C. Bauckhage. Network growth and the spectral evolution model. In *CIKM' 10.*
[19] J. Kunegis and A. Lommatzsch. Learning spectral graph transformations for link prediction. In *ICML' 10.*
[20] A. N. Langville and C. D. Meyer. *Google's PageRank and Beyond: The Science of Search Engine Rankings.* Princeton University Press, 2006.
[21] J. Leskovec. Standford network analysis project. *http://snap.standford.edu*, 2010.
[22] M. Li, B. M. Dias, I. Jarman, W. El-Deredy, and P. J. Lisboa. Grocery shopping recommendations based on basket-sensitive random walk. KDD' 09.
[23] P. Li, H. Liu, J. X. Yu, J. He, and X. Du. Fast single-pair simrank computation. In *SDM' 10.*
[24] D. Liben-Nowell and J. M. Kleinberg. The link-prediction problem for social networks. *JASIST*, 58(7):1019–1031, 2007.
[25] R. N. Lichtenwalter, J. T. Lussier, and N. V. Chawla. New perspectives and methods in link prediction. In *KDD' 10.*
[26] L. Lovasz. Random walks on graphs: A survey. *Combinatorics*, 2:1–46, 1996.
[27] L. Lu and T. Zhou. Link prediction in complex networks: A survey. *Physica A: Statistical Mechanics and its Applications*, 390(6):1150–1170, 2010.
[28] U. v. Luxburg, A. Radl, and M. Hein. Getting lost in space: Large sample analysis of the commute distance. In *NIPS'10.*
[29] M. E. J. Newman. Finding community structure in networks using the eigenvectors of matrices. *Phys. Rev. E*, 74(3), 2006.
[30] M. E. J. Newman. *Networks: An Introduction.* OXFORD University Press, 2010.
[31] W. PARRY. Intrinsic markov chains. *Transactions of the American Mathematical Society*, 112:55–66, 1964.
[32] M. Roth, A. Ben-David, D. Deutscher, G. Flysher, I. Horn, A. Leichtberg, N. Leiser, Y. Matias, and R. Merom. Suggesting friends using the implicit social graph. KDD '10, 2010.
[33] D. Ruelle. *Thermodynamic Formalism.* Addison-Wesley, Reading Mass., 1978.
[34] R. Sinatra, J. Gomez-Gardenes, R. Lambiotte, V. Nicosia, and V. Latora. Optimal random walks in complex networks with limited information. *arXiv:1007.4936v1*, 2010.
[35] A. J. Smola and R. I. Kondor. Kernels and regularization on graphs. In *COLT' 03.*
[36] D. J. Watts and S. Strogatz. Collective dynamics of 'small-world' networks. *Nature*, 393:409–410, 1998.
[37] L. Yen, F. Fouss, C. Decaestecker, P. Francq, and M. Saerens. Graph nodes clustering with the sigmoid commute-time kernel: A comparative study. *Data and Knowledge Engineering 68*, 68:338–361, 2009.
[38] L. Yen, A. Mantrach, and M. Shimbo. A family of dissimilarity measures between nodes generalizing both the shortest-path and the commute-time distances. In *KDD' 08.*

Exploiting Longer Cycles for Link Prediction in Signed Networks

Kai-Yang Chiang*
UT Austin
kychiang@cs.utexas.edu

Nagarajan Natarajan*
UT Austin
naga86@cs.utexas.edu

Ambuj Tewari*
UT Austin
ambuj@cs.utexas.edu

Inderjit S. Dhillon
UT Austin
inderjit@cs.utexas.edu

ABSTRACT

We consider the problem of link prediction in signed networks. Such networks arise on the web in a variety of ways when users can implicitly or explicitly tag their relationship with other users as positive or negative. The signed links thus created reflect social attitudes of the users towards each other in terms of friendship or trust. Our first contribution is to show how any quantitative measure of social imbalance in a network can be used to derive a link prediction algorithm. Our framework allows us to reinterpret some existing algorithms as well as derive new ones. Second, we extend the approach of [6], by presenting a supervised machine learning based link prediction method that uses features derived from longer cycles in the network. The supervised method outperforms all previous approaches on 3 networks drawn from sources such as Epinions, Slashdot and Wikipedia. The supervised approach easily scales to these networks, the largest of which has 132k nodes and 841k edges. Most real-world networks have an overwhelmingly large proportion of positive edges and it is therefore easy to get a high overall accuracy at the cost of a high false positive rate. We see that our supervised method not only achieves good accuracy for sign prediction but is also especially effective in lowering the false positive rate.

Categories and Subject Descriptors

H.4 [**Information Systems Applications**]: Miscellaneous ; J.4 [**Computer Applications**]: Social and Behavioral Sciences—*Sociology*

General Terms

Algorithms, Experimentation

*Equal contribution to the work.

Keywords

Link & Graph Mining, Web & Social Knowledge Management

1. INTRODUCTION

Many research problems in the analysis of networks, social or otherwise, have been tackled by modeling the presence or absence of relationships between pairs of entities using a graph where a relationship is simply indicated by a positively weighted edge. Recently, real-world networks have appeared that do not fit this simple description. In e-commerce sites such as Ebay, users of the network develop *trust* and *distrust* in *agents* in the network; websites such as Amazon let members express their likes and dislikes toward the purchased products; online review and news websites such as Epinions and Slashdot allow readers to approve or denounce reviews and articles; certain nodes in a computer network may be detected as *byzantine* by a sub-network, and communication through a byzantine node is considered unreliable. In all such cases, it is helpful to think of the edges between entities as being *signed* either positively or negatively.

The study of signed networks dates back to the early 1950s [1] where dislikes and distrusts were modeled as negative weight edges in a graph. A formal model encompassing different types of interpersonal relationships was proposed and notion of *balance* in signed graphs was defined.

We note that the nature and complexity of many graph problems change once negative edges are introduced. For example, the shortest-path problem in the presence of cycles with negative edges is known to be NP-hard. Consequently, solutions to problems in unsigned social networks are usually not immediately applicable to signed networks. In particular, signed link prediction has connections to social balance theory while no such connection exists for the standard (unsigned) link prediction task.

The proliferation of online *signed* networks, and the recent advances in social network analysis, including the problem of link prediction in particular, naturally led researchers to the problem of predicting the *sign* of a link in signed networks[3, 6]. We follow this line of work and consider the problem of predicting signs in a signed network. Our proposed methods for the problem are motivated by the *general theory of social balance*[1]. We build on the work of Leskovec et al.[6], driven by the realization that higher order cycles in a signed graph yield a "measure of imbalance" suggested by the general theory of social balance. We show how these measures can be successfully exploited for sign prediction. We also go beyond these simple measures of imbalance and propose a supervised machine learning approach that achieves state-of-the-art performance on datasets drawn from sources as diverse as Epinions, Slashdot and Wikipedia. Our largest network has more than 100k nodes and 800k edges. Our main contributions can be summarized as follows. First, we show how any quantitative measure of imbalance in a network can be used to derive a link prediction algorithm. We discuss different measures of imbalance that are derived from social balance theory and signed graph theory. In particular, we show that the *Katz* measure on a signed graph is quite naturally connected to a measure of imbalance. Second, we show that using measures of imbalance that depend on *higher order cycles* can improve the quality of sign prediction. The effect is more pronounced in the case of edges with zero *embeddedness*. The nodes of such edges, by definition, do not share any common neighbors. Third, our supervised learning approach to sign prediction uses features derived from longer cycles and achieves state-of-the-art performance. In particular, our method has smaller *false positive rate*, compared to the methods in [6]. Moreover, the performance improvement is consistent across diverse networks (in the sense of formation and composition of signed edges) such as Epinions, Slashdot and Wikipedia.

Our experiments with real-world networks show that not all relationships formed in a social network conform to the intuitions underlying social balance theory. Indeed, we find that real-world networks are too complex to be described by a simple formalism. Given the complexity of these networks, longer cycles seem to contain in them more useful information for predicting signs of links.

2. RELATED WORK

Signed networks have received attention in the last decade in the context of clustering and link prediction. The problem of predicting edge signs in a social network was first considered by Guha et al.[3], albeit in a slightly different setting. They develop a trust propagation framework to predict the trust (or distrust) between pairs of nodes. First, a combined matrix is derived from the adjacency matrix which captures all one-step propagations (corresponding to cases $k = 2$ and $k = 3$ in our k-cycle method). The propagated trusts and distrusts are then computed as a linear combination of powers of the combined matrix. They apply variants of their method on the Epinions network and find that higher iterations of propagation tend to have a beneficial effect on the accuracy of prediction.

Kunegis et al.[5] study the spectral properties of signed networks and use kernels derived from a signed variant of the graph Laplacian for link prediction. They also consider power sum of the adjacency matrix (up to degree 4) for link prediction. However, they do not propose any supervised learning approach that learns the coefficients in their models.

Leskovec et al.[6] first considered an explicit formulation of the sign prediction problem. Their prediction methods are based on the theory of social balance and status[7]. The idea is that the sign of an edge (i, j) should minimize the number of *unbalanced triangles* involving the edge (i, j), i.e. triangles with an odd number of negative edges (see Section 4). They also propose a supervised machine-learning formulation of the problem, and show that the features derived from different types of triangles, combined with first-order features of a node like the number of incoming positive edges, make better predictors of the edge sign. The prediction model is also shown to generalize fairly well across different online social networks. Their model, however, does not look beyond such local structures as triangles. These local features lead to impressive accuracies in the networks that they consider. Nevertheless, it is natural to ask if the acccuracy can be further boosted by considering higher order features.

3. PRELIMINARIES

For us, a graph will mean a signed graph unless otherwise stated. This formally means that $G = (V, E, \Sigma)$ where $V = \{1, 2, \ldots, |V|\}$ is a finite set of *nodes* or *vertices* of the graph. The set E consists of *edges* of the form $\{i, j\}$ or (i, j), for $i, j \in V$, depending on whether the graph is *undirected* or *directed* (we assume there are no self-loops). The third component of a graph is a mapping $\Sigma : E \to \{+1, -1\}$ giving a *sign* to each edge. We will assume that our graphs are connected (weakly connected if directed). We will use the terms 'network' and 'graph' interchangeably. An undirected graph has an associated *adjacency matrix* $A \in \{-1, 0, +1\}^{|V|\times|V|}$. For undirected graphs, A is symmetric, i.e. $A = A^T$, while for directed graphs it will not be symmetric in general. It will also be convenient to define the positive part A^+ and negative part A^- as: $A^+ := \max(A, 0)$, $A^- := \min(A, 0)$ where max/min are applied entry-wise. With these definitions, we have $A = A^+ + A^-$.

A *path* (of length or order k) in an undirected graph is a sequence $i_1, i_2, \ldots, i_{k+1}$ of vertices such that $\{i_j, i_{j+1}\}$ is an edge for $1 \le j \le k$. A *simple path* is a path with no repeated vertices. A *cycle* is a path with $i_1 = i_{k+1}$. A *simple cycle* is a cycle with no repeated vertices (except the first one). Similar definitions yield paths, simple paths, cycle and simple cycles in directed graphs. Denote the set of all order k cycles and simple cycles of a graph G by $C_k(G)$ and $SC_k(G)$ respectively. The *indicator* $\mathbf{1}[P]$ is 1 if predicate P is true and 0 otherwise. We let power take precedence over subscript, i.e. $A^k_{i,j}$ denotes $(A^k)_{i,j}$.

3.1 Problem set-up

We adopt the framework [3, 6] of predicting the sign of a single edge that has been suppressed, using the rest of the network. Formally, given a graph $G = (V, E, \Sigma)$, and a test edge $e_{\text{test}} \in E$, we want to predict $\Sigma(e_{\text{test}})$, using only the edges in $E - \{e_{\text{test}}\}$. When using a supervised machine learning approach it is convenient to think of $\{e' \in E - \{e_{\text{test}}\} : \Sigma(e') = +1\}$ and $\{e' \in E - \{e_{\text{test}}\} : \Sigma(e') = -1\}$ as the set of positive and negative examples respectively.

3.2 Basics of Social Balance Theory

We briefly review the rudiments of the theory of social balance. This theory rests on the premise that certain configurations of positive ('is a friend of' or 'trusts') and negative ('is an enemy of' or 'distrusts') edges between individuals are socially more plausible than others. A more detailed treatment can be found in [2, Chapter 5]. For example, in the case of three individuals a, b and c, the left two configurations below are more likely than the right two:

on the basis of sayings such as 'a friend of a friend is a friend' and 'an enemy of an enemy is a friend'. Accordingly, the first two triangles are called *balanced* while the latter two are said to be *unbalanced*. Formally, a complete undirected signed graph is called *balanced* iff all triangles in it are balanced. Of course, real world networks are not complete by any means. Hence, the notion of balance can be extended by using the idea of filling in missing entries. An undirected signed graph is called *balanced* iff it is possible to add signed edges to make it a balanced and complete graph. It turns out that this 'local' definition based on looking at triangles only is equivalent to a 'global' definition where we say that a graph is balanced if and only if its vertices can be divided into two mutually exclusive and exhaustive sets X and Y (with one of them possibly empty) such that all edges within X and within Y are positive while all edges with one end in X and the other in Y are negative.

The following theorem relates balance to the existence of simple cycles with an odd number of negative edges.

THEOREM 1. ([4, 1]) *A signed graph is balanced iff there are no simple cycles with odd number of negative edges.*

Motivated by this theorem, we call a cycle (simple or otherwise) *balanced* if it has an even number of negative edges and *unbalanced* otherwise.

4. METHODS BASED ON MEASURES OF SOCIAL IMBALANCE

The main idea developed in this section is that any quantitative measure of social imbalance in a graph can be used to design a link prediction algorithm. The sign prediction for a given edge is the one that minimizes the social imbalance in the resulting graph (once the signed edge has been added to the network).

In a complete graph, perfect balance, by definition, implies the absence of any unbalanced triangles. This motivates a simple measure of imbalance, namely the total number of unbalanced triangles in a graph. Thus, we define,

$$\mu_{\text{tri}}(G) := \sum_{\tilde{\sigma} \in SC_3(G)} \mathbf{1}[\tilde{\sigma} \text{ is unbalanced}] \quad (1)$$

A definition essentially similar to the one above appears in the recent work of van de Rijt [10, p. 103] who observes that the equivalence between $\mu_{\text{tri}}(G) = 0$ and G being balanced holds only for complete graphs.

For an incomplete graph, imbalance might manifest itself only if we look at longer simple cycles. Accordingly, we define a higher-order analogue of (1),

$$\mu_k^s(G) := \sum_{i=3}^{k} \beta_i \sum_{\tilde{\sigma} \in SC_i(G)} \mathbf{1}[\tilde{\sigma} \text{ is unbalanced}] \ . \quad (2)$$

where $k \geq 3$ and β_i's are coefficients weighting the relative contributions of unbalanced simple cycles of different lengths. If we choose a decaying choice of β_i, like $\beta_i = \beta^i$ for some $\beta \in (0, 1)$, then we can even define an infinite-order version $\mu_\infty^s(G)$ by setting $k = \infty$ above. It is clear that $\mu_\infty(\cdot)$ is a genuine measure of imbalance in the sense formalized by the following theorem which follows directly from Theorem 1).

THEOREM 2. *Fix a (possibly incomplete) graph G. Let $\beta_i > 0$ be any sequence such that $\mu_\infty^s(G)$ is well-defined. Then, $\mu_\infty(G) > 0$ iff G is unbalanced.*

This suggests that we could use $\mu_\infty(\cdot)$ as a measure of imbalance to derive link prediction algorithms. However, enumerating simple cycles of a graph is a hard problem. In particular, if we could count simple cycles of length n in a graph with n vertices in polynomial time, we would solve the NP-complete Hamiltonian cycle problem. To get around this computational issue, we slightly change the definition of $\mu_k(\cdot)$ to the following.

$$\mu_k(G) := \sum_{i=3}^{k} \beta_i \sum_{\sigma \in C_i(G)} \mathbf{1}[\sigma \text{ is unbalanced}] \ . \quad (3)$$

As before, we allow $k = \infty$ provided the β_i's decay sufficiently rapidly. The only difference between these definitions and the previous one is that here we sum over *all* cycles, not just simple ones. However, we still get a valid notion of imbalance as stated by the following result (proof will be given in a longer version of the paper).

THEOREM 3. *Fix a (possibly incomplete) graph G. Let $\beta_i > 0$ be any sequence such that $\mu_\infty(G)$ is well-defined. Then, $\mu_\infty(G) > 0$ iff G is unbalanced.*

The basic idea of using a measure of imbalance for predicting the sign of a given query link i, j, such that $i \neq j$ and $\{i, j\} \notin E$ is as follows. Given a graph G and query $\{i, j\}$ for $i, j \in V, i \neq j$, we construct two graphs: $G^{+(i,j)}$ and $G^{-(i,j)}$. These are obtained from G by augmenting its edge-set with $\{i, j\}$ and attaching a $+1$ and -1 sign to it respectively. Given a measure of imbalance, $\mu(\cdot)$, the predicted sign of $\{i, j\}$ is then simply:

$$\text{sign}\left(\mu\left(G^{-(i,j)}\right) - \mu\left(G^{+(i,j)}\right)\right) \ . \quad (4)$$

Note that, to be able to this quickly, we should use a $\mu(\cdot)$ for which the quantity (4) is efficiently computable. We now consider the measures mentioned in the previous subsection to ensure that this is indeed the case for them.

Somewhat surprisingly, for $\mu(\cdot) = \mu_3(\cdot)$, the prediction (4) simply amounts to computing the (i, j) entry in the matrix A^2 where A is the (signed) adjacency matrix of G. In fact, a more general result is true (proof will be given in a longer version of the paper).

THEOREM 4. *Let $G = (V, E, \Sigma)$ be an undirected signed graph and let $i \neq j$ be such that $\{i, j\} \notin E$. Let $G^{+(i,j)}$ and $G^{-(i,j)}$ be the augmented graphs as defined above. Then, for any $k \geq 2$,*

$$\sum_{\sigma \in C_k\left(G^{-(i,j)}\right)} \mathbf{1}[\sigma] - \sum_{\sigma \in C_k\left(G^{+(i,j)}\right)} \mathbf{1}[\sigma] = A_{i,j}^{k-1}$$

where $A \in \{-1, 0, +1\}^{|V| \times |V|}$ is the adjacency matrix of G.

Using Theorem 4, it is easy to see that

$$\text{sign}\left(\mu_k\left(G^{-(i,j)}\right) - \mu_k\left(G^{+(i,j)}\right)\right) = \text{sign}\left(\sum_{t=3}^{k} \beta_t A_{i,j}^{t-1}\right)$$

and that the above is true even for $k = \infty$. In the special case $\beta_k = \beta^{k-1}$ with $\beta < 1/\|A\|_2$, we can sum the above infinite series to get the Katz prediction rule for edge sign prediction: $\text{sign}\left(\left((I - \beta A)^{-1} - I - \beta A\right)_{i,j}\right)$. Katz has been successfully used as a link prediction method for *unsigned* networks [8] but here we see it reappearing for link prediction in *signed* networks from a social balance point of view. We find this connection between Katz and social balance intriguing and believe, to the best of our knowledge, that it has not been made before.

5. SUPERVISED METHOD BASED ON LONGER CYCLES

The methods derived from the measures of imbalance in the previous section rely on social balance theory for link prediction in signed networks. However, real world networks may not conform to the prediction of social balance theory or may do so only to a certain extent. To deal with this situation, we use measures such as Katz to derive *features* that can then be fed to a supervised machine learning algorithm along with the signs of the known edges in the network. We draw upon research in unsigned link prediction where the Katz measure has been empirically demonstrated to produce competitive results [8]. However, recent research [9] shows that learning the weights β_i based on supervised machine learning approaches tends to increase link prediction accuracy. It is thus natural to expect that the relative weights for cycles of various lengths may be better estimated by taking into account the evidence in the training data corresponding to the *given network*.

We pose the problem of predicting the sign of an observed link as a standard (binary) classification problem in machine learning, using positive and negative examples. Our training set consists of pairs $(e, \Sigma(e))$ where e ranges over edges whose signs are given to us and $\Sigma(e)$'s are the given signs. Given the dataset, we wish to learn a classifier that can predict the sign of a given test edge e_{test} that was not part of the training set.

We now extend the supervised learning approach of [6] by introducing features derived from *longer cycles*. In the process, we obtain supervised variants of the cycle-based sign prediction methods introduced in the previous section.

5.1 Features from Longer Cycles

Let us now describe the features of a *directed* edge $e = (i, j)$. Note that, unlike methods presented in Section 4, we here consider *directed* signed networks. Social balance theory has mostly been concerned with undirected network and hence the methods in Section 4 deal with undirected networks only. Here, we are weakening our reliance on social balance theory and can therefore naturally deal with directed graphs as well.

To motivate our longer cycle based features, let us first recall the feature construction used in Leskovec et al [6]. Fix an edge $e = (i, j)$. Consider an arbitary common neighbor (in an undirected sense) k of i and j. The link between i and k can be in 4 possible configurations: $i \xrightarrow{+} k$, $i \xleftarrow{+} k$ $i \xrightarrow{-} k$, or $i \xleftarrow{-} k$. Similarly, there are 4 possible configurations for the link between k and j. Thus, we can get a total of 16 features for the edge e by considering the number of common neighbors k in each of the $4 \times 4 = 16$ configurations.

This corresponds to a supervised variant of k-cycle method for $k = 3$. In terms of matrix powers, these sixteen features are nothing but the (i, j) entry in the sixteen matrices: $(A^{b_1})^{t_1} \cdot (A^{b_2})^{t_3}$ where $b_1, b_2 \in \{\pm\}$ and $t_i \in \{T, 1\}$. A criticism against using only these triangle-based features is that there could be many people in the social network who do not share friends. In fact, this is the case in most of the net-

Table 1: Network Statistics

	Epinions	Slashdot	Wikipedia
No. of nodes	131,828	82,144	7,065
No. of edges	840,799	549,202	103,561
Fraction of + edges	0.8529	0.7740	0.7884
Fraction of − edges	0.1471	0.2260	0.2116
Normalized MOI-3	0.0950	0.1335	0.2165

works that are used in [6]. The reason their method is able to predict well on such pairs is that they additionally use 7 "degree-type" features like in-degree and out-degree (and their signed variants). Thus, the prediction for edge with zero emdeddedness (embeddedness refers to the number of common neighbors of the vertices of an edge) relies completely on such degree based features. These degree features tend to introduce a bias in learning. For example, a node that is predisposed to make positive relationships, biases the classifier to predict positive relationships.

This criticism thus necessitates incorporating features from higher-order cycles. Generalizing the construction for $k = 3$ case, for the edge (i, j), the features can be obtained as the (i, j) entries in the 4^{k-1} matrices

$$\left(A^{b_1}\right)^{t_1} \cdot \left(A^{b_2}\right)^{t_2} \cdots \left(A^{b_{k-1}}\right)^{t_{k-1}}, \tag{5}$$

with $b_i \in \{\pm\}, t_i \in \{T, 1\}$.

Note that the number of features is exponential in k, and therefore it is not feasible to obtain features from arbitrarily long cycles. We use supervised higher order cycle (HOC) methods for $k \leq 5$ in the experiments.

The number of features can quickly become unmanageable, and computationally infeasible, as soon as k is beyond 5. While dimensionality of the feature space may be the primary concern, the combinatorial nature of the features also raises the following intuitive concern: the interpretability of features rendered by high-order cycles, say when $k = 6$, composed of different signs and directions, is a challenge. For example, it is intuitively hard to appreciate the difference between two walks $i \xrightarrow{+} k_1 \xrightarrow{+} k_2 \xrightarrow{-} k_3 \xrightarrow{+} k_4 \xrightarrow{+} j$ and $i \xrightarrow{+} k_1 \xrightarrow{+} k_2 \xleftarrow{-} k_3 \xrightarrow{+} k_4 \xrightarrow{+} j$.

With this realization, one way to reduce the number of features yet retain the information in longer cycles, is to consider the underlying undirected graph, ignoring the directions. In particular, the kth order features will be from the matrices $A^{b_1} \cdot A^{b_2} \cdots A^{b_{k-1}}$ with $b_i \in \{\pm\}$. Since we are considering the undirected graph, we ensure that the features are symmetric by summing features of the form $A^{b_1} A^{b_2}$ and $A^{b_2} A^{b_1}$. Thus the number of k-th order features to compute is reduced to $O(2^k)$ from $O(4^k)$. Though the number of features is still exponential in k, the construction of features becomes much easier for small values of k.

We use a simple logistic regression where the imbalance of an edge is modeled as a linear combination of the features, which are imbalances in cycles of various lengths and characteristics themselves. Let $\Phi : V \times V \to \mathbb{R}^p$ denote the feature map. We have, $P(\Sigma(u, v) = +1) = 1/(1 + \exp(-w_0 - \sum_{i=1}^{p} w_i \Phi_i(u, v)))$. The prediction for edge (u, v) is given by $\text{sign}(\langle w, \Phi(u, v)\rangle)$.

6. EXPERIMENTS

We consider three online social networks — Epinions, Slashdot and Wikipedia[6] (downloaded from `snap.stanford.`

Table 2: Accuracy of HOC Methods

	Epinions	Slashdot	Wikipedia
HOC-3	0.9014	0.8303	0.8424
HOC-5	0.9080	0.8469	0.8605

Table 3: False Positive Rate of HOC Methods

	Epinions	Slashdot	Wikipedia
HOC-3	0.4756	0.5575	0.5488
HOC-5	0.4441	0.5070	0.4817

edu). All the networks have explicit sign labels on the links. Refer to Table 1 for the statistics of the networks. Note that MOI-3 is normalized by the total number of triangles. Refer to [6] for description of the networks. We have 2 families of methods: one based on measures of imbalance (MOI) from Section 4 and the other based on the supervised machine learning approach involving higher order cycles (HOC) described in Section 5. Both families depend on a parameter $k \geq 3$ that denotes the order of the cycles that the method is based on. For MOI, we consider k up to 10 and for HOC we consider $k = 3, 4, 5$. Note that the set of features used by HOC-$(k+1)$ is a strict superset of the features used by HOC-k. We also remind the reader that MOI-3 and HOC-3 are the methods considered in [6].

We evaluate and compare MOI methods using a *leave-one-out* type methodology: each edge in the network is successively removed and the method tries to predict the sign of that edge using the rest of the network. For HOC methods, we resort to 10-*fold cross-validation*. We (randomly) created 10 disjoint test folds each consisting of 10% of the total number of edges in the network. For each test fold, the remaining 90% of the edges serve as the training set. For a given test fold, the feature extraction and logistic model training happens on a graph with the test edges removed. We report accuracies and false-positive rates by averaging them over the 10 folds.

6.1 Results

Our experiments on the three online social networks show that higher order cycles benefit the accuracy of sign prediction and lower the false positive rate. Furthermore, the results are consistent across the three diverse networks. Figure 2 shows the accuracy of MOI based methods. Note that the accuracy is shown for edges with embeddedness under certain threshold. Firstly, we see that accuracy is non-decreasing in embeddedness threshold. Next, it is clear that higher-order methods perform significantly better than MOI-3 (triangles) method. Finally, the performance boost is large for edges with low embeddedness. This is expected as edges of low embeddedness by definition do not have many common neighbors for their end-points, and higher-order cycles have relatively better information for such edges than others. We also observe from our experiments that beyond $k = 5$, the performance gain is not very significant.

Figure 1 shows the distribution of edge embeddedness in the data sets. Observe that a significant fraction of the edges have low embeddedness in all the networks. Thus, for a good fraction of edges, we observe a large increase in accuracy of higher-order MOI based methods, in all the data sets.

The results for the supervised HOC methods are shown in Tables 2 & 3 and Figure 3. In all the data sets, there is a small improvement in accuracy by using higher order cycles (HOC-5), as shown in Table 2. The false positive rate, however, reveals a more interesting phenomenon in Table 3. Indeed, higher order methods (such as HOC-5) significantly reduce the false positive rate as compared to that of HOC-3. However Figure 3 shows that, unlike MOI based methods, edge embeddedness does not seem to affect the decrease in false positive rate for HOC methods. We see this trend across all the data sets.

7. CONCLUSION

We see that longer cycles significantly benefit sign prediction, and do so consistently across many real-world networks. We presented a framework to obtain a link prediction algorithm, using any quantitative measure of imbalance. Higher order cycles came as a natural generalization of local triangles, and furthermore, the generalization is well-founded by the general theory of social balance. Finally, we observe that the edges appearing in real-world signed networks do not necessarily conform to the intuitions underlying the social balance theory, and longer cycles contain more useful information for predicting edge signs.

8. ACKNOWLEDGMENTS

This research was supported by NSF grant CCF-0916309 and DOD Army grant W911NF-10-1-0529.

9. REFERENCES

[1] D. Cartwright and F. Harary. Structure balance: A generalization of Heider's theory. *Psychological Review*, 63(5):277–293, 1956.

[2] D. Easley and J. Kleinberg. *Networks, Crowds, and Markets*. Cambridge University Press, 2010.

[3] R. Guha, R. Kumar, P. Raghavan, and A. Tomkins. Propagation of trust and distrust. In *WWW*, pages 403–412, 2004.

[4] F. Harary. On the notion of balance of a signed graph. *Michigan Mathematical Journal*, 2(2):143–146, 1953.

[5] J. Kunegis, S. Schmidt, A. Lommatzsch, J. Lerner, E. W. D. Luca, and S. Albayrak. Spectral analysis of signed graphs for clustering, prediction and visualization. In *SDM*, pages 559–570, 2010.

[6] J. Leskovec, D. Huttenlocher, and J. Kleinberg. Predicting positive and negative links in online social networks. In *WWW*, pages 641–650, 2010.

[7] J. Leskovec, D. Huttenlocher, and J. Kleinberg. Signed networks in social media. In *CHI*, pages 1361–1370, 2010.

[8] D. Liben-Nowell and J. Kleinberg. The link-prediction problem for social networks. *Journal of the American Society for Information Science and Technology*, 58(7):1019–1031, 2007.

[9] Z. Lu, B. Savas, W. Tang, and I. S. Dhillon. Supervised link prediction using multiple sources. In *ICDM*, pages 923–928, 2010.

[10] A. van de Rijt. The micro-macro link for the theory of structural balance. *Journal of Mathematical Sociology*, 35(1):94–113, 2011.

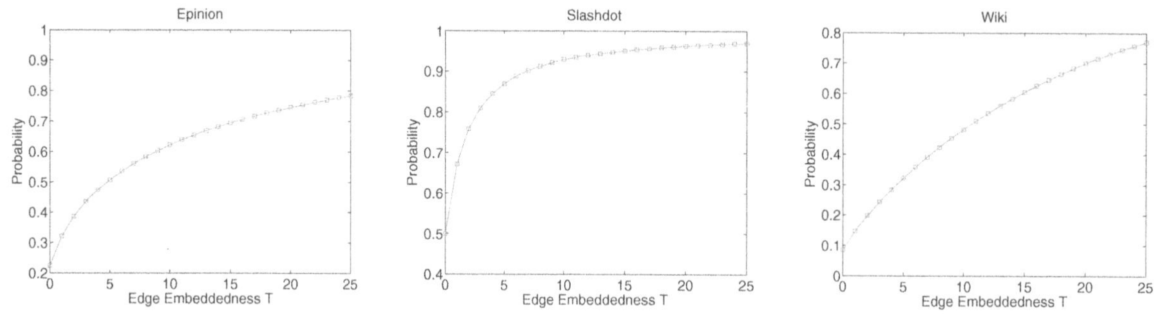

Figure 1: Cumulative Probability Distribution of Edge Embeddedness. These plots show the fraction of edges with embeddedness *no more* than T for various thresholds T. We see that these networks have a significant fraction of low embeddedness edges. For example, the fraction of edges with *zero* embeddedness (edges whose end-points do not share any common neighbor) is about 20%, 50% and 10% for Epinions, Slashdot and Wikipedia respectively.

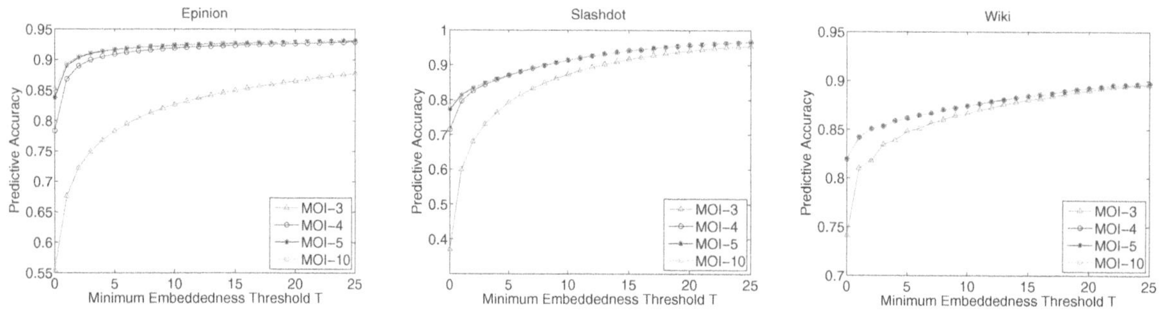

Figure 2: Accuracy of Measures of Imbalance (MOI) Based Methods for $k = 3, 4, 5, 10$. These plots show the accuracy of MOI-k methods for edges with embeddedness *at least* T for various thresholds T. We see that the difference in the performance of MOI-3 and higher order methods is larger when edges with lower embeddedness are considered. We also see that the improvement obtained by going beyond order 5 is not very significant.

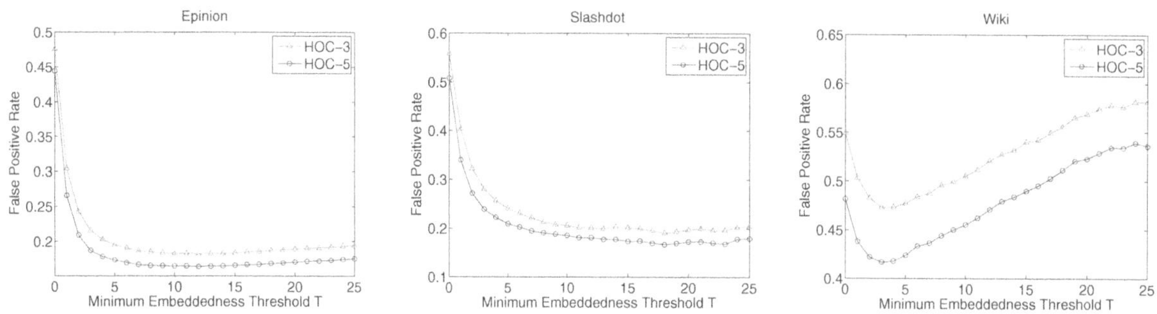

Figure 3: False Positive Rates of Higher Order Cycle (HOC) Methods for $k = 3, 5$. These plots show the false positive rate of HOC-k methods for edges with embeddedness *at least* T for various thresholds T. We see that considering higher order cycles has the benefit of significantly reducing false-positives while simultaneously achieving slightly better overall accuracy (see Table 2). However, unlike what we see for MOI methods, here the improvement does not seem to depend strongly on edge embeddedness. The false positive rates for HOC-4 are very similar to that of HOC-5 and hence are not shown.

Structural Link Analysis and Prediction in Microblogs

Dawei Yin Liangjie Hong Brian D. Davison
Department of Computer Science & Engineering, Lehigh University
Bethlehem, PA 18015 USA
{day207, lih307, davison}@cse.lehigh.edu

ABSTRACT

With hundreds of millions of participants, social media services have become commonplace. Unlike a traditional social network service, a microblogging network like Twitter is a hybrid network, combining aspects of both social networks and information networks. Understanding the structure of such hybrid networks and predicting new links are important for many tasks such as friend recommendation, community detection, and modeling network growth. We note that the link prediction problem in a hybrid network is different from previously studied networks. Unlike the information networks and traditional online social networks, the structures in a hybrid network are more complicated and informative. We compare most popular and recent methods and principles for link prediction and recommendation. Finally we propose a novel structure-based personalized link prediction model and compare its predictive performance against many fundamental and popular link prediction methods on real-world data from the Twitter microblogging network. Our experiments on both static and dynamic data sets show that our methods noticeably outperform the state-of-the-art.

Categories and Subject Descriptors: H.3.3 [Information Storage and Retrieval]: Information Search and Retrieval

General Terms: Algorithms, Experimentation,Performance

Keywords: link prediction, link analysis, Twitter

1. INTRODUCTION

The use of online social networks and social media in general has surged in recent years. In this work, we focus on the understanding of the use of one particular type of social service—that of the microblogging network. In microblog services such as Twitter, Yammer and Google Buzz, participants form an explicit social network by "following" (subscribing to) another user and thus automatically receive the (short) messages generated by the target user. Unlike some online social networks such as Facebook, LinkedIn or Myspace, a followed user has the option but not the requirement to similarly follow back. Thus, relationships in these social networks may be asymmetric, leading to three kinds of link relationships between users A and B. If A follows B, we say that A is a follower of B, and that B is a friend of A. If A and B both follow each other, we consider them mutual friends or reciprocal friends.

Thus, user B in a microblog service can generate messages, which are generally public and searchable, and any followers of B, such as A, will automatically receive those messages along with messages generated by all other users that A follows. The combination of multiple message intentions and asymmetry of connections has led some to call microblogging services such as Twitter "hybrid networks" [14, 22]. They are hybrid not just because they can carry multiple types of messages, but also because participants create links for multiple reasons—to be social (e.g., to connect online to existing offline social contacts) or to link to information sources. With multiple types of users, it may be difficult to understand how microblogging networks grow and evolve. In a hybrid social-information network, there are two viewpoints to consider. In an information network, the link prediction problem is like the recommendation problem, which is to recommend an information source to an information consumer. In a social network, the problem is to recommend friends to the users, as introduced by Liben-Nowell and Kleinberg [16]. If we can predict the next link that a user will likely create, we will 1) have a model of the user's interests that may be of value in recommending new links (e.g., as in Twitter's recently introduced "Who to follow" friend suggestions, and many third-party suggestion services) and in detecting communities; 2) be closer to modeling the network's overall growth processes; and, 3) be able to simplify the task of adding that link when the user wishes to do so.

In this paper, we analyze link structures in Twitter to predict future links. Our contributions are as follows. 1) We are the first to experimentally compare many popular link prediction methods in a microblogging network. Furthermore, we also compare with matrix factorization—a popular method of recommender systems. 2) We propose a novel structure-based approach to link prediction. Empirical results on ego-centric networks of Twitter users show that our method can outperform state-of-the-art methods on this task.

1.1 Related work

There are several fundamental kinds of link prediction methods, such as structural methods, random walk methods and supervised methods. Liben-Nowell et al. surveyed an array of methods for link prediction in online social networks [16, 17].

One branch of structural methods is based on the local structure, such as *common neighbors*, *Jaccard coefficient* and *Adamic/Adar* [1] which refines the simple counting features by weighting rarer features more heavily. The *preferential attachment* method supposes that the likelihood that a new edge involves node v is proportional to $\Gamma(v)$, the number of neighbors of v. Based on global structure information, Clauset et al. [4] present a general technique for inferring hierarchical structure from network data and show that the existence of the hierarchy can simultaneously explain and quantitatively reproduce many commonly observed topological properties of networks.

Another approach utilizes random walk methods such as *Rooted PageRank* [16, 17] which is a variation of PageRank [21] that measures the stationary probability of each node in a random walk that returns to the root with some probability in each step. Weng et al. [24] try to identify influential users of micro-blogging services by using LDA to analyze user interests. Yin et al. propose a method which augments the original graph with attribute nodes, and then uses random walk to calculate link relevance [26, 27]. *SimRank* [8] recursively defines the similarity of two nodes and can also be interpreted in terms of a random walk. The most recent random walk-like method is *PropFlow* [18] which calculates the probability that a restricted random walk starting at node v_i ends at v_j in l steps. Katz [10] proposes a path-based method, which defines a measure that sums over the collection of all paths from v_i to v_j, and assigns more weight to shorter paths. Recently, Backstrom et al. [2] proposed a supervised random walk method which combines information from the network structure with node and edge level attributes. Supervised learning then adjusts the weights on different attributes to guide a random walk on the graph.

In supervised methods, the link prediction problem is usually considered as a classification problem. Such methods extract features from training data and can include both topological features (as in [9]) and node features. Hasan et al. [7] use different kinds of features, such as proximity features, aggregated features and topological features, and also compare different kinds of classifiers. More recently, Lichtenwalter et al. [18] examine important factors in the link prediction problem and present a classification framework which employs their *PropFlow* as a feature.

If you consider link prediction as a recommendation problem, a popular method is matrix factorization [13, 12, 11, 19] where the algorithms find hidden features for users and items by factorizing the observation matrix. However, those methods are designed for a user-item pair, and never before used for link prediction in social network.

There is other related research about link prediction [20, 23] and hybrid networks. Kwak et al. [14] find that the relationship of following and being followed on Twitter is not reciprocal, unlike most other social networking sites such as Myspace and Facebook. Romero and Kleinberg [22] also introduce the hybrid network concept and explore the directed closure process in Twitter. Recently, Golder et al. [6] discuss prediction specifically in Twitter. They analyze several principles for link prediction, such as shared interests, shared followers, and mutuality. They also discuss their user study results in [5].

2. LINK PREDICTION

Here we introduce our prediction framework based on link structures. In a hybrid social-information network, structures can reflect many scenarios that may be useful for capturing users' interests and predicting potential links. In Figure 1, we can see some examples of various structural meanings: a) User v_u may be interested in v_c, because other similar users with v_u are following v_c. b) User v_u may want to follow v_c, because they may be friends with each other in real life and they are willing to use microblog as social networks. c) User v_u may want to follow v_c, because v_u is following other users which are following v_i while v_c is also following v_i and they may share the same interests. With these three examples, we

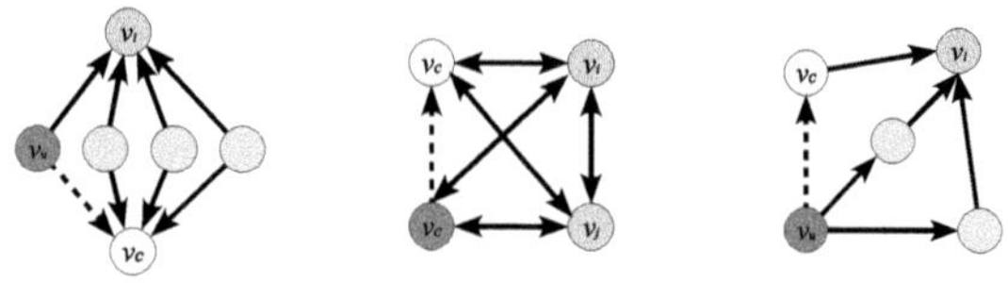

(a) (b) (c)

Figure 1: Examples of relationships between user v_u and candidate v_c.

have already seen some meanings of structures. We wish to design a model to exhaust such structural information for predicting new links.

Suppose that we want to recommend other users which user u may know or be interested in following. The problem we consider is that given a user u and the whole network G, what is the probability that user v_u follows user v_c: $P(v_u \rightarrow v_c|G)$. We will rank candidate users according to this equation, and the top N users will be recommended to user v_u. To calculate $P(v_u \rightarrow v_c|G)$, theoretically, each intermediate user/vertex v_i can contribute some structural information which represents two parts: the link structure between v_i and v_c and the link structure between v_u and v_i. Now let us define the set of target users to which we will recommend some friends V_u, the set of intermediate users which we will exhaust the structural information V_i, and the set of candidate users for recommendation V_c. Assuming that $P(v_u \rightarrow v_c|G)$ is the linear combination of all possible intermediate users/vertices' contribution, we have

$$P(v_u \rightarrow v_c|G) = \textstyle\sum_{v_i \in V_i} b_{v_i,v_c} \cdot a_{v_u,v_i}$$

Let b_{v_i,v_c} represent the contribution of the structural information between v_i and v_c, which can be considered as the strength of v_i's recommendation for v_c and a_{v_u,v_i} represent the contribution of the structural information between v_u and v_i, which can be considered as the score of v_u liking a recommendation of v_i. We will denote with A the matrix with elements $A_{v_u,v_i} = a_{v_u,v_i}$ and with A_{v_u} the column of A corresponding to v_u. Similarly, $B \in \mathcal{R}^{|V_i|\times|V_c|}$ with column vector B_{v_c}. Let $R_{v_u} = [r_{v_u,v_1}, r_{v_u,v_2}, ... r_{v_u,v_n}]$ represent the current friends snapshot of v_u in which $r_{v_u,v_i} = 1$ means v_i is a current friend of v_u and $r_{v_u,v_i} = 0$ means v_i is the current follower-only of v_u.

Elsewhere [25] we report that only 12% of follower-only users of all follower-only users become new friends; thus it is perhaps reasonable to use follower-only users as negative samples. Then,

$$\hat{R} = A^T B$$

In probabilistic view, we define the conditional distribution over the current friends.

$$p(R|A,B,\sigma^2) = \textstyle\prod_{v_u \in V_u} \prod_{v_c \in V_c} \left[\mathcal{N}(R|A_{v_u}^T B_{v_c}, \sigma^2)\right]^{I_{v_u,v_c}}$$

where $\mathcal{N}(R|A_{v_u}^T B_{v_c}, \sigma^2)$ is the probability function of the gaussian distribution with mean $A_{v_u}^T B_{v_c}$ and variance σ^2. I_{v_u,v_c} is the indicator function for selecting observed training data. For pair (v_u, v_c), if we use it as our training data, then $I_{v_u,v_c} = 1$, otherwise, $I_{v_u,v_c} = 0$. We also place zero-mean spherical Gaussian priors on the two structural parts A and B

$$p(A|\sigma_A^2) = \prod_{v_u \in V_u} \mathcal{N}(A_{v_u}|0, \sigma_A^2 \mathbf{I})$$

$$p(B|\sigma_B^2) = \prod_{v_c \in V_c} \mathcal{N}(B_{v_c}|0, \sigma_B^2 \mathbf{I})$$

The log of the posterior distribution over R,A and B is given by

$$
\begin{aligned}
&\ln p(A, B|R, \sigma^2, \sigma_A^2, \sigma_b^2) \\
=& -\frac{1}{2\sigma^2} \sum_{v_u \in V_u} \sum_{v_c \in V_c} I_{v_u,v_c}(R_{v_u,v_c} - A_{v_u}^T B_{v_c})^2 \\
& -\frac{1}{2\sigma_A^2} \sum_{v_u \in V_u} A_{v_u}^T A_{v_u} - \frac{1}{2\sigma_B^2} \sum_{v_c \in V_c} B_{v_c}^T B_{v_c} \\
& -\frac{1}{2}\left(\sum_{v_u \in V_u} \sum_{v_c \in V_c} I_{v_u,v_c} \right) \ln \sigma^2 - \frac{1}{2}|V_u||V_i| \ln \sigma_A^2 \\
& -\frac{1}{2}|V_c||V_i| \ln \sigma_B^2 + C
\end{aligned}
$$

where σ_A and σ_B control the smoothing factor of A and B. Let $\sigma_B = \sigma_A$, and then maximizing the log of the posterior distribution is equivalent to

$$
\begin{aligned}
\min_{A,B} \quad & \sum_{v_u} \sum_{v_c} I_{v_u,v_c}(R_{v_u,v_c} - A_{v_u}^T B_{v_c})^2 \\
& +\lambda_1(\|A\|_{Fro}^2 + \|B\|_{Fro}^2)
\end{aligned}
$$

where $\lambda_1 = \sigma^2/\sigma_A^2$, is actually the smoothing factor and $\|\cdot\|_{Fro}^2$ denotes the Frobenius norm. Next, we need to involve structural regularization into the objective function.

2.1 Structural regularization

Elsewhere [25] we show that more than 90% of new links go to people two hops away from user (the ego). Intuitively, if two users v_i and v_j are far away on the graph, that is, the shortest path between v_i and v_j is too long, their structural information can be ignored. We can define the set of the effective structures S^e. For example, if we define that the structures with only one hop are effective, the set of effective structures will be $S^e = \{\Leftarrow, \Rightarrow, \Leftrightarrow\}$ and if we define that all structures with up to two hops are effective, then the set of effective structures will be $S^e = \{\Leftarrow, \Rightarrow, \Leftrightarrow, \Rightarrow\Rightarrow, \Rightarrow\Leftarrow, \Rightarrow\Leftrightarrow, \Leftarrow\Leftarrow, \Leftarrow\Rightarrow, \Leftarrow\Leftrightarrow, \Leftrightarrow\Leftarrow, \Leftrightarrow\Rightarrow, \Leftrightarrow\Leftrightarrow\}$. Let S_{v_i,v_j} represent the set of all possible structures from v_i to v_j and $S^e_{v_i,v_j}$ represent the set of all effective structures from v_i to v_j—$S^e_{v_i,v_j} = S_{v_i,v_j} \cap S^e$. Thus, if $S^e_{v_u,v_i} = \emptyset$ where $v_u \in V_u$ and $v_i \subset V_i$, then let $a_{v_u,v_i} = 0$ and similarly, if $S^e_{v_i,v_c} = \emptyset$ where $v_i \in V_i$ and $v_c \in V_c$, then let $b_{v_i,v_c} = 0$.

Beginning at some user $v_u \in V_u$, intuitively, if the structures of $(v_u \leftrightsquigarrow v_i)$ and $(v_u \leftrightsquigarrow v_j)$ are similar or same, the contribution scores of a_{v_u,v_i} and a_{v_u,v_j} should be similar. Following this intuition, we make constraints on structural scores matrix A, and define a structural regularization function $\mathcal{S}(A)$ to constrain similar scores on similar structures.

$$
\mathcal{S}(A) = \frac{\sum_{v_u \in V_u} \sum_{v_i \in V_i} \sum_{v_j \in V_i} \mathcal{W}_{v_u}(v_i,v_j)(a_{v_u,v_i} - a_{v_u,v_j})^2}{\sum_{v_u \in V_u} \sum_{v_i \in V_i} \sum_{v_j \in V_i} \mathcal{W}_{v_u}(v_i,v_j)}
$$

where $\mathcal{W}_{v_u}(v_i, v_j)$ is the measurement of similarity on structures attached on v_u: the more similar the structures of $(v_u \leftrightsquigarrow v_i)$ and $(v_u \leftrightsquigarrow v_j)$ are, the higher value the $\mathcal{W}_{v_u}(v_i, v_j)$ is. There are many kinds of methods to measure the structural similarity. Here, We list two:

Binary weighting if $S^e_{v_u,v_i} = S^e_{v_u,v_j}$, then $\mathcal{W}_{v_u}(v_i, v_j) = 1$, otherwise $\mathcal{W}_{v_u}(v_i, v_j) = 0$.

Cosine weighting let $N_{S^e_{v_u,v_i}}$ represent the vector of quantified effective structures of $(v_u \leftrightsquigarrow v_i)$, that is, $N_{S^e_{v_u,v_i}} = [n_{v_u \Rightarrow v_i}, n_{v_u \Leftarrow v_i}, n_{v_u \Leftrightarrow v_i}, n_{v_u \Rightarrow\Rightarrow v_i} \cdots]$, where $n_{v_u \Rightarrow\Rightarrow v_i}$ is the number of $\Rightarrow\Rightarrow$ path from v_u to v_i. Then, the cosine similarity is calculated as $\mathcal{W}_{v_u}(v_i, v_j) = \frac{N_{S^e_{v_u,v_i}} \cdot N_{S^e_{v_u,v_j}}}{\|N_{S^e_{v_u,v_i}}\| \cdot \|N_{S^e_{v_u,v_j}}\|}$

We also notice that if we take $S^e = \{\Leftarrow, \Rightarrow, \Leftrightarrow\}$, the two kinds of weighting are equivalent, because $n_{v_u \Rightarrow v_i}$, $n_{v_u \Leftarrow v_i}$ and $n_{v_u \Leftrightarrow v_i}$ only can be 0 or 1. Similarly, we add the structural constraints to B, and we have

$$
\mathcal{S}(B) = \frac{\sum_{v_i \in V_i} \sum_{v_c \in V_c} \sum_{v_k \in V_c} \mathcal{W}_{v_i}(v_c,v_k)(b_{v_i,v_c} - b_{v_i,v_k})^2}{\sum_{v_i \in V_i} \sum_{v_c \in V_c} \sum_{v_k \in V_c} \mathcal{W}_{v_i}(v_c,v_k)}
$$

The objective function $\mathcal{O}$ becomes

$$
\begin{aligned}
\min_{A,B} \mathcal{O} \quad = \quad & \sum_{v_u \in V_u} \sum_{v_c \in V_c} I_{v_u,v_c}(R_{v_u,v_c} - A_{v_u}^T B_{v_c})^2 \\
& +\lambda_1 \|A_{v_u}\|_{Fro}^2 + \lambda_1 \|B\|_{Fro}^2 \\
& +\lambda_2 \mathcal{S}(A) + \lambda_2 \mathcal{S}(B) \qquad (1)
\end{aligned}
$$

where λ_2 is the structural factor tuning the weight of structural regularization. In the above model, we see the two parameters λ_1 controls the weight of smoothing and λ_2 controls the weight of regularization. The selected training links are represented by I_{v_u,v_c}.

2.2 Prediction in ego-centric networks

We call the above model the global model because the prediction is from the global network and performs collaborative filtering among all V_u. The global model will run on the whole graph to make predictions for a specific user and it will take a relatively long time to finish the computation; however, sometimes users perform interactive behaviors—such as requesting an instant recommendation. In this case, the global model may not work because of such long term computation. Secondly, the friendship network of some users may be already stable [25] and they may not want to add new friends.

It is necessary to make instant prediction for the users who are eager to get new friends. Unfortunately, directly reducing the model to fit the local structures of user v_u will cause overfitting. Thus, here we introduce a local model.

Considering the extreme case that only one user v_u requests new friends, the matrix R and A will reduce to only vectors R_{v_u} and A_{v_u} and a personalized method is necessary. We recall that the meaning of A and B, a_{v_u,v_i} can be considered as the probability of v_u trusting the recommendation of v_i and b_{v_i,v_c} can be considered as the probability of v_i recommending v_c. For b_{v_i,v_c}, because we know the current friendship network of v_u and also the structural information of v_i, we can make B personalized for v_u—B_{v_u}, that is, b_{v_u,v_i,v_c} means the probability of v_i recommending v_c for v_u, given the structure information of v_i. For some specific user v_u, we assume that v_u is interested in all his friends. Given the structure of some path between v_i and v_c $(v_i \leftrightsquigarrow v_c)$, we can use the following equation to get the approximation value of b_{v_u,v_i,v_c}:

$$
\beta_{v_u,v_c,v_i} = \frac{\sum_{v_k \in V_{v_u \rightarrow}} \mathcal{W}_{v_i}(v_c,v_k)}{\sum_{v_k \in V} \mathcal{W}_{v_i}(v_c,v_k)}
$$

where $v_u \in V_u$, $v_c \in V_c$ and $v_i \in V_i$. The above actually calculates the fraction of the number of v_u's friends who share similar structures with v_c over the number of all users who share similar structures with v_c. If the value β_{v_u,v_c,v_i} is larger, then there will be a larger probability that v_u will follow v_c. Then similarly as in section 2, for some specific targeting user v_u we let

$$p(A_{v_u}|\sigma_A^2) = \mathcal{N}(A_{v_u}|0, \sigma_A^2\mathbf{I})$$
$$p(B|\beta_{v_u}, \sigma_K^2) = \prod_{v_c \in V_c} \mathcal{N}(B_{v_c}|\beta_{v_u,v_c}, \sigma_B^2\mathbf{I})$$

Then we have the objective function $\mathcal{O}_{v_u}$ for v_u:

$$\min_{A,B} \mathcal{O}_{v_u} = \sum_{v_c \in V_c} I_{v_u,v_c}(R_{v_u,v_c} - A_{v_u}^T B_{v_c})^2 + \lambda_1 \|A_{v_u}\|^2 + \lambda_1 \|B - \beta_u\|_{Fro}^2 + \lambda_2 \mathcal{S}(A_{v_u}) + \lambda_2 \mathcal{S}(B) \quad (2)$$

2.3 Solving the model

Solutions for Equations 1 and 2 are quite similar. One simple method is gradient descent. Intuitively, the structure rarely contributes negative effects and usually a user v_u likes some kinds of users or does not care about some other kinds of users. In the quantified observed matrix R, we also use 1 for current v_u's friends and 0 to represent links that v_u does not care about. From the Section 2.2, we also involve a guidance value—β. All these reasons lead us to constrain A and B to be nonnegative. Nonnegative matrix factorization has been researched for many years [15, 3].

The objective function $\mathcal{O}$ and $\mathcal{O}_{v_u}$ in Eq. 1 and Eq. 2 are not convex in both A and B together and it is realistic to expect an algorithm to find the global minima. The process we use for solving $\mathcal{O}$ and $\mathcal{O}_{v_u}$ in Equations 1 and 2 is to use an iterative algorithm following the methods in in [15, 3] to derive multiplicative update rules. The proof by Lee and Seung [15] suggests that the objective function will be nonincreasing under such update rules.

3. EXPERIMENTS

In this section, we describe our prediction experiments. Our method is only based on structural information of the social graph; thus for comparison methods, we also mainly focus on structure-based methods which do not involve user properties or content.

3.1 Data set and evaluation

In link prediction experiments, we use the same 979 Twitter users as in [25] and their immediate neighbors (979 ego users and their neighbors) that were collected to build a network for the link prediction task. In total, there are 211,559 unique users. For our experiments, we employed two kinds of evaluation methods.

Static Evaluation. Based on the 979 users' ego network snapshot on April 5th 2010, for each target user whose number of friends is larger than ten, we remove five links to friends. The prediction task is then to use the pruned networks to find the missing links. This evaluation method is widely used in the link prediction literature [4, 26, 27]. We use this process both for parameter tuning and for model analysis.

Dynamic Evaluation. We also monitored the changes in the 979 users' friendships and recorded the new links established between April 5th and May 12th [25]. Here, the prediction task is based on the April 5th network snapshot to predict new friends in the following months.

For validation purposes, we also run our experiments on a second static Twitter data set (described below in Section 3.6). Precision, recall and F-measure are calculated in the standard manner, and our main measurement is the F-measure based in the break even point.

3.2 Baselines

In this section, we analyze and discuss simple predictors and principles to show the difficulty of this problem. Daily monitored data shows that more than 90% of new users are within two hops and also their relationship [25]. Golder et al. [6, 5] discuss link prediction in Twitter, analyzing several principles for link prediction, such as shared interests, shared followers, and mutuality. Romero and Kleinberg [22] also introduce the directed closure process in Twitter tie formation. Here, we re-implement and compare the simple predictors which are from the principles described in [22, 6, 5].

Method	Static	Dynamic
Shared followers	0.078	0.119
Shared friends	0.061	0.083
Shared mutual	0.074	0.086
Common neighbors	0.071	0.116
Katz (l=2)	0.094	0.086

Table 1: Simple predictor analysis (F-measure).

To represent the principle *Shared Interests*, we use the predictor: the number of shared friends. A shared interest is best represented by the relationship chain $v_u \rightarrow X \leftarrow v_c$. Similarly, *Shared Audience* ($v_u \leftarrow X \rightarrow v_c$) is measured by the number of shared followers. For *Transitivity* [6, 5] or the *Directed Closure Process* [22], we use Katz's methods with degree length $l = 2$, which is equivalent to the number of paths $v_u \rightarrow X \rightarrow v_c$. We also test *Shared Mutual Friends*. *Shared Neighbors* is just the count of the total number of neighbors (both friends and followers) without considering direction. The results are shown in Table 1.

From Table 1 we can see that all simple predictors provide similar performance—around .10 F-measure. We notice that the shared friends predictor performs worse than others, and that implies that two users sharing the same interests may not be particularly interested in following each other. Overall, simply using any single predictor cannot generate good results. Better methods are necessary.

3.3 Parameter analysis

In this section, we analyze our two models, and tune parameters on static data. In the experiments, we use the snapshots of the target user's friendship network to construct the observation matrix R: if user v_c is a friend of v_u, we will set the entry $r_{v_u,v_c} = 1$ and if user v_c is a follower-only of v_u, we will set the entry $r_{v_u,v_c} = 0$. Because we already know that more that 90% of new links are from second level neighbors, our effective structures are defined in one-hop; that is, each edge will have two parameters a and b respectively in A and B, and in the global model, it will generate prediction in two hops. In the local model, full structural information is captured in v_u's two-hop ego network. Initial values of A and B are all set to the same value. We finally find that when smoothing parameter $\lambda_1 = 100$ and regularization parameter $\lambda_2 = 100$ in the local model and $\lambda_1 = 1000$, $\lambda_2 = 100$ in the global model, the best performance is achieved. The model usually can converge within 10 iterations, and Figure 2(b) shows the performance changes as a function of iteration number. Because the current network is an ego-centric network which can provide full structural information, but the set of target users—V_u—is relatively small and may not provide good collaborative filtering, the performance of the local model is .197, which is better than the global model—.15. In the following, we use the local model for comparison.

Based on the local model and static data, we also analyze the effects of λ_1 and λ_2. Figure 2(a) shows the results. For the curve for λ_1, we set $\lambda_2 = 0$, and then tune λ_1 from 0 to infinity. We can see that it achieves the best performance when it is set to 100. We also note that when λ_2 is infinite, the model is reduced to the simple methods where links of the same type will share the same

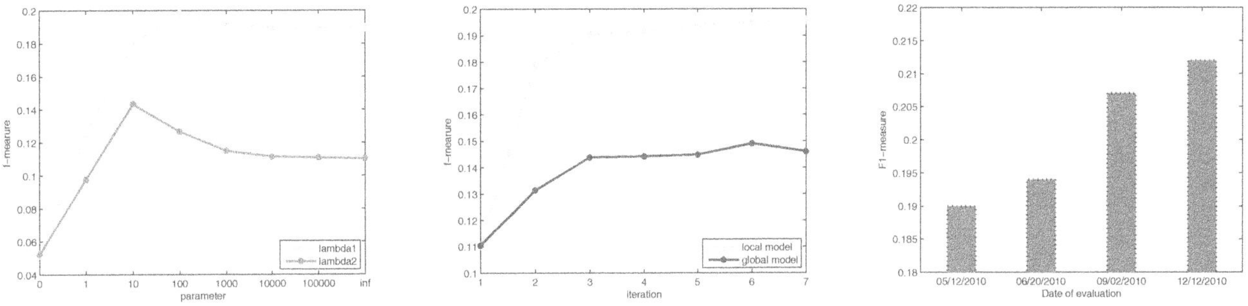

(a) Parameter analysis:F-measure as a function of $\lambda_1(\lambda_2 = 0)$ and $\lambda_2(\lambda_1 = 0)$

(b) F-measure as a function of No. of iterations

(c) Evaluation on different time periods

Figure 2: Experimental analysis

value. The performance of this model is still competitive, although its F-measure is lower than the best performance. Similarly, the performance of tuning λ_2 is shown in the same figure.

3.4 Comparing to link prediction methods

In this section, we compare recent and popular methods which have been already used widely in link prediction problem. Six methods are implemented for comparison. The *Common neighbors* method simply counts the number of common neighbors. The *Jaccard coefficient* is calculated through dividing the number of common neighbors by the total number of neighbors. *Adamic/Adar* [1] refines the simple counting features by weighting rarer features more heavily. *Preferential attachment* scores are the product of v_c in-degree and v_u out-degree. We also compare the latest method—*PropFlow* [18]. In both Katz's method [10] and PropFlow, we tune the parameters l from 1 to 5 in static data.[1] Finally, we compare them on real dynamic data. The results are shown in the Static and Dynamic columns of Table 2.

In static evaluation, the results of *PropFlow*, *Common Neighbors*, *Jaccard Coefficient* and *Adamic/Adar* are similar and *PropFlow* which is a relatively newer method, gets better results than the other five competitors. *Jaccard Coefficient* shows competitive results which is similar with *PropFlow*. Preferential Attachment fails to predict missing links. For Preferential Attachment, because it only depends on the in-degree of the candidates, in the case of the information producers (with higher in-degrees), it may work. However, in real world, we know that individual users are more prevalent than information producers. Thus, we can imagine the failure of Preferential Attachment. In dynamic evaluation, a point which we have to note is that unlike in static evaluation, the *Jaccard coefficient* works very well and even better than *PropFlow*. Within ego-networks, the *Jaccard coefficient* is a competitive method and also simple to calculate. We also find the failure of *Preferential Attachment*. Our method outperforms all other methods in both static evaluation and dynamic evaluation.

3.5 Comparing to matrix factorization

As mentioned earlier, another direction to solve the link prediction problem in a hybrid network is to use the techniques of the traditional recommender systems. Matrix Factorization is a popular method which is widely used in recommender systems [12, 13]. Here we employ the standard matrix factorization methods with smoothing. The observation matrix R is the same as the one in our model and the objective function is as follows.

$$\min_{A,B} \sum_{v_u \in V_u} \sum_{v_c \in V_c} I_{v_u,v_c}(R_{v_u,v_c} - A_{v_u}^T B_{v_c})^2 + \lambda(\|A\|_{Fro}^2 + \|B\|_{Fro}^2)$$

To solve this optimization, we used stochastic gradient descent. Based on the static data, we tune the number of hidden features from 20 to 300, find the optimal parameter for comparison and set $\lambda = 0.05$. The results are shown in the last row of Table 2. On the static data, matrix factorization only achieves around .09 F-measure but the performance of matrix factorization on real data is also competitive at .163. Our model can outperform the standard matrix factorization in both static data and dynamic data because our method essentially incorporates matrix factorization techniques with structural information.

3.6 Validating results

To test for sensitivity to our data set and sampling methods, we also ran our experiments on a subset of the large Twitter follow graph collected by Kwak et al. at KAIST [14]. We randomly sample 2,000 test users and extract their ego networks as in Section 3.3. There are, in total, 81,580 users and almost 10 million edges within this second test network. We again compared our methods with the other seven methods using the static dataset methodology. The results are shown in the rightmost column of Table 2 and are consistent with our earlier experiments. PropFlow is also better than other comparison methods. Our approach consistently outperforms all other tested methods.

Method	Static	Dynamic	KAIST
Our model	**0.197**	**0.190**	**0.127**
PropFlow	0.124	0.099	0.081
Katz	0.094	0.086	0.077
Jaccard coefficient	0.098	0.169	0.079
Adamic/Adar	0.090	0.128	0.069
Common neighbors	0.071	0.116	0.051
Pref. Attachment	0.012	0.012	0.023
Matrix factorization	0.082	0.163	0.074

Table 2: Comparing link prediction methods (F-measure).

[1] In their paper, they also proposed a supervised method. Here, we select PropFlow for two reasons: First, for Lichtenwalter et al.'s supervised methods, there are many parameters to tune and selecting features is also a problem. Second, in their paper, PropFlow is used as a feature, and for most supervised methods, our method can also be used as a feature.

3.7 Discussion

We have demonstrated many of the challenges of link prediction in a hybrid network and also noticed that the overall performance is relatively low, compared to results presented in some link prediction papers on other datasets. However, even when considering "social networks", most existing work does not directly examine online social networks, but rather networks of co-authorship or similarly constructed networks reflecting some social relationship or record of activity.

On the other hand, the links in an online social network may reflect relationships (friends, family) that are not visible in a record of activity, and in a microblogging network with hybrid characteristics is even more complex.

As a result, previous methods which may work well on traditional social networks or co-authorship networks may not work as well on hybrid networks. Our results shows that the F-measure of many popular methods on our real-world data is only around 0.10.

Another cause for low performance of link prediction is that the microblogging network continues to grow. Each day, there may be many new links created [25]. In our experiments, we only evaluate new links within the following one month, so performance may be underestimated. It is possible that users are actually interested in those predicted links but they may not create those links within the following one month due to the fact that users may not discover those potential friends in a short period of time. In other words, users may create those links later, after our initial evaluation period. We conduct a simple experiment to test this: we make predictions based on the same training data—the 04/05/2010 snapshot, but we evaluate on different snapshots from different times. Figure 2(c) shows the results, and we find that after 05/12/2010, target users continue to create links which we had predicted, so measured performance grows higher and higher.

Another thing we can notice is that performance on the three test sets are different. For example, matrix factorization works well on the dynamic data but not well on the static data. We can imagine that static evaluation and dynamic evaluation have different properties such that some methods are better suited for one or the other. For the prediction task, dynamic evaluation is a more accurate estimate of future performance than static evaluation. However, if recommendation is the true end goal, it is difficult to tell which (if any) is better without involving a user study.

4. SUMMARY

In this paper, we examined the link structure and link prediction task within the Twitter microblogging network. We proposed a novel personalized structure-based link prediction model and compared its predictive performance against many fundamental and popular link prediction methods on real-world data from the Twitter microblogging network. Our experiments on both static and dynamic data sets show that our methods noticeably outperform the state-of-the-art.

Acknowledgments

This material is based in part upon work supported by the National Science Foundation under Grant Number IIS-0545875. We thank Roger Nagel, Xiong Xiong, Xiaoguang Qi, Lifeng Shang and Yong Zhang for their suggestions. Finally, we thank Twitter for access to their service and Kwak et al. [14] for releasing their data.

5. REFERENCES

[1] L. A. Adamic and E. Adar. Friends and neighbors on the web. *Social Networks*, 25:211–230, 2001.

[2] L. Backstrom and J. Leskovec. Supervised random walks: predicting and recommending links in social networks. In *Proc. WSDM*, 635-644, 2011.

[3] D. Cai, X. He, X. Wang, H. Bao, and J. Han. Locality preserving nonnegative matrix factorization. In *Proc. IJCAI*, pages 1010-1015, 2009.

[4] A. Clauset, C. Moore, and M. E. J. Newman. Hierarchical structure and the prediction of missing links in networks. *Nature*, 453(7191):98-101, May 2008.

[5] S. Golder and S. Yardi. Structural predictors of tie formation in Twitter: Transitivity and mutuality. In *Proc. SocialCom*, pages 88-95, 2010.

[6] S. Golder, S. Yardi, M. Marwick, and d. boyd. A structural approach to contact recommendations in online social networks. In *Proc. 2nd Workshop on Search in Social Media (SSM)*, 2009.

[7] M. A. Hasan, V. Chaoji, S. Salem, and M. Zaki. Link prediction using supervised learning. In *Proc. of SDM workshop on Link Analysis, Counterterrorism and Security*, 2006.

[8] G. Jeh and J. Widom. SimRank: a measure of structural-context similarity. In *Proc. KDD*, pages 538-543, 2002.

[9] H. Kashima and N. Abe. A parameterized probabilistic model of network evolution for supervised link prediction. In *Proc. ICDM*, pages 340-349, 2006.

[10] L. Katz. A new status index derived from sociometric analysis. *Psychometrika*, 18(1):39-43, March 1953.

[11] Y. Koren. Factorization meets the neighborhood: a multifaceted collaborative filtering model. In *Proc. KDD*, pages 426-434, 2008.

[12] Y. Koren. Collaborative filtering with temporal dynamics. In *Proc. KDD*, pages 447-456, 2009.

[13] Y. Koren, R. M. Bell, and C. Volinsky. Matrix factorization techniques for recommender systems. *IEEE Computer*, 42(8):30-37, 2009.

[14] H. Kwak, C. Lee, H. Park, and S. Moon. What is Twitter, a Social Network or a News Media? In *Proc. WWW*, pages 591-600, 2010.

[15] D. D. Lee and H. S. Seung. Algorithms for non-negative matrix factorization. In *Proc. NIPS*, pages 556-562, 2001.

[16] D. Liben-Nowell and J. Kleinberg. The link prediction problem for social networks. In *Proc. CIKM*, pages 556-559, 2003.

[17] D. Liben-Nowell and J. Kleinberg. The link-prediction problem for social networks. *J. Am. Soc. Inf. Sci. Technol.*, 58(7):1019–1031, 2007.

[18] R. N. Lichtenwalter, J. T. Lussier, and N. V. Chawla. New perspectives and methods in link prediction. In *Proc. KDD*, 2010.

[19] B. Marlin. Modeling user rating profiles for collaborative filtering. In *Proc. NIPS*, 2003.

[20] T. Murata and S. Moriyasu. Link prediction of social networks based on weighted proximity measures. In *Proc. WI*, pages 85-88, 2007.

[21] L. Page, S. Brin, R. Motwani, and T. Winograd. The pagerank citation ranking: Bringing order to the web, 1998.

[22] D. Romero and J. Kleinberg. The directed closure process in hybrid social-information networks, with an analysis of link formation on twitter. In *Proc. ICWSM*, 2010.

[23] T. Tylenda, R. Angelova, and S. Bedathur. Towards time-aware link prediction in evolving social networks. In *Proc. 3rd Workshop on Soc. Net. Mining and Analysis (SNA-KDD)*, pages 1-10, 2009.

[24] J. Weng, E.-P. Lim, J. Jiang, and Q. He. TwitterRank: finding topic-sensitive influential twitterers. In *Proc. WSDM*, pages 261-270, 2010.

[25] D. Yin, L. Hong, X. Xiong, and B. D. Davison. Link formation analysis in microblogs. In *Proc. SIGIR*, pages 1235-1236, 2011.

[26] Z. Yin, M. Gupta, T. Weninger, and J. Han. LINKREC: a unified framework for link recommendation with user attributes and graph structure. In *Proc. WWW*, pages 1211-1212, 2010.

[27] Z. Yin, M. Gupta, T. Weninger, and J. Han. A unified framework for link recommendation using random walks. In *Proc. of the Int'l Conf. on Adv. in Social Net. Analysis and Mining (ASONAM)*, pages 152-159, 2010.

Temporal Link Prediction by Integrating Content and Structure Information

Sheng Gao, Ludovic Denoyer, Patrick Gallinari
LIP6 - UPMC
4 place Jussieu, 75005 Paris, France
{sheng.gao, ludovic.denoyer, patrick.gallinari }@lip6.fr

ABSTRACT

In this paper we address the problem of temporal link prediction, i.e., predicting the apparition of new links, in time-evolving networks. This problem appears in applications such as recommender systems, social network analysis or citation analysis. Link prediction in time-evolving networks is usually based on the topological structure of the network only. We propose here a model which exploits multiple information sources in the network in order to predict link occurrence probabilities as a function of time. The model integrates three types of information: the global network structure, the content of nodes in the network if any, and the local or proximity information of a given vertex. The proposed model is based on a matrix factorization formulation of the problem with graph regularization. We derive an efficient optimization method to learn the latent factors of this model. Extensive experiments on several real world datasets suggest that our unified framework outperforms state-of-the-art methods for temporal link prediction tasks.

Categories and Subject Descriptors

H.2.8 [**Database Management**]: Database applications—*Data Mining*; J.4 [**Social and Behavioral Sciences**]: Sociology

General Terms

Algorithms, Experimentation

Keywords

Temporal Link Prediction, Nonnegative Matrix Factorization, Graph Regularization

1. INTRODUCTION

Link prediction [7] is a generic task for the analysis of networked data which appears in many applications, such as Viral Marketing [15], Recommender systems [8], and Online Social Network Analysis [2]. The problem has mainly been considered from a static network point of view: given observed links in a network, infer the missing links [6]. Most real networks are however time-evolving in nature so that new relations between entities or new entities may appear at different times. For instance, one may be interested to conjecture whether individuals in a network will be linked by some relation in the future, even when no relation has been observed between them in the past. In this paper, we focus on the problem of temporal link prediction in time-evolving networks: given snapshots of a network for T time periods, can we predict the future link structure at time $T+1$ in the network? This task is illustrated in Figure 1. Note that temporal link prediction exploits the past history of link evolution provided by the state of the network at successive time slices. This is different from simply predicting future links (e.g. in a citation network predicting who will cite who) without considering the network evolution history, which could be considered as static link prediction.

Several approaches have been developed to predict future links in time-evolving networks. The mainstream developments, for example the pioneer work [12], or later papers [9], [1], consider only network topological information. However, taking into account the link structure only may lead to poor performance when there is few observed data. For example, social networks are usually very sparse and one needs additional information sources to capture the complex time-evolving patterns of link structure. Some authors like in [13] or [14] view link prediction as a binary classification problem and use both topological structure and node attributes as input into a classifier to decide whether two nodes will be linked in the future. Setting link prediction in a classification framework may cause severe overfitting problems due to the network sparsity and the imbalance between linked and unlinked pairs. To explicitly address these issues, we propose here a model based on a matrix factorization formulation, which exploits multiple information sources in the network in order to predict link occurrence probabilities as a function of time. The model may integrate three types of information: global network structure, content information of nodes if present and local proximity information. The multiple sources will provide additional information w.r.t. the link structure alone, and the regularized matrix factorization approach will be less prone to overfitting and less sensible to class imbalance than classification approaches.

Our contributions are the following: (1) we propose a framework for integrating the complementary information sources for the temporal link prediction problem. For this,

CIKM'11, October 24–28, 2011, Glasgow, Scotland, UK.

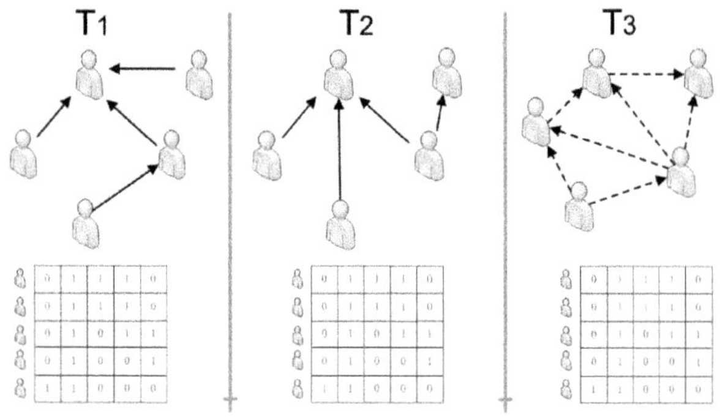

Figure 1: Example of temporal link prediction problem in time-evolving networks. Given time periods $T1$ and $T2$, we try to predict the link structure at $T3$ based on the network structure and node content information.

we exploit a latent matrix factorization method and make use of an efficient alternating iterative algorithm for learning the latent factors of nodes in the network. (2) Extensive experiments are conducted on several real world co-authorship datasets, and the proposed model is shown to outperform state-of-the-art methods for temporal link prediction problem on these datasets.

The paper is structured as follows. We first briefly introduce the problem definition and required background on latent matrix factorization model and graph regularization technique in Section 2. The proposed framework based on a graph regularized link matrix factorization and the training procedure are presented in Section 3. We describe experiments on several datasets and comparisons with state-of-the-art methods in Section 4. In Section 5 we present conclusions.

2. PROBLEM DESCRIPTION AND BACKGROUND

2.1 Problem Definition

The temporal link prediction problem is formally introduced as follows [1]: suppose we have a graph $\mathcal{G} = (\mathcal{V}, \mathcal{E})$, where $\mathcal{V} = \{x_i\}_{i=1}^N$ represents the set of nodes. Each node x_i has a set of associated content features denoted as $\mathbf{C}_i = \{C_{ij}\}_{j=1}^M$. Thus, the content matrix associated to the graph $\mathcal{G}$ is denoted as $\mathbf{C} \in \mathbb{R}^{N\times M}$. We consider that the nodes and their content do not change over time and that only the relations between nodes may evolve. A temporal graph series $\{\mathcal{G}_1, ..., \mathcal{G}_T\}$ can then be represented by a series of adjacency matrices $\{\mathbf{A}_t, t = 1, ..., T\}$, where $\mathbf{A}_t \in \mathbb{R}^{N\times N}$. For a pair of nodes x_i and x_j, let $\mathbf{A}_t(i,j) = 1$ when there is a link between x_i and x_j at time t, and $\mathbf{A}_t(i,j) = 0$ otherwise. Note that in this definition, $\mathbf{A}_t$ may be either symmetric or asymmetric, which respectively corresponds to undirected or directed graph.

Given such a series of T adjacency matrices $\{\mathbf{A}_1, ..., \mathbf{A}_T\}$ and a content matrix $\mathbf{C}$, the temporal link prediction problem is defined as the prediction of occurrence probabilities for links at time $T+1$. We will denote $\mathbf{Sc}$, the $N \times N$ predicted score matrix, whose element $\mathbf{Sc}(i,j)$ represents the predicted score for link (i,j):

$$\mathbf{Sc}_{T+1} = f(\mathbf{A}_1, ..., \mathbf{A}_T, \mathbf{C})$$

where f represents the link prediction model.

[1] We follow the terminology of problem definition in [9]

2.2 Latent Models

The proposed model in this paper integrates different information sources through. We build on the work of [17] which proposed a matrix factorization formalism by combining content and link information, and on the graph regularization models which have been introduced for collaborative filtering [8] in order to represent graph proximity. Our method combines the two ideas in a unique model. We first describe below these two ideas before introducing the proposed model in section 3.

2.2.1 *Latent Factorization Model for Combining Link and Content*

Zhu et al. [17] proposed a supervised matrix factorization model for combining link and content information for classification tasks. Both types of information are mapped onto a common low dimensional latent space. Let $\mathbf{A}$ and $\mathbf{C}$ respectively denote the link adjacency and content matrices for a given graph. The factorization problem can be formalized as follows:

$$\min_{U,S,V} J_{LFM} = \|\mathbf{A} - \mathbf{USU}^T\|_F^2 + \|\mathbf{C} - \mathbf{UV}^T\|_F^2$$

where $\|\cdot\|_F$ denotes the Frobenius norm. In $\|\mathbf{A} - \mathbf{USU}^T\|_F^2$, a tri-factorization is used in place of the classical bi-factor NMF [11]. The specific symmetric above form is utilized for approximating square matrices where rows and columns are indexed by the same element set (here the network nodes), whereas usual NMF method is used to approximate rectangular matrices where the two sets of elements are different. Each row $\mathbf{U}_i$ in the factor matrix $\mathbf{U} \in \mathbb{R}_+^{N\times K}$, can be considered as a low dimensional latent representation of the corresponding node x_i, which encodes the connectivity and content information of the individual node. The factor matrix $\mathbf{S} \in \mathbb{R}_+^{K\times K}$ provides the degree of freedom to make the matrix tri-factorization accurate. The rows of the factor matrix $\mathbf{V} \in \mathbb{R}_+^{M\times K}$, represent the projection of $\mathbf{C}$ onto the latent space.

2.2.2 *Graph Regularization Technique*

Graph regularization has been made popular for semi-supervised learning techniques exploiting data proximity information, i.e. the cluster assumption [16] [18]. The underlying idea is that in a metric space, similar points should have similar labels. This type of regularization has been used jointly with NMF for clustering in [4] and collaborative filtering in [8]. Let us denote $\mathbf{u}_i$ a feature vector associated to node x_i. For the Euclidean metric, the regularization constraint can be written as:

$$\mathcal{R} = \frac{1}{2}\sum_{i,j} \|\mathbf{u}_i - \mathbf{u}_j\|^2 \mathbf{W}_{ij}$$
$$= tr(\mathbf{U}^T(\mathbf{D} - \mathbf{W})\mathbf{U}) = tr(\mathbf{U}^T\mathbf{L}\mathbf{U})$$

where $tr(\cdot)$ denotes the trace of a matrix, $\{\mathbf{u}_1, ..., \mathbf{u}_N\}$ is a set of latent features, $\mathbf{W}$ is a similarity matrix between nodes. $\mathbf{L} = \mathbf{D} - \mathbf{W}$ is the graph Laplacian matrix with $\mathbf{D}$ being a diagonal matrix with diagonal elements $\mathbf{D}_{ii} = \sum_j \mathbf{W}_{ij}$ [5].

3. PROPOSED MODEL

Previous work on link prediction has made use of a unique information source, either topological features or node attributes. We propose here to integrate three network characteristics. To the best of our knowledge there is no similar prior work for temporal link prediction. We describe a condensed representation of the temporal graph series in section 3.1, the model specification with learning and inference procedures in section 3.2, and finally we provide a complexity analysis.

3.1 Temporal Link Structure

Given past snapshots of a network for T time periods, we need to capture the temporal dependencies of individual links and the global interlink dependencies. To do so, we will use here a simple weighted exponentially decaying model [1]. Let $\{A_t(i,j), t = t_0+1, ..., t_0+T\}$ be a time series of adjacency matrices on a sliding window of T successive temporal slices. We build an aggregate weighted link matrix as follows:

$$\mathbf{A}_{(t_0+1)\sim(t_0+T)}(i,j) = \sum_{t=t_0+1}^{t_0+T} \theta^{t_0+T-t} A_t(i,j) \qquad (1)$$

where the parameter $\theta \in [0,1]$ is the smoothing weight. In the final $\mathbf{A}_{(t_0+1)\sim(t_0+T)}$ matrix, the importance of $\mathbf{A}_t$ decreases together with the index t. $\mathbf{A}_{(t_0+1)\sim(t_0+T)}$ denoted as $\mathbf{A}$ for simplification from now on, will be used in the algorithm as a summarized information, describing the temporal evolution of the link structure.

3.2 Model Specification

3.2.1 Objective

The proposed model is based on a factor analysis framework for integrating the temporal link structure, content features and graph proximity information of nodes with the graph regularization technique. It combines the two ideas outlined in sections 2.2.1 and 2.2.2 into a joint latent model. The objective function is defined as:

$$\begin{aligned}\min_{U,S,V} J &= \|\mathbf{A} - \mathbf{USU}^T\|_F^2 + \alpha\|\mathbf{C} - \mathbf{UV}^T\|_F^2 + \lambda tr(\mathbf{U}^T\mathbf{LU}) \\ &= \sum_{i=1}^{N}\sum_{j=1}^{N}(\mathbf{A}_{ij} - (\mathbf{USU}^T)_{ij})^2 + \alpha\sum_{i=1}^{N}\sum_{j=1}^{M}(\mathbf{C}_{ij} - (\mathbf{UV}^T)_{ij})^2 \\ &+ \lambda tr(\mathbf{U}^T\mathbf{LU}) \\ s.t. \quad & \mathbf{U} \geq 0, \mathbf{S} \geq 0, \mathbf{V} \geq 0\end{aligned} \qquad (2)$$

where the factor matrices $\mathbf{U} \in \mathbb{R}_+^{N\times K}$, $\mathbf{S} \in \mathbb{R}_+^{K\times K}$, and $\mathbf{V} \in \mathbb{R}_+^{M\times K}$, are nonnegative. α and λ are parameters which can balance the influence of content information and graph proximity information in the joint model.

The first term $\|\mathbf{A}-\mathbf{USU}^T\|_F^2$ corresponds to the temporal link matrix factorization. The matrix tri-factorization form is used here to represent the fact that the rows and columns of link matrix $\mathbf{A}$ correspond to the same set of nodes. The link matrix $\mathbf{A}$ might be symmetric or asymmetric for respectively undirected or directed graph, and the corresponding factor matrix $\mathbf{S}$ will accordingly be a symmetric or asymmetric matrix. The second term $\alpha\|\mathbf{C}-\mathbf{UV}^T\|_F^2$ in Equation (2) is used to incorporate the content or semantic attributes of nodes, which play an important role in link prediction models [10] [14].

The regularization term $\lambda tr(\mathbf{U}^T\mathbf{LU})$ is employed to integrate the graph proximity information into the joint model, and acts as a constraint for the link matrix factorization. Different types of proximity information may be encoded into the weight matrix $\mathbf{W}$, such as *common neighbor* and *preferential attachment* measures (see section 4.2). Experimental results show that these local topological characteristics are useful for link prediction. Without loss of generality, we will use the *common neighbor* similarity matrix here.

3.2.2 Inference

After obtaining the latent factors $\mathbf{U}$, $\mathbf{S}$ and $\mathbf{V}$, the probability of a link existing between a pair of nodes can be obtained by an inner product of the latent factors $\mathbf{U}$ and $\mathbf{S}$, which produces the score matrix for predicting future link occurrence probabilities in time-evolving networks as follows:

$$\mathbf{Sc}_{T+1} = f(\mathbf{A}_{1\sim T}, \mathbf{C}, \mathbf{W}) = \mathbf{USU}^T \qquad (3)$$

3.2.3 Learning

For learning the proposed model, we use the alternating multiplicative updating algorithm [11], which warrants the nonnegativity of latent factors $\mathbf{U}$, $\mathbf{S}$ and $\mathbf{V}$ and provides an automatic step parameter selection. The objective function $J(U,S,V)$ in Equation (2) is not convex in $\mathbf{U}, \mathbf{S}$ and $\mathbf{V}$ together. The alternating updating algorithm optimizes the objective function with respect to one set of parameters while fixing the others, and then exchanges the roles of the parameter sets alternatively. This procedure will be repeated for several iterations until convergence.

To learn the factor matrix $\mathbf{U}$ while fixing the factor matrices $\mathbf{S}$ and $\mathbf{V}$, we will solve the following optimization problem:

$$\begin{aligned}\min_U J(\mathbf{U}) &= \|\mathbf{A} - \mathbf{USU}^T\|_F^2 + \alpha\|\mathbf{C} - \mathbf{UV}^T\|_F^2 \\ &+ \lambda tr(\mathbf{U}^T\mathbf{LU}) \\ s.t. \quad & \mathbf{U} \geq 0\end{aligned} \qquad (4)$$

The derivative of $J(\mathbf{U})$ with respect to $\mathbf{U}$ is:

$$\begin{aligned}\frac{\partial J(\mathbf{U})}{\partial \mathbf{U}} &= 2(\mathbf{USU}^T\mathbf{US}^T + \mathbf{US}^T\mathbf{U}^T\mathbf{US} - \mathbf{AUS}^T - \mathbf{A}^T\mathbf{US}) \\ &+ 2\alpha(\mathbf{UV}^T\mathbf{V} - \mathbf{CV}) + 2\lambda\mathbf{LU}\end{aligned}$$

Using the Karush-Kuhn-Tucker complementary condition for the nonnegativity of $\mathbf{U}$ and $\frac{\partial J(\mathbf{U})}{\partial \mathbf{U}} = 0$, we can get the following updating rule for $\mathbf{U}_{ij}$:

$$\mathbf{U}_{ij} \longleftarrow \mathbf{U}_{ij}\sqrt{\frac{[\mathbf{AUS}^T + \mathbf{A}^T\mathbf{US} + \alpha\mathbf{CV} + \lambda\mathbf{WU}]_{ij}}{[\mathbf{USU}^T\mathbf{US}^T + \mathbf{US}^T\mathbf{U}^T\mathbf{US} + \alpha\mathbf{UV}^T\mathbf{V} + \lambda\mathbf{DU}]_{ij}}} \qquad (5)$$

The latent factor matrices $\mathbf{S}$ and $\mathbf{V}$ can be learned in a way similar to the latent factor $\mathbf{U}$. The updating rules for learning $\mathbf{S}$ and $\mathbf{V}$ are respectively:

$$\mathbf{S}_{ij} \longleftarrow \mathbf{S}_{ij}\sqrt{\frac{[\mathbf{U}^T\mathbf{AU}]_{ij}}{[\mathbf{U}^T\mathbf{USU}^T\mathbf{U}]_{ij}}} \qquad (6)$$

$$\mathbf{V}_{ij} \longleftarrow \mathbf{V}_{ij}\frac{[\mathbf{C}^T\mathbf{U}]_{ij}}{[\mathbf{VU}^T\mathbf{U}]_{ij}} \qquad (7)$$

3.2.4 Convergence Analysis

Based on the above updating rules for latent factor $\mathbf{U}$ in Equation (5), $\mathbf{S}$ in Equation (6) and $\mathbf{V}$ in Equation (7), we can prove that the learning algorithm is convergent.

THEOREM 1. *Using the updating rules in Equation (5), Equation (6) and Equation (7), the objective function in Equation (2) will monotonically decrease, thus the learning algorithm converges.*

The proof is omitted here due to space limitation. [2]

3.2.5 Complexity Analysis

Since the alternating iterative updating algorithm is employed to learn the latent factors $\mathbf{U}$, $\mathbf{S}$ and $\mathbf{V}$, we can observe that in each iteration, the computational complexity for learning $\mathbf{U}$ is $O(NK^2)$, where N is the number of nodes in the network, K is the latent factorization dimensionality. The computational complexity required for learning $\mathbf{S}$ and $\mathbf{V}$ is $O(NK^2)$ and $O(NK)$ respectively. Typically, due to $K \ll N$, the overall complexity of the learning algorithm is $O(N)$, which provides the possibility for handling large scale networks.

4. EXPERIMENTS

4.1 Datasets

In the experiments, we examine how our proposed model behaves on real-world time-varying networks. We consider here four co-authorship networks extracted from arXiv archive for the years 1992 to 2002 [12]. These different networks come from different sections of arXiv: Condensed Matter (Cond-mat), General relativity and quantum cosmology (Gr-qc), High energy physics phenomenology (Hep-ph) and High energy physics theory (Hep-th). They will be exploited separately in the experiments.

4.2 Experimental Setup

We will introduce several baselines which are used for comparison with the proposed joint model:

Dependent Prediction method: which is a naive method that uses the most recent link graph A_{t_0+T} as the score matrix, i.e. $\mathbf{Sc}_{T+1} = \mathbf{A}_{t_0+T}$.

Weighted Dependent Prediction method: which is also a naive method that uses the weighted temporal link graph $\mathbf{A}_{(t_0+1)\sim(t_0+T)}$ as the score matrix, i.e. $\mathbf{Sc}_{T+1} = \mathbf{A}_{(t_0+1)\sim(t_0+T)}$.

Common Neighbor method: which simply evaluates the number of common neighbors in the temporal link graph $\mathbf{A}_{(t_0+1)\sim(t_0+T)}$ as the score in the score matrix, i.e., $\mathbf{Sc}_{T+1} = |\Gamma(i) \cap \Gamma(j)|$, where $\Gamma(i)$ is the set of neighbors of node i.

Preferential Attachment method [3]: which uses the product of node degrees in the link graph $\mathbf{A}_{(t_0+1)\sim(t_0+T)}$ as the score in the score matrix, i.e., $\mathbf{Sc}_{T+1} = |\Gamma(i)| \cdot |\Gamma(j)|$.

Katz method: which consists in summing over all paths between nodes of varying lengths in $\mathbf{A}_{(t_0+1)\sim(t_0+T)}$, exponentially damped by length to give short paths higher weights, i.e., $\mathbf{Sc}_{T+1} = \sum_{l=1}^{\infty} \beta^l \cdot |path_{i,j}^{<l>}|$, where $path_{i,j}^{<l>}$ is the set of paths of length l between nodes i and j.

NMF method [11]: which is directly applied on the temporal link matrix $\mathbf{A}_{(t_0+1)\sim(t_0+T)}$ to produce the score matrix using only the network structure information.

[2] See the supplementary information at the authors' website for the detailed proof.

GNMF method [4]: which combines the link structure with graph proximity information of nodes.

GRJMF method: this is our method. GRJMF holds here for Graph Regularized Joint Matrix Factorization.

The sliding window size for training the temporal model is set to $T = 3$ [3]. Since we start at Year 1992, we then evaluate all models on years from 1995 to 2002. To evaluate the performance, we use the AUC (score Area Under the receiver operating characteristic Curve), which is a robust measure for networked dataset [1], as the evaluation metric. For the experiments we evaluate the methods by repeating the process five times and report the average results.

4.3 Temporal Link Prediction Results

We compare the performance of different temporal link prediction models on the four co-authorship datasets. The parameters of the different methods have been manually tuned and we report here the best results obtained based on the optimal combination of many parameter settings. The dimensionality of the low dimensional factor representations, i.e. K, is also determined by the experiments. The results presented here have been obtained by using $K = 60$, $\alpha = 1$, $\theta = 0.4$ and $\lambda = 1$, and for the matrix factorization based methods the number of iterations has been set at 100. The influence of different parameter settings is studied in the next section.

The experimental results are shown in Table 1 for the temporal link prediction task. It can be observed that the best performing method among all the models is our proposed GRJMF model, which indicates that it can efficiently integrate the temporal link matrix, content information of nodes and graph proximity information to extract meaningful latent factors. Table 2 gives the detailed performance on every test year using different link prediction methods on Cond-mat dataset with the sliding time window of T=3 as an example. Among graph proximity information based models (i.e., CN, PA, Katz methods) the Katz method has the highest performance and is most often slightly better than the nonnegative matrix factorization based models (i.e., NMF and GNMF), which shows that the graph proximity information can provide useful topological features for temporal link prediction.

We also want to evaluate the contribution of multiple information sources (i.e., common neighborhood based graph proximity information and content information of nodes), in our model. Figure 2 gives the performances of variants of our proposed model on the different datasets: here GRJMF-L denotes the link matrix tri-factorization model which is the first term in GRJMF (i.e. $\alpha = 0$ and $\lambda = 0$). GRJMF-L+C denotes the model using link structure and content information (i.e. $\lambda = 0$), GRJMF-L+R denotes the link matrix factorization model using graph regularization while without content information (i.e. $\alpha = 0$), GRJMF-L+C+R denotes the graph regularized joint model with both link and content information. From the results, GRJMF-L is slightly lower than the other models, which is natural. GRJMF-L+C or GRJMF-L+R bring similar improvements w.r.t. GRJMF-L, while the integration of all the information sources in GRJMF-L+C+R contributes to an additional increase w.r.t. the last two models. The different sources thus bring com-

[3] Varying the value of sliding window size T leads to different prediction performances. $T = 3$ provided the best performance on the different test datasets.

Table 1: **Average AUC Performances using different methods averaged on the test years between 1995 and 2002 with the sliding time window of T=3. Best results are in bold and second best in italic.**

	DP	WP	CN	PA	Katz	NMF	GNMF	GRJMF
Cond-mat	0.6585	0.7068	0.6757	0.7152	0.7231	0.7195	*0.7261*	**0.7605**
Gr-qc	0.6288	0.6702	0.6375	0.6707	*0.7047*	0.6680	0.6756	**0.7588**
Hep-ph	0.6103	0.6549	0.6328	0.7112	*0.7649*	0.7323	0.7437	**0.7896**
Hep-th	0.6454	0.6911	0.6635	0.7216	*0.7518*	0.7133	0.7274	**0.7977**

Table 2: Average AUC Performances using different methods on Cond-mat dataset for each year. Best results are in bold and second best in italic.

Year	DP	WP	CN	PA	Katz	NMF	GNMF	GRJMF
1995	0.6306	0.6621	0.6490	0.7061	*0.7141*	0.6612	0.6683	**0.7186**
1996	0.6631	0.6962	0.6764	0.7028	*0.7122*	0.7094	0.7097	**0.7460**
1997	0.6086	0.6993	0.6451	0.7187	*0.7115*	0.6869	0.6907	**0.7374**
1998	0.6214	0.7133	0.6872	0.7074	0.7137	0.7293	*0.7360*	**0.7628**
1999	0.6864	0.7154	0.7142	0.7111	0.7330	0.7393	*0.7365*	**0.7979**
2000	0.6328	0.6987	0.6785	0.7004	0.7198	0.7083	*0.7284*	**0.7756**
2001	0.6870	0.7376	0.7177	0.7195	*0.7466*	0.7485	0.7403	**0.7876**
2002	0.7026	0.7322	0.7349	0.7277	0.7580	0.7466	*0.7598*	**0.8083**
Average	0.6585	0.7068	0.6757	0.7152	0.7231	0.7195	0.7261	**0.7605**

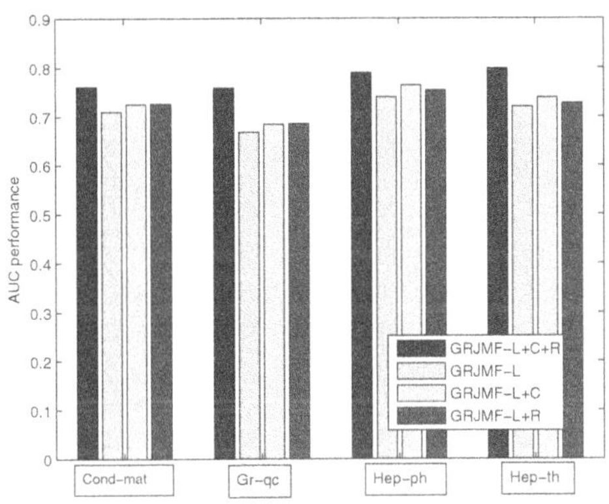

Figure 2: Average AUC performances on different datasets with variations of our proposed GRJMF model.

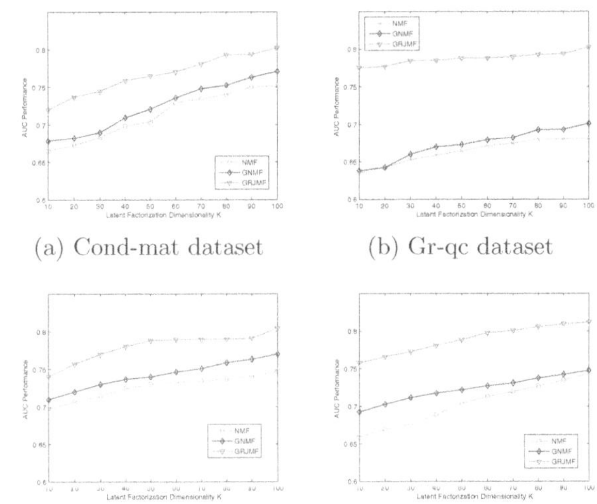

(a) Cond-mat dataset (b) Gr-qc dataset

(c) Hep-ph dataset (d) Hep-th dataset

Figure 3: Average AUC performances on different datasets using three latent matrix factorization based methods when varying K values.

plementary information and GRJMF-L+C+R model allows their integration in an efficient manner.

4.4 Impacts of Parameter Settings

We now study the influence of different parameter settings. We have conducted experiments with different values of the parameters: latent factorization dimensionality K, exponential smoothing weight α, content factorization parameter θ and graph regularization parameter λ.

Impact of K: Figure 3 shows the performance evolution of the matrix factorization based models when K varies from 10 to 100. In this range, the higher the dimensionality of the low-dimensional representation, the better the performance is. In order to achieve a compromise between complexity and performance we fixed K to 60 in the experiments.

Impact of α: We use here the Gr-qc dataset as an example to check the impact of various values on θ in Figure 4. The results on the other three datasets are similar. We can observe that increasing the value of θ tends to improve the prediction performance slightly by all the methods except for the Dependent Prediction method until $\theta = 0.4$, and that higher values of θ may decrease the performances.

Impact of θ: We vary the value of α in the range $[0, 2]$ to examine the impact of content information on the Gr-qc dataset as in Figure 5(a). When we set $\alpha = 0$, the proposed model reduces to the GNMF model (i.e. no content). It can be seen that content of nodes is indeed an important additional information source since the performance sharply increases as soon as this information is introduced and reaches best performance at around $\alpha = 1$. Based on the result in the experiments, we choose the optimal value $\alpha = 1$.

Impact of λ: We vary values of λ on $\{0.01, 0.1, 1, 10, 100\}$ to check the performance of the matrix factorization based

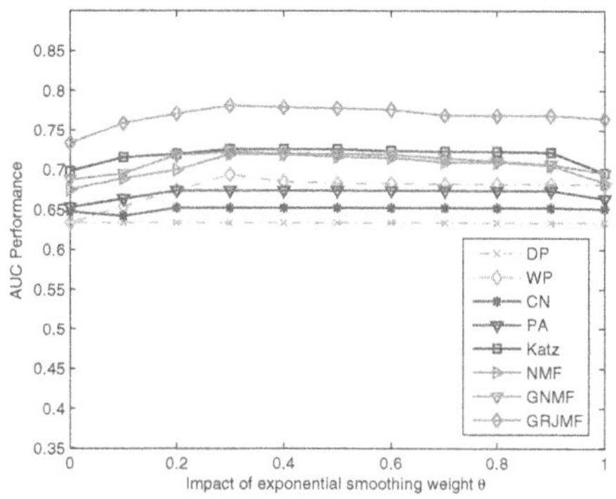

Figure 4: Average AUC performances on different values of θ using three matrix factorization based models on Gr-qc dataset.

models on the Gr-qc dataset when $\alpha = 1$. We omit this analysis for other datasets which exhibit a similar trend. Figure 5(b) demonstrates that λ slightly influences the prediction performance, confirming the relevance of the graph proximity information source. However, the effects are different on GNMF and GRJMF model. The performance of the former increases for the experiment range while the latter reaches a maximum and then slightly decreases. This could be explained by the need for a compromise between content and proximity information in the GRJMF model.

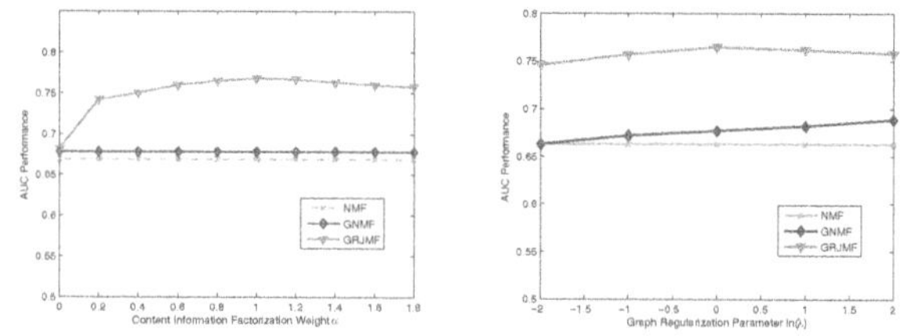

(a) Impact of α. (b) Impact of λ.

Figure 5: Average AUC performances on Gr-qc dataset using three matrix factorization based models when varying the values of α and λ.

5. CONCLUSION

In this paper we have focused on the problem of temporal link prediction in time-evolving networks, and have proposed a novel unified model which integrates three types of information: the global network structure, the content of nodes and the graph proximity information to capture the time-evolving patterns of links in the networks. The joint model is based on latent matrix factorization method and graph regularization technique. We also presented an efficient optimization procedure with the alternating iterative algorithm to learn the latent factors. The experimental analysis on several real world datasets suggest that our joint model can efficiently incorporate multiple information sources and provide a promising future for temporal link prediction task.

6. ACKNOWLEDGMENTS

The authors would like to thank the anonymous reviewers for their helpful feedback. This work was partially supported by the French National Agency of Research (the Fragrances-Project, ANR-08-CORD-008-01).

7. REFERENCES

[1] E. Acar, D. M. Dunlavy, and T. G. Kolda. Link prediction on evolving data using matrix and tensor factorizations. *ICDM Workshops*, pages 262–269, 2009.

[2] A. Adamic and E. Adar. Friends and neighbors on the web. *Social Networks*, 25:211–230, 2003.

[3] A. L. Barabasi and R. Albert. Emergence of scaling in random networks. *Science*, 286:509–512, 1999.

[4] D. Cai, X. He, X. Wu, and J. Han. Non-negative matrix factorization on manifold. *ICDM*, pages 63–72, 2008.

[5] F. Chung. Spectral graph theory. *American Mathematical Society*, 1997.

[6] A. Clauset, C. Moore, and M. Newman. Hierarchical structure and the prediction of missing links in networks. *Nature*, 453:98–101, 2008.

[7] L. Getoor and C. P. Diehl. Link mining: a survey. *ACM SIGKDD Explorations Newslett.*, 7:3–12, 2005.

[8] Q. Gu, J. Zhou, and C. Ding. Collaborative filtering: Weighted nonnegative matrix factorization incorporating user and item graphs. *SDM*, pages 199–210, 2010.

[9] Z. Huang and D. K. J. Lin. The time-series link prediction problem with applications in communication surveillance. *Info. Journal on Computing*, pages 286–303, 2009.

[10] H. Kashima, T. Kato, Y. Yamanishi, M. Sugiyama, and K. Tsuda. Link propagation: A fast semi-supervised learning algorithm for link prediction. *SDM*, pages 1099–1110, 2009.

[11] D. D. Lee and H. S. Seung. Algorithms for non-negative matrix factorization. *NIPS*, pages 556–562, 2000.

[12] D. Liben-Nowell and J. Kleinberg. The link prediction problem for social networks. *CIKM*, pages 556–559, 2003.

[13] J. O'Madadhain, J. Hutchins, and P. Smyth. Prediction and ranking algorithms for event-based network data. *SIGKDD Explor. Newsl,. Vol.7, No.2*, pages 23–30, 2005.

[14] C. Wang, V. Satuluri, and S. Parthasarathy. Local probabilistic models for link prediction. *ICDM*, pages 322–331, 2007.

[15] S. Wasserman and K. Faust. *Social Netwok Analysis: Methods and Applications.* Cambridge University Press, 1994.

[16] D. Zhou, O. Bousquet, T. N. Lal, J. Weston, and B. Scholkopf. Learning with local and global consistency. *NIPS*, 16:321–328, 2004.

[17] S. Zhu, K. Yu, Y. Chi, and Y. Gong. Combining content and link for classification using matrix factorization. *SIGIR*, pages 487–494, 2007.

[18] X. Zhu, Z. Ghahramani, and J. Lafferty. Semi-supervised learning using gaussian fields and harmonic functions. *ICML*, pages 912–919, 2003.

Towards Feature Selection in Network

Quanquan Gu
Department of Computer Science
University of Illinois at Urbana-Champaign
IL, 61801, USA
qgu3@illinois.edu

Jiawei Han
Department of Computer Science
University of Illinois at Urbana-Champaign
IL, 61801, USA
hanj@cs.uiuc.edu

ABSTRACT

Traditional feature selection methods assume that the data are independent and identically distributed (i.i.d.). However, in real world, there are tremendous amount of data which are distributing in a network. Existing features selection methods are not suited for networked data because the i.i.d. assumption no longer holds. This motivates us to study feature selection in a network. In this paper, we present a supervised feature selection method based on Laplacian Regularized Least Squares (LapRLS) for networked data. In detail, we use linear regression to utilize the content information, and adopt graph regularization to consider the link information. The proposed feature selection method aims at selecting a subset of features such that the empirical error of LapRLS is minimized. The resultant optimization problem is a mixed integer programming, which is difficult to solve. It is relaxed into a $L_{2,1}$-norm constrained LapRLS problem and solved by accelerated proximal gradient descent algorithm. Experiments on benchmark networked data sets show that the proposed feature selection method outperforms traditional feature selection method and the state of the art learning in network approaches.

Categories and Subject Descriptors

I.2.6 [**Artificial Intelligence**]: Learning; I.5.1 [**Pattern Recognition**]: Models

General Terms

Algorithms, Experimentation

Keywords

Feature Selection, Network, Graph Regularization, Laplacian Regularized Least Squares

1. INTRODUCTION

In many application of data mining, one is often confronted with very high dimensional data. It significantly increases the time and space complexity for processing the data. Moreover, in the presence of many irrelevant and/or redundant features, learning methods tend to over-fit and become less interpretable. One way to resolve this problem is feature selection [23] [8], which reduces the dimensionality by selecting a subset of features from the input feature set.

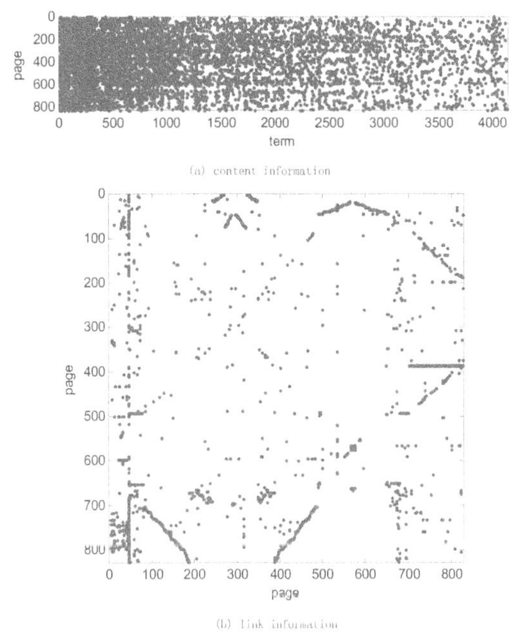

Figure 1: Sample data of WebKB (Cornell) dataset: (a) Content information (page-term co-occurrence matrix); (b) Link information (adjacenc matrix). Note that the adjacenc matrix is not s mmetric because the link has direction.

However, traditional feature selection methods [8] assume that the data are sampled i.i.d. from some unknown distribution. While in real world, there are tremendous amount of data which are distributing in a network. For example, in the classification of web pages, there are not only the content information within web pages, but also the hyper-links between the web pages. See Figure 1 for example. Figure 1 (a) shows the page-term matrix where the blue dot represents the occurrence of a term in a page. Figure 1 (b) shows the adjacency matrix of the pages, where the blue dot represents the link between pages. It is often the case that if there is a link from one page to another, then it is likely that these two pages are related. Another example is research paper classification. Besides the content information of each paper, a citation relation between two papers provides an evidence that they belong to the same topic. That is, if one paper cite another paper, or is cited by another one, then there is a high chance that the papers are belonging to the same topic. It can be seen that content information and link information complement each other. Hence, if one can utilize both the content information and link information in the network, one should achieve better classification result of the networked data than either using the content information or link information alone. In the past decade, there are quite a lot of works on learning in network along several directions. For example, combining content and link information for classification [6] [26] [12], learning based on graph regularization [2], collective classification of networked data [18], active learning for networked data [3] [19] and subspace learning in network [13]. However, feature selection for networked data is rarely touched. Traditional feature selection methods are not suited for networked data because the i.i.d. assumption no longer holds.

In this paper, based on the above motivation, we present a supervised feature selection method for networked data. It is built upon Laplacian Regularized Least Squares (LapRLS) [2]. The key idea is to use the least squares regression to fit the labels with respect to the content information, and adopt graph regularization [20] [25] to utilize the link information. We study graph regularization on both undirected graph and directed graph. The basic assumption of graph regularization is that if two nodes are linked in a network (or one node links another node), then their labels are likely to be the same. The proposed feature selection method aims at selecting a subset of features such that the empirical error of LapRLS is minimized. The resultant optimization problem is a mixed integer programming [4], which is difficult to solve. It is relaxed into a $L_{2,1}$-norm constrained LapRLS problem and solved by accelerated proximal gradient descent algorithm [15]. It is worth noting that we do not need to specify the number of features to select for the proposed feature selection method. It is implicitly controlled by a regularization parameter. Experiments on benchmark data sets indicate that the proposed method outperforms traditional feature selection method and the state of the art learning in network approaches.

The remainder of this paper is organized as follows. In Section 2, we review traditional feature selection methods and learning in network approaches. We present the feature selection method in Section 3. The experiments on benchmark data sets are demonstrated in Section 4. Finally, we draw a conclusion and point out the future work in Section 5.

1.1 Notation

The generic problem of supervised feature selection in network is as follows. Given a networked data set $\{(\mathbf{x}_i, y_i)\}_{i=1}^n$ where $\mathbf{x}_i \in \mathbb{R}^d$ is the feature vector of the i-th node, and $y_i \in \{1, 2, \ldots, c\}$ is the label of the i-th node, $\mathbf{A}$ is the adjacency matrix of the networked data, such that $A_{ij} = 1$ if there is a link from i-th node to the j-th node, and $A_{ij} = 0$ otherwise. For undirected graph, we have $A_{ij} = A_{ji}$. In other words, the adjacency matrix $\mathbf{A}$ is symmetric. For directed graph, the adjacency matrix $\mathbf{A}$ is asymmetric. The goal of feature selection is to find a feature subset of size m which contains the most informative features. We use $\mathbf{X} = [\mathbf{x}_1, \mathbf{x}_2, \ldots, \mathbf{x}_n] \in \mathbb{R}^{d\times n}$ to represent the data matrix, and $\mathbf{Y} \in \mathbb{R}^{n\times c}$ to represent the target label matrix, where $Y_{ik} = 1$ if $y_i = k$, and $Y_{ik} = 0$ otherwise. Given a matrix $\mathbf{W} \in \mathbb{R}^{d\times m}$, we denote the i-th row of $\mathbf{W}$ by $\mathbf{w}^i$, and the j-th column of $\mathbf{W}$ by $\mathbf{w}_j$. The Frobenius norm of $\mathbf{W}$ is defined as $||\mathbf{W}||_F = \sqrt{\sum_i^d ||\mathbf{w}^i||_2^2}$, the $L_{2,0}$-norm of $\mathbf{W}$ is defined as $||\mathbf{W}||_{2,0} = \text{card}(||\mathbf{w}^1||_2, \ldots, ||\mathbf{w}^d||_2)$, and the $L_{2,1}$-norm of $\mathbf{W}$ is defined as $||\mathbf{W}||_{2,1} = \sum_i^d ||\mathbf{w}^i||_2$. $\mathbf{1}$ is a vector of all ones with an appropriate length. $\mathbf{0}$ is a vector of all zeros. $\mathbf{I}$ is an identity matrix with an appropriate size.

2. RELATED WORK

In this section, we give a brief review of traditional feature selection methods and existing learning methods in network respectively.

2.1 Feature Selection

In feature selection [23], the features may be scored either dependent or independent on a classifier. In general, there are three families of approaches to score them: filter-based, wrapper-based, and embedded methods [8]. Filter-based methods score the features as a pre-processing step, independently of the classifier. The most representative filter-based methods include Information Gain (IG), χ^2 [23], Fisher score [17] [7] and so on. Wrapper-based methods score the features according to their prediction performance when used with the classifier. Finally, embedded methods combine feature selection with the classifier. While the design of embedded methods is tightly coupled with the specific classifier, they are often considered as more effective than filters and wrappers [8]. It is worth noting that the proposed feature selection method for networked data belongs to the family of embedded method, because it is specifically designed for Laplacian Regularized Least Squares (LapRLS) [2]. Feature selection methods rely on search strategies to guide the search for the "best" feature subset. While a large number of search strategies can be used, one is often limited to the greedy (forward or backward) strategies. The search for the "best" features in the proposed method is in a principled way rather than greedy.

2.2 Learning in Network

Learning in network has received increasing interest in the past decade. [6] proposed a missing-link model, which generalize probabilistic latent semantic analysis (PLSA) [10] to consider both content and link information. [26] proposed link-content matrix factorization (LCMF) method, which integrates content and link information into a matrix factorization framework. [12] proposed relation regularized matrix factorization (RRMF), which overcomes some limitations of LCMF. However, all the methods mentioned above are transductive learning methods [21]. Transductive learning methods work on the training and testing set together. They do not output a parametric classifier, hence they cannot generalize to new unseen data. When new data come, they need to re-learn based on the training and the testing data. This motivates inductive learning, which induces a parametric decision function in the whole sample space. [2] proposed Laplacian Regularized Least Squares (LapRLS) based on graph regularization. Although it is originally proposed for semi-supervised learning, it can be adapted to learning in network and works very well. [18] studied collective classification of networked data. [13] proposed probabilistic relation principle component analysis (PRPCA), which is the sate of the art subspace learning method in network. More recently, [3] [19] suggested active learning for networked data. On the other hand, there are some works such as modularity of network [16], which study how to measure the partition of a network. However, as far as we know, feature selection for networked data is still a rarely touched topic. This motivates the method presented in this paper.

3. THE PROPOSED METHOD

In this section, we will present a feature selection method for networked data. In detail, we first introduce Graph regularization and Laplacian Regularized Least Squares (LapRLS). Then we present the feature selection method in network, followed with its optimization algorithm and theoretical analysis.

3.1 Graph Regularization

Link information in network characterizes the structure of the network and relation between the nodes. In order to consider the link information, we turn to use *Graph Regularization* [20] [25], which is based on spectral graph theory [5]. Graph regularization has achieved great success in dimensionality reduction [1] [9] [22] and semi-supervised learning [27] [24] [2]. In the following, we will introduce graph regularization for both undirected graph and directed graph respectively.

3.1.1 Undirected Graph

For undirected network, the basic assumption of undirected graph regularization is: if two nodes are linked together, then their labels are likely to be the same. It can be mathematically formulated as [20]

$$
\begin{aligned}
& \frac{1}{2}\sum_{k=1}^{c}\sum_{ij}(\mathbf{w}_k^T\mathbf{x}_i - \mathbf{w}_k^T\mathbf{x}_j)^2 A_{ij} \\
= & \sum_{k=1}^{c}\sum_{i,j}\mathbf{w}_k^T\mathbf{x}_i A_{ij}\mathbf{x}_i^T\mathbf{w}_k - \sum_{k=1}^{c}\sum_{i,j}\mathbf{w}_k^T\mathbf{x}_i A_{ij}\mathbf{x}_j^T\mathbf{w}_k \\
= & \sum_{k=1}^{c}\sum_{i}\mathbf{w}_k^T\mathbf{x}_i D_{ii}\mathbf{x}_i^T\mathbf{w}_k - \sum_{k=1}^{c}\sum_{i,j}\mathbf{w}_k^T\mathbf{x}_i A_{ij}\mathbf{x}_j^T\mathbf{w}_k \\
= & \sum_{k=1}^{c}\mathbf{w}_k^T\mathbf{X}(\mathbf{D}-\mathbf{W})\mathbf{X}^T\mathbf{w}_k \\
= & \operatorname{tr}(\mathbf{W}^T\mathbf{X}\mathbf{L}\mathbf{X}^T\mathbf{W}), \qquad (1)
\end{aligned}
$$

where $\mathbf{L} = \mathbf{D} - \mathbf{A}$ is the graph Laplacian [5] and $\mathbf{D}$ is a diagonal matrix called degree matrix with $D_{ii} = \sum_j A_{ij}$. Note that in undirected graph regularization, $\mathbf{A}$ is symmetric.

3.1.2 Directed Graph

For directed graph, the undirected graph regularization in Eq.(1) does not work anymore since the adjacency matrix $\mathbf{A}$ is asymmetric. To revolve this problem, one way is to simply use $\mathbf{A} = \max(\mathbf{A}, \mathbf{A}^T)$. Another way is to use directed graph regularization [25] instead. An edge of a directed graph is an ordered pair (i, j) where i and j are the node indices. The in-degree of the i-th node is defined as $D_i^- = \sum_{j\to i} A_{ji}$, where $j \to i$ denotes the j-th node has a directed link pointing to the i-th node, while out-degree of the i-th node is defined as $D_i^+ = \sum_{i\to j} W_{ij}$, where $i \to j$ denotes the i-th node has a directed link pointing to the j-th node. Given the adjacency matrix $\mathbf{A}$ of a directed graph, we define a transition probability of random walk as $P_{ij} = A_{ij}/D_i^+$. It is obvious that it satisfies $\sum_j P_{ij} = 1$. Assume the stationary distribution for i-th node is π_i. Then it satisfies $\sum_i \pi_i = 1$ and $\pi_j = \sum_{i\to j}\pi_i P_{ij}$. The basic assumption of directed graph regularization is: if the i-th node link the j-th node, then their labels are likely to be the same. It is mathematically formulated as [25],

$$
\begin{aligned}
& \frac{1}{2}\sum_{k=1}^{c}\sum_{(i,j)}(\mathbf{w}_k^T\mathbf{x}_i - \mathbf{w}_k^T\mathbf{x}_j)^2\pi_i P_{ij} \\
= & \frac{1}{4}\sum_{k=1}^{c}\sum_{j}(\sum_{i\to j}(\mathbf{w}_k^T\mathbf{x}_i - \mathbf{w}_k^T\mathbf{x}_j)^2\pi_i P_{ij} \\
+ & \sum_{j\to i}(\mathbf{w}_k^T\mathbf{x}_j - \mathbf{w}_k^T\mathbf{x}_i)^2\pi_j P_{ji}) \\
= & \sum_{k=1}^{c}\sum_{j}\mathbf{w}_k^T\mathbf{x}_j\pi_j\mathbf{x}_j^T\mathbf{w}_k - \frac{1}{2}\sum_{k=1}^{c}\sum_{j}(\sum_{i\to j}\mathbf{w}_k^T\mathbf{x}_i\pi_i P_{ij}\mathbf{x}_j\mathbf{w}_k^T \\
+ & \sum_{j\to i}\mathbf{w}_k^T\mathbf{x}_j\pi_j P_{ji}\mathbf{x}_i\mathbf{w}_k^T) \\
= & \operatorname{tr}(\mathbf{W}^T\mathbf{X}(\mathbf{\Pi} - \frac{1}{2}(\mathbf{\Pi}\mathbf{P} + \mathbf{P}^T\mathbf{\Pi}))\mathbf{X}^T\mathbf{W}) \\
= & \operatorname{tr}(\mathbf{W}^T\mathbf{X}\mathbf{L}\mathbf{X}^T\mathbf{W}), \qquad (2)
\end{aligned}
$$

where $\mathbf{L} = \mathbf{\Pi} - \frac{1}{2}(\mathbf{\Pi}\mathbf{P} + \mathbf{P}^T\mathbf{\Pi})$ is graph Laplacian of directed graph, $\mathbf{\Pi}$ is a diagonal matrix with $\Pi_{ii} = \pi_i$ and $\mathbf{P}$ is the transition matrix of random walk.

3.2 Laplacian Regularized Least Squares

Till now, we have introduced the graph regularization on both undirected and directed graph. Since the proposed feature selection method is built up on Laplacian Regularized Least Squares (LapRLS), we will give a preliminary introduction here. In the setting of multi-class classification, LapRLS aims to learn c linear classifiers $f_k(\mathbf{x}) = \mathbf{w}_k^T\mathbf{x}, 1 \le k \le c$ by the following optimization problem,

$$
\begin{aligned}
\arg\min_{\mathbf{p},\mathbf{W}} \quad & \frac{1}{2}||\mathbf{X}^T\mathbf{W} - \mathbf{Y}||_F^2 + \frac{\lambda_A}{2}||\mathbf{W}||_F^2 \\
+ & \frac{\lambda_I}{2}\operatorname{tr}(\mathbf{W}^T\mathbf{X}\mathbf{L}\mathbf{X}^T\mathbf{W}), \qquad (3)
\end{aligned}
$$

where $\lambda_A, \lambda_I > 0$ are positive regularization parameters, $\mathbf{W} = [\mathbf{w}_1, \ldots, \mathbf{w}_c]$. More specifically, the first term in the above objective function is traditional least squares, which is able to fit the input content information and labels. The second term is Frobenious norm regularization on $\mathbf{W}$ which controls the complexity of the linear classifier. The third term is graph regularization as we introduced before. It can be either undirected graph regularization in Eq. (1) or directed graph regularization in Eq.(2). It is used to encode the link information of the network (undirected or directed).

The above problem has a closed form solution

$$
\mathbf{W}^* = (\mathbf{X}\mathbf{X}^T + \lambda_A\mathbf{I} + \lambda_I\mathbf{X}\mathbf{L}\mathbf{X}^T)^{-1}\mathbf{X}\mathbf{Y}. \qquad (4)
$$

Note that the inversion of the big matrix $\mathbf{X}\mathbf{X}^T + \lambda_A\mathbf{I} + \lambda_I\mathbf{X}\mathbf{L}\mathbf{X}^T$ is time consuming. Fortunately, it can be solved efficiently as a linear system equation.

Then the label of each data point $\mathbf{x}$ can be predicted by $l = \arg\max_k f_k(\mathbf{x})$.

3.3 Feature Selection in Network

In order to do feature selection, we introduce an indicator variable $\mathbf{p}$, where $\mathbf{p} = (p_1, \ldots, p_d)^T$ and $p_i \in \{0,1\}, i = 1, \ldots, d$, to represent whether a feature is selected or not. We further introduce a diagonal matrix diag($\mathbf{p}$). Then the input data matrix is now represented as diag($\mathbf{p}$)$\mathbf{X}$. In order to indicate that m features are selected, we constrain $\mathbf{p}^T\mathbf{1} = m$.

The proposed feature selection method aims at selecting a subset of features such that the empirical error of LapRLS is minimized. It can be mathematically formulated as

$$\begin{aligned} \arg\min_{\mathbf{p},\mathbf{W}} \quad & \frac{1}{2}||\mathbf{X}^T \text{diag}(\mathbf{p})\mathbf{W} - \mathbf{Y}||_F^2 + \frac{\lambda_A}{2}||\mathbf{W}||_F^2 \\ + \quad & \frac{\lambda_I}{2}\text{tr}(\mathbf{W}^T \text{diag}(\mathbf{p})\mathbf{X}\mathbf{L}\mathbf{X}^T \text{diag}(\mathbf{p})\mathbf{W}), \\ \text{s.t.} \quad & \mathbf{p} \in \{0,1\}^d, \mathbf{p}^T\mathbf{1} = m, \end{aligned} \tag{5}$$

where $\lambda_A, \lambda_I > 0$ are positive regularization parameters. It is worth noting that, when $\mathbf{p} = \mathbf{1}$, the proposed feature selection reduces to LapRLS in the input space. As a result, LapRLS can be seen as a special case of the proposed method without feature selection. We call Eq. (5) as *Feature Selection in Network* (FSNet). It is worth noting that the proposed method is heavily built upon LapRLS, so it is an embedded method.

As can be seen, the problem in Eq. (5) is a mixed integer programming [4], which is difficult to solve. In the following, we will relax it into a continuous optimization problem and present an efficient algorithm.

Suppose we find the optimal solution of Eq. (5), i.e., $\mathbf{W}^*$ and $\mathbf{p}^*$, then $\mathbf{p}^*$ is a binary vector, and diag($\mathbf{p}$)$\mathbf{W}$ is a matrix where the elements of many rows are all zeros. This motivate us to absorb the indicator variables $\mathbf{p}$ into $\mathbf{W}$, and use $L_{2,0}$-norm on $\mathbf{W}$ to achieve feature selection, leading to the following problem

$$\begin{aligned} \arg\min_{\mathbf{W}} \quad & \frac{1}{2}||\mathbf{X}^T\mathbf{W} - \mathbf{Y}||_F^2 + \frac{\lambda_A}{2}||\mathbf{W}||_F^2 \\ + \quad & \frac{\lambda_I}{2}\text{tr}(\mathbf{W}^T\mathbf{X}\mathbf{L}\mathbf{X}^T\mathbf{W}), \\ \text{s.t.} \quad & ||\mathbf{W}||_{2,0} \le m. \end{aligned} \tag{6}$$

Or equivalently the regularized problem,

$$\begin{aligned} \arg\min_{\mathbf{W}} \quad & \frac{1}{2}||\mathbf{X}^T\mathbf{W} - \mathbf{Y}||_F^2 + \frac{\lambda_A}{2}||\mathbf{W}||_F^2 \\ + \quad & \frac{\lambda_I}{2}\text{tr}(\mathbf{W}^T\mathbf{X}\mathbf{L}\mathbf{X}^T\mathbf{W}) \\ + \quad & \lambda||\mathbf{W}||_{2,0}, \end{aligned} \tag{7}$$

where $\lambda > 0$ is a regularization parameter. Note that it is difficult to give an analytical relationship between m and λ. Fortunately, such a relationship is not crucial for our problem. The objective function in Eq. (7) is a non-smooth and nonconvex function. We relax $||\mathbf{W}||_{2,0}$ to its convex hull [4], and obtain the following convex problem,

$$\begin{aligned} \arg\min_{\mathbf{W}} \quad & \frac{1}{2}||\mathbf{X}^T\mathbf{W} - \mathbf{Y}||_F^2 + \frac{\lambda_A}{2}||\mathbf{W}||_F^2 \\ + \quad & \frac{\lambda_I}{2}\text{tr}(\mathbf{W}^T\mathbf{X}\mathbf{L}\mathbf{X}^T\mathbf{W}) \\ + \quad & \lambda||\mathbf{W}||_{2,1}. \end{aligned} \tag{8}$$

In the following, we will present an algorithm for solving Eq. (8).

3.4 Proximal Gradient Descent

The most natural approach for solving the problem in Eq. (7) is the sub-gradient descent method [4]. However, its convergence rate is very slow, i.e., $O(\frac{1}{\epsilon^2})$ [15].

Recently, proximal gradient descent has received increasing attention in the machine learning community [11] [14]. It achieves the optimal convergence rate, i.e., $O(\frac{1}{\epsilon})$ for the first-order method and is able to deal with large-scale non-smooth convex problems. It can be seen as an extension of gradient descent, where the objective function to minimize is the composite of a smooth part and a non-smooth part. As to our problem, let

$$\begin{aligned} f(\mathbf{W}) &= \frac{1}{2}||\mathbf{X}^T\mathbf{W} - \mathbf{Y}||_F^2 + \frac{\lambda_A}{2}||\mathbf{W}||_F^2 \\ &+ \frac{\lambda_I}{2}\text{tr}(\mathbf{W}^T\mathbf{X}\mathbf{L}\mathbf{X}^T\mathbf{W}) \\ F(\mathbf{W}) &= f(\mathbf{W}) + \lambda||\mathbf{W}||_{2,1}. \end{aligned} \tag{9}$$

It is easy to show that $f(\mathbf{W})$ is convex and differentiable, while $\lambda||\mathbf{W}||_{2,1}$ is non-smooth but convex.

In each iteration of the proximal algorithm, $F(\mathbf{W})$ is linearized around the current estimate $\mathbf{W}_t$, and the value of $\mathbf{W}$ is updated as the solution of the following proximal gradient descent problem,

$$\mathbf{W}_{t+1} = \arg\min_{\mathbf{W}} G_{\eta_t}(\mathbf{W}, \mathbf{W}_t), \tag{10}$$

where $G_{\eta_t}(\mathbf{W}, \mathbf{W}_t)$ is defined as

$$\begin{aligned} G_{\eta_t}(\mathbf{W}, \mathbf{W}_t) &= f(\mathbf{W}_t) + \langle \nabla f(\mathbf{W}_t), \mathbf{W} - \mathbf{W}_t \rangle \\ &+ \frac{\eta_t}{2}||\mathbf{W} - \mathbf{W}_t||^2 + \lambda||\mathbf{W}||_{2,1}. \end{aligned} \tag{11}$$

In our problem, we have

$$\nabla f(\mathbf{W}_t) = \mathbf{X}\mathbf{X}^T\mathbf{W}_t - \mathbf{X}\mathbf{Y} + \lambda_A\mathbf{W}_t + \lambda_I\mathbf{X}\mathbf{L}\mathbf{X}^T\mathbf{W}_t. \tag{12}$$

The philosophy under this formulation is that if the optimization problem in Eq. (10) can be solved by exploiting the structure of the $L_{2,1}$ norm, then the convergence rate of the resulting algorithm is the same as that of gradient descent method, i.e., $O(\frac{1}{\epsilon})$, since no approximation on the non-smooth term is employed.

By ignoring the terms in $G_{\eta_t}(\mathbf{W}, \mathbf{W}_t)$ that is independent of $\mathbf{W}$, the optimization problem in Eq. (10) boils down to

$$\mathbf{W}_{t+1} = \pi_{\eta_t}(\mathbf{W}_t) = \arg\min_{\mathbf{W}} \frac{1}{2}||\mathbf{W} - \mathbf{U}_t||_F^2 + \frac{\lambda}{\eta_t}||\mathbf{W}||_{2,1}, \tag{13}$$

where $\mathbf{U}_t = \mathbf{W}_t - \frac{1}{\eta_t}\nabla f(\mathbf{W}_t)$. It can be further decomposed into c separate subproblems of dimension d

$$\mathbf{w}_{t+1}^i = \arg\min ||\mathbf{w}^i - \mathbf{u}_t^i||_2^2 + \frac{\lambda}{\eta_t}||\mathbf{w}^i||_2, \tag{14}$$

where $\mathbf{w}_{t+1}^i$, $\mathbf{w}^i$ and $\mathbf{u}_t^i$ are the i-th rows of $\mathbf{W}_{t+1}$, $\mathbf{W}$ and $\mathbf{U}_t$ respectively. It has a closed form solution [14] as follows

$$\mathbf{w}^{i*} = \begin{cases} (1 - \frac{\lambda}{\eta_t||\mathbf{u}_t^i||})\mathbf{u}_t^i, & \text{if } ||\mathbf{u}_t^i|| > \frac{\lambda}{\eta_t} \\ \mathbf{0}, & \text{otherwise.} \end{cases} \tag{15}$$

Thus, the proximal gradient decent in Eq. (10) has the same convergence rate of $O(\frac{1}{\epsilon})$ as gradient descent for smooth problem.

3.5 Accelerated Proximal Gradient Decent

To achieve more efficient optimization, we employ Nesterov s method [15] to accelerate the proximal gradient decent in Eq. (10), which owns the convergence rate as $O(\frac{1}{\sqrt{\epsilon}})$. More specifically, we construct a linear combination of $\mathbf{W}_t$ and $\mathbf{W}_{t+1}$ to update $\mathbf{V}_{t+1}$ as follows:

$$\mathbf{V}_{t+1} = \mathbf{W}_t + \frac{\alpha_t - 1}{\alpha_{t+1}}(\mathbf{W}_{t+1} - \mathbf{W}_t), \tag{16}$$

where the sequence $\{\alpha_t\}_{t\geq 1}$ is conventionally set to be $\alpha_{t+1} = \frac{1+\sqrt{1+4\alpha_t^2}}{2}$. For more detail, please refer to [11]. Here we directly present the final algorithm for optimizing Eq. (8) in Algorithm 1.

Algorithm 1 Feature Selection in Network

Initiali e: $\eta_0, \mathbf{W}_1 \in \mathbb{R}^{d\times m}, \alpha_1 = 1$;
repeat
  while $F(\mathbf{W}_t) > G_{\eta_{t-1}}(\pi_{\eta_{t-1}}(\mathbf{W}_t), \mathbf{W}_t)$ **do**
    Set $\eta_{t-1} = \gamma\eta_{t-1}$
  end while
  Set $\eta_t = \eta_{t-1}$
  Compute $\mathbf{W}_{t+1} = \arg\min_{\mathbf{W}} G_{\eta_t}(\mathbf{W}, \mathbf{V}_t)$
  Compute $\alpha_{t+1} = \frac{1+\sqrt{1+4\alpha_t^2}}{2}$
  Compute $\mathbf{V}_{t+1} = \mathbf{W}_t + \frac{\alpha_t - 1}{\alpha_{t+1}}(\mathbf{W}_{t+1} - \mathbf{W}_t)$
until convergence

3.6 Discussion

Once we obtain $\mathbf{W}$, we can obtain the selected features as follows. We calculate the score for each feature as

$$\text{score}(i) = \sqrt{\sum_j W_{i,j}^2}. \tag{17}$$

Then we select all those features whose score is nonzero.

Given the selected features, we can train a classifier such as regularized least squares (RLS) [17] or LapRLS on the reduced data to do classification. Since the proposed method is specifically designed for LapRLS, we use LapRLS as the classifier in our experiments. More importantly, we do not need to re-train a LapRLS using the selected features. We can use the learnt weight matrix $\mathbf{W}$ directly, because it is already a linear classifier based on the selected features.

It can be seen that one additional advantage of the proposed method is that we do not need to predefine the number of selected features, i.e., m. In fact, the number of features to select is implicitly controlled by the regularization parameter λ.

3.7 Convergence Analysis

The convergence property of Algorithm 1 is stated in the following theorem.

Theorem 3.1 *[15] Let $\{\mathbf{W}_t\}$ be the sequence generated by Algorithm 1, then for any $t \geq 1$ we have*

$$F(\mathbf{W}_t) - F(\mathbf{W}^*) \leq \frac{2\gamma L||\mathbf{W}_1 - \mathbf{W}^*||_F^2}{(t+1)^2}, \tag{18}$$

where L is the Lipschitz constant of the gradient of $f(\mathbf{W})$ in the objective function, $\mathbf{W}^* = \arg\min_{\mathbf{W}} F(\mathbf{W})$.

Theorem 3.1 shows that the convergence rate of the accelerated proximal gradient method is $O(\frac{1}{\sqrt{\epsilon}})$. The detail proof of the above theorem can be found in [15] [11].

4. EXPERIMENTS

In this section, we will evaluate the proposed method for web page classification and research paper classification. The task of the experiments is to classify the networked data based on their content information and link structure. We compare it with some state of the art methods.

4.1 Data Sets

We use the same data sets[1] used in [26] to evaluate our method.

WebKB data set contains about 6,000 web pages collected from the web sites of computer science departments of four universities (Cornell, Texas, Washington, and Wisconsin). Each web page is labeled with one out of seven categories: student, professor, course, project, staff, department, and "other". The characteristics about the WebKB data set are briefly summarized in Table 1.

Table 1: Description of the WebKB data set

Data Sets	#samples	#features	#links	#classes
Cornell	827	4134	1626	7
Texas	814	4029	1480	7
Washington	1166	4165	2218	7
Wisconsin	1210	4189	3200	6

Cora data set contains the abstracts and references of about 34,000 research papers from the computer science community. The task is to classify each paper into one of the subfields of data structure (DS), hardware and architecture (HA), machine learning (ML), and programming language (PL). The characteristics about the Cora data set are summarized in Table 2.

Table 2: Description of the Cora data set

Data Sets	#samples	#features	#links	#classes
DS	751	6234	1283	9
HA	400	3989	793	7
ML	1617	8329	4046	7
PL	1575	7949	4918	9

We can see that the dimensionality of the data is very high (thousands of words). In addition, the link in the above two data sets is in nature directed. In the following experiments, we study both undirected graph regularization and directed graph regularization. To use undirected graph regularization, we use a symmetric adjacency matrix, i.e., $\mathbf{A} = \max(\mathbf{A}, \mathbf{A}^T)$.

4.2 Methods

In order to evaluate the proposed feature selection methods, we compare it with the following baselines.

The first baseline is regularized least squares (RLS) [17], which is the state of the art classifier for i.i.d. data and is very related to LapRLS. In detail, RLS is applied in the following 3 settings.

[1] http://www.nec-labs.com/~zsh/files/link-fact-data.zip

- **RLS on content**: It ignores the link structure in the data, and applies RLS only on the content information in the original bag-of-words representation.
- **RLS on link**: It ignores the content information, and treats links as the features, i.e, the i-th feature is link to the i-th page.
- **RLS on content+link**: The content features and link features of the two methods above are concatenated to give the feature representation, then RLS is applied.

The second baseline is LapRLS [2], which is able to utilize both content information and link information. It can be seen as special case of the proposed method. That is, it does not do feature selection. So it uses all the original features. In detail, we adopt LapRLS in the following 2 scenarios.

- **undirected LapRLS**: It is LapRLS with undirected graph regularization in Eq.(1). We treat the networked data as undirected graph. That is, we set $\mathbf{A} = \max(\mathbf{A}, \mathbf{A}^T)$.
- **directed LapRLS**: It is LapRLS with directed graph regularization in Eq.(2).

The third baseline is a traditional feature selection method. We choose Fisher score [17] because previous study [7] showed that it is comparable to or even better than the other feature selection methods [23]. We first apply Fisher score to select features, then apply RLS in 3 ways as before. As a result, we get three methods: **FS+RLS on content**, **FS+RLS on link**, and **FS+RLS on content+link**. In addition, we are also interested in first applying Fisher score on the content information to select features, and then apply **undirected LapRLS** and **directed LapRLS**. We name these two methods as **FS+undirected LapRLS** and **FS+directed LapRLS**

The fourth baseline is probabilistic relation principle component analysis (PRPCA) [13] which is proposed recently. It is the state of the art subspace learning method in network. As we know, both subspace learning and feature selection can achieve dimensionality reduction. As a result, we are very interested in comparing the proposed method with PRPCA.

For the proposed feature selection method, i.e., FSNet, similar with LapRLS, we also evaluate it in two setting: **undirected FSNet** and **directed FSNet**. Note that we do not need to train a classifier after selecting the features, because FSNet not only selects the features, but also outputs a linear classifier, i.e., $\mathbf{W}$.

We did not compare the proposed method with the methods proposed in [25] [26] and [12] because these two methods are transductive learning method [21] rather than inductive learning methods. In other words, those methods utilize the testing data when training. Hence it is unfair to do comparison.

4.3 Parameter Settings

For RLS, we set $\lambda_A = 1$ on WebKB data set and $\lambda_A = 0.1$ on Cora Data set.

For undirected LapRLS and directed LapRLS, we simply fix $\lambda_A = 1$, and tune λ_I by searching the grid $\{0.001, 0.005, \ldots, 0.05, 0.1\}$.

For Fisher score, we select $\{50\ \ , 60\ \ , \ldots, 90\ \ \}$ of the original features (content, link, or content+link), and the best result is reported.

For PRPCA, according to [13], we set the dimensionality of the subspace to 50 and number of iterations to 5.

For undirected FSNet and directed FSNet, we fix $\lambda_A = 1$, and tune λ_I by searching the grid $\{0.001, 0.005, \ldots, 0.05, 0.1\}$. In addition, on WebKB data set, we set $\lambda = 1$, while on Cora data set, we use $\lambda = 0.001$. In the accelerated proximal gradient descent, there is a parameter γ. We simply set $\gamma = 1.1$.

We randomly split data into five folds and repeat the experiment for five times. For each time, we use one fold for testing, and the other four folds for training.

4.4 Study on Convergence

Before reporting the classification results, in this subsection, we first examine the convergence of the accelerated proximal gradient descent in Algorithm 1 and original proximal gradient descent. In Figure 2, we plot the objective function value in Eq. (8 with respect to the number of iterations on the WebKB (Cornell) data subset. The parameter setting is $\lambda_A = 1, \lambda = 1, \lambda_I = 0.01$. In the figure, the y-axis is the value of objective function and the x-axis denotes the iteration number.

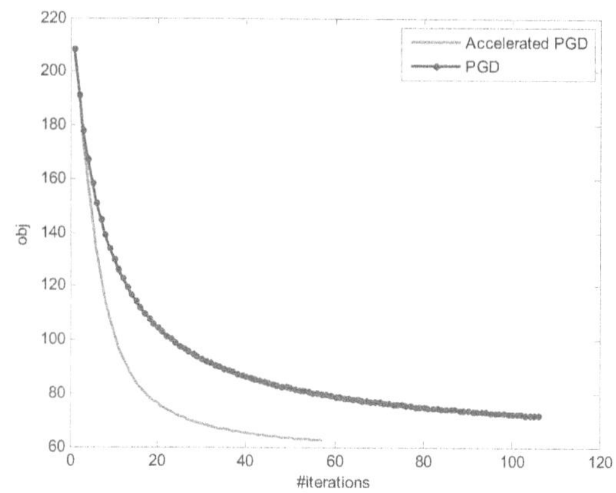

Figure 2: The objecti e function alue of FSNet with respect to the number of iterations for (a) accelerated proximal gradient descent and (b) proximal gradient descent on the WebKB (Cornell) data subset.

We can see that the accelerated proximal gradient descent (Accelerated PGD) converges faster than proximal gradient descent (PGD). In detail, the Accelerated PGD usually converges within 50 iterations, while the original PGD needs more than 100 iterations to converge on WebKB data sets. This is consistent with the theoretical result in Section 3.7. That is, the convergence rate of Accelerated PGD is $O(\frac{1}{\sqrt{\epsilon}})$, which is faster than that of PGD, i.e., $O(\frac{1}{\epsilon})$. Similar results can be observed on other data sets.

The experimental results of FSNet in the rest part are all achieved by accelerated proximal gradient descent. Note that given sufficient number of iterations, both accelerated proximal gradient descent and proximal gradient descent will converge to the same solution, because the optimization problem of FSNet in Eq. (8) is convex.

4.5 Study on the Weight Matrix $\mathbf{W}$

To get a better understanding of our approach, we plot the learnt weight matrix, i.e., $\mathbf{W}$ of our method and LapRLS on WebKB (Cornell) data subset in Figure 3. In the figure, (a) shows the weight matrix of LapRLS, while (b) shows the weight matrix of FSNet. The parameter settings are $\lambda_A = 1, \lambda_I = 0.01$ for LapRLS, and $\lambda_A = 1, \lambda_I = 0.01, \lambda = 1$ for FSNet. It can be seen that many rows of the weight matrix of FSNet are all zero, which leads to feature selection. We call it "row-sparsity". That means, the corresponding features are eliminated. In contrast, the weight matrix of LapRLS is not row-sparse, which is not able to do feature selection.

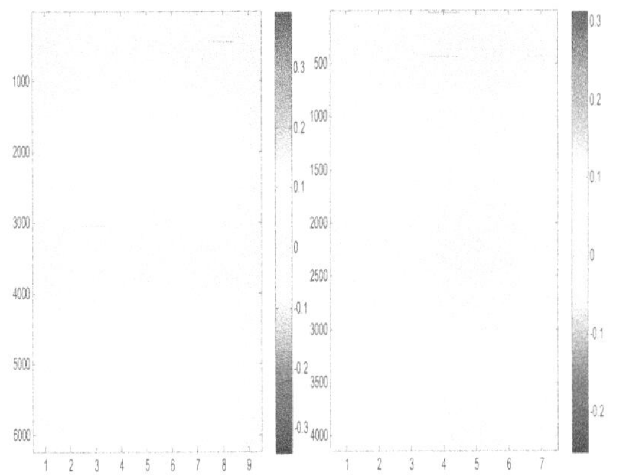

(a) LapRLS (b) FSNet

Figure 3: The weight matrix W of the learnt classifier: (a) LapRLS; (b) FSNet on WebKB (Cornell) data subset. For better iewing, please see it in colored pdf.

4.6 Classification Results

The classification results on WebKB data set and Cora data set are reported in Table 3 and Table 4 respectively. For clear comparison, we also show the results in Figure 4 and Figure 5.

It can be observed that:

1. The proposed method outperforms the baseline methods consistently on WebKB data set, while the proposed method outperforms the baseline methods on 3 out of 4 subsets in Cora data set.

2. The proposed method outperforms LapRLS, which can be seen as a special case of the proposed method without feature selection. This indicates that feature selection is crucial and beneficial for classification of networked data.

3. FS+LapRLS is inferior to FSNet. This is because that Fisher score is based on i.i.d. assumption, while the networked data violate this assumption. In contrast, FSNet is able to utilize both content and link information in a principled way. On the other hand, FS+LapRLS is no better than LapRLS. This is because Fisher score in FS+LapRLS cannot consider the link information, which is crucial for learning in network.

4. PRPCA also achieves very good result on WebKB data set. However, it is not as good as FSNet. The reason is that PRPCA is an unsupervised subspace learning method, while FSNet is a supervised method. Supervised dimensionality reduction methods are generally better than unsupervised methods for classification.

5. The reason why the proposed method is not as good as some baseline methods (RLS on content+link) on the Cora data set may be that the citation relation among papers is more complicated than hyper-link among web pages. Graph regularization may not be that useful to utilize the underlying information of citation. We will investigate other techniques to fully use the citation information in the future.

6. The proposed methods with undirected graph regularization and directed graph regularization achieve comparable results. We deem that FSNet with directed graph regularization will achieve better result than FSNet with undirected graph regularization because the link information in the two data sets is directed. However, they eventually achieve very similar results. As far as we know, there is no theoretical work on the comparison between undirected and directed graph regularization. This needs further study.

4.7 Sensitivity vs the Regularization Parameter λ_I

FSNet has three parameters, which are the regularization parameters, i.e., λ_A, λ_I and λ. In our experiments, we simply set $\lambda_A = 1$, and $\lambda = 1$ on WebKB data set while $\lambda = 0.001$ on Cora Data set. The only parameter needed to tune is λ_I. It controls the contribution of link information. Hence we investigate the classification accuracy with respect to the regularization parameter λ_I. We vary the value of λ_I, and plot the corresponding classification accuracy on the WebKB and Cora data sets in Figure 6 and Figure 7 respectively.

As can be seen, FSNet is not sensitive to the regularization parameter λ_I in a wide range of λ_I. In detail, FSNet achieves consistently better performance than LapRLS with the λ_I varying from 0.001 to 0.1 on both data sets. It is a very appealing property because we do not need to tune the regularization parameter painfully in the application.

5. CONCLUSION AND FUTURE WORK

In this paper, we proposed a feature selection method based on Laplacian Regularized Least Squares (LapRLS) for the data distributing in a network. We use linear regression to fit the content information, and use graph regularization to consider the link information. Then the feature selection method is casted as selecting a subset of features such that the training error of LapRLS is minimized. The resultant optimization problem is a mixed integer programming, which is difficult to solve. It is relaxed into a $L_{2,1}$-norm constrained least squares problem and solved by accelerated proximal gradient algorithm. Experiments on benchmark networked data show that the proposed method outperforms the state of the art methods.

In the future work, we will study other kinds of techniques to utilize the link information. For example, [16] proposed modularity to measure the strength of a partition for real-world networks by taking into account the degree distribution of nodes. It is shown to be effective in various kinds of complex networks. We will investigate how to incorporate modularity into our method.

Table 3: **Classification Accurac (%) on the four subsets of WebKB data set**

Data Sets	Cornell	Texas	Washington	Wisconsin
RLS on content	84.12±2.16	78.15±3.23	86.78±2.22	84.30±2.19
RLS on links	28.48±3.71	28.52±4.46	23.52±1.34	34.88±2.73
RLS on content+link	84.36±1.45	80.00±2.60	87.98±1.82	85.29±1.79
FS+RLS on content	84.12±2.07	78.27±2.97	86.09±2.03	84.05±2.18
FS+RLS on link	27.39±3.62	26.79±5.88	23.18±1.66	27.52±2.46
FS+RLS on content+link	84.85±1.42	79.75±3.64	87.73±2.24	85.12±2.13
undirected LapRLS	84.24±2.10	78.40±2.39	86.78±2.07	84.55±2.40
directed LapRLS	85.21±1.75	78.15±3.34	86.87±2.12	84.71±2.28
FS+undirected LapRLS	84.24±2.39	78.89±2.28	86.35±2.18	84.05±2.14
FS+directed LapRLS	85.21±1.95	78.40±3.18	86.18±1.95	84.13±2.27
PRPCA	86.30±2.89	81.85±1.83	89.87±1.62	88.93±2.03
undirected FSNet	**88.24±1.58**	84.69±1.34	**92.02±2.09**	**89.09±2.16**
directed FSNet	88.12±1.64	**84.81±1.61**	**92.02±2.09**	89.01±1.95

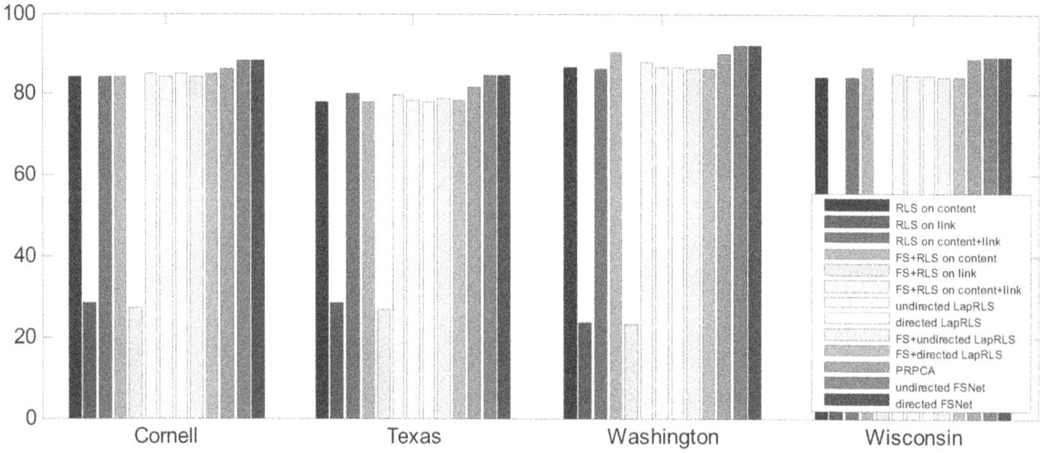

Figure 4: Classification accurac on the four subsets of WebKB dataset.

Table 4: **Classification Accurac (%) on the four subsets of Cora data set**

Data Sets	DS	HA	ML	PL
RLS on content	52.80±7.47	66.00±4.79	63.03±1.72	55.37±1.86
RLS on links	54.13±2.18	52.75±9.50	54.80±3.68	52.83±2.38
RLS on content+link	59.47±5.19	**79.50±5.05**	70.09±2.87	60.83±2.30
FS+RLS on content	54.00±5.60	66.00±4.79	63.10±1.30	55.37±1.86
FS+RLS on link	54.13±2.18	52.50±9.14	54.80±3.68	53.02±2.18
FS+RLS on content+link	59.73±6.51	75.50±7.10	70.09±2.87	60.83±2.30
undirected LapRLS	57.47±6.15	65.75±5.84	67.24±1.86	58.22±1.53
directed LapRLS	57.33±6.25	66.00±4.79	67.18±2.20	58.29±2.64
FS+undirected LapRLS	57.47±6.15	65.75±5.84	67.31±2.21	57.65±2.25
FS+directed LapRLS	57.33±6.25	66.25±4.59	67.37±1.99	58.10±1.88
PRPCA	53.07±4.80	68.25±3.60	68.36±2.41	54.98±2.41
undirected FSNet	**61.60±5.30**	67.50±5.59	**72.38±1.96**	61.52±2.92
directed FSNet	**61.60±5.30**	67.00±5.63	**72.38±1.96**	**61.52±2.59**

Acknowledgements

The work was supported in part by NSF IIS-09-05215, U.S. Air Force Office of Scientific Research MURI award FA9550-08-1-0265, and the U.S. Army Research Laboratory under Cooperative Agreement Number W911NF-09-2-0053 (NS-CTA). The views and conclusions contained in this document are those of the authors and should not be interpreted as representing the official policies, either expressed or implied, of the Army Research Laboratory or the U.S. Government. The U.S. Government is authorized to reproduce and distribute reprints for Government purposes notwithstanding any copyright notation here on. We thank the anonymous reviewers for their helpful comments.

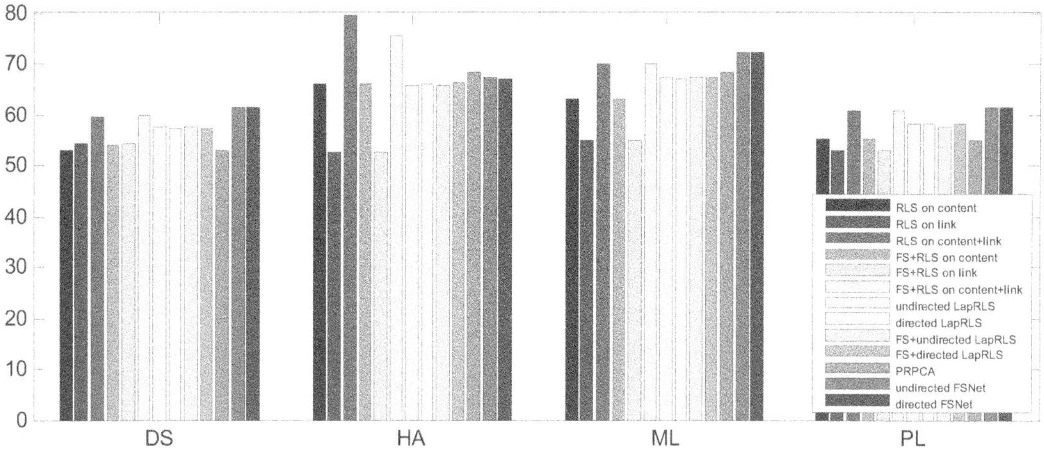

Figure 5: Classification accurac on the four subsets of Cora dataset.

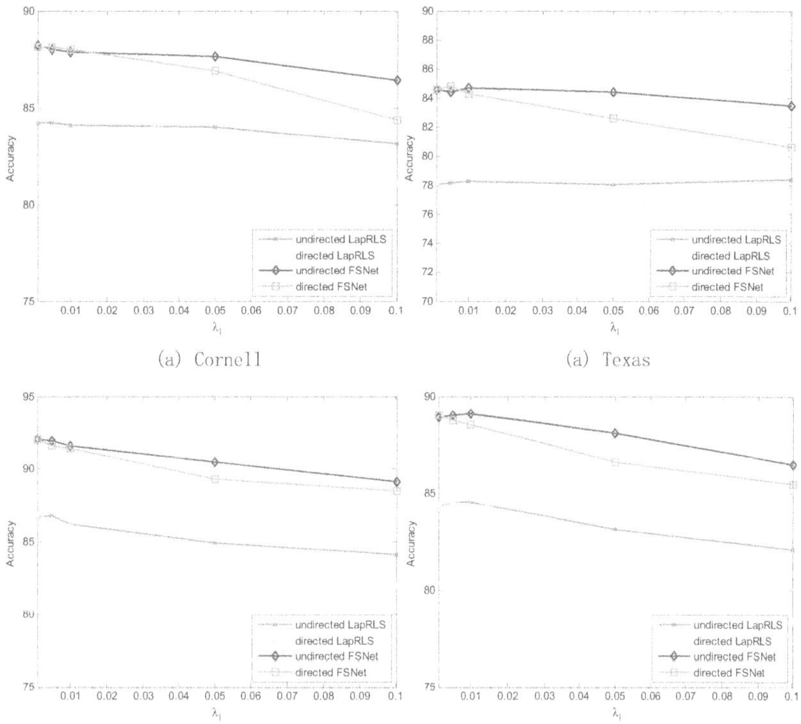

(a) Cornell (a) Texas

(c) Washington (d) Wisconsin

Figure 6: Classification accurac of LapRLS and FSNet with respect to the regulari ation parameter λ_I on the four subsets of WebKB dataset.

6. REFERENCES

[1] M. Belkin and P. Niyogi. Laplacian eigenmaps for dimensionality reduction and data representation. *Neural Computation*, 15(6):1373–1396, 2003.

[2] M. Belkin, P. Niyogi, and V. Sindhwani. Manifold regularization: A geometric framework for learning from labeled and unlabeled examples. *Journal of Machine Learning Research*, 7:2399–2434, 2006.

[3] M. Bilgic, L. Mihalkova, and L. Getoor. Active learning for networked data. In *ICML*, pages 79–86, 2010.

[4] S. Boyd and L. Vandenberghe. *Convex optimization.* Cambridge University Press, Cambridge, 2004.

[5] F. R. K. Chung. *Spectral Graph Theory.* American Mathematical Society, February 1997.

[6] D. A. Cohn and T. Hofmann. The missing link - a probabilistic model of document content and hypertext connectivity. In *NIPS*, pages 430–436, 2000.

[7] Q. Gu, Z. Li, and J. Han. Generalized fisher score for feature selection. In *Proceedings of the International Conference on Uncertainty in Artificial Intelligence*, 2011.

[8] I. Guyon and A. Elisseeff. An introduction to variable

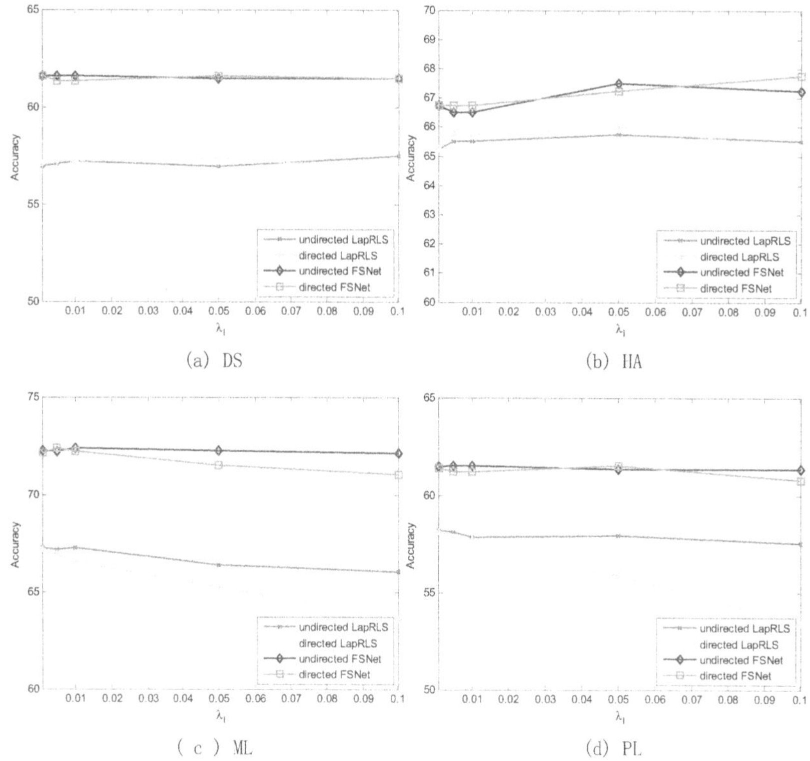

Figure 7: Classification accurac of LapRLS and FSNet with respect to the regulari ation parameter λ_I on the four subsets of Cora dataset.

and feature selection. *Journal of Machine Learning Research*, 3:1157–1182, 2003.

[9] X. He and P. Niyogi. Locality preserving projections. In *NIPS*, 2003.

[10] T. Hofmann. Unsupervised learning by probabilistic latent semantic analysis. *Machine Learning*, 42(1/2):177–196, 2001.

[11] S. Ji and J. Ye. An accelerated gradient method for trace norm minimization. In *ICML*, page 58, 2009.

[12] W.-J. Li and D.-Y. Yeung. Relation regularized matrix factorization. In *IJCAI*, pages 1126–1131, 2009.

[13] W.-J. Li, D.-Y. Yeung, and Z. Zhang. Probabilistic relational pca. In Y. Bengio, D. Schuurmans, J. Lafferty, C. K. I. Williams, and A. Culotta, editors, *Advances in Neural Information Processing Systems 22*, pages 1123–1131. 2009.

[14] J. Liu, S. Ji, and J. Ye. Multi-task feature learning via efficient $l_{2,1}$-norm minimization. In *Proceedings of the Twenty-Fifth Conference on Uncertainty in Artificial Intelligence (UAI 2009)*, 2009.

[15] Y. Nesterov. *Introductory Lectures on Convex Optimization: A Basic Course*. Kluwer Academic Publishers, 2003.

[16] M. E. Newman. Modularity and community structure in networks. *Proc Natl Acad Sci U S A*, 103(23):8577–8582, June 2006.

[17] P. E. H. R. O. Duda and D. G. Stork. *Pattern Classification*. Wiley-Interscience Publication, 2001.

[18] P. Sen, G. Namata, M. Bilgic, L. Getoor, B. Gallagher, and T. Eliassi-Rad. Collective classification in network data. *AI Magazine*, 29(3):93–106, 2008.

[19] L. Shi, Y. Zhao, and J. Tang. Combining link and content for collective active learning. In *CIKM*, pages 1829–1832, 2010.

[20] A. J. Smola and R. I. Kondor. Kernels and regularization on graphs. In *COLT*, pages 144–158, 2003.

[21] V. N. Vapnik. *The nature of statistical learning theory*. Springer-Verlag New York, Inc., New York, NY, USA, 1995.

[22] S. Yan, D. Xu, B. Zhang, H. Zhang, Q. Yang, and S. Lin. Graph embedding and extensions: A general framework for dimensionality reduction. *IEEE Trans. Pattern Anal. Mach. Intell.*, 29(1):40–51, 2007.

[23] Y. Yang and J. O. Pedersen. A comparative study on feature selection in text categorization. In *ICML*, pages 412–420, 1997.

[24] D. Zhou, O. Bousquet, T. N. Lal, J. Weston, and B. Schölkopf. Learning with local and global consistency. In *NIPS*, 2003.

[25] D. Zhou, J. Huang, and B. Schölkopf. Learning from labeled and unlabeled data on a directed graph. In *ICML*, pages 1036–1043, 2005.

[26] S. Zhu, K. Yu, Y. Chi, and Y. Gong. Combining content and link for classification using matrix factorization. In *SIGIR*, pages 487–494, 2007.

[27] X. Zhu, Z. Ghahramani, and J. D. Lafferty. Semi-supervised learning using gaussian fields and harmonic functions. In *ICML*, pages 912–919, 2003.

Practical Representations for Web and Social Graphs

Francisco Claude
University of Waterloo
Waterloo, Canada
fclaude@cs.uwaterloo.ca

Susana Ladra
Universidade da Coruña
A Coruña, Spain
sladra@udc.es

ABSTRACT

In this paper we focus on representing Web and social graphs. Our work is motivated by the need of mining information out of these graphs, thus our representations do not only aim at compressing the graphs, but also at supporting efficient navigation. This allows us to process bigger graphs in main memory, avoiding the slowdown brought by resorting on external memory.

We first show how by just partitioning the graph and combining two existing techniques for Web graph compression, k^2-trees [Brisaboa, Ladra and Navarro, SPIRE 2009] and RePair-Graph [Claude and Navarro, TWEB 2010], exploiting the fact that most links are intra-domain, we obtain the best time/space trade-off for direct and reverse navigation when compared to the state of the art. In social networks, splitting the graph to achieve a good decomposition is not easy. For this case, we explore a new proposal for indexing MP_K linearizations [Maserrat and Pei, KDD 2010], which have proven to be an effective way of representing social networks in little space by exploiting common dense subgraphs. Our proposal offers better worst case bounds in space and time, and is also a competitive alternative in practice.

Categories and Subject Descriptors

E.1 [**Data Structures**]: Graphs and networks; E.4 [**Coding and Information Theory**]: Data compaction and compression; H.3.3 [**Information Storage and Retrieval**]: Information Search and Retrieval

General Terms

Experimentation, Performance

1. INTRODUCTION

Graphs are a natural way of modeling connections among Web pages in a network or people according to a criteria like friendship, co-authorship, etc. Many algorithms that compute and infer interesting facts out of these networks work directly over these graphs. Some examples of this are Connected components, HITS [16], PageRank [21], spam-detection[22], among others. In social networks, graph mining also enables the study of populations' behavior. Successful graph mining not only enables segmentation of users but also prediction of behavior. Link analysis and graph mining remains an area of high interest and development.

These human-generated graphs are growing at an amazing pace, and their representation in main memory, secondary memory, and distributed systems are getting more and more attention. Furthermore, space-efficient representations for these graphs have succeeded at exploiting regularities that are particular to the domain. In the case of Web graphs the main properties exploited are the locality of reference, skewed in/out-degree, and similarity of adjacency lists among nodes of the same domain. In social networks, there is a tendency towards forming cliques in the network.

Hence, representing, compressing and indexing graphs become crucial aspects for the performance and in-memory processing when mining information from those graphs. In this work we focus on obtaining space-efficient in-memory representations for both, Web graphs and social networks. We follow the same notation across this paper. When talking about a graph $G = (V, E)$ we call $n = |V|$ the number of nodes and $m = |E|$ the number of edges.

For representing Web graphs, we present a structure that successfully combines the k^2-tree, proposed by Brisaboa et al. [7], and the RePair representation proposed by Claude and Navarro [11]. This new structure splits the graph in $t+1$ pieces, the first t ones correspond to sub-graphs formed by groups of domains. The last piece contains all the edges that point from one of the t sub-graphs to another one. This combination allows us to obtain the best cases for the k^2-tree, since most of the compression is gained inside domains and the query time is good when the matrix is dense.

Our second structure proposed corresponds to a new indexing technique for the MP_K linearization proposed by Maserrat and Pei [20]. This new indexing technique improves the time to obtain the in/out-neighbors of a node v from $O(\sum_{u \in N_v} deg(u))$ [1] to $O(\lg\lg n)$ per element retrieved, while obtaining a space that is bounded by the previous indexing proposal [20] plus lower order terms.

The experimental results show that for Web graphs we obtain a structure that improves upon the state of the art, achieving the best trade-off when we require both, direct and reverse navigation. In the domain of social networks,

[1] N_v corresponds to the neighbors of v and $deg(u)$ to the number of incoming/outgoing links to/from u.

our proposal improves upon previous results showing that it constitutes a competitive index for social networks. An interesting property of this last structure is that any practical advances in *rank/select* indexes for large alphabets [13, 9] would improve our representation. Our implementations are available at `http://webgraphs.recoded.cl/`.

2. RELATED WORK

In this section we describe the related work on Web graph and social networks representations, focusing on compact solutions that achieve little space while retaining basic navigational functionality. The first subsection covers Web graphs and presents in more detail the k^2-tree [7]. The next subsection presents results on social networks and relevant details about the representation proposed by Maserrat and Pei [20].

2.1 Compact Representations of Web Graphs

The best trade-off, for many years, was offered by the proposal of Boldi and Vigna [5]. They presented a highly engineered framework for managing Web graphs, exploiting the regularities of Web graphs, and at the same time offering fast access to any adjacency list. Later, Boldi et al. [4] proposed an improved method based on their original method. An alternative that permits a fast access to direct lists was proposed by Apostolico and Drovandi [1]. This representation depends only on their topology of the graph.

Another proposal, competing in the time/space trade-off, is the one by Claude and Navarro [11]. This approach represents the graph as a text, and then, by applying grammar based compression, they achieve a representation whose space consumption is similar to the one by Boldi and Vigna while the access time is considerably reduced. The particular method used is an approximate version of the well known Re-Pair compression method [11]. Claude and Navarro extended their work to support direct and reverse navigation [10]. This was later improved by Brisaboa et al. [7], who represent a binary matrix by using a succinct representation for trees [15] for a special kind of tree inspired in quad-trees. Their structure, called k^2-tree, achieves the smallest space reported so far when representing both graphs, direct and reverse. During the rest of this section, we focus on k^2-trees, providing information required in the rest of the article.

The k^2-tree method represents the adjacency matrix of the graph using a non-balanced k^2-ary tree. The method consists of a subdivision of the adjacency matrix into k rows and k columns of sub-matrices of size n^2/k^2. Each of the resulting k^2 sub-matrices will be a child of the root node and its value will be 1 iff in the cells of the sub-matrix there is at least one 1. A 0 child means that the sub-matrix has all 0s and hence the tree decomposition ends there. Once the level 1, with the children of the root, has been built, the method proceeds recursively for each child with value 1.

This construction allows us to represent the whole adjacency matrix with just two bit arrays: T (tree) and L (leaves). T stores all the bits of the k^2-tree except those in the last level. The bits are placed following a level-wise traversal. L stores the last level of the tree. Additionally, an auxiliary structure is created over T that allows the navigation through the compact representation of the tree.

To find the direct (reverse) neighbors of a node of the graph, the k^2-tree needs to locate which cells in a certain row (column) of the adjacency matrix have a 1. This is done with a top-down traversal that can be performed efficiently over the compact representation of the tree, requiring $O(1)$ time per node traversed in the tree.

While alternative compressed graph representations are limited to retrieving direct, and sometimes reverse, neighbors of a given node, the k^2-tree allows for more sophisticated forms of retrieval, such as range searches or checking whether two Web pages are connected or not without extracting the adjacency lists of the pages involved in the query.

2.2 Compact Representation of Social Networks

A Web graph can be regarded as an special case of social network, which describes a network of interconnected pages. Most Web graph compression techniques exploit properties that are exclusive from this particular class, and thus they do not extend well for other social networks.

There has been several attempts at approximating this reordering [4, 8], which turns to be NP-hard. The best result with this approach corresponds to the one by Chierichetti et al. [8]. They extend Boldi and Vigna's WebGraph framework [5] to compress social networks. They exploit the reciprocity exhibited in social networks to improve compression, using a scheme called *backlink* compression, and sort the nodes following a shingle-based ordering using the Jaccard coefficient to measure the similarity between nodes.

Another line is to exploit regularities such as clustering in the graph. One of the best results achieved, proposed by Maserrat and Pei [20], follows this approach. They propose a transformation called MP_K linearization and show how to index them in order to support direct and reverse navigation. Given a graph $G = (V, E)$, the MP_K linearization corresponds to a sequence S of node identifiers that satisfies the following property: For any $e = (u, v) \in E$, there exists a substring of length K in S, such that u and v appear in it.

This sequence, augmented with $2K$ bits per item, is enough to represent the whole graph. The structure proposed by Maserrat and Pei [20] works by storing this $2K$ bits per item in plain form, we call this string N, and storing an alternative sequence S_2, where $S_2[i] = p$ iff $p = \max(\min\{j|S[i] = S[j], j > i\}, \min\{j|S[i] = S[j], j \geq 0\})$. They add dummy nodes at the beginning in order to determine when a traversal of the list of occurrences of a given node finishes. Also, these dummy nodes allow us to start a traversal for a given node in $O(1)$. S is not represented.

3. K²-PARTITIONED

The main proposal of this paper consists in a simple combination of two existing Web graph compression techniques, the approach by Brisaboa et al. [7] and the one by Claude and Navarro [10, 11], which obtains striking practical space/time results, as we show in Section 5.

In order to combine both techniques, we partition the graph into $t+1$ pieces, $G_1, G_2, \ldots, G_{t+1}$. The first t of them correspond to non-overlapping squares along the diagonal of the binary matrix defining the graph. The last partition corresponds to all the ones outside the region defined by $G_1 \cup G_2 \ldots \cup G_t$.

As a simple example, consider a graph with t domains. A valid partition would consider every domain as defining a square in the matrix. The last graph generated contains all the links to external domains in the graph. In fact, this is what the partition scheme aims at, yet we want to be able to join small domains in order to amortize the extra cost of representing a separate graph.

This partition has many interesting advantages over handling the original graph. First, the representation of Brisaboa et al. works faster over smaller graphs, since the height of the tree is smaller; in addition, if the sub-graphs are roughly defined by domains, we do not expect to follow many empty paths through the trees. Besides being faster, we do not expect to lose too much compression, since most of the properties exploited are among nodes in the same domain, and we will enforce complete domains to land on the same sub-graph. Finally, we expect the last sub-graph (including all links not considered in the other sub-graphs) to be sparse, and thus not really an issue in terms of space.

3.1 Partitioning the Graph

We partition the graphs guided by the domains. The partition procedure receives a parameter M, and generates the splitting in a greedy fashion. It starts adding the alphabetically smaller domain to the current sub-graph, and continues adding domains to this partition, in alphabetic order, until at least M nodes are contained in the sub-graph (the size of the square is at least M^2). Then it creates a new sub-graph, and continues with the next domain in alphabetical order. Each of the sub-graphs generated by this process is stored independently, and then, all remaining edges are added to a matrix with the same size of the original graph ($n \times n$). This graph corresponds to G_{t+1}.

3.2 Internal Links

For the representation of the internal links we use the k^2-tree representation presented in [17]. It consists in a modification of the original algorithm where the last level of the k^2-tree is not represented in plain form, but compacted using the variable-length encoding scheme *Directly Addressable Codes* (DACs) [6]. This enables fast direct access to any leaf sub-matrix represented at the last level of the k^2-tree.

More concretely, we create a k^2-tree per each sub-graph G_j, $1 \leq j \leq t$, with the same parameters of k_L, where k_L is the k used in the last level. Then, we create a common vocabulary with the different $k_L \times k_L$ leaf sub-matrices that appear in the last level of the t partitions and compute their frequencies. We sort the vocabulary by frequency, and assign an integer value to each $k_L \times k_L$ sub-matrix: shorter integers are assigned to more frequent sub-matrices. Then, we compress the last level of each k^2-tree by representing the integers associated to those sub-matrices using DACs, which have been proved successfully for this scenario.

Hence, the representation of the internal links consists of an array of t k^2-trees, one per each sub-graph G_j, with $j \leq t$; the common vocabulary of leaf sub-matrices; and an array containing the offsets for each partition, that is, the node identifier of the first node of each sub-graph.

When a query involving internal links must be solved, a binary search is performed in the array of offsets to determine the sub-graph where the sought node is located, and then the query is translated to the corresponding k^2-tree.

Given that the k^2-tree plays the main role in representing the links of the graph, since most links are intra-domain, we call our combination k^2-partitioned.

3.3 External Links

We considered two representations for the graph representing the external links, both based on the approximate version [11] of the Re-Pair compression method [18].

The first one corresponds to the one proposed by Claude and Navarro [10], that supports direct and reverse navigation. The second is a simple modification of the original proposal by Claude and Navarro [11], that compresses both, the direct and the reverse graph, separately, but sharing the vocabulary among them, saving space over the naive representation that compresses both graphs independently.

The way this second approach works is the following: We compress the graphs $G_{t+1} = ([n] = \{1, 2, \ldots, n\}, E)$ and $G^R_{t+1} = ([n], E^R)$ by compressing the fictitious graph $G'_{t+1} = ([2n], E \cup S(E^R))$, where $S(E^R) = \{(n+i, j) | (i, j) \in E^R\}$. This allows us to compress both graphs at the same time, and generates only one dictionary, thus saving space. The query for direct neighbors does not change, and the reverse neighbors can be obtained by adding n to the node identifier and querying the direct neighbors in G'_{t+1}.

In our experiments we will use the second version, which proved to be faster and did not add much extra space.

4. INDEXING MP_K LINEARIZATIONS

As we have said, Web graph compression methods can be used for compressing social networks. However, the proposed method, k^2-partitioned, cannot be as successfully applied to social networks, since it is not usually possible to separate intra-host and inter-host links as clearly as for Web graphs. Hence, in this paper we study the MP_K linearizations to represent social networks.

It is a simple exercise to replace the pointers to the next occurrence of each symbol in the MP_k linearization by an index for sequences supporting rank, select and access.

The *rank* operation for symbol v and position p counts the number of occurrences of v in S up to position p (included). The *select* operation for a symbol v and position j computes the position where the j-th occurrence of v appears in S.

Using rank and select we can iterate over the occurrences of v in S by using $select_S(v, j)$ for $j = 1 \ldots rank_S(v, |S|)$. If we use the structure proposed by Barbay et al. [2], retrieving each position where v occurs takes $O(1)$ time and accessing a position takes $O(\lg \lg n)$ time.

To retrieve the reverse neighbors, a similar approach is valid, but we need to check the $2K$ adjacent positions to each occurrence of v to determine whether they point to v or not.

There are many proposals we can use to represent S offering different time/space trade-offs [2, 13, 19, 12, 14]. We can also improve the N_v term by paying $\lg(3)$ extra bits per symbol in S, by storing three different versions for the identifier of each node. This allows us to scan just the nodes relevant to each query and the time for direct neighbors becomes $O(\lg \lg n)$ per element retrieved. The time for reverse neighbors becomes $O(K \lg \lg n)$ per element retrieved. Note that we always know which part of the field in N we want to access in order to check, so we can always check if a node points to us in $O(1)$ given that we know both positions. When K is smaller than the word size w ($w = \Theta(\log n)$), we can do slightly better using tables to obtain the pointers to our position when retrieving the reverse neighbors, the $O(K)$ factor becomes $O(1 + K^2/\lg n)$.

Table 1: Description of the Web graphs used.

File	Pages	Links	Size (MB)
EU (2005)	862,664	19,235,140	77
UK (2002)	18,520,486	298,113,762	1,208
Arabic (2005)	22,744,080	639,999,458	2,528

THEOREM 1. *If an MP_K linearization (S, N) is represented with the string representation proposed by Barbay et al [2], we obtain an index that allows us to retrieve the direct neighbors of a node in $O(N_v \lg\lg n)$ time. The reverse neighbors can be computed in $O(N_v K \lg\lg n)$ time. The space requirement is $|S|H_0(S)+o(|S|)(1+H_0(S))+2K|S|$ bits, where H_0 corresponds to the zero-order entropy. By using $O(|S|)$ extra bits we can obtain $O(\lg\lg n)$ time per element retrieved for direct neighbors and $O(\min(K, 1+K^2/\lg n)\lg\lg n)$ time per element for the reverse ones.*

5. EXPERIMENTAL RESULTS

5.1 Experiments on Web Graphs

We ran several experiments over some Web graphs from the *WebGraph* project, some of them gathered by UbiCrawler [3]. These data sets are made available to the public by the members of the *Laboratory for Web Algorithmics*[2] at the *Univerita Degli Studi Di Milano*. Table 1 gives the main characteristics of the graphs used. The last column gives the size of a plain adjacency list representation of the graphs (using 4-byte integers).

The machine used in our tests is a 2GHz Intel®Xeon® (8 cores) with 16 GB RAM, and 580 GB Disk (SATA 7200rpm). It runs Ubuntu GNU/Linux with kernel version 2.6.24-28-server SMP (64 bits). We used the gcc compiler version 4.2.4 with `-O9` optimizations. The space achieved by our structures is measured in bits per edge (bpe), dividing the total space of the structure by the number of edges (i.e., links) in the graph. Time results measure average CPU user time per neighbor retrieved: We compute the time to search for the neighbors of all the web pages of the graph (in random order) divided by the total number of links retrieved.

We show in Section 5.1.2 the results of our technique, which outperforms the rest of the methods of the state of the art. These improved results are mainly caused by the partitioned representation of the internal links of the graphs. Hence, we first show some partial results when indexing only intra-host links, which helps us understand the benefits of our proposal.

5.1.1 Internal Links

In this section we show the advantages of representing the internal links separated by domains, using one k^2-tree for each sub-graph instead of using the original k^2-tree representation over the whole adjacency matrix of the web graph. Hence, we compare the compressed representation of the complete web graph obtained by the k^2-tree technique against the compressed representation of just the internal links using the proposed k^2-partitioned approach.

Table 2 illustrates the compression properties obtained by the two techniques, "k^2-tree all" and "k^2-partitioned" over the two larger web graphs described, using $M = 10000$ for the partition of Arabic and $M = 1000$ for UK. We also include a row for each web graph, "k^2-tree inlinks", which shows the time performance when we use the original k^2 technique representing the whole graph to retrieve just the internal links. This can be simulated by querying the neighbors of each web page within the range of page identifiers corresponding to its same domain, hence, we report the times to answer that range query for each web page.

Notice that we are comparing the space results for the original k^2-tree, which represents all the links of the web graph, with the results for k^2-partitioned when representing just the internal links. These intra-domains links constituted around the 90% of the total number of links depending on the graph. The space required by k^2-partitioned to represent those internal links is around 80-90% the space required by the original k^2-tree technique to represent the complete set of links. However, to compute the total space required by k^2-partitioned we must add the space of the external links, which may be less compressible than internal links. This causes that the total compression for k^2-partitioned approach will be close to the compression of the k^2-tree technique but not better, as we will see in Section 5.1.2.

The strength of k^2-partitioned approach consists in representing the internal links by building a separate k^2-tree for each sub-graph, as they become shorter. Moreover, it solves the main problem of k^2-tree approach, where the branches generated by external links may cause several unsuccessful top-down traversals over the tree. This behavior can be observed in Table 2. The average time to retrieve the internal links of a page is considerably faster for k^2-partitioned than retrieving all the links of a page using the original k^2-tree. The times obtained are around 5-20 times faster, as the average number of nodes traversed during the retrieval of the neighbors lists is one order of magnitude larger when using the original k^2-tree than when using k^2-partitioned. k^2-partitioned also obtains better times than retrieving just the internal links from the original k^2-tree.

Hence, excluding external links from the k^2-tree representation decreases the number of traversed nodes significantly, and thus the retrieval time. The experiments demonstrate the imperativeness of storing the external links separately.

5.1.2 Overall Representation

We now compare our combined representation, k^2-partitioned, with the most competitive solutions of the state of the art. Note that in this section we are indexing and searching the complete Web graph, using a k^2-tree approach for the intra-host links and a RePair approach for the inter-host links.

Figure 1 shows the space/time trade-off for retrieving direct neighbors over different graphs (reverse neighbors behave similarly). We measure the average time efficiency in μs/edge as before. We compare our compact representation, k^2-partitioned, with the original k^2-tree and the fastest proposal in [10] that computes both direct and reverse neighbors (`Re-Pair GMR`), as well as the original representation in [11] (`Re-Pair (dir+rev)`). A variant of Re-Pair GMR labeled `Re-Pair GMR (2)` is also included, where *access* operation is solved in constant time and *select* in time $O(\log\log n)$. Thus, `Re-Pair GMR` is faster for reverse neighbors (using constant-time select), and `Re-Pair GMR (2)` is faster on direct neighbors (using constant-time access). We also include

[2]http://law.dsi.unimi.it/

Table 2: Space time results of k^2-partitioned compared with k^2-tree method (just internal links).

Graph	Method	Links (%)	Space (bpe)	Time (μs/e)	Avg. trav. nodes
UK	k^2-tree all	100%	2.78	14.031	1,527.65
	k^2-tree inlinks	92.51%	-	1.174	71.64
	k^2-partitioned	92.51%	2.27	0.749	65.49
Arabic	k^2-tree all	100%	2.47	6.163	1,193.30
	k^2-tree inlinks	89.72%	-	1.217	139.78
	k^2-partitioned	89.72%	2.11	0.817	110.64

the `WebGraph (dir+rev)` alternative from Boldi and Vigna, using version 2.4.2 and the variant strictHostByHostGray, and Apostolico and Drovandi [1] `AD(dir+rev)`, version 0.2.1. In these two techniques, both the graph and its transpose are represented in order to achieve reverse navigation as well. Notice that `AD(dir+rev)` technique performs a reordering of the node identifiers based on the Breadth First Search (BFS) of the graph instead of the lexicographic order. This permutation of identifiers is not accounted for in the space results reported next. However, this mapping should be stored if we want to recover the graph with the original node identifiers.

We can observe that our new representation k^2-partitioned competes successfully with the other compression methods of the literature, especially for larger graphs. It achieves very compact spaces, smaller than the rest of the techniques except for the k^2-tree, which can obtain slightly better spaces at the expense of degrading its time efficiency in orders of magnitude. Hence, our proposed technique achieves the best space/time trade-off for Web graph representation when direct and reverse navigation are required.

5.2 Experiments on Social Networks

In this section we focus on compressing social networks. As k^2-partitioned makes heavy use of the `URLs` of the nodes, something non-existing in social networks, we consider the standard k^2-tree as a baseline for comparing space results.

The method implemented by Maserrat and Pei [20] is not available, thus we implemented our own linearization heuristic. Ours is much simpler than theirs, so we do not obtain the same numbers, still the index shows that it can compete against the other indexing method while offering a time guarantee. The heuristic we used to generate the MP_K linearization corresponds to simply adding the node with more in/out-going links from the last K nodes added so far. In case of a tie, we just chose one node at random. The value of K remains constant through the whole process.

Table 3 shows the social networks we used for our experiments. In Figure 2 we present the time/space tradeoff for our implementation, and we include the results for the WebGraph framework, `AD`, and k^2-trees. For the WebGraph framework, we add the space of the direct and reverse graphs compressed with standard parameters. In order to compare with the previous indexing method for MP_K linearizations, we implemented the index as proposed in [20]. Figure 2 includes these results as `MPk original`. We also include the results for the WebGraph framework, Apostolico and Drovandi technique and the k^2-trees.

We used wavelet trees without pointers [14, 9] to represent the *rank* and *select* data structure[3]. The time per element retrieved is around 8.5 to 20.33 microseconds. This is comparable with other Web graph representations. When compared to the original indexing for MP_K linearizations, we offer a new tradeoff where our version is slower in practice, but also smaller. For `Ljournal-2008` our approach is 4.96 times slower than the original proposal. Smaller ones are better exploited by the original indexing, since a *rank/select* operation does require more work than just traversing short lists; results for this case omitted due to lack of space.

[3]Available in libcds at http://libcds.recoded.cl

Crawl	Nodes	Edges	K
Web-Stanford	281,904	2,312,497	8
Web-Google	916,428	5,105,039	7
Ljournal-2008	5,363,260	79,023,142	4

Table 3: Data sets used for MP_k linearization.

6. CONCLUSIONS

We have shown two new compressed graph representations. The first one, k^2-partitioned, designed to represent Web graphs, provides the best space/time trade-off when compared to the state of the art on real crawls. Its simplicity contrasts with the remarkable results obtained. Our second proposal achieves competitive space compared to the results from Maserrat and Pei [20], and provides a time bound when retrieving an adjacency list that depends only on properties of the query node itself.

Both methods are designed to work in main memory, and they do not offer good access locality, thus are not recommendable for secondary memory. As previously mentioned [11], these compressed representations can also improve distributed systems from an economical point of view, since their smaller memory footprint allows us to represent the same data using fewer computers. In the case of k^2-partitioned, this is particularly interesting, since the partition of the graph could allow different computers to handle different domains, obtaining a natural division. This, of course, depends on the access patterns required by the system, when it is desirable to distribute the load across all computers.

Acknowledgments

The authors would like to thank Nieves Brisaboa, Ian Munro and Gonzalo Navarro for useful comments.

This work was funded in part by NSERC and David R. Cheriton Scholarships program (Francisco Claude), and by Ministerio de Ciencia e Innovación (grants TIN2009-14560-C03-02 and CDTI CEN-20091048) and Xunta de Galicia (grant 2010/17) (Susana Ladra).

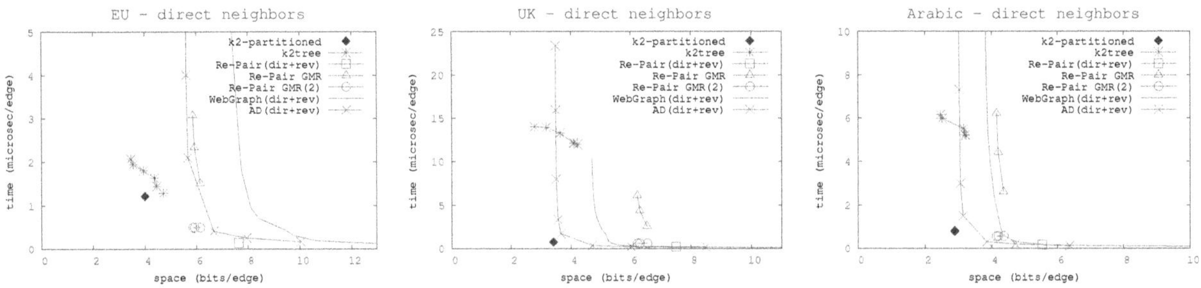

Figure 1: Space/time trade-off to retrieve direct neighbors for several Web graphs.

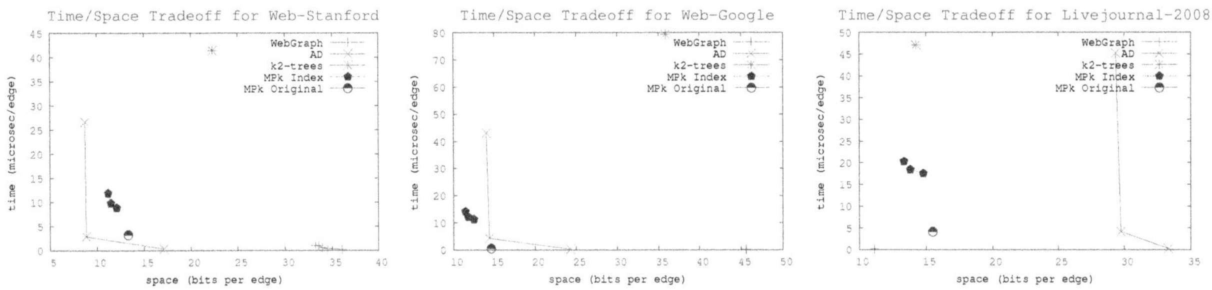

Figure 2: Space/time trade-off to retrieve direct neighbors for several social networks.

7. REFERENCES

[1] A. Apostolico and G. Drovandi. Graph compression by BFS. *Algorithms*, 2(3):1031–1044, 2009.

[2] J. Barbay, T. Gagie, G. Navarro, and Y. Nekrich. Alphabet partitioning for compressed rank/select and applications. In *Proc. ISAAC*, LNCS 6507, pages 315–326. Springer, 2010. Part II.

[3] P. Boldi, B. Codenotti, M. Santini, and S. Vigna. Ubicrawler: A scalable fully distributed web crawler. *Software: Practice & Experience*, 34(8):711–726, 2004.

[4] P. Boldi, M. Santini, and S. Vigna. Permuting Web graphs. In *Proc. WAW*, pages 116–126, 2009.

[5] P. Boldi and S. Vigna. The WebGraph framework I: Compression techniques. In *Proc. WWW*, pages 595–601, 2004.

[6] N. Brisaboa, S. Ladra, and G. Navarro. Directly addressable variable-length codes. In *Proc. SPIRE*, LNCS 5721, pages 122–130. Springer, 2009.

[7] N. Brisaboa, S. Ladra, and G. Navarro. K2-trees for compact web graph representation. In *Proc. SPIRE*, LNCS 5721, pages 18–30. Springer, 2009.

[8] F. Chierichetti, R. Kumar, S. Lattanzi, M. Mitzenmacher, A. Panconesi, and P. Raghavan. On compressing social networks. In *Proc. KDD*, pages 219–228. ACM, 2009.

[9] F. Claude and G. Navarro. Practical rank/select queries over arbitrary sequences. In *Proc. SPIRE*, LNCS 5280, pages 176–187, 2008.

[10] F. Claude and G. Navarro. Extended compact web graph representations. In *Algorithms and Applications (Ukkonen Festschrift)*, LNCS 6060, pages 77–91, 2010.

[11] F. Claude and G. Navarro. Fast and compact web graph representations. *ACM Transactions on the Web*, 4(4):article 16, 2010.

[12] P. Ferragina, G. Manzini, V. Mäkinen, and G. Navarro. Compressed representations of sequences and full-text indexes. *ACM Transactions on Algorithms*, 3(2):article 20, 2007.

[13] A. Golynski, I. Munro, and S. Rao. Rank/select operations on large alphabets: a tool for text indexing. In *Proc. SODA*, pages 368–373, 2006.

[14] R. Grossi, A. Gupta, and J. S. Vitter. High-order entropy-compressed text indexes. In *Proc. SODA*, pages 841–850, 2003.

[15] G. Jacobson. Space-efficient static trees and graphs. In *Proc. SFCS*, pages 549–554, 1989.

[16] J. Kleinberg, R. Kumar, P. Raghavan, S. Rajagopalan, and A. Tomkins. The Web as a graph: Measurements, models, and methods. In *Proc. COCOON*, LNCS 1627, pages 1–17, 1999.

[17] S. Ladra. *Algorithms and Compressed Data Structures for Information Retrieval.* PhD thesis, Department of Computer Science, University of A Coruña, 2011.

[18] J. Larsson and A. Moffat. Off-line dictionary-based compression. *Proceedings of the IEEE*, 88(11):1722–1732, 2000.

[19] V. Mäkinen and G. Navarro. Rank and select revisited and extended. *Theoretical Computer Science*, 387:332–347, 2007.

[20] H. Maserrat and J. Pei. Neighbor query friendly compression of social networks. In *Proc. KDD*, pages 533–542. ACM, 2010.

[21] L. Page, S. Brin, R. Motwani, and T. Winograd. The pagerank citation ranking: Bringing order to the web. Technical Report 1999-66, Stanford InfoLab, November 1999.

[22] H. Saito, M. Toyoda, M. Kitsuregawa, and K. Aihara. A large-scale study of link spam detection by graph algorithms. In *Proc. AIRWeb*. ACM Press, 2007.

Determining the Diameter of Small World Networks

Frank W. Takes
Leiden Institute of Advanced Computer Science
Leiden University, The Netherlands
ftakes@liacs.nl

Walter A. Kosters
Leiden Institute of Advanced Computer Science
Leiden University, The Netherlands
kosters@liacs.nl

ABSTRACT

In this paper we present a novel approach to determine the exact diameter (longest shortest path length) of large graphs, in particular of the nowadays frequently studied small world networks. Typical examples include social networks, gene networks, web graphs and internet topology networks. Due to complexity issues, the diameter is often calculated based on a sample of only a fraction of the nodes in the graph, or some approximation algorithm is applied. We instead propose an exact algorithm that uses various lower and upper bounds as well as effective node selection and pruning strategies in order to evaluate only the critical nodes which ultimately determine the diameter. We will show that our algorithm is able to quickly determine the exact diameter of various large datasets of small world networks with millions of nodes and hundreds of millions of links, whereas before only approximations could be given.

Categories and Subject Descriptors

G.2.2 [**Discrete Mathematics**]: Graph Theory;
J.4 [**Computer Applications**]: Social and Behavorial Sciences

General Terms

Algorithms, Experimentation, Measurement

Keywords

diameter, small world networks, social networks

1. INTRODUCTION

The *diameter* of a graph is defined as the length of the longest shortest path between any two nodes in the graph. Exact algorithms for calculating this diameter traditionally require running an All Pairs Shortest Path (APSP) algorithm for each node in the network, ultimately returning the length of one of the longest shortest paths that was found. While this will indeed return the exact diameter of the graph, complexity is in the order $O(n^3)$ for general weighted graphs and $O(mn)$ for sparse unweighted graphs (with n vertices and m edges). This naive solution for obtaining the diameter is clearly not feasible in extremely large graphs with for example millions of vertices and a billion edges.

We will study the diameter of *small world networks*: sparse networks that are most typically characterized by an average distance between two random nodes that grows only proportionally to the logarithm of the total number of nodes in the network [8]. Examples of small world networks that are frequently studied are web graphs [3], internet topology networks [7] and gene networks [2], but perhaps nowadays most well-known are the social networks [17]. A common type of social network is the (explicit) online social network [15], with Facebook, LinkedIn and Twitter as well-known examples. Implicit social networks include telephone call graphs, e-mail graphs [9] and scientific collaboration networks [4].

The diameter is a relevant property of a network for many reasons. For example in social networks, the diameter could be an indication of how quickly information reaches everyone in the network in the worst-case. Within a scientific collaboration network, a high diameter may indicate that there are groups of researchers that are not working together very closely. In an internet routing network, the diameter could reveal something about the worst-case response time between any two machines in the network.

An advantage of studying the exact diameter is that we can observe the actual path that realizes the diameter, a piece of information that we do not get when for example an approximation algorithm is used, or when the diameter is estimated by looking at only a sample of the network.

The main contribution of this paper consists of a new algorithm for determining the exact diameter of small world networks. Based on various lower and upper bounds and critical node selection strategies, we improve upon the straightforward APSP algorithm as well as upon existing approximation algorithms, obtaining the exact diameter of networks with millions of nodes in a matter of seconds or minutes. The performance is empirically verified on various large datasets of small world networks.

The rest of the paper is structured as follows. Section 2 introduces some definitions and an analysis of our problem's complexity, after which we will discuss related work in Section 3. We will use Section 4 to outline our algorithm for deriving the diameter of a graph, and discuss performance results in Section 5. Finally, Section 6 concludes.

CIKM'11, October 24–28, 2011, Glasgow, Scotland, UK.

2. PRELIMINARIES

In this section we will first consider some basic definitions related to graphs, distances, eccentricity, graph diameter and shortest path problems, and then give some insight in the complexity of determining these measures. After that we will briefly discuss small world networks.

2.1 Definitions

A graph $G(V, E)$ consists of a set $V = \{1, 2, \ldots, n\}$ of vertices and a set of edges $E \subseteq V \times V$. We will call them *nodes* and *links*, respectively. Throughout the paper we will use n to denote the number of nodes $|V|$, and for the number of links $|E|$ we use m. The distance $d(v, w)$ between two nodes $v, w \in V$ is defined as the length of the shortest path from v to w. This paper deals with *unweighted* graphs, and we will assume that our graphs are *undirected*, meaning that $(v, w) \in E$ iff $(w, v) \in E$ and thus $d(v, w) = d(w, v)$. The *degree* of a node v in an undirected graph is simply defined as the number of links connecting to that node. Finally, we assume our graph is *connected*, implying that for each $v, w \in V$, $d(v, w)$ is a finite number. We are now ready to define the two most important concepts used in this paper, node *eccentricity* and graph *diameter*:

Definition 1. The *eccentricity* of a node $v \in V$ is denoted by $\varepsilon(v)$ and defined as $\max_{w \in V} d(v, w)$: the longest shortest path starting at node v.

Definition 2. The *diameter* of a graph G is denoted by $\Delta(G)$ and defined as $\max_{v,w \in V} d(v, w)$, or equivalently as the maximum eccentricity over all nodes: $\max_{v \in V} \varepsilon(v)$. It is the longest shortest path length between any pair of nodes.

For convenience, we define two combinatorial problems that are frequently addressed in this paper and are tightly related to eccentricity. First, the *Single-source Shortest Path (SSP)* problem is the problem that deals with finding all shortest paths from a single source vertex $v \in V$ to all other nodes in the graph. For non-sparse graphs this problem has the traditional time complexity of $O(n^2)$ (Dijkstra's shortest path algorithm). When the graph is sparse and therefore more easily stored using an adjacency list, time complexity is bounded by $O(m \log n)$. In our unweighted case this can even be reduced to $O(m)$, as a Breadth First Search (BFS) from the starting node is sufficient to find all shortest paths. In essence, solving the SSP problem for a node means that we have found the eccentricity of that particular node.

Next, we can define the *All Pairs Shortest Paths (APSP)* problem as the problem of finding the shortest paths between all pairs of nodes of the graph, which increases the previous time complexity by a factor n to $O(n^3)$ for general weighted graphs, and $O(mn)$ for our sparse unweighted graphs. In essence, the maximum distance value that the APSP algorithm obtains, is the maximum eccentricity over all nodes and thus equal to the diameter of the graph. So if we solve the APSP problem, we have found the diameter.

2.2 Small World Networks

In this paper we will specifically look at the diameter of *small world networks*. A good overview of algorithmic properties of these networks, of which we will discuss a few, is given in [8]. First of all, small world networks are generally *sparse*: the total number of links m is very small compared to the maximum number of links $n(n-1)/2$. This may cause the reader to believe that nodes typically have very long shortest paths between them, as there are very few links in general. However, a second interesting characteristic is that even though the network is very sparse, the average distance between two nodes is very small. More specifically, this distance grows only proportionally to the logarithm of the total number of nodes. Typically, the node degree distribution of a small world network follows a power law: there are only a few nodes with a very large amount of connections, the so-called *hubs*, and there are many nodes with relatively few connections. In essence, hubs are functioning as bridges to realize a low average shortest path length. Lastly, small world networks generally contain one very large connected component which contains the vast majority of the nodes.

3. RELATED WORK

Most *exact* algorithms for finding the diameter are actually implementations of matrix multiplication that solve the APSP problem and thus also find the diameter. While these algorithms work well and have time complexity $O(n^{2.376})$ [18], they usually suffer from large hidden constants, and are often very unpractical. A lot of work has been done on the *estimation* of the diameter [1, 6]. Such estimation algorithms typically determine the diameter of any type of graph with some very small additive error, using significantly less computation time than the APSP algorithm. A method which is claimed to be leading in approximating the diameter, is the Approximate Neighborhood Function (ANF) by Palmer et al. [16], which claims to have an empirically verified accuracy of 7%.

In work which does not focus on actually determining the diameter, but where it is found only as a static property of the dataset, a *sample* of the network is frequently used to determine the diameter [10, 15]. A heuristic algorithm to estimate the diameter is described in [13] by Leskovec et al. In this work, the diameter is determined by, starting from a random node, repeatedly selecting the farthest node, meanwhile keeping track of the highest distance so far. If this value no longer increases after a certain number of iterations, a lower bound on the diameter has been found.

Work has also been done on variants of the diameter, such as the *effective diameter*, which is defined as the 90-th percentile of the cumulative distribution of shortest path lengths. Though this measure may appear more robust, it is claimed that the diameter and the effective diameter tend to exhibit qualitatively similar behavior [11]. We believe that the exact diameter is an elementary graph property worth computing, and will therefore focus solely on an exact approach to determine the precise diameter.

4. ALGORITHM

We will start with some observations about the eccentricity of neighboring nodes and how they influence the diameter. Then we describe our actual algorithm called BOUNDINGDIAMETERS, which makes use of these observations to improve upon the APSP algorithm. Next we discuss the algorithm's complexity and some optimization techniques.

4.1 Observations

If we calculate the eccentricity $\varepsilon(v)$ for some node v, we know that for all nodes w with $d(v, w) = k$, their eccentricity $\varepsilon(w)$ lies between $\varepsilon(v) - k$ and $\varepsilon(v) + k$. The upper bound follows because any node w at distance k of v can get to v in exactly k steps, and then reach any other node in at most $\varepsilon(v)$ steps. The lower bound can be derived in the same way, by interchanging v and w in the previous statement. In the "best" case, w is on some path that realizes the eccentricity of v, and has an eccentricity $\varepsilon(w)$ of only $\varepsilon(v) - k$. This lower bound can of course never be less than k itself: if the shortest path between v and w is equal to k, then $\varepsilon(w)$ is at least equal to k. More formally:

Observation 1. **Node eccentricity bounds**
If a node $v \in V$ has eccentricity $\varepsilon(v)$, then for all nodes w we have $\max(\varepsilon(v) - d(v,w), d(v,w)) \leq \varepsilon(w) \leq \varepsilon(v) + d(v,w)$.

We know that the diameter of a graph is equal to the maximum eccentricity over all nodes. Therefore, the maximum lower bound on the eccentricity over all nodes, is also a lower bound for the diameter. Similarly, the maximum upper bound on the eccentricity over all nodes can be seen as an upper bound on the diameter. The upper bound can even be made more tight by observing that this bound can be at most twice as big as the smallest eccentricity upper bound over all nodes, as observed in [14]. These observations can be formalized as follows:

Observation 2. **Diameter bounds**
Let $\varepsilon_L(v)$ and $\varepsilon_U(v)$ denote currently known lower and upper bounds for the eccentricity of node $v \in V$. For the diameter $\Delta(G)$ of a graph G it holds that $\max_{v \in V} \varepsilon_L(v) \leq \Delta(G) \leq \min(\max_{v \in V} \varepsilon_U(v), 2 * \min_{v \in V} \varepsilon_U(v))$.

We will denote the above lower and upper bounds on the diameter by Δ_L and Δ_U, respectively.

4.2 Algorithm

The bounds mentioned above can be used to refine the original APSP algorithm by reducing the number of eccentricity calculations, as only nodes that can actually contribute to the diameter bounds are considered. Pseudo-code for our algorithm is given in Algorithm 1.

After setting some initial values (lines 3–7), in the main while-loop, our algorithm repeatedly selects a node v (line 9) from the candidate set W, which initially contains all the nodes. The various mechanisms for selecting the next node to be examined are outlined in Section 4.4. The algorithm then calculates the eccentricity of that node v (line 10), and uses the result to update the lower and upper bound of the graph diameter (Δ_L and Δ_U, lines 11–12), cf. Observation 2. Next, the eccentricity bounds of all nodes in the candidate set W are updated (line 14–15) according to Observation 1. Then we determine which nodes (including v) can be removed from the set of candidates (line 17). This can happen either because a node's eccentricity is already known since the lower and upper bounds are identical (which is always the case for the current node v), or because a node can no longer "contribute" to the diameter of the graph by increasing the lower bound or decreasing the upper bound (line 16). Note that because we calculated the eccentricity of v, we know for each node w the distance $d(v,w)$. Finally, the algorithm stops when all nodes have been examined, or when the lower bound is equal to the upper bound (line 8). It then returns the lower bound of the diameter, which at that point contains the real value of the diameter (line 21).

Algorithm 1 BOUNDINGDIAMETERS

```
 1: Input: Graph G(V, E)
 2: Output: Diameter of G
 3: W ← V;    Δ_L ← −∞;    Δ_U ← +∞;
 4: for w ∈ W do
 5:     ε_L[w] ← −∞;
 6:     ε_U[w] ← +∞;
 7: end for
 8: while Δ_L ≠ Δ_U and W ≠ ∅ do
 9:     v ← SELECTFROM(W);              // cf. Section 4.4
10:     ε[v] = ECCENTRICITY(v);
11:     Δ_L = max(Δ_L, ε[v]);
12:     Δ_U = min(Δ_U, 2 * ε[v]);
13:     for w ∈ W do
14:         ε_L[w] = max(ε_L[w], max(ε[v] − d(v, w), d(v, w)));
15:         ε_U[w] = min(ε_U[w], ε[v] + d(v, w));
16:         if (ε_U[w] ≤ Δ_L and ε_L[w] ≥ Δ_U/2) or
               (ε_L[w] = ε_U[w]) then
17:             W ← W − {w};
18:         end if
19:     end for
20: end while
21: return Δ_L;
```

4.3 Complexity

Calculating the eccentricity of a node using the ECCENTRICITY() function (line 14) is the critical operation of our algorithm, as this requires running the previously mentioned $O(m)$ SSP algorithm. In the best case, we only have to calculate the eccentricity of *two* nodes v and w, only to find that $\varepsilon(w) = 2 * \varepsilon(v)$ (or vice versa), which means that the diameter is equal to $\varepsilon(w)$. In the worst case our algorithm needs to investigate the eccentricity of every single node, not improving the traditional APSP time complexity of $O(mn)$. An example of a graph in which *all* nodes have to be investigated in order to determine the diameter, is a graph where the nodes are connected through exactly one circle of edges, and will therefore all have identical eccentricity. In general, the eccentricity values of nodes in a network differ, and how much they differ will essentially determine the algorithm's performance, as larger differences in eccentricity values will result in tighter eccentricity bounds on surrounding nodes.

We claim that our algorithm specifically works well on small world networks, which we believe is due to power law degree distribution within such networks, as discussed in Section 2.2. A small world network has relatively few nodes with a very high degree (hubs), that will often (but not always) have a relatively low eccentricity value. The remainder of the nodes typically have a much lower degree, often (again, not always) resulting in a relatively high eccentricity value. Thus, due to the expected existence of a large diversity in eccentricity values of the nodes in a small world network, the bounds on the diameter will typically converge very quickly. Later on we will verify these claims empirically.

4.4 Selection Strategies

We will describe the different strategies that can be used to select the next node for which we want to calculate the eccentricity, essentially outlining the possible functionality of

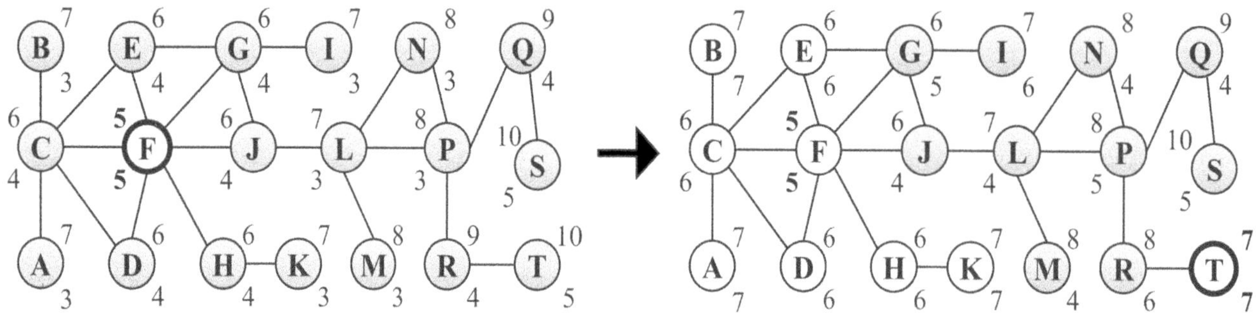

Figure 1: The path B-T realizes a diameter of length 7. Numbers beneath and above nodes denote lower and upper eccentricity bounds after first calculating the eccentricity of node F (left) and then node T (right).

the SELECTFROM() function that is called in line 12 of Algorithm 1. First notice how enumerating the nodes in some order, or selecting them at random, will in essence mean that we are executing the APSP algorithm, only now we discard nodes that can no longer contribute to the diameter bounds. While this will already improve upon the APSP algorithm, our main objective is to tighten the bounds of the diameter as quickly as possible in order to efficiently reduce the size of the set of candidate nodes. The strategy has to be easy to compute so that it does not influence the overall complexity.

The simplest strategy would be to select nodes based on their *degree*. This measure, known as *degree centrality*, is often suggested as a simple measure of the centrality of a node within a network, but is far from perfect with respect to eccentricity. For example, in Figure 1, node F has the highest degree (6 links) and eccentricity $\varepsilon(F) = 5$, whereas node J with lower degree 3 has eccentricity $\varepsilon(J) = 4$. The problem here is that degree centrality is merely a local measure. Therefore we suggest using the degree as a secondary selection mechanism only, for example to break ties in other methods, or to select the very first node to be examined.

4.4.1 *Eccentricity bound difference*

The *difference* between the lower and upper eccentricity bound could be an interesting feature, as it basically tells us how much we already know about the eccentricity of that node and its neighborhood. If for a certain node this difference is very big, determining its eccentricity may tighten the bounds of many nearby nodes.

4.4.2 *Interchanging eccentricity bounds*

Inspired by traditional branch-and-bound algorithms, we could choose to select nodes from the candidate set based on their their eccentricity lower bound or upper bound. To find nodes with high eccentricity, we select the node with the largest upper bound, and similarly we choose a node with a small lower bound to find nodes with a low eccentricity value. As our goal is to increase the lower bound and decrease the upper bound, we propose to *interchange* the selection of the node with the smallest lower bound and the node with the largest upper bound.

4.4.3 *Repeated Farthest Distance*

Another option is to select a node based on its distance to the previously investigated node, and then select a node with the highest distance. So essentially, starting from some initial node, we repeatedly select the farthest possible node. This is a variation of the heuristic presented in [13].

4.5 Example

We will give an example of how BOUNDINGDIAMETERS would determine the diameter of the graph depicted in Figure 1. As a selection strategy we alternately choose the largest upper bound and smallest lower bound, breaking ties by choosing the nodes with the highest degree. Any remaining ties are broken by choosing a random node. We will denote the a lower bound L and upper bound U by $[L; U]$.

The left situation of Figure 1 depicts the situation after the first iteration, where node F has been investigated. The diameter lower and upper bounds are now equal to $\Delta_L = \varepsilon(F) = 5$ and $\Delta_U = 2 * \varepsilon(F) = 10$, respectively. The current eccentricity bounds do not yet require us to remove any nodes from the candidate set. The eccentricity bounds after the second iteration are depicted in the right situation of Figure 1, where we have determined the eccentricity of node T, which is 7. The graph diameter now lies between $\Delta_L = 7$ and $\Delta_U = 10$. We can now remove A, B, C, D, E, H and K from the candidate list, as we have derived the exact eccentricity of these nodes (but without having calculated it explicitly). We can also remove node I and G, because they can no longer contribute to raising the lower bound or decreasing the upper bound.

For the third loop of our algorithm we calculate the eccentricity of node L, which is 4, lowering the diameter upper bound to $\Delta_U = 8$ and allowing us to update the eccentricity bounds to [4;5] for J, M and N, [5;5] for P, [4;6] for Q, [6;6] for R, [5;7] for S and finally [7;8] for the diameter Δ. We can now discard all nodes based on the same arguments as in the previous iteration, resulting in all nodes being visited, terminating the algorithm after only 3 eccentricity calculations, and returning the final value of the diameter: 7.

4.6 Optimizations

The size of the graph can be reduced by applying the following pruning strategy beforehand. For every node we can determine if removing its edges would disconnect the graph. If this is the case, and multiple identically structured small subgraphs remain, we can remove each but one of them, and still obtain the correct diameter value, assuming of course that a path that realizes the diameter of the graph does not run from one subgraph to another (pruned) subgraph. Therefore, the diameter of the pruned subgraph has to be smaller than $\Delta/2$. For example node C in Figure 1 is connected to two identical subtrees, namely nodes A and B. We could prune one of these subtrees, as they will both have identical eccentricity (bound) values. Similarly, P is connected to identical subtrees Q-S and R-T.

Dataset	Nodes	Links	Average Degree	Average Distance	Δ	Strategy 1	Strategy 2	Strategy 3	Nodes Pruned
AstroPhys [12]	17,903	396K	21	4.15	14	18	**9**	63	185
Enron [9]	33,696	362K	10	4.07	**13**	12	**11**	61	8,715
Flickr [15]	1,624,992	30.9M	18	5.38	24	10	**3**	7	553,242
Hyves	8,057,981	871M	112	4.75	25	40	**21**	44	446,258
LiveJournal [15]	5,189,809	97.4M	19	5.48	23	6	**3**	14	318,378
Orkut [15]	3,072,441	234M	76	4.16	10	357	**106**	389	27,429
Skitter [11]	1,696,415	22.2M	13	5.08	**31**	10	**4**	19	114,803
YouTube [15]	1,134,890	5.98M	5.3	5.32	24	2	**2**	2	399,553
Web [13]	855,802	8.64M	10	6.30	24	20	**4**	28	91,965
Wikipedia [5]	2,213,236	23.5M	11	4.81	18	21	**3**	583	947,582

Table 1: Comparison of different node selection strategies on various small world datasets.

5. EXPERIMENTS

This section starts with a brief description of our datasets, and then describes a measurement methodology for the different selection strategies described in Section 4.4. Next we will present and discuss the results of applying these strategies in our BoundingDiameters algorithm.

5.1 Datasets & Measurement Methodology

We will verify our algorithm on various datasets of small world networks. Characteristics of these datasets, such as the number of nodes, the number of directed links, the average degree, average node-to-node distance and the diameter Δ, are given in the first 6 columns of Table 1. Numbers are based solely on the largest connected component of each graph, therefore slight deviations from statistics presented in the original papers may be observed. The datasets Flickr, LiveJournal, YouTube, Web and Wikipedia are undirected versions of the original respective directed graphs.

In our experiments we will compare the three different selection strategies from Section 4.4, breaking ties as described in Section 4.5. The critical operation is the number of nodes for which we have to calculate the actual eccentricity, which will serve as our basis for comparison of the three strategies outlined in column 7 through 9 of Table 1. Note that the number of comparisons that the traditional APSP algorithm would perform, is equal to the second column, namely one eccentricity calculation for each node. Due to complexity issues (finding frequent subgraphs is NP-hard) we have chosen to only implement the simple optimization strategy (see Section 4.6) of pruning duplicate connected subgraphs consisting of one node. The number of pruned nodes using this technique is given in the last column of Table 1.

5.2 Results

The results in Table 1 clearly show that with only a few eccentricity calculations, our algorithm is able to determine the exact diameter of the datasets, with Strategy 2 as the best-performing node selection strategy. We expect this to be because interchanging the search for low and high eccentricity nodes basically means that we are interchanging the selection of a node in the dense and the peripheral part of the small world network, quickly lowering the upper bound and increasing the lower bound, respectively.

We believe the first strategy did not perform so well, because it only looked for unexplored areas of the graph, which is likely to be less effective when looking for extreme bound values that realize the diameter. The third method appeared to perform worse because it did not appear to find any low-eccentricity valued nodes that could lower the upper bound.

The last column shows how our optimization strategy is able to significantly reduce the size of the problem. This is not surprising; small world networks typically have many low degree nodes, and it is quite likely that many them of are linked to the same node, and can thus be pruned.

For the YouTube dataset, Strategy 2 only needs 2 eccentricity calculations to determine the diameter, demonstrating the best-case performance of our algorithm. It turned out that the node with the highest degree had eccentricity 12, causing nodes with bounds [12; 24] to exist, while another node had eccentricity 24, realizing bounds of [24; 24].

For the Orkut dataset, a relatively large number of eccentricity calculations was needed to determine the diameter. To further analyze this, it could be interesting to look at how quickly the amount of candidate nodes decreases over time. Therefore we show the number of unvisited nodes and the lower and upper bounds on the diameter during the execution of our algorithm using Strategy 2 on the Orkut dataset in Figure 2. After 16 calculations, another 90 calculations were needed to decide whether the diameter was equal to 9 or 10, and the number of nodes to be examined only decreases by 1 or 2 after each eccentricity calculation. Apparently the remaining unvisited nodes are positioned in the graph in such a way that the calculation of the actual eccentricity of these nodes can not be avoided using the neighboring bounds. Though it takes a while to find the exact diameter, tight bounds on the diameter are actually quickly available.

Although not related to our performance measurement methodology, we mention that one node eccentricity calculation takes only a few seconds in our C++ implementation on a standard 3.2GHz machine with 10GB of memory. This means that we are able to determine the exact diameter in a matter of seconds (or a few minutes in case of the Orkut dataset), which is very reasonable compared to for example approximation algorithms such as ANF [16].

As an interesting side result it turned out that, very often, the actual eccentricity has been found for a large portion of the nodes in the graph when the algorithm has terminated, because these node's eccentricity lower and upper bounds had become equal. For example, for the Orkut dataset, 777,257 actual eccentricity values (25%) were obtained, while only 106 values were explicity calculated. Also interesting to note is that the exact diameter that we obtain for the Enron and Skitter datasets deviates from the previously approximated values of 12 and 24, respectively.

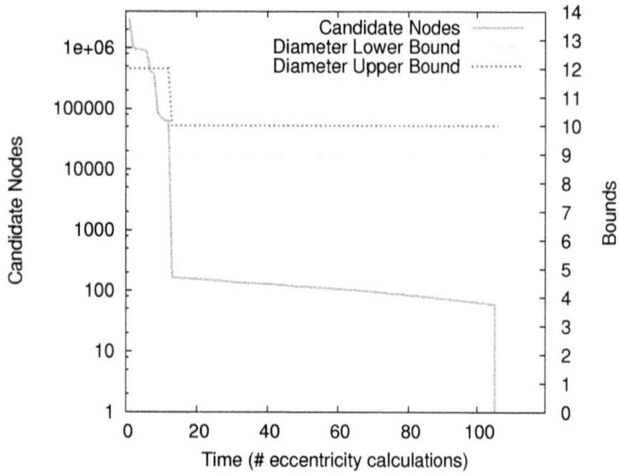

Figure 2: Orkut dataset – candidate nodes (left vertical axis; logarithmic) and lower and upper bounds (right vertical axis) vs. time (horizontal axis).

More information on the datasets used in this paper, the obtained diameter paths, and an implementation can be found at `www.liacs.nl/~ftakes/diameter/`.

6. CONCLUSION

We have shown that our algorithm, BoundingDiameters, is able to efficiently determine the exact diameter of small world networks, making use of lower and upper bounds on the eccentricity of the nodes and on the diameter itself. A proper selection strategy allows our algorithm to exploit the characteristic properties of small world networks. Moreover, we have outlined a pruning strategy which reduces the size of the problem. We have also shown that even when the diameter is not found very quickly, very tight bounds on the diameter are available after only a few iterations.

In future work we would like to investigate if our algorithm can be used to obtain the eccentricity of all nodes in the network, allowing us to study the exact eccentricity distribution of a graph. We also want to address the issue of determining the diameter of the strongly connected component of a directed graph. By using only the lower diameter bounds, significant improvements over the APSP algorithm are already observed. Last but not least, we hope to investigate how the exact diameter of small world networks behaves over time, and how our algorithm can be adjusted to adapt to changes in the network, i.e., the addition and deletion of nodes and links.

7. ACKNOWLEDGMENTS

This research is part of the COMPASS project, financed by NWO under grant number 612.065.926. We thank Hyves for making their anonymized friendship graph available.

8. REFERENCES

[1] D. Aingworth, C. Chekuri, and R. Motwani. Fast estimation of diameter and shortest paths (without matrix multiplication). In *Proceedings of the 7th Annual ACM-SIAM Symposium on Discrete Algorithms*, pages 547–553, 1996.

[2] R. Albert. Scale-free networks in cell biology. *Journal of Cell Science*, 118:4947–4957, 2005.

[3] R. Albert, H. Jeong, and A. Barabási. Internet: Diameter of the world-wide web. *Nature*, 401(6749):130–131, 1999.

[4] A. Barabási, H. Jeong, Z. Néda, E. Ravasz, A. Schubert, and T. Vicsek. Evolution of the social network of scientific collaborations. *Physica A: Statistical Mechanics and its Applications*, 311(3-4):590–614, 2002.

[5] C. Bizer, J. Lehmann, G. Kobilarov, S. Auer, C. Becker, R. Cyganiak, and S. Hellmann. DBpedia — A crystallization point for the web of data. *Web Semantics: Science, Services and Agents on the World Wide Web*, 2009.

[6] D. Dor, S. Halperin, and U. Zwick. All pairs almost shortest paths. *SIAM Journal on Computing*, 29(5):1740–1759, 2000.

[7] S. Jin and A. Bestavros. Small-world characteristics of internet topologies and implications on multicast scaling. *Computer Networks*, 50(5):648–666, 2006.

[8] J. Kleinberg. The small-world phenomenon: An algorithm perspective. In *Proceedings of the 32nd Annual ACM Symposium on Theory of Computing*, pages 163–170, 2000.

[9] B. Klimt and Y. Yang. The Enron corpus: A new dataset for email classification research. *Lecture notes in computer science 3201*, pages 217–226, 2004.

[10] J. Leskovec and C. Faloutsos. Sampling from large graphs. In *Proceedings of the 12th ACM International Conference on Knowledge Discovery and Data Mining*, pages 631–636, 2006.

[11] J. Leskovec, J. Kleinberg, and C. Faloutsos. Graphs over time: Densification laws, shrinking diameters and possible explanations. In *Proceedings of the 11th ACM International Conference on Knowledge Discovery and Data Mining*, pages 177–187, 2005.

[12] J. Leskovec, J. Kleinberg, and C. Faloutsos. Graph evolution: Densification and shrinking diameters. *ACM Transactions on Knowledge Discovery from Data*, 1(1):2, 2007.

[13] J. Leskovec, K. Lang, A. Dasgupta, and M. Mahoney. Community structure in large networks: Natural cluster sizes and the absence of large well-defined clusters. *Internet Mathematics*, 6(1):29–123, 2009.

[14] C. Magnien, M. Latapy, and M. Habib. Fast computation of empirically tight bounds for the diameter of massive graphs. *Journal of Experimental Algorithmics (JEA)*, 13:1–10, 2009.

[15] A. Mislove, M. Marcon, K. Gummadi, P. Druschel, and B. Bhattacharjee. Measurement and analysis of online social networks. In *Proceedings of the 7th ACM Conference on Internet Measurement*, pages 29–42, 2007.

[16] C. Palmer, P. Gibbons, and C. Faloutsos. ANF: A fast and scalable tool for data mining in massive graphs. In *Proceedings of the 8th ACM SIGKDD International Conference on Knowledge Discovery and Data Mining*, pages 81–90, 2002.

[17] S. Wasserman and K. Faust. *Social Network Analysis: Methods and Applications*. Cambridge Press, 1994.

[18] R. Yuster. Computing the diameter polynomially faster than APSP. *ArXiv e-prints, 1011.6181*, 2010.

Detecting Anomalies in Graphs with Numeric Labels

Michael Davis
mdavis05@qub.ac.uk

Weiru Liu
w.liu@qub.ac.uk

Paul Miller
p.miller@ecit.qub.ac.uk

School of Electrical and Electronic Engineering and Computer Science, Queen's University, Belfast, BT7 1NN, UK

George Redpath
gredpath@tycoint.com

CEM Systems, Airport Road West, Belfast, BT3 9ED, UK

ABSTRACT

This paper presents YAGADA, an algorithm to search labelled graphs for anomalies using both structural data and numeric attributes. YAGADA is explained using several security-related examples and validated with experiments on a physical Access Control database. Quantitative analysis shows that in the upper range of anomaly thresholds, YAGADA detects twice as many anomalies as the best-performing numeric discretization algorithm. Qualitative evaluation shows that the detected anomalies are meaningful, representing a combination of structural irregularities and numerical outliers.

Categories and Subject Descriptors: G.2.2 [Graph Theory]: Graph algorithms

General Terms: Algorithms

Keywords: graph mining, transactions, anomaly detection

1. INTRODUCTION

Graph representations are useful in many domains where data has a natural structure which cannot be easily represented as a set of attributes. Graphs are commonly used to represent complex structures such as social networks, biological or ecological processes and computer networks. Although graphs are often used to visualise networks for analysis by humans [9], machine learning techniques can improve on this by exposing knowledge hidden within the network structure. This paper presents a novel algorithm, YAGADA (Yet Another Graph-based Anomaly Detection Algorithm), to detect anomalies in labelled graphs.

Our research field is the security applications of network analysis, which include fraud detection and intrusion detection [5, 9]. In this paper, we analyse data from a physical Access Control System, of the type used to secure doors in buildings such as airports, power stations, hospitals and offices. The current generation of such systems can detect *suspicious events*—such as the use of an ID Card which has been reported stolen, or an attempt to physically force a door—but cannot detect *suspicious patterns*—transactions which are innocent in themselves but anomalous when considered in context: an airport technician who regularly hangs around in the baggage handling area; or a clerk who is spending an unusually long time on their own in the cash room.

There is little published research on mining physical Access Control databases. [2] presents four algorithms to detect suspicious patterns: temporal patterns ("zone overstay"); repetitive access patterns; displacement patterns; and out-of-sequence patterns. The patterns are detected by comparing timing values to a threshold. This produces a binary result ("normal" or "suspicious") but does not indicate the degree of suspiciousness. If the "normal" duration of stay varies (*e.g.*, at different times of day), a single parameter cannot represent this. Furthermore, the algorithms are based on domain knowledge. In contrast, our approach represents the transactions as a graph, using a single algorithm to detect both *structural anomalies* (unusual paths through the building) and *numeric anomalies* (unusual timing data).

Existing graph-based anomaly detection algorithms [5, 14] define "normal" patterns in terms of frequent substructures. Subdue [4] uses a greedy beam search to discover frequent substructures and evaluates them using the Minimum Description Length (MDL) principle. After compressing the graph, substructures which are more frequent have a shorter Description Length (DL): by implication, substructures with a high DL are more anomalous. [10] uses this principle as the basis of a heuristic to detect anomalies. Each substructure is evaluated on the basis of *how much* and *how soon* it is compressed by Subdue. GBAD [5] is a suite of three anomaly detection algorithms, also based on Subdue: GBAD-MDL detects anomalous modifications; GBAD-P (Probability) detects anomalous insertions; GBAD-MPS (Maximum Partial Substructure) detects anomalous deletions. The above algorithms operate on unweighted graphs with discrete vertex and edge labels. If the graph contains continuous (numeric) attributes, these cannot be incorporated and are therefore ignored. We can improve the accuracy of anomaly detection by incorporating the numeric attribute values.

A few algorithms take numeric edge weights into consideration. OddBall [1] operates on *egonets* but ignores vertex and edge labels. OddBall can therefore detect anomalous vertices with respect to their immediate neighbourhood, but cannot detect anomalous substructures. [8] applies three edge-weighting approaches to gSpan for transaction graph mining. The search space for frequent subgraph discovery is reduced, by assuming that high-weighted edges are more significant than low-weighted edges.

CIKM'11, October 24–28, 2011, Glasgow, Scotland, UK.

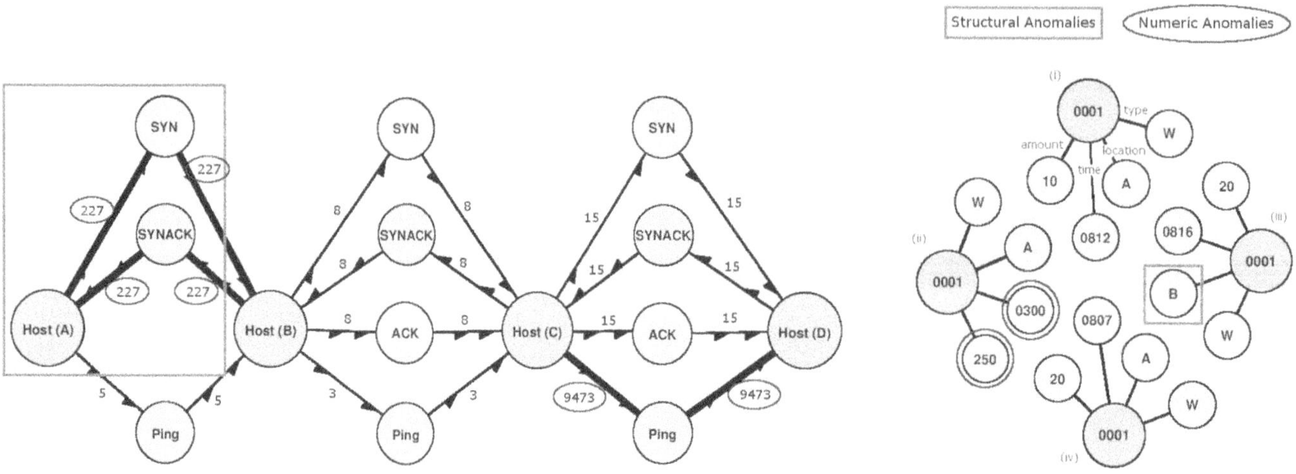

(a) Single large graph representing TCP SYN and ICMP PING network traffic, with two Denial of Service (DoS) attacks taking place.

(b) Each subgraph *(i)*–*(iv)* represents a bank transaction at an automated teller machine.

Figure 1: Detecting (a) anomalous substructures and (b) anomalous subgraphs

[6] extends GBAD-P to detect anomalies in graphs with continuous labels, by including the numeric values into the probability that a particular edge should exist. It is assumed that the values are distributed normally. YAGADA can detect anomalies without making such assumptions about the prior distribution of numeric values.

Two recent papers incorporate numeric labels in a more general way: [11] includes a discretization step before attempting frequent subgraph matching, using one of several unsupervised discretization methods. Seven methods are proposed to estimate the number of bins k. [13] is a brief outline of an extension to Subdue, which incorporates numeric values using frequency histograms. We evaluate these approaches in Sect. 4 and demonstrate that YAGADA outperforms these algorithms for anomaly detection.

The rest of this paper is organised as follows: Sect. 2 provides an overview of our approach to detecting anomalies in structural and numeric data. Sect. 3 presents the details of YAGADA. In Sect. 4, we evaluate YAGADA on a real-world Access Control database and compare YAGADA's performance against the algorithms discussed above. Our conclusions are presented in Sect. 5.

2. DETECTING ANOMALIES IN GRAPHS WITH NUMERIC LABELS

The example graphs in Fig. 1 contain both structural and numeric anomalies. Fig. 1a is a single large graph with discrete labels and numeric edge weights. Fig. 1b is a database of graph transactions with discrete and numeric attributes.

Fig. 1a shows a fragment of traffic in a TCP/IP network. Two types of interchange between the hosts in the network are shown: **ping** is used to test that another host is alive, and **SYN** is used to synchronise the order of TCP packets. SYN is a three-part exchange: after the TCP client sends the SYN request, the server acknowledges (SYNACK) and waits for the client acknowledgement (ACK).

The anomalies in the graph represent two common Denial of Service (DoS) attacks. The first is a SYN flooding attack, where a client starts many SYN exchanges but fails to send the final ACK, forcing the server to hold all its ports open. The second is a ping flooding attack, where the client consumes the server's bandwidth.

To illustrate how Subdue searches for anomalous substructures, we first define some formal properties of graphs:

Definition 1. A graph $G = (V, E)$ consists of a set of vertices (or nodes) V and edges E. $E \subseteq \{(v, w) : v, w \in V \times V\}$. Two vertices v and w are *adjacent* iff $(v, w) \in E$. If the tuple (v, w) is ordered, the graph is said to be *directed*, otherwise it is *undirected*.

Definition 2. A substructure $S = (V^S, E^S)$ is said to be *isomorphic* to G iff $V^S \subseteq V, E^S \subseteq E$. If $\forall(v, w) \in E \setminus E^S : v \notin V^S, w \notin V^S$, the substructure is *unconnected*. An unconnected substructure is also known as a *subgraph*.

Definition 3. The weight of each edge $e \in E$ is denoted by $\mathcal{W}(e) \in \mathbb{R}$. If $\forall e : \mathcal{W}(e) = 1$, the graph is *unweighted*, otherwise it is *weighted*.

Definition 4. For a graph G containing substructure S, the most frequent substructure is the one that minimises:

$$M(S, G) = DL(G|S) + DL(S) \tag{1}$$

where $DL(G|S)$ is the Description Length of G after compressing it with S and $DL(S)$ is the Description Length of S [4]. This implies that substructures with a high value of $M(S, G)$ are infrequent and therefore anomalous.

To illustrate structural anomaly detection, let G be the graph in Fig. 1a. Using Subdue's greedy beam search and MDL evaluation (Equation 1), we ascertain that the best frequent substructure S_1 is:

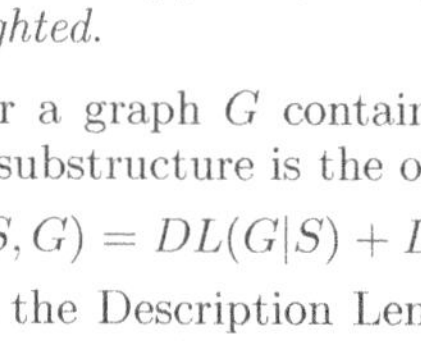

Note that Subdue operates on unweighted graphs, so $\mathcal{W}(e)$ was not taken into consideration. If we compress G with S_1, we obtain a new graph G_1:

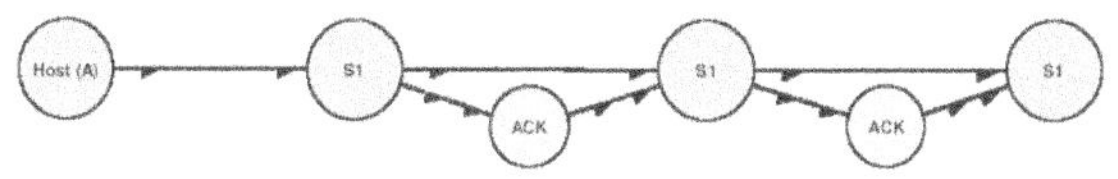

In the next iteration, we discover the best frequent substructure $S_2 = \{\ldots, (\text{ACK}, S_1)\}$. We compress G_1 with S_2, and evaluate the DL of the remaining substructures. The substructure with the highest DL is highlighted with a box in Fig. 1a. Subdue has discovered the SYN flooding attack, but not the ping flooding attack. Incorporating the numeric edge weights $\mathcal{W}(e)$ into Subdue does not help, as 3, 5 and 9473 will be considered as distinct discrete values, resulting in substructures which are all equally anomalous.

Our approach solves this problem by making a distinction between numeric values which are "normal" and those which are anomalous, and then incorporating that information into the graph. Stated more formally, we would like to alter G such that $\mathcal{W}(e)$ evaluates to a constant value q_0 for all $\{e \in E : e \text{ is normal}\}$, but evaluates to a set of values $q_i \in \mathbb{R}$ for $\{e \in E : e \text{ is anomalous}\}$. We will defer our discussion of how q_i is to be calculated until Sect. 3. For the purposes of this discussion, let us assume that we can create $G^a = G$, where $\mathcal{W}(e) = 227$ is replaced with q_1, $\mathcal{W}(e) = 9473$ is replaced with q_2 and all other edge weights are replaced with q_0. Now we can apply Subdue to the weighted graph G^a, treating the values q_i as discrete. We discover that the two most frequent substructures S_1^a and S_2^a are:

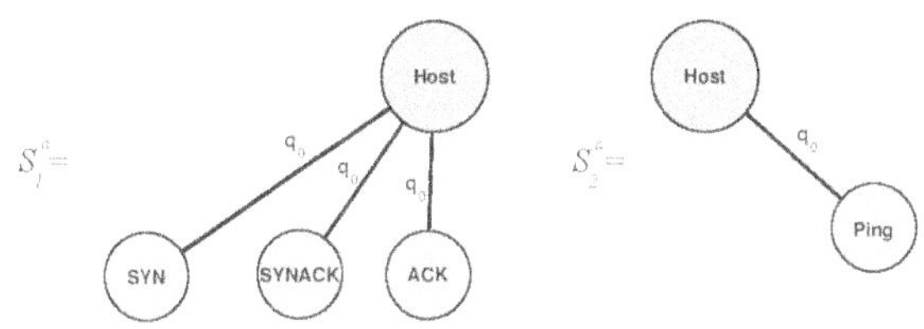

After compressing G^a with S_1^a and S_2^a, we obtain G_1^a:

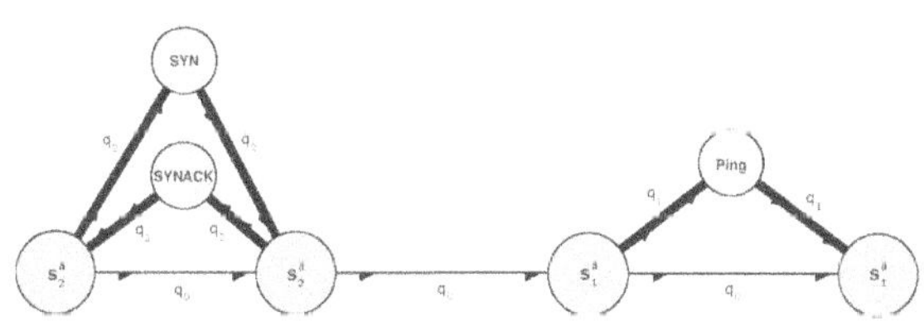

All of the normal substructures have been compressed away and only the anomalous substructures are left. As the DL of uncompressed substructures is always higher than the DL of compressed substructures, we can use $M(S_i^a, G^a)$ (Eq. 1) to measure the anomalousness of each substructure S_i^a.

We have demonstrated that replacing numeric edge weights with anomaly scores allows both structural and numeric anomalies to be detected in a weighted graph. We now extend this approach to the more general problem of labelled graphs. We formally define a labelled graph as follows:

Definition 5. Let L^V be the set of vertex labels and L^E be the set of edge labels. If $L^V \cup L^E = \emptyset$, the graph is *unlabelled*, otherwise it is *labelled*.

Definition 6. Let L^D be the set of discrete labels and L^N be the set of numeric labels, such that $L = L^V \cup L^E = L^D \cup L^N$. Let A^D be the set of discrete attribute values and $A^N \subset \mathbb{R}$ be the set of numeric attribute values, such that $A = A^D \cup A^N$. The label-to-value mapping function for vertices is denoted as:

$$\mathcal{L}_V : V \times (L^V \cap L^D) \to A^D,$$
$$\mathcal{L}_V : V \times (L^V \cap L^N) \to A^N$$

The label-to-value mapping function for edges $\mathcal{L}_E$ is defined in a similar manner. Edge weights can be considered as a special case of edge attributes: $\mathcal{W}(e) = \mathcal{L}_E(e, \text{"}weight\text{"})$.

Fig. 1b shows an example of a labelled graph which contains four graph transactions (subgraphs), $G_{(i)}$–$G_{(iv)}$. Each subgraph represents a cash withdrawal from a bank account. The "hub" vertex for each transaction is labelled with the account number (discrete). The hub is connected to four vertices labelled with the transaction type (discrete; **W** is a withdrawal), the physical location where the transaction took place (discrete; **A** or **B**), the time that the transaction took place (numeric) and the amount (numeric). This graph contains two anomalous subgraphs. Transaction *(ii)* took place at an unusual time of day and was for an unusual amount. Transaction *(iii)* took place in an unusual location.

Let G be the graph in Fig. 1b. We can use Subdue and calculate an anomaly score a_s for each subgraph G_s as:

$$a_s = 1 - \frac{1}{n}\sum_{i=1}^{n}(n - i + 1)\left(\frac{DL_{i-1}(G_s) - DL_i(G_s)}{DL_0(G_s)}\right) \quad (2)$$

where n is the number of iterations and $DL_i(G_s)$ is the description length of G_s after i iterations [10]. Ignoring numeric labels A^N, we find the best frequent substructures S_1 and S_2:

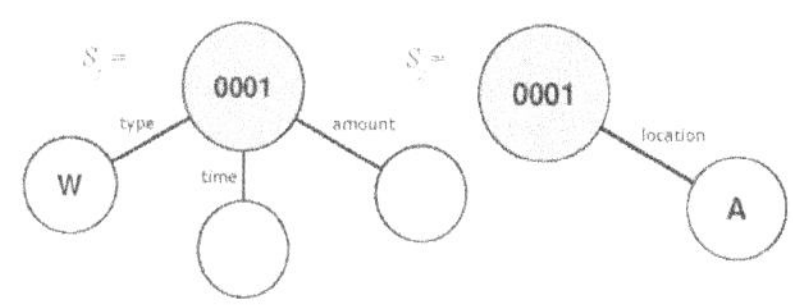

We compress G with S_1 and S_2 and evaluate a_s for all four substructures. As $G_{(i)}$, $G_{(ii)}$ and $G_{(iv)}$ are completely compressed, they have a lower anomaly score. $a_{(iii)}$ is the highest score, so we identify subgraph $G_{(iii)}$ as the most anomalous (highlighted with a box in Fig. 1b).

Once again, Subdue has correctly identified the structural anomaly but does not discover the numeric anomalies. Applying our approach, we map all numeric labels $l \in L^N$ to a constant value q_0 if they are "normal" and with a number q_i indicating the degree of anomalousness otherwise.

Thus we create a new graph G^b where $\mathcal{L}_V(G^b_{(ii)}, \text{"}amount\text{"}) = q_1$, $\mathcal{L}_V(G^b_{(ii)}, \text{"}time\text{"}) = q_2$ and all other numeric attributes take value q_0. Applying Subdue to G^b, we discover the best frequent substructures S_1^b and S_2^b are:

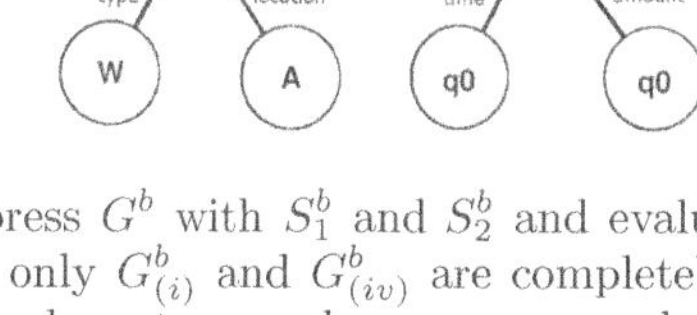

We compress G^b with S_1^b and S_2^b and evaluate a_s as before. Now, only $G^b_{(i)}$ and $G^b_{(iv)}$ are completely compressed and have the lowest anomaly scores $a_{(i)}$ and $a_{(iv)}$. The values for $a_{(ii)}$ and $a_{(iii)}$ are higher, correctly identifying both anomalous transactions.

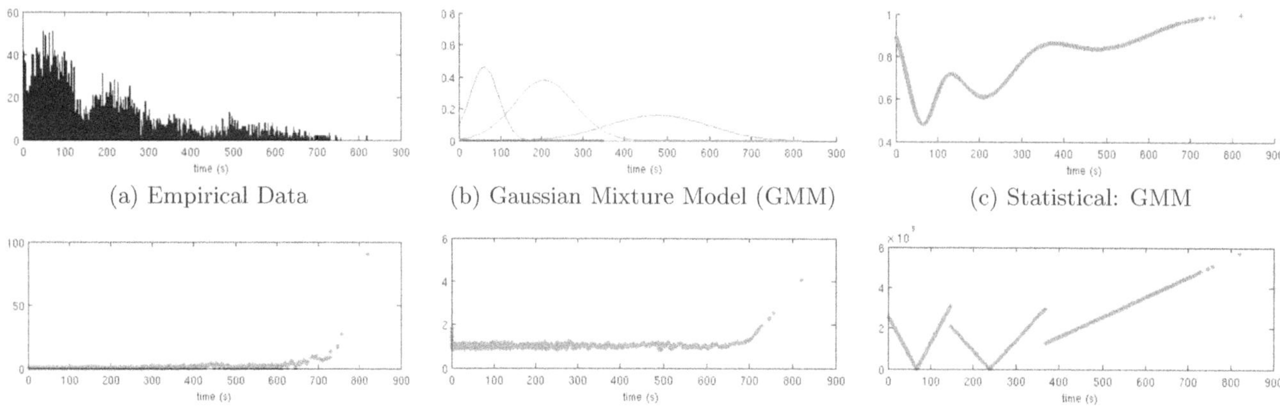

(a) Empirical Data (b) Gaussian Mixture Model (GMM) (c) Statistical: GMM

(d) Nearest Neighbour-based: k-dist (e) Density-based: LOF (f) Clustering-based: CBLOF

Figure 2: Comparison of methods for detecting numeric outliers

3. YAGADA: AN ALGORITHM TO DETECT STRUCTURAL AND NUMERIC ANOMALIES

In Sect. 2, we described the spirit of our approach and showed how anomaly scores for numeric attributes can be integrated into the graph structure. Now we consider how to calculate the anomaly scores q_i and present our algorithm for graph-based anomaly detection, YAGADA.

There are a number of well-known approaches for detecting outliers in numeric data sets. The simplest is to have a threshold t: if a numeric value $x > t$, it is considered anomalous [2]. This approach has several weaknesses: it requires some method of determining t; it cannot detect anomalies in the middle of the data range, only at the extremes; and the result is a binary—"normal" or "anomalous"—with no measure of the degree of anomalousness.

Fig. 2a shows a dataset $T = \{t_0, t_1, \ldots, t_n\}$, where each $t_i, 0 \leq i \leq n$ represents the elapsed time for a staff member to walk between a specific pair of physical Access Control sensors in an office building (see Sect. 4 for details of the dataset). It is obvious from visual inspection that there is more than one pattern of behaviour. These distinct patterns can be modelled as a mixture of K Gaussian distributions. The probability of observing t_i is:

$$P(t_i) = \sum_{j=1}^{K} \omega_{j,i} \cdot \eta(t_i, \mu_{j,i}, \sigma_{j,i})$$

where K is the number of distributions; $\omega_{j,i}$, $\mu_{j,i}$ and $\sigma_{j,i}$ are the weight, mean and standard deviation of the jth Gaussian in the mixture at time t_i; and η is a Gaussian pdf. The resulting Gaussian Mixture Model (GMM) is shown in Fig. 2b (with $K = 3$). In devising YAGADA, we compared four approaches to computing the anomaly score q_i:

Statistical: If we model the data using a GMM as shown above, $P(t_i \text{ is an outlier}) = 1 - P(t_i)$. The distribution of outlier scores for T is shown in Fig. 2c. Using this approach, we can set an anomaly threshold $0 \leq q_a \leq 1$ and define

$$q_i = \begin{cases} q_0 & \text{if } 1 - P(t_i) < q_a \\ 1 - P(t_i) & \text{otherwise} \end{cases}$$

GMMs can be rapidly computed using Expectation Maximisation. The main difficulty is selecting appropriate parameters: K and q_a must be calculated separately for each numeric label on every vertex and edge.

Nearest Neighbour-based: The above problem can be avoided by using a non-parametric approach, such as k-distances [12]. The distance is calculated from each t_i to its kth nearest neighbour. k is a global smoothing parameter and the selection of k is independent of the statistical distribution of T. Reasonable results are obtained with $k = 1$. Higher values of k reduce the sensitivity of detection. Fig. 2d shows the k-distances for T with $k = 10$. Samples in dense parts of the dataset have very small k-distances (close to 0). Outliers have k-distances which are orders of magnitude larger. Therefore we can define

$$q_i = \begin{cases} q_0 & \text{if k-distance}(t_i) \approx 0 \\ \text{k-distance}(t_i) & \text{otherwise} \end{cases}$$

The general k-distances algorithm has $\mathcal{O}(N^2)$ complexity, but various heuristics have been proposed to reduce this [12]. If T is one-dimensional and has been sorted (as in Fig. 2d), the complexity can be reduced to $\mathcal{O}(N)$.

Density-based: Using GMMs, we detect outliers with respect to the global distribution of T. With k-distances, we detect outliers with respect to the global density of T. If the density of the clusters is not uniform, both approaches will detect sparse clusters as anomalies. Local Outlier Factors (LOF) [3] calculates an anomaly score based on both the distance from and the relative density of the local neighbourhood. Samples belonging to a dense cluster or deep within a sparse cluster have $\text{LOF}(t_i) \approx 1$. Outliers have LOF values several times larger. Using LOF, we define

$$q_i = \begin{cases} q_0 & \text{if LOF}(t_i) \approx 1 \\ \text{LOF}(t_i) & \text{otherwise} \end{cases}$$

$\text{LOF}(T)$ is shown in Fig. 2e. Note that LOF has detected anomalies at the low end of the data range, which were not detected using k-distances. While LOF can detect anomalies very accurately, it suffers from $\mathcal{O}(N^2)$ complexity.

Cluster-based: CBLOF (Cluster-Based Local Outlier Factors) [7] is an efficient algorithm which detects outlierness relative to local clusters. Each cluster in the dataset is classified as "large" or "small" using two parameters, α and β. The outlier score $\text{CBLOF}(t_i)$ is the distance to the closest large cluster centroid. So samples in small or sparse clusters are more anomalous than those in big or dense clusters. To use CBLOF, we set an anomaly threshold q_a and define

$$q_i = \begin{cases} q_0 & \text{if CBLOF}(t_i) < q_a \\ \text{CBLOF}(t_i) & \text{otherwise} \end{cases}$$

$\text{CBLOF}(T)$ is shown in Fig. 2f, using k-means clustering with $k = 3, \alpha = 0.95, \beta = 2$. The distribution of anomaly values is similar to Fig. 2c: in fact, CBLOF has similar advantages and disadvantages to GMM. The complexity is generally low (depending on the chosen clustering algorithm), but the optimal values of k, α and β must be determined separately for each numeric label on every vertex and edge.

YAGADA must assign a constant value q_0 to normal values of t_i and an anomaly score q_i to numeric outliers. From our evaluation above, we see that a non-parametric approach is more suitable for unsupervised learning. Although LOF returned the most accurate results, its $\mathcal{O}(N^2)$ complexity made it unsuitable for use with large datasets. We therefore settled on K-Nearest Neighbours (k-distances) as the best trade-off between accuracy and efficiency. k-NN also has the property that it scales easily to multi-dimensional data. The choice of outlier detection algorithm is considered further in Sect. 5. Having chosen the outlier detection method, we can now present the complete algorithm for YAGADA:

Algorithm 1 YAGADA: detect anomalies in labelled graphs

Require: $G = (V, E, L^V, L^E, \mathcal{L}_V, \mathcal{L}_E)$
Return: Set of subgraphs $S = \{s_0, \ldots, s_n\}$; corresponding anomaly scores $A = \{a_0, \ldots, a_n\}$
1: Partition V into subsets $V_i : V = V_0 \cup V_1 \cup \ldots \cup V_{N-1}$, $\forall v, w \in V_i : v$ is the same type as w
2: **for all** $i : 0 \leq i < N$ **do**
3: **for all** $v \in V_i$ **do**
4: **let** $\mathcal{L}_V(v, \text{"anomaly score"}) = \text{Discretize}(v, V_i, \mathcal{L}_V)$
5: **end for**
6: **end for**
7: **let** $L^V = L^V \setminus L^N$
8: Partition E into subsets $E_j : E = E_0 \cup E_1 \cup \ldots \cup E_{M-1}$, $\forall (v, w), (x, y) \in E_j : (v, w)$ is the same type as (x, y)
9: **for all** $j : 0 \leq j < M$ **do**
10: **for all** $e \in E_j$ **do**
11: **let** $\mathcal{L}_E(e, \text{"anomaly score"}) = \text{Discretize}(e, E_i, \mathcal{L}_E)$
12: **end for**
13: **end for**
14: **let** $L^E = L^E \setminus L^N$
15: Execute Subdue(G) for *Limit* iterations
16: **for all** subgraphs $s \subset G$ **do**
17: Calculate anomaly score a_s by Eq. 2
18: **end for**

Algorithm 2 DISCRETIZE: calculate an anomaly score on the numeric attributes of a vertex or edge using k-distances

Require: $v, V, \mathcal{L}, k$
Return: Outlier score q_i
1: **let** $q_0 = 0$
2: **let** $FV = \mathcal{L}(V, L^N)$
3: **let** $fv_v = \mathcal{L}(v, L^N)$
4: **let** $fv_w = \text{k}^{\text{th}}$ nearest neighbour(fv, FV)
5: **let** $q = \text{distance}(fv_v, fv_w)$
6: **if** $q \approx 0$ **then**
7: **return** q_0
8: **else**
9: **return** q
10: **end if**

Algorithm 1 labels vertices with their anomaly score (lines 1–7). Vertices are partitioned so the attributes of vertices of the same type are considered together. The vertex type may be defined by its label (Fig. 1a) or by the type of edge it is connected to (Fig. 1b). The procedure is repeated for edges (lines 8–14). We then use Subdue to detect frequent substructures (line 15) and calculate the anomaly scores for the compressed graph (line 17). Algorithm 2 details the step of calculating the anomaly score from the numeric attributes. FV is a set of feature vectors created from the attributes of the vertices (or edges) under consideration (line 2). The dimensionality of FV is $|L^V \cap L^N|$ for vertices and $|L^E \cap L^N|$ for edges. fv_v, the feature vector for the current vertex, is compared to FV to find the k-distance to its kth nearest neighbour (lines 4–5). If the k-distance is normal, we return the constant q_0; otherwise, we use the k-distance as the measure of outlierness (lines 6–10).

Although a formal analysis of complexity is beyond the scope of this paper, we will comment briefly: we optimised the algorithm by pre-sorting T (average $\mathcal{O}(N \log N)$; worst case $\mathcal{O}(N^2)$), which allowed us to calculate k-distances in linear time. We also maintained a cache of k-distances for all attribute-value pairs.

4. EXPERIMENTS

In this section, we compare the performance of YAGADA to standard Subdue (ignoring the numeric attributes) and to three of the discretization approaches proposed for frequent subgraph discovery [11, 13]. Subdue discovers structural anomalies only and gives a baseline for comparison. The discretization approaches consider numeric attributes by sorting into ten bins of (a) Equal Frequency and (b) Equal Width, and (c) k-means clustering with $k = 10$. We compared to YAGADA using k-distances with $k = 10$.

The dataset for our experiments is from an Access Control system in a typical office building. There are 256 staff members and 155,100 Access Card transactions, representing all movements within the building over the course of 15 months. We reorganised the data into approximately 40,000 graph transactions (subgraphs), where each transaction represents the path taken by a specific user on a specific day. Each vertex represents a door sensor, and directed edges represent movements. We added a numeric attribute to each edge (v, w) for the elapsed time in seconds between presenting an Access Card at v and presenting it at w.

We applied each of the above approaches and used Eq. 2 to calculate an anomaly score $a = [0, 1]$ for every subgraph. Fig. 3 shows the results as a cumulative probability distribution. Most of the data—the "normal" part—has $a \lesssim 0.33$ (not shown): this represents the boundary between anomalous and normal transactions. Fig. 3 shows the relative performance of the five anomaly detection approaches: Subdue detects very few anomalies; KMeans performs somewhat better; EqualFreq and EqualWidth perform similarly, and YAGADA detects the most anomalies. At the upper part of the range ($a > 0.8$), YAGADA detects almost four times as many anomalies as the next best algorithm. In the mid-part of the range ($a > 0.65$), YAGADA detects approximately twice as many anomalies. This difference decreases with decreasing values of a, until at the boundary between normal and anomalous values ($a \approx 0.33$), the algorithms agree. This behaviour shows that while all algorithms may be discovering the same anomalous patterns, YAGADA detects them with much higher confidence, and provides much better discrimination between slightly anomalous and very anomalous patterns. Table 1 bears this out: of the top 10 anomalies discovered by any of the other four approaches, YAGADA detects all of them and in most cases assigns an anomaly score

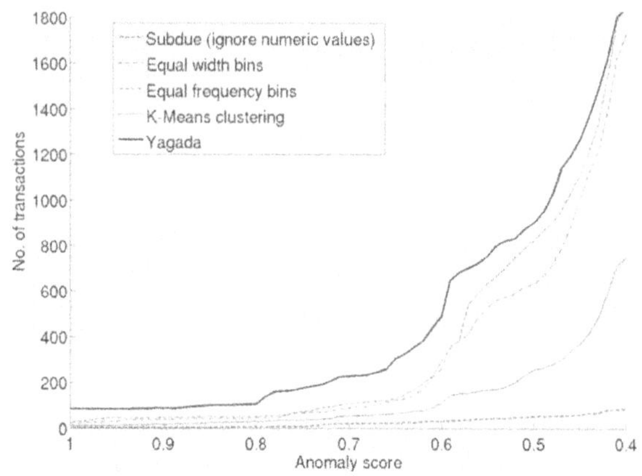

Figure 3: Cumulative Frequency Distribution showing transactions discovered as anomalous ($a \geq 0.4$)

Yagada	EqualFreq	EqualWidth	KMeans	Subdue
1.00	0.42	0.93	0.72	0.34
1.00	0.78	0.77	0.49	0.39
1.00	0.78	0.68	0.49	0.39
1.00	0.78	0.68	0.49	0.39
1.00	0.51	0.93	0.49	0.35
1.00	0.62	0.66	0.62	0.27
1.00	0.62	0.66	0.62	0.23
0.80	0.75	**0.81**	0.68	0.28
0.79	0.58	0.77	0.64	0.36
0.79	**0.96**	0.68	0.49	0.39

Table 1: Comparison of Top 10 Anomalies discovered by EqualFreq, EqualWidth and KMeans

which is greater than or similar to that produced by the best-performing of the alternative algorithms.

We also performed a qualitative analysis to confirm that the anomalies discovered by YAGADA are meaningful and useful. We examined a random sampling of anomalous patterns and checked that they were meaningful, such as failing to swipe at one sensor along a path. The patterns that YAGADA discovered with highest confidence were those which combined unusual paths with unusual timings.

We conclude that YAGADA is able to detect all of the anomalies which can be discovered using any of the alternative approaches, usually with greater confidence. YAGADA outperforms the other approaches as it uncovers a larger number of meaningful anomalies at the higher values of a.

5. CONCLUSIONS AND FUTURE WORK

In this paper, we presented YAGADA, an algorithm for detecting anomalies in graphs that consist of both structural data and numeric attributes. The novelty of our method is to replace numeric values in the graph with a constant q_0 if the value is normal, and an anomaly score q_i otherwise. When we subsequently search the graph for frequent substructures, q_0 will be incorporated into frequent patterns. The values q_i are infrequent and therefore substructures which contain $q_i \neq q_0$ are more anomalous. Our experiments demonstrate that calculating an outlier value for numeric attributes outperforms other numeric discretization methods for anomalous substructure discovery.

We evaluated several approaches to numeric anomaly detection and concluded that LOF and k-Nearest Neighbour (k-distances) were most suitable. These algorithms return an outlierness score close to some constant (0 or 1) for normal values, and much larger scores for anomalous values. k-distances was chosen over LOF due to its lower computational complexity. If we can make some assumptions about the data, it may be possible to devise a hybrid version of LOF. This would be an application-specific version of YAGADA, which trades off generality for improved performance and accuracy. As discretization is performed by a separate function, YAGADA lends itself to this kind of customization.

YAGADA combines the values for all numeric labels on a vertex or edge into a single feature vector. In our experiments, we had only one feature, elapsed time. YAGADA allows that we extend this into a 2-dimensional vector (*e.g.*, elapsed time and time of day) or multi-dimensional. As the number of dimensions is increased, so is the complexity of computing the k-distance between samples. The most efficient variant of k-distances is $\mathcal{O}(c^\delta + N)$, *i.e.* linear complexity with regard to the data size but exponential with regard to the number of dimensions δ. In our future work, we will evaluate whether k-distances is the most appropriate outlierness measure for multi-dimensional numeric data.

The algorithm demonstrated here is for use on static graphs, so it could be used for forensic analysis of graph transaction databases. We plan to extend the approach for on-line detection of anomalies using dynamic graphs.

6. REFERENCES

[1] L. Akoglu, M. McGlohon, and C. Faloutsos. Oddball: Spotting anomalies in weighted graphs. In *Advances in Knowledge Discovery and Data Mining*. Springer, 2010.

[2] R. P. Biuk-Aghai, Y.-W. Si, S. Fong, and P.-F. Yan. Security in physical environments: Algorithms and system for automated detection of suspicious activity. In *Workshop on Behavior Informatics 2010*. Springer, 2010.

[3] M. M. Breunig, H.-P. Kriegel, R. T. Ng, and J. Sander. LOF: Identifying density-based local outliers. *SIGMOD Rec.*, 29(2):93–104, 2000.

[4] D. J. Cook and L. B. Holder. Graph-based data mining. *IEEE Intelligent Systems*, 15:32–41, March 2000.

[5] W. Eberle and L. Holder. Mining for insider threats in business transactions and processes. In *Computational Int. and Data Mining, 2009*, pages 163–170, March 2009.

[6] W. Eberle and L. B. Holder. Discovering anomalies to multiple normative patterns in structural and numeric data. In *22nd International FLAIRS Conference*, 2009.

[7] Z. He, X. Xu, and S. Deng. Discovering cluster-based local outliers. *Pattern Recog. Letters*, 24(9–10):1641–1650, 2003.

[8] C. Jiang, F. Coenen, and M. Zito. Frequent sub-graph mining on edge weighted graphs. In *12th Int. Conf. on Data Warehousing and Knowledge Discovery*. Springer, 2010.

[9] F. Mansman, L. Meier, and D. A. Keim. Visualization of host behavior for network security. In *VIZSEC 2007*, Mathematics and Visualization. Springer, 2008.

[10] C. C. Noble and D. J. Cook. Graph-based anomaly detection. In *9th ACM SIGKDD International Conference on Knowledge Discovery and Data Mining*. ACM, 2003.

[11] G. Perez, I. Olmos, and J. A. Gonzalez. Subgraph isomorphism detection with support for continuous labels. In *23rd International FLAIRS Conference*, 2010.

[12] S. Ramaswamy, R. Rastogi, and K. Shim. Efficient algorithms for mining outliers from large data sets. *SIGMOD Rec.*, 29:427–438, May 2000.

[13] O. E. Romero, J. A. Gonzalez, and L. B. Holder. Handling of numeric ranges for graph-based knowledge discovery. In *23rd International FLAIRS Conference*, 2010.

[14] X. Yan and J. Han. gSpan: Graph-based substructure pattern mining. In *2002 IEEE International Conference on Data Mining*, ICDM '02, pages 721–724. IEEE, 2002.

Extracting Multi-dimensional Relations: A Generative Model of Groups of Entities in a Corpus

Ching-man Au Yeung*
ASTRI
3/F, Bio-informatics Centre
2 Science Park West Avenue, Hong Kong
albertauyeung@astri.org

Tomoharu Iwata
NTT Communication Science Laboratories
2-4 Hikaridai, Seika-cho, Soraku-gun
Kyoto, 619-0237, Japan
iwata.tomoharu@lab.ntt.co.jp

ABSTRACT

Extracting relations among different entities from various data sources has been an important topic in data mining. While many methods focus only on a single type of relations, real world entities maintain relations that contain much richer information. We propose a hierarchical Bayesian model for extracting multi-dimensional relations among entities from a text corpus. Using data from Wikipedia, we show that our model can accurately predict the relevance of an entity given the topic of the document as well as the set of entities that are already mentioned in that document.

Categories and Subject Descriptors

H.5.3 [**Group and Organization Interfaces**]: Web-based interaction; I.2.7 [**Natural Language Processing**]: Text analysis; I.7.1 [**Document and Text Editing**]: Languages

General Terms

Algorithms, Languages, Experimentation

Keywords

web mining, text mining, relations extraction, social network extraction

1. INTRODUCTION

Extracting relations among different entities from various data sources has been an important topic in data mining. Different types of relations are considered in the literature, such as co-authorship [15, 17] and social relations [13]. In fact, even when explicit relations are available among the entities concerned, it is still desirable to estimate the strengths of their relations [2, 20].

Previous works on relation extraction mainly focus on whether a relation exists between two entities. However, real world entities maintain relations that contain much richer information. A relation may only be defined in a particular context (topic). Taking social relations as an example, while Albert Einstein was closely related to other physicists, he, as a player of the violin, also maintained friendships with Fritz Kreisler and Bronislaw Huberman, two famous musicians.

While many methods for extracting relations exist, little attention has so far been given to the topic or context of the relations. We propose a hierarchical Bayesian model for extracting communities of entities under different topics from a text corpus. We assume that entities in a document are generated by picking a community, whose probability distribution depends on the topic distribution of the document. Our model is versatile and can be applied to extract relations among any type of entities found in a text corpus, such as persons and companies. Using data from Wikipedia, we show that our model can accurately predict the relevance of an entity given the topic of a document as well as the set of entities that are already mentioned in that document.[1]

We also demonstrate that our model and the results it generates open up new opportunities of analysing social networks and other relationships. The various distributions involving topics, communities and entities allow us to understand whether a particular entity is specialised or diverse in terms of its relations with other entities. This allows us to go beyond the limitations of abstract relations and gain more insight into the multi-dimensional nature of social relations.

2. RELATED WORK

One early systems for extracting social networks is the Referral Web system [11], which constructs a social network based on co-occurrences by crawling the Web. More recently, Matsuo *et al.* [13] propose using a Web search engine to extract relations among a group of academic researchers. Tang *et al.* [17] describe a framework for extracting research profiles and social relations of academic researchers. However, this type of works does not consider the fact that relations among people have different dimensions.

Cai *et al.* [6] propose methods for determining the relative weights of different types of relations in a social network. Tang and Liu [18] focus on classification of persons in a social network with the help of so-called 'latent social dimensions'. Tang *et al.* [16] describes a model of social influence among researchers in different topics, which can be

*This work described in this paper was carried out when Au Yeung was a research associate at the NTT Communication Science Laboratories in Kyoto, Japan.

[1]Wikipedia: `http://www.wikipedia.org/`

CIKM'11, October 24–28, 2011, Glasgow, Scotland, UK.

used to estimate how researchers influence one another in different topics. These works are related to our work in the sense that they attempts to model the multiple dimensions of relations. However, they are mainly designed to operate on well-defined network structures.

Topic modelling is used by some to model relations among persons. McCallum *et al.* presents the Author-Recipient-Topic (ART) model in [14] for analysing email communications. Wang *et al.* [19] propose the Group-Topic model to extract groups of people who have similar behaviours in some context, such as voting in the parliament. These works are similar to ours, but they are more specific and less suitable for the general objective we want to achieve.

Some other works explore ways to extract specific relations between two given entities (e.g. [1] and [5]). These methods aim at discovering specific semantic relations among entities. Chang *et al.* [7] propose a hierarchical Bayesian model for extracting this kind of specific relations in a principled way. While these methods are very useful, they are less applicable to large corpus because the number of possible relations increases dramatically as the number of entities increases.

Joshi and Gatica-Perez [10] propose to use probabilistic latent semantic analysis (PLSA) to obtain latent topics in news articles. The topic distributions are then used to estimate the probabilities of people in a particular topic. In contrast, our proposed method incorporates clustering of people into the process of topic modelling, and is therefore able to discover topics and communities that are more relevant to the relations among the people involved.

3. MULTI-DIMENSIONAL RELATIONS

We attempt to capture multi-dimensional relations by considering a generative process. In topic models such as LDA [4], each word in a document is generated by first sampling a topic and then by picking a word based on the word distribution of the topic. We propose the Community Topic Model that extends this idea by assuming that entities found in a document is also generated using a similar process. We note the following two important formulations of our proposed model: (1) Entities are generated by communities, which are generated by topics with distributions proportional to the topics of the words in the document, a formulation similar to the one described in [9]; (2) Entities are generated in pairs instead of one at a time.

The first formulation is based on the fact that different groups of entities may exist under the same topic. Adding the community latent variable would allow us to discover more coherent groups of entities. As for the second assumption, we design the model in such a way that for each community, entities are generated in pairs. This has the effect that each entity in a document is considered multiple times with all other entities, such that even in the same document an entity can be generated from different topics and communities. This increases the similarity between two entities when they appear together more frequently. We do not directly model every pair of relations. This is because this will result in exponential growth of parameters in the model. Entities that are assigned to the same community can be considered to be related to one another in that context.

3.1 The Community Topic Model

Figure 1 shows the graphical model representation of the proposed Community Topic Model, along with the descriptions of the symbols. Formally, our proposed model assume the following generative process of a corpus $\mathbf{D}$:

1. For each topic $k = 1, ..., T$:
   (a) Draw word probability $\phi_k \sim \text{Dir}(\beta)$.
   (b) Draw community probability $\lambda_k \sim \text{Dir}(\gamma)$.
2. For each community $g = 1, ..., G$:
   (a) Draw entity probability $\psi_g \sim \text{Dir}(\eta)$.
3. For each document j in $\mathbf{D}$:
   (a) Draw $\theta_j \sim \text{Dir}(\alpha)$.
   (b) For each word $i = 1, ..., W_j$:
      i. Draw a topic $k_{ij} \sim \text{Multinomial}(\theta_j)$.
      ii. Draw a word $w_{ij} \sim \text{Multinomial}(\phi_{k_{ij}})$.
   (c) For each pair of entities $r = 1, ..., R_j$:
      i. Draw a topic $c_{rj} \sim \text{Multinomial}(\left\{\frac{N_{kj}}{N_j}\right\}_{k=1}^{T})$
      ii. Draw a community $g_{rj} \sim \text{Multinomial}(\lambda_{c_{rj}})$.
      iii. Draw entities $y_{r_j 1}$ and $y_{r_j 2} \sim \text{Multinomial}(\psi_{g_{rj}})$.

To estimate the parameters of the model, we employ Gibbs sampling [8]. Let $\mathbf{w}$ be the words in the corpus, $\mathbf{z}$ be the topic assignment vector of words, $\mathbf{c}$ be the topic assignment vector of airs of entities, and $\mathbf{g}$ be the group assignment vector of pairs of entities. Firstly, we sample a topic for the i-th word in the j-th document conditioned on all other variables as follows:

$$P(z_{ij} = k|\mathbf{z}^{\neg ij}, \mathbf{w}, \mathbf{c}) \propto (N_{kj}^{\neg ij} + \alpha)\left(\frac{N_{kw_{ij}}^{\neg ij} + \beta}{N_k^{\neg ij} + V\beta}\right)\left(\frac{N_{kj}^{\neg ij} + 1}{N_{kj}^{\neg ij}}\right)^{M_{kj}}, \quad (1)$$

where $N_{kj}^{\neg ij}$ represents the number of times a word in document j is assigned to topic k, and $N_{kw_{ij}}^{\neg ij}$ represents the number of times the word w_{ij} is assigned to topic k in the whole corpus. The superscript $\neg ij$ indicates that the instance ij is excluded from the counting in the above variables. M_{kj} represents the number of times a pair of entities is assigned to topic k in document j. V is the total number of unique words in the corpus.

Next, we sample the a topic for the r-th pair of entities in the j-th document conditioned on all other variables as follows:

$$P(c_{rj} = l|\mathbf{z}, \mathbf{w}, \mathbf{c}^{\neg rj}, \mathbf{g}) \propto N_{lj}^{\neg rj}\left(\frac{M_{lg_{rj}}^{\neg rj} + \gamma}{M_l^{\neg rj} + G\gamma}\right), \quad (2)$$

where $M_{lg_{rj}}^{\neg rj}$ is the number of times the community g_{rj} is assigned the topic l in the whole corpus except the instance rj under consideration. G is the total number of unique communities.

Finally, we sample a community of a pair r of entities (a, b) in the j-th document conditioned on all other variables as follows:

$$P(g_{rj} = h|\mathbf{z}, \mathbf{w}, \mathbf{c}, \mathbf{g}_{\neg rj}) \propto (M_{c_{rj},h}^{\neg rj} + \gamma)\left(\frac{O_{ha}^{\neg rj} + \eta}{O_h^{\neg rj} + Y\eta}\right)\left(\frac{O_{hb}^{\neg rj} + \eta}{O_h^{\neg rj} + Y\eta + 1}\right), \quad (3)$$

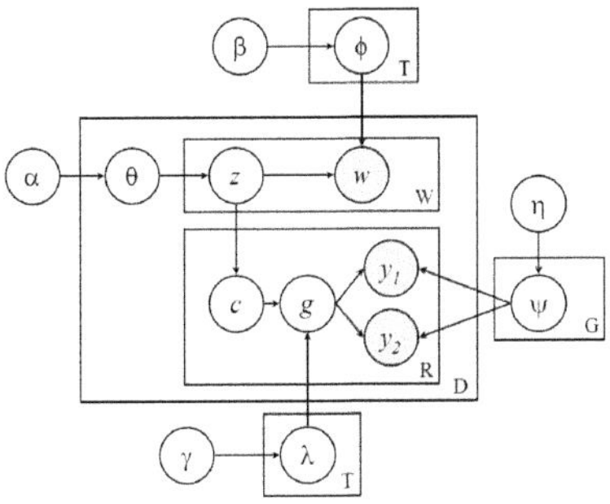

Symbol	Description
α, β, γ, η	parameters of Dirichlet distributions
θ, ϕ, λ, ψ	parameters of multinomial distributions
D	Number of documents
W	Number of words in a document
T	Number of topics
G	Number of communities
R	Number of pairs of entities in a document
z	topic of words
w	a word
c	topic of community
g	a community
y_1, y_2	entities

Figure 1: The graphical model representation of the proposed Community Topic Model.

where $O_{ha}^{\neg rj}$ is the number of times the entity a is assigned the community h in the whole corpus except the instance of rj under consideration. Y is the total number of unique entities in the corpus.

As we go through the Gibbs sampling process, the counting variables N, M and O are updated accordingly. We can then estimate the parameters of the model as follows.

$$\hat{\phi}_{wk} = \frac{N_{kw} + \beta}{N_k + V\beta}, \quad (4)$$

$$\hat{\theta}_{kj} = \frac{N_{kj} + \alpha}{N_k + K\alpha}, \quad (5)$$

$$\hat{\lambda}_{hl} = \frac{M_{lh} + \gamma}{M_l + K\gamma}, \quad (6)$$

$$\hat{\psi}_{yh} = \frac{O_{hy} + \eta}{O_h + Y\eta}. \quad (7)$$

4. DATA PREPARATION

Our main objective here is to experiment with extraction of topical communities and relations, and to investigate the performance of our proposed model. We choose Wikipedia as our data source, such that we can easily extract names of entities, such as persons and companies, based on some heuristic rules. This allows us to focus on the task of relation extraction, instead of worrying about named entity recognition. Our English Wikipedia dataset is obtained by downloading the XML dump file generated on 17th August, 2010.[2] It contains all current versions of the articles in the English Wikipedia at the time it was generated.

We carry out experiments on two different types of entities, namely persons and companies. To obtain a list of person names, we extract entities whose Wikipedia pages are assigned the following categories: 'YYYY births' and 'YYYY deaths'. Using this method, we obtain a total of 688,248 person names. Among all the articles, 1,055,611 articles contain one or more names from this list.

As we can see in Figure 2, the majority of person names appear only in a few articles. We extract only person names that appear most frequently to run our experiments. Arguably, the top persons are most interesting because they are more likely to be engaged in multi-dimensional relations with one another. Specifically, we generate three datasets, with the top 1,000, 2,000, and 3,000 person names respectively. For each of these, we obtain articles that mention 5 or more persons from the respective lists.

In addition, we also obtain a set of companies in Japan.

[2]http://dumps.wikimedia.org/enwiki/20100817/

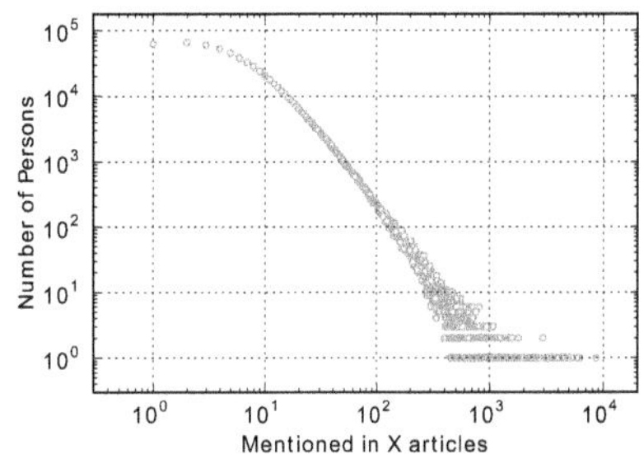

Figure 2: Number of articles in which a person is mentioned. Most persons are only mentioned in a few articles.

Dataset	No. of Entities	No. of Articles
Person-1000	1,000	6,932
Person-2000	2,000	12,783
Person-3000	3,000	37,314
JP-Companies	593	23,376

Table 1: Datasets extracted from the Wikipedia dump for use in our experiments.

We use this to demonstrate the applicability of our method on other types of relations. The list of companies names are collected from the article 'List of Companies of Japan', from which we extract a list of 593 company names. We find 23,376 articles that mention one or more of these companies.[3] Table 1 summarises the statistics of our datasets.

5. EXPERIMENTAL SETUP

Our aim is to study whether our model can capture accurately the relations between different entities. We evaluate our model using a practical task: predicting whether an entity is considered relevant in a particular context given a document and a list of other relevant entities. We carry out our experiments using the following procedures for each dataset.

1. From each article, an entity is randomly selected and put aside for testing.

2. Different models are trained on the training dataset, i.e. articles each with one entity removed.

[3]http://en.wikipedia.org/wiki/List_of_companies_of_Japan

3. For each article, we use the trained models to predict which entity is most likely to be included in this article (except the entities that are already found in the article).

4. The above procedures are performed for 10 trials for each dataset.

We measure performance by accuracy, which refers to the number of times the test entity appears in the top K candidates returned by a model, ranked by their probabilities. Let e_d be the test entity of article d, we define *accuracy* as follows.

$$accuracy(\Theta, K) = \sum_{d \in \mathbf{D}} \frac{|C_K(d, \Theta) \cap \{e_d\}|}{|D|}, \tag{8}$$

where Θ represents a trained model, $C_K(d, \Theta)$ is the set of top K candidates returned by Θ for document d. The value of accuracy ranges from 0 to 1. Ideally, relevant entities should receive high probability than irrelevant entities. Thus, a good model should achieve high accuracy for low values of K.

For comparison, we consider the following four different models in our experiments.

Co-occurrence Model.

This method considers only co-occurrence information and ignores the words that are found in the article. For each pair of entities (x, y), it estimates $P_e(y|x)$, the probability that y would be mentioned if x is already mentioned in an article. $P_e(y|x)$ can be estimated as follows.

$$P_e(y|x) = \frac{|D_x \cap D_y|}{|D_x|}, \tag{9}$$

where D_x and D_y represent sets of documents that contain the entities x and y respectively. This model can be used to predict the missing entity given a set X of entities that have already been mentioned in the article. A ranked list of candidates can be obtained by estimating the probability of an entity y using the following equation:

$$\begin{aligned} P(y|X) &= P(y|\{x_1, x_2, ..., x_n\}) \\ &\propto \sum_{x \in X} P_e(y|x). \end{aligned} \tag{10}$$

Co-occurrence + Word Model.

In this model, both word co-occurrence and entity co-occurrence for an entity are considered. For an entity y, in addition to $P_e(y|x)$ for x in all other entities, we also estimate $P_w(y|v)$ for every word v appearing in the corpus. $P_w(y|v)$ is estimated by:

$$P_w(y|v) = \frac{|D_y \cap D_v|}{|D_v|}, \tag{11}$$

where D_v represents the set of documents containing the word v. A ranked list of candidates is computed using the following equation:

$$\begin{aligned} P(y|X, V) &= P(y|\{x_1, x_2, ..., x_n\}, \{v_1, v_2, ..., v_m\}) \\ &\propto \sum_{x \in X} P_e(y|x) + \sum_{v \in V} P_w(y|v). \end{aligned} \tag{12}$$

Entity Topic Model.

This is a simplified version of the Community Topic Model. Every entity in a document is generated in a way similar to that of generating a word. A topic is first sampled from the topic distribution of the document, then an entity is sampled from $P(y|z)$, the entity distribution conditioned on the topic. This model conceptually resembles existing models in which both words and authors are directly generated from the topic sampled for the document. To generate a list of candidates for the task in our experiment, we estimate the probability $P(y|d)$ by the following equation:

$$P(y|d) = \sum_{z} P(y|z)P(z|d). \tag{13}$$

Community Topic Model.

Our model estimates the following distributions: $P(z|d)$ $(\hat{\theta}_{zd})$, $P(g|c)$ $(\hat{\lambda}_{gc})$ and $P(y|g)$ $(\hat{\psi}_{yg})$. To predict the missing entity for a given document, we can estimate $P(y|d)$, i.e. the probability of an entity given a document using the following equation:

$$P(y|d) = \sum_{g} P(y|g) \sum_{z} P(g|z)P(z|d) \tag{14}$$

in which we can use $P(g|c)$ to approximate $P(g|z)$, because c and z have the same distribution.

6. RESULTS AND ANALYSIS

6.1 Quantitative Result

Due to space limitation, we only present the results obtained by the worst and the best models for each datasets. Figure 3 shows the performances of the four models. We observe that the 'Co-occurrence + Word' model (Baseline 2) gives higher accuracy than the 'Co-occurrence only' model. This is expected as the former consider also the content of the articles. This consideration is of particularly importance when some special words are unique to an entity. Overall, we can see that the proposed model achieves the best results in all datasets. While we see that accuracy decreases as we have more entities and articles in the dataset (and thus the task becomes more difficult), our method still performs relatively better than other methods in all cases. The Entity Topic Model performance is comparable to the Community Topic Model in the JP-Companies dataset, but is consistently worse that the latter in the Person datasets. This shows clearly the advantage of incorporating a hierarchical structure (topics and communities) in the model.

6.2 Qualitative Analysis

We take a look at whether the model produces reasonable results by looking at two selected articles in the Person dataset, namely 'History of Films' and 'History of Philosophy'. These two articles are relatively long and mention many different persons. We remove these two articles from the Person-1000 dataset, and train a Community Topic Model using the rest of the articles. We then use the trained model to generate a list of person names for these two articles as follows.

Firstly, we estimate the topic distribution given an unseen

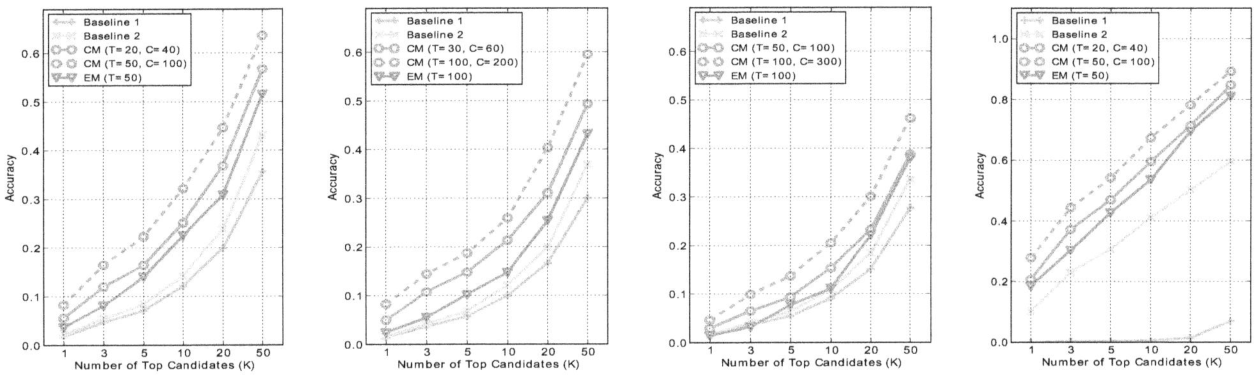

(a) Person-1000 (b) Person-2000 (c) Person-3000 (d) JP-Companies

Figure 3: Experimental results. CM refers to our proposed Community Topic Model, EM refers to the Entity Topic Model. We show the performance of the best EM, and also the worst and best CM.

1	**Alfred Hitchcock**	11	**Roman Polanski**
2	**Steven Spielberg**	12	**Akira Kurosawa**
3	**Francis Ford Coppola**	13	Robert Altman
4	**Martin Scorsese**	14	**Jean-Luc Godard**
5	**Quentin Tarantino**	15	**John Huston**
6	**George Lucas**	16	**Charlie Chaplin**
7	**Orson Welles**	17	Dennis Hopper
8	Clint Eastwood	18	John Ford
9	**Stanley Kubrick**	19	**Ingmar Bergman**
10	Woody Allen	20	Roger Ebert

(a) Article: 'History of Films'

1	**Immanuel Kant**	11	Augustine of Hippo
2	**Rene Descartes**	12	Friedrich Nietzsche
3	**Sigmund Freud**	13	**Galileo Galilei**
4	**Voltaire**	14	**Thomas Hobbes**
5	**Isaac Newton**	15	**Thomas Aquinas**
6	**John Locke**	16	**Francis Bacon**
7	Karl Marx	17	Johann Wolfgang von Goethe
8	**Charles Darwin**	18	Albert Einstein
9	Dante Alighieri	19	**Bertrand Russell**
10	**David Hume**	20	**Avicenna**

(b) Article: 'History of Philosophy'

Table 2: Top 20 person names generated for two selected articles. Names that already appear in the article are bolded.

article by

$$P(z|d) \propto \prod_{w} P(z|w) \tag{15}$$

where $P(z|w)$ can be obtained by using the Bayes' rule:

$$P(z|w) \propto P(w|z)P(z). \tag{16}$$

Next, we estimate $P(y|d)$, the probability of a person y given document d by

$$P(y|d) = \sum_{g} P(y|g) \sum_{z} P(g|z)P(z|d) \tag{17}$$

in which we can use $P(g|c)$ to approximate $P(g|z)$, because c and z have the same distribution. Using the above equation, we can then come up with a ranked list of person names based on the words appearing in an article.

Tables 2(a) and 2(b) show the top 20 person names generated by our model trained on the Person-1000 dataset with 100 topics and 200 communities. The names generated by the model match very well the topic of the two articles. For both articles, 14 out of the top 20 names are already mentioned in the articles. This shows that the model can accurately capture the associations between the persons and their relevant topics. Even for the names that are not found in the articles, they are actually highly relevant to the topics. For example, Clint Eastwood and Woody Allen are both well-known directors, and Karl Marx and Nietzsche are both important figures in the history of philosophy.

6.3 Multi-dimensionality of Relations

Our proposed model estimates the probability distribution of entities for each community. If an entity is associated with more than one topic, it will be assigned relatively high probabilities in multiple communities. This idea allows us to explore the *multi-dimensionality* of an entity.

Let $P(g|y)$ be the probability distribution of communities given a particular entity y. If y appears in only one very specific context (e.g. y is a tennis player), then $P(g|y)$ will have a single peak at the community involving tennis players. If y appears in two or more different contexts (e.g. y is both a politician and a science fiction writer), $P(g|y)$ will be multi-modal. This naturally points us to using *entropy* of the distribution as a measure of multi-dimensionality.

To measure the entropy of $P(g|y)$ of a particular y, we first need to obtain $P(g|y)$. While training the model we estimate $P(y|g)$, therefore, we can easily obtain $P(g|y)$ using the Bayes' rule:

$$P(g|y) = \frac{P(y|g)P(g)}{\sum_{g'} P(y|g')P(g')}. \tag{18}$$

$P(g')$ can be obtained by marginalising out c in $P(g|c)$, while $P(c)$ is approximated by $P(z) \propto \sum_d P(z|d)P(d)$. By computing the entropy of $P(g|y)$ for each y in the datasets, we can understand the multi-dimensionality of the entities.

Table 3 shows the top and bottom groups of entities in two of our datasets ranked by the entropy. For Person-1000, we find at the top of the list people who have their names associated with quite a number of topics. For example, Arnold Schwarzenegger is a well-known actor and politician. On the other hand, at the bottom we find mostly names of professional tennis players. We note that in general professional sportsmen and athletes have low entropy values.

Top 10	Bottom 10
Elvis Presley	Lisa Raymond
Michael Jackson	Rafael Nadal
Bob Dylan	Todd Woodbridge
James Brown	Leander Paes
Arnold Schwarzenegger	Mikhail Youzhny
David Bowie	Nikolay Davydenko
Woody Allen	Fernando Gonzalez
Elvis Costello	Fabrice Santoro
Johnny Cash	Daniel Nestor
William Shakespeare	Juan Carlos Ferrero

(a) Persons1000

Top 10	Bottom 10
Toho	SARD
Mitsui	Bones (studio)
All Nippon Airways	Gonzo (studio)
Softbank	Arc System Works
Japan Airlines	Dome (constructor)
Sumitomo	Pentax
Sony	Production I.G
Takenaka Corporation	Nismo
Mitsukoshi	Mugen Motorsports
Fujitsu	Mazdaspeed

(b) Japanese Companies

Table 3: The top and bottom entities ranked by entropy.

We observe similar and reasonable results in the list of Japanese companies. In the top group, we find mostly large corporations and conglomerates involved in a wide range of businesses, such as Sony and Sumitomo. On the other hand, in the bottom group, we find companies such as local banks that have very specific businesses.

7. DISCUSSION

We have demonstrated that our proposed model outperforms other models in predicting relevant entities given a document. We have also showed that it generates meaningful and reasonable results regarding the multi-dimensionality of the entities found in a corpus. Nevertheless, we are also aware of certain limitations of the models.

Firstly, in our model topics and communities are considered independent. However, two or more communities may be related to one another or they may form a hierarchical structure. We can extend the current model by considering the relations among topics/communities, using methods described in, for example, [3] and [12]. Secondly, we consider two entities to be related to each other if they appear in the same article. However, very often a long article contains multiple sections which are only weakly related to one another. We plan to consider only pairs of entities that appear within a certain window of text, or take into account the document structure of a Wikipedia article.

Regarding applications, our proposed model can be used to accurately predict relevant entities given the content of an article. Hence, an immediate idea of applying this model is to assist Wikipedia editors to develop existing articles by suggesting relevant but missing entities to an article. The model can even provide an explanation of why a certain entity is suggested. This will greatly facilitate editing of articles in Wikipedia.

8. CONCLUSIONS

We proposed a generative model of documents that takes into account the relations among entities appearing in the documents. The proposed model can be used to predict the relevance of an entity given a document more accurately than several other models. We also demonstrated how the model can be used to investigate multi-dimensional relations among entities. It also represents a more general approach to studying relations than existing works on heterogeneous networks, which require explicit information on how a particular type of network is formed.

9. REFERENCES

[1] Y. E. Agichtein. *Extracting relations from large text collections*. PhD thesis, Columbia University, New York, NY, USA, 2005.

[2] C.-m. Au Yeung and T. Iwata. Strength of social influence in trust networks in product review sites. In *WSDM'11*, pages 495–504, 2011. ACM.

[3] D. M. Blei and J. D. Lafferty. Correlated topic models. In *NIPS'05*.

[4] D. M. Blei, A. Ng, and M. Jordan. Latent dirichlet allocation. *JMLR*, 3:993–1022, 2003.

[5] D. T. Bollegala, Y. Matsuo, and M. Ishizuka. Relational duality: unsupervised extraction of semantic relations between entities on the web. In *WWW '10*, pages 151–160, 2010.

[6] D. Cai, Z. Shao, X. He, X. Yan, and J. Han. Mining hidden community in heterogeneous social networks. In *LinkKDD '05*, pages 58–65, 2005.

[7] J. Chang, J. Boyd-Graber, and D. M. Blei. Connections between the lines: augmenting social networks with text. In *KDD '09*, pages 169–178, 2009.

[8] T. L. Griffiths and M. Steyvers. Finding scientific topics. *PNAS*, 101:5228–5235, 2004.

[9] T. Iwata, T. Yamada and N. Ueda. Modeling Social Annotation Data with Content Relevance using a Topic Model. *NIPS'09*, 835–843, 2009.

[10] D. Joshi and D. Gatica-Perez. Discovering groups of people in google news. In *Proceedings of the 1st ACM international workshop on Human-centered multimedia*, pages 55–64, 2006.

[11] H. Kautz, B. Selman, and M. Shah. The hidden web. *AI magazine*, 18(2):27–36, 1997.

[12] W. Li and A. McCallum. Pachinko allocation: Dag-structured mixture models of topic correlations. In *ICML '06*, pages 577–584, 2006.

[13] Y. Matsuo, J. Mori, M. Hamasaki, K. Ishida, T. Nishimura, H. Takeda, K. Hasida, and M. Ishizuka. Polyphonet: an advanced social network extraction system from the web. In *WWW '06*, pages 397–406, 2006.

[14] A. McCallum, X. Wang, and A. Corrada-Emmanuel. Topic and role discovery in social networks with experiments on enron and academic email. *J. Artif. Int. Res.*, 30:249–272, October 2007.

[15] P. Mika. Flink: Semantic web technology for the extraction and analysis of social networks. *Journal of Web Semantics*, 3:211–223, 2005.

[16] J. Tang, J. Sun, C. Wang, and Z. Yang. Social influence analysis in large-scale networks. In *KDD '09*, pages 807–816, 2009.

[17] J. Tang, D. Zhang, and L. Yao. Social network extraction of academic researchers. In *ICDM 2007*, pages 292–301, 2007.

[18] L. Tang and H. Liu. Relational learning via latent social dimensions. In *KDD '09*, pages 817–826, 2009.

[19] X. Wang, N. Mohanty, and A. McCallum. Group and topic discovery from relations and their attributes. In *NIPS '06*, pages 1449–1456.

[20] R. Xiang, J. Neville, and M. Rogati. Modeling relationship strength in online social networks. In *WWW '10*, pages 981–990, 2010.

Distributed Social Graph Embedding*

Anne-Marie Kermarrec
INRIA Rennes - Bretagne Atlantique
Anne-Marie.Kermarrec@inria.fr

Vincent Leroy
Yahoo! Research
Barcelona, Spain
leroy@yahoo-inc.com

Gilles Trédan
Technische Universität Berlin
Deutsche Telekom Laboratories
gilles@net.t-labs.tu-berlin.de

ABSTRACT

Distributed recommender systems are becoming increasingly important for they address both scalability and the Big Brother syndrome. Link prediction is one of the core mechanism in recommender systems and relies on extracting some notion of proximity between entities in a graph. Applied to social networks, defining a proximity metric between users enable to predict potential relevant future relationships. In this paper, we propose SoCS (Social Coordinate Systems), a fully distributed algorithm that embeds any social graph in an Euclidean space, which can easily be used to implement link prediction.

To the best of our knowledge, SoCS is the first system explicitly relying on graph embedding. Inspired by recent works on non-isomorphic embeddings, the SoCS embedding preserves the community structure of the original graph, while being easy to decentralize. Nodes thus get assigned coordinates that reflect their social position. We show through experiments on real and synthetic data sets that these coordinates can be exploited for efficient link prediction.

Categories and Subject Descriptors

C.2.4 [**Distributed Systems**]: Distributed applications

General Terms

Design, Experimentation, Performance

Keywords

peer-to-peer, link prediction, embedding

1. INTRODUCTION

Peer-to-peer (P2P) networks are an appealing platform for social networks for they offer opportunities to increase the privacy of the users. In this paper, we address the problem of the distributed computation of *link prediction* [14]. Link prediction is a very important functionality in social network, as it assists users in finding new contacts in the social graph. Decentralized link prediction systems are appealing for two main reasons. First, many link prediction algorithms involves heavy computations and do not scale well with the size of the graph. As social networks now involve millions of users, a distributed approach enables each user to do his share of the computation, hence addressing the scalability problem. Second, some users are relunctant to let private companies handle their private data [5].

Building a distributed link prediction system is a challenging task. It requires to extract a notion of *proximity* between users in the whole social graph. The intuition is that only the *closest* entities to a given user guide his recommendations. Various data sources can be leveraged to establish this proximity, such as users' browsing/downloading/tagging behaviors. These approaches are however often application-dependent. Instead, we adopt a generic approach and solely exploit the social network of each user: only the relationships between friends are used to infer a social proximity measure. Although this measure could be exploited in multiple ways, a straightforward application is to suggest new friends to a user. This problem is typically referred to as *link prediction* [14]. In this paper, we address the challenge of decentralizing the proximity computation.

Most of the social graphs reflecting real life relationships exhibit a *community structure*. In other words, these graphs are often composed of smalls and internally well-connected subgraphs (the communities). *Bridges*, or *long links*, sparsely connect these communities. A user in a social network is typically connected to some communities such as her professional environment, her university friends, her childhood friends, etc. Connections between these communities may exist and the user precisely acts as a bridge between them. Extracting the community structure from a graph is crucial to guide a recommender system to predict links within the community. This extraction is however not straightforward and is a computationally expensive task that is hardly compatible with dynamic graphs. Moreover, the traditional definition of community, still under discussion, is fairly rigid: a vertex either belongs to a community or does not. This does not fit the current Internet setting. Overlapping communities have only been recently considered (see *e.g.* [17]). In this paper, we substitute the (tree-shaped) traditional community structure by a notion of community space, that we call *social* space. In this space, communities are no longer strictly defined as sets, but vertices from the same community belong to the same area. This definition allows vertices in the social space to be in the core or at the border of a community, as well as in multiple communities.

*This work is supported by the ERC Starting Grant, under the project GOSSPLE, number 204742.

In this paper, we introduce a novel decentralized algorithm based on (non-isometric) force based graph embedding to assist a link prediction system. More specifically, we propose SoCS (Social Coordinate Systems), a fully distributed graph embedding algorithm that embeds a social graph into a metric space. The embedding achieved by SoCS preserves the community structure of the input graph thus enabling to easily predict links. SoCS predicts links between vertices that turn out to be close in the social space but are not connected in the input graph. SoCS is a very simple algorithm, less than 20 lines of code. SoCS is based on a gossip protocol and does not require any vertex to have a global knowledge of the system.

As we show in the following, force based graph embedding is a natural candidate to distribution. Thus, our approach provides a sound basis for distributed link prediction systems. SoCS can be parameterized with any force-based model and we explore in this paper the application of two well-known energy models to generate a social graph embedding. We provide empirical evidence that the state-of-the-art force model as presented by theoreticians (the LinLog model [15]) is not necessarily the model providing the best results in a practical setting. Additionally, we obtain the surprising result that distributed versions of our protocol, that solely rely on local knowledge, often provide a better accuracy than their centralized counterparts. This demonstrates a connection with local non-linear dimensionality reduction algorithms. We evaluate SoCS in the context of a terrorist collaboration network, a co-authorship dataset, and a synthetic small-world Kleinberg topologies [11].

Our results show that SoCS is able to achieve social embedding: links removed from social networks are accurately predicted, and SoCS enables to clearly distinguish between short and long-range links in a small-world network. We also observe that SoCS is efficient and highly resilient to dynamics. Thus, SoCS is a perfect candidate to implement a contact recommender system in a P2P social network. The rest of the paper is organized as follows. In Section 2, we present background on graph embedding and force-based layout. We present SoCS in Section 3 and provide some experimental results in Section 4. Finally, we review related work in Section 5 and conclude in Section 6.

2. BACKGROUND

In this section, we present the link prediction problem and provide the background on graph embedding required to understand our decentralized protocol. We also introduce the two force models that we consider in this work.

2.1 Link Prediction

The link prediction problem, introduced in [14], consists in predicting the links that are likely to appear in a social network. Most of the existing approaches rely only on the structure of the graph to determine a similarity between users, and rank their predictions according to this similarity. Section 4, we evaluate SoCS against the three following algorithms. The graph shortest path (SP) and the number of common neighbors (CNSP) are used in [14]. In the case of CNSP, we first compute the shortest path between nodes, and then compare the number of common neighbors if the shortest path's length is 2. The hierarchical random graph (HRG) model, presented in [2], relies on the probability that two given nodes belong to the same community to predict links.

2.2 Graph Embedding

Consider $G(V, E)$, an undirected graph of $n = |V|$ nodes representing a distributed system. Let $\mathcal{P}$ be the *host* space and let $\dim \mathcal{P} = d$. A graph embedding is a *mapping* of the graph vertices to positions in the host space. In other words, each vertex gets assigned to a point in the host space.

Generally, the objective of graph embeddings is to preserve the original graph distances in the host space such that the graph shortest path distance between two nodes is equal to the distance between their respective images in the host space. If this property holds for any two nodes, the embedding is said *isometric*. Yet, our goal to achieve a social embedding is to precisely apply some distortion to extract the community structure of a graph so that edges within communities are shorter than those between communities. Therefore, in SoCS, we use low-dimensional host spaces ($d \ll n$): our goal is not to minimize the distortion, since an isometric embedding would not respect the community structure.

2.3 Force-based graph embedding

In this paper, we consider force-based embeddings (FBE), introduced by Eades [4]. Several variations have been proposed since. Intuitively, it is possible to explain the algorithm using a physical analogy: edges represent springs and nodes represent electrically equally charged particles. Edges (springs) attract the vertices they link, whereas vertices (particles) repulse each other. This is the physical system simulated by FBE algorithms. The embedding is achieved once the system reaches an equilibrium.

FBEs are iterative algorithms and rely on two kinds of forces that define the attractions and repulsions that each node is subject to in the host space. Initially, each node is placed at random in the host space. At each iteration of the algorithm, the forces are applied to the nodes. *Attractive* forces are always applied to a node by its *graph neighbors* whereas *repulsive* forces are applied by *all* nodes. Figure 1 illustrates this principle: node a is attracted by b, c and e, and repulsed by b, c, d, e and f. We denote by V_i the graph neighbors of the node i. Let P_i be the image (*i.e.* the position) of node i in the host space. Let $||\overrightarrow{P_iP_j}||$ be the distance between P_i and P_j, and let $\overrightarrow{e_{ij}}$ be the direction from P_i to P_j: $\overrightarrow{e_{ij}} = \frac{\overrightarrow{P_iP_j}}{||\overrightarrow{P_iP_j}||}$.

Following Noack's formalism [16], we define forces as proportional to some power of the distance between two images: attraction force $\overrightarrow{A_i}$ and repulsion force $\overrightarrow{R_i}$ applied to a node $i \in V$ are respectively defined as

$$\overrightarrow{A_i} = \sum_{j \in V_i} ||\overrightarrow{P_iP_j}||^{fa}.\overrightarrow{e_{ij}}, \qquad \overrightarrow{R_i} = -\sum_{j \in V} ||\overrightarrow{P_iP_j}||^{fr}.\overrightarrow{e_{ij}}.$$

Thus each couple (fa, fr), as respective parameters of the attraction and the repulsion forces, defines a new force model.

In this paper, we study two common FBE models. The first one is Noack's *LinLog* [15] defined by $(fa = 0, fr = -1)$, that is considered as the best force model to preserve the community structure of a graph. The second one is the carbon copy of physical Hooke's spring attraction and Coulomb's electrostatic repulsion forces (such as presented in [19]). We denote *HC* this model hereafter, defined by $(fa = 1, fr = -2)$.

3. SOCIAL COORDINATE SYSTEM (SOCS)

In this section, we describe how SoCS performs a distributed embedding of a social graph. For the sake of clarity, we hereafter add the adjective *social* to every element referring to the SoCS host space. For instance the host space of the embedding is designated as the *social space* and the distance in that space is designated as the *social distance*. Nodes that have close *social positions* are social neighbors. At this point it is particularly important to distinguish between the graph neighbors of a node (the friends of this node) and the social neighbors of this node, which are not necessarily the same. Indeed, SoCS will recommend to a node its closest social neighbors that are not already graph neighbors.

In a nutshell, each node that runs a SoCS instance (*i.e.* each graph node) regularly updates its position in the social space. Each node first gathers the positions of its graph and social neighbors. Then, using these positions, each node computes the forces that are applied to it, and derives its updated social position. The rest of the protocol is a gossip protocol that provides each node with a list of its social neighbors. This list of social neighbors is then used to compute new positions.

3.1 System model

SoCS is a peer-to-peer (P2P) algorithm that embeds a social graph and operates on a P2P overlay network. We consider a system of n nodes and assume a one-to-one mapping between the nodes of the social graph and the machines connected to the P2P network, hence we refer as node both to the machine connected to the network and to the logical entity in the social graph. The social graph is an input in SoCS, so each node is aware of its graph neighbors. In a dynamic social graph, the set of graph neighbors may vary during the execution. To join an existing SoCS P2P network, a node contacts its graph neighbors to establish connections. Traditionally, in FBEs, each node is assigned a random initial position. In SoCS, when a node first joins an existing network, its position is initialized at the barycenter of its graph neighbors.

3.2 Rationale

Let us consider the example graph on Figure 1. Assume that this graph represents *friendship* relations between people. Nodes d and f are both two hops away from a. From the shortest path perspective, they thus should be considered equally friends to a. Yet, it is very likely that d is *closer* to a since they have two friends in common, namely c and b. This could result in d having twice more chances than f of being invited to a's birthday party.

Such social information is typically what SoCS aims at capturing in the resulting social embedding: this is achieved since the attractive forces applied between c and b bring d closer to a in the social space. In addition, due to d's repulsions, c and b are closer to a than e. As a result, the list of friends of a in the resulting space is then ordered from the closest to the farthest: b and c, e, d, f.

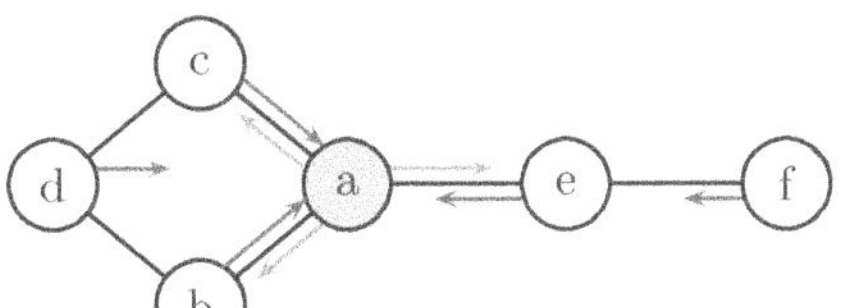

Figure 1: Example of a friendship social network

These results can be interpreted as follows: since (a, b, d, c) is a rectangle, it has more *cohesion* than a single line, and members of that structure get close positions. The generalization of this intuition is that nodes within the same community get closer positions than nodes from different communities. This is exactly the approach advocated by Noack, that recently bridged community detection and force-based graph embedding [16].

Link prediction algorithms are empowered by the knowledge of communities (see *e.g.* [2]). SoCS achieves such a social embedding, capturing, as the evaluation will confirm, the notion of clusters and communities by placing nodes of a community close to each other in the host space. Since links are more likely to appear between nodes of the same community, the social distance (*i.e.* the Euclidean distance over the social space) can be directly leveraged to predict links between nodes.

3.3 Local repulsions

In SoCS, in order to compute its position, a node needs to compute the sum of attractions and repulsions that apply to it. As explained in Section 2, attractions take into account the graph neighbors. Since a SoCS node is directly connected to all its graph neighbors, computing the attractions is straightforward. We now detail how repulsions are approximated and computed.

Computing repulsion forces based on all nodes is both extremely costly in a large system and hard to achieve in a decentralized way. Instead, SoCS only considers repulsion forces of the *close* nodes in the social space. This optimization was introduced by Fruchterman and Reingold [7] to reduce the time complexity of graph drawing algorithms. It is relevant for several reasons. First, in both force models (especially the HC model), the repulsion force quickly decreases with respect to the social distance between nodes: distant nodes' contribution to the force equilibrium is negligible. Second, we target link prediction. We aim at predicting links binding nodes that are socially close. Long social distances do not necessarily need to be precisely respected. We empirically show in Section 4 that considering only local repulsions provides better results while reducing the cost of the algorithm. Let $B(i, r)$ to be the set of i's r closest neighbors in P. SoCS discovers such neighbors and computes the following repulsion force:

$$\overrightarrow{R_i} = - \sum_{j \in B(i,r)} ||\overrightarrow{P_i P_j}||^{fr} . \overrightarrow{e_{ij}}.$$

3.4 The SoCS decentralized algorithm

SoCS is a fully decentralized algorithm: each node knows only a limited portion of the network, namely its graph neighbors and its social neighbors. SoCS relies on gossip to discover the social neighbors. Each node runs a clustering protocol, similar to [20], that we call the *Neighbors Peer Sampling* (NPS). The algorithm is very simple: each node maintains a list of its r closest social neighbors and communicates with them to share this information and discover closer nodes. Gossip protocols have been shown to be cheap, robust against churn, and to converge quickly [9].

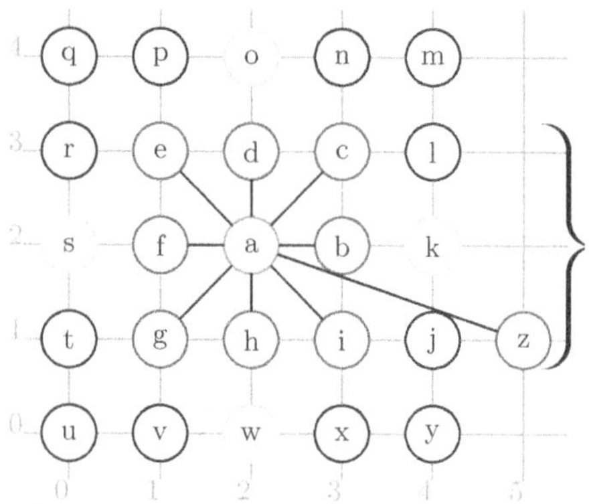

Figure 2: Kleinberg small-world grid

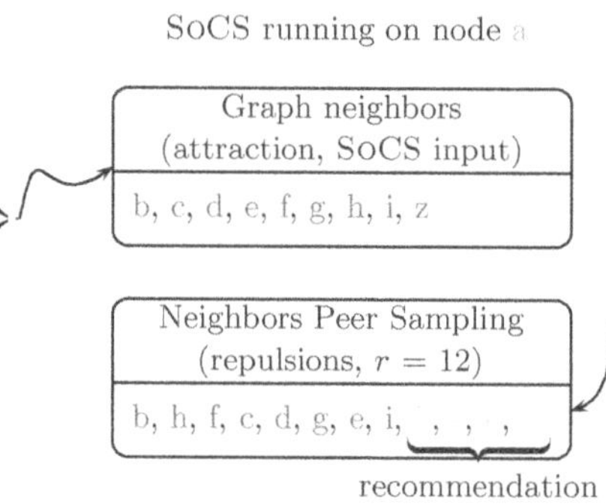

Figure 3: SoCS on node *a*

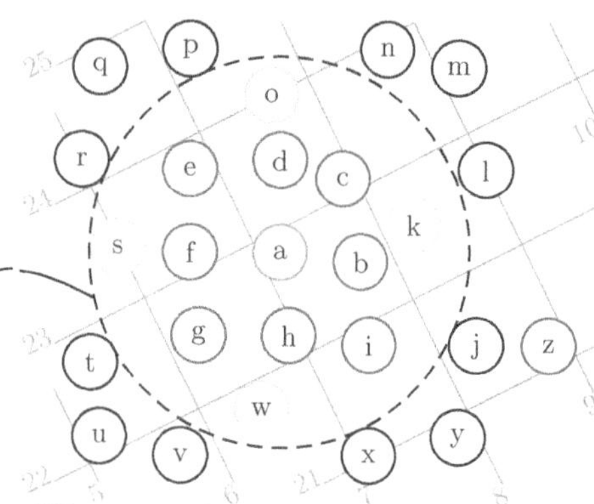

Figure 4: SoCS coordinates space

Algorithm 1 depicts the SoCS algorithm[1]. Lines 1 − 3 show initialization. In a static setting (G does not change over time), we assume that nodes are provided with a function `Converged()` that stops the execution of the protocol on a given node. For instance, a node that has not changed its position over the last couple of rounds, may stop. In a dynamic setting, `Converged()` always returns `false`. Two key parameters allow to tune the algorithm: the number of neighbors considered for computing the repulsions, r and the dimension of the host space, d. The impact of both parameters is detailed in Section 4.

Each node retrieves the lists of its social neighbors by calling `GetSocialNeighbors()` (this list is obtained from the NPS) and its graph neighbors by calling `GetGraphNeighbors()` (this list is extracted from the graph). Note that a node can be in both sets, and that the social neighbors list may only contain node positions instead of node identities.

Instead of computing directly a new node position, the presented algorithm computes a couple (speed, direction) toward the ideal position (lines 12 − 13). This improvement, also used in [7], allows a faster convergence by speeding up nodes in the early steps while avoiding oscillations during the late ones.

Figures 2,3 and 4 illustrate SoCS running on a small-world grid. They respectively illustrate Kleinberg's graph generation process, SoCS' input and ouptput on node a, and an illustration of SoCS' system-wide output. Blue nodes represent a's graph neighbors, green nodes represent a's predicted links.

Algorithm 1 Graph embedding algorithm, code for Node i

1: $P_i \leftarrow$ `GetBarycenter(GetGraph())`
2: $v_{prev} = 1$
3: $\overrightarrow{d}_{prev} \leftarrow$ new `RandomDirection()`
4: **while not** `Converged()` **do** ▷ Execute a cycle
5: $\quad \overrightarrow{d} \leftarrow \overrightarrow{0}$
6: $\quad$ **for** $j \in$ `GetGraphNeighbors()` **do**
7: $\quad\quad \overrightarrow{d} \leftarrow \overrightarrow{d} + ||\overrightarrow{P_iP_j}||^{fa}.\overrightarrow{e_{ij}}$ ▷ Compute attractions
8: $\quad$ **end for**
9: $\quad$ **for** $j \in$ `GetSocialNeighbors()` **do**
10: $\quad\quad \overrightarrow{d} \leftarrow \overrightarrow{d} - ||\overrightarrow{P_iP_j}||^{fr}.\overrightarrow{e_{ij}}$ ▷ Compute repulsions
11: $\quad$ **end for**
12: $\quad \overrightarrow{d} \leftarrow \overrightarrow{d}/||\overrightarrow{d}||$
13: $\quad v = (\frac{1}{2}.\cos(\overrightarrow{d}, \overrightarrow{d}_{prev}) + 1)v_{prev}$ ▷ Compute speed
14: $\quad \overrightarrow{d}_{prev} = \overrightarrow{d}$; $v_{prev} = v$
15: $\quad P_i = P_i + v.\overrightarrow{d}$ ▷ Move
16: **end while**

4. EXPERIMENTAL EVALUATION

We experiment SoCS through two different approaches. First, we measure SoCS' accuracy in a link prediction application using two different datasets: a computer science co-authorship graph (namely DBLP) and a terrorist interaction graph. We compare these results against some existing approaches. Then, in the second part of this section, we evaluate SoCS on synthetic small-world graphs. This setup provides a full knowledge of the desired social space and allows us to perform a more precise evaluation of SoCS, both in a static setting and in a dynamic network.

In our experiments, we evaluate the impact of SoCS' parameters, namely the number of repulsions applied to nodes (r, see Section 3.3), the force model (LinLog or HC, as described in Section 2.3), and the number of dimensions in the SoCS coordinates space. We show that, quite surprisingly, the configurations that achieve the best prediction quality are very close to the ones that perform well in a distributed environment. Finally, please note that, although SoCS is implemented in a java simulator, it runs in a fully distributed setting: each node is only provided with the list of its graph neighbors identities. In particular, SoCS does not rely on any assumption about the nature or the size of the graph.

4.1 SoCS link prediction quality

In this section, we consider two different social graphs. The first one is a terrorist association network [13] of 62 nodes and 152 edges, used in [2] to evaluate HRG. The second one is the DBLP dataset, from which we generate a co-author graph. We create an edge between the authors having at least one publication in common, while removing the authors that have less than 20 publications. We keep the largest connected component: 27,680 nodes connected by 211,078 edges. In order to perform the link prediction, we rely on the standard approach consisting in removing some edges from the graphs and trying to predict them. The edges removed are always selected at random, yet without disconnecting the graph.

We compare SoCS' performance with SP, CNSP and HRG (described Section 2.1). We consider the case of a static network: the social graph is not modified during the execution and SoCS runs until convergence. We use ROC curves, as well as the AUC measure to display the results.

Figure 8 displays the AUC of the link prediction on the

[1] Java binaries and complete source code are available: `http://www.irisa.fr/asap/coord`

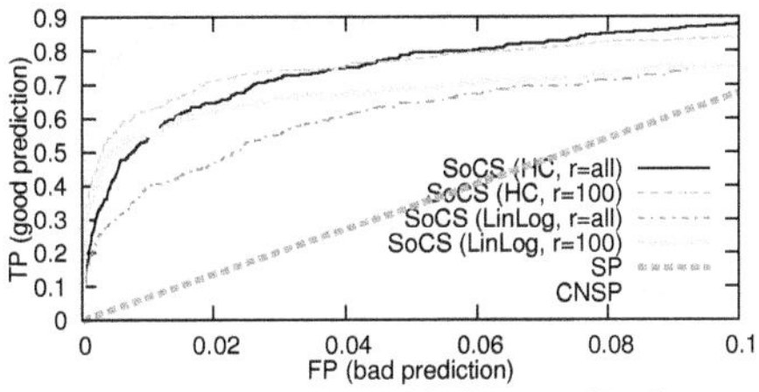

Figure 5: DBLP link prediction

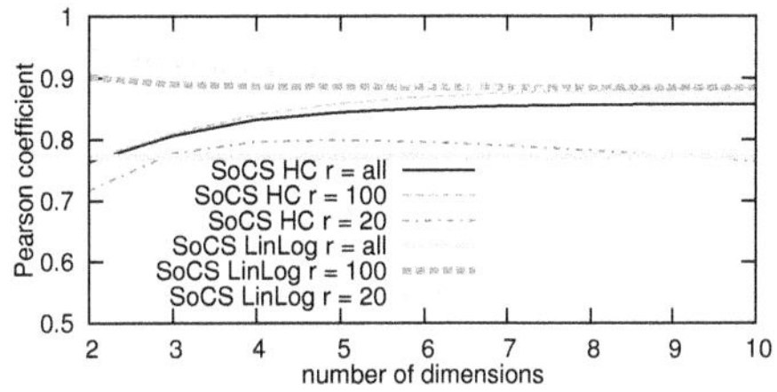

Figure 6: local Pearson coefficient on converged state

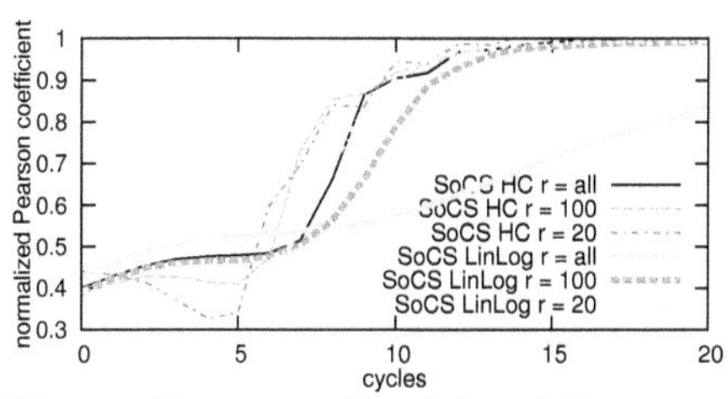

Figure 7: normalized local Pearson during cold start

terrorist association graph for an increasing number e of edges removed. We configure SoCS to use 10 dimensions. As already shown in [14], SP does not perform well, while CNSP is very accurate. We observe that SoCS performs best with the HC force model. It's also very interesting to notice that a lower value of r also improves the accuracy of the prediction. By reducing the amount of information gathered by each node, SoCS eliminates the impact of distant nodes and reduces the noise in the data: nodes get a better position. With HC, SoCS outperforms HRG at each level of sparsity.

The results obtained on the DBLP dataset, presented on Figure 5, confirm these observations. In that case, 1% of the edges were removed for prediction. We configure SoCS to use 20 dimensions. We were not able to evaluate HRG on this graph for the implementation provided by the authors quickly runs out of memory on a 16GB memory computer when applied to such a large graph. On smaller graphs, SoCS runs faster and uses much less memory than HRG.

Again, SoCS performs best in the HC force model with a small number of repulsions. This is a very positive indicator of SoCS' scalability, since repulsions consume bandwidth.

SoCS is always outperformed by CNSP. However, we argue that CN and SP both require the computation of all shortest paths, which has a prohibitive cost especially in a P2P environment facing churn: each node joining or leaving potentially impacts many shortest paths. In SoCS, nodes only exchange lists of neighbors in the SoCS coordinates space. Additionally, CNSP is known to perform very well in many social graphs [14], and we believe that the setup of this experiment largely favors the CNSP metric: scientific publications often have more than 2 authors, inducing a highly redundant common neighbors (CNSP) set. SP also outperforms SoCS after predicting 60% of the missing edges. However, similarly to a top-k ranking, we believe that first (say, 1%) predictions are the most important.

4.2 SoCS applied to a small-world network

In this section, we consider a synthetic small-world network. We rely on the Kleinberg model [11] to generate a small world network. In this model, nodes are first linked according to a lattice graph. These links represent short links. Then, long links are drawn between nodes representing the inter-community links. Figure 2 illustrates the process: node a has short links to nodes b to i, and a long link to z. We extract the resulting graph and use it as the SoCS input. All the results we present are averaged over 100 different randomly generated graphs.

e	SP	CNSP	HRG	SoCS HC		SoCS LinLog	
				$r = 20$	$r = all$	$r = 20$	$r = all$
1	.851	.914	.881	.899	.894	.869	.864
10	.841	.904	.884	.900	.896	.868	.864
20	.843	.888	.868	.883	.881	.854	.850
30	.837	.871	.859	.869	.869	.837	.835

Figure 8: Terrorist network link prediction AUC

4.2.1 *Static system evaluation*

After SoCS converged, it provides each node with a position in the social space, as illustrated on Figure 4. It is then possible to compute how closely the SoCS social coordinates match the ones in the grid used during the graph generation (Figure 2). We are not interested in the absolute value of the coordinates, nor by any scaling or rotation that could occur, as illustrated on Figure 4. Our goal is to have distances in the SoCS social space proportional to the ones in the grid. We first compute the Pearson correlation between all node pairs' distances. Contrary to the previous results, the best performance (0.95) is obtained with the LinLog force model and with a large value of r, and the performance slightly decreases when the number of dimensions increases. However, as observed in Section 4.1, the local positioning of nodes has much more impact on the quality of the link prediction than the accuracy of the distance between far away nodes. Hence, we define a second measure that we call the local Pearson coefficient. For each node, we compute the Pearson correlation by only considering the distances to graph neighbors, and we average this result over all the nodes. As Figure 6 shows, the best results are achieved through small values of r. Increasing the number of dimensions improves the results with HC, while Linlog performs better with a small d. These results confirm our experiments on link prediction: SoCS should be configured with a small r in order to generate an accurate short-range positioning without taking into account noise from distant nodes.

A second experiment consists in using SoCS to allow nodes to differentiate between short and long range links. This problem was posed by Kleinberg in [12] and was already theoretically addressed [6]. Due to space limitations, we do not present these results. SoCS provides an accurate and more flexible experimental approach to this problem.

4.2.2 *Dynamic system evaluation*

In this section, we consider SoCS in a dynamic system, typical of a deployed P2P network. Users may join and leave the system (aka churn), creating perturbations. SoCS relies on gossip protocols, which have been extensively studied within different churn conditions and have been shown to be very resilient, even in the case of massive failures. In SoCS, the arrival or departure of a node modifies the underlying social graph, therefore, the SoCS coordinates should be updated in order to reflect these modifications. In this section, we study the quality of the SoCS coordinates during different churn conditions.

We first consider the case of a "cold start". The 1,024 nodes of the small-world network simultaneously join, without running any intermediate SoCS coordinate adjustment. Figure 7 displays the normalized local Pearson coefficient for different SoCS configurations. The value 1 is obtained once the system has converged. The HC force model reaches stability much faster (8 cycles), than the LinLog one (up to 40 cycles). We also observe that the convergence time decreases with r. A massive churn scenario, in which half of the network converges and the other half simultaneously joins leads to the same observations, but with a faster convergence. Indeed, nodes joining the network leverage the other nodes' positions to obtain a fairly accurate initial placement. Regular churn, in which nodes join and leave the network at each cycle, has almost no impact on SoCS' precision. When r is low, the perturbations caused by churn only affect the few nodes that are socially close to the node leaving or joining. Such local perturbations are quickly absorbed.

These experiments show that the HC force model is more adapted to churn than LinLog. This is easily explained by the impact of repulsions: their weight is much lower in the HC model ($fr = -2$), so they generate less perturbations. Taking only the closes nodes into account, i.e. choosing a small r, is crucial for handling churn. It increases the convergence speed of SoCS and makes the system more resilient to churn. The previous experiments showed that a small r and the HC force model led to a better link prediction. Thus, SoCS does not suffer from its distributed nature, link prediction is inherently a distributed application in which each node considers its neighbors while ignoring the perturbation from the distant other nodes.

5. RELATED WORK

To the best of our knowledge, this paper presents the first distributed link prediction algorithm based on embeddings. As opposed to FBE, another approach to graph embedding relies on the graph eigenvectors [8]. A distributed algorithm to find these eigenvectors was proposed by Kempe and McSherry [10]. However, the application of this work to link prediction is not straightforward, and the stability of this algorithm when facing churn or dynamics of the graph has yet to be studied.

Assigning Internet coordinates to nodes in a fully distributed way is a problem that received a lot of attention. One of the most well known system is Vivaldi [3], a distributed protocol that aims to predict Round Trip Times (RTT) between nodes on the Internet. The main difference with our work is the goal (predicting RTTs) and the fact that we do not target isometric embeddings. Furthermore, in Vivaldi, nodes can easily compute, through a ping measure, their optimal distance to any given node and adjust their position accordingly. In SoCS, the nodes only have information about their graph neighbors and cannot do such a measure with respect to any node in the graph.

Another class of works that relate to SoCS is dimensionality reduction (DR). DR consists in discovering close items from a set of items described by highly dimensional data. These methods are heavily used in machine learning and recommender systems, where considering variables correlated in a manifold (such as the distances between cities of the Earth globe) is common. DR algorithms are used to flatten this data into a Euclidean space (a world map). The approach followed by these methods (*e.g.* KPCA, LMDS [1], LLE [18]) is to achieve DR while preserving the "local structure" of the data. Recently, Chen and Buja [1] pointed out the close link between graph drawing and non linear DR: SoCS can be seen as a non linear DR algorithm that "flattens" the social manifold. The importance of locality in nonlinear DR fits SOCS local repulsion approximation.

6. CONCLUSION

In this paper, we presented SoCS, a fully distributed algorithm for social graph embedding. SoCS distributes traditional force-based embedding algorithms to embed graphs while preserving their community structure [16]. SoCS exploits the benefits of the community structure knowledge for link prediction [2] to achieve meaningful recommendations in a social network. SoCS relies on gossip protocols to approximate the forces applied to the nodes and achieve scalability in large and dynamic graphs.

We extensively analyzed the performance of SoCS on both synthetic and real data. Our experiments show that SoCS is able to accurately assign social coordinates to nodes. The best results are obtained with configurations favoring the local accuracy over the global one. Not only does this setting improve the quality of the results, but it also offers better scalability and more resilience to churn.

SoCS can be used directly to predict links in a social network. In addition, this can form the basis for a more complete recommender system. Future work includes other force models evaluation, especially from their p2p applicability perspective, as well as achieving a better understanding of the algorithm parameter space. The privacy-protecting properties of SoCS have also to be studied.

7. REFERENCES

[1] L. Chen and A. Buja. Local multidimensional scaling for nonlinear dimension reduction, graph drawing, and proximity analysis. *JASA*, 104(485):209–219, 2009.

[2] A. Clauset, C. Moore, and M. Newman. Hierarchical structure and the prediction of missing links in networks. *Nature*, 453(7191):98–101, 2008.

[3] F. Dabek, R. Cox, F. Kaashoek, and R. Morris. Vivaldi: A decentralized network coordinate system. In *SIGCOMM*, pages 15–26, 2004.

[4] P. Eades. A heuristic for graph drawing. *Congressus Numerantium*, 42:149–160, 1984.

[5] A. Evfimievski, J. Gehrke, and R. Srikant. Limiting privacy breaches in privacy preserving data mining. In *PODS*, pages 211–222, 2003.

[6] P. Fraigniaud, E. Lebhar, and Z. Lotker. Recovering the Long-Range Links in Augmented Graphs. In *SIROCCO*, page 118, 2008.

[7] T. M. J. Fruchterman and E. M. Reingold. Graph drawing by force-directed placement. *SPE*, 21(11):1129–1164, 1991.

[8] K. M. Hall. An r-dimensional quadratic placement algorithm. *Management Science*, 17(3):219–229, 1970.

[9] M. Jelasity, S. Voulgaris, R. Guerraoui, A.-M. Kermarrec, and M. van Steen. Gossip-based peer sampling. *TOCS*, 25(3), 2007.

[10] D. Kempe and F. McSherry. A decentralized algorithm for spectral analysis. In *STOC*, pages 561–568, 2004.

[11] J. Kleinberg. The small-world phenomenon: An algorithmic perspective. In *STOC*, pages 163–170, 2000.

[12] J. Kleinberg. Complex networks and decentralized search algorithms. In *ICM*, volume 3, pages 1019–1044, 2006.

[13] V. Krebs. Mapping networks of terrorist cells. *Connections*, 24(3):43–52, 2002.

[14] D. Liben-Nowell and J. Kleinberg. The link-prediction problem for social networks. *ASIS&T*, 58(7), 2007.

[15] A. Noack. An energy model for visual graph clustering. In *Graph Drawing*, pages 425–436, 2003.

[16] A. Noack. Modularity clustering is force-directed layout. *Physical Review E*, 2009.

[17] G. Palla, I. Derényi, I. Farkas, and T. Vicsek. Uncovering the overlapping community structure of complex networks in nature and society. *Nature*, 435(7043):814–818, 2005.

[18] S. Roweis and L. Saul. Nonlinear dimensionality reduction by locally linear embedding. *Science*, 290(5500):2323, 2000.

[19] F. van Ham and J. J. van Wijk. Interactive visualization of small world graphs. In *INFOVIS*, pages 199–206, 2004.

[20] S. Voulgaris and M. V. Steen. Epidemic-style management of semantic overlays for content-based searching. In *EuroPar*, pages 1143–1152, 2005.

Classification and Annotation in Social Corpora using Multiple Relations

Yann Jacob
Laboratoire d'informatique de Paris 6
University Pierre et Marie Curie
Paris, France
yann.jacob@lip6.fr

Ludovic Denoyer
Laboratoire d'informatique de Paris 6
University Pierre et Marie Curie
Paris, France
ludovic.denoyer@lip6.fr

Patrick Gallinari
Laboratoire d'informatique de Paris 6
University Pierre et Marie Curie
Paris, France
patrick.gallinari@lip6.fr

ABSTRACT

We consider the problem of learning to annotate documents with concepts or keywords in content information networks, where the documents may share multiple relations. The concepts associated to a document will depend both on its content and on its neighbors in the network through the different relations. We formalize this problem as single and multi-label classification in a multi-graph, the nodes being the documents and the edges representing the different relations. The proposed algorithm learns to weight the different relations according to their importance for the annotation task. We perform experiments on different corpora corresponding to different annotation tasks on scientific articles, emails and Flickr images and show how the model may take advantage of the rich relational information.

Categories and Subject Descriptors

E.1 [**Data Structures**]: Graphs and networks; G.2.2 [**Graph Theory**]: Graph algorithms; I.2.6 [**Learning**]: Classification

General Terms

Algorithms, Experimentation, Performance

Keywords

Classification, Annotation, Networked Data, Social Networks

1. INTRODUCTION

The classification of linked semantic data occurs in many different contexts like Web page classification [17], document classification [5], Web spam detection [1], iamge or video annotation [6, 16], blog labeling [4]. In addition to the content element description, some form of relational information is available, and could be used as a complementary information source for classifying objects. Most existing works in this domain have considered that elements are connected with only one type of relation like authorship, friendship, etc... There are however many concrete problems for which several types of relations are available and could or must be exploited. Recently some work has started to develop in this direction. For example, [16] exploits the relations between different key frames represented by several modalities to annotate video shots, [15] performs protein classification using multiple protein networks. The main problem with these aproaches is that the content information is handled only through the computation of similarities between elements, and not used directly for classification. Moreover, these methods rely on complex optimization methods that are not well suited for large networks. We consider in the paper the problem of learning to annotate documents in content information networks, where the elements share multiple relations. This is one of the very first models for graph classification able to learn simultaneously from the content of the elements to be classified and from heterogeneous multiple relations between these elements. Experiments on different datasets allow us to evaluate the ability of the model to deal with a variety of contexts. The model is compared to mono-relational and multi-relational baselines methods and show both its ability to aggregate the information from the different types of relations, and also to efficiently mix the content and the structure for improving the classification.

The paper is organized as follows. In Section 3 we introduce a classical transductive framework for learning node scores in mono-relational graph data, in Section 4 we introduce the extension to multi-relational data, in Section 5 we present the results of experiments performed on different datasets and compared to baseline methods. Section 6 presents the related work.

CIKM'11, October 24–28, 2011, Glasgow, Scotland, UK.

2. NOTATIONS

We consider a multi-graph $G = (V, E)$. It is defined by:

- A set of N nodes $V = \{v_1, ...v_N\}$. We consider that nodes have a content information described by a feature vector. In the following, v_k will denote both the node and the feature vector associated to the node i.e $v_k \in \mathbb{R}^d$ where d is the dimension of the feature vector. Such a feature vector can be a histogram for an image or a word frequency histogram for a document.

- A set of edges $E = \bigcup_{k=1}^{R} E^{(k)}$ where $E^{(k)}$ is the set of edges of type k between the elements of V. R is the

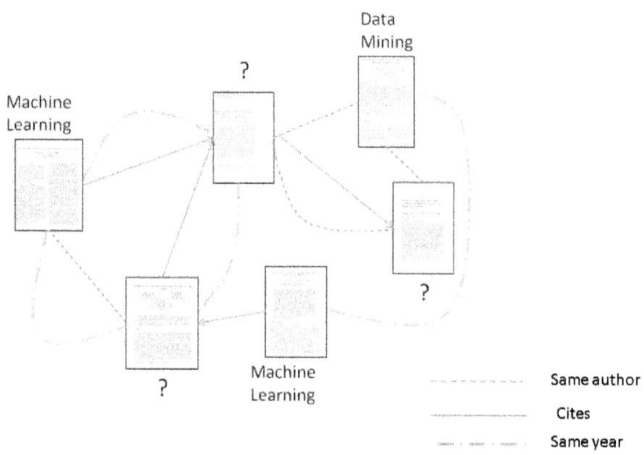

Figure 1: Transductive Multi-Relational Graph Labeling. The graph presents different types of edges modeling different relations (denoted by colours or dotted lines). Some nodes are already labeled (e.. Machine Learning) and some others have to be labeled by the model.

number of relations. E is a three dimensional tensor $E = \{w_{i,j}^{(k)}\}$ where $w_{i,j}^{(k)}$ is the weight of the edge of type k between node v_i and node v_j. If $w_{i,j}^{(k)} = 0$ then there is no relation of type k between v_i and v_j. Note that pairs of nodes can share multiple relations. N_e is the number of pairs of nodes with at least one relation.

We denote $V_\ell = \{v_1, ..., v_{N_\ell}\}$ the set of labeled nodes where N_ℓ is the number of labeled elements. For all these nodes, y_i is a known score associated to node v_i. The goal is to automatically compute a score $\hat{y}_i$ for the remaining unlabeled nodes $V_u = \{v_{N_\ell+1}, ..., v_N\}$, where $N_u = N - N_\ell$ is the number of unlabeled elements, using both the content of the nodes and the complex structure of the multi-graph. For $v_i \in V_\ell$, we set by definition $\hat{y}_i = y_i$.

In our transductive context, we consider that the scores of the labeled nodes are known during the whole process.

3. CLASSIFICATION IN MONO-RELATIONAL GRAPHS

3.1 Informal Description

We introduce below a general baseline transductive classifier for mono-relational graphs. We will use this model for our extension to multi-relational graphs in section 4. One considers that there are a set of labeled nodes and unlabeled nodes available. The goal is to score all unlabeled nodes using the information available from both labeled and unlabeled nodes.

Informally, our baseline operates in two steps. The first step consists in training a classical learning machine over the content of labeled nodes. This content only machine can be any type of classifier such as a perceptron, an SVM or a generative model. Once trained on the labeled nodes, it will be used to compute an initial score, $\bar{y}_i$, for all the unlabeled nodes of the graph. The second step consists in propagating these scores along the edges of the graph under the constraint that the propagated value should remain close to the initial scores computed in the first step. Propagation will smooth the cores so that graph neighbours tend to have similar scores. At the end of the process, the final score of a node is a balance between its content only score $\bar{y}_i$ and the scores of its neighbours. We detail below these two steps and then present in section 4 a model able to learn how to propagate the labels among different types of relations.

3.2 Propagation through Regularization for Mono-relational Graph

Classical propagation models have been developed for mono-relational graphs, i.e. $R = 1$. Most models [18, 3], rely on a smoothness assumption which considers that two connected nodes should have similar labels. This constraint is usually handled through a regularization term which enforces the smoothness. The loss function for these models has the general form:

$$L^{reg}(\hat{y}_1, ..., \hat{y}_N) = \frac{1}{N_u} \sum_{k=N_\ell+1}^{N} (\hat{y}_k - \bar{y}_k)^2 \quad \text{(term 1)}$$
$$+ \alpha \sum_{v_i, v_j \in N^2} w_{i,j}^{(1)} (\hat{y}_i - \hat{y}_j)^2 \quad \text{(term 2)} \tag{1}$$

where $\hat{y}_i$ is the predicted score of node v_i and α is a smoothness parameter. Here $w_{i,j}^{(1)}$ is the weight of the edge between v_i and v_j in a mono-relational graph. *Term 1* measures the error between the predicted score, and the content-only score on the unlabeled nodes. This term acts as a constraint so that $\hat{y}_i$ remains close to $\bar{y}_i$. This is a change wrt the classical formulation of transductive graph regularization which only consider propagation (i.e. term 2) and not content classifiers on the unlabeled nodes. *term 2* encourages smoothness. The final scores of the nodes are obtained through a minimization of this function:

$$\hat{y}^*_{N_\ell+1}, ..., \hat{y}^*_N = \underset{\hat{y}_{N_\ell+1} \dots \hat{y}_N}{\text{argmin}} \; L^{reg}(\hat{y}_{N_\ell+1} \dots \hat{y}_N) \tag{2}$$

4. LABEL PROPAGATION WITH MULTIPLE RELATIONS

4.1 Multi-relational model

We will describe now a new model able to learn to label in a multi-relational setting. This model learns an "optimal" linear combination of the different relation weights. It exploits a specific inference mechanism. We introduce the loss function in section 4.1.1, the inference technique in section 4.2 and the learning algorithm in 4.3.

4.1.1 Loss function

Instead of using directly the weights of the relations in the loss function as it is done in equation 1 through the $w_{i,j}^{(1)}$ factor, we will use a parametrized function $\psi_\gamma(i,j) \in [0;1]$ defined on each pair of nodes v_i, v_j where γ is the set of parameters of $\psi_\gamma(.,.)$. $\psi_\gamma(.,.)$ will be referred to as the *edge function* in the following. Its parameters will be learned from the data as described in part 4.3. This function will provide normalized weights in [0,1] for the different relation types. The loss function used in this model is $L^{multi}()$:

$$L^{multi}(\hat{y}_1 ... \hat{y}_N) = \frac{1}{N_u} \sum_{k=N_\ell+1}^{N} (\hat{y}_k - \bar{y}_k)^2 \quad \text{(term 1)}$$
$$+ \alpha \sum_{v_i, v_j} \psi_\gamma(i,j) (\hat{y}_i - \hat{y}_j)^2 \quad \text{(term2)} \tag{3}$$

$L^{multi}(\hat{y}_1, ...\hat{y}_N)$ has the same form as $L^{reg}(\hat{y}_1, ...\hat{y}_N)$ except that $w_{i,j}^{(1)}$ has been replaced by the $\psi_\gamma(i,j)$ function. Let us now describe this edge function.

4.1.2 *Edge function for multi-graphs*

Let us denote $\Phi(i,j)$ a feature vector that describes the different relations between v_i and v_j:

$$\Phi(i,j) = \begin{pmatrix} w_{i,j}^{(1)} \\ \vdots \\ w_{i,j}^{(R)} \end{pmatrix} \quad (4)$$

We define the edge function as a logistic function over the Φ vector:

$$\psi_\gamma(i,j) = \text{logit} < \gamma; \Phi(i,j) > \ = \text{logit} \sum_{r=1}^{R} \gamma_r . w_{i,j}^{(t)} \quad (5)$$

This setting considers that the edge function is defined with one parameter γ_r for each type of relation. This parameter reflects the importance of relation r for propagating the scores over unlabeled nodes. Note that in a single relation setting, it is equivalent to learning the smoothness hyperparameter. The logit function is used here for two reasons. First it forces the structural regularization term to be positive, second it prevents the γ coefficients from growing too much and acts in practice as a smooth constraint on the γ.

4.2 Inference

Inference consists in computing the predicted scores $\hat{y}^*_{N_\ell+1}, ...\hat{y}^*_N$ over the unlabeled nodes as the values that minimize L^{multi}:

$$\hat{y}^*_{N_\ell+1}, ...\hat{y}^*_N = \underset{\hat{y}_{N_\ell+1}, ...\hat{y}_N}{\text{argmin}} \ L^{multi}(\hat{y}_{N_\ell+1}, ...\hat{y}_N) \quad (6)$$

Note that this function only considers the unlabeled nodes, since for the training nodes we have $\hat{y}_i = y_i$.

We propose to solve the minimization of the function through an iterative algorithm based on a coordinate-wise descent method. This method consists in minimizing the L^{multi} function coordinate by coordinate. As $L^{multi}()$ is a convex function w.r.t $(\hat{y}_{N_\ell+1}, ...\hat{y}_N)$, the algorithm converges to the minimum of the function. At iteration t, one as to compute the minimum over a particular coordinate k knowing the predicted scores of all other nodes $\hat{y}_1^{(t)}, ..., \hat{y}_{k-1}^{(t)}, \hat{y}_{k+1}^{(t)}, ..., \hat{y}_N^{(t)}$. This minimum is found by solving the following equation:

$$\hat{y}_k^{(t+1)} = \underset{\hat{y}_k}{\text{argmin}} \ L^{multi}(\hat{y}_1^{(t)}, ..., \hat{y}_{k-1}^{(t)}, \hat{y}_k, \hat{y}_{k+1}^{(t)}, ..., \hat{y}_N^{(t)}) \quad (7)$$

This minimization is only computed for the unlabeled nodes and obtained when:

$$\frac{\partial L^{multi}(\hat{y}_{N_\ell+1}^{(t)}, ..., \hat{y}_{k-1}^{(t)}, \hat{y}_k, \hat{y}_{k+1}^{(t)}, ..., \hat{y}_N^{(t)})}{\partial \hat{y}_k} = 0 \quad (8)$$

The solution is thus:

$$\hat{y}_k^{(t+1)} = \frac{\frac{1}{N_u}\bar{y_k} + \alpha\left(\sum_{v_i}(\psi_\gamma(k,i) + \psi_\gamma(i,k))\hat{y}_i\right)}{\frac{1}{N_u} + \alpha\left(\sum_{v_i}(\psi_\gamma(k,i) + \psi_\gamma(k,i))\right)} \quad (9)$$

At each step, the new $\hat{y}_k^{(t+1)}$ value is a weighted average of the content value $\bar{y_k}$ and the $\hat{y}_i$ values of its neighbors. Hence, labels propagate via the relations while the content score is always present in the score combination. Note that the the algorithm uses a directed graph formulation (the two arcs (k,i) and (i,k) appear in the expression,) so that both undirected or directed edges could be used. The algorithm then consists in iterating equation 9 for any unlabeled node v_k until convergence.

4.3 Learning of the Structure Parameters

The goal here is to learn the parameters γ of the edge function. We consider that the content only parameters have been previously learned. Let us define $\Delta(\hat{y}_i, y_i)$, the cost of predicting score $\hat{y}_i$ instead of y_i using the proposed inference procedure. The empirical cost is defined over the labeled nodes as:

$$\forall v_k \in V_\ell, E(\gamma) = \frac{1}{N_\ell}\sum_{i=1}^{N_\ell} \Delta_\gamma(\hat{y}^*_k; y_k) \quad (10)$$

where $\hat{y}^*_k$ is obtained by using the inference procedure i.e:

$$\hat{y}^*_1, ...\hat{y}^*_{N_\ell} = \underset{\hat{y}_1, ...\hat{y}_{N_\ell}}{\text{argmin}} \ L^{multi}(\hat{y}_1, ...\hat{y}_{N_\ell}) \quad (11)$$

This function is difficult to minimize because it involves the minimization of an argmin function.

The structural parameters γ are learned on the labeled data. From the labeled subgraph, we generate one learning example for each node: it is composed of this node and its neighbours nodes. We then fit the γ parameters on these examples.

For labeled nodes, we would like to predict scores $\hat{y}_k^{(t+1)}$ as close as possible to the true score y_k of v_k. $\hat{y}_k^{(t+1)}$, computed through the inference procedure, will depend on the γ parameters (equation 9). We can optimize the γ values to obtain predicted scores close to real scores. Learning γ then consists in minimizing the prediction loss Δ defined for each labeled node v_k:

$$\gamma^* = \underset{\gamma}{\text{argmin}} \frac{1}{N_\ell} \sum_{k=1}^{k-N_\ell} \Delta_\gamma(\hat{y}^*_k; y_k) =$$

$$\underset{\gamma}{\text{argmin}} \sum_{k=1}^{k=N_\ell} \Delta\left(\frac{\frac{\bar{y_k}}{N_\ell} + \alpha\left(\sum_{v_i \in V_\ell}(\psi_\gamma(k,i) + \psi_\gamma(i,k))y_i\right)}{\frac{1}{N_\ell} + \alpha\left(\sum_{v_i \in V_\ell}(\psi_\gamma(k,i) + \psi_\gamma(i,k))\right)} - y_k \right) \quad (12)$$

This loss can be minimized by a classic gradient descent algorithm. We consider in this paper the use of a classical square-error loss for Δ.

4.3.1 *Complexity*

The complexity of our algorithm is : $O(N_\ell + N_e + N_u.N_e) = O(N_u.N_e)$ since $N_e >> 1$ and $N_u >> 1$. A mono-relational model (Step 1 and Step 3 only) has a complexity of $O((N_\ell + N_u.N_e).R) = O(N_u.N_e.R)$ (one model per relation). Our method is of the same order of practical complexity than mono-relational models and is faster in pratice. In the multi-class and multi-label settings, we learn one binary model per class for multi-relationnal and mono-relationnal algorithms. This multiplies both complexities by the number of classes, with the same analysis than above.

Dataset	Nodes	Edges	Rel.	Categories	Task
Cora	24 245	712 440	5	10	Monolabel
Flickr10	1 995	316 002	3	10	Multilabel
Flickr50	4 338	1 186 190	3	50	Multilabel
Emails	4 408	$\approx$ 1 M	4	15	Monolabel

Table 1: Statistics on datasets

5. EXPERIMENTS

5.1 Datasets

We have performed experiments on four datasets:

- The **Cora** dataset if a dataset of scientific articles with 10 thematic categories. The content of each node corresponds to the normalized TF-IDF vector of the abstract of the article. There are 5 corresponding relations involved in this dataset. The *Cite* relation between v_i and v_j is 1 iff article i cites article j. The *isCited* relation between v_i and v_j is 1 iff article j cites article i. The *sameAuthor* relation is 1 if two paper share a common author. We have also extracted two similarity relations: the *Title relation* is defined as the dot product between the normalized TF-IDF vector representing the title of two papers and the *Abstract relation* is the dot product between the normalized TF-IDF vector representing the abstract of two papers. For this dataset, the task is multi-class, monolabel classification.
- The **Flickr** dataset [12] corresponds to images and associated textual information extracted from Flickr. Each picture is described by a textual description found on Flickr and has been annotated with different tags. Images are connected with 4 different relations. The *Friendship* relation: two images are connected with weight 1 if the authors of the images are friends. The *Comment* relation: two images are connected with weight 1 if the same user has left comments on both images. The *SameMonth* relation: two images are connected with weight 1 if they have been published in the same period of 30 days. The task is multi-class, multilabel classification. We performed experiments on a version of the dataset with 10 possible tags and on another version with 50 possible tags.
- The **Email** dataset is a dataset of emails extracted from the emails of the authors of this article. The emails have been manually classified in 16 different emails folders. Each email is described by its textual content and two emails may be connected with 4 different types of relations. The *Authorship* relation: two emails are connected with weight 1 if they were sent by the same user. The *Recipient* relation: two emails are connected with weight 1 if they were sent to the same user. The *Copy* relation: two emails are connected with weight 1 if they shared the same user in copy. The *SameDay* relation: two emails are connected with weight 1 if they were sent the same day. The task here is multi-class classification.

Table 1 gives some basic statistics over the different corpora. While the presented model computes scores to the nodes of a binary multi-graph, we learn here one scoring model for each possible category of the classification problem. In the case of mono-label classification, the category with the higher score is assigned to the node. In multilabel, the scores of all the categories for each node are used to compute a precision @ n measure as explained below.

5.2 Models

In order to compare our approach with existing multi-relational methods that have been developped for structure only networks[1], we have performed two sets of experiments:

- The *Structure Only Experiments (SO)* make only use of the structure of the multi-graphs, without any content information. For these experiments, we have considered three different models. **The Mono-Relational model (SO-Mono)** which corresponds to the regularized model described in section 3.2 where $\alpha = +\infty$. This model only handles one type of relation at a time. Tests have been performed with all the different relations, one at a time, for each dataset. **The Multi-Relational model (SO-Multi)** which has been presented in section 4 with $\alpha = +\infty$ and allows us to consider simultaneously all relations. **The baseline model (Kato)** proposed by Kato et al. in [8] that automatically find a weighting scheme of the different types of relations by an alternate optimization algorithm (see part 6 for more details about the differences between our approach and this one).
- The *Structure and Content Experiments (SC)* where models can use both the content and the structure of the mutli-graphs. Here, we have compared also three different models. **The Mono-Relational model (SC-Mono)** which corresponds to the regularized model described in section 3.2. **The Multi-Relational model (SC-Multi)** model which has been presented in section 4. **The Content only model (SC-CO)** Note that it is equivalent to one of the two previous model with a α-value of 0.

5.3 Evaluation Measures

We divide our dataset in a training and a testing set. For the multiclass datasets, the results are evaluated using the classical micro-F_1 (miF_1) - and macro-F_1 (maF_1) measures. For the multi-label problems, we have also used the micro-F_1 and macro-F_1 by assigning a node to a category if its score is greater than 0. In order to evaluate how good the label ranking is for each node of the graph, we have also computed the precision at 1 (P@1) and precision at 3 (P@3) over the ordered list of labels. Three runs have been launched for each experiment and the results presented here are the average over these three runs. We have reported the best results with respect to the best α value.

5.4 Structure Only Experiments

Structure only experiments have been mainly done in order to compare our approach with state-of-the-art methods for multi-relational graph categorization. Results of the different models are presented in Table 2. First, one can see that the performance of the mono-relational model mainly depends on the type of relation used. The **Kato** model clearly outperforms the mono-relational models obtaining about 60% micro-F_1 for the same corpus. Depending on the

[1]These methods usually include any content information through the computation of similarity relations

Model	Train Size	Cora Corpus		Email Corpus		Flickr 10 Corpus				Flickr 50 Corpus			
		miF_1	maF_1	miF_1	maF_1	miF_1	maF_1	P@1	P@3	miF_1	maF_1	P@1	P@3
SO-Mono 1	5%	10.71	4.96	45.22	19.25	2.98	2.77	19.59	15.54	1.34	1.29	6.92	6.98
	10%	12.02	5.62	51.52	25.38	2.48	2.32	21.40	16.09	0.86	0.81	7.61	7.57
	25%	13.44	7.50	59.48	32.67	4.92	4.47	22.44	16.44	1.94	1.92	8.27	7.86
	50%	14.12	8.14	63.60	35.41	6.78	6.31	24.70	17.85	3.87	3.70	10.00	8.94
SO-Mono 2	5%	8.40	3.09	44.02	18.08	14.79	**14.24**	22.16	16.86	3.96	2.26	10.47	8.41
	10%	9.18	4.57	46.01	20.05	14.61	12.11	21.34	16.93	2.27	1.54	12.66	9.68
	25%	10.61	6.71	51.55	22.85	10.79	8.73	25.59	17.80	1.71	1.09	15.68	11.49
	50%	12.64	9.65	54.57	25.57	12.60	7.70	26.66	18.45	0.27	0.31	17.03	12.74
SO-Mono 3	5%	29.44	25.50	9.14	5.94	**16.45**	12.69	22.75	17.89	4.86	2.46	13.82	10.27
	10%	33.41	30.66	10.15	6.94	15.74	11.80	25.89	19.47	1.40	1.27	13.99	11.81
	25%	40.56	38.28	11.80	8.73	17.63	13.73	27.47	20.60	2.62	2.37	14.81	11.24
	50%	50.93	48.61	12.29	8.83	19.32	16.27	29.77	20.69	8.84	6.39	14.72	10.36
SO-Mono 4	5%	19.01	18.21	8.46	6.10	-	-	-	-	-	-	-	-
	10%	22.76	23.47	11.49	11.72	-	-	-	-	-	-	-	-
	25%	28.09	29.82	19.65	17.27	-	-	-	-	-	-	-	-
	50%	25.08	36.47	28.49	22.94	-	-	-	-	-	-	-	-
SO-Mono 5	5%	24.10	19.23	-	-	-	-	-	-	-	-	-	-
	10%	26.92	22.14	-	-	-	-	-	-	-	-	-	-
	25%	31.60	28.04	-	-	-	-	-	-	-	-	-	-
	50%	35.17	32.03	-	-	-	-	-	-	-	-	-	-
Kato	5%	57.02	46.12	63.10	25.14	12.06	7.39	26.89	18.46	2.45	1.24	26.02	**18.26**
	10%	60.72	53.50	64.74	28.42	8.85	5.70	28.22	20.48	1.17	1.06	27.96	18.86
	25%	**65.33**	59.99	70.85	**35.66**	11.72	8.03	31.32	21.91	2.53	1.79	35.18	**24.23**
	50%	**68.39**	**64.61**	73.71	38.78	13.25	9.18	33.91	23.03	8.90	5.94	**44.77**	**27.73**
SO-Multi	5%	**57.77**	**46.57**	**63.58**	**26.26**	8.02	6.30	**30.28**	**21.88**	**6.51**	**5.03**	**26.29**	17.52
	10%	**61.51**	**53.88**	**68.45**	**32.42**	**20.04**	**15.23**	**37.06**	**24.43**	**15.17**	**11.49**	**33.60**	**20.04**
	25%	64.51	**60.91**	**72.45**	34.20	**29.14**	**24.89**	**43.13**	**24.19**	**29.80**	**22.16**	**40.82**	23.88
	50%	65.64	60.75	**77.89**	**43.63**	**36.93**	**33.64**	**49.75**	**26.84**	**34.72**	**27.40**	43.58	24.54

Table 2: Performance of the different model on the Structure Only Experiments. SO-Mono n models corresponds to the SO-Mono model using relation number n. Bold performance correspond to the best model. '-' values correspond to relations that do not exist in the particular dataset.

Corpus	Train Size	Cora Corpus		Email Corpus	
		miF_1	maF_1	miF_1	maF_1
SC-Mono 1	5%	55.17	44.30	**64.31**	**29.37**
	10%	61.59	52.49	**70.74**	**33.13**
	25%	66.94	59.09	74.21	**37.73**
	50%	69.29	62.06	77.92	43.43
SC-Mono 2	5%	54.97	44.32	57.07	23.47
	10%	61.43	52.36	62.31	28.16
	25%	66.38	58.56	67.99	33.66
	50%	68.91	61.34	71.01	36.38
SC-Mono 3	5%	**60.74**	47.94	49.28	20.45
	10%	62.99	52.93	55.99	24.67
	25%	74.02	66.64	61.49	29.66
	50%	76.96	70.77	65.72	32.92
SC-Mono 4	5%	59.60	**48.67**	54.09	23.99
	10%	62.58	52.70	58.88	26.68
	25%	71.73	64.70	64.29	32.06
	50%	74.73	67.91	67.15	35.85
SC-Mono 5	5%	55.72	43.97	-	-
	10%	60.57	50.56	-	-
	25%	66.32	58.64	-	-
	50%	69.58	62.33	-	-
SC-CO	5%	56.70	44.18	50.32	22.48
	10%	60.44	51.22	56.03	24.19
	25%	66.70	59.41	60.90	28.75
	50%	69.26	62.52	64.91	33.64
SC-Multi	5%	59.21	46.55	61.82	23.95
	10%	**64.49**	**55.30**	66.92	25.52
	25%	**76.24**	**69.44**	**75.90**	35.25
	50%	**79.16**	**74.05**	**79.79**	**43.58**

Table 3: Performance of the different model on the Structure and Content Experiments. SC-Mono n models corresponds to the SC-Mono model using relation number n. Bold performance correspond to the best model.

dataset and on the training size, our approach often achieves at least as well as the Kato model, particularly when the number of training nodes is not too small. This is particularly true for the Flickr datasets where our model have a better precision at 1 and precision at 3, particularly when the size of the training set is small. These experiments show that the proposed algorithm learns well how labels do propagate. In this case, the multi-relational model is able to take advantage of the additional information brought by multiple relations and significantly outperforms other models.

5.5 Structure and Content Experiments

The results of the Structure and Content experiments are reported in table 3 for the Cora and the Email datasets. The results on Flickr are not illustrated here because the content of these datasets is not relevant enough for content-based classification and complex image classification techniques only achieves a performance close to the random model. From this table, on can see first that the simultaneous use of content and structure information greatly improves the performance of the different approaches. In the Cora corpus, our method also outperforms the best Mono-Relational model showing the ability of the SC-Multi model to both mix the information contained in the different types of relations, but also aggregate this information with the content of the nodes of the network. The performance increase with the training set size is quite intuitive since the multi-relational model being a little more complex needs more data to generalize well. The performance varies according to the corpus. For the e-mail corpus, the multi-relational model is equivalent to the best mono-relational model for most experiments. This is certainly due to the fact that the *Authorship* relation (SC-Mono 1) is clearly dominant over the other relations.

6. RELATED WORK

6.1 Graph based classification

Most work in this domain concerns learning in mono-relational graphs. As introduced before, there are from two main perspectives on this problem. The transducive approach followed in this paper, has been initially motivated by the semi-supervised learning problem and initiated by Zhou [18] and Belkin [3]. All these models rely on the minimization of an objective function combining a classical classification loss function on labeled data and a smoothness term like $L = \sum_{i,j} \omega_{i,j}(f_i - f_j)^2$ where f_i is the score of node i and $\omega_{i,j}$ is the weight of the edge between i and j. Note that [18] presents an interesting relation between regularized methods and a random walk formulation in the case of binary label propagation. The models are generally developped for undirected graphs, but some extensions for directed graphs have been proposed, e.g. [19]. The first general model that directly combines a content and a relational classifier is he recent paper [1]. Besides classification, graph models have been used for ranking [2] or re-ranking [13] for ad-hoc search and topic distillation. For the inductive setting, collective classification models are generally used. They can handle both content and structure information. These models include *Iterative Classification* [14], *Gibbs Sampling* [10], *Stacked Learning* [9] and SICA [11].

6.2 Multigraphs

Only a few works have considered multi-relational data and Multi-Graphs. [7] uses a weighted combination of kernels on relations. This approach produces a fully-connected graph, i.e. a n^2 complexity which is prohibitive for real data. [4] considers blog labeling in a multigraph setting where the weights are uniform and are not learned. [20] extend the ideas introduced in [19] to multigraphs. Here again, the model complexity is an issue. In an inductive context, different from the one considered here, [12] proposes a collective classification method for the annotation of multi-relational networked data. Kato et al. in [8] propose a simple EM-like algorithm that has been used as a baseline model in our experiments. Basically, the model learns to weight the different types of relations alternating node scores and edge weights optimization. They also provide a bayesian probabilistic interpretation of their model. Wang et al. in [16] propose a similar multi-graph regularization model for video annotation. Here again, and alternate EM like approach is used to learn a linear combination of graph laplacians. One key difference is that our model directly employs during training and inference both a node content classifier and a propagation along relations. Moreover, we do not need to set a prior on edge weights distribution, then the proposed model does not need an expensive hyperparameter search. Combined with the fact that we do not use alternate optimization procedures, the proposed method is considerably faster than state-of-the-art ones. Another advantage is that it may be used for both directed and undirected graphs. Experiments show that most of the time, the proposed model is as good as or outperforms the EM-like baseline.

7. CONCLUSION

We have proposed a model for multi-class, multi-label classification in multi graphs. This model relies on an original inference and learning algorithm. It includes as special cases different previously proposed mono-relational models. Moreover, in comparison to existing multi-relational methods, it considers both the structure and the content of multi-graphs and learning the weights of the different types of relations is made in one step instead of using alternate optimization techniques. Experiments performed on different datasets show the model's ability to extract relevant information from the rich relational information and to outperform baseline methods. Perspectives now lie in different extensions of this model and to an in depth analysis of its behavior.

8. ACKNOWLEDGEMENTS

This work was partially supported by the French National Agency of Research - ExDeus/Cedres, ANR-09-CORD-010-04, Projects.

9. REFERENCES

[1] J. Abernethy, O. Chapelle, and C. Castillo. Witch: A new approach to web spam detection. In *AIRWeb*. Citeseer, 2008.

[2] S. Agarwal. Ranking on graph data. In *ICML*, pages 25–32, New York, New York, USA, 2006. ACM.

[3] M. Belkin, P. Niyogi, and V. Sindhwani. Manifold regularization: A geometric framework for learning from labeled and unlabeled examples. *JMLR*, 7:2399–2434, 2006.

[4] S. Bhagat, G. Cormode, and I. Rozenbaum. Applying link-based classification to label blogs. *Adv. in Web Mining and Web Usage Analysis*, pages 97–117, 2009.

[5] M. Bilgic, G. M. Namata, and L. Getoor. Combining Collective Classification and Link Prediction. *Seventh IEEE Interna. Conf. on Data Mining Workshops (ICDMW 2007)*, pages 381–386, Oct. 2007.

[6] L. Cao, J. Luo, and T. Huang. Annotating photo collections by label propagation according to multiple similarity cues. In *MM*, pages 121–130, New York, New York, USA, 2008. ACM.

[7] H. Chen, L. Li, and J. Peng. Error bounds of multi-graph regularized semi-supervised classification. *Information Sciences*, 179(12):1960–1969, May 2009.

[8] T. Kato, H. Kashima, and M. Sugiyama. Integration of multiple networks for robust label propagation. In *SDM*, pages 716–726. Citeseer, 2008.

[9] Z. Kou and W. Cohen. Stacked graphical models for efficient inference in markov random fields. In *Proc. of SDM*, pages 533–538. Citeseer, 2007.

[10] S. Macskassy and F. Provost. A simple relational classifier. In *Proc. of the 2nd Workshop on MRDM*, pages 64–76. Citeseer, 2003.

[11] F. Maes, S. Peters, L. Denoyer, and P. Gallinari. Simulated iterative classification a new learning procedure for graph labeling. *Mach. Learn. and Know. Disc. in Databases*, pages 47–62, 2009.

[12] S. Peters, L. Denoyer, and P. Gallinari. Iterative Annotation of Multi-relational Social Networks. In *2010 Intern. Conf. on Advances in Social Networks Analysis and Mining*, pages 96–103. IEEE, 2010.

[13] T. Qin, T.-Y. Liu, X.-D. Zhang, D.-S. Wang, W.-Y. Xiong, and H. Li. Learning to rank relational objects and its application to web search. *Proc. of the 17th intern. conf. on World Wide Web*, page 407, 2008.

[14] P. Sen, G. Namata, M. Bilgic, L. Getoor, and B. Galligher. Collective classification in network data. *AI Magazine*, pages 1–24, 2008.

[15] K. Tsuda, H. Shin, and B. Schölkopf. Fast protein classification with multiple networks. *Bioinformatics*, 21(suppl 2):ii59, Sept. 2005.

[16] M. Wang, X.-S. Hua, R. Hong, J. Tang, G.-J. Qi, and Y. Song. Unified video annotation via multigraph learning. *Circuits and Systems for Video Technology, IEEE Transactions on*, 19(5):733 –746, may 2009.

[17] T. Zhang, A. Popescul, and B. Dom. Linear prediction models with graph regularization for web-page categorization. In *Proc. of the 12th ACM SIGKDD intern. conf. on Knowledge discovery and data mining*, pages 821–826. ACM, 2006.

[18] D. Zhou, O. Bousquet, T. Lal, J. Weston, and B. Schölkopf. Learning with local and global consistency. In *NIPS*, volume 1, pages 595–602, 2004.

[19] D. Zhou, J. Huang, and B. Schölkopf. Learning from labeled and unlabeled data on a directed graph. In *ICML*, pages 1036–1043, New York, USA, 2005. ACM.

[20] D. Zhou, J. Huang, and B. Scholkopf. Learning with hypergraphs: Clustering, classification, and embedding. *Adv. in NIPS*, 19(Figure 1):1601, 2007.

Plagiarism Detection Based on Structural Information

Efstathios Stamatatos
Dept. of Information and Communication Systems Eng.
University of the Aegean, Greece
stamatatos@aegean.gr

ABSTRACT
In this paper a novel method for detecting plagiarized passages in document collections is presented. In contrast to previous work in this field that uses mainly content terms to represent documents, the proposed method is based on structural information provided by occurrences of a small list of stopwords (i.e., very frequent words). We show that stopword *n*-grams are able to capture local syntactic similarities between suspicious and original documents. Moreover, an algorithm for detecting the exact boundaries of plagiarized and source passages is proposed. Experimental results on a publicly-available corpus demonstrate that the performance of the proposed approach is competitive when compared with the best reported results. More importantly, it achieves significantly better results when dealing with difficult plagiarism cases where the plagiarized passages are highly modified by replacing most of the words or phrases with synonyms to hide the similarity with the source documents.

Categories and Subject Descriptors
H.3.1 [**Content Analysis and Indexing**]

General Terms
Algorithms, Experimentation.

Keywords
Plagiarism detection, Stopwords, *n*-grams.

1. INTRODUCTION
A side effect of the rapid growth of online publishing of text in Internet media is that plagiarism became easier than ever. Plagiarism is particularly evident in journalism (i.e., newspapers, blogs) and academia (i.e., student reports, theses) [7]. As a result, significant parts or even entire documents are exact copies or modifications of a single or multiple original sources. While many plagiarism cases are easy to be found by human readers, the great volumes of suspicious and source texts demand automatic plagiarism detection tools to facilitate this process.

Automatic plagiarism detection comprises several tasks. The default scenario (aka *external plagiarism detection*) regards the identification of passages in suspicious documents as likely plagiarized and associate them with certain passages of source documents in a given reference collection [18,20]. *Intrinsic plagiarism detection* considers the case where no reference collection is available and the likely plagiarized passages in a suspicious document have to be extracted based on stylistic inconsistencies [23]. *Cross-lingual plagiarism detection* deals with the case where the suspicious and source documents are written in different natural languages [17]. *Text reuse* or *near-duplicate detection* is associated with plagiarism detection since it attempts to find documents that share most of their content and are derivatives of an original source [4,10]. However, it examines similarity on the document level. *Local text reuse* or *partial-duplicate detection* is closer to plagiarism detection where a very short passage may be copied in a long document [22,27]. In this task, the similarity is considered legitimate, so usually there is no attempt to hide it. As a result, it resembles the verbatim case of plagiarism detection.

One major concern in plagiarism detection is efficiency [21]. The suspicious documents should be exhaustively compared with any document in the reference collection which may be very large (i.e., the whole indexed Web). It is therefore necessary for the similarity estimation between a pair of documents to be based on simple measures. Additionally, plagiarism detectors should be able to capture local similarities where only a likely short passage is common in both documents. Given that the plagiarized and the original passages may not be exactly the same in case the plagiarist performed some kind of paraphrasing, the information used to represent texts should capture the similarity even when many words and word ordering are different [9].

Existing approaches in plagiarism detection are based on sequences of words or characters to represent texts [2,10,21]. The content words (e.g., nouns, adjectives, proper-names, etc.) are generally considered the most important information to identify local similarity in texts. Very frequent words conveying no meaning (i.e., stopwords) are usually excluded [6,9,10,18] or used to identify the position of important content terms [25].

It is a common practice in Information Retrieval (IR) to discard stopwords since they increase the size of index with many word occurrences. According to the *rule of 30*, the 30 most common words account for (roughly) 30% of the word tokens in a corpus [14]. However, efficient index compression methods can considerably decrease the size required by these occurrences. Moreover, the elimination of stopwords makes phrase queries more difficult or even impossible to be processed. As a result, modern IR systems, including many Web search engines, adopt full-text indexing [14]. Stopwords have been proved to be extremely useful in text mining tasks including authorship attribution [1] and text-genre detection [24] where the aim is to represent style rather than content. In plagiarism detection, it has been demonstrated that stopword removal considerably hurts the performance [6].

In this paper, we propose a novel plagiarism detection method that is based on structural rather than content information. Instead of following the common practice of eliminating stopwords, the

CIKM'11, October 24–28, 2011, Glasgow, Scotland, UK.

proposed method eliminates all the other tokens and is entirely based on the remaining stopword sequences to represent the syntactic structure of texts. It is shown that stopword n-grams are robust and accurate when used to capture local similarities between suspicious and original documents. Moreover, we propose an algorithm for detecting the exact plagiarized passage boundaries in suspicious and source documents. The presented results on a publicly-available corpus demonstrate that the performance of the proposed approach is competitive when compared with the best reported results on the same corpus. More importantly, our method achieves significantly better results when dealing with difficult plagiarism cases where the plagiarized passages are highly modified and most of the words or phrases have been replaced with synonyms.

The rest of this paper is organized as follows. The next section describes previous related work. Section 3 presents the proposed method in detail. The experimental settings and results are included in Section 4 while the conclusions drawn from this study and suggested future work directions are given in Section 5.

2. RELATED WORK

The majority of approaches to plagiarism detection adopt the same architecture [18]. First, to improve efficiency in large document collections, for each suspicious document a small set of candidate source documents is retrieved. This set is either of predefined or variable size according to the similarity between the documents. Then, a more detailed analysis between the suspicious document and each of the retrieved documents provides the requested passage boundaries. Finally, a post-processing step checks these detections and removes or merges some of them.

In order to detect the degree of similarity between documents, two basic approaches have been proposed. The first follows the typical IR methodology that considers the suspicious document (or parts of the document) as a query and attempts to rank documents in the reference collection according to their similarity with the query [9,10,16]. The similarity measures take into account relative word frequencies, document frequencies, and document lengths [15] while stopwords are usually discarded [9,10]. To take into account word substitutions by synonyms Gustafson et al. [9] proposes the use of word-correlation factors that measure frequency of co-occurrence and relative distance between pairs of terms in Wikipedia documents. The syntactic structure of sentences is more robust in cases of paraphrasing the plagiarized passages [26] but the required syntactic analysis considerably harms the efficiency.

The second basic family of approaches relies on document fingerprints comprising hashes of fixed-length chunks (aka *shingles*) in documents [21,22]. The complete set of chunks can be included in the document fingerprint (full fingerprinting) to optimize effectiveness or, alternatively, a chunk selection method can be applied to decrease storage requirements and optimize efficiency [21]. Some approaches define chunks so that to capture information about the content and the structure of a short piece of text. Usually they are character n-grams [21], word n-grams [2] or sentences [8,27]. Word n-grams can be sorted to be more flexible in small changes between the plagiarized and the source passages [11]. Theobald, et al., [25] use stopword positions to identify useful chains of content words in web pages. In contrast, Basile, et al. [3] consider chunks that are based on word-length sequences excluding any content information.

Provided a suspicious document is found to be similar with a source document, a scatter plot of the positions of all the matches found between the two documents can reveal the approximate passage boundaries [27, 28]. In case of verbatim plagiarism or partial-duplicate detection, these passages will be straight diagonal lines. To detect such passage boundaries, algorithms for finding diagonals of maximal length are appropriate [27]. However, in cases when the plagiarized passage is modified there is noise in these diagonal lines. A cluster of matches is produced and it is usual to have small gaps between adjacent areas that correspond to the same passage. To solve this problem, several methods have been proposed including sets of heuristic rules to identify and merge adjacent passages [3,11,12], Monte Carlo optimization to join adjacent matches [8], and application of clustering methods [28]. Although this kind of analysis has to be performed for relatively few source documents per suspicious document, it can harm the efficiency of the approach when its computational cost is high.

After the detection of passage boundaries, the post-processing step is used to filter the passage detections and eliminate or merge cases of short passages and overlapping or ambiguous (e.g., indicating the same plagiarized passage and different source passages) detections [11,12,16,28]. A final verification of similarity between the passages in the suspicious and the source documents has also been proposed [16]. The post-processing step is especially important for improving the precision of the plagiarism detection methods.

Recently, two competitions on plagiarism detection were organized addressing several plagiarism types, including external plagiarism, intrinsic plagiarism, and cross-lingual plagiarism [18, 20]. Evaluation corpora and methodologies have been released [19] providing the possibility to compare different approaches on the same testing ground. The focus of the evaluation in these competitions is on the exact detection of passage boundaries in plagiarized and source documents. Although the majority of the participants eliminated stopwords to increase the efficiency of document representation, the winning methods avoided explicitly removal of stopwords. The winner of the 2009 competition used character 16-grams [8] while the winner of the 2010 competition used (sorted) word 5-grams including all words with at least three characters [11].

3. THE PROPOSED METHOD

In this study, monolingual plagiarism detection is considered. Let D_x be a set of suspicious documents and D_s be the set of source documents (i.e., reference collection). The first task is to decide whether a suspicious document is plagiarized or non-plagiarized. In the former case, all the sources of plagiarism should be identified including source documents (a subset of D_s) and the exact boundaries of the plagiarized passages in both the suspicious and source documents. Furthermore, it is desirable to assign a score to each detected plagiarized passage to indicate the degree of plagiarism. This score can be used to sort the detected passages from exact copies to somehow related passages. The general architecture of the proposed method follows the state-of-the-art in this field [18].

3.1 Text Representation

The representation of texts according to the proposed method is based on stopword *n*-grams (SWNG). Given a document and a list of stopwords, the text is reduced to the appearances of these stopwords in the document. All the other tokens are discarded. As stopwords, in this study, we use a list of the 50 most frequent words of English (Table 1) extracted by the British National Corpus which includes about 90 millions tokens. Therefore, a text is first transformed to lowercase, then it is tokenized and all the tokens not belonging to the list of stopwords are removed. Finally, the *n*-grams of the remaining stopwords are produced. We call this set of SWNGs the *profile* of the document. Given a document *d*, the profile *P*(*n*,*d*) comprises all the stopword *n*-grams, i.e., analogous to the full-fingerprinting method [10]. The SWNGs in *P*(*n*,*d*) are ordered according to their first appearance in the document. The procedure of transforming text passages to a set of stopword *n*-grams is demonstrated in Figure 1.

Table 1. The list of 50 most frequent words of BNC corpus.

1. the	11. with	21. are	31. or	41. her
2. of	12. he	22. not	32. an	42. n't
3. and	13. be	23. his	33. were	43. there
4. a	14. on	24. this	34. we	44. can
5. in	15. I	25. from	35. their	45. all
6. to	16. that	26. but	36. been	46. as
7. is	17. by	27. had	37. has	47. if
8. was	18. at	28. which	38. have	48. who
9. it	19. you	29. she	39. will	49. what
10. for	20. 's	30. they	40. would	50. said

The intuition behind this representation is that stopword occurrences are usually associated with syntactic patterns. Therefore, sequences of stopwords reveal hints of the syntactic structure of the document that is likely to remain stable during the procedure of plagiarizing a passage. That is, when one attempts to plagiarize a particular passage of text and wants to cover their traits, the most usual act is to replace words and phrases with available synonyms. It is much more difficult to change the basic syntactic structure or rewrite large parts of the text. Stopwords are function words, that is they are content-independent and they do not convey any semantic information. They can usually be removed/replaced when the syntactic structure changes.

According to the terminology introduced in the work of Koppel, et al. [13], a language element (i.e., a word or a syntactic structure) is *unstable* when it can be replaced by other semantically equivalent elements. *Stability* of words can be regarded as the availability of synonyms. Given that definition, stopwords are words with high stability and, therefore, are likely to remain intact when someone attempts to slightly modify a text passage. In case the modification does not involve significant reordering of contents, long sequences of stopwords of the original passage are likely to also be included in the modified passage. Moreover, language diversity and language errors especially when the authors are non-native speakers can affect the stability of words. For example, the tokens 'plagiarize', 'plagiarise', 'pladgiarize', and 'plagarize' are some different (correct or erroneous) versions of the same content word. On the other hand, most speakers of the language are familiar with stopwords and since they are relatively short, they are less likely to contain errors.

Suspicious passage:	**Original passage:**
This came into existence likely from the deviance in the time-period of the particular billet. As the premier is to be nominated for not more than a period of four years, it can infrequently happen that an ample wage, fixed at the embarkation of that period, will not endure to be such to its end.	*This probably arose from the difference in the duration of the respective offices. As the President is to be elected for no more than four years, it can rarely happen that an adequate salary, fixed at the commencement of that period, will not continue to be such to its end.*

SWNG representation:	**SWNG representation:**
[this,from,the,in,the,of,the,as] —	[this,from,the,in,the,of,the,as]
[from,the,in,the,of,the,as,the] —	[from,the,in,the,of,the,as,the]
[the,in,the,of,the,as,the,is] —	[the,in,the,of,the,as,the,is]
[in,the,of,the,as,the,is,to] —	[in,the,of,the,as,the,is,to]
[the,of,the,as,the,is,to,be] —	[the,of,the,as,the,is,to,be]
[of,the,as,the,is,to,be,for] —	[of,the,as,the,is,to,be,for]
[the,as,the,is,to,be,for,not]	[the,as,the,is,to,be,for,it]
[as,the,is,to,be,for,not,a]	[as,the,is,to,be,for,it,can]
[the,is,to,be,for,not,a,of]	[the,is,to,be,for,it,can,that]
[is,to,be,for,not,a,of,it]	[is,to,be,for,it,can,that,an]
[to,be,for,not,a,of,it,can]	[to,be,for,it,can,that,an,at]
[be,for,not,a,of,it,can,that]	[be,for,it,can,that,an,at,the]
[for,not,a,of,it,can,that,an]	[for,it,can,that,an,at,the,of]
[not,a,of,it,can,that,an,at]	[it,can,that,an,at,the,of,that]
[a,of,it,can,that,an,at,the]	[can,that,an,at,the,of,that,will]
[of,it,can,that,an,at,the,of]	[that,an,at,the,of,that,will,not]
[it,can,that,an,at,the,of,that]	[an,at,the,of,that,will,not,to]
[can,that,an,at,the,of,that,will]	[at,the,of,that,will,not,to,be]
[that,an,at,the,of,that,will,not]	[the,of,that,will,not,to,be,to]
[an,at,the,of,that,will,not,to]	
[at,the,of,that,will,not,to,be]	
[the,of,that,will,not,to,be,to]	

Figure 1. An example of a plagiarism case and the proposed stopword n-gram representation (common 8-grams of the passages are indicated with lines).

The stability of stopwords is demonstrated in the example of Figure 1 where an original piece of text and a plagiarized version of it are given. Despite the fact that the plagiarized version is highly modified, many sequences of our list of 50 stopwords remain the same with those of the original document (the original and the plagiarized passage have 18 common 5-grams, 12 common 8-grams, and 6 common 11-grams of stopwords). This similarity is affected in the case the plagiarist rewrites significant parts of the passage. On the other hand, texts that are not associated are unusual to share long sequences of SWNGs since that would mean they share the same syntactic structure in consecutive sentences or entire paragraphs. The discussion in the following section shows that such coincidental similarity is rare.

3.2 Candidate Retrieval

The first important step in plagiarism detection is the retrieval of a subset of D_s that comprises the sources of likely plagiarism in a suspicious document. This procedure includes the exhaustive comparison of the suspicious document with any member of D_s to identify any local similarities. In general, the number of source documents for a given suspicious document is not known a priori. It could be none, a single, or multiple source documents. The most important issue here is to achieve a high recall since it is just the first step in the detection process and any source document missed will no further examined. On the other hand, a low precision score will affect the efficiency of the next steps.

Given the SWNG representation, our aim is to find common *n*-grams of stopwords between the suspicious and the source documents. The main question here regards the definition of an appropriate value of *n*. How long should the sequences of stopwords be so that to detect a similarity between a suspicious and a source document? Let n_1 be this value. Any common *n*-gram between a pair of documents with $n<n_1$ is considered not significant. A common *n*-gram with $n>=n_1$ suggests a match that is not coincidental. In that sense, the value of n_1 should be relatively high. On the other hand, beyond the case of verbatim plagiarism, when the plagiarized passages have been highly modified, we should not expect to find too long common sequences of stopwords. In those cases, a high value of n_1 would miss source documents including the originals of either short or highly modified plagiarized passages. Therefore, there is a trade-off between low and high values of n_1 for the candidate document retrieval task.

One common case of coincidental similarity between the sequences of stopwords of unrelated documents is when the sequence contains only specific, very frequent stopwords. These words are the first 6 most frequent stopwords (*the, of, and, a, in, to*) plus *'s*. An example is shown in Figure 2 where two unrelated text passages have exactly the same sequence of stopwords (11-gram). Such cases considerably increase the false positives of our approach. To avoid them, we need an additional constraint on the contents of the common *n*-grams found in the profiles of two documents. This constraint should not be too rigid so that similarities of short plagiarized passages are not filtered out. Let $C=\{the, of, and, a, in, to, 's\}$ be the set of the stopwords usually appear in coincidental matches. Let $d_x \in D_x$ and $d_s \in D_s$ while $P(n_1, d_x)$ and $P(n_1, d_s)$ are the corresponding profiles of these documents comprising SWNGs of length n_1. A match between these documents is detected when the following criterion is satisfied:

$$\exists g \in P(n_1,d_x) \cap P(n_1,d_s): member(g,C)<n_1-1 \wedge maxseq(g,C)<n_1-2 \quad (1)$$

where the functions $member(g,C)$ and $maxseq(g,C)$ return the number of stopwords of the *n*-gram *g* that belong to *C* and the maximal (longest) sequence of stopwords of *g* that belong to *C*, respectively. For instance, when $n_1=11$, a match *g* (i.e., a common 11-gram in the profiles of a suspicious and a source document) would indicate a possible plagiarism case only when *g* contains at least 2 stopwords not belonging to *C* (i.e., $member(g,C)<10$) and the longest sequence in *g* of stopwords belonging to *C* is less than 9. Note that the example of Figure 2 fails to satisfy both of these constraints since $member(g,C)=10$ and $maxseq(g,C)=10$.

The minutes of the committee record the motion of appreciation to the owners. Mr. Robert Bell of the old printing firm of that name made...

...the Fathers of the Church; the aesthetic mysticism of Plotinus, reborn to its greatest triumphs, during the classic period of German thought. Through the midst of these variously erroneous theories, that traverse...

Figure 2. Two unrelated text passages with the same sequence of stopwords.

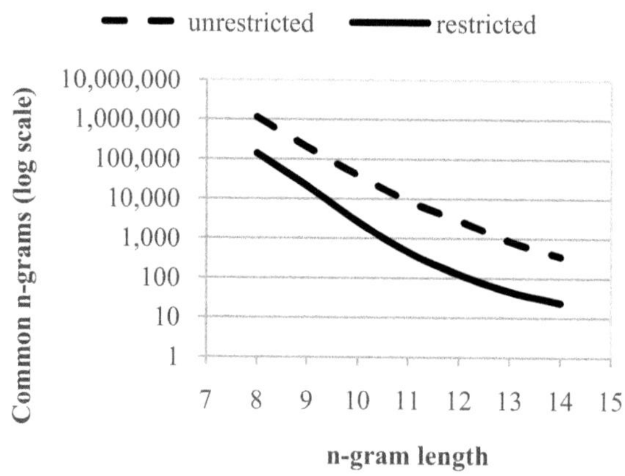

Figure 3. Number of common *n*-grams in a collection of 1,000 documents without any known case of plagiarism before and after applying criterion (1).

Figure 3 depicts the amount of common *n*-grams in a collection of 1,000 documents (a part of the corpus described in Section 4.1) without any known case of plagiarism before and after the application of criterion (1). The document length in this collection varies from 3,000 to 2.5 million characters. Apparently, this criterion significantly reduces the amount of coincidentally common *n*-grams. Note that usually there are many cases where two documents may share the same (short) passage (e.g. famous quotations) [12]. So, some long stopword *n*-grams are likely to be detected in some documents of any collection. This is further discussed in Section 3.4.

3.3 Passage Boundary Detection

When a set of source documents that match a suspicious document has been retrieved, the next step is to perform a more detailed analysis to estimate the exact boundaries of plagiarized passages in both the suspicious and the source documents. Let $D_{rx} \subseteq D_s$ denote the set of source documents that have been retrieved for the suspicious document d_x. Our aim is to find the common SWNGs in the profiles of d_x and each $d_s \in D_{rx}$ and build maximal sequences of them that correspond to text passages.

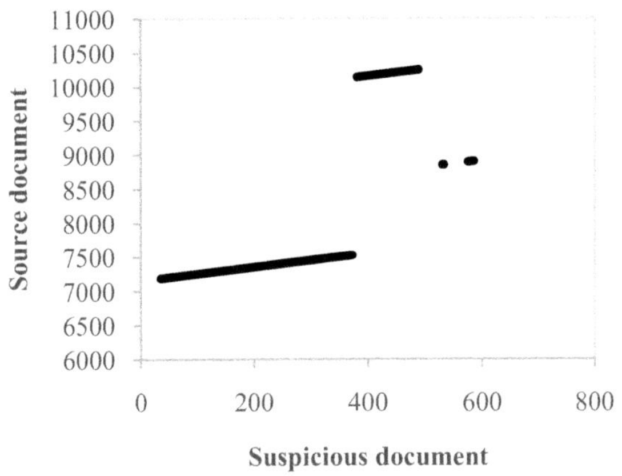

Figure 4. Scatter plot of the matched n-grams in verbatim plagiarism cases where the plagiarized passages are next to each other.

In case the plagiarized passage is an exact copy of the source document, the task is quite easy since exactly the same sequence of SWNGs will be included in both profiles and in the same order. Then, the scatter plot showing the matches between a suspicious and source document will be composed of diagonal lines. An example of verbatim plagiarism cases is given in Figure 4. However, when the plagiarized passage is highly modified there will be considerable noise (i.e., deviation from the diagonal line) and gaps between common SWNGs of the two profiles. The amount of noise and gaps depends on the value of n (order of n-grams) used in producing the profiles of the documents. The higher n is, the more gaps and noise will appear. Therefore, the long n-grams used to identify similarity between documents in the previous step (n_1) are not appropriate in the current step. We need shorter n-grams (of order n_2) so that more detailed matches between the documents to be captured. In order to avoid noise of coincidental matches of SWNGs due to n-grams containing only stopwords of C, we also need a criterion similar to (1) to exclude some uninformative SWNGs. However, to keep the gaps between common SWNGs low, this criterion should be more relaxed in comparison to (1). Let $P(n_2, d_x)$ and $P(n_2, d_s)$ be the profiles of the suspicious and source documents comprising stopword n_2-grams. A n_2-gram g is a match between these documents when the following criterion is satisfied:

$$g \in P(n_2,d_x) \cap P(n_2,d_s) \wedge member(g,C) < n_2 \quad (2)$$

where the function $member(g,C)$ returns the number of stopwords of the n-gram g that belong to C. Let $M(d_x,d_s)$ be the set of the matched n-grams between the profiles $P(n_2,d_x)$ and $P(n_2,d_s)$ of the suspicious and source documents. Members of $M(d_x,d_s)$ are ordered according to the first appearance of a match in the suspicious document. For example, in the case of the text passages of Figure 2, the ordered set of matches between the 8-grams of the plagiarized and the original passages are indicated with lines. That is, the first 8-gram of the plagiarized passage is identical with the first 8-gram of the original document, the 17th 8-gram of the plagiarized passage is identical with the 14th 8-gram of the original document, etc. Moreover, let M_1 and M_2 be the parts of M that correspond to the suspicious document and the source document, respectively. For instance, in the example of Figure 1, M_1={1, 2, 3, 4, 5, 6, 17, 18, 19, 20, 21, 22} while M_2={1, 2, 3, 4, 5, 6, 14, 15, 16, 17, 18, 19}. Therefore, consecutive M_1 values always increase while consecutive M_2 values may decrease as well. As shown in Figure 4 (scatter plot of M_1 vs. M_2) the boundaries of plagiarized passages are associated with big changes in consecutive values of M_1 and M_2. However, if these changes are not big enough they may correspond to gaps in noisy cases where the plagiarized passage is heavily modified.

```
Input: dx, a suspicious document
       ds, a source document
       n2, length of stopword sequences
       θg, threshold of maximum gap allowed
Output: a set of detections

detectPassageBoundaries(dx,ds,n2,θg)
Px=profile(n2,dx);
Ps=profile(n2,ds);
[M1,M2]=match(Px,Ps);
InitPlagPass=findPassages(M1,θg);
Detections=[];
PlagPassages=[];
for all Pi ∈ InitPlagPass
   Oi=subset(Pi,M2);
   OrigPassages=findPassages(Oi,θg);
   if size(OrigPassages)>1
      for all Oj ∈ OrigPassages
         Pj=subset(Oj,M1)
         PlagPassages=PlagPassages ∪ Pj;
      endfor
   else PlagPassages=PlagPassages ∪ Pi;
   endif
Detections=Detections ∪
          [PlagPassages, OrigPassages];
endfor
return Detections;
```

Figure 5. The proposed algorithm for detecting passage boundaries.

Another important problem in this task is when there are multiple plagiarized passages in a suspicious document and the distance between them is relatively low. This case is depicted in Figure 4, where the plagiarized passages are next to each other in the suspicious document (x-dimension). Note that this is not necessarily related with the distance of the original passages in the source document (y-dimension). Similarly, two original passages in the same source document can be close enough while the distance between the corresponding plagiarized passages in the suspicious document may be high.

To handle this problem in the detection of passage boundaries, we propose the following procedure. First, an initial set of passage boundaries of maximal length is detected in the suspicious document allowing small gaps to be included. Then, the corresponding passages in the source document are examined. In case a passage in the source document is not homogeneous (i.e., it comprises parts of the document with significant gaps between them) it splits into smaller passages. Finally, the passage boundaries in the suspicious document are determined based on these smaller passages of the source document. In more detail, the initial set of passage boundaries in the suspicious document is detected according to the following criterion:

$$m_i \in M_1(d_x,d_s): abs(diff(m_i)) > \theta_g \quad (3)$$

where the functions abs and $diff$ return the absolute value and the difference (derivative) and θ_g is a threshold that permits relatively small gaps to be included in the detected passage. If there are adjacent boundaries, they are joined to a single boundary. Each detected passage in the suspicious document (a subset of M_1 values) corresponds to a subset of M_2 values. However, a subset of M_2 values may correspond to different passages of the original document (i.e., the case depicted in Figure 4). Then, each $M_{2i} \subseteq M_2$, corresponding to a maximal subset of a detected passage in M_1 values, is examined to detect maximal passages of the original document. The boundaries of the source document passages are detected according to the following criterion:

$$m_i \in M_{2i}(d_x, d_s): abs(diff(m_i)) > \theta_g \quad (4)$$

where $M_{2i}(d_x,d_s)$ is a subset of M_2 that corresponds to an already detected plagiarized passage in the suspicious document. Gaps lower than θ_g are allowed in a passage. Again, if there are adjacent boundaries, they are joined to a single boundary. Finally, in case multiple passages are detected in the original document, the corresponding passage in the suspicious document is split accordingly to produce the final boundaries of the plagiarized passages. Note that this procedure detects boundaries in the sequence of *n*-grams. Let $<S_i, E_i>$ be the start and ending *n*-gram boundaries of a detected passage. These can be transformed into character boundaries by taking the position of the first character of the first word of S_i and the position of the last character of the last word of E_i.

The passage boundary detection algorithm is shown in Figure 5. The *profile* function extracts the stopword sequences from a text while *match* finds the matches between two texts according to criterion (2). The *findPassages* function detects passages of maximal length in a sequence of matched *n*-grams following the criteria (3) and (4) to estimate the passage boundaries, *size*(*X*) returns the size of the set *X*, and *subset*(*X*,*Y*) extracts a sequence of matched *n*-grams in document *X* that corresponds to a detected passage in document *Y*. The output detections are composed of the plagiarized passages and their corresponding original passages.

3.4 Post-processing

The procedure described so far, is based on SWNG representation and disregards all the words of the text not belonging to the set of the 50 stopwords. The detections obtained, especially in case they are short, should be checked to verify that the similarity of the detected plagiarized passage with the detected original passage is high, when the full text of the passages is taken into account. Moreover, we need a mechanism to assign scores to the detected plagiarism cases according to the degree of similarity with the original passages. This procedure should not be computationally expensive since it will be applied to full text of multiple passages. Moreover, it should be flexible so that to capture the similarity even in cases where the plagiarized passage is highly modified and contains many different words with respect to the original passage (i.e., the case of Figure 1).

Each detection is a 4-tuple $<t_x, d_x, t_s, d_s>$ that associates a plagiarized passage t_x in a suspicious document d_x with a passage t_s in an original document d_s. The presented approach examines the similarity between these passages by extracting the profile of character *n*-grams of each passage and calculating the amount of common *n*-grams in the two profiles. To normalize the form of the passages, all characters are transformed into lowercase and punctuation marks are removed. Let $P_c(n,t_x)$ and $P_c(n,t_s)$ be the character *n*-gram profiles (where multiple occurrences of the same *n*-gram are replaced by one single occurrence) of the detected passages in the suspicious and the original document, respectively. Then, the similarity between t_x and t_s is calculated as follows:

$$Sim(t_x, t_s) = \frac{|P_c(n_c,t_x) \cap P_c(n_c,t_s)|}{\max(|P_c(n_c,t_x)|, |P_c(n_c,t_s)|)} \quad (5)$$

where $|a|$ is the size of a. Note that in case the $P_c(n_c,t_x)$ and $P_c(n_c,t_s)$ are identical, the similarity measure is 1. This similarity measure resembles the *containment* measure [5]. However, the denominator ensures that if one of the profiles is much longer than the other, the similarity score is considerably reduced. This is especially useful to filter out cases where adjacent passages were erroneously merged. The choice of n_c is associated with the flexibility of the similarity measure. The longer the character *n*-grams are, the more they will be affected by changes in the plagiarized passage with respect to the original passage. Then, in case the similarity score is above a threshold θ_c the detected plagiarism case is considered true. Otherwise, it is removed from the set of detections. For n_c=3, the similarity of the text passages of the highly modified plagiarism case of Figure 1 is 0.59 while the similarity score of the two unrelated passages of Figure 2 is just 0.18.

Another problem that should be faced in the post-processing stage is the existence of many short passages in both the suspicious and source documents that are not plagiarized. Such passages are usually short and refer to famous quotations, sayings, poems, parts of the Bible, etc. [12]. A couple of examples are given below:

...for we have heard Him ourselves, and know that this is indeed the Christ, the Saviour of the world.

...He who of old would rend the oak, Deemed not of the rebound; Chained by the trunk he vainly broke, Alone, how looked he round!"

Ideally, such cases should not be reported as plagiarism acts. However, their identification among the set of detections is very difficult. Since they are usually almost identical in both the suspicious and the source documents, their similarity score would be very high. The same is true for verbatim plagiarism cases. As already mentioned, such passages are usually very short. Therefore, it is possible to apply a threshold θ_L to the length of the detected passages and filter out the vast majority of these. The length threshold is expected to also hurt the recall of the proposed approach since detected plagiarism cases of very short length will also be eliminated. If the aim is to find any similarities between a suspicious document and a set of source documents, no matter if they are plagiarism cases or not, this length threshold should not be applied.

4. EVALUATION

4.1 Corpus

Recently, in the framework of the PAN Workshop series, evaluation campaigns for plagiarism detectors were initiated [18, 20]. A corpus including multiple suspicious and source documents as well as many types of plagiarism cases was released in 2010 [19]. More specifically, the PAN 2010 Plagiarism Competition corpus[1] (PAN-PC-10) comprises 27,073 documents divided into a set of 15,925 suspicious documents and a set of 11,148 source documents. The length of the documents varies from one page to an entire book of several hundred pages. Half (7,972) of the

[1] http://www.uni-weimar.de/cms/medien/webis/research/corpora/pan-pc-10.html

suspicious documents are non-plagiarized. The other half of the suspicious documents contains 68,558 plagiarism cases that were inserted into randomly selected parts of the suspicious documents. Therefore, there are suspicious documents with only one plagiarized passage and other suspicious documents with dozens of plagiarized passages. 70% of the plagiarism cases refer to the external plagiarism detection task and the rest 30% refer to the intrinsic plagiarism detection task (the originals of the plagiarized passages were not taken from the source documents).

The external plagiarism detection cases have been produced either by humans (simulated) or computational tools (artificial) able to obfuscate a passage by replacing words and phrases with synonyms. In the latter case, it is possible to estimate the degree of obfuscation (high, low, or none). Additionally, 14% of the external plagiarism cases were produced by automatic translation tools that used source documents in Spanish and German. Since the proposed approach aims at the monolingual external plagiarism detection task we used the part of the PAN-PC-10 corpus that refers to this, that is, we excluded the suspicious documents with intrinsic or cross-lingual plagiarism cases. Note that each plagiarized document of PAN-PC-10 contains only one type of plagiarism to facilitate the extraction of a sub-corpus with a certain type of plagiarism cases. Some statistics of the corpus we used in this study are shown in Table 2.

4.2 Measures

For evaluating the produced detections, we use the recently proposed measures of *precision*, *recall* and *granularity* on the passage level [19]. In more detail, let S denote the set of plagiarism cases and R denote the set of detections. Then, macro-average precision and recall are defined as follows:

$$Prec(S,R) = \frac{1}{|R|}\sum_{r\in R}\frac{|\bigcup_{s\in S} s\cap r|}{|r|} \quad (6)$$

$$\mathrm{Rec}(S,R) = \frac{1}{|S|}\sum_{s\in S}\frac{|\bigcup_{r\in R} s\cap r|}{|s|} \quad (7)$$

where $s\cap r$ is the amount of overlapping characters between s and r when they share at least one character in both the suspicious and the source passage. Otherwise it is 0. These measures give equal weight to each plagiarism case regardless of its length. Additionally, they do not take into account the similarity score assigned by detectors to each plagiarism case.

In plagiarism detection, recall and precision do not give a complete picture of the effectiveness. In case a detector reports overlapping passages for the same plagiarism case or divides a long passage into shorter segments, recall and precision may be affected (increase). Therefore, we need an additional measure that takes these cases into account. Let $S_R \subseteq S$ be the cases detected in R and $R_s \subseteq R$ be the detections regarding the passage s. Then, the granularity measure is defined as follows:

$$\mathrm{Gran}(S,R) = \frac{1}{|S_R|}\sum_{s\in S_R}|R_s| \quad (8)$$

The minimum and ideal granularity value is 1. The larger the granularity is, the more (possibly overlapping) segments are detected for the same plagiarized passage. Precision, recall, and granularity can be combined to a single measure, *plagdet*, defined as follows:

$$\mathrm{plagdet}(S,R) = \frac{F_1}{\log_2(1+\mathrm{Gran}(S,R))} \quad (9)$$

Table 2. Details about the corpus used in this study.

Plagiarism type	Documents	Plagiarism Cases
Simulated	598	2,347
Artificial: High obfuscation	1,337	14,756
Artificial: Low obfuscation	1,354	14,883
Verbatim	1,728	17,423
Non-plagiarized	7,972	0
Total	12,989	49,409

Table 3. The parameter values used in this study.

Parameter	Value	Function
n_1	11	Stopword n-gram length to retrieve candidate documents
n_2	8	Stopword n-gram length to detect passage boundaries
n_c	3	Character n-gram length to measure similarity between passages
θ_g	100	Upper threshold (in SWNGs) of gap-length allowed in a passage
θ_c	0.5	Lower threshold of the similarity measure to keep a detection
θ_L	200	Lower limit (in characters) of the detected passage length

Table 4. Evaluation results for each processing step.

	Prec.	Recall	Gran.	Plagdet
Candidate retrieval	0.38	0.91	-	-
Passage boundary detection	0.23	0.85	1.02	0.36
Post-processing	0.94	0.83	1.01	0.88

where F_1 is the harmonic mean of precision and recall. Note that the *plagdet* measure was used to rank the candidates in the PAN competitions on plagiarism detection [18,20].

4.3 Results

To apply the presented approach to PAN-PC-10 corpus, a small part of it was first used to estimate the appropriate parameter settings. In more detail, the first 100 suspicious documents (containing non-plagiarized and plagiarized documents of any kind) and their corresponding source documents were used and various values for n-gram length and thresholds were tested. Our aim in these preliminary experiments was not to optimize the results for this specific sub-corpus but to estimate general parameter values that increase recall of the first steps and precision of the last steps. The parameter settings shown in Table 3 were selected and used in the experiments described below.

First, we examine the performance in each processing step. Table 4 shows the results after applying the candidate document retrieval, the passage boundary detection and the post-processing tasks. Note that, for the candidate retrieval task, recall and precision are calculated on the document level while granularity and *plagdet* are not defined. The final precision is very high while recall is lower indicating that many plagiarism cases are not

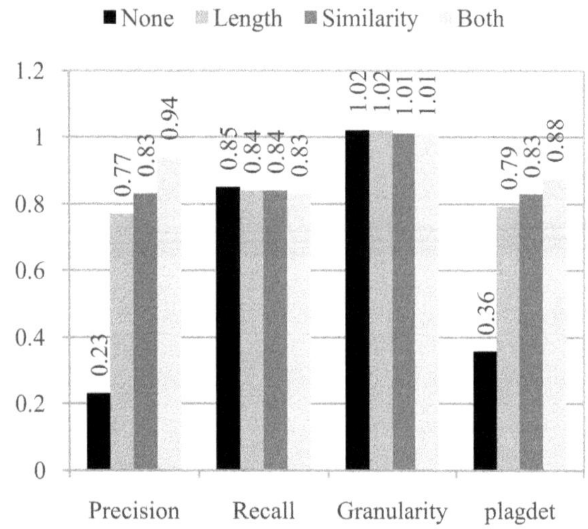

Figure 6. The contribution of the post-processing criteria (length threshold and similarity threshold) to the performance of the presented method.

detected but the provided detections are usually correct. Granularity remains low indicating that in the vast majority of the cases one passage is detected per plagiarism case. The first two steps achieve poor precision scores. However, the post-processing step significantly improves precision.

A more detailed look in the usefulness of the post-processing step is depicted in Figure 6. The performance attained by applying the similarity threshold and the length threshold separately or in combination is given. Apparently, each of these criteria is very important to significantly improve precision. This means that the vast majority of the wrong predictions of the passage boundary detection step correspond to very short passages with similar sequence of stopwords but essentially different content. The combination of these criteria further improves precision due to the elimination of short near-identical passages in suspicious and source documents that are not plagiarism cases (quotations, sayings, etc). Granularity is also improved. On the other hand, recall is slightly reduced.

Next, we examine the performance of the proposed approach in detecting certain plagiarism types. Table 5 shows the results when only simulated plagiarism, artificial plagiarism with high obfuscation, artificial plagiarism with low obfuscation, and verbatim cases are considered. For each type, we use the documents containing this kind of plagiarism (see Table 2) plus an equal number of non-plagiarized documents. This procedure was also followed in [18], so the presented results are directly compared with the performance of the participants in the PAN-10 plagiarism detection competition. The four top-performing participants are denoted as: PAN-10-1 [11], PAN-10-2 [28], PAN-10-3 [16], and PAN-10-4 [8]. The latter was the winner of the PAN 2009 competition using the same method in both competitions. As can be seen, the proposed approach is very competitive in all plagiarism types. It achieves better precision results in any case in comparison to the PAN-10 participants. On the other hand, recall is usually lower in comparison to top-performing approaches. Interestingly, in the most difficult cases of simulated plagiarism and artificial plagiarism with high obfuscation the attained performance is considerably better than the other approaches. This shows that the SWNG representation is better able to capture the structure of a text that remains roughly the same despite significant changes to hide the origin of the plagiarized passages.

5. CONCLUSIONS

Plagiarism detection in large document collections should be both efficient and effective. The former requires that the measures used to represent documents are easily available and capture local similarities so that to enable the identification of a short plagiarized passage within a long document. Moreover, the document representation measures should be flexible in modifications intentionally made by plagiarists to hide the similarity with the original passages. In contrast to the vast majority of the existing approaches that are (entirely or in part) based on content terms to represent documents, in this paper we presented a method that uses structural information acquired by a small list of stopwords.

It has been demonstrated that the stopword *n*-gram method is reliable when it is used to identify similarity in the document level. In addition, an algorithm for detecting exact passage boundaries was proposed. Its performance on a publicly-available corpus is competitive to state-of-the-art approaches achieving higher precision and slightly lower recall results. Interestingly, the proposed method achieves significantly better performance when it deals with difficult plagiarism cases where the plagiarized passage has been extensively modified. In such cases, usually many content words/phrases are replaced by synonyms. This act does not dramatically affect the main syntactic structure of the sentences and, consequently, many stopword sequences remain stable. Note that in these difficult plagiarism cases, content-based methods either cannot capture the similarity or require a more elaborate (and inefficient) analysis of texts. Obviously, when the plagiarist just borrows the ideas of some source documents and rewrites large parts of the passages, the stopword sequences are also affected. In such difficult cases, rare content terms or proper names seem more appropriate to capture the similarity between documents.

The proposed method is very easy to follow and requires minimal resources and text pre-processing cost. The parameter settings used in this paper were obtained manually using a small part of a heterogeneous corpus (i.e., in terms of document genre, document length, plagiarized passage length, and type of plagiarism). In case a more homogeneous corpus is available, machine learning techniques can also be used to acquire a more appropriate set of parameter values for that specific corpus. In this paper, we followed the full-fingerprinting approach where all the stopword *n*-grams are included in the fingerprint of a document. However, techniques that select a subset of stopword *n*-grams can also be applied to reduce the storage requirements and increase efficiency in very large document collections [21].

Provided that modern IR systems adopt full-text indexing, the presented method indicates an additional exploitation of the available information about stopword occurrences. Beyond the improvement in phrase queries, stopword occurrences can also be used to detect likely plagiarism cases. The proposed method can also be applied to detect near-duplicates. The presented document representation based on structural information can be combined with content information to improve the results in difficult plagiarism cases where significant parts of the plagiarized passage have been restructured. An open question regards the minimum

Table 5. Comparative performance results for several plagiarism types.

Plagiarism Type		SWNG	PAN-10-1	PAN-10-2	PAN-10-3	PAN-10-4
Simulated	Prec.	**0.89**	0.33	0.19	0.19	0.33
	Rec.	**0.27**	0.18	0.22	0.26	0.25
	Gran.	**1.00**	**1.00**	**1.00**	**1.00**	1.03
	plagdet	**0.41**	0.23	0.20	0.22	0.28
Artificial: High	Prec.	**0.97**	0.93	0.76	0.77	0.85
	Rec.	0.79	0.75	0.76	**0.81**	0.61
	Gran.	1.03	**1.00**	1.02	1.08	1.02
	plagdet	**0.85**	0.83	0.75	0.75	0.70
Artificial: Low	Prec.	**0.95**	0.93	0.81	0.78	0.82
	Rec.	0.84	**0.92**	0.85	**0.92**	0.66
	Gran.	**1.00**	**1.00**	1.22	1.10	1.01
	plagdet	0.89	**0.92**	0.72	0.79	0.73
Verbatim	Prec.	**0.96**	0.94	0.78	0.76	0.82
	Rec.	0.93	**0.96**	0.86	0.92	0.68
	Gran.	**1.00**	**1.00**	**1.00**	**1.00**	**1.00**
	plagdet	0.94	**0.95**	0.82	0.83	0.74

number of stopwords required to provide accurate results. Moreover, the contribution of each stopword in the detection procedure should be examined so that to form a list of the most effective stopwords for plagiarism detection. This is a language-dependent procedure since it concerns the definition and use of stopwords.

6. REFERENCES

[1] Arun, R., Suresh, V., and Madhavan, C.E.V. 2009. Stopword graphs and authorship attribution in text corpora. In *Proceedings of the IEEE International Conference on Semantic Computing*, 192-196.

[2] Barrón-Cedeño, A., and Rosso, P. 2009. On automatic plagiarism detection based on n-grams comparison. In *Proceedings of the 31th European Conference on IR Research on Advances in Information Retrieval*, pp. 696-700.

[3] Basile, C., Benedetto, D., Caglioti, E., Cristadoro, G., and Esposti, M.D. 2009. A plagiarism detection procedure in three steps: Selection, matches and "squares". In *Proceedings of the 3rd Workshop on Uncovering Plagiarism, Authorship and Social Software Misuse*, pp. 19–23.

[4] Bendersky, M. and Croft, W.B. 2009. Finding text reuse on the web. In *Proceedings of the 2nd International Conference on Web Search and Web Data Mining*, 262-271.

[5] Broder, A.Z. 1997. On the resemblance and containment of documents. In *Proceedings of the Compression and Complexity of Sequences*, 21-29.

[6] Ceska, Z. and Fox, C. 2009. The influence of text pre-processing on plagiarism detection. In *Proceedings of the Int. Conf. on Recent Advances in Natural Language Processing*, 55-59.

[7] Clough, P. 2003. *Old and New Challenges in Automatic Plagiarism Detection*. National UK Plagiarism Advisory Service.

[8] Grozea, C., Gehl, C., and Popescu, M. 2009. ENCOPLOT: Pairwise sequence matching in linear time applied to plagiarism detection. In *Proceedings of the 3rd Workshop on Uncovering Plagiarism, Authorship and Social Software Misuse*, 10-18.

[9] Gustafson, N., Pera, M.S., and Ng, Y.K. 2008. Nowhere to hide: Finding plagiarized documents based on sentence similarity. In *Proceedings of the IEEE/WIC/ACM Int. Conference on Web Intelligence and Intelligent Agent Technology*, 690-696.

[10] Hoad, T.C. and Zobel, J. 2003. Methods for identifying versioned and plagiarized documents. *Journal of the American Society for Information Science and Technology*, 54(3), 203-215.

[11] Kasprzak, J. & Brandejs, M. 2010. Improving the reliability of the plagiarism detection system - Lab report for PAN at CLEF 2010. In *Proceedings of the 4th Workshop on Uncovering Plagiarism, Authorship, and Social Software Misuse*.

[12] Kolak, O. and Schilit, B.N. 2008. Generating links by mining quotations. In *Proceedings of HT 2008*, 117–126.

[13] Koppel, M., Akiva, N., and Dagan, I. 2006. Feature instability as a criterion for selecting potential style markers. *Journal of the American Society for Information Science and Technology*, 57(11), 1519–1525.

[14] Manning, C.D., Raghavan, P., and Schütze, H. 2008. *Introduction to Information Retrieval*. Cambridge University Press.

[15] Metzler, D., Bernstein, Y., Croft, W.B., Moffat, A., and Zobel, J. 2005. Similarity measures for tracking information flow. In *Proceedings of the ACM Conference on Information and Knowledge Management*, 517-524.

[16] Muhr, M., Kern, R., Zechner, M., and Granitzer, M. 2010. External and intrinsic plagiarism detection using a cross-lingual retrieval and segmentation system - Lab report for PAN at CLEF 2010. In *Proceedings of the 4th Workshop on Uncovering Plagiarism, Authorship, and Social Software Misuse*.

[17] Potthast, M., Barrón-Cedeño, A., Stein, B., and Rosso, P 2011. Cross-language plagiarism detection. *Language Resources & Evaluation*, 45(1), 45-62.

[18] Potthast, M., Barrón-Cedeño, A., Eiselt, A., Stein, B., and Rosso, P. 2010. Overview of the 2nd international competition on plagiarism detection. In *Proceedings of the 4th Workshop on Uncovering Plagiarism, Authorship, and Social Software Misuse*.

[19] Potthast, M., Stein, B., Barrón-Cedeño, A., and Rosso, P. 2010. An evaluation framework for plagiarism detection. In *Proceedings of the 23rd International Conference on Computational Linguistics*.

[20] Potthast, M., Stein, B., Eiselt, A., Barrón-Cedeño, A., and Rosso, P. 2009. Overview of the 1st international competition on plagiarism detection. In *Proceedings of the 3rd Workshop on Uncovering Plagiarism, Authorship, and Social Software Misuse*, 1-9.

[21] Schleimer, S., Wilkerson, D.S., and Aiken, A. 2003. Winnowing: Local algorithms for document fingerprinting. In *Proceedings of the ACM SIGMOD International Conference on Management of Data*, 76-85.

[22] Seo, J., and Croft, W.B. 2008. Local text reuse detection. In *Proceedings of the 31st Annual International ACM SIGIR Conference on Research and Development in Information Retrieval*, 571-578.

[23] Stamatatos, E. 2009. Intrinsic plagiarism detection using character n-gram profiles. In *Proceedings of the 3rd Int. Workshop on Uncovering Plagiarism, Authorship, and Social Software Misuse*.

[24] Stamatatos, E., Fakotakis, N., and Kokkinakis, G. 2000. Text genre detection using common word frequencies. In *Proceedings of the 18th Int. Conf. on Computational Linguistics*, 808-814.

[25] Theobald, M., Siddharth, J., and Paepcke, A. 2008. Spotsigs: Robust and efficient near duplicate detection in large web collections. In *Proceedings of the 31st Annual International ACM SIGIR Conference on Research and Development in Information Retrieval*, 563–570.

[26] Uzuner, O., Katz, B., and Nahnsen, T. 2005. Using syntactic information to identify plagiarism. In *Proceedings of the ACL Workshop on Educational Applications*, 37–44.

[27] Zhang, Q., Zhang, Y., Yu, H., and Huang, X. 2010. Efficient partial-duplicate detection based on sequence matching. In *Proceedings of the 33rd Int. ACM SIGIR Conference on Research and Development*, 675-682.

[28] Zou, D. Long, W., and Ling, Z. 2010. A cluster-based plagiarism detection method - Lab report for PAN at CLEF 2010. In *Proceedings of the 4th Workshop on Uncovering Plagiarism, Authorship, and Social Software Misuse*.

Studying How the Past is Remembered: Towards Computational History through Large Scale Text Mining

Ching-man Au Yeung*
ASTRI
3/F Bio-informatics Centre
2 Science Park West Avenue, Hong Kong
albertauyeung@astri.org

Adam Jatowt
Graduate School of Informations, Kyoto University
Yoshida-honmachi, Sakyo-ku, Kyoto
606-8501, Japan
adam@dl.kuis.kyoto-u.ac.jp

ABSTRACT

History helps us understand the present and even to predict the future to certain extent. Given the huge amount of data about the past, we believe computer science will play an increasingly important role in historical studies, with computational history becoming an emerging interdisciplinary field of research. We attempt to study how the past is remembered through large scale text mining. We achieve this by first collecting a large dataset of news articles about different countries and analyzing the data using computational and statistical tools. We show that analysis of references to the past in news articles allows us to gain a lot of insight into the collective memories and societal views of different countries. Our work demonstrates how various computational tools can assist us in studying history by revealing interesting topics and hidden correlations. Our ultimate objective is to enhance history writing and evaluation with the help of algorithmic support.

Categories and Subject Descriptors

H.5.m [**Information Interfaces and Presentation**]: Miscellaneous; I.2.7 [**Natural Language Processing**]: Text analysis

General Terms

Algorithms, Languages, Experimentation

Keywords

computational history, news analysis, temporal analysis

1. INTRODUCTION

George Santayana, the famous Spanish American philosopher, once wrote, "Those who cannot remember the past are condemned to repeat it." It is hard to overestimate the importance of history of societies. History helps to bridge the present and the past, understand the present and even to predict the future to some extent. Studying the past and maintaining an awareness of national and international history serve many purposes such as educational, patriotic or political ones. Images of the past also commonly serve to legitimate a present social order [8].

Traditional historical methods and guidelines, according to which historians study the past and write histories, rely to a large extent on manual effort in amassing and investigating historical evidences. However, with the proliferation of digitalized historical sources such as newspaper archives, scanned books and other digital artifacts, it has become possible to employ a wide range of computational techniques in historical studies. Such an approach to historical studies, what we call *computational history*, would assist historians in analyzing massive amounts of data to obtain evidences that support various hypotheses and different correlations among events in the past. This will open up new research areas very much like computational linguistics [17] and, more recently, computational social science [15] have done.

Besides knowledge creation, computational history can also be used as a verification tool for evaluating the credibility of the existing historical knowledge. According to the meta-history view, history should not always be considered credible but rather requires a constant process of revision. This is because in many cases a "usable past" is often created to serve political and identity needs of nations. Since there is no "universal history", the remembered past, as being an intellectual product, calls for stringent analysis and criticism, and should remain in permanent evaluation [20]. The power of computational tools in processing huge amount of historical data will be desirable in this context.

In this paper, we focus on one important aspect of history, which is the perception of the past, or how the past is remembered. We achieve this by first collecting a large dataset of news articles about different countries from Google News Archive[1], and analyzing the data using computational and statistical tools such as topic modeling. We show that analysis of references to the past in news articles allows us to gain a lot of insight into the collective memories and societal views of different countries, such as what events or periods are of great importance to a country, and what were the reasons that triggered the remembering of the past at a particular time. The study of the collective remembering of

*Au Yeung contributed to this paper while he was at the NTT Communication Science Laboratories, Kyoto, Japan.

[1] http://news.google.com/archivesearch

CIKM'11, October 24–28, 2011, Glasgow, Scotland, UK.

the past using this methodology will help to understand the way in which societies retain their memories, modify them over time by recalling or eradicating particular events, and keep the memory of others. We also show the possibility of investigating the selectivity of social memories, as reflected in the differences between what have actually happened in the past with what is currently remembered.

Michel *et al.* [19] introduce "culturomics," an approach of studying the evolution of human culture by applying computers to analyze a huge dataset of digitalized books. We extend this idea to investigate history and collective memory. Our work is novel because we do not only focus on a particular period in the past (e.g. by analyzing documents created at that time), but attempt to study the *image* or *perception* of the past by analyzing references to the past in recent news articles. This generates even much more information and knowledge about our history.

This paper is structured as follows. In Section 2 we discuss works related to our project. In Section 3, we give an overview of our methodology. In Section 4, we present the results of statistical analysis and examination of retrospective views of the past using topic models. We discuss some applications of our work, its limitations and possible future research directions in Section 5. Finally, we conclude this paper in Section 6.

2. RELATED WORK

The use of computer to assist data analysis and mining hidden patterns in social sciences has attracted substantial attention in recent years. Lazer *et al.* write about computational social science [15], which aims at leveraging computational power to collect and analyze large datasets to reveal patterns of individual and group behaviors. This trend is in particular propelled by the explosive growth of digital data in recent years, ranging from digitalized historical archives, user-generated data on the Web, to huge amount of records of user interactions on social networking sites.

Some examples can be found in the literature recently. Michel *et al.* [19] have shown that analysis of n-grams from a huge corpus of digitalized books can be used to reveal trends in the development of the English language and usage of vocabulary over time. The recent work by Takahashi *et al.* [26] is an example of how one can measure the impact of historical persons using Wikipedia. Shahaf and Guestrin [23] propose an algorithm for discovering hidden connections and chains of events in news articles. There are also works on finding "across-time" synonyms [14][4] and comparing word senses over time [25] to support searching in document archives.

Historians and sociologists propose the concept of *collective memory* as the notion of societal remembrances of the past in contrast to individual memories composed of references to one's personal history [11]. Studies of collective memories have so far been limited to anecdotal analysis and interrogations of subjects. Given now the availability of huge amount of data about the past, we believe that our understanding of history can also benefit from the use of various computational tools. However, to the best of our knowledge, we are the first to attempt to apply computational methods on text corpora in order to study how the past is remembered and other related topics.

Several techniques in the field of computer science are actually relevant to computational history. These techniques include topic detection and tracking (TDT) [1], and temporal analysis. Topic detection and tracking focuses on developing methods for tracking changes in the popularity of topics over time given a text corpus. For example, Blei *et al.* [5] and Wang and McCallum [28] extend latent Dirichlet allocation (LDA) [6] to model topic evolution over time. Blei *et al.* assume that the topics in one year are dependent on the topics in the previous year, while Wang and McCallum assume that each topic has its own distribution over time.

A number of methods have also been proposed to cluster documents by temporal information. For example, Alonso *et al.* [2] propose to perform search result clustering by constructing a timeline for each document based on the temporal information extracted. Similarity of a pair of documents depends on how much their timelines overlap with each other. Qamra *et al.* [22] propose a time-sensitive and community-sensitive model for clustering blog posts, basing their model on a modified time-sensitive Dirichlet process [29]. In addition, Cooper *et al.* [9] describe a method for clustering photos based on their timestamps. Readers who are interested in an overview of the challenges and research directions related to temporal information extraction, processing and analysis should refer to the recent work by Alonso *et al.* [3].

In this work we rely on temporal information extraction from text collections, for which various methods have been proposed [16, 18, 24, 27]. Strötgen and Jannik [24] demonstrate a system for extraction, querying, storage, and exploration of spatio-temporal information stored in text documents. Our main focus is however not on the extraction of temporal infomarmation but on studying how it is used as a representation of collective memories of societies.

3. METHODOLOGY

Our aim is to apply computational methods to study history on a large scale, especially by analyzing huge corpora of documents that are dated and contain time expressions referred to the past. In this section, we describe our methodology in detail. Figure 1 shows an overview of the procedures we will follow in this paper.

3.1 Data Collection

To obtain data for our purpose of studying how the past is remembered, we first collected from Google News Archive[2] a dataset of news articles published in the period of 1990-2010. This period was chosen because for the majority of news articles in this period that are indexed in the archive, we were able to obtain the full texts in digital form from the Web, while most articles published earlier are only available in image format, which cannot be subject to text analysis.

News articles were collected by issuing 32 different country names as queries with the above time constraints to Google News Archive.[3] Table 1 shows the list of countries we used to collect our dataset. We decided to focus on countries because they are related to diverse topics and events. They also provide meaningful results when contrasted with one another. We note however that many other kinds of entities such as area names, company names and person names can

[2]`http://news.google.com/archivesearch`

[3]Our list includes names that are not countries (e.g. Hong Kong). However, to give a more concise discussion, we will refer to all these entities as countries in this paper.

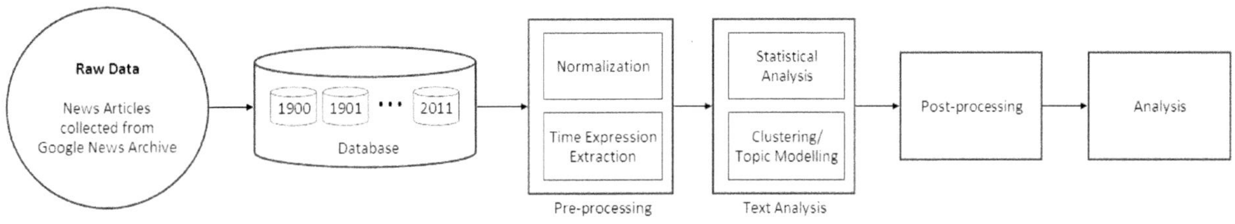

Figure 1: An overview of the methodology used in this study. Data are collected from an online news archive. Documents are then subjected to pre-processing and algorithms are applied to extract time expressions in the texts. Data mining techniques such as topic modeling are then applied to extract meaningful patterns from the data, which are used in further analysis.

Argentina	Australia	Austria	China
Egypt	France	Germany	Hong Kong
Iceland	India	Indonesia	Italy
Iran	Iraq	Ireland	Israel
Japan	New Zealand	Norway	Poland
Romania	Singapore	South Africa	South Korea
Soviet Union	Spain	Sweden	Switzerland
Taiwan	Tunisia	Turkey	United States

Table 1: The list of country names used in collecting news articles.

be used as the subjects of our investigation, and we plan to explore these possibilities in the future.

For each query, we gathered all the search results with links to the original articles, and downloaded their original Web pages. For a small percentage of news articles, we were unable to collect their full texts due to subscription restrictions and the lack of textual content. In these cases, we collected the article abstracts instead. On average each query resulted in 72K news articles. In total, our dataset consisted of 2.4 million news articles.

In addition to news articles published in the period of 1990-2010, we also created a reference dataset by collecting news articles in the period of 1900-1989. For each query listed in Table 1, we downloaded the snippets and titles of all articles published from 1900 to 1989 that are available in the Google News Archive. The purpose and use of this dataset will be further discussed in Section 4. All data collected were organized and indexed in a database for future analysis.

3.2 Pre-processing

News articles collected in the previous step were mainly in the form of Web pages. To extract useful parts from these pages, we processed each article such that HTML tags, JavaScript codes, and other non-content elements were removed. We then extracted the core part of the news articles based on identifying the largest chunk of text in each article. This heuristic worked well due to relatively simple layout of news articles. It allowed us not only to recover the main content of each news article, but also to remove many noisy temporal expressions such as copyrights dates or dates used for labeling archival content. We also discarded articles written in languages other than English using text categorization algorithm based on n-gram matching [7].

3.2.1 Extracting Temporal Expressions

A more important pre-processing task in our case is to extract temporal expressions from news articles. We need to know whether a document mentions something in the past and which time is mentioned. For example, we need to recognize the year 1945 in the sentence "The Second World War ended in 1945," in order to create an association between the year 1945 with the topic mentioned in the sentence.

To extract temporal expressions, we use the GUTime tagger [16], which is a temporal tagger for identifying and normalizing temporal expressions in text. It is one of the several components in the TARSQI toolkit [27], which can be used to extract events and their associations with temporal expressions. GUTime identifies temporal expressions in text and annotates them with the TimeML markup language which is ISO standard for robust specification of events and temporal expressions in natural language. Currently it is the most effective and state-of-the-art solution for the temporal information extraction and processing.

GUTime is able to detect both absolute and relative expressions. Absolute temporal expressions are defined as expressions that are unambiguously associated with a given time point or interval (e.g., 2nd November 1977, 1964). Relative temporal expressions, such as "last year" and "10 years ago", require a reference time expression called anchor in order to be converted into absolute time expressions. GUTime uses certain procedures to resolve relative temporal expressions such as using article timestamp and absolute dates that appear in the context of a relative expression. In this work we focus on both absolute and relative temporal references referring to past years. In our framework, for simplicity we use only temporal expressions of yearly granularity; we thus map references such as "2nd November 1977" or "March 1977" to "1977". However, we are aware that by this simplification some information is lost. In the future we plan to use temporal expressions with their original granularities.

Applying the GUTime tagger to our dataset, we extracted on average 19K temporal expressions that relate to the period 1900-1989 for a single country, and in total, 630K temporal expressions for all the countries. The period of 1900-1989 is the target time frame of our study.

3.3 Text Analysis

In order to obtain a summary of the topics mentioned in a corpus, latent Dirichlet allocation (LDA) [6] is commonly used. LDA is a generative model for obtaining the probability distributions of a chosen number of topics for both words and documents in the corpus. It assumes that each word in a document is generated by first picking a topic (from a set of finite number of topics) and then sampling a word from the word distribution of the selected topic. By training an

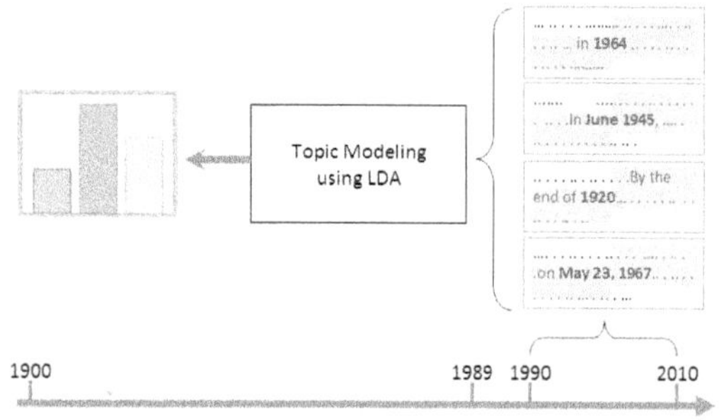

Figure 2: A diagram showing how we applied LDA on documents created by first extracting sentences containing temporal expressions. These temporal expressions were extracted from news articles published in the period of 1990-2010. The text around a temporal expression (the sentence containing it, the preceding and the next sentences) forms its context.

LDA model on a corpus, we will be able to obtain a set of topics with their word distributions, as well as the topic distribution of each document.

We are aware of some useful extensions of the original LDA model. For example, the Topic over Time (TOT) model described in [28] incorporates temporal information such that topic discovery is influenced not only by word co-occurrences but also the timestamps of the documents. However, since these more advanced models impose various time constraints when assigning words to topics, they are not suitable in our study. Instead, using a method similar to the one described in [12], we first use LDA to discover topics in news articles, and then perform post-hoc calculations to obtain different probability distributions related to the publication years of the news articles and the years in the past for further analysis.

We note an important consideration when applying LDA to our dataset. While a news article in general focuses on a specific topic, not all words are relevant when a particular temporal expression in the article is considered. Hence, to identify topics that are more likely to be about past events, we constructed a new document for each temporal expression identified in the dataset. Such a new document contains the sentence in which a temporal expression referring to the past was found, together with the preceding and following sentences. These sentences serve as the *context* of the temporal expression found. LDA was applied to these documents instead of the original news articles. Figure 2 depicts the idea of this procedure. Since LDA only returns the topic distribution of a document and the word distribution of a topic, we estimated other distributions, such as distributions of topics over the past years and over the recent years, for further analysis. The results are presented in the next section.

4. EXPERIMENTS AND ANALYSIS

4.1 Distribution of Past References

Firstly, we investigate to what extent different periods in the past are remembered. We expect to obtain a different picture for different countries. We also want to test and quantify the intuitive assumption that the distant past is on average remembered less than the recent past. From news articles published in the period of 1990-2010, we extracted all temporal expressions that refer to any year in the period of 1900-1989. Figures 3(a) and (b) show the distributions of these temporal expressions for some selected countries. We can see that depending on the country there are peaks at different years. These can be considered as years that are more remembered for the countries.

For example, if we look at the distributions of references for European countries in Figure 3(a), peaks can be found in the years during the Second World War for most countries. However, there are individual differences. For example, 1939 is the year of invasion of Poland by Germany, and it is particularly significant to Poland. On the other hand, 1933 marks the date of appointment of Hitler for Chancellor of Germany, and thus this year has a more special meaning to Germany. There are of course peaks referring to other events, although less prominent. For example, the peak in 1975 for Spain reflects the significance of the death of the dictator Francisco Franco. Sweden has a peak in 1958, when the country hosted the World Cup.

In Figure 3(b), we see a different picture. WWII is no longer a dominating event, although there is still a significant amount of references referring to its end. We can easily observe several important years in the Chinese history. For example, 1949 saw the end of the civil war in China, the founding of the People's Republic of China and the retreat of the Republic of China administration to Taiwan. In 1972, President Nixon visited China, which eventually led to the establishment of formal diplomatic relations between the US and China in 1979. The distribution of references for Hong Kong has a small peak in 1918, in which the Spanish Flu broke out. This is probably due to the fact that the city had several outbreaks of Avian Flu in 2003, and that the media referred to a related outbreak in the history when reporting these events.

Putting aside the occasional peaks in these graphs, we can see that they generally follow a similar shape. Figure 3(c) shows the graph averaged over all countries in our dataset. We notice that the decline in the number of past references resembles an exponential function. The graph can be compared to the well-known *forgetting curve* proposed by Ebbinghaus [10] to illustrate the decline of memory retention in time of individual persons.

We next investigate the change of the remembering patterns over time. The objective is to check whether the shape of the average remembering curve will change when it is plotted using data created in different time frames. We thus divide our dataset into four bins depending on the article publication date to represent every five consecutive years and we plot the average frequency over all the countries in Figure 3(d). The results confirm that the remembering pattern that we showed in Figure 3(c) is universal, at least over the time frame of 20 years. Naturally, the plot obtained for the first bin (1990-1994) results in the highest values due to its proximity to the period under analysis. However on a relative basis, the average shape of the function that governs remembering does not change much for the data extracted from different bins.

4.2 Remembering Topics/Events in the Past

In the previous section, we described analysis that gave us

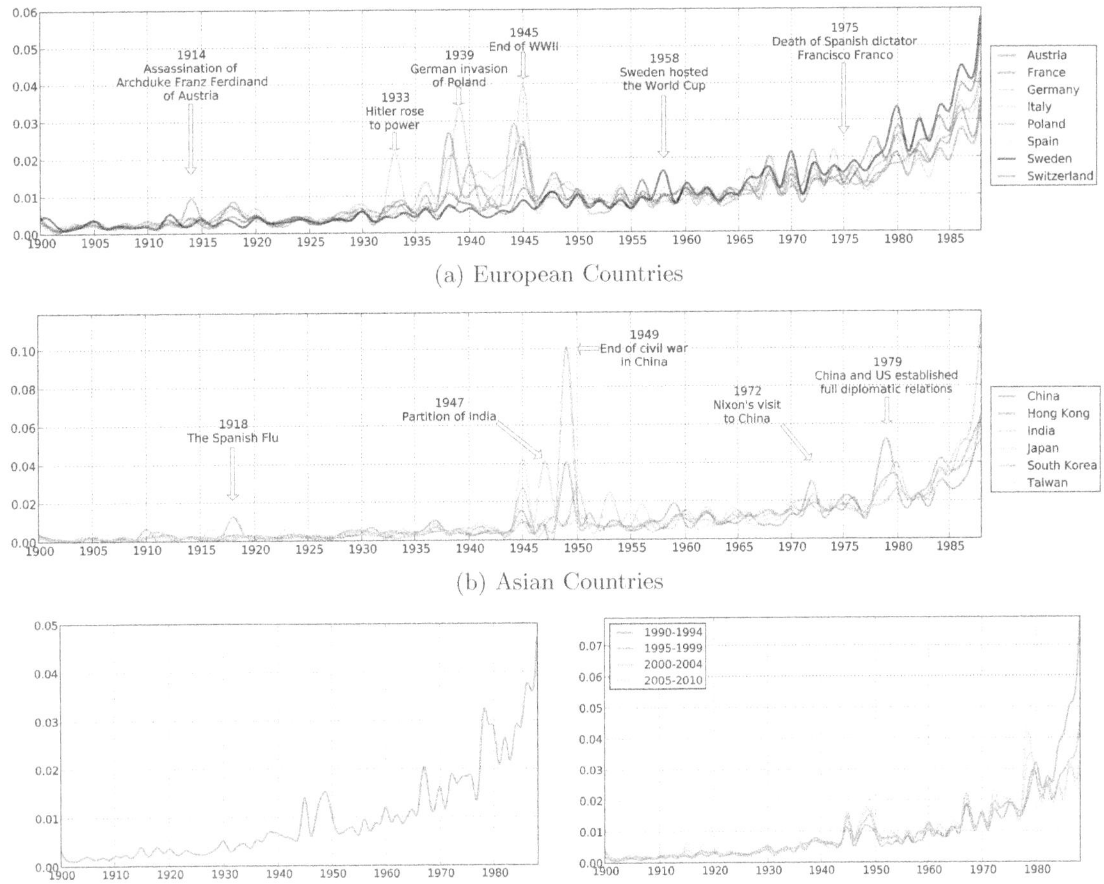

(a) European Countries

(b) Asian Countries

(c) Average across all countries

(d) Average for four different periods

Figure 3: The distribution of years mentioned in news articles that are related to different countries and are published in the period 1990-2010. (a) shows the graphs of some European countries, while (b) shows the graphs of some Asian countries. We observe a general decaying curve but also peaks at some eventful years for different countries. (c) shows the overall average distribution, and (d) shows the average distributions for four different periods of article publication dates.

a general picture of the characteristics of temporal references in news articles. However, we would like to go a step further to gain more insight into how the past is remembered. In particular, the graphs in Figure 3 only told us which years were mentioned more frequently than other years given a country, but they did not tell us why and when they were mentioned. We were able to name the events in Figure 3 only because we have some knowledge of the past. It would be very much desirable if we can identify automatically the topics associated with those years, and more interestingly, when and why were these topics and years mentioned in the news articles.

For this purpose, we now turn our focus to the topics or events mentioned in the news. We mainly rely on the results of topic modeling using LDA to perform post-hoc estimation of various probability distributions in order to study the relations between topics and years mentioned. Note that we use topics and events interchangeably here, although they are not strictly equivalent. However, since we choose a relatively large number of topics in running LDA, most topics do correspond to individual events. Incorporating event extraction analysis into our methodology will be considered in our future work.

LDA is a generative model of documents. Assume that we have a corpus $\mathcal{C}$ containing a set of documents, and each document d is represented by a bag of words. LDA assumes that every word in a document is generated by first picking a latent topic and then sampling from the distribution of words conditioned on the selected topic. Probability distributions obtained after training an LDA model include $P(w|z)$, the probability word w given topic z, and $P(z|d)$, the probability of topic z given document d.

In addition, we introduce the following notations. We use p to represent an article publication year in the period of 1990-2010, and y represent a year in the period of 1900-1989. For each country, we can estimate the distributions $P(y)$, $P(p)$ and $P(p, y)$ directly from the dataset by counting the occurrences of years in these periods. In the following, we combine these distributions with the distributions returned by LDA to perform various kinds of analysis.

We first focus on one country at a time and examine which years and topics are particularly important. Secondly, we investigate the differences between news articles in the past and news articles in recent years that refer to the past. Finally, we explore how topic modeling can be used to reveal the similarities between the histories of different countries.

4.2.1 Significant Years and Topics

Every country has her own historic moments and events. The significance of a particular year or a particular event to a country can, to certain extent, be measured by how frequently they are mentioned in the news. In the following, we examine how these characteristics of remembering can be revealed by making use of the results of topic modeling.

Our first step is to determine the significant years for a given country. This can be estimated in a straightforward way, by counting how many times each year has been mentioned in news articles in the respective dataset. Furthermore, we would like to know the reason why a particular year has been mentioned frequently. For this purpose, we estimate the topic distribution of each year in the past. Let $P(z|d)$ be the topic distribution of each document returned by LDA, and let D_y be the set of documents mentioning the year y. We can estimate the topic distribution of each year, i.e. $P(z|y)$ using the following equation:

$$P(z|y) = \frac{1}{|D_y|} \sum_{d \in D_y} P(z|d). \tag{1}$$

Table 2 shows the results of this experiment performed on 10 selected countries. For each country, we show the three most significant years, as well as a list of top words from the topic with the highest probability conditioned on the respective years. An immediate observation is that years related to WWII, such as 1939, 1944 and 1945, are significant to quite a number of countries on the list. This is expected since WWII involved most of the world's nations at that time and can be considered as one of the most significant events in the 20th century. However, similar to what we have discussed in Figure 3, we also observe obvious variations across different countries. The end of the civil war in 1949 tops the list of China, while for Spain the year 1975 in which the dictator Francisco Franco died is the most significant.

Overall, we observe that topic modeling is very useful in this case since it tells us clearly why a particular year is considered significant to a given country. It clearly demonstrates the power of computational tools in assisting historical studies. While some of the results are not too surprising given our general knowledge of the histories of these countries, not all of them are immediately obvious to a person who is not familiar with a country's past. We also note that the consideration of using only words appearing close to a temporal expressions in topic modeling results in very coherent topics in many cases.

4.2.2 Triggers of Remembering the Past

As we have mentioned above, the significance of a historic event can be context-dependent. The above analysis with the help of topics tells us the reason why a particular year is significant to a country. However, it does not tell us *when* a year in the past was recalled, and *what* triggered the recalling. A way to look into this characteristic is to see in what particular period of time was the event mentioned in the news. We can study this by estimating the probability distribution of the publication dates of news articles conditioned on a particular year in the past and the corresponding significant topic. We represent this probability distribution by $P(p|y,z)$, where p refers to a publication year. In our case, $1990 \leq p \leq 2010$. We use the following equation to estimate $P(p|y,z)$:

$$P(p|y,z) = \frac{P(p,y,z)}{P(y,z)} \tag{2}$$

$$= \frac{P(z|p,y)P(p,y)}{P(z|y)P(y)} \tag{3}$$

where $P(z|p,y)$ is estimated using equation similar to Equation 1, and $P(p,y)$ and $P(y)$ can be easily obtained by counting the number of documents published in year p and the number of documents mentioning year y.

Figure 4 shows the probability distribution over the twenty-year period for the most significant years and topics for four selected countries. As we have hypothesized, the distribution is not uniform. In other words, a historical event is usually mentioned more frequently in a particular period of time than in other periods. For example, for Japan the year 1972 was mentioned very frequently in the year 1998 (with high probability at $p = 1998$). This is because in both years the Winter Olympics was held in Japan.

For Japan, Germany and Poland, we observe peaks in the years 1995 and 2005 for the year 1945; obviously this reflects the fact that the end of WWII was remembered and mentioned more frequently in its 50th and 60th anniversaries. For China, the year 1949 was remembered relatively more in and after the year 2004. In 2004, Taiwan held its presidential election, which probably invoked various discussion postulating the development of the mutual relationship between China and Taiwan, and thus triggered the remembering of the end of the civil war in 1949.

To better assist the analysis of correlations between years in recent times and years in the past in context, we can use the topic model to generate topic distributions conditioned on a pair of past-recent years. In other words, we estimate $P(z|p,y)$, the topic distribution given a year in recent time (the publication date of a news article) and a year in the past. This can be estimated using the following equation:

$$P(z|p,y) = \frac{1}{|D_{p,y}|} \sum_{d \in D_{p,y}} P(z|d). \tag{4}$$

where $D_{p,y}$ represents the set of documents that were published in the year p and contain a reference to the year y.

Table 3 shows four examples of the most significant topics (by probability) for frequent pairs for four different countries. The context of the connections between two years is immediately understood by studying the topic words. For example, for Indonesia, 1975 and 1999 are both significant years regarding its relationship with East Timor, which was annexed by Indonesia in 1975 but claimed independence in 1999. On the other hand, the Polish Pope John Paul II, who was originally known by the name of Karol Wojtyla, was elected as the Pope in 1978 and passed away in 2005. He is considered a significant figure in Polish history.

4.2.3 Events Remembered and Forgotten

So far we have examined which topics and years were frequently mentioned in news articles of recent times. However, it is not uncommon that references to the past can be selective. In other words, while a year in the past was eventful, very often only few events were singled out and remembered after a long period of time. It might even be possible that

Country	Year	Top Words
Argentina	1978	world, cup, first, team, maradona, win, tournament, home, won, years
	1976	military, said, rights, human, dictatorship, argentine, government, years, war, people
	1974	pinochet, court, chile, chilean, regime, prats, death, charges, supreme, opponents
Australia	1975	east, timor, indonesia, australian, indonesian, invasion, timorese, sea, killed, agreement
	1974	world, cup, team, first, won, played, final, win, africa, tournament
	1980	states, united, australian, open, year, title, wimbledon, slam, grand, won
China	1949	taiwan, mainland, war, island, beijing, civil, communists, nationalist, government, chinese
	1972	president, visit, nixon, minister, beijing, years, relations, first, kissinger, trip
	1978	million, year, economic, billion, percent, growth, world, economy, years, population
France	1944	war, world, army, american, battle, soldiers, legion, served, veterans, french
	1940	war, french, german, germany, hitler, occupation, world, resistance, nazi, britain
	1968	killed, people, group, spain, attack, eta, basque, region, year, police
Germany	1945	war, world, end, day, second, declared, allies, europe, first, empire
	1939	soviet, poland, union, europe, war, eastern, western, czechoslovakia, polish, invaded
	1974	world, cup, final, england, team, first, won, second, win, football
India	1947	pakistan, kashmir, wars, fought, war, region, countries, independence, nations, territory
	1971	pakistan, bangladesh, war, military, pakistani, army, said, east, forces, report
	1962	china, border, war, chinese, relations, countries, beijing, area, territory, recently
Japan	1945	nuclear, hiroshima, atomic, bomb, nagasaki, weapons, august, dropped, bombs, bombing
	1972	world, tokyo, games, gold, won, cup, olympics, olympic, event, asian
	1980	percent, year, oil, million, said, yen, economy, cent, rate, billion
Poland	1939	war, hitler, germany, invasion, britain, invaded, france, german, september, world
	1945	camp, concentration, auschwitz, camps, nazi, death, nazis, sent, january, prisoners
	1980	communist, solidarity, walesa, gdansk, workers, movement, union, leader, government, lech
Spain	1975	franco, death, francisco, war, country, democracy, spanish, dictator, civil, dictatorship
	1968	basque, people, eta, group, killed, northern, campaign, state, independent, said
	1978	world, cup, european, team, club, championship, final, group, real, won
USA	1979	iran, said, relations, iranian, embassy, government, revolution, islamic, diplomatic, tehran
	1980	team, first, world, cup, olympic, time, games, americans, medal, won
	1972	president, treaty, soviet, nuclear, weapons, said, missile, union, washington, first

Table 2: Frequently mentioned years and topics in the news articles for different countries. For each country, we show the three most frequently mentioned years in the news articles, and the corresponding top words from the topic with the highest probability conditioned on the given year.

Country	p	y	Topic
Indonesia	1999	1975	east, timor, indonesian, portuguese, invaded, timorese, colony, invasion, territory, annexed
Israel	2009	1967	palestinian, state, said, hamas, borders, end, solution, abbas, final, negotiations
Italy	2009	1980	people, southern, region, naples, town, europe, earthquake, south, killed, die
Poland	2005	1978	pope, john, paul, catholic, krakow, church, visit, first, wojtyla, karol

Table 3: Topics for frequent pairs of past-recent years for four selected countries.

some events that were widely reported in the past eventually were forgotten over time.

To explore this characteristic, we run topic modeling over a combined dataset that contains both news articles from the recent times (1990-2010) and from the past (1900-1980).[4] Firstly, we present three examples (Figure 5) that visually compare two topic distributions, namely $P_p(z|y)$, the topic distribution given a year in the past based on past data, and $P_r(z|y) = \sum_{y' \in Y_r} P(z|y')P(y')$, the distribution given a year in the past based on recent data, where Y_r is the set of years in the period of 1990-2010.

[4]We use the reference dataset described at the end of Section 3.1. Note that we purposely limited the past period to 1900-1980 so as to have more distinct separation between the data from the past and data from the present in the subsequent analysis.

We observe from Figure 5 that there is an obvious difference between the two distributions. For the distribution obtained by running topic modeling on recent news articles, we usually observe a few spikes. These represent a few important topics/events in that particular year as judged in the recent times. However, while we also observe relatively high probabilities in a few topics in the distributions obtained from the news articles in the past, the distributions are generally more uniformly distributed. For example, referring to Figure 5(a), most news articles considered the year 1978 an important year after the Cultural Revolution in China, while at that time the attention of the media seemed to have focused on other events, such as the signing of the Treaty of Peace and Friendship between China and Japan.

Another observation is the difference between distributions in the past and in the recent times actually changes as we move towards the present times. For each year y in the period 1900-1980, we compute the KL-Divergence between the topic distributions $P_p(z|y)$ and $P_r(z|y)$. The results for two countries, China and Japan, are shown in Figure 6. An interesting observation can be made from this figure. In both cases we observe a gentle downward trend. This suggests that the difference between two distributions is becoming smaller as we move along the timeline. One explanation of this result is that news articles are more selective when mentioning events in the distant past. For example, only one or two topics related to the year 1905 may be frequently mentioned in the news in the recent times, while news articles may refer to more diverse topics related to the year 1980. This result seems to support the idea that attention would eventually focus on only a few topics/events that are considered significant as time passes.

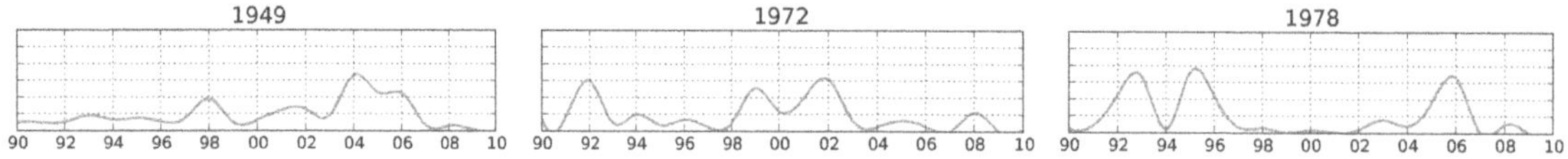

(a) China

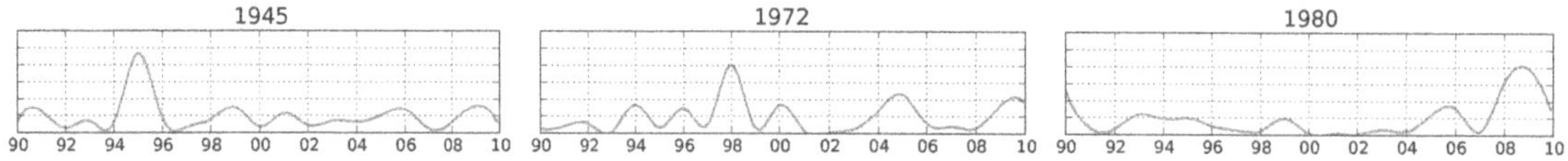

(b) Japan

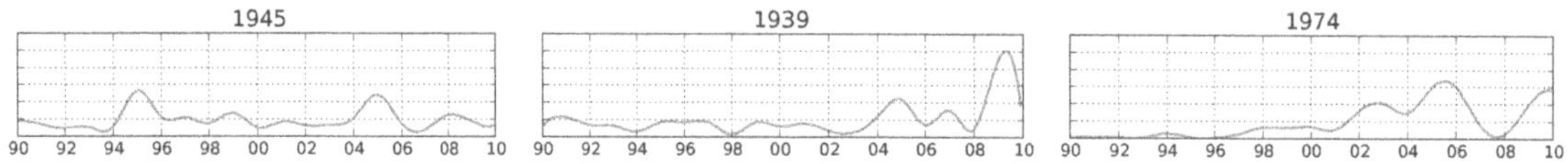

(c) Germany

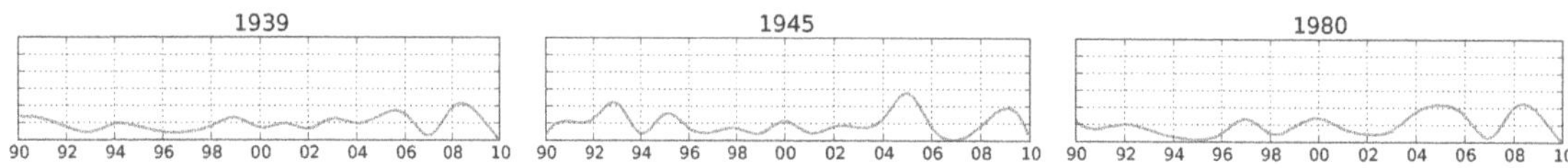

(d) Poland

Figure 4: The distribution of the years of publication for selected countries. For each selected country, we pick the three most frequently mentioned years in the past and then the topic with the highest probability given a year. We then estimate $P(p|y,z)$, the probability of the years of publication conditioned on the year in the past and the topic. In other words, the above graphs show the extent to which each year in the past and the corresponding topic was mentioned in the period of 1990 to 2010 (c.f. Table 2).

From an exploratory perspective, we note that it is also possible to contrast how historical entities such as persons were mentioned in documents in the past and how they are remembered in recent times. Figure 7 shows a comparison of the distribution of the term "Hitler" in past and recent news articles, with the targeting years in the period of 1900-1989. We can observe that the year 1933 has higher significance in the distribution obtained from the present articles than from the past articles. This can be explained by the fact that the year is now commonly recognized as the major turning point when Hitler rose to power. Also some other events from his early life are reflected in the graph generated from the recent articles.

4.2.4 *Historical Similarity of Countries*

One may say that a nation or a country is defined by its history. For some countries, their histories overlap one another from time to time, while others find their histories run on parallel lines. Looking at the histories of different countries thus represents one of the many ways to study the similarities and the relations between two countries. In this section, we try to explore how topic modeling allows us to discover countries with similar "historical narratives". Firstly, we pool data of all countries together and perform topic modeling using LDA. Using the result of topic modeling, we characterize each country with $P(z,y|c)$, the joint distribution of topics and years in the past conditioned on a country c. Similarity is then defined as the reciprocal of the KL-Divergence between the distributions of two countries.

Figure 8 shows the similarity matrix obtained based on the above method. One intuitive observation is that if countries are geographically close to one another, their historical views, or more exactly their perceptions of the past, are likely to be more similar to one another. For example, we observe high similarity among Germany, France, Italy and Poland. However, we also find that the similarity matrix is dominated by major events that are common across many countries, most noticeably WWII. Thus, it becomes difficult to determine the similarity among smaller countries such as Singapore and Iceland. We believe that several procedures can be used to reduce the dominating effect of major historical events, such as by performing pairwise comparison, or by normalizing the importance of different topics. We plan to investigate these possibilities in the future. For now, we observe that this approach is potentially useful in exploring historical similarity among countries.

5. DISCUSSION

We note that news articles only represent one source of data, and we do not exclude the usefulness of other data sources. One may consider that since the objective of a news article is to report a certain event of the present time, it may not necessarily reflect how people perceive the past. However, news articles are produced by the media which can be strongly influenced by the interests and attention of the people. Thus, while a reference to the past in a news article is usually invoked by a certain event that happens when the article is written, the reasons that a certain event in the past is mentioned are also tightly connected to the collective memory of the people. Hence, news articles represent a suitable proxy for studying how the past is remembered.

The application of computational tools such as topic modeling to assist historical studies can be used to answer many

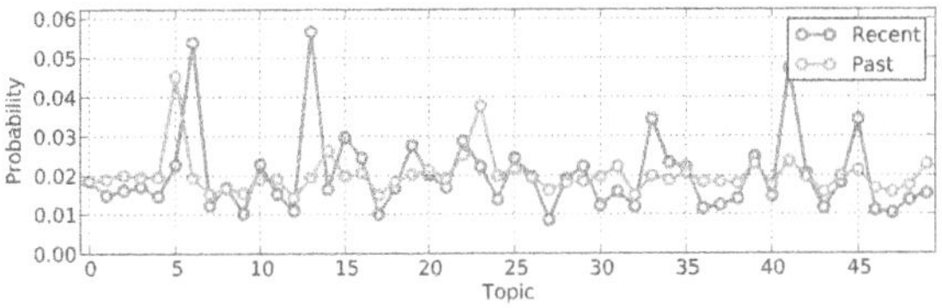

(a) China 1978

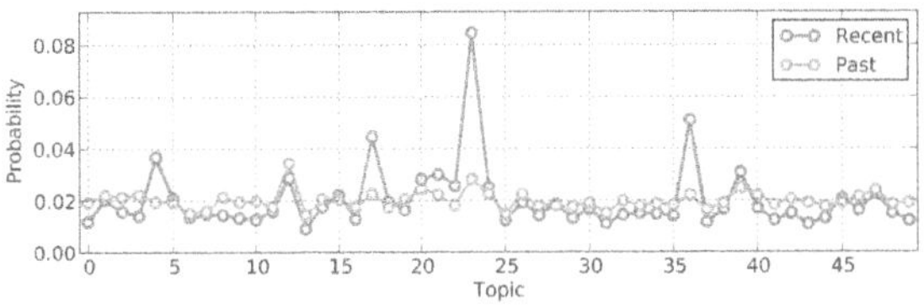

(b) Japan 1972

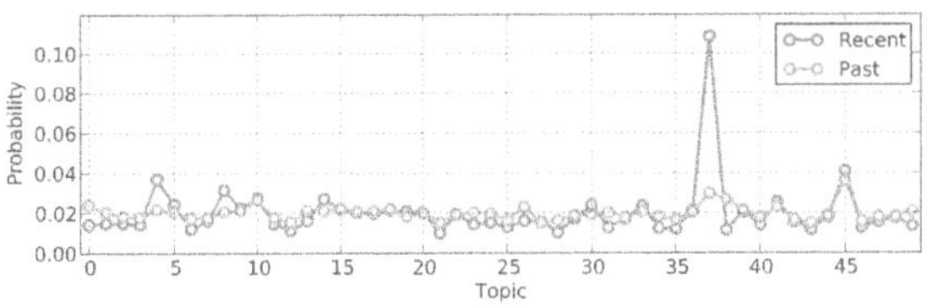

(c) Poland 1980

Figure 5: The distribution of topics for selected country-year pairs. For each country-year pair, we plot the distribution of topics conditioned on the recent years (1990-2010) and the particular year in the country-year pair. The graphs therefore reflect the differences between the topics/events happened in that particular year and the topics/events remembered in recent news articles when the particular year was mentioned.

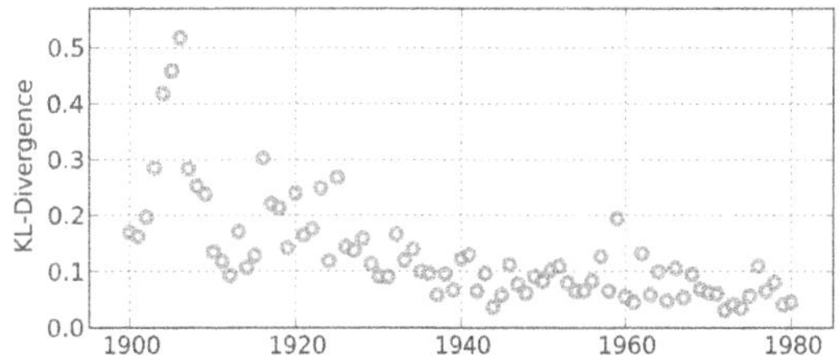

(a) China

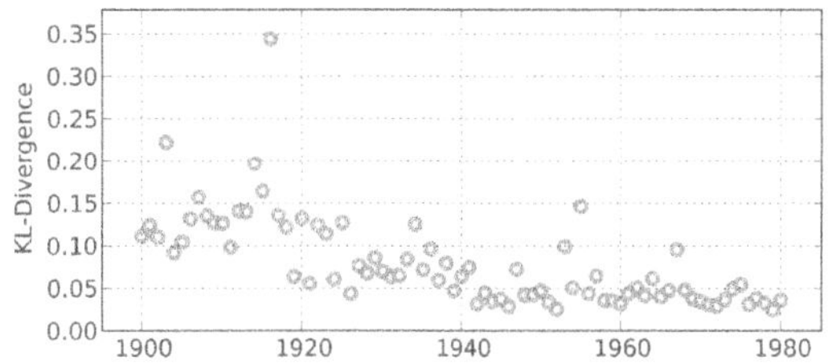

(b) Japan

Figure 6: Scatter plots of KL-Divergence between the distribution of topics in recent and past datasets for China and Japan. We observe in both cases that the difference between the two distributions decreases as we move towards the present time.

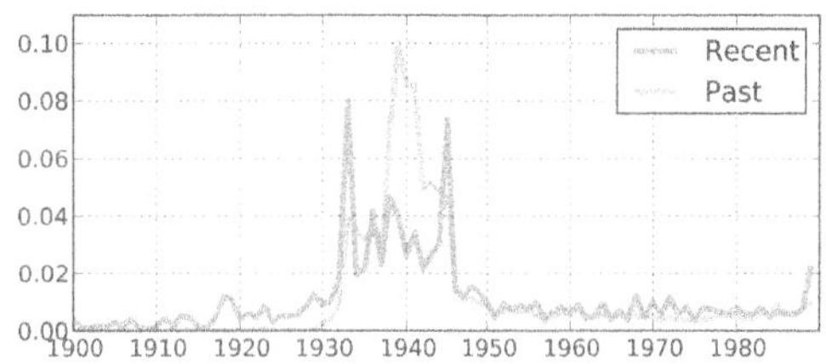

Figure 7: The distribution of occurrences of the word "Hitler" in articles about Germany. The "Recent" line refers to statistics obtained by analyzing the dataset we have collected, while the "Past" line refers to the normalized hit counts in each year returned by Google News Archive when "Germany" and "Hitler" are used together as a query.

more questions than those we have considered in this paper. We outline a few possible research directions.

Firstly, while news article provide the benefit of objectivity when compared to other genres like books or blogs, they only give part of the whole picture of the past and our perception of the past. To be more comprehensive, we plan to take other sources of data, such as magazines, textbooks, fictions, books and Web pages into consideration in the future.

As far as language is concerned, we only focused on news articles published in English this time. An even better way to probe the social memories of different countries is to analyze news articles and other datasets published in their own languages. It would be interesting to perform different kinds of analysis that compare and contrast the distributions of topics and periods obtained from different languages, thus revealing not only historical perspectives but also differences in cultural understanding.

Other computational tools can also help us gain more sight. For example, we can use sentiment analysis [21] to study whether the sentimental view on some historical events have changed over time, that is, whether people regard certain events with the same sentiment as they were seen at the time of their occurrence. By considering the source of data separately, we can even investigate the biases of these sources (e.g. newspapers vs. books). It is also desirable to explore new methods of text mining that are particularly suitable for computational history. For example, we may need algorithms to extract not only explicit references to the past (as in the form of temporal expressions such as past years), but also implicit historical references embedded in a text (e.g. mentions of historical persons, events).

In terms of applications, topic models can be used to assist the estimation of the *focus time* of Web documents, thus improving temporal information retrieval [3, 13]. Focus time (in contrast to document timestamp) is defined as the union of time periods to which the content of the document refers. For example, the focus time of an article about the attack on Pearl Harbor would be December 7th, 1941. Given topic models for each past year, one can estimate the focus time of a document by inspecting its probability distribution over topics. With the estimated focus time documents matching implicit time frames behind user queries can be retrieved.

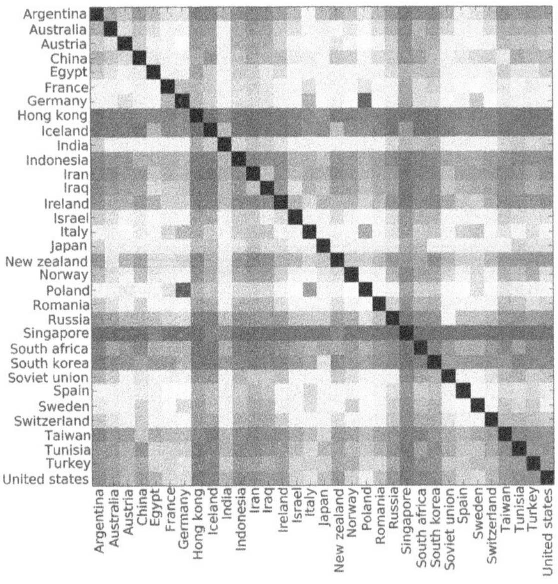

Figure 8: A similarity matrix of countries obtained by comparing their topic distributions in each year. A red cell indicates high similarity, while a blue cell indicates low similarity. Similarity is measured by the reciprocal of the KL-divergence between two topic distributions.

6. CONCLUSIONS

History plays an important role in our society. It is a subject that is taught since early stages of education in most nations. Computational history as a interdisciplinary field that aims at harnessing computational power to support history analysis is very appealing. In this paper, we described our effort in this direction in the context of collective social memories, and presented some interesting results obtained by applying text mining techniques to a large scale corpus of news articles. In the future, we plan to extend our work in the directions mentioned above.

7. ACKNOWLEDGMENTS

This research was partially supported by the MEXT Grant-in-Aid for Young Scientists B (#22700096) "Towards time-focused Web Search and Mining".

8. REFERENCES

[1] J. Allan. *Topic Detection and Tracking: Event-based Information Organization.* Kluwer Academic Publishers, Norwell, MA, USA, 2002.

[2] O. Alonso, M. Gertz, and R. Baeza-Yates. Clustering and exploring search results using timeline constructions. In *CIKM '09*, pages 97–106, 2009.

[3] O. Alonso, J. Strötgen, R. Baeza-Yates, and M. Gertz. Temporal information retrieval: Challenges and opportunities. In *TWAW '11*.

[4] K. Berberich, S. J. Bedathur, M. Sozio, and G. Weikum. Bridging the Terminology Gap in Web Archive Search. In *WebDB '09*, 2009.

[5] D. M. Blei and J. D. Lafferty. Dynamic topic models. In *ICML '06*, pages 113–120, 2006.

[6] D. M. Blei, A. Y. Ng, and M. I. Jordan. Latent dirichlet allocation. *J. Mach. Learn. Res.*, 3:993–1022, March 2003.

[7] W. B. Cavnar and J. M. Trenkle. N-Gram-Based Text Categorization. In *SDAIR-94*, pages 161–175, 1994.

[8] P. Conenrton. *How Societies Remember.* Cambridge University Press, 1989.

[9] M. Cooper, J. Foote, A. Girgensohn, and L. Wilcox. Temporal event clustering for digital photo collections. *ACM Trans. Multimedia Comput. Commun. Appl.*, 1:269–288, August 2005.

[10] H. Ebbinghaus. *Uber das Gedchtnis. Untersuchungen zur experimentellen Psychologie.* Duncker and Humblot, Leipzig, 1885.

[11] M. Halbwachs. *On collective memory.* The University of Chicago Press, 1992.

[12] D. Hall, D. Jurafsky, and C. D. Manning. Studying the history of ideas using topic models. In *EMNLP '08*, pages 363–371, 2008.

[13] A. Jatowt, Y. Kawai, and K. Tanaka. Calculating Content Recency based on Timestamped and Non-Timestamped Sources for Supporting Page Quality Estimation. In *SAC '11*, pages 1156–1163, 2011.

[14] N. Kanhabua and K. Nørvåg. Exploiting time-based synonyms in searching document archives. In *JCDL '10*, pages 79–88, 2010.

[15] D. Lazer *et al.* Computational social science. *Science*, 323(5915):721–723, 2009.

[16] I. Mani and G. Wilson. Robust temporal processing of news. In *ACL '00*, pages 69–76, 2000.

[17] C. Manning and H. Schutze. *Foundations of Statistical Natural Language Processing.* MIT Press, Cambridge, MA, 1999.

[18] B. Martins, H. Manguinhas and J. Borbinha. Extracting and Exploring the Geo-Temporal Semantics of Textual Resources. In *ICSC '08*, pages 1–9, 2008.

[19] J.-B. Michel *et al.* Quantitative Analysis of Culture Using Millions of Digitized Books. *Science*, 331(6014):176–182, January 2011.

[20] P. Nora. Between Memory and History. In *Representations*, volume 26, pages 7–25, 1989.

[21] B. Pang and L. Lee. Opinion Mining and Sentiment Analysis. *Found. Trends Inf. Retr.*, 2(1-2):1–135, 2008.

[22] A. Qamra, B. Tseng, and E. Y. Chang. Mining blog stories using community-based and temporal clustering. In *CIKM '06*, pages 58–67, 2006.

[23] D. Shahaf and C. Guestrin. Connecting the dots between news articles. In *KDD '10*, pages 623–632, 2010.

[24] J. Strötgen and G. Michael. TimeTrails: a system for exploring spatio-temporal information in documents. In *VLDB '10*, pages 1569–1572, 2010.

[25] N. Tahmasebi, K. Niklas, T. Theuerkauf and T. Risse. Using Word Sense Discrimination on Historic Document Collections. In *JCDL '10*, pages 89–98, 2010.

[26] Y. Takahashi, H. Ohshima, M. Yamamaoto, H. Iwasaki, S. Oyama, and K. Tanaka. Evaluating significance of historical entities based on tempo-spatial impacts analysis using wikipedia link structure. In *HT '11*, pages 83–92, 2011.

[27] M. Verhagen and J. Pustejovsky. Temporal processing with the tarsqi toolkit. In *COLING '08*, pages 189–192, 2008.

[28] X. Wang and A. McCallum. Topics over time: a non-markov continuous-time model of topical trends. In *KDD '06*, pages 424–433, 2006.

[29] X. Zhu, Z. Ghahramani, and J. Lafferty. Time-sensitive dirichlet process mixture models. Technical report, Carnegie Mellon University, 2005.

Combining Machine Learning and Human Judgment in Author Disambiguation*

Yanan Qian[1], Yunhua Hu[2], Jianling Cui[3], Qinghua Zheng[1], Zaiqing Nie[2],
[1] MOE KLINNS Lab and SKLMS Lab, Xi'an Jiaotong University, Xi'an 710049, P.R.China
[2]Microsoft Research Asia, No. 5 Danling Street, Haidian District, Beijing 100080, P.R China
[3] College of Software, Nankai University, Tianjin 300071, P.R China
ynqian@yahoo.cn, {yuhu, znie}@microsoft.com, jianlingcui@126.com, qhzheng@mail.xjtu.edu.cn

ABSTRACT

Author disambiguation in digital libraries becomes increasingly difficult as the number of publications and consequently the number of ambiguous author names keep growing. The fully automatic author disambiguation approach could not give satisfactory results due to the lack of signals in many cases. Furthermore, human judgment on the basis of automatic algorithms is also not suitable because the automatically disambiguated results are often mixed and not understandable for humans. In this paper, we propose a Labeling Oriented Author Disambiguation approach, called LOAD, to combine machine learning and human judgment together in author disambiguation. LOAD exploits a framework which consists of high precision clustering, high recall clustering, and top dissimilar clusters selection and ranking. In the framework, supervised learning algorithms are used to train the similarity functions between publications and a clustering algorithm is further applied to generate clusters. To validate the effectiveness and efficiency of the proposed LOAD approach, comprehensive experiments are conducted. Comparing to conventional author disambiguation algorithms, the LOAD yields much more accurate results to assist human labeling. Further experiments show that the LOAD approach can save labeling time dramatically.

Categories and Subject Descriptors

H.3.3 [**Information Storage and Retrieval**]: Digital Libraries; D.2.8 [**Database Management**]: Database applications

General Terms

Algorithms, Experimentation

Keywords

Author Disambiguation, User Contribution, Human Judgment

1. INTRODUCTION

In digital libraries, author disambiguation becomes increasingly difficult as the number of publications continuously grows and so does the number of authors with ambiguous names. Previous research aimed to solve the problem in a fully automatic way. Unfortunately, in current digital libraries, the information about publications is always insufficient, and the rapid increase of digital content also makes the manual creation of metadata highly costly. Fully automatic author disambiguation could not give satisfactory results in this situation. How to leverage limited human efforts to solve the author disambiguation problem becomes more and more important. In this paper, we propose a Labeling Oriented Author Disambiguation approach to solve the problem in a novel and efficient way.

We have been developing Microsoft Academic Search [1] to help scientists and students locate research publications. The publications include papers, books, patents, etc. By integrating information about tens of millions of publications from publishers, CrossRef and the web, we face serious author disambiguation problem. For example, in our system, we find that there are 117 different authors (before 24th Octber, 2010) named 'Lei Zhang'. Due to the incomplete and inconsistent nature of the data, it is impossible for fully automatic disambiguation algorithms to correctly assign the publications to all different 'Lei Zhang's.

A user contribution feature has recently been developed to change the situation. The feature supports users to manually correct the results output by fully automatic disambiguation algorithms. However, we find the manual labeling process is still very time-consuming and tedious. Given that in the large scale digital libraries the number of ambiguous names is huge, it is really not suitable for humans to correct errors made by the automatic algorithm.

In this paper, we propose a novel Labeling Oriented Author Disambiguation approach, called LOAD, to conquer the author disambiguation challenges in construction of digital libraries (or academic search engines) together with users. The key ideas are: 1) Find High Precision Clusters (HPCs) for each author to change the labeling granularity from individual publications to clusters; 2) Cluster the found HPCs into High Recall Clusters (HRCs) to place all publications of one author into the same cluster. Thus the labeling for one author can be limited within a narrow scope; 3) Select the best HPC in each HRC as the starting point to cover different important authors for labeling. Other similar HPCs can be re-ranked for further labeling.

To achieve the goals of the proposed LOAD approach, machine learning algorithms are used. First, we exploit a supervised learning algorithm to get similarity between publications, i.e., judge whether two publications belong to the same author. More specifically, two classifiers for HPC and HRC are trained respectively and various rich features are investigated. On the basis of learned sim-

*This work was conducted at Microsoft Research Asia when the first author visited there.

[1]http://academic.research.microsoft.com

CIKM'11, October 24–28, 2011, Glasgow, Scotland, UK.
Copyright 2011 ACM 978-1-4503-0717-8/11/10 ...$10.00.

ilarities, a clustering algorithm is further applied to generate final clusters. Comprehensive experiments are conducted to empirically verify the effectiveness of our proposed approach. One public dataset contains about 7,000 publications from DBLP and two internal datasets contains about 6,000 publications are used. Correct authors for all publications were labeled by manual. A typical conventional automatic author disambiguation algorithm is taken as the baseline. The results are obtained by applying the algorithm in the real-world academic search engine in which we do not know which names are ambiguous and which are unambiguous. Our algorithm achieves promising results on ambiguous names while keeps little harm to unambiguous names. For HPC, the experimental results show that it improves precision from 93.72% to more than 99% on average. For HRC, the recall is also improved from 75.43% to 91.85% on average. The results also show that the LOAD can improve the human labeling efficiency by about 10 to 30 times compared to the baseline.

The rest of the paper is organized as follows. Section 2 introduces related work. Section 3 describes motivation of our work. Section 4 explains the proposed approach and Section 5 presents experimental results. Section 6 concludes the paper with remarks while proposing future work.

2. RELATED WORK

Automatic Author Disambiguation for academic publications has gained continuous attention from research community for years. In this section, we will introduce related works of problem formulization, various frameworks and features used in automatic author disambiguation.

Most previous work formulized author disambiguation problem as a statistical learning problem. Han et al. formulated it as a clustering problem and solved it by a model-based k-means algorithm in [4] and by a K-way spectral clustering algorithm in [5]. They also viewed the problem as a classification problem in [6]. The main idea is to train a classifier to identify whether two publications belong to the same author. A graph partition based approach using Quasi-Clique is proposed by [2]. Treeratpituk and Giles [10] also proposed a random forest algorithm.

The framework for author disambiguation has also been studied comprehensively. On et al. [2] proposed a two-step framework which first divides publications into small blocks to reduce computational cost. Several work such as [1] focused on the blocking approaches. Fan et al. [3] proposed the graph-based framework for author disambiguation. However, performance issue in the graph framework is a big problem. Wang et al. [11] lightened the difficulty by changing clustering on papers to clustering on atomic clusters. But for digital libraries with millions of publications, graph based framework is still not the best choice. Huang et al. [7] proposed another two-step framework for large-scale author disambiguation. It learned the similarity function on pair of publications in the first step and performs clustering using the learned similarity in the second step. We adopt a similar framework and the difference is that we improve the framework by splitting its first step into high precision similarity learning and high recall similarity learning.

Features used in author disambiguation are also widely studied. Metadata including automatic extracted data are taken as features in many work [5, 10]. Tan et al. [9] introduced a useful feature named Inverse Host Frequency (IHF) by using search engine for author disambiguation. Song et al. [8] employed PLSA and LDA to get research topics for authors and then disambiguate them. All of the above work did not investigate the features related to high precision classification or high recall classification which are proposed in this paper.

3. MOTIVATION OF LOAD

3.1 Problems in Automatic Author Disambiguation

Fully automatic author disambiguation is infeasible due to the data quality problem and the data sparsity problem.

Data quality problem is very common in large scale digital libraries which often integrate data from different sources such as CrossRef, pdf files, and etc. However, such data often contain errors, conflict with each other, or have many variations. The data quality problem could confuse the automatic algorithms a lot and harm the disambiguation accuracy greatly.

Data sparsity problem means many publications lack necessary metadata information. For example, it is proved that email and affiliation are very useful for finding correct author. However, in our system, only about 10% publications have the email metadata and 23% have affiliation information. Without necessary signals, author disambiguation cannot be fully solved automatically.

3.2 Problems in Human Labeling after Automatic Disambiguation

One possible solution for fully solving the author disambiguation problem is to leverage human judgment to correct the errors of automatic algorithms. To valid the possibility, we perform a case study on authors named 'Lei Zhang'. The algorithm proposed in [6] is used before human labeling. 117 different authors are split into 141 clusters. Three human labelers were asked to correct the results. Finally they spent 7 hours on average to finish the task. Part (a) in Figure 1 illustrates the situation for human labeling. The human labeling process is very time-consuming for several reasons: First, publications in each cluster are not pure enough and human labelers still need to check them one by one. For example, the most diverse cluster contains publications from 27 different authors. This process is nearly equal to the fully manual labeling. Second, as one author's publications could be assigned to several different clusters, human labelers need to go through many clusters to find all results. For the 'Lei Zhang' from PolyU (Hongkong Polytechnic University), his publications are assigned to 8 different authors. So at least 8 clusters need to be checked one by one to finish the labeling.

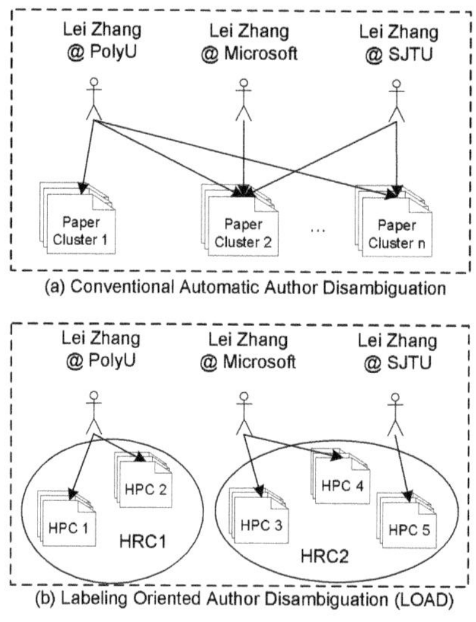

Figure 1: Comparison between Conventional Author Disambiguation and LOAD

From the discussions above, we can find that to fully solve the author disambiguation problem, we need to design an algorithm to assist human labeling efficiently from these perspectives: 1) Most ambiguous cases need to be solved by automatic author disambiguation before human labeling. 2) Human labeling need to be conducted on bigger granularity rather than on each individual publication. 3) Human labeling need to be limited within a narrow range rather than the whole publication list. 4) Human labeling need to be started from some good starting points.

4. OUR APPROACH

In this section, we propose an approach named LOAD for author disambiguation. First we provide an overview of the LOAD and how we formulate it. Then we study a key problem, i.e., the pairwise classification with rich features in LOAD.

4.1 Problem Description and Formulation

4.1.1 Description

We start from an example to show the framework in Figure 2. Step 0 is the initial state which shows several publications authored by 'Lei Zhang' at PolyU, 'Lei Zhang' at Microsoft, and 'Lei Zhang' at SJTU. In Step 1, all publications are clustered into 5 clusters. Notice that each HPC only contains publications of one author here. In Step 2, HPCs are further clustered into several HRCs. Publications of both 'Lei Zhang' at Microsoft and 'Lei Zhang' at SJTU are placed into the same cluster HRC_2. In Step 3, HPC_1 of 'Lei Zhang' at PolyU and HPC_4 of 'Lei Zhang' at Microsoft are selected as starting points for labeling. Human labeling starts from the

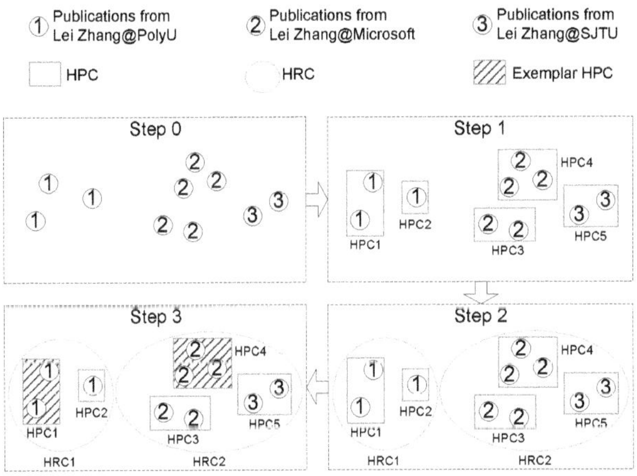

Figure 2: Working Process of Three Steps Framework

results of Step 3. Once we labeled HPC_1 in HRC_1 as publications of 'Lei Zhang' at PolyU, we can easily find his rest publications from HPC_2 in the same HRC. Meanwhile, once we labeled HPC_4 as publications of 'Lei Zhang' at Microsoft, HPC_3 is ranked higher for labeling. When all his publications are labeled, we can find that the rest publications in HPC_5 belongs exactly to 'Lei Zhang' at SJTU. The output of Step 3 is also shown as Part (b) in Figure 1. Comparing to the confused cases shown as Part (a) in Figure 1, Part(b) is much easier for human labeling. The comparison shows the benefit of our proposed LOAD approach intuitively.

The three-step framework of LOAD is: (1) High Precision Clustering: It tries to place one authors' publications into as fewer clusters as possible, while tries to keep all publications in each cluster written by the same author. Thus, human labeling can be conducted on clusters rather than on individual publications. (2) High Recall Clustering: It is conducted on the results of HPCs, it is different from HPC in two aspects: First, the goal of HRC is trying to put all publications of one author into the same cluster. Second, each HPC is totally contained in a HRC. (3) Top Dissimilar HPCs Selection and Ranking: after we get the HPCs and HRCs, we can select the best HPC in each HRC as the exemplar clusters for human labeling.

4.1.2 Formulation

Now we formulize the concepts and goals of LOAD in this section. Given a set of publications $X = \{x_1, x_2, \cdots, x_n\}$, each publication x_i has p authors $xa_i = \{xa_{i1}, xa_{i2}, \ldots, xa_{ip}\}$. Using the name blocking method described in [7], publications can be first clustered into blocks according to author name string similarity. So in each name block we only need to consider the disambiguation problem for one author name from each paper. We use $Y = \{y_1, y_2, \ldots, y_n\}$ to indicate the concerned author of related publications in X respectively, $y_i \in xa_i, i \in [1, n]$. Each y_i correspond to one of the real world authors $A = \{a_1, a_2, \ldots, a_h\}$. Then each step in LOAD can be formulized as follows.

High Precision Clustering

Assume n publications $X = \{x_1, x_2, \cdots, x_n\}$ are clustered into l clusters $C = \{c_1, c_2, \cdots, c_l\}$. The goal is to maximize the overall similarity V_{HPC} in Equation (1) while keeping the high precision of each cluster. The c_p and c_q here are HPC clusters.

$$\begin{aligned} V_{HPC} &= \sum_{p=1}^{l} \sum_{x_i, x_j \in c_p} S\left(x_i, x_j\right) \\ s.t. \quad & \forall p, x_i, x_j \in c_p, \; y_i = y_j \\ \forall i, j, p, q \quad & \max_{x_i \in c_p, x_j \in c_q, p \neq q} \left\{S(x_i, x_j)\right\} < \min_{x_i, x_j \in c_p} \left\{S(x_i, x_j)\right\} \end{aligned} \quad (1)$$

High Recall Clustering

The goal of step 2 is to place all publications of one author into only one cluster. It can be formulated in the similar way like the first step. We process high recall clustering by maximizing the similarity V_{HRC} in Equation (2) while ensuring the diversity between each cluster. The c_p and c_q here are the HRC clusters.

$$\begin{aligned} V_{HRC} &= \sum_{p=1}^{l} \sum_{x_i, x_j \in c_p} S\left(x_i, x_j\right) \\ s.t. \quad & \forall p, q, x_i \in c_p, x_j \in c_q, p \neq q, \; y_i \neq y_j \\ \forall i, j, p, q \quad & \max_{x_i \in c_p, x_j \in c_q, p \neq q} \left\{S(x_i, x_j)\right\} < \min_{x_i, x_j \in c_p} \left\{S(x_i, x_j)\right\} \end{aligned} \quad (2)$$

Top Dissimilar HPCs Selection and Ranking

For all HPCs in one HRC, we pick up the best HPC, i.e., HPC^* as an exemplar cluster for human labeling. We formally define the task in Equation (3). It means the HPCs with bigger size and higher overall inner similarity will have better chances of being selected. These exemplar clusters often corresponds to important authors for they often have more and correlated publications.

$$HPC^* = \arg\max_{c_p} \sum_{x_i, x_j \in c_p, i \neq j} S(x_i, x_j) \quad (3)$$

Once people select one HPC, the rest HPCs in that HRC can be re-ranked according to the similarity with the labeled HPC. The similarity can be calculated in Equation (4).

$$S(c_p, c_q) = \sum_{x_i \in c_p, x_j \in c_q, p \neq q} S(x_i, x_j) \quad (4)$$

Through the reranking approach, users need only to check whether top ranked HPC can be merged with labeled HPCs, which further reduces the human labeling efforts.

4.1.3 Learning Algorithms

The object function in Section 4.1.2 is a little difficult to learn, as our goal is to apply the algorithm in the large scale digital library, we need to find a less optimization but more efficient algorithm. In this section, we first analyze the formulations and simplify them into two sub-problems, the pairwise similarity learning problem and the clustering problem. Then we introduce the sub-problems respectively.

Formulations Simplification

We take Equation (1) as example to analysis how to simplify the optimization process. The goal of (1) is to place publications of the same author into the same cluster. At the same time, avoid to place publications of different authors into the same cluster. We propose to simplify the formulation into two steps by combining the approaches proposed by [2, 6, 7]. First, a similarity function between two publications is trained. Then, we can cluster the publications according to the similarity generated by the learned similarity function. Both Equation (1) and (2) can be approximated with these two steps. As explained in Section 4.1.1, HPC and HRC should be trained separately. Section 4.2 will discuss the details.

Pairwise Similarity Learning

Many previous work studied the problem of training a weighted similarity function [4, 5, 6, 7]. Our approach exploits the similar idea. The key problem is to find an adequate function which can represent the similarity/dissimilarity between the publication pairs. In the proposed approach, we view the similarity calculation between publication pairs as a classification problem. First, information about a publication pair is represented in a feature vector $\overrightarrow{x}$. Then a pairwise classification model is trained to judge whether the two publications are similar. We used the linear model showed in Equation (5) to compute the similarity for each paper pair. The weight $\overrightarrow{w}$ and threshold b are trained by SVM model through SVM-light toolkit [2].

$$f(\overrightarrow{x}) = <\overrightarrow{x}, \overrightarrow{w}> - b \tag{5}$$

Clustering

How to cluster publications efficiently in large scale digital libraries is a big challenge. In some previous work [11], the agglomerative clustering algorithm has been proved to be very effective and efficient. So we exploit it as our clustering algorithm. Yes we can also try more powerful clustering algorithms. However, to show the idea of our proposed approach, only this clustering algorithm is tried.

4.2 Pairwise Classification with Rich Features

In this section, we discuss in detail about how we conduct the high precision clustering and high recall clustering with rich features respectively. As explained in Section 4.1.3, the clustering algorithm used in both steps are the same. So we only focus on how to learn two classification models effectively here.

4.2.1 Features for High Precision Classification

Pairwise classification for HPC is to judge whether two publications are authored by the same person, so all features are defined via comparison of a pair of publications. In order to achieve high precision, we drill down features into different value scales. Two types of measures, i.e., SIF (Shared Item Frequency) and IPF (Inverse Publication Frequency) are also defined inspired by the idea of TF and IDF.

Suppose a publication has a list of metadata such as a list of coauthors and a list of references, we define SIF to represent the similarity of two lists I_1 and I_2:

$$SIF(I_1, I_2) = \frac{|I_1 \cap I_2|}{\sqrt{|I_1||I_2|}} \tag{6}$$

From another perspective, IPF is defined to discount the importance of common features. Suppose $A = I_1, I_2, \cdots, I_n$ is the set of all feature list, i is a feature that appears in one or several list, IPF_i is defined as follows:

$$IPF(i) = \log \frac{|A|}{|\{I_k : i \in I_k\}|} \tag{7}$$

The IPF to compare two lists is defined as the sum of shared IPF features.

$$IPF(I_1, I_2) = \sum_{i \in I_1 \cap I_2} IPF(i) \tag{8}$$

Referred to the above definitions, we adopted the strict comparison and IPF features of the metadata "name", "email", "affiliation" and "homepage" between two authors; also, the SIF and IPF features of "coauthor name", "coauthor email", "coauthor affiliation", "coauthor homepage", "title bigram", "reference" and "download link" are extracted. Besides, a binary feature "self citation" which represents whether one publication cited the other, or vice versa are extracted; the "publishing year" interval between two papers are also considered.

4.2.2 Features for the High Recall Classification

The high precision classifier aims at collecting high confidence signals while the high recall classifier aims at collecting as much signals as possible. The basic high recall features are in accordance with high precision features. Here, we only list the differences.

Email: We split the email into prefix and suffix by '@'. It is because some authors might change the email suffixes but tend to reserve the same prefixes. Besides, the email suffix might reflect the author's organization. When comparing, common email suffixes (e.g. @gmail.com, @yahoo.com) are removed.

Affiliation: The affiliation information is segmented and parsed into three groups: university, department and group name. We will compare these three groups of information separately. Some heuristic rules are defined to segment and parse the variations of affiliation information.

Homepage: Authors from the same organization often share the same domain for their homepage. Thus, 'homepage' is further split into domain and suffix for comparison.

Coauthor related feature: For the coauthor email, affiliation and homepage, similar parsing is performed to obtain more information.

Other features: for all other metadata, IPF features are removed to ensure a high recall.

5. EXPERIMENTS

5.1 Experiment Setup

5.1.1 Data Sets

Two internal data sets and one public data set are used in our experiments. Authors of publications were manually labeled by human experts.

CS data set: The CS(Case Study) data set is created when we conduct the case study for author disambiguation. Publications in this set are highly ambiguous. To avoid the case that the disambiguation algorithm might harm unambiguous authors, we also added some unambiguous authors here.

[2]http://svmlight.joachims.org/

UE data set: As mentions before, our system opens a feature for users to edit and correct author's publication list. All such user edited data are collected as UE(User Edited) data set.

DBLP data set: The DBLP (Digital Bibliography & Library Project) dataset is an open source data set[3]. There are 9,160 labeled publications in it. The publications without any metadata in our system are removed. After the cleaning, 7,434 publications are taken as the data set.

Basic statistics of three data sets are given in Table 1. As one author can have several different name variations, number of authors can be less than the number of names. UE is just the case.

Table 1: Statistical Information of Three Data Sets

Statistics	CS	UE	DBLP	*Total*
# of publications	1,322	4,624	7,434	*13,380*
# of names	54	1,199	739	*1,992*
# of authors	171	1,052	1,267	*2,490*
Avg/Max authors per name	3.96/117	1.01/6	1.71/17	*2.23/117*
Avg/Max names per author	1.25/4	1.15/5	1.00/2	*1.13/4*
Avg/Max publications per authors	7.73/323	4.40/131	5.89/129	*6.01/323*

5.1.2 Evaluation Metrics

As LOAD is to help users to edit the publication list, we evaluate it from several perspectives of user contribution.

First, we evaluate the results by using accuracy.

The evaluation measure is described in Equation (9).

$$Accuracy = \frac{\#\ fully\ correct\ clusters}{\#\ all\ clusters} \quad (9)$$

If one publication in the cluster is incorrect, the whole cluster will be taken as incorrect. For HPC cluster, if all publications in it belong to the same author, the cluster is counted as 'Correct', otherwise 'Incorrect'. For HRC cluster, if all authors in it have no publications in other clusters, this cluster is counted as 'Correct', otherwise 'Incorrect'.

Second, we evaluate the number of publications in HPCs and number of authors in HRCs.

For HPCs, to avoid the case that each HPC contains only one publication, we evaluate the number of publications in them. For HRCs, to avoid the case that all publications are placed into the same HRC, we evaluate the number of authors in them.

5.1.3 Baseline

We take the human labeling after conventional automatic author disambiguation as the baseline. In baseline, we reduce the two steps (clustering of HPCs and HRCs) in LOAD into one step, and then cluster the publications using the same algorithm in LOAD. Moreover, the baseline uses both HPC related and HRC related features. Strictly speaking, the baseline is more powerful than conventional automatic author disambiguation algorithms.

5.2 Evaluation of LOAD

5.2.1 Evaluate HPC and HRC

We first evaluate the accuracy by taking the whole cluster as a base unit. Results are shown in Table 2 and Table 3. Notice that the baseline methods in two tables are actually the same while the results are different because: Table 2 lists the results of finding "whether all publications in the cluster belong to the same author" while Table 3 lists the results of finding "whether all publications of authors can be find in the same cluster".

Table 2: Accuracy Comparison of HPC and Baseline

Method	CS	UE	DBLP	*Average*
HPC	99.80%	100.00%	99.94%	*99.91%*
Baseline	92.95%	95.94%	92.29%	*93.72%*

Table 3: Accuracy Comparison of HRC and Baseline

Method	CS	UE	DBLP	*Average*
HRC	87.80%	95.38%	92.38%	*91.85%*
Baseline	71.88%	80.67%	73.73%	*75.43%*

From the results we can see that the accuracy of both HPC and HRC are greatly improved comparing to the baseline. In three data sets, HPCs archive nearly 100% precision. HRCs also have much better accuracy than baseline.

The average publication number in each cluster for HPC, HRC, and baseline is shown in Table 4. The results of HRC are comparable with those in the baseline. We also compared the average author number in each cluster for HPC, HRC, and baseline. The results are shown in Table 5. Average author number in HRC is 1.43. That is to say, labelers only need to label one or two authors in each HRC.

Table 4: Comparison of Number of Publications in Clusters

Method	CS	UE	DBLP	*Average*
HPC	3.38	2.27	4.22	*3.29*
HRC	8.81	4.39	5.94	*6.38*
Baseline	5.81	3.71	5.47	*5.00*

5.2.2 Evaluate Human Labeling Efficiency

To investigate how much labeling time can be saved through LOAD, we compare it with two other methods, i.e., fully manual labeling and labeling after conventional automatic disambiguation (baseline). For simplicity, the comparison is performed in a publication list with the same author name. We take the total number of publication as n, number of authors as m, reading time for each publication as r, comparing time for each publication as c, d_i is the discount factor in the ith method.

In the first approach, human labelers need to go through all the publications. For each publication, they first need to read the basic information, and then compare the current publication's authorship with previous labeled authors. The reading time can be estimated as $O(r \cdot n)$ and comparing time as $O(c \cdot n \cdot m \cdot d_1)$ here.

In the second approach, as one cluster may contain several authors' publications while an author's publications may be assigned to several different clusters, labelers still need to conduct labeling on individual publications in all clusters. The reading time is still $O(r \cdot n)$ and the comparing time is $O(c \cdot n \cdot m \cdot d_2)$.

In the third approach (LOAD), labelers can view the whole HPC as one unit. Let average size of HPC be n_1, the estimated reading time will be $O(r \cdot n \cdot \frac{1}{n_1})$. Let average size of HRC be n_2, the average HPC number in each HRC becomes $\frac{n_2}{n_1}$. As the comparison can be limited within the HRC, the number of comparison is $(\frac{n_2}{n_1})^2$. Fortunately, HPCs are ranked in LOAD. So each unlabeled HPC need only to be compared with the previous labeled

[3]http://dblp.uni-trier.de/xml/

Table 5: Comparison of Number of Authors in Clusters

Method	CS	UE	DBLP	*Average*
HPC	1.01	1.00	1.02	*1.01*
HRC	1.82	1.21	1.26	*1.43*
Baseline	1.20	1.18	1.11	*1.16*

one. The number of comparison can be further approximated as $\frac{n_2}{n_1} \cdot d_3$. Finally the overall comparing time can be estimated as $O(c \cdot \frac{n}{n_2} \cdot \frac{n_2}{n_1} \cdot d_3) = O(c \cdot n \cdot \frac{1}{n_1} \cdot d_3)$.

Table 6 lists the estimated time for three methods. It also list the real labeling time for 'Lei Zhang'. Compared to the baseline, LOAD improves the label efficiency by about 11 times.

Table 6: Labeling Time Comparison

Approaches	Estimated Time	Labeling Time for 'Lei Zhang'
Manual	$O(r \cdot n + c \cdot n \cdot m \cdot d_1)$	102,000
Baseline	$O(r \cdot n + c \cdot n \cdot m \cdot d_2)$	26,400
LOAD	$O((r \cdot n \cdot \frac{1}{n_1} + c \cdot n \cdot \frac{1}{n_1} \cdot d_3)$	2,460

We also estimate the parameters during the case study to CS data set: $r = 15$, $c = 10$, $d_1 = 0.3$, $d_2 = 0.1$, and $d_3 = 0.3$, $n_1 = 4$, $n_2 = 9$. According to the estimated time, LOAD improves the label efficiency about 30 times compared to the baseline method for 'Lei Zhang'. The gap between estimated time and labeling time is due to that LOAD cannot get 100% HRC accuracy so extra efforts are needed. Anyway, roughly speaking, LOAD can improve the human labeling efficiency about 10 to 30 times.

5.3 Experiments for Pairwise Classification with Rich Features

Pairwise classification is very important for LOAD. We conduct further experiments to validate the effectiveness of the rich features for building the high precision and the high recall classifiers.

The pairwise classification is to judge whether two publications are written by the same author. Thus, publication pairs written by the same author are taken as positive instances, otherwise pairs with the same names but belong to different authors as negative instances. We combine both CS and UE data sets described in Section 5.1 as the new pairwise data set. About 2/3 instances are randomly selected for training and the rest for testing. The total positive pairs are 37,629, negative pairs are 241,178.

The experimental results for pairwise classification are shown in Table 7.

Table 7: Evaluation Results of Pairwise Classification

Parewise classifier	Precision	Recall
HPC	99.92%	99.44%
HRC	97.76%	99.65%

Both pairwise classifiers for HPC and for HRC achieve quite high precision and recall. Although the the error will be amplified with the increase of cluster size, the very accurate results of pairwise classification can help to get the high accuracy for final results for labeling.

6. CONCLUSIONS AND FUTURE WORK

This paper proposes a novel approach named LOAD to solve the author disambiguation problem together with users. The proposed approach follows a three-step framework which is very flexible and scalable for large scale author disambiguation in digital libraries. Comparing to conventional automatic disambiguation algorithms, LOAD can improve disambiguation accuracy greatly and save a lot of labeling time for human labelers.

There are several possible directions of future work. First, it would be interesting to design an iterative process for author disambiguation. Semi-supervised learning algorithms can then be imported to improve the accuracy. Second, we need to enlarge the feature sources to improve the automatic disambiguation accuracy. Also, more directly optimization algorithms can be applied to get better results.

7. ACKNOWLEDGEMENTS

We thank Microsoft Academic Search team for their encouragements and supports. We thank Hang Li and the anonymous reviewers for their comments to this paper.

8. REFERENCES

[1] M. Bilenko, R. J. Mooney, W. W. Cohen, P. D. Ravikumar, and S. E. Fienberg. Adaptive name matching in information integration. *IEEE Intelligent Systems*, 18(5):16–23, 2003.

[2] O. Byung-won, D. Lee, J. Kang, and P. Mitra. Comparative study of name disambiguation problem using a scalable blocking-based framework. In *ACM/IEEE Joint Conference on Digital Libraries*, pages 344–353, 2005.

[3] X. Fan, J. Wang, L. Bing, L. Zhou, and W. Hu. Ghost: an effective graph-based framework for name distinction. In *International Conference on Information and Knowledge Management*, pages 1449–1450, 2008.

[4] H. Han, H. Zha, and C. L. Giles. A model-based k-means algorithm for name disambiguation. In *International Semantic Web Conference*, 2003.

[5] H. Han, H. Zha, and C. L. Giles. Name disambiguation in author citations using a k-way spectral clustering method. In *ACM/IEEE Joint Conference on Digital Libraries*, pages 334–343, 2005.

[6] H. Han, H. Zha, C. Li, K. Tsioutsiouliklis, and C. L. GILES. Two supervised learning approaches for name disambiguation in author citations. In *ACM/IEEE Joint Conference on Digital Libraries*, pages 296–305, 2004.

[7] J. Huang, S. Ertekin, and C. L. Giles. Efficient name disambiguation for large-scale databases. In *Proceedings of the 10th European Conference on Principles and Practice of Knowledge Discovery in Databases*, pages 536–544, 2006.

[8] Y. Song, J. Huang, I. G. Councill, J. Li, and C. L. Giles. Generative models for name disambiguation. In *World Wide Web Conference Series*, pages 1163–1164, 2007.

[9] Y. F. Tan, M. yen Kan, and D. Lee. Search engine driven author disambiguation. In *ACM/IEEE Joint Conference on Digital Libraries*, pages 314–315, 2006.

[10] P. Treeratpituk and C. L. Giles. Disambiguating authors in academic publications using random forests. In *ACM/IEEE Joint Conference on Digital Libraries*, pages 39–48, 2009.

[11] F. Wang, J. Li, J. Tang, J. Zhang, and K. Wang. Name disambiguation using atomic clusters. In *Proceedings of the 9th International Conference on Web-Age Information Management*, pages 357–364, 2008.

Citation Count Prediction: Learning to Estimate Future Citations for Literature

Rui Yan
Dept. of Computer Science and Technology
Peking University
Beijing 100871, P. R. China
r.yan@pku.edu.cn

Jie Tang
Dept. of Computer Science and Technology
Tsinghua University
Beijing 100871, P. R. China
jietang@tsinghua.edu.cn

Xiaobing Liu
Dept. of Computer Science and Technology
Peking University
Beijing 100871, P. R. China
lxb@net.pku.edu.cn

Dongdong Shan
Dept. of Computer Science and Technology
Peking University
Beijing 100871, P. R. China
sdd@net.pku.edu.cn

Xiaoming Li
Dept. of Computer Science and Technology
Peking University
Beijing 100871, P. R. China
lxm@pku.edu.cn

ABSTRACT

In most of the cases, scientists depend on previous literature which is relevant to their research fields for developing new ideas. However, it is not wise, nor possible, to track all existed publications because the volume of literature collection grows extremely fast. Therefore, researchers generally follow, or cite merely a small proportion of publications which they are interested in. For such a large collection, it is rather interesting to forecast which kind of literature is more likely to attract scientists' response. In this paper, we use the citations as a measurement for the popularity among researchers and study the interesting problem of Citation Count Prediction (CCP) to examine the characteristics for popularity. Estimation of possible popularity is of great significance and is quite challenging. We have utilized several features of fundamental characteristics for those papers that are highly cited and have predicted the popularity degree of each literature in the future. We have implemented a system which takes a series of features of a particular publication as input and produces as output the estimated citation counts of that article after a given time period. We consider several regression models to formulate the learning process and evaluate their performance based on the coefficient of determination (R^2). Experimental results on a real-large data set show that the best predictive model achieves a mean average predictive performance of 0.740 measured in R^2, which significantly outperforms several alternative algorithms.

Categories and Subject Descriptors

H.3 [**Information Storage and Retrieval**]: Content Analysis and Indexing; I.2 [**Artificial Intelligence**]: Natural Language Processing—*Text analysis*

CIKM'11, October 24–28, 2011, Glasgow, Scotland, UK.

General Terms

Algorithms, Experimentation, Performance

Keywords

Citation count prediction, regression models, data engineering

1. INTRODUCTION

The rapid evolution of scientific research has been creating a huge volume of publications every year, and is expected to remain in this situation within the foreseeable future. Figure 1 shows statistics on a large literature database in Computer Science.[1] Figure 1.(a) visualizes the explosive increase on the volume of publications in the past years, in particular recent years. For example, the number of publications in 2009 almost triples than that of 10 year before. Effective scientific research requires keeping up with previous literature, but it is not wise, nor possible, for researchers to track all existed publications because the volume of literature collection grows extremely fast as mentioned. Therefore, researchers generally follow, or cite merely a small proportion of publications which they are interested in. An interesting phenomenon is that some of research papers are more likely to attract scientists' response than the others. If we use citation count as the popularity of papers among academia, we have the following observation in Figure 1.(b).

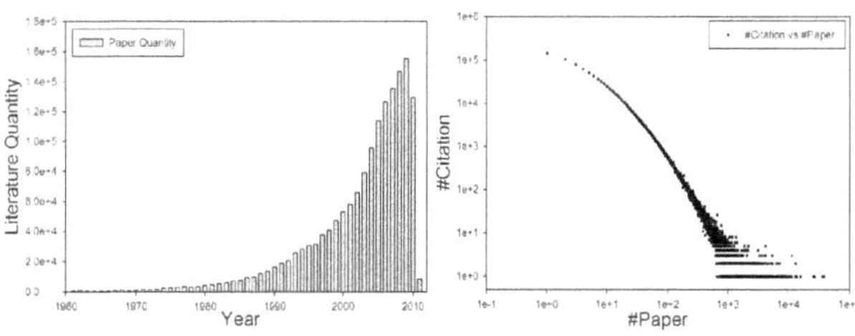

(a). The growing volume of literatures. (b). Distribution of literature citation.

Figure 1: Statistics of literature data from ArnetMiner.

[1] `http://arnetminer.org.`

It is natural to find that not all publications attract equal attention to academia. We show the citation distribution (the number of papers vs. citation counts) in the log-log plot of Figure 1.(b): the interests toward literature measured by citation counts is highly skewed. Not surprisingly, the plot follows a power law distribution. A power law relationship between two quantities x and y can be written as $y{=}ax^b$ where a and b are constants. We see that a huge number of research papers attract only a few citations, and a few research papers accumulate a large number of citations.

For the ever-growing literature collection, it is rather interesting to forecast which kind of literature is more likely to attract scientists' response. In this paper, we use the citation counts as a simple measurement for the popularity among researchers and the citation count is calculated by how many times a particular publication is cited by other articles. We study the interesting problem of Citation Count Prediction (CCP) to examine the correlative characteristics for popularity.

As a pilot study on learning to forecast future citations for literature, Citation Count Prediction faces with several challenges:

- The first challenge for CCP is to explore the truly effective features important to future citation counts from several aspects such as paper content, author expertise and venue impact. We introduce a series of features which are correlative with the number of future citations of literature;
- The second challenge for CCP is to combine all relevant features to identify the potentially interesting papers in a unified predictive model, linearly or non-linearly. Given multiple features relevant to popularity, i.e., citation counts in this study, we utilize several regression models to estimate future citations.

Our contributions are manifold by solving these challenges. In Section 2 we first define a series of features which correlate with citation counts. We then formulate citation count prediction as a learning problem and introduce several regression models to unify all possible features for prediction. We describe experiments and evaluations in Section 3, including performance comparisons and feature analysis. We briefly review previous works in Section 4 and draw conclusions in Section 5.

2. CITATION COUNT PREDICTION

2.1 Problem Definition

In this section, we first present several necessary definitions and a formal representation of the citation count prediction problem.

Citations. *Given the literature corpus* ***D****, the citation counts* $(C_T(.))$ *of a literature article* $\boldsymbol{d} \in D$ *is defined as:*

$$\begin{aligned} citing(d) &= \{d' \in D : d' cites\ d\} \\ C_T(d) &= |citing(d)| \end{aligned} \quad (1)$$

Learning task: Given a set of article features, $\vec{X} = x_1, x_2, \ldots, x_n$, our goal is to learn a predictive function f to predict the citation counts of an article d after a give time period Δt. Formally, we have

$$f(d|\vec{X}, \Delta t) \rightarrow C_T(d|\Delta t) \quad (2)$$

To learn the predictive model, we have investigated multiple relevant factors such as paper content, author expertise and venue impact. It is also important to find unified models which are able to consider all the features simultaneously. We introduce both aspects in the following subsections.

2.2 Feature Definition

2.2.1 *Topic Rank*

Topics have long been investigated as a significant feature for literature contents [11]. We utilize the unsupervised Latent Dirichlet Allocation [2] to discover topics for our corpus as it has been applied successfully to many content analysis tasks, and implementations are freely available[2]. We empirically train a 100-topic models on our corpus - the top words for a few of the sample topics are shown in Table 1.

Table 1: Top words from selected LDA sample topics after stopword removal.

Topic	Representative words
00	distribution probability value random probabilistic expected
09	query information search semantic retrieval document
12	mobile network wireless nodes communication device
84	data mining patterns analysis association set
97	programming formal language specification verification logic

Our topic feature works by inspecting the probability distribution over topics assigned to a literature article d. That is, for each of our 100 topics, our topic model calculates $p(topic_i|d)$, the inferred probability of topic i in document d. The topic distribution $\mathcal{T}(d)$ over all topics in document d is then:

$$\mathcal{T}(d) = \{p(topic_1|d), p(topic_2|d), \ldots, p(topic_{100}|d)\}$$

To calculate the total citation counts of a particular topic from article d, denoted by $C_T(topic_i|d)$, we distribute the citations of the article $C_T(d)$ according to the topic distribution $\mathcal{T}(d)$, i.e., $C_T(topic_i|d) = C_T(d) \times p(topic_i|d)$ and hence we obtain the citations of all 100 topics by using:

$$C_T(topic_i) = \sum_{d \in D} C_T(topic_i|d) \quad (3)$$

where D is the whole literature collection. We rank topics by average citation counts, namely topic "popularity".

2.2.2 *Diversity*

We obtain a notion of the breadth of an article from its topic distributions. This is important for identifying methodology papers, which are often cited by a wider topical range of articles. When an article has a vast range of audience, it is likely to be cited by authors from various research fields, and hence attract high citation counts. To measure the topical breadth of an article, we calculate the entropy of the document's topic distribution:

$$Diversity(d) = \sum_{i=1}^{|\mathcal{T}|=100} -p(topic_i|d) \cdot \log p(topic_i|d) \quad (4)$$

2.2.3 *Recency*

Temporal dimension has long been proved to be significant in literature studies [1, 19]. Intuitively, the citation counts accumulate as time passes by, thus a measure of the age of an article is assumed to be important. We include as a feature the number of years since the article was published. We expect a positive correlation on temporal recency - the longer an article is published, the more citations it may receive.

[2]We use Stanford TMT (`http://nlp.stanford.edu/software/tmt/`), with default settings for all model parameters.

2.2.4 H-Index

The h-index is useful which attempts to measure both the productivity and impact of the published work of a scientist [8]. The index is based on the set of the scientist's most cited papers and the number of citations received in others' publications. Besides, h-index has been proved to have measuring power of scientific output and impact of a researcher [8]. Therefore, we consider h-index as a candidate feature to predict citation counts.

2.2.5 Author Rank

We try to identify the correlation between author rank and average citation count. Sometimes, the "fame" of an author's name ensures the amount of citations. Each author has his/her own expectation of citation counts. We calculate all authors according to their average citation counts and assign each of them a unique rank position number.

2.2.6 Productivity

According to [1], authors have inclination to cite papers they have written themselves. Intuitively, the more productive an author is, the larger chances for his/her papers to be cited. We hence assume the productivity of an author is relevant to the citation counts, due to the self-citation behavior analysis from previous studies.

2.2.7 Sociality

From the author social factor studies in [1], researchers tend to cite papers from whom the author(s) have co-authored. Thus, it is natural to assume that the paper from a widely connected author has a larger probability to be cited by his/her wide variety of co-authors. A straightforward and simple measurement is to count the Number of Co-Authors (NOCA) and we assume the correlation between the number of co-authors and average citation counts.

2.2.8 Authority

A unique social network for academia is established from the "citing - cited" relationships among literature articles. Publications carry with author authorities: a widely cited paper indicates peer acknowledgements, and hence indicates authority. We transmit paper authority to all its authors. We first build a graph of $G_a(V, E)$, where V is the set of vertices and each vertex v_i in V represents a literature paper and E denotes the *citing-cited* linkage. The citing-cited graph has directions. The out-degrees measure how many times a paper is cited while in-degrees indicate the references of a particular paper. When there is a citing-cited relationship between two papers, we add a link into the graph. We use standard cosine similarity between two papers to weigh the linkage in the graph, i.e., $aff(v_i, v_j) = sim_{cos}(v_i, v_j)$. The transition probability between v_i and v_j is defined by normalizing the corresponding affinity weight as follows:

$$p(v_i, v_j) = \begin{cases} \frac{aff(v_i,v_j)}{\sum_{k=1}^{|V|} aff(v_i,v_k)} & \text{if } \sum aff \neq 0 \\ 0 & \text{otherwise} \end{cases} \quad (5)$$

We use the row-normalized matrix $M = M_{i,j_{|V|\times|V|}}$ to describe G_a with entry corresponding to the transition probability, i.e., $M_{i,j} = p(v_i, v_j)$. In order to make M be a stochastic matrix, the rows with all zero elements are replaced by a smoothing vector with all elements set to $\frac{1}{|V|}$. Based on the matrix M, the authority score of a paper d (denoted as $Authority(d)$) can be deduced from those of all other papers linked with it, which can be formulated in a recursive form as in the PageRank algorithm.

$$Authority(v_i) = \mu \sum_{j \neq i} Authority(v_j) \cdot M_{j,i} + \frac{1-\mu}{|V|} \quad (6)$$

where μ=0.85. We define the authority of an author a as:

$$Authority(a) = \sum_{d \in D_a} Authority(d) \quad (7)$$

where $D_a = \{d | author(d) = a\}$.

2.2.9 Venue Rank

Like authors, venues also have academic reputations. Based on our assumption, some venues have larger probability to be highly cited than others. We hereby investigate the venue impact on citations. Similar to the author rank pattern, prestigious venues attract more focus of researchers' attention. The reputation of a venue ensures the amount of citation as well.

2.2.10 Venue Centrality

Venues such as conferences or journals are connected by paper *citing-cited* linkage. We establish a venue connective graph $G_v(V, E)$ where V denotes the venues and the edges E denote the citing-cited relationships between venues. $G_v(V, E)$ also has directions: the out-degrees measure how many times a venue is cited by papers from other venues while in-degrees denote citations. The weight of each edge is calculated by the number of citations between two venues. Hence, the venue centrality can be calculated via a similar PageRank algorithm as Equation (6).

2.3 Predictive Models

2.3.1 Linear Regression (LR)

Linear regression attempts to model the relationship between two variables by fitting a linear equation to observed data. A linear regression line has an equation of the form **Y** = a + b**X**, where **X** is the explanatory variable and **Y** is the dependent variable. In our study, citation features are considered to be explanatory variables, and the predicted citation count is considered to be the dependent variable.

2.3.2 k-Nearest Neighbor (kNN)

The *k*-Nearest Neighbor algorithm is a method widely used in statistical estimation and pattern recognition for classifying objects based on closest training examples in the feature space by a majority common vote amongst its *k* nearest neighbors. The same method can be used for regression, by simply assigning the property value (in our case, citations) for the object (i.e., paper *d*) to be the average of the values of its *k* nearest neighbors to predict the value based on a similarity measure (e.g., distance functions such as cosine similarity). The neighbors are taken from a set of objects for which real citation counts are known.

Choosing the optimal value for *k* is best done by first inspecting the data. In general, a large *k* value is more precise as it reduces the overall noise; however, the compromise is that the distinct boundaries within the feature space are blurred. Based on performance tuning on the training set, we set *k*-NN as 5-NN empirically.

2.3.3 Support Vector Regression (SVR)

Statistical Learning Theory has provided a very effective framework for classification and regression tasks involving features. Support Vector Machines (SVM) are directly derived from this framework and they work by solving a constrained quadratic problem where the convex objective function for minimization is given by the combination of a loss function with a regularization term (the norm of the weights). There are two main categories for support vector machines: support vector classification (SVC) and support vector regression (SVR). SVM is a learning system using a high dimensional feature space. It yields prediction functions that are expanded on a subset of support vectors.

The model produced by SVR only depends on a subset of the training data, because the cost function for building the model ignores any training data that is close to the model prediction. Support Vector Regression is the most common application form of SVMs. An overview of the basic ideas underlying support vector machines for regression and function estimation has been given in details in [14].

2.3.4 CART Model

We then fit a Classification and Regression Tree (CART) model [3], in which a greedy optimization process recursively partitions the feature space, resulting in a piecewise-constant function where the value in each partition is fit to the mean of the corresponding training data. Folded cross-validation [12] is used to terminate partitioning to prevent over-fitting. Our model included 10 features summarized in the last section as predictors.

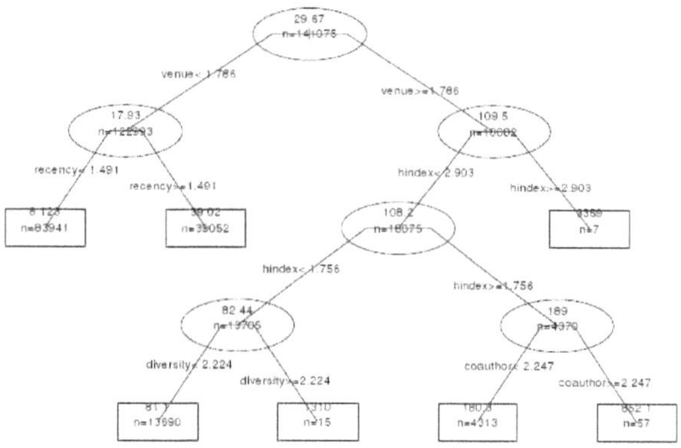

Figure 2: An example of regression tree for citation prediction.

Figure 2 shows the regression tree for one of the folds. Conditions at the nodes indicate partitions of the features, where the left (right) child is followed if the condition is satisfied (violated). Leaf nodes give the function value for the corresponding partition. Thus, for example, one of the leaves indicates that papers with *h-index*∈[1.756, 2.903) and *Sociality (NOCA)*<2.247 are predicted to have approximately 180 citation counts.

Thorough comparisons among all predictive methods and all features are examined in the experiments and evaluations.

3. EXPERIMENTS AND EVALUATION

3.1 Data Description

We perform citation prediction on the real-world data set[3], which is extracted from academic search and mining platform ArnetMiner [18]. It covers 1,558,499 papers from major Computer Science publication venues and has gathered 916,946 researchers for more than 50 years (from 1960 to 2011). The full graph of citation network contained in this data has 1,558,499 vertices (literature papers) and 20,083,947 edges (citations).

To predict the citation counts after one year, we randomly take 10,000 papers from the literature collection from Year 2009 as the test set, and another random 10,000 papers from the Year 2009 as the development set. Note that for all training and evaluation, we only used features calculated over previous years. For example, when predicting articles published in Year 2009, all the articles up through Year 2008 are processed, and only the articles from the Year 2009 are available (as test set). Thus, these time dependent features would only include papers published in 2008 and earlier. Structuring the evaluation in this way is more realistic - when presented with new coming articles, the system can only predict possible future citations based on the patterns it has previously observed. We take the same procedure to predict citation counts after 5 (and 10) years with 10,000 test papers and 10,000 development papers from Year 2005 (and Year 2000). For unobserved feature values, e.g., new authors or new venues, we use the minimum feature values instead of N/A: anything has a start. We compare predicted citation counts with actual citations from the test data.

[3]Downloaded from `http://arnetminer.org/citation`

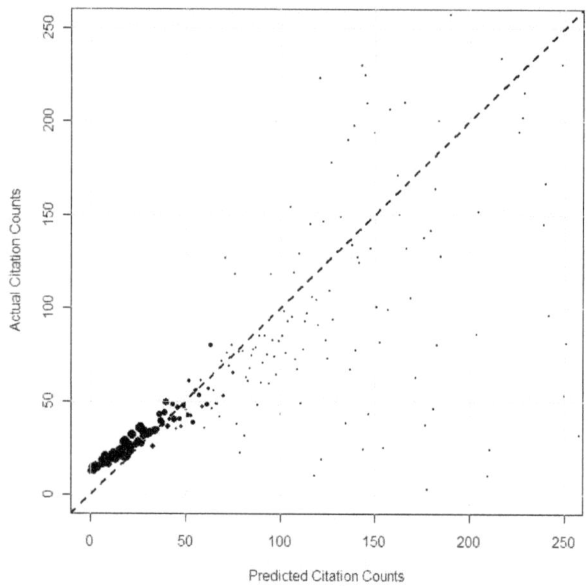

Figure 3: Actual vs. predicted citation counts: the performance for 10-Year CCP for Year 2000 with full features, regression = CART. The dotted line $y = x$ means the best result of predicted citation counts = actual citation counts.

3.2 Evaluation Metric

The coefficient of determination R^2 is used in the context of statistical models whose main purpose is the prediction of future outcomes on the basis of related features. It is the proportion of variability in a data set that is accounted for by the statistical model, which provides a measure of how well future outcomes are likely to be predicted by the model. The definition of R^2 is:

$$R^2 = \frac{\sum\limits_{d \in D_T} (C_{T\,ccp}(d) - C_T(D_T))^2}{\sum\limits_{d \in D_T} (C_T(d) - C_T(D_T))^2} \quad (8)$$

where $C_{T\,ccp}(d)$ is the predicted citations for article d in the test set D_T and $C_T(D_T) = \frac{1}{|D_T|} \sum_{d \in D_T} C_T(d)$ is the mean of the observed citation counts for an article in D_T. $R^2 \in [0, 1]$, and a larger R^2 indicates better performance and hence is desired.

Table 2: The performance of various prediction techniques for different feature combinations on the test set. "+" indicates the single feature group in isolation while "-" indicates the drop of the feature group from the full combination.

	1-Year CCP (Δt=1)				5-Year CCP (Δt=5)				10-Year CCP (Δt=10)			
Methods	LR	kNN	SVR	CART	LR	kNN	SVR	CART	LR	kNN	SVR	CART
+Content	0.093	0.055	0.097	0.100	0.102	0.061	0.103	0.105	0.122	0.101	0.147	0.155
+Author	0.541	0.515	0.537	0.549	0.572	0.567	0.583	0.571	0.598	0.581	0.603	0.611
+Venue	0.274	0.208	0.322	0.315	0.301	0.296	0.317	0.332	0.321	0.313	0.355	0.373
-Content	0.646	0.628	0.671	0.697	0.679	0.632	0.691	0.705	0.689	0.693	0.711	0.723
-Author	0.279	0.245	0.285	0.303	0.296	0.317	0.364	0.372	0.394	0.387	0.402	0.418
-Venue	0.571	0.551	0.548	0.562	0.582	0.575	0.585	0.589	0.612	0.606	0.631	0.643
Combined	0.664	0.607	0.625	0.683	0.706	0.640	0.719	0.752	0.767	0.725	0.755	0.786

3.3 Performance and Feature Analysis

The best predictive performance of 10-Year citation count prediction is shown in Figure 3, and the detailed results are summarized in Table 2 and 3. The size of the circles in Figure 3 indicates the number of points in each predicted citation counts. Most circles are gathered within in the range of [0, 50], indicating most of the papers have relatively low citations. The predicted citation counts will be overestimated for a short period of years. A possible explanation is that for papers with certain features (such as high *author rank*, high *venue rank*, etc.) are predicted to have high citations. To sum up, the system is not well performed in predicting short term impact but it is still of great significance because it is likely to estimate the long term citation counts for a paper more accurately, but the ultimate citations determine the achievements of literature.

Different predictive models have different performances on these three individual tasks in our experiments. In general, non-linear regression achieves better performance. From Table 2, we notice that kNN has the worst performance. The result is as expected because kNN merely seeks the most similar neighbors and takes the neighbors' citation counts as the predictive citations while utilizes little information from the enormous training data. LR, by linear combination of all features, and CART by non-linear regressions have comparable performances and proves the generality of our extracted features. CART performs best among these regression models in practice.

We then examine the different aspects of feature groups: paper content (feature 1-2), author expertise (feature 4-8) and venue impact (feature 9-10) in Table 2. Author expertise is proved to be the most influential feature group in citation count prediction, with the highest performance of R^2=0.611 in isolation and the lowest performance when left out from full feature combination. It is understandable that authors are likely to cite papers written by reputable and influential authors. Venue impact is also significant. Papers from prestigious venues are likely to be highly cited. Unexpectedly, paper content is proved to have the least significance, with the average performance of R^2=0.12 in isolation for CART. We assume (1) authors have biases to choose their bibliography: they sometimes merely consider author/venue reputation; (2) it seems that paper quality is represented by author/venue which create the paper. Influential authors or venues seem to overwhelm the impact of paper content itself; (3) it might also be due to the insufficient feature distilling for contents, e.g. using abstracts as approximation may not be enough for topic/diversity discovery.

We also conduct to a detailed experiment on all separate features in Table 3. We mark the most prominent performance of single features with asterisks in Table 3. The absence of *Author Rank*, *Venue Rank* and *H-Index* lead to unfavorable decrease.

Table 3: Feature analysis: R^2 result when with the pending feature ("+") in isolation (we mark the top 3 prominent features with asterisks), and the result in R^2 when dropped from the all-features model ("-").

Feature	+	−
Topic Rank	0.079	0.721
Diversity	0.157	0.645
Recency	0.101	0.677
H-Index	0.244*	0.536
Author Rank	0.486*	0.375
Productivity	0.198	0.613
Sociality (NOCA)	0.056	0.731
Authority	0.155	0.647
Venue Rank	0.337*	0.593
Venue Centrality	0.049	0.762

4. RELATED WORK

The measurement of citation count has long been a big concern for academia, and is heavily discussed by fundamental research journals (e.g. *Science*, *Nature* and *PNAS*) as further examinations of scientific achievements to distinguish significant ones. The yearly calculated *Impact Factor*, introduced by Eugene Garfield, is a measurement of citation counts of articles published in science journals and is still pervasive [6]. It is frequently used as a proxy for the relative importance of a journal within its field, with journals with higher impact factors deemed to be more important than those with lower ones and can be combined with other metrics such as popularity [15]. However, impact factor can not reflect the citations of individual papers [5] and hence needs a normalization from the audience of citing sides [20].

As to author aspects, the *h-index* is a useful index that attempts to measure both the productivity and impact of the published work of a scientist or scholar [8]. The index is based on the set of the scientist's most cited papers and the number of citations that they have received in other people's publications. H-index measures the impact of researchers and is directly related to publication citations.

However, both impact factor and h-index reflect the macro characteristics but the attractiveness of a specific collection (all papers from a particular author or venue) may be skewed by individuals. No previous work has focused on manipulation for individual papers, neither does any try to measure future citations of literatures. To the best of our knowledge, we are the first to formally research into future citation counts prediction for literatures.

Citation counts indicate the impact of authors, papers and venues, and several works have conducted to analyze citation behavior [1, 13] and perceive interesting discoveries. Sun *et al.* have investigated different impacts of author, venue and content features for clustering in these heterogeneous networks [16]. Through citation linkage, authors are found to affect to authors and paper contents [19, 17], and as well contents (such as topics) are influential to each other [11, 4]. We conduct to an extended examination of all these factors correlated with citation counts, with many more new features added. There do exist several prediction works for the literature world based on citation features, such as co-author prediction [10] and citation linkage prediction by collaborative filtering [9]. Other applications include literature search/recommendation system based on features and citation behaviors [1, 7].

Unlike previous studies, we formally research into a new predictive task of citation count prediction and what is more, we add more relevant features into consideration.

5. CONCLUSION AND FUTURE WORK

In this paper we present a novel task of Citation Count Prediction (CCP), which predicts the future citations for publications. Given a particular paper and its corresponding features relevant with citation patterns (such as paper content, author expertise and venue impact), CCP predicts its possible citation counts. We formally formulate CCP task as a learning problem utilizing several regression models, and evaluate the prediction performance by coefficient of determination (R^2).

From our experiments, we find that authors have biases in citing references. Author expertise and venue impact are the distinguishing factors for the consideration of bibliography, among which, *Author Rank*, *Venue Rank* make paper attractive. Content features in isolation are not predictive. In general, the prediction after a longer period can achieve the best accuracy (R^2=0.786 when $\Delta t = 10$). Currently, we consider a particular paper itself without considering any of its audience (citing papers). However, the impact of audience can also be modeled because once a paper is cited by an attractive audience, it is likely to be attractive as well. As considering the audience will result in a *multi-step diffusion* problem and increase the complexity in measurement. In this study, we do not consider the audience's characteristics when measuring the popularity of the cited literature, while it can be further studied in the future.

6. ACKNOWLEDGMENTS

The work was supported by the Natural Science Foundation of China (Grant No. 60933004 and No. 61073073), HGJ Grant No. 2011ZX01042-001-001, Chinese National Key Foundation Research (No. 60933013 and No. 61035004). Particularly, Rui Yan was supported by the MediaTek fellowship.

7. REFERENCES

[1] S. Bethard and D. Jurafsky. Who should I cite: learning literature search models from citation behavior. In *Proceedings of the 19th ACM international conference on Information and knowledge management*, pages 609–618. ACM, 2010.

[2] D. M. Blei, A. Y. Ng, and M. I. Jordan. Latent dirichlet allocation. *J. Mach. Learn. Res.*, 3:993–1022, March 2003.

[3] L. Breiman. *Classification and regression trees*. Chapman & Hall/CRC, 1984.

[4] L. Dietz, S. Bickel, and T. Scheffer. Unsupervised prediction of citation influences. In *Proceedings of the 24th international conference on Machine learning*, ICML '07, pages 233–240, New York, NY, USA, 2007. ACM.

[5] J. Dimitrov, S. Kaveri, and J. Bayry. Metrics: journal's impact factor skewed by a single paper. *Nature*, 466(7303):179–179, 2010.

[6] E. Garfield. Impact factors, and why they won't go away. *Nature*, 411(6837):522–522, 2001.

[7] Q. He, J. Pei, D. Kifer, P. Mitra, and L. Giles. Context-aware citation recommendation. In *Proceedings of the 19th international conference on World wide web*, WWW '10, pages 421–430, New York, NY, USA, 2010. ACM.

[8] J. Hirsch. An index to quantify an individual's scientific research output. *Proceedings of the National Academy of Sciences of the United States of America*, 102(46):16569, 2005.

[9] Z. Huang, X. Li, and H. Chen. Link prediction approach to collaborative filtering. In *Proceedings of the 5th ACM/IEEE-CS joint conference on Digital libraries*, JCDL '05, pages 141–142, New York, NY, USA, 2005. ACM.

[10] D. Liben-Nowell and J. Kleinberg. The link-prediction problem for social networks. *Journal of the American Society for Information Science and Technology*, 58(7):1019–1031, 2007.

[11] L. Liu, J. Tang, J. Han, M. Jiang, and S. Yang. Mining topic-level influence in heterogeneous networks. In *Proceedings of the 19th ACM international conference on Information and knowledge management*, CIKM '10, pages 199–208, New York, NY, USA, 2010. ACM.

[12] R. Picard and R. Cook. Cross-validation of regression models. *Journal of the American Statistical Association*, 79(387):575–583, 1984.

[13] A. Siddharthan and S. Teufel. Whose idea was this, and why does it matter? attributing scientific work to citations. In *HLT-NAACL*, pages 316–323, 2007.

[14] A. Smola and B. Schölkopf. A tutorial on support vector regression. *Statistics and computing*, 14(3):199–222, 2004.

[15] Y. Sun and C. Giles. Popularity weighted ranking for academic digital libraries. *Advances in Information Retrieval*, pages 605–612, 2007.

[16] Y. Sun, Y. Yu, and J. Han. Ranking-based clustering of heterogeneous information networks with star network schema. In *Proceedings of the 15th ACM SIGKDD international conference on Knowledge discovery and data mining*, KDD '09, pages 797–806, New York, NY, USA, 2009. ACM.

[17] J. Tang, J. Sun, C. Wang, and Z. Yang. Social influence analysis in large-scale networks. In *Proceedings of the 15th ACM SIGKDD international conference on Knowledge discovery and data mining*, KDD '09, pages 807–816, New York, NY, USA, 2009. ACM.

[18] J. Tang, J. Zhang, L. Yao, J. Li, L. Zhang, and Z. Su. Arnetminer: extraction and mining of academic social networks. In *Proceeding of the 14th ACM SIGKDD international conference on Knowledge discovery and data mining*, KDD '08, pages 990–998, New York, NY, USA, 2008. ACM.

[19] D. Zhou, X. Ji, H. Zha, and C. L. Giles. Topic evolution and social interactions: how authors effect research. In *Proceedings of the 15th ACM international conference on Information and knowledge management*, CIKM '06, pages 248–257, New York, NY, USA, 2006. ACM.

[20] M. Zitt. Citing-side normalization of journal impact: A robust variant of the Audience Factor. *Journal of Informetrics*, 4(3):392–406, 2010.

Extracting Cross References from Life Science Databases for Search Result Ranking

Anja Bachmann[1], Rene Schult[1], Matthias Lange[2] and Myra Spiliopoulou[1]
1 Faculty of Computer Science, Otto-von-Guericke-University Magdeburg, Germany
2 Research Group Bioinformatics and Information Technology, IPG Gatersleben, Germany
anja.bachmann@st.ovgu.de, {schult, myra}@ovgu.de, lange@ipk-gatersleben.de

ABSTRACT

Scholars in life sciences have to process huge amounts of data in a disciplined and efficient way. These data are spread among thousands of databases which overlap in content but differ substantially with respect to interface, formats and data structure. Search engines have the potential of assisting in data retrieval from these *structured* sources but fall short of providing a relevance ranking of the results that reflects the needs of life science scholars. One such need is to acquire insights to cross-references among entities in the databases, whereby search hits with many cross-references are expected to be more informative than those with few cross-references. In this work, we investigate to what extend this expectation holds. We propose *BioXRef*, a method that extracts cross-references from multiple life science databases by combining targeted crawling, pointer chasing, sampling and information extraction. We study the retrieval quality of our method and the relationship between manually crafted relevance ranking and relevance ranking based on cross-references, and report on first, promising results.

Categories and Subject Descriptors

H.2 [**Database Management**]: Data Mining; J.3 [**LIFE AND MEDICAL SCIENCES**]: Biology and genetics

General Terms

Theorie

Keywords

Ranking, search engines, outgoing cross references, life sciences

1. INTRODUCTION

As David Roos remarks "we are swimming in a rapidly rising sea of data" and there is no way to "keep from drowning" [?]. Fortunately, this pessimistic view has not become reality; people are comfortably using search engines to acquire speedily and precisely the information they need. However, general-purpose search engine solutions do not transfer to domain-specific search as in the life sciences, where not only the appearance of keywords matters but also the objects referenced in a document. We propose the search method *BioXRef* that assists search in life science databases by ranking search hits on the basis of the objects they reference.

Search in life science databases exhibits some fundamental differences from conventional search. First, links play a central role: not only a single article to a specific entity is of relevance, but all articles on this entity - though articles just mentioning this entity may be irrelevant. Second, life science databases are organized in different ways – usually around specific entity types (e.g. metabolomics). It is rather difficult to collect information on an entity if the database is organized across entities of a different type.

Third, and very importantly, the exploitation of links across entities in different databases is impeded by the lack of an agreed-upon convention for referencing data records.

For this reason scholars cannot take full advantage of cross references when they retrieve information on some entity (enzyme, gene, protein etc). Systems like GoPubMed [?] or ProMiner [?] use text mining methods to extract entities and other forms of relevant information (including types of interaction among entities, like "activation") in specific databases. Search engines like "Essic" [?] rank search results on the relevance of specific database fields and word combinations but these must have been defined in advance. Weighting and ranking search results on the amount (or importance) of cross references in each result is still an open issue.

In this study, we propose *BioXRef*, an algorithm that extracts cross references from multiple life science databases and thus sets the basis for an enhanced relevance ranking in search engines over biomedical data. Our method is backing the search engine LAILAPS [?] by taking a set of database entries as input, analyzing the entries and their attributes and identifying potential cross references in the same and in other databases. We describe *BioXRef* in section **??** after discussion related work in section **??**. In section **??**, we evaluate *BioXRef* on the search hits for a specific query, report on precision and recall, and concrete references retrieved for randomly selected hits. The last section concludes the study with a brief summary and outlook.

2. RELATED WORK

"Finding information in the WWW is not much of a challenge. Just head for Google or Entrez and get the related web page or database entry." This is being said among biologists who search information about a certain object [?]. However, issues like finding reliable information about the function of a protein, or identifying the protein that is involved in a certain activity of the cell cycle, are much more challenging tasks. One has to consider around 1,100

CIKM'2011, October 24–28, 2011, Glasgow, Scotland, UK.

life science databases and billions of database records [?][1]. Methods developed to rank natural language text or WWW-sites are not performing well on life science content and databases [?]. For example, the Google top-hit for "`arginase`" is a Wikipedia page.

Scholars of different disciplines apply different criteria to decide about the relevance of a database entry to a scientific task; a dentist has other relevance criteria than a plant biologist. Criteria like who published in which journal, for which organism, evidence scores, surrounding keywords etc. are of major importance and are used for query refinement. For some disciplines there exist even complete search guides, e.g. for dentists [?].

Some search algorithms over scientific databases use Term Frequency - Inverse Document Frequency (TF-IDF) for ranking. Apache-Lucene[2] is a popular implementation of this concept and is frequently used in bioinformatics as in LuceGene from the GMOD project [?] which is used for the EBI 'google' like search frontend EBeye. The TF-IDF approach works well but misses the semantic context between the database entries and the query. Another approach is probabilistic relevancy ranking [?] which shows promising results when combined to a user feedback system [?].

After choosing a ranking algorithm for a search engine, the next task is to define possible ranking criteria. Conventional search engines use several ranking criteria. Andrade and Silva consider the similarity between the result entry and the search query itself as a top-ranking criterion [?]. The importance of linkage in ranking has been put forward by PageRank, its variations and ranking extensions [?] which now constitute a mature field.

In their work [?] Lars J. Jansen et al. not only show the importance of text retrieval and information retrieval methods in life sciences, they also point out that such methods can be used for creating novel hypotheses by combining information of several papers. By further elaborating this thought we can suppose that combinations and linkages of several papers, websites or database entries are important.

Another approach is coming from Dennis Quan. He reinforces the statement that the retrieval of relevant information is the most important aspect of research, also in life sciences, and that information is often spread across multiple systems. Moreover Quan also pointed out that there are differences in "data formats, naming schemes and network protocols" [?]. For solving this problem he created a drug discovery dashboard called BioDash [?]. This approach mainly uses the linkage between different aspects and properties. Thus it is likely that references between entries could also be found by some algorithm.

There already are several approaches for solving this problem. Up to now cross references were detected by just picking the attribute named "cross references" or equals. In our context this is not possible, because the knowledge of semantics of particular database attributes, as known from Semantic Web approaches like RDF, is not a-priory given. An intuitive approach is to manually maintain a list of cross referencing attributes like BridgeDB [3] does. This link-database is a valuable asset but such an effort does not scale well to the number of databases to be linked. Hence, it leads to the question whether an automated approach is a feasible alternative of *complement*. *BioXRef* uses BridgeDB to identify links and use regular expressions for different databases.

[1]A list of life science databases and search engines can be found in http://en.wikipedia.org/wiki/List_of_biological_databases

[2]http://lucene.apache.org

[3]http://www.bridgedb.org/

3. THE *BioXRef* APPROACH

The core idea of our method *BioXRef* is that a document returned by a search for a specific entity (enzyme, protein, species etc.) is more informative if it contains many cross-references to other entities. Whilst the nature of each such cross-reference cannot be efficiently investigated by a search engine, the *number* of cross-references can be used as informativeness indicator when ranking the search results. Hence *BioXRef* scans each database entry to identify attributes that are potentially containing cross-references, uses sampling and thresholding to extract the most promising candidates and then detects the identifiers (IDs) of referenced entities within these attributes. Thus, *BioXRef* associates each database with a lookup table of cross references.

BioXRef is part of the LAILAPS [?] framework which we describe briefly below, before presenting the components of *BioXRef* in subsection ??.

3.1 The LAILAPS framework

The intention of the LAILAPS search engine is to find relevant data in non-integrated life science databases. LAILAPS loads and stores life science databases in an entity-attribute-value (EAV) [?] adapted database schema and computes an inverse text index using Apache-Lucene. In the publicly available systems (see Table ??), we provide protein synonyms extracted from UNIPROT/SWISSPROT [?] and a list of 46 keywords that are used as one feature of the feature model depicted in Table ??.

Table 1: LAILAPS Search Portals

Search Portal	*Records*	*Data Domain*
UniProt	1,215,553	protein annotation
IPK Databases [?]	287,252	EST annotation, plant phenotype, expression, metabolite, metabolism
DAWIS-M.D. [?]	9,461,855	disease, drug, ontology, protein metabolism, gene functions, compounds

The features shown on Table ?? reflect the aspects deemed important in general for search in life sciences. However, LAILAPS is a personalized search engine: a user may provide further synonyms and relevance-influencing keywords and LAILAPS trains a personalized neural network on the relevance ratings of each user for a training set of database entries (won with user-specific queries). For each entry we presented the 9-dimensional feature vectors to the user as input and the manually curated relevance scores constitute the network's output layer [?].

To check whether the indegree and outdegree of a database entry are appropriate as additional relevance features, we detect links from one entry to others and incorporate them to the ranking system of the search engine with *BioXRef* . We show that this increases the performance in relevance prediction.

3.2 The Components of *BioXRef*

BioXRef is depicted in Algorithm ??. It takes as input the LAILAPS database L (L actually consists of several databases), two sets of regular expressions $R1$ and $R2$, and a sampling rate S. $R1$ is the set of regular expressions for the databases from which we collect attributes; $R2$ contains regular expressions for a larger set of databases, in which we search for cross references. The specification of these databases and the parameter S are described later.

```
Algorithm 1: BioXRef algorithm
Data: A set of entries from several databases, L
A set of n regular expressions used for attribute search, R1
A set of m regular expressions used for cross reference detection, R2
A percental value used as sample size during attribute search and threshold computation, S.
Result: A lookup table T containing the identifiers of the cross references found for the database entries in L.
1  begin
2      T = ∅; attributeList = ∅;
3      for (each database D in L) do
4          threshold = getThreshold (D, R1, S); attributes = getAttributesFromSource(D,R1,S,threshold);
5          add to attributeList a new Map of attributes of D;
6      for (each entry e ∈ D and D ∈ L) do
7          entryID := ID of the currently treated entry; database := database from which current entry comes from
8          attrList = attributeList.getValue(database);
9          for (each attribute a ∈ attrList) do
10             aContent := content of the attribute (with primary key equal to attributeID) of the
               database entry (with primary key equal to the entryID) from database D;
11             IDList := getCrossReferences(aContent, R2);
12             for (each element x ∈ IDList) do if (x ∉ T) then add(x, T);
```

Table 2: Overview of the LAILAPS feature set

feature	description
F_1 : attribute	in which attribute the query term was found
F_2 : database	in which database the found entry is included
F_3 : frequency	the frequency of all query terms in the entry and attribute
F_4 : cooccurrence	express how close and in which order the query terms were found
F_5 : keyword	gives information, if good or bad keyword are present near to the query terms
F_6 : organism	to which organism the database entry relates to
F_7 : sequence length	the length of the sequence described by the database entry
F_8 : text position	which portion of the attribute is covered by the query term
F_9 : synonym	gives information if the hit was produced by an automatic synonym expansion

BioXRef returns a lookup table T: for each input database entry, T contains the identifiers of potential cross references.

For each database entry from L, *BioXRef* first extracts attributes from the database D where the entry came from (Line 4). The attributes expected to deliver many cross references are identified and considered further (Line 5, Lines 7ff). The list of cross references contributed by each attribute (Line 11) are placed in a lookup table (Line 12). The identification of attributes and the counting of expected cross references is based on regular expressions which we have collected and used heuristically, as explained in sequel.

3.2.1 Building a seed of regular expressions

When working with BridgeDB[4], we identified a list containing names of databases and their URLs, regular expressions for the formation of IDs and similar useful data. Such a regular expression can be used for pattern matching inside a database or across databases. The idea is that if there is a match within an attribute of a search hit (a single entry returned by the search engine) then this match is likely to be a cross reference to another database entry. We have built a list of 184 regular expressions.

3.2.2 Selecting databases for attribute search

In life sciences, we must deal with the interplay between recall and execution time. Ideally, all cross references should be found. However, searching with 184 regular expressions incurs a high overhead. Hence, we used KEGG "Link-only Databases" [5] as basis, and identified databases with at least one million links. The output set consisted of $DB_{attr=}${EMBL, GenBank, RefSeq, Uniprot, EGenes}; we have set the input parameter $R1$ to the set of regular expressions for these five databases. *BioXRef* (Algorithm **??**: Line 3) collects candidate attributes from these databases by invoking Algorithm **??**: getAttributesFromSource().

```
Algorithm 2: getAttributesFromSource
Data: A database D
A set of n regular expressions, R1
Sample size S used to compute a sample from D
A threshold that each attribute has to reach, threshold
Result: A list of attributes whose amount of cross references
        exceeds the threshold
1  begin
2      ResultList = ∅; D' = sample of D having size S
3      for (each attribute a of D) do
4          aID = primary key of a; CRef = 0
5          for (regexp ∈ R) do
6              if (matches(regexp, a) then CRef++
7          x.attributeID = aID
8          x.crossRefereneAmount = CRef
9          if (x.crossRefereneAmount > threshold) then
10             add (x, ResultList)
11     return ResultList
```

[4]http://www.bridgedb.org/

[5]http://www.genome.jp/dbget/linkdb.html

This subroutine identifies all attributes of each database (which contributes entries to our input database entries) and uses the set of regular expressions $R1$ to locate and count potential cross references for each attribute (Lines 5-8). If this count exceeds a threshold, the attribute and its anticipated number of cross references is added to the output (Lines 9-10). *BioXRef* uses the attributes and their indicatory counts to collect cross references from an *expanded* set of databases (cf. Algorithm **??**: Line 9), as explained next.

3.2.3 *Expanding the set of databases*

We have widened the search scope by identifying those KEGG databases with which the initial set DB_{attr} is linked. We came up with a set DB_{cross} of 18 databases. For this superset of DB_{attr}, we specified the set of regular expressions $R2$ (cf. Table **??**) which we use for cross reference detection.

The matching of identifiers from the detection of cross references is undertaken by Algorithm **??**: getCrossReferences(). Matching is possible per se, because the necessary regular expressions have already been identified (originally from BridgeDB) and associated with different databases.

Algorithm 3: getCrossReferences

```
Data: string ST representing the content of current attribute,
A set R2 of m regular expressions.
Result: A list containing the regular expression and the
        number of matches with it, IDList.
begin
  IDList = ∅
  substringArray = components of ST, split at
  semicolon, comma, equal sign, tab, enter or blank
  for (each regexp ∈ R2) do
    for (each s ∈ substringArray) do
      if (matches(regexp, s) then
        crossReferenceArray = [regexp, s]
        // s is an identifier of a foreign entry
        add (crossReferenceArray, IDList)
  return IDList;
```

3.2.4 *Sampling and threshold boundaries*

The complexity of detecting attributes with many cross references is $O(n^2)$, where n is the number of database entries. To keep execution time low, *BioXRef samples* over the input set of database entries D with sampling rate S, ans applies a lower boundary τ on the number of expected cross references that an attribute must have to be further considered.

The sampling parameter S is used as follows. We process the database entries in D to extract a first set of attributes (Line 3 of *BioXRef*), on the basis of which we collect cross references (Line 9 of *BioXRef*). Since the entries in D have some commonalities (in semantics and in the databases they appear in), *how many entries from D should we process* (in Line 4) *to identify all relevant cross references to the entries in D?* (in Line 11). We have experimented with different percentages S over D. The results are on Table **??**: we see that a small sample suffices to detect all 11 relevant attributes, although the number of processed attributes drops with the sample size. Even with 0.001 of the original set we identify 10 out of 11 attributes, hence we chose $S = 0.01$.

Finally, we applied a threshold τ, on the number of potential cross references that an attribute from the sample must have to be considered further (Line 9 of *BioXRef*). To compute this τ, we use

Table 4: Impact of sample size (percentage of D) on the number of processed attributes and relevant attributes

Sample size	Processed attributes	Relevant attributes
0.1	49	11
0.01	39	11
0.001	25	10

the number of entries in the database D, the sample percentage S over D, the number of distinct attributes appearing in D (let A_D be this set), and the cardinality of the set $R1$ of regular expressions:

$$\tau = \frac{|D| \times S}{|A_D| \times |R1|} \times c \qquad (1)$$

where c is a tuning parameter that helps personalizing the threshold, if the user considers the set of cross references returned by LAILAPS as too small or too large for her personal interests.

The reader may have noticed that the number of regular expressions is small. This is not always feasible. An altenrnative is to use a seed of identifiers instead of a seed of databases without associating these identifiers to a certain database. Then only the number of found foreign IDs is stored in a lookup table. Hence for a search query only one SQL-query is needed per result entry to figure the number of cross references that should be considered for ranking.

4. EVALUATION

We evaluated *BioXRef* for the detection and collection of cross references on a test set that contained result entries for the query "carotene 7,8-desaturase". We have chosen this query, because the search hits for it have already been inspected by users who provided relevance feedback. With their feedback, we organized the entries in the search output into three classes on "relevance": "high", "middle", "low". For creating our lookup table containing detected cross references we implemented a JAVA program and used an Oracle database as storage backend. Our test database D had 15,017,563 entries and $|A_D| = 63$ attributes. We considered 5 regular expressions and set $S = 0.01$. For threshold τ, we run preliminary tests to reach a proper number of attributes and set $c = 0.02$.

The most important aspect of rating an algorithm is its predictive performance. We selected three result entries of our test set randomly and inspected them to compute the true positive (TP), false positive (FP) and false negative (FN) values. In figure **??** we illustrate the evaluation of UniProt entry 6B1_AGRT4.

In Table **??** we show the absolute TP, FP and FN values together with the derived precision and recall. Best results are achieved for 6B1_AGRT4 where both precision and recall were more than 75%, while the results for ANGL5_HUMAN are comparably good. For AGRP_HUMAN both measures return lower values, although still higher than 50%. We found that some false positives were caused by regular expressions that matched publication year or mol weight. Since both pieces of information are of quite simple nature, such false positives can be easily dealt with.

Some regular expressions are similar, resulting in the same hit (positive) or miss (negative) being returned and counted more than once. We have permitted this, since it is not a priori clear whether such duplicates are more likely to be true or false positives.

We next checked for an association between the number of cross references an entry has, i.e. its outdegree, and the relevance of the entry as perceived by the human users. To this purpose, we used

Table 3: Regular expressions for ID detection

<table>
<tr><th>Database</th><th>Regular expressions for cross reference detection</th></tr>
<tr><td>DOI</td><td>$(doi\:)?\d{2}\.\d{4}/.*$</td></tr>
<tr><td>EMBL</td><td>\w+(_)?\d+(\.\d+)?\$</td></tr>
<tr><td>Entrez Gene, PubChem, PubMed, Taxonomy</td><td>\d+$</td></tr>
<tr><td>GenBank</td><td>(\w\d{5})|(\w{2}\d{6})|(\w{3}\d{5})</td></tr>
<tr><td>GeneOntology</td><td>GO:\d{7}$</td></tr>
<tr><td>InterPro</td><td>IPR\d{6}$</td></tr>
<tr><td>KEGG Genes</td><td>\w+:[\w\d\.-]*$</td></tr>
<tr><td>KEGG Orthology</td><td>K\d+$</td></tr>
<tr><td>PANTHER</td><td>PTHR\d{5}$</td></tr>
<tr><td>Pfam</td><td>PF\d{5}$</td></tr>
<tr><td>PIRSF</td><td>PIRSF\d{6}$</td></tr>
<tr><td>ProDom</td><td>PD\d+$</td></tr>
<tr><td>PROSITE</td><td>PS\d{5}$</td></tr>
<tr><td>RefSeq</td><td>(NC|AC|NG|NT|NW|NZ|NM|NR|XM|XR|NP|AP|XP|ZP) _\d+$</td></tr>
<tr><td>Uniprot/TrEMBL</td><td>$ \([A-N,R-Z][0-9][A-Z][A-Z, 0-9][A-Z, 0-9][0-9])
|([O,P,Q][0-9][A-Z,0-9][A-Z, 0-9][A-Z, 0-9][0-9])$</td></tr>
</table>

Table 5: Performance results for 3 randomly selected records

Entry name	TP	FP	FN	Precision	Recall
ANGL5_HUMAN	41	22	17	0.65	0.71
6B1_AGRT4	13	4	4	0.76	0.76
AGRP_HUMAN	54	40	33	0.57	0.62

a manually ranked set of 63 entries: they consist of search query results, ranking positions and relevance class specified by the user.

Figure 2: Relationship between outdegree of database entries (y-axis) and relevance class

In the boxplot of Figure ??, we juxtapose relevance class and outdegrees of the entries. The black bar in the middle of each box in Figure ?? presents the median of the class. The boxes represent the inner 50% of the data of the relevance class. As one can see, the medians $\tilde{x}$ of each relevance class have very similar values for the number of cross references. Except of the outlier in class "high", the outdegrees of the entries in the three classes show very similar distribution (cf. median, minimum, maximum values In Figure ??).

Figure ?? indicates that the number of references emanating from a database entry does not influence the relevance class of the entry. However, one must take into account that the sample contains only 63 entries, all of which were relevant to some extent; a random selection of entries might have shown a different distribution of outdegrees among the relevance classes. Second, prior knowledge about the number of cross references might have influenced the perception of the evaluators on the relevance of the entries. Further, the importance associated with some cross reference depends also on the user's expertise. Hence, we plan to study whether user feedback on relevance changes when cross references are used for scoring or not.

BioXRef is intended for a search engine (LAILAPS), so it is proper to investigate performance limitations. Finally we consider the execution time of *BioXRef*. Algorithm ?? contains a loop per database and one per entry but both loops can benefit from multi-threaded computation. On the other hand, searching for cross references of each entry in each database may be less efficient than crawling each database once for all entries. Hence, we intend to run experiments that test the efficiency of the method when the number of databases to be accessed per entry is changed when the number of cross references per entry in each database varies and as the size of the input dataset D increases. Such an experiment requires synthetic data, i.e. an appropriate data generator, which also takes the response time of individual databases into account. This was beyond the scope of this first proof-of-concept study.

5. CONCLUSION AND FUTURE WORK

We have presented *BioXRef*, a method that collects cross references of biomedical database objects with the intention to rank search hits with the number of cross references per hit. Our algorithm combines automated data crawling and information extraction without human intervention, with knowledge from existing life science databases, knowledge about links and regular expressions.

We have tested *BioXRef* on a test set of search query results that were manually categorized on relevance. The first results show that the algorithm performs well, achieving reasonable recall and precision. However, more tests are needed to shed light on the impact of different object types (e.g. protein, gene, enzyme) that are stored differently in each database. A thorough performance evalu-

```
ID   6B1_AGRT4               Reviewed;         207 AA.
AC   P0A3T0; P04031;
DT   23-OCT-1986, integrated into UniProtKB/Swiss-Prot.
DT   23-OCT-1986, sequence version 1.
DT   22-JUL-2008, entry version 11.
DE   RecName: Full=Protein 6b;
GN   Name=6b;
OS   Agrobacterium tumefaciens (strain Ach5).
OG   Plasmid pTiAch5.
OC   Bacteria; Proteobacteria; Alphaproteobacteria; Rhizobiales;
OC   Rhizobiaceae; Rhizobium/Agrobacterium group; Agrobacterium.
OX   NCBI_TaxID=176298;
RN   [1]
RP   NUCLEOTIDE SEQUENCE [GENOMIC DNA].
RX   MEDLINE=84207942; PubMed=6327292;
RA   Gielen J., de Beuckeleer M., Seurinck J., Deboeck F., de Greve H.,
RA   Lemmers M., van Montagu M., Schell J.;
RT   "The complete nucleotide sequence of the TL-DNA of the Agrobacterium
RT   tumefaciens plasmid pTiAch5.";
RL   EMBO J. 3:835-846(1984).
CC   -!- FUNCTION: Involved in tumor formation and increases auxin and
CC       cytokinin effects in host plants.
CC   -----------------------------------------------------------------------
CC   Copyrighted by the UniProt Consortium, see http://www.uniprot.org/terms
CC   Distributed under the Creative Commons Attribution-NoDerivs License
CC   -----------------------------------------------------------------------
DR   PIR; A04499; QQAG7T.
DR   InterPro; IPR006064; Glycosidase.
DR   Pfam; PF02027; RolB_RolC; 1.
PE   4: Predicted;
KW   Crown gall tumor; Plasmid.
FT   CHAIN         1    207       Protein 6b.
FT                                /FTId=PRO_0000064395.
SQ   SEQUENCE   207 AA;  23451 MW;  00896365CC1D065D CRC64;
     MTVANWQVRD LTLILRTGEM KSRLEQARTD FGALLSETVY FQPSAIRLGE FDDEYIHSRQ
     ELVYVYLRED IARQCALRRN LPSNSSNFGT MATAIPPWLM NARSLNRVMQ ERCDQGGLVN
     YYQGPHTNQF FLAIMPSNCF VRFGTDIINN ENYGFYARGG NYTEEGEDDD DEMDDEGEAG
     GAEPRECQIG NLINYPIIAL GSCDLSA
//
```

Figure 1: Example of a manual evaluated database entry from UniProt: the green boxes are correct predicted IDs, red boxes are false positive IDs and the blue boxes mark the false negative IDs. This mean, 13 true positives, 4 false positives and 4 false negatives.

ation with proper synthetic data is also planed for future work, most likely including the development of an appropriate data generator.

Future issues include alternative realizations, namely as part of a search engine, whereupon multi-threading looks promising, and as offline back-end that collects cross references for future ranking, whereupon bundling of accesses to each database may be needed. Finally, we want to investigate the correlation between cross-reference-based ranking and *perceived* relevance of each search result, by providing the new type of ranking as alternative to conventional ranking in an experiment with several users.

6. REFERENCES

[1] E. Agichtein, E. Brill, and S. Dumais. Improving web search ranking by incorporating user behavior information. In *SIGIR '06: Proceedings of the 29th annual international ACM SIGIR conference on Research and development in information retrieval*, pages 19–26, NY, USA, 2006. ACM.

[2] L. Andrade and M. J. Sílva. Relevance ranking for geographic ir. In *Workshop on Geographic Information Retrieval, Sigir'06*, 2006.

[3] A. Bairoch, R. Apweiler, C. H. Wu, W. C. Barker, B. Boeckmann, S. Ferro, E. Gasteiger, H. Huang, R. Lopez, M. Magrane, M. J. Martin, D. A. Natale, C. O'Donovan, N. Redaschi, and L. L. Yeh. The Universal Protein Resource (UniProt). *Nucleic Acids Research*, 33:154–159, 2005.

[4] J. Day. The quest for information: A guide to searching the internet. *Journal of Contemporary Dental Practice*, 2(4):033–043, 2001.

[5] A. Divoli, M. Hearst, and W. M. A. Evidence for Showing Gene/Protein Name Suggestions in Bioscience Literature Search Interfaces. In *Pacific Symposium on Biocomputing*, volume 13, pages 568–579, 2008.

[6] A. Doms and M. Schroeder. GoPubMed: exploring PubMed with the Gene Ontology. *Nucleic Acids Research*, 33:783–786, 2005.

[7] M. Y. Galperin and G. R. Cochrane. The 2011 Nucleic Acids Research Database Issue and the online Molecular Biology Database Collection. *Nucleic Acids Research*, 39, 2011.

[8] D. Hanisch, K. Fundel, H.-T. Mevissen, R. Zimmer, and J. Fluck. Prominer: rule-based protein and gene entity recognition. *BMC Bioinformatics*, 6:14, 2005.

[9] K. Hippe, B. Kormeier, T. Töpel, S. Janowski, and R. Hofestädt. DAWIS-M.D. - a data warehouse system for metabolic data. In *GI Jahrestagung (2)*, p. 720–725, 2010.

[10] N. C. Ide, R. F. Loane, and D. Demner-Fushman. Essie: A Concept-based Search Engine for Structured Biomedical Text. *Journal of the American Medical Informatics Association*, 14(3):253–263, 2007.

[11] IPK-Gatersleben. http://www.ipk-gatersleben.de/internet/infrastruktur/datenbanken.

[12] B. J. Jansen, A. Spink, J. Bateman, and T. Saracevic. Real life information retrieval: a study of user queries on the web. *SIGIR Forum*, 32:5–17, April 1998.

[13] M. Lange, K. Spies, C. Colmsee, S. Flemming, M. Klapperstück, and U. Scholz. The LAILAPS search engine: A feature model for relevance ranking in life science databases. *Journal of Integrative Bioinformatics*, 7(3):118, 2010.

[14] P. M. Nadkarni, L. Marenco, R. Chen, E. Skoufos, G. Shepherd, and P. Miller. Organization of Heterogeneous Scientific Data Using the EAV/CR Representation. *Journal of the American Medical Informatics Association*, 6(6):478–493, 1999.

[15] B. O'Connor, A. Day, S. Cain, O. Arnaiz, L. Sperling, and L. Stein. Gmodweb: a web framework for the generic model organism database. *Genome Biology*, 9(6):102, 2008.

[16] D. Quan. Improving life sciences information retrieval using semantic web technology. *Brief Bioinform*, 8:172,182, 2007.

[17] M. Richardson, A. Prakash, and E. Brill. Beyond pagerank: machine learning for static ranking. In *WWW '06: Proceedings of the 15th international conference on World Wide Web*, pages 707–715, NY, USA, 2006. ACM.

[18] D. S. Roos. Bioinformatics trying to swim in a sea of data. *Science*, 291(5507):1260–1261, 2001.

Extracting Collective Expectations about the Future from Large Text Collections

Adam Jatowt
Graduate School of Informatics, Kyoto University
Yoshida-honmachi, Sakyo-ku, Kyoto
606-8501, Japan
adam@dl.kuis.kyoto-u.ac.jp

Ching-man Au Yeung*
ASTRI
3/F Bio-informatics Centre
2 Science Park West Avenue, Hong Kong
albertauyeung@astri.org

ABSTRACT

News articles often contain information about the future. Given the huge volume of information available nowadays, an automatic way for extracting and summarizing future-related information is desirable. Such information will allow people to obtain a collective image of the future, to recognize possible future scenarios and be prepared for the future events. We propose a model-based clustering algorithm for detecting future events based on information extracted from a text corpus. The algorithm takes into account both textual and temporal similarity of sentences. We demonstrate that our algorithm can be used to discover future events and estimate their probabilities over time.

Categories and Subject Descriptors

H.3.3 [**Information Storage and Retrieval**]: Information Search and Retrieval

General Terms

Algorithms, Experimentation

Keywords

future-related information retrieval, temporal information

1. INTRODUCTION

Future related information can be found in textual documents such as newspapers, books and Web pages. They usually contain information such as plans, speculations, predictions and expectations and constitute an excellent source of what may happen in the future. However, the huge volume of information available makes it difficult for any person to detect all important future-related information manually, not to mention obtaining a clear picture of possible future scenarios.

In view of this challenge, we propose a framework for analyzing future-related information in a text corpus. Our goal is a system that can automatically extract future-related information from a large number of text documents, group related events and topics together and estimate the probabilities of these events based on the evidence found in the documents. We consider a query such as the name of a country, an enterprise, a celebrity or a well-known topic as the input of the system. To inform the design of our framework we first perform simple analysis of selected characteristics of future-related information (Section 3.3).

Our framework helps users understand the possible future scenarios associated with the entity given in the query based on the *collective image of the future* constructed from large textual collections. It should be noted however that our objective is not to predict the future per se. Instead, we propose a framework that can be used to provide the current view of the future that the society collectively expresses in large text collections.

Future forecasting has always been an important activity of humans and thus there should be many potential use cases for such a framework. In particular, a collective image of the future will be useful in various decision making scenarios. To name just a few, users wishing to invest in certain companies may be interested in their future perspectives and plans; fans of celebrities may want to know the schedules related to these persons; those who are considering moving to a certain city may want to know more about the development plans of the local government.

In the next section, we review related research works. Section 3 describes our dataset and presents some statistical analysis. In Section 4 we explain in detail our proposed framework. We describe several case studies and experiments in Section 5. Finally, we discuss some important issues regarding our work in Section 6, and conclude the paper in Section 7.

*Au Yeung contributed to this paper while he was at the NTT Communication Science Laboratories, Kyoto, Japan.

CIKM'11, October 24–28, 2011, Glasgow, Scotland, UK.

2. RELATED WORK

Our work is related to a number of areas including information extraction, information retrieval and data mining. While a lot of work has been done to process temporal information found in documents (e.g. [1][9]), relatively little research has been done specifically on future-related information. Baeza-Yates [2] is the first to talk about "future retrieval." He presents the idea of constructing a search engine that extracts future temporal expressions from news articles and represents documents using tuples of time segments and confidence probabilities of future events.

Jatowt *et al.* [4] summarizes future-related information in both Web pages and news articles. Two methods are proposed to generate summaries of future events. Firstly, information about a certain entity is agglomerated by issuing queries containing object names and future dates (e.g. 2020, 2030) to search engines. Secondly, news articles mentioning a periodical event are analyzed in order to discover its periodicity, which can be then used to predict the future occurrence of the event. This work further develops the above concepts by taking into account the uncertainty in a piece of future-related information, and by establishing a unified and model-based approach to cluster and summarize future-related information.

Kanhabua *et al.* [6] propose ranking model for predictions that takes into consideration their relevance. *Time Explorer* [8] is a search engine that lets users search in the future and analyze future evolution of topics. Kanazawa *et al.* [5] describe methods for retrieval and validity analysis of future-related information which is not associated with explicit future dates. Our task is different from the above works as we focus on estimating the probability of events based on the aggregated evidence of future-related expressions found in text collections.

3. DATA ANALYSIS

3.1 Data Collection

We collect from Google News Archive[1] a large dataset of news articles published in the period of 1990-2010. News articles are obtained by issuing 61 queries with sub-queries specifying the time of publication to the search engine, and collecting all the search results. Our queries can be classified into the following four categories: (1) countries (e.g. Sweden, India); (2) companies (e.g. Panasonic, Toyota); (3) Persons (e.g. Johny Depp, Putin); and (4) others (e.g. Internet, science).

For each query we collect all search results with links to the original news articles and their timestamps. All news articles are downloaded and subjected to preprocessing. In some cases we are unable to collect the full text of the news articles due to subscription or other restrictions. In these cases, we collect the abstracts instead. On average each query results in 60,000 news articles or about 2.4GB text. In total, our dataset consists of about 3.6 million news articles or 145GB text.

Each news article is processed so that HTML tags and other non-content elements are removed. Next, we extract the core part of the news articles following simple heuristics based on identifying the largest chunk of text in each article. In addition, to restrict our analysis to English news articles, we perform filtering to remove articles written in other languages by using a text categorization algorithm based on n-gram matching [3].

3.2 Temporal Information Extraction

In many cases when a possible future event is mentioned in a news article, a temporal expression (e.g. "next year" and "in 2020") can be found in the same sentence. In order to understand what events would happen in the future, we need to first extract temporal expressions from the news articles. We use the GUTime tagger [7], which is the most popular, state-of-the-art temporal tagger for identifying and normalizing temporal expressions in text.

GUTime is able to detect both absolute and relative expressions. Absolute temporal expressions are defined as expressions that are unambiguously associated with a given time point or interval (e.g., 1st March 1998, Jan 2003). Relative temporal expressions, such as "next year" and "10 years later", require a reference time expression called anchor in order to be converted into absolute time expressions.

3.2.1 Temporal Expression Modeling

Temporal expressions returned by GUTime have usually single values assigned to them. In this work we modeled each temporal expression as time interval $[t_b, t_e]$ with a granularity of days. For example, "June 2012" is represented by $[01-06-2012, 30-06-2012]$. Temporal expressions that contain hours are simply converted to daily granularity. The time interval representation allows us to properly consider the meaning of temporal prepositions associated with temporal expressions, such as "after", "between", "in", "from" and "at".

For more ambiguous temporal expressions we apply simple rules to determine their boundaries. For example, seasons are roughly mapped to different periods as follows: "spring" to "March to April", "summer" to "May to August", "fall/autumn" to "September to October" and "winter" to "November to February". In addition, expressions such as "beginning", "middle" and "end" of a given period (e.g., week, month, year) are modelled as respective time spans covering one third of the period, and expressions such as "the first half of" and "the second quarter of" are converted accordingly.

In total we extract 13.1 million temporal expressions, out of which 2.7 million refer to the future, 7 million to the past and 4.2 million to the present (with respect to the publication date of the articles). Present temporal expressions are defined as expressions whose time interval, $[t_b, t_e]$, is as follows $t_b \leq t_a \leq t_e$, where t_a denotes the article timestamp. Temporal expressions related to the future and the past are determined by the following constraints, respectively: $t_a < t_b$ and $t_a > t_e$.

3.3 Distribution of Temporal Expressions

Intuitively, articles are more likely to refer to the immediate future than to the distant future, simply because there is more information about the former. Figure 1 shows the average distribution of temporal expressions in the news articles in relation to their timestamps. The horizontal axis denotes the distance of the value of temporal expressions from the timestamps of the news articles in which they appear. Negative (positive) values indicate that the corresponding temporal expression refers to the past (future) when compared to the article timestamp. The vertical axis indicates the average number of temporal expressions referring to a given time point normalized by the number of news articles published in one month.

First, we can confirm the intuitive expectation that the average number of future and past references decrease as the absolute time difference between their time reference points and the publication date of the articles increases. We also observe that the number of future references is on average

[1] `http://news.google.com/archivesearch`

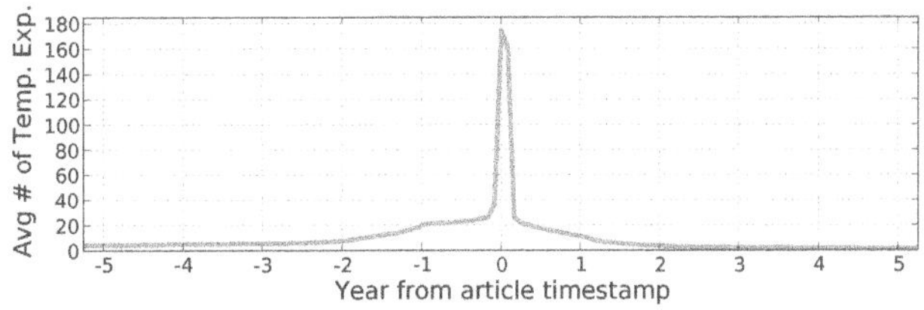

Figure 1: Distribution of temporal references.

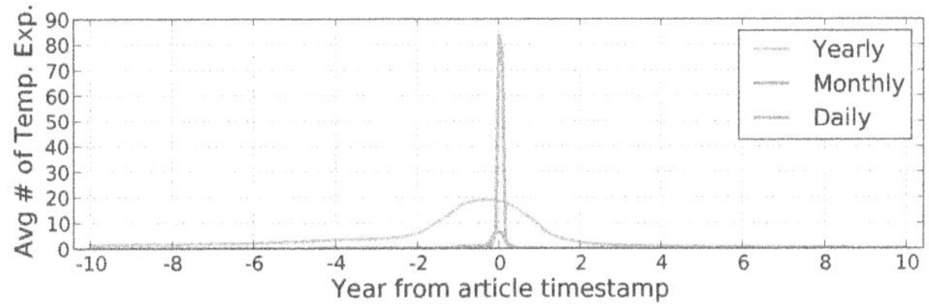

Figure 2: Distribution of temporal references according to their granularity.

smaller than that of past references (Figure 1). Another observation is that both the future and past parts of the curve decrease abruptly around the absolute values of two months, i.e. two months before and after the publication date of an article. The number of references does not change drastically beyond the 2 months from the present time.

We also investigate the usage of temporal expressions in terms of granularity (Figure 2). We categorize temporal expressions into daily, monthly and yearly depending on their minimal granularity. For example, "Monday", "tomorrow" and "17th February" are considered as daily-granularity expressions. "June" and "January 2003" are categorized into monthly expressions, while "2014" and "3 years later" are considered as yearly expressions. The graph follows our intuition that finer granularity expressions are used more often to refer to the nearer past and future. For example, it is relatively rare to use expressions of daily granularity for future or past time points that are further than 3 months from the news article publication date.

4. A FRAMEWORK FOR ANALYSIS OF FUTURE-RELATED INFORMATION

To analyze future-related information in a text corpus, we make use of a mixture model that clusters sentences based both on their *textual similarity* and *temporal similarity*. The idea is to obtain a set of clusters of sentences (presumably referring to some events in the future) such that each cluster refers to a coherent topic associated with a certain period in the future. At the same time, we also want to estimate the probability of an event (or more general a topic) happening in the future. Hence, each cluster will be associated with a probability distribution over time.

4.1 Probability Distribution of an Event over Time

When reporting events that have already happened, news articles usually provide the exact date and time of the events. However, for future events the temporal reference is usually uncertain and not all newspapers would agree on the exact time when a particular event will happen. For example, one newspaper may report that "Toyota is going to establish a new plant in Brazil in early 2012", while another may report that "Toyota's new factory in Brazil to be completed in 2011". While the two articles are probably referring to the same event, the temporal expressions are different. If we only consider the values of the temporal expressions, we will fail to cluster these two sentences together. To solve this problem, we map each temporal expression extracted from the text to a probability distribution over time. Specifically we consider the following four types of temporal expressions and suggest that they can be modeled by four different probability distributions based on their corresponding temporal modifiers.

1. A single time point (e.g. "In 2020 ...") is mapped to a Gaussian distribution.
2. An end date (e.g. "By the end of 2020 ...") is mapped to an increasing exponential distribution.
3. A start date (e.g. "from 2020 onwards, ...") is mapped to a decreasing exponential distribution.
4. A period (e.g. "... from 2015 to 2030.") is mapped to a uniform distribution.

4.2 Clustering with a Mixture Model

To group similar events together, we adopt a model-based clustering approach. We use the term "instances" to refer to the basic units in the clustering process. An instance consists of a sentence from which a temporal expression referring to the future is extracted, the probability distribution associated with the expression, and the surrounding text of that current sentence (the previous and the next sentences).

We approach this clustering task by considering a generative model of news articles. We assume that each instance extracted from the corpus is generated by first picking a topic cluster with certain probability, and then generating the terms and the temporal expression in the instance depending on the chosen topic cluster.

Formally, let the set of instances be D, and that each instance $d \in D$ is characterized by a bag of words W_d, and a probability distribution $P_d(t)$, which, as described in the previous section, reflects how likely the event mentioned in the instance would happen at different times. In addition, let Z be a set of topic clusters.

4.2.1 Basic Model-based Document Clustering

In a simple mixture model, in which documents are only characterized by a bag of words, the probability of a particular document being generated can be expressed as follows.

$$P(d) = \sum_{z \in Z} P(z) \prod_{w \in W_d} P(w|z)^{N_{w,d}} \tag{1}$$

where $N_{w,d}$ is the number of times a word w appears in document d, or it can be a score given to w with respect to d. A document is assumed to be generated by picking a particular topic cluster z and then generating terms from a probability distribution conditioned on the chosen topic.

However, we are not only interested in grouping instances that mention similar topics (e.g. putting all instances about Toyota's plans to build plants into one cluster). We are also interested in grouping instances that mention events that are likely to happen at about the same time. In other words, having similar words is not the only criterion when clustering the instances. We also want to consider the *temporal proximity* between the instances. Hence, we extend the above mixture model as follows.

4.2.2 Considering Temporal Proximity

To perform clustering based on temporal proximity, we need to put instances with similar probability distributions in the same cluster. We let $G_d(t)$ be the probability mass function of an instance d, and let $G_z(t)$ be the probability mass function of the topic z. Also, we define $H(d|z)$ as the probability that, given a certain cluster z, d has a probability distribution defined by the function $G_d(t)$. We define $H(d|z)$ as follows.

$$H(d|z) = \frac{h(d,z)}{\sum_z h(d,z)} \tag{2}$$

where

$$h(d,z) = \frac{1}{D_{KL}(G_d||G_z) + 1} \tag{3}$$

and $D_{KL}(G_d||G_z)$ represents the KL divergence between two probability mass functions. The intuition here is that $H(d|z)$ will be larger if the two probability mass functions are more similar, indicating that d has a high probability of belonging to the cluster z.

4.2.3 The Complete Model

To consider both the terms and the probability distributions of the instances, we propose the following mixture model which combines the two components described above.

$$P(d) = \sum_{z\in Z} P(z)(\prod_{w\in W_d} P(w|z)^{N_{w,d}} \times H(d|z)^{\alpha}) \tag{4}$$

where α is a parameter controlling the influence of temporal proximity in the clustering process.

Parameters can be estimated by using the EM algorithm. By iterating the E-step and the M-step until convergence, we obtain estimates of the parameters of the model. In the E-step, we estimate the probability $P(z|d)$ for each document.

$$P(z|d) \propto P(z) \times \prod_w P(w|z) \times H(d|z)^{\alpha} \tag{5}$$

In the M-step, we estimate the probability $P(w|z)$ and $G_z(t)$, the probability distributions over time for each topic, based on the soft clustering obtained in the E-step.

$$P(w|z) \propto 1 + \sum_w P(z|d) \times N_{w,d} \tag{6}$$

$$G_z \propto \sum_d G_d \times P(z|d) \tag{7}$$

An important parameter that needs to be tuned in our model is α. In order to take into account both textual and temporal similarities, the weight of the two components should be comparable. However, since the component of textual similarity depends on the number of words in the instance d, α should be chosen such that it is comparable to average number of words in the instances. Hence, we further define α as follows:

$$\alpha = \lambda \times \overline{N_d} \tag{8}$$

where $\overline{N_d}$ is the average number of words in the instances:

$$\overline{N_d} = \frac{1}{|D|} \sum_{d\in D} \sum_{w\in W_d} N_{w,d} \tag{9}$$

and λ is a parameter we can tune depending on how much weight we would like to put on the two components.

After the model is trained, we will be able to obtain the distribution of words for each topic ($P(w|z)$) as well as the probability distribution over time for each topic (G_z). These two pieces of information give us an idea of which topic is relevant in which period of time in the future.

4.2.4 Log-scale Timeline

In Section 3.3 we show that when a temporal expression refers to a time in the near future, it is likely to be a more specific one, while one that refers to a time in the far future is likely to be a rough indicator (e.g. only the year). To cater for this variation in the granularity of temporal expressions over time, we propose to transform the timeline from linear scale to log scale before performing the clustering process.

We assume that we are dealing with a discrete timeline, with the smallest division as a day. In a period given by $[t_1, t_2]$, we map a particular day t_x to a point t_l on the log-scale timeline spanning from 1 to 100 using the following equation:

$$t_l = \frac{\ln(t_x - t_1 + 1)}{\ln(t_2 - t_1 + 1)} \times 100 \tag{10}$$

After the transformation, days in the near future are more spread out and days in the far future will be more tightly packed together. In our experiments, we generate probability distributions for each instance after this transformation, and once we obtain the distributions of each cluster we transform the timeline back to a linear scale. In this way the events in the far future have distributions that are more spread out, indicating the higher uncertainty of these events.

5. EXPERIMENTS

Evaluating our proposed method is a challenging task because no benchmark dataset or ground truth is available. The results contain information about events or plans that were not yet realized at the time the news articles are published. Hence, it is difficult to perform quantitative evaluation. Instead, we carry out a set of case studies in order to demonstrate the effectiveness and some characteristics of our proposed method. We select three queries, namely "Germany", "Toyota" and "NASA", representing different categories of queries.

To perform the experiments, we extract news articles from our datasets that contain temporal expressions referring to a date or a period of time in or after 2011. Due to limited space here, we only present results with number of topics $|Z| = 50$ and $\lambda = 0.5$, by which we obtain reasonable results. Note that the output events are generated on the basis of 20-year old (1990-2010) collection of news articles, hence they are major events that have been usually "long-awaited" and are also scheduled in relatively far future.

5.1 Case Study: Germany

For the query "Germany", we extract 1,723 future temporal expressions. After the clustering process, quite a number of clusters are found to be associated with certain events about Germany in the future. The three largest clusters are shown in the follow table, and the corresponding probability distributions (G_z) are shown in Figure 3.

ID	Size	Frequent Terms
1	124	energy, emissions, percent, government, power, country, climate, nuclear, renewable, million
2	39	billion, government, debt, city, economic, eastern, percent, frankfurt, euros, supply
3	27	munich, bid, year, city, new, events, world, olympic, winter, games

Table 1: Top three clusters for "Germany".

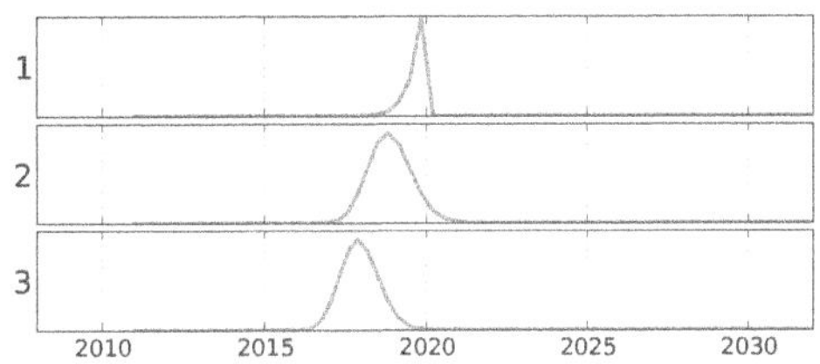

Figure 3: Probability distributions associated with the three clusters for "Germany".

Upon manual investigation of the sentences we observe that the first cluster is about energy and power consumption in Germany. In fact, this cluster is interesting because it consists of more than one topic. Firstly, there are reports about Germany's plan to cut emission to a certain level by 2020. There are also reports about Germany's plan to shut down all nuclear power plants in the country by 2020. The two topics are related and are usually mentioned together, therefore they are found in the same cluster. We also notice that the shape of the distribution of Cluster 1 is different from the other two (it is skewed to the left). This is because the year 2020 is usually mentioned in the way of "by 2020," therefore the distribution resembles an exponential rather than a Gaussian distribution.

On inspecting the instances belonging to Cluster 2, we find that they are mostly about western Germany's financial assistance to eastern Germany after unification. This long term project is scheduled to run until 2019, that is why we see a peak at 2019 in the probability distribution. On the other hand, the third cluster mostly contains sentences from news articles about Munich's bidding of the 2018 Winter Olympics.

5.2 Case Study: Toyota

For the query "Toyota", we extract 1,021 temporal expressions referring to the future.

ID	Size	Frequent Terms
1	129	new, company, car, hybrid, cars, motor, prius, vehicle, plans, electric
2	88	market, car, vehicles, plan, million, company, motor, year, share, vehicle
3	28	hybrid, vehicles, fuel, cars, company, market, global, year, million, prius

Table 2: Top three clusters for "Toyota".

We observe that the three clusters shown in Table 2 with their corresponding probability distributions in Figure 4 share

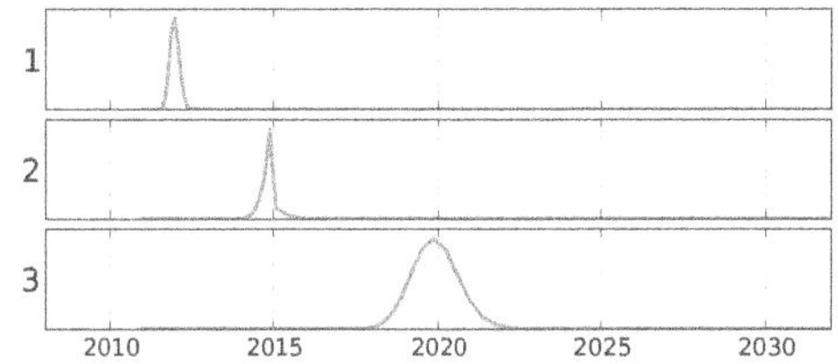

Figure 4: Probability distributions associated with the three clusters for "Toyota".

some common terms such as "hybrid", "electric" and "vehicles". However, they are actually referring to different events or plans about Toyota. The first cluster contains sentences in news articles about Toyota's plan to release both plug-in hybrid and battery electric cars in 2012, while the second cluster is about Toyota's plan to release hydrogen fuel cell vehicles by the year of 2015. Since many sentences in Cluster 2 are extracted from news articles that also discuss the projected market share of Toyota, terms such as "market" and "share" can be found in the cluster. Finally, Cluster 3 is about Toyota's plan to offer hybrid version for all of its models around 2020. This result suggests that our proposed method successfully group instances based not only on textual similarity but also the temporal expressions extracted from the text.

5.3 Case Study: NASA

Finally, we extract 2,499 temporal expressions referring to the future for the query "NASA".

ID	Size	Frequent Terms
1	276	moon, space, astronauts, return, mars, agency, president, lunar, program, new
2	139	space, launch, first, mission, shuttle, agency, flight, spacecraft, orion
3	82	earth, asteroid, space, apophis, mars, chance, hit, mission, propulsion, scientists

Table 3: Top three clusters for "NASA".

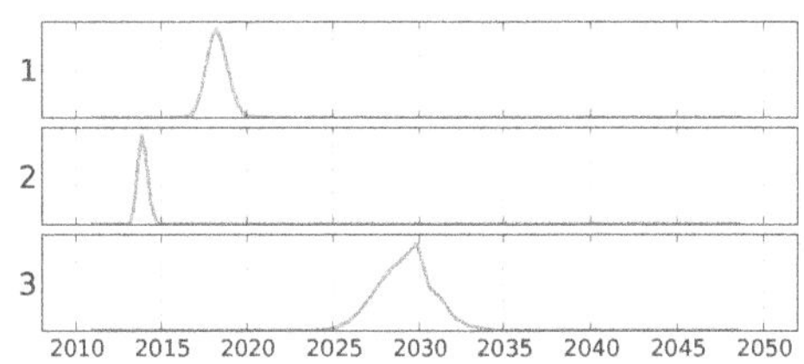

Figure 5: Probability distributions associated with the three clusters for "NASA".

This dataset mainly contains news articles about space programs and aerospace research conducted by NASA (see Table 3 and Figure 5). In the first cluster, we find news articles about NASA's plan to send manned spacecraft to the Moon again in 2018, thus we see a corresponding peak in that year in Figure 5.

Cluster 2 contains sentences from news articles about various plans of NASA to build spacecrafts. Ideally, different plans should be put into different clusters. However, since quite a lot of plans, such as a new space shuttle and the

Orion spacecraft, happen to be associated with the same period of time in the future (the year 2014), they are grouped into the same cluster. This suggests that depending on the topic we may have to give more weights to the terms instead of the temporal expressions in the clustering process.

Finally, Cluster 3 contains reports about the possibility that an asteroid called Apophis would hit the Earth in 2029. The probability distribution is much more spread out for this cluster, indicating high degree of uncertainty of this event. This is due to several reasons. Firstly, since we use a log-scale timeline during clustering, Gaussian distributions for years in the distant future as a result have a larger variance. Also, there were reports saying that the time of impact may be earlier or later. Finally, the cluster contains some sentences about the possible impacts of other asteroids in the surrounding years.

From the above three case studies, we can see that the proposed method gives reasonable and satisfactory results. In particular, we can obtain clusters that do not only contain instances that are about the same topic, but are also actually related to the same events. At the same time, we are aware of some limitations of our method. For example, in some cases when two events are highly related to each other and happen to be scheduled at about the same time, it becomes difficult to put them into different clusters, as in the case of "NASA".

6. DISCUSSIONS

The model proposed in this paper currently only takes into account some of the most important information found in the news articles. We believe several other factors can be utilized to achieve higher accuracy as shown below.

Information Freshness. Future-related information is inherently uncertain and continuously changing. Intuitively, the latest information should be more reliable than information published some time ago.

Source Credibility and Authority. Whether a piece of future-related information can be trusted is strongly related to the credibility and authority of the source. Hence, one may consider, for example, putting more emphasis on news articles from a major and reputable newspaper, and less on articles published in a blog.

Modal Expressions. It is common that modal expressions, which indicate different levels of certainty of the events, such as "may" or "is likely to" are used when news articles mention about future events. Hence, weighting instances by the modal expressions found near the temporal expressions is a potential method for improving accuracy.

Dependencies of Different Events. It is not uncommon to see sentences in the form of "A will occur if B and C happen". In other words, the probability of one event may be dependent on the probabilities of other events.

It should be noted that the above list is not exhaustive and is meant to provide a brief overview of some possible factors. In fact, our framework is flexible and can be easily extended to accommodate some of the above factors. For example, based on the credibility of the news sources and the modal expressions found in each instance, we can associate a score with each instance. We can then use these scores to weight the instances in the M-step when updating $P(w|z)$ and G_z.

While we show promising results, we are aware of certain limitations. We only focus on topics and events that are associated with temporal expressions. Therefore, a future topic/event is extracted only if it is mentioned together with some dates in the future. In fact, news articles also contain many references to future topics and events without mentioning when they are likely to happen [5]. The advantage of considering only time-referenced topics and events is that they allow us to estimate probability distributions over the timeline, and these references are more probable and credible as the time at which they will happen is more or less decided or agreed. On the other hand, we lose certain information about the complete picture of the future when we neglect topics or events that are not associated with any temporal expression.

7. CONCLUSION

Given the large amount of future-related information in text documents, it is possible to harness such data to construct a collective image of the future. We proposed a model-based framework for portraying collective images of the future, constructed based on numerous future-related information expressed in text collections. The framework supports users in understanding the currently planned or expected future events for a given query, be it a person, a company, a city or a country. We demonstrated its effectiveness on several examples of real world entities. Besides considering the additional factors mentioned in the previous section, we plan to improve our clustering algorithm and perform evaluation of larger scale in the future.

8. ACKNOWLEDGMENTS

We would like to thank Hang Li and Daxin Jiang for the discussions about this research. This research was partially supported by the MEXT Grant-in-Aid for Young Scientists B (#22700096) and by the Microsoft IJARC CORE6 Project "Mining and Searching the Web for Future-related Information".

9. REFERENCES

[1] O. Alonso, M. Gertz, and R. Baeza-Yates. Clustering and Exploring Search Results using Timeline Constructions. In *CIKM '09*, 97–106, 2009.
[2] R. Baeza-Yates. Searching the Future. In *MF/IR 2005*, 2005.
[3] W. B. Cavnar and J. M. Trenkle. N-Gram-Based Text Categorization. In *SDAIR '94*, 161–175, 1994.
[4] A. Jatowt, K. Kanazawa, S. Oyama and K. Tanaka. Supporting Analysis of Future-related Information in News Archives and the Web. In *JCDL '09*, 115–124, 2009.
[5] K. Kanazawa, A. Jatowt and K. Tanaka. Improving Retrieval of Future-related Information in Text Collections. In *WI '11*, 2011.
[6] N. Kanhabua R. Blanco and M. Matthews. Ranking Related News Predictions. In *SIGIR '11*, 755–764, 2011.
[7] I. Mani and G. Wilson. Robust Temporal Processing of News. In *ACL '00*, 69–76, 2000.
[8] M. Matthews *et al.* Searching through Time in the New York Times. In *HCIR '10*, 2010.
[9] A. Qamra, B. Tseng, and E. Y. Chang. Mining Blog Stories using Community-based and Temporal Clustering. In *CIKM '06*, 58–67, 2006.
[10] X. Zhu, Z. Ghahramani, and J. Lafferty. Time-sensitive Dirichlet Process Mixture Models. Technical report, Carnegie Mellon University, 2005.

Towards a Unified Solution: Data Record Region Detection and Segmentation*

Lidong Bing Wai Lam Yuan Gu
Department of Systems Engineering and Engineering Management
The Chinese University of Hong Kong
Shatin, Hong Kong
{ldbing, wlam, yuangu}@se.cuhk.edu.hk

ABSTRACT

Although the task of data record extraction from Web pages has been studied extensively, yet it fails to handle many pages due to their complexity in format or layout. In this paper, we propose a unified method to tackle this task by addressing several key issues in a uniform manner. A new search structure, named as Record Segmentation Tree (RST), is designed, and several efficient search pruning strategies on the RST structure are proposed to identify the records in a given Web page. Another characteristic of our method which is significantly different from previous works is that it can effectively handle complicated and challenging data record regions. It is achieved by generating subtree groups dynamically from the RST structure during the search process. Furthermore, instead of using string edit distance or tree edit distance, we propose a token-based edit distance which takes each DOM node as a basic unit in the cost calculation. Extensive experiments are conducted on four data sets, including flat, nested, and intertwine records. The experimental results demonstrate that our method achieves higher accuracy compared with three state-of-the-art methods.

Categories and Subject Descriptors

H.3.m [**Information Storage and Retrieval**]: Miscellaneous

General Terms

Algorithms, Performance, Experimentation

* The work described in this paper is substantially supported by grants from the Research Grant Council of the Hong Kong Special Administrative Region, China (Project Codes: CUHK4128/07 and CUHK413510) and the Direct Grant of the Faculty of Engineering, CUHK (Project Codes: 2050442 and 2050476). This work is also affiliated with the Microsoft-CUHK Joint Laboratory for Human-centric Computing and Interface Technologies.
We also acknowledge the help received from Gengxin Miao and Weiyi Meng who provided us some details of their experiments.

Keywords

Web Data Record Extraction, RST Structure, Web Information Integration

1. INTRODUCTION

The World Wide Web has been extensively developed since its first appearance two decades ago. The explosive growth and spread of the Web have resulted in a huge information repository, but yet it is still under-utilized due to the difficulty in automated information extraction (IE) caused by data heterogeneity. The task of Web IE differs largely from the traditional IE task which aims at extracting data from basically unstructured free text. In contrast, Web IE processes Web documents (or Web pages) which are semi-structured and coded with HTML tags. Furthermore, Web sites commonly employ pre-designed templates to format and present information units, known as *data records*, which have similar attributes or fields. For example, retailing Web sites usually run a server-side program to fill products' information, retrieved from back-end databases, in a pre-defined template to generate Web pages, which are referred to as deep or dynamic Web pages. Organizations also prefer to display its information in a structured way to facilitate easy browsing, such as list of chief staff, list of breaking events, etc. These pages are known as surface or static Web pages. Therefore, the structured information on the Web is tremendously popular and very valuable for various applications such as online market intelligence [5], data mashups [1], etc.

Some existing works adopt a supervised manner to perform the Web IE task [15, 28]. They need some pre-labeled pages as input to learn some extraction rules or wrappers. Some others adopt an unsupervised manner [3, 8, 17, 20, 22], which can extract desirable data without manually prepared training data. Considering the availability of single or multiple input pages from a particular Web site, Web IE systems can also be classified into single-page based methods and multiple-page based methods. Multiple-page based methods [3, 8, 15, 28] take several pages coming from the same Web site as input, and extract the underlying template or schema automatically by analyzing the differences and similarities of these pages. Single-page based methods [17, 20, 22] do not need several similar pages from the same Web site. Therefore, they are able to handle Web sites where multiple similar pages are not available. The work introduced in this paper is a single-page based and unsupervised framework, and it can detect the *record region* (*record section*) and segment the records simultaneously under a unified model. One

(a) A page fragment of company information.

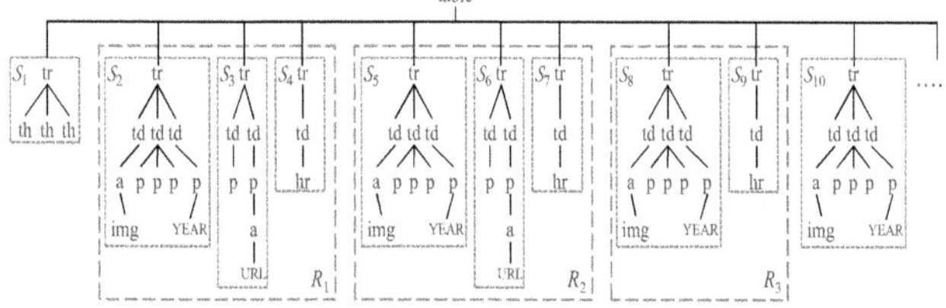

(b) DOM tree of the page in (a). $\mathcal{S}_i$ is a subtree, R_i is a record.

Figure 1: A page fragment and its DOM tree.

example of such kind of page is given in Figure 1(a). In some existing works, further post-processings are performed such as attribute alignment [26, 30] and labeling [24, 33]. These post-processings make the extracted data suitable for downstream applications.

Two basic observations on data record and record region are as follows: 1) A group of data records describing a set of similar objects are typically presented in a contiguous region, known as record region, of a page and are formatted using similar HTML tags; 2) A set of similar data records are formed by some child subtrees of the same parent node. Based on these observations, a natural way to detect record region and record boundary is to examine the similarity (or distance) between subtrees. This strategy is adopted by MDR, ViPER, and DEPTA. MDR [17] utilizes string edit distance to assess whether two adjacent subtree groups, named as *generalized nodes*, are a repetition of the same data type. ViPER [22] is another work which also calculates string edit distance of the subtree pairs to detect record region. Then it involves some visual information to segment a detected region into records. DEPTA [27] calculates tree edit distance between generalized nodes. In summary, MDR and DEPTA calculate similarity for the pairs of neighboring generalized nodes, while ViPER calculates similarity for every pair of subtrees.

The advantage of the above similarity-based approaches is that they are robust against optional fields or tags in a record, and can tackle the problem of approximate matching to identify repeating objects. However, one disadvantage is that the method of determining the granularity involved in the similarity calculation is not flexible. In a record region, records may contain different number of subtrees, as shown in Figure 1. Thus, the number of possible subtree combinations to compose records is exponential with respect to the number of subtrees. To tackle this problem, MDR and DEPTA introduce a concept known as generalized node, which contains several subtrees. The limitation of the MDR family methods [17, 26, 27] is the greedy search for the best generalized node combination, which is time consuming as noticed by other works [20, 22]. To speed up the greedy search, one inflexible constraint is introduced in their definition of record region. This constraint specifies that all generalized nodes must have the same length, i.e. the number of subtrees, in the same record region. This constraint will fail to handle some cases in which the records contain different number of subtrees. For the record region in Figure 1, MDR treats $\mathcal{S}_2 \cdots \mathcal{S}_7$ as one record region, and misses the record R_3. Noticing this limitation, ViPER only calculates the similarity for single subtree pairs and constructs a similarity matrix. Then with this matrix, some heuristic rules are employed to detect the record region. Another limitation of these existing methods is that they decompose record extraction into two separate steps, namely, record region detection, and record segmentation. The reason is that the calculated similarity or distance in region detection, namely, the edit distance of generalized nodes in MDR, and the similarity of pairwise subtrees in ViPER, cannot be utilized to decide record boundary directly, since the calculated information is not necessarily boundary related.

In this paper, we propose a unified method to tackle the record extraction task. A new search structure, named as **R**ecord **S**egmentation **T**ree (RST), is designed. Based on the RST structure, several key issues in record extraction are handled in a uniform manner. For example, whether the given region contains a record region, if so, from which subtree it starts, where it ends, and how to segment it into records. To obtain solutions for these issues, we develop several efficient search pruning strategies on the RST structure of a given region to identify the correct record segmentation. When a correct segmentation is successfully detected, it implies that the record region is also successfully obtained. Based on such approach, our method is able to combine the two steps in the existing works in a unified framework. An intuitive way to understand the advantage of our method is that if the region can be segmented into records having high pairwise record similarity, then we are confident that this region is a record region. At the same time, we also have high confidence on the record segmentation.

Another characteristic of our method which is significantly different from previous works is that it can effectively handle complicated and challenging data record regions such as embedded region and nested region. It is achieved by generating subtree groups dynamically from the RST structure during the search process. These groups may contain different number of subtrees which is determined by taking into account the records' features in the current region, whereas MDR and DEPTA pre-define a subtree grouping schema, i.e. generalized node, for all record regions. Furthermore, instead of using string edit distance or tree edit distance, we propose a token-based edit distance. Different tag names have different string length, thus using edit distance directly on tag name string is not suitable. In our token-based edit distance, each tag is counted as a basic unit in the edit cost calculation.

2. RELATED WORK

Structured data extraction from Web pages has been studied extensively. Early works on manually constructed wrappers [4, 18] were found difficult to maintain and be applied to different Web sites, because they are very labor intensive. Semi-automatic methods [2, 13, 14, 15, 16, 21, 28, 31, 32], known as wrapper induction, were proposed to tackle this problem. These methods need some labeled pages in the target domain as input to perform the induction. Thus, they still have limitation for large-scale applications. To overcome the above drawbacks, fully automatic methods have been developed. Methods such as MDR [17], DeLa [24], ViPER [22], and DEPTA [27] were designed to tackle record-level extraction task from a single input page. Our framework falls into this category, precisely, it is an automatic, record-level, and single-page based approach.

Techniques that address record extraction from a single page can be categorized into five categories: early methods based on heuristics [6, 10], repetitive pattern based methods [7, 24], similarity-based extraction methods [17, 22, 26], tag path based methods [20], and visual feature based methods [11, 19, 29]. Methods based on heuristic rules cannot be generalized well. Repetitive pattern based methods such as IEPAD [7] and DeLa [24] show some potential in solving this problem because similar templates are used in formatting the records, which make it feasible to mine some repetitive patterns as clues for locating records in the page. One limitation of such pattern mining approaches is that it is not robust against optional data and tags inserted into records.

The similarity-based approach tackles this limitation with approximate matching to identify repeating objects. MDR [17] and DEPTA [26] are such techniques, which utilize string or tree edit distance to assess whether two adjacent subtree groups are a repetition of the same data type. Our method also calculates the similarity between two groups of subtrees, but the designed RST structure makes the subtree grouping more flexible and better aligned with the record boundary. ViPER [22] is another work which computes the similarity of each pair of single subtrees to detect record region, then involves some visual perception to segment the detected regions into records.

Miao et al. investigate the tag paths in a Web page to perform record extraction [20]. They transform a DOM tree into pieces of tag paths, and cluster the paths according to the defined similarity measure to detect record regions. The limitation of this method is that it cannot take into account the record boundary information during region detection, and needs a separate step to segment records after region detection. Therefore, tag paths in the same records and paths among different records cannot be distinguished and treated differently. Inevitably, the accuracy of both steps will be affected. Furthermore, this method clusters the tag paths across the entire page, and does not consider the proximity relations of the paths. However, the same tag path may be used in different blocks of the page, even these blocks are far away from each other.

Although ViPER [22] and work by Miao et al. [20] utilize some visual information from rendered Web page to assist record segmentation, they depend on tag structure to detect record regions. In contrast, ViNTs [29] utilizes the visual information first to identify content regularity, and then combines it with tag structure regularity to generate wrappers. ViNTs cannot separate horizontally arranged records, e.g., nested records in a table, and identify multiple regions. Pure visual feature based methods include VENTex [11] and ViDE [19], and they are effective to extract records from pages with well organized visual features. Some other researchers employ pre-defined domain ontology [9] or automatically generated domain ontology [23] to assist the record extraction task.

3. BASIC OBSERVATIONS AND PROBLEM DEFINITION

In the Web page fragment given in Figure 1(a), the company information is organized in a "table", and each company corresponds to one data record. The table's DOM tree is given in Figure 1(b). We can see that the records share some common fields such as company description, investor, and established year. One can also notice that some records do not contain certain fields. For example, the third record does not have URL information. Furthermore, the records are formatted with similar HTML templates, and each record is composed of several rows in the table. We use $\mathcal{T}$ to denote the DOM tree given in Figure 1(b), and $\mathcal{T}$'s subtree sequence is denoted by $\mathbf{S}$, and an element in $\mathbf{S}$ is referred to as $\mathcal{S}_i$. In the DOM tree in Figure 1(b), $\mathcal{T}$ is "table", and $\mathbf{S}$ includes $\mathcal{S}_1$, $\mathcal{S}_2$, etc. $\mathcal{T}$ and $\mathcal{S}_i$ are also used to refer to the root nodes of the corresponding DOM trees. A fragment of the sequence $\mathbf{S}$ is denoted by $\mathcal{S}_{i..j}$ or $\mathcal{S}_i \cdots \mathcal{S}_j$, where $1 \leq i \leq j \leq |\mathbf{S}|$.

Considering the characteristics of data record and record region, previous works rely on two basic observations which are reviewed as follows:

OBSERVATION 1. *A group of data records describing a set of similar objects are typically presented in a particular region of a page and are formatted using similar HTML tags.*

OBSERVATION 2. *A group of similar data records being placed in a specific region is reflected in the tag tree by the fact that they are under one parent node, although we do not know which parent. It is very unlikely that a data record starts from an inner node of a child subtree and ends at an inner node of another child subtree of the parent node.*

Based on these two observations, existing works separate the record extraction task into two sub-tasks, namely, record region detection and record segmentation. In our framework, we propose a unified method which can tackle these two sub-tasks simultaneously. Returning to the example in Figure 1, given the subtree sequence $\mathbf{S}$ of the table $\mathcal{T}$, data record extraction aims at identifying the sequence $\mathcal{S}_{i..j}$ $(i < j)$ and a set of separating indexes $\mathbf{b}$ in which each $b_k \in \mathbf{b}$ *s.t.* $i < b_k \leq j$. The identified sequence $\mathcal{S}_{i..j}$ is a *record region*, and it is separated into *data records* by the indexes in $\mathbf{b}$. In the above example, the record region is $\mathcal{S}_{2..|\mathbf{S}|}$, and separating indexes set $\{4, 7, 9 \cdots\}$ indicates the boundary of records in this region. Thus, we know that the records are $\mathcal{S}_{2..4}$, $\mathcal{S}_{5..7}$, $\mathcal{S}_{8..9}$, etc. It is important to notice that a record region may not start from the first subtree of $\mathcal{T}$, and the length (number of subtrees) of different records may be different. In addition, some DOM trees may contain 0 or more than one regions. If there is no record region, no subtree sequence should be identified. If there are several regions, several subsequences of $\mathbf{S}$ should be identified.

4. RECORD SEGMENTATION TREE

Given a subtree sequence $\mathbf{S}$, we design a new search structure, named as Record Segmentation Tree (RST), to detect possible records in this sequence. Based on this search structure, the proposed algorithm can search and identify data records in the sequence. If some data records are identified, they naturally compose record regions. Therefore, region detection and record segmentation are performed simultaneously. For the convenience of interpretation, we use the

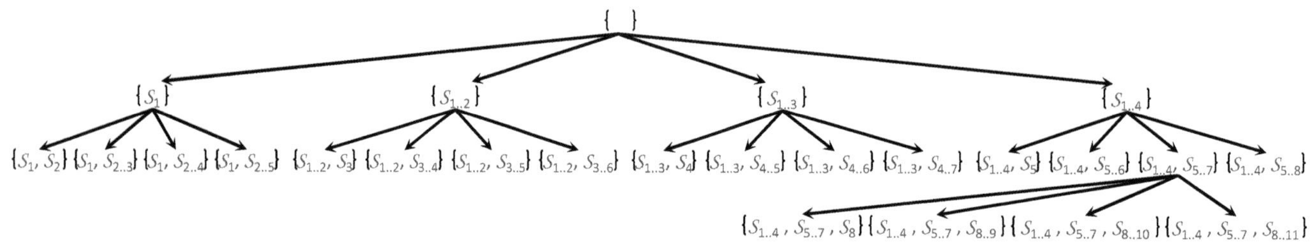

Figure 2: An example of basic record segmentation tree with $K = 4$.

subsequence starting from $\mathcal{S}_1$ to illustrate RST construction, as well as the subsequent algorithms. Our framework can detect the region starting from any subtrees in $\mathbf{S}$. We assume that one record at most contains K subtrees in $\mathbf{S}$.

4.1 Basic Record Segmentation Tree

DEFINITION 1. ***Record segmentation tree*** *is a search tree with the following properties:*

- *Each node $\mathbf{R}$ represents a possible record region. The root node represents an empty region.*
- *Each $\mathbf{R}$ covers a prefix subsequence $\mathcal{S}_{1..n}$ of $\mathbf{S}$, referred to as $\mathbf{S_R}$, where $0 \leq n \leq |\mathbf{S}|$, and has a separating indexes set $\mathbf{b}$ which segments $\mathcal{S}_{1..n}$ into records. Each record of $\mathbf{R}$ is denoted by R_i. The root has an empty prefix subsequence, i.e. $n = 0$, and an empty separating indexes set.*
- *Each $\mathbf{R}$ with $\mathcal{S}_{1..n}$ and $\mathbf{b}$ has at most K children. Each child of $\mathbf{R}$ covers $\mathcal{S}_{1..m}$ where $n+1 \leq m \leq \min\{n+K, |\mathbf{S}|\}$, and has a separating indexes set $\mathbf{b} \cup \{m\}$.*

From the above definition, it can been seen that each node is recursively defined with its parent node, and contains one more record. The record extraction task in $\mathbf{S}$ is transformed into a problem that searches a node in the RST structure which best matches with the true records in $\mathbf{S}$.

The segmentation tree with $K = 4$ is given in Figure 2. In this example, each node is labeled by its record set. For instance, the node $\mathbf{R} = \{\mathcal{S}_{1..4}, \mathcal{S}_{5..7}\}$ indicates that there are two records, namely, $R_1 = \mathcal{S}_{1..4}$, and $R_2 = \mathcal{S}_{5..7}$. The covered prefix is $\mathcal{S}_{1..7}$, and the separating indexes set is $\{4, 7\}$. $|R_i|$ denotes the length of R_i, and is equal to the number of subtrees it contains. For instance, $|R_1| = 4$, $|R_2| = 3$. We use $|\mathbf{R}|$ to denote the number of records in $\mathbf{R}$. $L_\mathbf{R}$ denotes the average length of the records in $\mathbf{R}$, calculated as $(\sum_{R_i \in \mathbf{R}} |R_i|)/|\mathbf{R}|$ or $|\mathbf{S_R}|/|\mathbf{R}|$.

4.2 Slimmed Segmentation Tree

In the same record region, it is almost impossible that the lengths of different records are significantly different, say some records contain only 1 subtree, while some others contain 5 subtrees. Based on this observation, we design a slimmed segmentation tree, in which the length of previous records is used to predict that of the next record. Suppose for a node $\mathbf{R}$ with $L_\mathbf{R} = 2$, we may think that it is impossible that a child of $\mathbf{R}$ has a new record with length 4 or more. Therefore, we only consider the children of $\mathbf{R}$ in which the new records' length is smaller than 4. Another observation is that when $L_\mathbf{R}$ is large, it is more probable that different records have a larger absolute length difference. For example, in a page in our experiment data set, the average length of the records is 7. Some records contain 4 subtrees, while some others contain 9 subtrees. Taking the above two observations into consideration, we introduce a slimmed version of segmentation tree.

DEFINITION 2. ***Slimmed segmentation tree*** *is a subgraph structure of the basic record segmentation tree. It keeps the first two layers of basic RST. Each child of a non-root node $\mathbf{R}$ with prefix sequence $\mathcal{S}_{1..n}$ has prefix sequence $\mathcal{S}_{1..m}$, where $n + (L_\mathbf{R} - \lfloor L_\mathbf{R}/2 \rfloor) \leq m \leq \min\{n + \min\{L_\mathbf{R} + \lceil L_\mathbf{R}/2 \rceil, K\}, |\mathbf{S}|\}$.*

An example is given in Figure 3, in which K is 5. It can be seen that in the third layer, we do not construct all possible children of a node $\mathbf{R}$ in the second layer. If $L_\mathbf{R}$ is smaller, we construct fewer number of children for it. Otherwise, we construct more.

4.3 Utilize RST in Record Extraction

Each node in RST is one possible segmentation of the record region starting from $\mathcal{S}_1$ in the sequence $\mathbf{S}$. According to the observation that the records in the same region are formatted using similar tags, the correct segmentation should be the node that achieves higher average pairwise record similarity. If we cannot find a node with pairwise record similarity greater than a pre-defined threshold, we may conclude that no record region exists starting from $\mathcal{S}_1$.

Precisely, given a DOM tree $\mathcal{T}$ and its subtree sequence $\mathbf{S}$, record extraction with the RST structure of $\mathbf{S}$ aims at finding a node $\mathbf{R}^*$ such that:

$$\mathbf{R}^* = \underset{\mathbf{R} \in \{\mathbf{R} | Q(\mathbf{R}) \geq \theta\}}{\operatorname{argmax}} |\mathbf{R}|, \tag{1}$$

where θ is a pre-defined threshold. $Q(\cdot)$ is the quality function of an RST node $\mathbf{R}$, which is defined as the average pairwise record similarity of records in $\mathbf{R}$:

$$Q(\mathbf{R}) = \frac{\sum_{R_i, R_j \in \mathbf{R} \ s.t. \ i<j} sim(R_i, R_j)}{|\mathbf{R}|(|\mathbf{R}| - 1)/2}, \tag{2}$$

where sim is a similarity function between two records. Let $\mathbb{R}^*$ denote $\{\mathbf{R} | Q(\mathbf{R}) \geq \theta\}$, each element in $\mathbb{R}^*$ is a node whose quality is not less than θ. Among these nodes in $\mathbb{R}^*$, the one with the maximum number of records is determined as the correct record region $\mathbf{R}^*$ starting from $\mathcal{S}_1$ in $\mathbf{S}$. If more than one nodes have the maximum number of records, we select the one with the best quality as $\mathbf{R}^*$. If $\mathbb{R}^* = \emptyset$, it means that no record region exists starting from $\mathcal{S}_1$.

For un-slimmed RST, when we expand it to layer $|\mathbf{S}|/K$, each inner node has K children. Thus, the total number of nodes in layer $|\mathbf{S}|/K$ is $K^{|\mathbf{S}|/K}$. In the slimmed version, suppose each inner node has $\hat{K}$ children on average, this number is $\hat{K}^{|\mathbf{S}|/K}$. Usually, in a possible record region, $|\mathbf{S}|$ is much larger than K. Constructing and searching such a segmentation tree is extremely time and space consuming because of its exponential size. Therefore, some search pruning strategies have been developed to allow efficient utilization of the RST structure.

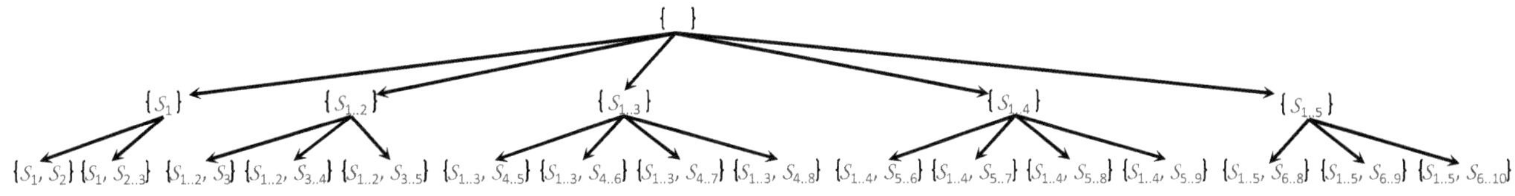

Figure 3: An example of slimmed segmentation tree with $K = 5$.

5. SEARCH PRUNING STRATEGIES

In this subsection, we introduce a threshold-based top k search that can prune the RST significantly, and reduce the complexity to $O(|\mathbf{S}|^2)$ without considering pairwise similarity computation of subtrees. Furthermore, instead of calculating the similarity of all record pairs in Equation 2, we may only check the similarity of a record and its nearest previous neighbors. Accordingly, the time complexity is further reduced to $O(|\mathbf{S}|)$.

5.1 Threshold-Based Top k Search

5.1.1 Initialization

In the beginning of RST construction, we have no idea about the record length in the given subtree sequence. The only information on hand is that each record has at most K subtrees. To attain a better starting, we fully expand the RST in the first 2 layers as shown in Figure 2. Each non-leaf node has K children in these layers. Then we have K^2 initial candidate nodes, denoted by $\tilde{\mathbb{R}}$, for future expansion and search. Note that K is very small, and the full expansion in the beginning will not cause much increasing of time complexity.

Before proceeding to the next layer of RST, we prune the candidates in $\tilde{\mathbb{R}}$ according to their quality, which is defined in Equation 2. For a particular node $\mathbf{R}$ in $\tilde{\mathbb{R}}$, it will be pruned if $Q(\mathbf{R}) < \theta'$. The meaning of θ' will be clear later. After the nodes with lower quality are pruned, if the number of retained nodes is more than a pre-defined threshold k, only the top k nodes with the best quality are retained, and denoted by $\mathbb{R}$. For example in Figure 2, the node $\{\mathcal{S}_1, \mathcal{S}_{2..5}\}$ is very likely to be pruned. If $\mathbb{R} = \emptyset$, then no region starting from $\mathcal{S}_1$ exists in $\mathbf{S}$.

5.1.2 Pruning Search

Suppose $\mathbf{R}$ is a node in $\mathbb{R}$, the last record in $\mathbf{R}$ is $\mathcal{S}_{i..n}$. We construct some children of $\mathbf{R}$, namely, $\mathbf{R} \cup \{\mathcal{S}_{n+1}\}, \mathbf{R} \cup \{\mathcal{S}_{n+1..n+2}\}, \cdots, \mathbf{R} \cup \{\mathcal{S}_{n+1..n+K}\}$. Then the similarity between newly generated records and the existing ones in $\mathbf{R}$ are calculated. Precisely, for each new record $\mathcal{S}_{n+1..m}$ ($n+1 \leq m \leq n+K$) and each $R \in \mathbf{R}$, $sim(\mathcal{S}_{n+1..m}, R)$ is calculated. Then, the quality of $\mathcal{S}_{n+1..m}$ is defined as:

$$Q(\mathcal{S}_{n+1..m}) = \frac{\sum_{R \in \mathbf{R}} sim(\mathcal{S}_{n+1..m}, R)}{|\mathbf{R}|}. \quad (3)$$

In the same way, each $\mathbf{R}$ in $\mathbb{R}$ is expanded, and the quality of each new record is calculated.

After the RST structure is expanded one more layer, a new pruning strategy different from that for $\tilde{\mathbb{R}}$ is adopted. For a new RST node $\mathbf{R} \cup \{\mathcal{S}_{n+1..m}\}$, if $Q(\mathcal{S}_{n+1..m}) \geq \theta'$ and $Q(\mathbf{R} \cup \{\mathcal{S}_{n+1..m}\}) \geq \theta$, $\mathbf{R} \cup \{\mathcal{S}_{n+1..m}\}$ is retained, otherwise it is pruned, where θ' is smaller than θ. The rationale behind this strategy is that some record, say $\mathcal{S}_{n+1..m}$, may have a larger difference compared with the previous records. But we assume that the difference should not be large. Precisely, $Q(\mathcal{S}_{n+1..m})$ should not be less than a looser threshold θ'. If this condition is met, we continue to check the quality of $\mathbf{R} \cup \{\mathcal{S}_{n+1..m}\}$. In this way, the search procedure can overcome the problems caused by some outlier records, meanwhile, the quality of the outliers is also bounded by θ'. Recall that we use θ' instead of θ in the pruning of the initial candidate nodes $\tilde{\mathbb{R}}$, it is because each element of $\tilde{\mathbb{R}}$ contains two records. For a particular $\mathbf{R}$, if no $\mathbf{R} \cup \{\mathcal{S}_{n+1..m}\}$ is retained after pruning, $\mathbf{R}$ is put into $\mathbb{R}^*$. Again, if the number of retained nodes is more than k, we keep the top k nodes with the best quality, and construct a new $\mathbb{R}$.

The above procedure is repeated on the new $\mathbb{R}$ until it is empty or the end of $\mathbf{S}$ is reached. Then we finish building an RST structure for $\mathbf{S}$ starting from $\mathcal{S}_1$, at the same time, $\mathbb{R}^*$ is also built. Note that the RST structure needs not reach $\mathcal{S}_{|\mathbf{S}|}$, which indicates that some subtrees in the end of $\mathbf{S}$ should not be included in the record region.

5.1.3 Retrospect with Short-term Memory

In the above expanding and pruning process, when examining the quality of a new record, all previous records are considered, as shown in Equation 3. This thorough retrospect is not only time consuming, but also unnecessary. Especially in the region with many records, the cost of such exhaustive comparison outweighs the benefit gained. We adopt a short-term memory retrospect strategy to reduce the computation workload. When a node is expanded one more layer, we only calculate the similarity between a new record and the nearest r previous records. Thus, in Equation 3, the number of pairwise similarity calculations is reduced from $|\mathbf{R}|$ to r. And in Equation 2, the cost of evaluating one node is reduced from $|\mathbf{R}|(|\mathbf{R}|-1)/2$ to $r|\mathbf{R}|$.

5.2 Complexity Analysis

The computation workload of pairwise record similarity calculation is related to the number of subtrees in the involved records. Hence, we use a finer unit to analyze the complexity of utilizing RST in record extraction.

In Section 5.1, when evaluating the quality of new records with Equation 3, we need to calculate the similarity between each existing record in $\mathbf{R}$ and each new record. The computation workload is:

$$|\mathbf{R}| \sum_{1 \leq l \leq K} (L_{\mathbf{R}} l) = \frac{K(K+1)|\mathbf{S_R}|}{2}, \quad (4)$$

where $L_{\mathbf{R}}$ is the average length of records in $\mathbf{R}$, $\mathbf{S_R}$ is the subtree sequence covered by $\mathbf{R}$, and $L_{\mathbf{R}} l$ indicates the computation needed for calculating the similarity between the records having $L_{\mathbf{R}}$ and l subtrees respectively. Thus, the computation workload of segmenting entire $\mathbf{S}$ is:

$$\sum_{1 \leq x \leq (\frac{|\mathbf{S}|}{L_{\mathbf{R}}} - 1)} (x \sum_{1 \leq l \leq K} (L_{\mathbf{R}} l)) = \frac{K(K+1)(\frac{|\mathbf{S}|}{L_{\mathbf{R}}} - 1)|\mathbf{S}|}{4}, \quad (5)$$

In the top k strategy, the overall computation needed is $kK(K+1)(|\mathbf{S}|/L_{\mathbf{R}}-1)|\mathbf{S}|/4$. In our framework, the method of calculating pairwise record similarity is a variant of edit distance. Due to the dynamic programming employed in edit distance, when calculating the distance matrix between two strings, the existing matrix between their prefix strings can be reused. In Equation 3, when calculating the similarity between $\mathcal{S}_{n+1..m}$ and an existing record R, the distance matrix between $\mathcal{S}_{n+1..m-1}$ and R can be reused. Consequently, the above workload can be further reduced to $k(K+1)(|\mathbf{S}|/L_{\mathbf{R}}-1)|\mathbf{S}|/4$. The value of k is usually smaller than K, and both k and K are small and can be treated as constants. Thus, the overall time complexity is $O(|\mathbf{S}|^2)$.

Under the strategy of short-term memory retrospect, the workload in Equation 5 becomes:

$$(\frac{|\mathbf{S}|}{L_{\mathbf{R}}}-1)r\sum_{1\leq l\leq K}(L_{\mathbf{R}}l)=\frac{rK(K+1)|\mathbf{S}|}{2}, \quad (6)$$

where r is the number of records retrospected from current layer. Similarly, the overall complexity can be further reduced to $r(K+1)|\mathbf{S}|/2$, which can be regarded as $O(|\mathbf{S}|)$.

For each sequence $\mathbf{S}$, MDR [17] has time complexity of $O(|\mathbf{S}|)$ to calculate the similarity among the same length generalized node. In MDR, only the adjacent generalized node pairs are considered in similarity calculation, which is similar to our retrospect strategy with $r=1$. ViPER [22] has time complexity of $O(|\mathbf{S}|^2)$ to construct the upper triangular similarity matrix of all subtree pairs. Note that the above time complexity is only the part needed by MDR or ViPER for record region detection, and they need another step to segment the detected region into records.

5.3 Composite Node Pruning

Suppose each subtree in $\mathbf{S}$ is one record, all RST nodes with the form $\{\mathcal{S}_{1..i},\mathcal{S}_{i+1..2i},\mathcal{S}_{2i+1..3i},\cdots\}$ $(1\leq i\leq K)$ have quite high quality. The reason is that the combination of i records is similar to that of the other i records. In some other cases, this kind of combination may even achieve higher quality than the correct record segmentation. For example, there are four records in a region $\mathbf{R}=\{\mathcal{S}'_1\mathcal{S}_2,\mathcal{S}'_3,\mathcal{S}'_4\mathcal{S}_5,\mathcal{S}'_6\}$, where the primed subtrees are matched ones in different records. The node $\mathbf{R}^c=\{\mathcal{S}'_1\mathcal{S}_2\mathcal{S}'_3,\mathcal{S}'_4\mathcal{S}_5\mathcal{S}'_6\}$ has a higher quality than $\mathbf{R}$. We call $\mathbf{R}^c$ a composite node of $\mathbf{R}$. Composite nodes will increase the computation workload and involve noise during RST search. To tackle this problem, after a period of search, say when all nodes in $\mathbb{R}$ exceed $\mathcal{S}_n$ in $\mathbf{S}$, we check the relation between the nodes in $\mathbb{R}$. If one node is a composite node of any other node, it is pruned. Note that for the node involving subtrees after $\mathcal{S}_n$, we only consider its records before $\mathcal{S}_n$ in the detection of composite node.

5.4 More Challenging Record Region Discussion

In this subsection, we discuss how several kinds of more challenging record regions can be handled with the proposed RST structure and search strategy.

5.4.1 Embedded Region and Non-continuous Region

Record region in $\mathbf{S}$ may not start from $\mathcal{S}_1$ because of the existence of header information, one example and its DOM tree are given in Figures 4(a) and 4(d). In the same way, the region also may not end at $\mathcal{S}_{|\mathbf{S}|}$. We name this kind of region as *embedded region*. The way to detect embedded regions in our framework is straightforward. In the beginning, we start from $\mathcal{S}_1$, and generate an initial set $\tilde{\mathbb{R}}_{\mathcal{S}_1}$. If all elements in $\tilde{\mathbb{R}}_{\mathcal{S}_1}$ are pruned, we move to $\mathcal{S}_2$, and repeat the above procedure. In this way, the header subtrees in the beginning are excluded. If $\mathbb{R}=\emptyset$ before coming to $\mathcal{S}_{|\mathbf{S}|}$, it means that there is some footer information which should not be treated as part of any record.

In some other cases, there may be more than one regions in $\mathbf{S}$. For example, in an on-line shopping Web page, $\mathbf{S}$ may contain two subsequences introducing new arrival products and featured products respectively. And they are separated by some other information. We name this kind of region as *non-continuous region*. The above procedure for dealing with embedded regions can also be applied to non-continuous region easily. After finishing one region detection, the detection algorithm will move on to the sequence of the remaining subtrees if there are some, and perform the search procedure again to detect the second region.

5.4.2 Nested Region

In some Web pages, the records are formatted in a nested manner. For example, the region formatted with <table>, each record is packed with one <td>, each <tr> has several <td>s. The region with <table> as root node is know as *nested region*. In our framework, with a top-down manner to scan the DOM tree, <table> is detected as a record region with <tr>s as records. Then, each <tr> is detected as a region with <td>s as records. After the <tr>s are detected as regions, along with the fact that these <tr>s have been detected as records of the same root node <table> in the preceding detection, we may postulate that the <table> is a nested region. To inspect our postulation, we compare the records, i.e., <td>s, from different <tr>s, and check whether they are similar. If so, we conclude the node <table> is a nested region. There are several other issues such as the orphan record detection in the last "row" will not be discussed here due to the limited space. Note that the above "table" is used to demonstrate the detecting process, our detection method does not rely on any particular tag.

5.4.3 Intertwine Records

Intertwine record, also known as *non-continuous record* in DEPTA [27], refers to the record whose attributes intertwine together with other records' attributes. One example and its DOM tree are given in Figures 4(b) and 4(e). Each record has 3 attributes, namely, image, title, and price, and these attributes scattered in 3 different subtrees (<tr>s). In our framework, the subtree sequence of <tr>s in the table is first passed to the record detection algorithm, and each successive non-overlapping 3-subtree segment is detected as one record. After that, each <tr> is passed to the detection algorithm, and detected as a region with each <td> as one record. Up to now, the above procedure resembles that of nested region detection. We continue to check the similarity between records in neighboring <tr>s, and they are found dissimilar to each other. Thus, we conclude that a intertwine region is detected, and the correct records can be generated by reassembling the detected regions. In this example, three regions (image 1, image 2), (title 1, title 2) and (price 1, price 2) are reassembled to generate records (image 1, title 1, price 1) and (image 2, title 2, price 2).

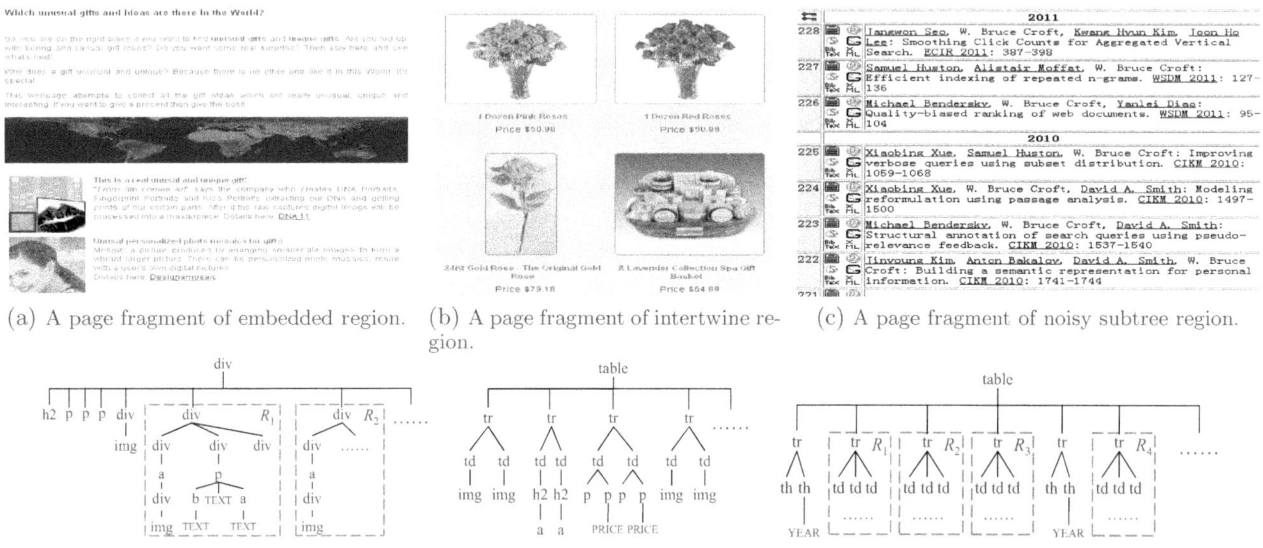

(a) A page fragment of embedded region. (b) A page fragment of intertwine region. (c) A page fragment of noisy subtree region.

(d) DOM tree of (a) (e) DOM tree of (b) (f) DOM tree of (c)

Figure 4: Several kinds of more challenging record regions.

5.4.4 *Noise Subtree Exclusion*

In Figures 4(c) and 4(f), a publication list is separated into different sections according to the published year. It can be regarded as a non-continuous region. Theoretically, with proper setting of thresholds, we can expect that publications in 2011 will be detected as the first region, and publications in 2010 will be detected as the second region. However, it is also possible that the year row 2011 fuses into record 228, and the year row 2010 fuses into record 225. If a record contains such noise subtrees, the similarity between this record and its context records becomes lower. Meanwhile, the number of subtrees in this record is more than that in others. Using these observations as clues, it is not difficult to exclude noise subtrees from records. Due to space limitation, we only outline the idea and omit the details. Basically, if some subtrees in the first record are detected as noise and excluded, we need to reexamine this record segmentation. The reason is that the polluted first record may lead to wrong segmentation of the region.

6. RECORD SIMILARITY MEASURE

In this section, we discuss the method used for measuring the similarity between two records (sequences of subtrees), in sequence **S**. There are mainly two existing approaches. One is string edit distance based [17, 22], the other is tree edit distance based [27]. In string edit distance based method, each subtree is encoded with a string which is obtained by traversing the subtree in pre-order, and appending the name of visited tag node to the string. Due to the fact that names of different tags may have different length, using the string of tag name directly is not suitable. In spite of this limitation, string edit distance can tackle repetitive fields properly by tandem repeats detection [22], as well as optional fields. In [27], top-down distance, which is a restricted version of tree edit distance, is employed to measure the distance between two subtrees. Its problem is that any crossing layers' operation is not permitted, making it unable to handle optional tags. On the other hand, the tree edit distance can overcome the limitation in string edit distance since it considers each DOM node as an inseparable unit. To adopt their good points and avoid the shortcomings, we propose a token-based edit distance method.

Table 1: Types of text node.

Type Name	Meaning	Priority
EMAIL	An email address	1
URL	A URL string	2
PRICE	Digital number with a currency symbol	3
TIME	Time in predefined format, such as hh:mm:ss	4
DATE	Date in predefined format, such as yyyy/mm/dd	5
YEAR	Four digits, arrange from 1900 to 2050	6
TEXT	Other kinds of text	7

6.1 Encoding Subtree with Tokens

Aiming at fixing the ill-formatted Web pages, some existing works [26, 27] introduce visual information from rendered Web page into DOM tree building. To avoid this time consuming rendering operation, we employ an HTML cleansing package, namely, HtmlCleaner[1], to clean the Web pages. Then the DOM structure of the cleaned page is built.

In the DOM tree, we have two kinds of nodes, namely, tag node and text node. Each tag node has a name such as "tr", "div", etc. A piece of visible text between a pair of ">" and "<" is regarded as a basic text unit, and normalized to a text node. Table 1 shows the types of text nodes defined in our framework. The priority indicates the order in which different types are attempted when normalizing a piece of text. Each subtree in the DOM is encoded with the sequence of node names in it, which is obtained by traversing the tree in pre-order. Each node name in the sequence is called one *token*, and it is an inseparable unit in similarity calculation.

6.2 Tandem Repeat Detection and Distance-based Measure

A typical characteristic of data records is that they vary in optional or repetitive fields. For example, a book record may have discounted price or not, and one author or several. An obvious disadvantage of edit distance computation is that repetitive and optional fields increase the edit cost.

[1] `http://htmlcleaner.sourceforge.net/`

As noticed by ViPER [22], similarity threshold is suitable to solve the problem caused by optional fields, but not suitable for repetitive fields. ViPER identifies *tandem repeats* in two strings before distance calculation, and allows zero cost for deletion and insertion inside additional repetitions.

In our token-based edit distance scenario, the above idea is also applicable. We implement the algorithm proposed by Gusfield et al. [12] to detect the tandem repeats. This algorithm utilizes suffix tree structure to identify the tandem repeats which are not longer than z in a sequence of length n in $O(n+z)$ time. The difference is that the basic unit in our sequences is token (node name), not single character. Thus we need to perform token comparison instead of character comparison in the detection of tandem repeats. Furthermore, if the token sequence is originated from several subtrees, it is constrained that tandem repeats are only detected in the token sequence of each single subtree. We refine the tandem repeats based edit distance proposed in ViPER [22] and make it suitable for the token scenario in our framework. For the details of tandem repeat detection and its application in edit distance, we would like to direct the readers to [12] and [22]. Then the calculated distance is normalized into the interval [0, 1], and the negative value of the normalized distance is added by 1. Thus, we obtain the record similarity measure used in our framework.

7. EXPERIMENTS

For evaluating the performance of our method and conducting comparison with existing methods, we attempt to use existing data sets and available implementation of existing methods. MDR implementation is available[2], which is able to deal with flat, nested, and intertwine records. Therefore, it was employed as the comparison baseline for all experiments. We used two existing data sets for testing the performance of our method on flat data record extraction. Besides MDR, we also compare with two other existing methods, namely, TPC [20], and ViNTs [29], whose experimental results are available on these data sets. Because no existing data set for nested or intertwine records is available, we collected one data set for each of them, and only compare our method with MDR. With respect to evaluation metrics, we employ the commonly used precision and recall. To avoid the evaluation bias brought in by pages with large number of records, both micro average and macro average are reported.

Given a Web page, our algorithm adopts a top down manner to scan its DOM tree for detecting records. For some pages, several record regions are detected. We first filter out the regions whose record size is smaller than 3, where the size of a record is defined as the number of leaf DOM nodes it has. After that, we employ the single-linkage agglomerative hierarchical clustering algorithm to cluster the remaining regions into different clusters. The algorithm starts with each region as an initial cluster which contains its records as the elements in it. The stopping similarity threshold is set to be θ'. After clustering, the cluster with the largest number of records is selected as the final result. We used a number of training pages collected separately to tune the parameter values in our framework. Finally, θ is set to 0.75, θ' is set to 0.65, K is set to 10, both k and r are set to 5.

[2] `http://www.cs.uic.edu/~liub/WebDataExtraction/`

Table 2: Experimental results on TB1.

		Ground	TP	FP	P-mi	R-mi	P-ma	R-ma
ALL	Our	864	855	21	.976	.990	.968	.974
	MDR	864	553	48	.920	.640	.594	.610
ALL/wrong	Our	851	843	16	.981	.991	.980	.977
	MDR	851	553	48	.920	.650	.620	.636
TPC used	Our	781	778	16	.980	.996	.977	.984
	TPC	781	NA	NA	NA	NA	.904	.931

Table 3: Experimental results on TB2.

		Ground	TP	FP	P-mi	R-mi	P-ma	R-ma
ALL	Our	968	953	10	.990	.985	.965	.958
	MDR	968	722	66	.916	.746	.693	.734
	ViNTs	968	934	11	.988	.965	.973	.950
ALL/wrong	Our	863	849	10	.988	.984	.961	.956
	MDR	863	722	66	.916	.837	.773	.819
	ViNTs	863	830	11	.987	.962	.970	.945

7.1 Flat Record Extraction

Our first data set is the testbed collected by Yamada et al. [25] which is available at `http://daisen.cc.kyushu-u.ac.jp/T` This testbed was also used by other works such as ViPER and TPC [20]. The testbed data has 253 Web pages from 51 Web sites randomly drawn from 114,540 Web pages with search forms. The data records in this testbed are manually labeled by the collectors, and results are also available online together with the data set. In our experiment, three sites are excluded because of nested records, garbled code, or ambiguous record annotation. Thus, we use the remaining 48 sites including 238 pages in total. TPC also conducted experiment on this testbed data set. The authors kindly provided us the Web site IDs in the subset they used, which contains 43 sites out of 48 sites we use. Therefore, without implementing their method, we can still conduct a fair comparison. Our second data set is the data set 3 used in ViNTs [29] which is available at `http://www.data.binghamton.edu:8080/vir` along with the details of ViNTs' performance on each page. Thus, we can conduct a comparison with ViNTs in more detail. This data set is originated from Omini [6] testbed collected by Buttler et al., which consists of more than 2,000 Web pages collected 50 Web sites. ViNTs took one random page per Web site to construct its data set 3. In our experiment, we exclude 2 pages because of the ambiguity on record annotation. Thus, our second data set contains 48 pages. The above two data sets are referred to as TB1 and TB2 respectively. We run MDR on both data sets with the default similarity threshold 60%, and extract the records reported. MDR could not produce output for 2 Web sites in TB1 and 5 pages in TB2 because the MDR program terminated abnormally. We report both results with and without these pages.

The experimental results on TB1 and TB2 are given in Tables 2 and 3 respectively. "ALL" refers to the entire page set used, "ALL/wrong" refers to the subset without the pages on which MDR program terminated abnormally, and "TPC used" refers to the subset used by the TPC method. "Ground" denotes the number of ground truth records, "TP" denotes the number of true positive given by a method, and "FP" denotes the number of false positive. "P-mi", "P-ma", "R-mi" and "R-ma" are the micro-averaged and macro-averaged precision and recall values respectively. "NA" means no corresponding result reported in TPC [20]. In P-ma calculation, if both TP and FP are 0 for a particular page, its precision is set to be 0.

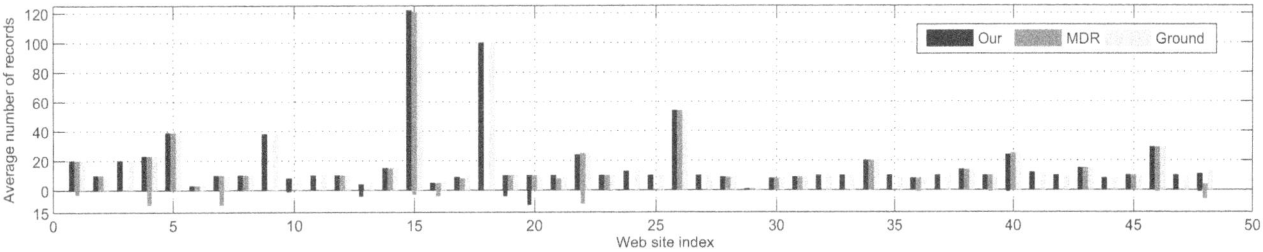

Figure 5: Extracted records for each site in TB1, the reported number is the average over the number of pages in the site. TP number and FP number are shown by the bars above and below the axis respectively.

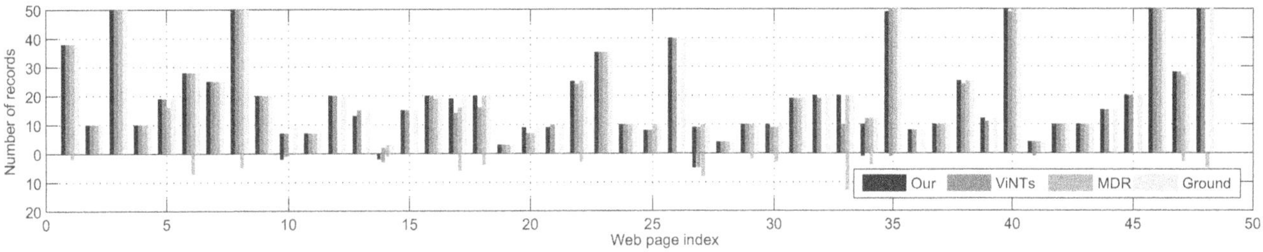

Figure 6: Extracted records for each page in TB2. The legend is the same as that in Figure 5.

On TB1, our method outperforms both MDR and TPC. The recall of our method is significantly better than that of MDR. In addition the precision of our method outperforms TPC about 7%. On TB2, the performance of our method is also much better than that of MDR. Compared with ViNTs, our method can extract more correct results, and achieve 2% improvement in R-mi. We can see that for MDR P-ma is much smaller than P-mi. It is because for some pages, although the MDR program terminated normally, it cannot give any output, thus both TP and FP are 0.

The details of the extracted records on TB1 and TB2 are given in Figure 5 and Figure 6 respectively. On TB1, our method outputs 10 false positives for site 20. After checking the pages manually, we find that each page in this site contains 10 recommended books on the right side bar. But the annotated ground truth only includes the books formatted with <table> in the center of the page. For this site, MDR only reports the books annotated. For site 35, we find that each field of a record is packed in a single subtree in **S**, such as id, title, URL, each of digest sentences, etc. Because different records have different number of subtrees, MDR fails to output any correct results. For site 48, each page contains more than one record regions, MDR only reports the largest one, and misses others. In Figure 6, we can see that for pages 17, 18 and 33, ViNTs misses some records. After checking these pages manually, we find that each of them has 3 or 4 regions. As reported by Zhao et al. [29], ViNTs is designed to extract records just from the major record region, it misses other smaller regions.

7.2 Nested and Intertwine Record Extraction

To collect data sets with nested and intertwine records, we investigated the online shopping Web sites one by one in an online shopping yellow page `http://www.toponlineshopping.com/`. There are 22 categories such as "Art & Collectibles" and "Beauty & Fragrances" in this page, and each category has about 6 sub-categories on average. Under each sub-category, we randomly selected 2 recommended Web sites. Instead of submitting queries to retrieve record pages, we directly clicked the navigation links in the home page, and obtained record pages. In this way, we successfully obtained record pages from 110 sites, and there are 50 sites adopting nested manner to present products, and 5 sites adopting intertwine manner. We downloaded 2 pages per nested site to construct the nested data set, thus it contains 100 Web pages. MDR terminated abnormally for one page in this data set. To construct the intertwine page set, we downloaded 3 pages per intertwine site, thus there are 15 pages in the intertwine data set.

Table 4: Experimental results on nested pages.

		Ground	TP	FP	P-mi	R-mi	P-ma	R-ma
ALL	Our	1293	1292	2	.998	.999	.997	.998
	MDR	1293	1141	90	.927	.882	.822	.867
ALL/wrong	Our	1284	1283	2	.998	.999	.997	.998
	MDR	1284	1141	90	.927	.889	.838	.884

Table 5: Experimental results on intertwine pages.

	Ground	TP	FP	P-mi	R-mi	P-ma	R-ma
Our	262	259	0	1	.989	1	.986
MDR	262	253	50	.835	.966	.898	.967

The experimental results for nested and intertwine page sets are given in Tables 4 and 5. Our method achieves nearly perfect results, while MDR misses many records in nested record extraction, and gives more false positives in both nested and intertwine record extraction. After checking the pages for which MDR misses all records manually, we found that these pages format the records in a very complicated manner. In 3 pages, each <td> contains another <table> to encapsulate the information of one record. In another page, each <td> even contains two layers of nested <table>s. Our method can tackle these pages correctly since it does not rely on any particular tag. Our final record selection process effectively excludes noise records, while MDR outputs more false positives.

8. CONCLUSIONS

In this paper, we present a novel approach to extract data records in a Web page. The proposed RST structure can be utilized to address several key issues in the record extraction task. The two essential sub-tasks, namely, record region detection, and record segmentation, are handled in a unified manner with the proposed search pruning techniques on the RST structure. Different from the existing similarity-based methods, our method examines the similarity between the dynamically generated subtree groups taking into account the characteristics of the current record region. Owing to the pruning strategies, our method has a comparative complexity compared with the existing methods. Furthermore, we propose a new similarity measure in which each DOM node is regarded as an inseparable unit. Together with the detected tandem repeats, our similarity measure can tackle optional and repetitive fields in records properly. Extensive experiments are conducted to evaluate the performance of our method. The results demonstrate that our method can achieve very superior results for the test data sets, and different kinds of records can be tackled effectively.

9. REFERENCES

[1] `http://www.programmableweb.com/`.

[2] B. Adelberg. Nodose - a tool for semi-automatically extracting structured and semistructured data from text documents. *SIGMOD Rec.*, 27:283–294, June 1998.

[3] A. Arasu and H. Garcia-Molina. Extracting structured data from web pages. In *SIGMOD '03*, pages 337–348, 2003.

[4] G. O. Arocena and A. O. Mendelzon. Weboql: restructuring documents, databases, and webs. *Theor. Pract. Object Syst.*, 5:127–141, August 1999.

[5] R. Baumgartner, G. Gottlob, and M. Herzog. Scalable web data extraction for online market intelligence. *Proc. VLDB Endow.*, 2:1512–1523, August 2009.

[6] D. Buttler, L. Liu, and C. Pu. A fully automated object extraction system for the world wide web. In *ICDCS '01*, pages 361–370, 2001.

[7] C.-H. Chang and S.-C. Lui. Iepad: information extraction based on pattern discovery. In *WWW '01*, pages 681–688, 2001.

[8] V. Crescenzi, G. Mecca, and P. Merialdo. Roadrunner: Towards automatic data extraction from large web sites. In *VLDB '01*, pages 109–118, 2001.

[9] D. W. Embley, D. M. Campbell, Y. S. Jiang, S. W. Liddle, D. W. Lonsdale, Y.-K. Ng, and R. D. Smith. Conceptual model-based data extraction from multiple-record web pages. *Data Knowl. Eng.*, 31:227–251, November 1999.

[10] D. W. Embley, Y. Jiang, and Y.-K. Ng. Record-boundary discovery in web documents. In *SIGMOD '99*, pages 467–478, 1999.

[11] W. Gatterbauer, P. Bohunsky, M. Herzog, B. Krüpl, and B. Pollak. Towards domain-independent information extraction from web tables. In *WWW '07*, pages 71–80, 2007.

[12] D. Gusfield and J. Stoye. Linear time algorithms for finding and representing all the tandem repeats in a string. *J. Comput. Syst. Sci.*, 69:525–546, December 2004.

[13] A. Hogue and D. Karger. Thresher: automating the unwrapping of semantic content from the world wide web. In *WWW '05*, pages 86–95, 2005.

[14] C.-N. Hsu and M.-T. Dung. Generating finite-state transducers for semi-structured data extraction from the web. *Inf. Syst.*, 23:521–538, December 1998.

[15] N. Kushmerick. Wrapper induction: efficiency and expressiveness. *Artif. Intell.*, 118:15–68, April 2000.

[16] A. H. F. Laender, B. Ribeiro-Neto, and A. S. da Silva. Debye - date extraction by example. *Data Knowl. Eng.*, 40:121–154, February 2002.

[17] B. Liu, R. Grossman, and Y. Zhai. Mining data records in web pages. In *KDD '03*, pages 601–606, 2003.

[18] L. Liu, C. Pu, and W. Han. Xwrap: An xml-enabled wrapper construction system for web information sources. In *ICDE '00*, pages 611–621, 2000.

[19] W. Liu, X. Meng, and W. Meng. Vide: A vision-based approach for deep web data extraction. *IEEE Trans. on Knowl. and Data Eng.*, 22:447–460, March 2010.

[20] G. Miao, J. Tatemura, W.-P. Hsiung, A. Sawires, and L. E. Moser. Extracting data records from the web using tag path clustering. In *WWW '09*, pages 981–990, 2009.

[21] I. Muslea, S. Minton, and C. A. Knoblock. Hierarchical wrapper induction for semistructured information sources. *Autonomous Agents and Multi-Agent Systems*, 4:93–114, March 2001.

[22] K. Simon and G. Lausen. Viper: augmenting automatic information extraction with visual perceptions. In *CIKM '05*, pages 381–388, 2005.

[23] W. Su, J. Wang, and F. H. Lochovsky. Ode: Ontology-assisted data extraction. *ACM Trans. Database Syst.*, 34:12:1–12:35, July 2009.

[24] J. Wang and F. H. Lochovsky. Data extraction and label assignment for web databases. In *WWW '03*, pages 187–196, 2003.

[25] Y. Yamada, N. Craswell, T. Nakatoh, and S. Hirokawa. Testbed for information extraction from deep web. In *WWW Alt. '04*, pages 346–347, 2004.

[26] Y. Zhai and B. Liu. Web data extraction based on partial tree alignment. In *WWW '05*, pages 76–85, 2005.

[27] Y. Zhai and B. Liu. Structured data extraction from the web based on partial tree alignment. *IEEE Trans. on Knowl. and Data Eng.*, 18:1614–1628, December 2006.

[28] Y. Zhai and B. Liu. Extracting web data using instance-based learning. *World Wide Web*, 10:113–132, June 2007.

[29] H. Zhao, W. Meng, Z. Wu, V. Raghavan, and C. Yu. Fully automatic wrapper generation for search engines. In *WWW '05*, pages 66–75, 2005.

[30] H. Zhao, W. Meng, and C. Yu. Mining templates from search result records of search engines. In *KDD '07*, pages 884–893, 2007.

[31] S. Zheng, R. Song, J.-R. Wen, and C. L. Giles. Efficient record-level wrapper induction. In *CIKM '09*, pages 47–56, 2009.

[32] S. Zheng, R. Song, J.-R. Wen, and D. Wu. Joint optimization of wrapper generation and template detection. In *KDD '07*, pages 894–902, 2007.

[33] J. Zhu, Z. Nie, J.-R. Wen, B. Zhang, and W.-Y. Ma. Simultaneous record detection and attribute labeling in web data extraction. In *KDD '06*, pages 494–503, 2006.

Fast Metadata-driven Multiresolution Tensor Decomposition*

Claudio Schifanella
University of Torino
Corso Svizzera 185 - 10149
Torino (Italy)
schi@di.unito.it

K. Selçuk Candan
Arizona State University
699 S. Mill Avenue 553
Tempe, AZ 85281
candan@asu.edu

Maria Luisa Sapino
University of Torino
Corso Svizzera 185 - 10149
Torino (Italy)
mlsapino@di.unito.it

ABSTRACT

Tensors (multi-dimensional arrays) are widely used for representing high-order dimensional data, in applications ranging from social networks, sensor data, and Internet traffic. Multi-way data analysis techniques, in particular tensor decompositions, allow extraction of hidden correlations among multi-way data and thus are key components of many data analysis frameworks. Intuitively, these algorithms can be thought of as *multi-way clustering* schemes, which consider multiple facets of the data in identifying clusters, their weights, and contributions of each data element. Unfortunately, algorithms for fitting multi-way models are, in general, iterative and very time consuming. In this paper, we observe that, in many applications, there is *a priori* background knowledge (or metadata) about one or more domain dimensions. This metadata is often in the form of a hierarchy that clusters the elements of a given data facet (or mode). In this paper, we investigate whether such single-mode data hierarchies can be used to boost the efficiency of tensor decomposition process, without significant impact on the final decomposition quality. We consider each domain hierarchy as a guide to help provide higher- or lower-resolution views of the data in the tensor on demand and we rely on these metadata-induced multi-resolution tensor representations to develop a multiresolution approach to tensor decomposition. In this paper, we focus on an alternating least squares (ALS) based implementation of the PARAllel FACtors (PARAFAC) decomposition (which decomposes a tensor into a diagonal tensor and a set of factor matrices). Experiment results show that, when the available metadata is used as a rough guide, the proposed multiresolution method helps fit PARAFAC models with consistent (for both dense and sparse tensor representations, under different parameters settings) savings in execution time and memory consumption, while preserving the quality of the decomposition.

*This work is partially supported by an NSF Grant #1043583 - 'MiNC: NSDL Middleware for Network- and Context-aware Recommendations'

Categories and Subject Descriptors

H.3.3 [**Information Search and Retrieval**]: Clustering

General Terms

Theory, Algorithms

Keywords

Tensor decomposition, multiresolution, PARAFAC

1. INTRODUCTION

Multidimensional arrays, i.e. tensors, are increasingly used for multi-way data representation in diverse of applications [1, 19]. Starting from their early use in psychometrics [31], multi-way analysis techniques, and in particular tensor decompositions, have been widely used in extraction of hidden correlations among multi-way data, in fields, such as information retrieval [7], sensor networks analysis [26], web ranking and analysis [28, 18].

Intuitively, tensor decomposition algorithms can often be thought of as *multi-way clustering* schemes, which consider, simultaneously, multiple facets of the data for identifying clusters, their weights, and contributions of each data element. Tensor decomposition techniques are often placed into three categories: the first group includes the Parallel Factors (PARAFAC) decomposition [10] (also called CANDECOMP [4]) and its extensions like PARAFAC2 [11], S-PARAFAC [12] and PARALIND [3] that decompose a tensor into a smaller diagonal tensor and a set of factor matrices, one for each dimension of the input tensor. In the second category we find models based on Tucker decomposition [30] that approximate the initial tensor into a core tensor and a set of matrices that represent subspaces of each dimension. The third group contains models like Multilinear Engine [21] and STATIS based multi-way models [25]. In the literature, there are various algorithms for fitting tensor decomposition models [23, 22, 15]. In particular, algorithms based on *alternating least squares (ALS)* estimate the decomposition one factor matrix at time, keeping other factors fixed; the process is repeated until the convergence condition is reached.

Unfortunately, algorithms for fitting multi-way models are, in general, very time consuming. In this paper, we observe that, in many applications, there is *a priori* background knowledge (or metadata) about one or more domain dimensions and this metadata is often in the form of a hierarchy that clusters the elements of a given data facet (or mode). We investigate whether such single-mode data hierarchies can help boost the efficiency of tensor decomposition process, without significant impact on the final decomposition quality. Intuitively, we consider each available domain hierarchy as a support that provides different views of the data, with varying resolutions along a single dimension. Using these different resolutions at different stages of the decomposition process, then, helps eliminate redundant work and save execution time.

In this paper we focus our attention on the Alternating Least Squares (ALS) based algorithms for fitting PARAFAC models, proposed by Carrol *et. al* [4] and Harshman [10]. We present a metadata-based multiresolution approach to ALS based PARAFAC. The algorithm enables the user to pick and choose among the available domain hierarchies, the approximation levels, as well as to vary target *convergence condition* for different levels of the input hierarchies to support tensor decomposition. The algorithm starts at a low resolution and identifies a decomposition for that resolution. Once the iterations for the given level is complete, the resulting decomposition is *expanded* and this expanded decomposition is used as a starting point for the next, higher resolution. This process is repeated one resolution at a time until all the selected levels of the hierarchy have been considered.

The proposed multi-resolution process increases the number of iterations of the algorithm; significant time savings are obtained because the initial iterations are much faster due to the lower resolution of the data. Moreover, the number of costly high resolution iterations are significantly reduced. Experiment results show that, when the available metadata is used as a rough guide (avoiding over-fitting to the lower resolution of the tensors), the proposed multiresolution method helps fit PARAFAC models with consistent (for both dense and sparse tensor representations, under different parameters settings) savings in execution time and memory consumption, while preserving the quality of the obtained decomposition. Experiments also show that the proposed method can leverage more than one uni-modal hierarchy to further reduce tensor decomposition times.

The structure of the paper is as follows. Section 2 provides an overview of the related works and introduces the tensor background knowledge and formalisms used along this paper. The details of the multiresolution algorithm are presented in Section 3, while Section 4 contains experimental evaluation. We conclude the paper in Section 5.

2. BACKGROUND AND RELATED WORKS

In this section we introduce the tensor notation, present background about operations on tensors and present other related works.

A tensor is a multidimensional array, where the *order* (also known as the number of ways or modes) N represents the number of dimensions. Following the notation reported in [19] vectors are represented by boldface lowercase letters (e.g. $\mathbf{a}$), matrices are denotated by boldface capital letters (e.g. $\mathbf{A}$), while tensors with order $N \geq 3$ are denoted by boldface Euler script letters (e.g. $\mathcal{X}$). Scalars are denoted by lowercase letters (e.g. a). Thus, an N-order tensor can be formalized as:

$$\mathcal{X} \in \mathbb{R}^{I_1 \times I_2 \times \ldots \times I_N}$$

The ith entry of a vector $\mathbf{a}$ is denoted by a_i, the element

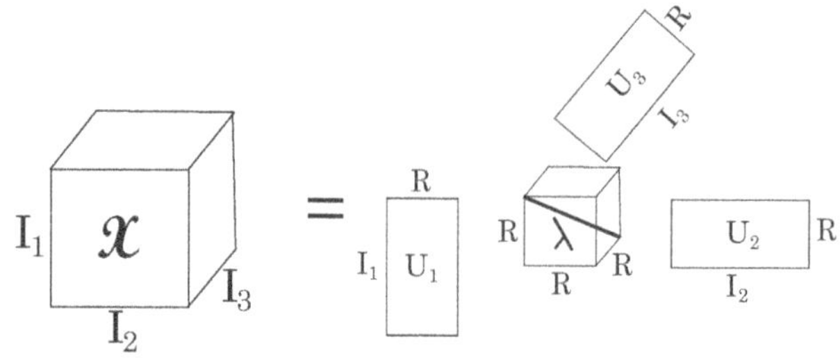

Figure 1: 3-way PARAFAC decomposition

(i, j) of a matrix $\mathbf{A}$ is denoted by a_{ij}, while the element (i, j, k) of a $3-order$ tensor $\mathcal{X}$ is represented by x_{ijk}.

Subarrays are formed when a subset of the indices is fixed. For example, if we want to identify the jth column of the matrix $\mathbf{A}$, we can write $\mathbf{a}_{:j}$. *Fibers* are defined by fixing every index of a tensor, but one. In a 3-order tensor we can identify column, row and tube fibers, denoted by $\mathbf{x}_{:jk}$, $\mathbf{x}_{i:k}$, $\mathbf{x}_{ij:}$. *Slices* are two-dimensional sections of a 3-order tensor, defined by fixing all but two indices. Horizontal, lateral, and frontal are denoted as $\mathbf{X}_{i::}$, $\mathbf{X}_{:j:}$, and $\mathbf{X}_{::k}$.

2.1 Tensor Decomposition

The two most popular tensor decompositions are the Tucker [30] and the PARAFAC/CANDECOMP [10, 4]. The Tucker decomposition approximates a tensor using a smaller tensor through a change of basis. Intuitively, the Tucker decomposition generalizes singular value matrix decomposition (SVD) to higher-dimensional matrices. One key difference is that Tucker fails to guarantee a unique and perfect decomposition. Instead, most approaches involve searching for orthonormal facet matrices and a core tensor that collectively minimize the decomposition error. For example, the High Order SVD approach first identifies the left eigenvectors (with the highest eigenvalues) of the lateral, horizontal, and frontal slices to construct the facet matrices.

CANDECOMP [4] and PARAFAC [10] decompositions (together known as the CP-decomposition) take a different approach and decompose the input tensor into a sum of component rank-one tensors: Given an input tensor $\mathcal{X}$ and a core size r, the PARAFAC decomposition finds r rank-one tensors in the form of $\lambda_i \mathbf{u}_i^{(1)} \circ \cdots \circ \mathbf{u}_i^{(N)}$, where r is a positive integer, $\mathbf{u}_i^{(d)} \in \mathbb{R}^{I_d}$ for $1 \leq i \leq r$ and $\circ$ represents the vector outer product. The decomposition approximates the tensor $\mathcal{X}$ by minimizing the value of

$$\left\| \mathcal{X} - \sum_{i=1}^{r} \lambda_i \mathbf{u}_i^{(1)} \circ \cdots \circ \mathbf{u}_i^{(N)} \right\|.$$

Alternatively, the decomposition can also be rewritten in terms of factor matrices (see Figure 1) as a combination of the vectors from the rank-one components as:

$$\mathcal{X} \approx [\![\lambda; \mathbf{U}^{(1)}, \mathbf{U}^{(2)}, \cdots, \mathbf{U}^{(N)}]\!] = \sum_{i=1}^{r} \lambda_i \mathbf{u_i}^{(1)} \circ \mathbf{u_i}^{(2)} \cdots \mathbf{u_i}^{(N)},$$

where $\lambda \in \mathbb{R}^R$ and $\mathbf{U}^{(i)} \in \mathbb{R}^{I_i \times R}$. PARAFAC can be considered as a special case of Tucker decomposition in which the core tensor λ is superdiagonal. Intuitively, as in SVD, PARAFAC enforces that the central matrix is diagonal; however, unlike in SVD the facet matrices are not guaranteed to be orthonormal.

PARAFAC_ALS($\mathcal{X}, r, tol, \mathcal{F}_{init}$)
Inizialize $\mathbf{U}^{(i)} i = 1 \ldots n$ to $\mathcal{F}_{init}$ (random if $\mathcal{F}_{init}$ is not present)
do
  $fit = \|\mathcal{X} - [\![\lambda; \mathbf{U}^{(1)}, \mathbf{U}^{(2)}, \cdots, \mathbf{U}^{(N)}]\!]\|$
  for $i = 1 \ldots N$ do
    $\mathbf{U}^{(i)} = \mathbf{X}^{(i)}[(\mathbf{U}^{(1)} \odot \ldots \odot \mathbf{U}^{(i-1)} \odot \mathbf{U}^{(i+1)} \odot \odot \ldots \odot \mathbf{U}^{(N)})^{\top}]^{\dagger}$
    normalize column of $\mathbf{U}^{(i)}$ (norms are stored in λ)
  end
  $fitchange = fit - \|\mathcal{X} - [\![\lambda; \mathbf{U}^{(1)}, \mathbf{U}^{(2)}, \cdots, \mathbf{U}^{(N)}]\!]\|$
while ($fitchange \geq tol$)
return $\mathcal{F} \equiv \lambda, \mathbf{U}^{(1)}, \ldots, \mathbf{U}^{(N)}$

Figure 2: The pseudo-code for alternating least squares fit algorithm for PARAFAC models [19]; $\odot$ represents the Khatri-Rao product [24]

2.2 Obtaining PARAFAC Decompositions

Many of the algorithms for fitting multi-way models are based on an iterative process that approximates the best solution until a convergence condition is reached.

Iterative Algorithms. The *alternating least squares* (ALS [32]) method is relatively old and has been successfully applied to the problem of tensor decomposition by Carrol *et al.* and Harshman [4, 10]. ALS is widely used as a building block in many applications for fitting PARAFAC and Tucker models [18, 27, 20]. ALS estimates, at each iteration, one factor matrix, maintaining other matrices fixed; this process is repeated for each factor matrix associated to the dimensions of the input tensor. Since our proposed multi resolution approach extends the basic ALS, in Figure 2 we present the pseudo-code of the standard ALS fitting for PARAFAC. The algorithm takes as input the data tensor $\mathcal{X}$, the number of factors r, a tolerance value tol (used as a stopping condition), and an *optional* initial factorization $\mathcal{F}_{init}$. The algorithms return the factor matrices and the elements of the resulting diagonal tensor λ.

Other alternation-based algorithms include the alternating slice-wise diagonalization (ASD) [15] and the self weighted alternating trilinear diagonalization (SWA-TLD) [6] algorithms: they improve fitting using objective functions that are not based on least squares.

Closed Form and Gradient-Based Algorithms. Non-Iterative approaches to tensor decomposition include closed form solutions, such as generalized rank annihilation method (GRAM) [22] and direct trilinear decomposition (DTLD) [23], which fit the model by solving a generalized eigenvalue problem. Gradient-based methods include the PMF3 algorithm that is based on a modified version of a Gauss-Newton method. An in depth study and comparison of these algorithms can be found in [29, 9].

Tensor Decomposition with External Knowledge. [8] presents FacetCube, a framework that allows users to incorporate prior knowledge in the non-negative Tucker decomposition process, with the primary goal of helping users enforce facets on certain data dimensions. In that work the metadata can be available in different forms. The first one is prior knowledge describing a subspace from which facets can be located. In the second one, the users require facets for some data dimensions be fixed. For example, in an $author \times reference \times keyword$ tensor, the paper shows how additional information on authors (i.e. the co-author relationship) can be leveraged in a recommendation system of references. In our multiresolution approach, instead, additional metadata are used to compute lower-level resolution representations of the input tensor, in order to speed up the decomposition process.

In a work probably most related to the approach presented in this paper, Kaarna *et al.* leverage a multiresolution approximation of the initial tensor in the ALS-based decomposition process [16] for image analysis. Authors recognize that two contiguous pixels in an image can be approximated down to a single pixel *since they are spatially correlated.* In particular, [16] relies on the hierarchical Integer Wavelet Transformations (IWT) to speed-up the decomposition process for image datasets. There are two main differences between [16] and the approach presented in this paper: First of all, unlike in [16], where the (wavelet) hierarchy relies in the inherent spatial correlation *internal to the data*, here we investigate the applicability of external metadata in supporting the tensor decomposition process. Secondly, unlike [16] where the data (i.e., image) tensor is inherently dense, we aim to also tackle sparse tensors (which are common in many applications, including social networks and graph structured data).

3. A MULTIRESOLUTION APPROACH FOR FITTING PARAFAC MODELS

As we pointed out in the Introduction, in this paper we observe that in general there may be external knowledge regarding how the domains represented by the individual tensor dimensions are hierarchically clustered (according to different clustering criteria). In this section we show how such background knowledge can be leveraged as a guide to help provide higher- or lower-resolution views of the data in the tensor on demand and develop a multiresolution approach to tensor decomposition.

3.1 Multiresolution Tensor Representation

Let D_i be the domain associated to the $i-th$ dimension of a tensor $\mathcal{X} \in \mathbb{R}^{I_1 \times I_2 \times \ldots \times I_N}$. Here, I_i is the cardinality of D_i, i.e., $D_i = \{d_{i,1}, d_{i,2}, \ldots, d_{i,I_i}\}$.

Clustering hierarchies capture different strategies along with the domain elements associated to the corresponding dimension can be grouped together. For example, if one dimension of the tensor is associated to the *users* accessing a given service, the corresponding domain elements may be clustered according to their age, according to the city/province/region/state where they live, or according to the preferences listed in their profiles. Let the tree H_i, of depth $depth_i$, be a hierarchical clustering defined on D_i (representing some semantic properties of the values associated to the corresponding tensor dimension). Let $nodes(H_i, l)$ be the set of nodes appearing at level l ($0 \leq l \leq depth_i$) in H_i. Note that the following holds:

- $|nodes(H_i, l)| < |nodes(H_i, j)|$ if $l < j$;
- let $n_{i,l,k}$ be the kth node at level l in the hierarchy H_i with $k = 1, \ldots, |nodes(H_i, l)|$ and $coverage(n_{i,l,k})$ be the set of leaves of the subtree rooted at $n_{i,l,k}$. Then, $coverage(n_{i,0,1}) = D_i$, i.e., the root of the hierarchy is a single cluster which covers the entire domain D_i, and $coverage(n_{i,l,k}) > coverage(n_{i,j,m})$ if $n_{i,l,k}$ is an ancestor of $n_{i,j,m}$.

We leverage the given domain hierarchical clustering strategy to define multiresolution representations of a given tensor. Intuitively, this representation leads to compact representations of the tensor, in which (multiple) tensor values of domain elements which are clustered together according to the given hierarchy are collapsed in a single value, which is seen as the representative of the entire cluster.

Given a domain D_i and a corresponding hierarchy H_i, the *representative selection function* is the function $repr_i : 2^{\mathbb{R}} \rightarrow \mathbb{R}$ which maps a set of real values (in the tensor, corresponding to the positions indexed by the elements clustered in H_i) to a single value, chosen as the representative of the cluster. Examples of representative selection functions include min, max, and average. Notice that for any given domain D_i and any clustering defined over it, multiple representative selection functions can be defined. When a dimension does not have an associated hierarchy, we denote this using $H_i = \perp$ and $repr_i = self$.

Definition 1. **Clustering embedding strategy.** Given a tensor $\mathcal{X} \in \mathbb{R}^{I_1 \times I_2 \times \ldots \times I_N}$, a clustering embedding strategy over $\mathcal{X}$ is a pair $S = \langle \pi, \{(H_1, repr_1, l_1), \ldots, (H_N, repr_N, l_N)\}\rangle$. Here π is a permutation over the indices of the tensor modes (describing the order in which clusterings are considered among different modes), each H_i is a clustering hierarchy defined on D_i, $repr_i$ is a corresponding representative selection function, and l_i is the clustering level adopted for the ith mode.

Given a tensor $\mathcal{X} \in \mathbb{R}^{I_1 \times I_2 \times \ldots \times I_N}$, and a set $\{H_1, \ldots, H_N\}$ of clustering hierarchies defined on the N domains associated to the tensor dimensions we define the corresponding multiresolution representation of $\mathcal{X}$ with respect to the set $\{H_1, \ldots, H_N\}$ as follows. Note that we first define uni-modal representation with respect to a single hierarchy and, then, extend this to multi-modal representation which considers multiple hierarchies simultaneously.

Definition 2. **Uni-modal multiresolution representation.** The multiresolution representation at level l_i with respect to the clustering hierarchy H_i and the representative selection function $repr_i$ of a tensor $\mathcal{X} \in \mathbb{R}^{I_1 \times I_2 \times \ldots \times I_N}$, is a function $\mathcal{U}_{H_i, repr_i, l_i}(\mathcal{X})$:

$$\mathcal{U}_{H_i, repr_i, l_i}(\mathcal{X}) : \mathbb{R}^{I_1 \times \ldots \times I_N} \rightarrow \mathbb{R}^{I_1 \times \ldots \times I_{i-1} \times I'_i \times I_{i+1} \ldots \times I_N},$$

where $I'_i = |nodes(H_i, l)|$. We also refer to $\mathcal{U}_{H_i, repr_i, l_i}(\mathcal{X})$ as $\mathcal{X}^{i, l_i}$ in shorthand:

- If $l_i \geq depth_i$, then $\mathcal{X}^{i, l_i} = \mathcal{X}$.
- Otherwise, let $C = \{C_1, \ldots, C_{|nodes(H_i, l_i)|}\}$ be the clustering induced by H_i at level l_i on the domain elements D_i. Let also the leaf-cardinality of the cluster C_h be denoted as $coverage(n_{i, l_i, h})$. Then, for $h = 1, \ldots, |nodes(H_i, l_i)|$, we have

$$\mathcal{X}^{i, l_i}_{j_1 \ldots j_{i-1} h j_{i+1} \ldots j_N} = repr_i(\{\mathcal{X}_{j_1 \ldots j_{i-1} k j_{i+1} \ldots j_N} \mid d_k \in C_h\}).$$

Intuitively, for any cluster $C_h \in C$ along the ith dimension, for all indices along the other modes, $|C_h|$ elements of the given tensor are collapsed and a single representative value, resulting from the application of the function $repr_i$ on the collapsed elements, appears in the l_i-resolution tensor.

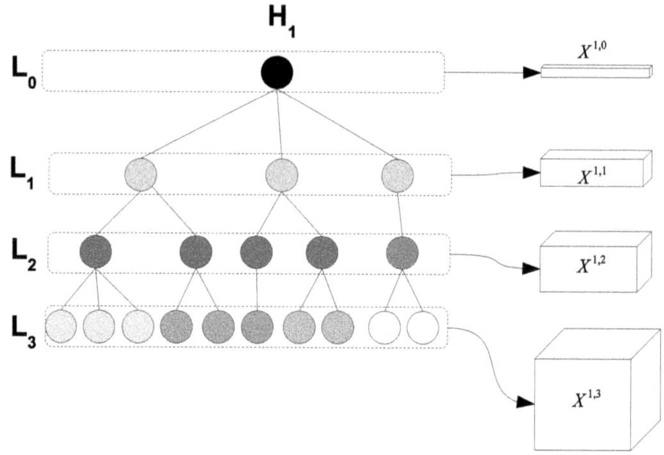

Figure 3: Hierarchy-based multiresolution representation

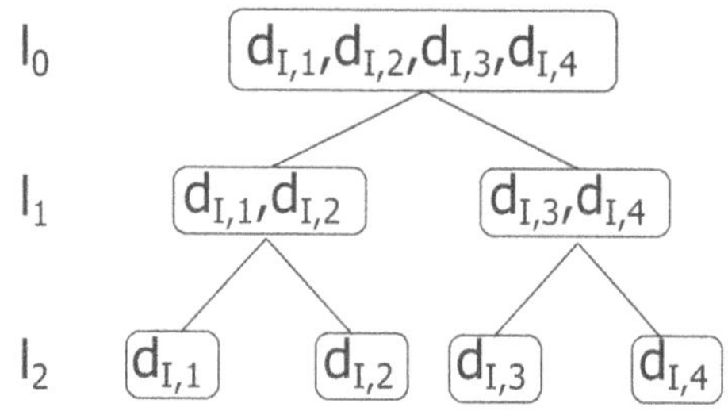

Figure 4: The example hierarchy H_I that encodes additional metadata.

Figure 3 is a visual representation of a uni-modal multiresolution representation of a 3-mode tensor. For example, if the domain associated to the considered hierarchy is a set of users, the multiresolution approach can be seen as hierarchically partitioning them in communities linked by a parent-child relationship.

Example 1. Let us consider the 3-mode I, J, K tensor $\mathcal{X} \in \mathbb{R}^{4 \times 2 \times 3}$:

$$\mathbf{X}_{1::} = \begin{bmatrix} 0 & 5 & 2 \\ 1 & 0 & 9 \end{bmatrix} \qquad \mathbf{X}_{2::} = \begin{bmatrix} 2 & 7 & 0 \\ 3 & 0 & 9 \end{bmatrix}$$

$$\mathbf{X}_{3::} = \begin{bmatrix} 0 & 2 & 3 \\ 1 & 0 & 4 \end{bmatrix} \qquad \mathbf{X}_{4::} = \begin{bmatrix} 2 & 0 & 3 \\ 3 & 0 & 6 \end{bmatrix}$$

Moreover, consider the hierarchy H_I depicted in Figure 4 that clusters elements of the dimension I and the *average* function as representative selection function. The tensor $\mathcal{X}^{I,1} \in \mathbb{R}^{2 \times 2 \times 3}$

$$\mathbf{X}^{I,1}_{1::} = \begin{bmatrix} 1 & 6 & 1 \\ 2 & 0 & 9 \end{bmatrix} \qquad \mathbf{X}^{I,1}_{2::} = \begin{bmatrix} 1 & 1 & 3 \\ 2 & 0 & 5 \end{bmatrix}$$

represents the lower-resolution representation at level 1 of the original tensor $\mathcal{X} = \mathcal{X}^{I,2}$.

Given the definition of uni-modal multiresolution representation, we can also define the multi-modal multiresolution representation as follows:

Definition 3. **N-modal multiresolution representation.** The multiresolution representation with respect to the clustering embedding strategy S =

```
1 PARAFAC_MR_ALS(X, H, R, ρ, r, tol)
1   S_ρ = clustering_strategy(X, H, R, π, ρ)
2   F^[ρ] = parafac_als(X^{S_ρ}, r, tol)
3   a = ρ
4   while (a > 0)
5     foreach U^(i)[a] not related to a compressed dimension
6       U^(i)[a-1] = U^(i)[a]
7     end
8     foreach U^(i)[a] related to a compressed dimension
9       U^(i)[a-1] = expand_factor(U^(i)[a], H)
10    end
11    F^[a-1] ≡ λ, U^(1)[a-1], ..., U^(N)[a-1]
12    load X^[a-1]
13    F^[a-1] = parafac_als(X^[a-1], r, tol, F^[a-1])
14    a = a - 1
15 end
16 return F^[0] ≡ λ, U^(1)[0], ..., U^(N)[0]
```

Figure 5: The pseudo-code of the multiresolution Alternating Least Squares fit for PARAFAC models.

$\langle \pi, \{(H_1, repr_1, l_1), \ldots, (H_N, repr_N, l_N)\}\rangle$ of the tensor $\mathcal{X} \in \mathbb{R}^{I_1 \times I_2 \times \ldots \times I_N}$, is the function $\mathcal{M}_S(\mathcal{X})$:

$$\mathcal{M}_S(\mathcal{X}) : \mathbb{R}^{I_1 \times I_2 \times \ldots \times I_N} \rightarrow \mathbb{R}^{I'_1 \times I'_2 \times \ldots \times I'_N},$$

where $I'_i = |nodes(H_i, l_i)|$. We also refer to $\mathcal{M}_S(\mathcal{X})$ as $\mathcal{X}^S$ in shorthand. $\mathcal{X}^S$ is inductively defined as follows: Let $\mathcal{X}^S_1 = \mathcal{X}^{\pi[1], l_{\pi[1]}}$, be the uni-modal multiresolution representation based on the first mode to be considered according to the permutation π specified in S. Then, we have $\mathcal{X}^S = \mathcal{X}^S_N$, where $\forall\ 1 < s \le N$, the multi-modal representation is defined, relying on the uni-modal definition, as follows:

$$\mathcal{X}^S_s = \left(\mathcal{X}^S_{s-1}\right)^{\pi[s], l_{\pi[s]}}.$$

3.2 Multiresolution PARAFAC

In this section we discuss how we leverage the multiresolution tensor representation to boost the efficiency of tensor decomposition process, without any significant impact on the final decomposition quality. The basic idea relies on the observation that the ALS algorithm [32] for PARAFAC tensor decomposition is an iterative process which starts from an initial randomly generated solution, on which each iterative step improves, until a satisfactory decomposition (i.e, an approximated decomposition differing not more than a predetermined threshold from an exact decomposition) of the given tensor is found.

Based on this, we expect that an "informed" initialization of the decomposition process could significantly reduce the computational cost of the iterative process. In particular, we choose to initialize the decomposition process with the approximate decomposition resulting from the ALS decomposition of a "simpler" (i.e., lower resolution) version of the given tensor. We show in Section 4 that the computational cost of this guided decomposition (including the cost of obtaining the lower resolution decomposition plus the cost of the iterative process starting from the initialization) is lower than the cost in the global decomposition from a randomly initialized iterative process.

Figure 5 contains the pseudo-code of the multiresolution-based algorithm. The algorithm takes as input the tensor, $\mathcal{X}$, the set of hierarchies, $\mathcal{H}$, the set of representative selection function, $\mathcal{R}$, the approximation levels to consider, ρ, the number of required factors r, and the convergence threshold (or tolerance value), tol, used as stopping condition.

The first step of the algorithm constructs a clustering strategy, $S_\rho = \langle \pi, \{(H_1, repr_1, depth_1 - \rho), \ldots, (H_N, repr_N, depth_N - \rho)\}\rangle$, for the lowest resolution level[1]. Here, $H_i \in \mathcal{H}$, $repr_i \in \mathcal{R}$, and π is a permutation of the indices. Let tensor $\mathcal{X}^{S_\rho}$ correspond to the representation of $\mathcal{X}$ at the lowest resolution based on this strategy.

Starting from this lowest-resolution tensor $\mathcal{X}^{S_\rho}$, the algorithm first computes a lowest-resolution factorization $\mathcal{F}^{[\rho]}$ by using the standard ALS fitting technique (line 2). This produces the (lowest-resolution) set of factor matrices $\{\mathbf{U}^{(i)[\rho]} 1 \le i \le N\}$, in which the matrix $\mathbf{U}^{(i)[\rho]}$ belongs to the tensor dimension I_i. The output factorization $\mathcal{F}^{[\rho]}$ will be used as the starting point of the next invocation of the ALS tensor decomposition, with $(\rho - 1)^{th}$ approximation.

In order to obtain the more detailed factorization corresponding to the $(a-1)^{th}$ approximation from $\mathcal{F}^{[a]}$, we need to transform the set of factor matrices by *expanding* the domains of the relevant dimensions – the number of elements of dimension that were not compressed by the strategy S are kept the same (lines 5-7). The *expand_factor*() function (line 9) expands the given factor matrix $\mathbf{U}^{(i)[a]}$ to the initial factorization of the corresponding higher-level factor matrix $\mathbf{U}^{(i)[a-1]}$. Let $N_{i,a} = nodes(H_i, depth_i - a)$ be the set of nodes at the ath approximation level for the hierarchy H_i; similarly, let $N_{i,a-1}$ be the set of nodes at the $(a-1)^{th}$ approximation level. For a given node, $n_h \in N_{i,a}$ let $children(n_h) \subseteq N_{i,a-1}$ be the corresponding set of children at the $(a-1)^{th}$ approximation level.

The *expand_factor*() function considers the dimensions of the tensor one at a time; i.e., for all $1 \le i \le N$, we have

$$\forall n_h \in N_{i,a} \quad \forall n_k \in children(n_h)$$
$$\left(\mathbf{U_{init}}^{(i)[a-1]}\right)_{j_1 \cdots j_{i-1} k j_{i+1} \cdots j_N} = expand_i\left(\left(\mathbf{U}^{(i)[a]}\right)_{j_1 \cdots j_{i-1} h j_{i+1} \cdots j_N}\right).$$

While the *expand$_i$* function can be domain specific, in the absence of addition information, it is intuitive to use the identity function:

$$\forall n_h \in N_{i,a} \quad \forall n_k \in children(n_h)$$
$$\left(\mathbf{U_{init}}^{(i)[a-1]}\right)_{j_1 \cdots j_{i-1} k j_{i+1} \cdots j_N} = \left(\mathbf{U}^{(i)[a]}\right)_{j_1 \cdots j_{i-1} h j_{i+1} \cdots j_N}.$$

Once the decomposition $\mathcal{F}^{[a-1]}_{init}$ is computed using the *expand_factor*() function described above, the algorithm loads the tensor $\mathcal{X}^{[a-1]}$ which represents the $(a-1)^{th}$ approximate resolution view of the original tensor and computes the ALS fitting starting from the initial factorization $\mathcal{F}^{[a-1]}_{init}$ to obtain $\mathcal{F}^{[a-1]}$. The algorithm ends when the highest level tensor factorization is computed and returns the corresponding final factorization $\mathcal{F}^{[0]}$ (line 16).

Note that the multiresolution algorithm shares with the standard Alternating Least Squares approach both time complexity class and memory consumption upper-bound.

[1] Note that ρ represents the number of considered levels of resolution. Given the hierarchy H_i, the algorithm considers the levels from $depth_i - \rho$ to $depth_i$.

Name	Type	Auth.	Conf.	Keyw.	Entries	Dens.
dblp128	dense	128	500	500	59K	0.186%
dblp256	dense	256	500	500	101K	0.158%
dblp512	dense	512	500	500	166K	0.130%
dblp2200	sparse	2.2K	1K	14K	927K	0.003%
dblp6600	sparse	6.6K	1K	14K	1.9M	0.002%
dblp20000	sparse	20K	1K	14K	3.5M	0.001%

Table 1: Properties of the datasets

4. EXPERIMENTAL EVALUATION

In this section we compare our metdadata driven, multiresoultion tensor decomposition method with the standard ALS Based PARAFAC decomposition.

4.1 Setup

We consider matrices with both dense and sparse representations. As reference software library, we used the Matlab Tensor Toolbox [2] by Kolda. All experiments are performed on a desktop with a dual core 2.5GHz processor and 4GB RAM. We repeated all experiments 20 times: all reported value represents the average value of all runs.

4.1.1 Experiment Parameters

In this section, we consider the effects of various problem and system parameters. These include

- size of the input tensor;
- tolerance (or convergence) value used to complete the overall decomposition iterative process;
- tolerance values used in the lower levels of resolution;
- number of resolution levels leveraged for the multiresolution approach;
- rank, r, of the decomposition;
- number modes for which there are external clustering encoded as hierarchies.

We evaluate the decomposition schemes against two key performance parameters: CPU time and quality [2]

$$1 - \frac{\sqrt{\|\mathcal{X}\|^2 + \|\hat{\mathcal{X}}\|^2 - 2innerproduct(\mathcal{X}, \hat{\mathcal{X}})}}{\|\mathcal{X}\|},$$

where $\hat{\mathcal{X}}$ is the tensor obtained by recomposing $\mathcal{F}$. The CPU time does not include the time to obtain different resolution versions of the input tensor.

4.1.2 Data Sets

In the experiments reported in this section, we used a set of 3-mode tensors of the form, *author* $\times$ *conference* $\times$ *keyword*, extracted from the publicly available DBLP data [14]. In particular, we selected the most prolific authors, the most used keywords, and the most popular conferences to construct data tensors with different properties. As mentioned earlier, we have considered both dense and sparse tensors. Table 1 presents the relevant properties of these datasets.

4.1.3 Metadata

For the three modes of the data tensor, we have considered the following hierarchies:

- *Conference Hierarchy*: We have obtained the hierarchy of conferences starting from [13].
- *Authors Hierarchy*: The hierarchy of authors is obtained by leveraging the co-author relationships among the authors (which is also available at DBLP). In particular, the hierarchy is obtained by iteratively partitioning the co-authors graph using the Metis [17] graph partitioning algorithm. We computed 7 levels of resolution for the dblp128 and dblp2200 data sets, 8 levels for dblp256 and dblp660 datasets, and 9 levels for dblp512 and dblp20000 data sets (to obtain these levels, we used an average branching factor of 2 for dense tensors, while for sparse data sets the average branching factor is set to 3).
- *Keyword Hierarchy*: The keyword hierarchy is obtained by first creating a similarity graph based on the set of articles containing at least one occurrence of a given pair of keywords. The keywords hierarchy is then obtained by iteratively partitioning the graph using Metis (we computed 9 levels of resolution, with a branching factor of 2).

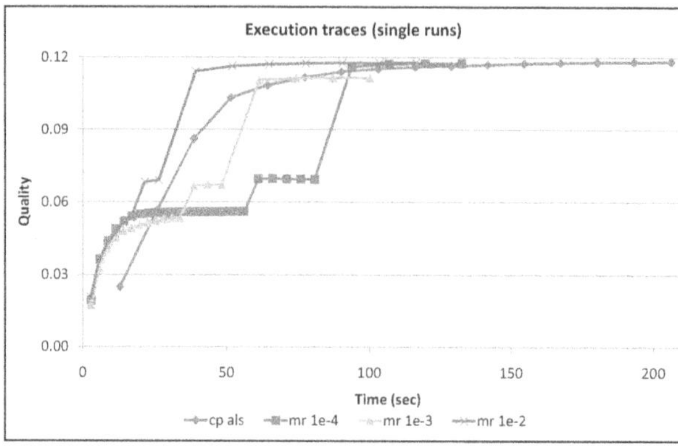

Figure 6: Different execution traces for dblp512 data set (sparse representation). The plots include standard ALS (with threshold 10^{-4}) and multiresolution approaches (using the last three levels of the authors hierarchy) for different *intermediate* tolerance values (10^{-4}, 10^{-3}, and 10^{-2} – the final tolerance value for the highest resolution level is 10^{-4} for all cases).

We note that each these hierarchies provide only uni-modal information. Note also that the domain hierarchies are *created intentionally* rough and noisy. Furthermore, they reflect different degrees of externality: the conference hierarchy is completely external to the DBLP data set, the author hierarchy is from DBLP, but not directly related to the data in the tensor, whereas the keyword hierarchy is created using document information, which (while not being directly represented in the tensor) relates the authors and the keywords in the DBLP data set.

4.2 Results

Before we provide a detailed analysis of the different problem and system parameters, we first analyze data preparation costs and provide sample execution traces to help observe the key advantages of the multi-resolution methods against the traditional ALS based tensor decomposition.

4.2.1 Data Preparation Costs

Data preparation involves the creation of multiple resolutions of the input tensor and thus depends on both the underlying representative selection function as well as the

number of approx. levels(ρ)	dblp512 dense, $166K$ entries	dblp20000 sparse, $3.5M$ entries
1	9.2 sec.	82.0 sec.
2	13.8 sec.	139.7 sec.
3	16.8 sec.	156.5 sec.
4	18.8 sec.	161.4 sec.
5	20.3 sec.	162.9 sec.
6	21.3 sec.	163.6 sec.
7	22.26 sec.	163.8 sec.

Table 2: Data preparation costs for different numbers of approximation levels (based on the authors hierarchy) for dense and sparse data sets

number, ρ, of approximation levels to be considered. Data preparation cost also depends on the number of nonzeros in the data as well as how the tensor is organized. Table 2 reports the data preparation costs both for dense `dblp512` (with $166K$ entries) and sparse `dblp20000` tensors (with $3.5M$ entries) with the average function, for different numbers of approximation levels. The sparse tensors are manipulated using the Matlab Tensor Toolbox [2] – except for the initial slicing of the data, which is not necessarily efficient in this library.

While the per-entry costs for sparse and dense tensor representations are comparable, they represent different relative overheads when considered along with the decomposition costs – this is because dense tensor decomposition is much costlier than the decomposition of sparse tensors. As we see in Section 4.2.3, the data preparation costs can largely be ignored when decomposing dense tensors. The same is not true for sparse tensors (Section 4.2.4). Therefore, in the case of sparse tensors, it is preferable to avoid data preparation for each decomposition tasks; instead, the multi-resolution decomposition over sparse tensors will be more effective if the data preparation costs can be amortized over multiple decompositions over the same tensor (e.g., for different subsets of modes or for different numbers of factors).

4.2.2 Sample Execution Traces

Consider Figure 6, which presents the tensor decomposition for the `dblp512` data set (dense representation). Here `cp-als` curve denotes the quality-time execution trace for the standard ALS scheme. Each marker on the curve corresponds to the end of an iteration and the beginning of the next one. As can be seen, ALS provides most of its improvements in its first few iterations; a significant portion of the overall time is spent seeking the target per-iteration quality difference (the convergence threshold is 10^{-4} in this case).

The figure also shows the quality-time execution traces for the multiresolution approach, using the deepest three levels of the authors hierarchy. In the figure there are three different multiresolution plots:

- `mr1e-4` corresponds to the case where the convergence threshold 10^{-4} is used for all data sets,
- `mr1e-3` is the case where a less precise, 10^{-3}, threshold is used as a stopping condition in the intermediary resolutions, but 10^{-4} is used in the final step, corresponding to the highest resolution and
- `mr1e-2` represents a rougher, 10^{-2}, in the intermediary steps and 10^{-4} in the final step.

The first thing to note is that there are more iterations when using the multiresolution approach. The algorithm performs a separate sequence of iterations for each selected level of the hierarchy – in this case, the lowest three levels, but each iteration is faster. Also, importantly, in deeper levels (i.e., higher resolutions, with costlier individual steps) much fewer iterations are necessary to reach the convergence threshold.

It is interesting to note that, convergence thresholds at the intermediary resolutions have significant impacts on the shape of the execution trace of the multi-resolution approach. In particular, requiring that the same threshold 10^{-4} as the high-resolution step at each level of the tree causes the multi-resolution approach to spend (unnecessarily) more time for the lower-resolution decompositions. Relaxing the threshold down to 10^{-3} and 10^{-2} significantly reduces the time spent for decomposing the lower-resolutions. In fact, in the `mr1e-2` case, the most relaxed (10^{-2}) intermediary convergence thresholds provide the best quality-time behavior and the multiresolution approach provides as good a final result quality as the standard ALS, but stops much quicker (with 10^{-4} at the leaf level as the standard ALS). This indicates that multi-resolution approach is able to leverage available external uni-model hierarchy to speed up the decomposition process, without negatively affecting the final quality. It also hints to the fact that neither the hierarchy, nor the intermediary decompositions step need to be perfect to have good decomposition performance.

In the rest of this section, we study the performance of the proposed scheme under different problem and system parameters to assess whether the trends observed in the above sample scenario extends to different situations.

4.2.3 Experiments with Tensors in Dense Form

We first consider decomposition of tensor matrices represented in dense form.

Tensor size. Figure 7 presents comparisons of the multiresolution algorithm with standard ALS for different tensor sizes. In these experiments, the tolerance is set to 10^{-4} in ALS as well as for multiresolution scheme (at intermediate levels as well as for the highest resolution). As the figure shows, the multiresolution approach provides gains in execution time for all sizes and the gains are especially larger for larger tensors. The figure also shows that the final quality of the multiresolution scheme matches the quality of the more traditional ALS scheme for all tensor sizes.

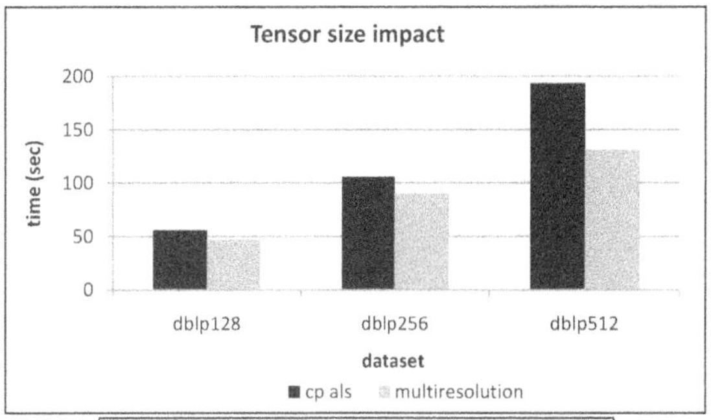

Quality	dblp128	dblp256	dblp512
cp als	0.180	0.143	0.119
multires	0.181	0.143	0.117

Figure 7: Impact of the tensor size (dense matrices, $r = 20$, only author hierarchy, 10^{-4} threshold; also for multi-resolution only the deepest three levels used; threshold is set to 10^{-4} for all resolutions)

Final convergence threshold (i.e., tolerance). In the

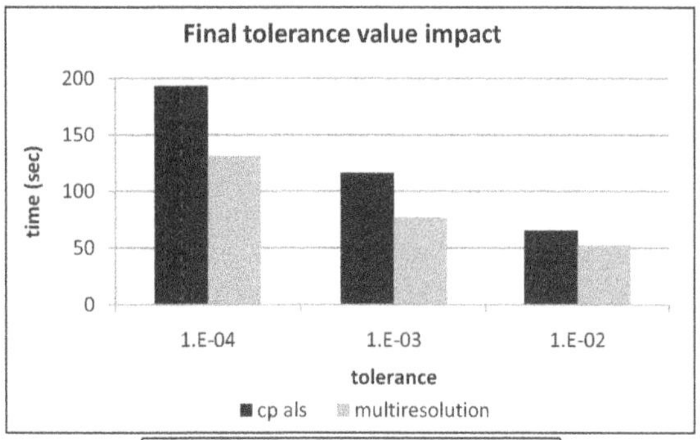

Quality			
	10^{-4}	10^{-3}	10^{-2}
cp als	0.119	0.118	0.108
multires	0.117	0.118	0.115

Figure 8: Impact of the final tolerance; i.e., stopping condition (dense matrices, $r = 20$, only author hierarchy, dblp512, deepest three levels of hierarchy)

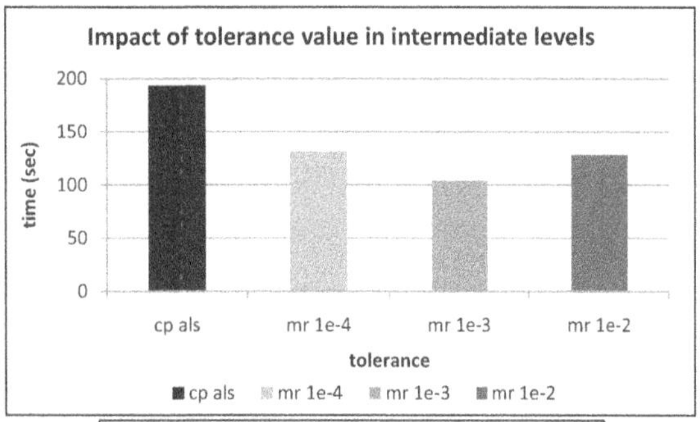

Quality			
cp als	mr 10^{-4}	mr 10^{-3}	mr 10^{-2}
0.119	0.117	0.116	0.118

Figure 9: Impact of tolerance values in the intermediate levels of resolution (dense matrices, $r = 20$, only author hierarchy, dblp512 data, deepest three levels of hierarchy)

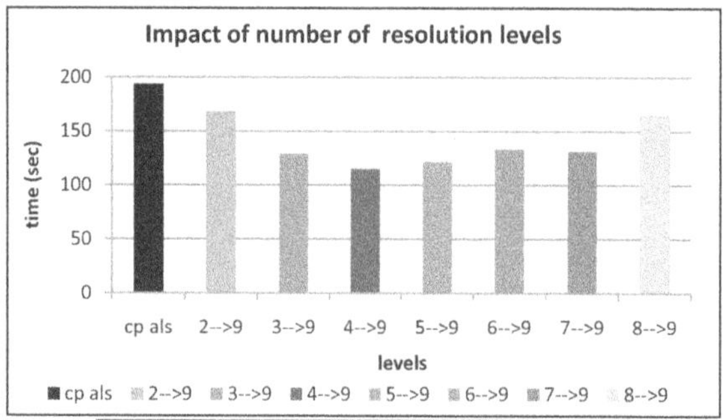

Quality				
cp als	$2 \to 9$	$3 \to 9$	$4 \to 9$	$5 \to 9$
0.119	0.118	0.118	0.117	0.118
	$6 \to 9$	$7 \to 9$	$8 \to 9$	
	0.117	0.117	0.119	

Figure 10: Impact of the number of resolution levels (dense matrices, $r = 20$, only author hierarchy, dblp512 data, tolerance 10^{-4} at all levels)

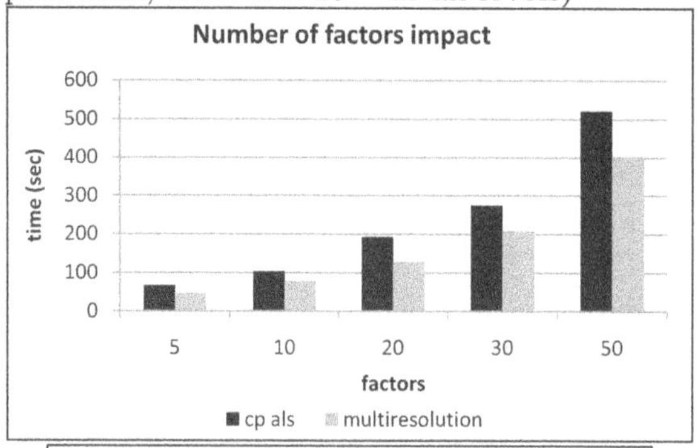

Quality					
	5	10	20	30	50
cp als	0.052	0.081	0.119	0.144	0.179
multires	0.050	0.079	0.118	0.141	0.178

Figure 11: Impact of the rank, r, of the decomposition (dense matrices, $r = 5, 10, 20, 30, 50$, only author hierarchy, dblp512 data, tolerance 10^{-4} at all levels, deepest three levels of hierarchy)

previous experiment, the stopping condition (tolerance) was set to 10^{-4} for ALS as well as for the multiresolution scheme. Figure 8 reports the results for the scenarios where the overall convergence thresholds range from 10^{-2} to 10^{-4}. As the figure shows, the gain in execution time is especially pronounced when the stopping condition is tighter; this is because ALS needs to spend a significant amount of time slowly approaching the convergence condition whereas the multiresolution approach converges faster.

It is important to note that in the traditional ALS, quality drops significantly (from 0.119 to 0.108) when the threshold is relaxed, whereas it is much more stable if the proposed multiresolution scheme is used (from 0.117 to 0.115).

Convergence conditions (i.e., tolerance) for intermediate levels. Figure 9 depicts the impact of using different convergence tolerances at intermediate levels of the multiresolution scheme (this figure provides a summary of the traces shown in Figure 6). Here, for multiresolution approaches, the final tolerance value is set to 10^{-4}, whereas the tolerance values at the intermediate levels are varied. We observe that the fastest execution is obtained when the thresholds at the intermediate resolutions are neither too tight, nor too lax. In terms of quality, however, as we have also seen in Figure 6, a relatively more lax threshold helps the multiresolution scheme avoid getting stuck at local optima.

Number of resolution levels. Figure 10 shows the impact of the number resolutions levels used in the multiresolution approach. As can be seen in the figure, there is a trade-off and the largest gains in execution time are obtained when the process is started at mid-height of the hierarchy: starting at levels closer to root (e.g., 2) causes the multiresolution algorithm to spend time searching for decompositions that are too imprecise to help effectively bootstrap lower levels; starting at levels too close to the leaves (e.g., 8), on the other hand, prevents the multiresolution scheme to properly leverage the available metadata. We note that quality-wise all cases perform similarly.

Target rank of the decomposition. Figure 11 shows that the proposed multiresolution approach consistently outperforms the traditional ALS based decomposition for all target decomposition ranks, even when the tolerance is set to 10^{-4} at all resolutions. The time gain ranges from $\sim 20\%$ to $\sim 30\%$. The multiresolution approach also matches the quality at all ranks.

Number of modes with available hierarchies. Finally, Figure 12 shows the impact of using more than one hierarchy

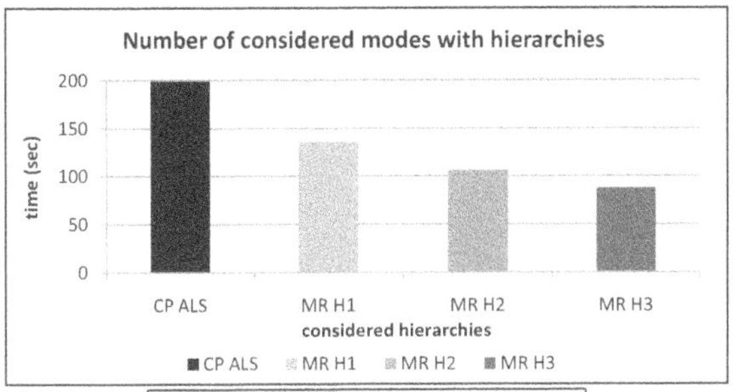

Quality			
cp als	mr h1	mr h2	mr h3
0.118	0.116	0.120	0.116

Figure 12: Impact of the number of modes with hierarchies (dense matrices, $r = 20$, `dblp512` data, tolerance 10^{-4} at all levels, deepest three levels of hierarchy). In `mr h1` only the hierarchy on authors is; `mr h2` also considers the keywords hierarchy and `mr h3` considers all three hierarchies.

	Tolerance values (i.e., stopping conditions)		
	leaf - 2	leaf - 1	leaf (highest res.)
mr444	10^{-4}	10^{-4}	10^{-4}
mr334	10^{-3}	10^{-3}	10^{-4}
mr224	10^{-2}	10^{-2}	10^{-4}

Table 3: Tolerance values used in experiments on sparse tensors

to support decomposition. As can be seen here, the more hierarchies are used, the faster the overall decomposition becomes. Moreover, the decomposition quality is minimally affected from the number of considered hierarchies.

4.2.4 *Experiments with Tensors in Sparse Form*

So far, we have reported experiment results on tensor represented in dense form. However, in many data sets of interest (such as social media graphs) tensors can be sparse and these can leverage tensor decomposition tools specifically designed to work for tensors with sparse encodings. Therefore, in this section, we also evaluate the multi-resolution approach on data sets with sparse representations as described in Table 1. In these experiments, we set the target rank r to 20 and the tolerance value for high resolution decomposition is set to 10^{-4}. For all data sets, we have considered the deepest three levels of the hierarchy and varied the thresholds for the different levels as reported in Table 3.

Bad news: As can be seen in Figure 13, when the tensor is sparse enough to rely on sparse tensor representations, the multiresolution approach does not necessarily provide time gains. This is because, when the tensors are represented in sparse form, decomposition cost tends to be a function of the number of non-zero entries [2]. Unfortunately, as reported in Table 4, reductions in tensor resolutions do not necessarily imply significant reductions in the number of tensor non-zero values and, therefore, time gains in the high resolution level do not always amortize the overhead incurred by at the lower resolutions. Thus, time gains are observed only when relatively lax thresholds (10^{-2}) are used at intermediate resolutions and, even then, gains are modest.

Good news: While this initially looks disappointing, we remember from the earlier experiments that *relaxing the precision at the lower resolutions by using a more relaxed convergence threshold could provide big boosts in execution time,*

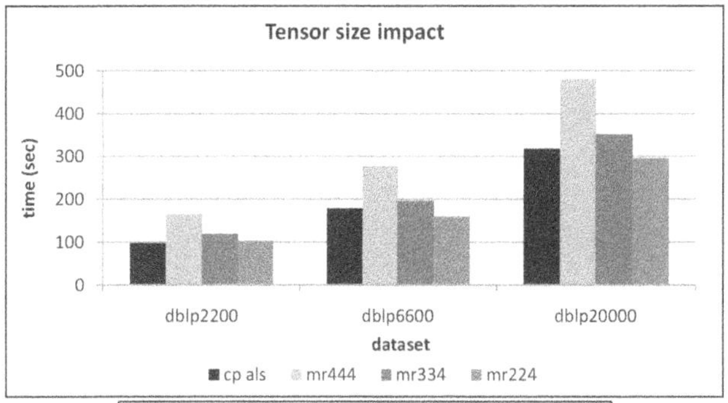

	Quality		
	dblp2200	dblp6600	dblp20000
cp als	0.055	0.042	0.035
mr444	0.053	0.042	0.034
mr334	0.053	0.042	0.034
mr224	0.053	0.042	0.034

Figure 13: Impact of the tensor size (sparse matrices, $r = 20$, only author hierarchy, 10^{-4} threshold; deepest three levels used)

Number of non-zero entries (for dblp2200)		
Leaf-2 (lowest res.)	Leaf-1	Leaf (highest res.)
802,032	853,138	927,663
Number of non-zero entries (for dblp6600)		
Leaf-2	Leaf-1	Leaf
1,572,440	1,685,556	1,862,769
Number of non-zero entries (for dblp20000)		
Leaf-2	Leaf-1	Leaf
2,819,233	3,060,544	3,463,212

Table 4: Number of non-zero entries at different levels of resolution

Number of non-zero entries with θ-cutoff (for dblp2200)						
Leaf-2			Leaf-1			Leaf
Initial	θ_1	Final	Initial	θ_1	Final	No cutoff
802,032	0.096	613,319	853,138	0.230	731,600	927,663
	0.109	540,300		0.229	507,519	
	0.132	226,074		0.238	186,379	
Number of non-zero entries with θ-cutoff (for dblp6600)						
Leaf-2			Leaf-1			Leaf
Initial	θ_2	Final	Initial	θ_2	Final	No cutoff
1,572,440	0.096	1,237,419	1,685,556	0.230	1,406,544	1,862,769
	0.109	1,083,064		0.310	1,001,005	
	0.132	460,251		0.450	340,733	
Number of non-zero entries with θ-cutoff (for dblp20000)						
Leaf-2			Leaf-1			Leaf
Initial	θ_3	Final	Initial	θ_3	Final	No cutoff
2,819,233	0.096	2,156,319	3,060,544	0.230	2,461,299	3,463,212
	0.109	1,852,138		0.310	1,697,666	
	0.162	827,287		0.380	705,163	

Table 5: Number of non-zero entries, with θ-cutoff, at different levels of resolution

without negatively affecting the final quality. This means that we might be able to eliminate the bottleneck by relaxing the number of non-zero entries considered in the lower resolution steps. To achieve this effect we introduced cutoffs, θ, for non-leaf levels and eliminated all entries smaller than θ from the tensors, creating less precise approximations of the original tensor at low resolutions. Table 5 shows the parameters used in the experiments. Note that we have experimented with very significant reductions in the number of non-zero entries. Figure 14 shows the performance results for these θ-cutoffs: as expected the more non-zero entries are removed in the low resolution steps, the faster becomes the decomposition, providing up to $\sim$ 40% gains in execution

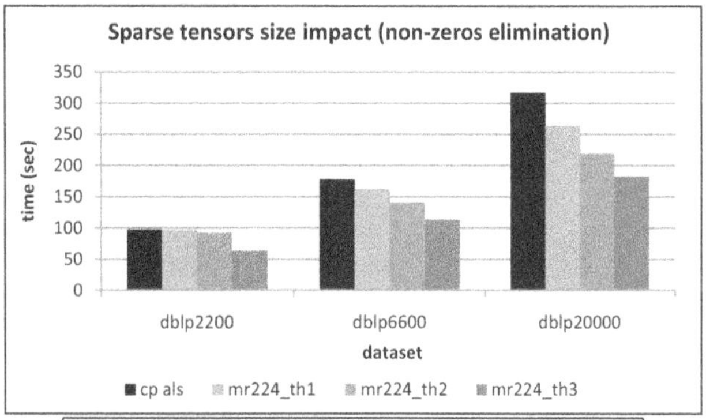

	Quality			
	cutoff	dblp2200	dblp6600	dblp20000
cp als		0.055	0.042	0.035
$mr224$	θ_1	0.053	0.042	0.034
$mr224$	θ_2	0.053	0.042	0.034
$mr224$	θ_3	0.053	0.042	0.034

Figure 14: Impact of the tensor size with θ-cutoff elimination of non-zero entries (sparse tensors, $r = 20$, only author hierarchy, 10^{-4} tolerance; deepest three levels used). See Table 5 for details of θ-cutoff values.

time. Most interestingly (and happily), the θ-cutoff based non-zero removal has close to zero impact on the quality of the final decomposition, rendering the proposed multiresolution approach very applicable for sparse tensors as well.

5. CONCLUSIONS

In this paper, we presented a metadata driven tensor decomposition approach which leverages uni-modal clustering hierarchies available a priori to significantly boost up the execution time of iterative alternating squares based PARAFAC decomposition. The experiment results showed that the time gains obtained by using external metadata do not come with undesirable reductions in the decomposition quality, even when the available metadata is imperfect and not directly representative of the tensor data.

6. REFERENCES

[1] E. Acar and B. Yener. Unsupervised multiway data analysis: A literature survey. *IEEE TKDE*, 21:6–20, 2009.

[2] B. W. Bader and T. G. Kolda. Efficient MATLAB computations with sparse and factored tensors. *SIAM Journal on Scientific Computing*, 30(1):205–231, 2007.

[3] R. Bro, R. A. Harshman, N. D. Sidiropoulos, and M. E. Lundy. Modeling multi-way data with linearly dependent loadings. *Journal of Chemometrics*, 23(7-8):324–340, 2009.

[4] J. Carroll and J.-J. Chang. Analysis of individual differences in multidimensional scaling via an n-way generalization of "Eckart-Young" decomposition. *Psychometrika*, 35:283–319, 1970.

[5] R. Cattell. Parallel proportional profiles and other principles for determining the choice of factors by rotation. *Psychometrika*, 9(4):267–283, 1944.

[6] Z.-P. Chen, H.-L. Wu, J.-H. Jiang, Y. Li, and R.-Q. Yu. A novel trilinear decomposition algorithm for second-order linear calibration. *Chemometrics and Intelligent Laboratory Systems*, 52(1):75 – 86, 2000.

[7] P. A. Chew, B. W. Bader, T. G. Kolda, and A. Abdelali. Cross-language information retrieval using parafac2. In *Proc. KDD '07* 143–152, 2007.

[8] Y. Chi and S. Zhu. Facetcube: a framework of incorporating prior knowledge into non-negative tensor factorization. In *Proc. CIKM '10*, 569–578, 2010.

[9] N. Faber, R. Bro, and P. K. Hopke. Recent developments in candecomp/parafac algorithms: a critical review. *Chemometrics and Intelligent Laboratory Systems*, 65(1):119 – 137, 2003.

[10] R. Harshman. Foundations of the parafac procedure: Models and conditions for an "explanatory" multi-modal factor analysis. *UCLA Working Pap. in Phonetics*, 16, 1970.

[11] R. Harshman. PARAFAC2: Mathematical and technical notes. *UCLA Working Pap. in Phonetics*, 22:30–44, 1972.

[12] R. Harshman, S. Hong, and M. E. Lundy. Shifted factor analysis – part i: Models and properties, 2003.

[13] http://en.wikipedia.org/wiki/List_of_computer_science_conferences. List of computer science conferences.

[14] http://www.informatik.uni trier.de/~ley/db/. The DBLP computer science bibliography.

[15] J.H. Jiang, H.L. Wu, Y. Li, and R.Q. Yu. Three-way data resolution by alternating slice-wise diagonalization (asd) method. *Journal of Chemometrics*, 14(1):15–36, 2000.

[16] A. Kaarna, A. Andriyashin, S. Nakauchi, and J. Parkkinen. Multiresolution approach in computing ntf. In *Proc. SCIA'07*, 334–343, 2007.

[17] G. Karypis and V. Kumar. A fast and high quality multilevel scheme for partitioning irregular graphs. *SIAM J. Sci. Comput.*, 20:359–392, 1998.

[18] T. Kolda and B. Bader. The TOPHITS model for higher-order web link analysis. In *Proc. SIAM Data Mining- Workshop on Link Analysis, Counterterrorism and Security*, 2006.

[19] T. G. Kolda and B. W. Bader. Tensor decompositions and applications. *SIAM Review*, 51(3):455–500, 2009.

[20] T. G. Kolda and J. Sun. Scalable tensor decompositions for multi-aspect data mining. In *Proc. ICDM*, 363–372, 2008.

[21] P. Paatero. The multilinear engine: A table-driven, least squares program for solving multilinear problems, including the n-way parallel factor analysis model. *J. of Comp. and Graphical Statistics*, 8(4):pp. 854–888, 1999.

[22] E. Sanchez and B. R. Kowalski. Generalized rank annihilation factor analysis. *Analytical Chemistry*, 58(2):496–499, 1986.

[23] E. Sanchez and B. R. Kowalski. Tensorial resolution: A direct trilinear decomposition. *J. of Chemometrics*, 4(1):29–45, 1990.

[24] A. Smilde, R. Bro, and P. Geladi. *Multi-way Analysis: Applications in the Chemical Sciences*. 2004.

[25] I. Stanimirova, B. Walczak, D. L. Massart, V. Simeonov, C. A. Saby, and E. D. Crescenzo. Statis, a three-way method for data analysis. application to environmental data. *Chemometrics and Intelligent Laboratory Systems*, 73(2):219 – 233, 2004.

[26] J. Sun, C. Faloutsos, S. Papadimitriou, and P. S. Yu. Graphscope: parameter-free mining of large time-evolving graphs. In *Proc. ACM KDD '07* 687–696, 2007.

[27] J. Sun, S. Papadimitriou, C.Y. Lin, N. Cao, S. Liu, and W. Qian. Multivis: Content-based social network exploration through multi-way visual analysis. In *SIAM-DM 09*, 2009.

[28] J.-T. Sun, H.-J. Zeng, H. Liu, Y. Lu, and Z. Chen. Cubesvd: a novel approach to personalized web search. In *Proc. WWW '05* 382–390, 2005.

[29] G. Tomasi and R. Bro. A comparison of algorithms for fitting the parafac model. *Comp.Stat.Data Anal.*, 50, 2006.

[30] L. Tucker. Some mathematical notes on three-mode factor analysis. *Psychometrika*, 31(3):279–311, 1966.

[31] L. Tucker. The extension of factor analysis to three-dimensional matrices. In H. Gulliksen and N. Frederiksen, ed., *Contributions to mathematical psychology.*, 110–127, 1964.

[32] F. Yates. The analysis of replicated experiments when the field results are incomplete. *J. Exp. Agric.*, 1:129, 1933.

Enabling Information Extraction by Inference of Regular Expressions from Sample Entities

Falk Brauer Robert Rieger Adrian Mocan Wojciech M. Barczynski
SAP AG, SAP Research
Chemnitzer Str. 48e
Dresden, Germany
{firstname.lastname} @sap.com

ABSTRACT

Regular expressions are the dominant technique to extract business relevant entities (e.g., invoice numbers or product names) from text data (e.g., invoices), since these entity types often follow a strict underlying syntactical pattern. However, the manual construction of regular expressions that guarantee a high recall and precision is a tedious manual task and requires expert knowledge.

In this paper, we propose an approach that automatically infers regular expressions from a set of (positive) sample entities, which in turn can be derived either from enterprise databases (e.g., a product catalog) or annotated documents (e.g., historical invoices). The main innovation of our approach is that it learns effective regular expressions that can be easily interpreted and modified by a user. The effectiveness is obtained by a novel method that weights dependent entity features of different granularity (i.e. on character and token level) against each other and selects the most suitable ones to form a regular expression.

Categories and Subject Descriptors

H.3 [**Information Storage and Retrieval**]: Content Analysis and Indexing—*Linguistic Processing*

General Terms

Algorithms

Keywords

Information Extraction, Machine Learning, Regular Expressions, Minimum Description Length

1. INTRODUCTION

Information extraction from textual data has various applications, such as semantic search [13] (e.g., to provide semantic facets for information retrieval systems) or preprocessing of documents to enable structured queries [9] (e.g., to process invoices automatically by assigning text fragments like an invoice number to the corresponding database column). Many entity types – especially in enterprise settings – can be extracted from texts using regular expressions that describe their syntactic patterns as a kind of formation rule. These entity types (codes, identifiers, etc.) occur most frequently in enterprise settings, because there is a strong need to identify entities like customers, invoices or products in a unique fashion.

Because the inherited patterns of identifier-like entities are often very distinctive, the exploitation of context information (e.g., words that occur frequently around entities within a corpus of annotated documents) is often not necessary. Thus, it is in many cases possible to construct effective regular expressions even though only a set of positive sample entities is available (e.g., derived from a database).

Examples of entity types, which may be extracted using regular expressions, some sample instances and likely effective regular expressions to extract unknown entities of the same type are shown in Table 1. Let us for instance consider the examples for software names depicted in Table 1.(a): Fireworks 4.0, Fireworks MX, Word 2010, Frontpage 2007 and Antivirus 2007. Possible regular expressions that capture their common features (i.e. syntactical patterns) are:

```
(R1)  .+ _ .+
(R2) [A-Za-z]+ _ .+
(R3) [A-Za-z]+ _ ((\{p}|[0-9])+|  [A-Z]+|   [0-9]+)
(R4) [A-Za-z]+ _ ([0-9]\{p}[0-9]| [A-Z]{2}| [0-9][4])
(R5) [A-Za-z]+ _ ([0-9]\.[0-9]|   [A-Z]{2}| 20[0-9]{2})
(R6) [A-Z][a-z]{3,8} _ (4\.0| MX| 2010| 2007)
(R7) (Fireworks| Word| Frontpage | Antivirus) _ .+
(R8) .+ _ (4\.0| MX| 2010| 2007)
```

The most general pattern is that they share two tokens, such as shown in (R1). In order to achieve a higher precision, we suggest describing the tokens in terms of token classes (see (R2) and (R3)), where the expression (\{p}|[0-9])+ describes tokens that consist of punctuations and numbers. For some sub-sequences of the samples a more fine grained representation with character classes will lead to a higher precision without any impact on the recall (for instance [0-9]\{p}[0-9] in (R4) as opposed to (\{p}|[0-9])+). However, it is not obvious how to decide which parts should be represented by token classes and which as character classes.

In order to achieve a high precision, dedicated subsequences of the samples should be kept in the final regular expression as they are. These sub-sequences may be shared across all instances of an entity type and increase the precision tremendously. For instance in (R5) the part 20[0-9]{2} expresses that multiple version qualifiers refer to the year of the software release, while (R6) shows that it might also be possible to consider fixed tokens.

Table 1: Example entities and potential regular expressions for extraction

<table>
<tr><th>(a) software</th><th>(b) notebook</th><th>(c) invoice number</th><th>(d) phone</th></tr>
<tr><td>Fireworks 4.0
Fireworks MX
Word 2010
Frontpage 2007
Antivirus 2007</td><td>z800
z800 AAB
d700 ASE
z40y
d50t ATX</td><td>11-093
#545465
2008-035465
2010.08338
2000.348</td><td>+1-734-936-6395
(313)593-5131
847.494.5626
212/949-8058
313/593-5131</td></tr>
<tr><td>[A-Z][a-z]$^+$ ([0-9]\.[0-9]|
[A-Z]{2}|20[0-9]{2})</td><td>(d|z)([0-9]0{2}|
[0-9]0[a-z]) ([A-Z]$^+$)?</td><td>(#[0-9]{6}|(([0-9]{2}|
20[0-9]{2})(−|\.)[0-9]$^+$)</td><td>(\(|\+)?[0-9]{1,3}\)?[0-9]{3}
(−|\.|/)([0-9]$^+$)(−|\.)?([0-9]$^+$)?</td></tr>
</table>

The examples (R7) and (R8) illustrate another difficulty. Usually, a formation rule that underlies a set of entities follows either a prefix- or suffix-like pattern. Thus, the most distinguishing features (e.g., fixed tokens or characters) occur either at the beginning of the names or at the end. For our example, even though software vendors will use a prefix-like pattern (software name followed by different version qualifiers), a more generic suffix-like pattern, is used across vendor boundaries to represent version qualifiers. Thus, having a set of sample entities from one vendor (indicating that only software entities from one vendor shall be extracted), we may end up with a regular expression such as (R7) - a software name with an arbitrary version qualifier. If we would consider software names of different vendors (indicating that we like to extract all software names), we will observe various overlapping version qualifiers and a rule such as (R8) will lead to a better extraction quality.

To tackle the challenges described above and automatically infer regular expressions that promise a high recall and precision, we present in this paper an approach that learns regular expressions by analyzing the given instances using the following processing steps:

1. the creation of pre- and suffix automatons that represent all overlapping syntactical features of the sample entities on different abstraction levels,
2. the identification of fixed patterns, i.e., tokens or characters that most likely occur at a certain position of unknown entities,
3. the selection of the best fitting feature representation from the different abstraction levels by adapting the minimum description length principle, and
4. the selection of the best fitting features from a pre- and suffix automaton to generate regular expressions.

The remainder of this paper is structured as follows: In the next section we discuss related work. We give an overview on statistical learning approaches, discuss the limitations of current rule learning techniques to features of one abstraction level and elaborate on related learning tasks in other research areas. Our method for inferring regular expressions is presented in Section 3 and 4. While in Section 3 we focus on abstracting from the sample entities by generating prefix and suffix automatons that capture all potential features, in Section 4 we elaborate on the methods for feature selection and regular expression generation. Finally, we demonstrate the applicability of our approach in Section 5. To show that our approach provides a similar performance as the best performing state-of-art machine learning techniques for extracting identifier-like entities, we compare the extraction quality of our approach to the one of the machine learning technique Conditional Random Fields. Furthermore, we show examples for learned regular expressions to demonstrate their readability.

2. RELATED WORK

In general one can distinguish learning algorithms in the area of information extraction into stochastic-statistical approaches and rule learning approaches. In the following, we give an overview on widely adopted stochastic models and elaborate on the limitations of current rule learning approaches to learn formation patterns for given sample entities. In the end of this section we discuss related learning approaches in other research areas such as data cleansing or DTD-schema inference.

Prominent stochastic-statistical models for information extraction are Hidden Markov Models (HMM), Maximum Entropy Markov Models (MEMM) or Conditional Random Fields (CRF) [16], which interpret a text as conditional probabilistic feature sequence (e.g., features like words, word shape, part-of-speech, character-n-grams, etc.). The generative nature of HMM restrict their application to feature representations of one abstraction level (e.g., word features OR character-n-grams) [10]. MEMM and CRF follow a discriminative approach and thus allow the combination of dependent feature types of different granularity into one model (e.g., word features AND character-n-grams). Recently [12] studied the bootstrapping of CRF-models by incorporating entity samples from pre-existing databases into the training process (still requiring a document corpus).

In general stochastic sequence models have two major drawbacks: First, there is no obvious way to train the above mentioned models in the absence of any document corpus, which is in principle possible with our approach if sample entities are available. Second, compared to rule based approaches, it is rather difficult to manually debug, modify and tune probabilistic models [16], which is often required in real world settings. Thus, rule based approaches are still the preferred choice in enterprise settings.

Many approaches have been developed in the past that tackled the problem of learning deterministic extraction rules from annotated document corpora (see [19, 16] for an overview). Traditional approaches can be classified according to the adapted learning principle: propositional learning (e.g., CRYSTAL [17] or TIMES [3]) or relational learning (e.g., SRV [6] or $(LP)^2$ [4]). The latter ones have the advantage that they can infer not only characteristic token features, but also relations among them. Both propositional learning and relational learning approaches encode the most discriminative token features of entities, features in their context and the relations among those features in a kind of logical expression.

More recent approaches such as proposed by WHISK [17], SPIES [20] or AliBaba [13] induce a kind of regular expressions that describe the sequential occurrence of token features in a text (usually in the scope of one sentence). Note that SPIES, similar to our approach, adapted the minimum description length principle (MDL). However, MDL is leveraged to determine the optimal combination of token features for extracting relationships among recognized entities, and not to select from features of different granularity.

Similar as for HMM, the feature space that can be leveraged by current rule learning approaches is limited to one token granularity (usually word features). This is usually adequate for the extraction of proper names (such as persons, organizations, genes, proteins), which requires the exploitation of context words, but not for the extraction of identifier-like entities. On the one hand, our approach complements previous rule learning techniques with a method to exploit dependent features of different granularity. On the other hand, it broadens the application of rule learning approaches to scenarios where only sample entities are given.

In the research area of information extraction, the closest related approach is ReLIE [11]. It optimizes regular expressions that are fed to the system by a user, by exploiting an annotated training corpus. Therefore, it transforms regular expressions, e.g., by adding negative lists (terms that should not be matched) until a (local) maximum with respect to recall and precision (i.e. F-measure) is reached. In contrast, our approach does not require such initial regular expressions. Therefore, our approach and [11] complement each other in situations where a training corpus is available. In summary, even though some previous approaches studied the application of prefix- and suffix patterns to extract unknown entities [18, 2], no approach has been proposed so far that weights dependent features of different granularity for a given set of sample entities to induce concise regular expressions for information extraction.

There are some other research areas that adapted MDL for the inference of regular expressions. Notable among those are approaches to infer a DTD-schema from a given set of XML-files [5, 7, 1]. However, MDL is used to determine cardinalities of elements within a schema. Thus their focus is the inference of sequentially re-occurring patterns rather than distinguishing the optimal abstraction level.

The most similar approach to ours was developed in the context of the data cleansing system "Potters Wheel" [15]. The basis of "Potters Wheel" are user defined domains, such as "⟨number⟩", "⟨time⟩" or "⟨word⟩", which are used to infer exactly one pattern (i.e. a sequential concatenation of domains) for a database column, such as "⟨number⟩⟨word⟩⟨time⟩" for instances like "19 January 06:45". Due to the different application domains, there are fundamental differences in the adaption of MDL. While [15] is meant to infer one general rule to detect outliers, our approach infers an arbitrary number of rules to provide robust extraction mechanisms that lead to a high extraction quality on unseen data. Thus the coverage of a rule with respect to the given instances is an important factor in the MDL-definition of [15], while our approach always covers all given instances. More importantly, abstraction levels or fixed instance sub-sequences are not taken into account by [15].

3. FEATURE EXTRACTION

The problem of inducing regular expressions from a given set of entities can be generalized as follows: Given a set of positive instances $\mathcal{I}$, we assume that there is an underlying grammar $\mathcal{G}$ that was used to generate those instances (formally: $\mathcal{I} \subseteq \mathcal{L}(\mathcal{G})$). The ultimate goal of our algorithm, which we denote as *infer*, is to approximate $\mathcal{G}$ by a regular grammar $\mathcal{G}^{\approx}$ such that $\mathcal{L}(\mathcal{G}^{\approx}) \approx \mathcal{L}(\mathcal{G})$ holds. Thereby, the approximation $\approx$ can be measured by the extraction quality, i.e. recall and precision. To summarize, we formalize the problem of inferring regular expressions (represented by $\mathcal{G}^{\approx}$) as follows:

$$infer : \mathcal{I} \mapsto \mathcal{G}^{\approx}, \mathcal{I} \subseteq \mathcal{L}(\mathcal{G}), \mathcal{L}(\mathcal{G}^{\approx}) \approx \mathcal{L}(\mathcal{G}), \quad (1)$$

A regular grammar can be represented by an automaton, which can be easily constructed and modified by computer programs. Thus automatons are frequently used in grammar inference problems [14]. We follow this approach and introduce in this section the construction of prefix and suffix automatons that capture all possible feature sequences of the given sample entities on different abstraction levels. Before, we introduce the feature types that should be considered by our approach or more precisely the alphabet (denoted as Σ) of the target grammar $\mathcal{G}^{\approx}$.

3.1 Feature Definition

The algorithm described in this paper is initialized by configuration of character classes. Let $\mathcal{K}_B$ be the set of basic characters (e.g., as defined in UTF-8[1]) that can be used in regular expressions of an information extraction system. Through defining disjunctive subsets of the characters, we can specify a set of character classes $\mathcal{K}_C$. We denote a character class by angle brackets (e.g., $\langle\cdot\rangle$) and refer in the remaining paper to the following standard configuration[2] for $\mathcal{K}_C$:

DEFINITION 3.1 (CHARACTER CLASSES).

$$\begin{aligned}
\mathcal{K}_C &:= \{\langle \text{NB}\rangle, \langle \text{UC}\rangle, \langle \text{LC}\rangle, \langle \text{SC}\rangle, \langle \text{WT}\rangle, \langle \text{OT}\rangle\},\\
\langle \text{LC}\rangle &:= \{a, b, c, \ldots, z\}\\
\langle \text{UC}\rangle &:= \{A, B, C, \ldots, Z\}\\
\langle \text{NB}\rangle &:= \{0, 1, 2, \ldots, 9\}\\
\langle \text{SC}\rangle &:= \{-, ,\$, /, *, \#, ., \ldots, ?\}\\
\langle \text{WT}\rangle &:= \backslash s
\end{aligned}$$

Therein, ⟨LC⟩ represents lower case characters, ⟨UC⟩ upper case characters, ⟨NB⟩ numbers, ⟨SC⟩ all special characters and ⟨WT⟩ arbitrary white spaces (space, tabulator, etc.). ⟨OT⟩ is a special character class ("others") that captures all not explicitly defined characters. The language formed by a character class, which is used for classifying the input character sequences later on, is defined as $L(\kappa_C) = \bigcup c, c \in \kappa_C, \kappa_C \in \mathcal{K}_C$.

On top of the character classes $\mathcal{K}_C$, we define a set of token classes, which we denote as $\mathcal{K}_T$. In the following we consider each character sequence that is bounded by a white space symbol (⟨WT⟩) or a special character (⟨SC⟩) as token. Each white space symbol and special character sequence is treated as a token on its own. Note, that it is possible to configure other tokenization methods for special use cases. To allow for arbitrary combinations of character classes in a token class (e.g., to describe something like [A-Za-z]+), we define them as follows:

DEFINITION 3.2 (TOKEN CLASSES). *The set of token classes $\mathcal{K}_T$ is defined by the power set of $\mathcal{K}_C$ except the empty set: $\mathcal{K}_T := 2^{\mathcal{K}_C} \setminus \emptyset$. A set in $2^{\mathcal{K}_C} \setminus \emptyset$ characterizes one token class.*

---

[1] ISO/IEC 10646-3:2003

[2] For simplification only ASCII characters are shown.

In the remainder of the paper we will denote a token class by the alternation of its underlying character classes and a Kleene plus (e.g. $\langle$UC|NB$\rangle^+$), wherein the order of character classes is arbitrary.

To classify token sequences with token classes, we have to define the corresponding language $L(\kappa_T), \kappa_T \in \mathcal{K}_T$. For token classes with only one element, we define its language by the Kleene closure of the character classes' language: $L(\kappa_T) = \kappa_Z^+, |\kappa_T| = 1, \kappa_Z \in \kappa_T$. The language definition for complex token classes, which are built from several character classes, is not straightforward because a character class language that could be expressed by [A-Za-z0-9]$^+$ inherits the language of [A-Za-z]$^+$. In order to avoid such inheritances, we define the languages of complex token classes to be disjunctive by excluding the languages of otherwise inherited token class languages. For instance we will get $L(\langle \text{UC}|\text{NB}\rangle^+) \equiv [\text{A-Z0-9}]^+ \backslash ([\text{A-Z}]^+ \cup [0\text{-}9]^+)$. Thus, we would classify input tokens such as '*AA*' $\in L(\langle \text{UC}\rangle^+)$ and '*A0A*'$\in L(\langle \text{UC}|\text{NB}\rangle^+)$, but '*AA*' $\notin L(\langle \text{UC}|\text{NB}\rangle^+)$. In practice such a definition of token class languages leads to the natural behavior that tokens that contain many different character classes will be treated as more specialized ones (since they occur less often) than tokens which are built of fewer character classes.

Having discussed feature types that are considered in the final regular expressions, we can define the alphabet Σ of the target grammar $\mathcal{G}^{\approx}$ as $\Sigma = \mathcal{K}_B \cup \mathcal{K}_C \cup \mathcal{K}_T$.

3.2 Prefix and Suffix Automatons

In order to come up with the target grammar $\mathcal{G}^{\approx}$ that is built upon the alphabet Σ, we have to extract all potential features from the sample instances and weight them against each other to determine the best fitting pattern description. The weighting is described in Section 4. In this sub-section, we describe how to generate automatons that capture all possible features of the sample instances. Therefore, we generate a prefix- and suffix automaton that describes the sequential occurrences of token classes as transition sequences and keep the respective tokens for each transition. In a next step we add for each token set that is underlying to a transition a parallel structure with respect to character classes.

The initial prefix and suffix automatons are generated using a sequence classification algorithm (see Algorithm 1). To generate the suffix automaton, we invert the character sequences of the given instances before running Algorithm 1. After tokenizing each input instance $i \in I$ in Algorithm 1, each token is classified with respect to the defined token classes $\mathcal{K}_T$ (based on the token class language definition). The corresponding token class is added to the respective token class sequence (see: $c_i \oplus \mathit{classify}(\mathit{token}, \mathcal{K}_T)$ in Algorithm 1). Finally, we get a set of pairs (denoted as C), which consists of token class sequences and the corresponding token sequence.

Algorithm: 1 token class feature extraction

Input: list of sample entities: I, token classes: $\mathcal{K}_T$
Output: token class sequences: C

```
C ← ∅
for all i ∈ I do
    c_i ← ∅    // token class sequence for i
    for all token ∈ tokenize(i) do
        c_i ⊕ classify(token, K_T)
    end for
    C ← (c_i, i)
end for
```

The automatons are generated through ordering the results of Algorithm 1 by classification sequences and iteratively building up a prefix (or suffix) tree automaton. In Figure 1 we illustrate an example prefix automaton (blue marked transitions) for the sample instances of notebook names shown in Table 1.(b). The transition labels for token classes are shown in Figure 1(a) (blue edges), while the underlying token sets are depicted in Figure 1(b). Note that we derive only one token class sequence for this simple example, while the examples from Table 1.(c) and Table 1.(d) will lead to more complex structures.

Next, we generate for each token class transition a parallel structure that describes character features. Therefore, we analyze the instance sub-sequences underlying a transition t, which we will denote in the following as I'_t. Each token $i'_t \in I'_t$ is classified with respect to the character class configuration $\mathcal{K}_C$ similar as explained for Algorithm 1. However, before encoding the character class sequences into the automaton, we apply an additional processing step to identify blocks of identical character classes with similar cardinality, e.g., to distinguish number sequences with three elements from such that have for instance two elements. The reason is that we would like to avoid treating sequences with different cardinalities as overlapping features in later processing steps (see Section 4.1).

We illustrate the blocking of character class sequences for the first tokens of the sample entities from Table 1.(b) in Mapping 2. The left matrix illustrates the tokens I'_t. We sort the resulting character class sequences and store them in a matrix as shown in the right part of Mapping 2. To derive a blocking as shown in Mapping 2, we mark identical character class sequences per row, e.g., the three occurrences of $\langle$NB$\rangle$ in the first row, and group in a second run identical character class sequences across row boundaries.

$$\begin{pmatrix} \text{z} & 8 & 0 & 0 \\ \text{z} & 8 & 0 & 0 \\ \text{d} & 7 & 0 & 0 \\ \text{z} & 4 & 0 & \text{y} \\ \text{d} & 5 & 0 & \text{t} \end{pmatrix} \mapsto \left(\begin{array}{c|cc} \langle\text{LC}\rangle & \langle\text{NB}\rangle\langle\text{NB}\rangle & \langle\text{NB}\rangle \\ \langle\text{LC}\rangle & \langle\text{NB}\rangle\langle\text{NB}\rangle & \langle\text{NB}\rangle \\ \langle\text{LC}\rangle & \langle\text{NB}\rangle\langle\text{NB}\rangle & \langle\text{NB}\rangle \\ \hline \langle\text{LC}\rangle & \langle\text{NB}\rangle\langle\text{NB}\rangle & \multicolumn{1}{|c}{\langle\text{LC}\rangle} \\ \langle\text{LC}\rangle & \langle\text{NB}\rangle\langle\text{NB}\rangle & \multicolumn{1}{|c}{\langle\text{LC}\rangle} \end{array}\right). \quad (2)$$

Next, we add states and edges by iterating the character block sequences as shown in Mapping 2 columnwise. Therefore, for each block, we encode a sequence of character class transitions into the previously generated automatons (see orange transitions in Figure 1(a)) and maintain in parallel the underlying character sets (orange transitions in Figure 1(b)).

4. FEATURE SELECTION

As result of the previous processing steps, we extracted features of different granularity from the given instances and encoded their sequences into a prefix- and suffix automaton. In this section, we discuss the selection of features that most likely represent the underlying formation rule of the given instances and shall be encoded into the final regular expressions. Therefore, we first describe in Section 4.1 how to compare features on instance level to those on class level (cf. Figure 1(a) vs. Figure 1(b)) by considering the instance sub-sequence distribution in an automaton.

In Section 4.2, we compare features on token level to those on character level (cf. blue vs. orange transitions in Figure 1) by adapting the minimum description length principle. As a result, we get a deterministic prefix and suffix automaton with feature sequences that can easily be trans-

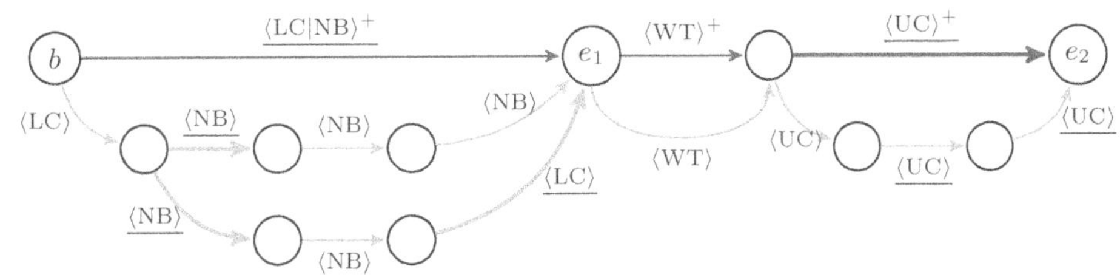

(a) *Features on class level:* token class features (blue) or character class features (orange).

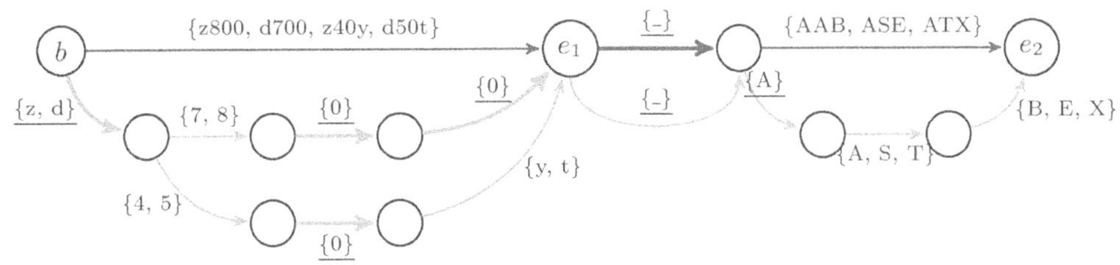

(b) *Features on instance level*: token feature sets (blue) / character feature sets (orange).

Figure 1: Example feature representation in a prefix automaton for the sample entities in Table 1.(b): The start state is labeled with b and possible end states with e_1 and e_2. Transitions describe the occurrences of features on class level (see 1(a)) and instance level (see 1(b)) for both token features (blue transitions) and character features (orange transitions). Underlined transition labels are selected after comparing instance and class level features (cf. Section 4.1), while thick marked transitions are selected after comparing token to character level features (cf. Section 4.2).

formed into regular expressions. In order to support heterogeneous instances, where some follow a prefix like pattern and others follow a suffix like formation rule (seeSection 1), we select per instance the most suitable feature sequence either from the prefix or suffix automaton, transform them into a regular expression and add them to the final rule set (if not yet present) as explained in Section 4.3.

4.1 Instance vs. Class Level Features

As mentioned before, to achieve a high precision during extraction, we would like to encode character or token sets into the regular expressions instead of their class representations. In order to judge whether a feature on instance level is very common, we compare the size of the instance set $|I'_t|$ attached to a transition t to the total number of instances that led to this transition (denoted as $A(I'_t)$). For instance for the first character level transition in Figure 1, we would get: $|I'_t| = |\{z, d\}| = 2$ and $A(I'_t) = 5$ (cf. Table 1.(b)).

Thus, if we derive a rather small ratio $|I'_t|/A(I'_t)$ compared to other transitions, it is more likely that the set of instance sub-sequences underlying such transitions will also occur in unknown instances. For instance if we have a prefix-like formation pattern such as shown in Figure 1, we will usually derive low values for $|I'_t|/A(I'_t)$ in the transitions that are close to the start state of the prefix automaton. However, since the ratios in different transition sequences may differ a lot, e.g., because the underlying instances follow different formation rules, we have to compare the derived values for a transition to those in their neighborhood.

We define the neighborhood in terms of preceding and succeeding transitions as follows: Let P be the set of transitions on the same abstraction level (token or character) that are predecessors of a transition t when traversing the automaton into the direction of the start state (b in Figure 1). Further, let S be all transitions that are reachable from a transition t when traversing the automaton into the direction of all possible end states (e.g., e_1 and e_2 for $t \equiv \{z, d\}$ in Figure 1(b)). That is, we use the mean ratio in the neighboring transitions to decide whether we are facing a low or high value for the ratio $|I'_t|/A(I'_t)$. The mean ratio, $E(|I'_t|/A(I'_t))$, is given by:

$$E\Big(\frac{|I'_t|}{A(I'_t)}\Big) = \frac{\sum_{p\in P}|I'_p| + |I'_t| + \sum_{s\in S}|I'_s|}{\sum_{p\in P}A(I'_p) + A(I'_t) + \sum_{s\in S}A(I'_s)} \quad . \quad (3)$$

We define the selection criteria, which incorporates a parameter $\beta \in (-1, 1)$ to allow engineers to influence the feature selection, as follows:

$$\frac{|I'_t|}{A(I'_t)} + \beta \leq E\Big(\frac{|I'_t|}{A(I'_t)}\Big). \quad (4)$$

In case Inequation 4 holds for a transition t, we select the token or character set I'_t as transition label. Otherwise we select the class representation as transition label (denoted as $\kappa_t \in \mathcal{K}_C \cup \mathcal{K}_T$). A high value of the parameter β will lead to fewer instance sets in the transition labels and thus to a higher recall, while a low value will lead to a higher precision. We consider two standard configurations: $\beta = 0.1$ (high recall) and $\beta = -0.1$ (high precision) and evaluate their performance in Section 5. As a result, we merged, figuratively speaking, the features shown in Figure 1(a) and Figure 1(b) into one single feature representation. Still, we maintain features on character and token level. For our running example in Figure 1, we would select – assuming a $\beta = 0.1$ – the underlined transition labels for further processing.

4.2 Token vs. Character Level Features

So far, we derived a prefix and suffix automaton that consist of a mix of instance and class labeled transitions. Still, we maintain transitions on token and character level (i.e. orange and blue marked transitions in Figure 1). In the following we discuss our adaption of the minimal description length principle (MDL) [8] to select the most promising abstraction layer to represent parts of the underlying sample instances, e.g., whether the last tokens of our samples in Figure 1 shall be represented by $\langle UC\rangle^+$ or its alternative on character level $\{A\} \rightsquigarrow \langle UC\rangle \rightsquigarrow \langle UC\rangle$.

The fundamental idea behind MDL is to compare different models, which describe a certain data structure, by means of their ability to compress the data. The underlying assumption is that the better a model describes the patterns within the data, the higher is the (approximated) compression rate. By incorporating the complexity of the model and its fitness to encode the actual data, MDL avoids over- and under-generation in a natural way. The measure to compare different models is the *description length*, which is commonly defined as follows:

DEFINITION 4.1 (DESCRIPTION LENGTH). *Let D be a dataset that can be described by a finite alphabet and M be a model describing the data. The description length $\mathcal{L}(D,M)$ to store D with M is defined as $\mathcal{L}(D,M) = \mathcal{L}(M) + \mathcal{L}(D|M)$, where $\mathcal{L}(M)$ is the description length to store the model M itself and $\mathcal{L}(D|M)$ is the description length that is required to encode the data D given M.*

In our case, we have to generate and compare all valid combinations of transitions (i.e. our alternative models), which we denote as $\mathcal{T}$. We start with the variant $T \in \mathcal{T}$ that encodes all instances with transitions on token level (e.g., $T \equiv \langle\text{LC}|\text{NB}\rangle^{+} \rightsquigarrow (\_) \rightsquigarrow \langle\text{UC}\rangle^{+}$ for Figure 1) and proceed with generating all variants by replacing some token transitions by alternatives on character level (e.g., $T \equiv \langle\text{LC}|\text{NB}\rangle^{+} \rightsquigarrow (\_) \rightsquigarrow (\{\text{A}\} \rightsquigarrow \langle\text{UC}\rangle \rightsquigarrow \langle\text{UC}\rangle))$. Thus, we get for the example shown in Figure 1 seven possible variants. For further explanation in the course of this sub-section, we list in Table 2 three of those variants, starting with a representation for transitions on token level in line 1, the combination that will turn out to be the most suitable one in line 2 and a representation on character level in line 3.

Table 2: Example description length for different abstraction level combinations for Figure 1

abstraction levels	$\mathcal{L}(T)$	$\mathcal{L}(I\|T)$	$\mathcal{L}(I,T)$
TL ⇝ TL ⇝ TL	26 bits	248 bits	274 bits
CL ⇝ TL ⇝ TL	62 bits	200 bits	262 bits
CL ⇝ CL ⇝ CL	72 bits	194 bits	266 bits
TL - token level, CL - character level			

The problem reduces, applying the MDL principle, to computing a description length $\mathcal{L}(D,M) = \mathcal{L}(I,T)$ for each set of transitions $T \in \mathcal{T}$, given the sample entities I. The description length definition shall implement the following heuristic: A high abstraction layer (i.e. many transitions on token level) shall lead to a low model description length $\mathcal{L}(T)$, but a rather high data description length $\mathcal{L}(I|T)$. Next, a lower abstraction level (i.e. many transitions on character level) shall lead to a high model description length $\mathcal{L}(T)$, but a rather low data description length $\mathcal{L}(I|T)$. With respect to instance feature sets, which more likely occur on a lower abstraction level, the description length definition shall lead to a higher model description length $\mathcal{L}(T)$, but a lower data description length $\mathcal{L}(I|T)$.

Model description length: In order to compute a description length for a model $T \in \mathcal{T}$, we can imagine a dictionary based compression. Thus, we, visually speaking, create a dictionary entry for each symbol in the transition labels and generate a code word that replaces a certain symbol in an transition label during an imagined compression step. To approximate the size of such a dictionary (i.e. the model description length), we have to consider two factors: the storage space for the actual symbol which is required for decoding a compressed transition sequence later on, and the storage space for the corresponding code word (i.e. a bit sequence that replaces a symbol). By the term 'symbol' we refer in the following either to a classification label, if we selected in the previous processing step a representation on class level, or a token or character in a transition label, if we selected a representation on instance level. We denote the set of symbols that are derived from a set of transitions T in the remaining paper as $S(T)$.

For the symbols themselves, we assume that each character of an instance feature $i'_t \in I'_t$ or likewise a class label requires 2^3 bits (e.g, $L(\langle\text{UC}\rangle^{+}) = 8$ bits). The storage space for one code word, that will be used to compress symbols $s \in S(T)$ later on, is computed by assuming an optimal entropy coding as: $H(s) = -\log_2 p(s), s \in S(T)$, where $p(s)$ is the probability that s occurs in T. Thus, in summary we get an approximated description length $\mathcal{L}(T)$ of:

$$\mathcal{L}(T) = \sum_{s \in S(T)} H(s) + L(s). \tag{5}$$

The second column of Table 2 illustrates some example values for $\mathcal{L}(T)$, given the running example from Figure 1.

Data description length: The description length $\mathcal{L}(I|T)$ that results from compressing the data I with the model $T \in \mathcal{T}$ should behave as follows: If there is indeed a prefix or suffix like pattern on character level with many overlapping features (e.g., as shown in the first sub-automaton on character level in Figure 1), the resulting description length $\mathcal{L}(I|T)$ should be rather low, compared to those on token level. Further, as mentioned above, the presence of instance features (which usually appear, with increasing β, first on character level) shall lead to a lower $\mathcal{L}(I|T)$ compared to a transition with a class label.

We start with a description length definition for one transition t and its underlying instance sub-sequences I'_t, which we denote as $L(I'_t|t)$. We have to consider two cases: First, if we have selected instance features as transition labels ($t \equiv I'_t$), we replace, visually speaking, the symbols by the previously derived code words. To reflect how many instances are covered by a certain code word, we assume a lossless compression, which means that we should be able to re-construct each individual instance sub-sequence. Therefore, we multiply the storage space of the corresponding code word $H(i'_t), i'_t \in I'_t$ with the total number (denoted as $A(i'_t)$) of the occurrences of a symbol within the instance sub-sequences. This leads to the following description length definition for one transition:

$$L(I'_t|t) = \sum_{i'_t \in I'_t} A(i'_t) \cdot H(i'_t) \ \ , t \equiv I'_t. \tag{6}$$

As a second case, we consider transitions that are labeled with a class feature $t \equiv \kappa_t, \kappa_t \in S(T), \kappa_t \in \mathcal{K}_C \cup \mathcal{K}_T$. A class feature label does not provide any exploitable information for lossless compression, but can be derived from the instance sub-sequences themselves. Thus, we encode only the instance set I'_t that led to $t \equiv \kappa_t$ without any compression and again consider one byte (2^3 bits) to store each character of each instance $i'_t \in I'_t$ in the code length $L(i'_t)$. Considering in addition the number of occurrences $A(i'_t)$, the description length $L(I'_t|t)$ for feature class labeled transitions is computed by the equation:

$$L(I'_t|t) = \sum_{i'_t \in I'_t} A(i'_t) \cdot L(i'_t), \ \ t \equiv \kappa_t, \kappa_t \in \mathcal{K}_C \cup \mathcal{K}_T, \tag{7}$$

To incorporate the structure of an automaton into $\mathcal{L}(I|T)$, we consider a factor to encode the transition sequences.

Therefore, we assume 2^3 bits to store each state (denoted as N_T) and define the description length $\mathcal{L}(I|T)$ as:

$$\mathcal{L}(I|T) = |N_T| \cdot 2^3 \text{ bits} + \sum_{t \in T, I'_t \in I} \mathcal{L}(I'_t|t), \tag{8}$$

Again, we show some example values for $\mathcal{L}(I|T)$, given the running example from Figure 1, in the third column of Table 2. The differences between the values for $\mathcal{L}(I|T)$ are rather low, because we considered only five instances in this minimal example.

Feature selection: Having computed the description length $\mathcal{L}(I,T) = \mathcal{L}(T) + \mathcal{L}(I|T)$ for each $T \in \mathcal{T}$, we get the minimum description length by:

$$\mathcal{L}_{min}(I, \mathcal{T}) = \min_{(T \in \mathcal{T})} \Big[\mathcal{L}(T) + \mathcal{L}(I|T)\Big]. \tag{9}$$

For further processing, we keep only the combination of transitions $T \in \mathcal{T}$ that led to $\mathcal{L}_{min}(I, \mathcal{T})$ (i.e., the combination in the second line of Table 2) from both the prefix and suffix automaton. Thus, we selected from the potential pattern descriptions as shown in Figure 1, the most suitable ones with respect to their complexity and fitness (i.e. the thick marked transitions in Figure 1) and get as result deterministic prefix and suffix automatons.

4.3 Regular Expression Generation

In order to allow for heterogeneous instances, where some follow a prefix like pattern and others follow a suffix like formation rule, we merge the results from the prefix- and suffix automaton. Therefore, we maintained for each end state in the automaton a pointer to the corresponding sample instances. In addition, during processing of the minimum description length (see Equation 9), we kept the computed description lengths for each path from the start state to each end state. To come up with the final set of regular expressions, we iterate over the input instances, choose the corresponding end states (e.g., e_1 for "z800" or e_2 for "z800 AAB" in Figure 1) in the prefix and suffix automaton and select the end state which led to the smallest description length. Thus, we get for each input instance a sub-automaton either from the prefix or suffix automaton, which is best suited to describe its pattern with respect to all other instances.

For our running example, we finally get two pattern descriptions from the prefix automaton (i.e., for e_1 and e_2 in Figure 1). We apply some simplification rules such as introducing cardinalities (denoted as curly brackets) if possible or merging of overlapping regular expressions. More complex sub-automatons on character level are encoded by the alternation of alternative transition sequences. Thus, we get only one expression for our running example: (z|d)(⟨NB⟩(0){2}|⟨NB⟩(0)⟨LC⟩)((_)⟨UC⟩$^+$){0, 1}, which can be expressed for instance in standard Java regular expression range syntax for easier readability as (d|z)([0-9]0{2}|[0-9]0[a-z]) (_[A-Z]$^+$)? (see also Table 1.(b)).

The generated regular expressions are ready-to-use to extract unknown entities that follow the same patterns as the given sample entities. The configuration of the algorithm can be adapted to any regular-expressions-based information extraction system. Furthermore, the generated regular expressions can be easily understood by users and tuned by an expert if required.

5. EXPERIMENTS

Our learning approach is intended for identifier-like entities that can be described by regular expressions. As discussed in Section 2, we are not aware of any other learning approach for rule based information extraction that supports the inference of regular expressions from given example entities and solves the problem of incorporating dependent features of different granularity. In our evaluation, we show that our approach generates easily understandable regular expressions and provides a comparable extraction quality to statistical approaches that leverage dependent features of different granularity. Therefore, we compare the extraction quality of our approach to results of the popular machine learning technique Conditional Random Fields (CRF) [10] and show examples of generated regular expressions. However, in contrast to our approach, CRF requires annotated documents for training and context information to determine entity boundaries. For comparison, we discuss the F_1-measure (harmonic mean of precision and recall). We assume that results are comparable if the F_1-measure difference is less than 0.15.

Table 3: Example rules (1) – see Figure 2 for extraction quality comparison to CRF and DICT

<table>
<tr><th colspan="2">Phone numbers (Invoices) - 3 of 28 rules</th></tr>
<tr><td>PAT-.1</td><td>(\+|\()(0621|...)(\)|-)(_)((4)⟨NB⟩{3}|⟨NB⟩{3})[...]
(06227|06205|...)(-|/)(_)⟨NB⟩+⟨WT⟩(4)⟨NB⟩{2}
(06227|06205|...)(-|/)(_)⟨NB⟩+⟨SC⟩⟨NB⟩+</td></tr>
<tr><td>PAT+.1</td><td>(\+|\()⟨NB⟩{1,5}(\)|-)(_)⟨NB⟩+⟨SC⟩⟨NB⟩+
⟨NB⟩{1,5}(-|/)(_)⟨NB⟩+⟨WT⟩⟨NB+⟩
(06227|06205|...)(-|/)(_)⟨NB⟩+⟨SC⟩⟨NB⟩+</td></tr>
<tr><th colspan="2">SWIFT-Codes (Invoices) - 2 rules</th></tr>
<tr><td>PAT-.1</td><td>(G|H|E|...)(C|A|B|...)[...](E|U|T|...)
(H|W|F|...)(V|S|A|...)[...](2|3|4|C|...)</td></tr>
<tr><td>PAT+.1</td><td>⟨UC⟩+
⟨UC|NB⟩+</td></tr>
<tr><th colspan="2">Invoice numbers (Invoices) - 3 of 7 rules</th></tr>
<tr><td>PAT-.1</td><td>(G|V|C|B|P|K)(H|S|D|B|O|K)(-|/)⟨NB⟩{4,9}
(2008|2009|0909|...)(-|\.)⟨NB⟩+(-)(47)⟨NB⟩{4}
(#)⟨NB⟩+</td></tr>
<tr><td>PAT+.1</td><td>⟨UC⟩{2}(-|/)⟨NB⟩{4,9}
(2008|...)(-|\.)⟨NB⟩+(-)⟨NB⟩+
(#)⟨NB⟩+</td></tr>
<tr><th colspan="2">Notebooks (Reviews) - 3 of 32 rules</th></tr>
<tr><td>PAT-.1</td><td>(HDX)(_)(1)⟨NB⟩⟨LC⟩
(Mini)(_)(10)⟨NB⟩{2}(_)⟨UC|LC⟩+
(Pavilion)(_)(z|d|t|x)(v|e|h|x)⟨NB⟩{2}(00)</td></tr>
<tr><td>PAT+.1</td><td>(HDX)(_)⟨NB|LC⟩+
(Mini)(_)⟨NB|LC⟩+(_)⟨UC|LC⟩+
(Pavilion)(_)⟨NB|LC⟩+</td></tr>
</table>

As CRF-implementation, we used the Stanford NLP toolkit[3] with a comparable feature combination. It considers: tokens in a context window of size 2, (overlapping) n-grams with a maximal length of 4 and a word shape feature (comparable to our configuration for token classes). For our approach, we tested the two standard configurations with $\beta = 0.1$ (high recall) and $\beta = -0.1$ (high precision).

We applied experiments on four (manually annotated) corpora from different domains and evaluated the performance for eight types of entities. Our method is trained with a randomly chosen subset of the annotated entities. We show the average results from multiple runs. To evaluate the performance with different training data sizes, we conducted experiments for 1%, 2%, 4%, ..., 64% and 100% of the available entities for training. For the CRF, we always

[3]http://nlp.stanford.edu/software/crf-faq.shtml

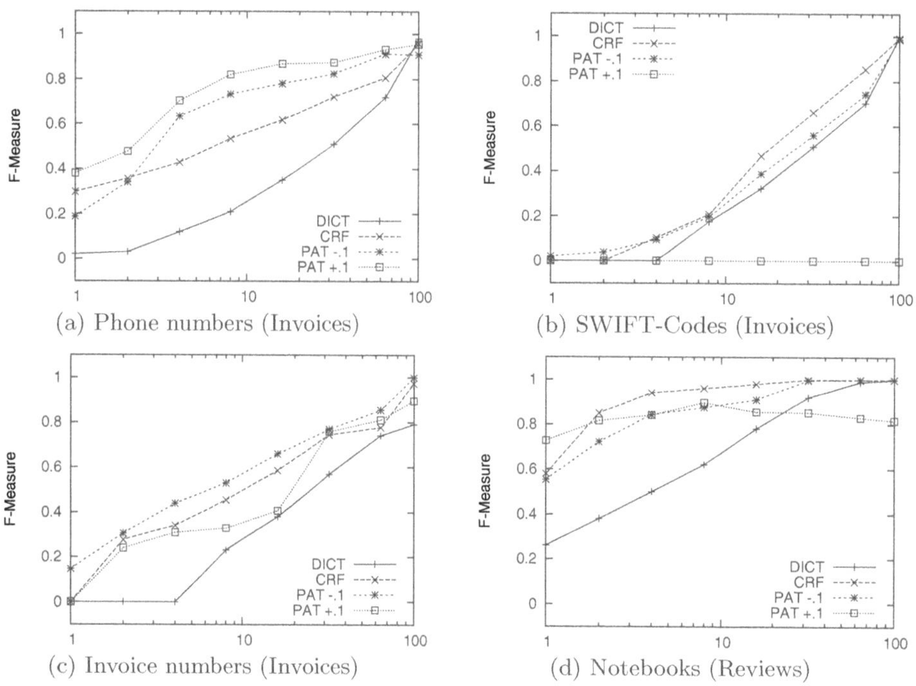

(a) Phone numbers (Invoices)

(b) SWIFT-Codes (Invoices)

(c) Invoice numbers (Invoices)

(d) Notebooks (Reviews)

Figure 2: Extraction quality (F_1-measure) with respect to the training data [%] (1)

used the whole document corpus in the training phase, but removed the text segments (entities and context) for those entities which were not selected as training samples.

Since we choose random sample entities from the documents for training (and not randomly selected example documents), it was difficult to implement a folding for cross-validation (especially with respect to the CRF). Instead, we always run the tests on the whole corpus (which contained the training data as well) and conducted experiments for a dictionary-based approach for comparison. The difference in the results of the evaluated method and the dictionary approach indicates how many additional, unknown entities were identified by an approach and is lowered by the number of false positive that were included in the results.

5.1 Document Corpora

In the following we briefly describe the used data sets and the entity types that were considered.

Invoices: To test the performance of our system in enterprise settings, we acquired a corpus of 103 real world paper invoices that were digitalized by an OCR-software. The corpus consists of invoices from different domains, such as from car dealers, hotels or IT-services. We evaluated the extraction of Swift-codes, invoice numbers and phone numbers. Note, that Swift-codes and invoice numbers usually occur in texts and databases in the same form. Thus our approach could train on a database as well. Phone numbers occur in texts usually with a reader friendly formatting.

Notebook reviews: To test the performance for product names, we used a corpus of notebook reviews[4]. The corpus contains 90 documents, each having a list of about 20 notebook names that should be extracted by the algorithms. The notebook names might occur in some product catalog in the same form.

SAP Forums: As another use case, we conducted experiments on user generated developer forum contents[5]. The goal was to extract mentioned Java exceptions (e.g., java.lang.NullPointerException) from 1,500 forum entries. The problem is that Java exceptions generally follow the syntax of class names in Java (which are also mentioned frequently in the forums), but have some distinguishing tokens.

ReLie corpus: The last corpus was provided by the authors of [11]. It contains about 80,000 text fragments that were extracted from 50,000 intranet sites, 50,000 web sites of the University of Michigan and 10,000 emails from the Enron data set[6]. The text fragments were selected using general regular expressions for phone numbers, software names and university course names. Finally, the corpus was annotated manually to distinguish false positives (with respect to the initial regular expressions) and correct matches.

We mentioned already in Section 2 that our approach and the one of [11] are complementary, because [11] optimizes a regular expression using a training corpus through transformations (e.g., by adding terms that shall not be matched). Thus, a direct comparison is not possible. Rather, a combination of our approach, rule learning approaches that incorporate context and [11] is a promising future integration problem to fully leverage annotated training corpora, if they are available.

5.2 Experimental Results

Figure 2 and 3 illustrate the results of our approach ($\beta = 0.1$ as *PAT+.1* and $\beta = -0.1$ as *PAT-.1*), of the CRF approach (see *CRF*) and the baseline method (*DICT*). Examples for generated regular expressions are shown in Table 3, 4 and 5. We use the same syntax as we used throughout this paper, shortened some alternations of instance features by "..." and cropped very long feature sequences by introducing "[...]". In this sub-section, will mainly investigate on the extraction quality and leave it to the experienced reader to decide on the simplicity of the generated rule sets.

The CRF-approach provides a high precision. Therefore,

[4]http://www.notebookreview.com

[5]http://www.sdn.sap.com

[6]http://www.cs.cmu.edu/ enron/

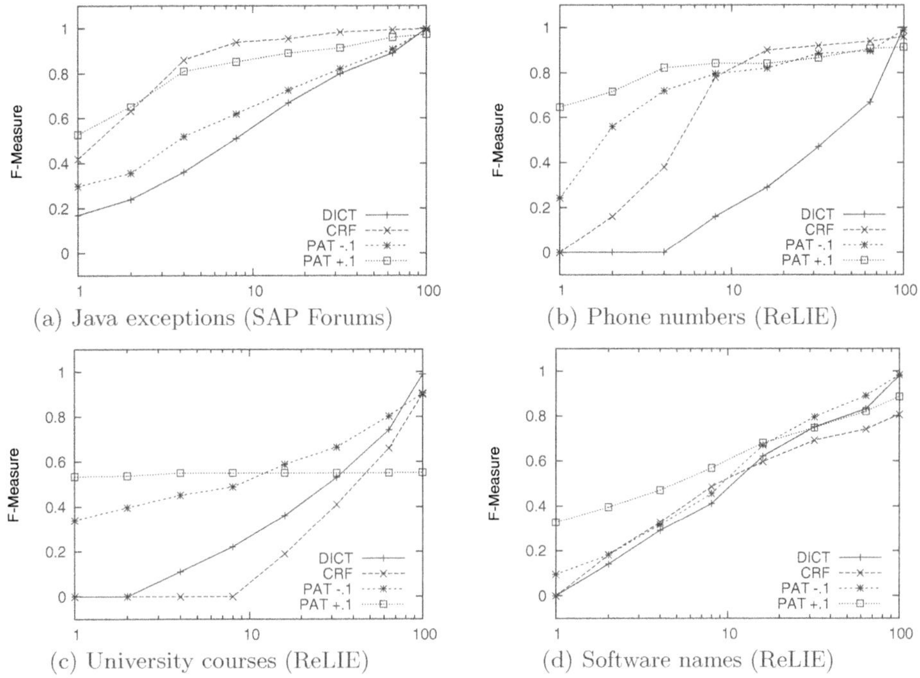

(a) Java exceptions (SAP Forums)
(b) Phone numbers (ReLIE)
(c) University courses (ReLIE)
(d) Software names (ReLIE)

Figure 3: Extraction quality (F_1-measure) with respect to the training data [%] (2)

Table 4: Example rules (2) – see Figure 3 for extraction quality comparison to CRF and DICT

Java exceptions (SAP Forums) - 4 of 23 rules	
PAT-.1	(java)(\.)(lang)(\.)⟨UC|LC⟩$^+$(Exception|Error|Message)
	(od|i)⟨UC|LC⟩$^+$(\.)⟨UC|LC⟩$^+$(\.)⟨UC|LC⟩$^+$(Exception|Error|Message)
	(com)(\.)(adobe)(\.)(ads)(\.)(operation)(\.)⟨UC|LC⟩$^+$(handle)⟨UC|LC⟩$^+$(Exception|Error|Message)
	⟨UC|LC⟩$^+$(\.)⟨UC|LC⟩$^+$(\.)⟨UC|LC⟩$^+$(Exception|Error|Message)
PAT+.1	⟨LC⟩{4}⟨SC⟩⟨LC⟩{4}⟨SC⟩⟨UC|LC⟩$^+$(Exception|Error|Message)
	⟨LC⟩$^+$⟨UC|LC⟩$^+$⟨SC⟩⟨UC|LC⟩$^+$⟨SC⟩⟨UC|LC⟩$^+$(Exception|Error|Message)
	⟨LC⟩$^+$⟨SC⟩⟨LC⟩$^+$⟨SC⟩⟨LC⟩$^+$⟨SC⟩⟨UC|LC⟩$^+$⟨LC⟩$^+$⟨UC|LC⟩$^+$(Exception|Error|Message)
	⟨UC|LC⟩$^+$⟨SC⟩⟨UC|LC⟩$^+$⟨SC⟩⟨UC|LC⟩$^+$(Exception|Error|Message)

we start comparing the results of CRF and the configuration $\beta = -0.1$. In the two use cases for extracting phone numbers (see Figure 2(a) and Figure 3(b)) as well as in the use case for university courses, *PAT-.1* outperforms *CRF* by far, given only a small training data set. In Figure 2(a) the difference is 0.24 and in Figure 3(b) 0.34 using 4% of the training data. With an increasing amount of training data, *CRF* adapts to the corpus and produces comparable results with respect to *PAT-.1*. Note that *CRF* produces poor results for Figure 3(c). In an advanced analysis of the results, it turned out that the classifier predicted in many cases a likelihood for being an entitiy that was slightly below the likelihood for not being an entity. However, a recombination and a different configuration of the used features did not lead to an improvement. We assume that a domain specific feature definition could improve the results significantly. In this use case *PAT-.1* performed very well and already leads to very good results using a training data size of 2% .

In the use case of extracting invoice numbers (see Figure 2(c)) and the one for notebook names (see Figure 2(d)), we can observe a very good, comparable performance of *PAT-.1* and *CRF*. In two other cases, namely the extraction of swift codes (see Figure 2(b)) and software names (see Figure 3(d)), we can also observe comparable results of *PAT-.1* and *CRF*, but a unsatisfactory performance compared to *DICT*. Again, we see in Figure 3(c) that performance of *CRF* is not optimal since the F_1-measure for 100% of the training data is only 0.81.

For the experiments concerning Java exceptions (see Figure 3(a)), we see that *PAT-.1* led to poor results compared to *CRF* (0.34 difference for 4% of the training data) because *CRF* implicitly encodes the re-occuring sequential patterns that occur in exception names (tokens separated by dots). In this case *PAT+.1* performs as well as *CRF* even though it is not aware of re-occuring sequential structures. Furthermore, *PAT+.1* turns out to perform best for the phone number entities (see Figure 2(a) and Figure 3(b)), because the syntactic structure is distinctive even though fewer instance features are considered. A similar behaviour can be seen for software names (see Figure 3(d)).

However, the configuration *PAT+.1* over-generates in other cases, e.g., for university course names (see Figure 3(c)) and especially for Swift-codes (Figure 2(b)), and leads to too abstract regular expressions (e.g., a expression like ⟨UC⟩$^+$ for Swift-codes). Therefore, the recall is with few training data rather high, but the precision does not improve significantly when supplying more training data.

In summary, we could show that in most of the cases our approach performs as well as the prominent CRF-approach (configured with comparable features) for the targeted classes of entity types. Furthermore, our approach leads in many cases (either with $\beta = -0.1$ or $\beta = 0.1$)

Table 5: Example rules (3) – see also Figure 3

<table>
<tr><th colspan="2">Phone number (ReLIE) - 3 of 7 rules</th></tr>
<tr><td>PAT-.1</td><td>(\(|\+)(1|313|...)(\.|\))(_)⟨NB⟩{3}(-)⟨NB⟩+
(1)⟨SC⟩(800)⟨SC⟩(723)⟨SC⟩⟨NB⟩+
⟨NB⟩{1,3}(_)⟨NB⟩{3}(-)⟨NB⟩+</td></tr>
<tr><td>PAT+.1</td><td>(\(|\+)(1|313|...)(\.|\))(_)⟨NB⟩+⟨SC⟩⟨NB⟩+
(1)⟨SC⟩(800)⟨SC⟩⟨NB⟩+⟨SC⟩⟨NB⟩+
⟨NB⟩{1,3}(_)⟨NB⟩{3}(-)⟨NB⟩+</td></tr>
<tr><th colspan="2">University courses (ReLIE) - 3 rules</th></tr>
<tr><td>PAT-.1</td><td>⟨UC|LC⟩+(_)⟨NB⟩+
⟨UC|LC⟩+⟨SC⟩(_)(271)
(G|H|U|M|...)(E|U|C|A|...)⟨UC⟩{1,8}(_)⟨NB⟩+</td></tr>
<tr><td>PAT+.1</td><td>⟨UC|LC⟩+(_)⟨NB⟩+
⟨UC|LC⟩+⟨SC⟩(_)⟨NB⟩+
⟨UC⟩+(_)⟨NB⟩+</td></tr>
<tr><th colspan="2">Software names (ReLIE) - 3 of 11 rules</th></tr>
<tr><td>PAT-.1</td><td>⟨UC|LC⟩+(_)(⟨NB⟩{1,2}|(200)⟨NB⟩)
⟨UC|LC⟩+(_)⟨UC|LC⟩+(_)(6|3|4|5)(\.)⟨NB⟩
⟨UC|LC⟩+(_)(8|6|3|4)(\.)⟨NB⟩</td></tr>
<tr><td>PAT+.1</td><td>⟨UC|LC⟩+(_)⟨NB⟩{1,4}
⟨UC|LC⟩+(_)⟨UC|LC⟩+(_)⟨NB⟩+⟨SC⟩⟨NB⟩+
⟨UC|LC⟩+(_)⟨NB⟩+⟨SC⟩⟨NB⟩+</td></tr>
</table>

to better results than CRF, even though it does not rely on context information (and can be trained in absence of a document corpus). In addition, users can understand and tune our regular expressions easily, which is extremely complicated for statistical machine learning approaches. Clearly, an integration of our approach with statistical approaches is straightforward since they support regular expression features. However, in order to keep the advantage of ease in traceability and manual tuning, an integration with other rule learning and optimization approaches appears more promising for extracting identifier-like entities in the presence of annotated training documents.

6. CONCLUSION

In this paper, we addressed the problem of inferring regular expressions, which can be easily understood by an user, from sample entities, e.g., derived from a database or an annotated document corpus, to extract unknown entities of the same type from text data. In principle, it does not require any (annotated) document corpus and extends therefore the applications of information extraction especially in enterprise settings, where usually a lot of structured data is available, as opposed to (annotated) training documents. Compared to previous rule learning approaches in information extraction, which are more suited to learning context information from training documents, our approach supports dependent features of different granularity, as opposed to a limitation to token features of one granularity.

An experimental study showed the applicability of our approach in different enterprise use cases and that it has a similar performance as the prominent approach of Conditional Random Fields (CRF) for use cases where annotated documents are available. Furthermore, it turned out that our approach leads often to a better performance than CRF for targeted class of identifier-like entities.

In future we would like to study – besides an integration with other learning approaches – the incorporation of higher abstraction levels and adapt our approach to the domain of web wrapper induction.

Acknowledgments

This work is supported by the FP7 EU Project 'ROBUST – Risk and Opportunity management of huge-scale BUSiness communiTy cooperation' [7] (contract no. ICT-257859).

7. REFERENCES

[1] G. J. Bex, F. Neven, T. Schwentick, and S. Vansummeren. Inference of concise regular expressions and dtds. *TODS*, 35(2):1–47, 2010.

[2] F. Brauer, R. Rieger, W. Barczynski, and A. Mocan. Regular language inference for domain-specific named entity recognition. In *IADIS WWW/Internet*, 2009.

[3] J. Y. Chai, A. W. Biermann, and C. I. Guinn. Two dimensional generalization in information extraction. In *AAAI*, pages 431–438, 1999.

[4] F. Ciravegna. Adaptive information extraction from text by rule induction and generalisation. In *IJCAI*, pages 1251–1256, 2001.

[5] H. Fernau. Algorithms for learning regular expressions from positive data. *Information and Computation*, 207(4):521–541, 2009.

[6] D. Freitag. Machine learning for information extraction in informal domains. *Machine Learning*, 39(2-3):169–202, 2000.

[7] M. N. Garofalakis, A. Gionis, R. Rastogi, S. Seshadri, and K. Shim. Xtract: A system for extracting document type descriptors from xml documents. In *SIGMOD*, pages 165–176, 2000.

[8] P. Grünwald. A tutorial introduction to the minimum description length principle. *CoRR*, math.ST/0406077, 2004.

[9] G. Kasneci, F. M. Suchanek, G. Ifrim, S. Elbassuoni, M. Ramanath, and G. Weikum. Naga: Harvesting, searching and ranking knowledge. In *SIGMOD*, pages 1285–1288. Association for Computing Machinery (ACM), 2008.

[10] J. D. Lafferty, A. McCallum, and F. C. N. Pereira. Conditional random fields: Probabilistic models for segmenting and labeling sequence data. In *ICML*, pages 282–289, 2001.

[11] Y. Li, R. Krishnamurthy, S. Raghavan, S. Vaithyanathan, and H. V. Jagadish. Regular expression learning for information extraction. In *EMNLP*, pages 21–30, 2008.

[12] I. R. Mansuri and S. Sarawagi. Integrating unstructured data into relational databases. In *ICDE*, page 29, 2006.

[13] P. Palaga, L. Nguyen, U. Leser, and J. Hakenberg. High-performance information extraction with alibaba. In *EDBT*, pages 1140–1143, 2009.

[14] R. Parekh and V. Honavar. Automata induction, grammar inference, and language acquisition. In *The Handbook of Natural Language Processing*, pages 727–764. Marcel Dekker Inc., New York, Ny, USA, 2000.

[15] V. Raman and J. M. Hellerstein. Potter's wheel: An interactive data cleaning system. In *VLDB*, pages 381–390, 2001.

[16] S. Sarawagi. Information extraction. *Foundations and Trends in Databases*, 1(3):261–377, 2008.

[17] S. Soderland. Learning information extraction rules for semi-structured and free text. *Machine Learning*, 34(1-3):233–272, 1999.

[18] P. P. Talukdar, T. Brants, M. Liberman, and F. Pereira. A context pattern induction method for named entity extraction. In *CoNLL*, pages 141–148, 2006.

[19] J. Turmo, A. Ageno, and N. Català. Adaptive information extraction. *ACM Computing Surveys*, 38(2):4, 2006.

[20] H. Yu, X. Zhu, M. Huang, and M. Li. Discovering patterns to extract protein-protein interactions from the literature: Part ii. *Bioinformatics*, 21(15):3294–3300, 2005.

[7] http://www.robust-project.eu

Mining Entity Translations from Comparable Corpora: A Holistic Graph Mapping Approach

Jinhan Kim†, Long Jiang‡, Seung-won Hwang†, Young-In Song‡, and Ming Zhou‡
†Pohang University of Science and Technology, Pohang, Republic of Korea
‡Microsoft Research Asia, Beijing, China
wlsgks08@postech.ac.kr, longj@microsoft.com, swhwang@postech.ac.kr,
yosong@microsoft.com, mingzhou@microsoft.com

ABSTRACT

This paper addresses the problem of mining named entity translations from comparable corpora, specifically, mining English and Chinese named entity translation. We first observe that existing approaches use one or more of the following named entity similarity metrics: entity, entity context, and relationship. Inspired by this observation, in this paper, we propose a new holistic approach, by (1) combining all similarity types used and (2) additionally considering relationship context similarity between pairs of named entities, a missing quadrant in the taxonomy of similarity metrics. We abstract the named entity translation problem as the matching of two named entity graphs extracted from the comparable corpora. Specifically, named entity graphs are first constructed from comparable corpora to extract relationship between named entities. Entity similarity and entity context similarity are then calculated from every pair of bilingual named entities. A reinforcing method is utilized to reflect relationship similarity and relationship context similarity between named entities. According to our experimental results, our holistic graph-based approach significantly outperforms previous approaches.

Categories and Subject Descriptors

I.2.7 [**Natural Language Processing**]: Machine Translation, Text Analysis; H.2.8 [**Database Application**]: Data Mining

General Terms

Languages, Experimentation

Keywords

Named Entity Translation, Graph Mapping

1. INTRODUCTION

Named entities (NE) normally refer to a range of concepts like people names, place names, organization names, product names, and so on. Large quantities of new named entities appear every day in newspapers, web sites, TV programs, and so on. However, their translations usually cannot be found in general purpose bilingual dictionaries. Automatic NE translation extraction is thus important to machine translation systems and cross-language information retrieval applications.

For this NE translation extraction task, early researches focused on finding NE correspondence in parallel sentences (or parallel corpora) [12, 7, 3]. Though such NE translation extraction from parallel corpora can achieve very high accuracy, obtaining large-scale parallel corpora is not a trivial task, especially for uncommon language pairs.

To avoid the high costs of obtaining parallel corpora, many researchers have switched to comparable corpora for building large scale bilingual lexicons. Comparable corpora refer to those texts that are not translations of each other but talk about the same or related topics. For instance, news articles published in different languages within the same period can be regarded as comparable corpora. The amount of comparable corpora is much larger than that of parallel corpora, and they are easier to obtain, which makes them a desirable source for large-scale bilingual lexicon building.

Table 1: Taxonomy of cross-language similarity metrics.

	Entity	Relationship
Using entity names	E	R
Using textual context	EC	

Existing work can be categorized, based on the types of similarity metrics used (Table 1):

- E: Entity names in the two corpora can be compared based on their phonetic similarity, *e.g.*, high phonetic similarity between Obama and Chinese translation of Obama, 奥巴马 (pronounced 'Aobama'), is evidence that they are translation pairs.
- EC: Entity Context, *i.e.*, common text surrounding named entity translation pair in the two corpora, can be compared. For example, Obama and 奥巴马, surrounded by words with the same meanings, such as 'president' and '总统', support the inference that they are translation pairs.
- R: Relationships between a NE pair in one corpus and a NE pair in other corpus, quantified by named entity co-occurrence, can be used as relational evidence that they are translation pair, *e.g.*, Barack and Michelle (巴拉克 and 米歇尔) frequently co-occur.

CIKM'11, October 24–28, 2011, Glasgow, Scotland, UK.

More specifically, early work applied E, using either rule-based phonetic similarity [19] or statistics-based phonetic similarity [11, 6]. However, pure E-based methods did not achieve satisfactory results, as some translations do not have similar pronunciation and there are also NEs with ambiguous pronunciation. In contrast, [15, 4] proposed to extract word translations from comparable corpora, to use EC. More EC-based approaches were proposed [2, 22, 8] adopting different context representation.

More recently, *holistic* approaches [16, 21] combining multiple similarity metrics have been proposed and outperformed preceding work. First, [16] combines E and EC using a language model and a probabilistic transliteration model respectively to find Chinese-English translation pair. In contrast, [21] combines E and R. As most NE translations do not appear in a general purpose bilingual word dictionary, [21] adopts an iterative approach to gradually refine R.

In this paper, we complete the picture, by (1) combining E, EC, and R, and (2) additionally considering RC, which is a missing quadrant in the taxonomy. Like EC, RC, Relationship Context, considers the textual context similarity between an English NE pair and a Chinese NE pair, *i.e.*, surrounding text explaining the relationship of the NE pair, as evidence for whether the two relationships are comparable. For example, Barack and Michelle described as couple in both corpora is a strong evidence.

Specifically, we first construct NE relationship graphs from comparable corpora and initialize pairwise translation similarity between bilingual NE pairs, using E and EC. We then iteratively reinforce the overall translation similarity until convergence using R and RC. Our experimental results suggest that our new holistic approach significantly outperforms previous state-of-art approaches.

To summarize, this paper has the following contributions:

1. We present a new named entity translation similarity metric, relationship context similarity (RC), to complete the taxonomy of cross-language named entity translation similarity metrics.

2. We propose a new holistic English-Chinese NE translation approach, by combining all translation similarity metrics (E, EC, R, and RC).

3. We perform various kinds of evaluations to present the effectiveness of our holistic approach by comparing with existing NE translation approaches.

The rest of this paper is organized as follows. Section 2 reviews existing work. Section 3 formally defines the problem and Section 4 then develops our framework. Section 5 reports experimental results and Section 6 concludes the paper.

2. RELATED WORK

As described earlier, existing work has focused on using entity context similarity (EC), entity similarity (E), and relationship similarity (R) for mining cross-language term translations from comparable corpora.

Early work applies entity similarity (E), using either rule-based phonetic similarity [19] or statistics-based phonetic similarity [11, 6, 17]. However, pure E-based methods did not achieve satisfactory results, as some translations do not have similar pronunciation and there are also NEs with ambiguous pronunciation. Meanwhile, [15, 4, 2, 22, 8] extracted translation pairs with high entity context similarity (EC) using word co-occurrences. More recently, holistic approaches combining two similarity notions have been studied, using E and EC [16, 1], and E and R [21] for computing overall similarity respectively. In this paper, we implemented [16] and [21] as baseline approaches, which we denote as Shao and You respectively from this point on.

More specifically, Shao [16] combines E and EC. For computing E, Shao uses a probabilistic pronunciation model for machine transliteration using expectation maximization (EM) algorithm. For computing EC, Shao uses a language model used in a typical information retrieval (IR) problem which considers each Chinese word as a query and each English word as a document using their context words. Each of these two models ranks English translation candidate words for each Chinese word. After that, Shao examines the top M English translation candidate words in both ranked lists, finds English words that appear in top M positions in both ranked lists, and selects the English word with the highest average rank position as the translation of the Chinese word.

On the other hand, You [21] combines E and R. For computing E, You computes edit distance (ED) between Chinese Pinyins and English strings as they are pronounced similarly. For R, You uses monolingual entity co-occurrences, crawled from entity search web sites. You develops an entity matching algorithm which initializes the translation similarity between named entities by using E and iteratively reinforces the translation similarity by using R. After the convergence of the reinforcement step, You extracts one-to-one matches maximizing the overall similarity by using greedy matching algorithm.

Our work generalizes these efforts by combining three notions (E, EC, and R) and by also considering relationship context similarity (RC), with the following distinctions from each.

Compared to Shao, our approach has at least two advantages. First, NEs co-occur frequently, and co-occurrence information is an important factor to determine NE translation. However, NE translation pairs rarely appear in a dictionary and thus are ignored in Shao. By iterative reinforcement in our approach, the correctly translated NEs can help us find the translations of their neighbors in the next iteration, which enables us to make use of most NEs and provide more accurate NE translations. Second, in Shao, the candidate ranking of a given NE is independent of the rankings of other NEs. It is very likely that one target language NE is considered the translation of many source language NEs (*i.e.*, one-to-many mapping). However, in our scenario, we want to find the best one-to-one mapping. That is, if Chinese NE is mapped to an English NE, it will not be mapped to other English NEs.

Compared to You, our approach has the following advantages: First, You gets named entities and their relationship similarity (R) directly from entity search web sites and thus cannot be easily extended to other languages; Second, since the entity search web sites only provide the co-occurrence relationship between NEs, it does not contain common words but only the related NEs, and thus may not be sufficient for finding the right translation; Third, when mapping NEs in the source and target graphs, You only considers relationship similarity (R) and ignore the relationship context similarity (RC), which may result in incorrect mapping.

Meanwhile, some existing work focuses on Web corpus [10, 14, 9], of a larger scale with higher asymmetry than comparable corpora, as an alternative resource to extract NE translations with promising results. However, these approaches require either crawling the corpus on a scale that cannot be easily hosted, or frequently issuing external queries to web search engines, both of which are costly.

3. PROBLEM STATEMENT

This section formally defines the problem and introduces the notations.

We abstract the NE translation mining problem as the matching of two NE relationship graphs extracted from the comparable corpora. More formally, we construct two graphs $G_e = (V_e, E_e)$ and $G_c = (V_c, E_c)$ from each English and Chinese corpus where V is a set of NEs (nodes) and E is a set of relationships (edges). Our goal is to populate a hard decision (or similarity) matrix $R*$, a $|V_e|$-by-$|V_c|$ matrix, where each $R*_{ij}$ denotes whether the two NEs $e_i \in V_e$ and $c_j \in V_c$ are translations of each other, *i.e.*, 1 if they are and 0 otherwise. As an intermediate goal, we populate a soft decision matrix R where each R_{ij} indicates the likelihood to be a translation.

Towards this goal of populating R, we holistically combine all the similarity notions used in the past– E, EC (Shao [16]), and R (You [21])– together with the new notion of RC.

R_0 using E and EC: A soft decision matrix R can be initialized by using pairwise entity similarity (E), as done in You. However, it cannot represent translation pairs with little phonetic similarity, *e.g.*, Jackie Chan and 成龙 (pronounced Cheng Long). To compensate for this weakness, we also consider entity context similarity (EC) around the NEs, as done in Shao. For example, if words like 'actor' co-occur frequently with Jackie Chan in the English corpus, the Chinese word for 'actor' is highly likely to co-occur with 成龙 in the Chinese corpus.

In order to consider E and EC, we first construct two $|V_e|$-by-$|V_c|$ translation similarity matrices, S^{E} and S^{EC}, for E and EC respectively. We then combine S^{E} and S^{EC} to build the initial soft decision matrix R_0.

R_∞ reflecting R and RC: You uses relationship similarity (R) between monolingual NE pairs in each corpus, which considers co-occurrences between NEs, to iteratively reinforce the soft decision matrix R. For instance, the Chinese translations of some NEs co-occurring frequently with 'Jackie Chan' in the English corpus, *e.g.*, 'Chris Tucker', are also likely to co-occur frequently with 成龙 in the Chinese corpus. As a result, if many English named entities co-occur with 'Jackie Chan' and their Chinese translations with 成龙, we can give a high similarity score for the NE translation pair ('Jackie Chan',成龙).

We take one step further to take advantage of the relationship context similarity (RC) between two monolingual NE pairs in the two corpora. In other words, the relationship between 'Jackie Chan' and 'Chris Tucker' can be represented by context words, co-occurring with these named entity pairs, such as 'Rush Hour'. Similarly, in G_c, context words for the translations of 'Jackie Chan' and 'Chris Tucker' can be collected, *e.g.*, the Chinese translation for 'Rush Hour'. The similarity of context words between two monolingual NE pairs in the two NE graphs, or RC, would give additional evidence that the right translation pairs have been found.

However, in order to consider R and RC, we must already know the translations of NEs, which makes this problem a chicken-and-egg dilemma. The nature of this problem therefore suggests an iterative process. That is, as we identify highly likely NE translation pairs from R_0, we can update these translated pairs to the named entity dictionary, such that, the remaining NEs can be updated to R_1 from this dictionary. From this update, we may identify more translation pairs, which we continue until pairwise similarity converges to R_∞.

This holistic approach complements the current state-of-the-art approaches, as summarized in Table 2.

Table 2: The similarity metrics used by current state-of-art approaches and our new holistic approach.

	E	EC	R	RC
Shao [16]	✓	✓		
You [21]	✓		✓	
Our holistic approach	✓	✓	✓	✓

4. OUR FRAMEWORK

As described in the previous section, our goal is to populate a hard decision matrix $R*$, using both entity-based (E and EC) and relationship-based (R and RC) similarities. Our framework consists of the following steps:

1. **Building NE graphs and initializing R_0:** building two NE relationship graphs, G_e and G_c, from comparable corpora and initializing a soft decision matrix R_0 by combining two entity-based similarity metrics, E and EC.

2. **Reinforcing into R_∞:** reinforcing the soft decision matrix (or translation similarity matrix) R by exploiting R and RC as additional evidence.

3. **Populating $R*$ from R:** generating a binary hard decision matrix $R*$ by using greedy matching algorithm.

We discuss each of these steps in the following sections respectively.

4.1 Initialization Step

This section discusses how we build two NE relationship graphs, G_e and G_c, from each English and Chinese corpus, and how we generate the initial soft decision matrix R_0 by combining two entity-based similarity metrics, E and EC.

4.1.1 Constructing NE Relationship Graphs

To extract the NE relationship information from the English and Chinese corpora, we first build two NE relationship graphs, $G_e = (V_e, E_e)$ and $G_c = (V_c, E_c)$, from each English and Chinese corpus where V is a set of NEs (nodes) and E is a set of relationships (edges) between NEs.

For mining V_e from the English corpus, we use a CRF-based English NE tagger. We then build an English relationship graph G_e, regarding an NE that appears more than δ times in the English corpus as a node and connecting two nodes (NEs) if the corresponding NE pair co-occurs more than δ times in the English documents in the corpus. We also build a Chinese graph G_c using the same approach after mining V_c from the Chinese corpus. We segment the Chinese corpus and identify NEs using a Chinese word breaker based on [5]. In this paper, we set $\delta = 20$ based on empirical observations.

4.1.2 Initializing R_0

We build the initial soft decision matrix R_0 by using two entity-based similarity metrics, E and EC. We first compute the entity similarity matrix S^{E} and the entity context similarity matrix S^{EC}. We then combine S^{E} and S^{EC} to generate R_0.

For computing the entity similarity matrix S^{E} between English NE e in V_e and Chinese NE c in V_c, we adopt the Edit-Distance (ED) between e and c used in You [21].

More specifically, we first convert c into its Pinyin form PY_c. Pinyin is the romanization representation of pronunciation of Chinese character. We then compute the string similarity between English string e and Chinese Pinyin PY_c, as English strings and Chinese Pinyins are pronounced similarly. To compute the string similarity, we use the Edit-Distance defined in You. Using the Edit-Distance score, entity similarity between English NE e_i and Chinese NE c_j is computed as:

$$S_{ij}^{\mathsf{E}} = 1 - \frac{ED(e_i, PY_{c_j})}{Len(e_i) + Len(PY_{c_j})}$$

where $e_i \in V_e$, $c_j \in V_c$, and $Len(e_i)$ and $Len(PY_{c_j})$ are the length of e_i and PY_{c_j} respectively.

For computing the entity context similarity matrix S^{EC}, we first define the entity context as the surrounding words w of the NE. Formally, let $d = \{w_1, w_2, ..., w_n\}$ be a given document which contains an English NE e in a corpus and l be the length of the entity context (or window size). When e is the ith word w_i in the document d, entity context word list is:

$$\{w_{i-\frac{l}{2}}, w_{i-\frac{l}{2}+1}, ..., w_i(=e), ..., w_{i+\frac{l}{2}-1}, w_{i+\frac{l}{2}}\}$$

In this paper, we set the length of the window size $l = 24$, based on empirical observations.

For the given English NE e, we aggregate all the context windows of e by summing up the occurrence of each context word w in the English corpus, and build N_e-by-N_w co-occurrence matrix where N_e is the number of English NEs and N_w is the number of context words. We then define a context association vector CA_e of NE e, using the Log-Odds (LO) association measure, which was the winner among all the context association metrics reported in [13], including chi-square and log-likelihood. The LO association measure between NE e and a single context word w is defined as:

$$LO(e, w) = \log \frac{(O_{11} + \frac{1}{2})(O_{22} + \frac{1}{2})}{(O_{12} + \frac{1}{2})(O_{21} + \frac{1}{2})}$$

where O_{ij} are the cells of the 2×2 contingency matrix of e and w. That is, O_{12} and O_{21} stand for the sum of co-occurrence matrix elements containing either e or w exclusively (*i.e.*, e but not w, or w but not e respectively), O_{11} for both and O_{22} for neither. CA_c can be similarly defined for Chinese NEs.

Now, we define the vector similarity between CA_e and CA_c, which shows the entity context similarity (EC) of English NE e and Chinese NE c, as CA_e and CA_c contain the relation score between NE and its context words. For such a computation, we need to "align" two vectors, such that scores in the same vector position correspond to the words of the same meaning, such as 'president' and '总统'. For this purpose, we use an English-Chinese word dictionary to align words with the same meaning.

Specifically, among entity context words of e and c, we stem the words and keep $w_e \in CA_e$ and $w_c \in CA_c$, only if the context word pair (w_e, w_c) appears as a translation in the dictionary. In other words, we prune out entity context words (1) if the English word does not appear in the dictionary or (2) its dictionary translation does not appear in the Chinese context. We also prune out stopwords and numbers as they do not add much contextual information.

However, as the context word translation pair may not map one-to-one to each other, there can be a word with multiple translations. In this case, we divide the association score among all possible translations: if w_e has two translations $w_c^{(1)}$ and $w_c^{(2)}$ with their occurrences in the Chinese corpus as n and m respectively, we divide w_e into $w_e^{(1)}$ and $w_e^{(2)}$ indicating the two different senses of the word, corresponding to $w_c^{(1)}$ and $w_c^{(2)}$ respectively. We then add new context association vector entries $CA_e(w_e^{(1)})$ and $CA_e(w_e^{(2)})$ as $CA_e(w_e) \times \frac{n}{n+m}$ and $CA_e(w_e) \times \frac{m}{n+m}$ respectively, then delete $CA_e(w_e)$. For example, if $CA_e = \{(w_e^a, 0.5), (w_e^b, 0.7)\}$ and w_e^a has two Chinese translations (w_c^{a1} and w_c^{a2}) with their occurrences in the Chinese corpus as 4 and 6 respectively, we remove $(w_e^a, 0.5)$ and add two new entries $(w_e^{a1}, 0.5 \times \frac{4}{4+6})$ and $(w_e^{a2}, 0.5 \times \frac{6}{4+6})$. As a result, new context association vector of NE e is $CA_e = \{(w_e^{a1}, 0.2), (w_e^{a2}, 0.3), (w_e^b, 0.7)\}$. We similarly refine context association vectors for Chinese words.

Once all context association vectors have been refined, we compute the cosine similarity between context association vector of English NE e_i and context association vector of Chinese NE c_j as:

$$S_{ij}^{\mathsf{EC}} = \frac{CA_{e_i} \cdot CA_{c_j}}{\|CA_{e_i}\| \cdot \|CA_{c_j}\|}$$

where $e_i \in V_e$ and $c_j \in V_c$.

Finally, we discuss how we combine S^{E} and S^{EC}. We first use min-max normalization for the values in S^{E} and S^{EC} into the same range of [0:1]. After that, we merge two similarity matrices using the following equation:

$$R_{ij} = S_{ij}^{\mathsf{E}} \times S_{ij}^{\mathsf{EC}}$$

where R_{ij} is the initial similarity score (R_{ij}^0) between English NE e_i and Chinese NE c_j.

4.2 Reinforcement Step

From the initial similarity matrix R_0, we iteratively reinforce R_{ij} of the nodes $i \in V_e$ and $j \in V_c$ from the matching similarities of their neighbor nodes u and v using relationship-based similarity metrics, R and RC.

The basic intuition is built on the assumption that two NEs with a strong relationship co-occur frequently in both corpora (R) with the similar context words (RC). In order to express this intuition, we formally define an iterative reinforcement model as follows. Let R_{ij}^t denote the similarity of nodes i and j at t-th iteration:

$$R_{ij}^{t+1} = \lambda \sum_{(u,v)_k \in B^t(i,j,\theta)} \frac{R_{uv}^t \times (S_{iu,jv}^{\mathsf{RC}})^\gamma}{2^k} + (1-\lambda) R_{ij}^0$$

where $B^t(i,j,\theta)$ is an ordered set which contains the best neighbor matching pairs between node i's neighbor u and node j's neighbor v, and $S_{iu,jv}^{\mathsf{RC}}$ is the RC similarity matrix element between edge $(i,u) \in E_e$ and edge $(j,v) \in E_c$ for the pair (u,v) listed in $B^t(i,j,\theta)$. We will discuss how we populate $B^t(i,j,\theta)$ later. γ is the parameter to control the weight of the RC similarity.

Our reinforce model is expressed as a linear combination of (a) relationship similarity and relationship context similarity $\sum(R_{uv}^t \times (S_{iu,jv}^{\mathsf{RC}})^\gamma)/2^k$ and (b) initial similarity R_{ij}^0. λ is the coefficient for interpolating the two terms.

Similar to entity context similarity S^{EC}, relationship context similarity S^{RC} is computed as the cosine similarity between two context association vectors, $CA_{(e,e')}$ and $CA_{(c,c')}$, defined for all English NE pairs and all Chinese NE pairs respectively. The differences are that we generate context association vector $CA_{(e,e')}$ based on the co-occurring context words from the documents where two NEs e and e' co-occur, and set the size of window l as the size of the given document. Similarly, we compute $CA_{(c,c')}$ and quantify the cosine similarity.

Algorithm 1 Find Common Neighbors (R^t, S^{RC}, i, j, θ, γ)

1: $B^t(i,j,\theta) \leftarrow \emptyset$
2: **for all** $(i,u) \in E_e$ and $(j,v) \in E_c$ **do**
3: $\quad SIM_{iu,jv} = R^t_{uv} \times (S^{\mathsf{RC}}_{iu,jv})^\gamma$
4: **end for**
5: $S \leftarrow Sort(SIM)$ {S is the ordered set of elements in SIM}
6: **for** $SIM_{iu,jv} \in S$ **do**
7: $\quad$ **if** $SIM_{iu,jv} < \theta$ **then**
8: $\quad\quad$ **return** $B^t(i,j,\theta)$
9: $\quad$ **end if**
10: $\quad$ **if** both u and v are not matched yet **then**
11: $\quad\quad B^t(i,j,\theta) \leftarrow B^t(i,j,\theta) \cup \{(u,v)\}$
12: $\quad$ **end if**
13: **end for**
14: **return** $B^t(i,j,\theta)$

In our reinforcement model, as evidence that English NE i is a translation of Chinese NE j, we consider the relationship similarity R between i and j. In R, we check the extent to which i and j share common neighbors using $B^t(i,j,\theta)$, which is an ordered set of the best matching translation pairs between neighbors of i and j, as similarly used in You [21] (Algorithm 1). More specifically, we consider the neighbor pair (u,v) with $R^t_{uv} \times (S^{\mathsf{RC}}_{iu,jv})^\gamma \geq \theta$, as a matching pair, where u is a neighbor of i and v is a neighbor of j (Line 6-13). But, instead of keeping all such pairs in $B^t(i,j,\theta)$, we make sure to eliminate many-to-many matches, by not adding (u',v'), if u' or v' appears in the pair with a higher matching score (Line 10-12). When $(u,v)_k$ is the pair in $B^t(i,j,\theta)$ with the k-th highest similarity score, we apply decaying coefficient $1/2^k$, to guarantee the convergence, as $\sum_{k=1}^{\infty} 1/2^k = 1$.

4.3 Matching Step

Once R converges to R_∞, we use R_∞ as a soft decision matrix, representing the likelihood of each bilingual NE pair being a translation, to generate a binary hard decision matrix $R*$, showing the one-to-one correspondence that is most likely. Such a problem can be stated as the maximum weighted bipartite matching problem and has been studied in [20]. However, computing the optimal matching solution incurs high computational cost. We thus approximate this problem using a greedy matching algorithm (Algorithm 2).

Algorithm 2 Greedy Matching Algorithm (R, θ)

1: $S \leftarrow Sort(R)$ {S is the ordered set of element R_{ij}}
2: **for** $R_{ij} \in S$ **do**
3: $\quad$ **if** both i and j are not matched yet **then**
4: $\quad\quad$ **if** $R_{ij} \geq \theta$ **then**
5: $\quad\quad\quad R*_{ij} = 1$ {i and j are matched}
6: $\quad\quad$ **else**
7: $\quad\quad\quad R*_{ij} = 0$ {i and j are not matched}
8: $\quad\quad$ **end if**
9: $\quad$ **else**
10: $\quad\quad R*_{ij} = 0$ {i or j are already matched}
11: $\quad$ **end if**
12: **end for**
13: **return** $R*$

Algorithm 2 works as follows: (1) Elements in the soft decision matrix R are sorted by the decreasing order of the similarity score R_{ij} (Line 1); (2) We check each element in S and set $R*_{ij} = 1$, if neither $i \in V_e$ nor $j \in V_c$ was selected and the similarity score R_{ij} is larger than the given threshold θ (Line 2-12), otherwise we set $R*_{ij} = 0$.

5. EXPERIMENTS

This section reports our experimental results to evaluate our proposed approaches. First, we report our experimental settings in Section 5.1. Second, we validate the effectiveness of our approaches over a real-life dataset in Section 5.2.

5.1 Experimental Settings

This section reports our experimental settings to evaluate our proposed approaches.

We used the same dataset (but with different time period) as Shao [16] did. For the English corpus, we used the English Gigaword Corpus (LDC2009T13) published by the Xinhua News Agency which contains news articles from January 2008 to December 2008. For the Chinese corpus, we used the Chinese Gigaword Corpus (LDC2009T27) also published by Xinhua News Agency during the same period. The English corpus contains 100,746 news documents and the Chinese corpus contains 88,029 news documents. As two corpora handle the news documents during the same period, they are regarded as comparable corpora in our experiments. From the English and Chinese corpora, we extracted person names by using NE taggers and built English and Chinese person name graphs independently as discussed in Section 4.

For the purpose of comparison, we implemented the following four existing approaches with ours:

- EC: Entity context-based approach which ranks NE candidates using word context similarity S^{EC}_{ij}.
- E: Entity name-based approach which ranks NE candidates using NE pronunciation similarity S^{E}_{ij}.
- Shao: Holistic approach which uses the average rank of NE candidates from two ranked lists computed by using EC and E [16].
- You: Holistic approach which initializes the translation similarity using E and iteratively reinforces the translation similarity using R from the two NE graphs [21].
- E+EC+R: Our approach without considering RC by setting $\gamma = 0$.
- E+EC+R+RC: Our approach considering RC setting non-zero γ.

We re-implemented You to use the same NE relationship graphs we extracted from the comparable corpora, and used the entity similarity (E) module of You for re-implementing Shao as well. In implementing EC, Shao, and our methods, we used an in-house English-Chinese general word dictionary containing more than 80,000 English-Chinese translation word pairs from Web resources such as online dictionaries to compute contextual similarities (EC and RC). As a result, this dictionary does not contain NE translation pairs and mainly consists of the pairs of general words.

For the main evaluation metrics, we used standard precision, recall, and F1 scores:

- Precision: the ratio of correctly returned translation pairs over returned translation pairs.
- Recall: the ratio of correctly returned translation pairs over the total number of correct translation pairs.

English Name	EC	E	E+EC+R	E+EC+R+RC
Fidel	菲德尔	费德勒	菲德尔	菲德尔
Trickett	孙晔	特里克特	特里克特	特里克特
Gbagbo	杜拉希	巴博	巴博	巴博
Amorim	拉夫罗夫	阿莫林	阿莫林	阿莫林
Federer	杰缅季耶娃	菲德尔	费德勒	费德勒
Kikwete	纳希德	斯科特	基奎特	基奎特
Mottaki	雅伯	摩加迪	穆塔基	穆塔基
Calderon	西梅翁	麦德林	卡尔德龙	卡尔德隆

Figure 1: The translation examples of person NEs. The shaded cells indicate the correctly translated pairs.

- F1-score: the harmonic mean of precision and recall.

$$\text{F1-Score} = 2 \times \frac{\text{Precision} \cdot \text{Recall}}{\text{Precision} + \text{Recall}}$$

We designed our experiments to follow the experiment setting used in most previous work (Shao and You) on name translation for fair comparison with them. Their settings aim to estimate a precision of name translations rather than recall, for which we need to ensure that the gold standard set has (a) sufficient amount of named entities in Chinese and English corpora and (b) such entities are not biased. To build ground truth on above conditions, we firstly selected 500 English person names randomly from all the person names extracted from the English corpus. Then, we hired an annotator to translate them into their Chinese translation names. These 500 English and Chinese named entity translation pairs were used for evaluation as ground truth. Among the 500 Chinese person name translations in the pairs, only 203 were matched to the person names extracted from our Chinese corpus. We used all 500 pairs to find the best parameters and computed the evaluation measures only using 203 matched pairs, as it is more suitable for real-life translation scenarios. This also follows Shao's [16] practice to make the results easy to compare.

In the evaluation, we optimized parameters as following: We used a fixed value of $\lambda = 0.15$ which is one of the robust parameter settings in [21]. We performed a 5-fold cross-validation by dividing 500 English-Chinese NE translation pairs into 5 groups (each group contains 100 NE translation pairs). We used four groups to optimize necessary threshold parameters of each method (for instance, θ in EC, E, You, and our two approaches, γ in our approach, and M value in Shao), and used the remaining group as a test dataset using optimized parameters. The optimal parameters were determined by the ones maximizing F1-scores.

5.2 Experimental Results

This section reports our experimental results using the evaluation datasets. In particular, we evaluated (1) the effectiveness of the overall framework using precision, recall, and F1-score by comparing our approaches with four existing approaches including two state-of-the art approaches [16, 21], (2) the effectiveness of our framework in terms of frequency of NEs, (3) the contribution of our reinforcement model, greedy matching algorithm, and parameters in improving NE translation quality, (4) other types of NEs using precision, recall, and F1-score, and (5) the effect of fuzzy matching. (In all experimental results, **Bold numbers** indicate the best performance for each metric).

5.2.1 Performance Comparison

We first evaluated the effectiveness of the overall framework using precision, recall, and F1-score by comparing our approaches with four existing approaches.

Table 3: The average precision, recall, and F1-score of each approach computed using 5-fold cross-validation. E+EC+R shows the best recall, and E+EC+R+RC shows the best precision and F1-score.

	Precision	Recall	F1 Score
EC	0.0819	0.2053	0.1160
E	0.3082	0.3255	0.3159
Shao	0.3000	0.3943	0.3379
You	0.3409	0.3965	0.3630
E+EC+R	0.4480	**0.6288**	0.5225
E+EC+R+RC	**0.5105**	0.5713	**0.5388**

Table 3 presents our experimental results. Our proposed approaches, E+EC+R and E+EC+R+RC, clearly outperform other approaches including both You and Shao. Specifically, E+EC+R shows the best recall, and E+EC+R+RC shows the best precision and F1-score. These performance improvements of ours over both You and Shao were statistically significant according to the Student's t-test at $P < 0.01$ level.

More specifically, E+EC+R performs significantly better than You and Shao. This result indicates that considering entity context similarity (EC) complements [21] by supplying more evidence for name translation, while considering relationship similarity (R) complements [16], and the reinforcement framework can effectively integrate them for name translation. Lastly, considering relationship context similarity (RC) was effective in terms of precision, but shows relatively lower recall compared to ours without RC (*i.e.*, E+EC+R). This can be explained by the sensitivity of RC to data sparsity– When data are sparse, *e.g.*, for rare name relationship pairs, the number of documents where such pairs co-occur is small and using RC may not be sufficiently precise to eliminate rare but relevant pairs (*i.e.*, low recall). However, when data are sufficiently abundant, RC can be a very effective device for precise name translation identification.

In addition, we present representative translation examples in Figure 1, where the shaded cells indicate the correctly translated pairs. We can observe that each notion of E, EC, R, and RC contributes to translation accuracy.

5.2.2 Impact of NE Frequency

In this section, we evaluated the performances of all approaches for high frequency and low frequency NEs to understand how the frequency of an NE affects the performances. To build high frequency and low frequency NE sets, we divided our 500 person NE evaluation dataset into two equally sized subsets according to the frequencies of their English corpus parts (top 250 NEs and bottom 250 NEs). The average numbers of frequency of high frequent NE set and low frequent NE set in our experiment are 213.62 and 27 respectively.

Table 4 presents our experimental results. *HF* shows the results of high frequent NEs and *LF* shows the results of low frequent ones. *Ratio* shows the "decreasing ratio" on the two subsets, *HF* and *LF*. To compute this, we divide the decrease from the score from the high frequency NEs to low frequency ones by the score from the high frequency NEs. That is, the lower decreasing ratio is, the

Table 4: Precision, Recall, F1 score of each approach using high frequent (*HF*) and low frequent (*LF*) NEs. In both high frequent and low frequent NEs, both of our approaches outperform all other approaches.

	Precision			Recall			F1 Score		
	HF	*LF*	*Ratio*	*HF*	*LF*	*Ratio*	*HF*	*LF*	*Ratio*
EC	0.1360	0.0480	0.6465	0.3063	0.1087	0.6451	0.1884	0.0667	0.6461
E	0.3364	0.2913	**0.1341**	0.3333	0.3261	**0.0217**	0.3348	0.3077	**0.0811**
Shao	0.3765	0.1535	0.5922	0.5766	0.4022	0.3025	0.4555	0.2222	0.5122
You	0.4845	0.2778	0.4267	0.4234	0.3804	**0.1015**	0.4519	0.3211	0.2895
E+EC+R	**0.5033**	**0.3939**	0.2173	**0.6847**	**0.5652**	0.1745	**0.5802**	**0.4643**	**0.1997**
E+EC+R+RC	**0.5274**	**0.4189**	**0.2059**	**0.6937**	**0.5326**	0.2322	**0.5992**	**0.4689**	0.2175

more robust the scheme is over varying NE frequencies. As the E approach does not use contextual similarity, its performance will not be affected by NE frequency. Considering this point, we also show the second lowest scores in **bold**.

As Table 4 shows, our approaches, E+EC+R and E+EC+R+RC, clearly outperform other approaches in both high frequent and low frequent NEs. The *Ratio* results also show that our approaches are relatively more robust over most frequencies.

5.2.3 Effectiveness of Reinforcement Model

We evaluated the contribution of our reinforcement model using MRR [18], the average of the reciprocal ranks of the query results as the following formula:

$$\text{MRR} = \frac{1}{|Q|}\sum_{q \in Q}\frac{1}{rank_q}$$

where q is a ground truth translation pair, Q is the set of ground truth translation pair, and $rank_q$ is the rank of the right translation answer in the list of translation candidates returned by our approach.

Specifically, we compared the MRR score of our framework using initial (or baseline) similarity matrix (R_0) with the score using reinforced similarity matrix (R_∞).

Table 5: MRR score of baseline and reinforced matrices using E+EC+R+RC. Our reinforcement model effectively improves MRR scores in all cases.

Set	MRR	
	Baseline R_0	Reinforced R_∞
$\gamma = 0.1$	0.7113	**0.7459**
$\gamma = 0.2$	0.7113	**0.7473**
$\gamma = 0.3$	0.7113	**0.7408**
$\gamma = 0.4$	0.7113	**0.7456**
$\gamma = 0.5$	0.7113	**0.7519**
$\gamma = 0.6$	0.7113	**0.7473**
$\gamma = 0.7$	0.7113	**0.7438**
$\gamma = 0.8$	0.7113	**0.7340**
$\gamma = 0.9$	0.7113	**0.7300**
$\gamma = 1.0$	0.7113	**0.7246**
Average	0.7113	**0.7411**

Table 5 summarizes our experimental results. We observed an increase in MRR scores in all cases after applying our reinforcement model, which indirectly shows the effectiveness of our reinforcement model. Note, as the initial matrix R^0 is not affected by γ, the MRR scores of all baselines are identical.

5.2.4 Effectiveness of Matching Approach

We also evaluated the effectiveness of matching a soft decision matrix R into a hard decision matrix $R*$, using precision, recall, and F1-score. As matching translations using R can occur one-to-many assignment problem, jointly finding translations for all source NEs can avoid many errors that may occur in Shao.

Table 6 shows the evaluation results of E+EC+R+RC. Our holistic approach using $R*$ shows consistently higher precision than R. The average number of returned translation pairs is 54.00 with R and 45.4 with $R*$. Among these pairs, the number of correctly returned pairs is 24.00 and 23.60 with R and $R*$ respectively. These results indicate that $R*$ can effectively filter some wrong translation pairs– on average, a 15.56% reduction of incorrect translation pairs.

In overall, E+EC+R+RC using $R*$ shows consistently higher F1-score which indicates our matching algorithm improves the translation quality.

5.2.5 Influences of Parameters

In this section, we study our performance over varying γ to see the effect of relationship context similarity (RC). We also varied θ for all γ values and found $\theta = 0.25$ to be optimal for most γ values, suggesting the robustness of our framework.

Table 7: Influence of the parameter γ of our approach E+EC+R+RC.

	Precision	Recall	F1-Score
$\gamma = 0.1$	0.4569	**0.6222**	0.5263
$\gamma = 0.2$	0.4741	0.6155	0.5349
$\gamma = 0.3$	0.4755	0.5990	0.5296
$\gamma = 0.4$	0.4892	0.5951	0.5364
$\gamma = 0.5$	0.4953	0.5800	0.5336
$\gamma = 0.6$	0.5017	0.5713	0.5338
$\gamma = 0.7$	0.5105	0.5713	**0.5388**
$\gamma = 0.8$	0.5137	0.5668	0.5384
$\gamma = 0.9$	**0.5193**	0.5583	0.5373
$\gamma = 1.0$	0.5141	0.5524	0.5321

Table 7 presents our results. A higher γ tends to lead to higher precision but lower recall, while a lower γ leads to high recall and low precision.

Table 6: Precision, Recall, F1-score of E+EC+R+RC using a soft decision matrix R and a hard decision matrix $R*$. $R*$ shows higher precision and F1-score, and R shows higher recall.

	E+EC+R+RC					
	Precision		Recall		F1 score	
	Using R	Using $R*$	Using R	Using $R*$	Using R	Using $R*$
$\gamma = 0.1$	0.3784	**0.4569**	**0.6300**	0.6222	0.4712	**0.5263**
$\gamma = 0.2$	0.3871	**0.4741**	**0.6233**	0.6155	0.4767	**0.5349**
$\gamma = 0.3$	0.3881	**0.4755**	**0.6069**	0.5990	0.4725	**0.5296**
$\gamma = 0.4$	0.4065	**0.4893**	**0.6029**	0.5951	0.4843	**0.5364**
$\gamma = 0.5$	0.4183	**0.4953**	**0.5917**	0.5800	0.4889	**0.5336**
$\gamma = 0.6$	0.4247	**0.5017**	**0.5792**	0.5713	0.4888	**0.5338**
$\gamma = 0.7$	0.4378	**0.5105**	**0.5792**	0.5713	0.4973	**0.5388**
$\gamma = 0.8$	0.4389	**0.5137**	**0.5753**	0.5668	0.4969	**0.5384**
$\gamma = 0.9$	0.4402	**0.5193**	**0.5629**	0.5583	0.4927	**0.5373**
$\gamma = 1.0$	0.4391	**0.5141**	**0.5550**	0.5524	0.4890	**0.5321**

In overall, when $\gamma = 0.7$, E+EC+R+RC shows the best F1-score.

5.2.6 *Other Type of NE*

To check the extension possibility of our approaches, we compared the performances of all approaches using the location type of named entities in the same corpora. We first extracted location type of NEs by using the same NE taggers. We then randomly selected 100 English location NEs from the English corpus and found their Chinese translations manually. As a result, 86 of their Chinese translations were found from the Chinese corpus. We used same parameters used in the person NE translation.

Table 8: The measure scores of all approaches computed using 100 location type of NEs. E+EC+R+RC outperforms all other approaches.

	Precision	Recall	F1 Score
EC	0.4684	0.4302	0.4485
E	0.6667	0.2558	0.3697
Shao	0.6557	0.4651	0.5442
You	0.4328	0.3372	0.3791
E+EC+R	0.6623	0.5930	0.6258
E+EC+R+RC	**0.6709**	**0.6153**	**0.6424**

Table 8 presents our experimental results. Compared to the Table 3, EC, E, and Shao show high precision (more than 50% precision improvement), while You shows the worst precision improvement. These results indicates that each translation similarity measure has a different contribution for different types of NEs– EC and E have big contribution for location type of NEs, and R has big contribution for person type of NEs.

As also shown in the Table 8, our proposed approaches, E+EC+R and E+EC+R+RC, clearly outperform other approaches. Specifically, E+EC+R+RC shows the best performance over all evaluation metrics. This result indicates that our approach, combining and optimizing many similarity metrics, is robust and effective in cross-type NE translation.

Figure 2 shows the difference of F1-score of each approaches. Our two approaches clearly outperform other approaches in cross-type NE translation.

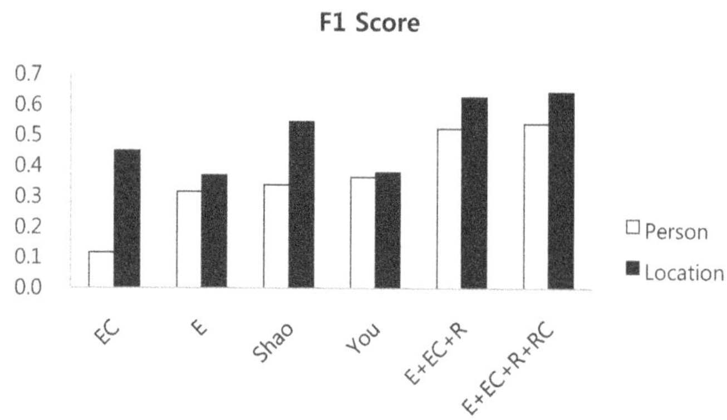

Figure 2: The difference of F1-Score between person type of NE and location type of NE.

5.2.7 *Fuzzy Matching*

In this section, we study our performances using fuzzy matching not exact matching. Fuzzy matching is the matching considering partial name match as the right translation. For example, if our approach returns a translation pair (Barack Obama, 奥巴马), the exact matching algorithm considers it as a wrong translation, as 奥巴马 is Obama not Barack Obama, while fuzzy matching algorithm considers it as a right translation.

Table 9 shows the evaluation results. Compared to the Table 7, fuzzy matching results show higher precision, but lower recall. It is because both of the number of pairs that have right translation and the number of correctly returned pairs are increased, but the former is larger than the latter.

6. CONCLUSION AND FUTURE WORK

This paper studies the problem of mining named entity translations from comparable corpora. Current state-of-the-art approaches are holistic, as they combine entity, entity context, and relationship similarity. In this paper, we propose a new holistic approach, by combining all similarity types used and additionally considering relationship context similarity between named entities. Specifically, named entity graphs are first constructed from comparable corpora. Entity and entity context similarities are then calculated from every

Table 9: The performance of E+EC+R+RC using fuzzy matching. Fuzzy matching results show higher precision but lower recall.

	Precision	Recall	F1-Score
$\gamma = 0.1$	0.5292	**0.4245**	0.4694
$\gamma = 0.2$	0.5506	0.4214	**0.4748**
$\gamma = 0.3$	0.5542	0.4127	0.4708
$\gamma = 0.4$	0.5709	0.4099	**0.4748**
$\gamma = 0.5$	0.5819	0.4012	0.4726
$\gamma = 0.6$	0.5859	0.3951	0.4691
$\gamma = 0.7$	0.5920	0.3922	0.4690
$\gamma = 0.8$	0.5963	0.3892	0.4681
$\gamma = 0.9$	**0.6037**	0.3835	0.4665
$\gamma = 1.0$	0.5991	0.3806	0.4627

pair of bilingual named entities. A reinforcing method is utilized to reflect relationship and relationship context similarities between named entities. According to our experimental results, our new holistic graph-based approach significantly outperforms previous approaches and is extensible for various types of NEs.

We leave the followings as future work:

- **Comparable Corpora**: Currently, we used English and Chinese Gigaword Corpora published by the Xinhua News Agency which contains news articles from January 2008 to December 2008. Though they can be regarded as comparable corpora, they do not always talk about the same or related topics. As a result, there can be some noises that disturb the NE translation quality. Using larger dataset can reduce the effect of noises and yield higher-quality NE translation. Building our approach using larger dataset remains as future work.

- **Measures**: To construct the context association similarity matrix, we used Log-Odd association measure and cosine similarity measure, as they were the winners among various kinds of measures reported in [13]. The quality of our approaches may improve by using other association measure and similarity measure. Testing the performances of our approaches using other measures remains as future work.

- **NEs with No Translation**: Some English names may not have translations in Chinese corpus and deciding whether the translation exists or not is a clear challenge. However, existing work focuses on finding the most likely translation and does not discuss or evaluate how to determine the case with no translation. Our model consider this "asymmetry" case, by discarding English names with similarity ranked under threshold θ, but did not compare with existing work as they are not designed for this problem. Evaluating the effectiveness of asymmetry pruning remains as future work.

Acknowledgments

This research was supported by Microsoft Research and the MKE (The Ministry of Knowledge Economy), Korea, under IT/SW Creative research program supervised by the NIPA (National IT Industry Promotion Agency) (NIPA-2010-C1810-1002-0003).

7. REFERENCES

[1] A. Baron and M. Freedman. Who is Who and What is What: Experiments in Cross-Document Co-Reference. In *Proceedings of the 2008 Conference on Empirical Methods in Natural Language Processing*, EMNLP '08. Association for Computational Linguistics, 2008.

[2] M. Diab and S. Finch. A statistical word level translation model for comparable corpora. In *Proc. of the Conference on Content-based Multimedia Information Access RIAO*, RIAO '00, 2000.

[3] D. Feng, Y. Lü, and M. Zhou. A New Approach for English-Chinese Named Entity Alignment. In *Proceedings of the 2004 Conference on Empirical Methods in Natural Language Processing*, EMNLP '04, pages 372–379. Association for Computational Linguistics, 2004.

[4] P. Fung and L. Y. Yee. An IR approach for translating new words from nonparallel, comparable texts. In *Proceedings of the 17th international conference on Computational linguistics - Volume 1*, COLING '98, pages 414–420. Association for Computational Linguistics, 1998.

[5] J. Gao, M. Li, and C.-N. Huang. Improved source-channel models for Chinese word segmentation. In *Proceedings of the 41st Annual Meeting on Association for Computational Linguistics - Volume 1*, ACL '03, pages 272–279. Association for Computational Linguistics, 2003.

[6] L. Haizhou, Z. Min, and S. Jian. A joint source-channel model for machine transliteration. In *Proceedings of the 42nd Annual Meeting on Association for Computational Linguistics*, ACL '04. Association for Computational Linguistics, 2004.

[7] F. Huang, S. Vogel, and A. Waibel. Automatic extraction of named entity translingual equivalence based on multi-feature cost minimization. In *Proceedings of the ACL 2003 workshop on Multilingual and mixed-language named entity recognition - Volume 15*, MultiNER '03, pages 9–16. Association for Computational Linguistics, 2003.

[8] H. Ji. Mining name translations from comparable corpora by creating bilingual information networks. In *Proceedings of the 2nd Workshop on Building and Using Comparable Corpora: from Parallel to Non-parallel Corpora*, BUCC '09. Association for Computational Linguistics, 2009.

[9] L. Jiang, S. Yang, M. Zhou, X. Liu, and Q. Zhu. Mining bilingual data from the web with adaptively learnt patterns. In *Proceedings of the Joint Conference of the 47th Annual Meeting of the ACL and the 4th International Joint Conference on Natural Language Processing of the AFNLP: Volume 2 - Volume 2*, ACL '09, pages 870–878. Association for Computational Linguistics, 2009.

[10] L. Jiang, M. Zhou, L.-F. Chien, and C. Niu. Named entity translation with web mining and transliteration. In *Proceedings of the 20th international joint conference on Artifical intelligence*, pages 1629–1634. Morgan Kaufmann Publishers Inc., 2007.

[11] K. Knight and J. Graehl. Machine transliteration. *Comput. Linguist.*, 24:599–612, December 1998.

[12] J. Kupiec. An algorithm for finding noun phrase correspondences in bilingual corpora. In *Proceedings of the 31st annual meeting on Association for Computational Linguistics*, ACL '93. Association for Computational Linguistics, 1993.

[13] A. Laroche and P. Langlais. Revisiting context-based projection methods for term-translation spotting in

comparable corpora. In *Proceedings of the 23rd International Conference on Computational Linguistics*, COLING '10. Association for Computational Linguistics, 2010.

[14] D. Lin, S. Zhao, B. V. Durme, and M. Pasca. Mining Parenthetical Translations from the Web by Word Alignment. In *Proceedings of the 46nd Annual Meeting on Association for Computational Linguistics*, ACL '08, pages 994–1002. Association for Computational Linguistics, 2008.

[15] R. Rapp. Automatic identification of word translations from unrelated English and German corpora. In *Proceedings of the 37th annual meeting of the Association for Computational Linguistics on Computational Linguistics*, ACL '99, pages 519–526. Association for Computational Linguistics, 1999.

[16] L. Shao and H. T. Ng. Mining new word translations from comparable corpora. In *Proceedings of the 20th international conference on Computational Linguistics*, COLING '04. Association for Computational Linguistics, 2004.

[17] P. Virga and S. Khudanpur. Transliteration of proper names in cross-language applications. In *Proceedings of the 26th annual international ACM SIGIR conference on Research and development in informaion retrieval*. ACM, 2003.

[18] E. M. Voorhees. The TREC question answering track. *Nat. Lang. Eng.*, 7:361–378, December 2001.

[19] S. Wan and C. M. Verspoor. Automatic English-Chinese name transliteration for development of multilingual resources. In *Proceedings of the 36th Annual Meeting of the Association for Computational Linguistics and 17th International Conference on Computational Linguistics - Volume 2*, ACL '98, pages 1352–1356. Association for Computational Linguistics, 1998.

[20] D. B. West. *Introduction to Graph Theory*. Prentice Hall, second edition, 2000.

[21] G.-w. You, S.-w. Hwang, Y.-I. Song, L. Jiang, and Z. Nie. Mining name translations from entity graph mapping. In *Proceedings of the 2010 Conference on Empirical Methods in Natural Language Processing*, EMNLP '10. Association for Computational Linguistics, 2010.

[22] K. Yu and J. Tsujii. Bilingual dictionary extraction from Wikipedia. In *Machine Translation Summit XII*, 2009.

Max Margin Learning on Domain-Independent Web Information Extraction

Bin Zhao
Machine Learning Department
Carnegie Mellon University
Pittsburgh, PA 15213
binzhao@cs.cmu.edu

Xiaoxin Yin
Microsoft Research
One Microsoft Way
Redmond, WA 98052
xyin@microsoft.com

Eric P. Xing
Machine Learning Department
Carnegie Mellon University
Pittsburgh, PA 15213
epxing@cs.cmu.edu

ABSTRACT

Domain-independent web information extraction can be addressed as a structured prediction problem where we learn a mapping function from an input web page to the structured and interdependent output variables, labeling each block on the page. In this paper, built upon an HTML parser of Internet Explorer that parses and renders a web page based on HTML tags and visual appearance, we propose a max margin learning approach for web information extraction. Specifically, the output of the parser is a vision tree, which is similar to a DOM tree but with visual information, i.e., how each node is displayed. Based on this hierarchical structure, we develop a max margin learning method for labeling each of its nodes. Due to the rich connections between blocks on the web page, we further introduce edges that connect spatially adjacent nodes on the vision tree, complicating the problem into a cyclic graph labeling task. A max margin learning method on cyclic graphs is developed for this problem, where loopy belief propagation is used for approximate inference. Experimental results on web data extraction show the feasibility and promise of our approach.

Categories and Subject Descriptors

I.2.6 [**Artificial Intelligence**]: Learning

General Terms

Algorithms, Performance

Keywords

Max Margin Learning, Web Information Extraction, Belief Propagation, Cutting Plane

1. INTRODUCTION

Web search has become a necessary part of our everyday life, and search engines such as *Google* and *Bing* can help us find the right web pages for majority of queries. However, the understanding of web pages by computers is still very limited. There have been studies on categorizing web pages [4], identifying the main entity of a page [5], and extracting particular types of information from pages [1]. But no approach can assign semantics to majority of contents on web pages. There have not been mature approaches for understanding the functionality and semantics of different sections of a web page. Even tasks such as distinguishing main contents from side contents (e.g., user comments, navigational bars, and advertisements) have remained tough challenges.

Figure 1: ***http://www.last.fm/music/Britney+Spears*** **(top portion), which contains a navigational bar at left, sections about** ***Similar Artists, Top Albums, Top Tracks, Videos, News, Listeners*** **and** ***Recent Activity.***

Figure 1 shows a web page about *Britney Spears* on last.fm. It has a typical layout among web pages covering multiple aspects of an entity. The entity name appears in bold at top, followed by a short biography. The page is divided into many sections, each having a title in red and bold font and contents under that. Each piece of content (e.g., an album, a song, or a video) occupies a small region containing text and possibly image/video that are close to each other. Without any knowledge about music, we can see this page is about *Britney Spears*, her similar artists include *Christina Aguilera* and *Lindsay Lohan*, her top albums include *Circus* and *Blackout*, etc. In fact we do not need to understand any word to get such information. For example, *http://www.lastfm.es/music/Ricky+Martin?setlang=es* contains a Spanish page about *Ricky Martin*. Even if we do not know Spanish at all, we can see his *Álbumes más escuchados (albums)* include *Ricky Martin* and *Vuelve*, and there are seven *Artistas similares (similar artists)* listed on the page.

CIKM'11, October 24–28, 2011, Glasgow, Scotland, UK.

If a human does not need to understand a page to extract such information, a computer can probably do it as well. A human tells the role of an element on a page mainly by its position, size, font, color, boldness, relative position to other elements, etc. All these features can be utilized by a machine learning algorithm, especially structured learning method which considers the relationships between related elements in a graph. In this paper we study the problem of *domain-independent web information extraction*, which aims at extracting information from a generic web page, with semantics provided by the page itself. Take the page in Figure 1 as an example. With existing approaches in [5] and [13], a computer is capable of figuring out that the main entity of this page is *Britney Spears*. Then our approach will be able to extract attributes and values. For example, *Top Albums* is an attribute of the main entity, and its values are *Circus*, *Blackout, etc.*

In this paper, domain-independent web information extraction is formulated as a structured prediction problem, with input as a web page and output as labeling for each block on the page. Specifically, we first use the HTML parser of Internet Explorer to parse and render a web page. The output of the parser is a vision tree, which is similar to a DOM tree but with visual information, i.e., how each node is displayed, such as the location and size of the surrounding rectangle of each node. Based on the web page parsing result, we build a hierarchical model, where nodes correspond to blocks on the page, and a smaller block residing in another block is represented as a child node of the node corresponding to that larger block. We first propose a hierarchical model where a node is only connected to its parent, and as a result, the hierarchical model for the web page is a tree. To label each node on this tree, we propose a max margin learning approach, where cutting plane method is used for parameter learning and a *Viterbi* decoding style approach is developed for inference. Moreover, due to the rich connections between blocks on the web page, we argue that modeling the web page structure as a tree encounters loss of crucial information, such as the adjacency relationship between attribute name block *Top Albums* and attribute value block *Circus* in Figure 1. Therefore, we further advance the model by introducing edges that connect spatially adjacent blocks in the hierarchical structure. The introduction of these edges complicates the structured prediction problem as the output structure is no longer a tree, but a cyclic graph. To perform inference on this graph, we introduce a loopy belief propagation method for approximate inference.

2. OVERVIEW OF OUR APPROACH

Our approach for domain-independent web information extraction could be separated into two steps. Given a web page, we first perform a web page segmentation that builds a hierarchical model for the page. Based on this hierarchical structure, a mapping function that maps the web page to a structured output is learned with max margin criterion.

2.1 Page Segmentation

We use the HTML parser of Internet Explorer to parse and render a web page. The output of the parser is a vision tree, which is similar to a DOM tree but with visual information, i.e., how each node is displayed. The vision tree provides the location and size of the surrounding rectangle of each node. For each leaf node containing text, image or another type of rich content, it provides the formatting information such as font, font-size, color, boldness, etc. Each node in the vision tree corresponds to a node in the original DOM tree. Sometimes the contents (especially textual contents) of a leaf node in the DOM tree may occupy multiple lines, and the vision tree will contain the display information for each line. As mentioned before, the display information such as position, font-size and boldness are very important for a human to understand the role of each piece of content on a web page, and similarly they are crucial for our system to label each node.

2.2 Structured Classification

Given the segmentation results, we formulate the web information extraction problem as a structured classification task, where the task is to assign labels for each node in the previously obtained vision tree. Given the predicted label for each node in the tree structure, useful information could therefore be extracted. Before getting into details of the structured prediction approach, we first define the label space employed in our approach. Specifically, there are mainly two types of nodes in the hierarchical structure corresponding to a web page, leaf nodes and non-leaf nodes. The leaf nodes correspond to those smallest blocks on the web page that have specific contents. On the other hand, the non-leaf nodes in the hierarchy structure define the structural layout of the web page by grouping leaf nodes and other non-leaf nodes.

2.2.1 Label Space for Leaf Nodes

Due to the definition of our information extraction problem, we only need to decide whether a leaf node is an attribute name, an attribute value or something else. It should be noted that we do not target to identifying the exact meaning of attribute name, like price, product name, date of birth, etc. In the information extraction problem, we only care about whether a leaf node is an attribute name, and exact meaning of the attribute name will be resolved in the query matching phase, which is beyond the scope of this paper. We also define labels for page title, navigational bar, page tail, images, etc. Anything not belonging to these classes is classified as *non_attribute*. Consequently, the leaf node label space is composed of 8 elements:

$$\mathcal{L}_{leaf} = \{attribute\_name, attribute\_value, non\_attribute, \\ image, nav\_bar, main\_title, page\_tail, image\_caption\}$$

2.2.2 Label Space for Non-Leaf Nodes

Non-leaf nodes in the web page hierarchical structure correspond to blocks composed of leaf nodes or other non-leaf nodes. We separate these non-leaf nodes into two groups: data record related nodes, and web page structural nodes. Specifically, the parent node of *attribute name* and *attribute value* nodes are *data record* nodes, and the node containing *data record* node as its descendent are also *data record* nodes. The web page structural nodes include navigational bar, advertisement, web page tail, etc. With the above definition, the non-leaf node label space could hence be defined as follows

$$\mathcal{L}_{nonl} = \{structure\_block, data\_record, nav\_bar\_block, \\ non\_attribute\_block, value\_block, page\_tail\_block, name\_block, \\ image\_block, image\_caption\_block, main\_title\_block\}$$

Specifically, *value_block* is the node whose children nodes are all labeled with *attribute_value* or *value_block*. For example, in Figure 1, the block right below *Top Tracks* containing a table of several tracks by *Britney Spears* is defined as a *value_block*. Moreover, *structure_block* denotes a large block containing multiple types of non-leaf blocks. Other labels are rather self-explanatory.

3. MAX MARGIN LEARNING IN STRUCTURED OUTPUT SPACE

In order to provide labels for each node in the hierarchical model of a web page, we employ structured max margin learning approach.

3.1 Problem Formulation

In supervised structured prediction problems, given input variables $\{\mathbf{x}_l\}_{l=1}^m \in \mathcal{X}$ and output variables $\{\mathbf{y}_l\}_{l=1}^m \in \mathcal{Y}$, it is generally infeasible to model each possible value of output $\mathbf{y}_l$ as an individual class. Moreover, multiple way dependencies might exist between the components of $\mathbf{x}_l$, between the components of $\mathbf{y}_l$, and between the components of $\mathbf{x}_l$ and $\mathbf{y}_l$ [7]. Therefore, a feature map $\Phi(\mathbf{x}_l, \mathbf{y}_l) : \mathcal{X} \times \mathcal{Y} \rightarrow \mathcal{R}^d$ that allows to capture these multiple way dependencies among the input and output variables is widely employed [7]. Specifically, a discriminant function $F : \mathcal{X} \times \mathcal{Y} \rightarrow \mathcal{R}$ is usually employed to map the feasible input-output pairs to a compatibility score of the pair. The response for input $\mathbf{x}$ is therefore computed as the one that maximizes this score over the set of all possible outputs [7],

$$h(x) = \arg\max_{\mathbf{y}\in\mathcal{Y}} F(\mathbf{x}, \mathbf{y}) \tag{1}$$

The score of an $(\mathbf{x}, \mathbf{y})$ pair is computed from local fragments. For example, in hidden Markov model, $\mathbf{x}$ is a chain, $\mathbf{y}$ provides label for each node in the chain $\mathbf{x}$ and a local fragment of $(\mathbf{x}, \mathbf{y})$ is a clique comprised of x_i and its labeling y_i.

Specifically, in structured SVM [7], a generalized linear model $F(\mathbf{x}, \mathbf{y}) = \langle \mathbf{w}, \Phi(\mathbf{x}, \mathbf{y}) \rangle$ is employed to decode the top-scoring output

$$\mathbf{y}^* = \arg\max_{\mathbf{y}\in\mathcal{Y}} F(\mathbf{x}, \mathbf{y}) = \arg\max_{\mathbf{y}\in\mathcal{Y}} \langle \mathbf{w}, \Phi(\mathbf{x}, \mathbf{y}) \rangle \tag{2}$$

for any input $\mathbf{x}$. To measure the accuracy of a prediction, a symmetric, non-negative loss function $\Delta : \mathcal{Y} \times \mathcal{Y} \rightarrow \mathbb{R}$ that details the distance between the true output variable $\mathbf{y}$ and the prediction is employed. Different from conventional SVM, where regularized 0-1 loss is minimized, structural SVM minimizes a loss function that could capture the complex structure within label variables $\mathbf{y}$ [2]. This is due to the fact that a label sequence with only one incorrect prediction is obviously more preferable than a label sequence with no correct predictions. Hence, the expected risk of f could be calculated as

$$R(f) = \int_{\mathcal{X}\times\mathcal{Y}} \Delta(\mathbf{y}, \arg\max_{\mathbf{y}} f(\mathbf{x}, \mathbf{y})) \mathrm{d}P_{\mathcal{X}\times\mathcal{Y}}(\mathbf{x}, \mathbf{y}) \tag{3}$$

where input-output pairs $(\mathbf{x}_l, \mathbf{y}_l)$ are generated *i.i.d.* according to some fixed distribution $P_{\mathcal{X}\times\mathcal{Y}}$. As $P_{\mathcal{X}\times\mathcal{Y}}$ is unknown, structured prediction is addressed by minimizing the empirical risk on the training input-output pairs $\{(\mathbf{x}_l, \mathbf{y}_l) \in \mathcal{X} \times \mathcal{Y} : l = 1, \ldots, m\}$, regularized with the inverse margin $||\mathbf{w}||^2$. Therefore, structured SVM could be formulated as follows [7]

$$\begin{aligned} &\min_{\mathbf{w}} \ \frac{1}{2}||\mathbf{w}||^2 + C\sum_{l=1}^{m} \xi_l \\ &s.t. \ \mathbf{w}^T\Phi(\mathbf{x}_l, \mathbf{y}_l) - \mathbf{w}^T\Phi(\mathbf{x}_l, \mathbf{y}') \geq \Delta(\mathbf{y}_l, \mathbf{y}') - \xi_l, \forall \mathbf{y}', \forall l \\ &\quad \xi_l \geq 0, \ \forall l \end{aligned} \tag{4}$$

In this paper, we define the loss function $\Delta(\mathbf{y}, \mathbf{y}')$ as the number of disagreements between $\mathbf{y}$ and $\mathbf{y}'$, i.e., $\Delta(\mathbf{y}, \mathbf{y}') = \sum_i \mathbb{I}(y_i \neq y_i')$, where $\mathbb{I}$ is the indicator function. The training phase of structural SVM targets to learn the weight vector $\mathbf{w}$, while in the inference phase, dynamical programming is usually employed to find the most compatible label structure with the underlying observation.

3.2 Definition of Feature Function $\Phi(\mathbf{x}, \mathbf{y})$

The definition of a proper parametric discriminant function F requires specifying the joint input output mapping $\Phi(\mathbf{x}, \mathbf{y})$, which extracts features from a web page/hierarchical structured labeling pair $(\mathbf{x}, \mathbf{y})$. In this section, we provide detailed definition of features extracted in our hierarchical model for web information extraction.

3.2.1 Feature Construction in General

Inspired by sequence prediction approaches, such as *hidden Markov model* and *conditional random field*, we define features for the two types of cliques in the hierarchical model respectively: cliques $\mathcal{C}^b$ covering observation-state node pairs and cliques $\mathcal{C}^p$ covering state-state node pairs. Note that in current hierarchical model, we only consider parent-child connections, resulting in the only group of state-state links connecting a node to its parent. Consequently, $\Phi(\mathbf{x}, \mathbf{y})$ is defined over the set $\mathcal{C} = \mathcal{C}^b \cup \mathcal{C}^p$ and its components could be categorized into two groups according to which type of cliques they are defined over. Specifically, each component defined over clique in $\mathcal{C}^b$ conjunctively combines an input attribute $\phi(\mathbf{x}_i)_d \in \mathcal{R}$ (i.e., the d-th entry for the feature vector $\phi(\mathbf{x}_i)$ of the i-th node in the graph) with a state l

$$\phi^b_{ld}(\mathbf{x}, \mathbf{y}) = \sum_{(\mathbf{x}_i, y_i)\in\mathcal{C}^b} \mathbb{I}_{[y_i=l]}\phi(\mathbf{x}_i)_d \tag{5}$$

where $(\mathbf{x}_i, y_i)$ is a node in the web tree structure. Besides, each component defined over clique in $\mathcal{C}^p$ deals with a pair of adjacent states y_i and y_j

$$\phi^p_{l\bar{l}}(\mathbf{x}, \mathbf{y}) = \sum_{(y_i, y_j)\in\mathcal{C}^p} \mathbb{I}_{[y_i=l]}\mathbb{I}_{[y_j=\bar{l}]} \tag{6}$$

3.2.2 Features of a Block in Isolation

We first define the features $\phi(\mathbf{x})$ extracted for each block $\mathbf{x}$ in the hierarchical structure.

- Leaf: whether the node is a leaf node. Since the leaf nodes and other nodes have different label spaces, this feature is important in choosing the proper label space;
- Spatial Features: $\{\frac{BlockCenter\_X}{PageWidth}, \frac{BlockCenter\_Y}{PageHeight}, \frac{BlockWidth}{PageWidth}, \frac{BlockHeight}{PageHeight}, \frac{BlockArea}{PageArea}\}$, this feature gives information about the spatial location of the block;
- Common Features for Leaf and Non-leaf Nodes: link number, presence and frequency of HTML tags, number of descendants (0 for leaf nodes);

- Leaf Node Specific Features: text length, text fonts, bold, italic, word count, number of images, image number, image size, the alternative text of an image element, link text length; for non-leaf nodes, these features will simply be set to 0;

As mentioned in the previous section, the feature representation for this block with label y is

$$\Phi^b(\mathbf{x}, y) = \mathbf{e}_y \otimes \phi(\mathbf{x}) \quad (7)$$

where $\mathbf{e}_y$ is a vector with all its elements being 0, except the y-th element being 1, and $\otimes$ is the Kronecker product.

3.2.3 Features Capturing the Relationship of a Block with Parent Block

Besides the aforementioned features extracted from each block independently, we also extract features that capture the relationship between connected nodes in the hierarchical structure. Specifically, this feature captures the label co-occurrence patterns for child and parent parent nodes. Therefore, we construct the following feature capturing the label co-occurrence pattern for a node s and its parent t in the hierarchical structure

$$\forall l, \bar{l}: \quad \phi^p_{st}(l, \bar{l}) = \mathbb{I}_{[y_s=l]}\mathbb{I}_{[y_t=\bar{l}]} \quad (8)$$

Since the root node has no parent, $\forall l, \bar{l} : \phi^p(l, \bar{l}) = 0$.

3.2.4 Aggregation of Features

All the features extracted at node i are simply stacked together to form $\Phi(\mathbf{x}_i, y_i)$. Finally, this feature map is extended to the entire hierarchical structure involving n nodes in an additive manner as

$$\Phi(\mathbf{x}, \mathbf{y}) = \sum_{i=1}^{n} \Phi(\mathbf{x}_i, y_i) \quad (9)$$

As a result of the two types of features in $\Phi(\mathbf{x}, \mathbf{y})$, we separate the weight vector $\mathbf{w}$ also into two independent groups $\mathbf{w}^b$ and $\mathbf{w}^p$, such that

$$\begin{aligned} F(\mathbf{x},\mathbf{y}) &= \langle \mathbf{w}, \Phi(\mathbf{x},\mathbf{y})\rangle \quad (10)\\ &= \langle \mathbf{w}^b, \Phi^b(\mathbf{x},\mathbf{y})\rangle + \langle \mathbf{w}^p, \Phi^p(\mathbf{x},\mathbf{y})\rangle \\ &= \sum_{(\mathbf{x}_i,y_i)\in\mathcal{C}^b} \langle \mathbf{w}^b, \Phi^b(\mathbf{x}_i, y_i)\rangle + \sum_{(y_i,y_j)\in\mathcal{C}^p} \langle \mathbf{w}^p, \Phi^p(y_i, y_j)\rangle \quad (11)\end{aligned}$$

3.3 Inference

Given a web page $\mathcal{X} = \{\mathbf{x}_1, \ldots, \mathbf{x}_n\}$ and learned parameter $\mathbf{w}$, we need to solve the following inference problem to obtain the optimal labeling $\mathbf{y}^*$

$$\begin{aligned} \mathbf{y}^* &= \arg\max_{y_1,\ldots,y_n \in \mathcal{Y}} \sum_{i=1}^{n} F(\mathbf{x}_i, \mathbf{y}_i) \quad (12)\\ &= \arg\max_{y_1,\ldots,y_n \in \mathcal{Y}} \sum_{i=1}^{n} \left[\langle \mathbf{w}^b, \Phi^b(\mathbf{x}_i, y_i)\rangle + \langle \mathbf{w}^p, \Phi^p(y_i, y_{\pi_i})\rangle\right]\end{aligned}$$

where π_i is the parent of node i. A closer look into the above formulation reveals that each term in $\langle \mathbf{w}^b, \Phi^b(\mathbf{x}_i, y_i)\rangle$ is independent of others, and could therefore be optimized separately. On the other hand, the terms in $\langle \mathbf{w}^p, \Phi^p(y_i, y_{\pi_i})\rangle$ are interdependent. However, as the only edges in the hierarchical structure are those connecting a node with its parent node, we could employ a Viterbi decoding approach that starts from the leaf nodes in the tree and traverses through the tree until reaching the root node. For each node, we define $\delta_i(y)$ for $\forall y \in \mathcal{Y}$ that stores the optimal value of terms in (12) involving the i-th node $\mathbf{x}_i$ with label y. Specifically, for a leaf node, $\delta_i(y)$ is defined as

$$\delta_i(y) = \langle \mathbf{w}^b, \Phi^b(\mathbf{x}_i, y)\rangle \quad (13)$$

On the other hand, for non-leaf node $\mathbf{x}_j$, $\delta_j(y)$ is defined as

$$\delta_j(y) = \langle \mathbf{w}^b, \Phi^b(\mathbf{x}_j, y)\rangle + \sum_{i\in\mathcal{C}(j)} \max_{y'\in\mathcal{Y}} \{\delta_i(y') + \langle \mathbf{w}^p, \Phi^p(y', y)\rangle\} \quad (14)$$

where $\mathcal{C}(j)$ is the set of nodes whose parent node is $\mathbf{x}_j$. Clearly, the δ function for a node is only computed when all its child nodes have been handled. The computation continues until the root node is reached. Among those $|\mathcal{Y}|$ values computed for the root node, the maximal one is selected and corresponding y is selected as the label for root node. After the root node has been handled, we perform a standard backtracking to obtain the optimal labeling for the entire hierarchical structure.

3.4 Parameter Learning

Learning parameter $\mathbf{w}$ requires solving a quadratic programming problem with exponential number of constraints. A standard approach for tackling this problem is cutting plane algorithm [7], a.k.a., constraint generation. Specifically, we construct a nested sequence of successively tighter relaxations of the original problem, and each optimization problem in this sequence could be efficiently solved via quadratic programming.

3.5 Connecting Spatially Adjacent Blocks

For a block on the web page, spatially adjacent blocks encrypt important information about its functionality and semantics. For example, in Figure 1, the blocks listing tracks of *Britney Spears* appear below the block *Top Tracks*, which serves as the attribute name for those blocks of track name. Correctly identifying the functionality of the block *Top Tracks* is of great help in assigning labels to those blocks below it, and vise versa. The aforementioned hierarchical model only encodes parent-child relationship, without any encryption of the relationship between spatially adjacent blocks. In this section, we improve the hierarchical model by introducing edges connecting adjacent blocks.

Specifically, for each leaf node in the web page parsing hierarchy, our approach finds its k nearest neighbor leaf nodes and adds edges between the leaf node and its k neighbors. After adding these edges, the hierarchical model for a web page becomes a cyclic graph, instead of a tree structure where edges only appear between parent-child nodes. Feature representation for this improved hierarchical model includes the two types of features defined previously for tree structure model. Moreover, we introduce one more group of features that directly model the relationship between spatially adjacent nodes.

3.5.1 Features Capturing the Relationship of a Block with Neighboring Nodes

This feature is designed to encrypt the relationship among labels for connected nodes. Therefore, a similar feature as used for parent-child relationship could be adopted here. Specifically, the feature captures the co-appearance pattern of labels for spatially adjacent blocks. If node i is connected to node j, we define the following boolean-valued feature for block pair (i, j)

$$\forall l, \bar{l}: \quad \phi^s_{ij}(l, \bar{l}) = \mathbb{I}_{[y_i=l]}\mathbb{I}_{[y_j=\bar{l}]} \tag{15}$$

We define the weight vector for this feature type as $\mathbf{w}^s$. With $\mathbf{w}^b$ and $\mathbf{w}^p$ defined similarly as in the tree structure model, the prediction function for this cyclic graph hierarchical model is

$$F(\mathbf{x},\mathbf{y}) = \langle \mathbf{w}^b, \Phi^b(\mathbf{x},\mathbf{y})\rangle + \langle \mathbf{w}^p, \Phi^p(\mathbf{x},\mathbf{y})\rangle + \langle \mathbf{w}^s, \Phi^s(\mathbf{x},\mathbf{y})\rangle \tag{16}$$

where $\Phi^b(\mathbf{x},\mathbf{y})$ captures features of a block itself, $\Phi^p(\mathbf{x},\mathbf{y})$ models the relationship between a block with its direct enclosing block, and $\Phi^s(\mathbf{x},\mathbf{y})$ represents features computed between spatially adjacent blocks. Assume the cyclic graph hierarchical model for a web page is $\mathcal{G} = (\mathcal{V}, \mathcal{E})$, where $\mathcal{V}$ is the set of nodes and $\mathcal{E}$ denotes the set of edges. Since both $\Phi^p(\mathbf{x},\mathbf{y})$ and $\Phi^s(\mathbf{x},\mathbf{y})$ model label co-occurrence patterns of connected nodes, we could unify these two types of features. Specifically, for each edge $e = (s, t) \in \mathcal{E}$ that connects two nodes s and t, define a feature $\phi^e(y_s, y_t)$ as

$$\forall l, \bar{l}: \quad \phi^e_{st}(l, \bar{l}) = \mathbb{I}_{[y_s=l]}\mathbb{I}_{[y_t=\bar{l}]} \tag{17}$$

Consequently, the prediction function becomes

$$F(\mathbf{x},\mathbf{y}) = \langle \mathbf{w}^b, \Phi^b(\mathbf{x},\mathbf{y})\rangle + \langle \mathbf{w}^e, \Phi^e(\mathbf{x},\mathbf{y})\rangle \tag{18}$$

3.5.2 *Inference*

Similar as the tree structured hierarchical model, given a web page $\mathcal{X} = \{\mathbf{x}_1, \ldots, \mathbf{x}_n\}$ and learned parameter $\mathbf{w}$, inference targets to finding the most probable labeling for each node on the page. Specifically, inference in the cyclic graph renders into solving the following problem

$$\begin{aligned}\mathbf{y}^* &= \arg\max_{y_1,\ldots,y_n \in \mathcal{Y}} F(\mathbf{x},\mathbf{y}) \\ &= \arg\max_{y_1,\ldots,y_n \in \mathcal{Y}} \sum_{i=1}^{n} \langle \mathbf{w}^b, \Phi^b(\mathbf{x}_i, y_i)\rangle + \sum_{(i,j)\in\mathcal{E}} \langle \mathbf{w}^e, \Phi^e(y_i, y_j)\rangle \end{aligned} \tag{19}$$

where the first term $\langle \mathbf{w}^b, \Phi^b(\mathbf{x}_i, y_i)\rangle$ computes features regarding a block in isolation, and $\langle \mathbf{w}^e, \Phi^e(y_i, y_j)\rangle$ computes features involving two nodes in the graph, either parent-child nodes or spatially adjacent nodes.

Different from the tree structured hierarchical model, where an exact inference based on Viterbi decoding could be employed, in the cyclic graph hierarchical model, exact inference would take exponential time. Therefore, we employ a loopy belief propagation algorithm in this section to perform approximate inference. Specifically, for nodes $\{\mathbf{x}_s\}$ with labels $\{y_s\}$, we define the following two functions

$$\begin{aligned} \psi_s(y_s) &= \langle \mathbf{w}^b, \Phi^b(\mathbf{x}_s, y_s)\rangle, \quad \forall s \in \mathcal{V} && (20) \\ \psi_{st}(y_s, y_t) &= \langle \mathbf{w}^e, \Phi^e(y_s, y_t)\rangle, \quad \forall (s,t) \in \mathcal{E} && (21) \end{aligned}$$

At each iteration, each node t passes a "message" to each of its neighbors $s \in \mathcal{N}(t)$, which is connected to t with edge $(s,t) \in \mathcal{E}$. This message, which we denote by $M_{ts}(y_s)$, is a function of the possible states $y_s \in \mathcal{Y}$. On the full graph $\mathcal{G}$, there are totally $2|\mathcal{E}|$ messages, one for each direction of each edge. This full collection of messages is updated according to the following recursion [10]

$$M_{ts}(y_s) \leftarrow \max_{y'_t}\{\psi_{st}(y_s, y'_t) + \psi_t(y'_t) + \sum_{u \in N(t)/s} M_{ut}(y'_t)\} \tag{22}$$

For tree-structured graphs, it can be shown that iterates generated by (22) will converge to a unique fixed point after a finite number of iterations. Given these messages $M_{ts}(y_s)$, a standard backtracking procedure could be used to find the most probable labeling variables $\mathbf{y}^*$. Moreover, this fixed point is precisely equal to the result obtained using the Viterbi decoding method introduced in previous sections for tree structured hierarchical model.

The idea of *loopy belief propagation* [10] is to run the above procedure on a graph with cycles. Specifically, message updates (22) can be applied at a node while ignoring the presence of cycles - essentially pretending that any given node is embedded in a tree. Due to the presence of cycles, information could flow many times around the graph. This approach is known to perform well in many real-world problems [6, 9, 8, 12, 11].

4. EXPERIMENTS

We test our web information extraction approach on two groups of experiments: labeling each block on the page and extracting attribute name-value pairs. The extraction of attribute name-value pairs is of particular interests as they cover the majority of search queries.

4.1 Data Set

We crawled 1000 web pages from around 200 web sites, covering a large variety of various domains. For the block-level prediction task, we provide detailed labels for each block in 50 randomly selected web pages, resulting in a total of 13640 blocks. Moreover, we also manually label all attribute name-value pairs in the 1000 crawled web pages.

4.2 Block-Level Prediction

The first experiment tests the performance of our approach in assigning semantic labels for each block on the web pages.

4.2.1 *Evaluation Criteria*

To evaluate block-level prediction results, we employ the following three criteria

- **Overall accuracy**. This calculates the mean classification accuracy of various algorithms on all categories.
- **Precision, Recall and F-measure on attribute-value and attribute-name nodes**.
- **Confusion matrix**. Finally, we calculate the confusion matrix for leaf node labels and non-leaf node labels, respectively.

Leave-one-out cross validation is performed on the training set to calculate these performance measures.

4.2.2 *Experimental Setups and Comparisons*

We use multi-class SVM [3] as baseline, and compare the block-level prediction performances of structured SVM with tree hierarchical structure and structured SVM on cyclic graphs. Table 1 compares the block-level prediction results of *multiclass SVM, structured SVM with tree hierarchical model (SVM-Tree)* and *structured SVM with cyclic graph hierarchical model (SVM-Cyclic)*. Specifically, overall accuracy on all categories, precision and recall on attribute name and value classes are provided. According to Table 1, both

Table 1: Block level prediction results(%)

	Multiclass SVM	SVM-Tree	SVM-Cyclic
Accuracy	52.11	71.93	**74.96**
pName	65.55	69.08	**72.62**
rName	12.13	69.83	**73.41**
pValue	52.55	70.69	**74.00**
rValue	35.78	75.41	**78.55**

Table 2: Confusion matrix for leaf nodes.

472	49	49	0	40	14	26	0
86	**1201**	160	2	126	0	48	0
10	14	**319**	10	46	0	18	0
0	0	1	**55**	3	0	0	0
70	228	327	54	**3266**	1	405	1
2	0	2	0	6	**1**	0	0
3	37	22	0	139	0	**637**	0
0	0	0	0	0	0	0	**0**

SVM-Tree and *SVM-Cyclic* algorithms achieve much higher accuracy than *multiclass SVM*, demonstrating the effectiveness of our structured prediction framework. Moreover, the results for *SVM-Cyclic* are roughly 3% higher than those for *SVM-Tree*. This shows that connecting spatially adjacent blocks in the hierarchical model improves our structured prediction framework, even though only edges connecting leaf nodes are incorporated in current model. Although no edges are adding between non-leaf blocks in *SVM-Cyclic*, connected leaf blocks affect the label assignment of their parent nodes through the child-parent edges in the model. With better prediction for the leaf nodes, prediction results for non-leaf nodes are also improved.

To better understand the prediction results, we also provide confusion matrix for *SVM-Cyclic*. Specifically, Table 2 shows confusion matrix for leaf node labels, with rows corresponding to predicted labels, and columns corresponding to manually generated true labels. The 8 leaf node labels are organized in the same order as in $\mathcal{L}_{leaf}$, from left to right, and from top to bottom. Similarly, Table 3 shows confusion matrix for non-leaf node labels. The 10 non-leaf node labels are organized in the same order as in $\mathcal{L}_{nonl}$, from left to right, and from top to bottom.

4.3 Attribute Name-Value Pair Extraction

Automatically assigning semantic labels on blocks of a web page reveals great promise for intelligent web page understanding. However, how to make use of the extracted data is also an interesting problem. In this section, we take a step further and focus on extracting attribute name and value pairs. For example, in Figure 1, *Top Albums* and *Blockout* compose an attribute name-value pair. Given the block-level prediction results, our algorithm matches each *attribute value* block with a "closest" *attribute name* block. In order to measure the closeness between two blocks, we define a distance measure composed of two parts: tree distance and Euclidean distance. Specifically, we define the tree distance as length of the shortest path connecting these two blocks in the tree hierarchical model. Moreover, Euclidean distance is calculated between centers of the two blocks. Finally, block distance is computed as a weighted sum of tree distance and Euclidean distance, i.e.,

$$d(B_s, B_t) = d_{Tree}(B_s, B_t) + \lambda d_2(B_s, B_t) \qquad (23)$$

where d_{Tree} is the tree distance, d_2 is the Euclidean distance and λ is a weight parameter. We label all attribute name and value pairs in 1000 web pages crawled from more than 200 web sites and apply the *SVM-Tree* approach for block-level prediction. We then match each *attribute value* block to the closest *attribute name* block. Using this approach for extracting attribute name-value pairs, we achieve precision of **56.91**%, and recall of **59.37**%.

Table 3: Confusion matrix for non-leaf nodes.

164	11	9	0	1	5	0	0	0	0
2	**263**	27	27	28	12	4	1	22	0
8	75	**2600**	427	76	119	7	92	46	1
0	3	74	**408**	7	32	0	8	1	0
0	17	43	22	**400**	14	0	4	58	0
2	1	27	5	0	**152**	0	0	2	0
0	0	0	0	0	0	**7**	0	0	0
0	1	15	1	0	0	0	**116**	0	0
0	6	8	21	27	14	3	1	**163**	0
0	0	0	0	0	0	0	0	0	**0**

5. CONCLUSIONS

In this paper, we propose a max margin learning approach for domain-independent web information extraction. Specifically, we propose a tree structured hierarchical model, and a cyclic graph hierarchical model. For both models, efficient inference and parameter learning methods are discussed. Experimental results for both block-level prediction and attribute name-value pair extraction demonstrate the effectiveness of our proposed method.

Acknowledgements

E. P. Xing is supported by NSF IIS-0713379, DBI-0546594, Career Award, ONR N000140910758, DARPA NBCH1080007 and Alfred P. Sloan Foundation.

6. REFERENCES

[1] E. Agichtein and L. Gravano. Snowball: extracting relations from large plain-text collections. In *Digital Libraries*, 2000.

[2] Y. Altun, I. Tsochantaridis, and T. Hofmann. Hidden markov support vector machines. In *ICML*, 2003.

[3] K. Crammer and Y. Singer. On the algorithmic implementation of multiclass kernel-based vector machines. *JMLR*, 2:265–292, 2001.

[4] T. Joachims. Text categorization with support vector machines: learning with many relevant features. In *ECML*, 1998.

[5] R. Mihalcea and A. Csomai. Wikify! linking documents to encyclopedic knowledge. In *CIKM*, 2007.

[6] K. Murphy, Y. Weiss, and M. Jordan. Loopy belief propagation for approximate inference: An empirical study. In *UAI*, pages 467–475, 1999.

[7] I. Tsochantaridis, T. Joachims, T. Hofmann, and Y. Altun. Large margin methods for structured and interdependent output variables. *JMLR*, 6, 2005.

[8] M. Wainwright, T. Jaakkola, and A. Willsky. Tree consistency and bounds on the performance of the max-product algorithm and its generalizations. *Statistics and Computing*, 14:143–166, 2004.

[9] M. Wainwright, T. Jaakkola, and A. Willsky. Tree-based reparameterization framework for analysis of sum-product and related algorithms. *IEEE Transactions on Information Theory*, 45(9):1120–1146, 2008.

[10] M. Wainwright and M. Jordan. *Graphical Models, Exponential Families, and Variational Inference.* Now Publishers Inc., 2008.

[11] Y. Weiss and W. Freeman. Correctness of belief propagation in gaussian graphical models of arbitrary topology. *Neural Computation*, 13:2173–2200, 2001.

[12] Y. Weiss and W. Freeman. On the optimality of solutions of the max-product belief propagation algorithm in arbitrary graphs. *IEEE Transactions on Information Theory*, 47(2):723–735, 2001.

[13] X. Yin, W. Tan, and C. Liu. Facto: A fact lookup engine based on web tables. In *WWW*, 2011.

Finding Dimensions for Queries*

Zhicheng Dou[1], Sha Hu[2], Yulong Luo[3], Ruihua Song[1], and Ji-Rong Wen[1]
[1]Microsoft Research Asia; [2]Renmin University of China; [3]Shanghai Jiaotong University
[1]{zhichdou, rsong, jrwen}@microsoft.com; [2]sally_555@163.com; [3]ronagon@gmail.com

ABSTRACT

We address the problem of finding multiple groups of words or phrases that explain the underlying query facets, which we refer to as query dimensions. We assume that the important aspects of a query are usually presented and repeated in the query's top retrieved documents in the style of lists, and query dimensions can be mined out by aggregating these significant lists. Experimental results show that a large number of lists do exist in the top results, and query dimensions generated by grouping these lists are useful for users to learn interesting knowledge about the queries.

Categories and Subject Descriptors

H.3.3 [**Information Storage and Retrieval**]: Information Search and Retrieval—*Clustering, Information filtering, Query formulation*

General Terms

Algorithms, Experimentation, Management, Measurement

Keywords

Query Dimension, Query Facet, Faceted Search, Query Suggestion, Entity, Query Reformulation, Query Summarization, User Intent, List Extraction

1. INTRODUCTION

We address the problem of finding query dimensions. A *query dimension*, which is similar to a dimension in data warehouses [19, 9], is a set of items which describe and summarize one important aspect of a query. Here a *dimension item* is typically a word or a phrase. A query may have *multiple* dimensions that summarize the information about the query from different perspectives. Table 1 shows dimensions for some example queries. For the query "watches", its query dimensions cover the knowledge about watches in five unique aspects, including brands, gender categories, supporting features, styles, and colors. The query "visit Beijing" has a dimension about popular resorts in Beijing (tiananmen square, forbidden city, summer palace, ...) and a dimension on several travel related topics (attractions, shopping, dining, ...).

Query dimensions provide interesting and useful knowledge about a query and thus can be used to improve search experiences in many ways. **First**, we can display query dimensions together with the original search results in an appropriate way. Thus, users can understand some important facets of a query without browsing tens of pages. For example, a user could learn different brands and categories of watches. We can also implement a faceted search [4, 14, 13] based on query dimensions. User can clarify their specific intent by selecting dimension items. Then search results could be restricted to the documents that are relevant to the items. A user could drill down to women's watches if he is looking for a gift for his wife. These multiple groups of query dimensions are in particular useful for vague or ambiguous queries, such as "apple". We could show the products of Apple Inc. in one dimension and different types of the fruit apple in another. **Second**, query dimensions may provide direct information or instant answers that users are seeking. For example, for the query "lost season 5", all episode titles are shown in one dimension and main actors are shown in another. In this case, displaying query dimensions can save browsing time. **Third**, query dimensions may also be used to improve the diversity of the ten blue links. We can re-rank search results to avoid showing the pages that are near-duplicated in query dimensions at the top. Query dimensions also contain structured knowledge covered by or related to the input keywords of a query, and thus they can be used in many other fields besides traditional web search, such as semantic search or entity search [10, 3, 5, 29, 35, 6]. There has been a lot of recent work on automatically building knowledge ontology on the Web [6, 29]. Query dimensions can become a possible data source for this.

We observe that important pieces of information about a query are usually presented in list styles and repeated many times among top retrieved documents. Thus we propose aggregating frequent lists within the top search results to mine query dimensions and implement a system called **QDMiner**. More specifically, QDMiner extracts lists from free text, HTML tags, and repeat regions contained in top search results, and groups them into clusters based on the items they contain. Compared to previous works on building facet hierarchies [4, 14, 13, 23, 11, 22, 31], our approach

*The work was done when the second and third author were visiting Microsoft Research Asia

CIKM'11, October 24–28, 2011, Glasgow, Scotland, UK.

Table 1: Example query dimensions (automatically mined by our proposed method in this paper). Items in each dimension are seperated by commas.

query: **watches** 1. cartier, breitling, omega, citizen, tag heuer, bulova, casio, rolex, audemars piguet, seiko, accutron, movado, fossil, gucci, ... 2. men's, women's, kids, unisex 3. analog, digital, chronograph, analog digital, quartz, mechanical, manual, automatic, electric, dive, ... 4. dress, casual, sport, fashion, luxury, bling, pocket, ... 5. black, blue, white, green, red, brown, pink, orange, yellow, ...
query: **lost** 1. season 1, season 6, season 2, season 3, season 4, season 5 2. matthew fox, naveen andrews, evangeline lilly, josh holloway, jorge garcia, daniel dae kim, michael emerson, terry o'quinn, ... 3. jack, kate, locke, sawyer, claire, sayid, hurley, desmond, boone, charlie, ben, juliet, sun, jin, ana, lucia ... 4. what they died for, across the sea, what kate does, the candidate, the last recruit, everybody loves hugo, the end, ...
query: **lost season 5** 1. because you left, the lie, follow the leader, jughead, 316, dead is dead, some like it hoth, whatever happened happened, the little prince, this place is death, the variable, ... 2. jack, kate, hurley, sawyer, sayid, ben, juliet, locke, miles, desmond, charlotte, various, sun, none, richard, daniel 3. matthew fox, naveen andrews, evangeline lilly, jorge garcia, henry ian cusick, josh holloway, michael emerson, ... 4. season 1, season 3, season 2, season 6, season 4
query: **flowers** 1. birthday, anniversary, thanksgiving, get well, congratulations, christmas, thank you, new baby, sympathy, fall 2. roses, best sellers, plants, carnations, lilies, sunflowers, tulips, gerberas, orchids, iris 3. blue, orange, pink, red, purple, white, green, yellow
query: **what is the fastest animals in the world** 1. cheetah, pronghorn antelope, lion, thomson's gazelle, wildebeest, cape hunting dog, elk, coyote, quarter horse 2. birds, fish, mammals, animals, reptiles 3. science, technology, entertainment, nature, sports, lifestyle, travele, gaming, world business
query: **the presidents of the united states** 1. john adams, thomas jefferson, george washington, john tyler, james madison, abraham lincoln, john quincy adams, william henry harrison, martin van buren, james monroe, ... 2. the presidents of the united states of america, the presidents of the united states ii, love everybody, pure frosting, these are the good times people, freaked out and small, ... 3. kitty, lump, peaches, dune buggy, feather pluckn, back porch, kick out the jams, stranger, boll weevil, ca plane pour moi, ... 4. federalist, democratic-republican, whig, democratic, republican, no party, national union, ...
query: **visit beijing** 1. tiananmen square, forbidden city, summer palace, temple of heaven, great wall, beihai park, hutong 2. attractions, shopping, dining, nightlife, tours, travel tip, transportation, facts
query: **cikm** 1. databases, information retrieval, knowledge management, industry research track 2. submission, important dates, topics, overview, scope, committee, organization, programme, registration, cfp, publication, programme committee, organisers, ... 3. acl, kdd, chi, sigir, www, icml, focs, ijcai, osdi, sigmod, sosp, stoc, uist, vldb, wsdm, ...

is unique in two aspects: (1) **Open domain**: we do not restrict queries in a specific domain, like products, people, etc. Our proposed approach is generic and does not rely on any specific domain knowledge. Thus it can deal with open-domain queries. (2) **Query dependent**: instead of a same pre-defined schema for all queries, we extract dimensions from the top retrieved documents for each query. As a result, different queries may have different dimensions. For example, although "lost" and "lost season 5" in Table 1 are both TV program related queries, their mined dimensions are different.

As the problem of finding query dimension is new, we cannot find publicly available evaluation datasets. Therefore, we create two datasets, namely UserQ, containing 89 queries that are submitted by QDMiner users, and RandQ, containing 105 randomly sampled queries from logs of a commercial search engine, to evaluate mined dimensions. We use some existing metrics, such as purity and normalized mutual information (NMI), to evaluate clustering quality, and use NDCG to evaluate ranking effectiveness of dimensions. We further propose two metrics to evaluate the integrated effectiveness of clustering and ranking.

Experimental results show that the purity of query dimensions generated by QDMiner is good. Averagely on UserQ dataset, it is as high as 91%. The dimensions are also reasonably ranked with an average NDCG@5 value 0.69. Among the top five dimensions, 2.3 dimensions are good, 1.2 ones are fair, and only 1.5 are bad. We also reveal that the quality of query dimensions is affected by the quality and the quantity of search results. Using more of the top results can generate better query dimensions.

The remainder of this paper is organized as follows. We briefly introduce related work in Section 2. Following this, we propose QDminer, our approach to generate query dimensions by aggregating frequent lists in top results, in Section 3. We discuss evaluation methodology in Section 4 and report experimental results in Section 5. Finally we conclude the work in Section 6.

2. RELATED WORK

Finding query dimensions is related to several existing research topics. In this section, we briefly review them and discuss the difference from our proposed method QDMiner.

2.1 Query Reformulation

Query reformulation is the process of modifying a query to get search results that can better satisfy a user's information need. It is an important topic in Web search. Several techniques have been proposed based on relevance feedback, query log analysis, and distributional similarity [1, 25, 2, 33, 28, 34, 36, 17]. The problem of mining dimensions is different from query reformulation, as the main goal of mining dimensions is to summarize the knowledge and information contained in the query, rather than to find a list of related or expanded queries. Some query dimensions include semantically related phrases or terms that can be used as query reformulations, but some others cannot. For example, for the query "what is the fastest animals in the world" in Table 1, we generate a dimension "cheetah, pronghorn antelope, lion, thomson's gazelle, wildebeest, ..." which includes animal names that are direct answers rather than query reformulations to the query.

2.2 Query-based Summarization

Query dimensions can be thought as a specific type of summaries that briefly describe the main topic of given text. Several approaches [8, 27, 21] have been developed in the area of text summarization, and they are classified into different categories in terms of their summary construction methods (abstractive or extractive), the number of sources for the summary (single document or multiple documents), types of information in the summary (indicative or informative), and the relationship between summary and query (generic or query-based). Brief introductions to them can be found in [16] and [12]. Similar to existing summarization systems, QDMiner aims to offer the possibility of finding the main points of multiple documents and thus save users' time on reading whole documents. The difference is that most existing summarization systems dedicate themselves to generating summaries using **sentences** extracted from documents, while we generate summaries based on frequent **lists**. In addition, we return **multiple groups** of semantically related items, while they return a flat list of sentences.

2.3 Entity Search

The problem of entity search has received much attention in recent years [10, 3, 5, 29, 15, 20, 32, 26]. Its goal is to answer information needs that focus on entities. The problem of mining query dimensions is related to entity search as for some queries, dimension items are kinds of entities or attributes. Some existing entity search approaches also exploited knowledge from structure of webpages [30, 35, 6, 15]. Finding query dimensions differs from entity search in the following aspects. Firstly, finding query dimensions is applicable for all queries, rather than just entity related queries. Secondly, they tend to return different types of results. The result of an entity search is usually a list of entities, their attributes, and associated homepages, whereas query dimensions are comprised of multiple lists of items, which are not necessarily entities.

2.4 Faceted Search

Faceted search is a technique for allowing users to digest, analyze, and navigate through multidimensional data. It is widely applied in e-commerce and digital libraries. A robust review of faceted search is beyond the scope of this paper. Most existing faceted search and facets generation systems [4, 14, 13, 23, 11, 22, 31] are built on a specific domain (such as product search) or predefined facet categories. For example, Dakka and Ipeirotis [11] introduced an unsupervised technique for automatic extraction of facets that are useful for browsing text databases. Facet hierarchies are generated for a whole collection, instead of for a given query. Li et al. proposed Facetedpedia [23], a faceted retrieval system for information discovery and exploration in Wikipedia. Facetedpedia extracts and aggregates the rich semantic information from the specific knowledge database Wikipedia. In this paper, we explore to automatically find *query-dependent* dimensions for *open-domain* queries based on a general Web search engine. Dimensions of a query are automatically mined from the top web search results of the query without any additional domain knowledge required. As query dimensions are good summaries of a query and are potentially useful for users to understand the query and help them explore information, they are possible data sources that enable a general open-domain faceted exploratory search.

3. OUR APPROACH

As the first trial of mining query dimensions, we propose to automatically mine query dimensions from the top retrieved documents and develop a system called **QDMiner**. QDMiner discovers query dimensions *by aggregating frequent lists* within the top results. We propose this method based on the following observations:

(1) Important information is usually organized in *list* formats by websites. They may repeatedly occur in a sentence that is separated by commas, or be placed side by side in a well-formatted structure (e.g., a table). This is caused by the conventions of webpage design. Listing is a graceful way to show parallel knowledge or items and is thus frequently used by webmasters.

(2) Important lists are commonly supported by relevant websites and hence repeat in the top search results, whereas unimportant lists just infrequently appear in results. This makes it possible to distinguish good lists from bad ones, and to further rank dimensions in terms of importance.

Experimental results in Section 5 confirm the above observations and demonstrate that the query dimensions mined by aggregating them are meaningful.

3.1 System Overview

We illustrate QDMiner in Figure 1. In QDMiner, given a query q, we retrieve the top K results from a search engine and fetch all documents to form a set R as input. Then, query dimensions are mined by the following four steps:

1. List Extraction Several types of lists are extracted from each document in R. "men's watches, women's watches, luxury watches, ..." is an example list extracted.

2. List Weighting All extracted lists are weighted, and thus some unimportant or noisy lists, such as the price list "299.99, 349.99, 423.99, ..." that occasionally occurs in a page, can be assigned by low weights.

3. List Clustering Similar lists are grouped together to compose a dimension. For example, different lists about watch gender types are grouped because they share the same items "men's" and "women's".

4. Dimension and Item Ranking Dimensions and their items are evaluated and ranked based on their importance. For example, the dimension on brands is ranked higher than the dimension on colors based on how frequent the dimensions occur and how relevant the supporting documents are. Within the dimension on gender categories, "men's" and "women's" are ranked higher than "unisex" and "kids" based on how frequent the items appear, and their order in the original lists.

In the remaining part of this section, we will describe the four modules in detail.

3.2 List Extraction

From each document d in the search result set R, we extract a set of lists $L_d = \{l'\}$ from the HTML content of d based on three different types of patterns, namely free text patterns, HTML tag patterns, and repeat region patterns.

3.2.1 Free text patterns

We extract all text within document d and split it into sentences. We then employ the pattern **item{, item}* (and|or) {other} item**, which is similar to that in [35], to extract all matched items from each sentence. In Example 1, the items in italic font are extracted as a list.

Example 1 We shop for gorgeous watches from *Seiko*, *Bulova*, *Lucien Piccard*, *Citizen*, *Cartier* or *Invicta*.

We further use the pattern **{^item (:|-) .+$}+** to extract lists from some semi-structured paragraphs. It extracts lists from continuous lines that are comprised of two parts separated by a dash or a colon. The first parts of these lines

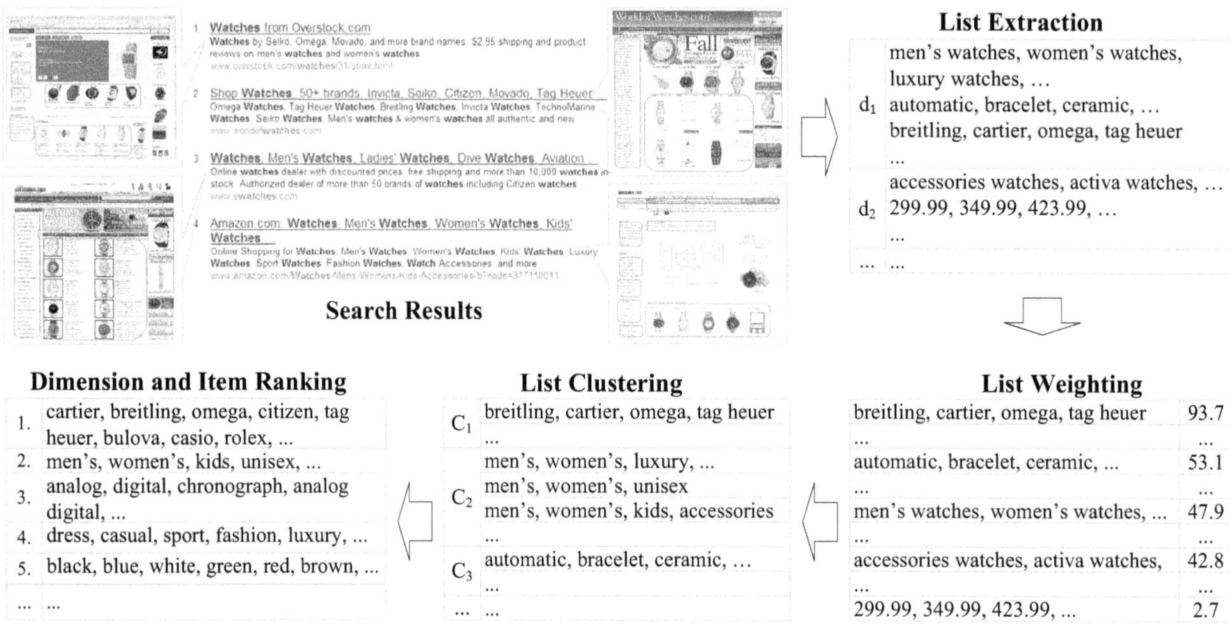

Figure 1: System overview of QDMiner

Table 2: Example HTML sources that contain lists

SELECT:
<select name="ProductFinder2" id="ProductFinder2" >
<option value="WatchBrands.htm"> *Watch Brands* </option>
<option value="Brands-Accutron.htm"> *Accutron* </option>
<option value="Brands-Bulova.htm"> *Bulova* </option>
<option value="Brands-Caravelle.htm"> *Caravelle* </option>
<option value="Brands-Seiko.htm"> *Seiko* </option></select>

UL:
<ul><li><a href="/rst.asp?q=dive"> *Dive* </a></li>
<li><a href="/rst.asp?q=titanium"> *Titanium* </a></li>
<li><a href="/rst.asp?q=automatic"> *Automatic* </a></li>
<li><a href="/rst.asp?q=quartz"> *Quartz* </a></li>
<li><a href="/rst.asp?q=gold"> *Gold* </a></li></ul>

TABLE:
<table width="100%">
<tr><td width="10%"></td><td> *White* </td></tr>
<tr><td></td><td height="20"> *Red* </td></tr>
<tr><td></td><td height="20"> *Black* </td></tr>
<tr><td></td><td height="20"> *Pink* </td></tr>
<tr><td height="4" colspan="2"></td></tr></table>

are extracted as a list. For instance, we extract all text in italic font in Example 2 as a list.

Example 2 ... are highly important for following reasons:
Consistency - every fact table is filtered consistently res...
Integration - queries are able to drill different processes ...
Reduced development time to market - the common dimensions are available without recreating the wheel over again.

3.2.2 HTML tag patterns

We extract lists from several list-style HTML tags, including SELECT, UL, OL, and TABLE. Example sources of these HTML tags can be found in Table 2. Extracted items are in italic.

SELECT For the SELECT tag, we simply extract all text from their child tags (OPTION) to create a list. Moreover, we remove the first item if it starts with some predefined text, such as "select" or "choose".

UL/OL For these two tags, we also simply extract text within their child tags (LI).

TABLE We extract one list from each column or each row. For a table containing m rows and n columns, we extract at most $m+n$ lists. For each column, the cells within THEAD or TFOOT tags are regarded as table headers and are dropped from the list. We also drop the first cell of each column when its cascading style[1] is different from other cells.

3.2.3 Repeat region patterns

We observe that peer information is sometimes organized in well-structured visual blocks in webpages. Figure 2 shows a repeat region of four blocks in repeated style. Each block contains a restaurant record that is comprised of four attributes: a picture, a restaurant name, a location description, and a rating. We can extract three lists from this region: a list of restaurant names, a list of location descriptions, and a list of ratings. Note that images are simply ignored in this paper.

To extract these lists, we **first** detect repeat regions in webpages based on vision-based DOM trees [7]. Here a repeat region is the region that includes more than one block, e.g., M blocks, with similar DOM and visual structures. We **then** extract all leaf HTML nodes within each block, and group them by their tag names and display styles. In the above example, all restaurant names have the same tag name (<a>) and displaying style (in blue color), and hence can be grouped together. Each group usually contains M nodes. Each two of them are from different blocks. **At last**, for each group, we extract all text from its nodes as a list.

3.2.4 Post-processing

We further process each extracted list l' as follows. We first normalize all items by removing useless symbol charac-

[1]http://www.w3.org/Style/CSS/

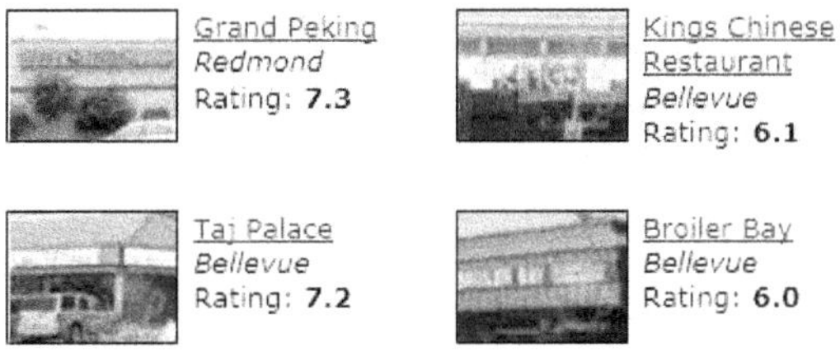

Figure 2: An example repeat region in a webpage

Table 3: Less informative list examples

	Items (separated by commas)
1	we recommend, my account, help
2	home, customer service, my account, tracking, faq's
3	read, edit, view history
4	movado 605635 luno two tone... 547.50 717.00 1 rating 1 review, movado museum strap 0690299... 225.00 395.00 1 rating, citizen calibre 2100 av0031... 299.00 350.99 11 ratings

ters, such as '[' and ']', and converting uppercase letters to lowercase. We then remove long items which contain more than 20 terms. At last, we remove all lists that contain less than two unique items or more than 200 unique items.

3.3 List Weighting

Some of the extracted lists are not informative or even useless. Some of them are extraction errors. Table 3 shows some sample lists for the query "watches". The first three lists are navigational links which are designed to help users navigate between webpages. They are not informative to the query. The fourth list is actually an extraction error: several types of information are mixed together.

We argue that these types of lists are useless for finding dimensions. We should punish these lists, and rely more on better lists to generate good dimensions. We find that a good list is usually supported by many websites and appear in many documents, partially or exactly. A good list contains items that are informative to the query. Therefore, we propose to aggregate all lists of a query, and evaluate the importance of each *unique* list l by the following components:

(1) S_{DOC}: **document matching weight.** Items of a good list should *frequently* occur in *highly ranked* results. We let $S_{\text{DOC}} = \sum_{d \in R}(s_d^m * s_d^r)$, where $s_d^m * s_d^r$ is the supporting score by each result d, and:

- s_d^m **is the percentage of items contained in** d. A list l is supported by a document d, if d contains some or all items of l. The more items d contains, the stronger it supports l. Suppose $|d \cap l|$ is the number of shared items in d and l, and $|l|$ is the number of items contained in list l, we let $s_d^m = \frac{|d \cap l|}{|l|}$.

- s_d^r **measures the importance of document** d. It is derived from ranks of documents in this paper. The documents ranked higher in the original search results are usually more relevant to the query, and hence they are more important. We simply let $s_d^r = 1/\sqrt{rank_d}$, where $rank_d$ is the rank of document d. The higher d is ranked, the larger its score s_d^r is.

(2) S_{IDF}: **average invert document frequency (IDF) of items.** A list comprised of common items in a corpus is not informative to the query. We calculate the average IDF value of all items, i.e., $S_{\text{IDF}} = \frac{1}{|l|} \cdot \sum_{e \in l} idf_e$. Here $idf_e = \log \frac{N - N_e + 0.5}{N_e + 0.5}$, where N_e is the total number of documents that contain item e in the corpus and N is the total number of documents. We use the ClueWeb09 collection[2], which includes about one billion webpages, as our reference corpus in counting N_e and N.

We combine these two components, and evaluate the importance of a list l by Equation (1).

$$S_l = S_{\text{DOC}} * S_{\text{IDF}} \tag{1}$$

Finally, we sort all lists by final weights for the given query. The first three lists in Table 3 are assigned low weights as they have low average invert document frequencies. The weight of the fourth list is also low. Its most items just appear in one document in top results; hence it has a low document matching weight.

3.4 List Clustering

We do not use individual weighted lists as query dimensions because: (1) An individual list may inevitably include noise. For example, the first item of the first list in Table 2, i.e., "watch brands", is noise. It is difficult to identify it without other information provided; (2) An individual list usually contains a small number of items of a dimension and thus it is far from complete; (3) Many lists contain duplicated information. They are not exactly same, but share overlapped items. To conquer the above issues, we group similar lists together to compose dimensions.

Two lists can be grouped together if they share enough items. We define the distance $d_l(l_1, l_2)$ between two lists l_1 and l_2 as $d_l(l_1, l_2) = 1 - \frac{|l_1 \cap l_2|}{\min\{|l_1|, |l_2|\}}$. Here $|l_1 \cap l_2|$ is the number of shared items within l_1 and l_2. We use the complete linkage distance $d_c(c_1, c_2) = \max_{l_1 \in c_1, l_2 \in c_2} d_l(l_1, l_2)$ to compute the distance between two clusters of lists. This means that two groups of lists can only be merged together when every two lists of them are similar enough.

We use a modified QT (Quality Threshold) clustering algorithm [18] to group similar lists. QT is a clustering algorithm that groups data into high quality clusters. Compared to other clustering algorithms, QT ensures quality by finding large clusters whose diameters do not exceed a user-defined diameter threshold. This method prevents dissimilar data from being forced under the same cluster and ensures good quality of clusters. In QT, the number of clusters is not required to be specified.

The QT algorithm assumes that all data is equally important, and the cluster that has the most number of points is selected in each iteration. In our problem, lists are not equally important. Better lists should be grouped together first. We modify the original QT algorithm to first group highly weighted lists. The algorithm, which we refer to as WQT (**Q**uality **T**hreshold with **W**eighted data points), is described as follows.

1. Choose a maximum diameter Dia_{max} and a minimum weight W_{min} for clusters.

2. Build a candidate cluster for the *most important point* by iteratively including the point that is closest to the group, until the diameter of the cluster surpasses the

[2] http://boston.lti.cs.cmu.edu/Data/clueweb09/

threshold Dia_{max}. Here the most important point is the list which has the highest weight.

3. Save the candidate cluster if the total weight of its points w_c is not smaller than W_{min}, and remove all points in the cluster from further consideration.

4. Recurse with the reduced set of points.

Recall that the main difference between WQT and QT is that WQT tries to get more neighbors for *important* points, and hence generated clusters are biased towards important data points. Suppose we have six lists: l_1 =(cartier, breitling, omega, citizen), l_2 =(breitling, omega, citizen, tag heuer), l_3 =(breitling, omega, citizen, movie, music, book), l_4 =(movie, music, book), l_5 =(music, book, radio), and l_6 =(movie, book, radio). Their corresponding weights satisfy: $S_{l1} > S_{l2} > S_{l3} > S_{l4} > S_{l5} > S_{l6}$. QT ignores their weights and generate a cluster (l_3, l_4, l_5, l_6) in the first iteration with $Dia_{max} = 0.6$, whereas WQT will generate a cluster (l_1, l_2, l_3) for list l_1. We prefer the second result, especially when S_{l_1} is much larger than S_{l_3}. In addition, WQT is more efficient than QT, as it just builds one candidate cluster while QT builds a candidate cluster for each remaining point.

In this paper, the weight of a cluster is computed based on the number of websites from which its lists are extracted. More specifically, $w_c = |Sites(c)|$ where $Sites(c)$ is the set of websites that contain lists in c. Note we use websites instead of webpages because webpages from the same website usually share the same page templates and contribute duplicated lists. We empirically set $Dia_{max} = 0.6$ and $W_{min} = 3$. $W_{min} = 3$ means that the lists of a qualified cluster are from at least three unique websites.

After the clustering process, similar lists will be grouped together to compose a candidate query dimension.

3.5 Dimension and Item Ranking

In this section, we evaluate the importance of dimensions and items, and rank them based on importance.

Based on our motivation that a good dimension should frequently appear in the top results, a dimension c is more important if: (1) The lists in c are extracted from more unique websites; and (2) the lists in c are more important, i.e., they have higher weights. We define S_c, the importance of dimension c, as follows.

$$S_c = \sum_{s \in Sites(c)} \max_{l \in c, l \in s} S_l \quad (2)$$

Here S_l is the weight of a list l. We sum up the maximum list weight from each website as dimension importance.

In a dimension, the importance of an item depends on how many lists contain the item and its ranks in the lists. As a better item is usually ranked higher by its creator than a worse item in the original list, we calculate $S_{e|c}$, the weight of an item e within a dimension c, by:

$$S_{e|c} = \sum_{s \in Sites(c)} w(c, e, s) = \sum_{s \in Sites(c)} \frac{1}{\sqrt{AvgRank_{c,e,s}}} \quad (3)$$

where $w(c, e, s)$ is the weight contributed by a website s, and $AvgRank_{c,e,s}$ is the average rank of e within all lists extracted from website s. Suppose $L(c, e, s)$ is the set of all lists in c that contain item e and are extracted from website s, we have $AvgRank_{c,e,s} = \frac{1}{|L(c,e,s)|} \sum_{l \in L(c,e,s)} rank_{e|l}$. $w(c, e, s)$ gets the highest score 1.0 when the item e is always the first item of the lists from s.

We sort all items within a dimension by their weights. We define an item e is a *qualified* item of dimension c if $S_{e|c} > 1$ and $S_{e|c} > \frac{|Sites(c)|}{10}$. Here $S_{e|c} > 1$ means that e is qualified if it is once the first item of lists from one website and also occurs in lists from at least another website. $S_{e|c} > \frac{|Sites(c)|}{10}$ means that it should be supported by at least 10% of all websites in this dimension. We only output qualified items by default in QDMiner.

Table 4: Statistics about human created dimensions

Item	UserQ			RandQ		
	Bad	Fair	Good	Bad	Fair	Good
#DimemsionsPerQ	4.4	5.3	4.9	2.1	2.1	2.9
#ItemsPerQuery	135	151	219	61	86	98
#ItemsPerDimension	31	29	45	30	40	33

4. EVALUATION METHODOLOGY

4.1 Data

We do not find any existing dataset available for evaluating the quality of query dimensions. Therefore, we build two datasets from scratch. First, we build an online service for finding dimensions, and invite some human subjects to issue queries about topics they know well. We collect 89 queries issued by the subjects, and name the set of queries as "UserQ". As asking users to produce queries concerning a topic that they are familiar with might induce a bias towards topics in which lists are more useful than general web queries, we further randomly sample another set of 105 English queries from a query log of a commercial search engine, and name this set of queries as "RandQ".

For each query, we first ask a subject to manually create dimensions and add items that are covered by the query, based on his/her knowledge after a deep survey on any related resources (such as Wikipedia, Freebase, or official web sites related to the query). We then aggregate the *qualified* items in the top *five* dimensions returned by all algorithms we want to evaluate, and ask the subject to assign unlabeled items into the created dimensions. New dimensions will be created for the items that are not covered by the existing dimensions.

For each human created dimension, we ask the subject who has created the dimension and four additional subjects to rate its usefulness in the following three levels:

`[Good/2]` - It is very useful and I like it;
`[Fair/1]` - It is just so so;
`[Bad /0]` - It is useless and I don't like it.

The rating that is most chosen by subjects is regarded as the final rating of the dimension. The higher one is used if two ratings are selected by the same number of subjects.

Table 4 shows the statistics about human labeled query dimensions. There are on average about 4.9 good dimensions and 5.3 fair dimensions for each query in the UserQ collection, while there are about 2.9 good dimensions and 2.1 fair dimensions for the RandQ collection. There are more dimensions and items in UserQ than in RandQ. This is because the queries in RandQ are randomly sampled from query logs. Some of them are too specific or noisy to have meaningful dimensions.

We find that the assessment of query dimensions is time-consuming and costly, even if we only assess the top five dimensions for each query. Each subject may spend up to an hour to completely assess a query.

4.2 Evaluation Metrics

The quality of query dimensions can be measured in the following two aspects:

Quality of clustering - Ideally, each dimension should only contain items reflecting the same facet of the query, and the items referring to the same information should not be separated into multiple dimensions. In this paper, we use several existing metrics [24], including Purity, NMI (Normalized Mutual Information), RI (Random Index), and F measure, to evaluate the quality of clusters.

Ranking effectiveness of dimensions - Obviously we aim to rank good dimensions before bad dimensions when multiple dimensions are found. As we have multi-level ratings, we adopt the nDCG measure (Normalized Discounted Cumulative Gain), which is widely used in information retrieval, to evaluate the ranking of query dimensions. Suppose that each output dimension c_i is assigned to a manually labeled class c'_i which covers the maximum number of items in c_i. The ranking quality of the top p dimensions is calculated by $\text{nDCG}_p = \frac{DCG_p}{IDCG_p}$ where $DCG_p = \sum_{i=1}^{p} DG_i$ and $IDCG_p$ is the ideal cumulative gain which is produced by the perfect ordering. DG_i is the discounted gain of the ith dimension. $DG_i = \frac{2^{r_i}-1}{\log_2(1+i)}$ if the rating of c'_i is r_i. In our problem, a ground truth class may be divided into multiple dimensions in automatic results. Hence DCG_p may exceed IDCG_p and nDCG may exceed 1 in some cases. To solve this problem, for each ground truth class c'_i, we only credit the *first* dimension that is assigned to it, and skip all later ones.

nDCG does not consider the quality of clustering which does influence user satisfaction. To evaluate the integrated effectiveness, we let $DCG_p = \sum_{i=1}^{p}(w_i \cdot DG_i)$ where w_i is a weight for each automatic dimension c_i, and propose two alternative nDCG measurements.

fp-nDCG - *purity aware nDCG.* fp-nDCG is also calculated based on the first appearance of each class. Different from the original nDCG, we further consider the purity of each dimension c_i by multiplying DG_i by the percentage of correctly assigned items, i.e., we let $w_i = \frac{|c'_i \cap c_i|}{|c_i|}$.

rp-nDCG - *recall and purity aware nDCG.* rp-nDCG is calculated based on all output dimensions. We weight each dimension by $w_i = \frac{|c'_i \cap c_i|}{|c_i|}\frac{|c'_i \cap c_i|}{|c'_i|}$. Here $\frac{|c'_i \cap c_i|}{|c'_i|}$ is the percentage of items in c'_i matched by the current output dimension c_i. rp-nDCG ranges from 0 to 1, and the best value 1 is achieved when all items are correctly classified into the right dimensions.

We calculate the above metrics based on the top five dimensions for each query, and then average them over all queries. We argue that ranking quality is generally more important than clustering quality for query dimensions. We prefer to generating useful dimensions that may contain a little noise rather than pure but useless dimensions.

5. EXPERIMENTAL RESULTS

5.1 Overall Results

We mine query dimensions based on top 100 results from a commercial search engine. Some samples of query dimensions have been shown in Table 1. We find that our generated top dimensions are usually meaningful and useful for users to understand underlying facets of queries.

Table 5: Statistics about mined query dimensions

Desc.	UserQ	RandQ
#queries	89	105
#results per query	99.8	99.5
#lists per document	44.1	37.0
#Items per list	9.7	10.1
#dimensions per query	32.1	21.6
#lists per dimension	7.1	6.4
#items/qualified items per dimension	20.8/7.5	23.7/8.7
#good/fair dimensions among top five	2.3/1.2	1.7/1

Table 6: Quality of mined query dimensions

Dataset	Purity	RI	F1	F5
UserQ	0.910	0.891	0.803	0.791
RandQ	0.922	0.849	0.770	0.738
	NMI	nDCG5	fp-nDCG5	rp-nDCG5
UserQ	0.818	0.691	0.636	0.212
RandQ	0.770	0.679	0.627	0.248

Table 5 shows some statistics about the generated query dimensions. On average for each query in UserQ, there are about 32.1 dimensions generated. Each dimension contains about 20.8 unique items, and 7.5 of them are classified as qualified ones. Among the top five dimensions, about 2.3 dimensions are labeled as good, and 1.2 ones are labeled as fair. The queries in RandQ have less lists and dimensions than UserQ. As we mentioned in Section 4, this is because some randomly sampled queries in RandQ are too specific or not well-formed.

We evaluate the top five query dimensions for each query, and show the results in Table 6. We find that:

(1) Clustering quality on the UserQ collection is good, with a high purity score (0.910) and reasonable scores of NMI, RI, F1, and F5. RandQ has a higher purity of 0.922 but a lower NMI of 0.770 than UserQ. This indicates that more small dimensions, which are from the same ground truth classes, are generated in RandQ than in UserQ. This may happen when the quality of search results is not good and there is not enough evidence to group similar lists.

(2) Rankings of query dimensions on both datasets are effective in terms of nDCG and fp-nDCG. rp-nDCG@5 values are relatively low on both datasets, which indicates that only a small percentage of human labeled items are returned in the output dimensions. This is caused by the following reasons. **Firstly**, some items do not appear in the top search results, and some of them are not presented in list styles. **Secondly**, we just evaluate *qualified* items for each dimension. Table 5 shows that only about 1/3 of items are predicted to be qualified. This may cause low item recall for all methods. **Thirdly**, it is difficult to enumerate all items. For example, there are hundreds of items within the labeled dimension "watch brands" for the query "watches". These items are collected from a large number of results generated by different algorithms, and it is not easy for one specific algorithm to enumerate all of them. **Fourthly**, some items in the labeled dimensions are actually variants of the same meaning. For example, "season one" and "season 1" are ex-

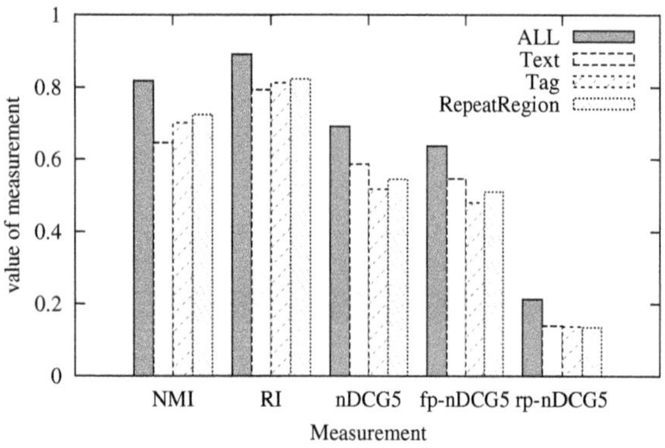

Figure 3: Effectiveness of different types of lists

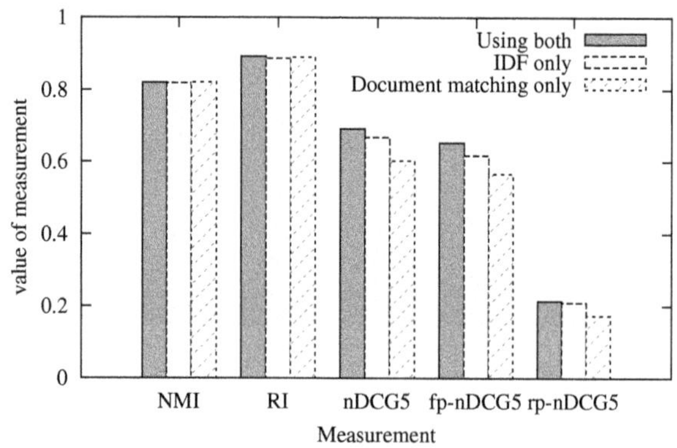

Figure 4: Experiments with list weighting methods

actly the same in meanings. These duplicated items may cause low recall if one algorithm can only return one of them. To overcome the issue, we plan to identify similar items in labeling dimensions in the future.

In the remaining parts of this paper, we only report the results on UserQ due to space limitations. In most experiments, we get the same conclusions on RandQ and UserQ.

5.2 Experiments with Different Types of Lists

As introduced in Section 3.2, we use three different types of patterns to extract lists from webpages, namely free text patterns (Text), HTML tag patterns (Tag), and repeat region patterns (RepeatRegion). In this section, we experiment with different types of lists, and investigate whether they are useful. Experimental results are shown in Figure 3. The figure indicates that the sole use of any type of list yields reasonable results, but a combination of them (series ALL) performs the best. This is intuitive because more lists provide more evidence for weighting important lists and generating better dimensions.

The repeat region based and HTML tag based query dimensions have *better clustering quality but worse ranking quality* than the free text based ones. By analyzing the data, we find that many lists appear in the header or the left region of webpages in well formatted HTML structures. They are originally designed to help users navigate between webpages, and hence we call them "navigational lists" in this paper. These navigational lists are easily extracted by HTML tag based or repeat region based patterns with high precision, but they are usually irrelevant to the query. The first two lists in Table 3 are such kinds of lists. Although we have punished them in Section 3.3, there are still some useless dimensions generated by aggregating them. The lists within free text of webpages, which are extracted based on simple sentence patterns, are short and sometimes noisy. However, they are generally more informative, and are more useful to users.

5.3 Experiments with List Weighting Methods

We integrate two different components, i.e., document matching weight and average invert document frequency (IDF), in evaluating the importance of a list in Section 3.3. In this section, we investigate whether these components are necessary and effective. We experiment with using only of them, and show the experimental results in Figure 4. The results indicate that clustering quality (in terms of NMI and RI) does not significantly change if each component is used or not. This confirms our previous conclusion that our WQT clustering algorithm performs well in most cases. In terms of ranking quality, we have the following findings:

(1) The quality of query dimensions significantly drops when IDF is not used (document matching only), which indicates that the average invert document frequency of items is an important factor. A list that contains common items in a corpus usually gets a high document matching score because most items also occur frequently in the top results of the query. It would be ranked high and generate a useless dimension if we did not consider IDF.

(2) Document matching weight is also helpful to improve the quality of query dimensions. Document matching weight does not affect the ranking of query dimensions as big as IDF. This is because in Equation (2) we use the number of websites (lists) in ranking query dimensions. Thus the function of document matching weight is partially overlapped.

5.4 Experiments with Clustering Algorithms

As introduced in Section 3.4, we use a modified QT clustering algorithm named WQT to group similar lists. In this section, we verify whether WQT is able to generate better query dimensions than QT. We generate query dimensions using both algorithms with different settings of maximum diameter Dia_{max}, and plot experimental results in Figure 5. This figure shows that WQT consistently outperforms QT with four different settings of maximum diameter. As WQT first generates clusters for important lists, it is proved to be able to generate better query dimensions than QT. The figure also indicates that our setting $Dia_{max} = 0.6$ is good for the WQT algorithm, as a lower value may generate less dimensions and a higher value may induce more noisy dimensions.

5.5 Experiments with Search Result Quantity

The top 100 search results are used in the above experiments. In this section, we experiment with various numbers of top results, ranging from 10 to 100, to investigate whether the quality of query dimensions is affected by the quantity of search results. Experimental results are shown in Figure 6. This figure shows that the number of results does affect the quality of query dimensions. Query dimensions become better when more search results are used. This is because more results contain more lists and hence can generate more dimensions. More results also provide more

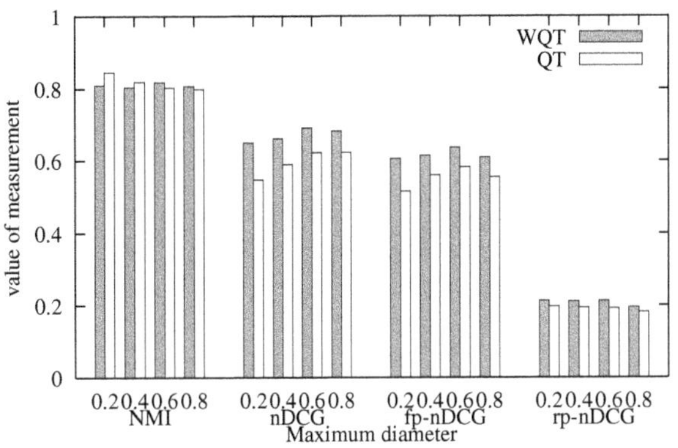

Figure 5: Effectiveness of clustering algorithms

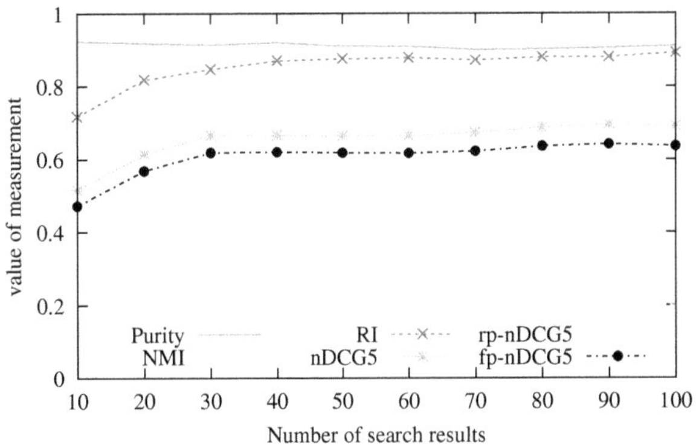

Figure 6: Experiments with search result quantity

evidence for voting the importance of lists, and hence can improve the quality of query dimensions. The figure also shows that the improvement of clustering quality becomes subtle when the number of results is larger than 50. Additional results may help discover more dimension items, but has less impact on the quality of query dimensions. Using top 50 results is already enough for the WQT algorithm to group similar lists into correct dimensions, and most valuable dimensions have already been found. Furthermore, the relevance of later search results also decreases, and the documents may contain less relevant or less useful lists.

In addition, we find that the purity of query dimensions (the red series in Figure 6) decreases a little bit when more results are used. This is because when a small number of results are used, some lists are not merged together but each of them individually has high purity. When similar lists are grouped based on more results, a part of purity may be sacrificed and the generated dimensions may inevitably include some noise from new lists.

5.6 Experiments with Search Result Quality

QDMiner is based on the assumption that most top results of a query are relevant. In this section, we investigate whether our dimension mining algorithms are significantly affected by the quality of search results. We experiment with the following configurations: (1) Top - using the original top K results; (2) TopShuffle - randomly shuffling the top K results; (3) Random - randomly selecting K results from the original 100 results and then shuffling them. In general, the

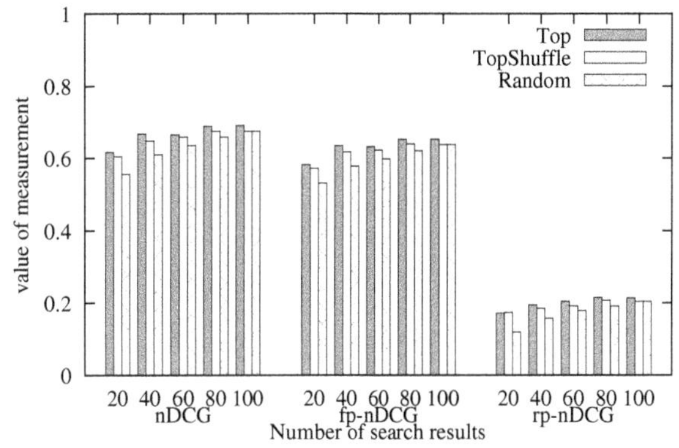

Figure 7: Results based on shuffled search results

Random method generates worse ranking than TopShuffle, and both perform worse than Top in ranking effectiveness.

Figure 7 shows that method Random is the worst among the three approaches. We find that Random generates much less dimensions than Top and TopShuffle. Consequently, the generated dimensions are usually less relevant to the query, and they also contain less qualified items. Some documents used by the Random method may have drifted to other irrelevant topics. Moreover, Figure 7 shows that shuffling the top results (TopShuffle) harms the quality of query dimensions. We assign larger weights for the lists that are extracted from the top-ranked documents in Equation (1). The TopShuffle method may cause the lists extracted from less relevant documents to be given higher weights, which finally affects the quality of query dimensions. All these results indicate that the quality of search results does affect query dimensions. Note that their clustering quality is comparable, and we skip them due to space limitations.

6. CONCLUSIONS AND FUTURE WORK

In this paper, we study the problem of finding query dimensions. We propose a systematic solution, which we refer to as QDMiner, to automatically mine query dimensions by aggregating frequent lists from free text, HTML tags, and repeat regions within top search results. We create two human annotated data sets and apply existing metrics and two new combined metrics to evaluate the purity and the ranking quality of query dimensions. Experimental results show that a large number of lists exist in the top search results. Meaningful and useful query dimensions are mined by aggregating these lists using QDMiner.

As the first approach of finding query dimensions, QDMiner can be improved in many aspects. For example, some semi-supervised bootstrapping list extraction algorithms can be used to iteratively extract more lists from the top results. Specific website wrappers can also be employed to extract high-quality lists from authoritative websites. Adding these lists may improve both accuracy and recall of query dimensions. Part-of-speech information can be used to further check the homogeneity of lists and hence improve the quality of query dimensions. We will explore these topics to refine QDMiner in the future.

We will also investigate some other related topics to finding query dimensions. Good descriptions of query dimensions may be helpful for users to better understand the dimensions. How to automatically generate meaningful descriptions is an interesting research topic. We also plan to utilize query dimensions to improve Web search. Some candidate directions include using query dimensions to improve search result diversity, using dimensions to provide structured query suggestions, and building a general faceted search system based on QDMiner.

7. REFERENCES

[1] J. Allan. Relevance feedback with too much data. In *Proceedings of SIGIR '95*, pages 337–343, 1995.

[2] P. Anick. Using terminological feedback for web search refinement: a log-based study. In *Proceedings of SIGIR '03*, pages 88–95, 2003.

[3] K. Balog, E. Meij, and M. de Rijke. Entity search: building bridges between two worlds. In *Proceedings of SEMSEARCH '10*, pages 9:1–9:5, 2010.

[4] O. Ben-Yitzhak, N. Golbandi, N. Har'El, R. Lempel, A. Neumann, S. Ofek-Koifman, D. Sheinwald, E. Shekita, B. Sznajder, and S. Yogev. Beyond basic faceted search. In *Proceedings of WSDM '08*, 2008.

[5] M. Bron, K. Balog, and M. de Rijke. Ranking related entities: components and analyses. In *Proceedings of CIKM '10*, pages 1079–1088, 2010.

[6] M. J. Cafarella, A. Halevy, D. Z. Wang, E. Wu, and Y. Zhang. Webtables: exploring the power of tables on the web. *VLDB*, 1:538–549, August 2008.

[7] D. Cai, S. Yu, J.-r. Wen, and W.-y. Ma. Vips: a vision-based page segmentation algorithm, 2003.

[8] Y. Chali and S. R. Joty. Unsupervised approach for selecting sentences in query-based summarization. In *FLAIRS Conference*, pages 47–52, 2008.

[9] S. Chaudhuri and U. Dayal. An overview of data warehousing and olap technology. *SIGMOD Rec.*, 26:65–74, March 1997.

[10] T. Cheng, X. Yan, and K. C.-C. Chang. Supporting entity search: a large-scale prototype search engine. In *Proceedings of SIGMOD '07*, pages 1144–1146, 2007.

[11] W. Dakka and P. G. Ipeirotis. Automatic extraction of useful facet hierarchies from text databases. In *Proceedings of ICDE '08*, pages 466–475, 2008.

[12] M. Damova and I. Koychev. Query-based summarization: A survey. In *S3T'10*, 2010.

[13] D. Dash, J. Rao, N. Megiddo, A. Ailamaki, and G. Lohman. Dynamic faceted search for discovery-driven analysis. In *CIKM '08*, 2008.

[14] M. Diao, S. Mukherjea, N. Rajput, and K. Srivastava. Faceted search and browsing of audio content on spoken web. In *Proceedings of CIKM '10*, 2010.

[15] O. Etzioni, M. Cafarella, D. Downey, S. Kok, A.-M. Popescu, T. Shaked, S. Soderland, D. S. Weld, and A. Yates. Web-scale information extraction in knowitall: (preliminary results). In *Proceedings of WWW '04*, pages 100–110, 2004.

[16] S. Gholamrezazadeh, M. A. Salehi, and B. Gholamzadeh. A comprehensive survey on text summarization systems. In *Proceedings of CSA '09*, pages 1–6, 2009.

[17] A. Herdagdelen, M. Ciaramita, D. Mahler, M. Holmqvist, K. Hall, S. Riezler, and E. Alfonseca. Generalized syntactic and semantic models of query reformulation. In *Proceeding of SIGIR'10*, 2010.

[18] L. J. Heyer, S. Kruglyak, and S. Yooseph. Exploring Expression Data: Identification and Analysis of Coexpressed Genes. *Genome Research*, 9(11):1106–1115, November 1999.

[19] W. H. Inmon. *Building the Data Warehouse,3rd Edition*. John Wiley & Sons, Inc., 3rd edition, 2002.

[20] Z. Kozareva, E. Riloff, and E. H. Hovy. Semantic class learning from the web with hyponym pattern linkage graphs. In *Proceedings of ACL'08*, 2008.

[21] B. Y.-L. Kuo, T. Hentrich, B. M. . Good, and M. D. Wilkinson. Tag clouds for summarizing web search results. In *Proceedings of WWW '07*, 2007.

[22] K. Latha, K. R. Veni, and R. Rajaram. Afgf: An automatic facet generation framework for document retrieval. In *Proceedings of ACE '10*, 2010.

[23] C. Li, N. Yan, S. B. Roy, L. Lisham, and G. Das. Facetedpedia: dynamic generation of query-dependent faceted interfaces for wikipedia. In *Proceedings of WWW '10*, pages 651–660. ACM, 2010.

[24] C. D. Manning, P. Raghavan, and H. Schtze. *Introduction to Information Retrieval*. Cambridge University Press, 2008.

[25] M. Mitra, A. Singhal, and C. Buckley. Improving automatic query expansion. In *Proceedings of SIGIR '98*, pages 206–214, 1998.

[26] V. Nastase and M. Strube. Decoding wikipedia categories for knowledge acquisition. In *Proceedings of AAAI '08*, pages 1219–1224, 2008.

[27] D. R. Radev, H. Jing, M. Stys, and D. Tam. Centroid-based summarization of multiple documents. *Information Processing and Management*, 40(6):919 – 938, 2004.

[28] S. Riezler, Y. Liu, and A. Vasserman. Translating queries into snippets for improved query expansion. In *Proceedings of COLING '98*, pages 737–744, 2008.

[29] S. Shi, H. Zhang, X. Yuan, and J.-R. Wen. Corpus-based semantic class mining: distributional vs. pattern-based approaches. In *Proceedings of COLING '10*, pages 993–1001, 2010.

[30] K. Shinzato and T. Kentaro. A simple www-based method for semantic word class acquisition. In *RANLP '05*, 2005.

[31] E. Stoica and M. A. Hearst. Automating creation of hierarchical faceted metadata structures. In *NAACL HLT '07*, 2007.

[32] R. C. Wang and W. W. Cohen. Iterative set expansion of named entities using the web. In *Proceedings of ICDM '08*, pages 1091–1096, 2008.

[33] R. W. White, M. Bilenko, and S. Cucerzan. Studying the use of popular destinations to enhance web search interaction. In *Proceedings of SIGIR '07*, 2007.

[34] J. Xu and W. B. Croft. Query expansion using local and global document analysis. In *Proceedings of SIGIR '96*, pages 4–11, 1996.

[35] H. Zhang, M. Zhu, S. Shi, and J.-R. Wen. Employing topic models for pattern-based semantic class discovery. In *Proceedings of ACL-IJCNLP '09*, 2009.

[36] Z. Zhang and O. Nasraoui. Mining search engine query logs for query recommendation. In *Proceedings of WWW '06*, pages 1039–1040, 2006.

Large-Scale Question Classification in cQA by Leveraging Wikipedia Semantic Knowledge

Li Cai, Guangyou Zhou, Kang Liu, and Jun Zhao
National Laboratory of Pattern Recognition,
Institute of Automation, Chinese Academy of Sciences
95 Zhongguancun East Road, Beijing 100190, China
{lcai, gyzhou, kliu, jzhao}@nlpr.ia.ac.cn

ABSTRACT

With the flourishing of community-based question answering (cQA) services like Yahoo! Answers, more and more web users seek their information need from these sites. Understanding user's information need expressed through their search questions is crucial to information providers. Question classification in cQA is studied for this purpose. However, there are two main difficulties in applying traditional methods (question classification in TREC QA and text classification) to cQA: (1) Traditional methods confine themselves to classify a text or question into two or a few predefined categories. While in cQA, the number of categories is much larger, such as Yahoo! Answers, there contains 1,263 categories. Our empirical results show that with the increasing of the number of categories to moderate size, the performance of the classification accuracy dramatically decreases. (2) Unlike the normal texts, questions in cQA are very short, which cannot provide sufficient word co-occurrence or shared information for a good similarity measure due to the data sparseness.

In this paper, we propose a two-stage approach for question classification in cQA that can tackle the difficulties of the traditional methods. In the first stage, we preform a search process to prune the large-scale categories to focus our classification effort on a small subset. In the second stage, we enrich questions by leveraging Wikipedia semantic knowledge to tackle the data sparseness. As a result, the classification model is trained on the enriched small subset. We demonstrate the performance of our proposed method on Yahoo! Answers with 1,263 categories. The experimental results show that our proposed method significantly outperforms the baseline method (with error reductions of 23.21%).

Categories and Subject Descriptors

H.3.3 [**Information Systems**]: Information Storage and Retrieval

General Terms

Algorithms, Experimentation, Performance

CIKM'11, October 24–28, 2011, Glasgow, Scotland, UK.

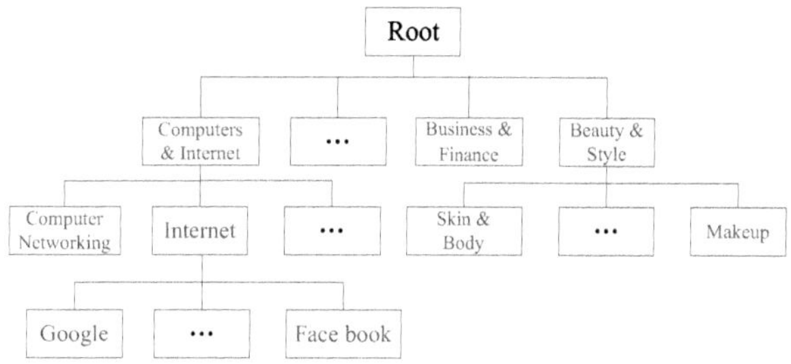

Figure 1: An example of Yahoo! Answers taxonomy.

Keywords

Question Retrieval, translation model, Wikipedia, Large-Scale Classification

1. INTRODUCTION

Community-based Question Answering (cQA) service is a particular form of online service for leveraging user-generated content, such as Yahoo! Answers [1] and Live QnA [2], which has attracted great attention from both academia and industry. Recently, efforts have been put to search similar questions [4, 22, 27] and recommend questions [3] in cQA. As a result, understanding the search and recommendation intent behind the questions issued by askers has become an important research problem. *Question Classification* (or *Question categorization*) is studied for this purpose by classifying user queried questions into a predefined target categories. Such category information can be used to help find the relevant questions in cQA archives [2]. An example of Yahoo! Answers taxonomy is shown in Figure 1. Unlike the traditional large-scale text taxonomy (e.g., Open Directory Project (ODP) and Yahoo! Directory), question classification in cQA is the task of classifying user queried questions into **predefined target categories at the leaf level**.[3]

Question classification in cQA is dramatically different from traditional text classification and factoid question classification from TREC QA. Directly applying these methods for question classification in cQA may lead to the following difficulties:

- Traditional methods confine themselves to classify a text [19]

[1]http://answers.yahoo.com/

[2]http://qna.live.com/

[3]Classifying a questions into the top level (e.g., Computer & Internet) is too coarse to contain a category like "Face book" (it is in "Computer & Internet\Internet") whose subtopics might be of interest to many users. These suggest the necessity of automatic fine-grained question classification in cQA.

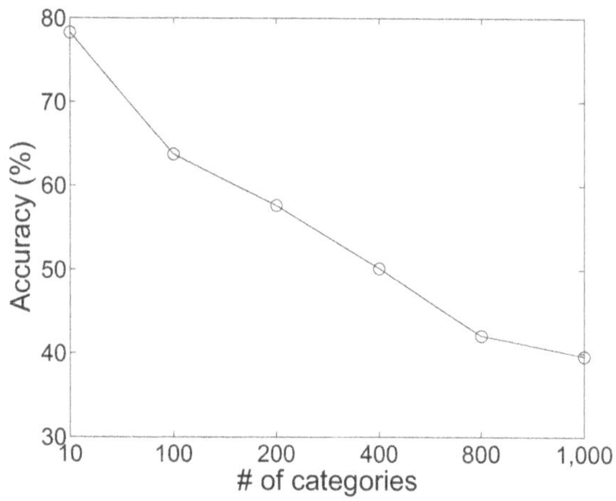

Figure 2: Number of categories vs. classification accuracy on validation data.

(benchmark collections, e.g., 20Newsgroups) or question [28] (e.g., TREC QA) into two or a few predefined categories. While in cQA, the number of categories is much larger than that in benchmark collections and TREC QA. For example in Yahoo! Answers, there contains 1,263 categories at the leaf level. Our empirical results show that with the increasing of the number of categories to a moderate size, the performance of the classification accuracy dramatically decreases. Figure 2 shows the classification accuracy vs. different number of categories on validation data using traditional methods.[4]

- Unlike the normal texts or documents, questions in cQA are usually much shorter, that is, they consist of only a few words for most questions. Because of the short lengths, they do not provide enough word co-occurrence or shared context for a good similarity measure. Therefore, traditional "bag of words" models usually fail to achieve satisfactory classification accuracy due to the data sparseness.

To address the above challenges, we propose a novel method that overcomes those difficulties and consequently improve the performance of question classification in cQA. As a first attempt to tackle the problem of large-scale category classification and data sparseness in cQA, we intend to answer the following questions: (1) For a given question, how to prune the large-scale categories into a much smaller subset of target category candidates? Therefore, we can build a local classification model on the small training data to optimize the performance for the target category candidates. (2) How to enrich questions by leveraging Wikipedia semantic knowledge in order to reduce the data sparseness? (3) How much improvement can we achieve using our proposed method? (4) Would our proposed method add too much computational burden and would it be possible to extend the idea for real world online services?

More specifically, our contributions are as follows.

- *To tackle the large-scale category classification problem*: We attempt to find a subset of categories related to a given question from the large-scale categories . Thus, the large-scale categories are pruned into a much smaller subset of target category candidates. It is intuitive that the classification performance on a smaller subset of target categories will be better than that on a larger set of categories, as shown in the experiments. For easy description, we call the above strategy as **search stage** in the rest of the paper (in Section 4).
- *To reduce the data sparseness*: We enrich questions by leveraging Wikipedia semantic knowledge due to the large coverage of concepts, rich semantic information and up-to-date content. However, Wikipedia is not a structural thesaurus like WordNet [12]. In this paper, we first build a *concept thesaurus* based on the semantic knowledge (synonym, hypernym, and associative concepts) extracted from Wikipedia. Then, we add the concepts into the questions for classification. For easy description, we call this strategy as **enrichment-based classification stage** in the rest of the paper (in Section 5).
- *To validate our proposed method*: We conduct experiments on Yahoo! Answers with 1,263 categories. Experimental results show that pruning the large-scale categories into a much smaller subset of target categories in the search stage can significantly improve the classification accuracy (i.e., eliminating more than 14.47% of errors) (see subsection 6.3.1). Moreover, enriching questions with Wikipedia concepts can further improve the accuracy (i.e., eliminating more than 12.31% of errors) (see subsection 6.3.2). Overall, training the classification model on the entire training data, the accuracy of our proposed method can achieve 52.20% on the test data, which is 23.21% error reductions over the baseline (see subsection 6.3.1). We also demonstrate that our proposed method does not add too much computational burden and it would be possible to extend for real world online services (see subsection 6.5).

The rest of this paper is organized as follows. In Section 2, we give a brief overview of related work. Section 3 presents our general framework. Section 4 describes the search stage to prune the large-scale target categories into a much smaller subset of target category candidates. Section 5 describes the enrichment-based classification stage with Wikipedia semantic knowledge. Experimental results are presented in Section 6. Finally, we conclude with ideas for future work.

2. RELATED WORK

Question classification in TREC QA has been intensively studied during the past decade. Many researchers have employed machine learning methods (e.g., maximum entropy and support vector machine) by using different features, such as syntactic features [28, 16] and semantic features [15]. However, these methods mainly focused on factoid questions and confined themselves to classify a question into two or a few predefined categories (e.g., "what", "how", "why", "when", "where" and so on). However, question classification in cQA is dramatically different from factoid question classification, as discussed in Section 1. Therefore, traditional methods may fail to achieve the satisfactory results.

Recently, Xue et al. [26] proposed a two-stage approach for large-scale text classification. In the search stage, a category-search algorithm is used to obtain category candidates for each document. Then in the classification stage, the classification model is trained on the small subset of the original taxonomy. Our approach stems from a similar motivation; however, we target the question classification in cQA. There are mainly two differences between our proposed methods and Xue et al. [26]. First, Xue et al. [26] obtain more training data by leveraging the structure information of ODP.

[4]The experiment is trained on the training data (2,000k questions) using traditional "bag of words" model (maximum entropy classifier) and tested on the validation data (10,000 questions)

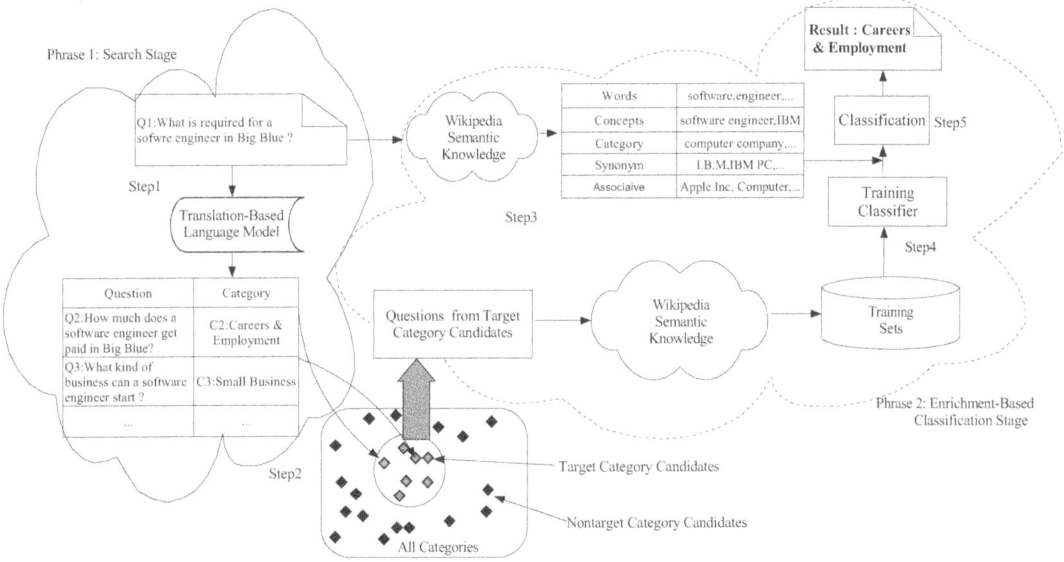

Figure 3: The general framework of our proposed approach.

In contrast, the taxonomy of Yahoo! Answers is not as deep as ODP, it is very difficult for us to utilize the structure information to collect more training data. Second, compared to the normal texts or documents in ODP, questions in cQA are very short, which leads to data sparseness. Therefore, data sparseness poses a great challenge in cQA.

To tackle the data sparseness, a variety of methods have been proposed in the literature. In general, these approaches can be divided into two categories. The first category is the basic representation of texts by exploiting phrases in the original texts from different aspects to preserve the contextual information [10, 20]. However, NLP technologies, such as parsing, are not employed as it is time assuming to apply such techniques to analyze the structure of the normal texts in detail. As a result, the methods fail to perform deep understanding of the original text.

The second category is to reduce the data sparseness by using the background knowledge. Hotho et al. [6] adopted various strategies to enrich text representation with synonyms and hypernyms from WordNet [12]. However, WordNet has limited coverage. Gabrilovich et al. [5] proposed a method to enrich documents with new features which are the concepts (Wikipedia titles) represented by the relevant Wikipedia articles. However, they do not make full use of the rich relations in Wikipedia such as hypernyms, synonyms and associated terms. Wang et al. [24] proposed to extract enrichment relations from Wikipedia and utilize the extracted relations to improve text classification. However, they treat the hypernyms and associative concepts equal with words in document.

3. THE GENERAL FRAMEWORK

In this section, we present the proposed framework for question classification in cQA. Our method works as follows. For a given question, the entire categories can be divided into two kinds: target category candidates and nontarget category candidates. For large-scale categories, the number of target category candidates for a question is much less than that of nontarget category candidates. Traditional classification methods only focus on building a global classification model to optimize the performance for all categories despite the fact that most of the categories may not be related to a given question. Our proposed approach can utilize such a property and thus focus on the categories related to the question. To this end, we extract a small subset of target category candidates from the large-scale categories by retrieving the semantically similar questions in the entire training data.

Then, we perform classification of the given question on these extracted small subset. However, unlike the normal texts or documents, questions in cQA are usually much shorter, that is, they consist of only a few words for most questions. Because of the short lengths, they do not provide enough word co-occurrence or shared context for a good similarity measure. Therefore, traditional "bag of words" model may fail to achieve satisfactory results due to the data sparseness. To reduce the data sparseness, we propose a novel method to enrich questions by leveraging Wikipedia semantic knowledge.

In order to illustrate the above ideas clearly, we give an example shown in Figure 3.

Step 1: Give question Q_1, we employ the state-of-the-art question retrieval model to get a list of semantically similar questions using, such as Q_2, Q_3, $\cdots$;

Step 2: The top-N most semantically similar questions are selected as related questions. Then we rank the target category candidates by counting the corresponding categories of these questions. The ranking is decided by the count of the categories. Finally, we can get a list of ranked target category candidates. Compared to the entire categories, this narrowing procedure helps reduce the number of target category candidates. In Figure 3, the target category candidates for question Q_1 are "Careers & Employment", "Small Business", "Software", $\cdots$;

Step 3: We enrich questions by leveraging Wikipedia semantic knowledge. Traditional "bag of words" representation is "software", "engineer", "big", "blue", $\cdots$. After mapping the given question into Wikipedia concept sets, Wikipedia concepts such as "IBM", "software engineer" can be identified from question Q_1. Moreover, semantic relations (synonym, hypernym, and associative relation) in Wikipedia are also used to expand the identified concepts (e.g., "software engineer", "IBM", "computer company", $\cdots$).

Step 4: We add the Wikipedia concepts into questions and build a local classification model for each given question.

Step 5: We add the Wikipedia concepts into the given question and classify the question using the trained local classification model.

4. SEARCH STAGE: RETRIEVAL THE TARGET CATEGORY CANDIDATES

In the search stage, we extract a small subset of target category candidates using the state-of-the-art question retrieval models.

For question retrieval, both translation-based language model (TRLM) [27] and syntactic tree matching (STM) [22] have gained state-of-the-art performance, while Ming et al. [14] compared the two methods and demonstrated that TRLM worked better than STM on the Yahoo! Answers data set. Therefore, we employ TRLM as state-of-the-art retrieval model to search the related questions.

4.1 Translation-Based Language Model

Translation-based language model (TRLM) is originally proposed to solve the lexical gap problem in question retrieval. The monolingual translation probabilities capture the lexical semantic relatedness between mismatched terms in the queried question and the historical questions in the training data. We employ TRLM to measure the semantic similarity between two questions q_1 and q_2. The similarity score function is similar to the retrieval function proposed by Xue et al. [27]:

$$P_{TRLM}(q_1|q_2) = \prod_{w \in q_1} P(w|q_2) \tag{1}$$

$$P(w|q_2)) = (1-\lambda)P_{mx}(w|q_2) + \lambda P_{ml}(w|Q) \tag{2}$$

$$P_{mx}(w|q_2) = \alpha \sum_{t \in q_2} P_{tr}(w|t)P_{ml}(t|q_2) + (1-\alpha)P_{ml}(w|q_2) \tag{3}$$

where $P(w|q_2)$, the probability that w is generated from question q_2 and smoothed using $P_{ml}(w|Q)$. $P_{ml}(w|Q)$, the prior probability that w is generated from the question collection Q. λ is the smoothing parameter. $P_{mx}(w|q_2)$ is the interpolated probabilities of $P_{ml}(w|q_2)$ and the sum of the probabilities $P_{tr}(w|t)$, weighted by $P_{ml}(t|q_2)$. P_{ml} is computed using the maximum likelihood estimator. $P(w|t)$ is the translation probability from word t to word w.

However, $P_{TRLM}(q_1|q_2)$ cannot well capture the semantic similarity between two questions q_1 and q_2 because the monolingual translation in cQA is not as strong as in the bilingual translation of SMT. We thus define a more effective method by taking the average of the two scores that switch the role of q_1 and q_2:

$$Score(q_1, q_2) = \frac{1}{2}(P_{TRLM}(q_1|q_2) + P_{TRLM}(q_2|q_1)) \tag{4}$$

We rank the semantically similar questions based on the score of $Score(q_1, q_2)$. For a given question, top-N most similar questions are selected as related questions. Then we rank the target category candidates by counting the corresponding categories of these questions. The ranking is decided by the count of the category. Finally, we can get a list of ranked target category candidates.

4.2 Learning Word Translation Probabilities

The performance of the TRLM will rely on the quality of the word-to-word translation probabilities. We follow the approach of Xue et al. [27] to the learn the word translation probabilities. In our experiments, question-answer pairs are used for training, and the GIZA++[5] toolkit is used to learn the IBM translation model 1. The training process can be accomplished through either as the source and the other as the target.

We employ $P(a|q)$ to denote the word-to-word translation probabilities with question q as the source and answer a as the target, and $P(q|a)$ denotes the opposite configuration. A simple method is to linearly combine the two translation probabilities for a source word and a target word as the final translation probability. Xue et al. [27] find that a better method is to combine the question-answer pairs used for training $P(a|q)$ with the answer-question pairs used for training $P(q|a)$, and to then use this combined set of pairs for learning the word-to-word translation probabilities.

[5]http://code.google.com/p/giza-pp/

5. ENRICHMENT-BASED CLASSIFICATION STAGE: ENRICHING QUESTIONS WITH WIKIPEDIA SEMANTIC KNOWLEDGE

In the search stage, we reduce the large-scale categories into a much smaller subset of target category candidates. In this Section, we propose a novel method to enrich questions using Wikipedia semantic knowledge to alleviate the data sparseness.

5.1 Wikipedia Thesaurus

Wikipedia is today the largest encyclopedia in the world and surpasses other knowledge bases in its coverage of concepts, rich semantic knowledge and up-to-date content. Recently, Wikipedia has gained a wide interest in IR community and has been used for many problems ranging from document classification [5, 23, 24] to text clustering [7, 8, 9]. Each article in Wikipedia describes a single topic: its title is a succinct, well-formed phrase that resembles a term in a conventional thesaurus [13]. Each article belongs to at least one category, and hyperlinks between articles capture their semantic relations as defined in international standard for thesauri [6]. These semantic relations include: equivalence (synonym), hierarchical relations (hypernym) and associative relation. However, Wikipedia is an open data resource built for human use, so it inevitable includes much noise and the semantic knowledge within it is not suitable for direct use in question classification in cQA. To make it clean and easy-to-use as a thesaurus, we first preprocess the Wikipedia data to collect Wikipedia concepts, and then explicitly derive relationships between Wikipedia based on the structural knowledge of Wikipedia.

5.1.1 Wikipeida Concept

Each article of Wikipedia describes a single topic and its title can be used to represent the concept, e.g., "United States". However, some articles are meaningless – it is only used for Wikipedia management and administration, such as "1980s", "List of newspapers", etc. Following the literature [7], we filter Wikipedia titles according to the rules describing below (titles satisfy one of below will be filtered):

- The article belongs to categories related to chronology, e.g., "Years", "Decades" and "Centuries".
- The first letter is not a capital one.
- The title is a single stopword.

5.1.2 Semantic Relations in Wikipedia

Wikipedia contains rich relation structures, such as synonym (redirect link pages), polysemy (disambiguation page), hypernym (hierarchical relation) and associative relation (internal page link). All these semantic relations express in the form of hyperlinks between Wikipedia articles [13].

Synonym:

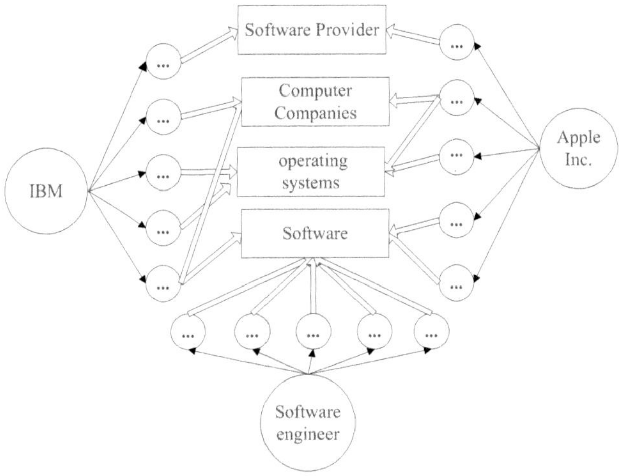

Figure 4: Out-link categories of the concepts "IBM", "Apple Inc." and "Software engineer".

Wikipedia contains only one article for any given concept by using redirect hyperlinks to group equivalent concepts to the preferred one. These redirect links cope with capitalization and spelling variations, abbreviations, synonyms, and colloquialisms. Synonym in Wikipedia mainly comes from these redirect links. For example, "IBM" is an entry with a large number of redirect pages: synonyms (I.B.M, Big blue, IBM Corporation). In addition, Wikipedia articles often mention other concepts, which already have corresponding articles in Wikipedia. The anchor text on each hyperlink may be different with the title of the linked article. Thus, anchor texts can be used as another source of synonym.

Polysemy:

In Wikipedia, disambiguation pages are provided for a polysemous concept. A disambiguation page lists all possible meanings associated with the corresponding concept, where each meaning is discussed in an article. For example, the disambiguation page of the term "IBM" lists 3 associated concepts, including "Inclusion body myositis", "Injection blow molding", and "International Business Machine".

Hypernym:

In Wikipedia, both articles (concepts) and categories belong to at least one category, and categories are nested in a hierarchical organization. The resulting hierarchy is a directed acyclic graph, in which multiple categorization schemes co-exist simultaneously [13]. To extract the real hierarchical relations from Wikipedia categories, we utilize the methods proposed in [18] to derive generic hierarchical relation from category links. Thus, we can get hypernym for each Wikipedia concept.

Associative Relation:

Each Wikipedia article contains a lot of hyperlinks, which express relatedness between them. As Milne et al. [13] mentioned that, links between articles are only tenuously related. For example, comparing the following two links: one from the article "IBM" to the article "Apple Inc.", the other from the article "IBM" to the article "Software engineer". It is clear that the former two articles are more related than the later pair. So how to measure the relatedness of hyperlinks within articles in Wikipedia is an important issue. In this paper, three measures have been introduced [24]: *Content-based*, *Out-link category-based* and *Distance-based*.

Content-based measure is based on the "bag-of-words" representation of Wikipedia articles. Clearly, this measure (denoted as S_{BOW}) has the same limitations of the "bag-of-words" approach since it only considers the words appeared in text documents.

Out-link category-based measure compares the out-link categories of two associative articles. The out-link category of a given article are the categories to which out-link articles from the original one belong. Figure 4 (a fraction of) the out-link categories of the associative concepts "IBM", "Apple Inc", and "Software engineer". The concepts "IBM" and "Apple Inc." share 37 out-link categories; "IBM" and "Software engineer" share 14 out-link categories; "Apple Inc." and "Software engineer" share 12 out-link categories. The larger the number of shared categories, the stronger the associative relation between the articles. To capture the similarity, articles are represented as vectors of out-link categories, where each component corresponds to a category, and the value of the ith component is the number of out-link articles which belong to the ith category. The cosine similarity is then computed between the resulting vectors and denoted as S_{OLC}. The computation of S_{OLC} for the concepts illustrated in Figure 4 gives the following values, which indeed reflect the actual semantic of the corresponding terms: $S_{OLC}(\textit{IBM, Apple Inc.}) = 0.517$, $S_{OLC}(\textit{IBM, Software engineer}) = 0.236$, $S_{OLC}(\textit{Apple Inc., Software engineer}) = 0.185$.

Distance-based measure captures the length of the shortest path connecting the two categories they belong to, in the acyclic graph of the category taxonomy. This measure is normalized by taking into account the depth of the taxonomy and denoted as D_{cat}.

Following [23], the overall strength of an associative relation between concepts can be written as:

$$S_{overall} = \lambda_1 S_{BOW} + \lambda_2 S_{OLC} + (1 - \lambda_1 - \lambda_2)(1 - D_{cat}) \quad (5)$$

where λ_1 and λ_2 reflect the relative importance of the individual measure. Using equation (5), we rank all the out-linked concepts for each given concept. Then we denote the out-link concepts with relatedness above certain threshold as associative ones for each given concept.

5.2 Mapping Questions into Wikipedia Concept Sets

To use the Wikipedia thesaurus to enrich questions, one of the key issues is how to map words in questions to Wikipedia concepts. Considering frequently occurred synonym, polysemy and hypernym in questions, accurate allocation of words in Wikipedia is really critical in the whole classification process.

Following Hu et al. [7], we build a phrase index which includes the phrases of Wikipedia concepts, their synonym, and polysemy in Wikipedia thesaurus. Based on the generated Wikipedia phrases index, all candidate phrases can be recognized in the web page. We use the Forward Maximum Matching algorithm [25] to search candidate phrases, which is a dictionary-based word segmentation approach. By performing this process, it is necessary to do word sense disambiguation to find its most proper meaning mentioned in questions if a candidate concept is a polysemous one. Wang et al. [24] proposed a disambiguation method based on document similarity and context information, and the implemented method show high disambiguation accuracy. We adopt Wang et al. [24]'s method to do word sense disambiguation for the polysemous concepts in the question.

Figure 5 shows an example of the identified Wikipedia concepts for question Q_1 using the above method. The phrase "software engineer" in Q_1 is mapped into Wikipedia concept "Software engineer", "Big Blue" in Q_1 is mapped into Wikipedia concept "IBM".

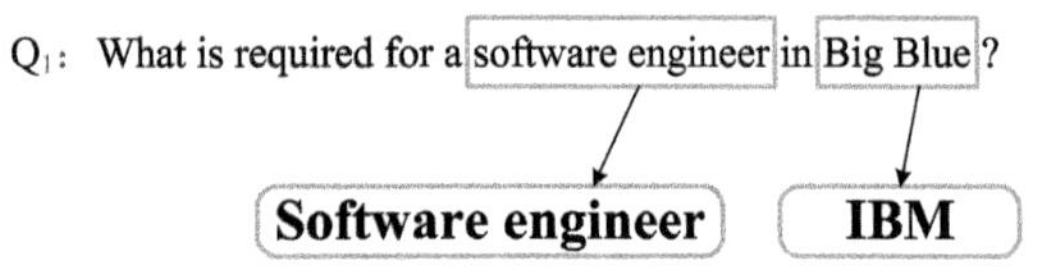

Figure 5: An example of the identified Wikipedia concepts for question Q_1.

5.3 Enriching Questions with Hypernyms

In Wikipedia, each concept belongs to one or more categories. Moreover, these categories are further belongs to more higher level categories, forming an acyclic category graph. The set of categories contained in the category graph of a given concept c is represented as $Cate(c) = \{cate_{c_1}, \cdots, cate_{c_m}\}$. In the category graph, a category may have several paths link to a concept. We calculate the distance $dis(c, cate_i)$ by the length of the shortest path from the concept c to the category $cate_i$.

As noted by Hu et al. [7], the higher level categories have less influence than those lower level categories since the lower level categories are more specific and therefore can depict the articles more accurate. In this paper, we present the influence of categories of γth layer on concept c as $Inf_\gamma(c)$ and define $lnf_1(c) = 1$. For higher levels of categories, we introduce a decay factor $\mu \in [0, 1]$. Thus, we have $lnf_\gamma(c) = \mu lnf_{\gamma-1}(c) = \mu^{\gamma-1} lnf_1(c)$. As each Wikipedia concept has more than one categories, and each category has more than one parent categories, a big γ will introduce too many categories. Therefore, we set $\gamma \leq 3$ in our experiments. Thus, for each concept c we can build a category vector $\mathbf{cate}_c = \{lnf(c, cate_{c_1}), \cdots, lnf(c, cate_{c_m})\}$, where $lnf(c, cate_{c_1}) = lnf_{dis}(c, cate_{c_i}(c))$ which indicates the influence of category $cate_{c_i}$ on concept c. For the collection C which contains all the concepts in question q, the corresponding category vector can be represented as $\mathbf{Cate}_q = \bigcup_{c \in C} \mathbf{cate}_c$.

Figure 6 shows an example of the first three level hypernyms for Wikipedia concept "IBM". For example in level 1, Wikipedia concept "IBM" has parent categories {"Computer hardware companies", "Multinatinal companies", "Cloud computing vendors"}. Thus, for concept c ="IBM", we can build a category vector $\mathbf{cate}_{\text{IBM}}$ = { ("Computer hardware companies", 1), ("Multinatinal companies", 1), $\cdots$, ("Cloud computing vendors", 1), ("Computer companies", 0.5), ("International business", 0.5), $\cdots$, ("Cloud computing", 0.5), ("Technology companies", 0.25), ("International economics", 0.25), $\cdots$, ("Centralized computing", 0.25), $\cdots$ }. Here, we set $\mu = 0.5$, as we tune the parameter on validation data in the experiment. For concept collection C = {"Software engineer", "IBM"} in Q_1, the corresponding category vector is represented as $\mathbf{Cate}_{Q_1} = \mathbf{cate}_{\text{Software engineer}} \bigcup \mathbf{cate}_{\text{IBM}}$.

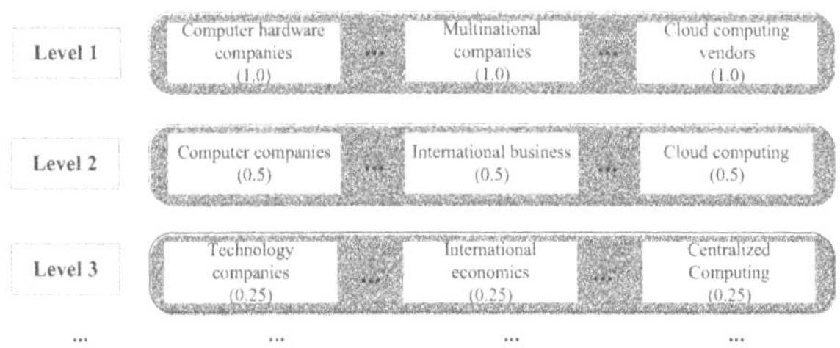

Figure 6: An example of the first three level hypernyms for Wikipedia concept "IBM".

5.4 Enriching Questions with Synonymies and Associative Concepts

To better relieve "bag of words" shortcomings, synonyms and associative concepts in Wikipedia can be used to include more related concepts to overcome the data sparseness. For each concept c in Wikipedia, a set of related concepts $\mathbf{rela}_c = \{(c_1, w(c_1, c)), (c_2, w(c_2, c)), \cdots, (c_k, w(c_k, c))\}$ are selected from its synonyms and associative concepts, in which c_k is the kth related concepts of c and $w(c_k, c)$ is the relatedness between c_k and c. The relatedness is defined as follows:

$$w(c_k, c) = \begin{cases} 1 & \text{if } c_k \text{ and } c \text{ are synonyms;} \\ S_{overall} & \text{if } c_k \text{ and } c \text{ are associative relations} \end{cases}$$

where $S_{overall}$ is defined by equation (5). For the collection C which contain all the concepts in question q, the corresponding synonym and associative vector can be represented as $\mathbf{SA}_q = \bigcup_{c \in C} \mathbf{rela}_c$.

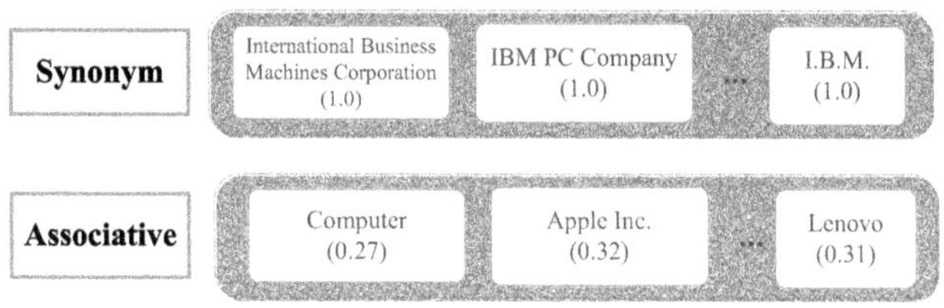

Figure 7: An example of the synonyms and associative concepts for Wikipedia concept "IBM".

Figure 7 gives an example of the synonyms and associative concepts for Wikipedia concept "IBM". For concept "IBM", a set of related concepts $\mathbf{rela}_{\text{IBM}}$ = {("International Business Machines Corporation", 1.0), ("IBM PC Company", 1.0), $\cdots$, ("I.B.M.", 1.0), ("Computer", 0.27), ("Apple Inc.", 0.32), $\cdots$, ("Lenovo", 0.31) }. For concept collection C = {"Software engineer", "IBM"} in Q_1, the corresponding synonym and associative vector can be represented as $\mathbf{SA}_q = \mathbf{rela}_{\text{Software engineer}} \bigcup \mathbf{rela}_{\text{IBM}}$.

5.5 Choosing Machine Learning Method

Many traditional classification methods, such as kNN, Naive Bayes, and more recent advanced models like maximum entropy (MaxEnt), SVMs can be used in our framework. Among them, we choose MaxEnt [1] because of the two main reasons [17]: (1) MaxEnt is robust and has been applied successfully to a wide range of NLP tasks, such as POS tagging, NER and parsing etc. It even performs better than SVMs and others in some special cases, such as classifying sparse data. (2) It is very fast in both training and testing. SVMs is also a good choice because it is powerful. However, the training and testing speed of SVMs are still a challenge to apply to almost real-time applications, especially for multi-classification problem. We train the MaxEnt classifier on the standard integrated data by using limited memory optimization (L-BFGS) [11]. As shown in recent studies, training using L-BFGS gives high performance in terms of speed and classification accuracy. For a given question q, we include the following feature vectors: "Words", "Hypernyms" $\mathbf{Cate}_q$, "Synonyms" and "Associative Concepts" $\mathbf{SA}_q$. An example of the feature vectors for question Q_1 in Figure 5 are shown in Table 1.

Table 1: An example of the feature vectors for question Q_1 in Figure 5.

Words	require(0.019), software(0.031), engineer(0.027), big(0.018), blue(0.022)
Hypernyms	Software engineering(1.0), Software engineers(1.0), Computer hardware companies(1.0), Cloud computing(0.5) International business(0.5), computer companies(0.5) Multinational companies(1.0), Technology companies(0.25) ...
Synonyms	International Business Machines Corporation(1.0), International Business Machines(1.0), IBM computer(1.0), IBM Corporation(1.0), I.B.M.(1.0), ...
Associative Concepts	Apple Inc.(0.32), IBM Personal Computer(0.60), Corporation(0.36), Computer science(0.47), software architecture(0.72), ...

6. EXPERIMENTS

6.1 Data Set

We collect questions from all categories at Yahoo! Answers. We use the *getByCategory* function in Yahoo! Answers API [6] to obtain QA threads from the Yahoo! site. The resulting question repository that we use for question classification contains 2,020,000 questions. Each question consists of three fields: "question", "description" and "answers". For question classification task, we use only the "question" field. There are 26 categories at the first level and 1, 262 categories at the leaf level. Each question belongs to a unique leaf category. Our task is to classify each question into a target leaf category. Table 2 shows the data distribution. Since the whole data set is too large, we select 10,000 questions as testing data. Furthermore, in order to tune the parameters, 10,000 additional questions are also selected as validation data, and the rest (2,000k) are selected as training data. Here, we select the test data and validation data in proportion to the number of questions and categories against the whole distribution to have a better control over a possible imbalance. Especially, the training and testing data are totally exclusive to make sure that the testing data are really difficult to classify. Before the experiments, we make some preprocessing: all the questions are converted into lower case. Each question is tokenized with a stop-word remover[7] and Porter stemming.[8] Besides, we also use one million question-answer pairs from another data set [9] for training the word translation probabilities. We perform a significant test, i.e., a t-test with a default significant level of 0.05 and measure the question classification performance by the accuracy values defined as follows:

$$Accuracy = \frac{\#\text{Correctly classified questions}}{\#\text{Total number of questions}} \quad (6)$$

6.2 Parameter Setting

The experiments use six parameters. The smoothing parameter λ in equation (2); α controls the self-translation impact in the translation-based language model in equation (3); the number of the category candidates returned in the search stage; λ_1 and λ_2 in equation (5); the decay factor μ; Following the literature, we set λ to 0.8 and α to 0.5 [14].

For the number of the category candidates returned in the search stage, we tune the parameter on the validation data and will show in the experiments. For decay factor μ, we perform an exhaustive grid search of step size 0.1 on [0, 1] to find the parameter on the validation data. To tune the parameters λ_1 and λ_2 in in equation (5), we conduct a method similar to Wang et al. [24]. First, we select 10 Wikipedia concepts randomly, and then extract all the out-linked concepts in the Wikipedia articles corresponding to the 10 concepts. To obtain the ground-truth, three annotators are asked to label all the linked concepts in the 10 articles to three levels (relevant:3, neutral:2, and not relevant:1). The annotating process is carried out independently among annotators. No one among the three annotators could access the annotating results of others. After annotating, each out-linked concept in the 10 articles is labeled with 3 relevance score, and we use the average value as the final value. For example, if one annotator labels two linked concepts as neutral and the other two label them as relevant, the the final score of the two linked concepts is 1.67 ($(1+2+2)/3$). Based on the labeled data, we can tune the parameters by performing an exhaustive grid search of step size 0.1 on [0, 1] to find the best results. As a result, we set $\lambda_1 = 0.4$ and $\lambda_2 = 0.5$ in the experiment.

Table 2: Number of questions in each first-level category

Category	#Size	Category	# Size
Arts & Humanities	86,744	Home & Garden	35,029
Business & Finance	86,846	Beauty & Style	37,350
Cars & Transportation	145,515	Pet	54,158
Education & Reference	80,782	Travel	205,283
Entertainment & Music	102,769	Health	132,716
Family & Relationships	34,743	Sports	214,317
Politics & Government	59,787	Social Science	46,415
Pregnancy & Parenting	43,103	Ding out	46,933
Science & Mathematics	89,856	Food & Drink	45,055
Computers & Internet	90,546	News & Events	20,300
Games & Recreation	53,458	Environment	11,276
Consumer Electronics	90,553	Local Businesses	51,551
Society & Culture	94,470	Yahoo! Products	150,445

6.3 Experimental Results

In this subsection, we conduct several experiments to demonstrate the effectiveness of our proposed method.

6.3.1 *The Effect of Search Stage*

To demonstrate the effect of search stage, we compare the following two methods:

- *BOW* (baseline): Traditional "bag of words" model with the binary weighting schema. The training process is performed on the entire training data.
- *Search_BOW*: In the search stage, top 8 categories are taken as target category candidates. The parameters are tuned on the validation data shown in subsection 6.4. Then we train the model on the much smaller training data using words as features.

Table 3 shows the experimental results. From the table, we can see that using the search stage can significantly improve the classification accuracy, that is, increasing from an accuracy of 37.75% of the baseline method (*BOW*) to 46.90% (*Search_BOW*) (i.e., eliminating more than 14.47% of error, row 1 vs. row 2). After performing a search stage, we can build a local model on the much smaller training data, thus optimizing the performance for the subset of target categories.

[6]http://developer.yahoo.com/answers/

[7]http://truereader.com/manuals/onix/stopwords1.html

[8]http://www.ling.gu.se/lager/mogul/porter-stemmer/index.html

[9]The Yahoo! Webscope dataset Yahoo answers comprehensive questions and answers version 1.0.2, available at http://reseach.yahoo.com/Academic_Relations.

Table 3: The effect of search stage

#	Methods	Accuracy (%)
1	*BOW*	37.75
2	*Search_BOW*	46.90

6.3.2 *The Effect of Enrichment-Based Classification Stage*

To demonstrate the effect of enrichment-based classification stage, we compare the following the methods:

- *Search_BOW*: This method is used as baseline, which has been discussed in subsection 6.3.1.
- *Search_BOW_HR*: We train the model on the much smaller training data using words and hypernym concepts as features.
- *Search_BOW_SA*: We train the model on the much smaller training data using words and synonyms and associative concepts as features.
- *Search_BOW_COB*: We train the model on the much smaller training data using words, hypernyms, synonyms and associative concepts as features.[10]

As described in Section 5, in order to reduce the data sparseness, we enrich questions with Wikipedia semantic knowledge. When enriching questions, we first identify the Wikipedia concepts in a question, and then enrich questions with new concepts introduced by the identified concepts. We have considered different strategies: adding hypernyms, adding synonyms and associative concepts. Here we demonstrate the effect of classification performance with questions of adding different kinds of concepts.

Table 4: The effect of adding hypernyms

#	Methods	Strategy	Accuracy (%)
1	*Search_BOW*	-	46.90
2	*Search_BOW_HR*	H_1	49.48
		H_2	48.64
		H_3	46.91
		H_4	45.83
		H_5	44.27

Table 4 demonstrates the performance of question representation with hypernyms. We first add the direct hypernyms (which are category names a candidate concept directly belongs to) for each identified concepts, and then hypernyms of both first and second level (which are parent category names of the direct category a identified concept belongs to), until hypernyms within 5 levels. In Table 4, "H_1" means adding direct hypernyms (first level) into questions; and "H_2" means adding hypernyms of both first and second level, so does for "H_3" to "H_4". Then we find that adding direct hypernyms achieves the best result on question classification, and adding more hypernyms of further levels even deteriorates the classification accuracy. The reason is that the higher level categories have less influence than the lower level categories since lower level categories are more specific and therefore can depict the articles more accurate.

[10]Following Hu et al. [9], document representation using Wikipedia alone does not perform well, so we do not provide the method in which the model only uses the Wikipedia concepts alone as features for comparison.

Table 5 shows the result of enriching questions with synonyms and associative concepts. In Table 5, "Synonyms" means adding synonyms into questions, "A_5" means adding 5 most associative concepts into questions, so does for "A_{10}" to "A_{20}". However, out of our expectation, adding synonyms fails to improve the classification accuracy. Since we cannot rank synonyms of a given mapped concepts, we just add all its synonyms into questions, which inevitably brings some noise into questions. We also find that adding 5 most associative concepts brings best performance, whereas adding more associative concepts even decreases the performance.

Table 5: The effect of adding synonyms and associative concepts

#	Methods	Strategy	Accuracy (%)
1	*Search_BOW*	-	46.90
2	*Search_BOW_SA*	Synonyms	43.88
		A_5	50.12
		A_{10}	49.91
		A_{15}	47.11
		A_{20}	46.35

Finally, we try to add both hypernyms and associative concepts together into questions and find that, when adding into questions direct hyponyms and 5 most associative concepts for each mapped concept, this strategy achieve a significant improvement (i.e., eliminating more than 9.98% of error, row 1 vs. row 2), as shown in Table 6.

Table 6: The effect of adding hypernyms and associative concepts

#	Methods	Strategy	Accuracy (%)
1	*Search_BOW*	-	46.90
2	*Search_BOW_COB*	H_1, A_5	52.20

Moreover, in order to demonstrate that question enrichment can effectively alleviate the data sparseness, we do another important experiment by training different classifiers on different sizes of training data ranging from 100k to 2,000k without using the search stage, and measure the accuracy on the test data. We make sure that the training and testing data are totally exclusive so that these data provide very limited context shared information. This makes the test data really difficult to be classified correctly if using traditional "bag of words" model. The results of this experiments are shown in Figure 8, where *BOW_COB* means adding direct hypernyms and 5 most associative concepts into questions without using the search stage, this method also built a global model on the entire training data. There are some clear trends in the result of Figure 8.

First, question enrichment with Wikipedia semantic knowledge can achieve an impressive improvement of accuracy, that is, increasing from an accuracy of 37.75% of the traditional "bag of words" method (*BOW*) to 45.41% (*BOW_COB*) (i.e., eliminating more than 12.31% of errors). This means that question enrichment can greatly reduce the data sparseness. Second, we can achieve a high accuracy even with a small amount of training data. When the sizes of training data changes from 100k to 2,000k, the accuracy with question enrichment changes slightly from 42.11% to 45.41%, while *BOW* accuracy increases nearly 7.33%, from 30.42% to 37.75%.

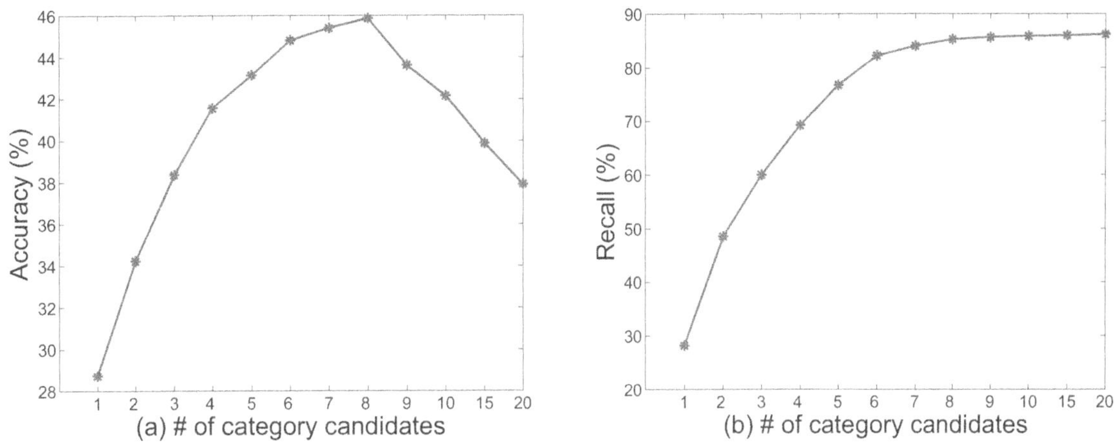

Figure 9: Classification performance and Recall on different number of category candidates on the leaf level.

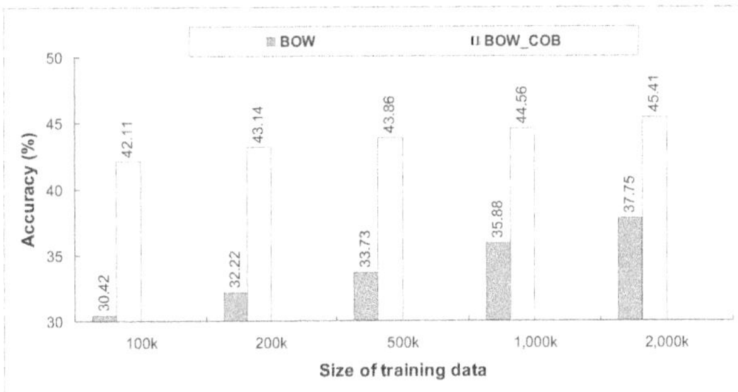

Figure 8: Classification accuracy on test data with different sizes of training data.

6.4 Category Candidate Number Selection

In the search stage, we use the state-of-the-art retrieval model TRLM to return different numbers of category candidates. we try to decide how many top ranked categories to be used to the category candidates are adequate. If we only choose one category, the two-stage method is reduced to the search stage only.

We perform the evaluation on the validation data. Our experimental result is presented in Figure 9. From Figure 9(a), we can see that too many categories also lead to involve in too many training data. As a result, large amount of training data may cause the data to be unbalanced and degrade the performance. From Figure 9(b), the more categories chosen by the search stage, the more likely we can find the correct target category. Here, the recall refers to the ratio of average correct target categories returned for each question using the search stage.

In summary, the performance increases significantly and obtain the best performance about 8 categories. Thus, the number of category candidates is set to 8 considering the trade-off between the recall and the performance. In this paper, we use the top 8 categories as the number of category candidates.

6.5 Running-Time Analysis

In this subsection, we analyze the time complexity of our approach. The learning translation-based language model (TRLM) and question indexing are conducted offline. The time complexity of online computation includes the following four steps: (1) use TRLM to retrieve the top-N most similar questions; (2) process the returned questions to get the category candidates; (3) train the classification model on the much smaller training data using words and Wikipeida concepts as features. (4) employ the classification model to classify the given question using words and Wikipeida concepts as features.

Table 7: Average running-time of each step for testing a given question (seconds)

Retrieval	training the model	classify a given question
0.105s	0.201s	0.017s

Table 7 shows the running-time of each step (averaged over the 10,000 questions in the testing data) on a PC with 8G of memory and a 2.5Ghz CPU of 8 core. We do not show the time for Step 2, since its running-time is negligable as compared to other steps. For example, when processing the returned questions to get the category candidates, the time for each question is about 10^{-5} seconds.

In summary, we observe that the average total time is 0.323 to process each given question. Therefore, the online time complexity is acceptable, and a question can be classified in real time (in the order of 10^{-1}), which indicate that our proposed method is practical and can be handle question classification in cQA efficiently.

7. CONCLUSIONS AND FUTURE WORK

In this paper, we propose a novel method to address the question classification in cQA by leveraging Wikipedia semantic knowledge. To tackle the large-scale category classification in cQA, we extract a small subset of target category candidates related to a given question by performing a search stage, thus the number of the target categories is reduced to a much smaller one. Then we enrich questions by leveraging Wikipedia semantic knowledge in the enrichment-based classification stage. Experimental results show that the classification accuracy of our proposed method significantly outperforms the traditional "bag of words" classification method on the entire large-scale categories (with error reductions of 23.12%).

As a first attempt to address the problem of large-scale category classification and data sparseness in cQA, there are several ways in which our approach might be improved: (1) A natural avenue for further research would be the development of more effective question retrieval methods (e.g., phrase-based translation model [29]) to improve the efficiency of the search stage. (2) We should try to meliorate the effect of adding synonyms by filtering "Redirect" links. After removing useless redirect links, such as spelling variations, adding synonyms into questions will not brings as much noise as before, and its effect could be better. (3) We will try to boost the question enrichment by leveraging YAGO [21] due to its high quality compared to Wikipedia.

8. ACKNOWLEDGMENTS

This work was supported by the National Natural Science Foundation of China (No. 60875041 and No. 61070106). We thank the anonymous reviewers for their insightful comments. We also thank Dr. Maoxi Li and Dr. Jiajun Zhang for suggestion to use the alignment toolkits, Dr. Xianpei Han for suggestion to use the Wikipedia Miner toolkit.

9. REFERENCES

[1] A. Berger, A. Pietra, and J. Pietra. A maximum entropy approach to natural language processing. *Computational Linguistics*, 22(1):39–71, 1996.

[2] X. Cao, G. Cong, B. Cui, and C. S. Jensen. A generalized framework of exploring category information for question retrieval in community question answer archives. In *WWW*, 2010.

[3] Y. Cao, H. Duan, C.-Y. Lin, Y. Yu, and H.-W. Hon. Recommending questions using the mdl-based tree cut model. In *WWW*, 2008.

[4] H. Duan, Y. Cao, C. Y. Lin, and Y. Yu. Searching questions by identifying questions topics and question focus. In *ACL*, pages 156–164, 2008.

[5] E. Gebrilovich and S. Markovitch. Overcoming the brittleness bottleneck using wikipedia: Enhancing text categorication with encyclopedia knowledge. In *IJCAI*, pages 1301–1306, 2006.

[6] A. Hotho, S. Staab, and G. Stumme. Wordnet improves text document clustering. In *SIGIR*, 2003.

[7] J. Hu, L. Fang, Y. Cao, H. Zeng, H. Li, Q. Yang, and Z. Chen. Enhancing text clustering by leveraging wikipedia semantics. In *SIGIR*, 2008.

[8] X. Hu, N. Sun, C. Zhang, and T.-S. Chua. Exploting internal and external semantics for the clustering of short texts using world knowledge. In *CIKM*, 2009.

[9] X. Hu, X. Zhang, C. Lu, E. K. Park, and X. Zhou. Exploiting wikipedia as external knowledge for document clustering. In *KDD*, 2009.

[10] G. Kumaran and J. Allan. Text classification and named entities for new event detection. In *SIGIR*, pages 297–304, 2004.

[11] D. Liu and J. Nocedal. On the limited memory bfgs method for large-scale optimization. *Mathematical Programming*, 45:503–528, 1989.

[12] G. Miller. Wordnet: a lexical database for english. *CACM*, 38:39–41, 1995.

[13] D. Milne, Q. Medelyan, and I. H. Witten. Mining domain-specific thesauri from wikipedia: a case study. In *IEEE/WIC/ACM WI*, 2006.

[14] Z.-Y. Ming, K. Wang, and T.-S. Chua. Prototype hierarchy based clustering for the categorization and navigation of web collection. In *SIGIR*, 2010.

[15] A. Moschitti, S. Quarteroni, R. Basili, and S. Manandhar. Exploiting syntactic and shallow semantic kernels for question/answer classification. In *ACL*, pages 776–783, 2007.

[16] T. Nguyen, L. Nguyen, and A. Shimazu. Using semi-supervised learning for question classification. *Journal of Natural Language Processing*, 15(1):3–21, 2008.

[17] X.-H. Phan, L.-M. Nguyen, and S. Horiguchi. Learning to classify short and sparse txt & web with hidden topics from large-scale data collections. In *WWW*, 2008.

[18] S. P. Ponzetto and M. Strube. Deriving a large scale taxonomy from wikipedia. In *AAAI*, 2007.

[19] F. Sebastiani. Machine learning in automated text categorization. *ACM Computing Surveys*, 34(1):1–47, 2002.

[20] D. Shen, J.-T. Sun, Q. Yang, and Z. Chen. Text classification improved through multigram models. In *CIKM*, 2006.

[21] F. M. Suchanek, G. Kasneci, and G. Weikum. Yago: A core semantic knowledge unifying wordnet and wikipedia. In *WWW*, 2007.

[22] K. Wang, Z. Ming, and T.-S. Chua. A syntactic tree matching approach to finding similar questions in community-based qa services. In *SIGIR*, 2009.

[23] P. Wang and C. Domeniconl. Building semantic kernels for text classification using wikipedia. In *KDD*, 2008.

[24] P. Wang, J. Hu, H.-J. Zeng, L. Chen, and Z. Chen. Improving text classification by using encyclopedia knowledge. In *ICDM*, pages 332–341, 2007.

[25] P. Wong and C. Chan. Chinese word segmentation based on maximum matching and word binding force. In *COLING*, 1996.

[26] G.-R. Xue, D. Xing, Q. Yang, and Y. Yu. Deep classification in large-scale text hierarchies. In *SIGIR*, 2008.

[27] X. Xue, J. Jeon, and W. B. Croft. Retrieval models for question and answer archives. In *SIGIR*, 2008.

[28] D. Zhang and W. S. Lee. Question classification using support vector machines. In *SIGIR*, 2003.

[29] G. Zhou, L. Cai, J. Zhao, and K. Liu. Phrase-based translation model for question retrieval in community question answer archives. In *ACL*, pages 653–662, 2011.

Hierarchical Tag Visualization and Application for Tag Recommendations

Yang Song
Microsoft Research
One Microsoft Way
Redmond, WA 98052, USA
yangsong@microsoft.com

Baojun Qiu
Computer Science & Engineering
Pennsylvania State University
University Park, PA 16802, USA
bqiu@cse.psu.edu

Umer Farooq
Microsoft Corp.
One Microsoft Way
Redmond, WA 98052, USA
umfarooq@microsoft.com

ABSTRACT

Social bookmarking sites typically visualize user-generated tags as tag clouds. While tag clouds effectively show the relative frequency and thus popularity of tags, they fail to convey two aspects to the users: (1) the similarity between tags, and (2) the abstractness of tags. We suggest an alternative to tag clouds known as tag hierarchies. Tag hierarchies are based on a minimum evolution-based greedy algorithm for tag hierarchy construction, which iteratively includes optimal tags into the tree that introduce minimum changes to the existing taxonomy. Our algorithm also uses a global tag ranking method to order tags according to their levels of abstractness as well as popularity such that more abstract tags will appear at higher levels in the taxonomy. Based on the tag hierarchy, we derive a new tag recommendation algorithm, which is a structure-based approach that does not require heavily trained models and thus is highly efficient. User studies and quantitative analysis suggest that (1) the tag hierarchy can potentially reduce the user's tagging time in comparison to tag clouds and other tag tree structures, and (2) the tag recommendation algorithm significantly outperforms existing content-based methods in quality.

Categories and Subject Descriptors

H.3.3 [**Information Storage and Retrieval**]: Information Search and Retrieval; I.5.3 [**Pattern Recognition**]: Clustering—*algorithms*

General Terms

Algorithms, Visualization, Experimentation

Keywords

hierarchical tag visualization, tag recommendation, minimum evolution criteria

1. INTRODUCTION

Social bookmarking systems, like Delicious[1] and Flickr[2], are one of the several systems that have been popularized by Web 2.0. Social bookmarking systems allow users to specify keywords or tags for web resources that are of interest to them, helping them to organize and share these resources with others in the community. The most prevalent way of displaying tags is using tag clouds, in which tags are organized in a two-dimensional array with (often) no particular order. Popular tags are typically expressed using larger font sizes or different colors.

While tag clouds offer a natural way of visually exploring the popularity of tags, it has failed to express two important information: (1) the similarity between different tags, and (2) the concept abstractness of different tags. Firstly, tag clouds cannot directly show how closely two tags are in its two-dimensional representation, which is quite important when users try to find relevant tags when performing tagging. Currently, most machine learning-based models for tag recommendations require a similarity measure of tags, e.g., tag co-occurrence or tag correlation [15, 8]. Since the representation of tag clouds can rarely help discovering tag similarities in this case, a lot of approaches have to resort to the content of the resources (e.g., the text of documents, the low-level features of images and so on) for learning models, which is known to be time-consuming [3, 13, 16].

Secondly, although some preliminary studies have tried to improve the tag clouds by clustering-based methods [9, 2], they are unable to observe the underlying concept abstractness of tags. For example, *programming* is a more abstract concept than *java*, which is in turn more abstract than *j2ee*. While more concrete tags give more specific descriptions of resources (e.g., j2ee based applications), more abstract tags provide a higher-level view of the underlying topics in the resources, which usually attract more interests from the general population. On the other hand, more abstract tags can also be (ambiguously) related to multiple topics. e.g., different users may use *tools* to annotate both resources about software or craftsman instruments. Consequently, simply clustering tags and displaying a 2-D array is not sufficient for abstract tags. As a result, it is important to understand the level of abstractness of tags, which can greatly help organizing and managing the user-expressed knowledge of a particular set of resources, as suggested by traditional approach of taxonomy learning. Since the unstructured representation of tag clouds is not capable of reflecting tag abstractness,

[1]http://delicious.com/
[2]http://www.flickr.com/

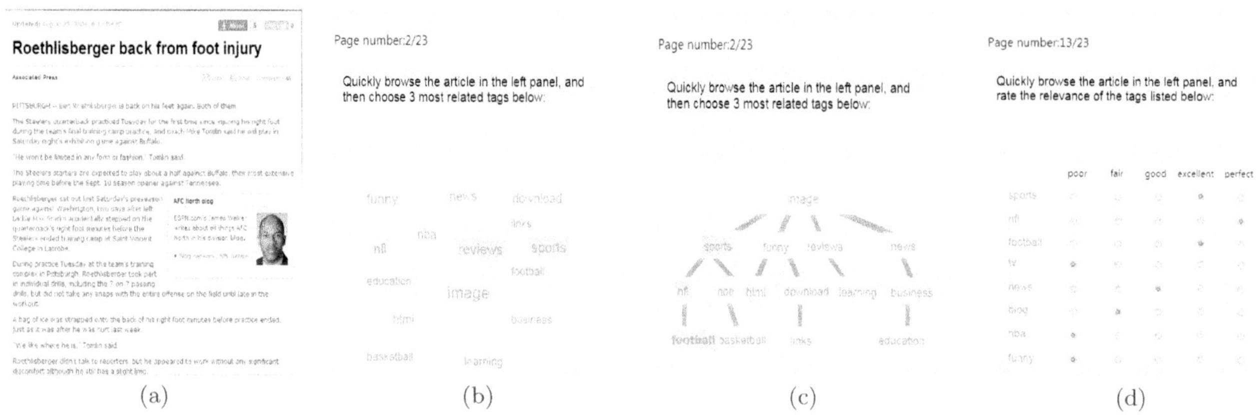

Figure 1: (a): A web page used in our user study. (b): Typical tag cloud expressed in current social bookmarking systems. (c): Tag tree based on a hierarchical tag representation using the minimum evolution criteria. (d): Judgers rates the tag relevancies. In (b) and (c), the highlighted tags are the most tagged ones.

having an alternative way of organizing and displaying tags is of imminent importance.

In this paper, we propose a novel framework to address both aforementioned issues in tag visualization. We suggest a hierarchical tag representation to visualize tags in a tree-structured taxonomy. In our representation, each node in the tree is a user-assigned tag, whose abstractness is controlled by its level in the tree. The edges in the tree reflect the closeness between tags, e.g., how often are they used to tag the same documents. We propose a principled way to construct the taxonomy by introducing the minimum evolution (ME) criteria from phylogenetics [6]. This structure offers a much richer knowledge representation than traditional tag clouds, thus can be potentially leveraged for many applications. As an extension to the tag hierarchy visualization, we derive an efficient tag recommendation algorithm using the tag taxonomy. The recommendation algorithm considers both the tag abstractness and the similarity between tag taxonomy and the resource content. Our algorithm is novel in the sense that it does not require training models that contain knowledge from previous seen documents.

Figure 1 illustrates one of the examples we tested during a user study. The same document is given to two sets of users with tag cloud and tag hierarchy respectively. Users are asked to find the most relevant tags as quickly as possible. It turned out that once the users have located *sports*, it only takes them 1.79 seconds to select *football* using tag hierarchy. While for tag cloud, users spend 3.56 seconds on average to locate the next tag. Besides being more efficient, tag hierarchy also results in more relevant tags being chosen, according to the user rating in terms of NDCG scores.

Specifically, this paper makes the following contributions:

• We propose an *unsupervised* approach to hierarchical tag visualization, which is a novel way to effectively exhibit both the similarity between tags, the level of abstractness and popularity for individual tags.

• We introduce two novel methods for ranking tags: information theoretic-based and learning-to-rank-based approaches, focusing on the popularity and the abstractness of tags respectively. We then combine the power of these two methods to assign global rankings to tags.

• We use a principled way to construct tree according to the minimum evolution (ME) criteria. Our greedy algorithm along with the minimum description length (MDL) guideline ensures that the tag hierarchy is calibrated to be balanced and well-organized into topics.

• We conducted a preliminary user study comparing tag clouds with tag trees. Results showed that the tagging time using tag trees was lesser than using tag clouds.

• Based on the hierarchical representation, we introduce a novel tag recommendation algorithm. Our algorithm is capable of matching a target document with one or more subtree of tags, then sorting the tags according to their correlations with the document. Comparing to previous approaches that require the content of the training documents for model learning, our framework does not involve any features from document contents, making it efficient and scalable.

It should be noted that although our proposal contains both tag visualization and recommendation, we put much more emphasis on the first part in this paper. Our biggest contribution is the visualization framework, while recommendation algorithm is a plus. Due to space limitations, we are unable to show all the details of our recommendation algorithm. Also, many other tag suggestion methods that we compare to during our study are not shown, so that we pick two most representative ones to present in this paper.

2. RELATED WORK

(ontology learning in folksonomies) Our work resembles that of ontology learning (OL) [4], where the objective is to construct a taxonomy of concepts as well as the relationship between them. Traditionally, OL is often studied in the context of natural language processing by annotating the concepts with labels, calculating the similarity between concepts via lexical and contextual similarities, and leveraging machine learning algorithms such as hierarchical clustering to construct a meaningful knowledge representation of concepts. Note that the labeling of terms in OL usually requires external resources. e.g., many of the existing approaches leveraged WordNet to collect hypernyms or synonyms for all terms in the documents [18]. Apparently, this guided approach is not suitable for tags since tags can be any arbitrary (novel) words which may not be found in WordNet or any other dictionaries. Comparatively, our work is a fully unsupervised approach that constructs the *tag ontology* by exploring the correlations between tags in an automatic fashion, without any human-labeling or external knowledge.

A similar tree-based tag hierarchy was studied in [5], where the authors used Jaccard coefficient to measure tag similarity and proposed a maximum spanning tree (MST) algorithm for tag hierarchy construction. While similar to our approach, the authors did not consider regularization which could cause the tree to be unbalanced.

(tag visualization) The most prevalent format of tag visualization is called *tag cloud* which represents tags in an ordered or random list. Popular tags are usually highlighted with larger font or unique colors. This representation is simply yet quite intuitive, allowing users to quickly discover popular topics they are interested in. This format is used by most popular web2.0 websites like Delicious and Flickr.

An alternative view of tags that aims at visualizing tag topics over time was proposed in [7]. It was used for Flickr photo-tag visualization by associating photos with the most user-tagged words. The application offers two different views of photo-tag pairs: list view and stream view.

Neither of the aforementioned two approaches considered the relationships between tags. A closer proposal to our approach was found in [9], where the authors proposed a two-dimensional layout for improving the display of tags. In their proposal, both tag popularity and tag correlations are considered so that similar tags can be displayed close to each other. However, the levels of abstractness of different tags are still missing in their representation.

The closest approach to ours so far is the greedy algorithm from Heymann [10]. The authors combined graph centrality theorem with tag similarity measurement to derive a greedy hierarchical method for visualization. While these two approaches seem identical, the underlying principle is quite different, as we shall discuss in Section 3.2.5.

(tag recommendations) Besides discovering more effective tag representations, extensive research attempts have been made recently on automatically recommending relevant tags based on the content of the resources (e.g., web pages, images, videos and so on) or the user interests.

Most of the existing tag recommendations methods are algorithmically equivalent to collaborative filtering techniques, where the goal is to first retrieve a set of similar documents from the corpus given a target document, then use the existing tags from these documents for recommendations [16, 8, 3, 11]. A list of successful tag recommendation methods have been posted on ECML/PKDD Discovery Challenge site[3]. The measurement of similarity between tags is usually the tag co-occurrence, i.e., the number of times tags were used to tag the same document. Other metrics of similarity include tag correlations, random-walk-based similarity and etc.

Overall, existing approaches of tag recommendation mainly aim at improving the relevance of recommended tags while ignoring the underlying structure of the tag taxonomy. This is mainly due to the heterogenous nature of tags where there is no principled way of modeling tag abstractness. In what follows, we propose our framework to address this issue.

3. OUR APPROACH

This section describes our framework of hierarchical tag visualization which consists of mainly two steps: (1) rank the tags across all documents, in which we combine the power of two ranking methods: information-theoretic based ranking and learning-to-rank based ranking, and (2) construct the tag tree iteratively given the ranked list of tags, where minimum evolution (ME) criteria is used to greedily add tags to the tree, with minimum description length (MDL) standard is control the optimal shape of the tree.

3.1 Global Tag Ranking

The first step of our approach is to rank tags according to their level of abstractness as well as popularity. e.g., "*programming*" has more abstract meaning than "*java*" thus should be ranked higher so that "*programming*" can appear at a higher level in the tree. In this paper, we leverage the following features for constructing global tag ranking:

- tag entropy $H(t)$: the entropy of a tag is defined as $H(t) = -\sum_1^N p(t_i)\log p(t_i)$, where the summation is over all N topics that the tag t belongs to, and $p(t_i)$ the probability that t appears in the ith topic. Tag entropy is a measurement of *specificity* where more general tags like "*fun*" should have higher entropies because they might appear in different topics, while tags like "*javascript*" are often more specific to a topic thus have lower entropies. A similar metric was proposed in [11]. Following [16], the most frequent tag in a document is treated as a topic and we calculate the entropies of all tags on the top 100 topics[4].
- tag raw count $C(t)$: the total number of appearance of tag t in a specific corpus. This generally indicates how popular a tag is during a certain time period, which usually follows a well-known long tail distribution.
- tag distinct count $D(t)$: the total number of documents tagged by t. The tag raw count shows the overall popularity of a tag but does guarantee the influence of the tag in different documents. A tag may be tagged many time on a specific document but not on others. Thus the tag distinct count offers a popularity measurement from a document perspective of view.

3.1.1 Information-Theoretic (IT) Tag Ranking

With the three features defined above, we introduce the *informativeness* of a tag t as follows:

$$I(t) = \frac{H(t)\cdot[D(t)\cdot\log(C(t)+1)]}{Z}, \qquad (1)$$

where the first term measures the specificity of t and the second term the popularity of t. Z is a normalization factor that ensures any $I(t)$ to be in (0,1). The second term is similar to the measurement of document-frequency and term-frequency in text retrieval applications. We empirically take the logarithm of $C(t)$ here to deemphasize its contribution since in practice, tag raw count is usually of several magnitudes larger than tag distinct count. A direct multiplication will thus over-credit $C(t)$. e.g., tag A is annotated 300 times but only in 2 documents, while tag B is annotated 50 times in 10 different documents. Directly multiply $C(t)$ and $D(t)$ would put tag A ahead of B but apparently B is more popular than A. Using our formula successfully eliminates this issue since tag B scores 56.72 while A only gets 16.46.

[3]http://www.kde.cs.uni-kassel.de/ws/dc09/

[4]Other numbers of topics are also tested which showed similar tag ranking results.

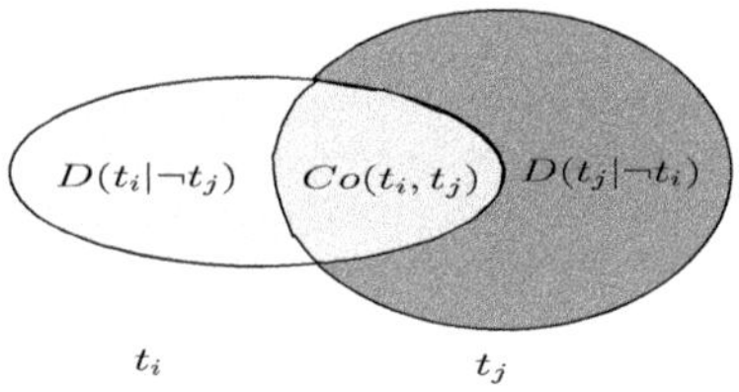

Figure 2: The relationship of two tags. ***Co*** **is the co-occurrence.** $D(t_i|\neg t_j)$ **is the relative appearance.**

While our information-theoretic approach bears some level of similarity with Heymann's entropy-based method [11], it should be noticed that the tag distinct count are apparently ignored in their approach. Since popular documents could potentially over-credit tags that appear many times in those documents but only a few times in less popular documents, it is important to consider both tag raw count and tag distinct count for a more accurate tag ranking.

3.1.2 Learning-to-rank (LETOR) based Tag Ranking

On the other hand, we construct an alternative tag ranking framework using the idea from learning-to-rank approach [14]. To be concrete, our training data are implicit feedbacks from users who performed tagging. Our objective is to learn an optimal weight vector for linear combination of features for ranking tags across all documents.

Figure 2 depicts a scenario of two tags' relationship. The middle part, $Co(t_i, t_j)$ indicates the number of times two tags t_i and t_j were used to tag same documents, while $D(t_i|\neg t_j)$ means the number of times t_i appeared in a document while t_j did not. Note that for any tag t_i, $D(t_i) = Co(t_i, t_j) + D(t_i|\neg t_j)$.

Intuitively, the relative occurrence of a tag t_i given the absence of another tag t_j is a strong indicator of higher abstractness of t_i than t_j. In our data set, we found that for example, $Co(programming, java) = 200$, $D(java|\neg programming) = 29$ and $D(programming|\neg java) = 239$. These statistics strongly indicates that "*programming*" is more abstract than "*java*", or say "*java*" is a kind of "*programming*".

Consequently, we can construct positive and negative training examples (x, y) automatically by discovering these pairs of tags from a given corpus $\mathcal{T}$. We construct

$$\text{for each } \; i, j \in \mathcal{T}, i < j$$
$$(x_k, y_k) = \begin{cases} (\{t_i - t_j\}, +1) & \text{if } t_i >_r t_j \\ (\{t_i - t_j\}, -1) & \text{if } t_i <_r t_j \\ \emptyset & \text{otherwise} \end{cases}$$
$$>_r \text{ is true when } D(t_i|\neg t_j)/D(t_j|\neg t_i) > \theta,$$
$$<_r \text{ is true when } D(t_i|\neg t_j)/D(t_j|\neg t_i) < 1/\theta. \qquad (2)$$

Here $\{t_i - t_j\}$ is the difference between feature vectors of two tags. In our case, we use the three features defined above, so $x_k \in \mathbb{R}^3$. And since we only consider binary classification, $y_k \in \{-1, +1\}$. Importantly, $>_r$ and $<_r$ define the pair-wise ranking preference. i.e., if the relative appearance of t_i is significantly more than t_j, we treated the pair $\{t_i - t_j\}$ as a positive example. Likewise, a negative example is constructed if t_i relatively appeared much less than t_j. For example, in the above case of "*programming*" (t_i) and "*java*" (t_j), $D(t_i|\neg t_j)/D(t_j|\neg t_i) = 8.24$ which we consider significant. In our experiment, we set $\theta = 2$ empirically.

IT Method	LETOR Method	Combination
web	reference	reference
tools	blog	tools
software	tool	web
web2.0	web	design
design	design	blog
reference	free	free
programming	cool	howto
blog	tutorial	tool
webdesign	news	software

Table 1: Top 10 ranked tags in Delicious using different ranking methods. IT = Information-theoretic, LETOR = Learning-to-rank. The combination uses a ratio of 0.5 as in eq.(5).

In our experiment, we constructed 532 training examples out of 3498 distinct tags in our experiment. For simplicity, we used a regularized logistic regression model for learning the optimal decision in this paper. Other advanced models such as Rank-SVM [14] remained to be explored in future work. Our model specifically maximizes the log-likelihood of the training data,

$$L(T) = -\sum_{i=1}^{N} \log g(y_i z_i) + C \sum_{j=1}^{M} w_j^2,$$
$$\text{where } g(z) = \frac{1}{1+e^{-z}}, \quad z_i = \sum_{m=1}^{M} w_m x_{im}. \qquad (3)$$

Here x_{im} is the value of the mth feature of the ith instance constructed using eq.(2), w_m is the weight value of that particular feature and the weight vector $\mathbf{w}$ is the parameter of the model. We used gradient decent to optimize $\mathbf{w}$ in model. After learning, we assign each tag a score

$$Lr(t_i) = w^T * t_i, \qquad (4)$$

and normalize Lr to be within $(0, 1)$.

It should be noted that although learning-to-ranking often requires *supervised* learning methods, the way we derive *labels* in our approach does not require any explicit human annotations.

3.1.3 Combine Two Ranking Methods

Since the aforementioned two ranking methods address different perspectives of tag importance, it is natural to combine the power from both of them. A linear combination is proposed here to calculate the final score for each tag:

$$S(t) = rI(t) + (1-r)Lr(t), r \in [0, 1]. \qquad (5)$$

Tags are then ranked according to $S(t)$ in a descending order. Table 1 shows the top 10 ranked tags for each of the methods and the combination uses a ratio of 0.5. This parameter will be tuned in our experiment.

3.2 Constructing Tag Hierarchy

The proposed construction of tag hierarchy is an iterative process that contains two primary operations at each step: (1) select appropriate tags to be included in the tree[5], and (2) choose the optimal position for those tags.

[5]Our method can be applied to other tag ranking methods as well, e.g., FolkRank [12].

3.2.1 *Iterative Tag Insertion*

We propose a greedy algorithm that iteratively includes tags from the ranked tag list to the hierarchical representation. Following the minimum-evolution (ME) criteria in phylogentics [6], our objective is to minimize the change (cost) of an existing tree when adding a new tree node. As such, we define the cost of a tree R to be the sum of distances between every pair of the nodes:

$$Cost(R) = \sum_{i<j, t_i, t_j \in R} d(t_i, t_j), \tag{6}$$

where the distance between two nodes are the shortest path ($\hat{P}(t_i, t_j)$) that connects them, through their lowest common ancestor ($LCA(t_i, t_j)$),

$$d(t_i, t_j) = \sum_{e(i,j) \in \hat{P}(t_i, t_j)} W(e(i, j)). \tag{7}$$

For example, in Figure 3, $d(t_1, t_2) = 0.7, d(t_3, t_5) = 0.9$. To specify the distance between two tags, we define the edge weight between two directly-connected tag nodes i and j as the normalized correlations of the tags t_i and t_j, i.e.,

$$W(e(i, j)) = \exp(-\frac{||t_i - t_j||^2}{\sigma^2}), \tag{8}$$

where σ is a radius parameter.

In general, our algorithm works as follows. During each iteration, we greedily choose the highest-ranked tag for inclusion to form a new tree. It is worth notice that not all tags are included in the tree. We discard those tags that have zero correlations with all existing tree nodes. The entire algorithm is sketched as in Algorithm 1.

3.2.2 *Optimal Position Selection*

The number of potential positions that a new tag can be added is equivalent to the number of existing nodes in the tree, which could become quite large when the tree grows. To limit the search space for the optimal insertion position, we make a restriction here that a new node t_{new} can not be added at a higher level than the current leaf nodes, i.e., if the tree has depth $L(R)$, t_{new} can only be inserted at level $L(R)$ or $L(R) + 1$. For example, in Figure 3, t_6 can only be added at the same level as of t_4 and t_5 or lower. Our restriction here is legitimate since the ranking of the tags are correlated to their abstractness, so that highly-ranked tags are more likely to be abstract. Under this guidance, we can reduce the search space significantly to $N(L(R) - 1) + N(L(R))$, where $N(i)$ indicates the number of nodes at level i.

Note that after the first step of tag ranking, more abstract tags are ranked at higher positions. Therefore, in our iteration insertion process, abstract tags will always be selected first and inserted at higher level of the tree, which makes our greedy selection process legitimate.

Once the search space is specified, it becomes easier to locate the optimal position for t_{new}. Mathematically, the optimal position for t_{new} thus can be found by minimizing the following criteria:

$$\begin{aligned} R_{new} &= \arg\min_{R'} \Delta Cost(R', R) = Cost(R') - Cost(R), \\ \text{where } R' &= R \cup t_{new}. \end{aligned} \tag{9}$$

The above optimization framework iteratively constructing an optimal tag hierarchy by adding one tag in each step.

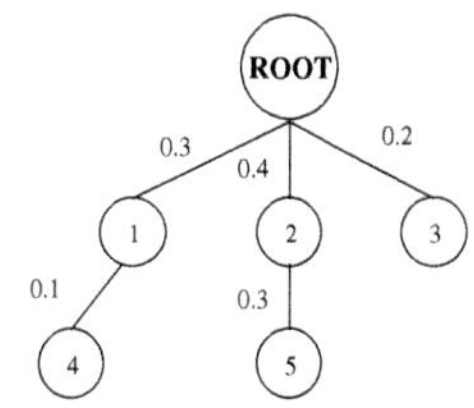

Figure 3: An example of tag representation of 5 tree nodes and a ROOT node.

This greedy method is quite efficient. Since in practice, only the cost difference ($\Delta Cost$) between two trees are required to be computed, the majority part of the tree remains unchanged so that the cost among the rest of the nodes usually does not change at all.

3.2.3 *Model Selection via Minimum Description Length*

There is an issue comes with the optimal selection criteria mentioned above. Since the nodes are chosen based on the co-occurrence with its parent node, it will then always have shorter distance to the parent node than others. Therefore, connecting the new node with its parent node always returns the optimal result. This could cause, in the worst case, all nodes to have only one child node while each level of the tree only contains one node (Such an example is shown in Figure 8(a), which will be discussed later).

To discourage such effort and make the tree more balance and meaningful, we introduce the idea of regularization, where we penalize the depth of the tree while minimizing the cost of adding new nodes.

This idea is similar to minimum description length (MDL) criteria [1], which has been widely used for model selection. The MDL principle states that the optimal model to encode a set of data essentially minimizes the number of bits that is required to transmit the data. To be specific, the MDL principle minimizes the objective function $L(M|D) + L(M)$, where the first term defines the explanation of the data D using model M, i.e., the likelihood. The second term corresponds to the length of the encoding under model M, i.e., model complexity. As a result, complex models are penalized. In our model, the first term controls the cost of introducing a new node, while the second term aims at reducing the height of the tree. i.e.,

$$\min \left(\Delta Cost(R', R) + \xi \frac{L(R')}{\log |R'|} \right), \tag{10}$$

where $L(R')$ and $|R'|$ indicate the depth and the total number of nodes in the new tree, respectively. Here ξ is a balancing factor between the two terms. The second term of eq(10), while penalizes the depth of the tree in general, encourages the increase of depth when the number of tree nodes at the same level becomes large. Since $L(R')$ remains a constant when the depth does not change, the insertion of new nodes will gradually increase the value of the denominator $\log |R'|$ and therefore decrease the value of the entire second term. Finally, the depth of the tree will increase when the second term exceeds a threshold.

3.2.4 *Tree Initialization*

We introduce a ROOT node for tree initialization. Because none of the top-ranked node can be treated as a parent node of all others as they all belong to different topics.

Algorithm 1 Tag Hierarchy Construction

```
Input Ranked tag list T = {t_1, ..., t_m}, tag correlation matrix
  Col(T) ∈ R^{m×m}
Initialize tag tree R ← ROOT
while L(R) ≤ 2
  add the top tag t' from T to R according to eq.(10)
  update W(e(ROOT, child)) according to eq.(11)
  T ← T\t'
  while sizeof(T) > 0
    extract top tag t' from T
    check the correlation of t' with R
    ∀t_k ∈ R, Col(t_k, t') = 0
      continue; (throw away t')
    else
      add t' to R according to eq.(10)
      T ← T\t'
  end while
end while
Output R
```

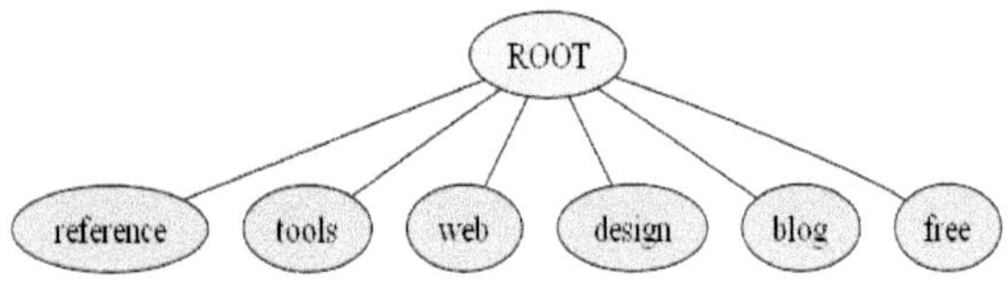

Figure 4: The ROOT node and the first level nodes in our data set. The first level corresponds to the highest level of topics for all tags.

Therefore, ROOT is a special node that controls the number of nodes at the initial level of the tree, which are *real* root nodes that break down the topics of a corpus at the highest level. Since there is no correlation between ROOT and other tags, we dynamically adjust the weights between ROOT and other tags according to the weights between its child nodes. We specify the distance to be equal to the maximum distance between any two child nodes,

$$W(e(ROOT, j)) = \max_{i<j, t_i, t_j \in R} W(e(i,j)) \quad i,j \in \text{child}(ROOT). \tag{11}$$

Under this criteria, once the first level of nodes are fixed and the tree grows to deeper levels, the distance between ROOT and other child nodes will not change. In practice, it helps constructing the initial topics in the tree hierarchy. Figure 4 shows the first level of nodes in our data set. A total of 6 topics are specified at the first level.

3.2.5 Comparison with Heymann's Hierarchy

Heymann proposed a tag hierarchy construction algorithm in [10] by leveraging graph centrality theorem and tag similarity measurement. Their method greedy's choose the most central tags from tag graph and added to the hierarchy. A tag can only be added as (1) a child node of the most similar tag node or, (2) a root node, depending on the similarity threshold. While the graph centrality theorem bears similarity with our global tag ranking algorithm, there are several fundamental differences:

- A tag is often added as a child node to its most similar node according to Heymann's algorithm. While in our algorithm, it often results in a sibling node. While it is arguable which guideline is more reasonable, we have observed a much clearer hierarchy by using our algorithm in practice. For example, *maps* is at the same level as *map* in our algorithm but treated as child node in their approach, same for *network*, *networking* and many other scenarios.
- Heymann's algorithm does not penalize the height of the tree by controlling the number of nodes at the same level. In practice, we observed that their algorithm is more likely to grow a deep tree than having multiple root nodes, considering for a high similarity threshold. This results in a skewed tree where the hierarchy no longer makes much sense (as an example in Fig. 8 (a)).

4. APPLICATION TO TAG RECOMMENDATIONS

While our tag visualization method offers an alternative view of underlying tag relationships to the traditional tag could representation, its hierarchial structure also provides a potential opportunity of recommending relevant tags for annotation. Traditional approaches of tag recommendations are usually equivalent to the idea of collaborative filtering, in which documents having similar contents with the targeting document are selected and their tags are used for recommendations. Although some researchers have proposed methods for real-time tag recommendations which work well in terms of efficiency [16], the cost of training the model and maintaining large amount of model parameters in memory is still quite expensive and may not be suitable for web-scale applications. In this section, we propose to simplify this recommendation process by leveraging the existing hierarchical tag structures without training an expensive model.

In our proposal, recommending relevant tags to a targeting document is equivalent to (1) retrieve a candidate *tag* list (instead of retrieving a candidate *document* list in traditional way), and (2) rank retrieved tags given a scoring function in terms of document-tag relevance. Our framework breaks down the retrieval of candidate list into three scenarios which will be discussed in the next section. Given a targeting document d with its textual content, as well as a set of prior user tags $\{\tilde{t}_1, ... \tilde{t}_k\}$ (documents with completely no prior tag information will be discussed later). We introduce a scoring function to measure document-tag relevance:

$$Score(d, t_i | \{\tilde{t}_1, ... \tilde{t}_k\}) = \alpha \sum_{j=1}^{k} W(\tilde{t}_j, t_i) + (1-\alpha) N(t_i, d), \tag{12}$$

where t_i is one of the candidate tags, $W(\tilde{t}_j, t_i)$ is the similarity between user-entered tag $\tilde{t}_j$ and t_i, $N(t_i, d)$ refers to the number of times tag t_i appears in document d. α is a balancing factor between two terms, so $\alpha \in [0, 1]$. This function addresses the similarity between candidate tags and user tags, as well as the relevance between candidate tags and the content of document d. Note that for applications like images and videos which does not contain textual contents, we could leverage the side-information such as user comments, related titles and so on, as proposed in [16]. Or we could simply set the balancing parameter $\alpha = 1$ to ignore the second term of eq.(12).

4.1 Candidates List Extraction

In the first scenario, we assume that document d only

Algorithm 2 Generating Candidate Tag List

```
Input tag tree R, target document d,
      list of user-entered tags T(d) = {t̃_1, ...t̃_k}
Initialize candidate(d) = ∅
If sizeof(T) = 0
  T(d) = top-K-words-in-d ∩ R
end if
  for each t̃_i ∈ T(d) (i = 1...k)
    do t_p = t̃_i.parent
     candidate(d).Add(t_p); t_p = t_p.parent;
    while(t_p ≠ ROOT)
   for each t_c ∈ t̃_i.childs
     candidate(d).Add(t_c)
   end for
  end for
Output candidate(d)[1...50]
```

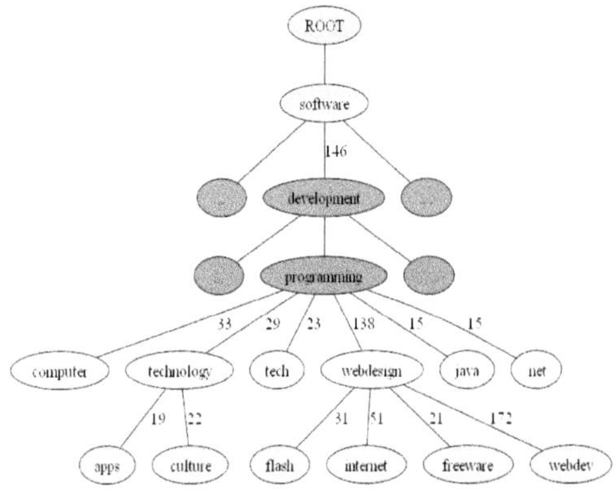

Figure 5: Subtree of *programming* are used for tag recommendation for programming related documents. The weights of the edge indicate the number of co-occurrence of two tags.

has one user-entered tag t_d. This basically involves finding the location of t_d in the tree (or location of the most lexically-similar tag), and recommending nearby tags. As an example, for t_d = "*programming*", Figure 5 shows part of the subtree for "*programming*", as well as its path to the ROOT, where the numbers beside the edges indicate the number of tag co-occurrence. The challenge here is whether the child nodes (more specific tags, like "*java*", "*.net*") of t_d or parent nodes (more general tags, like "*development*") should have the priority to be included in the list. In our framework, we set the size of candidate list to be sufficiently large (we empirically include 50 tags in the candidate list) to include as many relevant tags as possible. We treat parent nodes with higher priority and first include them to the candidate list, then perform a breadth-first search (BFS) to include the most relevant child nodes.

For documents with multiple user tags, e.g. *technology* and *webdesign* in Figure 5, we include the joint set of their candidate lists, and output the first 50 with the highest correlations. As a result, their common ancestors, *programming* and *development* will be more likely to be included.

The most common scenario, however, is a document d without any prior knowledge of user-tags. In this case, we leverage the top K most frequent words from d that appear in our tag list, and treat them as *pseudo* tags to extract candidate list. So that for each pseudo tag, we retrieve its candidate tree and combine all candidates together. Algorithm 2 summarizes our method for these three scenarios.

Note that we've been quite generous towards the inclusion of candidate tags for recommendation, which is an arguable factor against efficiency. However, in fact, the correlations of tags are pre-computed and thus can be looked up in constant time. Constructing the word frequency table for a document with F words costs $O(F)$ time. For each candidate tag, the total cost of ranking using eq.(12) is merely $O(K + F + F \log F)$, where K is the number of user-entered tags. Since both K and F are quite small in practice, our framework is fully capable of performing real-time tag recommendation with very little memory and computational cost.

5. EXPERIMENTS

In this section, we present empirical results which address (1) the efficiency of the tag hierarchy on helping users navigate through a large set of tags, and (2) the effectiveness of our tag recommendation algorithm on choosing the most relevant tags for annotations. In our experiments, we mainly focus on user tagging experience on web documents, including News articles, blog articles and so on.

5.1 Data Preparation

The most well-known tag repository of web documents is the Delicious web site, which currently has more than 5 million registered users with over 150 million tagged web pages. We crawled Delicious for a period of two months data from May 2008 to July 2008. We first subscribe to the RSS feeds of the top 100 most popular tags in Delicious tag cloud, and continuously crawl these tags to get the associated URLs. For each individual URL, we also retrieve all user tags and download its HTML content. Finally, we ended up with 43,113 unique tags with 36,157 distinct URLs. The data set in evaluation is approximately 3.6 GB.

For user study purpose, we cannot enumerate all combination of the parameters. Therefore, we set both r and α in eq.(5) and eq.(12) to be 0.5, $\xi = 0.7$ in eq.(10). The sensitivity of parameters will be discussed later in this section.

5.2 User Study

As a preliminary user evaluation, we sought to compare the efficiency and effectiveness of tag hierarchies with tag clouds and Heymann's tag tree representation [10]. First, efficiency was being measured by three time-related metrics: (1) time-to-first-selection: The time between the timestamp from showing the page, and the timestamp of the first user tag selection; (2) time-to-task-completion: the time required to select all tags for the task; (3) average-interval-between-selections: the average time interval between adjacent selections of tags. An additional metric considered is (4) deselection-count: the number of times a user deselects a previously chosen tag and selects a more relevant one.

We conducted a between-subjects design with 49 participants where half of the users were presented with one tag visualization method and the remaining users were presented with the other. The 49 users were selected randomly from the information and computer science departments at a large university, and engineers at a large software company. Technical users were sought because of their expected background in tagging. Table 2 shows the basic user information. Note that the size of users in our study is sufficient,

Male	Female	Average Years Using Computer	Average Tagging Experiences
30	19	14.2	2.1

Table 2: Statistics about user study. Tagging experiences are rated in 4-point Likert scale: *none (0)*, *a little (1)*, *some (2)* and *a lot (3)*.

which is supported by many previous literature [17] of user study, where much smaller sample sizes were used.

There were two phases to the experiment. In Phase I we compare our tag hierarchy and tag cloud. Users were asked to tag 10 random web documents from the Delicious data corpus. 15 tags were presented with each web document. Users were asked for select 3 tags that best described the web document. An example has been shown in Figure 1(b) at the beginning of the paper. Note that each user can only see either tag cloud or tag hierarchy. The 15 tags are selected based on Algo. 2. The *exactly* same set of tags are shown to users in both visualization methods so that quality of the recommended tags are same for all users. For the users chosen for tag cloud, we randomly serve them with (1) alphabetically ordered or (2) randomly ordered tag clouds. For the users chosen for tag hierarchy, we randomly serve them with (1) our result or (2) Heymann's approach [10].

5.3 Comparison of Tagging Efficiency

Table 3 and 4 list the results from Phase I study for all the 4 metrics. Overall, our method (MDL-Tree) outperforms all other three ones in all categories with statistical significance ($p < 0.01$). Some observations can be made: (1) users were faster in selecting tags using tag hierarchy than tag cloud. Both Heymann's tree and our method show significant less time in the time-to-task-completion metric. (2) assuming the two groups of users have similar reading speed, the time-to-first-selection metric indicates how fast the user can locate the most relevant tags once they finish reading. In this metric, we observe that our MDL-Tree requires the least time. Meanwhile, tag cloud organized alphabetically (Cloud-α) also exhibits better performance than random tag cloud (Cloud-Rand) as well as Heymann's Tree. (3) Once the user locates the first tag, tag tree shows better performance in average-interval-between-selections than tag cloud thanks to the tree structure. The reason behind this phenomenon is quite obvious: without the hierarchical structure which groups similar tags together, users have to scan the tag cloud every time when they need to find another relevant tag, which also explains why the deselection-count of tag clouds are much higher than tag trees.

Furthermore, we asked users to rate their tagging experience on the following 4-point Likert scale: *none*, *a little*, *some* and *a lot*. By removing the sophisticated users in the "a lot" category, the average time for users to tag using the MDL-Tree visualization was 494 seconds versus 643 seconds for the tag cloud visualization (Cloud-α), more than a 30% time advantage. Therefore, our experiment does show the potential for tag hierarchy visualization to be more efficient for tagging than the traditional tag clouds. Controlling for users' tagging experience can be incorporated in a subsequent experiment.

5.4 Evaluate Tag Recommendation Performance

In Phase II of our experiments, we evaluate the performance of our tag recommendation algorithm as in Algorithm 2 and eq.(12). For comparison, we implemented a content-based collaborative-filtering (CF) algorithm which is similar to one of the state-of-the-art P-Tag algorithm [3]. Since our candidate selection algorithm is a *content-free* recommendation method, we believe that the content-based CF method offers a strong baseline comparison. Specifically, the CF algorithm constructs a document-word matrix for all web pages in collection. For a new targeting web page, the algorithm finds the top m most similar web pages in collection by calculating the cosine similarities using word features. CF then recommends the most popular n tags within these m web pages to the targeting page. In our experiment, we fixed both m and n to be 5 for simplicity. Moreover, we also compare with one of the state-of-the-art algorithms in [16] which combines spectral clustering and mixture models for tag recommendation (noted as PMM).

To consider both the relevance of the recommended tags and their relative rankings, we use normalized discounted cumulative gain (NDCG) as the metric, which is a widely-used metric to evaluate the relevance of search engine result pages (SERP) given a set of user queries. We randomly sampled 10 pages from the data set and asked 49 users to measure the relevance of recommended tags. Each algorithm returns top 5 tags for relevance measurement. The tags are randomly ordered so that the judgers are not aware of the underlying algorithm or the relevance scores. Each tag is measured as one of the 5 levels: Perfect (score 5), Excellent (score 4), Good (score 3), Fair (score 2) and Poor (score 1). The NDCG of the tags given a web document with relevance scores $\{s(1), ...s(5)\}$ from a judge can be computed as $NDCG(w) = \frac{\sum_i (2^{s(i)}-1)/\log(i+1)}{Z(w)}$, where $Z(w)$ is a normalization factor corresponding to the ideal discounted cumulative gain, so that the $NDCG$ score will always be between 0 and 1. For each document, we average $NDCG$ from 49 judgements to get the average score.

Figure 7 demonstrates the strength of our method against the strong baseline approach and PMM. Overall, our algorithm beats the baseline in 9 out of 10 questions, and beats PMM in 8 out of 10 questions. We performed paired T-test with null hypothesis that both algorithm performs equally well. The alternative hypothesis is that our algorithm performs better in terms of NDCG (one-sided). The p-value from the statistical significance test is 0.001 comparing with the baseline, which indicates that the result is statistically significant. On average, our algorithm outscores the baseline by 21%. The p-value is 0.02 comparing with PMM–still shows statistically significance.

Furthermore, we break down the evaluation into different positions of recommendation. Here, we consider the quality of recommendation for the 1st tag as well as top-5 tags. Therefore, we measure the NDCG score at position 1 and 5, respectively. Figure 9 summarizes the two cases. Our algorithm has 0.79 NDCG score at position 1, indicating that in 79% of times, the first recommended tag by our algorithm is the most relevant one among all. Our algorithm also outperforms the baseline and PMM in both positions.

5.5 Discussion of Parameter Sensitivity

The regularization parameter ξ in eq.(10) plays an im-

#	Time-to-Task-Completion				Time-to-First-Selection			
	Cloud-α	Cloud-Rand	Heymann-Tree	MDL-Tree	Cloud-Alpha	Cloud-Rand	Heymann-Tree	MDL-Tree
1	59.5 ± 38.1	62.5 ± 32.1	61.3 ± 20.8	59.5 ± 21.6	41.81 ±18.8	40.53 ±22.1	51.09 ±19.3	35.55 ±18.5
2	73.5 ± 52.3	77 ± 51.7	37.5 ± 19.4	33 ± 16.6	41.03 ±15.0	35.98 ±23.8	36.6 ±14.4	38.24 ±17.1
3	57.3 ± 45.6	53.2 ± 47.3	39.2 ± 15.9	35.3 ± 16.0	35.7 ±17.8	38.74 ±21.9	46.1 ±21.7	37.47 ±14.5
4	61 ± 24.5	60.1 ± 20.6	49.6 ± 21.1	42.7 ± 17.9	37.54 ±17.5	45.31 ±20.4	51.83 ±19.7	36.01 ±14.2
5	38.2 ± 19.8	39.5 ± 17.4	37.2 ± 14.9	33.3 ± 13.9	31 ±17.6	35.83 ±24.8	40.28 ±19.6	39.47 ±18.5
6	46.6 ± 22.9	44.5 ± 20.9	43.25 ± 28.2	41.8 ± 25.2	38.2 ±18.7	38.83 ±20.9	47.88 ±17.1	36.99 ±14.5
7	88.2 ± 45.8	92.1 ± 49.7	69.9 ± 43.2	46.5 ± 25.8	38.64 ±19.8	40.57 ±19.1	42.76 ±20.5	35.74 ±17.9
8	50.4 ± 33.0	53.1 ± 30.3	50.2 ± 28.9	43.4 ± 28.6	38.02 ±16.1	41.07 ±21.6	44.5 ±20.7	38.26 ±14.9
9	45.8 ± 19.7	47.1 ± 18.3	42.2 ± 15.6	33 ± 13.7	36.15 ±20.3	41.52 ±18.2	47.18 ±14.5	34.09 ±18.7
10	46 ± 19.8	45.8 ± 17.9	37.8 ± 19.0	29.8 ± 11.1	38.52 ±18.8	38.67 ±25.6	41.69 ±14.5	41.44 ±17
Ave	56.65	57.49	46.815	**39.83**	37.661	39.705	44.991	**37.326**

Table 3: Results of Time-to-Task-Completion and Time-to-First-Selection metrics. Our method is named MDL-Tree. Less time indicates better performance.

#	Average-Interval-Between-Selections				Deselection-Count			
	Cloud-α	Cloud-Rand	Heymann-Tree	MDL-Tree	Cloud-α	Cloud-Rand	Heymann-Tree	MDL-Tree
1	1.7 ±1.1	2.7 ±0.8	2 ±1.7	2.2 ±0.6	0.7	0.4	0.3	0.1
2	2.6 ±0.8	1.4 ±1.3	1.9 ±1.1	1.8 ±0.7	0.6	0.4	0.5	0.5
3	2.4 ±0.7	1.7 ±0.7	1.5 ±1.6	1.9 ±0.3	0.4	0.6	0.5	0.5
4	2.2 ±1.4	1.7 ±1.3	1.8 ±0.5	0.8 ±0.5	0.5	0.6	0.3	0
5	2.4 ±0.8	2.2 ±1	1.7 ±0.7	1.4 ±0.4	0.6	0.6	0.2	0.1
6	2.1 ±1.5	2.2 ±1.7	2.4 ±0.9	1.8 ±0.7	0.7	0.6	0.6	0.3
7	2.3 ±1	2.7 ±1.3	1.6 ±0.7	1.7 ±0.6	0.7	0.4	0.5	0.2
8	2.5 ±1.3	1.7 ±1.3	1.9 ±1.2	1.6 ±0.6	0.6	0.6	0.6	0
9	1.8 ±0.8	2.8 ±0.6	1.7 ±0.5	0.9 ±0.4	0.7	0.5	0.2	0.4
10	2.7 ±0.9	1.7 ±0.7	1.8 ±1.4	1.2 ±0.4	0.6	0.7	0.5	0.2
Ave	2.27	2.08	1.83	**1.53**	0.61	0.54	0.42	**0.23**

Table 4: Results of Average-Interval-Between-Selections and Deselection-Count metrics. Our algorithm (MDL-Tree) outperforms others in both criteria ($p < 0.05$).

portant role in balancing the tree depth and the number of nodes at the same level. As mentioned above, without regularization, the tree could grow infinitely deep without expanding its child nodes at any level. By penalizing the tree depth properly following the MDL criteria, our model is capable of minimizing this issue. Figure 8 shows two bad tag tree construction due to the improper use of regularization. As indicated in the left graph (a), if the regularization is not leveraged (or slightly used), the objective function of eq.(10) will choose to grow the tree first instead of penalizing its height. On the other hand, if we penalize the height too much as in (b), the tree stops growing deeper but keep adding nodes to the current level. We found the range of [0.4, 0.7] best balancing these two factors. As our objective function in eq.(9) is equivalent to the maximum spanning tree (MST) used in [5], without proper regularization, MST is expected suffer the same problem in large taxonomy.

The next important parameter is the tuning parameter α in eq.(12), which controls the document-tag relevance by judging from two factors: the similarity between tags and the tag frequencies in the document content. To measure its sensitivity, we again resort to the $NDCG$ measurement used above. Figure 6 gives the contour plot of $NDCG@5$ as a function of α and ξ, where higher $NDCG$ scores indicate better performance. It can be observed that the highest $NDCG$ occurs when $\alpha = 0.7$ and $\xi = 0.5$. The best $NDCG@5$ is approximately 0.56. Recall that in our user study we set both parameters to be 0.5 which yielded a 0.51

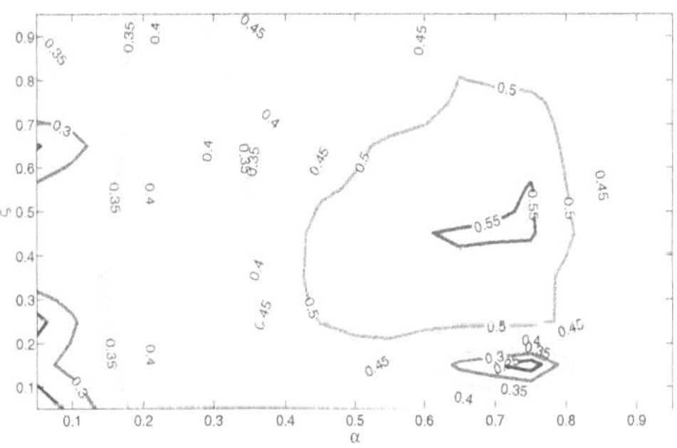

Figure 6: Parameter sensitivity of ξ and α in terms of $NDCG$ scores. The best combination is around $\alpha = 0.7$ and $\xi = 0.5$.

$NDCG$, close to the optimal combination. Overall, when α is in [0.4, 0.8], ξ in [0.4, 0.7], our method performs well.

Besides, the combination parameter in eq.(5) that combines two ranking methods decides the global ranking of tags. However, we did not find this parameter to be sensitive in practice. Although the global ranking of a tag determines the order of its inclusion into the hierarchy, what really matters, however, is the relative order between two tags. e.g., as long as "*programming*" is included in the tag hierarchy prior to "*java*", Algorithm 1 can optimize the objective function

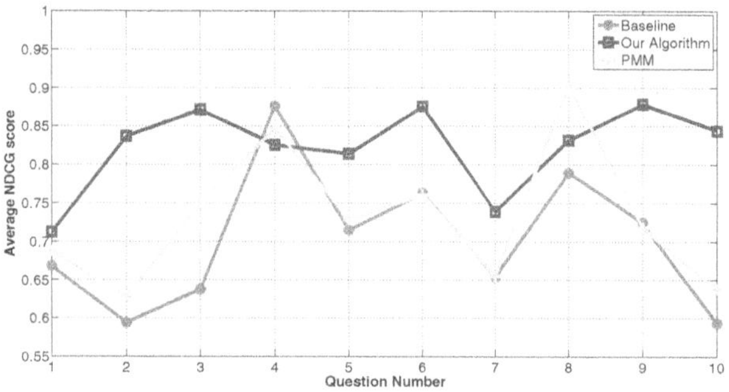

Figure 7: Comparison of algorithm performance in terms of NDCG scores. The improvement of our algorithm is significant to the baseline ($p<0.001$).

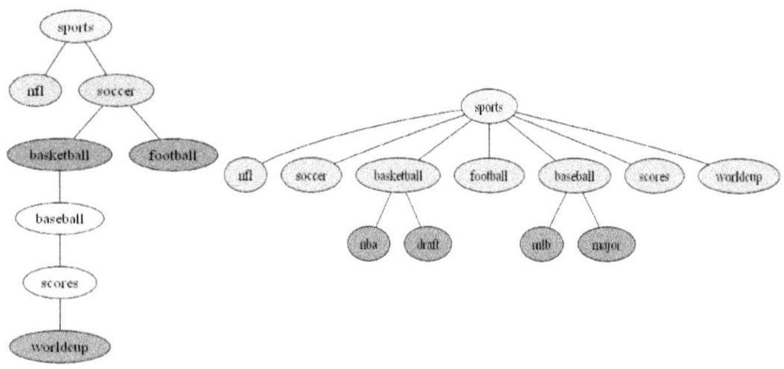

(a) (b)

Figure 8: Two bad examples of tree visualization without proper regularization. (a) $\xi = 0.1$. The tree grows too deep without expanding its children at the same level. (b) $\xi = 0.9$. The model penalizes too much on the depth and the tree grows too slowly.

and keep similar tags close with high probability. Due to space limitation this experiment is omitted here.

6. CONCLUSION AND FUTURE WORK

In this paper we proposed a novel visualization of tag hierarchy which addresses two shortcomings of traditional tag clouds: (1) unable to capture the similarities between tags, and (2) unable to organize tags into levels of abstractness. Our proposed method mimicked the principle of minimum evolution criteria and constructed tag hierarchy to overcome previous issues. A greedy algorithm was proposed to iterative select the best tags to be added in the tree. Along with the regularization method, our framework guaranteed a balanced tag hierarchy with well-organized topics.

We then proposed a taxonomy-based tag recommendation method which leveraged the tag hierarchy to find relevant tags. User study and quantitative analysis indicated that our visualization method can reduce the tagging time, especially for users with limited tagging experiences. Also, our tag recommendation algorithm outperformed a content-based recommendation method in NDCG scores.

In the future, we plan to investigate more advanced ranking methods for global tag ranking and compare with existing methods as well [12]. Document-specific tag hierarchy and personalized tag hierarchy are also under consideration.

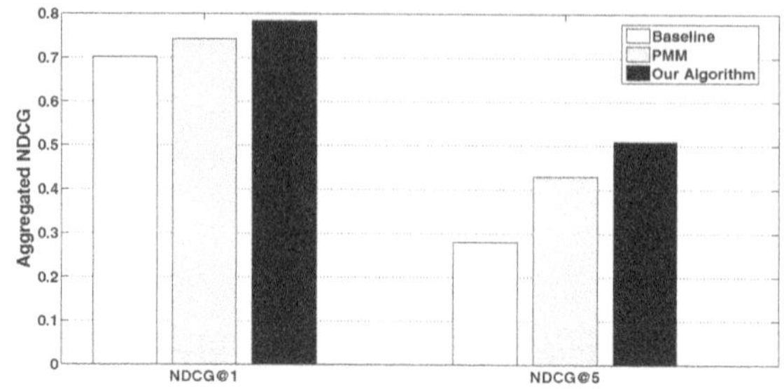

Figure 9: The performance of tag recommendation at position 1 and position 5.

7. REFERENCES

[1] A. Barron, J. Rissanen, and B. Yu. The minimum description length principle in coding and modeling (invited paper). pages 699–716, 2000.

[2] G. Begelman. Automated tag clustering: Improving search and exploration in the tag space. In *In Proc. of the Collaborative Web Tagging Workshop at WWWŠ06*, 2006.

[3] P. A. Chirita, S. Costache, W. Nejdl, and S. Handschuh. P-tag: large scale automatic generation of personalized annotation tags for the web. In *WWW '07*, pages 845–854.

[4] P. Cimiano, A. Hotho, and S. Staab. Learning concept hierarchies from text corpora using formal concept analysis. *Journal of Artificial Intelligence research*, 24:305–339, 2005.

[5] P. De Meo, G. Quattrone, and D. Ursino. Exploitation of semantic relationships and hierarchical data structures to support a user in his annotation and browsing activities in folksonomies. *Inf. Syst.*, 34(6):511–535, 2009.

[6] R. Desper and O. Gascuel. Fast and accurate phylogeny reconstruction algorithms based on the minimum-evolution principle. *Journal of Computational Biology*, 9(5):687–705.

[7] M. Dubinko, R. Kumar, J. Magnani, J. Novak, P. Raghavan, and A. Tomkins. Visualizing tags over time. In *WWW '06*, pages 193–202, New York, NY, USA, 2006.

[8] S. A. Golder and B. A. Huberman. Usage patterns of collaborative tagging systems. *J. Inf. Sci.*, 32(2):198–208, 2006.

[9] Y. Hassan-montero and V. H. solana A. Improving tag-clouds as visual information retrieval interfaces. In *Merída, InSciT2006 conference*, 2006.

[10] P. Heymann and H. Garcia-Molina. Collaborative creation of communal hierarchical taxonomies in social tagging systems. Technical Report 2006-10, April 2006.

[11] P. Heymann, D. Ramage, and H. Garcia-Molina. Social tag prediction. In *SIGIR '08*, pages 531–538, 2008.

[12] A. Hotho, R. Jäschke, C. Schmitz, and G. Stumme. Folkrank: A ranking algorithm for folksonomies. In *University of Hildesheim, Institute of Computer Science*, pages 111–114, 2006.

[13] D. Liu, X.-S. Hua, L. Yang, M. Wang, and H.-J. Zhang. Tag ranking. In *WWW '09*, pages 351–360, 2009.

[14] T.-Y. Liu. Learning to rank for information retrieval. pages 225–331, 2009.

[15] B. Markines, C. Cattuto, F. Menczer, D. Benz, A. Hotho, and G. Stumme. Evaluating similarity measures for emergent semantics of social tagging. In *WWW '09*, pages 641–650, New York, NY, USA, 2009. ACM.

[16] Y. Song, Z. Zhuang, H. Li, Q. Zhao, J. Li, W.-C. Lee, and C. L. Giles. Real-time automatic tag recommendation. In *SIGIR '08*, pages 515–522, New York, NY, USA, 2008.

[17] M. Toomim, S. M. Drucker, M. Dontcheva, A. Rahimi, B. Thomson, and J. A. Landay. Attaching ui enhancements to websites with end users. In *CHI '09*, pages 1859–1868.

[18] H. Yang and J. Callan. Metric-based ontology learning. In *ONISW '08*, pages 1–8. ACM, 2008.

Perspective Hierarchical Dirichlet Process for User-Tagged Image Modeling

Xin Chen[1] Xiaohua Hu[1] Yuan An[1] Zunyan Xiong[1] Tingting He[2] E.K. Park[3]

[1]College of Information Science and Technology, Drexel University, Philadelphia, PA 19104, USA

[2]Dept. of Computer Science at Central China Normal University, Wuhan, China

[3]California State University - Chico, Chico, CA 95929, USA

bruce.chen@drexel.edu thu@ischool.drexel.edu yuan.an@ischool.drexel.edu zx26@drexel.edu tthe@mail.ccnu.edu.cn ek.ek.park@gmail.com

ABSTRACT

In this paper, we proposed a perspective Hierarchical Dirichlet Process (pHDP) model to deal with user-tagged image modeling. The contribution is two-fold. Firstly, we associate image features with image tags. Secondly, we incorporate the user's perspectives into the image tag generation process and introduce new latent variables to determine if an image tag is generated from user's perspectives or from the image content. Therefore, the model is able to extract both embedded semantic components and user's perspectives from user-tagged images. Based on the proposed pHDP model, we achieve automatic image tagging with users' perspective. Experimental results show that the pHDP model achieves better image tagging performance compared to state-of-the-art topic models.

Categories and Subject Descriptors

I.2.6 [**Artificial Intelligence**]: Learning – *Parameter learning*; H.2.8 [**Database Management**]: Database applications – *Data mining*; *Image databases*; H.1.2 [**Models and Principles**]: User/Machine Systems – *Human factors, Human information processing*

General Terms

Algorithms, Experimentation, Human Factors, Design.

Keywords

Image tagging, Probabilistic generative model, Hierachical Dirichlet process, User perspective modeling

1. INTRODUCTION

The prevalence of digital imaging devices, such as digital cameras and digital video cameras, has brought an increasingly large amount of unlabeled multimedia data, especially unlabeled image data. To face the challenge of enormous explosion of unlabeled online image resources, it is important to achieve automatic image tagging for online image resources. The desirable image tagging system should not only be able to interpret the image content but also be able to integrate users' contextual information. Breakthroughs in automatic image tagging algorithms will help with organizing the massive amount of online image resources, promote developing and studying of image storage and retrieval systems, and serve for applications such as interest sharing among online image resource users.

CIKM'11, October 24–28, 2011, Glasgow, Scotland, UK.

Due to its social annotation nature, Flickr image tags have various functional purposes [6]. For example, the *topic* tags may refer to any object or person displayed in the picture, such as sky, lake, plant life; the *time* tags indicate the time when a picture was taken; the *location* tags provide information about sights, like which country it is from; the *type* tags include camera settings and photographic styles; the *usage context* tags suggest the context the picture was collected in, while the *self reference* tags contain highly personal information for the tagger himself, such as 'diamond class photographer'. Study on different tag categories suggests that *topic* and *location* are two most intensively used tag categories in Flick.com [6]. Further study in social tagging behavior suggests that the *factual* tags [7] (or the first five tag categories identified in [6]) are more closely related to resource content, while the *subjective* tags and *personal* tags are more influenced by users' perspectives. Generally speaking, compared to *subjective* and *personal* tags, *factual* tags are more relevant to image content. The *subjective* and *personal* tags, on the other hand, are usually free-form texts, but they also provide valuable contextual information of users' tagging preference which can be utilized to customize automatic image tagging for different users.

It should be noted that, some *factual* tags (which carry on the semantic meanings) are not visible from image contents. For example, the image content usually provides little clues about its location and it is not easy to infer the camera settings and photographic styles. Therefore, in automatic image tagging, one challenging problem is how to bridge over the "semantic gap" [4] between image features and high-level semantic meanings. Specifically, it requires identifying a set of image features that well preserve the semantic consistency of image content. It also requires using generative probabilistic models to infer the less visible semantic concepts (like locations) from the visible parts.

The Correspondence Latent Dirichlet Allocation (CorrLDA) model [1] has been intensively used to model image features with multiple types of associated semantic entities (such as tags) [8, 9]. However, the CorrLDA model requires specifying the exact number of mixture components. In real-world applications, the number of semantic components in an image is unknown. For example, a picture of clear blue sky tend to have less semantic components than an image showing a crowd of people in the street. Therefore, the Hieratical Dirichlet Process (HDP) model [5], a nonparametric extension of the LDA-based topic models, was proposed. It enables us to represent image content with unbounded number of semantic components, thus provides the flexibility of modeling different image categories in one generative process. In this paper, we extend the HDP model to deal with both users' perspective and the semantic components derived from image contents. We name the new model as 'perspective Hierarchical Dirichlet Process (pHDP) model' as it integrates the user's perspectives into the image tag generation process. The pHDP model introduces new latent variables to determine if an image tag is generated from user's perspectives or from the image contents. Experimental results show that the pHDP model not only generates useful information about semantic components and user perspectives from tagged images, but also achieves better performance in the task of automatic image tagging compared to state-of-the-art topic models.

The remainder of this paper is organized as follows. In Section 2, we review related works in generative topic models. In Section 3, we present the generative process of the proposed pHDP model. Section 4 provides the collapse Gibbs sampling algorithms for model estimation. Section 5 reports the experimental results of the automatic image tagging and compares our approach with several existing models. We conclude the paper in Section 6.

2. BACKGROUND AND RELATED WORK

2.1 Generative Models for Image Tagging

On automatic image tagging, one major task is to identify semantic mixture components from the co-existing image content and text descriptions. In the data mining and information retrieval community, there has been a long time focus on using probabilistic topic models to study the correlation between image and text descriptions. Specifically, the Correspondence LDA (CorrLDA) model [1], which imposes correspondence between text word and other semantic entities, provides a natural way to learn latent semantic components (topics) from image features and associate them with text descriptions. Many recent studies, including sophisticated topic models that associate image features with multiple types of semantic entities (such as protein entities [8], ontology-based biomedical concepts [9]), still follow a similar generative process to the prototype CorrLDA model. In CorrLDA model, each image document has different distribution over semantic mixture components; this feature provides the model a flexibility of adapting to different image contents. However, the CorrLDA model requires specifying the exact number of mixture components, which is fixed for each image document and remains unchanged during the model estimation. In practice, in order to get an optimal number, the researchers have to try out different mixture components numbers and make a choice by comparing the log-likelihood, perplexity and other criteria that indicate how good the model fits the data. The Hieratical Dirichlet Process (HDP) model [5], is a nonparametric extension of the Latent Dirichlet Allocation (LDA)-based topic models, it enables modeling documents with countable infinite mixture components, thus provides the flexibility of modeling images whose actual semantic component numbers are unknown.

2.2 Modeling User's Perspective

Study of social tagging in web-based applications has gained increased popularity in the data mining community. Specifically, several probabilistic generative models have been proposed to study users' tagging patterns [10, 11]. In [11], a topic-perspective (TP) model is proposed to infer how both users' perspective and the resource content relate to the generation of social annotations. It improves the generative process of social annotations by separating the tag generation process from the generation process of the resource content. While the resource content (such as text words) is only generated from resource topics, the social tags are generated by both resource topic and user perspective. In this model, the user perspective not only refers to the user's interest, but also covers the user's expertise, motivation, language and other personal factors.

3. MODELING USER-TAGGED IMAGES

In this section, we introduce the perspective HDP (pHDP) model for user-tagged images. We present graphical representation of pHDP model in Fig. 1. Following the convention in depicting graphical representation of topic models, we use round nodes to represent random variables, in which the white nodes stand for latent random variables, while the gray nodes denote observed ones during the model training. The rounded boxes are used to represent fixed hyper-parameters of the model, while the edges illustrate the conditional dependency in the generative process.

For clarity, we name each tagged image as a *document*. Some notations to be used in the two models are listed as follows: J is the number of image documents, K *and* K' (both are countable infinite) indicate the number of semantic mixture components; when K is a finite number, the models become LDA-like models. To represent the image content, we utilize the saliency features (including visual code-words [12] and MSER feature [13]) as a complement part of the holistic GIST features [3]. Our motivation comes from the fact that the mechanism of human visual perception allows for very rapid holistic image analysis to provide a coarse context of image scene (special layout model), yet it also gives rise to a small set of candidate salient locations in a scene (saliency model) that needs to be intensively studied [2]. In Fig. 1, N_j^t is the number of tags in document j, while N_j^v and N_j^r represent the total number of extracted visual code-words and MSER regions in document j, respectively. In the model, the holistic representation of an image is replicated *10* times to enable the posterior sampling, so N_j^h denoted the hth replication of the holistic image representation in document j. In both models, we assume fixed value for Dirichlet process concentration parameters α_0 and γ. We also assume symmetric priors α_u, ξv, ξ_t, η and ζ for Dirichlet distributions in the models. Detailed explanations of notations in following discussions are summarized in Table 1.

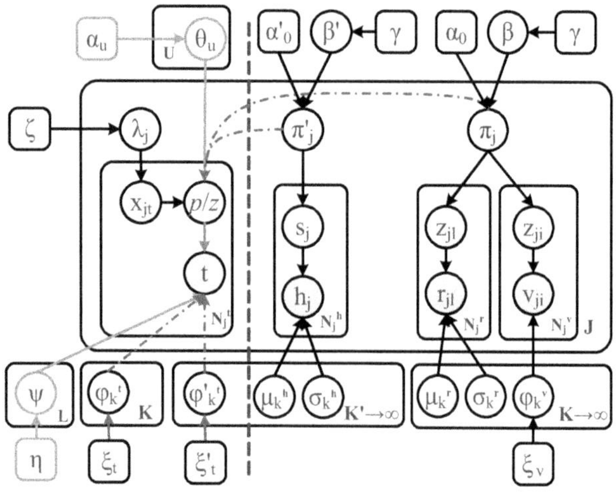

Fig. 1 Graphical representation of the perspective HDP (pHDP) model for user-tagged images

Table 1. Notations in proposed topic model

t, p, v, r, h	Instances of variables: t for tags, p for user's perspective, v for visual word, r for MSER feature, h for GIST feature
J, T, U, L	Number of documents, tags, users, user's perspectives
z_t, z_{ji}, z_{jl}, s_j	Indicators for semantic components.
K, K'	The number of components at a certain time point.
$N_j^v, N_j^r, N_j^t, N_j^h$	Number of visual words, MSER regions and tags, plus the replication number of GIST features in document j
$C_{vk}^{VZ}, C_{vk,-i}^{VZ}$	Number of times visual word v was assigned to semantic component k, with/without counting the current instance
C_{rk}^{RZ} $C_{rk,-i}^{RZ}$	Number of MSER feature vectors being assigned to component k, with/without counting the current instance
$C_{hk'}^{HS}$ $C_{hk',-i}^{HS}$	Number of GIST feature vectors being assigned to component k', with/without counting current instance.
$C_{pu,-q}^{PU}$	The number of times that perspective p is adopted by user u, except current instance;
$\tilde{n}_{j,-q}$	The number of tags in document $d=j$ generated from user's perspectives ($x_{jt}=2$), except current instance;
$n_{j,-q}$ $n'_{j,-q}$	The number of tags in document $d=j$ generated from semantic components ($x_{jt}=0,1$), except current instance
$C_{tp,-q}^{TP}$	The number of times that tag $t=q$ is generated from user's perspective p, except current instance;
$C_{tk,-q}^{TZ}, C_{tk',-q}^{TS}$	The number of times that tag $t=q$ is generated from semantic component k, k', except current instance;
α_0, γ	Concentration parameters of Dirichlet process.
$\varphi_k^t, \varphi'^t_k$	The tag distribution of semantic component k, k'.
φ_k^v	The visual word distribution of semantic component k
π_j	The document-level weights of semantic component indicators for document j
$\alpha_u, \xi_v, \xi_t, \eta, \zeta$	Hyper-parameters of Dirichlet distributions
$\mu^{(n)}_k, \sigma^{(n)2}_k$	Parameters of the nth Gaussian distribution with respect to the kth semantic component
$\overline{u}_{k,n}, s_{k,n}^2$	Sample mean and sample variance of the nth Gaussian distribution with respect to the kth semantic component
θ_u, ψ_p	The perspective distribution of user u, and the tag distribution of perspective p.
x, λ_j	Switch variable that decides the source of each tag and the document-level distribution of different x values
$\boldsymbol{\beta}$	The global weight of semantic component indicators across the corpora

As shown in Fig. 1, this model primarily comprises of two parts split by the dash line. The part on the right hand side is essentially the standard HDP model. The generative process of this part begins with drawing a global probability measure $G_0 \sim \mathrm{DP}(\gamma, H)$ and for each document j, draw a child Dirichlet process $G_j \sim \mathrm{DP}(\alpha_0, G_0)$. Following the stick-breaking construction, it is equivalent to firstly drawing a global weight $\boldsymbol{\beta} \sim \mathrm{GEM}(\gamma)$ for semantic component indicators k, then for each document j, draw the document-level weights of semantic component indicators $\boldsymbol{\pi}_j \sim \mathrm{DP}(\alpha_0, \boldsymbol{\beta})$. The data observations in document j are generated by repeatedly drawing semantic component indicator z_{ji} and z_{jl} from $\boldsymbol{\pi}_j$ and then draw each data observation (i.e. each MSER region and each visual code-word) from the conditional probability of the sampled semantic component.

The left half of the model is for the generation of image tags. As mentioned in Section 1, image tags have various functional purposes. For example, some tags (like most *factual* tags) are closely related to the contents displayed in images, while other tags (including *location* tags, *subjective* tags and *personal* tags) indicate user's contextual information as well as his/her subjective feelings and preferences, which we refer to as "user's perspectives". Accordingly, the generative process of user-tagged images should be able to take into account both user's perspectives and semantic components from image contents. In pHDP model, each tag t created by user u for document j can be either drawn from the semantic components associated with j's image content or from u's perspectives. To decide the source of each tag, a switch variable x is introduced. For each tag t in document j, the value of x_{jt} (which takes values 0-2) is sampled from a multinomial distribution λ_j (with a Dirichlet prior ζ). When the value of x_{jt} equals 0 or 1, the topical indicator of tag t is draw uniformly from the semantic components learned from the image contents (the red dashed arrows in Fig. 1 show this process). When x_{jt} equals 2, a user perspective p will be sampled from the perspective distribution θ_u for user u, and tag t will be drawn from the tag distribution ψ_p of perspective p (the blue arrows in Fig. 1 illustrate this procedure). The switch variable x plays a critical role in the pHDP model; it is a personalized factor that indicates in which extent the user's perspectives influence the tagging results. It provides the model a flexibility to determine if a specific image tag relates to the semantic components displayed in an image, or it relates to user's context information as well as his/her subjective feeling and preference (user's perspective). The generative process of the pHDP model is represented in Table 2.

Table 2. The generative process of proposed models

1. Draw a global weight $\boldsymbol{\beta} \sim \mathrm{GEM}(\gamma)$;
2. For each semantic component k, draw $\lambda_k \sim \mathrm{Beta}(1,\zeta)$, $\varphi_k^v \sim \mathrm{Dirichlet}(\xi_v)$, $\varphi_k^t \sim \mathrm{Dirichlet}(\xi_t)$;
3. For each semantic component k, sample Gaussian-parameters $\mu_{kh}, \sigma_{kh}, \mu_{kr}, \sigma_{kr}$ from sample mean and sample variance;
4. For each user u, sample $\theta_u \sim \mathrm{Dirichlet}(\alpha_u)$, for each user perspective p, sample $\psi_p \sim \mathrm{Dirichlet}(\eta)$;
5. For the jth document, draw $\boldsymbol{\pi}_j \sim \mathrm{DP}(\alpha_0, \boldsymbol{\beta})$, $\boldsymbol{\pi}'_j \sim \mathrm{DP}(\alpha_0, \boldsymbol{\beta}')$;
6. For the holistic scene representation of the jth tagged image ,
   a. sample scene component indicator $s_j = k \sim \mathrm{Discrete}(\boldsymbol{\pi}'_j)$,
   b. for the nth dimension of the GIST feature vector h_j
      i. sample $h^{(n)}_j \sim N(\mu^{(n)}_{kh}, \sigma^{(n)}_{kh}{}^2)$
7. For the ith of the N_j^v visual code-words in the jth document
   a. sample object component indicator $z_{ji}=k \sim \mathrm{Discrete}(\boldsymbol{\pi}_j)$
   b. sample its texton id $v_{ji} \sim \mathrm{Multinomial}(\varphi_k^v)$;
8. For the lth of the N_j^r MSER salient regions in the jth document
   a. sample object component indicator $z_{jl}=k \sim \mathrm{Discrete}(\boldsymbol{\pi}_j)$
   b. for the nth dimension of MSER feature vector r_{jl}
      i. *sample* $r^{(n)}_{jl} \sim N(\mu^{(n)}_{kr}, \sigma^{(n)}_{kr}{}^2)$
9. For each document j, sample $\lambda_j \sim \mathrm{Dirichlet}(\zeta)$;
10. For each tag t in document j created by user u;
    a. sample a switch variable $x \sim \mathrm{Multinomial}(\lambda_j)$;
    b. if ($x = 0$)
       Sample semantic component indicator $z_t \sim \mathrm{Discrete}(\boldsymbol{\pi}_j)$
       Sample a tag $t \sim \mathrm{Multinomial}(\varphi_k^t)$
    c. if ($x = 1$)
       Sample semantic component indicator $z_t \sim \mathrm{Uniform}(\boldsymbol{\pi}'_j)$
       Sample a tag $t \sim \mathrm{Multinomial}(\varphi'^t_k)$
    d. if ($x = 2$)
       Sample a perspective $p_t \sim \mathrm{Multinomial}(\theta_u)$;
       Sample a tag $t \sim \mathrm{Multinomial}(\psi_p)$;

4. GIBBS SAMPLING FOR THE MODEL ESTIMATION

In this section, we describe the Gibbs sampling scheme for the proposed pHDP model. The sampling scheme consists of two steps. The first step is sampling for semantic component indicators z as well as the corresponding HDP hyper-parameters β. In order to sample a HDP-like model, one may either follow the Chinese restaurant franchise (CRF) or use direct assignment [5]. In our work, the direct assignment is used (Table 3).

Table 3. The posterior sampling of semantic components

Preliminaries:

Suppose that at current stage of the sampling, only K of $L\to\infty$ semantic components have been assigned to the observations, define: $\beta_u = \sum_{k=K+1}^{\infty} \beta_k$, and $\gamma_r = \gamma / L$, $\gamma_u = \gamma(L-K) / L$, then we get: $\boldsymbol{\beta}=\{\beta_1,\ldots,\beta_k,\beta_u\}\sim\text{Dirichlet}(\gamma_r,\ldots,\gamma_r,\gamma_u)$.

Repeat for each data observation until convergence:

Sampling z (may either equals to an existing k or $k_{new}=K+1$)

Firstly, integrate out $\boldsymbol{\pi}_j$ to get the marginal probability $p(z|\boldsymbol{\beta})$:

$$p(\mathbf{z}\,|\,\boldsymbol{\beta}) = \int_{\pi_j} p(\mathbf{z}\,|\,\pi_j)p(\pi_j\,|\,\alpha_0,\beta)d\pi_j$$

$$=\prod_{j=1}^{J}\int_{\pi_j}\prod_{k=1}^{K}\pi_{jk}^{n_{jk}+\alpha_0\beta_k-1}\cdot\frac{\Gamma\left(\sum_{k=1}^{K}\alpha_0\beta_k\right)}{\prod_{k=1}^{K}\Gamma(\alpha_0\beta_k)}d\pi_j$$

$$=\prod_{j=1}^{J}\left[\frac{\Gamma(\alpha_0)}{\Gamma\left(\alpha_0+n_{j.}\right)}\cdot\prod_{k=1}^{K}\frac{\Gamma(\alpha_0\beta_k+n_{jk})}{\Gamma(\alpha_0\beta_k)}\right]$$

Secondly, get the posterior probability of z_{ji} given the data observations (not counting the current observation v_{ji})

$$p(z_{ji}=k\,|\,v_{ji},\mathbf{z}^{\text{-ji}},\mathbf{v}^{\text{-ji}},\boldsymbol{\beta}) \propto p(z_{ji}=k\,|\,\mathbf{z}^{\text{-ji}},\boldsymbol{\beta})p(v_{ji}\,|\,z_{ji},\mathbf{z}^{\text{-ji}},\mathbf{v}^{\text{-ji}},\boldsymbol{\beta})$$

$$\propto\begin{cases}(\alpha_0\beta_k+n_{jk}^{-ji})f_k^{-v_{ji}}(v_{ji})\\(\alpha_0\beta_k)f_{k_{new}}^{-v_{ji}}(v_{ji})\end{cases}$$

For visual word v_{ji}, $f_k^{-v_{ji}}(v_{ji})\propto\frac{C_{vk,-i}^{VZ}+\xi_v}{\sum_{v'=1}^{V}C_{v'k,-i}^{VZ}+V\xi_v}$, $f_{k_{new}}^{-v_{ji}}(v_{ji})\propto\frac{\xi_v}{V\xi_v}$

Similarly, for both MESR feature vector and GIST feature vector,

$$f_k^{-r_{ji}}(r_{ji})\propto\prod_n t_{C_{rk,-i}^{RZ}-1}(r^{(n)}\,|\,\overline{\mu}_{k,n},s_{k,n}^2/C_{rk,-i}^{RZ})$$

$$f_{k_{new}}^{-r_{ji}}(r_{ji})\propto\prod_n t_{C_{-i}^{RZ}-1}(r^{(n)}\,|\,\overline{\mu}_n,s_n^2/C_{-i}^{RZ})$$

in which $t_{n-1}\left(r^{(n)}\,|\,\overline{u},s^2/n\right)$ denotes the student-t density with mean $\overline{u}$, variance s^2/n and n-1 degree of freedom.

Sampling m (feasible when n_{jk}< 200)

For each j, the auxiliary variable m ($0\le m\le n_{jk}$) is sampled as:

$$p(m_{jk}=m\,|\,\mathbf{m}^{\text{-jk}},\mathbf{z},\boldsymbol{\beta})=\frac{\Gamma(\alpha_0\beta_k)}{\Gamma(n_{jk}+\alpha_0\beta_k)}s(n_{jk},m)(\alpha_0\beta_k)^m$$

in which $s(n,m)$ is defined as: $s(0,0)=s(1,1)=1$, $s(n,0)=0$, $s(n,m)=0$ for $m>n$, $s(n+1,m)=s(n,m-1)+ns(n,m)$

Sampling β: accumulate m_{jk} for all document j to get $m_{.1}$, $m_{.2}$, …, $m_{.K}$, then draw $\boldsymbol{\beta}\sim$ Dirichlet($m_{.1}$, $m_{.2}$, …, $m_{.K}$, γ)

The second step is sampling for switch variable x, perspective distribution θ_u, tag distribution φ_k, φ'_k and ψ. We derive the sampling equation of switch variable x_{jt} for each tag $t=q$ in document $d=j$ as follows:

$$p\left(x_{jt}=0,z_{jt}=k\,|\,t=q,\mathbf{z}_{\text{-q}},\mathbf{t}_{\text{-q}},\xi_t,\zeta\right)\propto$$
$$\frac{n_{j,-q}+\zeta}{n_{j,-q}+n'_j+\tilde{n}_j+3\zeta}\cdot\frac{C_{vk}^{VZ}+C_{rk}^{RZ}}{N_j^v+N_j^r}\cdot\frac{C_{tk,-q}^{TZ}+\xi_t}{\sum_{t'}C_{t'k,-q}^{TZ}+T\xi_t} \quad (1)$$

$$p\left(x_{jt}=1,z_{jt}=k'\,|\,t=q,\mathbf{z}_{\text{-q}},\mathbf{t}_{\text{-q}},\xi'_t,\zeta\right)\propto$$
$$\frac{n'_{j,-q}+\zeta}{n_j+n'_{j,-q}+\tilde{n}_j+3\zeta}\cdot\frac{C_{hk'}^{HS}}{N_j^h}\cdot\frac{C_{tk',-q}^{TS}+\xi'_t}{\sum_{t'}C_{t'k',-q}^{TS}+T\xi'_t} \quad (2)$$

$$p\left(x_{jt}=2,z_{jt}=p\,|\,t=q,\mathbf{z}_{\text{-q}},\mathbf{t}_{\text{-q}},\eta,\zeta\right)\propto$$
$$\frac{\tilde{n}_{j,-q}+\zeta}{n_j+n'_j+\tilde{n}_{j,-q}+3\zeta}\cdot\frac{C_{pu,-q}^{PU}+\alpha_u}{\sum_{p'}C_{p'u,-q}^{PU}+L\alpha_u}\cdot\frac{C_{tp,-q}^{TP}+\eta}{\sum_{t'}C_{t'p,-q}^{TP}+T\eta} \quad (3)$$

After a set of sampling processes based on the posterior distribution calculated above, other parameters can be sampled using the following equations:

$$\psi_p^{(t)}=\frac{C_{tp,-q}^{TP}+\eta}{\sum_{t'}C_{t'p,-q}^{TP}+T\eta},\qquad \varphi_{kt}^{(t)}=\frac{C_{tk,-q}^{TZ}+\xi_t}{\sum_{t'}C_{t'k,-q}^{TZ}+T\xi_t}$$

$$\varphi_{k't}^{(t)}=\frac{C_{tk',-q}^{TS}+\xi'_t}{\sum_{t'}C_{t'k',-q}^{TS}+T\xi'_t},\qquad \theta_u^{(p)}=\frac{C_{pu,-q}^{PU}+\alpha_u}{\sum_{p'}C_{p'u,-q}^{PU}+L\alpha_u}$$

$$\lambda_j^{(0)}=\frac{n_{j,-q}+\zeta}{n_j+n'_j+\tilde{n}_{j,-q}+3\zeta},\qquad \lambda_j^{(1)}=\frac{n'_{j,-q}+\zeta}{n_j+n'_j+\tilde{n}_{j,-q}+3\zeta}$$

$$\lambda_j^{(2)}=\frac{\tilde{n}_{j,-q}+\zeta}{n_j+n'_j+\tilde{n}_{j,-q}+3\zeta}$$

5. EXPERIMENTS AND RESULTS

In this section, we investigate the performance of the proposed pHDP model in automatic image tagging experiments using the MIR-Flickr dataset, which is composed of 25000 images covering a wide spectrum of image categories (contributed by a total of 9862 Flickr users). In total, there are 302447 tags, with a vocabulary size (number of unique tags) of 64037; thus the average number of tags per image is 8.94. In the image tagging experiment, we use a 50% subset of the MIR-Flickr collection as training data and the other 50% as testing data (with tags removed). On constructing the two subsets, we ensure that tagged images from the same user are equally split to both subsets. The values of global concentration parameter γ and the user perspective number L are determined by perplexity comparison on a serial of values. Other hyper-parameters (such as Dirichlet distribution priors: α_u, ξv, ξ_t, η and ζ) are set in prior and fixed during the experiments. The prediction of image tags for the testing images is achieved by performing another Gibbs sampling on testing images to estimate the document-level distribution of switch variable and semantic components, with a fixed set of semantic components and user perspectives estimated from the training dataset. On the convergence of Gibbs sampling, the probability of tagging an image j from user u with tag t_j is:

$$p(t_j)=p(x_{jt}=0,1)\sum_{k=1}^{K}p(t_j\,|\,z_k)p_{test}(z_k\,|\,j)+$$
$$p(x_{jt}=2)\sum_{l=1}^{L}p(t_j\,|\,p_l)p_{test}(p_l\,|\,u) \quad (4)$$

The performance is evaluated by perplexity and tagging accuracy.

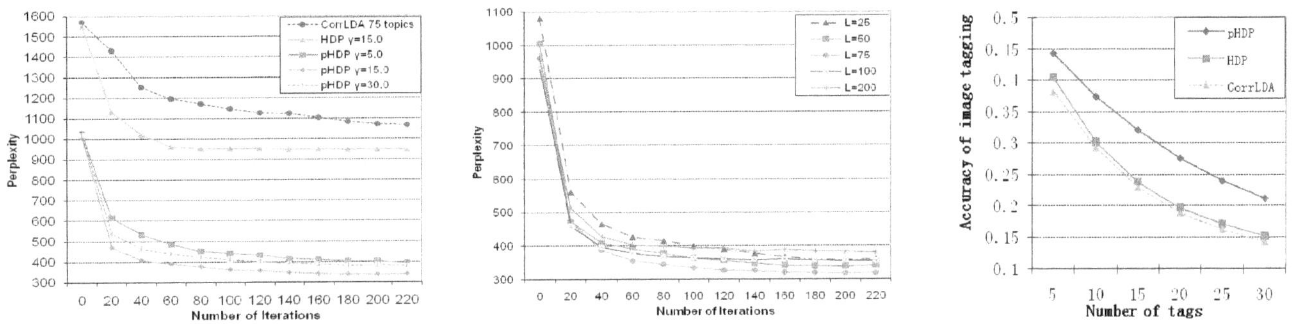

(a) Perplexity changing over iterations b) Perplexity as perspective number changing (γ=15.0) c) average image tagging accuracy

Fig. 2 The comparison of the proposed pHDP models and baseline models

5.1 Perplexity Comparison

The perplexity is a standard criterion for generative probabilistic models that evaluates how well the model predicts the testing data. The perplexity of a testing image dataset D_{test} is:

$$perplexity(D_{test}) = \exp\left[\frac{-\sum_{j=1}^{D_{test}} \log(p(\mathbf{t}_j))}{\sum_{j=1}^{D_{test}} N_j^t}\right] \quad (5)$$

The perplexity score for a model is the lower the better.

Fig. 2(a) shows the perplexity changing of the proposed pHDP model and baseline modes (CorrLDA model and HDP model) over the iterations during the Gibbs sampling process. We test pHDP model on a serial of γ values. For CorrLDA model and HDP model, we only show their perplexity scores under the optimal parameter settings (i.e. CorrLDA model with 75 topics and HDP model with γ=15.0). The results show that pHDP model achieve best performance with γ=15.0 and it outperforms both HDP model and CorrLDA model. Fig 2(b) represents the perplexity of pHDP model under different perspective numbers. The optimal perspective number is L=75.

5.2 Image Tagging Accuracy Evaluation

Using Eq. (4), we calculate the probability of tagging an image j from user u with different tags. Tags with highest probability are used for tagging. After that, the predicted top-ranked image tags are compared with the ground truth for validation. If a predicted tag finds exact match in the ground truth tags, it will be considered as one hit. The ratios of hit numbers over the predicted tag numbers are averaged to produce the final annotation accuracy.

Fig. 3 illustrates examples of image tagging results. Fig. 3(a) is an image shows a winter night in Toronto, Ontario, Canada. The ground truth image tags involve both *location* tags ('ontario', 'canada') and *topic* tags (such as 'clouds', 'lake', 'night', sky and 'water'). However, the image content alone provides little clues about the location. Further studies indicate that other images contributed by the same user are also tagged with 'ontario' and 'canada'. This may suggest that the user lives in Ontario, Canada and contribute pictures taken from the same location. During the pHDP modeling, this user contextual information is captured as a part of the user's perspectives. When tagging a new image from the same user, the pHDP model will smooth the document-level predictive tag distribution with user's perspective and allow for tagging with *location* tags (Fig. 3(a) and 3(b), highlighted in bold). Fig 3(c) is contributed a user from Malaysia. Similarly, the user contextual information is captured in user's perspectives. Thus the pHDP model succeeds in tagging image with both *location* tags (such as 'malaysia') and *type* tags (camera settings, like 'nikon'). As shown in Fig. 3(c), tags predicted by the pHDP model also involve *subjective* tag, like 'interestingness', which demonstrates that the pHDP model is also capable of modeling user's subjective feelings. As a comparison, the HDP model fails to predict either *location* tags or *subjective* tags since it only relies on image content to make tag predictions.

User ID: 17875539@N00
Title: City with Ice
Tags: toronto, torontoharbour, canada, ontario, clouds, lake, night, sky, structures, water, ice, winter, snow, frozen, city, cityscape, nikon, nikond200, cold, landscape, lake, water, outdoor, outdoorphotography, frost, frosty

Top ranked tag	Probability
canada	**0.0606**
ontario	**0.0597**
water	0.0523
sky	0.0474
lake	0.0427
toronto	**0.0322**
clouds	0.0295
outdoor	0.0257
structures	0.0232

tags predicted by pHDP

Top ranked tag	Probability
structures	0.0538
sky	0.0329
night	0.0265
transport	0.0230
clouds	0.0209
water	0.0173
sunset	0.0159
sea	0.0102
road	0.0097

tags predicted by HDP

(a) tagging results of image entitled 'City with Ice'

User ID: 17875539@N00
Title: Some say in ice
Tags: lake, night, ontario, toronto, torontoharbour, canada, ice, frozen, winter, dawn, morning, nature, sky, water, landscape, snow, nikon, nikond200, cold, cherrybeach, outdoor, natural, frost, frosty

Top ranked tag	Probability
sky	0.0458
canada	**0.0446**
ontario	**0.0439**
structures	0.0395
clouds	0.0244
water	0.0226
toronto	**0.0209**
sunset	0.0202
sea	0.0195

tags predicted by pHDP

Top ranked tag	Probability
sky	0.0375
structures	0.0306
clouds	0.0300
water	0.0199
sunset	0.0173
sea	0.0167
flower	0.0162
transport	0.0139
outdoor	0.0124

tags predicted by HDP

(b) tagging results of image entitled 'Some say in ice'

User ID: 9352758@N04
Title: Spread your wings and and fly away
Tags: female, people, portrait, tree, children, play, fun, windy, wind, fly, kid, girl, hair, malaysia, landscape, nikon, d50, movement, vacation, travel, diamond class photographer, an awesome shot

Top ranked tag	Probability
people	0.0631
female	0.0346
portrait	0.0305
flower	0.0239
outdoor	0.0427
nikon	0.0238
malaysia	**0.0227**
sky	0.0208
interestingness	0.0207

tags predicted by pHDP

Top ranked tag	Probability
people	0.0518
female	0.0290
portrait	0.0283
sky	0.0242
outdoor	0.0219
clouds	0.0213
tree	0.0187
flower	0.0156
water	0.0134

tags predicted by HDP

(c) tagging results of image entitled 'Spread your wings and and fly away'

Fig. 3 Illustration of automatic image tagging results

Fig 2(c) shows the overall image tagging accuracy (averaged over the testing dataset) of different models under their optimal parameter settings. It should be noted that the accuracy is calculated based on exact match, so it won't take into account the synonym tags. In other words, predicted tags like 'human' and 'female' will be considered as unmatched with respect to the ground truth tag 'girl'. According to the result, the HDP model doesn't show much improvement in the tagging accuracy compared to the CorrLDA model. It's reasonable because the CorrLDA model is in essence a finite case of HDP model. Under optimal parameter settings, their performance should be similar. The pHDP model, as it integrates the user perspective information, significantly outperforms both CorrLDA model and HDP model in predicting image tags for different users.

6. CONCLUSIONS

In this paper, we proposed a perspective Hierarchical Dirichlet Process (pHDP) model to deal with user-tagged image modeling. The contribution is twofold. Firstly, we associate image features with image tags. Secondly, we incorporate the user's perspectives into the image tag generation process and introduce new latent variables to determine if an image tag is generated from user's perspectives or from the image content. Therefore, the model is capable of extracting both embedded semantic components and user's perspectives from user-tagged images. Based on the proposed pHDP model, we achieve automatic image tagging with users' perspective. Experimental results show that the pHDP model achieves better image tagging performance compared to state-of-the-art topic models.

7. ACKNOWLEDGMENTS

This work was supported in part by NSF CCF 0905291, NSF CCF 1049864, NSFC 90920005.

8. REFERENCES

[1] D.M. Blei, and M.I. Jordan, Modeling annotated data The 26th annual international ACM SIGIR conference on Research and development in informaion retrieval, ACM, Toronto, Canada, 2003, pp. 127-134.

[2] Henderson, J.M. and Hollingworth, A. High level scene perception. Annual Review of Psychology, 50:243–271, 1999.

[3] C. Siagian and L. Itti, Rapid Biologically-Inspired Scene Classification Using Features Shared with Visual Attention, IEEE TPAMI, pp. 300-312, 2007.

[4] A. W. M. Smeulders, M. Worring, S. Santini, A. Gupta, and R. Jain, Content-based image rerieval at the end of the early years, IEEE Transactions on Pattern Analysis and Machine Intelligence, vol. 22, no. 12, pp. 1349–1380, 2000.

[5] Y. Teh, M. Jordan, M. Beal, and D. Blei. Hierarchical Dirichlet process. Journal of the American Statistical Association, 101(476):1566-1581, 2006

[6] K. Bischoff, C.S. Firan, W. Nejdl, and R. Paiu, Can All Tags be Used for Search?, CIKM'08, Napa Valley, California, USA, 2008, pp. 203-212.

[7] S. Sen, S.K.T. Lam, A.M. Rashid, D. Cosley, D. Frankowski, J. Osterhouse, F.M. Harper, and J. Riedl, Tagging, communities, vocabulary, evolution, CSCW'06, Banff, Alberta, Canada, 2006.

[8] Amr Ahmed, Eric P. Xing, William W. Cohen, Robert F. Murphy, Structured Correspondence topic models for mining captioned figures in biomedical literature, Proceedings of the 15th ACM SIGKDD International conference on Knowledge discovery and data mining, June 28-July 01, 2009, Paris, France.

[9] X. Chen, C. Lu, Y. An, and P. Achananuparp. Probabilistic Models for Topic Learning from Images and Captions in Online Biomedical Literatures. In the Proceedings of 18th ACM Conference on Information and Knowledge Management (CIKM'09)

[10] D. Zhou, J. Bian, S. Zheng, H. Zha, and C.L. Giles, Exploring Social Annotations for Information Retrieval, WWW 2008, Beijing, China, 2008, pp. 715-724.

[11] C. Lu, X. Hu, X. Chen and J. Park. The topic-perspective model for social tagging systems, The 16th ACM SIGKDD Conference on Knowledge Discovery and Data Mining (KDD'10), July 25-28, 2010, Washington D.C., USA. pp. 683-692.

[12] Sivic, J., Zisserman, A.: Video Google: A Text Retrieval Approach to Object Matching in Videos. International Conference on Computer Vision. (2003) 1470– 1477

[13] J. Matas, O. Chum, U. M., T. Pajdla. Robust wide baseline stereo from maximally stable extremal regions. In BMVC, 2002.

Asking What No One Has Asked Before: Using Phrase Similarities To Generate Synthetic Web Search Queries

Marius Paşca
Google Inc.
1600 Amphitheatre Parkway
Mountain View, California
mars@google.com

ABSTRACT

This paper introduces a method for automatically inferring meaningful, not-yet-submitted queries. The inferred queries fill some of the knowledge gaps between documents, on one hand, and known (i.e., already-submitted) queries, on the other hand. Thus, the inferred queries expand query logs and increase their coverage. New candidate queries are over-generated from known queries via phrase similarity data, then filtered against the set of known queries. The accuracy of the generated queries is computed using open-domain questions from standard question answering evaluation sets. Over the ranked lists of questions inferred for each of the evaluation questions, the precision reaches 0.9 at rank 50. The set of inferred queries is more than twice as large as the set of input queries.

Categories and Subject Descriptors

H.3.1 [**Information Storage and Retrieval**]: Content Analysis and Indexing; H.3.3 [**Information Storage and Retrieval**]: Information Search and Retrieval; I.2.6 [**Artificial Intelligence**]: Learning; I.2.7 [**Artificial Intelligence**]: Natural Language Processing

General Terms

Algorithms, Experimentation

Keywords

Query generation, synthetic queries, query templates, distributional similarities, Web search queries, query logs

1. INTRODUCTION

Background: Queries submitted collectively by Web search users indirectly convey human knowledge. Given the query *"how to replace a clutch on a honda civic"*, car enthusiasts would easily recognize that a particular car has parts that sometimes need replacement. Similarly, music aficionados would quickly interpret a query *"lyrics of yesterday beatles"* to refer to the lyrics of a particular song performed by a particular band. But not all queries lend themselves to easy interpretation. Indeed, queries take many forms, varying from relatively infrequent grammatically-structured, precise natural-language queries, to frequent noisy, underspecified, keyword-based queries. Throughout this continuum, the desire for better understanding of search queries is pervasive [7, 5], given its benefits towards better search results.

Motivation: If knowledge is generally prominent, users will eventually ask about it, especially as the number of users and the breadth of the available knowledge increase. But at a given time, an ever-growing document collection like the Web may capture more knowledge than has been asked about by search queries. Generating all meaningful queries that fill the knowledge gaps between documents, on one hand, and known (i.e., already-submitted) queries, on the other hand, is a daunting task. Manually compiling a comprehensive set of questions about a document or passage requires deep understanding of the document. Fortunately, some of the knowledge gaps are easier to fill than others. If a clutch is a replacement part on a *honda civic* and on a *truck*, it might be a replacement part on similar items including a *motorcycle* or *toyota yaris*, even if the query *"how to replace a clutch on a toyota yaris"* has not been submitted yet. Equally, if there are lyrics of *yesterday* and *hey jude*, there may be lyrics of *lovely rita* and *here comes the sun*, even if *"lyrics of here comes the sun beatles"* is not in the input set of queries.

Since inferred queries are new requests for knowledge derived from known requests for knowledge, they are useful in knowledge acquisition and access. For example, the development and training of specialized modules, such as those answering natural-language questions, benefit from the availability of additional inferred questions. In information extraction, methods operating over query logs rather than document collections benefit from a larger number of input queries, which increases the coverage of the extracted data. In Web search interfaces, inferred queries enrich the sets of queries displayed as potential completions based on what Web search users have typed so far, reducing the time to search result.

Contributions: We introduce a method for generating open-ended, not-yet submitted queries. The method aggregates known queries into query templates (e.g., *"lyrics of ⋆ beatles"*) associated with known phrase fillers (e.g., ⋆→{*yesterday, hey jude*}). The known phrase fillers of each query template are then expanded into new candidate phrase fillers. Queries generated in previous work have particular form (i.e., natural-language questions) and often require extensive linguistic processing of documents [14, 4]. In contrast, our method automatically generates new queries based on query analysis alone, as opposed to individual document analysis. This has the potential advantages of scalability and robustness with arbitrary, inherently-noisy queries. Furthermore, the method produces open-ended queries whose form resembles that of known queries, whether keyword-based or expressed in natural language. When

CIKM'11, October 24–28, 2011, Glasgow, Scotland, UK.

applied to a large set of anonymized search queries, the method generates more than twice as many new queries as there are input queries. The accuracy of the generated queries is computed over ranked lists of new phrase fillers generated for question templates corresponding to open-domain questions from standard question answering evaluation sets [18]. Precision over the evaluation set of question templates, for which new phrase fillers are generated, reaches 0.93 at rank 10 and 0.90 at rank 50.

2. GENERATING NEW QUERIES

Definitions: A query Q is a sequence of tokens Q=[q_1 q_2 .. q_i .. q_{N_Q}], submitted as a search query by Web users.

A query template T is a generalization of a set of queries that share a common prefix [q_1 q_2 .. q_{i-1}] and a common postfix [q_{j+1} .. q_{N_Q}]. The template is obtained by replacing the variable infix [q_i q_{i+1} .. q_j] from each query, with a generic template filler $\star$: T=[q_1 q_2 .. q_{i-1} $\star$ q_{j+1}.. q_{N_T}]. The template filler $\star$ is associated with the set of infixes, or phrase fillers, from the queries that contributed to it. Each of the contributing queries can be reconstructed from the query template.

A template signature T_S is a generalization of a set of query templates that, if their token sequences are reduced to token sets (i.e., ignoring the relative order of the tokens), become the same. Some tokens that belong to a fixed, global set of tokens deemed irrelevant may be discarded in the process. The template signature is associated with the query templates that contribute to it. Using these definitions, the processing stages of our method for generating new queries are described in the following.

Aggregation into Query Templates: Our method takes as input a set of Web search queries. The sequence of tokens available in each query is split into all combinations of triples of a prefix, non-empty infix and postfix. For example, *"lyrics of hey jude beatles"* is split into *lyrics*, *of hey jude*, *beatles*; *lyrics of*, *hey jude*, *beatles*; *lyrics of*, *hey*, *jude beatles*; etc. Resulting triples that share a common prefix and postfix are aggregated into a query template, where the input infixes are the known phrase fillers of the template:

$$\left.\begin{array}{l}\text{lyrics of come together beatles}\\ \text{lyrics of hey jude beatles}\\ \text{lyrics of yesterday beatles}\end{array}\right\}\text{“lyrics of } \star \text{ beatles”}$$

where the template filler $\star$ corresponds to the set of known phrase fillers, i.e., infixes from the input queries: {*yesterday*, *hey jude*, *come together*}. An input query may contribute to the creation of multiple query templates, via different infixes. For example, another template created from *"lyrics of yesterday beatles"* is *"lyrics of yesterday* $\star$*"*:

$$\left.\begin{array}{l}\text{lyrics of yesterday toni braxton}\\ \text{lyrics of yesterday leona lewis}\\ \text{lyrics of yesterday beatles}\end{array}\right\}\text{“lyrics of yesterday } \star\text{”}$$

Generation of Candidate Phrase Fillers: In order to generate new queries, we expand the set of known phrase fillers into additional candidate phrases that may fill the query template. The expansion of phrase fillers is similar to the task of instance set expansion [15, 20], with a few differences. First, the instance set (i.e., the known phrases) to be expanded is derived automatically from noisy search queries, rather than provided manually as a clean set of seed instances. This is a crucial difference, since the choice of the instance set to be expanded has been shown to greatly affect the outcome and quality of the expansion, even with "correct", manually selected seeds [15]. Second, the set of known phrases varies in size across templates, from very small to very large. Third, it is not necessarily semantically coherent since it can span disjoint, unrelated classes: it includes *first* and *exxon valdez*, for the template *"when was the* $\star$ *oil spill"*; and *fragile x syndrome* and *men and women*, for *"what is the life expectancy for* $\star$*"*. Fourth, the expansion needs to be performed at large scale, i.e., individually for all query templates created from the set of input queries.

As a prerequisite to generating candidate phrase fillers, distributionally similar phrases [11, 12, 15] and their scores are collected in advance. Let $DS(K_i)$ be the list of most distributionally similar phrases of a known phrase filler K_i from a query template T. Any phrase U from $DS(K_i)$ is considered as a candidate phrase filler U of the respective query template. The score of U relative to the entire set of known fillers $\{K_i\}_{i=1}^{N}$ (and therefore, relative to T) is:

$$Sim(U,T) = \frac{\sum_{i=1}^{N} DSscore(U,K_i)}{N} \tag{1}$$

where $DSscore(U,K_i)$ is the distributional similarity score [10] between U and K_i. For each template T, its candidate phrase fillers U are ranked in decreasing order of their scores. Known phrase fillers of T are discarded from the resulting list of candidate phrase fillers of T.

Filtering of Candidate Phrase Fillers: Candidate phrase fillers generated via distributional similarities are similar to known phrases only statically. To also take the context of the query template into account, the candidates are filtered using only the input queries:

1) A canonical, keyword-based template signature T_S is created from each template T. The process discards tokens from T that either are stop words, or are marked by a part-of-speech tagger [2] as prepositions (*of*, *for*), determiners (*the*, *an*), auxiliary verbs (*have*, *were*), or typical initial words in questions (*who*, *how*, *where*). The tokens not discarded are stemmed and ordered lexicographically in T_S. The same template signature may be shared by a large number of query templates:

$$\left.\begin{array}{ll}\text{“lyrics of } \star \text{ beatles”} & \text{“lyrics for } \star \text{ by the beatles”}\\ \text{“lyrics the beatles } \star\text{”} & \text{“}\star\text{ by beatles lyrics”}\\ \text{“beatles lyrics } \star\text{”} & \text{“lyrics } \star \text{ by the beatles”}\end{array}\right\}\text{“}\star\text{ beatl lyric”}$$

2) The list of candidate phrases of T is filtered, by retaining only known phrases of some other templates T' that share the same template signature T_S as T. For example, the unfiltered list of candidate phrases for the template *"lyrics of* $\star$ *beatles"* contains, among other phrases: *somehting*, *earlier today*, *last friday*, *gather together*, *eleanor rigby*, *two weeks ago*, *lucy in the sky with diamonds*, *strawberry fields forever*, *something else*, *here comes the sun*, *lovely rita*. Out of these phrases, *somehting*, *earlier today*, *last friday*, *gather together*, *two weeks ago*, *something else* are not among the known phrase fillers of any of the templates with the same signature as *"lyrics of* $\star$ *beatles"*. Therefore, these phrases are discarded from the candidate phrase fillers of *"lyrics of* $\star$ *beatles"*. In comparison, the query templates *"lyrics for* $\star$ *by the beatles"* and *"beatles lyrics* $\star$*"* have, among their known phrase fillers, the candidate phrases *eleanor rigby* and *lucy in the sky with diamonds*; and *here comes the sun* and *lovely rita* respectively. Therefore, these phrases are retained as candidate fillers of *"lyrics of* $\star$ *beatles"* after filtering.

A side effect of the filtering of candidate phrases is to effectively intersect vocabularies of candidate phrase fillers generated from documents, with vocabularies of known phrase fillers from queries. Indeed, candidate phrase fillers, generated from documents via distributionally similarities, are required to appear as known phrase fillers in other query templates of the same template signature.

The relative ranking of candidate phrases from the list of inferred unfiltered phrase fillers (before filtering) is preserved in the list of inferred filtered phrase fillers (after filtering). Each filtered phrase filler inferred for a query template corresponds to a new query, generated by filling the phrase into the slot filler of the query template.

Question Template (Original Question)	{Set of Known Fillers}: [Ranked List of Inferred Fillers]
what is the boiling point of ⋆ (What is the boiling point of water?)	{ch3br, caesium, engine oil, orange juice, gas,..}: [toluene, benzene, formic acid, acetonitrile, meoh, phenol, heptane,..]
when was the ⋆ oil spill (When was the Exxon Valdez Oil spill?)	{first, last, valdez, exxon valdez}: [past, torrey canyon, amoco cadiz, sea empress, braer, argo merchant, ixtoc,..]
what is the longest ⋆ in the human body (What is the longest bone in the human body?)	{organ, nerve, neuron, bone, cell,..}: [tendon, axon, bones]
who was the first african american to win the ⋆ (Who was the first African American to win the Nobel Prize in literature?)	{academy award, super bowl, medal of honor,..}: [tony award, grammy, grammy award, heisman, emmy, pulitzer, nobel,..]
how many home runs did ⋆ hit (How many home runs did Babe Ruth hit?)	{joe dimaggio, henry aaron, hank aaron, josh gibson, sammy sosa,..}: [albert pujols, chipper jones, ken griffey jr,..]
what ⋆ helps prevent osteoporosis (What mineral helps prevent osteoporosis?)	{}: []
how fast is ⋆ absorbed (How fast is alcohol absorbed?)	{birth control, sugar, thc, whey protein,..}: [aspirin, proteins]
what is the life expectancy for ⋆ (What is the life expectancy for crickets)	{lupus, fragile x syndrome, men and women,..}: [copd, epilepsy, sarcoidosis, schizophrenia, hemochromatosis, sle,..]
how old do you have to be to get married in ⋆ (How old do you have to be to get married in South Carolina?)	{france, connecticut, kentucky, kansas,..}: [united states, us,..]
where did ⋆ grow up (Where did Golda Meir grow up?)	{sarah palin, lamar odom, jimmy buffet}: [drew barrymore, dakota fanning, keyshia cole, beyonce knowles, fall out boy,..]

Table 1: Sample of phrase fillers present in (Known) or generated (Inferred) queries, for a selected subset of the evaluation set of 457 TREC question templates. The method infers phrase fillers for 246 out of the 475 question templates

3. EVALUATION

3.1 Experimental Setting

Data Sources: The experiments rely on a random sample of around 100 million fully-anonymized queries in English submitted by Web users to Google in 2010. Each query is accompanied by its frequency of occurrence in the query logs.

A phrase similarity repository is available, which is derived following [12, 15] from unstructured text available within a sample of around 200 million documents in English. The repository provides data for each of around 1 million phrases that occur as full-length queries in the input query logs. It contains ranked lists of the top 200 phrases computed to be the most distributionally similar, for each phrase. For example, the top distributionally similar phrases for *caesium* are *cesium, rubidium, strontium, barium, thallium, lanthanum* etc.

Evaluation Set of Question Templates: An evaluation set of question templates is compiled from the factoid evaluation questions of the TREC Question Answering track [19, 18] from 1999 through 2003. For this purpose, a random sample of 800 TREC questions is manually inspected. The inspection of a question may result in one of three possible outcomes. First, the question may be discarded, if the resulting question templates would be so general that generating additional new phrases to fill it would be trivial (too easy). This occurs for 158 of the 800 questions (e.g., for *"what is the location of lake champlain"* or *"what is a fuel cell"*). Alternatively, the question may be discarded, if the question is too specific to generate any new queries from its possible templates. This is the case for 139 of the 800 questions (e.g., for *"what cuban dictator did fidel castro force out of power in 1958"*, *"what did john hinckley do to impress jodie foster"* or *"in what year did joe dimaggio compile his 56-game hitting streak"*). Finally, the question may be retained and manually converted into a question template, by changing a phrase from the question into a slot filler. A total of 503 of the 800 questions are thus converted into 457 unique question templates. The left part of Table 1 shows a sample of the evaluation set of question templates, along with the questions from which they were derived.

Extraction Parameters: Any query template is created from at least two distinct input queries, such that the slot of a template is filled by at least 2 known phrases. To cap computational costs, at most 10,000 candidate phrases are retained per query template, out of the phrases generated from the set of known phrases based on the phrase similarity repository. For each known phrase, the 200 most similar phrases available in the phrase similarity repository are considered. During the mapping of query templates into canonical template signatures for the purpose of filtering candidate phrases, all tokens are stemmed using the Porter stemmer [16].

3.2 Quantitative Results

Relative Coverage for Inferred Queries: For query lengths from 1 to 10 and also for all query lengths, the graphs in Figure 1 compute percentages of counts of unique queries, relative to counts of unique, original queries available in the input query logs. The left graph is for the original queries. It captures the distribution of unique queries over query length in the input query logs. In particular, it shows that most of the input queries contain between 2 and 4 tokens: 21.6% (2 tokens), 31.7% (3 tokens), 23.7% (4 tokens), with an overall 100% (all tokens). The middle graph is for the subset of original queries that contribute to the creation of any query template and one of its known fillers. Because no query templates are created from queries containing a single token, the percentage for query length 1 is 0. The middle graph shows that many of the original queries do contribute to the creation of query templates: 15.6% (2 tokens), 25.9% (3 tokens), 19.2% (4 tokens) of all unique original queries. Overall, 76.7% (all tokens) of the original queries contribute to creating query templates, which in turn generate new queries. Since query frequency has a long tail distribution, the three quarters of the original queries covered by our query generation method include frequent queries as well as many rare queries.

The right graph in Figure 1 is for inferred filtered queries, which do not include any of the original queries among them. Even after filtering, the number of inferred queries exceeds the number of original queries at all query lengths, with the exception of query length 2: 16.3% (2 tokens), 56.3% (3 tokens), 70.1% (4 tokens), with an overall 224% (all tokens). Thus, the addition of the set of inferred queries to the set of original queries more than triples the size of the set of original queries. The relative query-count increase, from original queries (left graph) to inferred queries (right graph), is higher important for relatively longer queries: 2.4% to 9.1% (7 tokens), 1.2% to 3.4% (8 tokens), 0.6% to 1.2% (9 tokens).

As a more precision-oriented alternative to the right graph in Figure 1, a separate experiment generates new queries from only the top 50 (as opposed to all) inferred filtered phrase fillers per

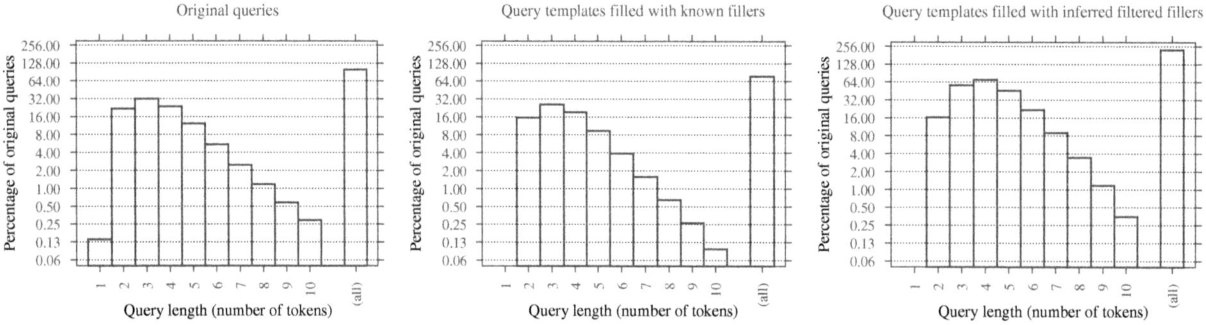

Figure 1: Number of unique queries of various lengths, shown as a percentage of the total number of unique original queries. Computed for the original query set (left graph), the query set obtained by filling each known phrase filler in its query template (middle graph), and the query set obtained by filling each inferred filtered candidate filler in its query template (right graph)

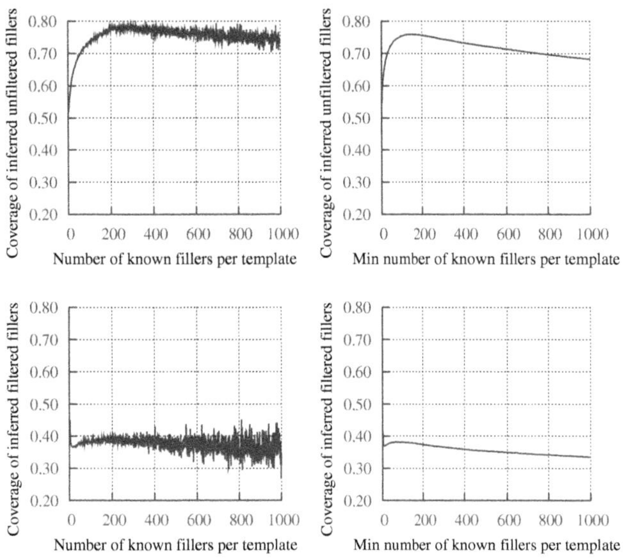

Figure 2: Coverage relative to known phrase fillers, for inferred unfiltered (upper graphs) or inferred filtered (lower graphs) phrase fillers, over templates containing a particular number (left graphs) or at least a particular number (right graphs) of known phrase fillers. Computed from the top 50000 inferred phrase fillers per template. For this computation only, known phrase fillers are not removed from the lists of inferred phrase fillers

query template. With this setting, the addition of the set of inferred queries almost doubles the size of the set of original queries, with 96% more queries.

Relative Coverage for Inferred Phrase Fillers: Because it is unfeasible to manually compile the exhaustive sets of phrases that can fill arbitrary query templates, we compute relative instead of absolute coverage. Figure 2 illustrates the coverage over all query templates, computed as the percentage of known fillers that occur among inferred fillers. Only for this computation, known fillers are not discarded from the ranked lists of at most 10,000 candidate fillers generated per query template. This is roughly equivalent to assessing to what extent candidate fillers generated from known fillers can recover known fillers that were to be missing. The left graphs of the figure show the relative coverage over query templates, when the absolute number of known phrase fillers per template increases. The right graphs correspond to a smoother version, in which the minimum number of known phrase fillers per template increases. The upper and lower graphs in the figure correspond to the coverage for inferred fillers before filtering and after filtering respectively. Naturally, filtering reduces relative coverage of known fillers, as shown by comparing the upper graphs against the respective lower graphs. Some of the known fillers (e.g., *men and women*) are not semantically similar to, and therefore may not be recovered from the similar phrases of, the other known fillers (e.g., *lupus*) of the template (e.g., *"what is the life expectancy for ⋆"*). This particularly affects query templates with few known fillers. Therefore, relative coverage in the upper graphs of Figure 2 is initially lower, but increases quickly as the (minimum) number of known phrase fillers for the template increases. For all graphs, coverage decreases slowly as the number of known fillers per template increases. The decrease is partly artificial, since an increase in the number of known fillers will cause more of the recovered known fillers to be ranked beyond the top 10,000 candidate fillers retained per query template.

Considering not all templates but just the evaluation set of 457 query templates, new queries are inferred (after filtering) for 246 of 457, i.e., 53% of the evaluation set. The average ratio of inferred phrase fillers vs. known phrase fillers is 290% or 159%, when computed over the subset of 246 or all 457 query templates respectively.

Forward Coverage for Inferred Queries: An additional experiment investigates the coverage of inferred queries, relative to queries submitted only later ("forward") in time. Concretely, forward coverage of inferred queries is measured relative to a separate "forward" sample of queries, used only for the purpose of this particular experiment. The forward sample consists in 100 million fully-anonymized queries in English, submitted collectively by Web users around 6 months later than the "main" query set (i.e., from which inferred queries are generated). Out of the forward query set, 55.6% of queries appear in the main query set. Conversely, almost half (44.4%) of the forward queries are new queries. More importantly, 8.6% of the queries in the forward query set are among the queries inferred from the main query set submitted 6 months earlier. In other words, 19.3% of the new queries in the forward query set can be inferred in advance from the main query set. Note that these queries represent only 3.5% of the set of inferred queries. Therefore, inferred queries capture queries submitted later in time, and also capture many other not-yet-submitted queries. If only the top 50 queries inferred per template are considered, the forward coverage numbers become 5.7% (instead of 8.6%) of forward

Label	Examples of *Question Template*: Phrase Filler
wrong	*what is the life expectancy for ⋆*: chinese crested
	when was the ⋆ oil spill: chernobyl nuclear
misspelled	*when did ⋆ enter the union*: illionis
	when was the ⋆ oil spill: exon valdez
okay	*what is the longest ⋆ in the human body*: bones
	how fast is ⋆ absorbed: proteins
correct	*what is the longest ⋆ in the human body*: tendon
	what is the boiling point of ⋆: toluene

Table 2: Correctness labels for the manual assessment of new phrases generated for query templates

Correctness	Percentage of Ranked Phrase Fillers							
	@5		@10		@20		@50	
	G_U	G_F	G_U	G_F	G_U	G_F	G_U	G_F
wrong	7.97	2.30	8.82	2.53	9.73	3.21	11.89	3.75
misspelled	5.28	1.43	5.24	1.68	5.16	1.68	5.08	1.63
okay	1.63	6.22	1.50	7.27	2.02	7.52	2.32	8.38
correct	85.12	90.05	84.44	88.52	83.09	87.59	80.71	86.24

Table 3: Comparative percentages of phrase fillers inferred for the evaluation question templates, whose correctness is deemed to be of a particular type from Table 2. Shown as an average over the subset of 246 question templates for which some phrase fillers were generated (G_U=inferred unfiltered candidate fillers; G_F=inferred filtered candidate fillers)

queries, and 12.8% (instead of 19.3%) of forward queries that are new queries.

3.3 Quality of Inferred Queries

Evaluation Procedure: The evaluation focuses on the assessment of accuracy of the ranked list of new phrases generated for each query template. Each phrase is manually assigned a correctness label within its respective query template, as shown in Table 2. A phrase is *correct*, if it is a meaningful filler of the template; *okay*, if it refers to a concept that would be a meaningful filler but as it stands grammatically disagrees with the template; *misspelled*, if it is a meaningful filler but is misspelled; or *wrong*, if it is not a meaningful filler.

Accuracy: Two experimental runs are evaluated, where new queries are generated by filling in a generated candidate phrase into its query template. In run **G_U**, the ranked lists of generated candidate fillers are unfiltered. Comparatively, in run **G_F**, the ranked lists of candidate fillers are automatically filtered.

The right part of the earlier Table 1 illustrates the ranked lists of filtered phrase fillers generated in run G_F, for a sample of the evaluation question templates. For example, the template *"what is the boiling point of ⋆"* has *caesium*, *orange juice* and *gas* among its known phrase fillers. The top fillers generated for it are *toluene* and *benzene*, which correspond to inferring the not-yet-submitted queries *"what is the boiling point of toluene"* and *"what is the boiling point of benzene"* respectively. No known fillers or inferred fillers are available for evaluation question templates such as *"what ⋆ helps prevent osteoporosis"*.

Table 3 illustrates how many of the phrase fillers are marked with each of the correctness labels from Table 2, at various ranks in the ranked lists of phrase fillers. Table 3 shows how, relative to G_U, run G_F reduces the counts of phrase fillers deemed as *wrong* and *misspelled*, but in doing so increases the number of phrase fillers deemed *okay*. More importantly, larger percentages of phrase fillers are deemed as *correct* for G_F than for G_U, across all ranks, e.g., around 90% vs. 85% at rank 5.

Inferred Query	Via Query Template
audio quality of ipod touch 3g	⋆ of ipod touch 3g
dress code at albert hall	dress code at ⋆
fly from paris to zagreb	fly from paris to ⋆
formatting decimal to string in c	⋆ decimal to string in c
how is the weather in key west in august	how is the weather in ⋆ in august
how to replace battery on imac	how to replace battery on ⋆
max speed of corvette zr1	⋆ of corvette zr1
pet supply stores in milwaukee	⋆ stores in milwaukee
what is the national flag of france	what is the ⋆ of france
when did reese witherspoon win the oscar	when did ⋆ win the oscar
where to buy t mobile phones without contract	where to buy ⋆ phones without contract

Table 4: Examples of queries inferred, after filtering (run G_F), from the input set of known queries

Table 4 shows a small sample of inferred filtered queries, derived via arbitrary query templates (i.e., templates that are not restricted to the evaluation set of question templates). Existing methods that extract instance attributes from queries can derive additional attributes from inferred queries (e.g., *audio quality* for *ipod touch 3g* from the inferred query *"audio quality of ipod touch 3g"*, or *max speed* for *corvette zr1* from the inferred query *"max speed of corvette zr1"*), which may not be otherwise derived from the set of known queries.

Discussion: Although unfiltered candidate fillers have good quality for many query templates, their filtering is useful. Meaningful fillers of a query template should be similar to the known fillers not only statically, but also in the context of the query template. Unfiltered candidate fillers satisfy only the first requirement: their computation relies only on the set of known fillers, and ignores the context introduced by the remainder of the query template. Intuitively, unfiltered candidates will have lower quality, whenever the context introduces additional constraints that are more difficult to derive by analyzing solely the set of known fillers. For example, both templates *"what year was ⋆ born"* and *"what dress size was ⋆"* take person names as fillers. However, the presence of *dress size* in the latter restricts its acceptable fillers mostly to feminine names - an important constraint that may be difficult to capture automatically just from the known fillers. Indeed, the top 10 unfiltered candidate phrases generated for the latter template include *cary grant* and *james dean*, which do not correspond to meaningful generated queries. The phenomenon is even more visible for templates like *"when was ⋆ 's founded"* and *"who directed the film ⋆"*. Both templates have a moderate number of known fillers, many of which happen to look like first names of people: *wendy*, *tiffany*, for the former; and *jack*, *anand*, for the latter. As a result, the unfiltered generated phrase fillers are skewed towards people first names, most of which are irrelevant for the respective templates. Although imperfect, filtering takes advantage of constraints imposed on the candidate phrases by the presence of the same keywords in other queries, to discard irrelevant candidate phrases.

4. RELATED WORK

Our method infers new queries by exploiting a particular type of relatedness between sets of known queries, on one hand; and new queries generated from the query template corresponding to those known queries, on the other hand. In this light, an inferred query is related to a known query, in that the former can be inferred from the latter by replacing a phrase with another phrase from the same semantic class, as approximated via phrase similarities. Unlike previous work in the related area of computing related queries for a given query, our method does not require the availability of user feedback, in the form of query sessions or user-specific information [13, 3] or clicks on search results [3]. It does not require large amounts of click information or other labeled data, and does not bias the generated queries towards typical substitutions made by Web searchers to their queries [8]. Moreover, it attempts to generate new queries that are meaningful by themselves, in addition to being useful in some internal system module or task. Queries are also aggregated into query templates in [17], in order to compute related queries for a given query. Our mapping of multiple query templates into the same template signature is a simpler alternative to previous work on bridging longer questions with their equivalent shorter queries [9, 6].

Other previous work shares the intuition that submitted search queries are influenced by and indicative of various semantic relations holding among full-length queries or query tokens. Semantic relations are untyped, similarity-based relations from query logs in [1], and hold among full-length queries. Untyped relations can also be identified among query tokens, for the purpose of query reformulation [21]. Among the classes of query substitutions defined in [8], our generation of new queries from known queries fits under the class of approximate rewriting, i.e., substitutions that replace part of the query with an alternative from the same category.

5. CONCLUSION

In this paper, redundancy within Web search queries allows for the generation of not-yet-submitted queries that correspond to meaningful user information needs. Redundancy is used in two ways: through different queries that specify the same properties or same relations of similar phrases; and through queries that have different degrees of verbosity (from natural-language to keyword-based) but essentially use the same keywords. The analysis of query logs is limited to queries considered in isolation from one another; no search-result clicks or query sessions are needed.

Because queries inferred in this paper resemble existing queries, and existing queries tend to be limited in length, arbitrarily complex questions are unlikely to occur among inferred queries. Ongoing work explores the generation of new queries via double-slot (*"what did ⋆ do to impress ⋆"*), as opposed to single-slot, query templates; the identification of new queries that should be discarded because the inferred phrase filler does not agree syntactically with the remainder of the query.

Acknowledgments

We would like to thank Lev Finkelstein, for suggestions and technical support; and Yangbo Zhu and Leonid Velikovich, for access to distributional similarity data.

6. REFERENCES

[1] R. Baeza-Yates and A. Tiberi. Extracting semantic relations from query logs. In *Proceedings of the 13th ACM Conference on Knowledge Discovery and Data Mining (KDD-07)*, pages 76–85, San Jose, California, 2007.

[2] T. Brants. TnT - a statistical part of speech tagger. In *Proceedings of the 6th Conference on Applied Natural Language Processing (ANLP-00)*, pages 224–231, Seattle, Washington, 2000.

[3] H. Cao, D. Jiang, J. Pei, Q. He, Z. Liao, E. Chen, and H. Li. Context-aware query suggestion by mining click-through and session data. In *Proceedings of the 14th ACM Conference on Knowledge Discovery and Data Mining (KDD-08)*, pages 875–883, Las Vegas, Nevada, 2008.

[4] M. Heilman and N. Smith. Good question! Statistical ranking for question generation. In *Proceedings of the 2010 Conference of the North American Association for Computational Linguistics (NAACL-HLT-10)*, pages 609–617, Los Angeles, California, 2010.

[5] J. Hu, G. Wang, F. Lochovsky, J. Sun, and Z. Chen. Understanding user's query intent with Wikipedia. In *Proceedings of the 18th World Wide Web Conference (WWW-09)*, pages 471–480, Madrid, Spain, 2009.

[6] S. Huston and B. Croft. Evaluating verbose query processing techniques. In *Proceedings of the 33rd International Conference on Research and Development in Information Retrieval (SIGIR-10)*, pages 291–298, Geneva, Switzerland, 2010.

[7] B. Jansen, D. Booth, and A. Spink. Determining the informational, navigational, and transactional intent of Web queries. *Information Processing and Management*, 44(3):1251–1266, 2008.

[8] R. Jones, B. Rey, O. Madani, and W. Greiner. Generating query substitutions. In *Proceedings of the 15h World Wide Web Conference (WWW-06)*, pages 387–396, Edinburgh, Scotland, 2006.

[9] J. Lee, S. Kim, Y. Song, and H. Rim. Bridging lexical gaps between queries and questions on large online qa collections with compact translation models. In *Proceedings of the 2008 Conference on Empirical Methods in Natural Language Processing (EMNLP-08)*, pages 410–418, Honolulu, Hawaii, 2008.

[10] L. Lee. Measures of distributional similarity. In *Proceedings of the 37th Annual Meeting of the Association of Computational Linguistics (ACL-99)*, pages 25–32, College Park, Maryland, 1999.

[11] D. Lin and P. Pantel. Concept discovery from text. In *Proceedings of the 19th International Conference on Computational linguistics (COLING-02)*, pages 1–7, Taipei, Taiwan, 2002.

[12] D. Lin and X. Wu. Phrase clustering for discriminative learning. In *Proceedings of the 47th Annual Meeting of the Association for Computational Linguistics (ACL-IJCNLP-09)*, pages 1030–1038, Singapore, 2009.

[13] Q. Mei, D. Zhou, and K. Church. Query suggestion using hitting time. In *Proceedings of the 17th International Conference on Information and Knowledge Management (CIKM-08)*, pages 469–477, Napa Valley, California, 2008.

[14] R. Mitkov and L. Ha. A computer-aided environment for generating multiple-choice test items. *Natural Language Engineering*, 12(2):177–194, 2006.

[15] P. Pantel, E. Crestan, A. Borkovsky, A. Popescu, and V. Vyas. Web-scale distributional similarity and entity set expansion. In *Proceedings of the 2009 Conference on Empirical Methods in Natural Language Processing (EMNLP-09)*, pages 938–947, Singapore, 2009.

[16] M. Porter. An algorithm for suffix stripping. *Program*, 14(3):130–137, 1980.

[17] I. Szpektor, A. Gionis, and Y. Maarek. Improving recommendation for long-tail queries via templates. In *Proceedings of the 20th World Wide Web Conference (WWW-11)*, pages 47–56, Hyderabad, India, 2011.

[18] E. Voorhees. Overview of the trec 2003 question answering track. In *Proceedings of the 12th Text Retrieval Conference (TREC-2003)*, pages 54–68, Gaithersburg, Maryland, 2003.

[19] E. Voorhees and D. Tice. Building a question-answering test collection. In *Proceedings of the 23rd International Conference on Research and Development in Information Retrieval (SIGIR-00)*, pages 200–207, Athens, Greece, 2000.

[20] R. Wang and W. Cohen. Automatic set instance extraction using the Web. In *Proceedings of the 47th Annual Meeting of the Association for Computational Linguistics (ACL-IJCNLP-09)*, pages 441–449, Singapore, 2009.

[21] X. Wang and C. Zhai. Mining term association patterns from search logs for effective query reformulation. In *Proceedings of the 17th International Conference on Information and Knowledge Management (CIKM-08)*, pages 479–488, Napa Valley, California, 2008.

Simultaneous Joint and Conditional Modeling of Documents Tagged from Two Perspectives

Pradipto Das
CSE Dept.
SUNY Buffalo
Buffalo, 14260
pdas3@buffalo.edu

Rohini Srihari
CSE Dept.
SUNY Buffalo
Buffalo, 14260
rohini@cedar.buffalo.edu

Yun Fu
CSE Dept.
SUNY Buffalo
Buffalo, 14260
yunfu@buffalo.edu

ABSTRACT

This paper explores correspondence and mixture topic modeling of documents tagged from two different perspectives. There has been ongoing work in topic modeling of documents with tags (tag-topic models) where words and tags typically reflect a single perspective, namely document content. However, words in documents can also be tagged from different perspectives, for example, syntactic perspective as in part-of-speech tagging or an opinion perspective as in sentiment tagging. The models proposed in this paper are novel in: (i) the consideration of two different tag perspectives - a document level tag perspective that is relevant to the document as a whole and a word level tag perspective pertaining to each word in the document; (ii) the attribution of latent topics with word level tags and labeling latent topics with images in case of multimedia documents; and (iii) discovering the possible correspondence of the words to document level tags. The proposed correspondence tag-topic model shows better predictive power i.e. higher likelihood on held-out test data than all existing tag topic models and even a supervised topic model. To evaluate the models in practical scenarios, quantitative measures between the outputs of the proposed models and the ground truth domain knowledge have been explored. Manually assigned (gold standard) document category labels in Wikipedia pages are used to validate model-generated tag suggestions using a measure of pairwise concept similarity within an ontological hierarchy like WordNet. Using a news corpus, automatic relationship discovery between person names was performed and compared to a robust baseline.

Categories and Subject Descriptors

I.2.7 [**Computing Methodologies**]: Artificial Intelligence—*Natural Language Processing*

General Terms

Algorithm, Experimentation

Keywords

Text mining, tag topic models, social media, classification and clustering

1. INTRODUCTION

This paper lays down a robust topic modeling framework to solve the problem of discovering latent topics from documents tagged from two different perspectives. Documents usually consist of at least two perspectives - a document level perspective and a word level perspective. The document level perspective often tries to summarize the contents as a small bag-of-words, while the other perspective tries to annotate the content in different ways. Tables 1, 2 and 3 show different examples of perspectives. In this paper, it is assumed that tags are non-hierarchical concepts. These concepts could be represented by words or by some other higher order representation that eventually denotes a concept. Many times, for e.g., in plain text documents, these two perspectives are not explicitly shown. However, documents hosted by today's interactive websites are a rich source of document tagging from at least two perspectives.

Word level tags	Image captions	Category labels
Syringa/0 (Lilac)/0 is/0 a/0 genus/0 of/0 about/0 ... Lilac/1 bushes/1 can/1 be/1 prone/1 to/1 powdery/1 mildew/1 disease/1 ... RHS/2 Dictionary/2 of/2 Gardening./2 Macmillan/2 ISBN/2 0-333-47494-5/2	Syringa josikaea, Syringa vulgaris shrub in flower, etc.	Syringa, Garden plants, Flowers, Shrubs

Table 1: Document with word level "Position" tags and document level image caption word tags [source: http://en.wikipedia.org/wiki/Syringa]

Table 1 shows an article on lilac flower in Wikipedia. Words in the document body annotated with a slash '/' denotes a word level perspective which in this case is position of the section in which the word appears. The section offsets are binned into three positions relative to the beginning of the document - begin(0), middle(1) and end(2). Positions signify the importance of the choice of words that constitute sections in a document. The document level perspective is assumed to be captured by the images which are described by the corresponding captions. In table 1, the third column represents the "ground truth" category labels which are a set of manually edited tags that summarize the Wikipedia article. With this structure of multimedia documents, several questions come to the forefront: "Could there be some way of using image captions to automatically suggest specific category labels for new articles? If so how good will those suggestions be? Further, can we discover latent topics or themes and label each theme with a multimedia object?" The generative process of word generation in these kinds of documents hinges on the following intuitions: Documents are distributions over latent topics. Latent topics, in turn, are distributions over observed document level tags and main content words such that the most probable observed variable ensembles for a topic are related through the assumptions of the generative process. For one particular assumption, a word conditioned on the word level tag observed at the word's position is sampled independently of the document level tags from a topic. The topic proportions for the document only depends on the expected number of document level tags and words being assigned to each topic through co-occurrence phenomenon. In another assumption, topics generate the document level tags first. Then a document level tag position is chosen and a word conditioned on the word level tag observed at the word's position is sampled from the corresponding topic in the position of the document level tag. For this second assumption, there is a conditioning of words to document level tags and is thus more intuitive from the document generation point of view. For example, a writer often "thinks" of a mental image/concept and then writes words that elaborate that image/concept. Although modeling multimedia Wikipedia articles served as the primary motivation for developing the proposed models, the models are extremely generic and had been applied to a variety of other datasets for different tasks. For brevity, the document level tags are dubbed DL tags and the word level tags are dubbed WL tags.

Table 2 shows an example where DL tags are abstracted at a level higher than words. In this example, the sample sentence in the table is an excerpt from a newswire article in the dataset used in the DUC2005 Summarization track[10]. The WL tags denote a particular named entity class like PERSON, LOCATION, ORGANIZATION, NUMBER, etc. being ascribed to each particular word or not. The DL tags, however, are indicative of discourse coherence markers. These markers were constructed following the technique used in [2]. Each word in the document is associated with a grammatical or semantic role (GSR in short) like named entities (ne), nouns (nn), adjectives (adj), verbs (vb), subjects (subj), objects (obj), etc. A GSR transition (GSRt in short) is a relation between the same normal form of a word that is either present in two contextual sentences or in a single sentence, e.g. a GSRt for the word "car" can be (car,*subj,obj*) leading to (car,$subj \rightarrow obj$) or (car,$subj \rightarrow -$) if the word "car" is not seen in the succeeding sentence. It is reported in [2] that a set of sentences with the same entities in roles like "subj," "obj," etc. are indicative of coherent passages. Although in [2], only entities are involved in GSRts, however, in this paper, words that are not entities are also considered since in quite a few cases, the foci of attentions are based not just on entities. *Thus, the document level perspective for DUC05 newswire data is that of syntactic coherence.* The proposed models are general enough to model documents arising out of such perspectives also.

Word level tags	Document level tags
Some 167/NE-NUM people were arrested in the US/NE-LOC , including a senior executive of Columbia/NE-LOC 's national bank .	$-\rightarrow$ne, ne$\rightarrow-$, $-\rightarrow$subj, subj$\rightarrow$subj, nn$\rightarrow$vb, vb$\rightarrow$vb, $-\rightarrow$adj, adj$\rightarrow-$, etc.

Table 2: Document with word level "Named Entity" tags and document level "syntactic role transition" tags

1.1 Representing Tags in Datasets

In all the experiments performed in the paper, three major datasets were considered. Also, all tags have a bag-of-words representation. For Wikipedia, only documents with images were collected. The category labels were not used as DL tags, rather the image caption words were used. Generally, if captions are not available, an initial preprocessing can be done using the work in [11]. The article title was also added to the DL tags. Each word in the main body of the article was tagged with "position" information of the sections they appeared in and were labeled as {*Begin, Begin_Middle, Middle, Middle_End, End*}.

Unprocessed Amazon product reviews from the dataset used in [7] (henceforth the AR dataset) was also used in the experiments. The words in each review were tagged with affect labels using a simple lexicon lookup from the dataset created in [9]. The lexicon consists of 2476 words that elicit human emotions in some form. The emotions were labeled with {*Unhappy, Unsatisfactory, Melancholic, Despair, Hopeful, Contended, Satisfied, Pleased, Happy, Untagged*} tags based on the maximum valence values of the affect words. Non-affect words were tagged as "*Untagged*". The AR dataset did not have product tags and hence the product name and the review title were used as "captions" for reviews which served as DL tags. Finally note that for WL tagging, a word can be conditioned on **only 1 tag**. Table 3 shows an example for the AR dataset used. The DUC (Document Understanding Conference) 2005 dataset consists of newswire articles organized in 50 folders or document sets (docsets) with each folder consisting of at least 25 sizable news reports. The documents were processed to extract named entities and roles of the words using the Stanford CoreNLP toolkit[1]. The GSRs were obtained using the dependency parse information. However, co-reference resolution was not performed due to unsatisfactory results. An example of this kind of tagging is shown in Table 2. Normal forms of the words were used e.g., "arrested" (verb) and "arrests" (noun) have the normal form "arrest". A total of 9 GSRs were chosen (Named Entities or ne, Subjects or subj, Objects or obj, Nouns or nn, Verb or vb, Adjective or adj, Adverb or adv, Other as ow and Null as –) resulting in a total of 81 GSRts. Note that if a word has several GSRs associated with it, only one is chosen using the priority rule: ne>subj>obj>nn>adj>vb>adv>ow. The task in the DUC2005 Summarization task was the creation of 250 word multi-document summaries for each of the docsets in response to the corresponding information needs. However, in this paper the docsets from DUC2005 dataset were used to validate entity-pair relationship discovery and not for summarization.

Word level tags	DL tags
What I like/CONTENDED is the exceptional zooming without loss/MELANCHOLIC in clarity.	compact camera, Ikon 550, 18X zoom {*Rating: 4.0*}

Table 3: Document with word level emotion tags and document level product feature tags

1.2 Improving Existing Tag Topic Models

Tag-topic models have been explored recently [16, 17, 1, 20] as ways of improving word-based topic models with ad-

[1] http://nlp.stanford.edu/software/corenlp.shtml

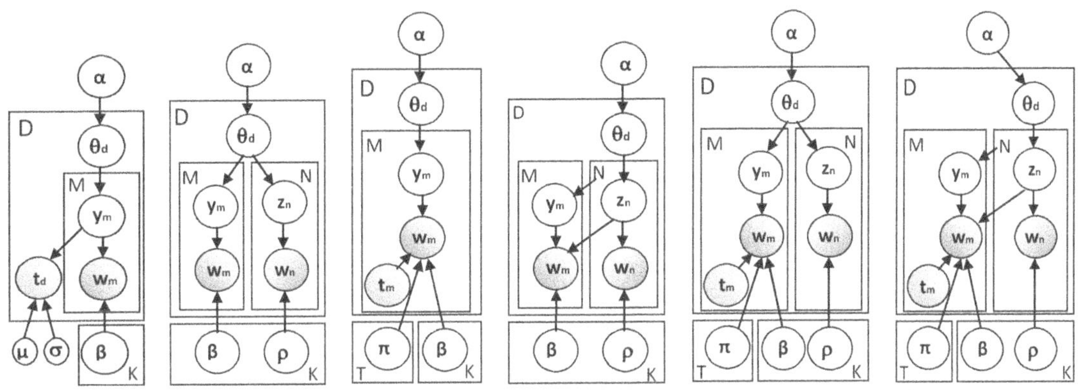

(a) supervised LDA model (b) MMLDA model (c) TagLDA model (d) corrMMLDA model (e) METag^2 LDA model (f) corrMETag^2 LDA model

Figure 1: Graphical model representations of one supervised topic model, two existing tag topic models, one extended tag topic model and two new tag squared topic models

ditional information in the form of tags, usually arising out of a **single** perspective. Existing mixture tag topic models [16, 17] (c.f. fig. 1b) can fit a number of latent topics to the documents without words and DL tags having direct correspondence with each other. However, there could be additional word level annotation information which are implicitly attributed to the words.

Thus existing tag topic models of documents focus either on document level tags[16, 17] or on word level tags[20] (c.f. fig. 1c). For models like those in [16, 17] (which are referred to as MMLDA - short for Multi(nomial) Multinomial LDA) each content word and DL tag is generated independently by choosing a topic and then choosing a content or DL tag. The expected number of words in the document's topic thus depends on the counts of both the content and the DL words ascribed to that topic. On the other hand, in the TagLDA model in [20] the content words are generated by choosing a topic and drawing a word from the topic's distribution but conditioned on the WL tag associated with that content word. This conditional aspect allows one to explore related words sharing the same semantic relatedness but along that particular condition or facet - for e.g. all "PERSON" named entities in a dataset that are semantically related through some hidden topic. Figures 1b and 1c show the existing tag topic models - MMLDA[16] and TagLDA[20]. The model in figure 1d was implemented in this study as an improvement over MMLDA following [4] for the text domain and is referred to as corrMMLDA. However, none of MMLDA, TagLDA or corrMMLDA addresses a tag space that is split across two different perspectives. The proposed TagSquaredLDA (abbreviated as Tag^{2}LDA) models: METag^{2}LDA model (ME is abbreviated form of Multinomial Exponential) (fig. 1e) and corrMETag^{2}LDA model (fig. 1f) allows topic modeling of documents with both DL and WL tags. Table 4 shows the relative merits and de-merits of each model discussed in this paper. Fig. 1a shows a supervised LDA topic model (sLDA)[5] that is only used for predictive power comparison on the AR dataset. Experiments reveal the improvements of the Tag^{2}LDA models over current tag topic models through reduced perplexity, or more predictive power for topical inference. Also an HMM type of model is not suitable for positional WL tagging, since, then during inference, there is nothing to *infer* on position "states" - they are implicit in any document.

Model Highlights	sLDA	MM LDA	Tag LDA	corr MM LDA	ME Tag^2 LDA	corr ME Tag^2 LDA
Generate words and DL tags from same topic?	×	√	×	√	√	√
Suggest related DL tags?	×	√	×	√	√	√
Associate words to DL tags probabilistically?	×	×	×	√	×	√
Decompose topics along WL tag dimensions?	×	×	√	×	√	√
Find topical-WLtag orientation of new documents ?	×	×	√	×	√	√
Document "label" prediction?	√	×	×	×	×	×

Table 4: Model features and their comparison

1.3 Applications and Quantitative Measures

Measuring model perplexity[6] is an established way of showing how good a model explains the observed data. Due to intractability issues, the lower bounds to the true log likelihoods on test data are also used which are directly proportional to perplexity measurements. However, while applying the models for a specific task, the goal is not only to measure held-out test data likelihood for a model. For example, for the Wikipedia data, it was important to have a quantitative measure of confidence between probable document tags from image captions and ground truth category labels. For this, a measure of semantic relatedness using path separation between concept pairs[14] in WordNet ontology was chosen as an evaluation tool. As an example, the connection between "fire_engines" and "fire_ extinguisher" can be described by a shortest path linking these two concepts in WordNet as "**fire_extinguisher** ↔ *device* ↔ *instrumentality* ↔ *container* ↔ *wheeled_vehicle* ↔ *self-propelled_ vehicle* ↔ *motor_vehicle* ↔ *truck* ↔ fire_engine" with a path length of 9 and a simple "inverse of path length" similarity score of 0.11. Under this measure, a value of 1 indicates exact match or parent/child relationship. Using this evaluation, users can be *explained* a "chain of reasoning" that relates a probable DL tag to a ground truth category label for a new document. For N suggested DL tags and C category word labels, scores for all possible $N \times C$ pairs P were obtained. The highest score served as a measure of DL tag suggestions. If a model captures caption words that happens to have shorter path distances to ground truth labels, then the model is scored higher. Note that WordNet is chosen since it is widely accepted - any other customized ontology can easily be pugged in depending upon the application. Also note that Newman et. al.[13] attempted to measure cohesiveness of topic "labels" consisting of top 10 high probability words, where the "results over WordNet are patchy at best." The WordNet evaluation presented here is not to measure topic cohesiveness but to measure and explain the goodness of a probable DL tag. Although measuring topic coherence is equivalent to measuring topic intrusion[8], the notion of a topic is only a mathematical convenience for a low-dimensional subspace that tries to capture the assumptions of the statistical generative model. So qualitatively, a topic is best interpreted by the task on which the model is adapted and its corresponding assumptions.

For the DUC2005 dataset where the WL tags came from named entity classes, all pairs of PERSON named entities from documents in each of the 50 docsets were collected. For a particular proposed Tag^{2}LDA model, hidden topics were inferred for these documents and pairs from top N entities from the "PERSON" facet of the topic were collected. Entity pairs that co-occur in a sentence were chosen as ground truth pairs that were strongly related - this is the baseline. The average of ratio of the counts of the PERSON entity pairs from topics to those from the baseline served as a quantitative measure of improvement over the latter in the entity relationship discovery application. Some qualitative results are shown in Table 8. Note that the same named entity can occur across multiple docsets. This is particularly true of NUMBER and LOCATION classes and entities related to governments.

2. RELATED WORK

Joint topic and tag analysis has been used in a some recent works including [16, 17, 20] which has culminated in the creation of variants of topic models like LDA[6]. Due to space constraints, the reader needs to be directed to [6] for a full description of the basic LDA model. The principle shortcoming of these papers are the use of a single tagging perspective - either document level tags **or** word level tags. While the models in [16] and [17] are essentially the same, the purposes of the models had been a little different. Both use generative models of words and document tags to discover latent topics. In [16] the topic-tag and the topic-word features were used to better cluster tagged documents. In [17] new documents were "folded-in" in the latent topic space and tags were predicted based on the inferred topic tag distribution. The work in [20] is useful in the sense that the topics are discovered w.r.t to words being conditioned on WL tags. A recent work on topic-perspective modeling has been done in [12] where the authors have tried to use perspectives as hidden states that represent a discreet distribution over tags. It is important to note that the "corrLDA" model referred to in [12] is not a true correspondence model as there happens to be no direct correspondence between words and tags. Further, although there is a connection between the user-perspective and perspective-tag distributions, the connections between the perspective-tag distribution and the topic-word/topic-tag distributions weakly depend on a binary switching variable. The sLDA[5] model discovers topics based on the ensembles of document contents and the response variables. The values of the response variables are explained by the frequency counts of the words in the corresponding documents only. The labeledLDA[15] model establishes a one-to-one correspondence to the latent topics and the actual document tags. This is done in a manner similar to imposing a non-uniform prior on the latent topic proportions per document[19]. Further the words in text are corresponded to topic labels which precludes any possibility of using WL conditional tags. The proposed Tag^{2}LDA models use both joint (words and DL tags) and conditional (words and WL tags) modeling, thereby allowing a richer document structure to be captured.

3. THE PROPOSED MODELS

This section introduces the model description and the model parameters for the Tag^{2}LDA models. In all model figures in fig. 1, the symbol notations and their meanings given in table 5 are adhered to. Note that in the Tag^{2}LDA

Symbol	Meaning ($r.v.$ = *random variable*)
D	total number of documents
N	total number of unique document level tags per document $d \in D$
M	total number of unique words per document $d \in D$
α	r.v. for Dirichlet prior for the document level topic proportions
θ_d	r.v. for document level latent topic proportions
ρ	r.v. for corpus level topic-DL_tag multinomial
β	r.v. for corpus level (marginal in figs. 1c, 1e and 1f) topic-word distribution
π	r.v. for corpus level marginal tag-word distribution
$\mathbf{z_n}$	indicator variable for DL topic proportion
$\mathbf{y_m}$ in figs. 1b, 1c and 1e	indicator variable for DL topic proportion
$\mathbf{y_m}$ in figs. 1d and 1f	indicator variable for DL tag correspondence
$\mathbf{w_n}$	r.v. for DL tag at position n; vocabulary size $corrV$
$\mathbf{w_m}$	r.v. for word at position m; vocabulary size V
t_m in figs. 1c, 1e and 1f	r.v. denoting tag at position m, on which word w_m is conditioned; vocabulary size T
t_d in fig. 1a	r.v. denoting observed response for document d
μ, σ in fig. 1a	r.v.s denoting mean and standard deviation for the observed response for document d[5]

Table 5: Symbols used in this paper and their meaning

models, $p(w_m|C = i, \boldsymbol{\beta}, \boldsymbol{\pi}, t_m)$, where $C = y_m$ or $C = z_{y_m}$, is not a simple topic multinomial anymore, but is distributed as

$$p(w_m|C = i, \boldsymbol{\beta}, \boldsymbol{\pi}, t_m) = \frac{\exp(\log \beta_{i,w_m} + \log \pi_{t_m,w_m})}{\sum_{v=1}^{V} \exp(\log \beta_{i,w_m} + \log \pi_{t_m,w_m})} \tag{1}$$

Note that each $\boldsymbol{\pi_t}$ is a distribution over V. Simplified Gibbs sampling using Multinomial-Dirichlet conjugacy cannot be applied in this setting since the distribution is not a multinomial anymore. Also note that for the correspondence models $y_m \sim Unif(N_d)$, short for Uniform distribution, as in [4]. The generative processes for the proposed Tag^{2}LDA models are illustrated below:

For each document $d \in 1, ..., D$
- Choose a topic proportion $\boldsymbol{\theta}|\boldsymbol{\alpha} \sim Dir(\boldsymbol{\alpha})$
- For each "document level" position n in document d
  - Choose topic indicator $z_n|\theta \sim Mult(\boldsymbol{\theta})$
  - Choose a "document level" tag $w_n|z_n = k, \boldsymbol{\rho} \sim Mult(\boldsymbol{\rho}_{z_n})$
- For each "word level" position m in document d
  - Choose $y_m \sim Unif(\mathbf{1}, ..., \mathbf{N})$ (for corrMETag^{2}LDA - fig. 1f)
  - *or* Choose $y_m|\theta \sim Mult(\boldsymbol{\theta})$ (for METag^{2}LDA - fig. 1e)
  - Choose a word $w_m|y_m, \mathbf{z}, \mathbf{t}, \boldsymbol{\beta}, \boldsymbol{\pi} \sim p(w_m|z_{y_m}, \boldsymbol{\beta}, \boldsymbol{\pi}, t_m)$ (fig. 1f)
  - *or* Choose a word $w_m|y_m, \mathbf{t}, \boldsymbol{\beta}, \boldsymbol{\pi} \sim p(w_m|y_m, \boldsymbol{\beta}, \boldsymbol{\pi}, t_m)$ (fig. 1e)

In the correspondence models, the DL perspective plays a significant role in the quality of topic coherence. For example, when the GSRt perspective (c.f. table 2) is chosen as a DL perspective, the topics will capture words that are both co-occurring and generated from similar roles. There could be a docset on "Global warming" which will tie together words like planet and ice based on co-occurrence alone. Consider another docset concerning discovery of ice on Pluto's surface. Thus, if the GSR of "ice" is taken to be a subject, then a "Global warming" topic can include Pluto as a probable word because of the GSRts for the word "ice" that involve "subj". This type of tagging is beneficial where the task is not to replicate the docset structure based on co-occurrence but to provide deeper insights into data for tasks such as summarization, relationship extraction, etc. This effect is hardly observed when the DL tags tersely summarize the main contents of the documents.

3.1 Latent variable inference

The Variational Bayesian Expectation Maximization algorithm [6, 3] has been used to maximize the lower bound to the true intractable likelihood of the data w.r.t. the model parameters. This section outlines the various updates of the latent variables and the parameters and subsection 3.3 outlines a general plan of implementation. To find as tight as possible an approximation to the log likelihood of the data (the joint and conditional distribution of the observed variables given the parameters), the KL divergence of an approximate factorized mean field distribution is minimized to the true posterior distribution of the latent variables given the data. A fully factorized q distribution with "free" variational parameters $\boldsymbol{\gamma}$, $\boldsymbol{\phi}$ and $\boldsymbol{\lambda}$ is imposed as

$$q(\boldsymbol{\theta},\mathbf{z},\mathbf{y}|\boldsymbol{\gamma},\boldsymbol{\phi},\boldsymbol{\lambda}) = \prod_{d=1}^{D} q(\boldsymbol{\theta_d}|\gamma_{\boldsymbol{d}})[\prod_{n=1}^{N_d} q(z_{d,n}|\boldsymbol{\phi_{d,n}}) \prod_{m=1}^{M_d} q(y_{d,m}|\boldsymbol{\lambda_{d,m}})]$$

and then optimal values of free variables and parameters are found by optimizing the lower bound on $\log p(\mathbf{w_m}, \mathbf{w_n}|\boldsymbol{\alpha}, \boldsymbol{\beta}, \boldsymbol{\rho}, \boldsymbol{\pi}, \mathbf{t})$. The variational functional to optimize can be shown to be (as in [3])

$$\mathcal{F} = E_q[\log p(\mathbf{w}_M, \mathbf{w}_N, \boldsymbol{\theta}, \mathbf{z}, \mathbf{y}|\boldsymbol{\alpha}, \beta, \boldsymbol{\rho}, \boldsymbol{\pi}, \mathbf{t})] - E_q[\log q(\boldsymbol{\theta}, \mathbf{z}, \mathbf{y}, |\boldsymbol{\gamma}, \boldsymbol{\phi}, \boldsymbol{\lambda})] \quad (2)$$

where $E_q[f(.)]$ is the expectation of $f(.)$ over the q distribution and $\mathcal{F}$ is the Expected Lower BOund (ELBO) to true likelihood. This ELBO is directly related to measuring perplexity[6]. In the following subsections, it is assumed that K is the number of topics, $\boldsymbol{\phi}$ to be free parameters of the variational DL_tag-topic distribution and $\boldsymbol{\lambda}$ to be the free parameters of the variational word-topic or word-DL_tag distributions. These free parameters are defined for every document $d \in D$. As in [6], the key inferential problem that is solved here is the learning of the posterior distribution of the latent variables given the observations and parameters of the models on data that are new on count proportions. Following the inequality, $\log(x) \leq \zeta^{-1}(x) + log(\zeta) - 1, \forall \zeta > 0$, the ELBO $\mathcal{F}$ is changed to further lower bounds $\mathcal{L}$ for the two models.

For the METag^{2}LDA model:

$$\mathcal{L}_{MM} = E_q[\log p(\boldsymbol{\theta}|\boldsymbol{\alpha})] + E_q[\log p(\mathbf{z_n}|\boldsymbol{\theta})] + E_q[\log p(\mathbf{w_n}|\mathbf{z_n}, \rho)] + E_q[\log p(\mathbf{y_m}|\boldsymbol{\theta})] + E_q[\log p(\mathbf{w_m}|\mathbf{y_m}, \beta, \boldsymbol{\pi}, \mathbf{t})] - E_q[\log q(\boldsymbol{\theta}, \mathbf{z}, \mathbf{y}, |\boldsymbol{\gamma}, \boldsymbol{\phi}, \boldsymbol{\lambda})] \quad (3)$$

The expression for $E_q[\log p(\mathbf{w_m}|\mathbf{y_m}, \beta, \boldsymbol{\pi}, \mathbf{t})]$ can be written as:

$$E_q[\log p(\mathbf{w_m}|\mathbf{y_m}, \beta, \boldsymbol{\pi}, \mathbf{t})] \geq \sum_{m=1}^{M_d}\sum_{i=1}^{K} \lambda_{m,i}(\log \beta_{i,w_{d,m}} + \log \pi_{t_{d,m},w_{d,m}}) - \sum_{m=1}^{M_d}\{\zeta_m^{-1}(\sum_{i=1}^{K}\sum_{v=1}^{V} \lambda_{m,i}\exp(\log \beta_{i,w_{d,m}} + \log \pi_{t_{d,m},w_{d,m}})) + \log \zeta_m^{-1} - 1\} \quad (4)$$

Using the new lower bound, the maximum likelihood estimations of the hidden variables in document d are as follows:

$$\zeta_m = \sum_{v=1}^{V}\sum_{i=1}^{K} \lambda_{d,m,i}\exp\{\log \beta_{i,v} + \log \pi_{t_{d,m},v}\} \quad (5)$$

$$\phi_{n,i} \propto \exp\left\{\psi(\gamma_i) - \psi(\sum_{j=1}^{K}\gamma_j) + \log \rho_{i,w_{d,n}}\right\} \quad (6)$$

$$\lambda_{m,i} \propto \exp\{\psi(\gamma_i) - \psi(\sum_{j=1}^{K}\gamma_j) + (\log \beta_{i,w_{d,m}} + \log \pi_{t_{d,m},w_{d,m}}) - \zeta_m^{-1}\sum_{v=1}^{V}\exp(\log \beta_{i,w_{d,m}} + \log \pi_{t_{d,m},w_{d,m}})\} \quad (7)$$

$$\gamma_i = \alpha_i + \sum_{n=1}^{N_d}\phi_{n,i} + \sum_{m=1}^{M_d}\lambda_{m,i} \quad (8)$$

For the corrMETag^{2}LDA model:

$$\mathcal{L}_{corrMM} = E_q[\log p(\boldsymbol{\theta}|\boldsymbol{\alpha})] + E_q[\log p(\mathbf{z_n}|\boldsymbol{\theta})] + E_q[\log p(\mathbf{w_n}|\mathbf{z_n}, \rho)] + E_q[\log p(\mathbf{y_m}|N)] + E_q[\log p(\mathbf{w_m}|\mathbf{y_m}, \beta, \boldsymbol{\pi}, \mathbf{t})] - E_q[\log q(\boldsymbol{\theta}, \mathbf{z}, \mathbf{y}, |\boldsymbol{\gamma}, \boldsymbol{\phi}, \boldsymbol{\lambda})] \quad (9)$$

The expression for $E_q[\log p(\mathbf{w_m}|\mathbf{y_m}, \beta, \boldsymbol{\pi}, \mathbf{t})]$ can be written as:

$$E_q[\log p(\mathbf{w_m}|\mathbf{y_m}, \beta, \boldsymbol{\pi}, \mathbf{t})] \geq [\sum_{m=1}^{M_d}\sum_{i=1}^{K}(\sum_{n=1}^{N_d}\lambda_{m,n}\phi_{n,i})(\log \beta_{i,w_{d,m}} + \log \pi_{t_{d,m},w_{d,m}}) - \sum_{m=1}^{M_d}\{\zeta_m^{-1}(\sum_{i=1}^{K}\sum_{v=1}^{V}(\sum_{n=1}^{N_d}\lambda_{m,n}\phi_{n,i})\exp(\log \beta_{i,w_{d,m}} + \log \pi_{t_{d,m},w_{d,m}})) + \log \zeta_m{}^{1} - 1\} \quad (10)$$

Using these lower bounds and the maximum likelihood estimations of the hidden variables in document d are as follows:

$$\zeta_m = \sum_{v=1}^{V}\sum_{i=1}^{K}(\sum_{n=1}^{N_d}\lambda_{m,n}\phi_{n,i})\exp\{\log \beta_{i,v} + \log \pi_{t_{d,m},v}\} \quad (11)$$

$$\phi_{n,i} \propto \exp\{\psi(\gamma_i) - \psi(\sum_{j=1}^{K}\gamma_j) + \log \rho_{i,w_{d,n}} + \sum_{m=1}^{M_d}\lambda_{m,n}(\log \beta_{i,w_{d,m}} + \log \pi_{t_{d,m},w_{d,m}}) - \sum_{m=1}^{M_d}\zeta_m^{-1}\lambda_{m,n}[\sum_{v=1}^{V}\exp(\log \beta_{i,w_{d,m}} + \log \pi_{t_{d,m},w_{d,m}})]\} \quad (12)$$

$$\lambda_{m,n} \propto \exp\{\frac{1}{N_d} + \sum_{i=1}^{K} \phi_{n,i}(\log \beta_{i,w_{d,m}} + \log \pi_{t_{d,m},w_{d,m}})$$
$$- \zeta_m^{-1}(\sum_{v=1}^{V}\sum_{i=1}^{K} \phi_{n,i} \exp(\log \beta_{i,w_{d,m}} + \log \pi_{t_{d,m},w_{d,m}}))\} \tag{13}$$

$$\gamma_i = \alpha_i + \sum_{n=1}^{N_d} \phi_{n,i} \tag{14}$$

$\zeta_m \geq 0$ is an additional free variable used in the Taylor expansion of $\log(x)$ to obtain a tractable second lower bound on the probability of word generation given the topic and tag parameters of the model. Note that ζ_m is defined for each document $d \in D$ and does not need to be initialized in the routines described in subsection 3.3.

3.2 Maximum Likelihood Parameter estimation

The expressions for the maximum likelihood of the parameters of the original graphical model using derivatives w.r.t the parameters of the functional $\mathcal{L}$ are obtained as follows: For the METag^{2}LDA model:

$$\rho_{i,j} \propto \sum_{d=1}^{D}\sum_{n=1}^{N_d}\sum_{j=1}^{corrV} \phi_{d,n,i}\delta(w_{d_n}, j) \tag{15}$$

$$\log\beta_{i,v} = \log\left(\sum_{d=1}^{D}\sum_{m=1}^{M_d} \lambda_{d,m,i}\delta(w_{d_m}, v)\right)$$
$$- \log\left(\sum_{d=1}^{D}\sum_{m=1}^{M_d} \zeta_{d,m}^{-1}\lambda_{d,m,i}\exp(\log \pi_{t_{d,m},v})\delta(w_{d_m}^{v})\right)$$
$$= \log(term_1^{\beta}) - \log(term_2^{\beta}) \tag{16}$$

$$\log\pi_{t,v} = \log\left(\sum_{d=1}^{D}\sum_{m=1}^{M_d}\sum_{i=1}^{K} \lambda_{d,m,i}\delta(w_{d_m}^{v})\delta(t_{d,m}^{t'})\right)$$
$$- \log\left(\sum_{d=1}^{D}\sum_{m=1}^{M_d} \zeta_{d,m}^{-1}\sum_{i=1}^{K} \lambda_{d,m,i}\exp(\log \pi_{t_{d,m},v})\delta(w_{d_m}^{v})\delta(t_{d,m}^{t'})\right)$$
$$= \log(term_1^{\pi}) - \log(term_2^{\pi}) \tag{17}$$

For the corrMETag^{2}LDA model:

$$\rho_{i,j} \propto \sum_{d=1}^{D}\sum_{n=1}^{N_d}\sum_{j=1}^{corrV} \phi_{d,n,i}\delta(w_{d,n}^{j}) \tag{18}$$

$$\log\beta_{i,v} = \log\left(\sum_{d=1}^{D}\sum_{m=1}^{M_d}(\sum_{n=1}^{N_d} \lambda_{m,n}\phi_{n,i})\delta(w_{d_m}^{v})\right)$$
$$- \log\left(\sum_{d=1}^{D}\sum_{m=1}^{M_d} \zeta_{d,m}^{-1}(\sum_{n=1}^{N_d} \lambda_{m,n}\phi_{n,i})\exp(\log \pi_{t_{d,m},v})\delta(w_{d_m}^{v})\right)$$
$$= \log(term_1^{\beta}) - \log(term_2^{\beta}) \tag{19}$$

$$\log\pi_{t,v} = \log\left(\sum_{d=1}^{D}\sum_{m=1}^{M_d}\sum_{i=1}^{K}(\sum_{n=1}^{N_d} \lambda_{m,n}\phi_{n,i})\delta(w_{d_m}^{v})\delta(t_{d,m}^{t'})\right)$$
$$- \log\left(\sum_{d=1}^{D}\sum_{m=1}^{M_d} \zeta_{d,m}^{-1}\sum_{i=1}^{K}(\sum_{n=1}^{N_d} \lambda_{m,n}\phi_{n,i})\right.$$
$$\left.\exp(\log \pi_{t_{d,m},v})\delta(w_{d_m}^{v})\delta(t_{d,m}^{t'})\right)$$
$$= \log(term_1^{\pi}) - \log(term_2^{\pi}) \tag{20}$$

where $\delta(x_z^y) = 1$ iff $x_z == y$ and 0 otherwise and $t' \in \{1, .., T\}$.

Since the updates for β and π are unconstrained, a Gaussian regularizer with 0 mean and constant standard deviation (set to 2 in this paper) is used for **every** $\beta_{i,v}$ and $\pi_{t,v}$. If $\boldsymbol{\beta}$ and $\boldsymbol{\pi}$ are in log space as $\boldsymbol{\beta}^{\ell}$ and $\boldsymbol{\pi}^{\ell}$, then $\mathcal{L}_{i,t}$ is transformed to

$$\widehat{\mathcal{L}}_{i,t} = \mathcal{L}_{i,t} - \frac{1}{2\sigma^2}(\sum_{v=1}^{V}\left(\exp(\beta_{i,v}^{\ell})\right)^2) - \frac{1}{2\sigma^2}(\sum_{v=1}^{V}\left(\exp(\pi_{t,v}^{\ell})\right)^2) \tag{21}$$

So, in the derivative of $\widehat{\mathcal{L}}$ w.r.t $\log\boldsymbol{\beta}$ or $\log\boldsymbol{\pi}$ results in a quadratic in $e^{\beta_{i,v}^{\ell}}$ or $e^{\pi_{t,v}^{\ell}}$ as $term_1^{(.)} - term_2^{(.)}\exp((.)) - \frac{1}{2\sigma^2}(2\times[\exp((.))]^2) = 0$ as a necessary condition for extrema, where $(.)$ is $\beta_{i,v}^{\ell}$ or $\pi_{t,v}^{\ell}$. For $\exp((.))$ to be ≥ 0, the positive root is taken as the only solution. So the solution becomes (letting $A = \exp((.))$),

$$2A = -\sigma^2 term_2^{(.)} + \sigma\sqrt{\sigma^2(term_2^{(.)})^2 + 4term_1^{(.)}} \tag{22}$$

which is ≥ 0. In the derivative of $\widehat{\mathcal{L}}$ w.r.t the log of β or π, if the regularizer is not used then convergence is not achieved[2]. **This derivation is different from that used in [20]**. Further, while initializing marginal statistics for $\boldsymbol{\beta}$ and $\boldsymbol{\pi}$, random initialization works best. A complete derivation of the extrema expressions for the hidden variables and model parameters cannot be shown due to space constraints. Note that number of Lagrange multipliers used in the optimization for $\phi_{d,n,i}$ is N_d, that for $\lambda_{d,m,i}$ or $\lambda_{d,m,n}$ is M_d and that for $\rho_{i,j}$ $j \in \{1, .., corrV\}$ is $corrV$. These free($\boldsymbol{\phi}$,$\boldsymbol{\lambda}$) and model($\boldsymbol{\rho}$) parameters follow multinomial distributions and hence sum to one.

3.3 Algorithms for Implementation

Algorithms 1, 2, 3 and 4 outline some computational procedures for implementing the model and corresponding time complexities (given as $[\mathcal{O}(.)]$). If a procedure is not defined, comments in $\{.\}$ explain the functionality of the procedures.

Algorithm 1 VB EM

```
if algorithm_mode == "training" then
    initialize_statistics(); {use seeded initialization for ρ
    and random initialization for β and π}
    vb_m_step();
end if
elbo_prev ← 0
elbo_current ← 0; iters ← 0
while converged ≥ EM_CONVERGED do
    elbo_current ← vb_e_step() {update hidden variables}
    vb_m_step() {update model parameters}
    converged ← (elbo_prev − elbo_current)/(elbo_prev)
    elbo_prev ← elbo_current; iters ←iters+1
end while [O(iters×(vb_e_step+vb_m_step))]
```

4. RESULTS AND DISCUSSIONS

This section shows the relative performances of the proposed models on DUC2005, Wikipedia and the Amazon Review (AR)[7] datasets (see subsection 1.1). The AR dataset was further processed to extract not more than 400 reviews per category. The reviews belong to 25 category labels including {apparel, software, magazine, food, etc.}. The Wikipedia documents were crawled using the special export url[3] mostly along the categories of {food, animal, countries,

[2] Authors thank Jordan Boyd-Graber for the hint on using regularizers

[3] http://en.wikipedia.org/wiki/Special:Export/<Wiki_article_name>

Algorithm 2 vb_e_step

zero_initialize_statistics();[$\mathcal{O}$(K.corrV+K.V+T.V)]
precompute_beta_and_pi_row_sums() {precompute $\sum_{v=1}^{V} \exp\{\log \beta_{i,v} + \log \pi_{t,v}\} \forall i \in \{1,...,K\}$ and $\forall t \in \{1,...T\}$ in an KxT matrix }[$\mathcal{O}$(K.T.V)]
$elbo\_current \leftarrow 0$
for $d = 0$ to D **do**
    $doc \leftarrow corpus \rightarrow document\_vec \rightarrow at(d)$
    elbo_current += doc_e_step(d, doc) {also accumulate $term_1^{\beta}$, $term_2^{\beta}$, $term_1^{\pi}$ and $term_1^{\pi}$ of the marginal statistics for β and $\pi \, \forall \, d, w_{d,m}$ and $t_{d,m}$ c.f. eqs. 16, 19, 17 and 20}
end for [$\mathcal{O}$(D(doc_e_step))]
return elbo_current;

Algorithm 3 doc_e_step

$\gamma_{d,i} = \alpha + \frac{\text{doc}\rightarrow total\_num\_words}{K}$ {If model is corrMETag^{2}LDA} {or}
$\gamma_{d,i} = \alpha + \frac{(\text{doc}\rightarrow total\_num\_words + \text{doc}\rightarrow total\_num\_corr\_words)}{K}$ {If model is METag^{2}LDA}
$\phi_{n,i} = \frac{1.0}{K}$
$\lambda_{m,i} = \frac{1.0}{K}$ {If model is METag^{2}LDA} {OR} $\lambda_{m,n} = \frac{1.0}{doc\rightarrow unique\_num\_corr\_words}$ {If model is corrMETag^{2}LDA}
$elbo\_current \leftarrow 0$; $v\_iter \leftarrow 0$
while not converged **do**
    update $\zeta_{d,m}$
    update $\phi_{d,n,i}$
    update $\lambda_{d,m,i}$ {If model is METag^{2}LDA} {OR} update $\lambda_{d,m,n}$ {If model is corrMETag^{2}LDA}
    $elbo\_current \leftarrow compute\_likelihood()$ {To compute likelihoods c.f. equations 3 for METag^{2}LDA and 9 for corrMETag^{2}LDA}
    update $\gamma_{d,i}$
    $v\_iter \leftarrow v\_iter + 1$
end while
return elbo_current; [$\mathcal{O}$(K+KN+KM+v_iter(MK+NK+MK+KN))] for METag^{2}LDA or [$\mathcal{O}$(K+NK+MN+v_iter(MKN+NKM+MKN+KN))] for corrMETag^{2}LDA

sport, war, transportation, natural, weapon, universe and ethnic groups}. The relative positions of the sections were binned into 5 categories which served as WL tags. Standard English stopwords were removed for the Wikipedia data and after processing, it contained 33,261 unique words and 6,902 unique DL tags (bag-of-words from image captions and Wikipedia article names). The AR dataset contained 6017 unique words and 4271 unique DL tags from product names and review titles after processing. Tags from the affect lexicon were used as WL tags. For both datasets, words occurring once or more than a thousand times across the entire corpus were also removed. Also note that the main document word vocabulary V and the document level tag vocabulary $corrV$ were processed independently using the same token processing rules but without any correspondence. To compare the proposed models with sLDA[5] on the AR data, all DL and WL tags were discarded for sLDA. Instead, the ratings served as values of the response random variables. For both the datasets the number of topics

Algorithm 4 vb_m_step

for all $i \in 1,..,K$, $v \in 1,..,V$ and $corr\_v \in 1,...,corrV$ **do**
    update $\rho_{i,corr\_v}$ from sufficient statistics
    update $\beta_{i,v}$ from marginal statistics
    update $\pi_{t,v}$ from marginal statistics
    update α {Follow the Newton-Raphson method in [6]}
end for [$\mathcal{O}$(K.corrV+K.V+T.V)]

K were set to $\{20, 50, 100, 200\}$. For the DUC2005 dataset, the DL tags were the GSRts found in respective documents and their counts (see subsection 1.1 for GSRts). Two types of WL tags were considered: word position bins like WL tags for Wikipedia dataset and named entity classes - PERSON, ORGANIZATION, LOCATION, NUMBER and MISC. Together, DL+WL tagging for DUC2005 data is named as GSRTPos and GSRTNe respectively (see fig. 2). Altogether, there were 36725 unique words for the DUC2005 dataset and 81 corresponding terms which were just the GSRts. K was set to $\{40, 60, 80, 100\}$ for the DUC2005 data based on human intuitions.

4.1 Model Perplexity

To measure predictive power of METag^{2}LDA and corrMETag^{2}LDA, a 10-fold cross validation was performed on the DUC2005 dataset. Figures 2a and 2c show the ELBO's (higher is better) on validation sets averaged over all folds. Figures 2b and 2d show the **minimum** of the differences in the ELBO's per topic across all folds for the corrMETag^{2}LDA model vs. corrMMLDA and METag^{2}LDA models. Clearly the differences prove that the improved performance of correspondence Tag^2 model is statistically significant. This is also intuitive since words in a document are always generated from a corresponding process, like visualizing an image or action role for a concept. There is a very slightly improved performance when the WL tags are chosen to be named entity classes.

The TagLDA model[20] was not compared for this dataset since the concept of multiple GSRts at the word level breaks down for TagLDA. However, empirically it is seen that the nature of DL tags influences the predictive power of the proposed Tag^{2}LDA models vs. TagLDA. For the DUC05 dataset, the DL tags were represented by coherence markers like "subj→subj" etc. as in [2]. Typically this type of marker groups variations like "landslide:subj→subj," "car:subj→subj" etc. under a common "subj→subj" abstraction. On the other hand, words like landslide and car signify concepts that allow for identifying specific centers in coherent sentences. In this respect, the WL perspective is more important (primary) over the more abstract DL perspective, the latter capturing a coarser notion of document level coherence. The counts of document level GSRts in the form of "GSR→GSR" do not allow for much variance to be exhibited by the documents at the DL perspective. This fits TagLDA better to the dataset at the cost of either ignoring abstract coherence markers altogether or discarding WL perspective and choosing only one coherence marker per word at WL annotation. However, if the document level GSRts are in the form "word:GSR→GSR", then the proposed models fit the data much better than TagLDA owing to the variance in the DL observations that are captured nicely in the topics along with the WL variations. The GSRts in the latter case

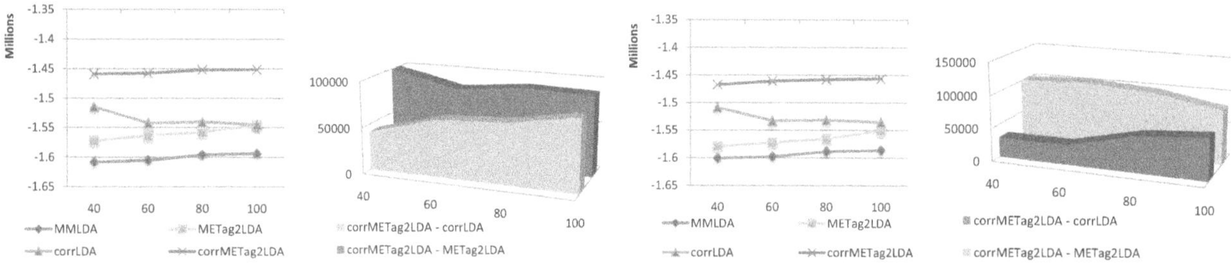

(a) (b) (c) (d)

Figure 2: Cross-Validation results on DUC05 newswire data (higher is better in 2a and 2c): (2a) ELBO-Validation DUC05 GSRTNe; (2b) Minimum of differences in ELBO across topics of corrMETag^{2}LDA to corrLDA and METag^{2}LDA for GSRTNe tagging; (2c) ELBO-Validation DUC05 GSRTPos; (2d) Minimum of differences in ELBO across topics of corrMETag^{2}LDA to corrLDA and METag^{2}LDA for GSRTPos tagging

cannot be considered as secondary to the WL perspective for document representation. Figures 3a, 3b, 4a and 4b also

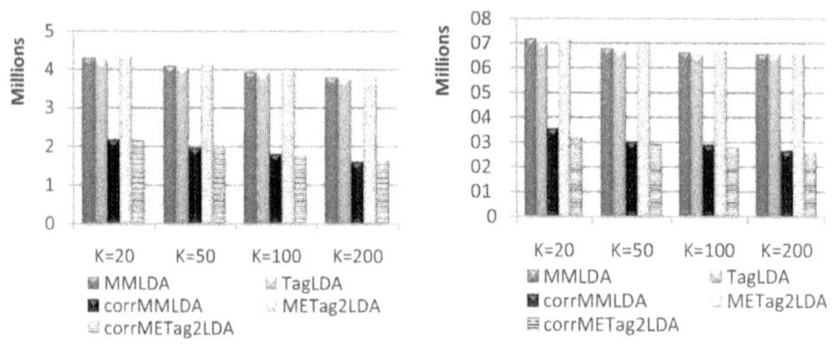

(a) (-)ELBO-Train Wiki (b) (-)ELBO-Test Wiki

Figure 3: Training and test negative ELBO plots of tag topic models on the Wiki data(Lower is better). In each K-group, the models from left to right are MMLDA, TagLDA, corrMMLDA, METag^{2}LDA and corrMETag^{2}LDA

show that in the presence of decent variations in DL tags, the corrMETag^{2}LDA model performs the best in terms of both training ELBO and test ELBO. The meaning of correspondence in terms of the bag-of-words model is to find important associations where the first word comes from a document and the second from DL tags in the same document. Table 6 shows some word correspondences that were obtained on test documents from Wikipedia (see rows with $\lambda_{m,n}^{(.)}$s). For the

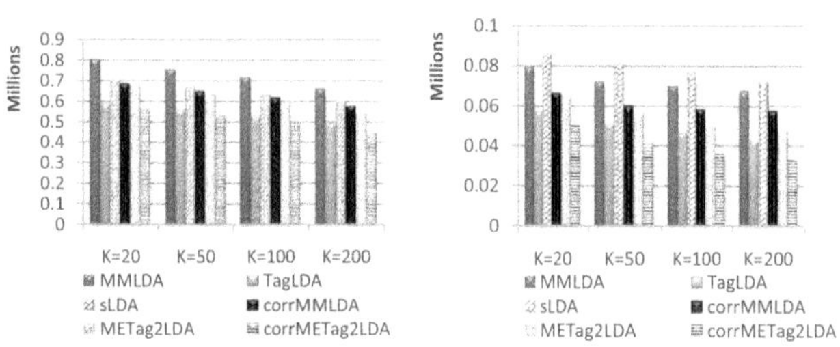

(a) (-)ELBO-Train AR (b) (-)ELBO-Test AR

Figure 4: Training and test negative ELBO plots of tag topic models on the Amazon Review(AR) data(Lower is better). In each K-group, the models from left to right are MMLDA, TagLDA, sLDA, corrMMLDA, METag^{2}LDA and corrMETag^{2}LDA

Wikipedia dataset, the mixture Multi-Multinomial (Exponential) class of models: MMLDA[16, 17] and METag^{2}LDA (fig. 1e) perform worst. TagLDA[20] performs a little better. This trend is seen on both the training and test sets. Note however that METag^{2}LDA does a simultaneous joint and conditional modeling of DL and WL tags w.r.t. the document's words. Thus it, along with corrMETag^{2}LDA, captures what MMLDA, corrMMLDA and TagLDA individually misses out. The ELBO trends of the correspondence class of LDAs are quite similar, with corrMETag^{2}LDA beating corrMMLDA. Again, this trend is seen on both the training and test sets. For the AR dataset, the corrMETag^{2}LDA model beats all other models convincingly in both the training and test set perplexities. The perplexity of MMLDA is the highest during training, followed by (supervised) sLDA[5] and the predictive power of sLDA decreases even further on the test set. In the AR dataset, TagLDA performs much better due to less variability in DL tags. The proposed corrMETag^{2}LDA combines the best of TagLDA and corrMMLDA to achieve the best predictive power on the AR dataset consisting mostly of very short review documents.

Table 6 shows some topics from Wikipedia dataset corresponding to the best performing corrMETag^{2}LDA model. Note that "positional facets" of topics 175 and 196 have been collapsed for space limitations. The test documents for these collapsed topics were the Wikipedia articles on "galaxy" and "fog". The learned $\boldsymbol{\beta}$ parameters contributing *marginally* to word generation are listed for the collapsed topics. Top suggested tags from image captions for the test documents also appear as the re-weighted $\boldsymbol{\rho}$ topic multinomial over all DL tags after document inference. Top correspondence tuples are listed as $\lambda_{m,n}$. For topics 54 and 76, notice how there is a "drift" from the beginning sections of the Wikipedia articles to the end sections. Words like "University Press, ISBN" have high mass on the "Middle_to_end" and the "End" facets of the topic 76. The image labels for topics are obtained from an inverted index of DL tags to thumbnailed image files. From figures 3 and 4, 200 topics are good fits to both the Tag^2 topic models for both Wikipedia and AR datasets.

Qualitative conditional topic distributions from the AR dataset (like the ones in table 6) are not shown in the paper due to space constraints. The nature of WL affect tags, though, needs some mention. The assignment of affect tags to review words based on maximum valence score do indeed make them orthogonal and one might choose not to use them at all in the modeling process. However, including such orthogonality do have some good uses. The conditioning of topics on the WL tags allows us to discover terms that might be related to tagged words through shared topics. For example, words like "advertisements," "ads," "listing," etc. that do not appear in [9] could receive higher probability mass for some topic (e.g. magazines) conditioned on "MELANCHOLIC" affect while it could receive higher probability mass for another topic (e.g. software) conditioned on "CONTENDED" affect thereby introducing a relaxation over orthogonal WL tagging constraints.

	Beginning →	Beginning To Middle →	Middle →	Middle To End →	End	Tag Suggestions	Correspondence	Image Labels
Topic54 (Artillery:Wars)	Firing, United, artillery, Army, century, guns, support, forced, targets, modern	Firing, artillery, United, guns. Army, targets, forced, century, operated, design, weapons, control	Firing, United, artillery, guns, targets, century, Army, modern, weapons, traditional, field, Battle	United, Firing, Army, weapons, guns, field, power, team, History, rockets, artillery, effective, numbers	targets, attacks, aircraft, design, combatants, radar, modern, small, capable, enemy, Electronic	artillery, guns, howitzer, French, century, Cannon,field, trajectories, PzH, self-propelled	(treating, soldiers) (construction, German) (construction, forge-welded) (postmodernism, Franco-Prussian) (demolitions, captured)	
	$\beta^{learned}_{54}$: Firing artillery guns. targets. United fuzes Army projectile mortars ammunition weapons shells. battery cannon modern							
Topic76 (Tofu:Food)	tofu, Chinese, Japanese, waters, China, Japan, century, origins, similar	tofu, Chinese, Japanese, Soy, Western, products, Asian, meat, important, milk, traditional, flavor	tofu, Chinese, Japanese, food, traditional, Western, cultures, meat, Asian, Korean, Dishes, Japan, soy	tofu, Press, Asian, fries, food, ancient, Western, play, Japanese, Ice, oil, cuisine, fresh, main, America, winter	Press, popular, cultures, China, deep, study, research, traditional, University, America, ISBN	tofu, sliced, China, water, soy, fresh, Provinces, Kong, milked, dishes, press, Hong, solid, soft, island, curds	(beans, dried) (beans, tofu) (suspended, solid) (palm, island) (feeling, sweet) (thinly, sliced) (stir-fries, hot) (canned, soya)	
	$\beta^{learned}_{76}$: tofu soy production Chinese milk firm texture flavor coagulated sauces soft Japanese "dĂšufu" fries Protein cooking fresh beans							
Topic175	$\beta^{learned}_{175}$: galaxy Star spiraled milky matter cluster Hubble gas Universe structure Formation elliptical active galactic nebula dwarf							
	ρ^{inf}_{175} : Galaxy, spiral, stars, Hubble, classification, Andromeda, rings, core, Great, compared							
	$\lambda^{(galaxy)}_{m,n}$: (Planet, Hubble) (Planet, object) (Planet, galaxy) (Herschel, Hubble) (ring, galaxy) (Heat, galaxy) (discoveries, Hubble)							
Topic196	$\beta^{learned}_{196}$: fog air Shadow Ice condensation light vapor Humidity layer temperature freeze particle cool waters moisture evaporation salt							
	ρ^{inf}_{196} : fog, Francisco, San, visible, high, temperature, streets, photo, Bai, lake, California, bridge, air							
	$\lambda^{(fog)}_{m,n}$: (dimensions, high) (beam, visible) (parallel, bridge) (droplets, fog) (combustion, temparature) (invisible, visible) (absorbed, air)							

Table 6: Topics and correspondences from the corrMETag²LDA for the Wikipedia data for $K = 200$

4.2 Automatically Evaluating Suggested Tags From Image Captions

For each of the Wikipedia test documents, top 5 predicted tags (coming from image captions and article names) were chosen. Following [14], the method described in section 1.3 was chosen as a quantitative measure of tag suggestion success. Figure 5a shows the relative values of the proposed Tag²LDA models for macro averages of maximum of best path distance scores for all test documents. Fig. 5a suggests that people ignore the specific contents of the documents while assigning a category label. The METag²LDA model, in spite of higher perplexity, performs a little better here because of the lack of specificity of suggested DL tags to the document contents. This shows that humans assign DL tags that belong to higher levels of abstraction. Nevertheless, the best DL tags suggested by both METag²LDA and corrMETag²LDA are only within 1 to 2 hops away from the ground truth tags based on a chosen WordNet ontology. Thus image captions in Wikipedia articles provide powerful clues for suggesting document tags. Table 7 shows "**explanations**" of the suggested **DL tags** to the ground truth *category labels* which is a desirable output of this type of evaluation. One could also use cross-document evidence trails[18] to measure semantic relatedness. It is to be noted here that the ontology chosen must be specific to the nature of the task. For example, in medical domain, WordNet is a poor choice for providing explanations to DL tag suggestions.

4.3 Automatically Evaluating Named Entity Relationship Discovery

For the DUC2005 data, the second column in the first, third and fifth rows of table 8 show selected PERSON entity pairs that were discovered to be related through some latent topics. The WL and DL tags for this purpose were named entity classes and GSRts. The first column in the first, third and fifth rows shows queries that serve as gists of the three docsets. To validate the discoveries the following experiment was devised: For each docset in the DUC2005 data, all entity pairs that were co-occurring in a sentence were counted and was treated to be a baseline measure of coverage for entity pairs that are related. Then a set of best topics were inferred for the documents in docsets by the Tag²LDA class of models. For each topic set, 2450 (=50x50-50)PERSON entity pairs were created out of the highly probable entities

Some concept pair evidence chains from domain ontology
spiral ↔ curve ↔ line ↔ shape ↔ attribute ↔ abstraction ↔ group ↔ collection ↔ *galaxy*
weapon ↔ persuasion ↔ communication ↔ act ↔ activity ↔ *occupation*
french ↔ sculptor ↔ artist ↔ creator ↔ person ↔ *modern*
soy ↔ legume ↔ herb ↔ vascular_plant ↔ plant ↔ organism ↔ person ↔ inhabitant ↔ Asian ↔ *Vietnamese*

Table 7: Sample evidence Chains for **DL Tag Suggestions** from image captions to *actual category labels* from the Tag² topic models

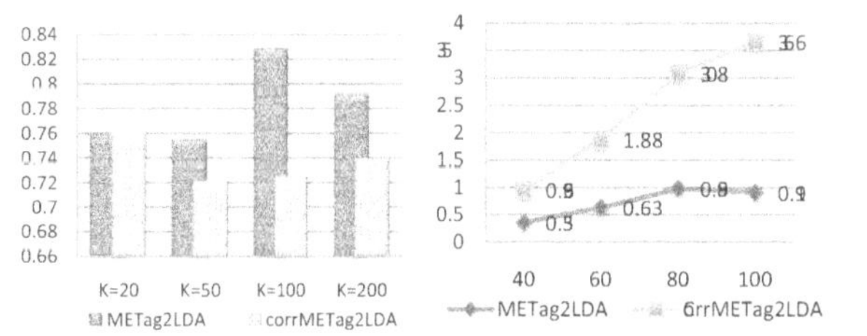

(a) (b)

Figure 5: (5a)The best ontological inverse path length measure between suggested DL tags from image captions and ground truth Wikipedia categories for the test set in fig. 3b and (5b) PERSON Named Entity-pair coverage ratio to baseline from DUC05 Newswire data

Nobel Prize Winners in Science & Economics	(John_Harsanyi, John_Nash) (Von_Neumann, John_Harsanyi) (Von_Neumann, John_Nash)
Last week the Nobel Prize for Economics was awarded to three 'game theorists': John Harsanyi, John Nash and Rheinhard Selten. What is game theory? Game theory is still a relatively young field. Von Neumann and Oskar Morganstern introduced many of the central ideas in a book published in 1944.	
Women in Parliaments	(Mrs_Margaret_Beckett, Ms_Ann_Taylor) (Mrs_Margaret_Beckett, Ms_Clare_Short) (Mrs_Margaret_Beckett, Ms_Harriet_Harman) (Mrs_Margaret_Beckett, Ms_Hilary_Armstrong) (Mrs_Margaret_Beckett, Ms_Jo_Richardson)
There are at present just four women occupants - Mrs Margaret Beckett, Ms Ann Clwyd, Ms Ann Taylor and Ms Jo Richardson - of the 18 shadow cabinet seats elected each year. The plan now being discussed by the group is to create a 'recommended' list of women candidates. Women would be asked to ensure that they included more than three votes for group members. Beneficiaries might include Ms Harriet Harman, Ms Clare Short, Ms Marjorie Mowlam and Ms Hilary Armstrong.	
VW/GM Industrial Espionage	(Bill_Clinton, Mr_Lopez) (Dorothea_Holland, Bill_Clinton) (Bill_Clinton, Ms_Holland)
It is believed US investigators have asked for, but have been so far refused access to, evidence accumulated by German prosecutors probing allegations that former GM director, Mr Lopez, stole industrial secrets from the US group and took them with him when he joined VW last year. This investigation was launched by US President Bill Clinton and is in principle a far more simple or at least more single-minded pursuit than that of Ms Holland. Dorothea Holland, until four months ago was the only prosecuting lawyer on the German case.	
Topic34(ORG): GM Opel EC General_Motors Harvard volkswagen Justice_Department World_Bank Volkswagen the_Times FBI	
Topic34(LOC): Germany Los_Angeles California UK german Washington Europe Brazil London Slovakia european U.S. New_York	
Topic34: GM Mr_Lopez group yesterday company german week official Mr_Piech work production charge car investigation prosecutor	

Table 8: DUC2005 dataset: Related PERSON named entity pairs and evidence from documents

appearing in the PERSON facet of the conditional topics. Note that for all entities A and B, two entity pairs (A,B) and (B,A) were created. Each docset had on average 2449 PERSON entity pairs and hence the number 2450. Note that John_Nash, Nash and Dr._Nash were treated as three separate entities. The graph in fig. 5b shows that the correspondence model is 3 times better than the robust baseline at the right number of fitted topics and using the abstract GSRt DL perspective. The second, fourth and sixth rows of table 8 show how topical context ties two entities together even though they do not occur in the same sentence. Rows 7, 8 and 9 show ORGANIZATION facet, LOCATION facet and *marginal* topic corresponding to the best topic for docset "VW/GM Industrial Espionage".

5. CONCLUSION

This paper proposes novel extensions to joint models of text and document level tags that makes use of conditional word level tags to better capture annotated document structure. The proposed Multinomial-Exponential Tag^{2}LDA models capture semantics of documents with domain knowledge coming from two different perspectives. The correspondence models also show impressive predictive power for inferring topics. Further, usefulness of the models have been explored with applications that provide deep insights into the data. Overall, it is possible to add domain knowledge from different perspectives, into topic models without sacrificing predictive power. Thus supervised models of data annotation can be made better without any intervention from topic models and still aid the latter in improving posterior inference. Adding **more than one** word level tag to each word or phrase, each being generated from a different perspective, is an important direction of research.

6. REFERENCES

[1] Shenghua Bao, Shengliang Xu, Li Zhang, Rong Yan, Zhong Su, Dingyi Han, and Yong Yu. Joint emotion-topic modeling for social affective text mining. *IEEE International Conference on Data Mining*, 0:699–704, 2009.

[2] Regina Barzilay and Mirella Lapata. Modeling local coherence: an entity-based approach. In *Proceedings of the 43rd ACL conference*, pages 141–148, 2005.

[3] Matthew J. Beal. *Variational Algorithms for Approximate Bayesian Inference*. PhD thesis, Gatsby Computational Neuroscience Unit, University College London, 2003.

[4] David M. Blei and Michael I. Jordan. Modeling annotated data. In *Proceedings of the 26th ACM SIGIR conf.*, pages 127–134, New York, NY, USA, 2003.

[5] David M. Blei and Jon D. Mcauliffe. Supervised topic models. In *NIPS*, volume 21, 2007.

[6] David M. Blei, Andrew Y. Ng, and Michael I. Jordan. Latent dirichlet allocation. *JMLR*, 3:993–1022, 2003.

[7] John Blitzer, Mark Dredze, and Fernando Pereira. Biographies, Bollywood, Boom-boxes and Blenders: Domain Adaptation for Sentiment Classification. In *Proceedings of the 45th ACL conf.*, pages 440–447, Prague, CZ, 2007.

[8] Jordan Boyd-Graber, Jonathan Chang, Sean Gerrish, Chong Wang, and David Blei. Reading tea leaves: How humans interpret topic models. In *NIPS*, 2009.

[9] M.M. Bradley and P.J. Lang. Affective norms for English words (ANEW): Stimuli, instruction manual and affective ratings. 1999.

[10] Hoa Trang Dang. Duc 2005: evaluation of question-focused summarization systems. In *Proceedings of the Workshop on Task-Focused Summarization and Question Answering*, SumQA '06, pages 48–55. ACL, 2006.

[11] Yansong Feng and Mirella Lapata. How many words is a picture worth? automatic caption generation for news images. In *Proceedings of the 48th ACL conf.*, pages 1239–1249, 2010.

[12] Caimei Lu, Xiaohua Hu, Xin Chen, Jung R. Park, TingTing He, and Zhoujun Li. The topic-perspective model for social tagging systems. In *Proceedings of the 16th ACM SIGKDD conf.*, pages 683–692, 2010.

[13] David Newman, Jey Han Lau, Karl Grieser, and Timothy Baldwin. Automatic evaluation of topic coherence. In *In proceedings of the NAACL conf.*, pages 100–108, Los Angeles, California, 2010.

[14] Ted Pedersen, Siddharth Patwardhan, and Jason Michelizzi. Wordnet::similarity - measuring the relatedness of concepts. In *AAAI*, pages 1024–1025, 2004.

[15] Daniel Ramage, David Hall, Ramesh Nallapati, and Christopher D. Manning. Labeled LDA: A supervised topic model for credit attribution in multi-labeled corpora. In *Proceedings of the 2009 EMNLP conf.*, pages 248–256, Singapore, 2009.

[16] Daniel Ramage, Paul Heymann, Christopher D. Manning, and Hector Garcia-Molina. Clustering the tagged web. In *Proceedings of the 2nd ACM WSDM conf.*, pages 54–63, 2009.

[17] Xiance Si and Maosong Sun. Tag-LDA for Scalable Real-time Tag Recommendation. *Journal of Computational Information Systems*, 2009.

[18] Rohini Srihari, Li Xu, and Tushar Saxena. Use of ranked cross document evidence trails for hypothesis generation. In *Proceedings of the 13th KDD conference*, pages 677–686, San Jose, CA, 2007.

[19] Hanna M. Wallach, David Mimno, and Andrew McCallum. Rethinking LDA: Why priors matter. In *NIPS*, 2009.

[20] Xiaojin Zhu, David Blei, and John Lafferty. Taglda: Bringing document structure knowledge into topic models. *UWisc Technical Report TR-1533*, 2006.

External Evaluation Measures for Subspace Clustering

Stephan Günnemann • Ines Färber • Emmanuel Müller ○ Ira Assent ◇ Thomas Seidl •

•RWTH Aachen University, Germany
{guennemann, faerber, seidl}@cs.rwth-aachen.de

○Karlsruhe Institute of Technology, Germany
emmanuel.mueller@kit.edu

◇Aarhus University, Denmark
ira@cs.au.dk

ABSTRACT

Knowledge discovery in databases requires not only development of novel mining techniques but also fair and comparable quality assessment based on objective evaluation measures. Especially in young research areas where no common measures are available, researchers are unable to provide a fair evaluation. Typically, publications glorify the high quality of one approach only justified by an arbitrary evaluation measure. However, such conclusions can only be drawn if the evaluation measures themselves are fully understood.

In this paper, we provide the basis for systematic evaluation in the emerging research area of subspace clustering. We formalize general quality criteria for subspace clustering measures not yet addressed in the literature. We compare the existing external evaluation methods based on these criteria and pinpoint limitations. We propose a novel external evaluation measure which meets the requirements in form of quality properties. In thorough experiments we empirically show characteristic properties of evaluation measures. Overall, we provide a set of evaluation measures that fulfill the general quality criteria as recommendation for future evaluations. All measures and datasets are provided on our website[1] and are integrated in our evaluation framework.

Categories and Subject Descriptors: H.2.8 Database management: Database applications [Data mining]

General Terms: Measurement, Experimentation

Keywords: data mining, high dimensional data, subspace clustering, projected clustering, evaluation

1. INTRODUCTION

For knowledge discovery in databases, fair and comparable evaluation of detected patterns is of major importance. For a thorough evaluation of mining techniques, it is essential to have objective methods that measure the quality of data mining results. In contrast to the subjective quality assessment by domain experts, these measures should provide an objective and comparable evaluation. This evaluation is important for quality assessment of novel methods vs. competing approaches but also for knowledge extraction based on the detected patterns. Evaluation completes the knowledge discovery process by providing more insights than a mere listing of patterns.

In this work we focus on evaluation measures for subspace clustering techniques [17, 9]. In general, *subspace clustering* or *projected clustering* aim at the detection of clusters in arbitrary subspace projections. While traditional clustering searches for clusters based on object similarity using all available attributes (full space), subspace clustering considers object similarity in any subset of the given attributes (subspaces). Several subspace clustering approaches have been proposed. They all show high quality results, especially on high dimensional data where traditional clustering approaches fail to detect clusters. Surveys [17, 9] or empirical studies [15, 13] provide some comparisons of subspace clustering approaches. However, all of these publications focus on the subspace clustering techniques and not on the specific characteristics of evaluation in this research area.

So far only few measures were developed specifically for subspace clustering. Instead, researchers borrowed measures from other areas, as information retrieval or classification without discussing their applicability and characteristics for subspace clustering. Thus, some measures may not be appropriate for subspace cluster evaluation. Furthermore, the differing use of measures leads to incomparable results. As illustrated in Fig. 1, comparing the hidden clusters (ground truth) and the detected clusters with two of these measures might yield contradicting results. Even for a single measure, users do not know how to interpret the results because they are not aware of its characteristics. The variety of evaluation measures used, usually reflect different aspects of the clustering results and hardly any of them allows a holistic evaluation. Overall, this situation leads to unfair comparisons of subspace clustering results.

In this paper we bridge the gap between individual evaluation measures. Besides evaluation challenges inherited by traditional clustering, we highlight specific core requirements for a systematic evaluation of subspace clustering results. Based on a given ground truth, traditional clustering measures evaluate the purity of clusters and the detection of all clustered objects. For subspace clustering we have further challenges: First, a high quality subspace clustering should also detect the correct subspaces in which objects are grouped. Second, subspace clusters might be reported redundantly in several subspaces. Last, objects may be part of multiple valid clusters.

As key contributions of this paper, we take a systematic approach to characterize the main *quality requirements for*

[1] http://dme.rwth-aachen.de/OpenSubspace/E4SC/

CIKM'11, October 24–28, 2011, Glasgow, Scotland, UK.

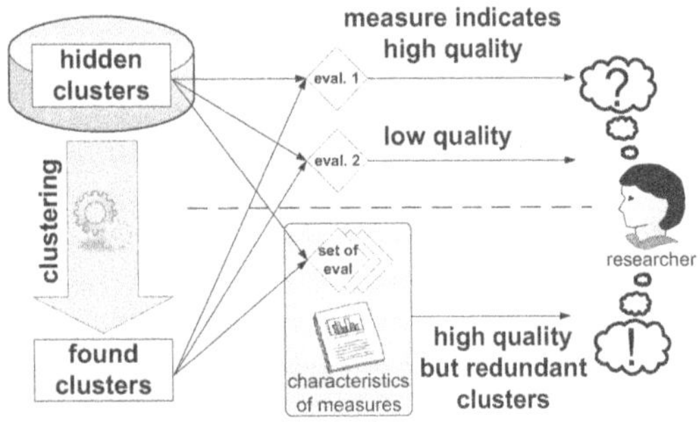

Fig. 1: Enhanced evaluation by insights into characteristics of evaluation measures [conflicting evaluation (top), meaningful interpretation (bottom)]

subspace clustering. We formalize all of these properties and we provide an *analysis of evaluation measures* used in recent publications [12, 18, 5, 11, 6, 14, 15, 13]. In addition, we propose an *enhanced evaluation measure* which meets these requirements. Based on our systematic comparison, we provide a *recommendation of measures* to be used in future evaluations. In conjunction with the *derived characteristics* in this paper, these measures can be used not only for evaluation but also for further knowledge extraction. Knowing about the characteristics of the measures, evaluation provides a reasoning about why poor results are observed (Fig. 1 (bottom)). This knowledge can be helpful for better parametrization or for improvement of the data mining algorithm itself.

2. SUBSPACE CLUSTER EVALUATION

Evaluation of clustering as unsupervised learning is challenging since the "correct" result is usually unknown. Several evaluation types have been proposed.

Evaluation Types. Evaluation based on domain experts is one possible type, used in application oriented evaluations. Here domain experts are consulted to manually evaluate each cluster. This evaluation provides more insight into the detected clusters but it is subjective and does not yield comparable results on benchmark data. Furthermore, it can only be applied for very small result sets. As a second evaluation type, internal evaluation measures are defined based on properties of the cluster definition e.g. the compactness of clusters (cf. k-means [10]). Such measures only reflect the relative adherence to the underlying cluster definition. They are thus typically used for those clustering paradigms trying to optimize a task specific objective function. For most clustering paradigms including subspace clustering such a general objective function is not defined, and thus, no internal measure is meaningful for all methods. Clustering methods adhering to different cluster definitions cannot be fairly evaluated w.r.t. a single internal measure. As a third type, external evaluation measures are used (e.g. for k-means [20]). They assume a ground truth, as provided by synthetic data or labeled data. External measures compare the detected clusters with this given ground truth, providing an objective quality assessment, independent of the cluster definition. In this work, we focus on external evaluation measures for subspace clustering. Before discussing the novel requirements induced by subspace clustering in Sec. 2, we review the general idea of external evaluation measures.

The "All and Only" Quality Criterion. External evaluation measures compare a given ground truth (ideal clustering) with the detected result set of found clusters. Intuitively, a measure should provide high quality values for a clustering that detects *all* hidden clusters, but also detects *only* the hidden clusters. This *all and only* property applies to several aspects in the evaluation of subspace clusters. We distinguish between the cluster level (single cluster) and the clustering level (overall set of clusters): First, on the cluster level, each found cluster should contain *all and only* objects of a single hidden cluster. Furthermore, each found subspace cluster should be detected in *all and only* the dimensions of the hidden subspace cluster. And second, on the clustering level, the overall set of detected clusters should contain *all and only* the hidden clusters.

Evaluation characteristics. We first introduce some basic notions for subspace cluster evaluation, before presenting the quality requirements that each measure should fulfill. An external measure evaluates the subspace clustering result that contains a set of subspace clusters, each representing a group of objects in a subset of the dimensions.

DEFINITION 1. *Subspace clustering result*
Given a set of dimensions Dim and a database DB, a subspace cluster $C = (O, S)$ is a set of objects $O \subseteq DB$ along with a set of relevant dimensions $S \subseteq Dim$. A subspace clustering result Res is a set of subspace clusters $Res = \{C_1, \ldots, C_k\}$ with C_i being a subspace cluster.

In Fig. 2 two exemplary subspace clusterings are illustrated. The x-axis denotes the dimensions and the y-axis the objects of the database. Each subspace cluster covers a specific set of objects and dimensions.

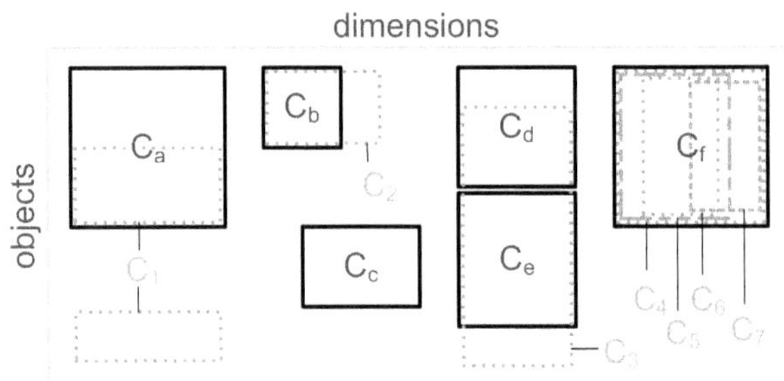

Subspace clustering 1: $\{C_1, C_2, \ldots, C_7\}$
Subspace clustering 2: $\{C_a, C_b, \ldots, C_f\}$

Fig. 2: Two exemplary subspace clusterings

External evaluation measures determine the quality of a clustering w.r.t. a ground truth. This ground truth represents a gold standard that should be recovered by the subspace clustering algorithms to the greatest extent.

DEFINITION 2. *Ground truth*
The ground truth Ground is a subspace clustering representing the perfect result.

In Fig. 2 we assume the ground truth to be given by $Ground = \{C_a, C_b, \ldots, C_f\}$ and the other clustering to be determined by a clustering algorithm. As indicated in Fig. 2, an object can belong to several subspace clusters. Also the relevant dimensions of clusters can overlap. Hence an object can be part of several clusters in a single dimension in the ground truth or in the clustering result, e.g. the ones of C_4 and C_5. Thus, a mandatory requirement for each measure is to handle overlapping subspace clusters. We denote this criterion as *overlap applicable.*

An evaluation measure for subspace clustering can formally be defined by:

DEFINITION 3. *Evaluation measure*
Given a set of dimensions Dim, a database DB, and the ground truth Ground of this data set; an evaluation measure is defined by

$$M : \mathcal{P}(Clus) \times \mathcal{P}(Clus) \rightarrow \mathbb{R}$$

where $Clus = \{(O, S) \mid O \subseteq DB, S \subseteq Dim\}$ *is the set of all possible subspace clusters. The quality of a clustering Res w.r.t. the ground truth is:* $M(Ground, Res)$.

In general, an external measure can be used as a similarity measure between two arbitrary clusterings. W.l.o.g., in our work all measures are normalized between 0 and 1, where 1 indicates the perfect quality, e.g. $M(Ground, Ground) = 1$ holds. Any errors in the result should be reflected in the value of M and hence an optimal value should only be achieved for identical clusterings. As depicted in Fig. 2, the clusters themselves can differ, i.e. the hidden clusters are not exactly recovered (C_b vs. C_2); but also the overall set of clusters can differ, i.e. the clusterings disagree (C_c). Overall, we discuss specific characteristics on the cluster level and on the clustering level. We start with the cluster level.

Object awareness. As in traditional clustering, we want to identify the correct object groupings of the hidden clusters. The found clusters should not mix several hidden clusters or obfuscate a hidden cluster by other objects, since the *purity* of a cluster is crucial. The cluster C_2 in Fig. 2 has perfect purity w.r.t. C_b regarding the objects, while the cluster C_3 mixes several hidden clusters and noise objects. Moreover, for a correct object grouping, it is also important to identify as many objects as possible of the hidden cluster, not just a few as the cluster C_1 w.r.t. C_a. Overall, for a good detection it is mandatory to group *all and only* the objects of the hidden cluster. If this is not fulfilled by the clustering result *Res* a measure M should determine a lower quality. We denote this property of a measure as *object awareness.*

Subspace awareness. For subspace clusters the set of relevant dimensions constitutes a major part of its information content. It is therefore important to identify the correct object group and *at the same time* the correct relevant dimensions. It is an indication of poor quality to find the hidden object group but in a totally different subspace. Consequently, we want to identify *all and only* the relevant dimensions of a subspace cluster of the ground truth. In Fig. 2 the cluster C_2 does not reflect the relevant dimensions of C_b perfectly. A measure fulfills the *subspace awareness* criterion if it punishes false or missing relevant dimensions.

Redundancy awareness. Both previous criteria are relevant for determining the quality of *single* subspace clusters. The following criteria will consider the clustering level. In subspace clustering, we analyze subspace projections of the data. For any subspace cluster definition fulfilling the anti-monotonicity criterion, all exponentially many subspace projections of a valid cluster are valid as well. A set of clusters sharing nearly all objects and relevant dimensions, however, induce redundancy and therefore obscure the true clustering result. A measure should punish clustering results that identify one ground truth cluster several times. Beside the true hidden cluster C_f/C_4, in Fig. 2 several redundant clusters are generated (C_5, C_6, C_7). In traditional clustering, redundancy does not occur due to full space clustering. In subspace clustering, however, several approaches suffer from this phenomenon [3, 16, 8]. Evaluation measures for subspace clustering have to take into account, that a redundancy polluted clustering is not the perfect clustering. Adding further clusters not represented by the ground truth must lead to lower quality. In extreme words: Simply generating all possible clusters must not yield the perfect quality. A measure accounting for this criterion is *redundancy aware.*

Identification awareness. Respectively, it is not optimal to miss some clusters of the ground truth. In Fig. 2 the cluster C_c is not identified at all; a measure should not determine perfect quality. For subspace clustering, this property is a challenge, which cannot be trivially adapted from traditional clustering. While in traditional clustering each object belongs to just one cluster, in subspace clustering objects can belong to several clusters due to their relevant dimensions. Missing clusters in traditional clustering can simply be identified by a non coverage of some objects. However, in subspace clustering all objects could be covered by the result, even if not all clusters are identified. This problem appears, e.g. in partitioning approaches that only detect disjoint subspace clusters [1, 2, 19, 21]. Overall, to be *identification aware*, a measure has to decrease the quality for every missing cluster of the ground truth.

Summarized, we introduce 4 criteria that evaluation measures for subspace clustering have to fulfill: object, subspace, redundancy, and identification awareness.

3. EVALUATION MEASURES

In this section we examine existing evaluation measures with regard to the 4 criteria. Only if a measure responds to all 4 respective clustering variations, substantial conclusions can be drawn out of its quality assessment. For measures that ignore at least one criterion, a low quality value still indicates a bad clustering solution. A high quality value, contrarily, does not necessarily indicate a good clustering result. Clearly, a measure where neither low nor high quality values allow any conclusions is inappropriate. This is the case for those, that do not handle mandatory requirements of subspace clustering like overlap applicability. An example is the *Entropy* measure [5, 15]. For a ground truth with overlapping clusters, the entropy will always indicate a quality below optimal, even if we compare the ground truth against itself. An optimal clustering that equals the ground truth should, however, always have optimal quality results.

In the following Sec. 3.1 we only consider those measures, that are overlap applicable. To the best of our knowledge, we include all evaluation measures in our comparison that are used in recent subspace clustering publications. For these we will examine the sensitivity w.r.t. our 4 criteria. As a result, we will get that none of the existing measures deals fairly with all criteria. We, therefore, propose a novel, simple quality measure for subspace clustering in Sec. 3.2.

3.1 Analysis of existing measures

For our analysis we assume *Res* to be the set of found clusters and *Ground* to be the ground truth. The objects of a cluster C are denoted with $O(C)$ and the set of relevant dimensions of C with $S(C)$ respectively.

3.1.1 F1 measures

One method for the evaluation of clustering results is the F1-measure. F1 formalizes the requirement that clusters in Res should represent the clusters in $Ground$. That is, a cluster $C_r \in Res$ should on the one hand have many objects in common with one of the hidden clusters $C_g \in Ground$, but on the other hand it should contain as few objects as possible that are not in this particular hidden cluster. These two constraints can be formalized by the terms precision and recall and represent the all and only constraint of object awareness.

$$recall(C_r, C_g) = \frac{|O(C_r) \cap O(C_g)|}{|O(C_g)|} = precision(C_g, C_r)$$

The F1-measure evaluates the matching of two clusters as the harmonic mean of precision and recall.

$$F1(C_r, C_g) = \frac{2 \cdot recall(C_r, C_g) \cdot precision(C_r, C_g)}{recall(C_r, C_g) + precision(C_r, C_g)}$$

Note that the relevant subspaces do not occur in the formal definition of F1, which is therefore not aware of subspaces. However, it is widely used in subspace clustering evaluation [12, 11, 13, 6, 14, 15]. For the overall matching of two *clusterings* P and Q the F1 measure is defined as:

$$F1^{Clus}(P, Q) = \frac{1}{|P|} \sum_{C_i \in P} \max_{C_j \in Q} \{F1(C_i, C_j)\}$$

Optimal quality is denoted by a value of 1, whereas 0 indicates the lowest quality. It is crucial that the function of $F1^{Clus}$ is not symmetric ($F1^{Clus}(P,Q) \neq F1^{Clus}(Q,P)$), even though it has not been discussed in the literature yet. The sum only iterates over clusters in P and thus clusters in Q are only considered if they match at least one cluster in P best. Clusters in Q besides these matches have no influence on the evaluation result at all. The measure is used as

$$M^{F1-R}(Ground, Res) := F1^{Clus}(Ground, Res)$$

in [4], where Res is the clustering that is considered only partially for the quality evaluation. Thus, this definition is not redundancy aware, since it is not capable of detecting the presence of false clusters. That is, for all clusterings $Res \supseteq Ground$ the quality result will always be optimal $M^{F1-R}(Ground, Res) = 1$. Thus, only the obtained recall w.r.t. the clusters in $Ground$ is assessed; hence the naming "$F1$-Recall" ($F1$-R).

In [12, 11, 13] results are evaluated by the counterpart definition

$$M^{F1-P}(Ground, Res) := F1^{Clus}(Res, Ground)$$

In this case, the ground truth has only limited influence on the quality assessment of F1. Therefore, the presented definition of F1 is not identification aware, as all clusterings $Res \subseteq Ground$ will always have the perfect quality outcome of $M^{F1-P}(Ground, Res) = 1$. Since only the obtained precision w.r.t. the clusters in $Ground$ is assessed, we chose the naming "$F1$-Precision" ($F1$-P).

In [6, 14, 15] a third definition was introduced, where clusters in Res are merged if their best matching cluster in $Ground$ is identical. The size of the resulting clustering Res' is thus adjusted to the size of $Ground$. For each cluster $\overline{C} \in Ground$ we get a new cluster $C' \in Res'$, such that:

$$O(C') := \bigcup_{C \in Res} \left\{ O(C) \mid \overline{C} = \underset{C_i \in Ground}{\operatorname{argmax}} \left\{ \frac{|O(C) \cap O(C_i)|}{|O(C_i)|} \right\} \right\}$$

A solution Res is evaluated based on the ground truth and the novel result Res':

$$M^{F1-Merge}(Ground, Res) := F1^{Clus}(Ground, Res')$$

Due to the merging of found clusters this measure does not detect whether found clusters split hidden clusters and is thus not object aware.

3.1.2 Accuracy

Another quality assessment is realized by the Accuracy measure [14, 7, 15]. The basic idea is to predict the hidden clusters based on the found clusters. The more accurate the hidden clusters are predicted, the better the ground truth is generalized by the identified clusters. For prediction, the method of classification is used. As the training data, bitvectors are given that represent the membership of the objects in the hidden clusters $C_i \in Res$. That is, each object o induces a bitvector of length $k = |Res|$ where the ith entry is 1 if $o \in C_i$. Based on these training data a decision tree classifier is built and the accuracy is determined (usually C4.5 with 10-fold cross validation).

Since classification accuracy depends on the training data, we can infer that impure clusters affect the quality of the result; the training data contains errors w.r.t. the ground truth. However, as a classifier tries to countervail these effects the object awareness of the measure is questionable: Even if an object was assigned to some wrong clusters, the classifier could be able to predict the correct hidden clusters for the object. Thus, the measure indicates high quality, even in the presence of errors in the clustering result. Obviously, this measure is also not subspace aware, because only the object sets are used for training. If a cluster is completely missed, the classifier cannot assign the objects to this cluster. Thus, the identification awareness is fulfilled.

3.1.3 RNIA

In [18] the first measures have been introduced that fulfill the subspace awareness criterion. The basic idea is to represent a cluster (O, S) as a single set T instead of a tuple. For this, each object $o_i \in O$ is not stored as the full-dimensional feature but for each dimension $d \in S$ an object $o_{i,d}$ is constructed. We denote these objects as micro-objects. Thus, a subspace cluster can be represented by its set of micro-objects

$$t(C) = \{o_{i,d} \mid o_i \in O(C) \wedge d \in S(C)\}$$

An x-dimensional cluster with y objects is represented by $x \cdot y$ micro-objects. Based on this representation, the RNIA (relative non-intersecting area) measure assesses whether the micro-objects of the ground truth are all and only covered by the clustering result. Formally, the union U of the micro-objects of both clusterings is determined and their intersection I is subtracted. The assumption is, that for a good clustering result U and I are nearly identical. Overall,

$$M^{RNIA}(Ground, Res) := (\,|U| - |I|\,) \;/\; |U|$$

with $U = U(Ground) \cup U(Res)$, $I = U(Ground) \cap U(Res)$, and $U(P) = \left[\bigcup_{C \in P} t(C)\right]$. To handle overlapping clusters, [18] presents a method to adapt the union and intersection. We use this version in our experiments and we plot the value $1.0-RNIA$ so that perfect quality corresponds to 1.0.

Obviously, the RNIA measure is subspace aware. The redundancy and identification awareness are also fulfilled, because errors w.r.t. these criteria have an influence on the union and intersection respectively. The drawback of RNIA is its lack of object awareness. The purity or recall of single clusters is not considered at all. RNIA simply checks whether a micro-object of the ground truth is also contained in *Res* and vice versa. If $U(Ground) = U(Res)$ holds, RNIA returns perfect quality; independent of how the single clusters behave. Splits or impurities of clusters remain undetected.

3.1.4 CE

The disadvantages of the RNIA measure were addressed by the CE (clustering error) measure [18]. The basic idea is to find a 1:1 mapping between the hidden and found clusters. Each cluster C_g of the ground truth is assigned to at most one cluster C_r of the result, and vice versa. For each mapped pair (C_g, C_r) the cardinality of their intersecting micro-objects is determined. Overall, those 1:1 mappings are chosen that result in the highest total sum over all cardinalities. This sum is denoted as D_{max}. By replacing the intersection I within RNIA by D_{max} we formally get the CE measure:

$$M^{CE}(Ground, Res) := (\,|U| - D_{max}\,)\; / \;|U|$$

We plot the values of $1.0-CE$ such that perfect quality equals to 1. CE fulfills the same quality criteria as RNIA. The object awareness is still not completely fulfilled. On the one hand, the 1:1 mapping penalizes clusters which split up in several smaller ones because the coverage of the cluster decreases. On the other hand, the impurity of clusters is still not considered; the intersection between two clusters is not influenced by additional, wrong objects. Thus, the object awareness is not adequately implemented.

3.2 The E4SC evaluation measure

The previously reviewed techniques have major drawbacks in at least one of the 4 awareness criteria. The gathered insights on subspace clustering allow us to define an external evaluation measure, that addresses all 4 criteria, for a holistic evaluation of subspace clusterings.

The terms of precision and recall assure the awareness of objects with full contentment. Thus, they build the basis of our new E4SC measure. By transforming subspace clusters to micro-object clusters, the object awareness is extended to dimensions. The definitions of recall and precision become:

$$recall_{SC}(C_r, C_g) = \frac{|t(C_r) \cap t(C_g)|}{|t(C_g)|} = precision_{SC}(C_g, C_r)$$

The harmonic mean of precision and recall now represents the all and only constraint for cluster objects as well as for relevant dimensions. On the cluster level this measure meets all requirements for subspace cluster evaluation.

$$F1_{SC}(C_r, C_g) = \frac{2 \cdot recall_{SC}(C_r, C_g) \cdot precision_{SC}(C_r, C_g)}{recall_{SC}(C_r, C_g) + precision_{SC}(C_r, C_g)}$$

The extension $F1_{SC}^{Clus}(P, Q)$ of this definition for the clustering level leads to

$$F1_{SC}^{Clus}(P, Q) = \frac{1}{|P|} \sum_{C_i \in P} \max_{C_j \in Q} \{F1_{SC}(C_i, C_j)\}$$

This formula exhibits a non-symmetry that we utilize for enhanced quality assessment. The non-symmetry of $F1_{SC}^{Clus}$ implicates a precision and recall relation itself – though on the cluster*ing* level. $F1_{SC}^{Clus}(Ground, Res)$ evaluates how well all of the hidden clusters were found; it can be denoted as the *recall of the clustering*. Contrarily, $F1_{SC}^{Clus}(Res, Ground)$ evaluates how well each of the found clusters represents one of the hidden clusters; thus, it can be seen as *precision of the clustering*. The combination of these derived precision and recall values by a harmonic mean represents the all and only constraint on the clustering level.

$$M^{E4SC}(P, Q) := \frac{2 \cdot F1_{SC}^{Clus}(P, Q) \cdot F1_{SC}^{Clus}(Q, P)}{F1_{SC}^{Clus}(P, Q) + F1_{SC}^{Clus}(Q, P)}$$

The novel measure of E4SC successfully adopts the idea of F1 for subspace clustering. The central idea of precision and recall has been transferred to the *level of subspace clusters* and by means of recurring averaging has also upgraded F1 to the *level of clustering*. E4SC stands out due to the complete consideration of all 4 criteria. Object awareness is realized by using precision and recall on cluster level. A maximal quality result thus reports pure and complete clusters in *Res* compared to *Ground*. As dimensions are treated as micro-objects, same holds for subspace awareness. Through the harmonic mean of $F1_{SC}^{Clus}(P, Q)$ and $F1_{SC}^{Clus}(Q, P)$, E4SC is able to consider lower quality due to redundant or missing identification of clusters. The recall $F1_{SC}^{Clus}(Ground, Res)$ of the clustering decreases if one cluster in *Ground* is not or insufficiently found by *Res*. The precision $F1_{SC}^{Clus}(Res, Ground)$ is low if clusters in *Res* are unrelated to the clusters in *Ground*. An optimal quality result thus also reports a pure and complete clustering *Res* with regard to *Ground*. The maximal quality value of $M^{E4SC}(Ground, Res) = 1$ indicates an optimal clustering w.r.t. all characteristics of subspace clustering.

Note that E4SC fulfills the following useful properties: symmetry, non-negativity and identity of indiscernibles. The symmetry property $M^{E4SC}(P, Q) = M^{E4SC}(Q, P)$ for all clusterings Q and P is valid by design. Since precision and recall values lie within the range $[0, 1]$, the harmonic mean does so too. Thus, E4SC fulfills the non-negativity and even stronger for all clusterings P and Q we get $M^{E4SC}(P, Q) \in [0, 1]$. At last, we prove the identity of indiscernibles, i.e. $P = Q \Leftrightarrow M^{E4SC}(P, Q) = 1$. This property is especially important since the perfect quality is only achieved if the two clusterings are identical. Any error in the clustering result, e.g. splits, redundancy, or inclusion of noise, leads to a decrease of the E4SC value.

Proof: $\Rightarrow$: It holds that $recall_{SC}(C, C) = 1$ and analogously $precision_{SC}(C, C) = 1$ since $t(C) \cap t(C) = t(C)$ and therefore also $F1_{SC}(C, C) = 1$. If $P = Q$ we have $\forall C_i \in P\ \exists C_j \in Q : C_i = C_j$ and since $F1_{SC}(C_r, C_g) \leq 1$ we get

$$\frac{1}{|P|} \sum_{C_i \in P} \max_{C_j \in Q} \{F1_{SC}(C_i, C_j)\} = \frac{1}{|P|} \sum_{C_i \in P} 1 = 1$$

Thus, $F1_{SC}^{Clus}(P, P) = 1$ and hence $M^{E4SC}(P, P) = 1$.

$\Leftarrow$: Assuming $P \neq Q$. W.l.o.g. there exists $C \in P$ and $C \notin Q$. It holds that $\forall C_j \in Q: F1_{SC}(C, C_j) < 1$ since either $recall_{SC}(C, C_j) < 1$ or $precision_{SC}(C, C_j) < 1$. Otherwise $C \in Q$ would hold. Thus

$$F1_{SC}^{Clus}(P,Q) \leq \frac{1}{|P|}\left(|P\backslash\{C\}| + \max_{C_j \in Q}\{F1_{SC}(C,C_j)\}\right)$$
$$< \frac{1}{|P|}\left(|P\backslash\{C\}| + 1\right) = 1$$

and hence the harmonic mean $M^{E4SC}(P,Q) < 1$ for $P \neq Q$. □

4. EXPERIMENTS

In our experiments, we highlight the characteristics of the evaluation measures w.r.t. errors in the clustering result. While all measures provide perfect quality for a perfect clustering, they show different behaviors on clustering errors. Given a ground truth *Ground* of hidden subspace clusters and a clustering result *Res* of found subspace clusters, we compare the measures' performance. In order to understand all properties of the measures under consideration, we first study them for different evaluation scenarios with synthetic data, where we are able to vary the degree of each error separately as illustrated in Fig. 3 (right). To study different characteristics, we emphasize a different error in each evaluation scenario. Each scenario is motivated by general errors produced by different clustering approaches. The thereby gained insights subsequently allow us to discuss some evaluations of real cluster algorithms on real world datasets. These experiments will reveal the dependency of the assessment of the vanquishing algorithm on the evaluation measure.

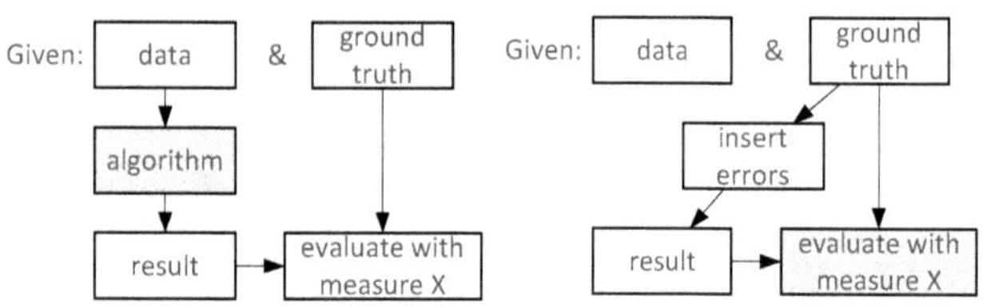

Fig. 3: Traditional workflow to evaluate *algorithms* (left) & novel workflow to evaluate *measures* (right)

Evaluation Setup. We created a benchmark database with 5000 objects and 30 dimensions. Objects are grouped in 9 subspace clusters, each with 9 dimensions and covering 500 objects. The ground truth for this synthetic data is given. In traditional evaluation to compare *different algorithms*, one uses each algorithm to obtain a clustering result and this result is compared with the ground truth by using a specific measure (cf. Fig. 3 (left)). In our work, however, we want to compare the characteristics of *different measures*. Thus, instead of using an arbitrary algorithm on the data, we systematically insert specific errors into the ground truth to obtain an (imperfect) clustering result. This insertion of errors corresponds to an algorithm that is not able to detect the perfect clustering on the data. However, we are now able to analyze each type of error separately leading to a more insightful analysis. Based on this clustering result, the different measures can be executed and their properties can be evaluated (cf. Fig. 3 (right)).

We created different clustering results based on our benchmark data, i.e. we insert different types of errors. Obviously, the perfect clustering result is simply the list of hidden subspace clusters ($Res = Ground$). This is the ideal baseline for all evaluation measures. However, we construct more realistic scenarios to analyze the sensitivity of the measures. For the first experiment, we split the hidden clusters into multiple found clusters regarding their objects, i.e. for each hidden cluster we partition its objects into x parts of equal size, thus getting x smaller clusters. For grid-based subspace clustering approaches [3, 16, 19, 21], this might happen due to discretization of the search space. Thus, we get a clustering result Res' that does not perfectly represent the ground truth. It is of major importance that evaluation measures are aware of such phenomena and show significantly lower quality if hidden clusters are split up. For the following experiments, we give short descriptions of the evaluation setup in the respective paragraph.

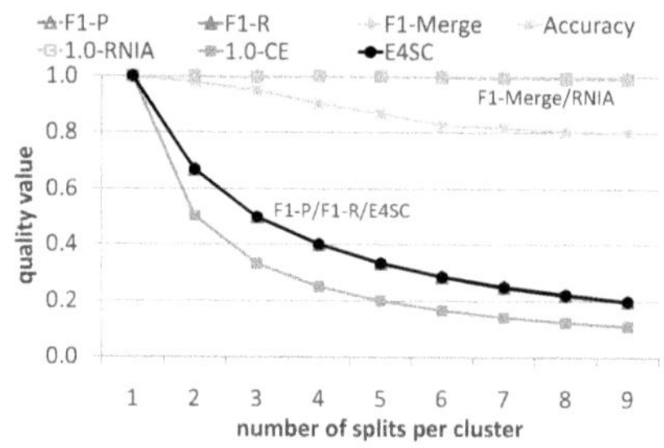

Fig. 4: Split of clusters

Object Awareness. Most measures compare the set of hidden objects with the found objects. Though, there are major differences in their sensitivity to *splits of clusters*. As depicted in Fig. 4, the measures RNIA and F1-Merge do not detect these errors and provide constantly perfect values. The merge operation of F1-Merge is a clear drawback as a split of clusters does not affect the overall quality. A similar argument holds for RNIA because this measure only assesses the coverage of the hidden clusters but not whether the objects belong to the correct clusters. The Accuracy measure can still identify a reasonable generalization for the data with the split parts; thus, the quality decreases only slightly.

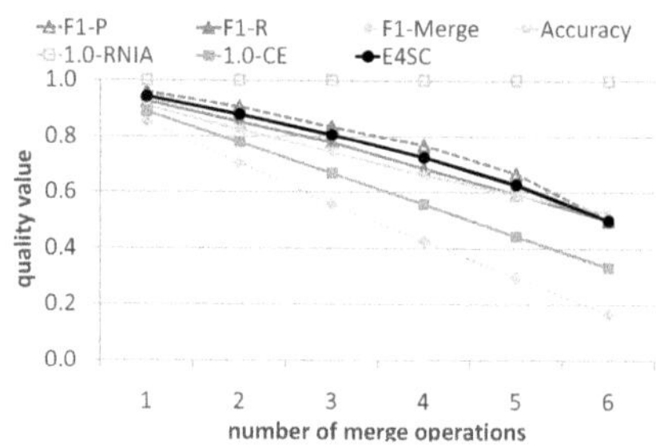

Fig. 5: Merge of clusters

Next, we perform a certain number of *merge operations* between the hidden clusters. This is a realistic scenario where clustering algorithms fail to separate two similar clusters, resulting in a bad purity of clusters. As depicted in Fig. 5, almost all measures detect this bad clustering and show decreasing values with increasing amount of merges.

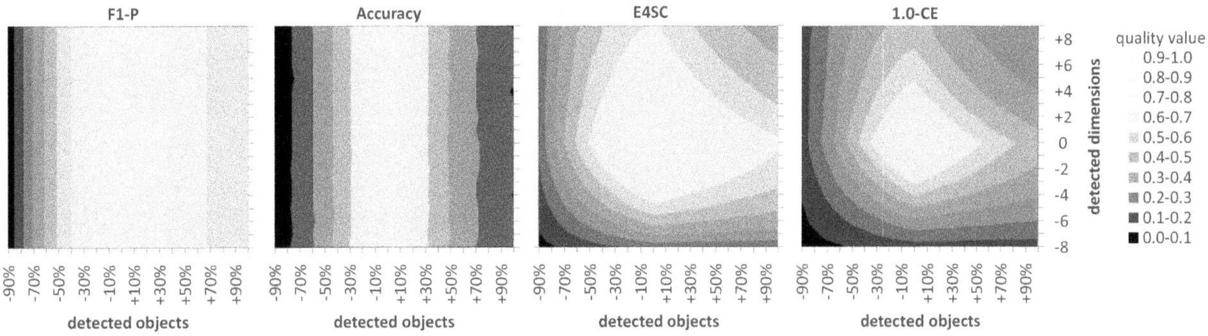

Fig. 6: Removal and adding of clustered objects and relevant dimensions

Only the RNIA measure is not affected by merged clusters due to the reason described above. Next, we consider object awareness for results produced by projected clustering methods [1, 2, 19, 21]; they *partition the data*. However, as we have overlapping hidden clusters, a partitioning of the data cannot be the perfect clustering result. The resulting quality values range from 0.735 (RNIA, CE) to 0.847 (F1 measures, E4SC). Thus, all measures show lower quality values as each object is assigned to exactly one cluster and not multiple ones.

Overall, the first experiments have shown that most measures are aware of the most basic properties of clustering quality. Missing objects due to partitioning, affects the quality of all measures. Splitting or merging clusters, affects all but the RNIA measure due to the simple coverage method.

Subspace Awareness. In the following experiments we consider errors in both, the detected object set and the dimension set, for each subspace cluster. We *remove/include objects and dimensions* respectively with a certain percentage. As depicted in Fig. 6, the perfect result is at the center of each figure (0% additionally included objects, 9 dimensions). For the x-axis 'detected objects' $-p\%$ means that $p\%$ of the objects were excluded from the found clusters and $+p\%$ refers to the amount of included objects. For the y-axis we added or removed dimensions compared to the perfect result respectively. We show four different measures (results of F1-R & F1-Merge are similar to the one of F1-P; the result of RNIA corresponds to the one of CE).

Obviously, F1-P and Accuracy, as measures without subspace awareness, are only affected by changes in the object set; however, they react differently. While F1-P still returns good qualities when adding many objects, the Accuracy measure is more sensitive and exposes the area of perfect quality more distinctly. Our novel E4SC measure and CE are affected also by changes in the dimension set. Beside this subspace awareness of CE and E4SC, we observe interesting characteristics. While in the area of perfect clustering both changes in the object and dimension set affect the overall quality to the same degree (nearly rectangular areas), this effect is not observed for extreme cases where e.g. most of the objects have been removed. For such extreme cases either the object set or the dimension set is dominating (rounded areas). Furthermore, the CE measure reacts more sensitive in this experiment, i.e. the quality values decrease faster than for E4SC. This property is especially observed in the first quadrant, where objects and dimensions are added.

Overall this experiment demonstrates the lack of subspace awareness in F1-P, F1-R, and F1-Merge. Their use in subspace clustering is meaningless or at least questionable. E4SC and CE simultaneously handle subspaces and object groups.

Set of detected clusters. While in the previous experiments we have analyzed different effects on the content of clusters, in the following we consider typical clustering errors such as completely missing clusters or detecting similar clusters multiple times.

In our first experiment, depicted in Fig. 7, we *remove one cluster* from the resulting clustering each time. We generated 9 hidden clusters, each with a different number of objects. By sorting the clusters based on their object size, such that to the left of the x-axis the smallest cluster is removed and to the right the largest one, we show the *effect of the cluster size*. We observe that CE, RNIA, and Accuracy are affected more by the exclusion of large clusters than by exclusion of small ones. These measures are biased w.r.t. the cluster size. All other measures are nearly not affected by the size of clusters; they are unbiased w.r.t. the size. A special case is F1-P, that shows perfect quality although clusters have not been detected. As F1-P maps each found cluster to one hidden cluster, it is not affected by missing clusters (cf. Sec. 3).

Next, we exclude not only one cluster but accumulate the *removal of several clusters*, starting by excluding the largest cluster until only one cluster remains in the found clustering. As depicted in Fig. 8, all measures except for F1-P show decreasing quality values. However, the slopes vary greatly. CE, RNIA and Accuracy show steep decrease in the first (large) clusters because removing large clusters is more critical for these measures. F1-R and F1-Merge measures show almost linear decrease; removing one additional cluster results in constant drop of the quality. Our E4SC measure, however, decreases more quickly with each additionally excluded cluster. That is, excluding two clusters is more than twice as bad as the removal of a single cluster; although we get in Fig. 7 a constant curve.

Both, missing a cluster but also detecting similar clusters in redundant projections, should lead to lower quality values. In the following experiment, we additionally add *redundant clusters* in lower dimensional projections as observed in several subspace clustering approaches [3, 16, 8]. The x-axis in Fig. 9 indicates the amount of redundant clusters. Starting by adding only the redundant 8 dimensional projections (of the original 9d clusters), we add more and more lower-dimensional ones. As illustrated, only CE, RNIA and E4SC are affected by redundancy; quality decreases while redundancy increases. However, CE & RNIA show a significant

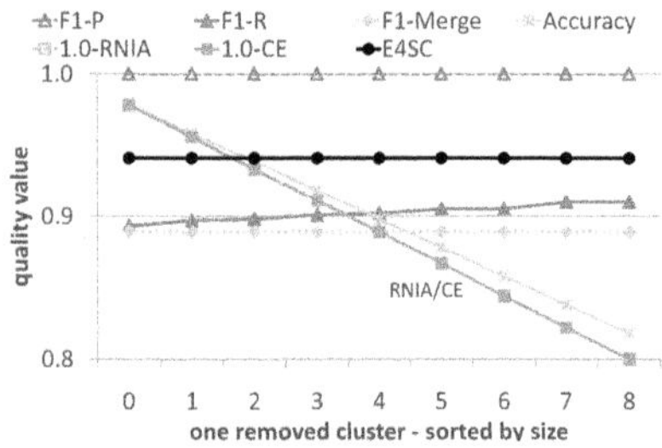

Fig. 7: Miss of single clusters

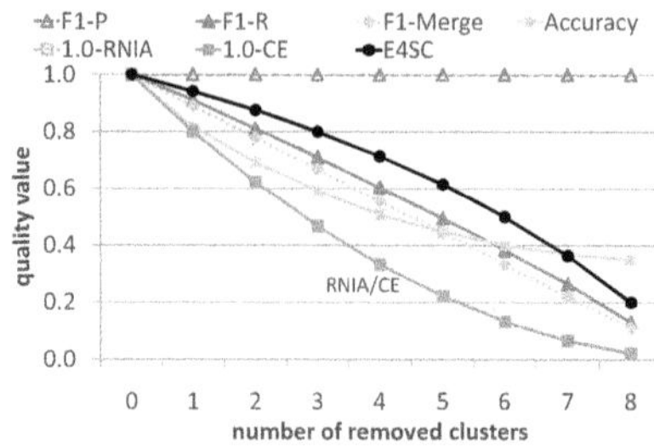

Fig. 8: Varying miss of clusters

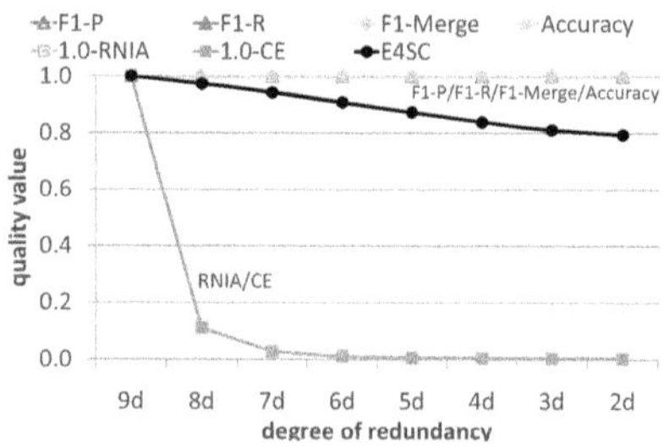

Fig. 9: Increasing redundancy

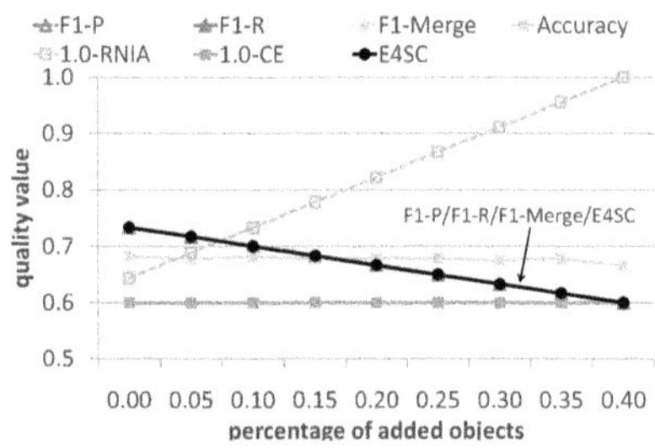

Fig. 10: Impurity of clusters

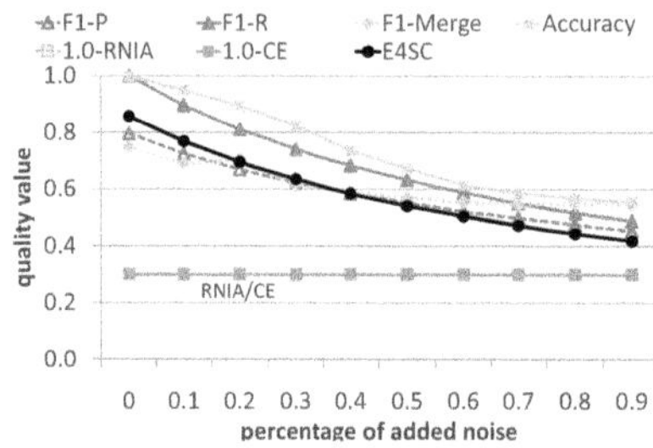

Fig. 11: Noise polluted clusters

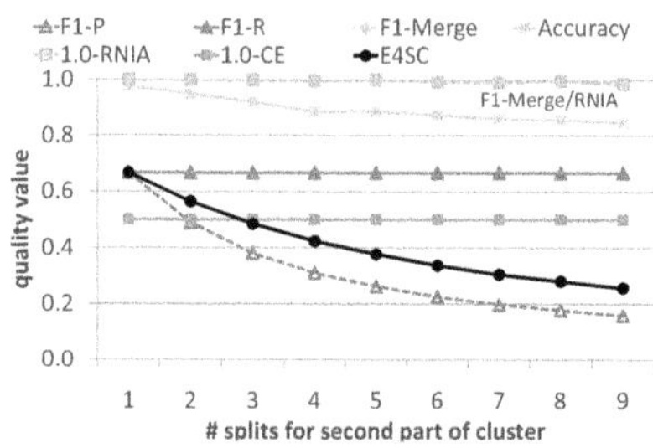

Fig. 12: Split in unequal parts

drop to almost zero quality already for redundancy in 6 to 8 dimensional clusters; we get no discriminable quality values after this point. Our E4SC measure shows continuously decreasing quality, down to the 1 dimensional redundant clusters, but remains in high quality ranges. CE and E4SC detect bad clusterings due to redundancy best.

Overall, these experiments have shown that F1-P, F1-R, and F1-Merge do not meaningfully assess the quality of redundancy polluted clusterings. Furthermore, F1-P is not able to detect a miss of clusters. For the criteria of redundancy and identification awareness the measures CE, RNIA and E4SC are preferable.

Sensitivity of measures. We created further evaluation scenarios to show the sensitivity of each measure. First, we created a clustering result where a certain fraction of the clustered objects is removed. This miss of objects is assessed as low quality by all measures in Fig. 10 as the leftmost values indicate. Afterwards, we progressively re-add objects to the clusters; however, not from the correct but different clusters. Thus, we increase the *impurity of the clustering results*. Most measures accurately show decreasing quality for impure clusterings in Fig. 10. CE and Accuracy, however, are almost not affected by this scenario. Because the largest part of the hidden cluster is still detected, adding incorrect objects does not influence their quality values. Even worse, the RNIA measure increases in quality since we cover more objects of the hidden clusters. Thus, these three measures are not sensitive to the impurity of clusterings.

Next, we simulate the effect of algorithms that are not able to detect *outliers*, i.e. algorithms enforcing an assignment of each object to a cluster. Thus, beside the hidden clusters we generate for the clustering result one single cluster that contains all *noise objects*. Most of the measures are influenced by this as the leftmost entries in Fig. 11 indicate. In the following, we relocate more and more objects from the noise-cluster to the hidden clusters. This phenomenon is typically observed in algorithms mixing up noise objects with the detected clusters. Clearly, the quality of the clustering should decrease because the true clusters are now polluted by noisy objects. However, CE and RNIA are not affected by noise as the hidden clusters are still covered and the purity is incidental. All other approaches show decreasing quality.

In the following experiment, we *split* each hidden cluster *not in equally large parts* but in one half of the cluster and an increasing fraction of further parts. While the large part seems to be the most valuable representation of the hidden cluster, the other parts hinder more and more the interpretation of the overall result set. As depicted in Fig. 12, most measures are not affected by this scenario because the major part of the hidden cluster is still found. F1-Merge and RNIA even show highest quality, ignoring the splits at all. Only F1-P and E4SC are aware of a decreasing quality.

Overall, for the core quality criteria we have shown that measures as F1-P, F1-R, F1-Merge, and Accuracy are not aware of subspace properties and fail in the very core of subspace cluster evaluation. Nevertheless, these measures are the most widely used ones in subspace clustering works. They are of interest where only object sets are relevant or given for the evaluation. Enhanced measures such as CE, RNIA, and E4SC consider also correct detection of subspaces. However, we have seen major differences in their evaluation. The RNIA measure is not affected by splits or merges of clusters. The CE measure shows high sensitivity to redundancy, while E4SC is sensitive to impure clusters, noise and split of clusters. In Fig. 13 we provide an overview of the measures and their characteristics.

Real world data and algorithms. The previous experiments aimed at an objective analysis of all error types separately. Enabled by a systematic transformation of a presumed set of ground truth clusters for synthetic data, an unaffected consideration for each error type was possible. The following consideration of real world data and clustering results of real algorithms will now provide the opportunity not only to prove but also to apply the newly won insights into the measures. For these real world experiments we used the publicly available clustering results of [15] and applied the discussed measures on them. Notice that the ground truth of real world data usually consists of a partitioning of

	F1-P	F1-R	F1-Mer.	Accu.	RNIA	CE	E4SC
object aware	+	+	-	-	-	-	+
subspace aware	-	-	-	-	+	+	+
redundancy aware	+	-	-	-	+	+	+
identifi. aware	-	+	+	+	+	+	+
split	+	+	-	+	-	+	+
merge	+	+	+	+	-	+	+
size unbiased	+	+	+	-	-	-	+
impurity	+	+	+	-	-	-	+
noise	+	+	+	+	-	-	+

Fig. 13: Characteristics of evaluation measures

the dataset and provides no subspace information with the partitions. Each table in Fig. 14 and 15 shows the quality values of different subspace clustering algorithms for one dataset [15]. For each measure we depicted the maximal and minimal values obtained for various parameter settings [15]. To fastly grasp the main tendency of the results we colored the quality values (gets darker with increasing quality). We only discuss Fig. 14 but similar observations can be drawn out for the other data sets in Fig. 15. As a first observation, each measure yields different quality values for the same algorithms. Consequentially, each measure assesses a different algorithm as vanquisher. This is hard to understand if one is not aware of the underlying characteristics of evaluation measures. Thus, further interpretation requires information about the measures' sensitivity as presented in this work.

Diabetes (size: 768; dim: 8)	F1		Accuracy		CE		RNIA		E4SC	
	max	min	max	min	max	min	max	min	max	min
CLIQUE	0.70	0.39	0.72	0.69	0.03	0.01	0.14	0.01	0.4	0.09
DOC	0.71	0.71	0.72	0.69	0.31	0.26	0.92	0.79	0.39	0.12
MINECLUS	0.72	0.66	0.71	0.69	0.63	0.13	0.89	0.58	0.14	0.09
SCHISM	0.70	0.62	0.73	0.68	0.08	0.01	0.36	0.09	0.11	0.08
SUBCLU	0.74	0.45	0.71	0.68	0.01	0.01	0.01	0.01	0.46	0.13
FIRES	0.52	0.03	0.65	0.64	0.12	0.00	0.27	0.00	0.1	0.06
INSCY	0.65	0.39	0.70	0.65	0.37	0.11	0.45	0.42	0.64	0.04
PROCLUS	0.67	0.61	0.72	0.71	0.34	0.21	0.78	0.69	0.45	0.25
P3C	0.39	0.39	0.66	0.65	0.56	0.11	0.85	0.22	0.57	0.57
STATPC	0.73	0.59	0.70	0.65	0.06	0.00	0.63	0.17	0.4	0.01

Fig. 14: Results for the measures on diabetes data

The coloring of the results reveals the rare differentiation of Accuracy, CE, and F1 since results only differ slightly and do not allow contrasty comparisons of different approaches. This effect is mainly due to the insensitivity of the measures to a variety of errors or, in the case of CE, the excessive punishment of redundancy and its size-bias. Only RNIA and E4SC show discriminative results between the approaches.

The evaluation results in Fig. 14 point out the importance of redundancy awareness. On average, the measures F1 and Accuracy, which are insensitive to redundancy, assign higher quality values to the resulting clusterings than CE, RNIA and E4SC. The worth of redundancy awareness becomes even more evident as we see that mainly the partitioning approaches DOC, MINECLUS, PROCLUS and P3C, whose results are not redundant by definition, have high values for CE, RNIA and E4SC. Only with these measures the benefit of non-partitioning subspace clustering approaches that successfully try to avoid redundancy, like INSCY and STATPC, is traceable as they yield better quality values than other approaches without redundancy model.

Overall, we see that our awareness criteria and the thorough evaluation on synthetic data helps to interpret quality assessment on real world data based on different measures. We also see that only measures fulfilling the majority of our 4 criteria are able to carry out significant quality assertions. The more error cases a measure is sensitive to (cf. Fig. 13), the higher is the quality assessment, and thus, the better the contrast of low and high quality ratings.

5. CONCLUSION

A fair and comparable quality assessment based on objective evaluation measures is a key component for knowledge discovery in databases. In this work, we provide an analysis of evaluation measures for the research area of subspace clustering. We show that novel criteria for a meaningful evaluation of subspace clustering algorithms are needed. Thus, we introduce four major criteria each measure has to fulfill: object, subspace, redundancy and identification awareness. Based on these categories, an analysis of existing measures identifies their drawbacks for applicability. Thus, we develop a novel evaluation measure that fulfills our general quality criteria. In an empirical study we highlight the characteristics for each measure in typical clustering scenarios.

As a conclusion, we recommend to use CE and E4SC measures in future evaluations as both highlight main subspace clustering properties. In combination with other measures such as RNIA they also bring out the reasons for bad clustering quality as depicted in Figure 10 where we observe a significant increase in RNIA while CE remains constant and E4SC decreases. This divergence in clustering evaluation measures indicates assignment of incorrect objects to the detected clusters. With such knowledge about the characteristics of measures, improvements of the clustering result and the algorithms itself can be fostered.

Our work lays the foundation for a fair evaluation of algorithms in the area of subspace clustering. Beside the analysis of measures, however, it is necessary to provide a set of benchmark data that is annotated with the hidden clustering structure. This is one challenge for future studies.

Acknowledgment. This work has been partly funded by the German Federal Ministry of Economics and Technology under project funding reference number 01MQ09014 and the UMIC Research Centre, RWTH Aachen University, Germany.

6. REFERENCES

[1] C. Aggarwal, J. Wolf, P. Yu, C. Procopiuc, and J. Park. Fast algorithms for projected clustering. In *SIGMOD*, pages 61–72, 1999.

[2] C. Aggarwal and P. Yu. Finding generalized projected clusters in high dimensional spaces. In *SIGMOD*, pages 70–81, 2000.

[3] R. Agrawal, J. Gehrke, D. Gunopulos, and P. Raghavan. Automatic subspace clustering of high dimensional data for data mining applications. In *SIGMOD*, pages 94–105, 1998.

[4] E. Amigó, J. Gonzalo, J. Artiles, and F. Verdejo. A comparison of extrinsic clustering evaluation metrics based on formal constraints. *Inf. Retr.*, 12(4):461–486, 2009.

[5] I. Assent, R. Krieger, E. Müller, and T. Seidl. DUSC: Dimensionality unbiased subspace clustering. In *ICDM*, pages 409–414, 2007.

Pendigits (size: 7494; dim: 16)	F1		Accuracy		CE		RNIA		E4SC	
	max	min	max	min	max	min	max	min	max	min
CLIQUE	0.30	0.17	0.96	0.86	0.06	0.01	0.20	0.06	0.2	0.2
DOC	0.52	0.52	0.54	0.54	0.18	0.18	0.35	0.35	0.23	0.13
MINECLUS	0.87	0.87	0.86	0.86	0.48	0.48	0.89	0.89	0.27	0.27
SCHISM	0.45	0.26	0.93	0.71	0.05	0.01	0.30	0.08	0.14	0.06
SUBCLU	--	--	--	--	--	--	--	--	--	--
FIRES	0.45	0.45	0.73	0.73	0.09	0.09	0.33	0.33	0.22	0.11
INSCY	0.65	0.48	0.78	0.68	0.07	0.07	0.30	0.28	0.17	0.02
PROCLUS	0.78	0.73	0.74	0.73	0.31	0.27	0.64	0.45	0.34	0.32
P3C	0.74	0.74	0.72	0.72	0.28	0.28	0.58	0.58	0.28	0.28
STATPC	0.91	0.32	0.92	0.10	0.09	0.00	0.67	0.11	0.64	0.01

Shape (size: 160; dim: 17)	F1		Accuracy		CE		RNIA		E4SC	
	max	min	max	min	max	min	max	min	max	min
CLIQUE	0.31	0.31	0.76	0.76	0.01	0.01	0.07	0.07	0.2	0.2
DOC	0.90	0.83	0.79	0.54	0.56	0.38	0.90	0.82	0.41	0.29
MINECLUS	0.94	0.86	0.79	0.60	0.58	0.46	1.00	1.00	0.42	0.3
SCHISM	0.51	0.30	0.74	0.49	0.10	0.00	0.26	0.01	0.26	0.15
SUBCLU	0.36	0.29	0.70	0.64	0.00	0.00	0.05	0.04	0.09	0.09
FIRES	0.36	0.36	0.51	0.44	0.20	0.13	0.25	0.20	0.28	0.21
INSCY	0.84	0.59	0.76	0.48	0.18	0.16	0.37	0.24	0.53	0.21
PROCLUS	0.84	0.81	0.72	0.71	0.25	0.18	0.61	0.37	0.31	0.2
P3C	0.51	0.51	0.61	0.61	0.14	0.14	0.17	0.17	0.2	0.2
STATPC	0.43	0.43	0.74	0.74	0.45	0.45	0.55	0.55	0.62	0.62

Vowel (size: 990; dim: 10)	F1		Accuracy		CE		RNIA		E4SC	
	max	min	max	min	max	min	max	min	max	min
CLIQUE	0.23	0.17	0.64	0.37	0.05	0.00	0.44	0.01	0.13	0.05
DOC	0.49	0.49	0.44	0.44	0.14	0.14	0.85	0.85	0.25	0.16
MINECLUS	0.48	0.43	0.37	0.37	0.09	0.04	0.62	0.34	0.12	0.12
SCHISM	0.37	0.23	0.62	0.52	0.05	0.01	0.43	0.11	0.11	0.09
SUBCLU	0.24	0.18	0.58	0.38	0.04	0.01	0.39	0.04	0.03	0.03
FIRES	0.16	0.14	0.13	0.11	0.02	0.02	0.14	0.13	0.03	0.03
INSCY	0.82	0.33	0.61	0.15	0.09	0.07	0.75	0.26	0.14	0.11
PROCLUS	0.49	0.49	0.44	0.44	0.11	0.11	0.53	0.53	0.13	0.13
P3C	0.08	0.05	0.17	0.16	0.12	0.08	0.69	0.43	0.25	0.21
STATPC	0.22	0.22	0.56	0.56	0.06	0.06	0.12	0.12	0.28	0.28

Liver-Dis. (size: 345; dim: 6)	F1		Accuracy		CE		RNIA		E4SC	
	max	min	max	min	max	min	max	min	max	min
CLIQUE	0.68	0.65	0.67	0.58	0.08	0.02	0.38	0.03	0.2	0.05
DOC	0.67	0.64	0.68	0.58	0.11	0.07	0.51	0.35	0.09	0.05
MINECLUS	0.73	0.63	0.65	0.58	0.09	0.09	0.68	0.48	0.06	0.05
SCHISM	0.69	0.69	0.68	0.59	0.04	0.03	0.45	0.26	0.12	0.11
SUBCLU	0.68	0.68	0.64	0.58	0.11	0.02	0.68	0.05	0.06	0.06
FIRES	0.58	0.04	0.58	0.56	0.14	0.00	0.39	0.01	0.22	0.01
INSCY	0.66	0.66	0.62	0.61	0.03	0.03	0.42	0.39	0.06	0.03
PROCLUS	0.53	0.39	0.63	0.63	0.26	0.11	0.66	0.25	0.36	0.36
P3C	0.36	0.35	0.58	0.58	0.55	0.27	0.96	0.47	0.68	0.68
STATPC	0.69	0.57	0.65	0.58	0.23	0.01	0.58	0.37	0.32	0.02

Glass (size: 214; dim: 9)	F1		Accuracy		CE		RNIA		E4SC	
	max	min	max	min	max	min	max	min	max	min
CLIQUE	0.51	0.31	0.67	0.50	0.02	0.00	0.06	0.00	0.21	0.16
DOC	0.74	0.50	0.63	0.50	0.23	0.13	0.93	0.33	0.18	0.17
MINECLUS	0.76	0.40	0.52	0.50	0.24	0.19	0.78	0.45	0.28	0.15
SCHISM	0.46	0.39	0.63	0.47	0.11	0.04	0.33	0.20	0.15	0.14
SUBCLU	0.50	0.45	0.65	0.46	0.00	0.00	0.01	0.01	0.38	0.26
FIRES	0.30	0.30	0.49	0.49	0.21	0.21	0.45	0.45	0.24	0.24
INSCY	0.57	0.41	0.65	0.47	0.23	0.09	0.54	0.26	0.18	0.14
PROCLUS	0.60	0.56	0.60	0.57	0.13	0.05	0.51	0.17	0.21	0.07
P3C	0.28	0.23	0.47	0.39	0.14	0.13	0.30	0.27	0.29	0.28
STATPC	0.75	0.40	0.49	0.36	0.19	0.05	0.67	0.37	0.25	0.12

Breast (size: 198; dim: 33)	F1		Accuracy		CE		RNIA		E4SC	
	max	min	max	min	max	min	max	min	max	min
CLIQUE	0.67	0.67	0.71	0.71	0.02	0.02	0.40	0.40	0.04	0.04
DOC	0.73	0.61	0.81	0.76	0.11	0.04	0.84	0.07	0.12	0.06
MINECLUS	0.78	0.69	0.78	0.76	0.19	0.18	1.00	1.00	0.12	0.08
SCHISM	0.67	0.67	0.75	0.69	0.01	0.01	0.36	0.34	0.01	0.01
SUBCLU	0.68	0.51	0.77	0.67	0.02	0.01	0.54	0.04	0.02	0.02
FIRES	0.49	0.03	0.76	0.76	0.03	0.00	0.05	0.00	0.02	0.01
INSCY	0.74	0.55	0.77	0.76	0.02	0.00	0.24	0.11	0.02	0.02
PROCLUS	0.57	0.52	0.80	0.74	0.51	0.11	0.65	0.43	0.48	0.16
P3C	0.63	0.63	0.77	0.77	0.04	0.04	0.19	0.19	0.03	0.03
STATPC	0.41	0.41	0.78	0.78	0.16	0.16	0.33	0.33	0.28	0.28

Fig. 15: Comparison of evaluation measures for different subspace clustering algorithms on real world data

[6] I. Assent, R. Krieger, E. Müller, and T. Seidl. INSCY: Indexing subspace clusters with in-process-removal of redundancy. In *ICDM*, pages 719–724, 2008.

[7] B. Bringmann and A. Zimmermann. The chosen few: On identifying valuable patterns. In *ICDM*, pages 63–72, 2007.

[8] K. Kailing, H.-P. Kriegel, and P. Kröger. Density-connected subspace clustering for high-dimensional data. In *SDM*, pages 246–257, 2004.

[9] H.-P. Kriegel, P. Kröger, and A. Zimek. Clustering high-dimensional data: A survey on subspace clustering, pattern-based clustering, and correlation clustering. *TKDD*, 3(1), 2009.

[10] Y. Liu, Z. Li, H. Xiong, X. Gao, and J. Wu. Understanding of internal clustering validation measures. In *ICDM*, pages 911–916, 2010.

[11] G. Moise and J. Sander. Finding non-redundant, statistically significant regions in high dimensional data: a novel approach to projected and subspace clustering. In *KDD*, pages 533–541, 2008.

[12] G. Moise, J. Sander, and M. Ester. P3C: A robust projected clustering algorithm. In *ICDM*, pages 414–425, 2006.

[13] G. Moise, A. Zimek, P. Kröger, H.-P. Kriegel, and J. Sander. Subspace and projected clustering: experimental evaluation and analysis. *KAIS*, 21(3):299–326, 2009.

[14] E. Müller, I. Assent, S. Günnemann, R. Krieger, and T. Seidl. Relevant subspace clustering: Mining the most interesting non-redundant concepts in high dimensional data. In *ICDM*, pages 377–386, 2009.

[15] E. Müller, S. Günnemann, I. Assent, and T. Seidl. Evaluating clustering in subspace projections of high dimensional data. *PVLDB*, 2(1):1270–1281, 2009.

[16] H. Nagesh, S. Goil, and A. Choudhary. Adaptive grids for clustering massive data sets. In *SDM*, 2001.

[17] L. Parsons, E. Haque, and H. Liu. Subspace clustering for high dimensional data: a review. *SIGKDD Explorations*, 6(1):90–105, 2004.

[18] A. Patrikainen and M. Meila. Comparing subspace clusterings. *TKDE*, 18(7):902–916, 2006.

[19] C. Procopiuc, M. Jones, P. Agarwal, and T. Murali. A monte carlo algorithm for fast projective clustering. In *SIGMOD*, pages 418–427, 2002.

[20] J. Wu, H. Xiong, and J. Chen. Adapting the right measures for k-means clustering. In *KDD*, pages 877–886, 2009.

[21] M. L. Yiu and N. Mamoulis. Frequent-pattern based iterative projected clustering. In *ICDM*, pages 689–692, 2003.

Behavior-driven Clustering of Queries into Topics

Luca Maria Aiello
Università di Torino
Torino, Italy
aiello@di.unito.it

Debora Donato
Yahoo! Labs
Sunnyvale, CA, USA
debora@yahoo-inc.com

Umut Ozertem
Yahoo! Labs
Sunnyvale, CA, USA
umut@yahoo-inc.com

Filippo Menczer
Indiana University
Bloomington, IN, USA
fil@indiana.edu

ABSTRACT

Categorization of web-search queries in semantically coherent topics is a crucial task to understand the interest trends of search engine users and, therefore, to provide more intelligent personalization services. Query clustering usually relies on lexical and clickthrough data, while the information originating from the user actions in submitting their queries is currently neglected. In particular, the *intent* that drives users to submit their requests is an important element for meaningful aggregation of queries. We propose a new intent-centric notion of topical query clusters and we define a query clustering technique that differs from existing algorithms in both methodology and nature of the resulting clusters. Our method extracts topics from the query log by merging *missions*, i.e., activity fragments that express a coherent user intent, on the basis of their topical affinity. Our approach works in a bottom-up way, without any a-priori knowledge of topical categorization, and produces good quality topics compared to state-of-the-art clustering techniques. It can also summarize topically-coherent missions that occur far away from each other, thus enabling a more compact user profiling on a topical basis. Furthermore, such a topical user profiling discriminates the stream of activity of a particular user from the activity of others, with a potential to predict future user search activity.

Categories and Subject Descriptors

H.3.3 [**Information Search and Retrieval**]: Clustering; H.3.5 [**Online Information Services**]: Web-based services

General Terms

Algorithms, Human factors

Keywords

Topic, Mission, User intent, User profiling, Query log

1. INTRODUCTION

Methods and algorithms for improving web search have been extensively studied in the last two decades. In the vast majority of the cases, such methodologies are query-centric, i.e., they exploit only the query itself to understand a user's intent and to provide relevant results. Only recently user search activity has been studied by looking at the entire set of actions she performs in order to satisfy a need. Such a line of research is based on the observation that users searching the web often perform a sequence, or chain, of queries with a similar information need [27]. Empirical studies have indeed shown that most of the needs are actually too complex to be satisfied by just one query [13]. Hence users are inclined to organize their search activity in so-called *missions*.

By way of example, let's consider the activity of a user who wants to purchase a vacuum cleaner. She will probably organize her queries in a number of sequential steps. Initially she starts acquiring information about available brands and models. In a second phase she will look for reviews and comparisons between different models with similar features. Finally, she will search for sellers who offer the chosen model at an advantageous price or with an extended guarantee. Each single step is a different granular task and the totality of tasks are meant to fulfill the "vacuum-cleaner purchase" need. In a similar scenario, an unsatisfied user who wants to return a vacuum cleaner is going to submit queries such as "returning shark navigator" or "dyson customer service." The two needs in this example concern particular aspects related to the same general topic "vacuum cleaner." We use the term *topic* in its acceptation of *mental object* or *cognitive content*, i.e., *the sum of what can be perceived, discovered or learned* about any real or abstract entity. In such a sense, topics naturally emerge from user search activity, since queries are issued to discover or learn facets (model, name, characteristics, pros and cons, price, seller's location, return policy) of a cognitive content (vacuum cleaner).

In this paper we present a methodology to extract topics from query logs. Our objective is inherently different from previous attempts to classify queries according to a predefined set of categories, because our definition of topic encompasses and outstrips the definition of category. Categories like shopping, sport, news, and finance can indeed be seen as the perspective or focus of a search mission in the context of a particular topic.

We propose a mission-based clustering technique to aggregate missions that are topically-related. As a first step we train a classifier to predict if two different missions have a similar topical connotation. The learned function takes as input two sets of queries and computes the probability that they are topically-related. Such a function is used as a similarity metric by an agglomerative algorithm to merge missions into large topical clusters.

The resulting topics would be useful in a number of different scenarios where great advantage can be derived by performing query categorization in a more natural, intent-driven fashion, without any constraint imposed by artificial categories. As an application of the methodology, we show how to build user profiles over topics and we use such profiles to predict user behavior.

The paper is organized as follows. In Section 2, we will give an overview of related work. Section 3 introduces terminology and presents the problem we aim to solve. Section 4 presents a semi-supervised classifier able to detect if two different missions belong to the same topic. A greedy agglomerative algorithm for topic extraction is illustrated in Section 5. The experimental framework and the results are respectively described in Sections 6 and 7. Section 8 presents an application of our methodology for user profiling.

2. RELATED WORK

Query chains, missions, goals. Previous work on query log mining has introduced general and widely used terms to define different structural features of the query log and behavioral aspects of the search engine users. Typically, sequences of query reformulations aimed to achieve the same atomic search need are referred as *query chains* [27]. More relaxed notions of coherence within the search session are represented by the concept of *logical session* [2] and *search mission* [20], namely a set of queries that express a complex search need, possibly articulated in smaller goals. Our work uses missions as atomic elements to build behavioral-driven query clusters.

Query clustering. Even if closely related to the document *topic extraction* task [29] or to multi-document summarization [4], where items from a textual corpus are summarized in one or more, possibly hierarchical [17] categories, our work gives a contribution to the *query clustering* area. Currently, query clustering is one of the hot topics in query log mining [6].

Grouping together queries with strong semantic relations is a task that is intrinsically harder than classic topic extraction or web document clustering [37], because of the short textual information contained into queries. Many approaches to query clustering rely on the computation of some notion of similarity between query pairs. When dealing with *query classification*, where the semantic categories are defined a-priori, it may be sufficient to compute the similarity based only on textual features to obtain good classification results [7]. Even classification based only on the so-called *clickthrough* data such as the information inside the result pages associated to the queries, can lead to good results [18]. However, if predefined concept categorizations or taxonomies are not available, lexical and content-based information taken separately are not sufficient to obtain good clusters. In this regard, an attempt to cluster queries from the Encarta user logs [33] showed that query-to-query similarity metrics that linearly combine textual features with click-through data can be used much more profitably in query clustering than single-attribute similarities. Similarly, hierarchical agglomeration of queries based on the similarity of their search result snippets (that mix words from the query and text from the page results) has also been profitably used [12].

Approaches focused only on the activity of single users, instead of the whole query log, are also interesting; in fact, it is clear that detecting the topics that can well shape the interests of the user is useful for personalization and recommendation. For instance, Song et al. [31] proposed a topic model able to extract most relevant themes from the user activity through probabilistic Latent Semantic Indexing [19]; once identified, such themes are used as a topical summarization of the user search history.

More recently, content-agnostic approaches based only on the relations between queries and clicked URLs have been explored. The idea is that similarity graphs between queries obtained by proper projections on the multiple dimensions of the query log accurately model semantic relations between queries [3, 9]. Many approaches of this kind represent the query-URL relation as a bipartite graph [6] and pick the densely connected components, like bicliques [36], as representative sets of similar queries or pages. *Query graphs* where queries are connected by some lexical or semantic relation are also commonly used. In order to overcome the problem of query ambiguity in topic detection, query graphs that introduce a lightweight query contextualization using the pairs $(sessionId, query)$ as nodes, instead of single queries, have also been proposed [32].

Graph clustering. In this work we use a graph-based model as baseline for our technique. This model relies on a network *community detection* algorithm to partition a graph of queries into topics. Community detection is an important branch of complex network analysis that received much attention in the recent past. One of the most known result in this field is the definition of the *modularity* as a global metric of goodness of clusters [26]. Even if finding maximum modularity partitions is an NP-complete problem [10], numerous algorithms based on suboptimal modularity maximization has been proposed, until the intrinsic resolution limit of modularity in cluster detection was discovered [16]. Lately, different fitness measures to define cluster quality have been introduced (e.g., [24]) and many recently proposed algorithms use local metrics to detect communities [15]. To our purpose, we will use a graph clustering algorithm that has been proved more effective than some of the main state of the art competitors [23].

3. DEFINITIONS

Query log. In a search engine context, search activity is typically recorded in a query log $\mathscr{L}$ defined as a set of tuples $\tau = \langle q, u, t, V, C\rangle$ containing the submitted query $q \in \mathscr{Q}$, an anonymized user identifier $u \in \mathscr{U}$, the time t when the action took place, the set of documents V returned by the search engine, and the set of clicked documents $C \subseteq V$ [8].

Missions. According to the original definition of Jones at al. [21], a *search mission is a related set of information needs, resulting in one or more goals.* In the example presented in the Introduction, "Purchasing a vacuum cleaner" is a mission that represents an intent that a user wants to satisfy. The three steps ("looking for models", "models comparison," and "sellers comparison") are the three sub-tasks (or goals) contained in the mission. All the queries in a missions have a strong topical coherence, which means that all

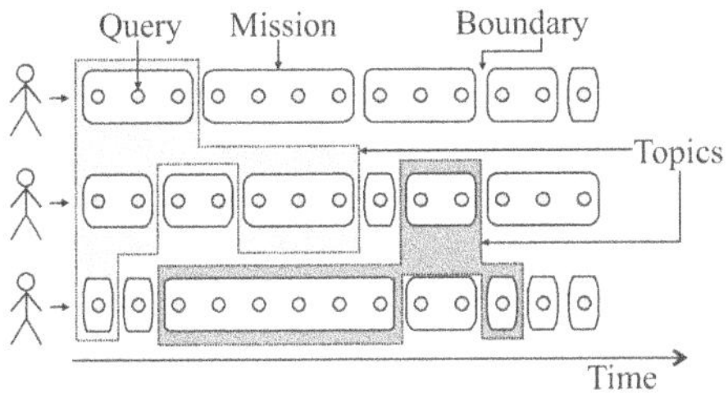

Figure 1: The activity of three search engine users partitioned at different levels. Every stream of user queries can be articulated in different missions that are aimed to satisfy a particular user intent. At a coarser level, topics can include missions from different users and also portions of activity originated by the same user at different times.

of them are issued with a main common objective. It has been observed [13] that search activities that take place in complex domains like "travel" or "health" often require several queries before complex user intents are fully satisfied.

Topics. Missions are characterized by a main objective and one or more sub-tasks related to the objective itself. For example, a mission devoted to organize a trip, has the travel itself as main objective and a number of functional sub-tasks (like booking the flight, reserving the hotel, finding a guided tour). Travel missions generated by different users are all characterized by the same main objective regardless the destination, the temporal order in which the sub-tasks are issued or even the recreational activities booked. In such a sense all the missions devoted to organize a travel can be seen as part of a same topic or *cognitive content.*

Missions within the same cognitive content are meant to fulfill one or more intents related to such a content. Here on, we use the term *topic* to define a *cognitive content that includes the sum of what can be perceived, discovered or learned about any real or abstract entity.* From an operational point of view, this means that a topic can be seen as the aggregation of all missions with the same cognitive content generated over time across different users. A sketch depicting the relation between queries, missions and topics can be found in Figure 1.

Our goal. Our primary objective is to define a methodology to aggregate different missions within the same cognitive content. This technique should be effective at different scales. In a individual perspective, it should be able to aggregate different but related missions of the same user, while in a wider context it can be used as a tool to cluster together all the missions that are topically coherent, across users. The method must not rely on predefined categorizations or taxonomies of user intent or topics.

4. MISSION SIMILARITY CLASSIFIER

According to the definitions given in Section 3, the concepts of mission and topic are strictly related to each other. In fact, sequences of queries that express coherently a single and well defined user intent must have a high degree of topical coherence. This strong connection allows us to use missions as fundamental building blocks for topics: distinct missions can be merged together if their semantic connotation is very similar. In the following, we first summarize the state of the art technique that we use to detect missions from the query log; then we describe a method that is able to effectively combine together pairs of topically-related missions.

4.1 Detection of search missions

To partition the user activity into missions we use the machine learning approach proposed by Donato et al. [13]. This method is able to detect the boundaries of a mission by analyzing the live stream of actions performed by the user on the search engine. This approach relies on a module based on a gradient boosted decision tree classifier [34], called the *mission detector*, that works at the level of query pairs. Given a set of features extracted from a pair of consecutive query log tuples τ_1, τ_2 generated by the same user, the mission detector indicates whether τ_2 is coherent with τ_1, from a topical perspective. When two queries are found to be incoherent, then a mission boundary is placed, so that the query log $\mathscr{L}$ is partitioned into missions containing one or more tuples.

The features used for the classifications come from three different domains: the *textual features*, that include different flavors of lexical similarity between the two queries, the *session features*, that measure several aspects of the click activity of the user in the time between the two queries and in the overall session, and the *time-related features* that take into account the inter-event time distance for some representative user actions. Using all of these feature together, the mission detector is able to reach a 95% accuracy in detecting boundaries on real user datastreams [13].

It has to be noted that missions identified by this method are semantically much narrower than topics, because queries in the same missions are not only constrained to be submitted by the same user, but they are also consecutive in time. Indeed, while a mission in theory can be fragmented in time, the mission detector by definition can only aggregate consecutive queries and, in practice, generates short-lived missions. Thus, the topical coherence constraints imposed on missions are much stronger than those that we require to be applied to topics.

4.2 Merging missions

Given the state of the art of mission boundary detection, it is possible to segment the user activity of every query log into missions. Furthermore, the strong topical coherence of queries inside the same mission can be exploited to generalize the approach used for mission boundary to a topic boundary detection. The idea is to use a new classifier, the *topic detector*, trained in semi-supervised fashion based on the data generated by the missions detector, to decide whether two query sets belong to the same topic. Its scheme is sketched in Figure 2.

Specifically, positive examples are automatically built by splitting missions in two consecutive query sequences and considering such two sequences as separate (sub)missions belonging to the same topic. Conversely, negative examples are formed by sets of queries belonging to consecutive missions of the same user, since we know they are topically unrelated because they are separated by the boundary placed by the mission detector. The topic detector is implemented with a Stochastic Gradient Boosted Decision Tree (GBDT) [35]. GBDT outputs the probability that the given sample is from

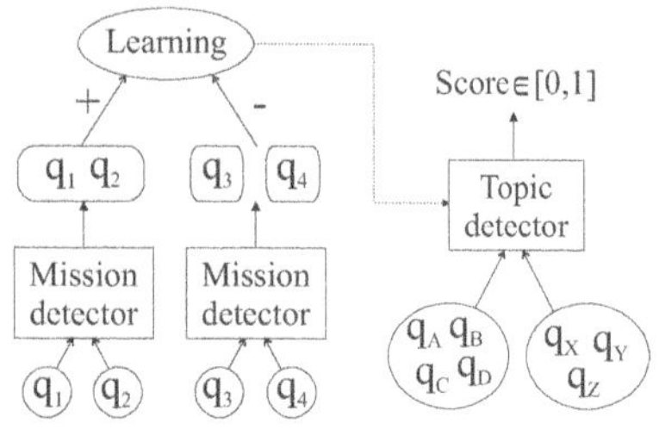

Figure 2: Training and application of the topic detector. Positive and negative examples for the learning phase are respectively missions and pairs of consecutive missions that are detected by the mission detector. Once trained, the topic detector can take in input any pair of query sets and compute a confidence score that can be interpreted as a topical similarity between the two sets.

the positive class; applied to our case, this is the probability that the two missions in input belong to the same topic. We can interpret this probability as a similarity score in $[0, 1]$ measuring the topical relatedness of the two sets and, consequently, the classifier can be seen as a *topical similarity function* $\mathscr{S}$.

The features given in input to the classifier are aggregated values over features computed from all the query pairs across two missions. Namely, given a (positive or negative) pair of missions m_1, m_2, all query pairs $q_1, q_2 | q_1 \in m_1 \wedge q_2 \in m_2$ are taken into account. Then, all the values of each feature are aggregated over all the pairs yielding four scores representing the average, standard deviation, minimum, and maximum values for that feature. For each query pair, features from three different categories are extracted[1]:

- **Lexical features**. Very often, similarity between the text of different queries denotes a strong semantic relation (e.g., "paris cheap travel" and "travelling to paris"). For this reason, we train the classifier using several lexical features such as length of common prefix and suffix, size of the intersection, edit distance, several similarity measures computed at word and character 3-grams level, and many others.

- **Behavioral features**. The behavior of users during the search activity gives much implicit information on the semantic relatedness of queries. For instance, if a user submits two queries in close succession, it is likely that the two queries are very related to each other, based on the assumption that the user activity is *bursty* [5] and events happening in the same burst are meant to accomplish the same task. However, since user behavior is very heterogeneous, it is necessary to aggregate behavioral information from several user sessions. We compute the average values of the behavioral features over a year of query log for each query pair q_1, q_2 such that q_2 has been observed at least once right after q_1 in the log.[2] The average time and the average number of clicks between two queries are examples of behavioral features.

- **Search result features**. Intuitively, the page result sets returned for a pair of topically-related queries will be topically related as well, to some extent. Thus, we consider a bunch of result-related features such as the intersection between result sets and the similarity between the vectors of the K most frequent words from a given content dictionary [1] appearing in the N top results.

[1]We do not report the complete list of features since they are commonly used in session analysis [20, 8].

[2]Behavioral features are defined only for successive query pairs observed at least 2 times. Else, a default value is used.

Algorithm 1 Iterative topic extraction

Require: Initial set of seed topics $\mathscr{T}_0$; similarity threshold $\theta \in (0, 1)$; termination threshold $\alpha \in (0, 1)$; topic similarity function $\mathscr{S} : \mathscr{T} \times \mathscr{T} \rightarrow [0, 1]$

$\mathscr{T}_{i+1} = \mathscr{T}_0$
repeat
  $\mathscr{T}_i = \mathscr{T}_{i+1} - T_0$; $\mathscr{T}_{i+1} = T_0$
  for $T_1 \in \mathscr{T}_i$ **do**
    $T_x = T_2 \in \mathscr{T}_{i+1} | \mathscr{S}(T_1, T_2) \geq \theta \wedge \mathscr{S}(T_1, T_2) \geq \mathscr{S}(T_1, T), \forall T \in \mathscr{T}_{i+1}$
    if a valid T_x has been found **then**
      $\mathscr{T}_{i+1} = \mathscr{T}_{i+1} - T_x + (T_x \cup T_1)$
    else
      $\mathscr{T}_{i+1} = \mathscr{T}_{i+1} + T_1$
    end if
  end for
until $\frac{|\mathscr{T}_i+1|}{|\mathscr{T}_i|} \leq \alpha$

We trained our topic detector using a balanced sample of 500K mission pairs extracted from random user sessions over the 2010 query log of the Yahoo! search engine. Results of 10-fold cross validation give an AUC value of 0.95, thus confirming that the topic detector is able to accurately discriminate between sets of queries that come from the same topic and those that do not.

One may think that the mission detector could have been used as-is to extract topics by means of detecting pairs of topically coherent queries among all the possible query pairs and iteratively clustering them. However, this approach has two main flaws. First, the computational effort to classify every possible query pair in $\mathscr{Q}$ is prohibitive given the dimension of real search query logs. Second, the mission detector is trained given query pairs that are adjacent realizations of the same user activity stream, while in topic extraction we are interested in comparing queries of different users, possibly in different times. On the other hand, classifying pairs of query sets allows us to leverage the mission data as an already available source. In any case, even if it were possible to classify every query pair, the clustering step would still require similarity computation for query sets.

5. GREEDY AGGLOMERATIVE TOPIC EXTRACTION

The topic similarity function $\mathscr{S}$ can be used iteratively to extract topics from the mission data. Consider a set $\mathscr{T}_0$ of *seed topics* where each topic contains only the set of queries submitted during a single user mission. This set is a very strict partition of the query corpus, where each partition is not only a coherent topic but it is the expression of an intent of a single user.

Our topic extraction algorithm is in the spirit of classic hierarchical agglomerative clustering [34]. As shown in the

Algorithm 1 pseudo-code, at any iteration i, the two sets $\mathscr{T}_i$ and $\mathscr{T}_{i+1}$ are considered. Initially, $\mathscr{T}_{i+1} = \{T_0\}$ and $\mathscr{T}_i = \{\mathscr{T}_0 - T_0\}$.

Each topic $T \in \mathscr{T}_i$ is compared with all topics $T_x \in \mathscr{T}_{i+1}$ through the function $\mathscr{S}(T, T_x)$; if topic similarity is below a certain threshold θ for all pairs, then T is moved from $\mathscr{T}_i$ to $\mathscr{T}_{i+1}$. Otherwise, the pair (T, T_x) with the highest score is greedily selected, T is removed from $\mathscr{T}_i$ and its elements are added to T_x, creating a broader topic. The algorithm is iterated as long as the relative decrease in the number of topics is large, or until $\frac{|\mathscr{T}_i+1|}{|\mathscr{T}_i|} > \alpha \in (0,1)$.

The complexity of a single iteration, in terms of number of computations of the $\mathscr{S}$ function, is $O(|\mathscr{T}_i|^2)$ and $\Omega(|\mathscr{T}_i|)$, since $\frac{|\mathscr{T}_i|^2-|\mathscr{T}_i|}{2}$ computations of the topic similarity are needed if no topics are merged, while just $|\mathscr{T}_i|$ comparisons take place if every topic merges into a single supertopic. The number of iterations needed depends on the stop condition α, but it is always bounded by $O(log(|\mathscr{T}_0|))$, thus leading to an overall algorithm complexity of $O(|\mathscr{T}_0|^2 \cdot log(|\mathscr{T}_0|))$.

Even if the number of iterations required is considerably smaller than the theoretical upper bound, in practice the quadratic complexity of computing $\mathscr{S}$ for every topic pair is still too costly for large query logs. However, the efficiency can be improved through a heuristic approach based on the observation that a very small portion of all possible topic pairs are actually merged in each iteration. To reduce the number of comparisons, the topic set $\mathscr{T}_i$ is partitioned into several smaller sets that are given in input to independent instances of Algorithm 1, so that the $\mathscr{S}$ function is applied only between elements inside the same partition and not across partitions. In addition to reducing the number of topic pairs considered, this approach enables a parallel implementation of the clustering algorithm, thus dramatically decreasing the actual computation time, even though the theoretical complexity remains the same. For brevity, in the following we will refer to our Greedy Agglomerative Topic Extraction algorithm using the acronym *GATE*.

The choice of a good *partitioning criterion* is crucial for the outcome of GATE. To maximize the number of topics merged at each iteration, partitions should contain topics that are more likely to be combined than randomly selected topics. This can be done by putting in the same partition topics that share some of the features given in input to the classifier used to compute topic similarity; for instance, topics can be partitioned on the most common character-level 3-gram that appears in their query sets, given that topics with some lexical similarity are more likely to be merged than random topics. The partition criterion can also possibly change at each iteration.

Aggregation on the basis of user identity is one of the most relevant to our study. If the first iteration of the algorithm is run keeping the missions of different users in different partitions, then the resulting agglomeration produces a minimal group of topically-coherent mission sets, called *supermissions*. These supermissions allow to define more compact profile of user activity on a topical basis.

6. EXPERIMENTAL SETUP

We extracted the total activity of $40K$ users from 3 months of the anonymized Yahoo! query log. Statistics for the data set are reported in Table 1. The queries in the log were sequentially grouped into 3,005,724 missions using the mission detector described in Section 4.1. The number of missions per user and number of unique queries per mission are broadly distributed with average values as in Table 1. The first iteration of GATE is performed with a user-based aggregation criterion, therefore the topics produced in the first iteration are supermissions. The average number of supermissions per user is 42, against the 57 missions per user, meaning that GATE can be used to compress the user description by nearly 30% on average.

Table 1: Dataset statistics

Unique queries (uq)	2,198,815
Missions (m)	3,005,724
Unique missions (um)	1,606,733
Avg uq per mission	1.72
Avg m per user	75
Avg um per user	57

In the rest of this section, we present OSLOM [23], a representative network-based clustering algorithm used for comparison with GATE. We then introduce the metrics used to compare such methodologies. The two methodologies are profoundly different, therefore a fair comparison is difficult. Nevertheless we show that our approach has a number of advantages when compared with OSLOM.

6.1 Baseline: Topic extraction through network clustering

We compare GATE with a content-agnostic query clustering algorithm based on query graphs. As mentioned in Section 2, graph-based clustering considers the queries as nodes and model relation between them with edges. Depending on the relation used, the query graph can assume different topologies and semantics [2]. The choice of comparing our method with a baseline from a different paradigm is motivated by the significant body of recent work and promising results using graph based approaches for query clustering. A thorough comparison between agglomerative clustering and graph based approaches is still missing in the context of query log mining.

The input to our baseline is a query graph based on the *click co-occurrence* relation, also known as *URL cover graph* [2]. Such graph models the topical relatedness of queries from the perspective of the common results to which they lead users: two queries are connected if users click on the same results. Edges are weighted depending on how many distinct clicked URLs are shared by the queries. In principle, several different query-query relations can be mapped onto a single query graph; for instance, it is quite common to mix lexical similarity and click co-occurrence (or other content-related similarity measures). In the present evaluation we consider a simple URL cover graph as input to our baseline.

To detect topically coherent clusters from the URL cover graph, we use a network *community detection* algorithm. Intuitively, the basic idea of community detection is to spot groups of nodes that have many connections with each other and few to the rest of the network, thus forming a dense cluster. Accordingly, a cluster on the URL cover graph would include a set of queries that have many more clicked URLs in common compared to all the other queries in the corpus.

Among the many community detection algorithms in the literature [15], we adopt the recently proposed OSLOM (`www.oslom.org`). This choice is motivated by its good performance over other state of the art algorithms on both synthetic benchmarks [22] and real network datasets [23]. Furthermore, unlike the vast majority of other community detection techniques, OSLOM automatically detects overlapping communities and hierarchies of clusters. This allows a more direct comparison with our greedy algorithm, which also outputs overlapping topics through a hierarchical agglomeration process.

OSLOM performs clustering based on the optimization of a local fitness function that measures the statistical significance of the detected cluster compared to a global randomized null model known as configuration model [25]. Clusters are detected by selecting several random seed nodes in the graph and finding the locally optimal clusters that include the seed nodes. Similar clusters found over different realizations of random seeds are then merged together, thus originating a minimal set of clusters that may overlap. The procedure is iterated over higher hierarchical levels by collapsing clusters into nodes. Iterations stop when no higher level clusters are found. For further details about the algorithm we refer to the original paper [23].

6.2 Metrics

In the following, we present the criteria used for a quantitative and qualitative comparison between the two methodologies. Although prior work has relied on human editors, manual evaluation for a huge corpus of topics is unfeasible, therefore here we focus on automatic evaluation metrics.

Clustering measures

The first group of metrics are meant to give a quantitative comparison of the two methods. We define three measures:

query set coverage: fraction of queries that the methodology is considering in the clustering phase;

singleton ratio: fraction of queries that remains isolated in singleton at the end of the iterative procedures;

aggregation ability: percent of topics that are aggregated in two consecutive iterations or in two consecutive hierarchical levels.

Cluster purity

The quality of a topic depends on its *purity*, or semantic coherence. When no ground truth about the correct composition of a topic is available, an automatic way to assess purity is to consider the results for all pairs of queries in a topic. We compare the result sets of two queries to assess how *related* they are, and average the relatedness over all pairs.

Perhaps the simplest way to establish the relatedness of two queries is to compare the result sets returned for each query and use the intersection to derive a measure of similarity [28, 14]. However, a more fine-grained criterion that uses the information inside the clickthrough result provides a more accurate evaluation basis. We construct a bag-of-words vector for each query, consisting of the *concepts* in the documents returned for this query. Concepts are selected using a predefined dictionary [1]. For a given query q and a concept dictionary D, Algorithm 2 computes the vector of concepts with their scores. The parameters are set to $k = 10$ and $K = 20$. The score of a term $t \in D$ depends on the number of documents in which the term t appears,

Algorithm 2 Algorithm to compute the concept vector

```
Require: Concept dictionary D, query q, parameters k, K
Retrieve set R of top-k results for q
T = Terms from D contained in R
Eliminate from T terms in q
for term t ∈ T do
    d(t) = number of results in which t appears
    r(t) = sum of ranks of the results in which t appears
    R(t) = ((k+1) d(t)) − r(t) / (d(t) k)
    S(t) = d(t) R(t) / k
end for
Return the K terms with highest score S(t)
```

where $R(t) = \frac{((k+1)\ d(t))-r(t)}{d(t)\ k}$ and $S(t) = \frac{d(t)\ R(t)}{k}$.

Table 2: Examples of the concept vector

Query	Terms in aboutness vector (ordered)
iphone	iphone, store, 4, camera, phone, apps, inc, facetime, mode, recording, software, 3gs, resolution, battery, shop, network, ios, 3g, broadband, ipod
iphone 4 reviews	phone, iphone, store, 4, camera, apple, reviews, apps, review, 3g, recording, model, inc, screen, resolution, ipad, coverage, network, photo, 3gs
toyota prius	hybrid, car, prius, toyota, mpg, photo, price, sales, specs, vehicle, yaris, cars, review, reviews, msrp, specification, milage, model, economy, research
toyota yaris	yaris, hatchback, car, price, hybrid, toyota, models, spec, mpg, liftback, dealer, model, vehicles, review, photo, reviews, city, prius, transmission,vehicle

and on the sum of ranks of those documents. Table 2 shows examples of two pairs of topical related queries, and their top concept terms ordered by descending score. Given the concept vectors of the queries that it contains, the concept vector of a topic is obtained by marginalizing all concept vectors and keeping the top concept terms.

Let us define the purity of a topic by considering all pairs of terms in the corresponding concept vector and measure how much they are related to each other on average. One could achieve this using the well-known pointwise mutual information (PMI) given by:

$$PMI(t_1, t_2) = \frac{f(t_1, t_2)}{f(t_1)f(t_2)}$$

where $f(t_1, t_2)$ is the number of queries that have both terms t_1 and t_2 in their concept vectors, and $f(t_1)$, $f(t_2)$ are the numbers of queries that have t_1 and t_2 in their concept vectors, respectively. One weakness of PMI is that it may become very unstable for a pair of rare terms. For example, if both $f(t_1)$ and $f(t_2)$ are small, a few coincidental co-occurrences may lead to a superficially high PMI value. To take this into account, we use the log-likelihood ratio, which is the expected value of the PMI:

$$\begin{aligned} LLR(t_1, t_2) &= p(t_1, t_2)PMI(t_1, t_2) + p(t_1, \overline{t_2})PMI(t_1, \overline{t_2}) \\ &+ p(\overline{t_1}, t_2)PMI(\overline{t_1}, t_2) + p(\overline{t_1}, \overline{t_1})PMI(\overline{t_1}, \overline{t_1}) \end{aligned}$$

where $\overline{t}$ denotes the set of all terms except t. LLR fixes the unstability problem of PMI. Note that when the marginal query frequencies $f(t_1)$ and $f(t_2)$ are small, the other terms in the LLR equation will start to dominate. Averaging LLR across all the pairs of terms in the topic concept vector, we obtain the log-likelihood ratio for the topic.

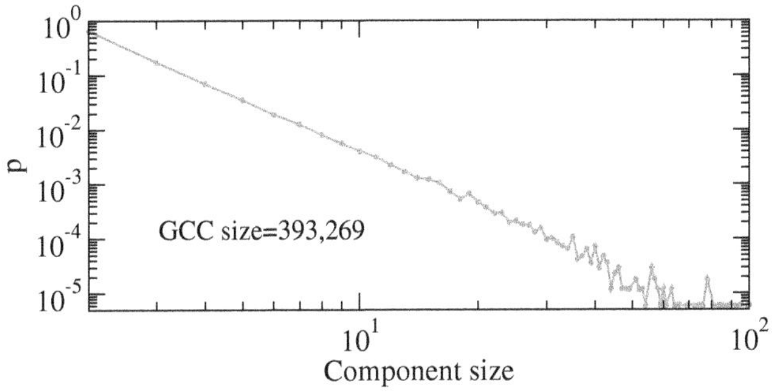

Figure 3: Distribution of connected components size in the query graph, except the giant connected component (GCC).

URL coverage

The topic LLR only focuses on the purity of the topic, which by itself is not too meaningful for the evaluation. A trivial solution of considering each query as a topic would yield very high topic LLR values. Similarly, one can easily cluster only synonymous queries, such as the query "facebook" and its misspellings, again leading to a high purity measure. Similar to singletons, such topics consisting of queries with almost identical results are not useful. To generate meaningful abstractions of the query space, it is desirable to aggregate related queries with different result sets. We therefore need a measure of *coverage* to complement purity, as suggested by previous work on clustering [30].

We measure the coverage by the number of unique URLs in the result sets for the queries in the topic. Given the 2010 query logs of the Yahoo! search engine, we extract all distinct URLs clicked by users for each query. To remove the tail of the clickthrough distribution, URLs that received less than 0.01 clickthrough rate are discarded. We define the coverage of a topic as the aggregate number of distinct URLs across the queries in the topic. Note that the trivial solutions of singleton topics or synonymous queries have very low coverage. Overall, our goal is to extract topics with both high purity and high coverage.

7. EXPERIMENTAL RESULTS

In this section we compare the two clustering algorithms according to the metrics presented in Section 6.2.

The GATE algorithm has a full query coverage on the dataset, because, by definition, every query can be found in at least one mission. Conversely, when dealing with graph-based clustering algorithms, the sparsity of the graph can lead to the emergence of isolated components that directly affect query coverage. In fact, since the vast majority of queries share very few clicked results, it turns out that the URL-cover graph is composed by a galaxy of tiny disconnected components. These little islands cannot be merged with other components due to lack of connections and, since they are mainly singletons, they do not represent any meaningful cluster just by themselves. The size distribution of the components in the URL-cover graph generated by our dataset is shown in Figure 3. We note that less than 400K queries are in the Giant Connected Component (GCC), thus leading to query set coverage below 0.2.

Figure 4 shows the distribution of the topic size with in-

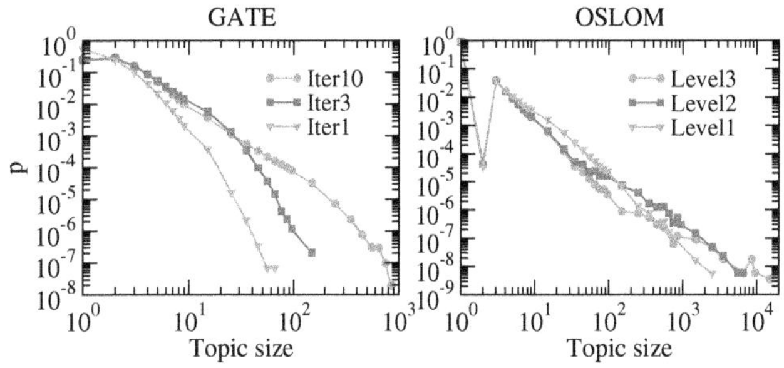

Figure 4: Distribution of topic size for GATE and

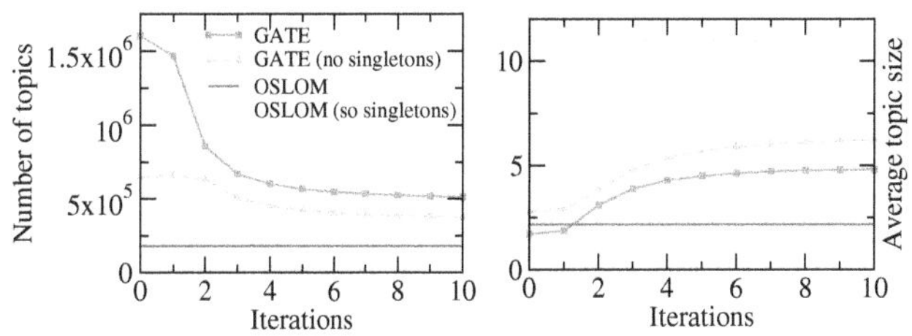

Figure 5: Number of topics and average topic size vs. GATE iterations. The values from the lowest hierarchical level of OSLOM are reported as a reference.

creasing number of iterations in GATE and in the three different hierarchical levels detected by OSLOM. The first thing to observe is that the singleton ratio in GATE decreases from 0.55 in the first iteration to 0.27 in the last one, while in OSLOM it remains stable around 0.88. Second, while in GATE the number of both medium-size (10-100) and big size (>100) topics grows with the iterations, in OSLOM the medium-size topics that are detected in the first hierarchical level tend to be merged in very large comprehensive and heterogeneous topics, with up to some tens of thousands queries. Note that the low frequency of size-2 topics in OSLOM is probably due to the tendency of the algorithm to merge dyads in larger clusters to optimize the partition fitness function.

Lastly, the aggregation ability of the two algorithms is shown in Figure 5. In GATE the number of topics decays quickly in the early iterations and then stabilizes, until the stop condition is reached. The final number of topics is around 500K, against the 180K found by OSLOM; recall that OSLOM only deals with the fewer queries in the GCC. The number of topics in the different hierarchical levels in OSLOM varies very slightly. Furthermore, the average size of OSLOM topics is more than double the size of the topics generated by GATE, mainly because of the presence of very large topics that skew the mean value.

Results on topic purity are shown in Figure 6. To check how the purity of the topic decreases with its size we computed the correlation between the topic size and LLR by averaging the LLR values of the topics with the same size:

$$\langle LLR_s \rangle = \frac{1}{|T \in \mathscr{T} : size(T) = s|} \sum_{T \in \mathscr{T} : size(T) = s} LLR(T).$$

As expected, the larger the topic, the more heterogeneous

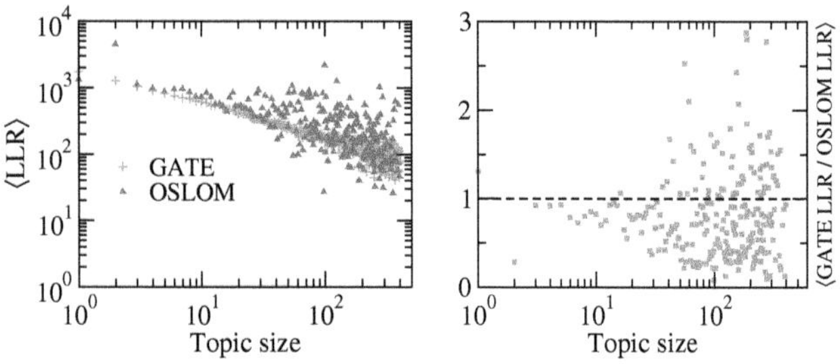

Figure 6: Left: Correlations between topics size and

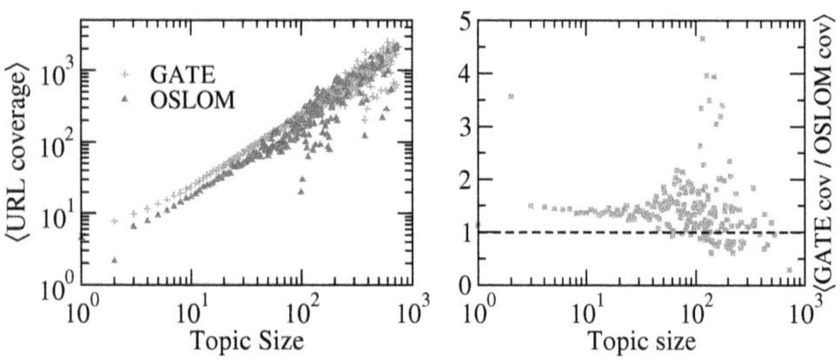

Figure 7: Left: Correlation between topic size and URL coverage. Right: Ratio between the two quantities.

the queries included, so we observe a negative correlation. OSLOM's topics have on average higher LLR than topics from GATE; this emerges clearly when computing the ratio between the average scores obtained by the two approaches for each topic size. This is mainly due to the fact that OSLOM generates many topics that include just concept *reformulations*, i.e., queries that are different from the lexical perspective but express exactly the same concept (e.g. "duran duran", "duan duran", "duran", etc.). As we remarked, such queries surely belong to the same cluster, but still they do not express a complex cognitive content. For this reason, it is necessary to complement the purity measure with the URL coverage. In Figure 7, the same analysis made for the URL coverage shows that the greedy algorithm has much higher coverage than OSLOM. If considering purity and coverage metrics separately is useful to learn the peculiarities of the two approaches, a joint measure that captures the tradeoff between the two scores is useful to compare the overall quality of the query clusters. Such unified measure can be obtained by multiplying the purity by the coverage for all the size classes of the topics and then comparing the resulting curves. Results in Figure 8 show that GATE outperforms OSLOM for all the medium-small topic sizes, that represent the great majority of topics. For clusters containing about 100 queries the two approaches are comparable, and only for some bigger, more rare topics OSLOM achieves the best performance.

To summarize, if we consider all the quality measures together, we can conclude that GATE leads to a better topical query clusters because it is able to process all the queries in the corpus, and most of the topics it generates have a better tradeoff between purity and coverage compared to OSLOM.

As a final remark we note that a fair comparison of the computational time needed by the two techniques is hard,

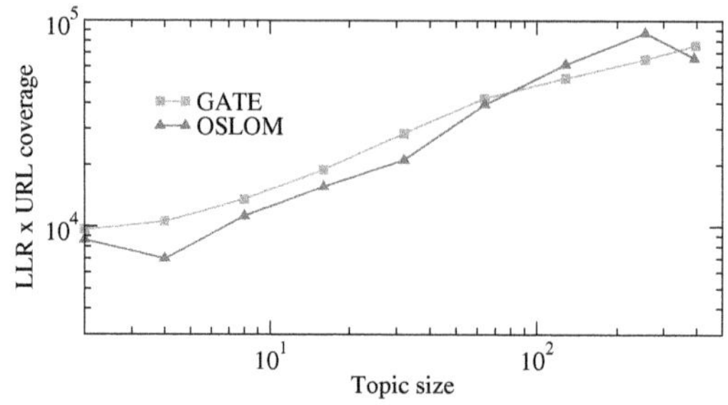

Figure 8: Trade-off between purity and URL coverage

first because OSLOM's theoretical complexity is difficult to estimate [23] and last because GATE can run in parallel while the current OSLOM implementation does not enable parallelism. However, we underline that parallelization is a strong advantage of GATE, because when dealing with real-life data sizes, it is hard to regard non-parallel algorithms as practical solutions for clustering web search queries.

8. USER PROFILING

A practical way to use the topics extracted from the query log is to profile users on a topical basis: each user can be described by the set of topics that match her queries. Since OSLOM has a small query coverage and allows only for an exact match between the user queries and the queries inside the clusters, it is not practical to employ it in profiling. Therefore, here we focus on user profiling based on our approach.

To build the profile of a user, we apply the topical similarity function $\mathscr{S}$ between the user missions and every topic that contain at least one query from that mission, then selecting the best match. Formally, let us define the topic that best matches mission m as:

$$T_m = \arg\max_{T \in \mathscr{T}} \mathscr{S}(m, T).$$

Given the best match scores, let us define the *topical profile* of a user u as a weighted vector over the topics matching her missions:

$$\mathscr{P}_u = \left\{ \left(T_m, \frac{\mathscr{S}(m, T_m)}{\sum_{m' \in \mathscr{M}_u} \mathscr{S}(m', T_{m'})} \right), \forall m \in \mathscr{M}_u \right\},$$

where $\mathscr{M}_u$ is the set of missions of user u. For a more compact user representation, supermissions can be used instead.

The topical profile can be used not only to detect the topics relevant to the user, but also to predict her future search goals. To check such a prediction potential, we perform an experiment to examine whether a user profile matches her future missions better than random missions from other users.

The match between a mission and a profile is performed by computing the $\mathscr{S}$ function between the mission and every topic in the profile, and scaling the resulting scores by the weights of the corresponding topics in the profile. This yields a vector of match scores over the profile topics. The match vector can be generalized to sequences of missions by averaging the elements of the vectors across the missions.

We produce the topical profile for the 40K users in the dataset starting from the 3 months of query log. For each

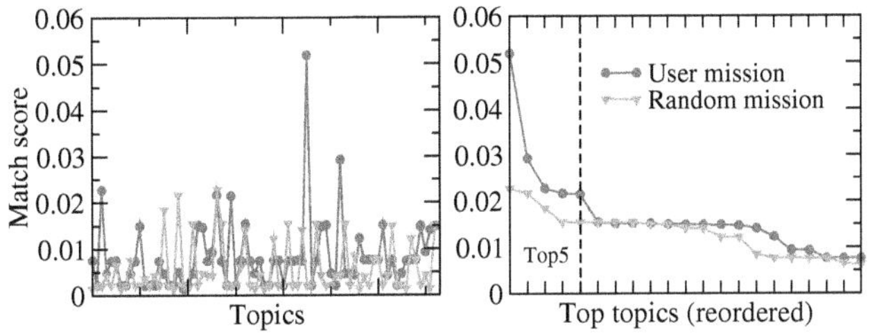

Figure 9: Example of match of missions sequences on a topical user profile. On the x axis are the topics in the profile; on the y axis are the match scores of the mission sequences for each topic. The sequence originated by the same user has more spikes compared to the sequence of the random user. When the values of the each curve are sorted, the best matching sequence is evident by looking at the top-N scores.

user we select two sequences of missions from the 30 days right after the 3 months considered. One sequence comprises of all the missions generated by the same user in the 30-day period. The other is a sequence of equal length generated by another user chosen at random among all other users.

Intuitively, a mission is likely to match at most a few of the several, possibly different topics in a user profile. Given this intuition, to decide which of the two sequences best matches the profile, we focus on the top-N ($N = 5$) elements of the match vectors between topic profile and mission sequences. We then apply a simple majority rule, i.e., which sequence has the most elements with higher match scores. This idea is exemplified by Figure 9.

Using this technique we are able to detect the user's own sequence in 65% of the cases. We stress that the mission sequences of randomly selected users are strongly biased toward high-frequency queries such as "facebook," "amazon," and so on. Since these are shared by a large number of users, any user profile is likely to match them, leading to a decay in detection performance. For this reason we divided the random sequences into three sets according to the average frequency of their queries. The accuracy rises to 72% when considering the sequences with lower frequency queries and drops to around 55% when considering the sequences with higher frequency queries. 65% success in prediction can be considered a good result. Even if the interest of a given user would presumably be quite stationary *within a particular domain*, in web search, where a much wider range of suitable topics is available, the user focus can be often inconstant in time, independent by past search sessions and made even more variable by bursty search activity triggered by external events (e.g., "Michael Jackson death"), hardly predictable by looking only at the user history. This issues make this prediction task much more difficult compared to domain-specific predicition or recomendation.

9. CONCLUSIONS

The *behavior* of the users in submitting queries to a search engine, including the implicit and explicit information that their actions reveal about their search intent, is a crucial element to determine what is the *topic* of a query or of a sequence of search actions. We introduce a novel definition of topic in the context of query log analysis and propose a topic extraction algorithm based on agglomerative clustering of sequences of queries that exhibit a coherent user intent. Our algorithm relies on a semi-supervised classifier that can tell if two query sets are topically coherent with excellent accuracy (AUC 0.95). We compare our method with a graph-based clustering baseline, showing its advantages on query coverage and on the trade-off between purity and resource coverage of the clusters. Finally, we define the *topical profile* of a user in terms of a topic vector that best defines the user search history. With our classifier we are able to discriminate a query sequence submitted by the profiled user from a random query sequence 72% of the time in the best case scenario.

One could consider more sophisticated baselines, for instance combining click co-occurrence with lexical similarity features, or even using query clustering algorithms based on alternative paradigms [7, 18, 11]. A more direct evaluation could be achieved with the golden standard of human judgments on the quality of the topics. A preliminary effort in this direction has pointed to the difficulty of human inspection of topic quality, as well as the challenge of identifying a suitable tradeoff between topic specificity and coverage.

This work opens several research directions. In particular, we are working on the formulation of a user-to-user similarity metric based on topics that can overcome the sparsity problem of similarity metrics based on exact query matches. Finally, we want to explore in greater depth the potential of the topical profiling technique to predict future search activity and provide novel search recommendation services.

10. REFERENCES

[1] P. Anick. Using terminological feedback for web search refinement: a log-based study. In *SIGIR '03*, 2003.

[2] R. Baeza-Yates. Graphs from search engine queries. In *SOFSEM'07: 33rd conference on Current Trends in Theory and Practice of Computer Science*, pages 1–8, Berlin, Heidelberg, 2007. Springer-Verlag.

[3] R. Baeza-Yates and A. Tiberi. Extracting semantic relations from query logs. In *KDD'07: 13th ACM SIGKDD international conference on Knowledge discovery and data mining*, pages 76–85, New York, NY, USA, 2007. ACM.

[4] N. Balasubramanian and S. Cucerzan. Automatic generation of topic pages using query-based aspect models. In *CIKM'09: 18th ACM conference on Information and knowledge management*, pages 2049–2052, New York, NY, USA, 2009. ACM.

[5] A. L. Barabasi. The origin of bursts and heavy tails in human dynamics. *Nature*, 435:207, 2005.

[6] D. Beeferman and A. Berger. Agglomerative clustering of a search engine query log. In *KDD'00: 6th ACM SIGKDD international conference on Knowledge discovery and data mining*, pages 407–416, New York, NY, USA, 2000. ACM.

[7] S. M. Beitzel, E. C. Jensen, D. D. Lewis, A. Chowdhury, and O. Frieder. Automatic classification of web queries using very large unlabeled query logs. *ACM Transactions on Information Systems*, 25, April 2007.

[8] P. Boldi, F. Bonchi, C. Castillo, D. Donato, A. Gionis, and S. Vigna. The query-flow graph: model and

applications. In *CIKM'08: Proceeding of the 17th ACM conference on Information and knowledge management*, pages 609–618, New York, NY, USA, 2008. ACM.

[9] I. Bordino, C. Castillo, D. Donato, and A. Gionis. Query similarity by projecting the query-flow graph. In *SIGIR'10*, pages 515–522. ACM, 2010.

[10] U. Brandes, D. Delling, M. Höfer, M. Gaertler, R. Görke, Z. Nikoloski, and D. Wagner. On Finding Graph Clusterings with Maximum Modularity. In *WG'07: Proceedings of the 33rd International Workshop on Graph-Theoretic Concepts in Computer Science*, Lecture Notes in Computer Science, 2007.

[11] H. Cao, D. Jiang, J. Pei, Q. He, Z. Liao, E. Chen, and H. Li. Context-aware query suggestion by mining click-through and session data. In *KDD'08: 14th ACM SIGKDD international conference on Knowledge discovery and data mining*, pages 875–883, New York, NY, USA, 2008. ACM.

[12] S.-L. Chuang and L.-F. Chien. A practical web-based approach to generating topic hierarchy for text segments. In *CIKM'04: 13th ACM international conference on Information and knowledge management*, pages 127–136, New York, NY, USA, 2004. ACM.

[13] D. Donato, F. Bonchi, T. Chi, and Y. Maarek. Do you want to take notes?: identifying research missions in Yahoo! search pad. In *WWW'10: 19th international conference on World wide web*, pages 321–330, New York, NY, USA, 2010. ACM.

[14] L. Fitzpatrick and M. Dent. Automatic feedback using past queries: social searching? In *SIGIR '97*, 1997.

[15] S. Fortunato. Community detection in graphs. *Physics Reports*, 486(3-5):75–174, 2010.

[16] S. Fortunato and M. Barthèlemy. Resolution limit in community detection. *Proceedings of the National Academy of Sciences*, 104(1):36–41, Jan 2007.

[17] S. Gollapudi and R. Panigrahy. Exploiting asymmetry in hierarchical topic extraction. In *CIKM'06: 15th ACM international conference on Information and knowledge management*, pages 475–482, New York, NY, USA, 2006. ACM.

[18] X. He and P. Jhala. Regularized query classification using search click information. *Pattern Recognition*, 41:2283–2288, July 2008.

[19] T. Hofmann. Probabilistic latent semantic indexing. In *SIGIR'99*, pages 50–57, 1999.

[20] R. Jones and K. L. Klinkner. Beyond the session timeout: automatic hierarchical segmentation of search topics in query logs. In *CIKM'08: Proceeding of the 17th ACM conference on Information and knowledge management*, pages 699–708, New York, NY, USA, 2008. ACM.

[21] R. Jones and K. L. Klinkner. Beyond the session timeout: automatic hierarchical segmentation of search topics in query logs. In *CIKM '08: 17th ACM conference on Information and knowledge mining*, pages 699–708, New York, NY, USA, 2008. ACM.

[22] A. Lancichinetti, S. Fortunato, and F. Radicchi. Benchmark graphs for testing community detection algorithms. *Physical Review E (Statistical, Nonlinear, and Soft Matter Physics)*, 78(4), 2008.

[23] A. Lancichinetti, F. Radicchi, J. J. Ramasco, and S. Fortunato. Finding statistically significant communities in networks. *PLoS ONE*, 6(4), 04 2011.

[24] J. Leskovec, K. J. Lang, A. Dasgupta, and M. W. Mahoney. Statistical properties of community structure in large social and information networks. In *WWW'08: Proceedings of the 17th international conference on World Wide Web*, pages 695–704, New York, NY, USA, 2008. ACM.

[25] M. Molloy and B. Reed. A critical point for random graphs with a given degree sequence. *Random Structures & Algorithms*, 6:161–179, March 1995.

[26] M. E. J. Newman and M. Girvan. Finding and evaluating community structure in networks. *Physical Review E*, 69, 2004.

[27] F. Radlinski and T. Joachims. Query chains: learning to rank from implicit feedback. In *KDD'05: 11th ACM SIGKDD international conference on Knowledge discovery in data mining*, pages 239–248, New York, NY, USA, 2005. ACM.

[28] V. V. Raghavan and H. Sever. On the reuse of past optimal queries. In *SIGIR '95*, 1995.

[29] G. Salton and M. J. McGill. *Introduction to Modern Information Retrieval*. McGraw-Hill, Inc., New York, NY, USA, 1986.

[30] L. Sarmento, A. Kehlenbeck, E. Oliveira, and L. Ungar. Efficient clustering of web-derived data sets. In *MLDM '09: 6th International Conference on Machine Learning and Data Mining in Pattern Recognition*, pages 398–412, Berlin, Heidelberg, 2009. Springer-Verlag.

[31] W. Song, Y. Zhang, T. Liu, and S. Li. Bridging topic modeling and personalized search. In *COLING'10: 23rd International Conference on Computational Linguistics: Posters*, pages 1167–1175, Stroudsburg, PA, USA, 2010. Association for Computational Linguistics.

[32] A. Veilumuthu and P. Ramachandran. Intent based clustering of search engine query log. In *CASE'09: 5th IEEE international conference on Automation science and engineering*, pages 647–652, Piscataway, NJ, USA, 2009. IEEE.

[33] J.-R. Wen, J.-Y. Nie, and Z. Hong-Jiang. Query clustering using user logs. *ACM Transactions on Information Systems*, 20:59–81, January 2002.

[34] I. H. Witten and E. Frank. *Data mining: practical machine learning tools and techniques with Java implementations*. Morgan Kaufmann, 1999.

[35] J. Ye, J.-H. Chow, J. Chen, and Z. Zheng. Stochastic gradient boosted distributed decision trees. In *CIKM'09: 18th ACM conference on Information and knowledge management*, pages 2061–2064, New York, NY, USA, 2009. ACM.

[36] J. Yi and F. Maghoul. Query clustering using click-through graph. In *WWW'09: 18th international conference on World wide web*, pages 1055–1056, New York, NY, USA, 2009. ACM.

[37] H.-J. Zeng, Q.-C. He, Z. Chen, W.-Y. Ma, and J. Ma. Learning to cluster web search results. In *SIGIR'04: 27th annual international ACM SIGIR conference on Research and development in information retrieval*, pages 210–217, New York, NY, USA, 2004. ACM.

Discovering Customer Intent in Real-time for Streamlining Service Desk Conversations

Ullas Nambiar, Tanveer Faruquie, L Venkata Subramaniam, Sumit Negi
IBM Research - India, New Delhi, India
{ubnambiar, ftanveer, lvsubram, sumitneg}@in.ibm.com

Ganesh Ramakrishnan
Dept of Computer Science and Engg, IIT Mumbai, India
ganesh@cse.iitb.ac.in

ABSTRACT

Businesses require the contact center agents to meet pre-specified customer satisfaction levels while keeping the cost of operations low or meeting sales targets, objectives that end up being complementary and difficult to achieve in real-time. In this paper, we describe a speech enabled real-time conversation management system that tracks customer-agent conversations to detect user intent (e.g. gathering information, likely to buy, etc.) that can help agents to then decide the best sequence of actions for that call. We present an entropy based decision support system that parses a text stream generated in real-time during a audio conversation and identifies the first instance at which the intent becomes distinct enough for the agent to then take subsequent actions. We provide evaluation results displaying the efficiency and effectiveness of our system.

Categories and Subject Descriptors

H.3.3 [**Information Search and Retrieval**]: Search process, Selection Process

General Terms

Algorithms, Design, Performance

Keywords

Real-time, Contact Center Conversation, Customer Intent Recognition

1. INTRODUCTION

Customer contact centers (also known as call centers) were started as a low-cost alternative to maintaining physical centers for serving existing customers of a business. However, with a view to increasing profits and to make maximum utilization of the agents time, other activities like lead generation, taking orders, etc. were slowly added to the tasks performed. In this paper, we present, *AgentAid* - a real-time audio conversation management system that will streamline service desk conversations by automatically recognizing customer intent regarding a service and immediately prompt the agent with relevant information. AgentAid is designed to help service desk agents in solving the customer's information need while ensuring operational effectiveness. AgentAid achieves this by prompting the agent, at appropriate time periods during the call, with information which is useful for successfully closing the call. This information could be in the form of queries which the agent can ask the customer to gain a better understanding of the customer's problem or product/service recommendations for effective cross-sell/up-sell. Two key aspects of the AgentAid system are *a)* The information which is displayed to the agent is generated in real time, i.e., as the agent-customer conversation is in progress *b)* The system, based on the conversation context, automatically generates this information without requiring any input from the agent. The AgentAid system consists of two main modules namely the *Decision Module* and the *Query Builder*.

The Decision Module's aim is to identify the *customer's intent* in real-time while an audio conversation between a customer and contact center agent is taking place. To do this, we start by converting the on-going call audio to text using an Automatic Speech Recognizer(ASR). We then segregate the streaming text into distinct portions and assign a set of predefined categories that reflect the intent of the customer. This is depicted in Figure 1 where the Decision Module has assigned call segment d_0 to d_1 to the *'Car unavailability issue'* category and d_2 to d_3 to the *'High rates'* category. The critical task for Decision Module is to identify *intent points* i.e. earliest point in the streaming conversation where the customer's intent becomes evident with reasonable degree of confidence. Once this is done and the call segment assigned a category (intent category) relevant information is fetched from the backend database using the *Query Builder* and presented to the agent. For instance, the moment the Decision Module detects (step [1] in Figure 1) that a particular call segment is of type *'Car unavailability issue'* it invokes the Query Builder (step [2] in Figure 1) and passes the relevant call context (i.e. portion of the ASR that was categorized as *'Car unavailability issue'* t_{25} to t_{42}). The Query Builder uses this call context to automatically build a query for the relevant backend (step [3] in Figure 1) database (e.g. database containing current fleet inventory at the location). The result of the query is then displayed to the agent in realtime (step [4] in Figure 1). In this paper, we describe in detail the *Decision Module* component of the AgentAid system. The *Query Builder* module of our system is explained in our previous work [21].

The intent identification is done by using a classifier that not only identifies customer's intent but also discovers the *intent points* - points at which intent changes. Typically classifiers make decisions after the entire document. However, a call center conversation can be visualized as a continuously evolving document that is stream-

CIKM'11, October 24–28, 2011, Glasgow, Scotland, UK.

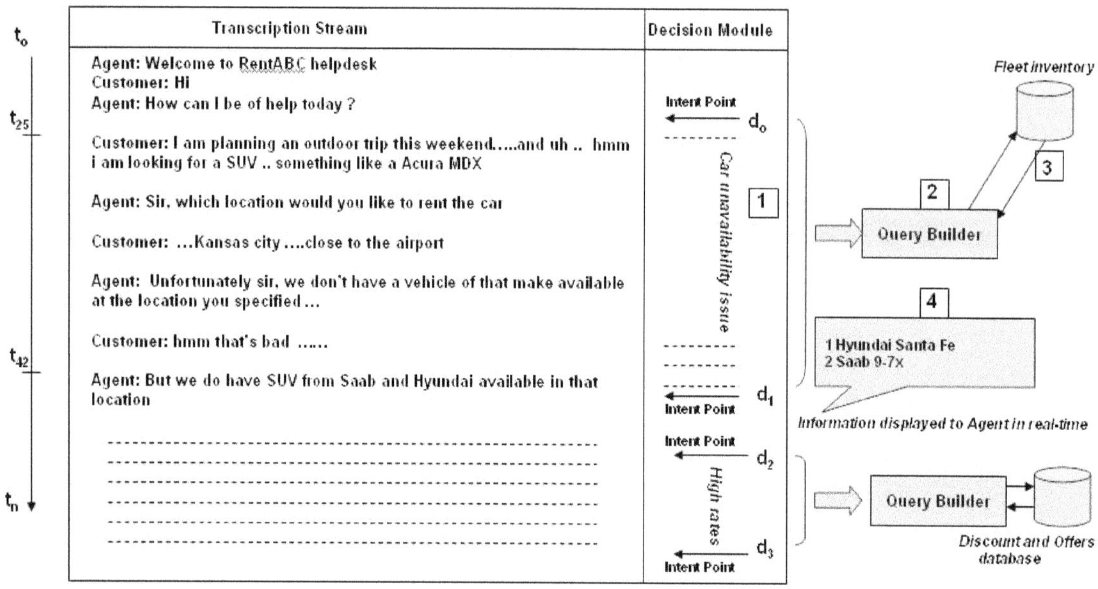

Figure 1: AgentAid system flow

ing into the system. Herein lies the *first challenge - The text stream is non-stationary i.e. distribution of features change with time and therefore the system must determine whether it has enough information to make the decision that an intent point has been reached and the call segment can be labeled with a pre-specified intent category.* Determining the customer's intent early in the call can help the agent take appropriate action (e.g. if the system prompts the agent that the customer's intent is to shop around for a good price it might be helpful to provide some kind of price comparison or offers upfront). Even if we can only narrow down to a broad intent category e.g. interested in *opening a checking account* and not to the particular type, *a student's checking*; the quicker mapping of information could help reduce the average time for the handling the call. The *second challenge* arises from the fact that the interactions between customer and agent is over a real-time audio call and therefore the customer expects satisfactory answers and suggestions in real-time. The *third challenge* is with respect to handling the high noise in audio to text translations done by most ASRs.

The remainder of the paper is organized as follows. In the next section, Section 2, we list related research efforts. In Section 3, we formulate the problem for efficiently finding customer intent in realtime conversation. We then show how we can assign intent categories and find intent points in Section 4. Section 5 presents detailed evaluation results over both synthetic and real-life data. We summarize our contributions in Section 6.

2. RELATED WORK

There exists prior work on building classifiers for call classification [16] and routing customer calls based on the customer response to an open ended system prompts such as, *"Welcome to xxx, How may I help you?"* [12]. In call classification and routing the complete call (document) is collected before a decision is made. In the case of online data streams where the individual class distribution does not remain stationary incremental learning is used [9]. The approach usually taken to capture non-stationarity is to take a time window or weigh the data depending on age or relevance. The size of the window tries to balance the adaptivity and generalization of the classifier [19]. The concept-adapting very fast decision tree learner [8] applies the very fast decision tree learner [4] to build the model incrementally using a sliding window of fixed size. Techniques to dynamically decide the window horizon to incorporate the relevance of the data stream have been proposed in [2]. Support Vector Machines (SVMs) have been used with a dynamic window size in [10]. The Incremental On Line Information Network [3] dynamically adjusts the window size and training frequency based on statistical measures.

In above methods the solution is to learn a classifier that forgets its past and learns the new distribution based on the changed concepts. This model is not suited in the call center conversation model where the document is evolving but a clear intent has not been established. Evolving the current state of classifier as more data streams in becomes necessary. To the best of our knowledge we are not aware of any prior work that looks at issues related to automatically finding intent points in real time conversations.

3. CLASSIFYING A CONVERSATION IN REAL-TIME

The primary challenge faced by AgentAid is to identify a particular conversational segment and classify it in realtime. Often the boundaries of these segments are fuzzy. For any real time call analysis, determining these boundaries quickly and effectively and making a classification decision is very important. The difficulty is compounded by the fact that segment boundaries are not available even at training time and often vary from call to call. In practice class labels for these particular segments are available only at the call level (i.e. entire document level) during training time. These labels are usually generated by contact center quality analysts as a post operational quality check exercise. The analysts after hearing portions of the call provide labeling at the call level only. In order to provide real time assistance to the agent we have to identify call segments and classify them as quickly as possible with high confidence. In the following section we describe an entropy based approach that identifies call segment boundaries (intent points) at which customer's intent changes even when no segment boundary information is available at training time. We further propose to use the intent points as a feedback loop to retrain the classifier on partial call segments so as to improve the accuracy of the classifier.

The Problem: In our system conversations of contact center agents are passed in real time through an ASR system which outputs streaming text corresponding to a transcription of the conversation. At the end of every speaker utterance the ASR outputs the word uttered by the speaker [6]. Hence, at a given time t_i the transcript of the conversation till t_i is available. When such text is passed to a classifier at the end of every word the classifier potentially has a new decision. It can alter the estimated confidence about the customer's intent at t_{i-1} or it can detect a completely new intent. We assume that words in a conversation $w_1 \ldots w_n$ are generated at time stamps $t_1 \ldots t_n$. Our classifier makes the decision based on the conditional probability model $p(C_x/a_1, a_2, \ldots, a_n)$ where $\hat{A} = a_1 \ldots a_n$ are features derived from the incoming words $w_1 \ldots w_n$ in the conversation and C_x takes on a value from the set of class labels $\mathcal{C}$. It is important to note that the features $\hat{A}$, necessary for classification, could all have been collected before the call reaches its end. In effect this means that even a partial call may be sufficient for the classifier to make a confident decision. Below we first define an *intent point* and then formally state the problem.

Intent Point: is the time instance t when the classifier has the least uncertainty $U(s_t)$ about the *intent category* to assign to the incoming conversation $s_t = w_1, w_2, \ldots, w_t$. Any decision made before or after this point has non-decreasing uncertainty.

Problem Definition: In text classification for (streaming) conversational text the intent identification cannot wait till the complete document has been seen. Hence, in conversational text the classifier needs to take two decisions: (1) the classification decision to determine the customer's intent in the conversation (2) the point in time where to take the classification decision (determining the intent point).

4. ENTROPY BASED IDENTIFICATION OF INTENT POINTS

In information theory, the information entropy or Shannon entropy of a random variable X is the measure of uncertainty associated with X. The information entropy $H(X)$ of a discrete random variable X, that can take values in the set $\{x_1, x_2, \ldots, x_n\}$ is defined to be

$$H(X) = E(I(X)) = \sum_{i=1}^{n} p(x_i) log_2 \left(\frac{1}{p(x_i)}\right) = -\sum_{i=1}^{n} p(x_i) log_2(p(x_i)) \quad (1)$$

where, $I(X)$ is the self information of X, which is itself a random variable and $p(x_i)$ is the probability mass function of X.

Let C_x be the class predicted for an instance x by a probabilistic classifier such as logistic regression [13]. C_x takes on a value from the set of class labels $\mathcal{C}$. The classifier associates a distribution with C_x. We use entropy of the class random variable C_x to measure the uncertainty $U(x)$ associated with the classification of x.

$$U(x) = -\sum_{C_x \ in\ \mathcal{C}} p(C_x) log_2(p(C_x)) \quad (2)$$

where, $p(C_x)$ is the posterior probability of class C_x for the instance x as predicted by the probabilistic classifier. A high value of $U(x)$ implies that the classifier is uncertain about the classification of instance x.

We make use of this uncertainty measure for determining the text segment that must be chosen from the test document to determine its class. To make computations feasible, we restrict the choice of text segments to multiples of units that are sentences. Further, we restrict the choice of segments to those that start at the beginning of the conversation. We refer to the segment comprising the first k sentences from a conversation S as s_k. For instance, given the conversation in Figure 1 we consider the following as candidate segments

$s_1 =$
<text name="Agent">Welcome to RentABC helpdesk</text>
$s_2 =$
<text name="Agent">Welcome to RentABC helpdesk< /text>
<text name="Customer">Hi</text>
$s_3 =$
<text name="Agent">Welcome to RentABC helpdesk</text>
<text name="Customer">Hi</text>
<text name="Agent">How can i be of help today ?</text>

Given a test conversation S consisting of N sentences, we consider two methods for determining its true class $C(S)$ on online streaming text

GlobalEntropy: This method is applicable when the entire conversation is made available before-hand, and the task is to determine segment that best determines the class label for the conversation. The best segment is determined by computing the uncertainty $U(S_i)$ of every segment s_i, $1 \leq i \leq N$ and finding the segment that has the lowest uncertainty.

$$C(S, GlobalEntropy) = C(s_k) \quad where\ s_k = \underset{s_i,\ 1 \leq i \leq N}{argmin}\ U(s_i) \quad (3)$$

where, $C(S, GlobalEntropy)$ is the class determined for the test instance S using the $GlobalEntropy$ method and $C(s_k)$ is the class determined for segment s_k using the probabilistic classifier that is being used. Further we define the quantity *Global Test Ratio* for a call as the ratio of $\frac{k}{N}$.

LocalEntropy: This method is applicable when the conversation is made available in a streaming manner and the task is to classify the conversation as quickly as possible. This method computes the uncertainty for the segment that has been seen so far and as soon as the uncertainty increases, it determines the class label based on the segment till the previous time instance.

$$C(S, LocalEntropy) = C(s_k) \quad where\ U(s_k) < U(s_{k+1}) \quad (4)$$

where, $C(S, LocalEntropy)$ is the class determined for the test instance S using the $LocalEntropy$ method. Further we define the quantity *Local Test Ratio* for a call as the ratio of $\frac{k}{N}$.

4.1 Incremental Classification

With streaming text the classifier incrementally updates its decisions. At every segment, the classifier has a decision, $p(C_x)$, and an associated Entropy value, $U(x)$. At some point into the stream the classifier has to decide on the "true" class. The relative entropy over the stream determines the point at which to make this decision. While we have presented our explanation based on a segment level stream it also holds for a word stream. It is possible that the LocalEntropy based segment detection may get stuck in a local minima, which can be determined by checking whether the LocalEntropy again dips after n words. If it does not dip we declare the decision at minima point. If a new minima is encountered in the look ahead zone we update the minima point and again look ahead.

4.2 Designing Segment Classifiers

We have so far taken the approach of building a classifier on the complete call (i.e. document) and then using the entropy to make decisions on partial documents. Below we consider an alternate model where the classifier learnt using partial data itself with the hope that it will perform better. Basically, we argue that depending on the class labels different portions of the call may be important. To classify whether the agent opens the call in a proper way, a classifier built on just the first portion of the call is sufficient. However, for separating calls where credit card details are asked versus those where the customer agrees to pay on delivery, the middle segment of the call may be important. So the same call may need to be classified into these different classes, where different classifiers can come into play on different segments of the call.

4.2.1 Order of Appearance of Features

The text stream for a conversation is non-stationary therefore features for specific tasks are limited to portions of the call. So for example, in most calls the features relating to greeting will occur at the beginning of the call and features relating to types of payment may appear in another portion of the call. The classifier makes a decision based on the conditional model $p(C_x/a_1, \ldots, a_n)$.

4.2.2 Incremental Learning

Learning a classifier on streaming text would mean that the classifier is updated with each new feature that appears. Earlier we hypothesized that a classifier built using the whole call reaches a "true" decision after seeing just a fraction of the call. This implies that the features needed for the classifier have all been collected at this point in the call which could be a fraction of the complete call. Given a collection T consisting of m conversations, we use the following method for determining the segment s_k that should be used for training the classifier:

TrainingCutOffPoint: The cut off segment is determined by computing the *Global Test Ratio*, G, for each call in the collection T. Based on this ratio we select $s_k = G \times N$ from each call to train the classifier.

4.3 Overcoming Errors in Transcript

The ability of our solution to suggest entities of interest is therefore dependent on how well it can handle the noise in the input. Generally, ASR systems are known to have 30-40% error in transcription of service desk conversations. ASRs have three components - *An acoustic model* that works at the level of phonemic sounds (sub word), a *lexical model* that defines the vocabulary and models how each word is formed from the phonetic sounds comprising it and a *language model* that organizes the words to model the structure of the language. A speech signal is converted into a sequence of words based on a search that is constrained using these three components [17]. ASR systems typically use a lexicon of over 60,000 words and the models are trained using a few hundred hours of speech data. Also the language models are modified to take into account the domain specific features [18]. For example, in calls relating to an IT help desk, there will be a lot of computer specific words, and these words are given higher weights.

Since, AgentAid is only focussing on the noun phrases, only errors introduced in the noun phrase transcription would affect the system. Moreover, as explained above, a domain specific vocabulary or controlled vocabulary can be used to tune the language model of the ASR to perform better for words appearing in the given vocabulary. Since, we are only interested in noun-phrases appearing in the transactional database of a particular business, we can build a business specific controlled vocabulary and tune the ASR systems to reduce error. Such vocabularies can be modified in time to reflect popular terms based on call transcription logs.

An added advantage of using a controlled vocabulary is the ability to overcome spelling errors in the transcript. Spelling errors can be reduced by consulting the controlled vocabulary and checking for similarity between the transcribed term and any element of the vocabulary. In our implementation, we use a graded *Levenshtein distance* [1] measure to map terms in transcript to those in the vocabulary. The grading is dependent on the length of the word.

5. RESULTS AND DISCUSSION

In the following, we present results of evaluations done to assess the Decision Module's effectiveness in detecting intent points during real-time audio conversations. Below we first describe the dataset used for evaluation and then present results of various evaluations done using it.

5.1 Datasets

We obtained automatic transcriptions of contact center dialogs from a car rental process using an ASR.The speech recognition system was trained on 40 hours of data comprising of calls sampled at 8KHz. The resultant transcriptions had a word error rate of about 40%. We used 527 calls from the car rental process for our experiments. These calls were labeled according to two criteria - 1) based on the reason for *non-booking* by a customer and 2) based on reason for call or *call-opening*. Non-booking here relates to a call where the customer didn't rent a car. A total of 9 labels such as *shopping around, high rates etc.* were assigned by contact center quality analyst as reasons for non booking. We call this the *non-booking* data-set. The second criteria was a *binary labeling* based on whether call was made for booking or to find out the rates. We refer to this as the *call-opening* data-set.

We also used a publicly available data-set, the *20NewsGroups* data-set to simulate a real-time stream and test our methods in a non car rental setting. We chose two classes, *talk.politics.mideast* and *talk.politics.guns*, and picked all the postings within these classes that had approximately 30 to 50 sentences. This resulted in 285 files being used for 'mideast' class and 327 files for 'guns' class. We appended 65 to 85 sentences to these postings by randomly picking these sentences from the remaining 18 classes of 20newsgroup data. The sentences for the postings are treated as being generated in a streaming manner. Construction of dataset in this way results in the decision boundary of the 'mideast' and 'guns' classes to be between 0.26 (30/115) and 0.43 (50/115) of the normalized duration of the call.

5.2 Entropy Based Selection of Intent Point

We conducted classification experiments for the tasks of *call opening intent point identification* using the *call-opening* data-set and *non-booking intent point identification* using the *non-booking* data-set. The objective was to evaluate how the different methods proposed in the paper perform for the intent point detection and intent classification task i.e. categorizing the intent behind non-booking (high rates, unavailability etc) and for the call-opening in-

[1]The Levenshtein distance between two strings is given by the minimum number of operations needed to transform one string into the other, where an operation is an insertion, deletion, or substitution of a single character.

tent detection i.e. whether the customer's intent is to do a booking or find out rates. We trained a logistic regression classifier[2] on complete call transcripts of all the 527 calls for each task. During the testing phase instead of classifying the complete call we classified the call incrementally where each unit of increment was a sentence as described in Section 4. For each such incremental segment, $s_1 \ldots s_k$, we computed the entropy.

Table 1: Accuracies for classifiers trained on different fractions of the call for call-opening intent classification

Call Fraction	Baseline Accuracy	Global Accuracy	Local Accuracy	Best Accuracy
0.2	70.96	80.64	80.64	93.54
0.4	70.96	87.09	87.09	96.77
0.6	74.19	80.64	77.42	93.55
0.8	70.97	80.64	77.42	93.54
1.0	77.41	80.64	80.64	83.87

5.3 Intent Classifier Design

In Tables 1, 2 and 3 we show the various accuracies for classifiers that have been trained on fractions of the call for call-opening intent classification, non-booking intent classification and 20newsgroup classification respectively. *Baseline accuracy* represents the case when the testing is done on the complete call. *Global accuracy* represents the accuracy when the segment is selected based on GlobalEntropy. The average global test ratio represents the fraction of the call where the global minima of the entropy lies on an average for the whole set. *Local accuracy* is what is actually used in real-time classification of conversational text. It is the accuracy when the segment is selected based on LocalEntropy. The average local test ratio is the fraction of the call one needs to see before making a classification decision. The *best accuracy* is the maximum classification accuracy for different segment lengths. The best accuracy is arrived at by computing the classification scores for different segment lengths and selecting that segment which gives the highest accuracy over the whole collection. The best accuracy is the upper bound that can be obtained for the given task using a given classifier. In all the tables we see that the best accuracy peaks when the classifier is trained on a fraction of the call.

Table 2: Accuracies for classifiers trained on different fractions of the call for non-booking intent classification

Call Fraction	Baseline Accuracy	Global Accuracy	Local Accuracy	Best Accuracy
0.2	27.50	42.5	42.5	67.5
0.4	40.00	55.00	50.00	70.00
0.6	52.50	55.00	55.00	77.50
0.8	45.00	50.00	50.00	67.50
1.0	52.50	55.00	55.00	67.50

5.4 Comparison with Classification by Humans

We also compared the entropy based intent point selection with the human decision making process. Given the streaming text output from the conversation, a human listener would perform the

[2]We chose logistic regression as a representative since it performs very well in practice and has been shown to be closely related to SVM [20] and AdaBoost [5].

Table 3: Accuracies for classifiers trained on different fractions of 20 NewsGroups Data

Call Fraction	Baseline Accuracy	Global Accuracy	Local Accuracy	Best Accuracy
0.2	87.50	91.07	91.07	96.42
0.4	89.28	92.85	91.07	96.42
0.6	94.64	96.42	96.42	98.21
0.8	96.42	96.42	96.42	98.21
1.0	89.28	92.85	91.07	96.42

Table 4: Comparing Intent Point Determination by Humans and Entropy Technique

Task	Av. Global Test Ratio	Human Test Ratio
call-opening intent Classification	0.47	0.25
non-booking intent Classification	0.60	0.5

classification after she has gathered enough evidence. For the call-opening intent classification task this decision point is at 0.25 and for non-booking intent classification task it is at 0.5. The human reaches close to 100% classification accuracy at this intent point. Also after this the classification accuracy remains at 100%. This is because once the human believes she has all the evidence required to reach a decision she does not change her mind. However, as shown in the results earlier our classifier achieves a high classification accuracy close to the intent point but after this intent point the accuracy actually goes down. In Table 4 we show the comparison between the intent point for classification done by a human and that determined by our method. Several observations can be made, namely - 1) A human classifier needs to see less of the call to make a final decision regarding the intent (i.e. the human intent point is earlier than that of our method). 2) For our method the classification accuracy is highest near the intent point and lesser before and after the intent point and 3) For a human classifier the classification accuracy reaches 100% at the intent point and remains at 100% even as more of the conversation is seen.

5.5 Higher Accuracy of ASR system with Controlled Vocabulary

The accuracy of a transcript is characterized by its *word error rate (WER)*. WER is measured as $\frac{S+D+I}{N} \times 100$ where N is the total number of words in the test set, and S, I and D are the total number of substitution, insertion, and deletion errors respectively. We also defined two other metrics, *Keyword Error Rate (KER)* and *Controlled Keyword Error Rate (CKER)*. Both KER and CKER are estimated similar to WER but differ over the set of words used for the measurement. KER is measured using all noun phrases appearing in the test set while CKER is measured using the noun phrases that appear in the controlled vocabulary. For our evaluation we randomly selected 501 call transcripts from the initial set of 527 call transcripts obtained from the car rental process. We looked at the Yahoo Auto Database [3] to determine a possible set of 300 words that could appear in a controlled vocabulary about cars.

We then measured, WER, KER and CKER using the automatically and manually generated transcripts. In addition, we also measured WER– where all stopwords were removed and CKER+ where we considered terms with a graded Levenshtein distance of 1 from the controlled vocabulary as similar to term in the vocabulary.

[3]http://autos.yahoo.com

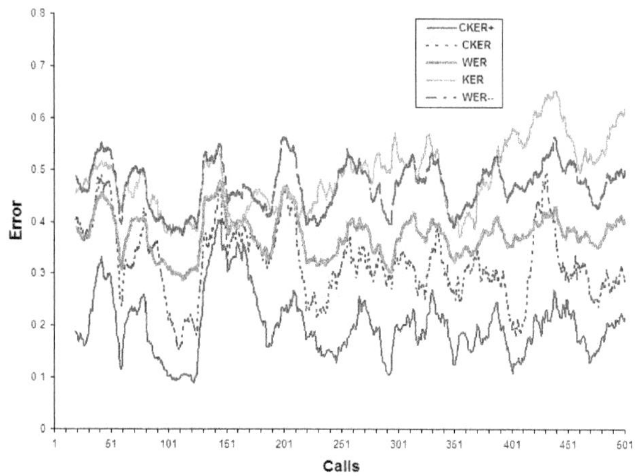

Figure 2: Comparison of WER, KER and CKER

Figure 2 compares the various error measurements for all the calls in our dataset. As expected the WER rate is around 30-35% for all the calls. However, CKER performs much better (25-30% error) than all the above and validates the assertion that ASR systems when tuned to domain specific words do improve the transcription accuracy.

6. CONCLUSION

In this paper we identify the need for identifying customer intent during a real-time call center conversation. We then presented details of the *AgentAid* conversation management system which prompts agents, at appropriate points during a real-time audio call, with information which is useful for successfully closing the call. Evaluation results demonstrate the ability of our system to efficiently and effectively identify customer intent, extract relevant information from backend database and prompt the agent about next steps. The results show our approach is able to overcome the errors introduced by Automatic Speech Recognition systems and is able to perform under strict response time constraints. To the best of our knowledge, AgentAid is the only conversation management system currently available for helping an agent during a real-time conversation. It can be implemented with minimal domain-specific setup and used by an agent with minimal training leading to reduced overall agent training costs.

7. REFERENCES

[1] S. Agarwal, S. Godbole, D. Punjani, S. Roy. 2007. How Much Noise Is Too Much: A Study in Automatic Text Classification. *Proceedings of IEEE International Conference on Data Mining*, Omaha, Nebraska, 3–12.

[2] C. Aggarwal, J. Han, J. Wang, P. S. Yu. 2004. On Demand classification of data streams. *Proceedings of the International Conferece on Knowledge Discovery and Data Mining*, Seattle, USA, 503–508.

[3] L. Cohen, G. Avrahami, M. Last, A. Kandel, O. Kipersztok. 2005. Incremental classification of nonstationary data streams. *ECML/PKDD-2005 International Workshop on Knowledge Discovery from Data Streams*, Portugal.

[4] P. Domingos, G. Hulten. 2000. Mining High-Speed Data Streams. *Proceedings of International Conference on Knowledge Discovery and Data Mining*, 71–80.

[5] Y. Freund, R. E. Schapire. 1996. Experiments in new boosting algorithm. *Prodeedings of the Thirteenth International Conference on Machine Learning*, 148–156.

[6] J. R. Glass, T. J. Hazen, I. L. Hetherington. 1999. Real-time telephone-based speech recognition in the Jupiter domain. *Proceedings of IEEE International Conference on Acoustics, Speech, and Signal Processing*, Phoenix, Arizona, 61–64.

[7] M. A. Hearst. 1994. Multi-paragraph segmentation of expository text. *Proceedings of IEEE International Conference on Acoustics, Speech, and Signal Processing*, Phoenix, Arizona, 61–64.

[8] G. Hulten, L. Spencer, P. Domingos. 2001. Mining Time-Changing Data Streams. *Proceedings of the Annual Meeting of the Association for Computer Linguistics (ACL)*, 9–16.

[9] I. Katakis, G. Tsoumakas, I. Vlahavas. 2006. Dynamic feature space and incremental feature selection for the classification of textual data streams. *ECML/PKDD-2006 International Workshop on Knowledge Discovery from Data Streams*, Berlin, Germany, 107–116.

[10] R. Klinkenberg, T. Joachims. 2000.Detecting concept drift with support vector machines. *Proceedings of International Conference on Machine Learning*, 487–494.

[11] K. Kummamuru, Deepak P., S. Roy, L. V. Subramaniam. 2008.Unsupervised Segmentation of Conversational Transcripts. *Proceedings of SIAM International Conference on Data Mining*, 834–845.

[12] H.-K. J. Kuo, C.-H. Lee. 2003. Discriminative training of natural language call routers. *IEEE Trans. on Speech and Audio Processing*, 11(1), 24–35.

[13] N. Landwehr, M. Hall, F. Eibe. 2003. Logistic Model Trees. *Proceedings of European Conference on Machine Learning*, Cavtat-Dubrovnik, Croatia, 241–252.

[14] Y. Park. 2007. Automatic call section segmentation for contact-center calls. *Proceedings of International Conference on Knowledge Discovery and Data Mining*, Lisbon, Portugal, 117–126.

[15] H. Takeuchi, L. V. Subramaniam, T. Nasukawa, S. Roy. 2007. Automatic Identification of Important Segments and Expressions for Mining of Business-Oriented Conversations at Contact Centers. *Proceedings of Empirical Methods on Natural Language Processing*, Prague, Czech Republic.

[16] M. Tang, B. Pellom, K. Hacioglu. 2003. Calltype classification and unsupervised training for the call center domain. *Proceedings of the Automatic Speech Recog. and Understanding Workshop*, St. Thomas, U S Virgin Islands, 204–208.

[17] M. Padmanabhan, G. Saon, J. Huang, B. Kingsbury, and L. Mangu. Automatic Speech Recognition Performance on a Voicemail Transcription Task. *IEEE Trans. on Speech and Audio Processing*, 10(7):433-442, 2002.

[18] H. Chevalier, C. Ingold, C. Kunz, C. Moore, C. Roven, J. Yamron, B. Baker, P. Bamberg, S. Bridle, T. Bruce, and A. Weader. Large-vocabulary speech recognition in specialized domains. *ICASSP-95*, May 9-12, 1995, Detroit, MI, USA.

[19] G. Widmer, M. Kubat. 1996. Learning in the presence of concept drift and hidden contexts. *Machine Learning*, 23(1), 69–101.

[20] V. N. Vapnik. 1995. *The nature of statistical learning theory*. Springer-Verlag, New York.

[21] U. Nambiar, H. Gupta, R. Balakrishnan and M. Mohania. 2008. Helping Satisfy Multiple Objectives during a Service Desk Conversation. *SIGMOD*, June 9-12, 2008, Vancouver, BC, Canada.

[22] T. Mitchell. 1997 Machine Learning. *McGraw Hill*.

Sparse Structured Probabilistic Projections for Factorized Latent Spaces

Xinquan Qu, Xinlei Chen
State Key Lab of CAD&CG
College of Computer Science, Zhejiang University
Hangzhou, China
{04dzjsqxq,endernewton}@gmail.com

ABSTRACT

Building a common representation for several related data sets is an important problem in multi-view learning. CCA and its extensions have shown that they are effective in finding the shared variation among all data sets. However, these models generally fail to exploit the common structure of the data when the views are with private information. Recently, methods explicitly modeling the information into shared part and private parts have been proposed, but they presume to know the prior knowledge about the latent space, which is usually impossible to obtain. In this paper, we propose a probabilistic model, which could simultaneously learn the structure of the latent space whilst factorize the information correctly, therefore the prior knowledge of the latent space is unnecessary. Furthermore, as a probabilistic model, our method is able to deal with missing data problem in a natural way. We show that our approach attains the performance of state-of-art methods on the task of human pose estimation when the motion capture view is completely missing, and significantly improves the inference accuracy with only a few observed data.

Categories and Subject Descriptors

I.2.6 [**Artificial Intelligence**]: Learning; I.5.1 [**Pattern Recognition**]: Models *Statistical*

General Terms

Algorithms, Experimentation, Performance

Keywords

Multi-view Learning, Factorized Latent Space, Sparse Structured Projections

1. INTRODUCTION

In machine learning, we usually meet cases where there are two or more disparate but related data sets. For example, the human pose data is composed of video information and motion capture information; in image retrieval applications, the data is consisted of various image features and surrounding texts. Effective consolidation of these data sets has been proved to be beneficial for many computer vision tasks. Particularly in this paper, we define data consolidation as to find a common latent representation for all data sets. Furthermore, this problem appears naturally in the multi-view learning problem, where the multiple data sets are refereed as different views of one object.

Canonical Correlation Analysis (CCA) aims to find linear transformations which maximize two views' correlation. And there has been work to put CCA into the more flexible probabilistic framework [2]. Other extensions include learning nonlinear transformations [9] in the RKHS, and learning a sparse projection matrix for easy interpretation [6]. Beside models based on CCA, there have been several nonlinear methods proposed [15, 4, 13, 17], which may be more robust than Kernel CCA [9] in noisy cases. However, they do not capture the view-dependent information, and therefore either totally fail to represent them, or mix them with the information shared by all views.

Some methods explicitly accounting the dependencies and independencies have been proposed. They factorize the latent space into shared part across all views and private part of each view. Among these approaches, some could be characterized as deterministic type [14, 7], and are proposed for predicting missing view based on observed views. One limitation of these methods is that they presume to know at least one complete view. Furthermore, these approaches all fail to utilize the partial observed information in views.

On the other hand, methods on factorizing the latent space into shared part and private parts in a probabilistic framework have been proposed [3, 1, 8]. Particularly, [8] firstly extracts the shared information across views by CCA, then learns the private information from the residuals. And the work of [3] can be regarded as its kennel extension. Since these methods use CCA or NCCA to capture the shared information, they inevitably inherit the defats of CCA. Another approach [1] imposes a sparse structure on the projection matrices for better interpretation, but this assumption may not work for missing view prediction task. What's more, these methods generally assume to know the

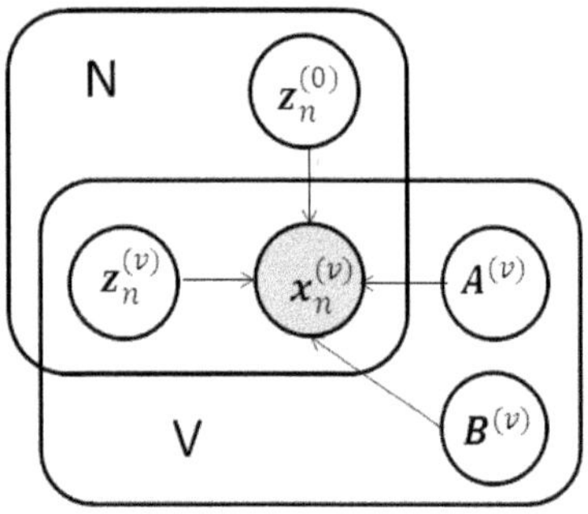

The corresponding graphical model for the latent variable learning of data $\mathbf{x}_n$. The data in each view $\mathbf{x}_n^{(v)}$ is a mix of two independent continuous components, the shared one $\mathbf{z}_n^{(0)}$ and the private one $\mathbf{z}_n^{(v)}$.

Figure 1: Graphical Model

dimension of the latent space, which is impractical in real-world applications.

In this paper, we build our model in the framework of the probabilistic interpretation of CCA, which is outlined by [2] and further extended by [8, 1]. Compared with previous approaches towards shared/private factorization, our model has three main contributions: (1). while previous extensions of CCA are generally sensitive to highly correlated noise, our model is more robust; (2). our model could learn the dimension of the latent space automatically without prior knowledge; (3). as a probabilistic model, our approach has an innate mechanism to deal with missing data problem. Detailed model will discussed in the later sections.

The remainder of this paper is organized as follows. In the next section, our model will be introduced. A parameter estimation and inference procedure will be provided in section 3 . In Section 4, we will give a through review of related methods. Section 5 is our experimental part. Finally, we will give the conclusion and discuss the future work in Section 6.

2. STRUCTURED PROJECTIONS FOR FACTORIZED LATENT SPACES

2.1 Proposed Model

The graphical model of our model is shown in Fig. 1. It is capable of dealing with the multi-view case, and explicitly considers the effects of private information in each view. Each data $\mathbf{x}_n$ has V representations as $\mathbf{x}_n^{(1)}, \mathbf{x}_n^{(2)}, \ldots, \mathbf{x}_n^{(V)}$. Furthermore, the data $\mathbf{x}_n$ in each view $\mathbf{x}_n^{(v)} \in \mathbb{R}^{P_v}$ is generated as a mix of a shared latent continuous vector $\mathbf{z}_n^{(0)} \in \mathbb{R}^{D_0}$, and a view-dependent (private) continuous latent vector $\mathbf{z}_n^{(v)} \in \mathbb{R}^{D_v}, v \in \{1, 2, \ldots, V\}$, such that:

$$\begin{aligned} &\mathbf{x}_n^{(v)} = \mathbf{A}^{(v)}\mathbf{z}_n^{(0)} + \mathbf{B}^{(v)}\mathbf{z}_n^{(v)} + \mu^{(v)} + \varepsilon^{(v)} \in \mathbb{R}^{P_v} \\ &\mathbf{A}^{(v)} \in \mathbb{R}^{P_v \times D_0}, \mathbf{B}^{(v)} \in \mathbb{R}^{P_v \times D_v} \\ &\mathbf{z}_n^{(0)} \sim \mathcal{N}(\mathbf{0}_{D_0}, \Lambda^{(0)}), \mathbf{z}_n^{(v)} \sim \mathcal{N}(\mathbf{0}_{D_v}, \Lambda^{(v)}), \end{aligned} \tag{1}$$

where $\mathbf{A}^{(v)}$ and $\mathbf{B}^{(v)}$ are projection matrices, $\mu^{(v)}$ is the view dependent mean, and $\varepsilon^{(v)} \sim \mathcal{N}(\mathbf{0}_{P_v}, \sigma^{(v)}\mathbf{I}_{P_v})$ is the white noise in view v. Here $\mathbf{0}_{p\times q}/\mathbf{1}_{p\times q}$ is the all-zero/all-one matrix in $\mathbb{R}^{p\times q}$, and $\mathbf{I}_p$ is the identity matrix in $\mathbb{R}^{p\times p}$, respectively.

To obtain a low dimensional latent variable, we choose a simple yet effective way as to impose a column sparsity structure on the projection matrices. In this way, with sufficient number of columns, the model can automatically determine the number of nonzero columns of $\mathbf{A}^{(v)}$,$\mathbf{B}^{(v)}$ and then adapt them to the data. To achieve the column sparsity, we impose an Automatic Relevance Determination (ARD) [18] prior on the columns of $\mathbf{A}^{(v)}$,$\mathbf{B}^{(v)}$ as follows:

$$\begin{aligned} &\mathbf{A}_j^{(v)} \sim \mathcal{N}(\mathbf{0}_{P_v}, \rho_j^{(v)}\mathbf{I}_{P_v}), \qquad j \in \{1, 2, \ldots, D_0\} \\ &\mathbf{B}_j^{(v)} \sim \mathcal{N}(\mathbf{0}_{P_v}, \gamma_j^{(v)}\mathbf{I}_{P_v}), \qquad j \in \{1, 2, \ldots, D_v\} \end{aligned}$$

On the other hand, we directly impose the ARD prior on the latent variables $\mathbf{z}^{(v)}$ to make them low dimensional. Therefore, the covariance matrices $\mathbf{\Lambda}^{(0)}, \mathbf{\Lambda}^{(1)}, \ldots, \mathbf{\Lambda}^{(V)}$ are diagonals. Note that if we restrict them to be nonzero diagonal, then the model reduces to Factor analysis. Furthermore, if we set $\mathbf{\Lambda}^{(V)}$ as identity, then the model reduces to Probabilistic PCA[19].

If the initial dimension of latent variables is set to be large, the model tends to over-fit since the residual variance $\sigma^{(v)}$ will approach zero. As a remedy to this problem, we impose a conjugate gamma prior on the inverse residual variance as $(\sigma^{(v)})^{-1} \sim \mathcal{G}(a, b)$. Here (a, b) could be regarded as regularization parameters.

2.2 Compact Reformulation of the Model

Before we give a detailed parameter estimation and inference procedure in section 3, we would like to first rewrite the above model in a more compact form. We denote the data in each view, the projection matrices and the latent variables as follows:

$$\begin{aligned} &\mathbf{X}^{(v)} = \left(\mathbf{x}_1^{(v)}, \mathbf{x}_2^{(v)}, \ldots, \mathbf{x}_N^{(v)}\right), \\ &\mathbf{C}^{(v)} = \left(\mathbf{A}^{(v)}, \mathbf{0}_{P_1\times D_1}, \ldots, \mathbf{B}^{(v)}, \ldots, \mathbf{0}_{P_V\times D_V}\right), \\ &\mathbf{z}_n = \left(\mathbf{z}_n^{(0)T}, \mathbf{z}_n^{(1)T}, \ldots, \mathbf{z}_n^{(V)T}\right)^T, \\ &\mathbf{Z} = (\mathbf{z}_1, \mathbf{z}_2, \ldots, \mathbf{z}_N), \end{aligned}$$

where N is the number of observations. The generative model can then be reformulated as follows:

$$\begin{aligned} &\mathbf{z}_n \sim \mathcal{N}(\mathbf{0}_D, \mathbf{\Lambda}), \\ &\mathbf{x}_n^{(v)}|\mathbf{z}_n \sim \mathcal{N}\left(\mathbf{C}^{(v)}\mathbf{z}_n, \sigma^{(v)}\mathbf{I}_P\right), \\ &\mathbf{\Lambda} = diag\left(\Lambda^{(0)}, \Lambda^{(1)}, \ldots, \Lambda^{(V)}\right) \\ &\mathbf{C}_j^{(v)} \sim \mathcal{N}\left(\mathbf{0}, \lambda_j^{(v)}\mathbf{I}\right), \quad j \in \{1, 2, \ldots, D\}, \end{aligned} \tag{2}$$

where $D = \sum_{v=0}^{V} D_v$ and $P = \sum_{v=1}^{V} P_v$. Note that we incorporate the column variance ρ and γ into τ. Additionally, we abuse the notation that if $\mathbf{C}_j^{(v)} = 0$, then $\lambda_j^{(v)} = 0$. The reason for this notation is that, $\mathbf{C}^{(v)}$ is initially dense, and we wish to learn a sparse column projection by setting columns not fitting to data to zero.

3. PARAMETER ESTIMATION AND INFERENCE

In this section we first derive an algorithm to estimate the parameters and latent variables. After that we give a inference procedure in case that some data of the measurements are missing.

3.1 Parameter Estimation

A traditional approach for parameter estimation is the renowned Expectation-Maximization (EM) algorithm, in which we treat $\mathbf{Z}$ as the missing variables, and other random variables as parameters to be estimated. We however, choose to directly take the Maximum Posteriori (MAP) of both $\mathbf{Z}$, the projection matrices $\mathbf{C}^{(v)}$ and the residual variance $\sigma^{(v)}$[1].

Now we write the log-likelihood function as follows:

$$\begin{aligned} L &= \log P(\mathbf{X}, \mathbf{Z}, \mathbf{C}, \Lambda, \tau, \sigma) \\ &= \sum_{v=1}^{V}\sum_{n=1}^{N} \log P\left(\mathbf{x}_n^{(v)}|\mathbf{z}_n, \mathbf{C}^{(v)}, \sigma^{(v)}\right) \\ &+ \sum_{i=1}^{D} \log P(\mathbf{Z}_{i,:}) + \sum_{v=1}^{V}\sum_{j=1}^{D} \log P(\mathbf{C}_j^{(v)}) + \sum_{v=1}^{V} \log P(\sigma^{(v)}), \end{aligned} \tag{3}$$

where $\mathbf{Z}_{i,:}$ denotes the i-th row of $\mathbf{Z}$. And each item expand as:

$$\begin{aligned} &\log P(\mathbf{x}_n^{(v)}|\mathbf{z}_n, \mathbf{C}^{(v)}, \sigma^{(v)}) = \\ &-\frac{1}{2}\log(2\pi) - \frac{1}{2}P_v \log(\sigma^{(v)}) - \frac{1}{2\sigma^{(v)}}\left\|\mathbf{x}_n^{(v)} - \mu^{(v)} + \mathbf{C}^{(v)}\mathbf{z}_n\right\|^2 \\ &\log P(\mathbf{Z}_{i,:}) = -\frac{1}{2}N\log(2\pi) - \frac{1}{2}N\log(\lambda_i) - \frac{1}{2\lambda_i}\|\mathbf{Z}_{i,:}\|^2 \\ &\log P(\mathbf{C}_j^{(v)}) = -\frac{1}{2}P_v \log(2\pi) - \frac{1}{2}P_v\log(\tau_j^{(v)}) - \frac{1}{2\tau_j^{(v)}}\left\|\mathbf{C}_j^{(v)}\right\|^2 \\ &\log P(\sigma^{(v)}) = -(a-1)\log\left(\sigma^{(v)}\right) + a\log(b) - \frac{b}{\sigma^{(v)}} - \Gamma(a). \end{aligned} \tag{4}$$

We directly use maximum likelihood to estimate λ and τ. By setting the derivative to be zero, we have:

$$\begin{aligned} \frac{dL}{d\lambda_i} = 0 \Rightarrow \quad & \lambda_i = \frac{1}{N}\|\mathbf{Z}_{i,:}\|^2 \\ \frac{dL}{d\tau_j^{(v)}} = 0 \Rightarrow \quad & \tau_j^{(v)} = \frac{1}{N}\left\|\mathbf{C}_j^{(v)}\right\|^2 \end{aligned} \tag{5}$$

Note that the above variance is directly related to the magnitude norm of rows of $\mathbf{Z}$ or columns of $\mathbf{C}$ respectively, and the ones not fitting to the data well will be driven to zero. This is the internal mechanics why our model could do automatic dimension determination.

By substituting the λ and τ in Eq.(3) with Eq.(4) and (5), and further discarding the constants, we then formulate it as a minimization problem:

$$\begin{aligned} \min_{\{\mathbf{C}^{(v)},\sigma^{(v)}\}_{v=1}^{V},\mathbf{Z}} &\sum_{v=1}^{V}(\frac{1}{2}P_v N + a - 1)\log\left(\sigma^{(v)}\right) \\ &+ \sum_{v=1}^{V}\frac{1}{\sigma^{(v)}}\left(\frac{1}{2}\left\|\mathbf{X}^{(v)} - \mu^{(v)}\mathbf{1}_{N\times P_v}^T - \mathbf{C}^{(v)}\mathbf{Z}\right\|_{Fro}^2 + b\right) \\ &+ N\sum_{i=1}^{D}\log\|\mathbf{Z}_{i,:}\| + \sum_{v=1}^{V}\sum_{j=1}^{D} P_v \log\left\|\mathbf{C}_j^{(v)}\right\|. \end{aligned} \tag{6}$$

We can directly solve problem Eq. (6) by the Majorization-Minimization (MM) algorithm [10]. For numerical stability, we can slightly modify the objective function of Eq. (6) by replacing the last two terms:

$$\begin{aligned} &N\sum_{i=1}^{D}\log\|\mathbf{Z}_{i,:}\| \to N\sum_{i=1}^{D}\log(\|\mathbf{Z}_{i,:}\| + \alpha), \\ &\sum_{v=1}^{V}\sum_{j=1}^{D} P_v \log\left\|\mathbf{C}_j^{(v)}\right\| \to \sum_{v=1}^{V} P_v \sum_{j=1}^{D}\log\left(\left\|\mathbf{C}_j^{(v)}\right\| + \alpha\right). \end{aligned} \tag{7}$$

where α is a regularization parameter. We denote the solution obtained in the t-th iteration as $\mathbf{Z}^{(t)}$, $\mathbf{C}^{(v,t)}$. In the $(t+1)$-th iteration, due to the concavity property, we can bound the last two terms in Eq. (eq:minreg) by the following inequation:

$$\begin{aligned} &\sum_{i=1}^{D}\log(\|\mathbf{Z}_{i,:}\| + \alpha) \le \\ &\quad \sum_{i=1}^{D}\left[\log\left(\left\|\mathbf{Z}_{i,:}^{(t)}\right\| + \alpha\right) - \frac{\|\mathbf{Z}_{i,:}\| - \left\|\mathbf{Z}_{i,:}^{(t)}\right\|}{\left\|\mathbf{Z}_{i,:}^{(t)}\right\| + \alpha}\right] \\ &\sum_{i=1}^{D} P_v \log\left(\left\|\mathbf{C}_j^{(v)}\right\| + \alpha\right) \le \\ &\quad \sum_{i=1}^{D} P_v\left[\log\left(\left\|\mathbf{C}_j^{(v,t)}\right\| + \alpha\right) - \frac{\left\|\mathbf{C}_j^{(v)}\right\| - \left\|\mathbf{C}_j^{(v,t)}\right\|}{\left\|\mathbf{C}_j^{(v,t)}\right\| + \alpha}\right]. \end{aligned} \tag{8}$$

Thus in the $(t+1)$-th iteration, what we need is to solve a weighted version of the Eq. (7):

$$\begin{aligned} \min_{\{\mathbf{C}^{(v)},\sigma^{(v)}\}_{v=1}^{V},\mathbf{Z}} &\sum_{v=1}^{V}(\frac{1}{2}P_v N + a - 1)\log(\sigma^{(v)}) \\ &+ \sum_{v=1}^{V}\frac{1}{\sigma^{(v)}}\left(\frac{1}{2}\left\|\mathbf{X}^{(v)} - \mu^{(v)}\mathbf{1}_{N\times P_v}^T - \mathbf{C}^{(v)}\mathbf{Z}\right\|_{Fro}^2 + b\right) \\ &+ N\sum_{i=1}^{D}\frac{\|\mathbf{Z}_{i,:}\|}{\left\|\mathbf{Z}_{i,:}^{(t)}\right\| + \alpha} + \sum_{v=1}^{V} P_v \sum_{j=1}^{D}\frac{\left\|\mathbf{C}_j^{(v)}\right\|}{\left\|\mathbf{C}_j^{(v,t)}\right\| + \alpha} \end{aligned} \tag{9}$$

According to [10], the MM algorithm is guaranteed to converge to a local optimum. In each iteration, the object function is not convex. Here we simply optimize one variable while fixing the other variables and the sub-optimization problem turns out to be convex. Moreover, note that although the optimization is not convex w.r.t. $\sigma^{(v)}$, it is convex w.r.t. its inverse.

[1]Since $\max_{\mathbf{Z}} \log P(\mathbf{X}, \mathbf{Z}) \ge E(\log P(\mathbf{X}, \mathbf{Z})|\mathbf{X})$, therefore taking the MAP of $\mathbf{Z}$ is a reasonable alternate to EM

3.2 Inference

An important application of multi-view learning is to infer unobserved views based on observed ones [7, 14]. And very frequently we may have partial information about the missing views. Unfortunately, many deterministic methods, such as [5, 14, 7] fail to utilize the partial observed data since their models can only deal with sound data. Here we treat it as a missing data problem and wish to utilize the incomplete information in inference.

We treat the latent variables $\mathbf{Z}$ and $\mu^{(v)}$ as parameters, and the missing data $\mathbf{X}_{mis}$ as latent variables. The EM algorithm is then applied. Denoting $\mathbf{X} = (\mathbf{X}_{ob}, \mathbf{X}_{mis})$, the corresponding object function is:

$$\min_{(\{\mu^{(v)}\}_{v=1}^{V}, \mathbf{Z})} \sum_{i=1}^{D} \frac{\|\mathbf{Z}_{i,:}\|^2}{\lambda_i} + \mathbb{E}_{X_{mis}}\left[\sum_{v=1}^{V} \frac{1}{2\sigma^{(v)}} \left\|\mathbf{X}^{(v)} - \mu^{(v)}\mathbf{1}_{N\times P_v}^{T} - \mathbf{C}^{(v)}\mathbf{Z}\right\|^2 \middle| \mathbf{Z}, \mathbf{X}_{ob}\right] \tag{10}$$

Note that $\mathbb{E}_{\mathbf{X}_{mis}}(\mathbf{X}_{mis}^{(v)}|\mathbf{Z}, \mathbf{X}_{ob})$ can be calculated according to $\mathbf{C}^{(v)}\mathbf{Z}$, and $\mathbb{E}_{\mathbf{X}_{mis}}(\mathbf{X}_{mis}^{(v)}\mathbf{X}_{mis}^{(v)T}|\mathbf{Z}, \mathbf{X}_{ob})$ can be deduce from $\mathbf{C}^{(v)}\mathbf{Z}\mathbf{Z}^T\mathbf{C}^{(v)}$. We omit the detailed computations here.

4. RELATED WORK

There has been some work taking emphasis on the structure of the latent space [7, 14, 3, 1, 8, 12]. That is, they all explicitly model the shared information across all views and private information for each view. Those models can all be formulated in a general generative model as

$$\mathbf{x}_n^{(v)} = f(\mathbf{z}_n^{(0)}) + g^{(v)}(\mathbf{z}_n^{(v)}) + \varepsilon^{(v)},$$

where f,$g^{(v)}$ could either be linear [7, 1, 8], or nonlinear functions, such as the functions in RKHS [3, 14, 12]. Existing work in the literature can also be characterized in two categories, namely probabilistic framework [1, 8, 12], or deterministic framework [7, 14, 3].

Both linear and kernel extensions on CCA to model the private information of views have been proposed in [3]. The key idea is that as CCA incorporates private information into the residuals, it explicitly extracts the view-dependent effects from the residuals. To be specific, it first applies CCA or kernel CCA to the data to calculate f and $\mathbf{z}_n^{(0)}$, and then optimize $g^{(v)}$ and $\mathbf{z}_n^{(v)}$ from the residuals. While it seems to be a good idea, this model inevitably inherits the drawbacks of CCA, i.e., sensitive to highly correlated noise.

Different from optimizing $f, \mathbf{z}^{(0)}$ and $g^{(v)}, \mathbf{z}^{(v)}$ step by step, a model iteratively optimizing the linear projections and latent variables has been proposed in [8]. In each inner iteration, it first models the shared information f and $\mathbf{z}^{(0)}$, and then extract the private information from the residuals. Unfortunately, this model essentially inheritress the drawbacks of CCA just as [3]. Their relationship is similar to the relationship between Maximum Likelihood (ML) and the EM optimization procedure for probabilistic CCA, therefore [8] behaves sensitively to correlated-noise as CCA.

In the model proposed by [1], the linear projection functions f and $g^{(v)}$ are simultaneously optimized. The key contribution of their model is to impose priors on the elements of projection matrices to incur sparsity, i.e. the ARD prior, which results in a model easy to interpret. However, their model only works well when the projection matrices are really sparse in the generative model, which is scarcely the case in practice. Furthermore, this model, together with the above two models all require to know the latent dimension beforehand, which is usually not possible in real applications.

The model introduced in [12] is quite similar to the kernel version proposed in [3], while it actually uses an ARD polynomial kernel function as the covariance function. Although the prior knowledge of the latent dimension is unnecessary here, the model still inherits limitations of CCA as [3, 8] do.

The model proposed by [14] encourages the private-shared factorization to be non-redundant by explicitly adding a penalty term to sKIE [17] and sGPLVM [4]. Although the resulting model has been shown to yield more accurate results in the context of human pose estimation, the optimization is computationally expensive. Furthermore, extension from two views to multiple views is non-trivial since the number of of shared/private latent spaces that need to be explicitly modeled grows exponentially with the number of views.

[7] casts the latent variable learning problem as a matrix decomposition task, and uses recent advances in the sparse coding in helping learning their representation. They introduces ℓ_p norm on the column of dictionary matrix for each view, and the ℓ_p norm also impose structured sparsity on the rows of the coefficient matrix. While this seems a good idea, their method lacks mechanism to deal with views with missing data, and thus implicitly require the training views to be complete. Furthermore, in case there is auxiliary information of target view, i.e. data motion view is partly available in human pose estimation, it is not straightforward to incorporate them into the inference process and thus the result is doomed to degrade.

Compared with the above models, our method avoids the noise sensitiveness of CCA. Furthermore, it can automatically detect the latent dimension without prior information. Finally, our method could deal with missing data in a natural way, which is either critical or beneficial in many multi-view learning applications.

5. EXPERIMENTS

In this section, we conduct experiments to evaluate the effectiveness of our approach. We first give synthetic examples for illustration of the properties of our method, and then apply it to the real application of human pose estimation.

5.1 Latent Space Factorization

To study the property of our method, we conducted the same toy experiment in [14, 7]. We show that our method can also correctly factorize a latent space into shared part and private part, even when the noise is highly correlated. We generated 100 points of two data streams containing one shared and one private information per view. Specifically, we used sinusoidal signals at different frequencies such that:

$$\mathbf{z}^{(0)} = \sin(2\pi t), \quad \mathbf{z}^{(1)} = \cos(\pi^2 t), \quad \mathbf{z}^{(2)} = \cos(2\sqrt{5}\pi t)$$

with t from the same interval $(-1, 1)$. Therefore, the ground-truth latent space is composed of 3 dimensions, 1 shared and 2 private. We then randomly projected the joint shared-private spaces $[\mathbf{z}^{(0)}, \mathbf{z}^{(1)}]$ and $[\mathbf{z}^{(0)}, \mathbf{z}^{(2)}]$ into two 20-dimensional

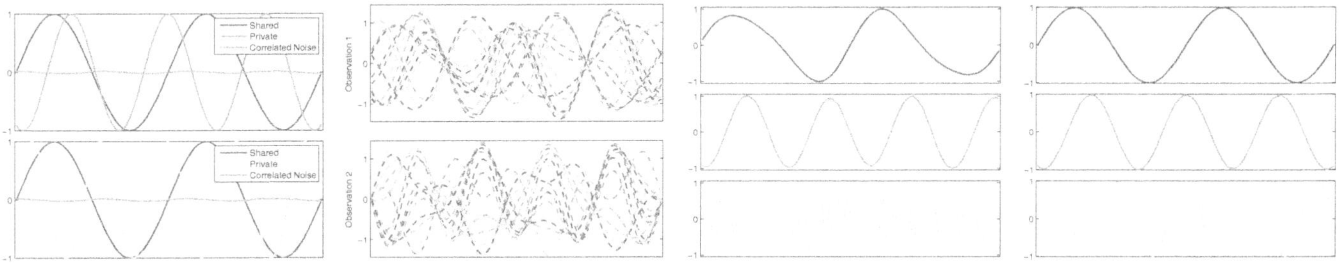

(a) Ground-truth of latent spaces

(b) Observed views

(c) Dimensions recovered by CCA

(d) 3-dimensional latent space recovered by our method

Figure 2: Synthetic example 2: latent spaces factorization

spaces respectively. Then both correlated noise $0.02\sin(3.6\pi t)$ and zero-mean Gaussian noise of variance 0.01 are added.

The ground-truth latent spaces together with correlated noise are depicted in Fig. 2(a), and the input views are depicted in Fig. 2(b). Fig. 2(c) shows the result obtained by CCA when the latent space is set by a priori to be 3-dimensional. We see that CCA recovers the shared signal, but mixes correlated noise as well. This phenomenon complies with the theoretical claim that approaches based on CCA would tend to be correlated-noise sensitive [8]. Fig. 2(d) depicts the reconstructed latent spaces for both views with our method, which clearly demonstrates the shared-private factorization.

5.2 Pose Estimation

We then apply our method to the problem of the human pose estimation on HumanEva dataset [16], which consists of Videos recorded by 7 cameras and motion capture data describing the *3D* locations of joints of a human skeleton. The video and the motion capture data have been synchronized and thus can be perceived as different representations for an object. Therefore, the task of pose estimation, i.e, infer the 3D poses from the 2D images, can be naturally formulated as a multi-view learning problem.

In our experiments, several methods that directly perform a regression from the images features to 3D poses were compared, namely linear regression (Lin-Reg), Gaussian Process regression with a linear kernel (GP-Lin). And we also implemented the Gaussian Process regression with an RBF kernel (GP-Rbf) as a competition method. Besides, we also implemented the method proposed in [7], which has been shown to outperform most multi-view learning methods for the task of human pose estimation on HumanEva. For clarity, we name their model FLSSP in short. By directly comparing our model to FLSSP, redundant comparisons with other existing algorithms [14, 11, 3, 4] are avoided. We use cross-validation to determine the regularization parameter for each algorithm.

We consider the walking and jogging video sequences of the first and second subject seen from the BW1 and BW2 camera. Since the objects move in circles, we used the first loop for training, and the remaining for testing. Each image is represented using a 100 dimensional integral HOG descriptoror 84 dimensional PHOG descriptor. In each test case, we have all together three views: two from the video recorded by BW1 and BW2, and one from the motion capture data. The standardized mean squared error (SMSE) is chosen as the metric function, since it's scale-invariant and thus easy for reproduction.

We treat the inference task as a missing data problem, in which we uniformly chose some features of the data points to be missing. In each trial, we varied the missing rate ζ, (the number of missing elements over the total number of elements in the data matrix), from 1 to 0.1. For each value, we sampled 20 different testing sets on the original inference framework. Fig. 3 and 4 show the mean error of the 20 trials.

We see that when the motion data is completely missing ($\zeta = 1$), our method is among the most promising methods. Since there is high ambiguity across the multiple views [3], the outstanding performance demonstrates the power of our model to factorize the intrinsic structure of the latent space.

Furthermore, our method effectively captured the structured information from the observed data, i.e. the error dropped dramatically as the missing rate decreased. For example, the estimation error reduces to about 1/2 with around 10% visible motion capture data in walking people with HOG features.

6. CONCLUSION

We have proposed a probabilistic model aiming at factorizing the latent space into shared part across views and private part for each view. By imposing ARD priors, we learn column sparse projection matrices. We have demonstrated the effectiveness of our approach on both synthetic data and the human pose estimation task. Currently, we are making two extensions. Since many multi-view learning data sets such as HumanEva are temporal, we are trying to capture the embedded time evolution in analogous to Kalman Filter. On the other hand, we are trying to develop a full Bayesian parameter estimation procedure.

7. REFERENCES

[1] C. Archambeau and F. Bach. Sparse probabilistic projections. In *Proceedings of the Conference on Neural Information Processing Systems (NIPS)*, volume 21. MIT Press, 2008.

[2] F. Bach and M. Jordan. A probabilistic interpretation of canonical correlation analysis. Technical report, Department of Statistics, University of California, Berkeley, 2005.

[3] C. Ek, J. Rihan, P. Torr, G. Rogez, and N. Lawrence. Ambiguity modeling in latent spaces. In *Proceedings of the International Conference on Machine Learning for*

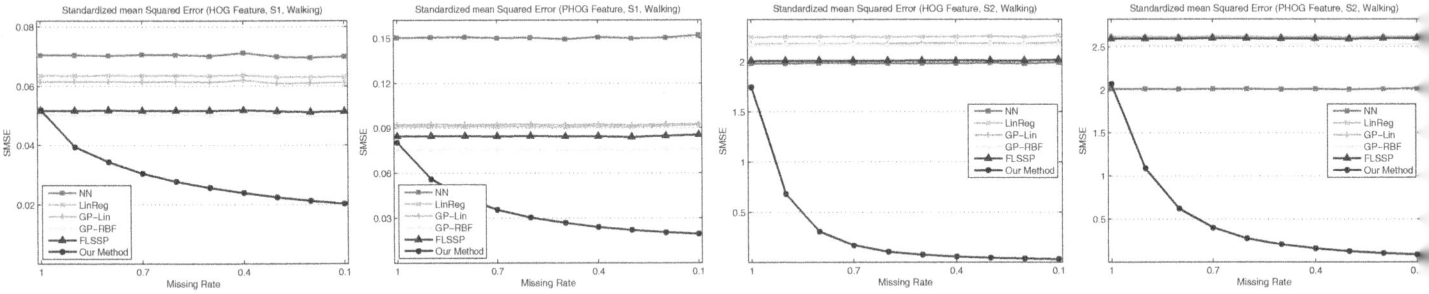

(a) S1_Walking+HOG (b) S1_Walking+PHOG (c) S2_Walking+HOG (d) S2_Walking+PHOG

Figure 3: SMSE of missing features with varying missing rate ζ: Walking

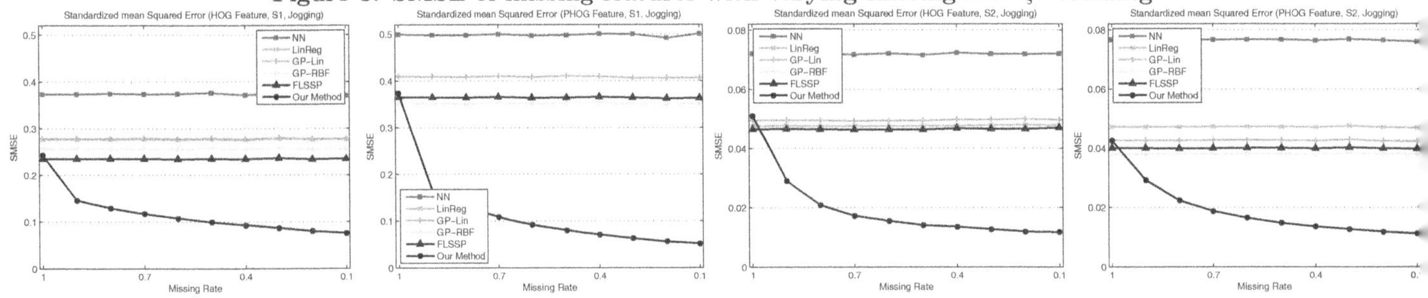

(a) S1_Jogging+HOG (b) S1_Jogging+PHOG (c) S2_Jogging+HOG (d) S2_Jogging+PHOG

Figure 4: SMSE of missing features with varying missing rate ζ: Jogging

Multimodal Interaction, pages 62–73. Springer-Verlag, 2008.

[4] C. Ek, P. Torr, and N. Lawrence. Gaussian process latent variable models for human pose estimation. In *Proceedings of the International Conference on Machine learning for Multimodal Interaction*, pages 132–143. Springer-Verlag, 2007.

[5] J. Fan, W. G. Aref, A. K. Elmagarmid, M.-S. Hacid, M. S. Marzouk, and X. Zhu. Multiview: Multilevel video content representation and retrieval. *J. Electronic Imaging.*

[6] D. Hardoon and J. Shawe-Taylor. Sparse canonical correlation analysis. *Machine Learning*, pages 1–23, 2008.

[7] Y. Jia, M. Salzmann, and T. Darrell. Factorized Latent Spaces with Structured Sparsity. In *Proceedings of the Conference on Neural Information Processing Systems (NIPS)*, volume 23. MIT Press, 2010.

[8] A. Klami and S. Kaski. Probabilistic approach to detecting dependencies between data sets. *Neurocomputing*, 72(1-3):39–46, 2008.

[9] M. Kuss and T. Graepel. The geometry of kernel canonical correlation analysis. Technical report, Max Planck Institution, 2003.

[10] K. Lange, D. Hunter, and I. Yang. Optimization transfer using surrogate objective functions. *Journal of Computational and Graphical Statistics*, 9(1):1–20, 2000.

[11] N. Lawrence. Gaussian process latent variable models for visualisation of high dimensional data. In *Proceedings of the Conference on Neural Information Processing Systems (NIPS)*, volume 16, pages 329–336. MIT Press, 2004.

[12] G. Leen. Context assisted information extraction. *PhD thesis, Univerisyt of the West of Scotland,*, 2008.

[13] R. Navaratnam, A. Fitzgibbon, and R. Cipolla. The joint manifold model for semi-supervised multi-valued regression. In *Proceedings of the IEEE International Conference on Computer Vision (ICCV)*, 2007.

[14] M. Salzmann, C. Ek, R. Urtasun, and T. Darrell. Factorized orthogonal latent spaces. In *International Conference on Artificial Intelligence and Statistics*, 2010.

[15] A. Shon, K. Grochow, A. Hertzmann, and R. Rao. Learning shared latent structure for image synthesis and robotic imitation. In *Proceedings of the Conference on Neural Information Processing Systems (NIPS)*, volume 18, pages 1233–1240. MIT Press, 2006.

[16] L. Sigal and M. Black. Humaneva: Synchronized video and motion capture dataset for evaluation of articulated human motion. Technical report, Brown Univertsity, 2006.

[17] L. Sigal, R. Memisevic, and D. Fleet. Shared kernel information embedding for discriminative inference. In *Proceedings of the IEEE Conference on Computer Vision and Pattern Recognition (CVPR)*, 2009.

[18] A. Tipping. Analysis of sparse Bayesian learning. In *Proceedings of the Conference on Neural Information Processing Systems (NIPS)*, pages 383–390. MIT Press, 2002.

[19] M. Tipping and C. Bishop. Probabilistic principal component analysis. *Journal of the Royal Statistical Society. Series B (Statistical Methodology)*, 61(3):611–622, 1999.

Automated Feature Generation from Structured Knowledge

Weiwei Cheng
University of Marburg
Germany
roywwcheng@gmail.com

Gjergji Kasneci
Microsoft Research
Cambridge, UK
gjergjik@microsoft.com

Thore Graepel
Microsoft Research
Cambridge, UK
thoreg@microsoft.com

David Stern
Microsoft Research
Cambridge, UK
dstern@microsoft.com

Ralf Herbrich
Microsoft Research
Cambridge, UK
rherb@microsoft.com

ABSTRACT

The prediction accuracy of any learning algorithm highly depends on the quality of the selected features; but often, the task of feature construction and selection is tedious and non-scalable. In recent years, however, there have been numerous projects with the goal of constructing general-purpose or domain-specific knowledge bases with entity-relationship-entity triples extracted from various Web sources or collected from user communities, e.g., YAGO, DBpedia, Freebase, UMLS, etc. This paper advocates the simple and yet far-reaching idea that the structured knowledge contained in such knowledge bases can be exploited to automatically extract features for general learning tasks. We introduce an expressive graph-based language for extracting features from such knowledge bases and a theoretical framework for constructing feature vectors from the extracted features. Our experimental evaluation on different learning scenarios provides evidence that the features derived through our framework can considerably improve the prediction accuracy, especially when the labeled data at hand is sparse.

Categories and Subject Descriptors

I.2.6 [**Artificial Intelligence**]: Learning

General Terms

Algorithms, Design, Experimentation

Keywords

query language, semantic features, structured knowledge

1. INTRODUCTION

Machine learning tasks often require identifying complex patterns from data and use these patterns to make appropriate decisions. For example, a typical task in supervised learning is to predict labels for unseen data items based on a training sample of labeled data items. The problem is often formulated as finding a function $f : \mathcal{X} \to \mathcal{Y}$ which maps objects $x \in \mathcal{X}$ to labels or target values $y \in \mathcal{Y}$. Typically, the problem is broken down into two steps.

1. Choose a fixed feature map $\phi : \mathcal{X} \to \mathcal{F}$ which takes input items $x \in \mathcal{X}$ and maps them to feature vectors $\phi \in \mathcal{F}$, where one often chooses $\mathcal{F} = \mathbb{R}^n$.
2. Define a (parameterized) class $\mathcal{H}$ of functions $h \in \mathcal{H}$ with $h : \mathcal{F} \to \mathcal{Y}$ and learn (the parameters of) the best function.

The predictive power of the learned classifier depends strongly on choosing a feature map ϕ that is informative with respect to the prediction task at hand. In the case of $\mathcal{F} \subset \mathbb{R}^n$ the components of the feature vector $\phi \in \mathcal{F}$ are referred to as features.

In the machine learning literature, the input items x have traditionally been identified with their feature representation $\phi(x)$, and often the second of the two problems above has been considered in isolation. This may be natural if the data set is already given in the form $(\phi_{(i)}, y_{(i)})$. However, for more and more large-scale learning problems that are typical for web-scale applications of machine learning, the situation is different. Consider, for example, the case of building a machine learning system for movie recommendation. The training data consists of users, movies and ratings (of movies by users). Suppose further that we are in possession of a knowledge base that contains information about users and movies. Instead of manually constructing and extracting user features and item features, would it not be great if we could specify a query that automatically constructs feature vector representations of users and items to be used by the machine learning system? Note, that the availability of such a mechanism would turn the knowledge base into a re-usable feature store that can provide different features for different applications.

The process of building appropriate features often involves two phases: A feature construction phase and a feature selection phase. In this paper, we will mainly be concerned with the question of how to construct good features from semantic knowledge bases. To this end we devise query patterns for constructing features from knowledge bases, in which the stored information is organized as entity-relationship-entity triples, e.g., in an RDFS representation.

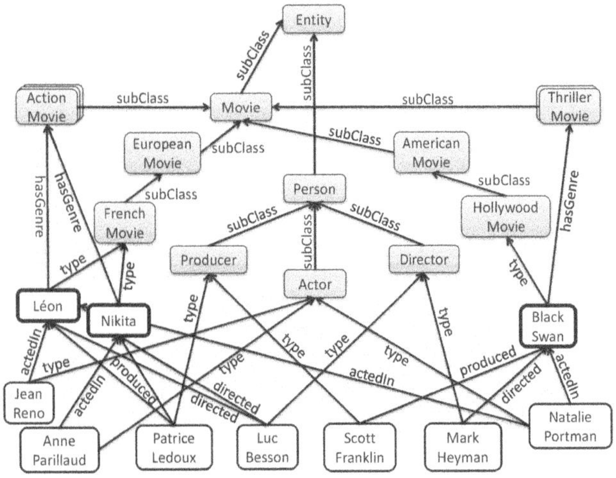

Figure 1: Sample knowledge graph from the YAGO knowledge base. The shaded nodes represent classes of entities, the remaining nodes represent individuals, and the edge labels represent relationships.

Such a knowledge base could be derived from a specific domain or from open, general-purpose RDF data sources such as YAGO [19], DBpedia [18], and LOD [17]. Figure 1 gives an example of a knowledge graph that organizes information about the movies "Léon", "Nikita" and "Black Swan" in the form of entities and relationships.

State-of-the-art knowledge bases typically have ontological components that organize entities into class-subclass hierarchies based on the *isA* or *type* and *subClass* relationships (see Figure 1). These taxonomic components are useful for understanding the roles of entities at different levels of abstraction. For example, a given movie may be in the class "French movies", which may be a sub-class of "European movies", which in turn could be a sub-class of "Movie". Other features about entities could be derived from their common relations to other entities, e.g., production dates, movie casts, costs, etc. Feeding these features to a suitable machine learning algorithm would enable it to learn a concept like user preference at the right level of abstraction from data. A framework that would allow the construction of this kind of features would be a significant step towards integrating the world of structured knowledge with that of machine learning.

2. RELATED WORK

The problem of improving predictive performance by incorporating structured knowledge has been addressed in previous work, especially in the fields of text classification and information retrieval [1, 2, 3, 4, 5, 6, 7, 8]. Despite a number of interesting results, the conclusions drawn from these works are multi-faceted, i.e., sometimes the structured knowledge is of benefit, and sometimes, even with carefully tuned NLP procedures and well-organized additional features, no clear empirical benefits are observed. The reasons for such negative observations are of course manifold and often task dependent. It is, however, worth noticing that most of the previous research in this realm focuses on semantics derived from the lexical level, which means that structured knowledge has been derived from the underlying text corpus by various parsing, pattern-matching, or other NLP techniques. Even when corpus-independent general-purpose knowledge sources are used (such as WordNet or other thesauri), the main features that are exploited are based on synonymy. For hypernymy-based features derived from general-purpose taxonomic thesauri, such as WordNet, it has been empirically shown that they can provide performance gains [1, 2, 8]. Along similar lines, [4, 5] provide preliminary evidence that class-oriented features derived from domain-specific knowledge bases can improve the underlying learning task. Therefore, we go one step further and advocate entity-relationship-oriented features with rich contextual and abstraction levels derived from related individuals and class-subclass hierarchies of state-of-the-art knowledge bases. In what follows, we discuss some of the previous work in more detail.

Scott et al. [1] incorporate the hypernymy information provided by WordNet into the Ripper rule learning system [9]. Tests on Reuter-21578 data show that the achieved improvement is category dependent. More specifically, when comparing with the conventional bag-of-words representation, the semantic features turn out to be effective for a small subset of categories. Later work, such as [8], by Kehagias et al., and [2], by Moschitti et al., follows the same line as [1], while taking more datasets and more classifiers into consideration. But neither [8] nor [2] provides sound evidence that the additional semantic features are attractive alternatives to the bag-of-words features. However, the authors of [2] have pointed out that the rather disappointing outcome of their analysis should not be taken as a general conclusion on the role of semantic features in classification tasks. It merely suggests that the elementary textual representation is very effective in many cases. And indeed, when the text is written consistently and the words are discriminative, there is not much room for improvement. However, more recent work, like [4], by Degemmis et al., and [5], by Bloehdorn et al., has reported more promising results. A key advantage of [4, 5] over earlier work is that the adapted features come from domain-specific ontologies. In [4], for example, background knowledge that is manually extracted from the Internet Movie Database (IMDb)[1] has improved the classification on the EachMovie dataset. Similarly, in [5] the MeSH thesaurus[2] (a tree-shape ontology that has been compiled out of the Medical Subject Headings of the United States National Library of Medicine) has led to better results than the more general WordNet in numerous cases, especially when medical knowledge is of interest.

Much of the related work done in the area of information retrieval has been in the context of query expansion techniques [3, 7]. Recent work by Lu et al. [6] proposes document and query-side processing to extract entity-oriented features. The proposed technique outperforms a major commercial web search engine[3] by 4% on average in terms of DCG@5.

Another domain in which structured knowledge has been widely adopted is question-answering. In [11], the usefulness of semantic features for such systems is well recognized and emphasized. Moreover, [10] points out that even simple question-answering approaches that use limited background knowledge can significantly improve a system's ability to find appropriate answers. This is also shown by the outstanding success of the Watson system [22], which exploits state-of-

[1]http://www.imdb.com/

[2]http://www.nlm.nih.gov/mesh/

[3]It was not pointed out which search engine it was.

the-art knowledge bases to compete with humans in the Jeopardy game.

2.1 Contributions

In all the above methods, the described semantic features are quite shallow; often they are derived from the underlying corpus through different NLP techniques, and when background knowledge is used, synonymy and hypernymy have been the main selection criteria. Furthermore, in those approaches that use background knowledge for feature generation, the construction of semantic features is somewhat ad-hoc, in that it does not follow a general and unified construction strategy. This makes the methods, from an evaluation point of view, incomparable (even when they use the same background knowledge) and often difficult to re-implement.

The contributions of this paper are the following.

- We introduce an expressive theoretical framework for constructing semantic features from a given knowledge base organized as a triple store. For a given entity, the framework allows the construction of entity-relationship-oriented features at different levels of abstraction.
- We discuss various strategies for incorporating the above features into a prediction model.
- Finally, we give experimental evidence for the effectiveness of semantic features constructed through the proposed framework.

The remainder of the paper is organized as follows. In Section 3.1 we introduce a graph-based query language for extracting entity-relationship-based features from a knowledge base. In Section 3.2 we present the theoretical framework for the construction of feature vectors and give an overview of viable methods for their applicability. The experimental evaluation of our approach is presented in Section 4.

3. SEMANTIC FEATURES

In the following we assume that we are given a corpus $\mathcal{C}$ over the elements of which we aim to make predictions (e.g., Web documents, tweets, movie descriptions, product reviews, etc.), a learning method $\mathcal{M}$ that expects semantic features about the entities that are recognized in $\mathcal{C}$, a knowledge base $\mathcal{K} = (\mathcal{G}, \mathcal{E}, \mathcal{R}, \mathcal{Q})$, where $\mathcal{E}$ and $\mathcal{R} \subset \mathcal{E}$ are the entities and relationships that are represented in $\mathcal{K}$, respectively, $\mathcal{G} \subseteq \mathcal{E} \times \mathcal{R} \times \mathcal{E}$ is the knowledge graph (of entity-relationship-entity triples) stored in $\mathcal{K}$, and $\mathcal{Q}$ represents a set of functions (or a query language) for querying the knowledge base. Furthermore, a basic assumption is that $\mathcal{E}(\mathcal{C}) \subset \mathcal{E}(\mathcal{K})$, where $\mathcal{E}(\mathcal{C})$ and $\mathcal{E}(\mathcal{K})$ denote the sets of entities in the corpus and in the knowledge base, respectively.

For the construction of semantic features, we start out with the following tasks. Given an entity $x \in \mathcal{E}(\mathcal{C})$ which has been recognized in the corpus, (1) use the knowledge base $\mathcal{K}$ to extract semantic features, (2) provide an automatic mechanism for constructing a vector $\phi(x)$ from the extracted features. For the first task, we propose a graph-based query formalism that builds on SPARQL [15], the W3C recommendation for querying RDF data; for the second task we provide a theoretical framework for constructing the desired feature vector.

3.1 Querying for Semantic Features

In the literature, there have been numerous proposals for query languages on graph-structured data. Most prominent among these are declarative languages such as SPARQL [15], Conjunctive Datalog, or NAGA [20]. Both SPARQL and NAGA have been designed for querying triple stores, which represent semantic networks. A query can be viewed as a semantic graph consisting of entities, relationships and variables. The variables of the query are substituted appropriately with entities or relationships by matching the given parts of the query and its structure with a subgraph from the underlying knowledge graph $\mathcal{G}$. Syntactic sugar aside, a basic query for the above languages can be defined as follows.

Definition 3.1. **Basic Query.** *A query over a set of variables $\mathcal{V}$ for a knowledge graph $\mathcal{G} \subseteq \mathcal{E} \times \mathcal{R} \times \mathcal{E}$ is a semantic connected graph $q \subseteq (\mathcal{E} \cup \mathcal{V}) \times (\mathcal{R} \cup \mathcal{V}) \times (\mathcal{E} \cup \mathcal{V})$.*

We see that a query is basically a graph, the edges of which are triples from the set $(\mathcal{E} \cup \mathcal{V}) \times (\mathcal{R} \cup \mathcal{V}) \times (\mathcal{E} \cup \mathcal{V})$. A query answer is defined as a subgraph of $\mathcal{G}$ that matches the query graph, or more specifically:

Definition 3.2. **Query Answer.** *An answer to a query q on a semantic graph $\mathcal{G}$ is a graph homomorphism $\sigma : q \mapsto \sigma_q \subseteq \mathcal{G}$ that preserves the given entity and relationships in q, and substitutes the variables with entities and relationships from $\mathcal{G}$.*

In addition, SPARQL provides useful mechanisms for performing projections or aggregations on the variables of the query. For example, for a query q a projection is defined as the set $\pi_{v_1,...,v_k}(q)$ of entities and relationships that are substituted for the variables $v_1, ..., v_k \in \mathcal{V}(q)$ of q in the query answers. In SPARQL this is enabled through a `SELECT` clause[4] (see also example in Section 3.1.1).

Another useful functionality of SPARQL is the aggregation on the results of a query q. The aggregation function is given by $\gamma_{f_1(v_1),...,f_k(v_k)}(\pi_{v_1,...,v_k}(q))$, where $v_1, ..., v_k \in \mathcal{V}(q)$ are variables of q and each f_i is an aggregation function (e.g., `COUNT, SUM, MAX, AVG`, etc.) that is applied to the entities or relationships substituted for the variable v_i. Additionally SPARQL provides useful operators such as `DISTINCT`, for removing duplicates, `UNION`, for building the union of results, `OPTIONAL`, for query edges that should be matched optionally, etc. For further information on the functionality of SPARQL we refer the reader to [15].

NAGA on the other hand does not support projection and aggregation but goes beyond the basic queries defined in 3.1 by allowing the definition of regular expressions over relationships in the query edges. More specifically a NAGA query is defined as follows.

Definition 3.3. **NAGA Query.** *Let $\mathit{RegEx}(\mathcal{R})$ be the set of all regular expressions over $\mathcal{R}$. A NAGA query over a set of variables $\mathcal{V}$ for a knowledge graph $\mathcal{G} \subseteq \mathcal{E} \times \mathcal{R} \times \mathcal{E}$ is a semantic connected graph $q \subseteq (\mathcal{E} \cup \mathcal{V}) \times (\mathit{RegEx}(\mathcal{R}) \cup \mathcal{V}) \times (\mathcal{E} \cup \mathcal{V})$.*

An answer to a NAGA query is defined similarly to Definition 3.2, with the difference that now entire paths from $\mathcal{G}$ can match the regular-expression of a query edge;

[4]In general the `SELECT` clause returns a multiset. The keyword `DISTINCT` can be used to remove duplicates.

this is the case when the sequence of relationship labels on an answer path matches the regular expression of the query edge. For an explicit definition of an answer to a NAGA query we refer the reader to [20].

The main point about NAGA queries is that they are useful when the relationships are transitive or when multiple relationships are of interest. For example, we could be interested in the query that asks for all genres and superclasses of the movie Black Swan in the knowledge graph. The corresponding NAGA query would be:

```
Black_Swan hasGenre|(type subClass*) ?x
```

In the above example, ?x represents a variable. The hasGenre relationship accesses the movie genres of Black Swan, type returns all direct classes of Black Swan, and subClass returns the superclasses of a given class. Finally, '|' reflects the "OR" condition in the query, and the Kleene star captures the transitivity of the subClass relationship. An answer to the above query would replace the variable ?x with a genre or a superclass of the movie 'Black Swan'. Assuming that Figure 1 represents the knowledge graph $\mathcal{G}$, a possible answer to the above query graph could be:

```
Black_Swan  type  Hollywood_Movie
Hollywood_Movie  subClass  American_Movie
American_Movie  subClass  Movie
```

For our goal of providing the user with a powerful tool for extracting meaningful graph-based features for entities, we need a query language that is expressive enough (e.g., enables the access of class and relationship information about entities in a transitive fashion) and thus allows us to select features at an adequate level of abstraction and granularity. To this end we combine the advantages of SPARQL with those of NAGA. Hence, we refer to the extension of SPARQL by the regular expression capabilities of NAGA as the *Extended SPARQL Query Language*, or ESPARQL for short.

We present some useful ESPARQL query patterns for feature construction in the following paragraph.

3.1.1 Exemplary Query Patterns

Suppose we were interested in all the entities from the knowledge graph $\mathcal{G}$ that are neighbors of an entity e that was recognized in the corpus $\mathcal{C}$. This could be useful for text classification tasks, when the underlying text corpus is sparse, and when the given entity has never been seen before. The corresponding query is shown below. Exemplary results to such queries on the YAGO knowledge base are given in Sections 3.2.2 and 4.3.2.

```
SELECT ?r ?x
WHERE { (e  ?r  ?x) UNION (?x  ?r  e) }
```

Note that the entity e might occur as a subject or an object in the triples of $\mathcal{G}$.

Another generic query for feature extraction is the one that asks for all superclasses of an entity e that was recognized in $\mathcal{C}$.

```
SELECT DISTINCT ?x
WHERE { e  type subClass*  ?x }
```

Note that we are using the regular expression type subClass* to access all the superclasses of e.

Now suppose that a movie m was recognized in the corpus $\mathcal{C}$. By using ESPARQL we can be precise about the semantic features we aim to extract for m. The example query below asks for the number of Oscar-winning actors or directors of m.

```
SELECT COUNT (DISTINCT ?x)
WHERE { ?x  starredIn|directed  m.
        ?x  hasWon  Oscar_Award  }
```

Another problem in classification is the case in which the feature representing a given entity does not generalize. For example, extrapolating a model of user behavior based on user IDs is often impossible. However, such a model could be derived if the IDs could be grouped by the social or geographical groups they belong to. A practical example is given when users are represented by IP addresses. A generic ESPARQL query pattern for generalizing the description of a user with ID u is depicted below.

```
SELECT ?y
WHERE { ?x  hasID  u.
         u  belongsToUserLocation  ?y.
        ?y  type subClass*  country  }
```

The above query enables the representation of users by their country information. In this example the user ID could be similar to an IP address and could belong to a specific country.

Note that all query patterns presented here are modular in nature and can be composed to derive richer semantic information from the knowledge base. Consequently, as we will see in the next section, our framework is modular as well. It allows the storage and composition of ESPARQL queries on demand (analogously to stored procedures). The question that we still need to answer is how to represent the semantic information extracted through ESPARQL queries adequately for a given learning task. This question is addressed in the next section.

3.2 Constructing Feature Vectors

Some of the most popular methods for solving supervised learning tasks, such as (generalized) linear models, k-nearest neighbors, kernel methods, etc., exploit a feature-based representation of the input data to deal with the prediction task. The typical computation that needs to be carried out by the above methods is the inner product between a weight vector $\mathbf{w}$ and a feature vector $\phi(x)$ for an input x, or between two feature vectors $\phi(x)$ and $\phi(y)$ (e.g., for computing a logit in logistic regression, a distance for a given 2-norm, or a polynomial kernel). In the spirit of [24], our goal is to provide a generic methodology for constructing such feature vectors from the semantic information that we extract from the knowledge base for a given entity.

Let $\mathcal{Y}$ be a set of target labels (i.e., categories). In our learning scenario we assume that the supervision is given by a training sample $S \subseteq \mathcal{E} \times \mathcal{Y}$. The goal is to find a mapping $\phi : \mathcal{E} \to \mathcal{F}$ from entities to feature vectors, so that traditional machine learning methods, such as the above, can be applied to the learning problem at hand.

Let $e \in \mathcal{E}$ be an entity that was recognized in the underlying corpus $\mathcal{C}$. Let $q(e)$ be an ESPARQL query for extracting semantic features of e. Let us further assume that $q(e)$ has k variables in the SELECT clause. Note that every variable of $q(e)$ takes values from $\mathcal{E}$ (where, as described in Section 3, $\mathcal{R} \subset \mathcal{E}$). Furthermore, the substitution of each variable in the SELECT clause is going to represent a semantic feature for e. Hence, q can be viewed as a mapping

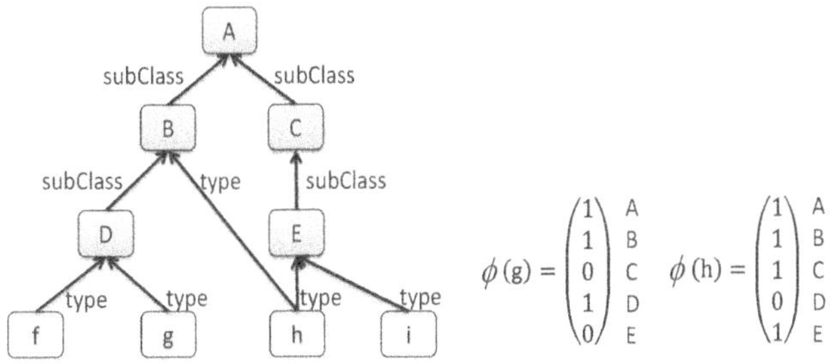

Figure 2: Example of a taxonomic knowledge graph with individuals f, g, h, i and types A, B, C, D, E. The feature vectors of g and h are shown on the left-hand side. Assuming that g and h are the entities from the training sample, the set $\mathcal{F}_S$ is given by the union of all their superclasses (i.e., {A, B, C, D, E}), as returned by the above query. A feature vector ϕ has a dimension for each element from $\mathcal{F}_S$. For each individual we set only those dimensions to 1 that represent superclasses of that individual.

$\mu : \mathcal{E} \to 2^{\mathcal{E}^k}$. The elements of $\mathcal{E}^k$ index the dimensions of the feature space $\mathcal{F} = \{0,1\}^{\mathcal{E}^k}$. Although the cardinality of $\mathcal{F}$ can be extremely large, in practice the features are derived from the training sample, which typically leads to a much smaller feature space. Hence, the effective feature space is given by:

$$\mathcal{F}_S := \{\mu(e) | (e, \cdot) \in S\}$$

Also note that often the domain of the knowledge base from which features are extracted can be restricted to the types of entities that are to be classified. For example if we are to classify movies, we would also like to extract semantic information from the knowledge base that is relevant and specific to movies. In summary the steps that are carried out by our framework in order to construct the feature vectors are the following:

1. Based on the training corpus $\mathcal{C}$ and the knowledge base $\mathcal{K}$ choose appropriate ESPARQL queries to extract semantic information about the entities of $\mathcal{C}$; the queries can be run on $\mathcal{K}$ or a restricted subset of $\mathcal{K}$ (see Section 3.2.2).
2. Unify the answer sets of the queries (for all entities from $\mathcal{C}$) to construct the set of semantic features that indexes the dimensions of the effective feature space $\mathcal{F}_S$.
3. The feature vector of an entity (which has the dimensionality of $\mathcal{F}_S$) can be built in the obvious way, by setting those dimensions which correspond to query answers for that entity to 1.

In the following, we show by means of examples how such feature vectors can be constructed and handled in practice.

3.2.1 Hypernymy-Based Feature Vectors

We start out by describing the simple case of constructing taxonomic (i.e., hypernymy-based) features. Suppose we have a knowledge base of individuals and all the classes they belong to. A sample knowledge graph is depicted in Figure 2. In order to extract all the hypernymy-based features for the entity h, we can run the following ESPARQL query $q(\text{h})$:

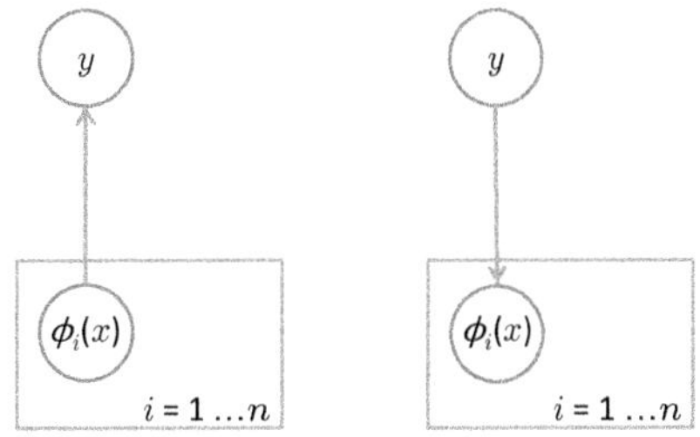

Figure 3: Difference between discriminative (left) and Naive Bayes model (right). The boxes represent n-fold replication of the feature values $\phi_i(x)$ for a given examples (x, y). Naive Bayes assumes independence of feature values given the label and hence leads to independent updates of weights, disregarding dependencies resulting from the ontological feature construction. This problem is avoided by discriminative models.

```
SELECT ?c
WHERE { h  type subClass*  ?c }
```

In Figure 2 we show how to construct hypernymy-based feature vectors for given entities. It is important to note that although these kinds of hypernymy-based vectors can be used by any of the mentioned supervised learning methods, they are best suited for methods that take the dependencies between the features into account. For instance, the Naive Bayes method does not consider these correlations and is thus expected to deliver a degraded performance. This is also shown empirically in our experimental section. It is relatively straight-forward to see that the subsumption of classes invalidates naive independence assumptions on the corresponding features. For example, on the taxonomy of Figure 2, a conditional independence assumption on the features $\phi_{\texttt{A}}$ and $\phi_{\texttt{B}}$ corresponding to the classes A and B, given a target label $y \in \mathcal{Y}$, would lead to $P(\phi_{\texttt{A}}, \phi_{\texttt{B}}|y) = P(\phi_{\texttt{B}}|\phi_{\texttt{A}}, y)P(\phi_{\texttt{A}}|y) = P(\phi_{\texttt{B}}|y)P(\phi_{\texttt{A}}|y)$. However $P(\phi_{\texttt{B}} = 1|\phi_{\texttt{A}} = 1, y) = 1$, hence $P(\phi_{\texttt{B}}|\phi_{\texttt{A}}, y) = P(\phi_{\texttt{B}}|y)$ if and only if $P(\phi_{\texttt{B}}|y) = 1$, which is in general not true. In Figure 3, we highlight the difference between discriminative models, which allow joint updates on weights, and Naive Bayes models whose conditional independence assumption on features leads to independent weight updates.

3.2.2 General Semantic Feature Vectors

Now consider the sample knowledge graph depicted in Figure 1. Suppose that the movies occurring there (i.e., Nikita, Léon, Black Swan) are movies from our training sample. Since in practice these kinds of knowledge bases can be very large, one can restrict the effective feature space by considering only types of entities that are relevant for the classification task at hand. A key concept for achieving this is given by the definition of a *restricted entity domain.*

DEFINITION 3.4. **Restricted Entity Domain.** *Let $T \subseteq \mathcal{E}$ be a set of types from a knowledge base $\mathcal{K} = (\mathcal{G}, \mathcal{E}, \mathcal{R}, \mathcal{Q})$. For a class $c \in T$, let D_c denote the set of entities that can be substituted for the variable* ?x *in the following ESPARQL query on $\mathcal{K}$:*

```
SELECT ?x
WHERE { ?x  subClass|(type subClass*)  c }
```

The restricted entity domain $\mathcal{D}_T$ *for T is defined as* $\mathcal{D}_T = \bigcup_{c \in T} D_c$.

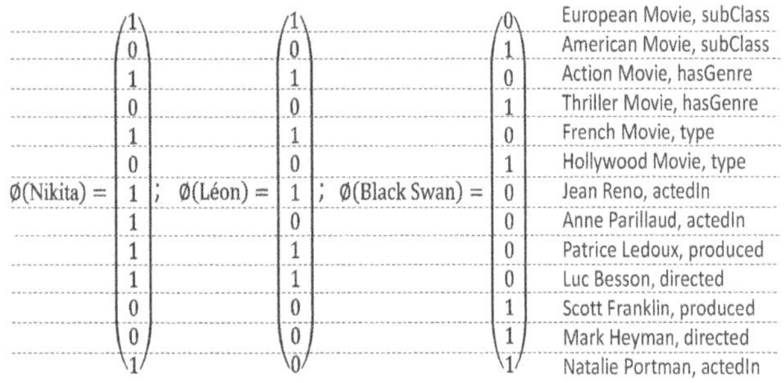

Figure 4: The elements in the union of the semantic neighborhood information (i.e., neighboring entities and relations) of the movies Léon, Nikita, and Black Swan index the dimensions of the effective feature space $\mathcal{F}_S$. Note that the higher semantic similarity between the movies Léon and Nikita is also reflected in the similarity between their semantic feature vectors.

For example, for the knowledge graph of Figure 1, we restrict the domain of entities to the types T={`Movie, Actor, Producer, Director`}. We then denote by $\mathcal{D}_T$ the *restricted entity domain* of all the subclasses and individuals of the classes in T.

With the restricted entity domain $\mathcal{D}_T$ from the above example, one possible way to construct the set $\mathcal{F}_S$ is by running two types of queries (1) a query to extract hypernymy-based features, similarly to above, and (2) a query to extract features about the semantic neighborhood of that entity, e.g.,

```
SELECT ?e ?r
WHERE { (m   ?r  ?e) UNION (?e  ?r  m) }
```

The results to these queries are then unified to construct feature vectors as depicted in Figure 4.

In practice, this kind of feature vectors will typically be very sparse. For example, if we use movie genres to classify movies, it is reasonable to expect every movie to belong to only a few from a long list of genres. Hence, for computational efficiency these vectors are implemented as sparse vectors. This way the complexity of the inner product is linear in the minimum number of dimensions set to 1 in one of the two corresponding vectors.

4. EXPERIMENTAL EVALUATION

In this section we evaluate the effectiveness of semantic features generated through the presented framework. For our experiments we use YAGO [19], a general-purpose knowledge base that was automatically constructed from Wikipedia, WordNet and other semi-structured Web sources. YAGO has been successfully used in many knowledge-oriented systems, such as the YAGO-NAGA project [21, 16], and most prominently in IBM's Watson [22], a system for answering Jeopardy questions.

In what follows, we empirically investigate two different learning tasks, recommendation and text classification. We first introduce the learning model that we have used and then describe the learning tasks and the datasets. The experimental results verify the hypothesis that semantic features are beneficial to predictive accuracy.

4.1 The Learning Model

As described in the previous section, each input instance (i.e., entity) x is formally represented by a sparse binary vector $\phi(x) = (\phi_1(x), \ldots, \phi_n(x))^T \in \mathcal{F}_S$.

In our model, the importance of the features in the vector $\phi(x)$ is represented by a weight vector $\mathbf{w} = (w_1, \ldots, w_n)$, where the component w_i reflects the importance of the feature $\phi_i(x)$. The model we use is a generalized linear Bayesian probit model, similar to the ones used in Matchbox [23] or AdPredictor [25]. This model computes a belief on the weights w_i, which is given by a Gaussian distribution with mean μ_i and variance σ_i^2. Hence, the state of the model is uniquely identified by vectors of means and variances of the weights, namely $\boldsymbol{\mu} = (\mu_1, \ldots, \mu_n)$ and $\boldsymbol{\sigma}^2 = (\sigma_1^2 \ldots \sigma_n^2)$. If we knew the real values of the weights w_i, we could compute a score $s(x) = \sum_{i=1}^{n} w_i \phi_i(x)$, which in turn could be used to derive the probability of a target label $y \in \mathcal{Y}$ given the score $s(x)$, i.e., $P(y|s(x))$. The probability of a weight is given by:

$$p(\mathbf{w}) = \prod_i \mathcal{N}(w_i; \mu_i, \sigma_i^2)$$

Since in our model the weights w_i are represented as Gaussian variables, the score $s(x)$ is represented as a Gaussian random variable as well:

$$p(s|\mathbf{w}, x) = \mathcal{N}\left(s; \sum_{i=1}^{n} \phi_i(x)\mu_i, \sum_{i=1}^{n} \phi_i(x)\sigma_i^2\right)$$

Finally, one can model the probability of label y as a probit function:

$$P(y \mid s) = \Phi\left(\frac{ys}{\beta}\right)$$

with noise variance β^2, where $\Phi(t) = \int_{-\infty}^{t} \mathcal{N}(t; 0, 1)\, dt$. For the update equations in such a model we refer the reader to [25].

Such a model has several advantages:

1. By jointly updating the beliefs on the weights of the features, it can capture and exploit dependencies between features. As discussed in Section 3.2.1, this is expected to yield a better performance than models that treat parameters independently (e.g., Naive Bayes) in the presence of hierarchical hypernymy-based features. This aspect is empirically demonstrated in our experiments.
2. As shown by [23, 25], the model can deal with large sparse vectors. Furthermore, the learning can be carried out in an incremental fashion, as in an online setting, which is important for practical concerns.
3. Finally, the above model can handle different feedback types, including absolute, binary, and ordinal [23]. This flexibility allows us to apply it to various learning tasks.

4.2 Test Case: Movie Feedback Prediction

4.2.1 The Task

The task consists in predicting the feedback that a user will give on a movie. We use the generalized linear probit model from above with user and movie IDs as basic features, and add semantic features on top. Note that this task is simpler than state-of-the-art (i.e., collaborative-filtering-style) recommendation, where based on a user-movie feedback matrix, user and movie affinities are estimated [26, 23].

These affinities can be used to estimate the probability of a movie being liked by a user. However, together with the probit model, the task we consider shifts the focus on the benefits of the different feature types.

The really interesting cases for this kind of feedback prediction are those for which there are very few users and movies in the training set. This is similar in spirit to recommendation scenarios in which the feedback of users on movies is very sparse, or in which there is no feedback at all. For example, usually users are interested in the most recent movies; for these, however, there are hardly any feedback labels, which makes the recommendation task very difficult. We refer to this problem as the cold-start problem.

With this in mind, in our experiments, we investigate the question whether the semantic features (for movies) generated by the proposed framework can improve the prediction accuracy.

4.2.2 The MovieLens Dataset

MovieLens is a commonly used movie recommendation dataset[5]. It contains 1,000,206 ratings of 3,952 movies by 6,040 users. Ratings are on an ordinal scale from 1 to 5. The dataset also provides some meta data including information about movies (e.g., cast, genre, etc.). As YAGO provides more comprehensive cast, genre and type information for movies, and to increase comparability, in our experiments, we neglect the meta data provided by MovieLens. Instead we use our framework to construct semantic features from YAGO. This is done by exploiting the movie titles provided by MovieLens. For a given movie title, a great deal of information can be retrieved from YAGO, such as its budget, release date, cast, genres, box-office information, etc. However, for the sake of a clear message, we only select the features regarding a movie's cast and type. For example, for the movie Black Swan, the following query

```
SELECT ?x
WHERE { ?x  actedIn  Black_Swan }
```

returns entities such as *Natalie_Portman*, *Mila_Kunis*, *Vincent_Cassel*, etc. Similarly, the query

```
SELECT ?x
WHERE { Black_Swan   hasGenre|(type subClass*)  ?x }
```

returns types and genres such as `Drama_Movie`, `Thriller_Movie`, `Tragedy_Movie`, `Ballet_Movie`, `American_Movie`, etc.

4.2.3 Experimental Results

For this experiment we consider two settings: (1) no semantic features are used; instead the model learns the bias of a user towards a movie by using user and movie IDs as features, (2) in addition, for movies, the model uses semantic features extracted from YAGO.

As expected, the semantic features provide better descriptions of the movies and are valuable in the learning process, especially in the case of very sparse feedback. In order to measure the prediction accuracy in such cold-start situations, we adopt the methodology of [13] and [23]. We divide the movies into two sets according to the release dates: a training set containing 50% of the movies and a test set containing the rest with newer release dates. First the linear probit model is trained on all ratings for the movies in the training set by taking the users who have rated those movies into account. Then, for each movie in the test set, we train the model further on a random subset L of its ratings, for $L = 0\%$ to 50%. We use the model to predict the rest of the ratings for that movie. Finally we report the mean absolute error (MAE), $|\hat{r}_i - r_i|$, where r_i is the true rating and $\hat{r}_i$ is the predicted rating. The experiments are repeated 10 times and the average results, together with corresponding standard derivations are summarized in Figure 5.

[5]http://www.grouplens.org/node/73

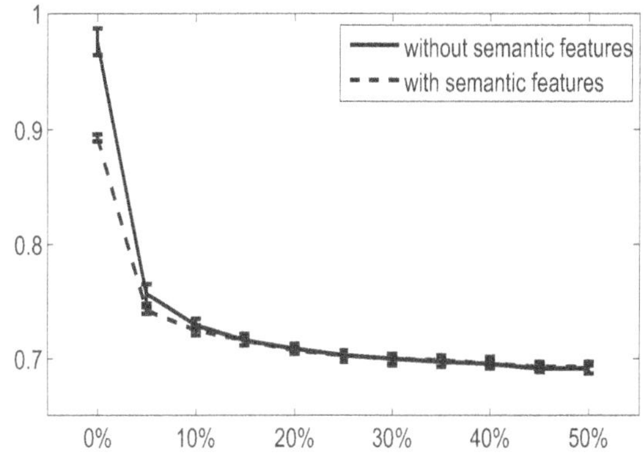

Figure 5: Mean absolute error (MAE) difference between two settings, with and without semantic features, for different values of L. It is important to note that these MAE results for semantic features are comparable to those of [26], which is a state-of-the-art recommendation system based on collaborative filtering. The MAE values of [26] range from 0.71 to 0.69, for $L = 5\%$ to $L = 75\%$ (see also [23]), whereas the values of the probit model with semantic features range from 0.74 to 0.69, for $L = 5\%$ to $L = 50\%$. This demonstrates the benefit of semantic features in combination with the linear probit model.

As expected, the improvement achieved by the semantic features is remarkable, especially when the ratings of a movie have not been largely revealed. For these cases the semantic features yield an improvement of almost 10% over the basic features. Such effectiveness, when dealing with the cold-start problem, is of particular interest for recommendation, as the service providers often experience the problem that users abandon their system and lose interest in returning due to the low quality of initial recommendations. We should also notice that the advantages of the semantic features start to become negligible when more and more ratings of a movie are observed. Finally, let us remark that the framework we propose has not reached its full potential yet. While there could be other meaningful semantic features for movie recommendation, we have only used the cast and type information. We hypothesize that semantic features for users could further improve the performance of the probit model. Furthermore, YAGO is rather a general-purpose knowledge base; better performance is expected when a more domain-specific knowledge base is used.

4.3 Tweet Classification

4.3.1 The Task

The classification task considered in this section is multi-label classification of tweets. More specifically, the goal is to assign the tweets to one or more of the nine

class	#instance	proportion
Business/Finance (BF)	2182	9.56%
Entertainment (E)	4235	18.56%
Lifestyle (LS)	4085	17.90%
Politics (P)	1199	5.25%
Science/Environment (SE)	789	3.45%
Sport (S)	1145	5.01%
Technology (T)	1880	8.23%
World Events (WE)	2122	9.30%
Other/Miscellaneous (OM)	12838	56.26%

Table 1: Statistics of the tweet classification dataset.

following categories: *Business/Finance (BF), Entertainment (E), Lifestyle (LS), Politics (P), Science/Environment (SE), Sport (S), Technology (T), World Events (WE), Other/Miscellaneous (OM).*

The problem with this task is that (since a tweet is restricted to 140 characters) tweets contain very few words, and many of those are often non-informative, especially when describing status updates. Moreover many tweets may contain words that have never been observed before (representing entities, such as new companies, products, upcoming celebrities, etc.). Semantic features for the entities recognized in the tweets can help mitigate such sparsity issues.

4.3.2 The Dataset

For a subset of tweets from the Twitter firehose, the categorizations were obtained using Amazon Mechanical Turk[6], and the results were manually verified by researchers from our lab. This dataset was collected and categorized for a personalized news service. For our experiments, a subset of the original dataset was selected, which contains 22,816 tweets with their class information. Table 2 shows three typical tweets from our training corpus. Some statistics of the dataset used in the experiments are shown in Table 1.

The sum of proportions is larger than 100%, since one tweet can simultaneously belong to more than one category. In this corpus the positive classes are often very sparse. Especially, the distribution of the classes is very unbalanced. For example in our dataset more than half of the instances belong to the category *Other/Miscellaneous*, while only less than 5% of them belong to *Science/Environment*. This is another reason (in addition to those presented in Section 4.3.1) why this tweet classification task is very challenging.

Conventional features in text classification are bag-of-words features, which can be extracted directly from the tweets. To obtain semantic features, we first apply an HMM-based entity recognition algorithm to locate terms which correspond to possible entities in a tweet. Then, the detected terms are mapped to the most likely entities in the YAGO knowledge base. This is done by means of a co-occurrence-based heuristics that exploits the YAGO *means* relation[7]. Once the entities have been recognized as YAGO entities, we use our framework to retrieve semantic features from YAGO. For example, by processing the first tweet in Table 2, *Bush* is recognized as an entity and is mapped by the above heuristics with high confidence to the YAGO entity George W. Bush. In this set of experiments we have used queries of the following kind:

[6]http://www.mturk.com/

[7]YAGO relates terms to an entity through the *means* relation if the terms refer to that entity.

	businessperson
	president
	person
governors_of_texas	politician
harvard_business_school_alumni	republican
harvard_university_alumni	scholar
phillips_academy_alumni	serviceman
presidents_of_the_united_states	skilled_worker
texas_republicans	worker
time_magazine_persons_of_year	corporate_executive
united_states_air_force_officers	executive
yale_university_alumni	governor
	leader
	military_officer
	administrator
	alumnus

Table 3: Some sample features obtained for the YAGO entity *George_W._Bush*. Left: neighboring entities; right: hypernyms.

```
SELECT ?x
WHERE { (George_W._Bush ?r ?x) UNION
        (?x ?r George_W._Bush) }
```

The above query retrieves all entities that are neighbors of George W. Bush from the knowledge base. For more general features, we make use of the YAGO type and subclass hierarchy and retrieve all hypernyms with the following query:

```
SELECT ?x
WHERE { George_W._Bush type subClass* ?x }
```

Some of the resulting semantic features are shown in Table 3.

4.3.3 Evaluated Learning Models

We evaluate the probit model on different feature settings for bag-of-words and semantic features; for the semantic features we look at the influence of hypernymy-based features. Because of their hierarchical and inclusive nature (e.g., a *president* is always a *person*), a naive independence assumption is in general invalid. To verify the hypothesis that the generalized linear probit model outperforms learning models with naive independence assumptions on these kinds of semantic features, we include the Naive Bayes model in our comparison. Finally, we compare the following five settings:

SH: probit model with bag-of-words and semantic features including hypernyms.

SnH: probit model with bag-of-words and semantic features excluding hypernyms.

BOW: probit model with only bag-of-word features.

NBSH: Naive Bayes with bag-of-words and semantic features including hypernyms.

NBBOW: Naive Bayes with only bag-of-word features.

The tests are carried out in a 10-fold cross validation. For each of the nine classes in the dataset, each learning model is trained and tested independently (often referred to as binary relevance by the multi-label learning community [12]). The

tweet	BF	E	LS	P	SE	S	T	WE	OM
Obama blames Bush for all of his misdeeds and then takes credit for the successful war in Iraq http://is.gd/e0iVM (via @PennyStarrDC)	0	0	0	1	0	0	0	1	0
A Modern Approach to an Ancient Game: The story behind The Path of Go http://bit.ly/g04KtA	0	0	0	0	1	0	1	0	0
@alex_ Good morning! How was the trip?	0	0	0	0	0	0	0	0	1

Table 2: Three typical training instances in tweet classification with associated labels.

predictions are evaluated with negative log-likelihood (NLL) and area under the ROC curve (AUC):

$$\text{NLL} = -\left(y_i \log(h(x_i)) + (1 - y_i)\log(1 - h(x_i))\right),$$

$$\text{AUC} = \frac{1}{|P|\,|N|} \sum_{x_i \in P} \sum_{x_j \in N} \omega(h(x_i) - h(x_j)),$$

where $y_i \in \{0, 1\}$ is the true class, and $h(x_i) \in [0, 1]$ is the the prediction of the method. P and N are the sets of positive and negative instances, respectively. $\omega(z)$ is defined as:

$$\omega(z) = \begin{cases} 1 & \text{if } z > 0, \\ 0.5 & \text{if } z = 0, \\ 0 & \text{if } z < 0. \end{cases}$$

While NLL is a commonly used classification loss, AUC measures the learner's ranking performance. When we randomly choose a positive instance and a negative one, AUC corresponds to the probability that the method ranks the positive instance ahead of the negative one.

4.3.4 Results

The results for the above settings, based on the NLL scores and AUC, are shown in Table 4 and Table 5. In both tables, the Friedman test shows a significant difference among these settings at α-level 0.1 [14].

Comparing the different settings for the probit model, the semantic features improve upon the bag-of-words features. For this learning task, however, it seems that hypernymy-based features are not very informative. Note that since the hypernymy information in YAGO is largely based on WordNet, our observations are consistent with the those of [1].

The performance across the different classes varies considerably. SnH is able to boost the performance for most classes. But for some classes, such as Technology and Politics, it seems very hard to improve. The tweets related to these topics are often about the latest developments and trends, and the recognized entities are not well-covered in YAGO. The performance of the Naive Bayes method is poor. Since the predictions of the Naive Bayes method are not well-calibrated and tend toward extreme values, the method suffers considerably in terms of NLL score. Furthermore, the Naive Bayes method fails to handle numerous correlated features as we expected. NBSH gives the worst results in our test.

5. CONCLUSION

Our work aims at bridging the gap between machine learning and semantic technologies. Along these lines, we presented a modular framework for automatically constructing semantic features from structured knowledge. While these features can be used with various learning algorithms, their hierarchical dependencies can be best exploited by learning methods that can capture these dependencies. Our experiments on movie recommendation and tweet classification give evidence for the improvement of predictive accuracy, especially in cold-start situations, when the data is sparse. Further improvement is conceivable if more accurate and more domain-specific knowledge bases are used. Therefore, we believe that future advances in the area of information extraction and knowledge base construction will pave the way for techniques such as the ones proposed in this paper.

6. REFERENCES

[1] Scott, S., Matwin, S.: Text Classification Using WordNet Hypernyms. In: Use of WordNet in Natural Language Processing Systems: Proceedings of the Workshop, pp. 45–51. Association for Computational Linguistics (1998)

[2] Moschitti, A., Basili, R.: Complex Linguistic Features for Text Classification: A Comprehensive Study. In: 26th European Conference on Information Retrieval Research, LNCS 2997, pp. 181–196. Springer (2004)

[3] Voorhees, E.: Using WordNet to Disambiguate Word Senses for Text Retrieval. In: 16th Annual International ACM SIGIR Conference on Research and Development in Information Retrieval, pp. 171–180. ACM (1993)

[4] Degemmis, M., Lops, P., Semeraro, G.: Learning Semantic User Profiles from Text. In: Advanced Data Mining and Applications, LNCS 4093, pp. 661–672. Springer (2006)

[5] Bloehdorn, S., Hotho, A.: Boosting for Text Classification with Semantic Features. In: Advances in Web Mining and Web Usage Analysis, LNCS 3932, pp. 149–166. Springer (2006)

[6] Lu, Y., Peng, F., Mishne, G., Wei, X., Dumoulin, B.: Improving Web Search Relevance with Semantic Features. In: 2009 Conference on Empirical Methods in Natural Language Processing, Vol. 2, pp. 648–657. Association for Computational Linguistics (2009)

[7] Voorhees, E.,: Query Expansion Using Lexical-Semantic Relations. In: 17th Annual International ACM SIGIR Conference on Research and Development in Information Retrieval, pp. 61–69. Springer (1994)

[8] Kehagias, A., Petridis, V., Kaburlasos, V., Fragkou, P.: A Comparison of Word- and Sense-Based Text Categorization Using Several Classification Algorithms. Journal of Intelligent Information Systems, Vol. 21(3), pp. 227–247. Kluwer Academic Publishers (2003)

[9] Cohen, W.: Fast Effective Rule Induction. In: 12th

class	SH	SnH	BOW	NBSH	NBBOW
Business/Finance	0.1663±.0083(3)	**0.1569±.0073**(1)	0.1637±.0076(2)	2.3281±.0575(4)	2.3511±.0350(5)
Entertainment	0.2993±.0057(2)	**0.2816±.0134**(1)	0.3000±.0117(3)	2.4119±.0795(5)	1.1625±.0358(4)
Lifestyle	0.3499±.0145(2)	**0.3402±.0058**(1)	0.3609±.0154(3)	2.3222±.0790(5)	1.2885±.0314(4)
Politics	0.1074±.0047(3)	0.1018±.0053(2)	**0.0990±.0042**(1)	5.1388±.0453(5)	3.7856±.0799(4)
Science/Environment	0.0935±.0076(2)	**0.0920±.0090(1)**	0.0938±.0069(3)	6.5148±.0654(5)	5.1472±.0691(4)
Sport	**0.0839±.0109**(1)	0.0874±.0087(3)	0.0862±.0029(2)	5.7259±.0407(5)	3.9350±.0608(4)
Technology	0.1311±.0068(3)	0.1272±.0084(2)	**0.1255±.0116**(1)	3.0432±.0728(5)	2.3635±.0588(4)
World Events	0.1752±.0056(2)	**0.1693±.0111**(1)	0.1783±.0078(3)	3.2537±.1058(5)	2.4399±.0555(4)
Other/Miscellaneous	0.4101±.0106(2)	**0.4054±.0073**(1)	0.4316±.0083(3)	1.0783±.0560(5)	0.8987±.0333(4)
average rank	2.22	1.44	2.33	4.89	4.11

Table 4: Comparison based on negative log-likelihood. Numbers in parentheses represent the rank of the methods in the corresponding class.

class	SH	SnH	BOW	NBSH	NBBOW
Business/Finance	.9238±.0101(3)	**.9395±.0090**(1)	.9335±.0094(2)	.8289±.0115(5)	.8947±.0133(4)
Entertainment	.8987±.0047(2)	**.9124±.0077**(1)	.8973±.0085(3)	.7984±.0150(5)	.8607±.0114(4)
Lifestyle	.8393±.0147(2)	**.8534±.0068**(1)	.8370±.0112(3)	.7554±.0140(5)	.7927±.0107(4)
Politics	.9464±.0129(3)	.9567±.0056(2)	**.9592±.0085**(1)	.8114±.0105(5)	.9004±.0133(4)
Science/Environment	.9051±.0266(3)	**.9251±.0136**(1)	.9153±.0137(2)	.7372±.0156(5)	.8239±.0178(4)
Sport	.9595±.0154(2)	**.9616±.0091**(1)	.9592±.0115(3)	.7869±.0214(5)	.8784±.0160(4)
Technology	.9484±.0122(3)	.9560±.0043(2)	**.9571±.0092**(1)	.8385±.0143(5)	.9138±.0107(4)
World Events	.9167±.0037(3)	**.9263±.0061**(1)	.9170±.0102(2)	.8226±.0138(5)	.8762±.0161(4)
Other/Miscellaneous	.8909±.0072(2)	**.8955±.0055**(1)	.8815±.0064(3)	.8458±.0110(5)	.8798±.0064(4)
average rank	2.56	1.22	2.22	5.00	4.00

Table 5: Comparison based on area under the ROC curve. Numbers in parentheses represent the rank of methods in the corresponding class.

International Conference on Machine Learning, pp. 115–123. Morgan Kaufmann (1995)

[10] McGuinness, D.: Question Answering on the Semantic Web. IEEE Intelligent Systems, Vol. 19(1), pp. 82–85. IEEE Computer Society (2004)

[11] Maybury, M. (Ed.): New Directions in Question Answering. AAAI Press (2004)

[12] Cheng, W., Hüllermeier, E.: Combining Instance-Based Learning and Logistic Regression for Multi-Label Classification. Machine Learning, Vol. 76, pp. 211–225. Springer (2009)

[13] Lam, X., Vu, T., Le, T., Duong, A.: Addressing Cold-Start Problem in Recommendation Systems. In: 2nd International Conference on Ubiquitous Information Management and Communication, pp. 208–211. ACM (2008)

[14] Demsar, J.: Statistical Comparisons of Classifiers over Multiple Data Sets. Journal of Machine Learning Research, Vol. 7, pp. 1–30. Microtome Publishing (2006)

[15] SPARQL Query Language for RDF. `http://www.w3.org/TR/rdf-sparql-query/`

[16] The YAGO-NAGA Project: Harvesting, Searching, and Ranking Knowledge from the Web. `http://www.mpi-inf.mpg.de/yago-naga/`

[17] W3C SweoIG: The Linking Open Data Community Project. `http://esw.w3.org/topic/SweoIG/TaskForces/CommunityProjects/LinkingOpenData`

[18] Bizer, C., Lehmann, J., Kobilarov, G., Auer, S., Becker, C., Cyganiak, R., Hellmann, S.: DBpedia: A Nucleus for a Web of Open Data. In: 6th International Semantic Web Conference, 2nd Asian Semantic Web Conference, pp. 722–735. Springer (2007)

[19] Suchanek, F. M., Kasneci, G., Weikum, G.: Yago: A Core of Semantic Knowledge. In: 16th International World Wide Web Conference, pp. 697–706. ACM Press (2007)

[20] Kasneci, G., Suchanek, F. M., Ifrim, G., Ramanath, M., Weikum, G.: NAGA: Searching and Ranking Knowledge. In: 24th International Conference on Data Engineering, pp. 953–962. IEEE (2008)

[21] Kasneci, G., Ramanath, M., Suchanek, F. M., Weikum, G.: The YAGO-NAGA Approach to Knowledge Discovery. In: SIGMOD Record, Vol. 37(4), pp. 41–47. ACM (2008)

[22] Ferrucci, D., Brown, E., Chu-Carroll, J., Fan, J., Gondek, D., Kalyanpur, A. A., Lally, A., Murdock, J. W., Nyberg, E., Prager, J., Schlaefer, N., Welty, C.: Building Watson: An Overview of the DeepQA Project. In: AI Magazine, Vol. 31(3), pp. 59–79. AAAI (2010)

[23] Stern, D., Herbrich, R., Graepel, T.: Matchbox: Large Scale Bayesian Recommendations. In: 18th International World Wide Web Conference, pp. 111–120. ACM (2009)

[24] Haussler, D.: Convolution Kernels on Discrete Structures. Technical Report (UCS-CRL-99-10), University of California at Santa Cruz (1999)

[25] Graepel, T., Candela, J. Q., Borchert, T. Herbrich, R.: Web-Scale Bayesian Click-Through Rate Prediction for Sponsored Search Advertising in Microsoft's Bing Search Engine. In: 27th International Conference on Machine Learning, pp. 13–20. Omnipress (2010)

[26] Lam, X. N., Vu, T., Le, T. D., Duong, A. D.: Addressing cold-start problem in recommendation systems. In: 2nd International Conference on Ubiquitous Information Management and Communication, pp. 208–211. ACM (2008)

Filtering and Clustering Relations for Unsupervised Information Extraction in Open Domain

Wei Wang[1]
wei.wang@cea.fr

Romaric Besançon[1]
romaric.besancon@cea.fr

Olivier Ferret[1]
olivier.ferret@cea.fr

Brigitte Grau[2]
brigitte.grau@limsi.fr

[1] CEA LIST, 18 route du Panorama, BP 6, Fontenay-aux-Roses, F-92265 France

[2] LIMSI, UPR-3251 CNRS-DR4, Bât. 508, BP 133, 91403 Orsay, France

ABSTRACT

Information Extraction has recently been extended to new areas by loosening the constraints on the strict definition of the extracted information and allowing to design more open information extraction systems. In this new domain of unsupervised information extraction, we focus on the task of extracting and characterizing *a priori* unknown relations between a given set of entity types. One of the challenges of this task is to deal with the large amount of candidate relations when extracting them from a large corpus.

We propose in this paper an approach for the filtering of such candidate relations based on heuristics and machine learning models. More precisely, we show that the best model for achieving this task is a Conditional Random Field model according to evaluations performed on a manually annotated corpus of about one thousand relations. We also tackle the problem of identifying semantically similar relations by clustering large sets of them. Such clustering is achieved by combining a classical clustering algorithm and a method for the efficient identification of highly similar relation pairs. Finally, we evaluate the impact of our filtering of relations on this semantic clustering with both internal measures and external measures. Results show that the filtering procedure doubles the recall of the clustering while keeping the same precision.

Categories and Subject Descriptors

H.3.3 [**Information Storage and Retrieval**]: Information Search and Retrieval—*clustering, information filtering, selection process*

General Terms

Algorithms, Experimentation

CIKM'11, October 24–28, 2011, Glasgow, Scotland, UK.

Keywords

Unsupervised information extraction, filtering, machine learning, clustering

1. INTRODUCTION

Traditionally, Information Extraction was considered from the viewpoint of the MUC (Message Understanding Conferences) paradigm [11]. According to this view, its objective is to extract pieces of information from texts for filling with a fixed role a predefined template. More recently, new forms of information extraction have been developed under the general idea of having more flexible ways to specify the information to extract from texts. Such information is generally defined as a configuration of relations between entities[1] with each relation being defined either as a handcrafted model (frequently a set of rules) or by a set of examples of relations in context that are used to train a statistical model. For an event such as an earthquake for instance, the extraction typically focuses on its location, its date, its magnitude and the damages it has caused and relies on the relations between these pieces of information and the mentions of the event [17]. This approach is globally a supervised or goal-driven approach. Weak forms of supervision have also been developed in this field. Work based on bootstrapping where, following [16], relations are first specified by a small number of examples or linguistic patterns [1], falls into this category. More recently, work related to the notion of *distant supervision* [23], in which relation examples are limited to pairs of entities without any linguistic form for relations, is also an example of such trend.

A reverse approach, called *unsupervised information extraction*, has also been explored during these last years. It aims at finding in texts relations between target entities or types of entities without any *a priori* knowledge concerning the type of the extracted relations. Furthermore, these relations can be clustered according to their similarity to be structured into meaningful sets. Work in this area can be considered according to three main viewpoints. The first one regards the unsupervised extraction of relations as a means for learning knowledge. This view has been developed both for learning "general world knowledge" through the concept of *Open Information Extraction* [2] applied for large-scale knowledge acquisition from the Web in [3] and in more re-

[1]Configuration that is often restricted to one relation.

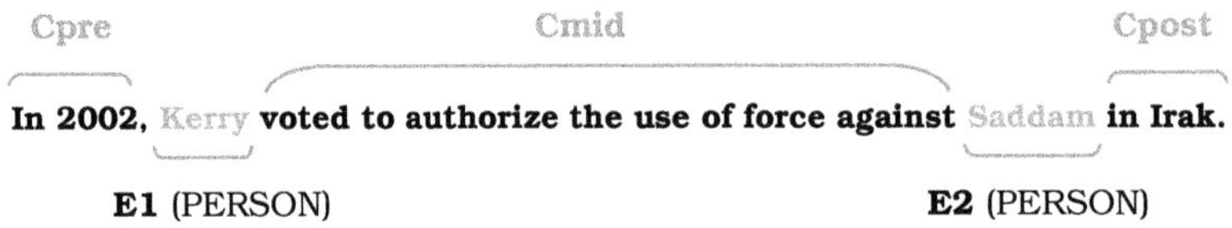

Figure 1: Example of extracted relation

stricted domains, as the biomedical domain, where such relation extraction is used for adding new types of relations between entities in an already existing ontology [6].

The two other viewpoints are more directly related to Information Extraction. The main one tackles the problem of making it possible for users to specify their information needs in a more open and flexible way. The *On-demand information extraction* approach [26], relying on [14] and extended by the notion of *Preemptive Information Extraction* [27], aims at inducing a kind of *template* from a set of documents that are typically retrieved by a search engine from queries that are representative of the information to extract. The same perspective can be found in [19] and, with a specific emphasis put on relation clustering, in [25].

Finally, the last viewpoint, less represented than the two others, considers unsupervised information extraction as a source of improvement for supervised information extraction. The supervised approach frequently depends on manually annotated corpora. As the task is complex, the annotation cost is high and these corpora are generally not very large. In this context, the results of an unsupervised approach can be used to extend the coverage of models learned from an annotated corpus. This idea is more specifically developed in [4] and is also present in [10].

Following the second viewpoint above, our work contributes to the definition of a more flexible information extraction scheme. Within this context, it tackles more particularly the problem of the filtering of extracted relations. The objective of such information extraction process is to discover new types of relations between entities by clustering relations, which requires as less noise as possible among the extracted relations. Hence, we first focus on the filtering procedure, whose objective is to determine whether a relation exists between two named entities in a sentence without any *a priori* knowledge about its type. Then, we evaluate the impact of such filtering on the clustering of large sets of relations and show that it leads to double its recall with the same precision.

2. OVERVIEW

The work we present in this article takes place in a larger context whose global objective is to develop an unsupervised information extraction process for addressing technology watch issues such as "tracking all events involving companies X and Y". This process is based on the extraction of relations defined initially by the co-occurrence of two named entities in a sentence, similarly to most of the works cited in the previous section[2]. The main idea behind these restrictions is to focus first on simple cases to counterbalance the difficulties raised by the unsupervised nature of the global approach. "Simple cases" means here relations whose arguments are rather easy to identify and relations whose linguistic expression is small enough to be easily delimited and to avoid coreference phenomena concerning their arguments.

More formally, candidate relations extracted from texts are characterized by two different kinds of information:

- a pair of named entities (E1 and E2);
- the linguistic form of the relation. It refers more precisely to the way the relation is expressed. As relation extraction is based on the presence of two named entities in a sentence, the linguistic form is made of three parts of this sentence:
  - *Cpre*: part before the first entity (E1);
  - *Cmid*: part between the two entities;
  - *Cpost*: part after the second entity (E2).

  The core expression of the relation is generally conveyed by *Cmid* while *Cpre* and *Cpost* are more likely to bring context elements that are used for detecting its similarity with other relations in the perspective of their clustering.

Figure 1 gives an example of relation with its constituents. It should be noted that such relation has a semi-structured form as one part of its definition – the pair of entities – is defined with elements coming from an already existing ontology while its other part only appears under a linguistic form.

The unsupervised information extraction process based on this notion of relation is defined by the following sequence of tasks:

- analysis of documents (linguistic preprocessing);
- extraction of candidate relations;
- filtering of extracted candidate relations;
- clustering of relations according to their similarity.

The linguistic preprocessing of documents aims at extracting the defining elements of relations. Hence, it includes named entity recognition for the target types of entities but also part-of-speech tagging and lemmatization for normalizing the three parts of the linguistic description of relations. It is achieved by the OpenNLP tools[3].

The step of candidate relation extraction involves very limited constraints: all pairs of named entities with the target types are extracted provided that the two entities appear in the same sentence with at least one verb between them. Table 1 illustrates the volume of the extracted candidate relations from a subpart of the AQUAINT-2 corpus containing news articles from 18 months of the newspaper *New*

[2] In some works such as [2], entities in relation are extended to any noun phrases.

[3] `http://opennlp.sourceforge.net`

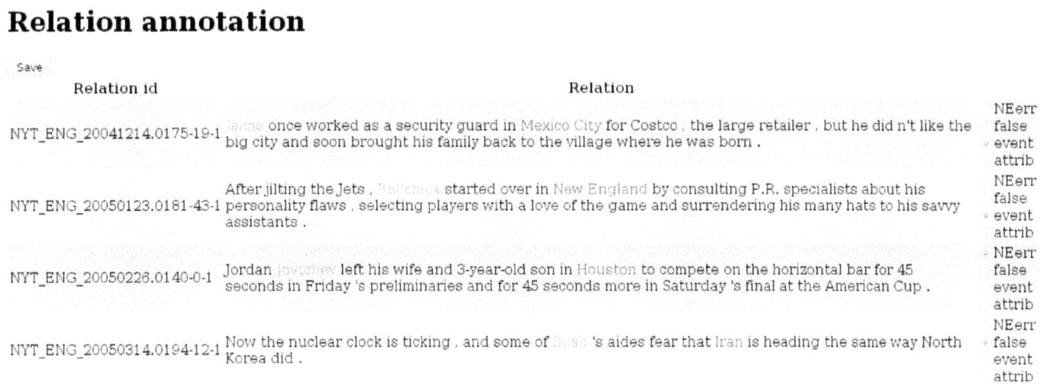

Figure 2: Interface for relation annotation

York Times. All our experiments in this article about relation filtering in section 3 and relation clustering in section 4 are based on this corpus and focus on relations involving persons (PER), organizations (ORG) or locations (LOC).

Table 1: Volume of extracted relations

Relation type	Number of relations
LOC – LOC	116,092
LOC – ORG	57,092
LOC – PER	78,845
ORG – LOC	71,858
ORG – ORG	77,025
ORG – PER	73,895
PER – LOC	152,514
PER – ORG	126,281
PER – PER	175,802

3. RELATION FILTERING

As a consequence of our relation extraction strategy, a significant number of candidates do not contain a true relation between their entities. This basic method, which can lead to good results in specific domains ([9] shows that 79% of extracted candidates using this heuristic are true relations in the biomedical domain), does not seem to be selective enough for open domain. Therefore, we added to this simple strategy a filtering procedure designed to determine the existence of a relation between two entities in a sentence.

3.1 Filtering Heuristics

We first defined more discriminative criteria to filter out sentences that do not contain a true relation between a pair of entities. In this perspective, three heuristics were tested:

- elimination of relations that contain a discourse related verb between the two entities (the list of verbs is currently limited to *to say* and *to present*). This aims at avoiding to extract a relation between the entities *Homgren* and *Allen* in a sentence like: "*Holmgren* said *Allen* was more involved with the team ...";
- the maximum distance between the two entities is limited to 10 words. Effective relations become very rare beyond this empirical limit;
- only one verb is allowed between the two entities, except auxiliary verbs (*be*, *have* and *do*): we discard sentences with a too complex syntactic structure between the entities as they tend to make the existence of a relation between them less likely.

The application of these three heuristics to relation extraction globally reduced the volume of candidate relations by about 50%. Table 2 presents in more details the filtering ratio of each relation type for a sample of 8,000 relations for each type. For each pair of entity types, the second column shows the numbers of relations filtered and kept using all the heuristics, as well as the ratio of kept relations. The three following columns give the number of filtered relations for each individual heuristic, considering that one relation may be filtered by more than one heuristic. The distance limit has obviously an important filtering effect but the only-one-verb limitation has an equally significant impact.

These filtering ratios only give quantitative information about the reduction of relation candidates. In order to evaluate the efficiency of this heuristic filtering in a reliable and feasible way, a subset of 50 randomly selected relations of each type were manually annotated to verify their validity with a Web interface (presented in Figure 2) generated by applying XSLT transformations to the XML representation of relations.

Table 3: Evaluation of filtering heuristics

Relation type	Filtered		Kept	
	true	false	true	false
LOC – LOC	1	49 (98%)	9 (18%)	41
LOC – ORG	4	46 (92%)	8 (16%)	42
LOC – PER	3	47 (94%)	2 (4%)	48
ORG – LOC	7	43 (86%)	14 (28%)	36
ORG – ORG	6	44 (88%)	20 (40%)	30
ORG – PER	4	46 (92%)	20 (40%)	30
PER – LOC	13	37 (74%)	40 (80%)	10
PER – ORG	12	38 (76%)	40 (80%)	10
PER – PER	5	45 (90%)	14 (28%)	36

The results of this annotation, presented in Table 3, show that a very high percentage of filtered relations are indeed false ones, which confirms the relevance of our filtering criteria. These results also show that the ratios of false relations

Table 2: Effect of the application of filtering heuristics on a sample of 8,000 relations

Relation type	filtered/kept	discourse	distance	one verb
LOC – LOC	4287/3713 (46%)	440	3548	2763
LOC – ORG	4097/3903 (49%)	488	3224	2650
LOC – PER	4790/3210 (40%)	1636	3352	2638
ORG – LOC	4225/3775 (47%)	643	3324	2869
ORG – ORG	4169/3831 (48%)	627	3123	2810
ORG – PER	4541/3459 (43%)	1541	3155	2859
PER – LOC	4209/3791 (47%)	905	3199	2813
PER – ORG	3888/4112 (51%)	952	2742	2566
PER – PER	4444/3556 (44%)	1290	3109	2741

after filtering remain important, especially those with LOC as first named entity type. This phenomenon can be explained by the fact that, in a true relation, the first entity should have an agent role in the sentence whereas location names often occur at the beginning of sentences in adverbial phrases. These cases could be detected using a deeper syntactic analysis but such analysis is too costly for the amount of data we process. Considering this observation, relations between entities involving a LOC as first entity are excluded from the following steps.

3.2 Filtering by Machine Learning

The results of Table 3 demonstrate the utility of our filtering heuristics. However, it also indicates that these heuristics are not sufficient to reach a high proportion of correct relations (*i.e.* high enough for the following steps of the unsupervised information extraction process). We present in this section an additional filtering method using statistical machine learning models. Training and test corpora for these models were built manually by annotating relations with the same interface as in Figure 2. More precisely, 200 relations for each of the 6 pairs of our target entity types were randomly selected and annotated. The annotation distinguished correct relations (*true*), incorrect relations due to a named entity recognition error (*NEerr*), and incorrect relations due to the absence of any effective relation (*false*). An additional distinction between the nature of the relations was also made (between attributive relations and event-related relations) but it was not exploited in this work. The results of this annotation are presented in Table 4.

Table 4: Results of manual annotation

Relation Type	true	NE errors	false
ORG – LOC	38% (77)	18% (35)	44% (88)
ORG – ORG	39% (78)	14% (28)	47% (94)
ORG – PER	36% (72)	18% (36)	46% (92)
PER – LOC	51% (102)	31% (62)	18% (36)
PER – ORG	60% (120)	18% (36)	22% (44)
PER – PER	41% (82)	20% (39)	40% (79)
All	44% (531)	20% (236)	36% (433)

The figures of Table 4 show that about 20% incorrect relations are caused by named entity errors. These relations were removed from the corpus to avoid introducing too much noise in the training data. The remaining corpus was composed of 964 relations, 531 of which were true and 433 were false. The resulting set of relation instances is well-balanced enough to avoid problems related to the training of classifiers with unbalanced data sets.

3.2.1 Non-Structured Local Feature Models

We first tested several models based on non-structured local features. Classically, we trained a Naive Bayes classifier, a Maximum Entropy classifier (MaxEnt), a Decision Tree and a Support Vector Machine classifier (SVM). The first three models were implemented using the tools provided by MALLET [22] while the last model was implemented with SVM^{light} [18].

The same set of features was used to train these four different classifiers:

- type of named entities E1 and E2;
- Part-of-Speech (POS) of words between the two entities, using a binary feature for each pair $< P_i, POS_i >$ (with P_i, the position of current word in *Cmid*), as well as bigrams of POS between the two entities, using a binary feature for each triplet $< P_i, POS_i, POS_{i+1} >$;
- POS for the two words before E1 and the two words after E2, both with unigrams and bigrams;
- POS sequence for words between E1 and E2: each possible sequence of 10 POS was encoded as a binary feature;
- number of tokens between E1 and E2;
- number of punctuation marks (comma, quotation mark, parenthesis ...) between E1 and E2.

3.2.2 Sequential Model for Machine Learning Filtering

As [4], we also tested a classifier based on the sequential tagging of each word in a sentence. Our representation of this sequential model is illustrated by Figure 3.

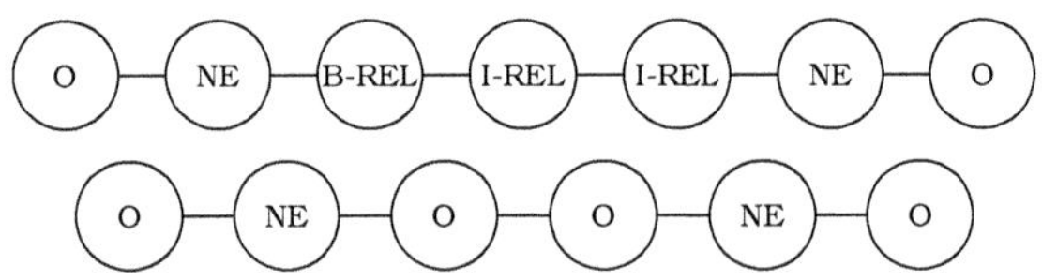

Figure 3: Sequential representation of sentence annotation

More precisely, each word is tagged with one of the four labels below, following the BIO encoding model introduced by [24]:

Table 5: Evaluation of statistical classifiers

Model	Accuracy	Precision	Recall	F_1-measure
Naive Bayes	0.637	0.660	0.705	0.682
MaxEnt	0.650	0.665	0.735	0.698
Decision Tree	0.639	0.640	0.784	0.705
SVM	0.732	0.740	0.798	0.767
CRF	0.745	0.762	0.782	0.771
[4]	/	0.883	0.452	0.598

- O: words not related to a relation or named entity;
- NE: named entity that defines a potential relation (E1 or E2);
- B-REL: first word after E1 inside a relation;
- I-REL: continuation of a relation after B-REL.

After their tagging, sentences containing true relations are labeled as the first configuration of Figure 3 (with a variable number of I-REL depending on the expression of the relation) whereas false relation sentences are labeled as the second one. In practice, a well-trained classifier should not generate configurations other than the two presented in Figure 3: for instance (O – NE – B-REL – O – O – NE – O) is not possible since B-REL is always followed by at least one I-REL in the training corpus.

This approach was implemented by a linear Conditional Random Fields (CRF) model, using the Wapiti [20] tool, and trained with the following set of features for each word of the sentence:

- POS of the current word, the previous one and the following one;
- bigrams of POS <POS_{i-1}, POS_i > , with i=-1,0,1 (0: current word; -1: previous word; 1: following word);
- entity type of the current word and the 6 previous and following words. This type is equal to NULL when the word is not a named entity.

3.2.3 *Evaluation of Statistical Filtering*

Considering the relatively small size of the annotated corpus, we used a 10-fold cross-validation to evaluate these different classifiers: the corpus was split into 10 equal parts, 9 of which being used for training and 1 for testing; the procedure is repeated 10 times so that each part is used for training and for test at least once. The results of Table 5 represent the average values on the 10 iterations of the standard measures of *Accuracy*, *Precision*, *Recall* and *F1-measure*.

Table 5 first shows that the SVM classifier obtains the best performance among the non-sequential models, which is a result generally obtained by similar works about relation extraction. It also shows that the CRF classifier slightly outperforms the SVM classifier, which confirms the advantage of the sequential model. Moreover, we note a balance between precision and recall for all types of classifiers. Compared with the results of [4] on the same subject (see the last line of the table), our results exhibit a better F1-measure, with a much better recall and a slightly lower precision. However, the work in [4] relies on more general entities than only named entities, which makes the task harder. As we have not enough room here for detailing the various relation representations and the different sets of features we have tested, we only present those achieving the best performance. However, it is interesting to notice, concerning the entities of relations, that removing the entity type as a feature and replacing it by a generic "NE" tag to mark the presence of a named entity only causes a slight decrease of the performance of the CRF classifier, with a F1-measure equal to 0.768. This indicates a promising extensibility of our classifier to other named entity types. Finally, as a consequence of the global results of this evaluation, the CRF model was adopted for the relation filtering part of our unsupervised information extraction method in the experiments of section 4.

3.3 Application of Relation Filtering

The extraction of relations is composed of three successive steps:

- initial extraction, only based on the the co-occurrence of two named entities with the target types and the presence of at least one verb in between;
- application of three filtering heuristics for eliminating a large number of false relations with a good precision;
- application of a machine learning filtering to distinguish more finely true relations from false ones.

Moreover, we observed the presence of a certain number of identical relations coming either from articles about the same subject or from very formatted expressions. Hence, we completed the filtering procedure with a final deduplication step for discarding these redundant relations. As there exists a superior boundary for the values of the similarity measure between relations, the implementation of this final step was based on the identification of pairs of relations with this maximal similarity value, which was done by relying on the same approach as for the clustering of relations in section 4 for evaluating the similarities between relations. For relations having this maximal similarity value, only one representative element was kept. We put this deduplication operation as the last step of the relation extraction process for two reasons: first, this procedure is more costly than the other filtering operations; second, it relies on the evaluation of relation similarity performed for relation clustering.

Table 6 shows detailed information for each step of relation filtering, starting from all candidate relations of Table 1. We can note that this filtering put aside a large number of the initially extracted relations but we have estimated that only 19.9% of these discarded relations result from erroneous decisions, with a global recall of the filtering procedure estimated to 0.553. Finally, the remaining volume is *a priori* sufficient for the next steps of our unsupervised information

Table 6: Relation volumes after each filtering step

	ORG-LOC	ORG-ORG	ORG-PER	PER-LOC	PER-ORG	PER-PER
initial extraction	71,858	77,025	73,895	152,514	126,281	175,802
heuristics	33,505 (47%)	37,061 (48%)	32,033 (43%)	72,221 (47%)	66,035 (52%)	78,530 (45%)
classifier CRF	16,700 (23%)	17,025 (22%)	12,098 (16%)	55,174 (36%)	50,487 (40%)	42,463 (24%)
deduplication	15,226 (21%)	13,704 (18%)	10,054 (14%)	47,700 (31%)	40,238 (32%)	38,786 (22%)

extraction process. Furthermore, as in [4], the context of our work is the processing of large text collections characterized by informational redundancy for which high-precision results are preferred to avoid too much noise.

4. RELATION CLUSTERING

4.1 Method

The objective of our work is to cluster similar relations in order to offer users a better view of existing relations between entities as in many articles in the domain of unsupervised information extraction [27, 25]. We have chosen for this clustering an approach similar to [14]: we only consider one level of clustering for gathering relations that share the same meaning (semantic clustering). The definition of this similarity of meaning is relatively loose: it does not only represent a strict notion of paraphrase or implication but is more related to the notion of information redundancy used in automated summarization.

The clustering method relies on two elements: a similarity measure between relations and a clustering algorithm that uses the pairwise similarities between relations. For the similarity measure, we chose the widely used *cosine* measure and applied it to a bag-of-words representation of relations. More precisely in our case, we only used the *Cmid* part of each relation in order to focus on its core meaning rather than on its context. The choice of the cosine measure was also justified by the results of preliminary experiments showing its superiority over the edit distance for a similar task.

Clustering algorithms often rely on a similarity matrix which can be costly to compute, in particular for larges sets of relations like the one we want to process (several tens of thousands of relations), since the number of similarities is quadratic with respect to the number of relations. Algorithms such as *k-means* are a little less costly since they only consider the similarities between the points and the centroids of current clusters but they require to fixed *a priori* the number of classes, which is hard to evaluate in our case (optimizing this number is possible but can lead again to a problem of complexity). We tackled this issue by using the *All Pairs Similarity Search* algorithm (APSS) [5] that allows to compute efficiently a similarity measure such as the cosine measure for all pairs of elements whose similarity value is above a given threshold. The efficiency of this algorithm relies on a series of optimizations in the indexing of the elements to compare that exploit the fixed threshold and the sparsity of the input vectors for reducing the number of comparisons to perform. In our experiments, this threshold was based on observations from the Microsoft Research Paraphrase Corpus [8]. This corpus contains a set of sentence pairs associated with an assessment indicating if they are paraphrases or not. We computed the cosine measure for all pairs of paraphrase sentences and chose to fix our threshold value to 0.45, which covers 3/4 of the similarity values between these sentences.

We then used the *Markov Clustering* algorithm [29] to create the final clusters of relations from the similarity matrix computed by the APSS algorithm. More precisely, this matrix, which is rather sparse, is directly transformed into a similarity graph by associating each relation with a node and each non-zero similarity with a weighted edge between two nodes. The Markov Clustering algorithm performs the partitioning of a graph by the means of a series of random walks on the graph. This algorithm converges quite fast in practice, which allows to deal with large graphs, and does not depend on a fixed number of clusters: its only parameter, *inflation*, controls the granularity of the clusters. In our experiments, we adopted the default inflation value of the MCL implementation[4].

4.2 Evaluation of Relation Clustering

We present in this section a quantitative evaluation of the relation clustering. Evaluation of clustering is a hard task because no gold-standard partitioning of the set of elements is available: such a reference would be too costly to build, considering we have tens of thousands of relations. The usual approach in this case is to evaluate the quality of the results obtained by manually looking at a particular set of clustering results. A major drawback of this kind of evaluation is that it relies on a specific clustering configuration and would require to perform the complete evaluation process again if the clustering technique changes. We wanted to have a more reproducible evaluation framework in order to compare clustering results with and without filtering and possibly with different filtering techniques.

We then propose to perform two evaluations of the clustering: the first one is an evaluation using internal criteria; the second one using external criteria, but only on a partial reference. On one hand, internal criteria for clustering evaluation allows to establish to which extent the clusters obtained correspond to the similarity measures between the relations [12]. More precisely, we use the internal criteria to test the hypothesis that the similarities in the relation space after filtering have a better distribution that the ones before filtering, then leading to a better clustering. On the other hand, external criteria allow to better take into account an actual evaluation of whether two relations in the same cluster belong to the same semantic relation. Since we do not have the possibility to create a gold-standard for the whole set of relations, we decided to create reference data for a selected subset of relations and evaluate how these relations are distributed among the different clusters.

4.2.1 *Clustering Evaluation with Internal Measures*

Among various internal measures for clustering evalua-

[4]http://micans.org/mcl

tion, we chose a measure of *expected density*, which is evaluated in [28] as the one having the best correlation with F-measure for documents clustering (the more usual measure of the *Dunn index* is said to be less stable).

Given a weighted graph (V, E, w) with a node set V, an edge set E and a weight function w, the density θ of the graph is defined by:

$$\theta = \frac{ln(w(G))}{ln(|V|)}$$

with $w(G) = |V| + \sum_{e \in E} w(e)$ and the weight function w defined by the relation similarity in our case.

Expected density can be computed by local and global graph density of clustering. For a set of result clusters $C = \{C_i\}$ with $C_i = (V_i, E_i, w)$, the expected density is defined by:

$$\rho = \sum_{i=1}^{|C|} \frac{|V_i|}{|V|} |V_i|^{\theta_i - \theta}$$

where $\frac{|V_i|}{|V|}$ intends to balance the difference of size of clusters. For taking into account the considerable difference of the collection size due to the filtering phase, we defined an expected density measure that is less dependent on the corpus size by loosening the exponential factor $|V_i|$, which is connected to the size of each cluster. Therefore, we used the following definition of expected density:

$$\rho' = \sum_{i=1}^{|C|} \frac{|V_i|}{|V|} \frac{\theta_i}{\theta}$$

A higher value of the measure ρ' implies a better clustering quality.

We also considered the *Connectivity* measure [13], another internal measure. Connectivity evaluates how many nearest neighbors are not clustered together. This measure is of particular interest for us since it is based on the same similarity graph that we are using for the clustering method. The connectivity measure is defined by:

$$c = \sum_{i=1}^{|V|} \sum_{j=1}^{p} x_{i, nn_i(j)}$$

where p denotes how many neighbors are taken into account, $nn_i(j)$ is the jth nearest neighbor of i and $x_{i,nn_i(j)}$ equals to 0 if i and $nn_i(j)$ are in the same cluster and equals to 1 otherwise.

As shown by its formal definition, connectivity also depends on corpus size. To avoid such dependence, we selected randomly a subset of the total corpus (5,000 relations were used for evaluation in our experiments). This measure is inverse compared to the expected density: a lower connectivity value indicates a better clustering.

Results of expected density measure and connectivity measure are presented in Table 7. The results with these two internal measures show that the filtering phase generally improves the clustering processing. Better clusters are generated from the filtered relations using the same clustering method. The two entity pairs which do not follow the same tendency are, for the expected density, ORG – LOC and PER – LOC. Since both share the same entity type *location*, this observation probably indicates a special behavior of these entities. Actually, as we stated in section 3, location entities are often included in adverbial phrases. When such a case happens, there is no real relation between the location entity and the other entity although, with the currently used similarity measure, phrases with similar location adverbials can be clustered together and obtain a good clustering score.

4.2.2 Clustering Evaluation with External Measures

The first results with internal measures demonstrate the interest of the filtering procedure. Then, we have tried to confirm this interest using external measures by comparing the clustering results with reference clusters. A partial reference has been built in three steps:

1. indexing of all relation candidates with a search engine;
2. querying of this index iteratively to locate interesting relations;
3. creation of relation clusters manually from the results of the queries.

More precisely, we first indexed the extracted relations with the search engine Lucene[5], using distinct fields for the text, the named entities and the entity types. This allows us to search relations with queries specifically targeting their first or second named entity (*E1*, *E2*), the types of these entities (*T1*, *T2*) or the linguistic constituents of relations *Cmid*, *Cpos* or *Cpre* (see relation example in Figure 1). We used this possibility by querying the index with various combinations of fields, in a first step to explore potential target relations between given named entities and entity types (*e.g.* with queries such as *E1=Bush*,*T2=*LOC), and then in a second step, to explore different named entities with target relations (*e.g.* with queries such as *T1=*PER, *Cmid contains "visit"*). After several iterations of these two steps, we obtained a set of relations mixing a large diversity of relations together with a significant number of similar relations. Based on these relations, we built manual clusters with a specific Web-based annotation tool.

Currently, our gold-standard reference concentrates on the relation type PER – LOC and contains 17 clusters with 253 relations, including relations such as, *come from*, *be going to*, *have a speech in*, *like*, etc. We present below some examples for the relation *grow up in*:

- *Pitcher Brandon Backe*, who grew up 50 miles from here in *Galveston* and dreamed of pitching for the Astros in the postseason, displayed a veteran's savvy with his varying speeds.
- Chief Justice Wallace B. Jefferson, a Republican, named *Pat Priest*, a retired Democratic judge from his hometown of *San Antonio*, to hear the case – but not before Jefferson's own multiple ties to DeLay's political operation were questioned.
- By the time he turned 10, *Levine* had performed as a soloist with his hometown *Cincinnati* Orchestra.

External measures like *Purity*, *Normalized Mutual Information* and *Rand Index* are well discussed in the literature (*e.g.* [21]). Given reference clusters with N relations, *Rand Index* is defined to check how all $N(N-1)/2$ pairs of relations are grouped. A clustering method should assign similar

[5]http://lucene.apache.org

Table 7: **Internal evaluation for relation clustering (best results are presented in bold)**

	Expected density		*Connectivity* ($p = 20$)	
	pre-filtering	post-filtering	pre-filtering	post-filtering
ORG – ORG	1.06	**1.13**	5335.7	**3450.8**
ORG – LOC	**1.13**	1.02	4458.7	**2837.6**
ORG – PER	1.09	**1.17**	3025.4	**1532.4**
PER – ORG	1.02	**1.06**	5638.0	**4620.0**
PER – LOC	**1.08**	1.07	5632.5	**4571.3**
PER – PER	1.13	**1.15**	3892.7	**2569.2**

Table 8: External evaluation for relation type PER – LOC

phase	*rand index*	*precision*	*recall*	F_1	*TP*	*FP*	*FN*	*TN*	*purity*	*MI*	*NMI*
pre-filtering	0.8863	0.5372	0.1271	0.2056	469	404	3221	27784	0.5540	1.6338	0.6008
post-filtering	0.8864	0.5280	0.2211	0.3117	866	774	3051	28979	0.5889	1.7216	0.6285

relations to the same cluster and separate dissimilar ones. Hence, there are four kinds of decisions. First, a true positive (TP) decision assigns two similar relations to the same cluster while a true negative (TN) one assigns two dissimilar relations to different clusters. TP and TN are both correct decisions. On the other hand, there are two incorrect decisions: false positive (FP) decisions, which assign two dissimilar relations to the same cluster, and false negative (FN) decisions, which assigns two similar relations to different clusters. The *Rand Index* measures the clustering accuracy, which is defined by:

$$RandIndex = \frac{TP + TN}{TP + FP + FN + TN}$$

F-measure can be defined in the same time, relying on the precision P and recall R:

$$P = \frac{TP}{TP + FP} \quad R = \frac{TP}{TP + FN} \quad F_\beta = \frac{(\beta^2 + 1)PR}{\beta^2 P + R}$$

We have computed the distribution of reference relations in clustering results for both the pre-filtering phase and the post-filtering phase. The results are presented in Table 8. These results show that the filtering procedure almost doubles the recall measure, from 0.1271 to 0.2211, while the precision is kept around 0.53. We can also see directly from this table that many more pairs of truly similar relations (TP) are found by the clustering method on the post-filtering corpus than on the pre-filtering corpus.

Rather than examining all pairs of relations, clustering quality can be measured directly at a cluster level. Purity and *Normalized Mutual Information* (NMI) are usually used for this purpose. A prerequisite of this approach is to assign each result cluster to the class (a reference cluster) with which it shares the largest number of relations. *Purity* is defined by:

$$purity(\Omega, \mathbb{C}) = \frac{1}{N} \sum_k \max_j |w_k \cap c_j|$$

where $\Omega = \{w_1, w_2, ...w_K\}$ is the set of result clusters and $\mathbb{C} = \{c_1, c_2, ..., c_J\}$ is the set of reference clusters.

Purity has a bias when the number of clusters is large: it is equal to 1 when each relation forms its own cluster. Normalized mutual information makes a trade-off between the number of clusters and their quality. It is defined by:

$$NMI(\Omega, \mathbb{C}) = \frac{MI(\Omega, \mathbb{C})}{(H(\Omega) + H(\mathbb{C}))/2}$$

$MI(\Omega, \mathbb{C})$ is the mutual information between Ω and $\mathbb{C}$, with the definition:

$$MI(\Omega, \mathbb{C}) = \sum_k \sum_j P(w_k \cap c_j) \log \frac{P(w_k \cap c_j)}{P(w_k) * P(c_j)}$$

where $H(\Omega)$ and $H(\mathbb{C})$ are respectively entropies of Ω and $\mathbb{C}$, defined as:

$$H(\Omega) = -\sum_k P(w_k) \log P(w_k)$$

where $P(w_k)$, $P(c_j)$ and $P(w_k \cap c_j)$ are respectively the probabilities of a relation being in a result cluster w_k, in a reference cluster c_j and in the intersection of the two. The probabilities are computed directly by counting the cardinalities of the clusters.

In the same way as for the *Rand Index* measure, we computed these measures for the result clusters obtained using relations extracted with or without the filtering phase. Evaluation results for *Purity* and *NMI* are illustrated in Table 8. The results show that both *Purity* and *Normalized Mutual Information* are improved by the filtering. In particular, the augmentation of *Purity* confirms the recall improvement observed with the *Rand Index* measure.

5. RELATED WORK

One of the specificities of the work we have presented in this article is to associate two types of work in the field of unsupervised information extraction, relation filtering and relation clustering, and to study the consequences of this association. Concerning relation filtering, our work is close to the work described in [4], with two main differences. First, relation arguments are restricted to named entities in our case, whereas such argument has more general form in [4] and can be any base noun phrase[6]. Second, [4] does not rely on manually annotated examples as we do but exploits examples built automatically from the successful parses of a

[6]Base noun phrases refer to noun phrases that do not contain nested noun phrases or modifiers such as prepositional phrases.

syntactic parser by applying a small set of heuristics. The possible impact of these two differences is not easy to predict as they tend to diverge in terms of effects. The first difference makes relation extraction more difficult in the case of [4] as it enlarges the set of possible relations to cover. However, restricting the possible relations to a subset of the successful parses of a syntactic parser clearly favors relations with a simple syntactic form whereas the limits of our reference relations are only set by a human annotation. Finally, the results of [4], a high precision but a low recall, can be explained as follows: because of the kind of entities it focuses on, [4] considers a large set of possible relations but the classifier it has developed is actually able to takes into account only a small subset of them because of the way it is trained. Our approach implements a more balanced choice between the set of relations we want to take into account and the set of relations we actually model, which globally leads to higher results. From a practical viewpoint, building the training examples automatically from the results of a syntactic parser as [4] did is of course an interesting choice to have a large training set without the cost of a human annotation but of course, this method heavily depends on both the availability and the quality of such parser in the target context (language, domain or type of texts).

Concerning relation clustering, the comparison with existing work raises two main issues. The first one is the scalability of the clustering process. Clustering algorithms frequently start from a similarity matrix that can be difficult to compute when the number of items to cluster is large. One way to overcome this difficult is to fix or to evaluate *a priori* the number of clusters to build. For instance, [30] sets arbitrarily the number of clusters according to the document set, [25] tests different values whereas [10] uses the Akaike Information Criterion to evaluate this number in one of its experiments. This problem is also bypassed in some works by limiting the number of relations to cluster, either directly or through the initial number of documents. [14] for instance only considers relations with at least 30 occurrences whereas experiments in [25] are limited to 4,000 relation occurrences and those in [30] to 526 Wikipedia documents. In our case, this issue is tackled by associating a filtering method for discarding explicitly false relations and the use of the APSS algorithm for evaluating efficiently the similarity of the remaining relations. This combination makes the use of a large spectrum of clustering algorithms possible.

The second important issue concerning relation clustering is the evaluation of its results. As mentioned in section 4.2, a direct evaluation of the built clusters and their content by human annotators as it was performed in [14] or in [30] cannot be achieved very often because of its cost. In particular, it does not fit the constraints resulting from the tuning of a system. It is why we have adapted and applied measures for the internal evaluation of clustering to the context of unsupervised information extraction, which was not done before to our knowledge. These measures were more specifically used for testing the impact of relation filtering and their conclusions appear as coherent with those of external measures, as illustrated in section 4.2.2. For our external evaluation, we have chosen as [25] to select a sample of relations and to cluster them manually to build a reference. More precisely, because of the very large number of relations we have, this selection was guided in our case by a search engine. Finally, the evaluation consists in determining to what extent relations that are part of a reference cluster are found in the same cluster in the evaluated clustering. Following [15], [10] adopts the same principle but uses as reference the relations annotated in a corpus in the context of a supervised information extraction task, more precisely, the Relation Mention Detection task of the ACE (Automatic Content Extraction) evaluation [7].

6. CONCLUSION AND PERSPECTIVES

In this paper, we have presented a work on relation filtering for unsupervised information extraction whose purpose is to determine if two entities occurring in the same sentence are linked by a relation without *a priori* knowledge about the relation type. This filtering is performed using both heuristic and machine learning techniques. Heuristic filtering is first used to remove the simple cases whereas machine learning techniques are used for more ambiguous cases. Evaluation of machine learning techniques shows that best results are obtained with CRF, compared with results obtained with SVM, MaxEnt or NaiveBayes classifiers. Our best performances are quite balanced between precision and recall and are better than the results reported in [4] (but their study is not limited to named entities, which makes the task more difficult). Applied to unsupervised information extraction, we have also showed, through an evaluation of relation clustering with both internal and external criteria, that this filtering is useful for a semantic clustering of the extracted relations.

The most direct perspectives of this work are about the clustering of relations. We will improve the external evaluation of the clustering using a larger set of annotated examples and try to have more evidences on the interest of such partial external evaluation by computing its correlation with a completely annotated reference. We also plan to use a more sophisticated clustering including two levels of clustering: a semantic clustering and a thematic clustering. Finally, we also consider applying this filtering process to improve a system for knowledge base population based on *distant supervision* by filtering out the candidate relations extracted from a corpus for learning linguistic relation patterns.

7. ACKNOWLEDGMENTS

This work was partly supported by the ANR FILTRAR-S project and the FP7 Virtuoso project.

8. REFERENCES

[1] E. Agichtein and L. Gravano. Snowball: Extracting relations from large plain-text collections. In 5th *ACM International Conference on Digital Libraries*, pages 85–94, San Antonio, Texas, USA, 2000.

[2] M. Banko, M. J. Cafarella, S. Soderland, M. Broadhead, and O. Etzioni. Open Information Extraction from the Web. In *Twentieth International Joint Conference on Artificial Intelligence (IJCAI-07)*, pages 2670–2676, Hyderabad, India, 2007.

[3] M. Banko and O. Etzioni. Strategies for Lifelong Knowledge Extraction from the Web. In 4th *International Conference on Knowledge Capture (K-CAP 2007)*, pages 95–102, Whistler, BC, Canada, 2007.

[4] M. Banko and O. Etzioni. The Tradeoffs Between Open and Traditional Relation Extraction. In *48th Annual Meeting of the ACL: Human Language Technologies (ACL-08: HLT)*, pages 28–36, Columbus, Ohio, 2008.

[5] R. J. Bayardo, Y. Ma, and R. Srikant. Scaling Up All Pairs Similarity Search. In *16th International Conference on World Wide Web*, pages 131–140, Banff, Alberta, Canada, 2007.

[6] M. Ciaramita, A. Gangemi, E. Ratsch, J. Saric, and I. Rojas. Unsupervised Learning of Semantic Relations between Concepts of a Molecular. Biology Ontology. In *International Joint Conference on Artificial Intelligence (IJCAI 2005)*, pages 659–664, Edinburgh, UK, 2005.

[7] G. Doddington, A. Mitchell, M. Przybocki, L. Ramshaw, S. Strassel, and R. Weischedel. The Automatic Content Extraction (ACE) Program – Tasks, Data, and Evaluation. In *4th Conference on Language Resources and Evaluation (LREC 2004)*, pages 837–840, 2004.

[8] B. Dolan, C. Quirk, and C. Brockett. Unsupervised Construction of Large Paraphrase Corpora: Exploiting Massively Parallel News Sources. In *20th International conference on Computational Linguistics (COLING 2004)*, pages 350–356, Geneva, Switzerland, 2004.

[9] M. Embarek and O. Ferret. Learning patterns for building resources about semantic relations in the medical domain. In *6th Conference on Language Resources and Evaluation (LREC'08)*, Marrakech, Morocco, 2008.

[10] E. González and J. Turmo. Unsupervised Relation Extraction by Massive Clustering. In *Ninth IEEE International Conference on Data Mining (ICDM 2009)*, pages 782–787, Miami, Florida, USA, 2009.

[11] R. Grishman and B. Sundheim. Design of the MUC6 evaluation. In *MUC-6 (Message Understanding Conferences)*, Columbia, MD, 1995. Morgan Kauffmann Publisher.

[12] M. Halkidi, Y. Batistakis, and M. Vazirgiannis. Cluster validity methods: part I. *ACM SIGMOD Record (Special Interest Group on Management of Data)*, 31:40–45, June 2002.

[13] J. Handl, J. Knowles, and D. B. Kell. Computational cluster validation in post-genomic data analysis. *Bioinformatics (Oxford, England)*, 21(15):3201–3212, August 2005.

[14] T. Hasegawa, S. Sekine, and R. Grishman. Discovering Relations among Named Entities from Large Corpora. In *42nd Meeting of the Association for Computational Linguistics (ACL'04)*, pages 415–422, Barcelona, Spain, 2004.

[15] H. Hassan, A. Hassan, and O. Emam. Unsupervised Information Extraction Approach Using Graph Mutual Reinforcement. In *2006 Conference on Empirical Methods in Natural Language Processing (EMNLP'06)*, pages 501–508, Sydney, Australia, 2006.

[16] M. Hearst. Automatic Aquisition of Hyponyms from Large Text Corpora. In *14th International Conference on Computational Linguistics (COLING'92)*, pages 539–545, Nantes, France, 1992.

[17] L. Jean-Louis, R. Besançon, and O. Ferret. Using Temporal Cues for Segmenting Texts into Events. In *7th International Conference on Natural Language Processing (IceTAL 2010)*, pages 150–161, Reykjavik, Iceland, 2010.

[18] T. Joachims. Making large-scale SVM learning practical. In B. Schölkopf, C. Burges, and A. Smola, editors, *Advances in Kernel Methods - Support Vector Learning*, pages 169–184. MIT Press, Cambridge, MA, 1999.

[19] H. H. Kathrin Eichler and G. Neumann. Unsupervised Relation Extraction From Web Documents. In *6th Conference on Language Resources and Evaluation (LREC'08)*, Marrakech, Morocco, 2008.

[20] T. Lavergne, O. Cappé, and F. Yvon. Practical Very Large Scale CRFs. In *48th Annual Meeting of the Association for Computational Linguistics (ACL 2010)*, pages 504–513, Uppsala, Sweden, 2010.

[21] C. D. Manning, P. Raghavan, and H. Schütze. *Introduction to Information Retrieval*. Cambridge University Press, New York, NY, USA, 2008.

[22] A. K. McCallum. MALLET: A Machine Learning for Language Toolkit. http://mallet.cs.umass.edu, 2002.

[23] M. Mintz, S. Bills, R. Snow, and D. Jurafsky. Distant supervision for relation extraction without labeled data. In *Joint Conference of the 47th Annual Meeting of the ACL and the 4th International Joint Conference on Natural Language Processing of the AFNLP*, pages 1003–1011, Suntec, Singapore, 2009.

[24] L. Ramshaw and M. Marcus. Text Chunking Using Transformation-Based Learning. In D. Yarowsky and K. Church, editors, *Third Workshop on Very Large Corpora*, pages 82–94, Cambridge, Massachusetts, USA, 1995.

[25] B. Rosenfeld and R. Feldman. Clustering for unsupervised relation identification. In *Sixteenth ACM conference on Conference on information and knowledge management (CIKM'07)*, pages 411–418, Lisbon, Portugal, 2007.

[26] S. Sekine. On-Demand Information Extraction. In *21st International Conference on Computational Linguistics and 44th Annual Meeting of the Association for Computational Linguistics (COLING-ACL 2006)*, pages 731–738, Sydney, Australia, 2006.

[27] Y. Shinyama and S. Sekine. Preemptive Information Extraction using Unrestricted Relation Discovery. In *HLT-NAACL 2006*, pages 304–311, New York City, USA, 2006.

[28] B. Stein, Sven, and F. Wißbrock. On Cluster Validity and the Information Need of Users. In *3rd IASTED International Conference on Artificial Intelligence and Applications (AIA'03)*, pages 404–413, 2003.

[29] S. van Dongen. *Graph Clustering by Flow Simulation*. PhD thesis, University of Utrecht, 2000.

[30] Y. Yan, N. Okazaki, Y. Matsuo, Z. Yang, and M. Ishizuka. Unsupervised Relation Extraction by Mining Wikipedia Texts Using Information from the Web. In *Joint Conference of the 47th Annual Meeting of the Association for Computational Linguistics and the 4th International Joint Conference on Natural Language Processing (ACL-IJCNLP 2009)*, pages 1021–1029, Suntec, Singapore, 2009.

Facilitating Pattern Discovery for Relation Extraction with Semantic-Signature-based Clustering

Yunyao Li
IBM Research - Almaden
650 Harry Road
San Jose, CA 95120
yunyaoli@us.ibm.com

Vivian Chu
IBM Research - Almaden
650 Harry Road
San Jose, CA 95120
vchu@cal.berkeley.edu

Sebastian Blohm *
Microsoft Corporation
Rablstr. 26, 81669 München,
Germany
sblohm@microsoft.com

Huaiyu Zhu
IBM Research - Almaden
650 Harry Road
San Jose, CA 95120
huaiyu@us.ibm.com

Howard Ho
IBM Research - Almaden
650 Harry Road
San Jose, CA 95120
ho@almaden.ibm.com

ABSTRACT

Hand-crafted textual patterns have been the mainstay device of practical relation extraction for decades. However, there has been little work on reducing the manual effort involved in the discovery of effective textual patterns for relation extraction. In this paper, we propose a clustering-based approach to facilitate the pattern discovery for relation extraction. Specifically, we define the notion of *semantic signature* to represent the most salient features of a textual fragment. We then propose a novel clustering algorithm based on semantic signature, S2C, and its enhancement S2C+. Experiments on two real-world data sets show that, when compared with k-means clustering, S2C and S2C+ are at least an order of magnitude faster, while generating high quality clusters that are at least comparable to the best clusters generated by k-means without requiring any manual tuning. Finally, a user study confirms that our clustering-based approach can indeed help users discover effective textual patterns for relation extraction with only a fraction of the manual effort required by the conventional approach.

Categories and Subject Descriptors

H.3.1 [**Information Storage and Retrieval**]: Content Analysis and Indexing—*Linguistic processing*; I.2.7 [**Artificial Intelligence**]: Natural language processing—*text analysis*

General Terms

Algorithms, Experimentation, Human Factors

Keywords

Information Extraction, Clustering, Pattern Discovery

*Work was done while visiting IBM Research - Almaden.

CIKM'11, October 24–28, 2011, Glasgow, Scotland, UK.

1. INTRODUCTION

Relation extraction refers to the task of detecting and classifying meaningful relations between two or more entities in text. For example, the text fragment "please call Alice from CompanyA Inc. at her cell phone (123) 456-7890" contains the EMPLOYEEOF relation "Alice from CompanyA Inc." and the PERSONPHONE relation "Alice ... at her cell phone (123) 456-7890". Relation extraction is important for many applications, ranging from information retrieval and question answering to text entailment.

Most information extraction systems rely on knowledge engineering or machine learning to generate the "task model" for relation extraction. In the knowledge engineering approach, the model is usually in the form of manually created extraction rules. In the machine learning approach, the model is learned automatically from a manually labeled training data in a supervised or semi-supervised fashion. The machine learning approach has been popular in the research community in recent years (e.g. [1, 5, 12, 24, 32, 39, 40]). At the same time, the knowledge engineering approach remains a widely adopted practical solution for relation extraction due to its transparency, customizability, and maintainability. These properties are highly valued by emerging enterprise text analytics applications (e.g. compliance and semantic search) [9, 11, 14, 31].

In the knowledge engineering approach, a developer creating rules for a binary relationship (e.g. pairs of PERSON and PHONENUMBER) typically starts by manually examining the contexts between the pairs. She then determines whether each pair forms a meaningful relation and manually discovers textual patterns indicating the desired relation. Finally she writes rules to incorporate the patterns observed. These rules, when applied to a training corpus, usually generate a large number of results. The developer examines a (typically small) sample of the results, and determines whether each one is positive or negative. She then discovers potential improvements to the rules by examining the relationship between the results, the original context strings, and the applicable patterns. She iterates through the process until she is satisfied with the precision and recall of the relation extraction annotator. The following example illustrates one step in this process.

EXAMPLE 1. PERSONPHONE. *An obvious pattern for identifying the* PERSONPHONE *relation is* "PERSON *followed by* 'at' *followed by a* PHONENUMBER *within the same sentence", represented as* P_1 = "⟨PERSON⟩ .* at .* ⟨PHONENUMBER⟩". *While* P_1

can correctly identify valid PERSONPHONE *relation such as "Alice at (123) 456-7890" and "Bob can be reached at (111) 222-3333", it not only produces incorrect matches such as "John's assistant at x1234" but also fails to identify correct matches such as "Jane's cell: (222) 333-4444". In order to account for precision and recall, a rule developer needs to refine P_1 (e.g. P_2 = "⟨PERSON⟩ (can be reached)? at .* ⟨PHONENUMBER⟩") as well as identifying additional patterns (e.g. P_3 = "⟨PERSON⟩'s (cell|office|home)? : ⟨PHONENUMBER⟩").*

As can be seen, this is an extremely tedious and error-prone manual process that can take days or even weeks of work to develop rules for a single relation. The focus of this work is to reduce the human effort involved in writing rules for relation extraction. In this paper, we propose a novel formulation of clustering algorithm called *Semantic-Signature Clustering* (short as S2C) to facilitate the discovery of patterns for relation extraction. In the rest of the section, we first summarize our contributions and then discuss in detail the related work.

1.1 Contributions

In a key departure from prior formulations, the clustering problem presented in this work not only clusters similar strings, but also generates meaningful patterns. These patterns are similar to the manually generated ones used in relation extraction rules. Our specific contributions are:

- A novel clustering problem consisting of clustering strings of relation candidates and generating clusterings that share the same pattern for relation extraction.
- Formulation of this clustering task as a three-step algorithm S2C, where each of these steps can be optimized individually with well-known techniques:
  - (Potentially offline) sequence mining & rule generation
  - Efficient rule application to generate semantic signatures
  - Efficient database-like grouping based on exact match
- Extensive experimental results over real-world data sets that showcase the effectiveness of S2C. The results include (1) improved precision and recall of relation extraction rules written with the assistance of S2C+ over product-quality relation extraction rules generated in a purely manual fashion; (2) S2C+ runs an order of magnitude faster than conventional k-means clustering for real-world relation extraction tasks.

Conventional text clustering algorithms (e.g. k-means [27]) are based on computing the similarity of context strings among each other or between each context string and a cluster representative. Context strings are mapped to a space (e.g. converted to a numeric vector) in which such a distance can be computed. For large scale relation extraction, both the numbers of context strings (depending on the size of the corpus) and potential clusters representatives (one needed for each way to express a relation) grow rapidly to large sizes and causes the number of comparisons to grow rapidly. As we will show later, our clustering method saves these comparisons by only requiring a rule-based local transformation on the context strings. Furthermore, unlike conventional clustering algorithms, our clustering method requires no extensive manual tuning on the parameters. To further motivate our approach, we now discuss prior work with a focus on related work in the area of clustering for relation extraction and the limitations of these techniques.

1.2 Related Work

Textual patterns play an important role in relation extraction [6, 21]. As discussed earlier, learning of patterns for relation extraction is typically a supervised process in learning-based systems or a tedious manual process in knowledge-engineering-based systems. Several semi-supervised systems were developed to enable relation extraction using a large unlabeled corpus and a small set of seeds [1, 4, 16, 18, 37].

A number of recent works focus on unsupervised relation identification. [20, 7] discover relations of co-occurring named entities by clustering based on the words that appear between each pair. [13] groups textual occurrences based on the so-called hook words and then uses statistical correlation between the related entities contained in the textual examples to generate meaningful groups. Another clustering based method was proposed by [33] where the goal is to identify relations by clustering pairs of entities. Classical sequence patterns are mined as part of this approach to generate features for clustering. The SNE system [25] clusters the subject-verb-object triples generated by an Open Information Extraction system[3] into semantically coherent relations by probabilistically modeling the triples in second-order Markov logic and applying a co-clustering algorithm.

While unsupervised relation identification can reduce the labor cost of semi-supervised systems by automatically generating seeds [34], little work has been done for the building of relation extraction patterns used by the knowledge-engineering-based systems. Our work seeks to fill this gap. It takes advantage of the unsupervised nature of clustering method similar to unsupervised relation identification, but with the goal of facilitating pattern discovery for relation extraction for knowledge-engineering-based systems. Our clustering method is configurable by the user using intuitive features, as the default clustering may or may not produce the granularity desirable to a user.

Our frequency-based pattern generation technique was motivated by the vGram approach [26] which performs fuzzy string matching by means of an automatically mined set of variable length subsequence. Our approach is based on a modification of the Apriori algorithm [2]. A similar approach is applied to web usage log mining in [29]. Their technique is based on task-specific pruning of the pattern candidate space. We extend their technique to mine interesting pairs of sequences. The underlying generalization of Apriori is described in [35]. An application of a more basic sequence mining technique to sentiment detection in texts can be found in [23].

2. OVERVIEW

In this work, we are primarily concerned with the task of clustering the contexts extracted from the vicinity of relation candidates to assist the discovery of patterns used for relation extraction. Once these clusters are formed the patterns may be generated either manually by an annotator developer or automatically by existing techniques such as [6, 16]. This second phase will not be discussed further here, but we do present user study results in the experimental section to demonstrate the effectiveness of the generated clusters in assisting annotator developers.

For pedagogical convenience, in the rest of the paper we restrict our attention to only consider binary relations and only context strings between the two entities in the relation. It will be obvious that the techniques presented here are applicable to more general situations. For example, the context string could include the complete sentence(s) in which the two entities appear, which may extend to the left and right of both entities.

Under the above restrictions, the clustering problem for a target

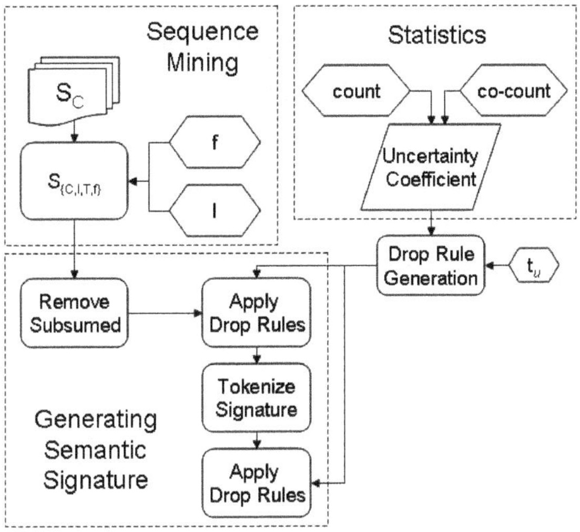

Figure 1: Flow chart for semantic signature generation

Input String	Relation Candidate c	Context String s_c
Nadia Ficara \n Event Manager \n tel: 555-3567	Nadia Ficara, 555-3567	\n Event Manager \n tel:
Bill can be reached at \n tel: 555-4567 early Monday morning.	Bill, 555-4567	can be reached at tel:
John can be found 555-4274	John, 555-4274	can be found

Figure 2: Example input, relation candidates and context strings

relation R can be described as follows. We are given two sets of entities E_1 and E_2, a set of relation candidates $C \subset E_1 \times E_2$, and a set of content strings S_C associated with C. Each string $s_c \in S_C$ is extracted from the vicinity of a candidate $c = (e_1, e_2) \in C$ according to predefined rules. The goal of the clustering task is to generate disjoint clusters $C = C_1 \cup C_2 \cup ... \cup C_n \cup O_t$ so that each cluster C_i is associated strongly with either R or its complement. These clusters serve as hints for positive and negative patterns for the relation R. The special cluster O_t (for "Orphan") is a conglomerate of all those clusters smaller than a threshold t.

Our strategy for generating these clusters is to associate each C_i with a distinct *Semantic Signature* G_i. This process (dubbed S2C) consists of two stages: (1) Generating first level semantic signatures; and (2) further clustering of these semantic signatures. The first stage utilizes the statistical correlations of the context strings. The second stage utilizes textual similarities of the context strings. These stages are described in Section 3 and 4 respectively.

3. SEMANTIC SIGNATURE GENERATION

The semantic signature generation stage consists of several steps, as illustrated in Figure 1. We describe details of each step in this section. Figure 2 provides three example inputs. We use data in the first row to construct a running example for this entire section. Figure 3 shows the results of the transformations in each step.

Step 1: Generating Frequent Sequences.

The goal of this step is to map the context strings to a reduced

Context string	\n Event Manager \n tel:
Frequent sequence set	{\n; manager \n tel:; \n tel:; tel }
After subsumed	{\n; manager \n tel: }*
After drop rule	{manager \n tel: }
After drop rule with split sequences	{\n; tel }

Figure 3: Example results of transformations in S2C

* The first "\n" (a line break character) in the context string is not subsumed because it is not part of the substring "Manager \n tel:".

set of sequences that are intended to capture the most salient features of the context strings. This mapping is done in the following process with three parameters: a tokenization procedure T, an integer l for maximum length of sequence, and an integer f for minimum frequency of the sequence. The steps are: (1) Tokenizing each context string s_c by T into a token sequence s. (2) Collecting all subsequences of s with length no more than l generated from all $s_c \in S_C$. (3) Retaining all those with at least f occurrences in the corpus. The result is a frequent sequence set $S_{C,T,l,f}$. In actual implementation, a single pass through the data is sufficient.

Step 2: Computing Correlation.

Once each context string is reduced to a set of sequences, we can collect statistics to compute the correlation between sequences. By discovering the correlation between sequences, similar sequences within the same set can be removed. This results in a semantic signature that represents the key elements of the context string. Different measure of correlation can be used in this step. In this paper, we choose *uncertainty coefficient* [38] to be the measure of correlation between two sequences.

For each ordered pair of frequent sequences x and y, the proportion of information in x that is shared with y can be measured by the uncertainty coefficient

$$U(x|y) = I(x, y)/H(x), \tag{1}$$

where $I(x, y)$ is the mutual information between x and y, and $H(x)$ is the entropy of x. If $U(x|y)$ is close to unity, dropping x in the presence of y will not remove a significant portion of available information. In practice, we can approximately compute $I(x, y) = p(x, y) \log \frac{p(x,y)}{p(x)\,p(y)}$, and $H(x) = -p(x) \log p(x)$, where $p(x)$ and $p(x, y)$ are the empirical probabilities of occurrences and co-occurrence. The definitions of $I(x, y)$ and $H(x)$ involve summing over the probabilities of occurrence and non-occurrence. However, since our interest here is only in the effect of occurrences of the sequences, and since the probability of non-occurrence is much larger than that of occurrence, terms for non-occurrences can be ignored.

Step 3: Generating Drop Rules.

For each pair of $x, y \in S_{C,T,l,f}$, if $U(x|y)$ is larger than a predefined threshold t we generate a "drop rule" $\text{DROP}(x|y)$. They are stored in decreasing order of corresponding $U(x|y)$. Figure 4 provides an example of some uncertainty coefficients and the corresponding drop rules generated. These will be used later in our running example.

Step 4: Removal of Subsumed Sequences.

To further remove noise from the semantic signature, we remove those sequences x in the presence of other sequences y if the origi-

x	y	$U(x\|y)$	$U(y\|x)$
manager	tel:	0.962	0.802
manager \n tel:	\n	0.762	0.553

(a) Example uncertainty coefficients

$U(x, y)$	Drop Rules
0.962	DROP(manager|tel:)
0.802	DROP(tel:|manager)
0.762	DROP(\n|manager \n tel:)

(b) Example drop rules generated with threshold $t = 0.75$ and stored order of $U(x|y)$

Figure 4: Example drop rule generation

Original Context Text	Semantic Signature
's number is	{number}
and her phone number is	{number}
; number:	{number}
's cell number	{number}
at	{at}
with at questions at	{at}
tomorrow at	{at}

Figure 5: Sample entries of two clusters generated by S2C

Size	Sample Original Context Text	Semantic Signature
19	's number is	{number}
2	\n\n Domestic Number:	{domestic number}
1	He said the number is	{number is}

Figure 6: Example of three similar clusters generated by S2C, which are merged into one cluster by S2C+

nal string for x is found within the original string of y. Simply put, if the original string of x is a substring of the original string of y, x is considered to be subsumed by y and thus removed from the sequence set.

Consider the example in Figure 3, where the given context string is "\n Event Manager \n tel:". The sequences {\n tel:} and {tel:} are subsumed by {manager \n tel:} since they are from the same substring. These are then removed. resulting the final sequence set {\n; manager \n tel:}.

Step 5: Applying the Drop Rules.

The drop rules are applied to remove non-informative sequences. As described earlier, these rules were generated to indicate that one sequence is not informative in the presence of another sequence. For instance, the current set {\n; manager \n tel:} results in {manager \n tel:} when the rule DROP(\n|manager \n tel) is applied.

The rules are applied in their stored order, which is determined by the correlation measure associated with each rule. Applying the drop rules in this order guarantees that the sequence with less useful information is dropped. For instance, if both DROP$(x|y)$ and DROP$(y|x)$ exist where DROP$(x|y)$ has a higher measure of uncertainty, then if the sequence set includes $\{x, y\}$, x is removed from the set and DROP$(y|x)$ has no effect. An example of this appears in the following step.

One may wonder why we chose to apply the drop rules after removing subsumed sequences, instead of before. When generating statistics, the results are generated based on the correlation between all pairs of sequences without considering the subsumed relationship. However, when applying the rules, we take a conservative approach and require a subsequence to be as important by itself as it is with other subsequences. If rules are applied before, essentially a higher weight is given to each subsequence and important sequences can be lost. Take, for example, the sequence set $\{a, ab, c\}$ where ab represent a sequence comprised of the subsequences a and b. If DROP$(c|a)$ is applied before subsumed, the resulting signature is $\{ab\}$ and c is lost. However, if subsumed is applied first, which removes a due to the presence of ab, the resulting signature is $\{ab, c\}$, preserving c. Only an explicit rule like DROP$(c|ab)$ would remove c.

Step 6: Applying the drop rules to split sequences.

For certain sequences, a second pass with the drop rules is required, after all larger sequences are split into subsequences of length 1. This captures cases where a sequence of length 1 is capable of describing the entire context string, but has been stored together with a second sequence of less importance.

For the previous sequence set {\n; manager \n tel:}, the only rule that would apply is D_1 =DROP(\n|manager \n tel:). However, by splitting the larger sequences, the rules in Figure 4, can now remove sequences that do not contribute meaningful information to the final semantic signature. Applying the rules, in stored order, results in a final sequence string of {\n; tel:}. Notice that when the rules are applied in stored order, {manager} was dropped as opposed to {tel:}.

Step 7: Clustering based on semantic signature.

We call the resulting sequence of tokens representing each context string the semantic signature of the original string.

Once we obtain the semantic signature of each context string for all the relation candidates, the clustering of context strings S_C is straightforward — all the relation candidates associated with the same semantic signatures form one cluster. Candidates with different semantic signatures are in different clusters. In addition, any cluster with size smaller than a predefined threshold t is reassigned to a special cluster O_t. We refer to this clustering method as S2C.

Figture 5 illustrates sample entries from two clusters of relation candidates generated by S2C. As can be seen, the entries in each cluster are indeed semantically similar to each other, as represented by their sematic signature, {number}, {at}, respectively.

4. CLUSTERING AND APPLICATION

In this section, we discuss the issues of applying the S2C results to assist in annotator development.

4.1 Merging of small groups based on string similarities

One remaining problem with the S2C algorithm is that the "Orphan" cluster O_t can be a non-trivial size. Recall that O_t is a conglomerate of all clusters with size smaller than t. It is clear that the content of O_t is very diverse and difficult to discover meaningful patterns from. Consequently, when O_t is large the resulting relational annotator developed with the help of this clustering may have a poorer recall. In order to reduce the size of O_t, we utilize the observation that the semantic signatures of many small clusters are often similar to those of larger ones. For instance, Figure 6 lists three different clusters created by S2C, with different but similar semantic signatures. If we merge some of the small clusters with larger ones, the total number of clusters stays the same, but the size of O_t will decrease. As long as the semantic signatures of the merged clusters are similar, the clusters can still assist the pattern discovery for relation extraction.

Merging small clusters into larger clusters, rather than simply discarding them, improves the results in two ways. First, after merging we still retain the set of original semantic signatures. This provides the user with very useful hints on the possible variations of semantic signatures. Second, the user can also drill down to all these clusters to see actual examples, which is a very crucial requirement in example-based rule development.

We measure the distance between two clusters by the distance between their respective semantic signatures, which are sets of token sequences. There are several ways to measure the (dis)similarity between them. For example, we can use the Jaccard distance on these two sets [22]. Given such a distance d, we proceed in the following steps: (1) For all the small clusters C that went into O_t, we look for those with size smaller than re-clustering threshold $t_s \leq t$. (2) If there exists a cluster C_j with size larger than $t_l \geq t$ such that $d(C, C_j) > s$, remove C from O_t to C_j. When there are multiple C_j satisfying the condition, we pick the largest among them. Other policies might be advantageous in certain aspects and further research is needed to quality them.

For example, when given $t_s = 3$, $t_l = 9$ and d the Jaccard Distance, the three clusters in Figure 6 are merged into one.

4.2 Complexity of the S2C and S2C+ algorithms

The computation in S2C involves several pass through the data points (context strings). In step 1 (generating frequent sequence), the set has $O(nml)$ cost, where n is the number of data points, m is the average number of tokens generated from each context string, and l is the maximum length subsequences allowed. Steps 2 and 3 (computing uncertainty coefficients and drop rules) have $O(ns^2)$ cost, where $s < ml$ is the average number of frequent subsequences for each context string. Seps 4 and 5 (removing subsumed subsequences and of applying drop rules) each also has $O(ns^2)$ cost. Step 6 (applying drop rules on split strings) has an $O(nms)$ cost. The final clustering step has $O(ns)$ cost. Therefore the total cost is $O(ns^2) + O(nms)$. Note that both m and s are only dependent on the distribution of the context strings and the parameters used in the algorithm. They do not depend on the size of the data set. Therefore the cost of this algorithm is essentially linear in the size of its input data.

The computation in S2C+ involves sweeping through the small clusters and computing their distance to each of the large clusters. The cost is $O(k_1 k_2 d)$, where k_1 and k_2 are the numbers of large and small clusters, and d is the cost of calculating a distance between two semantic signatures. If we choose the cutoff threshold t by limiting the number of large clusters to at most L, then the cost is bounded by $O(nLd)$. Since L and d are independent of the data size, the cost of S2C+ is also linear in the size of input data.

In summary the computational complexity of the S2C and S2C+ algorithms are both linear in the input data size.

In contrast, the k-means algorithm is known to have a complexity $O(Iknt)$, where I is the number of iterations, and t is the time needed to calculate the distance between two points.

4.3 User interface for utilizing the clustering results

We designed a novel GUI to facilitate the exploration of the clusters generated by S2C or S2C+ for pattern discovery [8]. See the screenshot in Figure 7. The basic idea is to allow a developer to quickly identify a cluster of interest based on its size and semantic signature and then have the ability to drill down and explore

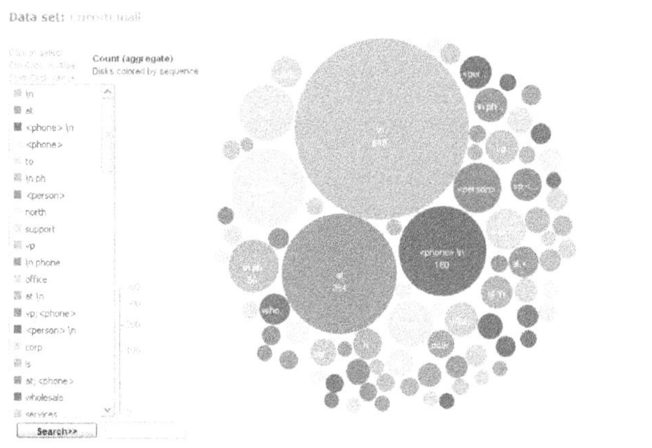

Figure 7: Screenshot of user interface

A bubble graph is used to represent the clusters. A bubble has a size proportional to that of its corresponding cluster and uses the semantic signature as its label.

the actual relation candidate contained by the cluster. In addition, through the GUI, the user should be able to exploit any labeling information available.

One of the most important design decision of the S2C system is that it can be a useful tool in the development cycle of annotator development. This imposes a constraint on system response time. As will be shown in the experimental section, S2C is at least an order of magnitude faster than k-means. In addition, as many of the steps in the S2C process are reusable, the actual responses time of S2C embedded in an annotator development environment is much shorter than the end-to-end running time. In many cases, the computation of frequent sequences and drop rules need to be computed only once. The user adjustable parameters are the thresholds for applying drop rules, for the orphan group, and for merging the small groups. Re-computation when these parameters change are almost instantaneous and are easily controlled in the GUI.

5. EXPERIMENTS

In this section, we present an empirical study of the S2C and S2C+ algorithms over two real-life data sets. The main goal of the study is answer the following questions: (1) Do the algorithms generate high quality clusters for relation extraction? (2) Are the algorithms effective in reducing manual effort in discovering textual patterns for high-quality relation extraction? (3) How do the algorithms compare with existing clustering algorithms, in both the quality of the clusters created as well as runtime performance?

5.1 Experimental Setup

5.1.1 Data Sets

For the experiments, we used two different real-life text corpora:

- **Bio**: A collection of 2,068 biographies from 456 SEC Form DEF 14A filings[1].
- **Email**: A collection of 37,939 email messages from the publicly available Enron collection [28].

The former contains formal clean text, while the latter contains mostly informal noisy messages.

[1]Tthe data set is now publicly available at URL.

5.1.2 Relation Extraction Tasks

For each data set, we chose a real-life relation extraction task that has been previously implemented for commercial products via a knowledge-based approach. Specifically, for the Bio data set, we chose the task of identifying POSITIONINORG and for the Email data set, we chose the task of identifying PERSONPHONE. The goal of our study is to compare the patterns produced manually, with ones crafted with the assistance of S2C and S2C+ in terms of the extraction quality of patterns as well as the amount of manual effort required to derive these patterns.

5.1.3 Gold Standard

We obtained the labeled data via the use of Amazon Mechanical Turk (MTurk), which has been shown to produce high quality annotations for a variety of natural language processing tasks [36]. Following the practice by [17], we first used existing state-of-the-art NER annotators [10] to identify *Person* and *PhoneNumber* over Email, *Position* and *Organization* over Bio. We then obtained noisy potential relation candidates by extracting ⟨ *Person*, *PhoneNumber*⟩ and ⟨*Position*, *Organization* ⟩ pairs from the data sets, with each pair of entities within 40 tokens of each other.[2] We then submitted each candidate along with its context as a Human Intelligence Task (HIT) to MTurk and asked the workers to select from three annotation options: the candidate (1) represents the relation, (2) does not represents the relation, or (3) not applicable.

We initially launched a pilot study with 100 HITs (i.e., 100 relation candidates). Upon the completion of the pilot and verification of the quality of the result, we then deployed the full study for all the relation candidates. Each HIT was assigned to five unique workers for a cost of $0.02 each. A total of 5171 HITs were submitted for Bio and 5771 HITS for Email. The majority vote of workers decided the final labeling. We also used known control answers to identify spurious responses and unreliable users to filter out noisy labels. Each rejected assignment was then resubmitted to MTurk until high quality answers were obtained.[3]

5.1.4 Comparison Study

In our experiments we evaluated both S2C and its enhancement S2C+ with $t_s = 3$ and $t_l = 10$. We also compared them to k-means [27], a popular generic clustering algorithm, using the implementation from WEKA [19]. Note that the results of k-means is sensitive to k, the number of clusters to be generated. Since we do not know about the optimal number of k, we set k of k-means to be the number of clusters found automatically by S2C and S2C+, denoted as k-means$_1$ and k-means$_2$ respectively. For all the clustering algorithms, we posed the threshold for orphan cluster $t = 5$ and move all the clusters with size smaller than t into a special orphan cluster.

5.1.5 Experimental Platform

We ran all our experiments on a Windows-based PC with Intel Core 2 Duo processor with a single core speed of 2.20GHz and total RAM of 3.0 GB.

5.2 Experiment 1: Quality of Clusters

We first examined the quality of the clusters generated by S2C and S2C+ in two aspects: (1) the total number of clusters that the algorithm generates, which determines the number of textual patterns required to develop the relation extraction annotator; (2) the overall quality of the clusters.

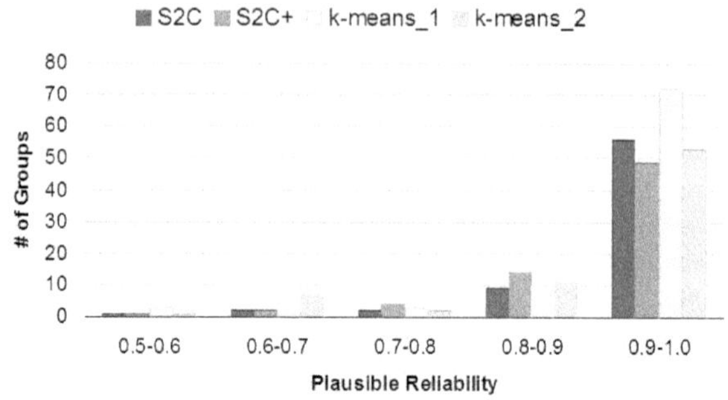

(a) By Number of Entries

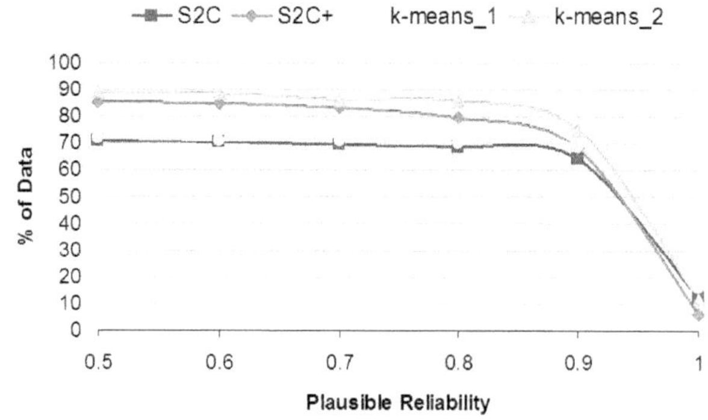

(b) By Percentage of Entries

Figure 8: Quality of clusters Generated by S2C, S2C+, k-means$_1$, and k-means$_2$ over Bio Corpus

k-means$_1$ and k-means$_2$ correspond to k-means with k being the cluster sizes found using S2C and S2C+ respectively.

5.2.1 Plausible Reliability

Intuitively, the quality of a cluster correlates with how reliable a (positive or negative) textual pattern can be generated based on the cluster. Therefore, given the precision of a cluster C $Precision(C) = \frac{|C \cap G|}{|C|}$, where G is the gold standard, the closer $Precision(C)$ to 1 or 0, the higher the quality of C. Following this intuition, we propose a new metric called *Plausible Reliability* (short as *PR*) to measure the quality of C, based on how close $P(C)$ is to 1 or 0, defined as follows:

$$PR(C) = \max(1 - Precision(C), Precision(C)) \quad (2)$$

Hence, the value of $PR(C)$ for a cluster C is between 0.5 and 1. The higher the value of $PR(C)$ is, the better the quality of C.

To measure the overall quality of a set of clusters $\mathcal{C} = C_0, ...C_n$, we can use their average PR, defined as follows:

$$Average\ PR(\mathcal{C}) = \frac{\sum_{i=0}^{n} |C_i| \times PR(C_i)}{\sum_{i=0}^{n} |C_i|} \quad (3)$$

5.2.2 Results over Bio

We first analyze the results obtained over Bio for the four different techniques. Figure 8(a) shows the histogram of clusters of

[2]For fair comparison, we used the same token boundary limit as that used in the existing annotators.

[3]We rejected 1.8% of the answers for the POSITIONINORG task over Bio and 5.1% of the answers for PERSONPHONE task over Email.

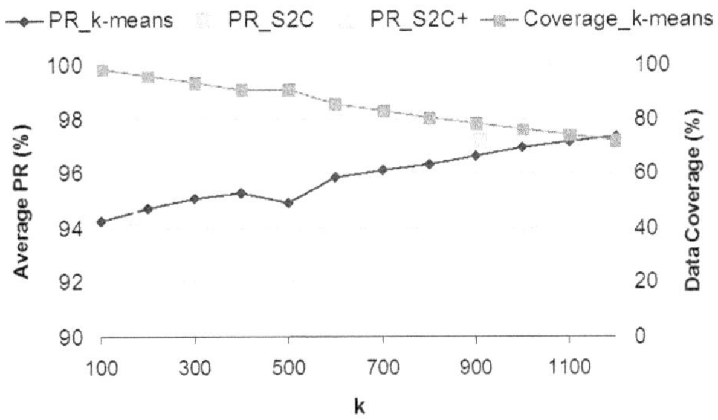

Figure 9: Average PR and data coverage of clusters generated by k-means with varying k

PR_{S2C} and PR_{S2C+} indicate the average PR of the clusters generated by S2C and S2C+ respectively.

different plausible reliability. For all four techniques, the number of clusters is not large, ranging from 70 for S2C and S2C+ and 89 for k-means$_1$. More importantly, the majority of the clusters (ranging from 68.5% for S2C+ to 80.0% for k-means$_1$) are high quality clusters with PR higher than 0.9. Furthermore, the vast majority of the clusters (around 90% across the board) are at least good clusters, i.e. clusters with PR higher than 0.8.

Another important aspect of the quality of the clusters is their coverage, especially of the high quality ones. Figure 8(b) depicts the distribution of data by plausible reliability. As we can see, the high quality clusters generated by all techniques cover the majority of the data (ranging from 72% to 76%). Furthermore, good quality clusters, i.e. clusters with PR higher than 0.8, cover the major of the remaining data. Recall that in the experiment, we provide k-means the cluster sizes found using S2C and S2C+ for k-means$_1$ and k-means$_2$ correspondingly. We found that on this data set, k-means$_1$ and k-means$_2$ produced higher number of high quality clusters than S2C and S2C+ respectively. We also found that the clusters produced by k-means$_1$ and k-means$_2$ have higher coverage than those produced by S2C and S2C+ respectively, but the advantage is very small.

We can see from Figure 8 that as expected, S2C+ has produced fewer high quality clusters than S2C, as more noise has been introduced into the clusters when merging small clusters with larger ones in S2C+. Meanwhile, we also observe that S2C+ has effectively reduced the size of the orphan cluster and evidently improved the coverage of the clusters over S2C.

Since the result of k-means is sensitive to the given value of k, in order to verify that the automatically found cluster sizes were reasonable parameters for k-means, we evaluated the performance of k-means on the Bio corpus with varying k-parameters. The results are summarized in Figure 9. As can be seen, the average PR of (weighted by the number of entries contained by each cluster) the clusters produced by k-means increases gradually with the increase of k, while the coverage of the clusters drops steadily as well. The graph also indicates that the size automatically discovered by S2C+ provides a good trade off between the coverage of the clusters and the overall quality of the clusters.

5.2.3 Results over Email

The performance of the algorithm over the Email set are analyzed similarly and the results are shown in Figure 10. Similar to their

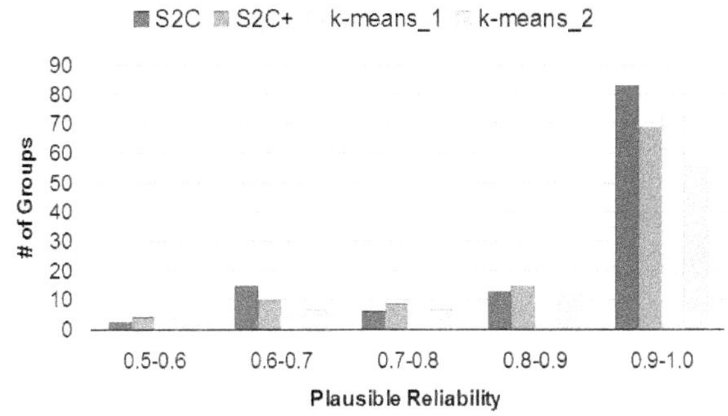

(a) By Number of Entries

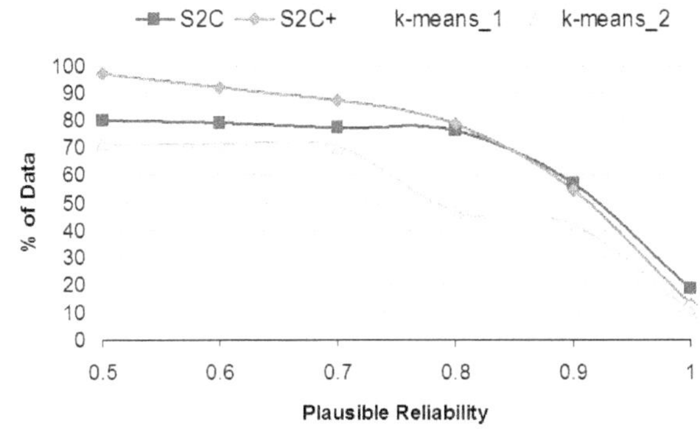

(b) By Percentage of Entries

Figure 10: Quality of clusters generated by S2C, S2C+, k-means$_1$, and k-means$_2$ over Email Corpus

k-means$_1$ and k-means$_2$ correspond to k-means with k being the cluster sizes found using S2C and S2C+ respectively.

performance over Bio, all algorithms generate relatively small numbers of clusters, with most being high quality clusters that together cover most data. Compared to the results over Bio, the number of high quality clusters generated by all techniques increases. However, their coverage drops considerably across the board. The drop is especially significant for k-means$_1$ and k-means$_2$, both from a coverage of lower 70% over Bio to that of lower 40% over Email. When taking good quality clusters into consideration, the coverage of k-means$_1$ and k-means$_2$ over Email remains lower than that over Bio. However, the coverage of S2C and S2C+ actual improves from around 70% on Email to nearly 80% on Bio.

S2C and S2C+ consistently outperform k-means$_1$ and k-means$_2$ respectively both in terms of the good quality clusters generated and in terms of the coverage of the clusters. The advantage is especially pronounced when we consider the coverage for clusters with PR higher than 0.8, where the coverage of good quality clusters of k-means$_1$ and k-means$_2$ is drastically lower than ones generated by S2C and S2C+. The decay of the performance of k-means$_1$ and k-means$_2$ on Email is not surprising — Email is much more noisy than Bio, and as a result, clustering blindly based on all the string content leads to less reliable clusters.

Once again, S2C+ does introduce noise to the clusters, with the coverage of high quality clusters dropping slightly from 56.8% to 54.5%. But at the same time, it effectively reduces the number of clusters that the developer needs to evaluate.

Semantic Signature	Pair	Example Context
at	Kristen Albrecht,x34763 Pamela Merchant,415-703-1404	please call Brent Price at x37647 or ⟨1⟩ at ⟨2⟩ ...Deputy Attorney General ; ⟨1⟩ ; at ⟨2⟩ or ...
number	Curt,713-230-7205 Andrea Walters, (281) 584-1405	...⟨1⟩'s number is ⟨2⟩... His assistant is ⟨1⟩ and her phone number is ⟨1⟩
\n ph	Doug Kinney,703-561-6339 Terrie James,713-853-7727	⟨1⟩ \n Ph: ⟨2⟩ ⟨1⟩ \n ph. ⟨2⟩

Figure 11: Sample clusters over Email: two candidate pairs for each cluster, and an example context for each pair.

5.3 Experiment 2: Effectiveness of S2C

Results of Experiment 1 indicate that S2C and S2C+ are able to automatically generate high quality clusters with good coverage without requiring manual tuning. Intuitively, the clusters generated, such as shown in Figure 11, should be able to help a rule developer generate high quality extraction patterns with reduced manual cost. To evaluate whether this main goal of our work is achieved, we conducted the following user study on the effectiveness of S2C algorithms.

In this experiment, each data set is randomly partitioned into 80% training and 20% test data. Two rule developers were asked to independently write the PERSONPHONE annotator for Email and POSITIONINORG annotator for Bio based on the clusters generated by S2C+ over the training data. To quantify the amount of manual effort involved in the annotator development, each developer was given 2 hours for each task. We then compared the extraction quality of the annotators developed with the help of S2C+ with the corresponding product-quality annotators developed previously using conventional purely manual approach over the entire data set.

The results are summarized in Table 1 and 2. As can be seen, even though the developer using the purely manual approach was given much longer time (2 to 3 weeks vs. 2 hours) than the developers using the S2C+-assisted approach, the extraction quality of the annotators created in the conventional approach ($Manual_{bio}$ and $Manual_{email}$) is significantly lower than that of the annotators developed with the assistance of S2C+ (S2C$_{bio}$ and S2C$_{email}$) in recall and F-measure [4]. In addition, the precision of the annotators developed by S2C-assisted approach is at least comparable to, if not better than, the precision of the conventional manual approach. Specifically, the precision of $Manual_{bio}$ is slightly better than that of S2C$_{bio}$, while the precision of $Manual_{email}$ is considerably lower than that of the annotator developed with assist of S2C (S2C$_{email}$). The results confirm that our S2C algorithms are indeed effective in reducing the manual effort required for developing high quality relation annotators.

In addition, Figures 12 and 13 show the progression of improvement each time the developer added a new pattern. As one can see, the recall on both data sets steadily increases while precision is held consistently high. Furthermore, Table 3 lists the quality results of the annotators over both training and test data on Bio. The quality of the annotator over the test data set are comparable to that over the training data set, implying that no over fitting has occurred.

5.4 Experiment 3: Running time

As discussed earlier, one motivation of our work on developing the new S2C-based clustering algorithms is to be able to produce clusters with high efficiency. We therefore also measured the runtime performance of k-means and S2C in our comparison study.

We found that for both Bio and Email, it took k-means at least one order of magnitude longer to return results than S2C or S2C+.

[4] β is set to 0.5 to reflect the practical emphasis on precision.

Table 1: Extraction quality over Bio

Annotator	Precision(%)	Recall(%)	$F_{0.5}$(%)
$Manual_{bio}$	98.37	53.68	84.33
S2C$_{bio}$ Expert 1	97.83	90.42	96.25
S2C$_{bio}$ Expert 2	98.20	84.86	95.21

Table 2: Extraction quality over Email

Annotator	Precision(%)	Recall(%)	$F_{0.5}$(%)
$Manual_{email}$	90.44	63.36	83.30
S2C$_{email}$ Expert 1	92.69	68.96	86.72
S2C$_{email}$ Expert 2	91.70	89.26	91.20

Table 3: Statistics for training set vs test set on Bio

Data Set	Precision(%)	Recall(%)	$F_{0.5}$(%)
Expert 1 Training	97.36	88.97	95.56
Expert 1 Test	97.83	90.42	96.25
Expert 2 Training	97.39	86.03	94.88
Expert 2 Test	98.20	84.86	95.21

For instance, over the Email corpus, it took k-means 50 minutes to generate all the clusters compared to the 5 minutes needed for S2C. Such long delay in generating results is problematic, since the clustering algorithms are embedded in an interactive annotator development tool where developers may desire to make changes to the configuration parameters to generate optimal clusters. Furthermore, S2C can often reuse the statistics previously computed to further speed up the cluster generation process based on various optimization techniques similar to database optimization. For instance, if the developer only makes the threshold for uncertainty coefficient stricter, the algorithm can determine that the only steps from drop rule generation need to be recomputed. Finally, k-means requires the user to run the clustering multiple times to find the optimal k-parameter and can potentially cause further delay in cluster generation.

We also observed that k-means tends to consume much more heap-based memory that S2C. When running our more complicated data set Email, often times k-means would not return a result because it would eventually consume over 1.5 GB of memory. In contrast, S2C never consumes over 1 GB of memory throughout our experiments. One reason is that our intermediate steps are saved to a database to conserve heap memory.

Given the fact that most of our annotator development are done on a laptop-based environment similar to the one used in our experiments, we can see that S2C is more suitable to assist the pattern

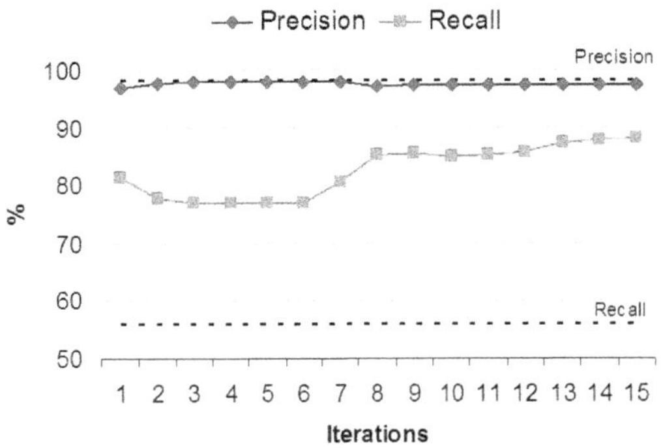

(a) Expert 1 Results

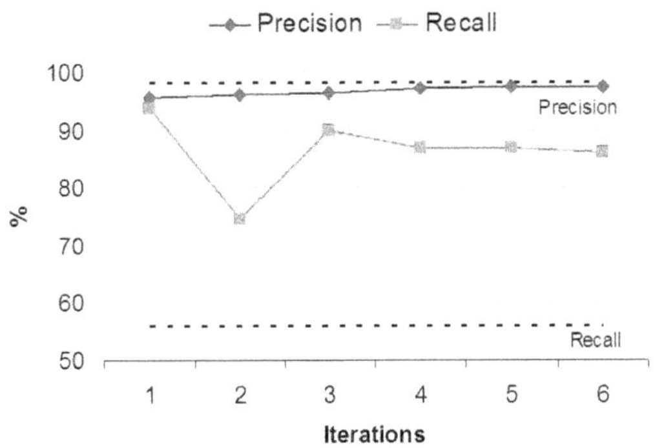

(b) Expert 2 Results

Figure 12: Changes of precision and recall of POSITIONINORG annotator over the iterations. The dotted lines are the results of the manually constructed annotators.

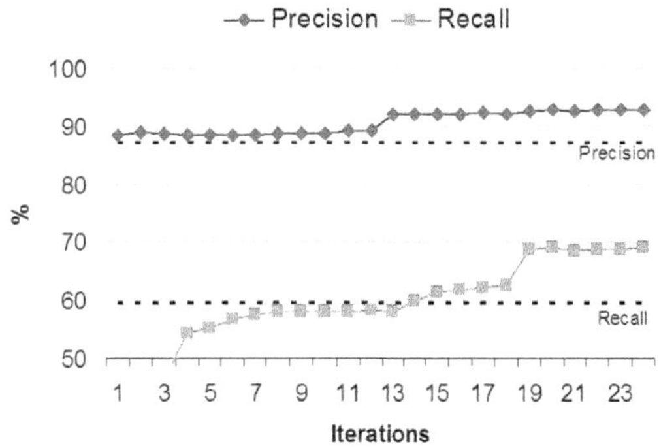

(a) Expert 1 Results

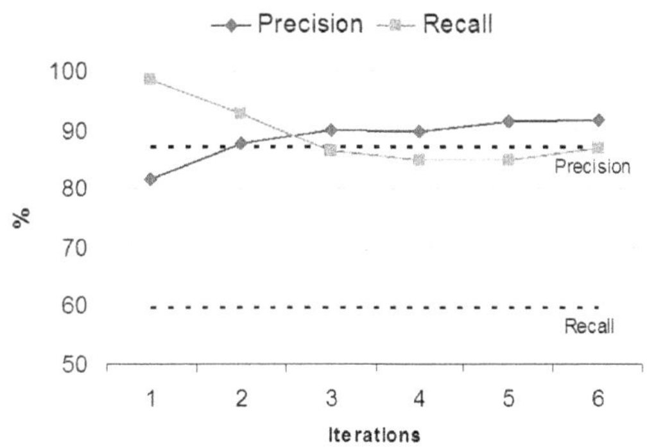

(b) Expert 2 Results

Figure 13: Changes of precision and recall of PERSONPHONE annotator over the iterations. The dotted lines are the results of the manually constructed annotators.

discovery task for relation extraction for both its faster response time and lower memory consumption.

5.5 Discussions of results

In Experiment 2, the annotators developed with the assist of S2C+ significantly outperform those developed in the conventional approach, while requiring a fraction of the development effort. The high quality clusters and their informative semantic signatures provided effectively assistance in the pattern discovery process, reducing the development time for a high-quality relation extraction annotator from weeks using the conventional purely manual approach[5] to merely hours using our new approach. Two additional issues were identified that may further speed up the development process, as will be discussed briefly in the following.

One issue concerns the usability of the clustering-based pattern discovery tool. Both expert annotator developers found that our GUI was effective in helping them understand and explore the clusters. However, they reported difficulty in keeping track of clusters that are already covered by their existing patterns, which resulted in wasted time developing additional patterns. One way to address this issue is to integrate the tool into the annotator development environment, so that the coverage of the patterns crafted by the developer is reflected automatically in the visualization of the clusters.

[5]According to an internal third-party report, the minimum amount of time required for the development of a product-quality relation annotator is 2 to 3 weeks.

The other issue is that while the semantic signature of a cluster provides valuable starting point for the generation of the patterns for the cluster, the actual pattern generation is still a manual process. A promising future direction is to generate those patterns in an automatic or semi-automatic fashion. As we have discussed in the relation work, there are a number of existing works on pattern induction based on a small number of seeds [4, 6, 15, 18, 30, 37]. It would be interesting to integrate those techniques into the context of a more interactive pattern discovery tool.

6. SUMMARY AND FUTURE WORK

We proposed a clustering-based approach to assist the pattern discovery process, and presented two novel algorithms, S2C and its enhancement S2C+, to automatically cluster relation candidates based on their semantic signatures. Our extensive experimental study has confirmed the practical impact of this approach — with the assist of the clusters, a rule developer can craft product-quality annotators for relation extraction with significantly lower manual effort than that required by the conventional manual approach. Furthermore, S2C and S2C+ not only run an order of magnitude faster with less memory required than k-means, they also generate clusters of a comparable or better quality.

As described earlier, we have fully implemented our semantic-signature-based clustering algorithms with a user-friendly GUI. In fact, this pattern discovery tool is being transferred into a commercial product. For future work, we plan to focus on the two issues discussed in Section 5.5 to further improve the usability of this tool and to explore the feasibility of automating the pattern generation process based on the clusters.

7. REFERENCES

[1] E. Agichtein and L. Gravano. Snowball: extracting relations from large plain-text collections. In *DL*, 2000.

[2] R. Agrawal and R. Srikant. Fast algorithms for mining association rules. In *VLDB*, 1994.

[3] M. Banko, M. J. Cafarella, S. Soderland, M. Broadhead, and O. Etzioni. Open information extraction from the web. In *IJCAI*, 2007.

[4] S. Brin. Extracting patterns and relations from the world wide web. In *WebDB*, 1999.

[5] R. Bunescu and R. Mooney. Learning to extract relations from the web using minimal supervision. In *ACL*, 2007.

[6] M. Califf and R. Mooney. Relational learning of pattern match rules for information extraction. In *ACL Workshop on Natural Language Learning*, 1997.

[7] J. Chen, D. Ji, C. L. Tan, and Z. Niu. Unsupervised feature selection for relation extraction. In *IJCNLP*, 2005.

[8] C.-F. Chiang, L. Chiticariu, V. Chu, S. Dasgupta, T. Goetz, H. Ho, R. Krishnamurthy, A. Lang, Y. Li, B. Liu, S. Raghavan, F. Reiss, S. Vaithyanathan, and H. Zhu. The SystemT IDE: An integrated development environment for information extraction rules. In *SIGMOD*, 2011.

[9] L. Chiticariu, R. Krishnamurthy, Y. Li, S. Raghavan, F. R. Reiss, and S. Vaithyanathan. Systemt: an algebraic approach to declarative information extraction. In *ACL*, 2010.

[10] L. Chiticariu, R. Krishnamurthy, Y. Li, F. Reiss, and S. Vaithyanathan. Domain adaptation of rule-based annotators for named-entity recognition tasks. In *EMNLP*, 2010.

[11] L. Chiticariu, Y. Li, S. Raghavan, and F. Reiss. Enterprise information extraction: Recent developments and open challenges. In *SIGMOD*, 2010.

[12] A. Culotta and A. McCallum. Confidence estimation for information extraction. In *HLT/NAACL*, 2004.

[13] D. Davidov and A. Rappoport. Unsupervised discovery of generic relationships using pattern clusters and its evaluation by automatically generated sat analogy questions. In *ACL-HLT*, 2008.

[14] A. Doan, R. Ramakrishnan, and S. Vaithyanathan. Managing information extraction: State of the art and research directions. In *SIGMOD*, 2006.

[15] D. Downey, O. Etzioni, S. Soderland, and D. Weld. Learning text patterns for web information extraction and assessment. In *AAAI Workshop on Adaptive Text Extraction and Mining*, 2004.

[16] O. Etzioni, M. Cafarella, D. Downey, A.-M. Popescu, T. Shaked, S. Soderland, D. S. Weld, and A. Yates. Unsupervised named-entity extraction from the web: An experimental study. *Artif. Intell.*, 165:91–134, 2005.

[17] M. R. Gormley, A. Gerber, M. Harper, and M. Dredze. Non-expert correction of automatically generated relation annotations. In *NAACL HLT Workshop on Creating Speech and Language Data with Amazon's Mechanical Turk*, 2010.

[18] M. A. Greenwood and M. Stevenson. Improving semi-supervised acquisition of relation extraction patterns. In *IEBeyondDoc*, 2006.

[19] M. Hall, E. Frank, G. Holmes, B. Pfahringer, P. Reutemann, and I. H. Witten. The weka data mining software: An update. *SIGKDD Explorations*, 11:10–18, 2009.

[20] T. Hasegawa, S. Sekine, and R. Grishman. Discovering relations among named entities from large corpora. In *ACL*, 2004.

[21] M. A. Hearst. Automatic acquisition of hyponyms from large text corpora. In *ACL*, 1992.

[22] P. Jaccard. Étude comparative de la distribution florale dans une portion des alpes et des jura. *Bulletin del la Société Vaudoise des Sciences Naturelles*, 37:547–579, 1901.

[23] N. Jindal and B. Liu. Mining comparative sentences and relations. In *AAAI*, 2006.

[24] N. Kambhatla. Combining lexical, syntactic, and semantic features with maximum entropy models for extracting relations. In *ACL*, 2004.

[25] S. Kok and P. Domingos. Extracting semantic networks from text via relational clustering. In *ECML/PKDD*, 2008.

[26] C. Li, B. Wang, and X. Yang. Vgram: Improving performance of approximate queries on string collections using variable-length grams. In *VLDB*, 2007.

[27] J. B. MacQueen. Some methods for classification and analysis of multivariate observations. In *Proc. of the 5th Berkeley Symp. on Math. Stat. and Prob.* UC Press, 1967.

[28] E. Minkov, R. C. Wang, and W. W. Cohen. Extracting personal names from email: applying named entity recognition to informal text. In *HLT/EMNLP*, 2005.

[29] A. Nanopoulos, D. Katsaros, and Y. Manolopoulos. A data mining algorithm for generalized web prefetching. *IEEE Trans. Knowledge and Data Engineering*, 15:1155–1169, 2003.

[30] D. Ravichandran and E. Hovy. Learning surface text patterns for a question answering system. In *ACL*, 2001.

[31] F. Reiss, S. Raghavan, R. Krishnamurthy, H. Zhu, and S. Vaithyanathan. An algebraic approach to rule-based information extraction. In *ICDE*, 2008.

[32] E. Riloff and R. Jones. Learning dictionaries for information extraction by multi-level boot-strapping. In *AAAI*, 1999.

[33] B. Rosenfeld and R. Feldman. Clustering for unsupervised relation identification. In *CIKM*, 2007.

[34] B. Rozenfeld and R. Feldman. High-performance unsupervised relation extraction from large corpora. In *ICDM*, 2006.

[35] L. Schmidt-Thieme and W. Gaul. Frequent generalized subsequences - a problem from web mining. In *Data Analysis, Scientific Modelling and Practical Application*. Springer, 2000.

[36] R. Snow, B. O'Connor, D. Jurafsky, and A. Y. Ng. Cheap and fast—but is it good?: evaluating non-expert annotations for natural language tasks. In *EMNLP*, 2008.

[37] M. Stevenson and M. Greenwood. A semantic approach to IE pattern induction. In *ACL*, 2005.

[38] H. Theil. On the estimation of relationships involving qualitative variables. *Amer. J. Sociology*, 76(1):103–154, 1970.

[39] D. Zelenko, C. Aone, and A. Richardella. Kernel methods for relation extraction. *JMLR*, 3:1083–1106.

[40] S. Zhao and R. Grishman. Extracting relations with integrated information using kernel methods. In *ACL*, 2005.

Finding All Justifications of OWL Entailments Using TMS and MapReduce

Gang Wu
Key Laboratory of Medical Image Computing (NEU), Ministry of Education, Shenyang 110004, China; College of Information Science and Engineering, Northeastern University, Shenyang 110004, China
wugang@ise.neu.edu.cn

Guilin Qi
School of Computer Science and Engineering, Southeast University, Nanjing 210096, China
gqi@seu.edu.cn

Jianfeng Du
Guangdong University of Foreign Studies, Guangzhou 510006, China; State Key Laboratory of Computer Science, Institute of Software, Chinese Academy of Sciences
jfdu@mail.gdufs.edu.cn

ABSTRACT

Finding all justifications of an OWL entailment is an important reasoning service for explaining logical inconsistencies. In this paper, we consider finding all justifications of an entailment in OWL pD^* fragment, which is a fragment of OWL that makes possible decidable rule extensions of OWL. We first propose a novel approach to find all justifications of OWL pD^* entailments using TMS and show the complexity of this approach. This approach is limited by the hardware capabilities of standalone systems. In order to improve its scalability to handle large scale semantic data, we optimize the proposed approach by exploiting the MapReduce technology. We implement our approach and the optimization, and do experiments on synthetic and real world data sets. Evaluation results show that our approach has the ability to scale to more than one billion triples.

Categories and Subject Descriptors

I.2.m [**Computing Methodologies**]: Artificial Intelligence

General Terms

Algorithms, Experimentation, Performance

Keywords

Justification, OWL, TMS, MapReduce

1. INTRODUCTION

The Web Ontology Language (OWL) is a standardized language for the Semantic Web. With the development of the Semantic Web, more and more OWL ontologies are published on-line, and are linked to each other in the Linked Open Data (LOD) project[1]. When these ontologies evolve or new links are created, it is important to ensure that logical inconsistency does not occur in the updated ontologies and in the linked ontologies. Finding all justifications of an entailment is an important reasoning service to help the users or domain experts to resolve logical inconsistencies when they occur. More generally, finding justifications can be useful to explain unwanted entailments of an OWL ontology.

In recent years, many approaches have been proposed for finding all justifications of an OWL entailment. These approaches can be roughly classified into two classes: one consists of approaches that are based on modification of a description logic reasoner, and the other consists of approaches that take a description logic reasoner as oracle to check satisfiability of an ontology. Existing approaches cannot handle large ontologies, for example, ontologies with more than one million triples. To improve the scalability of these approaches, some optimization techniques are developed by extracting a small module of an ontology that covers all justifications of an entailment. However, there is no evidence showing that the approaches optimized by module extraction techniques can scale to billions of triples. To provide explanation services for reasoning with large scale semantic data sets, like those in LOD, some novel optimization techniques are expected.

In this paper, we focus on a fragment of OWL, called OWL pD^* fragment [15]. The pD^* semantics is different from other OWL semantics based on description logics in that it provides a complete set of entailment rules represented as *if-then* rules. This semantics is important as large amounts of Web data can be expressed with OWL pD^*. Moreover, pD^* is the basis of OWL 2 RL [11], but it is much more concise and hence convenient for explaining our ideas. Scalable OWL reasoning is possible for OWL pD^* fragment as it has been implemented in MapReduce framework [16]. Therefore, it is one of the most important fragments of OWL that can be used to express semantic data. The rule-based feature of pD^* semantics inspires us to consider using Truth Maintenance Systems (TMS) [3] to find all justifications of an OWL entailment in pD^* semantics. TMS, also known as Reason Maintenance Systems, has been used to reason about and adapt to changes in a knowledge bases [13]. It has the ability of dealing with large search spaces efficiently [13].

In order to break the limitation of I/O and main memory, distributed computing techniques are widely exploited in data inten-

[1]`http://esw.w3.org/SweoIG/TaskForces/CommunityProjects/LinkingOpenData`

sive computing tasks involving Semantic Web applications. Although MapReduce and other distributed or parallel computing techniques have already emerged in the implementation of several inference engines, there is no work exploiting them to find all justifications of OWL entailments. Our second contribution is to use MapReduce technology to improve the scalability of our algorithm for finding all justifications using TMS. Our approach finds justifications in a MapReduce manner on a simplified Justification-based TMS (JTMS) which interacts with the first and only MapReduce-based OWL pD^* inference engine, WebPIE [16]. The experimental results on synthetic data and real world data show that our approach has the ability to scale to more than one billion triples.

2. PRELIMINARIES

2.1 OWL pD^* fragment

2.1.1 Syntax

An RDF graph is defined as a subset of the set **UB**×**UB**×**UBL**[2], where **U**, **B** and **L** represent the set of *URI references*, *Blank nodes*, and *Literals* respectively. Furthermore, **L** is composed of the set of plain literals L_p, well-typed literals L_t and ill-typed literals. The base element of an RDF graph is the *triple* which contains three components, i.e. the subject, the predicate, and the object, usually in the form of (s, p, o) with $s \in$**UB**, $p \in$**UB**, and $o \in$**UBL**. Given an RDF graph G, $T(G)$ is the set of elements in **UBL** that occur in the triples of G. The set of blank nodes of G is denoted as $bl(G) = T(G) \cap \mathbf{B}$. The vocabulary of G is denoted as $V(G) = T(G) \cap \mathbf{UL}$. If $bl(G) = \emptyset$, we say G is *ground*.

In [15], a subset of Ontology Web Language (OWL) vocabulary (e.g., `owl:sameAs`) is introduced, which extends the RDFS semantics and includes a subset of OWL vocabulary to so-call pD^* semantics. An ontology in the OWL pD^* fragment is a *generalized RDF graph*, which extends an RDF graph by allowing blank nodes in the predicate position and using a subset of OWL vocabulary. It guarantees a sound and complete entailment rule set. The set of rules, shown in Table 1, is introduced to define partial and full pD^* closures. The partial (or full) pD^* closure of a generalized RDF graph is computed by iteratively applying the rules on input triples until no new data derived, i.e., a fixpoint is reached [15, 16]. The entailment relation $\models$ between two generalized RDF graphs can then be equivalently defined by the partial pD^* closure.

2.1.2 Semantics

A *simple interpretation* I over a vocabulary V is a tuple $I = \langle R_I, P_I, E_I, S_I, L_I, LV_I \rangle$ where

1. R_I is a non-empty set, called the set of resources or the universe of I;

2. P_I is the set of properties, which is not necessarily disjoint from R_I;

3. $LV_I \subset R_I$ is the set of literal values, which contains at least all plain literals in $V \cap \mathbf{L}$;

4. E_I maps every property $p \in P_I$ to a subset of $R_I \times R_I$;

5. S_I maps each $t \in V \cap \mathbf{U}$ into $R_I \cup P_I$ that defines interpretation of URI references;

[2]We assume **U**, **B** and **L** fixed, and we concatenate the names to denote the union of them for ease. As in [15], we allow predicate to be blank node.

Table 1: Part of the OWL Horst rule set and compressed entailment justifications

Name	Antecedent	Consequent	Compressed Entailment Justification Label
p1	p rdf:type owl:FunctionalProperty, u p v, u p w	v owl:sameAs w	(v owl:sameAs w, **p1**, u p v)
p2	p rdf:type owl:InverseFunctionalProperty, v p u, w p u	v owl:sameAs w	(v owl:sameAs w, **p2**, v p u)
p3	p rdf:type owl:SymmetricProperty, v p u	u p v	(u p v, **p3**, v p u)
p4	p rdf:type owl:TransitiveProperty, u p w, w p v	u p v	(u p v, p4, u p w)
p7	v owl:sameAs w, w owl:sameAs u	v owl:sameAs u	(v owl:sameAs u, **p7**, v owl:sameAs w)
p8a	p owl:inverseOf q, v p w	w q v	(w q v, **p8a**, v p w)
p8b	p owl:inverseOf q, v q w	w p v	(w p v, **p8b**, v q w)
p11	u p v, u owl:sameAs x, v owl:sameAs y	x p y	(x p y, **p11**, u p v)
p12c	v rdfs:subClassOf w, w rdfs:subClassOf v	v rdfs:equivalentClass w	(v rdfs:equivalentClass w, **p12c**, v rdfs:subClassOf w)
p13c	v rdfs:subPropertyOf w, w rdfs:subPropertyOf v,	v rdfs:equivalentProperty w	(v rdfs:equivalentProperty w, **p13c**, v rdfs:subPropertyOf w)
p14a	v owl:hasValue w, v owl:onProperty p, u p w	u rdf:type v	(u rdf:type v, **p14a**, v owl:hasValue w)
p14b	v owl:hasValue w, v owl:onProperty p, u rdf:type v	u p w	(u p w, **p14b**, v owl:hasValue w)
p15	v owl:someValuesFrom w, v owl:onProperty p, u p x, x rdf:type w	u rdf:type v	(u rdf:type v, **p15**, x p w)
p16	v owl:allValuesFrom u, v owl:onProperty p, w rdf:type v, w p x	x rdf:type u	(x rdf:type u, **p16**, w p v)
D2	p rdfs:domain x, s p o	s rdf:type x	(s rdf:type x, **D2**, s p o)
D3	p rdfs:range x, s p o	o rdf:type x	(o rdf:type x, **D3**, s p o)
D5	p rdfs:subPropertyOf q, q rdfs:subPropertyOf r	p rdfs:subPropertyOf r	(p rdfs:subPropertyOf r, **D5**, p rdfs:subPropertyOf q)
D7	s p o, p rdfs:subPropertyOf q	s q o	(s q o, **D7**, s p o)
D8	s rdf:type rdfs:Class	s rdfs:subClassOf rdfs:Resource	(s rdfs:subClassOf rdfs:Resource, **D8**, s rdf:type rdfs:Class)
D9	s rdf:type x, x rdfs:subClassOf y	s rdf:type y	(s rdf:type y, **D9**, s rdf:type x)
D11	x rdfs:subClassOf y, y rdfs:subClassOf z	x rdfs:subClassOf z	x rdfs:subClassOf z, **D11**, x rdfs:subClassOf y
D12	p rdf:type rdfs:ContainerMembershipProperty	p rdfs:subPropertyOf rdfs:member	(p rdfs:subPropertyOf rdfs:member,
D13	o rdf:type rdfs:Datatype	o rdfs:subClassOf rdfs:Literal	(o rdfs:subClassOf rdfs:Literal, **D13**, o rdf:type rdfs:Datatype)
...	...	...	...

6. L_I maps each $t \in V \cap L_t$ into R_I that defines interpretation of typed literals;

If I is a simple interpretation of a vocabulary V, then I can also be treated as a function with domain V in the following way

$$I(a) = \begin{cases} a & a \in L_p \cap V \\ L_I(a) & a \in L_t \cap V \\ S_I(a) & a \in \mathbf{U} \cap V \end{cases} \quad (1)$$

Given a simple interpretation I and a partial function $A : \mathbf{B} \to R_I$, we can define a function I_A that extends the domain of I to the domain of A:

$$I_A(a) = \begin{cases} A(v) & v \in \mathbf{B} \cap \mathbf{dom}(A) \\ I(a) & a \in \mathbf{dom}(I) \end{cases} \quad (2)$$

Let G be an arbitrary RDF graph, we say I satisfies G if there is some function $A : bl(G) \to R_I$, such that for each triple $(s, p, o) \in G$, we have $I_A(p) \in P_I$ and $(I_A(s), I_A(o)) \in E_I(I_A(p))$. Intuitively, a triple (s, p, o) in a graph G is satisfied by the interpretation I, if p is interpreted as a property name, s and o are interpreted as resources, and the pair of resources assigned to (s, o) belongs to the extension of the interpreted property of p. Furthermore, blank nodes are treated as variables, e.g. the triple (x, p, o) with $x \in \mathbf{B}$ is satisfied by I if there is a function A maps x to $I(s)$, for some s such that (s, p, o) is satisfied by I.

A datatype d is composed by three parts: the lexical space $L(d)$, the value space $V(d)$ and the lexical-to-value mapping function $L2V(d) : L(d) \to V(d)$. Both $L(d)$ and $V(d)$ are non-empty sets. A datatype map is a partial function D from $\mathbf{U}$ to the set of datatypes. Given a datatype map D, the D-vocabulary is the domain $\mathbf{dom}(D)$ of D. The set of all well-typed D-literals with type in D is defined by $L_D^+ = \{(s, a) \in L_t : a \in \mathbf{dom}(D), s \in L(D(a))\}$.

If a simple interpretation I over the vocabulary *rdfV* $\cup$ *rdfsV* $\cup$ $\mathbf{dom}(D) \cup pV$ is said to be a pD^*-interpretation if I satisfies all D-constraints and P-constraints mentioned in [15]. Because of the space limitation, we do not list these constraints here. An RDF graph S is said to pD^* *entail* an RDF graph G, denoted as $S \models_p G$, if every pD^* interpretation that satisfies S also satisfies G.

The pD^* semantics can result in two kinds of logical inconsistencies: (1) two triples of the form v `owl:differentFrom` w and v `owl:sameAs` w; (2) three triples of the form v `owl:disjointWith` w, u `rdf:type` v, u `rdf:type` w.

2.2 Justification

In [8], the notion of justification is introduced to explain an OWL DL entailment. Formally, a justification of an entailment of an OWL DL ontology is a minimal set of axioms in the ontology that is responsible for the entailment. We adapt this notion as follows.

DEFINITION 1 (ONTOLOGY JUSTIFICATION). *Given a generalized RDF graph G and a triple α, suppose $G \models \alpha$. A subgraph J of G is an ontology justification for α, if $J \models \alpha$ and, for all $J' \subset J$, $J' \not\models \alpha$. The set of all ontology justifications of α is denoted as $\mathcal{J}^\alpha$.*

EXAMPLE 1. *Suppose there are two triples in the ontology.*

```
T1: <telephone, rdfs:domain, Person>
T2: <GraduateStudent83, telephone, "xxx-xxx-xxxx">
```

According to OWL pD^* Rule D2, i.e. (p `rdfs:domain` x, $s\ p\ o \Rightarrow s$ `rdf:type` x), a new triple `<GraduateStudent83, rdf:type, Person>` *(denoted as T3) can be inferred. In other words, it means that one and the only one of all justifications for $T3$ is $\{T1, T2\}$, i.e. $\mathcal{J}^{T3} = \{\{T1, T2\}\}$.*

2.3 Truth Maintenance Systems (TMS)

There have been variants of Truth Maintenance Systems (TMS) algorithms, such as JTMS, LTMS, ATMS, HTMS, and ITMS [1]. JTMS[3], i.e. justification-based TMS, is the basis of all the other variants, which uses "justifications" to record dependencies between propositions. Though the same term is used, the meaning of *justification* in TMS is different from that of ontology justification. Here, justification is used to represent an entailment (or called a rule instance for rule inference engines) that links between a derived fact and its antecedents [3, 13]. To distinguish these two terms with the same name, we call a justification in TMS an *entailment justification*. Formally, an entailment justification is a derivation of the form $A \Rightarrow \alpha$ where α is a proposition (also called a conclusion or consequent) and A is a set of propositions (also called antecedents) [2]. An entailment justification can be also written as an implication of the form $A \to \alpha$.

A TMS is built by calling specific *add-rule* functions from the inference engine [1]. Hence, all rule instances (entailments) processed by inference engine are recorded in TMS as entailment justifications. Usually, entailment justifications are organized as a dependency graph [5].

DEFINITION 2 (TMS DEPENDENCY GRAPH). *For a TMS $\mathcal{T}$, let $\mathcal{P}$ be the set of all propositions appearing in it and $\mathcal{R} = \{A \Rightarrow \alpha\}$ be the set of all entailment justifications (rule instances) in it, where $\alpha \in \mathcal{P}$ and $A \subseteq P$. A TMS dependency graph is a hypergraph $\mathcal{G}_\mathcal{T} = (V, \mathcal{E})$, where $V = \{v_p : p \in \mathcal{P}\}$ and $\mathcal{E} = \{(V_A, v_\alpha) : A \Rightarrow \alpha \in \mathcal{R}\}$. $\forall p \in \mathcal{P}$, $v_p \in V$ is called the node of the dependency graph corresponding to proposition p, and $V_A = \{v_p : p \in A\}$. For any $r \in \mathcal{R}$, $e_r \in \mathcal{E}$ is called the edge of the dependency graph corresponding to rule instance r, which may consist of more than two nodes, thus is a hyperedge.*

According to [10], the TMS dependency graph can be used to generate explanations for a proposition entailed by a set of propositions.

3. SIMPLIFIED JTMS FOR OWL pD^*

In this section, we first propose to exploit TMS to find all justifications of OWL pD^* entailments. On this basis, a compression technique is designed to simplify the traditional TMS labeling scheme.

3.1 JTMS for OWL pD^* Ontology Justification

Given a generalized RDF graph G, when calculating the closure of G, we can store a TMS dependency graph $\mathcal{G}$ by considering triples in G as propositions and pD^* inference rule instances as entailment justifications. The generation of $\mathcal{G}$ is complete when the closure of G is calculated. We have Theorem 1 if the TMS dependency graph $\mathcal{G}$ is acyclic.

THEOREM 1. *An acyclic JTMS dependency graph can be used to generate explanations for a triple in the closure of G by recursively traversing backwards from the node representing the triple through hyperedges.*

PROOF. Let the ontology justification for α to be $\mathcal{J}^\alpha$. Let v_α to be the node corresponding to α on the TMS dependency graph $\mathcal{G}_\mathcal{T}$.

If v_α has no parent node, obviously $\mathcal{J}^\alpha = \{\alpha\}$.

Otherwise, there must be at least one edge linking backwards to a set of nodes. Let the edge be e_r and the node set V be $V_A =$

[3]To facilitate the discussion, only the simplest type of TMS, Monotonic-JTMS, is considered in this paper since OWL semantics is monotonic.

$\{v_{\beta_1},...v_{\beta_k}\}$. Then, the entailment justification r can be written as $A \Rightarrow \alpha$, i.e.

$$\beta_1 \wedge ... \wedge \beta_k \Rightarrow \alpha. \tag{3}$$

Recursively, taking each node $v_{\beta_i} \in V_A$, traverse backwards until no nodes can be explored. As $\mathcal{G}_\mathcal{T}$ is acyclic, the recursive backwards traversal will definitely stop in finite steps. In other words, $\mathcal{T}$ is ensured to be *well-founded* [5]. Hence, in terms of propositional calculus, Equation 3 can be further expanded as shown in Equation 4 [5].

$$\xi_1 \wedge ... \wedge \xi_m \Rightarrow \alpha \tag{4}$$

where ξ_i is a premise.

As all the in-edges of a node are traversed, multiple explanations will be found. All explanations $\mathcal{E}$ for will be found if the traversal covers all possible branches of the search space on the dependency graph, which is ensured by the construction process of TMS $\mathcal{T}$.

According to Definition 1 and 2, $\mathcal{J}$ are the subset of dependency graph edge set $\mathcal{E}$ where $\forall \mathcal{J}_i, \mathcal{J}_j \in \mathcal{J}$, $\mathcal{J}_i \not\subset \mathcal{J}_j$ and $\mathcal{J}_j \not\subset \mathcal{J}_i$. □

Based on Theorem 1, we present an approach for finding all justifications of an OWL pD^* entailment.

Algorithm 1: FindOWLJustifications

input : Triple α; Dependency graph $\mathcal{G}_\mathcal{T}$
output: Set $\mathcal{J}$ containing all ontology justifications for α

1 **begin**
2   Put ($\mathcal{J}$,$\{\alpha\}$) ; // Init $\mathcal{J}$ with $\{\alpha\}$.
3   $\mathcal{J}' \leftarrow \emptyset$;
4   **while** $\mathcal{J}' \neq \mathcal{J}$ **do** // Find until no new found
5     $\mathcal{J}' \leftarrow \mathcal{J}$;
6   **for** $J_i \in \mathcal{J}$ **do**
7   **for** $a_j \in J_i$ **do**
8   **if** InEdges (Node (a_j))$\neq \emptyset$ **then**
9           $\mathcal{E} \leftarrow$ InEdges (Node (a_j));
10   **for** $e \in \mathcal{E}$ **do**
11   **if** *e is not marked* **then**
12   Remove (J_i, a_j);
13               $J_{i,e} \leftarrow J_i$; // Make a copy.
14               $V \leftarrow$ Antecedent (e);
15   **for** $v \in V$ **do**
16   Put ($J_{i,e}$, Triple(v));
17   Put ($\mathcal{J}$,$J_{i,e}$);
18   **if** a_j *is not in the original ontology* **then**
19   Remove ($\mathcal{J}$,J_i);
20   $\mathcal{J}' \leftarrow \mathcal{J}$; // Make a copy.
21   **for** $J_i \in \mathcal{J}$ **do** // Justifications from explanations
22   **for** $J_j \in \mathcal{J}$ **do**
23   **if** $J_i \subset J_j$ **then**
24   Remove ($\mathcal{J}'$,J_j);
25   **else if** $J_j \subset J_i$ **then**
26   Remove ($\mathcal{J}'$,J_i);
27   $\mathcal{J} \leftarrow \mathcal{J}'$;

In practical JTMS, specific data structures are used to support the traversing algorithm on the dependency graph. For our purpose, data structures on dependency graph nodes and edges are defined below. First, we uniquely label a node v_α with the corresponding triple α, and hence define two functions $Node(\alpha) = v_\alpha$ and $Triple(v_\alpha) = \alpha$ to get the other representation given one kind of representation. Secondly, we uniquely label an edge e_r with the form of (V_A, v_α) where entailment justification r satisfies that $A \Rightarrow \alpha$. We use another two functions $Antecedent(e_r) = V_A$ and $Consequent(e_r) = v_\alpha$ to return the set of antecedent nodes and the consequent node of r respectively. Furthermore, we use function $InEdges(v_\alpha)$ to get all the edges point to v_α. Algorithm 1 thus describes the algorithm to find all ontology justifications for OWL pD^* semantics based on JTMS.

There may exist cycles in the dependency graph, which unsatisfies the *well-foundedness* required by JTMS algorithms. Therefore, all cyclic dependencies, i.e. edges, should be marked before backwards traversal. Let V be the node set of $\mathcal{G}_\mathcal{T}$. The routine of marking cyclic dependencies can be implemented based on the depth-first search algorithm and executed once before Algorithm 1. The complexity of cyclic dependencies marking is $O(|V|^2)$ considering that the marking needs to visit all the nodes and the links between adjacent nodes, and the number of links between adjacent nodes is up to $|V|^2$.

Before performing finding all explanations, a set data structure $\mathcal{J}$ is initialized with $\{\alpha\}$ to store all explanations (and future ontology justifications) as shown in Line 2.

From Line 4 to Line 19, the algorithm recursively traverses the dependency graph reversely following incoming edges of all involved nodes that are not previously marked to cause cycles. Once a node is explored following certain incoming edge during the traversal, the triple corresponding to the node is replaced by a set of antecedent triples according to the label of the incoming edges. The replacement becomes a start point of a possible explanation for further expansion during the recursive traversal, and is put into $\mathcal{J}$. The recursion stops when no new explanations are put into $\mathcal{J}$. The worst-case of such a traversal is visiting all the nodes and the links between adjacent nodes of the dependency graph if implemented in dynamic programming, hence the complexity is $O(|V|^2)$.

There is a more complex situation that a triple may have a dual role of derivation and original in the ontology. For example, suppose that the original ontology consists of only three triples, `<A, rdfs:subClassOf, B>`, `<B, rdfs:subClassOf, C>`, and `<A, rdfs:subClassOf, C>`. Obviously, the justifications of `<A, rdfs:subClassOf, C>` include both `<A, rdfs:subClassOf, C>` itself and {`<A, rdfs:subClassOf, B>`, `<B, rdfs:subClassOf, C>`}. For this case, the triple should be kept a copy in the justification as the original ones in the ontology, rather than directly replaced by other triples as a derivation. This is shown in Line 18 and Line 19.

From Line 20 to Line 26, the algorithm computes all ontology justifications for α out of the explanations obtained formerly by removing all the supersets of each explanation that also appeared in $\mathcal{J}$. Obviously, the complexity is $O(\Sigma_{\forall J_i \in \mathcal{J}}|J_i|)$.

To sum up, the computation complexity of Algorithm 1 is $O(|V|^2 + \Sigma_{\forall J_i \in \mathcal{J}}|J_i|)$. From our experience, for a triple, both the count of all ontology justifications and the size of each individual ontology justification are relatively small compared with the size of nodes of the dependency graph. Therefore, we omit the last portion, and have $O(|V|^2)$.

3.2 Label Compression

Data manipulated in Algorithm 1 are mainly in triples. Take Example 2 for instance.

EXAMPLE 2. *For Example 1, triple T3 is obtained by substituting RDF terms for corresponding variable items of the rule as in Table 2. In other words, it means that one of the ontology justifications for* $T3$ *is* $\{T1, T2\}$ *as depicted in Figure 1.*

In the example, the entailment justification is labeled with $(\{T1, T2\}, T3)$. When expanded to triples, it turns to be ({`<telephone,`

Table 2: Variable bindings for OWL pD^* Rule $D2$

Rule	s	p	o	x
$D2$	GraduateStudent83	telephone	xxx-xxx-xxxx	Person

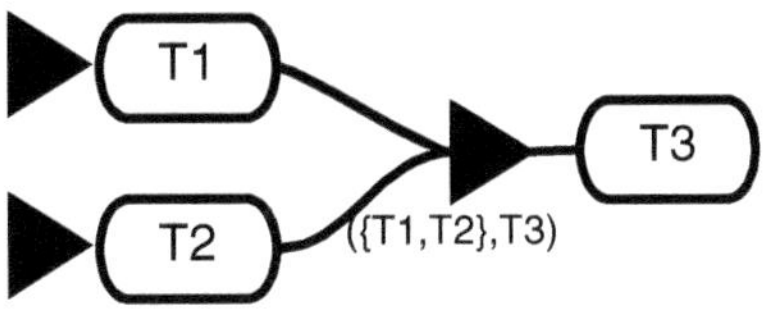

Figure 1: Dependency Graph Fragment: A black triangle is used to represent an entailment justification that links between the antecedents and the consequent as a hyperedge on the dependency graph. Nodes without incoming edges are premises for the entailment, e.g. $T1$ and $T2$.

`rdfs:domain, Person>`, `<GraduateStudent83, telephone, "xxx-xxx-xxxx">}`, `<GraduateStudent83, rdf:type, Person>`). RDF terms `telephone`, `Person`, and `GraduateStudent83` each appears twice in the label. Moreover, `rdfs:domain` and `rdf:type` are unchanged from any instance of Rule $D2$, thus they are not necessary to be recorded explicitly given the rule name. Apparently, there is a redundancy of 5 RDF terms compared with the RDF terms bound in Table 2. We will have a more compact data structure if it is possible to utilize such binding information to label an entailment justification.

DEFINITION 3 (RULE BINDING). *Given a generalized RDF graph G and a rule r with variables $x_1, ..., x_n$, a set of instances $v_1, ..., v_n$ to the variables is called a* Rule Binding *of r iff for rule instance r' obtained from r by replacing x_i by v_i, triples in the antecedent of r' can be entailed by G.*

THEOREM 2. *A rule binding can be used uniquely to determine an entailment justification, and vice versa.*

PROOF. Straightforward. □

Definition 3 and Theorem 2 enable us to label an entailment justification with a rule binding. It can be inferred that there will be $\frac{(RDFTerms\ \# - RuleBindings\ \#)}{RDFTerms\ \#}$ reduced when merely using rule binding to label an entailment justification compared with the traditional JTMS label.

To reduce the storage space consumption while improve the access speed, we propose a fixed length labeling scheme to represent the rule binding. A rule binding label is a 7-tuple (*Con-Sub, Con-Pre, Con-Obj, RuleName, Binding1, Binding2, Binding3*) where *Con-Sub*, *Con-Pre*, and *Con-Obj* are the subject, predicate, and object RDF terms of the consequent triple. *RuleName* indicates the rule schema in OWL pD^* rule set. *Binding1*, *Binding2*, and *Binding3* are the RDF terms appeared in the antecedents. In order to identify an original triple that has no antecedents in the ontology, the values of "RuleName", "Binding1", "Binding2", and "Binding3" in the rule binding label is set to be some invalid values, e.g. -1.

Six RDF terms are enough for recording a rule binding by investigating OWL pD^* rule set in Table 1. Table 1 summarizes most[4] of the rules in OWL pD^* rule set. In the fourth column, it gives the compressed entailment justification label based on the above rule binding labeling scheme. In order to rebuild the entailment justifications, it simply expends the binding labels according to Theorem 2 and Table 1. In our example, $\frac{(3+3+3)-(4+1)}{3+3+3} \approx 44\%$ is saved. For some rules, e.g. $p15$ and $p16$, the compression rate reaches up to $\frac{15-7}{15} \approx 53\%$.

[4]Some trivial rules are omitted similar to those in [16].

4. MAPREDUCE-BASED JUSTIFICATION FINDING FOR OWL PD^*

As discussed in the previous section, JTMS provides us a means of finding all ontology justifications on inferred data given corresponding inference engine. Although Algorithm 1 has a theoretically feasible complexity equal to that of DFS on dependency graphs, the scalability is limited by the capability of main memory and I/O of standalone systems. Distributed computing technologies will help on this point. WebPIE [16] is an open source Hadoop MapReduce framework based OWL pD^* inference engine that scales well even when dealing with large scale data sets. Thus, for OWL pD^* semantics, WebPIE is a possible appropriate choice of the inference engine to build our simplified JTMS on. Figure 2 shows the architecture of our MapReduce-based ontology justification finding system for OWL pD^*. For a generalized RDF graph, the ontology justification finding process can be divided into two phases, i.e. building phase and finding phase.

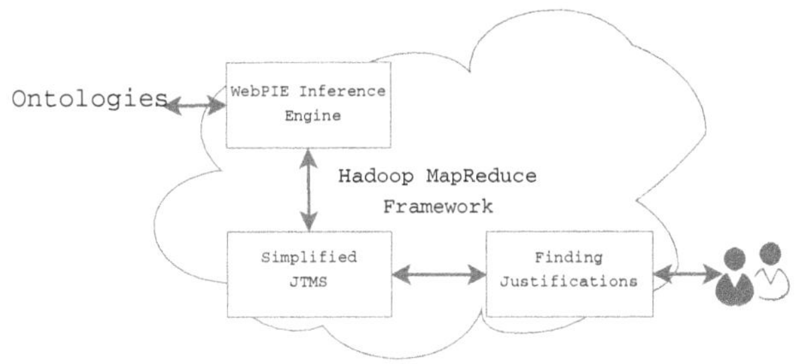

Figure 2: System Architecture

For the first phase, the simplified JTMS is built along with the forward inference process of WebPIE. Suppose WebPIE derives a triple $<s, p, o>$ by applying rule ρ on antecedents $<s_1, p_1, o_1>, \ldots$. Instead of simply output the derived triple $<s, p, o>$, our simplified JTMS records a binding label $<s, p, o, \rho, b_1, b_2, b_3>$ where b_1, b_2, and b_3 are RDF terms referred in the antecedents according to Definition 3 and Table 1. Note that the same triple derived by applying different rules or from different antecedents may result in different binding labels. Therefore, the count of labels stored in the simplified JTMS is equal to the count of edges in the dependency graph. The simplified JTMS is obtained once the forward inference of WebPIE comes to the iteration fixpoint. As no additional operations performed other than storing 7-tuples, the labeling operations does not affect the inference operation much.

Entering the second phase, users can initiate a MapReduce version of Algorithm 1 based on data from the simplified JTMS obtained during the previous phase. Analysis on Algorithm 1 shows that most of the time is spent on recursively traversing the dependency graph reversely and replacing triples with their antecedents. Hence, we design a MapReduce job, named `TracingJob` in Algorithm 2, to decompose and parallelize codes from Line 4 to Line 18 of Algorithm 1. Moreover, in order to return an explanation result as soon as possible, we design another job, `CollectingJob`, as well. The algorithm flow can be illustrated by Figure 3.

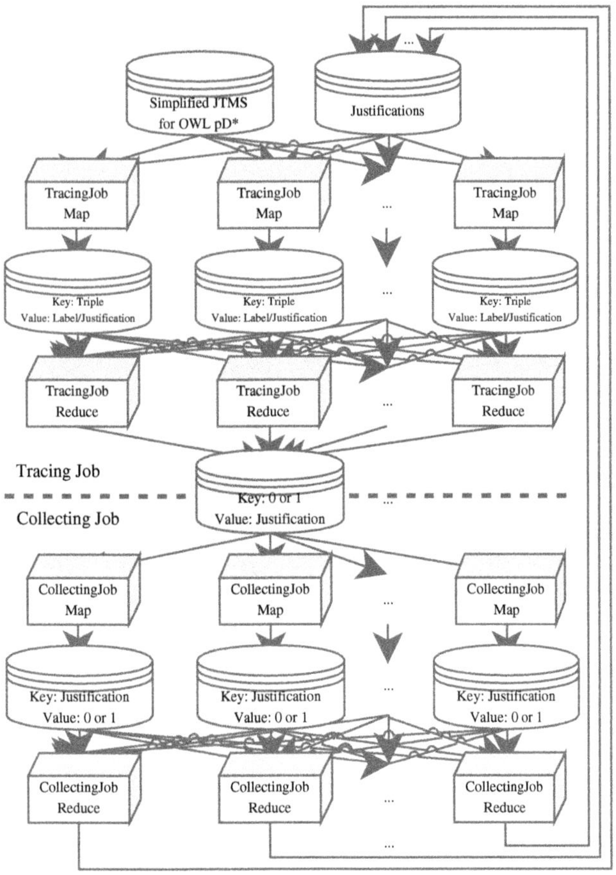

Figure 3: Algorithm Flow

Algorithm 2: MapReduceFindOWLJustifications

```
input : Triple α; Dependency Graph G
output: Set J containing all ontology justifications for α
begin
    Put (J, {α});
    repeat
        Set J and G as the inputs of TracingJob ;
        Set J as the inputs of CollectingJob ;
        J' ← J;
        TracingJob.waitForCompletion ();
        CollectingJob.waitForCompletion ();
    until J'==J;
    Minimize J ;        // See Algorithm 1 Line 19 25.
```

According to MapReduce programming specification, a job usually consists of two steps (functions). The *map* step decomposes the original problem into independent sub-problems, and then distributes them across machines. The *reduce* step collects and combines the outputs from the map step. The map step of `TracingJob` deals with two data sources, i.e. dependency graph $\mathcal{G}$ and explanations (future candidate ontology justifications) $\mathcal{J}$. For $\mathcal{G}$, a binding label $<s, p, o, \rho, b_1, b_2, b_3>$ will be distributed to some computation node by taking triple $<s, p, o>$ as decomposition key. For $\mathcal{J}$, an explanation $\{<s_1, p_1, o_1>, \ldots, <s_n, p_n, o_n>\}$ will be distributed n times by taking each triple $<s_i, p_i, o_i>$ as decomposition key. In this way, binding labels and explanations with the same triple value are grouped to the same computation node, which facilitates future expansion operations in `TracingJob`'s reduce step.

Algorithm 3: TracingJobReduce

```
   input : Triple key; Justifications or BindingLabels values
   output: Integer oKey; Justification oValue
1  begin
2      for value in values do
3          if value is a BindingLabel then
4              Put (bindings, value);
5          else // value is a Justification
6              Put (justifications,value);
7      if justifications.size()== 0 then
8          return ;   // The binding is not referenced.
9      if bindings.size() == 0 then
10         for just in justifications do
11             Write (1, just) ;          // Find a premise.
12     else
13         for binding in bingdings do
14             for just in justifications do
15                 for triple in just do
16                     if triple == key then
17                         Remove (just, triple);
18                 PutAll (just, Antecedent (binding));
19                 Write (0, just);
```

As shown in Algorithm 3, distributed expansion to explanations is implemented as joining binding labels and explanations on each involved triple. First, from Line 2 to 6, we build two lists for binding labels (`bindings`) and explanations (`justifications`) respectively as the operands of join operation. Then, we perform join operations accordingly. If `bindings` is empty, the triple *key* is a premise. If `justifications` is empty, the binding label is not relevant. Otherwise, a nested loop join is performed from Line 13 to 19.

During the map step of `CollectingJob`, it simply distributes the output of `TracingJob` by taking each explanation as decomposition key and integer 0 or 1 as value. And during the reduce step of `CollectingJob`, Algorithm 4, it sums the values being 1 for each explanation. An explanation is a candidate ontology justification iff the sum is equal to the count of triples in the explanation, otherwise the explanation needs further expansion.

Algorithm 4: CollectingJobReduce

```
input : Justification key; Integer List values (value 0 or 1)
output: Justification oKey; Null oValue
begin
    total ← 0;
    for value in values do
        total ← total + value;
    if total != key.size() then
        if total == 0 then
            Write (Null, key);
    else
        Put (J, key);
```

A comprehensive example as described in Example 3 may help to better understand the process of above algorithm flow.

EXAMPLE 3. *Given an RDF graph consisting of 7 triples as follows,*

```
T1: <Lecturer1, teacherOf, GraduateCourse46>
T2: <teacherOf, rdfs:range, Course>
T3: <_:genid13, owl:someValuesFrom, Course>
T4: <_:genid13, owl:onProperty, takesCourse>
T5: <GraduateStudent114, takesCourse,
    GraduateCourse46>
T6: <_:genid13, owl:someValuesFrom, GraduateCourse>
T7: <GraduateCourse46, rdf:type, GraduateCourse>
```

it will derive two more triples by calculating the closure of the graph.

```
T8: <GraduateCourse46, rdf:type, Course>
T9: <GraduateStudent114, rdf:type, _:genid13>
```

Hence, we can build a dependency graph as shown in Figure 4, and get a list of corresponding compressed rule binding labels as shown in Table 3.

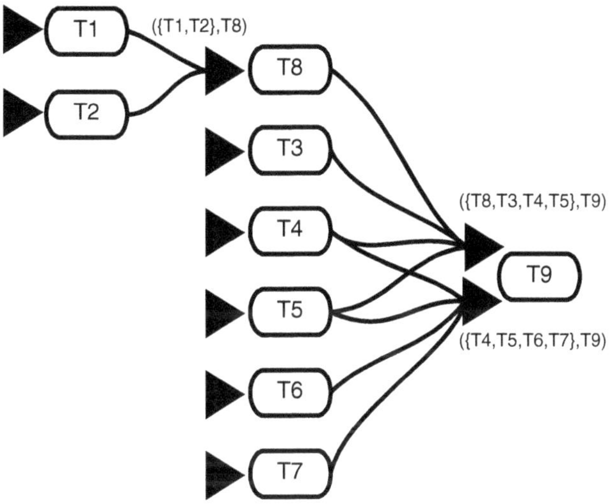

Figure 4: The Dependency Graph of Example 3

Suppose two map tasks and two reduce tasks are configured in our MapReduce framework. The process of finding all justifications of T9: `<GraduateStudent114, rdf:type, _:genid13>` *can be illustrated with Figure 5*

After three runs, the algorithm will output totally two justifications, J3={T4, T5, T6, T7} and J4={T1, T2, T3, T4, T5}. At the first run, T9 is used to initialize explanation J1={T9}. During the reduce step of tracing job, binding labels and explanations are joined on the key T9 with the values L9 and L10, which results in two replacements of J1, i.e. J2={T8, T3, T4, T5} and J3={T4, T5, T6, T7} correspondingly. As it cannot determine whether there exist labels to support tracing back from T3, T4, T5, T6, T7, and T8 currently, two key-value pairs with "0" as keys, i.e. <0, J2> and <0, J3>, are emitted to the next collecting job. During the collecting job at this run, explanations J2 and J3 are collected and counted, while no justification is output because of their unequal between the count and the size respectively. At the second run, J2 is further expand to be J4 with binding label L8 on T8, and output as pair <0, J4>. At the same time, J3 is determined to be one of the justifications of T9 because T4, T5, T6, and T7 are original triples from the RDF graph. Finally, at the last run, J4 is also output as another justifications of T9 because all elements in it are original triples.

Table 3: The Compressed Labels of Example 3

Label	*Con − Sub*	*Con − Pre*	*Con − Obj*	*RuleName*	*Binding1*	*Binding2*	*Binding3*	Triple
L1	Lecturer1	teacherOf	GraduateCourse46	-	-	-	-	T1
L2	teacherOf	rdfs:range	Course	-	-	-	-	T2
L3	_:genid13	owl:someValuesFrom	Course	-	-	-	-	T3
L4	_:genid13	owl:onProperty	takesCourse	-	-	-	-	T4
L5	GraduateStudent114	takesCourse	GraduateCourse46	-	-	-	-	T5
L6	_:genid13	owl:someValuesFrom	GraduateCourse	-	-	-	-	T6
L7	GraduateCourse46	rdf:type	GraduateCourse	-	-	-	-	T7
L8	GraduateCourse46	rdf:type	Course	D3	Lecturer1	teacherOf	GraduateCourse46	T8
L9	GraduateStudent114	rdf:type	_:genid13	p15	GraduateCourse46	takesCourse	Course	T9
L10	GraduateStudent114	rdf:type	_:genid13	p15	GraduateCourse46	takesCourse	GraduateCourse	T9

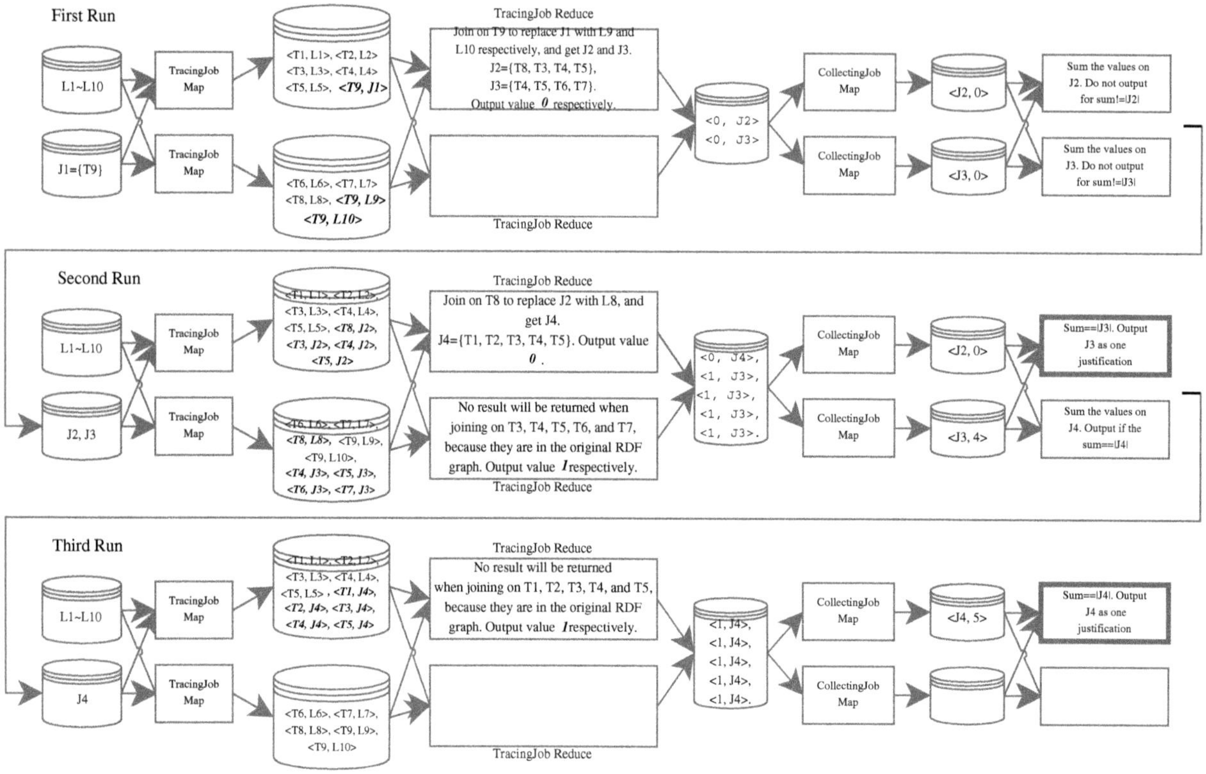

Figure 5: The flow of Example 3

5. EXPERIMENTS

In order to show the feasibility of our proposal, we implemented a prototype system based on the WebPIE inference engine which is built on top of Hadoop release 0.20.2. We set up a Hadoop cluster to conduct all experiments. The cluster consists of 9 commodity computers, one as the master (Intel Q8400 Core 2 Quad 2.66GHz processor, 4GB main memory, and 320GB SATA 7200rpm hard disk), and the others as the slaves (Intel E5400 Core 2 Duo 2.7GHz, 2GB main memory, and 320GB SATA 7200rpm hard disk). All computation nodes are connected via Gigabit Ethernet interconnect. The operating system is 32-bit Ubuntu 10.04. Hadoop heap size is set to be 2GB.

We did experiments on two groups of data sets. One of them consists of the synthetic data sets of LUBM [6], i.e., 1-university, 10-university, 100-university, 1000-university, 8000-university data set (denoted by LUBM-1, LUBM-10, LUBM-100, LUBM-1000, and LUBM-8000)[5]. The other consists of the DBpedia data sets[6].

5.1 Impact of Simplified JTMS Construction

We first investigated the impact of constructing the simplified JTMS on WebPIE inference engine on time cost and space consumption. In this experiment, all 8 slave nodes are involved. We assigned 16 map tasks and 16 reduce task for each job, i.e. 2 map tasks and 2 reduce tasks per slave node. In Figures 6 and 7, comparisons were made between inference processes with and without the simplified JTMS on time cost and space consumption respectively. As shown in Figure 6, using JTMS has almost no influence on the import time. The overhead of constructing a simplified JTMS mainly occurs at the inference phase of WebPIE. For any data set, although time cost of inference with simplified JTMS is higher than that without JTMS, they are of the same magnitude. The ratio of inference with JTMS to inference without JTMS is between 1.24 and 3.11 for this group of data sets. Similarly, according to Figure 7, the count of triples with and without JTMS are of the same magnitude too, and the ratio of sizes with and without JTMS is 2.72 for LUBM and is 8.74 for DBpedia. As a result of gzip compression,

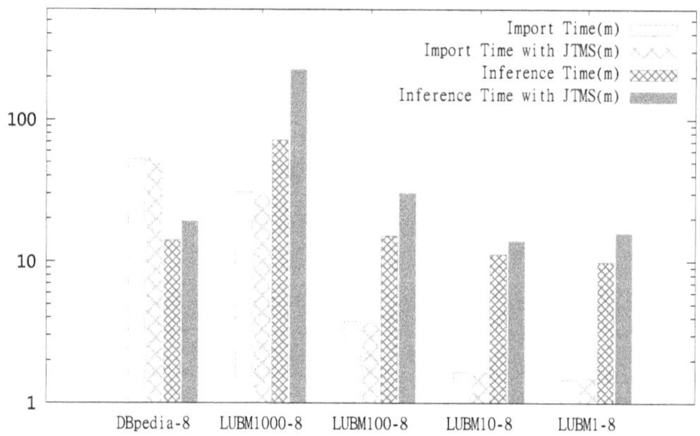

Figure 6: Comparisons on Import and Inference Time

[5]Total count of triples after derivation is approximately 82K, 1M, 11M, 110M, and 0.88 billion respectively.

[6]`http://downloads.dbpedia.org/3.6/en/`, accessed in Dec. 2010 (data sets *images*, *labels*, *long/short abstracts*, and *page links* are not included). Total count of triples after derivation is approximately 1M.

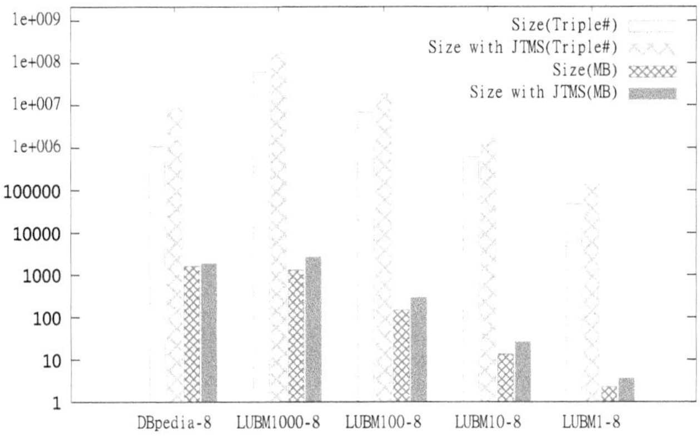

Figure 7: Comparisons on Space Consumption

the ratio of space consumption with and without JTMS is 2.0 for LUBM, and is 1.15 for DBpedia.

5.2 Scalability

Another evaluation objective is to show the scalability of our algorithm for finding justifications based on MapReduce. We take *speedup* as the evaluation measure, which is defined to be $\frac{Avg.\ justification\ time\ baseline}{Avg.\ justification\ time}$ [16]. In order to get the average justification time, we randomly selected 10 derived triples to perform our algorithm on each of them, and then computed the average value as the result. For LUBM-1000 data set, we increased the number of slave nodes from 1 to 8 every 2 times. When performing our algorithm on the data set using only 1 slave node, it failed with "out of heap size" error. Therefore, results on LUBM1000-1 are not available. Taking LUBM1000-2 as the baseline, the speedup has a growth trend. Table 4 gives the experimental results. Theoretically, the ideal speedup values are linear, i.e. speed scales linearly with the number of slave nodes. The proposed algorithm does not scale linearly for the data sets. The reason is that there exists basic platform startup overhead which prevents the linear characteristics of the system. The impact decays along with the increase of data set size and complexity. Experimental results on real world DBpedia data set are shown in Table 5.

Table 4: Speedup on LUBM-1000

DataSet	Time(min)	Speedup (Baseline: LUBM1000-2)
LUBM1000-2	39.25	1
LUBM1000-4	22.47	1.75
LUBM1000-8	16.98	2.31

Table 5: Speedup on DBpedia

DataSet	Time(min)	Speedup (Baseline: Dbpedia-1)
Dbpedia-1	11.78	1
Dbpedia-2	7.72	1.51
Dbpedia-4	6.26	1.88
Dbpedia-8	4.88	2.42

We also challenged the task of finding all justifications on billion triples utilizing Amazon Elastic Compute Cloud[7] (Amazon EC2) web service that provides configurable computational resources. Four *Large Type* Amazon EC2 instances were employed, each has 7.5 GB of memory, 4 EC2 Compute Units, 850 GB of local instance storage, and 64-bit platform. It took 10.85 hours to import all triples, and 58.6 hours to do inference on the triples and to construct the simplified JTMS. The average time cost to find all justifications is 1.5 hours.

5.3 Key Factor

Given an ontology and number of slaves, we observed that the execution time of finding justifications is only closely related to the number of iterations, but irrelevant to the number of justifications and the number of triples in each justification. For instance, Table 6 shows the experimental results for 10 different justification finding tasks executed on LUBM-1000 data set with 8 slave nodes. We investigated the execution time, number of justifications found, average number of triples in each justification, and count of iterations. The results essentially reflect our observations. As MapReduce exploits process-based parallel processing, memory objects are not easy to share between iterations. The objects have to be serialized on the disks, which becomes the bottleneck. Therefore, execution time is closely relevant to the number of iterations. An interesting observation is that the count of justifications does not affect the time consumption much. For instance, comparing the first line and the fourth line, there are 4 justifications for the first triple and 238 justifications for the fourth triple. However, it is slower to find all justifications for the former triple than that for the latter one. When looking into the log of this justification finding process, we found that all the justifications were output at the second run of the algorithm. The execution time was saved because no intermediate result need be written to the disks, and the expansion of justifications happened in parallel.

6. RELATED WORK

The first work on finding all justifications of an OWL ontology is proposed in [12]. Their approach is limited to $\mathcal{ALC}$ and is then extended to more expressive description logics in [9]. These approaches are based on the reasoning algorithm of a description logic, thus are often called glass-box approaches. Alternatively, there are some other approaches that treats a description logic reasoner as a "black-box" or an "oracle" and uses it to check satisfiability of an ontology (see [8] for example). These approaches are often called black-box approaches. Neither glass-box approaches nor black-box approaches can handle large scale OWL ontologies. Therefore, some optimization techniques and heuristic approaches are proposed. The main optimization techniques are modularization-based ones, which compute all justifications in a syntactic locality-based module [14] or a justification-preserving module [4] rather than in the whole ontology.

Our approach for finding all justifications of OWL pD^* entailments falls into the glass-box approaches. Since OWL pD^* semantics is different from other OWL semantics based on description logics, our approach is fundamentally different from existing glass-box approaches for finding all justifications in fragments of OWL DL. As for existing optimization techniques, although the modularization-based techniques can be applied to optimize finding all justifications of OWL pD^* entailments, it is still impractical in some cases where the extracted module is large, and it requires a mass of resources, including time and space, to extract the target module in a large scale OWL ontology.

[7]`http://aws.amazon.com/ec2/`

Table 6: Affecting Factors of Justifications Finding Time

	Time (min)	Iter. #	Just. #	Average Triples #	Entailment
1	23.3	4	4	2.5	<http://www.Department12.University743.edu/UndergraduateStudent416, rdf:type, Student>
2	21.97	4	4	2.5	<http://www.Department11.University153.edu/UndergraduateStudent40, rdf:type, Student>
3	18.15	3	7	3.71	<http://www.Department13.University444.edu/UndergraduateStudent108, rdf:type, _:genid16
4	17.8	3	238	3	<http://www.Department2.University135.edu, rdf:type, Organization>
5	17.42	3	6	4	<http://www.Department1.University270.edu/UndergraduateStudent416, rdf:type, _:genid16>
6	16.6	3	4	2.25	<http://www.Department14.University848.edu/UndergraduateStudent282,rdf:type, Person>
7	11.52	2	2	2	<http://www.Department15.University298.edu/FullProfessor8/Publication4, rdf:type, Publication>
8	11.42	2	1	2	<http://www.Department16.University645.edu, member, http://www.Department16.University645.edu/UndergraduateStudent307>
9	11.13	2	1	2	<http://www.Department17.University752.edu/GraduateCourse10, rdf:type, Course>
10	10.52	2	2	2	<http://www.Department1.University742.edu/Course5, rdf:type, Course>

7. CONCLUSIONS AND FUTURE WORK

Finding all justifications is critical for debugging an inconsistent ontology and providing explanations of unwanted entailments. In this paper, we proposed an approach to find all justifications of OWL entailments using TMS and MapReduce. With the help of TMS, the problem of finding justifications was converted to traversals on the dependency graph of TMS. Scalability was achieved by developing appropriate MapReduce algorithms. We analyzed the feasibility of the approach theoretically and empirically. Evaluation results show that our approach can scale to more than one billion triples. One of the applications of our work is to improve the quality of Web of Data produced in the LOD project, which can contain different errors such as logical inconsistencies [7].

One direction of our future work lies in adapting more complex TMS systems to deal with other OWL sub-languages. Furthermore, the evaluation is very preliminary due to our limited experimental conditions. To provide more convincing results, we will try larger or commercial Hadoop clusters (e.g. Amazon EC2), and provide extensional experimental results on data sets consisting of the large size of terminologies (T-Box) as well as those consisting of large number of instance data (A-Box). We also plan to study iterative MapReduce techniques to further improve our algorithm.

8. ACKNOWLEDGMENTS

Gang Wu is partially supported by the National Natural Science Foundation of China under grants 60903010, 61025007 and 60933001, the National Basic Research Program of China under grant 2011CB302206, the Natural Science Foundation of Jiangsu Province under grant BK2009268, and the Key Laboratory of Advanced Information Science and Network Technology of Beijing under grant XDXX1011. Guilin Qi is partially supported by Excellent Youth Scholars Program of Southeast University under grant 4009001011, the National Natural Science Foundation of China under grant 61003157, the Jiangsu Science Foundation under grant BK2010412, and the Key Laboratory of Computer Network and Information Integration (Southeast University). Jianfeng Du is partly supported by the National Natural Science Foundation of China under grant 61005043.

9. REFERENCES

[1] F. Bry and J. Kotowski. Reason Maintenance - State of the Art. Technical Report PMS-FB-2008-17, Institute for Informatics, University of Munich, 2008.

[2] J. de Kleer. An assumption-based tms. *Artif. Intell.*, 28(2):127–162, 1986.

[3] J. Doyle. A truth maintenance system. *Artif. Intell.*, 12(3):231–272, November 1979.

[4] J. Du, G. Qi, and Q. Ji. Goal-directed module extraction for explaining owl dl entailments. In *Proc. of ISWC'09*, pages 163–179, 2009.

[5] K. D. Forbus and J. de Kleer. *Building Problem Solvers*. The MIT Press, Cambridge, MA, USA, 1993.

[6] Y. Guo, Z. Pan, and J. Heflin. LUBM: A benchmark for OWL knowledge base systems. *Web Semantics: Science, Services and Agents on the World Wide Web*, 3(2-3):158–182, October 2005.

[7] A. Hogan, A. Harth, A. Passant, S. Decker, and A. Polleres. Weaving the Pedantic Web. In *Linked Data on the Web Workshop (LDOW2010) at WWW'2010*, 2010.

[8] A. Kalyanpur, B. Parsia, M. Horridge, and E. Sirin. Finding All Justifications of OWL DL Entailments. In *Proc. of ISWC/ASWC*, pages 267–280, Berlin, Heidelberg, 2007.

[9] A. Kalyanpur, B. Parsia, E. Sirin, and J. Hendler. Debugging unsatisfiable classes in OWL ontologies. *Journal of Web Semantics*, 3(4):268–293, 2005.

[10] D. Mattox, K. Smith, and S. C. Y. Lu. Tracking Causal Dependencies in an Active Object-Oriented Database. In *Proc. of DOOD*, pages 379–394, 1993.

[11] B. Motik, B. C. Grau, I. Horrocks, Z. Wu, A. Fokoue, and C. Lutz. OWL 2 web ontology language – profiles. http://www.w3.org/TR/owl2-profiles/, 2009.

[12] S. Schlobach and R. Cornet. Non-standard reasoning services for the debugging of description logic terminologies. In *Proc. of IJCAI'03*, pages 355–362. 2003.

[13] M. Stanojevic, S. Vranes, and D. Velasevic. Using Truth Maintenance Systems: A Tutorial. *IEEE Expert: Intelligent Systems and Their Applications*, 9(6):46–56, December 1994.

[14] B. Suntisrivaraporn, G. Qi, Q. Ji, and P. Haase. A modularization-based approach to finding all justifications for OWL DL entailments. In *Proc. of ASWC'08*, pages 1–15, 2008.

[15] H. J. ter Horst. Completeness, decidability and complexity of entailment for RDF Schema and a semantic extension involving the OWL vocabulary. *Web Semant.*, 3:79–115, October 2005.

[16] J. Urbani, S. Kotoulas, J. Maassen, F. van Harmelen, and H. Bal. OWL Reasoning with WebPIE: Calculating the Closure of 100 Billion Triples. In *Proc. of ESWC*, volume 6088, pages 213–227. Berlin, Heidelberg, 2010.

Estimating Selectivity for Joined RDF Triple Patterns

Hai Huang
Faculty of ICT
Swinburne University of Technology
VIC 3122, Australia
hhuang@swin.edu.au

Chengfei Liu
Faculty of ICT
Swinburne University of Technology
VIC 3122, Australia
cliu@swin.edu.au

ABSTRACT

A fundamental problem related to RDF query processing is selectivity estimation, which is crucial to query optimization for determining a join order of RDF triple patterns. In this paper we focus research on selectivity estimation for SPARQL graph patterns. The previous work takes the join uniformity assumption when estimating the joined triple patterns. This assumption would lead to highly inaccurate estimations in the cases where properties in SPARQL graph patterns are correlated. We take into account the dependencies among properties in SPARQL graph patterns and propose a more accurate estimation model. Since star and chain query patterns are common in SPARQL graph patterns, we first focus on these two basic patterns and propose to use Bayesian network and chain histogram respectively for estimating the selectivity of them. Then, for estimating the selectivity of an arbitrary SPARQL graph pattern, we design algorithms for maximally using the precomputed statistics of the star paths and chain paths. The experiments show that our method outperforms existing approaches in accuracy.

Categories and Subject Descriptors

H.2.4 [**Systems**]: Query processing

General Terms

Performance

Keywords

SPARQL Query Processing, Selectivity Estimation

1. INTRODUCTION

The Resource Description Framework (RDF) is a standard format for encoding machine-readable information on the Semantic Web. Recently, more and more data is being stored in RDF format. RDF data is a set of triples and each triple called statement is of the form (*subject*, *property*, *object*). RDF data can be represented as a graph with nodes representing resources or their property values and labeled arcs representing properties. This data representation is general and flexible. However, this fine-grained model leads to queries on RDF data with a large number of joins, which is an inherent characteristic of querying RDF data [1].

Since the use of RDF to represent data has grown dramatically over the last few years, query processing on RDF data becomes an important issue in realizing the semantic web vision. Some query languages such as SPARQL have been developed. As we know, accurate estimation of the result size of queries is crucial to query processing. Cost-based query optimizers use estimated intermediate result size to choose the optimal query execution plan.

As a SPARQL query has a large number of joins, estimating precisely the joined triple pattern is very important. Some work has been done in this area. In [4, 9] the join uniformity assumption is made when estimating the joined triple patterns with *bound* subjects or objects (i.e., the subjects or objects are concrete values). They assume that each triple satisfying a triple pattern is equally likely to join with the triples satisfying the other triple pattern. However, this assumption does not hold in many cases. And when the data are inconsistent with this assumption, it could cause a highly inaccurate estimation.

For example, in Figure 1, a SPARQL query is posed on an RDF database, which retrieves academic staff members and the courses they teach with some conditions. Suppose we want to estimate the selectivity $sel(t_1 \bowtie t_3)$ of the joined triple pattern $t_1 \bowtie t_3$. It would *overestimate* the result size $sel(t_1 \bowtie t_3)$ using the formula (1) proposed in [4] as follows:

$$sel(t_1 \bowtie t_3) = \frac{S_P}{|T|^2} \times sel(Income, \quad `\leq 70K\text{'}) \times sel(Position, \quad \text{`Prof.'})$$

where S_P is the result upper bound of the joined triple pattern (*?Z*, *Income*, *?W*)(*?Z*, *Position*, *?Y*) and $|T|$ is the number of triples in the database. $sel(Income$, '$\leq 70K$') and $sel(Position$, 'Prof.') are the object selectivities of t_1 and t_3. It assumes that each triple satisfying triple pattern t_1 is equally likely to join with triples satisfying triple pattern t_3. But in fact, the triple matching t_3 which indicates that the person is a professor, who is supposed to have higher income ('$> 70k$'). Thus, the triples matching t_1 are less likely to join with triples matching t_3.

There are two observations from this example. First, we

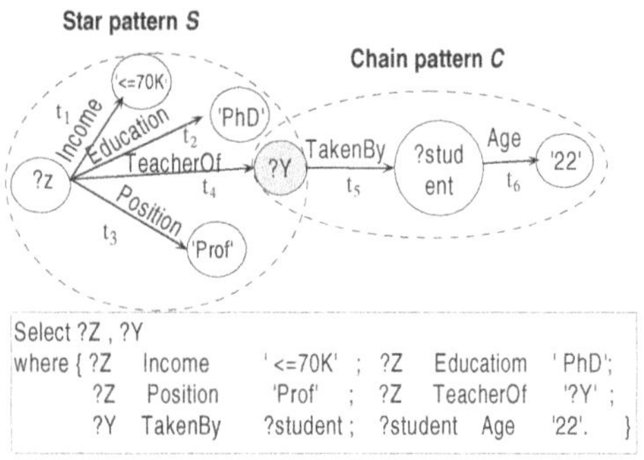

Figure 1: RDF SPARQL query

can observe that the join uniformity assumption is not applicable to those cases where properties have correlations (dependencies) with each other. In fact, this assumption is rarely satisfied in real data, so we need a more accurate model to relax this assumption for estimating the result size of a SPARQL query. Second, the query in Figure 1 is a composition of a chain query pattern and a star query pattern, and these two types of patterns are very common in SPARQL queries. It is desirable to find appropriate ways to estimate the selectivity of these common patterns.

Based on the observations, we propose new methods for selectivity estimation of SPARQL queries. The contributions of this paper can be summarized as follows:

- We study the star and chain patterns with correlated properties and propose two methods for estimating the selectivity of them respectively. For star query patterns, we construct Bayesian networks to compactly represent the joint probability distribution over values of correlated properties. And for chain query patterns, we build the chain histogram, which can obtain a good balance between the estimation accuracy and space cost.
- For an arbitrary SPARQL query represented as a composite graph pattern, we propose algorithms for maximally combining the statistics of chain paths and star paths that we have precomputed to estimate the overall selectivity of the graph pattern.
- We conduct experiments on both synthetic and real-world datasets show the effectiveness and performance of our approach.

The remainder of this paper is organized as follows. Section 2 introduces some preliminary knowledge. In Section 3 and Section 4, we propose two methods to estimate the selectivity of star and chain query patterns, respectively. Section 5 presents the algorithms for estimating the selectivity of arbitrary composite SPARQL graph patterns. Section 6 describes an experimental evaluation of our approach. Some related work is discussed in Section 7. At last, in Section 8 we conclude our work in this paper.

2. PRELIMINARY

A *triple* $(s, p, o) \in (I \cup B) \times (I \cup B) \times (I \cup B \cup L)$ is called an RDF triple, where I is a set of IRIs (Internationalized URIs), B a set of blank nodes and L a set of literals. In the triple, s is called subject, p the property (or predicate), and o the object or property value. An RDF *triple pattern* $(s, p, o) \in (I \cup V) \times (I \cup V) \times (I \cup V \cup L)$, where V is a set of variables disjoint from the sets I, B and L. An *RDF graph pattern* $G = (q_1, q_2, ..., q_n), q_i \in T$, where T is a set of triple patterns. A SPARQL query can be represented as an RDF graph pattern and called a SPARQL graph pattern.

Problem Definition. The problem that we tackle in this paper can be summarized as follows: *Given an RDF database D and a SPARQL graph pattern Q, we estimate the selectivity sel(Q) of Q.* $sel(Q)$ stands for the count of results in database D satisfying Q. In this paper, our interest is to estimate the selectivity of *joined triple patterns*, which will be discussed in the following sections.

3. ESTIMATION FOR STAR QUERY PATTERNS

In this section, we present the method of using Bayesian networks to estimate the selectivity of star query patterns.

3.1 Estimation for star patterns using Bayesian networks

Star query pattern that commonly occurs in SPARQL queries is used to retrieve entities with some constraints. It has the form of a number of triple patterns with different properties sharing the same subject variable. Normally, the properties involved in a star query patterns are correlated. For example, Figure 2 shows a star query pattern Q and the properties *Income*, *Education*, *Position*, *TeacherOf* are correlated. Thus, as shown in the introduction, the join uniformity assumption would cause a highly inaccurate selectivity estimation for star query patterns.

For estimating the selectivities of star query patterns precisely, we need some helpful statistics. In this paper, we precompute statistics for star paths. A star path is a set of properties which share the same domain. Given a star path with properties $prop_1, prop_2, \cdots, prop_n$, we use $(prop_1, prop_2, \cdots, prop_n)$ to denote. In Figure 2, Q_s(*Income*, *Education*, *Position*, *TeacherOf*) is a star path. Since the number of possible star paths could be huge (2^n, where n is the number of properties in the database), it is impossible to precompute statistics for all star paths. In this paper, we target the star paths in which properties are strongly correlated.

We assume that if a star path appears in the data graph *frequently* then the properties contained in this star path are strongly correlated. This assumption is also made in data mining field to find association rules. Using the algorithm presented in [9], we can find frequent star paths. A frequent star path is logically associated with a table R called cluster-property table [2] that contains a set of entities to be queried. For example, Figure 2 shows a cluster-property table of star path Q_s. Each row of the table is an academic staff with values of properties *Education*, *Income*, *Position* and *TeacherOf*. Note that different with [2], we do not store cluster-property tables for frequent star paths. More compressed structures would be constructed for selectivity estimation.

Given a frequent star path $Q_s(prop_1, prop_2, \cdots, prop_n)$ and its cluster-property table R, the selectivity of star query $Q(?x, prop_1, o_1)$ $(?x, prop_2, o_2) \cdots, (?x, prop_n, o_n)$ denoted by $sel(Q)$, can be computed as follows:

$$sel(Q) = \Pr(prop_1 = o_1, prop_2 = o_2, ..., prop_n = o_n) \cdot |R|$$

where $\Pr(prop_1 = o_1, prop_2 = o_2, ..., prop_n = o_n)$ denotes the joint probability distribution over object values of properties $prop_1$, $prop_2$, $\cdots$, $prop_n$ in table R and $|R|$ is the number of rows in the cluster-property table R.

Since the number of rows $|R|$ is easy to know, we will focus on computing the joint probability distribution $\Pr(prop_1 = o_1,\ prop_2 = o_2,\ \cdots,\ prop_n = o_n)$. Unfortunately, it is impossible to explicitly store $\Pr(prop_1 = o_1,\ prop_2 = o_2,\ \cdots,\ prop_n = o_n)$ because the possible combinations of property values would be exponential. Thus, we need an appropriate structure to approximately store the joint probability distribution information.

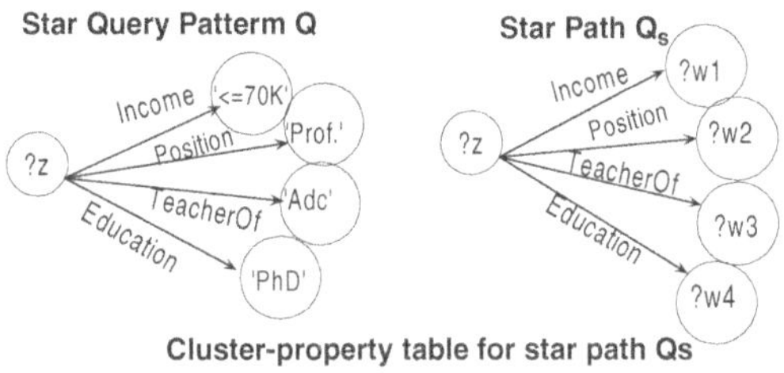

Cluster-property table for star path Qs

Subject	Education (Edu)	Position (Pos)	Income (Inc)	TeacherOf (TOf)
S_1	'PhD'	'Lecturer'	'<=70K'	'Preliminary course' (Prc)
S_2	'PhD'	'Lecturer'	'<=70K'	'Preliminary course' (Prc)
S_3	'PhD'	'Prof.'	'<=70k'	'Advanced course' (Adc)

Figure 2: Star path and star query pattern

The Bayesian network [3] can approximately represent the probability distribution over a set of variables using a little space. Bayesian networks make use of Bayes' Rule and conditional independence assumption to compactly represent the full joint probability distribution. Let X, Y, Z be three discrete valued random variables. We say that X is conditionally independent of Y given Z if the probability distribution of X is independent of the value of Y given a value for Z; that is:

$$\Pr(X = x_i | Y = y_j, Z = z_k) = \Pr(X = x_i | Z = z_k)$$

where x_i, y_j, z_k are values of variables X, Y, Z. The conditional independence assumptions associated with a Bayesian network and conditional probability tables (CPTs), determine a joint probability distribution. For example, in Figure 3, a Bayesian network is constructed on cluster-property table in Figure 2. We can see that properties *Education* and *Income* are conditionally independent given condition *Position*, which means if we already know the position of some person, knowing his education information does not make any difference to our beliefs about his income.

For a star query pattern Q with properties and object values $prop_1 = o_1$, $prop_2 = o_2$, $\cdots$, $prop_n = o_n$, given a Bayesian network β, we have:

$$Pr_\beta(prop_1 = o_1, prop_2 = o_2, ..., prop_m = o_n)$$
$$= \prod_{i=1}^{n} \Pr(prop_i = o_i \mid Parents(prop_i) = \vec{o_k})$$

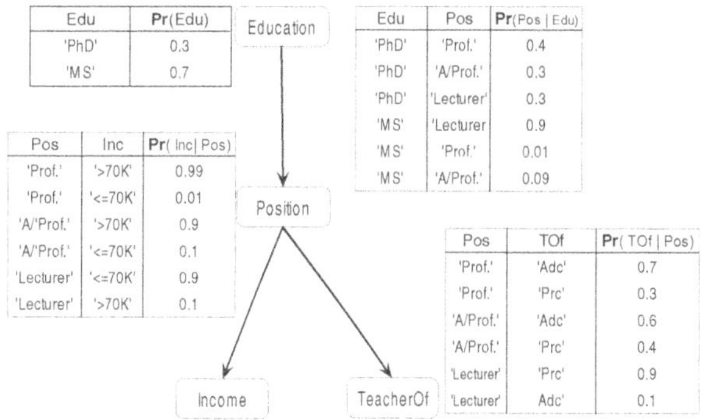

Figure 3: Bayesian Network

where $Parents(prop_i)$ denotes the set of immediate predecessors of $prop_i$ in the network and $\vec{o_k}$ denotes the set of values of $Parents(prop_i)$. Note that for computing $\Pr(prop_i \mid Parents(prop_i) = \vec{o_k})$, we only need to know the values of $prop_i$'s parent properties, which would save a lot of space in practice. So given the Bayesian network β, we can use $\Pr_\beta(prop_1 = o_1, prop_2 = o_2, ..., prop_n = o_n)$ to *approximately* represent $\Pr(prop_1 = o_1, prop_2 = o_2, ..., prop_n = o_n)$. We have:

$$\begin{aligned} sel(Q) &= \Pr(prop_1 = o_1, prop_2 = o_2, ..., prop_n = o_n) \cdot |R| \\ &\approx Pr_\beta(prop_1 = o_1, prop_2 = o_2, ..., prop_n = o_n) \cdot |R| \\ &= \prod_{i=1}^{n} \Pr(prop_i = o_i \mid Parents(prop_i) = \vec{o_k}) \cdot |R| \end{aligned}$$

Example 1. Given the star pattern Q(*?Z, income,* $\leq$*'70K'*) (*?Z, Education, 'PhD'*) (*?Z, Position, 'Prof.'*) (*?Z, TeacherOf, 'Adc'*) shown in Figure 2 and Bayesian network described in Figure 3, we compute the selectivity of Q as follows:

$$\begin{aligned} sel(Q) &= \Pr(Edu = \text{'PhD'}, Pos = \text{'Prof.'}, Inc \leq \text{'70K'}, \\ &\quad TOf = \text{'Adc'}) \cdot |R| \\ &= \Pr(Pos - \text{'Prof.'} \mid Edu = \text{'PhD'}) \\ &\quad \cdot \Pr(Inc \leq \text{'70K'} \mid Pos = \text{'Prof.'}) \\ &\quad \cdot \Pr(TOf = \text{'Adc'} \mid Pos = \text{'Prof.'}) \\ &\quad \cdot \Pr(Edu = \text{'PhD'}) \cdot |R| \\ &= 0.4 \cdot 0.01 \cdot 0.7 \cdot 0.3 \cdot |R| = 0.00084 \cdot |R| \end{aligned}$$

3.2 Learning Bayesian networks

To approximately represent the joint distribution of property values for selectivity estimation, we first generate the cluster-property tables for frequent star paths, and then Bayesian networks can be learned from these tables. From the Aprior property, we know that if a star path is frequent then its sub paths are also frequent. Given a frequent star path (p_1, p_2, p_3) and one of its sub path (p_1, p_3), if they have equal frequencies, namely $|(p_1, p_2, p_3)| = |(p_1, p_3)|$, it indicates that they have the same instance set. In this case, the information contained in the cluster-property table of path (p_1, p_3) is fully covered by the cluster-property table of path (p_1, p_2, p_3) and we do not need to generate the cluster-property table for path (p_1, p_3). Note that we will drop all cluster-property tables once Bayesian networks have been constructed.

Before building Bayesian networks, the property values

are first clustered into equi-width subsets (abstracted values). Bayesian network construction algorithms can be grouped into two categories: one category of algorithms uses heuristic searching methods to construct a model and then evaluates it using a scoring method [5, 6, 8]. The other category of algorithms constructs Bayesian networks by analyzing dependency relationships among nodes. The dependency relationships are measured by using some kind of conditional independence (CI) test. In this paper we adopt the algorithm in [7], which employs mutual information to measure how close the relationship between two variables. The mutual information $I(X, Y)$ of two variables X,Y is defined as follows:

$$I(X,Y) = \sum_{x,y} \Pr(x,y) log \frac{\Pr(x,y)}{\Pr(x) \cdot \Pr(y)}$$

and the conditional mutual information is defined as

$$I(X,Y|M) = \sum_{x,y,m} \Pr(x,y,m) log \frac{\Pr(x,y|m)}{\Pr(x|m) \cdot \Pr(y|m)}$$

where M is a set of observed variables. When $I(X, Y|M)$ is smaller than a threshold ϵ, X and X are conditionally independent and we also call X and X are *d-separated* by the condition set M.

The construction algorithm contains three steps. The first step is to compute mutual information of each pair of nodes as a measure of closeness, and creates a draft graph based on this information. The draft graph is a singly connected graph (a graph without loops). In the second phase, the algorithm adds edges when the pairs of nodes cannot be d-separated. In the third step, each edge of the Independent-map is examined using CI tests and will be removed if the two nodes of the edge can be d-separated. At the end of the third phase, the algorithm also carries out a procedure to orient the edges of the graph. For details on specific three steps, please see [7]. The time complexity of this algorithm is $O(n^4)$, where n is the number of properties involved in the cluster property table. In our problem, it requires that the conditional probability tables learned fit in a small amount of memory, therefore we restrict the threshold ϵ for space limit when building Bayesian networks.

4. ESTIMATION FOR CHAIN PATTERNS

The other kind of correlated properties commonly occur in SPARQL graph patterns is *chain path*. A chain path consists of a sequence of triple patterns where the object of a triple pattern is also the subject of the next triple pattern. For example, in Figure 4, *(?course, TakenBy, ?student)(?student, Age, ?age)* is a chain path. Note that triple patterns of a chain path have only unbound subjects and objects. Given a chain path with a sequence of properties $p_1, \cdots, p_n$, we use $(p_1\text{-}p_2\text{-}\cdots\text{-}p_n)$ to denote it. For instance, in Figure 4, (*TakenBy-Age*) is a chain path and tuples in the data graph matching this chain path fall in the subject-property matrix table [10] of this chain path.

A chain query pattern is a chain path with possible literal constraints on the start node (the subject of the first triple pattern) or end node (the object of the last triple pattern) in the chain path. For example, c_1 *(?course, TakenBy, ?student)(?student, Age, '22')* shown in Figure 4 is a chain query pattern. The straightforward way to estimate the selectivity of a chain query pattern is combining the selectivity of each triple pattern in the product form. Obviously, it would be highly inaccurate if the properties are correlated.

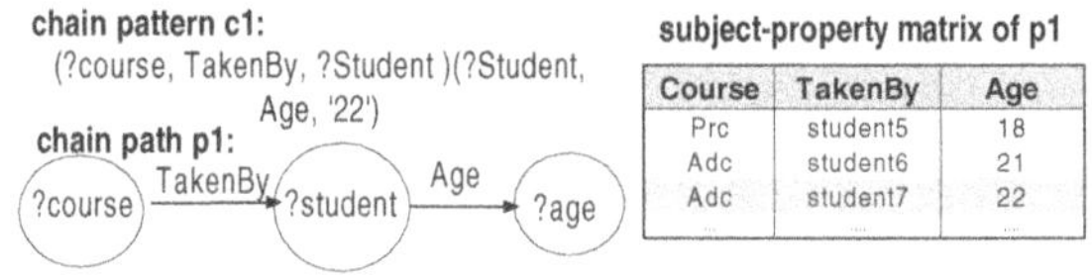

Figure 4: Chain path and chain query pattern

4.1 Constructing the histogram

We first select frequent chain paths and construct the histogram for them. For these frequent chain paths, we can construct a *chain frequency table CFT* (shown in Figure 5), which has two attributes: *Abstracted chain query pattern* and *Frequency*. The values of attribute *Abstracted chain query pattern* are abstracted chain query pattern descriptors consisting of frequent chain paths with possible value combinations of the start node and end node. Note that the possible values occurring on the start node and end node of paths are clustered into equi-width subsets called abstracted values. Each value of attribute *Frequency* is the count of tuples that match the abstracted chain pattern query in the data graph. We can see that each row of CFT indicates an abstracted chain query pattern with its frequency, so it is easy to get the selectivity of abstracted chain patterns from CFT. For example, the first tuple (*Prc/p1/20-22, 26*) of chain frequency table shown in Figure 5 indicates a chain query pattern (*'Prc', TakenBy, ?student*) (*?student, Age, '20-22'*) with its frequency *26*. However, chain frequency table CFT could be too large to fit in a small amount of main memory. Thus, we construct the new data structure called *chain histogram* to approximate the selectivity of chain query patterns.

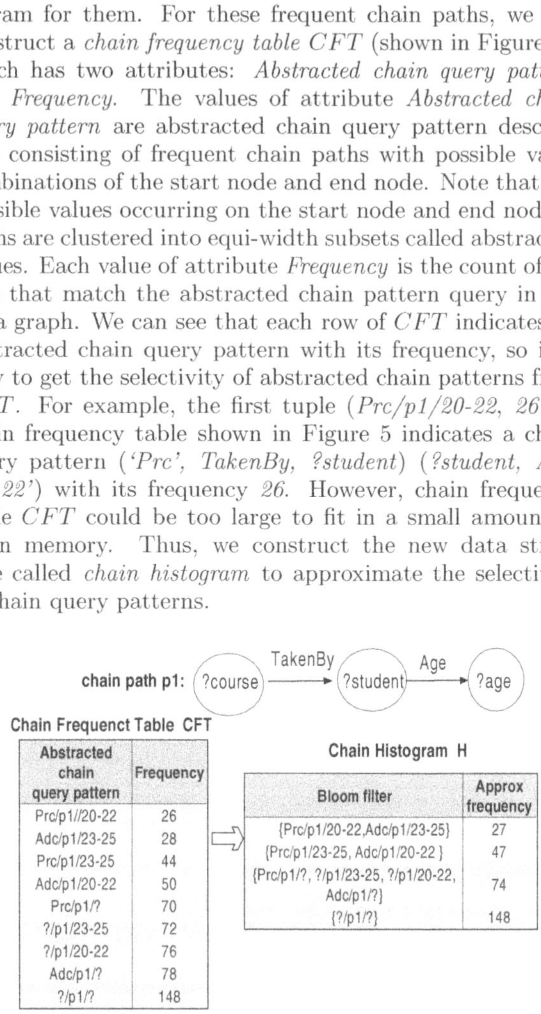

Figure 5: An example of the chain frequency table and the chain histogram. "?" indicates a variable.

We first group the abstracted chain query patterns in CFT into B buckets according to their frequencies. That means the abstracted chain query patterns with similar frequencies are grouped into one bucket, which is helpful to guarantee the accuracy of estimation. For example, in Figure 5, abstracted chain patterns (*Prc/p1/20-22*) and (*Adc/p1/ 23-25*) are grouped into one bucket since they have similar frequencies. For each bucket we only need to save the average frequency and its abstracted chain query pattern members. Given an abstracted chain query pattern and which bucket it belongs to, we can easily get the approximate frequency of this chain query pattern.

To space-efficiently store the elements of each bucket and accelerate the membership query processing, we employ the bloom filter technique. Bloom filter [11, 12] is a space-efficient probabilistic data structure that is used to test whether an element is a member of a set. Here we use bloom filters to store buckets and construct the chain histogram. An example of chain histogram is shown in Figure 5.

4.2 Estimation for chain patterns using the histogram

Given a chain query pattern C and a histogram H, for estimating the selectivity of C, we first map the basic level values of start node and end node of C to their abstracted values and generate the abstracted chain query pattern C_a. For example, if a chain query pattern *C(?course, Takenby, ?student)(?student, Age, '22')* is posed on the database, we map the value *'22'* to its abstracted value *'20-22'* and get the abstracted chain query pattern C_a*(?y, Takenby, ?student)(?student, Age, '20-22')*. The uniformity assumption is made here when computing the coefficient η between the selectivities of C and C_a. We can acquire the approximate selectivity of chain query pattern C_a from the chain histogram H. Note that though it is rare, it is possible that the pattern C_a is reported to fall in multiple buckets due to the false positive error of the bloom filter. In this case, we simply return the count of the first bucket which reports that the pattern C_a is its member. This process is given in Algorithm 1 *GetChainSel*. The time complexity of obtaining the selectivity of a chain pattern is $O(KB)$, where K is the maximal number of hash functions used in a bloom filter and B is the number of buckets (or bloom filters) in the chain histogram.

Algorithm 1 *GetChainSel*

Input: Chain pattern C, histogram H;
Output: The selectivity sel of chain pattern C;

```
Map chain query pattern C to C_a; {C_a is abstracted chain pattern of C}
Compute the coefficient η between C and C_a;
for all buckets b_k in H do
    if C_a falls into a certain bucket b_j then
        sel_a = b_j.frequency; {sel_a is the selectivity of C_a}
        return sel = η × sel_a;
return 0;
```

For example, given a chain query pattern (*?y, Takenby, ?student*) (*?student, Age, '22'*), we compute the selectivity of this chain query pattern as follows:

$$\begin{aligned} sel &= 1/3 \times sel(?/p1/20-22) \\ &= 1/3 \times 74 \approx 25; \end{aligned}$$

5. ESTIMATION FOR COMPOSITE GRAPH PATTERNS

In this section, we discuss how to estimate the selectivity of an arbitrary composite graph pattern with the maximum use of the precomputed statistics of star and chain paths.

5.1 Decomposition of SPARQL graph patterns

From previous sections, we know that the precomputed statistics of the star and chain paths can help to estimate the selectivity of star and chain query patterns respectively. As a SPARQL graph pattern SC (an example is shown in Figure 6) is a composite graph pattern, we decompose it into a set of star and chain query patterns and then use the precomputed statistics of star and chain paths to obtain the overall selectivity. For maximally using precomputed statistics, we hope to obtain a set of edge-disjoint precomputed star and chain paths as building blocks that constitute a subgraph SC' of graph pattern SC, which has the largest number of edges.

There is a special case we need to consider. A SPARQL query may include non-property-bound triple patterns. For this case, we remove such triple patterns from graph patterns (reserving join nodes) and estimate the selectivities of these triple patterns as single triple patterns. At last, we combine the selectivity of the whole graph pattern with the independent assumption.

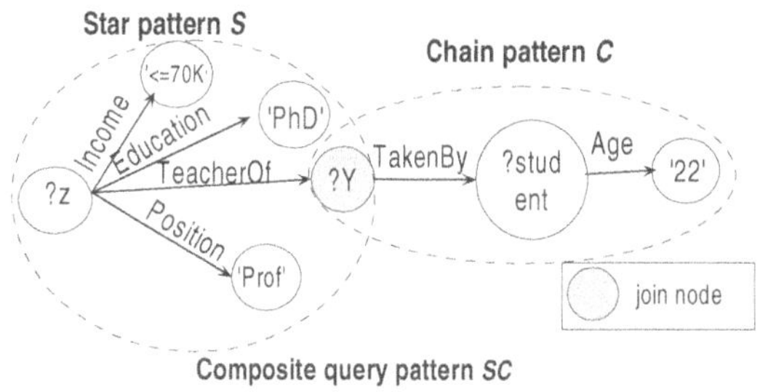

Figure 6: Composite graph pattern

We use PS to refer to the set of star and chain paths whose statistics have been precomputed. Removing a path p from graph Q, denoted by $Q \setminus p$, consists of removing all edges of p from Q, followed by removing all stand-alone nodes. Given a query pattern Q and precomputed path set PS, the *maximum path cover* of Q with respect to PS denoted by $Cov_{PS}(Q)$ is a subset of edge-disjoint paths in PS, which can constitute a subgraph Q' of Q such that Q' has the largest number of edges. Note that Q' could be Q itself.

Algorithm 2 *GreedyFindpathCover*

Input: Path set PS, Query Q;
Output: A maximum path cover set $Cov_{PS}(Q)$;

```
priority queue PQ = Ω, Cov_PS(Q) = Ω;
for all path p_k in PS do
    if p_k ⊆ Q then
        insert p_k to the priority queue PQ; {according to p_k's length}
while not empty(PQ) do
    remove(PQ, p_j);
    if p_j ⊆ Q then
        Cov_PS(Q) = Cov_PS(Q) ∪ p_j;
        Q = Q \ p_j;
    if Q is empty then
        return Cov_PS(Q);
return Cov_PS(Q);
```

Our problem is to obtain $Cov_{PS}(Q)$. It is similar to the classic *0-1 knapsack* problem: Given a set of items, each with a weight and a value, determine the number of each item to include in a collection so that the total weight is less than a given limit and the total value is as large as possible.

In our problem, the items are precomputed chain paths and star paths. For a chain or star path item, the value of this item is the length of the path and the weight is just the path since we use this path as a building block. Now, we need to determine the status for each path item ("picked" or "not picked") so that the picked edge-disjoint paths (or sub paths) can constitute a subgraph Q' of Q, which has the largest number of edges. The weight limit here is the query graph pattern Q.

Algorithm 3 *OptimalFC*

Input: A path array $PS[1..n]$,A boolean array flag[1..n], Graph pattern Q;
Output: A path cover set $Cov_{PS}(Q)$ of Q;

```
Initial flag [1..n]= false;
int maxNum = maxCov(n, Q); {get the number of edges
   covered, function maxCov(n, Q) is defined below}
for k := 1 to n do
   if flag[k] = true then
      add PS[k] to Cov_PS(Q);
return Cov_PS(Q);
Function int maxCov(n, Q);
if n = 0 or Q = Ω then
   return 0;
if path PS[n] ⊈ Q then
   return maxCov(n − 1, Q);
if maxCov(n − 1, Q) ⩽ edgeNum((PS[n]) + maxCov(n −
   1, Q \ PS[n]) then
   Q = Q \ PS[n];
   flag[n] = true ; {indicating that path PS[n] is picked}
   return maxCov(n − 1, Q \ PS[n]);
else
   return maxCov(n − 1, Q);
```

The straightforward way of finding $Cov_{PS}(Q)$ is to adopt greedy strategy (presented in Algorithm 2 *GreedyFindpathCover*), which is eager to use the longest paths in PS to constitute a subgraph of Q. The time complexity of the algorithm is $O(|PS| \cdot |E|)$, where $|PS|$ is the number of paths in PS and $|E|$ is the number of edges of Q. Due to the local optimum nature of the algorithm, *GreedyFindpathCover* would fail to achieve the global optimum (i.e., the maximum path cover of Q) in some cases. However this algorithm is still of interest because it provides an efficient way to find a path cover of Q when graph pattern Q is huge and dense.

Now we propose an optimal algorithm based on *dynamic programming*. Dynamic programming is a method for solving those problems which exhibit the property of *optimal substructures* by breaking them into overlapping subproblems. It is also applicable to our problem. Given a graph pattern Q, we represent PS as a path array $PS[1..n]$ that contains all precomputed chain paths, star paths. Let *maxCov(i,Q)* be the number of edges of subgraph Q' of Q such that Q' consists of edge-disjoint paths from $PS[1..i]$ and has the largest number of edges. Here we use the last item i and the remaining graph pattern (current weight limit) to index subproblems. $edgeNum(PS[j])$ indicates the edge number of path item j in PS. $maxCov(i, Q)$ can be obtained through combining the optimal solutions of its subproblems.

We have the following properties:

$$\begin{cases} .\ maxCov(0,Q) = 0; \\ .\ maxCov(i,Q) = 0,\ \text{if } Q \text{ is null graph;} \\ .\ maxCov(i,Q) = maxCov(i-1,Q),\ \text{if } PS[i] \nsubseteq Q; \\ .\ maxCov(i,Q) = Max(maxCov(i-1,Q), \\ edgeNum(PS[i]) + maxCov(i-1, Q \setminus PS[i])); \end{cases}$$

Obviously, when $i = 0$ or graph pattern Q is a null graph, $maxCov(i, Q) = 0$. If path $PS[i]$ is not a subgraph of Q, we drop $PS[i]$ and $maxCov(i, Q)$ is equal to its subproblem $maxCov(i-1, Q)$; otherwise, $maxCov(i, Q)$ is computed through comparing the values in two cases (where $PS[i]$ is picked or not picked). Based on these properties, we present the algorithm in Algorithm 3 *OptimalFC*. The time complexity of our optimal algorithm is $O(|PS| \cdot |Q|)$, where $|Q|$ is the number of subgraphs of Q, which is exponential to the number of edges of Q. In practice, if query graph pattern Q is sparse (i.e., the constituent vertices are of low degree) and not large, we can employ this optimal algorithm; otherwise, the greedy algorithm proposed can be used instead.

5.2 Joining a star pattern with a chain pattern

After a composite graph pattern is decomposed into a set of star and chain query patterns, how do we compute the selectivity of this graph pattern? To address this problem, let us first begin with a simple case shown in Figure 6.

In Figure 6, the composite graph pattern SC can be decomposed into a star query pattern S and a chain query pattern C whose corresponding star path and chain path have been computed. The variable $?Y$ is the join node. We use $val(C.Y)$ to refer to the value set of variable $C.Y$ and $val(S.Y)$ for variable $S.Y$. Our aim here is to estimate the selectivity of SC denoted by $sel(SC)$.

Using the Bayesian networks and the chain histogram constructed, we can get $sel(S)$ and $sel(C)$. However, estimating precisely the selectivity of SC is not trivial. A tuple s matching star query pattern S may not join with a tuple c matching chain query pattern C, since they may have different values on variable $?Y$. For estimating precisely the selectivity of SC, it is crucial to know the probability distributions over $val(S.Y)$ and $val(C.Y)$. However, obtaining the exact probability distributions of values over $val(S.Y)$ and $val(C.Y)$ is hard without executing the star query pattern S and chain query pattern C. Fortunately, the probability distribution of abstracted values on the join variable $?Y$ (target variable) can be inferred from the Bayesian network.

For example, suppose we have the Bayesian network shown in Figure 3 and we can infer the probability distribution of abstracted values over $val(S.Y)$ (i.e., the probability distribution over the object values of property *TeacherOf*(TOf for short) as follows:

$$\begin{aligned} & \Pr(TOf = \text{`Adc'} | Edu = \text{`PhD'}, Pos = \text{`Prof.'}, \\ & Inc \leq \text{`70K'}) \\ = \ & \Pr(TeacherOf = \text{`Adc'} | Pos = \text{`Prof.'}) = 0.7 \end{aligned}$$

$$\begin{aligned} & \Pr(TOf = \text{`Prc'} | Edu = \text{`PhD'}, Pos = \text{`Prof.'}, \\ & Inc \leq \text{`70K'}) \\ = \ & \Pr(TOf = \text{`Prc'} | Pos = \text{`Prof.'}) = 0.3 \end{aligned}$$

We can see that 70 percent of tuples matching pattern S have value "*Adc*" and 30 percent of tuples have value

"*Prc*" on variable $?Y$. Using the probability distribution over $val(S.Y)$, we can easily compute the selectivity of SC. Recall that we use the chain histogram to estimate the selectivities of chain query patterns. Now we take the values "*Adc*" and "*Prc*" as the values of start node of chain C separately, then test chain query patterns "Adc/C", "Prc/C" in the chain histogram and get the selectivities $sel(Adc/C)$ and $sel(Prc/C)$. Since bloom filter is efficient for answering set membership queries, this process is time efficient. At last, we can obtain the selectivity of SC as $0.7 \cdot sel(S) \cdot sel(Adc/C) + 0.3 \cdot sel(S) \cdot sel(Prc/C)$. This process is described in Algorithm 4 *ComSelStar-Chain*.

Algorithm 4 *ComSelStar-Chain*

Input: A composite graph pattern $SC(S \bowtie C)$ consisting of a chain pattern C and a star pattern S; Join node $?Y$;
Output: The selectivity of chain pattern SC;

```
count = 0;
for all abstracted values a_i over the join node Y do
    Compute the probability Pr(Y = a_i|M(S)); {M(S) are the observed values in S}
    count_1 = Pr(Y = a_i|M(S)) × sel(S); {compute sel(S) using formula (3)}
    count_2 = GetChainSel(a_i/C);
    count+ = count_1 × count_2;
return count;
```

Algorithm 5 *ComSelStar-Star*

Input: A composite graph pattern $S(S_1 \bowtie S_2)$ consisting of two star pattern S_1 and S_2, Join node Y;
Output: The selectivity of S;

```
count = 0;
for all abstracted values a_i over the join node Y do
    Compute the probability Pr(Y = a_i|M(S_1)), Pr(Y = a_i|M(S_2)) ; {M(S_1), M(S_2) are the observed values in S_1, S_2}
    count_1 = Pr(Y = a_i|M(S_1)) × sel(S_1);
    count_2 = Pr(Y = a_i|M(S_2)) × sel(S_2);
    count+ = count_1 × count_2;
return count;
```

5.3 Other cases

We have discussed the case where a composite graph pattern can be decomposed into one star pattern and one chain pattern. What if a composite graph pattern is decomposed into two star patterns (Figure 7(a)) or two chain patterns (Figure 7(b))? If a graph pattern $S(S_1 \bowtie S_2)$ is decomposed into two star patterns S_1 and S_2, we go through each possible abstracted value a_i on the join node $?Y$ of two star paths. Through inference on the Bayesian networks constructed, it is easy to acquire the probabilities $\Pr(Y = a_i|M(S_1))$ and $\Pr(Y = a_i|M(S_2))$ such that $M(S_1)$ and $M(S_2)$ are observed object values in two star patterns. We then get the selectivity of the composite graph pattern through cumulating the count of tuples from two star patterns which have the same values on the join node. The algorithm is described in Algorithm 5 *ComSelStar-Star*.

In the case where the graph pattern $C(C_1 \bowtie C_2)$ is decomposed into two chain query patterns C_1, C_2 that join on variable $?Y$, the method is similar (presented in Algorithm 6 *ComSelChain-Chain*). We go through each possible abstracted value a_i of the join node, and the selectivities of two chain query patterns with value a_i can be obtained using the chain histogram. $sel(C_1 \bowtie C_2|Y = a_i)$ is computed through combining $sel(a_i/C_1)$ and $sel(a_i/C_2)$ in the product form. At last, we cumulate $sel(C_1 \bowtie C_2|Y = a_i)$ with all possible abstracted values. Since bloom filter is quick to get the selectivities of two chain patterns, this method is also time efficient.

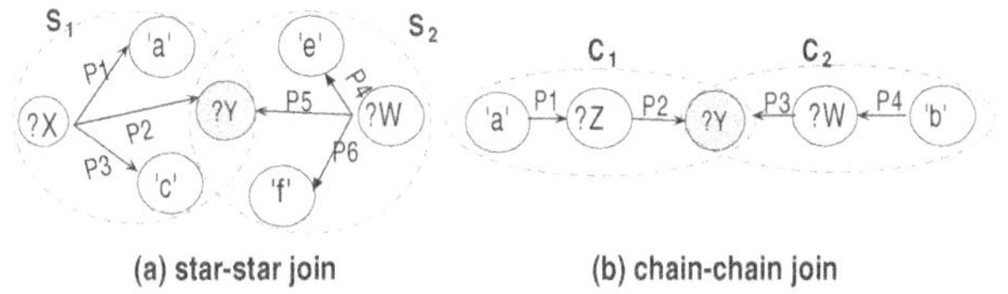

Figure 7: Join between chain patterns and star patterns, where "?Y" is the join node.

Algorithm 6 *ComSelChain-Chain*

Input: A composite graph pattern $C(C_1 \bowtie C_2)$ consisting of two chain patterns C_1,C_2; Join node Y;
Output: The selectivity of chain pattern C;

```
count = 0;
for all abstracted values a_i over the join node Y do
    count_1 = GetChainSel(a_i/C_1);
    count_2 = GetChainSel(a_i/C_2);
    count+ = count_1 × count_2;
return count;
```

Algorithm 7 *ComSelectivity*

Input: A query Q, a path cover set $Cov_{PS}(Q)$ of query Q;
Output: The selectivity $sel(Q)$ of query Q;

```
while ∃ two patterns p_i, p_j ∈ Cov_PS(Q) which can join together do
    p_ij = p_i ⋈ p_j;
    if p_i and p_j are star or chain patterns then
        sel(p_ij) = ComTwoPatterns(p_ij);
        Maintain a selectivity distribution table T_{p_ij} for p_ij;
    if p_i or p_j is a composite pattern then
        Compute sel(p_ij); {Using the chain histogram or inference on Bayesian networks and information provided by T_{p_i} or T_{p_j} }
        Maintain a selectivity distribution table T_{p_ij} for p_ij;
    Q = Q \ p_i \ p_j;
    Cov_PS(Q) = Cov_PS(Q) ∪ p_ij \ p_i \ p_j;
    if Q is Ω then
        return sel(Q) = sel(p_ij);
return sel(Q) = sel(p_ij) · ∏_{k=1}^{m} sel(pu_k); {pu_1...pu_m are uncovered single paths in Q }
Function ComTwoPatterns(p_ij)
if p_ij is a star-chain pattern then
    return ComSelStar-Chain(p_ij);
if p_ij is a chain-chain pattern then
    return ComSelChain-Chain(p_ij);
if p_ij is a star-star pattern then
    return ComSelStar-Star(p_ij)
```

Now we extend our method to the more general case where the path cover set $Cov_{PS}(Q)$ of query Q consists of multiple star patterns and chain patterns. We select two patterns p_i and p_j from $Cov_{PS}(Q)$ that can join together. Compute the selectivity for the composite pattern $p_{ij} = p_i \bowtie p_j$ maintain a selectivity distribution table $T_{p_{ij}}$ indicating the selectivity distributions over the possible abstracted values of the join node in p_{ij}. Iterate this process until there is only one composite graph pattern left in $Cov_{PS}(Q)$. For the part of Q that is not covered by $Cov_{PS}(Q)$, we deal with it as a set of single triple patterns and combine the results of them in the product form with the independence assumption. The formal description of this algorithm is presented in Algorithm 7 *ComSelectivity*.

6. EXPERIMENTS

6.1 Experiment Setup

We implemented the proposed algorithms. All algorithms are run on a windows XP professional operating system. The hardware is a PC with Intel Pentium 4 3.0GHz CPU, 4 GB memory.

#	Star Query Sets			Chain Query Sets			Composite Query Sets			
	Qs1	Qs2	Qs3	Qc1	Qc2	Qc3	Qsc1	Qsc2	Qsc3	Qsc4
# Queries	5	5	5	5	5	5	5	5	5	5
# Properties	2	3-4	>=5	2	3-4	>=5	<=5	6-7	8-9	>=10
# Literals	1-2	1-2	1-2	0-1	0-1	0-1	1-2	1-2	1-3	1-3

Figure 8: Query sets used in experiments.

Data sets. Both synthetic and real-world datasets are used in our experiments. In this paper, we present results on three datasets: (1) LUBM [13] is developed by Lehigh University; (2) SwetoDBLP [14] is a dataset describing real computer science bibliography information. (3) YAGO [15] consists of facts extracted from Wikipedia. Compared with the former two datasets, it is relatively heterogeneous. The details of three datasets are shown in Table 1.

Table 1: Statistics of datasets

#	LUBM	DBLP	YAGO
# Triples	25,511,071	11,014,618	40,114,899
# Instances	4,555,428	2,395,467	3,883,360
# Properties	43	45	93

Query Loads. There are three kinds of query patterns used in our experiments: star, chain and composite query patterns. Figure 8 shows some information about query sets used in the experiments. We use the seed queries (part of them are shown in Appendix) with some random literal values to generate different query sets.

Previous Techniques. We compare our method with two previous works: 1) In [4], the authors propose the selectivity estimation method PF based on the probabilistic framework. They build summary statistics of joined triple patterns for RDF data; 2) In [9], the authors propose the estimation method in RDF-3X system, which computes two kinds of statistics for selectivity estimation. The first one is called specialized histograms which assumes independence among predicates. The second statistics computes frequent join paths in the data.

Evaluation Method. We use *relative error RE* to present the performance of different techniques of selectivity estimation. Given a true selectivity *sel* and its estimate $\widetilde{sel}$, we use the relative error formula $RE(sel, \widetilde{sel}) = \frac{|sel-\widetilde{sel}|}{max(1,sel)}$ for positive queries ($sel > 0$) and negative queries ($sel = 0$).

6.2 Offline Evaluation

Learning Bayesian Networks. Before evaluating our methods for star query patterns, we first constructed Bayesian networks for frequent star paths in three datasets. For LUBM dataset, we constructed cluster property tables for 6 common star paths that correspond entities such as *Faculty, Student, Course* and so on. An entity may correspond several classes. Similarly, we constructed cluster property tables for 7 common star paths) in DBLP dataset. Then Bayesian networks are learned from these cluster property tables. Clearly, with the increase of space for storing learned Bayesian networks, the constructed Bayesian networks and CPTs are more accurate over the data. Due to the efficiency consideration, we set the space limit of each dataset for storing each Bayesian network to 16 KB. Some details about learning Bayesian networks are shown in Table 2. From Table 2, we can see that the learning time of Bayesian networks for three datasets are 127.3s, 232.2s, 2112.9s, respectively. In DBLP dataset, we have learned 7 Bayesian networks from cluster property tables and the largest cluster property table contains 362,907 tuples. However, the time of learning Bayesian network for this cluster property table is 72.2s, which is acceptable. For YAGO dataset, since the data is heterogeneous there are more frequent paths and we construct 100 Bayesian Networks for them.

Table 2: Some information about leaning Bayesian networks

#	LUBM	DBLP	YAGO
# Learned Bayesian Networks	6	7	100
# Maximum tuples in cluster property tables	100,532	362,907	161,496
# Properties in cluster property tables	2-9	2-8	2-8
Learning time (s)	227.3	372.7	2112.9
Space limit (KB) for storing each Bayesian Network	16	16	16

Constructing chain histograms. To employ our chain histogram based method to estimate the selectivity of chain patterns, we constructed chain histograms for chain paths of three datasets. The space limit for storing the chain histogram of each dataset is 16 KB. Some details of constructing chain histograms are shown in Table 3.

Table 3: Some information about chain histograms

#	LUBM	DBLP	YAGO
# Chain paths Contained	124	323	500
Length of chain paths	2-5	2-7	2-5
Constructing time (s)	179	357s	840s
Space limit (KB)	16	16	16

6.3 Estimation Accuracy

In this set of experiments, we study and compare the accuracy of different selectivity estimation methods. Figure 9

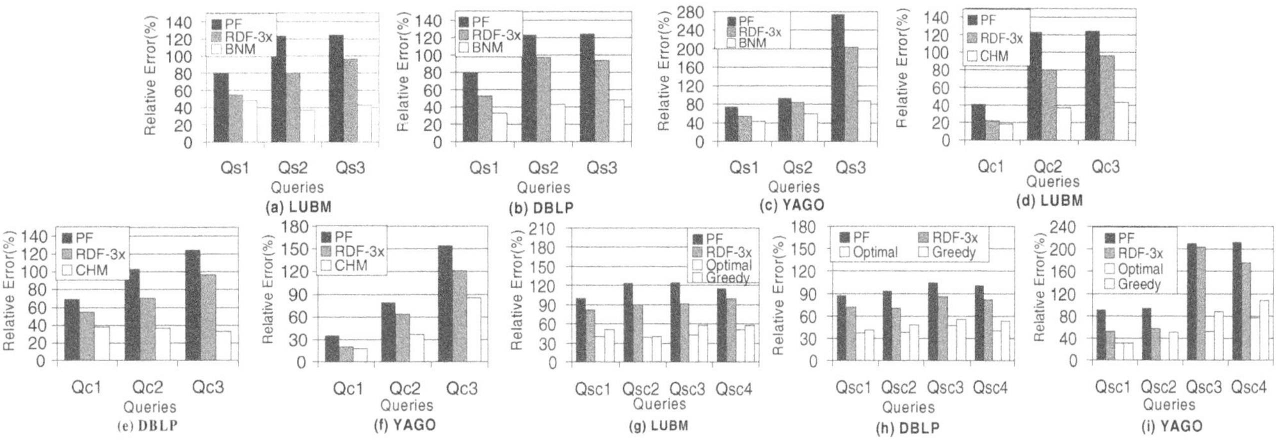

Figure 9: Relative errors for query patterns.

shows the accuracy of three methods for different query sets on three datasets. In all figures, X-axis are different query sets and Y-axis is the average relative error RE.

Performance of methods for star query patterns. In this experiment, we evaluate our method of selectivity estimation for star query patterns. For each dataset, 15 star query patterns are developed. They are grouped into 3 query sets: $Qs1$, $Qs2$, $Qs3$ (see Figure 8). $Qs1$, $Qs2$ and $Qs3$ contain star query patterns that have 2, 3 to 4, and more than 5 properties, respectively. Each query set contains 5 star query patterns. The relative errors of different methods on three datasets are shown in Figure 9(a), (b) and (c). "BNM" indicates our Bayesian network based selectivity estimation method for star query patterns.

From Figure 9(a), (b) and (c), we can see that our method for star patterns dominates the other methods because we capture the dependencies among properties in the queries. The RDF-3x method also have better results on query set $Qs1$ in which query patterns have the small number of properties and literal constraints. In this case, the join uniformity assumption does not affect much. Conversely, in query sets $Qs2$ and $Qs3$, queries have more properties and literal constraints. It is more likely that the join uniformity assumption affects the accuracy of estimation. Thus our Bayesian network based method obtains much better results on query sets $Qs2$ and $Qs3$ than the other two methods that adopt the join uniformity assumption.

Performance of methods for chain query patterns. From Figure 9(d), (e) and (f), we can see performance of methods on chain query patterns. For each dataset, 15 chain query patterns are developed. They are grouped into 3 query sets: $Qc1$, $Qc2$, $Qc3$ (See Figure 8 for more details). "CHM" indicates our chain histogram based method for estimating the selectivity of chain patterns. Our method dominates the other methods. The RDF-3x method also have better results on query set $Qc1$ in which the lengths of chain query patterns are relatively small. Conversely, in query sets $Qc2$ and $Qc3$, lengths of chain query patterns are longer. It is more likely that the join uniformity assumption affect the accuracy of estimation. Thus our method obtains much better results on query sets $Qc2$ and $Qc3$ than the other two methods.

Performance of methods for composite query patterns. In this experiment, we evaluate our method for composite query patterns. We develop 20 composite query patterns for each dataset. All these queries are also grouped into 4 query sets: $Qsc1$, $Qsc2$, $Qsc3$, $Qsc4$. Some details of query sets are shown in Figure 8. Figure 9(g), (h) and (i) show the results of four methods on three datasets, where "Greedy" and "Optimal" stand for two decomposition algorithms (shown in Algorithm 2 and Algorithm 3 respectively). Our methods obtain more accurate estimation since we construct the refined model when dealing with joined triple patterns and do not adopt join uniformity assumption. The optimal algorithm also outperforms the greedy algorithm because the latter may not find the maximum path cover of query patterns. And for the uncovered part of queries, greedy algorithm would adopt the independence assumption for selectivity estimation, which affects the estimation accuracy. However, figures show that Greedy algorithm still performs better than PF and RDF-3x methods.

6.4 Online Running Time

Table 4: Query Set

#	$Qsc1$	$Qsc2$	$Qsc3$	$Qsc4$
# Queries	5	5	5	5
# Edges	5	7	8	11

In this experiment, we study the on-line running time of our estimation methods adopting two decomposition algorithms: Greedy algorithm and Optimal algorithm on YAGO dataset which is relatively heterogeneous. Figure 10 shows the average running time of two methods as the average number of edge of query sets increases. The running time of the method with the Greedy algorithm reveals a slow growth with the increase of the average number of edge of queries sets. We can observe that the time cost is reasonable even when the average number of edge of query set $Qsc4$ rises to 11. Compared with the Greedy algorithm, the running time of the method with the Optimal algorithm is higher because the Optimal algorithm tries to find the maximum path cover of each composite query pattern. The time costs of two cases are close when graph patterns are small (the number of edge $\leqslant 8$), but the running time of Optimal algorithm rises significantly when the number of edge exceeds 8. It suggests the Greedy decomposition algorithm is preferable for larger and dense graph patterns.

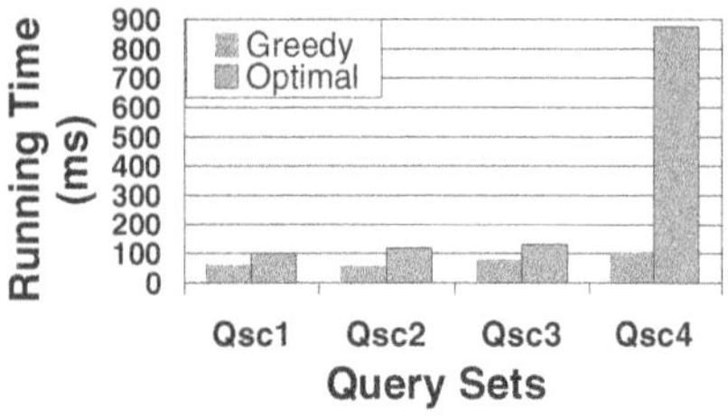

Figure 10: Online Running Time

7. RELATED WORK

Selectivity estimation is well studied in relational databases. Histogram is one of the most important statistical estimation data structure in relational DBMSs. [17] offers a latest, comprehensive survey on this subject. Join Synopses [16] enable accurate estimation by summarizing the combined join and value distribution across foreign-key joins of several tables. In our work, we estimate the composite graph patterns by summing over the possible abstracted values of the joined variables and do not have the restriction of foreign-key joins.

In [4], the authors propose the framework of static Basic Graph Pattern (BGP) optimization based on selectivity estimation. They devise a number of heuristics for the selectivity estimation of joined triple patterns. The heuristics range from simple variable counting techniques to more sophisticated selectivity estimation based on the probabilistic framework. In [9] the authors propose two kinds of statistics for selectivity estimation. The first one is a histogram, which is generic and can handle any kind of triple patterns and joins with independence assumption. The second statistics computes frequent join paths in the data, which are similar to our methods. Nevertheless, [4, 9] both take the join uniformity assumption when estimating the selectivity of joined triple patterns. We avoid this assumption and propose a more accurate estimation model that takes correlations among properties into account.

8. CONCLUSION

With the increasing amount of RDF data, efficient and scalable management of RDF data has become a fundamental challenge to achieve the semantic web vision. Selectivity estimation is critical to processing RDF queries efficiently. To address this problem, we employ the Bayesian network and chain histogram techniques for estimating the selectivity of star and chain query patterns. For an arbitrary composite graph pattern, the algorithm which combines the precomputed statistics of chain and star paths to estimate the overall selectivity is proposed. The experiments show that our method outperforms existing approaches in accuracy significantly. In the future, we will investigate the appropriate way to generalize our methods to support other applications in SPARQL query processing.

9. ACKNOWLEDGMENTS

This research was supported by the Australian Research Council Discovery Projects DP110102407 and DP0878405.

10. REFERENCES

[1] T. Neumann, G. Weikum: Scalable join processing on very large RDF graphs. In SIGMOD, pages: 627-640, 2009.

[2] K. Wilkinson et al. Efficient rdf storage and retrieval in jena2. In SWDB, 2003.

[3] Pearl, J.: Probabilistic reasoning in intelligent systems: Networks of plausible inference. San Mateo, CA: Morgan-Kaufmann, 1988.

[4] M. Stocker, A. Seaborne, Abraham Bernstein, Christoph Kiefer, Dave Reynolds: SPARQL basic graph pattern optimization using selectivity estimation. In WWW, pages:595-604, 2008.

[5] Wray L. Buntine: Operations for Learning with Graphical Models. In J. Artif. Intell. Res. (JAIR) 2: 159-225,1994.

[6] D. Heckerman, D. Geiger, D. Maxwell Chickering: Learning Bayesian Networks: The Combination of Knowledge and Statistical Data. In Machine Learning 20(3): 197-243, 1995.

[7] Jie C., D.A. Bell, W. Liu: Learning Belief Networks from Data: An Information Theory Based Approach. In CIKM, pages:325-331, 1997.

[8] G. F. Cooper, E. Herskovits: A Bayesian Method for the Induction of Probabilistic Networks from Data. In Machine Learning 9: 309-347, 1992.

[9] T. Neumann, G. Weikum: RDF-3X: a RISC-style engine for RDF. PVLDB 1(1): 647-659, 2008.

[10] E. I. Chong, S. Das, G. Eadon, and J. Srinivasan. An efficient SQL-based RDF querying scheme. In VLDB, pages:1216-1227, 2005.

[11] Bloom, Burton H: Space/time trade-offs in hash coding with allowable errors. Communications of the ACM 13 (7): 422-426, 1970.

[12] W. Wang, H. Jiang, H. Lu, J. X. Yu: Bloom Histogram: Path Selectivity Estimation for XML Data with Updates. In VLDB, pages:240-251, 2004.

[13] Y. Guo, Z. Pan, J. Heflin: An Evaluation of Knowledge Base Systems for Large OWL Datasets. In ISWC, page:274-288, 2004.

[14] B. Aleman-Meza, F. Hakimpour, I.B. Arpinar, A.P. Sheth: SwetoDblp Ontology of Computer Science Publications In: Web Semantics: Science, Services and Agents on the World Wide Web 5(3), pages:151-155, 2007.

[15] F. M. Suchanek, G. Kasneci, G. Weikum: Yago: a core of semantic knowledge. In WWW page:697-706, 2007.

[16] S. Acharya, P. B. Gibbons, V.Poosala, S. Ramaswamy: Join Synopses for Approximate Query Answering. In SIGMOD, pages:275-286, 1999.

[17] Y. E. Ioannidis: The history of histograms (abridged). In VLDB, pages:19-30, 2003.

APPENDIX

A. PART OF SEED QUERIES ON YAGO.

- Qs1: ?s hasProductionLanguage '%Random_Language%'. ?s type 'Movie'.
- Qs2: ?s yagoResource:interestedIn '%Random_Interest%'. ?s yagoResource:isCitizenOf '%Random_Country%'. ?s type 'Philosopher'.
- Qc3: ?x0 hasChild ?x1. ?x1 hasPredecessor ?x2. ?x2 hasPredecessor ?x3. ?x3 politicianOf ?x4. ?x4 hasCapital '%Random_City%'.
- Qsc2: ?s type wordnet_actor_109765278. ?s actedIn ?m1. ?m1 type 'movie'. ?m1 hasProductionLanguage 'English'. ?s directed ?m2. ?m2 type 'movie'. ?m2 hasProductionLanguage 'English'. ?s livesIn ?city. ?city locatedIn ?state. ?state locatedIn 'New_York'.

Efficient Resource Attribute Retrieval in RDF Triple Stores

Andreas Brodt, Oliver Schiller, Bernhard Mitschang
IPVS, Universität Stuttgart, Universitätsstraße 38, 70569 Stuttgart, Germany
{brodt, schiller, mitschang}@ipvs.uni-stuttgart.de

ABSTRACT

The W3C Resource Description Framework (RDF) is gaining popularity for its ability to manage semi-structured data without a predefined database schema. So far, most RDF query processors have concentrated on finding complex graph patterns in RDF, which typically involves a high number of joins. This works very well to query resources by the relations between them. Yet, obtaining a record-like view on the attributes of resources, as natively supported by RDBMS, imposes unnecessary performance burdens, as the individual attributes must be joined to assemble the final result records.

We present an approach to retrieve the attributes of resources efficiently. We first determine the resources in question and then retrieve all their attributes efficiently at once, exploiting contiguous storage in RDF indexes. In addition, we present an index structure which is specifically designed for RDF attribute retrieval. Our measurements show that our approach is clearly superior for larger numbers of attributes.

Categories and Subject Descriptors

H.2 [**Database Management**]: Systems—*Query processing*; H.3 [**Information Storage and Retrieval**]: Information Search and Retrieval—*Search process; Selection process*

General Terms

Performance, Algorithms

Keywords

RDF, SPARQL, triple store

1. INTRODUCTION

The W3C Resource Description Framework (RDF) is a data model for structured information that is gaining popularity in different application domains including life sciences, Web 2.0 platforms, and data integration tasks. RDF provides great flexibility towards any kind of schema and is even usable without a schema at all. RDF allows collecting data in a "pay-as-you-go"-fashion, starting with very little schema information and refining the schema later, as required. Thus, RDF allows breaking the traditional data engineering workflow of designing a schema first and populating it later. This suits RDF for scenarios such as community-based data collection, and in fact large knowledge bases from sources including Wikipedia have been built using RDF [2, 11].


```
(id1, title, "First Blood")
(id1, year, 1972)
(id1, author, id2)
(id2, firstName, "David")
(id2, lastName, "Morrell")
(id3, basedOn, id1)
(id3, title, "Rambo:  First Blood Part 1")
(id3, year, 1982)
(id3, length, "93 min")
(id4, actedIn, id3)
(id4, firstName, "Michael")
(id4, firstName, "Sylvester")
(id4, lastName, "Stallone")
(id4, yearOfBirth, 1946)
```

Listing 1: Sample RDF graph

RDF models data as a number of *(subject, predicate, object)*-triples: *subject* identifies the resource that is being described, *predicate* denotes a particular relation or attribute, and *object* is either another resource identifier, or a literal. The triples form a directed labeled graph that represents the resources with their relations and attributes. E.g., the triples in Listing 1 describe four resources: The novel "First Blood" (id1) by David Morrell (id2), on which the first Rambo movie (id3) is based, starring Sylvester Stallone (id4).

SPARQL [9] is a W3C-recommended language to query RDF graphs by graph pattern matching. At its core, a SPARQL query consists of triples containing at least one variable. We refer to such triples as *triple patterns*. The result is a table of variable bindings, such that the pattern exists in the queried RDF graph using the variable bindings in each result row. For instance, the SPARQL query in

```
SELECT ?first ?last WHERE {
   ?movie <title> "Rambo:  First Blood Part 1".
   ?actor <actedIn> ?movie.
   ?actor <firstName> ?first.
   ?actor <lastName> ?last.
}
```

Listing 2: Exemplary SPARQL query

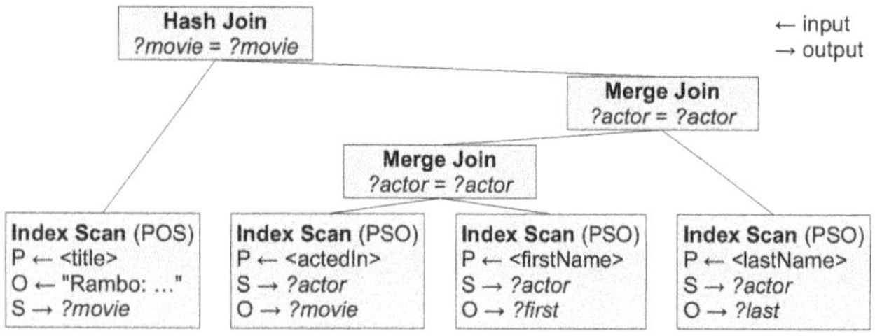

Figure 1: Canonical execution plan

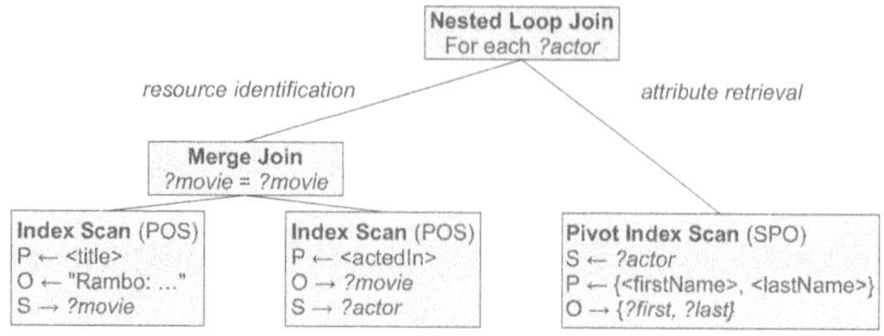

Figure 2: Execution plan following our approach

Listing 2 returns the first names and last names of all actors acting in the first Rambo movie. Executed on the RDF graph of Listing 1, the result would be a table with the columns "?first" and "?last", and two rows holding the values "Michael" and "Stallone", and "Sylvester" and "Stallone".

A system that manages RDF data cannot assume a defined schema in the general case. Thus, it possesses little knowledge about the higher-level structure of the data, e.g. entity types like "actor" or "movie". Hence, it can index and process the data only at triple-level. A common way to manage very large RDF data sets efficiently is to keep the triples in a single three-column table [7, 12, 4] with B^+-tree indexes in various (if not all) permutations and aggregations of *subject*, *predicate*, and *object*. Such an index efficiently returns all triples having one or two constant values at a given position, which precisely corresponds to a triple pattern. To combine these triples to the graph pattern defined in the query, joins are required. By carefully choosing indexes on the right triple permutation, index sort orders can frequently be exploited for efficient merge joins. Otherwise, hash joins can be used. We call this approach to generate an execution plan *canonical*, as it can be applied directly on any SPARQL graph pattern.

Figure 1 shows a canonical execution plan for the query of Listing 2. The query optimizer chose to use the predicate-subject-object (PSO) index, so that the triples corresponding to the triple patterns in lines 2, 3, and 4 are all sorted by their subject, i.e. the actor. This allows using two merge joins. The first triple pattern comes sorted by the movie, so a hash join is required to join it with the rest of the query.

Canonical execution plans are relatively easy to build and able to restrict intermediate results early, through a number of measures [8]. This makes them suitable for complex analytical queries on relationships between many resources; for instance, to identify all actors which acted in a movie which they also directed and which are married to the author of the novel on which the movie is based. However, canonical plans are not necessarily optimal for retrieving attributes of resources. Lines 3 and 4 in Listing 2 illustrate that SPARQL requires one triple pattern per attribute in order to query attributes, such as the first name. I.e., to retrieve n attributes of a resource, a query lists n triple patterns, which a canonical plan evaluates using n index scans and $n-1$ joins. Even though most often merge joins will be used to assemble the attributes to larger result tuples, these joins impact query performance severely for larger numbers of attributes.

In a record-based RDBMS, all attributes of a resource are stored contiguously on disk in the same record. Thus, the record can be retrieved in a single fetch operation and does not need to be assembled first. This is not possible for RDF because the schema is unknown. However, the subject-predicate-object (SPO) index is primarily sorted by subject, i.e., it stores all relations and attributes of a resource contiguously. By using the SPO index to retrieve attributes of a resource, a potentially large number of joins can be saved, without compromising the advantages of canonical plans for complex graph patterns.

In this paper we evaluate how the SPO index can be exploited to make resource attribute retrieval in RDF triple stores more efficient. We introduce our attribute retrieval approach (Section 2), discuss its integration into the query optimizer (Section 3), and present a dedicated index for attribute retrieval (Section 4). We evaluate our concepts (Section 5) and conclude with promising future research directions (Section 6).

2. ATTRIBUTE RETRIEVAL APPROACH

Canonical plans use the predicate-subject-object (PSO) index to retrieve *one* particular attribute, e.g. the first name, for *all* resources in the data set. Contrarily, the subject-predicate-object (SPO) index supports retrieving *all* attributes of *one* given resource without a join on the resource ID for every attribute. This is because the SPO index stores all triples with the same subject (i.e. resource ID) contiguously. On the other hand, it cannot easily identify the relevant triples without knowing the triple subject. The subject is a variable in every triple pattern that retrieves an attribute. Alternatively, scanning the SPO index top to bottom and joining the result with the remainder of the query is not an option, as this would scan the entire database.

We propose a processing model that splits SPARQL queries into two conceptual parts: *resource identification* and *attribute retrieval*. Resource identification determines the set R of qualifying resources. For each resource $r \in R$, attribute retrieval fetches the values of the attribute set A, as defined in the query.

2.1 The Pivot Index Scan Operator

To implement attribute retrieval using the SPO index, we designed the *pivot index scan* operator. It retrieves the values for a given resource r and attribute set A from the SPO index and pivots them into one or more result tuples in a single operation. The pivot index scan is designed for use under a nested loop join which connects resource identification with attribute retrieval. The nested loop join iterates on all identified resources, invokes the pivot index scan on each resource, and propagates all its result tuples. For the query of Listing 2, this results in an execution plan as shown in Figure 2: Resource identification determines the identifiers of all actors acting in the first Rambo movie. A nested loop join invokes attribute retrieval on each actor: a pivot index scan to look up the first name and the last name of each actor from the SPO index.

```
# B-tree search for resource r and smallest attribute a_min
scan ← SPO_Index.openScan(r, a_min)
(s, p, o) ← scan.firstTriple()
foreach a ∈ A do  # A is sorted in index order
  while s = r ∧ p < a do
      # Skip intermediate triple
      (s, p, o) ← scan.nextTriple()
  od
  if (s > r ∨ p > a) ∧ ¬isOptional(a)                    (*)
    then exit # r does not have all required attributes
  fi
  # Buffer all values for a
  do
     valueBuffer[a] ← valueBuffer[a] ∪ {o}               (**)
     (s, p, o) ← scan.nextTriple()
  while s = r ∧ p = a
od
```

Listing 3: Implementation of the pivot operation, which drives a scan on the SPO index (for brevity we assume the scan always returns a triple)

As shown in Figure 2, the pivot index scan takes a variable binding as input, which was produced by resource identification. During one run of the nested loop join, this variable binding is treated as a constant: it is the subject of the triples to look up from the SPO index. The second input for the pivot index scan is the set of attributes A, as defined in the query. Thus, the pivot index scan fetches a set of attributes for a given resource in a single invocation. Figure 2 shows that it possesses a set of output variables for this purpose: one for every attribute to retrieve.

Unlike other operators, the pivot index scan processes *sets* of triples rather than individual triples. Internally, it consists of two parts; an index scan and a pivot operation. First, the index scan looks up the first triple containing the resource r as subject, and the smallest attribute $a_{min} \in A$ as predicate from the SPO index. This requires the attributes in A to be sorted in the same order as they appear in the index. Then the pivot operation makes the index scan iterate through the triples of r, until the values for all attributes in A have been fetched, or all triples about r have been read. Listing 3 shows how the pivot operation selects all triples of the resource containing a predicate $p \in A$. The pivot operation projects the objects of these triples and buffers them.

2.2 Optional Attributes

SPARQL allows declaring parts of the query *optional*. This corresponds to a one-sided outer join in the relational model. I.e., the optional parts of a query will be evaluated and returned if they are found. Otherwise the projected variables from an optional query part produce NULL values, but do not cause a result tuple to be dismissed. If single triple patterns which retrieve attributes are declared optional, they can be evaluated in a pivot index scan. The pivot index scan operator would normally abort if it cannot find a triple containing a queried attribute for the current resource. To handle optional attributes, the query optimizer only needs to tell the pivot index scan which attributes are mandatory and which are optional. Listing 3 shows how a pivot index scan handles missing optional or mandatory attributes in the line marked with an asterisk (*).

2.3 Multi-Attributes

It is not at all safe to assume that a resource carries only one value for a particular attribute. There can be an arbitrary number of triples with the same subject and predicate, but with a different object. In this case, the predicate is a multi-attribute and the semantics of SPARQL require producing the cross product. For instance, the subject `id4` in Listing 1 carries two triples with predicate `firstName` and one triple with predicate `lastName`. Consequently, the query of Listing 2 produces two result tuples; one for each first name. It is important to note that the result of a pivot index scan is not one tuple, but a set of tuples.

A canonical plan automatically produces the cross product of multi-attributes when the joins assemble the attributes to larger result tuples. To preserve this behavior, the pivot index scan must buffer all values for each attribute $a \in A$ when it scans the triples of one resource. It must then calculate the cross product over these buffers in an explicit separate step. Listing 3 shows how a pivot index scan buffers the values indexed by attribute in the line marked with a double-asterisk (**). In a Volcano-style [5] operator implementation providing an open/next/close interface, the `open()` call has to scan the relevant triples and buffer the attribute values, as shown in Listing 3. It may then close the underlying index scan. The calls to `next()` then return the next combination of the cross product. The `close()` call discards the buffer.

2.4 Multiply Selected Attributes

SPARQL allows selecting an attribute of a resource more than once. This is particularly interesting in combination with multi-attributes and produces the cross product of all attribute values. For example, Listing 2 could be extended by the triple patterns in Listing 4 to return the cross product on all (ex-) wives of the actor.

This might seem a purely academic case at first, but in fact occurs not infrequently. The cross product on multiply selected attributes is often used to find a particular relation between all values. It is usually combined with a filter to ensure that resulting value pairs contain different values, i.e., `?spouse1 != ?spouse2` in the example. This way, one could determine whether two (ex-) wives of the actor share the same hobby or hair-color, for instance. Naturally, it is perfectly possible to simply query the cross product of the values as (part of) the query result.

A canonical plan will strictly map every triple pattern of the query to an index scan and create joins between them. It will equally apply this principle to triple patterns which retrieve the same attribute and the joins will automatically produce the cross product on the respective values.

A pivot index scan must replicate this behavior explicitly. As discussed above, it must buffer the values of multi-attributes and produce their cross product anyway. To create the cross product on a multiply selected attribute a, the query optimizer must inform the pivot index scan about the number k_a denoting how often to consider the values for a in the cross product. The pivot operation can be used as shown in

```
?actor <wasOrIsMarriedWith> ?spouse1.
?actor <wasOrIsMarriedWith> ?spouse2.
```

Listing 4: Triple patterns extending Listing 2 by a cross product on all values of one attribute

Listing 3. Only the cross product algorithm must consider the value buffer for a not just once, but k_a times.

Formally, this means that the set A of attributes to retrieve is really a *multi-set* in the general case. In the interest of a simpler presentation of this paper, we will nevertheless refer to A as a set. Consequently, by $|A|$ we do not really mean the number of distinct attributes to retrieve, but the number of triple patterns involved in attribute retrieval. This does not restrict the generality and applicability of our approach.

2.5 Related Work

The idea of a pivot operation transposing rows into columns is not new. Some RDBMS including Microsoft SQL server provide the *Pivot* and *Unpivot* data manipulation operators. Pivot transforms a set of rows into a set of fewer rows with additional columns. Unpivot is the reverse operation of Pivot [3]. [13] provides a formal characterization. When the set of columns is unknown in advance, a table can be implemented as a *property table* that is accessed using the Pivot operator. This is more flexible, as columns can be added as property rows of the form (id, propertyname, propertyvalue). This form is very similar to the RDF data model. Before Pivot and Unpivot were introduced, application programmers frequently used complex SQL statements with a nested subquery for every pivoted column [3]. These queries were inefficient and hard to optimize, and strongly resembled canonical execution plans for SPARQL queries.

The main difference to our pivot index scan operator is that Pivot must not produce multi-attributes, as the relational model does not allow them. For this purpose, Pivot takes an aggregation function which collapses multi-attributes into a single value. SPARQL, by contrast, requires returning the cross product on all multi-attribute values.

3. PLAN GENERATION

The classical bottom-up dynamic programming approach of System R [10] is well-suited to create canonical execution plans for SPARQL graph patterns. We first explain bottom-up plan generation for canonical plans, as implemented in [7]. Then we introduce our approach to extend such an optimizer so that it produces execution plans that use pivot index scans, if this is cheaper. We describe our cost model and an approach to cardinality estimation in presence of multi-attributes. Finally, we address selective attributes, which influence the set of selected resources in the query result.

3.1 Generating Canonical Plans

As illustrated in Figure 1, a graph pattern containing n triple patterns can be solved by a canonical plan which consists of n index scans and $n-1$ joins. Such a plan can be created using the following recursive rule: A plan which covers one triple pattern is an index scan. A plan covering $x > 1$ triple patterns is a join of two sub-plans covering a and b distinct triple patterns, respectively, with $a + b = x$. A plan covering $x = n$ triple patterns solves the query.

The canonical optimizer uses a table for dynamic programming, which contains all sub-plans produced so far. Thus, the table consists of n rows, where all plans in row x cover exactly x triple patterns. The plans of each row are grouped in sets of plans solving the same problem, i.e. covering the same triple patterns. First, the optimizer seeds the first row of the dynamic programming table with n sets of index scans. For every triple pattern, it generates an index scan on the index of every possible triple permutation, such that all possible sort orders are considered. E.g. for the second triple pattern of Listing 2, an index scan on the predicate-subject-object (PSO) index produces the triples sorted by actor, whereas using the POS index orders them by movie. Subsequently, the higher rows are populated incrementally. Every plan in row x is produced by joining one sub-plan from row a and one sub-plan from row b, with $a + b = x$. The two sub-plans must share a common variable to join on and their problems must not overlap, i.e., their sets of covered triple patterns must be disjoint. If both sub-plans are sorted on the join variable, a merge join is used; otherwise a hash join is created. As explained in [7], the optimizer should only accept a new plan for a problem, if is cheaper than all other plans of the same problem, or if it introduces a new sort order. Finally, the optimizer chooses the cheapest plan in row n.

3.2 Generating Plans with Pivot Index Scans

Before a pivot index scan can be created, the triple patterns which retrieve attributes have to be identified. For this purpose we sort the triple patterns by subject, predicate, and object. We order variables in the subject before constants, constants in the predicate before variables, and variables in the object before constants. This makes it easy to find set of triple patterns, which have (1) the same subject, (2) a variable subject, (3) a constant predicate, and (4) a variable object. As a side product, this sort order ensures that the set A of attributes to retrieve is sorted, which is later required by the pivot index scan, as described in Section 2. In addition, we require that the object (5) is listed in the `SELECT` clause of the query and (6) does not occur in any other triple pattern. Without condition (5), the object value does not need to be retrieved at all. Condition (6) ensures that the triple pattern is not involved in any joins and thus does not belong to the resource identification part of the graph pattern. Finally, we require that (7) every set contains at least two qualifying triple patterns; otherwise a pivot index scan would not save a join and definitely not benefit from storage locality.

Every such set of triple patterns for attribute retrieval can be solved by one pivot index scan. For each set, the predicates of the triple patterns constitute one set A and the pivot index scan covers $|A|$ triple patterns. As explained above, a canonical optimizer joins existing sub-plans to larger plans, starting with index scans as atomic plans. A pivot index scan is an atomic plan as well, but it covers more than one triple pattern. Thus, in addition to seeding the first row of the dynamic programming table with index scans, the optimizer must also generate pivot index scans in row $|A|$ for each set of triple patterns. When the bottom-up algorithm reaches row $x = |A| + b$, it generates a join between the pivot index scan and all sub-plans in row b. Naturally, these sub-plans must contain the variable which denotes the resource for which the pivot index scan retrieves the attributes. In addition to that, the optimizer must choose a nested loop join instead of a merge or hash join when it joins a pivot index scan. Also, the pivot index scan must become the right child of the join, i.e., it must occur inside the loop.

The nested loop join should occur near the root of the plan. It does, ideally, not restrict the cardinality of the query result (see Section 3.5), but might increase it through cross products quite a bit. Thus, executing the pivot index scan too early in the query plan causes an unnecessarily high number of intermediate result tuples. Moreover, it is in practice not invalid to assume the joins of the resource identification part of the query to be rather selective. Thus, query plans with early pivot index scans will be rated more expensive and eliminated by plans which use it later. The optimizer could, however, anticipate this and include the pivot index scans only towards the end. The bottom-up algorithm could ignore them until it reaches row $x = n - \sum_i |A_i|$, where $\sum_i |A_i|$ denotes the maximal amount of triple patterns covered by all possible pivot index scans.

3.3 Cost Model

A pivot index scan executes one B-tree lookup for every resource r that is produced by resource identification. Even if r does not carry all mandatory attributes, the pivot index scan only removes r from the query result *after* the B-tree lookup has been performed, as illustrated in Listing 3. We do not generally assume that the amount of scanned triples for each resource is significant. A pivot index scan rarely needs to access more than one leaf page of the SPO index for a single resource, as the triples can be compressed very well (we experienced about 4000 compressed triples in a single leave page using the method presented in [7]). The B-tree lookup costs for each resource will by far dominate the costs for sequentially scanning the respective triples. In addition, the cost of the nested loop join operator itself is negligible. Thus, if resource identification is estimated to produce $|R|$ resources with total costs $cost_{res.id.}$ and one B-tree lookup causes costs of $cost_{lookup}$, then the costs of the nested loop join over resource identification and a pivot index scan $cost_{nl}$ can be simply estimated as follows:

$$cost_{nl} = cost_{res.id.} + |R| * cost_{lookup}$$

This shows that plans using a pivot index scan are practically independent of the number of selected attributes $|A|$, but in turns do depend on $|R|$. Thus, it depends on the query and on the RDF data set, whether a pivot index scan should be favored over a canonical plan. Our plan generation approach always creates both possibilities and lets the cost model decide which plan is the cheapest.

3.4 Cardinality Estimation

Estimating the cardinality of a plan that uses our attribute retrieval approach is no different from general cardinality estimation, as cardinality depends on the queried data and not on the chosen execution plan. A pivot index scan evaluates a star-shaped graph pattern which comprises many triple patterns. Thus, a method to estimate cardinality of larger subgraphs is desirable, rather than estimating single triple patterns and combining them incrementally.

Characteristic sets [6] approximate star-shaped subgraphs in RDF data very well. They describe resources through their predicates, to characterize them in a similar way as entity types would. Thus, characteristic sets can be seen as some sort of "soft entity types". We introduce them here, as we will refer to them in the next section, too.

A characteristic set $S_C(s)$ of a triple subject s occurring in an RDF data set DS is defined as the set of predicates which are connected to s:

$$S_C(s) = \{p \mid \exists o : (s, p, o) \in DS\}$$

The set of all characteristic sets occurring in DS is consequently defined as follows:

$$S_C(DS) = \{S_C(s) \mid \exists p, o : (s, p, o) \in DS\}$$

Neumann and Moerkotte observed that the amount of characteristic sets in a real-world RDF data set is surprisingly low. They compute and store all characteristic sets for an RDF data set DS and count the resources belonging to each characteristic set S_C, denoted by $count_{S_C}(Res)$. To estimate the number of resources matching a star-shaped graph pattern, all characteristic sets have to be determined that fully include the predicates of the pattern. Summing up $count_{S_C}(Res)$ for all these characteristic sets, returns the number of resources matching the pattern.

The output cardinality equals this number of resources, conditioned there are no multi-attributes. Otherwise, the cross product over multi-attributes must be taken into account. To estimate multi-attributes, Neumann and Moerkotte compute $count_{S_C}(p)$ for each predicate p as the total sum of how often p occurred in a resource belonging to S_C. Thus, the average occurrence of p in a resource belonging to S_C is

$$\frac{count_{S_C}(p)}{count_{S_C}(Res)}.$$

For instance, in Listing 1 two resources (id2 and id4) belong to a characteristic set S_C that fully includes {*firstName*, *lastName*}, such that $\sum_{S_C} count_{S_C} = 2$. Within these two resources, the *firstName* predicate occurs three times, so $\sum_{S_C} count_{S_C}(firstName) = 3$. Thus, on average, these resources carry $\frac{3}{2}$ first names.

To estimate the output cardinality of a pivot index scan with subject variable $?s$, the set $P_Q(?s)$ of predicates which are connected to $?s$ in the query Q has to be determined:

$$P_Q(?s) = \{p \mid \exists o : (?s, p, o) \in Q\}$$

Is is important to note, that $P_Q(?s)$ must also include predicates which are not retrieved by the pivot index scan, but still connected to its subject variable in the query. Resources which do not possess these predicates will never reach the pivot index scan and are therefore irrelevant for output cardinality. Thus, for the query in Listing 2, $P_Q(?actor)$ is {*firstName*, *lastName*, *actedIn*}, even if the pivot index scan does not retrieve *actedIn*. Subsequently, all characteristic sets are determined which fully include $P_Q(?s)$. The occurrence counts of every predicate $p \in P_Q(?s)$ are summed up to $count(p)$ across all these characteristic sets, and their resource counts to $count(Res)$:

$$count(p) = \sum_{S_C \supseteq P_Q(?s)} count_{S_C}(p)$$

$$count(Res) = \sum_{S_C \supseteq P_Q(?s)} count_{S_C}(Res)$$

The output cardinality is $count(Res)$ times the factor by which the cross-product over multi-attributes increases the output. This factor can be estimated by multiplying the average occurrence of each predicate $p \in P_Q(?s)$, as described above. This, however, does not take multiply selected attributes into account, as discussed in Section 2.4. Thus—and this is a contribution beyond the cardinality estimation approach of [6]—every predicate must be considered in the cross-product estimation as often as the query selects it. I.e., in the product, the average occurrence of each predicate in the characteristic sets considered must be multiplied by its occurrence k_p in the query. Finally, we estimate the cardinality of a star-shaped graph pattern with subject variable $?s$ as

$$card(?s) = count(Res) * \prod_{p \in P_Q(?s)} \frac{k_p * count(p)}{count(Res)}.$$

3.5 Selective Attributes

The basic assumption of our approach is that resource identification, which determines the set R of qualifying resources, is highly selective. Also, attribute retrieval, which fetches the queried attribute values for each resource $r \in R$, is assumed to influence R very little. While this assumption intuitively holds for many cases, it is far from a given. It is not true, if only small fraction of R carries certain attributes of A. I.e. the *existence* of attributes is selective.

If, e.g., the following triple pattern was added to the SPARQL query of Listing 2, it would not return any results for the data set of Listing 1:

```
?actor <wonOscarForBestActorInYear> ?year.
```

Whereas most actors possess at least one first name and a last name, most actors (including Sylvester Stallone, at the time of writing of this paper) never win the academy award for the best actor in *any* year. Thus, `wonOscarForBestActorInYear` is very selective.

In a canonical execution plan, the joins between the index scans retrieving attributes will eliminate resources that lack a mandatory attribute. The optimizer will arrange joins over selective attributes early in the plan. And through sideways information passing [8], operators higher in the query plan may skip non-qualifying resources early. By contrast, a pivot index scan will only realize that a resource r lacks a mandatory attribute, when it has already found r in the SPO index—and the index lookup is the expensive part. Unlike the cascaded joins of a canonical plan, which are able to influence each other in a zig-zag fashion, a pivot index scan has no chance to influence resource identification.

3.5.1 Execution Plans for Selective Attributes

The only way to avoid failing index lookups in a pivot index scan due to selective attributes is to call it only on resources that possess all mandatory attributes in the first place. This means that resource identification must restrict R to such resources. The obvious solution is to remove a selective attribute a_{sel} from the set A of attributes which the pivot index scan retrieves, and to process it in the manner of a canonical plan: using a separate index scan on the PSO index and one join. The join is able to eliminate resources that lack a_{sel} early, so that they never reach the pivot index scan. We refer to this approach as "reduced" in our evaluation.

The separate index scan will return only resources which possess a_{sel}. It will also retrieve the corresponding attribute values. On the other hand, if the optimizer still chooses to use a pivot index scan, the scan will also find the values for a_{sel}, practically for free. So instead of removing the entire triple pattern that includes a_{sel} from the pivot index scan, it would be enough to ensure that every resource that enters attribute retrieval really possesses a_{sel}—without retrieving the value. For this, an index that only includes the predicate and the subject, but lacks the object value, would fully suffice.

The RDF-3X triple store [7] creates, in addition to the six possible triple permutations, also six *aggregated* indexes (SP*, PS*, OP*, ...). The aggregations project away one column

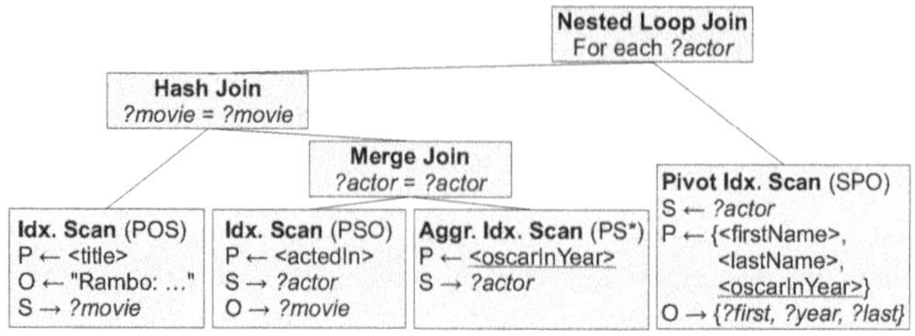

Figure 3: "Checked" execution plan for a selective attribute (oscarInYear)

of the triples and store the amount of resulting duplicates. E.g., the PS* index stores the number of triples in the data set with a particular predicate and subject. RDF-3X uses the aggregated indexes to evaluate triple patterns containing variables that are not used anywhere else in the query, i.e. their values are not required. It also uses the aggregated indexes for cardinality estimation of single triple patterns. Naturally, they are smaller than the full triple indexes.

Thus, instead of removing a_{sel} from the pivot index scan completely, as the "reduced" approach would, we can also add an index scan on the aggregated PS* index for a_{sel} to resource identification, as shown in Figure 3. The aggregated index scan returns less intermediate results than the full triple index and thus produces less join costs. Nevertheless, it is still able to restrict R on resources which possess a_{sel}. Finally, the pivot index scan will retrieve the values for a_{sel}, together with all other attribute values. We call this approach "checked", as the aggregated index scan checks the existence of the selective attribute.

3.5.2 Identifying Selective Attributes

To identify selective attributes, we need to characterize the resources that *enter* attribute retrieval. For this we take a look at the set P of predicates that are connected to this subject variable in the query, but not contained in the attribute list of the pivot index scan; i.e. $P \cap A = \emptyset$. For the query in Listing 2, P would be $\{actedIn\}$. In order to qualify for resource identification, a resource r must possess all predicates $p \in P$. Put differently, if r lacks any of these predicates, it never reaches attribute retrieval. Next, we need a method to determine, which other predicates these resources typically carry, once they possess all predicates $p \in P$. I.e. we need to characterize the resources based on the predicates in P. This is exactly what characteristic sets [6] do, as explained in Section 3.4.

First, we need to retrieve all characteristic sets in the RDF data set DS that fully include P. By summing up the number of resources belonging to these sets, $count_{S_C}(Res)$, we obtain an upper bound $card_P$ for the input cardinality $|R|$ of the pivot index scan.

$$card_P = \sum_{\substack{S_C \supseteq P \\ \wedge S_C \in S_C(DS)}} count_{S_C}(Res)$$

To see how each attribute $a \in A$ influences cardinality, we can similarly calculate the amount of resources which possess a, as well as all predicates in P:

$$card_a = \sum_{\substack{S_C \supseteq \{a\} \cup P \\ \wedge S_C \in S_C(DS)}} count_{S_C}(Res)$$

If $card_a \ll card_P$, then a is selective with respect to resources possessing all predicates in P. This means, that a pivot index scan likely performs many index lookups in vain, because many resources entering attribute retrieval lack a.

This approach only works if the query contains other triple patterns with constant predicates for the subject variable of the pivot index scan (otherwise $P = \emptyset$). If this is not the case, it is difficult to characterize the resources that enter attribute retrieval. Assuming statistical independence, we can still roughly determine selective attributes based on their general occurrence in the entire data set. For this we need to determine how many resources carry a particular attribute.

We can obtain this information using characteristic sets as well. For every retrieved attribute $a \in A$, we only need to determine every characteristic set S_C that includes a. By summing up $counts_{S_C}(Res)$ for all these sets, we obtain the number of resources in the data set that possess the attribute a. If one attribute returns significantly fewer resources than others, it is selective with respect to the entire data set.

The second approach assumes that resource identification selects resources that behave similarly to all other resources in the data set. In practice, selectivity of an attribute may depend quite heavily on the particular resources in question. E.g. the attribute `wonOscarForBestActorInYear` is utterly selective for actors or people in general, but much less for people honored with a star on the Hollywood Walk of Fame. Thus, we try to identify selective attributes using the characteristic sets that contain the predicates that are not retrieved by a pivot index scan. If this is not possible, we use general occurrence of each retrieved attribute in the data set.

4. ATTRIBUTE RETRIEVAL INDEX

Most RDF triple stores map the actual values of the triples to integer IDs, as they can be stored and processed much more efficiently than the strings, of which these values mostly consist [1, 7, 4]. Consequently, a dictionary must map every query result back to its string representation before returning it. This mapping step can cause significant overhead for large query results: we observed a fraction of over 90% of the total execution time for some queries.

Our attribute retrieval approach exploits locality of RDF triples about the same resource. It retrieves the attribute values from the SPO index to produce the final query result. Due to condition (6) in Section 3.2, these values cannot be involved in further operators of the query, i.e. they are simply returned for output. To save the mapping costs caused by the dictionary, we implemented a variant of the SPO index that does not store the integer IDs for the object values. Instead, it directly points to the external representation of the object value. Subject and predicate are still represented as IDs, because they are required for query processing, and because they are not an output of the pivot index scan. As a pivot index scan never searches by object value, the inner nodes of this attribute retrieval index are organized exactly as in the aggregated SP* index. I.e., they omit the triple object, which increases their fan-out by 25%.

The leaf nodes are specifically designed for the access pattern of a pivot index scan. The access pattern starts with the subject representing the resource in question and looks for its list of predicate/object pairs. After the predicate/object pairs have been found, the subject is no longer required. Thus, as shown in Figure 4 we store all subjects contiguously at the beginning of a leaf node. After each subject we store

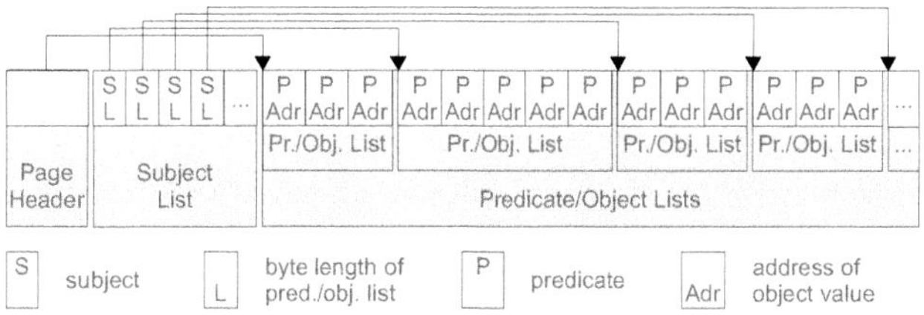

Figure 4: Leaf layout of the attribute retrieval index

the length (in bytes) of the subject's predicate/object list. We store the predicate/object list of each subject contiguously at a location further behind in the page. All predicates and objects are stored in the same page for all subjects, except for the last one. The last subject continues on the next page, if the page header indicates this. The page header also contains the in-page byte offset that points to the beginning of the first predicate-object list. At the same time, this offset marks the exclusive end of the subject list.

We use a simple compression technique for the leaf nodes. We use delta encoding for the subject list and for the predicates of each subject. Both are sorted integer IDs, which allows storing only the difference to their predecessor. This results in smaller integer numbers, which we store using 7-bit variable-length encoding. In most cases, this requires only one byte per subject or predicate. To point to the object values, we store the uncompressed page number and the in-page offset that identify the location where the dictionary stores the external value representation.

The storage addresses of the object values are longer than the internal IDs of the objects. Moreover, the addresses are not sorted. This makes the triples harder to compress than in the fully sorted SPO index. In our experiments, the compression rate was worse by a factor of about 2.2, compared to the compression method for the SPO index presented in [7]. Nevertheless, our compression technique for the attribute retrieval index stored the triples in roughly 50% of their uncompressed size. In addition, the attribute retrieval index is only intended for point queries, so the absolute index size is not primarily an issue. For point queries, it is much more important to access the relevant parts of the leaf nodes quickly, at which the attribute retrieval index excels.

When a pivot index scan searches for the attributes of a resource, it first locates the right leaf node through standard B-tree search. It opens the leaf node and reads the offset pointing to the end of the subject list. Then, it reads the (sorted) subject list sequentially until it finds the subject. The compressed subjects do not occupy much space, so that the linear search benefits from a good processor cache locality and can exploit hardware branch prediction well. For each subject, the pivot index scan reads the length of the corresponding predicate/object list. It adds the length to two total lengths; one including and one excluding the current subject. Added to the offset of the first predicate-object list, these lengths mark the offset where the current predicate-object list begins and ends in the page, respectively. The predicate-object list is processed as shown in Listing 3.

5. EVALUATION

We carried out an extensive performance evaluation to compare (1) canonical plans with execution plans that utilize

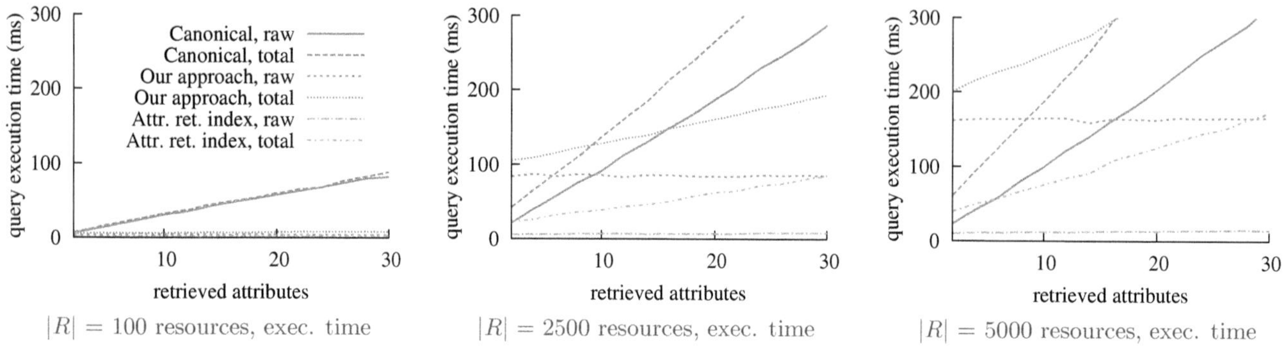

$|R| = 100$ resources, exec. time — $|R| = 2500$ resources, exec. time — $|R| = 5000$ resources, exec. time

$|R| = 100$ resources, page requests — $|R| = 2500$ resources, page requests — $|R| = 5000$ resources, page requests

Figure 5: Resources versus attributes: Query execution time and page requests

our attribute retrieval approach (2) on the "ordinary" SPO index and (3) on the attribute retrieval index.

5.1 Implementation

We implemented our attribute retrieval approach and integrated it into the RDF-3X [7] triple store, version 0.3.4, which is available as open source.[1] However, our approach is applicable for any triple store that indexes RDF data on a per-triple basis in several permutations (including the subject-predicate-object permutation, of course), which is the current state of the art.

In addition to adding a new logical and physical database operator, we had to modify the query optimizer, as described in Section 3.2. To integrate the attribute retrieval index, we also had to modify data import, and—most notably—large parts of the runtime system and the dictionary. As a consequence of the attribute retrieval index, intermediate query results no longer consist of dictionary IDs only. Instead, they may consist of IDs and addresses of object values. The runtime system must differ between both types, which makes the code quite a bit more complicated.

5.2 Test Setup

We generated artificial data, which allowed us to study different execution plans in a controlled way. Our test databases contained between 59.7 and 149.7 million triples, described 1 million resources, and occupied 6.6 to 15 GB of space.

We ran all test queries ten times consecutively on warm caches and measured the execution times. Our figures report the median of the ten test runs. In addition, we counted the logical page requests to get an impression on the main memory (if not disk) I/O behavior of the execution plans. Moreover, to examine only the physical database operators, we measured execution times and page requests both including and excluding the dictionary. I.e. in the latter case, the raw internal IDs and addresses were returned instead of resolving the external string representation of the values.

We ran all tests on a Dell Optiplex 755 equipped with an Intel Core2 Quad Q9300 CPU running at 2.50 GHz and 4 GB of main memory. We used two striped 250 GB SATA 3.0 GB/s hard drives spinning at 7.200 RPM. The test machine ran a 64 bit 2.6.31 Linux kernel.

5.3 Resources versus Attributes

The most important and most interesting question is, how the different execution plans behave for different amounts of queried resources $|R|$ and retrieved attributes $|A|$. To answer this, we ran a large series of queries on a database containing 1 million resources. Every resource carried exactly 30 attributes with random values, so that they can be assumed distinct. To simulate resource identification, we created 1000 resource groups of different sizes. The group members were chosen randomly. A resource is a member of a particular group, if it is connected to the group URI via the `inResourceGroup` predicate. This enabled us to select a defined amount of resources using a single triple pattern.

The test queries retrieved between $|A| = 2$ and $|A| = 30$ attributes. Figure 5 shows the results for $|R| = 100$, 2500, and 5000 resources, both retrieving only the *raw* internal IDs, and the *total* effort including the dictionary overhead. They lead to the following observations:

1. The raw figures of our approach and the attribute retrieval index are always simply horizontal lines. Thus, for a given number of resources $|R|$, our approach requires constant time and page accesses, independent of $|A|$. This is because it accesses all attributes of a resource from a contiguous memory area, so that it

[1] `http://www.mpi-inf.mpg.de/~neumann/rdf3x/`

effectively makes no difference, how many attributes it retrieves. The canonical plans scale linearly with $|A|$, as they require one join per retrieved attribute.

2. The difference between the raw and the total figures, i.e. the dictionary overhead, is the same for canonical plans and our approach on the SPO index. On the attribute retrieval index, the dictionary overhead is about 20% less for execution times and nearly 50% for page accesses. This is because it does not need to resolve the internal IDs of the attribute values.

3. The attribute retrieval index shows far better execution times than all other approaches for $|A| > 3$, both with and without the dictionary overhead. However, it accesses the identical amount of pages as our approach on the SPO index. Thus, the leaf page layout must make the difference. The attribute retrieval index only accesses a small part of every leaf page and only uncompresses what it needs to read. The other indexes must uncompress the entire page first.

4. The break-even-point of canonical plans and our approach on the SPO index is (in this evaluation) around

$$\frac{|R|}{|A|+1} \approx 300.$$

Higher values favor canonical plans, below our approach on the SPO index is faster. The attribute retrieval index was always faster than both of them for $|A| \geq 3$.

5.4 Multi-Attributes

As pointed out in Section 2.3, SPARQL returns the cross-product over multi-attributes. This results in exponentially growing results, if the number of retrieved attributes $|A|$ is increased. We ran large test series on databases similar to the one described in Section 5.3, except that every resource carried each attribute two, three, or four times, respectively.

For lower amounts of computed cross-products, the results were similar to those of Section 5.3. The more cross-products the multi-attributes caused, the closer the raw execution times of the different plans became (i.e. not counting dictionary overhead). For extremely high numbers of result tuples, the canonical plan showed faster raw execution times, even though it accessed significantly more pages. We presume that this is due to the more sequential memory access pattern of the streamlined merge joins that leads to better CPU cache-hit rates across the triples of different resources when computing the cross-products. A pivot index scan bears excellent memory locality for one resource, but it causes random memory access for different resources.

Figure 6 shows the raw execution times of one test series on a database with two multi-attributes. For 5000 resources, three attributes were retrieved once and a fourth attribute was selected two to eight times. It is observable, that the execution times become similar with high amounts of multiply-selected attributes. For lower amounts, however, our approach is more than an order of magnitude faster on the attribute retrieval index. The results are roughly comparable to a different test series on the same database that retrieved the same amount of distinct attributes, i.e. without multiply selected attributes. Thus, multiply selected attributes are hardly different from distinct selections, as long as the number of cross-products is the same.

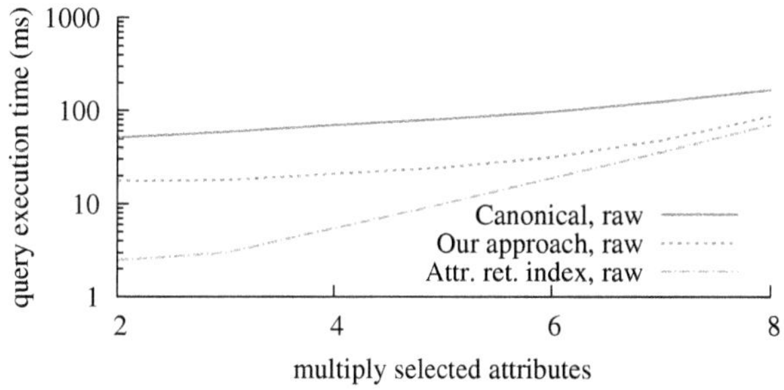

Figure 6: Two multi-attributes, $|R| = 5000$ resources, multiply selected attributes

5.5 Selective Attributes

As discussed in Section 3.5, naively applying our approach on attributes which only occur at a small fraction of resources will result in many failing index lookups. To measure this effect, we used the database of Section 5.3 and added 100 *selective* attributes, which occurred only at 0.1% to 10% of all resources. We randomly chose the resources which carried a selective attribute. Yet we ensured that the fraction of resources with selective attributes was the same for all resource groups. Also, for every selective attribute, every group contained at least one resource that carried the attribute.

Our queries retrieved four "ordinary" attributes, as in Section 5.3, and one selective attribute from different amounts of resources. Thus, if all attributes were always present, we would expect our approach to be superior up to about 1800 resources. We compared a canonical execution plan, a naive application of our approach, the "reduced" approach of Section 3.5.1, and the "checked" approach of Section 3.5.1.

Figure 7 shows the measured execution times and page requests for $|R| = 100$, 2500 and 5000 resources. As expected, the naive application of our approach is by far worse than the canonical plan, both for execution times and page requests. The "reduced" and "checked" plans, on the other hand, are more than twice as fast as the canonical plan and also request significantly fewer pages. The "checked" plan is always slightly better than the "reduced" plan.

6. CONCLUSIONS

The W3C Resource Description Framework (RDF) supports managing semi-structured data without a predefined database schema. RDF models data as triples which may represent a relation between two resources or an attribute of a resource. So far, the focus of most RDF query processors has been on finding complex graph patterns in RDF data based on the relations between resources. This typically involves a high number of joins. By contrast, obtaining a record-like view on the attributes of resources, as natively supported by record-based DBMS, imposes unnecessary performance burdens in these query processing models. They must join the individual attributes to assemble the final result records, as they do not differ between finding resources that match a graph pattern and retrieving resource attributes.

We proposed a processing model that splits queries to RDF data into two conceptual parts: *resource identification* and *attribute retrieval*. First, resource identification determines the resources of interest for the query. In a second step, attribute retrieval fetches the queried attributes in a single

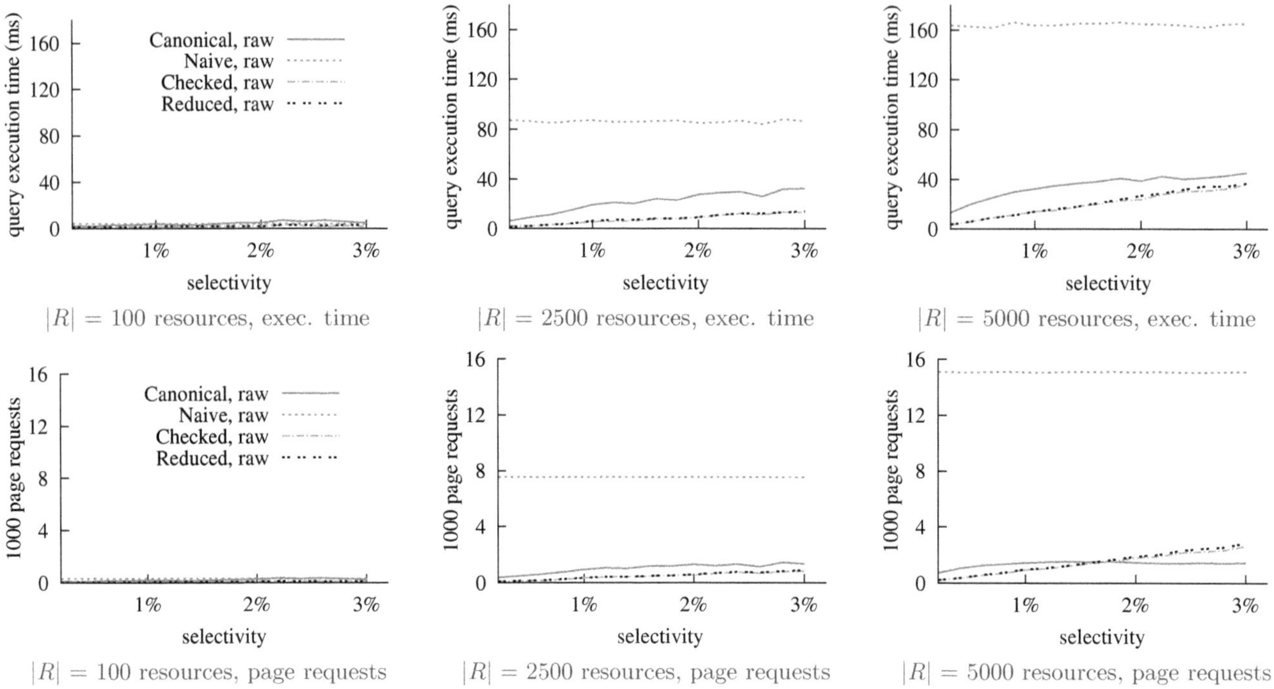

Figure 7: Selective attributes: Query execution time and page requests

step for each identified resource. For this, we exploit an index that stores all attributes of a resource contiguously, which saves a large number of joins. Most RDF stores already possess such an index anyway; they just do not exploit it in our proposed way. In addition to that, we proposed an index structure that is specifically designed for the access pattern of attribute retrieval. Our performance evaluation showed that our processing model is clearly superior for larger numbers of retrieved attributes and moderately large amounts of resources. Moreover, our attribute retrieval index further improves performance by large margins.

The underlying concept of our presented query processing model is not restricted to RDF data management. We believe that it is applicable on any decomposed storage model. It is an interesting challenge to apply it on other types of database systems, such as column-oriented databases or object databases, in the future.

Acknowledgments

We thank our students Tim Waizenegger and Bastian Reitschuster for strongly supporting our evaluation. Furthermore, we thank our colleagues Matthias Großmann, Carlos Lübbe and Nazario Cipriani for the fruitful discussions on the paper.

7. REFERENCES

[1] D. J. Abadi, A. Marcus, S. R. Madden, and K. Hollenbach. Scalable semantic web data management using vertical partitioning. In *VLDB*, 2007.

[2] S. Auer, C. Bizer, G. Kobilarov, J. Lehmann, R. Cyganiak, and Z. Ives. Dbpedia: a nucleus for a web of open data. In *ISWC/ASWC*, 2007.

[3] C. Cunningham, C. A. Galindo-Legaria, and G. Graefe. Pivot and unpivot: optimization and execution strategies in an rdbms. In *VLDB*, 2004.

[4] O. Erling and I. Mikhailov. RDF Support in the Virtuoso DBMS. *Networked Knowledge-Networked Media*, 2009.

[5] G. Graefe. Volcano—an extensible and parallel query evaluation system. *IEEE Trans. on Knowl. and Data Eng.*, 6, 1994.

[6] T. Neumann and G. Moerkotte. Characteristic sets: Accurate cardinality estimation for RDF queries with multiple joins. In *ICDE*, 2011.

[7] T. Neumann and G. Weikum. RDF-3X: a risc-style engine for RDF. *VLDB*, 2008.

[8] T. Neumann and G. Weikum. Scalable join processing on very large RDF graphs. In *SIGMOD*, 2009.

[9] E. Prud'hommeaux and A. Seaborne. SPARQL query language for RDF. Recommendation, W3C, 2008.

[10] P. Selinger, M. Astrahan, D. Chamberlin, R. Lorie, and T. Price. Access path selection in a relational database management system. In *SIGMOD*, 1979.

[11] F. M. Suchanek, G. Kasneci, and G. Weikum. Yago: A large ontology from wikipedia and wordnet. *Web Semantics: Science, Services and Agents on the World Wide Web*, 6, 2008.

[12] C. Weiss, P. Karras, and A. Bernstein. Hexastore: sextuple indexing for semantic web data management. In *VLDB*, 2008.

[13] C. M. Wyss and E. L. Robertson. A formal characterization of pivot/unpivot. In *CIKM*, 2005.

Effective Stratification For Low Selectivity Queries on Deep Web Data Sources

Fan Wang, Gagan Agrawal
Dept. of Computer Science and Engineering, The Ohio State University
Columbus OH 43210
wangfa@cse.ohio-state.edu, agrawal@cse.ohio-state.edu

ABSTRACT

We study the problem of estimating the result of an aggregation query with low selectivity when a data source only supports *limited data accesses*. Existing stratified sampling techniques cannot be applied to such a problem since either it is very hard, if not impossible, to gather certain critical statistics from such a data source, or more importantly, the *selective attribute* of the query may not be queriable on the data source. In such cases, we need an effective mechanism to stratify the data and form homogeneous strata with respect to the selective attribute of the query, despite not being able to query the data source with the selective attribute.

This paper presents and evaluates a stratification method for this problem utilizing a *queriable auxiliary attribute*. The breaking points for the stratification are computed based on a novel Bayesian Adaptive Harmony Search algorithm. This method derives from the existing Harmony search method, but includes novel *objective function*, and introduces a technique for dynamically adapting key parameters of this method. Our experiments show that the estimation accuracy achieved using our method is consistently higher than 95% even for 0.01% selectivity query, even when there is only a low correlation between the auxiliary attribute and the selective attribute. Furthermore, our method achieves at least a five fold reduction in estimation error over three other methods, for the same sampling cost.

Categories and Subject Descriptors

H.2 [**Database Management**]: Systems

General Terms

Algorithms

Keywords

Deep Web, Query Processing, Sampling Methods

1. INTRODUCTION

We study the problem of estimating the result of an aggregation query with *low selectivity* over a data source that only allows *limited access to data*, i.e. is limited with respect to the kind of queries it supports. By low selectivity, we refer to the queries with a selection predicate that is matched by only a very small fraction of the data. Data sources with limited access to data have been studied extensively in the context of data integration and query optimization [28, 6]. More recent examples of such data sources are the deep web data sources. With the rapid growth of the size and popularity of the data disseminated over the World Wide Web, a large portion of structured web data resides in the *deep web*. To access data in the deep web, a user must issue queries through the input interfaces of deep web data sources. Then, answers are returned to the user as dynamically generated HTML pages.

Deep web data sources often have limited data accessibility, from two different aspects. First, it is very hard, if not impossible, to obtain certain critical population statistics on deep web data. This is because many deep web data sources limit the number of queries a particular IP address can issue, or the number of data records can be returned, to protect their data from being completely downloaded, or to disallow a denial-of-service attack. Second, more importantly, deep web data can only be accessed through query interface made available on the data source's web page. Therefore, certain attribute of a query may not be directly queriable over the input interface of the deep web data source.

In this paper, we propose solutions to make *online aggregation* [17] feasible even for low selectivity queries over deep web data sources with limited data accessibility. Answering database queries by sampling has been extensively studied in the literature [18, 27, 5, 3, 4], including recent work on sampling methods and estimators for low selectivity queries [20]. However, these approaches are not directly applicable to a database that offers limited data access. Similarly, sampling deep web data sources has been a topic of recent interest [13, 11, 12]. However, sampling for low selectivity queries has not been studied in this work.

To further illustrate our problem, let us consider the following example. Suppose we have a data set as shown in Table 1. In this data set, we have 3 attributes and 10 records. We are considering the query $Q1$, which is

```
SELECT AVG(C)
FROM Table 1
WHERE B>15
```

Table 1: A Low Selectivity Query Example

A	B	C	A	B	C
50	1	58	32	1	30
60	2	79	51	2	40
59	3	63	70	3	24
52	2	100	**24**	**20**	**10**
40	1	2	**17**	**100**	**12**

CIKM'11, October 24–28, 2011, Glasgow, Scotland, UK.

The selection predicate of $Q1$ only accepts data records from Table 1 with the value of attribute B larger than 15. From Table 1, we observe that there are only 2 records that can be accepted by the selection predicate of $Q1$. The natural way of preparing to handle such low selectivity query is to use stratification [29]. Specifically, we can partition the entire data set into multiple sub-groups, called *strata*, such that the values of the selective attribute(s) of the query (attribute B in Table 1) are homogenous within each stratum. This objective is best achieved when the variability of the *partitioning attribute(s)*, in our case the selective attribute(s), is minimized within each stratum, and maximized across different strata. For answering the query shown above, we could have two strata, i.e., the last two records (in bold) in one stratum, and the rest eight records in the other. After stratification, we know that the query's selection predicate will favor certain strata. Then, those favored strata can be heavily sampled so as to obtain a better estimation for the query. More specifically, if a specified number of samples, n, are to be drawn from the data set, the number of samples selected from each stratum can be determined by existing sampling allocation methods, such as *Neyman allocation* [29] or *Bayes-Neyman allocation* [20].

Therefore, the critical problem is to find an *appropriate stratification*, i.e., to find multiple *breaking points* of the partitioning attribute on which the stratification is performed. In the literature, various methods have been proposed for this purpose, including *clustering based stratification* [29] and *outlier indexing* [3]. The above methods require knowledge of either the distribution or summary statistics of the partitioning attribute. While this information can be easily obtained for a relational database, this is not the case for a deep web source where the partitioning attribute is not directly queriable.

In statistical sampling, if the partitioning attribute is unknown or difficult to obtain, stratification can be performed based on an *auxiliary* attribute, which is *closely correlated* with the partitioning attribute [8]. Examples of methods which use a closely correlated auxiliary attribute include Dalenius and Hodges's method [9, 10], Ekman's rule [14], and Gunning and Horgan's geometric regression method [16]. However, all of the above methods have rigid requirements on the auxiliary attribute. For example, the auxiliary attribute and the partitioning attributes should be highly correlated and the variance of the auxiliary attribute is equal to the variance of the partitioning attribute [8], or the auxiliary attribute should be *uniformly* distributed within each stratum [14, 16]. In actual deep web data sources, these requirements are rarely satisfied. In our evaluation (Section 5), we actually show that the above methods do not achieve good estimation results for low selectivity queries on real data sets.

1.1 Problem Formulation and Our Contributions

In this paper, we have developed a *Bayesian Adaptive Harmony Search Stratification* algorithm for a non-queriable selective attribute based on an auxiliary attribute. We consider aggregation queries over deep web sources in the following format:

SELECT AVG($f_1(r.Target)$)
FROM R As r
WHERE $f_2(r.Sel)$

Here, $f_1()$ is any numerical function, $f_2()$ is a *selection predicate* with *low selectivity*, and $r.Target$ is the *target attribute* on which the aggregation is performed. If $r.Sel$ is directly queriable on the input query form of the deep web data source, the query can be answered trivially by specifying the selection predicate directly on the input query form. However, when $r.Sel$ is not directly queriable on the input query form, because of the limited query interface of a deep web data source, we require novel techniques.

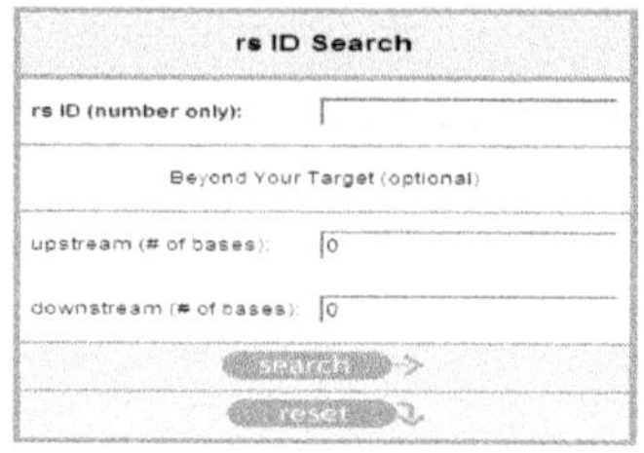

Figure 1: Input Query Form of SeattleSNP

A specific motivating example from the biology domain is as follows. Suppose we are interested in Single Nucleotide Polymorphisms (SNPs), which are promising for explaining the genetic contribution to certain rare diseases [1]. Biologists want to obtain the *average frequency of the SNPs related with a certain type of rare breast cancer*. In this example, the target attribute is *SNP frequency* and the selective attribute is *SNP function*. `SeattleSNP`[1] is a widely used deep web data source for searching SNP related information. The input interface of `SeattleSNP` is shown in Figure 1. As we can see from this figure, the SNP data can only be queried by SNP identifier and the chromosome range of a SNP. This limited query interfaces prohibits us from directly querying the selective attribute *SNP function* and performing stratification.

In our proposed approach, we take certain directly queriable attribute on the input query form, the *input attribute* $r.Input$, as the *auxiliary attribute*. We have developed an optimization to the recently proposed meta-heuristic algorithm, the *harmony search* algorithm [25], that we refer to as the *Bayesian Adaptive Harmony Search*. This algorithm finds robust stratification plans for the non-queriable selective attribute based on the auxiliary attribute. The stratification thus obtained can accurately reflects the distribution of the *hidden selective attribute*. In the above motivating example, we could use chromosome range as the auxiliary attribute to do stratification since there will be some correlation between the position of the chromosome on which a SNP is located and the function of the SNP.

Overall, our contributions are summarized as follows.

1. We have developed a novel stratification method to stratify a hidden selective attribute based on an auxiliary attribute. The stratification obtained from our algorithm accurately reflects the distribution of the hidden selective attribute even when the correlation between the auxiliary attribute and the selective attribute is weak.
2. Besides applying the idea of Harmony search to the stratification for low selectivity queries on the deep web, an important contribution of our work is an approach for automatically adapting the values of the parameters in the original harmony search algorithm based on the bayesian approach.
3. We experimentally show that the estimation accuracy, obtained with the same sampling cost, based on the stratification generated from our method is better than three existing methods by at least a factor of 5. Put another way, we incur much lower sampling cost to obtain the same level of accuracy. Furthermore, the estimation accuracy we obtained is consistently higher than 95% even for extremely low selectivity query (0.01% selectivity).

[1] http://pga.gs.washington.edu/

2. BACKGROUND

2.1 Stratification

In survey sampling, if the attribute we are interested in takes on different mean values in different *sub-populations*, we may be able to obtain more precise estimates to answer a given query by taking a *stratified sample* [29]. Stratified sampling is widely used for answering low selectivity queries [5, 3, 4, 20].

The first step in stratified sampling is *stratification*, i.e., to partition the data set R into k disjoint strata, with R_i representing the ith stratum. Then, we have $R = R_1 \cup R_2 \cup \ldots \cup R_k$. The attribute on which stratification is performed is refered to as the *partitioning attribute*. Specifically, suppose the partitioning attribute x has the range $[x_0, x_k]$, then we need to find $k-1$ breaking points within the range $[x_0, x_k]$, such that $x_0 < x_1 < x_2 < \ldots < x_{k-1} < x_k$. In this way, the data records whose attribute x fall into the range $[x_{i-1}, x_i]$ are in stratum R_i. Formally, we could consider a stratification of the partitioning attribute to be a *vector of breaking points*, for example, $Vector(x) = [x_0, x_1, \ldots, x_k]$.

As a specific example, we consider a datset that captures sales of used cars. Suppose we are interested in estimating the average price of used cars with mileage less than 50000. We could stratify the data set on the attribute `Mileage`. A possible stratification could be as follows: $[0, 10000]$, $[10000, 40000]$, $[40000, 100000]$, and $[100000, 300000]$. In this example, the breaking points are mileage 10000, 40000, and 100000.

When stratification is performed, the size of the stratified sample we need to choose from each stratum R_i can be determined by a *sample allocation method*, whihc will need to meet the constraint $\sum n_i = n$, where n_i is the number of samples we drawn from stratum R_i, and n is a pre-defined total number of samples.

In sampling a hidden data source, i.e. a data source supporting only a limited access, for a low selectively query, we also need determine the breaking points of the partitioning attribute for stratification. The key challenge we face is that the *selective attribute* of the query we are interested in, may not be directly queriable. As a result, stratification problem becomes significantly harder. The only option is to stratify or partition attribute with a queriable or an *auxiliary attribute*. Returning to the used car sale example, *target attribute* we are interested in is `Price`, and the the selective attribute is `Mileage`. Suppose `Mileage` cannot be queried on, and the input query form of the data source only provides direct access to the attribute `Year of Car`. Therefore, we need to take `Year of Car` as the *auxiliary attribute*, and create strata by choosing break points on these values. In choosing these break points, the key consideration is to be able to efficiently find sufficient number of *useful samples*, i.e. samples that meet the selection predicate based on `Mileage`, for the given low selectivity query.

2.2 Harmony Search

The harmony search (HS) algorithm is a meta-heuristic algorithm that was developed in 2005 [25]. Harmony search is a phenomenon-mimicking algorithm inspired by the improvisation process of musicians. In the HS algorithm, each musician (decision variable) plays (generates) a note (a value) for finding the best harmony (global optimum). Harmony search algorithm had been very successful in a wide variety of optimization problems [15, 25], and offers several advantages with respect to traditional optimization techniques [26].

Harmony search algorithm tries to find a vector X that optimizes (minimizes or maximizes) a certain objective function. The HS algorithm consists of the following five steps [25].

Step 1. Initialize the optimization problem and algorithm parameters. The optimization problem is specified as

$$\text{Minimize} \quad f(x_1, x_2, \ldots, x_N), x_i \in X_i, i = 1, \ldots, N$$

where $f(\mathbf{X})$ is the objective function; x_i is a decision variable in the vector X, X_i is the set of possible values (range) for each decision variable x_i, and N is the number of decision variables. To optimize the objective function, we need to specify the following harmony search parameters: the harmony memory size (the number of solution vectors in the harmony memory), harmony memory consideration rate ($HMCR$) and pitch adjusting rate (PAR). The $HMCR$ and PAR parameters both range from 0 to 1 and determine the generation of a new harmony vector. $HMCR$ indicates our confidence on the existing solutions in the current harmony memory. If $HMCR$ is set to be close to 1, it shows that we have high confidence that the existing solutions are close to the optimal one. However, if $HMCR$ is set to be close to 0, it means that we have low confidence on the existing solutions, and we are intend to obtain new solutions outside the current harmony memory. PAR indicates the likelihood we assign a random *shift* to the value of a decision variable. A large PAR indicates that we try to aggressively change the value of a decision variable, and a small PAR suggests otherwise.

Step 2: Initialize the harmony memory: The harmony memory HM is a $M \times N$ matrix, where N is the number of decision variables and M is the size of the harmony memory. In other words, the harmony memory contains M randomly initialized solution vectors of the objective function. An example of initialized harmony memory is shown as follows.

$$HM = \begin{bmatrix} x_1^1 & x_2^1 & \ldots & x_{N-1}^1 & x_N^1 \\ x_1^2 & x_2^2 & \ldots & x_{N-1}^2 & x_N^2 \\ \vdots & \vdots & \vdots & \vdots & \vdots \\ x_1^{M-1} & x_2^{M-1} & \ldots & x_{N-1}^{M-1} & x_N^{M-1} \\ x_1^M & x_2^M & \ldots & x_{N-1}^M & x_N^M \end{bmatrix}$$

Step 3: Improvise a new harmony from the harmony memory: A new harmony vector, $x' = [x_1', x_2', \ldots, x_N']$ is generated in a randomized fashion based on the value of the $HMCR$ and PAR parameters. Specifically, the value of the design variable x_i' can be chosen in two steps.

In the first step, we consider the harmony memory consideration rate, i.e., we choose an existing harmony or we generate a new harmony from an appropriate domain. Suppose we have a biased coin with head probability of $HMCR$, the value of x_i' is generated based on either of the following two outcomes of tossing the coin. If the head of the coin is up, the value of x_i' should be chosen from any value of the ith decision variable in the current harmony memory. If the tail of the coin is up, the value of x_i' should be chosen from any possible value within the range of the ith decision variable, which is X_i.

In the second step, for each x_i', we determine whether it should be pitch-adjusted by a random distance by considering the PAR parameter. Similarly, the value of x_i' can be either shifted by a random distance with the probability PAR, (i.e. not shifted with the probability $1 - PAR$).

Overall, the rule for generating a new value for x_i' is summarized as follows (*w/p* stands for *with probability*).

$$x_i' = \begin{cases} (x_i' \in \{x_i^1, \ldots, x_i^M\}) + \delta & \text{w/p HMCR} * \text{PAR}, \\ (x_i' \in X_i) + \delta & \text{w/p } (1 - \text{HMCR}) * \text{PAR}, \\ (x_i' \in \{x_i^1, \ldots, x_i^M\}) & \text{w/p HMCR} * (1 - \text{PAR}), \\ (x_i' \in X_i) & \text{w/p } (1 - \text{HMCR}) * (1 - \text{PAR}) \end{cases}$$

Step 4: Update harmony memory: If the new harmony vector is better than the worst harmony vector in the current harmony memory (in terms of the objective function value), the worst harmony vector in the harmony memory is replaced by the new harmony vector.

Step 5: Termination: The above iterative procedure is terminated until a *termination condition* is satisfied, for example, when the total number of iterations exceeds a threshold or when we achieve convergence in the objective function.

Our proposed Bayesian adaptive harmony search stratification algorithm derives from Harmony search. However, we had to address the following challenges. First, we need to map the stratification problem on a hidden data source to the harmony search model. Second, we had to develop an *objective function* that would be appropriate for low selectivity queries. Third, since execution time is critical while executing a query, we developed a Bayesian framework to dynamically update $HMCR$ and PAR parameters, and help the search converge faster. Details of these are presented in the next 2 sections.

3. ALGORITHM OVERVIEW

In this section, we give an overview of our entire algorithm. Our approach comprises of the following three steps. First, we map the stratification problem to the harmony search model. Second, we apply the harmony search algorithm to find the best stratification. To enable this step, we have developed a novel Bayesian adaptive framework to adjust the two parameters in the original harmony search algorithm, which are the harmony memory consideration rate and the pitch adjusting rate. The Bayesian adaptation method is detailed in Section 4. Finally, given the stratification obtained from the previous step, we apply a sample allocation method we have developed to allocate samples into each stratum.

3.1 Modeling Harmony Memory

To estimate the answer of a low selectivity query accurately, we need to find the best stratification of the selective attribute, from the view-point of most accurately reflecting its distribution and being able to efficiently obtain sufficient number of samples that match the selection predicate. Let us suppose a selective attribute has a distribution as illustrated in Figure 2(a). A good stratification of this selective attribute is illustrated by the vertical reference lines in the Figure 2(a). Suppose a low selectivity query asks for data with the values in the range between 1.2 and 1.8. Using the shown stratification, a sample allocation method could obtain good estimation result by heavily drawing samples from the last stratum, ($[1.2, 2.1]$).

As we have described earlier, our focus is on cases where the selective attribute is not accessible through the input interface of the deep web data source. In such a case, we use an attribute available in the input query form as the *auxiliary attribute*. Unlike many existing methods in statistics, we cannot assume that there be a strong correlation between the auxiliary attribute and the selective attribute, since this assumption is not likely to hold on real data sources. In Figure 2(b), the solid line shows the distribution of the selective attribute, and the dotted line shows the distribution of an auxiliary attribute. In this example, the correlation between them is 0.35. By applying our approach, we are trying to find a stratification of the auxiliary attribute (shown as the vertical lines in Figure 2(b)), which is sufficiently close to the stratification we could obtain for the selective attribute.

Harmony search can be viewed as a guided search process, which can stratify the auxiliary attribute in a way that we can efficiently obtain samples meeting the selection predicate, and accurately estimate the aggregation function. In Section 2, we had described that the harmony memory consists of a list of decision vectors. In our specific problem scenario, we consider each stratification of the auxiliary attribute as a decision vector. In other words, each decision variable in our case is a breaking point value in the range of the auxiliary attribute. For example, the stratification shown in Figure 2(b), $[0.25, 1.05, 1.25]$, is a decision vector in our harmony memory. In statistics literature, Cochran [7] concluded that in stratified sampling, there is typically not much further reduction in variance from having more than 6 strata. Based on this observation, in our implementation, the size of the decision vector is set to be 6, though clearly, our approach can apply in other cases as well.

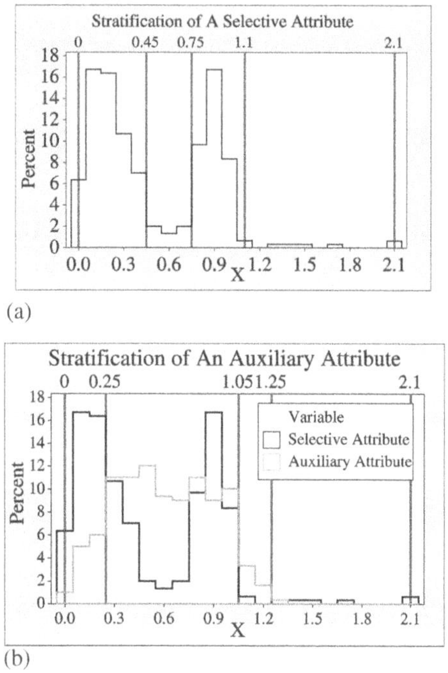

Figure 2: Example: Auxiliary Attribute Based Stratification: (a) Stratification for Selective Attribute, (b) Auxiliary Attribute Based Stratification

At the beginning, the initial harmony memory is randomly generated. Suppose there are M decision vectors in the harmony memory, i.e., the size of the harmony memory is M. Let the range of the auxiliary attribute be X. Then, each decision vector is generated in the following three steps. First, we generate a random number, denoted as k, between 1 and 6 using a uniform distribution. This is the number of strata represented by this decision vector. Second, we need to generate $k-1$ breaking points. Therefore, we generate $k-1$ random numbers within the range of the auxiliary attribute, which is X, using a uniform distribution. Each such generated number is a breaking point. Third, we form a decision vector of size 6 by ranking the $k-1$ breaking points in an increasing order and randomly inserting $6-k$ number of $*$. The $*$ indicates an empty position in the stratification.

The above procedure is repeated M times to initialize the harmony memory. An example of a harmony memory in our approach is shown as follows.

$$M = \begin{bmatrix} 0.2 & * & 0.5 & 0.8 & * \\ * & * & 0.8 & * & 1.5 \\ 0.4 & 0.9 & 1.3 & 1.5 & * \\ 0.2 & 1 & 1.4 & * & 1.8 \\ 0.3 & * & 1.2 & 1.5 & 1.9 \end{bmatrix}$$

The above harmony memory shows 5 stratification candidates (decision vectors). The first decision vector corresponds to the stratification of $[Min(X), 0.2]$, $[0.2, 0.5]$, $[0.5, 0.8]$, $[0.8, Max(X)]$, where X is the range of the auxiliary attribute.

3.2 Harmony Search and Objective Function

Given the initial harmony memory, our stratification search algorithm works as follows.

1. For each initial stratification candidate in the harmony memory, compute its *cost score*. The method for computing this metric will be described later. A stratification candidate with a lower cost score is preferred.
2. Generate a new stratification candidate according to the original harmony search algorithm described in Section 2.2. However, a key distinctive aspect of our work is that in the search algorithm, the two harmony search parameters, $HMCR$ and PAR, are adapted according to our Bayesian framework. This method will be described later in Section 4.
3. For each newly generated stratification candidate, compute its cost score, and update harmony memory using the newly generated stratification candidate.
4. Repeat the above procedure until either of the following two termination conditions is satisfied: 1). the number of iteration exceeds a pre-defined threshold, or 2). the average accuracy of the query obtained using the best stratification candidate in the current harmony memory is lower than a pre-defined threshold.

The method listed above clearly depends on the calculation of a cost or *objective function*, which evaluates the quality of the stratification. We now describe our method for evaluating the quality of stratification. More specifically, given a stratification vector $x = [x_1, x_2, \ldots, x_k]$ on an auxiliary attribute, our goal is to calculate the fitness of the stratification with respect to the distribution of the selective attribute.

In the traditional statistical methods, one prefers a stratification vector if the selective attribute of the data records in each stratum is homogenous. To test this condition, we could draw a random pilot sample of equal size from each stratum of the stratification, and compute the summation of the sample variance of the selective attribute of the pilot sample.

However, only considering the sum of variance condition is not sufficient for justifying a good stratification in our scenario, since the auxiliary attribute may not be highly correlated with the selective attribute. Thus, only using sum of variance may not ensure that we can efficiently obtain samples where the selection predicate will be true. Instead, we need to consider another measure in the objective function, which we call the *precision* of a stratification. The *precision* of a stratification is defined as the *percentage* of the pilot sample (from current stratification) that satisfies the low selective predicate specified in the given query. The *precision* of the ith stratum in a stratification is formally defined as $pre_i = \frac{|\{s_{ij} | f_2(s_{ij}) = true, s_{ij} \in \mathcal{S}_i\}|}{|\mathcal{S}_i|}$, where $\mathcal{S}_i$ is a simple random sample from the ith stratum. Recall that f_2 is the selection predicate in the query. Stratification that involves a higher precision can help us in finding more data records satisfying the low selectivity predicate.

Formally, given a stratification x, we draw a random pilot sample from each stratum R_i, and compute two measurements. The first one is σ_i^2, which is the sample variance, and the second one is pre_i, which is the precision. Then, the objective function for the stratification x is defined as

$$f(x) = \sum_{i=1}^{k} \frac{\sigma_i^2}{pre_i}$$

Clearly, the above approach involves a significant sampling overhead during stratification itself. However, the stratification obtained allows us to obtain samples matching the selection predicate more effectively. Our experiments show that despite this overhead, we can obtain the same number of samples matching the selection predicate with a lower sampling cost.

3.3 Sample Allocation

The problem of sample allocation is to determine the number of samples n_i that need to be drawn from each stratum R_i, so as to conduct the final estimation for the query. Suppose the total number of samples used to answer a query is pre-defined as n. Then sample allocation must satisfy the constraint $\sum_{i=1}^{k} n_i = n$. A widely used sample allocation method is *Neyman Allocation* [29]. The Neyman allocation states that the variance of the estimator is minimized when sample size n_i is proportional to the size of the stratum, N_i, and to the sample variance of the selective attribute in the stratum, σ_i^2. That is,

$$n_i = \frac{n}{\sum_{j=1}^{k} N_j \times \sigma_j^2} N_i \times \sigma_i^2$$

We can see that Neyman allocation only captures one measurement of our stratification objective function, the sample variance, but not the second measurement, the precision. Based on the description in Section 3.2, a stratum should be sampled more heavily if one of the following two conditions hold: 1) The values of the selective attribute in the stratum is more heterogenous, i.e., the sample variance of the selective attribute from the stratum is larger, and 2) The stratum covers more data records that satisfy the query's selective predicate, i.e., the stratum has a higher precision.

To capture the above two measurements, we propose a novel sample allocation method. In our method, the sample size n_i is proportional to the sample variance of the selective attribute in the stratum, and as well as the precision of the stratum. Formally,

$$n_i = \frac{n}{\sum_{j=1}^{k} \sigma_j^2 \times pre_j} \sigma_i^2 \times pre_i$$

4. BAYESIAN ADAPTATION

From the description of harmony search in Section 2, we know that two parameters are very important for the performance of the harmony search algorithm, since they enable new, probably better, harmony vectors into the harmony memory. These two parameters are *harmony memory consideration rate* ($HMCR$) and *pitch adjusting rate (PAR)*. As we explained earlier, $HMCR$ indicates the probability that a new harmony vector is generated using the current solution candidates in the harmony memory, and PAR indicates the probability that we shift the values of a newly generated harmony vector by a random distance.

In the original harmony search algorithm [25], these two parameters are fixed during the entire process, though their initial values are chosen carefully. In applying harmony search idea to query processing, efficiency (rate of convergence) is a critical issue. We observe that the values of these two parameters should be dynamically adapted to achieve faster convergence. Specifically, at the beginning of the algorithm, we want to bring in more new harmony vectors into the harmony memory, as the randomly generated initial harmony vectors are less likely to be good. Thus, a small value of $HMCR$ and a high value of PAR is preferred. As the algorithm progresses, the existing harmony vectors may be quite close to the global optima. If we still update the harmony memory aggressively, we may diverge from the optima. As a result, we may want $HMCR$ to become high and PAR to be low.

Figure 3 illustrates the adaptation pattern of $HMCR$ parameter on a dataset. In Figure 3, the x-axis represents the value of

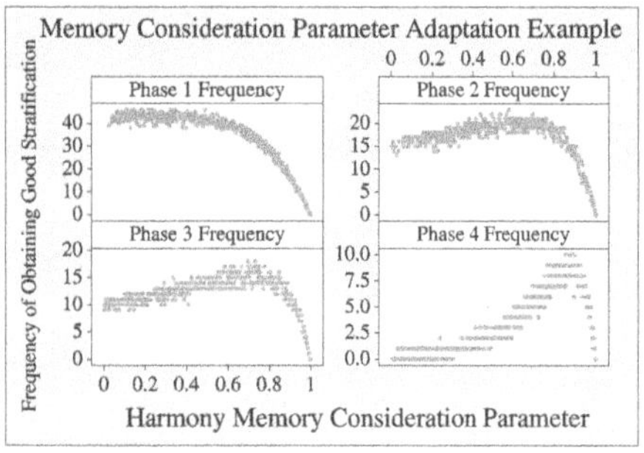

Figure 3: Example: adaptation Pattern of $HMCR$ Parameter

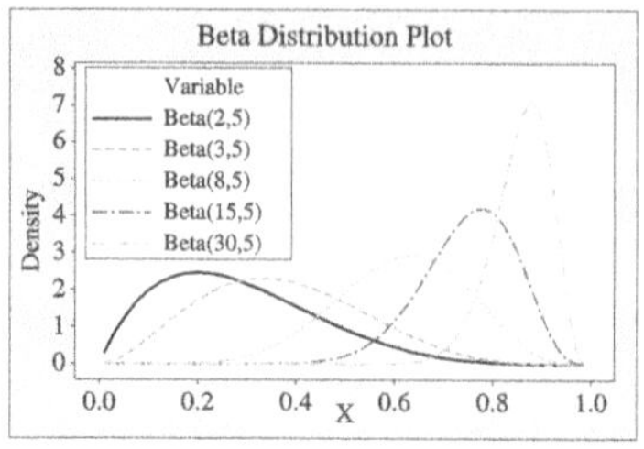

Figure 4: Beta Distribution Plot

$HMCR$, and the y-axis shows the percentage of newly generated harmony vectors having better objective function scores than the worst harmony vector in the current harmony memory. We show results for four phases of the execution of the algorithm, denoted as phase 1 (beginning) through phase 4 (end). During this experiment, the PAR is not changed. From Figure 3 we observe that, during the phase 1 the highest fraction of newly generated harmony vectors are better when $HMCR = 0.15$. During the phase 2, the peak occurs when $HMCR$ is around 0.55, at phase 3, $HMCR$ around 0.7 gives the best results, and at phase 4 (near the end of the harmony search algorithm), the best $HMCR$ value for generating better harmony vector is about 0.85. The PAR parameter has a similar trend as the $HMCR$ parameter.

While the above experiment demonstrates the benefit of increasing $HMCR$ during the execution of the algorithm, the desired adaptation pattern of the two parameters could vary depending upon the dataset and the query. Thus, in our approach, the adaptation pattern at each iteration is inferred from the statistics of the harmony vectors we obtained from the previous iteration of the algorithm. We now describe this method.

Bayesian Adaptation Overview: The Bayesian approach is a method which could let us estimate some unknown parameters (posterior distribution) based on prior knowledge or beliefs (prior distribution) [2]. In the Bayesian approach, based on a list of observed data y, we want to estimate an unknown parameter θ. The unknown parameter is usually in the form of a probability distribution $f(y|\theta)$. We could suppose θ has a prior distribution $\pi(\theta|\eta)$, where η is a vector of *hyperparameters*. Inference concerning θ is then based on its *posterior* distribution, given by

$$p(\theta|y,\eta) = \frac{f(y|\theta)\pi(\theta|\eta)}{\int f(y|u)\pi(u|\eta)du}$$

In our specific scenario, at each iteration of the harmony search algorithm, the data we can observe is the harmony parameter values ($HMCR$ and PAR) that generate better stratification candidates. The variable we want to estimate is the adaptation pattern of the these parameters.

Our Bayesian adaptive algorithm works as follows. We assume the adaptation patterns of the two harmony search parameters $HMCR$ and PAR follow the probability distribution $f_{HMCR}(HMCR|\theta)$ and $f_{PAR}(PAR|\theta)$. The parameter θ determines the adaptation pattern of the harmony parameters. θ is unknown and needs to be estimated. Next, we represent our belief in θ as a prior probability distribution.

In our method, we take a pilot sample from all possible values of the harmony parameters $HMCR$ and PAR, and select the ones, denoted as $HMCR_{opt}$ and PAR_{opt}, which generate the best stratification candidate with respect to the current harmony memory. $HMCR_{opt}$ and PAR_{opt} is our observed data. Based on our observed data $HMCR_{opt}$ and PAR_{opt}, we update the value of the unknown parameter θ, i.e., compute the *posterior distribution*. Finally, suppose the estimated value of the unknown parameter θ is $\hat{\theta}$, then the new adapted harmony search parameters $HMCR$ and PAR for the next iteration of the algorithm could be computed from the probability distribution $f_{HMCR}(HMCR|\hat{\theta})$ and $f_{PAR}(PAR|\hat{\theta})$.

We next describe our Bayesian adaptive approach for estimating $HMCR$ in detail. The adaptation for PAR parameter can be performed similarly.

Determining Probability Function $f_{HMCR}(HMCR|\theta)$: To apply Bayesian approach, we need to find a probability distribution which could reflect the pattern of the change of $HMCR$ during the entire procedure of harmony search. Learning from Figure 3, we know that the change of $HMCR$ has the following features. First, $HMCR$ ranges from 0 to 1, and second, $HMCR$ starts with small value and then increase along with the iterative procedure of harmony search. In statistics, the *Beta distribution* best mimics the above two features. The Beta distribution is a family of continuous probability distributions defined on the interval $(0, 1)$ parameterized by two positive shape parameters, typically denoted by α and β. Figure 4 shows the probability density function of Beta distribution with fixed $\beta = 5$ and varying α from 2 to 30.

Therefore, we use a Beta distribution with fixed β value to represent the probability function $f_{HMCR}()$. The change of the parameter α of the Beta distribution reflects the change of $HMCR$ during the iteration of the harmony search algorithm. Thus, the parameter α of the Beta distribution is the unknown parameter θ we need to estimate in our Bayesian adaptive method, and we use θ to represent the first parameter of a Beta distribution. Thus, to summarize, the probability function $f_{HMCR}(HMCR|\theta)$ is

$$f_{HMCR}(HMCR|\theta) = Beta(\theta, \beta)$$

Determining Prior Distribution and Bayesian Updates for θ: In Bayesian analysis, the value of θ is estimated after the values of $HMCR$ are observed. The *prior distribution* of θ expresses one's belief about θ before the data is observed. In other words, in our problem, the prior distribution indicates our belief on the value of θ even before the execution of the harmony search algorithm. We know that, for a Beta distribution with fixed β parameter, the shape of the Beta distribution is determined by the relation between the values of θ and β. If $\theta < \beta$, the peak of the Beta distribution occurs before $HMCR = 0.5$, and if $\theta > \beta$, the peak of the Beta distribution occurs after $HMCR = 0.5$. Furthermore, from Figure 3, we know that, roughly, $HMCR$ changes from small values (smaller than 0.5) to large values (larger than 0.5) during the execution of the harmony search algorithm. This suggests that a reasonable prior belief for θ will generate small $HMCR$ values. Formally, the prior distribution of θ is then:

$$\pi(\theta) = Uniform(0, \beta)$$

Now, for the parameter $HMCR$, we have the probability function $f_{HMCR}(HMCR|\theta)$ and the prior distribution $\pi(\theta)$. The posterior estimation for the unknown parameter θ could be computed using the following expression [2]

$$E^{\pi(\theta|HMCR)}[\theta] = \frac{\int \theta f_{HMCR}(HMCR|\theta)\pi(\theta)d\theta}{\int f_{HMCR}(HMCR|\theta)\pi(\theta)d\theta}$$

5. EVALUATION

In this section, we evaluate our Bayesian adaptive harmony search stratification algorithm. First, we examine the performance of our algorithm using datasets with different correlation between the auxiliary and the selective attributes, as well as using queries with different selectivity. Second, we compare the Bayesian adaptive version of our algorithm with a non-adaptive version of the algorithm. Finally, we compare our method with three other existing sampling methods. Here, we focus on two aspects: total sampling cost for obtaining the same number of samples meeting the selection predicate, and the accuracy achieved with the same sampling cost.

5.1 Data Sets

We have used 7 datasets, including five synthetic datasets and two real data sets.

Synthetic Data sets: These were generated using MINITAB[2], a statistical software package. We generated five datasets. As mentioned in Section 2, our method performs stratification on the selective attribute based on an auxiliary attribute, and therefore, the correlation between the auxiliary attribute and the selective attribute is important for our algorithm. These five synthetic datasets have different correlation values, i.e., 1, 0.85, 0.7, 0.5, and 0.3, respectively. Each synthetic dataset has 100,000 data records and 3 attributes, which are used as the auxiliary attribute, the selective attribute, and the target attribute, respectively.

US Census Dataset: The Census dataset, denoted as `IBQ`, comprises of the 2002 US Economic Census data on Wholesale Trade Product Lines listed by the Kind of Business. This dataset can be downloaded at American FactFinder[2]. We have 6 attributes and 24984 data records. We use `profit` as the target attribute, `sale` as the selective attribute, and `number of establishments` as the auxiliary attribute. An example low selectivity query that we could issue on `IBQ` dataset is "find the average profit of all kind of business whose sale amount during the year is smaller than $10,000." Suppose `sale` is not directly queriable, we need to answer the query based on the stratification generated for the `number of establishments` attribute. The correlation between the auxiliary attribute (`number of establishments`) and the selective attribute (`sale`) is 0.7.

Yahoo! Auto Data set: The Yahoo! Auto dataset, denoted as `Auto`, comprises of the data crawled from *http://autos.yahoo.com/*. Particularly, it includes the data on used cars from any model located within 50 miles of a zipcode address. This yields a dataset with 4000 data records. We consider `price` as the target attribute, `mileage` as the selective attribute, and `year` as the auxiliary attribute. An example low selectivity query that we could issue on `Auto` is "find the average price of the used cars with mileage smaller than 5000 miles." The correlation between the auxiliary attribute (`year`) and the selective attribute (`mileage`) is 0.56.

[2]http://www.Minitab.com

[2]http://factfinder.census.gov/

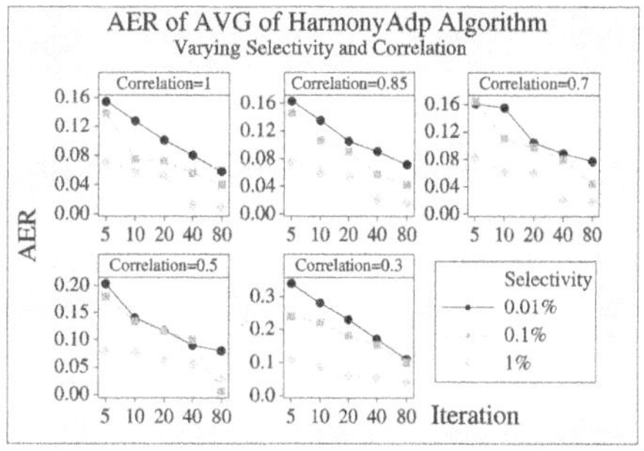

Figure 5: Evaluating HarmonyAdp on Different Datasets and Queries on Synthetic Data

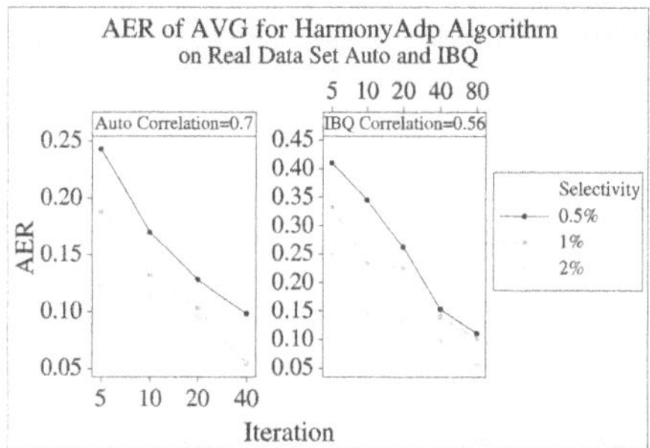

Figure 6: Evaluating HarmonyAdp on Different Datasets and Queries on Real World Data

5.2 Evaluation of Our Approach HarmonyAdp

In this experiment, we evaluate the performance of our approach on datasets with different correlation and queries with different selectivity. We first briefly describe how our experiment is conducted. For each query, we first find the stratification of the dataset using our method. Then, we draw a sequence of 5 independent random stratified samples using the sample allocation method proposed in Section 3.3. The query result is estimated independently using each stratified sample set. Finally, the average of the 5 independent estimation results are reports as the final estimation. All queries considered in our experiments are low selectivity queries with an aggregation function that averages the target attribute.

Throughout our experiment, we use Absolute Error Rate (AER) as our evaluation metric. AER reflects the accuracy of an estimator. For a variable with true value θ and estimated value $\hat{\theta}$, the AER of the estimator $\hat{\theta}$ is $AER(\hat{\theta}) = \frac{|\hat{\theta}-\theta|}{\theta}$.

Figure 5 shows the result on the 5 synthetic datasets, and Figure 6 shows the result on the 2 real world datasets. In Figure 5, each sub-figure shows the result on a dataset with different data correlation ranging from 1 to 0.3. The x-axis represents the number of iterations performed in the HarmonyAdp algorithm, and the y-axis is the AER of the query result estimation obtained. In this experiment, we consider three query selectivity values, which are 1%, 0.1%, and 0.01%.

From Figure 5, we have the following observations. First, as expected, with the increase in the number of iterations, the accuracy of the estimation results becomes higher for all correlation cases and all query selectivity values. When the number of iterations is around 40, corresponding to about 2000 samples (about 2% of dataset size), the estimation error rate for 1% selectivity query is below 5% for all cases, and even for 0.01% selectivity queries, the error rate is below 15%. This shows that our method HarmonyAdp is very appropriate for answering low selectivity queries using limited number of samples (i.e. only 2% of total size of the data). Second, for all data correlation cases, while the estimation accuracy decreases between the 1% and 0.01% selectivity queries, the difference between the error rate of 1% and 0.01% selectivity query is not significant. This shows that our approach is robust with respect to different query selectivity levels. Third, we observe that the error rates for queries of all selectivity levels do not vary too much across datasets with different data correlation. Even for a very low correlation, for example 0.3, the error rates achieved when the number of iteration is 40 range from 5% to 18% for different query selectivity. This shows that our method is also robust in terms of data correlation.

In Figure 6, the left sub-figure shows the result on `Auto` dataset, and the right sub-figure shows the result on `IBQ` dataset. Here, we consider three query selectivity levels 2%, 1%, and 0.5%. Here, we have similar observations as in Figure 5. For the `Auto` dataset, when the number of iteration is about 20 (7% of total data size), the error rates are always below 13% for all selectivity levels, and the error rates are about 8% for the 2% selectivity query. For the `IBQ` dataset, when the number of iteration is about 40 (8% of total data size), the error rates are always below 16% for all selectivity levels, and the error rates are about 10% for 2% selectivity query. The correlation of the `IBQ` date set is about 0.5, which is not very high. This further shows that our approach works quite well on real a dataset with relatively modest correlation.

5.3 Comparision Between Adaptive and Non-Adaptive Versions

In this experiment, we compare the performance of our Bayesian adaptive version of the algorithm, HarmonyAdp, with a non-adaptive version of the algorithm. In the non-adaptive version of the algorithm, denoted as SmartFixed, the $MHCR$ and PAR parameters are fixed to 0.8 and 0.5 respectively. These two parameter values are suggested (and used) in the original harmony search algorithm publication [25].

Figure 7 shows the results on all combinations of correlations and query selectivity values. From all the cases shown in Figure 7, we observe that, when the number of iteration is small, the error rate of the adaptive version is lower than the non-adaptive version, especially for queries with extreme low selectivity (such as 0.01%). However, with the increase of the number of iterations, the performance of the non-adaptive version becomes close to the adaptive version. This is an expected result, since the goal of the adaptive version is to achieve a good stratification faster.

Recall that we need extra samples to perform parameter adaptation, i.e. there is an additional cost for HarmonyAdp over SmartFixed in every iteration. Thus, we also examine the reduction in the total sampling cost achieved while meeting the same accuracy. We observe that the estimation accuracy of HarmonyAdp achieved at 10 iterations is very close to the estimation accuracy of SmartFixed achieved at 20 iterations in our experiments. For the synthetic data sets, the sample size is 50 in each iteration. The number of additional samples used in parameter adaptation is 340. Thus, the total sampling cost for 20 iterations for SmartFixed is 1000, whereas, for HarmonyAdp, it is 840. Thus, through the adaptive method we have introduced, there is a 16% reduction in the sampling cost to achieve the same quality of estimation. Similar results are also observed for the two real datasets.

5.4 Comparison with Three Other Methods

We now compare our method with three other methods. They are Leaps and Bounds stratification method [16] (denoted as L&B), Dalenius and Hodges stratification method [9, 10] (denoted as D&H),

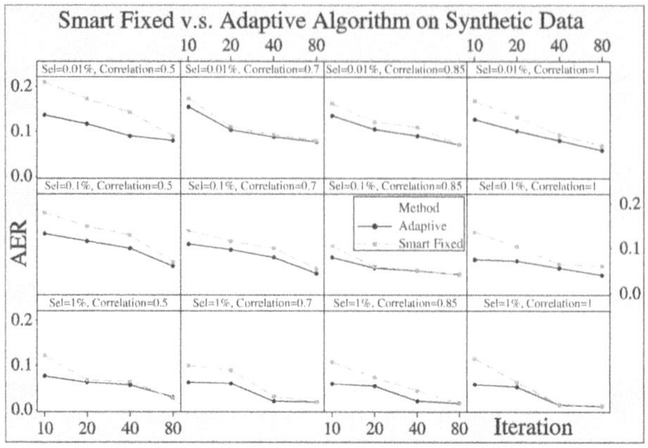

Figure 7: Comparing Adaptive and Non-Adaptive Algorithm

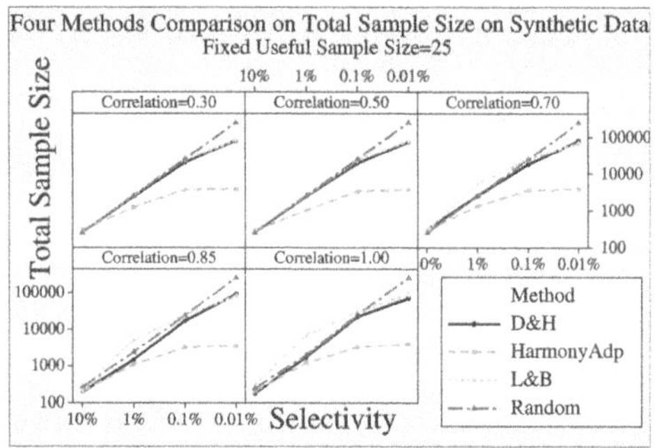

Figure 8: Four Methods Comparison on Total Sample Size on Synthetic Data

and No stratification (Random Sampling) method (denoted as Random). The L&B and D&H methods are classical optimal stratification methods from statistics literature and are both based on an auxiliary attribute.

Leaps and Bounds (L&B): This method assumes that the auxiliary attribute x is *strongly* correlated with y. Besides the correlation assumption, the L&B method is based on two more important assumptions, which are uniform distribution within stratum, and equal coefficients of variance in each stratum of the auxiliary attribute. While these three assumptions lead to a much simpler method, which does not require iteration. According to L&B, a L-stratum stratification on an auxiliary attribute is determined by the following stratum boundaries

$$k_h = ar^h, (h = 0, 1, \dots, L)$$

Dalenius and Hodges (D&H): As in the L&B method, the basic assumption of the D&H method is the existence of strong correlation between the auxiliary attribute and the unknown attribute. Furthermore, the D&H method also critically depends on the assumption that the distribution of the auxiliary attribute in each stratum is approximately uniform.

No Stratification (Random): This is a very simple method which does not stratify the dataset. Instead, we just select a random sample from the entire dataset and perform the estimation.

We conduct two experiments to compare our method HarmonyAdp with the these three methods. The first experiment is as follows. To answer low selectivity queries on the deep web, we will obviously prefer a method that can be more effective in obtaining records satisfying the selection predicate (refered to as *useful samples*). This

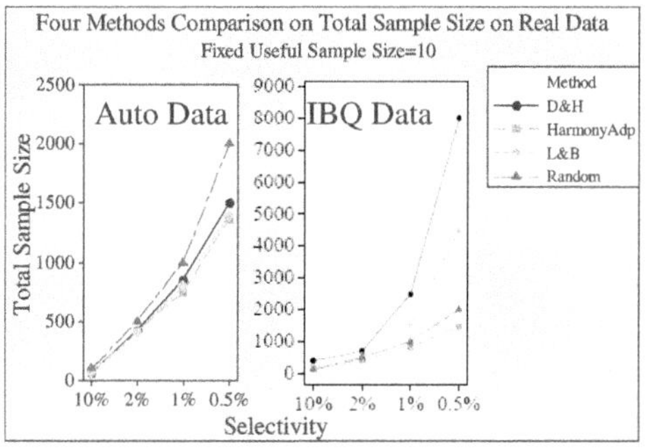

Figure 9: Four Methods Comparison on Total Sample Size on Real World Data

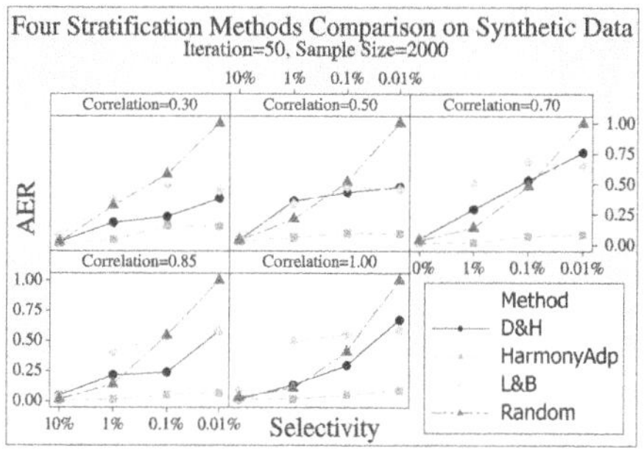

Figure 10: Four Methods Comparison on AER on Synthetic Data

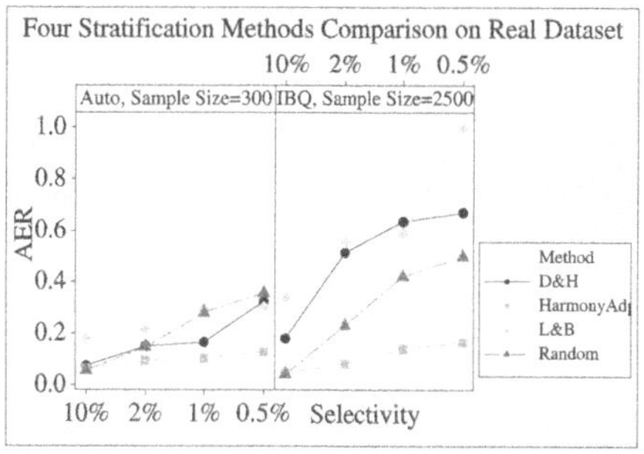

Figure 11: Four Methods Comparison on AER on Real World Data

is because the number of useful samples directly impacts the accuracy of the estimation, and because total querying cost over the deep web needs to be minimized. Therefore, in this experiment, we compare the *total number of samples* that need to be selected (i.e., the sampling cost involved), to obtain the same number of *useful samples*, across the four methods. For HarmonyAdp, the total number of samples includes the samples used in training our model and query estimation. Our goal is to show that HarmonyAdp is a useful method despite the sampling involved while training our model.

Figure 8 shows the results on synthetic data. Here, the number of useful samples obtained is fixed at 25. The Y-axis in Figure 8 is in logarithmic scale. We have the following observations. First, for *simpler* queries (10% selectivity), all four methods use nearly the same number of total samples to obtain 25 useful samples. Second, for more *challenging* queries (selectivity smaller than 10%), our algorithm only needs about one-tenth of the total number of samples to achieve the same number of useful samples. Third, with reducing selectivity of the queries, L&B, D&H, and the Random method have a linear increase in the total number of samples needed. However, the increase in total number of required samples is very small for our method. This shows that our stratification method is very effective for selecting samples satisfying the low selectivity clause. Figure 9 shows the results on real world data. For the `Auto` and `IBQ` dataset, the number of useful samples is fixed to be 10 in the experiment. We observe a similar pattern, i.e., our method always uses the least number of total samples to obtain a specified number of useful samples. Finally, in this experiment, we also compared the AER values achieved by the four methods when the number of useful samples is the same. As expected, all four methods obtain similar accuracy when aggregation is performed over the same number of useful samples.

In the second experiment, we compare the estimation accuracy obtained from the four methods when the *total sample size* is fixed to be the same for the four methods. For our method, the total sample size includes the samples used in training the harmony search model and the samples used in estimating query results. However, once the search model has been trained, we obtain more useful samples from fewer total number of samples. Figure 10 shows the results on synthetic datasets. Here, the sample size is fixed to be 2000 for all four methods (2% of total data size). Specifically, for our HarmonyAdp method, among the 2000 samples, 1500 are used in training, and 500 are used in query estimation. For other three methods, all 2000 samples are used in query estimation. We have the following observations. First, when the query selectivity is 10%, all of the methods achieve good results, across different correlation levels. Second, with a decrease in query selectivity, L&B, D&H and Random methods degrade severely, but our method only incurs a small reduction in accuracy. For 0.1% selectivity queries, HarmonyAdp outperforms other three method by a factor of 5 on the average. For 0.01% selectivity queries, the error rate of our method is consistently lower than 18%. Figure 11 shows the results on two real world datasets. For the `Auto` dataset, the sample size is fixed to be 300 (7% of the entire data) for all methods. Among these 300 samples, 50 samples are used for query estimation in HarmonyAdp. For the `IBQ` dataset, the sample size is fixed to be 2500 (10% of the entire data), and among the 2500 samples, 500 samples are used for query estimation in HarmonyAdp. From Figure 11, we can observe a similar pattern as in Figure 10.

It may be argued that comparison of our method with L&B and D&H methods is not a very fair one, since the latter two methods involve assumptions which did not hold true on these datasets. Similarly, random sampling is a very simple method, and it is not surprising that it does not do well on low selectivity queries. The primary conclusion, however, that we will like to make from our experiments is as follows. HarmonyAdp is the first effective method for answering low selectivity queries on data sources that allow only limited data accesses, and where the queriable attribute is not necessarily highly correlated with the selectivity attribute. Our experiments have demonstrated the robustness of our method when selectivity and/or correlation are decreased.

6. RELATED WORK

We now compare our work with existing work on related topics, including optimal stratification, answering queries over the deep web, answering low selectivity queries, and adaptive harmony search.

Optimal Stratification: The method of choosing the best boundaries that make strata internally homogenous is known as optimum stratification. Ideally, stratification should be done using the survey variable y. However, in many cases, y is unknown, and as a result, many stratification methods have been proposed to perform stratification based on an auxiliary variable x. The well-known cumulative root frequency method of stratum construction (D&H method), derived by Dalenius and Hodges [9, 10], depends critically on the assumption that the distribution of x in each stratum is approximate uniform. To further simplify the computation of the D&H method, Ekman [14] and Gunning and Horgan [16] have both proposed several other approximation methods. These methods are based on the Dalenius and Hodges's assumption, and even add more assumptions on the auxiliary variable x. As we have experimentally shown and analyzed in Section 5.4, these existing methods are not appropriate for our problem because of the following two reasons. First, when the correlation between the x and y is weak, the assumptions in these methods do not hold true. Second, these methods are not designed for low selectivity queries. There are stratification methods proposed for data following certain distribution, such as uniform and right triangular distributions [22], exponential [23] and triangular distribution [24]. However, in our problem, we need to handle dataset with an arbitrary and/or unknown distribution.

Answering Database (Low Selectivity) Queries Using Sampling: Answering database queries by sampling has been extensively studied in the literature [18, 27]. Chaudhuri *et al* [5, 3, 4] have conducted extensive studies on approximate aggregation queries answering using stratification. The approaches include partitioning the database into *fundamental regions* [4, 5] and generating outlier indexing [3]. The above approaches cannot be applied in the deep web scenario, as they need to know critical statistics or distribution about dataset. With support for only limited data accesses, as is the case on the deep web, this is not possible. Joshi *et al* designed sampling methods and estimators for low selectivity queries [20] using Bayesian-Neyman Allocation. The key difference between our work and their approach is that they only focus on allocating samples into stratum, whereas we also consider determining optimum stratification.

Answering Queries Over the Deep Web: The prominent work on deep web sampling and query answering includes online aggregation [17, 19] and hidden web sampler developed by Dasgupta *et al.* [13, 11]. In online aggregation, approximate answers for aggregation queries are generated and further refined when all data has been processed. Jermaine *et al* [19] proposed a scalable online aggregation method within the DBO engine. The hidden web sampler focuses on generating true random samples from the deep web. Recently, Dasgupta *et al* [12] developed a unbiased estimator for size and other aggregates over hidden web data sources. Their approach could use a small number of queries to produce unbiased estimates with a small variance. Joshi *et al* designed sampling methods and estimators for subset-based queries [21]. The key distinct aspect of our work is that we focus on handling low selectivity aggregation queries.

7. CONCLUSION

In this paper, we have studied the problem of estimating the result of an aggregation query with low selectivity on data sources that only support limited data access. The key challenge we have addressed is of stratification when the selective attribute is not directly queriable. Thus, we need to perform stratification on a queriable attribute, which may not necessarily be highly correlated with the selectivity attribute. We have developed a guided search method, which is motivated by the recently developed Harmony search model, to stratify the queriable attribute in a way that useful samples for a low selectivity query can be effectively obtained.

We have evaluated our method using both synthetic and real datasets. We show that the query estimation result using the stratification generated from our approach have a high accuracy (about 95%) for low selectivity queries, while querying only 2% of the data. The accuracy achieved using our method is higher than 85% even for extremely low selectivity queries (selectivity 0.01%). Furthermore, our method is robust even when the correlation between the auxiliary attribute and the selective attribute is relatively low.

8. REFERENCES

[1] A.J.Brookes. The Essence of SNPs. *Gene*, 234:177–186, 1999.

[2] James O. Berger. *Statistical Decision Theory and Bayesian Analysis*. Springer-Verlag, 1985.

[3] Surajit Chaudhuri, Gautam Das, Mayur Datar, Rajeev Motwani, and Vivek Narasayya. Overcoming limitations of sampling for aggregation queries. In *Proceedings of ICDE 1999*, pages 534–542, 1999.

[4] Surajit Chaudhuri, Gautam Das, and Vivek Narasayya. A robust, optimization-based approach for approximate answering of aggregate queries. In *Proceedings of SIGMOD 2001*, pages 295–306, 2001.

[5] Surajit Chaudhuri, Gautam Das, and Vivek Narasayya. Optimized Stratified Sampling for Approximate Query Processing. *ACM Transactions on Database Systems*, 32, 2007.

[6] Surajit Chaudhuri and Kyuseok Shim. Query optimization in the presence of foreign functions. In *VLDB '93: Proceedings of the 19th International Conference on Very Large Data Bases*, pages 529–542, San Francisco, CA, USA, 1993. Morgan Kaufmann Publishers Inc.

[7] W.G. Cochran. *Sampling Techniques*. New York: Wiley, 1977.

[8] T. Dalenius. The Problem of Optimum Stratification. *Skandinavisk Aktuarietidskrift*, pages 203–213, 1950.

[9] T. Dalenius and J. L. Hodges. The Choice of Stratification Points. *Skandinavisk Aktuarietidskrift*, pages 198–203, 1957.

[10] T. Dalenius and J. L. Hodges. Minimum Variance Stratification. *Journal of the American Statistical Association*, 54:88–101, 1959.

[11] Arjun Dasgupta, Gautam Das, and Heikki Mannila. Leveraging count information in sampling hidden databases. In *Proceedings of ICDE 2009*, pages 329–340, 2009.

[12] Arjun Dasgupta, Xin Jin, Bradley Jewell, Nan Zhang, and Gautam Das. Unbiased estimation of size and other aggregates over hidden web databases. In *Proceedings of SIGMOD 2010*, pages 855–866, 2010.

[13] Arjun Dasgupta, Nan Zhang, and Gautam Das. A random walk approach to sampling hidden databases. In *Proceedings of SIGMOD 2007*, pages 629–640, 2007.

[14] G. Ekman. An Approximation Useful in Univariate Stratification. *The Annals of Mathematical Statistics*, 30:219–229, 1959.

[15] Z. W. Geem, J. H. Kim, and G. V. Loganathan. Harmony Search Optimization: Application to Pipe Network Design. *International Journal of Model Simulation*, 22:125–133, 2002.

[16] P. Gunning and J. M. Horgan. A New Algorithm for the Construction of Stratum Boundaries in Skewed Populations. *Survey Methodology*, 30:159–166, 2004.

[17] Joseph M. Hellerstein, Peter J. Haas, and Helen J. Wang. Online aggregation. In *Proceedings of SIGMOD 1997*, 1997.

[18] W.-C. Hou, G. Ozsoyoglu, and B. K. Taneja. Statistical estimators for relational algebra expressions. In *Proceedings of PODS 1988*, pages 276–287, 1988.

[19] Christopher Jermaine, Subramaniam Arumugam, Abhijit Pol, and Alin Dobra. Scalable approximate query processing with the dbo engine. In *Proceedings of SIGMOD 2007*, pages 725–736, 2007.

[20] Shantanu Joshi and Christopher Jermaine. Robust stratified sampling plans for low selectivity queries. In *Proceedings of ICDE 2008*, pages 199–208, 2008.

[21] Shantanu Joshi and Christopher Jermaine. Sampling-Based Estimators for Subset-Based Queries. *The VLDB Journal*, 18:181–202, 2009.

[22] E. A. Khan, M. G. M. Khan, and M. J. Ahsan. Optimum Stratification: A Mathematical Programming Approach. *Calcutta Statistical Association Bulletin*, 52:323–333, 2002.

[23] M. G. M. Khan and M. J. Ahsan. Optimum Stratification for Exponential Study Variable under Neyman Allocation. *Journal of Indian Soc Agric Stats*, 59:146–150, 2005.

[24] M. G. M. Khan, N. Nand, and N. Ahmad. Determining the Optimum Strata Boundary Points Using Dynamic Programming. *Survey Methodology*, 34:205–214, 2008.

[25] Kang Seok Lee and Zong Woo Geem. A New Meta-Heuristic Algorithm for Continuous Engineering Optimization: Harmony Search Theory and Practice. *Computer Methods in Applied Mechanics and Engineering*, 194:3902–3933, 2004.

[26] M. Mahdavi, M. Fesanghary, and E. Damangir. An Improved Harmony Search Algorithm for Solving Optimizatoin Problems. *Applied Mathematics and Computation*, 188:1567–1579, 2007.

[27] F. Olken. *Random Sampling from Databases*. PhD thesis, 1993.

[28] Anand Rajaraman, Yehoshua Sagiv, and Jeffrey D. Ullman. Answering queries using templates with binding patterns (extended abstract). In *PODS '95: Proceedings of the fourteenth ACM SIGACT-SIGMOD-SIGART symposium on Principles of database systems*, pages 105–112, New York, NY, USA, 1995. ACM.

[29] John A. Rice. *Mathematical Statistics and Data Analysis*. Duxbury Press, 1995.

Finding Information Nebula over Large Networks

Lijun Chang, Jeffrey Xu Yu, Lu Qin, Yuanyuan Zhu
The Chinese University of Hong Kong
Hong Kong, China
{ljchang,yu,lqin,yyzhu}@se.cuhk.edu.hk

Haixun Wang
Microsoft Research Asia
Beijing, China
haixunw@microsoft.com

ABSTRACT

Social and information networks have been extensively studied over years. In this paper, we concentrate ourselves on a large information network that is composed of entities and relationships, where entities are associated with sets of keyword terms (kterms) to specify what they are, and relationships describe the link structure among entities which can be very complex. Our work is motivated but is different from the existing works that find a best subgraph to describe how user-specified entities are connected. We compute information nebula (cloud) which is a set of top-K kterms P that are most correlated to a set of user-specified kterms Q, over a large information network. Our goal is to find how kterms are correlated given the complex information network among entities. The information nebula computing requests us to take all possible kterms into consideration for the top-K kterms selection, and needs to measure the similarity between kterms by considering all possible subgraphs that connect them instead of the best single one. In this work, we compute information nebula using a global structural-context similarity, and our similarity measure is independent of connection subgraphs. To the best of our knowledge, among the link-based similarity methods, none of the existing work considers similarity between two sets of nodes or two kterms. We propose new algorithms to find top-K kterms P for a given set of kterms Q based on the global structural-context similarity, without computing all the similarity scores of kterms in the large information network. We performed extensive performance studies using large real datasets, and confirmed the effectiveness and efficiency of our approach.

Categories and Subject Descriptors

H.3 [**Information Storage and Retrieval**]: Miscellaneous

General Terms

Design, Management, Performance

1. INTRODUCTION

Social and information systems analysis plays an important role in modern knowledge discovery [12, 16, 14] to extract information and/or discover knowledge from large information networks [10]. In an information network, the two primary concepts are entities and relationships, where an entity is associated with information to describe the entity in a form of label, attributes, or a short description with a set of terms, and a relationship (or link) shows how two entities are related and the relationships among the entities can be very complex. Examples of information networks include the publication network [17], knowledge base [24], social networks [9], etc. In the literature, the existing work over information networks includes clustering, ranking, classification, data quality and search, as discussed in [10].

In this paper, we focus on an information network, $\mathcal{G}$, where entities are associated with a short description in a form of a set of terms, which we call keyword terms or simply kterms in short, that best describe the entities. We study a new problem on identifying a set of top-K kterms, P, that are most correlated to a set of user-specified kterms, Q, for $P \cap Q = \emptyset$, based on a goodness function such that every kterm in P is similar to every kterm in Q and the similarity is measured by a structural similarity over the complicated link structures among the entities in the large information network $\mathcal{G}$.

Our study is motivated by two reported studies [25, 14]. Tong and Faloutsos [25] and Kasneci et al. [14] find an informative connection subgraph (*CSG*) which best explains the relationships among a set of user-specified entities in an information network $\mathcal{G}$. Both the approaches effectively identify such informative connection subgraph following a goodness function. The identified subgraph is the best of many possible subgraphs to explain the relationships among user-specified entities, and the information (e.g. the kterms in our context) associated with entities is simply ignored. In our work, we study the relationships between kterms at the kterm level rather than at the entity level. Instead of finding a single best subgraph to explain the connectivities among entities, we find a set of top-K kterms P by exploring all possible subgraphs among entities that can possibly connect every kterm in P to every kterm in Q. It is worth noting that in [25, 14], the entities are explicitly given to identify the subgraph to explain the set of entities. In our problem, the kterms are given, there exist a large number of entities that may use some of kterms to describe themselves, and such entities may appear anywhere in the large information network $\mathcal{G}$. Our approach can be a complement of [25, 14].

Consider the semantic knowledge base *YAGO* (`http://www.mpi-inf.mpg.de/yago-naga/yago/`), which is a heterogeneous information network [10], an excerpt is shown in Fig. 1. Each node represents an entity, such as, a person, an organization, a country, etc. Based on the link structure among entities, suppose a user wants to know what the best is to connect {"Albert_Einstein", "Walther_Bothe"}. The *CSG* approach returns a subgraph induced

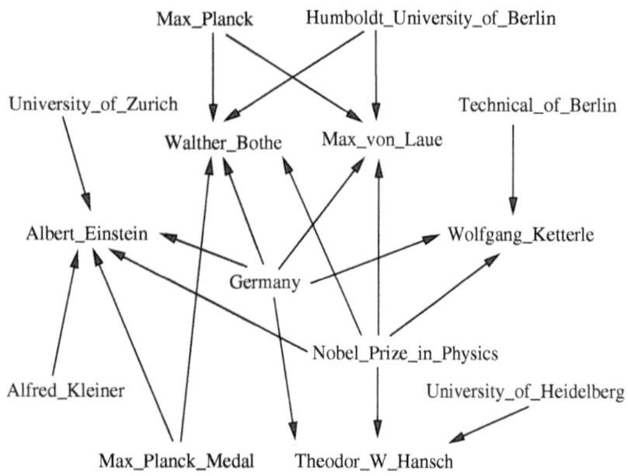

Figure 1: An Excerpt from *YAGO*

by the five nodes, "Albert_Einstein", "Walther_Bothe", "Germany", "Max_Planck_Medal", and "Nobel_Prize_in_Physics", which indicates that both "Albert_Einstein" and "Walther_Bothe" are from "Germany", and they are both Max Planck Medal and Nobel Prize winners. However, suppose a user wants to find similar scientists like $Q = \{$"Albert_Einstein", "Walther_Bothe"$\}$, the *CSG* approach cannot find "Wolfgang_Ketterle" and "Max_von_Laue", since the *CSG* is designed to identify the best subgraph to explain given entities. We consider $\{$"Albert_Einstein", "Walther_Bothe"$\}$ as kterms to describe two entities, and attempt to find the top-K kterms that are similar to $\{$"Albert_Einstein", "Walther_Bothe"$\}$ which include "Wolfgang_Ketterle" and "Max_von_Laue". Note that in this example, since all entities have unique labels (kterms), there are no obvious differences between entities and kterms. In other words, in this example, our goal can be seen as to find most related entities connected to $\{$"Albert_Einstein", "Walther_Bothe"$\}$.

Consider an information network, *DBLP-CP*, which is an induced subgraph of the *DBLP* dataset (`http://www.informatik.uni-trier.de/~ley/db/`). In *DBLP-CP*, a node represents a paper, and each edge reflects a citation relationship between two papers. A subgraph of *DBLP-CP* is shown in Fig. 2, e.g., $p_1, \cdots, p_{18}$ represents 18 papers, and the edge between p_2 and p_3 indicates that paper p_3 is cited by paper p_2. Each node is described using a set of kterms, e.g., "histogram" and "wavelet" as shown in Fig. 2(a), and the node p_{11} contains kterms "selectivity" and "histogram". Suppose a new graduate student wants to study a research topic related to data compression by submitting a query $Q = \{$"histogram", "wavelet"$\}$, which are known as two of the basic methods in data compression, and hopes to identify highly correlated kterms to Q. Under this scenario, each kterm in Q appears in several nodes. The top-3 kterm to be identified are $\{$"selectivity","practicality", "optimality"$\}$. It is worth noting that there are a large number of occurrence of kterms including "selectivity", "practicality", "optimality", as well as others. All such occurrences may be related to $Q = \{$"histogram", "wavelet"$\}$ via possible connections in the underneath information network. It is almost impossible to enumerate all such possible subgraphs with all possible combination of kterms, in order to compute the top-K kterms. For this example, the two approaches [25, 14] cannot be effectively used since the entities are not explicitly specified.

The main contributions of this paper are summarized below. First, we study a new problem of identifying top-K correlated kterms, P, in an information network $\mathcal{G}$ for a set of user-specified kterms Q. All possible kterms exhibited in $\mathcal{G}$ are taken into consideration for the top-K selection. We compute the top-K correlated kterms P regarding Q based on a global structural-context similarity between nodes in $\mathcal{G}$ without enumerating connection subgraphs. It is important to note that our approach is to measure correlated kterms using a global structural-context similarity but is independent of connection subgraphs. Among the link-based similarity measures [11, 13, 23], none of them consider similarity between two sets of nodes like we do in this work. Second, we propose two new top-K algorithms using the framework of the threshold algorithm [4, 5]. We study how to obtain sorted lists in different ways and how to optimize the threshold algorithms. Our algorithms avoid computing all pairs similarities, which is hard in large networks. Third, we propose an algorithm to build index for computing correlation scores, which optimizes the existing algorithm in both index construction time and index size. And we give a block-based index which reduces the I/O cost and memory requirement to hold the index in memory. Finally, we conducted extensive performance studies using large real datasets, and confirmed the effectiveness and efficiency of our approach.

ID	Labels
p_4	balancing *histogram optimality practicality* $\cdots$
p_7	join *synopses* approximate query answering $\cdots$
p_9	random sampling *histogram* construction $\cdots$
p_{10}	*wavelet histograms selectivity* estimation $\cdots$
p_{11}	*selectivity* estimation compressed *histogram* $\cdots$
p_{12}	*histogram* approximation set-valued $\cdots$
p_{16}	comparison *selectivity* estimators $\cdots$

(a) Labels on Nodes

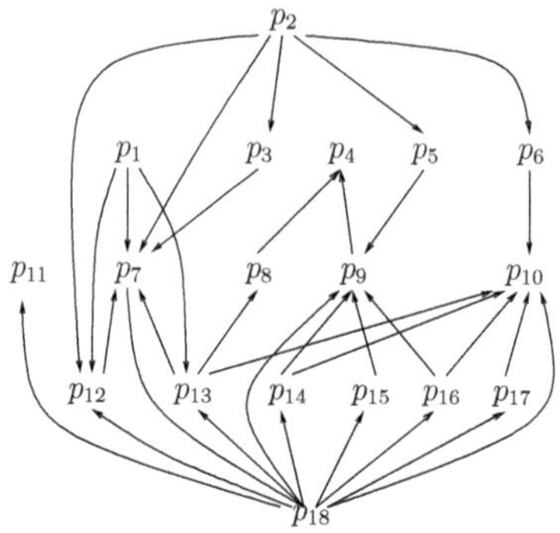

(b) Link Structure

Figure 2: A Subgraph from *DBLP-CP*

The remainder of the paper is organized as follows. We discuss our problem definition in Section 2. In Section 3, we give a solution overview. We discuss an extended network representation, and a naive algorithm to find correlated kterms for a query Q over extended network. We also give a 2-step solution with two algorithms, called CL-TOPK and IL-TOPK. The CL-TOPK algorithm is given in Section 4. The IL-TOPK is discussed in Section 5. We conducted experimental studies and discuss our findings in Section 6. The related works are discussed in Section 7. We conclude our paper in Section 8.

2. PROBLEM DEFINITION

We consider an information network, $\mathcal{G} = (\mathcal{V}, \mathcal{E}, \mathcal{K})$. $\mathcal{K}$ is the corpus of keyword terms (or simply kterms) contained in $\mathcal{G}$, and entities are described by kterms which are a small number yet important terms to describe entities. For a node $v \in \mathcal{V}$, let $\mathcal{K}(v)$ denote the set of kterms associated with v. Then $\mathcal{K} = \cup_{v \in \mathcal{V}} \mathcal{K}(v)$. For a kterm in the corpus, $t \in \mathcal{K}$, let $\mathcal{K}^{-1}(t)$ denote the set of nodes in $\mathcal{G}$ that contain t, i.e., $\mathcal{K}^{-1}()$ is the inverse of $\mathcal{K}()$. Note that, $|\mathcal{K}^{-1}(t)| \geq 1$ for any $t \in \mathcal{K}$, and $|\mathcal{K}^{-1}(t)| = 1$ if t is an entity. For a pair of nodes $u, v \in \mathcal{V}$, there may exist a directed edge from u to v, i.e., $\langle u, v \rangle \in \mathcal{E}$. Let $\mathcal{I}(v)$ denote the set of in-

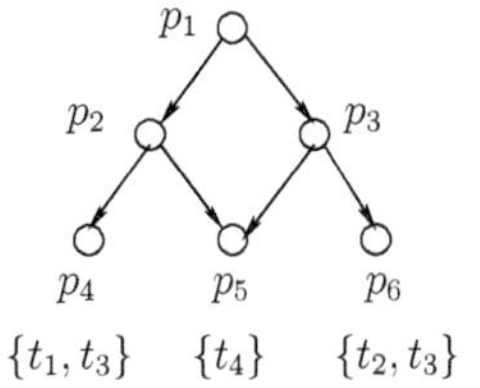

(a) Sample Network

node pair u, v	$sim(u, v)$
p_2, p_3	0.8
p_4, p_5	0.72
p_4, p_6	0.64
p_5, p_6	0.72

(b) SimRank Values

Figure 3: Information Network

neighbors of v, i.e., $\mathcal{I}(v) = \cup_{\langle u,v\rangle \in \mathcal{E}}\{u\}$, and $\mathcal{O}(v)$ denote the set of out-neighbors of v, i.e., $\mathcal{O}(v) = \cup_{\langle v,u\rangle \in \mathcal{E}}\{u\}$.

Example 2.1: Fig. 3(a) shows an information network $\mathcal{G}(\mathcal{V}, \mathcal{E}, \mathcal{K})$, where $\mathcal{V} = \{p_1, p_2, \cdots, p_6\}$. There are kterms contained in nodes p_4, p_5 and p_6, e.g., $\mathcal{K}(p_4) = \{t_1, t_3\}$, and $\mathcal{K}(p_5) = \{t_4\}$. The kterm corpus is $\mathcal{K} = \{t_1, t_2, t_3, t_4\}$. The set of nodes that contain t_3 is $\mathcal{K}^{-1}(t_3) = \{p_4, p_6\}$. The in-neighbors of p_5 is $\mathcal{I}(p_5) = \{p_2, p_3\}$. The out-neighbors of p_2 is $\mathcal{O}(p_2) = \{p_4, p_5\}$. □

We also consider entity names as one kind of kterms if they are explicitly given. For example, in Fig. 1, the entity names are listed, they are also treated as kterms, i.e., $\mathcal{K} = \{$"Albert_Einstein", "Germany", $\cdots\}$. For *DBLP-CP*, the kterms are explicitly given instead of entity names, i.e., $\mathcal{K} = \{$"histogram", "estimators", $\cdots\}$. In the following, we consider our problem in a kterm level instead of entity level.

Problem Statement: Given an information network $\mathcal{G}(\mathcal{V}, \mathcal{E}, \mathcal{K})$, a query Q consists of l kterms from $\mathcal{K}$, $\{k_1, \cdots, k_l\}$, and l weights corresponding to the kterms, $\{w_1, \cdots, w_l\}$, i.e., $Q = \{(k_1, w_1), \cdots, (k_l, w_l)\}$. Here, a weight is a positive value ≤ 1 and is 1 by default. The problem is to find an information nebula (cloud) P related to Q, which is a list of top-K kterms from $\mathcal{K}$ with $P \cap Q = \emptyset$.

In order to identify the top kterms similar to Q, we define a correlation score, $kcorr(Q, t)$, for each kterm $t \in \mathcal{K}$, which quantifies the similarity of t to Q in the information network $\mathcal{G}$.

$$kcorr(Q, t) = \sum_{(k_i, w_i) \in Q} w_i \cdot kcorr(k_i, t) \qquad (1)$$

where $kcorr(t_1, t_2)$ is a correlation score between two kterms t_1 and t_2 computed in $\mathcal{G}$.

In an information network, each kterm appears at nodes $\mathcal{K}^{-1}(t)$. Thus, the similarity between two kterms t_1 and t_2, $kcorr(t_1, t_2)$, should consider the similarity between the set of nodes containing t_1 and the set of nodes containing t_2. This is because that each similarity between one node from $\mathcal{K}^{-1}(t_1)$ and one node from $\mathcal{K}^{-1}(t_2)$ is a witness of the correlation between t_1 and t_2. Among the link-based similarity measures [11, 13, 23], none of them considers similarity between two sets of nodes. In SimRank [13], it defines the similarity between two nodes as an average of the similarities between their in-neighbors, which are two sets of nodes. Similarly, we define,

$$kcorr(t_1, t_2) = \frac{\sum_{i=1}^{|\mathcal{K}^{-1}(t_1)|} \sum_{j=1}^{|\mathcal{K}^{-1}(t_2)|} sim(\mathcal{K}_i^{-1}(t_1), \mathcal{K}_j^{-1}(t_2))}{|\mathcal{K}^{-1}(t_1)||\mathcal{K}^{-1}(t_2)|} \qquad (2)$$

Here, $\mathcal{K}^{-1}(t)$ denotes all nodes that contain the kterm t and $\mathcal{K}_i^{-1}(t)$ denotes the i-th element in $\mathcal{K}^{-1}(t)$. Also, $|\mathcal{K}^{-1}(t)|$ denotes the size of $\mathcal{K}^{-1}(t)$. Let $sim(u, v)$ denote a structural correlation measure of two nodes in a network, which will be discussed shortly. Eq. (2) computes the correlation between two kterms t_1 and t_2 by computing the average structural correlation ($sim(,)$) between every node that contains t_1 and every node that contains t_2 in the network $\mathcal{G}$.

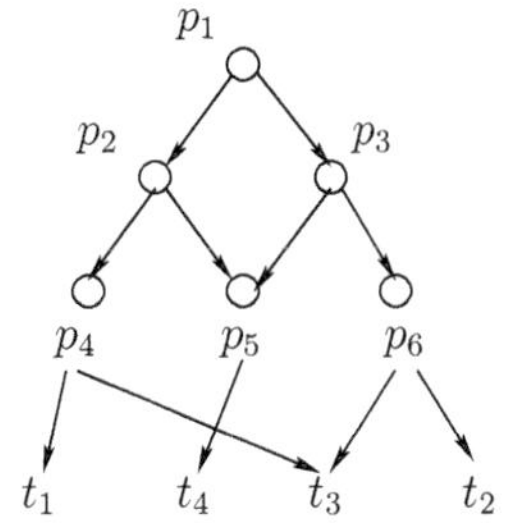

(a) Extended Network

node pair u, v	$sim(u, v)$
t_1, t_2	0.512
t_1, t_3	0.656
t_1, t_4	0.576
t_2, t_3	0.656
t_2, t_4	0.576
t_3, t_4	0.576

(b) SimRank Values

Figure 4: Extended Network

In this paper, for the similarity between two nodes u, v in $\mathcal{G}$, $sim(u, v)$ in Eq. (2), we adopt a structural-context similarity measure in the literature, SimRank [13]. SimRank is a popularly used measurement, which quantifies the similarity of a pair of nodes based on the link structures around these two nodes in the network. Let $sim(u, v)$ denote the similarity between two nodes u and v. u is always similar to itself, i.e., $sim(u, u) = 1$. Otherwise, it is defined in a recursive fashion as follows,

$$sim(u, v) = \frac{C}{|\mathcal{I}(u)||\mathcal{I}(v)|} \sum_{i=1}^{|\mathcal{I}(u)|} \sum_{j=1}^{|\mathcal{I}(v)|} sim(\mathcal{I}_i(u), \mathcal{I}_j(v)) \qquad (3)$$

where $\mathcal{I}_i(u)$ means the i-th element in $\mathcal{I}(u)$, $|\mathcal{I}(u)|$ is the number of elements in $\mathcal{I}(u)$, and C is a constant between 0 and 1. When the in-neighbor of u or v is empty, i.e., $\mathcal{I}(u) = \emptyset$ or $\mathcal{I}(v) = \emptyset$, Eq. (3) is not defined, and it is assigned with value 0. The SimRank value will always be between 0 and 1, i.e., $0 \leq sim(u, v) \leq 1, \forall u, v \in \mathcal{V}$. The SimRank values for node pairs in the network in Fig. 3(a) are shown in Fig. 3(b), where C is chosen as 0.8.

The similarity $sim(u, v)$ (see Eq. (3)) between two nodes in a network is defined as an average of the similarities of combinations of in-neighbors of u and in-neighbors of v. Meanwhile, our correlation score between two kterms, $kcorr(t_1, t_2)$ (see Eq. (2)), is also defined as an average of the similarities of combinations of nodes containing t_1 and nodes containing t_2. Thus, we can consider kterms in $\mathcal{K}$ as *kterm nodes*, and treat the nodes containing $t \in \mathcal{K}$, $\mathcal{K}^{-1}$, as in-neighbors of the kterm node t. Based on this, we can use the techniques of computing $sim(,)$ to compute our correlation score $kcorr(,)$. We define the *extended network*.

Extended Network: An extended network $\mathcal{G}^e = (\mathcal{V}^e, \mathcal{E}^e, \mathcal{K})$ is the information network $\mathcal{G} = (\mathcal{V}, \mathcal{E}, \mathcal{K})$ extended by kterm nodes and edges between kterm nodes and other nodes, i.e., $\mathcal{V}^e = \mathcal{V} \cup \mathcal{K}$ and $\mathcal{E}^e = \mathcal{E} \cup \{\langle v, t\rangle \mid t \in \mathcal{K} \wedge v \in \mathcal{K}^{-1}(t)\}$. For example, Fig. 4(a) shows the extended network of Fig. 3(a).

Although, in the extended network, each kterm in the query Q corresponds to exactly one node, the method used in [25] to compute a connection subgraph for a set of user-given nodes, cannot be applied to our extended network. The reasons are twofold. First, the methods in [25] work only on undirected graphs. However, if we treat the extended network as undirected, the similarity score between node-pairs may change dramatically. For example, in Fig. 4, the similarity of t_1 and t_2 is the lowest among all the kterm node-pairs. Based on the random walk with restart measure [25], $sim'(t_1, t_2)$ will be higher than $sim'(t_1, t_4)$ and $sim'(t_2, t_4)$, since p_4 and p_6 are now very similar to each other by the connection through t_3. Second, in order to find the global top-K correlated kterms, all connection subgraphs are needed, while [25] only finds one best connection subgraph.

In the extended network, we can compute $sim(,)$ for pairs of kterm nodes as shown in Fig. 4(b), using the techniques of computing SimRank. From Eq. (3) and Eq. (2), we know that $sim(t_1, t_2) = C \cdot kcorr(t_1, t_2)$ for any pair of kterm nodes. Then the correlation

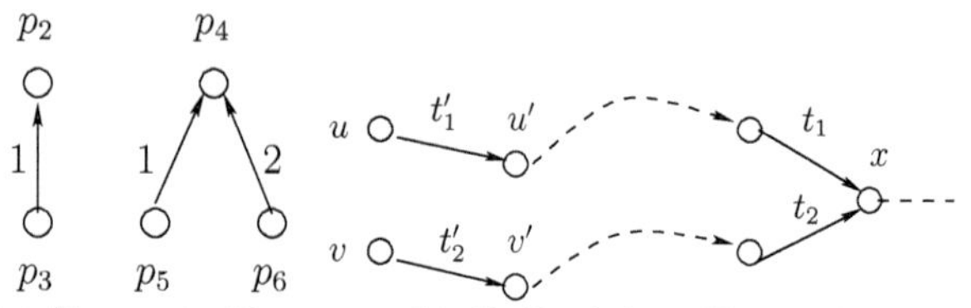

(a) Fingerprint Tree (b) SimRank from Fingerprint

Figure 5: Fingerprint and Compute SimRank

score of a kterm t to query Q can be rewritten as

$$kcorr(Q,t) = \frac{1}{C} \sum_{(k_i,w_i)\in Q} w_i \cdot sim(k_i,t) \tag{4}$$

With the extended network and Eq. (4), our approach finds top-K kterms based on $sim(,)$.

A Naive Algorithm: A naive algorithm, NAIVE, to compute top-K correlated kterms for a user-given query Q, can be designed to work as follows. It first gets the kterm corpus, $\mathcal{K}$, of $\mathcal{G}$, which consists of all the kterms appeared at nodes in $\mathcal{G}$. Then, it builds the extended network $\mathcal{G}^e$ as defined above. For each kterm t in $\mathcal{K}$ but not in the query Q, we compute a correlation score $kcorr(Q,t)$. Finally, the top-K correlated kterms can be identified.

In NAIVE, the most expensive computational cost comes from the $O(l \cdot |\mathcal{K}|)$ $sim(k_i,t)$ values computation, where l is the number of kterms in query Q. However, $|\mathcal{K}|$ can be of the same magnitude of $|\mathcal{V}|$, and it is impossible to compute the $O(l \cdot |\mathcal{K}|)$ $sim(k_i,t)$ values online, even for an information network with modest size, i.e., $n \geq 10,000$.

3. A 2-STEP APPROACH

The problem of computing SimRank for node-pairs in large networks is hard in general [21]. It is impractical to compute SimRank value for so many node-pairs on-line as illustrated in the NAIVE algorithm. We propose a two-step approach which makes use of the properties of fingerprint index [7]. In the first step, we process $\mathcal{G}$ (or more precisely fingerprint index of $\mathcal{G}$) to generate a set of sorted lists, $\mathcal{L} = \{L_1, L_2, \cdots\}$, where the definition of a list and the number of lists are determined by the specific algorithm. In the second step, we adopt the idea of *threshold algorithm* [4, 5] to compute top-K kterms over the set of sorted lists $\mathcal{L}$. The main issues are, how to define and obtain the set of lists $\mathcal{L}$, and how to optimize the threshold algorithm in our problem situation. We discuss the properties of fingerprint index in the following, and propose our algorithms in the next two sections. Note that the extended network is only used to illustrate the ideas, and does not need to be materialized.

3.1 Properties of Fingerprint

In the random surfer-pairs model, $sim(u,v)$ is equal to the expected first meeting distance of two independent random walks traveling backwardly starting from u and v respectively [13]. Let $\tau_{u,v}$ denote the random variable that is equal to the first meeting time of the random walks starting from u and v. $\tau_{u,v} = 0$ if $u = v$, and $\tau_{u,v} = \infty$ if the random walks do not meet. It shows in [13, 7] that, the equation $\mathbb{E}(C^{\tau_{u,v}}) = sim(u,v)$ holds.

Fogaras and Racz [7] generate a set of coalescing walks where each pair of walks will follow the same path after their first meeting time. With these coalescing walks, the equation $\mathbb{E}(C^{\tau_{u,v}}) = sim(u,v)$ still holds, since any pair of walks are independent until they first meet. A fingerprint index is designed to encode and store the set of random walks efficiently. Initially, a path of length zero is generated for each node in $\mathcal{G}$. Then it goes for L iterations to generate random walks up to length L. At each iteration i, all the paths travel one step backward by randomly choosing one of its in-neighbors. For all the paths that end at the same node, e.g., the paths starting from $u_1, \cdots, u_k$, a directed edge $\langle u_j, u_1\rangle$ with weight i is added to the fingerprint index for $2 \leq j \leq k$, and the paths starting from $u_2, \cdots, u_k$ are discarded. As an example, one fingerprint index for the network shown in Fig. 3(a) is shown in Fig. 5(a), the labels of the edges are their weights.

Let FPG denote the final graph obtained, it is a forest of rooted trees with edges towards the roots. FPG is of size $2n$, where $n = |\mathcal{V}|$. The FPG compactly encodes all-pairs first meeting time $\tau_{*,*}$, and $\tau_{u,v}$ can be computed using FPG. If u and v are in different trees in FPG, then $\tau_{u,v} = \infty$. Otherwise, u and v has one lowest common ancestor in FPG, let it be x, as shown in Fig. 5(b). Let $p(u,x)$ be the directed path from u to x, then $\tau_{u,v} = \max_{\langle a,b\rangle \in p(u,x)\cup p(v,x)} weight(\langle a,b\rangle)$, i.e., it is equal to the maximum weight among all the edges in the path from u or v to x. For example, in Fig. 5(a), $\tau_{p_2,p_5} = 0$, $\tau_{p_2,p_3} = \max\{0,1\} = 1$, and $\tau_{p_5,p_6} = \max\{1,2\} = 2$.

Note that, PSimRank [7], as a variant of SimRank, modifies SimRank by allowing random walks to meet with higher probability when they are close to each other, i.e., a pair of reverse random walks at u and v will advance to the same node in the next step with probability of Jaccard coefficient $\frac{\mathcal{I}(u)\cap\mathcal{I}(v)}{\mathcal{I}(u)\cup\mathcal{I}(v)}$ of their in-neighbors. PSimRank also has a recursive formula similar to Eq. (3) [7]. In our approach, we can use either SimRank or PSimRank as $sim(,)$.

4. A KTERM-LIST TOP-K ALGORITHM

From Eq. (4), we can see that the correlation score of a kterm t to query Q, $kcorr(Q,t)$, is a linear combination of $sim(k_1,t), \cdots, sim(k_l,t)$, and it is a monotonic function. Therefore, the general idea of threshold algorithm [4, 5] can be adopted here to compute top-K correlated kterms for a user-given query. We define a list for each query kterm $k_i \in Q$, $L_{k_i} = \{(t, sim(k_i,t)) \mid t \in \mathcal{K}\}$, which consists of kterms $t \in \mathcal{K}$ and their correlation scores to k_i. We call this *kterm-based lists*, as one list is defined for each query kterm. There are total l lists, $\mathcal{L} = \{L_{k_1}, \cdots, L_{k_l}\}$. The l lists should be computed in advance or on-demand. In order to adopt the idea of threshold algorithm, two interfaces are needed for each list. One is NEXT(L_{k_i}) which returns the next entry $(t, sim(k_i,t))$ in L_{k_i} with the highest $sim(k_i,t)$ value, and it corresponds to the sorted access of a list in the threshold algorithm. The other one is GET(L_{k_i}, t) which retrieves the $sim(k_i,t)$ value for kterm t, and it corresponds to the random access of a list in the threshold algorithm. Given l lists, and a sorted access interface (NEXT) and a random access interface (GET) for each list, the threshold algorithm [4, 5] can be used to find top-K correlated kterms for a user-given query.

CL-TOPK is shown in Alg. 1. Here, a priority queue $\mathcal{Q}$ is used to store potential results, each element in it is a kterm in $\mathcal{K}$ with its correlation score to the query Q as the key, i.e., $(t, sim(Q,t))$, and $\mathcal{Q}$ is a minimum queue so that the top element has the minimum key value. For simplicity, we access the l lists in a round-robin fashion, and each list has both sorted access interface (NEXT) and random access interface (GET). An upper bound of the correlation score of unseen kterm is maintained to terminate the algorithm earlier, denoted as $threshold$. We access the l lists in decreasing order, and an upper bound value of $sim(k_i,t)$ is maintained to be the last retrieved entry from L_{k_i} through interface NEXT, denoted as $L^u_{k_i}$. Then, the upper bound correlation score for any unseen kterms in $\mathcal{K}$ is bounded by the sum of $L^u_{k_i}$, i.e., $threshold = \sum_1^l L^u_{k_i}$. For each seen kterm $t \in \mathcal{K}$, its correlation score is computed based on

Algorithm 1 CL-TOPK $(\mathcal{G}, Q)$

Input: an information network $\mathcal{G}$, and a query Q.
Output: top-K kterms in $\mathcal{K}$ ranked with respect to $kcorr(Q, t)$.

Process $\mathcal{G}$ to generate l lists, $\mathcal{L} = \{L_{k_1}, \cdots, L_{k_l}\}$, and prepare $\text{NEXT}(L_{k_i})$ and $\text{GET}(L_{k_i}, t)$ for each list $L_{k_i} \in \mathcal{L}$;
Initialize a priority queue $\mathcal{Q}$ to be empty;
Initialize $threshold = \infty$;
while $\mathcal{Q}.\text{SIZE}() < K$ **or** $\mathcal{Q}.\text{TOP}() < threshold$ **do**
  Let L_{k_i} be the next list to be accessed, in a round robin fashion;
  $(t, sim(k_i, t)) \leftarrow \text{NEXT}(L_{k_i})$;
  for $j \leftarrow 1$ **to** l **and** $j \neq i$ **do**
    $sim(k_j, t) \leftarrow \text{GET}(L_{k_j}, t)$;
  Compute $kcorr(Q, t)$ based on Eq. (4);
  Update $\mathcal{Q}$ with $(t, kcorr(Q, t))$;
  Update $threshold$ with $sim(k_i, t)$;
Output the kterms in $\mathcal{Q}$;

Eq. (4), where $sim(k_i, t)$ for all l lists are retrieved through interface GET. The priority queue $\mathcal{Q}$ maintains the current top-K kterms among all the seen kterms. If the lowest correlation score in $\mathcal{Q}$ is no less than $threshold$, which means that none of the unseen kterms can have a correlation score larger than the lowest correlation score in $\mathcal{Q}$, then the K kterms stored in $\mathcal{Q}$ are guaranteed to be the top-K kterms in $\mathcal{K}$.

Note that, in CL-TOPK, it first generates l lists $\mathcal{L}$, then it works on $\mathcal{L}$ and discards the network $\mathcal{G}$. For each list $L_{k_i} \in \mathcal{L}$, the entries are accessed through two interfaces: NEXT and GET. To implement $\text{NEXT}(L_{k_i})$ and $\text{GET}(L_{k_i}, t)$, the entries $(t, sim(k_i, t)) \in L_{k_i}$ are ordered in non-increasing order according to $sim(k_i, t)$. For an information network with millions of nodes, no scalable algorithm in the literature can compute $sim(k_i, t)$ exactly for millions of pairs of nodes in practical time. Because the query kterms are contained in the kterm corpus, i.e., $Q \subset \mathcal{K}$, one may think of generating a list L_t for each $t \in \mathcal{K}$ off-line. However, it is impractical to generate and store the lists $\{L_t \mid t \in \mathcal{K}\}$, because it will take space $O(|\mathcal{K}|^2)$, where $\mathcal{K}$ contains millions of kterms.

To generate the l lists, $\mathcal{L} = \{L_{k_1}, \cdots, L_{k_l}\}$, efficiently on-line, we use an approximate algorithm to compute $sim(,)$, which is based on the fingerprint index as discussed in Section 3.1. It is worth noting that $sim(,)$ values computed using the fingerprint index are approximate values. Let N be the number of fingerprint indices (based on different random walks) used to improve the accuracy, denoted as $\text{FPG} = \{\text{FPG}_1, \cdots, \text{FPG}_N\}$, and $sim(,)$ can be computed as,

$$sim(u, v) = \frac{1}{N} \sum_{j=1}^{N} sim_j(u, v) \tag{5}$$

where $sim_j(u, v)$ is the $sim(,)$ value computed on FPG_j.

5. AN INDEX-LIST TOP-K ALGORITHM

In order to generate the lists, for each kterm $t \in \mathcal{K}$ and $k_i \in Q$, CL-TOPK needs to compute $sim(k_i, t) = \sum_{j=1}^{N} sim_j(k_i, t)$, which needs to access all the N copies of FPGS, thus it needs a lot of I/Os. In this section, we propose another formulation of lists $\mathcal{L}$, and an optimized top-k algorithm to efficiently find top-K correlated kterms directly from FPG.

In order to develop an efficient algorithm, we rewrite Eq. (4) by combining Eq. (5) as follows,

$$kcorr(Q, t) = \sum_{j=1}^{N} \frac{1}{C} \frac{1}{N} \sum_{(k_i, w_i) \in Q} w_i \cdot sim_j(k_i, t) \tag{6}$$

Algorithm 2 IL-TOPK (FPG, Q)

Input: fingerprint index $\text{FPG} = \{\text{FPG}_1, \cdots, \text{FPG}_N\}$ which is stored on disk, and a query Q.
Output: top-K kterms in $\mathcal{K}$ ranked with respect to $kcorr(Q, t)$.

1: PROCESS(FPG, Q);
2: Initialize a minimum priority queue $\mathcal{Q}$ to be empty;
3: Initialize $threshold = \infty$;
4: Initialize a sorted list ub to be empty;
5: **for** $i \leftarrow 1$ **to** N **do**
6:   $ub.\text{INSERT}((i, \infty))$;
7: **while** $\mathcal{Q}.\text{SIZE}() < K$ **or** $\mathcal{Q}.\text{TOP}() < threshold$ **do**
8:   $i \leftarrow ub.\text{FIRST}().id$;
9:   $(t, corr_i(Q, t)) \leftarrow \text{NEXT}(L_{F_i})$;
10:   **for** $j \leftarrow 1$ **to** N **and** $j \neq i$ **do**
11:     $kcorr_j(Q, t) \leftarrow \text{GET}(L_{F_j}, t)$;
12:   $kcorr(Q, t) \leftarrow \sum_{j=1}^{N} kcorr_j(Q, t)$;
13:   Update $\mathcal{Q}$ with $(t, kcorr(Q, t))$;
14:   Update $threshold$ with $kcorr_i(Q, t)$;
15:   Update the key of i in ub to be $kcorr_i(Q, t)$;
16: Output the kterms in $\mathcal{Q}$;

If we define a correlation score based on each FPG_j, such as,

$$kcorr_j(Q, t) = \frac{1}{C} \frac{1}{N} \sum_{(k_i, w_i) \in Q} w_i \cdot sim_j(k_i, t)$$

then, $kcorr(Q, t) = \sum_{j=1}^{N} kcorr_j(Q, t)$. Here, $kcorr(Q, t)$ is regarded as the global correlation score, and $kcorr_j(Q, t)$ (computed on FPG_j) is regarded as the local correlation score. We define a list for each FPG_j, denote as $L_{F_j} = \{(t, kcorr_j(Q, t)) \mid t \in \mathcal{K}\}$, which consists of kterms t and their local correlation scores $kcorr_j(Q, t)$ computed on FPG_j. We call this *index-based lists*, as one list is generated for each fingerprint index FPG_j. There are total N lists, i.e., $\mathcal{L} = \{L_{F_1}, \cdots, L_{F_N}\}$. In each list L_{F_j}, the entries $(t, kcorr_j(Q, t))$ are ordered according to $kcorr_j(Q, t)$. It is worth noting that, for each list L_{F_j}, only those kterms t with non-zero $kcorr_j(Q, t)$ values are of interest, the size of which usually is not large (e.g., in the order of hundreds to thousands). The interfaces for sorted access and random access of list L_{F_j} are $\text{NEXT}(L_{F_j})$ and $\text{GET}(L_{F_j}, t)$, respectively, where $\text{NEXT}(L_{F_j})$ gets the next entry $(t, kcorr_j(Q, t))$ from L_{F_j}, and $\text{GET}(L_{F_j}, t)$ retrieves the local correlation score of t computed on FPG_j.

The algorithm to compute top-K correlated kterms for a user-given query is shown in Alg. 2 (IL-TOPK). In IL-TOPK, Line 1, PROCESS(FPG, Q) generates N sorted lists, $\mathcal{L} = \{L_{F_1}, \cdots, L_{F_N}\}$ which will be discussed shortly. A sorted list ub is used to store the upper bound $kcorr_i(Q, t)$ for each list L_{F_i}. Each entry of ub consists of two fields, id and key, where id denote the list id and key denote the upper bound of the corresponding list. Entries in ub are sorted in deceasing order of key. Here, ub is used to determine the list on which the next sorted access should be. Different from CL-TOPK which accesses the l kterm-based lists in a round-robin fashion, we access the index-based list with highest upper bound in IL-TOPK, i.e., $ub.\text{FIRST}().id$. This is based on the fact that there are N lists in IL-TOPK, which is much larger than that of l lists in CL-TOPK, i.e., $N \gg l$. Thus, we can access the list that is more likely to have answers.

Theorem 5.1: *Let m denote the number of distinct kterms processed, i.e., it is the number of calls of* NEXT, *the time complexity of* IL-TOPK *is $O(m \cdot (N + \log K))$; the space complexity of* IL-TOPK *is $O(K + N)$.* □

Proof Sketch: For each kterm processed (Lines 9-12), it takes $O(N)$ time to compute $kcorr(Q, t)$. Here, we assume a hash index

Algorithm 3 OPTFINGERPRINT $(\mathcal{G}, N, L)$

Input: an extended network $\mathcal{G}$, N indicates the number of FPGs, and L indicates the length of random walks.
Output: N fingerprint graphs, $\text{FPG}_1, \cdots, \text{FPG}_N$.

1: **for** $i \leftarrow 1$ **to** N **do**
2:   Initialize FPG_i as $|\mathcal{K}|$ isolated nodes $t_1, \cdots, t_{|\mathcal{K}|}$;
3:   **for each** $t \in \mathcal{K}$ **do**
4:     $PathEnd[t] \leftarrow t$;
5:   **for** $j \leftarrow 1$ **to** L **do**
6:     Generate a random permutation δ with the n nodes in $\mathcal{V}$;
7:     **for each** $t \in \mathcal{K}$ **with** $PathEnd[t] \neq$ "stopped" **do**
8:       $PathEnd[t] \leftarrow \text{argmin}_{u \in \mathcal{I}(PathEnd[t])} \delta(u)$;
9:     **for each** set of nodes with the same $PathEnd$, $u_1, \cdots, u_k$ **do**
10:       Add edges $\langle u_2, u_1 \rangle, \cdots, \langle u_k, u_1 \rangle$ with weights j to FPG_i;
11:       Set $PathEnd[u_2], \cdots, PathEnd[u_k]$ to be "stopped";

is used to implement GET. Updating $\mathcal{Q}$ (Line 13) takes $O(\log K)$ time, because the size of $\mathcal{Q}$ is at most K. Updating ub (Line 15) takes $O(N)$ time, because ub is of size N. So the total time complexity is $O(m \cdot (N + \log K))$.

For the space complexity, IL-TOPK maintains a priority queue $\mathcal{Q}$ of size at most K, and a priority queue ub of size N. So it totally takes space $O(K + N)$. □

5.1 The IL-TOPK Implementation Details

In the following, we discuss some IL-TOPK implementation details. First, we show an optimization of the fingerprint index for our problem, which reduces both the index construction time and index size. We propose a general index structure to effectively store the N copies of the fingerprint index on disk. We give an algorithm to generate the N lists L_{F_i} efficiently based on our optimized fingerprint index.

Optimized Fingerprint: In PSimRank, to extend the random walks one step backwardly, instead of choosing one of its in-neighbors independently for all the paths, it first generates an independent random permutation δ on the nodes of $\mathcal{G}$. Then, the random in-neighbor for v is chosen as $\text{argmin}_{u \in \mathcal{I}(v)} \delta(u)$. We show an algorithm, called OPTFINGERPRINT, that directly generates the FPG on $\mathcal{G}$ efficiently in Alg. 3. Initially, FPG_i is initialized as $|\mathcal{K}|$ isolated nodes (Line 2). To expand the paths one step backwardly (Lines 7-8), a random permutation is generated first (Line 6). OPTFINGERPRINT generates only $|\mathcal{K}|$ random walks, while a naive generation of FPG on an extended network needs to generate $|\mathcal{K}| + |\mathcal{V}|$ random walks. With Alg. 3, the FPG generated is of size $2|\mathcal{K}|$. It is smaller than the size of FPG on $\mathcal{G}^e$, which is $2 \cdot (|\mathcal{K}| + |\mathcal{V}|)$. FPG generated by OPTFINGERPRINT contains all the information needed for our algorithm.

A New Block-Based Index Structure: With N copies of FPGs, the total index size is $O(N|\mathcal{K}|)$, where $|\mathcal{K}|$ is of same magnitude of $|\mathcal{V}|$. So it can not completely reside in main memory, we show data structures to store them on disk so that it can be efficiently retrieved and processed by the following query answering algorithms. Recall that, each FPG is a forest of rooted trees. We call a connected tree in a FPG as a *block*, denote as B, since the nodes in it should be stored in consecutive blocks on disk as they will be retrieved as a unit by any processing algorithm. Let the set of FPGs be $\text{FPG}_1, \cdots, \text{FPG}_N$. The index structure consists of *Global index*, where there exists only one for the whole index, and *In-block index*, where there exists one for each block, see Table 1.

For the *Global index*, it has two parts: a mapping between kterms and kterm ids (*kid*); and an inverted list of block ids (*bid*) for each kterm. Because kterms are strings, and they are more costly to store and process than integers, a unique *kid* is used to identify each kterm. In the beginning of query processing, all the input kterms are transformed to their *kids*. After the processing, the resulting *kids* are transformed to the corresponding kterms and output to users. Usually, the *kids* are from the corpus $\{1, 2, \cdots, |\mathcal{K}|\}$, where $|\mathcal{K}|$ is the size of the kterm corpus. For example, in Table 1, the kterm "algebra" has *kid* 47, and the kterm "algorithm" has *kid* 48.

Algorithm 4 PROCESS(FPG, Q)

Input: optimized fingerprint index $\text{FPG} = \{\text{FPG}_1, \cdots, \text{FPG}_N\}$ which is stored on disk, and a query Q.
Output: N sorted list $L_{F_1}, \cdots, L_{F_N}$.

1: Find and load l inverted lists *kid* → *bids* into main memory;
2: **for** $i \leftarrow 1$ **to** N **do**
3:   Let $\mathcal{B}$ be the set of *bids* belonging to FPG_i, in the l inverted lists;
4:   $L_{F_i} \leftarrow \emptyset$;
5:   **for each** $bid \in \mathcal{B}$ **do**
6:     Load the block of FPG_i that has block id bid into main memory, denote it as B;
7:     **for each** $t \in B$ **do**
8:       Compute $kcorr_i(Q, t)$ and insert $(t, kcorr_i(Q, t))$ into L_{F_i};
9:   Sort L_{F_i} to build a sorted list with $kcorr_i(Q, t)$ as the key;
10: Initialize a pointer for each list to point to the first entry;

Global index (one for the whole index)	
kterm ↔ *kid*	*kid* → *bids*
...	...
"algebra" ↔ 47	$47 \rightarrow \{(1, 10), (2, 15), \cdots, (N, 6)\}$
"algorithm" ↔ 48	$48 \rightarrow \{(1, 11), (2, 12), \cdots, (N, 17)\}$
...	...
"keyword" ↔ 1030	$1030 \rightarrow \{(1, 10), (2, 12), \cdots, (N, 8)\}$
...	...
In-block index (one for each block)	
kid ↔ *iid*	$\langle u, v \rangle, weight(\langle u, v \rangle)$
...	...
47 ↔ 10	$\langle 8, 10 \rangle, 3$
49 ↔ 11	$\langle 13, 11 \rangle, 2$
...	...
1280 ↔ 138	$\langle 7, 138 \rangle, 5$
...	...

Table 1: Example of Index Structure for Disk Store

In order to fast retrieve the corresponding block in each FPG_i that contains a specific kterm, an inverted list is built for each *kid*. Note that, a *kid* is contained in exactly one block in each FPG_i, and only the kterms in these blocks have non-zero correlation scores with it. For example, in Table 1, the kterm "algebra" with *kid* 47 has an inverted list, $\{(1, 10), (2, 15), \cdots, (N, 6)\}$, which means that the block id (*bid*) in each FPG_i that contains kterm "algebra" are, *bid* 10 in FPG_1, *bid* 15 in FPG_2, and *bid* 6 in FPG_N.

For each block $B \in \bigcup_{i=1}^{N} \text{FPG}_i$, we build an in-block index so that it can be processed efficiently. Recall that, each block is a reversed tree that all edges direct to the root. Furthermore, in a block B, the kterms contained are not with consecutive *kids*. In order to store and process a tree in memory effectively and efficiently, the nodes should be mapped to consecutive integers starting from 1. So we store a mapping between kterm ids (*kids*) and in-block ids (*iids*). Then, each edge is stored as *iid* of the start node , *iid* of the end node, and its weight. For example, in Table 1, *kid* 47 has *iid* 10, and *kid* 1280 has *iid* 138; the edge $\langle 8, 10 \rangle$ has weight 3, which means that the parent of *kid* 47 (with *iid* 10) is the node with *iid* 8.

List Sorting: PROCESS used in IL-TOPK is shown in Alg. 4. Given FPG and Q, it generates N lists, $\mathcal{L} = \{L_{F_1}, \cdots, L_{F_N}\}$. First, it loads the l inverted lists *kid* → *bids* (see Table 1), one for each user-specified query kterm, into main memory (Line 1). For each kterm, the *bids* in the inverted lists are those blocks in the corresponding FPG_i that contain it. Then, a sorted list L_{F_i} is built for each FPG_i (Lines 3-9). Let $\mathcal{B}$ be the set of *bids* belonging to FPG_i, which is found from the l inverted lists (Line 3). Note that, the size of $\mathcal{B}$ can be smaller than l, i.e., there can be more than one user-specified kterms in one block. Then L_{F_i} can be constructed from those blocks indicated by $\mathcal{B}$. For each block in $\mathcal{B}$ (Line 5), we first load the whole block into main memory (Line 6). For each kterm t in the block B (Line 7), $kcorr_i(Q,t)$ can be computed based on B, and the pair $(t, kcorr_i(Q,t))$ is inserted into list L_{F_i} (Line 8). As the kterms are inserted into L_{F_i} in random order, we have to sort it so that the kterms are ranked in non-increasing order with respect to the local correlation scores $kcorr_i(Q,t)$ (Line 9). Note that, after processing a block B (Lines 5-8), block B is discarded from memory.

After processing FPG, there are N lists $\mathcal{L}$, and they can reside in main memory since each list usually is not large. Also, only those N lists should be in memory. In order to call NEXT correctly, a pointer is constructed for each list, which points to the entry that should be returned when NEXT is called next time, and it is initialized to point to the first entry of the corresponding list. Each time when NEXT(L_{F_i}) is called, the entry pointed by the pointer is returned, and the pointer moves to the next entry in the list. GET(L_{F_i}, t) gets the local correlation score $kcorr_i(Q,t)$ for a kterm t, an in-memory index should be built to retrieve it efficiently, because the *kids* in a list L_{F_i} usually are not with consecutive integer ids.

Theorem 5.2: *Let n_i denote the size of list L_{F_i}, the time complexity of* PROCESS *is $O(\sum_{i=1}^{N}(n_i \cdot l \cdot L + n_i \log n_i))$, where l is the number of query kterms in Q and L is the maximum length of random walks in* FPG*; the space complexity of* PROCESS *is $O(\sum_{i=1}^{N} n_i + l \cdot N)$.* □

Due to space limit, we omit the proof.

Kterm-based lists vs Index-based lists: Recall that, kterm-based lists, $\{L_{k_1}, \cdots, L_{k_l}\}$, is used in CL-TOPK, which generates a list for each $k_i \in Q$, and index-based lists, $\{L_{F_1}, \cdots, L_{F_N}\}$, is used in IL-TOPK, which generates a list for each $FPG_i \in$ FPG. The number of lists in index-based lists is N, which is much larger than that of l kterm-based lists. However, there are advantages of the index-based lists. (1) The generation of index-based lists is more efficient. To generate a list L_{F_i}, only the related blocks, which is less than l, from FPG_i are needed. The related blocks from FPG_i usually are stored closely on disk, which is called the localization of index-based lists. (2) In generation of index-based lists, a block is loaded from disk at most once to compute correlation scores. While in kterm-based lists, a block will be loaded from disk multiple times, once for each query kterm $k_i \in Q$. (3) In order to enable sorted access on lists, entries in a list should be sorted. The size of a list in index-based lists is much smaller than that in kterm-based lists. Therefore, it is much more efficient for the index-based lists to be sorted than that of kterm-based lists.

6. EXPERIMENTS

We conducted extensive performance studies to test the algorithms proposed in this paper. We implemented our algorithms: CL-RR, IL-RR, and IL-BF. Here, CL-RR is for Alg. 1 which is kterm-list based, IL-RR is Alg. 2 with round robin access of the sorted lists, and IL-BF is for Alg. 2 which is index-list based. All algorithms were implemented in Visual C++ 2003, and all tests were conducted on a 2.8GHz CPU and 2GB memory PC running Windows XP.

We used two large real datasets, *DBLP*[1] and *YAGO*[2] [24] for testing. For *DBLP*, the network consists of two types of nodes, `Author` and `Paper`. Each node of type `Author` has a text attribute which stores the author name, and each node of type `Paper` has a text attribute which stores the title of the paper and the conference name of the paper. The kterms are author names and terms contained in paper titles. There are two types of relationships (edges) in *DBLP*, namely, author-write-paper relationship and paper-cite-paper relationship. After processing, the *DBLP* network consists of 2,120,264 nodes and 3,515,292 edges. The total number of distinct kterms and the average number of kterms per node are 445,314 and 5.05, respectively. We also extracted a subgraph from the *DBLP* network, denoted as *DBLP-CP*. It considers only paper-cite-paper relationship, and the papers from some top-ranked conferences are considered. The resulting *DBLP-CP* network consists of 6,705 nodes and 30,559 edges. The total number of distinct kterms and the average number of kterms per node are 4,723 and 6.0, respectively.

YAGO is a huge semantic knowledge base. Each node represents an entity, such as, a person, an organization, a city, etc. The text attribute of a node stores its name, and kterms are entity names. Each edge corresponds to a fact in *YAGO* knowledge base, such as, a person works at which university, a city belongs to which country. After processing, the *YAGO* network we used consists of 314,025 nodes and 398,257 edges. The total number of distinct kterms and the average number of kterms per node are 314,066 and 1.0, respectively.

6.1 Effectiveness Testing

To test the effectiveness of our algorithm, we used the implementation of IL-BF algorithm. We also tested the Center-Piece algorithm proposed in [25], denote as CePS[3], which returns a connection subgraph for a query Q which consists of entities. Since CePS does not scale to large graphs, in order to run CePS, we first extract a subgraph with 3k-7k nodes around the query entities. As the input graphs of CePS are undirected, we treat each edge as undirected in order to run CePS.

(Q1) {"Albert_Einstein", "Walther_Bothe"} on *YAGO*. The connection subgraph obtained by CePS is shown in Fig. 6(a), which indicates that both "Albert_Einstein" and "Walther_Bothe" are "Germany", and they both have won "Nobel_Prize_in_Physics" and "Max_Planck_Medal". However, CePS cannot find the persons in *YAGO* with similar relations as the two querying persons. The top-8 correlated persons returned by our approach are shown in Table 2. We also show in Fig. 6(b) the connection subgraph returned by CePS by adding the first two persons into Q. We know that both "Wolfgang_Ketterle" and "Max_von_Laue" are from "Germany" and have won "Nobel_Prize_in_Physics", and "Max_von_Laue" and "Walther_Bothe" have the same academic advisor "Max_Planck".

(Q2) {"Isabel_Sanford", "Nathan_Lane"} on *YAGO*. The top-8 correlated actors to the two actors in query are shown in Table 2. These returned actors have won similar awards with actors in Q, such as they have won "Emmy_Award", "Hollywood_Boulevard", and/or "Hollywood_Walk_of_Fame", as shown in Fig. 7. However, the CePS approach can only find the awards that "Isabel_Sanford" and "Nathan_Lane" have won, not actors with similar awards.

(Q3) {"histogram", "wavelet"} on *DBLP-CP*. The top-ranked kterms "synopses" denotes that both "histogram" and "wavelet" are meth-

[1]`http://www.informatik.uni-trier.de/~ley/db/`
[2]`http://www.mpi-inf.mpg.de/yago-naga/yago/`
[3]`http://www.cs.cmu.edu/~htong/work/CePS.zip`

$Q1$	$Q2$	$Q3$	$Q4$	$Q5$
Wolfgang_Ketterle	Vivian_Vance	synopses	discovering	Craig_Silverstein
Max_von_Laue	Nanette_Fabray	practicality	maximum	Michelle_Peterson
Theodor_W._hänsch	Tyne_Daly	rectangle	itemsets	David_Hecherman
J._Hans_D._Jensen	Imogene_Coca	fitting	association	Pini_Mogilevski
Leopold_Gmelin	Ron_Holgate	curve	rules	Bay-Wei_Chang
Max_Wolf	Loretta_Swit	approximation	matching	Takuhiro_Nagafuji
Johannes_Georg_Bednorz	Dick_Smothers	medians	episodes	Chung_T._Kwok
Harry_Rosenbusch	Henderson_Forsythe	selectivity	condensed	Brian_Milch

Table 2: Top correlated kterms returned by our approach

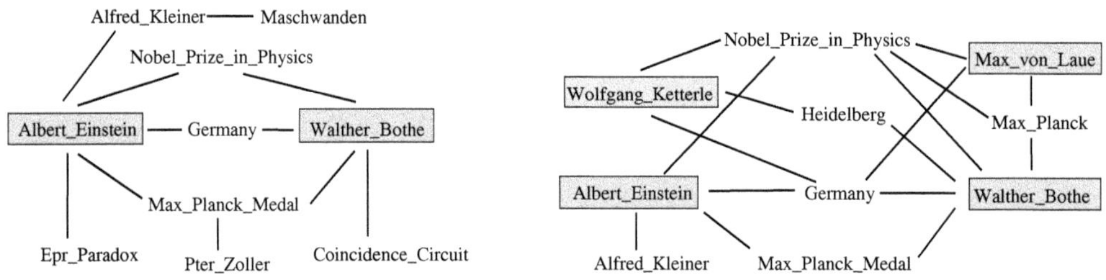

(a) CePS for $Q = \{AE, WB\}$ (b) CePS for $Q = \{AE, WB, WK, ML\}$

Figure 6: Subgraphs Obtained by CePS for Q1

ods to build synopses. "rectangle" and "medians" are approximation methods used in generating histograms and wavelets. "curve" "fitting" sometimes is used together with "histogram" and "wavelet" to get better results.

(Q4) {"frequent", "pattern", "mining"} on *DBLP-CP*. The top correlated kterms for this query are shown in Table 2. "discovering" has the same meaning as "mining", which is to discover frequent "itemsets" or frequent patterns from a database, or even to derive "association" "rules" from frequent itemsets. There are also some research papers about finding frequent "episode" patterns from sequential data.

(Q5) {"Sergey_Brin", "Larry_Page"} on *DBLP*, which is to discover the authors who have written papers with those two Google co-founders, or whose papers have similar citation patterns. The top authors are shown in Table 2. Among these eight authors, only "Craig_Silverstein", "Bay-Wei_Chang", and "Brian_Milch" are coauthors of "Sergey_Brin", while the other authors have written papers with similar citation patterns with the papers written by "Sergey_Brin" and "Larry_Page".

6.2 Efficiency Testing

For the efficiency testings, we report the query processing time and peak memory consumption for each test case. The query processing time of CL-RR, IL-RR, and IL-BF includes the time of processing the FPG index to build sorted lists and the time to find top-K kterms, and the time to build FPG index is the index construction time.

Parameter	Values	Default
Kterm Freq (p)	1, 2, 3, 4, 5	3
Kterm Num (l)	1, 2, 3, 4, 5	3
Return Num (K)	10, 20, 50, 100, 1000	50

Table 3: Parameters for Efficiency Testings

For each dataset, we select representative queries with different kterm frequencies. After removing all the stop words, let τ denote the maximum kterm frequency among all the kterms, the kterms are divided into five categories depends on their frequencies which are evenly divided between 0 and τ. For simplicity, we say a kterm

#	*DBLP*	*YAGO*
1	robust segmentation context	school village home
2	object oriented environment	ohio carolina minnesota
3	dynamic programming method study optimization	robert george michael paul wales
4	distributed web network	wisconsin illinois north
5	system design information	battle park south

Table 4: Query kterms used in Efficiency Testing (# is the kterms frequency)

is in category p ($p \in \{1, 2, 3, 4, 5\}$), if and only if its frequency is between $(p-1) \cdot \tau/5$ and $p \cdot \tau/5$.

For all the testings, we vary three parameters, namely, the kterm frequency (p), the query kterm number (l), and the number of kterms returned (K). The corresponding values for the three parameters are shown in Table 3 together with their default values. When varying the value of one parameter, the other two parameters take their default values. The query kterms selected for the datasets are shown in Table 4. When varying query kterm number l, the first l kterms from the default frequency category are selected.

Exp-1 (Testing on *DBLP* dataset): The time to construct indices for CL-RR and IL-BF algorithms are 32 minutes and 21 minutes, respectively. For *DBLP*, we test three algorithms: CL-RR, IL-RR, and IL-BF, where IL-RR has the same FPG index as IL-BF. The testing results are shown in Fig. 8. From Fig. 8(a) and Fig. 8(b), we know that the query processing time and peak memory consumption of all the three algorithms are not affected too much by the kterm frequency. Because the factors that affect the running time of IL-BF and CL-RR are the number of FPG indices (i.e., N) and the number of nodes in the index blocks that contain user-given kterms. Consistently, IL-BF takes less CPU time than IL-RR, and IL-RR takes less CPU time than CL-RR. IL-BF and IL-RR have the same index, and the same preprocessing algorithm. But, IL-BF accesses the N sorted lists in a best first manner, so it can stop earlier with less access of the lists. IL-RR outperforms CL-RR based on the fact that, the preprocessing algorithm for IL-RR is more efficient because it retrieves each block from disk only once. The memory consumption of CL-RR is less than that of IL-RR and IL-BF, which have almost the same memory consumption. This is because that the main memory consumption for CL-RR and IL-BF

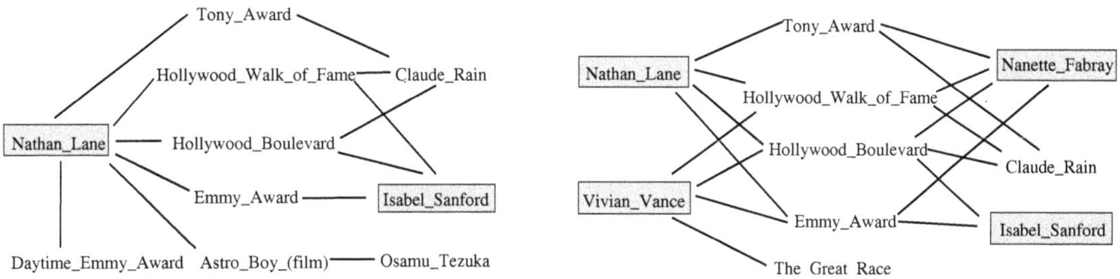

(a) CePS for $Q = \{IS, NL\}$ (b) CePS for $Q = \{IS, NL, VV, NF\}$

Figure 7: Subgraphs Obtained by CePS for Q2

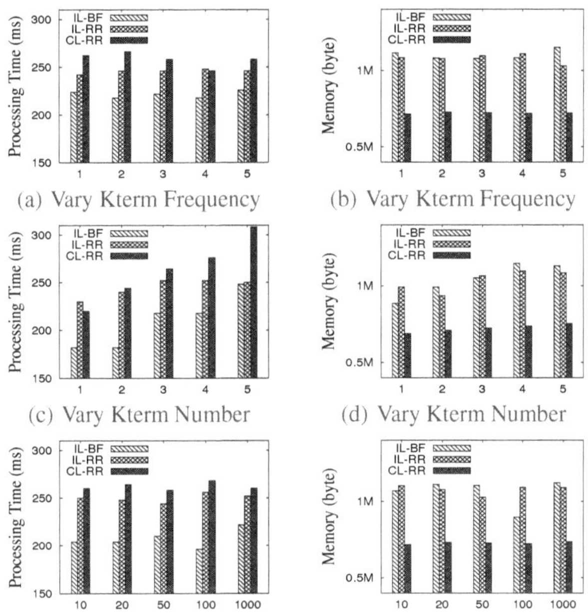

(a) Vary Kterm Frequency (b) Vary Kterm Frequency (c) Vary Kterm Number (d) Vary Kterm Number (e) Vary top-K (f) Vary top-K

Figure 8: Testing Results for the *DBLP* Dataset

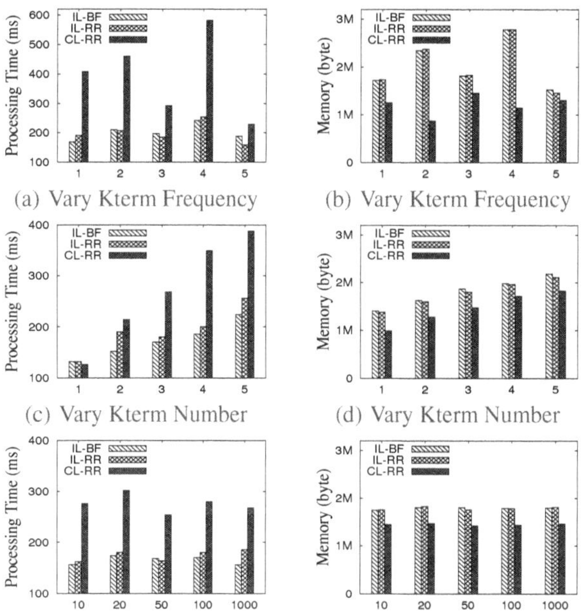

(a) Vary Kterm Frequency (b) Vary Kterm Frequency (c) Vary Kterm Number (d) Vary Kterm Number (e) Vary top-K (f) Vary top-K

Figure 9: Testing Results for the *YAGO* Dataset

algorithms are the l sorted lists and the $N(> l)$ sorted lists, respectively. When increasing the query kterm number, the CPU time and peak memory consumption of all the three algorithms increase, because the size of the sorted lists increases, as shown in Fig. 8(c) and Fig. 8(d). Fig. 8(e) shows that, when the top-K value increases, the CPU time of IL-BF increases while that of CL-RR and IL-RR almost remain the same. This is because that, the best first access makes IL-BF stop earlier when fewer results are desired. It also shows that round robin is inefficient when only a few results are desired.

Exp-2 (Testing on *YAGO* dataset): For this dataset, the time to construct indices for CL-RR and IL-BF algorithms are 4.2 minutes and 2.4 minutes, respectively. The testing results for IL-BF, IL-RR, and CL-RR are shown in Fig. 9, which have similar trends as that for *DBLP* dataset.

7. RELATED WORK

Our work is the first to find correlated kterms for a set of query kterms. It differs from other works in two aspects. First, one kterm can appear at many nodes in a graph. Second, we consider a global structural-context similarity between two sets of nodes in our correlation measure of two kterms. In the literatures, there are lots of work trying to find the best connection subgraph(s) to describe how the query terms are connected. Among them, query terms in [6, 25, 14] are entity names which correspond to unique nodes in a graph, while query terms in [3, 8, 2, 15] are kterms as our work. Instead of finding connection subgraphs, complementally, we find the correlated kterms surrounding the query kterms which is measured by a structural correlation score.

Finding Connection Subgraphs: Given an Entity-Relationship graph and a set of entities, the works in the literature return one (or a set of) connection subgraph (*CSG*), which is a subgraph describes the connection between query entities. Faloutsos et al. [6] proposed a delivered current based method to find a connection subgraph between two query nodes. To handle more than two query nodes, Tong and Faloutsos [25] proposed to find center-piece subgraph (CePS), which defines the proximity of a node t to node s as the probability that a random walk with restart from s will end at t. The center-piece subgraph consists of nodes whose proximity measures to all query nodes are high, and paths connecting to those query nodes. Kasneci et al. [14] first find a steiner tree between the query nodes, and then add nodes based on the probability that random walks from a node in the steiner tree to another node in the steiner tree will pass through it. In the above mentioned works, each query entity corresponds to a unique node in the graph.

Keyword Search: Keyword search in graphs finds small subgraphs which describe the connection between user-given keywords, where a keyword can appear at many nodes. The existing approaches define the cost of a subgraph based on the weights of edges. In [3, 8, 2, 15], they find a set of steiner trees with minimum costs. Exact [3] and approximate algorithms [8, 15] were studied. Dalvi et al. [2] considered external memory graphs. Qin et al. [22] return subgraphs (communities) for a keyword query. All these works aim at finding connection subgraph for a set of terms, based on the weights of edges. Our work is to find similar kterms for a set of user-given kterms based on the similarity between sets of nodes containing the corresponding kterms.

Link-Based Similarity Measures: One fundamental problem in graphs is to determine the similarity between node-pairs, which has a wide range of applications, such as link predication, graph clustering, etc. Liben-Nowell and Kleinberg [20] used similarity scores to predicate links between un-linked node-pairs, and reported that ensemble of paths performs the best. Examples of similarity measures of using the ensembles of paths are, personalized PageRank [11], SimRank [13], etc. In the personalized PageRank, the basic idea is to start a random walk from a node v, and at any setp the walk moves to a random neighbor with probability $1 - \alpha$ and is reset to the start node v with probability α. One characteristic of the personalized PageRank is that nodes close to the starting node will have higher stationary probability [23], and this is used to find connection subgraph for query nodes [25] and find relevant nodes for query keywords [12].

SimRank: SimRank was first proposed by Jeh et al. [13] to measure the similarity of two objects in a relationship graph based on the link structure. Iterative algorithms was proposed in [13]. Lizorkin et al. [21] gave an accuracy estimation for the number of iterations. Optimization techniques were also studied in [21] to reduce the computational cost for each iteration. A non-iterative method was proposed by Li et al. in [18]. Exact SimRank computation based on these techniques can only scale to graphs with thousands of nodes. Fogaras and Racz [7] proposed an index to scale the SimRank computation to graphs with millions of nodes, while the SimRank values computed are approximated values. Also, PSimRank was proposed in [7] to improve the quality of measuring node-pair similarity. As the data graph in our situation can have a size up to millions of nodes, we adopt the index proposed in [7]. However, the query in our work is different from that of [7], and the query answering techniques used in [7] can not be applied in our situation. A technique to efficiently compute SimRank value for a single-pair of nodes was proposed by Li et al. [19]. However, the technique can not be applied to our situation, because it has to compute SimRank values for millions of pairs of nodes. Variants of SimRank were proposed in the literature [26, 1]. P-RANK was proposed by Zhao et al. [26], which takes both in- and out-neighbors into consideration while SimRank only considers in-neighbors. Iterative algorithms were proposed to compute P-RANK values, so it does not scale to graphs with millions of nodes. Antonellis et al. [1] proposed SimRank++ for a weighted bipartite graph, which is an adaptation of SimRank to the special case of weighted bipartite graph.

8. CONCLUSION

In this paper, we studied knowledge discover from information networks which is composed of entities and relationships. Here, we consider the kterms associated with entities, and study the problem in the kterm level rather than entity level. We compute information nebula (cloud) which is a set of top-K kterms P that are most correlated to a set of user-specified kterms Q over a large information network. A global structural-context similarity between two sets of nodes is considered in our correlation measure of two kterms. We present efficient algorithms to find top-K kterms without computing correlation scores for all kterms in the information network. We conducted extensive performance studies using large real datasets, and confirmed the effectiveness and efficiency of our approach.

Acknowledgment: The work was supported by grants of the Research Grants Council of the Hong Kong SAR, China No. 419008 and 419109, and Microsoft Research Asia FY12-RES-OPP-002.

9. REFERENCES

[1] I. Antonellis, H. Garcia-Molina, and C.-C. Chang. Simrank++: query rewriting through link analysis of the click graph. *PVLDB*, 1(1), 2008.

[2] B. B. Dalvi, M. Kshirsagar, and S. Sudarshan. Keyword search on external memory data graphs. *PVLDB*, 1(1), 2008.

[3] B. Ding, J. X. Yu, S. Wang, L. Qin, X. Zhang, and X. Lin. Finding top-k min-cost connected trees in databases. In *Proc. of ICDE'07*, 2007.

[4] R. Fagin. Combining fuzzy information from multiple systems. *J. Comput. Syst. Sci.*, 58(1):83–99, 1999.

[5] R. Fagin, A. Lotem, and M. Naor. Optimal aggregation algorithms for middleware. *J. Comput. Syst. Sci.*, 66(4), 2003.

[6] C. Faloutsos, K. S. McCurley, and A. Tomkins. Fast discovery of connection subgraphs. In *Proc. of KDD'04*, 2004.

[7] D. Fogaras and B. Rácz. Scaling link-based similarity search. In *Proc. of WWW'05*, 2005.

[8] K. Golenberg, B. Kimelfeld, and Y. Sagiv. Keyword proximity search in complex data graphs. In *Proc. of SIGMOD'08*, 2008.

[9] M. Gomez-Rodriguez, J. Leskovec, and A. Krause. Inferring networks of diffusion and influence. In *Proc. of KDD'10*, 2010.

[10] J. Han, Y. Sun, X. Yan, and P. S. Yu. Mining knowledge from databases: an information network analysis approach (tutorial). In *Proc. of SIGMOD'10*, 2010.

[11] T. H. Haveliwala. Topic-sensitive pagerank. In *Proc. of WWW'02*, 2002.

[12] V. Hristidis, H. Hwang, and Y. Papakonstantinou. Authority-based keyword search in databases. *ACM Trans. Database Syst.*, 33(1), 2008.

[13] G. Jeh and J. Widom. Simrank: a measure of structural-context similarity. In *Proc.of KDD'02*, 2002.

[14] G. Kasneci, S. Elbassuoni, and G. Weikum. MING: mining informative entity relationship subgraphs. In *Proc. of CIKM'09*, 2009.

[15] G. Kasneci, M. Ramanath, M. Sozio, F. M. Suchanek, and G. Weikum. STAR: Steiner-tree approximation in relationship graphs. In *Proc. of ICDE'09*, 2009.

[16] A. Khan, X. Yan, and K.-L. Wu. Towards proximity pattern mining in large graphs. In *Proc. of SIGMOD'10*, 2010.

[17] M. Ley. DBLP - some lessons learned. *PVLDB*, 2(2), 2009.

[18] C. Li, J. Han, G. He, X. Jin, Y. Sun, Y. Yu, and T. Wu. Fast computation of simrank for static and dynamic information networks. In *Proc. of EDBT'10*, 2010.

[19] P. Li, H. Liu, J. X. Yu, J. He, and X. Du. Fast single-pair simrank computation. In *Proc. of SDM'10*, 2010.

[20] D. Liben-Nowell and J. M. Kleinberg. The link prediction problem for social networks. In *Proc. of CIKM'03*, 2003.

[21] D. Lizorkin, P. Velikhov, M. N. Grinev, and D. Turdakov. Accuracy estimate and optimization techniques for simrank computation. *PVLDB*, 1(1), 2008.

[22] L. Qin, J. X. Yu, L. Chang, and Y. Tao. Query communities in relational databases. In *Proc. of ICDE'09*, 2009.

[23] P. Sarkar and A. W. Moore. Fast nearest-neighbor search in disk-resident graphs. In *Proc. of KDD'10*, 2010.

[24] F. M. Suchanek, G. Kasneci, and G. Weikum. Yago: a core of semantic knowledge. In *Proc. of WWW'07*, 2007.

[25] H. Tong and C. Faloutsos. Center-piece subgraphs: problem definition and fast solutions. In *Proc. of KDD'06*, 2006.

[26] P. Zhao, J. Han, and Y. Sun. P-Rank: a comprehensive structural similarity measure over information networks. In *Proc. of CIKM'09*, 2009.

Efficient Methods for Finding Influential Locations with Adaptive Grids

Da Yan, Raymond Chi-Wing Wong, Wilfred Ng
The Hong Kong University of Science and Technology
Clear Water Bay, Kowloon, Hong Kong
{yanda, raywong, wilfred}@cse.ust.hk

ABSTRACT

Given a set S of servers and a set C of clients, an optimal-location query returns a location where a new server can attract the greatest number of clients. Optimal-location queries are important in a lot of real-life applications, such as mobile service planning or resource distribution in an area. Previous studies assume that a client always visits its nearest server, which is too strict to be true in reality. In this paper, we relax this assumption and propose a new model to tackle this problem. We further generalize the problem to finding top-k optimal locations.

The main challenge is that, even the fastest approach in existing studies needs to take hours to answer an optimal-location query on a typical real world dataset, which significantly limits the applications of the query. Using our relaxed model, we design an efficient grid-based approximation algorithm called FILM (Fast Influential Location Miner) to the queries, which is orders of magnitude faster than the best-known previous work and the number of clients attracted by a new server in the result location often exceeds 98% of the optimal. The algorithm is extended to finding k influential locations. Extensive experiments are conducted to show the efficiency and effectiveness of FILM on both real and synthetic datasets.

Categories and Subject Descriptors

H.2.8 [**Database Management**]: Database Applications—*Spatial databases and GIS*

General Terms

Algorithms, Design, Performance

1. INTRODUCTION

Optimal-location queries are important in a lot of real life applications. For example, a company can issue an optimal-location query to find an influential location to locate its next chain store, so as to maximize its potential revenue.

CIKM'11, October 24–28, 2011, Glasgow, Scotland, UK.

Informally, given a set S of servers and a set C of clients, an optimal-location query returns a location where a new server can attract the greatest number of clients. In the previous example, chain stores correspond to servers while customers correspond to clients, and the company wants to find a location that can maximize the number of customers attracted by its new chain store.

Optimal-location queries can also be used in many other applications, such as profile-based marketing and emergency schedules. However, most of the previous studies assume that the set of existing servers and clients are static, since even the state-of-the-art algorithm for processing optimal-location queries [1] takes hours to answer such queries on typical real world datasets. Thus, the existing approaches that have long response time are not practical to a fast-evolving environment, where the servers and clients may move, and the server and client sets may change as time goes by.

For instance, let us consider a military application where the location of each soldier and each military vehicle is tracked by GPS. Suppose there are medical workers, apparatus and instruments sufficient to set up 10 field hospitals, and the goal is to locate these field hospitals in a military area to serve as many soldiers as possible. As the battlefront changes over time, the locations of soldiers and vehicles will also change, and some field hospitals have to be relocated by military transport aircrafts.

Assume that there exists a coordination center, which is responsible for adjusting the location of a field hospital, if it finds that the hospital can no longer serve sufficient soldiers. Then, the center has to find the optimal location as soon as possible, since fast medical support is critical for the wounded soldiers. Instead of spending hours to run the existing algorithms to find an optimal location, it is more desirable to find a slightly less optimal location within a few seconds, so that the relocation of the hospital can be carried out in time. Thus, our goal is to find a near-optimal location efficiently.

To realize this goal, we propose an approximation algorithm called FILM that is able to return a small region, where each location is a sub-optimal one, within seconds to a couple of minutes, which is orders of magnitude faster than the state-of-the-art algorithm that returns an optimal one. We also consider the related problem of locating k new servers in order to maximize the total number of clients attracted by these servers "collectively". It is worth mentioning that [1] proposes to find k locations, each of which attracts as many clients as possible. However, since the k lo-

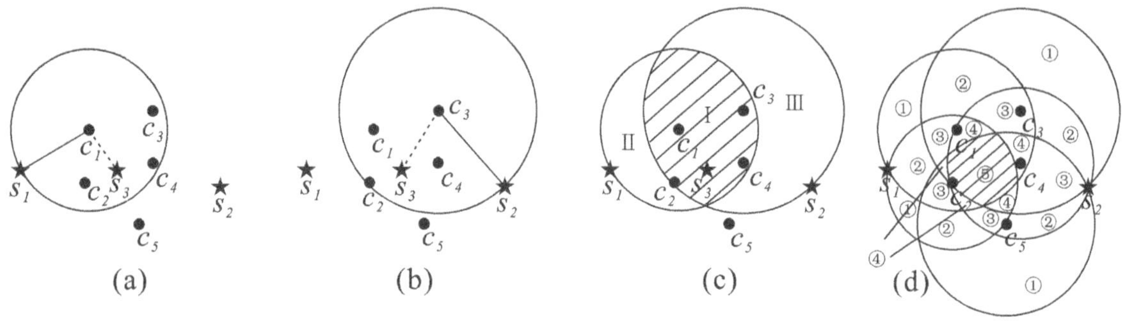

Figure 1: Illustrations of Nearest Location Circle (NLC)

cations are independently found in [1], they may share a lot of attracted clients and thus the total number of clients attracted "collectively" by these k locations may not be large. To solve this problem, we extend FILM to finding k influential locations that collectively attract as many clients as possible.

The rest of the paper is organized as follows: Section 2 formulates the problem of finding influential locations. Section 3 reviews the related work, with an emphasis on the state-of-the-art algorithm proposed recently. Our grid-based algorithm, FILM, is described in Section 4. Extensive experiments are conducted in Section 5 to evaluate the efficiency and effectiveness of FILM on both real and synthetic datasets. Finally, we conclude our paper in Section 6.

2. PROBLEM DEFINITION

2.1 Optimal-Location Query

We now use the example in Figure 1 to illustrate the idea of optimal-location queries. Figure 1(a) shows a spatial setting with a set of two servers (s_1 and s_2), and a set of five clients (c_1, c_2, c_3, c_4 and c_5). Suppose that we need to choose a location for a new server s_3. *Where should it go in order to attract as many clients as possible?* To answer this question, we first need to define the condition under which s_3 attracts client c_i as follows:

Definition 1 (ABUF). *The attraction buffer (ABUF) of a client $c \in C$, denoted $ABUF(c)$, is the union of all the locations where a new server s can attract c.*

Therefore, s_3 attracts c_i if and only if its location is within $ABUF(c_i)$. Previous work assumes that a client always visits its nearest server, which we call the *nearest neighbor assumption* (or the *NN assumption*). Under the NN assumption, when the distance metric is L_2-norm (Euclidean distance), the ABUF of a client is actually a circle as defined below:

Definition 2 (NLC). *The nearest location circle (NLC) of a client $c \in C$, denoted $NLC(c)$, is the circle centered at the location of c with radius $|c, NN(c)|$, where $NN(c)$ is the nearest neighbor of c in the server set S, and $|\cdot|$ stands for the Euclidean distance.*

We illustrate the concept of NLC by our running example in Figure 1. Assume that currently $S = \{s_1, s_2\}$, and thus S does not contain the new server s_3 to set up. Therefore, s_3 is not involved in the computation of the NLC of a client. Figure 1(a) shows the NLC of c_1 (note that c_1 is closer to s_1 than to s_2). However, if s_3 is set up at the location as shown in Figure 1(a), it becomes the new nearest neighbor (NN) of c_1 and thus attracts c_1. This gives rise to the following observation:

Observation 1. *If a new server is set up at a location within the NLC of a client $c \in C$, the server will attract c.*

The same principle also holds when the NLC of c_3 is considered (Figure 1(b)). When we consider only two clients c_1 and c_3, we have the corresponding NLCs as shown in Figure 1(c). In this figure, we can see that region II is only covered by c_1's NLC and thus a new server there will only attract c_1 but not c_3. Similarly, a new server in region III will attract c_3 but not c_1. In the overlapping region I, it is obvious that a new server there will attract both c_1 and c_3. In the region not covered by any NLCs, a new server there will certainly attract no clients. If we assume that there are only two clients c_1 and c_3, the optimal location for s_3 should be within region I. The above discussion can be formalized in the following observation:

Observation 2. *If a new server is set up at a location which is covered by the greatest number of NLCs, the new server will attract the greatest number of clients.*

We conclude that an optimal-location query should return a location which is covered by the greatest number of NLCs. Figure 1(d) shows a more complicated scenario by considering all the clients, namely $c_1, c_2, ..., c_5$. Their NLCs divide the whole space into a number of partitions. In Figure 1(d), each partition is marked with a number denoting the number of NLCs covering the partition. This number corresponds to the total number of clients who have interest in visiting a new server set up in this partition. Given a location l in this partition, we name this number as the *influence value* of l. Obviously, any point in the shaded region in Figure 1(d) is an optimal location.

Now, we generalize the concept of NLC in Observations 1 and 2 to any ABUF, and define the *influence value* of a location l based on ABUF:

Definition 3 (Influence Value). *Given a location l, the influence value of l, denoted $inf(l)$, is the number of clients $c \in C$ such that $l \in ABUF(c)$.*

Definition 4 (Optimal-Location Query). *Given a set S of servers and a set C of clients, the* optimal-location query *returns a location l such that $inf(l)$ is the maximum.*

With a straightforward extension we can also handle the more general case where each client $c \in C$ is associated with a weight $w(c)$. In this case, Definition 3 can be generalized as follows: given a location l, its influence value $inf(l) = \sum_{c \in C:\ l \in ABUF(c)} w(c)$, i.e., we compute the sum of the weights of the attracted clients rather than simply count the total number.

2.2 Finding Influential Location

Although optimal-location queries are useful in real life applications, it is expensive to compute the optimal location, which makes such queries not practical for fast-evolving environments. Another inherent limitation of such queries is that only one (optimal) location is returned as the answer, which is too restrictive. Thus, we propose to study a more general setting of the queries as follows: "finding k influential locations to locate k new servers so as to attract as many clients as possible". To our knowledge, this problem is still not formally addressed in the literature.

To support applications that require short response time, we propose an approximation algorithm called FILM, which is able to return a near-optimal location within seconds to a couple of minutes, and can support the top-k queries mentioned above.

The key to the design of FILM is a generalization of the concept of NLC. The traditional optimal-location queries studied in the previous work adopt NLC as the ABUF. However, the underlying assumption of the traditional optimal-location queries that a client always visits its nearest server (i.e., the NN assumption) may not hold in reality. For example, a restaurant that is 55 meters away from our home and serves better food is more likely to attract us, even if the nearest restaurant is 40 meters away, although we may be reluctant to go to a restaurant 500 meters away. This also holds for long distances. For example, for people living in the outskirt of a city who want to drive to a supermarket in the downtown area for shopping, a supermarket 5 miles away that sells more products is not less attractive than a supermarket 4 miles away.

In order to tolerate other close servers besides the NN, [1] proposes to set the radius of the NLC of a client c to $|c, \mathrm{NN}_k(c)|$, where $\mathrm{NN}_k(c)$ is the k-th nearest server of c, and k is a user-specified parameter. However, this radius relaxation still lacks flexibility: for one client, its second NN may be just a little farther away than its NN and the client is very likely to visit it, while for another client, its second NN may be times farther away than its NN, which deters the client from visiting it. We thus adopt a new NLC relaxation called *Relaxed NLC* (RNLC) defined as follows:

DEFINITION 5 (RNLC). *The relaxed nearest location circle (RNLC) of a client c is the circle centered at the location of c with radius* $(1+\alpha) \cdot |c, NN(c)|$, *where* $\alpha > 0$.

The parameter α in Definition 5 is a user-specified parameter that describes how far a client is willing to visit a server. If it is allowed to be set to 0, RNLC is reduced to NLC. However, note that Definition 5 requires $\alpha > 0$. Intuitively, Definition 5 states that a client is willing to visit a server whose distance is at most $(1+\alpha)$ times longer than the distance between the client and its nearest server.

Each client $c_i \in C$ can have an RNLC parameter α_i specific to it, and to differentiate from the traditional optimal-location queries that adopt NLC as the ABUF, we name the optimal-location queries that adopt RNLC as the ABUF to be *Relaxed Optimal-Location Queries*:

DEFINITION 6 (RELAXED OPTIMAL-LOCATION QUERY). *A relaxed optimal-location query is an optimal-location query given in Definition 4 that adopts RNLC as the ABUF.*

We develop a very efficient approximation algorithm (FILM) to the relaxed optimal-location queries. Although the parameter α can be different for different clients in the relaxed optimal-location queries, we use a fixed α for all clients and prove that as $\alpha \to 0^+$, the influence value of the result location of FILM converges to that of the traditional optimal-location query.

3. RELATED WORK

The optimal-location query was first studied by [2, 1]. [2] proposes an algorithm called *Arrangement*, whose time complexity is exponential to the number of clients, resulting in very poor scalability, while [1] proposes an efficient algorithm called *MaxOverlap* whose time complexity is polynomial to the number of clients. *MaxOverlap* is know to be the fastest algorithm for optimal-location queries. [1] reports that for a small dataset with 250 clients and 500 servers, the Arrangement algorithm runs for more than one day while MaxOverlap finishes the task within 0.1s.

The optimal-location query defined in [2, 1] is based on NLC instead of RNLC. In the following, we briefly introduce the underlying idea of MaxOverlap [1], as the following four steps:

- **Step 1 (NLC Construction):** For each client $c \in C$, find the NLC of c.
- **Step 2 (Intersection Point Computation):** For each pair of NLCs, find the intersection points between the boundaries of these two NLCs.
- **Step 3 (Point Query):** For each intersection point found in Step 2, find all NLCs covering this point.
- **Step 4 (Maximum Influence Value Finding):** find the intersection point which is covered by the greatest number of NLCs, and return the region which is the intersection of all those covering NLCs.

It is shown in [1] that the region returned by MaxOverlap corresponds to the optimal partition in which each location is an optimal one (e.g., the shaded region in Figure 1(d)).

Although MaxOverlap uses a pruning rule to avoid evaluating the intersection points that are guaranteed not to be optimal, it is still quite slow in practice. The time complexity of MaxOverlap is shown to be $O(|C| \log |S| + \ell^2 |C| + \ell |C| \log |C|)$ in [1], where ℓ is the average length of the overlapping lists of the clients. MaxOverlap is very expensive if ℓ is large, and since $\ell = O(|C|)$, the time cost of MaxOverlap is super-quadratic to the number of clients.

Unlike MaxOverlap that works on Euclidean distance, [6] uses Manhattan distance as the metric. In this case, the ABUF of a client is a square. [6] uses plane-sweep to evaluate the optimal-location query. Since [6] focuses on *constrained optimal-location query* that finds an optimal location within a query region rather than globally, it elaborates on the disk-based index to fetch only the ABUFs involved.

Note that MaxOverlap can easily be extended to handle the constrained optimal-location query, by filtering out the intersection points that are outside the query region.

Some recent work [4, 5] considers the capacity of each server. Other related work includes [8, 9, 10], all of which are based on the idea of *bichromatic reverse nearest neighbor* [7]. However, they find the most influential server among the existing servers, while we find an influential location for a new server, which is a fundamentally different problem from theirs.

4. FILM ALGORITHM

Although MaxOverlap [1] is the state-of-the-art algorithm for the evaluation of optimal-location queries, its efficiency is still far from satisfactory for most practical applications. This is because MaxOverlap needs to compute and evaluate a huge amount of intersection points between the boundaries of the NLCs. This observation reveals that, in order to find influential locations much more efficiently, we have to abandon the idea of checking the intersection points but to develop a new approach for finding such locations.

The idea of FILM is inspired by the way people solve the optimal-location query manually. If we are given a paper and a pencil, we will solve the optimal-location problem by drawing the NLCs of all clients and then find the most overlapped partition, as illustrated in Figure 1. Since the "paper" to draw on is a continuous space, and we need to find the most overlapped region/location within short time, we partition the "paper" space using grids and manipulate on the grid cells. FILM returns a grid cell in which each location is an influential one, as an approximation of the optimal location.

In the sequel, we first present in Section 4.1 our idea of FILM when there is only one grid partitioning imposed on the space. This paves the way of introducing the complete FILM algorithm in Section 4.2, where we show the necessity of using a hierarchy of multiple grids to improve the performance of finding an influential location.

4.1 Grid-based Algorithm

4.1.1 Basic Algorithm

Similar to MaxOverlap[1], the first step of FILM is also to obtain the NLCs of all the clients. To get the NLCs, we first bulk-load a balanced kd-tree on the server points in S, denoted as T_S^{kd}. Then, for each client $c \in C$, we find the server s nearest to c by an NN query on T_S^{kd} and get the NLC radius $|s, c|$. We adopt a kd-tree instead of an R*-tree since operations on kd-tree have time bounds. T_S^{kd} is freed from memory after we have computed all the NLCs, since it is no longer needed.

Algorithm 1 Basic Algorithm of FILM

1: **for each** client $c \in C$ **do**
2: Compute its NLC $NLC(c)$
3: **end for**
4: **for each** client $c \in C$ **do**
5: **for each** grid cell g that overlaps with $NLC(c)$ **do**
6: $counter(g) \longleftarrow counter(g) + 1$
7: **end for**
8: **end for**
9: **return** $\arg\max_g counter(g)$

After getting all the NLCs, we "draw" them on the grid partitioning of the space as shown in Algorithm 1, where each grid cell is a small square and its side length is called the *grid side length*. A counter $counter(g)$ is attached to each grid cell g to record the number of NLCs overlapping with the cell, which is initialized to 0. After all the NLCs are drawn, the grid cell with the maximum counter value is returned. In the cases where the clients are weighted, Line 6 of Algorithm 1 becomes $counter(g) \longleftarrow counter(g) + w(c)$, where $w(c)$ is the weight of client c.

4.1.2 Analysis

In this subsection, we justify that Algorithm 1 returns a grid cell in which each location is an influential one, and as the *grid side length* approaches 0, the influence value of a location in the result cell approaches the maximum influence value.

To prove this, we can view Algorithm 1 as an approximation algorithm to the relaxed optimal-location query defined in Definition 6. We now present the following theorem:

THEOREM 1. *If a grid cell g overlaps with the NLC of client c whose radius $r \geq \delta\varepsilon$ (ε is the grid side length, $\delta > 1$), then any location in g is within the RNLC of c with $\alpha \geq \frac{\sqrt{2}}{\delta}$.*

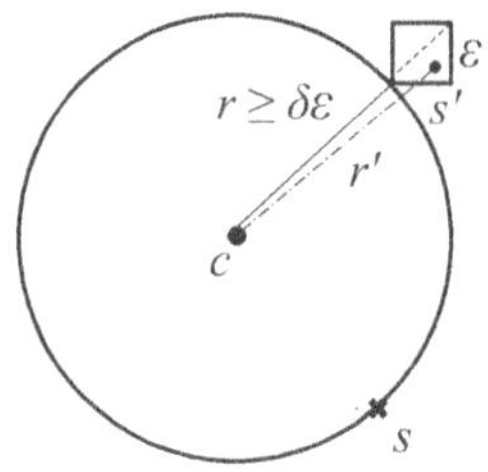

Figure 2: Illustration of Theorem 1

PROOF. To illustrate the idea of Theorem 1, Figure 2 shows the NLC of a client c, whose nearest server is s. Assume that the grid side length is ε and the radius of the NLC is $r \geq \delta\varepsilon$. Figure 2 is an extreme case for a grid cell g to overlap with the NLC of c. The point in g that is farthest from c is the upper right corner of g, denoted g_{ur}. It is obvious that, for any point s' in g, if we denote $d = |c, g_{ur}|$ and $d' = |c, s'|$, we have $d' \leq d$. Since $d = |c, g_{ur}| = r + \sqrt{2}\varepsilon$, we have $d' \leq r + \sqrt{2}\varepsilon$.

Note that Figure 2 is the ***extreme*** case, and for any grid cell g' closer to c than g (and hence overlaps with $NLC(c)$), we must also have $\forall s' \in g',\ |c, s'| \leq r + \sqrt{2}\varepsilon \leq r + \sqrt{2}(\frac{r}{\delta}) = (1 + \frac{\sqrt{2}}{\delta})r$.

Therefore, if a grid cell g overlaps with the NLC of c, then g is within the RNLC of c with $\alpha \geq \frac{\sqrt{2}}{\delta}$ (see Definition 5), which proves Theorem 1. □

The parameter δ in Theorem 1 has a straightforward geometric meaning: for a grid with grid side length ε, $\delta\varepsilon$ defines the lower bound of the radius of any NLC "drawn" on it. δ is also important for the grid hierarchy described later.

Next, we describe the relationship of our new parameter δ with the parameter α in Definition 5: Given the user-specified RNLC parameter α, we require $\delta \leq \frac{\sqrt{2}}{\alpha}$ according to Theorem 1. On the other hand, smaller grid side length

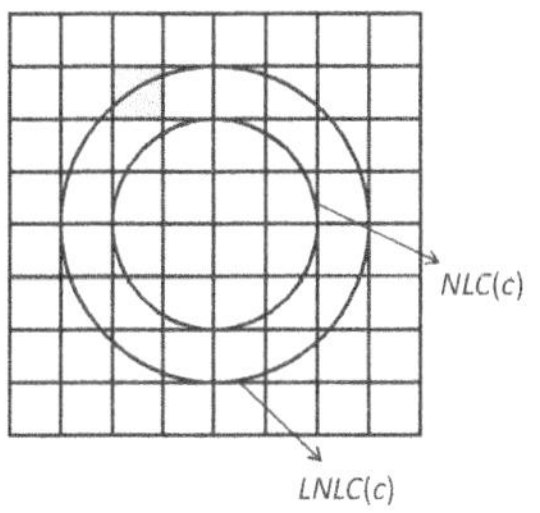

Figure 3: Underestimated Cell

ε leads to better approximation, and thus we want $\delta \le \frac{r}{\varepsilon}$ to be as large as possible. As a result, the optimal setting is $\delta = \frac{\sqrt{2}}{\alpha}$.

Although α is a more intuitive parameter that indicates the maximum distance a user can tolerate, we use δ as the user-specified parameter instead, due to its more straightforward geometric meaning. In fact, given α, we can always set $\delta = \frac{\sqrt{2}}{\alpha}$, and thus setting both parameters are essentially equivalent.

If a grid cell g does not overlap with the NLC of a client c, we do not add *counter*(g), although g may overlap with the RNLC of c (e.g., the gray cell in Figure 3). Therefore, the counter value of a grid cell g computed by our approach is a conservative estimation of the number of clients that a new server in g attracts, for the relaxed optimal-location query.

However, as $\delta \to +\infty$ ($\alpha = \frac{\sqrt{2}}{\delta} \to 0^+$), the boundary of RNLC approaches NLC and the probability that the above underestimation happens for a grid cell approaches 0. Therefore, we have the following theorem:

THEOREM 2. *The counter value of a grid cell g is a conservative estimation of the number of clients that a new server in g attracts, and this value approaches the exact value as $\delta \to +\infty$.*

Thus, the influence value of a location in the result cell of Algorithm 1 approaches the maximum influence value, as $\delta \to +\infty$.

4.1.3 Implementation Details

We first introduce our grid structure as shown in Figure 4. The whole space is divided into a number of grid cells with grid side length ε. Each cell is indexed by two integers $\langle i, j\rangle$, such that its lower left vertex coordinate is $(i\varepsilon, j\varepsilon)$. For example, Cells I, II, III, IV and V in Figure 4 are indexed as $\langle 0,0\rangle$, $\langle -1,0\rangle$, $\langle 1,0\rangle$, $\langle 0,1\rangle$ and $\langle -4,-4\rangle$, respectively.

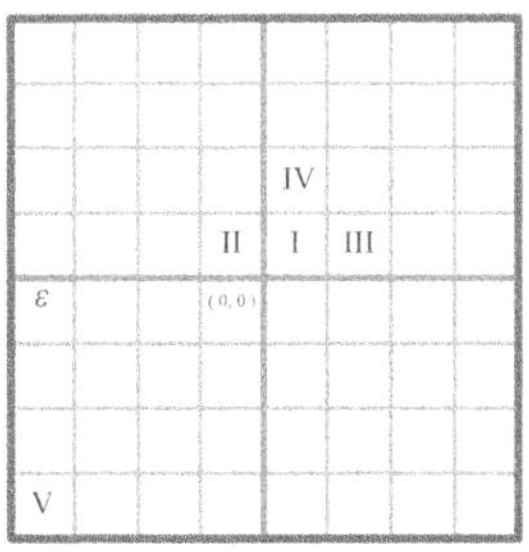

Figure 4: Grid Cell Indexing with Coordinates

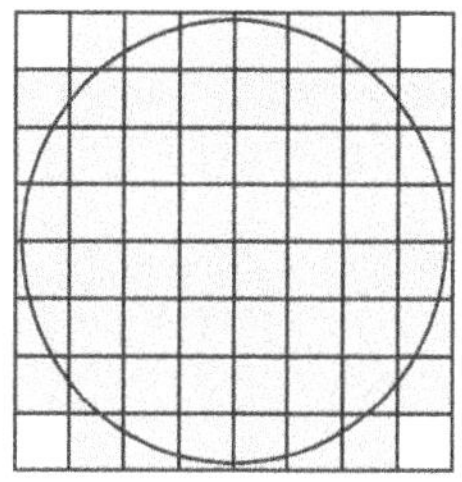

Figure 5: Grid Cells with Counters Added

Line 5 in Algorithm 1 aims at obtaining all the grid cells overlapping with an NLC. To find these cells efficiently, given an NLC with center $c = (x, y)$ and radius r, we define the *candidate cell set* of the NLC to be the set of cells $\{\langle i, j\rangle \mid \lfloor x - r\rfloor < i < \lfloor x + r\rfloor, \lfloor y - r\rfloor < j < \lfloor y + r\rfloor\}$. The round down operation $\lfloor x\rfloor$ is used because we index each cell by its lower left vertex.

For example, all the cells in Figure 5 compose the *candidate cell set* of the NLC in the figure. To see how to find this set, we note that the NLC has center $(0, 0)$ and radius r such that $3\varepsilon < r < 4\varepsilon$, and therefore the *candidate cell set* of the NLC is computed as $\{\langle i, j\rangle \mid \lfloor 0 - r\rfloor < i < \lfloor 0 + r\rfloor, \lfloor 0 - r\rfloor < j < \lfloor 0 + r\rfloor\} = \{\langle i, j\rangle \mid -4 < i < 3, -4 < j < 3\}$.

However, only the gray cells in Figure 5 are those that really overlap with the NLC. Therefore, after obtaining the *candidate cell set* of an NLC, we need a filtering step to find all the cells overlapping with the NLC. For each cell $g = \langle i, j\rangle$ in the *candidate cell set*, we determine whether it overlaps with an NLC with center $c = (x, y)$ and radius r, by checking whether $MINDIST(g, c) \le r$, where $MINDIST$ is defined similar to [11]:

$$MINDIST(g, c) = \sqrt{(x_g - x)^2 + (y_g - y)^2}$$

$$x_g = \begin{cases} i\varepsilon, \text{ if } i\varepsilon > x \\ i\varepsilon + \varepsilon, \text{ if } i\varepsilon + \varepsilon < x \\ x, \text{ otherwise} \end{cases}, \quad y_g = \begin{cases} j\varepsilon, \text{ if } j\varepsilon > y \\ j\varepsilon + \varepsilon, \text{ if } j\varepsilon + \varepsilon < y \\ y, \text{ otherwise} \end{cases}$$

Note that each grid cell can be represented as a key-value pair, where the key is the cell index $\langle i, j\rangle$ and the value is the counter of the cell. Since it may be extremely memory-inefficient to materialize all the cells in the grid (especially if the cells are very small compared to the whole space involved, or if most of the space is not covered by any NLC), we organize the cells by a balanced search tree, where for a cell $\langle i, j\rangle$, i serves as the primary key and j serves as the secondary key.

Only those cells that overlap with at least one NLC are stored in the tree. Algorithm 2 shows the operations done

Algorithm 2 Grid Cell Processing

```
if g overlaps with NLC then
    if g ∈ GRID then
        counter(g) ⟵ counter(g) + 1
    else
        Create grid cell g
        counter(g) ⟵ 1
        Insert g into GRID
    end if
end if
```

for each cell g in the already obtained *candidate cell set* and the NLC NLC in question, assuming $GRID$ to be the binary search tree storing the cells. Line 1 of Algorithm 2 is checked using $MINDIST$.

Although there are many efficient realizations of a balanced search tree (e.g., [12]), we simply use the "map" container from the C++ STL library, which is actually a red-black tree.

4.2 Adaptive Gird Hierarchy

To see the necessity of a hierarchy of multiple grid structures, let us first analyze the characteristics of NLCs on real datasets.

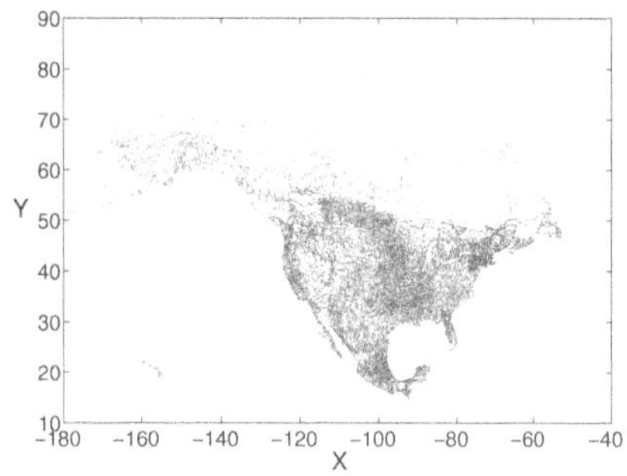

Figure 6: North American Dataset

Figure 6 shows the North American dataset from [14], where the 9203 red points are cultural landmarks and the 24493 blue points are populated places. We treat the cultural landmarks as servers and the populated places as clients, and assume that people tend to visit the cultural landmarks close to them. After all the NLCs are computed, we find that the radii of the NLCs span several orders of magnitude. For example, the smallest NLC of the North American dataset has radius 1.23×10^{-3} while the largest is 9.505. We find similar patterns in all the datasets we use.

As a result, if we use only one grid, of which the grid side length is suitable for the smallest NLC, "drawing" larger NLCs would involve quite a lot of cells, which degrades the performance. Thus, we need to adapt the grid structure to the NLC size automatically, which results in the grid hierarchy of FILM.

To achieve reasonable approximation quality, the grid cells we choose should be sufficiently small compared with the size of an NLC "drawn" on it. Therefore, we set a lower-bound to the size of any NLC handled by a grid as follows, where δ is the same parameter as in Theorem 1 and is the user-specified parameter of our grid hierarchy:

DEFINITION 7. *Given a grid structure with grid side length ε, any NLC that is "drawn" on it should have radius $r \geq \delta \cdot \varepsilon$.*

However, a grid structure of too fine granularity is not necessary for large NLCs, and will degrade the evaluation performance. Thus, we also set an upper-bound to the size of any NLC handled by a grid:

DEFINITION 8. *Given a grid structure with grid side length ε, any NLC that is "drawn" on it should have radius $r < \delta^2 \cdot \varepsilon$.*

To sum up, for a grid structure whose grid side length is ε, we only draw on it those NLCs with radius r satisfying $\delta \cdot \varepsilon \leq r < \delta^2 \cdot \varepsilon$.

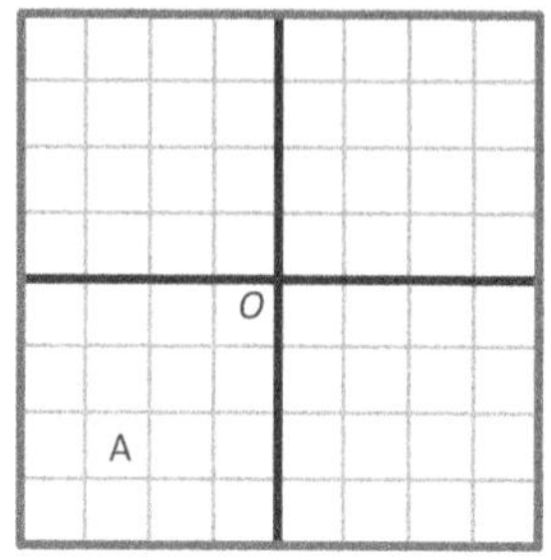

Figure 7: Two Consecutive Grids in the Hierarchy

FILM uses a set of grids such that consecutive grids have grid side lengths being different by a factor of δ. Figure 7 shows an example space with 2 consecutive grid structures, where $\delta = 4$ and the smaller grid side length ε_1 is of the lower level grid, and the large grid cells drawn with bold lines whose grid side length is $\varepsilon_2 = 4\varepsilon_1$ are of the higher level grid. Note that low level grids are just refinements of the upper level ones, e.g., each large grid in Figure 7 contains exactly $\delta^2 = 16$ small grids.

According to our grid hierarchy, each NLC is handled by exactly one grid structure in the hierarchy. For example, in Figure 7, the grid with grid side length ε_1 can only handle NLCs with radius $4\varepsilon_1 \leq r < 16\varepsilon_1$, and the grid with grid side length ε_2 can only handle NLCs with radius $4\varepsilon_2 \leq r < 16\varepsilon_2$, i.e., $16\varepsilon_1 \leq r < 64\varepsilon_1$.

4.2.1 *Algorithm for Mining k Influential Locations*

The algorithm of FILM consists of 2 steps: 1)build grid hierarchy from NLCs; and 2)evaluate the influence value estimation of each grid cell and pick the maximum one.

The first step is detailed as follows: The obtained NLCs are first sorted in non-decreasing order of the radius. Then a pass through the sorted list allocates the NLCs to the corresponding grids based on the bounds in Definition 7 and 8. The result of the first step is shown in Figure 8, where we obtain a list of grids (i.e., $GList$), and each grid element in $GList$ records: 1)len: the grid side length, 2)$[start, end]$: the set of NLCs allocated to the grid, and 3)$tree$: the binary search tree holding the grid cells of the grid, which is initialized to an empty tree.

An important issue is the choice of the value of the grid side length ε_{min} of the lowest level grid. We choose $\varepsilon_{min} = r_{min}/\delta$ where r_{min} is the radius value of the smallest NLC. In this way, the lowest level grid handles the NLCs with radius $\delta\varepsilon_{min} \leq r < \delta\varepsilon_{min}^2$, i.e., $r_{min} \leq r < \varepsilon_{min} \cdot r_{min}$.

After obtaining $GList$, the NLCs allocated to each grid are "drawn" on that grid as described in Section 4.1, and the counter information of the grid cells are stored in the binary search tree of that grid.

So far, the grid hierarchy has been constructed from the NLCs, and we are ready to evaluate the influence value estimation of each grid cell using our grid hierarchy —— a basic operation for the second step of FILM. The key to this operation is the following observation of our grid hierarchy:

OBSERVATION 3. *Given a grid cell $g = \langle i, j\rangle$ with grid side length ε, we can identify the cell in a upper level grid with grid side length ε' that contains g, as $g' = \langle\lfloor i\varepsilon/\varepsilon'\rfloor, \lfloor j\varepsilon/\varepsilon'\rfloor\rangle$.*

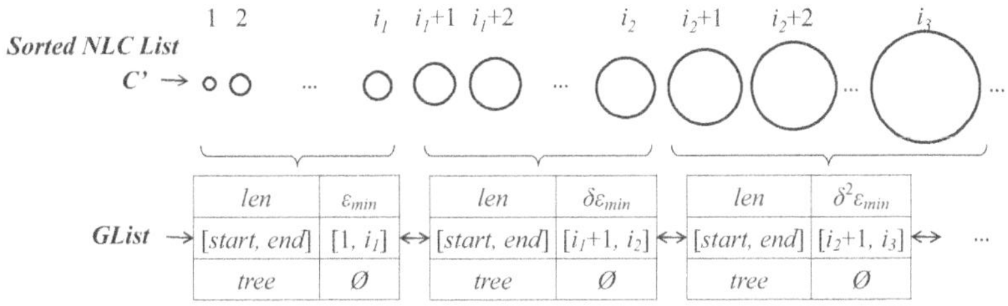

Figure 8: NLC Allocation to Grids

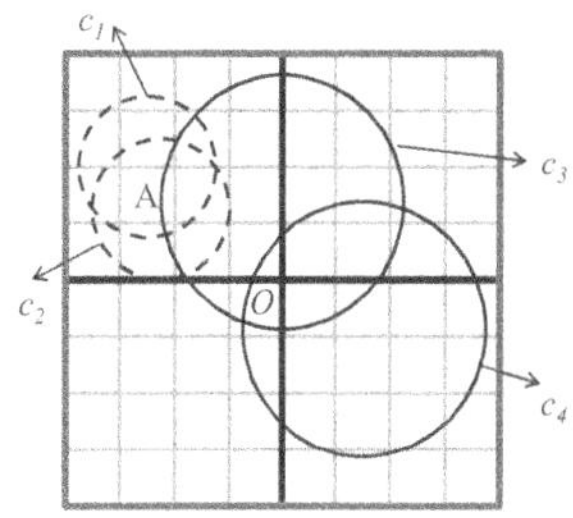

Figure 9: Estimation Integration Among Grids

We call g' the *covering cell* of g in this case. For example, the covering cell of Cell $A = \langle -3, -3 \rangle$ in Figure 7 is the lower left large cell: $\langle \lfloor -3\varepsilon_1/\varepsilon_2 \rfloor, \lfloor -3\varepsilon_1/\varepsilon_2 \rfloor \rangle = \langle \lfloor -3/4 \rfloor, \lfloor -3/4 \rfloor \rangle = \langle -1, -1 \rangle$. Therefore, our structure hierarchy allows us to find the covering cell of a grid cell in an upper level grid structure in O(1) time.

Since each grid only handles the NLCs of a subset $C' \subseteq C$ of the clients, the counter value of a grid cell g is just a conservative influence value estimation on this subset C'.

Figure 9 shows some NLCs on the grid hierarchy of Figure 7, where the two small NLCs c_1 and c_2 are drawn on the lower level grid, and the two large NLCs c_3 and c_4 are drawn on the higher level grid. After the grid hierarchy is built, the counter value of Cell A is 2 due to its overlap with c_1 and c_2, and the counter value of the upper left large cell (denoted as g_{ul}) is also 2 due to its overlap with c_3 and c_4.

The counter of Cell A does not take c_3 and c_4 into consideration. Note that c_4 does not even overlap with Grid A. However, the clients of c_3 and c_4 can also be attracted by a new server in Cell A. This is because c_3 and c_4 overlap with g_{ul}, the *covering cell* of Cell A, and according to Theorem 1, all the locations in g_{ul} are in the RNLCs of c_3 and c_4, including all the locations in Cell A.

Therefore, to get a conservative influence value estimation for cell g in terms of the whole client set C (for the relaxed optimal-location query), we need to sum up the counter values of all the covering cells of g in the upper level grids, besides the counter value of g. For example, the conservative estimation for Cell A in Figure 9 is the sum of its counter value and the counter value of g_{ul}, which is 2+2=4. The covering cell of g in an upper level grid can be identified in $O(1)$ using Observation 3. Algorithm 3 shows how the influence value estimation $\widehat{inf}(g)$ of cell g is computed.

Algorithm 3 Grid Cell Influence Value Estimation

```
    inf^(g) ⟵ counter(g)
    for each grid GRID of level higher than that of g do
        Find the covering cell g' of g in GRID
        if g' ∈ GRID then
            inf^(g) ⟵ inf^(g) + counter(g')
        end if
    end for
```

Algorithm 3 is executed on all the cells of all the grids in the hierarchy and the cell with maximum influence value estimation is returned.

However, a more general problem is to find k influential locations that collectively attracts the most clients. The exact problem can be viewed as a special case of the *maximum coverage problem*, where each intersection point between NLC boundaries corresponds to a subset of clients C that a new server there can attract, and the objective is to choose k such points(subsets) that covers as many clients in C as possible.

Although the *maximum coverage problem* is NP-hard [13], the greedy algorithm of choosing a subset which contains the largest number of uncovered elements at each stage, achieves an approximation ratio of $1 - \frac{1}{e}$ [13]. Inspired by this, FILM can be easily extended to find k influential grid cells by performing the following 2 steps at each stage, after the previous cell g_{pre} is picked: 1)find the NLCs overlapping with g_{pre}, and cancel them out from the grid hierarchy, and 2)pick the cell with maximum influence value estimation from the grid hierarchy as the next result cell. Algorithm 4 shows how an NLC NLC is canceled out from the the grid hierarchy, where we assume NLC is allocated to grid GD_{NLC}.

Algorithm 4 Cancel NLC out from the Grid Hierarchy

```
    for each grid GD of level not lower than GD_NLC do
        Find the candidate cell set of NLC in GD
        Pick the cells overlapping with NLC into set CELLS
        for each cell g ∈ CELLS do
            counter(g) ⟵ counter(g) − 1
        end for
    end for
```

Complexity Analysis: For NLC computation, it takes $O(|S| \log |S|)$ to construct the server kd-tree, and then for each client, an NN query is issued on the tree, with a total time of $O(|C| \log |S|)$. According to Definition 8, the *candidate cell set* size of any NLC is upperbounded by $\left(2 \cdot \frac{\delta^2 \cdot \varepsilon}{\varepsilon}\right)^2 = 4 \cdot \delta^4$. Therefore, for all $|C|$ NLCs, there are at most $n = 4 \cdot \delta^4 |C|$ cells stored in our grid hierarchy. For each of the n grids, we need to estimate its influence value using Algorithm 3, the time of which is bounded by $O(l \log n)$, where l is the number of grids in the hierarchy (typically around 6). To sum up, the time complexity of FILM is $O(|S| \log |S| + |C| \log |S| + n \cdot l \log n) = O(|S| \log |S| + |C| \log |S| + \delta^4 (\log \delta^4) l |C| + \delta^4 |C| l \log |C|)$, which is $O(|C| \log |C|)$ to the number of clients, much better than the super-quadratic time cost of MaxOverlap[1].

5. EXPERIMENTS

We have conducted extensive experiments on an AMD Opteron-based Linux CPU Server with 4×AMD Opteron 844 (1.8GHz) CPU and 8GB memory. We implemented

Table 1: Experimental Results on Real Datasets

		MaxOverlap_{NLC}		MaxOverlap_{RNLC}		FILM				
S	C	Exec Time	Influence	Exec Time	Influence	Exec Time	Inf_{RNLC}	Ratio_{RNLC}	Inf_{NLC}	Ratio_{NLC}
NA_{cl}	NA_{pp}	374.63 s	354	866.98 s	627	5.375 s	395	0.63	332	0.938
CA	GR	4379.65 s	1389	3685.37 s	1558	6.305 s	1460	0.937	1296	0.933
CA	GM	351916.73 s	3872	659814.0 s	5640	6.92 s	4369	0.775	3820	0.987

FILM in C++, and used the program of MaxOverlap provided by the authors of [1] for experimental comparison.[1]

The real datasets we used are obtained from R-tree Portal[14], which are summarized in Table 2. NA_{pp} and NA_{cl} contain 2D points representing the populated places and the cultural landmarks in North American, respectively. We also used the pre-processed real datasets adopted by [1], i.e., CA, GR and GM that contain 2D points representing geometric locations in California, Greece and Germany, respectively. On each dataset, we report our experimental results averaged over 10 runs.

Table 2: Summary of Real Datasets

S	$\|S\|$	C	$\|C\|$
NA_{cl}	9203	NA_{pp}	24493
CA	62556	GR	23268
CA	62556	GM	36334

As for the synthetic datasets, for each parameter configuration, we generated 5 independent sets of client and server points, and ran the program twice on each set. The reported results are averaged over the 10 runs.

Since we find that the experimental results on weighted clients are similar to those for the unweighted case, we only report the latter.

5.1 Experiments on Real Datasets

Table 1 shows our experimental results on the three datasets in Table 2 when the gird hierarchy parameter $\delta = 4$ (i.e., $\alpha = \frac{\sqrt{2}}{4}$). We denote by MaxOverlap_{NLC} the original MaxOverlap algorithm, and MaxOverlap_{RNLC} the modified MaxOverlap algorithm which uses RNLCs by expanding the radii of NLCs by $\alpha = \frac{\sqrt{2}}{\delta}$.

For FILM, we use inf_{RNLC} to denote the influence value estimation of the result cell, and define $ratio_{RNLC}$ as the ratio of inf_{RNLC} to the influence value of the result of MaxOverlap_{RNLC}, which measures the approximation quality of FILM to the relaxed optimal-location query.

To measure the result quality of FILM for the exact optimal-location query, we define inf_{NLC} to be the influence value of the center of the result cell of FILM. Since a user can pick any location in the result cell, we use the cell center to evaluate the result quality for simplicity.

Note that the center may not be the best choice, since many NLCs may just overlap with the boundary part of the cell. However, even in this case, their corresponding clients are still very likely to visit a server in the center since it is just a little farther than their nearest server, which is not considered by the conservative measure inf_{NLC}. We use the ratio of inf_{NLC} to the influence value of the result of MaxOverlap_{NLC} (i.e., the maximum influence) to evaluate the optimality of the result of FILM.

[1] http://www.cse.ust.hk/~raywong/code/maxRNN.zip

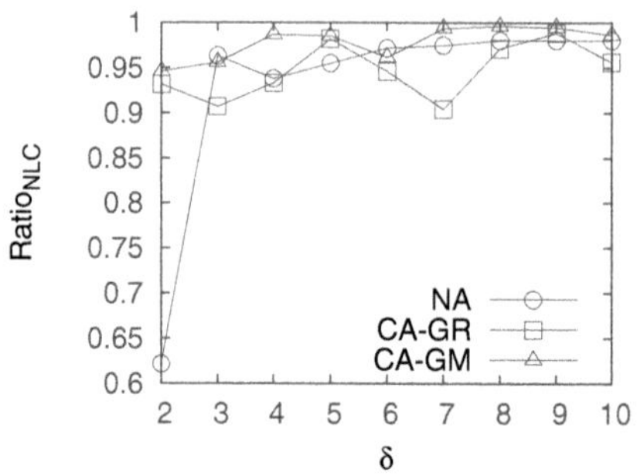

Figure 10: Approximation Quality on Real Datasets

From Table 1 we can see that the execution time of MaxOverlap is very sensitive to the data distribution. For example, MaxOverlap_{NLC} takes 4379.65s to compute the optimal location on CA–GR, but 351916.73s on CA–GM (over 80 times), despite the fact that the number of data points in GM is only 1.56 times that of GR. On the other hand, the execution time of FILM is very short and stable.

Theorem 2 only guarantees that FILM will be a good approximation algorithm for MaxOverlap_{RNLC} when δ is large. Thus, when $\delta = 4$ as in Table 1, $ratio_{RNLC}$ may not be close to 1 for some datasets (e.g., NA_{cl}-NA_{pp}). However, from $ratio_{NLC}$ we can see that FILM already approximates MaxOverlap_{NLC} well when $\delta = 4$, i.e., the center of the result cell of FILM is already a quite influential location when NLC is adopted as the ABUF.

Since our goal is to approximate MaxOverlap_{NLC} efficiently rather than to approximate MaxOverlap_{RNLC} for arbitrary δ, FILM works well in this sense and therefore we will focus on $ratio_{NLC}$ in the following discussion. As δ becomes larger, both $ratio_{RNLC}$ and $ratio_{NLC}$ approaches 1, but we cannot set δ too large because of the factor $O(\delta^4)$ in the time and space cost of FILM.

Fortunately, δ does not have to be very large to ensure good approximation quality. Figure 10 shows that Ratio_{NLC} approaches 1 as δ increases, and $\delta = 10$ is already sufficient for FILM to achieve over 98% of the maximum influence value.

There is a natural measurement of the memory usage of FILM, i.e., the total number of cells stored in the grid hierarchy (denoted N_{cell}). Since each grid cell is composed of a 2-integer index $\langle i, j \rangle$ and a counter, which consumes 12 bytes in a typical computer, the space cost of FILM can be approximated as $12 \times N_{cell}$ bytes.

Figure 13 shows the memory usage of FILM on the 3 real datasets, where we can see that N_{cell} increases fast with the increment of δ. Despite of this fact, a computer with gigabytes of memory like the one we use can easily handle FILM with δ up to 10, which is already sufficient to ensure good approximation.

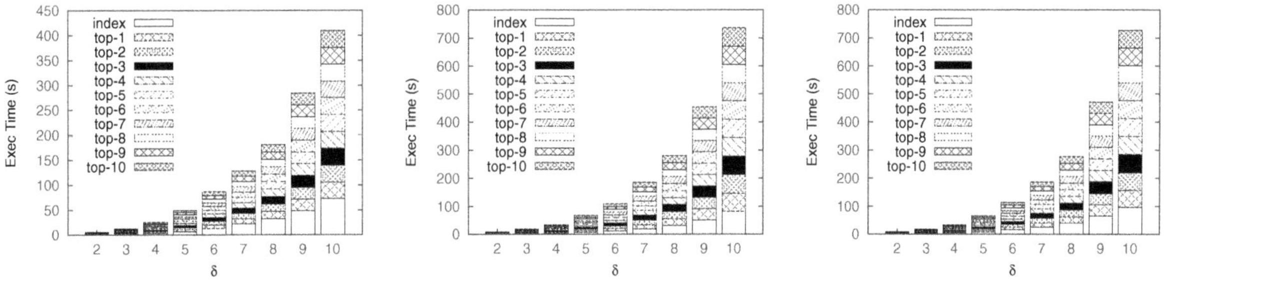

(a) NA (b) CA-GR (c) CA-GM

Figure 11: Execution Time on Real Datasets

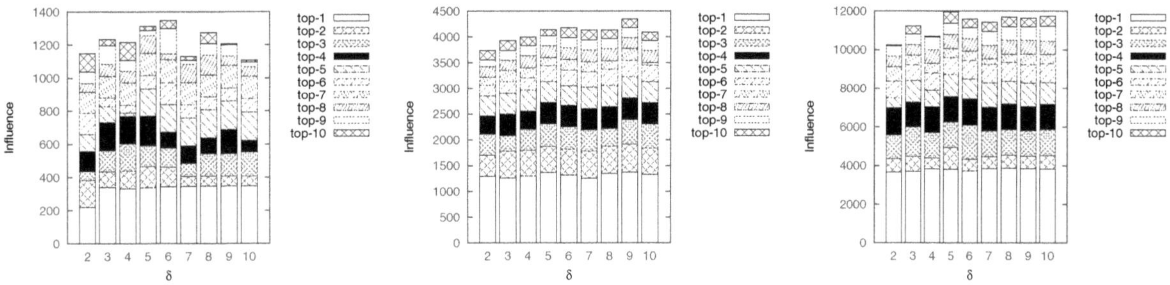

(a) NA (b) CA-GR (c) CA-GM

Figure 12: Influence Value on Real Datasets

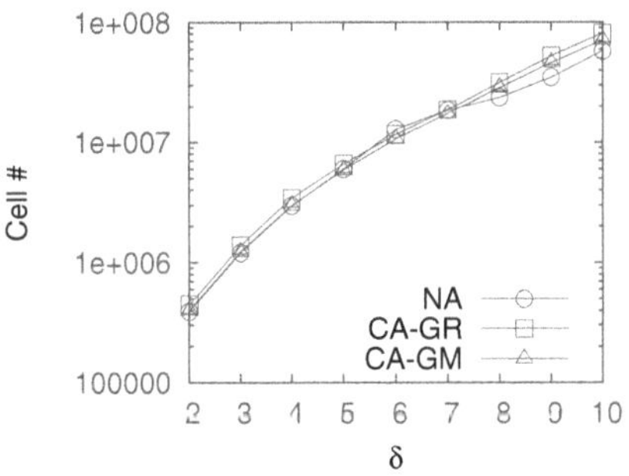

Figure 13: Memory Usage on Real Datasets

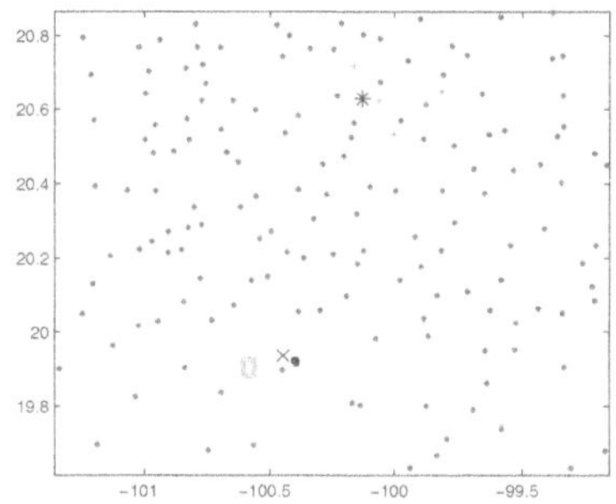

Figure 14: Top-1 Cells on North American Dataset

Figure 11 shows the running time of FILM on the 3 real datasets, where "index" denotes the time to construct the grid hierarchy, and "top-k" denotes the time to cancel out the $(k-1)$-th result cell (if $k > 1$) and find the k-th result cell from the grid hierarchy. We can see that the running time of FILM increases as δ increases, and that it takes FILM seconds to tens of seconds to return an influential cell depending on δ, which is considerably faster than MaxOverlap.

Figure 12 shows the result of FILM that finds k influential grid cells greedily on the 3 real datasets, where "top-k" denotes the number of new clients attracted by a server at the center of the k-th result cell. The number of clients attracted by the servers at the centers of the top-k cells increases with the increment of δ, although the influence value fluctuates at around $\delta = 6$. It is possible that if we randomly pick a location in each result cell rather than the cell center, there would be less fluctuation.

Figure 14 shows our results on NA_{cl}–NA_{pp} shown in Figure 6, where the red points are servers, the blue points are clients, the 'x' point is the intersection point returned by Max-Overlap$_{NLC}$, the '*' point is by Max-Overlap$_{RNLC}$, the green cell is the result of FILM when $\delta = 2$, the cyan cell is when $\delta = 4$, the magenta cell is when $\delta = 6$, the yellow cell when $\delta = 8$, and the black cell is when $\delta = 10$. We can see that the top-1 cell approaches 'x' from '*' as δ increases, which is also observed on CA-GR and CA-GM. Note that Figure 14 covers only 0.02% of the whole space in Figure 6.

5.2 Experiments on Synthetic Datasets

Since the effect of δ on the synthetic datasets is similar to that on the real datasets, we only report the results when $\delta = 4$. We generated the synthetic datasets by Uniform distribution or Gaussian distribution, and did two sets of experiments on them: 1)$|C| = |S|$, and 2) varying $|C|/|S|$.

In the first set of experiments, we set $|C| = |S| = 10^2$, 10^3, 10^4 and 10^5. The results show that it takes FILM more time on the more biased datasets of Gaussian distribution. For $|C| = |S|$, both the running time and memory usage of FILM are linear to the dataset size, and so is the running time of MaxOverlap.

We only show our experimental results for the second set of experiments in this subsection to save space. Since $|S|$ and $|C|$ are comparable on the real datasets we use, and in the real life $|C|$ tends to be much larger than $|S|$ for a server to serve many clients, we study the performance of FILM and MaxOverlap with varying $|C|/|S|$.

We set $|C| = 100000$ but use various $|S|$, the results of which are shown in Figures 15 and 16, where "FILM$_g$" denotes the results of FILM on datasets with Gaussian distribution, "RNLC$_u$" denotes the results of Max-Overlap$_{RNLC}$ on datasets with Unform distribution, "NLC$_g$" denotes the results of Max-Overlap$_{NLC}$ on datasets with Gaussian distribution, and so forth.

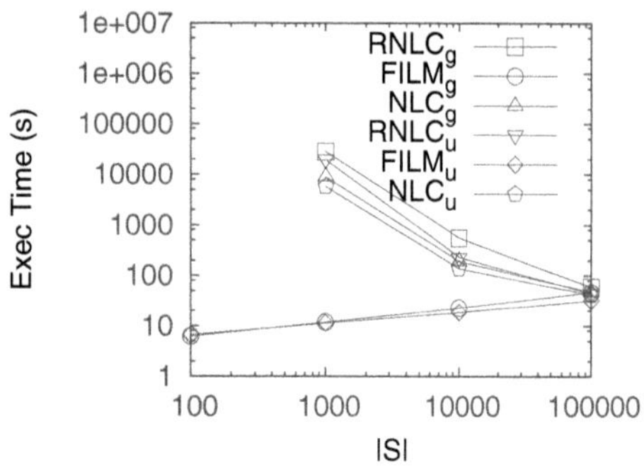

Figure 15: Execution Time on Synthetic Datasets

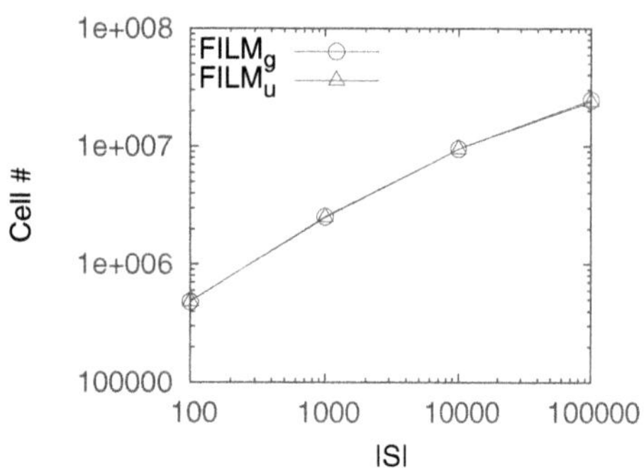

Figure 16: Memory Usage on Synthetic Datasets

We can see from Figure 15 that as $|C|/|S|$ becomes larger, Maxoverlap becomes much more expensive, while the time cost of FILM is insensitive to $|C|/|S|$. For example, when $|C|/|S| = 10$ (i.e., |S|=10000), Maxoverlap already takes hundreds of seconds, which is even worse as $|S|/|C|$ becomes larger (e.g., Maxoverlap takes over 28000s on "RNLC$_g$" when |S|=1000). When $|S| = 100$, MaxOverlap shows no trend to end after running for a week on any generated dataset of this configuration, and therefore these values are missing. The reason that large $|C|/|S|$ is expensive for MaxOverlap is that there are more intersection points to evaluate, since each NLC tends to be larger. On the other hand, FILM is even faster for small $|S|$ although the NLCs become larger, thanks to our grid structure that is adaptive to the NLC size.

6. CONCLUSION

We designed an efficient influential location miner called FILM, which returns a small grid cell in which all locations have an influence guarantee. In contrast to the existing approaches that return precisely an optimal location at the expense of long running time, our approach returns near-optimal locations in considerably less time. Thus, our approach is practical for many time-critical applications that require short response time of finding influential locations.

7. ACKNOWLEDGEMENTS

This work is partially supported by RGC GRF under grant number HKUST 618509 and grant number HKUST 621309.

8. REFERENCES

[1] R. C.-W. Wong, T. Ozsu, P. S. Yu, and A. W.-C. Fu. Efficient method for maximizing bichromatic reverse nearest neighbor. In *VLDB*, 2009.

[2] S. Cabello, J. M. Diaz-Banex, S. Langerman, C. Seara and I. Ventura. Reverse facility location problems. In *Canadian Conference on Computational Geometry*, 2005.

[3] N. Beckmann, H. Kriegel, R. Schneider and B. Seeger. The R*-Tree: An efficient and robust access method for points and rectangles. In *SIGMOD*, 1990.

[4] L. H. U, M. L. Yiu, K. Mouratidis, and N. Mamoulis. Capacity constrained assignment in spatial databases. In *SIGMOD*, 2008.

[5] R. C.-W. Wong, Y. Tao, A. W.-C. Fu, and X. Xiao. On efficient spatial matching. In *VLDB*, 2007.

[6] Y. Du, D. Zhang, and T. Xia. The optimal-location query. In *SSTD*, 2005.

[7] I. Stanoi, M. Riedewald, D. Agrawal, and A. E. Abbadi. Discovery of influence sets in frequently updated databases. In *VLDB*, 2001.

[8] B. C. Tansel, R. L. Francis, and T. Lowe. Location on networks: A survey. In *Management Science*, 1983.

[9] J. Krarup and P. M. Pruzan. The simple plant location problem: Survey and synthesis. In *European Journal of Operational Research*, 1983.

[10] T. Xia, D. Zhang, E. Kanoulas, and Y. Du. On computing top-t most influential spatial sites. In *VLDB*, 2005.

[11] T. Emrich, H.-P. Kriegel, P. Kröger, M. Renz, and A. Züfle. Boosting spatial pruning: on optimal pruning of MBRs. In *SIGMOD*, 2010.

[12] C. Kim, J. Chhugani, N. Satish, E. Sedlar, A. Nguyen, T. Kaldewey, V. Lee, S. Brandt, and P. Dubey. FAST: fast architecture sensitive tree search on modern CPUs and GPUs. In *SIGMOD*, 2010.

[13] D. S. Hochbaum. Approximating covering and packing problems: Set cover, vertex cover, independent set, and related problems. In *Approximation algorithms for NP-hard problems*, PWS Publishing Company, Boston, pp. 94-143, 1997.

[14] http://www.rtreeportal.org

Semi-Indexing Semi-Structured Data in Tiny Space

Giuseppe Ottaviano
Dipartimento di Informatica
Università di Pisa
ottavian@di.unipi.it

Roberto Grossi
Dipartimento di Informatica
Università di Pisa
grossi@di.unipi.it

ABSTRACT

Semi-structured textual formats are gaining increasing popularity for the storage of document collections and rich logs. Their flexibility comes at the cost of having to load and parse a document entirely even if just a small part of it needs to be accessed. For instance, in data analytics massive collections are usually scanned sequentially, selecting a small number of attributes from each document.

We propose a technique to attach to a raw, unparsed document (even in compressed form) a "semi-index": a succinct data structure that supports operations on the document tree at speed comparable with an in-memory deserialized object, thus bridging textual formats with binary formats. After describing the general technique, we focus on the JSON format: our experiments show that avoiding the full loading and parsing step can give speedups of up to 12 times for on-disk documents using a small space overhead.

Categories and Subject Descriptors

H.3.1 [**Information Storage and Retrieval**]: Content Analysis and Indexing—*Indexing methods*; E.4 [**Coding and Information Theory**]: Data Compaction and Compression

General Terms

Algorithms, Performance

Keywords

Semi-index, Semi-structured data, Succinct data structures

1. INTRODUCTION

Semi-structured data formats have enjoyed popularity in the past decade and are virtually ubiquitous in Web technologies: extensibility and hierarchical organization—as opposed to flat tables or files—made them the format of choice for documents, data interchange, document databases, and configuration files.

CIKM'11, October 24–28, 2011, Glasgow, Scotland, UK.

The field of applications of semi-structured data is rapidly increasing. These formats are making their way into the realm of storage of *massive* datasets. Their characteristics of being schema-free makes them a perfect fit for the mantra *"Log first, ask questions later"*, as the document schema is often evolving. Natural applications are crawler logs, query logs, user activity in social networks, to name a few.

In this domain JSON (*JavaScript Object Notation*, see [21]) in particular has been gaining momentum: the format is so simple and self-evident that its formal specification fits in a single page, and it is much less verbose than XML. In fact, both CouchDB[4] and MongoDB [24], two of the most used ([5, 25]) modern large-scale distributed schema-free document databases, are based on JSON, and Jaql [19] and Hive JSON SerDe [15] implement JSON I/O for Hadoop. These systems all share the same paradigm:

(*a*) Data is conceptually stored as a sequence of records, where each record is represented by a single (schema-free) JSON document.

(*b*) The records are processed in MapReduce [7] fashion: during the Map phase the records are loaded sequentially and parsed, then the needed attributes are extracted for the computation of the Map itself and the subsequent Reduce phase.

In part (*b*) the extracted data is usually a *small* fraction of the records actually loaded and parsed: in logs such as the ones mentioned above, a single record can easily exceed hundreds of kilobytes, and it has to be loaded entirely even if just a single attribute is needed. If the data is on disk, the computation time is dominated by the I/O.

A typical way of addressing the problem of parsing documents and extracting attributes is to change the data representation by switching to a *binary*, easily traversable format. For instance XML has a standard binary representation, Binary XML ([3]), and more sophisticated schemes that enable more powerful traversal operations and/or compression have been proposed in the literature (see [30]). Likewise MongoDB uses BSON, a binary representation for JSON. However, switching from a textual format to an ad-hoc binary format carries some drawbacks.

- In large-scale systems, the producer is often decoupled from the consumer, which gets the data through append-only or immutable, possibly compressed, distributed filesystems, so using simple self-evident standard formats is highly preferable.

- Binary data is not as easy to manually inspect, debug or process with scripting languages as textual data.
- If input/output is textual, back-and-forward conversions are needed.
- If existing infrastructure is based on textual formats, changing the storage format of already stored data can be extremely costly.

In fact, despite their advantages binary formats have not gained widespread adoption.

Surprisingly, even with a binary format it is not easy to support all the tree operations without incurring a significant space overhead. For example, BSON prepends to each element its size in bytes, enabling fast forward traversal by allowing to "skip" elements, but accessing the ith element of an array cannot have sublinear I/O complexity.

Our contribution. In this paper we introduce the notion of *semi-indexing* to speed up the access to the attributes of a textual semi-structured document without altering its storage format; instead, we accompany it with a small amount of redundancy.

A *semi-index* is a succinct encoding of the parse tree of the document together with a positional index that locates the nodes of the tree on the unparsed document. Navigation of the document is achieved by navigating the succinct parse tree and parsing on the fly just the leaf nodes that are needed, by pointing the parser at the correct location through the positional index. This way, a small part of the document has to be accessed: the I/O time is greatly reduced if the documents are large, and on a slow medium such as a disk or a compressed or encrypted filesystem. Specifically, the I/O time is proportional to the number of tree queries, regardless of the document size.

No explicit parsing tree is built, instead we employ a well-known balanced parenthesized representation and a suitable directory built on the latter. The resulting encoding is so small that it can be computed once and stored along with the document, without imposing a significant overhead.

We call our approach "semi-index" because it is an index on the *structure* of the document, rather than on its *content*: it represents a middleground between full indexing (where the preprocessing time and space can be non-negligible because the full content is indexed) and streaming (where data are not indexed at all).

The main novelty is that the document in its textual semi-structured format (or *raw data*) is not altered in any way, and can be considered a *read-only random access oracle*. The combination of *raw data + semi-index* can thus support the same operations as an optimized binary format, while maintaining the advantages of keeping the raw data unaltered.

- Backward-compatibility: Existing parsers can just ignore the semi-index and read the raw data.
- The semi-index does not need to be built by the producer: the consumer can build/cache it for later use.
- The raw data does not need to be given in explicit form, provided that a random-access primitive is given, while the semi-index is small enough that it can easily fit in fast memory. For example a compression format with random access can be used on the documents. We demonstrate this feature in the experimental analysis by compressing blockwise the data with *zlib*.

A semi-index can be engineered in several ways depending on the format grammar and the succinct data structures adopted for the purpose. Although the semi-indexing schema is general, we focus on a concrete implementation using JSON as the underlying format for clarity.

In our experiments (Section 6) we show that query time is very fast, and speedup using the precomputed semi-index on a MapReduce-like computation ranges from 2 to 12 times. Using a block-compressed input file further improves the running time when the document size is large, by trading I/O time for CPU time. This comes at the cost of a space overhead caused by the storage of the semi-index, but on our datasets the overhead does not exceed (and is typically much less than) around 10% of the raw data size.

When comparing against the performance of BSON, our algorithm is competitive on some datasets and better on others. Overall, raw data + semi-index is never worse than BSON, despite the latter is an optimized binary format.

To our surprise, even if the semi-index is built on the fly right before attribute extraction, it is faster than parsing the document: thus semi-indexing can be also thought of as a fast parsing algorithm.

The main drawback of the semi-index is that it has a fixed additive overhead of 150–300 bytes (depending on the implementation), making it unsuitable for very small individual documents. This overhead can be however amortized for a *collection* of documents. In our experiments we follow this approach.

In summary, our contribution in this paper is to show how to exploit our notion of semi-indexing to speed up sequential access to a collection of semi-structured documents in a very simple way. We believe that our paradigm is quite general and can be applied to other formats as well.

Paper organization. In Section 2 we compare our approach with existing literature. In Section 3 we review the tools and notations used in the paper. In Section 4 we overview a general technique to build and query the semi-index. In Section 5 we describe a specific representation for JSON, adopting some data structures from the state of the art ([2, 29]). In Section 6 we discuss the experimental results and the practicality of the approach. Finally, in sections 7 and 8 we introduce a different application of the technique and conclude giving future work directions.

2. RELATED WORK

A similar approach for comma-separated-values files is presented in [17]. The authors describe a database engine that skips the ordinary phase of loading the data into the database by performing queries directly on the flat textual files. To speed up the access to individual fields, a (sampled) set of pointers to the corresponding locations in the file is maintained, something similar to our *positional index*. This approach, however, is suitable only for tabular data.

Virtually all the work on indexing semi-structured data focuses on XML, but most techniques are easily adaptable to other semi-structured data formats, including JSON. For example, AgenceXML [6] and MarkLogic[16] convert JSON documents internally into XML documents, and Saxon [23] plans to follow the same route.

To the best of our knowledge, no work has been done on indexes on the *structure* of the *textual* document, either for XML or other formats. Rather, most works focus on providing indexes to support complex tree queries and queries on the *content*, but all of them use an ad-hoc binary representation of the data (see [13] for a survey on XML indexing techniques).

For the storage of XML data several approaches were proposed that simultaneously compress XML data while supporting efficient traversal, and they usually exploit the separation of tree structure and content (see [30] for a survey on XML storage schemes).

Some storage schemes employ succinct data structures: for example [8] uses a succinct tree to represent the XML structure, and [12] exploits compressed non-binary dictionaries to encode both the tree structure and the labels, while supporting subpath search operations.

The work in [35] is the closest to this paper, as it uses a balanced-parentheses succinct tree representation of the document tree, but like the others it re-encodes the contents of the document to a custom binary format and discards the unparsed form.

Industrial XML parsers such as Xerces2 [1] keep in memory only a summary of the tree structure with pointers to the textual XML, while parsing only the elements that are needed. This technique, known as Lazy XML parsing, needs however to scan the full document to parse the tree structure every time the document is loaded, hence the I/O complexity is no better than performing a full parse. Refinements of this approach such as double-lazy parsing [11] try to overcome the problem by splitting the XML file in several fragments stored in different files that link to each other. This however requires to alter the data, and it is also XML-specific. Besides, each fragment that is accessed has to be fully scanned. Semi-indexing is similar to lazy parsing in that a pre-parsing is used to speed up the access to the document, but the result of semi-index preprocessing is small enough that can be saved along the document, while in lazy parsing the preprocessing has to be done every time the document is loaded.

3. BACKGROUND AND TOOLS

3.1 JSON format

JSON (JavaScript Object Notation) is a small fragment of the Javascript syntax used to represent semi-structured data. A JSON *value* can either be an atom (i.e. a string, a number, a boolean, or a *null*), an *object*, or an *array*. An object is an unordered list of key/value pairs, where a key is a string. An array is an ordered list of values (so one can ask for the ith value in it). A JSON *document* is just a value, usually an object. The following figure shows an example of a JSON document and its parsing.

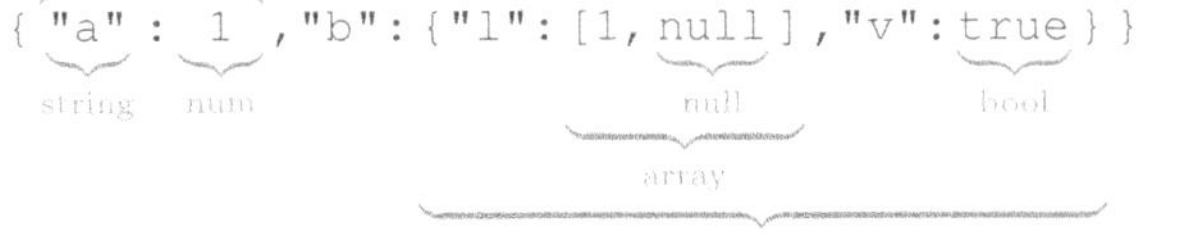

The document tree of a JSON value is the tree where the leaf nodes are the atoms and internal nodes are objects and arrays. The queries usually supported on the tree are the basic traversal operations, i.e. *parent* and *ith* child (and *labeled child* for objects). We use the Javascript notation to denote path queries, so for example in this document `a` is `1` and `b.l[1]` is `null`.

3.2 Succinct data structures

To encode and query the semi-index we employ succinct data structures. A succinct data structure stores the input data in the informational theoretical minimum number of bits, and still supports some given operations in constant time. We use two such data structures.

Elias-Fano encoding. The *Elias-Fano* representation of monotone sequences [9, 10] is an encoding scheme to represent a non-decreasing sequence of m integers in $[0..n)$ occupying $2m+m\lceil\log\frac{n}{m}\rceil+o(m)$ bits, while supporting constant-time access to the ith integer. The representation can be used to represent sparse bitvectors (i.e. where the number m of **1**s is small with respect to the size n of the bitvector), by encoding the sequence of the positions of the **1**s. In fact, the representation can support all the operations defined by Fully Indexable Dictionaries (FID, see [28]).

By analogy to FIDs, we call the access operation to the ith integer Select(i), and we denote its implementation in the pseudocode by `select`.

The scheme is very simple and elegant, and efficient practical implementations are described in [14, 27, 33][1].

BP. It is an acronym for *balanced parentheses*. They are inductively defined as follows: an empty sequence is BP; if α and β are sequences of BP, then also **(**α**)**β is a sequence of BP, where **(** and **)** are called *mates*. For example, **(()(()()))** is a sequence of BP. Note that a sequence of BP implicitly represents a tree, where each node corresponds to a pair of mates. BP sequences are represented as bitvectors, where **1** represents **(** and **0** represents **)**.

A sequence S of $2m$ BP can be encoded in $2m+o(m)$ bits [18, 26] so that the following operations, among others, are supported in constant or nearly-constant time.

- Access(i) returns $S[i]$; we denote its implementation with the square brackets operator `[]`.
- FindClose(i), for a value i such that $S[i] =$ **(**, returns the position $j > i$ such that $S[j] =$ **)** is its mate; we denote its implementation by `find_close`.
- FindOpen(i), for a value i such that $S[i] =$ **)**, returns the position $j < i$ such that $S[j] =$ **(** is its mate.
- Rank$_($(i) returns the pre-order index of the node corresponding to the parenthesis at position i and its mate; note that this is just the number of open parentheses before i, and we denote its implementation by `rank`.
- Excess(i) returns the difference between the number of **(**s and that of **)**s in the first $i+1$ positions of S. Note that since the parentheses are balanced this value is always non-negative, and it is easy to show that it equals 2Rank$_($(i) $- i$.
- Child(i, q) returns the parenthesis that opens the qth child of the node represented by the open parenthesis at position i.

4. SEMI-INDEXING TECHNIQUE

We illustrate our technique with the JSON document shown in the example of Section 3.1.

The most common way of handling textual semi-structured data is to *parse* it into an in-memory tree where the leaf

[1]In [27] the data structure is called *SDArray*.

nodes contain the parsed atoms. The tree is then queried for the requested attributes. Since the tree contains all the relevant data, the raw document is no longer needed, as shown in the figure below.

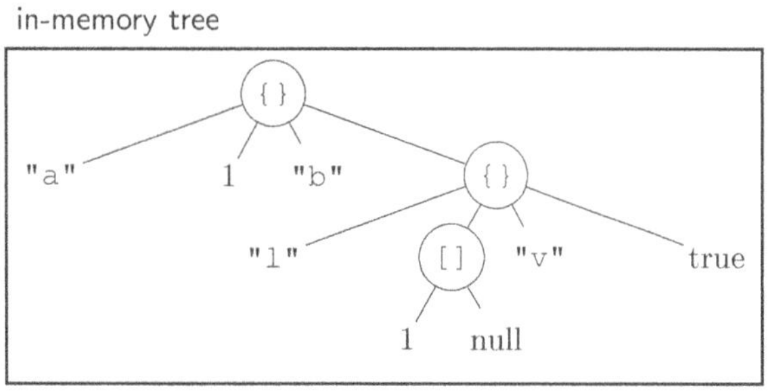


```
{ "a": 1, "b": { "1": [ 1, null ], "v": true } }
```

We would like to create a structure that allows us to navigate the document *without having to parse it*. One possible approach could be to dump the parse tree, and to replace the values in the nodes with *pointers* to the first character of their corresponding phrases in the document. This clearly requires to store also the raw data along with the resulting "thinner" tree.

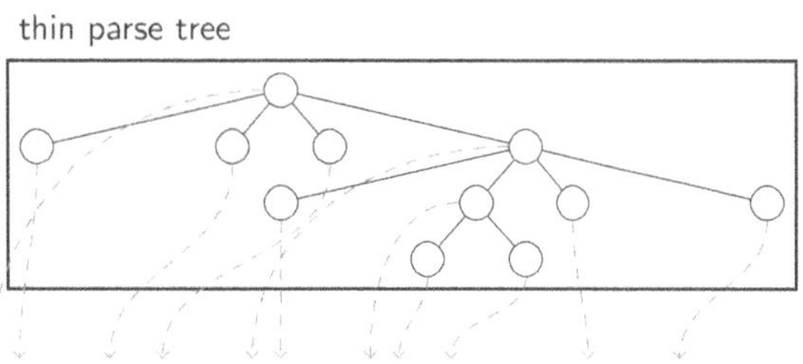


```
{ "a": 1, "b": { "1": [ 1, null ], "v": true } }
```

We can now navigate the parse tree, and parse just the values corresponding to the leaves that are actually needed. Note that if the grammar is LL(1)[2], we do not need to store the node type: it suffices to look at the first character of the node to recognize the production. So we are left with the tree data structure representing the topology of the parse tree, and a pointer for each node to the first character of its phrase in the raw text. This is very similar to the approach adopted by lazy parsers for XML.

Still, this requires building explicitly the parse tree every time the document is loaded. Instead, we will show how a quick scan of the document is sufficient to produce a sequence of balanced parentheses plus a bitvector as shown in the figure below (see Section 5 for details).

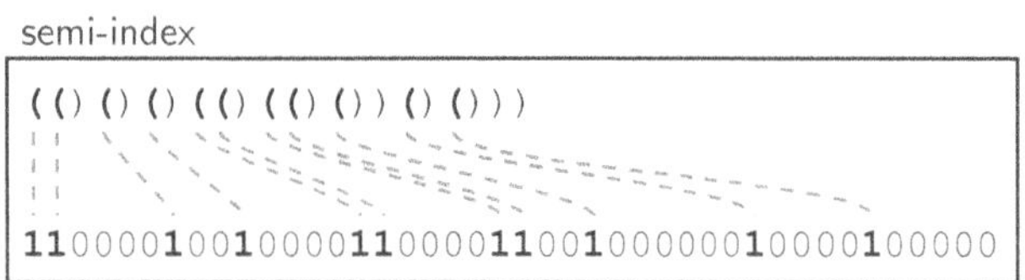


```
{"a": 1, "b": {"1": [1, null], "v": true}}
```

[2]Most semi-structured data formats are LL(1), including XML and JSON. If the grammar is not LL(1) an additional $\log P$ bits per node may be needed, where P is the number of productions.

This way we encode the same information as the thinner parse tree without parsing the document and building its parse tree. As we discuss in the experiments of Section 6, scanning is much faster than parsing. We merely store two binary sequences, encoding each parenthesis with a single bit, augmented with the machinery to support the operations described in Section 3.2. Besides, the binary sequence with the positions is sparse, so easy to encode in compressed format using very small space. Thanks to their small encoding, the two sequences can be computed just once and then be stored for future use.

This scheme can be applied to other formats. For instance, the XML semi-index would look like the following figure.

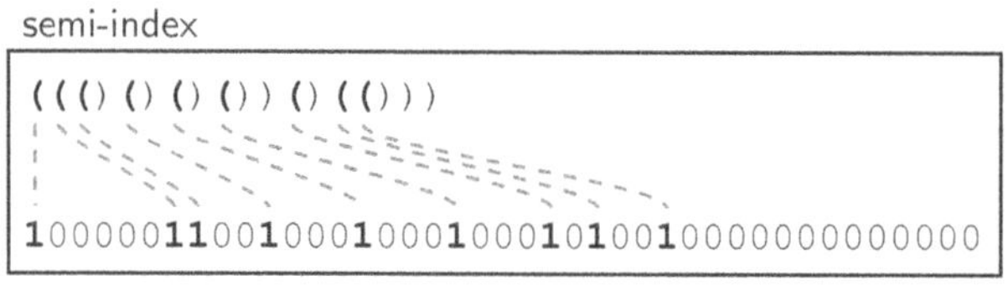


```
<entry␣id="1" cat="c">t1<b>t2</b></entry>
```

Our approach is to employ a set of succinct structures to replace the functionality of the thinner parse tree, and obtain faster construction and query time (see Section 6). We can thus define the *semi-index*.

Definition 4.1 *A* semi-index *for a document D is a succinct encoding of (i) the topology of the parse tree T of D, and (ii) the pointers that originate from each node of T to the beginning of the corresponding phrase in D.*

Let m denote the number of nodes in T. The general template to build the semi-index using an event parser is illustrated in Algorithm 1[3]. By *event parser* we mean a parser that simulates a depth-first traversal of the parse tree, generating an `open` event when the visit enters a node and a `close` event when it leaves it. (An example is the family of SAX parsers for XML.) If the event parser uses constant memory and is one-pass, so does Algorithm 1. Thus it is possible to build the semi-index without having to build an explicit parse tree in memory. In the pseudocode, *(i)* `bp` is the balanced parentheses tree structure, and *(ii)* `positions` is the Elias-Fano representation of the pointers.

```
def build_semi_index(s):
    positions = EliasFanoSequence()
    bp = BalancedParentheses()
    for event, pos in parse_events(s):
        if event == 'open':
            bp.append(1)
            positions.append(pos)
        elif event == 'close':
            bp.append(0)
```

Algorithm 1: Construction of semi-index using an event parser

For the construction algorithm to be correct we need the following observation.

[3]The pseudocode is actually working Python code, but we omitted the auxiliary functions and classes for the sake of presentation.

Observation 4.2 *The sequence of pointers in a pre-order visit of the parse tree T induces a non-decreasing sequence of m positions in D. In other words, the sequence of positions of* `open` *events in an event parsing is non-decreasing.*

Observation 4.2 allows us to use the Elias-Fano encoding, whose implementation is referred to as `EliasFanoSequence` in Algorithm 1, for the positions.

Algorithm 2 shows the pseudocode for some tree operations. Operation `get_node_pos` returns the position of the phrase in the document D corresponding to the node of T represented by the parenthesis at position `par_idx`. Operation `first_child` returns the position of the parenthesis corresponding to the first child of the current node. Operation `next_child` returns the position of the next sibling (if any).

```
def get_node_pos(bp, positions, par_idx):
    node_idx = bp.rank(node)
    pos = positions.select(node_idx)
    return pos

def first_child(bp, par_idx):
    return par_idx + 1

def next_sibling(bp, par_idx):
    next = bp.find_close(par_idx) + 1
    if bp[next]:
        return next
    else:
        return None
```

Algorithm 2: Some tree operations on the semi-index

We now discuss the space usage in our encoding. As shown in our example, the tree topology can be encoded with the balanced parentheses representation, thus taking $2m + o(m)$ bits. Nodes are identified by the open parentheses, so that $\text{Rank}_{(}(i)$ gives the pre-order index of node i.

The pointers can be thus encoded in pre-order by using the Elias-Fano representation, taking another $2m + m\left\lceil\log\frac{n}{m}\right\rceil + o(m)$ bits. Summing the two figures leads to the following lemma.

Lemma 4.3 *A semi-index of a document D of n bytes such that the parse tree T has m nodes can be encoded in*

$$4m + m\left\lceil\log\frac{n}{m}\right\rceil + o(m) \tag{1}$$

bits, while supporting each of the tree navigational operations in $O(1)$ time.

The bound in (1) compares favorably against an explicit representation of the tree T and its text pointers: even if space-conscious, it would require 2 node pointers plus one text pointer, i.e. $m(2\log m + \log n)$ bits. For example, for a reasonably sized 1MB document with density 0.2 (1 node for each 5 bytes on average), the size of the data structure would be 1.4MB, 140% of the document itself!

In practical implementation, the data structures that we adopt use approximately $5.5m + m\left\lceil\log\frac{n}{m}\right\rceil$ bits and have $O(\log n)$ complexity, but they are practically faster than data structures requiring theoretically constant time (see [2]). The encoding of the example above then takes 262kB, just 26.2% of the raw document. Even in case of a pathological high density document, i.e. $n = m$, the data structure would occupy $5.5m$ bits, i.e. an 68.7% overhead. Real-world documents, however, have very low densities (see Section 6).

5. ENGINEERING THE JSON *SEMI-INDEX*

In this section we describe a semi-index specifically tailored for JSON. It slightly deviates from the general schema presented in Section 4, since it exploits the simplicity of the JSON grammar to gain a few more desirable properties, as we will see shortly. As in the general scheme, we associate two bitvectors to the JSON document, `bp` and `positions`.

- The structural elements of the document, i.e. the curly brackets `{}`, the square brackets `[]`, the comma `,` and the colon `:` are marked in the bitvector `positions`, which is encoded with the Elias-Fano representation.
- For each structural element a pair of parentheses is appended to the `bp` (balanced parentheses) vector:
  - Brackets `{` and `[` open their own node (the *container*) and the first element of the list, so their encoding is `((`.
  - Brackets `}` and `]` close the last element of the list and their own node, so their encoding is `))`.[4]
  - Comma `,` closes the current element and opens the next, so its encoding is `)(`.
  - Colon `:` is treated like the comma, so key/value pairs are encoded simply as consecutive elements.

An example of the encoding is shown below: the JSON document (top), the `positions` bitvector (middle), and the `bp` bitvector (bottom). We implement `bp` as a binary sequence where `(` is encoded by `1`, and `)` is encoded by `0`.

```
{"a": 1, "b": {"l": [1, null], "v": true}}
100010010000010100010101000000110000100000011

(( )( )( )( (( )( (( )( )) )( )( )) ))
```

This encoding allows a very simple algorithm for the construction of the semi-index: a one-pass scan of the document is sufficient, and it can be implemented in constant space (in particular, no stack is needed). As a result, building the semi-index is extremely fast.

```
def build_semi_index(json):
    positions = EliasFanoBitVector()
    bp = BalancedParentheses()
    i = 0
    while i < len(json):
        c = json[i]
        if c in '[{':
            positions.append(1)
            bp.extend([1, 1])
        elif c in '}]':
            positions.append(1)
            bp.extend([0, 0])
        elif c in ',:':
            positions.append(1)
            bp.extend([0, 1])
        elif c == '"':
            # consume_string returns the position of
            # the matching '"'
            new_i = consume_string(json, i)
            length = new_i - i + 1
            i = new_i
            positions.extend([0] * length)
        else:
            positions.append(0)
        i += 1
```

Algorithm 3: Construction of JSON semi-index

[4]The empty object `{}` and array `[]` have encoding `(())`, so they are special cases to be handled separately in navigation.

Our ad-hoc encoding gives us two further features. First, each bit **1** in the bitvector `positions` is in one-to-one correspondence with pairs of consecutive parentheses in `bp`: there is no need to support a Rank operation to find the position in `bp` corresponding to a **1** in `positions`, as it is sufficient to divide by 2. Second, since the positions of closing elements (`}`, `]`, `,`) are marked in `positions`, it is possible to locate in constant time both endpoints of the phrase that represents a value in the JSON document, not just its starting position.

Navigation inside a JSON document is as follows. Finding a key in an object is performed by iterating its subnodes in pairs and parsing the keys until the searched one is found. The pseudocode for this operation can be found in `object_get`, Algorithm 4.

```
def get_pos(node):
    pos = positions.select(node / 2)
    pos += node % 2
    return pos

def object_get(json, node, key):
    # if node is odd, it is a comma, so skip it
    node += node % 2
    opening_pos = get_pos(node)
    if json[opening_pos] != '{':
        # not an object
        return None
    # empty objects are a special case
    if json[opening_pos + 1] == '}':
        return None

    node = node + 1
    node_pos = opening_pos + 1

    while True:
        if bp[node] == 0:
            return None
        node_close = bp.find_close(node)
        # node position after the colon
        val_open = node_close + 1
        # check if current key matches
        if parse(json, node_pos) == key:
            return val_open
        # otherwise skip to next key/value pair
        val_close = bp.find_close(val_open)
        node = val_close + 1
        # skip the comma
        node_pos = get_pos(node) + 1
```

Algorithm 4: Get position and object child by key

The query algorithm makes a number of probes to the JSON document that is linear in the fanout of the object. This is not much of a problem since the fanout is usually small. Otherwise, if it is possible to ensure that the keys are in sorted order, binary search can be used to reduce the number of probes to the logarithm of the fanout.

Array access can be done similarly with forward iteration through FindClose, with backwards iteration by jumping to the parenthesis closing the container and iterating on the contents with FindOpen, or with the ith child if `bp` supports it. In any case, at most 3 accesses to the JSON document are made: the I/O complexity is constant even if the runtime complexity may be linear.

We remark that in the design of the engineered JSON semi-index we have chosen simplicity over theoretical optimality. In general, other space/time/simplicity tradeoffs can be achieved by composing together other succinct data structures chosen from the vast repertoire in the literature, thus giving rise to a wide range of variations of the semi-indexing framework.

6. EXPERIMENTAL ANALYSIS

In this section we discuss the experimental analysis of the semi-index described in Section 5. The benchmark is aimed at the task of attribute extraction described in Section 1.

- Each dataset consists in a text file whose lines are JSON documents. The file is read from disk.
- The query consists in a list of key/index paths, to define which we use the Javascript notation. For instance given the following document

  ```
  {"a": 1, "b": {"v": [2, "x"], "l": true}}
  ```

  the query `a,b.v[0],b.v[-1]` returns `[1, 2, "x"]`, i.e. the list of the extracted values encoded as a JSON list. Note that negative indices count from the end of the array, so `-1` is the last element.
- Each benchmark measures the time needed to run the query on each document of the dataset and write the returned list as a line in the output file.

Implementation and testing details. The algorithms have been implemented in C++ and compiled with g++ 4.4. The tests were run on a dual core Intel Core 2 Duo E8400 with 6MB L2 cache, 4GB RAM and a 7200RPM SATA hard drive, running Linux 2.6.35 - 64bit. Before running each test the kernel page caches were dropped to ensure that all the data is read from disk. When not performing sequential scan, the input files were memory-mapped to let the kernel load lazily only the needed pages. For the construction of the semi-index each dataset is considered as a single string composed by the concatenation of all the documents, so a single semi-index is built for each dataset and stored on a separate file. The positions in the positional index are thus absolute in the file, not relative to each single document.

The source code used for the experiments is available at the URL `https://github.com/ot/semi_index`.

Succinct data structures. For the Select bitvectors and the Elias-Fano encoding we implemented the broadword techniques described in [33], in particular `rank9` for the Rank (used in the Excess primitive in BP) and a one-level hinted binary search for the Select. For the balanced parentheses we implemented the Range Min-Max tree described in [2]. With respect to the parameters described in the paper, we traded some space for speed using smaller superblock sizes. The excess forward and backward search on 64-bit words, that is in the inner loop of all the tree navigation operations, was implemented using a combination of lookup tables and broadword techniques to eliminate the branches.

Document compression. To simulate the behavior on compressed file systems we implemented a very simple block compression scheme which we call `gzra` (for gzipped "random access"). The file is split into 16kB blocks which are compressed separately with `zlib` and indexed by an offset table. On decompression, blocks are decompressed as they are accessed. We keep an LRU cache of decompressed blocks (in our experiments we use a cache of 8 blocks). The on-disk representation is not optimized—it may be possible to shave the I/O cost by aligning the compressed blocks to the disk block boundaries.

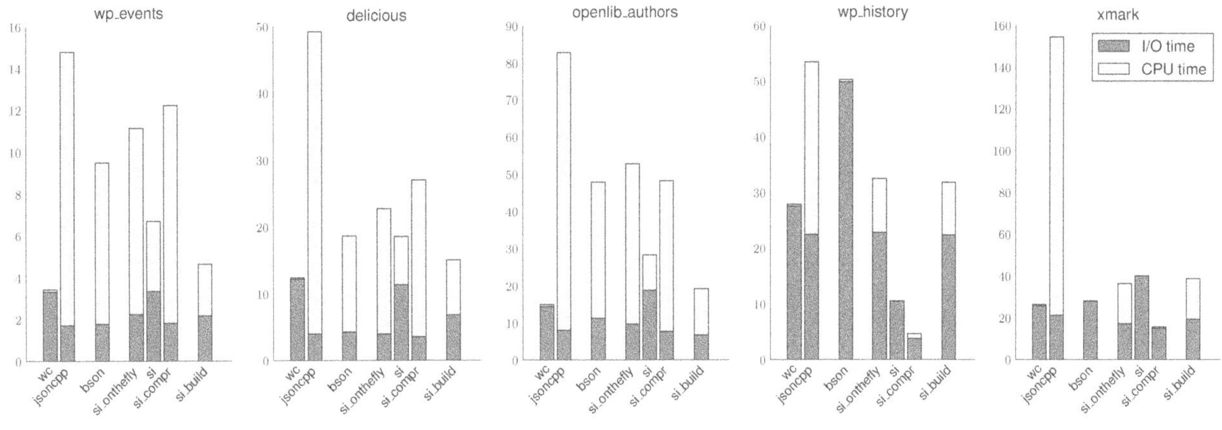

Figure 1: Wall clock times for each dataset as listed in Table 1. I/O time indicates the time the CPU waits for data from disk, while in CPU time the CPU is busy (and the kernel may be prefetching pages from disk).

Dataset	Wall clock time (seconds)						
	wc	jsoncpp	bson	si_onthefly	si	si_compr	si_build
wp_events	3.5	14.8 *(4.29)*	9.5	11.2 *(3.23)*	**6.7 *(1.94)***	12.2 *(3.55)*	4.7 *(1.35)*
delicious	12.4	49.3 *(3.96)*	18.7	22.8 *(1.83)*	**18.6 *(1.49)***	27.1 *(2.18)*	15.1 *(1.21)*
openlib_authors	15.0	82.9 *(5.52)*	48.0	53.0 *(3.53)*	**28.4 *(1.89)***	48.4 *(3.22)*	19.3 *(1.29)*
wp_history	28.0	53.5 *(1.91)*	50.3	32.6 *(1.16)*	10.6 *(0.38)*	**4.7 *(0.17)***	31.9 *(1.14)*
xmark	26.6	154.5 *(5.80)*	28.3	36.6 *(1.38)*	40.2 *(1.51)*	**15.9 *(0.60)***	38.9 *(1.46)*

Table 1: Running times for each dataset. Numbers in parentheses are the runtimes normalized on wc time. Numbers in bold are the ones within 10% from the best

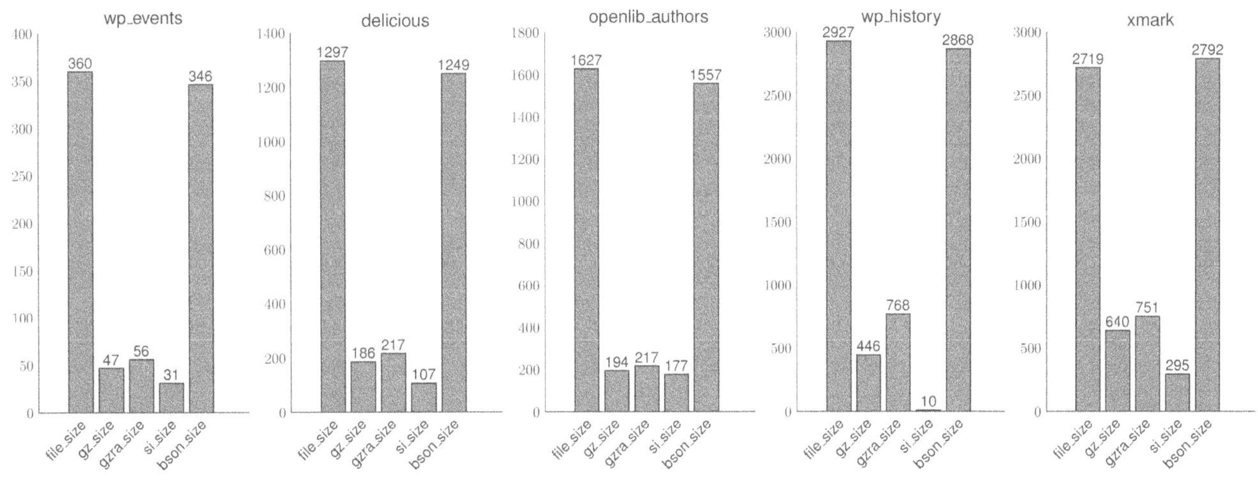

Figure 2: Space occupancy in MB of the file uncompressed (`file_size`), compressed with gzip (`gz_size`) and compressed with gzra (`gzra_size`), encoded in BSON (`bson_size`), and of the semi-index (`si_size`)

Dataset	Records	Average kBytes	Average nodes	Semi-index overhead
wp_events	1000000	0.36	24.82	8.85%
delicious	1252973	1.04	61.28	8.31%
openlib_authors	6406158	0.25	22.00	10.90%
wp_history	23000	127.27	203.87	0.34%
xmark	1000	2719.47	221221.48	10.86%

Table 2: Number of documents, average document size, average number of nodes, and semi-index space overhead (percent with respect to average document size) for each dataset used in the benchmark

Datasets. The experiments were performed on a collection of datasets of different average document size and density. On one extreme of the spectrum there are datasets with small document size (wp_events), which should yield little or no speedup, and very high density (xmark), which should give a high semi-index overhead. On the other extreme there is wp_history which has large documents and relatively small density. Specifically:

The Wikipedia data was obtained by converting to JSON the Wikipedia dumps [34], while we used the xmlgen tool from XMark [31] and converted the output to JSON to generate synthetic data of very high density.

- wp_events: Each document represents the metadata of one edit on Wikipedia.
- delicious [20]: Each document represents the metadata of the links bookmarked on Delicious in September 2009.
- openlib_authors [32]: Each document represents an author record in The Open Library.
- wp_history: Each document contains the full history of a Wikipedia page, including the text of each revision.
- xmark: Each document is generated using xmlgen from XMark with scale factor chosen uniformly in the range $[0.025, 0.075)$.

Queries. The queries performed on each dataset are shown in Table 3. We have chosen the queries to span several depths in the document trees (the XPath dataset xmark has deeper trees that allow for more complex queries). Some queries access negative indices in arrays, to include the contribution of the performance of backwards array iteration in our tests.

Dataset	Queries
wp_events	id timestamp title
delicious	links[0].href tags[0].term tags[-1].term
openlib_authors	name last_modified.value
wp_history	id title revision[0].timestamp revision[-1].timestamp
xmark	people.person[-1].name regions.europe.item[0].quantity regions.europe.item[-1].name open_auctions.open_auction[0].current

Table 3: Queries performed on each dataset

Testing. For each dataset we measured the time needed to perform the following tasks.

- wc: The Unix command that counts the number of lines in a file. We use it as a baseline to measure the I/O time needed to scan sequentially the file without any processing of the data.
- jsoncpp: Query task reading each line, and parsing it using the JSONCpp library [22] (one of the most popular and efficient JSON C++ libraries). The requested values are output by querying the in-memory tree structure obtained from the parsing.
- bson: Query task using data pre-converted to BSON.
- si_onthefly: Query task reading each line, building on the fly the semi-index, and using it to perform the queries. Note that in this case the semi-index is not precomputed.
- si: Query task using a precomputed semi-index from a file on disk.
- si_compr: Like si, but instead of reading from the uncompressed JSON file, the input is read from a gzra-compressed file.
- si_build: Construction of the semi-index from the JSON file.

Results. We summarize the running times for the above tests in Figure 1 and Table 1, and the space overhead in Figure 2 and Table 2, which also reports the statistics for each file in the dataset. We now comment in some detail these experimental findings.

A common feature on all the datasets is that the standard load-and-parse scheme using the JSONCpp library, and implemented as jsoncpp, has the worst performance. If time efficiency is an issue, the other methods are preferable.

BSON is a good candidate in this sense, since it uses preconverted data, as implemented in bson, and always runs faster than jsoncpp. It is interesting to compare bson with our methods, which also run faster than jsoncpp.

Consider first the situation in which we do not use any preprocessing on the data: when performing the queries, we replace the full parsing of the documents with an on-the-fly construction of the semi-index, as implemented in si_onthefly. As shown in our tests, si_onthefly performs remarkably well even if it has to load the full document, as the semi-index construction is significantly faster than a full parsing. Compared to bson, which uses a prebuilt index, the running times are slightly larger but quite close, and the I/O times are simlar. Surprisingly, for file wp_history, we have that si_onthefly is faster than bson: a possible reason is that in the latter the value sizes are interleaved with the values, causing a large I/O cost, whereas the semi-index is entirely contained in few disk blocks.

We now evaluate experimentally the benefit of using a prebuilt semi-index. The running times for si_build show that the construction of the semi-index is very fast, and mainly dominated by the I/O cost (as highlighted by the comparison with wc).

Using the pre-computed semi-index, si can query the dataset faster than bson, except for file xmark where it is slightly slower: as we shall see, when this file is in compressed format, the I/O time is significantly reduced. Also, on wp_history querying the last element of an array requires bson to scan all the file (as explained in the introduction), while si can jump to the correct position; overall si is 5 times faster than bson on this dataset. Note that contrarily to bson, si require less time than wc in some cases since it takes advantage of the semi-index to make random accesses to the file and retrieve just the needed bits.

The space overhead of the pre-built semi-index is reported in the last column of Table 2 and item si_size of Figure 2. The semi-index takes between 8% and 10% of the uncompressed input for all datasets except wp_history, where the overhead is practically negligible because data is sparse.

If the overall space occupancy is an issue, we can opt for a variant of our method si, as implemented in si_compr, where the dataset is kept compressed using the gzra format previously discussed. Note that this format, which is a variant of gzip, requires slightly more space but it allows for random block access to compressed data (e.g. compare items gz_size and gzra_size in Figure 2). When comparing to the space required by the binary format of bson (item bson_size in Figure 2), we obtain a significant saving, where the total space occupancy of the semi-index and the compressed dataset is the sum of the values of items gzra_size and size_size in Figure 2.

Regarding its time performance, si_compr is slighter slower than bson and si for sparse files, while it performs better for dense files such as wp_history and xmark: in the former case, the decompression cost dominates the access cost, while in the latter the I/O cost is dominant and the reduced file size improves it (still taking advantage of semi-indexing). This is also why si_compr is faster than wc on some files, and obtains a 12x speedup on wp_history over jsoncpp. Note that on xmark the running times of si and si_onthefly are comparable: the access pattern of the queries that we tested touches a large part of the file pages so there is no advantage in precomputing the semi-index, as (almost) all the file is accessed anyway.

Summing up, for each dataset at least one among si and si_compr has at least a 2x speedup. The graphs suggest that compression enables better performance as the average document size increases.

7. MEMORY-EFFICIENT PARSING

In this section we describe an alternative application of the semi-indexing technique.

A fully deserialized document tree takes often much more memory than the unserialized document itself. Hence in case of big documents it is very likely that the textual (XML or JSON) document fits in main memory but its deserialized version doesn't.

Industrial parsers such as Xerces2 [1] work around this problem by loading in memory only the tree structure of the document and going back to the unparsed document to parse the required elements. This approach however requires at least a pair of pointers per node, and usually much more. As shown in Section 4 for dense documents a pointer-based representation of the document tree can be more expensive than the document itself.

Since the construction of the semi-index is extremely fast, we suggest that a semi-index can be used in place of pointer-based data structures for lazy parsing.

Figure 3 shows the running times for jsoncpp and si construction and querying when the document is already in main memory, hence with no I/O is involved. Note that query times using the semi-index for in-memory documents are just 10 times slower than by accessing a fully deserialized tree using jsoncpp. This is very reasonable, since the query time includes the time to parse the leaf attributes once the semi-index has identified their position in the unparsed document.

Thus the semi-index can be used as an alternative to explicit or lazy parsing in applications where memory is a concern, for example on mobile devices.

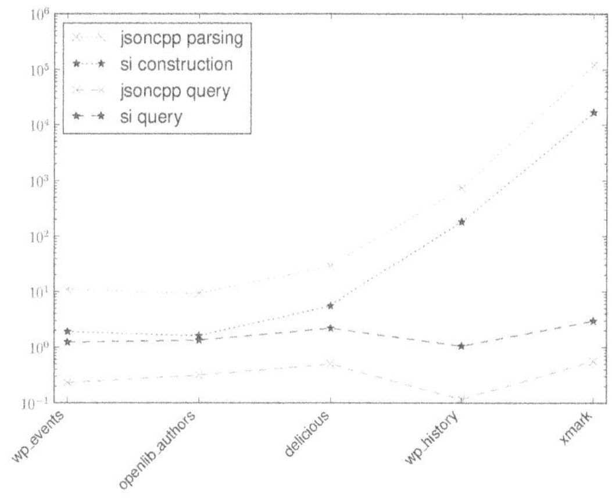

Figure 3: Timings (in microseconds, log-scale) for in-memory parsing and query operations.

8. CONCLUSIONS

We have described semi-indexing, a technique to build a data structure that enables navigation operations on textual semi-structured data without altering its representation. We engineered and implemented a specialization of the technique of the JSON format.

Our analysis demonstrates that the semi-index for JSON documents significantly outperforms the naive approach of parsing each document entirely, and has better performance than a binary format, without sacrificing too much storage space.

The technique we described only addresses basic traversal of the document tree. It would be interesting to devise more powerful semi-indexing schemes that support complex queries (à la XPath). Future work will focus on augmenting the semi-index with other structures to support new operations, while maintaining a small space overhead by exploiting the access to the raw document.

Acknowledgments

The authors would like to thank Luca Foschini for his insightful comments and suggestions on a preliminary draft.

9. REFERENCES

[1] Apache Xerces2 XML Parser. http://xerces.apache.org/xerces-j/.

[2] D. Arroyuelo, R. Cánovas, G. Navarro, and K. Sadakane. Succinct trees in practice. In *ALENEX*, pages 84–97, 2010.

[3] Binary XML. http://en.wikipedia.org/wiki/Binary_XML.

[4] CouchDB. http://couchdb.apache.org/.

[5] CouchDB in the wild. http://wiki.apache.org/couchdb/CouchDB_in_the_wild.

[6] A. Couthures. JSON for XForms. In *Proc. XMLPrague 2011*, 2011.

[7] J. Dean and S. Ghemawat. MapReduce: Simplified data processing on large clusters. In *OSDI*, pages 137–150, 2004.

[8] O. Delpratt, R. Raman, and N. Rahman. Engineering succinct DOM. In *EDBT*, pages 49–60, 2008.

[9] P. Elias. Efficient storage and retrieval by content and address of static files. *Journal of the ACM (JACM)*, 21(2):246–260, 1974.

[10] R. Fano. On the number of bits required to implement an associative memory. Memorandum 61. *Computer Structures Group, Project MAC, MIT, Cambridge, Mass., nd*, 1971.

[11] F. Farfán, V. Hristidis, and R. Rangaswami. 2LP: A double-lazy XML parser. *Inf. Syst.*, 34(1):145–163, 2009.

[12] P. Ferragina, F. Luccio, G. Manzini, and S. Muthukrishnan. Compressing and indexing labeled trees, with applications. *J. ACM*, 57(1), 2009.

[13] G. Gou and R. Chirkova. Efficiently Querying Large XML Data Repositories: A Survey. *IEEE Transactions on Knowledge and Data Engineering*, 19(10):1381–1403, 2007.

[14] R. Grossi and J. S. Vitter. Compressed suffix arrays and suffix trees with applications to text indexing and string matching. *SIAM J. Comput.*, 35(2):378–407, 2005.

[15] Hive JSON SerDe. http://code.google.com/p/hive-json-serde/.

[16] J. Hunter. A JSON Facade on MarkLogic Server. In *Proc. XMLPrague 2011*, 2011.

[17] S. Idreos, I. Alagiannis, R. Johnson, and A. Ailamaki. Here are my Data Files. Here are my Queries. Where are my Results? In *5th International Conference on Innovative Data Systems Research (CIDR)*, 2011.

[18] G. Jacobson. Space-efficient static trees and graphs. In *FOCS*, pages 549–554, 1989.

[19] Jaql. http://code.google.com/p/jaql/.

[20] JSON dump of Delicious bookmarks, September 2009. http://infochimps.com/datasets/delicious-bookmarks-september-2009.

[21] JSON specification. http://json.org/.

[22] JsonCpp. http://jsoncpp.sourceforge.net/.

[23] M. Kay. Ten Reasons Why Saxon XQuery is Fast. *IEEE Data Eng. Bull.*, 31(4):65–74, 2008.

[24] MongoDB. http://www.mongodb.org/.

[25] MongoDB Production Deployments. http://www.mongodb.org/display/DOCS/Production+Deployments.

[26] J. I. Munro and V. Raman. Succinct representation of balanced parentheses, static trees and planar graphs. In *FOCS*, pages 118–126, 1997.

[27] D. Okanohara and K. Sadakane. Practical entropy-compressed rank/select dictionary. In *ALENEX*, 2007.

[28] R. Raman, V. Raman, and S. R. Satti. Succinct indexable dictionaries with applications to encoding *n*-ary trees, prefix sums and multisets. *ACM Transactions on Algorithms*, 3(4), 2007.

[29] K. Sadakane and G. Navarro. Fully-functional succinct trees. In *SODA*, pages 134–149, 2010.

[30] S. Sakr. XML compression techniques: A survey and comparison. *J. Comput. Syst. Sci.*, 75(5):303–322, 2009.

[31] A. Schmidt, F. Waas, M. Kersten, M. J. Carey, I. Manolescu, and R. Busse. Xmark: A benchmark for xml data management. In *In VLDB*, pages 974–985, 2002.

[32] The Open Library, JSON dump of author records. http://infochimps.com/datasets/the-open-library.

[33] S. Vigna. Broadword implementation of rank/select queries. In *WEA*, pages 154–168, 2008.

[34] Wikipedia database dumps. http://download.wikimedia.org/.

[35] R. K. Wong, F. Lam, and W. M. Shui. Querying and maintaining a compact XML storage. In *WWW*, pages 1073–1082, 2007.

Evaluation of Set-based Queries with Aggregation Constraints

Quoc Trung Tran, Chee-Yong Chan, and Guoping Wang
Department of Computer Science, School of Computing
National University of Singapore
{tqtrung, chancy, wangguoping}@comp.nus.edu.sg

ABSTRACT

Many applications often require finding a set of items of interest with respect to some aggregation constraints. For example, a tourist might want to find a set of places of interest to visit in a city such that the total expected duration is no more than six hours and the total cost is minimized. We refer to such queries as SAC queries for "set-based with aggregation constraints" queries. The usefulness of SAC queries is evidenced by the many variations of SAC queries that have been studied which differ in the number and types of constraints supported. In this paper, we make two contributions to SAC query evaluation. We first establish the hardness of evaluating SAC queries with multiple count constraints and presented a novel, pseudo-polynomial time algorithm for evaluating a non-trivial fragment of SAC queries with multiple sum constraints and at most one of either count, group-by, or content constraint. We also propose a heuristic approach for evaluating general SAC queries. The effectiveness of our proposed solutions is demonstrated by an experimental performance study.

Categories and Subject Descriptors

H.2.8 [**Database Management**]: Database Applications

General Terms

Algorithms

Keywords

Set-based query, aggregation constraints

1. INTRODUCTION

Many database applications often require finding a set of items of interest with respect to some aggregation constraints. As an example, consider the following database relation which stores information about places of interest: $POI(\underline{name}, price, hour, type, city)$. Here, *name* refers to a place of interest located in *city* with a ticket fee of *price* dollars, *hour* refers to the recommended duration to spend at that place (in hours), and *type* refers to the category of the tourist place (e.g., museum, park). Suppose that Alice plans to find a tour package of places to visit from *POI* that satisfies the following requirements: (R1) all places are located in *NY* city, (R2) the total price is between \$300 and \$400, (R3) the expected duration is no greater than 10 hours, and (R4) the number of distinct types of places is maximized (to maximize diversity). Observe that Alice's request involves a simple filtering constraint, R1, and three aggregation constraints: two sum constraints (R2 and R3) and a count constraint, R4, to be maximized. The query's result consists of a collection of matching packages where each package is a set of places of interest that satisfy the four requirements.

Besides the "global" aggregation constraints illustrated by the above example, another very useful type of aggregation constraints are "local" *group-by aggregation constraints* that specify an aggregation constraint on specific subgroup(s) or all subgroups of the qualified sets, where a subgroup is defined with respect to an attribute list and optionally specific attribute values. As an example of a group-by count constraint on a specific group, Alice could require that there must not be more than two museum places in a matching package. In contrast, an example of a group-by sum constraint that is specified on each group is when Alice requires that the total visit duration to places of the same type does not exceed four hours.

Yet another useful type of set-based constraints are *content constraints* to specify the presence of certain attribute values (or tuples) in each qualified set. As an example, Alice could specify that each matching package must contain a visit to "Central Park".

We refer to such set-based queries with any combination of aggregation, group-by, and content constraints as `SAC` *queries*. The usefulness of `SAC` queries is evidenced by the variants of `SAC` queries (with different restrictions on the number and types of constraints permitted) that have been studied: OPAC queries for business optimization problems [4], student course planning in the CourseRank project [2], and item recommendations in shopping applications [1].

While `SAC` queries have many useful applications, the queries may not be easily expressed using SQL due to the fact that the qualified sets generally have different cardinalities and the maximum cardinality of the sets is data-dependent. More importantly, even when such complex queries can be

CIKM'11, October 24–28, 2011, Glasgow, Scotland, UK.

expressed and evaluated by SQL engines, their performance can be very poor as demonstrated by our experimental results. Indeed, the evaluation of general SAC queries involving any combination of aggregation, group-by aggregation, and content constraints is an NP-complete problem. Although a number of polynomial [2] and pseudo-polynomial time [4, 5] algorithms have been developed for evaluating simpler fragments of SAC queries, most of the proposed evaluation techniques are heuristic methods for more general SAC query fragments [1].

Contributions. We make two key contributions to the study of SAC query evaluation by addressing two open issues. First, there is the question of whether there exists other non-trivial fragments of SAC queries that can be evaluated in polynomial/pseudo-polynomial time. Currently, there are two fragments of SAC queries that are known to be amenable to efficient evaluation. First, SAC queries with one count constraint and at most one group-by count constraint, where the attribute(s) in the count and group-by constraint are the same, can be evaluated in polynomial time [2]. Second, SAC queries with any number of sum constraints and at most one group-by sum constraint can be evaluated in pseudo-polynomial time [5]. An open question that arises from this fact is: what is the complexity of evaluating SAC queries with more than one count constraint or with a combination of sum and count constraints? In this paper, we address this issue by first establishing that even for SAC queries with only two count constraints, the evaluation problem is already an NP-complete problem *in the strong sense*. Given this negative result for multiple count constraints, we next show that for the SAC query fragment with any number of sum constraints and at most one of either count, group-by, or content constraint, the evaluation problem has pseudo-polynomial time complexity, and we present a dynamic programming approach to evaluate this non-trivial SAC query fragment. Our second contribution is the proposal of a heuristic for evaluating general SAC queries with any combination of sum, count, group-by, and content constraints. The heuristic tries to find a solution that satisfies all the specified constraints but may return an approximate solution that meets only some of the constraints.

2. SAC QUERIES

A **S**et-based query with **A**ggregation **C**onstraints (or SAC query for short) can be expressed in terms of two components, $Q = (Q_{base}, C_{ans})$. Q_{base}, which is the base query of Q, is a conventional relational query that retrieves a set S_{base} of tuples, which serves as the base data for the SAC query. C_{ans} is a set of aggregation/group-by/content constraints such that each subset $S_{ans} \subseteq S_{base}$ that satisfies all the constraints in C_{ans} is a result of the SAC query Q.

The basic aggregation constraint in C_{ans} is a numeric constraint of the form "X *op* c", where X is some expression (to be described), *op* is one of the standard comparison operators ($=, \leq, \geq, <, >$), and c is a non-negative integer constant. The constraints permitted in C_{ans} are of the following five types:

(1) A **sum constraint** is a constraint on the sum of some attribute A_i in S_{ans}, denoted by $sum(A_i)$ *op* c.

(2) A **count constraint** is a constraint on the number of *distinct values* of a subset A' of the attributes in S_{ans}, denoted by $count(A')$ *op* c. When A' is a candidate key attribute of S_{ans}, the count constraint becomes a *cardinality constraint.*

(3) An **optimization constraint** is specified to maximize/minimize an aggregated value, and there are two forms of optimization depending on whether the aggregated value is bounded. A *bounded optimization constraint* is of the form "*opt* $(agg(X))$ *op* c", and an *unbounded optimization constraint* is of the form "*opt* $(agg(X))$". Here, *opt* is either *minimize* or *maximize*; *agg* is an aggregation operator (sum, count); X is either a single attribute (if *agg* is sum or count) or a sequence of attributes (if *agg* is count); and *op* is an non-equality comparison operator. As an example, the constraint $maximize(sum(A_i)) \leq c$ is a bounded optimization constraint on $sum(A_i)$, while the constraint $maximize(sum(A_i))$ is an unbounded optimization constraint on $sum(A_i)$.

(4) A **group-by constraint** is of the form $groupby(A', agg, B')$ *op* c, where A' and B' are subsets of attributes in S_{ans}, and *agg* is an aggregation operator (i.e., sum or count). The constraint requires that if S_{ans} is partitioned into groups of tuples having the same values for attribute(s) A', then each group must satisfy the aggregation constraint $agg(B')$ *op* c. In addition to this basic form of group-by constraint where the same count/sum constraint (i.e. c) is applied to each group, it is also possible to specify individual count/sum constraint for each group by explicitly listing the desired values of c's using the form: $groupby(A' = v_i, agg, B')$ *op* c_i.

(5) A **content constraint** is of the form $contain(A', V)$, where A' is a subset of attributes in S_{ans}, and V is a set of tuple values (of the same arity as the number of attributes in A'). The constraint requires that the projection of S_{ans} on A' must contain the set of tuples V.

In this paper, the SAC query fragment that we study allows C_{ans} to contain at most one group-by constraint. For other types of constraints, C_{ans} can contain any number of them[1]. Furthermore, the domain of the attribute involved in a sum or optimization constraint must contain non-negative values. For simplicity and without loss of generality, cardinality constraints are treated as a form of sum constraints (i.e., summing on a virtual attribute with a value of 1 for each tuple); therefore, we will not explicitly discuss cardinality constraints in this paper.

Since the problem of evaluating a SAC query is very hard in general, we focus on finding some answer for a given SAC query and leave the problems of ranking and/or finding top-k answers for SAC queries as part of our future work. We will use the tour package database illustrated in Figure 1 as our running example.

EXAMPLE 1. *Our example* SAC *query in the introduction can be expressed as follows: The base query* Q_{base} *corresponds to the SQL query: SELECT * FROM POI WHERE city = "NY", and the aggregation constraints are specified as follows: (R2)* $sum(price) \geq 300$, $sum(price) \leq 400$; *(R3)* $sum(duration) \leq 10$; *and (R4)* $maximize(count(type))$. *The additional local group-by count, local group-by sum, and content constraints discussed are specified, respectively, as follows:* $groupby(type = museum, count, *) \leq 2$, $groupby(type, sum, duration) \leq 4$, *and* $contain(name, \text{"Central Park"})$. □

[1]Note that when there are multiple optimization constraints, the query becomes a skyline query.

	name	price	hour	type	city
t_1	L1	50	2	museum	X
t_2	L2	70	3	park	X
t_3	L3	40	1	theatre	X
t_4	L4	25	2	museum	Y
t_5	L5	90	4	museum	Y
t_6	L6	20	1	shopping	Z

Figure 1: Running Example: Place of Interest (POI) relation

		city	hour	type
P_1	t_1	X	2	museum
	t_2	X	3	park
	t_3	X	1	theatre
P_2	t_4	Y	2	museum
	t_5	Y	4	museum
P_3	t_6	Z	1	shopping

(a) S_{base}

$SV_1 = \{1, 2, 3, 4, 5, 6\}$
$SV_2 = \{2, 4, 6\}$
$SV_3 = \{1\}$

(b) SV-sets

Figure 2: Partition POI using $city$ attribute

3. MULTI-SUM SAC QUERIES

With the exception of two fragments of SAC queries, namely, SAC queries with one count constraint and at most one group-by count constraint [2] and SAC queries with any number of sum constraints and at most one group-by sum constraint [5], most of the proposed techniques for evaluating more general SAC queries are heuristic solutions [1]. This raises the interesting open question of what is the complexity of evaluating SAC queries with more than one count constraint or SAC queries with a combination of sum and count constraints.

To address this issue, we first establish the following result on the evaluation of SAC queries with multiple count constraints; the proof is given elsewhere [6].

THEOREM 1. *Consider a* SAC *query Q where C_{ans} contains exactly two count constraints on two distinct attributes. The problem of evaluating Q is NP-complete.* □

Given the above negative result for SAC queries with multiple count constraints, we next ask the question of whether SAC queries with at most one count constraint can be efficiently evaluated. In this section, we show that for the SAC query fragment with any number of sum constraints and at most one of either count, group-by, or content constraint, the evaluation problem has pseudo-polynomial time complexity, and we present a dynamic programming approach to evaluate this non-trivial SAC query fragment. Our dynamic programming approach can also evaluate SAC query that includes any number of sum constraints and one count, one group-by, and one content constraint, where the attribute(s) used in these constraints are the same.

3.1 DP: Conceptual Approach

In this section, we present a novel, pseudo-polynomial time algorithm, termed DP, for evaluating SAC queries with any number of sum constraints and at most one of either count, group-by, or content constraint. For convenience, we refer to this SAC query fragment as *multi-sum* SAC *queries*.

To simplify the presentation, we first explain how DP evaluates a simpler subset of multi-sum SAC queries with multiple sum and a single count constraints, and then briefly discuss the generalization of DP to solve the general multi-sum SAC queries in Section 3.3.

For simplicity and without loss of generality, we explain the evaluation for a SAC query $Q = (Q_{base}, C_{ans})$ where C_{ans} contains the following two constraints on two attributes A and B and the domain of A contains integer values[2].

- Sum maximization constraint: $maximize(sum(A)) \leq K$, and
- Count constraint: $count(B) = m$.

Let ℓ denote the number of distinct B attribute values in S_{base}. Recall that S_{base} is the set of base data retrieved by the base query Q_{base}. DP is based on the following two-phase dynamic programming approach.

First, DP partitions S_{base} using the B attribute into ℓ partitions $P_1, \cdots, P_\ell$. For each partition P_i, DP derives $SV_i = \{V \in [1, K] \mid \exists\ P_{s,i} \subseteq P_i\ s.t. \sum_{t \in P_{s,i}}(t.A) = V\}$. We say that a value $V \in SV_i$ is the *representation* of a set $P_{s,i} \subseteq P_i$ iff $\sum_{t \in P_{s,i}}(t.A) = V$. Note that in general, V can represent more than one set $P_{s,i}$; however, DP only records one set $P_{s,i}$ that V represents. This task is a subset-sum problem that can be solved using dynamic programming.

In the next step, DP selects m SV_i sets and one value from each selected set SV_i so that the summation of these selected values is maximized and does not exceed K. This task can be solved using dynamic programming. Without loss of generality, assume that the selected sets in this step are $SV_1, \cdots, SV_m$; and the corresponding value selected in each SV_i is v_i, $i \in [1, m]$. Since each v_i represents a subset $P_{s,i} \subseteq P_i$, DP unions these $P_{s,i}$, $i \in [1, m]$, as the final answer S_{ans}. Clearly, S_{ans} has $count(B) = m$, as each $P_{s,i}$ "contributes" a distinct B value. Furthermore, S_{ans} has $sum(A)$ maximized without exceeding K because $\sum_1^m(v_i)$ is maximized and does not exceed K.

EXAMPLE 2. *Assume a user wants to find a package of places to visit from POI with the following two constraints: (1) $maximize(sum(hour)) \leq 7$, and (2) $count(city) = 2$.* DP *first partitions S_{base} into three partitions, P_1 to P_3, using city attribute, as shown in Figure 2(a).* DP *then derives the corresponding three sets, SV_1 to SV_3, shown in Figure 2(b). For instance, $v_{1,5} = 5 \in SV_1$, since $v_{1,5}$ represents for the subset $P_{1,s} = \{t_1, t_2\}$; i.e., $\sum_{t \in P_{1,s}}(t.hour) = 5$.*

In the next step, DP *selects SV_1 and SV_2; and chooses $5 \in SV_1$ and $2 \in SV_2$ where their summation is maximized and does not exceed 7. Since 5 represents for the set $P_{1,s} = \{t_1, t_2\}$ and 2 represents for the set $P_{2,s} = \{t_4\}$,* DP *unions $P_{1,s}$ and $P_{2,s}$ to return $S_{ans} = \{t_1, t_2, t_4\}$. Note that S_{ans} is not the only solution; another possible solution is $\{t_4, t_5, t_6\}$.* □

3.2 DP: Algorithm

We now elaborate on the details of DP for evaluating a SAC query involving two attributes A and B as given in Section 3.1. For simplicity and without loss of general-

[2]If the domain of A contains real values, DP approximates the real values by integer values.

ity, let the domain of the B attribute values in S_{base} be $dom(B) = \{1, 2, \cdots, \ell\}$[3].

For each $b \in dom(B)$, let S^b_{base} and $S^{\leq b}_{base}$ be a subset of S_{base} defined in Equations 1 and 2, respectively. Let $E[1 \cdots \ell, 1 \cdots K]$ be a two-dimensional matrix, where each cell $E[b, V]$ is a boolean value defined in Equation 3. Each row $E[b, .]$ is a subset-sum problem that can be solved with a time complexity of $O(K|S^b_{base}|)$. Therefore, the entire matrix E can be constructed in $O(K|S_{base}|)$.

Let $\mathcal{D}[1 \cdots \ell, 1 \cdots m, 1 \cdots K]$ be a three-dimensional matrix, where each cell $\mathcal{D}[b, d, V]$ is a boolean value defined in Equation 4.

$$S^b_{base} = \{t \in S_{base} \mid t.B = b\} \tag{1}$$

$$S^{\leq b}_{base} = \{t \in S_{base} \mid t.B \leq b\} \tag{2}$$

$$E[b, V] = true \text{ iff } \exists\, S \subseteq S^b_{base} \text{ s.t. } \sum_{t \in S}(t.A) = V \tag{3}$$

$$\mathcal{D}[b, d, V] = true \text{ iff} \exists\, S \subseteq S^{\leq b}_{base} \text{ s.t. } |\pi_B(S)| = d \wedge \sum_{t \in S}(t.A) = V \tag{4}$$

DP can find a solution if there exists a maximum value $V_{max} \leq K$ such that (1) $\mathcal{D}[\ell, m, V_{max}] = true$, and (2) for every value $V > V_{max}$, $\mathcal{D}[\ell, m, V] = false$. We have the following recurrence relation:

$$\mathcal{D}[b, d, V] = \mathcal{D}[b-1, d, V] \ \vee$$
$$\exists\, V' \in [1, V] \ s.t. \ (E[b, V'] = 1 \ \wedge \ \mathcal{D}[b-1, d-1, V-V'] = 1)$$

The recurrence relation indicates that $\mathcal{D}[b, d, V]$ can be derived from either (1) $\mathcal{D}[b-1, d, V]$ if we do not select any tuples from S^b_{base}, or (2) $\mathcal{D}[b-1, d-1, V-V']$ if we select a subset of tuples S' from S^b_{base} with $\sum_{t \in S'}(t.A) = V'$.

The computation of each $\mathcal{D}[b, d, V]$ requires at most V look up operations on the corresponding row $E[b, .]$ in the E matrix. Thus, the time to build matrix $\mathcal{D}$ in the worst case is $O(m\ell \sum_{V=1}^{K}(V)) = O(K^2 m\ell)$.

Deriving S_{ans}. In addition to the main matrix $\mathcal{D}$, DP uses another matrix $DTrace[\ell, m, K]$ that has the same dimensions as $\mathcal{D}$ to derive S_{ans}. Each cell $DTrace[b, d, V]$ is set to either (1) a value 0 if $\mathcal{D}[b, d, V]$ is derived from $\mathcal{D}[b-1, d, V]$, or (2) a value $V' > 0$ if $\mathcal{D}[b, d, V]$ is derived from $\mathcal{D}[b-1, d-1, V-V']$ and $E[b, V']$.

To derive a set of returned tuples S_{ans}, DP first determines the maximum value $V_{max} \leq K$ such that $\mathcal{D}[\ell, m, V_{max}] = true$. There are two cases to consider:

- If $DTrace[\ell, m, V_{max}] = 0$, then S_{ans} is the set of tuples that makes $\mathcal{D}[\ell-1, m, V_{max}] = true$.
- Otherwise, if $DTrace[\ell, m, V_{max}] = V'$, then S_{ans} is the union of the set of tuples that makes $D[\ell-1, m-1, V_{max} - V'] = true$ and the set of tuples that makes $E[\ell, V'] = true$.

The technique to derive a set of tuples that makes $E[\ell, V'] = true$ follows a standard procedure for solving the subset-sum problem. We briefly describe this procedure in the following.

[3]In general, we can easily map an arbitrary set of ℓ values into the set $\{1, 2, \cdots, \ell\}$.

Assume that $S^{\ell}_{base} = \{t_1, \cdots, t_y\}$. To compute $E[\ell, .]$, DP builds a two-dimensional matrix $F[1 \cdots y, 1 \cdots K]$ with the following recurrence equation:

$$F[i, V] = F[i-1, V] \ \vee \ F[i-1, V - t_i.A]$$

DP maintains another matrix, denoted as $FTrace[1 \cdots y, 1 \cdots K]$, that has the same dimensionality as F. Each $FTrace[i, V]$ keeps track of how $F[i, V]$ is derived; i.e., $FTrace[i, V]$ is set to either (1) $false$ if $F[i, V]$ is derived from $F[i-1, V]$; or (2) $true$, otherwise.

To find a subset S^{ℓ} of tuples that make $E[\ell, V] = true$, DP traces from $FTrace[y, V]$. If $F[y, V] = false$, then S^{ℓ} is the set of tuples that makes $F[y-1, V] = true$. Otherwise, if $F[y, V] = true$, then S^{ℓ} is the union of $\{t_y\}$ and the set of tuples that makes $F[y-1, V - t_y.A] = true$.

Complexity. The space complexity of DP is $O(K|S_{base}| + Km\ell)$ to keep the matrices for the recurrence relations in the main memory. The time complexity of DP is the summation of the following three components: (1) partitioning S_{base} based on B attribute (denoted by T_{part}), (2) computing E matrix, and (3) computing $\mathcal{D}$ matrix. To partition S_{base} based on the B attribute, Greedy augments the base query with an *ORDER BY* clause on B and evaluates this derived query to obtain the set of partitions of S_{base}. Thus, T_{part} is the time to execute the derived query on the DBMS. The time complexity of DP is, therefore, $O(T_{part} + K|S_{base}| + K^2 m\ell)$.

Approximation version of DP. When K and/or ℓ is large, the space required by DP might exceed the available main memory. In these cases, DP needs to reduce the space requirement by scaling down the domain values of the attribute used with the sum constraint (i.e., A attribute) by some factor c_f; thus, K will be replaced by K/c_f. The solution of DP is approximate in these cases.

3.3 DP: Generalization

The DP approach can be generalized to evaluate multi-sum SAC queries when C_{ans} includes more than one optimization constraint. The idea is to build a matrix for the dynamic programming technique similar to $\mathcal{D}$ and find all the "skyline" values in this matrix. In particular, assume C_{ans} includes $(n+1)$ constraints: $maximize(sum(A_i)) \leq K_i$ for $i \in [1, n]$, and $count(B) = m$. DP builds a $(n+2)$-dimensional matrix $\mathcal{D}[1 \cdots \ell, 1 \cdots m, 1 \cdots K_1, \cdots, 1 \cdots K_n]$. To derive a result set S_{ans}, DP finds all "skyline" cells $\mathcal{D}[\ell, m, V_1, \cdots, V_n] = 1$ such that there does not exist any tuple of values $(V'_1, \cdots, V'_n)$ where (1) $\mathcal{D}[\ell, m, V'_1, \cdots, V'_n] = 1$, (2) $V'_i \geq V_i$, for all $i \in [1, n]$, and (3) at least one of V'_i is strictly greater than V_i.

Similarly, the DP approach can be generalized to solve multi-sum SAC query when C_{ans} includes any number of sum constraints and at most one of either content or group-by constraint. The idea is also based on a two-phase dynamic programming approach. In the first phase, DP partitions S_{base} using attribute(s) for the content or group-by constraints and derives SV-sets for each partition of S_{base} with respect to the content or group-by constraints. The second phase manipulates the derived SV-sets to compute the answer set. The details are given elsewhere [6].

4. GENERAL SAC QUERIES

In this section, we examine the evaluation of general SAC

queries involving any combination of aggregation, group-by, and content constraints. By Theorem 1, it follows that this evaluation problem is NP-complete. We therefore present a heuristic solution, termed **Greedy**, to evaluate general SAC queries. An answer set computed by our heuristic could be suboptimal in the sense that the answer set does not satisfy all the required constraints.

For ease of presentation, our discussion is organized into three cases from the simplest to the most general case.

4.1 Count Constraints

We first discuss the simplest scenario where all the constraints in C_{ans} are count constraints. For simplicity and without loss of generality, we consider a SAC query with two count constraints: $count(B_i) = m_i$, $i \in [1, 2]$, where $m_1 \leq m_2$. Our Greedy heuristic is based on the following result.

LEMMA 1. *If there exists a subset $S_{count} \subseteq S_{base}$ that has $count(B_1) = m_1$ and $count(B_2) \geq m_2$, then there exists a subset $S_{ans} \subseteq S_{count}$ that has $count(B_1) = m_1$ and $count(B_2) = m_2$.*

Proof of Lemma 1. Given a subset $S_{count} \subseteq S_{base}$ that has $count(B_1) = m_1$ and $count(B_2) \geq m_2$, we first pick m_1 arbitrary tuples in S_{count} that have m_1 distinct B_1 values to put into S_{ans}. The number of distinct B_2's values in S_{ans} is currently not greater than m_1 and therefore is also not greater than m_2, since our assumption is $m_1 \leq m_2$. We then need to insert some tuples from $(S_{count} - S_{ans})$ into S_{ans} to increase the number of distinct B_2's values in S_{ans} into m_2. This task is accomplished by performing $m_2 - |\pi_{B_2}(S_{ans})|$ steps. In each step, we pick a tuple in $(S_{count} - S_{ans})$ to insert into S_{ans} in such a way that the number of distinct B_2's values in the resultant S_{ans} increases by 1. □

Using Lemma 1, Greedy will derive a set $S_{count} \subseteq S_{ans}$ that has $count(B_1) = m_1$ and $count(B_2)$ is as *large* as possible. The rationale is that if S_{count} has $count(B_2) \geq m_2$, then we can derive S_{ans} from S_{count} satisfying all the constraints. The details of Greedy are as follows.

Greedy first partitions S_{base} using the values of B_1 attribute, and performs m_1 iterations to insert m_1 partitions of S_{base} into S_{count}. At each iteration, Greedy considers all potential partitions in S_{base}, and chooses the "best" partition to insert into S_{count} such that the resultant S_{count} has the largest number of distinct B_2's values. After m_1 iterations, there are two cases to consider. If $|\pi_{B_2}(S_{count})| \geq m_2$, Greedy derives S_{ans} based on Lemma 1 such that S_{ans} satisfies all the count constraints from S_{count}. Otherwise, if $|\pi_{B_2}(S_{count})| < m_2$, Greedy returns $S_{ans} = S_{count}$ as an approximate result that does not satisfy the count constraint on B_2.

Complexity. The space complexity of Greedy is $O(|S_{base}|)$, since in the worst case, Greedy stores all distinct B_2 values in the main memory. The time complexity of Greedy is $O(T_{part} + T_{alg})$, where (1) T_{part} is the time to partition S_{base} based on B_1 attribute, and (2) T_{alg} is the time to derive S_{count} and then S_{ans}. Similar to DP, Greedy also augments the base query with an *ORDER BY* clause on B_1 and evaluates this derived query to obtain the set of partitions of S_{base}. We have $T_{alg} = m_1|S_{base}|$, since Greedy performs m_1 iterations and basically scans all tuples in S_{base} in each iteration.

EXAMPLE 3. *Consider a user who wants to find a tour package consisting of places of interest from two different cities and with three different types of activities.* Greedy *first derives a set S_{count} that has $count(city) = 2$ and $count(type)$ as large as possible. For this task,* Greedy *partitions $S_{base} = POI$ into three partitions using city attribute, as shown in Figure 2(a). In the first iteration,* Greedy *selects partition P_1 to put into S_{count}, since P_1 contains the largest number of distinct type values. In the second iteration,* Greedy *selects P_3 to put into S_{count}, since P_3 increases the number of distinct type values in S_{count} the most. Note that* Greedy *does not select P_2, since it does not help to increase $count(type)$ in S_{count}. Thus, $S_{count} = P_1 \cup P_3 = \{t_1, t_2, t_3, t_6\}$.*

Since S_{count} has $count(type) = 4$, Greedy *can derive the exact answer for this case. Using Lemma 1,* Greedy *first selects $t_1 \in P_1$ and $t_6 \in P_3$ to put into S_{ans} for $count(city) = 2$ in S_{ans}. Finally,* Greedy *puts t_2 into S_{ans}. Thus, $S_{ans} = \{t_1, t_2, t_6\}$.* □

Generalization. The other cases of count constraints involving inequality comparison operator can be reduced to the case of count constraints with equality operator. For instance, if the constraints are $count(B_1) \leq m_1$ and $count(B_2) \geq m_2$, we can use the above solution to find sets of tuples satisfying $count(B_1) = x$ and $count(B_1) = y$ for $0 \leq x \leq m_1$ and $m_2 \leq y \leq |B_2|$, where $|B_2|$ denotes the number of distinct B_2's values in S_{base}.

When there are more than two count constraints, assume these constraints are $count(B_i) = m_i$, $i \in [1, k]$ with $m_k = \max_{i=1}^{k}(m_i)$. As before, Greedy partitions S_{base} using B_1, $\cdots$, B_{k-1} attributes. At each iteration, Greedy selects one partition from S_{base} to insert into S_{ans} such that: (1) the constraints on B_1, $\cdots$, B_{k-1} can still be satisfied in the sense that $count(B_i) \leq m_i$ for $i \in [1, k-1]$, and (2) the number of distinct B_k values in the resultant S_{ans} is the largest. Greedy terminates the iteration when none of partitions satisfies both of these conditions.

4.2 Count & Sum Constraints

In this section, we consider the more complex scenario when there is a combination of count and sum constraints. For simplicity and without loss of generality, we consider a SAC query with two constraints: (1) $maximize(sum(A)) \leq K$ and (2) $count(B) = m$.

Our Greedy heuristic tries to satisfy the "easier" type of constraints before considering the "harder" constraints. Specifically, Greedy considers the constraints in the following order: count, sum, and finally the optimization constraint.

To satisfy the count constraint, Greedy can select an arbitrary subset $S_{count} \subseteq S_{base}$ that has $|\pi_B(S_{count})| = m$. Observe that the more tuples that S_{count} has, the more flexibility we have to select a subset of tuples from S_{count} to satisfy other constraints. Thus, Greedy finds S_{count} that has the cardinality as *large* as possible among all possible S_{count}'s. For this task, Greedy partitions tuples in S_{base} based on their B's values, and chooses m partitions that have the *largest* cardinalities to form S_{count}.

To satisfy the sum constraint, Greedy partitions tuples in S_{count} based on their B attribute values, and selects the tuple that has the smallest A value in each partition of S_{count} to insert into S_{ans}. If $\sum_{t \in S_{ans}}(t.A) > K$, it implies that any other subset of S_{count} will not satisfy both the count and sum constraints; therefore, **Greedy** returns S_{ans} as an approximate result in this case.

Finally, Greedy handles the optimization constraint by adding some tuples from $(S_{count} - S_{ans})$ into S_{ans}. This task is a subset-sum problem: select a subset of tuples from $(S_{count} - S_{ans})$ that has $max(sum(A)) \leq K - \sum_{t \in S_{ans}}(t.A)$. It is important to note that we cannot add any tuples from $(S_{base} - S_{count})$ into S_{ans} since it would increase the number of distinct B values in S_{ans} and violate the count constraint.

Complexity. The space complexity of Greedy is $O(K|S_{count}|)$ to maintain the matrix for dynamic programming in the last step. The running time of Greedy is $O(T_{part} + T_{SSP})$ where: (1) T_{part} is the time to partition S_{base} using B attribute and select m partitions that have the largest cardinalities, and (2) T_{SSP} is the running time of the solver for the subset-sum problem in the last step of Greedy. For T_{part}, Greedy augments the base query with the following: a *GROUP BY* clause on B, an *ORDER BY* clause on $COUNT(*)$, and a *LIMIT* clause to select the top-m highest cardinality partitions. For T_{SSP}, Greedy uses the conventional pseudo-polynomial algorithm to solve subset-sum problem. Thus, $T_{SSP} = O(K|S_{count}|)$.

EXAMPLE 4. *We reconsider Example 2 and use* Greedy *to solve the problem that finds a package having* $count(city) = 2$ *and* $maximize(sum(hour)) \leq 7$. Greedy *first partitions* S_{base} *using city attribute, and derives* $S_{count} = P_1 \cup P_2$*, which has the largest cardinality from all possible* S_{count}*'s.*

To satisfy the sum constraint, Greedy *selects* $t_3 \in P_1$ *and* $t_4 \in P_2$*, which has the smallest hour value to put into* S_{ans}*. Thus, we have* $\sum_{t \in S_{ans}}(t.hour) = 3$.

For the optimization constraint, Greedy *will select some tuples from* $S_{count} - S_{ans} = \{t_1, t_2, t_5\}$ *that have* $maximize(sum(hour)) \leq 4$ *to put into* S_{ans}*. Thus,* Greedy *will put* t_5 *into* S_{ans}*.*

In summary, $S_{ans} = \{t_3, t_4, t_5\}$ *and the solution of* Greedy *is turned out to be optimal in this case.* □

Generalization. The described algorithm can be generalized for cases where C_{ans} consists of any number of count and sum constraints, similar to the generalization described in Section 4.1. For instance, consider the situation with count constraints on attributes $A_1, \cdots, A_k$ and sum constraints $sum(B_i) < K_i$, for $i \in [1, \ell]$. Greedy first uses the described algorithm in Section 4.1 to derive S_{count} that satisfies the count constraints. At the end of this step, we can view S_{count} as being partitioned into n partitions using attributes $A_1, \cdots, A_k$. In the next step, Greedy selects one tuple in each partition of S_{count} to put into S_{ans}. The key point is how to select one tuple from each partition so that S_{ans} satisfies the sum constraint. Observe that if every selected tuple t in each partition has $t.A_i < K_i/n$, for $i \in [1, \ell]$, then these selected tuples together will satisfy all the sum constraints. Thus, our Greedy heuristic selects one tuple in each partition that satisfies the *largest* number of conditions "$t.A_i < K_i/n$" to put into S_{ans}.

4.3 General Case

In the general case when C_{ans} includes any combination of constraints, Greedy also follows the "easier-to-harder-constraint" principle so as to allow for more flexibility to satisfy all the constraints. In particular, Greedy considers the constraints in the following order: (1) content constraints, (2) count constraints, (3) sum constraints, and (4) group by together with optimization constraints. The absence of any constraints (e.g., count) allows Greedy to skip the corresponding step (e.g., skip the second step for count constraints). The details are given elsewhere [6].

5. BOUNDED SAC QUERIES

We now switch our attention to a special fragment of SAC queries, referred to as *bounded* SAC *queries*. A bounded SAC query has a bounded cardinality constraint to bound the cardinality of the qualified sets. As a simple example, Alice might be interested only in tour packages containing at most four places to visit. Bounded SAC queries are of interest because they can be processed using two existing approaches. In this section, we briefly describe these techniques, namely DirectSQL and MS, and compare these techniques against our proposed DP and Greedy in Section 6.

Since bounded SAC queries can be expressed directly using SQL, the first alternative evaluation method, denoted by DirectSQL, is to use relational database engines. Consider a SAC query Q with Q_{base} as "SELECT * FROM R" where there is a cardinality constraint in Q that sets the cardinality of qualified sets to a value k. Assuming that the key of relation R is an attribute *id*, Q can be expressed using SQL as follows:

SELECT $*$
FROM $R\ p_1, \cdots, R\ p_k$
WHERE $p_1.id < p_2.id$ AND $p_2.id < p_3.id$ AND $\cdots$
AND $p_{k-1}.id < p_k.id$ AND qualification

Here, qualification refers to the predicates that represent the remaining constraints in C_{ans}. Thus, each qualified set is returned as a tuple in the query's result. We now explain how to translate the various types of constraints in C_{ans} into SQL predicates.

Content constraint. For each content constraint of the form $content(A, v)$, DirectSQL needs to ensure that at least one instance p_i of R contains a tuple t that has $t.A = v$. The constraint can be expressed by the following SQL predicate: $(p_1.A = v$ or $\cdots$ or $p_k.A = v)$.

Sum constraint. A sum constraint of the form $sum(A) < K$ can be simply translated into the predicate: $(p_1.A + \cdots + p_k.A < K)$.

Count constraint. For a count constraint on an attribute A, we need to count the number of distinct values among $p_1.A, \cdots, p_k.A$. This can be achieved by using SQL's *case* construct to map each $p_i.A$ value to either 0 or 1 and comparing the sum of the mapped values against the desired count value. Specifically, each $p_i.A$ is mapped to 1 if the value of $p_i.A$ is not equal to any of the preceding $p_j.A$ values, $j < i$; otherwise, it is mapped to 0. For example, the count constraint "$count(A) = m$" is translated as follows:

(1 +
(case when $p_2.A \neq p_1.A$ then 1 or 0 end) + $\cdots$ +
(case when $p_k.A \neq p_1.A$ and $\cdots$ *and* $p_k.A \neq p_{k-1}.A$
then 1 or 0 end)) = m

Group-by constraint. Group-by constraints are translated similarly as count constraints using the *case* construct. For example, consider the group-by constraint $groupby(A, agg, B)$. For each $p_i.A$, $i \in [1, k]$, the translation considers other $p_j.A$, $j \neq i$, that has $p_j.A = p_i.A$ and performs the aggregation function *agg* on B attribute w.r.t. the tuples of p_i and p_j.

Table	# Tuples
adult	45222
part	200000
supplier	10000
track	10000000

Table 1: Sizes of Test Data sets (number of tuples)

Optimization constraint. An optimization constraint is translated essentially by sorting the query's result based on the aggregated attribute value and retrieving only the first tuple by using SQL's *ORDER BY* and *LIMIT* constructs.

For bounded SAC queries where the set cardinality is constrained to be a fixed value (e.g., $count(place) = 4$), a second alternative evaluation method is to apply a recently proposed technique MS [8]. The MS technique was actually designed for solving a more general problem, specifically finding preference sets (with multiple optimization constraints) over fixed-cardinality sets of items. However, the technique there can be used to evaluate bounded SAC queries as well. Further comments on MS are given in Section 7.

6. EXPERIMENTAL STUDY

In this section, we study the effectiveness and the efficiency of our proposed techniques to evaluate SAC queries. The algorithms compared include the dynamic programming approach, DP, that evaluates SAC queries with any number of sum constraints and at most one count, content, or group-by constraint; and Greedy, a heuristic approach for evaluating general SAC queries with any combination of constraints. In addition, we also compare DP and Greedy against two other methods for bounded SAC queries: (1) a direct approach using SQL queries, denoted by DirectSQL, and (2) the approach MS proposed in [8].

We used three real data sets for the experiments: Adult[4], TPCH (with a database size of 1GB), and a music data set containing 10,000,000 songs and 500,000 artists[5]. We used four test queries on Adult data set (Q_1 to Q_4), two queries (Q_5, Q_6) on TPCH data set, two queries (Q_7, Q_8) on the music data set, and another two queries Q_1' and Q_1'' that differ slightly from Q_1. Among these queries, Q_1 - Q_3 and Q_5 - Q_8 are multi-sum SAC queries, Q_4 is a general SAC query, and Q_1' and Q_1'' are bounded SAC queries. The test data and queries are given in Tables 1 and 2, respectively. The third column in Table 2 shows the number of tuples in the query result of the base query of each SAC query.

We used PostgreSQL 8.3 for our database system, and all algorithms (DP, Greedy, DirectSQL, and MS) were coded using C++ and compiled with GNU C++ compiler. Our experiments were conducted on a dual-core, 2.33GHz PC running Linux with 3.25GB of RAM and a 250GB hard disk.

6.1 Comparison between DP and Greedy

This section compares DP and Greedy to evaluate SAC queries in terms of the quality of computed results and the running time. Both methods are applicable for all test queries except for query Q_4, which is a general SAC query that consists of all kinds of constraints supported in this paper and cannot be handled by DP. We report the running times of these methods to return one result set for each test query.

[4]http://archive.ics.uci.edu/ml/datasets/Adult

[5]http://musicbrainz.org/

Quality of Computed Results. We measured the quality of a query result evaluation in terms of two metrics: (1) the number of query constraints that are satisfied by the computed result, and (2) the aggregate value returned for the optimization constraint. For all of our test queries, both DP and Greedy can find solutions that satisfy all the required constraints. Thus, we compare the quality of computed results for these test queries using the *ratio* between the aggregated value returned by DP over the aggregated value returned by Greedy, referred to as *relative* aggregated value of DP over Greedy. Since the optimization constraint in queries Q_1 to Q_8 is maximization, the higher the relative aggregated value of DP over Greedy, the better the solution of DP is in comparison with Greedy. The relative aggregated value of DP over Greedy for queries Q_1 to Q_8 are given in the second column in Table 3.

For queries Q_1 to Q_3, which involve small relations, DP returned optimal solutions while Greedy returned high-quality solutions; i.e., the aggregated values returned by Greedy are around 3% lower than the optimal values by DP.

Query Q_4 is an example of a general SAC query that contains all kinds of constraints supported in this paper and DP cannot handle. Thus, the DP result for Q_4 is not shown in Table 3. For this query, Greedy can find one set of tuples that satisfies all the constraints.

For queries that involve large data sets (Q_5 to Q_8), since the constructed matrices for the dynamic programming are too large to fit in the main memory, DP used its approximation version to scale down the domain values of the attributes used with the aggregated constraints (e.g., length, retail price attributes). For Greedy, with the heuristic strategy, Greedy first selected a set of tuples satisfying the count constraints, thus reducing the number of tuples to be considered by dynamic programming for the sum optimization constraints. Therefore, the solution of Greedy can be better than DP in these cases. In fact, the results of Greedy for Q_5 and Q_6 are slightly better than DP. For queries Q_7 and Q_8, both the number of involved tuples (3727521 tuples) as well as the number of distinct values of the attribute associated with the count constraint (270352 and 2003678 values, respectively) are large. Here, Greedy returns much better quality result than DP for Q_7 and Q_8. The aggregated values returned by Greedy are around 1.5 - 3.5 times larger than the ones by DP and are nearly equal to the maximum aggregated values required by the queries.

To study how far the aggregated values returned by Greedy and DP are from the optimal solutions, we varied the bounds on the aggregate values of queries Q_1 and Q_8. We report the results on queries Q_3 and Q_7 in Figure 3 (the same trends are observed for other queries). For Q_3, we vary the bounded optimal value from the set $\{500, 1000, 2000, 3000, 40000, 320000\}$. For Q_7, we vary the bounded value from the set $\{6\times10^6, 12\times10^6, 18\times10^6, 24\times10^6, 30\times10^6\}$. The results again show that when the matrices constructed by dynamic programming can fit in the main memory, the optimal value returned by DP is slightly better than Greedy. In contrast, when the matrices cannot be fit in main memory, the solution of Greedy is better than DP. For all cases, the optimal values obtained by Greedy are very close (e.g., more than 95%) to the bounded optimal values, which indicates that Greedy returns high quality solutions.

Query	Constraints	Size
Q_1	$Q_{base} = \pi_*(adult)$; $maximize(sum(edunum)) \leq 5000$; $count(race) = 2$	45222
Q_2	$Q_{base} = \pi_*(adult)$; $maximize(sum(edunum)) \leq 1000$; $groupby(nativecountry, count, *) \leq 5$	45222
Q_3	$Q_{base} = \pi_*(adult)$; $maximize(sum(capitalloss)) \leq 1000$; $2 \leq count(occupation) \leq 4$;	45222
Q_4	$Q_{base} = \pi_*(adult)$; $maximize(sum(capitalloss)) \leq 2000$; $count(nativecountry) = 2$; $count(race) = 2$ $content(nativecountry,$ "United-States"); $groupby(nativecountry, race, count, *) \leq 2$	45222
Q_5	$Q_{base} = \pi_*(part)$; $maximize(sum(retailprice)) \leq 80000$; $count(brand) = 4$	200000
Q_6	$Q_{base} = \pi_*\sigma_{acctbal>0}(supplier)$; $maximize(sum(acctbal)) \leq 150000$; $8 \leq count(nation) \leq 10$	9114
Q_7	$Q_{base} = \pi_*\sigma_{length>240000}(track)$; $maximize(sum(length)) \leq 30000000$; $count(artist) = 5$; content(artist, "Bob Dylan")	3727521
Q_8	$Q_{base} = \pi_*\sigma_{length>240000}(track)$; $maximize(sum(length)) \leq 18000000$; $4 \leq count(title) \leq 6$; content(title, "Jingles Bell")	3727521
Q'_1	$Q_{base} = \pi_*\sigma_{id\leq 60}(adult)$; $maximize(sum(edunum)) \leq 50$; $count(race) = 2$; $count(*) = x$	60
Q''_1	$Q_{base} = \pi_*\sigma_{id\leq 500}(adult)$; $maximize(sum(edunum)) \leq 1000$; $count(race) = 2$; $count(*) = x$	500

Table 2: SAC queries for experiments

Query	Relative aggregated value DP/Greedy	Running time (secs)	
		DP	Greedy
Q_1	1/1	7.7	7.5
Q_2	1/1	10	10
Q_3	1/0.97	2.3	1
Q_4	-	-	1
Q_5	0.98/1	11	8
Q_6	1/1	73	8
Q_7	0.64/1	70	28
Q_8	0.28/1	170	32

Table 3: Comparison between DP and Greedy

Cardinality value	Q'_1	Q''_1
4	0.8	0.56
5	1	0.65
6	1	0.71
7	1	0.75

Table 4: The relative aggregated value of Greedy over the optimal solution

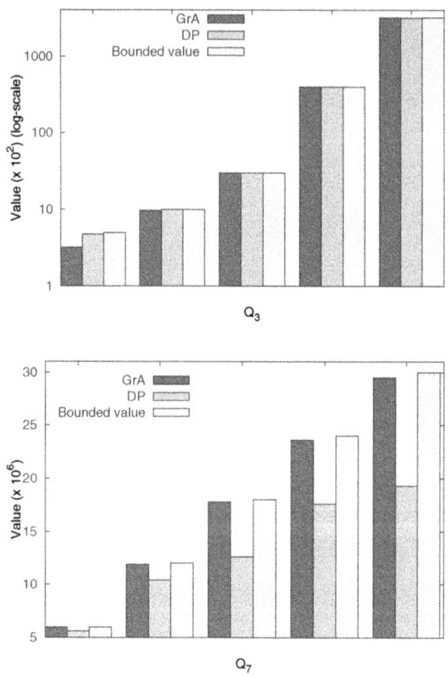

Figure 3: Optimal values obtained by DP and Greedy

Running Time. The third and fourth columns in Table 3 show the running time comparison between Greedy and DP, where Greedy runs 1.5 - 9 times faster than DP. The result is expected since Greedy is a heuristic solution.

6.2 Comparing DP, Greedy, MS and DirectSQL

In this section, we compare our proposed methods (DP and Greedy) against the direct approach that uses SQL queries, denoted by DirectSQL, and the method MS proposed in [8] for bounded SAC queries, which have a bounded cardinality constraint to bound the cardinality of the qualified sets. For this comparison, we used two queries Q'_1 and Q''_1, which are variants of query Q_1. The three methods (DP, MS, and DirectSQL) are able to find the optimal results for both queries Q'_1 and Q''_1.

First, we run these approaches for query Q'_1 by varying the set cardinality constraint value from 4 to 7; i.e., $x \in [4, 7]$. The Greedy approach returns rather good results; i.e., only for the cardinality 4, the relative aggregated value of Greedy over the optimal solution is 0.8; for the other cases, Greedy achieves the optimal aggregated values (the second column in Table 4). In terms of the running time, as shown in Figure 4(a), Greedy runs the most efficiently. For the other three methods, DP runs faster than MS and much faster than the direct approach (DirectSQL). Note that the number of tuples selected by the base query in Q'_1 is controlled to be small (i.e., 60) so that the DirectSQL approach can complete its evaluation within reasonable time. Observe that when the set cardinality value increases, the running times of DP and Greedy increase linearly; whereas the running times of MS and DirectSQL increase exponentially.

Second, we increase the maximum sum value in Q_1 to be 1000 and the number of selected tuples by the base query to be 500 to scale up the size of the matrices built by DP and the

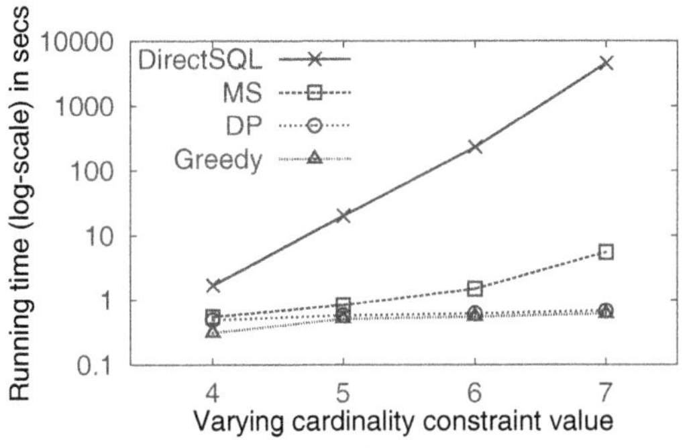

(a) Q_1'

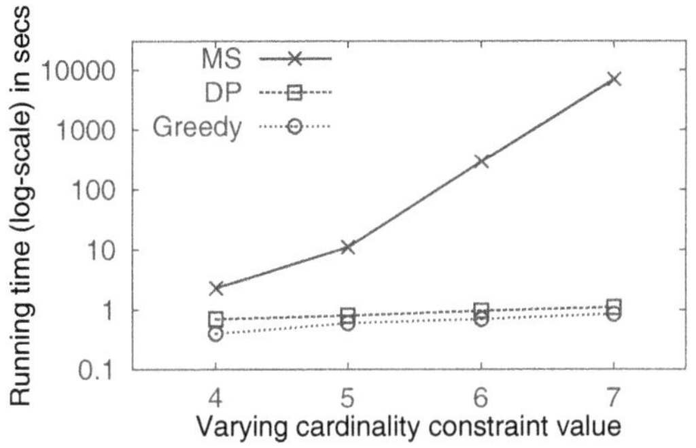

(b) Q_1''

Figure 4: The running time comparison between DP, Greedy, MS and DirectSQL

number of subsets to be considered by MS and DirectSQL. We denote this new query by Q_1''. For Q_1'', DirectSQL cannot finish in five hours, thus we do not record the results of DirectSQL in Figure 4(b). The relative aggregated value of Greedy over the optimal solution is in the range of 0.56 to 0.75 (the third column in Table 4). In terms of the running time as shown in Figure 4(b), Greedy still runs the most efficiently. DP runs much more efficiently than MS for this query, since the number of subsets considered by MS is large. For instance, for the case with $cardinality = 6$, the number of subsets of size six considered by MS is 3800000 and the running time is 5 minutes.

6.3 Summary

We have the following conclusions from our experimental study:

- DP can find optimal solutions for multi-sum SAC queries when its memory requirement is within the available main memory with a trade-off of slower running time compared to Greedy in the order of 1.5 - 9 times.

- The solutions found by Greedy have high quality and are better than these by DP when the memory requirement of DP exceeds the available main memory. Furthermore, Greedy runs very efficiently.

- For bounded SAC queries, both DP and Greedy run much more efficiently than the direct method (DirectSQL) of using SQL queries and MS method proposed for preferences involving fixed-cardinality sets [8].

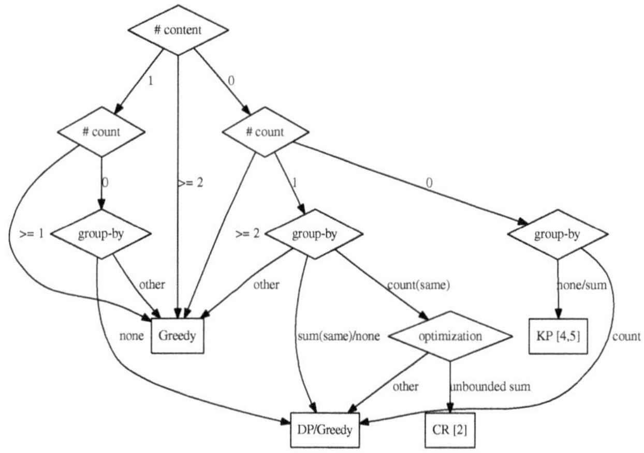

Figure 5: Evaluation Strategies for SAC Queries

7. RELATED WORK

The related work can be classified into two categories: work that are directly related to SAC queries [2, 4, 5] whose relationship to our work (DP and Greedy) is captured by the decision tree in Figure 5, and work that are related more broadly to set-based queries [1, 3, 7, 8] which involved constraints different from SAC queries.

SAC Queries. Several variants of SAC queries that have been studied differ in the number and types of constraints permitted. These work together with our techniques can be classified by the decision tree in Figure 5, where each leaf node represents the best evaluation technique for the fragment of SAC queries represented by the path of internal nodes which specify the permitted constraints. Specifically, "# contents" specifies the number of content constraints supported (0, 1, or ≥ 2), "# count" specifies the number of count constraints supported (0, 1, or ≥ 2), "group-by" specifies the type of group-by constraints supported (count, sum, none) and whether the attribute(s) used with group-by operators are the same (indicated by "same") or not (no explicit label) with the attribute(s) used with the count constraints, and "optimization" specifies the type of optimization constraints supported (unbounded sum, other).

KP refers to the classic knapsack problem techniques [5]: Given a set of items where each item j has a profit p_j and a weight w_j, the goal is to select a subset of items such that its total profit is maximized and its total weight does not exceed an input capacity value. A variant of KP was studied in [4] for solving optimization under parametric aggregation constraints (OPAC) query, which takes the following as inputs: (1) a relation $R(A_1, \cdots, A_n, P)$, (2) a set of parametric sum-aggregation constraints of the form $sum(A_i) \leq c_i$ with c_i as a parameter, and (3) a sum optimization constraint $sum(P)$ to be maximized. Given a parameterized OPAC query, [4] proposed an algorithm to construct indices to efficiently provide approximate answers with guarantee bound on its accuracy for any instantiated OPAC query with specific values for the parameters in the sum constraints.

A second variant of KP, which corresponds to the fragment of SAC queries with multiple sum and a single group-by-sum constraints, is the *multiple-choice* Knapsack problem [5]. This is useful in budgeting applications to select a set of projects to be funded such that the total cost for all projects is bounded by some limit, the total cost for projects belonging to the same department is bounded by another limit, and the total project profit is maximized. This problem can be solved in pseudo-polynomial time using a two-step dynamic programming approach [5] which is similar to our proposed DP. However, the formulation of the second dynamic programming stage in our DP is more complicated, since DP needs to take into account the count/content constraints, which [5] does not consider.

Another related work is the CourseRank (CR) project [2] which is motivated by course planning applications. CR considers constraints of the form "take at least a and at most b courses from a set S_i", where a and b are non-negative integers and S_i is a set of related courses (e.g. CS courses), and each course is associated with a use-preference score. For example, a student might be required to complete 2 or 3 courses from a given set of six math courses. Given such constraints, CR finds a set of courses that satisfies all requirements such that the number of selected courses is equal to some given value and the total score of the selected courses is maximized. A polynomial-time algorithm based on maximal flow was proposed for the CR problem [2].

Set-based Queries. There are also several work on set-based query evaluation [1, 3, 7, 8] but they differ from our work due to the types of constraints supported in the queries and/or the focus of the evaluation problem.

A related work, which is motivated by online shopping applications [1], examines the problem of recommending a set of "satellite items" (e.g., case, speaker) related to a given "center item" (e.g., iPhone). Given a budget B and a central item, [1] finds (approximately) all *maximal* sets of satellite items associated with the central item such that the cost of each maximal set does not exceed the given budget B. Different from [1], we do not consider "maximal set" constraints, which will make the problem of evaluating SAC queries even harder. However, SAC queries support other constraints (e.g., count, group-by, content) which [1] does not handle.

The work on making composite recommendations of a set of items is studied in [7], where each item is associated with both a rating value and a cost. The goal is to find the top-k sets of items such that the total cost of items in each set is no greater than a given budget, and a set with a higher total rating value is more preferable. Note that when $k = 1$, the problem setting is exactly the Knapsack problem. The problem addressed there, however, is based on an evaluation framework where the ratings of items are accessed via sorted access from some external recommending parties, while the costs of items are accessed via random access. [7] introduced a 2-approximation solution and a greedy algorithm to find top-k composite recommendations with the optimization goal to minimize the total access cost.

The work in [3] finds an optimal subset of a set of tuples according to a set preference, which is specified as either a TCP-net or a scoring function on a collection of set properties. A set property is based on the number of tuples satisfying a certain predicate (e.g., the number of tuples satisfying a predicate is greater than a given value). Two heuristic search algorithms (based on branch-and-bound and Constraint Satisfaction Problem) were proposed in [3]. There are two main differences between [3] and our work. First, [3] focuses on cardinality constraint and does not support other types of constraints considered in our work. Second, the algorithms developed for each work are different from the other.

Finally, there is also a recent related work on finding all subsets of a given fixed-cardinality from a relation that satisfy some user-specified preferences [8]. There are two main differences between the work in [8] and ours. First, [8] deals with sets of *fixed-cardinality*, whereas the sets retrieved by SAC queries can have varying cardinality. Second, [8] allows users to specify preferences over sets and the focus is on computing the skyline query result. However, as explained in Section 5, the technique in [8] can be applied to evaluate SAC queries with a fixed set cardinality.

In summary, although several related work have examined set-based queries or special fragments of SAC queries, our work on DP is the first pseudo-polynomial time algorithm for evaluating the non-trivial SAC query fragment with multiple sum and at most one of either count, group-by, or content constraint. Furthermore, our Greedy approach is the first heuristic to evaluate general SAC queries with any combination of count, sum, group-by, and content constraints. The Greedy heuristic tries to find a solution that satisfies all the specified constraints but may return an approximate solution that meets only some of the constraints.

8. CONCLUSION

In this paper, we have examined the evaluation of set-based queries with aggregation constraints (SAC queries), which are very useful for many data retrieval applications. We have presented two novel algorithms: DP, a pseudo-polynomial time algorithm for evaluating a non-trivial fragment of SAC queries involving multiple sum constraints and at most one of count, group-by, or content constraint; and Greedy, the first heuristic approach for evaluating general SAC queries. The effectiveness of our proposed solutions was demonstrated by an experimental performance study over real data sets. As part of our future work, we plan to integrate ranking/top-k pruning into SAC query evaluation.

Acknowledgements This research is supported in part by NUS Grant R-252-000-453-112.

9. REFERENCES

[1] S. Basu Roy, S. Amer-Yahia, A. Chawla, G. Das, and C. Yu. Constructing and exploring composite items. In *SIGMOD*, pages 843–854, 2010.

[2] B. Bercovitz, F. Kaliszan, G. Koutrika, H. Liou, A. Parameswaran, P. Venetis, Z. M. Zadeh, and H. Garcia-Molina. Social sites research through courserank. *SIGMOD Rec.*, 38(4), 2009.

[3] M. Binshtok, R. I. Brafman, S. E. Shimony, A. Martin, and C. Boutilier. Computing optimal subsets. In *AAAI*, pages 1231–1236, 2007.

[4] S. Guha, D. Gunopoulos, N. Koudas, D. Srivastava, and M. Vlachos. Efficient approximation of optimization queries under parametric aggregation constraints. In *VLDB*, pages 778–789, 2003.

[5] H. Kellerer, U. Pferschy, and D. Pisinger. *Knapsack Problems*. Springer, Berlin, Germany, 2004.

[6] Q. T. Tran, C.-Y. Chan, and G. Wang. Evaluation of set-based queries with aggregation constraints. Technical Report http://www.comp.nus.edu.sg/~tqtrung/sac-tech.pdf, National University of Singapore, August 2011.

[7] M. Xie, L. V. Lakshmanan, and P. T. Wood. Breaking out of the box of recommendations: from items to packages. In *RecSys*, pages 151–158, 2010.

[8] X. Zhang and J. Chomicki. Preference queries over sets. In *ICDE*, pages 1019–1030, 2011.

Index Structures and Top-k Join Algorithms for Native Keyword Search Databases

Günter Ladwig
Institute AIFB, Karlsruhe Institute of Technology
D-76128 Karlsruhe, Germany
guenter.ladwig@kit.edu

Thanh Tran
Institute AIFB, Karlsruhe Institute of Technology
D-76128 Karlsruhe, Germany
ducthanh.tran@kit.edu

ABSTRACT

For supporting keyword search on structured data, current solutions require large indexes to be built that redundantly store subgraphs called neighborhoods. Further, for exploring keyword search results, large graphs have to be loaded into memory. We propose a solution, which employs much more *compact index structures* for neighborhood lookups. Using these indexes, we reduce keyword search result exploration to the traditional database problem of top-k join processing, enabling results to be computed efficiently. In particular, this computation can be performed on data streams successively loaded from disk (i.e., does not require the entire input to be loaded at once into memory). For supporting this, we propose a *top-k procedure* based on the rank join operator, which not only computes the k-best results, but also selects query plans in a top-k fashion during the process. In experiments using large real-world datasets, our solution reduced storage requirements and also outperformed the state-of-the-art in terms of performance and scalability.

Categories and Subject Descriptors: H.2.4 [Database Management]: Systems

General Terms: Algorithms, Performance

Keywords: graph database, keyword search, top-k processing

1. INTRODUCTION

Today, we find on the Web not only textual documents but also a large amount of structured data. This includes metadata associated with Web pages, semi-structured data, and highly-structured information made publicly available such as Linked Data[1].

Especially for lay users, *keyword search* has been regarded as an effective mechanism because it helps to circumvent the complexity of structured query languages, and hide the underlying data representation. Without knowledge of the query syntax and data schema, users can obtain possibly complex structured results, including tuples from relational databases, XML data, data graphs, and RDF resources[4, 17]. As opposed to document retrieval, results in this structured data setting may encompass several resources that are connected over possibly very long paths (e.g. joined database tuples, XML trees, connected RDF resources).

There are two directions of research that aim at supporting this. First, there are *schema-based approaches* implemented on top of off-the-shelf databases ([5, 12, 13, 15]). These approaches find candidate networks, which represent valid join sequences that are employed as queries to retrieve the final results. The main advantage here is that the power and optimization capabilities of the underlying database engine can be fully utilized. Second, there are *schema-agnostic approaches* ([9, 4, 11]), which operates directly on the data. Since they do not rely on a schema, the applicability of these approaches is not limited to structured data. For instance, semi-structured RDF data [17] as well as the combination of structured, semi-structured and unstructured data [11] have been supported.

In this paper, we focus on the latter type, also called *native approaches*. Fig. 1 shows a data example, describing people ($p1 - p4$) and their relationships. For computing results of a query such as $\mathcal{Q}_1 = \{miller, corp\}$, a native approach firstly finds matching elements in the data graph, which are $miller = \{p1, p4\}$ and $corp = \{o1, o2\}$. Next, structures connecting these so-called *keyword elements* are explored. These structures constitute the query results, which are called Steiner trees [3], or *Steiner graphs* ([17, 11]).

Since the search space may be large, two main directions have been investigated for optimization. One is based on materializing paths [4]. The fastest solution proposed recently, called EASE, is based on materializing even more complex structures in the form of graphs, which capture entire neighborhoods of data elements [11]. The other direction is to improve the efficiency of the exploration algorithm ([9, 3]). The main drawbacks of current state-of-the-art is that materialized indexes [11], which redundantly store neighborhood information may become too large. Further, existing search strategies for efficient result exploration assume the entire data to be available in memory, a requirement that is too limited when the amount of data is large.

The index structures and algorithms proposed so far are very specific to the keyword search problem. In this work, we aim to reduce this problem to more standard database ones to leverage the vast body of existing work. In particular, we propose the concept of *native keyword search databases*, which solves the keyword search problem using two standard

[1] `http://linkeddata.org/`

CIKM'11, October 24–28, 2011, Glasgow, Scotland, UK.

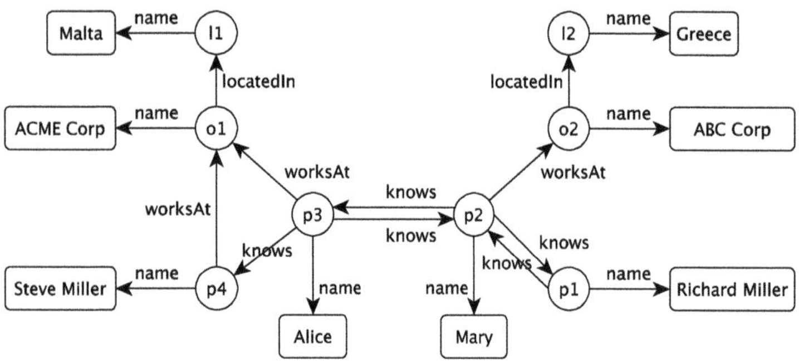

Query	Keywords
Q_1	"miller corp"
Q_2	"mary miller corp"
Q_3	"steve malta mary"

Keyword	Matching elements
corp	$\{o_1, o_2\}$
malta	$\{l_1\}$
mary	$\{p_2\}$
miller	$\{p_1, p_4\}$
steve	$\{p_4\}$

Figure 1: Example data graph, queries and keyword matching elements.

database operations, *data access* and *join*. Instead of loading the data entirely at once and exploring results in memory, keyword search is supported through a series of fine granular data access (path lookups) and join operations (path and graph joins). For supporting these operations, we build upon existing work on index structures and top-k join processing. The main contributions can be summarized as follows:

- We propose a new *processing strategy* for dealing with the keyword search problem that is based on the standard database operations data access and join.

- For efficient data access, we extend the *2-hop cover* concept ([16, 1]) to pre-compute and materialize the neighborhoods of data elements. Existing work indexes every maximal neighborhood, i.e., when it is not completely covered by one another [11]. In this work, we determine coverage at the level of paths, instead of graphs. Indexing only maximal paths reduces the space requirements.

- For efficient and scalable Steiner graph search, we propose an extension of the hash rank join [7] called *push rank join* to terminate early after the top-k results have been found. Instead of reading the entire graph into memory, this procedure operates on input streams.

- The main difference between join processing in keyword search and a standard database is that different query plans may lead to different, but also valid results. Instead of focusing on one single optimal plan, a large number of query plans have to be considered to generate all top-k answers. The *push-based top-k rank join procedure* proposed in this paper not only computes the best results according to one plan, but also selects plans in a top-k fashion during the process.

We evaluated our approach by comparing it to state-of-the-art native keyword search approaches ([11, 9]), using several large real-world datasets. Our solution reduced storage requirement (up to 86%) and improved scalability (by several factors) and performance (over 50% on average).

Outline. In Section 2 we present our data model and a formal definition of keyword search. Section 3 describes our extension of the 2-hop cover concept. In Section 4 we show how keyword queries can be answered using top-k join processing on the proposed data structures. Related work is presented in Section 5. In Section 6 we present the result of our evaluation. We conclude in Section 7.

2. OVERVIEW

This work deals with general graph structured data:

DEFINITION 1 (GRAPH STRUCTURED DATA). *Data is modeled as a directed, labeled graph $G(N, E)$ called* data graph, *where $N = N_E \uplus N_A$ is a set of* nodes, *conceived as the disjoint union of* entities *N_E and* attribute values *N_A, and $E = E_R \uplus E_A$ is a set of directed* edges, *where E_R are edges between entities called* relations, *and E_A are edges between an entity and an attribute value called* attributes. *The* length *of a path denotes the number of edges in the path. We use* distance *between u, w to denote the length of the shortest path between u and w. Two graph elements (nodes or edges) are* connected *if they appear together in a path (no matter the directions of edges in that path).*

In addition to graph-structured data such as RDF, this model can also be used to capture relational databases: a tuple captures an entity and its attribute values; and tuples with a foreign key relationship are connected via a relation edge.

Query keywords match entities' attribute value nodes, or labels of attribute or relation edges. Thus, keyword matches can always be associated with some entities. We call these matching entities *keyword elements*:

DEFINITION 2 (KEYWORD ELEMENT). *Given a keyword query K consisting of keywords $k_1, \ldots, k_n$, a node $n_k \in N_E$ is a* keyword element *for $k \in K$ iff there is $e(n_k, a) \in E$ and k matches any of the elements e, n_k or a (i.e., k matches edges that contain n_k in the "subject" position). The set of all keyword elements for k is N_k.*

For processing a keyword query, we firstly find keyword elements in the data graph. Then, we search for substructures, which connect the keyword elements. The most commonly used substructures are Steiner trees [9], i.e., minimal rooted trees in the data graph, which contains at least one keyword element for every keyword in the query. Instead of rooted trees, general graphs have also been used [17, 11]. This notion of Steiner graph is also employed in this paper:

DEFINITION 3 (KEYWORD QUERY ANSWER). *An* answer *to a keyword query $K = \{k_1, \ldots, k_n\}$ also called* Steiner graph *is a subgraph of G denoted as $G_S = (N_S, E_S)$, which satisfies the following conditions:*

- *For every $k \in K$ there is at least one keyword element $n_k \in N_S$. The set of keyword elements containing one for every $k \in K$ is $N_K \subseteq N_S$.*

- *For every possible pair $n_i, n_j \in N_K$ and $n_i \neq n_j$, there is a path $n_i \rightsquigarrow n_j$ such that every $n_i \in N_K$ is connected to every other $n_j \in N_K$.*

We call such a graph a d-length Steiner graph *when* direct paths, *i.e., paths that connect exactly two keyword elements n_i, n_j s.t. there is no other keyword element n_k in the path between n_i and n_j, have length d or less (we use $n_i \rightsquigarrow^d n_j$ to denote these paths).*

This notion captures the standard semantics of keyword query answers [9, 17]. Limited by its internal index structure, EASE [11] departs from this and employs an alternative semantics: while it also searches for Steiner graphs, it implicitly assumes one "center keyword element" that is connected to all other keyword elements over a maximum distance d. While this leads to a more restricted search space, results corresponding to the standard semantics may be missed. In this work, we support the standard semantics. The d-length restriction only implies that for every keyword element n_i in the Steiner graph, there is *at least one* other keyword element connected to it via a path of length d or less (i.e., the directly connected one), while all other keyword elements may be (indirectly) connected to it via longer paths.

The computation of top-k Steiner graphs typically requires a monotonic function for ranking. Widely used in keyword search is the score of a node calculated using a probabilistic IR model. Scores which measure nodes' prestige have also been incorporated – PageRank for instance [6]. Besides, keyword search solutions generally rest on the assumption that more compact Steiner graphs more likely match the user needs, i.e., the length of paths connecting two keyword elements has a negative effect on the rank. The solution proposed here is orthogonal to the ranking function being used. For ease of exposition, we use path length as the only metric:

DEFINITION 4. *Let G_S be a Steiner graph and P be the set of direct paths that connect its keyword elements, the* rank *of G_S is determined by $Score(G_S) = \sum_{p \in P} Score(p)$, where $Score(p) = \frac{1}{length(p)}$.*

The solution we propose is based on two main operations. For *data access*, a specialized index is employed to retrieve connecting paths for every pair of keyword elements. In a top-k fashion, these paths are then *joined* to construct the best ranked Steiner graphs.

3. D-LENGTH 2-HOP COVER

A 2-hop cover is a compact representation of connections in a graph that has been previously used to answer reachability and distance queries [16, 1]. In this work, we propose to leverage this concept for retrieving paths between two keyword elements. Our data graph is directed. However, while it is essential to find paths during the computation of Steiner graphs, the direction of the edges that establish these paths are irrelevant (have to be preserved only for outputting the actual results). For the efficient retrieval of paths, we propose the d-length 2-hop cover, which in contrast to the 2-hop cover employed in existing work, only considers paths up to length d. First, we define the neighborhood of a node u that captures paths from u to nodes in its vicinity:

DEFINITION 5 (NEIGHBORHOOD). *A* neighborhood *label (or short: neighborhood) $NB_u \subseteq G$ of a node $u \in N$ (also called the* center node *of NB_u) is the union set of nodes and edges that are connected to u via some paths. The set of paths between u and a node $w \in NB_u$ is denoted as $P(u, w)$, and its $Score(P(u, w))$ is defined as $max\{Score(p)|p \in P(u, w)\}$. The combined information is represented as a* path entry *(u, s, w) (or short: (u, w)), where u is the center node of NB_u, $w \in NB_u$ and $s = Score(P(u, w))$. A* d-neighborhood *of node u is the set of nodes and edges connected to u via paths of length d or less.*

DEFINITION 6 (d-LENGTH 2-HOP COVER). *A labeling of a graph $G = (N, E)$, which consists of a set of neighborhood labels is a* d-length 2-hop cover, *if the following two conditions hold for any two nodes $u, v \in N_E$: 1) if there is path of length d or less between u and v then $NB_u \cap NB_v \neq \emptyset$; 2) all paths of length d or less between the center nodes u and v are of the form $\langle u, \ldots, w, \ldots, v\rangle$, where $w \in NB_u \cap NB_v$ (w is called a* hop node*).*

This cover is used to find all paths of length d or less between two nodes by forming the intersection of their neighborhoods, i.e., the set of paths between u and v is $P(u, v) = \{p_{uw} + p_{wv} | w \in NB_u \cap NB_v, p_{uw} \in P(u, w), p_{wv} \in P(w, v), Length(p_{uw} p_{wv}) \leq d\}$.

3.1 Construction

The problem of constructing a 2-hop cover of minimal size has been reduced to the minimum set cover problem that is NP-hard [2]. Consequently, approximative algorithms are necessary for dealing with large graphs [16, 1]). The basic idea is as follows: in a greedy manner, one neighborhood is selected at every iteration to prune redundant paths in other neighborhoods. The goal is to reduce redundancy as much as possible, while preserving the 2-hop cover property.

We adopt existing algorithms in two directions. (1) Firstly we define a trivial d-length 2-hop cover for the keyword search setting, which is used as a basis for later pruning. (2) Then, the d-*length* restriction is taken into account during the pruning of paths. The detailed algorithm, complexity and proofs are presented in our report [10].

Basically, we observe that a trivial d-length 2-hop cover is simply the set of d-*neighborhoods*:

THEOREM 1. *The set of d-neighborhoods constructed for every node $u \in N$ in $G(N, E)$ is a valid d-length 2-hop cover.*

Proof Sketch: By definition, a d-neighborhood of a node u contains all nodes in $G(N, E)$ reachable from u via a path of length d or less. Thus, for all $u, v \in N$, $u \in NB_u$ and $v \in NB_v$, if $u \rightsquigarrow^d v$ then $u \in NB_v$ and $v \in NB_u$. Hence, $NB_u \cap NB_v$ must be not empty (this ensures condition 1). Further, we know the set $NB_u \cap NB_v$ contains hop nodes for all paths of length $2 \times d$ or less, which include all paths of length d or less (this ensures condition 2). □

Then, the following intuition is employed for pruning redundant paths captured by this trivial d-length 2-hop cover: Given two nodes $u, v \in N$ that are connected via the set of paths $P_{uv} = \langle u, \ldots, w, \ldots, v\rangle$ of length d or less, NB_u contains some "partial paths" $P_{wv} = \langle w, \ldots, v\rangle$ that are also in NB_v, and vice versa NB_v contains the parts $P_{uw} = \langle u, \ldots, w\rangle$ that are also in NB_u. Then, these parts are redundant in the sense that after removing P_{wv} from NB_u

and P_{uw} from NB_v, all the paths in P_{uv} are still preserved and can be computed via hop nodes in $NB_u \cap NB_v$.

The approximate algorithm for this consists of $|N-1|$ iterations. At each step, a neighborhood NB_i is selected (based on "pruning power" simply measured in terms of node counts), marked as complete, and used for pruning other neighborhoods not completed yet. Neighborhood pruning is discussed in the example below.

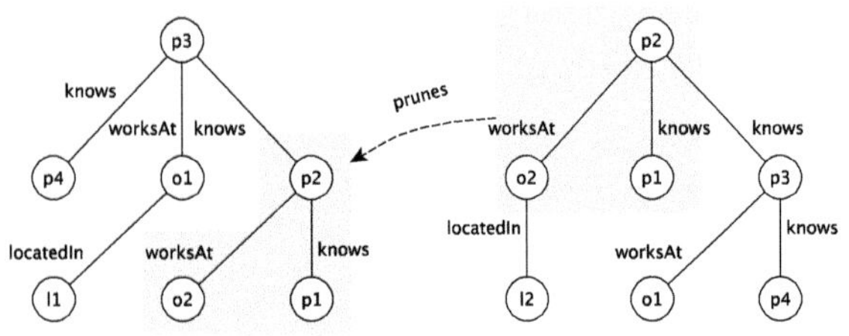

Figure 2: Pruning NB_{p_3} using NB_{p_2}

EXAMPLE 1. *Fig. 2 shows the two not yet pruned neighborhoods of p_2 and p_3. Here, we prune NB_{p_3} using NB_{p_2} by starting a simultaneous breadth-first search towards the leaf nodes from p_2. All edges in NB_{p_3} that also occur in NB_{p_2} are marked and later removed from NB_{p_3}. The part pruned this way is highlighted in Fig. 2.*

Note that the procedure here operates at the level of paths while existing work on keyword search applies pruning at the level of neighborhoods, i.e., a neighborhood is discarded only when it is completely covered by one another [11].

3.2 Storage

We store neighborhoods as well as the actual paths. We define the path and path entry indexes, which are used during the computation of Steiner graphs.

DEFINITION 7 (PATH ENTRY INDEX). *The* path entry index *I_{PE} maps nodes $u \in N$ to a list of* path entries *(u, s, w), sorted by $s = Score(P(u, w))$, where $w \in NB_u$.*

DEFINITION 8 (PATH INDEX). *The* path index *I_P maps a path entry (u, w) to a list of paths $P(u, w)$, sorted by $Score(p)$.*

Node	Entries
p_2	$(p_2, 2.0, p_2)$ $(p_2, 1.0, p_1)$ $(p_2, 1.0, p_3)$ $(p_2, 1.0, o_2)$ $(p_2, 0.5, l_2)$ $(p_2, 0.5, p_4)$ $(p_2, 0.5, o_1)$

Table 1: Example path entry index.

Center,Hop	Paths
p_2, p_1	1.0 $\langle p_1, knows, p_2\rangle$ 1.0 $\langle p_2, knows, p_1\rangle$
p_2, l_1	0.5 $\langle p_2, worksAt, o_2\rangle\langle o_2, locatedIn, l_1\rangle$
p_2, o_1	0.5 $\langle p_2, knows, p_3\rangle\langle p_3, worksAt, o_1\rangle$ 0.5 $\langle p_3, knows, p_2\rangle\langle p_3, worksAt, o_1\rangle$

Table 2: Example path index.

EXAMPLE 2. *Tab. 1 shows an index entry for node p_2 from the running example. It contains path entries from p_2 to all hop nodes in the neighborhood with their associated scores. Recall that this is simply the maximal score of paths from p_2 to a hop node. Tab. 2 shows an excerpt of the path index for nodes in the neighborhood of p_2. For example, the key (p_2, o_1) can be used to retrieve all paths (and their scores) from p_2 to o_1. In this case there are two such paths.*

4. KEYWORD QUERY PROCESSING

In this section we present the process of answering keyword queries using a d-length 2-hop cover.

4.1 Basic Join Operations

Given a keyword query K and its keyword elements N_K, the goal is to find Steiner graphs. The basic idea is to use the pruned neighborhoods of the d-length 2-hop cover to find paths between every pair of keyword elements and iteratively join them until they all are connected. For this, we (1) firstly perform *data access* operations to retrieve the neighborhoods for every keyword, called *keyword neighborhoods*, (2) then perform *neighborhood join* to merge two keyword neighborhoods to obtain a *keyword graph* and then successively (3) apply *graph joins* to combine a keyword neighborhood with a keyword graph.

DEFINITION 9 (KEYWORD NEIGHBORHOOD). *Given a keyword k and its keyword elements N_k, the* keyword neighborhood *NB_k of k is the union set of path entries retrieved from the index I_{PE}. It captures the neighborhoods of all keyword elements in N_k, i.e., $NB_k = \bigcup_{n \in N_k} I_{PE}(n)$.*

DEFINITION 10 (NEIGHBORHOOD JOIN). *Given two keyword neighborhoods NB_{k_1}, NB_{k_2}, the* neighborhood join *$\bowtie_{NB}$ combines two path entries (n_{k_1}, w) in NB_{k_1} and (n_{k_2}, w) in NB_{k_2} that match on w, i.e., $NB_{k_1} \bowtie_{NB} NB_{k_2} = \{(n_{k_1}, w) + +(n_{k_2}, w) | (n_{k_1}, w) \in NB_{k_1}, (n_{k_2}, w) \in NB_{k_2}, distance((n_{k_1}, w) + +(n_{k_2}, w)) \leq d\}$. The result $(n_{k_1}, w) + +(n_{k_2}, w)$ establishes a path between n_{k_1} and n_{k_2} with w being the hop node. A join of 2 or more path entries such as $(n_{k_1}, w) + +(n_{k_2}, w)$ form a* keyword graph *$G_K = (N_K, PE_K)$ with N_K subdivided into the two disjoint sets of center nodes N_K^C and hop nodes N_K^H. For every path entry $(n, w) \in PE_K$, we have $n \in N_K^C$ and $w \in N_K^H$.*

Based on this $\bowtie_{NB}$ operation, we provide Theorem 2 for computing results of 2-keyword queries.

THEOREM 2. *Given a 2-keyword query $K = \{k_1, k_2\}$ and the retrieved keyword neighborhoods NB_{k_1}, NB_{k_2}, the keyword graphs resulting from $NB_{k_1} \bowtie_{NB} NB_{k_2}$ are d-length Steiner graphs for K.*

Proof Sketch: In this 2-keywords setting, the set of all d-length Steiner graphs for $K = \{k_1, k_2\}$ is exactly the set of all paths of length d or less between the pairs of nodes $n_1 \in N_{k_1}, n_2 \in N_{k_2}$. By definition of the d-length 2-hop cover, the intersection $NB_{n_1} \cap NB_{n_2}$ contains the hop nodes for alls path of length d or less between n_1 and n_2. The neighborhood join $NB_{k_1} \bowtie NB_{k_2}$ leverages this, joining all paths in NB_{k_1} with paths in NB_{k_2} on the hop node $w \in NB_{n_1} \cap NB_{n_2}$. The result comprises all paths connecting the pairs of nodes $n_1 \in N_{k_1}, n_2 \in N_{k_2}$ that are of length d or less, i.e., all d-length Steiner graphs for K. □

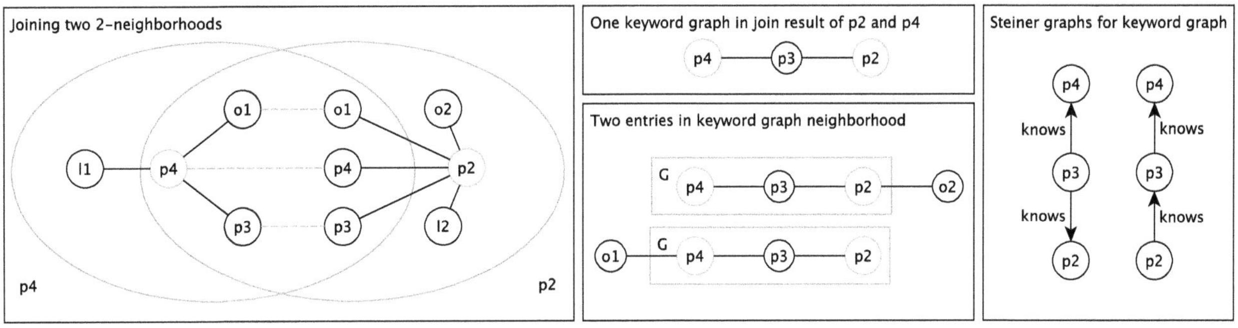

Figure 3: Join of 2-neighborhoods of p_2 and p_4 and (intermediate) results.

A keyword graph resulting from the neighborhood join contains only path entries in NB_{k_1} and NB_{k_2}, which connect the two keyword elements n_{k_1} and n_{k_2}. Thus, only hop nodes in these paths remain, while other nodes in the neighborhood of n_{k_1} and n_{k_2} have been eliminated during the process. For the subsequent graph join $\bowtie_G$, which takes a keyword graph G_K and a keyword neighborhood NB_k as inputs, these hop nodes still have to be considered because they might help in connecting G_K with NB_k. In order to include these candidates during the execution of $\bowtie_G$, a keyword graph is expanded with path entries discarded previously to obtain a keyword graph neighborhood:

DEFINITION 11 (KEYWORD GRAPH NEIGHBORHOOD). *Given a keyword graph $G_K = (N_K^C \uplus N_K^H, PE_K)$, the* keyword graph neighborhood NB_{G_K} *is a set of* graph entries *constructed from G_K and a path entry (n, w), i.e., $NB_{G_K} = \{G_K +\!\!+ (n, w) | (n, w) \in I_{PE}(n), n \in N_K^C\}$, where every $G_K + \!\!+ (n, w)$ forms a graph entry denoted as G_K^+.*

As a result of this expansion, each graph entry G_K^+ contains a "free" path entry (n, w), whose hop node w is yet not connected. Similar to $\bowtie_{NB}$, this hop node is used as the join attribute of the $\bowtie_G$ operation:

DEFINITION 12 (GRAPH JOIN). *Given a keyword neighborhood NB_{k_i} and a keyword graph neighborhood NB_{G_K}, the result of a* graph join $\bowtie_G$ *is the combination of path entries $(n_{k_i}, w) \in NB_{k_i}$ and graph entries $G_K^+(N_K, PE_K) \in NB_{G_K}$ defined as $NB_{k_i} \bowtie_G NB_{G_K} - \{G_K^+(N_K, PE_K) + \!\!+ (n_{k_i}, w) | \exists (n_{k_j}, w)((n_{k_j}, w) \in PE_K)\}$.*

The result of this operation is also a keyword graph, which however, connects more than two keyword elements via a number of path entries. For each entry, we use the path index to retrieve all paths between its center and hop nodes and join them along the edges of the keyword graph to construct the final Steiner graphs.

EXAMPLE 3. *Fig. 3 shows an example for processing the 2-neighborhoods of nodes p_2, p_4. The keyword neighborhoods have three hop nodes in common: p_3, p_4, o_1. The figure shows the keyword graph resulting from a join combination of path entries $(p_4, p_3), (p_2, p_3)$ and two entries of the resulting keyword graph neighborhood. Two Steiner graphs are generated from this keyword graph.*

4.2 Integrated Query Plan

A query K can be processed according to a *query plan*. It is a sequence of join operators $(\bowtie_{NB}^1, \bowtie_G^2, \ldots, \bowtie_G^{|K-1|})$, starting with the operator $\bowtie_{NB}$ joining two keyword neighborhoods (called base inputs), followed by $\bowtie_G$ operators that combine a base input with a graph. Since the base inputs represent elements retrieved for the keywords, a plan also represents a particular order of query keywords.

The principle difference to standard database join processing is that in keyword search, connections between two keywords are not known in advance. This is why typically, connections have to be explored at runtime by traversing edges of the data graphs that are loaded into memory. For this, efficient techniques for searching results in the data graph [9, 3], or pruning joined neighborhoods [11] have been proposed. For "searching" keyword search results via join processing, we observe there is no single optimal plan but different plans might produce different results, or even no results at all, as illustrated by Example 4.

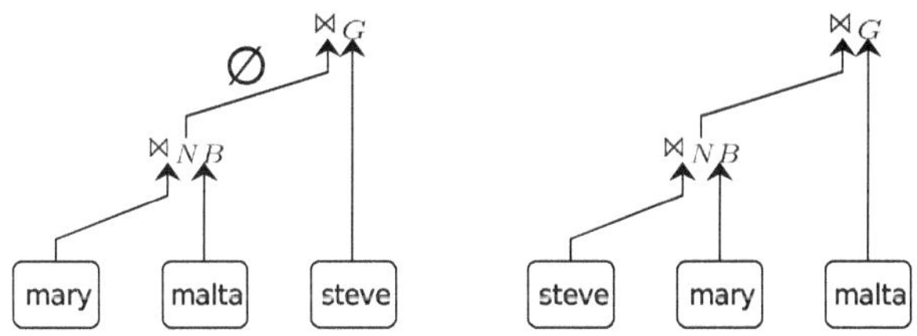

Figure 4: Two query plans for query Q_3.

EXAMPLE 4. *Consider query Q_3 from Fig. 1. For $d = 2$, keywords* steve *and* malta *are connected and* mary *is connected to* steve, *but not to* malta. *Fig. 4 shows two query plans for query Q_3. The first join on the keyword neighborhoods of* mary *and* malta *produces empty results as there are no paths of length d or less. However, results can be produced when the keyword neighborhoods of* steve *and* malta *or* steve *and* mary *are joined first.*

Now, we provide Theorem 3 to compute keyword search results for queries with more than 2 keywords, using an *integrated query plan*:

THEOREM 3. *Let G be the data graph, K be an n-keyword query, and $P(K)$ represents all permutations of keywords in the set K where each $p \in P(K)$ stands for a query plan, keyword graphs resulting from executing all $p \in P(K)$ capture all Steiner graphs for K that can be obtained from G.*

Proof Sketch: Let $N_K = \{N_{k_1}, \ldots, N_{k_i}\}$ be the set of keyword elements obtained for K. We must generate (1) all graphs from G, which (2) contain an element $n_{k_i} \in N_K$ for every $k_i \in K$, (3) all these keyword elements are pairwise connected, and (4) direct paths between two keyword elements are of length d or less. The integrated plan contains different orders of joins. Every join is either $\bowtie_{NB}$ or $\bowtie_G$. As both operations rest on the same concept of d-length 2-hop cover (i.e., join two path entries on a hop node), the resulting paths are of length d or less (4). Every plan joins every keyword element with one another, ensuring they all are pairwise (directly or indirectly) connected (3). Also, since every plan contains all keywords, (2) is trivially satisfied. Taken (2+3+4) together, we can conclude that every plan (i.e., order of join) results in Steiner graphs of one particular structure. Since the integrated plan contains all possible orders, Steiner graphs of all possible structures that may exist in the data graph are taken into account (1). □

As illustrated in Example 5, the integrated query plan consists of operators at levels $l = 0, \ldots, |K|$. Level 0 represents data access operators, employing $|K|$ base inputs. Level 1 to $|K-1|$ contain join operators. Only $\bowtie_{NB}$ operators are needed at level 1. Subsequent levels consist exclusively of $\bowtie_G$ operators, which always combine a graph with a base input such that there is a correspondence between level and the number of inputs, i.e., every join operator at level l consumes exactly $l+1$ base inputs. That is, operators at level $|K-1|$ have inputs for all query keywords in K. In fact, every operator at this level can be seen as representing one particular plan (i.e., particular order of keywords). Level $|K|$ has a single union operator that combines results from different plans.

The total number of join operators can be computed by taking all permutations of the set of base inputs K as the total number of join order plans and multiply this by $|K|-1$, which is the number of join operators for every plan. More precisely, the permutations of the set K represent only the upper bound. The number of join operators at level 1 is in fact $N(1) = C(|K|, 2) = |K|(|K|-1)/2$, which denotes all 2-combinations of the set $|K|$. At this level, where only $\bowtie_{NB}$ operators are applied, the order of the base inputs is not relevant (and thus it suffices to consider all 2-combinations instead of permutations). The order of the subsequent $\bowtie_G$ operations is however relevant and distinguishes one plan from another. At each subsequent level $l > 1$, l-permutations of the set $|K|$ have to be considered. These different orders however, share overlapping parts. To eliminate this redundancy and minimize the number of join operators, we employ join operators whose outputs can be connected to more than one subsequent operators at the next level. Based on this, we construct a join operator at level $l > 1$ by combining inputs of a possibly "shared" operator of the previous level with a base input not processed yet. Since the number of base inputs not processed by an operator at level $l-1$ is $|K|-l$, the number of join operators at level l is $N(l) = N(l-1)(|K|-l)$ (indicating all combinations of inputs from previous join operators and base inputs not processed yet). Thus, the total number of join operators is $N(K) = N(1) + \sum_{l=2}^{|K|-1}(|K|-l)N(l-1)$.

Complexity Given the number of join operators, the upper bound on complexity of keyword query processing can be established as follows. In worst case, the result of a join is the cross product of its inputs. Here, input size is given by the number of path entries in each keyword neighborhood, which can be calculated as $|N_k| \cdot b^d$ for each $k \in K$, where b is the average branching factor of the pruned d-neighborhood: b^d gives the number of paths in the neighborhood while $|N_k|$ denotes the total number of neighborhoods that can be obtained for a keyword k. The upper bound can then be calculated as $N(K) \cdot \max\{|N_k| \cdot b^d | k \in K\}^2$. Note that due to pruning at the level of paths, the branching factor of the neighborhoods is smaller than the one of the original graph.

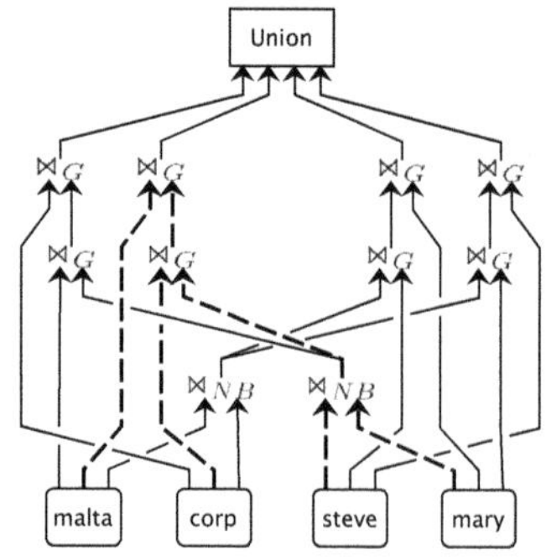

Figure 5: Excerpt of an integrated query plan.

EXAMPLE 5. *Fig. 5 shows an excerpt of the integrated query plan for a query of size 4. One subplan for the join order* ⟨*steve* $\bowtie_{NB}$ *mary* $\bowtie_G$ *corp* $\bowtie_G$ *malta*⟩ *is emphasized. The figure also shows that intermediate results such as the one produced by steve* $\bowtie_{NB}$ *mary is used for this as well as for one another plan.*

4.3 Top-k Keyword-Join Processing

Different top-k query processing techniques have been proposed to reach early termination after obtaining the top-k results [8]. Of particular interest in this context is the top-k join, which produces ranked join results without consuming all inputs [7].

A top-k join operator, also called *rank join*, takes two inputs that are sorted by the scores of their elements and iteratively processes them as data streams (i.e., no random access) to produce k top results. Crucial in top-k processing is the *threshold* T, an upper bound maintained for every join operator to capture the maximum score that can be achieved using as yet unprocessed input tuples. A join result can be reported if its score is higher than T. For a join between the inputs 1 and 2, $T = \max(Agg(s_1^{max}, \overline{s}_2), Agg(\overline{s}_1, s_2^{max}))$ where $Agg(\cdot)$ returns the score for the joined result, s_i^{max} denotes the best score of all tuples of input i, and $\overline{s}_i$ denotes the score of the tuple lastly seen from i. The last seen score and threshold decrease as new tuples are processed (because they arrive at a decreasing order of scores).

This concept of rank join is utilized for top-k query processing in a pull-based architecture: each operator in the query plan has a *next* method that is called to produce the next result (i.e., a reportable result whose score exceeds T); a tree-shaped query plan is employed where the root operator calls the next method of lower level operators, which in turn call next on the base inputs. Processing inputs this way is guaranteed to preserve the top-k property, i.e., the resulting k results have best scores. This follows directly from the notion of threshold, as results reported by the next methods have scores greater than T, and thus are guaranteed to have scores greater than all other result candidates that can be produced using remaining tuples.

Top-k Processing We adopt this top-k query processing to our setting, as early termination can avoid the processing of a possibly large amount of join operators in the integrated query plan. Further, implementing $\bowtie_G$ and $\bowtie_{NB}$ as *rank join* naturally enables us to treat data as input streams. Instead of loading large graphs into memory [11] at once, we use rank join to incrementally access and process streams of path entries. We note that the only difference to the standard query plan is that in the integrated query plan, the root is a union operator. We apply the notion of threshold to obtain a *rank union* operator in order to preserve the top-k property. The threshold of a union operator $\cup$ is defined as $T(\cup) = max\{T_{\bowtie} | \bowtie \in \cup_{\bowtie}\}$, where $T_{\bowtie}$ is the threshold of a rank join operator $\bowtie$, and $\cup_{\bowtie}$ is the set of all rank join operators that feed into $\cup$. A result for $\cup$ can be reported when its score is higher or equal to $T(\cup)$. Processing the integrated query plan with the rank version of our operators (i.e., operators with thresholds for result output) using the pull-based procedure discussed above [8], yields top-k results. We provide the following Theorem to capture this:

THEOREM 4. *Given a query K, the data G and a predefined parameter k, an integrated query plan consisting of rank operators produces a sorted list of k Steiner graphs $\{G_{S_1}, \ldots, G_{S_k}\}$ for K s.t. there exist no other Steiner graph G_{S_i} in G with $Score(G_{S_i}) > Score(G_{S_k})$.*

The proof for this essentially exploits the top-k property of the underlying rank operators. The intuition is this: the integrated query plan can be decomposed into a number of subplans, each represents a different join order for the keywords in K. Because every such subplan corresponds exactly to the notion of query plan used previously [8], the established top-k property holds in this case, providing the guarantee that every subplan yields the k best Steiner graphs (of one particular structure reflected by the join order). The rank union operator reports a top-k result only when its score equals or is higher than the maximum of the thresholds of the underlying rank join operators (subplans). This maximum threshold can be seen as a global threshold applied to results of all subplans. The top-k property is preserved because by definition, no subplan can produce further results with scores exceeding this global threshold.

Push-based Architecture The pull-based architecture [8] is "driven" by the final results. When called by the *next* method, each operator consumes its inputs until it is able to produce one result. Such an architecture is problematic in keyword query processing, as some operators of the integrated query plan may produce no results, which can only be determined after completely reading at least two base inputs. Detecting and avoiding these "broken operators" (and the subplans resulting from them) can improve efficiency. To this end, we propose a push-based architecture, which is "driven" by the data access operators instead of the results. These operators *push* their outputs into the join operators they are connected to, from where keyword graphs propagate upwards through the query plans. In contrast to pull-based architectures, control and data flow are in the same rather than opposite direction.

Operator Ranking Using such a push-based architecture, we can apply operator ranking to accommodate knowledge related to which operators are broken, which ones produce more results, or which ones produce results earlier than others. The ranking of operators determines its order during execution. That is, we propose not only to rank inputs and (partial) results, but also the join operators themselves. We associate rank join operators with a global score, which is estimated based on current results (R), and upper bound estimates for subsequent join operations to be performed on the remaining base inputs (NB_k).

DEFINITION 13 (OPERATOR RANK). *Given the results R of a $\bowtie_{Rank}$ operator and the remaining set NB_K of keyword neighborhoods not included in the inputs to $\bowtie_{Rank}$, the* global score *of $\bowtie_{Rank}$ is defined as $S = max\{Score(G_K)|G_K \in R\} + \sum_{NB_k \in NB_K} max\{Score(P)|P \in NB_k\}$.*

Query Execution The global score is used to guide query execution. When a join operator has results that can be pushed to the next operator, it is associated with an (updated) global score and becomes active. If there are no active join operators, the lower level data access operators are activated in a round-robin fashion, each pushing a path entry into all rank $\bowtie_{NB}$ operators they are connected to. If there are active operators, the operator with the highest global score pushes its results to subsequent operators until its result stack is empty, or another join operator has a better global score.

Detailed Algorithms Alg. 1 shows the query execution algorithm. First, the keyword elements N_k for all $k \in K$ are retrieved and their keyword neighborhoods are created. Priority queue J keeps track of all currently active join operators, sorted by their global scores. While the number of results is lower than k, the algorithm gets the best result (via the *topR* method) from the topmost push rank join (PRJ) operator *op* in the queue J. By calling the *push* method of every connected operators (retrieved via *nextLevelOps*), this result is propagated to the next level. Now we check if the second best result (the one not been pushed yet) passes the threshold to determine if *op* is still active, and add it back to the queue if this is the case. If no active operators are available, the base inputs are activated until at least one operator becomes active or all inputs are exhausted.

Algorithm 1: EvaluateQuery(K, I_{PE}, k)

Input: Keyword query K, k
Data: Queue J of active join operators, the integrated query plan IQP.

Retrieve N_k for all $k \in K$
Retrieve $NB_k \in NB_K$ for each N_k
while *number of final results* $< k$ **do**
  if $|J| > 0$ **then**
    op = J.pop()
    $NOps$ = IQP.nextLevelOps(*op*)
    foreach $nop \in NOps$ **do** nop.**push** (*op*.topR)
    op.active = $\exists op.secR(Score(op.secR) > op.T)$
    if *op.active* **then** Add *op* to J
  else
    Select next input NB_k
    $NOps$ = IQP.nextLevelOps(NB_k)
    foreach $nop \in NOps$ **do** nop.**push** (NB_k.topR)
    Add all active operators to J

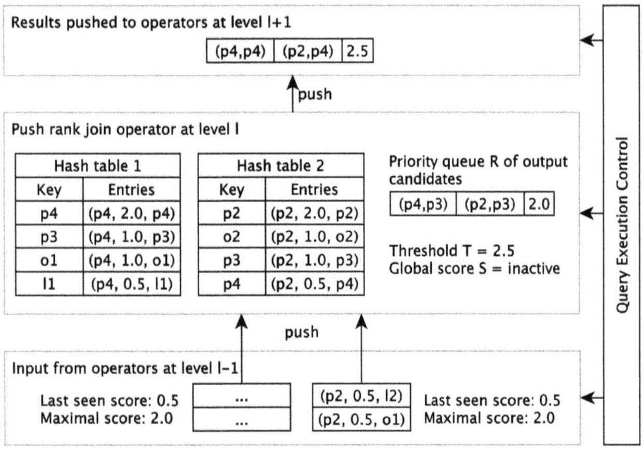

Figure 6: Keyword processing based on PRJ.

The employed PRJ shown in Alg. 2 is based on the hash rank join [7]: it also maintains a hash table for each input (H_1, H_2) for efficient lookup and computation of the join results J, and a threshold T (updated via the *threshold* method). Additionally, the PRJ operator also maintains the global score S. As previously defined, S is computed from the score of the currently best result and the maximum score of the combination of remaining base inputs that have not been joined during the process, i.e., are not part of the current results.

Algorithm 2: PRJ: Push(r)

Input: Pushed input element r
Data: Queue R of sorted results, hash tables H_1, H_2 for inputs, global score S
`// Use m,n to identify hash tables and inputs`
if *r is left input* **then** $m = 1$, $n = 2$
else $m = 2$, n=1
Insert r into hash table H_m
T = threshold()
J = probe H_n for valid joined results with keys of r
forall the $j \in J$ **do** insert j into R
if $|R| > 0$ **then**
  if $Score(this.topRes) > T$ **then**
    $this$.active = true
    Update S

EXAMPLE 6. *Fig. 6 shows a PRJ operator at level l, joining neighborhoods of p_2 and p_4. The inputs, i.e., path entries $(p_2, 0.5, l_2), (p_2, 0.5, o_1)$ from one operator and inputs (...) from other operators, are pushed from operators at level $l-1$. The two hash tables contain 4×2 elements already processed. One output with score 2.5 has been pushed to the next level. A candidate result with score 2.0 is in the queue. Because the last seen score is 0.5, $T = 2.0 + 0.5 = 2.5$. As the result has a score less than threshold T, it cannot be pushed to subsequent operators yet (is thus inactive). This may change subsequently because T may decrease when lower input scores are processed. The query execution controls the push operation: an operator is only activated to push its results if its global score S is the highest among all active operators.*

Note that the proposed modifications to the basic strategy, i.e., push-based execution in combination with operator-ranking, only aims at improving the efficiency. It has no effect on the top-k property. Essentially, because the same threshold checks are carried out, Theorem 4 must also hold in this case.

5. RELATED WORK

We discussed research work on neighborhood indexing [16, 1] and join processing [8, 7] that underlies our approach. We also provided an overview of existing keyword search solutions, which can be categorized into the categories of (1) schema-based ([5, 12, 13, 15, 14]) and (2) schema-agnostic ([9, 4, 11]) approaches. A similar distinction was made in a recent survey of keyword search in relational databases [18]. The capabilities of the underlying database engine can be fully utilized by the former approaches, while the applicability of the latter approaches is not limited to structured data that have well defined schemas. Our work follows the line of schema-agnostic approaches, aiming at providing keyword search support for different types of data, from structured to semi-structured up to unstructured data [11]. In particular, we compute Steiner graphs by operating directly on the data graph [11, 9, 17]. We make two kinds of contributions that are substantially different from previous work along this line: (1) previous strategies for searching Steiner graphs load the data graph into memory, and then find Steiner graphs by traversing graph edges [9], or pruning them [11]. Instead, we propose the use of join operations for this. (2) Further, for efficient data access, we propose an index that stores materialized paths in the neighborhoods of graph elements. While the concept of neighborhood is conceptually similar to the notion used by EASE [11], the data structure to implement it is more efficient because the employed strategies for neighborhood pruning is based on the more fine-grained notion of paths, instead of graphs. Further, this implementation enables us to conceive a neighborhood as a set of paths, enabling the search for Steiner graphs to be conducted via path-based join operations.

6. EVALUATION

Systems We compare our approach with an implementation of EASE [11], a state-of-the-art native keyword search solution. We also implemented the bidirectional search algorithm (BDS) [9]. We used two variants of our approach: KJ features operator ranking and KJU does not.

For all approaches, a Lucene keyword index is used to retrieve the top 300 matching keyword elements for each keyword of the query. The time needed for this is not counted as it is the same for all systems. For BDS, the exploration is performed directly on the data graph to obtain top-k Steiner graphs. For EASE, first all maximal 2-radius graphs, which contain at least one keyword element for every keyword, are identified. The union of these graphs computed for all query keywords is then loaded into memory, and pruned successively to obtain Steiner graphs.

All systems were implemented in Java 1.6 on top of Oracle Berkeley DB (Java Edition). Experiments were performed on a Linux system with two Intel Xeon 2.80GHz Dual-Core processors, a Samsung HE322HJ SATA 320GB disk and 8GB of main memory, 4GB of which were assigned

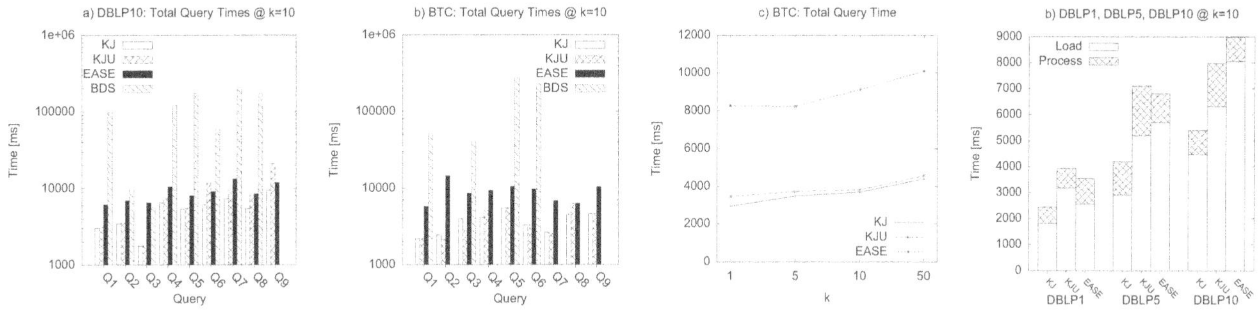

Figure 7: Evaluation results.

to the Java VM. Operating system caches were cleared after each query run.

Data and Queries We used a crawl of the Billion Triple Challenge 2009[2] (BTC) dataset, and 3 DBLP datasets from the SP2Bench benchmark [3] (DBLP) that vary in size, which we employ for the scalability experiment. Tab. 3 shows detailed statistics about the datasets and the size of the indexes for KJ (path entry index I_{PE} and path index I_P) and EASE. For each dataset, we created nine keyword queries of length 2 ($Q_1 - Q_3$), 3 ($Q_4 - Q_6$) and 4 ($Q_7 - Q_9$). Table 4 shows example queries for both datasets.

	Triples	I_{PE}	I_P	EASE
BTC	10M	237	890	7933
DBLP1	1M	42	76	234
DBLP5	5M	250	452	2201
DBLP10	10M	559	1004	7435

Table 3: Dataset and index statistics (index sizes in MB).

DBLP	BTC
"miller journal"	"event movie"
"press article 1988"	"album queen magic"
"journal medical article 1979"	"document iswc owl semantic 2009"

Table 4: Example queries for DBLP and BTC datasets.

Index Statistics For each dataset we created the path entry and path indexes with $d = 2$ for our approach and an index containing maximal 2-radius graphs for EASE. As discussed, the scale-free nature of Web data graphs makes values $d > 2$ impractical because neighborhoods become as large as the entire data graph. Note that unlike EASE, this is not such a strong limitation because paths between 2 keyword elements can still have lengths up to $|K - 1| \times d$ (instead of $2 \times d$).

Due to more fine-grained pruning, the KJ indexes were much smaller than the EASE indexes: for the DBLP datasets, the size of the KJ indexes was between 50% (DBLP1) and 21% (DBLP10) the size of the corresponding EASE indexes. For the BTC dataset, the difference was even larger: the KJ index was only 14% the size of the EASE index.

[2]`http://vmlion25.deri.ie/`
[3]`http://dbis.informatik.uni-freiburg.de/index.php?project=SP2B`

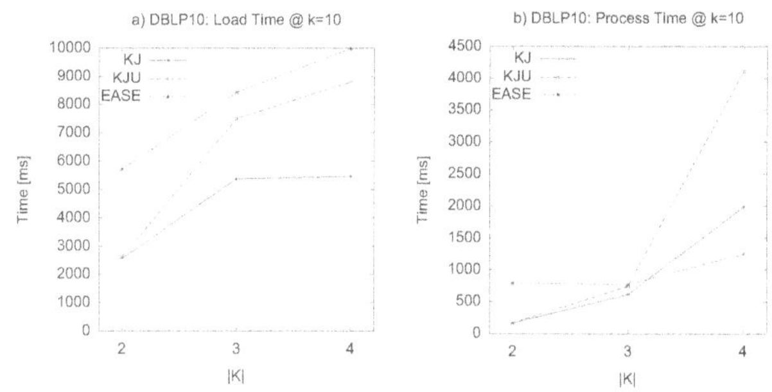

Figure 8: Evaluation results: load and process times for different keyword query lengths.

Overall Performance Fig. 7(a)+(b) show total query times for all queries on the DBLP10 and BTC datasets (missing values indicate timeouts). The performance of BDS was worse than all other systems on average (up to one order of magnitude for some queries). This suggests that the materialization strategies employed by other systems largely improve online performance. For both datasets, the performance of KJ was better than EASE for all queries. For DBLP10, and $k = 10$, the average total query times for KJ and EASE were 5.4s and 8.9s, respectively (BDS: 105.5s). On the BTC dataset with $k = 10$, the total times were 3.7s and 9.1s (BDS: 147.9s). This represents an improvement of 39% and 59%, respectively. However, the performance advantage of KJ compared to EASE decreases with longer queries. Whereas for $|K| = 2$ on DBLP10 with $k = 10$, EASE was on average 2.39 times slower than KJ, this factor decreased to 1.53 and 1.51 for $|K| = 3$ and $|K| = 4$, respectively. We will show later that the reason for that lies in the increased number of joins needed to process the search space resulting from the standard semantics of keyword search results that is larger than the one of EASE.

Top-k Processing Fig 7(c) shows query performance for different values of k for the BTC dataset. Clearly, query times for all systems increase with higher values of k.

Operator Ranking We compare KJ and KJU to examine the effect of operator ranking. Fig 7(c) shows that, on average, KJ with operator ranking was faster than KJU without operator ranking. We can see that the difference in query time between KJ and KJU decreases with larger values of k. For $k = 1$ KJU took 17% longer than KJ, whereas for $k = 50$ the difference was only 4%. This shows that operator ranking enables faster early result reporting, but also that the benefit decreases when more results are requested, which can be explained by the additional overhead introduced by operator ranking during query execution.

Scalability Fig. 7(d) shows overall query times for the three different DBLP datasets. The query time is split into the time for data access (load) and the time for join processing (process). We can see that data access makes up the main share of total time. For all datasets, KJ outperforms EASE. With respect to scalability, we found that the difference in performance between EASE and our system increases with larger datasets. On DBLP1, the smallest dataset, EASE was worse by a factor of 1.44. This increases with larger versions of the DBLP dataset, e.g. EASE was worse by a factor of 1.66 on DBLP10.

For an examination of the separate impact of data access (load) and data processing (process), Figure 8 illustrates a decomposition of query time.

Data Access Fig. 8 shows access times at different query lengths $|K|$ for DBLP with $k = 10$. For all systems, access times increase with longer queries. Again, we can see the positive effect of operator ranking, as access times for KJ do not increase as sharply as for KJU. For $|K| = 2$, both KJ and KJU exhibit similar access times, whereas for $|K| = 4$ KJU is 1.6 times worse than KJ. Access times for EASE are worse than KJ for all query lengths. This confirms that the more fine-grained path-level pruning implemented by KJ helps to focus on smaller neighborhoods. Further, this efficiency gain can also be attributed to the fact that instead of loading all entire neighborhoods (i.e., all matching 2-radius graphs), KJ only loads path entries necessary to compute top-k results.

Data Processing Fig. 8(b) shows processing times at different values for $|K|$. Clearly, processing times increase for larger values of $|K|$. However, this effect is more pronounced for KJ and KJU than for EASE. From $|K| = 2$ to $|K| = 4$, KJ's processing times increase by a factor 12.2 where EASE'times increase only by 1.6. This result is not surprising, given our approach supports the standard semantics whereas EASE assumes a center node. With more complex queries, the search space for KJ becomes larger. This is reflected in a higher number of query plans and join operators that have to be processed. Regardless of query length, EASE always operates on the union of the 2-radius graphs, and obtain results using the same pruning procedure.

Here, we can more clearly see the benefit of operator ranking: KJU's processing times are higher than KJ's times; this difference increases with $|K|$, indicating that operator ranking is beneficial when the queries are more complex.

7. CONCLUSION

We proposed a native keyword search database solution based on the basic operations data access and join. We introduced the d-length 2-hop index and a top-k procedure for implementing this database style processing. In experiments using large scale datasets, we showed that our solution consistently outperformed state-of-the-art solutions, i.e., it reduced storage requirement up to 86%, improved scalability by several factors, and improved performance by more than 50% on average. Further, our approach exhibits two main qualitative advantages. (1) While the exisiting solution requires large graphs to be loaded entirely into memory at once, the database style processing we propose operates data streams that are loaded successively. (2) Also, the semantics of the results supported is more general, leading to more results formed by longer paths. Whereas this work focuses on the efficiency of top-k keyword search processing, the question of how differences in semantics and scoring functions affect the quality of results is considered as the main future work.

Acknowledgements. The authors would like to thank Jörg Diederich for providing the DBLP query logs. Research reported in this paper was supported by the German Federal Ministry of Education and Research (BMBF) in the iGreen project (grant 01IA08005K).

8. REFERENCES

[1] J. Cheng and J. X. Yu. On-line exact shortest distance query processing. In *EDBT*, pages 481–492, Saint Petersburg, Russia, 2009. ACM.

[2] E. Cohen, E. Halperin, H. Kaplan, and U. Zwick. Reachability and distance queries via 2-hop labels. In *ACM-SIAM Symposium on Discrete algorithms*, pages 937–946, 2002.

[3] B. Ding, J. X. Yu, S. Wang, L. Qin, X. Zhang, and X. Lin. Finding top-k min-cost connected trees in databases. In *ICDE*, pages 836–845. IEEE, 2007.

[4] H. He, H. Wang, J. Yang, and P. S. Yu. Blinks: ranked keyword searches on graphs. In *SIGMOD Conference*, pages 305–316, 2007.

[5] V. Hristidis, L. Gravano, and Y. Papakonstantinou. Efficient ir-style keyword search over relational databases. In *VLDB*, pages 850–861, 2003.

[6] H. Hwang, V. Hristidis, and Y. Papakonstantinou. Objectrank: a system for authority-based search on databases. In *SIGMOD Conference*, 2006.

[7] I. F. Ilyas, W. G. Aref, and A. K. Elmagarmid. Joining ranked inputs in practice. In *VLDB*, pages 950–961, 2002.

[8] I. F. Ilyas, G. Beskales, and M. A. Soliman. A survey of top-k query processing techniques in relational database systems. *ACM Comput. Surv.*, 40(4), 2008.

[9] V. Kacholia, S. Pandit, S. Chakrabarti, S. Sudarshan, R. Desai, and H. Karambelkar. Bidirectional expansion for keyword search on graph databases. In *VLDB*, pages 505–516, 2005.

[10] G. Ladwig and T. Tran. Index structures and top-k join algorithms for native keyword search databases. Technical report, 2011. http://people.aifb.kit.edu/gla/tr/cikm_kwtopk.pdf.

[11] G. Li, B. C. Ooi, J. Feng, J. Wang, and L. Zhou. Ease: an effective 3-in-1 keyword search method for unstructured, semi-structured and structured data. In *SIGMOD Conference*, pages 903–914, 2008.

[12] F. Liu, C. T. Yu, W. Meng, and A. Chowdhury. Effective keyword search in relational databases. In S. Chaudhuri, V. Hristidis, and N. Polyzotis, editors, *SIGMOD Conference*, pages 563–574. ACM, 2006.

[13] Y. Luo, X. Lin, W. Wang, and X. Zhou. Spark: top-k keyword query in relational databases. In *SIGMOD Conference*, pages 115–126, 2007.

[14] L. Qin, J. Yu, and L. Chang. Ten thousand sqls: Parallel keyword queries computing. *PVLDB*, 3(1):58–69, 2010.

[15] L. Qin, J. X. Yu, and L. Chang. Keyword search in databases: the power of rdbms. In *SIGMOD Conference*, pages 681–694, 2009.

[16] R. Schenkel, A. Theobald, and G. Weikum. HOPI: an efficient connection index for complex XML document collections. In *EDBT*, pages 665–666. 2004.

[17] T. Tran, H. Wang, S. Rudolph, and P. Cimiano. Top-k exploration of query candidates for efficient keyword search on graph-shaped (rdf) data. In *ICDE*, 2009.

[18] J. X. Yu, L. Qin, and L. Chang. Keyword search in relational databases: A survey. *IEEE Data Eng. Bull.*, 33(1):67–78, 2010.

Optimized Processing of Multiple Aggregate Continuous Queries

Shenoda Guirguis [1], Mohamed A. Sharaf [2], Panos K. Chrysanthis [1], Alexandros Labrinidis [1]
[1]Department of Computer Science, University of Pittsburgh
[2]School of Information Technology and Electrical Engineering, The University of Queensland
{shenoda, panos, labrinid}@cs.pitt.edu, m.sharaf@uq.edu.au

ABSTRACT

Data Streams Management Systems are designed to support monitoring applications which require the processing of hundreds of Aggregate Continuous Queries (ACQs). These ACQs typically have different time granularities, with possibly different selection predicates and group-by attributes. In order to achieve scalability in the presence of heavy workloads, in this paper, we introduce the concept of *'Weaveability'* as an indicator of the potential gains of sharing the processing of ACQs. We then propose *Weave Share*, a cost-based optimizer that exploits weaveability to optimize the shared processing of ACQs. Our experimental analysis shows that *Weave Share* outperforms the alternative sharing schemes generating up to four orders of magnitude better quality plans. Finally, we describe a practical implementation of the *Weave Share* optimizer.

Categories and Subject Descriptors

H.2.4 [**Database Management**]: Systems—*Query Processing*

General Terms

Algorithms, Design, Experimentation, Performance

Keywords

Data Streams Management Systems, Aggregate Continuous Queries, Multiple Query Optimization, Weaveability, Shared Processing

1. INTRODUCTION

Data Stream Management Systems (DSMSs) were developed to be at the heart of every monitoring application, from environmental and network monitoring, to disease outbreak detection, financial market analysis and studying of cosmic phenomena (e.g., [3, 9, 1, 2, 21, 22]). DSMSs are designed to efficiently handle unbounded streams with large volumes of data and large numbers of continuous queries (i.e., exhibit scalability). Thus, optimizing the processing of multiple continuous queries is imperative for DSMSs to reach their full potential.

In all monitoring applications, hundreds of Aggregate Continuous Queries (ACQs) are typically registered [17] to monitor few input data streams. For example, a stock market monitoring application allows numerous users each to register several monitoring queries. For instance, traders interested in a certain stock might register ACQs to monitor the `average`, or `maximum`, volume trade in a certain period of time, e.g., the last 1, 8, or 24 hours. Meanwhile, decision makers might register monitoring queries for analysis purposes with coarse time granularity, e.g., the `average` volume trade in last week or month. Given the commonality of ACQs, and the high data arrival rates, optimizing the processing of ACQs is crucial for scalability.

In general, Multiple Query Optimization (MQO) is well known to be NP-hard for traditional database systems [19] as well as for DSMSs [25]. MQO techniques are typically based on heuristics that aim to share the processing of *common sub-expressions*. This raises the challenge of identifying which sub-expressions are beneficial to share, if any [27, 11]. However, the optimization of multiple ACQs goes beyond the classic identification of common sub-expressions to exploiting the window semantics and partial aggregation; this is the challenge we are addressing in this paper.

An ACQ is typically defined over a certain window of the input data stream, to bound its computations. For example, an ACQ that monitors the average volume trade of a stock index could be defined over a window of range 24 hours and slide 1 hour: every hour, the average volume trade in the past 24 hours is reported. Partial aggregation has been proposed to optimize the processing of ACQs [13, 14, 6] by minimizing the repeated processing of overlapping windows. Partial aggregation has also been utilized to share the processing of multiple similar ACQs with different windows, assuming it is always beneficial to share the partial aggregation [12].

The assumption that it is always beneficial to share is based on the premise that data arrival rate is the predominant factor in determining the sharing decision, where a high rate is always a precursor for plan sharing. It is also based on the observation that, in most practical applications, data streams do in fact exhibit a high rate. This approximation, however, considers only one facet of the problem (i.e., the characteristics of data streams) while diminishing the impact of the other facet (i.e., the characteristics of the registered queries). In this paper we argue that the properties of the installed ACQs are of equal importance in determining the sharing decision. In fact, we show that for many practical cases, sharing the partial aggregation phase of query plans could lead to a performance degradation even when data streams arrive at high rate.

To address this issue, we identify the trade offs in optimizing the shared processing of multiple ACQs and introduce the concept of *"Weaveability"* of ACQs. The *Weaveability* of a set of ACQs is an indicator of the potential gains from sharing their processing. The goal is then to design a multiple ACQs optimization technique that utilizes weaveability in the sharing decision. Exploiting weaveabil-

CIKM'11, October 24–28, 2011, Glasgow, Scotland, UK.

ity, however, involves three major challenges. First, given that the optimization problem at hand is NP-hard, the technique should efficiently search the exponential search space, while not sacrificing the quality of the optimized plans. Second, the technique should also efficiently handle the addition and deletion of ACQs as time advances. Finally, it should exploit the weaveability of ACQs with minimal overhead.

In this paper, we address all the above challenges and propose *Weave Share*, a cost-based multiple ACQs optimizer, which exploits weaveability to optimize the shared processing of ACQs. *Weave Share* considers all factors that affect the cost of the shared query plan. It selectively groups ACQs into multiple execution trees to minimize the total plan cost. We experimentally evaluate and analyze the performance of *Weave Share* in terms of quality of the generated plans using all possible settings of workload characteristics. Our experimental analysis shows that *Weave Share* generates up to orders of magnitude better quality plans compared to the alternative sharing schemes. In order to handle the addition and deletion of ACQs, we propose *Incremental Weave Share* that efficiently weaves the new ACQs into the execution trees of an existing plan, as long as the quality of the query plan is not compromised, i.e., remains within specified tolerance limits. Finally, we develop and experimentally evaluate a practical implementation and several optimizations that dramatically improve the efficiency of *Weave Share* in generating high quality plans.

Contributions: In summary, we make the following contributions:

- We introduce the concept of *"Weaveability."*
- We propose *Weave Share* and *Incremental Weave Share* cost-based multi ACQs optimizers.
- We develop practical implementation and several optimizations of the *Weave Share* optimizer.
- We experimentally evaluate our proposed techniques using simulation.

Road map: We summarize related work in Section 2 and describe the streams aggregation model in Section 3. We formalize the problem and introduce *Weaveability* in Section 4. We present *Weave Share* and its online version in Section 5. The evaluation platform and the quality of weave share plans are discussed in Sections 6 and 7, respectively. We present implementation optimizations in Section 8 and conclude in Section 9.

2. RELATED WORK

There is a rich literature on multiple query optimization (MQO) in traditional databases [20, 18, 16, 10, 23] as well as in data streams [23, 1, 24, 15]. Finding the optimal query plan in traditional databases is an NP-Hard problem [19]. Hence, cost-based heuristic approaches have been investigated [18, 8]. This is also the case in data streams. In the context of multiple ACQs optimization, two orthogonal approaches were proposed: *scheduling* and *partial aggregation*. In [7], a window-aware scheduling scheme was proposed to synchronize the re-execution times of similar ACQs to execute common parts only once.

Partial aggregation is the underlying principle for an efficient implementation of the aggregate continuous operator [13, 12]. The Panes [13] scheme splits the slide into equal sized fragments, to be processed using the partial aggregation operator. Paired windows [12] improves Panes by splitting the slide into exactly two fragments, minimizing the processing needed at the final-aggregation level. We assume the paired window scheme in our model, as discussed in the next section.

The work in [25, 26, 17] proposed a shared processing of multiple ACQs with different group-by attributes. The proposed scheme maintains fine-granularity ACQs called phantoms, or intermediate aggregations. The computation of these intermediate aggregations can then be shared among the different ACQs. While in [25, 26] the proposed techniques were designed for the architecture of Gigascope, a special purpose stream processing engine, they were generalized in [17]. In principle, the general idea of grouping ACQs in a hierarchy of intermediate ACQs is conceptually similar to the selective sharing technique underlying our proposed *Weave Share*. However, while the work in [17] focuses on optimizing the processing of multiple ACQs that have different *group-by attributes*, our work focuses on optimizing multiple ACQs that have different *window specifications*. These are two orthogonal problems.

3. STREAMS AGGREGATION

In this background section, we discuss window semantics of ACQs and partial aggregation, as per the current state of the art.

3.1 ACQ Semantics

An ACQ is defined over a window, which is specified in terms of two intervals: *range* (r) and *slide* (s). For example, an ACQ may compute the average stock price over the last hour (i.e., $r = 1$ hr) and update it every 30 minutes (i.e., $s = 30$ min). The range and slide intervals could be defined either as number of tuples or as a time interval. Here, we consider the more general time-based definition for both the range and slide; our contributions are applicable to the tuple-based definition. Producing a new window requires processing each tuple within the range. The slide interval defines how the window boundaries move over the input stream. For instance, when slide is less than range (sliding window), consecutive windows overlap and a single tuple will belong to more than one window instance. This is illustrated in the example below.

EXAMPLE 1. *Consider a stock monitoring application where the user is interested in the average trade volume in the past hour, and would like to be updated every ten minutes. The user then registers an ACQ with* $r = 1$ *hr and* $s = 10$ *min. Thus, a window boundary is reached every 10 min and an aggregation is performed over the tuples within the last hour. Hence, each input tuple is aggregated in six consecutive windows (=1 hr/10 min).*

In a straightforward implementation of ACQs, input tuples are buffered and once a window boundary is reached, the aggregate function is evaluated using the tuples that are within the range boundaries. Then as the boundaries are shifted, all tuples that fall outside the new boundaries are expired and discarded.

3.2 Partial Aggregation

Clearly the straight forward implementation of ACQs is inefficient. *Partial-aggregation* [13, 12] has been proposed to efficiently process ACQs. Under partial-aggregation, the final aggregate value is assembled from a set of partial aggregate values. For example, under partial aggregation an aggregate `COUNT(*)` is computed using (1) a `COUNT(*)` on each partition and (2) a `SUM(*)` over the partial counts. Clearly, partial aggregation is applicable over all distributive and algebraic aggregate functions that are widely used in database systems, such as: `MAX`, `COUNT`, `SUM`, etc.

In general, for a dataset G of disjoint fragments $g_1, g_2, ..., g_n$, an aggregate function A over G can be computed from a *sub-aggregate* function $\mathcal{S}$ over each dataset g_i and a *final-aggregate* function $\mathcal{F}$ over the partial aggregates. Formally,

$$A(G) = \mathcal{F}(\{\mathcal{S}(g_i) | 1 \leq i \leq n\}).$$

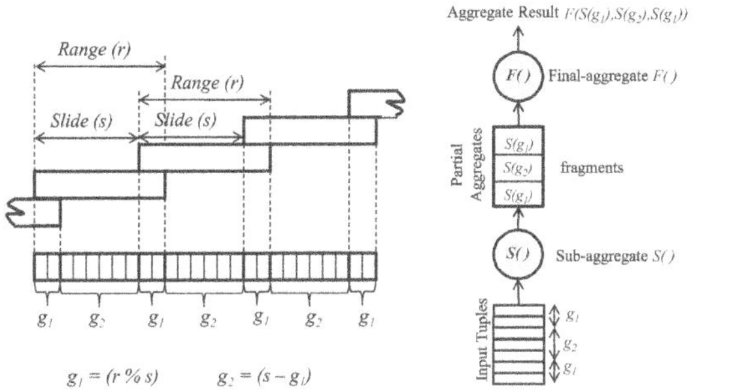

(a) Fragments (b) Plan

Figure 1: Paired Window Technique

Partial aggregation reduces the overall query processing cost by processing each input tuple only once by the sub-aggregate operator to produce partial aggregates. As the window slides, only partial aggregates are buffered and processed to generate new results. Clearly, smaller number of partial aggregates means fewer final aggregate operations. The *paired window* technique [12] (Figure 1(a)) partitions each slide into at most two *fragments* g_1 and g_2 (i.e., a pair). Hence, producing a final aggregate requires at most $\lceil 2 \times \frac{r}{s} \rceil$ operations, where $\frac{r}{s}$ is the number of slides per window and 2 is the maximum number of fragments per slide.

The bottom part of Figure 1(a) shows the set of input tuples, while the top part shows different overlapping window instances. Each *slide* is paired into exactly two *fragments* of length: g_1 and g_2, where $g_1 = r\%s$ and $g_2 = s - g_1$. Given this partitioning, the range consists of a sequence of $g_1, g_2, ..., g_1$ fragments, where the length of a paired window equals $g_1 + g_2 = s$. Note that if r is a multiple of s, then only one fragment is produced per slide. Figure 1(b) illustrates the query plan of the ACQ in Figure 1(a). The end of each fragment g_i represents an *edge*, where the tuples in g_i are assembled into a partial aggregate.

4. WEAVE SHARING OF MULTIPLE ACQs

In this section, we introduce the concept of *Weaveability* (Section 4.3), after first illustrating the trade-off involved in the shared processing of ACQs. We also discuss the challenges of optimizing the shared processing of multiple ACQs (Section 4.4).

4.1 Partial Aggregation Sharing Trade-off

The sharing of the partial aggregation among a set of n ACQs $\{q_1, q_2, ..., q_n\}$ with slides $\{s_1, s_2, ..., s_n\}$, respectively, involves three steps:

1. Multiple slides are integrated into a new *composite slide* (CS) of length equal to the least common multiplier of the individual slides (i.e., $CS = lcm(s_1, ..., s_n)$),
2. Each slide s_i is then stretched into a new slide s'_i of length CS, where the edges (i.e., end of each fragment) in each slide s_i are then copied and repeated to the length of s'_i (=repeated $\frac{s'_i}{s_i}$ times), and
3. The fragments in the composite slide are created by overlaying each edge from each individual slide s'_i onto the new composite slide CS, unless that edge already exists in CS (i.e., common edge).

While sharing the sub-aggregation operator reduces the cost at the sub-aggregation level, it might increase the processing needed at the final-aggregate level. To illustrate that trade-off, consider the following example.

EXAMPLE 2. *Consider two ACQs q_a and q_b with ranges $r_a = 12$ and $r_b = 10$, and slides $s_a = 9$ and $s_b = 6$ seconds, respectively. Hence,the fragments in q_a's slide are of length $g_{a,1} = 3$ and $g_{a,2} = 6$ and for q_b, the fragments are $g_{b,1} = 4$ and $g_{b,2} = 2$.*

If q_a and q_b are processed independently, their sub-aggregation operators will produce 2 fragments every 9 and 6 sec, respectively. That is, an *edge rate* (i.e., number of fragments generated per sec) of $E_a = 0.22$ and $E_b = 0.33$ edges per sec. Thus, the total final-aggregation operations performed per sec is 0.55.

Meanwhile, if q_a and q_b share their partial aggregation, then s_a and s_b are integrated into *composite slide* $CS_{a,b} = lcm(s_a, s_b) = 18$ and the union of edges in $CS_{a,b}$ will appear at times (3, 4, 6, 9, 10, 12, 16, 18). Hence, each of q_a and q_b would examine a combined edge rate of $E_{a,b} = 0.44$, resulting in more final-aggregation operations (0.88 per sec). This simple example clearly shows the presence of a trade-off in the shared processing of multiple ACQs.

We denote those two general methods above as *No Share* and *Shared*. The latter (i.e., *Shared*) is the core principle underlying the *Shared Time Slices (STC)* scheme [12]. Given that clear trade-off between these two extremes of sharing, our goal is to design a selective sharing scheme that groups ACQs into $1 \leq m \leq n$ groups, that is m execution trees, where the ACQs in each group are shared (as formalized in the next sections).

4.2 Formalization

Given a set of ACQs $Q = q_1, q_2, ..., q_n$ where r_j and s_j are the range and slide of each ACQ q_j, and given a grouping of the ACQs into m execution trees $t_1, t_2, ..., t_m$ where all ACQs of a tree t_i are shared, the cost, in terms of total number of aggregate operations per second, of each tree is computed by:

$$C_{t_i} = \lambda + E_i \Omega_i \qquad (1)$$

where λ is the data input rate and for a tree t_i, E_i is the edge rate (i.e., number of fragments generated per second) and Ω_i denotes the total number of final-aggregation operations performed on each fragment. Hence, for a set of shared ACQs $SQ = q_1, q_2, ..., q_k$ in a tree t_i, the total number of final aggregations is computed as:

$$\Omega_i = \sum_{j=1}^{k} \frac{r_j}{s_j} \qquad (2)$$

We refer to Ω_i as the *tree overlap factor* or *overlap factor* for short.

Thus the total cost of the query plan is simply the sum of the cost of the individual trees. Specifically, if the query plan contains m trees, then the total cost of the query plan is computed as:

$$C_{m\text{-}trees} = m\lambda + \sum_{i=1}^{m} E_i \Omega_i \qquad (3)$$

Note that the first term of Eq. 3 is the cost at the sub-aggregation level, whereas the second term is the cost at the final-aggregation level. The goal of our proposed *Weave Share* is to group the ACQs into a set of trees in a way that minimizes Eq. 3. That is, to strike a balance between the two components of the cost function. In particular, our objective is to find the most beneficial number of trees (i.e., m) as well as the best assignment of ACQs to each tree in order to provide the lowest execution time.

4.3 Weaveability

The affinity of ACQs, i.e., their similarity, is an important factor that determines whether it is beneficial to share two ACQs or not.

We refer to this affinity as the *weaveability* of ACQs. Specifically, given the paired-window processing scheme, two ACQs are said to be *perfectly weaveable* if the edges of both ACQs are identical. That is, when the two ACQs are shared, the edge rate does not increase for either of the ACQs. If the ACQs are not perfectly weaveable, the more *common* edges between the ACQs in their composite slide, the less the increase in edge rate for the ACQs when shared, hence the more *weaveable* they are. Thus, we define the degree of weaveability as follows.

DEFINITION 1. *Given two ACQs q_a and q_b with slides s_a and s_b, respectively, the degree of Weaveability of q_a and q_b ($\mathcal{WV}_{a,b}$) is the ratio of the number of common edges M_c in the composite slide $CS_{a,b} = lcm(s_a, s_b)$, to the total number of edges ($M_{a,b}$) in $CS_{a,b}$. Specifically,*

$$\mathcal{WV}_{a,b} = \frac{M_c}{M_{a,b}} \tag{4}$$

Note that the definition of weaveability is recursively applicable to two groups of shared ACQs, i.e., execution trees.

Sharing weaveable ACQs has the desirable property of minimizing the increase in final-aggregation cost since those weaved ACQs would have many common edges, which keeps the increase in edge rate of the final shared plan to a minimum. For example, for the two ACQs q_a and q_b (Example 2), with the set of edges of the composite slide (3, 4, 6, 9, 10, 12, 16, 18), the common edges are (12, 18). Thus, the weaveability $\mathcal{WV}_{a,b} = \frac{2}{8} = 0.25$, which is a relatively weak weaveability, and that explains why their shared tree encounter a high increase in the edge rate.

4.4 Challenges of Grouping Multiple ACQs

Grouping ACQs to multiple trees involves three major challenges. Namely: 1) designing a technique that effectively prunes the combinatorial search space, 2) handling the dynamic addition and deletion of ACQs over time, and 3) efficiently computing the weaveability with minimal overhead.

Towards the first challenge, grouping ACQs could be seen as first determining the optimal number of execution trees and then assigning ACQs to the trees. Thus, we have initially considered mapping our ACQ sharing problem to the generalized task assignment problem which is known to be NP-Hard [5]: the input is a set of heterogeneous machines and a set of tasks, where each task has a certain cost when processed on a certain machine. The output is an assignment of tasks to machines that minimizes the total cost.

This mapping, however, assumes the knowledge of number of machines (i.e., trees), which is not the case. Furthermore, even if we assume the knowledge of the optimal number of trees to use, the increase in processing cost when adding an ACQ to a tree is not constant as it depends on which other ACQs have already been assigned to that tree. This is simply true because the cost function in Eq. 3 involves the edge rate term, which depends on which ACQs are shared and the degree of weaveability of those ACQs.

Thus, we can not directly use any of the classical algorithms for solving the task assignment problem (e.g., Dynamic Programming) to solve our ACQ sharing problem. This is mainly because an optimal solution for a sub-problem is not necessarily a part of the optimal solution of the whole problem. In other words, there is no optimal substructure property.

Given the problem complexity discussed above, we have explored a suite of alternative algorithms towards the efficient sharing of ACQs. In this paper, we present *Weave Share*, an efficient heuristic that fully considers all cost factors in generating shared plans (Section 5).

```
Input: A set of n queries
Output: Weaved query plan P that consists of m execution trees
begin
  P ← Create an execution tree for each ACQ
  l ← n {current number of trees}
  (max-reduction, t1, t2) ← (0, −, −) {current tree-pair to merge}
  repeat
    for i = 0 to l − 1 do
      for j = i + 1 to l do
        temp ← cost-reduction-if-merging(ti, tj)
        if temp > max-reduction then
          (max − reduction, t1, t2) ← (temp, ti, tj)
        end if
      end for
    end for
    if max-reduction > 0 then
      merge(t1,t2)
      l ← l − 1
    end if
  until No merge is done
  Return P
end
```

Figure 2: The *Weave Share* Algorithm

The second challenge is the need for an online version of the algorithm that handles the addition and deletion of ACQs as time advances. To handle this challenge, we propose *Incremental Weave Share*, the online version of *Weave Share* that avoids the reconstruction of the query plan every time an ACQ is added or deleted. Both *Weave Share* and its online version are discussed in the following section (Section 5).

The third challenge (i.e., computing weaveability) stems from the complexity of counting the number of common edges between two different trees. This is because when merging two trees, there is no closed-form formula that determines the common edges. Specifically, this problem maps to small sieve theory problem which is a hard problem, and whose current solutions mostly deal with approximations and there is no closed formula to solve it [4]. Yet, the degree of weaveability directly determines the amount of increase in total processing cost (if any) when merging. To efficiently consider the weaveability while generating the shared plan, we propose several optimizations for the process of counting the number of common edges (Section 8).

5. THE WEAVE SHARE OPTIMIZER

5.1 Weave Share Algorithm

Our proposed *Weave Share* exploits weaveability to reap the benefits of cost reduction provided by sharing partial aggregation, while minimizing the increase in cost incurred at the final aggregation. Basically, *Weave Share* tries to group ACQs in multiple execution trees, where each tree contains only ACQs that *weave* best together.

To achieve our goal, *Weave Share* takes a global view of the execution plan as well as the objective function to minimize (i.e., Eq. 3). In particular, it simultaneously considers both of the cost components (i.e., partial- and final-aggregation) to group ACQs in multiple trees with minimum execution cost.

Weave Share (pseudo-code in Figure 2) takes as an input a set of ACQs $q_1, q_2, ..., q_n$ and produces a set of m shared trees where each tree contains one or more ACQs. Initially, the number of trees is equal to the number of individual queries, $m = n$ and each ACQ forms a separate tree, which is equivalent to the case of no sharing.

Weave Share advances towards sharing one step at a time in a greedy manner, where in each iteration two weaveable trees are

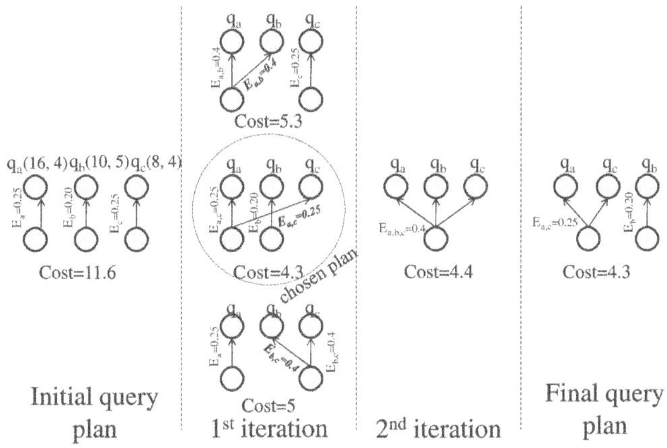

Figure 3: Example 3 - Iterations of *Weave Share*.

merged, reducing number of trees by one, until no more merging is beneficial. In particular, at each iteration, given a set T of l trees: $T = t_1, t_2, ..., t_l$ $(l \leq n)$, *Weave Share* estimates the benefits of merging all possible pairs of trees in T and merges the pair of trees that yields the maximum reduction in total cost.

Given Eq. 1, it is expected that for a pair of trees (t_x and t_y) to qualify for merging, they must satisfy either one or both of the following properties:

1. High degree of weaveability. The higher the degree of weaveability of the merged trees, the less the increase in the combined edge rate $E_{x,y}$ and the less the overall merged tree cost.

2. Low total overlap factor ($\Omega_{x,y} = \Omega_x + \Omega_y$), which is the total number of final-aggregation operations performed on each fragment in the new tree. Hence, the less the number of window instances, the less the number of final-aggregate operations performed on each edge (i.e., fragment).

The benefit (i.e., cost reduction) from merging t_x and t_y is:

$$\Delta(C_{x,y}) = \lambda + E_x\Omega_x + E_y\Omega_y - E_{x,y}\Omega_{x,y} \quad (5)$$

Note the term λ in Eq. 5 above denotes the savings at the sub-aggregation level. That is, each tuple is processed once instead of twice. The rest of the terms in the equation represents the savings in the final aggregation level.

Clearly, any two trees that exhibit the two properties above are good candidates for merging as they allow us to exploit the sharing of partial-aggregation while at the same time minimize the increase in final-aggregation. These are the main optimization criteria for *Weave Share*. We demonstrate how *Weave Share* iterations work using Example 3 below.

EXAMPLE 3. *Consider three queries q_a, q_b and q_c with sliding window specifications as follows: ranges 16, 10 and 8 and slides 4, 5 and 4, respectively. Additionally, consider an input rate $\lambda = 1.2$ tuples per second.*

Figure 3 shows the sequence of iterations performed by *Weave Share* as well as the resulting query plan. Figure 3 shows that initially, the number of trees is three, with no sharing. This results in a total cost of 11.6 based on Eq. 3 as shown in the figure (the calculations details are omitted for brevity). Next, the algorithm enters the main loop where it tries to merge the pair of trees that would reduce the cost the most.

In the first iteration, there are three possible pair-wise merges $< q_a, q_b >$, $< q_a, q_c >$, or $< q_b, q_c >$. Merging the pair $< q_a, q_c >$ leads to the maximal reduction in cost, reducing it to 4.3 aggregations per second according to Eq. 5. Thus, the algorithm merges them together into tree $t_{a,c}$ and proceeds to the next iteration.

In the second iteration, the only possibility is to merge $t_{a,c}$ with q_b. This, however, would lead to an increase in the cost to 4.4 aggregations per second. Since there is no room for improvement, *Weave Share* terminates the loop and returns the query plan it constructed: $t_{a,c}$ and q_b, where q_a and q_c are shared in $t_{a,c}$ and q_b is executed independently. Note that q_a and q_c *weave* well together, in the sense that all the edges of q_a exist in edges of q_c (i.e., common). This is due to the fact that their slides are equal. This results in no increase in the edge rate when they are merged and in turn, minimizes the overall execution cost.

5.2 Incremental Weave Share

In the previous section, we described the basic (offline) *Weave Share* algorithm, which constructs a query plan from scratch. In this section, we consider the online case where newly submitted ACQs are weaved into the current plan and the case of re-weaving existing trees after the deletion of some ACQs.

5.2.1 Adding New ACQs

Reconstructing the *Weave Share* query plan from scratch is one possible solution to handle the submission of a new set of ACQs into the system. In that solution, given an already existing set of ACQs Q in a *Weave Share* plan P and a set of new ACQs Q', *Weave Share* is invoked to generate a new weave share plan P' which includes the ACQs $Q \cup Q'$. This solution, however, has two drawbacks: 1) it incurs a large overhead since the algorithm is reinvoked to run from scratch whenever new ACQs are added, and 2) it might often lead to an unnecessary reconstruction since, in many cases, the new plan P' can be directly achieved from the current plan P.

To address the above drawbacks, we develop *Incremental Weave Share* which takes a more *lazy* approach for maintaining the weaved plan. This involves the following two steps:

1. Immediately incorporating new ACQs into the existing plan.

2. Reconstruct the query plan from scratch *only when needed.*

In this incremental version of *Weave Share*, a new tree t_{new} is created for each new ACQ q_{new} that is added to the system and *Weave Share* is invoked to merge t_{new} with the trees in the current plan P to generate a new incremental plan P''. Thus, among the existing trees, t_{new} will be merged with the one tree with which it weaves the best. The newly merged tree might be further merged with other trees in the plan if this is beneficial. This process continues until no further improvements are attainable.

The cost of the incremental plan P'' might, however, be worse than the plan P' which would be generated by the offline *Weave Share*. In order to detect the magnitude of that degradation, *Incremental Weave Share* maintains the *performance slope* of the *plan-cost curve*. This curve is basically a plot of the offline-generated plan cost vs. the number of ACQs. The points on the curve are obtained when a plan P' is generated from scratch.

As new ACQs are submitted to the system, the cost of P'' is compared with the extrapolated cost using the performance slope. If the difference percentage is more than a certain *deviation tolerance* threshold, which is a system parameter, a reconstruction phase is triggered and performed asynchronously. Specifically, for a *de-*

viation tolerance of ϵ, a reconstruction is triggered iff:

$$\frac{cost(P'')}{extrapolated\ cost\ using\ performance\ slope} - 1 > \epsilon \quad (6)$$

As such, the deviation tolerance value acts as a *knob* to control the reconstruction behavior. For instance, setting the tolerance to zero, resembles reconstructing the weaved plan whenever a new ACQ is added, whereas setting the tolerance to ∞ is equivalent to the case where no reconstruction is ever performed.

5.2.2 Deleting ACQs

We handle the deletion of existing ACQs similarly to the addition of new ACQs. Specifically, deleted ACQs are first removed from their respective tree, then each of those trees is then examined against all the other trees in the weaved plan for beneficial merging, i.e., if the merge would result in a reduction in the total cost of the updated plan. This process is repeated until no more improvements are attainable. Similarly to adding ACQs, given the performance slope and a tolerance factor, a reconstruction phase may be triggered depending on the degradation from the extrapolated cost.

5.3 Varying Predicates and Group-by

Weave Share can easily handle the case when different ACQs have different pre-aggregation filters (i.e., selection operators). For example, one query might monitor the average-volume of stock-trades that are higher than \$100, while another monitors the same for trades that are higher than \$500. To share the execution of such ACQs, we adopt the *Shared Data Shards* (SDS) technique [12].

Further, when different ACQs have different group-by attributes, *Weave Share* can utilize the techniques in [17, 26]. Specifically, each sub-aggregation operator can utilize a hash table based on the values of the union of all group-by attributes. When a fragment is due, proper hash table entries are combined together to form the fragment of each set of queries with identical group by attributes.

6. EXPERIMENTAL PLATFORM

We built a simulation platform in C++ to evaluate the quality of *Weave Share* plans. We validated our simulation model by reproducing same results trends as in [12] and running Exhaustive Search to find the optimal plan for small cases that we solved by hand[1]. Below, we list the different algorithms we compared with and describe the generated workload characteristics, experiments parameters (summarized in Table 1) and the performance metrics.

Algorithms: In addition to *Weave Share* and *Incremental Weave Share*, we implemented *Random*, *Shared* and *No Share* (base-line). We also implemented an obvious simplified version of the *Weave Share* algorithm, which we call *Insert-then-Weave*. *Insert-then-Weave* is a greedy heuristic that inserts ACQs, one at a time in an arbitrary order, to the tree that it weaves best with. After this phase, a weaving phase of merging the created trees (similar to *Incremental Weave Share*) follows.

Finally, we also adapted *Local Search* (LS), which is is a sub-optimal state space search algorithm. *LS* starts from an arbitrary initial state, i.e., grouping of ACQs. We used both *Random* and *No Share* to generate the initial states. In each iteration, *LS* moves towards the optimal solution by moving a single ACQ from one tree to another. In our experiments, we bound the number of iterations of *LS*, for each workload instance, to two, five or ten times the the number of iterations that *Weave Share* needed for that instance. Among these different options, *LS-NS-10x* (which starts from *No Share* initial state and uses ten times iteration's bound) was the best and we report its results.

[1]Other experiments with Exhaustive Search showed that *Weave Share* generates mostly optimal plans; for input rates/number of ACQs of 200/5, 300/10 and 400/15, *Weave Share* generated the optimal plan. In only one case, *Weave Share* generated the optimal number of trees but 3% more costly, due to different grouping of ACQs (*Shared* plan was 32% more costly in this case).

Table 1: Simulation Parameters

Parameter	Values
Slide Length (s)	[1 – 100000] using Zipf distribution
Slide Skewness	[0.0 – 3.3] (skewed to large-slide)
Max. Overlap Factor (Ω_{max})	[50 - 2000]
Overlap Factor	[1 – Ω_{max}]
Number of ACQs	[50 – 2000]
Input Arrival Rate	[0.5 – 1,000,000] tuples/sec.

ACQs: We generated ACQs with different specifications. The slide length (s) was drawn from a Zipf distribution over a discrete range. The discrete range depicts the real-world case of pre-specified (i.e., template) window specifications. The skewness of the Zipf distribution reflects the popularity of certain slide lengths. The range (r) for each ACQ is relative to its slide. That is, $r_i = \omega_i \times s_i$, where ω_i is the overlap factor. The overlap factor is uniformly distributed between 1.0 and Ω_{max}, which is a simulation parameter. In each experiment, we also changed the the number of ACQs and the input rate. The input rate values are chosen to cover a wide variety of different monitoring applications, ranging from phenomena monitoring (few tuples, or less per second) to high speed network monitoring (1M tuples/sec).

Dataset: We chose to use synthetic workload, which allows us to control the system parameters, in order to conduct detailed sensitivity analysis and gain better insight into the behavior of *Weave Share* by setting the parameters to cover all possible real scenarios.

Performance Metrics: We measured the quality of plans in terms of the cost of the plans as the number of aggregate operations per second (which also indicates the throughput). We chose this metric because it provides an accurate and fair measure of the performance, regardless of the platform used to conduct the experiments.

7. QUALITY OF WEAVE SHARE PLANS

7.1 Weave Share Performance

In this section we present our evaluation results, comparing *Weave Share* to other alternatives under different workload parameters.

7.1.1 Number of ACQs (Fig. 4 to 7)

Figures 4 and 5 show the cost of the *Weave Share* plan as the number of ACQs increases from 50 to 1000, for low (50 tuples/sec) and medium (300 tuple/sec) input rates, respectively. In both plots, the maximum overlap factor (Ω_{max}) is set to 50, and the slide skewness is 0.6. *Weave Share* always outperforms the best of all other algorithms. For instance, for 1000 ACQs, *Weave Share* outperforms *Insert-then-Weave* and *Shared* by three and four orders of magnitude, at low and medium input rates, respectively.

Note that *No Share* and *Random* generate the most expensive plans in both cases. *LS* did not find better plans than those generated by *Weave Share*, while incurring a very high overhead. Specifically, *LS-NS 10x* took thousand times the time needed by *Weave Share*. The reason is that an iteration of *LS* moves a single ACQ from a tree to another, while an iteration of *Weave Share* merges two trees, i.e., moves a group of ACQs at once. Thus, *Weave Share* reaches a reasonable sub-optimal solution much faster than *LS*.

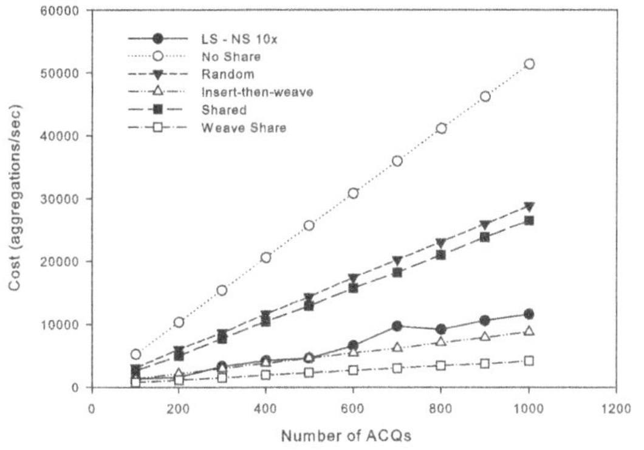

Figure 4: Impact of number of ACQs on cost for different policies under low input rate (50 tuples/sec)

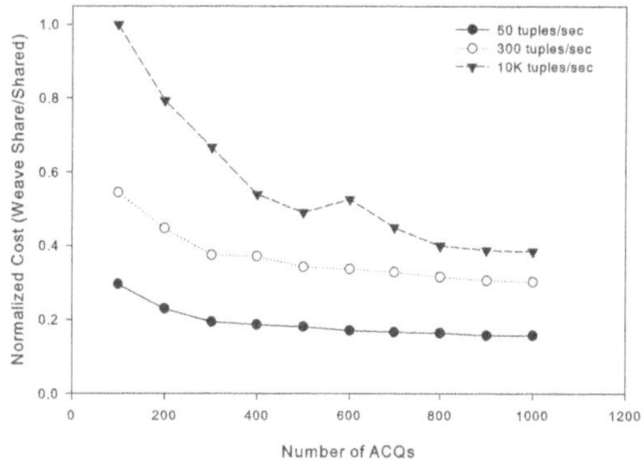

Figure 6: Impact of number ACQs on normalized cost under low, medium and high input rates

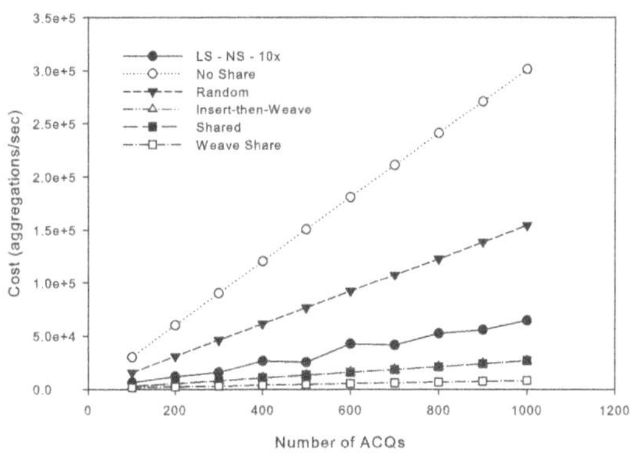

Figure 5: Impact of number of ACQs on cost for different policies under medium input rate (300 tuples/sec)

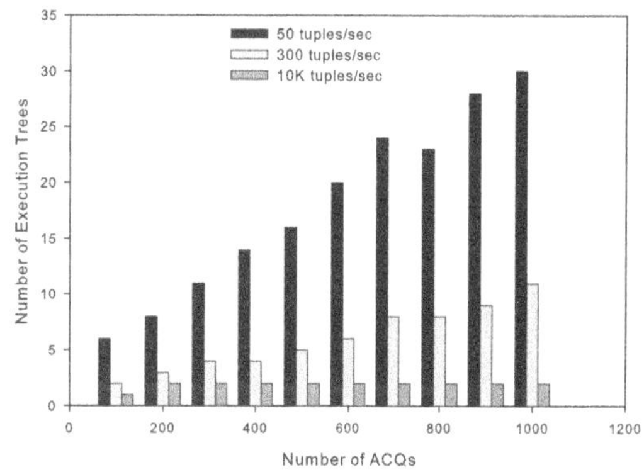

Figure 7: Number of Execution Trees for different number of ACQs under low, medium and high input rates

While *LS* and *Insert-then-Weave* perform better than *Shared* at low input rate (50 tuples/sec), *Shared* outperforms both at medium input rate (300 tuples/sec). For high input rate (10K tuples/sec), omitted for brevity, the relative performance of different algorithms was similar to the medium input rate case.

In Figure 6, we study the performance of *Weave Share* compared to *Shared*, for the low, medium and high input rates. Specifically, we plot the normalized cost of *Weave Share* plan to the cost of *Shared*, for the three input rates. The figure shows that as the number of ACQs increases, the gain provided by *Weave Share* increases. It also shows that even for high input rate (10K tuples/sec), as the number of ACQs increases, *Weave Share* outperforms *Shared*. For instance, at 1000 ACQs, for input rate of 10K tuples/sec, *Weave Share* reduces the cost by 62%.

The improvement of *Weave Share* over the best of other algorithms increases with the number of ACQs because the more ACQs, the more chances for *Weave Share* to selectively share ACQs that weave well together. Thus, limiting the increment in edge rate (E) and overlap factor (Ω) per merged tree, while still benefiting from sharing the partial aggregation. Finally, we notice in Figure 6 that for high input rate of 10K tuples/second and few number of ACQs, *Weave Share* performs identical to *Shared*, i.e., generates one tree. For such settings, the overhead at the partial aggregation level dominates that at the final-aggregation level.

Finally, Figure 7 shows the number of execution trees that were generated by *Weave Share* for the same settings as in Figure 6. As expected, the number of trees increases as the number of ACQs increases, while it decreases as the input rate increases. It also shows that for high input rate of 10K tuples/sec, *Weave Share* still generates more than one tree for more than 100 ACQs. This confirms our observation that the properties of the installed ACQs are as important as the input rate in determining the sharing decision.

7.1.2 Input Rate (Fig. 8)

In this experiment we study the sensitivity of *Weave Share* to the input rate. We report the normalized cost of *Weave Share* to that of *Shared* (here and in all the experiments hereafter) because *Shared* was the best alternative (in each experiment). We plot the normalized cost for different values of number of ACQs in Figure 8. The results in this plot are for a workload with Ω_{max} of 50 and slide skewness of 0.6.

Similar to the previous experiment, as the input rate increases, the performance of *Weave Share* approaches that of *Shared*. For instance, for 250 ACQs, the gain of *Weave Share* starts at 80% at input rate of 50 tuples/sec, and reaches 24% and 6% at input rates of 2K and 3K tuples/sec, respectively. For high input rate (10K tuples/sec), *Weave Share* still generates plans that are 12% and 24% less costly for 1000 and 2000 ACQs, respectively.

Weave Share also outperforms *Random*, *Insert-then-Weave*, *No Share* and *Local Search* by up to orders of magnitude. For instance, at input rate of 10K tuples/sec, *Weave Share* generates a plan that is more than 100 times less costly than the best of other plans.

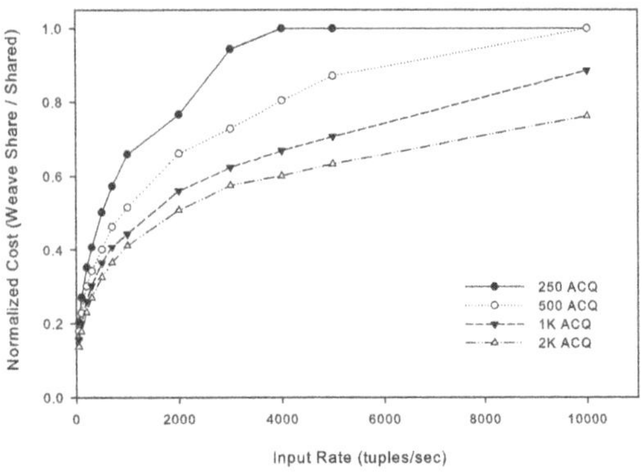

Figure 8: Impact of Input Rate on normalized cost for different number of ACQs

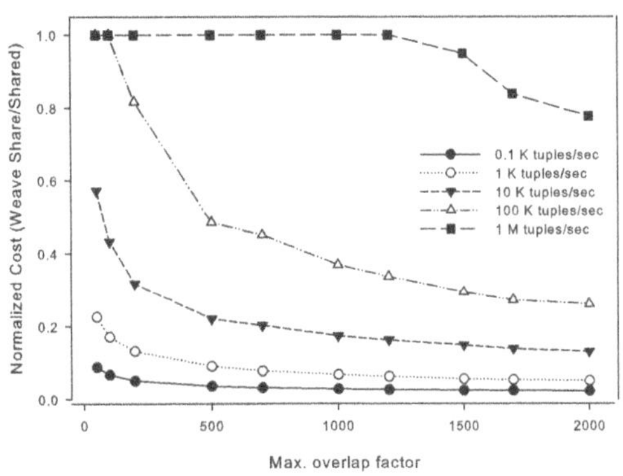

Figure 9: Impact of Maximum Overlap Factor on normalized cost for different input rates

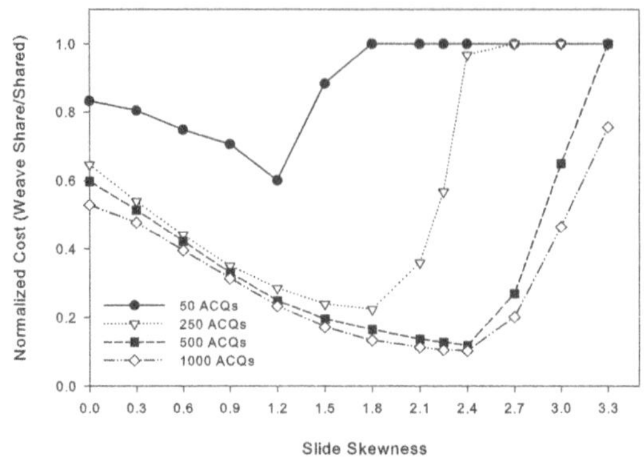

Figure 10: Impact of Slide Skewness on normalized cost for different number of ACQs

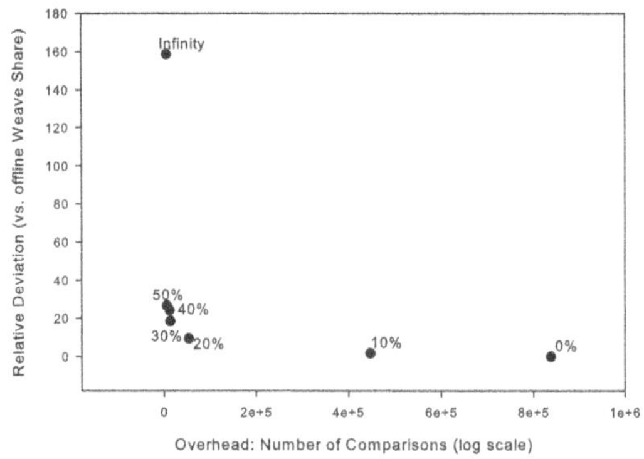

Figure 11: *Incremental Weave Share*: Deviation vs Overhead for different tolerance factor (ϵ).

7.1.3 Maximum Overlap Factor (Fig. 9)

In this experiment, we vary the maximum overlap factor (Ω_{max}) for different input rate values. Specifically, we set the input rate to 100, 1K, 10K, 100K and 1M tuples/sec. For all cases, the slide skewness was 0.6, and the number of ACQs was 2000. Recall that the overlap factor is the ratio between an ACQ's range and its slide. Hence, increasing the Ω_{max} increases the number of final-aggregations, but has no effect on partial-aggregation.

In Figure 9 we plot the normalized cost of *Weave Share* to *Shared*. As expected, as Ω_{max} increases from 50 to 2000, the gain provided by *Weave Share* increases. For example, consider the case of 100K tuples/sec. For small values of Ω_{max} (less than 200), *Weave Share* generates a single shared tree. For higher values of Ω_{max} (200 to 2000), *Weave Share* outperforms *Shared* by 19% to 74%. Recall that the overlap factor is multiplied by the edge rate in Eq.1, which is the cost of final-aggregation. Since *Weave Share* generates plans that consist of more than one tree, it keeps the maximum value of $E_i\Omega_i$ as small as possible. This is what enables *Weave Share* to outperform *Shared* for higher values of Ω_{max}.

7.1.4 Slide Skewness (Fig. 10)

In this experiment, we examine the slide distribution skewness parameter. By increasing the skewness, the query workload will contain more large-slide queries as generated by the Zipf distribution. Figure 10 shows the normalized cost of *Weave Share* to *Shared* for different number of ACQs, at input arrival rate of 100 tuple/second and maximum overlap factor of 10.

For all number of ACQs, we see that as the skewness increases, the relative gain provided by *Weave Share* increases. This continues until a global maximum gain is reached, where it starts to diminish until *Weave Share* performs similar to *Shared*. The reason is that initially, as the skewness increases the more large-slide ACQs we have, and hence the higher the *penalty* of sharing them with small-slide ACQs. *Weave Share* avoids this by selectively sharing ACQs that weave well together.

As the distribution becomes very skewed, most of the ACQs are large-slide ones, whereas small-slide ACQs gradually disappear. This means that grouping all in a single tree is the right choice. In this case, *Weave Share* captures this phenomenon and does share all ACQs. Figure 10 also shows that the more ACQs are in the system, the larger the maximum gain of *Weave Share* is.

7.2 Incremental performance

In this section, we study the performance of the *Incremental Weave Share* algorithm. For *Incremental Weave Share*, the tolerance factor is used to determine when to issue a reconstruction phase. A reconstruction phase is issued if the ratio of the current execution plan cost to the extrapolated cost using performance slope (given the learned plan-cost curve) exceeds the tolerance factor.

Figure 11 shows the overhead as number of comparisons versus the average relative error between the plan generated by *Incre-*

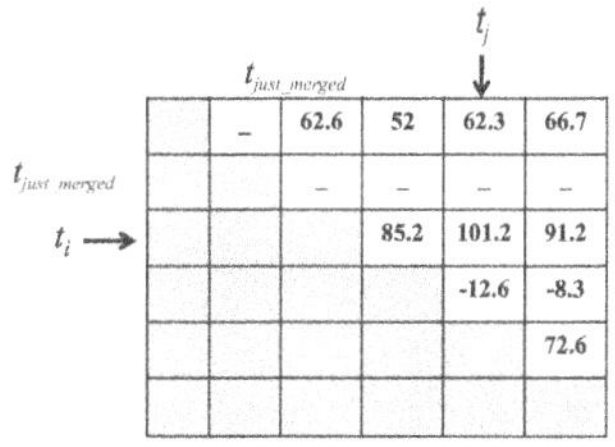

Figure 12: Cost Lookup Table

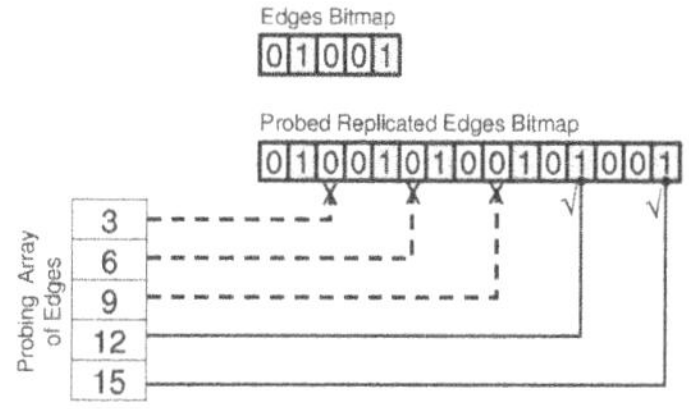

Figure 13: Edges Bitmap and Probing Process

mental Weave Share and the plan generated by the offline *Weave Share*, for different tolerance factor values (*the points' labels*). For instance, the point labeled as `Infinity` shows the incremental performance when no reconstruction is issued at all (tolerance = ∞). As expected, the figure shows that as the tolerance factor increases, the relative error increases while the overhead decreases. It also shows that the relative error is always less than or equal to the tolerance factor. From the above results, we conclude that a tolerance factor of 20% or 30% achieves a good balance between performance and overhead.

8. OPTIMIZING THE OPTIMIZER

Given a set of n ACQs, the time complexity of *Weave Share* algorithm is asymptotically $O(n^3)$. The algorithm starts with n trees and in each iteration it reduces the number of trees by one. Thus, in worst case, the algorithm needs n iterations. In each iteration i, $(n-i)^2$ comparisons are needed to find the pair of trees that yield the maximum benefit. Thus, the total time complexity is $O(n^3)$.

Computing the benefit of merging two trees (say t_x and t_y), requires calculating the new edge rate $E_{x,y}$ (Eq. 5). Given that there is no closed-form formula that determines the common edges as as discussed in Section 4.4, this is clearly an expensive operation which requires counting the set of common edges between the two trees, t_x and t_y.

Conceptually, to calculate the new edge rate resulting from merging t_x and t_y into tree $t_{x,y}$, we need to extend the steps needed for merging two ACQs (described in Section 4.1) as follows:

1. Set the composite slide $CS_{x,y}$ to be the least common multiple of the individual slides of all ACQs in t_x and t_y.

2. The edge count M'_x of the ACQs in t_x within the new composite slide $CS_{x,y}$ is computed as: $M'_x = M_x \frac{CS_{x,y}}{CS_x}$, where the last term is the number of times CS_x has been replicated. Similarly, the edge count M'_y of the ACQs in t_y is computed.

3. The composite edge count $M_{x,y}$ is computed as: $M_{x,y} = M'_x + M'_y - M_c$.

In order to compute the last step, we need to know the number of common edges in the composite slide (M_c) between t_x and t_y. This could be done by checking each edge in each ACQ in t_y to see if it is the same to any edge of any ACQ in t_x. Each one of those checks requires two comparisons. Specifically, to check if edge e of some ACQ in t_y is the same to some edge of ACQ q_i in t_x, we check if e is divisible by s_i, or if $e - g_{i,1}$ is divisible by s_i, as illustrated in the following example.

EXAMPLE 4. *Consider a tree with one query q_x that has slide $s_x = 5$ and fragments $g_{x,1} = 2$ and $g_{x,2} = 3$. Further consider a query q_y which has slide $s_y = 3$ and fragments $g_{y,1} = 0$ and $g_{y,2} = 3$. If q_x and q_y are to be merged, the common slide length is $CS_{x,y} = 15$, the edge counts of stretched q_x and q_y are $M'_x = 6$ and $M'_y = 5$, respectively. Hence, $M_{x,y}$ is 5 plus 6 minus the number of common edges (M_c), which is computed by checking each and every edge of q_y against those of q_x.*

The first edge in q_y is $e = 3$, which is not divisible by the slide of $s_x = 5$ nor is $e - g_{x,1} = 3 - 2 = 1$ divisible by $s_x = 5$. Hence, it is not a common edge and $M_{x,y}$ is kept at 11 edges. The current edge e is then advanced to next edge $e = 6$, and the two comparisons are performed and so on until $e = 12$, where $e - g_{x,1} = 12 - 2 = 10$ is divisible by $s_x = 5$, i.e., it is a common edge and the count is decremented. Similarly, at $e = C_{x,y} = 15$, e is divisible by s_x and the count is decremented once again.

This naive approach encounters a high overhead given that counting the edges process is repeated many times in the main loop of the algorithm, where, in each iteration, an edge count is needed for each pair of trees. We propose three optimizations that can dramatically minimize this overhead as discussed next.

8.1 Optimization I: Cost Lookup

The first optimization is to memoize the benefit (i.e., cost reduction) gained by merging two trees in a two dimensional array called *Cost Lookup* table. Thus, in the main loop of the algorithm, only the first iteration will compute the cost saving for each pair of trees. Next iterations will use the lookup table for all pairs, except those that involve the new merged tree from the previous iteration. Thus, the number of computations in each iteration i is reduced from $(n-i)^2$ to $(n-i)$ computations. This minimizes the number of pairs for which an edge count needs to be performed.

Figure 12 shows a possible instance of the Cost Lookup table. To check if merging two trees t_i and t_j is beneficial or not, we lookup the entry $Cost\_Lookup[i][j]$, which is 101.2 in this instance. This means that merging t_i with t_j would reduce the cost by 101.2 operations per second. Negative values mean that the merge would actually increase the cost. $t_{justmerged}$ is the merged tree in a previous iteration and that is why all its entries are nullified in order to be recomputed.

8.2 Optimization II: Edges Bitmap

The second optimization is to use a bitmap vector that acts as a hash table to represent the edges. The top part of Figure 13 shows the bitmap vector for an ACQ q_x with $s_x = 5$ and edges at locations 2 and 5 (i.e., fragments $g_{x,2} = 2$ and $g_{x,1} = 3$). Given the *Edges Bitmap* structure, finding the common edges between two trees requires to simply traverse the edges of one of the Edges Bitmap to probe the other, i.e., check if they exist in the other bitmap. This requires a number of probes equal to the number of edges in one of the trees, regardless of the number of ACQs in the other tree. Effectively, this optimization pre-computes and materializes the results of finding the common edges described in Example 4.

The Edges Bitmap is maintained as follows. When the tree has one query at most two edges are hashed into the bitmap. When adding a query to a tree, 1) new bitmap is created with length equal

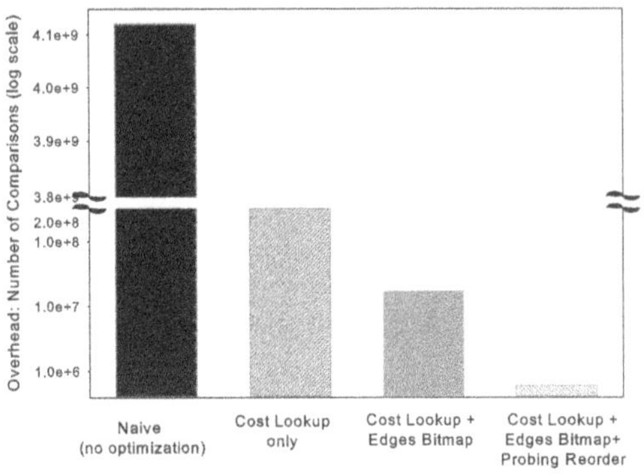

Figure 14: Optimizations' Benefits

to the new composite slide, 2) the old bitmap is replicated in this new bitmap and the previous count of edges is updated accordingly, and 3) the edges of the new query are hashed into the new bitmap, incrementing the edge counter only if no collision occurs.

8.3 Optimization III: Probing Reorder

Clearly, given the Edges Bitmap structure, the overall complexity of the algorithm will be affected by the choice of which bitmap to probe when counting common edges. Similar to join optimization, which uses the relation with fewer blocks to probe the other, we propose to use the tree with fewer edges (i.e., smaller edge rate) to probe the other. (this is illustrated in the lower part of Figure 13, where we used q_y which has 5 edges to probe q_x which has 6 edges). Specifically, the bitmap of the probed tree is replicated to the new composite slide, while the bitmap of the probing tree is used to generate an array of edges in the new composite slide. Edges in the array are then hashed into the bitmap of the probed tree, and if collision occurs, then the checked edge is common.

8.4 Impact of Optimizations

The impact of the above optimizations can be seen in Figure 14, where we report our run of *Weave Share* and its optimized versions for an experiment with 250 ACQs, input rate of 100 tuple/second, a slide skewness of 0.7 and a maximum overlap factor 10; we obtained similar results for different workload settings. The figure shows the overhead of the naive *Weave Share*, where no optimization is used, compared to the three optimization variants. In the first variant, only cost lookup is used. In the second variant, both cost lookup and edge bitmap are used and finally, in the third variant all three optimizations are used. Figure 14 (notice the log scale for the Y-axis) shows that each proposed optimization technique roughly adds one order of magnitude improvement over the naive implementation. Overall, with all three optimizations, *Weave Share* executes three orders of magnitude more efficiently.

9. CONCLUSIONS

In this paper, we introduced the concept of *Weaveability* of aggregate continuous queries (ACQs) that captures their potential for shared processing. We proposed *Weave Share*, a new cost-based multiple ACQs optimizer that selectively groups ACQs into multiple execution trees considering all cost factors, to minimize total cost. We also proposed *Incremental Weave Share* that supports dynamic query optimization when ACQs are added or deleted on demand. We experimentally evaluated and performed sensitivity analysis on the quality of the query plans generated by the *Weave Share*. The results show that *Weave Share* outperforms all alternative schemes. Finally, we developed practical implementation of *Weave Share* and experimentally illustrated their gains.

Acknowledgments This work was supported in part by NSF awards IIS-0534531 and IIS-0746696, an Andrew Mellon Predoctoral Fellowship, and Australian Research Council award DP110102777.

10. REFERENCES

[1] D. J. Abadi et al. Aurora: a new model and architecture for data stream management. *VLDBJ*, 12(2):120–139, 2003.

[2] D. J. Abadi et al. The design of the borealis stream processing engine. In *CIDR*, 2005.

[3] A. Arasu et al. STREAM: The stanford stream data manager. In *SIGMOD*, 2003.

[4] E. Bach, K. Pruhs. Personal communications, June 2010.

[5] M. R. Garey, D. S. Johnson. *Computers and Intractability; A Guide to the Theory of NP-Completeness*. WH.Freeman & Co., 1990.

[6] T. M. Ghanem et al. Incremental evaluation of sliding-window queries over data streams. *TKDE*, 19(1):57–72, 2007.

[7] L. Golab et al. Multi-query optimization of sliding window aggregates by schedule synchronization. In *CIKM*, 2006.

[8] G. Graefe, W. J. McKenna. The volcano optimizer generator: Extensibility and efficient search. In *ICDE*, 1993.

[9] M. A. Hammad et al. Nile: A query processing engine for data streams. In *ICDE*, 2004.

[10] R. Huebsch et al. Sharing aggregate computation for distributed queries. In *SIGMOD*, 2007.

[11] R. Johnson et al. To share or not to share? In *VLDB*, 2007.

[12] S. Krishnamurthy et al. On-the-fly sharing for streamed aggregation. In *SIGMOD*, 2006.

[13] J. Li et al. No pane, no gain: efficient evaluation of sliding-window aggregates over data streams. *SIGMOD Rec.*, 2005.

[14] J. Li et al. Semantics and evaluation techniques for window aggregates in data streams. In *SIGMOD*, 2005.

[15] S. Madden et al. Continuously adaptive continuous queries over streams. In *SIGMOD*, 2002.

[16] H. Mistry et al. Materialized view selection and maintenance using multi-query optimization. In *SIGMOD*, 2001.

[17] K. Naidu et al. Memory-constrained aggregate computation over data streams. In *ICDE*, 2011.

[18] P. Roy et al. Efficient and extensible algorithms for multi query optimization. In *SIGMOD*, 2000.

[19] W. Scheufele, G. Moerkotte. On the complexity of generating optimal plans with cross products. In *PODS*, 1997.

[20] T. K. Sellis. Multiple-query optimization. *TODS*, 13(1):23–52, 1988.

[21] Streambase, http://www.streambase.com, 2006.

[22] System S, http://domino.research.ibm.com/, 2008.

[23] S. D. Viglas, J. F. Naughton. Rate-based query optimization for streaming information sources. In *SIGMOD*, 2002.

[24] S. Wang et al. State-slice: new paradigm of multi-query optimization of window-based stream queries. In *VLDB*, 2006.

[25] R. Zhang et al. Multiple aggregations over data streams. In *SIGMOD*, 2005.

[26] R. Zhang et al. Streaming multiple aggregations using phantoms. *VLDBJ*, 19(4):557–583, 2010.

[27] J. Zhou et al. Efficient exploitation of similar subexpressions for query processing. In *SIGMOD*, 2007.

XQuery Optimization Based on Program Slicing *

Jesús M. Almendros-Jiménez
Dpto. de Lenguajes y Computación
Universidad de Almería
Carretera de Sacramento s/n
E-04120 Almería, Spain
jalmen@ual.es

Josep Silva
Dpto. de Sistemas Informáticos y Computación
Universitat Politècnica de València
Camino de Vera s/n
E-46022 Valencia, Spain
jsilva@dsic.upv.es

Salvador Tamarit
Dpto. de Sistemas Informáticos y Computación
Universitat Politècnica de València
Camino de Vera s/n
E-46022 Valencia, Spain
stamarit@dsic.upv.es

ABSTRACT

XQuery has become the standard query language for XML. The efforts put on this language have produced mature and efficient implementations of XQuery processors. However, in practice the efficiency of XQuery programs is strongly dependent on the ability of the programmer to combine different queries which often affect several XML sources that in turn can be distributed in different branches of the organization. Therefore, techniques to reduce the amount of data loaded and also to reduce the intermediate structures computed by queries is a necessity. In this work we propose a novel technique that allows the programmer to automatically optimize a query in such a way that unnecessary intermediate computations are avoided, and, in addition, it identifies the paths in the source XML documents that are really required to resolve the query.

Categories and Subject Descriptors

H.2 [**DATABASE MANAGEMENT**]: H.2.3 Languages—*Query languages*; F.3 [**LOGICS AND MEANINGS OF PROGRAMS**]: F.3.2 Semantics of Programming Languages—*Program analysis*

General Terms

Languages

Keywords

XQuery, Slicing, Query Optimization

*This work has been partially supported by the Spanish *Ministerio de Ciencia e Innovación* under grants TIN2008-06622-C03-02 and TIN2008-06622-C03-03, by the *Generalitat Valenciana* under grant PROMETEO/2011/052, and by the *Junta de Andalucía* under grant TIC-6114. Salvador Tamarit was partially supported by the Spanish MICINN under FPI grant BES-2009-015019.

1. INTRODUCTION

XQuery [21, 6] is a typed functional language devoted to express queries against XML documents. It contains *XPath* [2] as a sublanguage. *XPath* supports navigation, selection and extraction of fragments from XML documents. *XQuery* also includes *flowr* expressions (i.e. *for-let-orderby-where-return* expressions) to construct new XML values and to join multiple documents. The design of *XQuery* has been influenced by group members with expertise in the design and implementation of other high-level languages. *XQuery* has static typed semantics which is part of the *W3C* standard [6, 21].

XQuery has evolved into a widely accepted query language for XML processing and many XQuery engines have been developed [12, 8, 3, 14, 10, 16]. However, *memory consumption* and *execution time* remains a crucial bottleneck in query evaluation. Queries against large data sources require the improving of data loading and buffering together with XQuery optimization. Sometimes the refactoring of the XQuery or the pre-filtering of the source XML files is mandatory to be able to process large XML documents. As a matter of fact, standard XML processors have a maximum size in the XML documents they can process. Nevertheless, some XML documents such as the XML version of DBLP are very large and could require pre-processing and query optimization to be handled.

In this work we introduce a novel technique able to automatically project the portion of the input XML document that is needed to resolve a given XQuery expression (thus the remaining parts of the document are not loaded), and at the same time, it also allows us to optimize the XQuery itself with a refactoring process based on *program slicing*.

Program slicing is a general technique of program analysis and transformation whose main aim is to extract the part of a program (called slice) that influences or is influenced by a given point of interest [22, 20]. Program slicing has been traditionally based on a data structure called *program dependence graph* (PDG) [9] that represents all statements in a program with nodes and their control and data dependences with edges. Once the PDG is computed, slicing is reduced to a graph reachability problem, and slices can be computed in linear time.

Our slicing-based technique aims to provide an optimization method for XQuery. Given a (composed) query, we are able to detect those parts of the XQuery code which are not relevant for the output of the query. In addition, we are able to rewrite the query into a new one in which the irrelevant parts have been removed. Unfortunately, the PDG cannot be used with XQuery because the notion of statement is not applicable to functional languages. Therefore, firstly, we will define a notion of *XQuery Dependence Graph* (XDG) which is a labelled graph able to represent XQuery expressions. Secondly, we will describe how to transform an XDG in order to optimize an XQuery expression in such a way that only those expressions that contribute to the final result remain in the graph. The transformation consists on forward and backward propagation of data dependences together with an slicing procedure in order to detect the required paths in an XQuery expression. From the transformed XDG we extract a new optimized XQuery and, additionally, we deduce the parts of the documents used by the XQuery expression.

EXAMPLE 1. *The following composed query requests the* `customer` *elements obtained from a nested query in which all* `customer`, *and some* `provider` *elements are computed.*

```
Q1 =  for $i in (doc('File')/company)
      return <sales>{($i/customer, if ($i/provider='X')
                              then () else $i/provider)}</sales>
Q2 =  for $j in Q1
      return $j/customer
```

This query shows an example of query optimization. Given that the `provider` *elements are never used by Q2, they can be pruned from Q1 when they are composed. This produces an equivalent optimized query.*

The structure of the paper is as follows. Section 2 presents the related work. Section 3 introduces some preliminaries. The XDG is introduced in Section 4, and the slicing algorithms are presented in Section 5. Section 6 describes the implementation. Section 7 presents our experimental results. Finally, Section 8 concludes and presents future work.

2. RELATED WORK

There exist two major research lines concerning the optimization of XQuery. The first line tries to improve the processing of the XML input data. The second line operates over the source XQuery expressions transforming them to improve efficiency.

On one hand, XML document *loading* and *buffering* techniques have been studied in [17, 1, 4, 19]. The static *projection* technique of [17] of input XML documents implemented in the *Galax* [8] processor and refined in [1, 4] proposes that only the parts of the input documents relevant to query evaluation are loaded into memory. The projected documents are computed before query evaluation starts. In the case of [19], they distinguish *bulk* input data only used to generate the output from input data which are traversed in query evaluation, improving XML projection.

On the other hand, XQuery *optimization* techniques have been proposed. In [13], they describe a technique for *pruning* XQuery in order to improve composition based queries. Rather than projecting XML documents, they project XQuery sub-expressions with respect to other sub-expressions querying them. In other words, they propose the pruning of queries in which an (intermediate) result computed by means of a query is used as input of another query.

Our work follows the same line as [13] and [17], providing a query optimization technique based on query transformation which combines prunning and projection. However, our technique is much more precise because it uses a data dependence analysis that is performed bottom-up and top-down in the XQuery expression. Contrarily, their pruning technique is a bottom-up analysis that fails to prune many useless expressions as shown in the following XQuery expression:

```
for $j in (for $i in <A><B>...</B><C>...</C></A>
         return $i) return $j/B
```

Clearly, in this expression, the `C` elements are not necessary and can be removed. However, this simplification cannot be detected by their pruning technique (that would leave the query unchanged). The reason is that they only use a bottom-up analysis. Hence, when some inner subexpression is pruned, they do not have information about the outer subexpressions, thus missing pruning opportunities.

EXAMPLE 2. *The following query presented in [13] requests the* `close_auction` *elements obtained from a nested query in which the elements computed are* `open_auction` *elements enclosed by means of the label* `site`.

```
for $j in <site>{for $i in (doc('File1')/site)
                 return $i/open_auctions/open_auction
         }</site>
return for $k in (doc('File2')/site)
       where $j/person = $k/people/person
       return <common_auction>{$j/closed_auction}
              </common_auction>
```

The pruning technique in [13] would produce the following simplified query:

```
for $j in <site>{()}</site>
return for $k in (doc('File2')/site)
       where $j/person = $k/people/person
       return <common-auction>{()}</common-auction>
```

However, this simplification is suboptimal and it can be further optimized in our approach: the nested query does not compute `close_auction` *nor* `person` *elements and therefore the query can be completely pruned because the* `where` *clause cannot be satisfied (i.e., the final query should be the empty sequence* `()`*).*

In our technique, the same analysis performed to prune XQuery expressions provides the information needed to project the source XML documents. This means that with the XDG we can also project the XML documents that participate in the XQuery expression as it is done in [17]. Let us remark that the projecting technique of [17] is also improved here by means of our query optimization technique. For instance, in Example 1 `provider` elements will not be projected from the input XML document.

There has been previous attempts to define a PDG-like data structure for functional languages. The first attempt to adapt the PDG to the functional paradigm was [18] where they introduced the *functional dependence graph* (FDG). Unfortunately, FDGs are useful at a high abstraction level (i.e., they can slice modules or functions), but they cannot slice expressions and thus they are useless for XQuery. Another approach is based on the *term dependence graphs* (TDG) [7]. However, these graphs only consider term rewriting systems with function calls and data constructors (i.e., no complex structures such as let-expressions, for-expressions, if-then-else, etc. are considered). Finally, another use of program slicing has been done in [5] for Haskell. But in this case, no new data structure was defined and the abstract syntax tree of Haskell was used with extra annotations about data dependences.

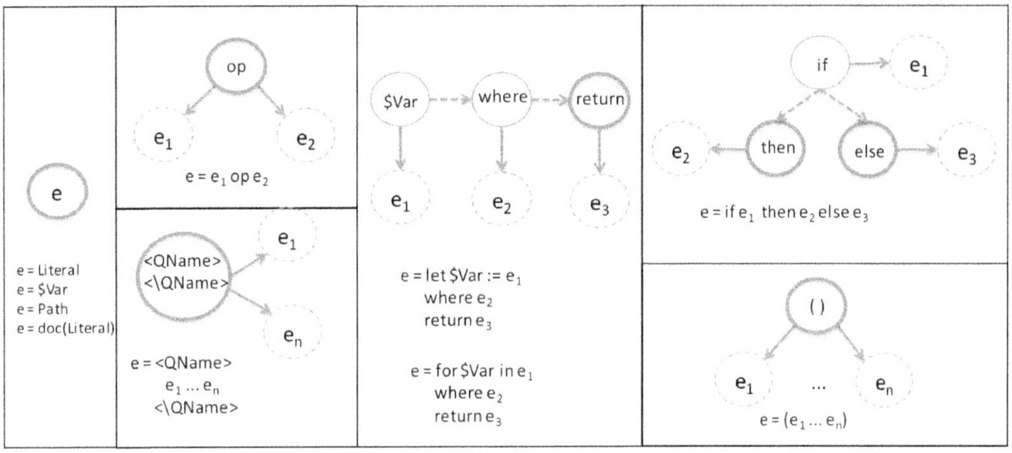

Figure 1: Graph Representation of XQuery Expressions

$Expr$	$::=$	$Literal$
	$\mid$	$(Expr_1, \ldots, Expr_n)$
	$\mid$	Var
	$\mid$	$doc(Literal)$
	$\mid$	$Path$
	$\mid$	for Var in $Expr$ (where $Expr$)? return $Expr$
	$\mid$	let Var := $Expr$ (where $Expr$)? return $Expr$
	$\mid$	if ($Expr$) then $Expr$ else $Expr$
	$\mid$	$Expr\ Op\ Expr$
	$\mid$	Tag
Tag	$::=$	$<QName>\ LExpr_1 \ldots LExpr_n\ <\backslash QName>$
$LExpr$	$::=$	$\{Expr\} \mid Literal \mid Tag$
$Path$	$::=$	$Expr\ \ (/QName)^+$
Var	$::=$	$\$VarName$
Op	$::=$	$< \mid > \mid = \mid + \mid - \mid * \mid / \mid and \mid or$

Figure 2: Syntax of XQuery expressions

3. PRELIMINARIES

For the sake of concreteness, in the rest of the paper we will consider the subset of the XQuery core language shown in Figure 2. We need to introduce a normalization process for XQuery expressions. This process ensures that (1) all variables defined in both let and for expressions are pairwise different, that is, they are renamed when they coincide; and (2) all *Path* expressions start with a variable. The normalization substitutes $e\ (/QName)^+$ by *let* $\$x := e$ *return* $\$x\ (/QName)^+$, whenever e is not a Var expression, where $\$x$ is a new variable, and e is recursively normalized.

Example 3. *The query of Example 1:*

```
for $j in for $i in (doc('File')/company)
      return <sales>{($i/customer, if ($i/provider='X')
                         then () else $i/provider)}</sales>
return $j/customer
```

is normalized as follows:

```
for $j in for $i in let $v := doc('File')
                       return $v/company
      return <sales>{($i/customer, if ($i/provider='X')
                         then () else $i/provider)}</sales>
return $j/customer
```

We define functions $first$, $suffix$ and $last$ to extract a portion of a normalized path as follows:
$first(\$x\ (/QName)^+) = \$x$,
$suffix(\$x\ (/QName)^+) = (/QName)^+$,
$last(\$x\ /QName_1 \ldots /QName_n) = QName_n$.

4. XQUERY DEPENDENCE GRAPHS

In this section we define the *XQuery dependence graph* (XDG). Such data structure is one of the main contributions of this work. It allows us to graphically represent XQuery expressions establishing data and control relations between subexpressions. Therefore, it is very useful for refactoring and, in particular, it is the basis of our slicing algorithms for XQuery. First, we define the *graph representation* of a XQuery expression.

Definition 1 (Graph Representation). *Given a normalized XQuery expression e, we represent e with a labelled graph $(\mathcal{N}, \mathcal{E}, \mathcal{F})$ where $\mathcal{N}$ are the nodes, $\mathcal{E} = (\mathcal{C}, \mathcal{S})$ are edges of two types: $\mathcal{C}$ the control edges, and $\mathcal{S}$ the structural edges, and $\mathcal{F}$ is a set of partial functions:*

$type:$	$\mathcal{N} \rightarrow \mathcal{T}$
$literal:$	$\mathcal{N} \rightarrow Literal$
$children:$	$\mathcal{N} \rightarrow \mathcal{P}(Nat \times \mathcal{N})$
$var:$	$\mathcal{N} \rightarrow Var$
$path:$	$\mathcal{N} \rightarrow Path$
$op:$	$\mathcal{N} \rightarrow Op$
$tag:$	$\mathcal{N} \rightarrow Tag$

The set $\mathcal{F}$ of partial functions defines the labels of each node in the graph. Function *type* returns the type of a node. $\mathcal{T}$ is the set of node types: *literal*, *seq*, *var*, *doc*, *path*, *letBinding*, *forBinding*, *where*, *return*, *if*, *then*, *else*, *op* and *tag*. Type *seq* represents a sequence of elements in a tuple or in a *Tag* element. Function *literal* is defined for nodes of type *literal* including elements *doc(literal)*. The partial function *children* is defined for nodes of type *seq* and *op*. It returns a set of pairs of the form (pos, n) where *pos* is the position in the sequence or operation of the expression represented

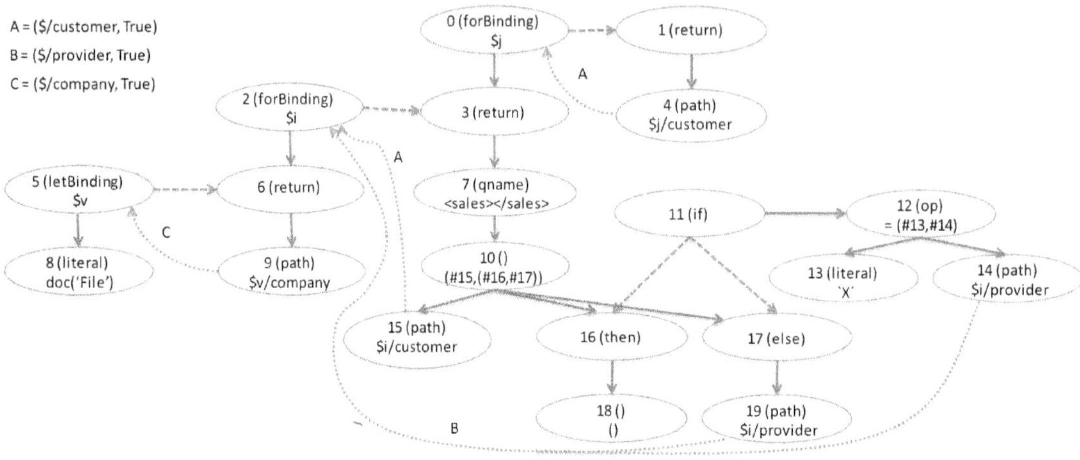

Figure 3: XQuery Dependence Graph of the running example

by node n. Function *var*, is defined for binding nodes (i.e, *forBinding* and *letBinding*) and represents the bound variable. The other functions are defined for nodes of type *path*, *op* and *tag*, respectively, and their results are straightforward. We denote by $f^{\mathcal{F}}$ the meaning that $\mathcal{F}$ assigns to the function f.

The graph representation of a XQuery expression is constructed compositionally according to the cases of Figure 1. In such representation, each graph has a *final node* (which has been graphically distinguished with a bold line) except *if-then-else* that has two final nodes. The nodes with a dashed line represent the graph associated to their subexpression, and all nodes connected to a dashed node are linked to the final nodes of the graph represented by the dashed node. We have graphically distinguished the two kinds of edges: *control edges* with a solid line, and *structural edges* with a dashed line. In addition, nodes are graphically represented including the information provided by means of the associated partial functions.

We are now in a position to define our main data structure called XQuery Dependence Graph (XDG). Essentially, the XDG augments the graph representation of a XQuery expression with the standard notion of data dependence of static analysis (see, e.g., [20]). Formally,

DEFINITION 2 (XQUERY DEPENDENCE GRAPH). *Given a XQuery expression e, the* XQuery Dependence Graph (XDG) *of e is a directed labelled graph $\mathcal{X} = (\mathcal{N}, \mathcal{E}, \mathcal{F})$ where $\mathcal{N}$ are the nodes and $\mathcal{E} = (\mathcal{C}, \mathcal{S}, \mathcal{D})$ are the edges. $(\mathcal{N}, \mathcal{E}', \mathcal{F}')$ is the graph representation of e being $\mathcal{E}' = (\mathcal{C}, \mathcal{S})$ with $\mathcal{C}$ the control edges, and $\mathcal{S}$ the structural edges. The set $\mathcal{D}$ represents* data edges. *We have a data edge from node n to n' iff $first(path(n)) = var(n')$. $\mathcal{F}$ is a set containing the functions in $\mathcal{F}'$ plus a partial function called* label *which returns a set of pairs of the form (Ppath, boolean) for each data edge, that is, label : $\mathcal{D} \to \mathcal{P}(Ppath \times boolean)$.*

In the previous definition *Ppath* denotes *partial paths* of the form: $Ppath = (\$ \mid QName)\ (/QName)^*$. Functions *first*, *suffix* and *last* can be also defined for partial paths. Given $pp = (\$ \mid QName)\ (/QName)^*$ we have: $first(pp) = (\$ \mid QName)$ and $suffix(pp) = (/QName)^*$; in addition, $last((\$ \mid QName)\ /QName_1 \ldots /QName_n) = QName_n$ if $n \geq 1$, and $(\$ \mid QName)$, otherwise.

Observe that the definition of XDG uses the standard notion of data dependence (see, e.g., [9]). In the case of XQuery the notion of variable definition and variable usage is similar to the other languages. In particular, variables are always defined in *forBinding* and *letBinding* nodes and they are used in any node that contains this variable (i.e., there exists a data edge from node n to n' when $first(path(n)) = \$v$ and $var(n') = \$v$). Observe that, thanks to the normalization process, no redefinition of a variable is possible, thus, all uses of a particular variable data-depend on the same variable definition.

The labels of the data edges are useful to know what information (i.e., partial paths) is required and provided by each node (i.e., **true** means that the partial path could[1] be provided by the node, and **false** means that it cannot be provided). Such labels represent complete or incomplete paths from a bound variable. The name of the bound variable does not need to be specified in edges, for this reason we have used the notation \$ in partial paths.

EXAMPLE 4. *The XDG of the normalized XQuery in Example 3 is shown in Figure 3 where nodes are identified with numbers. We have graphically represented the function children by means of sequences $(\#n_1, \ldots, \#n_k)$ representing the order of the children. The example contains five data dependence edges (the dotted edges) representing the request of* `$j/customer` *from the outermost* `for` *(A), the request of* `$i/customer` *(A) and* `$i/provider` *(B) from the innermost* `for`*, and the request of* `$v/company` *from the* `let` *expression (C). Let us remark that initially they are marked as* **true**, *but the proposed slicing algorithms will update such boolean values.*

5. SLICING XQUERY

In this section we describe how to transform a XDG in order to optimize an XQuery expression in such a way that only those expressions that contribute to the final result remain in the graph. From the final transformed XDG we can

[1]Whether the path is actually provided or not depends on the XML source.

(i) extract a new optimized query and (ii) deduce the parts of the source documents used by the query that are really needed.

The transformation is divided into two independent stages. In the first stage, all data dependences are *propagated* forwards and backwards in order to determine which expressions are needed and which of them are available. This process mainly affects data edges: labels of data edges are updated, and some new data edges can be also added or deleted. In the second stage, by means of an *slicing* procedure, those expressions that are useless are removed, and the graph is further transformed to ensure that the final XQuery expression is syntactically correct. In addition, there is a *garbage removal* procedure that can be applied before and after propagation and slicing procedures.

Now, we define some notation that will be used in the slicing algorithms. Given a XDG $\mathcal{G} = (\mathcal{N}, (\mathcal{C}, \mathcal{S}, \mathcal{D}), \mathcal{F})$:

(1) We use $ine_{\mathcal{E}}(n)$ and $oute_{\mathcal{E}}(n)$ to denote, respectively, the incoming and outgoing *edges* of a node $n \in \mathcal{N}$ belonging to a certain set $\mathcal{E}$:

$$ine_{\mathcal{E}}(n) = \{(n' \to n) \mid (n' \to n) \in \mathcal{E}\}$$
$$oute_{\mathcal{E}}(n) = \{(n \to n') \mid (n \to n') \in \mathcal{E}\}$$

Note that the set $\mathcal{E}$ is parameterizable; e.g., $ine_{\mathcal{S}}(n)$ denotes the incoming structural edges of n. Analogously, we use $inn_{\mathcal{E}}(n)$ and $outn_{\mathcal{E}}(n)$ to denote, respectively, the input and output *nodes* of a node n w.r.t. a certain set $\mathcal{E}$:

$$inn_{\mathcal{E}}(n) = \{n' \mid (n' \to n) \in \mathcal{E}\}$$
$$outn_{\mathcal{E}}(n) = \{n' \mid (n \to n') \in \mathcal{E}\}$$

(2) Function $reachable^{\mathcal{G}}(n)$, denotes the set of data and structural *edges* reachable from a node $n \in \mathcal{N}$:

$$reachable^{\mathcal{G}}(n) = \bigcup_{(n \to n') \in oute_{\mathcal{D} \cup \mathcal{S}}(n)} \{(n \to n')\} \cup reachable^{\mathcal{G}}(n')$$

(3) Finally, we denote by $init(\mathcal{G})$ the set of initial nodes of $\mathcal{G}$, which is defined as the set of binding nodes (i.e., *forBinding* and *letBinding*) that are not reachable from other binding nodes by traversing forwards data and structural edges. Formally:

$$\begin{aligned} init(\mathcal{G}) = \{n \in \mathcal{N} \mid\ & type^{\mathcal{F}}(n) \in \{letBinding, forBinding\} \\ & \wedge (\nexists n_{prev} \in \mathcal{N} : \\ & \quad type^{\mathcal{F}}(n_{prev}) \in \{letBinding, forBinding\} \\ & \quad \wedge\ n \in reachable^{\mathcal{G}}(n_{prev}))\} \end{aligned}$$

Observe that initial nodes of a graph $\mathcal{G}$ can be computed in linear time by traversing $\mathcal{G}$. As an example, in Figure 3 the only initial node is node 0.

5.1 Garbage removal

We can remove from the XDG all the *letBinding* nodes that are not the target of a data edge. Such bindings are useless in the XQuery expression: they represent variables that are declared and not used. Note that *forBinding* nodes cannot be removed because they can be useful for iteration even if they do not have incoming data edges. It provides our first optimization step, and in addition, it avoids to traverse such nodes in the next stages. Such garbage removal can be done in linear time with respect to the size of the XDG and it must be done before and after both stages of the transformation because the propagation of dependences and the slicing process itself could remove the incoming data edges of a *letBinding* node producing new garbage. The Algorithm 1 implements the garbage removal process.

Algorithm 1 Garbage Removal

Input: A XDG $\mathcal{G} = (\mathcal{N}, \mathcal{E} = (\mathcal{C}, \mathcal{S}, \mathcal{D}), \mathcal{F})$
Output: A XDG $\mathcal{G}'$
repeat
  $Garbage := \{n \in \mathcal{N} \mid type^{\mathcal{F}}(n) = letBinding \wedge ine_{\mathcal{D}}(n) = \emptyset\}$
  for each node $n \in Garbage$
    $\mathcal{G} := deleteFrom(n, \mathcal{G})$
until $Garbage = \emptyset$
return $\mathcal{G}$

Algorithm 2 deleteFrom Function

Function $deleteFrom(n, \mathcal{G} = (\mathcal{N}, \mathcal{E} = (\mathcal{C}, \mathcal{S}, \mathcal{D}), \mathcal{F}))$
  for each node $n_s \in (outn_{\mathcal{S}}(n) \cup inn_{\mathcal{C}}(n))$
    $\mathcal{G} := deleteFrom(n_s, \mathcal{G})$
  $\mathcal{E} := \mathcal{E} \backslash (ine_{\mathcal{S} \cup \mathcal{D}}(n) \cup oute_{\mathcal{D} \cup \mathcal{C}}(n))$
  $\mathcal{N} := \mathcal{N} \backslash \{n\}$
return $\mathcal{G}$

Note that, the removal of a *letBinding* node (and all its related nodes) is implemented with function *deleteFrom* in Algorithm 2. This function starts from a given node and removes recursively all the nodes reachable from them, following structural edges forwards and control edges backwards; it also removes all their structural/data edges. Observe also that the application of this function could produce new garbage and thus the process is repeated until no garbage exists in the XDG.

5.2 Propagating dependences

This phase propagates data dependences through the XDG. Such propagation must be done forwards and backwards.

Roughly speaking, the forward propagation says what (sub) paths *are required* by the expressions in the XQuery. And the backward propagation says which of these (sub)paths *could be provided* to the expressions that required them. Basically, propagation is as follows: the data dependences are represented by means of labelled edges in which a partial path is requested by a certain (sub)expression. The forward propagation starts from initial nodes and follows structural and data edges in order to (1) update labelled data edges with **false** whenever the partial path cannot be obtained, (2) delete useless data edges, and (3) add new data edges. The backward propagation updates the data edges from the forward propagation.

1. **Forward Algorithm** (see Algorithm 3):

   (i) The forward algorithm starts from the initial nodes and propagates forward partial paths of data edges.

Algorithm 3 Propagating Dependences Forwards

```
Input: A XDG 𝒢
Output: A XDG 𝒢'

for each node n ∈ init(𝒢) (i)
  𝒢 := propagateForward(n, 𝒢)
return 𝒢

Function propagateForward(n,𝒢=(𝒩,(𝒞,𝒮,𝒟),ℱ))
  nl := ∅
  for each edge e ∈ in_e𝒟(n)
    for each tuple (pp, bool) ∈ label^ℱ(e)
      fst := first(pp)
      suf := suffix(pp)
      case type^ℱ(n) of (ii)
      tag: if fst ∈ {tag^ℱ(n), $}
              then nl := nl ∪ {(suf, true) | suf ≠ ""}
                          ∪{($, true) | suf = ""}
              else label^ℱ(e) := (label^ℱ(e)\{(pp, bool)})
                          ∪{(pp, false)}
      path: if fst ∈ {last(path^ℱ(n)), $}
              then nl := nl ∪ {(path^ℱ(n)/suf, true)}
              else label^ℱ(e) := (label^ℱ(e)\{(pp, bool)})
                          ∪{(pp, false)}
      literal, op: if pp ≠ $
              then label^ℱ(e) := (label^ℱ(e)\{(pp, bool)})
                          ∪{(pp, false)}
      seq: if out_e𝒮(n) = ∅
              then label^ℱ(e) := (label^ℱ(e)\{(pp, bool)})
                          ∪{(pp, false)}
      otherwise: nl := nl ∪ {(pp, true)}
  if nl = ∅ then 𝒟 := 𝒟 \ out_e𝒟(n) (iv)
              for each node n_child ∈ out_n𝒮(n)
                  deleteFrom(n_child, 𝒢)
              return 𝒢
  else for each edge e ∈ out_e𝒮∪𝒟(n) (iii)
        𝒟 := 𝒟 ∪ {e}
        label^ℱ(e) := nl
      for each node n_child ∈ out_n𝒮∪𝒟(n)
        𝒢 := propagateForward(n_child, 𝒢)
      return 𝒢
```

(ii) For each data edge and each partial path of a data edge, it proceeds depending on the type of the node. Whenever the requested partial path does not match with the node, that is, for instance, the requested partial path is $p/...$ and the node has the form $/.../q$ or $< q > ... < /q >$, $p \neq q$, then it updates the partial path $p/...$ to **false**, that is, it adds the label ($p/...$,**false**) to the edge. Otherwise, it propagates forward **true** following the data and structural edges.

(iii) In addition, the forward propagation has to update partial paths. For instance, $p/q/r/...$ is propagated to the children of p/q by means of the partial path $r/...$.

(iv) When the forward propagation following data edges is not possible (e.g., we require a path p/q from an element p/r with $q \neq r$), the algorithm uses the auxiliary function *deleteFrom* (see Algorithm 2) to remove those nodes that are known to be useless.

Algorithm 4 Propagating Dependences Backwards

```
Input: A XDG 𝒢 = (𝒩, (𝒞, 𝒮, 𝒟), ℱ)
Output: A XDG 𝒢'

Pending := {n ∈ 𝒩 | in_e𝒟(n) ≠ ∅ ∧ out_e𝒟(n) ≠ ∅} (i)
for each node n ∈ Pending : Pending ∩ out_n𝒟(n) = ∅
(ii)
  𝒢 := propagateBackward(n, 𝒢)
  Pending := Pending\{n}
return 𝒢

Function propagateBackward(n,(𝒩,(𝒞,𝒮,𝒟),ℱ))
  nl:={(pp, true) ∈ label^ℱ(e) | e ∈ out_e𝒟(n)}∪
      {(pp, false) ∈ label^ℱ(e) | e ∈ out_e𝒟(n)∧
           ∀e' ∈ out_e𝒟(n) : ∄(pp, true) ∈ label^ℱ(e')}
  for each edge e ∈ in_e𝒟(n) (iii)
    for each tuple (pp, bool) ∈ label^ℱ(e)
      suf := suffix(pp)
      case type^ℱ(n) of
      tag: new := {(pp, bool') | (suf, bool') ∈ nl}
      path: new := {(pp, bool') |
                  (path^ℱ(n)/suf, bool') ∈ nl}
      otherwise: new := {(pp, bool') | (pp, bool') ∈ nl}
      label^ℱ(e) := (label^ℱ(e)\{(pp, bool)}) ∪ new
  return (𝒩, (𝒞, 𝒮, 𝒟), ℱ)
```

2. **Backward Algorithm** (see Algorithm 4):

(i) The backward algorithm updates backwards the labelled data edges from the forward propagation. It traverses all the nodes which are source and target of a data edge (the set represented with *Pending*).

(ii) However, it must be done with a certain order. Concretely, a node is analysed whenever its adjacent nodes have been already analysed (i.e., $n \in Pending$ such that $Pending \cap outn_{\mathcal{D}}(n) = \emptyset$).

(iii) The algorithm updates to **true** and **false** the dependences obtained with the forward algorithm. In addition, the updating has to rebuild partial paths, e.g., a partial path $r/...$ in a node p/q is propagated as $p/q/r/...$.

Let us remark that both propagation algorithms can be performed in linear time with respect to the size of the XDG.

EXAMPLE 5. *In Figure 4 we can see the forward and backward propagation of the normalized query in Example 3. $init(\mathcal{G}) = 0$, thus the forward propagation starts in node 0, propagating A until node 7. Then, B is propagated until nodes 15, 18 and 19 because only* `customer` *is required (i.e., the variable $j is paired with* sales*). Because node 19 only provides* `provider` *elements, and node 18 is the empty sequence, they cannot provide* `customer` *and thus they are updated to* **false** *(C). Moreover, because these nodes cannot provide required elements, the dependences that start from them are deleted. Note that the data edge from node 19 to node 2 has been deleted. The dependences (A) and*

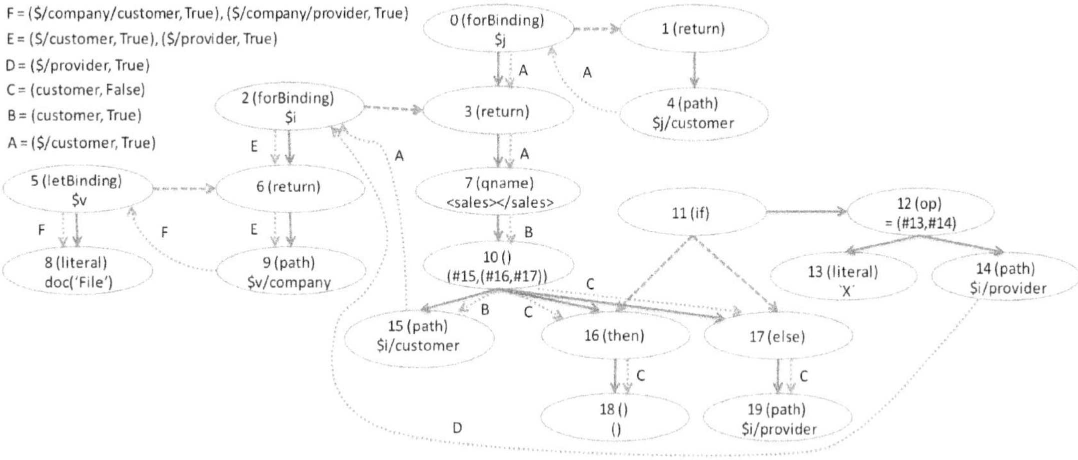

Figure 4: Forward and backward propagation of the running example

---

Algorithm 5 Slicing

Input: A XDG $\mathcal{G} = (\mathcal{N}, (\mathcal{C}, \mathcal{S}, \mathcal{D}), \mathcal{F})$
Output: A pruned XDG $\mathcal{G}'$
$Pending := \{n \in \mathcal{N} \mid$
$(in e_{\mathcal{D}}(n) \neq \emptyset \wedge \forall e \in in e_{\mathcal{D}}(n) : \nexists (pp, \mathbf{true}) \in label^{\mathcal{F}}(e))$
$\bigvee$
$(oute_{\mathcal{D}}(n) \neq \emptyset \wedge \forall e \in oute_{\mathcal{D}}(n) : \nexists (pp, \mathbf{true}) \in label^{\mathcal{F}}(e))\}$
(i)
for each node $n \in Pending : Pending \cap outn_{\mathcal{S} \cup \mathcal{D}}(n) = \emptyset$
(ii)
  $(\mathcal{G}, Pending') := slicingFrom(n, \mathcal{G})$ (iii)
  $\mathcal{C} := \mathcal{C} \backslash \{(n' \to n'') \in \mathcal{C} \mid n' \notin \mathcal{N} \vee n'' \notin \mathcal{N}\}$
  $Pending := (Pending \cup Pending') \backslash \{n\}$
return $\mathcal{G}$

(D) arriving to node 2 are also propagated forward (E) until node 9. This means that we only require elements `customer` *and* `provider` *from the* `company` *elements provided by node 9. Therefore, the dependence F is updated from E to express that node 9 only needs* `company/customer` *and* `company/provider` *elements. This is then propagated until node 8. In the backward propagation, the (B) dependences between nodes 10-16 and 10-17 are updated to* **false** *(C).*

5.3 Slicing algorithm

Once the dependences of the XDG have been propagated, the optimization technique uses a program slicing-based algorithm to produce a new optimised query.

3. **Slicing Algorithm** (see Algorithm 5):

   (i) The slicing algorithm removes nodes and edges from the XDG according to the partial paths that have been set to **false** by the forward/backward propagation algorithm. Those nodes that have at least one data edge and have all incoming or outgoing data edges with all paths labeled with **false** are removed. And, moreover, all nodes reachable from these nodes following structural and control edges are also removed.

   (ii) Nodes have to be analysed in a certain order to ensure efficiency: a node is analysed whenever the adjacents have been already analysed (i.e., $Pending \cap outn_{\mathcal{S} \cup \mathcal{D}}(n) = \emptyset$).

   (iii) The slicing algorithm uses function *slicingFrom* shown in Algorithm 6 (which in turn uses the auxiliary functions of Algorithms 2 and 7). Function *slicingFrom* is the responsible to remove nodes and edges, and it updates the set *Pending*. It distinguishes cases depending on the type of the node.

   Basically, it accurately removes the nodes of *Pending* following backward control edges (e.g., if a node of type *return* must be removed, then the associated nodes of types *where* and *forBinding* are also removed). An exception is *if-then-else* (removing a node of type *then* does not implies removing its associated node of type *if*). When a node is removed, all nodes reachable from it following structural edges are also removed. In some cases, the elimination of a node requires to rebuild the graph by replacing the children in the position of the parent, this is the functionality of the *replaceByChildren* function (see Algorithm 7).

EXAMPLE 6. *In the XDG of Figure 4 the slicing process starts from nodes 18 and 19 because all incoming data edges are labelled with* **false**. *In particular, the set Pending contains nodes 18 and 19 and thus Algorithm 5 performs, e.g., a call* $slicingFrom(18, \mathcal{G})$ *being* $\mathcal{G}$ *the XDG of Figure 4. Then, the case* $type^{\mathcal{F}}(n)$ = seq *of Algorithm 6 is executed with* $noNext$ = **true** *and hence, node 18 is removed and node 16 is included in pending. Then, e.g., it performs a call* $slicingFrom(19, \mathcal{G})$ *and the last* **if** *of Algorithm 6 is executed because* $allTrue = \emptyset$ *and hence, function* $deleteFrom$ *removes node 19. The next calls* $slicingFrom(16, \mathcal{G})$ *and* $slicingFrom(17, \mathcal{G})$ *produce the complete removal of the whole if-then-else. After unnormalization, the final result produced is optimal:*

```
Q1 =    for $i in (doc('File')/company)
        return <sales>{$i/customer}</sales>

Q2 =    for $j in Q1
        return $j/customer
```

Algorithm 6 SlicingFrom Function

Function slicingFrom($n,\mathcal{G}{=}(\mathcal{N},\mathcal{E}{=}(\mathcal{C},\mathcal{S},\mathcal{D}),\mathcal{F})$)
$next := outns_{\mathcal{S}}(n)$
$noNext := (next = \emptyset$
$\quad \bigvee(next = \{n_{next}\} \wedge type^{\mathcal{F}}(n_{next}) = \textsf{seq}$
$\quad \wedge outns_{\mathcal{S}}(n_{next}) = \emptyset))$
$allTrue := \{e \in (ine_{\mathcal{D}}(n) \cup oute_{\mathcal{D}}(n)) \mid \forall(pp, bool) \in label^{\mathcal{F}}(e) : bool = \textbf{true}\}$
if $type^{\mathcal{F}}(n) = \textsf{forBinding}$
$\quad \bigwedge(noNext \vee (allTrue = \emptyset \wedge ine_{\mathcal{D}}(n) \neq \emptyset))$
then let $n_r \in \mathcal{N} : ((n \rightarrow^* n_r) \in \mathcal{C} \wedge type^{\mathcal{F}}(n_r) = \textsf{return})$
$\quad$ **return** $(deleteFrom(n_r, \mathcal{G}), inns_{\mathcal{S}}(n_r))$
if $type^{\mathcal{F}}(n) = \textsf{letBinding} \wedge noNext$
then if $\exists n_w, n_r \in \mathcal{N} \; : \; (n \rightarrow n_w), (n_w \rightarrow n_r) \in \mathcal{C}$
$\quad$ **then** $\mathcal{G} := deleteFrom(n_w, \mathcal{G})$
$\quad$ **else** $\mathcal{G} := deleteFrom(n, \mathcal{G})$
$\quad\quad$ **let** $n_r \in \mathcal{N} : (n \rightarrow n_r) \in \mathcal{C}$
$\quad$ **return** $(replaceByChildren(n_r, \mathcal{G}), \emptyset)$
if $type^{\mathcal{F}}(n) = \textsf{where} \wedge noNext$
then let $n_p, n_r \in \mathcal{N} : (n_p \rightarrow n), (n \rightarrow n_r) \in \mathcal{C}$
$\quad$ **if** $type^{\mathcal{F}}(n_p) \in \{\textsf{forBinding}, \textsf{letBinding}\}$
$\quad$ **then return** $(deleteFrom(n_r, \mathcal{G}), inns_{\mathcal{S}}(n_r))$
$\quad$ **else** $\mathcal{G} = deleteFrom(n, \mathcal{G})$
$\quad$ **return** $(replaceByChildren(n_r, \mathcal{G}), \emptyset)$
if $type^{\mathcal{F}}(n) = \textsf{return} \wedge noNext$
then return $(deleteFrom(n, \mathcal{G}), inns_{\mathcal{S}}(n))$
if $type^{\mathcal{F}}(n) = \textsf{if} \wedge noNext$
then let $n_t \in \mathcal{N} \; : \; ((n \rightarrow n_t) \in \mathcal{C} \wedge type^{\mathcal{F}}(n_t) = \textsf{then})$
$\quad$ **let** $n_e \in \mathcal{N} \; : \; ((n \rightarrow n_e) \in \mathcal{C} \wedge type^{\mathcal{F}}(n_e) = \textsf{else})$
$\quad$ **let** $n_{child} \in \mathcal{N} \; : \; (n_t \rightarrow n_{child}) \in \mathcal{S}$
$\quad \mathcal{G} := deleteFrom(n_{child}, \mathcal{G})$
$\quad \mathcal{G} := (\mathcal{N} \backslash \{n, n_t\}, \mathcal{E} \backslash oute_{\mathcal{E}}(n), \mathcal{F})$
$\quad$ **return** $(replaceByChildren(n_e, \mathcal{G}), \; \emptyset)$
if $type^{\mathcal{F}}(n) \in \{\textsf{then}, \textsf{else}\} \wedge noNext$
then $type^{\mathcal{F}}(n_f) := \textsf{seq}$ and $children^{\mathcal{F}}(n_f) = \emptyset$
$\quad$ where n_f is a new node
$\quad \mathcal{G} = (\mathcal{N} \cup \{n_f\}, (\mathcal{C}, \mathcal{S} \cup \{(n \rightarrow n_f)\}, \mathcal{D}), \mathcal{F})$
$\quad$ **let** $n_{if} \in \mathcal{N} \; : \; (n_{if} \rightarrow n) \in \mathcal{C}$
$\quad$ **let** $n_t \in \mathcal{N} \; : \; ((n_{if} \rightarrow n_t) \in \mathcal{C} \wedge type^{\mathcal{F}}(n_t) = \textsf{then})$
$\quad$ **let** $n_e \in \mathcal{N} \; : \; ((n_{if} \rightarrow n_e) \in \mathcal{C} \wedge type^{\mathcal{F}}(n_e) = \textsf{else})$
$\quad$ **let** $n_{child_t} \in \mathcal{N} \; : \; (n_t \rightarrow n_{child_t}) \in \mathcal{S}$
$\quad$ **let** $n_{child_e} \in \mathcal{N} \; : \; (n_e \rightarrow n_{child_e}) \in \mathcal{S}$
$\quad$ **let** $n_{parent_t} \in \mathcal{N} \; : \; (n_{parent_t} \rightarrow n_t) \in \mathcal{S}$
$\quad$ **if** $type^{\mathcal{F}}(n_{child_t}) = type^{\mathcal{F}}(n_{child_e}) = \textsf{seq}$
$\quad\quad \wedge \; children^{\mathcal{F}}(n_{child_t}) = children^{\mathcal{F}}(n_{child_e}) = \emptyset$
$\quad$ **then** $\mathcal{G} := deleteFrom(n_t, \mathcal{G})$
$\quad\quad \mathcal{G} := deleteFrom(n_e, \mathcal{G})$
$\quad\quad \mathcal{G} := (\mathcal{N} \cup \{n_f\},$
$\quad (\mathcal{E} \backslash ine_{\mathcal{E}}(n_t) \cup ine_{\mathcal{E}}(n_e)) \cup (parent_t \rightarrow n_f) \in \mathcal{S}, \mathcal{F})$
$\quad$ **return** $(\mathcal{G}, \emptyset)$
if $type^{\mathcal{F}}(n) = \textsf{op}$
then if $next = \{n_{op}\} \wedge op^{\mathcal{F}}(n) = or$
$\quad$ **then return** $(replaceByChildren(n, \mathcal{G}), \emptyset)$
$\quad$ **if** $next \neq \{n_{op1}, n_{op2}\}$
$\quad$ **then return** $(deleteFrom(n, (\mathcal{N}, \mathcal{E}, \mathcal{F})), inns_{\mathcal{S}}(n))$
if $type^{\mathcal{F}}(n) = \textsf{seq}$
then if $noNext$
$\quad$ **then return** $((\mathcal{N} \backslash \{n\}, \mathcal{E} \backslash ine_{\mathcal{E}}(n), \mathcal{F}), inns_{\mathcal{S}}(n))$
$\quad$ **if** $next = \{n_{child}\}$
$\quad$ **then return** $(replaceByChildren(n, \mathcal{G}), \emptyset)$
$\quad$ **return** $(\mathcal{G}, \emptyset)$
if $allTrue = \emptyset$
then return $(deleteFrom(n, \mathcal{G}), inns_{\mathcal{S}}(n))$
return $(\mathcal{G}, \emptyset)$

Algorithm 7 replaceByChildren Function

Function $replaceByChildren(n, (\mathcal{N}, \mathcal{E}, \mathcal{F}))$
$\quad \mathcal{E} := \mathcal{E} \backslash ine_{\mathcal{C}}(n)$
$\quad$ **for each** $n' \in \mathcal{N} : (n \rightarrow n') \in \mathcal{S}$
$\quad\quad \mathcal{E} := \mathcal{E} \cup \{(n_p \rightarrow n') | (n_p \rightarrow n) \in \mathcal{E}\}$
$\quad\quad \mathcal{E} := \mathcal{E} \backslash \{(n \rightarrow n') \in \mathcal{E}\}$
$\quad \mathcal{N} := \mathcal{N} \backslash \{n\}$
return $(\mathcal{N}, \mathcal{E}, \mathcal{F})$

5.4 Projecting source documents

When the forward propagation process is finished, we can check all the data dependences of those nodes that represent an XML document (i.e., those labeled with *doc(Literal)*). These data dependences are a collection of paths that represent the information required by the query from this particular XML document. The projection $\mathcal{P}$ of the XML documents can be extracted from the XDG as follows:

$$\mathcal{P} = \{(literal^{\mathcal{F}}(n), \{pp \mid e \in ine_{\mathcal{D}}(n) \wedge (pp, true) \in label^{\mathcal{F}}(e)\}) \mid n \in \mathcal{N} \wedge type^{\mathcal{F}}(n) = doc\ \}$$

Each one of the computed pairs contains an input XML file and the paths required from this file.

The projection of XML documents can be done at any stage after the forward propagation. If it is computed immediately after the forward propagation, the result is equivalent to the projecting technique in [17]. If we compute it after the slicing phase, the result is much more precise because the projection takes advantage of the pruning analysis.

For instance, with the query of Example 2, the projection information that we get after the forward propagation is:

$$\{(File1, \emptyset), (File2, \{site/people/person\})\}$$

In contrast, the projecting information after the slicing phase is the empty set (no information is really needed from the XML sources).

6. IMPLEMENTATION

All the algorithms proposed have been implemented and integrated into a tool called *XQSlicer*. This tool allows us to automatically generate an XDG from a given XQuery expression. The tool has been implemented in Haskell. It has about 1000 LOC and generates XDGs in `dot` and `jpg` formats. The implementation is composed of eight different modules that interact to produce the final XDG:

Main This is the main module that coordinates all the other modules.

Parse Module used to transform XQueries to an internal representation.

Normalization This module automatically normalizes the expression introduced by the user.

Graph Creation Creates the initial graph (i.e., without propagation) according to Definition 1.

Propagation Performs backward and forward propagation as defined in Algorithms 3 and 4.

Slice Used to obtain the sliced graph after data propagation. It implements Algorithm 5.

Restore Contains all the needed functionality to produce the XQuery associated to a given XDG.

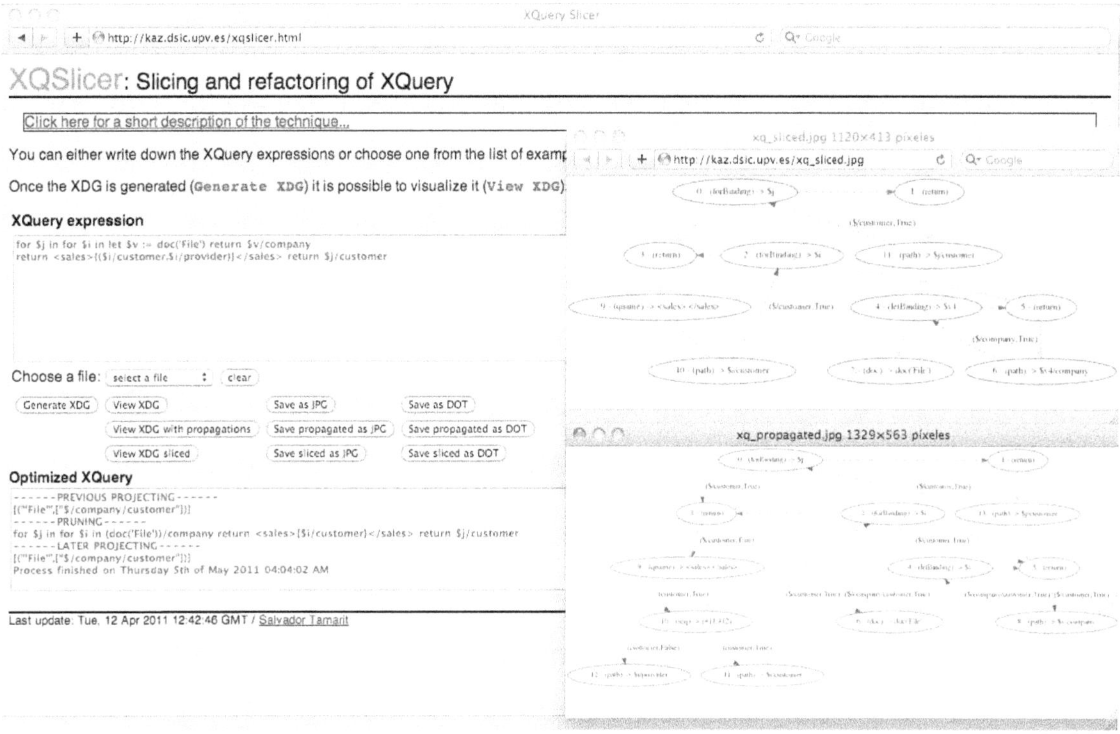

Figure 5: Screenshot of the online version of *XQSlicer*

Dot Generation To obtain a Dot file from a given XDG.

Utilities It contains common and auxiliary functions and tools used by the other modules.

There is an online version of *XQSlicer* that can be used to test the tool. This online version is publicly available at `http://kaz.dsic.upv.es/xqslicer.html`. Figure 5 shows a screenshot of the online version of *XQSlicer*. The user can either write down the initial XQuery expression or choose one from the list of available examples. Once the XDG is generated (Generate XDG) it is possible to visualize it (View XDG) and to save it as `jpg` or `dot` formats. The same options are available for the XDG with propagated dependences. And also for the sliced XDG. For instance, the XDGs in Figure 5 has been automatically generated by *XQSlicer* from the XQuery expression of Example 1. After the XDG is generated, the tool shows the final XQuery expression produced after the slicing process and the projecting information.

7. EXPERIMENTAL RESULTS

We tested our approach by means of the *BaseX* processor in a Intel machine of 1.60 GHz and 2 GB of RAM. We tested the following query:

```
for $j in <site>{
      for $i in (doc('File1')/site)
      where $i/people/person/@id = "X"
      return ($i/open_auctions/open_auction,
         for $k in (doc('File1')/site)
         return $k/closed_auctions/closed_auction,
         $i/people/person)
      }</site>
   return
      for $k in doc('File2')/site
where $j/person = $k/people/person
return
<common-auction>{$j/open_auction}</common-auction>
```

We used benchmarks for XML documents with (1) 100, (2) 1000, (3) 10000 and (4) 100000 records. Table 1 shows the execution time in ms.

Table 1: Execution Time

# Records	Pruned	Original
(1) 100	41,05	131,86
(2) 1000	99,92	3028,35
(3) 10000	447,09	264619,42
(4) 100000	3171,67	> 1 hour

This result shows that the proposed technique not only allows us to save memory by avoiding the computation, storage, and transfer of intermediate data structures. It also allows us to scale up with respect to the time needed to process the query. Note that the impact on time is very significative (from ms. to hours in the last case).

8. CONCLUSIONS

This work introduces a program slicing based technique to automatically optimize XQuery expressions. This is the first adaptation of program slicing to XQuery and it has the advantage that the dependence analysis performed allows us to project the source XML documents and to prune the XQuery expression. The technique is based on a data structure, the XDG, that is the adaptation to XQuery of the well-known PDG used in imperative languages. The definition of the XDG is by itself an important contribution of this work because it allows us to perform many other different static analyses and refactoring transformations for XQuery expressions that are expressed with this formalism. The way in which we have defined the XDG for XQuery could be easily adapted to other functional languages. In fact, we think that the slicing algorithms could be also adapted with slight modifications.

One important advantage of our technique is that it produces XQuery expressions that are executable. This means that other analyses and tools could use our transformation as a preprocessing stage simplifying the initial query and producing a more accurate and reduced expression that would predictably speed up the subsequent transformations.

Our proposed slicing technique can be extended in the future with some optimizations. For instance, in [11] they propose a *rewriting-based* optimization technique for XQuery in which they change the order of operations checking boolean conditions before constructing XML elements, and computing statically path expressions when they are applied to XML element constructors. In [15] they study under which conditions *query composition* can be eliminated and show a set of rules to this end. We think that the XDG can be used to improve these transformations.

9. REFERENCES

[1] V. Benzaken, G. Castagna, D. Colazzo, and K. Nguyên. Type-based XML projection. In *Proceedings of the 32nd International Conference on Very Large Databases*, pages 271–282. VLDB Endowment, 2006.

[2] A. Berglund, S. Boag, D. Chamberlin, M. Fernandez, M. Kay, J. Robie, and J. Siméon. XML path language (XPath) 2.0. *W3C*, 2007.

[3] P. A. Boncz, T. Grust, M. van Keulen, S. Manegold, J. Rittinger, and J. Teubner. Pathfinder: XQuery - The Relational Way. In *Proc. of the International Conference on Very Large Databases*, pages 1322–1325, New York, USA, 2005. ACM Press.

[4] S. Bressan, B. Catania, Z. Lacroix, Y. Li, and A. Maddalena. Accelerating queries by pruning XML documents. *Data & Knowledge Engineering*, 54(2):211–240, 2005.

[5] C. Brown. *Tool Support for Refactoring Haskell Programs*. PhD thesis, School of Computing, University of Kent, Canterbury, Kent, UK, 2008.

[6] D. Chamberlin, D. Draper, M. Fernández, M. Kay, J. Robie, M. Rys, J. Simeon, J. Tivy, and P. Wadler. *XQuery from the Experts*. Addison Wesley, Boston, USA, 2004.

[7] D. Cheda, J. Silva, and G. Vidal. Static slicing of rewrite systems. *Electron. Notes Theor. Comput. Sci.*, 177:123–136, June 2007.

[8] M. Fernández, J. Siméon, B. Choi, A. Marian, and G. Sur. Implementing XQuery 1.0: The Galax experience. In *Proceedings of the 29th International Conference on Very Large Databases-Volume 29*, pages 1077–1080. VLDB Endowment, 2003.

[9] J. Ferrante, K. Ottenstein, and J. Warren. The Program Dependence Graph and Its Use in Optimization. *ACM Transactions on Programming Languages and Systems*, 9(3):319–349, 1987.

[10] X. Franc. Qizx, a fast XML database engine fully supporting XQuery, 2003. `http://www.xmlmind.com/qizx/`.

[11] M. Grinev and M. Pleshachkov. Rewriting-based optimization for xquery transformational queries. In *Database Engineering and Application Symposium, 2005. 9th International*, pages 163–174. IEEE, 2005.

[12] C. Grün. BaseX. The XML Database, 2011. `http://basex.org`.

[13] B. Gueni, T. Abdessalem, B. Cautis, and E. Waller. Pruning nested XQuery queries. In *Proceeding of the 17th ACM Conference on Information and Knowledge Management*, pages 541–550. ACM, 2008.

[14] M. Kay. Ten reasons why Saxon XQuery is fast. *IEEE Data Eng. Bull*, 31(4):65–74, 2008.

[15] C. Koch. On the role of composition in XQuery. In *Proc. WebDB*, 2005.

[16] C. Koch, S. Scherzinger, and M. Schmidt. The GCX system: dynamic buffer minimization in streaming XQuery evaluation. In *Proceedings of the 33rd International Conference on Very Large Databases*, pages 1378–1381. VLDB Endowment, 2007.

[17] A. Marian and J. Simeon. Projecting XML Documents. In *Proc. of International Conference on Very Large Databases*, pages 213–224, Burlington, USA, 2003. Morgan Kaufmann.

[18] N. F. Rodrigues and L. S. Barbosa. Component identification through program slicing. In *In Proc. of Formal Aspects of Component Software (FACS 2005). Elsevier ENTCS*, pages 291–304. Elsevier, 2005.

[19] S. Scherzinger. Bulk data in main memory-based XQuery evaluation. In *Proceedings of the 4th International Workshop on XQuery Implementation, Experience and Perspectives*, pages 1–6. ACM, 2007.

[20] F. Tip. A survey of program slicing techniques. *Journal of Programming Languages*, 3(3):121–189, 1995.

[21] W3C. XML Query Working Group and XSL Working Group, XQuery 1.0: An XML Query Language. Technical report, www.w3.org, 2007.

[22] M. Weiser. Program slicing. In *Proceedings of the 5th International Conference on Software Engineering*, pages 439–449. IEEE Press, 1981.

Learning-based Relevance Feedback for Web-based Relation Completion

Zhixu Li[†], Laurianne Sitbon[‡], Xiaofang Zhou[†]
[†]School of Information Technology & Electrical Engineering
The University of Queensland, Brisbane, QLD 4072 Australia
[‡]Queensland University of Technology, Brisbane, QLD 4001 Australia
{zhixuli, zxf}@itee.uq.edu.au, laurianne.sitbon@qut.edu.au

ABSTRACT

In a pilot application based on web search engine called Web-based Relation Completion (WebRC), we propose to join two columns of entities linked by a predefined relation by mining knowledge from the web through a web search engine. To achieve this, a novel retrieval task Relation Query Expansion (RelQE) is modelled: given an entity (query), the task is to retrieve documents containing entities in predefined relation to the given one. Solving this problem entails expanding the query before submitting it to a web search engine to ensure that mostly documents containing the linked entity are returned in the top K search results. In this paper, we propose a novel Learning-based Relevance Feedback (LRF) approach to solve this retrieval task. Expansion terms are learned from training pairs of entities linked by the predefined relation and applied to new entity-queries to find entities linked by the same relation. After describing the approach, we present experimental results on real-world web data collections, which show that the LRF approach always improves the precision of top-ranked search results to up to 8.6 times the baseline. Using LRF, WebRC also shows performances way above the baseline.

Categories and Subject Descriptors

H.2.0 [**Database Management**]: General—*Security, integrity, and protection*; H.3.3 [**Information Storage and Retrieval**]: Information Search and Retrieval—*relevance feedback, retrieval models*

General Terms

Algorithms, Experimentation

Keywords

Web-based Relation Completion, WebRC

1. INTRODUCTION

As a pilot application based on web search engines, Web-based Relation Completion (WebRC) proposes to join two columns of entities in a given relation with the help of a web search engine. As shown in Figure 1, given two sets of entities in named relation and assuming we have little knowledge about the links between the two sets (merely examples of pairs linked by the relation), the task is to link every entity in one set to its corresponding entity in the other set. Previously the Relation Completion could only be processed manually by domain experts, which is quite expensive. Now with the rich knowledge available on the web, WebRC was proposed to mine web information to process the Relation Completion automatically. Several example scenarios that can use WebRC are given below:

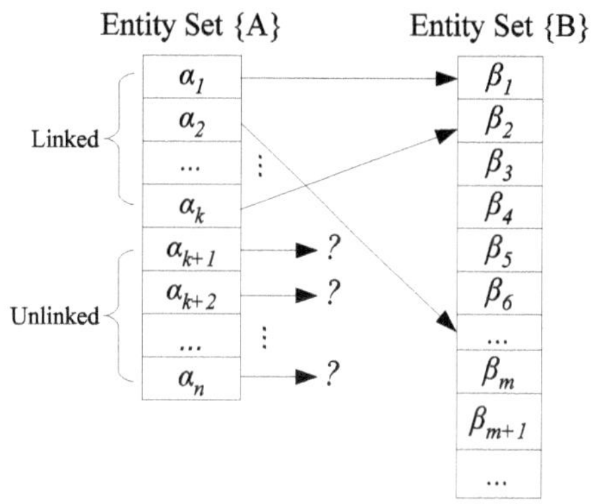

Figure 1: A Schematic Diagram of Relation Completion

Scenario 1: A research institution needs to evaluate its researcher's publication quality *w.r.t.* a given conference and journal ranking list, but most researchers do not provide the exact conference or journal names as per the ranking list within their publications lists.
Scenario 2: An on-line book store, which used to sell books only on the American market, is now trying to sell its books to non-English speaking countries such as Japan. Therefore, it needs to build a new book database in Japanese, with all books and authors' names translated into Japanese. However, they only have the English names of these books and authors, and literal translation is not acceptable since some books and authors already have popular and quite different names in Japanese.
Scenario 3: A head-hunting company needs to keep their database fresh, so they need to update, at least once a month, the employer, position, email address and office phone number of each person they are interested in. Web search engines with manual queries are the standard approach to maintain these databases, however, this is a very costly process.

In order to perform WebRC, a baseline search-based framework has been proposed recently [4]. By searching one given entity in the web search engine, it is assumed that its linked entity is mentioned in the neighbourhood of the given entity within the retrieved documents. This approach works for some real-world situations such as finding the conference where a given paper has been published (Scenario 1). Using top-ranked snippets[1] of searched web pages is enough to reach a good join result on this latter task (precision=0.873, recall=0.831) [4]. However, for some loosely-connected entity pairs such as an academic staff member and its employer university (which can be seen as a specific example of Scenario 3 above), it is expected that things become complicated in two respects. Firstly, the employer university is not always mentioned together with the staff member in the retrieved documents returned by the web search engine when querying with the staff member's name. Secondly, a university frequently mentioned with the staff member is not necessarily their employer. In this situation, we might need to process a large number of retrieved documents to find the right employer university of the staff member while noisy information will be brought in to weaken the join accuracy. The problem we have just illustrated is actually a gap between the search requirement and the search model of the web search engine. The search requirement for retrieving linked entities can be defined as: given an entity, the task is to retrieve documents containing the entity in named relation to the given one. However, if a query only contains the given entity, a web search engine also returns documents relevant to the given keywords, but not containing the relation nor the linked entity.

1.1 Approach

To improve the applicability and performance of WebRC, we propose in this paper the Relation Query Expansion (RelQE). In short, we propose to automatically expand the query with relation terms before submitting it to the web search engine, thus expecting that more documents containing the target entity (*ie.*, entity in the named relation to the query entity) will be returned among the top-K search results. We propose a novel Learning-based Relevance Feedback (LRF) approach for RelQE. The idea is to learn expansion terms for a given relation from a training set and then apply them to other queries for the same relation. Assuming an ideal training set[2] for entities in the given relation, the first step is to learn expansion terms for each query in the training set taken individually, where the LRF brings the positional and proximity information of terms into the adapted classic relevance model [3]. The second step is to select relation expansion terms from all queries' expansion term sets, where a cluster-based model is proposed. By selecting relation expansion terms according to their popularity amongst clusters, instead of queries, we can prevent the generation of expansion terms too specific for the relation.

1.2 Contributions

Our main contributions in this paper are summarized below:

- We motivate a novel application called Web-based Relation Completion (WebRC), which can be applied to various scenarios. In order to be able to apply WebRC to loosely-connected relations, we also motivate a new retrieval task called Relation Query Expansion (RelQE) on the client-side of web search engines, which aims to retrieve web documents containing entities in relation with a given one. With the help of RelQE, the performance of WebRC can be greatly improved compared to using the retrieval results obtained with unexpanded queries.

[1]Usually we only use snippets returned by web search engine instead of the original web pages *w.r.t.* time and space efficiency.

[2]By ideal training set, we mean the training set should be big enough, and its distribution is close to that of the test set

- We propose the Learning-based Relevance Feedback (LRF) approach to RelQE. Language models such as the positional model, semi-negative relevance feedback model as well as the cluster-based model are proposed.
- The experimental study based on several real-world data sets demonstrates the effectiveness of the proposed models.

After covering related work in Section 2, we formalize RelQE in Section 3. The LRF approach is introduced in Section 4. Then the results of experimental studies are provided in Section 5. Finally we provide the conclusion in Section 6.

2. RELATED WORK

The Relation Completion problem emerged from the Record Linkage problem, which has been studied extensively due to its importance in Data Cleaning. The difference between Record Linkage and Relation Completion is that there are common attributes between two sets of records in record linkage, so that some similarity functions such as edit distance and its variations [6] can be used to measure the similarity between each pair of records. However, in Relation Completion, we are talking about linking two sets of entities under a given relation, and we assume there is no common attribute that can be leveraged between the two sets.

In the natural language processing community, another line of related and well-studied problems are the analogy, metaphor and semantic relations classification problems [2], which mainly focus on recognizing or generating analogous string pairs under the same kind of relation such as (mason, stone) and (carpenter, wood). Most of the proposed approaches have used manually constructed lexicons and knowledge bases [7]. Differently, for Relation Completion, we assume there are already two sets of entities, and the task is to find pairs of entities between the two sets, which satisfy a predefined relation.

There are new trends on retrieving "objects", "entities" and their properties in both information retrieval communities and commercial systems [1]. There was even an entity track which defines related entity finding task and entity list completion task in TREC 2010. As a specific type of entity retrieval, expert finding has been proposed and important progress have been made since 2005 [9]. However, entity retrieval and expert finding aims at retrieving entities directly, while our work targets the retrieval of documents containing entities in a named relation to the given entity. Another line of work is the entity relation search, which focuses on searching relations between retrieved entities. Given the entity ranking results, entity relation search retrieves further details about the relationship between retrieved entities [9], which is also different from our task.

3. PROBLEM FORMALIZATION

Let $\mathcal{R}$ be a relation, which defines the relationship between two entities. If an entity x is in the relation $\mathcal{R}$ with entity y, then we say that (x, y) satisfies $\mathcal{R}$, denoted as $(x, y) \in \mathcal{R}$. Assuming two sets of entities A and B, for each entity α in A there must be an entity β in B such that $(\alpha, \beta) \in \mathcal{R}$. The task of Relation Completion is to find all pairs of entities between A and B that satisfy $\mathcal{R}$.

In order to perform Relation Completion we propose the Web-based Relation Completion (WebRC) framework. α and β still represent the two entity strings. By searching α in a web search engine, we retrieve web documents containing β, then recognize that β is the linked entity of α under $\mathcal{R}$. We call this kind of query a relation query of $\mathcal{R}$, which can be denoted as $\mathcal{R}$-query. For an entity α, its objective $\mathcal{R}$-query model (ignoring ranking) can be:

$$\theta_{\mathcal{R}}(\alpha) = \{D|\beta \subset D, (\alpha, \beta) \in \mathcal{R}, \beta \in B, D \in \mathcal{C}\} \quad (1)$$

where each document D contains β where (α, β) satisfies the relation $\mathcal{R}$. Documents are retrieved from the collection of web documents $\mathcal{C}$ indexed by the search engine under consideration.

On the other hand, the retrieval model of the mainstream keywords-based web search engines (ignoring ranking) can be expressed as:

$$\theta_{WSE}(Q) = \{D|Q \subseteq D, D \in \mathcal{C}\} \quad (2)$$

where each retrieved document D should contain the keywords from the query Q. This model expresses the constraint that all query terms have to appear in the documents retrieved by web search engine.

In order to use web search engines to solve our WebRC, we need to convert the $\mathcal{R}$-query model into the web search engine retrieval model. In order to do that, we propose the Relation Query Expansion (RelQE), which aims to find a set of expansion terms $E(\mathcal{R})$ for the relation $\mathcal{R}$. For each seed query α, by expanding it with each expansion term within the $E(\mathcal{R})$, the web search engine should returns less documents not containing β (noise), thus favouring the frequency of β in the retrieved documents. This conversion process can be represented as:

$$\theta_{\mathcal{R}}(\alpha) \sim \theta'_{\mathcal{R}}(\alpha) = \bigcup_{e_i \in E(\mathcal{R})} \theta_{WSE}(\alpha + e_i) \quad (3)$$

where e_i is an expansion term from $E(\mathcal{R})$, and $\theta_{WSE}(\alpha + e_i)$ means to use e_i to expand the query α before submitting it to the web search engine. In this paper, we only consider using one expansion term at a time and the combination of these expansion terms will be studied in future work. It is unlikely that $\theta'_{\mathcal{R}}(\alpha)$ is equal to $\theta_{\mathcal{R}}(\alpha)$ since there is virtually no way to that ensure all retrieved documents contain β without knowing β, but it should be a better approximation to $\theta_{\mathcal{R}}(\alpha)$ than the $\theta_{WSE}(\alpha)$.

4. LEARNING REL. EXPANSION TERMS

We now present the Learning-basd Relevance Feedback (LRF) approach for solving RelQE. Assume that we have a good enough training set $T = \{(\alpha_1, \beta_1), (\alpha_2, \beta_2), ..., (\alpha_m, \beta_m)\}$ of relation $\mathcal{R}$.

4.1 Learning Expansion Terms for Single Relation Query

To apply relevance feedback to an example pair $<\alpha, \beta>$, the documents retrieved through a web search engine are automatically assessed for relevance. For general queries, relevant documents are considered to be the top-k documents retrieved (pseudo-relevance feedback). But for the relation query, the relevant documents are those relevant to the relation, which consists of two entities. With a web search engine, the relevant documents containing both α and β can be retrieved by searching "α+β". For the remainder of this paper, consider $Q^{\mathcal{R}}$ to be an $\mathcal{R}$-query of searching α for β, while Q_+ refers to the query "α+β".

4.1.1 Adapted Classic Relevance Model

As a baseline model of learning expansion terms for single relation query, we adapt the classical relevance model [3], in which only relevance feedback is used to estimate the probability of an expansion term given the relation query $Q^{\mathcal{R}}$, *ie.*

$$P(e|Q^{\mathcal{R}}) = P(e|Q_+) \propto \frac{1}{|F_+|} \sum_{D \in F_+} P(e|D) \quad (4)$$

where $P(e|Q_+)$ is the probability of term e in the model of Q_+, F_+ is the positive relevance feedback set (relevant documents retrieved with search engine), $P(e|D)$ is the probability of the term e in document D, which can be estimated as:

$$P(e|D) = \frac{tf(e, D) + \mu P_{ML}(e|\mathcal{C})}{|D| + \mu} \quad (5)$$

where $tf(e, D)$ is the frequency of term e in document D, $P_{ML}(e|\mathcal{C})$ is the maximum likelihood estimation of the probability of e in the collection, $|D|$ is the length of the document D, and μ is the Dirichlet prior parameter of Dirichlet smoothing [8]. In our experiments, we use the term frequencies from the Web1T corpus to estimate $P_{ML}(e|\mathcal{C})$, and we set Dirichlet prior $\mu = 1500$.

4.1.2 Positional Model for Relevance Feedback

The adapted relevance model above selects expansion terms from the whole documents, which is most likely non-optimal since there are usually multiple topics and irrelevant information within a relevant document. Therefore we use a positional relevance model, which exploits the position and proximity information of terms as cues for assessing if a term is "close" enough to be used as an expansion term for the $\mathcal{R}$-query. Our positional relevance model is inspired by the one proposed by Lv *et. al.* [5],

$$P_p(e|D) = \frac{\sum_{i \in pos(\alpha,\beta,D)} P(e|D, i) + \mu P_{ML}(e|\mathcal{C})}{|D| + \mu} \quad (6)$$

where $pos(\alpha, \beta, D)$ is the set of positions where α and β appear together in D, with the distance between α and β is no larger than a given threshold δ_1. The $P(e|D, i)$ is the probability of term e in the proximity of the position i in document D, which can be simplified as:

$$P(e|D, i) = \begin{cases} 1.0 & \text{if } e \text{ occurs within } \delta_2 \text{ distance of } i \text{ in } D \\ 0.0 & \text{otherwise} \end{cases} \quad (7)$$

In our experiments, we set $\delta_1 = \delta_2 = 20$ such that we can have β in the snippet when we use e as the expansion term.

4.1.3 Mixture Model with Semi-Negative Relevance feedback

With the models above, we are likely to get the most distinctive terms between relevant documents and all other irrelevant documents on the Web. However, there is a specific subset of irrelevant documents that we should pay attention to. These documents are those containing the query entity α itself but not the target entity β. We call this subset of irrelevant documents Semi-Irrelevant Documents and consider that they express Semi-Negative Relevance Feedback (SNRF). Given the objective of RelQE, the improvement of $\theta'_{\mathcal{R}}(\alpha)$ over the $\theta_{WSE}(\alpha)$ lies on decreasing the number of semi-irrelevant documents in top-ranked retrieved documents. Besides, semi-irrelevant documents and relevant documents are likely to be similar, so it is necessary to have expansion terms that are effective in distinguishing relevant documents from semi-irrelevant documents.

With a web search engine, SNRF can be retrieved by searching "α-β". Here we let Q_- refer to the query "α-β". We have:

$$P_n(e|D) = \frac{tf(e, D) + \mu_n P_{ML}(e|Q_-)}{|D| + \mu_n} \quad (8)$$

where the Dirichlet prior μ_n is also set to 1500 in our experiments, $P_{ML}(e|Q_-)$ is the maximum likelihood estimation of term e in Q_-, which can be estimated as:

$$P_{ML}(e|Q_-) = \frac{1}{|F_-|} \sum_{D \in F_-} P(e|D) \quad (9)$$

where F_- is the set of SNRF retrieved with Q_-.

The probability of a term e appearing in the retrieved documents of $Q^{\mathcal{R}}$ is:

$$P(e|Q^{\mathcal{R}}) \propto \frac{1}{|F_+|} \sum_{D \in F_+} [\lambda P(e|D) + (1-\lambda) P_n(e|D)] \quad (10)$$

where the interpolation weight λ is set at 0.4 which is an optimal value in our experiments. Besides, if we use $P_p(e|D)$ instead of $P(e|D)$, we obtain the combined model of positional model and semi-negative model, which take both positional information and SNRF into account.

4.1.4 *Expansion Terms Verification*

In order to guarantee the quality of expansion terms for each example, we verify their validity. For an example pair such as (α, β), α is an unexpanded seed query. Each learned expansion term is used to expand the seed query in two ways: either the seed query plus the expansion term or the seed query minus the expansion term. Then we measure the accuracy of the top-ranked (top-100 is enough to reflect the performance) retrieved documents, P@N, *ie.* the proportion of documents containing β.

Expansion terms are then categorized into three categories according to their effectiveness: 1) positive terms that improve P@N evidently when added, and hurt it evidently when subtracted; 2) negative terms are those having the opposite effect; 3) neutral terms are all the remaining ones. We use a threshold to define if the improvement of P@N is evident. After this step, only positive terms will remain as expansion terms for each example pair.

EXAMPLE 1. *We compare the expansion terms learned for an example pair of the relation (Academic Staff, University) with the three models (threshold is set to 0.2). Also, we label positive expansion terms that can pass the verification process with boldfaced in Table1. In the verification process, a positive expansion term should improve the P@100 of a seed query by more than 30%.*

As we can see, the baseline model generates 20 expansion terms, of which only 7 pass the verification; with the positional model, 16 expansion terms are generated 7 positive terms; while with the positional+semi-negative model, only 14 expansion terms are generated with 6 passing the verification.

Table 1: The learned expansion terms for example pair with the baseline relevance model, or the positional model, or the combined positional and semi-negative mixture model, with boldfaced terms are those passed the verification.

(Person A, University of Cambridge)			
1. Baseline Model			
university	**cambridge**	dr	**college**
uk	books	**professor**	history
faculty	london	**education**	library
mr	economics	business	edited
publications	communications	email	profile
2. Positional Model			
cambridge	**university**	**college**	**faculty**
education	library	london	**uk**
professor	economics	business	studies
master	mr	communications	publications
3. Positional + Semi-Negative Model			
professor	**college**	communications	**education**
history	**faculty**	**cambridge**	**university**
economics	laboratory	master	london
mr	studies		

4.2 Selecting Expansion Terms

We consider how to generate $E(\mathcal{R})$ from the verified expansion terms of each example pair in the training set. Intuitively, the expansion term that belongs to more $\mathcal{R}$-queries has a higher priority to be selected into $E(\mathcal{R})$. Hence, a query-based relation query expansion model can be:

$$P(e|\mathcal{R}) = \sum_{Q_i^{\mathcal{R}} \in T} B(e, Q_i^{\mathcal{R}}) \quad (11)$$

where $B(e, Q_i^{\mathcal{R}}) = 1$ if e is a positive expansion term of $Q_i^{\mathcal{R}}$, or 0 otherwise.

However, this query-based model may give some specific expansion terms a higher score than less specific expansion terms. For example, terms like "London" and "Sydney" should have nothing to do with the (Academic Staff, University) relation. They come up as relation expansion terms because a number of examples take them as expansion terms (the reason being that some universities in the training examples are located in London or Sydney).

As an alternation, we propose a cluster-based query expansion model. In this model, we cluster all queries in the training set and then estimate the "coverage" of each expansion term amongst clusters, instead of queries. The purpose of query clustering is to reduce the influence of a possibly imbalanced distribution of examples. The cluster-based relation query expansion model is formalised with:

$$P(e|\mathcal{R}) = \sum_{C_i \in Clusters} B(e, C_i) \quad (12)$$

where $B(e, C_i)$ measures whether e is a positive expansion term of cluster C_i, which can be simplified as:

$$B(e, C) = \begin{cases} \lambda_2 \frac{N(e|C)}{|C|} + (1-\lambda_2) P(e|C) & \text{if } \frac{N(e|C)}{|C|} > t \\ 0 & \text{otherwise} \end{cases} \quad (13)$$

where $N(e|C)$ is the number of queries that have e as its expansion term in the cluster C. $P(e|C)$ is the probability that e is an expansion term for the cluster C_i, which can be estimated as:

$$P(e|C) = \frac{1}{|C|} \sum_{Q_i^{\mathcal{R}} \in C} P(e|Q_i^{\mathcal{R}}) \quad (14)$$

Other parameters in Equation 13 are: $|C|$ denotes the number of queries in the cluster, the interpolation weight λ_2 is set to 0.5 and the threshold t is set to 0.3, which are optimal in our experiments.

4.2.1 *Query Clustering*

The clusters are created with the hierarchical agglomerative clustering, in which the number of clusters is not predefined. The hierarchical agglomerative algorithm iteratively selects the closest pair of clusters to merge them into a new cluster until the similarity between the closest clusters drops below a given threshold.

Given two $\mathcal{R}$-queries Q_r (searching α_r for β_r), Q_s (searching α_s for β_s) under relation $\mathcal{R}$, the similarity between the two queries can be calculated as:

$$Sim(Q_r, Q_s) = 0.5 * Sim(\alpha_r, \alpha_s) + 0.5 * Sim(\beta_r, \beta_s) \quad (15)$$

where $Sim(\alpha_r, \alpha_s)$ and $Sim(\beta_r, \beta_s)$ are the similarities between the two query entities and the two target entities respectively. The similarity between two entities is based on context, which can be measured by:

$$Sim(\alpha_r, \alpha_s) = \begin{cases} 1.0 & \text{if } \alpha_r = \alpha_s \\ \sum_{w \in V} P(w|CT_{\alpha_r}) P(w|CT_{\alpha_s}) & \text{otherwise} \end{cases} \quad (16)$$

where V is the vocabulary of the whole collection, $P(w|CT_{\alpha_r})$ is the probability of w appearing in the context of α_r. The context of α_r can be approximated with words in the proximity of α_r in the positive relevance feedback set F_+ which are retrieved by $\alpha_r + \beta_r$, and similarly for $P(w|CT_{\alpha_s})$.

5. EXPERIMENTAL STUDY

5.1 Data Sets

In our experiments, three real-world data sets are used to evaluate the effectiveness of learning-based relevance feedback (LRF).

- **Academic Staff & University (AU):** *About 2.5k academic staff's full names and their universities are collected from 20 different universities. To build a larger university set, we also collect 500 university names from the SHJT world university ranking*[3].
- **Book & Author (BA):** *This data set contains more than 4.3k book titles collected from Google Books*[4]. *These books are of more than 20 different categories including education, history, bibliography, etc. We have also collected about 20k book writers' names (including the chief authors of the 4.3k books) from Google Books.*
- **Invention & Inventor (II):** *This data set contains 512 inventions' names with their chief inventors' full names (311 different people) from an inventor list*[5] *in Wikipedia.*

5.2 Experimental Setup

In all experiments, we use Google API[6] to retrieve documents and snippets from the web. The number of feedback documents we use for each query is fixed to 100, which is the maximum that the search engine returns at a time.

For learning expansion terms for each query, when there are more than 100 expansion terms generated, only the top 100 terms with the highest $P(e|Q)$ will be considered and verified. In the verification process for expansion terms, if a term can improve the P@100 of a query by more than 30%, it will be taken as a valid expansion term for the query. We adopt 30% since it has shown experimentally to be a good threshold to remove a great number of less effective expansion terms.

An arbitrary threshold would not be appropriate for selecting promising relation expansion terms since it is data-dependent. As a default setup, for each data set, the top-10 expansion terms with the highest score will be evaluated for each model. For all seed queries in a testing set, we use the same relation expansion terms to expand. Queries are expanded with only one expansion term at a time.

5.3 Effect of the Training Set Size

We perform experiments with several sizes of training set (|T|=2, 3, 5, 10, 30, 50, 80, 100, 120, 150). For each size, cross-validation is achieved by generating 5 different random sets for training, while all the remaining pairs in each data set are used for testing. The results are presented for learning expansion terms of single relation query with Combined Positional+Semi-Negative model.

As we can see in Figure 2, over the three data sets, the performance of Q-LRF improves dramatically when the size of the training set is smaller than 10, then improves slightly from 10 to 50. The performance stays relatively stable for training sets larger than 50 examples.

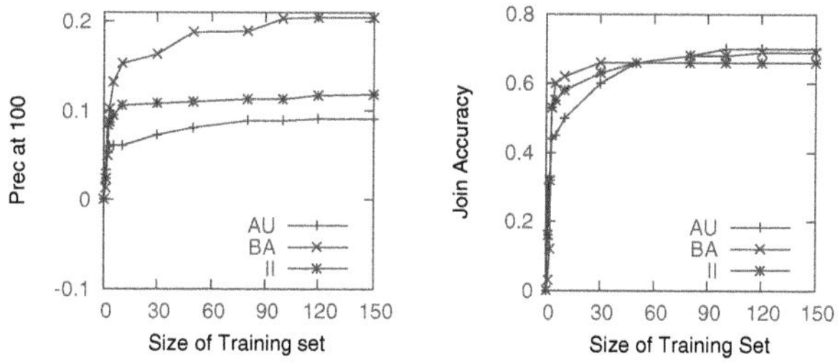

(a) The P@100 of Snippets (b) The Join results of WebRC

Figure 2: The effect of the quantity of training set to the P@100 of snippets of Q-LRF and the join accuracy of the WebRC for each dataset

Based on the observation of Figure 2, we set the default size of training set to 100 in the following subsections, since it is the most stable value to reach almost the best performance across all datasets. The remaining example pairs in each data set are used for testing. For each data set, we present the average results over 5 different random training set.

5.4 Evaluation for Single Relation Query

In this section, we evaluate the four models for learning expansion terms for a single relation query. As shown in Table 2, the classic model has by far the largest N_1 (the average number of expansion terms gen- erated for verification), but the ratio of its valid expansion terms N_2/N_1 (N_2 is the average number of remaining expansion terms after the verification process) is the lowest, which means that it generates the most expansion terms for single queries, but most of them cannot pass the verification process. Both Positional and Semi-Negative models generate less expansion terms, but the ratio of valid ones is higher than that of the classic model. The combined model generates the fewest terms and has the highest ratio of valid terms, which is the most optimal in terms of time for verifying the expansion terms. The positional and semi-negative models usually reach a higher P@100 and join accuracy than the classic model, which proves the effectiveness of the two models. The combined model in some cases even outperforms the positional model and semi-negative model taken individually.

In the following subsection, the combined Positional+Semi-Negative model will be set as the default model for learning the expansion terms of all single queries.

5.5 Evaluation of Relation Expansion Terms

Now we compare the performance of Query-based model (Q-LRF) and Cluster-based model (C-LRF) in selecting relation expansion terms. Here we set the similarity threshold ending the hierarchical agglomerative clustering algorithm to 0.8, which is an optimal value on both the quality of expansion terms and the outcome of WebRC.

The average precision of top-ranked documents retrieved with expanded queries (or unexpanded queries for the baseline) are listed in Table 3. As we can see, the cluster-based model works better than the query-based model in all cases. We also measure the join accuracy of WebRC by using top-ranked documents retrieved with expanded queries (or unexpanded queries for the baseline). As shown in Table 4, the join results with both C-LRF and Q-LRF reach much higher accuracy than the baseline, which demonstrates the effectiveness of our LRF approach. Additionally, C-LRF's per-

[3]http://www.arwu.org/
[4]http://books.google.com/
[5]http://en.wikipedia.org/wiki/List_of_inventors
[6]http://www.google.com

Table 2: The Comparison of N_1, N_2, N_2/N_1, the P@100 of documents retrieved with Q-LRF and the join accuracy of WebRC with the results of Q-LRF, based on the four different models for learning expansion terms of single relation query.

Acd. Staff & Univ.	N_1	N_2	N_2/N_1	P@100	Join
Classic	38.8	14.3	0.369	0.074	0.60
Positional	23.0	11.1	0.483	0.086	0.67
Semi-Neg.	32.6	13.5	0.414	0.087	0.68
Pos. + Semi-Neg.	**19.6**	**10.3**	**0.526**	**0.089**	**0.70**
Book & Author	N_1	N_2	N_2/N_1	P@100	Join
Classic	30.9	3.9	0.126	0.180	0.62
Positional	23.0	3.2	0.138	0.198	0.66
Semi-Neg.	23.1	3.3	0.143	0.201	**0.68**
Pos. + Semi-Neg.	**17.1**	**2.8**	**0.164**	**0.203**	**0.68**
Invention & Inventor	N_1	N_2	N_2/N_1	P@100	Join
Classic	42.3	19.3	0.456	0.110	0.61
Positional	26.1	14.5	0.556	0.112	0.64
Semi-Neg.	36.3	18.5	0.510	**0.113**	**0.66**
Pos. + Semi-Neg.	**23.2**	**13.7**	**0.591**	**0.113**	**0.66**

formances are always above Q-LRF's, which shows the advantage of estimating the "coverage" of expansion terms amongst clusters instead of queries.

The range of improvement of Q-LRF and C-LRF over the baseline mainly depends on the proportion of semi-negative documents in the top-ranked. This is illustrated by the massive improvement over unexpanded queries of Drug & Disease that have a very low P@100 (0.005). Besides, it is also affected by the expansion terms shared amongst different queries of the same relation. The P@N and Join@100 of Book & Author can also be greatly improved since books are usually better in sharing common expansion terms than query entities in other data sets.

Table 3: Average precision of top-ranked documents retrieved with unexpanded queries or expanded queries generated with Q-LRF or C-LRF models.

Acd. Staff & Univ.	P@10	P@50	P@100
Unexpanded	0.087	0.054	0.050
Q-LRF	0.094	0.074	0.089
C-LRF	**0.145**	**0.103**	**0.101**
Book & Author	P@10	P@50	P@100
Unexpanded	0.230	0.201	0.109
Q-LRF	0.242	0.241	0.203
C-LRF	**0.285**	**0.281**	**0.260**
Invention & Inventor	P@10	P@50	P@100
Unexpanded	0.115	0.108	0.105
Q-LRF	0.133	0.120	0.113
C-LRF	**0.146**	**0.123**	**0.114**

6. CONCLUSION

In this paper, a novel retrieval problem named Relation Query Expansion (RelQE) is motivated and formalized on the client-side of web search engines, which can be a crucial step in the scenario of Web-based Relation Completion (WebRC). To solve the RelQE problem, the Learning-based Relevance Feedback (LRF) approach is proposed, which learns common relation expansion terms from existing pairs in relation. According to the experimental results based on three real-world data sets, both Q-LRF and C-LRF are successful in learning high-quality relation expansion terms, which can be used to effectively improve the retrieval precision of top-ranked results by at most 8.6 times comparing to that of the unexpanded query search. At the same time, they greatly improve the join accuracy of WebRC for at least 37%, and sometimes even as high as 118%, comparing to that based on unexpanded query results. Besides, C-LRF usually works even better than Q-LRF, which proves the advantage of estimating the "coverage" of expansion terms among clusters instead of queries.

Table 4: Join accuracy of WebRC using top-ranked documents retrieved with unexpanded queries or expanded queries generated with Q-LRF or C-LRF models.

Acd. Staff & Univ.	Join@10	Join@50	Join@100
Unexpanded	0.33	0.38	0.41
Q-LRF	0.67	0.69	0.70
C-LRF	**0.70**	**0.72**	**0.73**
Book & Author	Join@10	Join@50	Join@100
Unexpanded	0.45	0.50	0.51
Q-LRF	0.54	0.66	0.68
C-LRF	**0.59**	**0.69**	**0.70**
Invention & Inventor	Join@10	Join@50	Join@100
Unexpanded	0.29	0.39	0.42
Q-LRF	0.56	0.58	**0.66**
C-LRF	**0.56**	**0.60**	**0.66**

7. REFERENCES

[1] S. Adafre, M. de Rijke, and E. Sang. Entity retrieval. *Proceedings of RANLP, Bulgaria, September*, 2007.

[2] R. French. The computational modeling of analogy-making. *Trends in Cognitive Sciences*, 6(5):200–205, 2002.

[3] V. Lavrenko and W. Croft. Relevance based language models. In *Proceedings of the 24th annual international ACM SIGIR conference on Research and development in information retrieval*, pages 120–127, 2001.

[4] Z. Li, L. Sitbon, L. Wang, X. Zhou, and X. Du. Approximate Membership Localization (AML) for Web-Based Join. In *Proceedings of the 19th International Conference on Information and Knowledge Management*, pages 1321–1324, 2010.

[5] Y. Lv and C. Zhai. Positional relevance model for pseudo-relevance feedback. In *Proceeding of the 33rd international ACM SIGIR conference on Research and development in information retrieval*, pages 579–586, 2010.

[6] S. Needleman and C. Wunsch. A general method applicable to the search for similarities in the amino acid sequence of two proteins. *Journal of molecular biology*, 48(3):443–453, 1970.

[7] P. Turney and M. Littman. Corpus-based learning of analogies and semantic relations. In *Machine Learning Journal, Volume 60, Numbers 1-3*, 2005.

[8] C. Zhai and J. Lafferty. A study of smoothing methods for language models applied to ad hoc information retrieval. In *Proceedings of the 24th annual international ACM SIGIR conference on Research and development in information retrieval*, pages 334–342, 2001.

[9] J. Zhu, A. de Vries, G. Demartini, and T. Iofciu. Evaluating relation retrieval for entities and experts. In *Proceedings of the SIGIR 2008 Workshop on Future Challenges in Expertise Retrieval (fCHER)*, 2008.

Categorising Logical Differences Between OWL Ontologies

Rafael S. Gonçalves
School of Computer Science
University of Manchester
Manchester, United Kingdom
goncalvj@cs.man.ac.uk

Bijan Parsia
School of Computer Science
University of Manchester
Manchester, United Kingdom
bparsia@cs.man.ac.uk

Ulrike Sattler
School of Computer Science
University of Manchester
Manchester, United Kingdom
sattler@cs.man.ac.uk

ABSTRACT

The analysis of changes between OWL ontologies (in the form of a *diff*) is an important service for ontology engineering. A purely syntactic analysis of changes is insufficient to distinguish between changes that have logical impact and those that do not. The current state of the art in semantic diffing ignores logically ineffectual changes and lacks any further characterisation of even significant changes. We present a diff method based on an exhaustive categorisation of effectual and ineffectual changes between ontologies. In order to verify the applicability of our approach we apply it to 88 versions of the National Cancer Institute (NCI) Thesaurus (NCIt), and demonstrate that all categories are realized throughout the corpus. Based on the outcome of the NCIt study we argue that the devised categorisation of changes is helpful for ontology engineers and their understanding of changes carried out between ontologies.

Categories and Subject Descriptors

I.2 [**Artificial Intelligence**]: Knowledge Representation Formalisms and Methods

General Terms

Theory, Experimentation

1. INTRODUCTION

The comparison of ontologies is a valuable service whether used as a subroutine in a version control system or to support users in understanding changes. Different diff methods vary in their sensitivity to changes: e.g., a diff method based on character differences will find that two notationally distinct serializations of the same ontology are radically different. If a diff method is too sensitive to irrelevant changes then the user will be faced with determining which reported changes are actually significant. On the other hand, a hard requirement is that the diff method does not miss any change of significance.

The OWL 2 specification [8] defines a high level notion of syntactic equivalence, so-called "structural equivalence" (and thus the associated notion of *structural difference*), which abstracts from certain neglectable changes such as the order of axioms or concrete syntax. A different syntactic approach is that of an edit-based diff, wherein change records are produced within the ontology editor being used, thereby capturing the history and intent of change, as implemented in Swoop [6]. The diffs mentioned so far, as well as PROMPTDIFF [9], do not perform any further characterisation of reported changes (e.g., whether these have logical impact). This forces the user to analyse each change in the diff, and determine whether it affects the set of entailments of an ontology; thus whether the change is logically *effectual*. When analysing a set of changes it would be useful to not only distinguish between those logically effectual and ineffectual ones, but also to characterise reported changes according to their impact. Certain classes of ineffectual changes are neglectable, e.g., order of conjuncts in an axiom. However other ineffectual changes provide useful insights, such as the introduction of redudant or rewritten axioms. Semantic diffs, such as CEX [7] or ContentCVS [4], regard all ineffectual changes as neglectable, though in general knowing the relative proportions of effectual and meaningful ineffectual changes gives us a better understanding of what has changed between ontologies. For example, if most changes are meaningfully ineffectual it might be a sign of wasted effort, and therefore it would be useful to know if and why this happens. Contrariwise, while those changes might be *logically* ineffectual, other tools might be sensitive to the variant syntactic forms. So on the one hand, syntactic diffs report without distinction both effectual and ineffectual changes, and on the other hand semantic diffs do not present ineffectual changes.

A major problem with the output of change sets is that the user is given a (possibly large) set of axioms (or terms) to analyse, with no indication as to what kind of change each of them represents. A reasonable presentation of changes will cluster changes according to relevant properties. In this paper we propose a diff method, which we refer to as *intentional difference*, incorporating a categorisation of changes. Our categorisation attempts to capture the impact of each change (e.g., whether it is a rewrite of another axiom). Aside from the intuitive appeal of categorised changes, these rectify a problem with existing diffs: the lack of source axioms. Thus users can see what was changed as well as the actual change.

For the purpose of verifying the suitability of our approach, we collected 88 versions of the National Cancer Institute (NCI) Thesaurus (NCIt) available in OWL, and conducted a diachronic study of the corpus. This study aimed at showing the computational feasibility of our approach and confirming that the devised categories are realized throughout the corpus. Additionally we investigate whether the proposed method helps us understand the evolution of the NCIt. Moreover we demonstrate how the devised categorisation can support change analysis by users.

CIKM'11, October 24–28, 2011, Glasgow, Scotland, UK.

2. PRELIMINARIES

We assume the reader to be reasonably familiar with ontologies and OWL, as well as the underlying description logics (DLs) [3], though detailed knowledge is not required. We do use the notion of entailment [2], which is identical to the standard first order logic entailment (an axiom α entailed by an ontology $\mathcal{O}$ is denoted $\mathcal{O} \models \alpha$). A *justification* $\mathcal{J}$ of a consequence α is a minimal subset of an ontology $\mathcal{O}$ that is sufficient for α to hold [5]. The *signatures* of an axiom α and an ontology $\mathcal{O}$ are denoted $\widetilde{\alpha}$ and $\widetilde{\mathcal{O}}$, respectively. We also use the notion of a *locality-based module* [1], and denote a $\bot$-*module* extracted from an ontology $\mathcal{O}$ for a set of terms (signature) Σ as $\bot\text{-}mod(\Sigma, \mathcal{O})$.

3. ONTOLOGY DIFFERENCE

The problem of computing the difference between pairs of ontologies has been approached both syntactically and semantically. We distinguish two major aspects of ontology diffing: *(i)* the detection of changes, and *(ii)* the presentation of changes to the user. We note that most effort has been largely dedicated to *(i)*. It is often the case that the output *(ii)* of diff operations is the set of axioms or terms in the diff. While this may reflect the desired detection of change, it does not necessarily convey sufficient information to the user w.r.t. the impact of changes.

3.1 Related Work and Diff Desiderata

Within the detection of changes *(i)*, one would expect a preliminary distinction of axioms in the diff according to their logical effectuality. As such, a purely syntactic change analysis does not suffice to achieve this. Standard semantic diff tools treat all ineffectual changes as neglectable. This goes too far, for example: consider the case where two ontologies differ in a substantial number of axioms, but the axioms in the diff are only equivalences rewritten into subsumptions. Semantic diffs would point out that there are no differences, which may seem counter-intuitive to the user since a shallow inspection of the ontologies would reveal a discrepancy in number of axioms. In this case the ineffectual changes point to possibly unnecessary work. Though if these were intentional, then other developers should be aware of it rather than rewriting the axioms once again. So for this kind of change we would expect a more granular analysis to be helpful.

The second fundamental aspect of any diff is the presentation of changes to the user *(ii)*. Currently ontology diffs return as the output an unstructured, uncharacterised set of changes. As a consequence the task of change analysis is not particularly appealing. Consider the fact that the average diff size across the NCIt corpus is over 6,000 changes; relying on current diff methods for change analysis would be frightening, to say the least. At this point it would be useful to determine further properties of individual changes which might help the user understand changes. A change could relate to, e.g, a newly introduced term, or an adjustment to the class hierarchy. Whatever it may be, the current state-of-the-art in ontology diffing does not carry out such a characterisation of changes.

In terms of computability, one would expect an ontology diff to be efficiently computable for OWL 2 ontologies.[2] CEX [7], e.g., computes differences efficiently only for a fragment of OWL.[3]

In Table 1 we summarise such useful features of an ontology diff, and whether existing approaches exhibit such desiderata. These properties motivate the diff method proposed in this paper, and our categorisation of changes according to their impact.

3.2 Diff Categories

Given the limitations of diff approaches described in Table 1, we address in this paper the problem of categorising changes between ontologies. We start with structural difference as it abstracts from some obviously pointless changes, and is part of the OWL W3C standard. The notion of structural difference is based on OWL's notion of structural equivalence (denoted $\equiv_s$) [8], and rules out differences that an otherwise syntactic equality based diff would detect, such as the concrete syntax of ontologies, the order of axioms or the order of disjuncts and conjuncts in an axiom. Furthermore we would like to distinguish between *(a)* axioms that do not alter the set of entailments between ontologies (ineffectual), and *(b)* those axioms that do (effectual). Structural difference does not realize this, and so we build on this notion with an effectuality test. The latter involves checking if changes in the first ontology are entailed by the second (and vice-versa). Finally, we devise a categorisation mechanism of these changes, in order to characterise their purported impact. Let us begin by defining how the change sets are obtained:

DEFINITION 1 (STRUCTURAL DIFFERENCE [4]). *The structural difference between $\mathcal{O}_1$ and $\mathcal{O}_2$ are the following sets:*

- $\text{Adds}(\mathcal{O}_1, \mathcal{O}_2) = \{\beta \in \mathcal{O}_2 \mid \nexists \alpha \in \mathcal{O}_1 \text{ s.t. } \alpha \equiv_s \beta\}$
- $\text{Rems}(\mathcal{O}_1, \mathcal{O}_2) = \{\alpha \in \mathcal{O}_1 \mid \nexists \beta \in \mathcal{O}_2 \text{ s.t. } \alpha \equiv_s \beta\}$

So if there is an axiom β s.t. $\beta \in \text{Adds}(\mathcal{O}_1, \mathcal{O}_2)$, this implies that $\beta \in \mathcal{O}_2 \setminus \mathcal{O}_1$, and analogously for $\text{Rems}(\mathcal{O}_1, \mathcal{O}_2)$. Intuitively $\text{Adds}(\mathcal{O}_1, \mathcal{O}_2)$ represent additions from $\mathcal{O}_1$ to $\mathcal{O}_2$, and $\text{Rems}(\mathcal{O}_1, \mathcal{O}_2)$ the removals. Based on these two sets, next, we distinguish between axioms in $\text{Adds}(\mathcal{O}_1, \mathcal{O}_2)$ (or $\text{Rems}(\mathcal{O}_1, \mathcal{O}_2)$) that affect the set of entailments of $\mathcal{O}_1$ (or $\mathcal{O}_2$). In other words, we distinguish between those axioms in the structural difference which are entailed by $\mathcal{O}_1$ (or $\mathcal{O}_2$), as follows:

DEFINITION 2. *The effectual and ineffectual changes between $\mathcal{O}_1$ and $\mathcal{O}_2$ are the following sets:*

- $\text{EffAdds}(\mathcal{O}_1, \mathcal{O}_2) = \{\beta \in \text{Adds}(\mathcal{O}_1, \mathcal{O}_2) \mid \mathcal{O}_1 \not\models \beta\}$
- $\text{EffRems}(\mathcal{O}_1, \mathcal{O}_2) = \{\alpha \in \text{Rems}(\mathcal{O}_1, \mathcal{O}_2) \mid \mathcal{O}_2 \not\models \alpha\}$
- $\text{IneffAdds}(\mathcal{O}_1, \mathcal{O}_2) = \text{Adds}(\mathcal{O}_1, \mathcal{O}_2) \setminus \text{EffAdds}(\mathcal{O}_1, \mathcal{O}_2)$
- $\text{IneffRems}(\mathcal{O}_1, \mathcal{O}_2) = \text{Rems}(\mathcal{O}_1, \mathcal{O}_2) \setminus \text{EffRems}(\mathcal{O}_1, \mathcal{O}_2)$

The resulting sets of ineffectual additions $\text{IneffAdds}(\mathcal{O}_1, \mathcal{O}_2)$ and removals $\text{IneffRems}(\mathcal{O}_1, \mathcal{O}_2)$ are composed of those axioms which do not change the set of entailments of $\mathcal{O}_1$ and $\mathcal{O}_2$, but were added or deleted, respectively. The effectual additions and removals, $\text{EffAdds}(\mathcal{O}_1, \mathcal{O}_2)$ and $\text{EffRems}(\mathcal{O}_1, \mathcal{O}_2)$, represent those axioms that have logical impact from $\mathcal{O}_1$ to $\mathcal{O}_2$ (and vice-versa).

While semantics diffs would consider all ineffectual changes as irrelevant, we here attempt to characterise meaningful ineffectual changes in order to get a sense of how relevant these are. For that purpose, we devise a categorisation of such axioms based on the reasons for the lack of impact, i.e. justifications. Note that this categorisation is not a partitioning of the set of ineffectual changes.

DEFINITION 3 (INEFFECTUAL CHANGE CATEGORISATION). *An axiom $\alpha \in \text{IneffRems}(\mathcal{O}_1, \mathcal{O}_2)$ is:*

- Rewritten, *if there is a justification $\mathcal{J}$ for α with $\mathcal{J} \cap \text{Adds}(\mathcal{O}_1, \mathcal{O}_2) \neq \emptyset$, and $\alpha \models \mathcal{J}$. If $\mathcal{J} \subseteq \text{Adds}(\mathcal{O}_1, \mathcal{O}_2)$ then α is a complete rewrite, otherwise a partial rewrite.*
- Strengthened, *if there is a $\mathcal{J}$ for α with $\mathcal{J} \cap \text{EffAdds}(\mathcal{O}_1, \mathcal{O}_2) \neq \emptyset$.*

---

[1] http://krizik.felk.cvut.cz/km/owldiff/

[2] Based on DLs up to $\mathcal{SROIQ}$ [3].

[3] Specifically acyclic $\mathcal{EL}$-terminologies [7].

- Redundant, *if there is a $\mathcal{J}$ for α with $\mathcal{J} \subseteq (\mathcal{O}_1 \cap \mathcal{O}_2)$. If $\mathcal{J} \subseteq (\mathcal{O}_1 \cap \mathcal{O}_2) \cup \text{IneffAdds}(\mathcal{O}_1, \mathcal{O}_2)$ then α is an avoided redundancy.*

For axioms $\beta \in \text{IneffAdds}(\mathcal{O}_1, \mathcal{O}_2)$, replace α, $\text{Adds}(\mathcal{O}_1, \mathcal{O}_2)$, $\text{EffAdds}(\mathcal{O}_1, \mathcal{O}_2)$ and $\text{IneffAdds}(\mathcal{O}_1, \mathcal{O}_2)$ with β, $\text{Rems}(\mathcal{O}_1, \mathcal{O}_2)$, $\text{EffRems}(\mathcal{O}_1, \mathcal{O}_2)$ and $\text{IneffRems}(\mathcal{O}_1, \mathcal{O}_2)$ respectively. In $\text{IneffAdds}(\mathcal{O}_1, \mathcal{O}_2)$ the label for the criteria of Strengthened *axioms changes to* Weakened *axioms.*

The term 'avoided redundancy' is used in the sense that, given a removed avoided redundancy $\alpha \in \mathcal{O}_1$, it would have been a redundancy in $\mathcal{O}_2$ if not removed. The ineffectual axiom categorisation returns possibly overlapping sets of axioms, as demonstrated in Section 3.3. Also we note that these categories are exhaustive, in such a way that for any axiom we have that it implies at least one of the defined categories. Consider an axiom α and ontologies $\mathcal{O}_1$ and $\mathcal{O}_2$, with $\alpha \in \mathcal{O}_1$ but $\alpha \notin \mathcal{O}_2$, and $\mathcal{O}_2 \models \alpha$. Then there must be a justification $\mathcal{J} \subseteq \mathcal{O}_2$ for α. If we have that $\mathcal{J} \subseteq (\mathcal{O}_1 \cap \mathcal{O}_2) \cup \text{IneffAdds}(\mathcal{O}_1, \mathcal{O}_2)$, then α is redundant, otherwise if we have that $\mathcal{J} \cap \text{EffAdds}(\mathcal{O}_1, \mathcal{O}_2) \neq \emptyset$, then α is strengthened.

The effectual changes are categorised according to the following definition:

DEFINITION 4 (EFFECTUAL CHANGE CATEGORISATION). *An axiom $\beta \in \text{EffAdds}(\mathcal{O}_1, \mathcal{O}_2)$ is categorised as follows:*

- *If $\widetilde{\beta} \subseteq \widetilde{\mathcal{O}}_1$, β is an element of:*
  - $\text{Strgth}(\mathcal{O}_1, \mathcal{O}_2)$, *if there exists an axiom $\alpha \in \text{Rems}(\mathcal{O}_1, \mathcal{O}_2)$ s.t. $\beta \models \alpha$.*
  - $\text{PAdd}(\mathcal{O}_1, \mathcal{O}_2)$, *otherwise, i.e., if there is no $\alpha \in \mathcal{O}_1$ s.t. $\beta \models \alpha$.*
- *If $\widetilde{\beta} \nsubseteq \widetilde{\mathcal{O}}_1$, let $T := \widetilde{\beta} \setminus \widetilde{\mathcal{O}}_1$. Then β is an element of:*
  - $\text{StrgthNT}(\mathcal{O}_1, \mathcal{O}_2)$, *if there exists an axiom $\alpha \in \text{Rems}(\mathcal{O}_1, \mathcal{O}_2)$ s.t. $\beta \models \alpha$.*
  - $\text{NewDesc}(\mathcal{O}_1, \mathcal{O}_2)$, *if we have that $\bot\text{-}mod(T, \{\beta\}) \neq \emptyset$.*
  - $\text{PAddNT}(\mathcal{O}_1, \mathcal{O}_2)$, *otherwise, i.e., if we have that $\beta \notin \text{NewDesc}(\mathcal{O}_1, \mathcal{O}_2)$ and there is no $\alpha \in \mathcal{O}_1$ s.t. $\beta \models \alpha$.*

$\text{Strgth}(\mathcal{O}_1, \mathcal{O}_2)$ represents strengthenings from $\mathcal{O}_1$ to $\mathcal{O}_2$, $\text{PAdd}(\mathcal{O}_1, \mathcal{O}_2)$ pure additions, and $\text{NewDesc}(\mathcal{O}_1, \mathcal{O}_2)$ new descriptions. Categories ending in 'NT' represent axioms that use new terms. For axioms $\alpha \in \text{EffRems}(\mathcal{O}_1, \mathcal{O}_2)$ replace β, $\mathcal{O}_1$, and $\text{Rems}(\mathcal{O}_1, \mathcal{O}_2)$ with α, $\mathcal{O}_2$, and $\text{Adds}(\mathcal{O}_1, \mathcal{O}_2)$, accordingly. We denote effectual removals as $\text{Weakng}(\mathcal{O}_1, \mathcal{O}_2)$ for weakenings and $\text{RetDesc}(\mathcal{O}_1, \mathcal{O}_2)$ for retired descriptions, while categories involving axioms with retired terms are followed by RT (e.g., $\text{PRemRT}(\mathcal{O}_1, \mathcal{O}_2)$ represents pure removals with retired terms).

Observe that the categories encompass two dimensions of changes; those changes involving new (or retired) terms, and changes involving shared terms between both ontologies (i.e. terms in $\widetilde{\mathcal{O}}_1 \cap \widetilde{\mathcal{O}}_2$). This duality of categories depending on the signature of axioms is illustrated in Table 2. We can see that there cannot be a strengthening which involves retired terms, or analogously a weakening involving new terms. Similarly new or retired descriptions are based on new or retired terms, accordingly.

Table 2: Effectual change categories.

Axiom terms	**Shared terms**	**New terms**	**Retired terms**
Strengthening	✓	✓	N/A
Weakening	✓	N/A	✓
Pure change	✓	✓	✓
New Description	N/A	✓	N/A
Retired Description	N/A	N/A	✓

3.3 Diff Walkthrough

In order to demonstrate the usefulness of the devised categories, let us compare ontologies $\mathcal{O}_1$ and $\mathcal{O}_2$, defined in Table 3.

Table 3: Example ontologies.

$\mathcal{O}_1$	$\mathcal{O}_2$	
$\alpha_1 : A \sqsubseteq C$	$\beta_1 : A \sqsubseteq B \sqcup C$	$\beta_9 : F \sqsubseteq G \sqcap I$
$\alpha_2 : B \sqsubseteq C$	$\beta_2 : A \sqsubseteq B$	$\beta_{10} : K \sqsubseteq \exists r.F$
$\alpha_3 : E \equiv D$	$\beta_3 : B \sqsubseteq C$	$\beta_{11} : D \sqsubseteq F \sqcap \exists s.A$
$\alpha_4 : D \sqsubseteq F$	$\beta_4 : E \sqsubseteq D$	$\beta_{12} : D \sqsubseteq F \sqcap \exists p.\top$
$\alpha_5 : F \sqsubseteq G$	$\beta_5 : D \sqsubseteq E$	$\beta_{13} : B \sqsubseteq K$
$\alpha_6 : G \sqsubseteq H \sqcap \exists s.H$	$\beta_6 : E \sqsubseteq B \sqcup \exists r.C$	
$\alpha_7 : F \sqsubseteq I$	$\beta_7 : D \sqsubseteq E \sqcup G$	
$\alpha_8 : F \sqsubseteq G \sqcap I \sqcap J$	$\beta_8 : G \sqsubseteq \exists s.H \sqcap H$	

From $\mathcal{O}_1$ and $\mathcal{O}_2$ we have the following structural differences:

◇ $\text{Adds}(\mathcal{O}_1, \mathcal{O}_2) = \{\beta_1, \beta_2, \beta_4, \beta_5, \beta_6, \beta_7, \beta_9, \beta_{10}, \beta_{11}, \beta_{12}, \beta_{13}\}$

◇ $\text{Rems}(\mathcal{O}_1, \mathcal{O}_2) = \{\alpha_1, \alpha_3, \alpha_4, \alpha_5, \alpha_7, \alpha_8\}$

Note that α_6 is not syntactically equal to β_8 ($\alpha_6 \neq \beta_8$), however they are structurally equivalent ($\alpha_6 \equiv_s \beta_8$). Therefore these axioms are not reported as changes. Given the sets of structural additions and removals from $\mathcal{O}_1$ to $\mathcal{O}_2$ we have that:

◇ $\text{EffAdds}(\mathcal{O}_1, \mathcal{O}_2) = \{\beta_2, \beta_6, \beta_{10}, \beta_{11}, \beta_{12}, \beta_{13}\}$

◇ $\text{EffRems}(\mathcal{O}_1, \mathcal{O}_2) = \{\alpha_8\}$

◇ $\text{IneffAdds}(\mathcal{O}_1, \mathcal{O}_2) = \{\beta_1, \beta_4, \beta_5, \beta_7, \beta_9\}$

◇ $\text{IneffRems}(\mathcal{O}_1, \mathcal{O}_2) = \{\alpha_1, \alpha_3, \alpha_4, \alpha_5, \alpha_7\}$

There are several ineffectual changes in the change set, while effectual changes are mostly additions (and a single removal). The

Table 1: Desiderata of ontology diffing approaches.

Properties	**Structural Diff**	**ContentCVS**	**CEX**	**OWLDiff**[1]	**PROMPTDIFF**	**Swoop Diff**
			Difference Detection			
Syntactic analysis	✓	✓	✗	✓	✓	✓
Semantic analysis	✗	✓	✓	✓	✗	✗
Effectively computable	✓	✓	✗	✓	✓	✓
OWL 2 adequacy	✓	✓	✗	✓	✗	✓
			Difference Output			
Axiom-based	✓	✓	✓	✓	✗	✓
Term-based	✗	✗	✓	✗	✓	✓
Change characterisation	✗	✗	✗	✗	✗	✗

Table 4: Categorisation of axioms in diff($\mathcal{O}_1$, $\mathcal{O}_2$).

Removals	Axioms	Pairing
Rewritten (I)	α_3	$\{\beta_4, \beta_5\}$
Strengthened (I)	α_1	$\{\beta_2, \beta_3\}$
	α_4	$\{\beta_{11}\}, \{\beta_{12}\}$
Redundant (I)	α_1	$\{\beta_2, \beta_3\}, \{\beta_1, \beta_3\}$
	α_3	$\{\beta_4, \beta_5\}$
	α_5, α_7	$\{\beta_9\}$
WeakeningRT	α_8	of $\beta_9 (\alpha_8 \models \beta_9 \wedge J \notin \widetilde{\mathcal{O}}_2)$
Additions	**Axioms**	**Pairing**
Rewritten (I)	β_9	$\{\alpha_5, \alpha_7\}$
Weakened (I)	β_9	$\{\alpha_8\}$
Redundant (I)	β_1	$\{\alpha_1\}$
	β_4, β_5	$\{\alpha_3\}$
	β_7	$\{\alpha_3\}, \{\alpha_4, \alpha_5\}$
	β_9	$\{\alpha_5, \alpha_7\}$
Strenthening	β_{11}	of α_4 $(\beta_{11} \models \alpha_4)$
StrentheningNT	β_{12}	of α_4 $(\beta_{12} \models \alpha_4 \wedge p \notin \widetilde{\mathcal{O}}_1)$
NewDescription	β_{10}	$K \notin \widetilde{\mathcal{O}}_1 \wedge \bot\text{-}mod(\{K\}, \{\beta_{10}\}) \neq \emptyset$
PureAddition	β_2	$\widetilde{\beta_2} \subseteq \widetilde{\mathcal{O}}_1 \wedge \beta_2 \notin \text{NewDesc}(\mathcal{O}_1, \mathcal{O}_2)$ $\wedge \nexists \alpha \in \mathcal{O}_1$ s.t. $\beta_2 \models \alpha$
PureAdditionNT	β_6	$K \notin \widetilde{\mathcal{O}}_1 \wedge \beta_6 \notin \text{NewDesc}(\mathcal{O}_1, \mathcal{O}_2)$ $\wedge \nexists \alpha \in \mathcal{O}_1$ s.t. $\beta_6 \models \alpha$
	β_{13}	$r \notin \widetilde{\mathcal{O}}_1 \wedge \beta_{13} \notin \text{NewDesc}(\mathcal{O}_1, \mathcal{O}_2)$ $\wedge \nexists \alpha \in \mathcal{O}_1$ s.t. $\beta_{13} \models \alpha$

changes are categorised as shown in Table 4, where ineffectual categories are labeled with (I).

Let us consider two ineffectual additions; β_9 is a rewrite of $\{\alpha_7, \alpha_5\}$, as well as an avoided redundancy (i.e., had it been added to $\mathcal{O}_1$ it would be redundant). The axiom is also weakened, due to α_8. This may seem like an unintentional change, since now we face a loss of information regarding J, which is no longer mentioned in $\mathcal{O}_2$. Such a change may be worth revising. The axiom β_1 is redundant, since we have from $\mathcal{O}_1$ that $A \sqsubseteq C$, which is also entailed from $\mathcal{O}_2$. Therefore the user can dispose of this axiom.

Bear in mind that the existence of a rewritten axiom from $\mathcal{O}_1$ to $\mathcal{O}_2$ does not imply that the same holds in the opposite direction. This is applicable to all categories. Also we can have that an axiom is in more than one category. Consider axiom α_1; a justification $\mathcal{J}_1$ for α_1 is $\mathcal{J}_1 = \{\beta_2, \beta_3\}$, which indicates a strengthening (since we have that $\beta_2 \in \text{EffAdds}(\mathcal{O}_1, \mathcal{O}_2)$), as well as a redundancy ($\beta_3 \in \mathcal{O}_1 \cap \mathcal{O}_2$). Another justification $\mathcal{J}_2 = \{\beta_1, \beta_3\}$ indicates a redundancy; $\beta_1 \in \text{IneffAdds}(\mathcal{O}_1, \mathcal{O}_2)$.

In terms of effectual changes there is only one removal, and six additions. The effectual removal (α_8) represents a weakening of β_9 with retired terms (J is not mentioned in $\mathcal{O}_2$). In the analysis of the ineffectual changes it was already noted that axiom α_8 should be revised. The pure additions appear to be adjustments to the class hierarchy, some associated with new terms in $\mathcal{O}_2$. Both axioms β_{11} and β_{12} are strengthenings of α_4, which suggests that they could be merged, especially since there is intra-axiom redundancy. Finally there is a new term K in $\mathcal{O}_2$ being described via axiom β_{10}.

Generally speaking, with such a categorisation it becomes conceivably more intuitive to navigate and understand sets of changes. In addition to this, we gathered from the analysis of ineffectual changes useful information about the changes between $\mathcal{O}_1$ and $\mathcal{O}_2$, e.g., that axiom α_4 is strenthened in two distinct, yet partially superfluous axioms (β_{11} and β_{12}). Similarly we discover that axiom β_9 is weakened, from α_8, which should be reconsidered as we now have that $\mathcal{O}_2 \not\models F \sqsubseteq J$ (J becoming a retired term).

4. CASE STUDY

In order to evaluate our approach to ontology diffing, we carried out a study of the NCIt corpus. We extracted all pairwise, consecutive diffs between NCIt versions, and show that all categories are instantiated throughout the corpus.

The NCIt archive[4] contains 88 versions of the ontology in OWL format, freely downloadable from the web. Two of these versions were unparsable (releases 05.03F and 05.04d) with the OWL API,[5] and consequently Protégé.[6] The experiment machine is an Intel Xeon Quad-Core 3.20GHz, with 12Gb DDR3 RAM dedicated to the Java Virtual Machine (JVM v1.5). The system runs Mac OS X 10.6.7, and all tests were run using the OWL API (v3.1). All gathered test data is available from `http://owl.cs.manchester.ac.uk/ncit`, a part of it is published on Google Public Data Explorer,[7] and can be visualised at `http://bit.ly/leZ6fM`.

[4] http://evs.nci.nih.gov/ftp1/NCI_Thesaurus
[5] http://owlapi.sourceforge.net/
[6] http://protege.stanford.edu/
[7] http://www.google.com/publicdata/home

Figure 1: Breakdown of effectual vs ineffectual removals (logarithmic scale, number of axioms).

Figure 2: Breakdown of effectual vs ineffectual additions (logarithmic scale, number of axioms).

Table 5: Sum of the results of diff($\mathcal{O}_i$, $\mathcal{O}_{i+1}$), for $1 \leq i \leq 86$.

Change type		Additions			Removals		
Effectual	*Axiom terms*	*Strengthening*	*New Description*	*Pure Addition*	*Weakening*	*Retired Description*	*Pure Removal*
	Shared terms	4,649	N/A	36,499	1,122	N/A	25,022
	New terms	4,948	170,095	69,333	N/A	N/A	N/A
	Retired terms	N/A	N/A	N/A	508	52,229	23,634
Ineffectual		*Rewrite*	*Weakened*	*Redundant*	*Rewrite*	*Strengthened*	*Redundant*
		115	8,576	4,186	114	30,370	8,012

4.1 Effectual vs Ineffectual Changes

The logical difference throughout the NCIt time-line consists of an average of 87% effectual changes, while the remaining are ineffectual (see Figures 1 and 2 and Table 5). There are, however, cases where the number of effectual and ineffectual changes is more balanced, such as $\mathcal{O}_{24}$ with 48% effectual changes, or $\mathcal{O}_{29}$ and $\mathcal{O}_{30}$ with 52% effectual changes out of all changes. Note that in $\mathcal{O}_{14}$ and $\mathcal{O}_{16}$ the number of effectual changes is (unusually) well above the number of ineffectual changes. In these two NCIt versions there is an annotation property and a data property both named "code", which in the version of the OWL API used results in the parsing of only data property assertions.[8]

Throughout the NCIt study we have excluded a class of ineffectual changes: changes to annotations. Since there are ontologies whose major focus is the annotations, as the NCIt, these represent a topic of study in themselves. E.g., in the NCIt the average proportion of axiomatic changes throughout the corpus is 15%, while the remaining are annotation changes. But for the purposes of this paper we focus on axiom changes only.

4.2 Ineffectual Changes

Throughout the corpus there is a high number of ineffectual removals, reaching values of 93% in $\mathcal{O}_{29}$ or 97% in $\mathcal{O}_{16}$, and with an average of 35% of all removals (see Figure 1). Out of these ineffectual removals 92% turned out to be strengthened axioms, which indicates a continuous refining of information throughout the corpus. E.g. $\mathcal{O}_{27}$ has 3,104 strengthened axioms out of 3,843 removals. There is a high number of removed redundancies as well, constituting 49% of ineffectual removals. This tells us that there is some pruning of redundant information going on in the corpus. Taking into account that only 23% of these removed redundancies are avoided redundancies, we see that there is some redundancy removal throughout. On average 5% of additions are ineffectual (see Figure 2), yet there are some high values such as 61% in $\mathcal{O}_{24}$. Among these, 73% are added redundancies, and 82% are weakened axioms. The latter occur typically due to adjustments in the class hierarchy. Despite being a high percentage, the number of ineffectual additions is generally low (see Table 5).

We also identified a number of rewrites in the corpus. Particularly in $\mathcal{O}_{33}$, there are 227 rewritten axioms. Upon inspecting the rewritten axioms, we noticed that these changes are not only syntactic but also trivial and easily detected. While ideally the underlying structural diff would not include these, at least with our categorisation and alignment with source axioms, it is easy to spot and recognize the triviality. In this version we also see a number of redundancies above average, with 202 removed redundancies and 157 added. Clearly certain ineffectual changes are in fact "refactorings", albeit in the case of strengthened and weakened axioms the refactoring would have to be of a set of axioms rather than a single axiom. Thus a strengthened axiom does not necessarily mean strengthening of the ontology since the change might either introduce a redundancy or redistribute information from other axioms. Consider an ontology $\mathcal{O}_1 = \{\alpha_1 : A \sqsubseteq B, \alpha_2 : A \sqsubseteq C\}$, and a change of α_1 into $A \sqsubseteq B \sqcap C$. The axiom α_1 was strengthened, but the resulting ontology $\mathcal{O}_2 = \{\alpha_1 : A \sqsubseteq B \sqcap C, \alpha_2 : A \sqsubseteq C\}$ was not. However, if we change $\alpha_2 \in \mathcal{O}_2$ into $A \sqsubseteq C \sqcap D$, then we can say both the axiom α_2 and the ontology $\mathcal{O}_2$ are strengthened.

We noted a somewhat high number of added redundancies in the corpus, with more incidence up until $\mathcal{O}_8$ (average of 166 added redundancies per comparison). However there are some outliars in the rest of the corpus, such as $\mathcal{O}_{35}$ with 174 added redundant axioms. The highest value found is in $\mathcal{O}_{17}$, where 482 redundant axioms were added. Upon investigating these axioms, we found that such added redundancies are, in many cases, entailments from previous versions. These entailments are those derived from the transitivity of the subclass relationship, but are not atomic subsumptions e.g. $\mathcal{O}_1 = \{\alpha_1 : A \sqsubseteq \exists r.B, \alpha_2 : C \sqsubseteq A\}$, $\mathcal{O}_2 = \{\alpha_1, \alpha_2, \alpha_3 : C \sqsubseteq \exists r.B\}$. From the example we see that α_3 is redundant; $C \sqsubseteq A$ suffices for $C \sqsubseteq \exists r.B$ to hold, yet entailments of this form constitute the majority of added redundancies.

[8]In turn, this lead to a mass-generation of individuals.

In cases where the number of ineffectual changes is quite high (e.g., $\mathcal{O}_{24}$ where 52% of changes are ineffectual, $\mathcal{O}_{27}$, $\mathcal{O}_{29}$ and $\mathcal{O}_{30}$ with 48% each) note that semantic diffs would significantly understate the amount of activity performed. While structural diff captures this, it does not analyse the logical impact of such changes.

4.3 Effectual Changes

We see in Figures 1 and 2 that the number of effectual changes is typically higher than the number of ineffectual changes. There are more additions than removals throughout the corpus, with an average of 60% additions versus 40% removals, which is hardly surprising for a constantly evolving ontology. Among the categories of effectual changes we discovered that the majority of these are new and retired descriptions. In terms of effectual additions the average of new descriptions is 60%, while retired descriptions average 51% of effectual removals. The highest values of new descriptions are in $\mathcal{O}_{14}$ (40,417), $\mathcal{O}_{16}$ (43,522) and $\mathcal{O}_{6}$ (18,912). This high number of new descriptions is unsurprising, as the terminology keeps increasing. We see in $\mathcal{O}_{15}$ and $\mathcal{O}_{6}$ high values of retired descriptions, with 39,584 in $\mathcal{O}_{15}$ and 11,835 in $\mathcal{O}_{6}$. This does not prove that such concepts were deleted, it could instead suggest a high number of concept renamings. Bear in mind that the number of changes in $\mathcal{O}_{14}$, $\mathcal{O}_{16}$, and adjacent versions is distorted by the parsing anomaly discussed in Section 4.1.

Strengthenings average around 4% of all additions, indicating refinements of concepts with additional constraints. There are cases where the number of strengthenings is high, such as $\mathcal{O}_{27}$ which has 142 with new terms and 1065 without. Also in $\mathcal{O}_{29}$ there are 102 strengthenings with new terms, and 891 without. It is natural that upon introducing new terms, others need to be re-described, thus explaining the strenghtenings with new terms.

Pure additions account for 37% of all additions, divided between 24% of additions with new terms and 13% without. The highest number of pure additions with new terms is in $\mathcal{O}_{25}$, with 11,746 axioms. This version also contains the most pure removals with retired terms, amounting to 10,645 axioms. With respect to pure additions with shared terms $\mathcal{O}_{80}$ contains the most, amounting to 4,489 axioms. Coincidently this same same version also has the highest number of pure removals with shared terms, with a total of 4,583 such axioms. Typically pure changes with shared terms suggest adjustments to the class hierarchy, while pure additions involving new terms point to the insertion of said terms and subsequent re-adjustment of the hierarchy accordingly.

The average of pure removals throughout the corpus is 47%, split between 23% with retired terms and 24% without. There are not as many weakenings in the corpus as there are strengthenings. This tells us that typically there is not much reduction of information from version to version. The average of weakenings (with or without retired terms) throughout is below 2% of all removals, with the highest value being 69% (739) in $\mathcal{O}_{24}$. The next version, $\mathcal{O}_{25}$, contains the highest number of weakenings with retired terms (508).

Table 5 demonstrates that all effectual categories are instantiated in the NCIt corpus. For instance the diff between versions $\mathcal{O}_{32}$ and $\mathcal{O}_{33}$ contains axioms in nearly all categories, with the exception of weakenings with retired terms.

5. DISCUSSION AND OUTLOOK

The diachronic study of the NCIt revealed that all the categories of changes occur throughout the corpus, providing indications as to the impact of changes. We showed that such categorisation of change sets is useful for change analysis, with particular benefits for division of labour by ontology engineers. By means of this categorisation we can group changes according to their impact, allowing users to shift their attention to specific types of changes, rather than going through a change set while inspecting both ontologies. With our correspondence of changes between ontologies we can show the changed axioms and what they are a change of. Consequently, by analysing changes in this way there is no need for constantly having to inspect ontologies manually. As such, we can support users in understanding the impact of their changes (or lack thereof), and refine these before publishing newer versions.

We found that ineffectual changes account for a significant amount of changes throughout the NCIt. Despite the fact that semantic diffs ignore these changes in their output, we show that they provide helpful modelling insights, and thus are worth examining. For instance we discovered a high number of redundant axioms in the NCIt, some of which could be disposed of. Also we found a number of structurally distinct ineffectual changes that are clearly neglectable: the rewrites in the NCIt. These indicate the need for improvement of the underlying diff. In general the inspection of ineffectual changes is helpful to prevent, e.g., re-doing work or introducing redundancy. Relying on semantic diffs one would be missing out on these meaningful ineffectual changes, which in turn could help users recognize the impact of certain types of change.

The next step in our study is to evaluate the diff tool with users. In particular we expect to confirm that the categorisation helps users in understanding changes between ontologies. In terms of further analysis of the NCIt corpus we intend to inspect the history of axioms, as in checking the progress of each axiom throughout the corpus since it was introduced (e.g., changes in constructors or strengthenings that the axiom went through). Another future survey involves checking for patterns of change throughout the corpus, e.g., if all strengthenings exhibit a common form.

6. REFERENCES

[1] B. Cuenca Grau, I. Horrocks, Y. Kazakov, and U. Sattler. Modular reuse of ontologies: Theory and practice. *J. of Artificial Intelligence Research*, 31:273–318, 2008.

[2] B. Cuenca Grau, I. Horrocks, B. Motik, B. Parsia, P. Patel-Schneider, and U. Sattler. OWL 2: The next step for OWL. *J. of Web Semantics*, 2008.

[3] I. Horrocks, O. Kutz, and U. Sattler. The even more irresistible $\mathcal{SROIQ}$. In *Proc. of KR-06*, pages 57–67, 2006.

[4] E. Jiménez-Ruiz, B. Cuenca Grau, I. Horrocks, and R. Berlanga Llavori. Supporting concurrent ontology development: Framework, algorithms and tool. *Data and Knowledge Engineering*, 70(1):146–164, 2011.

[5] A. Kalyanpur, B. Parsia, M. Horridge, and E. Sirin. Finding all justifications of OWL DL entailments. In *Proc. of ISWC/ASWC*, 2007.

[6] A. Kalyanpur, B. Parsia, E. Sirin, B. Cuenca Grau, and J. Hendler. Swoop: A Web ontology editing browser. *J. of Web Semantics*, 4(2):144–153, 2006.

[7] B. Konev, D. Walther, and F. Wolter. The logical difference problem for description logic terminologies. In *IJCAR-08*, volume 5195 of *LNCS*, 2008.

[8] B. Motik, P. Patel-Schneider, and B. Parsia. *OWL 2 Web Ontology Language: Structural Specification and Functional-Style Syntax*. W3C Cand. Rec., 11 June 2009. http://www.w3.org/TR/2009/CR-owl2-syntax-20090611/.

[9] N. F. Noy and M. A. Musen. PROMPTDIFF: A fixed-point algorithm for comparing ontology versions. In *Proc. of AAAI-02*, pages 744–750, 2002.

ReDRIVE: Result-Driven Database Exploration through Recommendations

Marina Drosou*
Computer Science Department
University of Ioannina, Greece
mdrosou@cs.uoi.gr

Evaggelia Pitoura
Computer Science Department
University of Ioannina, Greece
pitoura@cs.uoi.gr

ABSTRACT

Typically, users interact with database systems by formulating queries. However, many times users do not have a clear understanding of their information needs or the exact content of the database, thus, their queries are of an exploratory nature. In this paper, we propose assisting users in database exploration by recommending to them additional items that are highly related with the items in the result of their original query. Such items are computed based on the most interesting sets of attribute values (or faSets) that appear in the result of the original user query. The interestingness of a faSet is defined based on its frequency both in the query result and in the database instance. Database frequency estimations rely on a novel approach that employs an ϵ-tolerance closed rare faSets representation. We report evaluation results of the efficiency and effectiveness of our approach on both real and synthetic datasets.

Categories and Subject Descriptors

H.3.3 [**Information Storage and Retrieval**]: Information Search and Retrieval—*Query formulation, Search process*

General Terms

Algorithms, Experimentation, Design, Performance

1. INTRODUCTION

Typically, users interact with a database system by formulating queries. This interaction mode assumes that users are to some extent familiar with the content of the database and also have a clear understanding of their information needs. However, as databases get larger and become accessible to a more diverse and less technically-oriented audience, exploration or recommendation style database interactions seem attractive and useful.

A step towards this direction is offered by facet queries that provide a form of navigational search, where users restrict their results by selecting interesting facets of the original results (e.g., [11]). With facet search, users start with a general query and progressively narrow its results down to a specific item. Other related research includes addressing the *many-* or *empty-* answers problems. Approaches to the many-answers problem range from reformulating the original query so as to restrict the size of its result (for example, by adding additional constraints to it (e.g., [15]) to automatically ranking the query results and presenting to the user only the top-k most highly ranked among them (e.g., [7]). The empty-answers problem is commonly handled by relaxing the original query (e.g., [12]).

In this paper, we propose a novel exploration mode of interaction: we present to the users additional items which, although not part of the answer of their original query, may be of interest to them. This way users see information that they may be unaware that exists. For instance, when asking for movies directed by F.F. Coppola, we guide exploration by recommending movies by other directors that have directed movies similar to those of F.F. Coppola, i.e., with similar characteristics, such as, genre or production year. We also consider expanding the original query with additional attributes, by finding correlations with other relations. For example, when asking for the title of a movie, we also look into its genre or other characteristics.

The computation of recommended results is based on the most interesting sets of (attribute, value) pairs, called faSets, that appear in the result of the original user query. The *interestingness* of a faSet expresses how unexpected it is to see this faSet in the result. The computation of interestingness is based on the frequency of the faSet both in the user query result and in the database instance. Since computing the frequencies of faSets in the database instance on-line has prohibitively high cost, we opt to maintain statistics that allow us to *estimate* those frequencies when needed. More specifically, we propose a novel approach that is based on storing an ϵ-tolerance closed rare faSets representation as a summary of such frequencies and exploit these summaries to estimate the interestingness of the faSets that appear in the result of any given user query.

We also present a two-phase algorithm for computing the top-k faSets. In the first phase, the algorithm uses the precomputed statistics to set a frequency threshold that is then used to run a frequent itemset based algorithm on the result of the query. We evaluate the performance of our approach using both real and synthetic datasets.

The rest of this paper is organized as follows. Sec. 2 presents the overall framework, Sec. 3 its implementation and Sec. 4 an experimental evaluation. Finally, related work is presented in Sec. 5 and conclusions are offered in Sec. 6.

2. THE ReDRIVE FRAMEWORK

Let $\mathcal{D}$ be a relational database with n relations $\mathcal{R} = \{R_1, \ldots, R_n\}$ and $\mathcal{A}$ be the set of all attributes in $\mathcal{R}$. Without loss of generality, we assume that relation and attribute names are distinct. To locate items of interest, users pose queries.

*Supported by the research program "HRAKLEITOS II" co-funded by the European Union and National Sources.

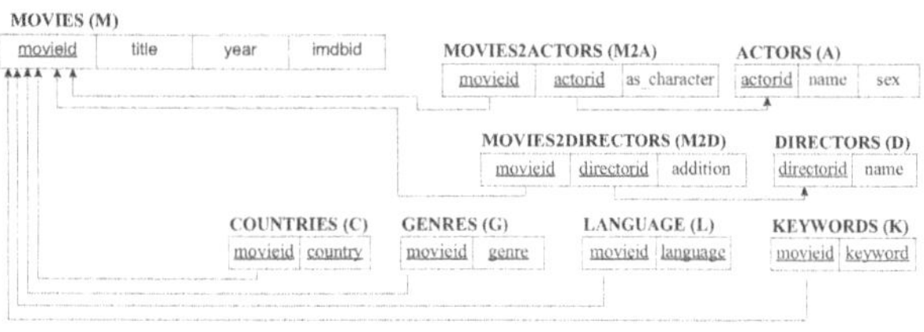

Figure 1: Movies database schema.

In particular, we consider Select-Project-Join (SPJ) queries of the following form:

SELECT $proj(Q)$
FROM $rel(Q)$
WHERE $sel(Q)$ **AND** $join(Q)$

where $rel(Q)$ is a set of relations, $sel(Q)$ is a conjunction of selection conditions, $join(Q)$ is a set of join conditions among the relations in $rel(Q)$ and $proj(Q)$ is the set of projected attributes. For simplicity, we shall focus on *equality* conditions, i.e., $sel(Q) = (A_1 = a_1) \wedge \ldots \wedge (A_m = a_m)$, $m \geq 1$, where $A_i \in \mathcal{A}$ and $a_i \in domain(A_i)$. The *result set*, $Res(Q)$, of a query Q is a relation with schema $proj(Q)$.

Since users must specify in their queries the conditions that the searched items need to satisfy, they must have a somewhat clear understanding of the information they are seeking. In this paper, we propose an exploratory way of discovering interesting information based on identifying potentially interesting pieces of information based on the initial result set and then using these pieces to explore the database further by recommending additional results to the users.

2.1 Interesting FaSets

Let us first define pieces of information in the result set:

DEFINITION 1 (FACET AND m-FASET). *A* facet *condition, or simply* facet*, is a condition of the form $(A_i = a_i)$, where $A_i \in \mathcal{A}$ and $a_i \in domain(A_i)$. An m-set of facets or m-faSet, $m \geq 1$, is a set of m facet conditions on m different attributes.*

We shall also use the term faSet when the size of the m-faSet is not of interest.

For a faSet f, we use $Att(f)$ to denote its attributes. Let t be a tuple from a set of tuples S with schema R; we say that t satisfies a faSet f, where $Att(f) \subseteq R$, if $t[A_i] = a_i$, for all facets $(A_i = a_i) \in f$. We call the percentage of tuples in S that satisfy f, *support* of f in S. In the following, we use the term faSet to mean both the conditions and the list of the associated values appearing in the conditions.

Example: Consider the movies database in Fig. 1 and the query and its corresponding result set in Fig. 2. Then {*G.genre = "Drama"*} or simply {*"Drama"*} is a 1-faSet and {*M.year = "1972"*, *G.genre = "Drama"*} or simply {*"1972"*, *"Drama"*} is a 2-faSet.

We are looking for interesting pieces of information at the granularity of a faSet: this may be the value of a single attribute (i.e., a 1-faSet) or the values of m attributes (i.e., an m-faSet).

Example: Consider the example in Fig. 2, where a user poses a query to retrieve movies directed by F.F. Coppola. {*"Drama"*} is a 1-faSet in the result that is likely to interest the user, since it is associated with many of the movies directed by F.F. Coppola. The same holds for the 2-faSet {*"1983"*, *"Drama"*}.

To define faSet relevance formally, we take an IR-based approach and rank faSets in decreasing order of their odds of being relevant to a user information need. For a user information need u_Q expressed through a query Q, let R_{u_Q} be the set of tuples that are relevant to u_Q and $\overline{R_{u_Q}}$ be the

```
SELECT D.name, M.title, M.year, G.genre
FROM D, M2D, M, Gs
WHERE D.name = "F. F. Coppola"
    AND D.directorid = M2D.directorid
    AND M2D.movieid = M.movieid
    AND M.movieid = G.movieid
```

D.name	M.title	M.year	G.genre
F. F. Coppola	The Godfather III	1990	Drama
F. F. Coppola	The Rainmake	1997	Crime
F. F. Coppola	The Godfather	1972	Drama
F. F. Coppola	Rumble Fish	1983	Drama
F. F. Coppola	The Conversation	1974	Thriller
F. F. Coppola	The Outsiders	1983	Drama
F. F. Coppola	Supernova	2000	Thriller
F. F. Coppola	Apocalypse Now	1979	Drama

Figure 2: Example query and result set.

set of tuples that are not relevant to u_Q. Then, the relevance score of a faSet f for u_Q is defined as:

$$\frac{p(R_{u_Q}|f)}{p(\overline{R_{u_Q}}|f)}$$

where $p(R_{u_Q}|f)$ (resp. $p(\overline{R_{u_Q}}|f)$) is the probability that a tuple satisfying f is relevant (resp. not relevant) to u_Q. Using the Bayes rule we get:

$$\frac{p(f|R_{u_Q})p(R_{u_Q})}{p(f|\overline{R_{u_Q}})p(\overline{R_{u_Q}})}$$

Since $p(R_{u_Q})$ and $p(\overline{R_{u_Q}})$ have the same value for all faSets, and thus do not affect their ranking, they can be ignored.

We make the assumption that all relevant to u_Q results are those that appear in $Res(Q)$, thus $p(f|R_{u_Q})$ is equal with the probability that f is satisfied by a tuple in the result set, written $p(f|Res(Q))$. Similarly, $p(f|\overline{R_{u_Q}})$ is the probability that f is satisfied by a tuple that is not relevant, that is, a tuple that does not belong to the result set. We make the logical assumption that the result set is small in comparison with the size of the database, and approximate the non-relevant tuples with all tuples in the database, that is, all tuples in the global relation, denoted by $\mathcal{D}$, with schema $\mathcal{A}$. Based on the above motivation, we provide the following definition for the relevance of a faSet:

DEFINITION 2 (INTERESTINGNESS SCORE). *Let Q be a query and f be a faSet with $Att(f) \subseteq proj(Q)$. The interestingness score, $score(f, Q)$, of f for Q is defined as:*

$$score(f, Q) = \frac{p(f|Res(Q))}{p(f|\mathcal{D})}$$

The term $p(f|Res(Q))$ is estimated by the support of f in $Res(Q)$, that is, the percentage of tuples in the result set that satisfy f. The term $p(f|\mathcal{D})$ is a global measure that does not depend on the query. It serves as an indication of how frequent the faSet is in the whole dataset, i.e., it measures the discriminative power of f.

Example: In the example in Fig. 2, *"Drama"* appears more frequently than *"Thriller"* in the result set. However, if *"Thriller"* appears only a handful of times in the database, then it would be considered more interesting than *"Drama"*.

In general, a faSet stands out when it appears more frequently in $Res(Q)$ than expected. Clearly, the $sel(Q)$ part of a query is also a faSet. Therefore, another way of interpreting the interestingness score of f for Q is as the confidence of the association rule: $sel(Q) \rightarrow f$. High confidence indicates a strong dependency of the faSet f on the selection conditions of Q.

Finally, note that in particular, for a faSet f with $Att(f) \subseteq Att(sel(Q))$, that is, for a faSet that includes only attributes whose values are specified in the selection conditions, it holds that $score(f, Q) \geq 1$, since $p(f|Res(Q)) = 1$.

Attribute Expansion: Def. 2 provides a means of ranking the various faSets that appear in the result set of a query Q and discovering the most interesting among them. However, there may be interesting faSets that include attributes not in $proj(Q)$ and thus do not appear in $Res(Q)$. For example take a query Q that just returns the titles of movies directed by F.F. Coppola. All faSets appear only once in the result set of Q. However, including for instance the relation "Countries" in $rel(Q)$ (and modifying $join(Q)$ accordingly) may disclose interesting information, e.g., that many of the movies directed by F.F. Coppola are related to Romania.

To this end, we extend the definition of interestingness to include faSets with attributes not in $proj(Q)$, by introducing an extended query Q' with the same $sel(Q')$ as the original query Q but with additional attributes in $proj(Q')$ and additional relations in $rel(Q')$.

DEFINITION 3 (EXTENDED INTERESTINGNESS SCORE). *Let Q be a query and f be a faSet with $Att(f) \subseteq \mathcal{A}$. The interestingness score of f for Q is equal to:*

$$score(f, Q) = \frac{p(f|Res(Q'))}{p(f|\mathcal{D})}$$

where Q' is an SPJ query with $proj(Q') = proj(Q) \cup Att(f)$, $rel(Q') = rel(Q) \cup \{R' \mid A_i \in R', \text{for } A_i \in Att(f)\}$, $sel(Q') = sel(Q)$ and $join(Q') = join(Q) \wedge$ (joins with $\{R' \mid A_i \in R', \text{for } A_i \in Att(f)\}$).

2.2 Exploratory Queries

Besides locating interesting faSets, we also use interesting faSets to discover additional pieces of data that are potentially related to the user needs. In particular, we aim at constructing exploratory queries that retrieve results strongly correlated with those of the original user query Q by replacing the selection conditions, $sel(Q)$, of Q with related ones. Recall that a high interestingness score for f means that the confidence of $sel(Q) \rightarrow f$ is high, indicating replacing $sel(Q)$ with f, since $sel(Q)$ seems to impose f.

For example, by replacing $sel(Q)$ of Q in Fig. 2 with its interesting faSet {*"Drama"*}, we get the exploratory query:

```
SELECT D.name
FROM D, M2D, M, G
WHERE G.genre = 'Drama'
 AND D.directorid = M2D.directorid
 AND M2D.movieid = M.movieid
 AND M.movieid = G.movieid
```

which retrieves other directors that have also directed drama movies, which is an interesting value appearing in the original query result set.

DEFINITION 4 (EXPLORATORY QUERY). *Let Q be a user query and f be an interesting faSet for Q. The exploratory query $\hat{Q}$ that uses f is an SPJ query with $proj(\hat{Q}) = Attr(sel(Q))$, $rel(\hat{Q}) = rel(Q) \cup \{R' \mid A_i \in R', \text{for } A_i \in Att(f)\}$, $sel(\hat{Q}) = f \wedge \neg\, sel(Q)$ and $join(\hat{Q}) = join(Q) \wedge$ (joins with $\{R' \mid A_i \in R', \text{for } A_i \in Att(f)\}$).*

Then, interesting faSets for the exploratory $\hat{Q}$ are recommended to the user. Clearly, one can use the interesting faSets in the results of an exploratory query to construct other exploratory queries. This way, users may start with an initial query Q and gradually discover other interesting information in the database through results attained by applying exploratory queries progressively. ions.

Framework Overview: In summary, ReDRIVE database exploration works as follows. Given a query Q, the top-k most interesting faSets for Q are computed and presented to the users. Such faSets may be either interesting pieces (sub-tuples) of the tuples in the result set of Q or extended tuples that include additional attributes not in the original result. Interesting faSets are further used to construct exploratory queries that lead to discovering additional information related to the initial user query. This process may be repeated for each exploratory query.

3. TOP-K FASETS COMPUTATION

In this section, we present algorithms for finding interesting faSets. In particular, first, we present an approach to maintaining statistics for estimating $p(f|\mathcal{D})$ for each faSet f. Then, we present a two-phase algorithm for computing the top-k most interesting faSets for a query Q. Proofs omitted can be found in [9].

3.1 Estimation of $p(f|\mathcal{D})$

To compute the interestingness of a faSet f for a query Q according to Def. 2 (resp. Def. 3), we need to compute two quantities: $p(f|Res(Q))$ (resp. $p(f|Res(Q'))$) and $p(f|\mathcal{D})$. Whereas $p(f|Res(Q))$ (resp. $p(f|Res(Q'))$) is different for each Q, and thus needs to be computed on-line, $p(f|\mathcal{D})$ is the same for all user queries. The straightforward approach would be to also compute $p(f|\mathcal{D})$ on-line for each query Q, by counting for each examined faSet f the number of database tuples that satisfy it. Given the large number of such faSets and the size of the database, the cost of such computations may become prohibitively expensive. We propose pre-computing and storing some form of information that will allow us to estimate $p(f|\mathcal{D})$, thus avoiding such on-line computations. Next, we discuss available options.

Let m_{max} be the maximum number of projected attributes of any user query, i.e., $m_{max} = |\mathcal{A}|$. An exhaustive approach would be to generate all possible faSets of size up to m_{max} and pre-compute their support in $\mathcal{D}$. Such an approach, however, is infeasible even for small databases due to the exponential number of possible faSets.

A first approach is to pre-compute and store the support of all 1-faSets in $\mathcal{D}$. Then, assuming that facet conditions are satisfied independently from each other, the support of a higher-order m-faSet is equal to:

$$p(f|\mathcal{D}) = p(\{A_1 = a_1, \ldots, A_m = a_m\}|\mathcal{D}) = \prod_{i=1}^{m} p(\{A_i = a_i\}|\mathcal{D})$$

This approach requires maintaining information for a relatively small number of faSets, i.e., $\sum_{A_i \in \mathcal{A}} |domain(A_i)|$ faSets. However, the independence assumption is unrealistic in real-world applications.

Now, let us assume that we maintain the support of all faSets up to size ℓ. In this case, we can attain a more accurate estimation of the support of a high-order m-faSet f, $m > \ell$, using a more sophisticated method such as Iterative Proportional Fitting (IPF) [4] used in [15]. The supports of low-order faSets provide some knowledge for the distribution of the supports of high-order faSets. IPF is based on the Principle of Maximum Entropy, which states that, since there is no reason to bias the estimated distribution towards any specific form, then the estimation should be as close to the uniform distribution as possible. The maximum entropy criterion smooths the estimated distribution. This may lead to the loss of interesting information. Consider for example that the faSets {*G.genre* = *"Sci-Fi"*}, {*M.year* = *"2000"*}, {*M.year* = *"2005"*} have similar supports, while the supports of {*G.genre* = *"Sci-Fi"*, *M.year* = *"2000"*} and {*G.genre* = *"Sci-Fi"*, *M.year* = *"2005"*} differ a lot. IPF (for $\ell = 1$) will estimate similar values for these two faSets.

Maintaining ϵ-Tolerance Closed Rare FaSets.

We propose a different form of statistics aiming at capturing fluctuations in the support of related faSets. To do this, we extend the notion of δ-tolerance frequent itemsets [8] and define ϵ-tolerance closed rare faSets.

Preliminaries: In data mining, the term *itemset* refers to a set of items. An itemset is said to be *frequent* in a dataset if its frequency is above a specific threshold. Otherwise it is called *rare*. Clearly, an m-faSet is an itemset whose items are facets. An itemset $\{A_1 = a_1, \ldots, A_m = a_m\}$ appears in exactly the same set of tuples that satisfy the m-faSet $f = \{A_1 = a_1, \ldots, A_m = a_m\}$. Therefore, we say that a faSet f is *frequent* (resp. *rare* (RF)) for a set of tuples S if its support in S is above (resp. below) a specific threshold. Also, we define a faSet f to be *closed rare* (CRF) for S if it is rare and has no proper subset f', $f' \subset f$, such that, f' has the same support as f in S. A faSet f is *minimal rare* (MRF) for S, if it is rare and has no subset f' such that f' is rare for S.

Statistics based on ϵ-tolerance: Maintaining the support of a number of representative faSets can assist us in estimating the support of a given faSet f. Generally, faSets that appear frequently in the database $\mathcal{D}$ are not expected to be interesting, even if they appear often in the result of user queries, since this is expected. Therefore, it is useful to maintain information about the support of rare faSets in $\mathcal{D}$. We use $count(f, S)$ to denote the absolute number of appearances of a faSet f in a set of tuples S.

If we maintain the MRFs, we can derive all corresponding RFs but not their actual support, while if we keep the CRFs we can retrieve these supports as well. However, the number of $CRFs$ is in practice very large, since any RF that has a distinct support is a CRF. Thus, our goal is to store a tunable amount of rare faSets from which we will be able to retrieve a bounded estimation of the support of a given faSet in the database. This is achieved by relaxing the definition of CRFs to maintain only those RFs whose support differs from their rare subsets based on a threshold ϵ. In particular, we define *ϵ-tolerance closed rare faSets* (ϵ-CRFs) as follows:

DEFINITION 5 (ϵ-CRF). *A faSet f is called ϵ-CRF for a set of tuples S, if and only if, it is rare for S and it has no proper immediate rare subset f', i.e., $|f'| = |f| - 1$, such that, $count(f', S) < (1 + \epsilon)\ count(f, S)$, where $\epsilon \geq 0$.*

Intuitively, a rare faSet f is an ϵ-CRF if, even if we increase its count by a constant ϵ, all its subsets still have a larger frequency than f. This means that f has a different frequency from all its subsets and cannot be estimated (or represented) by any of them.

Let us assume that a set of ϵ-CRFs is maintained for some value of ϵ. We denote this set C. An RF f either belongs to C or not. If $f \in C$, then the support of f is stored and its count is readily available. If not, then, according to Def. 5, there is some subset of f that belongs to C whose support is close to that of f. We use $C(f)$ to denote the faSet in C that is the most suitable one to estimate the count of f, i.e., the largest subset of f in C. The following lemma holds:

LEMMA 1. *Let C be a set of ϵ-CRFs for a set of tuples S and f be a faSet, $f \notin C$. Then, there exists f', $f' \in C$, such that, $count(f', S) \leq \phi\ count(f, S)$, where $\phi = (1 + \epsilon)^{(|f|-|f'|)}$.*

To provide estimations, each ϵ-CRF is stored along with its *frequency extension* defined as follows:

DEFINITION 6 (FREQUENCY EXTENSION). *Let C be a set of ϵ-CRFs for a set of tuples S and f be a faSet in C. Let also $\mathcal{X}(f)$ be the set of all RFs represented in C by f. Then, $X_i(f) = \{x | x \in \mathcal{X}(f) \wedge |x| - |f| = i\}$, $1 \leq i \leq m$, where $m = \max\{i | X_i(f) \neq \emptyset\}$. The frequency extension of f for i, $1 \leq i \leq m$, is defined as:*

$$ext(f, i) = \frac{\sum_{x \in X_i(f)} \frac{count(x,S)}{count(f,S)}}{|X_i(f)|}$$

Intuitively, the frequency extension of f for i is the average count difference between f and all the faSets that f represents whose size difference from f is equal to i. Given a faSet f, the estimation of $p(f|\mathcal{D})$, denoted $\tilde{p}(f|\mathcal{D})$, is:

$$\tilde{p}(f|\mathcal{D}) = count(C(f), S) \cdot ext(C(f), |f| - |C(f)|)$$

It holds that:

LEMMA 2. *Let f be an ϵ-CRF. Then, $\forall i$, it holds that $\frac{1}{\phi} \leq ext(f, i) \leq 1$, where $\phi = (1 + \epsilon)^i$.*

It can be shown that the estimation error is bounded by ϕ, i.e., by ϵ. More specifically, let f be an RF and $|f| - |C(f)| = i$. The estimation error for $p(f|\mathcal{D})$ is bounded as follows:

$$\frac{1}{\phi} - 1 \leq \frac{\tilde{p}(f|\mathcal{D}) - p(f|\mathcal{D})}{p(f|\mathcal{D})} \leq \phi - 1$$

3.2 The Two-Phase Algorithm

Given a query Q, our goal is to locate the k faSets with the highest interestingness scores. Clearly, the brute-force method of generating all possible faSets in $Res(Q)$ and computing their score is exponential on the number of distinct values that appear in $Res(Q)$. Applying an a-priori approach for generating and pruning faSets is not applicable either, since *score* is neither an upwards nor a downwards closed measure. Recall that, a measure d is *upwards closed* if for any two sets S and S', $S \subseteq S' \Rightarrow d(S) \leq d(S')$ and *downwards closed* if $S \subseteq S' \Rightarrow d(S) \geq d(S')$.

PROPOSITION 1. *Let Q be a query and f a faSet. $score(f, Q)$ is neither an upwards nor a downwards closed measure.*

This implies that we cannot employ any subset or superset relations among the faSets of $Res(Q)$ to prune the search space.

As a baseline approach to reduce the number of examined faSets of $Res(Q)$, we consider only the most frequent faSets of $Res(Q)$, motivated by the fact that faSets that appear in $Res(Q)$ frequently are likely to be highly interesting to the user. To this end, we apply an adaptation of a frequent itemset mining algorithm to generate all frequent faSets of $Res(Q)$, that is, all faSets with support larger than some pre-specified threshold $minsupp_f$. Then, for each frequent faSet f, we use the maintained statistics to estimate $p(f|\mathcal{D})$ and compute $score(f, Q)$.

This baseline approach has the problem of being highly dependent on $minsupp_f$. A large value of $minsupp_f$ may lead to losing some less frequent in the result but very rarely appearing in the database faSets, whereas a small value may result in a very large number of candidate faSets being examined. Therefore, we propose a Two-Phase Algorithm (TPA), described next, that addresses this issue by setting $minsupp_f$ to an appropriate value so that all top-k faSets are located without generating redundant candidates. TPA assumes that the maintained statistics are based on keeping rare faSets of the database $\mathcal{D}$. Let $minsupp_r$ be the support threshold of the maintained rare faSets.

In the first phase of the algorithm, all facet conditions, or 1-faSets, that appear in $Res(Q)$ are located. TPA checks which rare faSets of $\mathcal{D}$, according to the maintained statistics, contain only facet conditions from $Res(Q)$. Let X be the set of faSets. Then, in one pass of $Res(Q)$, all faSets of $Res(Q)$ that are supersets of some faSet in X are generated and their support in $Res(Q)$ is measured. For each of the located faSets, $score(f, Q)$ is computed. Let s be the kth highest score among them. TPA sets $minsupp_f$ equal to $s \times minsupp_r$ and proceeds to the second phase where it executes a frequent itemset mining algorithm with threshold equal to $minsupp_f$. Any faSet in $Res(Q)$ less frequent than $minsupp_f$ has score smaller than the kth faSet located in the first phase and thus can be safely ignored. To see this, let f be a faSet examined in the second phase of the algorithm. Since the score of f has not been computed in the first phase, then $p(f|\mathcal{D}) > minsupp_r$. Therefore, for $score(f, Q) > s$ to hold, it must be that $p(f|Res(Q)) > s \times p(f|\mathcal{D})$, i.e., $p(f|Res(Q)) > s \times minsupp_r$. TPA is shown in Alg. 1.

Algorithm 1 Two-Phase Algorithm (TPA).

Input: Q, $Res(Q)$, k, C, $minsupp_r$ of C.
Output: The top-k interesting faSets for Q.

$S \leftarrow \emptyset$, $A \leftarrow$ all 1-faSets of $Res(Q)$
for all faSets $f \in C$ **do**
  if all 1-faSets $g \subseteq f$ are contained in A **then**
    $f.score = score(f, Q)$, $S \leftarrow S \cup \{f\}$
  end if
end for
for all tuples $t \in Res(Q)$ **do**
  generate all faSets $f \subseteq t$, s.t. $\exists\, g \in S$ with $g \subset f$
  for all such faSets f **do**
    $f.score = score(f, Q)$, $S \leftarrow S \cup \{f\}$
  end for
end for
$minsupp_f \leftarrow$ (k^{th} highest score in S) $\times$ $minsupp_r$
$candidates \leftarrow$ frequentFaSetMiner($Res(Q)$, $minsupp_f$)
for all faSets f in $candidates$ **do**
  $f.score = score(f, Q)$, $S \leftarrow S \cup \{f\}$
end for
return The k faSets in S with the highest scores

4. EXPERIMENTAL RESULTS

In this section, we present experimental results of the deployment of our approach. We use two real datasets: (i) "AUTOS", a single-relation database consisting of 41 characteristics for 15,191 used cars from Yahoo!Auto [2] and (ii) "MOVIES", a database with 13 relations whose sizes range from around 10,000 to almost 1,000,000 tuples, containing information extracted from the Internet Movie Database [1]. We use also synthetic datasets consisting of a single relation with 5 attributes and 1,000 tuples, taking values generated using a zipf distribution from a 5-value domain.

Statistics Generation: First, we evaluate the proposed method for maintaining statistics based on ϵ-CRFs in terms of (i) storage, measured as the number of stored faSets and (ii) generation time. We report results for all intermediate computation steps, i.e., locating MRFs, RFs and CRFs. We base our implementation for locating MRFs and RFs on the MRG-Exp and Arima algorithms [18] and use an adapted version of the CFI2TCFI algorithm [8] for producing ϵ-CRFs. For a given $minsupp_r$, all MRFs are located. However, locating all RFs is inefficient due to the exponential nature of algorithms such as Apriori. To overcome this, we use a *random walk* based approach [10]: instead of producing all RFs, we produce only a subset of them discovered by random walks initiated at the MRFs.

Table 1(a) reports the number of produced faSets for different values of $minsupp_r$ and ϵ. In the reported results, we kept the number of random walks fixed (equal to 20). As ϵ increases, an ϵ-CRF represents faSets with larger support differences and, thus, the number of maintained statistics decreases. As $minsupp_r$ increases, more faSets of the database are considered to be rare and, thus, the number of maintained faSets should also increase. However, this is not always the case because of the random walks technique employed to retrieve RFs. Note also that the number of ϵ-CRFs is much smaller than the number of RFs, even for values of ϵ as low as 0.5. For comparison, we also report the number of 2-faSets (Table 1(b)with id attributes excluded) that could alternatively be used for estimating frequencies, as discussed in Sec. 3, which is considerably large for the real databases. Finally, in terms of execution time, the main overhead was induced by the stage of generating RFs which can take up many minutes, while all other stages require a couple of seconds for all datasets (see [9] for details).

Estimation Accuracy: Next, we evaluate the accuracy of estimating the support of rare faSets using the support of the stored ϵ-CRFs. For this, we employ our synthetic datasets and probe our statistics to retrieve estimations for the frequency of 10 rare faSets for each possible size. We observed that, even though we do not maintain the complete set of ϵ-CRFs, because of our random walks approach, the estimation error remains low and below the theoretical bound. For example, for $\epsilon = 0.9$, and $minsupp_r = 10\%$, the absolute error was 3.0 to 4.0 on average. The same holds for the real datasets (see [9] for details).

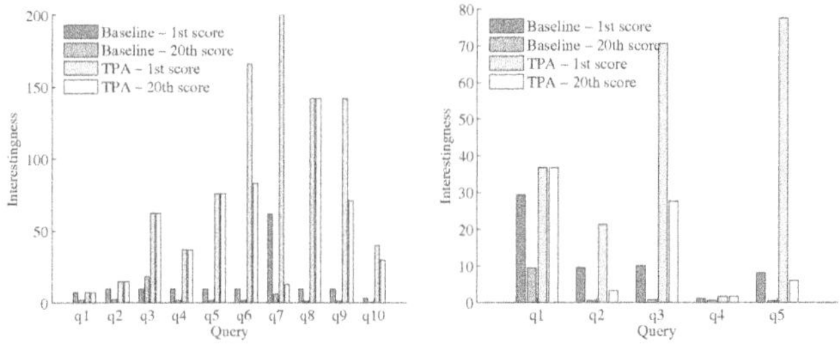

(a) ZIPF (b) AUTOS

Figure 3: Baseline vs. TPA.

We also experimented using IPF. This approach turned out to be very inefficient for estimating the frequency of rare faSets. This was mainly due to two reasons. Take for example rare 3-faSets. When they consist of rare 2-faSets, their estimated support was too small (most often equal to zero) due to the maximum entropy principle that tends to considers faSet co-occurrences independent. On the other hand, when rare 3-faSets consist of frequent 2-faSets, their support was over-estimated (often at a ten-fold order).

Top-k FaSet Discovery: We compare the baseline and the Two-Phase (TPA) algorithms. For the synthetic datasets, we generate random queries, while for the real databases we use predefined queries selected so that their result sets include various combinations of rare and frequent faSets. Fig. 3 shows the 1st and 20th highest ranked interestingness score retrieved. For TPA we set $k = 20$ and for the baseline approach we start with a high $minsupp_f$ and gradually decrease it until we get at least 20 results. TPA retrieves more interesting faSets, mainly due to the first phase where rare faSets in $Res(Q)$ are examined. For the reported results ϵ was equal to 0.5. In general, the value of ϵ did not affect the interestingness scores of the top-k results considerably. In most cases TPA located k results during phase one and, thus, phase two was not executed.

Exploring the two Real Databases: We experimented with the exploration of the real databases. Due to space limitations, we just present two of our observations about the acquired results. For example, take a query in the AUTOS database about car models with navigation systems which is a query whose result set includes many rare faSets, all having a high interestingness score, e.g., the car models "*Land Rover Discovery II HSE7*" and "*Mercedes-Benz G55 AMG*". Expanding the query towards the "state" attribute reveals interesting faSets not present in the original result, such as the "*Land Rover Range Rover*" model in VA and the "*Cadillac*" model in DE, suggesting that such combinations are highly related with navigation systems but only in specific states. As another example take the query in the MOVIES database for the countries and genres of movies directed by F.F. Coppola. FaSet {"*Switzerland*", "*Sci-Fi*"} is retrieved as the most interesting, since this is extremely rare in the database, and it is very interesting that it was located by the user query. Another highly ranked faSet for this query is {"*Romania*"} (and its supersets).

5. RELATED WORK

In this paper, we have proposed a novel database exploration model. A common exploration technique is *faceted search* (e.g., [14, 11]), where query results are classified into different multiple categories, or facets, and the user refines

Table 1: Number of FaSets.

$minsupp_r$	# MRFs	# RFs	# CRFs	# ϵ-CRFs $\epsilon = 0.1$	$\epsilon = 0.3$	$\epsilon = 0.5$	$\epsilon = 0.7$	$\epsilon = 0.9$
ZIPF								
5%	186	2983	2283	2283	2177	1319	778	243
10%	145	3402	2639	2639	2505	1541	881	254
20%	54	3238	2547	2547	2443	1556	876	154
AUTOS								
5%	2106	2960	2737	2715	2683	2617	2547	2446
10%	2014	2856	2606	2591	2561	2486	2437	2338
20%	1960	2654	2421	2398	2365	2278	2231	2126
MOVIES								
5%	11533	11809	11787	11787	11783	11757	11730	11630
10%	11537	11820	11803	11803	11798	11768	11734	11621
20%	11538	11826	11802	11802	11799	11776	11750	11643

(a)

# 1-faSets	# 2-faSets
ZIPF	
25	250
AUTOS	
17664	851954
MOVIES	
67094	561223

(b)

these results by selecting one or more facet condition. Our approach is different in that we do not tackle refinement, instead, our goal is to discover other interesting results related to the results of the original query. There is also some relation to *query reformulation*, where a query is relaxed or restricted when its results are too few or too many respectively, using term rewriting or query expansion to increase recall and precision (e.g., [15]). Again, our aim is locating interesting results that are highly related to the results of the original query. Besides restricting the query, another common method of addressing the too-many answers problem is ranking its results and presenting only the top-k ones to the user. This line of research is extensive; the work most related to ours is research on *automatically ranking* the results [7, 3]. Besides addressing a different problem, our approach is also different in that the granularity of ranking is at the level of faSets as opposed to whole result tuples. We also propose a novel method for frequency estimation. In terms of the interestingness score, similar measures have been used in the literature, such as unexpectedness [21] and χ^2 [5].

Yet another method of exploring results relies on *why queries* that consider the presence of unexpected tuples in the result and *why not* queries that consider the absence of expected tuples in the result. For example, ConQueR [19] proposes posing follow-up queries for *why not* by relaxing the original query. In our approach, we find interesting faSets in the result based on their frequency and other faSets highly correlated with them. Another line of research considers how to *"output" a query* whose execution will yield results equivalent to a given result set [20, 16]. Our work differs in that we do not aim at constructing queries to match given result sets but rather guiding the users towards novel results.

Finally, in some respect, exploration queries may be seen as *recommendations*. In a previous position paper [17], we have discussed various approaches for making recommendations in relational databases. Extending database queries with recommendations has been studied in two recent works, namely [13] and [6]. In [13], a general framework and a related engine are proposed for the declarative specification of the recommendation process. Recommendations in [6] are based on the past behavior of similar users, whereas we consider only the content of the database and the result.

6. CONCLUSIONS

In this paper, we introduced ReDRIVE, a novel database exploration framework for recommnding to users items which may be of interest to them although not part of the results of their original query. The computation of such additional results is based on identifying the most interesting sets of (attribute, value) pairs, or faSets, that appear in the result of the original user query. The computation of interestingness is based on the frequency of the faSet in the query result and in the database instance. We also proposed a frequency estimation method based on storing an ϵ-CRF representation and a two-phase algorithm for computing the top-k faSets. There are many directions for future work, such as, extending our work to more general types of facet conditions and considering that a history of previous database queries and results exists.

7. REFERENCES

[1] The Internet Movie Database. http://www.imdb.com.

[2] Yahoo!Auto. http://autos.yahoo.com.

[3] S. Agrawal, S. Chaudhuri, G. Das, and A. Gionis. Automated ranking of database query results. In *CIDR*, 2003.

[4] Y. M. Bishop, S. E. Fienberg, and P. W. Holland. *Discrete Multivariate Analysis: Theory and Practice*. Springer, 2007.

[5] S. Brin, R. Motwani, and C. Silverstein. Beyond market baskets: Generalizing association rules to correlations. In *SIGMOD*, 1997.

[6] G. Chatzopoulou, M. Eirinaki, and N. Polyzotis. Query recommendations for interactive database exploration. In *SSDBM*, 2009.

[7] S. Chaudhuri, G. Das, V. Hristidis, and G. Weikum. Probabilistic information retrieval approach for ranking of database query results. *ACM Trans. Database Syst.*, 31(3), 2006.

[8] J. Cheng, Y. Ke, and W. Ng. delta-tolerance closed frequent itemsets. In *ICDM*, 2006.

[9] M. Drosou and E. Pitoura. ReDRIVE: Result-driven database exploration through recommendations, TR 2011-10. *Computer Science Dept., Univ. of Ioannina*, 2011.

[10] D. Gunopulos, R. Khardon, H. Mannila, S. Saluja, H. Toivonen, and R. S. Sharm. Discovering all most specific sentences. *ACM Trans. Database Syst.*, 28(2), 2003.

[11] A. Kashyap, V. Hristidis, and M. Petropoulos. Facetor: cost-driven exploration of faceted query results. In *CIKM*, 2010.

[12] N. Koudas, C. Li, A. K. H. Tung, and R. Vernica. Relaxing join and selection queries. In *VLDB*, 2006.

[13] G. Koutrika, B. Bercovitz, and H. Garcia-Molina. Flexrecs: expressing and combining flexible recommendations. In *SIGMOD*, 2009.

[14] S. B. Roy, H. Wang, G. Das, U. Nambiar, and M. K. Mohania. Minimum-effort driven dynamic faceted search in structured databases. In *CIKM*, 2008.

[15] N. Sarkas, N. Bansal, G. Das, and N. Koudas. Measure-driven keyword-query expansion. *PVLDB*, 2(1), 2009.

[16] A. D. Sarma, A. G. Parameswaran, H. Garcia-Molina, and J. Widom. Synthesizing view definitions from data. In *ICDT*, 2010.

[17] K. Stefanidis, M. Drosou, and E. Pitoura. "You May Also Like" results in relational databases. In *PersDB*, 2009.

[18] L. Szathmary, A. Napoli, and P. Valtchev. Towards rare itemset mining. In *ICTAI (1)*, 2007.

[19] Q. T. Tran and C.-Y. Chan. How to conquer why-not questions. In *SIGMOD*, 2010.

[20] Q. T. Tran, C.-Y. Chan, and S. Parthasarathy. Query by output. In *SIGMOD*, 2009.

[21] K. Wang, Y. Jiang, and L. V. S. Lakshmanan. Mining unexpected rules by pushing user dynamics. In *KDD*, 2003.

Information Re-finding by Context: A Brain Memory Inspired Approach *

Tangjian Deng, Liang Zhao, Ling Feng
Tsinghua National Laboratory for Information Science and Technology
Dept. of Computer Science and Technology
Tsinghua University, Beijing 100084, China
dtj@cs.tsinghua.edu.cn
zhaoliang0415@gmail.com
fengling@tsinghua.edu.cn

Wenwei Xue
Nokia Research Center, Beijing, China
wayne.xue@nokia.com

ABSTRACT

Re-finding what we have accessed before is a common behavior in real life. Psychological studies show that context under which information was accessed can serve as a powerful cue for information recall. *"Finding the sweet recipe that I read at the hotel on the trip to Africa last year"* is a context-based re-finding request example. Inspired by users' recall characteristics and human memory, we present a context memory model, where each context unit links to the data created/accessed before. Context units are organized in a clustering and associative manner, and evolve dynamically in life cycles. Based on the context memory, we build a recall-by-context query model. Two methods are devised to evaluate context-based recall queries. Our experiments with synthetic and real data show that evaluation exploring the use of context associations can get the best response time.

Categories and Subject Descriptors

H.3.3 [**Information Search and Retrieval**]: Search process

General Terms

Algorithms, Design

Keywords

human memory, context, information re-finding

1. INTRODUCTION

Motivation. To re-access information one has come across occasionally or intentionally before is very common in daily lives. Teevan *et al.* [17] once analyzed a one-year Web log of 114 users and found that 40% of queries are re-finding requests. A similar finding was obtained by [15] that over 58% of Web pages accessed are re-visits to pages previously seen, based on the analysis of 6-week usage data of 23 users.

Information re-finding is different from finding. There is uncertainty in the latter because users don't know enough information, while re-finding is a more directed process as users have seen the information before [3]. A general way to support re-finding is to maintain query logs [2]. However, because of users' dim memories of the past (as evidenced in [16], original queries were remembered wrongly 28% due to miss-remembering or forgetting), sometimes it is a difficult and time-consuming task to re-find what they want by simply entering keywords of the previous information content.

Inspiration by Human Memory. Psychological studies show that context under which information was accessed before can serve as a powerful cue for information recall, as it is easier to remember than detailed content itself [9]. For example, it may be hard to recall a *recipe*'s detail accessed one year ago, but the associated contexts *last year, at a hotel, traveling to Africa*, etc. may leave a deeper impression, and can thus serve as cues to re-find target information.

Life scientists discovered that there is a kind of memory mechanism called *episodic memory* in a human brain, which enables people to be consciously aware of earlier experiences under context [19]. It is the episodic memory that receives and stores information about temporally dated episodes or events, together with their temporal-spatial relations [18]. The memory trace, which is the central representation of the to-be-remembered event, is a multi-dimensional collection of elements, features, or attributes [20]. The retrieval of episodic memories involving an interaction between a retrieval cue and a memory trace, is a cue dependent process that reflects the temporal contiguity and the semantic relationship of the cue and the target entities [14].

Our Work. Inspired by the human memory retrieval mechanism, we build a link between the information and its previous accessing context instance, represented as a multi-dimensional vector. A context memory contains a large volume of associated context instances organized in clusters. To mimic the amnesia characteristic of human memory, we bind each context instance with a dynamic life-cycle degradation policy. Memory reinforcement is also incorporated by adjusting the degradation speeds of context instances.

*The work is funded by National Natural Science Foundation of China (60773156, 61073004) and Chinese Major State Basic Research Development 973 Program (2011CB302203-2).

Based on the context memory, we build a recall-by-context model to support users' re-finding queries, where a query is indeed a context instance, and a ranked list of the matched context instances is an *intermediate* result that links to the information accessed before as the *final* result. We explore the use of context clusters and associations for efficient processing of context-based re-finding queries. Our experiments on synthetic and real data show that the association link enables the best response time and scalability due to its index-like role. We also examine three similarity ranking functions and find out their little influence upon results ranking. The contributions of the paper are summarized as follows.

- We present a brain memory inspired, context-based information re-finding framework, which enables users to re-find results accessed before by relevant contexts.
- We build a context memory model, which specifies clustering and associative structures of context instances, as well as their dynamic life-cycle evolution strategies.
- We build a recall-based querying-by-context model based on the context memory model, and evaluate several querying methods and ranking methods.

The rest of the paper is organized as follows. We review some closely related work in Section 2. In Section 3, we present the context memory model, followed by a context-based re-finding model in Section 4 describing several query evaluation methods, and report corresponding performance in Section 5. We conclude the paper in Section 6.

2. RELATED WORK

Web Search. Mayer [11] made a good survey on the existing approaches and tools for web re-visitation. Typical techniques to assist Web re-finding include bookmarks, history lists, search engines, etc. Google's *Web History* [1] keeps users' Web activity data such as search requests and clicked pages and classifies them into different topics such as Web, images, news, etc., and allows users to browse or search their historically accessed pages. Teevan [16] built a search engine which can support not only finding of new information but also re-finding of old information. Morris *et al.* [12] developed a *SearchBar* to organize a user's Web access history in a hierarchy, including user's recent search topics, queries, results visited and user's notes. By browsing the hierarchy, the user can re-acquire previous search information (such as queries, results visited, and their notes).

Personal Information Management. Dumais *et al.* [6] developed a system *Stuff I've Seen* to facilitate personal information re-use. It builds an index for what a person has seen, and uses file-type, access date, and author for filtering and sorting results. Context and memory cues are also taken into account to enhance content-based personal information searching [8, 5]. Chen *et al.* [4] built a desktop search system *iMecho* exploiting semantic associations among files to enhance full-text search, where the associations are mined from contents such as *similar-to* relation and users' such operations as *jump-to, copy-from, same-task,* etc. Li and Meng proposed a query method to re-find referenced files, given some file items as input. They identified three types of reference relations based on users' sequence operations, such as *adjacent, inclusive,* and *lineage* relations, based on which three adjacency matrixes of file items are produced. Query results can thus be computed by multiplying the entry vector with the matrixes [10].

While great efforts have been made to explore contextual cues for re-finding, this study draws inspirations from human memory and aims at a more general context-based re-finding framework, and consequently the query model against a well-organized and evolving context memory.

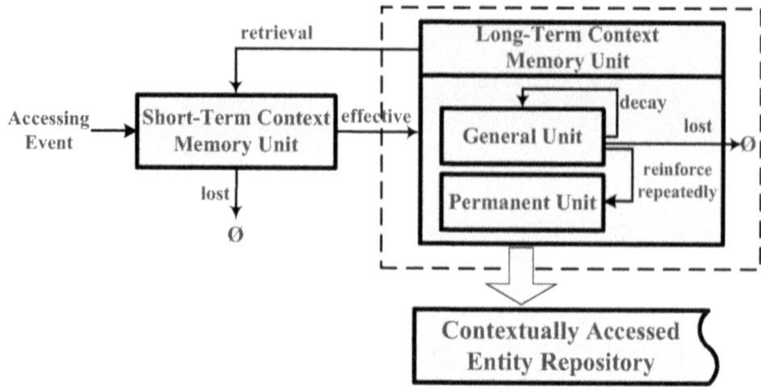

Figure 1: The framework of context memory

3. CONTEXT MEMORY

To support context-based information re-finding, the first thing to do is to build a context memory model.

3.1 Context Memory Framework

We mimic human memory and organize our context memory into a *short-term context memory unit* (SCM) and a *long-term context memory unit* (LCM), as shown in Figure 1. There are two types of memory units in LCM: **permanent** and **general**. The former records life-long experiences and is immutable, while the latter will decay.

In the study, the circumstance under which a user's information access occurs is called an *access context.* Contexts can be either internal *user*-related (like user name, activity, etc.) or external *environment*-related (like place, surrounding people, etc.) [7]. If the accessed information (like an article) is of interest to the user, a linkage between the access context instance and the information is created and together with the detail of information content, is stored into the *contextually accessed entity repository.*

Context memory is dynamic and information transits across the two memory units as showed in Figure 1. This paper focuses on the long-term context memory unit (abbreviated as context memory for short) where contexts will decay gradually in life-cycles. We describe its static structure and dynamic evolution in detail in the following subsections.

3.2 Static Structure of Context Memory

3.2.1 Contextual Attribute and Context

Access context is comprised of n contextual attributes $(A_1, A_2, \ldots, A_n)$. The domain of each attribute forms a hierarchy of levels of abstraction that can be viewed as a lattice $(H, \prec_h)$, where $H{=}(h_1, h_2, \ldots, h_{s-1}, ALL)$ of s levels with the *levelId* $(1, 2, \ldots, s\text{-}1, s)$, and $\prec_h$ is a partial order among the levels of H, such that $(h_1 \prec_h h_i \prec_h ALL)$, $1 < i < s$. Figure 2 depicts two hierarchy examples for contextual attribute *Time* and *Location*. A weight in [0, 1] expresses the *hierarchical similarity factor* between two consecutive hierarchical levels h_i and h_{i+1} in H, denoted as $s_{i,i+1}$.

Definition 1. Let c and c' be two contextual attribute values of A. Assume function $h(A, v)$ returns the hierarchical level id of v. c' is called an *ancestor* of c, denoted as $c \prec_a c'$

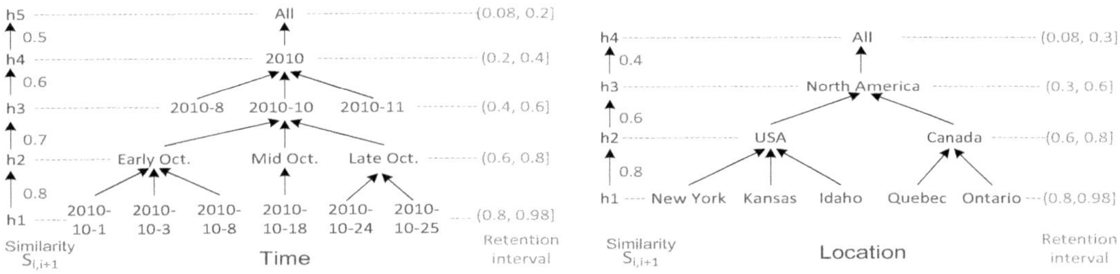

Figure 2: An example of contextual hierarchies for *Time* and *Location*.

(reversely, c is called a *descendant* of c'), if and only if $h(A,c) < h(A,c')$ and there exists an upward path from c to c'.

Definition 2. Given two contextual attribute values $c, c' \in Dom(A)$, let $k = h(A,c)$, $k' = h(A,c')$. The similarity between c and c' denoted as $sim(A,c,c')$ is defined as follows:
(1) if $c = c'$, $sim(A,c,c') = 1$;
(2) if $c' \prec_a c$, $sim(A,c,c') = \prod_{i=k'}^{k-1} s_{i,i+1}$;
(3) if $c \prec_a c'$, $sim(A,c,c') = \prod_{i=k}^{k'-1} s_{i,i+1}$;
(4) if c and c' have a common ancestor p, let $m = h(A,p)$, $sim(A,c,c') = \prod_{i=k}^{m-1} s_{i,i+1} \cdot \prod_{j=k'}^{m-1} s_{j,j+1}$

The above definition is quite intuitive. The similarity between two contextual attributes is subject to their distances at hierarchical levels. It is easy to show that if $c_1 \prec_a c_2$ and $c_2 \prec_a c_3$, then $sim(A,c_1,c_3) < sim(A,c_2,c_3)$.

3.2.2 Context Instance

A context instance is an instantiation of its n contextual attributes, represented as a tuple $C = (c_1, c_2, \ldots, c_n)$, where $c_i \in Dom(A_i)$ for every $1 \le i \le n$. Based on the similarities of their respective contextual attribute values, we can measure the similarity of two context instances $C = (c_1, c_2, \ldots, c_n)$ and $C' = (c'_1, c'_2, \ldots, c'_n)$ as follows.

$$Sim(C,C') = \sqrt{\frac{1}{n}\sum_{i=1}^{n} sim^2(A_i, c_i, c'_i)}$$

Definition 3. Assume context is an n-dimensional vector $(A_1, A_2, \ldots, A_n)$, let $C = (c_1, c_2, \ldots, c_n)$ and $C' = (c'_1, c'_2, \ldots, c'_n)$ be two context instances.
(1) C is **equal to** C', denoted as $C' = C$, if and only if $\forall i \in \{1,2,\ldots,n\}$ $(c'_i = c_i)$.
(2) C is **more general** than C', denoted as $C' \prec C$, if and only if $\forall i \in \{1,2,\ldots,n\}$ $((c'_i \prec_a c_i) \vee (c'_i = c_i)) \wedge (C \ne C')$.
(3) C is **associated with** C' on contextual attribute A_i, denoted as $C \xleftrightarrow{A_i} C'$, if and only if $sim(A_i, c_i, c'_i) \ge \theta$, where θ is a threshold value set beforehand.

Definition 4. Centered around a **representative contextual attribute value** $r \in Dom(A)$, a set of context instances form a **cluster**, denoted as $CC(A,r)$, where for $\forall C = (c_1, c_2, \ldots, c_n) \in CC(A,r)$ $sim(A, c_i, r) \ge \delta \wedge (c_i \in Dom(A)) \wedge ((c_i = r) \vee (c_i \prec_a r))$, where δ is a clustering threshold value in [0,1].

Definition 5. A **context memory snapshot** is a graph $CM = (V_{CC}, E_{CC})$, where V_{CC} is a set of vertices (representing context instance clusters) and E_{CC} is a set of edges on vertices (representing association relationships of context instances). The graph varies with time goes by, that is, it's a function of time to some extent.

3.3 Dynamic Evolution of Context memory

To measure the degradation of contextual attribute value $c \in Dom(A)$, we employ a modified exponential-power function [13], denoted as $R(A,c,t)$ to express c's **retention strength** after elapsing time t. A real number $r \in [0,1]$ is used to represent the retention strength for each value, which is clearly remembered if r approaches 1 and tends to be forgot when close to 0.

$$R(A,c,t) = \begin{cases} r_0 \cdot 1 & \text{if } r_0 > \theta_{max} \\ r_0 \cdot e^{-\lambda\sqrt{t}} & \text{if } \theta_{min} \le r_0 \le \theta_{max} \\ r_0 \cdot 0 & \text{if } r_0 < \theta_{min} \end{cases}$$

where r_0 is the initial value of retention strength, λ is the decay rate coefficient, θ_{max} and θ_{min} are two thresholds.
• If $(r_0 > \theta_{max})$: the retention degree of the value remains unchanged, corresponding to the permanent LCM.
• If $(r_0 < \theta_{min})$: the retention degree is set to 0, corresponding to the SCM.
• If $(\theta_{min} \le r_0 \le \theta_{max})$: the retention degree is weakened as time passes, corresponding to the general LCM.

For a contextual attribute A, different retention ranges are allocated to different hierarchical levels as shown in Figure 2 and particularly, the union of all the exclusive retention ranges in a hierarchy is $[\theta_{min}, \theta_{max}]$. if $R(A,c,t) \in (\theta_{i-1}, \theta_i]$ at $t = t_0$, and $R(A,c,t') \in (\theta_{j-1}, \theta_j]$ at $t' = t_0 + \Delta t$, $(1 \le i < j \le s)$, then c will degrade from h_i to h_j. When a value c of attribute A is recalled by a user, r_0 is increased by a percentage of δ_r and λ is decreased by a percentage of δ_λ, thus slowing down the degradation speed.

4. CONTEXT-BASED INFORMATION RE-FINDING

Context-based re-finding differs from database querying in three aspects. Firstly, request formulation is based on contextual attributes rather than database contents. Secondly, query target is context memory snapshot rather than database. Thirdly, an *intermediate* query result is a ranked list of context instances, with their linked information accessed before as the *final* query result.

4.1 Context-based Re-Finding Model

A **context-based re-finding query** can be denoted as a function $RF(Q,CM) = \langle C_1, C_2, \ldots, C_m \rangle$, where Q is the query request formulated as a context instance, CM is the query target that is the context memory snapshot, and the intermediate query result is a ranked list of context instances in CM, $\langle C_1, C_2, \ldots, C_m \rangle$, whose ranking is determined by a ranking function. For the final result generation via the accessing context instances is quite straightforward, we focus on the evaluation of the intermediate context instances result in the following discussion.

In the study, we consider three ranking methods based on simple similarity, weighted similarity, and negative dissimilarity between Q and C. Let $Q = (q_1, q_2, \ldots, q_n)$, and $C = (c_1, c_2, \ldots, c_n)$ without loss of generality.

Ranking by simple similarity. Use the similarity function defined above to rank context instances in the memory snapshot against Q.

$$Rank(Q, C) = Sim(Q, C) = \sqrt{\frac{1}{n}\sum_{i=1}^{n} sim^2(A_i, q_i, c_i)} \quad (1)$$

Ranking by weighted similarity. A weight vector $(w_1, w_2, \ldots, w_n)$ is used to state the precise degrees of Q's contextual attribute values, where $w_i \in [0, 1]$, $\sum_{i=1}^{n} w_i = 1$.

$$Rank(Q, C) = \sqrt{\sum_{i=1}^{n} w_i \cdot sim^2(A_i, q_i, c_i)} \quad (2)$$

Ranking by negative dissimilarity. The similarity between Q and C can also be calculated via their dissimilarity: $Dissim(Q, C) = 1 - \min_{i=1}^{n} sim(A_i, q_i, c_i)$.

$$Rank(Q, C) = 1 - Dissim(Q, C) = \min_{i=1}^{n} sim(A_i, q_i, c_i) \quad (3)$$

4.2 Processing of Context-based Re-Finding

A query may or may not exactly match to a context instance in CM. Three kinds of matching between Q and C (denoted as $C \dashv Q$) are considered and included in the re-finding result: 1) *exactly matching* ($Q = C$); 2) *specifically matching* ($C \prec Q$); and 3) *generally matching* ($Q \prec C$).

A straightforward way to re-find information by Q is to scan CM, and get those three kinds of matching context instances, and return them after ranking. Apparently, this naive solution takes $O(n \cdot |CM|)$ time cost in the dominate matching part, and can't scale-up well with a large volume of existing and consistently incoming context instances in the memory. Efficient re-finding strategies are needed.

4.2.1 Cluster-based Re-Finding Approach

For each contextual attribute A_i, we can get a set of context instance clusters as follows:

1) Identifying a representative attribute value r for a new cluster $CC(A_i, r)$. Find the un-clustered context instance whose contextual attribute value of A_i situates at the highest hierarchical level, and take the value as r.

2) For each un-clustered context instance C in CM, if its attribute value equals to r or is descendant of r, and its similarity to r is no less than a cluster threshold δ, then put C into $CC(A_i, r)$, where $CC(A_i, r) = \{C | (C \in CM$ is un-clustered$) \wedge ((c_i \prec_a r) \vee (c_i = r)) \wedge sim(A_i, c_i, r) \geq \delta\}$.

3) Repeat 1) and 2) until all instances are clustered.

Now we obtain n cluster sets $CL(A_1), CL(A_2), \ldots, CL(A_n)$, where $CL(A_i) = \{CC(A_i, r_1), CC(A_i, r_2), \ldots, CC(A_i, r_m)\}$ $(1 \leq i \leq n)$, m is the total number of clusters in $CL(A_i)$ and $CC(A_i, r_j)$ is a context instance cluster for every $1 \leq j \leq m$. The obtained clusters in this way are exclusive.

After clustering, we can then check the matching of Q on a cluster base. We call $CC(A_i, r)$ a *candidate cluster* of Q, if it contains instances that may match Q, i.e., satisfying one of the following conditions: (1)$r = q_i$; (2) $r \prec_a q_i$; and (3) $q_i \prec_a r$. As Q may indicate n attribute values for matching, we choose the attribute value leading to the least number of candidate clusters to start matching. After filtering out candidate clusters based on the selected attribute value, we further examine whether each of their instances, C, matches the rest attribute values of Q. If yes, we put C into the result list; and discard it, otherwise. The pseudocode of cluster-based re-finding is shown in Algorithm 1.

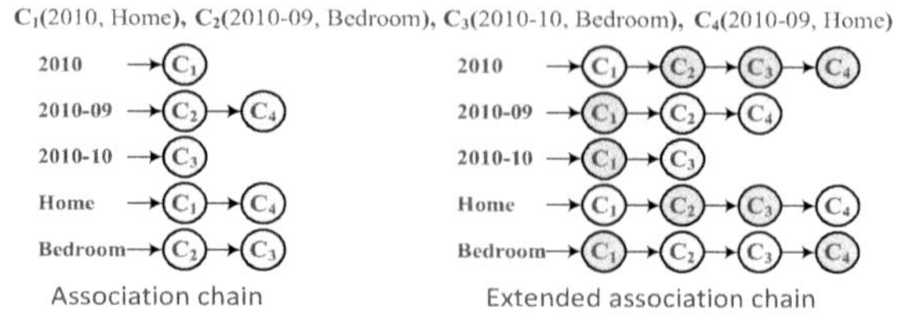

Figure 3: Association chains of context instances

Algorithm 1 Cluster-δ-based Re-finding

Input:
A context memory snapshot CM and query Q
Output:
A ranked list of context instances L that match Q

1: $L \leftarrow \emptyset$;
2: $A_i \leftarrow$ SelectAtt($CLUSTER\text{-}SET$, Q);
//select the starting attribute value, $CLUSTER\text{-}SET = \{CL(A_1), CL(A_2), \ldots, CL(A_n)\}$
3: **for** each $CC(A_i, r_s) \in CL(A_i)$ **do**
4:   **if** $(r_s = q_i) \vee (r_s \prec_a q_i) \vee (q_i \prec_a r_s)$ **then**
5:     **for** each $C \in CC(A_i, r_s)$ **do**
6:       **if** $(C = Q) \vee (C \prec Q) \vee (Q \prec C))$ **then**
7:         Add C to L;
8: $L \leftarrow Rank(L, Q)$;
9: **return** L;

Correctness. The exclusive candidate clusters contain all possible context instances that match Q. This is obvious, as for any context instance C, $C \dashv Q$ implies that $(r_s = q_i) \vee (r_s \prec_a q_i) \vee (q_i \prec_a r_s)$, which is the filtering condition.

Time Complexity Analysis. Selection of a starting contextual attribute A_i (line 2) takes O(n). Filtering out matching contextual instances (line 3-7) takes O($n \cdot |CL(A_i)| \cdot |CC(A_i, r_s)|$). Therefore, the time complexity of the algorithm is O($n \cdot |CL(A_i)| \cdot |CC(A_i, r_s)|$). Apparently, it depends on the number of clusters and the size of clusters, which are sensitive to the clustering threshold δ.

4.2.2 Association-based Re-Finding Approach

We also explore context associations to re-find information. For each contextual attribute A_i, we build for every value v an association chain $Chain(A_i, v)$, which consists of all the context instances with the same attribute value of A_i. Figure 3 shows four context instances in the memory snapshot, and a few chains are illustrated in the left of it. To facilitate exactly, specifically, and generally matching between the query and context instances, we extend association chains to include all the ancestors and descendants according to the contextual attribute hierarchies, and obtain $EChain(A_i, v)$, so that for $\forall C \in EChain(A_i, v)$, $(c_i \prec_a v)$ or $(v \prec_a c_i)$ or $(c_i = v)$, as shown in the right of Figure 3.

Given a query Q, we start from the extended association chain of the shortest length, and then check the matching of each chained context instance against other contextual attribute values requested in Q. Algorithm 2 gives the pseudocode of association-based re-finding approach.

Algorithm 2 Association-based Re-finding

Input:
A context memory snapshot CM and query Q
Output:
A ranked list of context instances L that match Q

Let $EChain(A_k, v)$ be an extended association chain for every $(1 \leq k \leq n)$ and $(v \in Dom(A_k))$.
$L \leftarrow \emptyset$;
$A_i \leftarrow argmin_{k=1}^{n} Length(EChain(A_k, q_k))$;
for each $C \in EChain(A_i, q_i)$ **do**
  if $(C = Q) \vee (C \prec Q) \vee (Q \prec C)$ **then**
    Add C to L;
$L \leftarrow Rank(L, Q)$;
return L;

Correctness. As all the context instances that possibly match Q are included in the selected chain $EChain(A_i, v)$ which is of the shortest length, the result list contains all matching context instances.

Time Complexity Analysis. Selection of the shortest extended association chain takes $O(n)$. Checking whether a context instance in the selected association chain matches Q takes $O(n \cdot Length(EChain(A_i, q_i)))$. So the total time cost is $O(n \cdot Length(EChain(A_i, q_i)))$.

5. PERFORMANCE STUDY

We examine the performance of the two re-finding algorithms on both synthetic and real data sets. We evaluate their scalability in terms of query response time on large-scaled synthetic data, and their applicability on a small-scaled real data set. We study the influence of context degradation on query quality through the two widely adopted precision and recall measurements:

$$precision = \frac{num\_of\_true\_context\_instances\_being\_matched}{num\_of\_matched\_context\_instances}$$

$$recall = \frac{num\_of\_true\_context\_instances\_being\_matched}{num\_of\_true\_context\_instances}$$

5.1 Experiments on Synthetic Data

We first build a complete contextual attribute hierarchies, each of which contains approximately 1000 nodes and totally 7 hierarchical levels. To generate a context memory snapshot that is a set of context instances, we randomly pick up an attribute value from each hierarchy, and combine them to form an n-dimensional context instance. For each context memory snapshot, we generate 100 re-finding queries, each of which is an n-dimensional context instance. We bind a weight with each attribute in the query, and some attribute values may be missing. For each query, we indicate a true context instance that the user is looking for.

Context Degradation and Reinforcement. Each attribute of a context instance has its own initial retention factor r_0 and decay rate λ, and decays independently based on the function $R(A, c, t)$, where $\theta_{max} = 0.98$, $\theta_{min} = 0.08$. The attribute value will be brought into the permanent unit if $r > \theta_{max}$ while deleted if $r < \theta_{min}$. When all the attributes are deleted, the context instance will die out. Every time a value degrades, there is a probability (0.05 in the experiments) the context instance gets reinforced, *i.e.*, λ is decreased 10% and r_0 is increased 5%. Figure 4 shows the

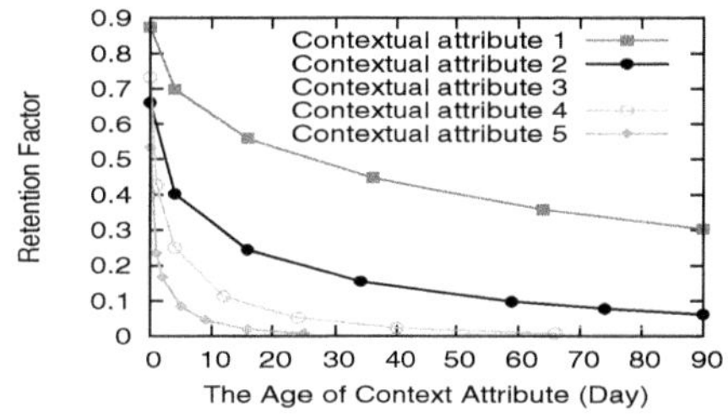

Figure 4: Change of memory retention strengths under different (r_0, λ)s

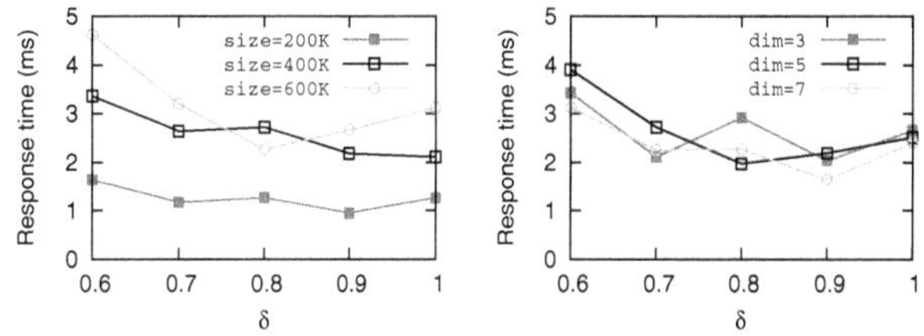

(a) dimension number = 4 (b) memory size = 400K

Figure 5: Query response time versus clustering threshold δ

change of retention strengths of attribute values under different (r_0, λ)s as time elapses, where $A_1(0.87, 0.11)$, $A_2(0.66, 0.25)$, $A_3(0.38, 0.32)$, $A_4(0.73, 0.54)$, $A_5(0.53, 0.82)$.

Response Time. We run 100 queries on different-scaled context memory snapshots, and calculate the average response time of the *cluster*-based and *association*-based approaches. The clustering threshold δ is set to 0.9 (Figure 5 shows the *cluster*-based approach gets the best response time when δ=0.9). We examine the behaviors of these two algorithms by varying the number of context instances in a 4-dimensional memory snapshot from 100K to 600K (Figure 6(a)), and varying the dimensional number from 2 to 7 (Figure 6(b)) under $size$ = 400K, respectively.

The association-based method performs consistently better than the cluster-based one does, thanks to its effective index-like association chains constructed in advance. Both methods take more time to re-find context instances along with the growth of the memory size. However, increasing the contextual dimension number dim hardly affects the response time of both. This might be due to the fact that both methods have already appropriately organized the context instances beforehand and the increase of dim just incurs a little bit more time to match the involved attribute values.

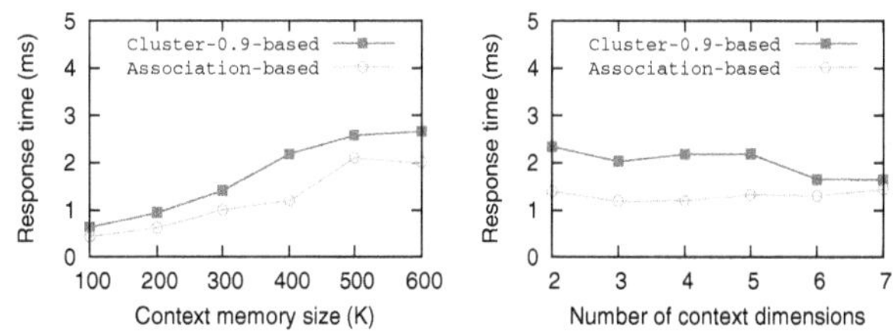

(a) dimension number = 4 (b) memory size = 400K

Figure 6: Re-finding response time on synthetic data

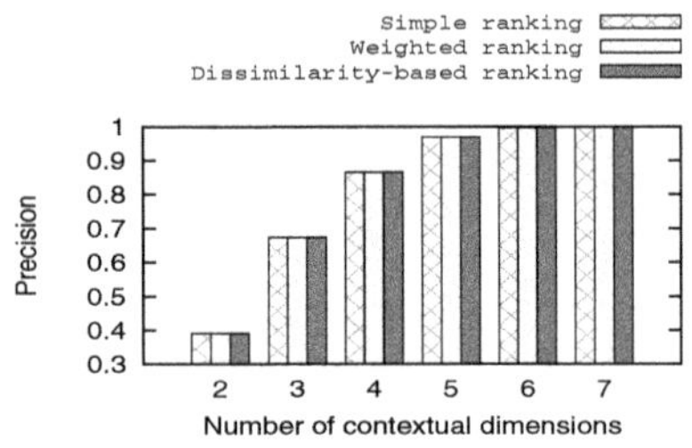

(a) Synthetic data

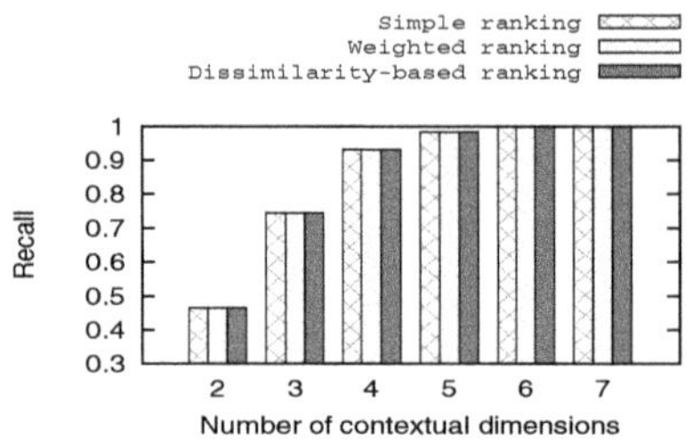

(b) Synthetic data

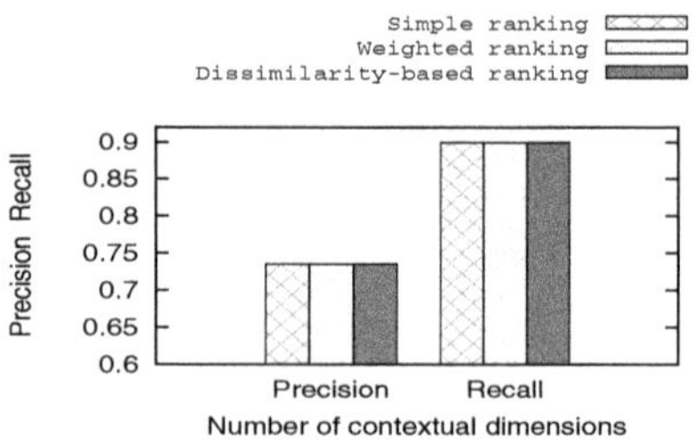

(c) Real data

Figure 7: Query precision and recall

Query Quality. We evaluate the query quality through recall and precision measurements. Three ranking methods described in Section 4.1 are tested. It is interesting to note their very similar behaviors. We execute 100 queries over the synthetic data set of memory size = 400K, and compute the average precision and recall rates. Along with the increase of dimension number from 2 to 7, both precision and recall get improved, as shown in Figure 7(a) and 7(b). This is contributed to two factors: 1) with more contextual dimensions, more query conditions are imposed, leading to a better query quality; and 2) more dimensional attribute values of a context instance participate the degradation makes the chance that the context instance gets lost out of the memory become smaller, leading to a better query quality.

5.2 Experiments on Real Data

We collect from the IE browser 1000 typical URLs that a user visited during the past 4 weeks. Since pieces of extremely aged URL information is too obscure for the user to remember and his/her attempts to re-find become less, we just extract a sample covering not a too long time span. Linked to each URL is the access context instance that contains 4 attribute values *visit time, Web site, topic,* and *visit purpose*. We raise three type of queries: 1) 2 effective dimensions (*ALL, Web site, topic, ALL*); 2) 3 effective dimensions (*ALL, Web site, topic, visit purpose*); and 3) 4 effective dimensions (*visit time, Web site, topic, visit purpose*). For each type, 20 queries are put forward and tested. Due to the small-scaled real data set, we only evaluate the re-finding query quality. Figure 7(c) shows that memory degradation may not throw away wanted instances, but may bring more irrelevant context instances into the query result.

6. CONCLUSION

In this paper, we present a context-based information refinding framework to enable users to re-find information by accessing context. Inspired by human memory we build a context memory model, based on which we build a context-based re-finding model and present two algorithms to process a context-based re-finding request. Our experiments show that the association-based strategy has the faster response time than cluster-based strategy has. We also examine the influence of memory degradation on query quality.

There are some interesting topics to be explored in the future. While appropriate degradation of context memory can reduce storage demands and improve query performance, too fast or too slow degradation must be avoided. Feedbacks from users could help make proper decisions. Dynamically tuning of the degradation is also worthwhile to explored.

7. REFERENCES

[1] Google web history. http://www.google.com/history.
[2] E. Adar, J. Teevan, and S. T. Dumais. Large scale analysis of web revisitation patterns. In *CHI*, 2008.
[3] R. Capra, M. Pinney, and M. A. Perez-Quinones. Refinding is not finding again. Technical report, Computer Science, Virginia Tech., August 2005.
[4] J. Chen, H. Guo, W. Wu, and W. Wang. imecho: An associative memory based desktop search system. In *CIKM*, 2009.
[5] Y. Chen and G. Jones. Integrating memory context into personal information re-finding. In *the 2nd Symposium on Future Directions in Information Access*, 2008.
[6] S. Dumais, E. Cutrell, J. Cadiz, G. Jancke, R. Sarin, and D. C. Robbins. Stuff i've seen: a system for personal information retrieval and re-use. In *SIGIR*, 2003.
[7] L. Feng, P. M. Apers, and W. Jonker. Towards context-aware data management for ambient intelligence. In *DEXA*, 2004.
[8] M. Fuller, L. Kelly, and G. J. F. Jones. Applying contextual memory cues for retrieval from personal information archives. In *PIM Workshop at CHI*, 2008.
[9] M. Lamming and M. Flynn. "forget-me-not"-intimate computing in support of human memory. In *FRIEND21 International Symposium on Next Generation Human Interface*, 1994.
[10] Y. Li and X. Meng. Supporting context-based query in personal dataspace. In *CIKM*, 2009.
[11] M. Mayer. Web history tools and revisitation support: A survey of existing approaches and directions. *Foundations and Trends in HCI*, 2(3):173–278, 2009.
[12] D. Morris, M. R. Morris, and G. Venolia. Searchbar: a search-centric web history for task resumption and information re-finding. In *CHI*, 2008.
[13] D. C. Rubin and A. E. Wenzel. One hundred years of forgetting : A quantitative description of retention. *Psychological Review*, 103(4):734–760, 1996.
[14] M. D. Rugg and E. L. Wilding. Retrieval processing and episodic memory. *Trends Cogn. Sci.*, 2000.
[15] L. Tauscher and S. Greenberg. How people revisit web pages: empirical findings and implications for the design of history systems. *International Journal of Human Computer Studies*, 47:97–137, 1997.
[16] J. Teevan. The re:search engine: simultaneous support for finding and re-finding. In *UIST*, 2007.
[17] J. Teevan, E. Adar, R. Jones, and M. A. S. Potts. Information re-retrieval: repeat queries in yahoo's logs. In *SIGIR*, 2007.
[18] E. Tulving. *Elements of episodic memory.* Oxford University Press, 1983.
[19] E. Tulving. What is episodic memory? *Current Directions in Psychological Science*, 2(3):67–70, 1993.
[20] E. Tulving and D. M. Thomson. Encoding specificity and retrieval processes in episodic memory. *Psychological Review*, 80(5):359–380, 1973.

Semantic Data Markets: A Flexible Environment for Knowledge Management *

Roberto De Virgilio
Università Roma Tre, Italy
devirgilio@dia.uniroma3.it

Giorgio Orsi
University of Oxford, UK
giorgio.orsi@cs.ox.ac.uk

Letizia Tanca
Politecnico di Milano, Italy
tanca@elet.polimi.it

Riccardo Torlone
Università Roma Tre, Italy
torlone@dia.uniroma3.it

ABSTRACT

We present NYAYA, a system for the management of Semantic-Web data which couples a general-purpose and extensible storage mechanism with efficient ontology reasoning and querying capabilities. NYAYA processes large Semantic-Web datasets, expressed in multiple formalisms, by transforming them into a collection of *Semantic Data Kiosks*. NYAYA uniformly exposes the native meta-data of each kiosk using the Datalog$^{\pm}$ language, a powerful rule-based modelling language for ontological databases. The kiosks form a *Semantic Data Market* where the data in each kiosk can be uniformly accessed using conjunctive queries and where users can specify user-defined constraints over the data. NYAYA is easily extensible and robust to updates of both data and meta-data in the kiosk and can readily adapt to different logical organization of the persistent storage. The approach has been experimented using well-known benchmarks, and compared to state-of-the-art research prototypes and commercial systems.

Categories and Subject Descriptors

H.2.4 [**Database Management**]: Query Processing, Rule-based databases; H.2.3 [**Database Management**]: Query languages

General Terms

Management, Performance, Experimentation

Keywords

ontological databases, Datalog$^{\pm}$, query rewriting, query answering, semantic data management, semantic web

*This research has been partially funded by the European Commission, Programmes IDEAS-ERC, Projects no.227977-SMScom and no. 246858-DIADEM and from the Oxford Martin School's grant no. LC0910-019-Extreme and Ubiquitous Computing.

CIKM'11, October 24–28, 2011, Glasgow, Scotland, UK.

1. INTRODUCTION

Ever since Tim Berners Lee presented the design principles for Linked Data[1], the public availability of Semantic Web data has grown rapidly. Today, many organizations and practitioners are all contributing to the "Web of Data", building RDF repositories either from scratch or by publishing, in RDF, data stored in traditional formats. The adoption of ontology languages such as RDFS and OWL supports this trend by providing the means to semantically annotate Web data with meta-data, enabling ontological querying and reasoning. Despite the fact that storing, reasoning over, and querying large datasets of semantically annotated data in a flexible and efficient way represents a challenging area of research and a profitable opportunity for industry [16], semantic applications using RDF and linked-data repositories set performance and flexibility requirements that, in our opinion, have not yet been satisfied by the state of the art of data-management solutions. In particular, current semantic data-management systems present some common shortcomings: (i) they usually operate within a language-dependent framework, implementing the reasoning and query-processing algorithms for a specific ontology language; (ii) they hardly adapt to requirements of changing the underlying physical organization (e.g., for optimization purposes); (iii) to bring the expressiveness and performance desiderata to terms, most systems unnecessarily restrict the allowed combination of ontology-modeling constructs, although in many cases decidability and tractability of reasoning and query answering are syntactically identifiable on a per-ontology basis.

We discuss possible solutions to these problems by presenting NYAYA[2], an environment for Semantic-Web data management which provides – in the same order as above – (i) flexible and uniform ontology-reasoning and querying capabilities over semantic data sets expressed in different formalisms, (ii) an efficient and, most importantly, general and extensible storage policy for Semantic-Web datasets, which can adapt to different query engines, exploiting their optimization strategies, (iii) the possibility to syntactically check whether the meta-data in a given repository can be queried efficiently and to use the subset of the language that keeps the complexity of the process at the required level. The last aspect is particularly significant. Suppose for instance that the combined use of two language constructs could potentially lead to undecidability or to a complexity increment;

[1] `http://linkeddata.org/`

[2] Nyaya is the name of the school of logic in the Hindu philosophy.

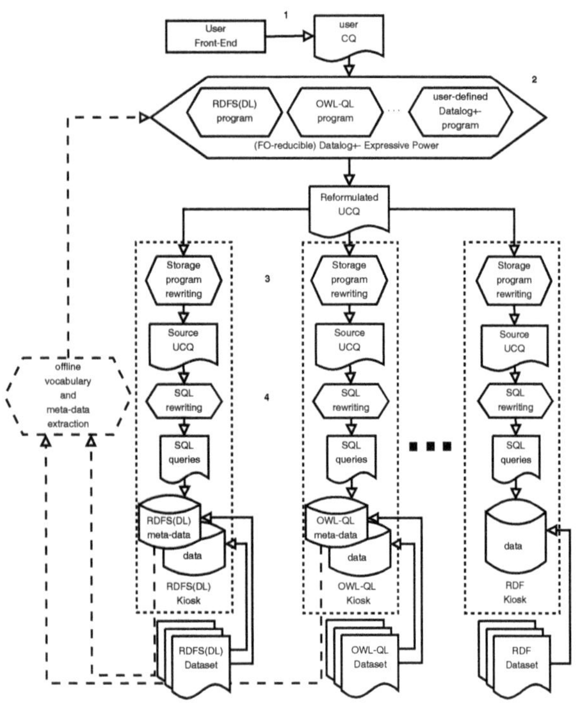

Figure 1: A Semantic Data Market

normally, with a Semantic Web language the two constructs would not appear in the language together, thus severely reducing expressiveness. Conversely, NYAYA does not restrict a-priori the language but checks each set of meta-data for decidability and tractability.

Reasoning and querying in NYAYA is based on Datalog$^{\pm}$ [5, 6], a family of rule-based languages that extends Datalog [8] to allow a controlled class of unsafe rules, i.e., rules with existentially quantified variables in their heads. Datalog$^{\pm}$ captures the most common ontology languages for which query answering is tractable, and provides efficiently-checkable, syntactic conditions for decidability and tractability. To our knowledge, this is the first full and generic implementation of a Datalog$^{\pm}$ engine.

NYAYA allows the construction of persistent repositories of Semantic-Web data that we call *Semantic Data Kiosks*. As shown at the bottom of Figure 1, a kiosk is populated by importing an available RDF dataset, possibly coupled with constraints defined on its content expressed in some Semantic-Web language such as RDF(S) and OWL (or variants thereof). In order to allow inferencing, native vocabularies and meta-data are extracted and represented as (first-order) Datalog$^{\pm}$ constraints. In addition, the entities of a kiosk are mapped to their actual representation in the storage by means of a set of non-recursive Datalog rules called *storage program*. This enables the separation of concerns between, on the one hand, the reasoning and query-processing algorithms and, on the other hand, the logical organization of the storage, which can be changed without affecting querying. A collection of kiosks constitutes what we call a *Semantic Data Market*, a place that exposes the content of all the kiosks in a uniform way and where users can issue queries and collect results, possibly by specifying additional constraints over the available data using Datalog$^{\pm}$. An important aspect of NYAYA is its flexibility. First, whenever a fresh Semantic-Web source is made available, a new kiosk can be easily built from it by extracting its meta-data and importing its data; in this way, its content is promptly available to the users of the semantic data market. Second, if a user wants to query the same kiosk by adopting a different set of constraints, the query is automatically reformulated accordingly and issued to the kiosk.

Summarizing, our main contributions are the following:

- the definition of the Semantic Data Kiosk, an extension of the standard Knowledge Base where the ontological constraints and the logical organization of persistent information are uniformly represented in the same language;
- the associated efficient and model-independent storage mechanism for Semantic-Web data, which guarantees the separation of concerns between the reasoning capabilities and the underlying organization of data;
- a powerful rule-based inference and query-answering engine over massive data sets based on Datalog$^{\pm}$, whose efficiency is confirmed by our experimental results over widely accepted benchmarks.

The rest of the paper is organized as follows. Section 2 presents the notion of semantic data kiosk and the adopted storage and querying techniques of NYAYA. Section 3 discusses related literature, while Section 4 illustrates the implementation of NYAYA and the experiments that allowed us to evaluate NYAYA's performance. Finally, Section 5 draws some conclusions and delineates our future work.

2. SEMANTIC DATA MARKETS

Semantic Data Kiosk. The basic building block of NYAYA has three components:

1. an *ontological program* Σ_O, made of a set of Datalog$^{\pm}$ [5, 6] rules over a collection of first-order predicates $\mathcal{O}$, called *ontology predicates*, that represent the ontological entities of the current application;
2. a *storage program* Σ_S, made of a set of full TGDs having, as head, a (single) atom with predicate in $\mathcal{O}$ and, as body, a conjunction of atoms over a set of first-order predicates $\mathcal{S}$, called *storage predicates*, that represent constructs of the metamodel $\mathcal{M}$;
3. a database D over $\mathcal{S}$.

A *Semantic Data Market* is just a collection of Semantic Data Kiosks.

Storage. Following an approach for the uniform management of heterogeneous data models [2], in NYAYA data and meta-data are extracted from the sources and represented using a *meta-model* $\mathcal{M}$ made of a generic set of *constructs*, each of which represents a primitive used in a concrete Semantic-Web language (such as RDF, RDFS and OWL). This has two main advantages: (i) it provides a framework in which different Semantic-Web languages can be handled in a uniform way and (ii) it allows the definition of *language-independent* reasoning capabilities. The constructs of $\mathcal{M}$ are chosen by factoring out common modeling primitives of different models. For instance, $\mathcal{M}$ includes the construct CLASS that is used in both RDFS and OWL to represent a set of resources having common characteristics. Each construct is associated with an identifier, a name, a set of *features*, and a set of references to other constructs. NYAYA relies on a relational implementation of the meta-model where each construct corresponds to a relational table. The approach is easily extensible; for instance, generalization hi-

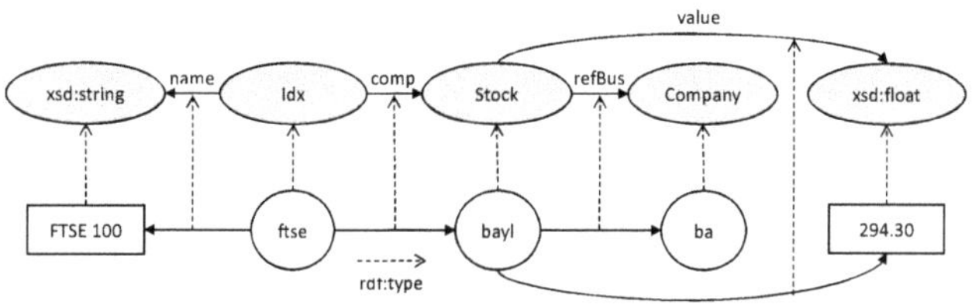

Figure 2: A running example.

erarchies can be added to $\mathcal{M}$ by specifying constructs that capture the notions of subclass and subproperty [2].

As an example, the RDF/RDFS stock-exchange scenario of Figure 2 is represented using $\mathcal{M}$ as illustrated in Figure 3 (where some fields are omitted for the sake of readability). The example involves three classes: `Stock`, `Company`, and

CLASS	
ID	**Name**
30	Idx
31	Stock
32	Company

I-CLASS		
ID	**URI**	**ClassID**
60	ftse	30
61	bayl	31
62	ba	32

OBJECTPROPERTY			
ID	**Name**	**Subject ClassID**	**Object ClassID**
20	comp	30	31
21	refBus	31	32

I-OBJECTPROPERTY			
ID	**I-Subject ClassID**	**I-Object ClassID**	**Object PropertyID**
50	60	61	20
51	61	62	21

DATAPROPERTY			
ID	**Name**	**ClassOID**	**TypeID**
10	name	30	string
11	value	31	float

I-DATAPPROPERTY			
ID	**I-ClassID**	**Value**	**DataPropertyID**
40	60	FTSE 100	10
41	61	294.30	11

Figure 3: Representation of the running example in the meta-model used for data storage.

`Idx`, which models financial indexes. Each class is represented by a tuple in the CLASS table. The instances of these classes, namely `ftse` (the financial index FTSE 100), `bayl` (the British Airways PLC stock) and `ba` (the British Airways company), are represented by tuples in the I-CLASS table. The relationships `comp` and `refBus`, modeling the stock composition of a financial index and the company related to each stock respectively, are represented by tuples in the OBJECTPROPERTY table. Similarly, the attribute `name` of a financial index and the attribute `value` of a stock are represented in the DATAPROPERTY table. Instances of these relationships are represented in the I-OBJECTPROPERTY and I-DATAPROPERTY tables, respectively. In particular, the `bayl` stock, which is a component of the financial index `ftse`, refers to the `ba` company and has value `294.30` pounds. Note that data and meta-data are managed in a uniform way. In Section 4 we illustrate the indexing and partitioning techniques adopted to guarantee good performance when the above tables become very large.

Ontological and storage programs. The top half of Table 1 shows a possible terminological knowledge over the stock-exchange scenario illustrated above. The first constraint specifies that each stock index must have a name, while the second one specifies that a stock has a value, a reference business (`refBus`), and it is part of a financial index. The third constraint specifies that a stock is a particular form of financial instrument (`FinIns`), and the following one defines a new class representing investments. The last

Table 1: Semantic Data Kiosk: Stock Exchange

	Datalog$^\pm$ rules
$\Sigma_\mathcal{O}$	idx(X) $\rightarrow \exists Y$name(X,Y). stock(X) $\rightarrow \exists YZW$ value(X,Y), comp(X,Z), idx(Z), refBus(X,W), company(W). stock(X) $\rightarrow$ finIns(X). investment(X) $\rightarrow \exists YZW$ product(X,Y), stock(Y), buyer(X,Z), qty(X,W). company(X) $\rightarrow \exists Y$ market(X,Y). loan(X) $\rightarrow$ finIns(X). company(X), buyer(Y,X) $\rightarrow$ marketActor(X). comp(X,Y) $\rightarrow$ stock(X). comp(X,Y) $\rightarrow$ idx(Y). loan(X), stock(X) $\rightarrow \perp$. (NC) comp(X,Y) $\wedge$ comp(X,Z) $\rightarrow$ Y=Z. (EGD)
$\Sigma_\mathcal{S}$	idx(X) $\leftarrow$ I-CLASS(Z_0,X,Z_1), CLASS(Z_1,'Idx'). comp(X,Y) $\leftarrow$ I-OBJECTPROPERTY(Z_0,Z_1,Z_2,Z_3), I-CLASS(Z_1,X,Z_6), I-CLASS(Z_2,Y,Z_7), OBJECTPROPERTY(Z_3,'comp',Z_4,Z_5). name(X,Y) $\leftarrow$ I-DATAPROPERTY(Z_0,Z_1,Y,Z_2), DATAPROPERTY(Z_2,'name',Z_3,Z_4), I-CLASS(Z_1,X,Z_5).

two constraints are: (i) a negative constraint specifying that loans and stocks are disjoint classes, and (ii) a functional constraint on the relationship `comp`. The bottom half of Table 1 provides three examples of storage-program rules for the class `idx`, the object property `comp` and the data property `value`, respectively. These rules describe how concepts, roles and attributes of the ontology are represented in the meta-model used for storage and are automatically derived when a new semantic data kiosk is built.

Querying. Let us now consider a semantic data kiosk $\mathcal{K} = (\Sigma_\mathcal{O}, \Sigma_\mathcal{S}, D)$. Querying K requires to consider both the constraints in $\Sigma_\mathcal{O}$ and in $\Sigma_\mathcal{S}$.

In NYAYA querying and reasoning are reduced to conjunctive query answering under *first-order reducible constraints* [17], i.e., given a query q, it is possible to construct a first-order query q_{rew} such that for every database D the answers to q over D given the constraints in $\Sigma_\mathcal{O} \cup \Sigma_\mathcal{S}$ are answers of q_{rew} over D (i.e., the query q_{rew} "embeds" the constraints in $\Sigma_\mathcal{O} \cup \Sigma_\mathcal{S}$). This class of constraints corresponds to the class of all the non-recursive Datalog programs for which data-complexity of query answering with respect to a fixed query and a fixed set of rules is in uniform AC^0 [15]. This allows NYAYA to delegate both reasoning and querying to the underlying relational database engine thus obtaining the same efficiency as for traditional database queries. Notice that the rules of $\Sigma_\mathcal{S}$ always constitute a safe and non-recursive Datalog program. Therefore, if $\Sigma_\mathcal{O}$ is FO-reducible then conjunctive-query answering over D under $\Sigma_\mathcal{O} \cup \Sigma_\mathcal{S}$ is also FO-reducible [10], implying that the organization of the data in the persistent storage does not affect the complexity of query answering. Based on this result, the construction of a new Semantic Data Kiosk from a fresh data source requires only to check for FO-reducibility of its meta-data. This check needs also to be applied whenever a user introduces a new user-defined Datalog$^\pm$ program to be used on top of an existing stored dataset.

NYAYA provides an implementation of two FO-reducible members of the Datalog$^\pm$ family: Linear Datalog$^\pm$ [5], and Sticky Datalog$^\pm$ [6]. Both languages are strictly more expressive than DL-*Lite* [7], the best-known language for tractable ontology-based data access and thus together offer a powerful formalism for expressing ontological constraints. Let Q be a user conjunctive query expressed in Datalog-like syntax over a semantic data kiosk. Following Figure 1, the processing of a query Q against a semantic data kiosk $\mathcal{K} = (\Sigma_{\mathcal{O}}, \Sigma_{\mathcal{S}}, D)$ proceeds as follows.

1. The CQ Q is reformulated using the rules in $\Sigma_{\mathcal{O}}$ by applying TGD-Rewrite [11], a backward-chaining resolution algorithm that produces a perfect rewriting $Q_{\mathcal{O}}$ of Q with respect to $\Sigma_{\mathcal{O}}$. By virtue of the FO-reducibility of Sticky and Linear Datalog$^{\pm}$, $Q_{\mathcal{O}}$ is a union of conjunctive queries.

2. Every $Q^i_{\mathcal{O}} \in Q_{\mathcal{O}}$ is rewritten in terms of the storage tables using the rules in $\Sigma_{\mathcal{S}}$. For each $Q^i_{\mathcal{O}}$, the result is another CQ $Q^i_{\mathcal{S}}$ that is perfect rewriting of $Q^i_{\mathcal{O}}$ with respect of $\Sigma_{\mathcal{S}}$. The union of all the $Q^i_{\mathcal{S}}$ forms a perfect rewriting $\hat{Q}$ of Q with respect to $\Sigma_{\mathcal{O}} \cup \Sigma_{\mathcal{S}}$.

3. The query $\hat{Q}$ is rewritten in SQL and executed over the underlying DBMS.

Consider the Semantic Data Kiosk in Table 1 and the query $Q: \ Q(A) \leftarrow name(C, A), comp(B, C), stock(B)$ retrieving the names of the financial indexes with at least one quoted stock (i.e., a sanity check query). After the application of the steps above, the final query is easily translated into the following SQL statement to be executed on the underlying relational database.

```
SELECT DP.Value
FROM I-OBJECTPROPERTY AS OP
     I-DATAPROPERTY as DP
WHERE DP.I-ClassID = OP.I-ObjectClassID AND
      OP.ObjectPropertyID = '20' AND
      DP.DataPropertyID = '10'
```

This dramatic simplification is due to the fact that the knowledge of the meta-model allows us to eliminate a high number of automatically generated subqueries, reducing the number of joins to be executed, with a noticeable improvement in performance.

3. RELATED WORK

Existing systems for the management of Semantic-Web data can be discussed according to two major issues: *storage* and *querying*.

Considering the storage, two main approaches can be identified: the first focuses on developing *native storage systems* (such as AllegroGraph[3] or OWLIM[4]) to exploit ad-hoc optimisations, while the second (e.g., Sesame[5], TAP[6], Jena[7], Virtuoso[8] and the semantic extensions implemented in Oracle Database 11g R2 [9]) make use of traditional DBMSs, *e.g.* relational and object-oriented. Generally speaking, native storage systems are more efficient in terms of load and update time, whereas the adoption of mature data management systems has the advantage of relying on consolidate and effective optimisations. Indeed, a drawback of native approaches consists in the need for re-thinking query-optimization and transaction-processing techniques. Differently from the other approaches, NYAYA provides a *general-purpose* storage policy for Semantic-Web data sets that allows the uniform management of different ontological formalisms and language-independent reasoning capabilities. A rule-based mapping between the ontological entities and their representation in the storage separates concerns between the query-processing algorithms and the physical organization of data, which can be changed without affecting querying. Our current relational implementation takes advantage of RDBMS optimization techniques based on indexing and partitioning.

On the querying side, if we assume the absence of ontological constraints, the efficiency of query processing depends only on the logical and physical organization of the data and on the query language complexity. However reasoning is a fundamental requirement of Semantic-Web applications, and efficient reasoning algorithms are now available for several ontology languages based on description logics. A first family of systems [4, 19, 18] materialises all the inferences; this dramatically improves query-processing performance, but loading time is inflated because all the complexity of reasoning is deferred to the loading time and could potentially generate an exponential blow-up of space occupation. Moreover, update management is also critical since the inferred data must be updated accordingly. Full materialisation is therefore suitable for stable data sets, especially when the query patterns are known in advance. A second class of systems [1, 14, 3, 12] including NYAYA executes inferencing on-the-fly through *intensional query reformulation*, thus the complexity of query processing depends on both the logical organisation of the data and the expressiveness of the adopted data language and of the queries. This approach has many advantages: in the first place, space occupation is reduced to the minimum necessary to store the data set and it is possible to define a suitable trade-off for inference materialisation depending on which queries are executed most frequently. Another advantage is the robustness to updates: since inferences are computed every time, there is no need for incremental updates. The major drawback of on-the-fly inferencing is the impact of reasoning time on query processing. In NYAYA, the separation between the ontological entities and the organization of data allow us to push the rewriting up to the level of the persistent storage, increasing the efficiency of query answering. In addition, the Datalog$^{\pm}$ language adopted in NYAYA allows to test decidability and tractability of query answering for a given ontology in polynomial time.

4. EXPERIMENTS

One of the most interesting contributions of NYAYA is its overall efficiency that makes it appealing for general-purpose applications. In this section we provide a detailed experimental evaluation that supports this claim.

NYAYA has been implemented in Java and its inference component has been built by extending the IRIS Datalog engine[9]. Oracle 11g R2 has been used for the persistent storage, exploiting the native referential partitioning technique of the DBMS. In particular, tables storing instance-level predicates are horizontally partitioned with respect to the foreign keys that refer to the tables storing schema-level predicates. A prototype implementation of NYAYA is available on the Web[10]. We compared NYAYA with two well-known representatives of semantic-data management systems that rely on full materialization: BIGOWLIM[11] and

[3] http://www.franz.com/products/allegrograph/
[4] http://www.ontotext.com/owlim/
[5] http://www.openrdf.org/
[6] http://tap.stanford.edu/.
[7] http://jena.sourceforge.net/
[8] http://virtuoso.openlinksw.com/

[9] http://www.iris-reasoner.org/
[10] http://pamir.dia.uniroma3.it:8080/nyaya/
[11] http://www.ontotext.com/owlim/big/

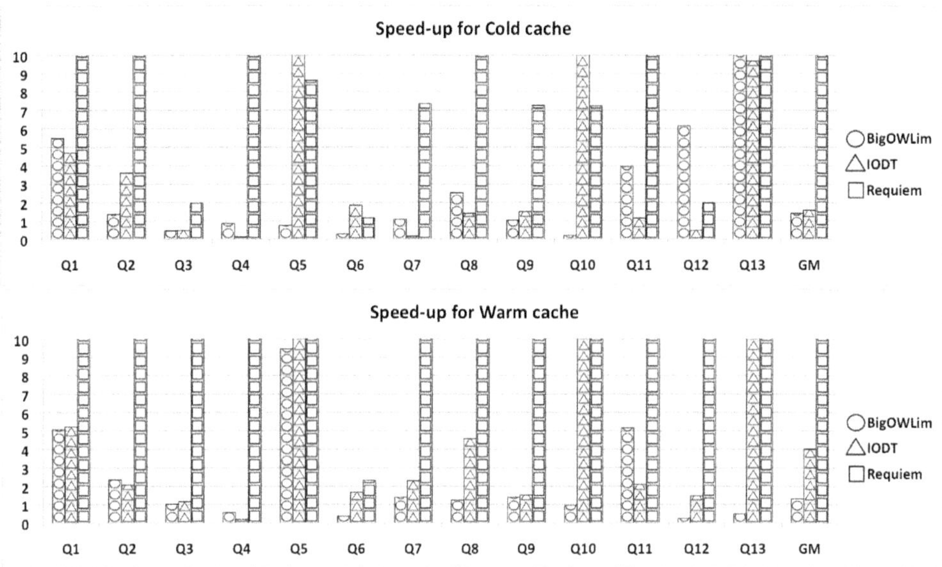

Figure 4: Performance ratio on UOBM50 between other semantic-data management systems and Nyaya

Table 2: Data Loading

	BigOWLim	IODT	Nyaya
LUBM(50)	8 (mins)	77 (mins)	9,18 (mins)
UOBM(50)	18 (hours)	65 (hours)	0,5 (hours)
Wikipedia3	71 (hours)	181 (hours)	2,38 (hours)

IODT[12]. In particular, we used BigOWLim v.3.3 over the File System, and IODT v.1.5 equipped with the Scalable Ontology Repository (SOR). In addition, we compared the rewriting technique of Nyaya with the on-the-fly inferencing mechanisms of REQUIEM [14] over the Nyaya storage meta-model, since REQUIEM does not rely on a specific back-end. All the experiments have been performed on a dual-quad core 2.66GHz Intel Xeon, running Linux RedHat, with 8 GB of memory, 6 MB cache, and a 2-disk 1Tbyte striped RAID array. In our experiments we used two widely-accepted benchmarks: LUBM[13] and UOBM [13], for which we considered an instance of 12.8 million triples. Since the expressiveness of the meta-data in the above data sets exceeds the one of Datalog$^\pm$ (i.e., OWL-Lite for LUBM and OWL-DL for UOBM), in our experiments we manually produced the FO-reducible approximation of the constraints for all the data sets. These approximations are available on the Nyaya Web site for the reproducibility of the experiments. We have also used Wikipedia3, a conversion of the English Wikipedia[14] into RDF. This is a monthly updated data set containing around 47 million triples. The expressiveness of its meta-data completely falls within that of Datalog$^\pm$ so no adaptations were made. The performance of the systems has been measured with respect to: (i) data loading, (ii) querying and reasoning, and (iii) maintenance.

Data loading. As shown in Table 2, Nyaya behaves much better than IODT and BigOWLim. Actually, the main advantage of our approach is that we execute pure data loading while the other systems have to pre-compile the knowledge-base to materialize it, producing a very large (and possibly exponential) number of tuples to be stored. The loading time for BigOWLim degrades dramatically from LUBM to UOBM (135 times slower) due to the increasing complexity of the meta-data, and from LUBM to Wikipedia3 (532 times slower), due to the large set of facts. Moreover our framework exploits the storage meta-model presented in Section 2 which allows a parallel execution of data import into the DBMS. BigOWLim has to process all the triples in memory while IODT needs to maintain complex block indexes. Since for REQUIEM we used our storage model, a comparison with it is not meaningful here.

Querying and reasoning. We performed *cold-cache* experiments (by dropping all file-system caches before restarting the systems and running the queries) and *warm-cache* experiments (without dropping the caches). We repeated all the tests three times and measured the mean execution times. Three phases of the query process have been considered: *preprocessing*, *execution* and *traversal*. In the preprocessing phase BigOWLim loads statistics and indexes in main memory, while Nyaya and REQUIEM compute the rewriting of queries. IODT does not require preprocessing.

We executed the sets of queries included in the LUBM and UOBM benchmarks (they are not reported here due to space limitation). A significant result is the *speed-up* between our approach and the others. We computed the speed-up for all data sets as the ratio between the execution time of each competitor approach P, and that of our approach Nyaya, or briefly as $S = {}^{t_P}/_{t_{\text{Nyaya}}}$. The speed-up for UOBM is reported in Figure 4. The vertical axis is the speed-up S computed for each competitor approach while on the horizontal axis we have the 13 queries. We also report the geometric mean (GM) of speed-up values for both cold-cache and warm-cache experiments. In general BigOWLim performs better than IODT, and Nyaya performs very well with respect to both of them: for cold-cache experiments, the mean Nyaya is 1,6 times and 1,9 times faster than BigOWLim and IODT respectively. For some queries BigOWLim and IODT are faster than our system since the query rewriting produces a large number of CQs to be executed. In these cases we have $S < 1$. Actually, we are currently investigating

[12]http://www.alphaworks.ibm.com/tech/semanticstk
[13]http://swat.cse.lehigh.edu/projects/lubm/
[14]http://labs.systemone.net/wikipedia3

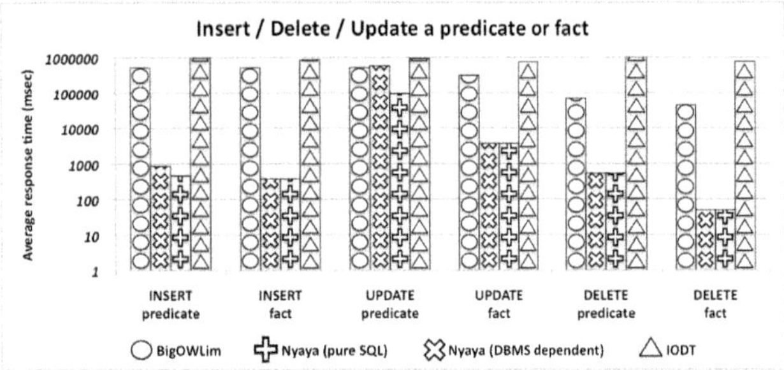

Figure 5: Maintenance of a kiosk

further optimization techniques to significantly reduce this number. NYAYA is 25 times faster than REQUIEM (for the sake of readability in Figure 4 the maximum value on the vertical axis is 10). This is due to the query rewriting phase of REQUIEM, that is the most expensive operation of the overall process. In [10] we reported in detail performance evaluation of each query. We omit the results for LUBM because the systems present a similar behavior.

In the experiments done on the Wikipedia3 data set, NYAYA behaved in general better than the other systems, while IODT performed better than BIGOWLIM. This is due to the significant amount of data to process, although the set of ontological constraints are simpler in this case. For space limitations, the details have been presented in [10].

Maintenance. In these last experiments we tested maintenance operations in terms of insertion (deletion) of new (old) terms or assertions, and update of existing terms or assertions. Figure 5 shows the performance of each system for update operations of data and meta-data over the LUBM, UOBM and Wikipedia data sets. As for data loading, the comparison with REQUIEM is meaningless. We considered the mean response times (in msec) to insert, delete and update a meta-data predicate (i.e., a concept, a role or an attribute) or a fact in the database. The results show how NYAYA outperforms the other systems when dealing with insertions and deletions of both data and meta-data. In fact, in both BIGOWLIM and IODT the insertion a new predicate or a fact entails re-compiling a (possibly exponential) number of tuples referring to the new predicate while in NYAYA this simply requires an insertion or a deletion of a single-tuple. On the other hand, the update of an existing predicate needs to be propagated in order to satisfy the constraints. As a consequence, the complexity of this task depends on the amount of data stored in the database. In this respect, Figure 5 shows the behavior of NYAYA in the case of meta-data updates when pure-SQL operations are used (i.e., independently of the DBMS) and when optimized partition-maintenance functions provided by the specific DBMS are adopted.

5. CONCLUSION AND FUTURE WORK

In this paper we presented NYAYA, a system for the uniform management of different repositories of Semantic Web data. This work opens a number of interesting and challenging directions of further research. A natural step is to further extend NYAYA to deal with non-FO-reducible languages like *Guarded* Datalog$^{\pm}$ [5]. Moreover, on a different front, it would be interesting to exploit NYAYA for supporting also the reconciliation and the integration of the data of the Semantic Data Market.

6. REFERENCES

[1] A. Acciarri, D. Calvanese, G. de Giacomo, D. Lembo, M. Lenzerini, M. Palmieri, and R. Rosati. QuOnto: Querying ontologies. In *AAAI*, pages 1670–1671, 2005.

[2] P. Atzeni, P. Cappellari, R. Torlone, P. Bernstein, and G. Gianforme. Model-independent schema translation. *VLDB J.*, 17(6):1347–1370, 2008.

[3] C. Beeri, A. Levy, and M. Rousset. Rewriting queries using views in description logics. In *PODS*, pages 99–108, 1997.

[4] B. Bishop, A. Kiryakov, D. Ognyanoff, I. Peikov, Z. Tashev, and R. Velkov. OWLIM: A family of scalable semantic repositories. *J. of Web Semantics*, 2(1):33–42, 2011.

[5] A. Calì, G. Gottlob, and T. Lukasiewicz. A general datalog-based framework for tractable query answering over ontologies. In *PODS*, pages 77–86, 2009.

[6] A. Calì, G. Gottlob, and A. Pieris. Advanced processing for ontological queries. In *VLDB*, pages 554–565, 2010.

[7] D. Calvanese, G. de Giacomo, D. Lembo, M. Lenzerini, and R. Rosati. Tractable reasoning and efficient query answering in description logics: The DL-Lite Family. *J. of Automated Reasoning*, 39(3):385–429, 2007.

[8] S. Ceri, G. Gottlob, and L. Tanca. What you always wanted to know about Datalog (and never dared to ask). *IEEE TKDE*, 1(1):146–166, 1989.

[9] E. Chong, S. Das, G. Eadon, and J. Srinivasan. An efficient SQL-based RDF querying scheme. In *VLDB*, pages 1216–1227, 2005.

[10] R. De Virgilio, G. Orsi, L. Tanca, and R. Torlone. Reasoning over large semantic datasets. Technical Report RT-DIA-149, University Roma Tre, 2009.

[11] G. Gottlob, G. Orsi, and A. Pieris. Ontological queries: Rewriting and optimization. In *ICDE*, 2011.

[12] C. Lutz, D. Toman, and F. Wolter. Conjunctive query answering in the description logic $\mathcal{EL}$ using a relational database system. In *IJCAI*, pages 2070–2075, 2009.

[13] L. Ma, Y. Yang, Z. Qiu, G. T. Xie, Y. Pan, and S. Liu. Towards a complete OWL ontology benchmark. In *ESWC*, pages 125–139, 2006.

[14] H. Pérez-Urbina, B. Motik, and I. Horrocks. Tractable query answering and rewriting under description logic constraints. *J. of Applied Logic*, 8(2):151–232, 2009.

[15] M. Vardi. On the complexity of bounded-variable queries. In *PODS*, pages 266–276, 1995.

[16] R. D. Virgilio, F. Giunchiglia, and L. Tanca, editors. *Semantic Web Information Management - A Model-Based Perspective*. Springer Verlag, 2010.

[17] K. Wang and L. Yuan. First-order logic characterization of program properties. *IEEE TKDE*, 6(4):518–533, 1994.

[18] Z. Wu, G. Eadon, S. Das, E. I. Chong, V. Kolovski, M. Annamalai, and J. Srinivasan. Implementing an inference engine for rdfs/owl constructs and user-defined rules in oracle. In *ICDE*, pages 1239–1248, 2008.

[19] J. Zhou, L. Ma, Q. Liu, L. Zhang, Y. Yu, and Y. Pan. Minerva: A scalable owl ontology storage and inference system. In *ASWC*, pages 429–443, 2006.

Advancing the Discovery of Unique Column Combinations*

Ziawasch Abedjan
Hasso-Plattner-Institut
Potsdam, Germany
ziawasch.abedjan@hpi.uni-potsdam.de

Felix Naumann
Hasso-Plattner-Institut
Potsdam, Germany
naumann@hpi.uni-potsdam.de

ABSTRACT

Unique column combinations of a relational database table are sets of columns that contain only unique values. Discovering such combinations is a fundamental research problem and has many different data management and knowledge discovery applications. Existing discovery algorithms are either brute force or have a high memory load and can thus be applied only to small datasets or samples. In this paper, the well-known GORDIAN algorithm [9] and "Apriori-based" algorithms [4] are compared and analyzed for further optimization. We greatly improve the Apriori algorithms through efficient candidate generation and statistics-based pruning methods. A hybrid solution HCA-GORDIAN combines the advantages of GORDIAN and our new algorithm HCA, and it outperforms all previous work in many situations.

Categories and Subject Descriptors

H.2.8 [**Database Management**]: Database applications

General Terms

Algorithms

Keywords

unique, apriori, functional dependency, key discovery

1. UNIQUE COLUMN COMBINATIONS

Unique column combinations are sets of columns of a relational database table that fulfill the uniqueness constraint. Uniqueness of a column combination K within a table can be defined as follows:

DEFINITION 1. *Given a relational database schema* $R = \{C_1, C_2, \ldots, C_m\}$ *with columns* C_i *and an instance* $r \subseteq C_1 \times \ldots \times C_m$, *a column combination* $K \subseteq R$ *is a* unique, *iff*

$$\forall t_1, t_2 \in r : (t_1 \neq t_2) \Rightarrow (t_1[K] \neq t_2[K])$$

Unique discovery has high significance in several data management applications, such as data modeling, anomaly detection, query optimization, and indexing. Discovered uniques are good candidates for primary keys of a table. Therefore some literature refers to them as "candidate keys" [8]. The term "composite key" is also used to highlight the fact that they comprise multiple columns [9]. We want to stress that the detection of *uniques* is a problem that can be solved exactly, while the detection of *keys* can only be solved heuristically. Uniqueness is a necessary precondition for a key, but only a human expert can "promote" a unique to a key, because uniques can appear by coincidence for a certain state of the data. In contrast, keys are consciously specified and denote a schema constraint.

An important property of uniques and keys is their minimality. Minimal uniques are uniques of which no strict subsets hold the uniqueness property:

DEFINITION 2. *A unique* $K \subseteq R$ *is* minimal, *iff*

$$\forall K' \subset K : (\exists t_1, t_2 \in r : (t_1[K'] = t_2[K']) \wedge (t_1 \neq t_2))$$

In principle, to identify a column combination K of fixed size as a unique, all tuples t_i must be scanned. A scan has a runtime of $O(n)$ in the number n of rows. To detect duplicate values, one needs either a sort in $O(n \log n)$ or a hashing algorithm that needs $O(n)$ space. Non-uniques are defined as follows:

DEFINITION 3. *A column combination* K *that is not a unique is called a* non-unique.

Discovering all uniques of a table or relational instance can be reduced to the problem of discovering all minimal uniques. Every superset of a minimal unique is also a unique. Hence, in the rest of this paper the discovery of all uniques is synonymously used for discovering all minimal uniques. The exponential complexity is caused by the fact that for a relational schema $R = \{C_1, \ldots, C_m\}$, there are $2^m - 1$ subsets $K \subseteq R$ that can be uniques. Actually, even the result size of the problem can be exponential. In the worst case, there can be $\binom{m}{\frac{m}{2}}$ minimal uniques, each consisting of $\frac{m}{2}$ columns.

The contributions of this paper toward efficient unique detection are:

1. We analyze, discuss, and categorize existing algorithms and their strengths and weaknesses.
2. We introduce the new algorithm HCA and show how a bottom-up algorithm can be optimized by applying the concept of apriori candidate generation, statistics-driven pruning, and ad-hoc inference of FDs.
3. Furthermore, we present an elegant combination of HCA with the well-known GORDIAN algorithm [9], named HCA-GORDIAN, gaining even more efficiency.

2. RELATED WORK

Although the topic of finding or inferring composite keys and functional dependencies appeared ever since there are

*A full version of this paper is available at [1]

CIKM'11, October 24–28, 2011, Glasgow, Scotland, UK.

relational databases, there are only a few known approaches to the problem of discovering all minimal uniques of a table. These are discussed in detail in Sec. 3. In the broader area of meta data discovery however, there is much work related to the discovery of functional dependencies (FD). In fact, the discovery of FDs is very similar to the problem of discovering uniques, as uniques functionally determine all other individual columns within a table. There are several approaches for FD discovery [3, 6]; some include approximative solutions [5, 7]. Most new ideas in this research field follow either an Apriori or level-wise partitioning approach and require exponential runtime.

On the other hand, knowledge of FDs can be exploited for runtime-efficient unique discovery. Saeidian and Spencer present an FD-based approach that supports unique discovery [8]. They showed that given a minimal set of FDs , any column that appears only on the left side of the given FDs must be part of all keys and columns that appear only on the right side of the FDs cannot be part of any key. This insight cannot be used in the context of our work, as we assume no prior knowledge of functional dependencies, indexes, or semantic correlations. However, in Sec. 4 we show that our new algorithm HCA is able to infer some FDs on the fly and use them for apriori classification of some column combinations.

3. ALGORITHMIC FOUNDATIONS

In this section, the most important approaches to unique discovery are introduced, distinguishing two different classes: Row-based algorithms are based on a row-by-row scan of the database for all column combinations. The second class, column-based algorithms, contains algorithms that check the uniqueness of a column combination on all rows at once. Such column combinations are generated iteratively and each of them is checked only once.

Gordian: A Row-based Approach. Row-based processing of a table for discovering uniques requires multiple runs over all column combinations as more and more rows are considered. It benefits from the intuition that non-uniques can be detected without considering all rows of a table. A recursive unique discovery algorithm that works this way is GORDIAN [9]. The algorithm consists of three parts: *(i)* Preorganize table data in form of a prefix tree. *(ii)* Find maximal non-uniques by traversing the prefix tree. *(iii)* Compute minimal uniques from maximal non-uniques. The prefix tree has to be stored in main memory. Each level of the tree represents one column of the table whereas each branch stands for one distinct tuple. Non-unique discovery is performed by a depth-first traversal of the tree for discovering maximum repeated branches, which constitute maximal non-uniques. Maximal non-uniques can be defined as follows:

DEFINITION 4. *A non-unique* $K \subseteq R$ *is* maximal, *iff all of its strict supersets* $K' \supset K$ *are unique.*

After the discovery of all maximal non-uniques, GORDIAN computes all minimal uniques by generating minimal combinations that are not covered by any of the maximal non-uniques. In [9] it is stated that this step needs only quadratic time in the number of minimal uniques, but the presented algorithm implies cubic runtime. The generation of minimal uniques from maximal non-uniques marks a serious bottleneck of the algorithm in case of large numbers of maximal non-uniques. Indeed, our experiments showed that in most cases the unique generation dominates the entire algorithm. Furthermore, the approach is limited by the available main memory and must be used on samples for approximate solutions when dealing with large data sets.

Apriori: A Column-based Approaches. The problem of finding minimal uniques is comparable to the problem of finding frequent itemsets [2]. The well-known Apriori approach is applicable for minimal unique discovery, working bottom-up as well as top-down. With regard to the powerset lattice of a relational schema the Apriori algorithms generate all relevant column combinations of a certain size and verify those at once. Figure 1 illustrates the powerset lattice for the running example in Tab. 1. The effectiveness and theoretical background of those algorithms is discussed by Giannela and Wyss [4]. They call their family of algorithms "Apriori-based", while in fact they make only minimal use of the Apriori idea.

first	last	age	phone
Max	Payne	32	1234
Eve	Smith	24	5432
Eve	Payne	24	3333
Max	Payne	24	3333

Table 1: Example data set

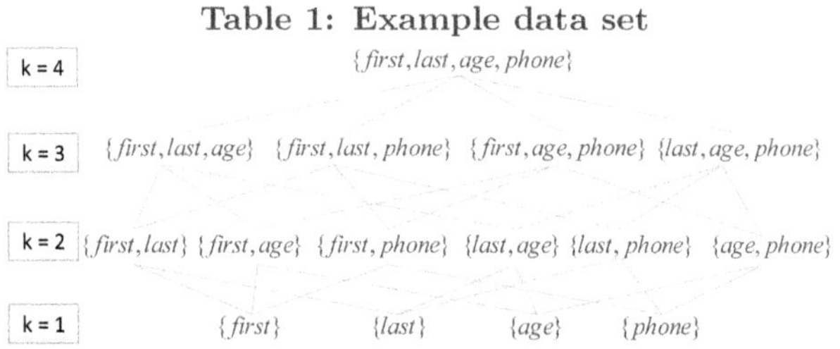

Figure 1: Powerset lattice for the example table

Bottom-up unique discovery indicates here that the powerset lattice of the schema R is traversed beginning with all 1-*combinations* to the top of the lattice, which is the $|R|$-*combination*. The prefixed number k of k-*combination* indicates the size of the combination. The same notation is used for the more specific terms k-*unique* and k-*non-unique*. The algorithm begins with checking the uniqueness of all individual columns. If a column is a unique, it will be added to the set of uniques, and if not it will be added to the list of *1-non-uniques*. The next iteration steps are based on the so-called candidate generation. A k-*candidate* is a potential k-*unique*. In principle, all possible k-*candidates* need to be checked for uniqueness. Effective candidate generation leads to the reduction of the number of uniqueness verifications by excluding apriori known uniques and non-uniques.

4. THE HCA APPROACH

In the following, we introduce the Histogram-Count-based Apriori Algorithm (HCA), an optimized bottom-up algorithm, which outperforms GORDIAN given a threshold of minimum average distinctness. The algorithm is based on the bottom-up algorithm presented in 3. We improve the algorithm by applying an efficient candidate generation, consideration of column statistics as well as ad-hoc inference and use of FDs. Finally, we describe how the advantages of our approach can be combined with advantages provided by GORDIAN for a hybrid solution.

4.1 Efficient Candidate Generation

Candidate generation is a crucial point for both bottom-up and top-down approaches. The more candidates can be pruned apriori, the fewer uniqueness checks have to be performed and the better runtime will be achieved. Given a set of k-*non-uniques*, the naïve approach for generating $(k+1)$-*candidates* is to add non-contained 1-*non-uniques* to a k-*non-unique* [4]. The disadvantage of this approach is that repeated candidates may be generated: Given the example in Tab. 1, the combination {*first,phone*} would be identified as unique after the second pass of the algorithm. In the same pass, the combinations {*first,last*}, { *first,age*}, {*last,age*}, {*last,phone*}, and {*age,phone*} would be identified as non-uniques. In the third pass, the naive candidate generation would generate the 3-*candidates* including {*first,last,age*} by adding *age* to {*first,last*} , {*first,age,last*} by adding *last* to {*first,age*}, and {*last,age,first*} by adding *first* to {*last,age*}. These candidates are equal sets and their generation leads to unnecessary runtime overhead.

Furthermore, candidate generation faces another significant problem. Considering the running example, the generated 3-*candidates* would include {*first,last,phone*} by adding *phone* to { *first,last*} and {*first,age,phone*} by adding *phone* to {*first,age*}. Knowing that {*first,phone*} is a minimal unique, {*first,last,phone*} and {*first,age,phone*} are redundant uniques and their verification is futile.

Our candidate generation (Alg. 1) benefits from all optimizations of the classical apriori candidate generation in the context of mining association rules [2], so that repeated and redundant candidates are indeed pruned apriori.

The intuition behind our candidate generation is that a $(k+1)$-*unique* can only be a minimal iff all of its strict subsets are non-uniques. In other words, a $(k+1)$-*unique* can only be a minimal if the set of k-*non-uniques* contains all of the candidate's k-*subsets*. Because a minimality check is much cheaper than a verification step, we perform this step already within candidate generation. This is done by creating the union of every two k-*non-uniques* that are equal in the first $k-1$ columns (line 5). For the correctness of this operation, it is necessary that the columns are sorted lexicographically. We illustrate sorted sets using square brackets: $[C_1, C_2 \ldots]$. The sorting can be achieved by considering the order during the generation. 2-*candidates* are generated by cross-combination of all 1-*non-uniques*. Each new combination is sorted by a less-equal comparison of its two members. In candidate generations of later passes, the sorting is maintained by retaining the first $k-1$ columns in the preexisting order and a single comparison of the non-equal kth column of the two combined k-*non-uniques* (line 8).

A $(k+1)$-*combination* is not generated if there are no two k-*non-uniques* that conform exactly in the first $k-1$ columns. This is correct because it indicates that one k-*subset* is not a non-unique. Regarding our example from before, the redundant candidate [*first,last,phone*] would not be generated because it requires the occurrence of the sorted subsets [*first,last*] and [*first,phone*] as k-*non-uniques* that equal in the first column. However, [*first,phone*] as a previously discovered unique is missing.

A final minimality check on all remaining candidates prunes all redundant $(k+1)$*uniques*. Due to the inherent sortation of the non-uniques, the second important benefit of our candidate generation is the avoidance of repeated candidates.

4.2 Statistics-based Pruning

Real-world data contains semantic relations between column entries, such as correlations and functional dependencies (FDs). Knowledge of such relations and dependencies can be used to reduce the number of uniqueness checks. Unfortunately, these dependencies are usually not known. Based on retrieved count-distinct values and value frequencies, HCA is able to discover some FDs on the fly. In addition, knowledge of the number of distinct values of column combination and their value distribution allows further pruning by apriori non-unique detection.

HCA is based on a hybrid verification scan that retrieves either the number of distinct values and the histogram of value frequencies of a combination or only the number of distinct values. A candidate is a unique if it contains as many distinct values as there are tuples in the table or if all value frequencies are 1. Regarding our example, column *last* contains the frequencies 1 and 3 for "Smith" and "Payne" respectively. It is a non-unique, because one value frequency is above 1. The retrieval of the histogram is still in $O(n \cdot log(n))$, because retrieving distinct count values and value frequencies need only a sort and a followup scan as it is needed by the duplicate detection approach.

Ad-Hoc Inference of Functional Dependencies. The first benefit of the count-based approach is that FDs can be identified. A functional dependency $X \rightarrow A$ allows us to conclude uniqueness statements: Given combinations $X, Y \subseteq R$ and a column $A \in R$, $\{X, Y\}$ is a unique if $\{A, Y\}$ is a unique and $X \rightarrow A$. In addition, if $\{A, X\}$ is a non-unique and $A \rightarrow B$, then $\{B, X\}$ is also a non-unique. These statements hold because the dependent side of an FD contains at most as many distinct values as the determinant side. For a column combination X and a column A, it holds $X \rightarrow A$ iff the number of distinct values of X equals the number of distinct values in the combination $\{A, X\}$.

HCA, illustrated in Alg. 2, retrieves those dependencies for all 1-*non-uniques* that are contained by the verified 2-*non-uniques*(line 35). In later iterations, for each member of a k-*candidate* it is scanned whether the column is part

Algorithm 1 CANDIDATEGEN

Require: *nonUniques* of size k
Ensure: *candidates* of size $k+1$
1: **for** $i \leftarrow 0$ to $|nonUniques| - 1$ **do**
2:   **for** $j \leftarrow i+1$ to $|nonUniques| - 1$ **do**
3:     *non-unique1* $\leftarrow$ *nonUniques*$[i]$
4:     *non-unique2* $\leftarrow$ *nonUniques*$[j]$
5:     **if** *non-unique1*$[0 \ldots k-2]$ = *non-unique2*$[0 \ldots k-2]$ **then**
6:       *candidate* $\leftarrow$ new $k+1$-sized list
7:       *candidate* $\leftarrow$ *non-unique1*$[0 \ldots k-2]$
8:       **if** *non-unique1*$[k-1]$ <*non-unique2*$[k-1]$ **then**
9:         *candidate*$[k-1]$ $\leftarrow$ *non-unique1*$[k-1]$
10:         *candidate*$[k]$ $\leftarrow$ *non-unique2*$[k-1]$
11:       **else**
12:         *candidate*$[k-1]$ $\leftarrow$ *non-unique2*$[k-1]$
13:         *candidate*$[k]$ $\leftarrow$ *non-unique1*$[k-1]$
14:       **end if**
15:       **if** ISNOTMINIMAL(*candidate*) **then**
16:         **continue**
17:       **end if**
18:       *candidates*.ADD(*candidate*)
19:     **end if**
20:   **end for**
21: **end for**
22: **return** *candidates*

of a discovered FD and if so which of the previously defined conclusions can be applied for the combination with the substituted member. So, it is possible to skip scans of *k-candidates* that were apriori classified through FDs.

The FD-based pruning takes place after each verification of a current candidate by looking for all substitutions that are possible using an existing FD (lines 23 and 28). The futility check in line 14 is performed to omit candidates that were already covered by FDs. Regarding our running example, it holds *phone* → *age*. Thus, knowing that {*first,phone*} is a non-unique, {*age,first*} must be a non-unique, too. On the other hand knowing that {*age, first,last*} is a unique {*first,last,phone*} must be a unique, too.

Algorithm 2 HCA Algorithm

```
Require: m columns
Ensure: Uniques
 1: for currentColumn in columns do
 2:   if isUnique(currentColumn) then
 3:     Uniques.add(currentColumn)
 4:   else
 5:     nonUniqueColumns.add(currentColumn)
 6:     storeHistogramOf(currentColumn)
 7:   end if
 8: end for
 9: currentNonUniques ← nonUniqueColumns
10: for k ← 2 to |nonUniqueColumns| do
11:   k-candidates ←candidateGen(currentNonUniques)
12:   currentNonUniques ← new empty list
13:   for candidate in k-candidates do
14:     if isFutile(candidate) then
15:       continue;
16:     end if
17:     if prunedByHistogram(candidate) then
18:       currentNonUniques.add(candidate)
19:       continue;
20:     end if
21:     if isUnique(candidate) then
22:       Uniques.add(candidate)
23:       for each FD k-candidate→ candidate do
24:         Uniques.add(k-candidate)
25:       end for
26:     else
27:       currentNonUniques.add(candidate)
28:       for each FD candidate → k-candidate do
29:         currentNonUniques.add(k-candidate)
30:       end for
31:       storeHistogramOf(candidate)
32:     end if
33:   end for
34:   if k = 2 then
35:     retrieveFDs()
36:   end if
37: end for
38: return Uniques
```

Count- and Histogram-based Pruning. Another benefit of the count- and histogram-based approach is the apriori identification of non-uniqueness of a *k-candidate* by considering the value frequencies of its combined $(k-1)$-*non-unique* subsets. The union of two non-unique combinations cannot be a unique if the product of the count-distinct values of these combinations is below the instance cardinality. In a more general case, it is sufficient to identify a value within one of the $(k-1)$-*non-uniques* that has a higher frequency than the number of distinct values within the other $(k-1)$-*non-unique*. In our running example, the 2-*candidate* {*last,age*} can be pruned because the value frequency of "Payne" is 3 and therefore higher than the number of distinct values in *age*, which is only 2. In case the value with the highest frequency equals the number of distinct values of the other $(k-1)$-*non-unique*, we compare the next highest value frequency with the count distinct value of a modified view of the other $(k-1)$-*non-unique*. In the modified view each frequency is decreased by 1 so that it can be assumed that each distinct value was combined once with the more frequent value.

This approach has two drawbacks: *(i)* Such constellation of value frequencies appears only in early passes of the algorithm; *(ii)* histograms must be stored in memory. The remedy for the two drawbacks is to perform histogram retrieval only for single columns (line 6) and to store only count-distinct values in later passes. In line 17, for each generated *k-candidate*, it is checked whether one of the two combined $(k-1)$-*non-uniques* has a lower count-distinct value than a value frequency of the additional *k*th column. Note, for an apriori identified non-unique there will be no count-distinct value that can be used in the next pass. Thus, the pruning takes place in at most every second pass of the algorithm.

4.3 Combination of GORDIAN and HCA

In Sec. 3, we stated that the unique-generation part of the GORDIAN algorithm is inefficient if the number of discovered non-uniques is high. By profiling the runtime of GORDIAN we could identify the unique generation as the bottleneck. At the same time the non-unique discovery consumed only a fraction of the runtime. Thus, an intriguing idea is to interlace the non-unique discovery of GORDIAN with the candidate generation of HCA.

We combined GORDIAN with HCA by performing the non-unique discovery of GORDIAN on a smaller sample of the table and executing HCA on the entire table. Non-uniques discovered within a sample of a relational instance are also non-uniques for the complete instance and can be used for pruning candidates during the HCA part of the algorithm. It is thus possible to smooth the worst case of the bottom-up algorithm by skipping non-uniques identified by GORDIAN, and simultaneously to avoid GORDIAN's bottleneck of unique generation.

5. EVALUATION

We tested HCA and HCA-GORDIAN against GORDIAN itself and the basic bottom-up, top-down and Hybrid Apriori approaches introduced in Sec. 3. We implemented two different versions of the bottom-up algorithm: The approach identified by "BU Apriori" uses the candidate generation in Alg. 1, and a naïve approach labeled as "Naïve BU" generates candidates without pruning redundant non-minimal uniques. The "Naïve BU" is actually the implementation of the bottom-up algorithm proposed by Giannella and Wyss [4].

The algorithms were tested on synthetic data as well as real-world data. All algorithms are self-implemented in Java 6.0 on top of a commercial relational database. The experiment platform had the following properties:

- Windows Vista (32 Bit) Business™
- Pentium (R) Dual-Core CPU E5200 @2.50 GHz
- JRE limited to 1 GB RAM

5.1 Synthetic Data

We compared the algorithms with regard to increasing number of rows, columns, average distinctness. Additional important parameters for the algorithms are the number of uniques and their average size. Unfortunately, both values are only available after a successful completion of one algorithm. The generation of random data with specific number and size of uniques is probably as hard as the problem of discovering the minimal uniques and is an important challenge for future work. Nevertheless we also analyze these values when looking at the runtime of each algorithm.

Influence of Number of Rows. We generated multiple tables with 20 columns differing in the row-count. Note, the bigger the table, the lower the average distinctness might be, because the possibility of repeated values increases with increasing number of tuples. So, for the table with 10,000 tuples the average distinctness is 47%, while for the table with 200,000 tuples the value is 3%. Figure 2 illustrates the runtime of all algorithms with regard to row-counts between 10,000 and 200,000. In addition to the number of tuples, the number of uniques for each data set is denoted below the number of rows.

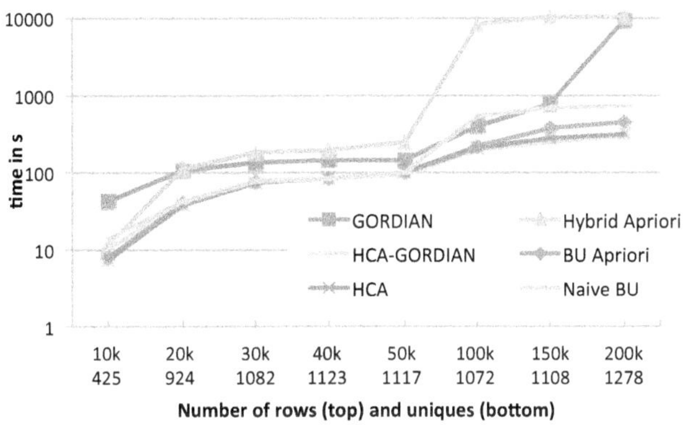

Figure 2: Runtime with respect to increasing number of rows on datasets with 20 columns

The Top-Down Algorithm is omitted in the diagram because its runtime was by magnitudes worse than GORDIAN. As all uniques in these experiments are combinations of only few columns, a bottom-up approach discovers all of them, earlier. The Hybrid Apriori Algorithm performs worse than the bottom-up approaches, but still better than the Top-Down Algorithm. The HCA-GORDIAN performed clearly better than GORDIAN. This is probably due to the fact that the relatively high number of uniques slows down the unique generation step of GORDIAN, which is avoided in HCA-GORDIAN. HCA-GORDIAN performed the preprocessing with GORDIAN for non-unique discovery always on a 10,000 tuple sample. On the data sets with more than 100,000 tuples, both HCA and HCA-GORDIAN perform at least 10% better than BU Apriori, which does not perform HC-based pruning. Note, the bottom-up approaches with our efficient candidate generation performed always at least 25% better than the Naïve BU. On the datasets with more than 100,000 rows, the performance gain was above 60%. Furthermore, all bottom-up algorithms outperform GORDIAN on all of these data sets.

Table 2 denotes the maximum memory usage of the algorithms on the table with 100,000 rows. GORDIAN performs clearly worse than all other algorithms. The Apriori approaches perform best and are nearly equal. The memory usage of the HCA-GORDIAN algorithm is due to the prefix tree on sample data higher than HCA.

Algorithm	Memory Usage
GORDIAN	534 MB
HCA-GORDIAN	71 MB
HCA	20 MB
Bottom-Up Apriori	19 MB
Hybrid Apriori	20 MB

Table 2: Memory usage for 100,000 tuples, 20 columns and 7.5% average distinctness

Influence of Number of Columns. Theoretically, the runtime of any algorithm is exponential in the number of columns, in the worst case. The algorithms have been tested on data sets consisting of 15 to 25 columns. The data sets each consist of 10,000 tuples and hold an average distinctness of about 5%. The experimental results are presented in Fig. 3. As expected, the runtime of all algorithms increases with the number of columns, but the incline of the curves is far smaller than exponential. GORDIAN again performs worse than all bottom-up approaches. The remarkable runtime decrease on the data set with 20 columns is due to the decrease of the number of uniques from 1,712 to 1,024. This is a good example for the unpredictability of the runtime of GORDIAN because of its high dependence on the number of existing uniques. For the datasets with more than 21 columns, the runtime of GORDIAN exploded.

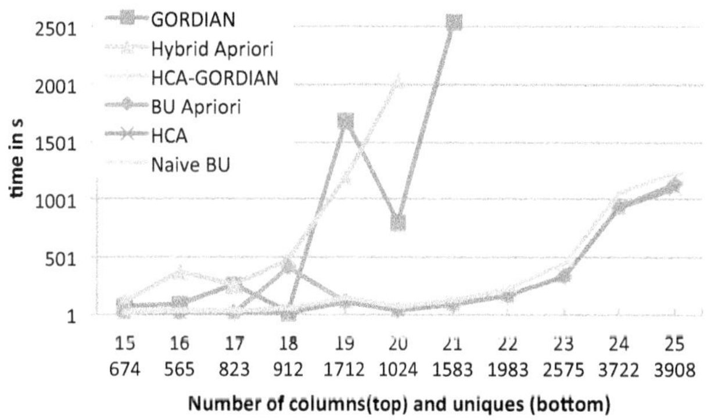

Figure 3: Runtime with respect to column numbers

Influence of Average Distinctness. The higher the average distinctness of all columns, the smaller is the size of minimal uniques – in the extreme case, already individual columns are unique. Thus, also the number of uniques is expected to be low. On the other hand, if the average distinctness is very low, minimal uniques become very large – in the extreme case only the entire relation is a unique. Again, the number of uniques is expected to be low. In between, the number of uniques is expected to be higher. This behavior can be observed in the generated data sets: Figure 4 shows the observed average numbers of minimal uniques for different average distinctnesses (five datasets each) and the observed average runtimes for data sets with 15 columns and 10,000 tuples.

Considering Fig. 4, all algorithms perform better on data with high average distinctness. For GORDIAN, the opposite case is expected as it is based on discovering non-uniques: Lower distinctness should result in faster discovery of non-uniques and better runtime for GORDIAN. However, low distinctness is accompanied by higher number of uniques and

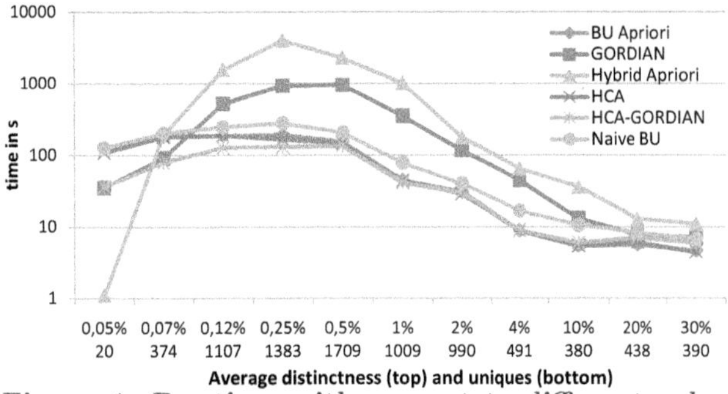

Figure 4: Runtime with respect to different values of average distinctness

non-uniques, which leads to more overhead during unique generation. This can be observed among the distinctness values between 0.12% and 2%, where the average unique size was 7, which is about one half of the number of columns. In fact, the Bottom-Up Algorithm, HCA, HCA-GORDIAN, and even the Naïve BU performed better in this range. Vice versa, the Hybrid Apriori Algorithm performed worst. Regarding the distinctness range below 0.12%, GORDIAN outperforms the bottom-up algorithms. The Hybrid Apriori Algorithm outperforms all other algorithms in this range due to the fact that the average size of uniques is 12 and Hybrid Apriori checks uniques of this size earlier than all other algorithms. That means that the Top-Down Apriori Algorithm would have performed even better. HCA-GORDIAN consistently performs better or at least as good as HCA and GORDIAN.

5.2 Real World Data

Real world data may differ in its nature from domain to domain. Table 3 lists four real world tables that were downloaded from the data collecting website `factual.com`. Table 4 presents the runtime results for these data sets. HCA and HCA-GORDIAN outperformed GORDIAN on all tables where only one unique was to be discovered, because their bottom-up approach discovers single column uniques very fast. Especially the experiment on the "National File" table shows the disadvantage of GORDIAN with regard to scalability, because the prefix tree did not fit into 1GB main memory. The NFL Stats data set that contains also multi-column uniques shows that there are data where GORDIAN still performs best. However, the hybrid solution HCA-GORDIAN is not remarkably worse.

Table	tuples	columns	uniques
US places	195,762	19	1
National file	1,394,725	20	1
NFL Stats	42,589	14	10

Table 3: Real world tables with statistics

Table	GORDIAN	HCA-GORDIAN	HCA
US places	64.13 s	15.389 s	9.232 s
National file	too large	114.919 s	130.239 s
NFL Stats	79.26 s	86.345 s	263.513 s

Table 4: Real world tables with runtime results

Summary. All algorithms show strengths and weaknesses for different value distributions, size and number of uniques. Efficient candidate generation leads to remarkable runtime improvement of the bottom-up algorithms. The HC-based pruning methods improve the algorithms on large data sets with low average distinctness. HCA-GORDIAN is a significant improvement of the basic HCA having large tables. HCA-GORDIAN performs better than GORDIAN when the number of detected non-uniques is high. GORDIAN performs best on data with low average distinctness and small number of uniques. The HCA approaches are much more memory efficient than GORDIAN.

6. CONCLUSIONS AND FUTURE WORK

In this paper we elaborated the concepts of uniques and non-uniques, the effects of their size and numbers, and showed strengths and weaknesses of existing approaches. We introduced the new bottom-up algorithm HCA, which benefits from apriori candidate generation and data- and statistic-oriented pruning possibilities. Furthermore, we showed a simple way of combining HCA and GORDIAN for even better runtime results. A more detailed analysis of these approaches and their optimizations is provided as a technical report [1]. The results of this paper constitute further open directions. The most important issue for further research is *approximate unique discovery*. As HCA is a statistics-based approach, it allows further optimizations based on statistics-driven heuristics for approximate solutions.

Another open issue is the need for a flexible and efficient data generator that should be able to generate a table that contains a fixed number of uniques of a certain size and holds specific value distributions for all columns. Thus, it is possible to evaluate and benchmark algorithms for special cases that might occur. Finally, the recent proposals for column stores call for unique discovery solutions that benefit from features of a column-based DBMS. Here, the column-based approach HCA is a promising candidate.

7. REFERENCES

[1] Z. Abedjan and F. Naumann. Advancing the discovery of unique column combinations. Technical Report 51, Hasso-Plattner-Institute Potsdam, Germany, 2011.

[2] R. Agrawal and R. Srikant. Fast algorithms for mining association rules in large databases. In *Proceedings of the International Conference on Very Large Databases (VLDB)*, pages 487–499, San Francisco, CA, 1994.

[3] P. A. Flach and I. Savnik. Database dependency discovery: a machine learning approach. *AI Commun.*, 12:139–160, August 1999.

[4] C. Giannella and C. Wyss. Finding minimal keys in a relation instance. `http://citeseerx.ist.psu.edu/viewdoc/summary?doi=10.1.1.41.7086`, 1999. Last accessed on 2010-09-29.

[5] Y. Huhtala, J. Kaerkkaeinen, P. Porkka, and H. Toivonen. TANE: an efficient algorithm for discovering functional and approximate dependencies. *The Computer Journal*, 42(2):100–111, 1999.

[6] M. Kantola, H. Mannila, K.-J. Räihä, and H. Siirtola. Discovering functional and inclusion dependencies in relational databases. *International Journal of Intelligent Systems*, 12:591Ű–607, 1992.

[7] V. Matos and B. Grasser. SQL-based discovery of exact and approximate functional dependencies. *SIGCSE Bull.*, 36(4):58–63, 2004.

[8] H. Saiedian and T. Spencer. An efficient algorithm to compute the candidate keys of a relational database schema. *The Computer Journal*, 39(2):124–132, 1996.

[9] Y. Sismanis, P. Brown, P. J. Haas, and B. Reinwald. Gordian: efficient and scalable discovery of composite keys. In *Proceedings of the International Conference on Very Large Databases (VLDB)*, pages 691–702, 2006.

Continuously Monitoring The Correlations of Massive Discrete Streams

Yueguo Chen[1], Wei Wang[2], Xiaoyong Du[1,2], Xiaofang Zhou[1,3]
[1]Key Laboratory of Data Engineering and Knowledge Engineering (Renmin University of China), MOE, China
[2]School of Information, Renmin University of China, Beijing, China
[3]University of Queensland, QLD 4072 Australia
{chenyueguo,wangwei.info,duyong}@ruc.edu.cn, zxf@uq.edu.au

ABSTRACT

The problem of monitoring the correlations of discrete streams is to continuously monitor the temporal correlations among massive discrete streams. A temporal correlation of two streams is defined as a *tracking* behavior, i.e., the most recent pattern of one stream is very similar to a historical pattern of another stream. The challenge is that both the tracking stream and the tracked stream are evolving, which causes the frequent updates of the correlation-ships. The straightforward way of monitoring correlations by brute-force subsequence matching will be very expensive for massive streams. We propose techniques that are able to significantly reduce the number of expensive subsequence matching calls, by continuously pruning and refining the correlated streams. Extensive experiments on the streaming trajectories show the significant performance improvement achieved by the proposed algorithms.

Categories and Subject Descriptors

H.2.8 [**Database Management**]: Database Applications-Data Mining

General Terms

Algorithms, Performance

Keywords

stream correlation, trajectory tracking

1. INTRODUCTION

Discrete streams, the streams of discrete numbers, are ubiquitous in many applications such as digital communication, logistics systems and environmental monitoring. Although many streams are time series of numerical data, they can however be transformed into discrete data, to improve the performance of stream processing. In this paper, we are interested in applications where a large volume of discrete streams are frequently updated when new discrete numbers continuously feed to the streams. The problem we want to address is to online monitor the lagged correlations among those evolving discrete streams, i.e., to continuously monitor the correlated streams of any given query stream. In this problem setting, a stream r is a correlated stream of a query stream s if s is repeating a historical pattern of r. If r is a correlated stream of s, r is called a tracked stream, and s is called a tracking stream. A pattern is a subsequence of significant length within a stream.

The problem of correlated stream detection is useful in monitoring streams that present similar evolving patterns, and making decisions timely on the tracking streams based on the past experience of the tracked streams. Exampling applications include trajectory monitoring and sensor networks. For example, in computer games, monitoring the trajectories of characters is very useful in identifying the objectives of characters. It may bring benefits such as advanced game AI and efficient sharing dynamic game contents.

This paper is mainly focused on discrete trajectory applications, although the proposed techniques can also be applied to other types of discrete streams. Monitoring the correlated streams is achieved by discovering the *tracking* behavior among streams, i.e., to find correlated (similar) patterns for the most recent pattern of each query stream. It is basically a subsequence matching problem which can be straightforwardly addressed by existing subsequence matching techniques [10, 12]. However, subsequence matching will be extremely expensive because an update of the query pattern will trigger the subsequence matching process of the query pattern against a huge number of long streams. The cost will be more expensive when approximate string matching distances (e.g., edit distance) are applied for evaluating the similarities between patterns. It will be not scalable if every update triggers the correlated stream detection process from scratch.

In this paper, we propose techniques that are able to effectively and continuously bound the distances for subsequence matching. Candidate streams are incrementally refined so that most of the complex subsequence matching processes can be postponed.

2. RELATED WORK

Subsequence matching attempts to locate matching subsequences within a long sequence with respect to a short query sequence [4]. Traditionally, it is studied by assuming that the long sequences are fixed and stored in time series database. Sliding windows of fixed width are applied to extract a large number of local patterns from the long sequences [4, 9]. Pattern detection on streams is different from

CIKM'11, October 24–28, 2011, Glasgow, Scotland, UK.

finding matching subsequences of long database sequences. It tries to detect matching subsequences within long streams. Examples are BRAID [13] and SPIRIT [11]. Streaming pattern detection on DTW distance has been studied in [12]. The matching subsequences are continuously monitored by cumulating DTW distances in a continuous manner. Note that, although many of the above techniques are focused on numerical streams, they can however be adapted to find matching subsequences in discrete streams. We apply the idea of [12] to the edit distance for matching discrete streams as our baseline solution.

Approximate string matching is typically preferred for matching strings because it is error tolerant. Some surveys of approximate string matching can be found in [6]. One type of string similarity measures use the set similarity (e.g., Jaccard similarity [1]) of tokens to evaluate the similarity of two strings, where the positions of tokens are ignored. Another type of string similarity measures use the number of operations to transform one string to the other, e.g., edit distance and Hamming distance. Edit distance has been widely used in many recent studies of approximate string matching [3, 8, 7], we use it as an exampling distance, although our techniques can be applied to many other distances.

Li et al. [8] showed that many string distances can be effectively bounded using the q-grams (tokens) within two strings. Many list-merging search and similarity join algorithms [1, 5, 7] have been proposed to speed up approximate string matching. MergeSkip [7] is one of them to efficiently retrieve similar strings of a given query by effectively pruning most non-similar strings in the process of merging token inverted lists. It has been shown [7] that MergeSkip is an very efficient solution for filtering approximate strings. We therefore use it as a baseline of filtering candidate correlated streams in our problem.

3. PRELIMINARIES

3.1 Problem Definition

A stream r is a window of sequential data items most recently generated. It can be denoted as $r = \{r[b], r[b+1], \ldots, r[e]\}$, where $r[b]$ is the earliest data item recorded in r, $r[e]$ is the latest data item of r, and i is the index of data item $r[i]$. As a stream, new data items will be continuously appended to r. Meanwhile, to limit the memory usage of recording historical data items in r, those outdated data items will be removed from r timely. The memory window size of the stream r is denoted as $n = e - b + 1$. We consider the applications where there are a large number of discrete streams $R = \{r\}$. To capture the temporal correlation-ship, we say that the stream s is correlated to the stream r if the most recent pattern of s is similar to a historical pattern of r. We denote the most recent pattern (the most recent w data items) of a stream s as $\vec{s}$. It implies the current tendency of a stream. In our problem, $\vec{s}$ is treated as a query pattern every time the query stream s updates.

DEFINITION 1 (CORRELATED PATTERN). *Given the most recent pattern $\vec{s}$ of a stream s, a subsequence $\bar{r}$ (in the memory window of r) of another stream r is a correlated pattern of $\vec{s}$ if the distance between $\vec{s}$ and $\bar{r}$ is small enough, i.e., $d(\vec{s}, \bar{r}) \leq \varepsilon$, where ε is a given threshold.*

Note that the distance function $d()$ can be any distance of discrete sequences. However, in this paper, we focus on string edit distance. In our problem, to capture the *tracking* behavior (i.e., the *lagged* correlation between two patterns), temporal constraints are required between data items of $\vec{s}$ and $\bar{r}$. After the edit operations, two strings $\bar{s}'$ and $\bar{r}'$ are identical only if $\bar{s}'[i] = \bar{r}'[i]$ and $\bar{s}'[i].t \geq \bar{r}'[i].t$ ($s[i].t$ is the time stamp of $s[i]$), for $i = 1, \ldots, |\bar{s}'| = |\bar{r}'|$. Consequently, we modify the edit distance as a time-constraint edit distance. Given two strings $\bar{s}$ and $\bar{r}$ of length m and n respectively, the time-constraint edit distance of $\bar{s}$ and $\bar{r}$ is defined as $d(\bar{s}, \bar{r}) = M[m][n]$, where $M[i][j]$ is computed as follows:

$$M[i][j] = \min \begin{cases} M[i-1][j] + 1 \\ M[i][j-1] + 1 \\ M[i-1][j-1] + d(\bar{s}[i], \bar{r}[j]) \end{cases} \quad (1)$$

where $M[0][j] = j, 0 \leq j \leq n; M[i][0] = i, 0 \leq i \leq m$. For any two data items x and y, $d(x, y)$ is defined as:

$$d(x, y) = \begin{cases} 1 & x! = y \text{ or } x.t < y.t \\ 0 & otherwise \end{cases}$$

DEFINITION 2 (CORRELATED STREAM). *Given the most recent pattern $\vec{s}$ of a stream s, if another stream r contains a correlated pattern of $\vec{s}$, we say that r is a correlated stream of s, denoted as $s \rightarrow r$.*

Based on above definitions, the online correlated stream monitoring problem is defined as: given a set of streams R, and a query stream s ($s \in R$ or not), we want to continuously monitor a subset $R(s) = \{r | s \rightarrow r, r \in R, r \neq s\}$, whenever the query stream s updates.

3.2 Brute-force Subsequence Matching

Discrete streams can be treated as evolving strings. Therefore, the problem of monitoring correlated streams can then be modeled as an online substring matching problem. By applying some advanced subsequence matching techniques proposed in [12], the complexity of checking whether one stream r is the correlated stream of s can be $O(nm)$. We use it as a baseline of detecting correlated streams $R(s)$ of the query stream s, which is a brute-force subsequence matching process shown in Algorithm 1. Given N streams, the complexity of Algorithm 1 is $O(Nnm)$.

Algorithm 1 Brute-force subsequence matching

Input: $\vec{s}$, the most recent pattern of a stream s
Input: R, the set of all evolving streams
Input: ε, matching threshold
Output: $R(s)$, the set of correlated streams of s

```
R(s) = ∅;
for each r ∈ R, r ≠ s do
  int prev,cur,dis[w + 1];
  for (x = 0; x ≤ w; x + +) do
    dis[x] = x;
  for (y = 1; y ≤ n; y + +) do
    prev=0;
    for (x = 1; x ≤ w; x + +) do
      t = d(s[x], r[y]);
      cur=min(dis[x − 1] + t, dis[x] + 1, prev + 1);
      dis[x − 1] = prev;
      prev = cur;
    if (prev ≤ ε) then
      insert r into R(s);
    else
      dis[w] = cur;
```

Note that the baseline solution does not support the incremental computation of $R(s)$ for a given stream s. Whenever

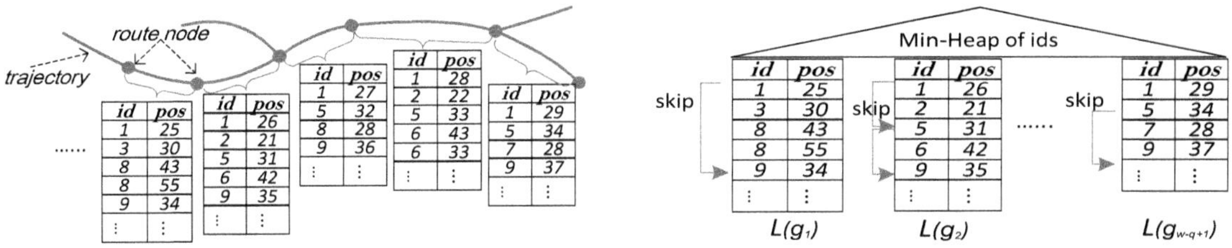

(a) Inverted lists of 2-grams (b) Merge counting using SkipMerge

Figure 1: Illustration of counting inverted lists by MergeSkip

a new data item feeds to s, $R(s)$ has to be re-computed from scratch, although $R(s)$ may change slightly due to the insertion of a new data item.

4. CORRELATED STREAM FILTERING

To effectively bound the edit distance, we propose to use the q-grams of streams. A q-gram of a string $\bar{s}$ is a substring (of the length q) of $\bar{s}$. Given a string of $\bar{s}$, the set of all q-grams of $\bar{s}$ is denoted as $G(\bar{s})$. The total number of q-grams in $G(\bar{s})$ is actually $|G(\bar{s})| = |\bar{s}| - q + 1$. Let the edit distance of two strings $\bar{s}$ and $\bar{r}$ be $d(\bar{s}, \bar{r})$, the number of all common q-grams of $\bar{s}$ and $\bar{r}$ be $|G(\bar{s}) \cap G(\bar{r})|$. It can be easily proved that $d(\bar{s}, \bar{r}) \cdot q \geq \max(|G(\bar{s})|, |G(\bar{r})|) - |G(\bar{s}) \cap G(\bar{r})|$.

LEMMA 1. *For two streams s and r, if $s \to r$, then $|G(\vec{s}) \cap G(r)| \geq w + 1 - (\varepsilon + 1)q$.*

PROOF. Since $s \to r$, there must be a substring $\bar{r}$ within r, that $d(\vec{s}, \bar{r}) \leq \varepsilon$. $d(\vec{s}, \bar{r}) \cdot q \geq \max(|G(\vec{s})|, |G(\bar{r})|) - |G(\vec{s}) \cap G(\bar{r})|$, i.e., $|G(\vec{s}) \cap G(r)| \geq \max(|G(\vec{s})|, |G(\bar{r})|) - \varepsilon \cdot q$. Because $\max(|G(\vec{s})|, |G(\bar{r})|) \geq |G(\vec{s})| = w - q + 1$, then $|G(\vec{s}) \cap G(r)| \geq w - q + 1 - \varepsilon \cdot q = w + 1 - (\varepsilon + 1) \cdot q$. □

Lemma 1 provides a lower bound of $|G(\vec{s}) \cap G(r)|$ to guarantee that $s \to r$ is satisfied. It therefore allows us to effectively prune the costly subsequence matching between $\vec{s}$ and r if $|G(\vec{s}) \cap G(r)| < t$. To achieve such a pruning mechanism, we therefore need to monitor the number of common q-grams between the most recent pattern $\vec{s}$ and the other streams. We denote the set of all streams having at least t common q-grams of $G(\vec{s})$ as $C(s) = \{r \,|\, |G(\vec{s}) \cap G(r)| \geq t\}$. It is obvious that $R(s) \subseteq C(s)$.

4.1 Sorted Merge Counting

As the streams evolve, the q-grams of the streams continuously update. Counting the number of common q-grams between the most recent patterns and streams is a stream join problem. One way to efficiently count common q-grams in stream scenario is to maintain an inverted list of streams for each q-gram g, recording the streams that recently generate g. Figure 1(a) shows an example. The inverted list of a gram is a list of elements with each element consists of two parts: the *id* of the stream, and the position of the first data item of a gram occurrence in the stream. All the elements are sorted by their *ids* and positions in turn. As such, all sorted inverted lists can be maintained by a B^+-tree, with the tandem of stream *id* and gram position (*pos*) as the key. The outdated elements of an inverted list can be removed from the index based on the *pos* attribute or an additional *timestamp* attribute.

Given a most recent pattern $\vec{s}$, and the inverted lists of all its q-grams, the number of common q-grams that the other streams have can be computed by a merge counting algorithm (called MergeSkip in [7]) over the sorted inverted lists of $G(\vec{s})$. Every time a new data item feeds to s, a new q-gram is generated in $G(\vec{s})$. In the meanwhile, an outdated gram need to be removed from $G(\vec{s})$. This will trigger a new merge counting process. However, the MergeSkip algorithm is not a continuous algorithm that is able to incrementally maintain the counts for $|G(\vec{s}) \cap G(r)|$ when stream updates. Each update process requires to scan and merge $w - q + 1$ inverted lists, even though for two consecutive most recent patterns $\vec{s_1}$ and $\vec{s_2}$, where $\vec{s_2}[i] = \vec{s_1}[i+1]$ (for $i = 1, \ldots, w-1$), there will be $w - q$ inverted lists to be repeatedly scanned.

4.2 Continuous Counting

To efficiently maintain $C(s)$, we design an algorithm that is able to continuously count the number of common q-grams among streams. For each query stream s, a counting list (denoted as $A(s)$) is maintained that records all streams having common q-grams of $G(\vec{s})$, sorted by the stream *ids*. An entry in the counting list $A(s)$ corresponds to a stream r. A list of common q-grams between $\vec{s}$ and $G(r)$ are maintained for each entry, sorted by the positions of grams in $G(\vec{s})$. Each entry r in the counting list $A(s)$ consists of the *id* of r and a pointer to a gram list.

If $g_s \in G(\vec{s})$ has a number of common q-grams in a stream r, there will be an entry for g_s, in the gram list of r. The first column of the gram list records the position of g_s. In addition to the position of g_s, an entry of the gram list also records the position of the oldest common gram and that of the newest common gram of g_s in the stream r. If there is only one common gram of the gram g_s, the positions in the last two columns will be the same. Because duplicated grams from the same r have been reduced, each gram list will at most contain $|G(\vec{s})|$ elements.

Upon the detection of a new q-gram from a stream s, the updates of the $A(s)$ and the candidate stream set $C(s)$ are conducted following the process given in Algorithm 2 (shorted as the CC algorithm). It basically merges $A(s)$ with the inverted list $L(g_i)$ of the most recent gram of s. For a stream r that is newly discovered from $L(g_i)$, a new entry will be created in $A(s)$. Otherwise, a new entry will be appended in the gram list of the corresponding entry of the stream r, in $A(s)$. If multiple common grams of r are detected, only the position l_p is updated. When scanning each entry of $A(s)$, we will check and remove its outdated grams (in terms of s_p) in its gram list. Because entries in the gram list is sorted based on s_p, the outdated checking is very efficient. Once the size of a stream entry of $A(s)$ is no less than t, a candidate stream will be discovered. On the other hand, if all entries in the gram list are outdated, the stream entry will be removed from $A(s)$. Compared to the MergeSkip algorithm where $|G(\vec{s})|$ lists are merged, the CC algorithm only needs to merge two lists. It is therefore more efficient than the merge counting algorithm, especially when w is large.

Algorithm 2 Continuous counting (CC)

Input: g_i, the new detected gram of the stream s due to the attachment of the new data item $s[i]$.
Input: $A(s)$, the counting list of the stream s.
Input: t, the minimal common q-grams that a candidate stream should have.
Output: $C(s)$

$C(s) = \emptyset$
let $a = A(s)[1]$ be current entry of the counting list $A(s)$
let $l = L(g_i)[1]$ be current entry of the inverted list $L(g_i)$
while either $A(s)$ or $L(g_i)$ is not scanned out **do**
  if $l.id < a.id$ or $A(s)$ is scanned out **then**
    create a new stream entry a'
    $a'.id = l.id$
    $a'.insert(i, l.pos)$ //insert a gram entry into the gram list of a'
    insert a' into the counting list $A(s)$
    let $a = a'$
    l advances in $L(g_i)$
  else
    remove outdated grams from a's gram list
    if $l.id = a.id$ **then**
      $a.insert(i, l.pos)$
      l advances in $L(g_i)$.
    if $a.size \geq t$ **then**
      insert $a.id$ into $C(s)$, affiliated with the minimal f_p and the maximal l_p of a's gram list.
    else if $a.size = 0$ **then**
      remove a from $A(s)$.
    if $l.id > a.id$ **then**
      a advances in $A(s)$

5. CORRELATED STREAM REFINEMENT

The filtering algorithms discussed above generate candidate streams ($C(s)$) that need to be further refined because they may not be true correlated streams of s. It is likely that the set $C(s)$ updates slightly when stream s only updates a few data items. If every candidate stream in $C(s)$ needs to be checked by an expensive subsequence matching process each time s is updated, there will be too much redundant computation. We propose an algorithm to achieve incremental refinement of the candidate streams in $C(s)$.

Given a substring $\bar{s}$ and a string r, let $\mathbf{d}(\bar{s}, r) = \min_{\bar{r}} d(\bar{s}, \bar{r})$. We use $s[b_s : e_s]$ to denote a subsequence of s starting at the position b_s and ending at the position e_s. We have the following lemmas (proof is not given due to the space limits) that support the incremental refinement of $C(s)$.

LEMMA 2. *Let $\vec{s} = s[b_s : e_s]$, $\vec{s}' = s[b_s + 1 : e_s + 1]$ which is one entry shift of the previous most recent pattern $\vec{s}$, we have $\mathbf{d}(\vec{s}', r) \geq \mathbf{d}(\vec{s}, r) - 1$.*

Lemma 2 has the following corollary:

COROLLARY 1. *If $\mathbf{d}(\vec{s}, r) = \delta > \varepsilon$, r can be a correlated stream of s only if after at least $\delta - \varepsilon$ data items feed to s.*

LEMMA 3. *Let $\bar{s} = s[b_s : e_s]$, $\bar{r} = r[b_r : e_r]$, $\bar{s}' = s[b_s + 1 : e_s + 1]$, $\bar{r}' = r[b_r + 1 : e_r + 1]$. We have $d(\bar{s}', \bar{r}') \leq d(\bar{s}, \bar{r}) + 1$. If $s[e_s + 1] = r[e_r + 1]$, we have $d(\bar{s}', \bar{r}') \leq d(\bar{s}, \bar{r})$.*

COROLLARY 2. *Suppose there is a correlated pattern $\bar{r} = r[b_r : e_r]$ of $\vec{s} = s[b_s : e_s]$ such that $d(\vec{s}, \bar{r}) \leq \varepsilon$, when $\vec{s}$ is updated to $\vec{s}' = s[b_s + 1 : e_s + 1]$, if $s[e_s + 1] = r[e_r + 1]$ and $r[b_r + 1]$ is not outdated, then $s \rightarrow r$ still remains.*

Let $\bar{r}' = r[b_r + 1 : e_r + 1]$. According to Lemma 3, in this case, $d(\vec{s}', \bar{r}') \leq d(\vec{s}, \bar{r}) \leq \varepsilon$. Therefore, $s \rightarrow r$ remains. This allows us to delay the computation of $\mathbf{d}(\vec{s}, r)$ for a previously valid $s \rightarrow r$, if $s[e_s + 1] = r[e_r + 1]$ and $r[b_r + 1]$ is not outdated. Moreover, such a delay can be transmitted if the condition always holds when $\vec{s}$ advances.

COROLLARY 3. *Suppose there is a correlated pattern $\bar{r} = r[b_r : e_r]$ of $\vec{s} = s[b_s : e_s]$ such that $d(\vec{s}, \bar{r}) \leq \varepsilon$, when $\vec{s}$ is updated to $\vec{s}' = s[b_s + 1 : e_s + 1]$, if $s[e_s + 1] \neq r[e_r + 1]$ and $r[b_r + 1]$ is not outdated, then $d(\vec{s}', \bar{r}') \leq d(\vec{s}, \bar{r}) + 1$.*

Corollary 3 can be easily proved based on Lemma 3. It allows us to delay the computation of $\mathbf{d}(\vec{s}, r)$ for a previously valid $s \rightarrow r$ if $\mathbf{d}(\vec{s}, r)$ is small enough, even though $s[e_s + 1] = r[e_r + 1]$ does not hold.

Algorithm 3 Incremental refinement (IR)

Input: $C(s)$, the candidate correlated stream set of s.
Input: $V(s)$, the list of candidate correlated streams that have been refined for the stream s, sorted by ids.
Output: $R(s)$, the correlated stream set of s

$R(s) = \emptyset$
let $v = V(s)[1]$ be current entry of the list $V(s)$
let $r = C(s)[1]$ be current entry of the candidate stream in $C(s)$, sorted by the stream ids.
while $C(s)$ is not scanned out **do**
  if $r.id < v.id$ or $V(s)$ is scanned out **then**
    v' = refine($\vec{s}$, r)
    insert v' into $V(s)$
    r advances in $C(s)$
  else if $r.id = v.id$ **then**
    if $v.t = T$ {previously a correlated stream} **then**
      if $r[v.b_r + 1]$ is not outdated **then**
        if $s[v.p_s + 1] = r[v.e_r + 1]$ **then**
          insert r into $R(s)$
          $v.p_s{+}{+}$, $v.p_r = \langle b_r{+}{+}, e_r{+}{+} \rangle$
        else
          $v.dis{+}{+}$
          if $v.dis > \varepsilon$ **then**
            v'=refine($\vec{s}$, r), update v' as v
      else
        v'=refine($\vec{s}$, r), update v' as v
    else
      $v.d = v.d - 1$ {previously not a correlated stream}
      if $v.d \leq \varepsilon$ **then**
        v'=refine($\vec{s}$, r), update v' as v
    r advances in $C(s)$
    v advances in $V(s)$
  else
    remove v from $V(s)$
    v advances in $V(s)$

refine($\vec{s}$, r)

1. compute $dis = \mathbf{d}(\vec{s}, r)$ by subsequence matching. r is constrained as a subsequence derived from Algorithm 2.
2. create a new refining node v
3. **if** $dis \leq \varepsilon$ **then**
4.   insert r into $R(s)$
5. $v.t = T$, $v.d = dis$
6. $v.p_s = e_s$, $v.p_r = \langle b_r, e_r \rangle$
7. **else**
8. $v.t = F$, $v.d = dis$
9. return v

Based on the above three corollaries, we propose the incremental refinement (IR) algorithm in Algorithm 3. It achieves the efficient incremental refinement of candidate correlated streams by delaying the actual subsequence matching process to the time when correlation-ship of two streams is able to change.

6. EXPERIMENTAL STUDY

Because the baseline solution (Algorithm 1) of brute-force subsequence matching is very expensive, we do not plot its results in our experimental results. Therefore, the comparative approaches are some alternatives of the filtering and refining algorithms. For filtering, we have two alternatives: the MergeSkip algorithm (labelled as M) and the CC algorithm (labelled as C). For refining, we either use the proposed incremental refining (IR) algorithm (labelled as R), or directly use the subsequence matching algorithm (labelled as S) for refining all candidate streams. As such, we derive four alternatives by combining them: CR, MR, CS, MS. The best approach we propose to use is the CR approach, which is the combination of CC and IR.

6.1 Experiment Setup

We use trajectories generated from a road network generator [2] as the original dataset. The generator can guarantee the positions of the objects are reported whenever they pass through a node of the network. As such, we are able to convert the position of a node into a discrete number. We choose the map of 'San Francisco Bay Area', which is the largest map provided by the generator. For each stream (trajectory), we generate about 280 data items in average. The performance test starts when trajectories have been updated 100 times in average. The test lasts for a duration where 50 updates happen for a stream in average. During the test period, we treat each stream as a query stream. The performance is measured as an average update cost of an update (a new data item appended) of one stream, which is averaged over all streams during the test period. We compare the cost mainly in two types: the computational cost and the ratio of subsequence matching calls. For the computational cost of each approach, we measure the running time of both the filtering (including the index updates) algorithm and the refining algorithm. For the ratio of subsequence matching calls, we measure the following ratios: $|C(s)|/|R|$, $|R(s)|/|R|$, and $\#calls/|R|$ (the number of actual subsequence matching calls).

We run all experiments on an Intel Core 2.0GHz machine with 3GB memory, running Linux 2.6.28 system. The algorithms are implemented by GNU C++. To guarantee the efficiency, all data are maintained in memory. The default parameters are set as $|R| = 10k$, $w = 12$, $\varepsilon = 2$, $n = 50$, $q = 2$ (gram size).

6.2 Experiment Results

Before discussing the results of these parameters respectively, we should note that the performance of our baseline solution (Algorithm 1) is much more expensive (in 3-4 orders of magnitude) than the alternatives shown in our experiments. This is very reasonable because from Figure 3 we can see that most of subsequence matching calls can be pruned by applying the filtering and refining algorithms. We therefore do not show the results for the baseline algorithm in those figures showing the experimental results.

6.2.1 *Scalability test by varying* $|R|$

We can see from Figure 2(a) that, the CPU time of the 4 approaches linearly increases as the stream set enlarges. When considering only the refining algorithm, we can see that the approaches (CR and MR) with the IR algorithm can achieve around 2-3 times faster than those (CS and MS) without it. When considering only the filtering algorithm, we can see that the CC algorithm (CR and CS) is around 2.5 times faster than the MergeSkip algorithm (MR and MS). As a result, the CR can achieve around 3 time overall performance improvement than the MS baseline. Note that although an update of a query can be addressed in around only $1m$ seconds when $|R| = 100K$, if every stream need to be monitored, the total cost for an update of all streams (100K) will be around 100 seconds, which is very expensive.

Figure 3(a) shows that the filtering algorithms achieve very tight lower bound distance for pruning un-correlated streams. Almost all (more than 99.5%) un-correlated streams can be pruned during the filtering process. Figure 3(a) also shows that the IR algorithm can also prune a large percentage of subsequence matching calls that cannot pruned in the filtering phase. This explains why the IR algorithm improves the over performance. The ratio of subsequence matching calls changes slightly when $|R|$ changes.

6.2.2 *The impact of query window size* w

Figures 2(b) and 3(b) shows the impact of query window size w. We can see that, with the enlargement of w, the pruning power of both the filtering algorithms and the refining algorithm increases. As a result, the CR approach can be as fast as 4 times of the MS baseline. Although the pruning power increases when w is enlarged, the overall computational cost of each approach still increases. This is because, the basic computational cost of a subsequence matching call increases with the enlargement of w. We can also find that the relative cost of the filtering algorithms over the IR algorithm increases when w is enlarged, especially for the MergeSkip algorithm. This is because the MergeSkip algorithm requires to scan $w - q + 1$ inverted lists.

6.2.3 *The impact of matching threshold* ε

On another dimension, we enlarge the matching threshold ε which determines the correlations of patterns and find that (Figures 2(c) and 3(c)) the computational cost of the 4 approaches increases slightly with the enlargement of ε. Meanwhile, the pruning power of filtering and refining algorithms drops slightly, which is reasonable.

6.2.4 *The impact of the gram size* q

By varying the gram size q, we find that (Figures 2(d) and 3(d)) the best pruning power is achieved when $q = 2$. As a result, the four alternative solutions achieve their best running performance when $q = 2$. This is reasonable because according to Lemma 1, the larger the q, the less the minimal number of common grams t required for candidate correlated streams, and the looser the bounds derived from Lemma 1. That explains why the pruning power of $q = 2$ is slightly better than that of $q = 3$. However, when $q = 1$, the pruning power is the worst. This is because the direction information of trajectories is lost when $q = 1$. It also explains that many false positive candidates are generated by filtering algorithms when $q = 1$. Based on this study, we choose $q = 2$ as the default value of q in other experiments.

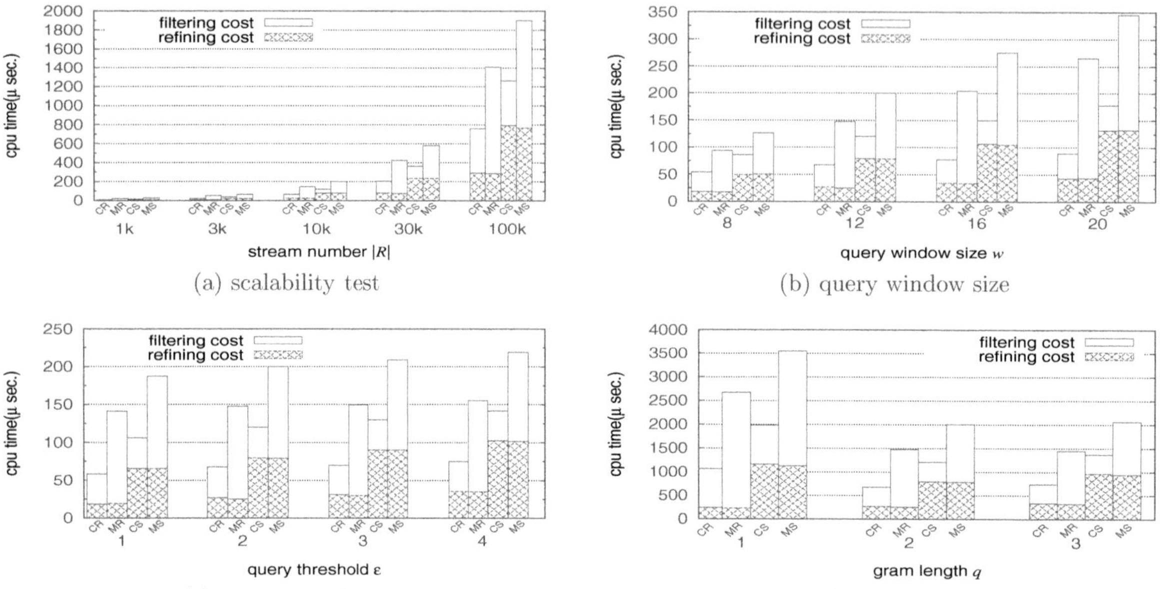

(a) scalability test (b) query window size

(c) query thresholds (d) gram size

Figure 2: Computational cost for various parameter settings

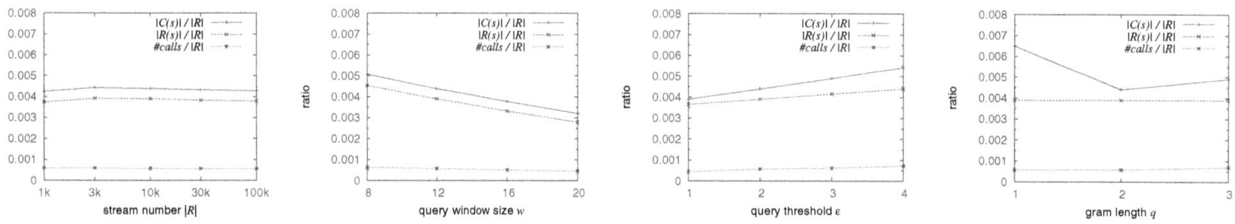

(a) scalability test (b) query window size (c) query thresholds (d) gram size

Figure 3: Ratio of subsequence matching calls for various parameter settings

7. CONCLUSION

To the best of our knowledge, this is the first work on monitoring the correlations of discrete streams where both the tracked streams and the tracking streams evolve. We proposed two algorithms (CC and IR) to achieve efficiency for monitoring correlated streams. The experimental studies show that based on the tight bound derived from the q-grams, the CC algorithm can effectively filter most of the un-correlated streams. In the refining phase, we propose techniques that are able to effectively postpone the expensive subsequence matching calls. The experimental results demonstrate the advantages of the proposed algorithms.

8. ACKNOWLEDGMENTS

This work is partially supported by NSFC under the grant No. 61003085, and HGJ PROJECT 2010ZX01042-002-002-03.

9. REFERENCES

[1] A. Arasu, V. Ganti, and R. Kaushik. Efficient exact set-similarity joins. In *VLDB*, pages 918–929, 2006.

[2] T. Brinkhoff. A framework for generating network-based moving objects. *GeoInformatica*, 6(2):153–180, 2002.

[3] K. Chakrabarti, S. Chaudhuri, V. Ganti, and D. Xin. An efficient filter for approximate membership checking. In *SIGMOD Conference*, pages 805–818, 2008.

[4] C. Faloutsos, M. Ranganathan, and Y. Manolopoulos. Fast subsequence matching in time-series databases. In *SIGMOD Conference*, pages 419–429, 1994.

[5] M. Hadjieleftheriou, A. Chandel, N. Koudas, and D. Srivastava. Fast indexes and algorithms for set similarity selection queries. In *ICDE*, pages 267–276, 2008.

[6] M. Hadjieleftheriou and C. Li. Efficient approximate search on string collections. *PVLDB*, 2(2):1660–1661, 2009.

[7] C. Li, J. Lu, and Y. Lu. Efficient merging and filtering algorithms for approximate string searches. In *ICDE*, pages 257–266, 2008.

[8] G. Li, D. Deng, and J. Feng. Faerie: Efficient filtering algorithms for approximate dictionary-based entity extraction. In *SIGMOD Conference*, 2011.

[9] Y.-S. Moon, K.-Y. Whang, and W.-S. Han. General match: a subsequence matching method in time-series databases based on generalized windows. In *SIGMOD Conference*, pages 382–393, 2002.

[10] G. Navarro. A guided tour to approximate string matching. *ACM Comput. Surv.*, 33(1):31–88, 2001.

[11] S. Papadimitriou, J. Sun, and C. Faloutsos. Streaming pattern discovery in multiple time-series. In *VLDB*, 2005.

[12] Y. Sakurai, C. Faloutsos, and M. Yamamuro. Stream monitoring under the time warping distance. In *ICDE*, pages 1046–1055, 2007.

[13] Y. Sakurai, S. Papadimitriou, and C. Faloutsos. Braid: Stream mining through group lag correlations. In *SIGMOD*, 2005.

Multiple Keyword-based Queries over XML Streams

Felipe C. Hummel, Altigran S. da Silva
Universidade Federal do Amazonas
Manaus, Brazil
{fch, alti}@dcc.ufam.edu.br

Mirella M. Moro, Alberto H. F. Laender
Universidade Federal de Minas Gerais
Belo Horizonte, Brazil
{mirella, laender}@dcc.ufmg.br

ABSTRACT

In this paper, we propose that various keyword-based queries be processed over XML *streams* in a *multi-query processing* way. Our algorithms rely on parsing stacks designed for simultaneously matching terms from several distinct queries and use new query indexes to speed up search operations when processing a large number of queries. Besides defining a new problem and novel solutions, we perform experiments in which aspects related to performance and scalability are examined.

Categories and Subject Descriptors

H.2 [**Database Management**]: Miscellaneous

General Terms

Algorithms, Performance, Experimentation

Keywords

Keyword-based Queries, XML Streams

1 Introduction

As the Web continues to grow in size and complexity, users tend to focus their attention to on-the-fly updates (such as news and RSS feeds) rather than on archived information. In this context, XML is the standard for many of such applications, which usually employ XML dissemination techniques. Such techniques involve two distinct tasks: filtering of documents according to the users' information needs [2, 7], and routing matched documents to those users [4, 12]. Instead of evaluating queries over stored data, the system must evaluate queries over *streams* of documents.

In such a context, users describe their needs in profiles composed of one or more queries. Without loss of generality, in this paper, we abstract the concept of profile and refer to each query individually. Queries are usually specified with XML query languages, such as XQuery and XPath, which allow querying on both the data structure and data values using predicates with exact semantics. Therefore, users formulating queries must have some knowledge of the XML documents that compose the stream.

CIKM'11, October 24–28, 2011, Glasgow, Scotland, UK.

However, within the Web environment, it is common to have XML documents storing values in a textual format. This makes the retrieval of (text) values based on predicates with exact semantics extremely difficult, aggravated by the existence of many disparate data sources. Even for applications with few sources, given the lively nature of the Web, new sources can come and go anytime. Hence, in order to retrieve the desired information, users have to know (1) the exact structure of the documents provided by each data source and (2) the exact values represented on the textual contents.

An alternative approach to using XML query languages is to employ more *intuitive* keyword-based queries [5, 6, 10]. The main advantage of this approach is to allow users with disparate interests posing queries in an informal way, without caring about document structure or schema anymore. However, only very recently, this approach was adapted to the context of XML streams, where there is no document storage, pre-processing, statistics, or indexes available [11].

Using keyword-based queries can solve the problems of knowing the structure and using exact predicates, but a third problem arises in the stream context: there is a large number of users and documents flowing on the Web. Here, processing *one query* per document traversal or *one query* per stream (as in [11]) is not efficient. Ideally, we would like to process *multiple* queries over one single traversal of each document on the stream. Finally, even though such an idea is employed for XPath based queries over streams [12], there is no work on multiple query processing over XML streams with *keyword-based semantics*.

Thus, in this paper we tackle a novel and very relevant problem: *processing multiple keyword-based queries over XML streams*. We propose two new algorithms for simultaneously processing several keyword-based queries over XML streams. They rely on parsing stacks and query indexes specially designed to allow the simultaneous matching of terms from different queries. We present experiments in which aspects concerning performance and scalability are examined and discussed. The results show that our algorithms are effective on processing thousands of queries in a single pass over XML streams.

Next, we discuss related work (Section 2), introduce our multi-query procedure (Section 3), describe our two new algorithms (Section 4) and our experiments (Section 5), and then present our conclusions (Section 6).

2 Related Work

XML Keyword Search. Using keywords to query XML databases has been extensively studied. XSEarch [3] adopts an intuitive concept of *meaningfully related sets of nodes* based on the relationship of the nodes with its ancestors (on the graph). XRANK [5] presents an adaptation of Google's PageRank to XML documents

Query	Formulation	Specification
q_1	*Author::Porter Type::Novel*	s_a
q_2	*Author::Porter Novel*	s_a
q_3	*Porter Type::Novel*	s_a, s_b
q_4	*Porter Novel*	s_a, s_b
q_5	*Title::Porter Type::Novel*	s_b
q_6	*Title::Porter Novel*	s_b
q_7	*MP3:: Publisher::MP3*	s_c

Table 1: Examples of keyword-based queries.

for computing a ranking score for the answer trees. XSeek [6] proposes a query processing strategy over the notion of entities inferred from DTDs. The aforementioned approaches work on *stored* XML databases. The work in [11] and [1] took the first steps towards processing keyword-based queries over XML *streams*. Specifically, [11] adapts two traditional algorithms for keyword-based queries over streams and [1] performs their experimental analysis. However, those algorithms evaluate queries in a *single-query fashion* (i.e., *one* query per time over the stream).

XML Streams. Recent research on XML streams (dissemination, filtering and routing) has aimed at building large-scale, distributed systems [2, 4, 7, 12]. Most of those are concerned with performance aspects and optimize the filtering process [2, 7], the message delivering and the routing network [4, 12]. We focus on two different facets: (1) improving the flexibility of query specification and (2) alleviating users dependency on possible schema details of multiple document providers. Both facets are guaranteed by using keyword-based queries to express the user's intentions. In order to deal with multiple XML schemas, two approaches are very common: to apply query rewriting [13] and to use global schemas [8]. Using keyword-based queries over XML streams frees the user from knowing the (possible multiple) source schemas. As a consequence, there is no need for mediators, rewritings or global schemas.

3 Processing Multiple Queries

This section details the types of query considered in this work and gives an overview of our multi-query procedure as well as of the data structures used.

Current approaches for processing keyword-based queries over XML data consider queries that specify constraints on the textual content or on both the textual and the labels of each XML element. Thus, we assume a simple keyword-based query language, with syntax borrowed from [3] and [11], defined as follows.

A keyword-based query q over an XML document stream is a list of query terms (also denoted search terms) $\langle t_1, \ldots, t_m \rangle$. Each query term is of the form: ℓ*::k*, ℓ*::*, *::k*, or *k*, where ℓ is an element label and k a keyword. A node n within a document d satisfies a query term of the form: ℓ*::k*, if n's label is equal to ℓ and the textual content of n contains the keyword *k*; ℓ*::*, if n's label is equal to ℓ; *::k*, if the textual content of n contains the keyword *k*; *k*, if n's label is equal to *k* or the textual content of n contains the keyword *k*. We also assume that the keyword-based queries are evaluated against documents using the well-known SLCA semantics[1].

To illustrate our query language, consider the following query specifications:

s_a: *New novels written by Porter*
s_b: *New novels having "Porter" in their title*
s_c: *New books in MP3 format by publisher named "MP3"*

Table 1 presents possible keyword-based query formulations that fulfill these query specifications[2]. These keyword queries were intentionally built to illustrate our algorithms and are targeted to streams containing book releases. Moreover, they illustrate different scenarios regarding the user's knowledge about the XML labels. In queries q_1 and q_5 the user knows the labels and employs query terms of the form ℓ*::k*, where each keyword k is qualified with a node label ℓ. In queries q_2, q_3 and q_6 the user knows only some labels while in query q_4 the user has no knowledge at all (no labels are used). Notice that q_3 and q_4 are ambiguous, i.e., they may represent both requirements s_a and s_b. This is an inherent collateral effect of using keyword-based queries. Also notice that in query q_7, the term *MP3::* is an example of a pure structural condition where XML subtrees must contain an element with label *MP3*.

Procedure MultiQuery
Input: A stream of XML documents D
1. **let** $Q = q_1, \ldots, q_n$ be a set of queries from users' profiles
2. **while** D is not empty **do**
3. get a new document d_j from D
4. S.clear() {initialize the stack}
5. $\langle r_1, \ldots, r_n \rangle$:= SAX_Parsed(d_j,$\langle q_1, \ldots, q_n, \rangle$,S)
6. **return** $r_1, \ldots, r_n$
7. **end while**

Figure 1: General Multi-Query Procedure.

Figure 1 describes our general multi-query procedure. A set of queries Q (from users' profiles) are processed against a stream D of documents. Upon its arrival, each document d_j in D is individually processed (Lines 3 to 6). The results found within this document are collected and returned (Lines 5 and 6). This is accomplished at the same time for all queries q_i and results are individually collected in each r_i. A result includes the full path and the Dewey Code [9] of the SLCA resulting node of d_j, if any.

Each document d_j in D is processed by a SAX parser, which generates five types of event for a document: *startDocument()*, *startElement(tag)*, *characters(text)*, *endElement(tag)* and *endDocument()*. Our algorithms then work by means of SAX *Callback Functions* for those events. The parser is called to action in Line 5 of the procedure.

Parsing Stack. As the SAX parser traverses the document in an in-order fashion, each visited node is associated with an entry in a stack S, which we call the *Parsing Stack*. Each entry is popped from the stack when its corresponding node and all its descendants have been visited. To support the recursive processing of a document, each entry in the parsing stack handles the following information: (1) the label of the element corresponding to the entry; (2) a bitmap called CAN_BE_SLCA, which contains one bit for each query q_i being evaluated (3) a set used_queries containing the IDs of the queries whose terms include keywords present in the element (or its descendants), either as labels or as in values; (4) which keywords from these queries have occurred in the corresponding document node and its descendants.

Notice that, without loss of generality, we assume that labels are unique per type of element in each document. For instance, in one single document, the label `Author` is always used to represent a book author and not a paper author.

Query Index. During the traversal of a document, it is necessary to look for keywords that occur in text elements or labels. As we expect to process a large number of queries, our algorithms rely on *query indexes* in order to avoid looking up each query individually. The indexing structures we use are adaptations of inverted lists. Each index entry represents a query term and refers to queries in which this term occurs, making a distinction between structural (label) and non-structural (value) query terms.

Notice that, as in any inverted list, query indexes are generated beforehand from the set of queries posed by users. Tackling new queries requires the query indexes to be rebuilt. This is a simple task that does not require any effort from users or developers. Moreover, it is reasonable to expect that the set of queries posed by users is stable, while documents keep arriving through streams.

[1]Actually, any other LCA-based semantics could also be used.
[2]Attributes can be easily handled with no significant overhead.

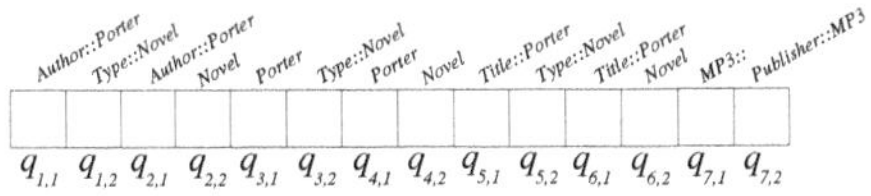

Figure 2: query_bitmap used by KStream.

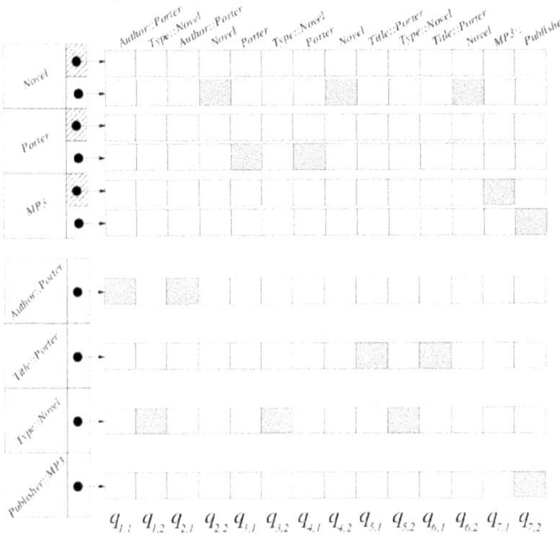

Figure 3: query_index used by KStream.

```
Callback Function KStream.Start
Input: Parsing stack S, XML node e being processed
 1. ℓ := label(e)
 2. push(sn) {create new stack entry}
 3. sn.label := ℓ
 4. for all q_i ∈ set of queries being processed do
 5.     sn.CAN_BE_SLCA[q_i]:= true
 6. end for
 7. N := number of terms in all queries being processed
 8. sn.query_bitmap[0,...,N-1] := false
 9. if ℓ is indexed in query_index then
10.     {Gets from the index the bitmap corresponding to ℓ}
11.     m_bitmap := query_index[ℓ].labels_bitmap
12.     Q := query_index[ℓ].labelOcurrences
13.     add Q to sn.used_queries
14.     sn.query_bitmap := sn.query_bitmap or m_bitmap
15. end if

Callback Function KStream.Text
Input: Parsing stack S, XML node e being processed
 1. ℓ := label(e)
 2. sn := *top(S) {sn points to the top entry in the stack}
 3. K := set of tokens in node e
 4. for all k ∈ K do
 5.     if k is indexed in query_index then
 6.         {Gets from the index the bitmap corresponding to k}
 7.         m_bitmap := query_index[k].values_bitmap
 8.         Q := query_index[k].keywordOcurrences
 9.         add Q to sn.used_queries
10.         sn.query_bitmap := sn.query_bitmap or m_bitmap
11.     end if
12. end for

Callback Function KStream.End
Input: Parsing stack S, the XML node e being processed
 1. sn := pop(S) {pops the top entry in the stack to sn}
 2. tn := *top(S) {tn points to the top entry in the stack}
 3. tn.CAN_BE_SLCA:=tn.CAN_BE_SLCA and sn.CAN_BE_SLCA
 4. add sn.used_queries to tn.used_queries
 5. sn.query_bitmap := sn.query_bitmap or tn.query_bitmap
 6. for q ∈ sn.used_queries do
 7.     let j be the first query term from q in sn.query_bitmap
 8.     let k + 1 be the number of query terms in q
 9.     COMPLETE := and sn.query_bitmap[t_j, ..., t_{j+k}]
10.     if sn.CAN_BE_SLCA[q] and COMPLETE then
11.         q.results := q.results ∪ { sn }
12.         tn.CAN_BE_SLCA[q]:= false
13.         remove q from tn.used_queries
14.     end if
15. end for
```

Figure 4: KStream Callback Functions.

4 Proposed Algorithms

Our proposed algorithms run as SAX callback functions on the general procedure described in Figure 1. The first one, KStream, employs one single bitmap for representing all queries being processed. The second one, CKStream, optimizes space consumption by compacting the bitmap representation. These algorithms are described next.

4.1 KStream Algorithm

Before describing KStream, we present the main data structures it uses. Information about which keywords from each query have occurred in an XML node (and its descendants) is kept using a bitmap stored on the stack entry corresponding to such a node. This bitmap is called query_bitmap and each of its bits is associated with one search term from each query q_i. When the corresponding term occurs in the current node (or in its descendants), this bit is set to **true**. For example, considering the queries in Table 1, Figure 2 illustrates the query_bitmap used by KStream when processing those queries. In this figure, each cell $q_{i,j}$ refers to the j-th term of query q_i. The size of the query_bitmap is equal to the number of terms in all queries.

While processing a node, the query_bitmap is built based on information of which queries mention keywords occurring in labels or values present on such a node. This information is kept on a *query index*. In KStream, this index comprises inverted lists, in which entries refer to bitmaps. As illustrated in Figure 3, for each keyword entry in this index, two bitmaps with the same size of query_bitmap are used. The first, labels_bitmap, keeps track of terms related only to labels ℓ, (i.e., ℓ:: and ℓ), while the second, values_bitmap, handles occurrences of terms related only to values k (i.e., ::k and k). Each bit associated with an occurrence of a term is set to *true* (these bits are grayed in the figure). Search terms of the form ℓ::k are treated differently, and their inverted lists use a single bitmap for the same purpose. An auxiliary indexing structure is used to speed up the search for queries that contain a certain term.

KStream consists of three callback functions, each one for a distinct event. Function KStream.Start handles *starElement* events, KStream.Text handles *characters* events and KStream.End handles *endElement* events. These functions are presented in Figure 4.

In function KStream.Start, a new stack entry is created to handle the current XML node. For this entry, the CAN_BE_SLCA bitmap (Line 5) and the query bitmap are initialized (Line 8). While CAN_BE_SLCA bits are set to *true*, bits in query_bitmaps are set to *false*. Then, the algorithm searches the query index for queries in which the label of the node being processed occurs in search terms of types ℓ:: and ℓ (Line 11), to retrieve from the query_index the bitmap that tracks the occurrences of the label ℓ in queries, if any. The matching queries are marked by a bitwise **or** operation between the labels bitmap (m_bitmap) from the inverted list and the query_bitmap in the stack entry (Line 14). Notice that all queries used in this step have their references added to the used_queries set. This way, the callback function KStream.End only needs to check these queries, instead of the whole set of submitted queries.

In function KStream.Text, for each keyword found in the text (Line 3), it searches the query index for queries that contain any of these keywords (Line 7). Next, a bitwise **or** operation is performed between m.values_bitmap from the inverted list and query_bitmap in the stack entry (Line 10). However, this time, the function looks in the index for search terms of types ℓ::k, ::k and k.

Finally, function KStream.End pops the current entry sn out of the stack and creates a reference to the new top entry on the stack tn (Lines 1 and 2). Notice that this new top entry tn corresponds to the parent of the XML node whose entry stack sn was just popped out. Moreover, this function needs to propagate the information stored in sn to tn. Specifically, this propagation involves: performing an **and** operation between sn and tn CAN_BE_SLCA bitmaps (Line 3), adding all queries from the sn used_queries set to the tn used_queries set (Line 4), and updating the query_bitmaps from tn according to query_bitmaps from sn to keep track of which queries match with its corresponding XML node (and its descendants), which is done by an **or** between the bitmaps of the used queries on the popped entry and the corresponding bitmaps (i.e., relative to the same queries) in the top entry (Line 5).

Function KStream.End is also responsible for checking whether the node corresponding to the popped entry sn is to be added to the set of results of some query q (q.results). For this, two conditions must be satisfied (Line 10). First, all terms in the query must be present in this node, or in some of its descendant nodes. In this case, we say that the query is *complete*. This is verified by computing an and over the bits in sn.query_bitmap that correspond to each specific query (Line 9). Second, the document subtree rooted at the node corresponding to sn must satisfy the SLCA semantic for the query. This is verified by using the bit associated to this query in the CAN_BE_SLCA bitmap. Recall that this bitmap is also recursively constructed considering the CAN_BE_SLCA bitmap of the descendant nodes (Line 3). If these conditions are satisfied, the node is added to the set of results of the query q. Also, tn.CAN_BE_SLCA[q] is set to false to indicate that none of its ancestors can be an SLCA result, since this node already is (because it is lower than any of its ancestors).

4.2 CKStream Algorithm

CKStream was designed for condensing redundant information on search terms occurring in more than one query. In KStream, we use N bits to represent the same search term in N different queries. Instead, CKStream uses only *one* bit for each distinct search term in all queries. Thus, each stack entry includes a different configuration for the query_bitmap, in which a bit is associated with each *distinct* query term. Figure 5 illustrates the query_bitmap used by CKStream when processing the queries in Table 1.

As a consequence, in the query index the entry corresponding to a term t needs only to store the position of the bit corresponding to this term in the query_bitmap, as illustrated in Figure 5.

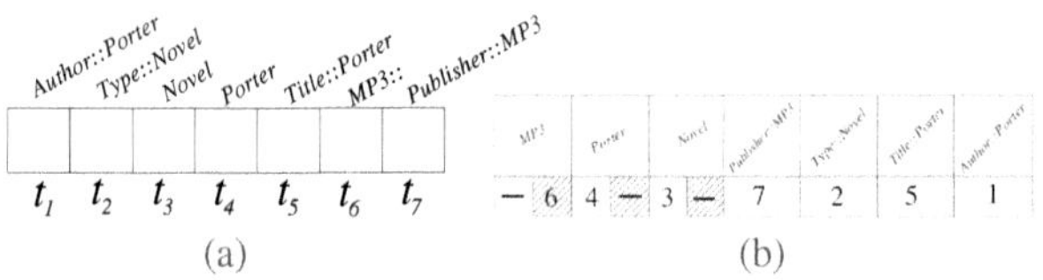

Figure 5: query_bitmap (a) and query_index (b) used by CKStream.

Like KStream, CKStream also uses an auxiliary index to speed up the search for queries that contain a certain term.

Functions CKStream.Start, CKStream.Text and CKStream.End are presented in Figure 6. CKStream.Start searches the query_index for the current node's label ℓ, obtaining the positions associated with the entry corresponding to this label (Line 9). Then, it sets to *true* the bit position associated with this occurrence in the query_bitmap of the new stack entry (Line 13). Similarly, CKStream.Text searches the query index and sets *true* to the corresponding bits. Notice that terms of the form ℓ::k are handled in this function and receive a specific treatment.

Finally, CKStream.End looks for *complete* queries, i.e., those in which all search terms are satisfied by the node being processed (or by its decedents). The main distinction from KStream.End is that the bits corresponding to query terms are not necessarily contiguous in sn.query_bitmap. Hence, it requires the position of the bits corresponding to search terms used in each query to be known. This is accomplished by using an auxiliary structure, which is built with a single pass over all queries. Building the auxiliary structure happens simultaneously with the construction of the query_index.

```
Callback Function CKStream.Start
Input: Parsing stack S, the XML node e being processed
 1. ℓ := label(e)
 2. push(sn) {create new stack entry}
 3. sn.label := ℓ
 4. for all q_i ∈ queries being processed do
 5.    sn.CAN_BE_SLCA[q_i]:= true
 6. end for
 7. N := number of distinct terms in all queries being processed
 8. sn.query_bitmap[0,...,N-1] := false
 9. q := query_index[ℓ].asLabel {q gets the position of term ℓ}
10. Q := query_index[ℓ].labelOccurrences
11. add Q to sn.used_queries
12. if q ≥ 0 then
13.    sn.query_bitmap[q] := true
14. end if
```

```
Callback Function CKStream.Text
Input: Parsing stack S, the XML node e being processed
 1. ℓ := label(e)
 2. sn := *top(S) {sn points to the top entry in the stack}
 3. K := set of tokens in node e
 4. for all k ∈ text do
 5.    {q gets the position of of term k}
 6.    q := query_index[k].asKeyword
 7.    Q := query_index[k].keywordOcurrences
 8.    add Q to sn.used_queries
 9.    if q > 0 then
10.       sn.query_bitmap[q] := true
11.    end if
12.    {q gets the position of of term ℓ::k}
13.    q := query_index[ℓ::k].asLabeledKeyword
14.    Q := query_index[ℓ::k].keywordOcurrences
15.    add Q to sn.used_queries
16.    if q ≥ 0 then
17.       sn.query_bitmap[q] := true
18.    end if
19. end for
```

```
Callback Function CKStream.End
Input: Parsing stack S, the XML node e being processed
 1. sn := pop(S) {pops the top entry in the stack to sn}
 2. tn := *top(S) {tn points to the top entry in the stack}
 3. tn.CAN_BE_SLCA:=tn.CAN_BE_SLCA and sn.CAN_BE_SLCA
 4. add sn.used_queries to tn.used_queries
 5. sn.query_bitmap := sn.query_bitmap or tn.query_bitmap
 6. for q ∈ sn.used_queries do
 7.    let {j_1,...,j_N}) the positions of the bits corresponding to terms from
       query q in query_bitmap
 8.    COMPLETE := sn.query_bitmap[j_1] and ...
       and sn.query_bitmap[j_N]
 9.    if sn.CAN_BE_SLCA[q] and COMPLETE then
10.       q.results := q.results ∪ { sn }
11.       tn.CAN_BE_SLCA[q]:= false
12.       remove q from tn.used_queries
13.    end if
14. end for
```

Figure 6: CKStream Callback Functions.

5 Experimental Results

We now report experiments that consist in processing streams of XML documents against all posed queries simultaneously and measuring the time spent and the memory consumption. In the first experiment, we analyze how the algorithms handle an increasing number of keyword-based queries. In the second one, we observe the behavior of the algorithms as the number of search terms in each query increases.

5.1 Setup

The algorithms were implemented using Java and the SAX API from Xerces Java Parser. The query indexes and other data structures are kept entirely in memory. All experiments were performed in an Intel Dual Core 2.0Ghz computer with 3 GB of memory on Linux.

Three distinct datasets were used: (1) *ICDE* – metadata from papers published in the proceedings of the ICDE conference, extracted from DBLP; (2) *ISFDB*[3] – bibliographic data from fiction books available on the ISFDB Web site; (3) *SIGMODR* – data from

[3] http://www.isfdb.org

the table of contents of SIGMOD Record issues. We organized the data on ICDE papers by year of publication into a stream of 14 different XML documents, from 1995 to 2008. Similarly, in ISFDB, we separated books published between 2000 and 2009 into a stream of 10 different XML documents. Finally, we organized SIGMODR into as stream of 18 XML documents, each containing data from a single issue. Details on the three datasets are presented next in Table 2.

Dataset	Docs	Avg. Height	# Elem.	Avg. Nodes	Avg. Objects
ICDE	14	2	12	2073	119
ISFDB	10	2	11	41637	4110
SIGMODR	18	7	13	1697	167

Table 2: Details of the datasets used in the experiments.

SIGMODR has the deepest documents. In ISFDB and ICDE, most book and paper elements are flat. Regarding the number of distinct elements, notice that elements that have different full paths from the root node are considered distinct. ISFDB dataset has the largest XML documents. Hence, this stream has much more objects and elements than the other two. Furthermore, although ICDE has, on average, more elements than SIGMODR, the latter has more sub-trees that characterize objects.

We randomly generated sets of queries using data from each dataset. For example, using data from ISFDB, the following query could be generated: "*Author*::*jose* ::*saramago Title*::*blindness*". Depending on the experiment, we generate different sets of queries by varying the number and the type of terms to appear in the queries.

We measured, for each dataset, the time spent for processing all XML documents on a given stream. This excludes the time spent to create the query indexes, which is done only once when the operations start. Similarly, we measured the average memory usage while processing each XML document.

5.2 Varying the Number of Queries

We here analize how the algorithms handle an increasing number of queries. We use as a baseline a simple multi-query extension of the algorithm proposed in [11], which processes a single query over XML streams. Like in the original proposal, in this baseline, each element of the stack has one bitmap for each query. However, in order to allow multi-query processing, a query index is used to speed up the search.

We submitted up to 40,000 queries, each with up to 4 terms. We observed (in preliminary experiments) that searching for keywords in node values (e.g., $\ell::k$, $::k$ or k) presents no performance impact when using one type of query over the other. Hence, this experiment includes only query terms as $::k$. Figure 7 presents the comparison of time and memory spent by the algorithms over each of the datasets.

The time curves show a clear advantage of KStream and CKStream over the baseline. Both use a single bitmap for simultaneously matching terms of several queries against data on the nodes, whereas the baseline algorithm represents each query by an specific bitmap. Comparing the three datasets, the time performance in ISFDB is uniformly worse. This is explained because the documents in this dataset are larger, i.e., there are more nodes that need to be processed. Also, the performance of the algorithms over the ICDE dataset is slightly better than their performance over the SIGMODR dataset. This is due to the number of nodes that satisfy the queries, which is larger in SIGMODR than in ICDE.

Regarding memory consumption, the better performance of KStream pays the price of poor memory usage in comparison with the baseline and CKStream. This is due to the large bitmap structures allocated for each entry in the query index. Indeed, due to such a structure, KStream memory usage increases quadratically to the number of query terms. On the other hand, the baseline and CKStream have similar memory performance.

5.3 Varying the Number of Terms

Here, we aim to verify how our algorithms scale with the number of distinct terms, since this is an important factor in both time and space consumption. The experiment compares the impact of using queries with 2, 4 and 6 terms. We argue that 6 is a reasonable limit for the number of terms one typically uses when specifying a query. For each algorithm, we submitted an increasing number of up to 40,000 queries. In here, queries use only terms of the form $::k$. Figures 8 and 9 present, respectively, the comparison of time and memory spent by each algorithm over each of the datasets.

As expected, the performance is affected by the increase in the number of terms. This effect is even bigger in the ISFDB dataset, whose documents have more nodes. Nonetheless, both KStream and CKStream scale well with the number of queries and the number of query terms, even considering that their space and time performances have some degradation. Specifically regarding memory usage, again as expected, KStream suffers a larger impact than CKStream due to the increasing of the number of terms.

6 Conclusions

In this paper, we introduced the problem of processing multiple keyword-based queries over XML streams and proposed two new algorithms for addressing it. We performed comprehensive experiments to demonstrate their behavior regarding memory usage and processing time. The results show that both algorithms have a similar behavior in terms of processing time, although KStream performs slightly faster than CKStream. Regarding memory consumption, KStream excessive costs may be an impediment for its use in some cases. On the other hand, CKStream offers a good compromise between performance and memory usage, which makes it the best choice in real world scenarios.

Acknowledgments. This work was partially funded by CNPq, CAPES and FAPEMIG, Brazil.

7 References

[1] E. G. Barros, M. M. Moro, and A. H. F. Laender. An Evaluation Study of Search Algorithms for XML Streams. *J. Information and Data Management*, 1(3):487–502, 2010.

[2] S. Chen et. al. Scalable Filtering of Multiple Generalized-Tree-Pattern Queries over XML Streams. *IEEE Trans. Knowl. Data Eng.*, 20(12):1627–1640, 2008.

[3] S. Cohen et.al. XSEarch: A Semantic Search Engine for XML. In *Proc. of VLDB*, 2003.

[4] Y. Diao, S. Rizvi, and M. J. Franklin. Towards an Internet-Scale XML Dissemination Service. In *Proc. of VLDB*, 2004.

[5] L. Guo et.al. XRANK: Ranked Keyword Search over XML Documents. In *Proc. of SIGMOD Conf.*, 2003.

[6] Z. Liu and Y. Chen. Identifying meaningful return information for XML keyword search. In *Proc. of SIGMOD Conf.*, 2007.

[7] M. M. Moro, P. Bakalov, and V. J. Tsotras. Early Profile Pruning on XML-aware Publish-Subscribe Systems. In *Proc. of VLDB*, 2007.

[8] Y. Ni and C. Y. Chan. Dissemination of heterogeneous XML data in publish/subscribe systems. In *Proc. of CIKM*, 2009.

[9] I. Tatarinov et.al. Storing and querying ordered XML using a relational database system. In *Proc. of SIGMOD Conf.*, 2002.

[10] A. Termehchy and M. Winslett. Keyword Search for Data-Centric XML Collections with Long Text Fields. In *Proc. of EDBT*, 2010.

[11] Z. Vagena and M. M. Moro. Semantic Search over XML Document Streams. In *Proc. of DATAX*, 2008.

[12] Z. Vagena, M. M. Moro, and V. J. Tsotras. RoXSum: Leveraging Data Aggregation and Batch Processing for XML Routing. In *Proc. of ICDE*, 2007.

[13] C. Yu and L. Popa. Constraint-based XML query rewriting for data integration. In *Proc. of SIGMOD Conf.*, 2004.

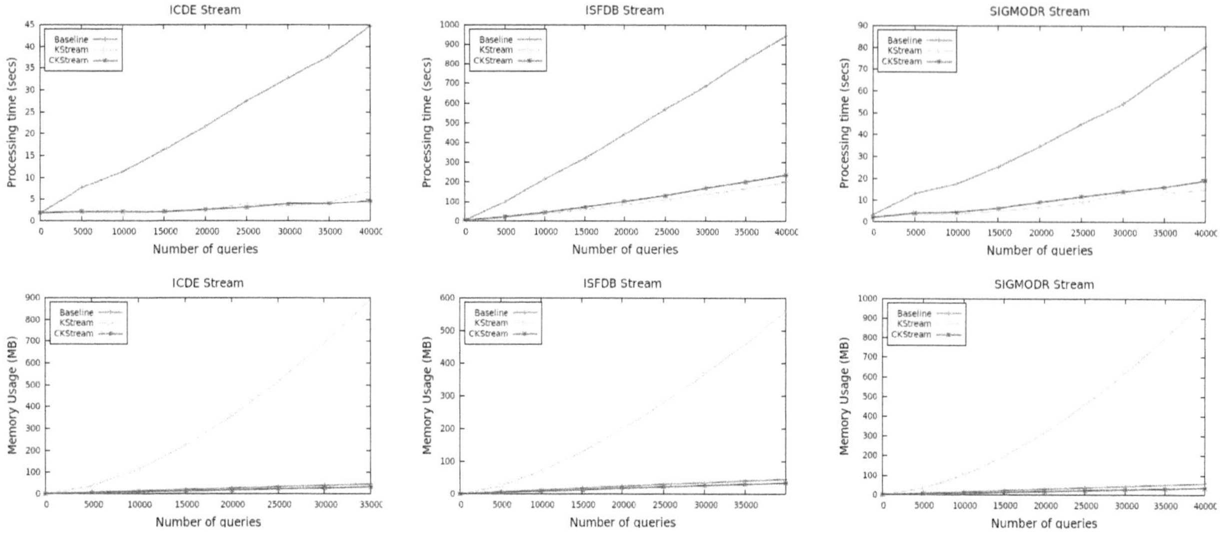

Figure 7: Varying the number of queries: time (top) and memory spent (bottom) for each algorithm in each dataset.

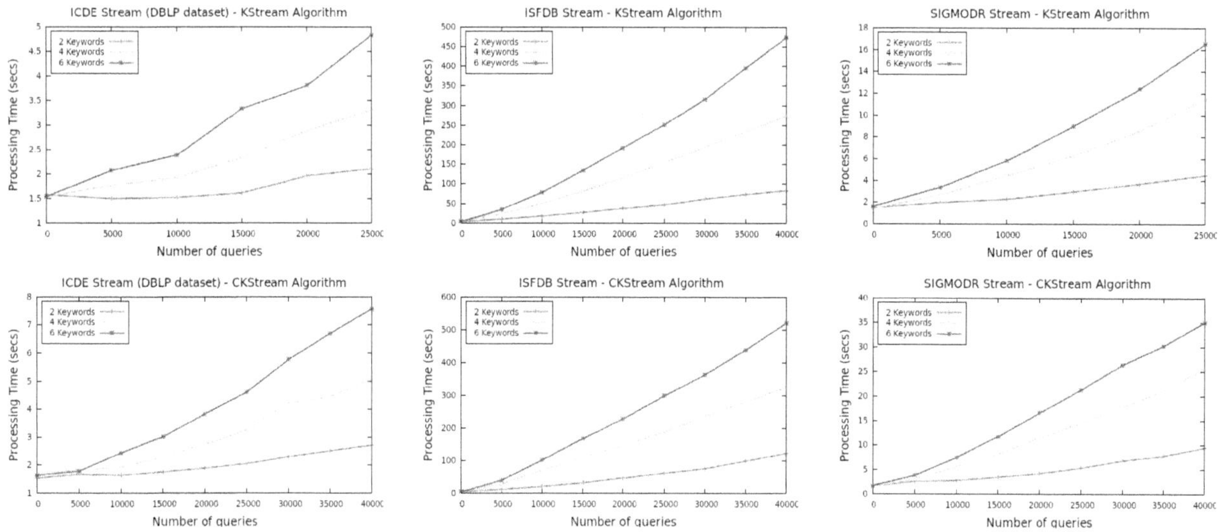

Figure 8: Using queries with 2, 4 and 6 terms: processing time for the three datasets.

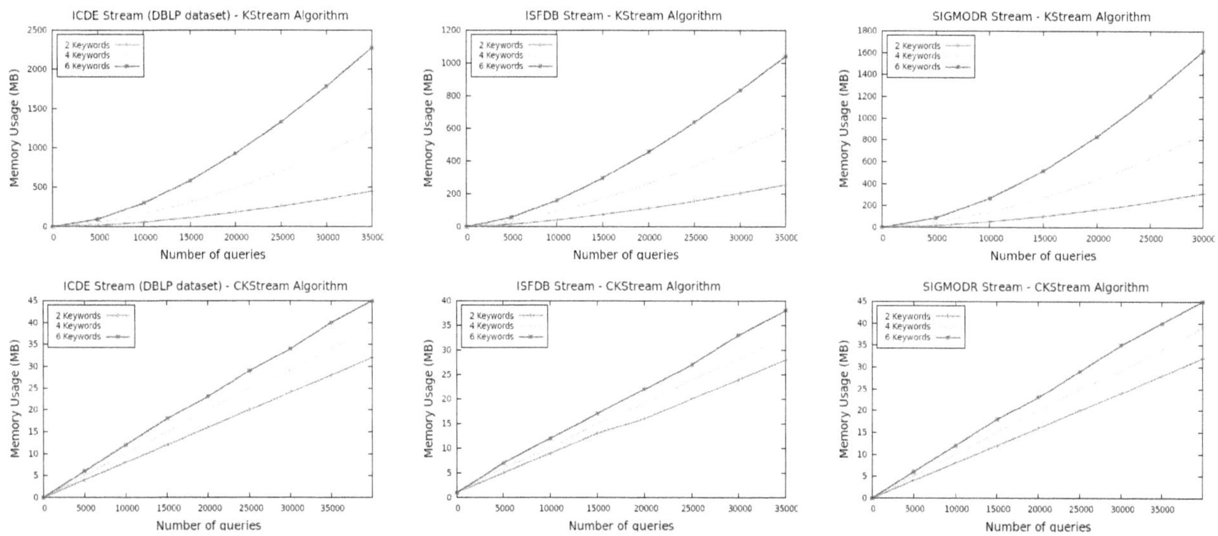

Figure 9: Using queries with 2, 4 and 6 terms: memory used for the three datasets.

Authentication of Location-based Skyline Queries

Xin Lin[†§], Jianliang Xu[§], Haibo Hu[§]
[†]Department of Computer Science, East China Normal University, Shanghai, China
[§]Department of Computer Science, Hong Kong Baptist University, Kowloon Tong, Hong Kong
xlin@cs.ecnu.edu.cn {xujl,haibo}@comp.hkbu.edu.hk

ABSTRACT

In outsourced spatial databases, the location-based service (LBS) provides query services to the clients on behalf of the data owner. However, if the LBS is not trustworthy, it may return incorrect or incomplete query results. Thus, authentication is needed to verify the soundness and completeness of query results. In this paper, we study the authentication problem for location-based skyline queries, which have recently been receiving increasing attention in LBS applications. We propose two authentication methods: one based on the traditional MR-tree index and the other based on a newly developed MR-Sky-tree. Experimental results demonstrate the efficiency of our proposed methods in terms of the authentication cost.

Categories and Subject Descriptors

H.2.4 [**Database Management**]: Query Processing

General Terms

Algorithm, Experimentation, Performance

Keywords

Data Outsourcing, Skyline Query, Authentication

1. INTRODUCTION

The past decade has seen tremendous amount of research efforts in spatial database technology. In practice, spatial databases from various sources (e.g., land surveys, traffic management, and environmental monitoring) are often outsourced to a service provider (i.e., LBS) because the agencies collecting such data (e.g., governments or non-profit organizations) are usually not able to support advanced query services [7]. However, such an outsourcing model brings a great challenge in query processing. Since the LBS is not the real owner of data, clients may want to authenticate the *soundness* and *completeness* of query results: soundness means that the original data is not modified by the LBS, while completeness means that no valid result is missing. This leads to a problem known as *authenticated query processing* [2, 3].

Figure 1: Authenticated Query Processing

A general framework of authenticated query processing is shown in Fig. 1. Before outsourcing a spatial dataset to the LBS, the data owner (DO) builds an authenticated data structure (ADS) of the dataset. To support efficient query processing, the ADS is often a tree-like index structure, where the root is signed by the DO using her private key. The LBS server keeps the spatial dataset, as well as the ADS and its root signature. For each user query, the LBS server returns the query results, the root signature, as well as a verification object (VO) that is constructed based on the ADS. The correctness of the query results can be verified by the client using the returned VO, the root signature, and the DO's public key.

There have been several studies that focused on authenticated processing of location-based queries [7, 8, 9]. However, the existing approaches are confined to proximity based queries, including range queries [7], nearest-neighbor (NN) queries [9], and shortest-path queries [8]. These queries are not sufficient to the LBS applications that need to consider both spatial and non-spatial attributes of queried objects. A typical example is finding nearby car parks with cheap parking fees, where the distance is a spatial attribute and the parking fee is a non-spatial attribute. In this scenario, a multi-criterion query is clearly more appealing than a conventional spatial query that considers the distance only.

Among various multi-criterion queries, location-based skyline is considered one of the most useful queries and has received considerable attention in LBS research (e.g., [6, 10]). The dynamic nature of spatial attributes makes location-based skyline queries unique and challenging. Take the above carpark-finding scenario for example. The distance from a client to a carpark varies with the location of the client. Therefore, the skyline results would be different with respect to different query locations. In the literature, several algorithms have been proposed to answer location-based skyline queries [6, 10]. However, no existing work has considered authenticated processing of such queries.

In this paper, we study the authenticated location-based

skyline problem and propose two methods. The first method is based on a generic ADS, namely MR-tree [7], that indexes spatial objects with an authenticated R-tree structure. We develop efficient algorithms to construct the VO for each location-based skyline query on the LBS server and to verify the query results on the client. In the second method, we observe that the solution space of spatial objects can be pre-computed in a form of *skyline scopes*. Thus, we propose a new ADS, called MR-Sky-tree, which indexes the skyline scopes of spatial objects (rather than the objects themselves). By doing so, both the VO construction time and the VO size can be reduced notably. Although MR-Sky-tree costs more time in building the index structure than MR-tree, its run-time performance is attractive for static or infrequently updated datasets (e.g., carparks, hotels, and points-of-interest).

On the whole, our contributions made in this paper can be summarized as follows:

- We identify the problem of authenticated location-based skyline queries that arises in outsourced spatial databases. To the best of our knowledge, this is the first work that studies this problem.
- We propose a basic MR-tree-based method for authenticated location-based skyline queries. We also propose a solution-based MR-Sky-tree to index the skyline scope of each object. Given a location-based skyline query, by employing the MR-Sky-tree, not only the VO can be quickly constructed but also its size is reduced notably.
- We conduct extensive experiments to evaluate the performance of the proposed methods and algorithms. The results show that our methods and algorithms perform well under various system settings.

The rest of this paper proceeds as follows. Section 2 gives some background and preliminaries of the problem to be studied. We present the MR-tree-based method in Sections 3. In Section 4, we propose the MR-Sky-tree method. The proposed methods and algorithms are experimentally evaluated in Section 5. Finally, this paper is concluded in Section 6.

2. BACKGROUND AND PRELIMINARIES

In this section, we give the formal definition of location-based skyline queries (LSQs) and present some background on the related authentication problem.

2.1 Location-based Skyline Queries (LSQs)

We consider a set of data objects O. Each object $o \in O$ is associated with a 2D spatial location attribute (denoted by $o.x$ and $o.y$) and several non-spatial attributes (e.g., parking fee and service quality, denoted by $o.A_i$ for the i-th non-spatial attribute). In this paper, we employ the Euclidean distance metric to measure the spatial proximity.

DEFINITION 1. ***(Non-Spatial Dominance)*** *Given two objects o and o', if o' is no worse than o on all non-spatial attributes, then we say o' non-spatially dominates o, and o' is a non-spatial dominator of o. Formally, it is denoted as $o' \lhd o$. The set of o's non-spatial dominator objects is denoted as $Dom(o)$.*

DEFINITION 2. ***(Dominance)*** *Given a query point q and two objects o and o', if (1) o' non-spatially dominates o, and (2) o' is closer to q than o (i.e., o' also spatially dominates o), then we say o' dominates o w. r. t. the query point q. Formally, it is denoted as $o' \lhd_q o$.*

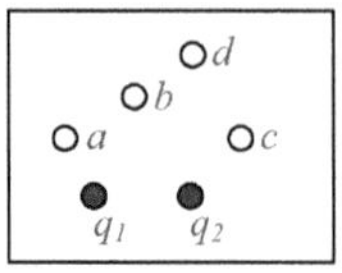

Carpark	Park fee	Service quality
a	15	4
b	13	5
c	14	5
d	18	3

Figure 2: An Example of LSQ

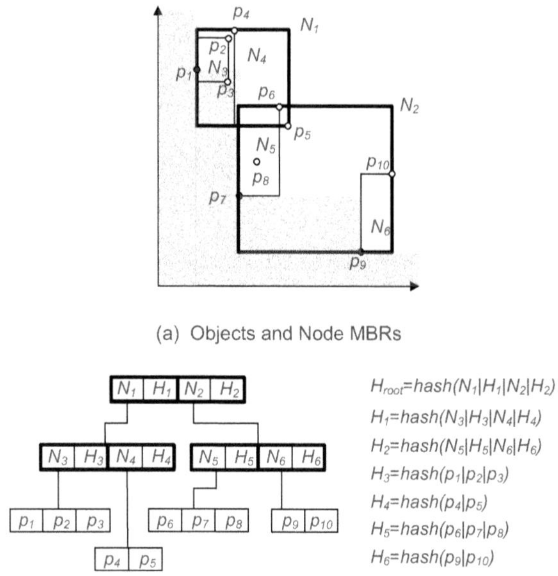

(a) Objects and Node MBRs

(b) MR-Tree

Figure 3: An Illustration of MR-Tree

DEFINITION 3. ***(Location-based Skyline Query (LSQ))*** *Given an object set O, the location-based skyline of a query point q is a subset of O, $LSQ(O, q)$, in which each object is not dominated by any other object in O w. r. t. q.*

Fig. 2 shows an example of LSQ about the aforementioned carpark-finding scenario. Suppose we have four carparks (i.e., a, b, c, and d) and two query points (i.e., q_1 and q_2). The non-spatial attributes of the four carparks are shown in the table, where low parking fee and high service quality are preferred. If the query is issued at q_1, the LSQ result is $\{a, b\}$ because c is dominated by b and d is dominated by both a and b; if the query is issued at q_2, the LSQ result is $\{b, c\}$ because they dominate a and d but not each other.

Given an LSQ query, the authentication problem is how to construct the VO for the client to verify the correctness of the query results. It involves three related issues (refer to Fig. 1): i) ADS design on the data owner; ii) dynamic VO construction for each LSQ query on the LBS server; iii) result verification based on the received VO on the client.

2.2 Query Authentication and MR-Tree

Authenticated query processing has been studied for a long time. Most prior work on query authentication is based on an ADS called Merkle B-tree (MB-tree) [2]. Yang *et al.* [7] first introduced this problem to the spatial database domain and studied the authentication of spatial range queries. They proposed an authenticated index structure called MR-tree, which combines the ideas of MB-tree and R-tree. Fig. 3

exemplifies the index structure of MR-tree. The data objects are shown in Fig. 3(a). As shown in Fig. 3(b), each leaf node in the MR-tree is identical to that of R-tree, which stores pointers pointing to actual data objects. The digest of a leaf node is obtained by hashing the concatenation of the binary representations of all objects in the node. Each internal node contains a number of entries in the form of (ptr_i, MBR_i, H_i),[1] where ptr_i, MBR_i, and H_i are the pointer, the minimum bounding rectangle, and the digest of the i-th child, respectively. The digest of an internal node summarizes the MBRs and digests of all children nodes (e.g., H_1 and H_2 in Fig. 3(b)). The use of digests makes possible the pruning of index nodes in the VO while being able to verify the correctness of query results.

In [7], the authors also provided a baseline solution to authenticating general skyline queries. The basic idea is to convert a skyline query to a range query. Assuming the skyline results are p_1, p_7, and p_9 as shown in Fig. 3(a). To construct the VO, the LBS server only needs to process a range query with the shaded area as the query range because all objects in the blank area are dominated by at least one skyline object. However, this solution is effective only for static skyline queries, but not for LSQs where query points are dynamic. Although it can be adapted to LSQs, it is less efficient than our two proposed methods, as will be shown in the performance evaluation (Section 5). In the following sections, we present the proposed methods for the LSQ authentication problem.

3. BASIC MR-TREE-BASED METHOD

In this section, we develop a basic authentication method by leveraging the existing MR-tree as the ADS. A naive approach is to return the whole MR-tree (see Fig. 3 for an example) excluding the digests as the VO, along with the signature of the root node. Thus, the client can authenticate the integrity of the received MR-tree by the root's signature, and then perform local query processing over the MR-tree to verify the correctness of the skyline results. However, the drawback of this approach is that the VO size is too large. In the following, we propose to reduce the VO size by pruning some index nodes in the MR-tree, without affecting the result verification ability.

Before presenting the detailed algorithm, we introduce a notion of *mindist* between a data object/index node and a query point. Without loss of generality, we assume that a lower value is preferred for any non-spatial attribute by a skyline query.

DEFINITION 4. ***(Mindist)*** *For an object o and a query point q, the mindist is defined as:* $mindist(o, q) = dist_S(o, q) + \sum_i o.A_i$, *where* $dist_S(o, q)$ *is the distance between o and q in the spatial dimension. For an index node m and a query point q, the mindist is defined as:* $mindist(m, q) = min\_dist_S(m, q) + \sum_i \min_{o \in m} o.A_i$, *where* $min\_dist_S(m, q)$ *is the minimum distance between m and q in the spatial dimension (see Fig. 4 for an illustration), and* $\min_{o \in m} o.A_i$ *is the minimum value in the i-th non-spatial dimension over all objects covered by m.*

[1]In the actual implementation, all the digests of a node can be stored in a separate page and pointed by the node. In this way, the original R-tree structure is not modified.

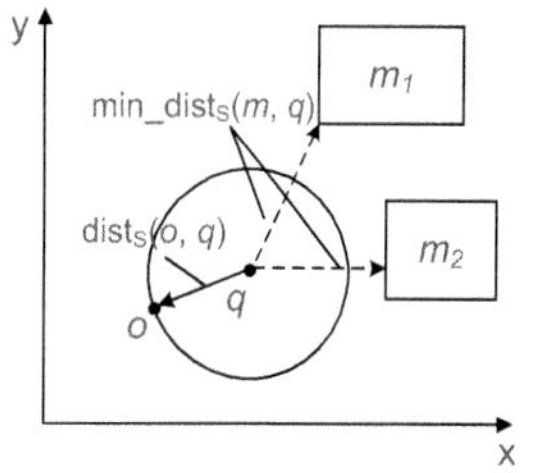

Figure 4: $dist_S(o, q)$ **and** $min\_dist_S(m, q)$

Algorithm 1 VO Construction in the Basic Method

INPUT: Root of MR-tree *mrRoot*; Query Point q
OUTPUT: Skyline Set S; VOTree *voTree*

1: $S \leftarrow \emptyset$
2: initialize *voTree* with *mrRoot* (excluding the digest)
3: insert *mrRoot* into a min-heap $\mathcal{H}$ ordered by *mindist*
4: **while** $\mathcal{H}$ is not empty **do**
5:   get the top element e from $\mathcal{H}$
6:   **if** e is an index node **do**
7:     **if** e is dominated by some object in S **do**
8:       prune e and keep its digest in the parent node
9:     **else**
10:       insert e's children into $\mathcal{H}$ and *voTree*
11:   **if** e is an object **do**
12:     **if** e is not dominated by any object in S **do**
13:       $S \leftarrow S \cup \{e\}$

Given an object o and a region R, if and only if o dominates all objects covered by R, we say o dominates R. Then, the following lemmas are obtained [4]:

LEMMA 1. *Given a query point q, if an object o dominates another object o′, we must have* $mindist(o, q) < mindist(o', q)$; *if an object o dominates a region R, we must have* $mindist(o, q) < mindist(R, q)$.

LEMMA 2. *Any data object added to a candidate skyline set based on a traversal of MR-tree in ascending order of mindist is guaranteed to be a final skyline result.*

Lemma 2 implies that only a single scan of objects is needed to find the skyline results if the MR-tree is traversed in ascending order of *mindist*. Based on these two lemmas, the VO construction algorithm is developed in Algorithm 1. The VO and skyline objects are recorded in the data structures *voTree* and S, respectively. Initially, S is empty, and *voTree* contains only the root (excluding the digest) of the MR-tree (Lines 1–2). We also maintain a min-heap $\mathcal{H}$ to keep the index nodes and objects to be scanned in the order of *mindist* (Line 3). In the loop iteration, each time the top element e is popped up from $\mathcal{H}$ (Lines 4–5). In the case where e is an index node, if it is dominated by some object in S, then this node will be pruned from *voTree* and we only keep its digest in the parent node (Lines 6–8); otherwise all children of this node will be inserted into $\mathcal{H}$ and *voTree* (Lines 9-10). In the case where e is a data object, if e is not dominated by any object in S, then e is added to S (Lines 11–13).

We use a simple example to illustrate the process of this algorithm. Suppose we have a number of objects $a - l$ as listed in Table 1. Each object includes one spatial (x and y) and two non-spatial (A_1 and A_2) attributes. Assume the

Obj.	x	y	A_1	A_2	Obj.	x	y	A_1	A_2
a	0	18	8	14	g	16	43	74	80
b	24	20	16	31	h	43	23	41	61
c	33	13	28	39	i	45	18	89	16
d	38	17	88	22	j	56	11	76	11
e	34	24	75	68	k	46	22	22	55
f	19	17	32	38	l	12	23	17	25

Table 1: An Object Set

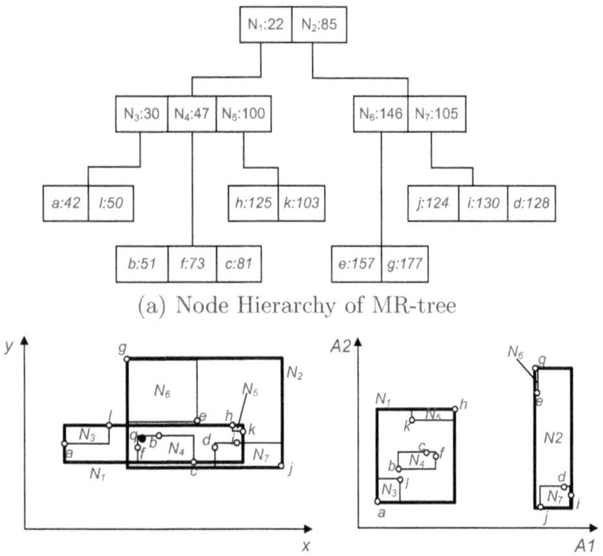

(a) Node Hierarchy of MR-tree

(b) Spatial Dimension (c) Non-Spatial Dimensions

Figure 5: MR-Tree Structure of Our Example

location of the query point q is (20, 20). Fig. 5(a) shows the MR-tree structure. In each node, for illustration, the *mindist* value is marked on the right side of the colon, where the decimal fraction is omitted. Fig. 5(b) visualizes the spatial information of objects $a - l$ and the query point q. The non-spatial attributes are visualized in Fig. 5(c). When running Algorithm 1, the data structures including the min-heap $\mathcal{H}$, skyline set S, and *voTree* will change step by step (see Table 2). In the beginning, *voTree* will be gradually expanded from the root (steps (1)–(3) in Fig. 6). Then, object a pops up from $\mathcal{H}$ and becomes the first skyline result. After that, as N_4 is not dominated by a, the objects under N_4 are inserted into $\mathcal{H}$ and *voTree* (step (4) in Fig. 6)). Next, objects l, b, f, c pop up from $\mathcal{H}$ and the skyline set is updated to $\{a, b, f, l\}$. This process continues until we examine N_5. As N_5 is dominated by object a both spatially (Fig. 5(b)) and non-spatially (Fig. 5(c)), it is pruned from *voTree* (step (6) in Fig. 6). Similarly, N_6 is dominated by object b and hence pruned when we examine it in the last step of Fig. 6.

We now describe the result verification process on the client. To verify the soundness and completeness of skyline results, we should examine two facts: 1) all objects in the result set S are not dominated by each other; 2) no skyline result is missed (i.e., *voTree* is complete and sound; all non-result objects and pruned MBRs are dominated by some object in S). The completeness and soundness of *voTree* can be guaranteed by comparing the signature of the root signed by the data owner and the digest dynamically computed from the *voTree* received by the client.

Min-Heap $\mathcal{H}$	Skyline Set S	VOTree (Fig. 6)
N_1, N_2		(1)
N_3, N_4, N_2, N_5		(2)
a, N_4, l, N_2, N_5		(3)
l, b, f, c, N_2, N_5	$\{a\}$	(4)
N_2, N_5	$\{a, b, f, l\}$	(4)
N_5, N_7, N_6	$\{a, b, f, l\}$	(5)
N_7, N_6	$\{a, b, f, l\}$	(6)
j, d, i, N_6	$\{a, b, f, l\}$	(7)
N_6	$\{a, b, d, f, j, l\}$	(7)
$\emptyset$	$\{a, b, d, f, j, l\}$	(8)

Table 2: Changes of Data Structures

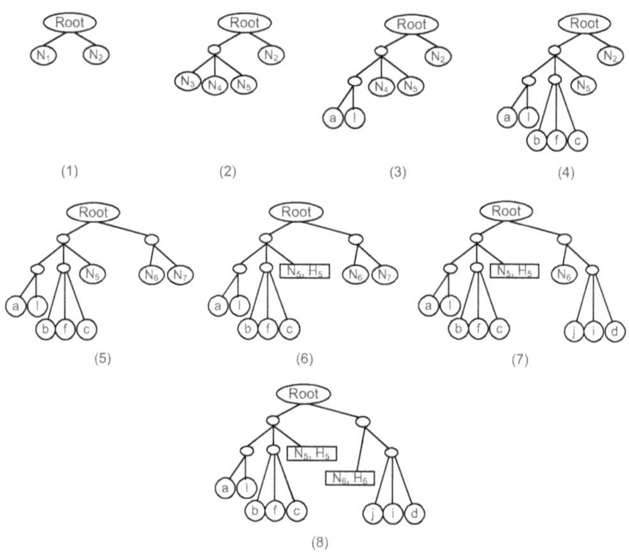

Figure 6: Changes of VOTree

4. MR-SKY-TREE METHOD

In essence, the MR-tree-based method computes the location-based skyline LSQ(O, q) on the fly. For static datasets, the data owner may alternatively precompute the skyline or at least its outline for the entire space. In this section, we propose such a solution-based method.

First, we introduce a notion of *skyline scope* for each queried object. The skyline scope of each object o is defined as the spatial area in which o will contribute to the skyline results.

DEFINITION 5. ***(Skyline Scope)*** *For an object $o \in O$, its skyline scope in a 2D plane P is denoted as $SS(o) = \{q \mid q \in P \wedge o \in LSQ(q, O)\}$, where $o \in LSQ(q, O)$ means $\forall m \in Dom(o)$, $dist_S(o, q) < dist_S(m, q)$.*

If Dom(o) is empty, i.e., o has no non-spatial dominators, then o must be a skyline result of any query point q. That is, o's skyline scope is the entire space. Otherwise, o will only be a skyline result of q if it is closer to q than all of its non-spatial dominators. The skyline scope of the latter is essentially the Voronoi cell of o in the object set $\{o\} \cup$ Dom(o). Fortunately, the Voronoi cell be computed using a divide-and-conquer algorithm, with a time complexity of O$(|O| log |O|)$ [1].

With skyline scopes computed, a location-based skyline

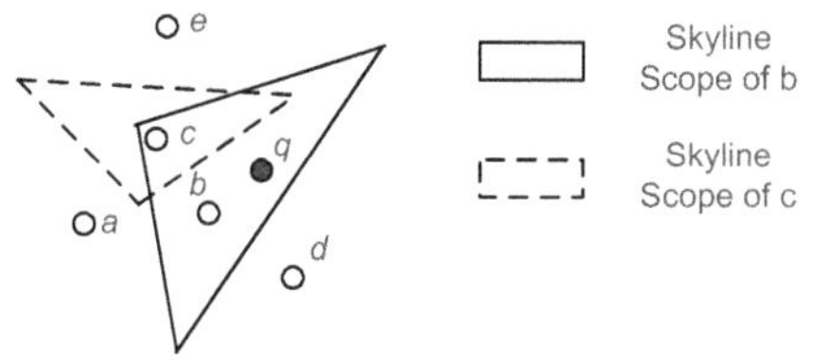

Figure 7: Skyline Scopes

Algorithm 2 VO Construction in the MR-Sky-tree Method

INPUT: Root of MR-Sky-Tree *mrRoot*; Query Point q
OUTPUT: Skyline Set S; VOTree *voTree*

```
1: S ← ∅
2: initialize voTree with mrRoot (excluding the digest)
3: insert mrRoot into a queue Q
4: while Q is not empty do
5:    get the top element e from Q
6:    insert e's children into voTree
7:    if e is an index node do
8:       for each child c of e do
9:          if c covers q do
10:            insert c to Q
11:         else
12:            prune c and keep its digest in the parent node
13:   else // e is a leaf node
14:      for each child c of e do
15:         if c covers q do
16:            S ← S ∪ {c}
```

---

can be computed by finding the objects whose skyline scopes cover the query point q. Fig. 7 shows an example, where a, d, and e have no non-spatial dominators, $a \lhd b \lhd c$, $d \lhd b \lhd c$, $e \lhd b \lhd c$. Hence, the skyline scopes of a, d, and e are the whole space, and the skyline scopes of b and c are enclosed by the corresponding perpendicular bisectors as shown in the figure. Since the query point q is covered by the skyline scopes of a, b, d, and e, the skyline result set is $\{a, b, d, e\}$.

To support query authentication, all skyline scopes should be inserted into an MR-tree as data points. We call this special solution-based index as MR-Sky-tree. Then, the original location-based skyline query is reduced to a point-location query on the MR-Sky-tree. Algorithm 2 shows the VO construction procedure. Specifically, it checks, from root and downwards, whether each child of an MR-Sky-tree node covers the query point. If it does, the child is inserted to a queue $\mathcal{Q}$ for further checking (Lines 9–10). Otherwise, the child is pruned and its MBR and digest are inserted into the final VO for verification (Lines 11–12).

Fig. 8 shows an example. The MR-Sky-tree structure is shown in Figs. 8(a) and 8(b). Assume that a query point q is only inside of a and c's skyline scopes. The root node is visited first, followed by its children nodes N_1 and N_2. As N_1 covers q while N_2 does not, N_1's children N_3 and N_4 are visited next, while N_2's MBR and digest (N_2, H_2) are inserted to *voTree*. At Level 1, N_3 and N_4 both cover the query point q; so their children, objects a, c, b, d are visited. While $\{a, c\}$ are the final skyline objects, the final *voTree* is shown in Fig. 8(c).

To verify this result, the client checks the following three facts: 1) the skyline scopes of all objects in the result set should cover the query point q; 2) no MBRs of pruned nodes

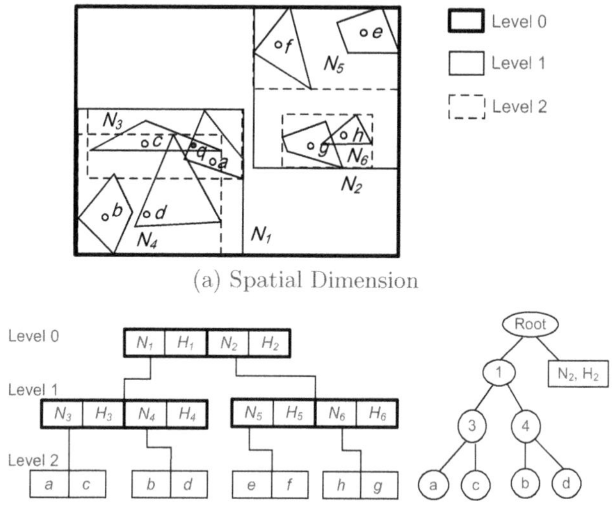

(a) Spatial Dimension

(b) MR-Sky-Tree Hierarchy (c) Final VOTree

Figure 8: MR-Sky-Tree

and skyline scopes of non-result objects cover q; 3) the root signature matches the digest computed from *voTree*. The fact 3 ensures the soundness of results, and facts 1-3 ensure the completeness of results.

5. EXPERIMENTS

5.1 Experiment Setup

In this section, we evaluate the performance of our proposed methods and algorithms through experiments. The spatial object set used in the experiments contains 2,249,727 objects representing the centroids of the street segments in California [5]. All testing datasets draw objects randomly from this set. The data space is normalized to a 100,000 Unit × 100,000 Unit square, where 1 Unit represents about 1 meter. The non-spatial attribute values of these objects are synthesized with a uniform distribution in the interval [0, 100,000]. The page size is 4K bytes and the size of each object is 320 bytes. The hashing function we choose is SHA-512, so the size of each digest is 64 bytes.

We measure the performance with three metrics: index construction time, query processing time, and client verification time. We compare the basic MR-tree-based method (denoted as *Basic*) and the MR-Sky-tree method (denoted as *Sky*). In addition, we implement a baseline method (denoted as *Baseline*), which is a modification of ARQ [7]. It finds the skyline results by the dynamic BBS algorithm [4] and then uses the shaded area like in Fig. 3 as a query range to obtain the VO. In theory, the VO size and verification time of the baseline algorithm are the same as those of the MR-tree-based method, while their query processing times are different since the MR-tree-based method integrates skyline result computation and VO construction.

We conducted our experiments on a workstation (Intel Xeon E5440 2.83GHz CPU) running on Ubuntu Linux Operating System. The simulation codes were written in Java (JDK 1.6). Each measurement is the average result over 100 queries.

5.2 Index Construction Time

Firstly, we measure the ADS index construction time of

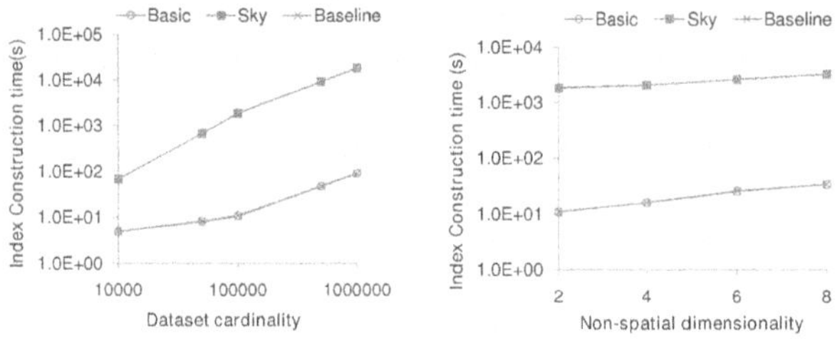

(a) (b)

Figure 9: Index Construction Time

each method. The results are shown in Fig. 9. Since Baseline is also based on MR-tree, its index construction time is the same as that of Basic. As expected, Sky costs much more index construction time than Basic and Baseline because it incurs the computation of the skyline scopes of all objects. Nonetheless, even when the cardinality reaches 1,000,000, its index construction can finish within 5 hours.

5.3 Query Processing Time

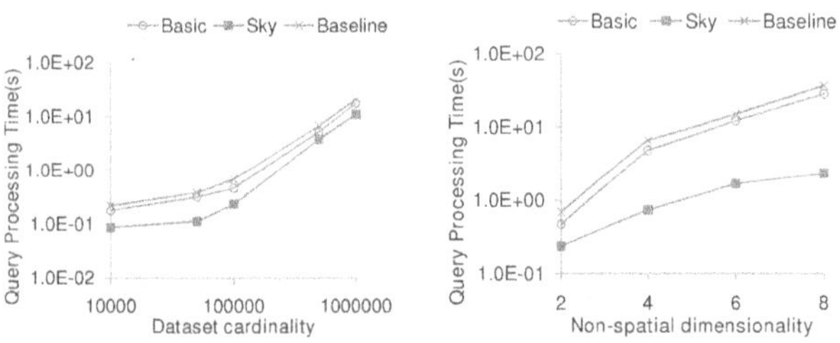

(a) (b)

Figure 10: Elapsed Time for Query Processing

Fig. 10 shows the results for query processing time, which includes the time for both skyline result computation and VO construction. We observe that Sky performs the best, e-specially as the non-spatial dimensionality increases. This is because the cardinality of the skyline result set soars as non-spatial dimensionality increases (from 39 for 2 non-spatial attributes to about 28,000 for 8 non-spatial attributes). The query processing time sharply increases in the Basic and Baseline methods, as the skyline objects distribute dispersedly in all dimensions. In contrast, Sky already precomputes the solution in the non-spatial dimensions during index construction, and the skyline scopes of data objects are always 2D regardless of the non-spatial dimensions. Besides, Sky is faster than Baseline because it integrates VO construction into skyline result computation.

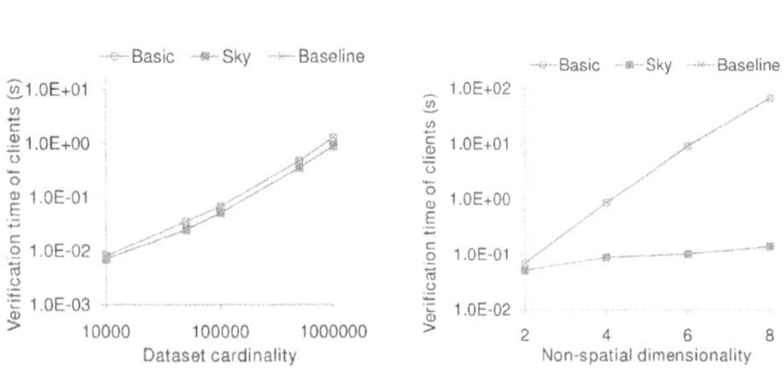

(a) (b)

Figure 11: Client Verification Time

5.4 Client Verification Time

Fig. 11(a) shows Basic and Baseline incur a slightly longer verification time than Sky for all dataset cardinality settings. Regarding the non-spatial dimensionality, Fig. 11(b) shows the costs of Basic and Baseline increase significantly with increasing dimensionality, due to the larger number of skyline results. On the other hand, Sky keeps a relatively stable verification time. This is because the skyline scopes are already precomputed and thus not much affected by the dimensionality.

6. CONCLUSIONS

In this paper, we have studied the problem of authenticated processing of location-based skyline queries. We have proposed two methods for VO construction and result verification: one is based on the existing MR-tree and the other is based on a novel solution-based MR-Sky-tree. The experiments show that the MR-Sky-tree method performs the best in terms of the authentication cost. However, as it needs more time to build/maintain the MR-Sky-tree index, this method is more suitable for static or infrequently updated datasets. For dynamic datasets, the MR-tree-based method is preferred. As for future work, we will extend the authentication problem to continuous skyline queries and road networks.

Acknowledgments

This work is supported by GRF Grants HKBU211510 & HKBU210811 and NSFC Grant 60903169. Lin Xin's research is also supported by the Fundamental Research Funds for the Central Universities and the Opening Project of Shanghai Key Laboratory of Integrated Administration Technologies for Information Security (No. AGK2008004).

7. REFERENCES

[1] M. Berg, O. Cheong, and M. Kreveld. Computational Geometry: Algorithms and Applications. Third Edition, Chapter 7, *ISBN: 978-3-540-77973-5*, 2008.

[2] F. Li, M. Hadjieleftheriou, G. Kollios, and L. Reyzin. Dynamic Authenticated Index Structures for Outsourced Databases. In *Proc. SIGMOD*, 2006.

[3] H. Pang, A. Jain, K. Ramamritham, and K.-L. Tan. Verifying Completeness of Relational Query Results in Data Publishing. In *Proc. SIGMOD*, 2005.

[4] D. Papadias, Y. Tao, G. Fu, and B. Seeger. An Optimal and Progressive Algorithm for Skyline Queries. In *Proc. SIGMOD*, 2003.

[5] R-tree Portal. [Online] http://www.rtreeportal.org/.

[6] M. Sharifzadeh and C. Shahabi. The Spatial Skyline Queries. In *Proc. VLDB*, 2006.

[7] Y. Yang, S. Papadopoulos, D. Papadias, and G. Kollios. Authenticated Indexing for Outsourced Spatial Databases. *VLDB Journal*, 18(3), 2009.

[8] M. L. Yiu, Y. Lin, and K. Mouratidis. Efficient Verification of Shortest Path Search via Authenticated Hints. In *ICDE*, pp. 237-248, 2010.

[9] M. L. Yiu, E. Lo, and D. Yung. Authentication of Moving kNN Queries. In *ICDE*, 2011.

[10] B. Zheng, C. K. Lee, and W.-C. Lee. Location-Dependent Skyline Query. In *MDM*, 2008.

Matching Query Processing in High-Dimensional Space *

Chunyang Ma #1 Yongluan Zhou †2 Lidan Shou #3 Dan Dai #4 Gang Chen #5

#Department of Computer Science
Zhejiang University, China
{[1]mcy, [3]should, [4]daidanhere, [5]cg}@zju.edu.cn

†Department of Mathematics and Computer Science
University of Southern Denmark, Denmark
[2]zhou@imada.sdu.dk

ABSTRACT

In many applications, such as online dating or job hunting websites, users often need to search for potential matches based on the requirements or preferences imposed by both sides. We refer to this type of queries as matching queries. In spite of their wide applicabilities, there has been little attention devoted to improve their performance. As matching queries often appear in various forms even within a single application, we, in this paper, propose a general processing framework, which can efficiently process various forms of matching queries. Moreover, we elaborate the detailed processing algorithms for two particular forms of matching queries to illustrate the applicability of this framework. We conduct an extensive experimental study with both synthetic and real datasets. The results indicate that, for various matching queries, our techniques can dramatically improve the query performance, especially when the dimensionality is high.

Categories and Subject Descriptors

H.2.8 [**Database Management**]: Database Applications—*Spatial databases and GIS*

General Terms

Algorithm, Management, Performance

Keywords

Matching, High-dimensional, Index

1 Introduction

Many matching services allow users to search for matching counterparts based on the requirements and/or preferences of both parties. Below are a few examples:

Case 1: Each subscriber of an online dating website has some personal properties such as age, stature, weight, income, hobbies, etc. At the same time, he or she has some requirements for the potential partners, characterized as ranges of age, weight, income, etc. When a user, say Tom, searches for potential partners on the website, it is desirable to return a list of candidates such that the candidates meet Tom's requirements and Tom fulfills the requirements imposed by the candidates as well.

Case 2: Nowadays home exchange is a very popular vacation alternative where you allow someone else to stay at your home while you stay in theirs during a vacation. Users of a website that provides this service would provide information of their houses as well as their requirements for the residences that they would like to exchange with. Suppose a young couple in Beijing plan a vacation in Shanghai. Then the website should provide the couple the candidate houses that meet most of the couple's requirements and, at the same time, the couple's house can match requirements imposed by those houses' owners.

Case 3: Consider a job hunting website. Information of each open position on the website consists of the properties of the job, such as job category, title, salary, office locations, etc., as well as the requirements for job applicants, including education level, major, age, and so on. When a person searches for jobs on this website, he will input his personal information, including education level, age, major, etc., and his expectation on the jobs that he would like to find, such as salary, working locations, etc. The desirable results returned by the website should be the openings that meet most of his requirements and are looking for someone like him.

We refer to the queries in the aforementioned examples as *matching queries*. This type of queries is usually specified as a query object, which is associated with a number of attributes, together with a list of matching conditions. Each data object in the database also has a number of attributes and a list of conditions. Unlike traditional queries, such as range queries, whose processing only needs to check whether the data objects are within the query region, the processing of matching queries needs to determine if both the data object and the query object can match each other's conditions.

Besides the new query semantics, there are a couple of additional challenges in processing matching queries. First, the data type here is more complicated than traditional spatial data types, such as point data or region data. Instead, each data object in the above applications can be modeled as a combination of a point and a region that represent the data object's attributes and matching conditions respectively. Moreover, the point and the region could be in different domain spaces. For example in case 3, the attributes of an open position could be in a domain space consisting of job category, title, salary and locations; meanwhile, the required qualifications for the job applicants could be specified in a space with three dimensions: education level, age and major. This problem imposes extra challenges in building index on the data to speed up the queries.

Second, matching queries could exist in different forms even in a single application. For instance, in the job finding application, it is desirable to allow the users to choose whether they only want the jobs that satisfy all their conditions or they want a list of jobs, which may not meet all the conditions but are ranked by "how well" the conditions are met. To realize this, a uniform indexing and process-

*This work is supported in part by the National Science Foundation of China (NSFC Grant No. 60803003, 60970124).

CIKM'11, October 24–28, 2011, Glasgow, Scotland, UK.

ing framework could simplify the implementation and maintenance of the system.

Motivated by the above observations, we propose a matching query processing framework in this paper. In the framework, a single index is built on the joint space of the data object's attributes and matching conditions. Note that in real applications, the user data and matching conditions can easily contain and involve dozens of attributes respectively. So the attribute space or the condition space alone, not to mention the joint space, is often high-dimensional. To overcome the curse of dimensionality, we transform each object into a single point in the joint space associated with several auxiliary parameters and then we map the point into a one-dimensional key value. The resulting key value as well as the auxiliary parameters are stored within a B^+-tree like index. The framework also provides a generic query evaluation algorithm template, with which the system can evaluate various specific forms of matching queries in a uniform way by plugging in the appropriate functions.

Furthermore, we develop detailed algorithms for two specific forms of matching queries and show how they can be fit into the uniform processing framework. Finally, we perform an extensive experimental study on both real and synthetic datasets. The results show that our algorithms consistently outperform the other alternative methods, especially when the dimensionality is high.

The rest of the paper is organized as follows. Section 2 reviews the related work. Section 3 presents the data model and query definitions. The uniform indexing and processing framework as well as the detailed processing algorithms for the specific queries are described in Section 4 and Section 5 respectively. Section 6 reports the results of an extensive experimental study of our proposals. Section 7 concludes the paper.

2 Related Work

In this section we first review the spatial assignment problem in Section 2.1. Second, we review existing multi-dimensional indexes in Section 2.2.

2.1 Spatial Assignment Problems

The most famous spatial assignment problem is known as the Stable Marriage Problem (SMP)[12, 2, 8, 5, 7, 6].

The SMP is mainly involved in applications of resource assignment, where there is always a centralized management system. The SMP in these applications focuses on centrally assigning all objects from two different datasets into 1-1 pairs to achieve certain global stableness. After centralized assignment, each object is given a determined resource without personal choices. On the contrary in this paper we do not compel all objects to be assigned. Our goal is to provide customers good matching options and leave the decision to them. The matching query addressed in this paper is based on users' individual demands and is a different problem from the SMP.

Further more, since the SMP focuses on achieving global stableness, the techniques proposed for SMP cannot achieve the goal of the matching queries proposed in this paper.

2.2 Spatial Indexes

The R*-tree is the state-of-art index for multi-dimensional objects. The R*-tree is optimized for range queries. The main concern about R*-tree is that it cannot scale to high-dimensional data well [11].

Many existing studies attempt to break the curse of dimensionality[4, 11, 1, 13, 3]. However these high-dimensional indexes are only designed for point data and cannot handle data objects in more complicated forms. And there is no straightforward way to directly adapt any of them to index objects modeled in this paper.

3 Problem Formulation

3.1 Data model

A data model should represent the attributes and matching conditions of objects at the same time.

First let D_a denotes the number of attributes of each object, then the attributes of an object X can be modeled as a hyper-point in a D_a-dimensional attribute domain space.

Each object is also associated with a number of matching conditions. Let D_c denotes the number of dimensions that each object has matching conditions on and then the matching conditions of an object X can be modeled inside a D_c-dimensional condition domain space. In particular, each condition is represented as a tolerant range in the domain of one of the counterpart's attributes.

In many applications, users may have different preferences among different attributes. We model the preferences of users as different weights on different attributes.

Next, we give the formal definition of an object.

DEFINITION 1. *An object X is represented as $\{P_X, R_X, W_X\}$, where $P_X = \{p_{X,1}, p_{X,2}, \ldots, p_{X,D_a}\}$ is the attribute point in a D_a-dimensional attribute space, $R_X = \{[l_{X,1}, u_{X,1}], [l_{X,2}, u_{X,2}], \ldots, [l_{X,D_c}, u_{X,D_c}]\}$ is the tolerant range in a D_c-dimensional condition space and $W_X = \{w_{X,1}, w_{X,2}, \ldots, w_{X,D_c}\}$ contains the weight of each dimension of R_X.*

3.2 Query definition

Given a database where the attributes of objects are in a D_a-dimensional attribute space and conditions are in a D_c-dimensional condition space, a **query object** Q is a triplet, $\{P_Q, R_Q, W_Q\}$, where P_Q is a point in the D_c-dimensional condition space, R_Q is a rectangle in the D_a-dimensional attribute space and W_Q contains weights of each dimension of R_Q.

In this section we define two specific types of matching queries, the full matching query and the tolerant top-k matching query.

3.2.1 The full matching query

A *full matching query* is defined as follows:

DEFINITION 2. ***Full matching query (FMQ)***
Given a database DB and a query object Q, a full matching query returns every object X from DB that P_X is inside R_Q in the attribute space and P_Q is inside R_X in the condition space.

An object X is the answer of a FMQ of Q iff for each dimension i in the attribute space $p_{X,i}$ is inside $[l_{Q,i}, u_{Q,i}]$ and for each dimension i in the condition space $p_{Q,i}$ is inside $[l_{X,i}, u_{X,i}]$.

3.2.2 The tolerant top-k matching query

Next we introduce the *tolerant top-k matching query* (TKMQ), where a ranking is imposed on a data object based on "how tightly" it and the query match each other's tolerant ranges. We refer to the "tightness" of the match between a data object and a query as the tolerant matching coefficient and it is formally defined as follows:

DEFINITION 3. *Given an object X and a query object Q, the **tolerant matching coefficient between** X **and** Q, denoted as $\mathscr{M}_t^{X \bowtie Q}$, is defined as*

$$\mathscr{M}_t^{X \bowtie Q} = \sum_{i=1}^{D_a} (\delta_{X,i} \cdot w_{Q,i}) + \sum_{i=1}^{D_c} (\delta_{Q,i} \cdot w_{X,i}) \qquad (1)$$

where

$$\delta_{X,i} = \begin{cases} 1 & \text{if } p_{X,i} \in [l_{Q,i}, u_{Q,i}] \\ 0 & \text{otherwise} \end{cases}$$

and

$$\delta_{Q,i} = \begin{cases} 1 & \text{if } p_{Q,i} \in [l_{X,i}, u_{X,i}] \\ 0 & \text{otherwise} \end{cases}$$

The $\mathscr{M}_t^{X \bowtie Y}$ can be viewed as the weighted number of dimensions that X and Q meet each other's matching conditions. Next we give the formal definition of the tolerant top-k matching query.

DEFINITION 4. ***Tolerant top-k matching query (TKMQ)*** *Given a database DB, a query object Q and an integer k, a tolerant top-k matching query returns a set S which consists of k objects from DB so that for any object $X \in S$ and any object $Y \in DB - S$, $\mathscr{M}_t^{Q \bowtie X} \geq \mathscr{M}_t^{Q \bowtie Y}$.*

A TKMQ answer object X does not have to match Q in all dimensions but just matches Q in more dimensions than others. Usually TKMQs are issued when there are no or not enough objects in the databases that totally matches with the query but users still want adequate choices.

4 The Query Processing Framework

In this section, we present our matching query processing framework, *PROM* (*PRO*cess various forms of *M*atching queries). *PROM* joins the attribute space and the condition space of the objects together and then builds index structure and processes matching queries in the joint space. In particular, we first propose an efficient and intuitive index technique utilized by *PROM* in Section 4.1. Then in Section 4.2 we summarize the general query processing procedure of *PROM*.

4.1 The Index Structure

The index is built in a $(D_a + D_c)$-dimensional domain space which is the joint space of the attribute space and condition space of objects. In particular the first D_a dimensions are corresponding to the attribute space and the last D_c ones are corresponding to the condition space. In the rest of the paper, we use D_J to denote the dimensionality of the joint space, i.e. $D_J = D_a + D_c$.

The index is built in the following three steps:

Step 1. For each object $X = \{P_X, R_X, W_X\}$, we represent the attribute point P_X and tolerant range R_X with a D_J-dimensional rectangle, which is $X^{D_J} = \{[p_{X,1}, p_{X,1}], \ldots, [p_{X,D_a}, p_{X,D_a}], [l_{X,1}, u_{X,1}], \ldots, [l_{X,D_c}, u_{X,D_c}]\}$. Let $C_X = \{c_{X,1}, \ldots, c_{X,D_J}\}$ denote the center of X^{D_J}, then $c_{X,i} = p_{X,i}$ when $i \in [1, D_a]$ and $c_{X,i} = (l_{X,i-D_a} + u_{X,i-D_a})/2$ when $i \in [D_a + 1, D_J]$. Furthermore, let r_X be the maximum distance between C_X and the bounds of X^{D_J} in each dimension, then $r_X = \max_{i=1}^{D_c}(u_{X,i} - l_{X,i})/2$. We call r_X the **radius** of X. In addition let ω_X denote the maximum weight of W_X, so that $\omega_X = \max_{i=1}^{D_c} w_{X,i}$. Therefore we transform X into a single point in the joint space associated with two auxiliary parameters.

Step 2. As mentioned earlier, the joint space is often of high dimensionality. Therefore in the second step for each object X we employ certain mapping technique to map the D_J-dimensional center point C_X into a one-dimensional key value. Note that any mapping technique, such as iDistance [3], the Pyramid [1] and P$^+$-tree [13] can be used here. We will not go into details of the mapping techniques due the space limit.

Step 3. After the second step, each object X is represented as combination of a key value and two auxiliary parameters, i.e. r_X and ω_X. In the third step we index these information of objects with one tree structure. Note that all existing mapping techniques employ B$^+$-tree to index objects' $keys$. We also employ B$^+$-tree due to its simplicity and small size. However traditional B$^+$-tree can only index objects based on one key value. In order to index

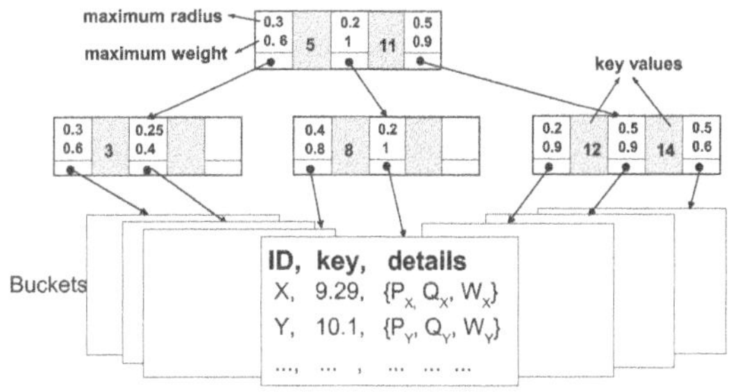

Figure 1: Data structure of the advanced B$^+$-tree.

$keys$ together with the radiuses and maximum weights, we modify the node structure of B$^+$-tree. The data structure of the new advanced B$^+$-tree is shown in Figure 1. In each tree node, besides the key values (shadowed in grey in the figure), we also store a radius and a weight of each child, which is the maximum radius and maximum weight of all objects in the subtree of that branch. A leaf node serves as a bucket, containing the objects with key values falling in a range determined by $keys$ stored in its father node.

4.2 The Processing Algorithm Template

Algorithm 1 presents the processing algorithm template for matching queries. Note that when constructing the index, the center points of objects are all mapped into the one-dimensional space of the key values. Accordingly, given a matching query, we also need map the matching query into the same one-dimensional space. To achieve this we first transform the matching query into one or more range queries, since range queries can be easily mapped into one-dimensional space. This transformation is dependent on the exact query type, whose details will be presented in the following section. For each range query, we map it into an interval of one-dimensional $keys$ in the same way as we handle the objects' center points. These key intervals are then stored in a list L_{key}. This whole process is done in a function $GetKeyInterval(\,)$, which is different for each type of matching query.

Then *PROM* visits the advanced B$^+$-tree from the root node down to the leaf nodes. In order to check as few objects as possible, we search the advanced B$^+$-tree in a "best-first" manner. That means the node whose subtree has the highest possibility of containing matching objects will be visited before the others. Finally, when a leaf node is visited, each object in the corresponding leaf node is checked to see if it is a match.

Specially, we maintain a max heap H in the memory. The entries in H are in the form of $(N, N.value)$, where N is a tree node and $N.value$ is N's ranking value in H. $N.value$ indicates the likelihood that the objects in N's subtree satisfy the query.

The way to calculate $N.value$ is different for different query types. (1) For ranking matching queries, such as TKMQ, $N.value$ is usually a bound of the ordering value of objects in N's subtree. For example, for TKMQs, $N.value$ is the upper bound of matching coefficient of objects in the subtree. Large $N.value$ means that objects in N's subtree may have high matching coefficients and high likelihood to be answers of the query. (2) For non-ranking matching queries, $N.value$ is a Boolean value. For instance, in FMQ, if there are possible matching objects in N's subtree, we set $N.value = 1$. Otherwise, we set $N.value = 0$. More details of the estimation of $N.value$ will be presented in the next section.

Initially we push the root node with $N_{root}.value = \infty$ into H. Afterwards we always visit the node N in the top entry $(N, N.value)$ of H, since N has the greatest ranking value and hence is most likely to contain answers in the subtree.

If N is a non-leaf node, for each child node of N, denoted as N_{child}, we compute $N_{child}.value$ and push it into H. $N_{child}.value$ is computed by a function $GetRankValue(\,)$, which works by directly comparing the key interval of N_{child} with the key intervals in L_{key}. The function $GetRankValue(\,)$ is different for different types of matching queries.

If N is a leaf node, for each object X in N we check if X is a matching object. If yes, we put X into the answer list L_{ans}.

A value V_{thres} is used to indicate when to stop visiting the nodes in H. (1) For ranking matching queries (top-k queries), V_{thres} is the kth maximum ordering value of the objects in the current answer list. The process stops when $N.value$ is no larger than V_{thres}, which indicates no unvisited object can have higher rank than the current answers. For example, for TKMQs, V_{thres} is always the kth maximum matching coefficient of the current objects in the answer list L_{ans}. The visiting process stops when the top entry in H has a $N.value$ no greater than V_{thres}, which means no unvisited objects can have a matching coefficient greater than the current k objects in L_{ans}. (2) For non-ranking queries, V_{thres} is set to 0. The visiting process stops when no nodes in H have $N.value = 1$, which means no more nodes can have matching objects in their subtrees.

Algorithm 1: MatchingQuery(Q)

```
Create empty lists L_ans and L_key.
Create a max heap H.
L_key ← GetKeyInterval( ).
V_thres ← 0.
PushHeap(H, (N_root, ∞)).
while H is not empty and top(H).value > v_thres do
    (N, N.value) ← PopHeap(H).
    if N is a non-leaf node then
        for each child of N do
            N_child.value ← GetRankValue(N_child, L_key).
            PushHeap(H, (N_child, N_child.value)).
    else
        for each object X in N do
            if X is an answer then
                L_ans ← L_ans ∪ X.
                Update V_thres.
return L_ans
```

With the above algorithm template, for each particular query type, we only need to implement the appropriate function $GetKeyInterval(\,)$ and $GetRankValue(\,)$. In the next section, we will show how these functions can be designed for two example queries.

5 Processing matching queries

5.1 Processing FMQs

FMQ.GetKeyInterval(Q)

Given a query Q, *PROM* transforms a FMQ into a number of range queries and pre-computes key intervals for these range queries in the following way.

First, we transform P_Q and R_Q into a rectangle in the data objects' joint space and we can get $\overline{Q^{D_J}} = \{[l_{Q,1}, u_{Q,1}], \ldots, [l_{Q,D_a}, u_{Q,D_a}], [p_{Q,1}, p_{Q,1}], \ldots, [p_{Q,D_c}, p_{Q,D_c}]\}$. Let $\overline{Q^{D_J}}(r)$ be an extension of $\overline{Q^{D_J}}$ that extends the last D_c dimensions of $\overline{Q^{D_J}}$ by r on both side, then $\overline{Q^{D_J}}(r)=\{[l_{Q,1}, u_{Q,1}], \ldots, [l_{Q,D_a}, u_{Q,D_a}], [p_{Q,1}-r, p_{Q,1}+r], \ldots, [p_{Q,D_c}-r, p_{Q,D_c}+r]\}$. Now we can decide if an object X is a full matching answer of Q based on the following theorem.

THEOREM 1. *Given an object X with C_X and r_X, if C_X is not inside $\overline{Q^{D_J}}(r_X)$ in the joint space, X cannot be a full matching answer of Q.*

The proof of Theorem 1 is omitted due to space limits. Based on Theorem 1, given a query Q, a full matching query is equivalent to searching every object X with its center C_X inside an extension rectangle of $\overline{Q^{D_J}}$, which is $\overline{Q^{D_J}}(r_X)$.

Note that r_X is the radius of a data object X and different objects have different radiuses. Intuitively it is not feasible to get the extension of $\overline{Q^{D_J}}$ corresponding to radiuses of all the data objects during query processing. So we pre-extend $\overline{Q^{D_J}}$ according to some catalog radiuses. In particular, suppose r_{max} is the maximum radius of all objects. Then we uniformly choose T values from $(0, r_{max}]$ as the **catalog radiuses**, denoted as $\{r_0, r_1, \ldots, r_{T-1}\}$, where $r_j < r_{j+1}$ and $r_{T-1} = r_{max}$. For each catalog radius r_j, we have $\overline{Q^{D_J}}(r_j)$. Each of these extended rectangle $\overline{Q^{D_J}}(r_j)$ is then treated as a range query. Particularly, for each $\overline{Q^{D_J}}(r_j)$ we compute its corresponding key interval, denoted as $[key_j^-, key_j^+]$, in the same way as we handle the objects' center points. All key intervals are stored in the form of $(r_j, [key_j^-, key_j^+])$ into a list L_{key}.

FMQ.GetRankValue(N_{child}, L_{key})

Note that for FMQs, the ranking value $N_{child}.value$ is a Boolean value, where 1 means that there may be matching objects in the subtree of N_{child} and 0 means that no matching can be found in the subtree. In particular, we decide if there can be matchings in N_{child}'s subtree based on the following lemma.

THEOREM 2. *Given a child node N_{child} associated with the maximum radius r_{child} and key interval $[key^-_{child}, key^+_{child}]$, objects in the subtree of N_{child} cannot be full matching answers of Q, if there is a radius r_j in L_{key} that $r_j \geq r_{child}$ and r_j's corresponding key interval $[key_j^-, key_j^+]$ does not intersect $[key^-_{child}, key^+_{child}]$.*

The proof of Theorem 2 is omitted due to the space constraint. Based on Theorem 2, for each child node N_{child} associated with r_{child} and $[key^-_{child}, key^+_{child}]$, we compute $N_{child}.value$ in the following way. Let r_{chosen} be the minimum catalog radius that is no less than r_{child} and $[key^-_{chosen}, key^+_{chosen}]$ be the key interval corresponding to r_{chosen} in L_{key}. If $[key^-_{chosen}, key^+_{chosen}]$ intersects $[key^-_{child}, key^+_{child}]$, we set $N_{child}.value = 1$. Otherwise, $N_{child}.value = 0$.

5.2 Processing TKMQs

TKMQ.GetKeyInterval(Q)

A TKMQ returns objects that match with Q in most dimensions. *PROM* transforms this problem into a number of range queries in the joint space in the following way.

Let $\overline{Q^{D_J}}(r, i)$ be an extension of $\overline{Q^{D_J}}(r)$ in the joint space which extends the boundaries of $\overline{Q^{D_J}}(r)$ to cover the whole domain in all dimensions except dimension i. Then given $\overline{Q^{D_J}}(r) = \{[l_{Q,1}, u_{Q,1}], \ldots, [l_{Q,D_a}, u_{Q,D_a}], [p_{Q,1}-r, p_{Q,1}+r], \ldots, [p_{Q,D_c}-r, p_{Q,D_c}+r]\}$, for each dimension i ($i \in [1, D_a]$), $\overline{Q^{D_J}}(r, i)$ equals $\{[0, 1], \ldots, [l_{Q,i}, u_{Q,i}], \ldots, [0, 1]\}$ and for each dimension i ($i \in [D_a+1, D_J]$), $\overline{Q^{D_J}}(r, i)$ is $\{[0, 1], \ldots, [p_{Q,i-D_a} - r, p_{Q,i-D_a} + r], \ldots, [0, 1]\}$. Then we have the following theorem.

THEOREM 3. *Given an object X with C_X and r_X, for each dimension i in the attribute space ($i \in [1, D_a]$), $p_{X,i}$ is inside $[l_{Q,i}, u_{Q,i}]$ iff C_X is inside $\overline{Q^{D_J}}(r_X, i)$ in the joint space; for each dimension i in the condition space ($i \in [1, D_c]$), $p_{Q,i}$ is inside $[l_{X,i}, u_{X,i}]$ only if C_X is inside $\overline{Q^{D_J}}(r_X, D_a+i)$ in the joint space.*

The proof of Theorem 3 is omitted due to space constraint. Based on Theorem 3 for TKMQs, *PROM* transforms the problem of determining if X and Q match each other in each dimension into a

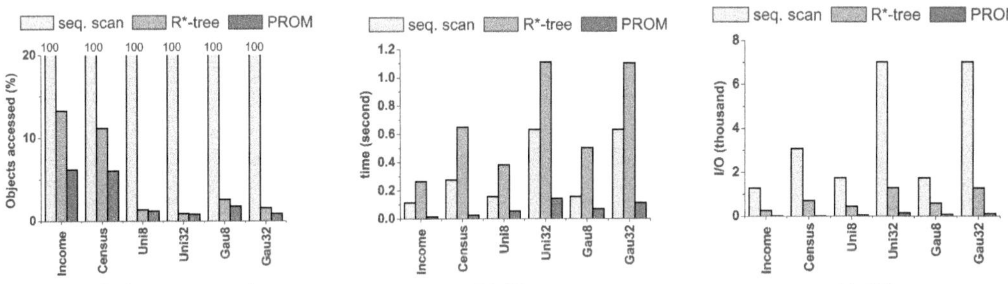

(a) Objects accessed (b) Time (c) I/O

Figure 2: The performance of FMQs.

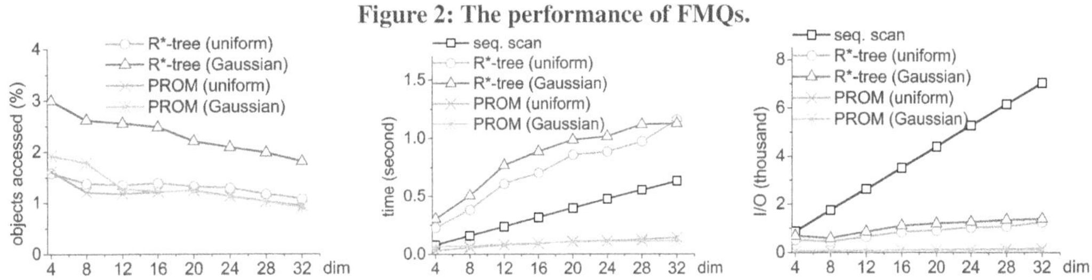

(a) Objects accessed (b) Time (c) I/O

Figure 3: Effect of dimensionality for FMQs.

number of subproblems, each of which is to determine if C_X is inside $\overline{Q^{D_J}}(r_X, i)$ for a dimension i in the joint space.

We also choose T catalog radiuses $\{r_0, r_1, \dots, r_{T-1}\}$ from $(0, r_{max}]$ in the same way as we handle FMQs in the previous subsection. Then, for each catalog radius r_j and each dimension i $(i \in [1, D_J])$, we have a range query whose range is $\overline{Q^{D_J}}(r_j, i)$. For each $\overline{Q^{D_J}}(r_j, i)$ we compute its corresponding key interval, denoted as $[key^-_{i,j}, key^+_{i,j}]$. All intervals of keys are stored in the form of $(i, r_j, [key^-_{i,j}, key^+_{i,j}])$ into a list L_{key}.

Note that for $i \in [1, D_a]$, given two catalog radiuses r_j and $r_{j'}$, $\overline{Q^{D_J}}(r_j, i) = \overline{Q^{D_J}}(r_{j'}, i)$. So for each dimension i $(i \in [1, D_a])$ after computing the key interval corresponding to $\overline{Q^{D_J}}(r_0, i)$, the key intervals corresponding to $\overline{Q^{D_J}}(r_j, i)$ for other catalog radiuses do not need further computation.

TKMQ.GetRankValue(N_{child}, L_{key}**)**

The ranking value of each child node N_{child} is the upper bound of the tolerant matching coefficients of objects in the subtree of N_{child}. For each N_{child}, we initially set $N_{child}.value = 0$. Then let r_{chosen} be the minimum catalog radius that is no less than r_{child}. For each dimension i, we check if $[key^-_{i,chosen}, key^+_{i,chosen}]$, the corresponding key interval of r_{chosen} in L_{key}, intersects $[key^-_{child}, key^+_{child}]$. If yes, for $i \in [1, D_a]$ $N_{child}.value = N_{child}.value + w_{Q,i}$ and for $i \in [D_a + 1, D_J]$ $N_{child}.value = N_{child}.value + \omega_{child}$.

6 Experiments

6.1 Experiment Settings

All the experiments are run on a desktop PC with a 2.66GHz CPU and 4GB RAM. The page size is set to 4096 bytes.

We use both real and synthetic datasets. Details of the datasets and query generation are given in Section 6.2.

We conduct comparative performance study of both types of matching queries in Sections 6.3 and 6.4. We compare *PROM* based approach with the R*-tree based approach and sequential scan. All three approaches are implemented using C++ language. Particularly, we employ the P^+-tree technique [13] as the mapping technique for *PROM* in this paper, since the mapping technique of P^+-tree is the latest and most efficient one.

We process matching queries with support of the R*-tree in the following ways. First we represent each object $X = \{P_X, R_X, W_X\}$ with a D_T-dimensional rectangle $X^{D_T} = \{[p_{X,1}, p_{X,1}], \dots, [l_{X,1}, u_{X,1}], \dots, [w_{X,1}, w_{X,1}], \dots\}$, where $D_T = D_a + 2D_c$. Then we use a D_T-dimensional R*-tree to index the transformed rectangles of objects. To process FMQs, we search the R*-tree from the root node to find all objects with transformed rectangles that intersect R_Q in the first D_a dimensions and P_Q in dimensions from dimension $D_a + 1$ to dimension $D_a + D_c$. To process TKMQs, we search the R*-tree following a "best-first" manner in a similar way as processing TKMQs based on the *PROM*.

6.2 Generating Datasets and Queries

Real Data. We downloaded two datasets from [9, 10]. The US Census (1990) data set contains 2,458,285 samples drawn from the full 1990 census sample. We use a subset of 50,000 samples in our experiments. The Adult Income data set contains the information of personal income of 48,842 adults drawn from the 1994 Census database. Both real datasets contain only point data. We obtain objects in our paper by attaching a range, with weights on each dimension, to each point data. Specially we let the dimensionality of the attribute space and the condition space be the same.

Synthetic Data. We first generate a dataset containing d-dimensional points which follow certain distribution (uniform or Gaussian). Then we construct our objects based on these datasets in the same way as described above. Without additional specification, the basic information of real and synthetic datasets in our experiments are listed in Table 1.

Table 1: Experiment datasets.

Dataset	Type	Cardinality	Dimensionality
Adult Income	real	48,842	6
Census	real	50,000	14
Uni8 / Gau8	synthetic	50,000	8
Uni32 / Gau32	synthetic	50,000	32

Queries. The query object of a matching query is an object randomly chosen from the database. For every experiment, we run 100 queries and the result presented is the average on 100 queries. We measure the pruning power, query processing time and the number of disk page accesses (I/O). The pruning power is measured by the percentage of objects we need access during the query processing.

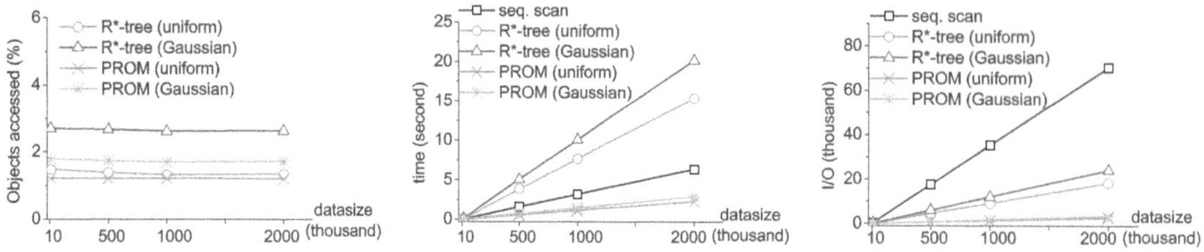

(a) Objects accessed (b) Time (c) I/O

Figure 4: Effect of dataset cardinality for FMQs.

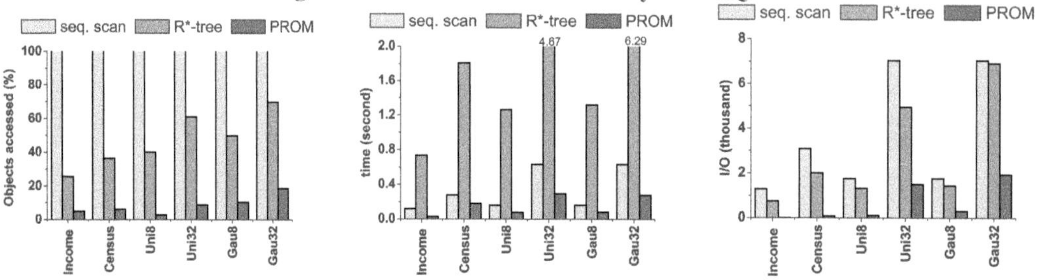

(a) Objects accessed (b) Time (c) I/O

Figure 5: The performance of TKMQs.

6.3 FMQ Performance

The results of FMQs on all datasets in Table 1 are demonstrated in Figure 2. As shown by the results, the pruning power of R*-tree is only a little worse than *PROM*. However during query processing a large percentage of nodes of R*-tree are visited, which causes high I/O cost and time cost due to high cost of random accesses of these nodes. The speedup of *PROM* compared to the R*-tree reaches up to 24 times during these experiments (Census dataset). To summarize, *PROM* beats both other techniques in terms of pruning power, total precessing time and the number of I/O accesses.

We also construct two sets of experiments on synthetic data to investigate the impact of dimensionality and dataset cardinality on the query performance, respectively. The results are shown in Figure 3 and 4. Note that the pruning power of both *PROM* and R*-tree increases as the dataset dimensionality increases. This is because when the width of tolerant range on each dimension is fixed, the selectivity of a FMQ decreases as the dimensionality increases. Both the query processing time and the number of I/O of *PROM* increase linearly as the dataset dimensionality and cardinality increase, which proves that *PROM* scales very well in terms of dimensionality and dataset cardinality. And it beats both other techniques in all aspects in this set of experiments.

6.4 TKMQ Performance

The default value of k is 10 in this set of experiments. As shown in Figure 5(a), the pruning power of *PROM* is much better than the R*-tree. On all datasets more than 80% objects are pruned by *PROM*. And with the R*-tree, 70% objects are left in the worst case (Gau32 dataset). This explains the huge improvement of *PROM* in terms of query processing time and number of I/O accesses, as shown in Figure 5(b) and 5(c).

We also construct two sets of experiments on synthetic data to investigate the impact of the dimensionality and dataset cardinality. In these experiments the comparative order of these techniques remains the same. Specially, the improvement of *PROM* compared to the other two approaches enhances as the dimensionality increases. Due to the space constraint, detailed results are omitted here.

7 Conclusion

In this paper, we formulate the problem of matching queries, which has a wide applicability in many applications. To facilitate the accommodation of multiple types of matching queries in an application, we propose a processing framework, *PROM*, which is composed by an efficient index and a query processing template. With this framework, one can easily extend the query types that can be supported by the system. Moreover, we conduct a detailed analysis of two specific types of matching queries and show how the processing algorithms of these queries can be developed within our framework. Finally, we conduct an extensive experimental study on both real and synthetic datasets to prove the efficiency of our proposal. The experimental results suggest that our algorithms can outperform the other alternatives significantly.

8 References

[1] S. Berchtold, C. Böhm, and H.-P. Kriegel. The pyramid-technique: Towards breaking the curse of dimensionality. In *SIGMOD*, 1998.

[2] A. Corral, Y. Manolopoulos, Y. Theodoridis, and M. Vassilakopoulos. Closest pair queries in spatial databases. In *SIGMOD*, 2000.

[3] H. V. Jagadish, B. C. Ooi, K.-L. Tan, C. Yu, and R. Zhang. idistance: An adaptive b^+-tree based indexing method for nearest neighbor search. *TODS*, 2005.

[4] B. C. Ooi, K.-L. Tan, C. Yu, and S. Bressan. Indexing the edges - a simple and yet efficient approach to high-dimensional indexing. In *PODS*, 2000.

[5] Y. Tao, K. Yi, C. Sheng, and P. Kalnis. Efficient and accurate nearest neighbor and closest pair search in high-dimensional space. *TODS*, 2010.

[6] L. H. U, N. Mamoulis, and K. Mouratidis. Efficient evaluation of multiple preference queries. In *ICDE*, 2009.

[7] L. H. U, N. Mamoulis, and K. Mouratidis. A fair assignment algorithm for multiple preference queries. *PVLDB*, 2009.

[8] L. H. U, M. L. Yiu, K. Mouratidis, and N. Mamoulis. Capacity constrained assignment in spatial databases. In *SIGMOD*, 2008.

[9] UCI repository of machine learning databases. http://archive.ics.uci.edu/ml/datasets/US+Census+Data+%281990%29.

[10] UCI repository of machine learning databases. http://archive.ics.uci.edu/ml/datasets/Adult.

[11] R. Weber, H.-J. Schek, and S. Blott. A quantitative analysis and performance study for similarity-search methods in high-dimensional spaces. In *VLDB*, 1998.

[12] R. C.-W. Wong, Y. Tao, A. W.-C. Fu, and X. Xiao. On efficient spatial matching. In *VLDB*, 2007.

[13] R. Zhang, B. C. Ooi, and K.-L. Tan. Making the pyramid technique robust to query types and workloads. In *ICDE*, 2004.

Answering Label-Constraint Reachability in Large Graphs *

Kun Xu
Peking University
Beijing, China
xukun@icst.pku.edu.cn

Lei Zou †
Peking University
Beijing, China
zoulei@cse.ust.hk

Jeffrey Xu Yu
The Chinese Univ. of Hong Kong
Hong Kong, China
yu@se.cuhk.edu.hk

Lei Chen
Hong Kong Univ. of Sci. & Tech.
Hong Kong, China
leichen@cse.ust.hk

Yanghua Xiao
Fudan University
Shanghai, China
shawyh@fudan.edu.cn

Dongyan Zhao
Peking University
Beijing, China
zdy@icst.pku.edu.cn

ABSTRACT

In this paper, we study a variant of reachability queries, called *l*abel-*c*onstraint *r*eachability (LCR) queries, specifically, given a label set S and two vertices u_1 and u_2 in a large directed graph G, we verify whether there exists a path from u_1 to u_2 under label constraint S. Like traditional reachability queries, LCR queries are very useful, such as pathway finding in biological networks, inferring over RDF (*r*esource *d*escription *f*ramework) graphs, relationship finding in social networks. However, LCR queries are much more complicated than their traditional counterpart. Several techniques are proposed in this paper to minimize the search space in computing path-label transitive closure. Furthermore, we demonstrate the superiority of our method by extensive experiments.

Categories and Subject Descriptors

H.4 [**Information Systems Applications**]: Miscellaneous; H.2.8 [**Database Management**]: Database Applications—*Graph Database*

General Terms

Algorithm

†corresponding author: Lei Zou, zoulei@icst.pku.edu.cn

*Lei Zou and Dongyan Zhao were supported by NSFC under Grant No.61003009 and RFDP under Grant No. 20100001120029. Jeffrey Xu Yu was supported by RGC of the Hong Kong SAR under Grant No. 419008 and 419109. Lei Chen's research is partially supported by HKUST SSRI11EG01 and NSFC No.60003074. Yanghua Xiao was supported by the NSFC under Grant No.61003001 and RFDP under Grant No. 20100071120032.

CIKM'11, October 24–28, 2011, Glasgow, Scotland, UK.

1. INTRODUCTION

The growing popularity of graph databases has generated many interesting data management problems. One important type of queries over graphs are *reachability queries* [1, 2, 3, 4, 5, 6]. Specifically, given two vertices u_1 and u_2 in a directed graph G, we want to verify whether there exists a directed path from u_1 to u_2. There are many applications of reachability queries, such as, pathway finding in biological networks [7], inferring over RDF (*r*esource *d*escription *f*ramework) graphs [8], relationship finding in social networks [9]. There are two extreme solutions to answer reachability queries. One approach is to materialize the full transitive closures of G, enabling one to answer reachability queries efficiently. In the other extreme, one can perform DFS (*d*epth-*f*irst *s*earch) or BFS (*b*reath-*f*irst *s*earch) over graph G until reaching the target vertex, or the search process cannot be continued. Obviously, these two methods cannot work in a large graph G, since the former needs $O(V^2)$ space to store the transitive closure (large index space cost), and the latter needs $O(V)$ time in answering reachability queries (slow query response time). The key issue in reachability queries is how to find a good trade-off between the two basic solutions. Therefore, many algorithms have been proposed, such as 2-hop [1, 10, 11], GRIPP [2], path-cover [5], tree-cover [2, 6], pathtree [3] and 3-hop [4], to address this issue.

In many real applications, edge labels are utilized to denote different relationships between two vertices. For example, edge labels in RDF graphs denote different properties. We can also use edge labels to define different relationships in social networks. In this paper, we study a variant of reachability queries, called *l*abel-*c*onstraint *r*eachability (LCR) queries, which are originally proposed in [12]. Conceptually, LCR query verifies some specified type of relationships between two vertices. Here, we give a motivation example to demonstrate the usefulness of LCR queries.

Let us consider an inference example in RDF Schema (RDFS for short) dataset in Figure 1. Assume that we want to verify whether $\langle freshman \rangle$ is a subclass of $\langle people \rangle$. The traditional database system can simply answer *no*, since there exists no triple ($\langle freshman \rangle$, *rdfs:subclass*, $\langle people \rangle$). However, due to RDFS semantics, "rdfs:subclass" is a tran-

<freshman>	rdfs:subclassof	<student>
<student>	rdfs:subclassof	<people>
<Lucy>	rdf:type	<freshman>
<Lucy>	:studyIn	<PKU>
<PKU>	rdf:type	<school>

(a) RDF Dataset

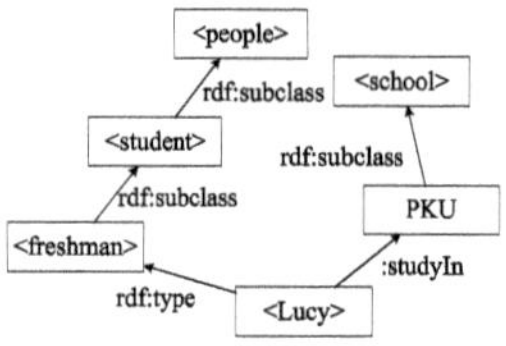

(b) RDF Graph

Figure 1: Inference VS. LCR Query

sitive property. Therefore, given two triples (⟨*freshman*⟩, *rdfs:subclass*, ⟨*student*⟩) and (⟨*student*⟩, *rdfs:subclass*, ⟨*people*⟩), we can infer that (⟨*freshman*⟩, *rdfs: subclass*, ⟨ *people*⟩). Therefore, the correct answer should be *yes*. This kind of queries are called *inference queries*. Obviously, it is prohibitive to materialize all inferred facts, according to RDFS reasoning rules, in a very large RDF dataset. Actually, some inference queries can be reduced into LCR queries over RDF graphs. For example, the above example can be transformed into the following LCR query: verifying whether there exists a directed path from entry ⟨*freshman*⟩ to ⟨*people*⟩ in the RDF graph, where all edge labels along the path are "rdfs:subclass".

Although LCR queries are quite useful, it is non-trivial to answer LCR queries over a large directed graph. Traditional indexing methods can only verify reachability without considering how the connection is made between two vertices [12]. Furthermore, the traditional transitive closure does not contain path labels.

In order to address LCR queries efficiently, we make the following contributions in this work:

1) For LCR queries, we propose a method to transform an edge-labeled directed graph into an *augmented DAG* by representing the maximal strongly connected components as *bipartite graphs*. Then, based on the augmented DAG, we propose a method to compute transitive closure efficiently.

2) We re-define the "distance" of a path and propose a Dijkstra-like algorithm to compute single-source path-label transitive closure. We prove the optimality of our algorithm.

3) Extensive experiments confirm that our method is faster than the existing ones by orders of magnitude. For example, given a random network satisfying ER model with 100K vertices and 150K edges, the method in [12] consumes 277 hours for index building. However, given the same graph, our method only needs 0.5 hour for indexing building. Furthermore, our method can work well in a very large RDF graph (Yago dataset) having more than 2 million vertices and 6 million edges and 97 edge labels.

2. BACKGROUND

2.1 Problem Definition

DEFINITION 2.1. *A directed edge-labeled graph G is denoted as $G = \{V, E, \sum, \lambda\}$, where (1) V is a set of vertices, and (2) $E \subseteq V \times V$ is a set of directed edges, and (3) $\sum$ is a set of edge labels, and (4) the labeling function λ defines the mapping $E \to \sum$.*

Given a path p from u_1 to u_2 in graph G, the path-label *of p is denoted as $L(p) = \bigcup_{e \in p} \lambda(e)$, where $\lambda(e)$ denotes e's edge label.*

Given a graph G in Figure 2, the numbers inside vertices are *vertex IDs* that we introduce to simplify description of the graph; and the letters beside edges are *edge labels*. Considering path $p_1 = (1, 2, 5)$, the path-label of p_1 is $L(p_1) = \{ac\}$.

DEFINITION 2.2. *Given two vertices u_1 and u_2 in graph G and a label constraint (set) $S = \{l_1, ..., l_n\}$, we say that u_1 can reach u_2 under label constraint S (denoted as $u_1 \overset{S}{\to} u_2$) if and only if there exists a path p from u_1 to u_2 and $L(p) \subseteq S$.*

DEFINITION 2.3. (Problem Definition) *Given two vertices u_1 and u_2 in graph G and a label set $S = \{l_1, ..., l_n\}$, a* l*abel-constraint* r*eachability (LCR) query verifies whether u_1 can reach u_2 under the label constraint S, denoted as $LCR(u_1, u_2, S, G)$.*

For example, given two vertices 1 and 6 in graph G in Figure 2 and label constraint $S = \{ac\}$, it is easy to know that 1 can reach 6 under label constraint S, i.e., $LCR(1, 6, S, G) =$ true, since there exists path $p_1 = \{1, 2, 5, 6\}$, where $L(p_1) \subseteq S$. If $S = \{bc\}$, query $LCR(1, 6, S, G)$ returns false.

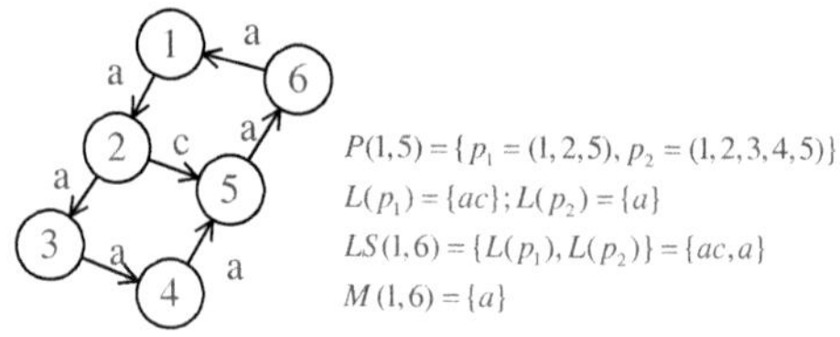

Figure 2: A Running Example

DEFINITION 2.4. *Given two vertices u_1 and u_2 in graph G, $P(u_1, u_2)$ denotes all paths from u_1 to u_2. The* path-label set *from u_1 to u_2 is defined as $LS(u_1, u_2) = \{L(p) | p \in P(u_1, u_2)\}$.*

Consider two paths $(1, 2, 3, 4, 5, 6)$ and $(1, 2, 5, 6)$ in $P(1, 6)$, where $L(1, 2, 3, 4, 5, 6) \subseteq L(1, 2, 5, 6)$. Obviously, if path $(1, 2, 5, 6)$ can satisfy some label constraint S, path $(1, 2, 3, 4, 5, 6)$ can also satisfy S. Therefore, path $(1, 2, 5, 6)$ is *redundant* (Definition 2.5) for any LCR query.

DEFINITION 2.5. *Considering two paths p and p' from vertex u_1 to u_2, respectively, if $L(p) \subseteq L(p')$, we say $L(p)$* covers *$L(p')$. In this case, p' is a* redundant *path, and $L(p')$ is also* redundant *in the path-label set $LS(u_1, u_2)$.*

DEFINITION 2.6. *The* minimal path-label set *from u_1 to u_2 in graph G is defined as $M_G(u_1, u_2)$, where 1)$M_G(u_1, u_2) \subseteq LS(u_1, u_2)$; and 2) there exists no redundant path-label in $M_G(u_1, u_2)$; and 3) path-labels in $M_G(u_1, u_2)$ cover all path labels in $LS(u_1, u_2)$.*

DEFINITION 2.7. *Given two vertices u_1 and u_2 and a label constraint (set) S, we say $M_G(u_1, u_2)$* covers *S if and only if there exists a path p from u_1 to u_2, where $S \supseteq L(p)$ and $L(p) \in M_G(u_1, u_2)$.*

DEFINITION 2.8. *Given a graph G,* path-label transitive closure *is a matrix $M_G = [M_G(u_1, u_2)]_{|V(G)| \times |V(G)|}$, where $u_1, u_2 \in V(G)$, and a* single-source path-label transitive closure *is a vector $M_G(u, -) = [M_G(u, u_i)]_{1 \times |V(G)|}$, where $u_i \in V(G)$.*

When the context is clear, we also say *transitive closure* instead of *path-label transitive closure* for short. Furthermore, for ease of presentation, we borrow two operator definitions (*Prune* and $\odot$) from reference [12].

$Prune(\cdot)$ is defined as $Prune(LS(u_1, u_2)) = M_G(u_1, u_2)$, which means removing all redundant paths. In Figure 2, $Prune(LS(1{,}6) = \{a, ac\}) = M_G(1, 6) = \{a\}$, since $a \subseteq ab$.

$(\cdot) \odot (\cdot)$ is defined as follows: $\lambda(\overrightarrow{u_1u_2}) \odot M_G(u_2, u_3) = \{\lambda(\overrightarrow{u_1u_2}) \bigcup L(p_1), \lambda(\overrightarrow{u_1u_2}) \bigcup L(p_2), ...\}$, where $L(p_i) \in M_G(u_2, u_3)$ and $\lambda(\overrightarrow{u_1u_2})$ denotes the label of edge $\overrightarrow{u_1u_2}$.

It is easy to prove that $M_G(u_1, u_3) = Prune(\bigcup_{u' \in V(G)} \{\lambda(\overrightarrow{u_1u'}) \odot M_G(u', u_3)\})$. Analogously, we also define $\lambda(\overrightarrow{u_1u_2}) \odot M_G(u_2, -)$.

An extreme approach to answering LCR queries is to materialize transitive closure M_G. At run time, given a query $LCR(u_1, u_2, S, G)$, LCR queries can be answered by simply checking $M_G(u_1, u_2)$. However, computing M_G is much more complicated than traditional transitive closure. Before the formal discussion, we introduce the following theorem, which forms the basis of our algorithm and performance analysis.

THEOREM 2.1. *(Apriori Property) Given one path p, if one of its subpaths is redundant, p must be redundant.*

2.2 Existing Approaches

LCR queries are proposed in [12]. Generally speaking, the method in [12] employs a spanning tree T and a partial transitive closure NT to compress the full transitive closure. Specifically, a spanning tree T is found in the graph G. Based on T, we partition all pairwise paths into three categories P_n and P_s and P_e. All paths in P_n contains all pairwise paths whose starting edges and end edges are both non-tree edges. All paths in P_s (and P_e) contains all pairwise paths whose starting (and ending) edges are tree-edges. In Figure 3, (4,5,6,1) is a path in P_n, since $\overrightarrow{4,5}$ and $\overrightarrow{6,1}$ are non-tree edges. $NT(u, v)$ contains all path labels between u and v in P_n. We can re-construct $M_G(u, v)$ by Equation 1. Therefore, we can re-construct the full transitive closure by the spanning tree T and partial transitive closure $NT = \{NT(u, v), u, v \in V(G)\}$.

$$M_G(u, v) = \{\{L(P_T(u, u'))\} \odot NT(u', v') \odot \{L(P_T(v', v))\} | u' \in Succ(u) \text{and} v' \in Pred(v)\} \quad (1)$$

where u' is reachable from u in the spanning tree T and $L(P_T(u, u'))$ denotes the corresponding path label in T; and v' can reach v in the spanning tree T and $L(P_T(v', v))$ denotes the corresponding path label in T.

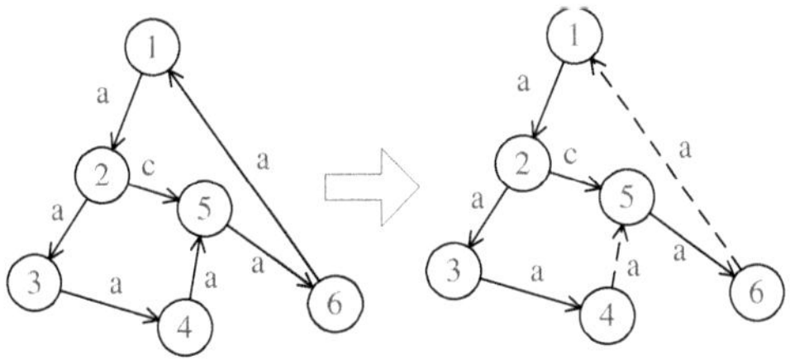

Figure 3: An Example of Tree-Cover

Obviously, different spanning trees will lead to different NT. In order to minimize the size of NT, authors introduce "weight" $w(e)$ for each edge e, where $w(e)$ reflects that if e is included in a spanning tree, the number of path-labels that can be removed from NT. Therefore, they propose to use the maximal spanning tree in G. However, it is quite expensive to assign exact edge weights $w(e)$. Thus, they propose a sampling method. For each sampling seed (vertex), they compute single-source transitive closure, based on which, they propose some heuristic methods to define edge weights.

However, there are two limitations of their method in [12]. First, similar with the counterpart methods in traditional reachability queries [6, 3], a single spanning tree cannot compress the transitive closure greatly, especially in dense graphs. Consequently, NT may be very large. Second, in order to find the optimal spanning tree T, authors propose an algorithm to compute single-source transitive closure for each sampling seed (vertex). However, the search space in their algorithm is not minimal, i.e., containing a large number of redundant paths, which affect the performance greatly. The above two problems (large index size and expensive index building process) affect the scalability of the method in [12].

Since computing single-source transitive closure is also a building block in our method, we argue that our method is optimal in terms of search space. In order to understand the superiority of our method, in the full version of this paper [13], we analyze the algorithm in [12]. Due to space limit, the details are omitted in this paper.

In [14], Fan et al. add regular expressions to graph reachability queries. Specifically, given two vertices u_1 and u_2, the method in [14] verifies whether there exists a directed path P where all edge labels along the path satisfy the specified regular expression. Obviously, LCR query is a special case of the problem in [14]. Fan et al. propose a bi-directional BFS algorithm at runtime. We can utilize the method in [14] for LCR queries. Given two vertices u_1 and u_2 over a large graph G and a label set S, two sets are maintained for u_1 and u_2, respectively. Each set records the vertices that are reachable from (resp. to) u_1 (resp. u_2) only via edges of labels in S. We expand the smaller set at a time until either the two sets intersect, or they cannot be further expanded (i.e., unreachable). The problem of this method lies in its large search space. The search strategy in [14] is different from traditional BFS algorithm, since one vertex may be visited multiple times in bi-directional BFS algorithm [14].

3. COMPUTING TRANSITIVE CLOSURE

As mentioned earlier, compared with traditional transitive closure, it is much more challenging to compute *path-label transitive closure* (Definition 2.8). This section focuses computing path-label transitive closure efficiently. We first propose a Dijkstra-like algorithm to compute single-source transitive closure efficiently (Section 3.1). Obviously, it is very expensive to iterate single-source transitive closure computation from each vertex in G to compute M_G. In order to address this issue, we propose *augmented DAG* (aDAG for short) by representing all strongly connected components as *bipartite graphs*. The aDAG-based solution is discussed in Section 3.2.

3.1 Single-Source Transitive Closure

This subsection discusses how to compute single-source transitive closure efficiently, since it is a building block in our aDAG-based solution. As discussed in Section 2.2, the method in [12] is not optimal. The key problem is that some redundant paths are visited before their corresponding non-redundant paths. In order to address this issue, we propose a Dijkstra-like algorithm. As we know, in each step of Dijkstra's algorithm, we always access one un-visited vertex that has the minimal distance from the origin vertex. In our algorithm, we redefine "distance". A *distance* of a path p is defined as *the number of distinct edge labels* in p instead of the sum of edge weights. Then, according to the distance definition, we adopt the Dijkstra-like algorithm to compute single-source transitive closure. This algorithm can guarantee that all redundant paths must be visited after their corresponding non-redundant paths. Therefore, all redundant paths can be pruned from the search space (Theorem 3.1).

Heap H	Path Set RS
Step 1. [{a}, (1,2) , 2];	[{a}, (1,2), 2];
Step 2. [{a}, (1,2, 3), 3]; [{ac}, (1,2,5), 5];	[{a}, (1,2,3), 3];
Step 3. [{a}, (1,2, 3, 4), 4]; [{ac}, (1,2,5), 5];	[{a}, (1, 2,3,4), 4];
Step 4. [{a}, (1,2, 3, 4,5), 5]; ~~[{ac}, (1,2,5), 5];~~	[{a}, (1, 2,3,4,5), 5];
Step 5. [{a}, (1,2,3,4,5,6), 6]	[{a}, (1,2,3,4,5,6), 6]

Figure 4: Algorithm Process

Given a graph G in Figure 2, Figure 4 demonstrates how to compute $M_G(1,-)$ from vertex 1 in our algorithm (i.e., Algorithm 1). Initially, we set vertex 1 as the source. All vertex 1's neighbors are put into the heap H. Each neighbor is denoted as a *neighbor triple* $[L(p), p, d]$, where d denotes the neighbor's ID, p specifies one path from source s to d, and $L(p)$ is the path-label set of p. All neighbor triples are ranked according to the *total order* defined in Definition 3.1. Since $[\{a\}, (1,2), 2]$ is the heap head (see Figure 4), it is moved to path set RS. When we move the heap head T_1 into path set RS, we check whether T_1 is *covered* (Definition 3.2) by some neighbor triple T_2 in RS (Line 5 in Algorithm 1). If so, we ignore T_1 (Lines 5-6); otherwise, we insert T_1 into RS (Lines 7-8).

DEFINITION 3.1. *Given two neighbor triples* $T_1 = [L(p_1), p_1, d_1]$ *and* $T_2 = [L(p_2), p_2, d_2]$ *in the heap* H, $T_1 \leq T_2$ *if and only if 1)* $|L(p_1)| < |L(p_2)|$*; or 2)* $|L(p_1)| = |L(p_2)|$*, the orders of* T_1 *and* T_2 *are arbitrarily defined.*

DEFINITION 3.2. *Given one neighbor triple* $T_1 = [L(p_1), p_1, d_1]$, T_1 *is* redundant *if and only if there exists another neighbor triple* $T_2 = [L(p_2), p_2, d_2]$*, where* $L(p_1) \supseteq L(p_2)$ *and* $d_1 = d_2$*. In this case, we say that* T_1 *is* covered *by* T_2.

DEFINITION 3.3. *Given two neighbor triple* $T_1 = [L(p_1), p_1, d_1]$ *and* $T_2 = [L(p_2), p_2, d_2]$*, if* p_1 *is a parent path (or a child path) of* p_2*, we say that* T_1 *(or* T_2*) is a* parent neighbor triple *(or a* child neighbor triple*) of* T_2 *(or* T_1*).*

Then, we put all child neighbor triples (Definition 3.3) of $[\{a\}, (1,2), 2]$ into heap H. Considering one neighbor of vertex 2, such as vertex 3, we put neighbor triple $[\{a\} \cup L(\overrightarrow{2,3}) = \{a\}, (1,2,3), 3]$ into H, where $(1,2,3)$ is $(1,2)$'s child path. Analogously, we put $[\{a\} \cup L(\overrightarrow{2,5}) = \{ac\}, (1,2,5), 5]$ into H. When we insert some neighbor triple $T'[L(p'), p', d']$ into H, we first check whether p' is a non-simple path. If so, we ignore T' (Lines 10-11). Furthermore, we also check whether there exists another triple T'' that has existed in H and T' is *covered* by T'', or T' covers T'' (Lines 12-15). If T' is *covered* by T'', we ignore T'; otherwise, T' is inserted into H. If T' covers some triple T'' in H, T'' is deleted from H. At Step 2, the heap head is $[\{a\}, (1,3), 3]$, which is moved to path set RS.

Iteratively, we put all child neighbor triples of $[\{a\}, (1,3), 3]$ into heap H. At Step 4, we find that $[\{ac\}, (1,2,5), 5]$ is covered by $[\{a\}, (1,2,3,4,5), 5]$. Therefore, we remove $[\{ac\}, (1,2,5), 5]$ from H. Figure 4 illustrates the whole process. All paths and path-labels in RS are non-redundant. According to RS, it is straightforward to obtain $M_G(1,-)$. Note that, our algorithm stops the infection from the redundant path to its child paths (Theorem 3.1). For example, path $(1,2,5,6)$ is pruned from search space in our algorithm.

Algorithm 1 Single-Source Transitive Closure Computation

Require: Input: A graph G and a vertex u in G;
Output: A compressed path tree $C\text{-}PT(u)$.
1: Set u as the source. Set answer set $RS=\phi$ and heap $H=\phi$.
2: Put all neighbor triples of u into H.
3: **while** $H \neq \phi$ **do**
4: Let $T_1 = [L(p_1), p_1, d]$ to denote the head in H.
5: **if** T_1 is covered by some neighbor triple T_2 in RS **then**
6: Delete T_1 from H
7: **else**
8: Move T_1 into RS
9: **for** each child neighbor triple $T'[L(p'), p', d']$ of T_1 **do**
10: **if** p' is a non-simple path **then**
11: continue
12: **if** T' is *not* covered by some neighbor triple T'' in H **then**
13: Insert T' into H
14: **if** T' covers some neighbor triple T'' in H **then**
15: Delete T'' from H
16: According to paths in RS to build $C\text{-}PT(u)$.

THEOREM 3.1. *Given a vertex* u *in graph* G*, the following statements about Algorithm 1 hold:*

1. *(correctness) Any non-redundant path beginning from vertex* u *can be found in path set RS in Algorithm 1.*
2. *(optimality) Given any redundant path* p'*, if one of* p'*'s parent paths is also redundant,* p' *is pruned from the search space in Algorithm 1.*

3.2 Computing Transitive Closures

Given a graph G, a straightforward method to compute transitive closure M_G is to repeat Algorithm 1 from each vertex in G. Obviously, it is inefficient to do that. Intuitively, given two adjacent vertices u_1 and u_2, most computations in Algorithm 1 for u_1 and u_2 are the same to each other. Therefore, an efficient algorithm should employ the property. Usually, a directed graph G is transformed into a DAG by coalescing each strongly connected component into a single vertex to compute transitive closure efficiently. However, this method cannot be used for LCR queries, since it may miss some edge labels. Instead, we propose an *augmented DAG D* by representing all strongly connected components as bipartite graphs. Then, we can compute single-source transitive closure $M(u,-)$ according to the reverse order of D. During the computation, $M(u,-)$ is always transmitted to its parent vertices in D. In this way, redundant computation can be avoided.

Specifically, we first identify all maximal connected components in graph G, denoted as $C_1, ..., C_m$. For each C_i $(i = 1, ..., m)$, we compute local transitive closure in C_i (denoted as M_{C_i}) by iterating Algorithm 1 for each vertex in C_i. For example, given a graph G in Figure 5(a), one maximal connected component C_1 is identified in G. We compute M_{C_1} for C_1. Then, we represent a maximal connected component C_i as a bipartite graph $B_i = (V_{i_1}, V_{i_2})$, where

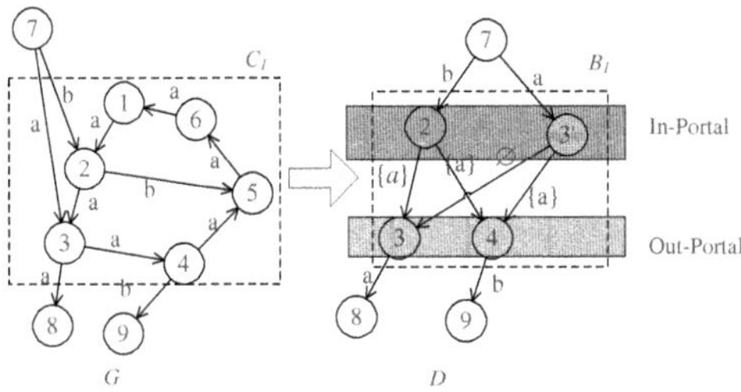

Figure 5: Augmented DAG

V_{i_1} contains all *in-portal* vertices in C_i and V_{i_2} contains all *out-portal* vertices in C_i. A vertex u in C_i is called as an in-portal if and only if it has at least one incoming edge from vertices out of C_i. A vertex u in C_i is called as an out-portal if and only if it has at least one outgoing edge to vertices out of C_i. If one vertex u is both an in-portal and an out-portal, it has two instances u and u' that occur in V_{i_1} and V_{i_2}, respectively. For any two vertices $u_1 \in V_{i_1}$ and $u_2 \in V_{i_2}$, we introduce a directed edge u_1 to u_2, whose edge label is $M_{C_i}(u_1, u_2)$. For example, a bipartite graph B_1 corresponding to C_1 is given in Figure 5(b). Finally, we replace all maximal connected components C_i by the corresponding bipartite graph B_i. In this way, we can get a graph D, as shown in Figure 5(b). We can prove that D must be a DAG. In this paper, we call it *augmented DAG* (aDAG for short). Note that, given a vertex u in C_i, if $u \notin D$, u is called an *intra vertex*, such as vertices 1,5 and 6 in Figure 5(a).

Algorithm 2 aDAG-Based Compute Local Transitive Closure

Require: Input: A graph G and its corresponding aDAG D;
 Output: M_G.
Identify all maximal connected component C_i.
Employ Algorithm 1 to compute local transitive closure M_{C_i} for each C_i.
Build aDAG D by replacing C_i by the bipartite graphs B_i.
Perform Topological Sorting Over D. Set $M_G(u,-) = \{\phi, ..., \phi\}$ for each vertex u.
for each vertex u according to the reverse topological order **do**
  for each child c_i of u **do**
    $M_G(u,-) = Prune(M_G(u,-) \bigcup Prune(\lambda(\overrightarrow{uc_i}) \odot M_G(c_i,-)))$
for each maximal connect component C_i **do**
  for each intra-vertex $u \in C_i$ **do**
    $M_G(u,-) = M_{C_i}(u,-)$
    for each out-portal u_i in V_{2_i} **do**
      $M_G(u,-) = Prune(M_G(u,-) \bigcup Prune(M_{C_i}(u,u_i) \odot M_G(u_i,-)))$
  for each vertex $u' \notin C_i$ **do**
    for each intra-vertex $u \in C_i$ **do**
      for each in-portal u_i in V_{1_i} **do**
        $M_G(u',u) = Prune(M_G(u',u) \bigcup Prune(M_G(u',u_i) \odot M_{C_i}(u_i,u)))$

Algorithm 2 lists the pseudo code to compute transitive closure for aDAG D. First, we perform topological sorting over D. Initially, for all vertices u in G, we set $M(u,-) = \{\phi, ..., \phi\}$. Then, we process each vertex according to the reverse topological sort. If a vertex u has n children c_i, for each c_i, we update $M_G(u,-) = Prune(M_G(u,-) \bigcup Prune(\lambda(\overrightarrow{uc_i}) \odot M_G(c_i,-)))$ iteratively. In this way, we can obtain $M_G(u,-)$ for each vertex u in aDAG D.

Now, we need to consider "intra vertices" in each cluster C_i, such as vertices 4 and 7 in Figure 5. Given an intra vertex u in C_i, we initialize $M_G(u,-) = M_{C_i}(u,-)$. Then, for each out-portal u_i in V_{2_i}, we update $M_G(u,-) = Prune(M_G(u,-) \bigcup Prune(M_{C_i}(u,u_i) \odot M_G(u_i,-)))$ iteratively.

Consider any one vertex $u' \notin C_i$. Given an intra vertex u in C_i, we compute $M_G(u',u)$ as follows: Initially, we set $M_G(u',u) = \phi$. For each in-portal u_i in V_{1_i}, we update $M_G(u',u) = Prune(M_G(u',u) \bigcup Prune(M_G(u',u_i) \odot M_{C_i}(u_i,u)))$ iteratively.

As we know, 2-hop labeling technique is proposed to compress traditional transitive closure [1, 10]. We also extend the labeling technique to compress the path-label transitive closure.

DEFINITION 3.4. *A 2-label-hop coding over a graph G assigns to each vertex u ($\in V(G)$) a code $C(u) = (C_{in}(u), C_{out}(u))$, where the entries in $C_{in}(u)$ and $C_{out}(u)$ are in form of $\{(w, M_G(w,u)\}$ and $\{(w, M_G(u,w)\}$, respectively.*

DEFINITION 3.5. *A 2-label-hop coding over a graph G is called* complete *if and only if Equation 2 holds.*

$$\begin{aligned} &\forall u_1, u_2 \in V(G), \forall S \in \textstyle\sum^+ \\ &u_1 \xrightarrow{S} u_2 \Leftrightarrow \exists w, w \in C_{out}(u_1) \wedge w \in C_{in}(u_2) \\ &\wedge(\exists L(p_1), L(p_1) \in M_G(u_1,w) \wedge S \supseteq L(p_1)) \\ &\wedge(\exists L(p_2), L(p_2) \in M_G(w,u_2) \wedge S \supseteq L(p_2)) \end{aligned} \quad (2)$$

where $L(p_1)$ denotes one path label-set from u_1 to w, and $L(p_2)$ denotes one path label-set from w to u_2.

4. EXPERIMENTS

In this section, we evaluate our methods over both random networks and real datasets, and compare them with the existing solution the sampling-tree method in [12]. Specifically, we experimentally study the performance of three approaches: 1) the *sampling-tree method* proposed in [12]; 2) we compute path-label transitive closure method by Algorithm 2 and compress it by 2-label-hop technique. Then, based on 2-label-hop codes, we can answer LCR queries. This method is called *transitive closure method*; 3) the *bi-directional BFS* proposed in [14]. Our methods are implemented using C++, and our experiments are conducted on a P4 3.0GHz machine with 2G RAM running Ubuntu Linux.

4.1 Datasets

There are two types of synthetic datasets to be used in our experiments: Erdos Renyi Model (ER) and Scale-Free Model (SF). ER is a classical random graph model. It defines a random graph as $|V|$ vertices connected by $|E|$ edges, chosen randomly from the $|V|(|V|-1)$ possible edges. In our experiments, we vary the density $\frac{|E|}{|V|}$ from 1.5 to 5.0, and vary $|V|$ from 1K to 10K. SF defines a random network with $|V|$ vertices satisfying power-law distribution in vertex degrees. In our implementations, we use the graph generator *gengraphwin* (http://fabien.viger.free.fr/liafa/generation/) to generate a large graph G satisfying power-law distribution. Usually, the power-law distribution parameter γ is between 2.0 and 3.0 to simulate real complex networks [15]. Thus, default value of parameter γ is set to 2.5 in this work. In order to study the scalability, we also vary $|V|$ in SF networks from 1K to 10K. The number of edge labels ($|\Sigma|$) is 20. The distribution of labels is generated according to uniform distribution.

Table 1: Performance VS. $|V|$ in ER Graphs

|V| density = 1.5	2-Label-Hop Codes			Sampling-Tree method			Bi-directional BFS (Memory-based)
	IT	IS	QT	IT	IS	QT	QT
	sec.	KB	ms.	sec.	KB	ms.	ms.
1K	15	415	0.01	113	13725	0.05	0.01
2K	23	1396	0.01	493	51020	0.09	0.02
4K	217	4920	0.02	3680	78920	0.10	0.02
6K	623	9000	0.03	5689	92890	0.15	0.03
8K	964	13200	0.03	9290	100890	0.18	0.04
10K	5065	33000	0.04	100560	123450	0.29	0.05

Table 2: Performance VS. Graph Density in ER Graphs

density |V|=10K	2-Label-Hop Codes			Sampling-Tree method			Bi-directional BFS (Memory-
	IT	IS	QT	IT	IS	QT	QT
	sec.	MB	ms.	sec.	MB	ms.	ms.
2	6860	26.3	0.08	123890	95.6	0.31	0.05
3	11112	102.3	0.09	378563	232.7	0.53	0.09
4	25347	160	0.12	F	F	F	0.15
5	33169	186	0.23	F	F	F	0.18

Note: F denotes "fail due to memory crash" or "cannot finish index building in 48 hours"

We also employ two real graph datasets (Yeast, Small-Yago) in our experiments, which are provided by authors in [12]. More details about the two datasets and more experiments are given in the full version of this paper [13].

4.2 Performance of Transitive Closure Method

In this section, we use Algorithm 2 to compute transitive closure for a graph G. Then, we use 2-label-hop coding technique to compress the transitive closure. We report index construction time (IT), index size (IS) and average query response time (QT) for the experiments on the synthetic datasets. Note that, the default query constraint size ($|S|$) is $30\% \times |\sum| = 6$. Furthermore, we also compare our method with the sampling tree method. Note that, in the following experiments, we always randomly generate 10000 queries to evaluate query performance. QT is reported as the average response time for one query. In these experiments, we evaluate the performance with regard to graph size, graph density and label constraint size $|S|$. Furthermore, we also test the performance of bi-directional BFS in Table 1. Since bi-directional BFS does not need offline processing, thus, we only report QT in the following experiments.

Exp1. Varying Graph Size ($|V|$) on ER graphs. In this experiment, we fix the density $\frac{|E|}{|V|}$=1.5 and label constraint size $|S|$=6 and vary $|V|$ from 1,000 to 10,000 to study the performance by varying graph sizes. Table 1 reports the detailed performance, such as, index sizes (IS), index building times (IT) and average query response time (QT). From Table 1, we know that transitive closure method is faster than the sampling-tree method in offline processing by orders of magnitude. For example, when $|V|$ =1K, transitive closure method only spends 15 seconds to build index, but the sampling-tree method needs 113 seconds. The index size of our method is much smaller than that in the sampling-tree method. Furthermore, our query performance are also better than the sampling tree method. From Table 1, we know that memory-based bi-directional BFS is also very fast for LCR queries. However, this method is not scalable with regard to graph size due to its exponential time complexity.

Exp2. Varying Density ($\frac{|E|}{|V|}$) on ER graphs. In this experiment, we fix $|V|$=10,000 and vary the density $\frac{|E|}{|V|}$ from 2 to 5 to study the performance of our method in dense graphs. From Table 2, we know that the index building time and index size increase when varying $\frac{|E|}{|V|}$ from 2 to 5 in both methods. Furthermore, the sampling tree method cannot finish index building in 48 hours when $\frac{|E|}{|V|} \geq 4$. From Table 2, we know that transitive closure method has better scalability with regard to the graph density $\frac{|E|}{|V|}$ than the sampling tree method. Actually, the two methods both need to compute $M_G(u, -)$ (i.e., single-source transitive closure). As proven in Theorem 3.1, our method has the minimal search space, but the search space in the sampling tree method is not minimal. Thus, large search space affects the salability of the sampling tree method.

5. CONCLUSIONS

In this paper, we address label-constraint reachability (LCR) queries over large graphs. Theoretically, we propose several methods to optimize path-label transitive closure computing. We also demonstrate the superiority of our method by extensive experiments.

6. REFERENCES

[1] E. Cohen, E. Halperin, H. Kaplan, and U. Zwick, "Reachability and distance queries via 2-hop labels," *SIAM J. Comput.*, vol. 32, no. 5, 2003.

[2] S. Trißl and U. Leser, "Fast and practical indexing and querying of very large graphs," in *SIGMOD*, 2007.

[3] R. Jin, Y. Xiang, N. Ruan, and H. Wang, "Efficiently answering reachability queries on very large directed graphs," in *SIGMOD*, 2008, pp. 595–608.

[4] R. Jin, Y. Xiang, N. Ruan, and D. Fuhry, "3-hop: a high-compression indexing scheme for reachability query," in *SIGMOD*.

[5] H. V. Jagadish, "A compression technique to materialize transitive closure," *ACM Trans. Database Syst.*, vol. 15, no. 4, 1990.

[6] H. Wang, H. He, J. Y. 0001, P. S. Yu, and J. X. Yu, "Dual labeling: Answering graph reachability queries in constant time," in *ICDE*, 2006.

[7] S. Lu, F. Zhang, J. Chen, and S.-H. Sze, "Finding pathway structures in protein interaction networks," *Algorithmica*, vol. 48, no. 4, 2007.

[8] J. P. McGlothlin and L. R. Khan, "Rdfkb: efficient support for rdf inference queries and knowledge management," in *IDEAS*, 2009.

[9] J. Zhu, Z. Nie, X. Liu, B. Zhang, and J.-R. Wen, "Statsnowball: a statistical approach to extracting entity relationships," in *WWW*, 2009.

[10] J. Cheng, J. X. Yu, X. Lin, H. Wang, and P. S. Yu, "Fast computing reachability labelings for large graphs with high compression rate," in *EDBT*, 2008.

[11] R. Bramandia, B. Choi, and W. K. Ng, "Incremental maintenance of 2-hop labeling of large graphs," *IEEE Trans. Knowl. Data Eng.*, vol. 22, no. 5, 2010.

[12] R. Jin, H. Hong, H. Wang, N. Ruan, and Y. Xiang, "Computing label-constraint reachability in graph databases," in *SIGMOD*, 2010.

[13] L. Zou, K. Xu, J. X. Yu, L. Chen, Y. Xiao, and D. Zhao, "Answering label-constraint reachability in large graphs," Peking University, Tech. Rep., 2011. [Online]. Available: http://www.icst.pku.edu.cn/intro/leizou/TR/labelConstraintQuery.pdf

[14] W. Fan, J. Li, S. Ma, N. Tang, and Y. Wu, "Adding regular expressions to graph reachability and pattern queries," in *ICDE*, 2011.

[15] Réka Albert and Albert-László Barabási, "Statistical mechanics of complex networks," *Reviews of Mordern Physics*, vol. 74, pp. 47–97, 2002.

The List Viterbi Training Algorithm and Its Application to Keyword Search over Databases

Silvia Rota
DII - University of Modena and Reggio Emilia, Italy
silvia.rota@unimore.it

Sonia Bergamaschi
DII - University of Modena and Reggio Emilia, Italy
sonia.bergamaschi@unimore.it

Francesco Guerra
DEA - University of Modena and Reggio Emilia, Italy
francesco.guerra@unimore.it

ABSTRACT

Hidden Markov Models (HMMs) are today employed in a variety of applications, ranging from speech recognition to bioinformatics. In this paper, we present the List Viterbi training algorithm, a version of the Expectation-Maximization (EM) algorithm based on the List Viterbi algorithm instead of the commonly used forward-backward algorithm. We developed the batch and online versions of the algorithm, and we also describe an interesting application in the context of keyword search over databases, where we exploit a HMM for matching keywords into database terms. In our experiments we tested the online version of the training algorithm in a semi-supervised setting that allows us to take into account the feedbacks provided by the users.

Categories and Subject Descriptors

H.3.3 [**Information Storage and Retrieval**]: Information Search and Retrieval—*Search process; Retrieval models*

General Terms

Algorithms, Experimentation, Performance

Keywords

Hidden Markov Model, List Viterbi algorithm, Keyword Search over Databases, Relational Databases, Metadata

1. INTRODUCTION

Hidden Markov Models (HMMs) have been largely used in the last thirty years for modeling stochastic processes, with several applications that range from the field of speech recognition to computational biology. The most common training approaches for HMMs, e.g., Bayesian, maximum likelihood, are batch algorithms that require multiple passes through the dataset to converge. These algorithms perform the training offline using a training dataset previously collected that needs to match as close as possible the run-time conditions. When such a training dataset is not available in advance and/or the run-time conditions vary over time, we need to resort to an online training algorithm. In online approaches the model parameters are continuously updated every time a new piece of data is collected without the need to store previously seen information. Therefore, the HMM performances improve over time and adapt to changing conditions [7].

Training algorithms for HMM are typically based on Expectation-Maximization (EM) procedures, where the model parameters are iteratively estimated following a two-step process [8]. In this paper, we propose a version of the EM training algorithm, the List Viterbi training algorithm, that bases the expectation step on the List Viterbi algorithm. List Viterbi [12] produces a ranked list of the K sequences of states that have the highest probability of having generated a given sequence of observations. Consequently, the estimation process is based on the top-K maximum likelihood state sequences and a state optimized joint likelihood function is employed during the maximization step. We developed both the batch and online versions of the training algorithm.

For evaluating the approach, we propose the application of the algorithm in the context of keyword search over databases. Keyword queries have become popular since they allow non-expert users to easily formulate queries even without any knowledge about how the data is structured in the source. Nevertheless, existing approaches rely on a-priori instance-analysis that scans the whole database and constructs some indexing structure which is later used during run time to identify the parts of the database in which each keyword appears. Consequently, these approaches cannot easily be applied in web environments where a complete access to the database instance is not always possible, and the data are subject to frequent update.

In this field, we developed KEYRY (From KEYwords to queRY) [4], a system exploiting a HMM for mapping user keywords into database terms (names of tables and attributes, domains of attributes). The KEYRY parameters are "static", i.e. they are defined in the bootstrap phase exploiting some database metadata. In this paper, we extend KEYRY by coupling it with the online version of the List Viterbi training algorithm, thus making the system able to learn by the use, exploiting the users' feedbacks for improving its performance. The approach has been largely evaluated in a semi-supervised setting that allows us to take into account different levels of feedbacks provided by the users. The experimental results show that the algorithm improves its ranking performance during time and requires a small amount of data for training.

The remainder of the paper is as follows. Section 2 introduces our approach that has been applied in Section 3 for solving keyword-based queries over relational databases. Section 4 is about related work and Section 5 proposes the results or our experiments. Finally, in Section 6 we sketched out some conclusion and future work.

CIKM'11, October 24–28, 2011, Glasgow, Scotland, UK.

2. PROPOSED APPROACH

We introduce a version of the EM algorithm, called List Viterbi training algorithm, which can be seen as a "K winners take all" algorithm since only the top-K state sequences are considered in the objective function. Following the formalism adopted in [8, 7], we propose the batch and online versions of the algorithm.

Let $O = \{O_1, O_2, \ldots O_L\}$ be a dataset of L mutually independent observations. A single observation $O_l = (o_1, o_2, \ldots, o_T)$ is composed of a sequence of observed symbols and has an arbitrary length T. A correspondent sequence of states of the same length is denoted as $Q_l = (q_1, q_2, \ldots, q_T)$. We assume to use a HMM $\lambda = (A, B, \Pi)$ composed of a finite number N of states $S = \{s_1, s_2, \ldots, s_N\}$ and having the parameters defined as follows:

$$A = \{a_{ij} = P(q_{t+1} = s_j | q_t = s_i)\}, 1 \leq i \leq N, 1 \leq j \leq N$$
$$B = \{b_i(v_m) = P(o_t = v_m | q_t = s_i)\}, 1 \leq i \leq N, 1 \leq m \leq M$$
$$\Pi = \{\pi_i = P(q_1 = s_i)\}, 1 \leq i \leq N$$

where M represents the number of observable symbols. A more detailed technical background on HMMs can be found in the tutorial [11].

The List Viterbi algorithm is a dynamic programming algorithm that was initially used for the decoding of convolutional codes [13]. The algorithm has also been applied, using a different formulation, to HMMs in order to solve the following problem:

Given a HMM λ and an observation sequence $O_l = (o_1, o_2, \ldots, o_T)$ find the ordered list of the K state sequences $\hat{Q}_l^k = (q_1^k, q_2^k, \ldots, q_T^k), 1 \leq k \leq K$ which have the highest probability of generating O_l

In other words, the algorithm generalizes the well-known Viterbi algorithm finding the top-K maximum likelihood state sequences (MLSSs) instead of the single MLSS found by the original Viterbi algorithm [11].

We assume to use a training dataset O composed of L mutually independent records. Without loosing generality, we consider each record composed of a sequence of observations and we present the unsupervised versions of the algorithm (batch and online). The supervised versions of the algorithm can be straightforwardly derived from the unsupervised: in this case the E-step relies on the correct state sequences that are given in the training dataset, instead of estimating the top-K MLSSs. Given the assumption that the observations are mutually independent, the distribution over the state sequence outputs used in the E-step $\tilde{P}^{(z)}(Q)$ can be decomposed as the product of the distributions over the single records:

$$\tilde{P}^{(z)}(Q) = \prod_{l=1}^{L} \tilde{P}_l^{(z)}(Q_l)$$

2.1 Batch List Viterbi training algorithm

The batch version of the algorithm performs each EM iteration using the whole training dataset O. During the E-step, the top-K MLSSs $\hat{Q}_l^{k(z)}$ are computed for each record l using the List Viterbi algorithm.

$$\hat{Q}_l^{k(z)} = \arg \overset{(k)}{\max_{Q_l}} P(O_l, Q_l | \lambda^{z-1}), 1 \leq l \leq L, 1 \leq k \leq K$$

The distribution $\tilde{P}$ is constrained to assume value zero to all state sequences but the top-K MLSSs. For the top-K sequences, $\tilde{P}$ assigns the probability calculated by the List Viterbi algorithm normalized by the sum of the top-K MLSS probabilities.

$$\tilde{P}_l^{(z)}(Q_l) = \begin{cases} \dfrac{\overset{(k)}{\max_{Q_l}} P(O_l, Q_l|\lambda^{(z-1)})}{\sum_{k=1}^{K} \overset{(k)}{\max_{Q_l}} P(O_l, Q_l|\lambda^{(z-1)})} & \text{iff } Q_l = \hat{Q}_l^{k(z)} \\ 0 \text{ iff } Q_l \neq \hat{Q}_l^{k(z)} & \text{where } 1 \leq k \leq K \end{cases} \quad (1)$$

In the maximization step the model parameters are chosen to maximize a state-optimized log likelihood function that takes into account only the top-K MLSSs.

$$\begin{aligned} \lambda^{(z)} &= \arg\max_{\lambda} E_{\tilde{P}^{(z)}}[logP(O, Q|\lambda)] \\ &= \arg\max_{\lambda} \sum_{l=1}^{L} E_{\tilde{P}_l^{(z)}}[logP(O_l, Q_l|\lambda)] \\ &= \arg\max_{\lambda} \sum_{l=1}^{L}\sum_{k=1}^{K} logP(O_l, \hat{Q}_l^{k(z)}|\lambda) \end{aligned} \quad (2)$$

The number of iterations required for convergence depends on the specific dataset used for the training and can be calculated using cross validation.

2.2 Online List Viterbi training algorithm

In the online version of the algorithm, each iteration is performed over a single record, or a small groups of records, at a time. Thus, the algorithm requires only a single pass through the dataset and there is no need to store the past records. Each iteration consists of a partial update of the distribution $\tilde{P}$ and the parameters λ. The information provided by each record O_l is exploited immediately instead of waiting to process the other records in the dataset, as in the batch version. This speeds up the convergence of the algorithm, which is a crucial aspect in online applications. We present here the formalization of the algorithm for the unsupervised scenario, where only a single record is utilized in each iteration. The formalization of the case where m records are processed at each step is straightforward.

Given some guess for the initial distributions $\tilde{P}_l^{(0)}$ and the parameters $\lambda^{(0)}$, the algorithm proceeds as follows. Assuming that a single record n is selected from the training dataset at iteration z, in the E-step the top-K MLSSs are only computed for the n-th record, while the MLSSs of the other records are kept equal to the ones calculated in the previous iteration.

$$\hat{Q}_n^{k(z)} = \arg\max{}_{Q_n}^{(k)} P(O_n, Q_n|\lambda^{t-1}), 1 \leq l \leq L, 1 \leq k \leq K$$
$$\hat{Q}_j^{k(z)} = \hat{Q}_j^{k(z-1)}, j \neq n, 1 \leq k \leq K$$

The distribution $\tilde{P}$ is calculated as in the batch version (1), but since the top-K MLSSs are partially computed, $\tilde{P}$ is only partially updated.

The maximization step is performed using the distribution partially updated during the E-step (2). We will show in our experiment that this version of the algorithm converge quikly, even only using fractions of the whole training dataset.

2.3 Training using discrete observations

In the case where the observations assume discrete values, i.e., there exists a finite number M of observable symbols $V = \{v_1, v_2, \ldots, v_M\}$ as in our applicative scenario, the emission probability distribution at each state s_i can be represented using a multinomial distribution. Let us introduce the following variables:

$$\xi_t(i, j) = P(q_t = s_i, q_{t+1} = s_j | O, \lambda)$$

$$\gamma_t(i) = \sum_{j=1}^{N} \xi_t(i,j)$$

where, given an observation dataset O and a HMM λ, $\xi_t(i,j)$ represents the probability of entering state s_i at time t and state s_j a time step later. Summing over j, we obtain $\gamma_t(i)$, i.e. the probability of entering state s_i at time t. Using these variables, the E-step of the batch algorithm can be stated as estimating, i.e. counting, the following quantities:

$$\sum_{t=1}^{T-1} \xi_t^{(z)}(i,j) = \text{\# transitions from } s_i \text{ to } s_j$$

in the top-K MLSSs $\hat{Q}_l^{k(z)}, 1 \leq l \leq L$, found by the List Viterbi algorithm.

$$\sum_{t=1}^{T-1} \gamma_t^{(z)}(i) = \text{\# transitions starting from } s_i$$

in the top-K MLSSs $\hat{Q}_l^{k(z)}, 1 \leq l \leq L$. During the M-step, the parameters of the HMM are re-estimated using the quantities previously calculated:

$$\pi_i^{(z)} = \gamma_1^{(z)}(i) = \text{\# times in state } s_i \text{ at time } t = 1$$

$$a_{ij}^{(z)} = \frac{\sum_{t=1}^{T-1} \xi_t^{(z)}(i,j)}{\sum_{t=1}^{T-1} \gamma_t^{(z)}(i)} = \frac{\text{\# transitions from } s_i \text{ to } s_j}{\text{\# transitions from } s_i}$$

$$b_i^{(z)}(v_m) = \frac{\sum_{t=1}^{T} \gamma_t^{(z)}(i,m)}{\sum_{t=1}^{T} \gamma_t^{(z)}(i)} = \frac{\text{\# times in } s_i \text{ observing } v_m}{\text{\# times in state } s_i}$$

In the online version of the algorithm only the n-th observation O_n is processed at each iteration. Thus, the sufficient statistics are accumulated during time:

$$\sum_{t=1}^{T-1} \xi_t^{(z)}(i,j) = \text{\# transitions from } s_i \text{ to } s_j + \sum_{t=1}^{T-1} \xi_t^{(z-1)}(i,j)$$

$$\sum_{t=1}^{T-1} \gamma_t^{(z)}(i) = \text{\# transitions from } s_i + \sum_{t=1}^{T-1} \gamma_t^{(z-1)}(i,j)$$

Note that the HMM parameters can be initialized at $z = 0$ randomly or using some initial guess on the distribution. In our applicative scenario we use heuristic rules to initialize them, as explained in Section 3.2.

3. SEARCHING OVER DATABASES WITH LIST VITERBI

Keyword search over databases is a hot challenging topic that has recently received a considerable attention. In this paper, we model the keyword search process with a HMM and we apply the List Viterbi algorithm for enabling keyword-based searches over relational databases in cases where the access to the instances is precluded. We conceive the searching process as a two-step approach where firstly the keyword query is analyzed for discovering its intended meaning, and then a ranked set of SQL queries, expressing the discovered meaning according to the database structure, is formulated. Our approach relies on the knowledge about the database schema for providing an initial HMM parameter estimate and for formulating correct SQL queries. We employ the online version of the List Viterbi training algorithm to improve the HMM performances taking into account both the users' feedbacks and a query log.

3.1 The problem statement

Each keyword represents some piece of information that has been modeled in the database as data or metadata. We call *configuration* the description of what each keyword models in a specific data source and to which metadata/data may be associated to. In general, there are many possible configurations for a keyword query: the same keyword may be retrieved as domain value of several attributes, or may be at the same time part of the domain of an attribute and name of some schema element. As usual in these approaches, a score is computed for each configuration, representing its likelihood of describing the user intended meaning.

We define as *database vocabulary* V_D the set of all the tables and all the attributes and their respective domains in a database D. We distinguish two subsets of the database vocabulary: the *schema vocabulary* V_{SC}, i.e. the list of the database tables and attributes, and the *domain vocabulary* V_{DO}, i.e., the attribute domains. We call as *database term* a generic element of V_D.

We assume that: (i) each keyword cannot have more than one meaning in the same configuration, i.e., it is mapped into only one database term; and (ii) every keyword is relevant to the database content, i.e., keywords always have a correspondent database term. Furthermore, while modeling the keyword-to-database term mappings, we also assume that every keyword denotes an element of interest to the user, i.e., there are no stop-words or unjustified keywords in a query.

Answering a keyword query over a database D means finding the SQL queries that describe its possible semantics in terms of the database vocabulary. Each such SQL query is referred to as an *interpretation* of the keyword query in database terms. An interpretation is based on a configuration and includes in its clauses all the database terms that are part of the configuration. A more detailed elaboration on the issues related to the query formulation is out of the scope on this paper. In the following, we will study the application of HMMs to the computation of configurations.

3.2 Computing configurations with a HMM

We model the process for computing configurations using a HMM, where the keywords inserted by the user are the observable part of the process, while the correspondent database terms are the unknown variables that have to be inferred. An initial HMM parameter estimate is defined by means of some heuristic rules that are based on the database schema [4].

By means of these parameters, the HMM is able to work without any training set, and is used to compute the top-K configurations by applying the *List Viterbi* algorithm. List Viterbi produces a ranked list of the K sequences of states that have the highest probability of having generated a given sequence of observations. This is equivalent of finding, given a keyword query $KQ = (k_1, k_2, \ldots, k_l)$, the top-K sequences of database terms $SDT = (sdt_1, sdt_2, \ldots, sdt_l)$ that best represent the intended meaning of the query, i.e, the top-K configurations.

Is important to note that keyword queries are composed of free text while the observations in a HMM are constrained to assume a fixed number M of possible symbols. For this reason, the majority of the applications in the literature [11] assumes a closed vocabulary of possible symbols that is known in advance. However, in our applicative scenario, this assumption is not realistic since it is not possible to predict all the possible keywords that the users will request to the system. Moreover, since we assume that the database instance is not available, we cannot use it to extract a closed keyword vocabulary. We adopt, instead, an open world assumption where the observation symbols are not known a-priori and their number M can vary during time. Therefore, the multinomial distributions used to represent the emissions take into account the new keywords that the users type during time. This implies that, when a new symbol is inserted, the size of the vocabulary M is increased and the previously calculated probabilities are normalized. Our experiments empirically show that, even after removing the closed world assumption, the algorithm converges fast and achieves high performances.

4. RELATED WORK

A theoretical framework that permits the study of variations of the EM algorithm, including incremental versions, has been proposed in [8]. In this work, the EM algorithm is viewed as maximizing a joint function of the parameters and of the distribution over the hidden variables that justify the partial E-step employed in the online versions. Following this work, in [7] an online version of the segmental K-means algorithm has been derived and implemented in a speech recognizer. Our approach extends these works in order to take into account for training the top-k MLSSs calculated by the List Viterbi algorithm.

There has been already a number of different systems that consider keyword searching over structured or semi-structured data. Well-known systems include BANKS, DISCOVER, DBXplorer, QUICK, SQAK, PerK, DivQ and many others presented in various surveys [5, 16]. Their typical approach is to perform an off-line preprocessing step that scans the whole data instance and constructs an index, a symbol table or some structure of that kind which is later used at run-time to identify the parts of the database in which each keyword appears. After that, they perform a path discovery algorithm to find the different ways in which these tables are connected. In contrast to all these approaches, our system is able to achieve similar results without the need of accessing and scanning the dataset instance.

A related field is keyword disambiguation where several approaches have been developed. For example, in [1] an incremental technique based on WordNet and Description Logics is proposed, in [14] context and ontologies are exploited for removing ambiguity, and in [9] attribute disambiguation enables faceted searches.

To the best of our knowledge, HMMs have been applied in field related to the keyword search over databases only in [10], where a HMM has been exploited for performing keyword query cleaning. Nevertheless, the approaches differ in several aspects: in particular, [10] requires to access the database instance for setting the HMM parameters and its training is based on a gradient based optimization algorithm. Moreover we propose an extensive evaluation of our approach in different domains. Finally, Keymantic [2, 3] has goals similar to ours but it follows a fundamentally different approach. It handles the keyword search as a bipartite graph assignment problem and finds the solutions using an extended version of the Hungarian algorithm.

5. EXPERIMENTAL EVALUATION

The evaluation of keyword-based search engines is a difficult task, mainly due to the lack of standard evaluation criteria and benchmarks allowing the comparison with other approaches [15]. Only recently, [6] proposed a benchmark composed of 3 datasets and 50 queries for each one of them and evaluated some of the most popular searching systems against it according to four metrics (the number of top-1 relevant results, the reciprocal rank, the mean average precision and the 11-point interpolated average precision). Nevertheless, a direct comparison of our approach against this benchmark is substantially unfair, since we are interested in finding configurations, i.e. associations of keywords to database terms. Moreover, the benchmark, and the existing searching techniques, assume the availability of the data instance, thus making the comparison based on unequal footing.

In the following, our approach is evaluated according to three perspectives: a) the convergence speed, i.e. how many queries are required for training the systems; b) the effectiveness of the approach, i.e. how much the system outputs are relevant to the user's information need; c) the time performances, i.e. the time required by the algorithm for generating the configurations.

Datasets. For the evaluation of our approach we used three databases: *IMDB*[1], *Mondial*[2] and *UNIV*. *IMDB* and *Mondial* have been frequently used for the experiments of keyword search systems [6]. The database *UNIV* is a fragment of an internal database used in our department for managing research and teaching activities. The databases are respectively composed of 197, 303 and 131 terms.

The construction of a query training dataset is a critical task since synthetic keyword queries do not resemble the actual distribution of information needs, and, on the other hand, self-authored queries have a strong potential for bias. Moreover, query logs cannot be used for evaluation, since they are missing the intended meaning of the users' queries required for measuring the algorithm performances. Finally, it is difficult to have a sufficient number of queries formulated by independent third parties with a description of their intended meaning. For this reason, we adopted a mixed approach, that exploited a small dataset of queries provided by independent users for creating a large dataset. In particular, we asked a small set of real users (29) to provide keyword queries for these databases alongside a natural language explanation of what they were looking for. We obtained a total of 44, 76 and 99 queries for the IMDB, Mondial and UNIV database respectively. A database expert translated each natural language explanation of what the user was looking into a configuration, obtaining a reference to evaluate the results returned by our system. These configurations have been exploited by a software application as a template for the generation of new keyword queries, having the same structure, but different values that are extracted from the database. For the evaluation we adopted a 10-fold cross validation approach, where each fold is composed of 10000 keyword queries. In each fold, 9000 queries are used as training dataset, as described in the experiments in Section 5.1, and 1000 as test dataset, as described in the experiments in Section 5.2. We performed the experiments for each fold, and we computed the result as the average of the results obtained in each fold.

Setup. The experiments in this section were performed on a Windows machine with a 2.27GHz Centrino Duo vPro 32bit and 3GB of RAM. The system is implemented in C++.

5.1 Convergence speed

We expect that our application will be used for querying unknown databases where little or no information about the queries previously submitted to the system is available for the training. In such case, the implicit feedback provided by the user selecting an answer among the top-K returned by the system can be used for the training as supervised data. In this specific applicative scenario, there is only one correct answer provided by the user. Nevertheless, the algorithm can be used also when the feedback is a set of answers. In other cases, a small set of queries along with their configurations could be available and used for a supervised initial training phase. In absence of such an information, the top-K results are used as unsupervised data for the training.

[1] http://www.imdb.com/

[2] http://www.dbis.informatik.uni-goettingen.de/Mondial/

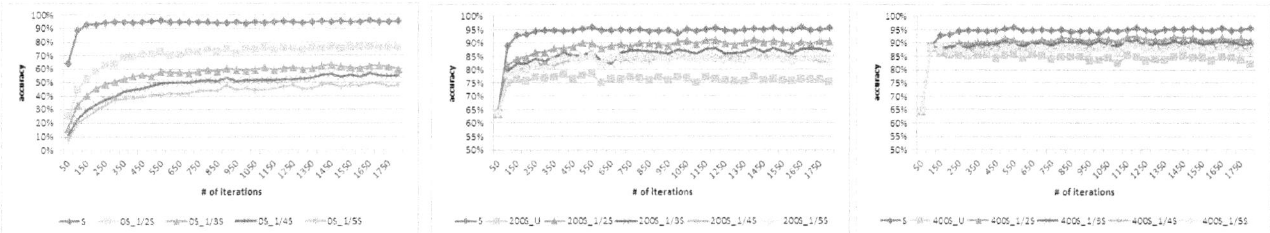

(a) Learning curve without any query supervised (b) Learning curve with the first 200 queries supervised (c) Learning curve with the first 400 queries supervised

Figure 1: Learning curve with different training settings

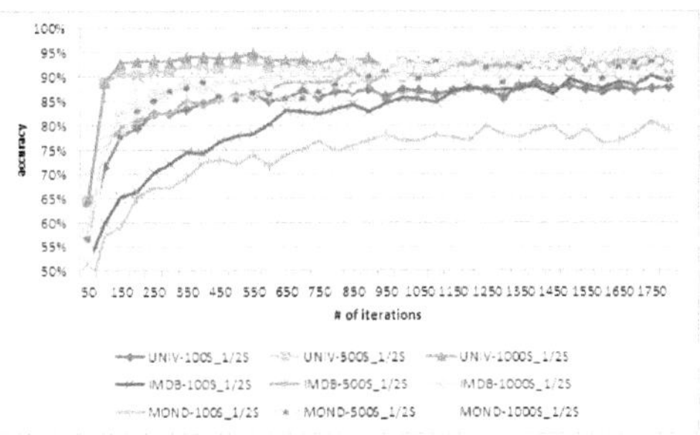

(a) Learning curve

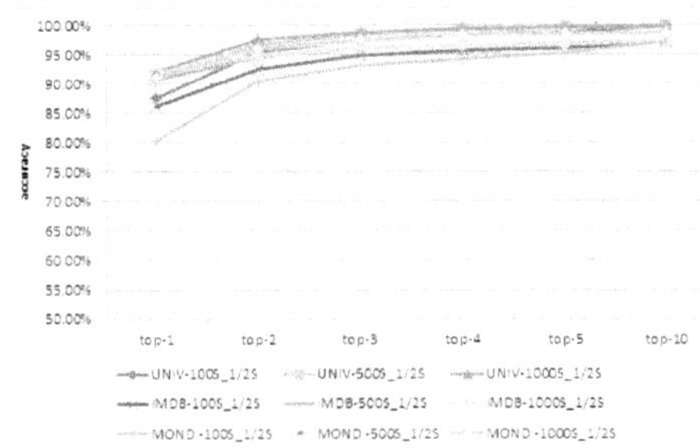

(b) Accuracy

Figure 2: Experiments against the 3 databases

We conducted the training with an initial phase of supervised data and after that a semi-supervised training is adopted to simulate the users' behavior (we assume that the users' feedbacks are not always available). We also tested the supervised algorithm, which is a reference point for the performances.

In Figure 1 we experimented the approach against the *UNIV* database, taking into account the accuracy as percentage of correct answers with rank 1 and different amounts of supervised initial training queries, ranging from 0 (see Figure 1(a)) to 400 queries (see Figure 1(c)). In the semi-supervised phase, different levels of user feedback have been considered. In particular, we considered scenarios where the user provides a feedback for 1 out of 2, out of 3, out of 4, and out of 5 results respectively. Note that, in Figure 1, a label of a series with the format ###S_1/X means that there is a supervised initial training set of ### queries and after there is a user feedback for 1 out of X queries (i.e., 1 out X queries in the dataset is supervised); ###S_U means that after ### queries supervised the approach is unsupervised; S means that the approach is completely supervised. We used small blocks of 5 records for each iteration of the online algorithm, thus generating 1800 iterations of the algorithm, as shown in figure.

The results show that a small initial set of supervised queries is useful for achieving a good training. Figure 1(a) for example

	UNIV	IMDB	Mondial
100	0.927	0.905	0.87
500	0.949	0.934	0.946
1000	0.955	0.941	0.944

Table 1: MRR comparison among the 3 databases

shows that with an initial set of 100 supervised queries and a user feedback about 1 out of 2 results, the system converges after 500 iterations on values with an accuracy greater than 85%. With a larger set of initial supervised queries, the algorithm converges faster and the effects of the user feedbacks are less marked (see Figure 1(c)). However, a small amount of supervised training data is necessary because an a-priori semantics to be learned by the system is associated to each HMM state, i.e., it represents a specific database term.

Obviously, the learning curves are different in different domains. In Figure 2(a), a comparison between the *UNIV*, the *Mondial*, and the *IMDB* database is shown. As expected, the larger number of terms in the *IMDB* and *Mondial* databases requires a larger dataset for converging. Nevertheless, the algorithm converges fast.

5.2 Approach effectiveness

In order to evaluate the effectiveness of the approach, we tested the algorithm with different training settings and we measured how many times the configuration expected by the user was part of the first, second, ..., tenth results computed by the algorithm. Figure 3 shows[3] the results of this experiment considering the *UNIV* database after the training represented in Figure 1. The worst results are obtained in absence of a supervised initial training set as shown in Figure 3(a). In this test condition, the differences in the amount of user feedbacks during the training vary the accuracy on the first answer from 48% (users have provided a feedback on 1 out of 5 queries) to 75% (the feedback was about 1 out of 2 queries).

The importance of the user feedbacks decreases with the number of supervised initial queries. There is no substantial difference among the training conditions if we consider the cases where the user expected results are in the top-10 results provided by the algorithm as shown in Figure 3.

The Mean Reciprocal Rank (MRR) provides a concise indicator about the effectiveness of the approach. The comparison of the MRR values computed against the three databases in Table 1 shows that increasing the database dimension, the number of records in the training dataset needs to increase for obtaining the same performances. This is motivated by the direct relationships between the number of database terms and number of parameters in the HMM. Nevertheless, in all the settings we obtained good results,

[3]This figure has the same legenda of Figure 1. See Section 5.1 for further details.

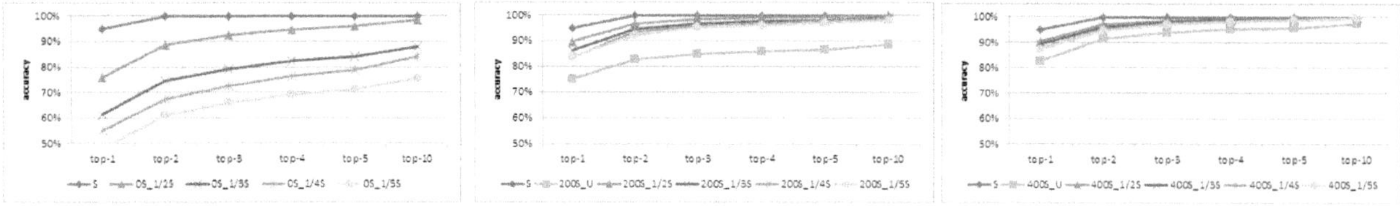

(a) Training settings without any query supervised (b) Training settings with the first 200 queries supervised (c) Training settings with the first 400 queries supervised

Figure 3: Effectiveness in different training settings

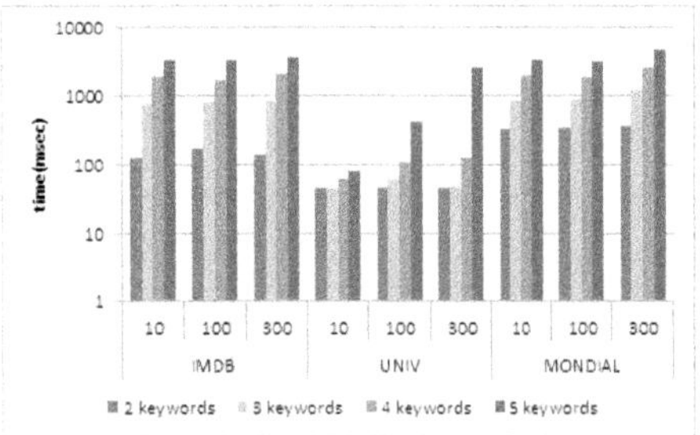

Figure 4: Time performances

even compared with the ones obtained by other approaches in similar domains [6].

5.3 Time performances

We studied the time performance in answering keyword queries of the system with respect to three different parameters: the number of keywords in a query, the number of configurations to compute and the number of the database terms. The results, depicted in figure 4, show performances consistent with the computational complexity of the List Viterbi algorithm $O(lKd^2)$, where l is the number of keywords, K the number of results and d the number of database terms. In the experiments above, we did not report the time needed to actually execute the queries on the database, but only for computing the configurations in order to avoid having the query engine performance blurring the results.

6. CONCLUSION AND FUTURE WORK

In this paper, we proposed the batch and the online version of *List Viterbi training*, a version of the EM algorithm that, for each query in the dataset, considers for training only the top-K MLSSs generated by List Viterbi. List Viterbi and List Viterbi training have been applied to a hot challenging scenario such as keyword-based searching system over relational databases. The experimental results showed that List Viterbi training fast converges to high accuracy levels after a small number of iterations and that List Viterbi provides an effective and the efficient solution to the keyword-based search problem.

Future work will be devoted to the application of the approach to multiple distributed data sources, where solving a keyword query implies to find the data sources relevant for the queries (since they provide a result to all or part of the query), defining a query plan and fusing the obtained result in a unique answer.

Acknowledgment

This work was partially supported by the project "Searching for a needle in mountains of data" (http://www.dbgroup.unimo.it/keymantic/).

7. REFERENCES

[1] S. Bergamaschi, P. Bouquet, D. Giacomuzzi, F. Guerra, L. Po, and M. Vincini. An incremental method for the lexical annotation of domain ontologies. *Int. J. Semantic Web Inf. Syst.*, 3(3):57–80, 2007.

[2] S. Bergamaschi, E. Domnori, F. Guerra, R. T. Lado, and Y. Velegrakis. Keyword search over relational databases: a metadata approach. In *Proceedings of the ACM SIGMOD 2011, Athens, Greece, June 12-16, 2011*. ACM, 2011.

[3] S. Bergamaschi, E. Domnori, F. Guerra, M. Orsini, R. T. Lado, and Y. Velegrakis. Keymantic: Semantic keyword-based searching in data integration systems. *PVLDB*, 3(2):1637–1640, 2010.

[4] S. Bergamaschi, F. Guerra, S. Rota, and Y. Velegrakis. A hidden markov model approach to keyword-based search over relational databases. In *to appear in ER*. Springer, 2011.

[5] S. Chakrabarti, S. Sarawagi, and S. Sudarshan. Enhancing search with structure. *IEEE Data Eng. Bull.*, 33(1):3–24, 2010.

[6] J. Coffman and A. C. Weaver. A framework for evaluating database keyword search strategies. In *CIKM 2010, Toronto, Canada, Oct. 26-30, 2010*, pages 729–738. ACM, 2010.

[7] V. Digalakis. Online adaptation of hidden markov models using incremental estimation algorithms. *Speech and Audio Processing, IEEE Transactions on*, 7(3):253 –261, may 1999.

[8] R. Neal and G. E. Hinton. A view of the em algorithm that justifies incremental, sparse, and other variants. In *Learning in Graphical Models*, pages 355–368. Kluwer Pub., 1998.

[9] J. Pound, S. Paparizos, and P. Tsaparas. Facet discovery for structured web search: a query-log mining approach. In *SIGMOD Conference*, pages 169–180. ACM, 2011.

[10] K. Q. Pu. Keyword query cleaning using hidden markov models. In M. T. Özsu, Y. Chen, and L. C. 0002, editors, *KEYS*, pages 27–32. ACM, 2009.

[11] L. R. Rabiner. A tutorial on Hidden Markov Models and selected applications in speech recognition. In *Proceedings of the IEEE*, volume 77, pages 257–286, 1989.

[12] N. Seshadri and C.-E. Sundberg. List Viterbi decoding algorithms with applications. *Communications, IEEE Transactions on*, 42(234):313 –323, feb/mar/apr 1994.

[13] N. Seshadri and C.-W. Sundberg. Generalized viterbi algorithms for error detection with convolutional codes. In *GLOBECOM '89., IEEE*, pages 1534 –1538, nov 1989.

[14] R. Trillo, J. Gracia, M. Espinoza, and E. Mena. Discovering the semantics of user keywords. *J. UCS*, 13(12), 2007.

[15] W. Webber. Evaluating the effectiveness of keyword search. *IEEE Data Eng. Bull.*, 33(1):54–59, 2010.

[16] J. X. Yu, L. Qin, and L. Chang. *Keyword Search in Databases*. Morgan & Claypool Publishers, 2010.

Context-based People Search in Labeled Social Networks

Cheng-Te Li[1], Man-Kwan Shan[2], Shou-De Lin[1]
Graduate Institute of Networking and Multimedia, National Taiwan University, Taipei, Taiwan [1]
Department of Computer Science, National Chengchi University, Taipei, Taiwan [2]
d98944005@csie.ntu.edu.tw, mkshan@cs.nccu.edu.tw, sdlin@csie.ntu.edu.tw

ABSTRACT

In online social networking services, there are a range of scenarios in which users want to search a particular person given the targeted person one's name. The challenge of such people search is *namesake*, which means that there are many people possess the same names in the social network. In this paper, we propose to leverage the query contexts to tackle such problems. For example, given the information of one's graduation year and city, the last names of some individuals, one may wish to find classmates from his/her high school. We formulate such problem as the *context-based people search*. Given a social network in which each node is associated with a set of labels and given a query set of labels consisting of a targeted name label and other context labels, our goal is to return a ranking list of persons who possess the targeted name label and connects to other context labels with minimum communication costs through an effective subgraph in the social network. We consider the interactions among query labels to propose a grouping-based method to solve the context-based people search. Our method consists of three major parts. First, we model those nodes with query labels into a group graph which is able to reduce the search space to enhance the time efficiency. Second, we identify three different kinds of connectors which connecting different groups, and exploit connectors to find the corresponding detailed graph topology from the group graph. Third, we propose a Connector-Steiner Tree algorithm to retrieve a resulting ranked list of individuals who possess the targeted label. Experimental results on the DBLP bibliography data show that our grouping-based method can reach the good quality of returned persons as a greedy search algorithm at a considerable outperformance on the time efficiency.

Categories and Subject Descriptors

H.2.8 [**Database Management**]: Database Applications – *Data mining*. H.3.3 [**Information Storage and Retrieval**]: Information Search and Retrieval – *Information Filtering*.

General Terms

Algorithms, Performance, Design.

Keywords

People Search, Social Network, Context-based Search.

1. INTRODUCTION

In online social networking services such as Facebook, Twitter, and LinkedIn, it is essential to provide people search which searches for an individual by name. However, if the query name is a namesake, especially if there exist millions of individuals share the query name, it would be difficult to find the target person over social networking services.

CIKM'11, October 24–28, 2011, Glasgow, Scotland, UK.

One approach is the *context-based people search* which search for an individual not only by name of the target, by also by the social contexts of the target. The user specified social contexts may be the first names of target's friends, the last names of target's classmates, the hobbies of the target's colleagues, hometowns of target's relatives, and so on. These social contexts are *labels* associated with each individual in social networking services.

The idea of the proposed context-based social search is illustrated by Figure 1. Each person is associated with labels, where some have many labels and others provide few labels or only their user names (e.g., Angel). It can be observed that there are three people named Sam and two named Mary. The weights on the edges indicate the communication cost between two people. Higher weights indicate that the people tend to have a casual acquaintance, whereas lower values imply that they are more familiar with one another. If someone seeks to find a friend named "Mary" who has a friend named George and a colleague familiar with Java, the expected result by our context-based people search *individual search* is "Mary-1," rather than "Mary-2." Another example is to find an individual named "Sam" who had learned the "C++" programming language with his old friend "Robert" in his hometown "Boston", the expected target would be "Sam-1," who is connected with "James", "Jane" and "Robert." Not only they meet the query labels but also interact with each other in an effective manner (with minimal costs).

Given a social network, how to find the individual who is the most relevant to some user-interested social contexts? Specifically, given an arbitrary set of labels as queries in a social network (e.g., an acquaintance network in Facebook), in which each individual is characterized by some set of labels, how can we efficiently find the individual who has strong direct or indirect relationships to all of the query labels?

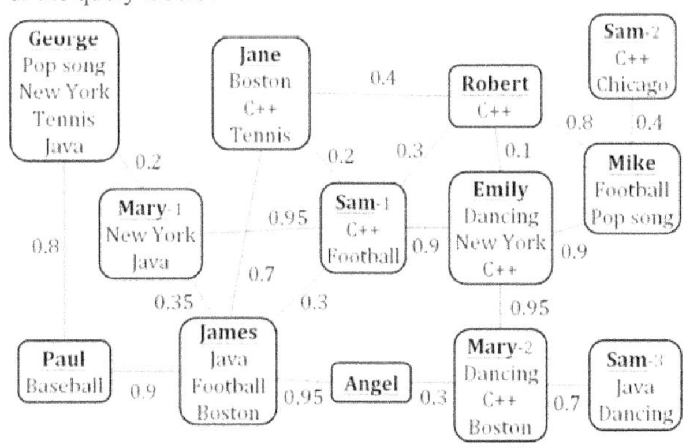

Figure 1. A social network with labels on each person. Labels include name, interest, skill, and hometown. Note that we append "-number" to individuals to distinguish between people with the same name (e.g. Mary-1, Mary-2).

To perform such search tasks in current social networking services containing considerable numbers of people, we have to address two critical and universal issues: *commonality* and *incompleteness*. Commonality indicates that there are a large number of individuals sharing common labels in the network. An obvious illustration is the presence of popular given names, such as Mary, James, and John. Moreover, there are even more people possessing the same labels, such as interests, hometowns, schools, and graduation years. Incompleteness means that users in social networking sites usually do not (necessarily) provide complete information about themselves. Some enthusiastic members of online social networks fill in all their details, whereas others may only be willing to display their names or a few labels. To address the issues of commonality and incompleteness in real-life social networks, we propose to leverage the user-given social contexts with the social interactions to achieve a context-based social search: (1) for commonality, individuals with the same names can be distinguished by context attributes in the network; (2) for incompleteness, we can also make conjectures about individuals who provide limited information to their social circles.

In the literature, search tasks in the social contexts of Web 2.0, called *social search*, refer to many different aspects. Among these diverse perspectives on the term *social search*, the viewpoint of Kleinberg [5], who defines it as searching over a social graph to find the set of individuals closest to a given user, is the most relevant to our context-based people search. In addition, some commercial solutions to people search, such as Wink [13] and Intelius [14], have also been developed to provide search over online social networking sites. These people search services aim at exploiting social information such as tagging, voting, and profiles to find people related to any given individual. However, existing search services over social networks do not tackle the commonality issue, that is, that there are usually many people with the same names. In addition, they assume that the social information, including personal attributes and user tagging, is complete. Nevertheless, in real-life social networking, it is infeasible to collect complete personal profiles from all users.

In this paper, we propose, formally define, and efficiently and effectively solve the context-based people search problem for a labeled social network. Given a social network in which each node is associated with a set of labels and a user query consisting of a set of required labels, our goal is to find the individual that satisfies the query requirements while minimizing the communication costs. We define the communication cost as the sum of the weights on the edges in a minimum spanning tree connecting both the required labels and the found individual in a direct or indirect manner.

The central idea of the solution to solve the problem of context-based people search is to leverage the effective interactions of query labels. We propose a grouping-based method consists of three major parts. First, we group those nodes with the same query labels and transform the original social network into a group graph which can be regarded as high-level view for the interactions between groups. The group graph is able to reduce to graph space and provides an effective guidance for search tasks. Second, we identify three kinds of connectors which connecting different groups in the social network. The connectors can be regarded as key points controlling the bottleneck of cost in the final subgraph and allowing a more effective graph search. Finally, we propose a Connector-Steiner algorithm to compose the ranked list of effective connection subgraphs as the resulting context-based communities.

2. CONTEXT-BASED PEOPLE SEARCH

[Definition 1] (Labeled Social Network) Let $A=\{a_1,...,a_m\}$ be a universe of m labels. A *labeled social network* is defined as an undirected and weighted graph $G=(V, E)$. Each node i in $V=\{1,...,n\}$ is an individual that possesses a set of labels $X_i \subseteq A$. Each edge (i, j) in E captures the interaction between two individuals. The weight on each edge (i, j) represents the communication cost between individuals i and j. Note that edges with low (high) weights represent high (low) communication costs between two nodes. For example, in a social network, if two people share more interests, the weight of their edge is correspondingly lower.

[Definition 2] (Communication Cost) Given a labeled social network $G=(V, E)$ and $V'\subseteq V$, the *communication cost* of V' is defined as the sum of the weights of edges of the *minimum spanning tree* on the induced subgraph $G[V']$, denoted by $CC(V')$.

[Definition 3] (Context-based Query) A query for the context-based people search consists of a set of labels, which consists of a targeted label $t\in A$ (i.e., the first name of the targeted person) and more than one context labels (e.g., the names or labels of the targeted one's friends) provided by the users.

Given a labeled social network $G=(V, E)$ and a search task T consisting of a particular first name label to indicate the targeted person and a set of context labels $\{a_1,..., a_r\}\subseteq A$, the *context-based people search* problem is to return a ranking list of persons in which each retuned person connects to the query labels with minimum communication cost. Specifically, we aim to find a set of individuals $V'\subseteq V$ that is connected by a subgraph $G[V']$ such that (1) $T\subseteq \{X_i, i\in V'\}$ and (2) the communication cost $CC(V')$ is minimized. And for the ranking result, a ranked list is returned based on the communication cost.

3. THE APPROXIMATED METHOD: *ApxSteiner*

For the context-based people search in a labeled network, a simple approach is to exploit the Steiner tree algorithm. The minimum *Steiner tree problem* is to find a connected subgraph that connects some required nodes with minimum sum of edge weights. We can add the query labels as nodes in the labeled social network, and designate these nodes of query labels as the required ones in the Steiner tree problem. Using existing solutions to the minimum Steiner tree problem, a subgraph with minimum cost can be derived, and the individual with the targeted label in the resulting subgraph is reported as an answer person. Repeating such process up to N times and sort the returned answer persons based on their costs, a ranked list of N answer persons can be derived.

We first review the *Steiner tree problem*. Given an undirected graph with non-negative costs on edges, the nodes in this graph are separated to the *terminal/required vertex set* T and the *Steiner vertex set* S. The Steiner tree problem is to find the minimum-cost spanning tree in the given graph; the found tree must contain all nodes in the terminal set T and any subset of the Steiner nodes. Since the Steiner tree problem is a NP-hard problem, several approximation algorithms had been proposed. Here we modify the greedy algorithm in [6] to find the minimum Steiner tree. This algorithm starts by randomly selecting a node as a seed in the required (terminal) set T. Then at each step, a single terminal node v^* from T is incrementally added to the current solution V'. Each v^* is determined by the minimum distance to V', which contains nodes that have already been added to the solution set.

4. THE PROPOSED METHOD: *GrpSteiner*

We propose to perform the context-based people search by grouping nodes based on query context labels to provide effective and efficient search. Our method consists of seven steps. The first step is a *label-based node grouping* that collects individuals into groups according to each query label. The second step is to identify three kinds of *connectors* between groups. The connectors play key roles to construct an effective group graph. By exploiting the connectors, the third step is to construct the *group graph*, in which linkages capture the critical interactions between groups. To realize the group graph, the fourth step is to embed the topological information only relates to the query labels into the *relevance graph*. The fifth step aims to construct the *label relevance graph* which integrates the social interactions with the query context labels to guide the search. To allow more effective and efficient search result, in the sixth step, we propose to find the *crucial label* as the seed node for the following Steiner tree algorithm. In the seventh step, by using the derived seed label and the identified connectors, we propose and apply the *Connector-Steiner tree algorithm* to find an *effective subgraph* of individual for the query labels. According to the targeted label and the communication cost on the effective subgraph, we perform a *weight enhancement* mechanism to return a *ranked list* of individuals who satisfy the targeted label.

4.2 Label-based Node Grouping

The first step is to group the individuals in the labeled social network according to the query labels. A *group*, with respect to one of the query labels, for example, a_i, is a connected subgraph in which each individual node contains at least a_i. We denote the group of a certain query label as *grp*. Note that for a query label a_i, it can have more than one group since there could exist multiple disconnected subgraphs belonging to a_i.

Figure 2 shows an example of grouping for the query labels a_1, a_2, and a_3, in which a_1 is the targeted label. Each group is surrounded by a dotted region. We can observe two groups correspond to label a_1. These two groups are separated components since they have no interactions. In addition, node *i* belongs to two groups because *i* contains both a_1 and a_2. Nodes *m* and *q* do not belong to any of groups because they contain none of the three query labels.

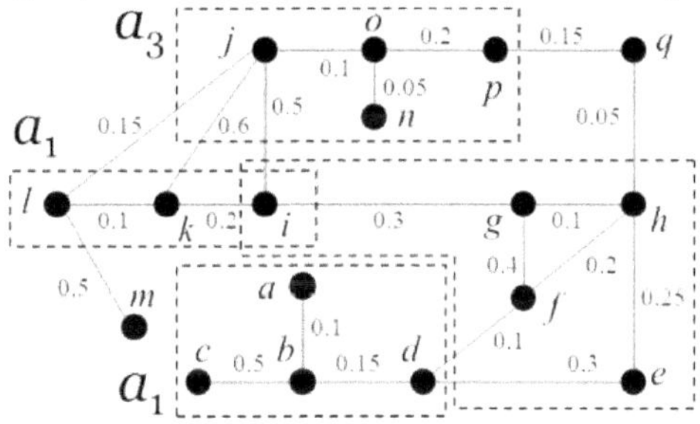

Figure 2. The label-based node grouping for the labeled social network, where there are three query labels a_1, a_2, and a_3 and a_1 is the targeted label specified by users.

4.3 Connector Identification

Based on the result of label-based node grouping, we can further distinguish different roles of individuals in a social network, especially for the *connectors* that take charge of connecting groups. According to the interaction behaviors between groups, there are three kinds of connectors: the overlap connector, the direct connector, and the indirect connector.

[Definition 3] (Overlap Connector) Given the label-based groups, if a node *v* belongs to more than one groups, it is called an *overlap connector*. The set of overlap connectors is denoted by *OC*.

In Figure 2, node *i* is the overlap connector since it contains multiple query labels, a_1 and a_2, and belong to multiple groups.

[Definition 4] (Direct Connector) Given the label-based groups, for each edge $e=(u, v)\in E$ in the social network $G=(V, E)$, if $u\in grp_{ai}$, $v\in grp_{aj}$, and $a_i \neq a_j$, then *u* and *v* are the direct connectors of grp_{ai} and grp_{aj} respectively. The set of direct connectors in a network is denoted by *DC*.

Director connectors are those end nodes of a bridge edge which connects two different groups. If a node belongs to one group and directly link to another, it is direct connectors of that group. For example, in Figure 2, for the group of label a_3, its direct connector is node *j*. It directly links to groups of label a_1 and a_2 respectively. Note that although node *i* is an overlap connector, it is also a direct connector because it directly link to group of a_3.

[Definition 5] (Inter-Mediator) Given the label-based groups, if a node *v* belongs to no groups (contain no query labels), it is called an inter-mediator. The set of inter-mediators is denoted by *IM*.

For example, in Figure 2, node *q* is an inter-mediator because it does not contain any of query labels a_1, a_2, and a_3.

[Definition 6] (Indirect Connector) Given the label-based groups, for a path $p=(v_1,...,v_{n-1},v_n)$ ($n>2$) in the social network $G=(V,E)$, if $v_1\in grp_{ai}$, $v_n\in grp_{aj}$, $a_i\neq a_j$ and $\forall j\in\{2,...,n-1\}$, $v_j\in IM$, then v_1 and v_n are the *indirect connectors* for grp_{ai} and grp_{aj} respectively. The set of indirect connectors in a network is denoted by *IC*.

Indirect connectors are those end nodes of a path (|path|>1) where nodes other than the end points do not contain any query labels. For example, in Figure 2, *p* and *h* are the indirect connectors for the groups of label a_3 and a_2 respectively.

4.4 Group Graph Construction

We have aggregated individuals into groups based on query labels. But the underlying interactions among groups have not yet been modeled. The group interactions are essential for finding effective communications of groups with respect to the query labels. If we can construct the *group graph* with lower costs to connect groups, it will guide the following search algorithm to have resulting subgraph with lower cost and cardinality. In this subsection, we exploit the benefits of the priority principle of connectors for constructing the group graph in an effective manner.

[Definition 7] (Group Graph) A *group graph* $H=(V_H, E_H)$ is a weighted graph constructed using query labels from the labeled social network $G=(V, E)$, where V_H is a finite set of *group nodes*, and $E_H \subseteq V_H\times V_H$ is a finite set of *group links*.

[Definition 8] (Group Node) *Group nodes* are defined according to query labels. For a query label $a_i\in T$, the group node $grp_{ai}\in V_H$ contains a set of nodes $V'(grp_{ai}) \subseteq V$ in *G* and must satisfy (1) $\forall u\in V'(grp_{ai})$, $a_i\subseteq X_u$, (2) the nodes in $V'(grp_{ai})$ form an induced connected subgraph $G[V'(grp_{ai})]$.

[Definition 9] (Group Link) A *group link* $e_H\in E_H$ is defined on two group nodes grp_{ai} and grp_{aj} in G_H, such that the corresponding induced subgraphs of these two group nodes, $G[V'(grp_{ai})]$ and $G[V'(grp_{aj})]$, are reachable from one another. Note that a group link between two induced subgraphs in *G* can be overlapped, direct, or indirect connection.

To have an effective group graph, we follow the priority of connectors, i.e., "overlap first, direct second, and indirect finally", to construct the group graph. The algorithm for group graph construction is shown in Algorithm 1. This algorithm starts by isolating all group nodes, and then constructs the group graph based on the priority of connectors in turn until the group graph is connected. For the example in Figure 2, the group graph is shown in Figure 3(a), where the circles represent the group nodes.

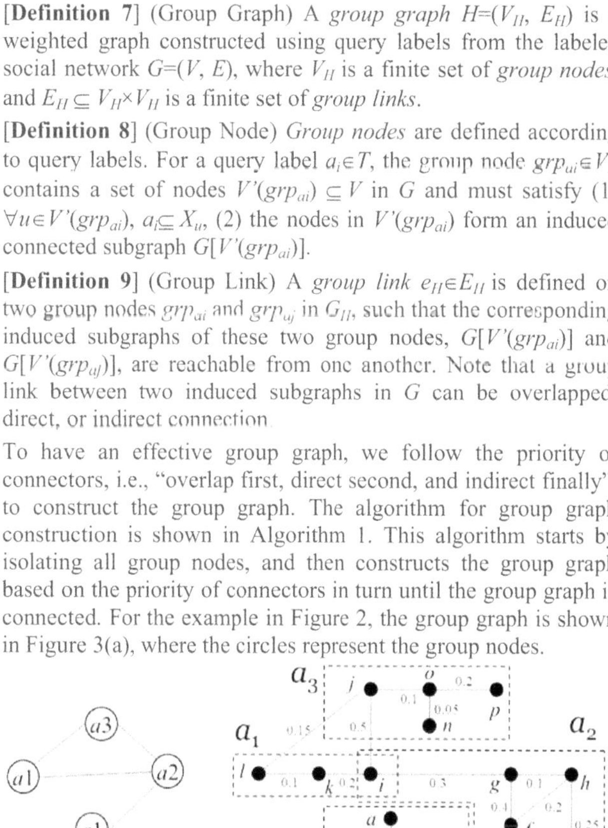

Figure 3. (a) The group graph constructed from Figure 2. (b) The relevance graph of Figure 3(a).

Algorithm 1. Group Graph Construction

Input: The labeled social network $G=(V,E)$; the set of all group nodes GRP; the set of groups that v_i involves R_{vi}; the sets of overlap, direct, and indirect connectors OC, DC, and IC.

Output: A connected group graph $H = (V_H, E_H)$.

$V_H \leftarrow V_H \cup \{v_H = grp_{ai} \in GRP\}$.
for each $v_i \in OC$ **do**
  $\{e_H\} \leftarrow (grp_x, grp_y)$, where $grp_x \in R_{vi}$, $grp_y \in R_{vi}$, and $x \neq y$.
  $E_H \leftarrow E_H \cup \{e_H\}$.
  if H is connected **do**: return H.
for each $e=(v_i,v_j) \in E$ and $v_i \in DC$ and $v_j \in DC$ **do**
  $\{e_H\} \leftarrow (grp_x, grp_y)$, where $grp_x \in R_{vi}$, $grp_y \in R_{vj}$, and $x \neq y$.
  $E_H \leftarrow E_H \cup \{e_H\}$.
  if H is connected **do**: return H.
$h \leftarrow 1$.
while (true) **do**
  for each h-hop path $(v_i,...,v_j)$ $v_i \in IC$ and $v_j \in IC$ **do**
    $\{e_H\} \leftarrow (grp_x, grp_y)$, where $grp_x \in R_{vi}$, $grp_y \in R_{vi}$, $x \neq y$.
    $E_H \leftarrow E_H \cup \{e_H\}$.
    if H is connected **do**: return H.
  $h \leftarrow h + 1$.

4.5 Relevance Graph Realization

We restore the corresponding graph topology in the original social network. We call this restored graph topology as the *relevance graph* G_R (i.e., relevant to query labels). In other words, we aim to obtain the induced graph of nodes contained in the group nodes. The restoration process from the group graph to the relevance graph consists of two steps. The first is to restore the group nodes. For each group node, we find the induced subgraph in the original social network corresponding to all nodes contained in it. The second is for the group links. For group links derived from overlap connectors, it is unnecessary to be processed since they have belonged to at least one group. For group links derived from direct connectors, there exists more than one bridge edge. For example, in Figure 2, there are three bridge edges between group nodes a_1 and a_3. We find the bridge edges with the lowest costs and add them into the relevance graph. For group links derived from indirect connectors, the h-hop paths found in Algorithm 1 are added into the relevance graph. For the example in Figure 3(a), the corresponding relevance graph is shown in Figure 3(b).

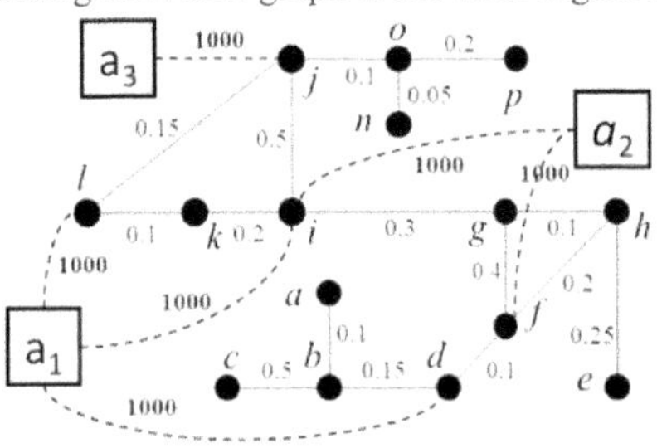

Figure 4. The label relevance graph for the previous example.

4.6 Label Relevance Graph Construction

To facilitate the people search considering query labels, we then embed these query labels into the relevance graph. By regarding each query label as a node, we add the query labels into the relevance graph and add edges to connect each query label node to nodes of connectors that possess that label. For these newly added edges between label nodes and connectors, we associate a positive weight higher than the sum of all weights in the social network. Eventually, a *label relevance graph* $G^{LR} = (V^{LR}, E^{LR})$ will be constructed. For example, the label relevance graph for Figure 3 is shown in Figure 4, where the squares represent the label nodes and the dotted lines represent the edges between label nodes and the corresponding connectors. In addition, we assign the new added edges a large weight. Note that the nodes corresponding to the query labels will serve as seeds to perform the search algorithm in the following subsection.

4.7 Seed Label Selection for Steiner Algorithm

To find the individuals with lower communication cost, our approach then finds the Steiner tree in the label relevance graph as the resulting context-based subgraph for people search. Given the label relevance graph $G^{LR} = (V^{LR}, E^{LR})$, the query labels as the terminal node set T, and the Steiner nodes are the nodes $V^{LR} \setminus T$, our goal is to find an effective subgraph $G^{LR}[U]$ with minimum communication cost CC(U), where $U \subseteq V^{LR}$. The node with the targeted label in $G^{LR}[U]$ will be reported as a returned person.

We start the graph search by selecting a label node randomly from the label relevance graph. However, some experimental studies show that the seed node plays an important role for minimizing communication cost of the derived subgraph. If a good seed node is selected, the communication cost can be lowered. We propose the *connective degree* to measure the effectiveness of label nodes in the label relevance graph. The label node with the highest connective degree will be selected as the seed node to perform the greedy Steiner tree algorithm. We first define the ε-neighborhood of a label node.

[Definition 10] (ε-Neighborhood) The *ε-neighborhood* of a node $v \in V^{LR}$ is the set of nodes $N_\varepsilon(v)=\{u_i \mid 1 \leq PathLength(v, u) \leq \varepsilon, u \in V\}$.

[Definition 11] (Connective Degree) Given the label nodes in the label relevance graph and the three sets of connectors OC, DC, and IC, the *connective degree* of a label node v is defined as $CDegree(v)=|N_\varepsilon(v) \cap OC| \times \alpha_{OC} + |N_\varepsilon(v) \cap DC| \times \alpha_{DC} + |N_\varepsilon(v) \cap IC| \times \alpha_{IC}$, where the parameters α_{OC}, α_{DC}, and α_{IC} are used to control the effectiveness of different kinds of connectors. In the work, ε is set as 2, α_{OC} is set as 0.7, α_{DC} is set as 0.2, and α_{IC} is set as 0.1.

Algorithm 2. Connector-Steiner Tree Algorithm with Ranking.

Input: The graph $G^{LR} = (V^{LR}, E^{LR})$; a search task consists of a targeted label t and a set of context labels $T = \{a_1,...,a_r\}$; the number of people search results to be returned n.

Output: A ranked list of nodes $P=<(p_1,CC_1)...,(p_n,CC_n)>$.

for $k = 1$ to n **do**
  $U_k \leftarrow s$, where $s \in T$ and s is picked by *connective degree*.
  while $(T \setminus U_k) \neq \phi$ **do**
    $v^* \leftarrow \text{argmin}_{u \in T \setminus U_k} Dist(u, U_k)$ in G^{LR}.
    if $Path(v^*, U_k) \neq \phi$ **then**
      $U_k \leftarrow U_k \cup \{Path(v^*, U_k)\}$.
  $U_k \leftarrow U_k \setminus \{a_1, ..., a_r\}$.
  $p \leftarrow \{v_i \mid v_i \in U_k$ **and** $t \in X_i$ **and** $v_i \neq p_j, j=1,...,k\text{-}1\}$.
  $weight(e_i=(v_i, t)) \leftarrow weight(e_i=(v_i, t)) \times$LARGEVALUE(=1000).
  $LIST \leftarrow (p, CC(U_k))$.
Sort $LIST$ according to $CC(U_k)$ and return as the ranked list of nodes $P=<(p_1,CC_1),...,(p_n,CC_n)>$, where $CC_1<CC_2<, ..., <CC_n$.

4.8 Connector-Steiner Algorithm with Ranking

Given the label relevance graph G^{LR}, and the set of query label nodes $\{a_1,...,a_r\}$ of the search task T, we propose the Connector-Steiner Tree algorithm to find a list of effective connection subgraph with respect to the query labels. We propose a *weight enhancement* mechanism, which increases the edge weights between each answer node and the targeted label nodes. Specifically, when each time an effective subgraph is constructed, we identify the node with the targeted label and regard it as one answer person. Then we replace the edge weight between the returned person and the targeted label node with a larger value. Such weight enhancement is capable of guiding the following Steiner tree searches to choose other persons with the targeted label as other answers. Each time when an answer person is returned, we also record the cost of the current effective subgraph as the effectiveness of such answer. Eventually, we obtain a list of answer persons with their costs. By sorting such list based on the costs, a ranked list of effective subgraphs can be derived as the results. The detailed is shown in Algorithm 2.

Figure 5 shows the round-1 and round-2 effective subgraphs for the query search task $T=\{a_1,a_2,a_3\}$ and the targeted label is a_1, using the label relevance graph of Figure 4. For the round-1 result, the highlighted nodes $\{i, j, k, l\}$ and red edges $\{(i, k), (k, l), (l, j)\}$ compose the effective subgraph with the minimum cost 0.15+0.1+0.2=0.45. Node l that satisfies the targeted label a_1 is reported as the answer person with cost=0.45. Before the end of 1st round, the algorithm enhances the edge weight between the node l and the label node a_1 to be 1000×1000. For the round-2 result, the highlighted nodes $\{i, j\}$ with the green edge (i, j) compose the effective subgraph with cost=0.5. Node i satisfies the targeted label is reported as the answer person with cost=0.5. If we designate to have n=2 results, eventually, the ranking list will be <(l, 0.45), (i, 0.5)> (i.e., l is the rank-1, i is the rank-2).

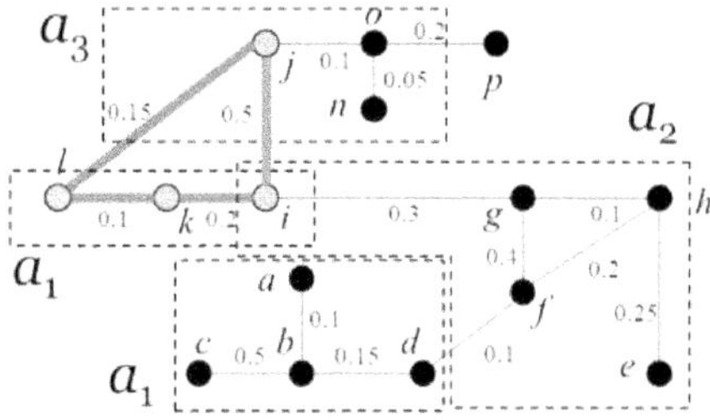

Figure 5. The round-1 and round-2 effective subgraphs derived by the proposed Connector-Steiner Tree algorithm is highlighted as the red and green ones respectively. Recall the targeted label is a_1. The round-1 answer person is node l with cost=0.45 while the round-2 answer is node i with cost=0.5.

5. EVALUATIONS

We conduct experiments to test the effectiveness and efficiency of the proposed method for tackling the context-based people search in a social network. By comparing our grouping-based method (**GrpSteiner**) to the original greedy Steiner tree algorithm (**ApxSteiner**), the experimental results demonstrate that our GrpSteiner performs as well as ApxSteiner in terms of ranking performance, and takes significantly less search time.

5.1 The DBLP Bibliography Data

We conduct the experiments on the DBLP bibliography database. The snapshot on December 31, 2010 of information retrieval and data mining related conferences (including KDD, ICDM, SDM, PAKDD, PKDD, ICML, CIKM, WWW, SIGIR, ACL, SIGMOD, VLDB, PODS, ICDE, EDBT, and ICDT) is used. We construct the labeled social network using co-authorship between authors. The set of labeled nodes consists of authors who have co-authored at least three papers. The label set X_i of each author i consists of his/her first names and keywords of textual terms (removed the stop words) occurring in the paper titles of at least three papers titles that he or she co-authored. Two authors are connected in the network if they co-authored at least three papers. There are a total of 10,443 authors and 25,354 edges. We compute the edge weights (i.e., communication costs) using the *Jaccard coefficient*. The formula of computing edge weights is given as: $w(i,j) = 1 - (|P_i \cap P_j|/|P_i \cup P_j|)$, where P_i is the set of papers of i.

5.2 Experiment Design

Evaluation Measures. The goals of the experiments are to evaluate the effectiveness and efficiency between the proposed grouping-based Steiner algorithm (GrpSteiner) and the original greedy Steiner tree algorithm (ApxSteiner). The effectiveness is measured by calculating the ranked position of the ground-truth targeted person in the returned ranking list. Specifically, for a query consisting of a set of context labels and the first name of the target person t_i, when a search method returns a ranking list of persons, we find the ranked position of the ground-truth targeted person, denoted by $rank(t_i)$. Given a set of N search queries, we compute the average value of ranked positions of targeted persons, $AvgRank=(\Sigma_{i=1...N}\, rank(t_i))/N$. On the other hand, the efficiency is measured by averaging the execution time (seconds) of search queries. Note that the ranked list of original Steiner algorithm (ApxSteiner) is generated by performing the algorithm n times and sorts the results by the communication costs, in which we apply the abovementioned *weight enhancement* mechanism when each resulting person is returned.

Generating Targeted Person with Context Labels. We simulate how users perform people search in a social network to generate a set of N the ground-truth targeted persons with the query sets of context labels. For each targeted person, we produce a set of $\boldsymbol{k}$ context labels for the search process. The generation procedure is given as the following. First, we sort the frequency of first names in the compiled DBLP co-authorship network, and derive a set of highly-frequent first names S_f by setting a first-name threshold τ_f. The same process is applied to derive a set of highly-frequent keywords S_w. using a keyword threshold τ_w. To impose the namesake effect which is what we mainly concern, we set $(\tau_F, \tau_K) = (30, 250)$ in the experiments. Second, we randomly pick a first name from S_f, and then randomly pick a person i with this first name. We regard such individual i as a ground-truth targeted person and his/her first name as one of the query context labels. Third, using the social network, we perform Breath-first search up to r steps starting from t_i, and obtain a set of neighboring persons S_r. And then we randomly select $\boldsymbol{k}$-1 persons from S_r. For each selected person j, it has an equal probability to choose either his/her first name or one of his/her possessed keywords as a query context label. The neighboring step r is set to be 2 because in real-life cases it is less possible for users to employ far information about the targeted person for people search. Repeating the above second and third parts up to N times, we can attain N ground-truth targeted persons with the corresponding N $\boldsymbol{k}$-sized sets of context labels as the search queries. Here we set N to be 200.

Evaluation Plan. The experiments are divided into two parts to demonstrate the effectiveness and efficiency from diverse points of views. First, to investigate how the number of provided context information affects the performance, we vary the number of the query context labels $\boldsymbol{k}$ = 3, 4, ..., 10. Note that among $\boldsymbol{k}$ context labels, one is the first name of the ground-truth targeted person t_i and the other $\boldsymbol{k}$–1 ones are either the first names or the keywords in t_i's neighbors. Second, to examine how the ratio between the first-name and keyword context labels affects the performance, we fix $\boldsymbol{k}$=6 and vary the ratio of "*#NameLabel* versus *#KeywordLabel*" as 1:5, 2:4, ..., 5:1.

5.3 Experimental Results

Number of Context Labels. The results of varying the number of query context labels are shown in Figure 6(a) and 6(b) for the average rank and time efficiency respectively. For the average rank in Figure 6(a), we can find our GrpSteiner and the original ApxSteiner algorithms have very similar performance under different numbers of context labels. In details, which the number of query contexts are lower, both methods become slightly worse (i.e., average ranks are up to 2.5). As the numbers of query context labels increase, the average ranks generally decrease toward 2.0. This indicates both methods can averagely return the ground-truth targeted person within top-2 returned persons. On the other hand, for the time efficiency of execution time (in seconds) in Figure 6(b), our GrpSteiner significantly outperforms the ApxSteiner method, especially when the number of query context labels gradually becomes higher. We believe such good efficiency is due to that the grouping mechanism successfully reduces the graph search space so that the execution of our Connector-Steiner Tree algorithm is more efficient to find the results.

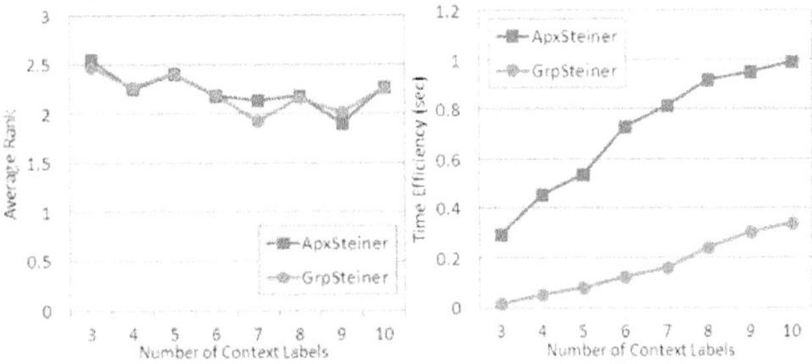

(a) (b)

Figure 6. (a) Varying the number of query context labels (b) Varying the number of query context labels to show the average ranks of both our GrpSteiner and ApxSteiner.

#Keyword-#FirstName Ratio. We present the average rank and time efficiency by varying the ratio between #KeywordLabel and #FirstNameLabel. In Figure 7(a), we find the effectiveness of both GrpSteiner and ApxSteiner is well-performed and similar. Averagely both can find the ground-truth targeted person within around top-three returned persons. In more details, as the number of query keyword labels increases, the average ranks of both methods gradually raise from about 2.0 to 2.75, which indicates both needs more returns to catch the answers. We think such effect results from that the query with more keyword labels will produce higher potentials to allow those with the same keyword labels usually connect to one another in the relevance graph. Therefore the graph search, which aims to minimize the communication cost, will be guided toward different directions that are away from the targeted person. In contrast with confusing the search based on keyword labels, when the number of first name labels increases, the effectiveness becomes better. It is due to that those people with the same first names are usually hard connected to each other in the relevance graph, and thus are able to provide accurate guidance of graph search toward the targeted person. On the other hand, for the time efficiency in Figure 7(b), no matter what the ratio become, our GrpSteiner generally outperform the ApxSteiner. And, likewise, as the number of query keyword labels increases, more connections among those with the same keywords will make the search take more time.

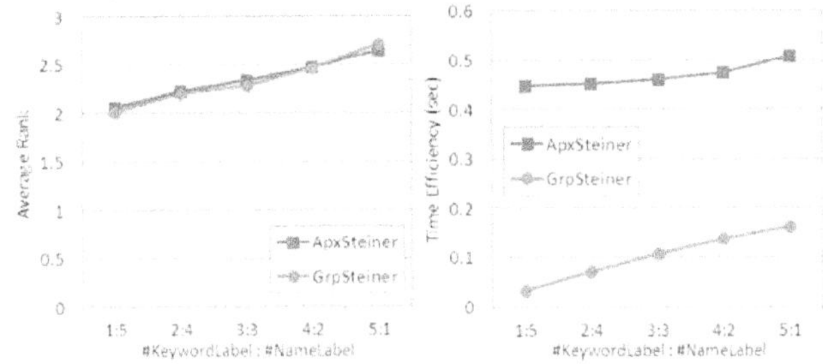

(a) (b)

Figure 7. Varying the #KeywordLabel: #FirstNameLabel ratio to show (a) the average ranks. (b) the time efficiency.

6. RELATED WORKS

Existing work on social search originates from the IR field, and they focus on optimizing Web search using social content such as voting, tagging and bookmarking [2][12]. Since social annotations provided by the public are usually good summaries for web pages, some ranking methods, such as *SocialPageRank* [2] and *HubRank* [3], have been proposed to enhance the search quality. In addition, some works [1][4][9][10][11] categorize the annotations into diverse types of entities and exploit the relationships among these heterogeneous sources to perform multifaceted entity search. However, they neglect the underlying social network among the users. On the other hand, few works [5][7][8] describe social search methods to find individuals by considering the social relationships among people. Vieira et al. [8] modify the shortest path among individuals as a ranking function to recommend relevant friends for a single user. Their method cannot be used to perform people search based on querying users or other labels. Though Schendel et al. [7] retrieve relevant items satisfying a given set of user-given query tags in a social tagging network, the communication cost among these individuals is ignored, so their method cannot be applied to our context-based people search.

7. CONCLUSION

In this paper, we propose and formally define the problem of context-based people search in a labeled social network. Given a labeled social network and a set of query labels consists of a targeted label and other context labels, we aim to return a ranking list of persons who possess the targeted label and connects to other context labels with minimum communication costs through certain effective subgraph. Considering the namesake challenge, we propose to leverage context information with the potential interactions between the targeted person and such context labels to tackle the people search in a social network. Experiments on the DBLP bibliography data demonstrate the excellent quality of our found ranked results and take significantly less execution time comparing to a greedy approximation algorithm.

REFERENCES

[1] E. Amitay, D. Carmel, N. Har'El, S. Ofek-Koifman, A. Soffer, S. Yogev, and N. Golbandi. Social Search and Discovery Using a Unified Approach. *ACM HT 2009*, 199–208, 2009.

[2] S. Bao, G. Xue, X. Wu, Y. Yu, B. Fei, and Z. Su. Optimizing Web Search Using Social Annotations. *WWW 2007*, 501–510.

[3] K. Chakrabarti, V. Ganti, J. Han, and D. Xin. Ranking Objects Based on Relationships. *SIGMOD 2006*, 371–382.

[4] J. Davitz, J. Yu, S. Basu, D. Gutelius, and A. Harris. iLink: Search and Routing in Social Networks. *KDD 2007*, 931–940.

[5] J. Kleinberg. Social Networks, Incentives, and Search. *SIGIR 2006*, 210–211.

[6] T. Lappas, K. Liu, and E. Terzi. Finding a Team of Experts in Social Networks. *KDD 2009*, 467–475.

[7] R. Schenkel, T. Crecelius, M. Kacimi, S. Michel, T. Neumann, J. X. Parreira, and G. Weikum. Efficient Top-k Querying over Social-Tagging Networks. *SIGIR 2008*, 523–530.

[8] M. V. Vieira, B. M. Fonseca, R. Damazio, P. B. Golgher, D. D. C. Reis, and B. Ribeiro-Neto. Efficient Search Ranking in Social Networks. *CIKM 2007*, 563–572.

[9] X. Wang, J. T. Sun, and Z. Chen. SHINE: Search Heterogeneous Interrelated Entities. *CIKM 2007*, 583–292.

[10] X. Wang, J. T. Sun, Z. Chen, and C. Zhai. Latent Semantic Analysis for Multiple-type Interrelated Data Objects. *SIGIR 2006*, 236–243.

[11] W. Xi, E. A. Fox, W. Fan, B. Zhang, Z. Chen, J. Yan, and D. Zhuang. SimFusion: Measuring Similarity Using Unified Relationship Matrix. *SIGIR 2005*, 130–137.

[12] Y. Yanbe, A. Jatowt, S. Nakamura, and K. Tanaka. Can Social Bookmarking Enhance Search in the Web? *JCDL 2007*, 107–116.

[13] Wink People Search. http://wink.com/

[14] Intelius People Search. http://search.intelius.com/

On Benchmarking Data Translation Systems for Semantic-Web Ontologies*

Carlos R. Rivero, Inma Hernández, David Ruiz, Rafael Corchuelo
University of Sevilla, Spain
{carlosrivero, inmahernandez, druiz, corchu}@us.es

ABSTRACT

Data translation, also known as data exchange, is an integration task that aims at populating a target model using data from a source model. This task is gaining importance in the context of semantic-web ontologies due to the increasing interest in graph databases and semantic-web agents. Currently, there are a variety of semantic-web technologies that can be used to implement data translation systems. This makes it difficult to assess them from an empirical point of view. In this paper, we present a benchmark that provides a catalogue of seven data translation patterns that can be instantiated by means of seven parameters. This allows us to create a variety of synthetic, domain-independent scenarios one can use to test existing data translation systems. We also illustrate how to analyse three such systems using our benchmark. The main benefit of our benchmark is that it allows to compare data translation systems side by side within a homogeneous framework.

Categories and Subject Descriptors

H.2.5 [**Information Systems**]: Heterogeneous Databases

General Terms

Performance

Keywords

Data exchange, Semantic Web and ontologies

---

*Supported by the European Commission (FEDER), the Spanish and the Andalusian R&D&I programmes (grants TIN2007-64119, P07-TIC-2602, P08-TIC-4100, TIN2008-04718-E, TIN2010-21744, TIN2010-09809-E, TIN2010-10811-E, and TIN2010-09988-E).
A technical report and an implementation regarding this paper are available at:
`http://tdg-seville.info/carlosrivero/DTSBench`

1. INTRODUCTION

The most widespread data models in current databases are relational and nested relational, which include relational and semi-structured schemata [3]. However, there is an steady shift towards modelling data by means of semantic-web ontologies [15], which build on the RDF, RDF Schema and OWL ontology languages for modelling structure and data, and the SPARQL query language to query these data [2].

Existing databases comprise a variety of heterogeneous models, created by different organisations for different purposes, and there is a need to integrate them [3, 12]. In the bibliography, there exist various data integration tasks. Data translation, also known as data exchange, is one of these tasks that aims at populating a target model using data of a source model [6, 7, 13].

Our focus in this paper is on data translation systems using semantic-web ontologies that build on standard query engines, i.e., systems that perform the data translation task by executing a number of queries that extract data from the source model, transform them, and load the result into the target model [3, 10, 12].

Currently, there exists a variety of semantic-web technologies that are suitable to implement the data translation task, e.g., Jena, TDB, Oracle, or Pellet to mention a few. This makes it difficult to assess them from an empirical point of view. It is important to notice that some of these technologies are data translation systems by themselves, e.g., Oracle. However, other technologies need to be combined to form a data translation system, e.g., TDB needs to be combined with a reasoner like Pellet.

In the bibliography, there is a benchmark that focuses on data translation systems for nested relational models [1]; however, it cannot be straightforwardly applied to semantic-web ontologies due to a number of inherent differences with nested relational models [11, 13]. In addition, there are several benchmarks in the bibliography to test semantic-web technologies, namely: [14] focuses on evaluating the performance of SPARQL engines; [5] focuses on both loading ontologies and executing SPARQL queries; [16] focuses on the performance of the Oracle reasoner; LUBM [9] takes into account loading ontologies, executing SPARQL queries, and reasoning. Unfortunately, none of these benchmarks focuses on data translation problems, i.e., they do not provide source and target ontologies, and a number of queries to perform the data translation task.

In this paper, we present a benchmark for testing data translation systems that provides a catalogue of seven data translation patterns. These patterns are common integration problems that occur frequently in practice. Note that this catalogue is not meant to be exhaustive: the patterns described in this paper are based on our experience regarding information integration, and they are the starting point to a community effort on extending them. Furthermore, we provide seven parameters to build synthetic scenarios, which are instantiations of the data translation patterns.

The expected benefit of our benchmark is that it provides a homogeneous framework that allows to compare data translation systems in the context of semantic-web ontologies side by side, thus alleviating the decision of software engineers on adopting a specific data translation system to solve particular integration problems. As far as we know, this is the first benchmark in the bibliography to test such systems. Finally, we illustrate how to analyse three data translation systems using our benchmark and we draw a number of conclusions from this experimental analysis.

This paper is organised as follows: Section 2 presents the data translation task. Section 3 describes our catalogue of data translation patterns. In Section 4, we present the input and output of our benchmark. In Section 5, we evaluate a number of data translation systems using our benchmark. Section 6 presents the related work. And, finally, Section 7 recaps on our main conclusions.

2. THE DATA TRANSLATION TASK

The data translation task between OWL ontologies comprises five steps when it is performed by means of SPARQL queries (cf. Figure 1), namely:

1. Loading: This step consists of loading the source and target ontologies and the set of SPARQL queries from files into appropriate internal models of semantic-web technologies.

2. Reasoning over source: This step is optional and deals with making the knowledge explicit over the source ontology. Note that SPARQL only deals with plain RDF and does not implement RDFS/OWL semantics, therefore, this step may be mandatory in some integration problems.

3. Query executing: This step consists of executing the set of SPARQL queries over the source ontology to produce instances of the target ontology. Note that this step may be performed by every SPARQL query engine, and the result is the same regardless the execution order of queries.

4. Reasoning over target: This step is also optional and it deals with making the knowledge explicit over the target ontology.

5. Unloading: This final step deals with saving the target ontology into a file.

3. DATA TRANSLATION PATTERNS

A data translation pattern represents a common and relevant integration problem that should be supported by every data translation system. Furthermore, each pattern represents an intention of change as occurs in the ontology evolution context, i.e., when an ontology changes in response to a certain need [8].

Data translation patterns may be instantiated into a number of scenarios, each of which is a three element tuple (S, T, Q), in which S is the source ontology, T is the target ontology, and Q is a set of SPARQL queries to perform the data translation task.

Our benchmark provides a catalogue of seven data translation patterns that usually occur in the context of information integration. To devise them, we have leveraged our experience on real-world information integration problems regarding digital libraries (SwetoDBLP and OAEI's 101), semantic web services (OWL-S and MSM), film reviews (DBpedia and Revyu), and ontology evolution (DBpedia 3.2 and DBpedia 3.6). Without an exception, the data translation patterns described in this section occur frequently in these problems.

Below, we present our data translation patterns, which are illustrated in Figure 2. The source ontology is on the left side and the target on the right side; the arrows represent correspondences between entities of both source and target ontologies. Keep in mind that these correspondences are only visual aids to help readers understand the intention of change behind each scenario [4]. In this notation, classes, data properties and object properties are represented as circles, squares and pentagons, respectively. In addition, subclasses are represented between brackets, the domain of a property is represented by nesting the property in a class, and the range is represented between '<' and '>'. Note that *src:* and *tgt:* prefixes are used for the source and target ontologies, respectively. Note also that we omit SPARQL queries due to space limitations.

Lift Properties: The intention of change is that the user wishes to extract common properties to a superclass in a hierarchy. Therefore, the data properties of a set of subclasses are moved to a common superclass. In the example, *src:name* and *src:birth* data properties are lifted to *tgt:name* and *tgt:birth*, respectively.

Sink Properties: The intention of change is that the user wishes to narrow the domain of a number of properties. Therefore, the data properties of a superclass are moved to a number of subclasses. In the example, *src:name* and *src:birth* data properties are sunk to *tgt:name* and *tgt:birth*, respectively.

Extract Subclasses: The intention of change is that the user wishes to specialise a class. Therefore, a class is split into several subclasses and data properties are distributed amongst them. In the example, every instance of *src:Person* is transformed into an instance of *tgt:Person*. Note that, after performing the data translation task in this example, all target instances are of type *tgt:Person*. However, if the knowledge is made explicit, every instance of *tgt:Person* with a data property instance of *tgt:paper* is also an instance of type *tgt:Author*.

Extract Superclasses: The intention of change is that the user wishes to generalise a class. So, a class is split into several superclasses, and data properties are distributed amongst them. Note that, after performing the data translation task in this example, all target instances are of type *tgt:Author*, which are implicitly instances of *tgt:Person* too.

Extract Related Classes: The intention of change is that the user wishes to extract a number of classes based on a single class. Therefore, the data properties of a class are split into a number of new classes, which are related to the original one by a number of object properties. In the example, the source class *src:Paper* is split into two target classes

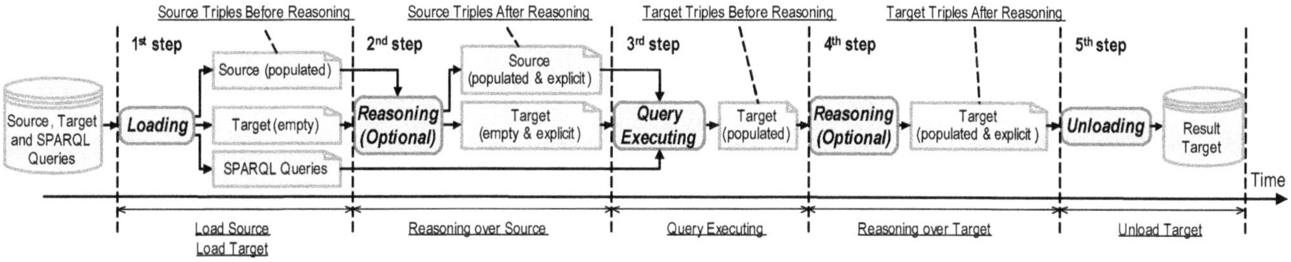

Figure 1: Steps of the data translation task

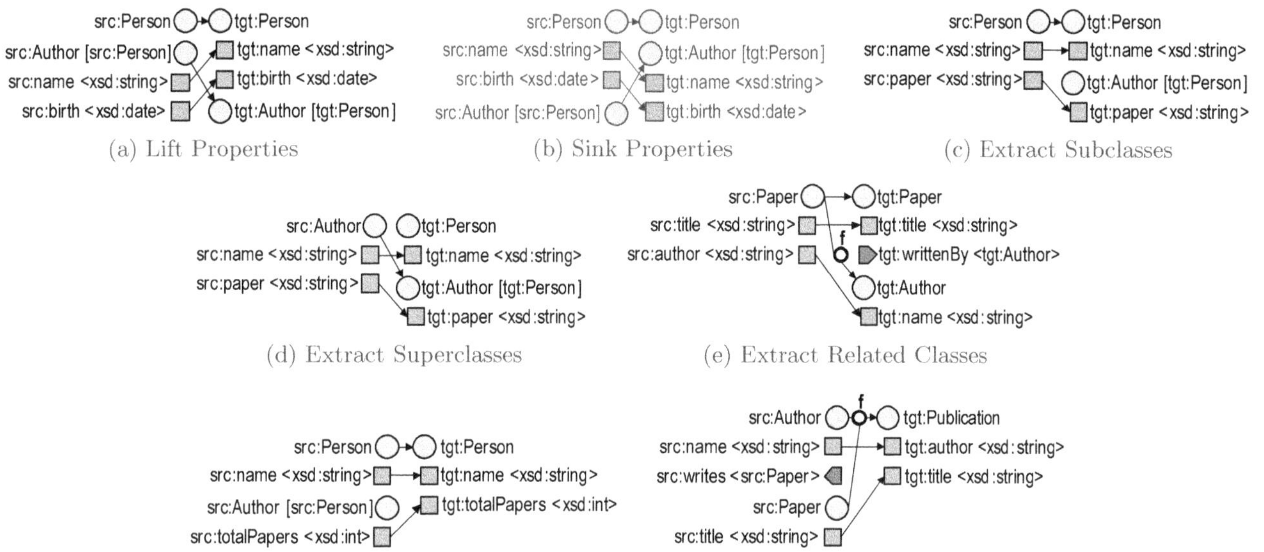

(a) Lift Properties (b) Sink Properties (c) Extract Subclasses

(d) Extract Superclasses (e) Extract Related Classes

(f) Simplify Specialisation (g) Simplify Related Classes

Figure 2: Data translation patterns of our benchmark

called *tgt:Paper* and *tgt:Author* that are related by object property *tgt:writtenBy*. Note that instances of *tgt:Author* are generated by means of function f over the instances of *src:Paper*.

Simplify Specialisation: The intention of change is that the user wishes to remove a hierarchy of classes. So, a set of specialised classes are flattened into a single class. In the example, *src:Person* and *src:Author*, which is an specialisation of *src:Person*, are simplified into *tgt:Person*.

Simplify Related Classes: The intention of change is that the user wishes to join a set of classes that are related by object properties. Therefore, several source classes, which are related by a number of object properties, are transformed into one class that aggregates them. In the example, for every instance of *src:Author* and *src:Paper* related by *src:writes*, a new instance of *tgt:Publication* is generated.

4. THE BENCHMARK

A benchmark, amongst other properties, should be scalable and the results that it produces should be deterministic and reproducible. To fulfill these properties, we introduce a number of parameters to control the automatic instantiation of our data translation patterns. Furthermore, we describe the measures that we are able to compute.

4.1 Input

Our benchmark takes a number of input parameters that allow to tune both structure and data of source and/or target ontologies. Note that, thanks to these parameters, our benchmark generates synthetic ontologies in both structure and data, which are domain-independent. Note also that the structure of ontologies we generate are trees, each of which comprises, at least, a single root class.

Structure parameters are used to tune the structure of these ontologies, which are the following:

- Levels of classes (L): number of relationships (specialisations or object properties) from the root to each leaf in the source or target ontologies, $L \in \mathbb{N}$.
- Number of related classes (C): number of classes related to each class by specialisation or object properties, $C \in \mathbb{N}$.
- Number of data properties (D): the total number of data properties of the source and target ontologies, $D \in \mathbb{N}$.

Consequently, L allows to scale the structure of ontologies in depth, C in width, and D allows to scale the number of data properties for a particular scenario. L and C may be applied over both source and target ontologies, which is the case of the Lift Properties and Sink Properties patterns; over the target ontology only, i.e., the Extract Subclasses, Extract Superclasses and Extract Related Classes patterns; or over the source ontology only, i.e., the Simplify Specialisation and Simplify Related Classes patterns. Note that structure parameters also affect the SPARQL queries generated by our benchmark, since they vary depending on the structure of the source and target ontologies. Note also that the total number of classes an ontology comprises is computed by the following formula:

$$\sum_{i=0}^{L} C^i.$$

Regarding data parameters, they are used to tune the instances of the source ontology. Note that the goal of the data translation task is to populate the target ontology; therefore, these parameters are only applied to the source ontology since the target ontology remains unpopulated. Data parameters are the following:

- Number of individuals (I): number of individuals (instances of *owl:Thing*) that the populated ontology contains, $I \in \mathbb{N} \backslash \{0\}$.
- Number of types (I_T): number of types that each individual has, $I_T \in \mathbb{N}$.
- Number of data properties (I_D): number of data property instances that a given individual has as domain, $I_D \in \mathbb{N}$.
- Number of object properties (I_O): number of object property instances that a given individual has as domain, $I_O \in \mathbb{N}$.

Note that we may compute the number of data triples that a populated ontology comprises by means of the following formula: $Triples = I + II_T + II_D + II_O$.

4.2 Output

The measures that our benchmark is able to compute are underlined in Figure 1. These measures are the following:

1) Time and memory consumed by loading and unloading ontologies: they represent the time and memory consumed by the data translation system when the source and target ontologies are loaded from files into internal representations, and when the target ontology is unloaded for this internal representation into a file. Note that data translation systems have uneven performance when loading ontologies [5, 9, 14, 16]; in this case, we are able to test if the time a system takes to load an ontology depends only on the number of instances or also on its structure.

2) Time and memory consumed by reasoning over source and/or target ontologies: these measures represent the time and memory consumed by the data translation system when making the knowledge explicit over source and/or target ontologies. In this case, we are able to test if the reasoning time of a data translation system depends on the number of triples and/or the structure of the ontology.

3) Number of triples before and after reasoning: when making the knowledge explicit, there is usually an increment of triples. These measures compute the triples of the ontologies before and after reasoning; in this case, the number of generated triples tests the expressivity of a system.

4) Time and memory consumed by query executing: they represent the time and memory consumed by the data translation system when executing the set of SPARQL queries over the source ontology to generate target data. In this case, we are able to test how the number of triples of the source ontology have influence over the execution time. Furthermore, the structure of the ontology has also influence over this time since a complex ontology structure entails a large number of triple patterns in the SPARQL queries.

5. EVALUATION

In this section, we evaluate three data translation systems based on our benchmark, which are the following: System 1 comprises Jena and Pellet, System 2 is formed by TDB and Oracle, and System 3 comprises TDB and Pellet. Jena and TDB are used to load/unload ontologies and to execute SPARQL queries. In these technologies, ontologies and queries are stored and executed in main memory and the file system, respectively. Furthermore, Pellet and Oracle perform reasoning in main memory and a database schema, respectively.

In the following, we use three tests over the previous data translation systems and we describe evidences that arise from the analysis of the results. In this evaluation, we executed the experiments on a machine with a four core Intel Xeon 3.00 GHz CPU and 16 GB RAM, running on Windows Server 2008 (64-bits) and JRE 1.6.0. The execution times on which we report are the result of averaging 25 actual executions, leaving out outliers on both the left and right 5% tails of the distributions.

The first test evaluates the performance of data translation systems when scaling the structure of the source and/or target ontologies in depth. Therefore, in this test, we fix all structure and data parameters except L, which ranges from 1 to 25 by 1. The rest of parameters are as follows: $\{C = 1, D = 25, I = 2500, I_T = 5, I_D = 5, I_O = 5\}$.

The second test evaluates the performance of these systems when scaling the structure in width; so the parameters are equal to the previous test except C, which ranges from 1 to 25 by 1, and $L = 1$. Finally, the third test evaluates the performance of these systems when scaling the data of ontologies. In this case, the parameters are fixed as in the previous tests, except $\{L = 1, C = 1\}$ and I, which ranges from 500 to $5,050$ by 175.

Note that the values of the parameters were selected to generate non-trivial ontologies. In this context, the number of triples in the ontologies of these tests ranges from $3,500$ triples to $80,000$ triples, roughly. The results after performing the tests are shown in Figures 3, 4 and 5, which present the time to perform the data translation task in the Y axis, and the varying input parameter in the X axis.

From our experimental analysis we can draw the following conclusions:

- Systems 1 and 3 perform similarly for all tested scenarios. Consequently, as long as the ontologies involved fit in memory, there does not seem to be any differences between using Jena and TDB.
- Systems 1 and 3 seem to perform linearly in both L and C.
- It seems that neither L nor C have an impact on the

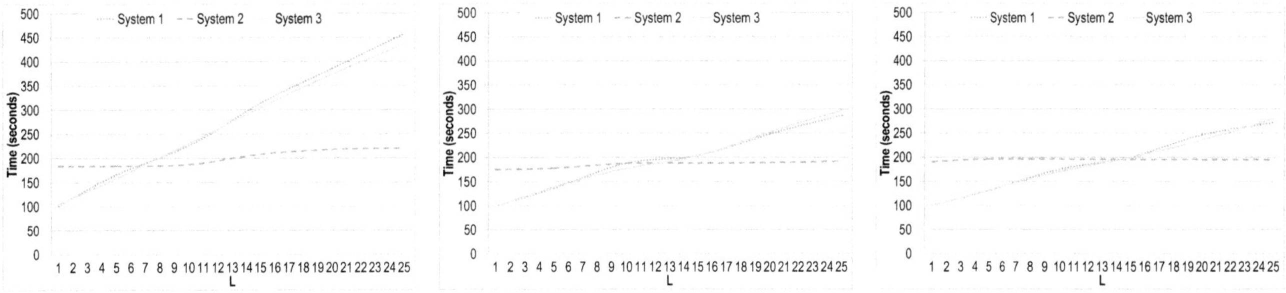

(a) Lift Properties (b) Extract Subclasses (c) Simplify Specialisation

Figure 3: Scaling in depth

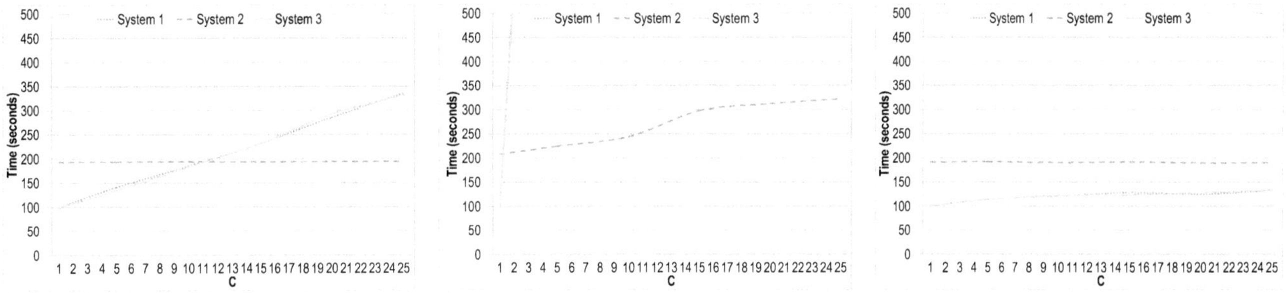

(a) Extract Superclasses (b) Extract Related Classes (c) Simplify Specialisation

Figure 4: Scaling in width

performance of System 2, which seems almost invariant to changes to these parameters.

- System 2 seems to outperform the others when L and I vary. The result is similar when C varies, the only exception is the Simplify Specialisation pattern. The reason is that Pellet outperforms Oracle when performing reasoning over these scenarios.

- Systems 1 and 3 seems to perform exponentially when I varies. Meanwhile, System 2 seems to perform linearly in this case. The reason is that TDB and Oracle are optimised to work with large sets of triples. Therefore, when these triples are increased from 8,000 to 16,000 (between $I = 1000$ and $I = 2000$), TDB and Oracle manage resources that perform linearly beyond this point.

6. RELATED WORK

In the bibliography, there exist benchmarks for data translation systems and semantic-web ontologies.

Regarding data translation benchmarks, Alexe et al. [1] devised a benchmark that is used to test data translation systems in the context of nested relational models. Unfortunately, this benchmark is not suitable in our context since semantic-web ontologies have a number of inherent differences with respect to nested relational models [11, 13].

Regarding benchmarks for semantic-web ontologies, Guo et al. [9] presented LUBM, a benchmark to compare systems that support semantic-web ontologies, which is based on the university domain. This benchmark provides a single ontology, a data generator algorithm that allows to create scalable synthetic data, and fourteen SPARQL queries of the SELECT type. Note that this benchmark is similar to our benchmark; however, it has a number of crucial differences:

- LUBM focuses on a single ontology. Contrarily, our benchmark focuses on data translation problems that comprise source and target ontologies, and a number of queries to perform the data translation task.

- LUBM provides a data generator to populate an ontology in the university context with synthetic data. On the contrary, our benchmark is domain-independent and it allows to tune the structure and data of source and target ontologies for each pattern instantiation.

- LUBM provides fourteen SPARQL queries of the SELECT type. Our benchmark provides a query generator that allows to automatically build synthetic queries to perform the data translation task. Furthermore, our SPARQL queries are of the CONSTRUCT type, which are suitable to perform this task.

Furthermore, other benchmarks for semantic-web ontologies[1] focus on analysing the performance of the steps of the data translation task in isolation, and they cannot be used to test the data translation task as a whole.

Wu et al. [16] presented the experience of the authors when implementing an inference engine for Oracle. This engine implements the RDFS and OWL entailments, i.e., it performs reasoning over RDFS and OWL ontologies. Furthermore, they presented a performance study based on two examples: LUBM, which data range from 6.7 to 133.7 million triples, and UniProt, which comprises 5 million triples.

[1] http://esw.w3.org/RdfStoreBenchmarking

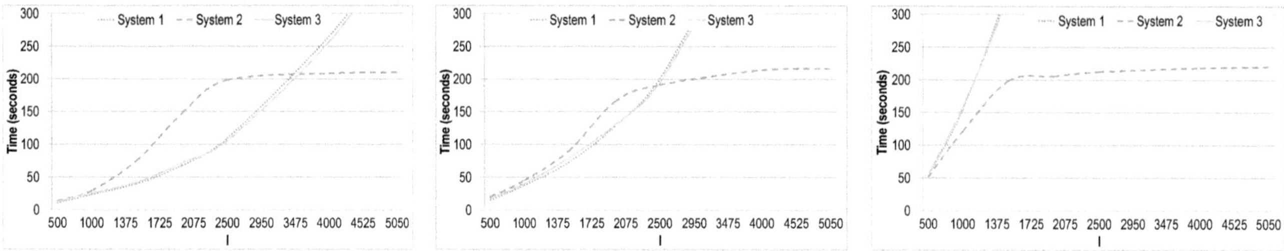

(a) Sink Properties (b) Extract Related Classes (c) Simplify Related Classes

Figure 5: Data scaling

Bizer and Schultz [5] presented BSBM, a benchmark to compare the performance of SPARQL queries using native RDF stores and SPARQL-to-SQL query rewriters. Their benchmark focuses on an e-commerce use case, and they provide a data generator and a test driver: the former allows to create large datasets and it offers RDF and relational outputs to compare the approaches; the latter emulates a realistic workload by simulating multiple clients that concurrently execute queries. The benchmark consists of twelve SPARQL queries that are divided in ten SELECT queries, one DESCRIBE query, and one CONSTRUCT query.

Schmidt et al. [14] presented SP^{2}Bench, a benchmark to test SPARQL query management systems, which is based on DBLP and comprises both a data generator and a set of benchmark queries in SPARQL. They study the DBLP dataset to generate a realistic set of synthetic data by measuring probability distributions for certain attributes, e.g., authors or cites in articles or papers. The benchmark comprises seventeen queries that are divided in fourteen SELECT queries and three ASK queries.

7. CONCLUSIONS

In this paper, we present a benchmark to test data translation systems in the context of semantic-web ontologies. As far as we know, this is the first benchmark in the bibliography in such a context. Existing benchmarks are not suitable to test these systems since they focus on nested relational models, which are not applicable to semantic-web ontologies due to a number of inherent differences with nested relational models; or they do not focus on data translation problems, so they do not provide source and target ontologies and a number of queries to perform this task.

Our benchmark provides a catalogue of seven data translation patterns that represent common and relevant integration problems that should be supported by every data translation system. Furthermore, our benchmark is able to instantiate these patterns based on seven parameters that allow to control the generation of both the structure and data of ontologies. In this paper, we also evaluate three data translation systems based on our benchmark.

Finally, the main benefit of this benchmark is that it provides a homogeneous framework that allows to compare empirically data translation systems side by side, thus alleviating the decision of software engineers on adopting these systems to solve integration problems.

8. REFERENCES

[1] B. Alexe, W. C. Tan, and Y. Velegrakis. STBenchmark: towards a benchmark for mapping systems. *PVLDB*, 1(1):230–244, 2008.

[2] G. Antoniou and F. van Harmelen. *A Semantic Web Primer, 2nd Edition*. The MIT Press, 2008.

[3] P. A. Bernstein and L. M. Haas. Information integration in the enterprise. *Commun. ACM*, 51(9):72–79, 2008.

[4] P. A. Bernstein and S. Melnik. Model management 2.0: manipulating richer mappings. In *SIGMOD*, pages 1–12, 2007.

[5] C. Bizer and A. Schultz. The Berlin SPARQL benchmark. *Int. J. Semantic Web Inf. Syst.*, 2009.

[6] C. Drumm, M. Schmitt, H. H. Do, and E. Rahm. Quickmig: automatic schema matching for data migration projects. In *CIKM*, pages 107–116, 2007.

[7] R. Fagin, P. G. Kolaitis, R. J. Miller, and L. Popa. Data exchange: semantics and query answering. *Theor. Comput. Sci.*, 336(1):89–124, 2005.

[8] G. Flouris, D. Manakanatas, H. Kondylakis, D. Plexousakis, and G. Antoniou. Ontology change: classification and survey. *Knowledge Eng. Review*, 23(2):117–152, 2008.

[9] Y. Guo, Z. Pan, and J. Heflin. LUBM: A benchmark for OWL knowledge base systems. *J. Web Sem.*, 3(2-3):158–182, 2005.

[10] L. M. Haas, M. A. Hernández, H. Ho, L. Popa, and M. Roth. Clio grows up: from research prototype to industrial tool. In *SIGMOD*, pages 805–810, 2005.

[11] B. Motik, I. Horrocks, and U. Sattler. Bridging the gap between OWL and relational databases. *J. Web Sem.*, 7(2):74–89, 2009.

[12] L. Popa, Y. Velegrakis, R. J. Miller, M. A. Hernández, and R. Fagin. Translating web data. In *VLDB*, pages 598–609, 2002.

[13] C. R. Rivero, I. Hernández, D. Ruiz, and R. Corchuelo. Generating SPARQL executable mappings to integrate ontologies. In *ER*, 2011.

[14] M. Schmidt, T. Hornung, G. Lausen, and C. Pinkel. SP^{2}Bench: A SPARQL performance benchmark. In *ICDE*, pages 222–233, 2009.

[15] N. Shadbolt, T. Berners-Lee, and W. Hall. The semantic web revisited. *IEEE Intelligent Systems*, 21(3):96–101, 2006.

[16] Z. Wu, G. Eadon, S. Das, E. I. Chong, V. Kolovski, J. Srinivasan, and M. Annamalai. Implementing an inference engine for RDFS/OWL constructs and user-defined rules in oracle. In *ICDE*, pages 1239–1248, 2008.

I/O-Efficient Algorithms for Answering Pattern-Based Aggregate Queries in a Sequence OLAP System

Chun Kit Chui, Ben Kao
Department of Computer Science,
The University of Hong Kong
{ckchui, kao}@cs.hku.hk

Eric Lo
Department of Computing,
The Hong Kong Polytechnic University
ericlo@comp.polyu.edu.hk

Reynold Cheng
Department of Computer Science,
The University of Hong Kong
ckcheng@cs.hku.hk

ABSTRACT

Many kinds of real-life data exhibit logical ordering among their data items and are thus sequential in nature. In recent years, the concept of *Sequence OLAP* (S-OLAP) has been proposed. The biggest distinguishing feature of S-OLAP from traditional OLAP is that data sequences managed by an S-OLAP system are characterized by the subsequence/substring patterns they possess. An S-OLAP system thus supports *pattern-based* grouping and aggregation. Conceptually, an S-OLAP system maintains a *sequence data cube* which is composed of *sequence cuboids*. Each sequence cuboid presents the answer of a pattern-based aggregate (PBA) query. This paper focuses on the I/O aspects of evaluating PBA queries. We study the problems of *joining plan selection* and *execution planning*, which are the core issues in the design of I/O-efficient cuboid materialization algorithms. Through an empirical study, we show that our algorithms lead to a very I/O-efficient strategy for sequence cuboid materialization.

Categories and Subject Descriptors: H.2.0 [Database Management]: General

General Terms: Design

1 Introduction

Sequence data is ubiquitous. Examples include workflow data, data streams and RFID logs. Techniques for processing various kinds of sequence data have been studied extensively in the literature (e.g., [13, 14, 11, 1, 2, 15]). Recently, issues related to warehousing and online analytical processing (OLAP) of archived sequence data (e.g., stock ticks archive, passenger traveling histories) have received growing attentions [6, 5, 10]. In particular, [10] developed a sequence OLAP system (called S-OLAP) that efficiently supports various kinds of pattern-based aggregate queries.

While traditional OLAP systems group data tuples based on their *attribute values*, an S-OLAP system groups sequences based on the *patterns* they possess. Common aggregate functions such as `COUNT/SUM/AVG` can then be applied to each group. The resulting aggregate values form the cells of a so-called sequence data cuboid, or *s-cuboid*.

Since an s-cuboid displays the aggregate values of sequences that are grouped by the patterns they possess, one can view an s-cuboid as the answer to a *pattern-based aggregate (PBA) query*. To illustrate PBA queries and s-cuboids, let us consider the sequence data set shown in Figure 1. The dataset models a collection of passenger traveling records registered by the Washington DC's metro system. The records are captured electronically by *SmarTrip*, which is an RFID-card-based stored-value e-payment system. Each row in Figure 1 shows a sequence of passenger events. An event consists of a number of attributes, such as *Time*, *Station*, *Action* and *Amount*. For example, the event [t_9; Wheaton; exit; 1.9] of passenger 623 indicates that the passenger exited Wheaton Station at time t_9 and paid \$1.9 dollars for his trip.

Figure 2 shows a PBA query "(X, Y, Y, X), `COUNT`" and a few cells of the resulting s-cuboid. A PBA query "T, F" consists of two components: A pattern template T (e.g., (X, Y, Y, X)) and an aggregate function F (e.g., `COUNT`). A pattern template is a sequence of pattern symbols (e.g., X, Y) defined over an attribute $\mathcal{A}$ of event records. The pattern symbols are instantiated by the values of $\mathcal{A}$ to generate various *patterns*. Data sequences are grouped based on the patterns. Finally, the function F is applied to each sequence group to derive aggregate values.

For example, the pattern template (X, Y, Y, X) defined on the *Station* attribute specifies that passenger sequences are grouped together if they have traveled round-trip between stations X and Y (i.e., he first entered station X and exited station Y in his first trip, and then entered station Y and come back to station X in the next). The symbols X and Y are instantiated with various station names to form patterns, such as (Clarendon, Pentagon, Pentagon, Clarendon). Data sequences that possess a given pattern are grouped into a cell[1]. Each data sequence gives a value (or *measure*) to be aggregated. For example, a passenger sequence could be associated with the amount of fare paid, or simply '1' if we only care about the cardinality of a cell. The aggregate function F is then applied to the values of the sequences of each cell to obtain an aggregate value of the cell. In this paper, if P represents a pattern (e.g., (Clarendon, Pentagon, Pentagon, Clarendon)), we use $C(P)$ to denote the cell of pattern P (i.e., $C(P)$ = the set of sequences containing pattern P), and we use $F(C(P))$ to denote the aggregate value of the cell. An s-cuboid consists of all the aggregate

CIKM'11, October 24–28, 2011, Glasgow, Scotland, UK.

[1] A data sequence may contain more than one pattern. A sequence can, therefore, belong to multiple cells.

values of the cells derived from all possible instantiations of the pattern template. For example, Figure 2 shows that there are 16,289 sequences that possess the pattern (Clarendon, Pentagon, Pentagon, Clarendon). In our notation: $\texttt{COUNT}(C((\text{Clarendon, Pentagon, Pentagon, Clarendon}))) = 16{,}289$. Given a PBA query (e.g., "(X, Y, Y, X), COUNT"), our goal is to evaluate the query by computing all the cells of the corresponding s-cuboid (e.g., all the cells and their COUNTs listed in Figure 2).

In [10], a basic implementation of an S-OLAP system is presented. In that study, data sequences were indexed by inverted lists. Given a pattern P, its inverted list $L[P]$ is a list of sequence id's such that each sequence s listed in $L[P]$ contains the pattern P. An s-cuboid cell $C(P)$ can thus be represented by the inverted list $L[P]$. The inverted list of a pattern can be obtained by *joining* the lists of its sub-patterns. This process allows PBA queries to be evaluated efficiently. For example, consider the query pattern template (X, Y, Z, X). To materialize an s-cuboid cell, say, $C((a, b, c, a))$, one can intersect (or "join") the inverted lists $L[(a, b, c)]$ and $L[(c, a)]$ (if these lists are available). This is because a sequence that contains the pattern (a, b, c, a) must contain the sub-patterns (a, b, c) and (c, a). (We will present the details of this list-joining procedure in Section 3.)

For large sequence databases, the inverted lists are long and should be stored on external storages. The I/O cost of retrieving the inverted lists for computing an s-cuboid is a dominating factor in PBA query processing. The objective of this paper is to study the I/O issues in evaluating PBA queries and to propose I/O-efficient query processing algorithms. We identify the following two I/O issues.

First, in [10], a *static* joining plan is used for computing an inverted list. More specifically, given a pattern P, the inverted list $L[P]$ is always materialized by joining $L[P_1]$ and $L[P_2]$, where P_1 and P_2 are the length-($|P|$-1) prefix and length-2 suffix of P, respectively. For example, we always compute $J_1 : L[(a, b, c)] \bowtie L[(c, a)]$ to obtain $L[(a, b, c, a)]$. We observe that multiple joining plans are usually available for materializing an inverted list. For example, to compute $L[(c, a, b, c)]$, we can do either $J_2 : L[(c, a, b)] \bowtie L[(b, c)]$ or $J_3 : L[(c, a)] \bowtie L[(a, b, c)]$. Note that the advantage of the latter plan, J_3, is that it shares the same joining lists with J_1. Hence, when evaluating a PBA query with the pattern template (X, Y, Z, X), only two joining lists (namely, $L[(a, b, c)]$ and $L[(c, a)]$) are retrieved to materialize the inverted lists that correspond to the two cells $C((a, b, c, a))$ and $C((c, a, b, c))$. On the other hand, if J_2 were picked over J_3, four joining lists are retrieved, doubling the I/O cost. In this paper, we show that the choice of joining plans has big impacts on the I/O cost of query processing. We study the *Joining Plan Selection Problem* (JPS) — given a pattern template T and the set of all instantiated patterns $\mathcal{I}$ of T, which joining plans shall be picked to materialize the inverted lists of the patterns in $\mathcal{I}$? As we will see in Section 4, the JPS problem is NP-hard. We propose an effective heuristic algorithm, GPS, for solving the JPS problem. We will show that GPS is comparable to the best approximation algorithm, LP, in terms of minimizing the I/O cost while at the same time GPS executes about 5 times faster than LP.

Second, we observe that the order in which cuboid cells are materialized significantly affects the size of the memory buffer required in query processing. For example, consider the two joining plans J_1 and J_3 for materializing the cells $C((a, b, c, a))$ and $C((c, a, b, c))$, respectively. These two

Pid	*Event Sequence*
...	...
28	⟨ [t_4;Clarendon;enter;0], [t_7;Pentagon;exit;1.9], [t_9;Pentagon;enter;0], [t_{10};Clarendon;exit;1.9] ⟩
...	...
623	⟨ [t_1;Pentagon;enter;0], [t_9;Wheaton;exit;1.9] ⟩
...	...

Figure 1: A sequence data set $\mathcal{D}$

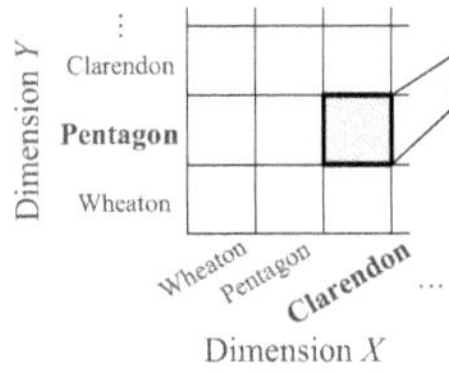

(X, Y, Y, X)	COUNT
(Clarendon, Pentagon, Pentagon, Clarendon)	16,289
(Clarendon, Wheaton, Wheaton, Clarendon)	2,654
...	...
(Rockville, TwinBrook, TwinBrook, Rockville)	5
...	...
(Pentagon, Wheaton, Wheaton, Pentagon)	6,543

Figure 2: A PBA query and its s-cuboid

plans use the same joining lists $L[(a, b, c)]$ and $L[(c, a)]$. If J_1 is executed first, then J_3 should be executed soon after, before the required joining lists get swapped out of the memory buffer. We study the *Execution Planning Problem* (EP) — given a set of joining plans, how shall we order the execution of the plans so that even a small memory buffer is enough to avoid repeated retrievals of joining lists? We propose the REP scheduling algorithm, which generates execution orders that result in a very small memory buffer requirement.

The rest of the paper is organized as follows. Section 2 discusses some related works. Section 3 reviews the basic algorithm for evaluating PBA queries using inverted indices on data sequences. Section 4 discusses the JPS problem and presents the GPS algorithm for selecting low-cost joining plans. Section 5 discusses the EP problem and presents the REP scheduling algorithm. Section 6 evaluates the performance of the algorithms through an experimental study. Finally, Section 7 concludes this paper.

2 Related Work

Sequence data processing has been studied extensively in the literature. The PREDATOR system [13] was first proposed to store and query sequence data based on the object-relational model. The DEVise system [11] addressed sequence data processing based on the relational model. To query sequence data, [12] developed an extension to SQL, called SQL-TS, to express various kinds of pattern-based queries. Beyond native sequence data processing, recently, the processing of live stream data (e.g., [1, 2, 4, 16]) and the online analytical processing (OLAP) of RFID workflow data [6, 5] have attracted a lot of attention. Nonetheless, none of these works address the problem of pattern-based grouping and analysis.

The concept of Sequence OLAP was first introduced in [10]. The paper presented an S-OLAP architecture, a formulation of PBA queries, and the idea of s-cuboids as answers to PBA queries. It also put forward six S-OLAP operations, which transform an s-cuboid to another by manipulating the pattern template of a PBA query. For example, the APPEND operation extends a pattern template (e.g., (X, Y, Y, X)) by adding a pattern symbol at the end of the template (e.g., (X, Y, Y, X, Z)). These S-OLAP operations allow an analyst to incrementally modify his PBA query, exploring a sequence data cube in a manner that is similar to the application of traditional OLAP operations such as *rollup* and *drill-down*.

The query model proposed in [10] has served as a foundation to other Sequence OLAP research. For example, variants of the PBA query model, such as iceberg and top-k queries [3], have been proposed. In [3], pruning algorithms that avoid the processing of non-top-k cells are studied. We remark that the I/O-efficient algorithms we propose in this paper are also applicable to those query model variants.

Another piece of work on pattern-based sequence analysis is given in [9]. Given a set of standing patterns and an event data stream, the objective is to determine the occurrences of the standing patterns in the data stream. An aggregate function is then applied to those occurrences to obtain summary statistics of the patterns. In [9], an interesting algorithm CHASE is proposed which intelligently exploits the similarity of the standing patterns so that the processing of these patterns can be efficiently done.

3 Evaluating PBA queries with inverted indices

In this section we describe the inverted index structure and the basic s-cuboid materialization algorithm (BASIC) using inverted indices. The BASIC algorithm is based on the inverted lists proposed in [10] except that we add positional information into the lists to facilitate join result verification. (We will elaborate on this verification process shortly.) For reference, symbols that are frequently used in our discussion are shown in Table 1.

T	A pattern template.
m	Length of T.
P	A pattern.
I^T	An inverted index for template T.
$L[P]$	An inverted list of pattern P.
L_{MAT}	The set of all materialized inverted lists.
$\Phi(I^T)$	A set of selected joining plans for materializing I^T.
$\mathcal{L}$	The set of joining lists used in the selected joining plans for materializing I^T.
$cost(\Phi(I^T))$	Total number of disk blocks occupied by the joining lists in $\Phi(I^T)$.
$\mathcal{L}_{buf}$	The set of inverted lists cached in memory buffer.

Table 1: Frequently used symbols

An inverted index consists of a set of inverted lists. An inverted list, $L[P]$, is associated with a length-m pattern P = $(v_1, \ldots, v_m)$. Each element (v_i) in pattern P is a value chosen from the domain of an event attribute. The inverted list $L[P]$ is a list of *postings* which record the occurrences of P in the sequence dataset. Each posting is of the form (s_i: $p_1, \ldots, p_{f_i}$), where s_i is a sequence identifier, f_i is the number of occurrences of P in s_i, and $p_1, \ldots, p_{f_i}$ are the starting positions at which pattern P occurs in s_i. Given a pattern template T, the inverted index I^T is the set of inverted lists $L[P]$ such that pattern P is an instantiation of the template T. Figure 3 shows three example inverted indices: $I^{(X,Y,Y)}$, $I^{(Y,X)}$ and $I^{(X,X)}$. For instance, the first inverted list l_1 in $I^{(X,Y,Y)}$ indicates that sequences $s2$, $s27$ and $s34$ all contain the pattern (Clarendon, Pentagon, Pentagon)[2]. The first posting ($s2$:1,4) indicates that there are two occurrences of the pattern in sequence $s2$ at positions [1..3] and [4..6].

[2]Symbols in a pattern template are unbound variables. So, the inverted indices $I^{(X,Y)}$ and $I^{(Z,U)}$ are the same. Multiple occurrences of the same variable in a template, however, have the same binding. So, $I^{(X,X)}$ and $I^{(X,Y)}$ are different.

$I^{(X,Y,Y)}$
l_1: L[(Clarendon, Pentagon, Pentagon)] = {(s2:1,4), (s27:3), (s34:1)}
⋮
l_3: L[(Pentagon, Rockville, Rockville)] = {(s4:5,8)}
l_4: L[(Pentagon, Suitland, Suitland)] = {(s15:3)}
⋮
l_5: L[(Wheaton, Pentagon, Pentagon)] = {(s23:7), (s26:1,4,12,16)}

$I^{(Y,X)}$
l_6: L[(Clarendon, Pentagon)] = {(s2:1,4), (s27:1,3,19), (s34:1)}
⋮
l_7: L[(Pentagon, Glenmont)] = {(s16:2,7,9), (s25:6), (s18:6,12)}
l_8: L[(Pentagon, Clarendon)] = {(s1:1,3), (s27:5), (s34:16), (s40:6)}
⋮
l_9: L[(Glenmont, Pentagon)] = {(s6:1), (s7:4,11), (s8:2,6,12), (s50:7)}
l_{10}: L[(Glenmont, Wheaton)] = {(s19:4,14), (s21:8)}

$I^{(X,X)}$
l_{11}: L[(Clarendon, Clarendon)] = {(s3:2,8,12), (s4:5,22), (s16:19,32)}
l_{12}: L[(Deanwood, Deanwood)] = {(s5:2,9), (s7:2,12,17)}
⋮
l_{13}: L[(Pentagon, Pentagon)] = {(s2:2,5), (s27:2,4,16), (s34:2,19)}
⋮
l_{14}: L[(Wheaton, Wheaton)] = {(s67:7,14), (s86:2,8,11)}

Figure 3: Inverted indices

An S-OLAP query can be evaluated (or equivalently an s-cuboid can be constructed) from a set of inverted indices. For example, given the set of inverted indices shown in Figure 3, the PBA query "(Y, X), COUNT" can be evaluated as follows. First the inverted index $I^{(Y,X)}$ is retrieved. For each pattern P that is an instantiation of (Y, X), the inverted list $L[P]$ in $I^{(Y,X)}$ gives the sequences that contain P. These sequences thus form one cell of the s-cuboid and the cardinality of $L[P]$ gives the aggregate value of the cell. For example, the value of the cell C((Pentagon, Clarendon)) is 4 because the inverted list l_8 contains four sequences.

Evaluating a PBA query with a pattern template T thus requires the index I^T. If I^T is not available, it can be materialized by joining the indices of shorter templates. In particular, I^T can be obtained by joining the inverted indices I^{T_1} and I^{T_2}, where T_1 and T_2 are the length-(m-1) prefix and the length-2 suffix of T, respectively. (If I^{T_1} is not available, it is recursively constructed.) For example, the inverted index $I^{(X,Y,Y,X)}$ can be materialized by joining $I^{(X,Y,Y)}$ and $I^{(Y,X)}$. We denote this index join by $I^{(X,Y,Y,X)} = I^{(X,Y,Y)} \bowtie I^{(Y,X)}$. For this join, an inverted list $L[(v_1, v_2, v_2, v_1)] \in I^{(X,Y,Y,X)}$ is obtained by considering the joining lists $L[(v_1, v_2, v_2)] \in I^{(X,Y,Y)}$ and $L[(v_2, v_1)] \in I^{(Y,X)}$. More specifically, if a sequence s appears in a posting of $L[(v_1, v_2, v_2)]$ with a starting position i and in another posting of $L[(v_2, v_1)]$ with a starting position $i + 2$, then s is recorded in a posting of $L[(v_1, v_2, v_2, v_1)]$ with a starting position i. We use $L[(v_1, v_2, v_2, v_1)] = L[(v_1, v_2, v_2)] \bowtie L[(v_2, v_1)]$ to denote this join operation. For example, the inverted list L[(Clarendon, Pentagon, Pentagon, Clarendon)] is obtained by considering l_1 and l_8. From the lists, we see

```
Algorithm BuildIndex
Input: A pattern template T = (X_1, ..., X_m).
Output: An inverted index I^T.
if all inverted lists in I^T are materialized
    return I^T;
T_1 = (X_1, ..., X_{m-1}), T_2 = (X_{m-1}, X_m).
BuildIndex (I^{T_1}).
for all pattern P instantiated from T
    if L[P] is not materialized
        P_1 = (v_1, ..., v_{m-1}), P_2 = (v_{m-1}, v_m).
        L[P] = L[P_1] ⋈ L[P_2].
return I^T.
```

Figure 4: A recursive algorithm for materializing an inverted index

that $s27$ at position 3 is in l_1 and $s27$ at position 5 is in l_8, so the posting ($s27$:3) is added to $L[(v_1, v_2, v_2, v_1)]$.

We note that in evaluating a PBA query, the S-OLAP system will materialize a number of inverted indexes. These materialized indexes can be stored on disks to facilitate the processing of future PBA queries. Also, the system can be pro-active in pre-computing some inverted indexes. In this paper we assume that all indexes of length-2 pattern templates are materialized. This approach is similar to bigram indexing in document retrieval systems. Our assumption is thus a reasonable one. Algorithm 4 shows the recursive algorithm BuildIndex that computes an inverted index I^T given a pattern template T. Our Basic algorithm for evaluating a PBA query "T,F" first invokes BuildIndex to obtain I^T. Then, the aggregation function F is applied to the sequences of each inverted list in I^T to compute the aggregate values of the s-cuboid cells.

4 Joining Plan Selection (JPS)

The Basic algorithm uses a *static* joining plan. More specifically, each inverted list $L[P] \in I^T$ is materialized by joining lists $L[P_1]$ and $L[P_2]$, where P_1 and P_2 are the length-(m-1) prefix and the length-2 suffix of P, respectively. We call this the (m-1) $\bowtie$ 2 *joining plan*. For example, Basic materializes the list $L[(a, b, b, a)]$ by:

$$(m-1) \bowtie 2 \text{ plan: } L[(a,b,b,a)] = L[(a,b,b)] \bowtie L[(b,a)].$$

If $L[(a, b, b)]$ is not available, Basic will recursively materialize $L[(a, b, b)]$ first by computing $L[(a, b)] \bowtie L[(b, b)]$. (Recall that we assume all inverted lists of length-2 patterns are materialized. So, no further recursive calls are needed.) We note that other than the (m-1) $\bowtie$ 2 joining plan, there are many others to choose from. For example, $L[(a, b, b, a)]$ can be obtained by:

$$J_2 : L[(a,b,b,a)] = L[(a,b)] \bowtie L[(b,b,a)].$$

In many cases, these alternate joining plans incur lower I/O costs, especially if their joining lists (e.g., $L[(a, b)]$ and $L[(b, b, a)]$) are readily available. For instance, if a query "(Y, Y, X), F" has been processed, then the list $L[(b, b, a)]$ would have been materialized. Now, if the user modifies the pattern template to (X, Y, Y, X) (i.e., by prepending a symbol X to his previous query), then the inverted list $L[(a, b, b, a)]$ will have to be materialized. Note that the joining list $L[(b, b, a)]$ is available for executing Plan J_2 to obtain $L[(a, b, b, a)]$. However, the joining list $L[(a, b, b)]$, required by the (m-1)$\bowtie$ 2 plan, is not. Plan J_2 is thus better than the static plan executed by Basic in this case. This advantage is especially significant if the list $L[(b, b, a)]$ is cached in main memory due to the execution of the query (Y, Y, X).

An interesting question is which plan we shall pick to achieve fast query processing. As another motivating example, consider materializing the inverted index $I^{(X,Y,X,Y)}$. Let $L[(a, b, a, b)]$ be an inverted list in the index. To materialize this list, we can consider two plans:

$$J_3 : \; L[(a,b,a,b)] = L[(a,b,a)] \bowtie L[(b,a,b)] \text{ or}$$
$$J_4 : \; L[(a,b,a,b)] = L[(a,b,a)] \bowtie L[(a,b)].$$

If we pick Plan J_3, then the two lists $L[(a, b, a)]$ and $L[(b, a, b)]$ (if materialized) will be retrieved from disk and cached. Note that (b, a, b, a) is another instantiation of the template (X, Y, X, Y) and so the list $L[(b, a, b, a)]$, which can be obtained by $L[(b, a, b)] \bowtie L[(a, b, a)]$, needs to be materialized as well. Since the two joining lists are cached, the materialization of $L[(b, a, b, a)]$ does not require any extra I/O. On the other hand, Plan J_4 does not offer similar benefit. J_3 is thus more I/O efficient.

Given a length-m pattern P, the number of joining plans for materializing the list $L[P]$ is exponential w.r.t. m. Considering all possible joining plans is thus expensive and in many cases an overkill. For efficiency, we limit our search space and consider only *binary* joining plans: $L[P] = L[P_1] \bowtie L[P_2]$ that satisfy the following conditions:

C1: P_1 is a length-x prefix of P, i.e., $P_1 = (v_1, \ldots, v_x)$, where $2 \leq x < m$.

C2: P_2 is a length-(m-y+1) suffix of P, i.e., $P_2 = (v_y, \ldots, v_m)$, where $2 \leq y \leq x$.

C3: $L[P_1], L[P_2] \in L_{MAT}$, where L_{MAT} is the set of inverted lists that have been materialized.

A joining plan that satisfies all three conditions is called a *candidate joining plan*. Conditions C1 and C2 ensure that the prefix pattern P_1 overlaps with the suffix pattern P_2. Hence, we do not consider, e.g., $L[(a, b, b, a)] = L[(a, b)] \bowtie L[(b, a)]$ as a candidate plan. Condition C3 further restricts candidate plans to those whose joining lists are all materialized. When there are no candidate joining plans, we fall back to the (m-1) $\bowtie$ 2 scheme[3].

With the restriction, there are $O(m^2)$ candidate joining plans for the materialization of each inverted list [3]. Our objective is to select a set of joining plans to materialize all the lists in a given inverted index I^T such that the I/O cost of retrieving the joining lists is minimized. We call this problem the *joining plan selection problem* (JPS).

We tackle the JPS problem by formulating it as an instance of the *minimum weight multi-colored subgraph problem* (MWMCSP) [7]. Since MWMCSP is NP-hard, we propose a heuristic algorithm GPS (Greedy Plan Selection) to obtain an approximate solution. Our experiment results show that GPS is as effective as the best approximation algorithm while at the same time it has a much smaller running time. We now describe the problem formulation and the GPS algorithm.

To materialize an inverted list $L \in I^T$, we need to select a candidate joining plan, say, $L = L_1 \bowtie L_2$, and retrieve the joining lists (L_1 and L_2) from disk. Let $\Phi(I^T)$ be the set

[3]That is, P_1 and P_2 are the length-(m-1) prefix and the length-2 suffix of P, respectively. In this case, $L[P_1]$ will have to be recursively materialized first (see BuildIndex).

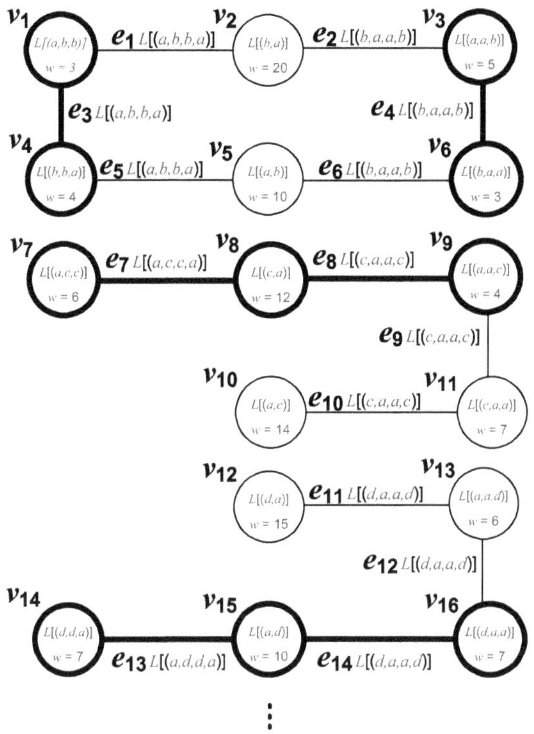

Figure 5: The graph G for template $I^{(X,Y,Y,X)}$

of selected joining plans for materializing all the lists in I^T. Also, let

$$\mathcal{L} = \cup_{(L=L_p \bowtie L_q)\in\Phi(I^T)}\{L_p, L_q\}$$

be the set of joining lists to be retrieved from disk. We make two assumptions: (A1) there is at least one candidate joining plan (that satisfies the three conditions C1 to C3) for each inverted list in I^T, and (A2) there is enough memory buffer to hold all joining lists in $\mathcal{L}$. Assumption A1 ensures that the set $\Phi(I^T)$ is complete and well-defined. Assumption A2 implies that no joining list needs to be retrieved from disk twice (due to swapping) in materializing I^T. The I/O cost of materializing I^T using the set of joining plans $\Phi(I^T)$, denoted by $cost(\Phi(I^T))$, is given by:

$$cost(\Phi(I^T)) = \sum_{L_x\in\mathcal{L}} b(L_x), \qquad (1)$$

where $b(L_x)$ is the number of disk blocks needed to store the inverted list L_x. We will relax the two assumptions (A1, A2) later and discuss how we handle cases in which the assumptions do not hold.

Given an inverted index I^T, our goal is to find a $\Phi(I^T)$ that minimizes $cost(\Phi(I^T))$. We model this optimization problem as a graph problem. Let $\mathcal{C}(I^T)$ be the set of all candidate joining plans for all the inverted lists in I^T. That is, a joining plan $(L = L_p \bowtie L_q) \in \mathcal{C}(I^T)$ iff $L \in I^T$ and the plan satisfies the conditions C1-C3. Since our desired output $\Phi(I^T)$ contains exactly one candidate joining plan for each inverted list in I^T, we have $\Phi(I^T) \subseteq \mathcal{C}(I^T)$. Now, we construct a graph $G = (V, E)$ as follows. First, for each L_x that is a joining list of some joining plan in $\mathcal{C}(I^T)$, a vertex v_{L_x} is created in V. A weight $w(v_{L_x}) = b(L_x)$ is assigned to v_{L_x}. Next, for each joining plan $(L = L_p \bowtie L_q) \in \mathcal{C}(I^T)$, an edge e_L, labeled L, is created in E connecting vertices v_{L_p} and v_{L_q}. The weight $w(e_L)$ of edge e_L is the sum of the weights of its end vertices, i.e., $w(e_L) = w(v_{L_p}) + w(v_{L_q})$. Figure 5 shows part of the graph constructed for materializing the inverted index $I^{(X,Y,Y,X)}$. For illustration purpose, only the joining plans of six inverted lists (e.g., $L[(a,b,b,a)]$) are shown in the figure. In the graph, the edge e_1 (labeled $L[(a,b,b,a)]$) connects v_1 and v_2 (labeled $L[(a,b,b)]$ and $L[(b,a)]$, respectively). This edge represents a joining plan $(L[(a,b,b)] \bowtie L[(b,a)])$ for $L[(a,b,b,a)]$. Note that $w(e_1) = 3+20 = 23$, so the I/O cost of retrieving the joining lists to execute e_1 is 23 disk blocks. Edges e_3 and e_5 represent two other joining plans for materializing $L[(a,b,b,a)]$.

Note that a set of selected plans $\Phi(I^T)$ is equivalent to a set of $|I^T|$ edges of distinct labels in G, where $|I^T|$ denotes the number of inverted lists in I^T. Also, it is easy to see that $cost(\Phi(I^T)) = \sum_{L_x\in\mathcal{L}}(w(v_{L_x}))$. If we consider each distinct edge label as a distinct "color" (e.g. The edges e_1, e_3 and e_5 in Figure 5 are of the same edge label $L[(a,b,b,a)]$.), then finding a $\Phi(I^T)$ with the smallest $cost(\Phi(I^T))$ is equivalent to finding a subset E' of E such that (1) all edges in E' are of distinct colors, (2) all colors are covered by E' and (3) the total weight of the end vertices of the edges in E' is minimized. This problem is MWMCSP [7].

In Figure 5, an optimal solution for the graph is highlighted. For instance, e_3 is picked indicating that the joining plan $L[(a,b,b)] \bowtie L[(b,b,a)]$ should be used to materialize $L[(a,b,b,a)]$. The sum of the weights of the vertices in this optimal solution is 61, which means that materializing the inverted index requires 61 disk block accesses.

The MWMCSP problem is NP-hard. The state-of-the-art approximation algorithm for the problem is based on the LP-rounding technique [7]. The algorithm (let's call it LP) has a $\Omega(d^2k)$ running time, where d is the number of inverted lists in I^T and k is the number of candidate joining plans for each inverted list in I^T. For efficiency, we propose a greedy algorithm, GPS, which runs in $O(dk)$ time. Since in practice $d \gg k$, GPS is much more efficient than LP. Our experiments show that GPS generally yields a cost $(cost(\Phi(I^T)))$ that is comparable to the one obtained by LP (See Figure 9a). GPS is therefore as effective as LP.

Given the graph G, GPS selects the joining plans one at a time. For each $L[P] \in I^T$, GPS picks the edge e whose weight $w(e)$ is the smallest among all the edges labeled $L[P]$. Intuitively, this means that the joining plan picked requires the least number of disk block accesses among all the available candidate plans for $L[P]$. For example, in Figure 5, edge e_3 is picked for $L[(a,b,b,a)]$ because $w(e_3) = 7$, which is the smallest among all candidate plans for $L[(a,b,b,a)]$ ($w(e_1) = 23$ and $w(e_5) = 14$).

Once an edge $e = (u,v)$ is selected, GPS performs two steps: (1) it removes all the edges labeled $L[P]$ from G and (2) it sets $w(u) = w(v) = 0$ and the weights of any edges that are incident to either u or v are updated accordingly. The second step is done to reflect that the joining lists represented by vertices u and v have been retrieved. If they are cached, future executions of any other joining plans that require either u or v as a joining list do not incur any additional I/O. For example, suppose GPS picks e_7 to materialize $L[(a,c,c,a)]$. After that, GPS sets $w(v_8)$ to 0, and update $w(e_8)$ to 0+4 = 4. Later, when GPS compares the three edges (plans) for materializing $L[(c,a,a,c)]$ (i.e., e_8, e_9 and e_{10}), e_8 will be picked because its weight is the smallest. Algorithm 6 shows the GPS algorithm.

Algorithm GPS
Input: The graph G created from I^T.
Output: A set of selected joining plans $\Phi(I^T)$.

```
for all L[P] ∈ I^T, if L[P] ∉ L_MAT
    Add e = (u, v) with the minimum weight among all
    edges labeled L[P] to Φ(I^T);
    Remove all other edges labeled L[P] from G;
    Set w(u) = w(v) = 0;
return Φ(I^T).
```

Figure 6: GPS

In our discussion so far, we have assumed that for each inverted list $L[P] \in I^T$, there is at least one candidate joining plan for $L[P]$ (and so there is at least one edge labeled $L[P]$ in G). If that is not the case, we fall back to the (m-1) $\bowtie$ 2 joining plan. Recall that all length-2 inverted lists are materialized in our system. So, to make the (m-1) $\bowtie$ 2 plan a candidate plan (that satisfies condition C3), we need to first materialize the list $L[P_1]$, where P_1 is the length-(m-1) prefix of P. We consider all inverted lists in I^T and collect all the length-(m-1) prefixes of those lists that are without a candidate joining plan into a set $\mathcal{S}$. All the lists in $\mathcal{S}$ would then have to be materialized first. We can achieve that by simply executing Algorithm 6 recursively, replacing the set I^T by $\mathcal{S}$.

Another assumption we have made is that the memory buffer is big enough to cache all the lists in $\mathcal{L}$ (i.e., all the joining lists of the selected plans). This assumption implies that each required joining list is retrieved from disk only once even if it is used for multiple joins. For example, in Figure 5 the joining list $L[(c, a)]$ (vertex v_8) is retrieved once for computing both $L[(a, c, c, a)]$ (e_7) and $L[(c, a, a, c)]$ (e_8). With this assumption, the formula given in Equation 1 correctly captures the I/O cost ($cost(\Phi(I^T))$) of materializing the inverted index I^T. For large datasets and a small memory buffer, the assumption may not hold. A joining list retrieved may be swapped out of the buffer before it is needed again to execute another join. In that case, the joining list is retrieved again and additional I/O is paid. To avoid such redundant I/O, we should wisely schedule the execution order of the joining plans. For example, the execution of the plan e_7 should be followed soon by the execution of e_8 while the common joining list v_8 is still residing in the buffer. Given $\Phi(I^T)$, the set of selected joining plans for materializing I^T, we call the problem of scheduling the execution order of the plans so as to avoid redundant I/O as much as possible the *execution planning problem* (EP).

5 Execution Planning (EP)

Given a set of selected joining plans ($\Phi(I^T)$), we can construct a graph $G' \subseteq G$ that contains all and only the edges in $\Phi(I^T)$. (See Figure 7 for an example G'.) To tackle the EP problem, we propose a scheduling algorithm REP (Rule-based Execution Planning), which determines an execution order of the edges (joining plans) in G'. REP follows three scheduling rules (to be discussed shortly). Given a joining list L_x, it may be required for the execution of multiple joins. (For example, in Figure 7, the joining list $L[(a, b)]$ (v_6) is required by four joins (e_4, e_5, e_8 and e_9).) When the first of such joins, say J_1, is executed, L_x is retrieved and placed in the buffer. After the last of such joins, say J_2, is done, L_x can be released from the buffer and need not be retrieved again. Let us call the time span between the executions of J_1 to J_2 *the span of* L_x. To avoid redundant I/O, we should avoid swapping a joining list out of the buffer during its span. To achieve that, we should shorten a list's span as much as possible so that the chances of a buffer overflow occurs during the list's span, which may lead to a swap-out of the list, is small. Also, a short span implies that the memory occupied by the list can be released earlier and so buffer overflow is less likely to occur. The three scheduling rules we will present next are based on this *short-span principle.*

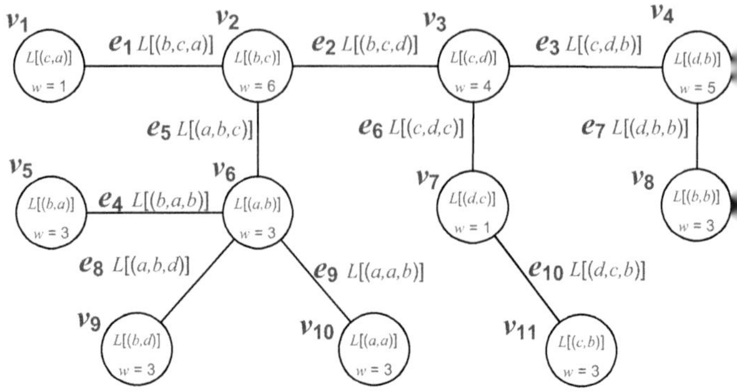

Figure 7: An example G'.

Since our scheduling algorithm REP operates on the graph G', in the following discussion, we describe REP in terms of *vertices* and *edges*, with the understanding that a "vertex" refers to a "joining list" and an "edge" refers to a "joining plan". Let $\mathcal{L}_{buf}$ be a memory buffer where joining lists are cached. Given a set of selected joining plans $\Phi(I^T)$ (equivalently, the graph G'), the REP algorithm prioritizes the plans (equivalently, the edges in G') by applying the following rules in order:

R1: An edge e_i is executed ahead of another edge e_j if more joining lists (end vertices) of e_i are cached in $\mathcal{L}_{buf}$ than those of e_j. For example, a plan with both of its joining lists cached in $\mathcal{L}_{buf}$ is executed before another plan that has only one of its joining lists cached. With Rule R1, REP tries to finish executing all the joins that require the lists cached in $\mathcal{L}_{buf}$ early and to delay bringing in new lists into the buffer. The former aims at terminating the spans of the lists in $\mathcal{L}_{buf}$ early and the latter aims at starting the spans of the not-yet-retrieved lists late. Intuitively, this strategy tends to shorten lists' spans in general.

R2: If two edges e_i and e_j are tied w.r.t. Rule R1, they have the same number of joining lists in $\mathcal{L}_{buf}$. In this case, REP executes e_i ahead of e_j if the joining lists (end vertices) of e_i are of smaller degrees than those of e_j. We call this strategy *smallest-degree-first.*[4] Note that a joining list (vertex), say v, of large degree implies that it is involved in many joins (edges). The span of v is thus generally large. Bringing v to the buffer early would extend its span and allow it to hog the memory for an extensive period of time, making the buffer more likely to overflow. REP thus prefers executing edges that involve "small-degree" vertices first.

R3: An edge e_i is executed ahead of another edge e_j if the total size of the joining lists that have to be retrieved from disk for e_i is smaller than that for e_j. For example, consider edges e_3 and e_6 in Figure 7. If v_3 is in $\mathcal{L}_{buf}$, then executing e_3 and e_6 requires the retrievals of v_4 and v_7, respectively. Since

[4]See Algorithm REP, Figure 8, for details.

Algorithm REP
Input: $\Phi(I^T)$ (as represented by a graph $G' = (E', V')$).
Output: An execution order of the joins in $\Phi(I^T)$.
$\mathcal{L}_{buf} = \emptyset$;
AssignScore(G');
while $E' \neq \emptyset$
  $e(u, v)$ = lowest-scored edge in G';
  $\mathcal{L}_{buf} = \mathcal{L}_{buf} \cup \{u, v\}$;
  $E' = E'$ - e;
  if $deg(u) = 0$ **then** $\mathcal{L}_{buf} = \mathcal{L}_{buf}$ - $\{u\}$;
  if $deg(v) = 0$ **then** $\mathcal{L}_{buf} = \mathcal{L}_{buf}$ - $\{v\}$;
  update edge scores due to the removal of e;

Algorithm AssignScore
for each edge $e(u, v) \in E'$
  $R1(e)$ = number of joining lists in e that is not in $\mathcal{L}_{buf}$;
  $R2(e) = \sum\{deg(x)$, where $x \in \{u, v\} \wedge x \notin \mathcal{L}_{buf}\}$;
  $R3(e) = \sum\{|x|$, where $x \in \{u, v\} \wedge x \notin \mathcal{L}_{buf}\}$;
  $score(e) = \langle R1(e), R2(e), R3(e) \rangle$;
Sort all e's in ascending order of $score(e)$, with $R1$, $R2$ and $R3$ being the primary, secondary, and tertiary sort keys, respectively.

Figure 8: REP

$w(v_7) < w(v_4)$, e_6 is executed ahead of e_3. By preferring joining plans that request shorter joining lists, REP avoids bringing large lists into the buffer early. This lowers the chances and extent of buffer overflow.

The REP scheduling algorithm is shown in Figure 8. To illustrate, let us apply REP on the graph G' shown in Figure 7. Initially, $\mathcal{L}_{buf} = \emptyset$, so Rule R1 does not apply. According to Rule R2, either edge e_7 or e_{10} should be executed first because their end vertices are of the lowest degrees. REP applies Rule R3 to break the tie and selects e_{10} first because the total weight of its end vertices is 1+3=4, which is smaller than that of e_7 (5+3=8). When e_{10} is being executed, $\mathcal{L}_{buf} = \{v_7, v_{11}\}$. After e_{10} is done, v_{11} is released from the buffer because it is no longer needed by any other plans. By Rule R1, e_6 is executed next, since it is the only plan that has a joining list in $\mathcal{L}_{buf}$. After that, $\mathcal{L}_{buf} = \{v_3\}$. Now e_2 and e_3 are tied w.r.t. Rule R1. Since e_3's end vertices are of lower degrees, it is executed next. Now, $\mathcal{L}_{buf} = \{v_3, v_4\}$. By Rule R2, e_7 is executed ahead of e_2, and so on.

Note that joining lists are moved into and out of $\mathcal{L}_{buf}$ as plans are executed. To avoid redundant I/O, we need enough memory to store the largest $\mathcal{L}_{buf}$. For our toy example, this *memory requirement* is 12 disk blocks. As a comparison, if one executes the joins in the order $e_1, e_2, \ldots, e_{10}$, the buffer requirement is 21 disk blocks, which is much more than that required by the execution order generated by REP. We remark that one may come up with other scheduling rules. The ones we have presented (R1-R3) are examples which show that intelligently scheduling the plans' execution order can significantly reduce the size of the memory requirement. With limited buffer space, this benefit translates to more I/O-efficient query processing.

6 Experimental evaluation

This section presents the results of the experiments we conducted on our prototype S-OLAP system. The prototype was implemented in JAVA 1.6 on a machine with a 2.83GHz

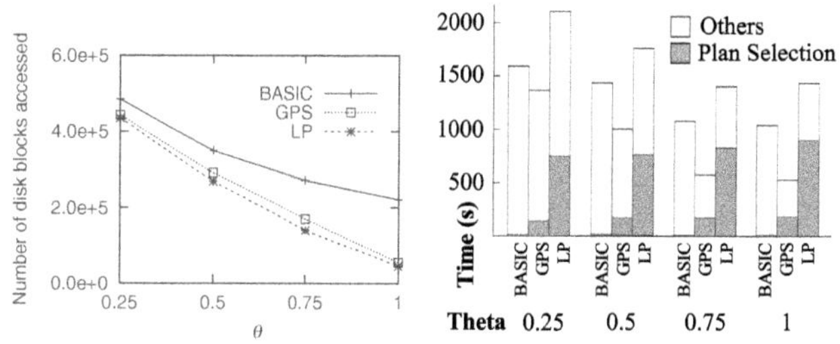

(a) I/O cost vs θ. (b) Execution time (s) vs θ.

Figure 9: Comparing JPS algorithms (real data)

Intel Core 2 Duo CPU and 4GB RAM running Linux 2.6.24 kernel. In the experiments, we set the disk block size to 1KB. We use least-recently-used (LRU) as the replacement policy for the joining list buffer ($\mathcal{L}_{buf}$). Experiments are done on both real data and synthetic data. We focus on the two I/O-aware algorithms, namely, GPS and REP and study their efficiency and effectiveness in reducing the I/O cost of query evaluation compared with the BASIC algorithm

6.1 Experiments on Real Data

The real sequence data is a clickstream and purchase dataset of Gazelle.com, a legwear and legcare web retailer. The data was prepared by [8] for KDD Cup 2000. Each tuple in the data file is a visitor click event (sorted by user sessions). The original data is 238.9MB large and consists of 164,364 click events. Each event is captured by 215 attributes. Three example attributes are *session-id*, *request-time* and *page-category*. These attributes identify a user session, its first access time, and the accessed page, respectively. We cleaned the data manually and removed click sequences that were generated from web crawlers (e.g., user sessions with thousands of clicks). After this step, an event database of 148,924 click events was obtained forming 50,524 sequences.

The query workload consists of 100 random queries. A pattern template T is randomly generated for each query Pattern symbols are defined on the attribute *page-category*, whose domain consists of 24 distinct values. To generate a template T, we first pick a length m, which is uniformly distributed over the range $[3 \ldots 6]$. Next, the number of distinct pattern symbols n in T is randomly picked uniformly over the range $[1 \ldots \min\{m, 4\}]$. Finally, a pattern template is randomly selected from all possible pattern templates of length m with n distinct symbols (e.g., the template (X, Y, Y, X) is of length 4 with 2 distinct symbols). We use `COUNT` as the aggregate function. Table 2 shows the query parameters and their default values.

Query Parameter	Notation	Default
Template length	m	$[3 \ldots 6]$
Number of distinct pattern symbols	n	$[1 \ldots \min\{m, 4\}]$

Table 2: Query Workload Parameters

6.1.1 *Joining plan selection (JPS) algorithms*

We first evaluate algorithms for the JPS problem. They are (1) BASIC, which uses the static $(m-1) \bowtie 2$ joining plans, (2) LP, which selects joining plans by solving the MWMCSP problem using LP-rounding technique, and (3) GPS, which solves MWMCSP using a greedy strategy.

Given an inverted index I^T, a JPS algorithm selects one candidate joining plan for each inverted list in I^T. Recall that a candidate joining plan is one whose joining lists are both materialized (i.e., in L_{MAT}). The set L_{MAT} thus determines how many candidate joining plans are available for the selection algorithms to choose from. This, in turn, affects the set of selected plans $\Phi(I^T)$ and its I/O cost $cost(\Phi(I^T))$.

Let $\mathcal{P}$ be the set of all possible joining plans for materializing the inverted lists in I^T (i.e., those that satisfy Conditions C1 and C2). For example if $L[(a,b,b,a)] \in I^T$, then $L[(a,b,b,a)] = L[(a,b)] \bowtie L[(b,b,a)]$ is a plan in $\mathcal{P}$. Let JL be the set of all joining lists that appear in the plans of $\mathcal{P}$, and let JL_i be those whose patterns are of length i (e.g., $L[(a,b)] \in JL_2$ and $L[(b,b,a)] \in JL_3$). Recall that we assume all lists of length-2 patterns are pre-computed, therefore, $JL_2 \subseteq L_{MAT}$. Further, let $JL' = JL - JL_2$ be the set of all other joining lists. Define $\theta = |JL' \cap L_{MAT}|/|JL'|$, i.e., the fraction of the joining lists in JL' that are materialized. Our first experiment studies the performance of the JPS algorithms as θ varies. Note that when $\theta = 0$, only joining lists of length-2 patterns are materialized; when $\theta = 1$, all joining lists in JL are materialized and so all plans in $\mathcal{P}$ are candidate plans (satisfying Condition C3) for the algorithms to pick. In this experiment, we use a large memory buffer so that joining lists retrieved do not get swapped out of the buffer during query processing.

Figure 9(a) shows the number of disk blocks accessed by the three algorithms as θ varies from 0.25 to 1. Although not shown in the figure, when $\theta = 0$, all three algorithms access the same number of disk blocks. To see why, consider any list $L[P] \in I^T$ to be materialized. If $m = 3$, pattern P consists of three symbols and so only one candidate plan, $L[P] = L[P_1] \bowtie L[P_2]$, where P_1 and P_2 are the length-2 prefix and the length-2 suffix of P, exists. Any JPS algorithm will execute this plan. If $m \geq 4$, then no candidate plans are available because any such plan requires some joining lists whose patterns are length-3 or longer. These lists are not materialized because $\theta = 0$. In this case, the JPS algorithms are recursively invoked to materialize $L[P']$, where P' is the length-(m-1) prefix of P, first. By induction, when $\theta = 0$, all three JPS algorithms retrieve the same lists from disk to execute the same joins. They thus have the same I/O cost.

As θ increases, more joining lists are materialized. This has two effects. First, it is more likely that at least one candidate plan is available for materializing $L[P]$ and so no recursive calls of the JPS algorithms are needed to obtain the (m-1)-prefix list. This explains why the I/O costs of all three algorithms go down as θ increases. Second, there are more candidate plans available for GPS or LP to choose. It is thus more likely that these smart algorithms are able to pick some sets of low-cost plans. This explains why the gaps between BASIC and GPS or LP widen as θ increases. This I/O cost reduction is very significant, particularly when θ is large. For example, when $\theta = 1$, the I/O costs under LP and GPS are about 1/5 of BASIC's. We remark that in practice, the joining lists in JL are often materialized and available. This is especially true if the user is exploring the s-cube space by incrementally modifying his PBA query, for example, by adding a symbol to extend the query pattern template. In this case, inverted lists of shorter patterns are materialized due to the evaluation of previous queries.

Note that the curves for LP and GPS are very close to each other throughout the whole range of θ in Figure 9(a). This shows that the set of joining plans selected by GPS is as good

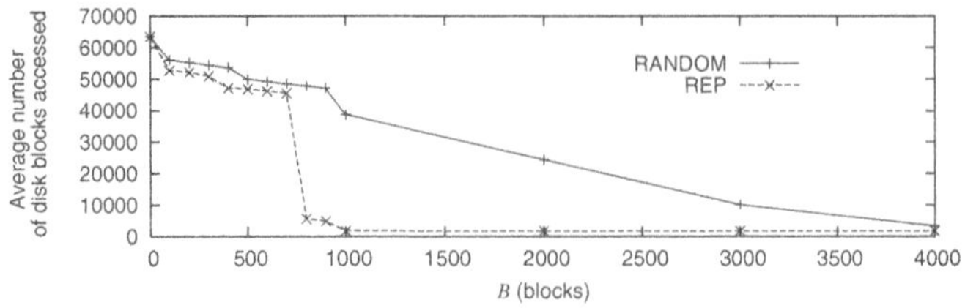

Figure 10: Comparing EP algorithms (real data)

as that of LP in terms of I/O cost. However, LP is much slower than GPS. Figure 9(b) shows the query execution times of the three algorithms, with the fraction attributable to plan selection (e.g., solving MWMCSP) shaded. From the figures, we see that GPS is much more efficient than LP. We also see that LP spends so much time in plan selection that it is counter productive. On the other hand, due to its relatively low computation overhead, GPS gives a much lower overall query processing time.

6.1.2 Execution planning (EP) algorithms

Our second experiment evaluates execution planning (EP) algorithms. Given a set of selected joining plans $\Phi(I^T)$ obtained by GPS, we consider two algorithms for determining the joins' execution order. They are (1) REP, our rule-based planner, and (2) RANDOM, which executes the joins in $\Phi(I^T)$ in some random order. Recall that the join execution order affects the amount of redundant I/O when the memory buffer is limited (see Section 5). Therefore, we compare the I/O costs of REP and RANDOM for processing our query workload under different buffer sizes (B). In this experiment, we set $\theta = 0.5$.

Figure 10 shows the average number of disk blocks accessed by our system per query under REP and RANDOM. When there is no joining list buffer (i.e., $B = 0$), a joining list that participates in k joins is retrieved from disk k times, regardless of the joins' execution order. Therefore, REP and RANDOM have the same I/O cost. As B increases, we see that the curve for REP drops sharply from 45,600 blocks (when $B = 700$) to 5,600 blocks (when $B = 800$). This shows that REP is very successful in putting joins that share common joining lists together so that even a small buffer allows joining lists to be effectively cached. This significantly avoids redundant I/O. On the other hand, the curve for RANDOM drops at a much lower rate — only when B is increased to about 4000 does its I/O cost reach the level of REP. The per-query memory requirement under RANDOM is thus 5 times bigger than that of REP. Moreover, when the per-query buffer is small (e.g., when $B = 1{,}000$), the I/O cost under REP is 1/21 of RANDOM. This experiment shows that our rule-based execution planner REP is very effective.

6.2 Experiments on Synthetic Data

To further evaluate our techniques, we have also carried out experiments on synthetic data and synthetic query workloads. The synthetic sequence data generator is controlled by four parameters: L, M, α, and D. Specifically, a synthetic dataset consists of D sequences. To generate a data sequence s, we first determine its length l, which is randomly generated from a Poisson distribution with mean L. Symbols in sequence s are picked from a domain of M symbols. The first symbol of s is randomly selected according to a

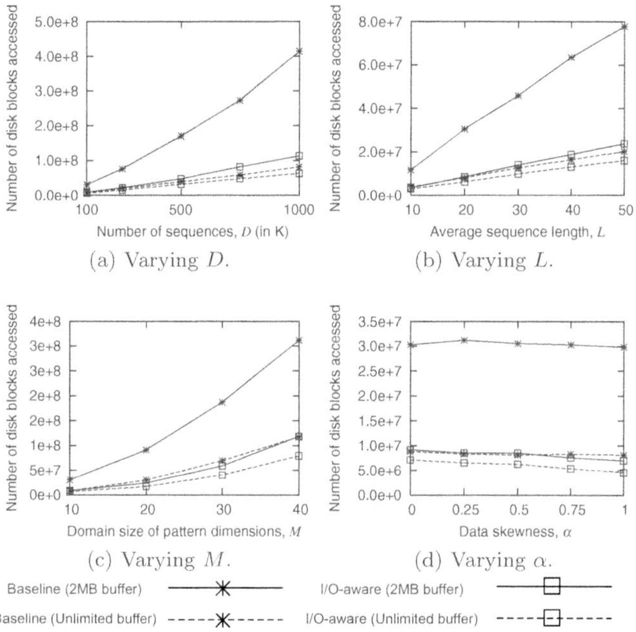

Figure 11: Varying Data Characteristics.

Zipf distribution with skew factor α. Subsequent events are generated according to a Markov chain of order one. Each probability vector in the transition probability matrix follows a Zipf distribution. Table 3 shows the parameters and their default values.

parameter	notation	default value
Number of sequences	D	100,000
Average number of events per sequence	L	20
Domain size of pattern dimension	M	10
Data skewness	α	0.5

Table 3: Synthetic data parameters and default values

In the following discussion, we use "I/O-aware" to refer to the applications of our two I/O-cognizant techniques, i.e., GPS and REP. We use "Baseline" to refer to the I/O-oblivious alternative, which uses BASIC for the JPS problem and RANDOM for the EP problem. We compare the I/O-aware approach with Baseline by varying the four parameters listed in Table 3. When we vary one parameter, the other three are fixed at their default values. The query workload is generated in the same manner as in the real-data experiments with $\theta = 0.5$. We use "number of disk blocks accessed" as the performance metrics. In each experiment, two performance curves are displayed for each approach: one for a limited buffer scenario (2MB allocated to each query) and another for an unlimited buffer scenario. Section 6.2.1 shows the results of varying the data characteristics and Section 6.2.2 shows the results of varying the query characteristics.

6.2.1 Varying data characteristics

Varying D. Figure 11(a) shows the results of varying the dataset size (D) from 100K sequences to 1M sequences. When D increases, the joining lists become longer (more sequences contain a certain pattern) and the I/O cost of retrieving them is higher. From the figure, we see that our I/O-aware approach performs much better than the Baseline approach. For example, at D = 1M sequences and with a 2MB per-query buffer, the I/O cost of I/O-aware is about 4 times smaller than that of Baseline. This is because the memory requirement of Baseline exceeds the given buffer. Joining lists are often swapped out of the buffer due to overflow even if these lists are needed for the execution of more joins later. This leads to redundant I/O and hence a high I/O cost. The I/O-aware approach, on the other hand, has a small memory requirement, which allows it to work comfortably over a small buffer. As a result, the performance of I/O-aware under a limited 2MB buffer is comparable to that of Baseline under unlimited buffer.

Varying L. Figure 11(b) shows the results of varying the average sequence length. A longer sequence contains more patterns. Therefore, with longer sequences in the dataset, a pattern is expected to occur in more data sequences. This results in larger inverted lists and hence larger I/O costs. The effect is thus very similar to that of increasing D. Again, we see that I/O-aware performs much better than Baseline, especially when buffer space is limited. For example, I/O-aware is 3.3 times faster than Baseline when $L = 50$.

Varying M. Figure 11(c) shows the results of varying the domain size of the pattern symbols. Given a pattern template T that contains n distinct symbols, the number of cells in the s-cuboid (or equivalently, the number of lists in I^T) is M^n. A larger M therefore implies more inverted lists to be materialized resulting in a higher I/O cost. This explains why the curves in Figure 11(c) go up as M increases. Again, the I/O-aware approach outperforms Baseline by a wide margin.

Varying α. Figure 11(d) shows the the results of varying the data skewness. When data is more skewed (larger α), some patterns occur much more frequently than others. As a result, the sizes of the inverted lists vary significantly from one pattern to another. Different joining plans, which involve different joining lists, are therefore likely to incur very different costs. Our I/O-aware approach, which employs GPS as a smart join-plan-selection algorithm, is able to select low-cost plans in general. This explains why the curves for our I/O-aware approach drop as α increases. On the other hand, Baseline uses a static (m-1) $\bowtie$ 2 strategy and is not able to take advantage of the availability of lower-cost plans. Its performance is thus not very sensitive to α.

6.2.2 Varying query characteristics

Varying n. Figure 12(a) shows the I/O costs of Baseline and I/O-aware as the number of distinct pattern symbols (n) in the query workload (e.g., $n = 2$ for the query template (X, Y, Y, X)) varies from 1 to 4. In this experiment, the query template length m is fixed at 4. Again, we see that I/O-aware is more I/O efficient. Figure 12(b) shows the *I/O speedup* defined as the I/O-cost of Baseline over that of I/O-aware. For example, when $n = 4$ and with a 2MB per-query buffer, I/O-aware achieves a 3.4 times speedup in I/O over Baseline. Note that n is the number of distinct pattern symbols so when n increases, there are more cells in the s-cuboid. Therefore, the system needs to materialize more inverted lists and hence the I/O costs generally increase as shown in Figure 12(a). When $n = 4$, we observe that I/O-aware significantly outperforms Baseline in the limited buffer scenario. The reason is that in this experiment $m = 4$ and so when $n = 4$, there is only one query template, say, (W, X, Y, Z). Note that all four symbols in the template are distinct and

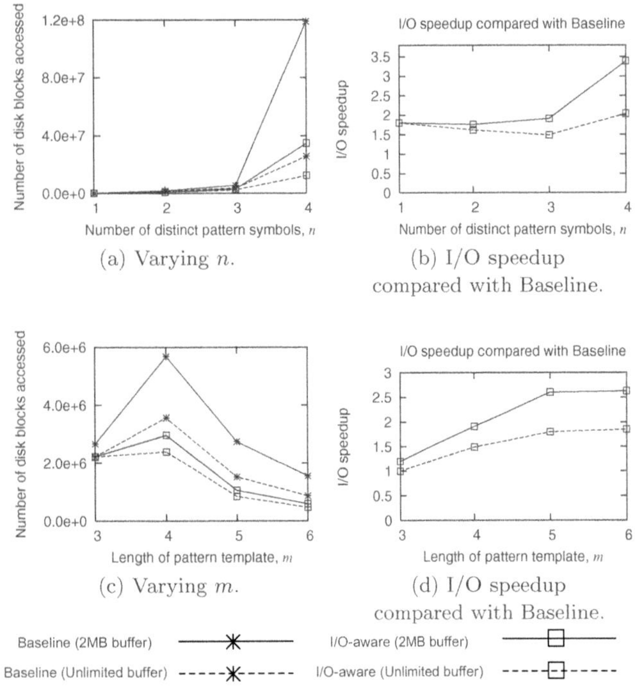

Figure 12: Varying query characteristics.

therefore they are not restricted to the same binding in the instantiations. As a result, any joining list retrieved for one join can be heavily reused in many others. For example, after we execute the join $L[(a,b,c,d)] = L[(a,b,c)] \bowtie L[(c,d)]$, the joining list $L[(a,b,c)]$ retrieved can be used to execute any join of the form $L[(a,b,c,*)] = L[(a,b,c)] \bowtie L[(c,*)]$, where $*$ is any value of the pattern symbol domain. In this case, our REP algorithm tends to schedule the executions of these joins close together so that the span of $L[(a,b,c)]$ is small. The Baseline approach, however, adopts a RANDOM strategy for the EP problem, which cannot effectively utilize the buffer cache to avoid redundant I/O when it is given a limited buffer. The curve of Baseline thus rises sharply when n=4 in the limited buffer scenario.

Varying m. Figure 12(c) shows the I/O costs as the length of the pattern templates (m) varies from 3 to 6. In this experiment, the number of distinct pattern symbols is 3 and $\theta = 0.5$. Note that $m = 3$ is a special case for which only one candidate plan, $L[P] = L[P_1] \bowtie L[P_2]$, where P_1 and P_2 are the length-2 prefix and the length-2 suffix of P, exists. Therefore both Baseline and I/O-aware select the same joining plan. This explains why both Baseline and I/O-aware have similar I/O costs when $m = 3$. We also observe that I/O-aware outperforms Baseline in the entire range of m. The reason is that given an inverted list $L[P] \in I^T$, Baseline attempts to materialize it using the (m-1) $\bowtie$ 2 joining plan. If this plan is not available (i.e., the joining list whose pattern is the (m-1)-prefix of P is not materialized yet), Baseline will have to recursively materialize the prefix-pattern list first (which may require further recursive joins, e.g. to materialize the (m-2)-prefix list of P, etc.). On the other hand, since I/O-aware considers any possible joining plans in addition to the (m-1) $\bowtie$ 2 one, it is very likely that some of the possible plans are available (i.e., their joining lists are materialized). In this case, I/O-aware can avoid the costs of executing recursive joins. The I/O cost of I/O-aware is thus significantly smaller than that of Baseline.

Figure 12(d) shows the I/O speedup achieved by I/O-aware over Baseline. We observe that the saving increases as m increases. It is because the number of possible joining plans is proportional to m^2. So, a larger m implies more candidate joining plans for I/O-aware to choose from. This allows I/O-aware to pick a low-cost plan.

7 Conclusion

This paper studied the problem of sequence cuboid materialization. In particular, we studied the joining plan selection problem and the execution planning problem. We proposed the GPS algorithm and the REP algorithm to solve the two problems, respectively. Through extensive experiments, we showed that our I/O-aware algorithms significantly reduce the I/O cost of query processing.

Acknowledgement

This work was supported by the Research Grants Council of Hong Kong (GRF Projects 513508, 711309E and 713008E). We would like to thank the anonymous reviewers for their insightful comments.

8 References

[1] Brian Babcock, et al. Models and issues in data stream systems. In *PODS*, 2002.
[2] Jianjun Chen, et al. NiagaraCQ: a scalable continuous query system for internet databases. *SIGMOD Rec.*, 2000.
[3] Chun Kit Chui, et al. Supporting ranking pattern-based aggregate queries in sequence data cubes. In *CIKM*, 2009.
[4] Lukasz Golab, et al. Issues in data stream management. *SIGMOD Record*, 2003.
[5] Hector Gonzalez, et al. FlowCube: Constructing RFID FlowCubes for Multi-Dimensional Analysis of Commodity Flows. In *VLDB*, 2006.
[6] Hector Gonzalez, et al. Warehousing and Analyzing Massive RFID Data Sets. In *ICDE*, 2006.
[7] Mohammad Taghi Hajiaghayi, et al. Minimum multicolored subgraph problem in multiplex PCR primer set selection and population haplotyping. In *International Conference on Computational Science (2)*, 2006.
[8] Ron Kohavi, et al. KDD-Cup 2000 organizers' report: Peeling the onion. *SIGKDD Explorations*, 2000.
[9] Mo Liu, et al. E-cube: Multi-dimensional event sequence processing using concept and pattern hierarchies. In *Technical Report, WPI-CS-TR-09-08*. The Worcester Polytechnic Institute, 2009.
[10] Eric Lo, et al. OLAP on Sequence Data. In *SIGMOD*, 2008.
[11] Raghu Ramakrishnan, et al. SRQL: Sorted Relational Query Language. In *SSDBM*, 1998.
[12] Reza Sadri, et al. Optimization of sequence queries in database systems. In *PODS*, 2001.
[13] Praveen Seshadri, et al. Sequence query processing. In *SIGMOD*, 1994.
[14] Praveen Seshadri, et al. The design and implementation of a sequence database system. In *VLDB*, 1996.
[15] Fusheng Wang, et al. Temporal management of RFID data. In *VLDB*, 2005.
[16] Chen Yixin, et al. Multi-dimensional regression analysis of time-series data streams. In *VLDB*, 2002.

Tractable XML Data Exchange via Relations

Rada Chirkova
Department of Computer Science
North Carolina State University
chirkova@csc.ncsu.edu

Leonid Libkin
School of Informatics
University of Edinburgh
libkin@inf.ed.ac.uk

Juan L. Reutter
School of Informatics
University of Edinburgh
juan.reutter@ed.ad.uk

ABSTRACT

We consider data exchange for XML documents: given source and target schemas, a mapping between them, and a document conforming to the source schema, construct a target document and answer target queries in a way that is consistent with source information. The problem has primarily been studied in the relational context, in which data-exchange systems have also been built.

Since many XML documents are stored in relations, it is natural to consider using a relational system for XML data exchange. However, there is a complexity mismatch between query answering in relational and XML data exchange, which indicates that restrictions have to be imposed on XML schemas and mappings, and on XML shredding schemes, to make the use of relational systems possible.

We isolate a set of five requirements that must be fulfilled in order to have a faithful representation of the XML data-exchange problem by a relational translation. We then demonstrate that these requirements naturally suggest the inlining technique for data-exchange tasks. Our key contribution is to provide shredding algorithms for schemas, documents, mappings and queries, and demonstrate that they enable us to correctly perform XML data-exchange tasks using a relational system.

Categories and Subject Descriptors
H.2.5 [**Heterogeneous Databases**]: Data translation

General Terms
Algorithms, Theory

Keywords
Data Exchange, XML, XML Shredding, Inlining

1. Introduction

Data exchange is the problem of finding an instance of a target schema, given an instance of a source schema and a schema mapping, that is, a specification of the relationship between the source and the target. Such a target instance should correctly represent information from the source instance under the constraints imposed by the target schema, and should allow one to evaluate queries on the target instance in a way that is semantically consistent with the source data. The problem has received much attention in the past few years, with several surveys already available [21, 9, 8].

The general setting of data exchange is this:

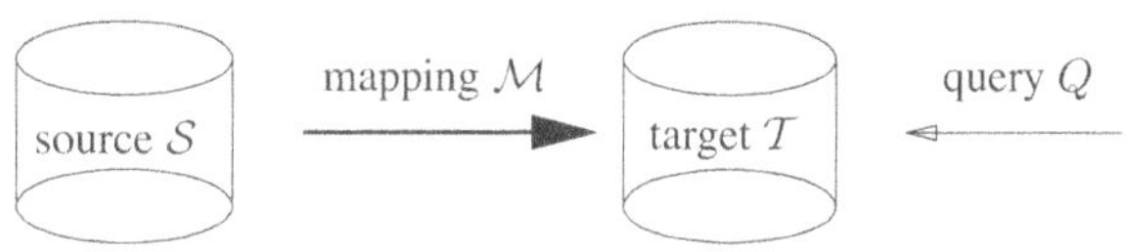

We have fixed source and target schemas, an instance $\mathcal{S}$ of the source schema, and a mapping $\mathcal{M}$ that specifies the relationship between the source and the target schemas. The goal is to construct an instance $\mathcal{T}$ of the target schema, based on the source and the mapping, and answer queries against the target data in a way consistent with the source data.

The mappings rarely specify the target instance completely, that is, for each source $\mathcal{S}$ and mapping $\mathcal{M}$, there could be multiple target instances $\mathcal{T}_1, \mathcal{T}_2, \ldots$ that satisfy the conditions of the mapping. Such instances are called *solutions*. The notion of query answering has to account for their non-uniqueness. Typically, one tries to compute *certain answers* $\text{CERTAIN}_{\mathcal{M}}(Q, \mathcal{S})$, i.e., answers independent of a particular solution chosen. If Q produces relations, these are usually defined as $\bigcap_i Q(\mathcal{T}_i)$. Certain answers must be produced by evaluating some query – not necessarily Q but perhaps its *rewriting* Q_{rewr} over a particular solution $\mathcal{T}$, so that $Q_{\text{rewr}}(\mathcal{T}) = \text{CERTAIN}_{\mathcal{M}}(Q, \mathcal{S})$.

Thus, the key tasks in data exchange are: (a) choosing a particular solution $\mathcal{T}$ among $\{\mathcal{T}_1, \mathcal{T}_2, \ldots\}$ to materialize, and (b) finding a way of producing query answers over that solution by running a rewritten query Q_{rewr} over it. Usually one builds a so called *universal* solution [12, 8]; these solutions behave particularly nicely with respect to query answering.

These basics of data exchange are independent of a particular model of data. Most research on data exchange, however, occurred in the relational context [12, 13, 21, 8] or slight extensions [32, 18]; the first paper that attempted to extend relational results to the XML context was [6], and a few followups have since appeared [4, 3]. They all concentrate on the algorithmic aspects of query answering and constructing solutions, with the main goal of isolating tractable cases. The problem these papers do not address is *how XML data exchange can be implemented*?

Previous work on algorithms for XML data exchange has tacitly assumed that one uses a native XML DBMS such as [19]. However, this is not the only (and perhaps not even the most common) route: XML documents are often stored in relational DBMSs. Note that it is natural and in many cases desirable to be able to use the established relational technology to solve the considerably more recent and not as well understood XML data-exchange task. In fact, many ETL products claim that they handle XML data simply by producing relational translations (known as *shredding* [22]). This leads to a two-step approach:

- first shred XML data into relations;
- then apply a relational data-exchange engine (and publish the result back as an XML document).

The approach seems very natural, but the key question is whether it will *work correctly*. That is, are we guaranteed to have the same result as we would have gotten had we implemented a native XML data-exchange system? We answer this question in this paper.

To state more precisely the main question addressed in this paper, assume that we have a translation $\sigma(\cdot)$ that can be applied to (a) XML schemas, (b) XML documents, (c) XML schema mappings, and (d) XML queries. Then the concept of *correctness* of such a translation is shown below:

$$\begin{array}{lccccc} \mathrm{XML:} & \text{source } \mathcal{S} & \xrightarrow{\text{mapping } \mathcal{M}} & \text{target } \mathcal{T} & \xrightarrow{\text{query } Q} & \text{answer} \\ & \Big\downarrow \text{shred} & & \Big\downarrow \text{shred} & & \Big\downarrow \text{shred} \\ \mathrm{Relations:} & \sigma(\mathcal{S}) & \xrightarrow{\quad \sigma(\mathcal{M}) \quad} & \sigma(\mathcal{T}) & \xrightarrow{\quad \sigma(Q) \quad} & \text{answer} \end{array}$$

That is, suppose we start with an XML document $\mathcal{S}$ and an XML schema mapping $\mathcal{M}$. In a native system, we would materialize some solution $\mathcal{T}$ over which we could answer queries Q.

But now we want a relational system to do the job. So we shred $\mathcal{S}$ into $\sigma(\mathcal{S})$ and then apply to $\sigma(\mathcal{S})$ the translation of the mapping $\sigma(\mathcal{M})$ to get a solution – which itself is a shredding of an XML solution – so that the answer to Q could be reconstructed from the result of the query $\sigma(Q)$ over that relational solution.

The idea seems simple and natural on the surface, but starts looking challenging once we look deeper into it. Before even attempting to show that the relational translation faithfully represents the XML data-exchange problem, we need to address the following.

Complexity mismatch. Without restrictions, there *cannot be a faithful representation* of XML data exchange by a relational system. Indeed, it is well known that positive relational-algebra queries can be efficiently evaluated in relational data exchange [12, 21, 8], but even for simple XML analogs of conjunctive queries finding query answers can be coNP-hard [6]. So any claim that a relational data-exchange system correctly performs XML data exchange for arbitrary documents and queries is bound to be wrong. We thus need to identify the cases that can be handled by a relational system.

Which shredding scheme to use? There are several, that can roughly be divided into two groups: those that do not take the schema information into account (e.g., the edge representation [14], interval codings [33], and other numbering schemes [30]), and those that are based on schemas for XML, such as variants of the inlining technique [28, 22]. Since in data-exchange scenarios we start with two schemas, it seems more appropriate to apply schema-based techniques.

Target constraints. In relational data exchange, constraints in target schemas are required to satisfy certain acyclicity conditions; without them, the chase procedure that constructs a target instance does not terminate [12, 21, 8]. Constraints imposed by general XML schema specifications need not in general be even definable in relational calculus, let alone be acyclic [20]. We thus need to find a shredding technique that enables us to encode targets schemas by means of constraints that guarantee chase termination.

As for the complexity issue, the work on the theory of XML data exchange has identified a class of mappings for which efficient query answering is possible [6, 4, 3]. The schemas (say, DTDs), have rules of the form $db \to book^*$, $book \to author^*\ subject$ (we shall give a formal definition later), and the mappings transform patterns satisfied over the source into patterns satisfied over targets. Observe that these mappings (just as nested-relational tgds [15, 27]) are strictly more expressive than relational tgds; see the Related-Work section for a discussion.

This restriction suggests a relational representation to use. Going with the edge representation [14] is problematic: first, each edge in an XML pattern used in a mapping will result in a join in the relational translation, making it inefficient, and second, enforcing even a simple schema structure under that representation takes us out of the class of target constraints that relational data-exchange systems can handle. Verifiably correct translations based on numerical encodings [30, 33] will necessarily involve numerical and/or ordering constraints in relational translations of mappings, and this is something that relational data exchange cannot handle at the moment [21, 8] (beyond simple ordering constraints [2]).

One translation scheme however that fits in well with restrictions identified in [6, 4, 3] is the *inlining* scheme. It works very well for DTDs of the "right" shape, and its output schemas involve only acyclic constraints, which is perfect for data-exchange scenarios.

Desiderata for the translation We now formulate some basic requirements for the translation σ, in order to be able to achieve our goals described in the diagram above.[1] We need the following:

Requirement 1: translation of schemas A translation $\sigma(D)$ that, when applied to a DTD of a special form, produces a relational schema that only has acyclic constraints, which can be used in a relational data-exchange setting.

Requirement 2: translation of documents A translation $\sigma_D(\cdot)$ for a DTD D that, when applied to document T conforming to D, produces relational database $\sigma_D(T)$ of schema $\sigma(D)$.

Requirement 3: translation of queries For a DTD D, a translation $\sigma_D(Q)$ of (analogs of) conjunctive queries so that $\sigma_D(Q)\big(\sigma_D(T)\big) = Q(T)$ (that is, the result of $Q(T)$ can be computed by relational translations).

Requirement 4: translation of mappings For a mapping $\mathcal{M}$ between a source DTD D_s and a target DTD D_t, its translation $\sigma(\mathcal{M})$ is a mapping between $\sigma(D_s)$ and $\sigma(D_t)$ that preserves universal solutions. That is:

(a) Each σ_{D_t}-translation of a universal solution for T under $\mathcal{M}$ is a universal solution for $\sigma_{D_s}(T)$ under $\sigma(\mathcal{M})$; and

(b) Each universal solution for $\sigma_{D_s}(T)$ under $\sigma(\mathcal{M})$ contains[2] a σ_{D_t}-translation of a universal solution of T under $\mathcal{M}$.

Requirement 5: query answering For (analogs of) conjunctive queries over trees, computing the answer to Q under $\mathcal{M}$ over a source tree T is the same as computing a $\sigma(\mathcal{M})$-solution of $\sigma(T)$, followed by evaluation of $\sigma(Q)$ over that solution, as is normally done in a relational data-exchange system.

Satisfaction of these five requirements would guarantee that we have a *correct* relational translation of an XML data-exchange problem, which would guarantee correct evaluation of queries. The

[1] In the next sections we formalize each desideratum.

[2] We cannot require the equivalence, as relational solutions are open to adding new tuples and thus cannot always be translations of trees; we shall discuss this later.

relational approach to XML data exchange, which we propose in this paper, satisfies all the five requirements.

For the choice of the query language, one has to be careful since the definition of certain answers depends on the output of the queries. We consider two classes of conjunctive queries over trees. The first is tree patterns that output tuples of attribute values. These are the queries most commonly considered in XML data exchange [6, 4, 3] because for them we can define certain answers as the usual intersection $\text{CERTAIN}_{\mathcal{M}}(Q, \mathcal{S}) = \bigcap_i Q(\mathcal{T}_i)$. The second is a simple XML-to-XML query language from whose queries output *trees*. It is essentially the positive fragment of FLWR expressions of XQuery [31]. For outputs which are XML trees, the intersection operator is no longer meaningful for defining certain answers. Instead, we use recent results of [11] that show how to define and compute certain answers for XML-to-XML queries.

Contributions We provide a relational approach to solve two of the most important problems of XML data-exchange settings: materializing solutions and answering queries. Our specific contributions are as follows. First, we introduce an architecture for XML data exchange using relational vehicles, with a focus on correct evaluation of (analogs of) conjunctive queries on XML data. Second, we identify a class of XML schema mappings and a shredding mechanism that allows us to overcome the complexity mismatch. Third, we provide algorithms for relational translation of schemas, XML documents, schema mappings, and queries in our proposed architecture. Finally, we prove the correctness of the translations: namely, we show that they satisfy the above five requirements, and thus enable us to use relational data exchange systems for XML data-exchange tasks. Since the computational complexity of our proposed algorithms is quite low, and their correctness has been established, we believe this paper makes a case for using relational technology for provably correct XML data exchange.

Related work In recent years, significant effort has been devoted to developing high-performance XML database systems, and to building tools for data exchange. One major direction of the XML effort is the "relational approach", which uses relational DBMSs to store and query XML data. Documents could be translated into relational tuples using either a "DTD-aware" translation [29, 28] or a "schemaless" translation. The latter translations include the edge [14] and the node [33] representations of the data. Indexes could be prebuilt on the data to improve performance in relational query processing, see, e.g., [30, 33]. Constraints arising in the translation are sometimes dealt with explicitly [7, 23]. See [17] for a survey of the relational approach to answering XML queries.

The work on data exchange concentrated primarily on relations, see [8, 21] for surveys and [26, 27] for system descriptions. Mappings for the XML data exchange problem were studied in [6, 4]; it was noticed there that the complexity of many tasks in XML data exchange is higher than for their relational analogs, which suggests that restrictions must be imposed for a relational implementation. The problem of exchanging XML data was also studied in [15, 27], which give translations of documents and DTDs into nested-relational schemas, and then show how to perform XML data exchange under this translation. Most RDBMSs, however, do not provide support for nested relational schemas, and, thus, specific machinery has to be developed in order to implement this translation under a strictly relational setting. Moreover, XML mappings considered in this paper are strictly more expressive than nested-relational mappings, and every nested-relational data exchange setting can be efficiently transformed into an equivalent XML data exchange setting. Thus, the results of this paper may aid towards the development of a relational implementation for both XML and nested-relational data exchange.

Outline Key definitions are given in Section 2. Section 3 provides translations of schemas and documents and shows that they fulfill Requirements 1 and 2. Section 4 states the main concepts of relational and XML data exchange. Section 5 provides translations of mappings and queries, and shows that Requirements 3, 4, and 5 are fulfilled. Section 6 studies queries that output XML trees.

2. Preliminaries

Relational schemas and constraints. A *relational schema*, or just *schema*, is a finite set $\mathbf{R} = \{R_1, \ldots, R_k\}$ of relation symbols, possibly with a set of integrity constraints (*dependencies*). Constraints used most often in data exchange are equality- and tuple-generating dependencies [12, 21, 8], but for our purposes it will suffice to consider only *keys* and *foreign keys*. If R is a relation over attributes U, and X is a set of attributes, then X is a key of R if no two tuples of R coincide on X-attributes (that is, for all tuples $t_1, t_2 \in R$ with $t_1 \neq t_2$ we have $\pi_X(t_1) \neq \pi_X(t_2)$). If R_1 and R_2 are relations over sets of attributes U_1 and U_2, respectively, then an inclusion constraint $R_1[X] \subseteq R_2[Y]$, where $X \subseteq U_1$ and $Y \subseteq U_2$ are of the same cardinality, holds when $\pi_X(R_1) \subseteq \pi_Y(R_2)$. We further say that a foreign key on the attributes of $R_1[X] \subseteq_{FK} R_2[Y]$ holds if the inclusion constraint $R_1[X] \subseteq R_2[Y]$ holds, and Y is a key of R_2.

With each set of keys and foreign keys, we associate a graph in which we put an edge between attributes A and B if there is a constraint $R_1[X] \subseteq_{FK} R_2[Y]$ with $A \in X$ and $B \in Y$. If this graph is acyclic, we say that the set of constraints is *acyclic*. A schema is acyclic if its constraints are acyclic. In data exchange, one often uses a more technical notion of weak acyclicity: it includes some cyclic schemas for which the chase procedure still terminates. For us, however, the simple concept of acyclicity will suffice, as our translations of schemas only produce acyclic constraints.

XML documents and DTDs Assume that we have the following disjoint countably infinite sets: El of element names, Att of attribute names, and Str of possible values of string-valued attributes. All attribute names start with the symbol @.

An *XML tree* is a finite rooted directed tree $T = (N, G)$, where N is the set of nodes and G is the set of edges, together with

1. a labeling function $\lambda : N \to El$;
2. attribute-value assignments, which are partial functions $\rho_{@a} : N \to Str$ for each $@a \in Att$; and
3. an ordering on the children of every node.

A DTD D over El with a distinguished symbol r (for the root) and a set of attributes Att consists of a mapping P_D from El to regular expressions over $El - \{r\}$, usually written as productions $\ell \to e$ if $P_D(\ell) = e$, and a mapping A_D from El to 2^{Att} that assigns a (possibly empty) set of attributes to each element type. For notational convenience, we always assume that attributes come in some order, just like in the relational case: attributes in tuples come in some order so we can write $R(a_1, \ldots, a_n)$. Likewise, we shall describe an ℓ labeled tree node with n attributes as $\ell(a_1, \ldots, a_n)$.

A tree T conforms to a DTD D (written as $T \models D$) if its root is labeled r, the set of attributes for a node labeled ℓ is $A_D(\ell)$, and the labels of the children of such a node, read from left to right, form a string in the language of $P_D(\ell)$.

A class of DTDs In this paper we consider a restriction on DTDs called *nested-relational DTDs* [1, 6], a class of DTDs that naturally represent nested relational schemas such as the ones used by the Clio data-exchange system [26]. The reason for using them is that outside of this class, it is very easy to construct instances of

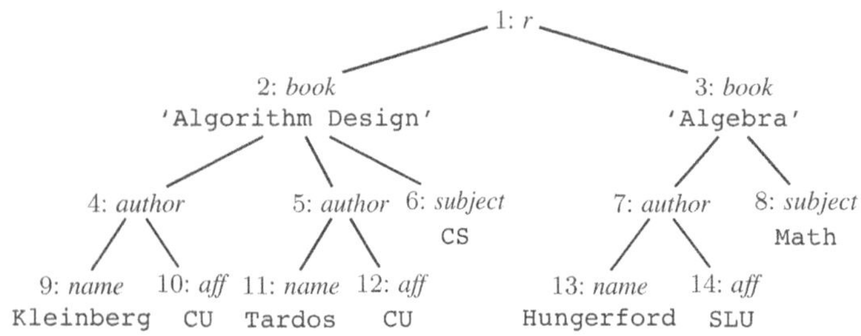

(a) Tree T

$$\begin{array}{lcl} r & \rightarrow & book^* \\ book & \rightarrow & author^*\ subject \\ author & \rightarrow & name\ aff \\ A_D(book) & = & @title \\ A_D(subject) & = & @sub \\ A_D(name) & = & @nam \\ A_D(aff) & = & @aff \end{array}$$

(b) DTD D

Figure 1: The XML tree T conforms to D

XML data-exchange problems that will exhibit coNP-hardness of answering conjunctive queries (which are known to be tractable in practically all instances of relational data exchange), see [6].

A DTD D is *non-recursive* if the graph $G(D)$ defined as $\{(\ell,\ell') \mid \ell'$ is mentioned in $P(\ell)\}$ is acyclic. A non-recursive DTD D is *nested-relational* if all rules of D are of the form $l \to \tilde{l}_0 \dots \tilde{l}_m$ where all the l_i's are distinct, and each $\tilde{l}_i$ is one of l_i and l_i^*. From now on, unless otherwise noted, all DTDs are assumed to be nested-relational. We also assume, without loss of generality, that the graph $G(D)$ is not a directed acyclic graph (DAG) but a tree. (One can always unfold a DAG into a tree by tagging occurrences of element types with the types of their predecessors.)

EXAMPLE 2.1. Figure 1(a) shows an example of an XML tree. In the Figure, the node identifiers precede the corresponding labels of each node in T; we omit the attribute names and only show the attribute values of each node. In addition, Figure 1(b) shows an example of a nested relational DTD. Moreover, it is easy to see that the tree T of Figure 1(a) conforms to D. □

3. Translations of schemas and documents

We now review the *inlining* technique [28], provide a precise definition of the translation, and show that it satisfies our **Requirements 1** and **2**. The main idea of inlining is that separate relations are created for the root and each element type that appears under a star, and other element types are inlined in the relations corresponding to their "nearest appropriate ancestor". Each relation for an element type has an ID attribute that is a key, as well as (for non-root) a "parent-ID" attribute that is a foreign key pointing to the "nearest appropriate ancestor" of that element in the document. All the attributes of a given element type in the DTD become attributes in the relation corresponding to that element type when such a relation exists, or otherwise become attributes in the relation for the "nearest appropriate ancestor" of the given element type.

We begin with a formal definition of the *nearest appropriate ancestor* for the element types used in D. Given a nested-relational DTD $D = (P_D, A_D, r)$, we "mark" in $G(D)$ each element type that occurs under a star in P_D. In addition, we mark the root element type in $G(D)$. Then, for a given element type ℓ, we define the *nearest appropriate ancestor* of ℓ, denoted by $\mu(\ell)$, as the closest marked element type ℓ' in the path from the root element to ℓ in the graph $G(D)$. The inlining schema generation is formally captured by means of the procedure INLSCHEMA below.

EXAMPLE 3.1. Consider again DTD D in Figure 1(b). The relational schema INLSCHEMA(D) is as follows:

R_r(<u>`rID`</u>)
R_{book}(<u>`bookID`</u>,`@title,rID,subID,@sub`)
R_{author}(<u>`authID`</u>,`bookID,nameID,afID,@nam,@aff`)

Keys are underlined; we also have the following foreign keys: $R_{book}(\texttt{rID}) \subseteq_{FK} R_r(\texttt{rID})$ and $R_{author}(\texttt{bookID}) \subseteq_{FK} R_{book}(\texttt{bookID})$. □

Procedure INLSCHEMA(D)

Input : A nested relational DTD D.
Output: A relational schema $\mathbf{S}_D$ and a set of integrity constraints Δ_D

Set $\mathbf{S}_D = \emptyset$ and $\Delta_D = \emptyset$
for each *marked element type ℓ of D:*
add to $\mathbf{S}_D$ a relation R_ℓ, with attributes:

$$attr(R_\ell) = \begin{cases} id_\ell & \\ A_D(\ell) & \\ id_{\mu(\ell)} & \mid \text{ if } \ell \neq r. \\ id_{\ell'} & \mid \ \mu(\ell') = \ell, \ell' \text{ is not marked,} \\ A_D(\ell') & \mid \ \mu(\ell') = \ell, \ell' \text{ is not marked.} \end{cases}$$

endfor
for each *relation R_ℓ in $\mathbf{S}_D$:*
add to Δ_D the constraint stating that id_ℓ is key of R_ℓ and, if $\ell \neq r$, the foreign key

$$R_\ell[id_{\mu(\ell)}] \subseteq_{FK} R_{\mu(\ell)}[id_{\mu(\ell)}].$$

endfor
add to Δ_D the dependency (stating the uniqueness of the root)

$$\forall \bar{y} \forall \bar{z} R_r(x, \bar{y}) \wedge R_r(x', \bar{z}) \rightarrow x = x'.$$

return ($\mathbf{S}_D, \Delta_D$)

The following shows that our **Requirement 1** is satisfied.

PROPOSITION 3.2. *For every nested relational DTD D, the output of* INLSCHEMA*(D) is an acyclic relational schema.*

Shredding of XML documents. We now move to the shredding procedure. Given the inlining INLSCHEMA(D) $= (\mathbf{S}_D, \Delta_D)$ of a DTD D, and an XML tree T conforming to D, we use the algorithm INLDOC to *shred* T into an instance of the relational schema $\mathbf{S}_D$ that satisfies the constraints in Δ_D. Let us first explain this translation by means of an example.

EXAMPLE 3.3. Recall tree T from Figure 1(a) and DTD D from Figure 1(b). Figure 2 shows relations R_{book} and R_{author} in the shredding of T. □

To present the algorithm, we define the *nearest appropriate ancestor* $\mu(n)$ of a node n of an XML document T that conforms to a DTD D, as follows. Mark each node n of T such that $\lambda(n)$ is starred in D, as well as the root of T. Then $\mu(n)$ is the closest marked node n' that belongs to the path from the root to n. In the following algorithm, and for the remainder of the paper, we denote by id_n the relational element representing the node n of a tree T.

bookID	@title	rID	subID	@sub
id_2	'Algorithm Design'	id_1	id_6	CS
id_3	'Algebra'	id_1	id_8	Math

(a) Relation R_{book} in INLDOC(T, D)

authID	bookID	nameID	afID	@nam	@af
id_4	id_2	id_9	id_{10}	'Kleinberg'	CU
id_5	id_2	id_{11}	id_{12}	'Tardos'	CU
id_7	id_3	id_{13}	id_{14}	'Hungerford'	SLU

(b) Relation R_{author} in INLDOC(T, D)

Figure 2: Shredding of T into INLSCHEMA(D)

Procedure INLDOC (T, D)

Input : A nested relational DTD D and an XML tree T that conforms to D.

Output: A relational instance of the schema INLSCHEMA(D).

for each *marked node n of T:*

Let ℓ be the label of n; Add to the relation R_ℓ of I a tuple that contains elements

$$\begin{cases} id_n & \\ \rho_{@a}(n) & \mid \quad @a \in A_D(\ell) \\ id_{\mu(n)} & \mid \quad \text{if } \ell \neq r \\ id_{n'} & \mid \quad \mu(n') = n, n' \text{ is not marked.} \\ \rho_{@a}(n') & \mid \quad \mu(n') = n \text{ , } @a \in A_D(\lambda(n')) \text{ and} \\ & \quad\;\; n' \text{ is not marked} \end{cases}$$

where the identifiers and attributes values for each of the elements $id_{n'}$, $id_{\mu(n)}$ and $\rho_{@a}(n')$ coincide with the position of the attributes for $id_{\lambda(n')}$, $id_{\mu(\ell)}$ and $A_D(\lambda(n'))$ of R_ℓ.

endfor

return I

The following proposition shows our **Requirement 2** is satisfied.

PROPOSITION 3.4. *Let D be a DTD, and T an XML tree such that $T \models D$. Then* INLDOC(T, D) *is an instance of the schema computed by* INLSCHEMA(D).

4. Relational and XML Data Exchange

We now quickly review the basics of relational data exchange and introduce XML schema mappings that guarantee tractable query answering.

Relational Data Exchange A schema mapping $\mathcal{M}$ is a triple $(\mathbb{S}, \mathbb{T}, \Sigma)$, where $\mathbb{S}$ is a source schema, $\mathbb{T} = (\mathbf{T}, \Delta_\mathbf{T})$ is a target schema with a set of constraints Δ_T, and Σ is a set of *source-to-target dependencies* that specify how the source and the target are related. Most commonly these are given as source-to-target tuple generating dependencies (st-tgds):

$$\varphi(\bar{x}) \rightarrow \exists \bar{z}\, \psi(\bar{x}, \bar{z}), \qquad (1)$$

where φ and ψ are conjunctions of relational atoms over $\mathbb{S}$ and $\mathbb{T}$, respectively.

In data-exchange literature, one normally considers instances with two types of values: constants and nulls. Instances $\mathcal{S}$ of the source schema $\mathbb{S}$ consist only of constant values, and nulls are used to populate target instances $\mathcal{T}$ when some values are unknown.

An instance $\mathcal{T}$ of $\mathbb{T}$ (which may contain both constants and nulls) is called a *solution* for an instance $\mathcal{S}$ of $\mathbb{S}$ under $\mathcal{M}$, or an $\mathcal{M}$-*solution*, if every st-tgd (1) from Σ is satisfied by $(\mathcal{S}, \mathcal{T})$ (that is, for each tuple $\bar{a}$ such that $\varphi(\bar{a})$ is true in $\mathcal{S}$, there is a tuple $\bar{b}$ such that $\psi(\bar{a}, \bar{b})$ is true in $\mathcal{T}$).The set of all $\mathcal{M}$-solutions for $\mathcal{S}$ is denoted by SOL$_\mathcal{M}(\mathcal{S})$ (or SOL$(\mathcal{S})$ if $\mathcal{M}$ is understood).

Certain answers and canonical universal solution The main difficulty in answering a query Q against the target schema is that there could be many possible solutions for a given source. Thus, for query answering in data exchange one normally uses the notion of certain answers, that is, answers that do not depend on a particular solution. Formally, for a source $\mathcal{S}$ and a mapping $\mathcal{M}$, we define CERTAIN$_\mathcal{M}(Q, \mathcal{S})$ as $\bigcap\{Q(\mathcal{T}) \mid \mathcal{T} \in$ SOL$_\mathcal{M}(\mathcal{S})\}$.

Building all solutions is impractical (or even impossible), so it is important to find a particular solution $\mathcal{T}_0 \in$ SOL$_\mathcal{M}(\mathcal{S})$, and a rewriting Q_{rewr} of Q, so that CERTAIN$_\mathcal{M}(Q, \mathcal{S}) = Q_{\text{rewr}}(\mathcal{T}_0)$.

Universal solutions were identified in [12] as the preferred solutions in data exchange. Over them, every positive query can be answered, with a particularly simple rewriting: after Q is evaluated on a universal solution $\mathcal{T}_0$, tuples containing null values are discarded. Even among universal solutions there are ones that are most commonly materialized in data-exchange systems, such as the *canonical solution* CANSOL$_\mathcal{M}(\mathcal{S})$, computed by applying the chase procedure with constraints Σ and $\Delta_\mathbf{T}$ to the source instance $\mathcal{S}$. If all the constraints in $\Delta_\mathbf{T}$ are acyclic (in fact, even a weaker notion suffices), such a chase terminates and computes CANSOL$_\mathcal{M}(\mathcal{S})$ in polynomial time [12].

Note that our **Requirement 4** relates universal solutions in relational and XML data exchange; in particular, we do not insist on working with the canonical solutions, and others, such as the core [13] or the algorithmic constructions of [25] can be used as well.

Towards XML schema mappings: patterns To define XML schema mappings, we need the notions of schemas and source-to-target dependencies. The notion of schema is well understood in the XML context. Our dependencies, as in [6, 4, 3] will be based on *tree patterns*. Patterns are defined inductively as follows:

- $\ell(\bar{x})$ is a pattern, where ℓ is a label, and $\bar{x}$ is a (possibly empty) tuple of variables (listing attributes of a node);
- $\ell(\bar{x})[\pi_1, \ldots, \pi_k]$ is a pattern, where $\pi_1, \ldots, \pi_k$ are patterns, and ℓ and $\bar{x}$ are as above.

We write $\pi(\bar{x})$ to indicate that $\bar{x}$ is the tuple of all the variables used in a pattern. The semantics is defined with respect to a node of a tree and to a valuation of all the variables of a pattern as attribute values. Formally, $(T, v) \models \pi(\bar{a})$ means that π is satisfied in node v when $\bar{x}$ is interpreted as $\bar{a}$. It is defined as follows:

- $(T, v) \models \ell(\bar{a})$ if v is labeled ℓ and its tuple of attributes is $\bar{a}$;
- $(T, v) \models \ell(\bar{a})[\pi_1(\bar{a}_1), \ldots, \pi_k(\bar{a}_k)]$ if
  1. $(T, v) \models \ell(\bar{a})$ and
  2. there exist children $v_1, \ldots, v_k$ of v (not necessarily distinct) so that $(T, v_i) \models \pi_i(\bar{a}_i)$ for every $i \leq k$.

We write $T \models \pi(\bar{a})$ if $(T, r) \models \pi(\bar{a})$, that is, the pattern is witnessed at the root.

EXAMPLE 4.1. Consider tree T from Figure 1(a), and the tree pattern $\pi(x, y) = r[book(x)[author[name(y)]]]$, which finds books together with the names of their authors. Then it is easy to see that $T \models \pi($`'Algorithm Design'`, `Tardos`$)$. In fact, evaluation of $\pi(x, y)$ over T returns the tuples (`'Algorithm Design'`, `Tardos`), (`'Algorithm Design'`, `Kleinberg`), and (`'Algebra'`,`Hungerford`). □

Given a DTD D and a tree pattern π, we say that π is *compatible* with D if there exists a tree T that conforms to D and a tuple of attribute values $\bar{a}$ such that $T \models \pi(\bar{a})$. In general, checking compatibility of patterns with DTDs is NP-complete [10], but for the DTDs we consider here it can be easily done in polynomial time.

EXAMPLE 4.2.[Example 4.1 continued] The pattern $\pi(x, y)$ is compatible with the DTD D of Figure 1(b). On the other hand, the pattern $\pi'(x) = r[author(x)]$ is not, because no tree consistent with D can have a child of r labeled as *author*, or an *author*-labeled node with an attribute. □

Remark More general patterns have been considered in the literature [5, 24, 10, 4, 3]; in particular, they may involve descendant navigation, wild cards for labels, and sibling order. However, [6, 4, 3] showed that with these features added, query answering in data exchange becomes intractable even for very simple queries. In fact, the restrictions we use in our definition were identified in [6] as essential for tractability of query answering. Note that the same restriction was imposed to queries when transforming XML data into nested-relational schemas [15, 27].

XML schema mappings As our descriptions of XML schemas we shall use DTDs (since for complex schemas, query answering in data exchange is known to be intractable [6], and DTDs will suffice to capture all the known tractable cases). Source-to-target constraints will be given via patterns.

Formally, an *XML schema mapping* is a triple $\mathcal{M} = (D_S, D_T, \Sigma)$, where D_S is the source (nested relational) DTD, D_T is the target (nested relational) DTD, and Σ is a set of *XML source-to-target dependencies* [6], or XML stds, of form

$$\pi(\bar{x}) \to \pi'(\bar{x}, \bar{z}), \tag{2}$$

where π and π' are tree patterns compatible with D_S and D_T, respectively.

As in the relational case, target trees may contain nulls to account for values not specified by mappings. Given a tree T that conforms to D_S, a tree T' (over constants and nulls) is an $\mathcal{M}$-solution for T if T' conforms to D_T, and the pair (T, T') satisfies all the dependencies (2) from Σ. The latter means that for every tuple $\bar{a}$ of attribute values from T, if T satisfies $\pi(\bar{a})$, then there exists a tuple $\bar{b}$ of attribute values from T' such that T' satisfies $\pi'(\bar{a}, \bar{b})$. The set of all $\mathcal{M}$-solutions for T is denoted by $\text{SOL}_{\mathcal{M}}(T)$.

EXAMPLE 4.3. Consider the data-exchange scenario $(D, D_T, \mathcal{M})$ given by the DTDs D and D_T of Figures 1(b) and 3(b), respectively, and where $\mathcal{M}$ is specified by the dependency

$$r[book(x)[author[name(y)]]] \to r[writer[name(y), work(x)]],$$

that restructures book-author pairs as writer-work. It can be shown that the XML tree T' in Figure 3(a) is an $\mathcal{M}$-solution for T. □

5. XML data exchange using relations

We now provide algorithms for implementing XML data exchange via relational translations. Since we have already shown how to translate DTDs and documents, we need to present translations of stds of mappings and queries. Both of them are based on translating patterns into relational conjunctive queries. We first concentrate on that translation. Then we show how to extend it easily to mappings and queries, and prove the correctness of the translations. This will complete our program of using a relational system for XML data exchange in a semantically correct way.

Inlining tree patterns. The key ingredient in our algorithms is a translation of patterns π compatible with a DTD D into a *conjunctive query* INLPATTERN(π, D) over the relational schema INLSCHEMA(D). Very roughly, it can be viewed as this:

1. View a pattern $\pi(\bar{x})$ as a tree T_π in which some attribute values could be variables;
2. Compute the relational database INLDOC(T_π, D) (which may have variables as attribute values);
3. View INLDOC(T_π, D) as a tableau of a conjunctive query; the resulting query is INLPATTERN(π, D).

The algorithm is actually more complicated because INLDOC cannot be used in Step 2; we shall explain shortly why.

Towards defining INLPATTERN, observe that each tree pattern $\pi(\bar{x})$ can be viewed as an XML document $T_{\pi(\bar{x})}$, in which both values and variables can be used as attribute values. It is defined inductively as follows: $T_{\ell(\bar{x})}$ is a single-node tree labeled ℓ, with $\bar{x}$ as attribute values, and if π is $\ell(\bar{x})[\pi_1(\bar{x}_1), \ldots, \pi_k(\bar{x}_k)]$, then the root of T_π is labeled ℓ and has $\bar{x}$ as attribute values. It also has k children, with the subtrees rooted at them being $T_{\pi_1(\bar{x}_1)}, \ldots, T_{\pi_k(\bar{x}_k)}$.

However, even for a pattern $\pi(\bar{x})$ compatible with a DTD D, we may not be able to define its inlining as the inlining of $T_{\pi(\bar{x})}$, because $T_{\pi(\bar{x})}$ need not conform to D. For example, if a DTD has a rule $r \to ab$ and we have a pattern $r[a]$, it is compatible with D, but $T_{r[a]}$ does not conform to D, as it is missing a b-node. Hence, the procedure INLDOC cannot be used 'as-is' in our algorithm.

Nevertheless, we can still mark the nodes of $T_{\pi(\bar{x})}$ with respect to D and define the nearest appropriate ancestor exactly as it has been done previously. Intuitively, the procedure INLPATTERN shreds each node of $T_{\pi(\bar{x})}$ into a different predicate, and then joins these predicates using the nearest appropriate ancestor.

Procedure INLPATTERN(π, D)

Input : A DTD D, a tree pattern $\pi(\bar{x})$ compatible with D.
Output: Conjunctive query over INLSCHEMA(D).

for each *node* v *of* $T_{\pi(\bar{x})}$ *of form* $\ell(\bar{x}_v)$:
Construct a query $Q_v(\bar{x}_v)$ as follows:

if v is marked **then**

$$Q_v(\bar{x}_v) := \exists id_v \exists id_{\mu(v)} \exists \bar{z} R_\ell(id_v, \bar{x}_v, id_{\mu(v)}, \bar{z}),$$

where $\bar{z}$ is a tuple of fresh variables, and the positions of variables id_v, $\bar{x}_v$ and $id_{\mu(v)}$ are consistent with the attributes id_ℓ, $A_D(\ell)$ and $id_{\mu(\ell)}$ respectively in *attr*(R_ℓ).
If $\ell = r$, then Q_v does not use $id_{\mu(v)}$.

else (v is not marked):
set v':=$\mu(v)$, ℓ':=$\lambda(v')$, and let $Q_v(\bar{x}_v)$ be

$$\exists id_{v'} \exists id_{\mu(v')} \exists id_v \exists \bar{z} R_{\ell'}(id_{v'}, id_{\mu(v')}, id_v, \bar{x}_v, \bar{z}),$$

where $\bar{z}$ is a tuple of fresh variables, and the positions of the variables $id_{v'}$, $id_{\mu(v')}$, id_v and $\bar{x}_v$ are consistent with the attributes $id_{\ell'}$, $id_{\mu(\ell')}$, id_ℓ and $A_D(\ell)$ respectively in *attr*$(R_{\ell'})$. If $\ell' = r$, then Q_v does not use $id_{\mu(v')}$.

endfor
return $\bigwedge_{v \in T_{\pi(\bar{x})}} Q_v(\bar{x}_v)$.

Note that the compatibility of π with D ensures that INLPATTERN is well defined. That is, (1) every attribute formula of the form $\ell(\bar{x})$ only mentions attributes in $A_D(\ell)$, and (2) for all nodes $v, v' \in T_{\pi(\bar{x})}$, if v' is a child of v, then $\lambda(v') \in P_D(\lambda(v))$.

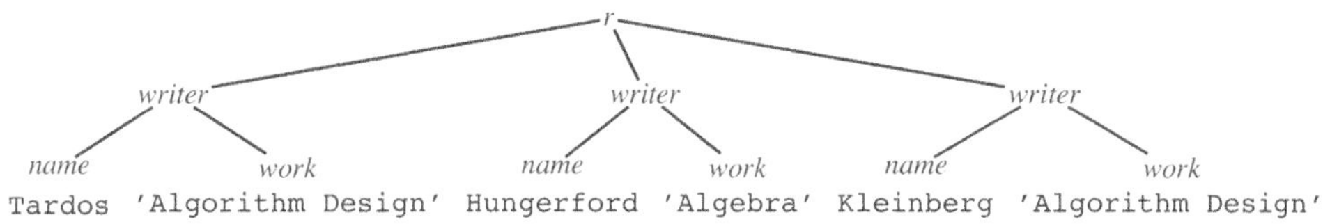

(a) Target Tree T'

$$
\begin{array}{lcl}
r & \to & writer^* \\
writer & \to & name\ work^* \\
A_D(name) & = & @nam \\
A_D(work) & = & @title
\end{array}
$$

(b) Target DTD D_T

Figure 3: Tree T' is an $\mathcal{M}$-solution for T

Correctness. Given a pattern $\pi(\bar{x})$, the evaluation of π on a tree T is $\pi(T) = \{\bar{a} \mid T \models \pi(\bar{a})\}$. The following proposition shows the correctness of INLPATTERN.

PROPOSITION 5.1. *Given a nested relational DTD D, a pattern π compatible with D, and a tree T that conforms to D, we have $\pi(T) = \text{INLPATTERN}(\pi, D)(\text{INLDOC}(T, D))$.*

That is, the inlining of π, applied to the inlining of T, returns $\pi(T)$.

Conjunctive queries over trees. We use the language that is essentially conjunctive queries over trees [6, 16, 10] with navigation along the child axis.

The language $\mathcal{CTQ}$ is obtained by closing patterns under conjunction and existential quantification:

$$Q \;:=\; \pi \mid Q \wedge Q \mid \exists x\, Q,$$

where π is a fully specified tree-pattern formula. The semantics is straightforward, given the semantics of patterns defined above: $Q(\bar{a}) \wedge Q'(\bar{b})$ is true iff both $Q(\bar{a})$ and $Q'(\bar{b})$ are true, and $\exists x\, Q(\bar{a}, x)$ is true iff $Q(\bar{a}, c)$ is true for some value c. The output of Q on a tree T is denoted by $Q(T)$.

We say that a query Q is compatible with the DTD D if every pattern used in it is compatible with D.

The inlining of queries Q compatible with D is given by the recursive algorithm INLQUERY below.

Procedure INLQUERY (Q, D)

Input : A DTD D, a query Q compatible with D.
Output: A conjunctive query over INLSCHEMA(D)

if $Q = \pi$ **then**
  return INLPATTERN(π, D)
else if $Q = Q_1 \wedge Q_2$ **then**
  return INLQUERY(Q_1, D) $\wedge$ INLQUERY(Q_2, D)
else if $Q = \exists x Q_1$ **then**
  return $\exists x$ INLQUERY(Q_1, D)

Now we show that every query Q in $\mathcal{CTQ}$ can be computed by its inlining on the inlining of its input (assuming, of course, compatibility with a DTD). In other words, **Requirement 3** is satisfied.

THEOREM 5.2. *Given a DTD D, a tree T that conforms to it, and a compatible query Q, we have*

$$Q(T) \;=\; \text{INLQUERY}(Q, D)(\text{INLDOC}(T, D)).$$

Inlining XML schema mappings We use our transformation of tree patterns to define the procedure INLMAP, that, given source and target DTDs D_S and D_T, transforms an XML mapping $\mathcal{M}$ into a relational mapping INLMAP($\mathcal{M}$,D_S,D_T) specified with a set of source-to-target tuple generating dependencies.

Correctness While one could be tempted to ask for a translation that preserves all solutions, such a result need not hold. The relational mapping INLMAP uses null values to represent the shredded

---

Procedure INLMAP ($\mathcal{M}$, D_S, D_T)

Input : An XML mapping $\mathcal{M}$ from a source DTD D_S to a target DTD D_T.
Output: A relational mapping from INLSCHEMA(D_S) to INLSCHEMA(D_T).

Set INLMAP($\mathcal{M}, D_S, D_T$) := $\emptyset$
for *dependency* $\pi(\bar{x}) \to \exists \bar{z} \pi'(\bar{x}, \bar{z})$ *in* $\mathcal{M}$ **do**
  INLMAP($\mathcal{M}, D_S, D_T$) := INLMAP($\mathcal{M}, D_S, D_T$) $\bigcup$ $\{\text{INLQUERY}(\pi, D_S)(\bar{x}) \to \exists \bar{z}\ \text{INLQUERY}(\pi', D_T)(\bar{x}, \bar{z})\}$
end
return INLMAP($\mathcal{M}, D_S, D_T$)

---

nodes of XML trees, and thus we should only consider solutions whose null values have not been renamed. However, relational solutions are open to renaming of nulls. This intuition can be formalized by means of the universal solutions, which are the most general among all solutions, and thus do not permit null renaming. Furthermore, one typically materializes a universal solution, as these solutions contain all the information needed to compute certain answers of conjunctive queries. This motivates the restriction of our **Requirement 4** to universal solutions.

The theorem below shows that parts (a) and (b) of **Requirement 4** hold. Note that in part (b), relational universal solutions are only required to contain a shredding of an XML universal solution. This is because relational solutions are also open to adding arbitrary tuples, which need not reflect a tree structure of an XML document.

THEOREM 5.3. *a) Let $\mathcal{M} = (D_S, D_T, \Sigma)$ be an XML schema mapping and T an XML document that conforms to D_S. If T' is an $\mathcal{M}$-universal solution for T, then its inlining INLDOC(T', D_T) is an INLMAP($\mathcal{M}, D_S, D_T$)-universal solution for INLDOC(T, D_S).*
b) Let $\mathcal{M} = (D_S, D_T, \Sigma)$ be an XML schema mapping, and T an XML document that conforms to D_S. Then for every INLMAP($\mathcal{M}, D_S, D_T$)-universal solution R for INLDOC(T, D_S) there exists an $\mathcal{M}$-universal solution T' such that INLDOC(T', D_T) is contained in R.

Answering XML queries using relational data exchange. The semantics of query answering in data exchange, both relational and XML [12, 21, 8, 6, 4], is defined by means of certain answers. That is, given a schema mapping $\mathcal{M} = (D_S, D_T, \Sigma)$, a tree T that conforms to D_S, and a conjunctive tree query Q that is compatible with D_T, the *certain answers of Q for T under $\mathcal{M}$*, denoted by CERTAIN$_{\mathcal{M}}(Q, T)$, is the set of tuples that belong to the evaluation of Q over every possible $\mathcal{M}$-solution for T, that is, $\bigcap\{Q(T') \mid T'$ is an $\mathcal{M}$-solution for $T\}$. Note that our queries return sets of tuples, so we can talk about the intersection operator.

It was shown in [6, 4] that, for conjunctive tree queries and mappings using nested-relational DTDs, computing certain answers for a given source tree T is solvable in polynomial time. Thus, for the classes of mappings and queries we consider, there is no complexity mismatch between relational and XML data exchange. The next theorem shows that our translation is correct with respect to query answering, that is, our **Requirement 5** is satisfied.

THEOREM 5.4. *Let $\mathcal{M} = (D_S, D_T, \Sigma)$ be an XML schema mapping. Then, for every XML tree T that satisfies D_S and for every conjunctive tree query Q, the certain answers of Q for T under $\mathcal{M}$ and the certain answers of* INLQUERY(Q, D_T) *for* INLDOC(T, D_S) *over* INLMAP$(\mathcal{M}, D_S, D_T)$ *coincide:*

$$\text{CERTAIN}_{\mathcal{M}}(Q,T) = \text{CERTAIN}_{\text{INLMAP}(M)}(\text{INLQUERY}(Q, D_T), \text{INLDOC}(T, D_S)).$$

This result, combined with the standard procedure of evaluating conjunctive queries in relational data exchange, also gives us an algorithm for computing certain answers.

COROLLARY 5.5. *Under the conditions of Theorem 5.4,* CERTAIN$_{\mathcal{M}}(Q,T)$ *can be obtained by the following procedure:*

1. *run* INLQUERY(Q, D_T) *on an* INLMAP$(\mathcal{M}, D_S, D_T)$*-universal solution for* INLDOC(T, D_S)*;*
2. *discard all tuples that contain null values.*

6. XML-to-XML Queries

Up to now, we have only considered queries that output tuples of attribute values. In this section, we shall focus on proper XML-to-XML query languages, that is, queries that output XML trees.

Some immediate questions arise when dealing with these formalisms in a data exchange context. Let $\mathcal{M} = (D_S, D_T, \Sigma)$ be an XML schema mapping, T be a tree conforming to D_S, and $\mathcal{Q}$ be an XML-to-XML query. Since the evaluation of $\mathcal{Q}$ over T returns an XML tree, we cannot define certain answers as $\bigcap\{\mathcal{Q}(T')) \mid T'$ is a solution for $T\}$, since the meaning of the intersection operator for XML documents is not clear.

To overcome this problem, we use recent results from [11] which showed how to define certain answers for queries returning XML trees, and how to use them in data exchange context. The key idea of [11] is to use tree patterns to define information contained in documents, and to use them to represent compactly the certain knowledge from the collection $\{\mathcal{Q}(T')) \mid T'$ is a solution for $T\}$. More precisely, if Π is a set of tree patterns which are matched by every tree $Q(T')$, we look for a small set Π_0 of patterns that is equivalent to Π as a description of certain answers. By equivalence we mean that a tree matches every pattern in Π iff it matches every pattern in Π_0. If the set Π_0 is finite, then its patterns can be put together to create a tree with nulls, which we then view as the certain answer.

We shall not need additional details of the construction; instead we shall use a result from [11] that tells us how certain answers can be computed for a specific XML-to-XML query language. The language, called TQL (to be defined shortly), is inspired by XQuery's FLWR expressions, and is restricted to positive features (i.e., no negation). The key result from [11] is the following:

PROPOSITION 6.1 ([11]). *Let $\mathcal{M} = (D_S, D_T, \Sigma)$ be an XML schema mapping, Q a TQL query, and T a tree that conforms to D_S. If T' is an $\mathcal{M}$-universal solution for T, then* CERTAIN$_{\mathcal{M}}(Q,T) = Q(T')$.

Given this result, we now do the following. We provide a formal definition of the TQL language of [11], which can express XML-to-XML analogs of relational conjunctive queries. We then show how to adapt the machinery we have previously developed for evaluating certain asnwers over a universal solution. Note that for this new translation, a TQL query Q returning trees needs to be translated into a *set* of relational queries generating views that define the shredding of the tree $Q(T)$.

6.1 TQL queries

TQL queries [11] are inspired by the FLWR (for-let-where-return) expressions of XQuery [31], but they only use positive features. The key construct is $\textsf{for}\ \pi(\bar{x})\ \textsf{return}\ q(\bar{x})$, where $\pi(\bar{x})$ is a pattern and $q(\bar{x})$ is a query that defines a forest expression. Formally, the syntax of forest expressions is

$$\begin{array}{rcl} q(\bar{x}) & ::= & \epsilon \\ & | & \ell(\bar{a}, \bar{x}')[q'(\bar{x}'')] \\ & | & q'(\bar{x}'), q''(\bar{x}'') \\ & | & \textsf{for}\ \pi(\bar{a}, \bar{x}, \bar{y})\ \textsf{return}\ q'(\bar{x}, \bar{y}) \end{array}$$

where ℓ ranges over node labels, $\bar{a}$ over constant attribute values, and $\bar{x}$ etc are tuples of variables.

A TQL query Q is an expression of the form $r[q]$, where q is a forest expression without variables. To define the semantics of this language, we first define inductively the forest $[\![q(\bar{x})]\!]_{T,v}$, for a valuation v of all variables in $\bar{x}$ as attribute values. We use the notation $\ell(\bar{a})[f]$ for a tree whose root is labeled ℓ and carries a tuple of attributes $\bar{a}$, and f is the forest of subtrees below the root.

$$\begin{array}{rcl} [\![\epsilon]\!]_{T,v} & = & \epsilon \text{ (empty forest)} \\ [\![\ell(\bar{a}, \bar{x}')[q'(\bar{x}'')]]\!]_{T,v} & = & \ell(\bar{a}, v(\bar{x}'))[[\![q']\!]_{T,v}] \\ [\![q'(\bar{x}), q''(\bar{x}'')]\!]_{T,v} & = & [\![q']\!]_{T,v} \cup [\![q'']\!]_{T,v} \end{array}$$

$$[\![\textsf{for}\ \pi(\bar{a}, \bar{x}, \bar{y})\ \textsf{return}\ q'(\bar{x}, \bar{y})]\!]_{T,v} =$$

$$\bigcup \{[\![q']\!]_{T,v'} \mid v' \text{ extends } v \text{ and } T \models \pi(\bar{a}, v'(\bar{x}), v'(\bar{y}))\}$$

For a tree T and a query $Q = r[q]$, the evaluation $Q(T)$ of Q over T is defined as the tree $r[[\![q]\!]_T]$, i.e., the forest $[\![q]\!]_T$ under root r.

EXAMPLE 6.2. Recall the tree T from figure 1(a). The tree T' from figure 3(a) can also be obtained as the transformation $Q(T)$ resulting from the evaluation of a TQL query Q over T, where $Q = r[q]$, and q is defined as

$$\textsf{for}\ r/book(x)/author/name(y)\ \textsf{return} \quad writer[name(y), work(x)] \qquad (3)$$

For the sake of readability, we use the / operator to denote the child axis in tree patterns. □

6.2 Inlining TQL queries

If Q is a TQL query, then, to be able to define its inlining translation, we need to specify a DTD for trees $Q(T)$. Note that TQL queries define the shape of their outputs, and at the same time do not put restrictions on the number of appearances of labels. Hence it is natural to define the DTD for outputs of Q as a *starred* DTD D_Q, whose shape is determined by Q, and where each element type except the root occurs under the Kleene star.

More precisely, for a forest expression q, we define a forest F_q inductively as follows: F_ε is the empty forest; $F_{\ell[q']}$ is $\ell[F_{q'}]$; $F_{q' \cup q''} = F_{q'} \cup F_{q''}$, and $F_{\textsf{for}\ \pi\ \textsf{return}\ q'} = F_{q'}$. For $Q = r[q]$ we let $T_Q = r[F_q]$.

Then D_Q is a non-recursive DTD that has a rule $p \rightarrow c_1^* \cdots c_n^*$ for each node p in T_Q with children labelled $c_1, \ldots, c_n$. As usual, we require that D_Q be acyclic and we assume without loss of generality that $G(D_Q)$ is a tree.

EXAMPLE 6.3.[Example 6.2 continued] Recall query $Q = r[q]$. Then, T_Q is the XML tree given by $r[writer[name, work]]$, and thus D_Q contains productions $r \rightarrow writer^*$, $writer \rightarrow name^*\, work^*$, $name \rightarrow \epsilon$ and $work \rightarrow \epsilon$. □

Before showing the algorithm INLTQL, we need to introduce some features that will be used in the algorithm. Consider again query (3) and DTD D_Q in examples 6.2 and 6.3. For each pair of attributes that satisfy $r/book(x)/author/name(y)$, the query Q creates a subtree $writer[name(y), work(x)]$ in the tree $Q(T)$. Thus, the relational translation would need to create one tuple in the relations corresponding to *writer*, *name* and *work* for each pair of attributes x, y that satisfy the relational translation of the pattern $r/book(x)/author/name(y)$ in the instance INLDOC(T).

Thus, in the relational translation we need a way to associate each particular *writer* wih a particular *name* and *work*. One possible way of doing this is by creating a (Skolem) function f that associates with each pair $(name, work)$ a unique identifier for the corresponding *writer*. Thus, the function f must be defined in such a way that $f(book, name)$ is different for each different pair $(name, work)$. We enforce this requirement by letting each term $f(\bar{a})$ represent a distinct constant $c_{f(\bar{a})}$.

We will define our translation algorithm inductively. The key procedure TQLSTEP for the inductive step is described below. Its inputs, in addition to a query and a DTD, include a conjunctive query corresponding to the conjunction of patterns in the query, and a function term corresponding to the parent in the tree $Q(T)$ (for example, when creating views for relation R_{work}, we would input the identifier $f(x, y)$ of the parent node labelled *writer*). This is illustrated by the example below.

EXAMPLE 6.4.[Example 6.3 continued] Assume that query $Q = r[q]$ of examples 6.2 and 6.3 is posed over T under schema D. The following views define the translation for Q:

$R_r(f_r)$:= true
$R_{writer}(f_{writer}(x, y), f_r)$:=
INLQUERY$(r/book(x)/author/name(y), D)$
$R_{name}(f_{name}(x, y), f_{writer}(x, y), y)$:=
INLQUERY$(r/book(x)/author/name(y), D)$
$R_{work}(f_{work}(x, y), f_{writer}(x, y), x)$:=
INLQUERY$(r/book(x)/author/name(y), D)$

Notice how each tuple in relations R_{name} and R_{work} is set to reference the correct tuple in relation R_{writer}. □

Procedure TQLSTEP(Q, D, φ, t)

Input : A forest expression $q(\bar{x})$, a DTD D, a conjunctive query $\varphi(\bar{x})$ and a skolem term t.
Output: A set of views over INLSCHEMA(D_Q).

if $q(\bar{x}) ::= \epsilon$ **then**
  return $\emptyset$
else if $q(\bar{x}) ::= q'(\bar{x}'), q''(\bar{x}'')$ **then**
  return TQLSTEP$(q', D, \varphi, t) \cup$ TQLSTEP(q'', D, φ, t)
else if $q(\bar{x}) ::= \ell(\bar{a}, \bar{x}')[q'(\bar{x}'')]$ **then**
  Let f be a fresh skolem function. Define view V as $R_\ell(f(\bar{x}), t, \bar{a}, \bar{x}')$:= INLQUERY(φ, D), or just $R_\ell(f(), t, \bar{a})$:= true if $\varphi = \emptyset$.
  return $\{V\} \cup$ TQLSTEP$(q', D, \varphi, f(\bar{x}))$
else if $q(\bar{x}) ::=$ for $\pi(\bar{a}, \bar{x}, \bar{y})$ return $q'(\bar{x}, \bar{y})$ **then**
  Let $\varphi'(\bar{a}, \bar{x}, \bar{y}) = \varphi(\bar{x}) \wedge \pi(\bar{a}, \bar{x}, \bar{y})$.
  return TQLSTEP(q', D, φ', t)

To define the inlining translation INLTQL, we simply need a Skolem term for the root of the tree, as the basis for the inductive procedure TQLSTEP.

Procedure INLTQL(Q, D)

Input : A TQL query $Q = r[q]$ and a DTD D.
Output: A set of views over INLSCHEMA(D_Q).

Create a 0-ary function f_r.
return TQLSTEP$(Q, D, \emptyset, f_r())$

A TQL query Q is compatible with a DTD D if all the patterns used in Q are compatible with D. The following proposition shows that INLTQL satisfies an analog of **requirement 3** for queries that outputs trees.

PROPOSITION 6.5. *Given a DTD D, a TQL query Q compatible with D, and and a tree T that conforms to D, we have that* INLDOC$(Q(T), D_Q)$ = INLTQL$(Q, D)($INLDOC$(T))$*, up to renaming of nulls.*

That is, the set of views INLTQL(Q, D) applied to the inlining of T yields the same answer as the inlining of $Q(T)$.

Translating relations back into XML

To complete the translation, we need an algorithm to publish back the relational data as an XML document. This is done by means of the algorithm PUBREL. We say that an instance I of INLSCHEMA(D) *D-represents* a tree T that conforms to D if I = INLDOC(T, D).

Procedure PUBREL(D, I)

Input : A DTD D and an instance I that D-represents some tree.
Output: An XML tree T that is D-represented by I.

for each *node ℓ of $G(D)$, traversed as Depth-first-search* **do**
  for each *tuple t of R_ℓ in I with elements n, $\bar{a}$ and n' corresponding to attributes id_n, $A_D(\ell)$ and $id_{\mu(n)}$*. **do**
    for every *non-starred node ℓ' of $G(D)$ such that $\mu(\ell') = \ell$, and elements n'' and $\bar{b}$ in t corresponding to attributes $id_{\ell'}$ and $A_D(\ell')$* **do**
      Create a node n'' in T labelled ℓ', with attributes $\bar{b}$, in a parent-child scheme that resembles $G(D)$.
    endfor
    Add to T a node n labelled ℓ, with attributes $\bar{a}$, with n' as ancestor, according to the parent-child sequence defined by $G(D$ (no parent if $\ell = r$).
  endfor
endfor
return T

This algorithm will only work for relational instances that represent shredded documents. The following proposition shows its correctness.

PROPOSITION 6.6. *Given a DTD D and a relational instance I of* INLSCHEMA(D)*, it is the case that* INLDOC(PUBREL(D, I)) = I.

6.3 TQL queries in XML data exchange

Combining the previously mentioned result in [11] with the correctness of the algorithms we presented we conclude that **requirements 1-5** are satisfied for data exchange with XML-to-XML queries:

THEOREM 6.7. *Let $\mathcal{M} = (D_S, D_T, \Sigma)$ be an XML schema mapping. Then, for every XML tree T that satisfies D_S and for every TQL query Q, the certain answers of Q for T under $\mathcal{M}$ and the certain answers of* $\text{INLTQL}(Q, D_T)$ *for* $\text{INLDOC}(T, D_S)$ *over* $\text{INLMAP}(\mathcal{M}, D_S, D_T)$ *coincide:*

$$\text{INLDOC}(\text{CERTAIN}_{\mathcal{M}}(Q,T), D_Q) = \text{CERTAIN}_{\text{INLMAP}(\mathcal{M})}(\text{INLTQL}(Q, D_T), \text{INLDOC}(T, D_S)).$$

Remark: The notion of certain answers naturally (component-wise) extends to queries computing multiple relations.

Theorem 6.7 and Proposition 6.6 give us a way of computing $\text{CERTAIN}_{\mathcal{M}}(Q,T)$. First, compute $\text{CERTAIN}_{\text{INLMAP}(M)}(\text{INLTQL}(Q, D_T), \text{INLDOC}(T, D_S))$ by materializing views $\text{INLTQL}(Q, D_T)$ over the canonical solution for $\text{INLDOC}(T, D_S)$ and then use the procedure PUBREL to output it as the tree $\text{CERTAIN}_{\mathcal{M}}(Q,T)$.

7. Concluding Remarks

Our technique provides a relational approach to solve two of the most important problems of XML data-exchange settings: materializing solutions and answering queries. The diagram below summarizes this. In a pure XML setting, we can start with a document T and use a mapping $\mathcal{M}$ to find a (universal) solution T'_{univ}, over which we can then answer a query Q to produce certain answers.

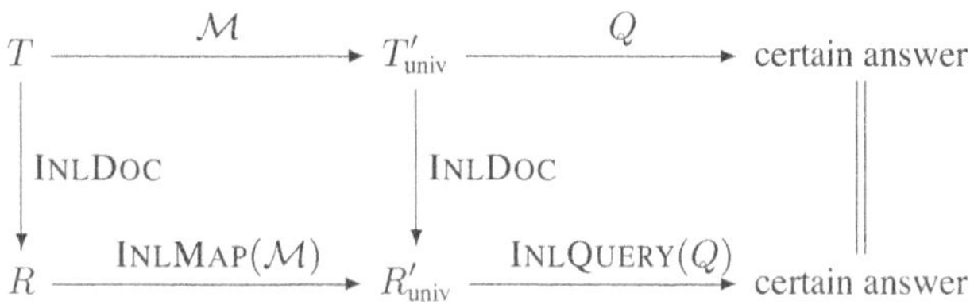

Using the translation INLDOC of documents, we generate a relational instance R, on which the translation of the mapping $\text{INLMAP}(\mathcal{M})$ generates a universal solution R'_{univ}. This solution is a shredding, via INLDOC, of a universal XML solution, and also conforms to the shredding of source DTD. Finally, we apply the standard technique [12] for evaluating queries in relational data exchange to the query translation $\text{INLQUERY}(Q)$ or $\text{INLTQL}(Q)$ to produce the correct answers, in the latter case with the possibility of using PUBREL to publish back the results into XML.

Implementing our proposed algorithms for use in practical systems would be straightforward using their specifications given in this paper. A natural next step is to evaluate XML data-exchange systems using relational data storage and implementations of our algorithms. We are currently working on this direction.

We finish with a remark about the possibility of allowing operators ? and $+$ in DTDs, as well as a choice operator for representing multiple choices. We say that a non-recursive DTD D is an *extended nested relational* DTD if all rules of D are of the form $\ell \to \tilde{\ell}_0 \ldots \tilde{\ell}_m$, or $\ell \to \ell_0 + \ldots + \ell_m$, where all the ℓ_i's and $\tilde{\ell}_i$'s are distinct, and each $\tilde{\ell}_i$ is one of $\ell_i, \ell_i?, \ell_i^*$ or ℓ_i^+ (as usual $\ell?$ stands for $\ell|\epsilon$ and ℓ^+ for $\ell\ell^*$).

The procedure INLSCHEMA can be extended to these DTDs. For each element ℓ that is under the operator ?, the transformation creates a special relation ℓ that references the relation of the nearest appropriate ancestor of ℓ. Furthermore, the transformation for a rule of the form $\ell_1 \to \ell_2^+$ can be defined by including a dependency that ensures that there is at least one tuple in the relation R_{ℓ_2} for each tuple in R_{ℓ_1}. Finally, for the choice operator $\ell \to \ell_0 + \ldots + \ell_m$ the transformation would create one relation R_ℓ for each possible choice of $\ell_0, \ldots, \ell_m$. Then, it is possible to extend all the procedures in a way that still satisfies **requirements 1-5** under extended nested relational DTDs.

8. References

[1] S. Abiteboul, L. Segoufin and V. Vianu. Representing and querying XML with incomplete information. *TODS*, 31(1) (2006), 208-254
[2] F. Afrati, C. Li, V. Pavlaki. Data exchange in the presence of arithmetic comparisons. In *EDBT 2008*, pages 487-498.
[3] S. Amano, C. David, L. Libkin, F. Murlak. On the tradeoff between mapping and querying power in XML data exchange. In *ICDT 2010*.
[4] S. Amano, L. Libkin, F. Murlak. XML schema mappings. In *PODS 2009*, pages 33-42.
[5] S. Amer-Yahia, S. Cho, L. Lakshmanan, D. Srivastava. Tree pattern query minimization. *VLDB J.* 11 (2002), 315–331.
[6] M. Arenas, L. Libkin. XML data exchange: consistency and query answering. *J. ACM* 55(2): (2008).
[7] A. Balmin and Y. Papakonstantinou. Storing and querying XML data using denormalized relational databases. *VLDB J.*, 14:30–49, 2005.
[8] P. Barceló. Logical foundations of relational data exchange. *SIGMOD Record* 38(1): 49–58 (2009).
[9] P. A. Bernstein, S. Melnik. Model management 2.0: manipulating richer mappings. *SIGMOD'07*, pages 1-12
[10] H. Björklund, W. Martens, T. Schwentick. Conjunctive query containment over trees. In *DBPL 2007*, pages 66-80.
[11] C. David, L. Libkin, F. Murlak. Certain answers for XML queries. In *PODS 2010*, pages 191-202.
[12] R. Fagin, P. G. Kolaitis, R. Miller, L. Popa. Data exchange: semantics and query answering. *TCS* 336(1): 89–124 (2005).
[13] R. Fagin, P. G. Kolaitis, and L. Popa. Data exchange: getting to the core. *ACM TODS* 30(1):174–210, 2005.
[14] D. Florescu, D. Kossman. Storing and querying XML data using a RDBMS *IEEE Data Engineering Bulletin* 22(3): 27–34, 1999.
[15] A. Fuxman, M. Hernández, H. Ho, R. Miller, P. Papotti, L. Popa. Nested mappings: schema mapping reloaded. *VLDB'06*, pages 67-78.
[16] G. Gottlob, C. Koch, K. Schulz. Conjunctive queries over trees. *JACM* 53(2): 238-272, 2006.
[17] G. Gou and R. Chirkova. Efficiently querying large XML data repositories: A survey. *IEEE TKDE*, 19:1381–1403, 2007.
[18] M. Hernández, H. Ho, L. Popa, A. Fuxman, R. Miller, T. Fukuda, P. Papotti. Creating nested mappings with Clio. In *ICDE 2007*.
[19] H. V. Jagadish, S. Al-Khalifa, A. Chapman, L. Lakshmanan, A. Nierman, S Paparizos, J. Patel, D. Srivastava, N. Wiwatwattana, Y. Wu, C. Yu. TIMBER: A native XML database. *VLDB Journal* 11(4): 274-291, 2002.
[20] N. Klarlund, T. Schwentick, D. Suciu. XML: model, schemas, types, logics, and queries. In *Logics for Emerging Appl. of Databases 2003*.
[21] Ph. Kolaitis. Schema mappings, data exchange, and metadata management. In *PODS 2005*, pages 61-75.
[22] R. Krishnamurthy, R. Kaushik, J. Naughton. XML-to-SQL query translation literature: state of the art and open problems. In *XSym'03*.
[23] R. Krishnamurthy, R. Kaushik, and J. Naughton. XML views as integrity constraints and their use in query translation. In *ICDE'05*.
[24] L. Lakshmanan, G. Ramesh, H. Wang, Z. Zhao. On testing satisfiability of tree pattern queries. *VLDB 2004*, pages 120–131.
[25] G. Mecca, P. Papotti, S. Raunich. Core schema mappings. In *SIGMOD 2009*, pages 655-668.
[26] R. Miller, M. Hernández, L. Haas, L. Yan, H. Ho, R. Fagin, L. Popa. The Clio project: managing heterogeneity. *SIGMOD Record*, 30 (2001).
[27] L. Popa, Y. Velegrakis, R. Miller, M. Hernández, R. Fagin. Translating Web data. In *VLDB 2002*, pages 598–609.
[28] J. Shanmugasundaram, et al. Relational databases for querying XML documents: limitations and opportunities. *VLDB'99*, pages 302-314.
[29] J. Shanmugasundaram, et al. A general techniques for querying XML documents using a relational database system. *SIGMOD Record*, 30:20–26, 2001.
[30] I. Tatarinov, et al. Storing and querying ordered XML using a relational database system. In *SIGMOD'02*, pages 204–215.
[31] XQuery 1.0: An XML Query Language. http://www.w3.org/TR/xquery.
[32] C. Yu, L. Popa. Constraint-based XML query rewriting for data integration. In *SIGMOD 2004*, pages 371-382.
[33] C. Zhang, et al. On supporting containment queries in relational database management systems. In *SIGMOD'01*, pages 425–436.

A Parallel Algorithm for Computing Borders

Nicolas Hanusse*
LaBRI
University of Bordeaux. France
CNRS. UMR5800
hanusse@labri.fr

Sofian Maabout*
LaBRI
University of Bordeaux. France
CNRS. UMR5800
maabout@labri.fr

ABSTRACT

The *border* concept has been introduced by Mannila and Toivonen in their seminal paper [20]. This concept finds many applications, e.g maximal frequent itemsets, minimal functional dependencies, emerging patterns between consecutive database instances and materialized view selection. For large transactions and relational databases defined on n items or attributes, the running time of any border computations are mainly dominated by the time T (for standard sequential algorithms) required to test the *interestingness*, in general the frequencies, of sets of candidates.

In this paper we propose a general parallel algorithm for computing borders whatever the application is. We prove the efficiency of our algorithm by showing that: (i) it generates exactly the same number of candidates as the standard sequential algorithm and, (ii) if the interestingness test time of a candidate is bounded by Δ then for a multi-processor shared memory machine with p cores, we prove that the total interestingness time $T_p < T/p + 2\Delta n$. We implemented our algorithm in the maximal frequent itemset (MFI) mining setting and our experiments confirm our theoretical performance guarantee.

Categories and Subject Descriptors

H.2.8 [**Database Management**]: Database Applications-Datamining

General Terms

Algorithm, Performance.

1. INTRODUCTION

Let us first recall the definition of *borders* as it has been introduced in [20]. Let $\mathcal{O}$ be a set of objects, $\mathbf{r}$ be a database and q be a predicate evaluating the *interestingness* of $O \subseteq \mathcal{O}$ over $\mathbf{r}$. In other words, $q(O, \mathbf{r}) = True$ iff O is interesting. On the other hand, let $\sqsubseteq$ be a partial order between the subsets of $\mathcal{O}$. The border of $\mathcal{O}$ with respect to $\mathbf{r}$, q and $\sqsubseteq$ is the set of subsets $O \subseteq \mathcal{O}$ such that (i) $q(O, \mathbf{r}) = True$ and (ii) there is no $O' \neq O$ such that $O \sqsubseteq O'$ and $q(O', \mathbf{r}) = True$. We illustrate this notion by the following examples:

- Let $\mathcal{O}$ be a set of items and $\mathbf{r} = \{O_1, \ldots, O_m\}$ be a transactions database defined as a multi-set with $O_j \subseteq \mathcal{O}$ for $1 \leq j \leq m$. The support of $O \subseteq \mathcal{O}$ is the number of transactions $O_j \in \mathbf{r}$ such that $O \subseteq O_j$. Let σ be a support threshold. We define $q(O, \mathbf{r}) = True$ iff $support(O, \mathbf{r}) \geq \sigma$. By considering $\sqsubseteq$ as the set inclusion relationship, the border of $\mathcal{O}$ in this context is actually the set of maximal frequent itemsets. The problem of extracting maximal frequent itemsets (MFI's) has been studied for a long time (see e.g. [3, 4, 12, 11, 28]). The most efficient implementations follow a depth first strategy which we will explain later in Section 3.1.

- Let $\mathbf{r}$ be relational table and let $\mathcal{A}$ be its set of attributes. Let $A \in \mathcal{A}$ and $\mathcal{O} = \mathcal{A} \backslash \{A\}$. A set of attributes $O \subseteq \mathcal{O}$ is interesting (i.e $q(O, \mathbf{r}) = True$)) iff $\mathbf{r}$ satisfies the functional dependency $O \to A$. Finding the minimal subsets O of $\mathcal{O}$ such that $\mathbf{r} \models O \to A$ aims at finding the border of $\mathcal{O}$ by considering $O \sqsubseteq O'$ iff $O \supseteq O'$. Hence, finding the minimal non trivial functional dependencies (FD's) satisfied by a relation turns to be a border computation. Again, extracting the exact or approximate FD's has attracted a real interest either for query optimization or database reorganization (see e.g [16, 19, 23, 27]. [27] is among the most efficient algorithms designed for this purpose this why it has been adapted in [8] for mining conditional FD's. One should notice that this algorithm also follows a depth first strategy.

- Let $\mathcal{O}$ be a set of items. If $I \in \mathcal{O}$ then $I.price$ denotes the price of I. Let $\mathbf{r}$ be a table containing the price of each item I. $O \subseteq \mathcal{O}$ is interesting (i.e $q(O, \mathbf{r}) = True$)) iff $\sum_{I \in O} I.price \leq \sigma$ where σ is a budget threshold. If $\sqsubseteq$ denotes the set inclusion relationship, then the border with respect to $q, \mathbf{r}$ and $\sqsubseteq$ is the maximal subsets of $\mathcal{O}$ whose prices (the sum of their elements prices) do not exceed threshold. This problem has been studied in [25] in an e-commerce application where a customer searches for a product by providing his/her budget. The system returns not only the searched product but

*This work has been partially supported by the project ANR ALADDIN from the French Ministery of Research.

CIKM'11, October 24–28, 2011, Glasgow, Scotland, UK.

also suggests other related items while not exceeding the customer's budget.

Other recent applications of borders can be found e.g. in [22] where it is used to characterize the emerging parts of a datacube between two consecutive states, in [15] for datacube partial materialization and in [21] for extracting the most interesting attributes w.r.t. a query log.

However, computing borders is a very time consuming task. Indeed, [13] shows that it is NP-Hard. Therefore, either we rely on heuristics to optimize the computation (for example, the way we traverse the search space), try to approximate the result (for example, by using probability arguments) or exploit parallelism (data and/or task parallelism). [20] proposed a general level-wise algorithm for computing the borders when q is *anti-monotone*. Recall that q is anti-monotone iff whenever $q(O, \mathbf{r}) = False$ then $q(O', \mathbf{r}) = False$ for each $O' \sqsupseteq O$. In the three examples above, one may easily check that q is anti-monotone. The main parts of any border computations algorithms are the candidates management and the interestingness tests. Whatever is the underlying data structure (tables, FP-trees, ...), the interestingness test time for one candidate is between 1 (atomic test) and $O(mn)$ (scan of the whole table of m entries containing at most n values). It turns out that for large datasets, in practice, the interestingness tests is the most consuming task. The algorithm of [20], akin to A priori [2], turns to be inefficient in practice in that it tests much more candidates than the algorithms following a depth first strategy (DFS). The reason is that DFS exploits the anti-monotone property up and downward to prune the candidates. In order to parallelize DFS algorithms, the immediate solution would be to partition the data and each time we have to check the interestingness of a candidate, we test it in parallel in every part then we combine the results. The problem here is that we have no guarantee that doing so, the time required is not more than that of a sequential algorithm, e.g. for MFI mining, prefix trees [14] are often used to summarize the data and it may happen that each tree corresponding to a part has the same size as the global one. Therefore, the performance of the parallel version is much worse than the sequential one. To sum up, no existing parallel computations of borders provides a theoretical guarantee to run faster than sequential executions.

1.1 Contribution

Our starting point is a new proposition of a parallelization of DFS algorithms based on an on-line scheduling of *independent* sets of candidates. To our knowledge, it is the first parallel algorithm that provides some guarantee of performance with respect to the running time. More precisely, we present a partitioning of the candidates into at most $2n - 1$ ordered equivalence classes then we provide an algorithm that picks candidates from one class at each iteration and evaluates the interestingness of them in parallel. The performance of the algorithm is proven by showing that during its execution, it generates exactly the same candidates as those considered by the baseline **DFS** algorithm (described in Section 3.1). Let T be the interestingness test time required by **DFS**. Let Δ be the maximal time needed for testing one candidate. Then for or a multi-processor shared memory machine of p cores, we prove that the total interestingness time $T_p < T/p + 2\Delta n$. Since $2\Delta n$ is in general much less than T/p, the speed up of our algorithm is in practice almost perfect.

To make our results more concrete and without loss of generality, in the rest of the paper we will concentrate on the MFI mining problem. This makes the comparison with related works easier.

1.2 Paper Organization

In the next section we recall some related work on MFI extraction. After giving some notations, we describe more precisely the DFS algorithm in section 3.1. Then, we give our algorithm **MineWithRounds** in section 4 and prove some of its properties. We discuss data distribution in section 5.1 and we conclude this paper by section 6 where we show some of the experiments we conducted on real and synthetic data sets. Future work is described in section 7.

2. RELATED WORK ON MFI MINING

The algorithms for extracting MFI's proposed so far can be divided into three categories: DFS algorithms (e.g Mafia [4], GenMax [11], DepthProject [1], FPmax* [12]and PADS [28]), BFS (e.g Pincer search [18] and MaxMiner [3]) and those based on dualization (e.g Dualize and Advance [13, 26]). Even if the MFI extraction problem is not recent, it continues to motivate the suggestion of new algorithms. After a flourishing number of such algorithms, the community of researchers decided to organize the FIMI workshops (2003 and 2004) especially devoted to compare these algorithms and their implementations. Indeed, the analytical comparison of all these proposals turned to be quite difficult. The experiments have confirmed this difficulty since, for example, depending on data distribution and minimal support thresholds, almost each algorithm turned to behave better than the others under some circumstances. [9] proposed data classification depending on MFI and minimal infrequent itemsets distributions (also called the negative border) as a classification criterion of data sets and hence explained some of the performance results obtained with state of the art algorithms.

To the best of our knowledge, two parallel algorithms [5, 7] have been proposed so far. [5] partitions the data and parallelizes the support computation of each candidate by using MaxMiner [3]. Due to its BFS strategy, MaxMiner does compute the support of more candidates than DFS algorithms. [7] guesses a set of MFI's candidates by considering all branches of the prefix tree summarizing the data. If a branch is frequent then it is an MFI otherwise it is intersected with other non frequent candidates to generate new ones. Due to the usage of the tree structure, this technique is hardly adaptable to other contexts, e.g. FD mining. The following is a summary of the limitations of each category:

- For DFS algorithms, the problem is essentially that at any time, there is a single candidate. This is interesting for the memory requirement but does not easily allow to compute many supports in parallel.

- For level wise algorithms, the problem is the number of generated candidates: it can be much larger than those processed by DFS algorithms. This is because they do not exploit the downward pruning property: an itemset included in an already found frequent itemset cannot be maximal.

- Dualization requires hyper graph transversal calculations which are often very time consuming [6].

2.1 DFS versus BFS

DFS and BFS have the same worst case time complexity, even if in practice DFS behaves better. To illustrate this, let $\mathcal{I} = \{A, B, C, D, E\}$ be a set of items. The search space may be represented by the lexicographic tree of $\mathcal{I}$ which is depicted in Figure 1. Suppose that the border is $\{ABCD, E\}$.

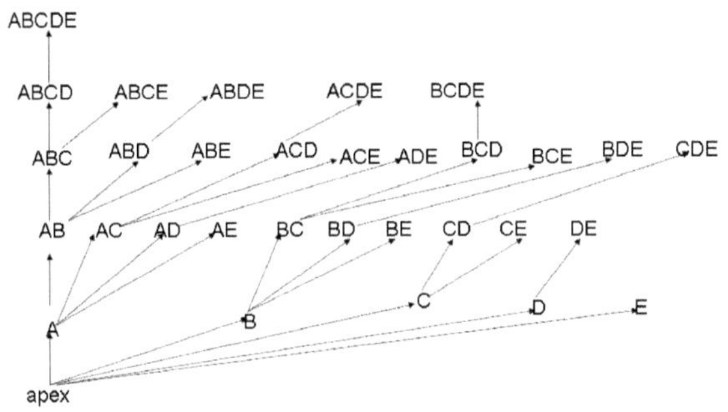

Figure 1: The lexicographic tree of $\{A, B, C, D, E\}$

DFS will compute the support of all supersets of E. Hence, for a border of size 2, **DFS** may compute $O(2^{n-1})$ supports where n is the number of items. For the same case, **BFS** does not test all supersets of E but does test all subsets of $ABCD$. Thus both algorithms make the same number of tests. Suppose now that the border is $\{ABCDE\}$. **DFS** will *climb* the left most branch until $ABCDE$. Hence, it computes n supports while **BFS** computes the support of all subsets of $ABCDE$ thus 2^n supports. Note however that from a parallel programming point of view, since **BFS** is level wise, at each level it may compute the supports of all candidates in parallel. Therefore, from a theoretical point of view, if we have p processors where p is the maximal number of candidates we may generate in a level i.e., $\binom{n}{n/2}$, both algorithms behave the same. So, from the number of data scans point of view, both DFS and BFS are similar.

The advantage of DFS over BFS algorithms can be easily explained: the algorithms for extracting MFI's try to exploit the anti-monotonicity in order to prune the search space in two ways:(i) Upward pruning: eliminating those itemsets which are supersets of infrequent itemsets and (ii) Downward pruning: no need to compute the frequency of an itemset whenever one of its supersets is already found frequent. Since BFS cannot exploit downward pruning, it generates more candidates than DFS.

3. PRELIMINARIES

We first define a total order among the items.

Definition 1 (Item Rank). *Let $\lhd$ be a total order on the items appearing in the transaction data base. If I is an item, then $Rank(I) = r$ iff $|\{J \mid J \lhd I\}| = r - 1$.*

Example 1. *Let $\mathcal{I} = \{A, B, C, D\}$ be the set of items. Suppose that $\lhd$ is the alphabetical order. Then $Rank(A) = 1, Rank(B) = 2, \ldots, Rank(D) = 4$.*

Without loss of generality, in the rest of the paper the order $\lhd$ is equivalent to the alphabetical order. We also will consider only *ordered itemsets* i.e., if $I = I_1 I_2 \ldots I_k$ is an k-itemset then $j < \ell \Leftrightarrow I_j \lhd I_\ell$. For example, ACD is an ordered itemset while DAC is not. As usual, from the order $\lhd$ we can define the lexicographic order between itemsets as follows: Let $I = I_1 I_2 \ldots I_m$ and $J = J_1 J_2 \ldots J_\ell$ two ordered itemsets. Then $I \prec J$ iff there exists p such that $I_k = J_k$ for $k < p$ and $I_p \lhd J_p$. For example $ABD \prec B$. Moreover, we say that I is an ancestor of J iff $I \supseteq J$ and I is a parent of J iff I is a $J's$ ancestor and $|I| = |J| + 1$. For example, ABC is an ancestor of B while AB is a parent of B. With respect to an itemset I and to the order $\prec$ we distinguish two kinds of ancestors (resp. parents): those that precede I, called *left ancestors*, and those that follow it, called *right ancestors*. For example, AB and BC are both parents of B. Since $AB \prec B \prec BC$, then AB is a *left parent* of B while BC is a *right parent* of B. We say that a set of itemsets $\mathcal{S}$ *covers* an itemset I iff $\mathcal{S}$ contains an ancestor of I. We define the *position* of an itemset I, denoted $Pos(I)$, as the rank of I with respect to the order $\prec$. More precisely,

Definition 2. *Let $(2^{\mathcal{I}}, \prec)$ be the ordered set of itemsets. $Pos(I) = |\{J \mid J \prec I\}|$.*

For example, if $\mathcal{I} = \{I_1, \ldots, I_n\}$ and $I_1 \lhd I_2 \lhd \cdots \lhd I_n$ then $Pos(\{I_1\}) = 1$ (I_1 follows $\emptyset$), $Pos(\{I_n\}) = 2^n - 1$ and $Pos(\{I_1, I_2\}) = 2$. From these definitions, the structure of the lexicographic tree should be clear: $\mathcal{T}$ is the lexicographic tree of a set of items $\mathcal{I}$ iff the root of $\mathcal{T} = \emptyset$ (or apex) and for each itemset $I \subseteq \mathcal{I}$ all the right ancestors of I belong to the subtree of $\mathcal{T}$ rooted at I.

Finally, let $I = I_1 \ldots I_m$ be an ordered itemset. The successor of I, denoted $Successor(I)$, is the itemset $J = I_1 \ldots I_m I_k$ such that $rank(I_k) = rank(I_m) + 1$. Clearly, not all itemsets have a successor. For example, if $\mathcal{I} = \{A, B, C, D, E\}$ then $Successor(AC) = ACD$ while AE does not have a successor (leaves of the lexicographic tree).

3.1 Pure Depth Traversal

We start with a simple algorithm for extracting MFI's. Despite its simplicity, this algorithm provides some nice properties. It computes less supports than any BFS algorithm. Moreover, we claim that any candidate and borders update can be performed in constant time. This DFS algorithm traverses the so called lexicographic tree. We assume that the itemsets are coded by a binary vector $V(n)$ where $V[j] = 1$ means that item I_j is present and $V[j] = 0$ otherwise. We note the set of MFI's as $\mathcal{B}$ where $\mathcal{B}$ stands for Border. The parameters n and σ are respectively the total number of items and the support threshold. The integer i is a position index in the vector V. The algorithm is called by initializing i to 1, $\mathcal{B}$ as empty set and all positions of V as 0.

There are two critical operations in this algorithm: the covering test (line 3) and the support test (line 7). The covering test may require the comparison of V to all elements of $\mathcal{B}$. One heuristic has been proposed to optimize this step in [11] by maintaining a *local* subset of $\mathcal{B}$ where the test is performed. Furthermore, most DFS like algorithms use some optimizations in order to reduce the number of covering tests, e.g. candidates reordering: the parents of an itemset are reordered by increasing support[1] i.e., the order $\lhd$ is changed dynamically [11, 4] or exploit previously obtained

[1]Note that this makes these algorithms not pure DFS algorithms.

```
Procedure DFS(integer i)
  Input: integer i
  Output: The MFI set B
  if i ≤ n then
  |  V[i] ← 1;
  |  if B covers V then
  |  |_ DFS(i + 1);
  |  else
  |  |  if support(V) ≥ s then
  |  |  |  Add V to B;
  |  |  |  Remove from B the subsets of V;
  |  |  |_ DFS(i + 1);
  |  |_
  |  V[i] ← 0;
  |_ DFS(i + 1);
```

MFI's in order to prune some branches [28]. For support computation, data structures like FP-trees and FP-arrays [12], diffsets [11] and bitmaps/bitvectors [4] have been proposed. Finally, *look ahead* heuristic first proposed in [3] has been adopted by most algorithms.

In the next section, we introduce a new algorithm which traverses the search tree in such a way that the advantages of both depth and breadth strategies are kept i.e., efficiently mining of long patterns and "small" number of transaction data base scans.

4. MINE WITH ROUNDS

As we have seen in the previous section, **DFS** processes *sequentially* the set of itemsets following the lexicographic order $\prec$. From time to time, it makes jumps that correspond to upward pruning. In this section we propose a new algorithm which *mimics* **DFS** and whose rationale consists in triggering the processing of an itemset *as soon as possible* i.e., whenever we respect the $\prec$ order, we will obtain no new information about the status of this itemset. More precisely, suppose that I has just been processed and let J be an itemset such that $I \prec J$. We want to start the processing of J whenever none of the itemsets K such that $I \prec K \prec J$ is able to provide new information about I.

For example, consider the itemsets AB and B from figure 1. Once AB is processed, we can start the processing of B. Indeed, either AB is frequent and in this case B is covered[2] or AB is not frequent and in this case none of the itemsets whose position is between AB and B i.e, $[ABC \dots AE]$, will provide a new insight about B. Figure 2 illustrates this. The shaded region contains the itemsets whose processing is useless for gaining information about itemset B once AB is processed.

The principle of the proposed algorithm consists in processing several itemsets in parallel. Roughly speaking, we partition the set of itemsets into rounds $\mathcal{R}_1, \dots, \mathcal{R}_d$ such that an itemset is processed during the ith round if it belongs to $\mathcal{R}_i$. Let us now formalize our partitioning procedure.

DEFINITION 3 (DEPTH FIRST PARTITIONS). *Let $(\mathcal{R})_{i\geq 1}$ be a partition of $2^{\mathcal{I}}$. $\mathcal{R}$ is a Depth First Partition (DFP) of $2^{\mathcal{I}}$ with respect to $\prec$ if and only if for each itemset I,*

[2]Processing B in this situation means just discarding it as a candidate.

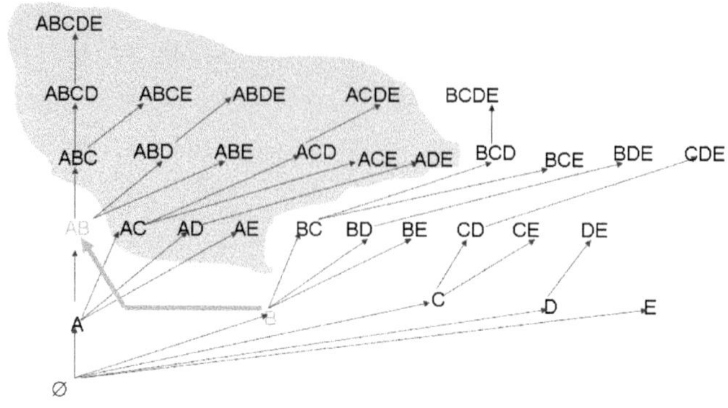

Figure 2: Useless itemsets for B once AB is processed.

1. *$I \in \mathcal{R}_k$ and I has a successor $\Leftrightarrow$ $Successor(I) \in \mathcal{R}_\ell$ where $\ell > k$ and*
2. *$I \in \mathcal{R}_k \Leftrightarrow \forall$ left parent I' of I, $I' \in \mathcal{R}_l$ where $l < k$.*

To simplify the notation, we will talk about the DFP of $\mathcal{I}$ instead of $2^{\mathcal{I}}$. Intuitively, the two conditions above simply say that (1) the successor relationship must be satisfied by a DFP (an itemset must be processed before its ancestor) and (2) the left parents of I must satisfy the $\prec$ relationship (they must be processed before I). The obvious DFP of $\mathcal{I}$ is the one with $2^n - 1$ parts and $I \in \mathcal{R}_j \Leftrightarrow Pos(I) = i$. In order to maximize parallelism while respecting the DFS, we want the *smallest* partition in terms of the number of parts. We say that a DFP $\mathcal{R}$ is smaller than $\mathcal{R}'$ iff $|\mathcal{R}| < |\mathcal{R}'|$ where $|\mathcal{R}|$ denotes the number of parts in $\mathcal{R}$.

EXAMPLE 2. *Let $\mathcal{I} = \{A, B, C\}$. One can easily check that $\mathcal{R} = \{\{A\}, \{AB\}, \{B\}, \{ABC\}, \{AC, BC\}, \{C\}\}$ and $\mathcal{R}' = \{\{A\}, \{AB\}, \{B\}, \{ABC\}, \{AC\}, \{BC\}, \{C\}\}$ are both DFP's. $\mathcal{R}$ is smaller than $\mathcal{R}'$.*

The following theorem shows that there exists a unique smallest DFP.

THEOREM 1. *Let Π be the set of DFP's we can define over $(\mathcal{I}, \prec)$. Let $\mathcal{R} \in \Pi$ s.t $\mathcal{R}$ has the least number of parts, then there is no other $\mathcal{R}' \in \Pi$ such that $|\mathcal{R}| = |\mathcal{R}'|$ and $\mathcal{R} \neq \mathcal{R}'$.*

Let us denote by $\widehat{\mathcal{R}}$ the smallest DFP of $(\mathcal{I}, \prec)$. Now we give a constructive way to obtain $\widehat{\mathcal{R}}$.

THEOREM 2. *Let $\widehat{\mathcal{R}} = \{\mathcal{R}_1, \dots, \mathcal{R}_m\}$ and $I = I_1 \dots I_k$ be an ordered k-itemset such that $rank(I_k) = r$. Then $I \in \mathcal{R}_i \Leftrightarrow 2r - k = i$.*

From here on, *Round*(I) denotes the round where I belongs. As a consequence of the above theorem, we have the following properties.

COROLLARY 1. *Let $\widehat{\mathcal{R}}$ be the smallest DFP of $\mathcal{I}$ where $|\mathcal{I}| = n$. Then*

- *the number of rounds $|\widehat{\mathcal{R}}|$ is $2n - 1$.*
- *Let $J^1, \dots, J^k$ be the right parents of I and $H^1, \dots, H^\ell$ be its left parents. Then*
  - *$Round(H^i) = Round(I) - 1$ for $1 \leq i \leq \ell$ and*
  - *$Round(J^i) = Round(I) + (2i - 1)$ for $1 \leq i \leq k$*

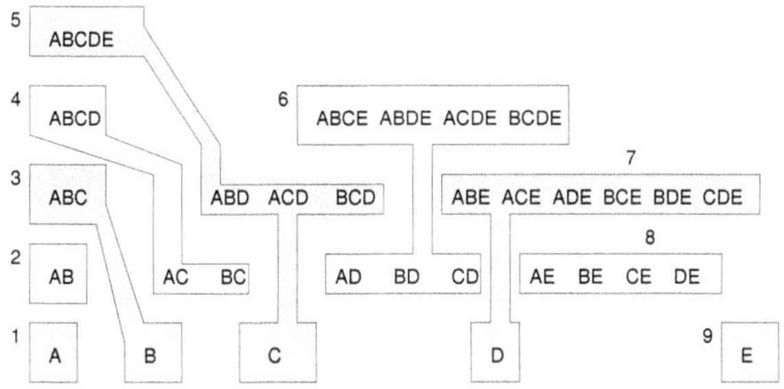

Figure 3: Rounds assignment

EXAMPLE 3. *Let $\mathcal{I} = \{A, B, C, D, E\}$ be the set of items. Then, the round of each itemset is depicted in Figure 3.*

We now describe the **MineWithRounds** which uses the partitioning defined before. Intuitively, it uses a loop which considers at each iteration the itemsets of the corresponding round. We use the following data structures: $\mathcal{C}$ is an array of sets of itemsets sets. $\mathcal{C}[i]$ is the set of candidates to be processed during round i and $\mathcal{B}$ is the set of MFI's found so far. The right children of ABC are AC and BC (just not consider its prefix). The right sibling of ABC is ABD (just replace the last item, here C, by its successor, here D). Note that if $Round(I) = i$ and J is the right sibling of I then $Round(J) = i + 2$. Intuitively, the algorithm proceeds

Algorithm 1: MineWithRound for mining MFI's

1 $\mathcal{C}[1] \leftarrow \{I_1\}$;
2 $k \leftarrow 1$;
3 **while** $k \leq 2n - 1$ *and* $\mathcal{C}[k] \neq \emptyset$ **do**
4   **foreach** $I \in \mathcal{C}[k]$ **do**
5   `// Loop executed in parallel`
6   **if** $support(I) \geq \sigma$ **then**
7   Add I to $\mathcal{B}$;
8   Remove the left child I' of I from $\mathcal{B}$;
9   Add the right parent I'' of I to $\mathcal{C}[k+1]$;
10   **else**
11   Add the right children of I to *Children*;
12   Add the right sibling of I to $\mathcal{C}[k+2]$;
13   **foreach** $I \in \mathcal{C}[k+1]$ **do**
14   `// Loop executed in parallel`
15   **if** *I is covered by $\mathcal{B}$* **then**
16   Remove I from $\mathcal{C}[k+1]$;
17   **foreach** $I \in$ *Children* **do**
18   `// Loop executed in parallel`
19   **if** *I is not covered by $\mathcal{C}[k+1] \cup \mathcal{B}$* **then**
20   Add I to $\mathcal{C}[k+1]$;
21   $k \leftarrow k + 1$;

as follows: If a candidate $I \in \mathcal{C}[k]$ is found frequent, then its parent is a candidate for the next iteration $k+1$. If I is infrequent then (i) its right children are *potential* candidates for the next iteration $k+1$ and (ii) its sibling is a *potential* candidate for iteration $k+2$. To explain the covering tests, suppose AC and BC are candidates tested during the same round. Suppose AC is frequent but not BC. Thus AC generates its parent ACD as a future candidate and BC generates both C (its right child) and BD (its sibling). Note that since C is covered by ACD, there is no need to consider it as a future candidate.

In lines 15 and 19, we make a covering test with respect to the whole current $\mathcal{B}$. We optimized this test as follows: we considered a prefix tree structure with a header table to manage the border[3]. Each new discovered MFI is a branch that has to be inserted in the tree. Doing so, we do not need to remove the left child of a new discovered MFI (line 8 is actually needless); we just use it as a prefix of the new branch, e.g. if ACE is just discovered, then there is certainly a branch in the tree whose prefix is AC, then inserting ACE by using this branch will "remove" the child AC. Now let H be the header table and $I = I_{j1} \ldots I_{jm}$ be a potential candidate for which we want to make the coverage test. It suffices to traverse the nodes of the tree corresponding to I_m starting from the last inserted one (newest) back to the older ones. Each time, I is compared to the path from the current node to the tree root. This traversal is stopped as soon as an inclusion is found (I is covered) or a node whose depth is less than the size of I (I is not covered). Figure 4 illustrates this. The underlined part represents the depth of each node. The nodes are sorted from right to left in the descending order of their depth. Fortunately, this list of

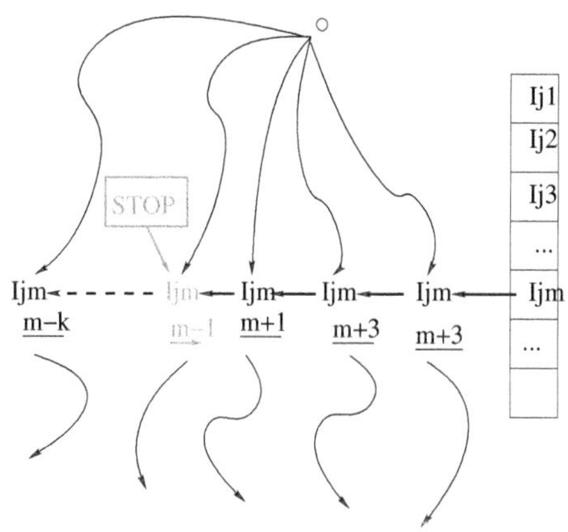

Figure 4: Coverage test for $I = I_{j1} \ldots I_{jm}$

nodes does not need to be sorted each time a new node has to be inserted. Indeed, we have the following lemma.

LEMMA 1. *Let I_j be an item and let $L(I_j)$ be the list of nodes related to I_j in the FP-tree serving for storing the border. Assume that d is the maximal depth of the nodes in $L(I_j)$ at iteration i. Now suppose that at iteration $i+1$ we add a new element I' to the border and that I' contains I_j. If the insertion of I' into the tree requires the creation of a new node ν for I_j then $Depth(\nu) \geq d$.*

Thus, it suffices to consider insertions of new nodes in the front of the list to keep it sorted in depth descending order making coverage tests faster.

In our implementation, the **Foreach** loops in lines 4, 13 and 17 are executed in a parallel fashion. The first one essentially tests the support, the second checks the coverage of the sibling candidates that have been generated during iteration $k - 1$ and the last one tests the coverage of the

[3]We do not recall this structure due to space limitation. The interested reader can find it in [14].

children that have been generated during iteration k. It is worthwhile to note that there are barriers between these loops, i.e. the second loop cannot start before the first has finished.

The following theorem, which is our main result, compares the performance of the above algorithm with DFS.

THEOREM 3. **DFS** *and* **MineWithRounds** *perform exactly the same number of support computations.*

PROOF. (Sketch) It suffices to note that **DFS** does compute the support of an itemset I if and only if (i) all left children of I are frequent and (ii) none of the left parents of I is frequent. These two conditions are verified by **MineWithRounds**. □

As a consequence, we can state the theoretical speed up with respect to the number of available processing units.

COROLLARY 2. *Let T and T_p be respectively the computations times of* **DFS** *and* **MinWithRounds** *when p processors are available. Then*

$$\frac{T}{p} \leq T_p \leq \frac{T}{p} + (2n-1)\Delta$$

Where n is the total number of items and Δ is the maximal time needed for one support computation.

PROOF. First, suppose that the time needed for computing the interestingness of each candidate is the same and let us denote it by t. Let r_i be the number of candidates tested during round i and $r = \sum_i r_i$. Clearly, $T = t \times r$. When p processors are available, the computation time of iteration i is $\tau_i = \lceil \frac{r_i}{p} \rceil * t$. Hence, $T_p = \sum_i \tau_i \leq (r/p + 2n - 1) * t = T/p + (2n-1)t$.

In the more realistic setting, the required testing time of a candidate interestingness is not always the same. Hence, we can bound the formula above by replacing t by the maximal time Δ and we obtain $T_p \leq T/p + (2n-1)\Delta$. □

Note that, since in general the number of candidates r is much larger than n, $(2n-1) * \Delta$ can be neglected with regard to T/p. Hence, the speed up of **MineWithRounds** is almost perfect. The worst case is when $r_i \mod p = 1$, e.g. suppose $p = 16$ and $r_i = 33$. Suppose that the 33rd test takes $2sec$ and the others take $1sec$. Then, the sequential algorithm requires $34sec$. With p cores, the first 32 candidates are processed within $2sec$ while the last candidate requires $2sec$ by itself so a total of $4sec$. Hence, the speed up is $34/4 = 8.5$. Note that if we had 47 candidates and it is the 47th one which requires $2sec$ then the parallel total time is again $4sec$ and the speed up is this time equal to $48/4 = 12$.

The following example illustrates the MFI's computation with our algorithm.

EXAMPLE 4. *Let $\mathcal{I} = \{A, B, C, D, E\}$ and suppose that the maximal frequent itemsets are $\{ABDE, BC\}$. Figure 5 shows candidates generation. The arrows show candidates generation. For example, A is found frequent in round 1, therefore its parent AB is generated as a candidate. ABC is found infrequent during round 3, so its sibling ABD is generated together with its right children AC and BC. Dashed arrows show candidates that have been generated and immediately removed because they turned to be covered. For example, in round 4, AC is found infrequent so its right children C is generated but this one is covered by BC. The same remark holds for the sibling AD of AC which is first generated for round 6 then removed because meanwhile (during round 5) ABD is found frequent. Note that in this small example just two iterations contain more than one candidate, namely iterations 4 and 5. Thus, with 2 processors just there rounds will benefit from parallelism. We will come back to this remark in Section 6 to explain the obtained speed ups.*

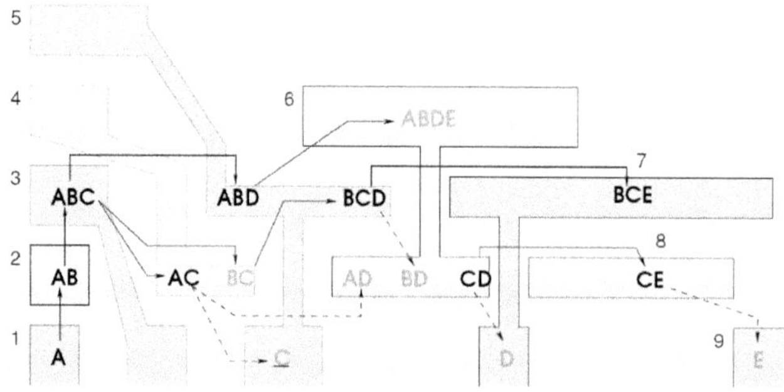

Figure 5: Rounds assignment and MineWithRounds MFI's computation

5. EXTENSIONS

In this section we discuss some extensions one can envision for our algorithm. The first one considers data distribution and the second concerns the application of the algorithm in the functional dependency mining setting.

5.1 Data Distribution

An obvious implementation of our algorithm when data is distributed is to consider one distinguished node as the *master* and the others are *slaves*. The master is responsible of the candidates and the border management while the slaves compute the interestingness on their respective local data. At each iteration, (1) the master sends all candidates to all slaves, (2) each slave computes the local support of all candidates, (3) each slave sends its results to the master, (4) the master combines the partial results to find the global *interesting* candidates, (5) it updates the border and (6) it generates new candidates

In the MFI setting, the communication complexity is the total size of messages. Let r_i be the the number of candidates processed during iteration i and p be the number of slaves. At each iteration i the master sends a message of size r_i to the slaves and each slave notifies the master with a message of length r_i. Thus the total communication cost is $2p \sum_{i=1}^{2n-1} r_i$. Of course, other implementations are possible, e.g., instead of computing the support of each candidate by every slave, we let the later to make this computation only if the already computed support is not sufficient to make the candidate frequent. This will reduce the overall computation time. As one can see, our proposal of candidates partitioning is orthogonal to the way data is distributed. In fact, it leads itself easily to Map-Reduce setting.

5.2 Mining Functional Dependencies(MFD)

The adaptation of our algorithm to the case of MFD is straightforward. Given a relational schema $R(A_1, \ldots, A_n)$ and an instance r of R we want the dependencies of the form $X \to A_i$ satisfied by r such that X is minimal, i.e., there is no $Y \subset X$ such that $r \models Y \rightarrow A_i$. Let us first introduce some notations. Let $\mathcal{A} = \{A_1, \ldots, A_n\}$ and $\mathcal{A}_i = \mathcal{A} \backslash \{A_i\}$. We also note $\bar{X}_i = \mathcal{A}_i \backslash X$, i.e. the complement of X in $\mathcal{A}$. It is known that $r \models X \rightarrow A_i$ iff $|r_X| = |r_{X \cup \{A_i\}}|$. Hence, our algorithm can be rewritten as shown in Algorithm 2. The reader may notice the very small modifications of Algorithm 1. Clearly, the result of this algorithm satisfies the following: $X \in \mathcal{B}[i] \Leftrightarrow r \models \bar{X}_i \rightarrow A_i$ and this dependency is minimal.

Algorithm 2: Minimal FD's

```
1  foreach A_i ∈ 𝒜 do
2      𝒞[1] ← ∅;
3      k ← 1;
4      while k ≤ 2n − 1 and 𝒞[k] ≠ ∅ do
5          foreach X ∈ 𝒞[k] do
6              // Loop executed in parallel
7              if r ⊨ X̄_i → A_i then
8                  Add X to ℬ[i];
9                  Remove the left child X′ of X from ℬ[i];
10                 Add the right parent X″ of X to 𝒞[k + 1];
11             else
12                 Add the right children of X to Children;
13                 Add the right sibling of X to 𝒞[k + 2];
14         foreach X ∈ 𝒞[k + 1] do
15             // Loop executed in parallel
16             if X is covered by ℬ[i] then
17                 Remove X from 𝒞[k + 1];
18         foreach X ∈ Children do
19             // Loop executed in parallel
20             if X is not covered by 𝒞[k + 1] ∪ ℬ[i] then
21                 Add X to 𝒞[k + 1];
22         k ← k + 1;
```

6. PARALLEL IMPLEMENTATION AND EXPERIMENTS

6.1 Experiment Setting

We implemented our algorithm using C++ and the STL library together with OpenMP [24] a multi-shared programming API. OpenMP makes it very easy to exploit new multi-core architecture by just adding compilation directives. Our tests were conducted on a machine equipped with two quad-core Intel Xeon X5570 2.93GHz processors running under Redhat Linux enterprise release version 5.4. Thanks to their multi-threading ability, these processors can execute concurrently two threads per core. Therefore, we were able to launch up to 16 threads. The machine has 48G RAM while the caches are respectively L1=32K, L2=256K and L3=8G. We checked the correctness of our implementation by comparing its results with those presented by Flouvat[4].

We present the results we obtained with six well known datasets: Chess, Mushroom, T10I4D100K, T40I10D100K, Kosarak and Webdocs. Their respective characteristics are described in Table 1. With each dataset, we varied the minimal support threshold σ and with every such value, we varied the number of parallel threads executed for every **Foreach** loop in the algorithm (the same number of threads for the three loops). This number varies from 1 to 16 as a power of 2. In order to gain load balancing, we used the *dynamic scheduling* of openMP. This option means that if for example we have to compute in parallel the support of ℓ itemsets by using m threads, then the first m itemsets are assigned randomly to the m threads and as soon as one thread terminates its computation, the system will assign to it a new task, i.e., a new itemset for which the support computation has to be done.

[4] `pages.univ-nc.nc/~flouvat/rprojects.html`

Dataset	# trans.	# Items	Avg. transact. length
Chess	3196	75	37
Mushroom	8124	119	23
T10I4D100K	10^5	10^3	10
T40I10D100K	10^5	10^3	40
Kosarak	$\sim 10^6$	40348	8
Webdocs	$\sim 1.7 * 10^6$	$\sim 5.3 * 10^6$	178

Table 1: Data description.

6.2 Results Analysis

For each data set, we measured the time devoted to each of the three loops present in our algorithm (cf. Algorithm 1). The first loop essentially computes the support of a set of candidates while the two remaining loops make covering tests: One of them (line 17) tests the coverage of the candidates that have been generated as children of non frequent itemsets and the other (line 13) tests the candidates that have been generated as siblings. In our main theoretical result (Corollary 2, we claimed that when the time devoted to support computation or more generally to interestingness test is the dominating time, the speedup of our algorithm is almost perfect. The experiments not only confirm this result but also show that when this test is not very time consuming we still get interesting speed ups.

Figure 6 shows some of the obtained results. For each dataset, we consider two support thresholds and for each, there is one subfigure showing the time repartition over the three loops as well as the time of the sequential part of the algorithm. The second subfigure shows the speedup of each loop as well as the total speedup. The X_axis of each figure represents the minimal support value concatenated to the number of threads. For example, in subfigure 6(a), 140K_16 means that the minimal threshold is 140K and the number of threads is 16.

6.3 General Remarks

Subfigures in the first and third columns of Figure 6 show that time repartition is quite different from one data set to another. In general, the larger is the dataset and more time is devoted to support computation. Time repartition depends also on data density as well as the support threshold. Another general remark is that sibling coverage test time is in general negligible w.r.t. the rest. This shows that its parallelization is not worthwhile in general. Despite our algorithm does not provide any performance guarantee on the candidate management part, we generally observe an interesting speedup for the covering tests.

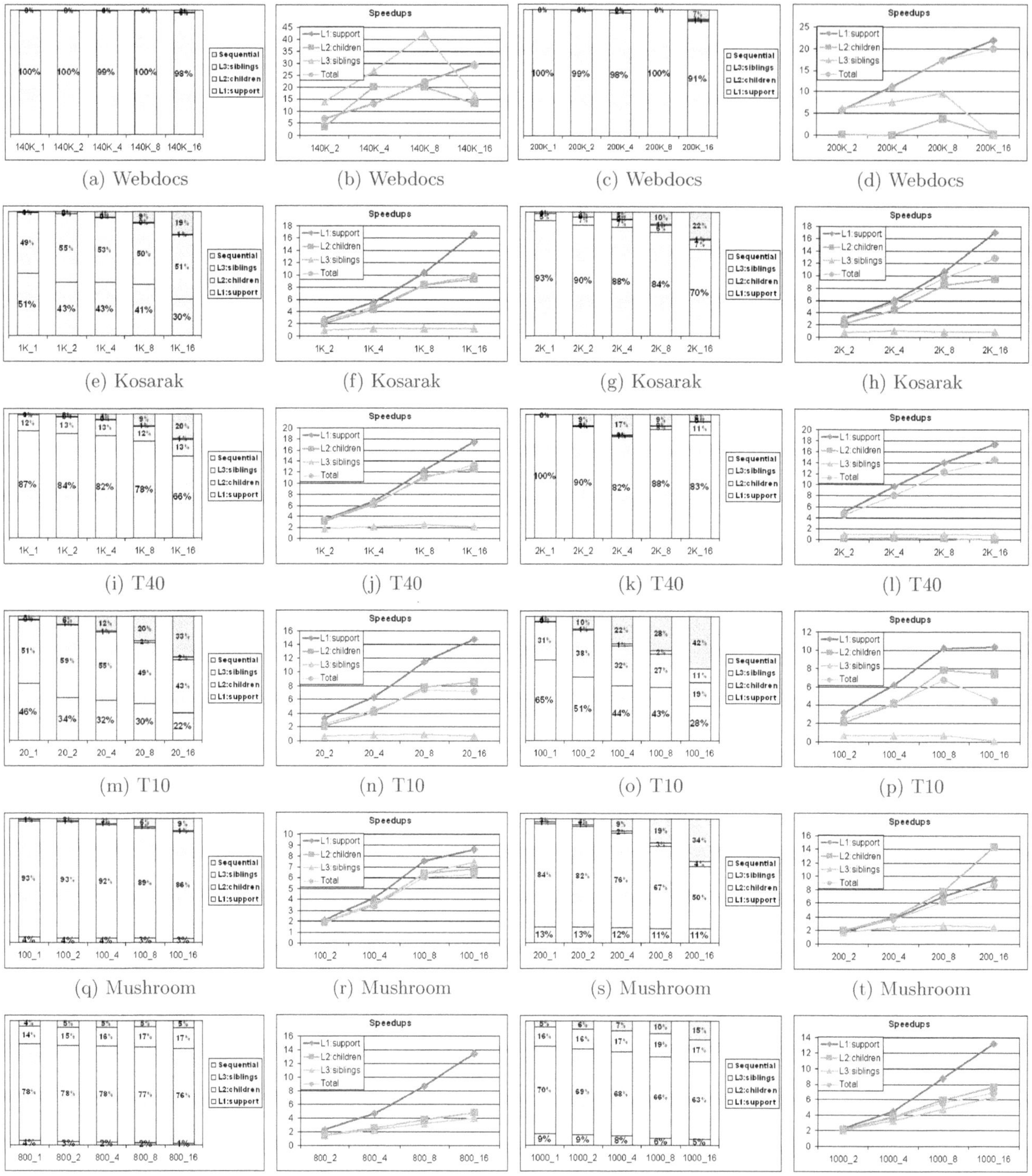

(a) Webdocs (b) Webdocs (c) Webdocs (d) Webdocs

(e) Kosarak (f) Kosarak (g) Kosarak (h) Kosarak

(i) T40 (j) T40 (k) T40 (l) T40

(m) T10 (n) T10 (o) T10 (p) T10

(q) Mushroom (r) Mushroom (s) Mushroom (t) Mushroom

(u) Chess (v) Chess (w) Chess (x) Chess

Figure 6: Time repartition and speed ups

Webdocs. With this dataset, more than 90% of the time is consumed by the support computation (Figures 6(a) and 6(c)). Hence, the speed up of the overall execution is almost equal to the support computation speed up. A noticeable remark at this stage is the values mentioned in Figures 6(b) and 6(d). Indeed, Figure 6(b) shows a total speedup of 30 while the number of threads is 16. Recall that the number of physical cores is 8. This is explained by data locality. Indeed, when two threads access the same data, the system will first check the different levels of the cache before making an access to the memory.

Kosarak. Even if this data set is quite large, we notice that the proportion of time devoted to support computation is comparable to the time spent in covering tests when the minimal support σ is set to $1K$ (Figure 6(e)). This is not the case when $\sigma = 2k$. and 6(g)). We note however that the speedup for support computation is in both cases almost perfect(Figures 6(f) and 6(h)). Finally, even if the support calculation uses only half of the total time, the total speed up is interesting.

T40I10D100K. This dataset is of medium size but is denser than T10I4D100K. Figures 6(i) and 6(k) show that support computation time is important. Nevertheless, we do not reach the same speed ups as those with Webdocs. Nevertheless, the total execution time is almost always divided by the number of threads.

T10I4D100K. The average length of the transactions of this data set is 10. Hence, maximal frequent itemsets are rapidly reached when DFS is used (note that in Kosarak, this average length is even lower). This makes support computation not very time consuming, even when the minimal support is set to 20) thanks to the summarization capacity of the FP-trees.

Mushroom and Chess. Both these datasets are small. Thus, it is not surprising to find that support computation is negligible w.r.t. candidates management.

6.4 Number of Tested Candidates

We conducted some experiments so that to check whether this simple DFS algorithm performs much worse than the theoretical lower bound [20]. It is proven that any algorithm which computes the set of MFI's has to check the support of at least each MFI and each *minimal infrequent itemset*. This second set if also called the negative border. More precisely, if $\mathcal{M}^+$ and $\mathcal{M}^-$ are respectively the positive and the negative borders, then any algorithm computing the MFI's needs to make more than $|\mathcal{M}^+ \cup \mathcal{M}^-|$ support computations. Figure 7 shows the ratios between the number of support computations made by **DFS** and $|\mathcal{M}^+ \cup \mathcal{M}^-|$. In general the number of support computations is not much more than the theoretical lower bound. To our knowledge, there is no algorithm in the literature providing a proven linear or at least a polynomial upper bound of the support computations number w.r.t. $|\mathcal{M}^+ \cup \mathcal{M}^-|$.

6.5 MineWithRounds vs. PADS

As a final experiment, we present the execution time of PADS [28] which is, to our best knowledge, the most efficient implementation of a sequential MFI mining algorithm compared to that of **MineWithRounds**. PADS is not a *pure* DFS implementation in that it uses several heuristics to reduce computation time, e.g., each time a candidate is found frequent, all its right parents are evaluated and reordered w.r.t their increasing support. Hence, the $\prec$ order is dynamically and continuously modified. Figure 8 shows the execution times w.r.t. support thresholds. Both implementations have been executed on the same machine as before. The time needed to load the data and to construct the FP-trees is not taken into account. One should however notice that our execution time is measured when 16 threads are executed in parallel. It however took about 2 minutes for both implementations to start the mining procedure. When

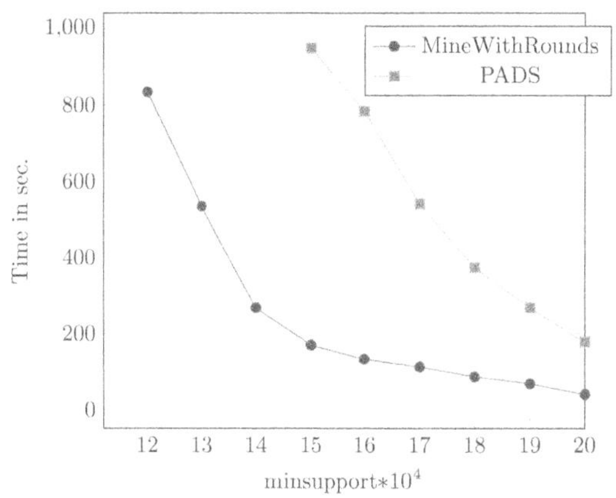

Figure 8: Execution times for PADS and MineWithRounds with Webdocs

the minimal support is less or equal to 140000 PADS had a segmentation fault. To be complete, we should mention that our implementation is naive in that we used the C++ STL library which makes it very easy to program prototypes but if we want to fine tune the optimizations, as in PADS, one should program his/her own data structures.

7. CONCLUSION

We presented a general algorithm for computing borders. Our results are valid independently of the actual type of border as soon as the mined patterns are sets of objects and the interestingness property is anti-monotone. With the generalization of multi-core CPU's and their cache management, some proposals fine tuned the previous techniques so that data caching and pre-fetching become effective [10]. The proposal of an efficient parallel algorithm for building the FP-trees has already been proposed by [17] but the authors did not parallelize the mining process. With our work, we make a step further in exploiting modern multi-core architectures. Our experiments show that without necessarily using very sophisticated optimization techniques, we are able to have execution times much better than state of the art implementations. Parallelizing algorithms that extract other kinds of patterns e.g. sequences, trees or graphs is a natural extension of the present work, e.g. [29] use a lexicographic order for mining frequent graphs. With the *Round* function, one may partition the subgraphs such that they can be processed in parallel. In a distributed setting, i.e. when the data itself is distributed, communications overhead becomes

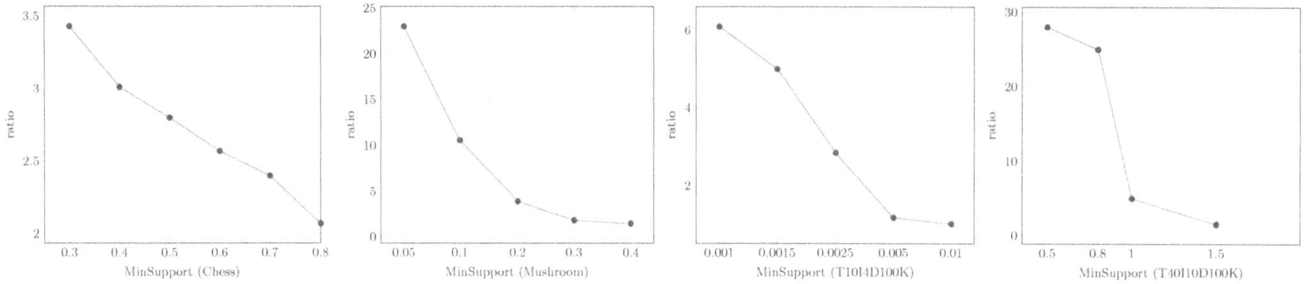

Figure 7: (Number of support computations)/$|\mathcal{M}^+ \cup \mathcal{M}^-|$

a bottleneck thus our algorithm could have to be adapted. Finally, extending our algorithm to mine in parallel conditional functional dependencies [8] is an interesting direction of future work.

Aknowledgments. We are grateful to the anonymous reviewers for their valuable suggestions that helped us for ameliorating the presentation of this work.

8. REFERENCES

[1] R. Agarwal, C. Aggarwal, and V. Prasad. Depth first generation of long patterns. In *SIGKDD Conf.*, 2000.

[2] R. Agrawal and R. Srikant. Fast algorithms for mining association rules in large databases. In *VLDB Conf.*, 1994.

[3] R. Bayardo. Efficiently mining long patterns from databases. In *SIGMOD Conf.*, 1998.

[4] D. Burdick, M. Calimlim, and J. Gehrke. MAFIA: A maximal frequent itemset algorithm for transactional databases. In *ICDE Conf.*, 2001.

[5] S. M. Chung and C. Luo. Efficient mining of maximal frequent itemsets from databases on a cluster of workstations. *KAIS journal*, 16(3), 2008.

[6] T. Eiter, G. Gottlob, and K. Makino. New results on monotone dualization and generating hypergraph transversals. *SIAM Journal of Computing*, 32(2), 2003.

[7] M. El-Hajj and O. Zaïane. Parallel leap: Large-scale maximal pattern mining in a distributed environment. In *ICPADS Conf.*, 2006.

[8] W. Fan, F. Geerts, J. Li, and M. Xiong. Discovering conditional functional dependencies. *IEEE TKDE*, 23(5):683–698, 2011.

[9] F. Flouvat, F. D. Marchi, and J. Petit. A thorough experimental study of datasets for frequent itemsets. In *ICDM Conf.*, 2005.

[10] A. Ghoting, G. Buehrer, S. Parthasarathy, D. Kim, A. Nguyen, Y. Chen, and P. Dubey. Cache-conscious frequent pattern mining on modern and emerging processors. *VLDB J.*, 16(1):77–96, 2007.

[11] K. Gouda and M. Zaki. GenMax: An efficient algorithm for mining maximal frequent itemsets. *DMKD Journal*, 11(3), 2005.

[12] G. Grahne and J. Zhu. Fast algorithms for frequent itemset mining using FP-Trees. *IEEE TKDE journal*, 17(10), 2005.

[13] D. Gunopulos, R. Khardon, H. Mannila, S. Saluja, H. Toivonen, and R. Sharm. Discovering all most specific sentences. *ACM TODS journal*, 28(2), 2003.

[14] J. Han, J. Pei, Y. Yin, and R. Mao. Mining frequent patterns without candidate generation: A frequent pattern tree approach. *DMKD*, 8(1):53–87, 2004.

[15] N. Hanusse, S. Maabout, and R. Tofan. A view selection algorithm with performance guarantee. In *EDBT Conf.*, 2009.

[16] Y. Huhtala, J. Kärkkäinen, P. Porkka, and H. Toivonen. Tane: An efficient algorithm for discovering functional and approximate dependencies. *Comput. J.*, 42(2), 1999.

[17] E. Li and L. Liu. Optimization of frequent itemset mining on multiple-core processor. In *VLDB Conf.*, 2007.

[18] D. Lin and Z. Kedem. Pincer search: A new algorithm for discovering the maximum frequent set. In *EDBT Conf.*, 1998.

[19] S. Lopes, J.-M. Petit, and L. Lakhal. Efficient discovery of functional dependencies and armstrong relations. In *EDBT Conf.*, 2000.

[20] H. Mannila and H. Toivonen. Levelwise search and borders of theories in knowledge discovery. *DMKD Journal*, 1(3), 1997.

[21] M. Miah, G. Das, V. Hristidis, and H. Mannila. Standing out in a crowd: Selecting attributes for maximum visibility. In *ICDE Conf.*, 2008.

[22] S. Nedjar, A. Casali, R. Cicchetti, and L. Lakhal. Emerging cubes: Borders, size estimations and lossless reductions. *Information Systems*, 34(6), 2009.

[23] N. Novelli and R. Cicchetti. Fun: An efficient algorithm for mining functional and embedded dependencies. In *ICDT Conf.*, 2001.

[24] OpenMP. www.openmp.org.

[25] S. B. Roy, S. Amer-Yahia, A. Chawla, G. Das, and C. Yu. Constructing and exploring composite items. In *SIGMOD Conf.*, 2010.

[26] K. Satoh and T. Uno. Enumerating maximal frequent sets using irredundant dualization. In *Discovery Science Conf. proceedings*, 2003.

[27] C. M. Wyss, C. Giannella, and E. L. Robertson. Fastfds: A heuristic-driven, depth-first algorithm for mining functional dependencies from relation instances. In *DaWaK Conf.*, 2001.

[28] K. W. X. Zeng, J. Pei and J. Li. PADS: a simple yet effective pattern-aware dynamic search method for fast maximal frequent pattern. *KAIS Journal*, 20(3), 2009.

[29] X. Yan and J. Han. gSpan: Graph-based substructure pattern mining. In *ICDM Conf.*, 2002.

Supporting Queries Spanning Across Phases of Evolving Artifacts using Steiner Forests*

Siarhei Bykau
University of Trento
bykau@disi.unitn.eu

John Mylopoulos
University of Trento
jm@disi.unitn.eu

Flavio Rizzolo
Carleton University
flavio@scs.carleton.ca

Yannis Velegrakis
University of Trento
velgias@disi.unitn.eu

ABSTRACT

The problem of managing evolving data has attracted considerable research attention. Researchers have focused on the modeling and querying of schema/instance-level structural changes, such as, addition, deletion and modification of attributes. Databases with such a functionality are known as temporal databases. A limitation of the temporal databases is that they treat changes as independent events, while often the appearance (or elimination) of some structure in the database is the result of an evolution of some existing structure. We claim that maintaining the causal relationship between the two structures is of major importance since it allows additional reasoning to be performed and answers to be generated for queries that previously had no answers.

We present here a novel framework for exploiting the evolution relationships between the structures in the database. In particular, our system combines different structures that are associated through evolution relationships into virtual structures to be used during query answering. The virtual structures define "possible" database instances, in a fashion similar to the possible worlds in the probabilistic databases. The framework includes a query answering mechanism that allows queries to be answered over these possible databases without materializing them. Evaluation of such queries raises many interesting technical challenges, since it requires the discovery of Steiner forests on the evolution graphs. On this problem we have designed and implemented a new dynamic programming algorithm with exponential complexity in the size of the input query and polynomial complexity in terms of both the attribute and the evolution data sizes.

Categories and Subject Descriptors

H.m [**Information Systems**]: Miscellaneous

General Terms

Algorithms, Performance

*Work partially supported by the ERC Advanced Grant project "Lucretius"

CIKM'11, October 24–28, 2011, Glasgow, Scotland, UK.

Keywords

Data evolution, Probabilistic Databases; Graph Algorithms

1. INTRODUCTION

Advances in information and telecommunication technologies of the last two decades have allowed organizations and individuals alike to develop large scale data collections and make them available on-line. These collections are often about entities that persist over time and the changes that occur to their attributes/relationships. Considerable effort has gone toward the development of advanced solutions for managing the evolution of schemas[1, 22, 21], data [5, 23, 3, 19] and schema transformations [27, 26, 13]. Temporal databases are one of the outcomes of this effort, where the notion of versioning has been central [4, 6]. In temporal databases, users have the ability to access and query snapshots of the data at different points in time.

Unfortunately, such work fails to capture the full spectrum of evolutionary phenomena. Specifically, those approaches are founded on the assumption that the nature of each real world entity represented in the database persists over time, e.g., students are added, modified, and eventually deleted, but never become professors, with a direct link between the student tuple and the professor one. As such, evolution amounts only to temporal changes of attributes/relationships [1, 5, 21]. Evolution of an entity that spans different concepts (e.g., student to professor, research lab to independent corporate entity) are unaccounted for. And so are evolution phenomena where one entity is split into several (e.g., Germany splitting into East and West Germany at the end of WW II), or the other way around (e.g., East and West Germany amalgamating into one entity at the end of the Cold War). The result of this is that historical queries, such as "give me all the heads-of-state of Germany between 1800 and 2000" are hard to deal with, as they essentially require hand-coding of the history of Germany into several queries to be processed separately. Note that this may look similar to terminology evolution [25], i.e., using different terms to describe the same real world entity at different points in time, but it actually goes far beyond that.

This form of evolution finds a natural fit in Dataspace Systems [10, 16] that are anchored on the notion of an entity. Such entities may split/merge or otherwise evolve during their lifetime. Modeling and supporting evolution relationships for historical query processing finds many additional real-world applications. For instance, modern historians will be able to model and study the chains of human achievements and developments, e.g., how the concept of biotechnology evolved from its beginnings as an agricultural technology to the current notion that is coupled to genetics and molecular biology. Educators will better track how courses evolve and how the material and educational objectives for a course

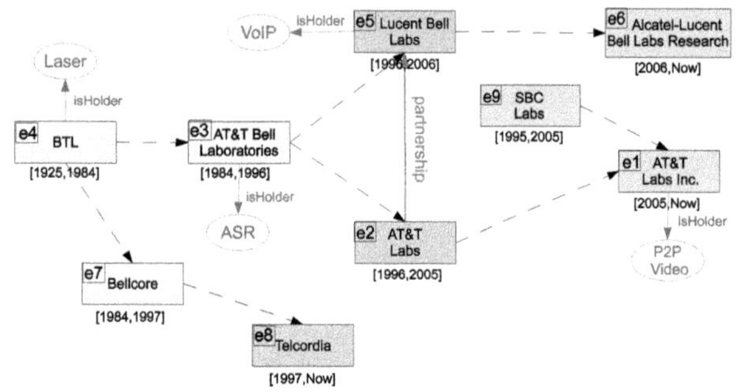

Figure 1: The history of the AT&T Labs.

are "transferred" and become associated with another. Finally, biologists will become more effective in studying the evolution of a species by querying the dependencies and changes that have taken place since the beginning of life on earth.

We have previously presented a formal foundation for modeling evolution [24]. This paper focuses on the query facilities required for our proposal and on algorithmic and performance issues. Specifically, our contributions in this paper are as follows: (i) we formally describe new semantics of query answering in which answers are returned from virtual instances constructed on-the-fly by merging series of entities representing different evolution phases of a real-world object into one; (ii) we introduce the concept of Steiner forest as a mean of finding the optimal mergings that need to be done to answer a query and devise a dynamic programming algorithm for solving it; (iii) we present an efficient indexing technique that facilitates the above queries, and we show effective evaluation methods; (iv) we experimentally evaluate our findings on some large publicly available dataset.

The remainder of the paper is structured as follows. Section 2 provides a motivating example and sketches our solution. Sections 3 presents our modeling framework and formally defines queries and evaluations. Section 4 shows the query evaluation strategy and Section 5 describes the Steiner forest algorithm. The optimization techniques are presented in Section 6. The experimental evaluation results are shown in Section 7. Finally, we conclude in Section 8.

2. MOTIVATING EXAMPLE

Consider AT&T, a company that over the years has gone through a large number of break-ups, merges and acquisitions. Its famous Bell Labs where many great innovations took place, had a similar fate. It was founded in 1925 under the name Bell Telecommunication Laboratories (BTL). In 1984, it was split into Bellcore (to become Telcordia in 1997) and AT&T Bell Laboratories. The latter existed until 1996 when it was split into Bell Labs, that was bought by Lucent, and to AT&T Labs. The Lucent Bell Labs became Alcatel-Lucent Bell Labs Research in 2006 due to the take-over of Lucent by Alcatel. Furthermore, due to the take-over of AT&T by SBC in 2005, the AT&T Labs were merged with the SBC Labs to form the new AT&T Inc. Labs. Despite being research labs of different legal entities, Lucent and AT&T Labs have actually maintained a special partnership relationship. All the different labs have produced a large number of inventions, as the respective patents can demonstrate. Examples of such inventions are the VoIP (Voice over Internet Protocol), the ASR (Automatic Speech Recognition), the P2P (Peer-to-Peer) Video and the laser. A graphical illustration of the above can be found in Figure 1 where the labs are modeled by rectangles and the patents by ovals.

Assume now a temporal database that models the above information as illustrated in Figure 1, and consider a user who is interested in finding the lab that invented the laser and the ASR patent. It is true that these two patents have been filed by two different labs, the AT&T Bell Labs and the AT&T Labs Inc. Thus, the query will return no results. However, it can be noticed that the latter entity is an evolution of the former. It may be the case that the user does not have the full knowledge of the way the labs have changed or in her own mind, the two labs are still considered the same. We argue that instead of expecting from the user to know all the details of the evolution granularity and the way the data has been stored, which means that the user's conceptual model should match the one of the database, we'd like the system to try to match the user's conceptual model. This means that the system should have the evolution relationships represented explicitly and take them into account when evaluating a query. In particular, we want the system to treat the AT&T Bell Labs, the AT&T Labs Inc, and the AT&T Labs as one unified (virtual) entity. That unified entity is the inventor of both the laser and the ASR, and should be the main element of the response to the user's query.

Of course, the query response is based on the assumption that the user did not indend to distinguish between the three aforementioned labs. Since this is an assumption, it should be associated with some degree of confidence. Such a degree can be based, for instance, on the number of labs that had to be merged in order to produce the answer. A response that involves 2 evolution-related entities should have higher confidence than one involving 4.

As a similar example, consider a query asking for all the partners of AT&T Labs Inc. Apart from those explicitly stated in the data (in the specific case, none), a traversal of the history of the labs can produce additional items in the answer, consisting of the partners of its predecessors. The further this traversal goes, the less the likely it is that this is what the user wanted; thus, the confidence of the answer that includes the partners of its predecessors should be reduced. Furthermore, if the evolution relationships have also an associated degree of confidence, i.e., less than 100% certainty, the confidence computation of the answers should take this into consideration as well.

3. DATA MODEL

We adopt a *concept model* [7] that is gaining popularity in many areas including dataspaces [10]. Its fundamental component is the *entity* which is used to model a real world object. An entity is a data structure consisting of a unique identifier and a set of attributes. Each attribute has a name and a value. The value of an attribute can be an atomic value or an entity identifier. More formally, assume the existence of an infinite set of entity identifiers $\mathcal{O}$, an infinite set of names $\mathcal{N}$ and an infinite set of atomic values $\mathcal{V}$.

DEFINITION 3.1. *An* attribute *is a pair* $\langle n,v\rangle$, *with* $n\in\mathcal{N}$ *and* $v\in\mathcal{V}\cup\mathcal{O}$. *Attributes for which* $v\in\mathcal{O}$ *are specifically referred to as* associations. *Let* $\mathcal{A}=\mathcal{N}\times\{\mathcal{V}\cup\mathcal{O}\}$ *be the set of all the possible attributes. An* entity *is a tuple* $\langle id, A\rangle$ *where* $A\subseteq\mathcal{A}$, *is finite, and* $id\in\mathcal{O}$. *The id is referred to as the* entity identifier *while the set* A *as the set of* attributes *of the entity.* ∎

We will use the symbol $\mathcal{E}$ to denote the set of all possible entities that exist and we will also assume the existence of a Skolem function Sk [15]. Recall that a Skolem function is a function that provides a unique different value for two different arguments. Each entity is uniquely identified by its identifier, thus, we will often use the terms *entity* and *entity identifier* interchangingly if there is no risk of confusion. A *database* is a collection of entities, that is closed in terms of associations between the entities.

DEFINITION 3.2. *A* database *is a finite set of entities* $E\subseteq\mathcal{E}$ *such that for each association* $\langle n, e'\rangle$ *of an entity* $e\in E$: $e'\in E$. ∎

As a query language we adopt a datalog style language. A query consists of a head and a body. The body is a conjunction of atoms. An atom is an expression of the form $e(n_1{:}v_1,\ n_2{:}v_2,\ \ldots,\ n_k{:}v_k)$ or an arithmetic condition such as $=$, $\leq$, etc. The head is always a non-arithmetic atom. Given a database, the body of the query is said to be true if all its atoms are true. A non-arithmetic atom $e(n_1{:}v_1,\ n_2{:}v_2,\ \ldots,\ n_k{:}v_k)$ is true if there is an entity with an identifier e and attributes $\langle n_i, v_i\rangle$ for every i=1..k. When the body of a query is true, the head is also said to be true. If a head $e(n_1{:}v_1,\ n_2{:}v_2,\ \ldots,\ n_k{:}v_k)$ is true, the answer to the query is an entity with identifier e and attributes $\langle n_1{:}v_1\rangle$, $\langle n_2{:}v_2\rangle$, ..., $\langle n_k{:}v_k\rangle$.

The components e, n_i and v_i, for i=1..k of any atom in a query can be either a constant or a variable. Variables used in the head or in arithmetic atoms must also be used in some non-arithmetic atom in the body. If a variable is used at the beginning of an atom, it is bound to entity identifiers. If the variable is used inside the parenthesis but before the ":" symbol, it is bound to attribute names, and if the variable is in the parenthesis after the ":" symbol, it is bound to attribute values. A variable assignment in a query is an assignment of its variables to constants. A *true assignment* is an assignment that makes the body of the query true. The answer set of a query involving variables is the union of the answers produced by the query for each true assignment.

EXAMPLE 3.3. *Consider the query:*
$\$x(isHolder{:}\$y)$:-$\$x(name{:}'AT\&TLabsInc.', isHolder{:}\$y)$ *that looks for entities called "AT&T Labs Inc." and are holders of a patent. For every such entity that is found, an entity with the same identifier is produced in the answer set and has an attribute isHolder with the patent as a value.* ∎

In order to model evolution we need to model the lifespan of the real world objects that the entities represent and the evolution relationship between them. For the former, we assume that we have a temporal database, i.e., each entity is associated to a time period; however, this is not critical for this work so we will omit that part from the following discussions. To model the evolution relationship, on the other hand, we consider a special association that we elevate into a first-class citizen in the database. We call this association an *evolution relationship*. Intuitively, an evolution relationship from one entity to another is an association indicating that the real world object modeled by the latter is the result of some form of evolution of the object modeled by the former. In Figure 1, the dotted lines between the entities illustrate evolution relationships. A database with evolution relationships is an *evolution database*.

DEFINITION 3.4. *An* evolution database *is a tuple* $\langle E,\Omega\rangle$, *such that* $\langle E\rangle$ *is a database and* Ω *is a partial order relation over* E. *An* evolution relationship *is every association* $(e_1, e_2)\in\Omega$. ∎

Given an evolution database, one can construct a directed acyclic graph by considering as nodes the entities and as edges its evolution relationships. We refer to this graph as the *evolution graph* of the database.

Our proposal is that entities representing different evolution phases of the same real world object can be considered as one for query answering purposes. To formally describe this idea we introduce the notion of *coalescence*. Coalescence is defined only on entities that are connected through a series of evolution relationships; the coalescence of those entities is a new entity that replaces them and has as attributes the union of their attributes (including associations).

DEFINITION 3.5. *Given an evolution database* $\langle E,\Omega\rangle$, *The* coalescence *of two entities* $e_1{:}\langle id_1,A_1\rangle$, $e_2{:}\langle id_2,A_2\rangle\in E$, *connected through an evolution relationship* ev *is a new evolution database* $\langle E',\Omega'\rangle$ *such that* $\Omega'=\Omega-ev$ *and* $E'=(E-\{e_1,e_2\})\cup\{e_{new}\}$, *where* $e_{new}{:}\langle id_{new},A_{new}\rangle$ *is a new entity with a fresh identifier* $id_{new}=Sk(id_1,id_2)$ *and* $A_{new}=A_1\cup A_2$. *Furthermore, each association* $\langle n,id_1\rangle$ *or* $\langle n,id_2\rangle$ *of an entity* $e\in E$, *is replaced by* $\langle n,id_{new}\rangle$. *The relationship between the two databases is denoted as* $\langle E,\Omega\rangle \xrightarrow{ev} \langle E',\Omega'\rangle$ ∎

The Skolem function that we have mentioned earlier defines a partial order among the identifiers, and this partial order extends naturally to entities. We call that order *subsumption*.

DEFINITION 3.6. *An identifier* id_1 *is said to be* subsumed *by an identifier id, denoted as* $id_1\dot{\prec}id$ *if there is some identifier* $id_x\neq id$ *and* $id_x\neq id_1$ *such that* $id=Sk(id_1,id_x)$. *An entity* $e_1=\langle id_1,\ A_1\rangle$ *is said to be* subsummed *by an entity* $e_2=\langle id_2,\ A_2\rangle$, *denoted as* $e_1\dot{\prec}e_2$, *if* $id_1\dot{\prec}id_2$ *and for every attribute* $\langle n,v_1\rangle\in A_1$ *there is attribute* $\langle n,v_2\rangle\in A_2$ *such that* $v_1=v_2$ *or, assuming that the attribute is an association,* $v_1\dot{\prec}v_2$. ∎

Given an evolution database $\langle E,\Omega\rangle$, and a set $\Omega_s\subseteq\Omega$ one can perform a series of consecutive coalescence operations, each one coalescing the two entities that an evolution relationship in the Ω_s associates.

DEFINITION 3.7. *Given an evolution database* $D{:}\langle E,\Omega\rangle$ *and a set* $\Omega_s=\{m_1, m_2, \ldots, m_m\}$ *such that* $\Omega_s\subseteq\Omega$, *let* D_m *be the evolution database generated by the sequence of coalescence operations* $D\xrightarrow{m_1}D_1\xrightarrow{m_2}, \ldots, \xrightarrow{m_m}D_m$. *The* possible world *of* D *according to* Ω_s *is the database* D_{Ω_s} *generated by simply omitting from* D_m *all its evolution relationships.* ∎

Intuitively, a set of evolution relationships specifies sets of entities in a database that should be considered as one, while the possible world represents the database in which these entities have actually been coalesced. Our notion of a possible world is similar to the notion of a possible worlds in probabilistic databases [8]. Direct consequence of the definition of a possible world is the following theorem:

THEOREM 3.8. *The possible world of an evolution database* $D{:}\langle E,\Omega\rangle$ *for a set* $\Omega_s\subseteq\Omega$ *is unique.* ∎

Due to this uniqueness, a set Ω_s of evolution relationships of a database can be used to refer to the possible world.

According to the definition of a possible world, an evolution database can be seen as a shorthand of a set of databases, i.e., its possible worlds. Thus, a query on an evolution database can be seen as a shorthand for a query on its possible worlds. Based on this observation we define the semantics of query answering on an evolution database.

DEFINITION 3.9. *The evaluation of a query* q *on an evolution database* D *is the union of the results of the evaluation of the query on every possible world* D_c *of* D. ∎

For a given query, there may be multiple possible worlds that generate the same results. To eliminate this redundancy we require every coalescence to be well-justified. In particular, our principle is that no possible world or variable assignment will be considered, unless it generates some new results in the answer set. Furthermore, among the different possible worlds that generate the same results in the answer set, only the one that requires the smaller number of coalescences will be considered. To support this, we define a subsumption relationship among the variable assignments across different possible worlds and we redefine the semantics of the evaluation of a query.

$x	$y	Possible World	Answer	Cost
e1	P2P Video	∅	e1(isHolder:"P2P Video")	0
Sk(e1,e2)	**P2P Video**	**e1,e2**	**Not generated**	**1**
Sk(e1,e2,e3)	**P2P Video**	**e1,e2,e3**	**Not generated**	**2**
Sk(e1,e2,e3)	ASR	e1,e2,e3	Sk(e1,e2,e3)(isHolder:"ASR")	2
Sk(e1,e2,e3,e4)	Laser	e1,e2,e3,e4	Sk(e1,e2,e3,e4)(isHolder:"Laser")	3
...	...	...	...	...

Table 1: A fraction of variable assignments for Example 3.11.

DEFINITION 3.10. *Let h and h' be two variable assignment for a set of variables X. h' is said to be* subsumed *by h, denoted as $h'{\subseteq}h$ if $\forall x{\in}X$: $h(x){=}h'(x){=}constant$, or $h(x){=}e$ and $h'(x){=}e'$, with e and e' being entities for which $e'{\prec}e$ or $e{=}e'$. Given an evolution database D, let $\mathcal{W}$ be the set of its possible worlds. The answer to a query q is the union of the results of evaluating q on every database in $\mathcal{W}$. During the evaluation of q on a database in $\mathcal{W}$, true variable assignments that are subsumed by some other true variable assignment, even in other possible worlds, are not considered.* ∎

It is natural to assume that not all possible worlds are equally likely to describe the database the user has in mind when she was formulating the query. We assume that the more a possible world differs from the original evolution database, the less likely it is to represent what the user had in mind. This is also in line with the minimality and well-justification principle described previously. We reflect this as a reduced confidence to the answers generated by the specific possible world and quantify it as a score assigned to each answer. One way to measure that confidence is to count how many evolution relationships have to be coalesced for the possible world to be constructed. The evolution relationships may also be assigned a weight reflecting the confidence to the fact that its second entity is actually an evolution of the first.

EXAMPLE 3.11. *Consider again the query of Example 3.3. and assume that it is to be evaluated on the database of Figure 1. Table 1 illustrate a set of true variable assignments for some of the possible worlds of the database. The possible world on which each assignment is defined is expressed through its respective set Ω_s. The fourth column contains the result generated in the answer set from the specific assignment and the last column contains its respective cost, measured in number of coalesces that are required for the respective possible world to be generated from the evolution database. Note that the second and the third assignment (highlighted in bold), are redundant since they are subsumed by the first.* ∎

The existence of a score for the different solutions, allows us to rank the query results and even implement a top-k query answering. The challenging task though is how to identify in an efficient way the possible worlds and more specifically the true variable assignments that lead into correct results.

4. QUERY EVALUATION TECHNIQUES

4.1 The naive approach

The straight forward approach in evaluating a query is to generate all the possible worlds and evaluate the query on each one individually. In the sequel, generate the union of all the individually produced results, eliminate duplication and remove answers subsumed by others. Finally, associate to each of the remaining answers a cost based on the coalescences that were performed in order to generate the possible world from which the answer was produced, and rank the answers according to that score. The generation of all possible worlds is a time consuming task. For an evolution database with an evolution graph of N edges, there are 2^N possible worlds. This is clearly a brut force solution, not desirable for online query answering.

4.2 Materializing all the possible worlds

Since the possible worlds do not depend on the query that needs to be evaluated, they can be pre-computed and stored in advance so that they are available at query time. Of course, as it is the case of any materialization technique, the materialized data need to be kept in sync with the evolution database when its data is modified. Despite the fact that this will require some effort, there are already well-known techniques for change propagation [3] that can be used. The major drawback, however, is the space overhead. A possible world contains all the attributes of the evolution database, but in fewer entities. Given that the number of attributes are typically larger than the number of entities, and that entities associated with evolution relationships are far fewer than the total number of entities in the database, we can safely assume that the size of a possible world will be similar to the one of the evolution database. Thus, the total space required will be 2^n times the size of the evolution database. The query answering time, on the other hand, will be 2^n times the average evaluation time of the query on a possible world.

4.3 Materializing only the maximum world

An alternative solution is to generate and materialize the possible world D_{max} generated by performing all possible coalescences. For a given evolution database $\langle E, \Omega \rangle$, this world is the one constructed according to the set of all evolution relationships in Ω. Any query that has an answer in some possible world of the evolution database will also have an answer in this maximal possible world D_{max}. This solution work has two main limitations. First it does not follow our minimalistic principle and performs coalescences that are not needed, i.e., they do not lead to any additional results in the result set. Second, the generated world fails to include results that distinguish difference phases of the lifespan of an entity (phases that may have to be considered individual entities) but the approach coalesces them in one just because they are connected through evolution relationships.

4.4 On-the-fly coalescence computations

To avoid any form of materialization, we propose an alternative technique that computes the answers on the fly by performing coalescences on a need-to-do basis. In particular, we identify the attributes that satisfy the different query conditions and from them the respective entities to which they belong. If all the attributes satisfying the conditions are on the same entity, then the entity is added in the answer set. However, different query conditions may be satisfied by attributes in different entities. In these cases we identify sets of entities for each one of which the union of the attributes of its entities satisfy all the query conditions. For each such a set, we coalesce all its entities into one if they belong to the same connected component of the evolution graph. Doing the coalescence it is basically like creating the respective possible world; however, we generate only the part of that world that is necessary to produce an answer to the query. In more details, the steps of the algorithm are the following.

[Step 1: Query Normalization] We decompose every non-arithmetic atom in the body of the query that has more than one condition into a series of single-condition atoms. More specifically, any atom of the form $x(n_1{:}v_1, n_2{:}v_2, \ldots, n_k{:}v_k)$ is decomposed into a conjunction of atoms $x(n_1{:}v_1), x(n_2{:}v_2), \ldots, x(n_k{:}v_k)$.

[Step 2: Individual Variable Assignments Generation] For each non-arithmetic atom in the decomposed query, a list is constructed that contains assignments of the variables in the respective atom to constants that make the atom true. Assuming a total of N non-arithmetic atoms after the decomposition, let L_1, L_2, ..., L_N be the generated lists. Each variable assignment actually specifies the part of the evolution database that satisfies the condition described in the atom.

[Step 3: Candidate Assignment Generation] The elements of the lists generated in the previous step are combined together to form complete variable assignments, i.e., assignments that involve every variable in the body of the query. In particular, the cartesian product of the lists is created. Each element in the cartesian product is a tuple of assignments. By construction, each such tuple will contain at least one assignment for every variable that appears in the body of the query. If there are two assignments of the same attribute bound variable to different values, the whole tuple is rejected. Any repetitive assignments that appear within each non-rejected tuple is removed to reduce redundancy. The result is a set of variable assignments, one from each of the tuples that have remained.

[Step 4: Arithmetic Atom Satisfaction Verification] Each assignment generated in the previous step for which there is at least one arithmetic atom not evaluating to true, is eliminated from the list.

[Step 5: Candidate Coalescence Identification] Within each of the remaining assignments we identify entity-bound variables that have been assigned to more than one values. Normally this kind of assignment evaluates always to false. However, we treat them as suggestions for coalescences, so that the assignment will become a *true assignment* (ref. previous Section). For each assignment h in the list provided by Step 4, the set $\mathcal{V}_h=\{V_{x_1}, V_{x_2}, \ldots, V_{x_k}\}$ is generated, where V_x is the set of different entities that variable x has been assigned in assignment h. In order for the assignments of variable x to evaluate to true, we need to be able to coalesce the entities in V_x. To do so, these entities have to belong to the same connected component in the evolution graph of the database. If this is not the case, the assignment h is ignored.

[Step 6: Coalescence Realization & Cost Computation] Given a set $\mathcal{V}_h=\{V_{x_1}, V_{x_2}, \ldots, V_{x_k}\}$ for an assignment h among those provided by Step 5, we need to find the minimum cost coalescences that need to be done such that all the entities in a set V_i, for $i=1..k$, are coalesced to the same entity. This will make the assignment h a *true* assignment, in which case the head of the query can be computed and an answer generated in the answer set. The cost of the answer will be the cost of the respective possible world, which is measured in terms of the number of coalescences that need to be performed. Finding the required coalescences for the set $\mathcal{V}_h$ that minimizes the cost boils down to the problem of finding a Steiner forest [12].

EXAMPLE 4.1. *Let us consider again the query of Example 3.3. In Step 1, its body will be decomposed into two parts:* $\$x(name{:}'AT\&TLabsInc.')$ *and* $\$x(isHolder{:}\$y)$. *For those two parts, during Step 2, the lists* $L_1=\{\{\$x=e1\}\}$ *and* $L_2=\{\{\$x=e1, \$y='P2PVideo'\}, \{\$x=e3, \$y='ASR'\}, \{\$x=e4, \$y='Laser'\}, \{\$x=e5, \$y='VoIP'\}\}$ *will be created. Step 3 creates their cartesian product* $L=\{\{\$x=e1, \$x=e1, \$y='P2PVideo'\}, \{\$x=e1, \$x=e3, \$y='ASR'\}, \{\$x=e1, \$x=e4, \$y='Laser'\}, \{\$x=e1, \$x=e5, \$y='VoIP'\}\}$. *The only attribute bound variable is* $\$y$ *but this is never assigned to more than one different value at the same time so nothing is eliminated. Since there are no arithmetic atoms, Step 4 makes no change either to the list L. If for instance, the query had an atom* $\$y\neq'VOIP'$ *in its body, then the last element of the list would have been eliminated. Step 5 identifies that the last three elements in L have the entity bound variable* $\$x$ *assigned to two different values; thus, it generates the candidate coalescences:* $V_1=\{e1, e3\}$, $V_2=\{e1, e4\}$ *and* $V_3=\{e1, e5\}$. *Step 6 determines that all three coalescences are possible. Entities* e1, e2 *and* e3 *will be coalesced for* V_1, e1, e2, e3 *and* e4 *for* V_2, *and the* e1, e2, e3 *and* e5 *for* V_3. ∎

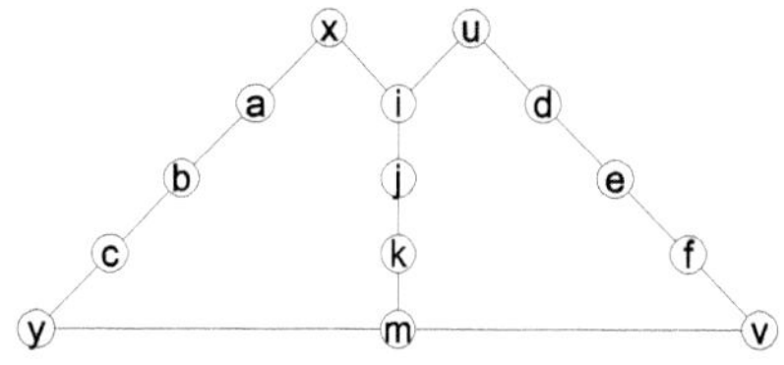

Figure 2: An illustration of the Steiner forest problem.

5. STEINER FOREST ALGORITHM

The last step of the evaluation algorithm presented in the previous section takes as input a set of entity sets and needs to perform a series of coalesce operations such that all the entities within each set will become one. To do so, it needs to find an interconnect on the evolution graph among all the entities within each set. Note that the interconnect may involve additional entities not in the set that unavoidably will also have to be coalesced with those in the set. Thus, it is important to find an interconnect that minimizes the total cost of the coalescences. The cost of a coalescence operation is the weight of the evolution relationship that connects the two entities that are coalesced. Typically, that cost is equal to one, meaning that the total cost is actually the total number of coalescence operations that need to be performed. For a given set of entities, this is known as the problem of finding the Steiner tree [11]. However, given a set of sets of entities, it turns out that finding the optimal solution, i.e., the minimum cost interconnect of all the entities, is not always the same as finding the Steiner tree for each of the sets individually. The specific problem is found in the literature as the Steiner forest problem [12].

The difference in the case of the Steiner forest is that edges can be "used" by more than one interconnect. More specifically, the Steiner tree problem aims at finding a tree on an undirected weighted graph that connects all the nodes in a set and has the minimum cost. In contrast to the minimum spanning tree, a Steiner tree is allowed to contain intermediate nodes in order to reduce its total cost. The Steiner forest problem takes as input sets of sets of nodes and needs to find a set of non-connected trees (branches) that make all the nodes in each individual set connected and the total cost is minimal, even if the cost of the individual trees are not always the minimal. We refer to these individual trees with the term *branches*. Figure 2 illustrates the difference through an example. Assuming that we have the graph shown in the figure and the two sets of nodes $\{x,y\}$ and $\{u,v\}$. Clearly, the minimum cost branch that connects nodes x and y is the one that goes through the nodes a, b and c. Similarly the minimum cost branch that connects u and v is the one that goes through the nodes e, f and g. Each of the two branches has cost 4 (the number of edges in the branch), thus, the total cost will be 8. However, if instead we connect all the four nodes x, y, u and v though the tree that uses the nodes i, j, k and m, then, although the two nodes in each set are connected with a path of 5 edges, the total cost is 7.

Algorithm 1 Steiner tree algorithm

Input: graph G,$f : E \rightarrow \mathbb{R}^+$, groups $\mathcal{V}= V_1, \ldots, V_L$
Output: ST for each element in $flat(\mathcal{V})$
1: Q_T: priority queue sorted in the increasing order
2: $Q_T \Leftarrow \emptyset$
3: **for all** $s_i \in maxflat(\mathcal{V})$ **do**
4:   enqueue $T(s_i, \{s_i\})$ into Q_T;
5: **end for**
6: **while** $Q_T \neq \emptyset$ **do**
7:   dequeue Q_T to $T(v, \mathbf{p})$;
8:   **if** $\mathbf{p} \in flat(\mathcal{V})$ **then**
9:     $ST(\mathbf{p}) = T(v, \mathbf{p})$
10:   **end if**
11:   **if** ST has all values **then**
12:     **return** ST
13:   **end if**
14:   **for all** $u \in N(v)$ **do**
15:     **if** $T(v, \mathbf{p}) \oplus (v, u) < T(u, \mathbf{p})$ **then**
16:       $T(u, \mathbf{p}) \Leftarrow T(v, \mathbf{p}) \oplus (v, u)$;
17:       update Q_T with the new $T(u, \mathbf{p})$;
18:     **end if**
19:   **end for**
20:   $\mathbf{p}_1 \Leftarrow \mathbf{p}$;
21:   **for all** $\mathbf{p}_2$ s.t. $\mathbf{p}_1 \cap \mathbf{p}_2 = \emptyset$ **do**
22:     **if** $T(v, \mathbf{p}_1) \oplus T(v, \mathbf{p}_2) < T(v, \mathbf{p}_1 \cup \mathbf{p}_2)$ **then**
23:       $T(u, \mathbf{p}_1 \cup \mathbf{p}_2) \Leftarrow T(v, \mathbf{p}_1) \oplus T(v, \mathbf{p}_2)$;
24:       update Q_T with the new $T(u, \mathbf{p}_1 \cup \mathbf{p}_2)$;
25:     **end if**
26:   **end for**
27: **end while**

Formally, the *Steiner forest* problem is defined as follows. Given a graph $G = \langle N, E \rangle$ and a cost function $f : E \rightarrow \mathbb{R}^+$, alongside a set of groups of nodes $\mathcal{V}= V_1, \ldots, V_L$, where $V_i \subseteq N$, find a set $C \subseteq E$ such that C forms a connected component that involves all the nodes of every group V_i and the $\sum_i f(c_i) \mid c_i \in C$ is minimal.

The literature contains a number of approximate solutions [2][18][14] as well as a number of exact solution using Dynamic Programming [11][9][20] for the discovery of Steiner trees. However, for the Steiner forest problem (which is known to be NP-hard [12]) although there are approximate solutions [12], no optimal algorithm has been proposed so far. In the current work we are making a first attempt toward that direction by describing a solution that is based on dynamic programming and is constructed by extending an existing Steiner tree discovery algorithm.

To describe our solution it is necessary to introduce the set $flat(\mathcal{V})$. Each element in $\flat((\mathcal{V}))$ is a set of nodes created by taking the union of the nodes in a subset of $\mathcal{V}$. More specifically, $flat(\mathcal{V})= \{U \mid U{=}\bigcup_{V_i \in S} V_i$ with $S{\subseteq}\mathcal{V}\}$. Clearly $flat(\mathcal{V})$ has 2^L members. We denote by $maxflat(\mathcal{V})$ the maximal element in $flat(\mathcal{V})$ which is the set of all possible nodes that can be found in all the sets in $\mathcal{V}$, i.e., $maxflat(\mathcal{V}){=}\{n \mid n{\in}V_1{\cup}\ldots{\cup}V_L\}$.

Our solution for the computation of the Steiner forest consists of two parts. In the first part, we compute the Steiner trees for every member of the $flat(\mathcal{V})$ set, and in the second part we use the computed Steiner trees to generate the Steiner forest on $\mathcal{V}$.

The state-of-the-art optimal (i.e., no approximation) algorithm for the Steiner tree problem is a dynamic programming solution developed in the context of keyword searching in relational data [9]. The algorithm is called the Dynamic Programming Best First (DPBF) algorithm and is exponential in the number of input nodes and polynomial with respect to the size of graph. We extend DPBF in order to find a *set* of Steiner trees, in particular a Steiner tree for every element in $flat(\mathcal{V})$. The intuition behind the extension is that we initially solve the Steiner tree problem for the $maxflat(\mathcal{V})$ and continue iteratively until the Steiner trees for every element in $flat(\mathcal{V})$ has been computed. We present next a brief description of DPBF alongside our extension.

Let $T(v, \mathbf{p})$ denote the minimum cost tree rooted at v that includes the set of nodes $\mathbf{p}{\subseteq}maxflat(\mathcal{V})$ Note that by definition, the cost of the tree $T(s, maxflat(\mathcal{V}))$ is 0, for every $s{\in}maxflat(\mathcal{V})$.

Trees can be iteratively merged in order to generate larger trees by using the following three rules.

$$T(v, \mathbf{p}) = min(T_g(v, \mathbf{p}), T_m(v, \mathbf{p})) \quad (1)$$

$$T_g(v, \mathbf{p}) = min_{u \in N(v)}((v, u) \oplus T(u, \mathbf{p})) \quad (2)$$

$$T_m(v, \mathbf{p}_1 \cup \mathbf{p}_2) = min_{\mathbf{p}_1 \cap \mathbf{p}_2 = \emptyset}(T(v, \mathbf{p}_1) \oplus T(v, \mathbf{p}_2)) \quad (3)$$

where $\oplus$ is an operator that merges two trees into a new one and $N(v)$ is the set of neighbour nodes of node v. In [9] it was proved that these equations are dynamic programming equations leading to the optimal Steiner tree solution for $maxflat(\mathcal{V})$ set of nodes. To find it, the DPBF algorithm employs the Dijkstra's shortest path search algorithm in the space of $T(v, \mathbf{p})$. The steps of the Steiner tree computation are shown in Algorithm 1. In particular, we maintain a priority queue Q_T that keeps in an ascending order the minimum cost trees that have been found at any given point in time. Naturally, a *dequeue* operation retrieves the tree with the minimal cost. Using the greedy strategy we look for the next minimal tree which can be obtained from the current minimal. In contrast to DPBF, we do not stop when the best tree has been found, i.e. when the solution for $maxflat(\mathcal{V})$ has been reached, but we keep collecting minimal trees (lines 7-10) until all elements in $flat(\mathcal{V})$ have been computed (lines 11-13). To prove that all the elements of $flat(\mathcal{V})$ are found during that procedure, it suffices to show that our extension corresponds to the finding of all the shortest paths for a single source in the Dijkstra's algorithm. The time and space complexity for finding the Steiner trees is $O(3^{\sum l_i} n + 2^{\sum l_i}((\sum l_i + logn)n + m))$ and $O(2^{\sum l_i} n)$, respectively, where n and m are the number of nodes and edges of graph G, and l_i is the size of the ith set V_i in the input of set $\mathcal{V}$ of the algorithm.

Once all the Steiner trees for $flat(\mathcal{V})$ have been computed, we use them to find the Steiner forest for $\mathcal{V}$. The Steiner forest problem has an optimal substructure and its subproblems overlap. This means that we can find a dynamic programming solution to it. To show this, we first we consider the case for $L{=}1$, i.e., the case in which we have only one group of nodes. In that case finding the Steiner forest is equivalent to finding the Steiner tree for the single set of nodes that we have. Assume now that $L{>}1$, i.e., the input set $\mathcal{V}$ is $\{V_1, \ldots, V_L\}$, and that we have already computed all the Steiner forests for every set $\mathcal{V}'{\subset}\mathcal{V}$. Let $SF(\mathcal{V})$ denote the Steiner forest for an input set $\mathcal{V}$. We do not know the exact structure of $SF(\mathcal{V})$, i.e. how many branches it has and what elements of $\mathcal{V}$ are included in each. Therefore, we need to test all possible hypotheses of the forest structure, which are 2^L, and pick the one that has minimal cost. For instance, we assume that the forest has a branch that includes all nodes in V_1. The total cost of the forest with that assumption is the sum of the Steiner forest on V_1 and the Steiner forest for $\{V_2, \ldots, V_L\}$ which is a subset of $\mathcal{V}$, hence it is considered known. The Steiner forest on V_1 is actually a Steiner tree. This is based on the following lemma.

LEMMA 5.1. *Each branch of a Steiner forest is a Steiner tree.*

Algorithm 2 Steiner forest algorithm

Input: $G = \langle N, E\rangle$, $\mathcal{V}= \{V_1, \ldots, V_L\}$,$ST(s)$ $\forall s \in flat(\mathcal{V})$
Output: $SF(\mathcal{V})$

for all $V_i \in \mathcal{V}$ **do**
  $SF(V_i) = ST(V_i)$
end for
for $i = 2$ to $L - 1$ **do**
  for all $H \subset \mathcal{V}$ and $\mid H \mid = i$ **do**
    $u \Leftarrow \infty$
    for all $E \subseteq H$ and $E \neq \emptyset$ **do**
      $u \Leftarrow min(u, ST(maxflat(E)) \oplus SF(H \setminus E))$
    end for
    $SF(H) \Leftarrow u$
  end for
end for
$u \Leftarrow \infty$
for all $H \subseteq \mathcal{V}$ and $H \neq \emptyset$ **do**
  $u \Leftarrow min(u, ST(maxflat(H)) \oplus SF(\mathcal{V} \setminus \mathcal{H}))$
end for
$SF(\mathcal{V}) \Leftarrow u$

PROOF. This proof is done by contradiction. Assuming that a branch of the forest is not a Steiner tree, it can be replaced with a Steiner tree and reduce the overall cost of the Steiner forest. This means that the initial forest was not minimal. □

We can formally express the above reasoning as:

$$SF(\mathcal{V}) = \min_{H \subseteq V}(ST(maxflat(H)) \oplus SF(\mathcal{V} \setminus H)) \quad (4)$$

Using the above equation in conjunction with the fact that $SF(\mathcal{V})=ST(V_1)$, if $\mathcal{V}=\{V_1\}$, we construct an algorithm (Algorithm 2) that finds the Steiner forest in a bottom up fashion. The time and space requirements of the specific algorithm are $O(3^L - 2^L(L/2-1)-1)$ and $O(2^L)$, respectively. Summing this with the complexities of the first part, it gives a total time complexity $O(3^{\sum l_i}n+2^{\sum l_i}((\sum l_i+logn)n+m))+3^L-2^L(L/2-1)-1)$ with space requirement $O(2^{\sum l_i}n + 2^L)$

6. QUERY EVALUATION OPTIMIZATION

In the case of top-k query processing there is no need to actually compute all possible Steiner forests to only reject some of them later. It is important to prune as early as possible cases which are expected not to lead to any of the top-k answers. We have developed a technique that achieves this. It is based on the following lemma.

LEMMA 6.1. *Given two sets of sets of nodes $\mathcal{V}'$ and $\mathcal{V}''$ on a graph G for which $\mathcal{V}' \subseteq \mathcal{V}''$: $cost(SF(\mathcal{V}')) \leq cost(SF(\mathcal{V}''))$.*

PROOF. The proof is based on the minimality of a Steiner forest. Let SF(V') and SF(V'') be Steiner forests for V' and V'', with costs w_1 and w_2, respectively. If $cost(SF(\mathcal{V}'')) \leq cost(SF(\mathcal{V}'))$, then we can remove $V'' \setminus V'$ from V'' and cover V' with a smaller cost forest than $SF(V')$, which contradicts the fact that $SF(V')$ is a Steiner forest. □

To compute the top-k answers to a query we do the following steps. Assume that $B = \{\mathcal{V}_1, \ldots, \mathcal{V}_n\}$ is a set of inputs for the Steiner forest algorithm. First, we find the $B_{min} \subseteq B$ such that for each $\mathcal{V}' \in B_{min}$ there is no $\mathcal{V}'' \in B$ such that $\mathcal{V}' \subset \mathcal{V}''$. Then, we compute the Steiner forest for each element in B_{min}. According to Lemma 6.1 and the construction procedure of B_{min} we ensure that the the Top-1 is among the computed Steiner forests. We remove the input which corresponds to that Top-1 answer from B and then we continue with the computation of Steiner forests to update B_{min}. The above steps are repeated until k answers have been found.

7. EXPERIMENTS

To evaluate the efficiency and effectiveness of our approach we performed two kinds of experiments. First we studied the behavior of the Steiner forest discovery algorithm in isolation, and then we evaluated the performance of the query answering mechanism we have developed and which uses internally the Steiner forest algorithm. We also studied the effectiveness of our optimization technique for top-k query answering.

In the experiments we used both synthetic and real data. We used the term *non-evolution* data to refer to entities and attributes, and the term *evolution* data to refer to the the evolution relationships and more generally to the evolution graph. We noticed that in the real datasets, the non-evolution data were much larger than the evolution data and we maintained a similar analogy during our synthetic data generation.

For the synthetic data generation we used the Erdös-Rényi graph generator [17] which can produce random graphs for which the probability to have an edge between two nodes is constant and independent of other edges. Since many real world data follow a power law distribution, for the non-evolution synthetic data we used the Zipf's distribution. In our own implementation of the Zipfian distribution, as a rank we considered the number of occurrences of an attribute-value pair in the entire dataset (e.g., if the attribute $\langle State, CA\rangle$ appeared 15 time, its rank was 15). This allowed us to model the fact that there are few frequent attribute-value pairs and the majority are rare attributes. The real corpora that we used had similar properties. We will refer to the synthetic dataset generated using this method as *ER-SYNTH*.

For real dataset we used an extract from the trademark corpora which is available from the United States Patent and Trademark Office[1]. The trademarks are a kind of intellectual property which may belong to an individual or a company. If the owner of some trademark changes, the trademark has to be re-registered accordingly. Analyzing the trademark owner lists we could extract sequences of companies that have registered the same trademark, and we used this as an indication for evolution. We constructed the evolution graphs by considering each such a pair as an evolution relationship. The dataset we generated that way from the UPTSO files contained approximately 16K unique companies, 200K attributes (the information about companies such as name, place where it is registered and so on), and an evolution graph with 573 components of sizes between 5 and 373. To make the dataset extracted from real data even richer, i.e., with components of higher complexity, we used two graph merging strategies. In the first, a new evolution component is constructed by connecting two components through an artificial evolution relationship edge between two random nodes from the two components. We refer to this kind of merge as *CHAIN*, because it creates a chain of source graphs. In the second strategy, two components are merged, by choosing an arbitrary node from one component and then adding evolution relationship edges to some random node of every other component. We refer to this method as *STAR*. Datasets generated using these methods will be denoted as *REAL-CHAIN* and *REAL-STAR*, respectively.

The naive evaluation strategies that were described in Sec-

[1]http://www.uspto.gov/

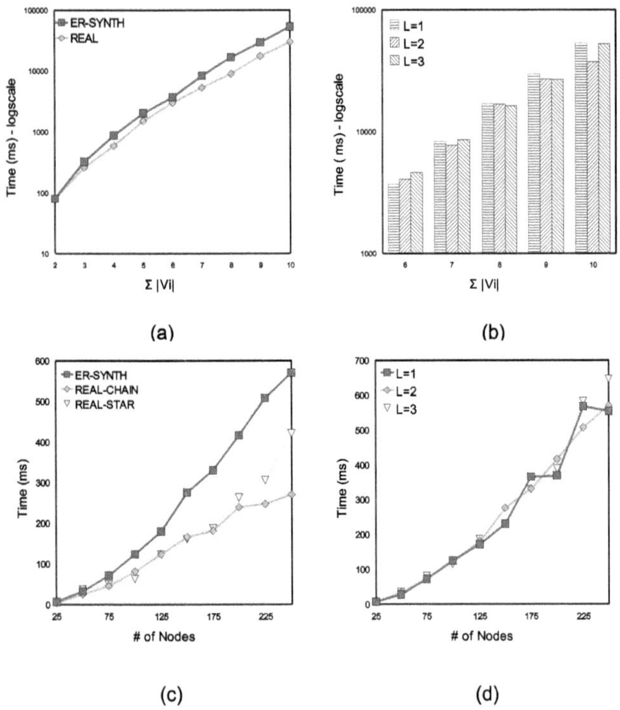

Figure 3: Steiner forest discovery performance

tions 4.1 and 4.2 are omitted from the discussion since their high complexity makes them practically infeasible to implement. In some sense, the naive case corresponds to the brute force way of finding a minimal Steiner forest, which is exponential in the size of evolution graph.

The experiments were all carried out on a 2.4GHz CPU and 4G memory PC running MS Windows Vista.

7.1 Steiner Forest

To study in detail the Steiner forest algorithm we performed two kinds of experiments. First, we studied the scalability properties of the algorithm for varying inputs, and then the behavior of the algorithm for graphs with different characteristics.

Scaling the Input. Recall that the input to the Steiner forest algorithm is the set $\mathcal{V}=\{V_1,\ldots,V_L\}$. In this experiment we studied the query evaluation time with respect to the size of the input. By size we considered two parameters: (i) the total number of elements in the sets of $\mathcal{V}$, i.e., the $\sum_{i=1}^{L}|V_i|$; and (ii) the number of the groups, i.e., the value L.

For the former, we started with L=1 and we scaled the $\sum|V_i|$ (which in this case is actually equal to $|V_1|$) from 2 to 10. For each size the average evaluation time of 25 random queries was recorded. The queries were evaluated both on synthetic and on real data. The synthetic graph was obtained using the Erdös-Rényi method and had $n = 57$ nodes and $m = 65$ edges. The real dataset graph was the one described previously. The results of this experiment are presented in Figure 3(a). The exponential grows in time (note that the time is presented on a logarithmic scale) with respect to a query size is consistent with the theoretical complexity of the Steiner forest algorithm.

To study how the parameter L affects the query execution time we kept the $\Sigma_{i=1}^{L}|V_i|$ constant but modified the number of the sets L from 1 to 3, and then we repeated the experiment for values of $\sum_{i=1}^{L}|V_i|$ from 6 to 10 (we assumed that a minimal set size was 2). The results of the average of 25 random query execution times are reported in Figure 3(b). The characteristics of the graph were the same as those in the previous experiment. The current experiment showed that the execution time depends fully on the $\sum_{i=1}^{L}|V_i|$ and not on L itself. This means that within a reasonable range of query sizes the number of forest branches does not have any influence on the performance.

Scaling the Graph. In this experiment we studied the Steiner forest discovery time with respect to the size of the graph. We used three kinds of graph data: *ER-SYNTH*, *REAL-CHAIN* and *REAL-STAR*, with sizes from 25 to 250 nodes with a step of 25.

For the synthetic dataset the number of edges and nodes was almost the same. We generated 25 random inputs to the Steiner forest problem with $L = 2$ and $|V_1|$=3, and $|V_2|$=3. The results of this experiment are presented in Figure 3(c). The query evaluation time has a linear trend as expected, and it was interesting that the execution time was always less than a second..

We also studied the scalability of the algorithm in terms of the parameter L. For three queries with $\sum|V_i| = 6$ and L=1, 2 and 3 we varied the evolution graph size from 25 to 250 with step 25. The graph we used was the *ER-SYNTH* with the same number of nodes and edges as before. The results are shown in Figure 3(d), where it can be observed that the scalability of the algorithm depends on the total number of elements in the sets in the input set $\mathcal{V}$, i.e., the $\sum_{i=1}^{L}|V_i|$, and not on the number of forest branches, i.e., the number L, at least for values of $\sum_{i=1}^{L}|V_i|$ up to 10.

7.2 Query Evaluation

Apart from experimenting with the Steiner forest algorithm in isolation, we run a number of experiments to evaluate the query answering mechanism we have developed for evolution databases. The query evaluation time depends not only on the evolution graph size and structure but also on the size and structure of the whole evolution database. First, we analyzed the behaviour of the system with respect to the query size. The query size is determined by the number of distinct variables, and their number of occurrences in the query. We started with a 1-variable query and we observe its behavior as size increases.. Then, we tested the scalability of the query evaluation mechanism as a function of the evolution graph only. Finally, we studied the scalability as a function of the data (i.e., attributes and associations) and we found that their distribution (but not their size) can dramatically affect the performance of the system.

In the synthetic data generation, we generated values that were following the Zipfian distribution for the attributes/associations. We controlled the generation of the *ER-SYNTH* dataset through four parameters, and in particular, the *pool of entities*, the *exponent* that is used to adjust the "steepness" of the Zipfian distribution, the *number of elements* that describes the maximum frequency of an attribute or association, and the *number of attributes*.The values of the parameters for the synthetic data are chosen to coincide with those of the real corpora.

Scaling the Query. We considered a number of 1-variable queries with a body of the form:

$$\$x(attr_1{:}value_1),\ldots,\$x(attr_N{:}value_N)$$

and we performed a number of experiments for different values of N, i.e., the number of atoms in the query. For every atom we randomly chose an attribute-value pair from a pool of available distinct attribute name/value pairs. The *ER-SYNTH* graph that was generated had 57 nodes and 65 edges. The results are shown in

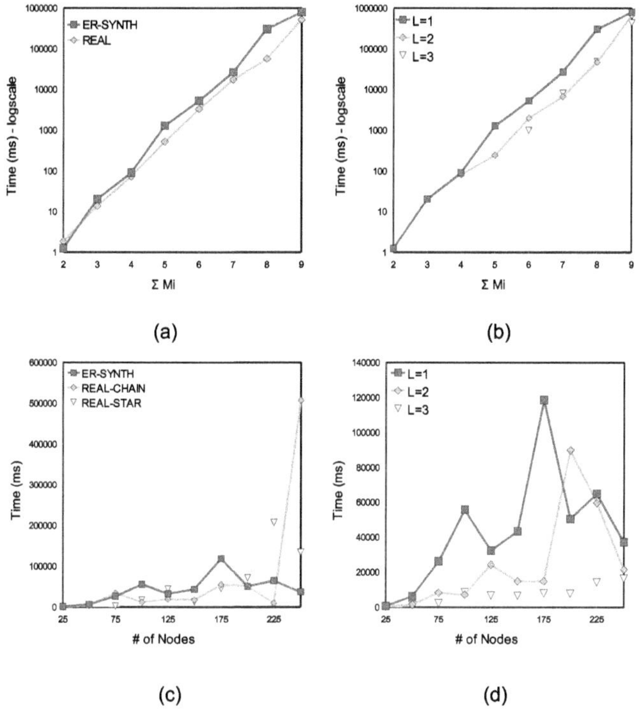

Figure 4: Query evaluation performance

Figure 4(a). The same figure includes the results of the query evaluation on the real dataset that had a size similar to the synthetic. For the generation of their non-evolution data we had the exponent set to 3, the number of elements parameter set to 15 and their total number was 537. The results of the Figure 4(a) are in a logarithmic scale and confirm the expectation that the query evaluation time is growing exponentially as the number of variables in the query grows. If we compare these results with those of the Steiner forest algorithm for the respective case, it follows that the integrated system adds a notable overhead on top of the Steiner forest algorithm execution time. This is was due to the number of coalescence candidates and the number of Steiner forests that needed to be computed in order to obtain the cost of the elements in the answer set. Although the parameters for the generation of the synthetic and real data coincided, their trends were different, as Figure 4(c) illustrates.

We further tested how the number of entity variables in the query affect the performance. Note that we are mainly interested in the entity-bound variables. Let M represent the number of distinct entity-bound variables in the query, and M_i the number of appearances of the i-th variable in the query. Note that the number of distinct variables will require to solve a Steiner forest problem in which the input $\mathcal{V}=\{V_1,\ldots,V_L\}$ will have $L=M$ and $|V_i|=M_i$, for each $i=1..M$. The total number of variable appearances in the query will naturally be $\sum_{i=1}^{M} M_i$.

In the experiment, we chose a constant value for the $\sum_{i=1}^{M} M_i$ and we run queries for $M=1$, 2 or 3. As a dataset we used the *ER-SYNTH* with 57 nodes and 65 edges. 537 attributes were generated with the exponent parameter having the value 3 and the number of elements parameter to have the value 15.A total of 53 synthetic associations were also generated with the exponent parameter having the value 3, and the number of elements parameter to have the value 10. We used 25 randomly generated queries for each of the 3 M values, and took their average execution time. We did multiple runs of the above experiments for different values of $\sum_{i=1}^{M} M_i$ between 4 and 10. The outcome of the experiments is shown in Figure 4(b) in a logarithmic scale. Clearly, the number of branches in a forest did not affect the query evaluation time, i.e., queries with many variables showed the same increase in time as the 1-variable query for the same $\sum_{i=1}^{M} M_i$.

Scaling the Data. In this experiment we examined the query evaluation time with respect to the size of the evolution graph. As evolution data, we used both real and synthetic sources. Regarding the real data, we used a series of graphs (and their attributes as non-evolution data) with sizes from 25 to 250 with step 25. The number of edges was 110% of the number of nodes for all graphs. For the real dataset we used both the *REAL-CHAIN* and the *REAL-STAR* data. For each graph we generated 25 random queries with 3 distinct variables, i.e., $M=3$, and each variable had $M_1=2$, $M_2=2$ and $M_3=3$ appearances in the query, and we measured the average time required to evaluate them. As a synthetic dataset the *ER-SYNTH* was used, generated to be the same size as before but with the following Zipfian distribution parameters: exponent 3, number of elements 15 and number attributes 10 times more than the number of nodes. Note that we did not generate associations because the trademark dataset did not have any association that we could use as a guide. Figure 4(c) depicts the results of this experiment. It shows that there is a linear growth of time which is is accompanied with an increasing oscillations which can be explained by the growing exponent of non-evolution data, i.e. the number of coalescence candidates may become too large for evolution graphs with considerable size.

Furthermore, we studied how the query evaluation time scales for different values of M, i.e. for different distinct variables but with the same total number of variable appearances in the query (i.e., the $\sum_{i=1}^{M} M_i$). We used the *ER-SYNTH* dataset again with sizes from 25 to 250, using a step 25. The number of evolution relationships was 110% of the number of entities. For each case, we generated 25 random queries with $M=1$ having $M_1=6$, $M=2$ having $M_1=3$, and $M_2=3$ and finally, $M=3$ having $M_1=3$, $M_2=2$, and $M_3=2$. We executed these queries and measured the average evaluation time. The non-evolution data was following the Zipfian distribution with exponent 3, the number of elements was 15 and the total number of attributes was 10 times more that the number of nodes (entities). For the associations, the exponent was 3, the number of elements was 10 and their total number was 5 times more that the respective number for nodes. The results are presented in Figure 4(d). Similarly to the previous experiment, we observed a linear growth with increasing oscillations.

Evolution scalability for different forest structures. We further examined how the number of evolution graph components influence the query evaluation time. For this purpose, we generated data using *ER-SYNTH*, and in particular 5 datasets of evolution graphs with a total size of 300 nodes and 330 edges. The sets had 1, 2, 3, 4 and 5 evolution graphs respectively. For each set we run 25 random queries with two distinct variables ($L = 2$) that were appearing in the query 3 times each, i.e., $M_1=3$ and $M_2=3$ and measured their average execution time. As non-evolution data, we generated attributes and associations with varying exponent parameter, 2.5, 3 and 3.5. The total number of elements and attributes/associations were 15 and 1000 in one case, while it was 10 and 100 in the other. Figure 5(a) contains a table with the query evaluation time for each number of branches and exponent values. From the result, we could observe the dramatic decrease in time with respect to the number of evolution graph components. This can be explained by the fact that the query evaluation "smeared" across a number of evolution

# of Branches	s=2.5	s=3.0	s=3.0
1	93,845	44,098	35,382
2	2,400	1,414	4,686
3	374	637	485
4	485	20	91
5	124	260	16

(a)

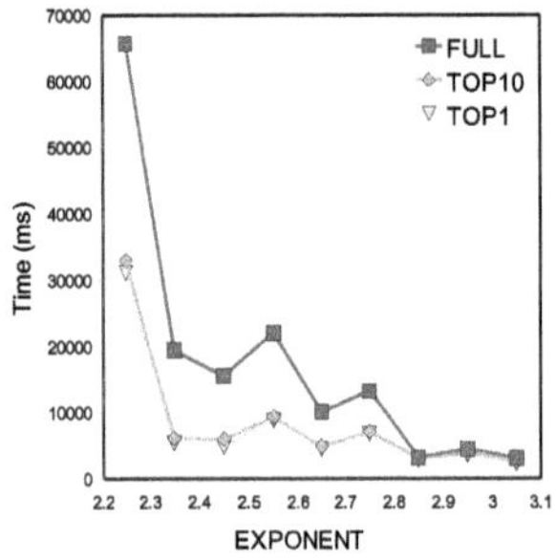

(b)

Figure 5: Query evaluation time for graphs with different numbers of connected components and for varying exponent of data distribution

graph components where each evaluation time becomes considerably small.

Data distribution dependency. Finally, we studied the properties of the system in relation to the data distribution parameter, namely the exponent of Zip's distribution. The query optimizer described in Section 6 was taken into consideration here and we analyzed how the non-evolution data were affecting the top-k query answering. For this experiment we used the following input parameters: 25 random queries with M=2 distinct variables, and M_1=3 and M_2=3 respective appearances of each distinct variable in the query. We used an *ER-SYNTH* dataset, the evolution graph of which had $n = 57$ nodes and $m = 65$ evolution edges. We also had 10000 attributes distributed over 30 entities, and 1000 associations distributed over 15 entities. The exponent we used varied from 2.25 to 3.05 with a step of 0.1. The results of the specific experiment are presented in Figure 5(b). For small exponents the difference between regular query answering and the top-10 or top-1 was significant. To justify this, recall that the number of pruned candidates depends on how different are the input sets in the Steiner forest algorithm input (ref. Section 6), thus, when the exponent is small the input sets share many entities.

8. CONCLUSION

In this work we presented a novel framework for dealing with evolution of entities at different granularity levels. We have made first class citizens of the system associations between entities indicating that they represent the same real world object but in different evolution phases. We have designed and implemented a technique that allows query answering over such databases even if the evolution model that the user has in mind is of different granularity than the one used in the database. The solution required the computation of a Steiner forest. For the later we have presented a novel algorithm for computing its optimal solution. Finally, we have performed a number of extensive experimental evaluation to determine the efficiency of our technique.

References

[1] J. Banerjee, W. Kim, H. Kim, and H. F. Korth. Semantics and implementation of schema evolution in object-oriented databases. In *SIGMOD*, pages 311–322, May 1987.

[2] Gaurav Bhalotia, Arvind Hulgeri, Charuta Nakhe, Soumen Chakrabarti, and S. Sudarshan. Keyword searching and browsing in databases using banks. In *ICDE*, pages 431–440, 2002.

[3] J. Blakeley, P. A. Larson, and F. W. Tompa. Efficiently Updating Materialized Views. In *SIGMOD*, pages 61–71, 1986.

[4] P. Buneman, S. Khanna, K. Tajima, and W. Tan. Archiving scientific data. In *SIGMOD*, pages 1–12, 2002.

[5] S. Chawathe, S. Abiteboul, and J. Widom. Representing and Querying Changes in Semistructured Data. In *ICDE*, pages 4–19, 1998.

[6] S. Chien, V. J. Tsotras, and C. Zaniolo. Efficient Management of Multiversion Documents by Object Referencing. In *VLDB*, pages 291–300, 2001.

[7] N. N. Dalvi, R. Kumar, B. Pang, R. Ramakrishnan, A. Tomkins, P. Bohannon, S. Keerthi, and S. Merugu. A web of concepts. In *PODS*, pages 1–12, 2009.

[8] Nilesh Dalvi and Dan Suciu. Efficient query evaluation on probabilistic databases. volume 16, pages 523–544, Secaucus, NJ, USA, 2007. Springer-Verlag New York, Inc.

[9] Bolin Ding, J Xu Yu, Shan Wang, Lu Qin, Xiao Zhang, and Xuemin Lin. Finding Top-k Min-Cost Connected Trees in Databases. *ICDE*, pages 836–845, 2007.

[10] X. Dong and A. Y. Halevy. Indexing dataspaces. In *SIGMOD*, pages 43–54, 2007.

[11] S E Dreyfus and R A Wagner. The Steiner problem in graphs. *Networks*, 1(3):195–207, 1972.

[12] Elisabeth Gassner. The Steiner Forest Problem revisited. *Journal of Discrete Algorithms*, 8(2):154–163, June 2010.

[13] A. Gupta, I. S. Mumick, and K. A. Ross. Adapting Materialized Views after Redefinitions. In *SIGMOD*, pages 211–222, 1995.

[14] Hao He, Haixun Wang, Jun Yang 0001, and Philip S. Yu. Blinks: ranked keyword searches on graphs. In *SIGMOD Conference*, pages 305–316, 2007.

[15] R. Hull and M. Yoshikawa. ILOG: Declarative Creation and Manipulation of Object Identifiers. In *VLDB*, pages 455–468, 1990.

[16] E. Ioannou, W. Nejdl, C. Niederee, and Y. Velegrakis. Onthe-Fly Entity-Aware Query Processing in the Presence of Linkage. *PVLDB*, 3(1):429–438, 2010.

[17] Richard Johnsonbaugh and Martin Kalin. A graph generation software package. In *SIGCSE*, pages 151–154, 1991.

[18] Varun Kacholia, Shashank Pandit, Soumen Chakrabarti, S. Sudarshan, Rushi Desai, and Hrishikesh Karambelkar. Bidirectional expansion for keyword search on graph databases. In *VLDB*, pages 505–516, 2005.

[19] A. M. Keller. Algorithms for Translating View Updates to Database Updates for Views Involving Selections, Projections, and Joins. *SIGMOD*, March 1985.

[20] B. Kimelfeld and Y. Sagiv. New algorithms for computing steiner trees for a fixed number of terminals. http://www.cs.huji.ac.il/ bennyk/papers/steiner06.pdf.

[21] B. S. Lerner. A Model for Compound Type Changes Encountered in Schema Evolution. *ACM TODS*, 25(1):83–127, March 2000.

[22] P. McBrien and A. Poulovassilis. Schema Evolution in Heterogeneous Database Architectures, A Schema Transformation Approach. In *CAiSE*, pages 484–499, 2002.

[23] F. Rizzolo and A. A. Vaisman. Temporal XML: modeling, indexing, and query processing. *VLDB Journal*, 17(5):1179–1212, 2008.

[24] F. Rizzolo, Y. Velegrakis, J. Mylopoulos, and S. Bykau. Modeling Concept Evolution: A Historical Perspective. In *ER*, pages 331–345, 2009.

[25] N. Tahmasebi, T. Iofciu, T. Risse, C. Niederée, and W. Siberski. Terminology Evolution in Web Archiving: Open Issues. In *IWAW*, Sep 2008.

[26] Y. Velegrakis, R. J. Miller, and J. Mylopoulos. Representing and Querying Data Transformations. In *ICDE*, pages 81–92, 2005.

[27] C. Yu and L. Popa. Semantic Adaptation of Schema Mappings when Schemas Evolve. In *VLDB*, pages 1006–1017, 2005.

Provenance-Based Refresh in Data-Oriented Workflows*

Robert Ikeda
Computer Science Department
Stanford University, USA
rmikeda@cs.stanford.edu

Semih Salihoglu
Computer Science Department
Stanford University, USA
semih@cs.stanford.edu

Jennifer Widom
Computer Science Department
Stanford University, USA
widom@cs.stanford.edu

ABSTRACT

We consider a general workflow setting in which input data sets are processed by a graph of transformations to produce output results. Our goal is to perform efficient *selective refresh* of elements in the output data, i.e., compute the latest values of specific output elements when the input data may have changed. We explore how *data provenance* can be used to enable efficient refresh. Our approach is based on capturing one-level data provenance at each transformation when the workflow is run initially. Then at refresh time provenance is used to determine (transitively) which input elements are responsible for given output elements, and the workflow is rerun only on that portion of the data needed for refresh. Our contributions are to formalize the problem setting and the problem itself, to specify properties of transformations and provenance that are required for efficient refresh, and to provide algorithms that apply to a wide class of transformations and workflows. We have built a prototype system supporting the features and algorithms presented in the paper. We report preliminary experimental results on the overhead of provenance capture, and on the crossover point between selective refresh and full workflow recomputation.

Categories and Subject Descriptors

H.4.1 [**Information Systems Applications**]: Office Automation—*workflow management*

General Terms

Algorithms, Management

1. INTRODUCTION

Consider a *workflow* in which input *data sets* are fed into an acyclic graph of *transformations* to produce output data sets. Examples include data warehouse ETL (*extract-transform-load*) processes [19], scientific data analyses [4, 11, 18], and information extraction pipelines [6]. Suppose the input data sets have been modified since the workflow was run, but the workflow has not been rerun on the modified input (for reasons outlined below). However, suppose we would like to *selectively refresh* one or more elements in the output data, i.e., compute the latest values of particular output elements based on the modified input data.

Selective refresh can be useful in any workflow that involves expensive, batch operations, for the following reasons:

- *Eager propagation*, i.e., rerunning the workflow whenever the input changes, may be prohibitively expensive, especially if the input data is modified frequently.
- Eager propagation may be overkill: Users may not care about each input update, or about all of the output data elements.

With selective refresh, we can avoid the expense of recomputing an entire output data set frequently, when all we need is a few up-to-date output values after the input has undergone some changes.

Our challenge is to perform selective refresh efficiently in a general setting. To avoid unnecessary work during the refresh of an output element, we must understand where the element came from in the input data, and how to rerun just the relevant computation to refresh the element. At the same time, we want to support refresh for workflows constructed from a wide class of possible transformations. Thus, we do not limit ourselves to well-understood transformations such as relational queries, or specific types of data elements. Rather, we define and consider *data-oriented workflows*, where all we require is some understanding of the behavior and relationships of individual data elements constituting the inputs and outputs of each transformation.

Clearly, data *provenance* (also called *lineage*) is highly relevant to our problem, since it captures where data came from and how it was derived [1, 4, 7, 18]. There has been a large body of work in lineage and provenance over the past two decades (Section 1.1), but we are unaware of any previous work that formalizes the refresh problem or exploits provenance for selective refresh in a general workflow environment. In this paper, we explore how provenance can be used to enable correct and efficient refresh. Our contributions are as follows:

- In Section 2, we present a formal foundation for individual transformations and their provenance.
- In Section 3, we formalize the refresh problem in terms of provenance. We specify a refresh procedure for single transformations, and we identify the properties of transformations and provenance that are required for correct refresh.
- In Section 4, we extend our formalization and refresh procedure to data-oriented workflows. We identify an additional provenance property necessary for the "transitive" workflow refresh procedure to produce correct refreshed data.

*This work is supported by the National Science Foundation under grants IIS-0414762 and IIS-0904497 and by a KAUST research grant.

- In Sections 5 and 6, we extend our formalism and algorithms to support transformation types that were excluded, for presentation development, from Sections 3 and 4.
- In Section 7, we discuss how refresh can still be performed (albeit less efficiently) in workflows for which the provenance property identified in Section 4 does not hold.
- In Section 8, we describe the prototype system we have built that supports refresh in data-oriented workflows. We explain the features and limitations of the current system, how the user interacts with the system, and how provenance-based refresh is supported.
- In Section 9, we report preliminary experimental results on the overhead of provenance capture, and on the crossover point between selective refresh and full workflow recomputation.

The remainder of this section covers related work and introduces a running example. In Section 10 we conclude and describe future work.

1.1 Related Work

There has been a large body of work in lineage and provenance over the past two decades. Surveys are presented in, e.g., [4, 7, 18], and formal models for provenance are presented in, e.g., [1, 2, 5, 9, 10, 13]. Provenance in the context of schema mappings is studied in [8, 12, 20]. None of these papers exploits provenance for selective refresh in a general workflow environment.

There also has been a large body of work in *incremental view maintenance*: the efficient propagation of base data modifications, usually in a relational setting [3, 14]. Our work considers general workflows, rather than relational views. Also, in contrast to the view-maintenance problem, selective refresh considers efficiently computing the up-to-date value of individual output elements, rather than keeping the entire view up to date by propagating changes made to the base data.

Reference [15] provides a framework to explain "missing" answers in queries. There is some high-level similarity between how explanations provided by their framework are created and how we support efficient refresh using data provenance. However, the details are quite different, and their framework supports SQL queries rather than general workflows.

Reference [12] considers the problem of "update exchange" between data peers linked by mappings. A subproblem they address is determining when a derived data element is no longer valid, but they do not provide a means to selectively refresh out-of-date values. Also, transformations in [12] are restricted to those that can be expressed in Datalog.

1.2 Running Example

We present a running example, designed to illustrate challenges and solutions throughout the paper. Consider *Jen*, a genetic counselor who runs a workflow, shown in Figure 1, to calculate her patients' genetic risk profiles. The workflow's input data sets are two lists of URLs: PatientURLs and DNAURLs. PatientURLs point to the patients' genetic test results, recording the patients' DNA sequences at certain DNA locations. DNAURLs identify XML documents describing disease risks associated with specific DNA location-sequence combinations. The workflow involves the following transformations:

- Transformations **PatientDL** and **DNADL** download files located at the URLs in data sets PatientURLs and DNAURLs. They produce directories RawPatientData (abbreviated RP) and RawDNAData (RD), respectively.
- Transformations **PExtract** and **RiskExtract** extract data from the downloaded files into tables: PatientDNA (PD) has attributes for patient name (name), DNA location (loc), and DNA sequence (seq). Table DNARisks (DR) has attributes for DNA location (loc), DNA sequence (seq), disease, and risk.
- Transformation **Join** joins tables PatientDNA and DNARisks on attributes loc and seq, then projects away the join attributes to produce table PatientRisks (PR) with attributes name, disease, and risk.
- Transformation **Filter** selects from PatientRisks those records with risk $>$ 0.5, producing final output HighPatientRisks.

Figure 2 shows sample input data sets along with all intermediate data, and finally output table HighPatientRisks. (The figure also includes *provenance predicates* and *forward filters*, described in Sections 2 and 5, respectively.) The starred data elements are for reference in the following scenario.

Before seeing a patient, Jen refreshes relevant records in table HighPatientRisks. As an example, we show how our approach efficiently refreshes Denise's heart disease record, i.e., element #2 in table HighPatientRisks. There are two main steps:

(1) Backward-tracing: To refresh a given output element, first one-level provenance is used to trace transitively from the output element to its relevant input elements. Starting with HighPatientRisks element #2, provenance enables tracing backward one step to obtain element #3 in table PatientRisks. From this element, another step is traced backward, resulting in PatientDNA element #4 together with DNARisks element #2. This process continues, to elements *Denise.xml* in RawPatientData and *2-aga.xml* in RawDNAData, and finally to input elements PatientURLs #3 and DNAURLs #2. Details of how provenance supports backward-tracing in general will be presented in Sections 3–6.

(2) Forward-propagation: Now that the relevant input elements have been found, they are propagated forward. Transformations **PatientDL** and **DNADL** are rerun on input elements PatientURLs #3 and DNAURLs #2 respectively to download the latest data from the web. The resulting elements are then sent through transformations **PExtract** and **RiskExtract**. Suppose that when **RiskExtract** is run on the latest downloaded data, the risk value for DNARisks element #2 has changed from 0.8 to 0.6. Further forward-propagation through transformations **Join** and **Filter** sets Denise's new heart-disease risk in HighPatientRisks to 0.6. Note if the new value were $\leq$ 0.5, then after the **Filter** transformation Denise's record would disappear, a situation that is also captured by refresh. Details of when forward-propagation works correctly, and how, will be covered in Sections 3–6.

The remainder of the paper formalizes the basic building blocks and techniques demonstrated in this example, covering a wide class of data types, transformations, and workflows.

2. FOUNDATIONS

2.1 Transformations

Let a *data set* be any set of data *elements*. We are not concerned about the types of individual data elements; we treat them simply as members of a data set. A *transformation* T is any procedure that takes one or more data sets as input and produces one or more data sets as output. As can be seen in the running example, we do not limit ourselves to transformations expressible in relational algebra or SQL. For now, we will consider transformations that take a single data set as input and produce a single output set; we

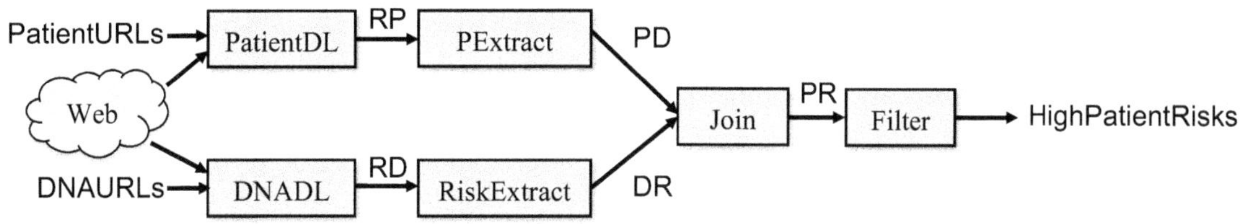

Figure 1: Genetic risk workflow example.

PatientURLs

	url
1	genetic.com/dl/00501
2	genetic.com/dl/00502
3	genetic.com/dl/00503
4	genetic.com/dl/00504

DNAURLs

	url
1	dnarec.com/1/aaa
2	dnarec.com/2/aga
3	dnarec.com/2/ttt
4	dnarec.com/3/gcc

RawPatientData (RP)

file	
Bob.xml	p: url contains '00501'
Carl.xml	p: url contains '00502'
Denise.xml	p: url contains '00503'
Earl.xml	p: url contains '00504'

RawDNAData (RD)

file	
1-aaa.xml	p: url contains '1/aaa'
2-aga.xml	p: url contains '2/aga'
2-ttt.xml	p: url contains '2/ttt'
3-gcc.xml	p: url contains '3/gcc'

PatientDNA (PD)

	name	loc	seq	
1	Bob	1	aaa	p: file = 'Bob.xml', f: loc = 1
2	Carl	2	ttt	p: file = 'Carl.xml', f: loc = 2
3	Carl	3	ggg	p: file = 'Carl.xml', f: loc = 3
4	Denise	2	aga	p: file = 'Denise.xml', f: loc = 2
5	Earl	2	ata	p: file = 'Earl.xml', f: loc = 2
6	Earl	3	gcc	p: file = 'Earl.xml', f: loc = 3

DNARisks (DR)

	loc	seq	disease	risk	
1	1	aaa	heart	0.6	p: file = '1-aaa.xml'
2	2	aga	heart	0.8	p: file = '2-aga.xml'
3	2	ttt	liver	0.4	p: file = '2-ttt.xml'
4	3	gcc	lung	0.7	p: file = '3-gcc.xml'

PatientRisks (PR)

	name	disease	risk	
1	Bob	heart	0.6	p^{PD}: name='Bob' ∧ loc=1 ∧ seq='aaa', p^{DR}: loc=1 ∧ seq='aaa'
2	Carl	liver	0.4	p^{PD}: name='Carl' ∧ loc=2 ∧ seq='ttt', p^{DR}: loc=2 ∧ seq='ttt'
3	Denise	heart	0.8	p^{PD}: name='Denise' ∧ loc=2 ∧ seq='aga', p^{DR}: loc=2 ∧ seq='aga'
4	Earl	lung	0.7	p^{PD}: name='Earl' ∧ loc=3 ∧ seq='gcc', p^{DR}: loc=3 ∧ seq='gcc'

HighPatientRisks

	name	disease	risk	
1	Bob	heart	0.6	p: name = 'Bob' ∧ disease = 'heart'
2	Denise	heart	0.8	p: name = 'Denise' ∧ disease = 'heart'
3	Earl	lung	0.7	p: name = 'Earl' ∧ disease = 'lung'

Figure 2: Genetic risk workflow sample data with provenance predicates. (*'s indicate elements relevant to HighPatientRisks element #2.)

will generalize to *multi-input* transformations in Section 6. (*Multi-output* transformations do not introduce any interesting challenges, and are thus omitted.) For any input data set I, we say that the application of T to I resulting in an output set O, denoted $T(I) = O$, is an *instance* of T.

2.2 Provenance

In general a transformation may inspect the entire input data set to produce each element in the output set, but in most cases there is a more fine-grained relationship between the input and output data elements: an output data element may have been derived from a small subset of the input data elements (maybe only one). Given a transformation instance $T(I) = O$ and an output element $o \in O$, *provenance* identifies the input data elements that contributed to o's derivation.

There has been a great deal of work on defining and capturing provenance for specific understood types of transformations [5, 7, 10], and some work describing properties of "opaque" transformations and how they relate to provenance [9]. Our goal in this paper is not to expand or improve upon any of that work, but rather to develop a formal framework and algorithms for the refresh problem that can exploit those definitions and techniques.

For generality, we only require that provenance for each output data element can be obtained by applying a predicate on the input:

DEFINITION 2.1 (PROVENANCE PREDICATES). Consider a transformation instance $T(I) = O$. We require that each output element $o \in O$ be annotated with a *provenance predicate* p. The elements of I satisfied by predicate p, i.e., the result of *tracing query* $\sigma_p(I)$, constitute o's provenance for instance $T(I) = O$. □

We do not impose any restrictions on provenance predicates, except that they can be applied to choose elements from data sets. Also note that our use of the relational notation $\sigma_p(I)$ for tracing queries is for convenience and familiarity only; data set I need not be a conventional relation.

Predicates give us a very general notion of provenance, and a full treatment of how provenance predicates are obtained is beyond the scope of this paper. Note, however, that provenance in the form of pointers to specific data elements, as in [2] and other work, can be specified as predicates selecting on identifiers or keys. (In this case "evaluating a tracing query" would likely be implemented as simple pointer-chasing.) Provenance for basic relational operators [5, 7, 10] is naturally expressed as predicates, e.g., for a *group-by aggregation* operator, provenance predicates select relevant input elements based on grouping value. Most of the numerous transformation types covered in [9] are amenable to the provenance-predicate approach. Although it's possible some less conventional forms of provenance may not be captured by predicates, we believe this formalization is a useful and general starting point.

Formally, we now assume that the output of each transformation instance produces a set of pairs: $T(I) = O = \{\langle o_1, p_1\rangle, \ldots, \langle o_n, p_n\rangle\}$, combining output elements and their provenance predicates.

EXAMPLE 2.1. Our running example data in Figure 2 includes provenance predicates, denoted p. Table PatientDNA includes additional predicates labeled f, which will be explained in Section 5. Table PatientRisks includes pairs of provenance predicates, since there are two input data sets to its transformation (Section 6). All of the remaining tables have a single provenance predicate for each output element, according to our definition. In all of them it can be seen easily that the predicate p associated with each output element o, when applied to the input table for o's transformation, produces the appropriate provenance for o. □

In our running example, it happens that provenance predicates always select a single input element, but this property is not required in our approach. In general, provenance predicates may select any number of input elements, up to the entire input data set.

3. ONE-TRANSFORMATION REFRESH

In this section, we specify a provenance-based refresh procedure for single transformations, and we identify two properties of the transformations and their provenance that are required for the procedure to work correctly. These properties also yield insights into the meaning of refresh in the presence of provenance.

But first, ignoring provenance for a moment, consider refresh for a single transformation T. Suppose input I has been modified to I^{new}, and we would like to refresh an output element o that was produced by $T(I)$. The refreshed value of o should be the element o' in $T(I^{new})$ that "corresponds" to o, if one exists. (In this paper we assume refresh of a single output element produces either a single refreshed element or no element at all, but not several elements. We intend to relax this assumption in future work.) Note that for refresh to even be well-defined, we need to formalize when an element o' in $T(I^{new})$ corresponds to the element o being refreshed.

One way to make refresh well-defined is to declare one or more output attributes as an immutable key. Then, given an output element o in $T(I)$, the refreshed value of o is the element o' in $T(I^{new})$ with the same key, if one exists.

EXAMPLE 3.1. Consider output directory RawDNAData in Figure 2. Intuitively, the file name is an immutable key. To refresh a file in RawDNAData, we could rerun transformation **DNADL** on list DNAURLs, then look for the output file whose file name matches the file we wish to refresh. □

While immutable keys make for a convenient definition, unfortunately performing refresh based on immutable keys typically requires full recomputation of the output data set in order to find the refreshed element. Our goal is to avoid unnecessary computation while performing selective refresh.

Consider as an alternative the following refresh procedure based on provenance. For the remainder of the paper we assume each transformation T has a (possibly infinite) *input domain* $\mathbb{I}_T$, specifying T's allowable input sets.

PROCEDURE 3.1 (PROVENANCE-BASED REFRESH). Consider transformation instance $T(I) = O$, and suppose input data set $I \in \mathbb{I}_T$ has been modified to $I^{new} \in \mathbb{I}_T$. To refresh an output element $\langle o, p\rangle \in O$ there are two steps:

1. *Backward-tracing:* Run tracing query σ_p on I^{new} to find the subset of I^{new} associated with provenance predicate p.
2. *Forward-propagation:* Apply T on $\sigma_p(I^{new})$ to compute the new value $\langle o', p'\rangle$. If the result is empty, o has no refreshed value. □

EXAMPLE 3.2. Suppose we wish to refresh RawDNAData element *2-aga.xml*. Instead of rerunning transformation **DNADL** on the entire input data set as suggested in Example 3.1, Procedure 3.1 first finds the provenance of the element being refreshed: Provenance predicate p (url contains '2/aga') is applied to the input set DNAURLs to obtain DNAURLs element #2. Next transformation **DNADL** is applied to the selected element only, which yields the refreshed RawDNAData element. □

Example 3.2 is more efficient than Example 3.1, but does Procedure 3.1 always work? We identify two requirements on transformations and provenance under which it does.

The first restriction requires that each provenance predicate indeed captures the relevant input data subset for its output element.

REQUIREMENT 3.1 (PROVENANCE CORRECTNESS). Consider any transformation instance $T(I) = O$ for $I \in \mathbb{I}_T$, and any $\langle o, p\rangle \in O$. Then $T(\sigma_p(I)) = \{\langle o, p\rangle\}$. □

For *many-one* (and therefore *one-one*) transformations and their provenance, this requirement is natural. We will adapt the requirement to also capture *many-many* transformations, but for presentation purposes we defer this topic to Section 5.

All of the transformations in our running example satisfy Requirement 3.1, with two exceptions: **PExtract** is a many-many transformation that requires the additional machinery introduced in Section 5, and **Join** is a multi-input transformation requiring some (minimal) additional machinery covered in Section 6.

The second requirement is more subtle, and more central to our approach:

REQUIREMENT 3.2 (PROVENANCE AS KEY). Consider any transformation instance $T(I) = O$ for $I \in \mathbb{I}_T$, and any $\langle o, p\rangle \in O$. Then for any $I' \in \mathbb{I}_T$, if $T(\sigma_p(I')) \neq \emptyset$, then $T(\sigma_p(I')) = \{\langle o', p\rangle\}$ for some o', and $\langle o', p\rangle \in T(I')$. □

This requirement intuitively states that when input changes, even if there is a new value for an old output element based on its provenance, the provenance predicate remains unchanged. Not only does this condition enable efficient refresh, it also identifies what it means for an output element based on new input to be the refreshed version of an old output element:

> *Effectively, we are treating provenance as the immutable key that coordinates new and old values of output elements.*

In our running example, and in other workflows we have looked at [9, 10], it is natural for transformations to output provenance predicates such that Requirement 3.2 is satisfied, and for provenance to act as an immutable key.

The following property, which follows directly from Requirement 3.1, further solidifies the key analogy by observing that provenance predicates are unique (under set semantics) within each output data set:

PROPERTY 3.1 (UNIQUE PROVENANCE). Consider any transformation instance $T(I) = O$ for $I \in \mathbb{I}_T$, and any $\langle o, p\rangle \in O$. There is no $\langle o', p\rangle \in T(I)$ with $o' \neq o$. □

Now let us return to our refresh procedure and see how Requirements 3.1 and 3.2 guarantee that Procedure 3.1 works correctly, under the provenance-as-key approach. Recall, to refresh an output element $\langle o, p\rangle \in T(I)$ after input I has been modified to I^{new}, Procedure 3.1 computes $T(\sigma_p(I^{new}))$.

- First suppose $T(\sigma_p(I^{new}))$ produces an empty result. Then there should be no $\langle o', p\rangle$ in $T(I^{new})$, i.e., no new output with provenance predicate p, thus corresponding to o. If there were such an $\langle o', p\rangle$, then by Requirement 3.1, $T(\sigma_p(I^{new})) = \{\langle o', p\rangle\}$, contradicting the fact that $T(\sigma_p(I^{new}))$ is empty.
- Now suppose $T(\sigma_p(I^{new}))$ is non-empty. Requirement 3.2 guarantees that $T(\sigma_p(I^{new})) = \{\langle o', p\rangle\}$ for some o', and that $\langle o', p\rangle$ is a valid output element in $T(I^{new})$. Thus, o' is the refreshed value for o.

4. REFRESH FOR WORKFLOWS

Consider any transformations T_1 and T_2. As usual, each transformation takes a data set from its domain as input, and it produces as output a data set annotated with provenance predicates. The *composition* $T_1 \circ T_2$ of the two transformations first applies T_1 to an input data set $I_1 \in \mathbb{I}_{T_1}$ to obtain *intermediate* data set I_2. It then applies T_2 to the data portion (omitting provenance predicates) of I_2 to obtain output data set O. We assume transformations T_1 and T_2 are only composed when the data elements output by T_1 are guaranteed to satisfy the input domain of T_2.

Composition is associative, so we denote the linear composition of n transformations as $T_1 \circ T_2 \circ \cdots \circ T_n$. We refer to such a composition as a *data-oriented workflow*, or *workflow* for short. In Section 6, we extend our formalism and algorithms to cover workflows where transformations may have multiple input data sets. (As mentioned in Section 2, transformations with multiple output sets do not introduce any complexities, and therefore are omitted from this paper.) Our running example in Figure 1 is a workflow composed of six transformations, with one of them taking multiple inputs.

Consider a workflow $T_1 \circ T_2 \circ \ldots \circ T_n$. A *workflow instance* is the application of the workflow to an input $I_1 \in \mathbb{I}_{T_1}$. Let $I_{i+1} = T_i(I_i)$ for $i = 1..n$. We assume $I_{i+1} \in \mathbb{I}_{T_{i+1}}$ for $i = 1..n-1$. The final output data set is I_{n+1}. We denote this workflow instance as $(T_1 \circ T_2 \circ \ldots \circ T_n)(I_1) = I_{n+1}$.

Our goal is to selectively refresh an output element of an arbitrary workflow instance, when input data sets may have been modified. The following workflow refresh algorithm is a recursive extension of the single-transformation refresh Procedure 3.1.

ALGORITHM 4.1 (WORKFLOW REFRESH). Consider a workflow instance $(T_1 \circ T_2 \circ \ldots \circ T_n)(I_1) = I_{n+1}$. Suppose I_1 has been modified to $I_1^{new} \in \mathbb{I}_{T_1}$. Algorithm *workflow_refresh* recursively refreshes output element $\langle o, p\rangle \in I_{i+1}$:

---

workflow_refresh($\langle o, p\rangle \in I_{i+1}$) :
  if $i = 1$ **then return** $T_1(\sigma_p(I_1^{new}))$
  else { $S = \sigma_p(I_i)$;
    $S' = \bigcup_{\langle o', p'\rangle \in S}$ *workflow_refresh*($\langle o', p'\rangle \in I_i$);
    return $T_i(S')$ }

EXAMPLE 4.1. We revisit the original example from Section 1.2, now using *workflow_refresh* to refresh (Denise,heart,0.8) (element #2) in HighPatientRisks. The **else** branch of the algorithm traces backward one step by applying provenance predicate p (name='Denise' $\wedge$ disease='heart') to table PatientRisks, yielding element #3. This element is then refreshed recursively: The algorithm traces backward another step by applying provenance predicates to PatientDNA and DNARisks (requiring our extension for multi-input transformations; see Section 6), yielding elements #4 and #2 respectively. The recursive refresh continues until the initial transformations **PatientDL** and **DNADL** are reached, for which the **if** branch selects elements #3 and #2 from input sets PatientURLs and DNAURLs respectively.

As the recursion unwinds, the algorithm forward-propagates each refreshed element. Transformations **PatientDL** and **DNADL** are run on PatientURLs element #3 and DNAURLs element #2, yielding refreshed values for elements *Denise.xml* in RawPatientData and *2-aga.xml* in RawDNAData. **PExtract** and **RiskExtract** are then run on these refreshed elements. Suppose, as in Section 1.2, the refreshed value for DNARisks element #2 now has risk=0.6. After the unwinding recursion runs **Join** and **Filter** on refreshed elements, we finally get the refreshed value of HighPatientRisks element #2, with Denise's heart disease risk set to 0.6. □

In Section 3 we identified properties of transformations and provenance required for the single-transformation refresh procedure to work correctly. Are the same properties sufficient for the recursive algorithm to work correctly? It turns out we need to restrict the composition of transformations and their provenance to ensure correctness; we call this requirement *workflow safety*.

We first provide intuition for workflow safety, then formalize it. Consider $T_1 \circ T_2$ applied to input $I_1 \in \mathbb{I}_{T_1}$. Let $I_2 = T_1(I_1)$ and $O = T_2(I_2)$. Suppose I_1 has been modified to $I_1^{new} \in \mathbb{I}_{T_1}$. Let $I_2^{new} = T_1(I_1^{new})$, i.e., I_2^{new} is what would be produced by running transformation T_1 on the entire new input set. Consider any element $\langle o, p\rangle$ in the original output set O. Safety requires that the set of elements in o's "new provenance," $\sigma_p(I_2^{new})$, is equal to the set obtained by refreshing each element in o's "old provenance," $\sigma_p(I_2)$.

REQUIREMENT 4.1 (WORKFLOW SAFETY). Consider any workflow instance $(T_1 \circ T_2 \circ \ldots \circ T_n)(I_1) = I_{n+1}$. Every T_i must be *safe with respect to* T_{i-1}, $i = 2..n$, defined as follows. Consider any $I'_{i-1} \in \mathbb{I}_{T_{i-1}}$. Let $I'_i = T_{i-1}(I'_{i-1})$. For any $\langle o, p\rangle \in T_i(I_i)$, we must have $\bigcup_{\langle o', p'\rangle \in \sigma_p(I_i)} T_{i-1}(\sigma_{p'}(I'_{i-1})) = \sigma_p(I'_i)$. □

With extensions to the safety definition to be introduced in Sections 5 and 6 for many-many and multi-input transformations, the workflow in our running example satisfies Requirement 4.1. However, there are some reasonable workflows where safety is not satisfied, as illustrated by the following example.

EXAMPLE 4.2. Consider a workflow $T_1 \circ T_2$ that takes an input set I_1 with attributes salesperson, city, and sales_in_Euros. T_1 converts sales_in_Euros to sales_in_Dollars, with output provenance predicates selecting on salesperson. T_2 then sums sales_in_Dollars grouped by city, with output provenance predicates selecting on city.

Suppose the original input I_1 has two salespeople from Paris, Amelie and Jacques, selling 10 Euros each. The output I_2 of transformation T_1 contains (Amelie,Paris,13) and (Jacques,Paris,13) (at generous 2010 exchange rates), and the final output is (Paris,26). Now suppose I_1 is modified to I_1^{new}, with an additional salesperson (Marie,Paris,20). Safety requires equality of the following two procedures:

1. Compute the provenance of (Paris,26) in intermediate data set I_2, then refresh the resulting values. Predicate city='Paris' applied to I_2 yields (Amelie,Paris,13) and (Jacques,Paris,13); refreshing does not change their values.
2. Update the intermediate data set to $I_2^{new} = T_1(I^{new})$, then compute the provenance of (Paris,26) in I_2^{new}. I_2^{new} contains Marie as well as Amelie and Jacques, so applying predicate city='Paris' gives us a different result from case 1. □

Intuitively, a workflow is unsafe if, in some intermediate data set I, full forward-propagation of modified input would cause "insertions" into a subset of I that comprises the provenance of a data element in the next data set. These insertions will be missed when we perform backward-tracing, since we only refresh existing elements in intermediate data sets.

Provenance predicates for relational transformations typically yield safe workflows, but aggregation is an example of a transformation that can cause a workflow to be unsafe, if it is not the first transformation in a workflow, or if groups can grow as a result of input modifications. In Section 7 we discuss one way of handling unsafe workflows that allows us to retain some of the advantages of selective refresh without compromising correctness.

We now show that *workflow_refresh* correctly refreshes output elements, when Requirements 3.1, 3.2, and 4.1 all hold. The argument hinges on the following theorem.

THEOREM 4.1 (RECURSIVE REFRESH THEOREM). Consider a workflow instance $(T_1 \circ T_2 \circ \ldots \circ T_n)(I_1) = I_{n+1}$ satisfying Requirement 4.1. Given any element $\langle o, p \rangle \in I_{i+1}$ for $i \geq 1$, *workflow_refresh*$(\langle o, p \rangle) = T_i(\sigma_p(I_i^{new}))$.

Proof. We prove the theorem by induction on i. For the base case of $i = 1$, consider any $\langle o, p \rangle \in I_2 = T_1(I_1)$. By the first line (**if** case) of Algorithm 4.1, *workflow_refresh*$(\langle o, p \rangle \in I_2) = T_1(\sigma_p(I_1^{new}))$.

Now suppose the theorem holds for $i = k-1$, $k > 1$; we show it holds for $i = k$. Consider element $\langle o, p \rangle \in I_{k+1}$. *workflow_refresh* computes the following two sets: $S = \sigma_p(I_k) = \{\langle o_1, p_1 \rangle \ldots \langle o_m, p_m \rangle\}$ and $S' = \bigcup_{\langle o_i, p_i \rangle \in S}$ *workflow_refresh*$(\langle o_i, p_i \rangle)$. By the inductive hypothesis, each *workflow_refresh*$(\langle o_i, p_i \rangle) = T_{k-1}(\sigma_{p_i}(I_{k-1}^{new}))$. Thus, $S' = \bigcup_{\langle o_i, p_i \rangle \in \sigma_p(I_k)} T_{k-1}(\sigma_{p_i}(I_{k-1}^{new}))$. By Requirement 4.1, the right-hand side of the last expression is equal to $\sigma_p(I_k^{new})$. Since the last line of *workflow_refresh* returns $T_k(S')$, *workflow_refresh* returns $T_k(\sigma_p(I_k^{new}))$, which completes the proof. □

To understand what the theorem is saying, consider a workflow instance $(T_1 \circ T_2 \circ \ldots \circ T_n)(I_1) = I_{n+1}$ and a final output element $\langle o, p \rangle \in I_{n+1}$. Suppose I_1 is updated to I_1^{new}. Theorem 4.1 says that running *workflow_refresh* on $\langle o, p \rangle$ is equivalent to computing I_n^{new} by pushing input I_1^{new} through every transformation except the last one, then running T_n on o's "new provenance," $\sigma_p(I_n^{new})$.

With this theorem, we see that the same arguments given in Section 3 for the correctness of single-transformation refresh carry over to the general workflow case: Running *workflow_refresh* logically reduces to running single-transformation refresh of T_n on the new input set I_n^{new}. Since T_n satisfies Requirements 3.1 and 3.2, the arguments in Section 3 show that *workflow_refresh* returns the correct refresh of an element: If it returns empty, there is no element in the new output set with provenance predicate p. If it returns an element $\langle o', p' \rangle$, then $p' = p$ and $\langle o', p \rangle$ is the unique element in I_{n+1}^{new} with predicate p.

5. MANY-MANY TRANSFORMATIONS

So far we have required $T(\sigma_p(I)) = \{\langle o, p \rangle\}$ for any $\langle o, p \rangle \in O$ in any transformation instance $T(I) = O$ (Requirement 3.1). This requirement effectively limits us to transformations that are many-one or one-one. We now weaken this requirement, only insisting $\langle o, p \rangle \in T(\sigma_p(I))$. Let us see how weakening the requirement captures more transformations (specifically allowing one-many and many-many transformations) but complicates the picture.

EXAMPLE 5.1. In our running example, **PExtract** is a one-many transformation. Consider refreshing (Earl,3,gcc) (element #6) in PatientDNA through transformation **PExtract**. Using Refresh Procedure 3.1 for single transformations, provenance predicate file='Earl.xml' is applied to RawPatientData, producing input element *Earl.xml*. Suppose when transformation **PExtract** is then run on *Earl.xml*, two elements are produced, (Earl,2,aaa) and (Earl,3,ttt) (indicating corrected DNA sequences at locations 2 and 3), both with provenance predicate file='Earl.xml'. How do we know which of these elements, if any, corresponds to the one we are trying to refresh? □

To solve the problem illustrated in this example, we require that for many-many (and therefore one-many) transformations, output elements include not only provenance predicates, but also *forward filters*. The forward filter for an output element o is applied after forward-propagating o's provenance, to select from multiple output elements the one corresponding to o. In Example 5.1, a suitable forward filter for output element #6 is loc=3, capturing the fact that element #6 describes Earl's DNA sequence at location 3. Note that all of the forward filters for table PatientDNA (denoted f in Figure 2) select on attribute loc, since locations are unique within each set of elements for a given name.

It is not hard to generalize our entire framework to support many-many transformations using forward filters. We require each transformation instance to produce triples instead of pairs: $T(I) = O = \{\langle o_1, p_1, f_1 \rangle, \ldots, \langle o_n, p_n, f_n \rangle\}$. (By implicitly assuming all f_i=True for many-one transformations, our extension is fully "backward compatible" with everything in the paper thus far.) To refresh an element $\langle o, p, f \rangle \in O$, we add a third step to Procedure 3.1 that applies forward filter σ_f to the result from Step 2, i.e., the overall refresh operation is $\sigma_f(T(\sigma_p(I^{new})))$.

All of the formalism and intuitive arguments in Sections 3 and 4 extend quite easily to incorporate forward filters, generally replacing $\langle o, p \rangle$ with $\langle o, p, f \rangle$ and $T(\sigma_p(I))$ with $\sigma_f(T(\sigma_p(I)))$. Note that in Requirement 3.2 (*Provenance as Key*), by extending each output pair to include a forward filter f, we are effectively treating provenance predicates and forward filters together as immutable keys, i.e., only the p-f pairs need be unique, not provenance predicates alone. Full details of the extension for many-many transformations are given in an online technical report [16].

6. MULTI-INPUT TRANSFORMATIONS

For presentation purposes, so far we have assumed each transformation has one input data set. The extension for transformations with multiple input sets is straightforward and intuitive: Each output element carries a separate provenance predicate for each of its transformation's input sets. Now a transformation instance is $T(I_1, I_2, \ldots, I_m) = O$, and O consists of extended triples: $\{\langle o_1, (p_1^1, \ldots, p_1^m), f_1\rangle, \ldots, \langle o_n, (p_n^1, \ldots, p_n^m), f_n\rangle\}$. (We obtain full "backward compatibility" with everything in the paper thus far by setting $m = 1$.) Refresh proceeds in a similar manner as before, except during backward-tracing m provenance predicates are evaluated on their corresponding input data sets, and during forward-propagation the transformation is run on the m input subsets.

EXAMPLE 6.1. From our running example, to refresh (Carl,liver,0.4) (element #2) in PatientRisks, provenance predicate p^{PD} (name='Carl' $\wedge$ loc=2 $\wedge$ seq='ttt') is applied on PatientDNA to obtain element #2, and provenance predicate p^{DR} (loc=2 $\wedge$ seq='ttt') is applied on DNARisks to obtain element #3. These elements are forward-propagated as the two inputs to transformation **Join**, yielding the refreshed value of PatientRisks element #2. □

We can easily adapt all of the formalism from Sections 3–5 to handle multi-input transformations. In general we replace p with $p_1, \ldots, p_m$, and $T(\sigma_p(I))$ with $T(\sigma_{p_1}(I_1), \ldots, \sigma_{p_m}(I_m))$. In Requirement 3.2 (*Provenance as Key*), we now treat the entire combination of $p_1, \ldots, p_m, f$ as the immutable key. In Requirement 4.1 (*Workflow Safety*), we require each transformation to be safe with respect to all of its predecessor transformations in concert. Full details are given in an online technical report [16].

7. UNSAFE WORKFLOWS

In Section 4 we introduced *safe workflows* (Requirement 4.1), and our refresh algorithms thus far require workflow safety. For now, we suggest one simple mechanism that allows refresh in unsafe workflows to still make some use of our algorithms.

Consider a workflow instance $(T_1 \circ T_2 \circ \ldots \circ T_n)(I_1) = I_{n+1}$. (Our argument generalizes easily to workflows with multi-input transformations.) Suppose the workflow is unsafe at T_k for some k, $1 < k \leq n$, but the rest of the workflow is safe. (More generally, consider the largest k such that the workflow is unsafe at T_k.) Suppose I_1 has been modified to I_1^{new}. To support correct refresh of output elements in I_{n+1}, we can first bring intermediate data set I_k up-to-date by sending the entire modified input I_1^{new} through all transformations up to T_{k-1}, producing I_k^{new}. Then we can treat I_k^{new} as if it were the first input data set (and T_k the first transformation), performing refresh as normal: backward-trace from I_{n+1} to I_k, then forward-propagate through to I_{n+1}.

In this setting, we would certainly want to keep track of when I_k^{new} is up-to-date, perhaps even propagating input modifications through the first $k-1$ transformations eagerly. Combining eager propagation with on-demand refresh is an interesting direction of future work.

8. SYSTEM PROTOTYPE

We have built a prototype system that implements all features and algorithms presented in this paper. This system, built initially

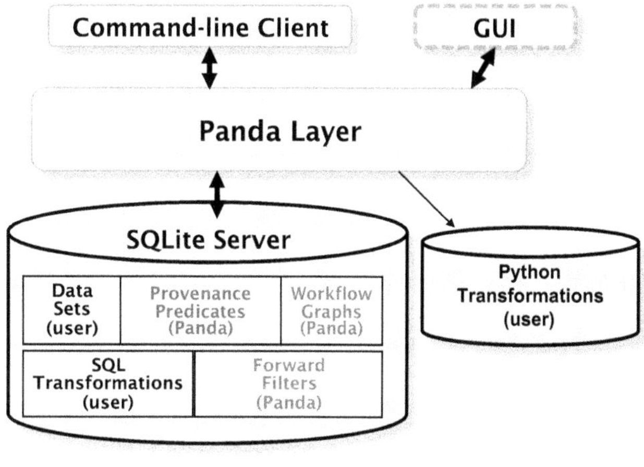

Figure 3: Architecture of the prototype Panda system.

to support refresh, has been evolving into a more ambitious system we call *Panda* (for *Provenance and Data*), supporting several other aspects of provenance and data in addition to refresh [17]. In this paper we focus our system description on features relevant to refresh. For the time being, all data sets handled by Panda are encoded in relational tables, but as we have seen, our formal underpinnings and algorithms do not rely on the relational model.

The high-level architecture of the Panda system is shown in Figure 3. The main backend is a **SQLite** server, storing all data sets, relational (SQL) transformations, provenance, and workflow information. The Panda system supports "opaque" transformations programmed in Python; they are stored separately in files.

Users interact with Panda through a simple command-line interface; we intend to build a GUI in the near future. There are three types of user commands: (1) Creating or modifying input data sets; (2) Creating transformations that generate newly-defined data sets from existing ones, to build up workflows; (3) Refresh commands. The *Panda Layer* processes all user commands: It stores workflow graphs and their transformations, creates and maintains auxiliary provenance tables, generates provenance predicates and forward filters for output elements, and runs the refresh algorithms.

In the remainder of this section we briefly discuss how Panda handles transformations specified in Python, transformations specified as SQL queries, and finally Refresh commands.

8.1 Python Transformations

The Panda system currently supports Python transformations that output provenance predicates with each output element. As an example, consider adding transformation **PatientDL** as we build up our running example workflow (Figure 1). The user writes a Python script **patientdl.py** that takes as its argument a list of URLs, and returns the set of XML documents located at the URLs, with corresponding provenance predicates. The user then appends transformation **PatientDL** to the workflow with the following command:

```
Create Dataset RawPatientData
As Python 'patientdl.py' on PatientURLs
```

In response to this command, the Panda Layer: (1) Creates the new data set RawPatientData; (2) Inserts a record into the Workflow table connecting PatientURLs to RawPatientData via Python script **patientdl.py**; (3) Creates a provenance-predicate table RawPatientData_PP for RawPatientData; (4) Runs **patientdl.py** on PatientURLs, inserting the resulting elements and corresponding provenance-predicate records into tables RawPatientData and RawPatientData_PP, respectively.

For many-many transformations, the Python script also needs to create a forward filter for each output element. Then, step (3) above also creates a forward-filter table, and step (4) also inserts a record for the forward filter.

8.2 SQL Transformations

The Panda system also supports transformations specified as SQL queries, including queries/transformations involving multiple input tables. Provenance predicates are created automatically for SQL transformations, following known definitions and techniques [5, 7, 10]: Single-table **Select** statements are one-one, so their output provenance predicates can select on declared keys from the input data set. Multi-table **Select** statements generate provenance predicates for each input table separately as described in Section 6, again relying on declared keys. Finally, **Group-by** queries generate provenance predicates based on the grouping attribute(s).

The command to create a new SQL transformation is similar to the command shown in Section 8.1, except **As** is followed by a SQL query, whose **From** clause must refer to already-defined tables. The steps performed by the Panda Layer are also similar to those outlined in Section 8.1; forward filters are never needed since SQL queries cannot produce many-many transformations.

8.3 Refresh

When workflows are created and run, Panda stores everything needed to support selective refresh: provenance predicates and intermediate data sets for backward-tracing; transformations and forward filters for forward-propagation. The Panda system assumes that all transformations, provenance, and workflows satisfy the requirements specified in this paper. Automatically detecting when the requirements are satisfied—particularly the most interesting requirement of workflow safety—is an important area of future work.

Under the assumption of all requirements being satisfied, Panda supports selective refresh using the exact algorithms given in this paper. When an output element o is refreshed, if a new value o' is produced then Panda automatically replaces o with o'. If the refresh results in an empty set, then o is deleted. However, we leave a visible "tombstone" for o with its associated provenance predicate (and forward filter if present). Then, if desired we can refresh the tombstone at a later time and possibly discover that further input modifications have created a new value for o.

9. EXPERIMENTS

The primary goal of our empirical study was to determine, for varying workflow characteristics, when it is advantageous to perform selective refresh as opposed to rerunning the entire workflow. Specifically, how many refreshes can we perform before their aggregate running time—including the extra time spent to capture provenance—exceeds that of complete recomputation?

While eventually we plan to experiment with a suite of workflows, for this preliminary empirical study we used our running example workflow described in Section 1.2, with fabricated data. Transformations **Join** and **Filter** use SQL, while transformations **PatientDL**, **DNADL**, **PExtract**, and **RiskExtract** were coded in Python. We indexed the intermediate data sets so that our provenance predicates could be evaluated efficiently. All of our experiments were run using the Panda system (Section 8) on a MacBook Pro laptop (2.4 GHz Intel Core 2 Duo, 4 GB memory, 150 GB storage, Mac OS X 10.4). To study how different workflow characteristics impact the overhead of provenance capture and the performance of refresh, we ran experiments for varying data sizes and varying transformation costs.

Our performance results are summarized as follows:

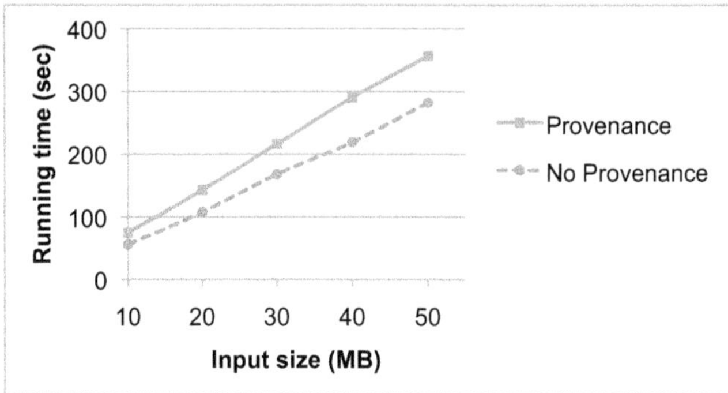

Figure 4: Time overhead of provenance capture, vary input size.

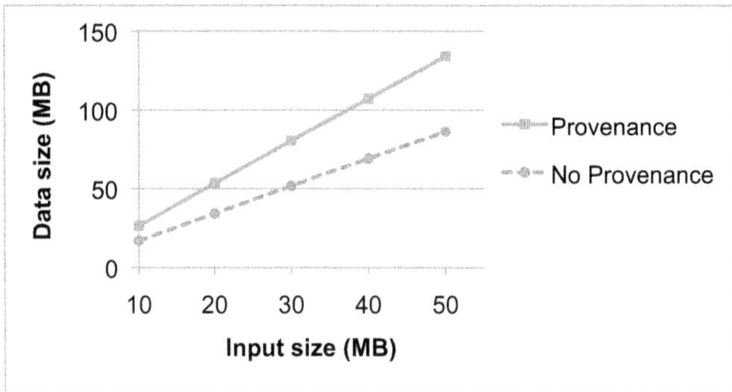

Figure 5: Space overhead of provenance capture, vary input size.

- The time and space overhead of provenance capture is proportional to the time and space required by workflow execution, which in turn is proportional to the amount of input data. We observed roughly 30% time overhead and 56% space overhead for various input sizes to capture provenance while executing the workflow.
- Not surprisingly, the relative time overhead of provenance capture and provenance tracing decreases as individual transformations get more expensive. Thus, selective refresh is most advantageous for workflows with relatively expensive transformations.
- In our experiments, we were able to refresh between 52% and 70% of the data elements in the output data set before the running time (including provenance capture) exceeded that of complete recomputation. The crossover point was independent of input data size, but became more favorable for selective refresh as transformations got more expensive.

9.1 Overhead of Provenance Capture

Figure 4 shows the time overhead of provenance capture for varying input data sizes. Comparing the running times of workflow computation with and without provenance, we see that the time overhead is roughly proportional to the amount of input data, ranging from 27% to 34%

Figure 5 shows the space overhead of provenance capture for varying input data sizes. We totaled all data involved in the workflow, including intermediate data, with and without provenance. Storing provenance, which includes provenance predicates and forward filters, incurred a 56% overhead across all input data sizes. Note the space overhead would be considerably lower for "wider" data elements; our fabricated data elements are relatively small.

Next we measured the impact of transformation cost on time overhead of provenance capture. We modified the two transformations that download data from the web, **PatientDL** and **DNADL**, to

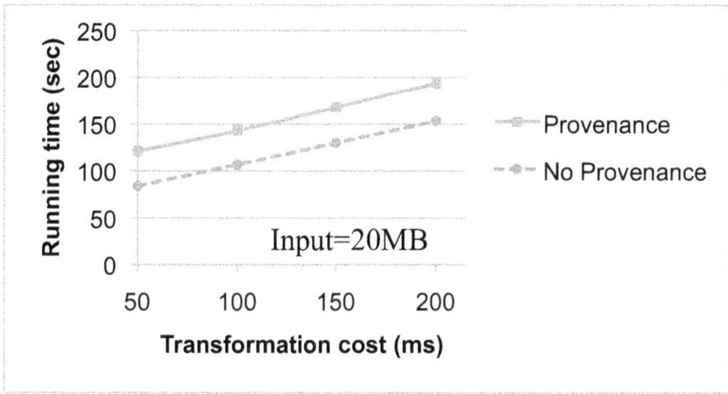

Figure 6: Time overhead of provenance capture, vary transformation cost.

perform local downloads instead, and we instrumented them with a configurable delay. Figure 6 shows the time overhead of provenance capture, varying the costs of (i.e., the delays in) transformations **PatientDL** and **DNADL**. We can see that the larger the transformation costs, the lower the relative time overhead of provenance capture; e.g., time overhead is 42% at 50ms vs. 26% at 200ms. Intuitively, when transformations are more expensive, provenance capture plays a smaller role.

9.2 Crossover Point for Refresh

Our next experiments identify the crossover point between selective refreshes (including provenance capture) and full recomputation (without provenance capture). For starters, the two lines in Figure 7 plot the running times of:

1. **Recompute:** Time required to fully (re)compute the workflow.
2. **Refresh:** Total time to selectively refresh a varying fraction of the output data elements. To make a fair comparison, we added the time overhead of provenance capture to the total time.

In this experiment we used an input size of 20 MB and the original transformation costs for **PatientDL** and **DNADL**. From Figure 7 we see that we can capture provenance and then refresh over 60% of the data elements in the output data set before the total running time exceeds that of recomputation. Obviously, selective refresh is most advantageous when only a small subset of the output elements are refreshed, however in our experiment a significant fraction of output elements needed to be refreshed before we observed no advantage at all.

Figure 8 shows the crossover point (in terms of percentage of refreshed elements) between selective refresh and full workflow recomputation when we vary the input size. This line is approximately constant, indicating that the relationship between selective refresh and workflow recomputation is independent of input data size. Figure 9 shows the impact of transformation costs on the crossover point. The input data size is 20 MB, and the transformation costs are varied as described above for Figure 6. Here the crossover point becomes more favorable for selective refresh as transformations get more expensive: we can refresh 52% at 50ms versus 70% at 200ms before refresh time exceeds recomputation. Like with provenance capture, as transformations get more expensive, we are not surprised to see a decrease in the relative cost of provenance tracing.

9.3 Unsafe Workflows

All of the reported experiments were conducted using our running example, which is a *safe* workflow. Although we have not yet run experiments on unsafe workflows, until we develop more sophisticated techniques for handling them, we don't expect any

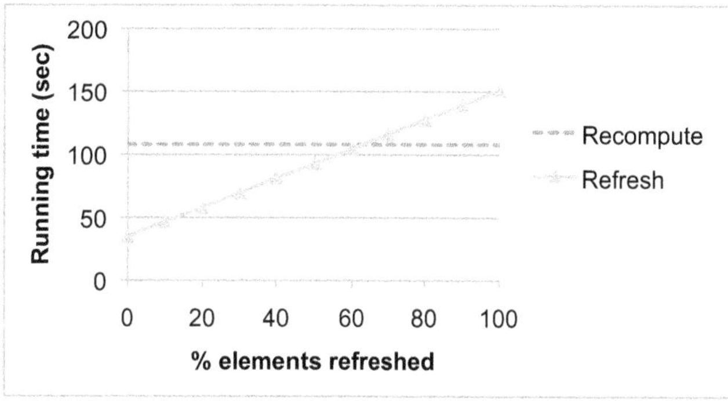

Figure 7: Recomputation and refresh costs.

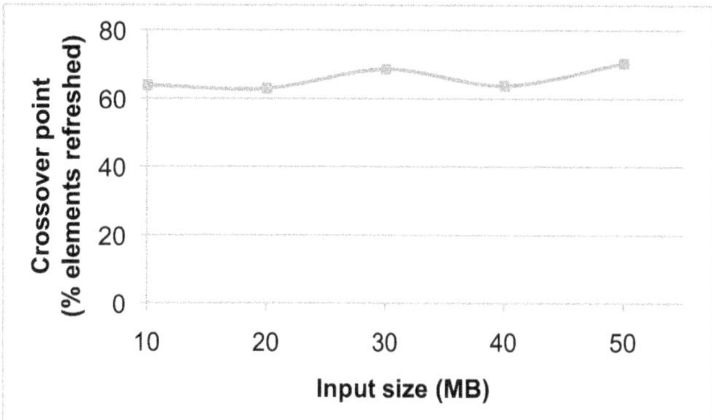

Figure 8: Crossover point between selective refresh and workflow recomputation, vary input size.

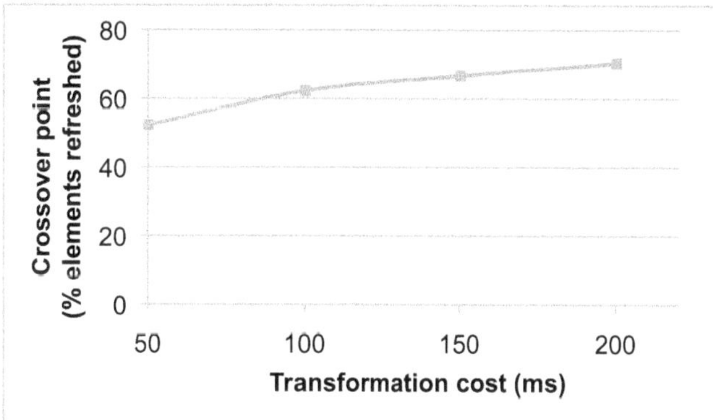

Figure 9: Crossover point between selective refresh and workflow recomputation, vary transformation cost.

significant surprises or insights. Recall from Section 7 that currently we propose handling unsafe workflows with a simple hybrid approach: perform workflow computation for the unsafe portion of the workflow, and selective refresh for the rest. Since this solution combines the two computations we've measured, we would expect a hybrid result: the crossover point for unsafe workflows will be less favorable towards selective refresh, with the amount of crossover "shift" determined by the percentage of the workflow that is unsafe.

10. CONCLUSIONS AND FUTURE WORK

We presented a formal foundation and algorithms for efficient selective refresh of output elements in data-oriented workflows. We identified properties of transformations, provenance, and workflows that are required for the algorithms to perform refresh correctly, and we discussed how the algorithms can be adapted to handle unsafe workflows. We described the prototype system we have built that supports the features and algorithms presented in the paper, and we reported some experimental results. There are several directions for future work:

- **Verifying requirements:** Currently we rely on workflow creators to ensure that their transformations and workflows satisfy the properties required for correct refresh. We would like to develop static and/or dynamic tests to check the requirements for a given workflow. We also intend to explore more precisely the general classes of transformations, provenance, and workflows that are guaranteed to satisfy the requirements.
- **Relaxing requirements:** We would like to offer solutions when some of the requirements and assumptions made in this paper are not satisfied. For example, the rudimentary solution offered in Section 7 for unsafe workflows can probably be improved upon, and we don't yet have a formalism and algorithms that capture the case when refreshing a single value logically results in multiple values.
- **Automatic generation of provenance predicates:** As discussed in Section 2.2, there has been a large body of work on generating provenance predicates automatically for relational transformations [5, 7, 10]. However, automatic or semi-automatic generation of provenance predicates for general transformations is an interesting, largely open problem.
- **Integrating refresh with eager propagation:** In its current form, the workflow refresh algorithm may unnecessarily repeat work that may be shared between individual refreshes invoked during the recursion. We hope to come up with an algorithm that can take advantage of all information obtained about new values during a refresh operation. More generally, we plan to expand our prototype into a system that can perform a combination of eager and lazy refresh in response to user needs.
- **Stability guarantees:** Currently we assume that input data may change at any time, so selective refresh must always perform full backward-tracing. Furthermore, we always perform forward-propagation, under the assumption the data has changed. If the system monitors changes and can make guarantees about data stability—both input data and, when possible, intermediate data—we can use this information to avoid unnecessary work.
- **Special settings:** In this paper we have considered a very general environment where provenance is tracked at the level of individual data elements and individual transformations. Our goal was to lay the foundations for selective refresh for a wide class of data-oriented workflows. In some settings, the refresh problem might be simplified and/or made more efficient when special properties hold. For example, often schema-level provenance relationships are known for transformations [9]. Currently, we require schema-level provenance to be encoded as provenance predicates on each data element. This approach works, but it is unnecessarily cumbersome when all predicates take the same form. Also, with additional information, sometimes it is possible to "fold together" provenance for multiple transformations [9], eliminating the need for intermediate results and making refresh more efficient.

11. REFERENCES

[1] The Open Provenance Model — Core Specification (v1.1). Dec. 2009. http://eprints.ecs.soton.ac.uk/18332/.

[2] O. Benjelloun, A. Das Sarma, A. Halevy, and J. Widom. ULDBs: Databases with uncertainty and lineage. In *VLDB*, 2006.

[3] J. A. Blakeley, P.-A. Larson, and F. W. Tompa. Efficiently updating materialized views. In *SIGMOD*, 1986.

[4] R. Bose and J. Frew. Lineage retrieval for scientific data processing: a survey. *ACM Comput. Surv.*, 37(1), 2005.

[5] P. Buneman, S. Khanna, and W.-C. Tan. Why and where: A characterization of data provenance. In *ICDT*, 2001.

[6] C.-H. Chang, M. Kayed, M. R. Girgis, and K. F. Shaalan. A survey of web information extraction systems. *IEEE Trans. on Knowl. and Data Eng.*, 18(10), 2006.

[7] J. Cheney, L. Chiticariu, and W.-C. Tan. Provenance in databases: Why, how, and where. *Foundations and Trends in Databases*, 1(4), 2009.

[8] L. Chiticariu and W.-C. Tan. Debugging schema mappings with routes. In *VLDB*, 2006.

[9] Y. Cui and J. Widom. Lineage tracing for general data warehouse transformations. *The VLDB Journal*, 12(1), 2003.

[10] Y. Cui, J. Widom, and J. L. Wiener. Tracing the lineage of view data in a warehousing environment. *ACM TODS*, 25(2), 2000.

[11] S. B. Davidson and J. Freire. Provenance and scientific workflows: challenges and opportunities. In *SIGMOD*, 2008.

[12] T. J. Green, G. Karvounarakis, Z. G. Ives, and V. Tannen. Update exchange with mappings and provenance. In *VLDB*, 2007.

[13] T. J. Green, G. Karvounarakis, and V. Tannen. Provenance semirings. In *PODS*, 2007.

[14] A. Gupta and I. S. Mumick. Maintenance of materialized views: Problems, techniques, and applications. *IEEE Data Engineering Bulletin*, 18(2), 1995.

[15] M. Herschel and M. A. Hernández. Explaining missing answers to SPJUA queries. *VLDB*, 2010.

[16] R. Ikeda, S. Salihoglu, and J. Widom. Provenance-based refresh in data-oriented workflows. Technical report, Stanford University, available at http://ilpubs.stanford.edu:8090/962/.

[17] R. Ikeda and J. Widom. Panda: A system for provenance and data. *IEEE Data Engineering Bulletin*, September 2010.

[18] Y. L. Simmhan, B. Plale, and D. Gannon. A survey of data provenance in e-science. *SIGMOD Rec.*, 34(3), 2005.

[19] P. Vassiliadis, A. Simitsis, and S. Skiadopoulos. Conceptual modeling for ETL processes. In *DOLAP*, 2002.

[20] Y. Velegrakis, R. J. Miller, and J. Mylopoulos. Representing and querying data transformations. In *ICDE*, 2005.

Ranking Support for Keyword Search on Structured Data using Relevance Models

Veli Bicer
FZI Forschungszentrum Informatik
Haid-und-Neu-Str. 10-14
76131, Karlsruhe, Germany
bicer@fzi.de

Thanh Tran
Institute AIFB
Geb. 11.40, KIT-Campus Süd
76128, Karlsruhe , Germany
thanh@kit.edu

Radoslav Nedkov
disy Informationssysteme GmbH
Erbprinzenstr. 4-12
76133, Karlsruhe, Germany
radoslav.nedkov@disy.net

ABSTRACT

Keyword query processing over structured data has gained a lot of interest as keywords have proven to be an intuitive mean for accessing complex results in databases. While there is a large body of work that provides different mechanisms for computing keyword search results efficiently, a recent study has shown that the problem of ranking is much neglected. Existing strategies employ heuristics that perform only in ad-hoc experiments but fail to consistently and repeatedly deliver results across different information needs. We provide a principled approach for ranking that focuses on a well-established notion of what constitutes relevant keyword search results. In particular, we adopt *relevance-based language models* to consider the structure and semantics of keyword search results, and introduce novel strategies for *smoothing* probabilities in this structured data setting. Using a standardized evaluation framework, we show that our work largely and consistently outperforms all existing systems across datasets and various information needs.

Categories and Subject Descriptors

H.3.3 [**Information Storage and Retrieval**]: Information Search and Retrieval—*Retrieval models, Relevance feedback*; H.2.8 [**Database Management**]: Database applications

General Terms

Theory,Algorithms

Keywords

Relevance Models, Keyword Search, Structured Data

1. INTRODUCTION

Keyword query processing over structured data has gained a lot of interest as keywords have proven to be an intuitive mean for accessing information and the amount of available structured data increases rapidly, especially in the realm of Web databases. Keyword search helps to circumvent the complexity of structured query languages, and hide the underlying data representation. Without knowledge of the query syntax and data schema, users can obtain complex structured results, including tuples from relational databases, XML data, data graphs, and RDF resources [1, 5, 3, 18]. As opposed to standard keyword search where retrieval units are single documents, results in this setting may encompass several resources that are connected over possibly very long paths (e.g. joined database tuples, XML trees, RDF resources connected over paths of relations).

Although much attention has been focused on finding efficient techniques to process keyword queries and to retrieve the structured data in these settings, only a small number of dedicated work can be found on the ranking of results and understanding their relevance to the user information need. One main direction is the use of Information Retrieval (IR) inspired TF-IDF ranking [11, 12]. Another direction is proximity search where the goal is to minimize the distance between data elements matching the keywords [1, 5]. For computing this weight of paths (distance), a PageRank-based metric is often incorporated for including the node prestige [5]. While high-quality results have been reported in the ad-hoc evaluations of these approaches, a recent study [2] that specifically focuses on benchmarking the effectiveness of keyword search ranking strategies has revealed serious problems: in contrast to previously published results, there is no ranking strategies that is clearly superior, and effectiveness results are much worst than those reported when using a principled approach for assessing relevance and a broader spectrum of queries.

The major shortcomings of previous work can be summarized as follows: the minimal distance heuristic behind proximity search is rather convenient for the efficient computation of results but does not directly capture relevance. The adoption of IR-based ranking proposed so far is also problematic because unlike document ranking, the score of a result in this setting is an aggregation of several resources' scores. Combining resources with high "local scores" however, does not always guarantee highly relevant final results [12]. Recent evaluation results [2] suggest that the proposed normalization methods [11, 12] are not effective in dealing with this issue. More importantly, previous work implicitly assumes that relevance is completely captured by the keyword query that is mostly short and ambiguous. We consider this assumption to be too strong especially in this

CIKM'11, October 24–28, 2011, Glasgow, Scotland, UK.

setting, where users might not be aware of the underlying structure and terminology of the database and thus, cannot specify "complete queries".

In this work, we make the following contributions: (1) we propose the use of Relevance Models (RM) for dealing with the ranking of structured results in keyword search. RM has been used for document ranking [8], which is a probabilistic model that directly captures the notion of relevance behind documents and queries. Primarily, it is employed as a form of query expansion, where relevance (and the query model) is constructed based on the set of documents obtained from an initial query run, i.e., via pseudo-relevance feedback (PRF). While it has shown to be effective in dealing with document ranking, the use of RM has not been studied in this keyword search setting before. (2) We adopt this model, with the goal of obtaining a representation more fine-grained than the original RM that can also exploit the structure of the PRF results. That is, instead of relying on the possibly short and ambiguous query, we use a model of relevance derived from both the content and structure of PRF results. (3) We introduce smoothing strategies that exploit the specific structure and semantics of the underlying data to obtain better estimates of probabilities that make up the RM. (4) We proposed a relevance-based ranking function that employs this adopted RM for ranking standalone as well as aggregated structured results. In particular, we show that this ranking function not only provides a principled way for the aggregation of "local scores", but also, it is monotonic. This is a crucial design issue because only monotonic functions are compatible with existing top-k techniques proposed for the efficient computation of keyword search results. (5) As opposed to previous ad-hoc experiments, we employ the general framework recently proposed for evaluating keyword search ranking strategies [2]. To the best of our knowledge, this is the first work that – based on a standardized evaluation – largely and consistently outperforms all existing systems across datasets and information needs in terms of precision, recall and MAP.

Structure. We introduce the readers to the problem of computing and ranking structured results for keyword queries in Section 2. Then, our approach for ranking is discussed in detail in Section 3. Section 4 contains results of the experiments. We discuss related work in Section 5 and conclude in Section 6.

2. KEYWORD SEARCH ON STRUCTURED DATA

In this section, we provide the definition of our keyword search problem an present an overview of existing approaches.

2.1 Problem Setting

Keyword search approaches have been proposed for dealing with different kinds of data, including relational, XML and RDF data. Generally speaking, the underlying data can be conceived as a directed labeled data graph $G = (V, E)$, where V is a disjoint union ($V = V_R \uplus V_A$) of resource nodes (V_R), and attribute nodes (V_A), and $E = E_F \uplus E_A$ represents a disjoint union of relation edges also called foreign key edges (E_F) that connect resource nodes, and attribute edges (E_A) that link between a resource node and an attribute node. In the following, we denote all attributes of the resource $r \in V_R$ as $\mathcal{A}(r)$, the attributes reachable from r via the edge e as $\mathcal{A}(r, e)$, and all the outgoing edges of r as $\mathcal{E}(r)$. This model closely resembles the graph-structured RDF data model (omitting special features such as RDF blank nodes). The intuitive mapping of this model to relational data is as follows: a database tuple captures a resource, its attributes, and references to related resources in the form of foreign keys; the column names correspond to edge labels. Example data and its corresponding data graph is shown in Figure 1.

The user query Q is a set of keywords $(q_1, ..., q_m)$. A keyword matches a resource node r if it matches any of the attribute nodes $\mathcal{A}(r)$, or any of the edges $\mathcal{E}(r)$. An answer to the user query Q is a minimal rooted directed tree that can be found in the data graph, which contains at least one matching resource for every keyword in Q. This is commonly referred to as a Steiner tree [1, 5]. In this work, we use the term *Joined Resource Tree* (JRT) to make clear that an answer is a joined set of resources represented as $JRT = \{r_1, \ldots, r_n\}$. In recent work, subgraphs have also been considered as keyword answers [18], instead of trees. While this difference in semantics requires more advanced mechanisms for result computation, we will show that this aspect is orthogonal to the problem of *keyword search result ranking* studied in this paper: given a user query, the goal here is to rank Steiner trees (or graphs) according to the user's perceived degrees of *relevance*. In other words, we want to produce a ranking of keyword search results that corresponds to the degree to which they *match the user information needs.* Unlike previous approaches which employ ad-hoc notions of relevance, and conducted different (and rather ad-hoc) experiments to assess this relevance, we aim to provide a principled approach to modeling and dealing with relevance, and will follow the general evaluation framework for evaluating ranking strategies as proposed recently [2].

2.2 Keyword Search Result Computation

Clearly, the main difference of keyword search on structured data and the traditional keyword search on documents is that instead of one single document, a Steiner tree may encompass several resources (e.g. database tuples, documents, RDF resource descriptions) that are connected over a possibly very long path of foreign key relationships.

There are *schema-based approaches* implemented on top of off-the-shelf databases ([4, 11, 12]). Basically, a keyword query is processed by mapping keywords to elements of the database. Then, candidate networks are computed from the schema, which represent valid join sequences (Steiner tree templates) that can be used to connect computed keyword elements. Formal structured queries are derived from candidate networks that finally, are evaluated using the underlying database engine. The main advantages of this approach is that the power and optimization capabilities of the underlying database engine can be fully utilized for computing structured results.

The *schema-agnostic approaches* ([5, 3, 10]) operate directly on the data. Since they do not rely on a schema, the applicability of these approaches is not limited to structured data. For instance, schema-agnostic approaches have been proposed for dealing with semi-structured RDF data [18] as well as the combination of structured, semi-structured and unstructured data [10]. Also here, keyword elements have to be identified first. Then, Steiner trees are iteratively com-

Person

id	name	birthplace
p1	Audrey Hepburn	Ixelles, BE
p2	Cate Blanchett	Melbourne, AUS
p3	Kate Winslet	Reading, UK
p4	Katharine Hepburn	Connecticut, USA

Character

pid	mid	cname
p1	m1	Princess Ann
p2	m2	Katharine Hepburn
p3	m3	Iris Simpkins

Movie

mid	title	plot
m1	Roman Holiday	Princess Ann (Audrey Hepburn) is a royal princess of a country
m2	The Aviator	Hughes and Hepburn go to a holiday, play golf and fly together ..
m3	The Holiday	Iris swap her cottage for the holiday along the next two weeks ..

(a)

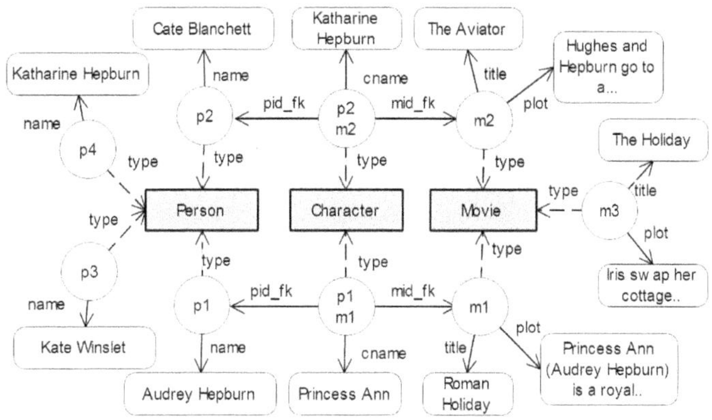

(b)

Figure 1: a) An example database from IMDB and b) its corresponding data graph (partially shown).

puted by exploring the underlying data graph that is mostly held in memory. For the query "Blanchett Aviator" for instance, this graph is simply the path between $p2$ and $m2$ in Fig. 1. Various kinds of algorithms have been proposed for the efficient exploration of data graphs, which might be very large (e.g. bidirectional search [5]).

While this large body of work on result computation is in principle orthogonal to the problem of ranking, there is one critical issue to be considered. Namely, existing approaches employ top-k processing techniques to focus only on the best results in order to terminate as early as possible. In particular, top-k processing terminates when the score of the k-best result obtained so far is guaranteed to be at least as high as the maximum score that can be achieved with the remaining candidates. The score of a result (i.e., a JRT), is typically defined as an aggregation of scores of the individual resources. The upper bound guarantee that is necessary for top-k can be ensured, when the overall score monotonically increases as more resources are added to the result during the process. In other words, existing top-k techniques assume the ranking function to be monotonic, a requirement we aim to satisfy so that our proposal can be used in combination with this previous work.

2.3 Keyword Search Result Ranking

The main idea behind ranking is to (1) assign each resource r in the JRT a score $Score(r)$, and then to combine the individual scores using a monotonic aggregation function $agg(\cdot)$ to obtain the final score $Score(JRT)$. Most commonly used is the IR-style ranking function adopted from TF-IDF based ranking. For instance, Discover [11] uses the sum of individual TF-IDF scores obtained via pivoted normalization weighting [16]:

$$\begin{aligned} Score(JRT) &= \sum_{r \in JRT} Score(r), \\ Score(r) &= \sum_{v \in r, Q} weight(v,r) * weight(v,Q), \\ weight(v,r) &= \frac{ntf}{ndl} * idf, \\ ntf &= 1 + ln(1 + ln(tf)), \\ ndl &= (1-s) + s * \frac{dl}{avgdl}, \\ idf &= ln\frac{N}{df+1}, \end{aligned} \quad (1)$$

where ntf is the normalized term frequency (the normalized number of occurrences of v in r), df is the document frequency (the number of r containing the term v), N is the total number of resources in the collection, idf is the inverse document frequency, dl is the length measured as the number of terms contained in r, $avgdl$ is the average length in the collection, s is a constant usually set to 0.2, and ndl is the normalized document length.

In fact, Discover adopts this weighting via four different normalization methods. The goal is to obtain customized (1) idf and (2) ndl values, and to introduce (3) inter-document weight normalization as well as (4) Steiner tree size normalization. They are motivated by the facts that in this scenario, each column text has different vocabularies and thus shall be treated as a single collection, a Steiner tree is actually an "aggregated resource" and thus requires additional normalization beyond the resource level, and similar to document length, the size of the tree shall have an effect on relevance.

The last factor is very specific to this keyword search setting. Closely related to this Steiner tree size metric is the length of "root to matching nodes" paths [3], or "leaf to center nodes" paths [18]. All these metrics aim to capture the goal of what is known as proximity search, i.e., to minimize the distance between search terms (matching resource nodes) in the data graph. Applying this heuristic yields higher scores to those Steiner trees that are more compact. Intuitively speaking, the assumption here is that trees with more closely related matching nodes more likely capture the intended information need.

Besides IR-style scores defined for matching nodes (IR), and scores representing the distances between nodes in the result (proximity), the third category of scores commonly used is node prestige derived via PageRank [5]. Further, while most scoring functions are designed to be monotonic, examples can be constructed where the resulting ranking contradicts human perception [12]. This gives rise to non-monotonic aggregation functions [12] that however, preclude the large body of existing query processing algorithms.

We note that these existing ranking strategies capture ad-hoc and often debatable intuitions of what supposed to be relevant. Traditionally, IR ranking (i.e., the probability ranking principle [19]) aims to maximize performance by ranking documents based on the posterior probability that they belong to the relevant class. That is, an explicit notion of relevance is employed, and specific approaches vary in their attempt to estimate word probabilities in this class. While the discussed TF-IDF normalizations [11] – and other existing IR-style ranking strategies [12] – intuitively make sense for the introduced examples, they lack a general account for relevance, i.e., it is not clear whether the resulting weights correspond to word probabilities in the relevant class. Also, while the distance-based heuristic used for proximity search is convenient from the computational point of view (as the keyword search problem can be reduced to the shortest-path problem [3]), it does not directly capture relevance in this sense.

An extensive evaluation of existing ranking strategies [2] suggests that no existing schemes is best for search effectiveness (contradicting previous ad-hoc evaluations). Proximity search that incorporates node prestige tends to be slightly more effective than IR-style ranking. Overall, the authors found that previously reported results were "abnormally well", which they attribute to non-standard relevance definitions coupled with very general queries. Further, non-monotonic ranking yields no appreciable difference such that the derived recommendation is "cheap ranking schemes should be used instead of complex ones that require completely new query processing algorithms". In light of these results, we will now present a principled approach to keyword search ranking that enables the reuse of out-of-the-box techniques for result computation.

3. RELEVANCE BASED RANKING

In this section, we present an IR-style ranking strategy. Instead of TF-IDF ranking and the ad-hoc normalization of weights proposed previously, we employ a principled method based on the use of language models that represent documents and queries as multinomial distributions over terms. In particular, we advocate the use of RM [8], aiming to directly capture the relevance behind the user query and documents.

3.1 Relevance Model

As a generic framework, RM is based on the generative relevance hypothesis that assumes for a given information need, queries and documents relevant to that need can be viewed as random samples from the same underlying generative model. Formally, an RM is defined as the function

$$RM_{\mathbf{R}}(v) = P(v \mid r_1, .., r_m) = \frac{P(v, r_1, .., r_m)}{P(r_1, .., r_m)}, \qquad (2)$$

where R captures the notion of relevance. The selection of R is highly critical for the effectiveness of the RM. Using a set F of PRF documents (i.e., documents obtained using the query Q) as an approximation of R, and assuming that query terms $q_i \in Q$ are independent, Lavrenko and Croft defined RM as

$$RM_F(v) \approx P(v \mid Q) = \sum_{D \in F} P(D)P(v \mid D) \prod_{q_i \in Q} P(q_i \mid D). \qquad (3)$$

Given a collection of documents C and the vocabulary of terms V, the score of a document $D \in C$ is based on its cross-entropy from the relevance model RM_F, defined as

$$H(RM_F \parallel D) = \sum_{v \in V} RM_F(v) \log P(v \mid D), \qquad (4)$$

where $P(v \mid D)$ is defined as

$$P(v \mid D) = \lambda_D \frac{n(v, D)}{\mid d \mid} + (1 - \lambda_D) P(v \mid C). \qquad (5)$$

Here, $n(v, D)$ is the count of the word v in the document, $\mid d \mid$ is the document length, and $P(v \mid C)$ is the background probability of v.

Intuitively speaking, relevance is modeled as a distribution over words obtained from PRF documents. This can be seen as a kind of query expansion. However, the difference is that instead of adding a few additional terms to the query, the relevance model here assigns a probability value to every term in the vocabulary V. Given the relevance and document as language models, cross-entropy is used as a similarity measure. Note that while constructing the document language model, the background collection probability is used for smoothing, which can be seen as a method for normalizing the document-specific probability of a term v.

3.2 Edge-specific Relevance Model

Given a user query $Q = (q_1, ..., q_m)$, we follow the RM approach to construct RM from a set of artifacts that is assumed to be close to the query. To achieve this, we use a *keyword index* over the data graph that index resources along with their attributes. Conceptually, this index can be seen as a query-resource map used for evaluating the multi-valued function $f : Q \to 2^{V_R}$. A standard inverted index is used for its implementation: every node $r \in V_R$ is treated as a document and document terms correspond to labels of attribute nodes $a \in \mathcal{A}(r)$. Further, we store edge labels in the index such that every term actually carries the information $(r, e, a) \in V_R \times E_A \times V_A$. After an initial

words	RM_q^{name}	$RM_q^{character}$	RM_q^{title}	RM_q^{plot}
hepburn	0.30	0.17	0.02	0.11
holiday	0.02	0.03	0.5	0.1
audrey	0.14	0.02	0.01	0.06
katharine	0.12	0.12	0.02	0.03
princess	0.01	0.01	0.02	0.1
roman	0.01	0.01	0.26	0.03
...	...	...	...	...

Table 1: Example ERM for the query "Hepburn Holiday"

run of the query Q over the keyword index, we obtain a PRF set of resources $F_R = \{r_1, ..., r_n\}$. Based on this, we construct an edge-specific relevance model (ERM) for each unique attribute edge e as

$$RM_{F_R}^e(v) = \frac{\sum_{r \in F_R} P_{r \xrightarrow{e} a}(v \mid a) \prod_{i=1}^m P_{r \xrightarrow{*} a}(q_i \mid a)}{\sum_{r' \in F_R} \prod_{i=1}^m P_{r' \xrightarrow{*} a}(q_i \mid a)}, \qquad (6)$$

where $P_{r \xrightarrow{e} a}(v \mid a)$ represents the probability of observing a word v in the edge-specific attribute a (i.e., the attribute that is connected to r over e) and $P_{r \xrightarrow{*} a}(v \mid a)$ is the probability of observing the word in all the attributes of r. In fact, $P_{r \xrightarrow{*} a}(v \mid a)$ can be rewritten in the form of $P_{r \xrightarrow{e} a}(v \mid a)$ as

$$P_{r \xrightarrow{*} a}(v \mid a) = \sum_{e \in \mathcal{E}(r) \subseteq E_A} P_{r \xrightarrow{e} a}(v \mid a) P(e \mid r), \qquad (7)$$

where $P(e \mid r)$ denotes the weight of edge e among all the edges of r. In particular, we estimate this by considering the length of the attributes of the edge as

$$P(e \mid r) = \frac{\sum_{a \in \mathcal{A}(r,e)} |a|}{\sum_{e' \in \mathcal{E}(r) \subseteq E_A} \sum_{a' \in \mathcal{A}(r,e')} |a'|}. \qquad (8)$$

A trivial way to estimate the edge-specific attribute probabilities, $P_{r \xrightarrow{e} a}(v \mid a)$, is to consider every attribute as a document and to use a maximum likelihood estimation, $P^{ML}_{r \xrightarrow{e} a}(v \mid a)$, which is proportional to the count of the word v in an attribute a. However, such an estimation is problematic because it would assign zero probabilities to those words not occurring in the attribute. This may result in an underestimation of probabilities of the missing words. We will discuss later in Section 3.4 how to address this by applying a structure-based smoothing method to $P_{r \xrightarrow{e} a}(v \mid a)$.

Example. Consider the query "Hepburn Holiday" on the example data graph in Fig. 1. The keyword index returns the PRF resources $F_R = \{m1, p1, p4, m2, p2m2, m3\}$, each matches one or more query keywords. Based on this, we construct an ERM as illustrated in Table 1. Note the probabilities of the words vary for different edges. For example, "hepburn", and "audrey" are important words for the *name* or *plot* attributes, whereas "holiday" is given more emphasis as a movie *title*.

Compared to RM (equation 3), ERM (equation 6) takes the specific structures of the results into account. ERM is thus a more fine-grained approximation of relevance. It can be considered as analogous to form-based keyword search on databases in which the user is required to enter different keywords to different fields of the form. By processing the PRF set F_R of an initial query run, we are able to exploit the structure of the returned resources. This for instance, may capture attribute types such as *name*, *city*, *comment* etc. without any user intervention. Structures that can be incorporated might emerge from different resources with varying types of attributes.

3.3 Edge-Specific Resource Model

The basic retrieval unit here is a resource (a tuple) since the final results are obtained by combining resources (joining tuples) into an aggregated result. In order to calculate a final aggregated score and utilize an efficient top-k algorithm, we need to be able to assign each resource a score using our ranking mechanism. In order to achieve that, we construct a resource model that assign probabilities to the word in the vocabulary w.r.t. a given resource r. This is similar to the document model in standard IR approaches. The difference is that also structure information (the edges) is exploited for the estimation of word probabilities. We define an edge-specific resource model as

$$RM^e_r(v) = (1 - \lambda_r) P_{r \xrightarrow{e} a}(v \mid a) + \lambda_r P_{r \xrightarrow{*} a}(v \mid a). \qquad (9)$$

Here, the probability of a word for a specific edge e of r is approximated as smoothed probabilities controlled by λ_r. Actually, the parameter λ_r is critical for our ranking to indicate the weight of the edge-specific attributes. A small λ_r means less smoothing and more emphasis on the edge-specific attribute (more emphasis on the terms of the attribute), and more emphasis on the terms of the entire resource (terms in all attributes) otherwise.

The score of a resource is then calculated based on the cross-entropy between the relevance model obtained for the query (RM_{F_R}) and the resource model (RM_r) as

$$Score(r) \; = \; \sum_{e \in E} \alpha_e \sum_{v \in V} RM^e_{F_R}(v) \log RM^e_r(v), \qquad (10)$$

where α_e is a parameter that allow us to control the importance of different edges in the scoring.

3.4 Smoothing

Note that the core probabilities of both RM_{F_R} and RM_r is $P_{r \xrightarrow{e} a}(v \mid a)$. Smoothing is a well-known technique to address data spareness and improve the accuracy of language models, which we apply to obtain a better estimate for $P_{r \xrightarrow{e} a}(v \mid a)$. Traditional smoothing methods mainly use the global collection probabilities. In our case, the global collection simply comprises all attributes in the database. One deficiency of such a global smoothing is that it does not reflect the structure information that is available in this case. As an example, the smoothing probability of the word "Washington" in the *name* attribute "Denzel Washington" should not consider the probability of that word in the *city* attribute, since "Washington" can be highly frequent as a *city* but not as a *name*.

A general framework for smoothing is presented in [13], which consists of the tuple $\{S, f_u, \tilde{f}_u, w(u), w(u,v)\}$, where $S = (V_S, E_S)$ is the smoothing graph, f_u is the smoothed probabilities of the vertexes $u \in V_S$, $\tilde{f}_u$ is the non-smoothed (initial) probabilities of $u \in V_S$, $w(u)$ captures the weights indicating the importances of $u \in V_S$, and $w(u,v)$ stands for the weights of the edges $(u,v) \in E_S$.

Different instantiations of this framework result in different smoothing strategies. We adopt this by using the data graph G for S. The goal is to estimate the edge-specific attribute probabilities $f_u = P_{r \xrightarrow{e} a}(v \mid a)$. While $w(u)$ is set to be uniform, $\tilde{f}_u$ is computed via maximum likelihood as $P^{ML}_{r \xrightarrow{e} a}(v \mid a) = \frac{n(v,a)}{|a|}$, where the nominator is the count of v in a and the denominator denotes the length of a. Then, we obtain the smoothed probability

$$P_{r \xrightarrow{e} a}(v \mid a) = (1 - \lambda_a) P^{ML}_{r \xrightarrow{e} a}(v \mid a) + \lambda_a \sum_{a' \in \mathcal{N}(a)} \frac{w(a,a')}{Deg(a)} P_{r \xrightarrow{e} a}(v \mid a')$$

where $\mathcal{N}(a)$ is the neighborhood of a and:

$$Deg(a) = \sum_{a' \in \mathcal{N}(a)} w(a, a')$$

This notion of neighborhood in the case of structured data is illustrated in Fig. 2. More formally, given $a \in \mathcal{A}(r,e)$, a' is said to be in the neighborhood of a, $a' \in \mathcal{N}(a)$, iff:

- a and a' shares the same resources, i.e., $a' \in \mathcal{A}(r, e')$ for all edges $e' \in \mathcal{E}(r) - \{e\}$ (*Type 1*),
- resources of a and a' are of the same type, i.e., $a' \in \mathcal{A}(r', e)$ where $(r, type, c), (r', type, c) \in E$ (*Type 2*),

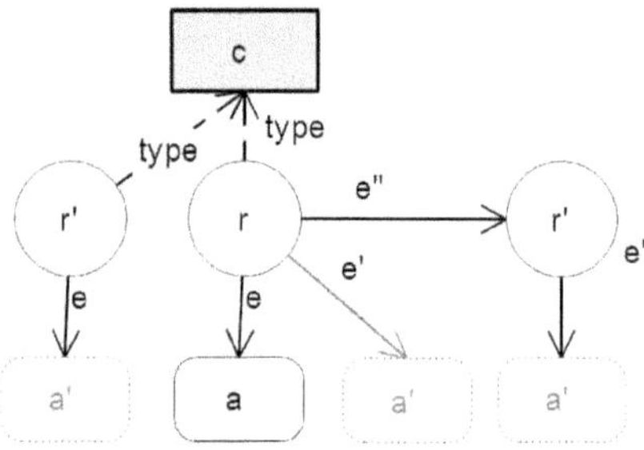

Figure 2: The neighborhood of attribute a.

- resources of a and a' are connected over a foreign key, i.e., $a' \in \mathcal{A}(r', e')$, where $(r, e'', r') \in E_F$ (*Type 3*).

The weight of these three types of attributes ($i \in \{1, 2, 3\}$) are determined separately as

$$w_i(a, a') = \frac{\gamma_i + \sigma(sim(a, a'))}{\gamma_i + 1} \quad \forall i \in \{1, 2, 3\} \tag{11}$$

Here, $\sigma(.)$ is sigmoid function, $sim(a, a')$ is the content-based similarity of the two attributes, and $\gamma_1, \gamma_2, \gamma_3$ are the control parameters for each type. A commonly used instantiation of $sim(a, a')$ is the cosine similarity that we also employ in our experiments.

3.5 Ranking

Ranking in this setting is concerned with JRT, which is a joined set of resources. We provided equation 10 for ranking individual resources. For ranking a set of resources, the same scoring function is applied. However, in this case, $RM^e_r(v)$ in equation 10 actually stands for the set of resources $r_m \in JRT$, defined as

$$RM^e_{JRT}(v) = \sqrt[m]{RM^e_{r_1}(v) \ldots RM^e_{r_m}(v)}. \tag{12}$$

A critical issue for the efficient computation of results is that such an aggregated scoring function, which combines scores from more than two resources are monotonic:

DEFINITION 1. (Score Monotonicity) *Let Q be the query, and $JRT = \{r_1, \ldots, r_n\}$ and $JRT' = \{r'_1, \ldots, r'_n\}$ be two results to Q. An aggregated scoring function is* monotonic *if it satisfies the following condition: if $Score(r_i) \leq Score(r'_i)$ for all $0 \leq i \leq n$, then $Score(JRT) \leq Score(JRT')$.*

We now show that the proposed ranking satisfies this:

THEOREM 1. *The scoring function defined in equation 10 is monotonic with respect to the aggregation of resources defined in Equation 12.*

Proof:

$$\begin{aligned} & Score(JRT) \\ = & \sum_{e \in E} \alpha_e \sum_v RM^e_{F_R}(v) \log \sqrt[m]{RM^e_{r_1}(v) \ldots RM^e_{r_m}(v)} \\ = & \frac{1}{m} \sum_{e \in E} \alpha_e \sum_v RM^e_{F_R}(v) \left[\log RM^e_{r_1}(v) + \ldots + \log RM^e_{r_m}(v)\right] \\ = & \frac{1}{m} \sum_{e \in E} \alpha_e \sum_v RM^e_{F_R}(v) \log RM^e_{r_1}(v) + \ldots + \\ & \sum_{e \in E} \alpha_e \sum_v RM^e_{F_R}(v) \log RM^e_{r_m}(v) \\ = & \frac{1}{m}(Score(r_1) + \ldots + Score(r_m)) \end{aligned}$$

Clearly, $\frac{1}{m}(Score(r_1) + \ldots + Score(r_m))$ is monotonic. □

Example. Continuing with our example query "Hepburn Holiday", the keyword search algorithm firstly obtains the matching resources $F_R = \{m1, p1, p4, m2, p2m2, m3\}$. Based on this, several JRTs are constructed in a bottom-up top-k fashion. They are found based on exploring foreign key paths between these elements. Table 2 shows two of these paths (between p_1 and m_1, and between p_2m_2 and m_2) and two example JRTs resulting from these. During this computation, the scoring function defined in equation 10 is used both to compute the individual scores *Score(r)* (e.g. of p_1 and m_1) and *OurScore*, which indicates the combined score in Table 2 (e.g. of $\{p_2, m_2\} \rightarrow m_2$). Note the difference of our ranking scheme and the ones using proximity and TF-IDF. Proximity alone would assign $\{p_2, m_2\} \rightarrow m_2$ the highest score simply because it is the most compact answer. The two results tie in terms of TF-IDF scores. Our approach ranks $p_1 \leftarrow \{p_1, m_1\} \rightarrow m_1$ first, recognizing that "Hepburn" is an important term for *name* and "Holiday" is an important term for the *title* of movies.

4. EXPERIMENTS

Due to ad-hoc style evaluation, results of previous keyword search ranking were found to be abnormally well. Aiming at making results more conclusive and comparable, we exactly follow the framework for evaluating keyword search ranking strategies proposed recently [2]. For completeness, we will now summarize the data, queries and experimental settings proposed for this kind of evaluation.

4.1 Datasets

We use three different datasets, two of which are derived from two popular and large websites (Wikipedia and IMDb). IMDb data proposed for keyword search evaluation [2] is actually a subset from the original IMDb database, containing information about more than 180.000 movies. This is because several keyword search systems require data to be completely loaded into memory, and thus cannot scale to large datasets. The complete Wikipedia contains more than 3 milion articles. For the same reason, only a selection of more than 5500 articles was used. All tables unrelated to articles or users were excluded, and the PageLinks table was augmented with an additional foreign key to explicitly indicate referenced pages. The third dataset is MONDIAL, which represents the counterpoint to the other two because compared to them, it is smaller in size but more complex in terms of structure. It captures geographical and demographic information from the CIA World Factbook, the *International Atlas*, the TERRA database, and other web sources. The relational version for PostgreSQL was downloaded. Wikipedia contains more text than IMDb, which in turn, has more text then MONDIAL. In other words, while

JRT	$r \in JRT$	$tf_{hepburn}$	$tf_{holiday}$	$Score(r)$	$TF-IDF$	$Proximity$	Our Score
	p_1	1	0	0.36			
$p_1 \leftarrow \{p_1, m_1\} \rightarrow m_1$	$\{p_1, m_1\}$	0	0	0.10	3.0	3	0.22
	m_1	1	1	0.18			
$\{p_2, m_2\} \rightarrow m_2$	$\{p_2, m_2\}$	1	0	0.12	3.0	2	0.19
	m_2	1	1	0.26			

Table 2: Compare TF-IDF, proximity and our scores for the query "Hepburn Holiday".

MONDIAL can be seen as a structured database, Wikipedia is rather a structured document collection.

4.2 Queries

Clearly, performance may vary widely across information needs for the same document collection. Traditionally, fifty information needs are regarded as the minimum for evaluating retrieval systems. Accordingly, 50 queries were proposed [2] for each dataset to cover distinct information needs that vary in complexity. The maximum number of terms in any query is 7 and the average number of terms is 2.91. Among these different queries, there are two important types that were investigated in detail. There are the (1) *"TREC-style" queries* which are Wikipedia topics most similar to those encountered at TREC. Terms of these queries are present in many articles, yet most of those articles are not relevant. For instance, the query "smallpox vaccination" asks for information about the one who discovered/invented the smallpox vaccine. Finding out which articles are relevant and how they vary in the degree of relevance is the problem here. (2) The other type comprises *"single-resource"* queries which ask for exactly one resource. It has been reported that this type of queries constitute the most common type of query posed to existing search engines. For instance the query "rocky stallone" asks for the film in which the actor Sylvester Stallone plays the character Rocky.

4.3 Measuring the Degree of Relevance

Relevance is assessed based on the specified information needs. Binary relevance judgments are used such that all relevant results are equally desirable. Firstly, SQL queries are constructed to capture the information needs. Then, one single expert judges all results that can be obtained for these queries. Three metrics are employed to compare systems. (1) We use the number of *top-1 relevant results*, which is defined as the number of queries for which the first result is relevant. (2) *Reciprocal rank* is simply the reciprocal of the highest ranked relevant result for a given query. These measures aim to capture the quality of the top-ranked results. As the third metric, we use *average precision*, which also takes the order into account. For a query, it is defined as the average of the precision values calculated after each relevant result is retrieved (and assigning a precision of 0.0 to any relevant results not retrieved). Mean average precision (MAP) averages this single value across queries to obtain one single measure across different levels of recall and different types of information needs. These metrics are calculated based on the top-50 results returned by each system.

Table 3 provides a summary of the statistics of the data, the query workload, and the relevant results for each dataset.

4.4 Baseline Systems

We compare the results against systems, which have shown

Dataset	Size	Rel.	Tuples	$\lvert Q \rvert$	$\lvert \bar{q} \rvert$	$\lvert \bar{R} \rvert$
Mondial	9	28	17,115	50	2.04	5.90
IMDb	516	6	1,673,074	50	3.88	4.32
Wikipedia	550	6	206,318	50	2.66	3.26

Table 3: Characteristics of the three datasets and query workload. Size in MB, number of relations and tuples, total number of queries $\lvert Q \rvert$, average number of terms per query $\lvert \bar{q} \rvert$, and average number of relevant results per query $\lvert \bar{R} \rvert$.

to provide best results in the previous evaluation [2]. There are *BANKS* [1] and *Bidirectional* [5], which represent the category of ranking strategies that make use of proximity and node prestige. The IR-style (TF-IDF based) ranking is implemented by *Efficient* [4], *SPARK* [12] and Covered Density [2] (*CD*). *SPARK* is the one that features a non-monotonic function. It has been found [2] that for single-resource queries, proximity in combination with node prestige perform well (compared to IR-style ranking). This is because this scheme prefers the smallest result that satisfies the query (i.e., it prefers less complex JRTs referring to only one single resource) while IR-style ranking scheme prefers larger results that contain additional instances of the search terms. *BANKS* and the like are the best ones on the Mondial dataset, outperforms the IR approaches on the IMDb dataset, and tie for the second most effective on Wikipedia. While this type of systems also provides reasonable effectiveness for the TREC-style queries, they are outperformed by systems implementing IR-style ranking. In particular, *Efficient* shows the best MAP result among all systems – for the set of Wikipedia topics used in the experiment. Further, SPARK reported results were not supported by previous finding, suggesting that the use of non-monotonic ranking function may not be beneficial after all.

4.5 Results

The goal of the experiment is to find out how the proposed ranking (*RM-S*) compares to the best systems on TREC-style as well as single-resource queries. We will firstly discuss the overall results, and then investigate these two types of queries in more detail.

4.5.1 Overall Results

Figure 3 summarizes the overall effectiveness of each system across different information needs in terms of MAP values. We see that the overall effectiveness varies considerably across the three datasets. On average, the best three systems are *Bidirectional*, *CD* and *RM-S*. In particular, our proposed ranking *RM-S* shows very convincing results. It consistently outperforms all systems across datasets. MAP values are above 0.78 and for the MONDIAL dataset, it is even over 0.9. For the IMDb dataset, MAP is close to 0.3

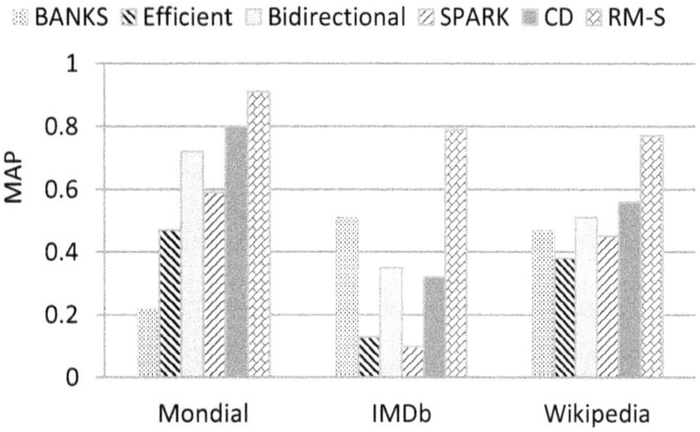

Figure 3: MAP across systems and datasets.

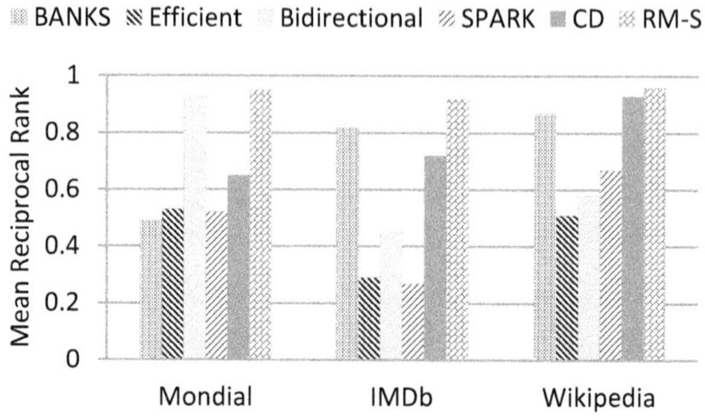

Figure 4: Reciprocal rank for single-resource queries.

higher then the second best system. These results are very encouraging, given the experiments have been conducted in a standardized way using real world datasets and a large set of queries. Also very important for practical purposes is the fact that the best systems including *RM-S* do not require non-monotonic ranking (as advocated by SPARK), and thus can be used in combination with state-of-the-art approaches for the efficient computation of keyword search results.

4.5.2 Single-Resource Queries

Figure 4 shows the mean reciprocal rank for each system for queries where exactly one resource is relevant. Performance of systems vary for this type of queries. As already reported in the previous study, *Bidirectional* and *BANKS* perform relatively well, outperforming the standard TF-IDF based systems such as *Efficient* and *SPARK* on average. *BANKS* achieves poor performance on the IMDb dataset but very good performance on the MONDIAL dataset, while *Bidirectional* exhibits more consistent performance. Our approach clearly shows best performance. It outperforms other approaches across all datasets, with mean reciprocal rank values being consistently above 0.91. We found out that TF-IDF based ranking tends to prefer complex results, which contain a large number of mentions of query terms. Thus, there are high rank results, which contain a large number of resources (each possibly containing mentions of several query terms). These results are however not relevant in this case because the queries target a single resource. In particular, the JRT size normalization (inspired by the document length normalization used in TF-IDF based ranking) [11] introduced to address this issue seems to be not as effective[1] as the more aggressive proximity-based scheme [1], which simply focuses on minimizing the tree size and finding compact results.

In light of these arguments, it seems surprising that *RM-S*, which does not incorporate this tree-size heuristic at all, achieves best results even in this case. Based on the query and the PRF results, it constructs a model of relevance and performs ranking entirely based on this model. Thus, while

[1]The performance of [11] is not shown because it is similar to *Efficient* in concept but worse in performance. It is also based on TF-IDF but employes additional normalization strategies to accommodate for differences in the keyword search setting.

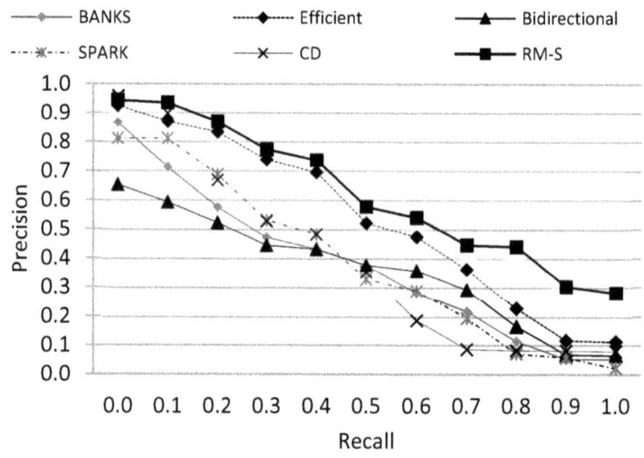

Figure 5: Precision-recall for TREC-style queries on Wikipedia.

RM-S can accommodate for and exploit the possibly varying structures of the PRF results, it does not directly assume that more compact results are necessary better. We believe the key here is that *RM-S* is able to make better estimates of the structure (i.e., the set of attributes) and the content (i.e., the terms) that make up relevant results (independent of their size). For instance for the IMDb query "rocky stallone", TF-IDF based ranking finds many movies but the one with Silvester Stallone as actor and Rocky as character is not the highest ranked one because the term "rocky" and "stallone" appear more frequently in the other movies. Also here, proximity based ranking fails because there is one movie with a character name that matches "rocky stallone". This one is ranked best because its JRT size is smaller compared to the JRT of the result with Rocky as character and Stallone as actor. In this case, *RM-S* is able to find PRF results where "stallone" appears as term in the attribute *actor* and "rocky" appears in the attribute *character*. Based on the resulting ERM, it successfully makes the guess that relevant results should have the attribute *actor* with terms such as "stallone" and "sylvester", and the attribute *character* with terms like "rocky" and "balboa".

4.5.3 TREC Queries

The results for this type of queries are shown in Figure

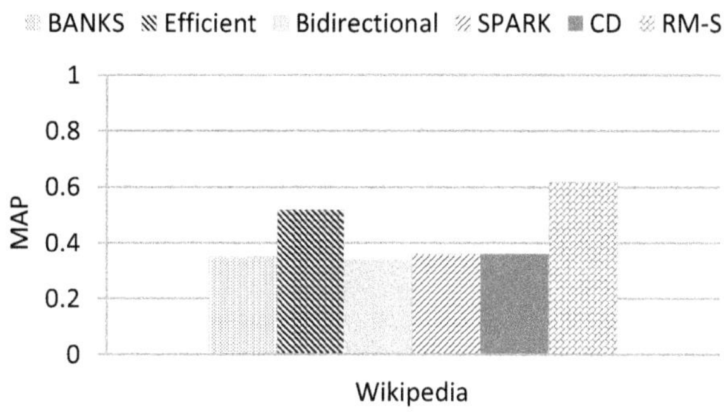

Figure 6: MAP for TREC-style queries on Wikipedia.

5 and Figure 6. While Figure 6 shows the overall performance, Figure 5 provides a breakdown into different levels of precision and recall. These results suggest that ranking schemes based on proximity and prestige do not perform well. *BANKS* is the best one in this category with precision close to 0.9 at the lowest recall level. Its precision however drops precipitously at higher recall levels. Expectedly, TF-IDF ranking performs better, with *Efficient* being the one with best performance in terms of MAP, and most stable performance across the entire precision-recall curve. In this category, *SPARK* performs best at low levels of recall. However, its precision drops sharply as recall increases over 0.1.

Also for this type of queries, our approach yields good results, providing best MAP (0.62) and stable performance over the entire precision-recall curve. It closely matches the performance of *SPARK* at the lowest level of recall, and consistently outperforms all approaches at higher recall levels. Up to recall level of 0.7, its performance is similar to the one of *Efficient*. It however provides much more stable performance at recall levels above that. In fact, we expect our approach to provide better recall (at the same level of precision) because using the relevance model is conceptually similar to query expansion. Terms and attributes, which make up relevant results are not limited to the ones specified in the query. Thus, relevant results can be determined even when they do exactly contain the query terms. For the query "smallpox vaccination" for instance, the resulting relevance model also contains terms such as "louis", "pasteur", "1794" and "virus". Surprising is however the fact that this does not come at the expense of precision. We believe that this is due to the fine-grained structure of the relevance model we employ, which reduces noises in the query expansion process. For instance, results are only deemed relevant when they contain the term "louis" in the attribute *inventor*.

4.5.4 *Parameters*

There is a number of parameters that we set experimentally based on the effectiveness of the ranking results. In particular, the PRF set of documents is $|F_R| \in \{5, 10, 25, 50, 75\}$, and the smoothing parameters for the edge-specific attribute properties $P_{r \xrightarrow{e} a}(v \mid a)$ are $\lambda_r \in \{0.1, 0.2, ..., 0.9\}$ and $\lambda_a \in \{0.1, 0.2, ..., 0.9\}$. We sweep over values for finding the best configuration of these parameters. Further, α_e is set to be uniform in all the experiments.

We analyze the sensitivity of MAP w.r.t. the smoothing parameter λ_a and control parameters $\gamma_1, \gamma_2, \gamma_3$ of Equation 11. We first fix the control parameters and show in Figure 7 how MAP changes according to the value of λ_a for the Wikipedia dataset. We see that MAP values are relatively high at low levels of smoothing, i.e., are best for λ_a in the range between 0.2 and 0.5. This means that while smoothing based on the structure of the data helps to improve performance, it should not be overemphasized. For a fixed $\lambda_a = 0.3$, we investigate the sensitivity of each control parameter by fixing the other two (based on best performance such that fixed values are $\gamma 1 = 0.8, \gamma 2 = 0.1$ and $\gamma 3 = 0.6$). As illustrated in Fig. 8, best performance can be achieved when more emphasis is put on Type 1 and Type 3 and less on Type 2.

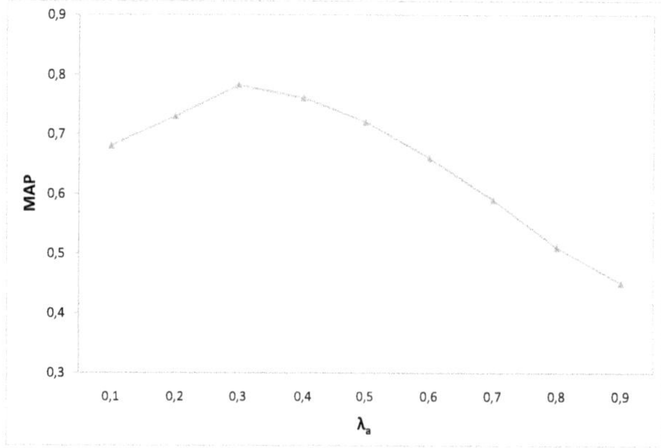

Figure 7: Sensitivity to smoothing interpolation parameter λ_a on Wikipedia.

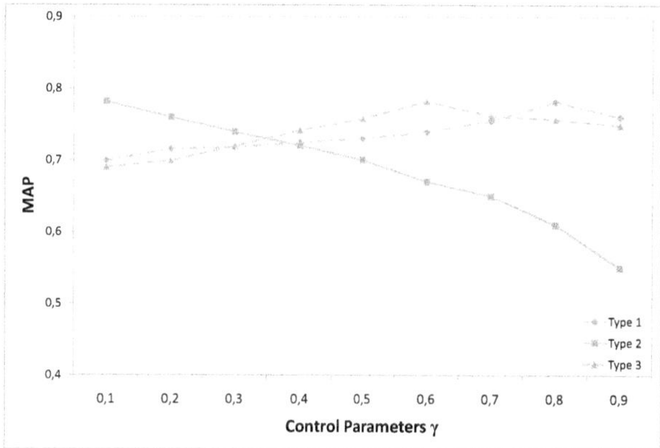

Figure 8: Sensitivity to control parameters of smoothing on Wikipedia ($\lambda_a = 0.3$).

5. RELATED WORK

Finding and ranking relevant resources is the core problem in the Information Retrieval community, for which different approaches have been investigated. The model we use here originates from the concept of language models [15], which have been proposed for modeling resources and queries as multinomial distributions over vocabulary terms, and for ranking based on the distance of the two models (e.g. using KL-divergence [20] or cross entropy [8] as measures for distance). More precisely, the foundation of our work is established by Lavrenko et al., who propose relevance-based language models to directly capture the relevance behind document and queries. Further, the structure of results as well as queries have been incorporated into language models. For instance, combinations of language models constructed from fields of documents have been proposed for structured document retrieval [21], and combinations of attribute-level language models have been employed for the retrieval of complex Web objects [14] and semistructured XML data [6]. Also, structure information has been exploited for constructing structured relevance models [9] (SRM). This is the one mostly related to ERM. The difference is that while SRM consists of models derived from the structure specified in the query, ERM is derived from results obtained from unstructured keyword search. Also, the goal of SRM is to predict values of empty fields, whereas ERM targets the ranking of keyword search on structured data. In this setting, scores have to be combined from several resources (tuples), using a monotonic aggregation function. Thus, while ERM is similar to SRM in concept, the way it is constructed and how it is used are different.

The smoothing method we use represents an instantiation of an existing framework [13]. We adopt it to the case of structured data and show how the local neighborhood of resources can be exploited to obtain smoothed estimations of the edge-specific attribute probabilities. This technique is clearly different to existing work that instead, uses the local corpus structure of documents (e.g. document clusters, neighbors etc.) [7, 17].

Throughout the paper, we discussed existing approaches including various adoptions of IR-style ranking [11, 12] that focus on the problem of keyword search on structured data. However, we note that this is the first work that investigates the use of language models. Instead of employing questionable normalizations and heuristics, we provide a principled approach that directly models the relevance behind queries and results.

6. CONCLUSION

Keyword search on structured data is a popular problem for which various solutions exist. We focus on the aspect of keyword search result ranking, providing a principled approach that employs language models to capture results, queries and the relevance behind them. A recent study has shown that existing heuristics and normalizations proposed for this problem exhibit good results only in the previous adhoc experiments, but fail to deliver consistent performance across different information needs and datasets, and especially, do not deliver stable performance across the precision-recall curve (low precision at higher recall levels). Through a standardized evaluation, we show that our approach delivers superior results, largely outperforming all existing systems in terms of precision, recall and MAP. Further, we formally show that the ranking function is monotonic. This is of great value in practice, enabling the proposed ranking scheme to be used in combination with state of the art approaches for the efficient computation of results.

7. REFERENCES

[1] B. Aditya, G. Bhalotia, S. Chakrabarti, A. Hulgeri, C. Nakhe, Parag, and S. Sudarshan. Banks: Browsing and keyword searching in relational databases. In *VLDB*, pages 1083–1086, 2002.

[2] J. Coffman and A. C. Weaver. A framework for evaluating database keyword search strategies. In *CIKM*, pages 729–738, 2010.

[3] H. He, H. Wang, J. Yang, and P. S. Yu. Blinks: ranked keyword searches on graphs. In *SIGMOD Conference*, pages 305–316, 2007.

[4] V. Hristidis, L. Gravano, and Y. Papakonstantinou. Efficient ir-style keyword search over relational databases. In *VLDB*, pages 850–861, 2003.

[5] V. Kacholia, S. Pandit, S. Chakrabarti, S. Sudarshan, R. Desai, and H. Karambelkar. Bidirectional expansion for keyword search on graph databases. In *VLDB*, pages 505–516, 2005.

[6] J. Kim, X. Xue, and W. B. Croft. A probabilistic retrieval model for semistructured data. In *ECIR*, pages 228–239, 2009.

[7] O. Kurland and L. Lee. Corpus structure, language models, and ad hoc information retrieval. In *Proceedings of the 27th annual international ACM SIGIR conference on Research and development in information retrieval*, pages 194–201. ACM, 2004.

[8] V. Lavrenko and W. B. Croft. Relevance-based language models. In *SIGIR*, pages 120–127, 2001.

[9] V. Lavrenko, X. Yi, and J. Allan. Information retrieval on empty fields. In *HLT-NAACL*, pages 89–96, 2007.

[10] G. Li, B. C. Ooi, J. Feng, J. Wang, and L. Zhou. Ease: an effective 3-in-1 keyword search method for unstructured, semi-structured and structured data. In *SIGMOD Conference*, pages 903–914, 2008.

[11] F. Liu, C. T. Yu, W. Meng, and A. Chowdhury. Effective keyword search in relational databases. In *SIGMOD Conference*, pages 563–574, 2006.

[12] Y. Luo, X. Lin, W. Wang, and X. Zhou. Spark: top-k keyword query in relational databases. In *SIGMOD Conference*, pages 115–126, 2007.

[13] Q. Mei, D. Zhang, and C. Zhai. A general optimization framework for smoothing language models on graph structures. In *SIGIR*, pages 611–618, 2008.

[14] Z. Nie, Y. Ma, S. Shi, J.-R. Wen, and W.-Y. Ma. Web object retrieval. In *WWW*, pages 81–90, 2007.

[15] J. M. Ponte and W. B. Croft. A language modeling approach to information retrieval. In *SIGIR*, pages 275–281, 1998.

[16] A. Singhal, C. Buckley, and M. Mitra. Pivoted document length normalization. In *SIGIR*, pages 21–29, 1996.

[17] T. Tao, X. Wang, Q. Mei, and C. Zhai. Language model information retrieval with document expansion. In *HLT-NAACL*, 2006.

[18] T. Tran, H. Wang, S. Rudolph, and P. Cimiano. Top-k exploration of query candidates for efficient keyword search on graph-shaped (rdf) data. In *ICDE*, pages 405–416, 2009.

[19] M. Wechsler and P. Schäuble. The probability ranking principle revisited. *Inf. Retr.*, 3(3):217–227, 2000.

[20] C. Zhai and J. D. Lafferty. A risk minimization framework for information retrieval. *Inf. Process. Manage.*, 42(1):31–55, 2006.

[21] L. Zhao and J. Callan. A generative retrieval model for structured documents. In *CIKM*, pages 1163–1172, 2008.

Efficient Similarity Search: Arbitrary Similarity Measures, Arbitrary Composition

Dustin Lange   Felix Naumann
Hasso Plattner Institute, Potsdam, Germany
firstname.lastname@hpi.uni-potsdam.de

ABSTRACT

Given a (large) set of objects and a query, similarity search aims to find all objects similar to the query. A frequent approach is to define a set of base similarity measures for the different aspects of the objects, and to build light-weight similarity indexes on these measures. To determine the overall similarity of two objects, the results of these base measures are composed, e. g., using simple aggregates or more involved machine learning techniques. We propose the first solution to this search problem that does not place any restrictions on the similarity measures, the composition technique, or the data set size.

We define the *query plan optimization problem* to determine the best query plan using the similarity indexes. A query plan must choose which individual indexes to access and which thresholds to apply. The plan result should be as complete as possible within some cost threshold. We propose the approximative *top neighborhood algorithm*, which determines a near-optimal plan while significantly reducing the amount of candidate plans to be considered. An exact version of the algorithm determines the optimal solution. Evaluation on real-world data indicates that both versions clearly outperform a complete search of the query plan space.

Categories and Subject Descriptors

H.3 [**Information Storage and Retrieval**]: Information Search and Retrieval

General Terms

Algorithms

1. INTRODUCTION

Many commercial applications maintain a person/customer data set that typically contains information such as the name, the date of birth, and the address of individuals that are somehow related to the company. Often, queries against this data set have to be answered extremely fast, e. g., to process online orders or to support call centers. In many cases queries may contain information that differs from the information stored in the data set. For example, there may be typos, outdated values, or sloppy data or query entries. A good search application needs to handle these errors effectively while returning results as fast as possible.

For these and similar problem settings, a common approach is to define several similarity measures for different aspects of the problem. These customized similarity measures focus on calculating the similarity of an aspect as effectively as possible. For example, in the person data use case, we have different similarity measures for the name of a person, for the address, and for the birth date. In the case of image similarity search, one could have different similarity measures for the color, the structure, and the textures of images [11].

To combine such similarity measures, there exist different approaches, such as the weighted sum or the minumum/maximum. Recent approaches employ machine learning techniques to learn an optimal combination of similarity measures [2, 18]. In our person data use case, we compared SVMs, decision trees, and logistic regression as combination techniques and decided for logistic regression after thorough evaluation.

Our goal is now to perform efficient search based on a set of similarity measures and an *arbitrary* composition technique. We assume that we can create a set of similarity indexes that provide efficient access to the set of records based on the defined similarity measures above a parameterizable threshold (e. g., $sim_{\mathsf{FirstName}} \geq \phi$ for an arbitrary, but fixed $\phi \in [0, 1]$). There are many approaches to create indexes for specific similarity measures, such as different string similarity measures [15, 16, 21]. For the general case, Christen et al. propose a blocking approach to precompute similarities [6]. (We later sketch how our query plan optimization approach can be exploited to optimize the required blocking criterion.)

Apart from the similarity indexes, we do not place any restrictions on the similarity measures or the composition technique. Thus, we cannot apply any of the excellent techniques for similarity search in specific data spaces, such as metric space [20] or vector space [3]. Instead, we consider our similarity measures as black boxes and want to find an efficient method for searching with them.

In this paper, we focus on range queries: Given an overall similarity measure $sim_{Overall}$, a fixed similarity threshold

$\phi_{Overall}$ (the range), a query q, and a record set R, the task is to find all records $r \in R$ with $sim_{Overall}(q, r) \geq \phi_{Overall}$.

1.1 Filter-and-Refine Search

To perform efficient similarity search with an arbitrarily composed similarity measure, we apply a filter-and-refine approach. Given a query, we first filter the entire set of records to derive a set of probably relevant records. For this step, we need one similarity index for each base similarity measure in the filter. We apply filter criteria on these indexes (e.g., *all records with* $sim_{\mathsf{FirstName}} \geq 0.9$ as well as *all records with* $sim_{\mathsf{LastName}} \geq 0.8$) and then combine the filtered sets (e.g., the *intersection* of records with similar FirstName and LastName).

In the refine phase, we calculate the exact similarity (with the combined similarity measure) of the query to each of the records that survived the filtering. The result then contains the set of records above the predetermined threshold for overall similarity ($\phi_{Overall}$).

The filter criterion (which operates on the base similarity measures) is an approximation of the overall similarity measure (which composes the base similarity measures). The key to success is to optimize the filter criterion – it should be as concise, but as complete as possible. For as many cases as possible, the filtered list of records should contain the correct similar records; the number of missing similar records should be as low as possible. Additionally, this list should be as short as possible, i. e., the number of incorrect matches that are unnecessarily compared to the query record should be as low as possible. In this paper, we define metrics to evaluate filter criteria and algorithms to derive a good filter criterion in a general setting. In the following, we refer to the filter criterion as *query plan* (to access the similarity indexes) in analogy to query plans in database systems (to access tables and indexes).

In Fig. 1, we illustrate the analogy between our approach and query processing in DBMS. In contrast to database systems, we only support one kind of query: similarity range queries with a fixed range. Thus, we only need to determine a single optimal plan for these queries. Similar to database systems, we first gather statistics about the data and generate a set of possible query plans. We optimize each query plan thresholds and need to handle the trade-off between costs and completeness (while a DBMS is only interested in the cheapest plan as every computed plan yields complete results). We select the overall best query plan based on these criteria and then create the appropriate index structures for efficient access.

1.2 Contributions

The contributions of this paper are:

- Definition of the novel *optimization problem* for efficient similarity search with arbitrarily composed similarity measures using similarity indexes. In contrast to earlier work, we do not place any restrictions on the similarity measures, the composition technique, or the data set size.
- Definition of *performance metrics* to evaluate query plans for accessing similarity indexes
- Exact and approximative *algorithms* for optimization of query plans based on the specified metrics. The approximate version evaluates only a small fraction of the valid query plans and still determines near-optimal plans. Both versions clearly outperform a complete search of the query plan space.
- An *evaluation* on a large real-world person data set from Schufa, the largest German credit agency (66m records, 2m queries)

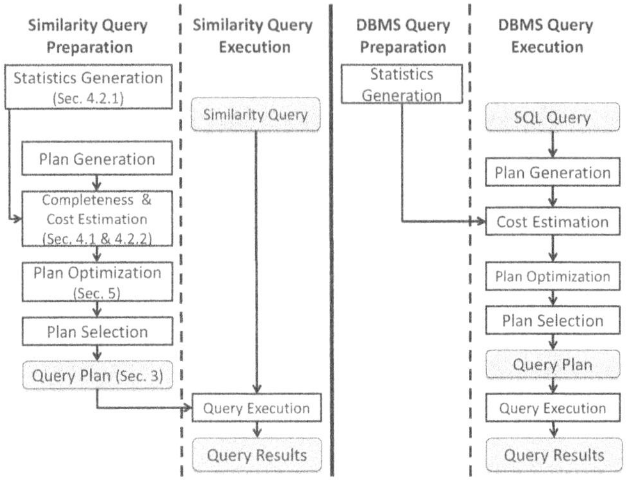

Figure 1: Comparison of our approach with a DBMS architecture

The remainder of this paper is structured as follows: In Sec. 2 we describe related work in the area of similarity search. A description of the problem setting can be found in Sec. 3. We propose evaluation metrics for query plans in Sec. 4. Section 5 contains a description of our proposed query plan optimization algorithms. We apply an optimized query plan to a large real-world data set and present results in Sec. 6. The paper concludes in Sec. 7 with an outline of future work.

2. RELATED WORK

In the field of similarity search there is a variety of approaches for specific cases of similarity measures and data. If the data can be transformed into a vector space (feature space), the search of similar objects can be reduced to the search of close vectors. A popular similarity measure is the Euclidean distance. For an overview on approaches to this setting, we refer the reader to the excellent survey [3]. For another well-explored space, the metric space, the similarity measure needs to fulfill the metric requirements, while the data can have arbitrary form. In this setting, the triangular inequality can be exploited to efficiently reduce the search space [5, 20].

Another relevant similarity search approach has been suggested by Fagin [9]. The presented algorithm retrieves the top k elements by accessing the list of elements in order of their similarity to the query object regarding different aspects (e. g., order all pictures by their similarity to *blue* and *round*). The approach only works for a very limited set of basic composition techniques for the overall similarity measure; thus, Fagin's algorithm cannot be applied in our setting with arbitrarily composed similarity measures.

Deshpande et al. suggest an index structure for non-metric similarity measures that exploits inverted indexes (*similarity lists*) for all values [7]. As stated by the authors, their index structure AL-Tree is only suitable for attributes with very small numbers of distinct values. In our setting with possibly millions of distinct values per attribute, this approach is infeasible. As none of the aforementioned approaches are applicable to our problem, we cannot empirically compare with them.

An area related to similarity search is duplicate detection [8, 14, 19]. For a given set of records, the task is to determine all duplicate entries, i. e., all sets of records that refer to the same real-world entity. For similarity search, too, the problem is to find similar entries, but only for one query object. Duplicate detection is often run in a batch processing job, while similarity search usually requires an answer very fast for a satisfying user experience.

Christen et al. [6] propose to determine similar records *before* inserting a new record into a database, thus preventing the insertion of duplicate records beforehand. Similar to our approach, they exploit a set of similarity indexes. To determine the overall similarity, the authors propose to calculate the sum of the base similarity values, while our approach allows to use *any* combination technique as the composite similarity measure. Our approach tackles the main question that remains unanswered: Which similarity indexes should be created and queried with which thresholds?

A common approach to duplicate detection is blocking, i. e., similar records are grouped into blocks, and then all records within each block are compared to each other [17]. The problem of finding the best blocking criterion is similar to that of finding the best query plan for similarity indexes. In our setting, the blocking predicates are similar to the attribute predicates for which we optimize the thresholds. Michelson and Knoblock suggest a machine learning approach to learn blocking schemes, i. e., selected attributes for blocking as well as similarity measures [13]. Bilenko et al. determine an optimal blocking criterion by modeling the problem as red-blue set cover problem [1]. Both approaches can only decide whether the predefined blocking attribute candidates are contained in the optimal blocking criterion or not. In contrast to these approaches, our proposed algorithm supports the optimization of thresholds involved in similarity predicates (not only boolean contained/not-contained decisions). By exploiting the monotonicity property of these thresholds and defining neighborhoods of query plans, we can quite efficiently traverse the threshold space. Chaudhuri et al. determine duplicates by calculating the union of similarity joins [4]. They reduce the problem of finding the best similarity join predicate to the maximum rectangle problem. In a second step, they union the optimal join predicates. We handle both aspects in a unified approach of finding the best disjunction of conjunctions of similarity predicates. Their approach requires the specification of negative points (in their case: non-duplicates) as training data, which is not helpful in the similarity search setting (where for a given query almost all records are irrelevant and thus negative examples). As we cannot rely on these negative examples in our setting, we need a more sophisticated cost estimation. With a more expensive evaluation function for query plans, we also need a suitable algorithm for efficiently traversing the solution space (and saving the evaluation of unpromising query plans).

3. PROBLEM DEFINITION

In this section, we define basic notations for composed similarity measures and the problem to optimize a query plan for efficient search with them (during the filter phase).

3.1 Composed Similarity Measures

We follow the common and proven notion of defining individual similarity measures for different attributes and attribute types; for instance, dates are compared differently than names or addresses. These individual similarities are subsequently combined to define the global similarity of two records.

We first split the problem of measuring the similarity of two records into smaller subproblems. We define a set of **base similarity measures** $sim_p(r_1, r_2)$, each responsible for calculating the similarity of a specific attribute p of the compared records r_1 and r_2 from a set R of records that is a subset of a universe U of possible records. In our use case, we have the functions $sim_{\mathsf{FirstName}}$, sim_{LastName}, $sim_{\mathsf{BirthDate}}$, sim_{City}, and sim_{Zip}. All base similarity measures can be chosen independently. For example, we could use Jaro-Winkler distance for $sim_{\mathsf{FirstName}}$ [19], the relative distance between dates for $sim_{\mathsf{BirthDate}}$, and numeric difference for sim_{Zip}. We assume the domain of the similarity measures to be between 0 and 1, with 1 representing identity and 0 dissimilarity of the compared record parts:

$$sim_p : (U \times U) \rightarrow [0, 1] \subset \mathbb{R} \tag{1}$$

A **composed similarity measure** uses the base similarity measure to derive an overall similarity judgement. For example, a weighted sum of the base similarity measures is one composition technique. Other techniques involve machine learning approaches, such as logistic regression, decision trees, and support vector machines. Learnable similarity measures have been addressed by several researchers [2, 18]. We make no assumptions whatsoever on the composed similarity measure other that it is composed of base similarity measures.

3.2 Query Plan Optimization

A base similarity measure **predicate** $sim_p(q, r) \geq \phi_p$ covers all records $r \in R$ for which the similarity to the query record $q \in U$ calculated with the base measure sim_p is at least ϕ_p. In the following, we abbreviate this predicate to $p \geq \phi_p$ and refer to base similarity measure predicates as attribute predicates (due to our running example, in which each base similarity measure covers one attribute).

A **query plan template** is a combination of attribute predicates (with yet unassigned threshold variables) with the logical operators conjunction and disjunction. We require query plan templates to be in disjunctive normal form (DNF), since this form is popular [1, 4] and easy to understand and modify. Note that all logical combinations of attributes can be expressed in DNF. A query plan template combines N attribute predicates and has the form:

$$\bigvee \bigwedge p_i \geq \phi_{p_i} \tag{2}$$

with $1 \leq i \leq N, \forall i : 0 \leq \phi_{p_i} \leq 1$.

Once all threshold variables in a query plan template are assigned a value, we call this a **query plan**. An example for a query plan that covers all records with similar FirstName and Zip or LastName and BirthDate is the following:

$$\begin{aligned}&(\mathsf{FirstName} \geq 0.9 \wedge \mathsf{Zip} \geq 1.0)\\ \vee\ &(\mathsf{LastName} \geq 0.8 \wedge \mathsf{BirthDate} \geq 0.85)\end{aligned}$$

To evaluate query plans, we define different performance metrics. Given a set of positive training examples for query/result record pairs, the **completeness** $comp(qp)$ of a query plan qp is the expected proportion of correct query/result record pairs that are covered by qp. The **costs** $costs(qp)$ of a query plan qp is the expected average number of records in R that are covered by qp. Completeness and costs are described and analyzed in detail in Sec. 4.

Given a set R of records and a cost threshold C, the **query plan optimization problem** is to find the query plan qp that maximizes $comp(qp)$ with $costs(qp) < C$. We analyze problem properties and describe our approach to solve the problem in Sec. 5.

4. EVALUATING QUERY PLANS

In this section, we discuss how we evaluate a query plan. We evaluate based on two dimensions: **(1) Completeness:** How many matches can be found with this query plan? **(2) Cost:** How large is the cardinality of an average query result with this query plan? In general, we want to maximize completeness within an upper bound for cost. How to find such best plans is topic of the following Sec. 5.

4.1 Completeness Estimation

For a given query plan, we want to estimate how complete the results will be. We express completeness of a query plan as the proportion of query/result record pairs from a set of positive training record pairs that are covered by the plan (i. e., for which the similarity of query and result records are above the query plan thresholds). Completeness is thus the probability that a correct result to a query will be found with the query plan. In the following, we describe how to gather training data and estimate completeness with it.

4.1.1 Gathering Training Data

To estimate the completeness a query plan, we need a set $T \subseteq U \times U$ of positive training examples for query/result record pairs. There are two main options to gather training data: (1) We have a (preferably large) set of queries with correct answers. (2) We use virtual training data.

(1) Real training data: In our use case, we have a set of 2m queries, most of them with results manually labeled as correct. This is the ideal situation, where we can rely on a manually labeled set of query/result record pairs.

(2) Virtual training data: The first case relies on manually determining sets of query/result record pairs. Since this is often a costly task, one can also create virtual training data. For one training instance, our only concern is whether the overall similarity measure judges that the instance is relevant based on its base similarity values. Thus, we can make up base similarity values (without creating a real query/result pair). We can determine whether these base similarity values would lead to a correct match (if the composed similarity measure computes an overall similarity value above $\phi_{Overall}$). If yes, we have created a positive training instance without the need for real training data. We leave for future work the definition of an algorithm that efficiently traverses the space of possible base similarity values. Inspiring work comes from the domain of learning logical expressions in DNF with membership-query algorithms [12].

4.1.2 Estimation

With positive training instances $T \subseteq U \times U$ at hand, we can estimate completeness of a query plan qp. The function $covers_{qp}(q,r)$ evaluates to *true* iff the pair $(q,r) \in U \times U$ is covered by qp (i. e., if the query plan predicates are fulfilled).

$$comp(qp) = \frac{|\{(q,r) \in T \mid covers_{qp}(q,r)\}|}{|T|} \qquad (3)$$

Our basic algorithm to calculate $comp(qp)$ for given qp and T is very simple: We iterate over the list T and count all query/result record pairs that are covered by qp. Since there is a potentially large amount of base similarity value combinations that are checked multiple times, we speed up the basic algorithm with a more efficient data structure: For each distinct base similarity value combination, we save its count, thus eliminating all "duplicate" combinations. In addition, we further reduce the number of value combinations by rounding to two decimal places. Distinct combinations with the same rounded combinations are accumulated. In our use case, we can reduce the amount of value combinations to be checked from 2.0m to 4.4k (a reduction rate of 99.8 %).

4.2 Cost Estimation

The second evaluation criterion for query plans is the involved costs. We need to estimate how many result records we can expect on average when applying a query plan to the entire data set.

For cost estimation we do not require training data, because we only exploit information from the distribution of attribute values in the complete record set R. A naive approach to estimate query plan costs would be to sample a set $S \subseteq R$ of records, exactly determine the costs for this sample by comparing each record in S to each record in R, and then average the determined costs. In our use case, exactly determining costs for one record would take several hours. As we need to analyze a large set of query plans during the query plan optimization phase, we need a more efficient procedure. Thus, we precalculate attribute similarity histograms with which we can quickly estimate costs of complete query plans.

In the following, we first describe how we derive similarity histograms for determining the amount of similar records regarding one attribute. After that, we explain how to combine attribute costs to estimate costs for query plans involving multiple attributes.

4.2.1 Similarity Histograms

We want to estimate the cardinality of the predicate $p \geq \phi_p$, i. e., how many records in our database have at least a similarity of ϕ_p regarding the attribute p with respect to a random query? To derive a generic query plan, this estimation needs to be independent of specific values. We rather want a general estimation for each attribute.

To achieve this, we first create a similarity histogram for several values of the attribute. For each analyzed value, we calculate the similarity to all other values of the attribute. Figure 2 shows a distance histogram for the last name "Lange". A reading example is: For LastName ≥ 0.9, there are 172,000 records with a last name with minimum similarity 0.9 to "Lange". The solid line is the cumulated number of similar values up to a total of 66m records with a similarity of at least zero.

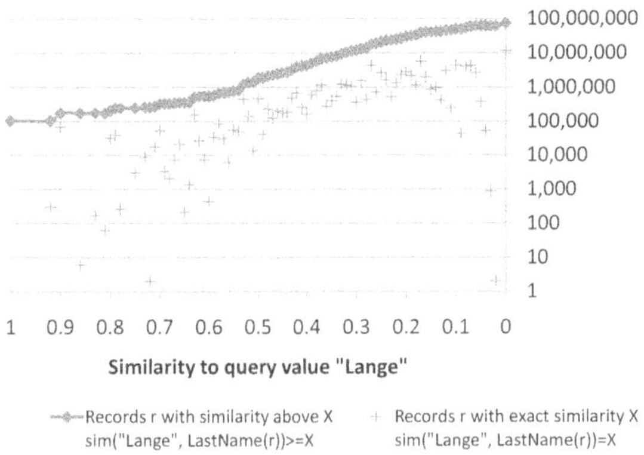

Figure 2: Similarity histogram for attribute LastName for value "Lange"

We then calculate the average of the created similarity histograms. For each possible similarity, we average the measured numbers of records with similar values. The resulting similarity histograms for our attributes are shown in Fig. 3. For the attributes FirstName, LastName, and City, we can see rather smooth curves. The curves for BirthDate and Zip are stepped, because all values have an equal length, and only few errors can occur. These curves allow estimations such as "for FirstName ≥ 0.7, we can expect 500k records with similar values, on average".

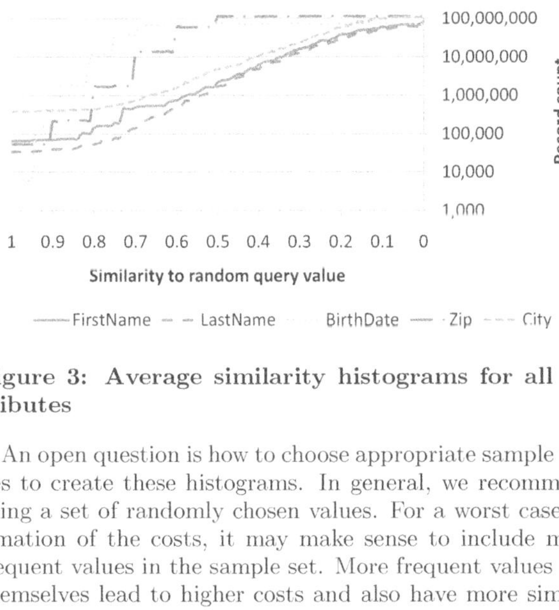

Figure 3: Average similarity histograms for all attributes

An open question is how to choose appropriate sample values to create these histograms. In general, we recommend using a set of randomly chosen values. For a worst case estimation of the costs, it may make sense to include more frequent values in the sample set. More frequent values will themselves lead to higher costs and also have more similar values (as we empirically validated). Regarding the sample size, we empirically determined that a set of 100 randomly chosen elements is sufficient in our use case (for a population of 66m elements, a confidence interval of $\pm 10\%$, and a probability of 95%, 96 elements are necessary).

4.2.2 *Combining Attribute Estimations*

Using the similarity histograms, we are able to estimate the cardinality of a complete query plan. In a nutshell, we estimate the costs of a query plan qp for a random query $q \in U$ by estimating the probability that a randomly chosen element $r \in R$ is covered by qp. We multiply the probability with the cardinality of the complete record set to determine expected average costs:

$$costs(qp) = |R| * P(covers_{qp}(q, r) \mid q \in U, r \in R) \quad (4)$$

By calculating costs using probabilities, we are able to easily handle conjunctions and disjunctions in the query plans with probability theory.

In the following, we abbreviate the probability that a randomly chosen element $r \in R$ is covered by an attribute predicate $p \geq \phi_p$ in $P(covers_{p \geq \phi_p}(q, r) \mid q \in U, r \in R)$ as $P(p \geq \phi_p)$ and any conjunctions and disjunctions accordingly.

We first estimate the probability that an element is in the set of records determined with a *conjunction*, such as LastName $\geq 0.9 \wedge$ City ≥ 0.95. For two attributes a and b with thresholds ϕ_a and ϕ_b we want to estimate the probability $P(a \geq \phi_a \wedge b \geq \phi_b)$. To resolve the joint probability, we distinguish between attributes that are statistically dependent or independent, for ease of calculation. (Although we would theoretically be able to calculate all joint distributions, this would consume a significant amount of time and space.) In our case, we observe that City and Zip are dependent and that each attribute is dependent on itself (this is relevant if a conjunction contains several predicates on the same attribute); all other attributes are independent from each other. If dependent attributes are not known in advance, these can be determined with statistical independence tests such as the χ^2-test. To estimate joint probabilities of dependent attributes, we assume the worst case: the two predicates completely overlap, i. e., the records covered by one predicate are completely covered by the second predicate. Thus, we estimate the probability of the predicates' conjunction as the minimum of the probabilities of two predicates (and accordingly for three or more overlapping predicates). For statistically independent attributes, we simply calculate the product of the predicate probabilities. Thus, for two predicates we have:

$$P(a \geq \phi_a \wedge b \geq \phi_b) = \begin{cases} P(a \geq \phi_a) P(b \geq \phi_b), \\ \qquad \text{if } a \text{ and } b \text{ are independent}, \\ min(P(a \geq \phi_a), P(b \geq \phi_b)), \\ \qquad \text{else} \end{cases} \quad (5)$$

For more than two attributes, we accordingly resolve joint probabilities of statistically dependent attributes and then calculate the product of the remaining predicate probabilities of independent attributes.

With the similarity histograms, we can estimate the individual predicate probabilities as:

$$P(p \geq \phi_p) = \frac{|\{r \in R | p \geq \phi_p\})|}{|R|} \quad (6)$$

Note that the randomness regarding queries is already covered by the attribute costs estimations. As described above, for each attribute we selected several values from R as example queries and averaged their real costs.

In a final step, we estimate the probability of a *disjunction* of conjunctions. For the union of two sets, we can calculate the cardinality as the sum of the cardinalities of the two sets less the intersection of them. The same applies for probabilities. For example, we want to estimate $P(a \geq \phi_a \vee b \geq \phi_b)$

and have:

$$P(a \geq \phi_a \vee b \geq \phi_b) = P(a \geq \phi_a) + P(b \geq \phi_b) - P(a \geq \phi_a \wedge b \geq \phi_b) \quad (7)$$

The remaining probabilities contain only conjunctions and can be estimated as described above. For the general case of n conjunctions c_i in the disjunction $\bigvee_{i=1}^{n} c_i$, the principle of inclusion and exclusion gives us:

$$P\left(\bigvee_{i=1}^{n} c_i\right) = \sum_{k=1}^{n}(-1)^{k-1} \sum_{\substack{T\subset\{1,\ldots,n\},\\ |T|=k}} P\left(\bigwedge_{t\in T} c_t\right) \quad (8)$$

With these estimations, we can accurately and efficiently estimate the costs of any query plan in DNF.

4.3 Evaluation of Cost Estimation

To analyze the quality of our cost estimation model, we compare estimated and observed costs for a set of query plans templates. We generated *all* query plan templates with one or two disjunctions of conjunctions that involve two or three attributes each. We required the conjunctions to contain different sets of attribute, while overlapping of attributes in the conjunctions was allowed. Overall, we analyzed 210 query plan templates.

We randomly selected 100 queries as test objects for which we can quickly count the exact number of records with the values given in the query using an inverted index. With this method, we can count exact matches (i. e., all similarity thresholds in the query plans are set to 1.00). This allows the evaluation of the quality of the probability model. (For the quality of the similarity histograms, we rely on statistical guarantees that we have enough training examples for calculating average frequencies.)

In Fig. 4, we show estimated and average observed costs for the analyzed query plans. Optimal estimations would result in points arranged at a diagonal line with $y = x$ (shown as model line in the graph). We observe that our estimations are quite close to the observed frequencies for all considered plans. Our cost model, albeit not perfectly accurate, seems to be a good estimator for average costs of different query plans.

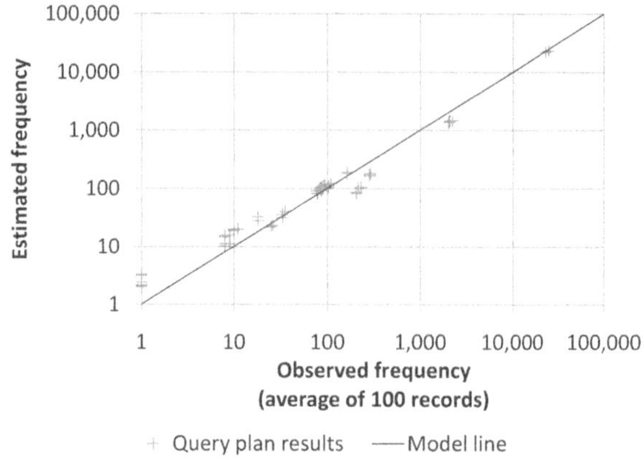

Figure 4: Comparison of observed and estimated frequencies for the 210 generated query plans. Example: For the query plan BirthDate $\geq 1 \wedge$ City ≥ 1, our estimation is 22 records, and the observed average frequency is 25 records.

5. QUERY PLAN OPTIMIZATION

Based on the performance metrics defined in the previous section, we want to find the best query plan, i. e., the plan with highest completeness below a cost threshold. We iterate over the set of all possible query templates and then optimize thresholds for each query plan template. We thus have one optimal query plan per query plan template. From these query plans, we can simply select the overall best query plan.

In the remainder of this section, we discuss the problem of optimizing the thresholds of one query plan template. For a given query template containing n attribute predicates, each attribute predicate's threshold can be set to one of v values. Thus, the complexity of a complete search is $O(v^n)$, i. e., exponential in terms of attribute predicates. For example, for 6 attribute predicates, each with 101 possible threshold values (0.00 to 1.00), there are $101^6 \approx 1$ trillion possible query plans. As we need to calculate both completeness and costs for each plan to be analyzed, this large set of possible plans is infeasible to be analyzed completely; thus, more efficient algorithms are required.

We begin this section with observations regarding the distributions of completeness and costs and then discuss algorithms for exact and approximative optimization of query plans.

5.1 Observations

To better understand the problem space, we first analyze the distribution of completeness and costs. For the exemplary query plan template

$$\text{FirstName} \geq \phi_{\text{FirstName}} \wedge \text{LastName} \geq \phi_{\text{LastName}}$$

we evaluated all possible query plans, i. e., all possible threshold values for $\phi_{\text{FirstName}}$ and ϕ_{LastName}. We show the resulting comparison distribution in Fig. 5 and the cost distribution in Fig. 6.

In the cost distribution diagram, we can see that query plans with lower thresholds have higher costs. This is not surprising, as lower thresholds result in at least as many or more covered records as a higher threshold. For decreasing thresholds, we observe that costs grow exponentially. We can especially see that only few query plans in the upper right corner have acceptable costs; as we will see later, more complex plans with disjunctions of conjunctions in the query plan templates achieve better results (i. e., higher completeness with lower costs).

The distribution of completeness shows that lower thresholds result in higher completeness. While this insight is also not surprising, the growth of completeness is quite different from the cost distribution. Already with the highest thresholds (i. e., only exact matches are found), we can cover the vast majority of the 2m training query/result record pairs. The increase in found matches is high for higher thresholds, but for lower thresholds, the increase dwindles. This confirms our intuition: The last percentages of completeness (recall) are the most difficult to resolve.

The monotonicity observations can be generalized for any combination of similarity measures. Any query plan with thresholds (ϕ_x, ϕ_y) has at least the costs and the completeness of any query plan with thresholds $(\phi_{x'}, \phi_{y'})$ with $\phi_{x'} <$

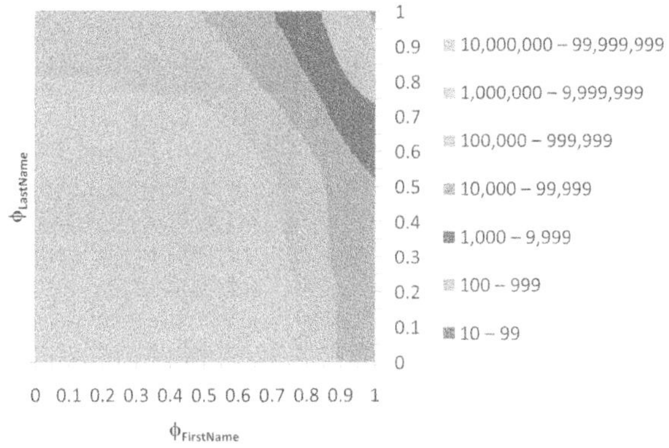

Figure 5: Distribution of costs for query plan template FirstName $\geq \phi_{\text{FirstName}} \wedge$ LastName $\geq \phi_{\text{LastName}}$

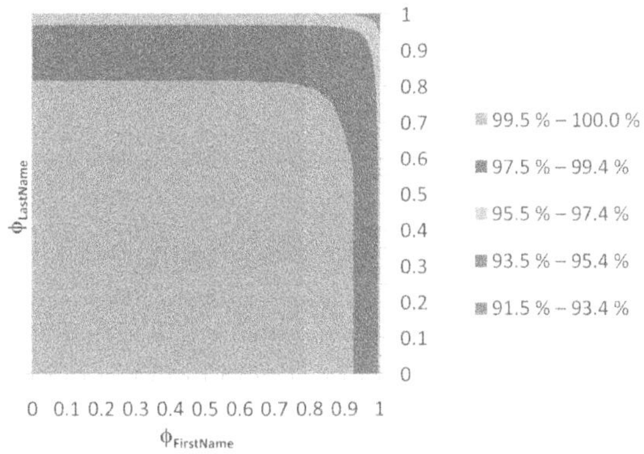

Figure 6: Distribution of completeness for query plan template FirstName $\geq \phi_{\text{FirstName}} \wedge$ LastName $\geq \phi_{\text{LastName}}$

ϕ_x or $\phi_{y'} < \phi_y$. Note that Chaudhuri et al. make similar observations and also exploit the monotonicity property in their algorithm [4]. In our case we do not know completeness and cost of the query plans in advance, so we solve a different problem with an entirely different approach.

From the cardinality distribution diagram, we can derive the space of all valid query plans, i. e., all plans with costs at most as high as the predefined cost threshold C. For the two-dimensional case, we can think of a line that separates all valid query plans from the invalid ones. From the monotonicity observations, we can infer that such a line always exists and that we can ignore any combinations below this line. Thus, we consider only the combinations above this line without discarding valid combinations. In our following algorithms, reaching this line will be regarded as stopping criterion.

5.2 Top Neighborhood Algorithm

An described above, an algorithm that analyzes all possible query plans for a query plan template is infeasible. Keep in mind that we do not know completeness and cost for any query plan in advance. We need an algorithm that efficiently navigates through the solution space: The algorithm should only evaluate as few query plans as possible and determine an overall good solution.

The general idea of the **top neighborhood algorithm** is to start with the plan with highest thresholds (in our case, all thresholds are set to 1, which corresponds to the top-right corner of Figs. 5 and 6), then follow promising plans in its neighborhood (the top plans), until we reach the valid query plan separation line. The result is then the plan with highest completeness (and lowest cost, respectively) found so far. In the following, we describe the algorithm in greater detail.

The start plan must be the one with highest thresholds, since any other plan for starting could make it impossible to find the best solution due to our downwards search approach.

We define the neighborhood of a plan to help us navigate the threshold space. A query plan qp has a **neighborhood** $N(qp)$ that contains all query plans that can be constructed by lowering one thresholds of qp by one step (e. g., by 0.01). For example, the neighborhood of a plan with two thresholds ϕ_a and ϕ_b has two elements:

$$\begin{aligned} N(a \geq \phi_a \wedge b \geq \phi_b) &= \{a \geq \phi_a - 0.01 \wedge b \geq \phi_b, \\ &\quad a \geq \phi_a \wedge b \geq \phi_b - 0.01\} \end{aligned}$$

The neighborhood thus defines all possible directions to traverse the solution space given one query plan. We define the neighborhood only for lower thresholds and thus higher completeness (and also higher costs), since we traverse the threshold space from higher to lower thresholds.

In each iteration of our algorithm, we have a **window** $W = \{q_1 \dots q_n\}$ of n query plans that are currently regarded. We extend the neighborhood concept to windows by defining the set of all neighborhood plans for the plans in W as $N(W) = \bigcup_{qp \in W} N(qp)$. We then select a subset of these plans: the t plans with highest completeness (and lowest costs, if there are several plans with equal completeness; if there are more than t eligible plans, a random selection is made). We call this set the **top t neighborhood** $T_t(W)$. Only plans with costs below the cost threshold C are contained in this set.

The cost threshold C also determines the **stopping criterion** of our algorithm. If the top t neighborhood contains only plans with costs above C, then the algorithm terminates and returns the best plan found so far. Otherwise, the algorithm continues with a new iteration by setting $W := T_t(W)$ (t is thus also the maximum window size).

Note that the algorithm is optimal regarding the number of times a query plan is evaluated. In each iteration, the window contains only plans with the same amount of applied threshold lowering steps (compared to the initial plan). Since the union of the generated plans is calculated before evaluating them, no query plans are evaluated more than once.

In Fig. 7, we illustrate one iteration of the algorithm by means of an exemplary query plan template with two thresholds. Note that the illustration is similar to the measured completeness distribution in Fig. 6. The diagram shows the search space of all valid plans, i. e., all plans with acceptable costs (which we do not know in advance). The current window consists of two plans. The neighborhood of the window contains three plans, two of which (with *comp=38*) are selected as the top 2 neighborhood and thus form the new window for the next iteration.

Exact algorithm. The parameter t allows us to turn the approximative top neighborhood algorithm into an exact

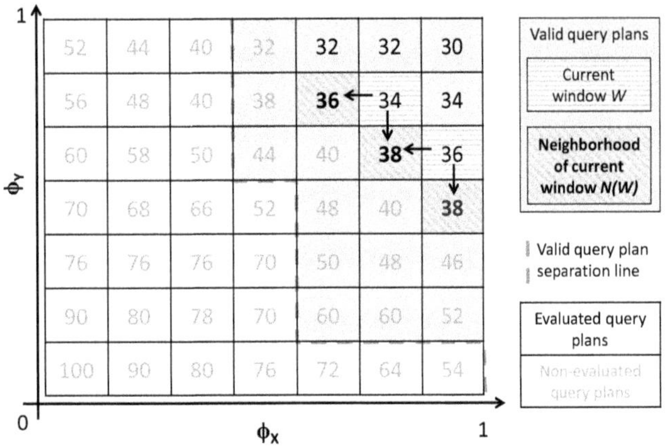

Figure 7: Application of top neighborhood algorithm to exemplary completeness estimations (in percent) for two thresholds ϕ_X, ϕ_Y in a query plan template

algorithm for finding the optimal query plan. By setting $t = \infty$, we do not limit the window size and thus evaluate *all* valid query plans. Still, we avoid the evaluation of a number of query plans: those with costs above C. Regarding the search space coverage, this exact algorithm is thus a better approach than a brute force search over all possible query plans. A disadvantage is the higher memory requirement, since all evaluated query plans of an iteration need to be kept in memory.

Complexity. The complexity of the top neighborhood algorithm depends on the number of necessary iterations as well as the number of generated query plans per iteration. A worst case estimation for the number of necessary iterations assumes that all thresholds need to be lowered to their lowest possible value. The number of iterations is thus limited by the number of all possible thresholds of all predicates of the query plan template. The number of generated plans per iteration is determined by the top neighborhood size (and thus maximum window size) t and the number of predicates in the query plan template (for which one threshold can be lowered in an iteration). Thus, the complexity of the top neighborhood algorithm is linear in the following parameters:

- the number of predicates in the query plan template
- the number of possible thresholds of all predicates
- the top neighborhood size t

5.3 Evaluation

To evaluate the top neighborhood algorithm, we analyzed the behavior of the algorithm on our data set with 2m (correct) query/result record pairs. We ran the algorithm for three randomly chosen query plan templates with different numbers of predicates and varied the parameter t. Figure 8 shows the results. For comparison, the first line of each table shows the results for exact matching (i. e., all thresholds are set to 1) as baseline, and the last line contains the result of the exact version of our algorithm (with $t = \infty$). We refer to the result of the exact algorithm as the optimal plan, since no better plan can be found with the given query plan template.

For all analyzed templates, a small value for t is sufficient to find a plan with near-optimal completeness (only a few of the 2m records are missing). For all analyzed values of t, we can see a significant improvement over the baseline results for exact matching. In general, a larger value for t results in larger completeness. The numbers of evaluated query plans also confirm the linearity of the algorithm regarding t and the query template complexity (i. e., the number of predicates as well as the number of thresholds per predicate; this cannot be distinguished in this experiment).

With growing query plan templates (i. e., more predicates), the results become more complete, since the template is more expressive. In general, the thresholds of a more complex predicate are higher in order to satisfy the cost constraint.

The more complex the query plan, the larger the number of saved query plan evaluations: For the template with six predicates, we consider only less than a percent of the *valid* query plans. For all templates, we only evaluate a fraction of *all* possible plans. Even the exact version of our algorithm with unlimited t considers only 16% of the possible plans for the small template and 0.6% for the large template. For the large template and $t = 200$, still only less than a ten thousandth of all possible plans have been evaluated.

To summarize, the results show that the top neighborhood algorithm determines a near-optimal plan while evaluating only a fraction of the possible query plans. We have measured similar results for other query plan templates.

6. REAL-WORLD SIMILARITY SEARCH

In addition to the experiments for individual aspects of our approach in earlier sections, we also ran an experiment on the complete data set with the overall optimal query plan.

To determine the overall optimal query plan for our data set, we used the set of query plan templates from the experiment in Sec. 4.3. This set contains *all* query plan templates with one or two disjunctions of conjunctions that involve two or three attributes each. We required the conjunctions to contain different sets of attributes, while overlapping of attributes in the conjunctions was allowed. For each of the 210 query plan templates, we ran our top neighborhood algorithm with $t = 100$ (a window size that results in acceptable runtime of our algorithm) and $C = 1000$ (a cost threshold that is acceptable for our use case). We selected the overall best query plan for this experiment.

As test queries, we randomly selected 50,000 queries from our test data set. We ran these queries with different search settings and show the results (completeness and cost as defined in Sec. 4) in Table 1.

The first line shows a basic result when searching for only those records where all attribute values of the query exactly match the values in the record. This shows that 87 % of the queries are "easy" to answer, since the corresponding correct matches in the record set do not contain any differences to the query. The costs for queries with this search settings are quite low, since there is usually at most one such exactly matching record.

We then tried to answer the same set of queries with the query plan that turned out to be optimal regarding completeness (according to our top neighborhood algorithm). We first did an exact search with this plan (line 2 in Ta-

t	Evaluated query plans	Fraction of **valid** plans	Fraction of **all** plans	Completeness
Baseline	1 (all thresholds set to 1)	0.310%	0.049%	93.1599%
5	173	53.560%	8.543%	98.7725%
10	276	85.449%	13.630%	99.0643%
20	323	100.000%	15.951%	99.0643%
∞	323	100.000%	15.951%	99.0643%

(a) Results for query plan template with *two* predicates ($A \wedge B$). The number of possible query plans is 2,025.

t	Evaluated query plans	Fraction of **valid** plans	Fraction of **all** plans	Completeness
Baseline	1 (all thresholds set to 1)	0.004%	0.000%	99.3322%
5	573	2.438%	0.171%	99.9154%
10	818	3.480%	0.245%	99.9619%
20	1,802	7.666%	0.539%	99.9604%
50	5,364	22.819%	1.605%	99.9826%
100	9,399	39.984%	2.813%	99.9861%
200	16,825	71.574%	5.036%	99.9880%
∞	23,507	100.000%	7.035%	99.9905%

(b) Results for query plan template with *four* predicates ($(A \wedge B) \vee (C \wedge D)$). The number of possible query plans is 334,125.

t	Evaluated query plans	Fraction of **valid** plans	Fraction of **all** plans	Completeness
Baseline	1 (all thresholds set to 1)	0.000%	0.000%	99.3633%
5	1,335	0.033%	0.000%	99.9275%
10	2,657	0.065%	0.000%	99.9786%
20	5,007	0.122%	0.001%	99.9786%
50	11,440	0.280%	0.002%	99.9845%
100	20,672	0.505%	0.003%	99.9892%
200	37,141	0.908%	0.005%	99.9936%
∞	4,092,574	100.000%	0.605%	99.9994%

(c) Results for query plan template with *six* predicates ($(A \wedge B) \vee (C \wedge D) \vee (E \wedge F)$). The number of possible query plans is 676,603,125.

Figure 8: Evaluation results of top neighborhood algorithm for different query plan templates

Search setting	**Completen.**	**Cost**
(1) Exact search with all attributes	87.28%	0.8
(2) Exact search with overall best query plan	99.47%	37.8
(3) Optimized similarity search with overall best query plan	99.98%	551.7
(4) No filtering	100.00%	66m

Table 1: Search performance of different search settings

ble 1). In comparison to the first search setting where all attribute values were required to exactly match, this plan only requires that one of two conjunctions (of two attributes each) match. The result shows that the majority of the remaining records can be found with this setting, but that the average costs are also higher for this setting (again compared to search setting (1)).

By applying the top neighborhood algorithm, we optimized the thresholds of the query plan. Line 3 in Table 1 shows that we achieve even better results than for search setting (2). The completeness is near 100 %. As already pointed out, the last couple of records are the most difficult to find. This query plan thus has higher costs, but they are still below the cost threshold of $C = 1000$.

For comparison, we also show that comparing the query to each record in our data set (line 4 in Table 1) would result in perfect completeness, but also in costs of 66m, which is clearly infeasible. Our optimized query plan exploits the cost limit best and is thus an appropriate choice for efficient similarity search in the given data set.

7. CONCLUSION AND OUTLOOK

We introduced a novel approach to efficient similarity search for composed similarity measures. We showed how to efficiently compute completeness and costs, two important performance metrics for query plans based on a set of similarity indexes. The resulting trade-off between completeness and costs has been solved with the approximative top neighborhood algorithm. We showed that the algorithm efficiently determines near-optimal query plans for real-world data.

Further applications. Our proposed algorithm for optimizing query plans can also be adapted to determine a good blocking criterion. Blocking is a simple approach to improve efficiency of duplicate detection [17]. Another application scenario is the creation of a similarity index for an attribute predicate $sim_p \geq \phi_p$: We create blocks of similar values of the attribute p and then compare only the values in the blocks with each other. For each attribute value v_1, we store all values v_2 with $sim_p(v_1, v_2) \geq \phi_p$ in a sorted list for efficient access. To optimize this process, a blocking criterion needs to be defined with which as many similar values and as few dissimilar values as possible are within each block and are thus compared. The completeness of the blocking criterion should be high, and the costs should be low, similar to the formulation of the query plan optimization problem.

Our algorithm can be applied to this setting as follows: Instead of query plan templates, our algorithm now optimizes *blocking criterion templates* that may also include boolean blocking predicates. An example for a blocking criterion is:

$$(\mathsf{CommonPrefix} \geq 3) \vee (\mathsf{CommonNGrams} \geq 2)$$

This blocking criterion means that in a first blocking run, all values with a common prefix of length 3 are compared, and in a second blocking run, all values with a at least two common n-grams are compared (this approach is called multi-pass blocking [10]). Blocking criteria may also contain conjunctions, similar to query plans.

Costs of a blocking criterion are calculated as the average number of similar values for a given "query" value (to create a complete similarity index, all values will be "queried" for similar values). Similar to the description for query plans in Sec. 4.2, we can sample some values and calculate the average number of values covered by the blocking criteria for an appropriate range of blocking predicate thresholds. To create training data for *completeness* estimation, we can sample some attribute values and then compare these to all other values. In contrast to the similarity search problem (where there is usually only a very small set of objects similar to a query), there is usually a large set of values in the same block. The *top neighborhood algorithm* can work with these estimations; it starts with a very rigorous blocking criterion (with high thresholds and thus small blocks) and then lowers the thresholds until a predefined cost threshold is reached.

Future work. We leave for future work the following research directions:

- *Frequency-adaptive query plans:* We aim to develop a framework that optimizes query plans at query time with information about the frequencies of the attribute values in the query. Based on this information, a good query plan needs to be selected very fast.

- *Virtual training data:* To apply our algorithm to data sets without sufficient training data, we want to develop an algorithm for generating training data based solely on the composite similarity measures.

Acknowledgments

We thank Schufa Holding AG for supporting this work. We especially thank Stephan Springob, Boris Zerban, and Michael Stolz for their valuable input.

8. REFERENCES

[1] M. Bilenko, B. Kamath, and R. J. Mooney. Adaptive blocking: Learning to scale up record linkage. In *Proc. of the Intl. Conf. on Data Mining (ICDM)*, pages 87–96, Hong Kong, China, 2006.

[2] M. Bilenko and R. J. Mooney. Adaptive duplicate detection using learnable string similarity measures. In *Proc. of the ACM Intl. Conf. on Knowledge Discovery and Data Mining (SIGKDD)*, pages 39–48, Washington, DC, USA, 2003.

[3] C. Böhm, S. Berchtold, and D. A. Keim. Searching in high-dimensional spaces: Index structures for improving the performance of multimedia databases. *ACM Computing Surveys*, 33:322–373, September 2001.

[4] S. Chaudhuri, B.-C. Chen, V. Ganti, and R. Kaushik. Example-driven design of efficient record matching queries. In *Proc. of the Intl. Conf. on Very Large Databases (VLDB)*, pages 327–338, Vienna, Austria, 2007.

[5] E. Chávez, G. Navarro, R. Baeza-Yates, and J. L. Marroquín. Searching in metric spaces. *ACM Comput. Surv.*, 33(3):273–321, 2001.

[6] P. Christen, R. Gayler, and D. Hawking. Similarity-aware indexing for real-time entity resolution. In *Proc. of the Intl. Conf. on Information and Knowledge Management (CIKM)*, pages 1565–1568, Hong Kong, China, 2009.

[7] P. M. Deshpande, D. P, and K. Kummamuru. Efficient online top-k retrieval with arbitrary similarity measures. In *Proc. of the Intl. Conf. on Extending Database Technology (EDBT)*, pages 356–367, Nantes, France, 2008.

[8] A. K. Elmagarmid, P. G. Ipeirotis, and V. S. Verykios. Duplicate record detection: A survey. *IEEE Transactions on Knowledge and Data Engineering (TKDE)*, 19(1):1–16, 2007.

[9] R. Fagin. Fuzzy queries in multimedia database systems. In *Proc. of the Symposium on Principles of Database Systems (PODS)*, pages 1–10, Seattle, WA, USA, 1998.

[10] M. A. Hernández and S. J. Stolfo. Real-world data is dirty: Data cleansing and the merge/purge problem. *Data Mining and Knowledge Discovery*, 2:9–37, 1998.

[11] Q. Iqbal and J. K. Aggarwal. Combining structure, color and texture for image retrieval: A performance evaluation. In *Proc. of the Intl. Conf. on Pattern Recognition (ICPR)*, pages 438–443, Quebec City, Canada, 2002.

[12] J. C. Jackson. An efficient membership-query algorithm for learning dnf with respect to the uniform distribution. *J. Comput. Syst. Sci.*, 55:414–440, December 1997.

[13] M. Michelson and C. A. Knoblock. Learning blocking schemes for record linkage. In *Proc. of the National Conf. on Artificial Intelligence (AAAI)*, pages 440–445, Boston, MA, USA, 2006.

[14] F. Naumann and M. Herschel. *An Introduction to Duplicate Detection*. Synthesis Lectures on Data Management. Morgan & Claypool Publishers, 2010.

[15] G. Navarro. A guided tour to approximate string matching. *ACM Comput. Surv.*, 33:31–88, March 2001.

[16] G. Navarro and R. Baeza-Yates. A hybrid indexing method for approximate string matching. *Journal of Discrete Algorithms*, 1:2000, 2001.

[17] H. Newcombe. Record linkage: the design of efficient systems for linking records into individual and family histories. *American Journal of Human Genetics*, 19:3, 1967.

[18] S. Sarawagi and A. Bhamidipaty. Interactive deduplication using active learning. In *Proc. of the ACM Intl. Conf. on Knowledge Discovery and Data Mining (SIGKDD)*, pages 269–278, Edmonton, Alberta, Canada, 2002.

[19] W. E. Winkler. The state of record linkage and current research problems. Technical report, Statistical Research Division, U.S. Census Bureau, 1999.

[20] P. Zezula, G. Amato, V. Dohnal, and M. Batko. *Similarity Search - The Metric Space Approach*. Springer, 2006.

[21] Z. Zhang, M. Hadjieleftheriou, B. C. Ooi, and D. Srivastava. Bed-tree: an all-purpose index structure for string similarity search based on edit distance. In *International Conference on Management of Data*, pages 915–926, Nagpur, India, 2010.

Learning to Rank Results in Relational Keyword Search

Joel Coffman
University of Virginia
Charlottesville, VA
jcoffman@cs.virginia.edu

Alfred C. Weaver
University of Virginia
Charlottesville, VA
weaver@cs.virginia.edu

ABSTRACT

Keyword search within databases has become a hot topic within the research community as databases store increasing amounts of information. Users require an effective method to retrieve information from these databases without learning complex query languages (viz. SQL). Despite the recent research interest, performance and search effectiveness have not received equal attention, and scoring functions in particular have become increasingly complex while providing only modest benefits with regards to the quality of search results. An analysis of the factors appearing in existing scoring functions suggests that some factors previously deemed critical to search effectiveness are at best loosely correlated with relevance. We consider a number of these different scoring factors and use machine learning to create a new scoring function that provides significantly better results than existing approaches. We simplify our scoring function by systematically removing the factors with the lowest weight and show that this version still outperforms the previous state-of-the-art in this area.

Categories and Subject Descriptors

H.3.3 [**Information Storage and Retrieval**]: Information Search and Retrieval; H.2.4 [**Database Management**]: Systems—*Relational databases*

General Terms

Design, Experimentation, Performance

Keywords

relational keyword search, ranking

1. INTRODUCTION

The success of web search engines has made keyword search the preferred method for individuals to discover and to retrieve information [12] as evidenced by the 4 billion keyword searches performed daily [14]. Given the ubiquity of the search text box, it is natural to extend the keyword search paradigm to support other sources of information, including semi-structured data (e.g., XML) and relational data.[1] Many data-driven websites store information in relational databases; periodically crawling their content inevitably results in outdated information appearing in search results. While websites commonly provide a means to search their content, such facilities often are inferior to Internet search engines or constrain searches by supporting only the simplest queries (e.g., find articles whose titles are like ...). Hence, a niche exists for systems that search databases like Internet search engines search the web.

A decade of academic research has led to a number of systems that extend the keyword search paradigm to relational data, but we are not aware of any of these systems that are actively used outside the academic community. We posit that this transition has not occurred due to a host of challenges that plague research in this field. First, the evaluation of many systems remains ad hoc, and results do not seem to generalize to other datasets and query workloads. Second, many systems propose algorithms to improve performance while also adopting new functions for scoring results, and existing evaluations tend to focus on the former while ignoring the latter. Third, extant literature has not dealt with the numerous issues that surround different ranking functions. For example, although one ranking function might be shown empirically to provide higher quality search results, studies have not investigated which factors in the scoring function are responsible for the improvement.

In this paper, we focus on this last issue by examining existing ranking methods and by investigating the importance of different factors in these scoring functions. Our work is timely because many researchers to date have relied on intuition to create new scoring functions. For example, many systems assume that the relevance of a search result is negatively correlated with the total edge weight of a result. However, the literature contains little evidence for this relationship, and in this paper, we show that total edge weight is actually positively correlated with relevance. We couple our analysis of existing scoring functions with machine learning to create a new ranking scheme.

Machine learning is preferable to deriving a new scoring function by hand due to machine learning's ability to consider many potential factors and to provide confidence measures

[1]In this paper, we focus on keyword search within relational databases, and due to length, we omit the numerous techniques for searching semi-structured data.

CIKM'11, October 24–28, 2011, Glasgow, Scotland, UK.

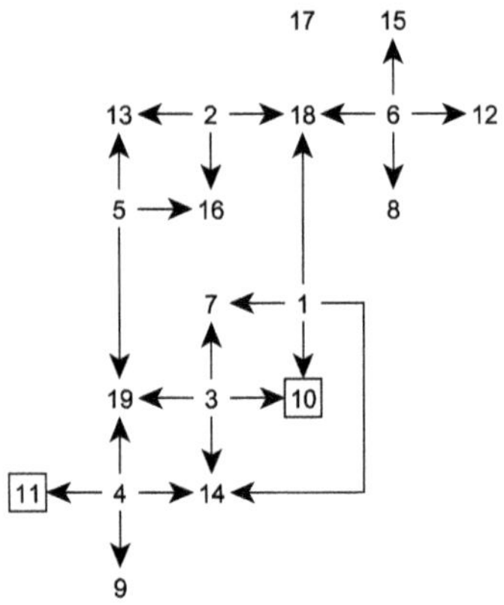

Postings	
actor	→ 14
ark	→ 18
composer	→ 17
connery	→ 11
crusade	→ 19
director	→ 16
ford	→ 10
harrison	→ 10
indiana	→ 7, 19
jones	→ 7, 9, 19
last	→ 19
raiders	→ 18
sean	→ 11
...	

Figure 1: Example of an IMDb data graph (left) and a portion of its inverted index (right).

for its results. Moreover, scoring functions typically include a number of parameters that have previously been tuned by researchers using a small number of test queries. It is reasonable to believe that significant improvement is possible simply by applying better tuning methodologies (e.g., via machine learning). In our evaluation using a diverse set of datasets and queries, we show that our scoring function, which includes many factors identified in existing work, significantly improves upon the retrieval effectiveness of state-of-the-art systems.

1.1 Example of Relational Keyword Search

As an example of relational keyword search, consider the data graph and the portion of its associated inverted index shown in Figure 1. Furthermore, assume that the user wants to identify the relationship between "Harrison Ford" and "Sean Connery" (e.g., to determine if they have appeared together in any films). To start, the inverted index must be scanned to identify nodes (tuples) that contain the search terms. In our example, nodes 10 and 11 both match disjoint subsets of the search terms. Hence, it is not appropriate to return each individual node as a search result because each node by itself does not address the relationship between the search terms. Search heuristics are typically used to identify these relationships. In this case, nodes 10 and 11 are related by the path 10–3–**14**–4–11 and by the path 10–3–**19**–4–11. These two relationships can be described loosely as "both are actors" (10–3–**14**–4–11) and "both appeared in the film *Indiana Jones and the Last Crusade*" (10–3–**19**–4–11).

The aforementioned steps cover the *enumeration* of search results. Enumeration is distinct from *ranking*, where the list of results is ordered by each result's estimated relevance to the user's information need. In our example, the latter result (both appeared in the film *Indiana Jones and the Last Crusade*) should appear before the former (both are actors). The existing literature includes a host of different ranking strategies, but little analysis of why particular strategies perform better than others.

1.2 Contributions and Outline

In this paper, we use machine learning to investigate the importance of different factors when ranking search results. The major contributions of this work are as follows.

- We review existing scoring functions and show that they have become increasingly complex over the past decade. More recent scoring functions introduce additional features that increase the number of free parameters, but previous work does not address issues related to tuning these parameters.
- We use ordinal regression to learn a linear function for scoring search results. Our scoring function significantly outperforms existing systems at high recall levels.
- We simplify our scoring function by reducing the total number of factors that are included and show that many factors can be eliminated without significantly sacrificing search quality.
- We compare our simplified scoring function against more conventional alternatives. Even though the alternatives are computationally more expensive, they do not improve search quality.

The remainder of this paper is organized as follows. In Section 2, we present background material—existing scoring functions and how to use machine learning to weight the features of a scoring function. Section 3 describes the creation of our scoring function. We evaluate our scoring function against an established benchmark for relational keyword search and show that it outperforms existing systems. Section 4 analyzes our scoring function, compares it to alternatives, and discusses the limitations of our approach. In Section 5, we review related work. Finally, we conclude and describe future work in Section 6.

2. BACKGROUND

This section starts by examining existing functions for scoring search results. Our objective is to underscore the variety of schemes that have been proposed and to illustrate the complexity of existing scoring functions. We also present machine learning as a technique to derive appropriate weights for the features in a scoring function.

2.1 Existing Scoring Functions

Tables 1 and 2 summarize the features advocated by systems that propose a novel scoring scheme. Many systems are omitted from these tables because they address performance

Table 1: Summary of scoring functions used by proximity search systems. Systems that do not propose an alternative scoring function are omitted (i.e., each row contains at least one unique definition •).

System	Features: $\|N\|$	Features: $weight(e)$	Features: $weight(n)$	Factors: $\sum_e weight(e)$	Factors: $\sum_n weight(n)$	Parameters
BANKS [1]	○	•	•	•	•	1
DISCOVER [19]	○					0
BANKS-II [22]		•	•	•	•	1
DPBF [10]		○		•		0
BLINKS [17]		•	○	•	•	3
EASE [31]		○		•		0
Golenberg *et al.* [16]		•		○		2

Legend

•	unique definition	$n \in N$	nodes in result
○	uses existing definition	e	edge in result

Table 2: Summary of IR-style scoring functions used for relational keyword search. The factors *ntf*, *ndl*, and *idf* are components of pivoted normalization weighting; ⊕ indicates the combination of attribute scores.

System	Features: $\lvert N\rvert$	Features: $\overline{\lvert N\rvert}$	Features: $\lvert N'\rvert$	Factors: *nsize*	Factors: L^2 *norm*	Factors: *ntf*	Factors: *ndl*	Factors: *idf*	Factors: ⊕	Parameters
DISCOVER-II [18]	○			○		○	○	○	●	1
Liu *et al.* [32]	○	○		●		○	●	●	●	2
SPARK [33]	○		○	●	●	○	●	●	○	4
EASE [31]						●	○	●	○	1

Legend

●	unique definition	N	nodes in result
○	uses existing definition	$\overline{\lvert N\rvert}$	average result size
⊕	attribute combination	N'	non-leaf nodes

issues (i.e., enumeration) rather than ranking. Space prevents us from presenting the actual scoring functions and a detailed discussion of the differences among the systems.[2] Instead, distinctions are indicated in the tables where a unique definition (•) differs from previous work instead of using an existing technique (○) to score results. Each row of the table contains at least one unique element. For example, although Golenberg *et al.* [16] reuse DPBF's scoring function [10] (see Table 1), they propose an alternative method to assign edge weights.

The number of "features" (that is, atomic values from a search result, user's query, or database) has increased steadily as the various scoring functions distinguish between a search result's root, leaves, interior nodes, etc. Accompanying this increase is a rise in the number of "factors" (that is, values derived from one or more features). As the number of factors increases so does the total number of free parameters, which are used to weight the importance of each factor in the final scoring function. This is problematic because tuning these parameters is expensive, requiring exploration of a low-dimensional grid of possible parameter values or heuristics that partially explore many dimensions [45]. Unfortunately, the existing literature does not suggest that these experiments are being conducted by researchers.

2.2 Machine Learning

Machine learning offers an alternative to creating scoring functions by hand and also may be used to determine the relative weights of different factors. In this case, the goal of machine learning is to determine the weight of each feature that maximizes the relevance of results. Such work is described as *ordinal regression*, which predicts the ranking of search results. Ordinal regression lies between classification—that is, predicting a categorical variable (e.g., relevant or non-relevant)—and regression—that is, predicting a real number as a function of inputs.

Given a document collection $C = \{d_1, d_2, \ldots, d_n\}$ and query Q, the objective of an IR system is to provide a ranking σ that optimally orders the documents according to their relevance to Q. A support vector machine (SVM) is a type of large-margin classifier, which attempts to maximize the decision boundary between classes. We use a *ranking SVM* in this work. The goal of a ranking (or ordinal regression) SVM is to learn a function f such that for any d_i, d_j

$$f(\phi(q, d_i)) > f(\phi(q, d_j)) \Rightarrow \sigma(d_i) > \sigma(d_j)$$

where $\phi(q, d)$ is the feature vector of the query and a document d and $\sigma(d)$ is the position of d in the optimal ranking. Let P be the set of pairs (i, j) where $\sigma(d_i) > \sigma(d_j)$. Formally, a ranking SVM optimizes

$$\min_{\vec{w}, \xi_{ij} \geq 0} \frac{1}{2} \vec{w}^T \vec{w} + \frac{C}{P} \sum_{(i,j) \in \mathcal{P}} \xi_{ij}$$

subject to

$$\forall (i, j) \in P, \vec{w}^T f(\phi(q, d_i)) \geq \vec{w}^T f(\phi(q, d_j)) + 1 - \xi_{ij}$$

where $\vec{w}$ is the decision hyperplane that separates different classes (ranks) and ξ is a slack variable that allows for training errors. The function f identifies the ideal weights for each feature by minimizing the number of pairs that are swapped (with regard to the optimal ranking) when training the SVM.

3. MODEL

This section describes the creation and evaluation of our model for scoring relational keyword search results.

3.1 Features

The features included in any scoring function should be efficient to compute and highly correlated with the ideal ranking of the search results [16]. From our review of existing scoring functions, we identified 10 different features that are used in 8 different factors. Some features included in previous work cannot be computed efficiently. For example, calculating the average number of nodes in the set of results ($\overline{\lvert N\rvert}$) requires enumerating all results for each query. Including this feature in a scoring function immediately precludes top-k query processing schemes.

We derive 12 different factors from the features present in existing scoring functions. Our additional factors revolve around simple ways to combine multi-valued features (e.g., averaging the edge weights). Table 3 lists all our factors. Note that some of our factors subsume the features shown in Tables 1 and 2. For example, pivoted normalization weighting [42] includes *ntf*, *ndl*, and *idf* factors. Rather than considering these factors in isolation, we only use their combination in pivoted normalization weighting, which is a state-of-the-art scoring function [41].

Our factors are generally a superset of those included in previous work, but we do not explore all the variations of these factors that appear in the literature because doing so would greatly expand the search space. For example, there are nearly 100 different formulations of pivoted normalization weighting alone if all the proposed factors are considered independently. In addition, several factors have been created to improve the tractability of enumerating search results (e.g., distinct root semantics [17, 22]), and these factors are typically compared to more traditional methods for scoring results (in this case, minimizing the total edge weight), which we do include.

Given the variety of existing techniques to calculate the value of each factor, we chose one instead of exploring all the alternatives. We use BLINKS's formula for deriving the

[2]For additional coverage of this material, we refer the reader to an extended version of this paper [8].

Table 3: Correlations between factors and the relevance of results ($p < 0.01$). Larger absolute values indicate stronger correlations.

Factor	r	ρ	τ
$\|N\|$	-0.007	-0.041	-0.045
$\|E\|$	-0.007	-0.041	-0.045
$\min weight(e)$	-0.096	-0.039	-0.036
$\max weight(e)$	0.149	0.243	0.215
$\sum weight(e)$	0.048	0.142	0.123
$\overline{weight(e)}$	0.113	0.172	0.154
$\min weight(n)$	0.043	0.008	0.005
$\max weight(n)$	-0.097	-0.009	-0.010
$\sum weight(n)$	-0.095	0.035	0.026
$\overline{weight(n)}$	-0.095	0.031	0.024
pivoted normalization	0.264	0.389	0.310
Euclidean (L^2) distance	-0.132	-0.219	-0.207

weights of edges in the data graph:

$$weight(e) = \ln(1 + out(u)) \quad (1)$$

where e is an edge from u to v and $out(u)$ is the outdegree of u. Node weights are computed using the PageRank algorithm [2], which is the most common method in the literature. Pivoted normalization's document-related factors are computed over an entire search result and collection statistics are taken from the entire database. Unlike traditional IR, the collection (and consequently its statistics) is not well-defined when searching semi-structured and relational data.[3] Our decision to use statistics from a complete search result and the entire database follows Robertson *et al.*'s previous work [38] and techniques from XML retrieval [5].

Correlating Scoring Factors with Relevance

Before we present the creation of our learned scoring function, we present the correlation between each factor and the relevance of search results. We consider three different measures of the correlation between each factor and relevance: Pearson's r, which measures the degree of linear relationship [39]; Spearman's p, which measures the degree of dependence with any monotonic function [43]; and Kendall's τ, which is the number of bubble-sort swaps required to transform one list into another [26]. Kendall's τ is perhaps the best metric for comparing ordinal correlations [20], but we also report Pearson's r and Spearman's p because they are more common. In general, the trends are similar regardless of the measurement used.

Table 3 summarizes our findings. Note that none of the correlations are particularly strong although all the values are significant at the 0.01 level. Pivoted normalization weighting is moderately correlated with relevance. The Euclidean distance (which is 0 if the result contains all terms present in the query Q and 1 if the result does not contain any query terms) has one of the most negative correlations. These two results are not altogether unsurprising because pivoted normalization is a state-of-the-art scoring function and the Euclidean distance is a very coarse measure of relevance. While most relevant results will contain all the query terms, the converse is not true: a result is not relevant just because it contains the query terms—it must address the query's underlying information need.

The correlations for our different edge weight factors is extremely surprising. Note that the table simply uses the raw values of each factor. In contrast, proximity search systems minimize the weight of results. Hence, we expect a larger total edge weight ($\sum weight(e)$) to be *negatively* correlated with relevance or—stated conversely—a smaller sum should be positively correlated with relevance. Our results indicate the exact opposite: results with higher weights are more likely to be relevant than results with smaller weights! This result differs substantially from the conventional wisdom in this field, and we will return to it in our discussion of our scoring function in Section 4 and in the appendix.

3.2 Creation

We use 10-fold cross validation [27] to mitigate the threat of overfitting our scoring function. In 10-fold cross validation, the data is randomly partitioned into 10 different folds (subsets). Training uses 9 of the folds (that is, 90% of the original data), and the model is tested against the final fold. This process is repeated so each fold is used exactly once to test the model.

We use SVM^{rank} [21] to learn the weight for each factor in our scoring function. SVM^{rank} is designed to efficiently solve ordinal regression problems and operates on a set of training instances. The training instances are derived from potential query results, and each instance consists of a feature vector of all the factors that we include in our scoring function and the ideal rank of the result.

Because different enumeration algorithms have been shown to omit results [16], we pool the top-1000 results returned by 9 different systems [1, 7, 10, 17, 18, 19, 22, 32, 33] to create the set of training instances. Pooling ensures that we consider as many different query and result semantics as possible and increases the generality of our scoring function.

Binary relevance judgments are distributed as part of the test collection. While these judgments would be sufficient to train a classifier, they are not suitable for ordinal regression, and the limited number potentially could diminish training effectiveness. We augment the binary relevance judgments with marginal relevance judgments of the results returned by each system. Given a large number of factors and available training instances (see Table 4), a SVM may fail to terminate within a timely fashion. We give the SVM 1% of the available training instances and ignore the remainder. This subset always includes all the ideal (completely relevant) results and—if possible—at least as many marginally relevant and irrelevant results as the number of ideal results to ensure the training set covers the gamut of available relevance judgments.

3.3 Evaluation

We use a publicly available evaluation benchmark in our experiments. We briefly describe the datasets and queries but refer the reader to its original description [6] for additional details.

The evaluation workload includes three datasets: MONDIAL, the Internet Movie Database (IMDb), and Wikipedia.

[3] It is straightforward to show that calculating exact collection statistics in the context of relational keyword search requires violating desirable properties of the original IR scoring function [18, 32], estimation [33], or enumeration of all possible search results *a priori* [31].

Table 4: Characteristics of the evaluation datasets and number of training instances available.

	Evaluation		Training
Dataset	Tuples	Size (MB)	Instances
MONDIAL	17K	10	33500
IMDb	1.7M	427	132175
Wikipedia	200K	378	119969

Two datasets (IMDb and Wikipedia) are derived from popular websites. The MONDIAL database [34] contains geographical, political, and demographic information.The IMDb database, which is a subset of the original, was constructed from the IMDb's plain text files using IMDbPY 4.1. The Wikipedia database is drawn from the English Wikipedia and includes all the articles chosen for the 2008–2009 Wikipedia schools DVD. Table 4 summarizes the characteristics of the datasets.

The query workload distributed with the benchmark comprises 50 synthetic information needs for each dataset. While these information needs are not sampled from search engine query logs, they are designed to be representative of the types of queries users submit to search engines. In particular, the statistics of the supplied queries are similar to those encountered by web search engines.

Examining the existing binary relevance judgments suggests that they should be viewed as the *ideal recall-base* for each query. The ideal recall-base includes all non-overlapping results [29]. In recent years, evaluation forums have moved toward marginal relevance judgments, and systems should return results in decreasing order of their estimated marginal relevance. Hence, we extend the supplied relevance judgments by creating the *full recall-base*, which includes all results that have any relevance to the query. We construct the full recall-base by pooling the results returned by each system, and any result that completely overlaps an ideal result is judged marginally relevant.[4] We adopt the practice used at the Initiative for the Evaluation of XML retrieval (INEX) workshop for assigning relevance scores: the marginal relevance of a result is the ratio of relevant information to the total information [29, 30]. Issues related to overlap have been investigated in the context of XML retrieval [25] so we do not explore them further in this paper.

3.3.1 Metrics

We use a variety of metrics to evaluate our work. Precision is the ratio of the number of relevant documents retrieved to the total number of documents retrieved. When computing precision, we define the set of relevant results to include all results that have any relevance—i.e., they may only be marginally relevant to the query.

Precision @ k (P@k) is the mean precision value at a fixed retrieval depth (e.g., the first 10 results returned by a system). Mean reciprocal rank (MRR) is the reciprocal of the rank of the first relevant result retrieved by a system. Although neither of these metrics is robust, we report them to enable more direct comparison with previous evaluations. Average precision (AP) is the mean of the precision values calculated after each relevant result is returned. Any relevant result not retrieved receives a score of 0. Mean average precision (MAP) averages this value across all queries to compute a single-valued measurement of retrieval effectiveness. Normalized discounted cumulative gain (nDCG) was designed for evaluations with non-binary (i.e., marginal) relevance assessments. The family of cumulative gain metrics rewards systems that return results in the order of their relevance to the query.

Because our focus is ranking search results, we do not address the runtime performance or efficiency of any system. Result enumeration is largely orthogonal to ranking, and our objective in this paper is to investigate scoring results.[5]

3.3.2 Systems

We compare our learned scoring function, SVM rank, to 9 other relational keyword search systems. We implemented 6 systems (BANKS [1], DISCOVER [19], DISCOVER-II [18], Liu *et al.* [32], SPARK [33], and cover density ranking (CD) [7]) ourselves and obtained implementations of the other 3 systems (BANKS-II [22], DPBF [10], and BLINKS [17]). While we would like to compare our scoring function against all other systems described in the literature, little sharing of their source code hampers this objective.

All the systems adhere to their original description[6] although we did correct a number of minor deficiencies that we found in their specification or implementation. For each system, we set all tuning parameters to the values suggested by the authors. If a system failed due to exhausting virtual memory ($>$ 2.7 GB), our results include anything output prior to the error. A system's omission from a table or figure indicates that no query returned even a single result on that particular dataset.

3.3.3 Results

Table 5 presents our results for P@k. Our results are similar to those previously reported [6]; the minor deviations are due to our full recall-base, which increases the total number of relevant results. On MONDIAL and Wikipedia, SVM rank lags slightly behind the best systems for P@1, but it scores best for P@10. However, SVM rank falters on the IMDb dataset, scoring only half as well as the best systems, which is likely due to their slight variations on our scoring factors. For example, BANKS uses a different edge weighting scheme than SVM rank. We note that SVM rank outperforms the systems that share exactly the same factors.

The results for MRR (Table 6) are very similar to the results of P@k. In fact, the relative performance of each system compared to the others is largely unchanged from P@1. SVM rank continues to provide excellent performance on the MONDIAL and Wikipedia datasets but is only average for IMDb.

In Figure 2, we present MAP (left) for each system and dataset. SVM rank nearly doubles the performance of any previous system on the MONDIAL dataset and also outscores the other systems for Wikipedia queries. On the IMDb dataset, SVM rank is edged out by cover density ranking.

[4] Unlike XML, which is tree-structured, relational keyword search systems create result trees from a data graph. We define two results as overlapping when one is a subset of the other and not when they merely share tuples in common.

[5] In some instances, combining enumeration and ranking (i.e., enumerating the top-k results in the order their final ranking) improves performance; we leave this task for future work due to the intricacies involved in their integration.

[6] The implementation of Liu *et al.*'s work [32] does not include phrase-based ranking.

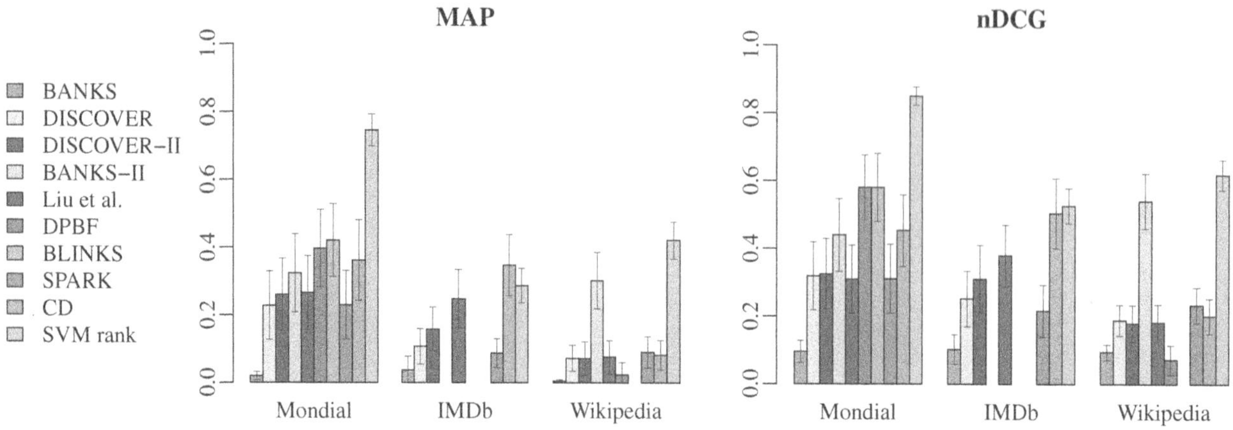

Figure 2: MAP ($\in [0, 1]$, higher is better) and NDCG ($\in [0, 1]$, higher is better) for each system and dataset. Systems are ordered by date of publication, top to bottom in the legend and left to right in the graphs. Omitted bars indicate that the system failed to retrieve *any* results for any query. The error bars provide 95% confidence intervals for the mean.

Cover density ranking uses a unique scoring scheme that differs dramatically from other systems and includes features not considered in our model. The results for MAP are considerably lower than those of P@k and MRR due to many systems failing to enumerate all the relevant results (e.g., due to different search semantics). Unlike P@k and MRR, these results differ dramatically from those previously reported [6],

Table 5: P@k ($\in [0, 1]$, higher is better) for the systems on each dataset; the best score for each dataset is bolded. Omitted values indicate that the system failed to retrieve *any* results for any query.

$k = 1$

System	Mondial	IMDb	Wikipedia
BANKS [1]	0.420	**0.540**	0.500
DISCOVER [19]	0.620	0.140	0.120
DISCOVER-II [18]	0.580	0.120	0.180
BANKS-II [22]	0.720		0.500
Liu *et al.* [32]	0.660	0.400	**0.640**
DPBF [10]	0.740		0.020
BLINKS [17]	0.720		
SPARK [33]	0.560	0.100	0.280
Cover Density [7]	**0.780**	0.380	0.540
SVM rank	0.753	0.220	0.540

$k = 10$

System	Mondial	IMDb	Wikipedia
BANKS [1]	0.132	0.206	0.094
DISCOVER [19]	0.385	0.120	0.140
DISCOVER-II [18]	0.417	0.166	0.173
BANKS-II [22]	0.442		0.190
Liu *et al.* [32]	0.429	**0.440**	0.227
DPBF [10]	0.438		0.048
BLINKS [17]	0.594		
SPARK [33]	0.375	0.114	0.216
Cover Density [7]	0.588	0.388	0.452
SVM rank	**0.744**	0.221	**0.540**

which again is attributable to using our full recall-base in lieu of the ideal recall-base supplied with the evaluation framework.

Figure 2 also shows nDCG (right) for each system and dataset. In terms of the relative rank of each system, these results are similar to MAP. However, nDCG is designed to reward systems that rank more relevant results ahead of less relevant results. We see several examples of systems that significantly improve under nDCG; indeed every system improves at least slightly compared to MAP. SVM rank shows a moderate boost in its measured effectiveness; this improvement is sufficient for SVM rank to edge cover density ranking as the best system on the IMDb dataset, which indicates that SVM rank is more likely than cover density ranking to rank more relevant results ahead of less relevant results.

4. DISCUSSION

In this section, we analyze the linear function that we used to score search results. We show that many features may be eliminated without having a significant impact on search quality. We also discuss the limitations of our approach.

Table 6: MRR ($\in [0, 1]$, higher is better) for the systems on each dataset; the best score for each dataset is bolded. Omitted values indicate that the system failed to retrieve *any* results for any query.

System	Mondial	IMDb	Wikipedia
BANKS [1]	0.488	**0.608**	0.558
DISCOVER [19]	0.676	0.196	0.241
DISCOVER-II [18]	0.647	0.202	0.394
BANKS-II [22]	0.781		0.591
Liu *et al.* [32]	0.683	0.446	**0.748**
DPBF [10]	0.825		0.111
BLINKS [17]	0.771		
SPARK [33]	0.627	0.171	0.492
Cover Density [7]	**0.849**	0.456	0.619
SVM rank	0.834	0.332	0.613

Table 7: **Comparison (nDCG) of SVM rank trained using different cross folds. The "baseline" is graphed in Figure 2.**

	nDCG		
Dataset	baseline	μ	σ
MONDIAL	0.849	0.862	0.006
IMDb	0.527	0.525	0.002
Wikipedia	0.618	0.621	0.007

4.1 Analysis of Model

Using machine learning to create our scoring function potentially introduces several sources of error in our results. We consider these sources to show that their effect is negligible before moving on to feature selection.

4.1.1 Sensitivity

As mentioned previously, we use cross validation to train and to test our scoring function. Because cross validation requires randomly partitioning the query workload, it is possible that the partitions bias the results. To investigate this possibility, we compare retrieval effectiveness across 10 different random partitions (i.e., we repeat the cross validation 10 times). The results are shown in Table 7. As evidenced by the table, different cross folds do not significantly impact our results.

A second source of possible error in our results stems from using a fraction of the available training instances. Table 8 provides the search effectiveness from different percentages of training instances where we randomize the set of training instances included at each level. Because we ensure that all the ideal results are retained for each query, doubling the percentage does not exactly double the number of training instances. The table also shows that increasing the number of training instances increases the time required to train the model, from approximately 5 minutes (per fold) for 0.5% to almost 20 minutes for 3.0%. However, the impact that the training percentage has on search effectiveness is negligible. MAP sees moderate improvement when moving from 0.5% to 3.0%, but the impact on nDCG is much smaller.

4.1.2 Feature Selection

Feature selection tries to reduce the number of factors in the scoring function without significantly impacting search effectiveness. We start with our baseline scoring function that includes 12 different factors and then identify the factor with the lowest weight (that is, it contributes least to the final ranking) and train a new model without that factor. This process is then repeated.

Table 8: Average number of training instances and average training time across all cross-folds for different percentages of training instances. MAP and nDCG improve only slightly with more training instances.

	Training		Effectiveness	
%	Instances	Time (s)	MAP	nDCG
0.5	2279	298	0.457	0.657
1.0	3430	321	0.489	0.663
2.0	5909	550	0.509	0.664
3.0	8453	1024	0.516	0.667

While greedy backward selection is non-optimal—finding the optimal requires searching all possible combinations of factors [28]—it does provide a simple measure of the importance of each factor. We note that there is overlap among our factors: a principal component analysis shows that 98% of the variability can be attributed to 6 different components. Hence, we should be able to remove a number of factors without significantly impacting search quality.

Table 9 shows nDCG as we remove factors from our scoring function. Note that the number of factors removed is cumulative—i.e., the first variation is SVM rank without $\max weight(n)$ and the second variation is SVM rank without $\max weight(n)$ and without $\sum weight(n)$. The final variation, SVM rank (minimal), includes the factors *not* appearing in the table: $\min weight(n)$ and pivoted normalization. As evidenced by the table, retrieval effectiveness remains largely unchanged as several factors are removed. However, performance drops precipitously when the fourth factor (the Euclidean distance between a result and the query) is removed. This impact is most noticeable for the MONDIAL dataset. We posit that this factor is very noisy, having almost no impact for many queries but is very important for a few.

We can remove all but two factors from our scoring function without seriously impacting search effectiveness. Retrieval effectiveness actually improves on the Wikipedia dataset as we eliminate additional features. This trend is not completely surprising given that pivoted normalization weighting was developed by the IR community to score lengthy text documents and the Wikipedia articles are most similar to this use case.

4.2 Comparison with Alternative Functions

If we take the order in which we remove features (see Table 9) to be indicative of their importance, we would conclude that node weights (with the exception of the minimum node weight, which is included in SVM rank (minimal)) are relatively unimportant when ranking search results. Similarly, the total sum of edge weights is the first edge-based factor to be dropped. This result clashes sharply with conventional wisdom in this field. In particular, all proximity search systems attempt to rank search results in order of their total edge weight. Strangely enough, we find that other factors (e.g., the minimum edge weight) are more indicative of relevance as evidenced by its stronger correlation with relevance (see Table 3) and by its longer retention in feature selection. We hope that this opens the door for future debate regarding the design of new scoring functions.

In Figure 3, we consider our two versions of SVM rank and two alternatives that score search results more conventionally. We compare SVM rank (minimal), which includes only 2 factors ($\min weight(n)$ and pivoted normalization), to one using pivoted normalization and $\sum weight(e)$ and to one using $\sum weight(n)$ and $\sum weight(e)$. Both of these scoring functions are more similar to those proposed in previous work. The weights for the various factors are determined using SVM^{rank}; hence, the alternatives may be viewed as a rough upper bound of the search effectiveness of existing techniques. As evidenced in the figure, both SVM rank and SVM rank (minimal) always outperforms the more conventional scoring functions. We conclude—contrary to the established norm in this area—that ranking results by their total edge weight

Table 9: Comparison of retrieval effectiveness when removing factors (listed in Table 3) from the scoring function. The factors that have been removed are *cumulative*—i.e., the second variation of SVM rank (the 3rd row of the table) does not include $\max weight(n)$ **or** $\sum weight(n)$**. SVM rank (minimal) includes the 2 factors that were *not* removed:** $\min weight(n)$ **and pivoted normalization. It is the same as the next-to-last row of the table (but is duplicated for clarity). The best score for each dataset is bolded.**

Removal		Mondial			IMDb			Wikipedia		
			Improvement			Improvement			Improvement	
Order	Factor	NDCG	Δ	%	NDCG	Δ	%	NDCG	Δ	%
SVM rank		0.849	—	—	**0.527**	—	—	0.618	—	—
1	$\max weight(n)$	0.854	0.005	0.6	0.525	-0.002	-0.4	0.627	0.009	1.5
2	$\sum weight(n)$	**0.866**	**0.017**	**2.0**	0.515	-0.012	-2.3	0.630	0.012	1.9
3	$\overline{weight(n)}$	0.855	0.006	0.7	0.518	-0.009	-1.7	0.616	-0.002	-0.3
4	Euclidean (L^2) distance	0.673	-0.177	-20.8	0.454	-0.073	-13.6	0.560	-0.058	-7.7
5	$\sum weight(e)$	0.681	-0.169	-19.9	0.464	-0.063	-12.0	0.576	-0.042	-6.8
6	$\|N\|$	0.679	-0.170	-20.0	0.446	-0.081	-15.4	0.580	-0.038	-6.1
7	$\max weight(e)$	0.676	-0.173	-20.4	0.456	-0.071	-13.5	0.573	-0.045	-7.3
8	$\overline{weight(e)}$	0.691	-0.158	-18.6	0.469	-0.058	-9.4	**0.634**	**0.016**	**2.8**
9	$\|E\|$	0.711	-0.139	-16.4	0.494	-0.033	-6.3	0.619	0.001	0.2
10	$\min weight(e)$	0.772	-0.077	-9.1	0.495	-0.032	-6.1	0.623	0.005	0.8
SVM rank (minimal)		0.772	-0.077	-9.1	0.495	-0.032	-6.1	0.623	0.005	0.8

is not an ideal ranking scheme. This conclusion overturns general intuition and questions the importance of algorithms that attempt to enumerate results in the order of their total edge weight. We refer the interested reader to the appendix for further discussion of this result.

4.3 Threats to Validity

There are several factors that may have impacted our evaluation. First, our results are dependent on our evaluation datasets. As mentioned previously, our evaluation includes 3 diverse datasets with a large query workload for each so the likelihood that our results generalize to other databases is high. Second, we do not address the enumeration of results in this work. A variety of enumeration algorithms has already been proposed; it would be straightforward to marry our scoring function with any one of these algorithms.

Our work uses a linear SVM to fit a linear function for scoring results. This decision follows naturally from most existing relational keyword search scoring functions, which are linear. In contrast, most scoring functions used by the IR community are non-linear and include—for example—logarithmic damping of term frequency and inverse document frequency. Although our edge weighting scheme is non-linear, we combine all our factors linearly, and it is certainly possible for a different combination function to provide even better results.

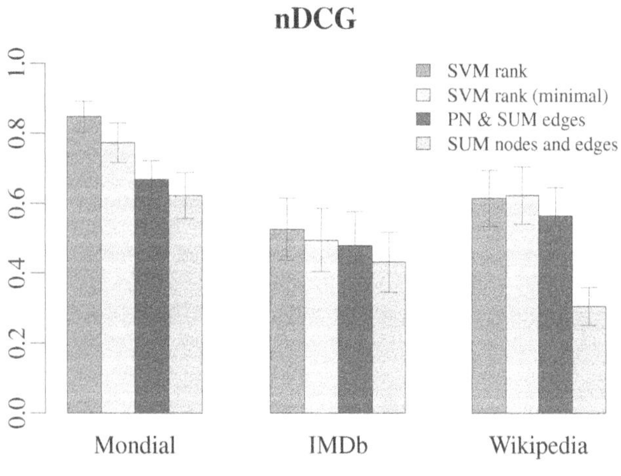

Figure 3: Comparison of retrieval effectiveness among SVM rank and traditional scoring functions proposed in the literature.

5. RELATED WORK

A dichotomy exists within relational keyword search systems. Proximity search endeavors to minimize the distance between search terms within a data graph. While minimizing the total edge weight is NP-hard [36] (it is equivalent to the group Steiner tree problem [11]), different semantics allow more efficient enumeration of results. Schema-based approaches identify search results by executing queries against the relational database, and many of these systems have adopted IR-style scoring functions to rank the search results. Yu *et al.* [46] provide an excellent survey of relational keyword search.

BANKS [1] proposed the backward expanding search heuristic to enumerate search results. BANKS-II [22] uses the bidirectional search heuristic to alleviate performance problems. DPBF [10] finds the optimal group Steiner tree via a dynamic programming algorithm. BLINKS [17] creates a two-level index to improve enumeration performance. EASE [31] precomputes all r-radius Steiner graphs within a data graph and ranks search results with both structural compactness and IR-style scoring factors. Golenberg *et al.* [16] enumerate search results in approximate order by height rather than weight. Dalvi *et al.* [9] investigate keyword search on data graphs that do not fit within main memory. STAR [23] provides a pseudo-polynomial time algorithm to identify search results.

DISCOVER [19] was an early system that executed SQL queries to identify potential search results. DISCOVER-II [18] adopted pivoted normalization for ranking search results and also provided efficient query processing algorithms. Liu *et al.* [32] proposed a variety of modifications and additional factors for pivoted normalization. SPARK [33] proposed new query processing techniques to handle its non-monotonic scoring function. Qin *et al.* [35] address query processing techniques under different query semantics. Structured cover density ranking [7] ranks search results in decreasing order of their coordination with the query terms.

The major focus for much of this previous work is the enumeration of search results. The significant amount of work on enumeration algorithms complements our work, for our scoring function can be used to re-rank results following their enumeration (as proposed by Golenberg *et al.* [16]). We note that further improvements in enumeration algorithms are likely when the scoring function need not minimize the total edge weight of results. Coffman and Weaver [6] analyze the various ranking schemes that appear in the literature. SVM rank outperforms 9 of 11 existing ranking schemes. The primary reasons that we did not compare our work to the remaining scoring functions are little sharing of source code and significant reimplementation effort.

To the best of our knowledge, using machine learning to explore how to weight different factors when scoring search results has not been previously investigated in the context of relational keyword search. Machine learning in IR is a well-studied topic. Sebastiani [40] provides an overview of automated text categorization. Joachims [20] applies ordinal regression to clickstream data and shows that the learned function outperforms existing search engines. Burges *et al.* [3] and Richardson *et al.* [37] also apply learning to rank to web search. Cao *et al.* [4] address how to adapt ranking SVMs to document retrieval. Geng *et al.* [13] consider the problem of feature selection and proposes an approach based on the importance and similarity of the various features. Joachims [20] and Richardson *et al.*'s [37] work is closest to our own, but our context and the features that we consider both differ. Incorporating Cao *et al.*'s work [4] on ranking SVMs would have undoubtedly improved our search effectiveness for P@k and MRR, the instances where SVM rank was only comparable to existing systems.

6. CONCLUSION AND FUTURE WORK

Although many scoring functions for relational keyword search have been proposed in the literature, relatively little work has considered their effectiveness when ranking results. Instead, researchers have relied on intuition and anecdotal evidence without extensive experiments to determine whether or not various factors are indicative of relevance. In this work, we consider factors that have been previously proposed in the literature, and we show that many existing scoring functions—indeed complete systems—have been constructed around factors that are not highly correlated with relevance. The best example is identifying group Steiner trees, which is the goal of many systems. We use machine learning to create a new scoring function, which outperforms existing approaches. Finally, we simplify our scoring function by eliminating all the features except the minimum node weight and pivoted normalization and show that it continues to outperform existing approaches.

In the future, we would like to investigate the variation in search effectiveness from different formulations of the same feature. For example, different methods for assigning edge weights in the data graph could alter our results; we note that this question has not been addressed by any previous work in this field. We would also like to investigate non-linear scoring functions.

As a challenge to the research community, differentiating the separate steps of enumeration and ranking would lend clarity to these largely orthogonal issues. In particular, research focused on enumeration algorithms should reuse existing scoring functions (to the greatest extent possible) so as not to merge evaluations of performance with search effectiveness. Likewise, new ranking schemes should not only be compared to existing systems, but an analysis of the various factors (i.e., their impact on search effectiveness) should also be provided.

7. ACKNOWLEDGMENTS

Ray Buse provided insight on how to conduct this study and helpful comments regarding drafts of this paper. We thank Ding *et al.* and He *et al.* for sharing implementations of systems that we included in our evaluation.

References

[1] G. Bhalotia, A. Hulgeri, C. Nakhe, S. Chakrabarti, and S. Sudarshan. Keyword Searching and Browsing in Databases using BANKS. In *ICDE '02*, pages 431–440, February 2002.

[2] S. Brin and L. Page. The anatomy of a large-scale hypertextual Web search engine. *Computer Networks and ISDN Systems*, 30(1-7):107–117, 1998.

[3] C. Burges, T. Shaked, E. Renshaw, A. Lazier, M. Deeds, N. Hamilton, and G. Hullender. Learning to Rank using Gradient Descent. In *ICML '05*, pages 89–96, 2005.

[4] Y. Cao, J. Xu, T.-Y. Liu, H. Li, Y. Huang, and H.-W. Hon. Adapting Ranking SVM to Document Retrieval. In *SIGIR '06*, pages 186–193, 2006.

[5] C. L. A. Clarke. Controlling Overlap in Content-Oriented XML Retrieval. In *SIGIR '05*, pages 314–321, 2005.

[6] J. Coffman and A. C. Weaver. A Framework for Evaluating Database Keyword Search Strategies. In *CIKM '10*, pages 729–738, October 2010.

[7] J. Coffman and A. C. Weaver. Structured Data Retrieval using Cover Density Ranking. In *KEYS '10*, pages 1–6, June 2010.

[8] J. Coffman and A. C. Weaver. Learning to Rank Results in Relational Keyword Search. Technical Report CS-2011-06, University of Virginia, 2011.

[9] B. B. Dalvi, M. Kshirsagar, and S. Sudarshan. Keyword Search on External Memory Data Graphs. *PVLDB*, 1(1):1189–1204, 2008.

[10] B. Ding, J. X. Yu, S. Wang, L. Qin, X. Zhang, and X. Lin. Finding Top-k Min-Cost Connected Trees in Databases. In *ICDE '07*, pages 836–845, April 2007.

[11] S. E. Dreyfus and R. A. Wagner. The Steiner Problem in Graphs. *Networks*, 1(3):195–207, 1971.

[12] S. Fox. Search engines. Technical report, Pew Internet and American Life Project, July 2002. `http://www.pewinternet.org/Reports/2002/Search-Engines.aspx`.

[13] X. Geng, T.-Y. Liu, T. Qin, and H. Li. Feature Selection for Ranking. In *SIGIR '07*, pages 407–414, 2007.

[14] Global Search Market Grows 46 Percent in 2009. `http://www.comscore.com/Press_Events/Press_Releases/2010/1/Global_Search_Market_Grows_46_Percent_in_2009`, January 2010.

[15] R. Goldman, N. Shivakumar, S. Venkatasubramanian, and H. Garcia-Molina. Proximity Search in Databases. In *VLDB '98*, pages 26–37, August 1998.

[16] K. Golenberg, B. Kimelfeld, and Y. Sagiv. Keyword Proximity Search in Complex Data Graphs. In *SIGMOD '08*, pages 927–940, June 2008.

[17] H. He, H. Wang, J. Yang, and P. S. Yu. BLINKS: Ranked Keyword Searches on Graphs. In *SIGMOD '07*, pages 305–316, June 2007.
[18] V. Hristidis, L. Gravano, and Y. Papakonstantinou. Efficient IR-style Keyword Search over Relational Databases. In *VLDB '03*, pages 850–861, September 2003.
[19] V. Hristidis and Y. Papakonstantinou. DISCOVER: Keyword Search in Relational Databases. In *VLDB '02*, pages 670–681. VLDB Endowment, August 2002.
[20] T. Joachims. Optimizing Search Engines using Clickthrough Data. In *KDD '02*, pages 133–142, 2002.
[21] T. Joachims. Training linear SVMs in linear time. In *KDD '06*, pages 217–226, August 2006.
[22] V. Kacholia, S. Pandit, S. Chakrabarti, S. Sudarshan, R. Desai, and H. Karambelkar. Bidirectional Expansion For Keyword Search on Graph Databases. In *VLDB '05*, pages 505–516, August 2005.
[23] G. Kasneci, M. Ramanath, M. Sozio, F. M. Suchanek, and G. Weikum. STAR: Steiner-Tree Approximation in Relationship Graphs. In *ICDE '09*, pages 868–879, March 2009.
[24] G. Kasneci, F. M. Suchanek, G. Ifrim, M. Ramanath, and G. Weikum. NAGA: Searching and Ranking Knowledge. In *ICDE '08*, pages 953–962, April 2008.
[25] J. Kekäläinen, M. Junkkari, P. Arvola, and T. Aalto. TRIX 2004 – Struggling with the Overlap. In N. Fuhr, M. Lalmas, S. Malik, and Z. Szlávik, editors, *Advances in XML Information Retrieval*, volume 3493 of *LNCS*, pages 145–162. Springer, 2005.
[26] M. Kendall. A New Measure of Rank Correlation. *Biometrika*, 30(1/2):81–93, June 1938.
[27] R. Kohavi. A Study of Cross-Validation and Bootstrap for Accuracy Estimation and Model Selection. In *IJCAI*, volume 2, pages 1137–1143, 1995.
[28] R. Kohavi and G. H. John. Wrappers for feature subset selection. *Artificial Intelligence*, 97(1–2):273–324, 1997.
[29] M. Lalmas, G. Kazai, J. Kamps, J. Pehcevski, B. Piwowarski, and S. Robertson. INEX 2006 Evaluation Measures. In N. Fuhr, M. Lalmas, and A. Trotman, editors, *Comparative Evaluation of XML Information Retrieval Systems*, volume 4518 of *LNCS*, pages 20–34. Springer, 2007.
[30] M. Lalmas and A. Tombros. INEX 2002 - 2006: Understanding XML Retrieval Evaluation. In C. Thanos, F. Borri, and L. Candela, editors, *Digital Libraries: Research and Development*, volume 4877 of *LNCS*, pages 187–196. Springer, 2007.
[31] G. Li, B. C. Ooi, J. Feng, J. Wang, and L. Zhou. EASE: An Effective 3-in-1 Keyword Search Method for Unstructured, Semi-structured and Structured Data. In *SIGMOD '08*, pages 903–914, June 2008.
[32] F. Liu, C. Yu, W. Meng, and A. Chowdhury. Effective Keyword Search in Relational Databases. In *SIGMOD '06*, pages 563–574, June 2006.
[33] Y. Luo, X. Lin, W. Wang, and X. Zhou. SPARK: Top-k Keyword Query in Relational Databases. In *SIGMOD '07*, pages 115–126, June 2007.
[34] W. May. Information Extraction and Integration with FLORID: The MONDIAL Case Study. Technical Report 131, Universität Freiburg, Institut für Informatik, 1999.
[35] L. Qin, J. X. Yu, and L. Chang. Keyword Search in Databases: The Power of RDBMS. In *SIGMOD '09*, pages 681–694, June 2009.
[36] G. Reich and P. Widmayer. Beyond Steiner's problem: A VLSI oriented generalization. In M. Nagl, editor, *Graph-Theoretic Concepts in Computer Science*, volume 411 of *LNCS*, pages 196–210. Springer Berlin / Heidelberg, 1990.
[37] M. Richardson, A. Prakash, and E. Brill. Beyond PageRank: Machine Learning for Static Ranking. In *WWW '06*, pages 707–715, 2006.
[38] S. Robertson, H. Zaragoza, and M. Taylor. Simple BM25 Extension to Multiple Weighted Fields. In *CIKM '04*, pages 42–49, November 2004.
[39] J. L. Rodgers and W. A. Nicewander. Thirteen Ways to Look at the Correlation Coefficient. *The American Statistician*, 42(1):59–66, February 1988.
[40] F. Sebastiani. Machine Learning in Automated Text Categorization. *ACM Computing Surveys*, 34:1–47, March 2002.
[41] A. Singhal. Modern Information Retrieval: A Brief Overview. *IEEE Data Engineering Bulletin*, 24(4):35–42, December 2001.
[42] A. Singhal, J. Choi, D. Hindle, D. Lewis, and F. Pereira. AT&T at TREC-7. In *TREC-7*, pages 239–252, November 1999.
[43] C. Spearman. The Proof and Measurement of Association between Two Things. *The American Journal of Psychology*, 15(1):72–101, January 1904.
[44] F. M. Suchanek, G. Kasneci, and G. Weikum. YAGO: A Core of Semantic Knowledge. In *WWW '07*, pages 697–706, 2007.
[45] M. Taylor, H. Zaragoza, N. Craswell, S. Robertson, and C. Burges. Optimisation Methods for Ranking Functions with Multiple Parameters. In *CIKM '06*, pages 585–593, November 2006.
[46] J. X. Yu, L. Qin, and L. Chang. *Keyword Search in Databases*. Morgan and Claypool Publishers, 1st edition, 2010.

APPENDIX

Justification for Minimizing Total Edge Weight

To the best of our knowledge, Goldman *et al.* [15] first proposed proximity search in databases. Intuitively, users want results that are more closely related to be ranked ahead of results that are less closely related. For example, if two nodes are connected by a single edge, this relationship is stronger than one that requires multiple edges and intermediary nodes. Goldman *et al.* [15] do not consider search effectiveness in their evaluation, but BANKS [1] provides anecdotal evidence that total edge weight is correlated with relevance. In NAGA [24] and STAR [23], Kasneci *et al.* claim that a Steiner-tree-based scoring function is correlated with relevance.

We cannot immediately reconcile these claims with our results, but we have identified three possible factors that might account for this discrepancy. First, Kasneci *et al.* search the YAGO knowledge base [44], which includes millions of facts connected by predefined relationships. Its structure is considerably different from the graphs created from a relational database, and NAGA's evaluation [24] did not include graphs created from relational data. Second, NAGA [24] does indicate that its weighting of graph edges (based on the strength of its beliefs regarding each relationship) outperforms BANKS's scoring function [1], which cannot capture the informativeness of different relationships. Hence, alternative edge weighting schemes might produce different results. BANKS significantly outperforms SVM rank on the IMDb dataset for the highest ranked results (see the P@1 and MRR results), and one possible reason is its different method for assigning edge weights. A formal examination of these different edge weighting schemes would undoubtedly be useful for future work in this area. Third, the general intuition—results should be composed of closely related tuples—seems valid, particularly for identifying the *most relevant* result, but it may not be as good at identifying marginally relevant results, which would cause it to perform worse at higher recall levels (e.g., on MAP and nDCG). Again, a formal study of this phenomenon seems prudent for future work in this area.

Adding Structure to Top-K: From Items to Expansions

Xueyao Liang
Dept. of Computer Science,
Univ. of British Columbia
liangxue@cs.ubc.ca

Min Xie
Dept. of Computer Science,
Univ. of British Columbia
minxie@cs.ubc.ca

Laks V.S. Lakshmanan
Dept. of Computer Science,
Univ. of British Columbia
laks@cs.ubc.ca

ABSTRACT

Keyword based search interfaces are extremely popular as a means for efficiently discovering items of interest from a huge collection, as evidenced by the success of search engines like Google and Bing. However, most of the current search services still return results as a flat ranked list of items. Considering the huge number of items which can match a query, this list based interface can be very difficult for the user to explore and find important items relevant to their search needs. In this work, we consider a search scenario in which each item is annotated with a set of keywords. E.g., in Web 2.0 enabled systems such as flickr and del.icio.us, it is common for users to tag items with keywords. Based on this annotation information, we can automatically group query result items into different expansions of the query corresponding to subsets of keywords. We formulate and motivate this problem within a top-k query processing framework, but as that of finding the top-k most important expansions. Then we study additional desirable properties for the set of expansions returned, and formulate the problem as an optimization problem of finding the best k expansions satisfying all the desirable properties. We propose several efficient algorithms for this problem. Our problem is similar in spirit to recent works on automatic facets generation, but has the important difference and advantage that we don't need to assume the existence of pre-defined categorical hierarchy which is critical for these works. Through extensive experiments on both real and synthetic datasets, we show our proposed algorithms are both effective and efficient.

Categories and Subject Descriptors

H.3.4 [**Information Storage and Retrieval**]: Systems and Software - Information Networks

General Terms

Algorithms

Keywords

Top-*k* Query Processing, Top-*k* Query Expansions, Semantic Redundancy, Efficiency, Keywords and Tags

CIKM'11, October 24–28, 2011, Glasgow, Scotland, UK.

1. INTRODUCTION

Keyword based search interfaces are extremely popular as a means for efficiently discovering items of interest from a huge collection, as evidenced by the success of search engines like Google [5], Bing [2] and Yahoo! [7]. However, most of the current search services still return results as a flat ranked list of items. As has been found by a recent study [8], this list-based interface can make it very difficult for the user to explore and find important items relevant to their search needs. We claim that *automatically grouping search results into semantically independent "topics" can significantly enhance the usability of the results*. Below, we discuss a few motivating examples to illustrate this point.

Consider an academic search engine like Google Scholar [1]. Though it works perfectly for those queries which target a specific paper, when handling a general purpose query like "find all papers which are relevant to the topic of database histogram", the search engine returns a huge list of papers ranked by their relevance to the query. This ranked list is difficult for user to work from for exploring papers related to the query and efficiently finding the papers they want. It is clear that the user may benefit significantly if the search service can automatically group all the papers into semantically independent "topics". As a second example, consider search on social annotation websites like Del.icio.us [3] and Flickr [4]. These websites have rich user generated metadata for each item, however current search engines on these websites only utilize them to generate a ranked list of items for a query based on keyword relevance. In case of Del.icio.us, search results are presented using a faceted interface, but this is based on expanding the user's keyword query with one of a fixed set of tags. E.g., searching on the tag "programming" returns more than 1.3 million hits on Del.icio.us, however, only three single word tags "ajax", "software" and "javascript" are suggested to expand the query, while many other useful expansions such as "c++ programming tutorial" and "database programming language" cannot be found on the interface. As a third example, consider a community question answering forum like Quora [6]. A user may wish to search the Q&A in Quora using keywords and it is often helpful for the system to present the search results in an automatically grouped form, where different groups somehow correspond to different "subtopics" of the "topic" that the user may have questions about.

Indeed, to help users explore the returned search results, current search engines like Google, Bing and Yahoo! often add to the search result interface a set of facets, like publishing time, size of document, price etc. Faceted interfaces can greatly facilitate user navigation through the results. However, these facets are often predefined, and may not capture the attributes of the item which are the most important. E.g., for Google Scholar, current facets for the search results contain only types of publication and publication date, whereas the users may want to explore "topics" of papers among the search results. Similar comments apply to the other two example search scenarios above.

Our problem is similar in spirit to recent works on automatic facets generation [19], but has the important difference and advantage that we don't need to assume the existence of pre-defined categorical hierarchy which is critical for these works. Indeed, in the applications we consider such as above, we cannot assume any prior taxonomy.

Motivated by these drawbacks of current search result interfaces, we consider a search scenario in which each item is annotated with a set of keywords. These can be keywords associated with papers or tags assigned to items by users of social annotation systems or keywords occurring in question and answers in Q&A systems. Based on this annotation information, we want to automatically group query result items into different expansions of the query corresponding to subsets of keywords. Items may have a number of attributes, either explicitly stored or computed, which can signify their importance or utility to the user. E.g., papers have citation score, pagerank of their authors, etc. In social annotation systems, popularity of items and pagerank of the annotator can be important attributes. Finally, in a system like Quora, we have attributes like importance scores of questioner or answerer, number of people interested in a question, etc. Intuitively, the expansions that we wish to return to a user should be driven by how important the items are that match an expansion and how many such important items match it. This raises the problem of what expansions of a query should we show the user? We formulate and motivate this problem within a top-k query processing framework, but as that of finding the top-k most important expansions, where the importance or utility of an expansion is driven by the utility of the items matching it.

We make the following contributions:

- We introduce the problem of finding top-k high quality expansions (Section 2).
- We first propose a naïve algorithm for this problem and then discuss its limitations and propose a significant improvement leveraging the lattice structure of expansions (Section 3).
- We consider some semantic issues with directly returning the top-k high quality expansions, and propose several different algorithms for improving the quality of the returned results (Section 4).
- Through extensive experiments on both real and synthetic datasets, we demonstrate that our proposed algorithms have excellent performance and very good quality (Section 5).

Related work is discussed in Section 6. We summarize the work in Section 7 and discuss open research problems.

2. PROBLEM DEFINITION

Consider a set of items $S = \{t_1, ..., t_n\}$, each item $t_i \in S$ being associated with a set of m attributes $\{a_1, ..., a_m\}$. We denote the value of t_i on attribute a_j as $t_i.a_j$, and assume without loss of generality that all values on attribute a_j are normalized to [0, 1], $j \in 1...m$. Attributes of an item t_i correspond to t_i's "utility" to a user, and in this work, without loss of generality, we assume large attribute values are preferred, so larger the value larger the utility. The overall *utility* of an item t_i, denoted $u(t_i)$, is captured by a weighted sum of its values on all attributes, i.e., $u(t_i) = \sum_{j \in 1...m} w_j \times t_i.a_j$, where w_j is a positive weight associated with attribute a_j. These weights may be chosen by a user or the system may learn the "best" weights from user behavior using models like linear regression [10].

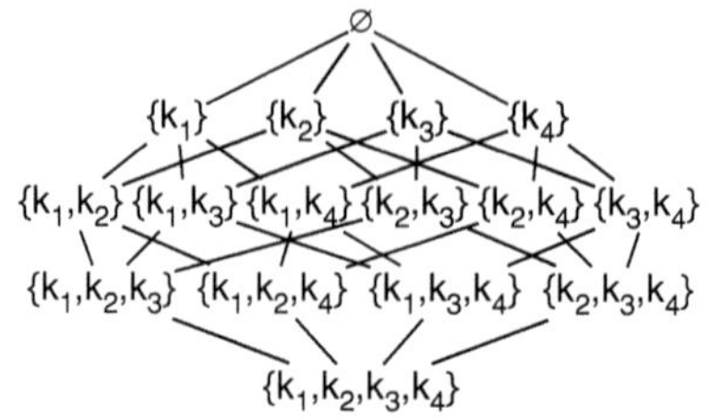

Figure 1: Lattice structure of expansions.

We assume each item $t_i \in S$ is also associated with a set of l keywords or tags $\{k_1, ..., k_l\}$ which summarize the contents of t_i. We denote the set of keywords associated with an item t_i as $\mathrm{Kw}(t_i)$. A query Q in our system is a set of keywords, $Q = \{k_1, ..., k_p\}$. An item t *matches* query Q iff $Q \subseteq \mathrm{Kw}(t)$. The answer to Q, denoted S_Q, is then the set of matching items in S, i.e., $S_Q = \{t \mid t \in S, Q \subseteq \mathrm{Kw}(t)\}$.

As mentioned in the introduction, the number of items matching a query Q can often be huge, and merely returning the top-k matching items may not help the user find the items they are most interested in. So we want to group items into different expansions of Q and return high quality expansions. Let K denote the set of all keywords in the system. We call a subset of keywords $e \subseteq K - Q$ an *expansion*[1] of Q. The size of an expansion e, $|e|$, is the number of keywords in e. Let the set of all possible expansions for Q be E_Q, then given an expansion $e \in E_Q$, we say an item $t \in S$ *matches* e if $Q \cup e \subseteq \mathrm{Kw}(t)$. Let S_e denote the set of matching items for e, then we have $S_e = \{t \mid t \in S, Q \cup e \subseteq \mathrm{Kw}(t)\}$.

Given a query Q, all possible expansions of Q can be organized as a lattice based on the *subset-of* relationship, E.g., Figure 1 shows the lattice structure of all possible expansions for $K - Q = \{k_1, ..., k_4\}$. We will shortly define the quality of an expansion, and we will show in Section 3.2 that this lattice structure can be used to improve the efficiency of our algorithm for determining high quality expansions.

Intuitively, the importance of an expansion e can be captured by aggregating the utilities of items which match e. Let g be a monotone aggregation function which calculates the overall utility or quality of expansion e, i.e., define $u(e) := g(\{u(t) \mid t \in S_e\})$. Then we can define our top-k expansion problem as follows.

DEFINITION 1 (TOP-k EXPANSIONS). *Given a set S of items and a keyword query Q, find the top-k expansion set $E_k = \{e_1, ..., e_k\}$ s.t. $\forall e \in E_k$ and $\forall e' \in E_Q - E_k$, $u(e) \geq u(e')$.*

The intuition is that in response to a user query, we want to return the best quality expansions where the quality of an expansion is monotonically determined by the utility of the items matching it.

The set of annotations used in this paper is summarized in Table 1. Below, we give an example of an aggregation function with certain desirable properties.

2.1 Determining Importance of An Expansion

To determine the utility $u(e)$ of expansion e, a natural idea is to use a monotone function to aggregate utility values of all items which can match e. However, this approach means for every expansion, we may need to retrieve all items that are relevant to this expansion which can be prohibitive considering the huge size of matching items. Besides, low quality items matching e intuitively should not determine its importance. So we will only consider top-

[1]Note, actually the real expansion is $Q \cup e$ but for technical convenience, we deal with the part of the expansion outside Q.

Symbol	Description
t	an item in the system
S	a set of items
$t.a$	attribute a's value of an item t
w	the weight associated with an attribute
$u(t)$	the utility value of an item t
k	a keyword
K	the set of all possible keywords
$\mathcal{L}_K$	the lattice of all possible keywords K
$\mathcal{L}$	the partially materialized lattice
Kw(t)	the set of keywords associated with t
Q	a query which is composed of a set of keywords
S_Q	the set of matching items for query Q
e	an expansion
E_Q	the set of all possible expansions for query Q
S_e	the set of matching items for expansion e
$u(e)$	the utility value of an expansion e
V_{S_e}	the multiset of utility values of all items matching e
$\mathcal{L}_K(e)$	the sub-lattice induced by e
E_t	all possible expansions of t
e_t	the largest size expansion in E_t

Table 1: Annotations

N matching items for determining importance of an expansion e, where N is a parameter that is tuned for each application.

Let $V_{S_e} = \{u(t) \mid t \in S_e\}$ be the multiset of utility values of all items matching e. We will apply a function top_N to V_{S_e} which retrieves the top-N highest utility values from V_{S_e}. Then to determine the importance of e, we will sum up all values in $top_N(V_{S_e})$, so $g(S_e) := \sum_{v \in top_N(V_{S_e})} v$. It is clear that $g(S_e)$ satisfies the desired properties for determining the importance of an expansion, as $g(S_e)$ will be large when there are high quality items matching e and also when the number of these high quality items is large.

It can be easily shown that the aggregation function g defined is *subset-monotone*, which means for two expansions e_1 and e_2, if $S_{e_1} \subseteq S_{e_2}$, then $g(e_1) \leq g(e_2)$. And it is worth noting that the algorithms proposed in this work can be easily adapted to other subset-monotone score functions.

On top of the basic top-k expansion problem, we will want to impose some additional desirable properties for the k expansions returned by our algorithms. In Section 4, we study these properties and propose additional algorithms which can return expansions satisfying these properties.

3. BASIC ALGORITHM

In this section, we present two algorithms for finding top-k expansions. In order to facilitate both algorithms, we assume m inverted lists are materialized, one each for the m attributes, where for each inverted list, items are sorted in the non-increasing order of their value on the corresponding attribute.

3.1 Naïve Algorithm

Inspired by the NRA algorithm proposed in [13], a naïve way of generating top-k expansions can be described as follows: 1. access items in the non-increasing order of their attribute value; 2. for each matching item accessed, enumerate all possible expansions and update their lower bound and upper bound utility value; 3. stop the iterative process once top-k expansions have been identified. The pseudo-code for the above process is given in Algorithm 1.

In Algorithm 1, all attribute lists are accessed in a round-robin fashion (line 4), and for each matching item t obtained from list I_a, we will enumerate the set E_t of all possible expansions (line 5–7).

Consider an expansion $e \in E_t$, let SS_e be the current set of accessed items which can match e. Then for each $t \in SS_e$, because all attribute values are normalized to $[0, 1]$ and items are accessed in the non-increasing order of their attribute values, similar to the NRA algorithm [13], we can determine the lower bound on t's utility $\underline{u}(t)$ by summing up all current accessed attribute values of t, and we can determine its upper bound utility $\bar{u}(t)$ by summing up all accessed attribute values of t along with the last accessed values of other attributes in the inverted lists.

Then because of the subset-monotonicity of the score function g, the lower bound utility $\underline{u}(e)$ for expansion $e \in E_t$ can be calculated as a sum of all values in $top_{min(N,|SS_e|)}(\{\underline{u}(t) \mid t \in SS_e\})$. And the upper bound utility $\bar{u}(e)$ of an expansion e can be estimated by considering both SS_e and the maximum utility value which can be achieved by any unseen items. Let the last accessed values on each of the m attribute lists be $\bar{v}_1, ..., \bar{v}_m$ respectively, then because items are accessed in the non-increasing order of their attribute value, an "imaginary" item t' with m attribute values $\bar{v}_1, ..., \bar{v}_m$ must have the maximum value that can be achieved by any unseen items. So the upper bound utility of e can be estimated as the sum of all values in $top_N(\{\bar{u}(t) \mid t \in SS_e\} \cup \{u(t'_1), ..., u(t'_N)\})$. where $t'_1, ..., t'_N$ are N imaginary items which have the same utility as t'.

After the lower and upper bounds for all expansions in E_t have been updated (line 8–10), we can estimate the upper bound utility for all possible unseen items by summing up the values of N maximum possible imaginary items (updateUpperBound($\emptyset$) in line 12).

Henceforth, by the value of an expansion, we mean its utility value. Let EQ be the expansion query which contains the set of expansions of Q that have been materialized by the algorithm at a given point. We can rank all expansions in EQ by their lower bound values. Let EQ_k be the top-k expansions in EQ and UB' be the maximum upper bound value of an expansion in $EQ - EQ_k$, then the maximum of UB' and the upper bound value for all unseen items determines the overall upper bound value UB (line 11–12). If the lower bound value for the kth expansion in EQ_k is already larger than UB, the algorithm can be safely terminated, exactly in the spirit of NRA.

Algorithm 1: TopExp-Naive(Q, I, g, k)

```
1  EQ ← expansion queue;
2  UB ← upper bound threshold;
3  while |EQ| < k OR u(EQ.k^th expansion) < UB do
4      I_a ← getNextListRR();
5      t ← I_a.getNextItem();
6      if Q ⊈ Kw(t) then continue;
7      E_t ← enumerateExpansion(Kw(t) − Q);
8      foreach e ∈ E_t do
9          if e ∉ EQ then EQ.push(e);
10         e.updateLower&UpperBound(t, g);
11     UB' ← maximum upper bound value of an expansion in
           EQ − EQ_k;
12     UB ← MAX(UB', updateUpperBound(∅));
```

The correctness of Algorithm 1 easily follows from the fact that both lower bound and upper bound of an expansion are correct. And to assess the performance of Algorithm 1, we borrow the notion of *instance optimality* as proposed by Fagin et al. in [13].

Definition 2. **Instance Optimality:** *Let $\mathcal{A}$ be a class of algorithms that make no random accesses to the m inverted lists, and let $\mathcal{I}$ be a class of problem instances. Given a non-negative cost measure cost(A, I) of running algorithm $A \in \mathcal{A}$ over $I \in \mathcal{I}$, an algorithm $A \in \mathcal{A}$ is* instance optimal *over $\mathcal{A}$ and $\mathcal{I}$ if for every*

$A' \in \mathcal{A}$ *and every* $I \in \mathcal{I}$ *we have* $cost(A, I) \leq c \cdot cost(A', I) + c'$, *for constants* c *and* c'. *Constant* c *is called the optimality ratio.*

Let the cost of an algorithm for the top-k expansion problem be determined by the number of items accessed, we first show the following result.

LEMMA 1. *Given any instance* I *of the top-k expansion problem and any algorithm* A *with the same access constraints as TopExp-Naive, assume* A *accesses* x *items, then TopExp-Naive will access at most* $m \times x$ *items.*

PROOF. (Sketch) Assume another algorithm $B \in \mathcal{A}$ stops in list I_a after accessing x items, then it must be true that at the time when B stops, the current utility of the kth maximum utility expansion e_k will have its utility larger than or equal to the upper bound utility of all generated non-result expansions and all possible unseen expansions. This is because otherwise, we can come up with an configuration of the remaining unseen items such that we can have an expansion of which the utility is larger than e_k. Then it is clear that our algorithm TopExp-Naive will also stop at the same position in list I_a. By considering the fact there are m lists in total, we can infer that the total number of items accessed by TopExp-Naive is at most $m \times x$, for the scenario where B accesses x items in list I_a, zero item in other lists, and TopExp-Naive accesses x items in each list. □

THEOREM 1. *Let* $\mathcal{I}$ *be the class of all top-k expansion problem instances, and* $\mathcal{A}$ *be the class of all possible algorithms that find the top-k expansions, that are constrained to access items sequentially in non-increasing order of their attribute values, then TopExp-Naive is instance optimal over* $\mathcal{A}$ *and* $\mathcal{I}$ *with an optimality ratio of* m.

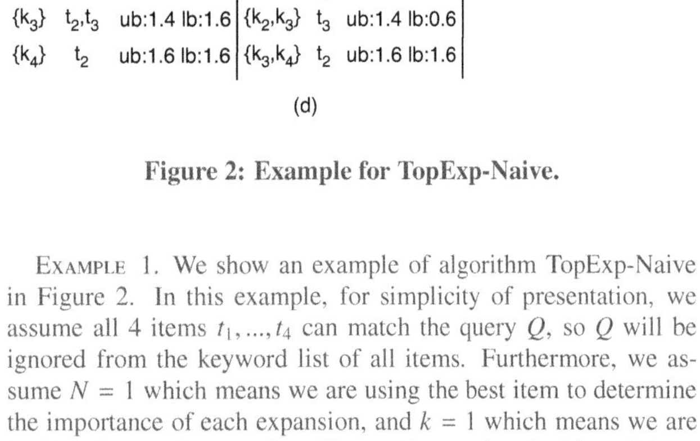

Figure 2: Example for TopExp-Naive.

EXAMPLE 1. We show an example of algorithm TopExp-Naive in Figure 2. In this example, for simplicity of presentation, we assume all 4 items $t_1, ..., t_4$ can match the query Q, so Q will be ignored from the keyword list of all items. Furthermore, we assume $N = 1$ which means we are using the best item to determine the importance of each expansion, and $k = 1$ which means we are looking for top-1 expansion. Keywords associated with each item are shown in Figure 2 (a), and each item in the example has two attributes a_1 and a_2. The inverted lists for these two attributes are shown in Figure 2 (b).

As described in TopExp-Naive, the algorithm will enumerate all possible expansions for each item accessed, e.g., after t_1 is accessed, $\{k_1\}$, $\{k_2\}$ and $\{k_1, k_2\}$ will be generated, and their utility bound values will be updated using the attribute value of t_1. For this case, because only $t_1.a_1$ is known, we know $\bar{u}(t_1) = 1.9$ and $\underline{u}(t_1) = 0.9$, these will be the upper and lower bound utility value for all three expansions. After we have accessed the first two items of both lists, the expansions generated are shown in Figure 2 (c), while the items contained in each generated expansion and the utility bound values for each generated expansion are shown in Figure 2 (d). It is clear that at this moment, the upper bound utility for all generated expansions is 1.6, the upper bound utility for all unseen expansions is 1.4 (sum of the last accessed utility value from each list) and the lower bound utility for expansions $\{k_3\}$, $\{k_4\}$ and $\{k_3, k_4\}$ are all 1.6, so we can stop the algorithm now and return any one of these three expansions. □

3.2 Improved Algorithm

One serious drawback of the naïve algorithm is that every time an item t containing keywords Kw(t) is accessed, all $2^{|\text{Kw}(t)-Q|}$ possible expansions for this item are explicitly enumerated and their bounds are maintained. In this section, we propose an efficient algorithm which can leverage the lattice structure of expansions to avoid enumerating and maintaining unnecessary expansions. We also address the challenge of determining the bounds of unseen (unmaterialized) expansions, which is necessary for early termination of the top-k algorithm.

3.2.1 Avoiding Unnecessary Expansions

Given a query Q and a newly accessed item t, let $e_t = \text{Kw}(t) - Q$ be the largest size expansion in E_t, then the naïve algorithm will enumerate all possible expansions of t by considering all non-empty subsets of e_t. However, this may not be necessary. E.g., let $K_{<t}$ be the set of keywords which have been seen before t; if $\forall k \in K_{<t}, k \notin e_t$, we just need to maintain one single expansion e_t, as all other expansions generated from e_t will have the same current matching itemset as e_t and thus the same lower and upper bounds as e_t. This indicates that there are opportunities to avoid the expansion enumeration process for each newly accessed item.

Let $\mathcal{L}_K$ be the lattice of all possible keywords K. For an expansion $e \in \mathcal{L}_K$, we let $\mathcal{L}_K(e)$ denote the sub-lattice *induced* by e, i.e., $\mathcal{L}_K(e) = \{e' \mid e' \subseteq e\}$. For a newly accessed item t, the naïve algorithm will enumerate all expansions $e \in \mathcal{L}_K(e_t)$, however, as discussed above that this isn't always necessary.

The idea of the new algorithm can be described as follows. Let $\mathcal{L}$ denote a partially materialized lattice which contains the set of expansions generated so far before the current item t. If $\exists e \in \mathcal{L}$ s.t. $e = e_t$, then it is clear we just need to update the lower bound and upper bound utilities of all existing expansions in $\mathcal{L}$ which are subsets of e_t. Otherwise, all expansions in $\mathcal{L}$ will correspond to different sets of items compared with e_t, so we need to first generate the expansion e_t and update its lower bound and upper bound utility. Then we consider the following two cases: 1. if $\forall e \in \mathcal{L}, e \cap e_t = \emptyset$, then all $e' \in \mathcal{L}_K(e_t)$ correspond to the same set of items, their lower bound and upper bound utilities are the same, and we just need to maintain one expansion e_t which can concisely represent all expansions in $\mathcal{L}_K(e_t)$; 2. On the other hand, if there exists an expansion $e \in \mathcal{L}$ s.t. $e \cap e_t \neq \emptyset$, then *for each such expansion* e, we need to further consider the following three sub-cases:

1. if $e \subseteq e_t$, we don't need to generate additional expansions, but we need to update the lower bound and upper bound utility of e since item t also contributes to every sub-expansion e of e_t.
2. if $e_t \subseteq e$, similar to case 1, we don't need to generate additional expansions; and since t cannot contribute to e, we don't need to update utility bounds of e.

Algorithm 2: TopExp-Lazy(Q, I, g, k)

```
1  UB ← upper bound threshold;
2  ℒ ← partial materialized lattice structure;
3  while |EQ| < k OR u(EQ.k^th expansion) < UB do
4      I_a ← getNextListRR();
5      t ← I_a.getNextItem();
6      if Q ⊈ Kw(t) then continue;
7      e_t ← Kw(t) − Q;
8      if e_t ∈ ℒ then
9          foreach e ∈ {e | e ∈ ℒ ∧ e ⊆ e_t} do
10             e.updateLower&UpperBound(t);
11     else
12         TQ ← temporary update expansion queue;
13         TQ.push(e_t);
14         while ¬ TQ.empty() do
15             e = TQ.pop();
16             E_l ← {e' | e' ∈ ℒ ∧ (∄e'' ∈ ℒ : e' ⊂ e'')};
17             foreach e_l ∈ E_l ∧ e_l ∩ e ≠ ∅ do
18                 E ← {e' | e' ∈ ℒ ∧ e' ⊆ e_l};
19                 if ∃e' ∈ E s.t. e' ⊈ e ∧ e ⊈ e' then
20                     Find all e' ∈ E s.t. e' ⊈ e ∧ e ⊈ e' and
                       (∄e'' ∈ E : e' ⊂ e'' ∧ e'' ⊈ e ∧ e ⊈ e'');
21                     TQ.push(e ∩ e');
22             if e ∉ ℒ then ℒ.add(e);
23         foreach e ∈ ℒ ∧ e ⊆ e_t do
24             e.updateLower&UpperBound(t);
25     UB ← upper bound value of the (k + 1)^th expansion in ℒ;
26     UB ← MAX(UB, getUpperBound(∅));
```

3. if $e \not\subseteq e_t$ or $e_t \not\subseteq e$, let $e' = e \cap e_t$, then it is clear that $S_{e'} \neq S_e$ and $S_{e'} \neq S_{e_t}$, which means we need to generate a new expansion e' and update its utility bounds accordingly.

3.2.2 Bounds for Unseen Expansions

Since we don't explicitly maintain all possible expansions for each item accessed, this will create a challenge for determining lower bound and upper bound utilities for all possible expansions. For all expansions which are maintained in $\mathcal{L}$, the lower bound and upper bound are determined as discussed in Section 3.1. For each remaining expansion e not materialized in $\mathcal{L}$, depending on the position of e in the lattice $\mathcal{L}_{\mathcal{K}}$, we need to consider the following two cases:

- $\nexists e' \in \mathcal{L}$ s.t. $e \subset e'$. This means we haven't accessed any item which corresponds to this expansion. The utility upper bound of e in this case is the same as the maximum possible utility of an unseen expansion, as discussed in Section 3.1.

- $\exists e' \in \mathcal{L}$ s.t. $e \subset e'$. This means we have already accessed some items which correspond to this expansion. Then we must be able to find a smallest such expansion $\hat{e} \in \mathcal{L}$ s.t. $e \subset \hat{e}$, and $\forall e' \in \mathcal{L}$, if $e \subset e'$, then $\hat{e} \subseteq e'$. To see this, suppose $e', e'' \in \mathcal{L}$ are distinct expansions such that $e \subset e'$ and $e \subset e''$. From Section 3.2.1, it follows that for $e''' = e' \cap e''$, we have $S_{e'''} \neq S_{e'}$ and $S_{e'''} \neq S_{e''}$, so e''' should be generated as a new expansion before e, and this expansion has the property that it is a subset of both e' and e'', and it is a superset of e. It follows that the smallest superset expansion $\hat{e}$ must exist in $\mathcal{L}$. So after $\hat{e}$ is found, we know e and $\hat{e}$ currently correspond to the same set of items, then e's utility bound will be the same as $\hat{e}$. This means that we don't need to explicitly consider this expansion when using the utility bounds to determine whether the algorithm can stop.

Example 2. Consider the lattice in Figure 1 and assume we have only materialized two expansions $e_1 = \{k_1\}$ and $e_2 = \{k_1, k_2, k_3\}$. Then for an expansion $e_3 = \{k_2, k_4\}$, because there is no such materialized expansion $e' \in \mathcal{L}$ s.t. $e_3 \subset e'$, then we know we haven't accessed any item which corresponds to this expansion. So we only need to consider its upper bound utility, which is the maximum possible utility for all possible expansions. And for another unmaterialized expansion $e_4 = \{k_1, k_2\}$, we can find out that $e_4 \subset e_2$, so e_4 and e_2 correspond to the same set of items, and e_4's utility bounds are the same as those of e_2. □

So the general idea of our *lazy expansion generation* based algorithm is that we only need to maintain expansions which correspond to a *unique* set of items. For a set of expansions which are matched by the same set of items, we can simply represent them using the largest expansion in the set.

3.2.3 Lazy Expansion Algorithm

The pseudo-code for the lazy expansion generation based algorithm is given in Algorithm 2. Similar to TopExp-Naive, TopExp-Lazy iteratively retrieves items from the attribute lists (line 4–6). However, unlike TopExp-Naive, *we maintain only necessary expansions in the partially materialized lattice* $\mathcal{L}$. For a newly accessed item t, if e_t has already been generated by a previous item, we simply update the itemset and lower/upper utility bounds of the corresponding expansions which contain this item (line 8–10). Otherwise, as discussed above, we may need to generate some additional expansions which correspond to a unique matching itemset (line 11–24). The procedure works as follows. First, we identify from $\mathcal{L}$ all *leaf expansions* E_l which are maximal expansions, i.e., they are not included in other expansions in $\mathcal{L}$ (line 16). Then for each leaf expansion $e_l \in E_l$, if e_t doesn't overlap with e_l, we can ignore all expansions which are subsets of e_l as they can't overlap with e_t either (line 17). If e_l overlaps with e_t, then we search the set E of expansions in $\mathcal{L}$ which are subsets of e_l: if there is an expansion $e' \in E$ s.t. $e' \not\subseteq e_t$ and $e_t \not\subseteq e'$, then we need to find all of the largest such expansions e' in E, and as described in Section 3.2.1, for each of them, a new expansion $e' \cap e_t$ needs to be inserted to $\mathcal{L}$ as it corresponds to a unique set of matching items, so we will recursively insert this new expansion into $\mathcal{L}$ (line 19–21).

The procedure for updating lower bound and upper bound utilities for each expansion is very similar to TopExp-Naive. However, because in TopExp-Lazy each expansion may represent more than one expansion, in order to determine which expansions in the expansion buffer $\mathcal{L}$ are current top-k expansions, we need to calculate for each expansion $e \in \mathcal{L}$ the exact number of ungenerated expansions which have the same utility bounds as e. The pseudo-code for this procedure are listed in Algorithm 3 and Algorithm 4.

The idea of Algorithm 3 is that we first find from $\mathcal{L}$ the expansion set ST_e of which the expansions are subset of e (line 1), we prune away those expansions in ST_e of which a superset is also present in ST_e (line 2–3), then for the pruned expansion set ST_e, we can use the classical *inclusion-exclusion principle* to count the total number of expansions covered by ST_e (line 4). Algorithm 4 is a simple implementation of the counting procedure.

Example 3. Figure 3 shows an example that illustrates how Algorithm TopExp-Lazy works. The configuration of this example, including query, item attributes, item attribute values, keywords of

Algorithm 3: updateCount($\mathcal{L}$, e)

1 $ST_e \leftarrow \{e' \mid e' \in L \wedge e' \subset e\}$;
2 $ST'_e \leftarrow \{e' \mid e' \in ST_e \wedge \exists e'' \in E \rightarrow e' \subset e''\}$;
3 $ST_e = ST_e - ST'_e$;
4 $count \leftarrow$ countGeneratedExpansions(ST_e);
5 e.count $\leftarrow 2^{|e|} - count - 1$;

Algorithm 4: countGeneratedExpansions(ST_e)

1 $count \leftarrow 0$;
2 **for** *outeridx from 2 to* $|ST_e|$ **do**
3     $ST'_e = \emptyset$;
4   **for** *inneridx from 1 to outeridx - 1* **do**
5   ST'_e.insert($ST_e[outeridx] \cap ST_e[inneridx]$);
6     $ST''_e \leftarrow \{e' \mid e' \in ST'_e \wedge \exists e'' \in E \rightarrow e' \subset e''\}$;
7     $ST'_e = ST'_e - ST''_e$;
8   **if** ST'_e*.hasOverlap()* **then**
9   *count* += countGeneratedExpansions(ST'_e);
10   **else**
11   **foreach** $e' \in ST'_e$ **do**
12   *count* += $2^{|e'|}$-1;

each item and parameters k, N, is the same as Example 1. However, because we are using the lazy expansion generation based algorithm, we don't need to enumerate all possible expansions for each item accessed. E.g., when the first item t_1 is accessed, we only need to generate expansion $\{k_1, k_2\}$ and don't need to generate expansions $\{k_1\}$ and $\{k_2\}$, as they correspond to the same current set of matching items as $\{k_1, k_2\}$. The utility bound values for $\{k_1, k_2\}$ will be the same as in the TopExp-Naive algorithm, and again we don't need to maintain these utility bound values for $\{k_1\}$ and $\{k_2\}$ since they are the same as for $\{k_1, k_2\}$. After accessing two items from each lists, the expansions materialized for TopExp-Lazy are shown as bolded expansions in Figure 3 (c). Compared with TopExp-Naive, it's worth noting that 5 expansions don't need to be maintained. At this point, similarly to TopExp-Naive, the algorithm can also stop as the top expansion $\{t_3, t_4\}$'s lower bound utility is already larger than or equal to the maximum upper bound utility for all expansions.

Note that for the lazy expansion generation based algorithm, for each expansion which needs to materialized, we need to use Algorithm 3 to count how many expansions correspond to the same set of items. E.g., after accessing t_3 in the inverted list of a_2, we need to consider how many expansions are "covered by" the current expansion $\{k_1, k_2, k_3\}$. Algorithm 3 will first find all materialized expansions which are subsets of $\{k_1, k_2, k_3\}$, for this case, $\{k_1, k_2\}$ and $\{k_3\}$. Then as in line 4 of Algorithm 3, Algorithm 4 will be called to enumerate the number of non-empty expansions covered by these two expansions. Because there is no overlap between $\{k_1, k_2\}$ and $\{k_3\}$, in line 10–12 of Algorithm 4, we can simply sum up the number of non-empty expansions covered by these two expansions, which is 4. Then this number will be used to determine the number of non-empty expansions covered by $\{k_1, k_2, k_3\}$ in line 5 of Algorithm 3, which is 3 ($\{k_1, k_2, k_3\}$, $\{k_1, k_3\}$ and $\{k_2, k_3\}$).

Figure 3 (d) shows all the expansions that should be considered and whether they are "covered by" some other expansions in the lattice. Compared with Figure 2 (d), it is clear that the lazy expansion generation based algorithm will maintain just one expansion for each set of expansions which correspond to the same set of items. □

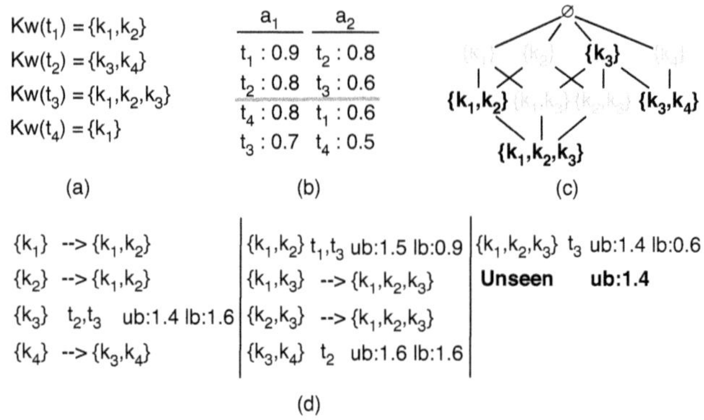

Figure 3: Example for TopExp-Lazy.

4. SEMANTIC OPTIMIZATION

Though algorithms described in Section 3 can correctly find expansions which have the k highest utility, there are two kinds of issues with these algorithms. First, the basic algorithm will favor small expansions (i.e., fewer keywords) as these expansions have more matching items than larger expansions. Second, in the returned top-k expansions, it may happen that two expansions have the subset-of relationship, which is not ideal. Indeed, we would like the resulting expansions to have little overlap with each other.

In this section, we propose two solutions to remedy the above drawbacks. In Section 4.1, we will study weighting schemes which can penalize expansions that are either too small or too large. Then in Section 4.2, we propose to find the k most interesting expansions which don't have overlap with each other.

4.1 Weighting Expansions

It is clear that expansions which have small size (e.g., "XML") correspond to "general topics" which are related to the query, whereas expansions which have large size (e.g., "XML, schema, conformance, automata") correspond to "specific topics" which are related to the query. To help users quickly locate interesting information from the returned results, intuitively neither too general topics nor too specific topics should be returned early, so we want to favor those expansions which are neither too large nor too small.

We assume there is a function $f_w : \mathbb{N} \rightarrow \mathbb{R}$ (where $\mathbb{N}/\mathbb{R}$ denote the sets of natural/real numbers) which can return the weight $f_w(p)$ for an expansion of size p. The intuition is that f_w penalizes too small and too large expansions for we expect them to be intuitively too general or too specific. Then we can use this function to weight the utility of all expansions under consideration. In this work, we consider the Gaussian function $f_w(p) = e^{-\frac{(x-\mu)^2}{2\sigma^2}}$. The mean μ of f_w is set as the most ideal size of an expansion and the variance σ can be adjusted by the system for different problem instances.

So how are the top-k algorithms impacted? For TopExp-Naive, the weighting function can be simply applied to the utility bounds of each expansion enumerated, and other parts of the algorithm won't be affected. However, for TopExp-Lazy, for each materialized expansion $e \in \mathcal{L}$, the unmaterialized expansions which have the same set of matching items as e have the same utility bounds as e when no weighting is applied. But once weighting is applied, these expansions may have different utility bounds depending on the size. E.g., consider that there is only one materialized expansion $e = \{k_1, k_2\}$ in $\mathcal{L}$ and let the lower and upper utility bounds of e be $\underline{u}(e) \times f_w(2)$ and $\bar{u}(e) \times f_w(2)$ respectively. Then for expansions $\{k_1\}$ and $\{k_2\}$, though they correspond to the same set of matching items as e, their lower and upper utility bounds are $\underline{u}(e) \times f_w(1)$ and $\bar{u}(e) \times f_w(1)$ respectively.

So for the weighted lazy expansion generation based algorithm, for a set E of expansions which correspond to the same set of matching items, we may need to maintain multiple expansions where the number of expansions to be maintained depends on the size of the largest expansion in E. For an expansion e, Algorithm 5 and Algorithm 6, which are adapted from Algorithm 3 and Algorithm 4, can be used to count for each possible expansion size, the number of expansions which correspond to the same set of matching items as e. These counts can be utilized along with the weighting function to determine the corresponding lower and upper utility bounds.

Algorithm 5: updateCount(λ, e)

$ST_e \leftarrow \{e' \mid e' \in L \wedge e' \subset e\}$;
$ST'_e \leftarrow \{e' \mid e' \in ST_e \wedge \exists e'' \in E \rightarrow e' \subset e''\}$;
$ST_e = ST_e - ST'_e$;
$vec_c \leftarrow$ a new count vector of size $|e|$;
for *expsize from 1 to* $|e|$ **do**
    $vec_c[expsize] = \binom{|e|}{expsize}$;
$vec_c \leftarrow$ countGeneratedExpansions(ST_e, vec_c);
e.count = vec_c;

Algorithm 6: calculateSameLBExpansionVec(ST_e, vec_c)

for *outeridx from 2 to* $|ST_e|$ **do**
    $ST'_e = \emptyset$;
    for *inneridx from 1 to outeridx - 1* **do**
        ST'_e.insert($ST_e[outeridx] \cap ST_e[inneridx]$);
    $ST''_e \leftarrow \{e' \mid e' \in ST'_e \wedge \exists e'' \in E \rightarrow e' \subset e''\}$;
    $ST'_e = ST'_e - ST''_e$;
    if ST'_e*.hasOverlap()* **then**
        countGeneratedExpansions(ST'_e, vec_c);
    else
        for *expsize from 1 to* $|e|$ **do**
            foreach $e' \in ST'_e$ **do**
                $vec_c[expsize] = vec_c[expsize] - \binom{|e'|}{expsize}$;

4.2 Path Exclusion based Algorithm

To lessen the semantic overlap between different expansions returned to the user, intuitively we may not want to return two different expansions e_1 and e_2, such that either $e_1 \subset e_2$ or $e_2 \subset e_1$. Note that there can be many sets of expansions satisfying this pairwize comparability, and the set of highest utility expansions may not satisfy this property. So in order to guarantee the quality of the expansions returned, we want to maximize the sum of the utilities for the set of expansions returned under the constraint that the expansions returned should satisfy the pairwise comparability.

Definition 3. *(Maximum k Path-Exclusive Expansion) Given a set S of items and a keyword query Q, find the top k-expansion set* $E_k = \{e_1, ..., e_k\}$ *s.t.* $\forall e_i, e_j \in E_k$, $i \neq j$, $e_i \not\subset e_j$, $e_j \not\subset e_i$, *and* $\sum_{e \in E_k} u(e)$ *is maximized.*

Let $\mathcal{L} = \{e_1, ..., e_n\}$ be the set of all expansions materialized by the algorithm. Consider a weighted undirected graph $G = (Vtx, Edg)$, with nodes $Vtx = \mathcal{L}$ where each node e_i is associated with a weight $u(e_i)$, i.e., the utility of e_i. Whenever two expansions $e_i, e_j \in Vtx$ are such that either $e_1 \subset e_2$ or $e_2 \subset e_1$, Edg contains the edge (e_i, e_j). Then it is straightforward to show that the maximum k path-exclusive expansion problem is NP-hard by a direct reduction from the *maximum weighted independent set* problem [18].

A simple greedy algorithm for the maximum weighted independent set was proposed by [18]: repeatedly select a node in G with minimum weighted degree in each iteration and add it to the current solution; then delete this node and all of its neighbors from the graph; stop when all nodes are removed from G. It has been proven in [18] that this algorithm gives a $\max(\delta_w, 1)$-approximation, where $\delta_w = \max_{H \subseteq G} \min_{v \in V(H)} d_w(v, H)$, $d_w(v, H)$ is defined as $\frac{ww(N_G(v))}{ww(\{v\})}$, $ww(S)$ denotes the sum of weights of a set of nodes S, and $N_G(v)$ is the set of neighbors of v in G.

Furthermore, if we rank all generated expansions by their upper bound utility, because items are accessed in the non-increasing order of their attribute values, it is clear that the sum of the top-k expansions' upper bound utilities is an upper bound for the value of all possible k path-exclusive expansions.

So based on this information, we propose the following algorithm called Top-PEkExp, which can be used to calculate an approximate solution for the maximum k path-exclusive expansion problem. In Top-PEkExp, similar to the previous algorithms, we iteratively retrieve items from the attribute lists (line 3–5), then we use TopExp-Lazy to generate necessary expansions in $\mathcal{L}$ (line 6). The set of expansions in $\mathcal{L}$ are sent to the greedy algorithm for the maximum weighted independent set problem (line 7), and if the result is already larger than $\frac{1}{\alpha}$ of the maximum upper bound utility, for some constant $\alpha > 1$ that is chosen by the system, we can stop the algorithm (line 8–11).

Algorithm 7: Top-PEkExp(Q, I, g, k)

1 $\mathcal{L} \leftarrow$ partial materialized lattice structure;
2 **while** *true* **do**
3     $I_a \leftarrow$ getNextListRR();
4     $t \leftarrow I_a$.getNextItem();
5   **if** $Q \not\subseteq$ Kw(t) **then** continue;
6   Generate necessary expansions using TopExp-Lazy;
7     $R^G \leftarrow$ GreedyMWIS($\mathcal{L}$);
8     $E_{topk} \leftarrow k$ expansions in $\mathcal{L}$ which have the largest upper bound utilities;
9     $U^* = sum_{e \in E_{topk}} \bar{u}(e)$;
10   **if** $u(R^G) \geq \frac{1}{\alpha} \times U^*$ **then**
11   **return**

It is clear that Algorithm Top-PEkExp can correctly return an α approximate answer for the maximum k path exclusive expansion problem. However, because we are using a greedy algorithm for calculating the k path exclusive expansions in each iteration, there may exist a better algorithm, e.g., which utilizes an exact algorithm, which can find an α approximate answer much earlier compared with our Top-PEkExp algorithm. This would trade more work done per iteration for achieving early termination. We leave a detailed study of optimal algorithms for the maximum k path exclusive expansion problem for future work.

5. EXPERIMENTS

In this section we will discuss the performance of our proposed algorithms. We use synthetic datasets to demonstrate the relative efficiency, scalability, and memory savings of various algorithms with respect to the naive algorithm. We also use a real dataset to demonstrate the quality of the expansions returned by our algorithms.

5.1 Experiment Setup and Data Sets

The goal of our experiments is two-fold: (i) Evaluate the efficiency and scalability of the algorithms proposed in this paper. (ii) Evaluate the quality of the expansions discovered by various algorithms. The experiments are done on a Xeon 2.5GHz Dual Core Windows 7 machine with 4GB RAM. All algorithms are implemented in Java using JDK/JRE 1.6.

We use two kinds of datasets in our experiments. First, we generated synthetic datasets to compare the performance of various algorithms with the naive algorithm. The metrics we used for the comparison include the running time, number of items accessed and number of expansions generated during the process. We generated 5 synthetic datasets with size from 8000 to 12000, and for all these datasets, attributes and keyword values are sampled from a power law distribution $x = e^{-\beta}$ with $\beta = 2$, which is in accordance with our observation in the real datasets.

The second dataset is a partially crawled dump of the ACM Digital Library. We obtained the items by combining result paper lists of 3 queries: (1) "xml" (2) "histogram" (3) "privacy". We chose these queries because they are all representative interesting research fields in the database community and also feature a good number of publications. The attributes we use for each paper are the average author publication number and the citation count. Values of both attributes are normalized into the range [0, 1]. For each paper, we extract its keywords from the title, keywords list and abstract. Stop words are removed and also stemming is done on all the keywords obtained. For each paper under consideration, we select the top 15 BM25 scored [20] keywords as its topic keywords. A manually created mapping table is used to map similar keywords into a common keyword, namely the most frequent among them. Note that some recent work on tag clustering/recommendation [22] can be leveraged to automate the creation of the mapping table.

After preprocessing, there are in total 48656 papers in the dataset, and 9000 distinct topic keywords. The quality of the expansions (keywords) generated is manually evaluated by domain experts consisting of grad students, who investigated the top expansions discovered, and checked whether the keywords make sense for the field.

5.2 Efficiency Study

First, the efficiency comparison of various algorithms on the synthetic datasets with fixed N and k is presented in Figure 4 A ($N = k = 10$). Note that for the path exclusive algorithm, we choose $\alpha = 0.1$ and $\alpha = 0.3$ as two settings for the algorithm. The running time, the number of items accessed and the number of expansions generated during execution of these algorithms are presented in Figure 4 A(1)-A(3) respectively.

For running time, both TopExp-Lazy and TopExp-LazyW (Weighted TopExp-Lazy) run much faster than the baseline TopExp-Naive algorithm. And the running time of PekExp based algorithms highly depend on the α parameter chosen.

For the number of items accessed, TopExp-LazyW, TopExp-Lazy and TopExp-Naive access roughly the same number of items. And for PekExp based algorithms, the number of items accessed may vary depending on the parameter α. With relatively small α, PekExp accesses significantly less items compared with other algorithms, hence much more efficient. Through our observation, for small α, PekExp usually stops very soon, and as we will illustrate in the next section, the quality of the expansions returned by PekExp based algorithms are also comparable compared with other algorithms. If the application needs immediate response in most cases and tolerable for occasion failure, PekExp would be a reasonable choice from the aspect of efficiency.

For the number of expansions generated, while accessing the same number of items, both TopExp-LazyW and TopExp-Lazy generate much less expansions than TopExp-Naive does. This could significantly lessen the space required and the related computations of generating and updating expansions. For TopExp-LazyW and TopExp-Lazy, the weighted algorithm takes more time and generates more expansions. This is because the weighted algorithm needs to keep different bounds for expansions which correspond to the same set of seen items but with different number of keywords. However, the space and time cost is still reasonable considering the flexibility we could achieve by customizing the weights.

In Figure 4 B(1)-B(3), we show efficiency comparison of the algorithms with k ranging from 10 to 15(number of items=10000, $N = 10$). With larger k, more information needs to be kept for the top expansions, so the updating cost is higher. Furthermore, because more items need to be accessed before the algorithm stop, the algorithm needs longer running time. This coincides with what shows in Figure 4 B(1)-B(2). The only exception is PekExp-alpha= 0.3, for this setting, the number of items accessed and the running time may decrease as k increases. This is because that as k grows, the upper bound of the top-k expansions will drop much faster as more low utility value expansions are included.

Similarly, in Figure 4 C(1)-C(3), we compare the algorithms with N ranging from 10 to 15(number of items=10000, $k = 10$). With larger N, because we need to keep track of more items to determine the bounds for each expansion, we could expect longer running time, more items to be accessed and more expansions to be generated.

We can conclude from these plots that the performance of our proposed algorithms are very robust with respect to different settings, and the performance of the algorithms grows linearly with respect to the size of the dataset, so these algorithms can easily scale to larger datasets. Furthermore, it is clear that the TopExp-Lazy algorithms (weighted and unweighted) always outperform the TopExp-Naive algorithm. PekExp based algorithms is an exception to these observations. With proper configuration it could give good performance, but generally the performance varies depending on the value selected for the parameter α.

5.3 Quality of the Generated Expansions

The quality of the expansions generated can be measured by the quality of the keywords of each top expansion. In Table 2, we show the top-20 expansions generated by the TopExp-Lazy and PekExp (shown as Path-exclusive in Table 2) algorithms on the ACM Digital Library dataset, as well as the corresponding keywords for the 3 selected queries for which expansions were generated. By manually analyzing the expansions generated, we can see that TopExp-Lazy works fairly well in generating expansions related to major subtopics of each query. E.g., for the query "histogram", according to the survey [17], the two most important applications of histogram techniques in databases have been "selectivity estimation" and "approximate query answering". For both topics we can find corresponding expansions in the list of expansions generated, e.g. "select", "approxim". Furthermore, Approximation is an established application of histograms, which constitutes a large portion

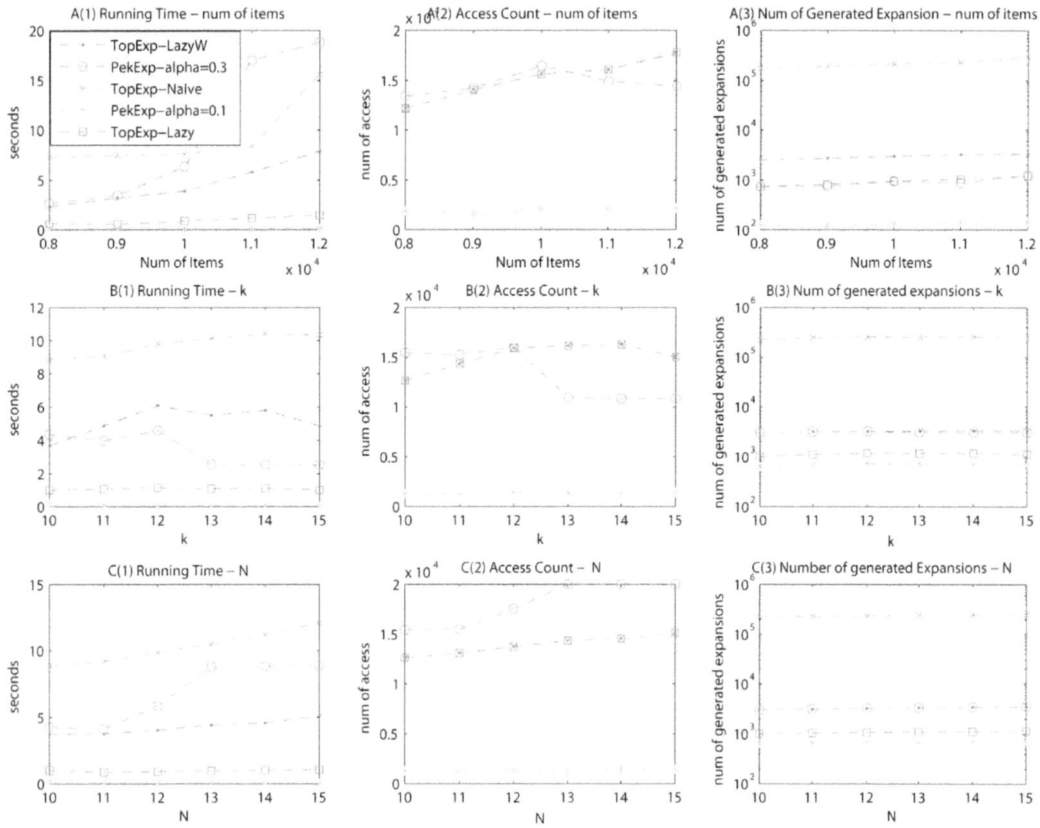

Figure 4: Efficiency experiments

of [17]. Indeed, accordingly we can see various low level expansions like "approxim wavelet", "approxim olap" and so on. Notice that other expansions of "histogram" also correspond to important aspects in the survey. For example, "multi-dimension" histogram is a relatively new and important subfield of histogram, and "optim" refers to an important application of approximation using histogram – query optimization. So in general, the expansions generated can cover most important aspects of the survey. Similar results can be observed for the other two queries as well.

While the quality of expansions returned by TopExp-Lazy are quite good, as can be found in Table 2, these expansions may contain redundant information. E.g., for query "histogram", the expansions returned include both the high level expansion "approxim" and low level (i.e., more refined) expansions "approxim wavelet", "approxim olap". Similarly, for query "privacy", we have "anonym" returned along with "anonym protect" and "anonym k", and for query "xml", we have "query" returned along with "query xpath" and "query store". Our path exclusive algorithm can avoid this problem by making sure that no expansion in the returned result set is a subset of other expansions in the result, thus avoiding such redundancy. By a manual inspection of the list of expansions in Table 2, it is easy to see that such redundancy is avoided by PekExp and also that the set of expansions returned by the that algorithm can also cover most of the important expansions for each query.

In sum, while both TopExp-Lazy and PekExp provide good quality results in terms of meaningful and most important expansions of queries on a real data set, as demonstrated by our experiments, PekExp has the added advantage that it can avoid redundancy in the returned expansions.

6. RELATED WORK

The area of top-k query processing has been studied extensively in the past several years [16]. Most of the top-k algorithms are based on the TA and NRA family of algorithms and their variants or enhancements [13]. The majority of them assume a monotone aggregation function for combining scores of items for different attributes. For each attribute, a non-increasing score-sorted list of items is maintained. In [11], Chakrabarti et al. consider the problem of finding top-k entities in a document corpus, where the score of an entity is defined as a weighted aggregation of the scores of its related documents. The proposed algorithm is similar to our naïve algorithm for the top-k expansion problem, and both algorithms are extensions of the NRA algorithm. However, the number of entities arising in [11] can be considered as a constant, whereas in our context, the number of expansions is exponential w.r.t. the total number of keywords, which can be huge. Thus, it is critical to generate the expansions as lazily as possible.

Our top-k expansion problem is also related to the recent efforts on faceted search [23, 15]. Li et al. [19] propose the problem of automatic generation of top-k facets for query results on Wikipedia. However, their work makes crucial use of a pre-defined category hierarchy in Wikipedia whereas we don't need to make such assumptions. In fact, as mentioned in the introduction, for the applications we consider, this assumption *cannot* be made.

Citation recommendation is another area where previous works [12, 9, 14, 12] often generate results as a ranked list of documents. By contrast, in our work we automatically group all the results into different expansions, and return to the user the top-k interesting expansions along with the relevant items.

histogram		privacy		xml	
TopExp-Lazy	Path-Exclusive	TopExp-Lazy	Path-Exclusive	TopExp-Lazy	Path-Exclusive
approxim	optimal	preserve mining	mining preserve	dtd conform	twig
bucket	approxim wavelet	anonym protect	anonym protect	twig holist	join
select	approxim olap	preserve	mining rule	query	ancestor-descend parent-child
optim	multi-dimension	mining	anonym mining	query xpath	conform
wavelet	approxim stream	anonym publish	individual	dtd	dtd tractable
approxim wavelet	approxim summary	anonym	perturb reconstruct	twig pattern	decide
approxim olap	frequency	anonym k	disclose disclosure	index	dissemin secure
multi-dimension	provable	protect individual	breach	access control	sql store
approxim stream	cost select	protect	mining reconstruct	holist pattern	typecheck
maintain	maintain remark	mining rule	access	dtd schema	node
approxim optim	alloc bucket	locat cloak	k	secure	encrypt secure
bucket multi-dimension	maintain size	access control	mining protect	index twig	control enforce
attribute	join select	mining anonym	control	query store	dynamic query
approxim construct	bucket workload-aware	anonym attack	location-based	twig	index subsequence
approxim summary	bucket reconstruct	anonym locate	categorize	query index	extension select
query	approxim near	locate	vertice	join	native timber
construct	predict range	individual	microdata quasi-identify	ancestor-descend parent-child	secure subject
sample	interval partition	disclosure	pose preserve	index holist	portion secure
frequency	build maintain	preserve anonym	anonym multi-dimension	conform	prevalence secure
stream summary	prohibit self-tuning	reconstruct perturb	scheme secret	holist	index indice

Table 2: Expansions generated by various algorithms.

In [21], the authors propose a way to facilitate the search process by suggesting interesting additional query terms. To measure the interestingness of an additional query term or keyword, they proposed the surprising score which is based on the co-occurrence of two keywords. Compared with our work, they don't consider the overlap between different sets of query keywords. Besides, their score function needs to access all items which are relevant to the query. Since this cannot be calculated at the query time in a scalable manner, they instead propose an approximate solution.

7. CONCLUSION

In this paper, we started with the observation that years after search engines first came into being, most current search services still return results as a flat ranked list of items, which is not ideal for users to easily get to the items they are really interested in. We studied the problem of how to better present search/query results to users. We considered a search scenario in which each item is annotated with a set of keywords and is equipped with a set of attributes, and proposed novel ways to automatically group query result items into different expansions of the query, corresponding to subsets of keywords. We proposed various efficient algorithms which can calculate top-k expansions, and we also studied additional desirable properties for the set of expansions returned, from a semantic perspective, whereby certain redundancies in the expansions returned can be avoided. With a detailed set of experiments, we not only demonstrated the performance of the proposed algorithms, we also validated the quality of the expansions returned by doing a study on a real data set. It is interesting to explore more desirable properties of the expansions returned, and to investigate more efficient algorithms which can return high quality expansion set and can handle the web scale.

8. ACKNOWLEDGEMENT

This work was supported in part by the Institute for Computing, Information and Cognitive Systems (ICICS) at UBC.

9. REFERENCES

[1] http://scholar.google.com.

[2] http://www.bing.com.

[3] http://www.delicious.com.

[4] http://www.flickr.com.

[5] http://www.google.com.

[6] http://www.quora.com.

[7] http://www.yahoo.com.

[8] Sihem Amer-Yahia. I am structured: Cluster me, don't just rank me. In *BEWEB*, 2011.

[9] Steven Bethard and Dan Jurafsky. Who should i cite: learning literature search models from citation behavior. In *CIKM*, pages 609–618, New York, NY, USA, 2010. ACM.

[10] Christopher M. Bishop. *Pattern Recognition and Machine Learning*. Springer, 2006.

[11] Kaushik Chakrabarti, Venkatesh Ganti, Jiawei Han, and Dong Xin. Ranking objects based on relationships. In *SIGMOD*, pages 371–382, New York, NY, USA, 2006. ACM.

[12] Michael D. Ekstrand, Praveen Kannan, James A. Stemper, John T. Butler, Joseph A. Konstan, and John T. Riedl. Automatically building research reading lists. In *ACM RecSys*, pages 159–166, New York, NY, USA, 2010. ACM.

[13] Ronald Fagin, Amnon Lotem, and Moni Naor. Optimal aggregation algorithms for middleware. *JCSS*, 66(4):614–656, 2003.

[14] Qi He, Jian Pei, Daniel Kifer, Prasenjit Mitra, and Lee Giles. Context-aware citation recommendation. In *WWW*, pages 421–430, New York, NY, USA, 2010. ACM.

[15] Marti A. Hearst. Clustering versus faceted categories for information exploration. *Commun. ACM*, 49:59–61, April 2006.

[16] Ihab F. Ilyas, George Beskales, and Mohamed A. Soliman. A survey of top-k query processing techniques in relational database systems. *ACM Comput. Surv.*, 40(4), 2008.

[17] Yannis Ioannidis. The history of histograms (abridged). In *VLDB*, pages 19–30. VLDB Endowment, 2003.

[18] Akihisa Kako, Takao Ono, Tomio Hirata, and Magnús M. Halldórsson. Approximation algorithms for the weighted independent set problem. In *WG*, pages 341–350, 2005.

[19] Chengkai Li, Ning Yan, Senjuti Basu Roy, Lekhendro Lisham, and Gautam Das. Facetedpedia: Dynamic generation of query-dependent faceted interfaces for wikipedia. In *WWW*, pages 651–660, 2010.

[20] S. E. Robertson, S. Walker, and M. M. Hancock-Beaulieu. Okapi at trec-3. In *TREC-3*, pages 109–126. NIST, 1994.

[21] Nikos Sarkas, Nilesh Bansal, Gautam Das, and Nick Koudas. Measure-driven keyword-query expansion. *PVLDB*, 2(1):121–132, 2009.

[22] Yang Song, Ziming Zhuang, Huajing Li, Qiankun Zhao, Jia Li, Wang-Chien Lee, and C. Lee Giles. Real-time automatic tag recommendation. In *SIGIR*, pages 515–522, New York, NY, USA, 2008. ACM.

[23] Roelof van Zwol, Börkur Sigurbjornsson, Ramu Adapala, Lluis Garcia Pueyo, Abhinav Katiyar, Kaushal Kurapati, Mridul Muralidharan, Sudar Muthu, Vanessa Murdock, Polly Ng, Anand Ramani, Anuj Sahai, Sriram Thiru Sathish, Hari Vasudev, and Upendra Vuyyuru. Faceted exploration of image search results. In *WWW*, pages 961–970, New York, NY, USA, 2010. ACM.

TEXplorer: Keyword-based Object Search and Exploration in Multidimensional Text Databases

Bo Zhao, Xide Lin, Bolin Ding, Jiawei Han
Department of Computer Science, University of Illinois at Urbana Champaign
{bozhao3, xidelin2, bding3, hanj}@illinois.edu

ABSTRACT

We propose a novel system TEXplorer that integrates keyword-based object ranking with the aggregation and exploration power of OLAP in a text database with rich structured attributes available, *e.g.*, a product review database.

TEXplorer can be implemented within a multi-dimensional text database, where each row is associated with structural dimensions (attributes) and text data (*e.g.*, a document). The system utilizes the *text cube* data model, where a *cell* aggregates a set of documents with matching values in a subset of dimensions. Cells in a text cube capture different levels of summarization of the documents, and can represent objects at different conceptual levels.

Users query the system by submitting a set of keywords. Instead of returning a ranked list of all the cells, we propose a *keyword-based interactive exploration framework* that could offer flexible OLAP navigational guides and help users identify the levels and objects they are interested in. A novel *significance measure* of dimensions is proposed based on the distribution of *IR relevance* of cells. During each interaction stage, dimensions are ranked according to their significance scores to guide drilling down; and cells in the same cuboids are ranked according to their relevance to guide exploration. We propose efficient algorithms and materialization strategies for ranking top-k dimensions and cells. Finally, extensive experiments on real datasets demonstrate the efficiency and effectiveness of our approach.

Categories and Subject Descriptors

H.3.3 [**Information Systems**]: Information Storage and Retrieval

General Terms

Algorithms

1. INTRODUCTION

Nowadays the web is deeply integrated with database technologies, and one important trend is that much more free texts generated on the web are associated with structured attributes which are either automatically extracted or recognized by human experts. For example, many shopping websites display technical attributes of their products, *e.g.*, Brand, Model, Price, along with customer reviews about the products, so users can conveniently specify those structured attributes to refine their results. Structured data coexist with texts also in many other domains, such as medical reports, system bug reports, *etc.* Therefore, developing novel systems that can efficiently manage such *multidimensional textual data* and provide effective methods for users to explore and understand the data has become a demanding need.

Intuitively, users should be able to query multi-dimensional text databases by specifying values that match the dimensions and keywords that match the texts. Keyword search has been developed in RDBMSs [4], and traditional keyword search systems are effective if users only care about the top relevant tuples, but when the relevant results are many, it could be difficult for users to digest the results and come up with more accurate queries to refine the results. However, if rich structured dimensions are available, they can be naturally utilized to organize the results and give users possible refinement. One example is faceted search systems [15, 17, 6, 11, 12, 10, 2], which show structured facets that are associated with relevant documents in their interfaces, and facets can be interactively selected by users to further refine the search results. Moreover, to further guide user exploration, some systems [17, 6, 11] rank facets based on their proposed measures to promote those dimensions and attributes that are more effective in helping users navigate to their desired results. For example, DynaCet [17] focuses on minimizing the number of facets users need to select to reach the most relevant documents.

Faceted search offers users much more flexibility to explore the results by specifying various facet refinement, however, we should notice in faceted search attributes are mainly treated as filtering conditions and the results displayed to users are still individual relevant tuples, which means the relevance computation, if there is any, still stays at the tuple level. However, individual tuples may not be exactly what users are looking for in many scenarios, instead, users may be more interested in finding the relevance objects, which can be represented by certain aggregation of the tuples. For example, when a user searches for "light-weighted laptop" on Amazon, usually she is not looking for specific review documents that mention the keywords, but some laptop brands or models that reviewers generally think are light-weighted. In this case, faceted search that returns the relevant documents may not be very helpful, instead, we need a framework that supports object-level relevance and navigation.

Past works on entity and object search [5, 1, 3] have justified the effectiveness of aggregating relevant tuples into high-level objects. And recently, [7, 22] target on supporting more flexible aggregation in multidimensional databases, *i.e.*, any combination of the

CIKM'11, October 24–28, 2011, Glasgow, Scotland, UK.

structured attributes correspond to an object at a certain level. In data cubes built on top of the databases, [22] searches for the minimum cells covering the query, while TopCells [7] ranks all the cells based on IR relevance functions. However, all these systems output results in a ranked list, which as we have argued is not ideal for user digestion and exploration, and the fact that ranked objects are in different levels could give more difficulties to users. Therefore, an exploration mechanism suitable for higher-level objects needs to be developed.

With such motivation, in this work we propose TEXplorer, *a keyword-based interactive OLAP framework* that incorporates keyword search with the aggregation and exploration functionalities that are essential in OLAP systems (Figure 1 compares TEXplorer with existing keyword search systems). In TEXplorer, we adopt the strengths of object search and faceted search by utilizing structured attributes in two aspects: first, as in object/entity search they represent high-level objects which individual tuples can be aggregated into; and second as in faceted search they are ranked and displayed to users to facilitate informative navigation of the results.

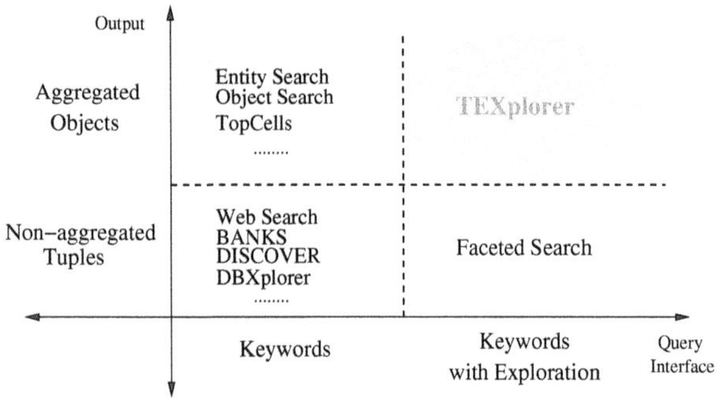

Figure 1: Roadmap of Keyword Search Systems

Moreover, to enable smooth exploration experience, TEXplorer employs a *text cube* data model as presented in [7], so that objects, *i.e.*, cells in the cube, at different levels can be efficiently aggregated. When a keyword query comes, the relevance of each object/cell is aggregated from the relevance scores of tuples belonging to the cell, so that objects in same dimension subspaces can be ordered by relevance, and we further propose a significance measure for ranking different dimension subspaces, which indicates to users which subspaces are more likely to contain desired objects. To interactively explore the results, users can drill down to a dimension with high significance to look at the objects in the corresponding subspace, then they can select an object with high relevance and advance to the next interaction stage, where sub-objects are computed only from tuples belonging to the selected object. Example 1.1 explains the user interaction with concrete details.

EXAMPLE 1.1. *(Motivating Example) Given a customer review database of laptops, each review document is associated with several structural attributes of the laptop being reviewed, e.g., Brand, CPU, Screen, OS, Video Card and Weight, etc.*

Figure 2 shows a running example of TEXplorer. A customer Kate wants to buy a powerful laptop suitable for gaming. Using our system, she could submit a keyword query "powerful, gaming".

Suppose at the beginning, the system returns Kate a list of dimensions ordered by significance: Screen, Brand, Video Card, etc. The Screen dimension will be on the top if we infer from review data it is the most important factor for choosing gaming laptops. Within the Screen subspace different screen objects are ranked according to relevance, e.g. 15" LED will be the most relevant one if reviews about laptops with this screen have the highest aggregated relevance score.

Kate can drill down the Screen dimension and select 15" LED, then in the second stage, the rest dimensions and objects in each dimension are re-ranked only based on reviews for laptops that have the selected screen type. Then this time she could drill down to the top 2 "Video Card" dimension if she feels video cards are more important to her, after which she will be prompted to the third stage to make more refinements. At each stage, Kate can modify her keyword query and the system will re-rank the current records based on the updated query; Kate can also choose to roll back to any previous stages and explore other subspaces.

To summarize, we identify the contributions of this paper are:

- We propose a *keyword-based interactive exploration framework*, which integrates keyword search with OLAP aggregation and exploration, and supports most state-of-the-art IR models for relevance computation.
- We introduce a novel measure, *significance*, to effectively rank dimensions and facilitate informative user exploration based on relevance scores.
- We identify the major computational challenges in our system and propose pre-computation strategies, as well as ranking algorithms that efficiently retrieve top-k dimensions/cells.

Organization We will introduce the data model, *text cube*, and identify the major tasks of TEXplorer in Section 2. Section 3 introduces our *significance* measure. Section 4 proposes pre-omputation strategies and efficient algorithms for ranking dimensions and cells. Section 5 reports experimental study. Section 6 discusses related work, and finally Section 7 concludes this paper.

2. PROBLEM DEFINITION

In this section, we first introduce the *text cube* data model, in Section 2.1, then define the problems we need to address in Section 2.2.

2.1 Data Model: Text Cube

In an n*-dimensional text database* $\mathcal{DB}$, each tuple t can be represented by a *document* d and an object with n *structural dimensions* $\mathcal{A}_1, \mathcal{A}_2, \ldots,$ and $\mathcal{A}_n$, *i.e.*, $t = (a_1, a_2, \ldots, a_n, \mathsf{d})$. Each dimension corresponds to one attribute of the object, *e.g.*, Brand, Model, *etc.* We let $t_{\mathcal{A}_i} = a_i$, and $t_{\mathcal{D}} = \mathsf{d}$ denote the *value* of *dimension* $\mathcal{A}_i$ and document of the tuple respectively.

A *text cube* can be built on top of the multidimensional text database in order to support OLAP operations on the text data. The model was first introduced in [16]. Our system utilizes text cube so we briefly introduce several important concepts as follows.

A *cell* in the text cube is denoted as $C = (v_1, v_2, \ldots, v_n : \mathsf{D})$, where $v_i \in \mathcal{A}_i \cup \{*\}$. $v_i = *$ means the dimension $\mathcal{A}_i$ is *aggregated* in C (v_i can take any value in $\mathcal{A}_i$). D is the set of documents in the tuples of $\mathcal{DB}$ whose dimension values match C. We call this set D the *aggregated document* of the cell C. Let $C_{\mathcal{A}_i}$ denote v_i, and $C_{\mathcal{D}}$ denote D. A cell is called *empty* if $C_{\mathcal{D}} = \varnothing$.

A *cuboid* is a group of cells having the same non-$*$ dimensions. A cuboid with m non-$*$ dimensions is called an m*-dim cuboid*. Cell C' is a *child* of cell C iff $\exists i$, s.t. $C_{\mathcal{A}_i} = *$, and $C'_{\mathcal{A}_i} \in \mathcal{A}_i$, and $\forall j \neq i : C_{\mathcal{A}_j} = C'_{\mathcal{A}_j}$. Specifically, if $\mathcal{A}$ is the only one dimension that is aggregated in C but has non-$*$ value in C', we call C' the $\mathcal{A}$*-child* of C. Let $\mathsf{chd}(C')$ denote the set of (non-empty) children of C', and $\mathsf{chd}_{\mathcal{A}}(C')$ denote the set of (non-empty) $\mathcal{A}$-children of C'.

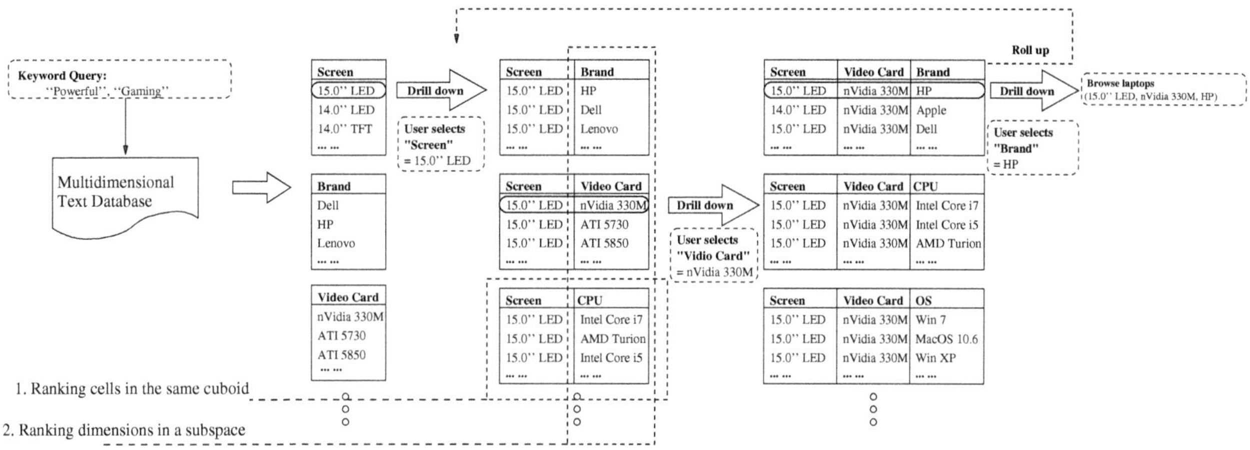

Figure 2: Keyword-based Interactive Exploration in TEXplorer

2.2 Tasks of TEXplorer

After introducing our data model, in this section we will formally define the major tasks of TEXplorer. As explained in Example 1.1 and Figure 2, at any interactive stage, if users would like to further drill down to a more detailed level, they need to decide: (i) which dimension to drill down; and (ii) which cell in the drilled down cuboid to further explore. Hence, two major tasks of TEXplorer are (i) ranking candidate dimensions by the significance measure; and (ii) for each dimension, ranking children cells in the corresponding subspace by relevance. We give formal definitions of these two problems as follows:

2.2.1 *Ranking Dimensions for Drilling Down*

Given a cell C (being explored by the user), for any aggregated dimension $\mathcal{A}_i$ of C, we define the *significance* of $\mathcal{A}_i$ w.r.t. the keyword query q, denoted by $\mathsf{Sig}_{\mathcal{A}_i}(\mathsf{q}, C)$. Our goal is to rank all the aggregated dimensions of C according to $\mathsf{Sig}_{\mathcal{A}_i}(\mathsf{q}, C)$, or provide the top-$k$ ones.

EXAMPLE 2.1. *Consider the example in Figure 2. When the cell (Screen = 15.0" LED) is being explored and query is "gaming, powerful", the drilling down dimensions are ranked as Brand, Video Card, CPU, ... This implies, for laptops with 15.0" LED screens, Brand, Video Card and CPU are the most important factors that are related to gaming experience. The user can choose a dimension to drill down based on the system outputs as well as her own intention and preference.*

Providing a ranked list of top-k significant dimensions is important, especially when the number of dimensions is large, to help users explore the data more effectively. Otherwise, users who do not have much knowledge about the domain, *e.g.*, laptops, could waste a lot more time looking into all possible subspaces. Even for domain experts, such data-oriented ranking can also benefit the analysis of the correlation between structured attributes and keywords in the texts. For example, in a TEXplorer built on aviation report databases, aviation safety analysts can query specific problems mentioned in pilot reports by several keywords and find what dimensions, *e.g.*, location, weather, time, *etc*, are the most important factors that are potentially related to the problem.

Note that although the roles are similar, the significance measure in TEXplorer is designed with quite different intuitions from facet ranking measures in faceted search systems. Since we focus on the ranking and exploration of relevant objects rather than individual tuples given a keyword query, our significance measure is more appropriate for this goal by exploiting the distributions of relevance scores of objects and tuples. We will formally define the significance measure in Section 3.

2.2.2 *Ranking Cells in the Same Cuboid*

Given a cell C (being explored by the user) and an aggregated dimension $\mathcal{A}_i$ of C, we want to rank all the $\mathcal{A}_i$-children of C according to the relevance $\mathrm{Rel}(\mathsf{q}, C)$ efficiently, or provide the top-k relevant ones.

EXAMPLE 2.2. *Consider the second stage in Figure 2, when the user decides to drill down from the cell C: (Screen = 15.0" LED), for C's Brand-children, we need to rank them according to their relevance to the keyword query, in the order of, e.g., (Screen = 15.0" LED, Brand = HP), (Screen = 15.0" LED, Brand = Dell), and so on. Similarly, we also rank C's Video Card-children, CPU-children, and so on. Note we only rank cells within the same cuboid.*

Different from [22, 7], where all the cells in the whole cube are ranked together, we focus on ranking cells (objects) in the same cuboid (subspace), which not only makes the ranking more meaningful in semantics, but also enables our system to adopt much more IR relevance models that could potentially increase accuracy.

Recall a cell C aggregates the documents in $C_{\mathcal{D}}$, so the relevance of C w.r.t. a query q, *i.e.*, $\mathrm{Rel}(\mathsf{q}, C)$, is actually the relevance of a set documents. Previous studies in IR [8] propose two general relevance models for this problem. The first one is called "large document model": simply concatenating all the documents in the set into a pseudo document, and computing the relevance of such pseudo document. The second is "small document model": computing the relevance of each individual document and aggregating the scores using an aggregate function, e.g., the average function:

$$\mathrm{Rel}(\mathsf{q}, C) = \frac{1}{|C_{\mathcal{D}}|} \sum_{\mathsf{d} \in C_{\mathcal{D}}} \mathrm{rel}(\mathsf{q}, \mathsf{d}) \qquad (1)$$

where $|C_{\mathcal{D}}|$ is the number of documents in $C_{\mathcal{D}}$, and $\mathrm{rel}(\mathsf{q}, \mathsf{d})$ is the relevance of a document d w.r.t. q.

The two relevance models have their own advantages. One limitation of previous methods [22, 7] is that they are restricted to specific relevance functions. For example, TopCells [7] can only support the "small document model" due to its efficiency issue. But in TEXplorer, we can efficiently support both models. In the rest of the paper, we will use the average model (Equation 1) to denote the relevance of a cell only for the ease of explanation.

For the document relevance $\text{rel}(q, d)$, TEXplorer is not restricted to a specific form of document relevance function either. We support the class of document relevance in a more general form of:

$$\text{rel}(q, d) = \sum_{w \in q} \text{IDF}_w \cdot \text{TFW}_{w,d} \cdot \text{QTW}_{w,q} \tag{2}$$

where IDF_w is the inverted document frequency factor of term $w \in q$, $\text{TFW}_{w,d}$ is the term frequency factor of w in document d, and $\text{QTW}_{w,q}$ is the query term frequency factor of w in q.

Most state-of-the-art relevance functions fit into the above form, such as Okapi BM25, pivoted normalization, and some language modeling approaches [21]. Moreover, user relevance models [12] can also be implemented in TEXplorer to take users' interaction as feedback and make the ranking more personalized. For example, documents in a cell may be less relevant if a user rolls up after visiting the cell. We will not explain more details since the relevance function for ranking documents and objects is not the contribution of this paper, since we intend to design a general framework that can utilize any IR relevance measure.

3. SIGNIFICANCE OF A DIMENSION

In this section, we introduce a novel *significance* measure to help users determine which dimension to drill down when exploring a cell. For a cell C and an aggregated dimension $\mathcal{A}_i$, $\mathcal{A}_i$-children of C are obtained by drilling down $\mathcal{A}_i$ from C. The significance of drilling down dimension $\mathcal{A}_i$ w.r.t. a keyword query q is defined based on the following two intuitions.

i) **How distinctive are top relevance cells?** The overall relevance of documents in C is constant given the query q, then if for some dimension $\mathcal{A}_i$, relevant documents are aggregated in a way that some cells are very relevant while the others are not, it implies $\mathcal{A}_i$ is discriminative w.r.t. q, and therefore $\mathcal{A}_i$ is more interesting to look into. For example, if reviews of (Brand = Lenovo, Model = ThinkPad) laptops are highly relevant to query "long battery life" while reviews of (Brand = Lenovo, Model = IdeaPad) are not, then users might be more interested in drilling down dimension Model from cell (Brand = Lenovo) than those dimensions where top relevance cells are not very distinctive.

ii) **How consistent are documents within each cell?** Now consider the documents in each of the $\mathcal{A}_i$-children of C. If these documents are consistent w.r.t. q, *i.e.*, they are either all relevant to q or all irrelevant to q, then it implies the relevance of this cell is of high confidence. For example, if we drill down dimension Color from a cell (Brand = Lenovo), and documents in every children cell are not very consistent w.r.t. the query {"battery", "long", "time"}, then it probably means Color is not a very meaningful dimension to drill down.

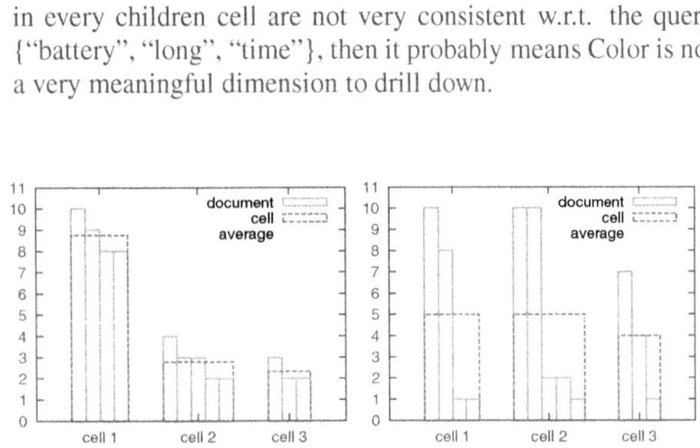

(a) High Significance (b) Low Significance

Figure 3: Example of Significance Scores

Figure 3 illustrates the significance scores for two dimensions. The height of the bars indicate the relevance of the documents and cells. In the first dimension, top cells are more distinguished from others and documents are more consistent within each cell, and therefore the first dimension will have higher significance score.

Now we can formally introduce the significance measure. To capture our first intuition, we define *cell variance* $\text{CV}_{\mathcal{A}_i}(q, C)$ as how much the relevance of each of C's $\mathcal{A}_i$-children deviates from the relevance of C, weighted by the number of documents in each $\mathcal{A}_i$-child, since intuitively larger cells should have higher weights:

$$\text{CV}_{\mathcal{A}_i}(q, C) = \frac{\sum_{C' \in \text{chd}_{\mathcal{A}_i}(C)} |C'_{\mathcal{D}}| \cdot (\text{Rel}(q, C') - \text{Rel}(q, C))^2}{|\text{chd}_{\mathcal{A}_i}(C)| - 1} \tag{3}$$

To capture our second intuition, we define the *document variance* $\text{DV}_{\mathcal{A}_i}(q, C)$ as how much the relevance of each document in C deviates from the relevance of the $\mathcal{A}_i$-child of C which contains that document. And *inverted document variance* $\text{IDV}_{\mathcal{A}_i}(q, C)$ is the reciprocal of $\text{DV}_{\mathcal{A}_i}(q, C)$, so higher IDV implies higher consistency of documents within each $\mathcal{A}_i$-child of C:

$$\text{IDV}_{\mathcal{A}_i}(q, C) = \frac{|C_{\mathcal{D}}| - |\text{chd}_{\mathcal{A}_i}(C)|}{\sum_{C' \in \text{chd}_{\mathcal{A}_i}(C)} \left(\sum_{d \in C'_{\mathcal{D}}} (\text{rel}(q, d) - \text{Rel}(q, C'))^2 \right)} \tag{4}$$

If the average relevance model (Equation 1) is used, treating each cell as a document group, CV is actually the *variance of group means*, and DV is the *mean of with-in group variances*. We define a more general form here so other relevance models can also be plugged in.

We will consider a dimension more significant if the CV and IDV are both high. On the other hand, a dimension with higher CV is also more likely to have lower IDV, since the documents in this cuboid tend to be inconsistent. Therefore, similar to the well-known TF-IDF mechanism, we penalize high CV scores based on IDV scores by using the product of the two as our measure, *i.e.*, we define the significance as:

$$\text{Sig}_{\mathcal{A}_i}(q, C) = \text{CV}_{\mathcal{A}_i}(q, C) \cdot \text{IDV}_{\mathcal{A}_i}(q, C) \tag{5}$$

Statistical Meaning of Sig Actually our proposed significance measure $\text{Sig}_{\mathcal{A}_i}$ has some intrinsic relationship to the *F-ratio*, which is often used in *ANOVA* test [13] in statistics. All the documents in a cell C are partitioned into its $\mathcal{A}_i$-children for a drilling down dimension $\mathcal{A}_i$. If we associate each of the $\mathcal{A}_i$-children with a relevance distribution, we can regard the relevance scores of documents in each of the $\mathcal{A}_i$-children as samples drawn from this distribution. If the average relevance model (1) is used, $\text{Sig}_{\mathcal{A}_i}$ as defined in (5) is actually the *F-ratio*, which measures how significantly these relevance distributions are different from each other. The higher *F-ratio* is, the more significantly these distributions are different. And in this paper we generalize its form so other relevance models can also be used to compute $\text{Sig}_{\mathcal{A}_i}$.

4. RANKING ALGORITHMS

In this section, we focus on designing efficient algorithms for the two computational tasks: ranking most significant dimensions and most relevant cells in each dimension. In the previous section, we can see that our significance measure depends on the relevance scores of children cells in each dimension, so the ranking of relevant cells can be naturally implemented within the framework of ranking dimensions. Therefore, in the discussion of our proposed algorithms we mainly focus on computing the top-*k* significant dimensions. We identify two major computational challenges of this problem and proposed the corresponding solutions:

- Each document belongs to one children cell in each drill-down dimension. Therefore, in order to rank children cells in every dimension and compute the Sig score, every relevant document needs to be aggregated multiple times to different cells. However, we find the cell relevance scores are *pre-computable*, therefore we can materialize some statistics offline in the Text Cube, so that online query-dependent aggregation can be performed very efficiently.

- The Sig measure requires aggregated statistics from all the relevant documents. Hence, to compute the exact scores all relevant documents need to be scanned, which could be costly on large scale corpus. To solve this problem, we focus on finding top-*k* solutions, *i.e.*, if only top-*k* significant dimensions are desired we can just scan a very small number of documents. We identify our top-*k* problem is very different from existing ones, and by exploiting some good properties of our problem, we could achieve stronger pruning power than previous top-*k* algorithms.

4.1 MultiAccess Algorithm

The first algorithm is the baseline approach. Equation (3) and (4) show that, given the cell C (currently visited by users) and the keyword query q, the Sig score of dimension $\mathcal{A}_i$ depends on: i) relevance of C, and every $\mathcal{A}_i$-child of C; ii) relevance of every document in C, *i.e.*, $\mathrm{rel}(\mathsf{q}, \mathsf{d})$; iii) some query independent factors: $|C'_{\mathcal{D}}|$, $|C_{\mathcal{D}}|$, and $|\mathsf{chd}_{\mathcal{A}_i}(C)|$.

For the query independent factors, we can pre-compute and materialize them in the Text Cube, so that we do not have to scan all the documents in C on-the-fly. However, we still need to scan every *relevant* document when the query comes. Moreover, each relevant document should be aggregated to all the cells C' it belongs to for computing $\mathrm{Rel}(\mathsf{q}, C')$. After we scan all the relevant documents, exact significance scores can be computed and the dimensions with top-*k* highest scores will be output. Because multiple aggregation operations are performed for each relevant document, we call this algorithm MultiAccess.

Algorithm 1 MultiAccess Algorithm

Input: keyword query q, starting cell C, parameter k.

```
d = FetchNextRelevant(q, C);
while d is not NULL do
    Update C with d;
    for each aggregated dimension A_i of C do
        Update d's cell C' ∈ chd_{A_i}(C) with d;
    d = FetchNextRelevant(q, C);
for each aggregated dimension A_i of C do
    Compute Sig_{A_i}(q, C);
Output dimensions A_i with the top-k highest Sig_{A_i}(q, C);
```

Analysis Suppose there are m different aggregated dimensions in C, and n relevant documents, then the time complexity of the MultiAccess algorithm is $O(m \times n)$. When n is very large, this algorithm runs very slow. Also notice that if we do not pre-compute the query-independent factors like the number of documents in C, then those factors can only be computed by scanning all documents in the cell, meaning the time complexity for every query is $O(m \times |C_{\mathcal{D}}|)$, which is not acceptable.

4.2 OneAccess Algorithm

One major overhead of the MultiAccess algorithm is that multiple aggregation operations are performed for each relevant document. To alleviate this problem, we naturally exploit the precomputability of the scores by materializing some statistics about the terms offline in the Text Cube, so that when online queries come, the scores can be computed based on materialized results very efficiently.

From Equation (5) we can see the only factor that causes multiple aggregation of documents is the relevance of children cells of C, *i.e.*, $\mathrm{Rel}(\mathsf{q}, C')$. Since users could query on any cell in the Cube, we now discuss how to precompute relevance signals for any cell in the Text Cube.

Precomputation of Relevance To compute the relevance of a cell C w.r.t. a keyword query q, without any precomputation, we need to scan each document in $C_{\mathcal{D}}$ at least once. In the following, we show that, for the general form of cell relevance defined in Section 2.2.2, we need only $O(1)$ space per term in each cell for precomputation, so that the relevance of the cell C, $\mathrm{Rel}(\mathsf{q}, C)$, can be computed in $O(|\mathsf{q}|)$ time.

For the "small document" cell relevance model defined in (1), we can rewrite it as follows:

$$\mathrm{Rel}(\mathsf{q}, C) = \frac{1}{|C_{\mathcal{D}}|} \sum_{\mathsf{d} \in C_{\mathcal{D}}} \sum_{w \in \mathsf{q}} \mathsf{IDF}_w \cdot \mathsf{TFW}_{w,\mathsf{d}} \cdot \mathsf{QTW}_{w,\mathsf{q}}$$

$$= \frac{1}{|C_{\mathcal{D}}|} \sum_{w \in \mathsf{q}} \mathsf{IDF}_w \cdot \mathsf{QTW}_{w,\mathsf{q}} \cdot \left(\sum_{\mathsf{d} \in C_{\mathcal{D}}} \mathsf{TFW}_{w,\mathsf{d}} \right)$$

Let $\mathsf{TFW}_{w,C} = \sum_{\mathsf{d} \in C_{\mathcal{D}}} \mathsf{TFW}_{w,\mathsf{d}}$. If for each term w, we precompute IDF_w, and in each cell C, we precompute $\mathsf{TFW}_{w,C}$, then from the above equation, $\mathrm{Rel}(\mathsf{q}, C)$ can be computed in $O(|\mathsf{q}|)$ time.

For the "large document model", the precomputation is straightforward: we concatenate the documents in each cell offline and store the pseudo document in the cell. Computing $\mathrm{Rel}(\mathsf{q}, C)$ is then equivalent to computing the relevance of the pseudo document, which takes $O(|\mathsf{q}|)$ time.

The precomputaion needs O(1) space per term for each cell, so the total space cost of the text cube is $O(|V| \times |Cube|)$, where $|V|$ is the size of the vocabulary, and $|Cube|$ is the number of non-empty cells in the Cube, bounded by $2^m \times$#(Base Cells), m is the number of dimensions. For a text database that does not have very high number of dimensions, *e.g.*, 10 dimensions, but have a large number of documents, the number of non-empty cells is comparable to the number of documents, so the extra space needed is comparable to the size of inverted index built on the document collection, which is quite affordable.

Moreover, there have been extensive studies on reducing the space cost and supporting efficient query processing in a *partial materialized* cube [16, 20], where only some cells of the cube are precomputed and the rest ones can be efficiently computed online based on them. Those techniques can be easily implemented in our system to further save the storage, since the measures stored in the text cube satisfy the *distributive* property [16]. In the remainder of the paper, however, we assume our cube is fully materialized since how to reduce the space is not the main focus of this work.

Online Computation We have showed with precomputation the relevance of cells can be computed very efficiently on-the-fly. And based on those scores we can compute the cell variance $\mathsf{CV}(\mathsf{q}, C)$ (3) directly. Next, we further decompose the $\mathsf{IDV}(\mathsf{q}, C)$ and rewrite Equation (5):

$$\mathsf{Sig}_{\mathcal{A}_i}(\mathsf{q}, C) = \frac{\mathsf{CV}_{\mathcal{A}_i}(\mathsf{q}, C) \cdot (|C_{\mathcal{D}}| - |\mathsf{chd}_{\mathcal{A}_i}(C)|)}{\sum\limits_{C' \in \mathsf{chd}_{\mathcal{A}_i}(C)} (|C'_{\mathcal{D}}| \mathrm{Rel}(\mathsf{q}, C')^2 - 2S_{C'} \mathrm{Rel}(\mathsf{q}, C')) + SS_C} \tag{6}$$

where $S_{C'} = \sum_{\mathsf{d} \in C'} \mathrm{rel}(\mathsf{q}, \mathsf{d})$, and $SS_C = \sum_{\mathsf{d} \in C} \mathrm{rel}(\mathsf{q}, \mathsf{d})^2$.

$S_{C'}$ is the sum of the relevance scores of documents in cell C', so it can also benefit from the precomputation. In fact, $S_{C'}$ just equals to $|C'_{\mathcal{D}}| \cdot \mathrm{Rel}(\mathsf{q}, C')$ if the average relevance model (1) is used. Then the only factor left unknown in Sig is SS_C, the sum of squares of each document's relevance score. And this factor can not be easily pre-computed unless bigrams are considered, which would cause too much storage overhead. Therefore, in the online query processing we still need to scan all relevant documents, but this time we only need $O(1)$ operation for each document to compute SS_C. We call this algorithm OneAccess.

Algorithm 2 OneAccess Algorithm

Input: keyword query q, starting cell C, parameter k.

Compute $\mathrm{Rel}(\mathsf{q}, C)$;
for each aggregated dimension $\mathcal{A}_i$ of C **do**
  for each $C' \in \mathsf{chd}_{\mathcal{A}_i}(C)$ **do**
    Compute $\mathrm{Rel}(\mathsf{q}, C')$;
d = FetchNextRelevant(q, C);
while d is not NULL **do**
  $SS_C = SS_C + \mathrm{rel}(\mathsf{q}, \mathsf{d})^2$;
  d = FetchNextRelevant(q, C);
for each aggregated dimension $\mathcal{A}_i$ of C **do**
  Compute $\mathsf{Sig}_{\mathcal{A}_i}(\mathsf{q}, C)$ using SS_C, *etc*;
Output dimensions $\mathcal{A}_i$ with the top-k highest $\mathsf{Sig}_{\mathcal{A}_i}(\mathsf{q}, C)$;

Analysis Since for each relevant document OneAccess only needs $O(1)$ operation, the time complexity is $O(n + m)$, if there are n relevant documents and m dimensions. When m or n is large, OneAccess will be significantly faster than MultiAccess. Another benefit of OneAccess is that the relevance of cells can be computed without scanning any document, so the ranking of top cells in each dimension can be performed very efficiently.

4.3 OneAccess+ Algorithm

OneAccess needs to scan all relevant documents once in order to compute the exact significance scores. However in the case only top-k dimensions are desired by users, we do not have to compute the exact scores if the top-k is guaranteed.

Specifically, in OneAccess+ we progressively fetch documents in the descending order of their relevance scores, which can be easily supported by the underlying full text search component. Then we can estimate the upper and lower bounds of the scores, and rank all dimensions in two lists: $\mathcal{L}_{UB}$ and $\mathcal{L}_{LB}$, based on their upper bounds and lower bounds respectfully. We update the bounds and the ranked lists every time we fetch new documents. When the top-k dimensions with highest values in $\mathcal{L}_{UB}$ and $\mathcal{L}_{LB}$ are the same, and the k-th lower bound is greater than or equal to the $(k+1)$-th upper bound, it means no dimension in $\mathcal{L}_{UB}$ that ranks lower than k could eventually win any top-k dimension in $\mathcal{L}_{LB}$, *i.e.*, the top-k is guaranteed and the algorithm can stop.

Upper and Lower Bounds of Sig As we have discussed in the OneAccess algorithm, all factors in (6) can be computed efficiently from offline materialized scores without scanning any relevant documents, except the sum of squares of document relevance scores $SS_C = \sum_{\mathsf{d} \in C} \mathrm{rel}(\mathsf{q}, \mathsf{d})^2$. So if we treat factors that have been calculated as constants, it is easy to see the Sig score monotonically decreases with SS_C. Also we know the documents can be fetched in a non-increasing order of their relevance. Based on these facts, we can derive the upper and lower bounds of Sig as follows.

Suppose at the current step we are accessing the i-th document, then an obvious lower bound $\underline{SS_C}$ is given by the current SS_C score we have aggregated:

$$\underline{SS_C} = \sum_{j=1}^{i} \mathrm{rel}(\mathsf{q}, \mathsf{d}_j)^2 \tag{7}$$

Then the Sig score computed by using lower bound $\underline{SS_C}$ is the upper bound.

To derive the upper bound of SS_C, we first need to know the number of relevant documents for the current query. While the exact number is not easy to get without scanning all the relevant documents, the total number of documents in the current starting cell $C_{\mathcal{D}}$ is obviously too loose. The solution is we can offline compute and materialize the document frequency of w in C, *i.e.*, number of documents in C that contain w, denoted as $df_{w,C}$. Then for each w in the query q, the sum of $df_{w,C}$ gives an upper bound of the number of relevant documents. And since we know the relevance of future documents is not greater than the current $\mathrm{rel}(\mathsf{q}, \mathsf{d}_i)$. The upper bound of SS_C can be estimated by:

$$\overline{SS_C} = \sum_{j=1}^{i} \mathrm{rel}(\mathsf{q}, \mathsf{d}_j)^2 + (\min\{\sum_{w \in \mathsf{q}} df_{w,C}, |C_{\mathcal{D}}|\} - i) \cdot \mathrm{rel}(\mathsf{q}, \mathsf{d}_i)^2 \tag{8}$$

And the lower bound of Sig can be computed using $\overline{SS_C}$.

Algorithm 3 OneAccess+ Algorithm

$\mathcal{L}_{UB}$ and $\mathcal{L}_{LB}$: ranked lists of dimensions (in the non-increasing order of upper bound and lower bound of $\mathsf{Sig}(\mathsf{q}, C)$ respectfully)

Input: keyword query q, starting cell C, parameter k.

Compute $\mathrm{Rel}(\mathsf{q}, C)$;
for each aggregated dimension $\mathcal{A}_i$ of C **do**
  for each $C' \in \mathsf{chd}_{\mathcal{A}_i}(C)$ **do**
    Compute $\mathrm{Rel}(\mathsf{q}, C')$;
d = FetchNextRelevant(q, C);
while d is not NULL **do**
  Update $\overline{SS_C}$ and $\underline{SS_C}$;
  for each aggregated dimension $\mathcal{A}_i$ of C **do**
    Update $\overline{\mathsf{Sig}_{\mathcal{A}_i}}(\mathsf{q}, C)$ using $\underline{SS_C}$;
    Update $\underline{\mathsf{Sig}_{\mathcal{A}_i}}(\mathsf{q}, C)$ using $\overline{SS_C}$;
    Update $\mathcal{L}_{UB}$ and $\mathcal{L}_{LB}$;
  if $\mathcal{L}_{UB}[1..k] == \mathcal{L}_{LB}[1..k]$ and $\mathcal{L}_{LB}[k].score \geq \mathcal{L}_{UB}[k+1].score$ **then**
    break;
  d = FetchNextRelevant(q, C);
Output top-k dimensions $\mathcal{L}_{UB}[1..k]$;

Analysis OneAccess+ exploits upper and lower bounds of the significance scores to enable early termination of the algorithm when top-k is guaranteed. When the bounds are tight, and k is small, it could lead to more efficient execution than MultiAccess and OneAccess. However, every time we get a new relevant document, the upper and lower bounds for each dimension should be updated, which takes $O(m)$, and the ranked lists may need to be adjusted, which takes expected $O(m \log m)$ time. Hence the time complexity of OneAccess+ is $O(n \cdot m \log m)$ for n relevant documents and m dimensions, which is worse than OneAccess. Several heuristics could be applied to improve the running time, *e.g.*, only updating the bounds after fetching a batch of t documents.

4.4 OneAccess++ Algorithm

OneAccess+ deploys standard top-k stop conditions which work for general ranking functions [3]. However, our top-k problem is quite different from previous top-k aggregation problems [3, 1, 14]. In previous problems, each object is aggregated from a set of tuples in the database, and to get the top-k objects, the algorithms give higher priorities to the promising objects so that their exact scores can be computed first. However, in our problem, the Sig scores for different dimensions depend on all relevant documents in the cell. Computation of the exact scores requires scanning all the relevant documents, which is what we want to prevent.

More specifically, for the Sig score in Equation (6), if all pre-computable factors are already calculated, they can be treated as constant. Therefore, the significance scores for different dimensions can be simplified as a series of functions with different parameters but the same variable, which is the unknown factor SS_C (it is unknown before all relevant documents are scanned):

$$\mathsf{Sig}_{\mathcal{A}_i}(SS_C) = \frac{p_{\mathcal{A}_i}}{q_{\mathcal{A}_i} + SS_C} \tag{9}$$

Then we can exploit a good property of this family of functions to achieve stronger pruning power.

PROPERTY 1. *$f^1, f^2, \ldots, f^n$ are a series of functions of x. For any two functions f^s and f^t ($1 \leq s < t \leq n$), there exists no $x_i < x_k < x_j$, s.t. $f^s(x_i) < f^t(x_i)$, and $f^s(x_j) < f^t(x_j)$, but $f^s(x_k) > f^t(x_k)$.*

Property 1 says if the values of any two functions at x_i, x_j rank in the same order, then such order remains for the values of the two functions at any point between x_i and x_j. It is equivalent to say that any two functions do not cross more than once between any x_i and x_j.

According to Equation (9), $\mathsf{Sig}_{\mathcal{A}_i}(SS_C)$ represents a family of functions of SS_C. And it is easy to verify that any two functions in this family with different parameters can only have at most one intersection, *i.e.*, $\mathsf{Sig}_{\mathcal{A}_i}(SS_C)$ satisfies Property 1.

Now we give the lemma which is the key of this OneAccess++ algorithm.

LEMMA 1. *Given a series of functions of x: $f^1, f^2, \ldots, f^n$ that satisfy Property 1. If x is bounded between $lower(x)$ and $upper(x)$, and f functions with top-k highest values at $lower(x)$ are the same as f functions with top-k highest values at $upper(x)$; then the top-k remain the same at any point x between $lower(x)$ and $upper(x)$.*

PROOF. Let us assume the lemma is not true, *i.e.*, there exists a function f', s.t. f' is not in top-k either at $lower(x)$ nor at $upper(x)$, but in top-k at some point x' which is between $lower(x)$ and $upper(x)$. Then there must exist a function f'' which is in top-k at both $lower(x)$ and $upper(x)$, but $f''(x') < f'(x')$. On the other hand, since the values of f'' are greater than f' at both $lower(x)$ and $upper(x)$, and Property 1 is satisfied for all functions in the series, we can derive that $f''(x') > f'(x')$. Contradiction. □

Since $\mathsf{Sig}_{\mathcal{A}_i}(SS_C)$ is a series of functions of SS_C satisfying Property 1, and SS_C is bounded by its lower bound $\underline{SS_C}$ and upper bound $\overline{SS_C}$. Therefore the real top-k $\mathsf{Sig}_{\mathcal{A}_i}(SS_C)$ scores are achieved when SS_C reaches the exact value, which is some point between $\underline{SS_C}$ and $\overline{SS_C}$. Lemma 1 tells us, if the top-k dimensions $\mathcal{A}_i$ with highest $\mathsf{Sig}_{\mathcal{A}_i}(\underline{SS_C})$ and $\mathsf{Sig}_{\mathcal{A}_i}(\overline{SS_C})$ are the same, then they are the real top-k dimensions.

Therefore, our OneAccess++ algorithm is generally the same as OneAccess+. The only difference is the stop-condition for top-k. OneAccess++ stops as soon as the top-k dimensions in the lower bound and upper bound lists are the same. The condition that the k-th lower bound is greater than or equal to the $k+1$-th upper bound is no longer required. Since the stop condition is relaxed, OneAccess++ is guaranteed to be more efficient than OneAccess+. Also note that OneAccess++ will generate the exactly same top-k results as OneAccess+.

Algorithm 4 OneAccess++ Algorithm

$\mathcal{L}_{UB}$ and $\mathcal{L}_{LB}$: ranked lists of dimensions (in the non-increasing order of upper bound and lower bound of $\mathsf{Sig}(\mathsf{q}, C)$ respectfully)
Input: keyword query q, starting cell C, parameter k.

```
Compute Rel(q, C);
for each aggregated dimension A_i of C do
    for each C' ∈ chd_{A_i}(C) do
        Compute Rel(q, C');
d = FetchNextRelevant(q, C);
while d is not NULL do
    Update \overline{SS_C} and \underline{SS_C};
    for each aggregated dimension A_i of C do
        Update \underline{Sig_{A_i}}(q, C) using \underline{SS_C};
        Update \overline{Sig_{A_i}}(q, C) using \overline{SS_C};
        Update L_UB and L_LB;
    if L_UB[1..k] == L_LB[1..k] then
        break;
    d = FetchNextRelevant(q, C);
Output top-k dimensions L_UB[1..k];
```

Analysis Since OneAccess++ is generally the same as OneAccess+ except the stop condition is different, the time complexity of the two algorithms are identical. But in practice, OneAccess++ is guaranteed to be faster.

5. EXPERIMENTS

In this section, our goal is to (i) verify the effectiveness of our ranking mechanisms and (ii) analyse the performance of our proposed algorithms, and storage of the text cube.

Dataset We crawled customer reviews for laptops from Google Products[1]. The dataset has 26,418 reviews, 920 laptops, and 11 dimensions: Audio Card, Battery Run Time, Brand, Screen Type, Color, Weight, Operating System, CPU, Hard Drive, Main Memory and Video Card.

Environment Setup All experiments were done on a machine running Windows 7 Professional, with a Inter Core Duo T9300 processor, 4GB main memory, and 80G hard disk. The algorithms were implemented in C++ and compiled with Microsoft Visual C++ 2008.

5.1 Effectiveness

In this section we focus on studying the effectiveness of our proposed significance measure for ranking dimensions. For the relevance functions of documents and cells, there have been extensive studies in the field of information retrieval, and TEXplorer can

[1]http://products.google.com

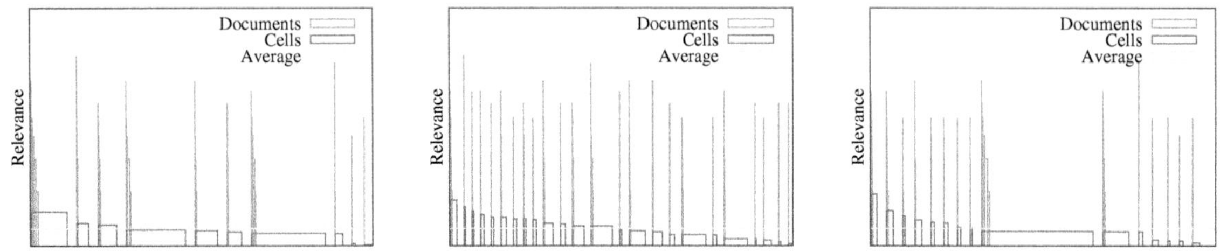

(a) Sig: Brand (b) Indg: Weight (c) Intr: CPU

Figure 4: Top-1 dimension given by Sig, Indg, and Intr for query "stylish beauty cool fashion"

flexibly adopt most state-of-the-art relevance models. Therefore we will not focus on evaluating different relevance functions. In the following experiments, we use Okapi BM25 [21] for document relevance and the average model (Equation 1) for cell relevance, which work quite well on our dataset.

Measures in Faceted Search We compare our significance measure with the dimension ranking functions in two recent faceted search systems [17, 6] defined as follows:

i) [17] targets on building decision trees with minimum height on the tuples, so that users' efforts to reach each individual tuple can be minimized. The Indg score of dimension $\mathcal{A}_i$ measures the number of *indistinguishable* pairs of tuples if choosing $\mathcal{A}_i$ as the root, and the algorithm greedily selects the dimension with minimum Indg to build the tree.

$$\mathsf{Indg}_{\mathcal{A}_i}(\mathsf{q}, C) = \sum_{C' \in \mathsf{chd}_{\mathcal{A}_i}(C)} \left(\sum_{\mathsf{d}_i, \mathsf{d}_j \in C'_{\mathcal{D}}} \mathrm{rel}(\mathsf{q}, \mathsf{d}_i) \times \mathrm{rel}(\mathsf{q}, \mathsf{d}_j) \right) \tag{10}$$

ii) [6] estimates the probability of the query results using a *hypergeometric distribution*: let $|C_{\mathcal{D}}|$ be the number of documents in $C_{\mathcal{D}}$, and $|C_{\mathcal{D}}(\mathsf{q})|$ be the numbers of relevant documents w.r.t. q in $C_{\mathcal{D}}$. For an $\mathcal{A}_i$-child of C, say C', if we randomly sample $|C_{\mathcal{D}}(\mathsf{q})|$ documents from $C_{\mathcal{D}}$, the p-value of getting at least $|C'_{\mathcal{D}}(\mathsf{q})|$ documents from $C'_{\mathcal{D}}$ in the sample can be written as:

$$p_{\mathcal{A}_i, C'}(\mathsf{q}, C) = 1 - \sum_{s=0}^{|C'_{\mathcal{D}}(\mathsf{q})|-1} \frac{\binom{|C'_{\mathcal{D}}|}{s}\binom{|C_{\mathcal{D}}|-|C'_{\mathcal{D}}|}{|C_{\mathcal{D}}(\mathsf{q})|-s}}{\binom{|C_{\mathcal{D}}|}{|C_{\mathcal{D}}(\mathsf{q})|}} \tag{11}$$

A smaller p-value indicates it is less likely to get the results by chance, and therefore the cell C' is more *interesting*. And the overall *interestingness* of a dimension $\mathcal{A}_i$ is the aggregation of p-values of the top-k interesting $\mathcal{A}_i$-children of C:

$$\mathsf{Intr}_{\mathcal{A}_i}(\mathsf{q}, C) = -\sum_{t=0}^{k} \log p_{\mathcal{A}_i, C'_t}(\mathsf{q}, C) \tag{12}$$

We can see the two measures defined above more focus on the tuple level results. Indg targets on distinguishing individual tuples, which may not be very effective for users to understand the data if they are more satisfied with higher level aggregated results. The p-value and Intr utilize the distribution of result tuples, but the relevance scores of tuples and cells are not considered at all. Therefore, these two measures may not be well suited for our tasks in TEXplorer.

Case Studies We issue a keyword query "stylish beauty cool fashion" on all documents in our dataset. The top-1 dimension ranked by Sig is Brand, and the corresponding top relevant cell is (Brand = Apple), which is quite reasonable since Apple laptops are well-known for the stylish design. However, the Brand dimension only ranks the 9th and the 10th according to Indg and Intr respectively, while the top-1 dimensions according to those two measures are Weight and CPU, which are quite difficult to interpret.

Figure 4 plots the documents and cells for each top-1 dimension. Height of red and blue bars indicates the relevance of documents and cells, and the green bar represents the average relevance of all the documents, which remains the same. Width of the blue bars represents the number of documents in the cells. In Figure 4(a), we can see the top (Brand=Apple) cell dominates other cells and the documents are rather consistent compared to the other two dimensions, and therefore its Sig score is very high. Figure 4(b) shows Indg tends to give higher scores to dimensions that have more cells but each cell has less documents, so that the number of filtered tuples is maximized after users select one cell. However, the results lack semantic interpretation if users prefer higher level objects rather than individual tuples. Intr does not utilize the relevance scores at all. Although in our experiments cell (Brand=Apple) has quite high p-value compared to other Brand-children, more CPU-children get higher p-values and thus the CPU dimension ranks top-1, which is not very meaningful either.

Query	Sig	Indg	Intr
game player	Screen Type (16" TFT)	Weight	Processor
runtime error	OS (MaxOS 10.5)	Weight	Display Type
slow response	Processor (Celeron M353)	OS	Video
long hour	Battery Time (9.5 hour)	Color	Processor

Table 1: Top-1 Dimensions given by Sig, Indg and Intr

We can show the effectiveness of our method using several more queries. The top-1 dimensions given by the three measures Sig, Indg and Intr are put in Table 1. For our proposed Sig measure we also show the top relevant cell in the corresponding subspace. Results of Sig are generally more meaningful than the other two measures. Take the first query for instance, Screen Type is very important to gaming, and the top relevant cell is a fairly large screen, meaning users who bought this screen mentioned gaming experience more frequently in their reviews. However, Indg and Intr still rank Weight and Processor as the top-1 dimensions, same as the results of a quite different query in Figure 4, which is probably because these two measures do not utilize much the distribution of the relevance scores.

Quantitative Evaluation To quantitatively justify the effectiveness of our method, we adapt the most popular IR evaluation mechanism: labelling dimensions as relevant or non-relevant for a given query and compute several measures such as precision and MAP against the results. We want to compare with other state-of-the-art systems and see whether our system can provide immediate helpful guides, so in this experiments, we evaluate the first stage of the exploration (immediately after keyword query issued). To get the ground truth, we choose 20 common queries and ask 3 users to label which dimensions are meaningful w.r.t. the queries. Then we take the intersection of their labelled sets as the ground truth, which is quite conservative but can ensure us labelled dimensions are really relevant. Actually, we found the 3 users agree on more than 90 percent of the dimensions, which means the meaningful dimensions are quite obvious given a certain keyword query. For example, for the query "stylish", Brand is obviously a relevant dimension.

Then we compute two most important measures in IR evaluation: mean average precision (MAP) and the precision at top 3 against the dimensions output by Sig, Indg, and Intr measures. Table 2 shows the averaged results over 20 queries: unsurprisingly Sig achieves the best MAP and precision among the three measures by a significant margin; the MAP of Intr and Indg are close while the precision of Intr is higher than Indg.

-	Sig	Indg	Intr
MAP	**0.662**	0.430	0.468
Precision@3	**0.467**	0.233	0.367

Table 2: MAP and Precision@3 of Sig, Indg and Intr

5.2 Efficiency

Now we analyse the performance of the proposed algorithms. In the experiments we issue 10 queries of length 3 and compare the average running time and visited documents of each algorithm. Note that for fair comparison we do not count the time of loading index and fetching relevant documents, since all algorithms assume it is efficiently supported by underlying full text search modules. We also loop the algorithms for multiple times and take the average in order to measure the running time more accurately.

Efficiency vs. Number of Documents To verify the scalability of the algorithms, we take 4 samples of 4901, 9802, 14703, 19604 documents from our dataset and run the algorithms on the 4 samples and the whole dataset with 26418 documents. All 11 dimensions are considered, and the k is set to 3 for top-k algorithms.

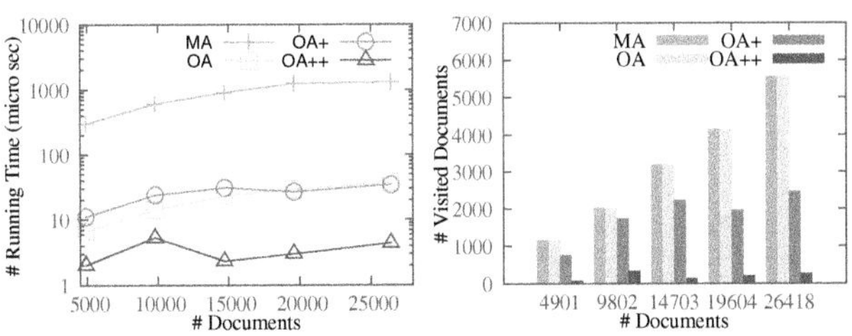

(a) Running Time (b) Visited Documents

Figure 5: Performance for Different # Documents

If we look at the number of visited documents in Figure 5(b). MultiAccess and OneAccess always visit all the relevant documents as expected, which grow linearly with the number of all documents in the database. OneAccess+ visits less documents by utilizing the upper and lower bounds of Sig to compute the top-k dimensions, and the documents OneAccess+ accesses grow slower than the total number of relevant documents, which means the pruning power of OneAccess+ becomes stronger as the size of the database increases. OneAccess++ visits significantly less documents than all the other three algorithms, and the number is almost stable. This verifies the unique property of our top-k problem does deliver stronger pruning power. Also note that top-k algorithms OneAccess+ and OneAccess++ also has a good property that they may actually visit less documents when the total number of document increases, because when there are more relevant documents it is possible that the gap between top-k results and the rest becomes larger, so the algorithms can confidently stop earlier.

For the running time shown in Figure 5(a), MultiAccess is slower than OneAccess even they visit the same number of documents, since multiple aggregation is performed for each document in MultiAccess. Also notice that OneAccess+ is also slower than OneAccess on the smallest samples because of the overhead for updating the bounds and maintaining the top-k lists. When the size of the database is large, the pruning power begins to dominate and therefore OneAccess+ becomes slightly faster than OneAccess. OneAccess++ is consistently the fastest as expected, and it generally runs more than 10 times faster than OneAccess and OneAccess+ except for the first two smaller samples. This again verifies the good performance of OneAccess++.

Efficiency vs. Top-k In this experiment, we vary the length of the top list, *i.e.*, k, and evaluate the efficiency for each algorithm. All the documents in the dataset and all 11 dimensions are considered. We evaluate 10 queries of length 3 and report the average running time and number of visited documents in Figure 6.

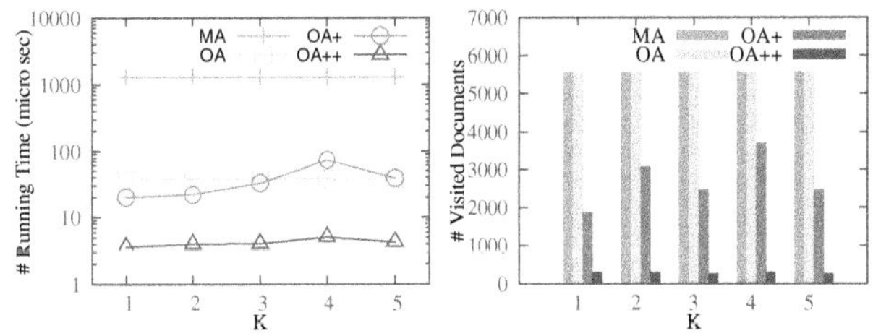

(a) Running Time (b) Visited Documents

Figure 6: Performance for Different Top K

First Figure 6(b) shows MultiAccess and OneAccess always visit all the relevant documents, which do not change for different k. The number of documents OneAccess+ accesses fluctuates, since it may be difficult to predict the stop condition of OneAccess+, but OneAccess+ still visits less documents than MultiAccess and OneAccess. Among all the algorithms, OneAccess++ accesses the least documents, and the performance is quite stable for different k compared to OneAccess+. The running time in Figure 6(a) shows the same trend as Figure 6(b), and the running time of OneAccess++ is consistently the fastest among all the algorithms.

5.3 Storage

We now examine the space overhead of the text cube in our system. We use all the 11 dimensions and vary the number of documents to build the cube, and compare its size with inverted index built on the document collection (Figure 7). Although the size of text cube is several times larger, it increases much slower w.r.t. the number of tuples, which means the summarization power of text cube becomes stronger when the size of original databases gets larger. Given in our experiments we are only able to get a small portion of the real world customer review data, we could image the size of text cube would be comparable with inverted index on much larger datasets, in which sense our solution is quite scalable.

Also notice there have been extensive studies on saving the space of a data cube using partial materialization [16, 20]. Since it is not the main focus in this paper, we construct the full cube in the experiments. However, those techniques can be easily applied to reduce the space substantially.

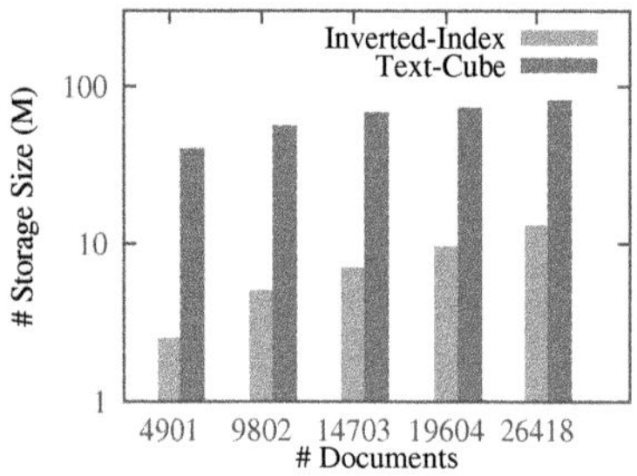

Figure 7: Space Overhead vs. Documents

6. RELATED WORK

Faceted Search Faceted search systems [17, 6, 11, 12, 10, 2, 15] allow users to flexibly select structured attributes to refine the search results. Facets are ranked based on number of associated documents [10], estimated user effort [17, 11], or p-value of the results [6]. Some systems dynamically generate facets from data [2, 15] or build personalized relevance models [12]. As we have mentioned, TEXplorer is different from previous faceted search systems because it focuses on keyword-based ranking and exploration of aggregated objects rather than individual documents. None of the previous facet ranking measures consider the distribution of IR relevance scores as we do and our experiments show the proposed Sig measure is more effective for our task.

Discovery-driven OLAP Systems In traditional data cubes, discovery driven OLAP mechanisms [18] can find surprising or unexpected cells in the cube. [19] further supports matching candidate subspaces by keywords and then dynamically suggests facets by measuring surprising or correlated aggregates of categorical or numerical attributes. TEXplorer is different in the sense that we care about the relevance of cells and correlated dimensions, rather than the distribution of categorical or numerical values in the database. And we target on the most common search behaviors: we suppose users who issue the keyword queries are always interested in the most relevant objects rather than surprising ones, because objects with rather low relevance could still get high surprise scores.

Object Ranking in Database Ranking of aggregated documents for keyword queries have been developed in relational databases [1, 3] and data cubes [22, 7]. TEXplorer ranks objects in the same subspaces so that the comparison is more meaningful, and the interactive exploration framework organizes different subspaces and rankings in an effective way.

Our algorithms of ranking top-k dimensions are related to top-k query processing in database [9, 14, 3]. [14] supports ad-hoc ranking aggregation for the group-by operations in SQL. The mechanism of progressively aggregating scores to each group is proposed so that the top-k groups can be computed efficiently. [3] also proposes aggregation-based top-k generation and pruning strategies. We identify the unique property of our top-k problem and our algorithms achieve stronger pruning power.

7. CONCLUSION

In this work, we propose a novel system TEXplorer that allows users to perform keyword search and OLAP-style aggregation and exploration of the objects in a text cube built on a multidimensional text database. A novel significance measure is proposed to rank dimensions. Top relevant objects/cells in each dimension subspace are also ranked for users to select. We develop top-k algorithms and materialization strategies to accelerate the ranking. Extensive experimental studies verify the scalability of our methods and the effectiveness of our proposed significance measure. TEXplorer can be potentially implemented on top of many text databases like Amazon to improve user experience.

8. ACKNOWLEDGMENTS

The work was supported in part by HP Lab Innovation Award, NASA NRA-NNH10ZDA001N, and the U.S. Army Research Laboratory under Cooperative Agreement No. W911NF-09-2-0053 (NS-CTA).

9. REFERENCES

[1] A. Angel, S. Chaudhuri, G. Das, and N. Koudas. Ranking objects based on relationships and fixed associations. In *EDBT*, 2009.

[2] O. Ben-Yitzhak, N. Golbandi, N. Har'El, R. Lempel, A. Neumann, S. Ofek-Koifman, D. Sheinwald, E. J. Shekita, B. Sznajder, and S. Yogev. Beyond basic faceted search. In *WSDM*, 2008.

[3] K. Chakrabarti, V. Ganti, J. Han, and D. Xin. Ranking objects based on relationships. In *SIGMOD Conference*, 2006.

[4] Y. Chen, W. Wang, Z. Liu, and X. Lin. Keyword search on structured and semi-structured data. In *SIGMOD Conference*, 2009.

[5] T. Cheng, X. Yan, and K. C.-C. Chang. Entityrank: searching entities directly and holistically. In *VLDB*, 2007.

[6] D. Dash, J. Rao, N. Megiddo, A. Ailamaki, and G. M. Lohman. Dynamic faceted search for discovery-driven analysis. In *CIKM*, 2008.

[7] B. Ding, B. Zhao, X. Lin, J. Han, and C. Zhai. Topcells: Keyword-based search of top-k aggregated documents in text cube. In *ICDE*, 2010.

[8] J. L. Elsas, J. Arguello, J. Callan, and J. G. Carbonell. Retrieval and feedback models for blog feed search. In *SIGIR*, 2008.

[9] R. Fagin, A. Lotem, and M. Naor. Optimal aggregation algorithms for middleware. *J. Comput. Syst. Sci.*, 66(4), 2003.

[10] M. Hearst, A. Elliott, J. English, R. Sinha, K. Swearingen, and K.-P. Yee. Finding the flow in web site search. *Commun. ACM*, 2002.

[11] A. Kashyap, V. Hristidis, and M. Petropoulos. Facetor: Cost-driven exploration of faceted query results. In *CIKM*, 2010.

[12] J. Koren, Y. Zhang, and X. Liu. Personalized interactive faceted search. In *WWW*, 2008.

[13] R. Kuehl. *Design of Experiments: Statistical Principles of Research Design and Analysis*. Duxbury Press, 2000.

[14] C. Li, K. C.-C. Chang, and I. F. Ilyas. Supporting ad-hoc ranking aggregates. In *SIGMOD Conference*, 2006.

[15] C. Li, N. Yan, S. B. Roy, L. Lisham, and G. Das. Facetedpedia: dynamic generation of query-dependent faceted interfaces for wikipedia. In *WWW*, 2010.

[16] C. X. Lin, B. Ding, J. Han, F. Zhu, and B. Zhao. Text cube: Computing ir measures for multidimensional text database analysis. In *ICDM*, 2008.

[17] S. B. Roy, H. Wang, G. Das, U. Nambiar, and M. K. Mohania. Minimum-effort driven dynamic faceted search in structured databases. In *CIKM*, 2008.

[18] S. Sarawagi, R. Agrawal, and N. Megiddo. Discovery-driven exploration of olap data cubes. In *EDBT*, 1998.

[19] P. Wu, Y. Sismanis, and B. Reinwald. Towards keyword driven analytical processing. In *SIGMOD Conference*, 2007.

[20] D. Xin, J. Han, X. Li, and B. W. Wah. Star-cubing: Computing iceberg cubes by top-down and bottom-up integration. In *VLDB*, 2003.

[21] C. X. Zhai and G. Hirst. *Statistical Language Models for Information Retrieval*. Morgan & Claypool Publishers, 2008.

[22] B. Zhou and J. Pei. Answering aggregate keyword queries on relational databases using minimal group-bys. In *EDBT*, 2009.

The Quality of the XML Web

Steven Grijzenhout
University College London
Department of Management Science and Innovation
Gower Street
London WC1E 6BT, United Kingdom
steven.grijzenhout.10@ucl.ac.uk

Maarten Marx
ISLA, Informatics Institute
University of Amsterdam
Science Park 904
1098 XH Amsterdam, The Netherlands
maartenmarx@uva.nl

ABSTRACT

We collect evidence to answer the following question: Is the quality of the XML documents found on the web sufficient to apply XML technology like XQuery, XPath and XSLT? XML collections from the web have been previously studied statistically, but no detailed information about the quality of the XML documents on the web is available to date. We address this shortcoming in this study. We gathered 180K XML documents from the web. Their quality is surprisingly good; 85.4% is well-formed and 99.5% of all specified encodings is correct. Validity needs serious attention. Only 25% of all files contain a reference to a DTD or XSD, of which just one third is actually valid. Errors are studied in detail. Automatic error repair seems promising. Our study is well documented and easily repeatable. This paves the way for a periodic quality assessment of the XML web.

The full paper and all data are publicly available at the url http://data.politicalmashup.nl/xmlweb.

Categories and Subject Descriptors

H.m [Information Systems]

General Terms

Measurement, Reliability, Standardization.

Keywords

XML, XML Web, Schemas, Data Quality.

1. INTRODUCTION

In this study we look at the prospects of using XML technology for information extraction and integration tasks on XML data found on the World Wide Web. Without becoming specific we refer to the multitude of these tasks as Extract-Transfer-Load (ETL) tasks [35]. Examples of ETL subtasks are data harvesting, text extraction, structure extraction, text mining [25], data de-duplication [14], data exchange (from one schema to another) [13] and data publishing (from one format (e.g. XML) to another (e.g., RDF or relational)).

Apart from the actual collecting of data from the web, all of these tasks can be expressed in the three XML query languages, XPath 2.0, XSLT 2.0 and XQuery 1.0. Not only can these tasks be expressed in these languages, when the input is XML it is desirable to do so for a number of reasons. XSLT and XQuery programs are largely declarative. The semantics of the languages is clear and well-defined. The languages are vendor and software independent, developed and maintained by a committed community and became W3C standards. The immense success of SQL shows the great software engineering benefits of working with such programming languages. Maintainability of code is crucial for ETL tasks as they are typically applied in a changing environment not under control of the developers of the ETL code. The LixTo [17] suite of web-extraction tools is built on these principles. A recent addition to the Lixto tools is OXPath [15], an extension of XPath which allows declarative extraction of the deep web.

CIKM'11, October 24–28, 2011, Glasgow, Scotland, UK.

Whether it is *feasible* to use XML technology for ETL tasks depends on many factors. This is out of the scope of this study. Here we only look whether it is *possible*. That is, is the quality of the XML documents found on the web sufficient to apply XML technology?

Another reason to study the XML web is the new XQIB, *XQuery In the Browser*, initiative (http://www.xqib.org/). XQIB is an alternative to JavaScript. Obviously it needs XML of good quality.

Previous studies on HTML showed that the vast majority of HTML documents (around 95%) on the web did not comply with the standards set by the World Wide Web Consortium [11][32][33]. For XML, studies that measure basic quality indicators (like being syntactically correct) on arbitrary XML data from the web have not been performed yet. There are several empirical studies on XML but they either use data from repositories or have very small samples and always contain only well-formed XML (Cf. Section 2).

Unhappy with this omission and frustrated by our own efforts of using XML tools for a large data integration project we set ourselves the following research goal:

> Create a corpus of XML documents and accompanying schemas that is representative of the web, evaluate which part is ready to be processed with XML tools, and evaluate the prospects of automatic error correction for the other part. In addition, process, document and store the corpus in such a manner that our study can easily (e.g., yearly) be repeated.

The paper describes the created collection (Section 3), and the evaluation of its quality (Section 4). We also created a corpus of schemas in the three XML schema languages and evaluated their inter-translatability (Section 4.3). The remainder of this introduction consists of our operationalization of XML-quality and an overview of the main results. Related work is presented in Section 2.

1.1 Basic quality requirements

One can only apply XML tools to XML files if they satisfy a few basic but important properties. As XML is a self-describing format, these properties all state that files should not lie about themselves concerning some aspect X. We looked at three aspects: a file should not lie about its encoding, it should not state that it is XML when it is not, and it should not lie about its validity with respect to a schema. More precisely,

1. The document should be encoded using a single encoding that is stated in the document.
2. The document should be well formed XML.
3. If the file references a schema, that should be useful and truthful. This means that
    a. the URI identifying the schema should be resolvable. Also all included schema files should be resolvable recursively;
    b. all these schemas are syntactically correct, and
    c. the file is valid with respect to the schema(s).

We collected almost 180K unique XML files from the web from almost 100K websites with a total size of 40GB. We now summarize the main results. Our first result states that encodings do not pose a real problem as 99.5% had a correctly specified encoding. The other results are neatly summarized in Figure 1.

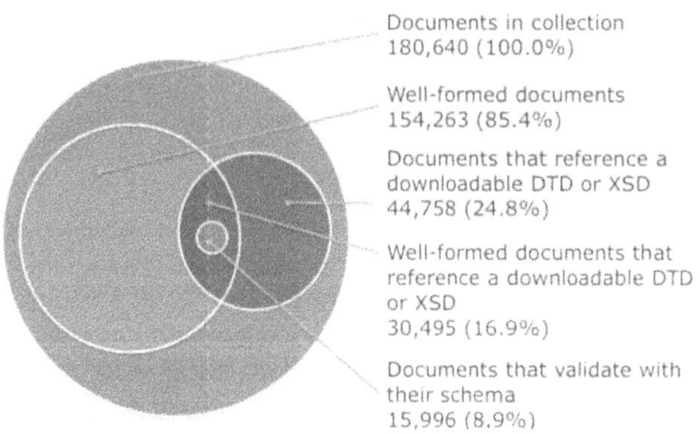

Figure 1. Summary of the Quality of the XML Web.

If we pick a random XML document there is a 14.6% chance that it is not well-formed. This is much better than could be expected from earlier studies on HTML. Interesting is the position of the subset of documents that reference a DTD: 66.4% is not well-formed, almost five times more than on average. It seems that the addition of a DOCTYPE declaration is often added to hide their own poor quality.

Validity is rare on the web. Just over 10% of the well-formed documents are also valid. If we zoom in on validity we see very different patterns for DTD and XML Schema. We go through the three possible problems. The first problem is to reference a schema that cannot be retrieved. This happened in 12.5% of all references to a DTD. Things get subtle once one realizes that DTDs can also include other DTDs, and these have to be retrieved as well. Of the 5410 include statements in DTDs in our corpus, 33% could not be downloaded. Includes in XML Schema behave much better: of 2110 includes only 23 could not be retrieved. XML documents which claim to be valid with respect to an XML Schema behave very well: they have 99% chance of being well-formed, which is much better than the average 85.6%. Figure 2 and Figure 3 show those files that reference a schema but could not be validated. The figures present the causes for non-validation.

The differences are remarkable. Files referencing a DTD are for 73% not valid just because they are not even well-formed. For XML Schemas this cause of error is negligible. Conversely, 31% of all XML Schema validity errors are due to a schema that is useless because it is not even syntactically correct. This happens in only 4% of the DTD-errors.

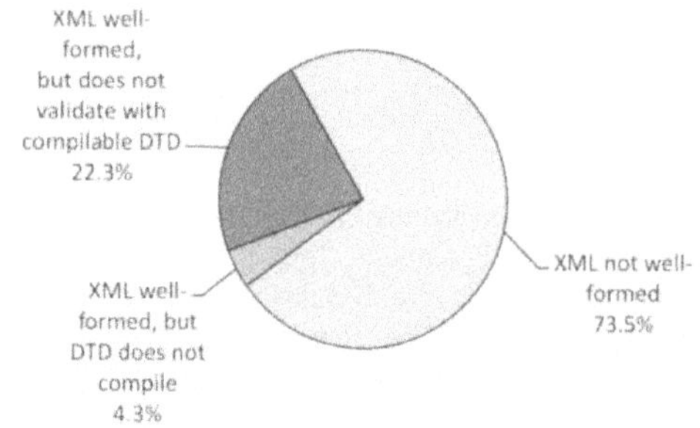

Figure 2. Distribution of causes for non-validation: DTD.

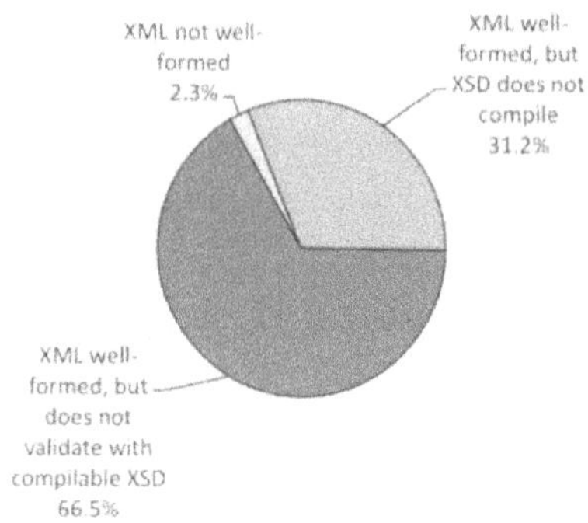

Figure 3. Distribution of causes for non-validation: XSD.

1.2 Main contributions

Our main contribution is an up-to-date and reliable estimate of the quality of the state of the XML web in 2010. Our second contribution consists of an extensive analysis of the type of errors that compromise the quality of the XML web. As they are mostly Pareto distributed we believe this can be used to guide research into automatically repairing errors.

Our third contribution is the collected data itself. All data is made publicly available in a uniform format at the url http://data.politicalmashup.nl/xmlweb. All referenced schema files are (recursively) locally available. Information about headers, encodings, and errors of each XML file is stored in a relational database that is also available. Also all scripts and settings for crawling and analyzing the collection are available and well-documented. This makes our study easily repeatable. We hope that this is a start of a longitudinal XML collection. Of course we also hope to see a steady improvement of the quality of the XML web.

Our fourth contribution consists of a corpus of 8000 schema files in the four main schema languages. We analysed their inter schema translatability with James Clark's Trang (http://www.thaiopensource.com/relaxng/trang.html).

2. BACKGROUND

Data quality is a research field established by Wang and Madrick and matured into a field with an own ACM journal [26]. Within the categorization of data quality research described in [26], our study is concerned with assessment and uses an empirical method. Ultimately we study whether XML data from the web is 'fit for use' by XML technologies. The idea to measure data quality as data being 'fit for use' by data consumers goes back to [39].

A large number of descriptive studies on XML have been conducted. There are three main themes identifiable in the literature, which will be discussed accordingly: studies on XML collections; studies on the quality of the HTML web; and studies on XML schema languages.

2.1 Studies on XML collections

Studies on XML document collections mainly differ in sample data [38]. A study has been done on 200,000 publicly available XML documents from the Xyleme repository [30]. This collection contains only well-formed XML documents. Another study used a number of XML collections, consisting of 16,534 documents and accounting for a total size of 20 Gigabytes [31]. The collections include well-known docbook samples, XML bibles, RDF samples and IMDb collections

2.2 Studies on HTML web quality

Several surveys on the quality of HTML documents on the web exist [32][11][5][33]. Although XML's predecessor HTML differs greatly in applicability, these studies are relevant because of their approach. The differences in sample collections and quality measures do not make a large difference in results. All indicate a poor quality of the HTML web: a mere 6.5% [5], 5% [10], 4% [33] and 3% [32] of the HTML documents complied with W3C's HTML standards.

2.3 Studies on XML schema languages

XML schemes (DTD, XML Schema (abbreviated as XSD), Relax NG) have been studied in a number of ways. Firstly, XML schemes are studied in relation to XML collections. As we have seen above, only a small percentage of documents reference a schema [30][31]. As is the case with HTML files, the syntax of most DTD files is incorrect [12][36]. This is generally also the case for XML Schema [8]. Secondly, the properties of XML schemas are studied [12][21][36]. Thirdly, work has been done in developing metrics to measure the properties of DTDs [21] and XML Schemas [29]. These metrics might be interesting to use in future versions of quality analysis. Lastly, research is done in comparing the use of the different XML schema languages. The three languages are incomparable in expressive power and their effect when validating. In our study we look at these differences in expressive power from a pragmatic point of view: how often can schemas be inter-translated using an existing schema translator (Cf. Section 4.3)?

3. DATA

We briefly describe the collections of XML and schema files, and how they were obtained. More detail can be found on the webpage where all data can be downloaded.

3.1 Desired Data

The population of the data in this study is the subset of the web made of XML documents only [3]. The actual amount of files in the XML web is unknown. Obtaining an estimate of its size is intrinsically difficult [1]. The size of the population is, however, irrelevant in calculating a representative sample size. Unfortunately, collecting XML documents from the web is often not a simple random sample. Because of this, it is not possible to calculate a required sample size. We decided to harvest as many XML documents from the web as possible. The objective of our study is to assess the quality of the XML Web, and a large collection will maximize the probability that errors are included in the collection. Our data collection process does not access the Hidden Web [34]. As a consequence, our collections will not contain any data from the Hidden Web.

3.2 Description of Data

The XML collection contains 180,640 XML files. The total file size of the collection is 40 Gigabytes. The largest file in the collection is 683.7 Megabytes, and the smallest is 1 byte. The average file size is approximately 223 Kilobytes. The number of documents that has a duplicate is only 1296. The URLs in the collection allow us to describe the distribution of XML documents on the web. We clustered our XML files into the zones, consisting of generic Internet domains and geographical regions, defined by Barbosa et al. [3]. Figure 4 shows the partition of our dataset in zones.

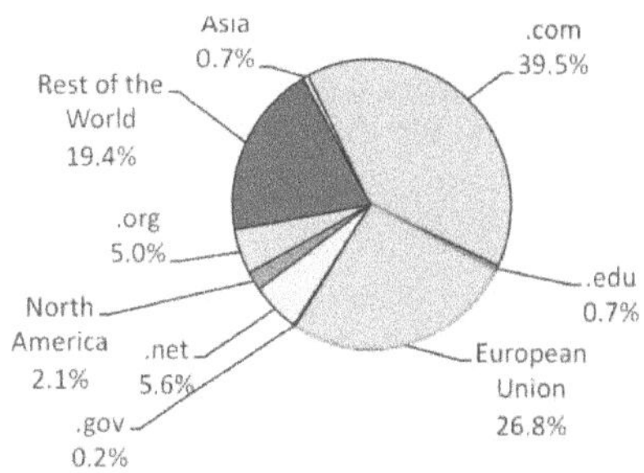

Figure 4. Distribution of web sites by Zone.

The ability to reference a schema is one of the most important features of XML. We focused on DTDs and XSDs because they are used most often, and they are uniformly referenced in XML documents. DTDs were downloaded by extracting the system identifier in the XML document header. All external referenced document includes have been downloaded recursively. Our collection contains 24,426 (13.5%) files with a reference to a DTD. The DTD schemas contained a total of 5410 includes of other DTDs or entity documents. These have been downloaded recursively, and the original schemas have been modified to include the locally downloaded included schemas. 1786 (33.0%) of them failed to download. The thus obtained collection contains 1375 DTDs. The collection contains 24,087 files with a reference to an XSD (13.3%). We could download 437 unique XSDs.

Apart from collecting schema files that were referenced in an XML file, we also collected schema files directly. In this way we could also harvest Relax files. In total we have 3078 DTDs, 4141 XSDs, 338 Relax NGs in XML and 337 Relax NGs in the compact syntax.

3.3 Data Collection

The data were collected in the following 4 steps:

1. Crawl a list of URLs of XML documents from Yahoo and Google,
2. Download the content of each URL,
3. Organize the collection,
4. Determine duplicates.

For each URL, we store the URL, the HTTP header, the actual XML file, and recursively all schema files it references.

The list of URLs was created using a modified version of the crawler from [8]. The crawler executes several keyword queries with the filetype restricted to XML. Only Yahoo and Google can limit search to XML files. The results of these two steps are described in Table 1.

Table 1. Statistics of URL List and Downloading

Filetype	Unique URLs in List	Files Downloaded	Loss Percentage	Last File Downloaded
XML	188,332	180,640	4.08%	2010-07-17

The resulting collection was organized in a MySQL database. For each file, the database stores its URL, its HTTP header, a list of its duplicates in the collection, information on the encoding, lists of all recursively referenced schemas, and all well-formedness and validity errors. The actual files are saved on disk with the appropriate id as its filename. Duplicates were not removed from the dataset, but rather a relation of duplicate content was inserted into the database.

4. QUALITY OF XML ON THE WEB

In three sections we look at the basic quality requirements outlined in Section 1.1: character encoding, well-formedness and validity. We are not only interested in the amount of errors but also whether a small amount of error-types is responsible for a large amount of errors. We also report correlations between errors and other variables.

4.1 Encoding

We checked whether documents lie about their encoding. Of every document in the collection, we checked whether the encodings as specified either in the HTTP header, in the encoding attribute in the XML declaration or in Content-Type meta tag (often used in XHTML documents) was compliant with the document. Our main result is that 99.47% of all specified encodings is correct. Further details are in the full paper.

4.2 XML Well-formedness

We use the libxml2 parser to check whether a document is wellformed. We created a modified version of the XML parser libxml2. The main change was to make the error output uniform for all errors. The modified version of libxml2 distinguishes four different error levels: No error, Warning, Recoverable error and Fatal error. Files with only recoverable errors can still be parsed. The modified version of libxml2 also categorizes the error that occurred. We found 74 different error categories.

We note that libxml2 is not meant to collect statistics on the number of errors in a not well-formed XML file. It often happens that the parser outputs a large amount of errors while fixing just one makes the document well-formed. We however believe that the output is still useful for giving directions to research on automatic error repairmen.

26,377 different files (14.6% of the collection) had at least one fatal error. Figure 5 lists the 10 most common errors. Note that a document may have many errors, so the total sum is higher than the number of bad XML files. 'Opening and ending tag mismatch' is encountered in most documents (16,996 docs) followed by 'Premature end of data in tag' (14,250 docs). Third is an unknown encoding (11,615 docs). This last error does not necessarily have to be a fatal error, as libxml2 allows specifying the encoding of a document manually.

The distribution of errors across error categories follows a Pareto distribution. The Pareto Chart in Figure 6 shows the first nine error categories. Approximately 20% of the error categories (9 from a total of 74) account for 99% of the fatal errors.

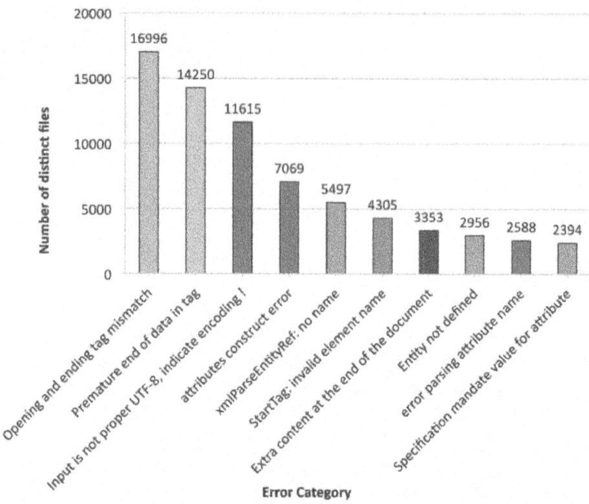

Figure 5. Top Ten Fatal Error Categories.

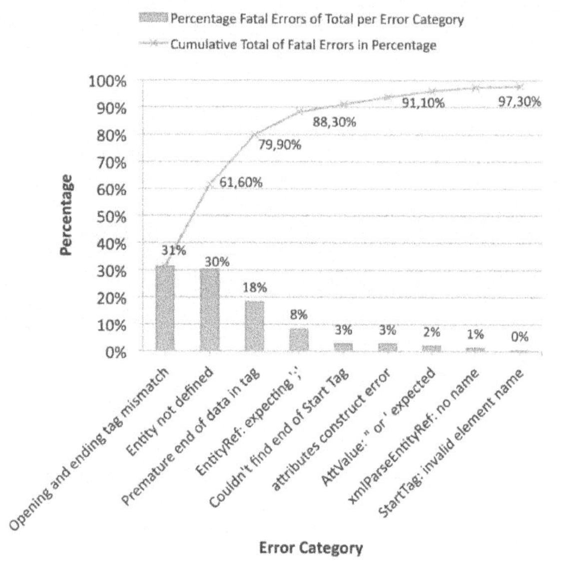

Figure 6. Pareto Chart of Fatal Errors per Error Category.

As indicated above, an error occurring need not mean that it is responsible for the file being not well-formed. Still, 5708 documents (21.6% of all documents with a fatal error), contain only one fatal error. Also here, 'Opening and ending tag mismatch' is most often (25.1%) responsible for not being well-formed.

We checked whether some internet zones were over- or under-represented in errors but found no significant deviations from Figure 4.

4.3 XML Validity

This section discusses the results about validity testing with respect to DTDs and XSDs.

4.3.1 Bad schemas

Figure 2 and Figure 3 give a breakdown of the reasons for non-validity of the files that reference a DTD or XSD. With both DTD and XSD being referred to in roughly 24K files there are large differences in their validity scores. Over half of the XML files with an XSD is actually valid, in contrast to less than 10% for files referencing a DTD. On the other hand, over half of the documents with a DTD is itself not even wellformed. With XSD, this occurs less than 1%. The most interesting case of invalidity occurs when all perquisites are satisfied. Here the two schema languages behave rather alike, with one sixth (DTD) and one fourth (XSD) of the files falling in this class.

4.3.2 Geographic distribution

We looked whether validity errors were over or under represented in certain domains and found one significant deviation. The .edu and .gov domains behave well compared to the rest: 2, respectively .4% of all files come from these domains, but of all files that refer to a well-formed DTD they contribute 11 and .9%, respectively.

4.3.3 Most common errors

First we look at errors in DTDs. A total of 28 different errors have been found, of which the top ten is shown in Figure 7.

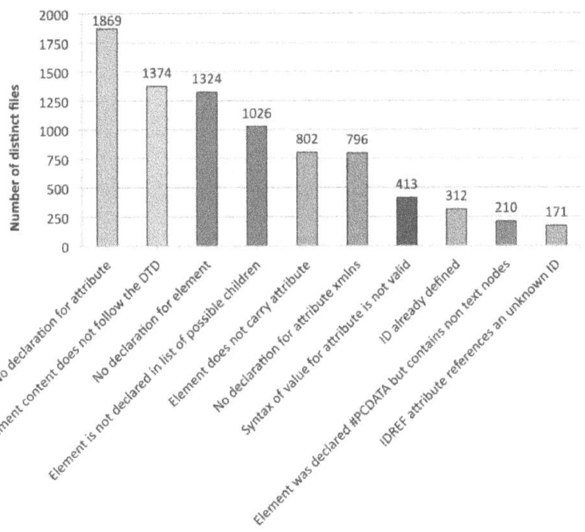

Figure 7. Top Ten Recoverable Error Categories in DTD validation based on occurrence in files.

The first two error-types are an indication that the data is in fact richer than the schema describes. If an application is built on the schema it can thus simply ignore the extra information. The third error type is problematic for parsers, and potentially difficult to repair automatically. It contains a lot of errors concerning CDATA, for instance that a text node is encountered where only element nodes are allowed. Some schemas have an obvious default element in which to wrap forbidden text nodes. E.g., in XHTML, text is forbidden under the body-element, and could be wrapped in a p-element.

This leads us to ask which DTDs have errors across the largest number of different files. The top of the list is dominated by W3C DTDs. For details, see the full paper.

For XSDs we see very much the same picture. 93% of all validation errors are of type 'this element is not expected'. Because XSDs can, in contrast to DTDs, also restrict the type of values, one could expect many type-errors. In fact these are uncommon: less than 5% of all errors and occurring in around 10% of all invalid files.

4.3.4 The good guys and the bad guys

Though not of direct practical value, it is fun to see which background variables correlate strongly with (in)validity. We looked at file size, domain extension, encoding and the type of webserver used for the site. Details are in the full paper.

The Content-Length HTTP header is an interval variable, but not normally distributed (Kolmogorov-Smirnov test. *Sig value* < 0.05. N = 131,831). We use Spearman's rho to determine if there is a relationship between file size and validation of the document. There indeed is a statistically significant but weak relationship, $r(131{,}831) = .214, p < .01$.

Regarding base domain, we did a binary logistic regression analysis. The produced model does indicate that domain name extension is statistically significant and explains variations in validity of the documents (χ^2=6087.791, df=334, $p < 0.01$). We found 33 domain name extensions with a statistically significant ($p < 0.05$) effect. The 5 bad guys are '.jp', '.org.au', '.cat', '.gov.uk', '.gov.br'. They are 3.2, 5.1, 3.6, 3.6 and 9.4 times more likely to be invalid than to be valid. The rest are good guys, ranging from 2.226 (.gov) to 24.750 (.im) more likely to be valid than invalid.

All seven statistically significant domain name extensions in the educational and academic domains (containing .edu or .ac) are more likely to be valid than invalid. In contrast, documents from governmental domains in the USA are more likely to be valid (.gov), while documents from two other governmental domains are less likely to be valid (.gov.br and .gov.uk). An other interesting fact is that documents from the .uk domain are generally almost 2.5 times more likely to be valid than invalid, while documents from the governmental domain in the uk (.gov.uk) are 3.6 times more likely to be invalid than valid. It might indicate that documents from the British government are of poorer quality than other documents originating in the UK

Does it matter for validity whether a site uses a commercial (Microsoft's ISS) or an open source (Apache) server? The effect is significant but extremely small: documents served by an Apache server are 1.07 times more likely to be valid than documents that are server by Microsoft IIS.

The encoding of a file has a minor effect on validity. The only statistically significant effects we found are for windows125(1|2) which is twice more likely to be invalid and iso88591 which is 2.5 times more likely to be valid.

4.3.5 Translations between schema languages

Because our collection does not contain any Relax NG schemas we also crawled schema files directly. Combined with the schema's already found we created a collection of 3087 DTDs, 4141 XSDs, 337 Relax NGs in compact syntax and 338 Relax NG's in XML. All schemas are syntactically correct. All data and results are at http://data.politicalmashup.nl/xmlweb/trang.html.

While XSDs allow expressions that cannot be expressed in DTD syntax, these extras are rarely used in practice [7][8]. We wondered whether available schema translation software could support these findings on our dataset. We used James Clark's Trang as it can translate between all three schema languages except from XSD. The results are that Trang translates 88% of the DTDs to the other two languages and that 30% of the Relax schemas can be translated to DTD and 96% to XSD. The surprisingly low 88% seems due to Trang, not to the use of DTD features the other languages cannot handle. The University of Dortmund is working on an improved translator based on [16], which can also translate from XSD.

5. CONCLUSIONS

Our results show that it is possible to do ETL tasks on 'XML' files solely using XML query and transformation languages. Only 14.6% is not truly XML and the distribution of errors is promising for (semi-)automatic repair. Of course ETL development would become much easier and far more robust when restricted to valid XML. Here the quality of the XML web needs drastic improvement as less than 10% is valid. Although it is hard to compare our data with previous studies, the growth of referenced XSDs and the fact that files with an XSD tend to be twice as often valid as those with a DTD seems a positive development. We have set up our study in such a way that it can easily be replicated in the future. Hopefully we can measure an upward trend in validity.

The distribution of XML syntax errors follows an 80-20 law which make them amenable to automatic error repairing techniques. Validation errors occur because schemas do not compile or because the XML is not valid. This shows that work on (semi-)automatic learning DTDs or XML Schemas from XML documents is useful [6][9]. Most validation errors occur because there is an element or attribute used that is not defined in the schema. This could mean that either the schema is not correct or a wrong name is used in the XML. Schema learning techniques may be expanded to schema repairing techniques. Techniques used in data-deduplication and learning schema mappings seem useful to repair XML documents in this case.

6. REFERENCES

[1] Abiteboul, S., & Vianu, V. (1997). Queries and Computation on the Web. ICDT '97: *Proceedings ICDT* (pp. 262-275).

[2] Azze-Eddine, M., Samia, K.-B., & Douniazed, A. H. (2004). XML-DFG : A Dynamic Forms Generator for XML Valid DTD Document. *RIST*, 14 (2), 15-26.

[3] Barbosa, D., Mignet, L., & Veltri, P. (2005). Studying the XML Web: Gathering Statistics from an XML Sample. *World Wide Web*, 8 (4), pp. 413-438.

[4] Beatty, P., Dick, S., & Miller, J. (2008, Mar/Apr). Is HTML in a Race to the Bottom? A Large-Scale Survey and Analysis of Conformance to W3C Standards. *IEEE Internet Computing*, 12 (2), pp. 76-80.

[5] Beckett, D. (1997). 30% accessible - a survey of the UK Wide Web. *Computer Networks and ISDN Systems*, 29 (Nos 8-13), pp. 1367-75.

[6] Bex, G.J., Gelade, W., Neven, F. & Vansummeren, S. Learning deterministic regular expressions for the inference of schemas from XML data. WWW 2008: 825-834

[7] Bex, G. J., Martens, W., Neven, F., & Schwentick, T. (2005). Expressiveness of XSDs: from practice to theory, there and back again. *: Proceedings WWW* (pp. 712-721

[8] Bex, G. J., Neven, F., & Bussche, J. V. (2004). DTDs versus XML Schema: A Practical Study. *Proceedings WebDB '04* (pp. 79-84).

[9] Bex, G. J., Neven, F., Schwentick, T., & Tuyls, K. (2006). Inference of concise DTDs from XML data. *: Proc. VLDB '06* (pp. 115-126).

[10] Chen, B., & Shen, V. Y. (2006). Transforming Web Pages to Become Standard-Compliant through Reverse Engineering. *: Proceedings W4A '06*. pp. 14-22.

[11] Chen, S., Hong, D., & Shen, V. (2005). An experimental study on validation problems with existing HTML web pages. *Proceedings ICOMP'05*. (pp. 373-379).

[12] Choi, B. (2002). What are real DTDs like? *Proceedings WebDB '02*, (pp. 43-48).

[13] Doan, A., & Halevey, A. (2005). *AI Magazine*, Vol. 26, pp. 83-94.

[14] Elmagarmid, A., Ipeirotis, P., & Verykios, V. (2007). Knowledge and Data Engineering, *IEEE Transactions on*, 19 (1), pp. 1-16.

[15] Furche T., Gottlob G., Grasso G., Schallhart Ch., Sellers A. 2011. OXPath: A Language for Scalable, Memory-efficient Data Extraction from Web Applications. In *Proceedings VLDB 2011*.

[16] Gelade, W., Idziaszek, T., Martens, W. & and Neven, F. (2010) Simplifying XML Schema: Single-Type Approximations of Regular Tree Languages. Proc. PODS 2010.

[17] Gottlob, G., Koch, Ch., Baumgartner, R., Herzog, M. & Flesca, S. 2004. The Lixto data extraction project: back and forth between theory and practice. In *Proceedings* PODS '04 (pp. 1-12).

[18] Guerrini, G., Mesiti, M., & Rossi, D. (2005). Impact of XML schema evolution on valid documents. *Proc. WIDM '05* (pp. 39-44).

[19] Hackett, S., Parmanto, B., & Zeng, X. (2004). Accessibility of Internet websites through time. *SIGACCESS Access. Comput.*, 32-39.

[20] Harold, E. R. (2001). *XML Bible*. New York , NY, USA: John Wiley & Sons, Inc.

[21] Klettke, M., Schneider, L., & Heuer, A. (2002). Metrics for XML Document Collections. *XMLDM Workshop*, (pp. 162-176). Prague.

[22] Kosek, J., Kratky, M., & Snasel, V. (2003). Struktura realnych XML dokumentu a metody indexovani. *ITAT 2003: Workshop on Information Technologies Applications and Theory*. High Tatras, Slovakia.

[23] Lawrence, S., & Giles, C. L. (2000, Spring). Accessibility of information on the Web. *Intelligence*, 11 (1), pp. 32-39.

[24] Lee, D., & Chu, W. W. (2000). Comparative analysis of six XML schema languages. *SIGMOD Rec.*, 29 (3), 76-87.

[25] Liu, B. (2007). *Web Data Mining*. Springer.

[26] Madnick, S., Wang, R., Lee, Y. & ZHU, H. (2009) Overview and framework for data and information quality research. *Journal of Data and Information Quality*.1 (1), pp. 2.1-2.22.

[27] Martens, W., Neven, F., & Schwentick, T. (2005). Which XML schemas admit 1-pass preorder typing? *Proc.s ICDT* (pp. 68-82).

[28] Martens, W., Neven, F., Schwentick, T., & Bex, G. J. (2006). Expressiveness and complexity of XML Schema. *ACM Trans. Database Syst.*, 31 (3), 770-813.

[29] McDowell, A., Schmidt, C., & Yue, K.-B. (2004). Analysis and Metrics of XML Schema. *Proc. SERP '04* (pp. 538-544).

[30] Mignet, L., Barbosa, D., & Veltri, P. (2003). The XML Web: a First Study. *Proceedings WWW '03* pp. 500-510.

[31] Mlynkova, I., Toman, K., & Pokorny, J. (2006). *Statistical Analysis of Real XML Data Collections* (Technical Report). Charles University, Faculty of Mathematics and Physics, Department of Software Engineering, Prague, Czech Republic.

[32] Ofuonye, E., Beatty, P., Dick, S., & Miller, J. (2010). Prevalence and classification of web page defects. *Online Information Review*, 34 (1), 160-174.

[33] Pollach, I., Pinterits, A., & Treiblmaier, H. (2006). Environmental Web Sites: An Empirical Investigation of Functionality and Accessibility. *Proceedings of the 39th Hawaii International Conference on System Sciences*. IEEE.

[34] Raghavan, S., & Garcia-Molina, H. (2001). Crawling the Hidden Web. *Proceedings VLDB '01* (pp. 129-138

[35] Rahm, E., & Do, H.H. (2000). *Data Cleaning: Problems and Current Approaches*, 23 (4)

[36] Sahuguet, A. (2001). Everything You Ever Wanted to Know About DTDs, But Were Afraid to Ask. *Proc. WebDB* (pp. 171-183).

[37] Sundaresan, N., & Moussa, R. (2001). Algorithms and programming models for efficient representation of XML for Internet applications. *Proceedings WWW '01* (pp. 366-375).

[38] Toman, K., & Mlynková, I. (2006). XML Data - The Current State of Affairs. *Proceedings of XML Prague '06 conference*, (pp. 87-102).

[39] Wang, R. & Strong, D. Beyond accuracy: What data quality means to data consumers. *J. Manag. Inf. Syst.* 12(4) pp. 5-34.

[40] W3C. (2004, 02 10). *World Wide Web Consortium (W3C)*. Retrieved 04 05, 2010, from RDF - Semantic Web Standards: http://www.w3.org/RDF

Context-based Entity Description Rule for Entity Resolution

Lingli Li, Jianzhong Li, Hongzhi Wang, Hong Gao
Department of Computer Science, Harbin Institute of Technology
Harbin, China
lwsbrr@gmail.com, lijzh@hit.edu.cn, wangzh@hit.edu.cn, honggao@hit.edu.cn

ABSTRACT

In this paper, we consider the entity resolution(ER) problem, which is to identify objects referring to the same real-world entity. Prior work of ER involves expensive similarity comparison and clustering approaches. Additionally, the quality of entity resolution may be low due to insufficient information. To address these problems, by adopting context information of data objects, we present a novel framework of entity resolution, context-based entity description (CED), to make context information help entity resolution. In our framework, each entity is described by a set of CEDs. During entity resolution, objects are only compared with CEDs to determine its corresponding entity. Additionally, we propose efficient algorithms for CED discovery and CED-based entity resolution. We experimentally evaluated our CED-based ER algorithm on the real DBLP datasets, and the experimental results show that our algorithm can achieve both high precision and recall as well as outperform existing methods.

Categories and Subject Descriptors
H.3.3 [**Information Storage and Retrieval**]: Information Search and Retrieval –*Clustering, Information filtering.*

General Terms
Algorithms.

Keywords
entity resolution, context-based, data cleaning

1. INTRODUCTION

Entity resolution (ER) is the process of identifying objects that refer to the same real-world entity. ER is one of the most important problems in data cleaning and arises in many applications. For example, in publications, two identical author names may represent different persons and an author may have different name spellings; same address might have multiple entries due to different spelling; a person can have quite different descriptions on web.

Because of its importance, ER has attracted general attention in the literatures. Most algorithms and frameworks of ER involve two steps. One is similarity comparison between objects [1], the other is clustering objects [5-7], in which objects in the same cluster represent the same entity. Even though existing methods can perform ER effectively in many cases, these ER approaches have the following limitations.

- *Lack of consideration of updating.* In many systems, the number of objects increases rapidly. Unfortunately, current ER approaches seldom consider the update problem. Both comparing new objects with old ones and re-clustering are quite expensive.
- *Expensive Time Complexity.* Computing the similarity between pairs of objects is too expensive when the data size becomes large. Moreover, since the similarity relationship between objects is not transitive, after the pair-wise matching between objects, the clustering step has to be involved next, which is also an expensive operation.
- *Order dependent.* Since the similarity relationships are not transitive, the results of ER can be order dependent, which means if different matching orders are selected; the clustering results might be different as well. As the result, inconsistency exists in ER results.
- *Sensitive to training data.* For learning-based strategies of ER [3, 4], they usually assume the training data is similar to the test data. In real world, since data can be obtained from various sources continuously, this assumption cannot always be guaranteed.
- *Monotonicity assumption of similarity functions.* The similarity functions can be divided into two kinds. One is feature-based similarity, the other is relational similarity. Most approaches of ER are based on feature similarity comparison between object pairs. They are all based on the intuition of the monotonicity of similarity, which means that the matching pairs in real world are more similar in features than the non-matching pairs. We will soon use Example 1 to show that this intuition is incorrect sometimes. Differently with feature similarity, [5-7] focus on the relationships among objects. They solve the ER problem on a relationship graph, which requires a quite large space and as far as we know, they are not as efficient as feature-based similarity approaches.

We use Example 1 to illustrate the limitations of prior work.

Table 1 Objects for Example 1

ID	coauthor	coauthor	coauthor
o_1	*Qi Zhang*		
o_2	*Jian Pei*	*Hye-Chung Kum*	*Dean Duncan*
o_3	*Jian Pei*	*Xuemin Lin*	*Yidong Yuan*
o_4	*Jian Pei*	*Xuemin Lin*	*Wenjie Zhang*
o_5	*Jian Pei*	*Xuemin Lin*	*Wenjie Zhang*
o_6	*Qi Zhang*	*Mei Wang*	*Hongtao Xu*
o_7	*Jian Pei*	*Baile Shi*	*Jian Xu*
o_8	*Jian Pei*	*Baile Shi*	*Chen Wang*
o_9	*Jian Pei*	*Baile Shi*	*Chen Wang*

This paper is partially supported by National Science Foundation of China under Grant No. 61003046, No. 61111130189. Key Program of the National Natural Science Foundation of China under Grant No.60933001, No.61033015

CIKM'11, October 24–28, 2011, Glasgow, Scotland, UK.

Example 1. In Table 1, there are 9 objects o_1-o_9 describing 9 publications of authors named "Wei Wang". For the interests of space, we omit some other coauthors and conferences. Even though these objects are all named "Wei Wang", they do not refer to the same author. From the information obtained from the homepages of these authors, o_1 and o_2 represent the author in *UNC*, denoted as e_1; o_3-o_5 represent the author in *UNSW*, denoted as e_2; o_6-o_9 represent the author in *Fudan University*, denoted as e_3. It is a natural way to measure the similarity between object pair (o_i, o_j) with the size of intersection of coauthors between o_i and o_j[2], denoted as $Sim(o_i, o_j)$. Thus we can get the following cases that are not coincident to the truth.

- $Sim(o_1, o_2) = 0$, $Sim(o_1, o_6) = 1$, where o_1 and o_2 are a match and o_1 and o_6 are a non-match.
- $Sim(o_6, o_7) = Sim(o_6, o_8) = Sim(o_6, o_9) = 0$, where o_6 matches with o_7- o_9.
- $Sim(o_5, o_7) = Sim(o_5, o_8) = Sim(o_5, o_9) = 1$, where o_5 does not match with o_7- o_9.

In this example we observe that, parts of the matching pairs have lower similarities than non-matching pairs. Additionally, pair-wise ER requires comparison between each object pair. Even though similarity join algorithms [8-9] can accelerate the processing in database, for new-coming object, such comparisons are still required. In contrast, if we have the rule-based entity descriptions for e_1-e_3 shown in Table 2,

Table 2 Entity descriptions for Example 1

ent	descriptions
e_1	*<coauthor>Qi Zhang*∧¬*<coauthor>Baile Shi*
	<coauthor>Hye-Chung Kum
e_2	*<coauthor> Xuemin Lin*
e_3	*<coauthor>Baile Shi*
	<coauthor>Mei Wang

we compute the similarity between object o and entity e denoted as $Sim(o, e)$ by counting the number of rules of e been matched by o, i.e., for object o_1, *<coauthor>Qi Zhang*$\in o_1$ while *<coauthor>Baile Shi*$\notin o_1$, thus o_1 matches the rule *<coauthor>Qi Zhang*∧¬*<coauthor>Baile Shi* of e_1, so $Sim(o_1, e_1) = 1$. The worst cost of comparison between rule and object is much smaller than the cost of object comparison.

Therefore based on the feature descriptions of entities, the ER problem can be reduced to a pair-wise matching problem between object and entity descriptions. Since entity descriptions are highly extracted information from the objects representing the same entity, thus comparing objects with entity descriptions has a lower cost than object comparison; the result accuracy will also be better, since entity descriptions include more comprehensive information than object. Thus the pair-wise matching between object and entity will be more efficient, scalable and effective than pair-wise matching between objects. Moreover, the pair-wise matching between object and entity has advantages of both pair-wise matching and clustering, such as easy to implement; amenable to incremental and distributed processing; and accurate of result.

Contributions We propose a novel tool, Context-based Entity Description (CED), to describe entity features based on contexts of objects representing identical entity and we formalize the ER problem based on CEDs (Sect. 2.1). Properties of entity description rules are also been discussed (Sect. 2.2). Based on the definition of entity description rules, we present an efficient ER algorithm by comparing objects with entity description rules (Sect. 3.1). In order to describe entity effectively, conditions of entity description rules are discovered. Based on these conditions, we develop an entity description rule discovery algorithm (Sect. 3.2). Extensive experiments verified the effectiveness and efficiency of our algorithms on real data sets (Sect. 4).

2. Context-based Entity Description (CED)

As discussed in Section 1, context information may help more effective entity resolution. In this section, we will discuss Context-based Entity Description (CED).

2.1 Definitions

An instance of an entity is called an ***object***. For structured data, an object is a record; for unstructured data, an object is a phrase; while for semi-structured data such as XML, an object is an element.

The information related to an object is called the ***context*** of the object. For structured data, the context of an object is the values of other attributes in the same record. For unstructured data, the context of an object is the text near the phrase. For XML data, the context of an object o can be defined as the set of elements satisfying,

$$C(a) = \{e \mid dis(LCA(a, e), e) < K\},$$

where $dis(a, b)$ is the distance between elements a and b, $LCA(a, b)$ is the least common ancestors of a and b and K is a predefined threshold.

By the extraction of values and their position information from context, an *object o* can be represented as follows,

$$o = \{<a_1>b_1, <a_2>b_2, \ldots, <a_n>b_n\},$$

i.e, o= *{<author>Wei Wang, <author>Ning Jin, <conference>CIKM}*.

In the description of an object o, each $<a_i>b_i$ in o is defined as a ***feature element***, where a_i is a place constraint and b_i is a value, i.e. t = *<author>"Qi Zhang"* means value "Qi Zhang" should appear in value of the attribute *author*.

Similarly, by discovering common feature elements of the objects referring to an entity e, e can be described as a set of feature elements. With the consideration of distinguishing from other entities, the conjunctions and negations will enhance the express power of the description. Based on the discussion, we define the Context-based Entity Description (CED).

Definition 1(CED) a CED r is defined recursively,

- a feature element t is a CED
- if r is a CED, then $\neg r$ is a CED
- if r_1 is a CED and r_2 is a CED, then $r_1 \wedge r_2$ is a CED
- if r_1 and r_2 are CEDs, then $r_1 \vee r_2$ is a CED

Examples of CEDs on various data types are shown as follows.

Example 2. We denote the entity of *Wei Wang* in *Fudan* as e_1, the entity of *Wei Wang* in *UNC* as e_2. The CEDs for e_1 and e_2 as follows:

- r_1 = *<author> "Baile Shi"*
- r_2= *<author> "Qi Zhang"* ∧ ¬(*<author> "Baile Shi"*)
- r_3 = *<dis=100bytes> "Baile Shi"*

r_1 and r_2 are instances of CEDs on semi-structured or structured data and r_3 is an instance of CED on unstructured data. For a CED r, the ***length*** of r, denoted as $|r|$, is the number of feature elements in r, i.e. in Example 2, $|r_1|=|r_3|=1$, $|r_2|=2$.

Based on the CED and feature-based description of objects, the judgment of whether an object o matches a CED r is represented as a Boolean function ***match rule*** *M(o, r)*. *M(o, r)* returns *true* when *o* matches *r*, otherwise *M(o, r)* returns *false*. And the matching condition between *o* and *r* is defined recursively as following where *t* is an atom feature description,

- if $r=t$, *o* matches *r* if and only if $t \in o$,
- if $r = \neg r_1$, *o* matches *r* if and only if *o* does not match r_1,
- if $r = r_1 \wedge r_2$, *o* matches *r* if *o* matches r_1 and *o* matches r_2,
- if $r = r_1 \vee r_2$, *o* matches *r* if *o* matches r_1 or *o* matches r_2.

Considering the difference of importance of attributes, different CEDs may have different weights. We further describe an entity *e* with a set *R* of CEDs and a cost function *W*, denoted by $e=(R, W)$, where $W(r)$ represents the weight of *r* which describes the confidence of object *o* referring to *e* if *o* satisfies *r*. The larger the value of $W(r)$ is, the more possible the object satisfying *r* represents *e*.

For simplicity, in the following of the paper, we use *entity* instead of *entity description*. The possibility of an object referring to an entity is computed with similarity function described as following.

Definition 2(similarity function) For a given entity $e=(R, W)$ *and* an object *o*, the similarity function of *o*, *e* is defined as:

$$Sim(o, e)=\Sigma\ M(o, r)*W(r),\ r\in R.$$

Given two objects o_1, o_2, if they have identical or similar representations, they are an ***ambiguous object pair***. Given a set *O* of objects, if $\forall o_i \in O$, $\exists o_j \in O$ satisfying o_i and o_j are an ambiguous object pair, we call that *O* is an ***ambiguous object set***. Since from the representation, objects referring to different entities can be distinguished directly, we focus on the ER problem for each ambiguous object set in *O*. For simplicity, in the following, the object set we discussed all refer to the ambiguous object sets.

Definition 3 (CED-ER model) Given a set *O* of objects, a set *E* of entities and a similarity threshold θ, a valid classification result $C = CED\text{-}ER(R)$ satisfies that, for $\forall object\ o_i \in O$,

- if $maximal\{Sim(o, e_j)\} < \theta$ then $C(o_i) = \phi$,
- Otherwise, $C(o)=argmax\{Sim(o, e_j)\}$.

Our main idea is for each object *o*, to find the entity *e* which matches *o* most and if $Sim(o,e)$ is larger than θ, *o* is deemed to present *e*, otherwise, *o* is not similar enough to any entity.

2.2 Correctness Verification

In this section, we study the properties of CEDs required by ER. As defined in Definition 1, each atom element in a CED is a bool variable and each CED is represented as a Boolean expression. Thus the problem of determining whether $\exists$object *o*, satisfying *o* matches a CED *p* is reduced to a *satisfiable problem* of the Boolean expression by truth assignment as the judgment of the atom feature element.

For two CEDs *p* and *q*, we say *p* ***dominates*** *q* (denoted as $p \leq q$) if $\forall$object *o*, if *o* matches *p* then *o* matches *q*. If $p \neq q$ and $p \leq q$, then we say *p* ***strongly dominates*** *q*, denoted as $p < q$.

Proposition 1 *For two satisfiable CEDs p and q, if p dominates q, they must satisfy the constraint that* $\exists$*CED p' satisfying that* $p=q \wedge p'$.

For two satisfiable CEDs *p* and *q*, we say *p* ***conflicts*** with *q* if $p \wedge q$ is *unsatisfiable*.

Proposition 2 *For two satisfiable CEDs p and q, if p conflicts with q, then* $\exists$ *CED p' satisfying that* $p = \neg q \wedge p'$.

We say a set R of CEDs satisfies the ***independency property*** if there is no *conflict* and no *domination* in *R*, which means *R* should satisfy:

- there is no feature element *t* satisfying that $\exists\ r_i, r_j \in R$, $r_i \neq r_j$, $r_i \leq t$ and $r_j \leq \neg t$
- there is no two CEDs r_i, $r_j \in R$, $r_i \neq r_j$, satisfying $r_i \leq r_j$.

We define an entity $e=(R, W)$ as a ***logical valid entity*** if R satisfies the independency property. Given a set *E* of entities, *E* is a ***logical valid entity set*** if each entity is a *logical valid entity* and there is no *domination* between CEDs, which means *E* should satisfy:

- $\forall e_i \in E$, e_i is a logical valid entity,
- $\forall e_i, e_j \in E$, $e_i = (R_i, W_i)$, $e_j = (R_j, W_j) \in E$, $e_i \neq e_j$, e_i and e_j satisfy that there is no two CEDs *p*, *q*, $p \in R_i$, $q \in R_j$, satisfying that $p \leq q$.

In order to guarantee a good performance of ER problem, CED-ER enforces the following two conditions:

- *Each entity should be a logical valid entity.*
  Since in the ER problem, when we compute the similarity between entity *e* and object *o*, we sum up the weights of all the matching CEDs with *o* of *e*. Therefore, the CEDs of *e* should satisfy independency property.
- *An entity set should be a logical valid entity set.*
  For e_i, e_j, if $\exists\ p \in R_i$, $q \in R_j$, satisfying that $p \leq q$, and $W(p) < W(q)$, then for an object *o* representing e_i, *o* will always be deemed to represent e_j if *o* matches *p*; unless *o* also matches some other CEDs in e_i to increase the similarity between *o* and e_i. Thus the independency property of CEDs is violated.

For the interest of space, the proofs of the following propositions are eliminated.

Proposition 3 *Given an entity* $e=(R, W)$, $\forall r \in R$, *there is a disjunctive normal form(DNF) r' which is equivalent with r.*

Proposition 4 $\forall$*entity* $e=(R, W)$ *can be converted to an equivalent (R', W') with R' as a DNF set.*

According to Proposition 4, for an entity $e=(R, W)$, we can modify *e* into *(R', W')*, where each CED $p\in R'$ do not contain logical OR($\vee$), thus *p* can be written as $p=t_1\wedge\ldots\wedge t_i\wedge\neg t_{i+1}\wedge\ldots\wedge\neg t_k$. Therefore in the following paper, the CEDs we discussed all do not contain logical OR.

Proposition 5 We have the following time complexity results.

- The time complexity of checking whether there is a dominate relationship between two CEDs *p*, *q* is $O(|p|+|q|)$.
- The time complexity of checking whether there is a conflict relationship between two CEDs *p*, *q* is $O(max\{|p|,|q|\})$.
- The time complexity of logical valid judgment for an entity $e = (R, W)$ is $O(|R|^2*max\{|r|\}, r \in R)$.
- For a set *E* of entities, the worst time complexity of identifying whether *E* is valid is $O(|E|^2)$.

3. Leveraging CED for Entity Resolution

3.1 U-CED algorithm for ER

In this section , we present U-CED algorithm of using CEDs to perform ER. The pseudo code of U-CED is shown in Algorithm

1. U-CED is a pair-wise matching strategy between object and entity based on CEDs. The algorithm has two phrases. First, for each object o_i, we compute the similarity between o_i and each entity (lines 2-5). Then the entity e_j with the biggest value of similarity with o_i is selected as the entity o_i referring to (lines 6-7).

Algorithm 1 U-CED

Input: a set O of objects, a set E of entities, and a similarity threshold θ
Output: a classification C of O

1 for i←1 to $|O|$ do
2 $Sim(o_i,e_j)=0$;
3 for j ←1 to $|E|$ do
4 For each CED $r \in R_j$ do
5 if o_i matches r then $Sim(o_i,e_j)$+= $W(r)$;
6 if $Sim(o_i, FindMatch(o_i)) > \theta$ then $C(o_i)=FindMatch(o_i)$;
7 else $C(o_i)=\phi$;
8 Return C;

The function $FindMatch(o)$ is to find entity e satisfying,

$Sim(o, e) = maximal\{Sim(o,e_j)\}\ 1 \le j \le |E|$.

Complexity We suppose the maximal length of a CED is l_{max}, the maximal number of CEDs in an entity is R_{max}, the time complexity of Algorithm 1 is $O(|O|*|E|*l_{max}*R_{max})$.

3.2 CED discovery

In this section, we present a discovery strategy of CED set. The training data for CED discovery can be obtained by manually labeling on objects or by extracting from reliable data sources such as Wikipedia, personal homepages, databases and so on, by utilizing IR techniques. Before the introduction of CED discovery problem, we introduce some notations used in this subsection.

The goal of CED discovery is to find valid CED sets. Therefore, we discuss what are valid CED sets. For a CED r of entity e, we say r is a ***valid CED*** of e on object set O, if r satisfies that $\forall o \in O$, if o matches r then o represents e. In another word, r can only be matched by the objects representing e. We define this property of valid CED as ***uniqueness property***. For a CED r, the number of objects in object set O which matches CED r is the ***frequency*** of r on O, denoted as $frq(r)$. A CED r is a ***pCED*** if r is in the form of $t \wedge t'$ or t, where t and t' are feature elements. $\forall pCED\ r$, $|r|$ is no more than 2, besides, there is no $\neg$ in r. A CED r is an ***nCED*** if r is in the form of $t \wedge \neg t_1 \wedge \neg t_2 ... \wedge \neg t_k$ with t and t_1-t_k as feature elements. Based on above concepts, the valid entity set is defined as follows.

Definition 4 (valid entity set) Given a set O of objects, a classification C of O and an entity set E, E is a valid entity set if E satisfies the following conditions:

1. E is a logical valid entity set;
2. $\forall e = (R, W) \in E$ satisfies that $\forall r \in R$ is a valid CED of e on O;
3. $\forall e = (R, W) \in E$ satisfies that $\forall r \in R$, r is a pCED or r is a nCED;
4. $\forall e = (R, W) \in E$ satisfies that $\forall r \in R$, if r is a nCED, $r = t \wedge \neg t_1 \wedge \neg t_2 ... \wedge \neg t_k$ then $\exists$ pCED $r' \in R$, satisfying $r' = t \wedge t'$.

The first two conditions are intuitive. The reasons of condition 3 and condition 4 are explained as follows.

pCED is intuitive and easy to describe entity feature, however, when we can not discover enough feature elements to distinguish an entity from others, nCEDs have to be used. The reason of limiting the maximal length of CED is to guarantee that the feature elements we picked is representative enough. Actually, the longer the rule is, the less representative the rule is. Condition 4 guarantees the correctness of the CEDs generated by Algorithm 3. Otherwise, the uniqueness property of valid CED will be violated.

Now we present the model of CED-discovery in Definition 5.

Definition 5 (CED-discovery model) Given an object set O, a classification C of O and a threshold θ, the valid result of CED-discovery is an entity set E satisfying:

- *E is a valid entity set on O*
- *$\forall e=(R, W) \in E$ satisfies $\forall pCED\ r \in R, frq(r) \ge \theta$*

We can see that, pCED is the core rules which describes entity features, however nCED is just a complementary of pCED. In order to generate pCEDs, finding the feature elements in pCEDs are the key problem of CED discovery.

In order to discover useful feature elements for pCED, we define two metrics of relevance between feature element t and entity e. Based on the properties and inspired by TF/IDF model in IR, we use two parameters GF and ITF defined as follows to measure the relevance between feature element and entity.

Given an object set O and an entity set E, for an entity $e \in E$ and a feature element t, we have,

$GF(t, O(e))=\Sigma w(t,o_i),\ o_i \in O(e),\ O(e)$ *is the object set representing* e,

where $w(t, o_i) = 1$ if and only if o_i matches t, otherwise, $w(t, o_i)=0$.

$$TF(t)= \Sigma u(t, e_i),\ e_i \in E,\ ITF(t) = 1/TF(t)$$

where $u(t, e_i)=1$ if and only if $\exists o_j$, $o_j \in O(e_i)$ and o_j matches t, otherwise, $u(t, e_i)=0$.

According to the definitions, $GF(t, O(e))$ is the frequency of t on $O(e)$. $ITF(t)$ is the inverse frequency of t on entity set. Thus for a feature element t and an entity e, the larger the values of $GF(t, O(e))$ and $ITF(t)$ are, the more relevant t is to e. Then we formalize the problem of generating ***Candidate Feature Element(CFE)***s of pCED as follows.

Definition 6 (CFE discovery model) Given a set O of objects, a classification C of O, a threshold θ of GF, and a threshold of ITF, θ_{ITF}, the valid result is a set T of CFEs satisfying:

- $\forall$ feature element $t \in T$, $ITF(t) \ge \theta_{ITF}$
- $\forall$ feature element $t \in T$, $\forall$entity e, if $t \in T(e)$, then $GF(t, O(e)) \ge \theta$, where $T(e)$ is the CFE set of e.

Based on this model, we present the GenCFE algorithm of discovering CFEs for pCEDs in Algorithm 2. In lines 1-3, we initialize T and Cla, where T stores the feature element set of each entity at first, and Cla is a family with each set $C_E \in Cla$ containing all the objects referring to entity e. In lines 4-5, we compute the values of TF and GF and stores them in TF and GF.

Algorithm 2 GenCFE

Input: a set O of objects, a classification C of O, thresholds θ and θ_{ITF}.
Output: $R=(GF, ITF, T, I)$

1 for each $o \in O$ do
2 $T[C(o)]= T[C(o)] \cup Split(o)$;
3 $Cla[C(o)]$.insert(o)
4 $TF=ComputeTF(T,Cla)$;
5 $GF=ComputeGF(T,Cla)$;
6 for i←1 to $|Cla|$ do

```
        for each feature element t∈ T[i] do
                if 1/TF(t) ≥ θ_ITF && GF(t, i) ≥ θ then I(t).insert(i);
                else T[i].delete(t);
Return (T, GF, TF, I);
```

In Algorithm 2, the function *Split(o)* is to transform object *o* into a feature element set.

Complexity analysis We suppose the maximal number of feature elements in an object *o* is o_{max}, since $|Cla|=|E|$, the worst time complexity of Algorithm 2 is $O(|E|*|O|*o_{max})$. If $|E|$ is considered as a constant, thus the time complexity of Algorithm 2 is linear to the size of data.

Then we present GenCED, the CED generation algorithm with CFEs generated by GenCFE. The pseudo code is shown in Algorithm 3. In this algorithm for generating *p*CEDs, we consider how to combine CFEs in order to satisfy the uniqueness property of CEDs. If a CFE *t* already satisfies uniqueness property, *t* becomes a *p*CED directly; otherwise, we should identify whether *t* can combine with other feature element *t'*. If $t \wedge t'$ satisfies both uniqueness property and $frq(t \wedge t') \geq \theta$, $t \wedge t'$ is a *p*CED. All the valid combinations should be found in this way.

As a complementary of *p*CEDs, once a *p*CED in the form of $t \wedge t'$ of entity *e* is generated, for other entity *e'* which also has *t* as a CFE, corresponding *n*CED in form of $t \wedge t'$ is generated for *e'*. We use Example 3 to illustrate the relationship between *n*CEDs and *p*CEDs.

Example 3. There are three entities e_1, e_2 and e_3. Suppose they share a CFE *t*.

The *p*CEDs of e_1-e_3 are as follows:

*p*CEDs of e_1: $t \wedge t_1$, $t \wedge t_2$; *p*CEDs of e_2: $t \wedge t_3$; *p*CEDs of e_3: $t \wedge t_4$.

Then the corresponding *n*CEDs of e_1-e_3 are as follows:

*n*CEDs of e_1: $t \wedge \neg t_3 \wedge \neg t_4$; *n*CEDs of e_2: $t \wedge \neg t_1 \wedge \neg t_2 \wedge \neg t_4$; *n*CEDs of e_3: $t \wedge \neg t_1 \wedge \neg t_2 \wedge \neg t_3$.

The flow of GenCED is as follows: In line1 we run GenCFE to obtain CFEs; then in lines 4-5, for each CFE *t* in each entity, all the possible *p*CEDs and corresponding *n*CEDs containing *t* are generated by function *Add*; before *p*CEDs are stored in *R*, line 6 checks whether there is a dominate relationship, the dominated rules are excluded from the results; in lines 7-11, *n*CEDs are stored in *R*.

Algorithm 3 GenCED

Input: a set *O* of objects, a classification *C* of *O*,Thresholds θ_{ITF}.

Output: a set *E* of entities

```
1    (T, GF, ITF, I)=Gen_CFE();
2    for k←1 to |E| do
3        for each t_i∈T[k] do
4            if I(t_i).size=1 then W(t_i)=GF(t_i,k); R.insert(t_i);
5            else (P(t_i), N(t_i))=Add(t_i,k);
6            for each t_j∈P(t_i) do if t_j∉R then R.insert(t_i∧t_j);
7            CED r= t_i;
8            for each t_j∈N(t) do r=r∧¬t_j;
9            for each j∈I(t_i) do
10               W(r)+=ComputeGF(r,k);
11               R[j].insert(r);
12       e_i=(R, {W(r)|r∈R});
13   E.insert(e_i);
14   Return E;
15   Add(t_i,k)
16   for each t_j(j>i) in T[k] do
17       W(t_i∧t_j)+=ComputeGF(t_i∧t_j,k);
18       If ComputeITF(t_i∧t_j)=1 && W(t_i∧t_j)≥θ then P.insert(t_j);N.insert(t_j);
19   Retun (P,N);
```

Complexity analysis We suppose the maximal length of *n*CEDs is l_n, the maximal number of CFEs in an entity is l_e, the maximal value of GF of CFEs is gf_{max}, and the maixmal value of TF of CFEs is tf_{max}. If tf_{max} and l_n are viewed as constants, the time complexity of Algorithm 3 is $O(|E|* l_e^2 * gf_{max})$ in the worst case.

CED optimization strategy As mentioned before, there are two ways of obtaining CEDs. No matter the CEDs are obtained manually or by learning from training data, CEDs can never capture the full feature information of entities due to continuously new-coming objects. Taking author identification as an example, people may change their research areas or teams. Due to lack of new feature descriptions, running U-CED directly on the new-coming object set can hardly achieve good performance. However, the classification result of U-CED can provide us new feature information of entities. Based on this classification, we can discover new entity description rules using GenCED, which leads to a better accuracy.

4. Experimental Evaluation

Experimental Setting Our experiments were run on a 2.67 GHz Intel(R) Core 2 processor with 4GB of RAM. The operation system is Microsoft Windows 7. Since author identification is one of the most difficult ER problems, and current ER approaches we discussed in section 1 result in the low accuracy and efficiency in author identification problem. Thus we evaluate our algorithm P-CED with CED optimization strategy involved on DBLP[11]. For simplicity, for a given name s, we use *pub(s)* to denote the set of publications which include *s* as an author name, *aut(s)* to denote the set of authors with name *s*. In order to evaluate the effectiveness of our algorithms, we select 10 representative author names shown in Table 3.

Table 3. Names corresponding to multiple authors

ID	name	#pub	#aut	ID	name	#pub	#aut
A_1	*jing wang*	115	11	A_6	*ping zhang*	164	4
A_2	*yan liu*	118	10	A_7	*hui wang*	171	11
A_3	*jian zhang*	147	8	A_8	*xin zhang*	173	13
A_4	*lei chen*	149	4	A_9	*jun yang*	202	9
A_5	*jun sun*	152	7	A_{10}	*wei wang*	421	25

In our experiments, we randomly choose n_i = *maximal {1, 20%*#pub}* publications from the test data as the training data.

Measures Similar to [10, 5], we measure the accuracy of P-CED by precision, recall and f-score.

4.1 Comparison with GHOST

As far as we know, GHOST[5] is the best author identification algorithm both in accuracy and efficiency. Therefore, we compare our algorithm and the comparison results are shown in Table 4, in which we use PC to denote P-CED for short. We can make the following observations from these results.

We can see that GHOST shows a slight boast in precision. However, the result shows P-CED is more robust than GHOST. Besides, P-CED achieves a better performance of precision in average. P-CED offers considerably better recall than GHOST. As mentioned in [5], inadequate relationship may result in low similarity of two tuples, which may cause them to be separated into two clusters by GHOST. However, we can see this situation can hardly affect the recall result of P-CED. This shows how robust P-CED is again. We can see that P-CED can be executed significantly more efficiently than GHOST. The time complexity of GHOST is O(|*O*|*log|*O*|), while our algorithm is approximate linear to |*O*|.

Table 4. Performance Comparison(PC vs GHOST)

ID	precison		recall		f-score		run time(s)	
	GHOST	PC	GHOST	PC	GHOST	PC	GHOST	PC
A_1	1.00	1.00	0.19	.93	0.32	.96	1.19	.05
A_2	1.00	1.00	0.16	**.79**	**0.28**	**.88**	.96	.04
A_3	1.00	0.98	0.91	.95	0.95	.96	.85	.05
A_4	1.00	0.97	0.90	.97	0.95	.97	1.07	.04
A_5	1.00	1.00	0.60	.95	0.75	.97	1.58	.06
A_6	1.00	0.96	**0.13**	.98	0.23	.97	.93	.04
A_7	1.00	**0.89**	0.26	.87	0.42	.88	.83	.04

4.2 Impact factors of Quality

In order to test the impact of training data size on accuracy, we pick two names, "jian zhang" and "ping zhang". By the default setting of training data size, "jian zhang" has the worst accuracy result and "ping zhang" gets the best result. From Figure 1 we observe that, for both names, the accuracy result can reach a high value even when the size of training data is small. With the growth of the training data size, the recall increases gradually, while precisions are insensitive to the training data size.

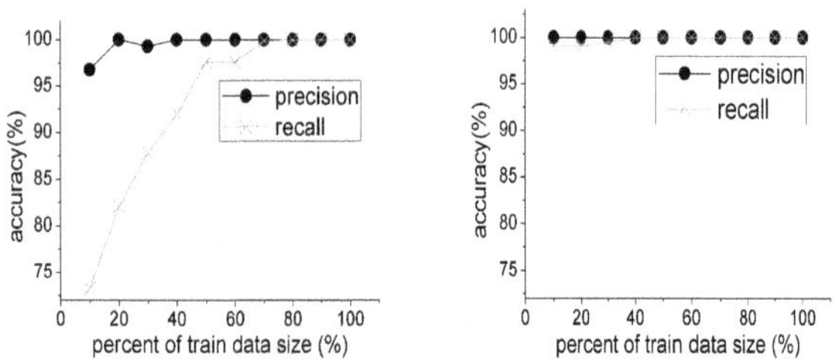

(a) jian zhang **(b)ping zhang**

Figure 1. Training data size impact on accuracy

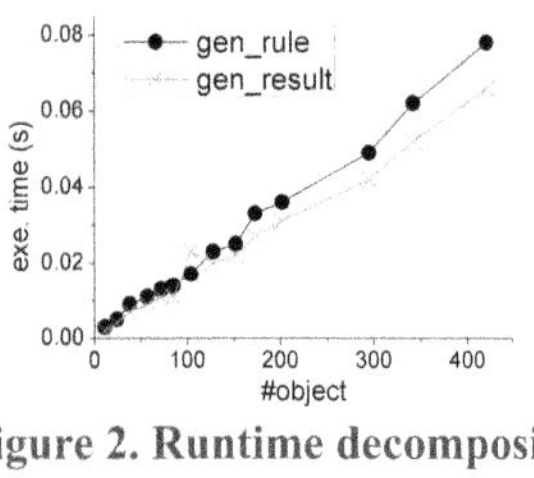

Figure 2. Runtime decomposition

4.3 Efficiency and Scalability

In Figure 2, we test the impact of number of tuples on efficiency. In order to vary the values of numbers of publications of each name, we pick 14 names with publication numbers varying from 11 to 421. From Figure 2, it can be observed that the run time is approximately linear to the number of objects. This result is in accordance with our time complexity analysis in section 2.

From the experimental results, we can draw following conclusions.

P-CED is flexible than GHOST. P-CED neither care about whether the authors having the same name unlikely have similar research area nor assume authors seldom change their research teams or labs.

P-CED is insensitive to the size of the training data. Due to the contribution of new CEDs been discovered, P-CED only requires a small size of training data. Even when the training data size is small, P-CED can get a high accuracy.

P-CED has both good scalability and high efficiency. The experiments show that with the increase of size of data, the runtime of PC increase approximately linearly.

5. Conclusions

Current ER approaches mostly based on object comparison and similarity functions. This paper addressed the limitations of comparison between objects on ER, and developed a strategy based on comparison between object and entity. We present a context-based entity description rule (CED) to describe the features of entity. Thus the ER problem is reduced to that for each object, to identify the entity which is most similar with the object. We develop a CED-based algorithm for ER problem and present a CED discovery strategy. We experimentally evaluated our algorithm on real data set, and the experimental results show that our algorithm can achieve a good performance in accuracy and outperforms existing algorithm both in efficiency and accuracy.

6. ACKNOWLEDGMENTS

Thanks for the help on experiments by Jianyong Wang in Tsinghua University.

7. REFERENCES

[1] N. Koudas, S. Sarawagi, and D. Srivastava: Record linkage: similarity measures and algorithms. SIGMOD 2006.
[2] W. W. Cohen: Integration of heterogeneous databases without common domains using queries based on textual similarity. SIGMOD 1998.
[3] S. Chaudhuri, B.-C. Chen, V. Ganti, and R. Kaushik: Example-driven design of efficient record matching queries. VLDB 2007.
[4] A. Arasu, S. Chaudhuri, and R. Kaushik: Learning string transformations from examples. VLDB 2009.
[5] Xiaoming Fan, Jianyong Wang, Xu Pu, Lizhu Zhou, Bing Lv: On Graph-Based Name Disambiguation. J. Data and Information Quality 2(2): 10 (2011).
[6] Bansal, N., Blum, A., Chawla, S.: Correlation clustering. In: FOCS, p. 238(2002).
[7] Chaudhuri,S., Ganjam, K., Ganti, V., Motwani, R.: Robust and efficient fuzzy match for online data cleaning. SIGMOD 2003.
[8] Chuan Xiao, Wei Wang, Xuemin Lin, Jeffrey Xu Yu: Efficient similarity joins for near duplicate detection. WWW 2008: 131-140.
[9] Chuan Xiao, Wei Wang, Xuemin Lin, Haichuan Shang: Top-k Set Similarity Joins. ICDE 2009: 916-927.
[10] Xiaoxin Yin, Jiawei Han, Philip S. Yu: Object Distinction: Distinguishing Objects with Identical Names by Link Analysis. ICDE 2007.
[11] http://dblp.uni-trier.de/

Cost-Efficient Repair in Inconsistent Probabilistic Databases

Xiang Lian, Yincheng Lin, and Lei Chen
Department of Computer Science and Engineering
The Hong Kong University of Science and Technology
Hong Kong, China
{xlian, lycheng, leichen}@cse.ust.hk

ABSTRACT

Due to the ubiquitous data uncertainty in many emerging real applications, efficient management of probabilistic databases has become an increasingly important yet challenging problem. In particular, one fundamental task of data management is to identify those unreliable data in the probabilistic database that violate integrity constraints (e.g., functional dependencies), and then quickly resolve data inconsistencies. In this paper, we formulate and tackle an important problem of repairing inconsistent probabilistic databases efficiently by value modification. Specifically, we propose a repair semantic, namely *possible-world-oriented repair* (PW-repair), which partitions possible worlds into several disjoint groups, and repairs these groups individually with minimum repair costs. Due to the intractable result that finding such a PW-repair strategy is NP-complete, we carefully design a heuristic-based greedy approach for PW-repair, which can efficiently obtain an effective repair of the inconsistent probabilistic database. Through extensive experiments, we show that our approach can achieve the efficiency and effectiveness of the repair on inconsistent probabilistic data.

Categories and Subject Descriptors

H.2.0 [**Database Management**]: Systems—*General*; H.3.0 [**Information Systems**]: Information Storage and retrieval—*General*

General Terms

Algorithms, Design, Experimentation, Performance, Theory

Keywords

Inconsistent probabilistic database, possible-world-oriented repair

1. INTRODUCTION

Recently, a wide spectrum of real applications often require integrating data from multiple sources (e.g., the Web, public or enterprise databases). Due to various reasons such as misspellings, integration precisions, and subjective opinions from people, inconsistencies, errors, or conflicts may emerge in the integrated data, violating integrity constraints like functional dependencies. Such dirty data may lead to serious consequences, for example, annually costing US businesses 600 billion dollars [11, 12]. Therefore, it has been recognized as an important task for the data integration system to effectively manage inconsistencies in databases.

HID	AC	Zip	Loc.	Rating	t_i.p
t_1	44	20000	L_1	5	.6
t_2	44	30000	L_2	4	1
t_3	44	40000	L_2	3	.7
t_4	44	10000	L_1	3	.8

Table 1: Illustration of an Inconsistent Probabilistic Database, hotel**.**

Possible World $pw(\mathcal{D})$	**Probability** $Pr\{pw(\mathcal{D})\}$
$pw_1(\mathcal{D}) = \{t_2\}$	$(1-.6) \times 1 \times (1-.7) \times (1-.8) = .024$
$pw_2(\mathcal{D}) = \{t_1, t_2\}$	$.6 \times 1 \times (1-.7) \times (1-.8) = .036$
$pw_3(\mathcal{D}) = \{t_2, t_3\}$	$(1-.6) \times 1 \times .7 \times (1-.8) = .056$
$pw_4(\mathcal{D}) = \{t_2, t_4\}$	$(1-.6) \times 1 \times (1-.7) \times .8 = .096$
$pw_5(\mathcal{D}) = \{t_1, t_2, t_3\}$	$.6 \times 1 \times .7 \times (1-.8) = .084$
$pw_6(\mathcal{D}) = \{t_2, t_3, t_4\}$	$(1-.6) \times 1 \times .7 \times .8 = .224$
$pw_7(\mathcal{D}) = \{t_1, t_2, t_4\}$	$.6 \times 1 \times (1-.7) \times .8 = .144$
$pw_8(\mathcal{D}) = \{t_1, t_2, t_3, t_4\}$	$.6 \times 1 \times .7 \times .8 = .336$

Table 2: Possible worlds of hotel **in Table 1.**

While previous works [8, 3, 5, 21, 9] on resolving inconsistencies by the database repair usually assume that the underlying data are precise, real-world data, however, are often uncertain and imprecise. Table 1 depicts an example of a small database containing the records (tuples) of 4 hotels $t_1 \sim t_4$. The table schema is:

$$\text{hotel(HID, AC, Zip, Loc., Rating)},$$

where each tuple has attributes: hotel id (HID), area code (AC), zip code (Zip), location in the area (Loc.), and the rating (Rating).

In addition, hotel records in Table 1 may possibly expire in reality (e.g., the hotel closes). Thus, we associate each tuple t_i with an attribute t_i.p ($\in [0, 1]$), indicating the probability that the hotel entity still opens (exists) currently. As a result, Table 1 exactly corresponds to a probabilistic database [10], where each tuple (hotel) t_i appears in the real world with an *existence probability* $t_i.p$.

In the literature of probabilistic databases [10], we usually consider the *possible worlds* semantics, where each possible world $pw(\mathcal{D})$ is a materialized instance of the probabilistic database $\mathcal{D}$ that can occur in reality. Table 2 shows all the 8 possible worlds, $pw_1(\mathcal{D}) \sim pw_8(\mathcal{D})$, of Table 1, where each tuple either exists or does not exist in a possible world.

In the table, tuples t_1 and t_4 in possible worlds $pw_7(\mathcal{D})$ and $pw_8(\mathcal{D})$ have the same area code AC ("44") and hotel location Loc. ("L_1"), however, they have distinct zip codes Zip (i.e., "20000" and "10000", respectively), which violates a functional dependency (FD):

$$\text{AC, Loc.} \rightarrow \text{Zip}.$$

Thus, we say that tuples t_1 and t_4 are inconsistent with each other in possible worlds $pw_7(\mathcal{D})$ and $pw_8(\mathcal{D})$. Similarly, t_2 and t_3 are also inconsistent in possible worlds $pw_5(\mathcal{D})$, $pw_6(\mathcal{D})$, and $pw_8(\mathcal{D})$, violating the FD above.

In order to resolve such inconsistencies, we may need to repair data in possible worlds by attribute value modifications. In our

CIKM'11, October 24–28, 2011, Glasgow, Scotland, UK.

example, in possible worlds $pw_7(\mathcal{D})$ and $pw_8(\mathcal{D})$, we can set attribute Zip of both inconsistent tuples t_1 and t_4 to a value, "20000" or "10000"; in possible worlds $pw_5(\mathcal{D})$, $pw_6(\mathcal{D})$, and $pw_8(\mathcal{D})$, we can also modify zip codes of t_2 and t_3 to a value, "30000" or "40000". Thus, one critical yet challenging issue arises, that is, how to efficiently determine repaired attribute values and resolve inconsistencies, especially in possible worlds of probabilistic data.

One straightforward method is to repair each possible world of the inconsistent probabilistic database, by applying the existing repair techniques on inconsistent certain data [5]. However, since there are an exponential number of possible worlds on probabilistic data, the total number of repairs can be also exponential in the worst case. Clearly, this repair method is inefficient or even infeasible, in terms of the repair time and space cost. Moreover, the resulting (many) versions of repaired data are also inconvenient for the usage (e.g., answering queries) in practical applications.

Inspired by the inefficiency of the straightforward method, as a preliminary work for the repair in inconsistent probabilistic databases, we propose repair semantics, *possible-world-oriented repair* (PW-repair). A PW-repair classifies possible worlds into k (disjoint) groups, namely, *possible world groups* (PWGs), and obtains one repair for each PWG, such that the PW-repair cost in possible worlds of PWGs is minimum. Intuitively, instead of repairing every possible world, the PW-repair repairs a much smaller number, k, of PWGs, which trades the effectiveness for (space/time) efficiency, where k is a controllable parameter that is specified by users.

Unfortunately, we prove that the problem of finding a PW-repair with the minimum repair cost (via value modification) is NP-complete and intractable. Therefore, in this paper, we will design a greedy algorithm for the PW-repair, which can efficiently obtain repairs with low repair costs in PWGs.

We make the following contributions in this paper.

1. We formalize the PW-repair problem which repairs inconsistent probabilistic data in Section 2.
2. We prove in Section 3.1 that our PW-repair problem is NP-complete and intractable.
3. We propose in Sections 3.2 $\sim$ **??** an efficient greedy approximation approach for PW-repair.
4. We conduct extensive experiments to confirm the efficiency of our proposed repair approach in Section 4.

In addition, Section 5 reviews previous works on repairs in inconsistent certain databases, and query answering in probabilistic databases. Section 6 concludes this paper.

2. PROBLEM DEFINITION

2.1 Preliminary

Probabilistic Databases [10]: A probabilistic database $\mathcal{D}$ contains a set of N *x-tuples* t_1, t_2, ..., and t_N, where each x-tuple t_i ($1 \leq i \leq N$) consists of a single or multiple (mutually exclusive) *alternatives* t_{ij} ($1 \leq j \leq l_i$). Each alternative t_{ij} is associated with an existence probability $t_{ij}.p$, where $\sum_{j=1}^{l_i} t_{ij}.p \leq 1$.

For the sake of clear presentation, throughout this paper, we assume that the probabilistic database contains single-alternative x-tuples (i.e., $l_i = 1$ for all i). For brevity, we will use tuple t_i to represent either x-tuple or the single alternative t_{i1} of an x-tuple when the context is clear.

Possible Worlds: A *possible world* $pw(\mathcal{D})$ of a probabilistic database $\mathcal{D}$ is a materialized instance of $\mathcal{D}$ that may occur in reality. Each x-tuple has at most one alternative appearing in a possible world.

Symbol	Description
$\mathcal{D}$	a probabilistic database containing N tuples
$\mathcal{D}^R$	a repaired probabilistic database (i.e., $\mathcal{D} \oplus \Delta(\mathcal{D})$)
$\mathcal{PW}(\mathcal{D})$	the set of *possible worlds*, $pw(\mathcal{D})$, in $\mathcal{D}$
t_i	an x-tuple (or a single alternative in t_i) in probabilistic databases
$t_{ij}.p$	the existent probability of tuple t_{ij}
$t_{ij}.w(A)$	the confidence (weight) that attribute A in tuple t_{ij} is correct
Σ	a set of functional dependencies in the form $X \rightarrow A$

Table 3: Symbols and descriptions.

DEFINITION 2.1. (*Possible Worlds, $pw(\mathcal{D})$*) *A possible world, $pw(\mathcal{D})$, is a subset of probabilistic database $\mathcal{D}$ such that each x-tuple t_i has at most one alternative in $pw(\mathcal{D})$. The appearance probability, $Pr\{pw(\mathcal{D})\}$, that $pw(\mathcal{D})$ occurs is:*

$$Pr\{pw(\mathcal{D})\} = \prod_{\forall t_{ij} \in pw(\mathcal{D})} t_{ij}.p \cdot \prod_{\forall t_i \notin pw(\mathcal{D})} (1 - \sum_{j=1}^{l_i} t_{ij}.p), \quad (1)$$

where l_i is the number of alternatives in x-tuple t_i.

Table 2 shows 8 possible worlds (and their appearance probabilities) of the probabilistic database in Table 1.

Inconsistent Probabilistic Databases: In an inconsistent probabilistic database, tuples are often inconsistent with each other (e.g., violating FDs) [14]. Following the practice of US national statistical agencies [13, 22], we assume that each attribute A of a tuple $t_i \in \mathcal{D}$ is associated with a *weight*, $t_i.w(A) \in [0, 1]$, which reflects the confidence that attribute $t_i[A]$ is correct. Similar to [18], we assume that tuples (attributes) are from independent data sources. Table 3 summarizes the commonly used symbols in this paper.

Functional Dependencies (FDs): An FD, $X \rightarrow A$, indicates that any two tuples, t and t', with the same value on attribute X (i.e., $t[X] = t'[X]$) should also have equal values on attribute A (i.e., $t[A] = t'[A]$).

2.2 Repairing Inconsistent Probabilistic Databases

Possible-World-Oriented Repair (PW-Repair): To resolve inconsistencies, we propose PW-repair by considering attribute value modifications in possible worlds with *minimal repair* semantics [5].

DEFINITION 2.2. (*PW-Repair in Inconsistent Probabilistic Databases*) *Given an inconsistent probabilistic database $\mathcal{D}$, and a set, Σ, of FDs in the form of $X \rightarrow A$, a possible-world-oriented repair (PW-Repair) divides all possible worlds, $pw(\mathcal{D})$, of $\mathcal{D}$ into k (≥ 1) disjoint possible world groups (PWGs), PWG_1, PWG_2, ..., and PWG_k, and for each PWG PWG_i ($1 \leq i \leq k$), obtains a repaired database $\mathcal{D}^{R_i}$ by attribute value modification, such that 1) $\mathcal{D}^{R_i}$ is consistent in any possible world of PWG_i, and 2) the PW-repair cost,* Repr_{PW}, *is minimized, where*

$$\text{Repr}_{\text{PW}} = \sum_{i=1}^{k} \left(\sum_{\forall pw(\mathcal{D}) \in PWG_i} Pr\{pw(\mathcal{D})\} \cdot \left(\sum_{\forall t \in pw(\mathcal{D})} cost(t, t^{R_i}) \right) \right), \quad (2)$$

and $t^{R_i} \in \mathcal{D}^{R_i}$ is the repaired tuple of $t \in \mathcal{D}$.

The function $cost(t, t^{R_i})$ in Eq. (2) is defined as:

$$cost(t, t^{R_i}) = \sum_{\forall A \in attr(\mathcal{D})} \left(t.w(A) \cdot \frac{dist(t[A], t^{R_i}[A])}{max\_dist(A)} \right) \quad (3)$$

where $dist(\cdot, \cdot)$ is a distance function to measure the distance between two attribute values, and $max\_dist(A)$ is the maximum deviation of the repaired value from original one.

The PW-Repair Semantics: In Definition 2.2, the PW-repair divides all possible worlds into disjoint partitions (i.e., PWG_i), each of which contains possible worlds with similar repairs. Then, a repair is carried out on each PWG PWG_i, such that the resulting repaired database $\mathcal{D}^{R_i}$ is consistent, and the PW-repair cost (given by Eq. (2)) is the lowest. Note that, here the partitioning of possible worlds can be arbitrary, thus, an exhaustive search of PW-repair would incur rather high cost. Therefore, in this paper, we will design an efficient PW-repair approach, which quickly finds a good partitioning strategy with low PW-repair cost.

Parameter k: The parameter k in Definition 2.2 represents the number of PWGs for PW-repair, which is assumed to be a user-specified constant parameter.

PW-Repair Cost, Repr_{PW}*:* The PW-repair cost, Repr_{PW}, in Eq. (2) is given by the summation of repair costs in k possible world groups, $PWG_1 \sim PWG_k$, using k versions of data repairs, $\mathcal{D}^{R_1} \sim \mathcal{D}^{R_k}$, respectively. For each PWG_i ($1 \leq i \leq k$), we compute the summed value modification cost of all tuples that appear in possible worlds $pw(\mathcal{D})$ of PWG_i (i.e., $\sum_{\forall t \in pw(\mathcal{D})} cost(t, t^{R_i})$), and sum up these costs weighted by appearance probabilities $Pr\{pw(\mathcal{D})\}$.

Value Modification Cost, $cost(t, t^{R_i})$*:* For a particular tuple t in possible worlds, the value modification cost, $cost(t, t^{R_i})$, from t to t^{R_i} is shown in Eq. (3), which sums up the weight, $t.w(A)$, of attribute $t[A]$ times (normalized) value distances before and after the repair (w.r.t. $\mathcal{D}^{R_i}$), for all attributes A (i.e., $\sum_{\forall A \in attr(\mathcal{D})} (t.w(A) \cdot \frac{dist(t[A], t^{R_i}[A])}{max\_dist(A)})$). Intuitively, smaller weight $t.w(A)$ (i.e., lower data accuracy) and less attribute modification cost will indicate lower repair cost. We notice that this function (i.e., $cost(t, t^{R_i})$) was also used as a measure to evaluate the repair cost on the tuple level in certain databases [5]. Here, in Eq. (2), we utilize it to calculate the repair cost of a tuple t in a possible world $pw(\mathcal{D})$.

Applications: The PW-repair can be used in many practical applications to improve the quality of real-world probabilistic data. In the application of data integration, we need to merge two distinct data sources via the join operator. The join results might be associated with existence probabilities due to inaccurate join attributes, which thus form a probabilistic database. In the application of the information extraction, we extract data (tuples) from Web pages. Each tuple t_i is associated with a probability $t_i.p$, indicating the chance that the Web page is still valid (not expired), and an extraction accuracy $t_i.w(A)$ of attributes in t_i. In these applications, data are usually probabilistic and inconsistent (in possible worlds). Our PW-repair can exactly resolve inconsistencies by providing k repaired versions of the probabilistic database, where each version is specific for a group of possible real-world scenarios (i.e., PWGs).

After the PW-repair, we can use the k resulting repairs to answer queries in real applications. In particular, for any query, we can first find a PWG that contains the real world by checking the expiration status of those partitioning tuples w.r.t. PWGs, and then select the repaired database corresponding to this PWG for query processing.

3. POSSIBLE-WORLD-ORIENTED REPAIR

3.1 Intractable Results

We next present intractable results for our PW-repair problem under functional dependencies in inconsistent probabilistic databases, showing that this problem is NP-complete and not tractable.

LEMMA 3.1. *Given an inconsistent probabilistic database $\mathcal{D}$, a set Σ of functional dependencies, and a constant ε, the problem of determining whether there exists a PW-repair of $\mathcal{D}$ whose repair cost is at most ε is NP-complete.*

Proof. Please refer to Appendix A. □

Lemma 3.1 shows that the PW-repair problem is not tractable. Thus, it is necessary to propose heuristic-based greedy approximation approaches to find good PW-repairs with low costs.

ERB(A, {X→A}) ERB(A, {Y→A}) ERB(A, {X→A, Y→A})

id	X	Y	A	$t_i.p$
t_1	1	1	3	0.8
t_2	1	1	3	0.7
t_3	1	0	4	0.2
t_4	2	0	6	0.6
t_5	2	0	7	0.5
t_6	3	4	8	0.9
t_7	3	4	9	0.4

(a) $ERB(A, \{X \to A\})$ and $ERB(A, \{Y \to A\})$

id	X	Y	A	$t_i.p$
t_1	1	1	3	0.8
t_2	1	1	3	0.7
t_3	1	0	4	0.2
t_4	2	0	6	0.6
t_5	2	0	7	0.5
t_6	3	4	8	0.9
t_7	3	4	9	0.4

(b) $ERB(A, \{X \to A, Y \to A\})$

Figure 1: An example of identifying equivalence repair blocks (w.r.t. 2 functional dependencies: $X \to A$ and $Y \to A$).

3.2 Identifying Equivalence Repair Blocks

To facilitate our heuristic-based approach of repairing probabilistic data, we first define a notion of the basic repair unit, namely *equivalence repair block* (ERB). Specifically, an ERB, $ERB(A, \{\sigma_1, ..., \sigma_n\})$, for attribute A is defined as a set of tuples whose attribute A that should be modified to the same value after the repair, inferred from FDs σ_1, ..., and σ_n in Σ, where $\sigma_i : U_i \to A$. Moreover, each ERB $ERB(A, \{\sigma_1, ..., \sigma_n\})$ is associated with a set of candidate repairing values for attribute A, denoted as $V(A, \{\sigma_1, ..., \sigma_n\}) = \{t_i[A] \mid \forall\, t_i \in ERB(A, \{\sigma_1, ..., \sigma_n\})\}$.

ERBs for a Single FD: For a single FD $X \to A$, an ERB, $ERB(A, \{(X = v) \to A\})$, for attribute A is given by a set of tuples $\{t \mid \forall t,\, t[X] = v\}$, for a particular value v of attribute X. Intuitively, $ERB(A, \{(X = v) \to A\})$ contains all tuples that have the same attribute value v in X, and their A values are also expected to be the same after the repair, due to FD $X \to A$. As an example in Figure 1(a), under $X \to A$, we have 3 ERBs, that is, $ERB(A, \{(X = 1) \to A\}) = \{t_1, t_2, t_3\}$, $ERB(A, \{(X = 2) \to A\}) = \{t_4, t_5\}$, and $ERB(A, \{(X = 3) \to A\}) = \{t_6, t_7\}$.

ERBs for Multiple FDs: Given more than one FD, we may need to merge ERBs of different FDs. As an example, in Figure 1(a), in addition to $X \to A$, we have another FD $Y \to A$, where $X \neq Y$. The resulting 3 ERBs under $Y \to A$ are given by $ERB(A, \{(Y = 1) \to A\}) = \{t_1, t_2\}$, $ERB(A, \{(Y = 0) \to A\}) = \{t_3, t_4, t_5\}$, and $ERB(A, \{(Y = 4) \to A\}) = \{t_6, t_7\}$.

Since $t_2, t_3 \in ERB(A, \{(X = 1) \to A\})$ in Figure 1(a), we have $t_2[A] = t_3[A]$. Similarly, since $t_3, t_4 \in ERB(A, \{(Y = 0) \to A\})$, it holds that $t_3[A] = t_4[A]$. Thus, by the equality transition, we know $t_2[A]$, $t_3[A]$, and $t_4[A]$ should be assigned with the same value after the repair. In other words, their residing ERBs $ERB(A, \{(X = 1) \to A\})$ and $ERB(A, \{(X = 2) \to A\})$ (or equivalently, $ERB(A, \{(Y = 1) \to A\})$ and $ERB(A, \{(Y = 0) \to A\})$) should be merged into one ERB, in which tuples should have the same value of attribute A. As shown in Figure 1(b), the merged ERB contains tuples $t_1 \sim t_5$, and can be denoted as $ERB(A, \{(X, Y) \in \{(1, 1), (1, 0), (2, 0)\} \to A\})$. Furthermore, the candidate values for attribute A are $\{3, 4, 6, 7\}$, that is, the union of value sets $V(A, \{(X = 1) \to A\})$ ($i.e.$, $\{3, 4\}$) and $V(A, \{(X = 2) \to A\})$ ($i.e.$, $\{6, 7\}$).

Identification of ERBs: To identify ERBs under multiple FDs, we first find those dependent attributes A that appear on the RHS of FDs. Then, for each attribute A, we identify ERBs by considering relevant FDs one by one. That is, for an FD $\sigma_i : U_i \to A$, if a set, W_j, of tuples that agree on attribute(s) U_i belong to more than one (previously assigned) ERB, then we need to merge tuples in these ERBs, and update their candidate repairing values (via union) for the resulting merged block.

Repair Order: By considering each attribute as a vertex and the determination relationship among attributes from FDs as edges, we can construct a directed acyclic graph (DAG). In this paper, we use

id	X	A	$t_i.p$
t_1	1	1	0.9
t_2	1	2	0.3
t_3	1	3	0.2

Figure 2: An example of the PWG partitioning in PW-repair (w.r.t. functional dependency $X \rightarrow A$).

the *topological order* of vertices (attributes) in the DAG of FDs as the repair sequence on attributes. Intuitively, with this order, each tuple attribute will not be repaired more than once.

3.3 Partitioning Possible Worlds

Since the PW-repair problem is NP-complete (see Lemma 3.1), in this subsection, we propose an efficient heuristic-based approach, which partitions all the possible worlds of an inconsistent probabilistic database $\mathcal{D}$ into disjoint PWGs, such that the repaired data in PWGs can achieve low PW-repair costs.

Illustrative Example of Partitioning Possible Worlds: We illustrate our heuristics of partitioning possible worlds using an example in Figure 2, where a small probabilistic database $\mathcal{D}$ contains 3 tuples t_1, t_2, and t_3, following a functional dependency $X \rightarrow A$, and all weights, $t_i.w(A)$, of $t_i[A]$ are assumed to be 0.5. In this example, we can see that due to the functional dependency $X \rightarrow A$, the tuple set, $\{t_1, t_2, t_3\}$, forms an ERB.

Let us first consider the case where all possible worlds of $\mathcal{D}$ form one group, PWG_1 (i.e., $k = 1$). In this case, the PW-repair with $k = 1$ will obtain one repaired database $\mathcal{D}^R$ for PWG_1 that modifies all values of attribute A to a single value 1 ($= t_1[A]$). It is worth noting that, we still have the chance to further obtain lower repair cost. As an example in Figure 2, in a possible world $pw(\mathcal{D}) = \{t_2, t_3\}$ where t_1 (with $t_1[A] = 1$) does not exist, our PW-repair (with $k = 1$) will always modify $t_2^R[A] = t_3^R[A] = 1$, with the repair cost 0.35 ($= 0.5\times(2-1)\times0.3+0.5\times(3-1)\times0.2$). However, in fact, attribute A's value "1" never appears in this possible world $pw(\mathcal{D})$, and a lower repair cost (i.e., 0.1) can be achieved in $pw(\mathcal{D})$ if we modify attribute A of tuple t_3 to "2" ($= t_2[A]$).

Based on the observation above, in some possible world of the database, attributes of tuples might be assigned with a repairing value that does not appear in this possible world, which may lead to high PW-repair cost. Therefore, our strategy of partitioning possible worlds is based on heuristics of reducing such a repair cost.

Specifically, for PW-repair with $k = 2$, we can divide all the possible worlds into 2 disjoint groups, PWG_1 and PWG_2. PWG_1 includes all possible worlds that contain t_1, whereas PWG_2 contains possible worlds where t_1 does not appear. Intuitively, during the PW-repair, we perform a repair for each PWG individually. The repair in PWG_1 has candidate repairing values 1, 2, and 3 for attribute A. For PWG_2, since t_1 does not appear in possible worlds of PWG_2, candidate repairing values are 2 and 3, and exclude value "1" ($= t_1[A]$). This way, a lower repair cost can be obtained.

Sub-Blocks: Next, we introduce a notion, namely *sub-block*, based on which we can apply our strategy to the PWG partitioning in PW-repairs. Note that, in Definition 2.2, possible worlds can be arbitrarily partitioned into k groups. However, since to find the partitioning with the minimum repair cost is NP-complete (Lemma 3.1), we can only give an approximate approach, which assumes that the sub-block is the basic partitioning unit in PW-repair.

Assume that we have identified m ERBs for an attribute A (as mentioned in Section 3.2), where the subscript i of ERB_i is an index for ERBs, and we omit symbols of FDs in $ERB_l(A, \{\sigma_1, ..., \sigma_n\})$ when the context is clear. Each ERB, $ERB_l(A)$, has a_l distinct candidate repairing values, $v_{l1} \sim v_{la_l}$. Without loss of generality, we denote a *sub-block*, $sub\_ERB_{lj}(A)$, as a subset of tuples in an ERB, $ERB_l(A)$, with the same value v_{lj} of attribute A.

In the example of Figure 2, we have one ERB, $ERB_1(A)$, which contains 3 sub-blocks, that is, $sub\_ERB_{11}(A) = \{t_1\}$, $sub\_ERB_{12}(A) = \{t_2\}$, and $sub\_ERB_{13}(A) = \{t_3\}$.

The PWG Partitioning Strategy: Our PWG partitioning strategy is as follows. We will always select some sub-block, $sub\_ERB_{lj}(A)$, in the database, and divide possible worlds according to the criterion whether or not possible worlds in PWGs contain tuples in sub-block $sub\_ERB_{lj}(A)$.

As in the example of Figure 2, we can partition possible worlds of $\mathcal{D}$ into two groups, based on the (non-)existence of sub-block $sub\_ERB_{11}(A)$ ($= \{t_1\}$). That is, we can obtain two PWGs, PWG_1 having tuple t_1, and PWG_2 without t_1.

3.4 Approximation Approach

In the sequel, we will propose an approximation approach, namely *the greedy algorithm* (GA), to obtain a PW-repair with sub-optimal minimum repair cost.

Greedy Algorithm: Our greedy algorithm aims to obtain k repaired databases $\mathcal{D}^{R_i}$, each with the attribute value setting to v_{lj_i} in $ERB_l(A)$ ($1 \leq l \leq m$ and $1 \leq j_i \leq a_l$), and associated with a PWG, PWG_i, which can approximately minimize the PW-repair cost (given by Eq. (2)).

<u>*Base Case:*</u> First, we consider the base case where the number, k, of PWGs is equal to 1. For the convenience, we denote the minimum PW-repair cost in Eq. (2) (for $k = 1$) on all possible worlds of $\mathcal{D}$ (i.e., treated as one PWG) as function $\widehat{\mathsf{Repr}_{\mathsf{PW}}}(\mathcal{D}, 1)$.

Since the original formula of $\mathsf{Repr}_{\mathsf{PW}}$ in Eq. (2) involves an exponential number of possible worlds, we now reduce its computational cost by condensing the possible worlds of $\mathcal{D}$. Specifically, we have:

$$\widehat{\mathsf{Repr}_{\mathsf{PW}}}(\mathcal{D}, 1) = \sum_{l=1}^{m} \min_{\forall v_{lj}} \left\{ \sum_{\forall t \in ERB_l(A)} \left(t.p \cdot t.w(A) \cdot \frac{dist(t[A], v_{lj})}{max\_dist(A)} \right) \right\}. \quad (4)$$

In particular, the formula above sums up the smallest repair cost in each ERB, which is given by first taking every possible repairing value v_{lj} in $ERB_l(A)$, and then selecting the one with the smallest cost. By condensing possible worlds, the repair cost in each ERB can be obtained by summing up the term $t.p \cdot t.w(A) \cdot \frac{dist(t[A], v_{lj})}{max\_dist(A)}$ for all tuples t in the ERB, where v_{lj} is one candidate repairing value of A. This way, while computing the minimum PW-repair cost where $k = 1$, we can also obtain a PW-repair mechanism on ERBs (when the minimum PW-repair cost is achieved).

<u>*Recursive Function:*</u> To obtain PW-repairs, we propose a greedy approximation approach that partitions possible worlds into k disjoint groups, and achieves low PW-repair cost $\widehat{\mathsf{Repr}_{PW}}$ of Repr_{PW} in Eq. (2), given by a recursive function:

$$\begin{aligned}
\widehat{\mathsf{Repr}_{\mathsf{PW}}}(\mathcal{D}, k) = \min \Big\{ & min_{i=1}^{k-1} \big\{ (1 - \Pi_{\forall t \in sub_ERB_{11}(A)}(1 - t.p)) \quad (5)\\
& \cdot \widehat{\mathsf{Repr}_{\mathsf{PW}}}(\mathcal{D}\text{-}sub_ERB_{11}(A) \mid sub_ERB_{11} \text{ exists}, i) \\
& \underline{(\bigstar \text{ for } PWG_1 \sim PWG_i)} \\
& + \Pi_{\forall t \in sub_ERB_{11}(A)}(1 - t.p) \\
& \cdot \widehat{\mathsf{Repr}_{\mathsf{PW}}}(\mathcal{D} - sub_ERB_{11}(A), k - i) \big\}, \\
& \underline{(\blacklozenge \text{ for } PWG_{i+1} \sim PWG_k)} \\
& \widehat{\mathsf{Repr}_{\mathsf{PW}}}(\mathcal{D} - sub_ERB_{11}(A), k) \\
& - \sum_{i=1}^{k} max\{0, repr_cost_1 - repr_cost_2\} \Big\} \\
& \underline{(\blacktriangle \text{ for } PWG_1 \sim PWG_k)}
\end{aligned}$$

where $\widehat{\mathsf{Repr}_{\mathsf{PW}}}(\mathcal{D}, 1)$ is given by Eq. (4), $\mathsf{Repr}_{\mathsf{PW}}(\emptyset, k) = 0$, and $\mathsf{Repr}_{\mathsf{PW}}(\mathcal{D}, k) = 0$ (if $2^a < k$ holds, given the number, a, of sub-blocks in $\mathcal{D}$). Moreover, variable $repr\_cost_1$ is the repair cost on ERB $ERB_1(A)$, which uses the repairing value of PWG_i for tuples in $(ERB_1(A) - sub\_ERB_{11}(A))$; variable $repr\_cost_2$ is the minimum repair cost in $ERB_1(A)$ (under possible worlds in $PWG_i \times \{\forall pw(sub\_ERB_{11}(A))\}$) using the repairing value v_{11} in $sub\_ERB_{11}(A)$).

Intuitively, $\widehat{\mathsf{Repr}_{PW}}(\mathcal{D}, k)$ in Eq. (5) aims to recursively find a good partitioning strategy on possible worlds of $\mathcal{D}$, with a low PW-repair cost, and decides PW-repairs $\mathcal{D}^{R_i}$, as well as their associated possible world groups PWG_i.

Specifically, within the outer $\min\{\cdot\}$ operator of Eq. (5), the first term considers dividing all possible worlds of $\mathcal{D}$ into two parts, $PWG_1 \sim PWG_i$ (denoted as ★) and $PWG_{i+1} \sim PWG_k$ (denoted as ♦), according to the (non-)existence of tuples in the sub-block, $sub\_ERB_{11}(A)$, where $1 \leq i \leq k-1$.

Furthermore, the second term (denoted as ▲) in $\min\{\cdot\}$ of Eq. (5) corresponds to the case where all PWGs are not partitioned at the sub-block $ERB_{11}(A)$. Thus, to compute the PW-repair cost, we first obtain the repair cost on the remaining data, $\mathcal{D}$-$sub\_ERB_{11}(A)$, at which k PWGs, $PWG_1 \sim PWG_k$, are split. Then, since the repair in $ERB_1(A)$ using the repairing value v_{11} in $sub\_ERB_{11}(A)$ may produce lower repair cost for some PWGs, we thus update the obtained cost above, as shown in ▲ of Eq. (5).

Therefore, the function in Eq. (5) will recursively take the smaller cost value (as well as selecting PW-repairs in PWGs where the value is achieved) between terms (★ + ♦) and (▲).

We illustrate the pseudo-code for the PW-repair procedure, namely GA_PW_Repair, in Figure 3.

```
Procedure GA_PW_Repair {
  Input: an inconsistent probabilistic database D, a set Σ of FDs
  Output: k disjoint PWGs PWG_i, and their PW-repaired databases D^{R_i}
  (1) PWG_0 = {∀pw(D)};
  (2) for (inconsistent) attribute A in topological order
  (3)     for each PWG, PWG_i
  (4)         use the greedy approach in Eq. (5) to obtain k(A) disjoint PWGs,
              PWG_l(A), in PWG_i and their repairs D^{R_l} with low repair costs
                      // ∪_{l=1}^{k(A)} PWG_l(A) = PWG_i
  (5) return PWGs PWG_l and D^{R_l} (1 ≤ l ≤ k)
}
```

Figure 3: The greedy algorithm of PW-repair in inconsistent probabilistic databases.

4. EXPERIMENTAL STUDY

In this section, we evaluate the efficiency and effectiveness of our repair approach in inconsistent probabilistic databases, on both real and synthetic data. For the real data, we crawl the zip codes and city name [*http://www.aresllc.com/zip-codes-finder/*] in the United States. We also have another real census data [*http://nationalatlas.gov/atlasftp.html*] containing the state name and the percentage of mothers in each city/county who smoked during pregnancy for different race groups during the period 1995-1999. We join these two tables on attribute city/county name, and obtain a large joined table. Since different states may have the same city/county name in our data, some join results thus violate the FD $Zip \rightarrow State$. For synthetic data, under an FD: $X \rightarrow A$, we first generate numerical values for attribute X within domain $[1, 100]$, following *Uniform* or *Zipf distribution* (with skewness 0.8). Then, for tuples t with the same value $t[X]$, we randomly produce a value (with the same distribution as X) for $t[A]$. Moreover, we associate each tuple t with an existence probability $t.p \in [p_{min}, p_{max}]$ ($[0.5, 1]$ by default).

To evaluate the quality of our PW-repair, similar to [9], we randomly add noises to original data, changing $(100 \cdot \theta)\%$ attribute values by adding a random noise within $[-5, 5]$ in synthetic data (or changing characters in strings of real data with maximum DL-metric 4), where θ is the noise rate. To indicate the accuracy, for each attribute $t[A]$ with noises, we generate a random weight $t.w(A)$ within $[0, 0.5)$; for that without noises, we assign a random weight $t.w(A)$ in $[0.5, 1)$. We measure the quality of our PW-repair in terms of *recall* and *precision*, where recall is the ratio of the number of correctly repaired noises to the total number of noises we add, and precision is the ratio of the number of correctly repaired noises to the total number of changed values made by repair algorithms. Since we repair on a probabilistic database $\mathcal{D}$, we first materialize r possible worlds $pw(\mathcal{D})$ (i.e., select tuple t to $pw(\mathcal{D})$ with probability $t.p$), where r is set to $1,000$ by default. For PW-repair, we will use the repaired database $\mathcal{D}^{R_i}$ that corresponds to PWG_i containing $pw(\mathcal{D})$. Then, we average recalls and precisions over all the tested possible worlds $pw(\mathcal{D})$ (weighted by their probabilities $Pr\{pw(\mathcal{D})\}$) as our measures.

data sets	PW-repair precision	PW-repair recall	PW-repair time (sec)	Baseline time (sec)
Uni	96%	92.6%	2.992	2.916×10^{6987}
$Zipf$	77%	70%	3.2204	3.926×10^{6987}
$census$	78%	84%	4.25	3.035×10^{789}

Table 4: PW-repair vs. Baseline ($k = 5$) Under an FD: $X \rightarrow A$.

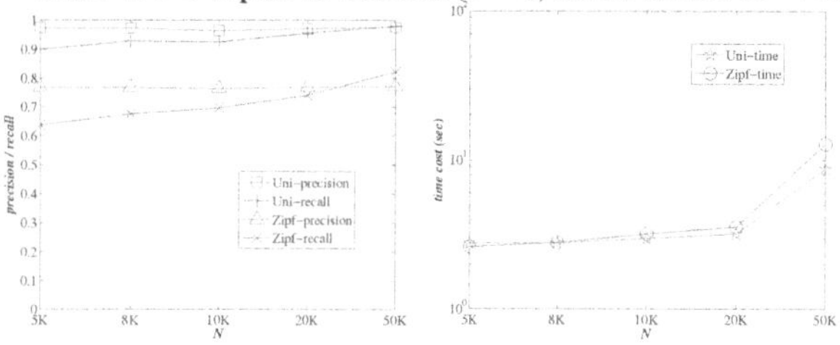

(a) *precision / recall* (b) *time cost*

Figure 4: PW-repair performance vs. data size N.

Further, we also use the *time cost* to measure the execution time of finding PW-repairs. We compare the time cost of our PW-repair with that of a baseline method, $Baseline$, which enumerates all the Par_Num partitioning strategies, computes the PW-repair cost for each strategy, and selects the one with the smallest PW-repair cost. Due to exponential number of partitioning strategies, we estimate the time cost of $Baseline$ by first taking 100 random partitioning strategies, and then obtaining the PW-repair time, T_s, for these 100 strategies. Thus, the estimated time cost is $\frac{Par\_Num \cdot T_s}{100}$.

Below, we test the performance of PW-repairs under the FD: $X \rightarrow A$. All our experiments are conducted on a PC with Core(TM)2 Duo 3GHz CPU with 3G memory.

4.1 Performance vs. Data Sets

Table 4 depicts the recall, precision, and time cost of our PW-repair on both real and synthetic data, where $k = 5$, $m = 500$, $\theta = 0.5\%$, and $N = 10K$. In the table, recall and precision of PW-repair remain high (i.e., 70%-96%), whereas $Baseline$ has 100% recall but much lower precision due to the exponential number (about $10^{790} \sim 10^{6987}$) of candidates. The time cost of our greedy algorithm is about 3-4 seconds, which significantly outperforms $Baseline$. This is because $Baseline$ has to enumerate an exponential number of partitioning strategies, which incurs high cost. The results on real/synthetic data confirm that PW-repair is efficient and produces data with high precision and recall.

4.2 Performance vs. Data Size N

Figure 4 tests the scalability of our repair approach by varying the data size N from $5K$ to $50K$, where $k = 5$, $m = 500$, and $\theta = 0.5\%$. With larger data size, the recall and precision increase, which indicates the good scalability against the data size. Moreover, the total repair time cost increases for large data size N. This is reasonable, since larger data size may incur more sub-blocks, which make the greedy algorithm more costly.

For data sets with other parameter values (e.g., different values of θ, m, N, or r) or with multiple FDs, the experimental results are similar, and thus we will not report them.

5. RELATED WORK

An inconsistent database contains inconsistent tuples that violate integrity constraints such as functional dependencies. In literature [3, 14], many existing works on inconsistent databases assume that the underlying data are certain and precise. The notion of *minimal repair* was first introduced by Arenas et al. [3], which manipulates inconsistent data such that a consistent database is obtained with the smallest *repair cost*, defined as the symmetric difference of databases before and after the repair. In contrast, our work considers a more complex scenario in probabilistic database where data are unreliable and uncertain. Thus, we have to re-define the repair cost for such inconsistent probabilistic data, as well as designing efficient and effective repairing techniques.

The repair models [12] can be classified into 3 categories: X-repair [8] allowing tuple deletions only, S-repair [3] with both tuple insertions and deletions, and U-repair [21, 5, 9] considering tuple value updates. In this paper, we consider the U-repair semantics by value modification in the probabilistic database. The repair-key operation in MayBMS [2] repairs the table that violates key constraints by removing a minimum subset of tuples, whereas our work considers the U-repair with the attribute value modification.

Andritsos et al. [1] considered the repair under the key constraint by joining multiple dirty databases, where each tuple is associated with a probability, indicating the confidence that this tuple is clean. In contrast, our work considers the repair by attribute value modification under FDs in possible worlds of inconsistent probabilistic databases. Lian and Chen [16] studied consistent query answering in inconsistent probabilistic databases by aggregating answers over all possible repairs, whereas this work directly modifies attribute values of tuples with the minimal repair semantics.

In the literature of probabilistic databases [10], there are many existing systems that manage probabilistic and uncertain data, for example, MystiQ [6], Orion [7], TRIO [4], MayBMS [2], MCDB [15], and BayesStore [20]. Most existing works assume consistent probabilistic data, and focus on query answering [17, 19] with the guaranteed accuracy of answers. Our work explores PW-repairs to resolve inconsistencies in possible worlds of probabilistic data.

6. CONCLUSIONS

In this paper, we study an important problem of repairing an inconsistent probabilistic database by value modification, under functional dependencies. We formalize and tackle the PW-repair problem, which repairs over groups of possible worlds in the database, minimizing the PW-repair cost. Due to the NP-completeness of this problem, we propose a greedy algorithm to achieve the PW-repair with a low cost. Extensive experiments have been conducted to demonstrate the efficiency of our PW-repair approach.

Acknowledgments

Funding for this work was provided by RGC NSFC JOINT Grant under Project No. N_HKUST61 2/09, HKUST RPC10 EG13, and NSFC Grant No. 60736013, 60803105, 60873022, and 60903053.

7. REFERENCES

[1] P. Andritsos, A. Fuxman, and R.J. Miller. Clean answers over dirty databases: A probabilistic approach. In *ICDE*, 2006.

[2] L. Antova, C. Koch, and D. Olteanu. MayBMS: Managing incomplete information with probabilistic world-set decompositions. In *ICDE*, 2007.

[3] M. Arenas, L. Bertossi, and J. Chomicki. Consistent query answers in inconsistent databases. In *PODS*, 1999.

[4] O. Benjelloun, A. Das Sarma, A. Y. Halevy, and J. Widom. ULDBs: Databases with uncertainty and lineage. In *VLDB*, 2006.

[5] P. Bohannon, W. Fan, M. Flaster, and R. Rastogi. A cost-based model and effective heuristic for repairing constraints by value modification. In *SIGMOD*, 2005.

[6] J. Boulos, N. N. Dalvi, B. Mandhani, S. Mathur, C. Ré, and D. Suciu. Mystiq: a system for finding more answers by using probabilities. In *SIGMOD*, 2005.

[7] R. Cheng, S. Singh, and S. Prabhakar. U-DBMS: A database system for managing constantly-evolving data. In *VLDB*, 2005.

[8] J. Chomicki and J. Marcinkowski. Minimal-change integrity maintenance using tuple deletions. *Inf. Comput.*, 197(1/2), 2005.

[9] G. Cong, W. Fan, F. Geerts, X. Jia, and S. Ma. Improving data quality: consistency and accuracy. In *VLDB*, 2007.

[10] N. N. Dalvi and D. Suciu. Efficient query evaluation on probabilistic databases. *VLDB J.*, 16(4), 2007.

[11] W. W. Eckerson. Data quality and the bottom line: Achieving business success through a commitment to high quality data. *The Data Warehousing Institute*, 2002.

[12] W. Fan. Dependencies revisited for improving data quality. In *PODS*, 2008.

[13] I. Fellegi and D. Holt. A systematic approach to automatic edit and imputation. *J. American Statistical Association*, 71(353), 1976.

[14] A. Fuxman, E. Fazli, and R. Miller. ConQuer: efficient management of inconsistent databases. In *SIGMOD*, 2005.

[15] R. Jampani, F. Xu, M. Wu, L. L. Perez, C. Jermaine, and P. J. Haas. Mcdb: a monte carlo approach to managing uncertain data. In *SIGMOD*, 2008.

[16] X. Lian, L. Chen, and S. Song. Consistent query answers in inconsistent probabilistic databases. In *SIGMOD*, 2010.

[17] C. Re, N. Dalvi, and D. Suciu. Efficient top-k query evaluation on probabilistic data. In *ICDE*, 2007.

[18] F. Sadri. Reliability of answers to queries in relational databases. *TKDE*, 3(2), 1991.

[19] M. A. Soliman, I. F. Ilyas, and K. C. Chang. Top-k query processing in uncertain databases. In *ICDE*, 2007.

[20] D. Z. Wang, E. Michelakis, M. Garofalakis, and J. Hellerstein. Bayestore: Managing large, uncertain data repositories with probabilistic graphical models. In *VLDB*, 2008.

[21] J. Wijsen. Database repairing using updates. *TODS*, 30(3), 2005.

[22] W. E. Winkler. Methods for evaluating and creating data quality. *Inf. Syst.*, 29(7), 2004.

Appendix

A. Proof of Lemma 3.1

Proof. We aim to reduce the repair problem in a certain database (which is NP-complete [5]) to our PW-repair problem in an inconsistent probabilistic database. Specifically, in [5], it has been proved that the minimum-cost repair under FDs in an inconsistent certain database is NP-complete. Thus, by setting k to 1 and existence probabilities of tuples to 1 (with $O(1)$ cost), the solution to PW-repair in the probabilistic database can exactly solve that in the certain database [5]. In other words, the problem in [5] can be reduced to our PW-repair problem. Hence, our PW-repair problem is NP-complete. □

Approximate Tensor Decomposition within a Tensor-Relational Algebraic Framework*

Mijung Kim
Arizona State University
Tempe, AZ 85287, USA
mijung.kim.1@asu.edu

K. Selçuk Candan
Arizona State University
Tempe, AZ 85287, USA
candan@asu.edu

ABSTRACT

In this paper, we first introduce a tensor-based relational data model and define algebraic operations on this model. We note that, while in traditional relational algebraic systems the join operation tends to be the costliest operation of all, in the tensor-relational framework presented here, tensor decomposition becomes the computationally costliest operation. Therefore, we consider optimization of tensor decomposition operations within a relational algebraic framework. This leads to a highly efficient, effective, and easy-to-parallelize `join-by-decomposition` approach and a corresponding KL-divergence based optimization strategy. Experimental results provide evidence that minimizing KL-divergence within the proposed `join-by-decomposition` helps approximate the conventional `join-then-decompose` scheme well, without the associated time and space costs.

Categories and Subject Descriptors

H.2.4 [**Database Management**]: Systems—*Query processing, Relational databases*; H.3.3 [**Information Storage and Retrieval**]: Information Search and Retrieval—*Information filtering*

General Terms

Algorithms, Experimentation, Measurement

Keywords

Tensor-based Relational Model, Tensor Relational Algebra, Approximate Tensor Decomposition

*This work is supported by an NSF Grant #1043583 - 'MiNC: NSDL Middleware for Network- and Context-aware Recommendations'

1. INTRODUCTION

Relational data have various representations. The *relational model* [7] represents the data as sets of tuples, where each tuple is an instance in the attribute domain; the model also encodes the functional dependencies between the attributes. The *vector model* [12] maps each attribute to a dimension in an n-dimensional space and represents each tuple as a point in this space (a natural representation when attributes are totally ordered). The *tensor model*, on the other hand, maps each attribute to a mode in an n-dimensional array where each possible tuple is a cell.

Thanks to their simplicity in modeling high-dimensional data and the availability of various mathematical tools (such as tensor decompositions) that support multi-aspect analysis of such data, tensors are widely used in many application domains including scientific data [2, 5, 8, 14] and sensor data [13]. Tensor-based data representation and tensor analysis are also increasingly popular in emerging fields, such as social network analysis [4, 6]. CANDECOMP/PARAFAC (CP) [5, 8] and Tucker [14] models are the two most widely used tensor decompositions generalized as high-order linear tensor factorizations. Since tensor decomposition is a costly process, to address the high computational cost of this very useful operation, many recent works focused on scalable implementation of tensor decompositions [13, 10].

Note that these decompositions can be interpreted probabilistically, if additional constraints (nonnegativity and summation to 1) are imposed. In the case of the CP decomposition, for example, each nonzero element in the core can be thought of as a cluster and the values of entries of the factor matrices can be interpreted as the conditional probabilities of the entries given clusters. Recently [6] proposed a nonnegative tensor factorization model using probabilistic interpretation incorporated by users' prior knowledge.

Spectral analysis of tensor data is often preceded by a tensor decomposition operation, which involves partitioning a large tensor into a smaller core tensor (i.e., spectral coefficients) and factor matrices (i.e., basis matrices) that represent different facets of the data for multi-aspect analysis: each factor matrix describes one specific aspect of the data, whereas the core tensor describes the strength (e.g., amount of correlation) of the relationships between these distinct data dimensions. Because of these properties, tensors have emerged as useful representations for relational data.

Given a tensor based representation of the data, we can manipulate it in several ways, including tensor algebra [9] and relational algebra [7]. Tensor algebra includes operators, such as addition, multiplication of a mode with a vector

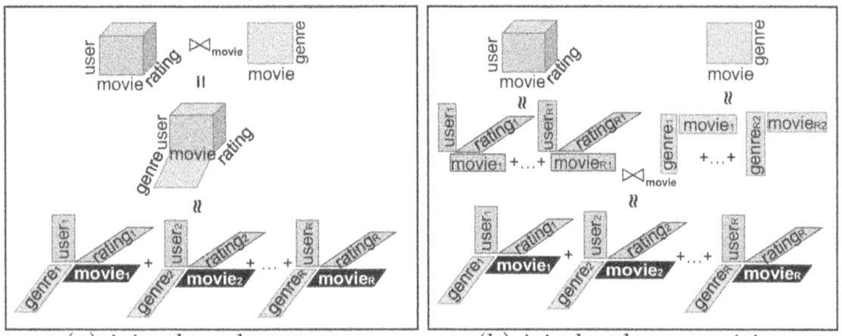

(a) join-then-decompose (b) join-by-decomposition

Figure 1: (a) Join-then-decompose: Rank-R CP decomposition of the tensor obtained by joining (`user, movie, rating`) **and** (`movie, genre`) **relations. (b) Join-by-decomposition: Rank-R_1 CP decomposition of** (`user, movie, rating`) **relation and rank-R_2 CP decomposition of** (`movie, genre`) **relation are combined on the** `movie` **mode into Rank-R CP decomposition of the joined tensor.**

or a matrix, inner product of tensors, and the norm of a tensor. Relational algebra, on the other hand, manipulates relational data using operators such as projection, selection, Cartesian-product, and set operators.

1.1 Contributions of this Paper

Common tensor operations (such as scalar addition/multiplication and tensor addition/multiplication) are well understood. However there is little prior research on efficient implementation of complex and semantically-rich data operations, such as *joins*, in conjunction with tensor analysis operations, such as *decompositions*.

In this paper, we first introduce a tensor-based relational data model and define relational algebraic operations on this model. We then note that, while in traditional relational algebraic systems the join operation tends to be the costliest operation of all, in the tensor-relational framework presented here, tensor decomposition becomes the computationally costliest operation. Therefore, we next consider optimization of tensor decomposition operations within a relational algebraic framework.

EXAMPLE 1.1. *Consider two relations described as tensors*[1]*: a 3-mode relational tensor of* `(user, movie, rating)` *and 2-mode relational tensor of* `(movie, genre)`.

Let us assume that we have an application that requires us to first combine these two relations based on the `movie` *attribute and then obtain the decomposition of the integrated tensor: Figure 1(a) illustrates how we would first combine these two relational tensors on the* `movie` *attribute into a 4-mode multi-relational tensor* `(user, rating, movie, genre)` *and then perform a tensor decomposition. In the rest of the paper, we refer to this scheme as the* `join-then-decompose` *scheme. Note that this combined tensor is higher-dimensional than both input tensors, therefore its decomposition is likely to be much more expensive than the decompositions of the two original input tensors. Therefore, an alternative processing scheme would involve first decomposing the input tensors into their spectral components and then combining these into the decomposition of the joined tensor. Figure 1(b) illustrates this* `join-by-decomposition` *scheme.*

[1]Since we use a tensor model to describe relational data, the corresponding terms in the tensor and the relational model (e.g., a relation and a tensor, an attribute and a mode, etc) can be used interchangeably throughout the paper.

In the above example, since the costliest operation is the decomposition and the join operation increases the number of modes of the tensor, we argue that the `join-by-decomposition` scheme will be more efficient than the conventional `join-then-decompose` scheme.

However, even if our argument is true, a number of challenges remain. First of all, tensor decomposition can be seen as discovering the eigen-basis of the given tensor and a mapping of the input data onto these eigen-bases. While this eigen-bases representation is very useful when a fixed basis for analysis is not available, it also poses challenges when integrating decompositions of multiple tensors: since each tensor has its *own* eigen-bases, combining different decompositions to obtain the decomposition of the joined tensor is not straightforward. Secondly, unlike the decomposition of the joined tensor, which captures the relationships between all four modes (`user`, `movie`, `rating`, and `genre`) simultaneously in the above example, the individual decompositions of the input tensors capture the relationships of the partial subsets of these four modes. As a result, it is important to select a `join-by-decomposition` strategy that will best *approximate* the conventional `join-then-decompose` strategy.

Since in nonnegative CP tensor decomposition,

- the elements of the core tensor can be seen as clusters of the data and
- each entry, U_{ij}, can be seen as the conditional probability $P(U_i|C_j)$ of the i_{th} element of mode U to belong to the j_{th} cluster, C_j,

we propose to obtain rank-R decomposition of the joined tensor by combing two rank decompositions whose ranks are the factors of R such that $R_1 \times R_2 = R$.

This is intuitive in that if the clusters of the first data set are highly correlated with the clusters of the second data set, then when combined these will lead to less than $R_1 \times R_2 (= R)$ clusters that the user seeks. Relying on this observation, we seek R_1 and R_2 decompositions of the input tensors that lead to clusters that are *independent* relative to the join attributes. In particular, we propose a KL-divergence based measure to quantify the difference between the conditional probability distributions implied by the factor matrices and pick the R_1 and R_2 decompositions which minimize this measure based on the conditional probabilities of the entries of the join mode. This leads to a highly efficient, effective, and easy-to-parallelize algorithm for `join-by-decomposition` strategy.

2. TENSOR-BASED RELATIONAL MODEL

As we mentioned earlier, tensors have been used for representing and manipulating relational data. For example, [4] presents a multi-way clustering framework which operates on relational data represented in the form of multi-mode tensor. Note that, like [4], most existing works assume that the available data has been pre-integrated into a single multi-mode tensor, which can then be manipulated using tensor operations. In practice, however, data rarely exists in a pre-integrated form and its lifecycle (from collection to analysis) involves various integration and other manipulation steps. In this section, we present a relational model for data represented as tensors.

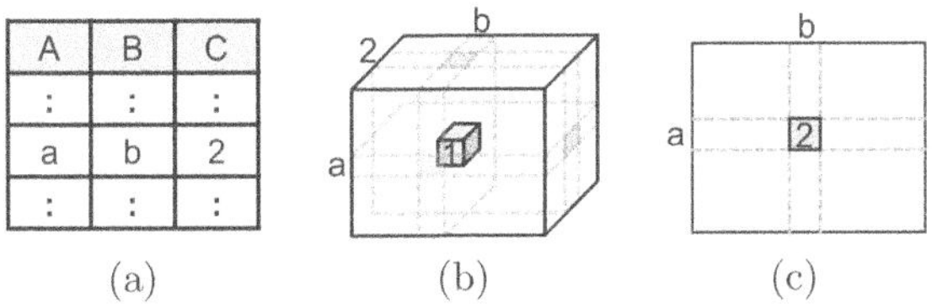

Figure 2: (a) A sample relation, (b) an occurrence tensor, and (c) the value tensor (assuming that the attribute set $\{A, B\}$ is a candidate key for the relation)

2.1 Types of Tensors Representing Relations

Let $A_1, \ldots, A_n$ be a set of attributes in the schema of a relation, R, and $D_1, \ldots, D_n$ be the attribute domains. Let the relation instance $\mathcal{R}$ be a finite multi-set of tuples, where each tuple $t \in D_1 \times \ldots \times D_n$.

Occurrence Tensor. We define an *occurrence tensor* $\mathfrak{R}_o$ corresponding to the relation instance $\mathcal{R}$ as an n-mode tensor, where each attribute $A_1, \ldots, A_n$ is represented by a mode. For the ith mode, which corresponds to A_i, let $D'_i \subseteq D_i$ be the (finite) subset of the elements such that

$$\forall v \in D'_i \ \exists t \in \mathcal{R} \ s.t. \ t.A_i = v$$

and let $idx(v)$ denote the rank of v among the values in D'_i relative to an (arbitrary) total order, $<_i$, defined over the elements of the domain, D_i. The cells of the *occurrence tensor* $\mathfrak{R}_o$ are such that

$$\mathfrak{R}_o[u_1, \ldots, u_n] = 1 \leftrightarrow \exists t \in \mathcal{R} \ s.t. \forall_{1 \leq j \leq n} \ idx(t.A_j) = u_j$$

and 0 otherwise. Intuitively, each cell indicates whether the corresponding tuple exists in the multi-set corresponding to the relation or not (Figures 2(a) and (b)).

Counting Tensor. Note that the relation instance $\mathcal{R}$ is a finite *multi-set* of tuples; i.e., there can be two tuples, t_a and t_b, in $\mathcal{R}$ such that $\forall_{1 \leq j \leq n} \ t_a.A_j = t_b.A_j$. We define the corresponding n-mode *counting tensor*, $\mathfrak{R}_c$, such that

$$\mathfrak{R}_c[u_1, \ldots, u_n] = |\{t \in \mathcal{R} \mid \forall_{1 \leq j \leq n} \ idx(t.A_j) = u_j\}|$$

Intuitively, each cell counts the number of corresponding tuples in the multi-set corresponding to the relation.

Value Tensor. Let again $A = \{A_1, \ldots, A_n\}$ be the set of attributes in the schema of the relation, R. In the relational model, a *candidate key* of the relation R is defined as a subset, K, of the attributes that uniquely determines the tuple. More formally,

$$\forall t_a, t_b \in \mathcal{R} \, (\forall_{A_i \in K} t_a.A_i = t_b.A_i) \ \rightarrow \ (\forall_{A_i \in A} t_a.A_i = t_b.A_i)\,.$$

Given a relation R with an attribute set $A = \{A_1, \ldots, A_n\}$ and a candidate key $K = \{A_{K(1)}, \ldots, A_{K(m)}\} \subset A$, let $X = \{A_{X(1)}, \ldots, A_{X(n-m)}\}$ denote the set of remaining attributes; i.e., $(X \cup K = A) \ \wedge \ (X \cap K = \emptyset)$. Then, for this relation, we define the corresponding *value tensor* as an m-mode tensor, $\mathfrak{R}_v$, such that

$$\begin{aligned}\mathfrak{R}_v[u_1, \ldots, u_m] = \langle v_1, \ldots, v_{n-m} \rangle \ s.t. \\ \exists t \in \mathcal{R} \ s.t. \forall_{A_{K(i)} \in K} \ idx(t.A_{K(i)}) = u_i \ \wedge \\ \forall_{A_{X(i)} \in X} \ t.A_{X(i)} = v_i.\end{aligned}$$

If $K = A$, then the value tensor is not defined. Intuitively, in this case, each mode corresponds to an attribute in the candidate key of the relation and each cell represents the values of the attributes determined by the corresponding instance of the candidate key. Figure 2(c) presents an example.

Tensor Conversion. Note that a counting or value tensor can be converted into an occurrence tensor by adding an additional mode, which represents the *count* in the counting tensor or the *value* in the value tensor, respectively. Let $\mathfrak{P}$ be a counting or value tensor; the mapping $occ(\mathfrak{P})$ gives the corresponding occurrence tensor. Similarly, given a candidate key K, an occurrence tensor, $\mathfrak{P}$, can be converted into a value tensor, $val(\mathfrak{P}, K)$.

2.2 Tensor Relational Algebra

Next, we introduce tensor relational algebra operations to manipulate relations represented as tensors. Let $\mathfrak{P}$ and $\mathfrak{Q}$ be two tensors, representing relation instances $\mathcal{P}$ and $\mathcal{Q}$, with attribute sets, $A^P = \{A^P_1, \ldots, A^P_n\}$ and $A^Q = \{A^Q_1, \ldots, A^Q_m\}$, respectively. In the rest of this section, we denote the index of each cell of $\mathfrak{P}$ as $(i_1, i_2, ..., i_n)$; similarly, the index of each cell of $\mathfrak{Q}$ is denoted as $(j_1, j_2, ..., j_m)$. The cell indexed as $(i_1, \ldots, i_n)$ of $\mathfrak{P}$ is denoted by $\mathfrak{P}[i_1, \ldots, i_n]$ and the cell indexed as $(j_1, \ldots, j_m)$ of $\mathfrak{Q}$ is denoted by $\mathfrak{Q}[j_1, \ldots, j_m]$.

Selection (σ). In relational algebra, the *selection* operation is an operation which takes as input a single relation and a condition, φ, and returns all the tuples in the relation satisfying the given condition:

$$(t \in \sigma_\varphi(\mathcal{P})) \ \leftrightarrow \ (t \in \mathcal{P}) \wedge \varphi(t).$$

Given an occurrence or counting tensor $\mathfrak{P}$ and a selection condition, φ, we define the *condition tensor*, $\mathfrak{C}_\varphi$, as a tensor of the same dimensions as $\mathfrak{P}$, such that for $i_1, i_2, ..., i_n$, if $\varphi(i_1, i_2, ..., i_n)$, then $\mathfrak{C}_\varphi[i_1, i_2, ..., i_n] = 1$ and $\mathfrak{C}_\varphi[i_1, i_2, ..., i_n] = 0$, otherwise. Given the condition tensor, $\mathfrak{C}_\varphi$, the tensor selection operation for the given occurrence or counting tensor $\mathfrak{P}$ is defined as

$$\sigma_\varphi(\mathfrak{P}) \stackrel{\text{def}}{=} comp(\mathfrak{P} * \mathfrak{C}_\varphi),$$

where $*$ is the cell-wise product of $\mathfrak{P}$ and $\mathfrak{C}_\varphi$ and $comp()$ is the compaction operator which eliminates all-0 slices from the resulting tensor to ensure that the elements along all modes correspond to attribute values that occur in at least one tuple satisfying the selection condition.

If $\mathfrak{P}$ is a value tensor with candidate key K, on the other hand, the selection operation is defined as

$$\sigma_\varphi(\mathfrak{P}) \stackrel{\text{def}}{=} val(comp(occ(\mathfrak{P}) * \mathfrak{C}_\varphi), K).$$

Projection (π). In relational algebra, the *projection* operation takes as input a single relation R with an attribute set, $A^P = \{A^P_1, \ldots, A^P_n\}$, and an attribute set $A = \{A_{a_1}, \ldots, A_{a_k}\} \subseteq A^P$ and maps the relation into a new relation $\pi_A(\mathcal{R})$ with the attribute set A such that

$$\forall t \in \mathcal{R} \ \exists t' \in \pi_A(\mathcal{R}) \ s.t. \ \forall_{A_{a_h} \in A} \ t'.A_{a_h} = t.A_{a_h}.$$

The corresponding tensor projection operator eliminates all the modes that do not belong to the target attribute set A; i.e., given $\mathfrak{P}$ with an attribute set, A^P, and the projection attribute set $A \subseteq A^P$, the result is a new tensor $\pi_A(\mathfrak{P})$ with the attribute set A. More specifically, if $\mathfrak{P}$ is an occurrence tensor, then

$$\pi_A(\mathfrak{P})[i_{a_1}, ..., i_{a_k}] = 1 \ \leftrightarrow \ \exists \mathfrak{P}[\ldots, i_{a_1}, \ldots, i_{a_k}, \ldots] = 1.$$

On the other hand, if $\mathcal{P}$ is a counting tensor, then

$$\pi_{\mathrm{A}}(\mathcal{P})[i_{a_1},...,i_{a_k}] = \sum_{(...,i_{a_1},...,i_{a_k},...)} \mathcal{P}[\ldots, i_{a_1}, \ldots, i_{a_k}, \ldots].$$

As before, if $\mathcal{P}$ is a value tensor, we can define the projection by first converting it into an occurrence tensor:

$$\pi_{\mathrm{A}}(\mathcal{P}) = val(\pi_{\mathrm{A}}(occ(\mathcal{P})), \mathrm{K}).$$

Cartesian product ($\times$). Given two relations $\mathcal{P}$ and $\mathcal{Q}$, with attribute sets, $\mathrm{A}^P = \{\mathrm{A}_1^P, \ldots, \mathrm{A}_n^P\}$ and $\mathrm{A}^Q = \{\mathrm{A}_1^Q, \ldots, \mathrm{A}_m^Q\}$, the *cartesian product* operator returns a new relation, $\mathcal{P} \times \mathcal{Q}$, with an attribute set $\{\mathrm{A}_1^P, \ldots, \mathrm{A}_n^P, \mathrm{A}_1^Q, \ldots, \mathrm{A}_m^Q\}$:

$$t \in \mathcal{P} \times \mathcal{Q} \leftrightarrow \exists_{t_1 \in \mathcal{P}} \exists_{t_2 \in \mathcal{Q}}\ t = concat(t_1, t_2).$$

If we consider two occurrence or counting tensors, $\mathcal{P}$ and $\mathcal{Q}$, as inputs, we can define the tensor relational algebraic cartesian product simply in terms of the outer product of the two input tensors:

$$\mathcal{P} \times \mathcal{Q} \stackrel{\text{def}}{=} \mathcal{P} \otimes \mathcal{Q}.$$

As before, for value tensors, we can define the cartesian product by first converting the tensors into occurrence tensors:

$$\mathcal{P} \times \mathcal{Q} = val((occ(\mathcal{P}) \times occ(\mathcal{Q})), K_P \cup K_Q).$$

Join ($\bowtie$). In relational algebra, given two relations $\mathcal{P}$ and $\mathcal{Q}$, and a condition φ, the *join* operation is defined as a cartesian product of the input relations followed by the selection operation. Therefore, given two relational tensors $\mathcal{P}$ and $\mathcal{Q}$, and a condition φ, we can define their join as

$$\mathcal{P} \bowtie_{\varphi} \mathcal{Q} \stackrel{\text{def}}{=} \sigma_{\varphi}(\mathcal{P} \times \mathcal{Q}).$$

Given two relations $\mathcal{P}$ and $\mathcal{Q}$, with attribute sets, $\mathrm{A}^P = \{\mathrm{A}_1^P, \ldots, \mathrm{A}_n^P\}$ and $\mathrm{A}^Q = \{\mathrm{A}_1^Q, \ldots, \mathrm{A}_m^Q\}$, and a set of attributes $\mathrm{A} \subseteq \mathrm{A}^P$ and $\mathrm{A} \subseteq \mathrm{A}^Q$, the *equi-join* operation, $\bowtie_{=,\mathrm{A}}$, is defined as the join operation, with the condition that matching attributes in the two relations will have the same values, followed by a projection operation that eliminates one instance of A from the resulting relation. Therefore, the equi-join operation can also be defined in terms of the basic tensor relational operators described earlier.

2.3 Challenge: Query Plans with Joins and Decompositions

As in the case of relational algebra, a query (or data manipulation) plan can be visualized as a tree, where the leaves of the tree are the input tensors and each node of the tree is a tensor relational operation, selecting, projecting, or joining its inputs.

However the tensor-relational operations are part of a larger framework that involves other tensor operations, such as tensor decompositions. In fact, in most cases, the tensor relational operations precede a tensor decomposition operation to manipulate the data into a form ready for the context of the analysis.

This situation is especially aggravated when the decomposition operation is preceded by a join operation which increases the number of modes of the tensor to be decomposed. Since tensor decomposition cost is exponential in the number of modes of the input tensor, data integration through joins tends to increase the cost of the whole plan significantly and even renders the whole query infeasible if sufficient resources and time are not available.

3. APPROXIMATELY EVALUATING TENSOR DECOMPOSITIONS WITHIN JOIN PLANS

In order to obtain *approximate* decompositions of joined tensors, `join-by-decomposition` scheme works as follows: as illustrated in Figure 1(b), to construct a rank-R decomposition of the joined tensor, we consider two integers, R_1 and R_2, such that $R_1 \times R_2 = R$ and we find rank-R_1 and rank-R_2 decompositions of the two input tensors. We then combine these two decompositions along the given factor matrix which corresponds to the join attribute in the equi-join operation (the process is trivially extended to the case where there are multiple equi-join attributes in the query). Intuitively, we treat each diagonal element in the core tensor as a cluster and the factor matrices as the conditional probabilities of the attribute values along the modes belonging to the given clusters.

Let us consider two 3-mode relational tensors, $\mathcal{P}$ and $\mathcal{Q}$, with $u \times l \times m$ and $u \times b \times s$ dimensions, respectively, and an equi-join operation on the first mode of these tensors (note that for simplicity, we assume that both modes have u slices along the join attribute, representing the common values for the two relations along the equi-join attribute. The rank-R_p and rank-R_q CP decompositions of $\mathcal{P}$ and $\mathcal{Q}$ are as follows:

$$\mathcal{P}_{u \times l \times m} = \sum_{r=1}^{R_p} \lambda_r \circ U_r \circ L_r \circ M_r, \quad \mathcal{Q}_{u \times b \times s} = \sum_{r=1}^{R_q} \lambda_r^{'} \circ U_r^{'} \circ B_r \circ S_r.$$

Note that (if decompositions are nonnegative and tensors are properly normalized) the equation for $\mathcal{P}$ can be interpreted probabilistically as

$$\mathcal{P}_{u \times l \times m} = \sum_{r=1}^{R_p} P(C_r^p) \sum_{i=1}^{u} P(U_i|C_r^p) \sum_{j=1}^{l} P(L_j|C_r^p) \sum_{k=1}^{m} P(M_k|C_r^p).$$

Here C_*^p are the clusters of $\mathcal{P}$; analogously, the equation for $\mathcal{Q}$ can also be interpreted probabilistically.

Let us denote the equi-join tensor $\mathcal{P} \bowtie_{=,\mathrm{U}} \mathcal{Q}$ as $\mathcal{X}$. Similarly to the input tensors $\mathcal{P}$ and $\mathcal{Q}$, we can also probabilistically interpret the rank-R decomposition of $\mathcal{X}$:

$$\mathcal{X}_{u \times l \times m \times b \times s} = \sum_{r=1}^{R} P(C_r^x) \sum_{i=1}^{u} P(U_i|C_r^x) \sum_{j=1}^{l} P(L_j|C_r^x) \sum_{k=1}^{m} P(M_k|C_r^x) \sum_{f=1}^{b} P(B_f|C_r^x) \sum_{g=1}^{s} P(S_g|C_r^x),$$

where C_*^x are the clusters of the joined tensor. Note that if the R_p and R_q clusters of the input tensors are independent from each other and $R_p \times R_q = R$, we can rewrite this in terms of the clusters and membership probabilities of the input tensors as

$$\hat{\mathcal{X}}_{u\times l\times m\times b\times s} = \sum_{r_p=1}^{R_p}\sum_{r_q=1}^{R_q} P(C^p_{r_p})P(C^q_{r_q})$$
$$\sum_{i=1}^{u} P(U_i|C^p_{r_p})P(U_i|C^q_{r_q})$$
$$\sum_{j=1}^{l} P(L_j|C^p_{r_p})\sum_{k=1}^{m} P(M_k|C^p_{r_p})$$
$$\sum_{f=1}^{b} P(B_f|C^q_{r_q})\sum_{g=1}^{s} P(S_g|C^q_{r_q}).$$

This gives us a way to reconstruct the decomposition of the join tensor directly from the decompositions of the input tensors, which are much cheaper to obtain. However, this reconstruction makes sense only if the clusters of the input tensors are independent from each other:

$$P(C^x_{r_p,r_q}) = P(C^p_{r_p}\wedge C^q_{r_q}) = P(C^p_{r_p})P(C^q_{r_q}),$$
$$P(U_*|C^x_{r_p,r_q}) = P(U_*|C^p_{r_p}\wedge C^q_{r_q}) = P(U_{r_p}|C^p_{r_p})P(U_{r_q}|C^q_{r_q}),$$
$$P(L_*|C^x_{r_p,r_q}) = P(L_*|C^p_{r_p}\wedge C^q_{r_q}) = P(L_*|C^p_{r_p}),$$
$$P(M_*|C^x_{r_p,r_q}) = P(M_*|C^p_{r_p}\wedge C^q_{r_q}) = P(M_*|C^p_{r_p}),$$
$$P(B_*|C^x_{r_p,r_q}) = P(B_*|C^p_{r_p}\wedge C^q_{r_q}) = P(B_*|C^q_{r_q}),$$
$$P(S_*|C^x_{r_p,r_q}) = P(S_*|C^p_{r_p}\wedge C^q_{r_q}) = P(S_*|C^q_{r_q}).$$

Otherwise, there will be a nonzero difference between $\mathcal{X}$ and $\hat{\mathcal{X}}$. Next we describe how to minimize the approximation error, $\|\mathcal{X}-\hat{\mathcal{X}}\|$. The natural approach to minimize the approximation error involves searching for input clusters (i.e., decompositions of the input tensors) that are the most independent relative to the join attribute.

This presents two challenges: first of all, we need to enumerate pairs of ranks that multiply to R and then obtain the corresponding decompositions of the input tensors $\mathcal{P}$ and $\mathcal{Q}$. As we will see in the experiment section (Section 4), while this involves enumeration of multiple (low-modal) decompositions, the overall cost of the process is often much less than the cost of decomposing the (high-modal) joined tensor. Secondly, given a pair of rank-R_p and rank-R_q decompositions of $\mathcal{P}$ and $\mathcal{Q}$, this requires a measure to quantify the independence of the clusters relative to the join attribute. The problem is that the term $P(U|C^p_{r_p}\wedge C^q_{r_q})$ requires counting joins falling within a cluster given by the decomposition of the joined tensor; but this is not known.

Intuitively, independence of the two input clusterings relative to the join attribute implies that given a join element U_j that connects clusters C^p_a and C^q_b of the inputs, another join element U_l is neither more likely or less likely to connect these two clusters. More specifically, given the join elements in C^p_a, we would expect to see the distribution of the corresponding C^q_* to be uniformly distributed. Similarly, given the join elements in C^q_b, the distribution of the corresponding C^p_* should be uniform. Therefore, we can quantify the independence of the input clusters relative to the join attribute by using the KL-divergence of the conditional probability distributions:

$$\Delta(p,q) = \sum_b KL[P(C^p_*|C^q_b), uniform] + \sum_a KL[P(C^q_*|C^p_a), uniform].$$

Therefore, given the set $\mathcal{R}$ of all possible combinations of rank decompositions that lead to a rank-R decomposition of the joined tensor, we find the pair which leads to the smallest Δ value.

4. EXPERIMENTAL RESULTS

In this section, we present experimental results assessing the efficiency and effectiveness of the proposed `join-by-decomposition` scheme relative to the `join-then-decompose` approach.

4.1 Experimental Setup

We use two data sets - movie rating data and Enron email data sets. The movie rating data set is obtained from [1] and consists of 100,000 movie ratings of 983 users for the 1682 movies. From this data set, we created one pair of relations, `(user, movie, rating)` and `(movie, genre)`, and their joined tensor `(user, rating, movie, genre)`, and the other pair, `(movie, user, rating)` and `(user, occupation)`, and their joined tensor `(movie, rating, user, occupation)`. We experimented with 20 subsets of these relations of different sizes. We obtained the Enron email data set from [11]. This subset consists of email exchanges among 184 email addresses during 44 months, which becomes one relation `(month, from_email, to_email)`. We created a second relation consisting of the employee information associated with the email addresses `(to_email, position)`. These two relations join into `(month, from_email, to_email, position)` of the size $44\times 184\times 184\times 8$. We experimented with rank-9 and rank-12 decompositions.

We use MATLAB Tensor Toolbox [3] to manipulate a relational tensor as a sparse tensor. For nonnegative CP decomposition, we employ the N-way Toolbox for MATLAB [2]. Our experiments ran on Pentium(R) Dual-Core CPU E5800 @3.20GHz with 4GB of RAM.

Our evaluation criteria include *running time ratio* which is the ratio of the running times of `join-by-decomposition` and `join-then-decompose`, and *fit ratio* defined as

$$\text{fit ratio} = \frac{1-\frac{\|\mathcal{X},\hat{\mathcal{X}}\|_F}{\|\mathcal{X}\|_F}}{1-\frac{\|\mathcal{X},\hat{\hat{\mathcal{X}}}\|_F}{\|\mathcal{X}\|_F}},$$

where $\mathcal{X}$ is the joined tensor, $\hat{\mathcal{X}}$ is the tensor obtained by re-composing the `join-then-decompose` tensor, and $\hat{\hat{\mathcal{X}}}$ is the tensor obtained by re-composing the `join-by-decomposition` tensor.

4.2 Results

Efficiency. Figure 3 shows that the proposed `join-by-decomposition` scheme becomes much cheaper relative to the traditional `join-then-decompose` scheme as the tensor size and the number of nonzero entries (i.e., relation size) increase. This is because, while the `join-by-decomposition` scheme needs to perform multiple nonnegative CP decompositions to select the best, each one is done much faster than the decomposition of the joined tensor.

Here it is important to note that one key disadvantage of the traditional `join-then-decompose` scheme is the amount of resources it requires to complete its operation. In our experiments, the `join-then-decompose` scheme was infeasible (with our experimental setup) for the joined tensors with the number of nonzero entries which was greater than 60,000

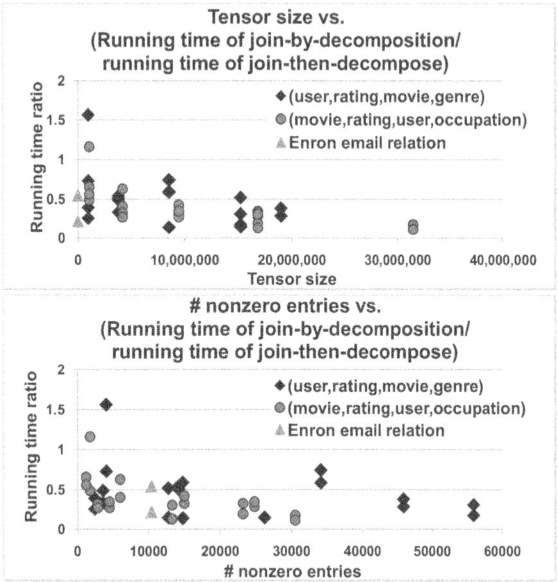

Figure 3: Relative running times of join-by-decomposition compared with join-then-decompose schemes against (a) tensor sizes and (b) numbers of nonzero entries (i.e., relation sizes)

since the main memory required for nonnegative CP decomposition for these relational tensors is beyond the capability of our hardware/software setting. The proposed `join-by-decomposition` scheme, however, did not have this shortcoming since it decomposes much smaller input tensors.

Effectiveness. Now we examine the effect of the factor of the relation size (i.e., number of nonzero entries) to the fit ratio of the joined tensor (see Figure 4). The fit ratio starts somewhat low between 0.4 and 0.7 when the number of nonzero entries are less than 10,000 however the fit ratio increases as the number of nonzero entries increases. More notably, the fit ratio of the relation `(movie, rating, user, occupation)` shows a steep increase and reaches to a value higher than 0.9 when the number of nonzero entries is about 15,000. On the other hand, the fit ratio of the relation `(user, rating, movie, genre)` reaches to 0.8 when the number of nonzero entries is around 60,000. In the two movie relations we have experimented, the clusters of the pair `(movie, rating, user)` and `(movie, genre)` were less independent than the clusters of the pair `(movie, user, rating)` and `(user,occupation)` because, generally, a movie rating of a user can be more affected by the movie genre than the user occupation; i.e., the latter one is likely to show higher inde- pendence among the clusters of the input relations. Indeed, the average KL-divergence measure for the selected combinations for the `(user, rating, movie, genre)` relation was 601.5; for the `(movie, rating, user, occupation)` relation, on the other hand, the average KL-divergence for the selected combinations was only 5.55.

We also observed that the average correlation, which indicates how the fit ratio changes with the KL-divergence measure, was as expected, strongly negative: **-0.7**. This shows that the (inverse of the) KL-based measure captures the likelihood of a given combination to produce high degrees of fit and the proposed KL-measure is effective in optimizing the quality of `join-by-decomposition` plans.

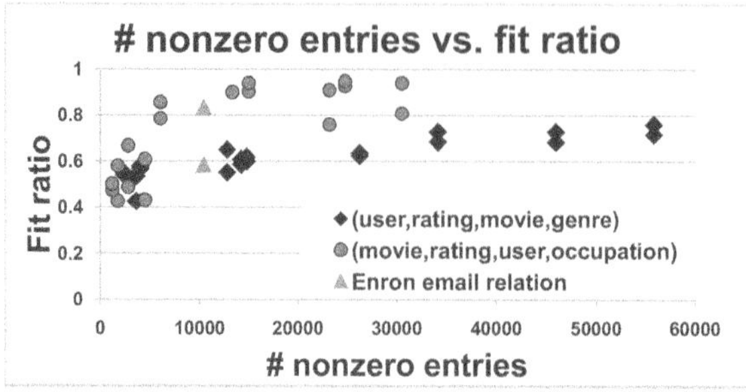

Figure 4: #nonzero entries of joined relations vs. fit ratio of join-by-decomposition of the relations

5. CONCLUSIONS

Lifecycle of most data includes various operations, such as capture, integration, projection, decomposition, and data analysis. In this paper, we first presented a tensor-based relational data model and introduced relational algebraic operations for this model. Since in the proposed tensor-relational framework, tensor decomposition is often costlier than other operations on the data, including joins, we proposed a highly efficient, effective, and easily parallelizable `join-by-decomposition` strategy for approximately evaluating decompositions within a relational plan, which is optimized based on KL-divergence. Experimental results confirmed that the efficiency and effectiveness of the proposed `join-by-decomposition` scheme compared to the `join-then-decompose` approach.

6. REFERENCES

[1] Movielens dataset from GroupLens research group. http://www.grouplens.org.

[2] C. A. Andersson and R. Bro. The N-way Toolbox for MATLAB. Chemometrics & Intelligent Laboratory Systems. 52 (1):1-4, 2000. http://www.models.life.ku.dk/source/nwaytoolbox/.

[3] B. W. Bader and T. G. Kolda. MATLAB Tensor Toolbox Version 2.2, Jan. 2007. http://csmr.ca.sandia.gov/ tgkolda/TensorToolbox/.

[4] A. Banerjee, S. Basu, and S. Merugu. Multi-way clustering on relation graphs. In SIAM Int. Conf. on Data Mining, 2007.

[5] J. D. Carroll and J. J. Chang. Analysis of individual differences in multidimensional scaling via an N-way generalization of 'Eckart-Young' decomposition. Psychometrika, 35:283-319, 1970.

[6] Y. Chi and S. Zhu. FacetCube: A framework of incorporating prior knowledge into non-negative tensor factorization. In CIKM '10: Proceeding of the 19th ACM Conference on Information and knowledge management, 2010.

[7] E. F. Codd. A Relational Model of Data for Large Shared Data Banks, in Communications of the ACM, 1970.

[8] R. A. Harshman. Foundations of the PARAFAC procedure: Models and conditions for an "explanatory" multi-modal factor analysis, UCLA working papers in phonetics, 16:1-84, 1970.

[9] T. G. Kolda and B. W. Bader. Tensor decompositions and applications, SIAM Review, 51:3, in press.

[10] T. G. Kolda and J. Sun. Scalable Tensor Decompositions for Multi-aspect Data Mining. ICDM 2008: Proceedings of the 8th IEEE International Conference on Data Mining, 363-372, 2008.

[11] C. E. Priebe, J. M. Conroy, D. J. Marchette, and Y. Park. Enron data set, 2006. http://cis.jhu.edu/ parky/Enron/enron.html.

[12] G. Salton, A. Wong, and C. S. Yang. A vector space model for automatic indexing, Communications of the ACM, v.18 n.11, 613-620, 1975.

[13] C. E. Tsourakakis. Mach: Fast randomized tensor decompositions. CoRR, abs/0909.4969, 2009.

[14] L. R. Tucker. Some mathematical notes on three-mode factor analysis. Psychometrika, 31, 1966.

RFID Data Analysis using Tensor Calculus for Supply Chain Management

Roberto De Virgilio † and Franco Milicchio ‡
Dipartimento di Informatica e Automazione
Università Roma Tre, Rome, Italy
† dvr@dia.uniroma3.it ‡ milicchio@dia.uniroma3.it

ABSTRACT

In current trends of consumer products market, there is a growing significance of the role of retailers in the governance of supply chains. RFID is a promising infrastructure-less technology, allowing to connect an object with its virtual counterpart, *i.e.*, its representation within information systems. However, the amount of RFID data in supply chain management is vast, posing significant challenges for attaining acceptable performance on their analysis. Current approaches provide hard-coded solutions, with high consumption of resources; moreover, these exhibit very limited flexibility dealing with multidimensional queries, at various levels of granularity and complexity. In this paper we propose a general model for supply chain management based on the first principles of linear algebra, in particular on *tensorial calculus*. Leveraging our abstract algebraic framework, our technique allows both quick decentralized on-line processing, and centralized off-line massive business logic analysis, according to needs and requirements of supply chain actors. Experimental results show that our approach, utilizing recent linear algebra techniques can process analysis efficiently, when compared to recent approaches. In particular, we are able to carry out the required computations even in high memory constrained environments, such as on mobile devices. Moreover, when dealing with massive amounts of data, we are capable of exploiting recent parallel and distributed technologies, subdividing our tensor objects into sub-blocks, and processing them independently.

Categories and Subject Descriptors

H.2.7 [**Database Management**]: [Data warehouse and repository]; I.1.4 [**Symbolic and Algebraic Manipulation**]: Applications

General Terms

Management, Performance, Experimentation

Keywords

Supply chain, algebraic models, multidimensional analysis.

CIKM'11, October 24–28, 2011, Glasgow, Scotland, UK.

1. INTRODUCTION

A supply chain is a complex system for transferring products or services from a supplier to a final customer. In the management of a supply chain, main retailers are investing in new technologies in order to boost the information exchange. To this aim, RFID, the Radio-Frequency Identification, is a recent potential wireless technology, which enables a direct link of a product with a virtual one within information systems. Currently, RFID tags attached to products store an identification code named EPC, used as a key to retrieve relevant properties of an object from a database, usually within a networked infrastructure. An RFID application usually generates a stream of tuples, usually called *raw data*, of the form of a triple (e, l, t), where e is an EPC, l represents the location where an RFID reader has scanned the e object, and t is the time when the reading took place. Other properties can be retrieved, *e.g.*, temperature, pressure, and humidity. A single tag may have multiple readings at the same location, thus potentially generating an immense amount of raw data. Therefore, a simple data cleaning technique consists in converting raw data in *stay records* of the form (e, l, t_i, t_o), where t_i and t_o are the time when an object enters or leaves a location l, respectively.

In this manuscript, we address the challenging problem of efficiently managing the tera-scale amount of data per day, generated by RFID applications [2, 3, 8, 13], focusing on stay records as the basic block to store RFID data. Recently, two models have been proposed: a *herd* and a *single* model. The former [8] proposes a warehousing model observing that usually, products move together in large groups at the beginning, and continue in small herds towards the end of the chain: this allows the aggregation and reduces significantly the size of the database. On the contrary, the latter [13] focuses on the movement of single, non grouped tags, defining query templates and path encoding schemes to process tracking and path oriented queries efficiently. Both of these approaches present limited flexibility dealing multidimensional queries at varying levels of granularity and complexity. To exploit the compression mechanism, such proposals have to fix the dimensions of analysis in advance and implement *ad-hoc* data structures to be maintained. It is not known in advance whether objects are sorted and grouped, and therefore, it is problematic to support different kinds of high-level queries efficiently.

Contribution. Leveraging such background, this paper proposes a general model of supply chains, mirrored with a formal *tensor* representation (*i.e.* a generalization of linear forms, usually represented by matrices) and endowed with specific operators, allowing both quick decentralized on-line processing, and centralized off-line massive business logic analysis, according to needs and requirements of supply chain actors. Our model and operations, inherited by linear algebra and tensor calculus, is therefore theoretically sound, and its implementation may benefit of several numerical libraries developed in the past. Additionally, due to the properties of our tensorial model, we are able to attain two significative features: the possibility of conducting computations in memory-constrained environments such as on mobile devices, and exploiting modern parallel and distributed technologies, owing to the possibility for matrices, and therefore tensors, to be dissected into several chunks, and processed independently (*i.e.*, also on-the-fly).

Outline. Our manuscript is organized as follows. In Section 2 we will briefly recall the available literature, while Section 3 will be devoted to the introduction of tensors and their associated operations. The general supply chain model, accompanied by a formal tensorial representation is supplied in Section 4, subsequently put into practice in Section 5, where we provide the reader a method of analyzing RFID data within our framework. We benchmark our approach with several test beds, and supply the results in Section 6. Finally, Section 7 sketches conclusion and future work.

2. RELATED WORK

In a real scenario, great lapse and huge amounts of data are generated. To this aim, knowledge representation techniques focus on operating deep analysis in such systems. There exists two main approaches to the management of RFID data: the processing is performed off-line, once RFID data are aggregated, compressed and stored [8, 13]. An alternative approach consists in warehousing RFID data and performing multidimensional analyses on the warehouse. The focus here is on data compression techniques and on storage models with the goal of achieving a more expressive and effective representation of RFID data. A straightforward method is to provide a support to path queries (*e.g.*, find the average time for products to go from factories to stores in Seattle) by collecting RFID tag movements along the supply chain. Usually, the tag identifier, the location and the time of each RFID reading is gathered and stored in a huge relational table. Gonzalez et al. [8] have presented a new storage model, based on a data warehousing approach, in which items moving together are grouped and data analysis is preformed in a multidimensional fashion, as it happens in a typical data warehouse. Finally, Lee et al. have proposed an effective path encoding approach to represent the data flow representing the movements of products [13]. In a path, a prime number is assigned to each node and a path is encoded as the product of the number associated with nodes. Mathematical properties of prime numbers guarantee the efficient access to paths.

As we have noticed in the Introduction, a major limitation of the majority of these approaches have to fix the dimensions of analysis in advance to exploit *ad-hoc* data structures to be maintained. It follows that, in many application scenario the compression loses its effectiveness and the size of tables does not be reduced significantly. Moreover, most of the approaches presented in this section present a limited flexibility when multidimensional queries, at varying levels of granularity and complexity, need to be performed.

3. PRELIMINARY ISSUES

The following paragraphs will be devoted to a brief recall of tensor representations, which is preliminary to the introduction of our model in the ensuing sections. We take for granted notions and notations of *groups*, *vector spaces*, *matrix rings*, and for a thorough review of vector spaces and tensors, we refer the reader to [11], [1] [10], and [12].

Tensors. Tensors arise as a natural extension to linear forms. Linear forms on a vector space $\mathbb{V}$ defined over a field $\mathbb{F}$, and belonging to its *dual space* $\mathbb{V}^*$, are maps $\phi : \mathbb{V} \to \mathbb{F}$ that associate to each pair $\phi \in \mathbb{V}^*$, and $v \in \mathbb{V}$, an element $e \in \mathbb{F}$. This is usually denoted by the *pairing* $\langle \phi, v \rangle = e$, or by definition, with a *functional* notation, *i.e.*, $\phi(v) = e$. Such mapping exhibits the linearity property, *i.e.*, $\langle \phi, \alpha v + \beta w \rangle = \alpha\langle \phi, v\rangle + \beta\langle \phi, w\rangle$. Generalizing the concept of linearity, we hence may introduce the following:

Definition 1 (Tensor). *A tensor is a multilinear form ϕ on a vector space* $\mathbb{V}$, i.e., *a mapping*

$$\phi : \underbrace{\mathbb{V} \times \ldots \times \mathbb{V}}_{k-\text{times}} \longrightarrow \mathbb{F}, \tag{1}$$

the form ϕ assumes also the name of tensor of rank k *(or rank-k tensor).*

As with linear forms, one possible representation of a tensor is with elements of the *matrix ring.* Therefore, a rank-k tensor may be represented by $M \in \mathbb{M}_{i_1 i_2 \ldots i_k}(\mathbb{F})$, that is a k-dimensional matrix with elements in $\mathbb{F}$.

Definition 2 (Hadamard Product). *The* Hadamard product *of two vectors $v, w \in \mathbb{V}$ is the* entry-wise *product of their components,* i.e.,

$$v \circ w = r, \quad \textit{such that} \quad r_i := v_i w_i\,. \tag{2}$$

Since a tensor of rank k will henceforth be denoted by a multidimensional matrix, we shall simplify notations by a variant of *Einstein's notation.* Such variant will be employed wherever a summation occurs: where we encounter two identical indices in a given expression, a summation on that index is implicitly defined. Let us consider for example, a notable form, the *inner product* $(\cdot)$ between two vectors, known also as *scalar product.* We mention in passing that an inner product arises in defining a particular class of rank-2 tensors: symmetric (or Hermitian) positive-definite forms. If we consider a standard cartesian metrics, *i.e.*, an orthonormal basis [11], the inner product notation can be written leveraging the summation notation described above: $v \cdot w = \sum_j v_j w_j =: v_j w_j$. As with linear applications, represented by matrices, tensors may be applied to elements of vector spaces, giving rise the following:

Definition 3 (Application). *The* application *of a k-ranked tensor ϕ, represented by the matrix $M \in \mathbb{M}_{i_1 i_2 \ldots i_k}(\mathbb{F})$, to a vector $v \in \mathbb{V}$ is a rank $k-1$ tensor represented by the matrix $\widetilde{M}$:*

$$\widetilde{M}_{i_1 \ldots i_{j-1} i_{j+1} \ldots i_k} := M_{i_1 \ldots i_j \ldots i_k} v_{i_j}\,. \tag{3}$$

The reader should notice that the previous definition of *application* is a generalization of the common matrix-vector product. In other terms, applying a tensor to a vector simply "eats" one dimension, as evidenced by the indices in the previous definition. Following a standard algebraic practice, indices may be rendered more intelligible when dealing with a tiny number of dimensions, *e.g.*, do not exceed 4 dimensions: in this case, instead of using $M_{i_1 i_2 i_3 i_4}$, we will employ the easier notation of M_{ijkl}.

EXAMPLE 1. *Let us consider a rank-3 tensor ϕ represented by the matrix $M \in \mathbb{M}_{333}(\mathbb{R})$ and a vector $v \in \mathbb{R}^3$:*

$$M = \left(\begin{pmatrix} 1 \\ 1 \\ 1 \\ 2 \\ 2 \\ 2 \\ 3 \\ 3 \\ 3 \end{pmatrix} \begin{pmatrix} 1 \\ 1 \\ 1 \\ 2 \\ 2 \\ 2 \\ 3 \\ 3 \\ 3 \end{pmatrix} \begin{pmatrix} 1 \\ 1 \\ 1 \\ 2 \\ 2 \\ 2 \\ 3 \\ 3 \\ 3 \end{pmatrix} \right), \; v = \begin{pmatrix} 0 \\ 1 \\ 0 \end{pmatrix}.$$

The result of the application of ϕ to v is a rank-2 tensor

$$\langle \phi, v \rangle = M_{ijk} v_i = \begin{pmatrix} 2 & 2 & 2 \\ 2 & 2 & 2 \\ 2 & 2 & 2 \end{pmatrix}.$$

DEFINITION 4 (KRONEKER TENSOR). *The rank-k tensor $\delta_{i_1 i_2 \ldots i_k}$, whose matricial representation is $M_{i_1 i_2 \ldots i_k} = 1$ iff $i_1 = i_2 = \ldots = i_k$, is called* Kroneker tensor.

Kroneker tensor is well known in diverse fields ranging from computer science to economics, and it is commonly known as *Kroneker delta*. Moreover, with the canonical duality between forms and vectors [11], it is common to employ the very same symbol for a vector specification, *e.g.*, $v \in \mathbb{R}^3$, with $v = \delta_2 = (0\ 1\ 0)^t$. Note as the notation δ_2 does not contain any reference to the dimension, due to any lack of ambiguity, since here $\delta_2 \in \mathbb{R}^3$; this notation means that each component in a position different from 2 has value 0, while the component in position 2 has value 1.

DEFINITION 5 (MAP). *The* map *is a function with domain a pair constituted by a function and a vector space, and codomain a second vector space:*

$$\text{map} : \mathbb{V}^* \times \mathbb{V} \to \mathbb{W}, \tag{4}$$

which associates to each component of a vector, the result of the application of a given function to the component itself:

$$\text{map}(f, v) = w, \quad w_i := f(v_i),$$

with $f : \mathbb{V} \to \mathbb{W}$, $v \in \mathbb{V}$, and $w \in \mathbb{W}$.

4. RFID DATA MODELING

This section is devoted to the definition of a general model capable of representing all aspects of a given supply chain. Our overall objective is to give a rigorous definition of a supply chain, along with few significant properties, and show how such representation is mapped within a standard tensorial framework.

4.1 A General Model

Let us define the set $\mathcal{E}$ as the set of all EPCs, with $\mathcal{E}$ being finite. A *property* of an EPC is defined as an application $\pi : \mathcal{E} \to \Pi$, where Π represents a suitable property codomain. Therefore, we define the application of a property $\pi(e) := \langle \pi, e \rangle$, *i.e.*, a property related to an EPC $e \in \mathcal{E}$ is defined by means of the pairing EPC-property; a property is a surjective mapping between an EPC and its corresponding property value. A *supply chain* is defined as the product set of all EPCs, and all the associated properties. Formally, let us introduce the family of properties π_i, $i = 1, \ldots, k + d < \infty$, and their corresponding sets Π_i; we may therefore model a supply chain as the product set

$$\mathcal{S} = \mathcal{E} \times \Pi_1 \times \ldots \times \Pi_{k-1} \times \Pi_k \times \ldots \times \Pi_{k+d}. \tag{5}$$

We highlight the indices employed in the definition of the supply chain. The reader should notice as we divided explicitly the first k spaces $\mathcal{E}, \Pi_1, \ldots, \Pi_{k-1}$, from the remaining ones. As a matter of fact, properties may be split into two different categories: *countable* and *uncountable* ones. By definition, a set A is *countable* if there exists a function $f : A \to \mathbb{N}$, with f being injective; for example, every subset of natural numbers $U \subseteq \mathbb{N}$ is countable (possibly infinite), and relative and rational sets, $\mathbb{Z}$ and $\mathbb{Q}$, respectively, are countable.

4.2 Properties

In the following we will focus on some of the properties related to EPCs, *i.e.*, we will model some codomains Π and their associated features.

Location. Let us briefly model the *location* associated to an EPC. It is common to employ a GPS system in order to track the position on earth, however, any fine-grained space is sufficient to our purposes. In particular, being the earth homeomorphic to a 3-sphere, any ordered triple of real numbers suffices, leading us to the following definition:

DEFINITION 6 (LOCATION). *Let $\mathcal{L}$ be the set of ordered tuples $\ell := (\ell_1, \ell_2, \ell_3)$, with $\ell_1, \ell_2, \ell_3 \in \mathbb{R}$. We name $\mathcal{L}$ as* location set, *ℓ_1, ℓ_2 and ℓ_3 as* location coordinates.

A commonly employed coordinate system is the GPS location, *i.e.*, latitude and longitude, with an additional altitude coordinate. However, in many cases the altitude has no influence from an applicative point of view, thus leading the location to be defined by a couple of real numbers, or better, $\ell = (\ell_{lat}, \ell_{long}, \ell_{alt} \equiv 0)$. Some standard representation of locations abstract their geographical information, preferring to employ a simple mapping between locations and a subset of natural numbers, representing the *location identifier*. Which representation is more suitable to an application, is a matter of choice with respect to the domain of the problem.

Time. In order to model a temporal interval relative to a product (EPC), we resort to an ordered couple of elements from the ring of real numbers. This suffices to specify, *e.g.*, the *entry* and *exit* time of a product from a given location. With this point of view, we model time as follows:

DEFINITION 7 (TIME). *Let $\mathcal{T}$ be the set of ordered couples $\tau := (t_i, t_o)$, with $t_i, t_o \in \mathbb{R}$. We name $\mathcal{T}$ as* time set, *t_i and t_o as* incoming *and* outcoming timestamps, *respectively.*

We highlight the fact that time spaces need not to be modeled as real numbers: in fact, natural numbers may also be suitable within a particular context, *e.g.*, employing UNIX timestamps. However, our model aims at generality, and therefore the real ring is the most appropriate choice, being $\mathbb{N}$a proper subset of the real numbers ring.

DEFINITION 8 (INNER SUM). *Let us define the* inner sum *of two time elements $\tau_1 = (t_i^1, t_o^1)$, $\tau_2 = (t_i^2, t_o^2)$ as the operator $\oplus : \mathcal{T} \times \mathcal{T} \to \mathcal{T}$:*

$$\tau_1 \oplus \tau_2 := \left(\min(t_i^1, t_i^2), \max(t_o^1, t_o^2) \right).$$

With the above operator, we have that $(\mathcal{T}, \oplus)$ assumes the algebraic structure of an abelian group. Such operation allows us to rigorously model the "addition of products": the overall timeframe of two products is, in fact,

DEFINITION 9 (LIFETIME). *We define as* lifetime *the linear form $\lambda : \mathcal{T} \to \mathbb{R}$ defined as follows:*

$$\langle \lambda, \tau \rangle := t_o - t_i, \quad \tau = (t_i, t_o) \in \mathcal{T}.$$

Due to the linearity, we are allowed to construct equivalence classes in $\mathcal{T}$ as follows:

$$[\widetilde{\tau}] := \{\tau \in \mathcal{T} : \langle\lambda, \tau\rangle = \langle\lambda, \widetilde{\tau}\rangle\} . \qquad (6)$$

The *canonical representative elements* of the above equivalence classes are defined as $(0, t_o)$, with $t_o \in \mathbb{R}$.

Definition 10 (Admissible time). *Given a time element $\tau \in \mathcal{T}$, we say that $\tau = (t_i, t_o)$ is* admissible *iff*

$$\langle\lambda, \tau\rangle > 0, \text{ with } t_i, t_o > 0 .$$

4.3 Tensorial Representation

Let us now introduce a formal *tensorial framework* capable of grasping all properties related to a supply chain, as proposed in Section 4.1. As previously outlined, we divide properties into two categories, *countable* and *uncountable* spaces. This separation allows us to represent countable spaces with natural numbers, therefore mapping their product space to $\mathbb{N}^k$, while leaving the product space of all uncountable properties into a collective space $\mathbb{U}$:

$$\mathcal{S} = \underbrace{\mathcal{E} \times \Pi_1 \times \ldots \times \Pi_{k-1}}_{\mathbb{N}^k} \times \underbrace{\Pi_k \times \ldots \times \Pi_{k+d}}_{\mathbb{U}} . \qquad (7)$$

Such mapping will therefore introduce a family of injective functions called *indexes*, defined as:

$$\mathrm{idx}_i : \Pi_i \longrightarrow \mathbb{N} , \qquad i = 1, \ldots, k-1 . \qquad (8)$$

When considering the set $\mathcal{E}$, we additionally define a supplemental index, the *EPC index function* $\mathrm{idx}_0 : \mathcal{E} \rightarrow \mathbb{N}$, consequently completing the map of all countable sets of a supply chain $\mathcal{S}$ to natural numbers. It should be hence straightforward to recognize the tensorial representation of a supply chain:

Definition 11 (Tensorial Representation). *The* tensorial representation *of a supply chain $\mathcal{S}$, as introduced in equation (5), with countability mapping as in (7) is a multilinear form*

$$\Sigma : \mathbb{N}^k \longrightarrow \mathbb{U} . \qquad (9)$$

A supply chain can be therefore rigorously denoted as a rank-k tensor with values in $\mathbb{U}$, mapping countable to uncountable product space.

4.4 Implementation

Preliminary to describing an implementation of our supply chain model, based on tensorial algebra, we pose our attention on the practical nature of a supply chain. Our treatment is general, representing a supply chain with a tensor, *i.e.*, with a multidimensional matrix. Several other approaches are available in literature on the same topic, with a graph being the preferred supply chain model [7]. These models are thoroughly represented by our tensorial approach, due to the well known mapping between graphs and matrices (cf. [4]). However, a matrix-based representation need not to be *complete*. Supply chain rarely exhibit completion: practical evidence [7] suggests that products, identified by their EPC, for example, seldom present themselves in every location. The same consideration applies also to other properties, in particular, to countable properties. Hence, our matrix effectively requires to store only the information regarding connected nodes in the graph: as a consequence, we are considering sparse matrices [5], *i.e.*, matrices storing only non-zero elements.

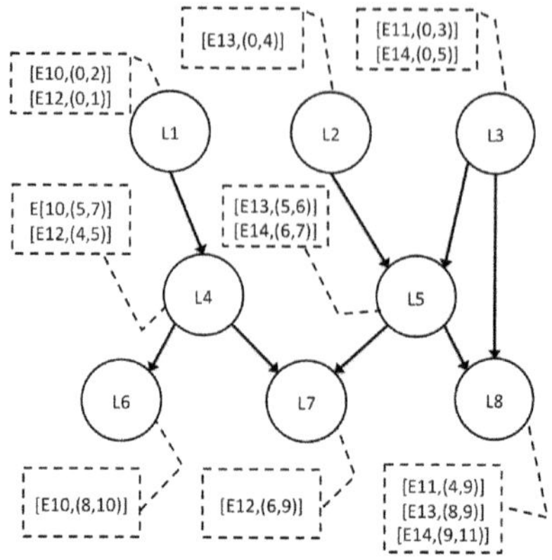

Figure 1: An example supply chain represented by a directed graph. Callouts represent lists of tuple constituted by an EPC with the associated time (t_i, t_o).

Notation. A sparse matrix may be indicated with different notations (cf. [14] and [5]), however, for simplicity's sake, we adopt the *tuple notation*. This particular notation declares the components of a tensor $M_{i_1 i_2 \ldots i_k}(\mathbb{U})$ in the form of

$$\mathcal{M} = \Big\{ \{i_1 i_2 \ldots i_k\} \rightarrow u \neq 0 , u \in \mathbb{U} \Big\} , \qquad (10)$$

where we implicitly intended $u \neq 0 \equiv 0_{\mathbb{U}}$. As a clarifying example, consider a vector $\delta_4 \in \mathbb{R}^5$: its sparse representation will be therefore constituted by a single tuple of one component with value 1, *i.e.*, $\{\ \{4\} \rightarrow 1\ \}$.

Example 2. *Let us consider the supply chain pictured in Figure 1, described tensorially by $\Sigma : \mathbb{N}^2 \rightarrow \mathcal{T}$, whose representative matrix is as follows:*

$$\begin{pmatrix} (0,2) & \cdot & \cdot & (5,7) & \cdot & (8,10) & \cdot & \cdot \\ \cdot & \cdot & (0,3) & \cdot & \cdot & \cdot & \cdot & (4,9) \\ (0,1) & \cdot & \cdot & (4,5) & \cdot & \cdot & (6,9) & \cdot \\ \cdot & (0,4) & \cdot & \cdot & (5,6) & \cdot & \cdot & (8,9) \\ \cdot & \cdot & (0,5) & \cdot & (6,7) & \cdot & \cdot & (9,11) \end{pmatrix}$$

where, for typographical simplicity, we omitted $0_{\mathcal{T}} = (0,0)$, denoted with a dot. For clarity's sake, we outline the fact that Σ is a rank-2 tensor with dimensions 5 (i.e. the rows), 8 (i.e. the columns). In fact, the EPC and locations sets are, respectively

$$\mathcal{E} = \{E10, E11, E12, E13, E14\} ,$$
$$\Pi_1 = \{L1, L2, L3, L4, L5, L6, L7, L8\} ,$$

where $\mathrm{idx}_0(E10) = 1$, $\mathrm{idx}_0(E11) = 2$, $\ldots$, $\mathrm{idx}_0(E14) = 5$, *and similarly* $\mathrm{idx}_1(L1) = 1$, $\ldots$, $\mathrm{idx}_1(L8) = 8$. *In the sparse representation we have* $\{\{1,1\} \rightarrow (0,2), \{1,4\} \rightarrow (5,7), \ldots, \{5,8\} \rightarrow (9,11)\}$.

Remarks. Due to the distributivity of products with respect to summations, we actually may *split* a matrix in submatrices, carry out the application and finally, thanks to the associativity, add the partial results obtaining the correct solution. For example, if $A \in \mathbb{M}_{22}(\mathbb{R})$, and $v \in \mathbb{R}^2$ being a suitable vector, the matrix can be divided in two (or more) sub-matrices, thus giving the ability to perform computations independently, as $Av = (A' + A'')v = A'v + A''v$. When performing $A'v$, we actually do not need any information regarding the subsequent A'' matrix and vice versa, and as a result, we may choose not to store its elements in memory. Additionally, multiplication of a sparse matrix (or tensor) with a vector has a *sub-quadratic* computational complexity (cf. [5]), and even *quasi-linear* asymptotic complexity [9]. On a final note, being the two multiplications independent from one another, we are capable of exploit recent parallel and distributed technologies, parallelizing multiplication and then *reducing* by summation their partial results.

5. RFID DATA ANALYSIS

Based on our conceptual framework, in this section we will provide a method to analyze RFID data represented by a tensor. With reference to the example provided in Section 4, in the following we simplify our notation, employing two countable sets, EPC $\mathcal{E}$ and location $\mathcal{L}$ indexes, in that order, and the uncountable time set $\mathcal{T}$, *i.e.*, a matrix M_{ij}: i referring to EPCs, and j being the index of locations. Such choice of attributes introduce no limitations on the generality of our approach, due to the fact that, in essence, applying a tensor to a vector means summing all the components sharing an index, regardless of ranks and dimensions.

5.1 Tracking Query

A *tracking query* finds the movement history for a given tag identifier $e \in \mathcal{E}$. We can comfortably perform the query efficiently, using the model described in Section 4, by applying the tensor application. Therefore, given $i = \text{idx}(e)$, we build a Kroneker vector as a vector δ_i, with $|\delta_i| = |\mathcal{E}|$, and finally apply of the rank-2 tensor represented by M_{ij} to δ_i:

$$r = M_{ij}\delta_i .$$

For instance, referring to the example pictured in Figure 1, let us consider the tag $E13$, we have $i = \text{idx}(E13) = 4$, and therefore our vector will be $\delta_4 = \{\{4\} \to 1\}$. Consequently, the resulting vector will be

$$r = M_{ij}\delta_4 = \{\{2\} \to (0,4), \{5\} \to (5,6), \{8\} \to (8,9)\} ,$$

or in another notation, $L2 \to L5 \to L8$.

5.2 Path Oriented Query

A *path oriented query* returns the set of tag identifiers that satisfy different conditions. Following the query templates given in [13], we subdivide path oriented queries into two main categories: *path oriented retrieval* and *path oriented aggregate* queries. The former returns all tags covering a path satisfying given conditions, while the latter computes an aggregate value. It is possible to formulate a grammar for these queries, similar to XPath expressions; in particular, path oriented retrieval and path oriented aggregate queries are respectively indicated as follows:

$$L_1[\text{cond}_1]//L_2[\text{cond}_2]//\ldots//L_n[\text{cond}_n] , \tag{11a}$$

$$L_1[\text{cond}_1]/L_2[\text{cond}_2]/\ldots/L_n[\text{cond}_n] , \tag{11b}$$

where $L_1, \ldots L_n$ is the *path condition*, *i.e.*, the sequence of locations covered by the tag, and cond_i is the *info condition*; for more information about such expressions, we refer the reader to [13]. A path condition expresses *parenthood* between locations, indicated as L_i/L_j, or *ancestry* with $L_i//L_j$; an info condition, on the other hand, indicates conditions on tag properties, *e.g.*, $StartTime$ and $EndTime$.

Path Oriented Retrieval. In our framework, a path oriented retrieval query as in (11a) is easily performed by exploiting the tensor application coupled with the Hadamard product. Given the location set $\mathcal{L}$, for each $z = \text{idx}(L_k)$, with $k = 1, \ldots, n$, we create a Kroneker vector δ_z and subsequently apply the rank-2 tensor, resulting in a set of vectors $r_z = M_{ij}\delta_j$, where for typographical reasons, we dropped the subscript intending $\delta \equiv \delta_z$. Finally, we apply the condition function to each r_z employing the map operator. This yields a set of vectors

$$\widetilde{r_z} = \text{map}(\text{cond}_z, r_z) , \qquad \text{cond}_z : \mathbb{N}^k \times \mathbb{U} \longrightarrow \mathbb{F} ,$$

whose Hadamard multiplication generates the final result:

$$\bar{r} = \widetilde{r_1} \circ \ldots \circ \widetilde{r_n} ,$$

reminding the reader that only non-zero values are stored, and therefore given as a result of a computation. The cond functions, as indicated above, are maps between properties of supply chains and a suitable space $\mathbb{F}$, *e.g.*, natural numbers for a boolean result. For an example, referring to Figure 1, let us consider the query

$$L3[StartTime > 0]//L8[EndTime - StartTime < 4] .$$

In this case, given $\text{idx}(L3) = 3$ and $\text{idx}(L8) = 8$, we build δ_3 and δ_8, and generate the partial results

$$r_3 = M_{ij}\delta_3 = \{\{2\} \to (0,3), \{5\} \to (0,5)\}$$

$$r_8 = M_{ij}\delta_8 = \{\{2\} \to (4,9), \{4\} \to (8,9), \{5\} \to (9,11)\}$$

where evidently the application was performed along the second dimension, *i.e.*, for each $\delta \in \{\delta_3, \delta_8\}$, we compute $M_{ij}\delta_j$. Finally, subsequent to mapping conditions on the results, in this case $\text{cond}_3 = t_i(\cdot) > 0$ and $\text{cond}_8 = \langle\lambda, \cdot\rangle < 4$, we obtain the correct outcome $\bar{r} = \widetilde{r_3} \circ \widetilde{r_8} = \{\{5\} \to (9,11)\}$, *i.e.*, $E14$.

Considering parenthood as in (11b) instead of ancestry, *i.e.*, L_i/L_j, we briefly sketch the fact that such query does not, in fact, differ from the above, except for one particular: each resulting EPC, when subject to a tracking query, produces a sparse vector whose *length*, *i.e.*, the number of non-zero stored elements, is exactly equal to the number of locations under analysis.

Path Oriented Aggregate. Path oriented aggregate queries may be represented as $\langle f, Q\rangle =: f(Q)$ where f is an *aggregate function*, *e.g.*, average or minimum, and Q is the result of a path oriented retrieval query. Therefore, let $\bar{r_Q}$ be the result of Q, and let f be a function defined on vectors of supply chain elements, we simply have that a path aggregate may be expressed as $f(\bar{r_Q})$. Referring to Figure 1, let us consider the query expressed in the grammar of [13]

$$\langle AVG[L8.StartTime], //L8\rangle ,$$

it is easily performed by applying the function $f := \text{average}(t_i)$ to the outcomes of the path oriented retrieval query on $L8$, resulting in $\bar{r} = \text{average}(\{4,8,9\}) = 7$.

6. EXPERIMENTS

We performed a series of experiments aimed at evaluating the performance of our approach, reporting the main results in the present section.

Environment. Our benchmarking system is a dual core 2.66 GHz Intel with 2 GB of main memory running on Linux, where we implemented our framework[1] in C++ within the Mathematica 8.0 computational environment. Our results have been compared to the ones from the approach in [13], tested against a generated synthetic RFID data in terms of stay records, and considering products moving together in small groups or individually, a behavior called *IData* in [13]: data production followed the same guidelines on a supply chain of 100 locations. Finally the complete data set comprises 10^5, $5 \cdot 10^5$, 10^6, $5 \cdot 10^6$, and 10^7 stay records. In the following, we will denote our tensorial approach T, while the proposed one in [13] with P.

[1] A prototype implementation is available at `http://pamir.dia.uniroma3.it:8080/SimpleWebMathematica`

Results. Performances have been measured with respect to data loading and querying. Referring to the former, the main advantage of our approach is that we are able to perform loading without any particular relational schema, when compared to P, where a schema coupled with appropriate indexes have to be maintained by the system. In this case, loading execution times are 0.9, 11, and 113 seconds, for sets of 10^5, 10^6, and 10^7 stay records, respectively; on the contrary, P timings were in order of minutes and hours. Another significant advantage of T relies in memory consumption: we need 13, 184, and 1450 MB to import the above mentioned sets; as a side-note, we highlight the fact that the 10^7 set required a division in smaller blocks, *e.g.*, 10^6, due to the limited memory at disposal. With respect to query execution, T presents a similar behavior and advantages with respect to P, for both time and memory consumption. We performed *cold-cache* experiments, *i.e.*, dropping all file-system caches before restarting the systems and running the queries, and repeated all the tests three times, reporting the average execution time. As in [13], we formulated 12 queries to test the two systems as reported in [6]. In brief, Q1 is a tracking query, Q2 to Q5 are path oriented retrieval queries, while Q6 to Q12 are path oriented aggregate queries. Due to the nature of P, we were able to perform a comparison only on centralized off-line massive analysis.

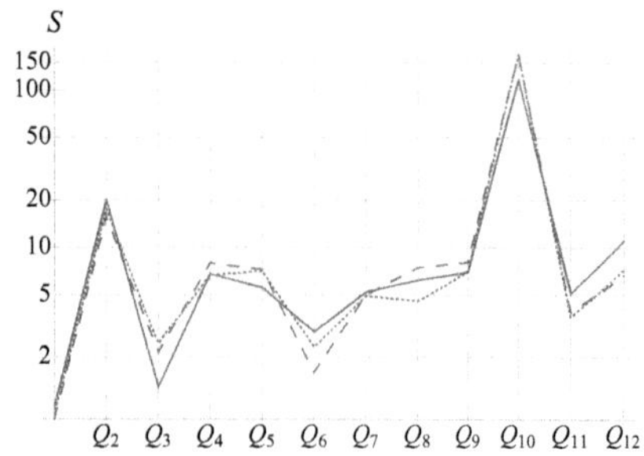

Figure 2: Speed-up logarithmic graph for all queries with 10^5 (solid), 10^6 (dashed), and 10^7 (dotted).

A significant result is the *speed-up* between the two approaches, as shown in Figure 2; again, Q1 label is dropped due to typographical causes. We computed the speed-up for all data sets as the ratio between the execution time of P, and that of our approach T, or briefly $S = {}^{t_P}/_{t_T}$. In general, T performs very well with respect to P in any dataset, particularly for queries related to the object transition, *e.g.*, Q2, Q4, Q5, Q10. The query performance of T is on the average 19 times better than that of P, 150 times on the maximum, *i.e.*, Q10. Another strong point of T is a very low consumption of memory, due to the *sparse matrix* representation of tensors and vectors. Figure 3 illustrates the main memory consumption of each query with respect to 10^5, 10^6, and 10^7 stay records. On the average, tracking queries require very few bytes of memory for any dataset, path oriented queries few KBytes, topping 1 MB for 10^7. Results demonstrate how our approach can be used in a wide range of applications, where devices with limited calculus resources may process large amount of data in an efficient and effective way.

7. CONCLUSION AND FUTURE WORK

We have presented an abstract algebraic framework for the efficient and effective analysis of RFID data in supply chain management. Our approach leverages tensorial calculus, proposing a general model that exhibits a great flexibility with multidimensional queries, at diverse granularity and complexity levels. Experimental results proved our method efficient when compared to recent approaches, yielding the requested outcomes in memory constrained architectures. For future developments we are investigating the introduction of reasoning capabilities, along with a thorough deployment in highly distributed Grid environments. In addition, we are about to test our model on mobile devices, comprising more complex properties and queries.

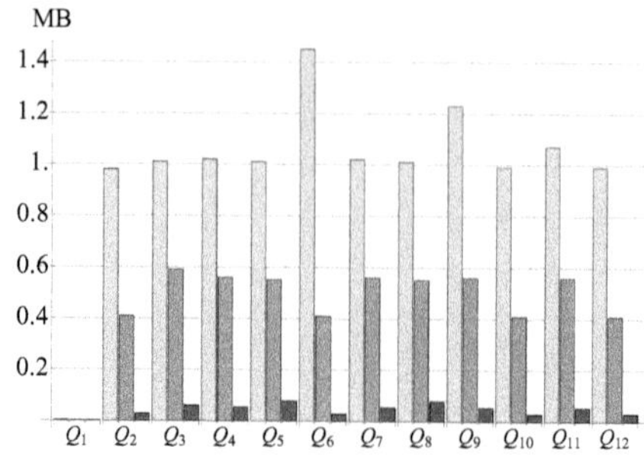

Figure 3: Main memory consumption for each query: black bars refer to 10^5, dark gray to 10^6, and light gray to 10^7 data size.

8. REFERENCES

[1] R. Abraham, J. E. Marsden, and T. Ratiu. *Manifolds, Tensor Analysis, and Applications*. Springer, 1988.

[2] R. Angeles. Rfid technologies: supply-chain applications and implementation issues. *Information Systems Management*, 22(1):51–65, 2005.

[3] Y. Bai, F. Wang, P. Liu, C. Zaniolo, and S. Liu. Rfid data processing with a data stream query language. In *ICDE*, 2007.

[4] A. Bondy and U. S. R. Murty. *Graph Theory*. Graduate Texts in Mathematics. Springer, 2010.

[5] T. A. Davis. *Direct Methods for Sparse Linear Systems*. SIAM, 2006.

[6] R. De Virgilio and F. Milicchio. Tensor calculus for rfid data management. Technical Report RT-DIA-182, University Roma Tre, 2011.

[7] R. Derakhshan, M. E. Orlowska, and X. Li. Rfid data management: Challenges and opportunities. In *RFID*, pages 175–182, 2007.

[8] H. Gonzalez, J. Han, X. Li, and D. Klabjan. Warehousing and analyzing massive rfid data sets. In *ICDE*, 2006.

[9] F. G. Gustavson. Two fast algorithms for sparse matrices: Multiplication and permuted transposition. *ACM Trans. Math. Softw.*, 4(3):250–269, 1978.

[10] J. H. Heinbockel. *Introduction to Tensor Calculus and Continuum Mechanics*. Trafford Publishing, 2001.

[11] K. M. Hoffman and R. Kunze. *Linear Algebra*. Prentice Hall, 1971.

[12] B. Jancewicz. The extended grassmann algebra of $\mathbb{R}^3$. In W. E. Baylis, editor, *Clifford (geometric) algebras with applications to physics, mathematics, and engineering*. Birkhäuser Boston, 1996.

[13] C.-H. Lee and C.-W. Chung. Efficient storage scheme and query processing for supply chain management using rfid. In *SIGMOD*, pages 291–302, 2008.

[14] O. Osterby and Z. Zlatev. *Direct Methods for Sparse Matrices*. Springer, 1983.

Spreadsheet-based Complex Data Transformation

Vu Hung, Boualem Benatallah
Sydney, UNSW, Australia
{vthung,boualem}@cse.unsw.edu.au

Regis Saint-Paul
CREATE-NET, Italy
regis.saint-paul@create-net.org

ABSTRACT

Spreadsheets are used by millions of users as a routine all-purpose data management tool. It is now increasingly necessary for external applications and services to consume spreadsheet data. In this paper, we investigate the problem of transforming spreadsheet data to structured formats required by these applications and services. Unlike prior methods, we propose a novel approach in which transformation logic is embedded into a familiar and expressive spreadsheet-like formula mapping language. Popular transformation patterns provided by transformation languages and mapping tools are supported in the language via formulas. Consequently, the language avoids cluttering the source spreadsheets with transformations and turns out to be helpful when multiple schemas are targeted. We implemented a prototype and evaluated the benefits of our approach via experiments in a real application. The experimental results confirmed the benefits of our approach.

Categories and Subject Descriptors

D.2.12 [**Interoperability**]: Data mapping

General Terms

Design, Languages

Keywords

Data transformation, Spreadsheets

1. INTRODUCTION

Spreadsheets are ubiquitous tools used for the storage, analysis and manipulation of data [14]. There are several reasons for their popularity. Spreadsheet-based data management offers important flexibility in data formatting over a tabular grid [2]. Data can be organized according to subjective importance, preferences, and styles (e.g., by placing important data in the top-left corner or placing related elements of data next to each other). Furthermore, spreadsheets offer a simple, but effective formula language using spatial relationships that shield users from the low-level details of traditional programming [8, 15]. To use the language, a user only needs to master two concepts, namely cells as variables and functions for expressing relations between cells. Consequently, spreadsheets are widely used by millions of knowledge workers (e.g., accountants, project managers, teachers) who play a key role in critical enterprise activities [6].

Given the ubiquity and utility of spreadsheets, it is increasingly necessary to allow data stored in spreadsheets to interact with external applications and services [1]. There has been a proliferation of online spreadsheet-like applications including Google Spreadsheets [2] and Zoho Spreadsheet [3]. To enable other applications to consume or generate spreadsheet data, some of these applications provide Web service interfaces (APIs). The authors in [6] report that spreadsheets often serve as hubs for organizing and manipulating information, which is later transferred to other services for archiving or processing.

In this paper, we consider the problem of transforming spreadsheet data into structured formats required by external applications and services (i.e., *spreadsheet-based data transformation*). We believe that facilitating interoperation between spreadsheets, applications and Web services will profoundly improve the effectiveness of information and services management in a variety of domains. However, the problem is challenging because of the nature of spreadsheets: (i) the data they contain does not conform to a predefined schema; (ii) there may be a mismatch between the organization of spreadsheet data and the structure expected by an external application. For example, the spreadsheet in Figure 1(a) contains data arranged in a table while the schema used by a bar chart (Figure 1(d)) consists of a list of labels, each comprising a list of bars.

Mainstream solutions to data transformation rely on specifying mappings between elements of the source and target schemas to transform a source instance to the target format [5]. However, there are many cases in which the schema of the source instance is unknown and transformation is performed directly from the source instance to the target format. For example, end-user visualization websites [16, 1] let users upload a data set (i.e., a source instance) and assist

CIKM'11, October 24–28, 2011, Glasgow, Scotland, UK.

[1] http://www.altova.com/mapforce/excel-mapping.html
[2] http://docs.google.com
[3] http://sheet.zoho.com/

	A	B	C	D	E	F	G
1							
2		**Country**	**Confirmed Cases**	**Deaths**	**Infection Rate**	**Death Rate**	**Population**
3		US	46329	593	163.64	1.88	314659000
4		Australia	36888	185	1,732.40	8.69	21293000
5		Mexico	32950	236	53.57	2.15	109610000
6		Thailand	23867	160	3.98	2.36	67764000
7		Germany	19893	3	2.84	0.04	82167000
8		...	...	...	...	...	...

(a)

```
PieChart
  Pies [ ]
    Pie
      Name =B3:B14
      Value =D3:D14
```

(b)

```
ScatterPlot
  Dots [ ]
    Dot
      X =C3:C195
      Y =E3:E195/10
      Label =B3:B195
      Size =G3:G195
```

(c)

```
BarChart
  Labels [ ]
    Label
      Name =C2
      Bars [ ] =B3:C22
        Bar
          X =B3:B22
          Y =C3:C22
```

(d)

Figure 1: (a) The Swine Flu data set; (b) *Pie Chart* schema; (c) *Scatter Plot* schema; (d) *Bar Chart* schema

them in transforming it to the format required by a given visualization type (e.g., chart, map, and timeline) with its own target schema.

There are three main existing approaches. The first approach, namely *schema-based*, allows users to specify schemas of spreadsheets via a layout specification language [7], and then transformation can be performed at *schema level* using either low-level transformation languages (e.g., XSLT), or high-level mapping tools, such as Clio [5], Clip [10], and +Spicy [9]. However, users must learn a new language, e.g., by creating correspondences between the source and target elements and annotating those correspondences with one or more unfamiliar functions (e.g., functions of XSLT/XQuery, Java) in the case of mapping tools [13]. This flowchart-like mapping interface is cluttered when schemas are large and mappings are complex [12]. On the contrary, spreadsheet users are familiar with formulas and an incremental approach to building applications with instant feedback [15].

The second approach, namely *column-based*, enables users to specify simple mappings between spreadsheet columns and target attributes (atomic elements) via drag-and-drop operations [11, 4]. This approach requires direct correspondences between spreadsheet column contents and the values of target attributes. For example, after dragging attribute `Y` of scatter plot (Figure 1(c)) onto source column `Infection Rate` (Figure 1(a)), the values of the column are *copied* to values of the attribute. Such straightforward correspondences, however, are unlikely when the target application and the spreadsheet have been developed independently. For instance, while the infection rate is expressed per million in the source, the target scatter plot expects a rate of per one hundred thousand. To correct this issue, the source spreadsheet must be modified, e.g., the values of column `Infection Rate` must be changed.

The third approach, visualization specific, supports simple mappings in the context of visualization [16]. It compares atomic types of source columns and target attributes of visualization types to suggest mappings to users. For example, to visualize the Swine Flu data set (Figure 1(a)) using a pie chart (Figure 1(b)), one of five candidate columns `Confirmed Cases`, `Deaths`, `Infection Rate`, `Death Rate`, `Population` can be mapped to attribute `Value` since all of them have the same type float. Similar to the column-based approach, source column data directly corresponds to the values of target attributes.

In summary, all three approaches suffer from *at least* one of the following drawbacks: (i) Existing programming experience of spreadsheet users (e.g., spreadsheet formulas with instant feedback at each step) is not leveraged; (ii) The transformation may be tedious to accomplish since it can involve multiple manipulations on the spreadsheet. It can also clutter the original organization of the spreadsheet with transformations. This issue may be aggravated if users need to interact with several different target applications, e.g., if requesting quotations by interacting with various supplier Web services or if targeting several visualizations as depicted in Figure 1.

To address these issues, we propose a novel approach, namely TranSheet, which enables users to perform mappings via a familiar and expressive spreadsheet-like formula language. The main contributions of this paper are as follows:

- A spreadsheet-like formula language is designed for specifying mappings between spreadsheet data and the target schema. In terms of expressiveness, we demonstrate that popular transformation patterns provided by transformation languages (e.g., XSLT/XQuery) and mapping tools [3], that are relevant to spreadsheet-based data transformation, are supported in the language via formulas. This enables the language to avoid cluttering the spreadsheet with transformations and it turns out to be helpful when multiple schemas are targeted (Section 3).
- We implemented a prototype and evaluated the expressiveness and mapping generalization of TranSheet in two real applications. The experimental results show that our language is expressive and flexible enough to support numerous practical spreadsheet-based data transformation scenarios (Section 4).

2. DATA MODEL

Spreadsheet data model. A spreadsheet is modeled as a two-dimensional matrix of cells. We use the coordinate $\langle x, y\rangle$ to denote the cell corresponding to column x and row y. While x is numbered starting from 1 and can also be denoted using capital letters, y is denoted by numbers. For example, cell $\langle 1, 5\rangle$ can also be denoted as cell A5. Each cell has an atomic value with associated type τ_a: τ_a ::= $empty|int|float|string|datetime$. The type *empty* represents the special case of an empty cell.

Target data model. We focus on transformation of spreadsheet data to XML, which is a popular standard for heterogeneous data exchange [13]. We use the nested relational model proposed in [5, 10]. Note that it is straightforward to convert XML to JSON, which is a standard format for Web mashups. A schema is modeled as a set of typed labels (i.e., elements) τ_t: τ_t ::= τ_a | $SetOf[l_i{:}\tau_t^i]$ | $Rcd(l_1{:}\tau_t1, \ldots, l_n{:}\tau_t^n)$ where l_is are label names and τ_t^is are their respective types. The symbol $SetOf$ represents repeating elements as an unordered set of the same label and *Rcd* represents tuples. For user interface presentation, we use an equivalent notation illustrated in Figure 2(b), where the symbol [ ] is used to denote the $SetOf$ construct.

	A	B	C	D	E
1	**0042**				
2	*Ford Prefect*	*Addison*	*Sydney*	*NSW*	
3	75.64	150	Beer		
4	5.26	2	Towel		
5	4.32	1	Babel Fish		
6					
7	**0525**				
8	*Arthur Dent*	*Evans*	*Melbourne*	*VIC*	
9	2.75	1	Towel		
10		...			

(a) Source spreadsheet with hierarchical representation of orders

```
QuoteRequest
  Account
    Login ="MyLogin" {MyLogin}
    Password ="MyPass" {MyPass}
  Orders [ ] (1 item)
    Order
      Id =A1 {0042}
      ShipTo
        FirstName =left(A2,search(' ', A2)) {Ford}
        LastName =right(A2,len(A2)-search(' ',A2)) {Prefect}
        Address =concatenate(B2,' ',C2,' ',D2) {Addison...}
      OrderDetails [ ] (3 items)
        OrderLine
          Quantity =B3:B5*10 {1500, 20, ...}
          ProdName =C3:C5 {Beer, Towel, ...}
          Price =round(A3:A5,0) {76, 5, ...}
```

(b) Schema view with mappings for order 0042

Figure 2: A spreadsheet and its mapping specification

Types	Transformation patterns
Value mapping	*Copying, Derivation, Constant Value Generation, Merging, Splitting*
Structural mapping	*Nesting, Filtering, Sorting, Grouping with aggregation, Join and Cartesian product, Union/Intersect/Minus, Branching*

Table 1: Transformation patterns of TranSheet

3. FORMULA MAPPING LANGUAGE

While atomic labels hold actual values, structural labels control the structural information of schema. Thus, we consider two kinds of mappings, namely *value mapping* (map one or more cells to an atomic label) and *structural mapping* (map a range of cells to a *SetOf* label). A mapping formula has the form `l =formula`, where `l` is a target label and `formula` is a spreadsheet formula. Due to space limitations, we demonstrate mainly via examples that popular transformation patterns provided by transformation languages (e.g., XSLT/XQuery) and mapping tools [3] are supported in our language via formulas (Table 1). A full description of the language's semantics can be found in [17].

3.1 Value mapping

3.1.1 Copying

This pattern simply copies a cell value to a target value of a label. For example, in Figure 2(b), we have the following mappings: `Id`=A1 copies the value corresponding to A1 to the value of `Id`. Instant feedback for the mapping is provided in the curly brackets {*0042*} adjacent to label `Id`; `ProdName`=C3:C5 copies three values of cells C3, C4, and C5 to the values of label `ProdName`. In the last example, a *mono-dimensional range* expression is associated to an atomic label. In spreadsheet programming, range expressions are only used as function parameters (e.g., for computing the total sum of a collection of cells). TranSheet, however, leverages the familiarity users have with the range notation to conveniently express mappings of schema labels with cell collections called *range formulas*. A range formula is valid only for an atomic label that has a *SetOf* label as ancestor. To show that the `OrderDetails` label allows repetition of label `ProdName`, the text "*(3 items)*" (the number of label `ProdName`) is displayed as an additional metadata.

Special care needs to be taken for range formulas associated with atomic labels. Suppose that instead of the mapping shown in Figure 2(b), the user inputs the mapping formulas `Quantity`=B3:B17 (15 `Quantity` items) and `ProdName`=C3:C5 (3 `ProdName` items). Taken together, these two mapping formulas violate the schema constraint which states that the target document should contain the same number of `Quantity` and `ProdName` labels.

3.1.2 Constant Value Generation

In some special cases, a constant must be copied to a target value where the constant value is independent of the source. For example, in Figure 2(b) the mapping formulas `Login`="MyLogin" and `Password` ="MyPass" associate constants to the values of `Login` and `Password`, respectively.

3.1.3 Derivation

This kind of mapping allows users to use one or more Excel-like functions on strings (e.g., *upper, lower, trim*), numbers (e.g., "+", "*", "-", "/", *abs, ceiling, round*), and dates (e.g., *date, time, hour*) to bring the format of a cell value to the required format of a target value. For example, in Figure 2(b): Mapping `Quantity`=B3:B5*10 uses a range formula to state that values of `Quantity` correspond to three values in the spreadsheet multiplied by 10; Mapping `Price`=round(A3:A5,0) rounds values in the range A3:A5 to the nearest integers and copies to values of `Price`.

3.1.4 Merging

This pattern merges multiple cell values into one value of a target label. For example, in Figure 2(b), the mapping formula `Address`=concatenate(B2," ",C2," ",D2) merges the values of three cells B2, C2, D2, which contain information on street, city, state, respectively, into the value of label `Address` with delimiters whitespace " " using Excel-like function *concatenate*.

3.1.5 Splitting

This kind of mapping is used when splitting one cell value into one or multiple target values. For example, mapping formulas `FirstName`=left(A2, search(" ", A2)) and `LastName`=right(A2, len(A2)-search(" ",A2)) in Figure 2(b) split the value of cell A2, which contains information on customer name, into the values of labels `FirstName` and `LastName` according to the whitespace " " using Excel-like functions *left, search, right,* and *len.*

3.2 Structural mapping

3.2.1 *Formula inheritance*

When using a structural mapping l_s=f, formula f is interpreted in terms of mapping formulas associated with the atomic children labels of structural label l_s. To intuitively illustrate this formula inheritance, the structural mapping OrderDetails=B3:C5 in Figure 2 is interpreted in terms of lower level mapping formulas in the following two steps:

$$\texttt{OrderDetails}=\text{B3:C5}$$
$$\Downarrow$$
$$\texttt{OrderLine}=\text{B}\langle i\rangle\text{:C}\langle i\rangle, \quad 3 \le i \le 5$$
$$\Downarrow$$
$$\texttt{Quantity}=\text{B}\langle i\rangle, \texttt{ProdName}=\text{C}\langle i\rangle, \quad 3 \le i \le 5$$

As can be seen, by using formula inheritance, the atomic children labels **Quantity** and **ProdName** of label **OrderDetails** obtain values from ranges (columns) B3:B5 and C3:C5.

3.2.2 *Defaults of structural mapping*

Figure 3 presents a simple structural mapping **Orders** =A2:E50, where several orders are organized in a single denormalized table (nested table). The interpretation process, as presented so far, uses certain defaults: (i) TranSheet assumes that data is organized in a table with attributes as columns and tuples as rows; (ii) TranSheet also takes advantage of the same ordering of columns in the source spreadsheet and target atomic labels (e.g., quantity comes "before" product name in both the spreadsheet and the target schema). These defaults can be overridden: the first by using function *transpose* to indicate that a table is represented with attributes as row and tuples as column; the second by the *schema restructuring* features described in [17].

3.2.3 *Nesting*

The mapping illustrated in Figure 3 is potentially ambiguous since two distinct target instances are possible: either (i) grouping products per order, as could be expected, or (ii) mimicking the data organization of the spreadsheet document with as many order labels as there are products. In this example, both generated documents satisfy the mapping specification as well as the target schema. However, the document where products are grouped per orders is often desirable [5]. By default, the target document is nested according to order identifier, first name, and last name.

3.2.4 *Filtering*

This kind of structural mapping allows users to select data from a set of source tuples according to specific filtering conditions. For example, in Figure 3 the user wants to select orders from the source whose product name is equal to "Towel" and quantity is greater than 1. This can be obtained by associating a filtering predicate *filterexp* to the structural mapping **Orders** = A2:E50. *Filterexp* is a combination of Excel-like logical functions *AND*, *OR*, and *NOT*. For example, the following mapping is employed for the above example: **Orders** =A2:E50[AND(D2:D50="Towel", E2:E50>1)]

3.2.5 *Sorting*

This kind of structural mapping allows users to sort tuples in the source spreadsheet according to values of columns. It is defined via function *sort(column1, order1, column2, order2,...)*, where $column_i$ is a column specified by a one-dimensional range, and $order_i$ is the corresponding sorting order of $column_i$ with value "ascending" or "descending". For example, the list of orders in Figure 3 can be sorted according to product name in ascending order, and then according to quantity in descending order as follows:

Orders =A2:E50[sort(D2:D50, ascending, E2:E50, descending)]

3.2.6 *Grouping with aggregation*

In this example, the user wants to group the source spreadsheet in Figure 3(a) by order identifier, first name, and last name. Excel-like aggregate functions (e.g., *count*, *sum*, *avg*, *min*, and *max*) can then be used together with grouping to calculate values for product name and quantity in each group. The target schema to be mapped is as follows:

```
Target
  Orders [ ] =A2:E50[groupby(A2:A50, B2:B50, C2:C50)]
    Order
      Id {0042, 0525, ...}
      FirstName {Ford, Arthur, ...}
      LastName {Prefect, Dent, ...}
      ProdName =count(D2:D50) {3,2, ...}
      Quantity =max(E2:E50) {150,20, ...}
```

The following mappings are employed: **Orders** =A2:E50[groupby(A2:A50, B2:B50, C2:C50)] where function *groupby(column1, ...)* groups a set of tuples according to values in columns $column_1$, $column_2$, and so on. This structural mapping is then refined at leaf level on atomic labels **ProdName** and **Quantity**; **ProdName** =count(D2:D50) counts the number of products for each order; **Quantity** =max(E2:E50) finds the maximum value in the set of quantities associated with an order.

3.2.7 *Join*

Suppose that the source spreadsheet in Figure 3(a) is divided into tables A2:C6 and D2:F3 where table A2:C6 contains order details and table D2:F3 contains customer information:

	A	B	C	D	E	F
1	OrderID	ProdName	Quantity	ID	FName	LName
2	42	Beer	180	42	Ford	Prefect
3	42	Towel	2	525	Arthur	Dent
4	42	Fish	1			
5	525	Towel	1			
6	525	Teabags	20			

The two above tables are joined according to order identifiers and mapped to the target schema in Figure 3(b). This can be achieved via function *join(table1, table2, joincondition)* where *table1* and *table2* are two tables defined by two-dimensional ranges and *joincondition* is an optional condition to join these two tables. We have the following mappings:

Orders =join(D2:F3, A2:C6, D2:D3=A2:A6)
Id =D2:D3; **FirstName** =E2:E3; **LastName** =F2:F3
OrderDetails =B2:C6

When *joincondition* is missing, a full Cartesian product is computed between the two tables.

3.2.8 *Union/Intersect/Minus*

Function *union* allows users to union two tables with the corresponding signature *union(table1, table2,...)*, where *table1*, *table2*,... are tables to be unioned. By default, union is duplicate-eliminating. For example, the user wants to union the following two tables with duplicate removal and map them to the target schema shown in Figure 3(b):

	A	B	C	D	E
1	*OrderId*	*FirstName*	*LastName*	*ProdName*	*Quantity*
2	0042	Ford	Prefect	Beer	150
3	0042	Ford	Prefect	Towel	2
4	0042	Ford	Prefect	Babel Fish	1
5	0525	Arthur	Dent	Towel	1
6	0525	Arthur	Dent	Tea Bags	20
7			...		

(a) Tabular representation of orders

```
QuoteRequest
  Orders [ ] =A2:E50 (49 items)
    Order
      Id {0042, 0525, ...}
      ShipTo
        FirstName {Ford, Arthur, ...}
        LastName {Prefect, Dent, ...}
      OrderDetails [ ]
        OrderLine
          ProdName {{Beer, Towel, ...}, ...}
          Quantity {{150, 2, ...}, {1, 20, ...}, ...}
```

(b) Mapping specification

Figure 3: A tabular representation of orders and its corresponding transformation

	A	B	C	D	E	F
1	42	Ford	Prefect	Beer	150	
2	42	Ford	Prefect	Towel	2	
3	42	Ford	Prefect	Babel Fish	1	
4						
5	525	Arthur	Dent	Towel	1	
6	525	Arthur	Dent	Tea Bags	20	

The following structural mapping is associated with label `Orders`: `Orders`=union(A1:E3, A5:E6). Other set operators intersect and minus can be specified via functions *intersect(table1, table2,...)* and *minus(table1, table2,...)*.

3.2.9 Branching

This kind of mapping allows users to map different sets of data to a target label depending on the outcome of a preset condition. It is specified via Excel-like function *if(condition, value_if_true, value_if_false)*. For example, suppose that there is an additional attribute, namely `Description`, located right below element `Quantity` of the target schema in Figure 3(b) to indicate whether the quantity of an order item is small or large. The following mapping is used:
`Description` =if(E2:E50>20, "large", "small")

That is if the quantity of an order item is greater than 20, then attribute `Description` is assigned "large"; otherwise it is associated with "small".

3.2.10 Composition and refinement of mappings

A *complex transformation* is typically composed of multiple patterns of structural and value mappings. For example, the user can perform sorting and then filtering in Figure 3: `Orders` =A2:E50[sort(D2:D50, ascending), D2:D50="Towel"].

Additionally, a formula specified on a label may collide with a formula inherited from one of its ancestor labels. Regarding mapping `Orders`=A2:E50 in Figure 3, the user can see that, by inheritance, the values associated to label `ProdName` are {*150, 2, ...*} which is a copy of the quantity column of the spreadsheet. However, the user expects that values of label `Quantity` should correspond to values of this column multiplied by 10. In such situation, the user can specify mapping formulas at structural labels and refine them at a lower level (e.g., leaf level). These will have precedence over the values derived by the automated mechanism. For instance, mapping `Quantity`=E2:E50*10 is used to correct the problem.

4. IMPLEMENTATION AND EXPERIMENTS

Architecture. TranSheet has been implemented as an Excel plug-in using C# 3.0 and Visual Studio 2008. The architecture of TranSheet consists of the following main components: (i) GUI enables users to specify mappings via formulas. While spreadsheet data is imported using the built-in functionality of Excel, target schemas are imported using

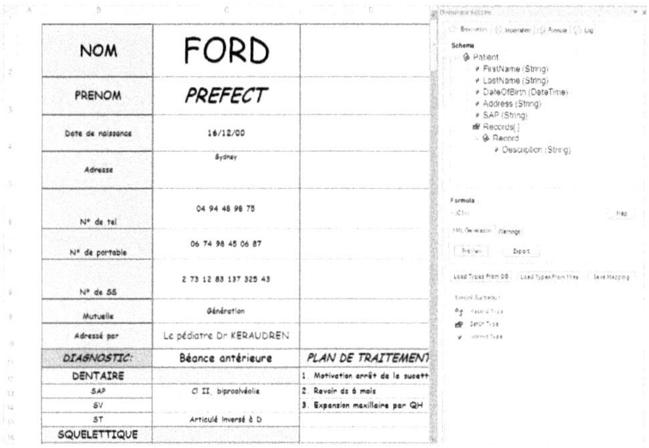

Figure 4: TranSheet user interface

TranSheet functionality; (ii) Mapping interpretation engine takes mapping formulas from GUI and generates XQuery; (iii) Execution engine is responsible for executing XQuery and then returning the transformation result to GUI for validation. TranSheet currently employs the open-source execution engine Saxon [4].

User interface. The user interface of TranSheet is shown in Figure 4. While the left side corresponds to the source spreadsheet, the target schema is located in the Excel task pane on the right. To specify a mapping, the user selects a target label and enters a formula into the formula editor located in the task pane. Instant feedback for the mapping is then displayed adjacent to the target labels.

Experiments. We selected 5 real data sets from the public repositories of Australian government agencies [5] and ManyEyes [1]. The *NSW Crime* dataset is a table showing crimes level in New South Wales - Australia by offence type, month and local government area from 1995 to 2009 with 184 columns and 10541 rows. The *Economic Stimulus Package* data set contains national building - economic stimulus plan projects of Australia with 29 columns and 4271 rows. The *School Locations* data set consists of addresses of schools in Victoria - Australia with 12 columns and 2294 rows. The *Frog Atlas* contains various kinds of frogs in South Australia recorded at different places with 13 columns and 6732 rows. The *expensive cities* data set indicates the most expensive cities in the world from 2002 to 2009 with 9 columns and 144 rows. Our test schemas are five structurally different

[4]http://saxon.sourceforge.net/
[5]http://data.australia.gov.au/

visualization types *Pie Chart*, *Scatter Plot*, *Bar Chart*, *Map* of ManyEyes [16, 1], and *Time Line* of the SIMILE project [6].

Eight popular mapping scenarios commonly used by the ManyEyes community for visualization [1, 16] are considered in these experiments (copying, merging, derivation, splitting, sorting, filtering, grouping with aggregation, and nesting). Detailed information can be found on in [17].

Prior to implementing these mapping scenarios, we familiarized ourselves with all functionalities offered by EXM and ManyEyes. For each mapping scenario, if it can be implemented using a system, we record manipulation operations on the source data set, if any.

In a nutshell, TranSheet can implement all mapping scenarios using mapping formulas without modifying data sets. On the other hand, both EXM and ManyEyes need multiple manipulations on data sets to accomplish the mapping scenarios. EXM generally requires fewer manipulations than ManyEyes and multiple manipulations of EXM can be done using graphical wizards. This is because Excel provides many advanced features to support data manipulation. However, EXM cannot implement mapping scenario nesting. While EXM supports only one nesting level in the target schema, a bar chart consists of two nesting levels.

EXM supports copying by dragging target attributes onto columns containing local government area and crimes in December 2009. In the case of ManyEyes, while the column containing local government area is selected from 4 candidates to map with the text target attribute, the column containing crimes in December 2009 is selected from 180 candidates to map with the numeric target attribute. However, 10530 unwanted rows must be deleted for both tools. TranSheet supports copying via either range formulas.

To implement derivation, EXM and ManyEyes require 6731 values in the sighting date column must be converted to the mm/dd/yyyy format. Similarly, a new column is inserted and its values are changed in the case of the splitting or merging scenario to store splitting/merging values. TranSheet supports derivation, merging, and splitting via applying functions on range formulas.

EXM requires fewer manipulations than ManyEyes in implementing sorting and filtering since Excel provides graphical wizards for users to implement these mapping scenarios. The user needs to perform these manually in the case of ManyEyes. TranSheet supports filtering and sorting by performing structural mappings via formulas or wizards.

To implement grouping with aggregation using EXM, a new table is created with 2 columns and 5 rows, in which each row contains a program type and its average funding. In the case of ManyEyes, the user must create a new table and then deletes 29 old columns to avoid default grouping. TranSheet supports this mapping scenario by grouping the data set according to program type and then using the aggregate function *average*.

Since EXM does not support nesting, we only consider ManyEyes. To implement this scenario using ManyEyes, a new table with is created with 2 columns and 69 rows, where each row contains different types of crimes in October 2009, except the header row. In addition, 184 old columns must be deleted. TranSheet supports nesting by mapping range formulas to 2 attributes of the bar chart.

[6]http://www.simile-widgets.org/

5. RELATED WORK AND DISCUSSION

Transformation Languages and Mapping Tools. A language for the description of spreadsheet content as a series of relational tables is proposed in [7]. Once defined, the schema can be used with either low-level transformation languages (e.g., XSLT/XQuery) or visual mapping tools (e.g., Clio [5], Clip [10], and +Spicy [9] to perform transformation. However, spreadsheet users must learn a new complex language to perform transformations and their existing programming experience is not leveraged. By contrast, TranSheet provides a familiar spreadsheet-like formula mapping language.

Exportation of spreadsheet data. Several existing approaches support the exportation of spreadsheet data to structured formats [11, 4, 16]. Regarding these approaches, data representation or structural mismatches between a source spreadsheet and target XML schema are addressed by modifying the spreadsheet document before exportation. Most of the transformation logic is embedded in modifications of the source spreadsheet. By contrast, TranSheet separates the transformation logic from source manipulations through the notion of mapping formulas. The benefits are increased expressiveness and preservation of the original source.

Since a significant amount of the world's data is stored in spreadsheets, we believe TranSheet has numerous applications in data exchange for both desktop and Web-based environments. Additional interesting features of TranSheet, including mapping generalization and mapping formula interpretation, can be found in [17].

6. REFERENCES

[1] Manyeyes. http://many-eyes.com/.

[2] R. Abraham and M. Erwig. Header and unit inference for spreadsheets through spatial analyses. In *VLHCC '04*.

[3] B. Alexe, W.-C. Tan, and Y. Velegrakis. Stbenchmark: towards a benchmark for mapping systems. *VLDB'08*.

[4] B. Brauer. Next evolution of data integration into microsoft excel. Technical report, StrikeIron Inc., 2006.

[5] A. Fuxman, M. A. Hernandez, H. Ho, R. J. Miller, P. Papotti, and L. Popa. Nested mappings: schema mapping reloaded. In *VLDB '06*.

[6] C. Jensen, H. Lonsdale, E. Wynn, J. Cao, M. Slater, and T. G. Dietterich. The life and times of files and information: a study of desktop provenance. In *CHI'10*.

[7] L. Lakshmanan, S. Subramanian, N. Goyal, and R. Krishnamurthy. On querying spreadsheets. In *ICDE'98*.

[8] B. Liu and H. V. Jagadish. A spreadsheet algebra for a direct data manipulation query interface. In *ICDE '09*.

[9] G. Mecca, P. Papotti, and S. Raunich. Core schema mappings. In *SIGMOD'09*.

[10] A. Raffio, D. Braga, S. Ceri, P. Papotti, and M. A. Hernández. Clip: a visual language for explicit schema mappings. In *ICDE'08*.

[11] F. Rice. Creating xml mappings in excel 2003. Technical report, Microsoft Corporation, 2005.

[12] G. G. Robertson, M. P. Czerwinski, and J. E. Churchill. Visualization of mappings between schemas. In *CHI '05*.

[13] M. Roth, M. A. Hernandez, P. Coulthard, L. Yan, L. Popa, H. C.-T. Ho, and C. C. Salter. Xml mapping technology: making connections in an xml-centric world. *IBM Syst.J.'06*.

[14] C. Scaffidi, M. Shaw, and B. Myers. Estimating the numbers of end users and end user programmers. In *VLHCC '05*.

[15] J. Tyszkiewicz. Spreadsheet as a relational database engine. *SIGMOD'10*.

[16] F. B. Viegas, M. Wattenberg, F. van Ham, J. Kriss, and M. McKeon. Manyeyes: a site for visualization at internet scale. *IEEE Trans Vis Comput Graph*, 2007.

[17] H. T. Vu. *Spreadsheet-based complex data transformation*. PhD thesis, CSE-UNSW, 2011.

High Efficiency and Quality: Large Graphs Matching

Yuanyuan Zhu†, Lu Qin†, Jeffrey Xu Yu†, Yiping Ke†, Xuemin Lin‡

†The Chinese University of Hong Kong, {yyzhu,lqin,yu,ypke}@se.cuhk.edu.hk

‡University of New South Wales & NICTA, lxue@cse.unsw.edu.au

ABSTRACT

Graph matching plays an essential role in many real applications. In this paper, we study how to match two large graphs by maximizing the number of matched edges, which is known as maximum common subgraph matching and is NP-hard. To find exact matching, it cannot handle a graph with more than 30 nodes. To find an approximate matching, the quality can be very poor. We propose a novel two-step approach which can efficiently match two large graphs over thousands of nodes with high matching quality. In the first step, we propose an anchor-selection/expansion approach to compute a good initial matching. In the second step, we propose a new approach to refine the initial matching. We give the optimality of our refinement and discuss how to randomly refine the matching with different combinations. We conducted extensive testing using real and synthetic datasets, and will report our findings.

Categories and Subject Descriptors

H.2.8 [**Database management**]: Database applications—*Data mining*; G.2.2 [**Discrete mathematics**]: Graph theory—*Graph algorithms*

General Terms

Algorithm, Theory, Performance

Keywords

Graph Matching, Maximum Common Subgraph, Vertex Cover

1. INTRODUCTION

Graph data proliferates in a wide variety of applications, including social networks in psycho-sociology, attributed graphs in image processing, food chains in ecology, electrical circuits in electricity, road networks in transport, protein interaction networks in biology, topological networks on the Web, etc. Graph data processing has attracted great attention from both research and industrial communities.

Graph matching plays an essential role in many applications. In biochemistry, the genome of an organism is represented as a graph with genes as nodes and the metabolic pathway is represented as another graph with enzymes as nodes. These two graphs are then matched to identify FRECs (functionally related enzyme clusters) that reveal important biological features of the organisms [14]. In medicine, the electroencephalogram (EEG) signal can be transformed into a graph with the extracted energy bursts as nodes. Graph matching is applied to the comparison of two EEG signals to analyze different brain activities in terms of latency, frequency, energy, and activated areas [5]. In video indexing, a region adjacency graph (RAG) is constructed to represent an object, where the nodes are segmented regions in video frames. Graph matching between two RAGs can be used to retrieve similar objects in video-shot collections [8].

In the literature, a number of algorithms have been proposed for graph matching including exact matching [20, 13, 11] and approximate matching [21, 7, 3, 9, 12, 15, 23, 17]. The exact approaches are able to find the optimal matching at the cost of exponential running time, while the approximate approaches are much more efficient but can get poor matching results. More importantly, most of them can only handle small graphs with tens to hundreds of nodes. As an indication, exactly matching two undirected graphs with 30 nodes may take 100,000 seconds. It is important to note that real-world networks nowadays can be very large. The existing approaches cannot efficiently match graphs even with thousands of nodes with high quality.

In this paper, we study the problem of matching two large graphs, which is formulated as follows. Given two graphs G_1 and G_2, we find a one-to-one matching between the nodes in G_1 and G_2 such that the number of the matched edges is maximized. The optimal solution to the problem corresponds to the maximum common subgraph (*MCS*) between G_1 and G_2, which is an NP-hard problem, and has been studied in decades. It is known to be very difficult to find a high quality approximate matching efficiently even for small graphs. In order to meet the needs of handling large graphs for graph matching and analyzing, we propose a novel approximate solution with polynomial time complexity while still attaining high matching quality.

The main contributions of this paper are summarized below. We propose a novel two-step approach, namely, matching construction and matching refinement. In the matching construction, we propose a new anchor-selection/expansion approach to compute an initial matching. We give heuristics to select a small number of important anchors using a new similarity score, which measures how two nodes in two different graphs are similar to be matched by taking both global and local information of nodes into consideration. We compute a good initial matching by expanding from the anchors selected. The expansion is based on structural similarity among the neighbors of nodes in two graphs. In the matching refinement, we propose a new approach to refine the initial matching. The novelty of our refinement is as follows. First, we refine a matching M to a

CIKM'11, October 24–28, 2011, Glasgow, Scotland, UK.

better one which is most likely to exist and can be identified. Second, we consider the efficiency, and focus on a subset of nodes to refine while giving every node in the graphs a chance to be refined. We show the optimality of our refinement. We also show how to randomly refine matchings with different combinations. Our refinement can improve the matching quality with small overhead. We conducted extensive testing using real and synthetic datasets, and confirmed the quality and efficiency of our approach. The average ratio of our approximate matching to the exact matching is above 90%, while the computational cost is less than 1% compared to the state of the art exact algorithms. This is a big step compared to all the approximate algorithms to match large graphs in the literature.

The rest of the paper is organized as follows. Section 2 discusses some related work. Section 3 gives the problem statement. Section 4 and Section 5 discuss the matching construction and matching refinement. Section 6 shows the performance results. Section 7 concludes this paper.

2. RELATED WORK

Graph matching can be divided into two categories, namely, exact graph matching and approximate graph matching.

For exact graph matching, in the literature, most of the algorithms use backtracking (refer to Ullmann's algorithm for subgraph and graph isomorphism [20]). Existing solutions on finding maximum common subgraph mainly focus on maximum common node induced subgraph, and most techniques can hardly be used for maximum common edge induced subgraph. Among them, Mcgregor [13] proposes a backtracking search method for finding maximum common subgraph. An improved backtracking algorithm is given in [11] with time complexity $O(m^{n+1} \cdot n)$. Abu-Khzam et al. in [1] propose an algorithm that combines backtracking and vertex cover enumeration to solve the maximum common node induced subgraph problem. There are also some other works to calculate the maximum common node induced subgraph by finding the maximum clique in the association graph [16, 10, 19]. The complexity of the maximum clique approach is no better than backtracking.

For approximate graph matching, there are three categories: propagation based method, spectral based method, and optimization based method. The propagation based method is introduced in [6]. It is based on the intuition that two nodes are similar if their respective neighborhoods are similar. IsoRank [18] extends the propagation based method by adding the weight of propagation. Spectral based method aims to represent and distinguish structural properties of graphs using eigenvalues and eigenvectors of graph adjacency matrices. It is based on the observation that if two graphs are isomorphic, their adjacency matrices will have the same eigenvalues and eigenvectors. Since the computation of eigenvalues can be solved in polynomial time, it is used by a lot of works in graph matching [21, 7, 3, 9, 12, 15, 23]. Among these works, Umeyama [21] uses the eigendecomposition of adjacency matrices of the graphs to derive a simple expression of the orthogonal matrix that optimizes the objective function. However, such method is only suitable for graphs with the same number of nodes. [7] extends Umeyama's work to match two graphs of different sizes by choosing the largest k-eigenvalues as the projection space. Knossow [9] improves the matching result by performing eigendecomposition on the Laplacian matrix since it is positive and semidefinite. Heat-kernel [23] is used to embed the nodes of the graph into vector-space based on the graph-spectral method, and the correspondence matrix between the embedded points of two graphs is computed by a variant of the Scott and Longuet-Higgins algorithm. The optimization based method aims to model graph matching as an optimization problem and solve it. The representative algorithms include PATH [25] and GA [24]. In PATH [25], the graph matching problem is formulated as a convex-concave programming problem and approximately solved by starting from the convex relaxation and then iteratively solves the convex-concave programming problem by gradually increasing the weight of the concave relaxation and following the path of solutions thus created. GA [24] is a gradient method based approach, which starts from an initial solution and iteratively chooses a matching in the direction of a gradient objective function. A survey can be found in [17].

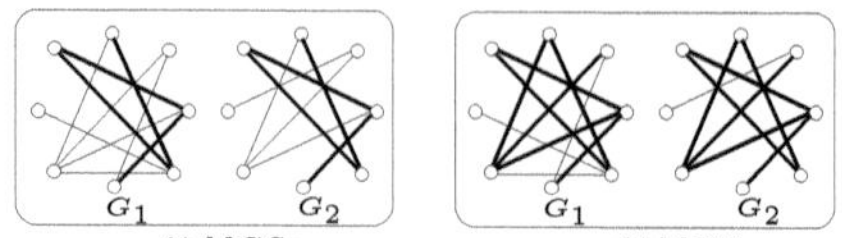

(a) $MCSv$ (b) $MCSe$

Figure 1: *MCSv* **and** *MCSe*

3. PROBLEM STATEMENT

In this paper, we deal with undirected and unlabeled graphs, which are difficult to match, because they do not have any label information to assist graph matching. For a graph $G(V, E)$, we use $V(G)$ to denote the set of nodes and $E(G)$ to denote the set of edges.

Definition 3.1: Graph/Subgraph Isomorphism. Graph G_1 is isomorphic to graph G_2, if and only if there exists a bijective function $f : V(G_1) \to V(G_2)$ such that for any two nodes $u_1 \in V(G_1)$ and $u_2 \in V(G_1)$, $(u_1, u_2) \in E(G_1)$ if and only if $(f(u_1), f(u_2)) \in E(G_2)$. G_1 is subgraph isomorphic to G_2, if and only if there exists a subgraph G' of G_2 such that G_1 is isomorphic to G'. □

Definition 3.2: Maximum Common Subgraph. A graph G is the maximum common subgraph (*MCS*) of two graphs G_1 and G_2, denoted as $\mathsf{mcs}(G_1, G_2)$, if G is a common subgraph of G_1 and G_2, and there is no other common subgraph G', such that G' is larger than G. □

The *MCS* of two graphs can be disconnected, and there are two kinds of *MCS*s, namely, maximum common node induced subgraph (*MCSv*) and maximum common edge induced subgraph (*MCSe*). The former requires *MCS* to be the node induced subgraph of both G_1 and G_2, and G' is larger than G iff $|V(G')| > |V(G)|$. The latter requires *MCS* to be the edge induced subgraph of both G_1 and G_2, and G' is larger than G iff $|E(G')| > |E(G)|$. Fig. 1 shows the difference between *MCSv* and *MCSe*. Given two graphs G_1 and G_2. Fig. 1(a) shows the *MCSv* of G_1 and G_2, whereas Fig. 1(b) shows the *MCSe* of G_1 and G_2. As can be seen from this example, *MCSe* can possibly get more common substructure for two given graphs. In this paper, we adopt *MCSe* since it can possibly get more common substructure for two given graphs, and we use *MCS* (mcs) to denote *MCSe*. Finding *MCS* is NP-hard.

Definition 3.3: Graph Matching. Given two graphs G_1 and G_2, matching M between G_1 and G_2 is a set of pairs $M = \{(u, v) | u \in V(G_1), v \in V(G_2)\}$, such that for any two pairs $(u_1, v_1) \in M$ and $(u_2, v_2) \in M$, $u_1 \neq u_2$ and $v_1 \neq v_2$. The optimal matching M of two graphs is the one with the largest number of matched edges. Finding the optimal matching M is the same as *MCS*. □

Problem Statement: We aim to compute the optimal matching M for two given graphs G_1 and G_2. For a given matching M, we evaluate its quality by computing $score(M)$ as follows.

$$score(M) = \frac{\sum_{(u_1,v_1) \in M} \sum_{(u_2,v_2) \in M} e_{u_1,u_2} \times e_{v_1,v_2}}{2} \quad (1)$$

where $e_{u,v} = 1$ if there is an edge between u and v, and $e_{u,v} = 0$,

Algorithm 1 match(G_1, G_2)

```
A ←anchor-selection (G1,G2);
M ← anchor-expansion (G1, G2, A);
M ← refine(G1, G2, M);
return M;
```

otherwise. Obviously, finding the optimal matching M is actually to find a matching with the maximum $score(M)$, and the maximum $score(M)$ is $|E(\mathsf{mcs}(G_1, G_2))|$.

MCS problem is NP-hard, and it is known to be very difficult to obtain a tight and even useful bound in the past decades. For the quality of the result, [2] give a bound $O(n^2)$ based on the number of mis-matched edges, where n is the size of the larger graph. It means that it may mis-match all the edges. [16] provides an upper bound for the size of the *MCS*, which is computed by sorting the degree sequences of two graphs separately followed by summarizing the corresponding smaller degrees. The bound is almost the smaller graph, without considering any structural information of the two graphs, which does not provide much information. In [2], the time complexity is $O(n^6 L)$, where L is the size of LP model formulated for graph matching (at least n). It cannot even handle graphs with more than 100 nodes.

In this paper, we propose a novel approach to solve the graph matching problem, which includes two steps: matching construction and matching refinement. In the matching construction step, we construct the initial matching M by identifying anchors of two graphs G_1 and G_2 followed by expanding from the anchors. We do so based on a new similarity between nodes in the two different graphs which combines both global and local information of nodes. In the matching refinement step, we refine the initial matching. We prove that our refinement is efficient and can generate a matching with good quality. The framework of the algorithm is shown in Algorithm 1 and is self-explained. We discuss the first step in Section 4, and the second step in Section 5.

4. MATCHING CONSTRUCTION

In this section, we discuss how to select anchors and how to expand from the selected anchors to obtain the initial matching M for two graphs G_1 and G_2, using a new node similarity matrix S. The node similarity between $u \in G_1$ and $v \in G_2$ is very important because it indicates how likely the two nodes will be matched when computing the matching M.

4.1 Global and Local Node Similarity

Let G_1 and G_2 be two graphs. The new node similarity matrix S we propose takes both global and local node similarities into consideration when matching nodes in two graphs.

$$S[u, v] = S_g[u, v] \times S_l[u, v] \tag{2}$$

Here, S is a $|V(G_1)| \times |V(G_2)|$ matrix, in which the element $S[u, v] \in [0, 1]$ represents the similarity of two nodes, u in G_1 and v in G_2. S is based on S_g and S_l, where S_g measures global similarity between u and v in the entire graphs G_1 and G_2, and S_l measures local similarity between u and v in their neighborhoods. We will introduce an existing global similarity below followed by the discussion on our new local similarity in this section.

Global node similarity: In the literature, the global similarity for nodes in two graphs can be the spectral based similarity. The representative study is Umeyama's work [21] which is improved by [9]. Suppose G_1 and G_2 are two undirected graphs with the same number of nodes n. The Laplacian matrix $L_{n\times n}$ of graph G with

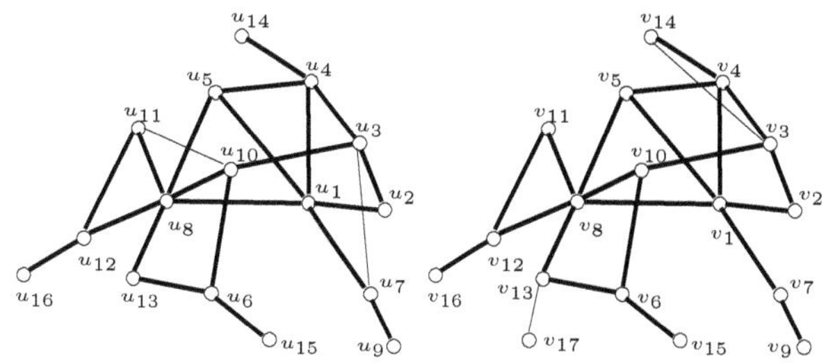

(a) Graph G_1 (b) Graph G_2

Figure 2: Two Graphs

n nodes is defined as $L = D - A$, where A is the adjacency matrix and D is the diagonal degree matrix. $A[u_1, u_2] = 1$ if $(u_1, u_2) \in E(G)$, and 0 otherwise. $D[u_1, u_1] = \sum_{(u_1,u_2)\in E(G)} A[u_1, u_2]$. We denote the Laplacian matrices of G_1 and G_2 as L_1 and L_2 respectively. Suppose the eigenvalues of L_1 and L_2 are $\alpha_1 \geq \alpha_2 \geq \cdots \geq \alpha_n$ and $\beta_1 \geq \beta_2 \geq \cdots \geq \beta_n$ respectively. Since L_1 and L_2 are symmetric and positive-semidefinite, we have $L_1 = U_1 \Lambda_1 U_1^T$ and $L_2 = U_2 \Lambda_2 U_2^T$, where U_1 and U_2 are orthogonal matrices, and $\Lambda_1 = diag(\alpha_i)$ and $\Lambda_2 = diag(\beta_i)$. If G_1 and G_2 are isomorphic, there exists a permutation matrix P such that $PU_1\Lambda_1U_1^TP^T = U_2\Lambda_2U_2^T$. Let $P = U_2D'U_1^T$ where $D' = diag(d_1, \cdots, d_n)$ and $d_i \in \{+1; -1\}$ accounts for the sign ambiguity in the eigendecomposition. When G_1 and G_2 are isomorphic, the optimum permutation matrix is P which maximizes $tr(P^T\bar{U}_2\bar{U}_1^T)$, where $\bar{U}_1$ and $\bar{U}_2$ are matrices which have the absolute value of each element of U_1 and U_2, respectively. When the numbers of nodes in G_1 and G_2 are not the same, we only choose the largest c eigenvalues [9]. Let $c = \min\{|V(G_1)|, |V(G_2)|\}$, and $\bar{U}'_1$ and $\bar{U}'_2$ be the first c columns of $\bar{U}_1$ and $\bar{U}_2$ respectively, the global similarity matrix can be computed with Eq. (3).

$$S_g = \bar{U}'_1\bar{U}'^T_2 \tag{3}$$

Here, $S_g[u, v] \in [0, 1]$ is the global node similarity between the node u in $V(G_1)$ and the node v in $V(G_2)$.

Example 4.1 shows an example of matching the two graphs using the global node similarity.

Example 4.1: Consider the two graphs in Fig. 2. We first compute their global node similarity matrix S_g. We construct a bipartite graph G_b with $|V(G_1)| + |V(G_2)|$ nodes, and for any $u \in V(G_1)$ and $v \in V(G_2)$, we add an edge $(u, v) \in E(G_b)$ with weight $S_g[u, v]$. We compute the maximum weight bipartite matching of G_b and get the matching as $M = \{(u_1, v_1), (u_2, v_2), (u_3, v_7), (u_4, v_4), (u_5, v_5), (u_6, v_{12}), (u_7, v_{13}), (u_8, v_8), (u_9, v_{17}), (u_{10}, v_{10}), (u_{11}, v_3), (u_{12}, v_6), (u_{13}, v_{14}), (u_{14}, v_{15}), (u_{15}, v_{16}), (u_{16}, v_9)\}$. In this way, the number of matched edges is 10, which is far away from the optimal solution $\mathsf{mcs}(G_1, G_2)$, 21 (bold edges in Fig. 2). Comparing to the optimal solution, u_3 is mismatched to v_7 because they have a high global similarity, but obviously, the local structure near u_3 and the local structure near v_7 differ much. □

The global node similarity gives a node similarity measure from the global point of view. However, when G_1 and G_2 are not sufficiently similar to each other, using global node similarity only is not sufficient to get a good matching because the global node similarity does not consider the local information for nodes in two graphs. We need a local node similarity.

Local node similarity: For any node v in graph G and $k \geq 0$, we define the k-neighborhood of v, $N_k(v)$, as the set of nodes in $V(G)$ such that $v \notin N_k(v)$ and for any $u \in N_k(v)$, the shortest distance from v to u is no more than k. The shortest distance is defined as the number of edges in the shortest path from v to u.

The k-neighborhood subgraph of v in G, denoted as G^k_v, is defined as the induced subgraph over $N_k(v) \cup \{v\}$ in G. For two nodes $u \in V(G_1)$ and $v \in V(G_2)$, we measure their local node similarity by comparing the k-neighborhood subgraphs of them. Suppose $d(u)$ and $d(v)$ are the degrees of node u and v in G_1 and G_2 respectively, and suppose $d_{1,1}, d_{1,2}, \cdots$ is the degree sequence of node set $N_k(u)$ in G^k_u sorted in non-increasing order, and $d_{2,1}, d_{2,2}, \cdots$ is the degree sequence of node set $N_k(v)$ in G^k_v sorted in non-increasing order. Let $n_{min} = \min\{|N_k(u)|, |N_k(v)|\}$. We define a $|V(G_1)| \times |V(G_2)|$ local node similarity matrix S_l as follows.

$$S_l[u,v] = \frac{(n_{min} + 1 + D(u,v))^2}{(|V(G^k_u)| + |E(G^k_u)|)(|V(G^k_v)| + |E(G^k_v)|)} \quad (4)$$

$$D(u,v) = \frac{\min\{d(u), d(v)\} + \sum_{i=1}^{n_{min}} \min\{d_{1,i}, d_{2,i}\}}{2} \quad (5)$$

Here, $D(u,v)$ consists of two parts. The first part $\min\{d(u), d(v)\}$ is the ideal contribution of edges when matching u with v, and the second part $\sum_{i=1}^{n_{min}} \min\{d_{1,i}, d_{2,i}\}$ is the ideal contribution of edges when matching nodes in $N_k(u)$ with nodes in $N_k(v)$. We show that S_l has the following properties. (1) $0 \leq S_l[u,v] \leq 1$. (2) $S_l[u,v] \geq \frac{(|V(\mathsf{mcs}(G^k_u, G^k_v))| + |E(\mathsf{mcs}(G^k_u, G^k_v))|)^2}{(|V(G^k_u)| + |E(G^k_u)|)(|V(G^k_v)| + |E(G^k_v)|)}$. (3) If G^k_u and G^k_v are isomorphic, and u is matched to v in the optimal matching of G^k_u and G^k_v, we have $S_l[u,v] = 1$. (4) If G^k_u is subgraph isomorphic to G^k_v, and u matches v in the optimal matching of G^k_u and G^k_v, we have $S_l[u,v] = \frac{|V(G^k_u)| + |E(G^k_u)|}{|V(G^k_v)| + |E(G^k_v)|}$.

Example 4.2 shows an example of matching two graphs using S.

Example 4.2: Reconsider the graphs in Fig. 2. Let $k = 2$. We construct a bipartite graph G_b with $|V(G_1)| + |V(G_2)|$ nodes, and for any $u \in V(G_1)$ and $v \in V(G_2)$, we add an edge $(u,v) \in E(G_b)$ with weight $S[u,v]$ (instead of $S_g[u,v]$). We compute the maximum weight bipartite matching of G_b and get the matching $M = \{(u_1,v_1), (u_2,v_2), (u_3,v_3), (u_4,v_4), (u_5,v_5), (u_6,v_{12}), (u_7,v_{13}), (u_8,v_8), (u_9,v_{17}), (u_{10},v_{10}), (u_{11},v_{14}), (u_{12},v_6), (u_{13},v_{11}), (u_{14},v_{15}), (u_{15},v_9), (u_{16},v_{16})\}$. The number of edges matched is 13 which is better than 10 when only using the global similarity. But it is still much less than the optimal solution, 21. □

A problematic approach to compute M using S: Umeyama [21] computes a matching M by applying the Hungarian algorithm to the node similarity matrix, which can be with S we newly proposed or S_g given in [21]. Using all the similar node pairs computed, a matching M can be found. In order to compute a matching, Umeyama constructs a bipartite graph G_b that includes $|V(G_1)| + |V(G_2)|$ nodes. For any node $u \in V(G_1)$ and node $v \in V(G_2)$, an edge (u,v) is added to G_b with weight $S[u,v]$ (or $S_g[u,v]$). The maximum weight bipartite matching of G_b leads to a matching M of graphs G_1 and G_2. Such an approach has two drawbacks. (1) Similarity optimality does not mean matched edge optimality, while our aim is to maximize the number of matched edges in two graphs. It is possible that two nodes are very similar in terms of S (or S_g) but the two nodes do not have many incident edges that help to increase the number of matched edges. (2) This approach only considers the matching of individual nodes in two graphs, and does not consider whether the nodes around them can be well matched when it matches two nodes. In other words, matching $u \in V(G_1)$ with $v \in V(G_2)$ does not consider whether the nodes around u and v can be matched using the maximum weight bipartite matching.

4.2 Anchor Selection and Expansion

In our approach, we solve the two drawbacks as follows. Instead of matching all the nodes, we first match some important nodes as anchors. Every two anchors matched have high similarity and large degrees, and can contribute a large number of matched edges. Then, we expand from the anchors to match the other nodes using the local similarity S_l as the measure. Thus, our solution consists of two steps, namely, anchor selection and anchor expansion.

Algorithm 2 anchor-expansion $(G_1, G_2, \mathcal{A})$

Input: two graphs, G_1 and G_2, and the anchor pairs $\mathcal{A}$;
Output: graph matching M;
$M \leftarrow \mathcal{A}$; $\mathcal{Q} \leftarrow \emptyset$; $\mathcal{S}_1 \leftarrow \emptyset$; $\mathcal{S}_2 \leftarrow \emptyset$;
for all $(u,v) \in \mathcal{A}$ **do**
  $\mathcal{S}_1 \leftarrow \mathcal{S}_1 \cup \{u\}$; $\mathcal{S}_2 \leftarrow \mathcal{S}_2 \cup \{v\}$; $\mathcal{Q} \leftarrow \mathcal{Q} \cup (N(u) \times N(v))$;
while $\mathcal{Q} \neq \emptyset$ **do**
  remove (u,v) from Q with the largest similarity $S_l[u,v]$;
  if $u \notin \mathcal{S}_1$ **and** $v \notin \mathcal{S}_2$ **then**
    $M \leftarrow M \cup \{(u,v)\}$; $\mathcal{S}_1 \leftarrow \mathcal{S}_1 \cup \{u\}$; $\mathcal{S}_2 \leftarrow \mathcal{S}_2 \cup \{v\}$; $\mathcal{Q} \leftarrow \mathcal{Q} \cup (N(u) \times N(v))$;
return M;

The anchors selected play two important roles in matching construction. (1) The matching anchors contribute a large number of edges to the matching M. (2) The anchors are the references to start with when matching the other nodes. The algorithm for anchor selection (line 1 in Algorithm 1) is illustrated below. First, we compute the similarity matrix S (Eq. (2)). Second, we sort the pairs (u,v) for all $u \in V(G_1)$ and $v \in V(G_2)$ in the decreasing order of $S[u,v]$. Third, we select (u,v) from the sorted pairs list as matched anchors, if they satisfy the following two conditions: (1) $\min\{d(u), d(v)\} \geq \delta$, where δ is the larger average degree of the two graphs, i.e., $\delta = \max\{\frac{2 \times |E(G_1)|}{|V(G_1)|}, \frac{2 \times |E(G_2)|}{|V(G_2)|}\}$, and (2) $S[u,v] \geq \tau$, where τ is a threshold and generally $\tau > 0.5$.

Example 4.3: Consider the two graphs in Fig. 2. Suppose $\tau = 0.94$, we get the anchor pairs to be $\mathcal{A} = \{(u_1,v_1), (u_8,v_8)\}$. The pair (u_9, v_{17}) is not selected because it destroys the degree constraint, even though it satisfies the similarity constraint . Expanding from the pair (u_9, v_{17}) to match other pairs is a bad choice. □

We illustrate the anchor expansion algorithm (Algorithm 2) to obtain a matching M. Let $\mathcal{A}$ be the anchor pairs (u,v) selected already. Initially, $M = \mathcal{A}$. Let $N(u)$ and $N(v)$ denote the immediate neighbors of u and v in graphs G_1 and G_2 respectively. For every matched pair (u,v) in the initial M, we put all $(N(u) \times N(v))$ pairs in a queue $\mathcal{Q}$, where $\mathcal{Q}$ is the set of candidate matching pairs sorted in decreasing order of their local similarity. In an iterative manner, we remove the pair (u,v) with the largest local similarity $S_l[u,v]$ (Eq. (4)) from $\mathcal{Q}$. If both u and v have not been matched before, we add (u,v) to M and put their all $(N(u) \times N(v))$ immediate neighbor pairs into $\mathcal{Q}$ for further consideration. We repeat it until $\mathcal{Q} = \emptyset$.

The example of anchor expansion is given below.

Example 4.4: Given the two graphs in Fig. 2. After we get the set of anchor pairs $\mathcal{A} = \{(u_1,v_1), (u_8,v_8)\}$. Using Algorithm 2, we can construct our matching $M = \{(u_1,v_1), (u_2,v_7), (u_3,v_3), (u_4,v_4), (u_5,v_5), (u_6,v_6), (u_7,v_2), (u_8,v_8), (u_9,v_9), (u_{10},v_{10}), (u_{11},v_{13}), (u_{12},v_{12}), (u_{13},v_{11}), (u_{14},v_{14}), (u_{15},v_{15}), (u_{16},v_{16})\}$. The number of matched edges is 18. □

5. MATCHING REFINEMENT

The initial matching M is computed using the heuristics that matches the anchors first followed by matching the nodes around the anchors in a top-down fashion. The heuristics used cannot guarantee that all the anchors are correctly matched. In this section, we propose a new approach to refine the initial matching M. It is

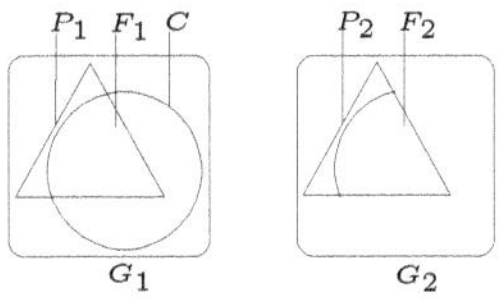

Figure 3: Vertex Cover Refinement

important to note that our strategy is to refine the initial matching and is not to find a completely new matching. By refinement, we mean the following two things. First, we are not to explore all possibilities without a goal when we refine a matching. In other words, we refine a matching M to a better one which is most likely to exist and can be identified. Second, we consider the efficiency when refining a matching. In our approach, each time we focus on a subset of nodes to refine by excluding a subset of nodes and including a subset of nodes. The set of nodes to be excluded from refinement at one time is neither large nor small. Also we give every node in the graphs a chance to be refined.

5.1 Vertex Cover Based Refinement

We use a vertex cover C to refine a matching M. A vertex cover C of a graph G is a subset of nodes in $V(G)$, i.e., $C \subseteq V(G)$, such that for every edge $(u, v) \in E(G)$, we have $u \in C$ or $v \in C$. A minimum vertex cover of graph G is a vertex cover with the minimum number of nodes. A vertex cover C of G is a minimal vertex cover, if there does not exist a vertex cover C' of G such that $C' \subset C$. A set of nodes C is a vertex cover of graph G if and only if its complement $I = V(G) - C$ is an independent set of G. Here, an independent set I of G is a subset of nodes in $V(G)$, i.e., $I \subseteq V(G)$, such that for any $u \in I$ and $v \in I$, $(u, v) \notin E(G)$.

Below, we introduce some notations we use to refine a matching M based on vertex cover. Suppose we match two graphs G_1 and G_2, and M is a matching found. Let P_1 and P_2 be the matched nodes in G_1 and G_2 respectively using the matching M. For any $(u, v) \in M$, we have $u \in P_1$ and $v \in P_2$. Given a cover C of G_1, we use F_1 to denote $C \cap P_1$. For any subset of nodes $S \subseteq P_1$, we use $M[S]$ to denote the corresponding matched part of S in P_2 using matching M. For any subset of nodes $S \subseteq P_2$, we use $M^{-1}[S]$ to denote the matched part of S in P_1 using matching M. Let $F_2 = M[F_1]$. The relationships among G_1, G_2, P_1, P_2, F_1, F_2 and C are illustrated in Fig. 3.

Vertex cover plays an important role when we match two graphs G_1 and G_2. It allows us to focus on one graph G_1, with the assistance of its vertex cover. The intuition is as follows. By definition, a vertex cover of G_1 is the set of nodes that covers all possible edges in G_1. This implies that a node in a vertex cover can possibly have many edges to cover (or possibly have many matched edges with another graph G_2).

A vertex cover C of G_1 divides $V(G_1)$ into three parts, $F_1 = C \cap P_1$, $C - F_1$ and $V(G_1) - C$. The implications are given below. The nodes in F_1 are most likely to lead to good matches, based on the definition of vertex cover. We exclude nodes in F_1 to refine. We include nodes in $V(G_1) - C$ to refine, because the complement of the vertex cover $V(G_1) - C$ is an independent set such that there are no edges between any two nodes in $V(G_1) - C$. Such a property makes it possible to apply some efficient polynomial algorithms for optimizing the matching. For $C - F_1$, we will first discuss how to refine by excluding nodes in $C - F_1$, and then discuss how to include nodes $C - F_1$ to refine.

Remark 5.1: *The size of a vertex cover for a graph is usually neither too large nor too small. It can not be too large, because a graph contains a considerable number of nodes that are independent with each other, and the complement of such nodes forms a vertex cover. For example, if G is a star graph, it has a vertex cover of size 1; if G is a tree, it has a vertex cover of at most $\lfloor \frac{|V(G)|}{2} \rfloor$; if G is a bipartite graph, it has a vertex cover of at most $\lfloor \frac{|V(G)|}{2} \rfloor$. It can not be too small, because it must guarantee that all edges in the graph will be covered by at least one node in the vertex cover. In our experiments, the average size of the vertex covers is 53.1% to the number of nodes in the graph.* □

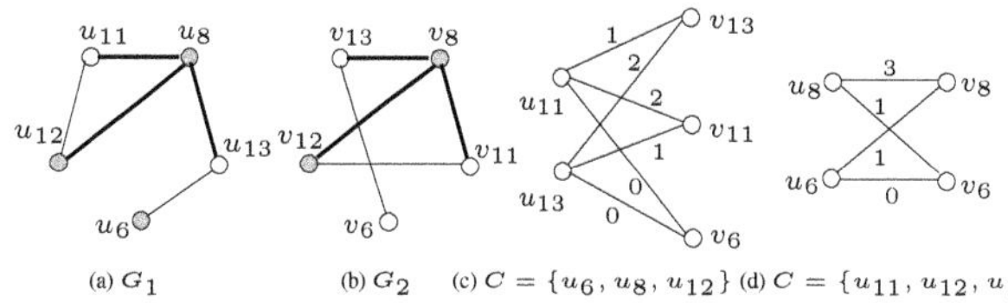

Figure 4: Vertex Cover Refinement Example

5.2 Refinement and Its Optimality

Given two graphs G_1 and G_2, a matching M, and a vertex cover C of G_1, we give a refinement $M^+(C)$ of M, and show its optimality below.

First, we show how to obtain a refinement $M^+(C)$ of M. We build a complete weighted bipartite graph G_b. On one side G_b includes the nodes in $V(G_1) - C$, and on the other side G_b includes the nodes in $V(G_2) - F_2$. For any node $u \in V(G_1) - C$ and node $v \in V(G_2) - F_2$, we add an edge (u, v) in $E(G_b)$, and the weight of the edge (u, v) is defined as follows.

$$w(u, v) = |M[N(u) \cap F_1] \cap (N(v) \cap F_2)| \tag{6}$$

where $N(u)$ and $N(v)$ are the sets of immediate neighbors of u and v in graphs G_1 and G_2 respectively. Intuitively, $w(u, v)$ is the contribution of the matched edges if we match u in graph G_1 with v in graph G_2. Next, we find the maximum weighted bipartite matching M_b of G_b using the Hungarian algorithm, such that the total weight of edges in M_b is maximized. We obtain our new matching $M^+(C)$ as follows.

$$M^+(C) = (M \cap (F_1 \times F_2)) \cup M_b \tag{7}$$

where $F_1 \times F_2$ is the cartesian product of F_1 and F_2. It includes all pairs (u, v) such that $u \in F_1$ and $v \in F_2$.

Example 5.1: Continue with Example 4.4. To make it more simple, let's only consider part of the matching in the initial matching. Suppose the first graph in Fig. 4(a) is the partial graph induced by nodes $\{u_6, u_8, u_{11}, u_{12}, u_{13}\}$ in G_1, and the second graph in Fig. 4(b) is the partial graph induced by nodes $\{v_6, v_8, v_{11}, v_{12}, v_{13}\}$ in G_2. In the initial matching M generated in Example 4.4, only three edges are matched, which is showed as the bold edges in Fig. 4(a) and Fig. 4(b). We have $P_1 = \{u_8, u_{11}, u_{12}, u_{13}\}$ and $P_2 = \{v_8, v_{11}, v_{12}, v_{13}\}$. Suppose $C = \{u_6, u_8, u_{12}\}$, we have $F_1 = C \cap P_1 = \{u_8, u_{12}\}$ and $F_2 = M[F_1] = \{v_8, v_{12}\}$. In the bipartite graph G_b, the left part consists of the nodes in $V(G_1) - C$, which is $\{u_{11}, u_{13}\}$, and the right part consists of the nodes in $V(G_2) - F_2$, which is $\{v_6, v_{11}, v_{13}\}$. The graph G_b is shown in Fig. 4(c). For the edge (u_{11}, v_{11}), its weight is 2 because if we match node u_{11} with node v_{11}, 2 edges will be matched in the original graphs, i.e., edge (u_{11}, u_8) is matched to edge (v_{11}, v_8), and edge (u_{11}, u_{12}) is matched to edge (v_{11}, v_{12}). The maximum weighted bipartite matching of G_b is $M_b = \{(u_{11}, v_{11}), (u_{13}, v_{13})\}$. Thus we can improve the number of matched edges from 18 to 20. Similarly, we can refine matching pairs $\{(u_2, v_7), (u_7, v_2)\}$ to $\{(u_2, v_2), (u_7, v_7)\}$ such that it improves the number of matched edges to 21, which is the optimal value in this example. □

Second, we give the optimality of $M^+(C)$ over a matching space

Algorithm 3 select-random-cover (G)

Input: a graph G;
Output: a randomly selected minimal cover of G;

1: $\mathcal{L} \leftarrow$ shuffled nodes in $V(G)$; $C \leftarrow \emptyset$;
2: **for all** $u \in L$ **do**
3:     **if** $\exists(u, v) \in E(G)$, s.t. $v \notin C$ **then** $C \leftarrow C \cup \{u\}$;
4: **for all** $u \in C$ **do**
5:     **if** $C - \{u\}$ is a vertex cover of G **then** $C \leftarrow C - \{u\}$;
6: **return** C;

Algorithm 4 refine (G_1, G_2, M)

Input: two graphs G_1 and G_2, and the matching M;
Output: a refined matching M;

1: **while** M is updated or it is the first iteration **do**
2:     **for** $i = 1$ **to** X **do**
3:         $G \leftarrow$ random selection between G_1 and G_2;
4:         $C \leftarrow$ select-random-cover (G);
5:         compute $M^+(C)$;
6:         **if** $score(M^+(C)) > score(M)$ **then** $M \leftarrow M^+(C)$;
7: **return** M;

Algorithm 5 refine (G_1, G_2, M)

Input: two graphs G_1 and G_2, and the matching M;
Output: a refined matching M;

1: **while** M is updated or it is the first iteration **do**
2:     **for** $i = 1$ **to** X **do**
3:         $G_F \leftarrow$ random selection between $G_1[P_1]$ and $G_2[P_2]$;
4:         $F \leftarrow$ select-random-cover (G_F);
5:         compute $M^*(F)$;
6:         **if** $score(M^*(F)) > score(M)$ **then** $M \leftarrow M^*(F)$;
7: **return** M;

$\mathcal{M}$. The space $\mathcal{M}$ is a set of matchings between nodes in G_1 and G_2, such that for any matching M', $M' \in \mathcal{M}$ if and only if $M' \cap (F_1 \times F_2) = M \cap (F_1 \times F_2)$ and $M' \cap ((C - F_1) \times V(G_2)) = \emptyset$. For the matching M, a matching $M' \in \mathcal{M}$, if and only if the matching for nodes in F_1 is not changed and the matching for nodes in $C - F_1$ is $\emptyset$. The second condition can also be expressed as $M'[C - F_1] = \emptyset$.

Theorem 5.1: *Suppose* $min = \min\{|V(G_1)| - |C|, |V(G_2)| - |F_2|\}$ *and* $max = \max\{|V(G_1)| - |C|, |V(G_2)| - |F_2|\}$, *then we have (1)* $|\mathcal{M}| = \sum_{i=0}^{min} \frac{min! \times max!}{i! \times (min-i)! \times (max-i)!}$ *and* $\frac{max!}{(max-min)!} \leq |\mathcal{M}| \leq (max+1)^{min}$, *(2)* $M \in \mathcal{M}$, *(3)* $M^+(C) \in \mathcal{M}$ *and (4)* $M^+(C)$ *is optimal in* $\mathcal{M}$. □

The proof sketch is given in the Appendix.

Theorem 5.1 shows that the size of $\mathcal{M}$ is exponentially large. Both M and $M^+(C)$ are elements in $\mathcal{M}$, and $M^+(C)$ is the optimal matching for all matchings in $\mathcal{M}$. It implies that $M^+(C)$ is the best among a large number of matchings in $\mathcal{M}$ and $score(M^+(C)) \geq score(M)$. For two graphs with 2000 nodes each, the number of nodes in a vertex cover can be assumed as 1,000 (50%) reasonably. According to Remark 5.1, $M^+(C)$ is the best among a factorial of 1,000 (1,000) possible matchings.

5.3 Randomly Refine Excluding $C - F_1$

If M itself is an optimal matching in $\mathcal{M}$, or the selected vertex cover C includes most nodes in G_1 that are not well matched, it is possible that $M^+(C)$ cannot improve M. As an example, suppose $C = \{u_{11}, u_{12}, u_{13}\}$, in Example 5.1, then the new bipartite graph G_b is the one shown in Fig. 4(d). In other words, using the maximum weighted bipartite matching of G_b, the matching $M^+(C)$ might be the same with M. The reason is that the mismatched nodes are excluded by the vertex cover C to refine. We give an approach based on two strategies to solve such a problem. (1) Making C smaller, such that more mismatched nodes can be included and thus can be used to refine. (2) Iteratively refining the current matching using different vertex covers, such that every mismatched node will have a chance to be included to refine. The first strategy is based on the following Lemma.

Lemma 5.1: *For any two vertex covers* C_1 *and* C_2 *of* G_1, *if* $C_1 \subseteq C_2$, *then* $score(M^+(C_1)) \geq score(M^+(C_2))$. □

The proof sketch is given in the Appendix.

In order to make C small, a straightforward way is to find the minimum vertex cover of G_1. This method is not practical for two reasons. (1) Finding a minimum vertex cover of a graph is NP-hard. (2) In a minimum vertex cover, the mismatched nodes do not have a chance to be included to refine. To avoid these, we use a minimal vertex cover instead, because (1) a minimal vertex cover is easy to be found, and (2) the number of different minimal vertex covers for a graph is much larger than the number of different minimum vertex covers. Thus, a minimal vertex cover gives the mismatched nodes in a minimum vertex cover more chances to be refined.

The approach to randomly select a minimal vertex cover of graph G is shown in Algorithm 3. First, in line 1, we shuffle all nodes in the graph and put them into a list $\mathcal{L}$, such that any permutation of $V(G)$ has the same probability in $\mathcal{L}$. In line 2-3, we find a vertex cover of G by adding node in $\mathcal{L}$ one by one. For any node to be added, we add it into the vertex cover if and only if it contributes at least one edge to the currently covered edges (line 3). Line 4-5 makes the current vertex cover minimal by removing those useless nodes, such that the removal of such nodes does not influence any edge currently covered. The following lemma shows that, for any minimal cover C of a graph G, there are considerable number of ways for Algorithm 3 to generate C.

Lemma 5.2: *For any minimal vertex cover* C *of graph* G, *there are at least* $|C| \times |V(G) - C|$ *permutations of* $V(G)$, *such that Algorithm 3 generates* C. □

The proof sketch is given in the Appendix.

The main refine approach is an iterative algorithm shown in Algorithm 4. We iteratively update the current matching until the matching is not improved in a certain iteration. In each iteration (line 2-6), we try X times to find a new random minimal vertex cover C (line 4), generate the matching $M^+(C)$ using the method introduced above (line 5), and update the current matching if $M^+(C)$ is a better matching (line 6). Here, X is a constant (≥ 1) in order to avoid selecting a bad cover to terminate the whole process. In our experiments, when $X = 5$ and $X = 10$ over 92% and 99% of the nodes have a chance to be included to refine. We use $X = 5$. Note that in line 3, we choose C to be a vertex cover of either G_1 or G_2 with the same probability to increase the randomness.

Theorem 5.2: *The time complexity of Algorithm 4 is* $O(m \cdot n^3)$, *for* $m = \min\{|E(G_1)|, |E(G_2)|\}$ *and* $n = \max\{|V(G_1)|, |V(G_2)|\}$. □

The proof sketch is given in the Appendix.

Theorem 5.2 shows an upper bound of the time complexity for Algorithm 4. In practice, the processing time for the algorithm is much smaller than the upper bound because the initial matching M has already matched a lot of edges.

5.4 Randomly Refine Including $C - F_1$

In this section, we show that $M^+(C)$ can be further improved. Recall that in our previous approach to compute $M^+(C)$, the nodes in $C - F_1$ of G_1 are excluded to refine. In order to refine the

Table 1: The PN dataset

Graph	g1	g2	g3	g4	g5
$\|V\|$	118	443	1,454	1,723	5,300
$\|E\|$	179	590	1,923	2,394	6,094

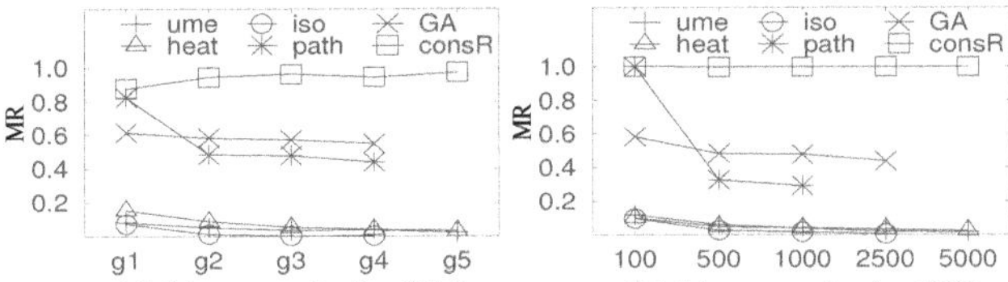

(a) Vary graph size(PN) (b) Vary graph size(SF)

Figure 5: Vary Graph Size

nodes in $C - F_1$, we build a new weighted bipartite graph G_b^* as follows. On one side G_b^* includes all nodes in $V(G_1) - F_1$, and on the other side G_b^* includes all nodes in $V(G_2) - F_2$. For any node $v \in V(G_1) - F_1$ and node $u \in V(G_2) - F_2$, there is an edge $(u, v) \in E(G_b^*)$ with weight defined in Eq. (6). Suppose the maximum weighted bipartite matching of G_b^* is M_b^*, the new matching $M^*(F_1)$ is defined as follows.

$$M^*(F_1) = (M \cap (F_1 \times F_2)) \cup M_b^* \quad (8)$$

We define a matching space $\mathcal{M}^*$ as follows. For any matching M' between graphs G_1 and G_2, $M' \in \mathcal{M}^*$ if and only if $M' \cap (F_1 \times F_2) = M \cap (F_1 \times F_2)$ and $F_1 \cup (V(G_1) - P_1 - M'^{-1}[V(G_2) - P_2])$ is a vertex cover of G_1. We have the following theorem.

Theorem 5.3: *$\mathcal{M} \subseteq \mathcal{M}^*$ and suppose $M^*_{\mathcal{M}}$ is the optimal solution among all matchings in $\mathcal{M}^*$, we have $score(M^*(F_1)) \geq score(M^*_{\mathcal{M}}) \geq score(M^+(C))$.* □

The proof sketch is given in the Appendix.

Theorem 5.3 implies that the new space $\mathcal{M}^*$ is larger than the space $\mathcal{M}$ in refinement excluding $C - F_1$, and the new matching $M^*(F_1)$ is no worse than the optimal matching in $\mathcal{M}^*$. This implies that $score(M^*(F_1)) \geq score(M^+(C))$, where $M^+(C)$ is the optimal matching in $\mathcal{M}$. It is worth noticing that the cover C of G_1 does not participate in the construction of $M^*(F_1)$ directly. The matching $M^*(F_1)$ can be computed as long as F_1 is generated, and F_1 can be computed easily by the following lemma.

Lemma 5.3: *Suppose $G_1[P_1]$ is the subgraph of G_1 induced by P_1. If C is a vertex cover of G_1, then $C \cap P_1$ is a vertex cover of $G_1[P_1]$, and if C_{P_1} is a vertex cover of $G_1[P_1]$, then there exists a vertex cover C of G_1 such that $C_{P_1} \subseteq C$.* □

The proof sketch is given in the Appendix.

Based on Lemma 5.3, we can derive that the vertex cover of $G(P_1)$, F_1, is enough generate $M^*(F_1)$. Our new refinement algorithm is shown in Algorithm 5 which is the refine used in Algorithm 1. We use $X = 5$. Comparing to Algorithm 4, there are two major modifications. The first is about the cover computing in line 3-4, instead of computing the cover of G_1 (or G_2 if we select G_2 as the first graph in line 3), we only compute the vertex cover of $G_1[P_1]$ (or $G_2[P_2]$). For the second modification, instead of computing $M^+(C)$, we compute our new matching $M^*(F)$.

6. PERFORMANCE STUDIES

We compare our algorithms, cons (matching construction only) and consR (matching construction plus matching refinement), with five state of the art graph matching algorithms: ume, heat, iso, path, and GA. Here, ume is the improved Umeyama algorithm in [21, 9], and heat, iso, path, and GA are the algorithms proposed in [23], [18], [25], and [24], respectively. We implement ume, heat

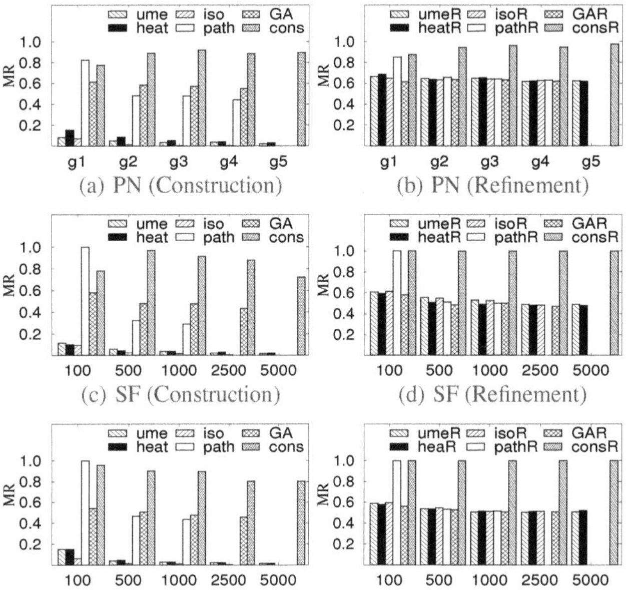

(a) PN (Construction) (b) PN (Refinement)

(c) SF (Construction) (d) SF (Refinement)

(e) ER (Construction) (f) ER (Refinement)

Figure 6: Vary Initial Matching

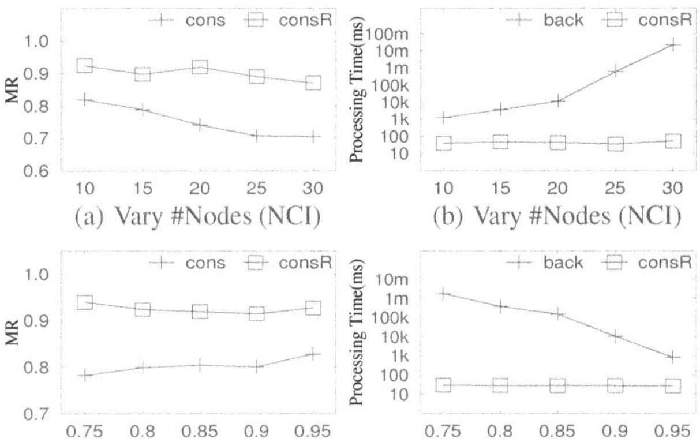

(a) Vary #Nodes (NCI) (b) Vary #Nodes (NCI)

(c) Vary Optimal Solution (NCI) (d) Vary Optimal Solution (NCI)

Figure 7: Test the NCI dataset

and our algorithm using Visual C++ 2005 and Matlab R2009a. The C++ part calls Matlab to compute the eigenvalues and eigenvectors of the matrix, and executes the rest of the algorithm in C++. For iso, path, and GA, we download the source code of the graph matching package GraphM[1]. All tests were conducted on a 2.66GHz CPU and 3.43GB memory PC running Windows XP.

We evaluated the algorithms using both real and synthetic datasets. The real datasets include the Power Network and the NCI dataset. The synthetic datasets are generated using two models, namely, Scale-Free/Power Law Model and Erdos Renyi Model. We use software Pajek[2] to generate graphs under these two models.

Power Network (PN) is the electrical power grid of the western US selected from the University of Florida Sparse Matrix Collection[3]. The nodes are generators, transformers, and substations, and the edges are the high-voltage transmission lines between them. The graphs are proved to be power law networks [22, 4]. The dataset contains graphs with number of nodes varying from 39 to 5,300. The information of graphs used in our testing is shown in Table 1.

[1] http://cbio.ensmp.fr/graphm/

[2] http://vlado.fmf.uni-lj.si/pub/networks/pajek/

[3] http://math.nist.gov/MatrixMarket/data/Harwell-Boeing/bcspwr/bcspwr.html

Table 2: Processing Time Comparison (PN)

Graph	g1	g2	g3	g4	g5
selection (sec)	0.047	0.453	20.406	33.109	1,221.578
expansion (sec)	0.016	0.078	1.109	0.968	32.921
refinement (sec)	0.046	0.719	6.812	10.453	205.045
consR (sec)	0.109	1.250	28.327	44.530	1459.544
ume (sec)	0.047	0.484	20.625	33.412	1561.578
heat (sec)	0.109	2.063	72.794	116.467	4117.504
iso (sec)	0.12	2	185	57	-
path (sec)	14	411	11700	22200	-
GA (sec)	1	8	150	253	-

NCI dataset (NCI) contains the compound structures from the National Cancer Institute Open Database[4]. The NCI dataset contains 233,281 connected graphs. The average node number is 21.17 and the average node degree is 2.2. According to the number of nodes in a graph, we selected 5 groups, containing graphs with node numbers 10 ± 4, 15 ± 4, 20 ± 4, 25 ± 4, and 30 ± 4, respectively.

Scale-Free/Power Law Model (SF) is a network model whose node degrees follow the power law distribution or at least asymptotically. We generate graphs with node numbers 100, 500, 1,000, 2,500, and 5,000, respectively, with default value 1,000. The average node degree is 4.

Erdos Renyi Model (ER) is a classical random graph model. It defines a random graph as N nodes connected by M edges that are chosen randomly from the $N(N-1)/2$ possible edges. We generate graphs with node numbers 100, 500, 1,000, 2,500, and 5,000, respectively, with default value 1,000. The average node degree is 4.

For NCI, since each graph is small, we can compute the optimal matching for each pair of graphs using backtracking method. For graphs in other datasets, it is impossible to compute the optimal matching. Therefore, for any graph G_1, we generate G_2 by randomly inserting/deleting a certain percent of nodes/edges followed by shuffling all nodes. The average percentage is 0.2. We set the parameters used in our algorithms as follows. For threshold τ used in anchor selection, we traversal interval [0.5, 1] with step size 0.02 and choose the one that generate the best result in matching construction. For k in the k-neighborhood definition, we vary it from 0 to 4 and find $k = 2$ achieves the best result in most cases. Thus we set k to 2 in the experiment.

We use matching ratio as our measure for the matching quality, which is computed as $MR = \frac{actual\ matched\ edges}{optimal\ matched\ edges}$.

6.1 Comparison with the Approximate Algorithms

Vary Graph Size: We vary the number of nodes in the graphs from 100 to 5,000 and test the matching ratio of each algorithm on PN, SF, and ER. The results for PN and SF are shown in Fig. 5(a) and Fig. 5(b). The results for ER dataset share the same patterns. For all cases, the matching ratios for ume, heat and iso algorithms are no larger than 0.2. It is because all the three algorithms get the matching by maximizing the total weight of the similarity matrix and consider little about their neighborhood information of two nodes. When the numbers of nodes are no large than 120, the performance of path is similar to consR, and reaches a matching ratio above 0.9. When the sizes of the graphs increase, the matching ratio of path decrease. GA performs better than path for large graphs, but still much worse than consR in all cases. When the sizes of the graphs are above 2,500, iso, path, and GA can not generate a result for some cases under our current computing environment. path even can not generate a result for graphs with more than 2,000 nodes.

[4]http://cactus.nci.nih.gov/download/nci/

Table 3: Sensitivity of Randomness

Graph	g1	g2	g3	g4	g5
average MR	0.860	0.950	0.961	0.949	0.975
standard deviation	0.008	0.008	0.002	0.003	0.002

Vary Initial Matching: We compare ume, heat, iso, path, and GA with our matching construction algorithm cons. Fig. 6(a) shows the results for PN. In most cases, cons performs best among all algorithms. The only exception is the case when the numbers of nodes in graphs are smaller than 120, where path performs better than cons. Fig. 6(b) shows the results by applying our matching refinement algorithm to these five algorithms. Accordingly, they are denoted as umeR, heatR, isoR, pathR, and GAR. For ume, heat, and iso, the matching ratios increase 0.5 after refinement in all cases. Our consR algorithm performs best in all cases after refinement even for the case when the numbers of nodes in the graphs are smaller than 120. Fig. 6(c) and Fig. 6(d) show the testing results for SF. Our algorithms perform best both before and after refinement in all cases. The results for ER are shown in Fig. 6(e) and Fig. 6(f). The performances for ER are similar to those in SF.

Efficiency Testing: We test the efficiency of the algorithms with PN. The processing time is shown in Table 2. We divide the whole processing time of our algorithm into three phases, namely, selection, expansion and refinement, denoting the processing time for anchor selection, anchor expansion, and matching refinement respectively. The processing time for consR is the sum of the time for all the three phases. For the three phases, in all cases, the most costly part is anchor selection, because it involves calculating the eigenvalues for matrices. In all test cases, our consR algorithm is faster than iso, heat, path, and GA, and is similar to ume. For the largest graph g5, the total processing time for consR is smaller than 25 minutes, while heat needs more than one hour and iso, path, and GA even can not generate a result under our current computing environment.

6.2 Comparison with the Exact Algorithm

With NCI, we randomly select 10 pairs of graphs from each group of graphs with different node numbers. For each pair, we compute the optimal matching by backtracking using the best upper bound introduced in [16]. For each group, we record the average processing time for backtracking and our algorithm as well as the average matching ratio in the two steps of our algorithm. The results are shown in Fig. 7(a) and Fig. 7(b). When node number increases from 10 to 30, the processing time of backtracking increases from 1 to 100,000 seconds and consR algorithm consumes ≤ 0.1 second in all cases. The average accuracy (matching ratio) for cons is 0.8 and the average accuracy for consR is 0.95.

We randomly select 1,000 pairs from the group of graphs with 20 ± 4 nodes. For each pair, we compute the ratio of the optimal matched edges to the size of the smaller graph, and vary the ratio from 0.75 to 0.95. For each ratio, we compute the average processing time and average accuracy of our algorithm. The results are shown in Fig. 7(c) and Fig. 7(d). When the ratio increases from 0.75 to 0.95, the processing time of the backtracking algorithm decreases from 10,000 seconds to 1 second. This is because when the ratio is large, the upper bound used to cut branches in the backtracking is tight [16], thus the algorithm stops early. Our consR algorithm consumes no more than 0.1 second in all cases. The average accuracy (matching ratio) for our cons algorithm is 0.8 and the average accuracy for our consR algorithm is 0.95.

6.3 Sensitivity of Randomness(PN)

In the refinement step, each vertex cover is randomly selected. In order to test the sensitivity of such randomness, for each test case, we run our program for 100 times, and calculate their average match ratio (MR) as well as the standard deviation of the 100 match ratios. The average match ratio (MR) and the standard deviation for the PN dataset are shown in Table 3. For each test case, the standard deviation is very small. It means that no matter how the vertex covers are randomly selected, the program will generate almost the same result. There are two reasons. First, the nodes that largely influence the stability of results are those with large degrees, and with high probability such nodes will be selected in a vertex cover. Second, our refinement algorithm is an iterative algorithm and it stops when converged. In each iteration, every vertex cover has chances to be refined. The results for SF and ER datasets are similar with those in the PN dataset.

7. CONCLUSION

In this paper, we study how to find matching of two large graphs or how to score how similar two large graphs can be in terms of the possibly max number of matched edges. This is known to be NP-hard. We give a new two-step approach which ensures high efficiency and high quality. We conducted extensive testing using real and synthetic datasets, and confirmed the quality and efficiency of our approach.

Acknowledgments The work was supported by grants of the Research Grants Council of the Hong Kong SAR, China No. 419008 and 419109.

8. REFERENCES

[1] F. N. Abu-Khzam, N. F. Samatova, M. A. Rizk, and M. A. Langston. The maximum common subgraph problem: Faster solutions via vertex cover. In *AICCSA*, pages 367–373, 2007.

[2] H. A. Almohamad and S. O. Duffuaa. A linear programming approach for the weighted graph matching problem. *IEEE Trans. Pattern Anal. Mach. Intell.*, 15(5):522–525, 1993.

[3] X. Bai, H. Yu, and E. R. Hancock. Graph matching using spectral embedding and alignment. In *ICPR*, pages 398–401, 2004.

[4] A. Barabási and R. Albert. Emergence of scaling in random networks. *Science*, 286(5439):509, 1999.

[5] M. Bernard, N. Richard, and J. Paquereau. Functionnal brain imaging by eeg graph-matching. In *IEEE EMBS Conference*, 2005.

[6] V. D. Blondel, A. Gajardo, M. Heymans, P. Senellart, and P. V. Dooren. A measure of similarity between graph vertices: Applications to synonym extraction and web searching. *Siam Review*, 46(4):647–666, 2004.

[7] T. Caelli and S. Kosinov. An eigenspace projection clustering method for inexact graph matching. *IEEE Trans. Pattern Anal. Mach. Intell.*, 26(4):515–519, 2004.

[8] F. Chevalier, J.-P. Domenger, J. Benois-Pineau, and M. Delest. Retrieval of objects in video by similarity based on graph matching. *Pattern Recognition Letters*, 28(8):939–949, 2007.

[9] D. Knossow, A. Sharma, D. Mateus, and R. Horaud. Inexact matching of large and sparse graphs using laplacian eigenvectors. In *GbRPR*, pages 144–153, 2009.

[10] I. Koch. Enumerating all connected maximal common subgraphs in two graphs. *Theor. Comput. Sci.*, 250(1-2):1–30, 2001.

[11] E. B. Krissinel and K. Henrick. Common subgraph isomorphism detection by backtracking search. *Softw., Pract. Exper.*, 34(6):591–607, 2004.

[12] W.-J. Lee and R. P. W. Duin. An inexact graph comparison approach in joint eigenspace. In *SSPR/SPR*, pages 35–44, 2008.

[13] J. J. McGregor. Backtrack search algorithms and the maximal common subgraph problem. *Softw., Pract. Exper.*, 12(1):23–34, 1982.

[14] H. Ogata, W. Fujibuchi, S. Goto, and M. Kanehisa. A heuristic graph comparison algorithm and its application to detect functionally related enzyme clusters. *Nucleic Acids Research*, 28(20):4021–4028, 2000.

[15] H. Qiu and E. R. Hancock. Graph matching and clustering using spectral partitions. *Pattern Recognition*, 39(1):22–34, 2006.

[16] J. W. Raymond, E. J. Gardiner, and P. Willett. Rascal: Calculation of graph similarity using maximum common edge subgraphs. *Comput. J.*, 45(6):631–644, 2002.

[17] K. Riesen, X. Jiang, and H. Bunke. Exact and inexact graph matching: Methodology and applications. *Managing and Mining Graph Data*, pages 217–247, 2010.

[18] R. Singh, J. Xu, and B. Berger. Pairwise global alignment of protein interaction networks by matching neighborhood topology. In *RECOMB*, pages 16–31, 2007.

[19] W. H. Suters, F. N. Abu-Khzam, Y. Zhang, C. T. Symons, N. F. Samatova, and M. A. Langston. A new approach and faster exact methods for the maximum common subgraph problem. In *COCOON*, pages 717–727, 2005.

[20] J. Ullmann. An algorithm for subgraph isomorphism. *JACM*, 23(1):42, 1976.

[21] S. Umeyama. An eigendecomposition approach to weighted graph matching problems. *IEEE Trans. Pattern Anal. Mach. Intell.*, 10(5):695–703, 1988.

[22] D. Watts and S. Strogatz. Collective dynamics of 'small-world' networks. *Nature*, 393(6684):440–442, 1998.

[23] B. Xiao, E. R. Hancock, and R. C. Wilson. A generative model for graph matching and embedding. *Computer Vision and Image Understanding*, 113(7):777–789, 2009.

[24] M. Zaslavskiy, F. R. Bach, and J.-P. Vert. Global alignment of protein-protein interaction networks by graph matching methods. *Bioinformatics*, 25(12), 2009.

[25] M. Zaslavskiy, F. R. Bach, and J.-P. Vert. A path following algorithm for the graph matching problem. *IEEE Trans. Pattern Anal. Mach. Intell.*, 31(12):2227–2242, 2009.

APPENDIX

Proof sketch of Theorem 5.1: We prove it step by step.

(1) To make things simple and without loss of generality, we assume $|V(G_1)|-|C| \leq |V(G_2)|-|F_2|$, then $min = |V(G_1)|-|C|$ and $max = |V(G_2)| - |F_2|$. Since $V(G_1) - C$ and $V(G_2) - F_2$ are the included parts of G_1 and G_2 respectively, we only consider the number of different matchings between $V(G_1) - C$ and $V(G_2) - F_2$. Suppose in $V(G_1) - C$, there are i nodes that participate in the matching in $\mathcal{M}$, there are C^i_{min} different selections of the i nodes, and for each selection, there are P^i_{max} different matchings between the i nodes and nodes in $V(G_2) - F_2$. There are totally $C^i_{min} \times P^i_{max}$ different matchings for a certain i. Since $i \in [0, min]$, the total number of different matchings is $|\mathcal{M}| = \sum_{i=0}^{min} C^i_{min} \times P^i_{max} = \sum_{i=0}^{min} \frac{min! \times max!}{i! \times (min-i)! \times (max-i)!}$. When $i = min$, we have $|\mathcal{M}| \geq C^i_{min} \times P^i_{max} = \frac{max!}{(max-min)!}$. If we remove the constraint that different nodes in $V(G_1) - C$ must match different nodes in $V(G_2) - F_2$, each node in $V(G_1) - C$ will have $max + 1$ choices include max nodes in $V(G_2) - F_2$ and an empty match. The number of different relaxed matchings is then changed to $(max + 1)^{min}$ which is an upper bound of $|\mathcal{M}|$.

(2) We only need to prove that M satisfies the two conditions of $\mathcal{M}$. For the first condition, obviously, $M \cap (F_1 \times F_2) = M \cap (F_1 \times F_2)$. For the second condition, the part $C - F_1$ is the nodes in C that are not matched in M, so $M[C - F_1] = \emptyset$. As a result, $M \cap ((C - F_1) \times V(G_2)) = \emptyset$.

(3) We need show that $M^+(C)$ satisfies the two conditions of $\mathcal{M}$.

- For the first condition, we have $M^+(C) \cap (F_1 \times F_2) = ((M \cap (F_1 \times F_2)) \cup M_b) \cap (F_1 \times F_2) = (M \cap (F_1 \times F_2)) \cup (M_b \cap (F_1 \times F_2))$. Since M_b only includes nodes in $V(G_1) - C$ and $V(G_2) - F_2$, we have $M_b \cap (F_1 \times F_2) = \emptyset$. As a result, $M^+(C) \cap (F_1 \times F_2) = M \cap (F_1 \times F_2)$.
- For the second condition, $M^+(C) \cap ((C - F_1) \times V(G_2)) = ((M \cap (F_1 \times F_2)) \cup M_b) \cap ((C - F_1) \times V(G_2)) = ((M \cap (F_1 \times F_2)) \cap ((C - F_1) \times V(G_2))) \cup (M_b \cap ((C - F_1) \times V(G_2)))$. $(M \cap (F_1 \times F_2)) \cap ((C - F_1) \times V(G_2)) = \emptyset$ because $M \cap ((C - F_1) \times V(G_2)) = \emptyset$ is already proved in (2) and $M_b \cap ((C - F_1) \times V(G_2)) = \emptyset$ due to the fact

that M_b does not contain any nodes in $C - F_1$. As a result, $M^+(C) \cap ((C - F_1) \times V(G_2)) = \emptyset$.

(4) For any matching $M' \in \mathcal{M}$ we define a matching M'_b as $M'_b = M' \cap ((V(G_1) - C) \times (V(G_2) - F_2))$. We use $score_b(M_b)$ to denote the total weight for the bipartite matching M_b of the bipartite graph G_b. We claim (a) M'_b is a bipartite matching of G_b, (b) $score(M') = score_b(M'_b) + score(M \cap (F_1 \times F_2))$ and (c) $score(M^+(C)) = score_b(M_b) + score(M \cap (F_1 \times F_2))$.

- For (a), it is obvious because of two reasons. (1)M'_b only contains the nodes in $V(G_1) - C$ and $V(G_2) - F_2$, which is exactly the set of nodes in G_b. (2) Any edge in M'_b is also an edge of G_b since G_b is a complete bipartite graph.
- For (b), we have $score(M') = score(M' \cap ((C \cup (V(G_1) - C)) \times (F_2 \cup (V(G_2) - F_2)))) = score((M' \cap (C \times F_2)) \cup (M' \cap (C \times (V(G_2) - F_2))) \cup (M' \cap ((V(G_1) - C) \times F_2)) \cup (M' \cap ((V(G_1) - C) \times (V(G_2) - F_2))))$. Since $C \times F_2$, $C \times (V(G_2) - F_2)$, $(V(G_1) - C) \times F_2$ and $(V(G_1) - C) \times (V(G_2) - F_2)$ are mutually exclusive with each other, we have $score(M') = score(M' \cap (C \times F_2)) + score(M' \cap (C \times (V(G_2) - F_2))) + score(M' \cap ((V(G_1) - C) \times F_2)) + score(M' \cap ((V(G_1) - C) \times (V(G_2) - F_2)))$. Since $M'[F_1] = F_2$ and $M'[C - F_1] = \emptyset$, we have $M'[C] = M'[F_1] \cup M'[C - F_1] = F_2$, and thus $M' \cap (C \times (V(G_2) - F_2)) = \emptyset$. Since $M'^{-1}[F_2] = F_1$ and $F_1 \subseteq C$, we have $M' \cap ((V(G_1) - C) \times F_2) = \emptyset$. We also have $M' \cap (C \times F_2) = M' \cap (((C - F_1) \cup F_1) \times F_2) = (M' \cap ((C - F_1) \times F_2)) \cup (M' \cap (F_1 \times F_2)) = M' \cap (F_1 \times F_2)$. The last equation is due to $M' \cap ((C - F_1) \times F_2) = \emptyset$ because $M'[C - F_1] = \emptyset$. Now we can derive $score(M') = score(M' \cap (F_1 \times F_2)) + score(M' \cap ((V(G_1) - C) \times (V(G_2) - F_2))) = score(M \cap (F_1 \times F_2)) + score(M'_b)$ since $M' \cap (F_1 \times F_2) = M \cap (F_1 \times F_2)$. We only need to prove $score(M'_b) = score_b(M'_b)$. Since $V(G_1) - C$ is a independent set which only have edges with C and C is the excluded part of the matching M', we can derive that $score(M' \cap ((V(G_1) - C) \times (V(G_2) - F_2)))$ only consists of the contributions of the edges $(u, v) \in E(G_1)$ such that $u \in C$ and $v \in V(G_1) - C$. From the construction of G_b, the contribution for each $v \in V(G_1) - C$ in M' is just the weight $(v, M'[v])$ in the bipartite graph G_b. This implies $score(M'_b) = score_b(M'_b)$.
- For (c), it can be easily derived from (b) because $M^+(C) \in \mathcal{M}$ and $M_b = M^+(C) \cap ((V(G_1) - C) \times (V(G_2) - F_2))$. We now prove(4). Since M_b is the maximum weight bipartite matching of G_b, we have $cost_b(M_b) \geq cost_b(M'_b)$, therefore $score(M^+(C)) = score_b(M_b) + score(M \cap (F_1 \times F_2)) \geq score_b(M'_b) + score(M \cap (F_1 \times F_2)) = score(M')$. As a result, $M^+(C)$ is the optimal solution in $\mathcal{M}$.

The theorem holds. □

Proof sketch of Lemma 5.1: Suppose $\mathcal{M}(C_1)$ and $\mathcal{M}(C_2)$ are the matching spaces generated by C_1 and C_2 respectively. We use $F_1(C_1)$, $F_1(C_2)$, $F_2(C_1)$, and $F_2(C_2)$ to denote F_1 generated by C_1, F_1 generated by C_2, F_2 generated by C_1, and F_2 generated by C_2, respectively. Since we have $F_1(C_1) \subseteq F_1(C_2)$ and $F_2(C_1) \subseteq F_2(C_2)$, we need show $\mathcal{M}(C_2) \subseteq \mathcal{M}(C_1)$. For any $M' \in \mathcal{M}(C_2)$, we have $M' \cap (F_1(C_2) \times F_2(C_2)) = M \cap (F_1(C_2) \times F_2(C_2))$ and $M' \cap ((C_2 - F_1(C_2)) \times V(G_2)) = \emptyset$. Since $F_1(C_1) \times F_2(C_1) \subseteq F_1(C_2) \times F_2(C_2)$, we can derive $M' \cap (F_1(C_1) \times F_2(C_1)) = M \cap (F_1(C_1) \times F_2(C_1))$. We also have $C_1 - F_1(C_1) \subseteq C_2 - F_1(C_2)$, thus $M' \cap ((C_1 - F_1(C)) \times V(G_2)) = \emptyset$, and accordingly $M' \in \mathcal{M}(C_1)$. As a result, $\mathcal{M}(C_2) \subseteq \mathcal{M}(C_1)$. Since $M^+(C_1)$ and $M^+(C_2)$ are the optimal solutions in $\mathcal{M}(C_1)$ and $\mathcal{M}(C_2)$ respectively, we have $score(M^+(C_1)) \geq score(M^+(C_2))$. □

Proof sketch of Lemma 5.2: We construct the $|C| \times |V(G) - C|$ permutations as follows. For each permutation, we put C in the front in any order followed by $V(G) - C$ in any order. The number of such permutations is $|C| \times |V(G) - C|$. Now we prove for any such permutation, Algorithm 3 can generate C. Since C is minimal, in the first $|C|$ loops of line 2-3 of Algorithm 3, the conditions in line 3 are all satisfied, and in the last $|V(G) - C|$ loops of line 2-3, the conditions in line 3 are all unsatisfied because C is already a vertex cover of G. So after the loop in line 2-3, C is generated. Since C is already minimal, the loop in line 4-5 will eliminate no node. Thus, Algorithm 3 can generate C. □

Proof sketch of Theorem 5.2: Algorithm 4 is the main refinement. The while loop in line 1 will repeat for at most m times because the optimal solution can match at most m edges and in each loop, the number of edges for the latest solution will be increased for at least 1. In each loop, the dominate part is finding the maximum weight bipartite matching using the Hungarian algorithm which can be done in $O(n^3)$. Since X is a constant, the total time complexity for Algorithm 4 is $O(m \cdot n^3)$. □

Proof sketch of Theorem 5.3: For $\forall\ M' \in \mathcal{M}$, we have $M' \cap (F_1 \times F_2) = M \cap (F_1 \times F_2)$ and $M'[C - F_1] = \emptyset$. The first condition is the same as the first condition of $\mathcal{M}^*$. Since $M'[C - F_1] = \emptyset$, we have $(C - F_1) \cap M'^{-1}[V(G_2) - P_2] = \emptyset$. We also have $(C - F_1) \cup M'^{-1}[V(G_2) - P_2] \subseteq V(G_1) - P_1$, accordingly, $C - F_1 \subseteq V(G_1) - P_1 - M'^{-1}[V(G_2) - P_2]$, and thus $C \subseteq F_1 \cup (V(G_1) - P_1 - M'^{-1}[V(G_2) - P_2])$. Since C is a vertex cover of G_1, $F_1 \cup (V(G_1) - P_1 - M'^{-1}[V(G_2) - P_2])$ is a vertex cover of G_1, hence we have $M' \in \mathcal{M}^*$. Thus $\mathcal{M} \subseteq \mathcal{M}^*$ holds.

We now prove that $score(M^*(F_1)) \geq score(M^*_{\mathcal{M}})$. Suppose $C^* = F_1 \cup (V(G_1) - P_1 - M^{*-1}_{\mathcal{M}}[V(G_2) - P_2])$, we know C^* is a vertex cover of G_1. Since $M^*_{\mathcal{M}}[V(G_1) - P_1] \subseteq V(G_2) - P_2$, we have $M^*_{\mathcal{M}}[C^* - F_1] = M^*_{\mathcal{M}}[V(G_1) - P_1 - M^{*-1}_{\mathcal{M}}[V(G_2) - P_2]] = \emptyset$, so $M^*_{\mathcal{M}} \in \mathcal{M}$ using vertex cover C^*. This implies $score(M^*_{\mathcal{M}}) = score(M \cap (F_1 \times F_2)) + score_b(M_b)$ (see the proof of Theorem 5.1), where M_b is the maximum weight bipartite matching of G_b generated by C^*. We also have $score(M^*(F_1)) \geq score(M \cap (F_1 \times F_2)) + score_b(M^*_b)$. Since $G_b \subseteq G^*_b$, we have $score(M^*(F_1)) \geq score(M \cap (F_1 \times F_2)) + score_b(M^*_b) \geq score(M \cap (F_1 \times F_2)) + score_b(M_b) = score(M^*_{\mathcal{M}})$.

We last prove $score(M^*_{\mathcal{M}}) \geq score(M^+(C))$. This can be derived directly from $\mathcal{M} \subseteq \mathcal{M}^*$ since $M^*_{\mathcal{M}}$ is optimal in $\mathcal{M}^*$ and $M^+(C)$ is optimal in $\mathcal{M}$. □

Proof sketch of Lemma 5.3: We first prove that if C is a vertex cover of G_1, then $C \cap P_1$ is a vertex cover of $G_1[P_1]$. Suppose $C \cap P_1$ is not a vertex cover of $G_1[P_1]$, then there exists an edge $(u, v) \in E(G_1[P_1])$ such that $u \notin C \cap P_1$ and $v \notin C \cap P_1$. Note that C is a vertex cover of G_1, we have $u \in C$ or $v \in C$. Without loss of generality, we suppose $u \in C$, since $u \notin C \cap P_1$, we have $u \in C - (C \cap P_1)$, this contradicts with $u \in V(G_1[P_1])$. Accordingly, we prove $C \cap P_1$ is a vertex cover of $G_1[P_1]$.

We then prove that if C_{P_1} is a vertex cover of $G_1[P_1]$, then there exists a vertex cover C of G_1 such that $C_{P_1} \subseteq C$. We only need to prove that $C = C_{P_1} \cup (V(G_1) - P_1)$ is a vertex cover of G_1. For any $(u, v) \in E(G_1)$, if $u \in P_1$ and $v \in P_1$, (u, v) is covered by C because C_{P_1} is a vertex cover of $G_1[P_1]$. Otherwise, without loss of generality, we suppose $u \notin P_1$, then $u \in V(G_1) - P_1 \subseteq C$, so (u, v) is also covered by C. As a result, all edged in $E(G_1)$ can be covered by C, thus C is a vertex cover of G_1. □

DELTA: Indexing and Querying Multi-labeled Graphs

Jiong Yang, Shijie Zhang, and Wei Jin
EECS Department, Case Western Reserve University
Cleveland, OH, USA
jiong.yang@case.edu, shijie.zhang@case.edu, wei.jin@case.edu

ABSTRACT

With the emergence of social networks and computational biology, more data are in the forms of multi-labeled graphs, where a vertex has multiple labels. Since most algorithms focus only on single labeled graphs, these algorithms perform inefficiently when applied to multi-labeled graphs. In this paper, we investigate the problem of subgraph indexing and matching in the multi-labeled graphs. The label set on a vertex is transformed into a high dimensional box. The R-tree is employed to store and index these boxes. The vertex matching problem can be transformed into spatial range queries on the high dimensional space. In addition, we study two types of queries: location and existence queries. In this paper, detailed algorithms are provided to process these two types of queries. Real and synthetic data sets are employed to demonstrate the efficiency and effectiveness of our subgraph indexing and query processing methods.

CATEGORIES H.3.1 Content Analysis and Indexing

GENERAL TERMS Algorithms, Theory

KEYWORDS Multiple labeled graphs, R-Tree, Subgraph query

1. INTRODUCTION

With the emergence of bioinformatics and social sciences, a large amount of data can be represented as graphs. There is an increasing interest in developing fast indexing and querying algorithms that operate on graphs. Most algorithms can only work on single labeled graphs, e.g., a vertex has only one label, while many real world graphs are multi-labeled. The following are some examples.

In protein interaction networks, vertices representing proteins, an edge is added between two proteins if an interaction exists between them. The label of the vertex is the protein's function annotations, e.g., gene ontology terms. The ontology consists of three domains: (1) cellular component, the parts of a cell or its extracellular environment; (2) molecular function, the elemental activities of a gene product at the molecular level, such as binding or catalysis; and (3) biological process, operations or sets of molecular events with a defined beginning and end, pertinent to the functioning of integrated living units: cells, tissues, organs, and organisms. Thus, protein interaction networks are better to be modeled as multi-labeled graphs than single labeled graphs.

Another challenging problem in computational biology is to search for a well-characterized pathway in a less studied model organism. One approach to identify pathways across multiple species would be the utilization of protein domains and familial information based on domains. A protein domain is a part of protein sequence and structure that has the functional component of the protein sequence. The domain information can be used to classify known proteins into familial relationships. In other words, these domains and the familial information can be used as labels to annotate the protein. One application is to query for pathways from well studied model organisms. Such an approach would be quite useful since during evolution, many of the domains remain intact, with alterations in various other parts of the protein sequences.

In software engineering, system dependence graphs [7] that model the dependency among statements of a program generally have multiple attributes. A node representing a statement containing an expression, such as an assignment statement or a conditional branch point, may have multiple attributes such as, an attribute representing the *abstract syntax tree* (AST) of the expression and the source code location. A subgraph may represent a code defect (bug) [13]. By locating the bug in the code, the software engineer can find possible bugs in a program.

In a typical online social network, users being vertices, an edge is added between two users if they are friends, relatives, colleagues, etc. A vertex may have multiple labels describing the user's personal information, e.g., age, gender, occupation, hometown, martial status, etc. A subgraph in this context may represent a group of people with special relationships or connections.

In the above applications, the database graph can be characterized as a multi-labeled graph. There are a set of $gval$ categories of labels associated with each vertex. For each category C_i, a vertex may have a specified label or a non-specified label. Figure 1 shows an example of a multi-labeled graph where each vertex has three specified labels and two query graphs where each vertex has one or two specified labels. The goal is to find match(es) of the query graph in the database graph.

Indexing has been a popular method in subgraph matching. In most of these work [12, 21, 20, 18], the neighborhood information is used to find mapping from a query vertex v to a database vertex u. The main idea is that if u is a match of v, the neighborhood of u has to contain that of v. For example, let $NH_G(u, k)$ be the set of vertices that are k hops/edges away from u in G. In order to qualify u a match of v, the labels of vertices in $NH_G(u, k)$ have to be a superset of the labels of vertices in $NH_Q(v, k)$. In the context of

CIKM'11, October 24–28, 2011, Glasgow, Scotland, UK.

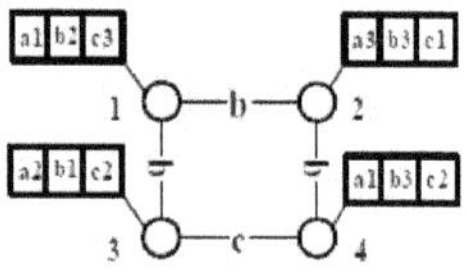

(a) G ($gvl = 3$)

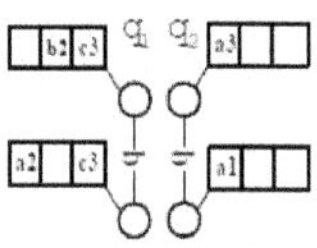
(b) Query Graphs

Figure 1: The Database Graph and Query Graph

single vertex label graphs, the subset/superset relationship can be easily computed. Even when the set is very large, some probabilistic data structure, e.g., bloom filter [20] can be used to compute the subset relationship efficiently and accurately.

The multi-labeled graph presents a unique challenge: how to find one neighborhood contains another.One method is to take the union of all labels in a neighborhood. For example, if there are two vertices in $NH_G(u,k)$ and their labels are $\{a_1, b_1, c_1\}$ and $\{a_2, b_2, c_2\}$. Then the overall label set in $NH_G(u,k)$ is $\{a_1, a_2, b_1, b_2, c_1, c_2\}$. By taking the union, the problem becomes the superset/subset computation again, for which existing methods could be applied. However, this would introduce a large amount of false positives. For instance, let's assume that $NH_Q(v,k)$ has one vertex with labels $\{a_1, b_2\}$. u would be considered a match for v under the union label scheme. However, it should not be since $\{a_1, b_2\}$ is not a subset of either vertex label set in $NH_G(u,k)$. The union approach does not work because in the multi-label graphs, what we want to find is not whether a set of labels is a subset of another set, but is really a **containment** problem, which could be stated as following. For two given sets of sets $\mathcal{A}$ and $\mathcal{B}$, for every set B in $\mathcal{B}$, whether there exists a set A in $\mathcal{A}$ such that A is a superset of B.

A novel method is proposed in this paper to address the neighborhood containment problem. The label set of every vertex in G is transformed into a gvl dimension box in the R^{gvl} space, where each dimension corresponds to a category of labels. If a vertex has a specified label at category C_i, then in the corresponding dimension, the label set is mapped to a specific value. On the other hand, for an unspecified category C_i, the label set is mapped into a range $[min, max]$ on the corresponding dimension where min and max are the minimum and maximum mapped values for any label in category C_i. Under this transformation scheme, if a label set X is a superset of another label set Y, then the box corresponding to X should be contained within the box corresponding to Y. Now the problem of neighborhood containment becomes the problem of range queries at a high dimension space. Thus, the R-tree [6] is used to store and index these transformed boxes in the high dimension space. As a result, the neighborhood containment problem can be solved efficiently, which leads to an efficient vertex matching procedure.

The neighborhood containment only considers set relationship, but not the matches. For example, $NH_G(u,k)$ has two vertices with labels $\{(a_1, b_1), (a_2, b_2)\}$. $NH_Q(v,k)$ has two vertices with labels $\{(a_1), (b_1)\}$. In this case, the label sets in $NH_G(u,k)$ contain those in $NH_Q(v,k)$, but there could not exist a mapping from all vertices in $NH_Q(v,k)$ to vertices in $NH_G(u,k)$ since a *collision* occurs, e.g., both vertices in $NH_Q(v,k)$ are mapped to the same vertex in $NH_G(u,k)$. In a single labeled graph, a collision may occur only if the label of two query vertices are the same and thus, collisions do not occur often. However, in a multi-label graph, a graph vertex may have a large number of labels. It is much more common that multiple query vertices (even with different sets of labels) may be mapped into the same database vertex, which leads to more collisions as shown in the example. In this paper, a bipartite matching pruning process is devised to remove the false containment due to collisions. The vertices in $NH_G(u,k)$ are put in the group of vertices L while the vertices in $NH_Q(v,k)$ are put in the group of vertices R. There is a directed edge from a vertex u in L to a vertex v in R if the label set of u is a superset of that of v. If the maximum flow mf in the bipartite graph is the same as the number of vertices in R, then there exists a set of true disjoint matches from all vertices in $NH_Q(v,k)$ to vertices in $NH_G(u,k)$. On the other hand, if $mf < |R|$, then it is a false positive containment due to label set collisions.

Among many graph based applications, one of the most important query task is to check whether a given query graph is a subgraph of the database graph or not. For example, a software engineer may want to find whether a program contains a bug and a biologist may want to find whether a protein interaction network contains a special pathway motif. After it has been determined that a graph contains a particular subgraph pattern, a user may further wish to locate all matches of the pattern. These are two related, but different types of queries:

Existence Query: Checking whether a query graph is subgraph isomorphic to a database graph.

Location Query: Finding all matches of a query graph in a database graph.

Most recent research in subgraph matching has been focused on location queries [12, 21, 20, 18]. Little attention has been paid on processing the existence queries in a large graph. Although these two types of queries are highly related, there are some fundamental differences. Since all matches need to be identified, it is unnecessary to develop an order to search the candidate matches in the location queries. On the other hand, for the existence queries, it is beneficial to first search the candidate partial matches that have a high possibility to become a true complete match. Therefore, a breadth-first search style algorithm is developed for the process of location queries while a depth-first style search is used for the process of existence queries. Furthermore, due to the different natures of these two types of queries, specific query vertex and graph vertex search orders are designed to accelerate the matching process.

The DELTA, for in<u>d</u>exing and qu<u>e</u>rying in mu<u>lt</u>i-labeled gr<u>a</u>phs, is provided in this paper. DELTA constructs an index structure for multiple-labeled graphs and provide a query processing method to answer both location and existence queries. The main contributions of this paper are as follows: (1) The multi-label graph matching problem is first proposed in this paper. (2) The wild card label (i.e. don't care) can be used as either query or database graph vertex label, which could not be used in previous work. (3) Based on the nature of vertex label set, a novel approach that transforms each vertex label set into a high dimension box is proposed. The R-tree data structure is employed to store and index these boxes. (4) A bipartite matching pruning technique is proposed to detect the false positive matches due to label set collisions. (5) Two types of queries: location and existence queries are investigated. Different search orders are developed for these two types of queries. (6) By applying DELTA to real applications and synthetic data sets, we show the efficiency and scalability of the DELTA method over existing alternative approaches.

The remainder of this paper is organized as follows. Section 2 discusses the related work. Section 3 defines the preliminary concepts and presents the problem statement. Section 4 and 5 describe our indexing mechanism, and the query processing algorithms, respectively. Experimental results are presented in Section 6. The final conclusions are drawn in Section 7.

2. RELATED WORK

The existence query is more common in the context of graph indexing instead of subgraph indexing. In the graph indexing problem, there are a set of database graphs and a query graph. The goal is to identify the set of graphs which are the supergraphs of the query graph. Usually, the database graph is small, e.g., with hundreds of vertices. Many pruning strategies have been proposed. The most common method is the frequent discriminative substructure based filtering. The approaches in this category apply data mining techniques to extract some discriminating substructures, then build an inverted index for each feature. Query graph q is denoted as a set of features, the pruning power of which depends on the set of selected indexed features. With the inverted indices, the complete set of candidates can be discovered. Many algorithms have been proposed to improve the effectiveness of the selected features, using features as frequent graphs, frequent trees and their combinations, such as Closure-tree[8], gIndex[16], TreePi[17], FG-Index[3] and Tree+δ[22]. Closure-tree uses the graph closure concept to organize the database graphs into a tree, where each node is a database graph. Database graphs with similar topologies are put as siblings. A pseudo subgraph isomorphism test is performed by checking the existence of a semi-perfect match from vertices in the query graph to vertices in a data graph (or graph closure). In gIndex, the authors propose a "discriminative ratio"for features. Only frequent and discriminative subgraphs are chosen as indexed features. In TreePi, due to the manipulation efficiency of trees, frequent and discriminate subtrees are chosen as feature set. The frequent sub-graphs and edges are used as indexed features in FG-Index. In Tree+δ, the author use frequent free trees and a small number of discriminative subgraphs as indexed features.

The location query problem commonly exists in the subgraph matching domain, which is to find all occurrences of a given query graph in the database graph. In this problem domain, database graphs are usually large, e.g., tens of thousands or more vertices. In GraphGrep [12, 5], the authors propose to use all paths up to $maxL$ length as indexed features. It also builds inverted index for each path. In TALE [14], an approximate matching method is proposed for large query graphs based on neighborhood units. In Graphs-at-a-time [9], the authors introduce a pattern matching method based on a combination of techniques: use of neighborhood subgraphs and profiles, joint reduction of the search space, and optimization of the search order. In GADDI [18] and SUMMA [19], a distance index based method is developed to process location queries. The authors in [19] and [20] propose to build a set of neighborhood indices for each database vertex. The index contains the labels of vertices in the neighborhood. The bloom filter is used in [20] to represent the vertex labels in a neighborhood. These neighborhood indices can be used to generate matches between query vertices and database vertices. In [23, 2, 15], algorithms are presented on how to process pattern match queries, which are similar to location queries.

In all the above work (existence queries or location queries), the graphs are assumed to be single-labeled graphs and these methods could not be directly applicable to the multi-labeled graphs. Therefore, it is necessary to develop a novel method for multi-labeled graphs.

3. PRELIMINARIES

In this section, we introduce the fundamental definitions used in this paper and give the formal problem statement. This paper investigates the subgraph indexing and querying methods for undirected and unweighted multi-labeled graphs. Without a loss of generality, it is easy to extend our methods to directed and weighted multi-labeled graphs.

DEFINITION 1. *A* ***multi-labeled graph*** *G is a five element tuple $G = \{V, E, \Sigma_V, \Sigma_E, L_G\}$ where V is a set of vertices and $E \subseteq V \times V$ is a set of edges. Σ_V and Σ_E are the sets of vertex and edge labels, respectively. Each vertex label is composed of gvl categories of labels, while any edge label is composed of only one label. Vertex label can be absent for any vertex in any category. The labeling function L_G defines the mappings $v \rightarrow \{l_v \mid l_v \in \Sigma_V\}$ and $e \rightarrow \{l_e \mid l_e \in \Sigma_E\}$.*

Figure 1 (a) shows an example multi-labeled graph. In this example, each vertex has three labels. Therefore, $gvl = 3$ in this graph. In the paper, we assume that any vertex label in category C_i cannot be the same as any vertex label in another category C_j and all graphs studied in this paper are multi-labeled graphs.

DEFINITION 2. *Given a database graph G, a connected query graph $Q = (V_q, E_q, \Sigma_{V_q}, \Sigma_{E_q}, L_q)$, a subgraph of G $m = (V_m, E_m, \Sigma_{V_m}, \Sigma_{E_m}, L_m)$ is a* ***match*** *of Q in G if and only if there exists a bijection $f : V_q \rightarrow V_m$, s.t.,*

- $\forall\, u \in V_Q,\ L_Q(u) \subseteq L_m(f(u))$,
- $\forall\, u, v \in V_Q, (u, v) \in E_Q \Leftrightarrow (f(u), f(v)) \in E_m$,
- $\forall\, (u, v) \in E_Q,\ L_Q(u, v) = L_m(f(u), f(v))$.

If at least one match of Q can be found in G, Q is **subgraph isomorphic** *to G.*

Since labels from different categories can not be the same, in order for the labels of a query vertex v to be a subset of those of a database vertex u, the following has to be true. If v has a specified label l_i in category C_i, then the C_i category label of u has to be l_i also. As an example, query graph q_1 in Figure 1 (b) is not subgraph isomorphic to graph G in Figure 1 (a), because the vertex in the bottom with label $\{a_2, c_3\}$ cannot be a subset of the labels of any vertex in G. Query graph q_2 is subgraph isomorphic to G. In these query graphs, an empty box means the vertex label is absent (unspecified) for this vertex in this category.

Problem Statement: Given a large database graph G, a set of query graphs, we aim to construct an index, and efficiently process two types of queries with the help of the indexed information. These two types of queries are (1) **existence query**: whether a query graph is subgraph isomorphic to the database graph, i.e., there is at least one match of the query graph exists in the database graph; and (2) **location query:** find all matches of the query graph in G.

Suppose the database graph G has $|V|$ vertices and $|E|$ edges, we assign each vertex a unique integer from 1 to $|V|$ as its **vertex ID**, and each edge a unique integer from 1 to $|E|$ as its **edge ID**. In Figure 1 (a), the vertex ID is illustrated near each vertex.

For example, suppose the database graph is G in Figure 1, the result of existence query of q_1 is false, while it is true for q_2. No match will be outputted when processing location query for q_1, while two different matches will be outputted for q_2.

One of the pruning techniques used by many existing methods [20, 21, 14] is the neighborhood set relationship. We define the k neighborhood of a vertex in the following manner.

DEFINITION 3. *Given a database graph G, a vertex v in G, and a non-negative integer k, k-neighborhood of v in G (denoted as $NH_G(v, k)$) is a set of vertices u such that there exists a k edge path between u and v.*

For instance, in Figure 1 (a), $NH_G(1,0) = \{1\}$ while $NH_G(2,1) = \{1,4\}$. Furthermore, we denote $NL_G(v,k)$ to be the set of label sets of vertices in $NH_G(v,k)$. $NL_G(2,1)= \{\{a_1,b_2,c_3\}, \{a_1,b_3,c_2\}\}$. Intuitively, in order for a query vertex v to be matched to a database graph vertex u, for every non-negative integer k, the k-neighborhood of v in Q should be contained in that of u in G. In a single labeled graph, both $NL_G(u,k)$ and $NL_Q(v,k)$ are sets of labels. To determine whether $NL_Q(v,k)$ is contained in $NL_G(u,k)$, we only need know whether $NL_Q(v,k) \subseteq NL_G(u,k)$, which can be determined efficiently. Even with very large size of $NL_G(u,k)$, by employing a bloom filter [20], the set relationship can be determined with $O(|NL_Q(v,k)|)$ complexity at a very high accuracy. However, determining containment relationship becomes a complicated process in multi-label graphs since both $NL_G(u,k)$ and $NL_Q(v,k)$ are sets of label sets. The **containment** relationship between sets of sets is defined as follows.

DEFINITION 4. *Given two sets of sets $\mathcal{A} = \{A_1, A_2, \ldots, A_n\}$ and $\mathcal{B} = \{B_1, B_2, \ldots, B_m\}$ where A_i $(1 \leq i \leq n)$ and B_j $(1 \leq j \leq m)$ are sets of elements in the form of $\{l_1, l_2, \ldots\}$. $\mathcal{A}$* ***contains*** *$\mathcal{B}$ if for every $B_j \in \mathcal{B}$, there exists a $A_i \in \mathcal{A}$ such that $B_j \subseteq A_i$.*

For instance, $\{\{1,3\},\{2,4\}\}$ is contained in $\{\{1,2\},\{1,3,\}, \{2,4\}\}$, but is not contained in $\{\{1,2,3\},\{1,4\}\}$. Based on this definition, the computation of set containment becomes a complicated process. In addition, the bloom filter no longer could be applied. We will present an efficient computing the set containment in the next section.

Furthermore, some database graphs and query graphs may have edge labels. Thus, edge labels can be used as a pruning or search tool for indexing and query processing. Since the edge label information can be easily adapted in the index and query processing without significant modification of the algorithms, we will omit how to handel and utilize the edge label information in the remainder of this paper. The focus of this paper is to deal with multiple labeled vertices and the method to process the existence and location queries.

4. INDEX CONSTRUCTION

Our index structure is essentially for finding the matches between query vertices and database vertices. As in much existing work, the neighborhood containment is one of the most popular methods. Due to the nature of multi-label vertices, the existing methods could not be directly applied in computing the neighborhood containment. A novel method of transforming labels of a vertex into a high dimensional box is introduced.

4.1 Neighborhood Containment Computation

Let $gval$ be the number of categories of labels for each vertex. The most straight forward method to find whether a set of sets $NL_G(u,k)$ contains another set of sets $NL_Q(v,k)$ is the following. For every set Y in $NL_Q(v,k)$, we compare Y with every set in $NL_G(u,k)$. If there exists a set X in $NL_G(u,k)$ such that $Y \subseteq X$, then $NL_G(u,k)$ contains $NL_Q(u,k)$. The complexity of this step is $O(gval\times\ |NL_G(u,k)|\ \times|NL_Q(v,k)|)$. The cardinality of $NL_G(u,k)$ is approximately equal to $(d_G)^k$ where d_G is the degree of G. In most applications, d_G ranges from less than 10 to over 100. Thus, when k is small, e.g., 1, the running time of the straight forward method is tolerable. To effectively find an accurate candidate match set for a query vertex v, it is beneficial to compare the neighborhood vertex label sets for multiple k. Some of the k values could be more than 1. In this case, the straight forward method may be too costly, especially the candidate vertex generation process needs to be invoked many times. (It has to be invoked for every query vertex.) As a result, in the DELTA framework, we propose a novel method for efficiently computing the set containment.

The set of labels of a vertex $(l_1, l_2, \ldots, l_{gval})$ is mapped into a box in a $gval$ dimensional space $\mathcal{R}^{gval}$ in the following manner. Let f_i be a function that maps an ith category label into an integer. Also denote max_i and min_i be the largest and smallest mapped integers for ith category labels. The label set $(l_1, l_2, \ldots, l_{gval})$ is mapped to a box in the form of $((L_1, M_1), (L_2, M_2), \ldots, (L_{gval}, M_{gval}))$ where $L_i = M_i = f_i(l_i)$ if l_i is specified. Otherwise, $L_i = min_i$ and $M_i = max_i$. For instance, the label set $(a_1, b_3, \emptyset)$ where $\emptyset$ represents an unspecified label, is transformed into a box of three dimension $((1,1),(3,3),(1,1000))$ assuming $f_1(a_1) = 1$, $f_2(b_3) = 3$, $min_3 = 1$, and $max_3 = 1000$.

The vertex labels of a particular neighborhood of a database vertex u $(NL_G(u,k))$ can be considered as a set of boxes in the $\mathcal{R}^{gval}$ space. To find whether $NL_Q(v,k)$ is contained in $NL_G(u,k)$, we need to determine for each vertex label set L_i in $NL_Q(v,k)$, whether there exists a set in $NL_G(u,k)$ that is a superset of L_i. To achieve this, each label set in $NL_Q(v,k)$ is also transformed into a box in the same manner as the label sets in $NL_G(u,k)$. For two label vertex sets X and Y with $gval$ categories of labels, X is a *superset* of Y if and only if the transformed box of X is *within* the transformed box of Y. The following is the formal description of the property.

PROPERTY 1. *For two vertex label sets $X = (x_1, x_2, \ldots, x_{gval})$ and $Y = (y_1, y_2, \ldots, y_{gval})$. The transformed $gval$ dimension boxes of X and Y are $X_{box} = ((x_1^{low}, x_1^{up}), \ldots, (x_{gval}^{low}, x_{gval}^{up}))$ and $Y_{box} = ((y_1^{low}, y_1^{up}), \ldots, (y_{gval}^{low}, y_{gval}^{up}))$, respectively. X is a superset of Y if and only if X_{box} is within Y_{box}, i.e., for each i $(1 \leq i \leq gval)$, $y_i^{low} \leq x_i^{low} \leq x_i^{up} \leq y_i^{up}$.*

Proof: First we prove that if X is a superset of Y, then X_{box} is within Y_{box}. Since X is a superset of Y, for each category i that Y has a specified label y_i, X also has the same specified label, i.e., $x_i = y_i$. Thus, $y_i^{low} = x_i^{low} = x_i^{up} = y_i^{up}$. For each category i that Y does not have a specified label $(y_i = \emptyset)$, X either has a specified label or a null label. In either case, it is within (min_i, max_i) which is the transformed range of y_i.

Now we prove that if X_{box} is within Y_{box}, then X is a superset of Y. Based on the transformation, for each dimension i, there two situations for x_i^{low} and x_i^{up}, either (1) $x_i^{low} = x_i^{up}$ (x_i is specified) or (2) $x_i^{low} = min_i$ and $x_i^{up} = max_i$ (x_i is unspecified). In order for X_{box} is within Y_{box}, for every unspecified category i, y_i has to be unspecified either so that $y_i^{low} = min_i$ and $y_i^{up} = max_i$. For every specified x_i, y_i is either unspecified or $y_i = x_i$ so that $y_i^{low} \leq x_i^{low} \leq x_i^{up} \leq y_i^{up}$. Therefore, X is a superset of Y.

For every transformed box X from $NL_Q(v,k)$, if we can find X encompasses some box from $NL_G(u,k)$, then $NL_G(u,k)$ contains $NL_Q(v,k)$. This essentially is the problem of range queries in a high dimension space. To efficiently perform these operations, an index structure is discussed in the next subsection.

4.2 Index structure

The index consists of two parts. The first part is the *vertex label index* and the second is the *neighborhood index*.

4.2.1 Vertex Label Index

We index the vertex label information by using a fully inverted index for all labels. For every possible vertex label l_a, the list L_a of vertices which has l_a as one of their labels is kept. To accelerate the query process, the vertices in the list are sorted in the ascending order according to the vertex IDs.

For every specified label l_a of a query vertex v, the list of vertices that have the label l_a is retrieved. Since v may have several specified labels, multiple vertex lists are retrieved. A database vertex u has the superset labels as v only if u appears in all these retrieved lists. Thus, we need join these lists, i.e., finding vertices that exist in all retrieved lists. Since the vertices are sorted according to the ascending order of the vertex IDs, the join process can be done by a linear scan through all the retrieved lists. These vertices are put into $S(v)$ as the candidate matches for v.

4.2.2 *Neighborhood Index*

The neighbor index is constructed for each database vertex u. For each u, there are multiple neighborhoods, each of which corresponds to a particular k. For a given vertex u and k, the neighborhood index contains two parts: (1) the number of vertices in $NH_G(u,k)$ and (2) the label sets of vertices in $NH_G(u,k)$.

Since the vertex label sets in a neighborhood is essentially a set of high-dimension boxes, the R-tree [6] is chosen as the index structure. For each vertex u and k, an R-tree is built to index the transformed boxes in label sets of vertices in $NH_G(u,k)$. Since the R-tree is a very well known spatial indexing structure, we omit the procedures on how to construct and use the R-tree in this paper. With the R-tree index structure, the complexity of finding whether a box contains any box in $NH_G(u,k)$ is $O(\lceil \log |NH_G(u,k)| \rceil)$. Since $|NH_G(u,k)| = O(d_G^k)$, the complexity is $O(k \log d_G)$. Therefore, the total complexity for computing the set containment of $NL_Q(v,k)$ in $NL_G(u,k)$ is $O(k \times d_G \times |NL_Q(v,k)|)$, which is much lower than the straight forward containment computation especially with $k > 1$.

With small k, e.g., $k = 1$, the number of label sets in $NH_G(u,k)$ is small. Although the complexity of the R-tree method is lower, it may not be worthwhile to use this method due to overheads. Based on our experiments, we found that when the cardinality of $NL_G(u,k)$ is less than 50, comparing to the straight-forward set containment computation, the R-tree index is not cost effective. Since d_G is usually between 10 and 100 in many real applications, the straight forward set containment computation is more efficient with $k = 1$ in most cases. Thus, with $k = 1$, the label sets of $NH_G(u,k)$ are stored as a linked list. On the other hand, with $k \geq 2$, the label sets of vertices in $NH_G(u,k)$ are transformed into a set of high-dimension boxes and stored in an R-tree.

With more neighborhoods for each database vertex, the pruning power is greater. However, this comes at a price of larger index size since more neighborhoods need to be stored. In addition, the cardinality of $NH_G(u,k)$ grows exponentially with respect to k. We have performed experiments on the pruning effects with different values of k and found that the pruning is the most cost effective with $k = 2$. Thus, in this paper, we choose the maximum value of k to be 2.

5. QUERY PROCESSING AND OPTIMIZATIONS

In this paper, we investigate two types of queries: the location queries and existence queries. These two types of queries are highly related, but with some important differences. In the existence queries, we only need find one match while in the location queries, we need find all matches. Thus, for the location queries, a breath-first search order is devised to find all matches. On the other hand, the depth-first search order is employed for the existence queries since this is more efficient to find one match.

The graph matching process consists of the following steps. (1) For each query vertex v, we find the candidate set of graph vertices that are possible matches to v based on the index described in the previous section. (This step is the same for both types queries.) (2) Next, the match(es) of the query graph Q is discovered. For the location queries, the matches of Q are discovered in a breadth-first manner. We first find all candidate matches M_1 of one query vertex v. Next, we add another vertex v' to v, then all matches M_2 of the pattern with these two query vertices are discovered based on M_1. This process continues until the query pattern consists of all query vertices or no match could be found.

On the other hand, for the existence query, the match is discovered in a depth-first manner. We also start from one query vertex, at this procedure only one match of the single vertex pattern is discovered and the match grows until one complete match of Q is located. If a partial match could not grow any more, we trace back and start to grow from another partial match. These steps are presented in details in the remainder of this section.

5.1 Finding Candidate Vertices

The inverted index presented in the previous section is used to find candidate vertex matches for each vertex in the query graph Q. First the vertex label index is used. Secondly, the neighborhood index is used for further pruning. This formal algorithm is described in Algorithm 1.

Algorithm 1 Build_Candidate(q, G)

Input: query graph q, database graph G
Output: candidate vertex match sets S, vertex matching order $orderQueue$ of q

```
for each vertex v_i in q do
    for each label l_j in v_i do
        retrieve the vertex list containing l_j by the inverted index
    end forS(i) ← intersectionofallthevertexlists
end for
for each vertex u_k in S(i) do
    if ! u_k's one-hop neighborhood contains v_i's then
        remove u_k
    else if ! u_k's two-hop neighborhood contains v_i's by u_k's R
    Tree index then
        remove u_k
    else if the two-hop neighborhoods fail to pass Bipartite
    Matching then
        remove u_k
    end if
end for
build orderQueue by the size of each set in S
return S and orderQueue
```

For each query vertex v, we first find the set database vertices $S(v)$ that have the vertex labels as a superset of those of v by the Vertex Label Index.

To refine $S(v)$, the neighborhood indices of v is used. For $k = 1$, the straight-forward containment computation method is used: For each vertex label set Y in $NH_Q(v,k)$, we scan through the list for $NH_G(u,k)$ to see whether Y is a subset of some label sets in $NH_G(u,k)$. On the other hand, for $k \geq 2$, the R-tree is used to store vertex label sets in $NH_G(u,k)$. For each label set $Y \in NL_Q(v,k)$, Y is transformed to a high dimension box and find whether there exists a vertex label set in $NH_G(u,k)$ contained in Y. If Y does not contain any vertex label set, then u could not be a match to v and is removed from $S(v)$. If for every k, $NH_G(u,k)$ contains $NH_Q(v,k)$, then u remains in $S(v)$.

Bipartite Graph Matching Pruning

In a multi-labeled database graph, a database vertex may have up to $gval$ specified labels. On the other hand, a query vertex usually has much less number of specified labels. It is possible that the label set of one database vertex is a superset of the label sets of multiple query vertices. For instance, assume that the label set of vertices in $NH_G(u,k)$ are $\{(2,3,5), (3,7,9)\}$ and the label sets of vertices in $NH_Q(v,k)$ are $\{(2,3), (3,5)\}$. In this case, $NH_Q(v,k)$ is contained in $NH_G(u,k)$. However, u cannot be matched to v since the two vertices in $NH_Q(v,k)$ can only be mapped into a single vertex in $NH_G(u,k)$. To further prune the false matches, the **bipartite matching** process is introduced.

When determining $NH_G(v,k)$ containing $NH_G(u,k)$, for each vertex $Y_i \in NH_G(u,k)$, the label sets of vertices in $NH_G(u,k)$ that are a superset of Y_i are identified. Thus, a bipartite graph B is constructed. B consists of two types of vertices L and R. Each vertex in $NH_G(u,k)$ is a vertex in L while every vertex in $NH_q(v,k)$ is a vertex in R. There is an edge from a vertex (l) in L to a vertex (r) in R if the labels of l is a superset of those of r. B can be considered as a flow network while each edge has a capacity of 1. The maximum number of disjoint matches in B (from vertices in L to vertices in R) is equal to the maximum flow of B, which can be easily solved by the Ford-Fulkerson algorithm [4]. If the maximum flow is equal to $|R|$, then every vertex in $NH_Q(v,k)$ can be mapped into a different vertex in $NH_G(u,k)$ so that u could be a candidate match to v and remain in $S(v)$. Otherwise, u could not be a match to v and it is removed $S(v)$.

Figure 2 shows an example of this pruning. The vertices in L are these from $NH_G(u,k)$ while vertices in R are from $NH_Q(v,k)$. The maximum flow is 2. Since there are three vertices in R, it means that there could not exist a one to one mapping from vertices in $NH_Q(v,k)$ to vertices in $NH_G(u,k)$. As a result, u could not be a match to v.

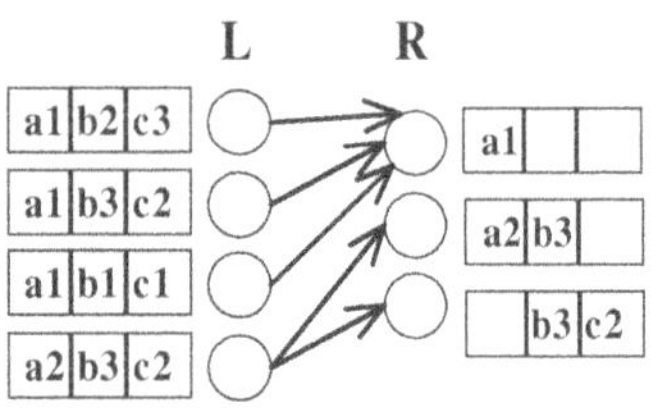

Figure 2: The bipartite graph matching pruning

The complexity of the Ford-Fulkerson algorithm is $O(|NL_G(u,k)|^2 \times |NL_Q(v,k)|)$. Although the bipartite matching can reduce false positive matches for a query vertex, it also could incur extra computation. In the empirical studies, we will show the effects of this pruning method.

5.2 Processing Location Query

After the matches for each query vertex are discovered, the next step is to assemble the vertex matches to form the complete matches of Q. As mentioned before, a breadth-first search style method is adapted for the processing of location queries. The formal location query algorithm is presented in Algorithm 2.

In general, a partial query pattern P is maintained. Denote P_i be an i-vertex subgraph of the query pattern Q. Initially, P_1 consists of a single vertex. After discovering all matches M_1 of P_1, one query vertex v is added into P_1 to obtain a new partial query pattern P_2. Next, the matches of P_2 are generated based on M_1. The process

Algorithm 2 Query_Locations($q, G, orderQueue, S$)

Input: query graph q, database graph G, vertex matching order $orderQueue$ of q, candidate vertex match sets S
Output: All matches of q in G.

```
v ← orderQueue.remove(), P ← P + v
for each vertex v_i in S(v) do
  matchesQueue.push(v_i)
end for
while !matchesQueue.empty() do
  if orderQueue.size()==0 then
    return matchesQueue
  end if
  v ← orderQueue.remove()
  P ← P + v
  n ← matchesQueue.size()
  for i = 0; i < n; ++i do
    m ← matchesQueue.remove()
    for each vertex v_i in S(v) do
      if v_i matches m then
        matchesQueue.push(m + v_i)
      end if
    end for
  end for
end while
```

continues until either (1) P_i includes all vertices in Q or (2) there does not exist any match for P_i.

There are two challenges for this algorithm: (1) which vertex should be added into P_i and (2) how to obtain the matches M_{i+1} of P_{i+1} based on M_i. We start by explaining how to choose a vertex to be added into P_i, i.e., the growth order of the query pattern. It is beneficial to add a vertex that is adjacent to some vertex in P_i since the relationship (edges) between the newly added vertex and vertices in P_i can be used to prune the matches. This means that P_i is always connected. There may be multiple adjacent vertices to vertices in P_i. So which vertex should be chosen?

During the matching process, after generating a partial match m_i with i vertices, we try to add one more database vertex (match of query vertex v) to m_i. However, no match could be found. This means that m_i could not grow to the complete match of Q. As a result, the computation on generating the partial match m_i is wasted. To minimize the wasted partial matches, it is beneficial to first match these vertices with low likelihood to be matched so that these wasted partial matches would not be generated at the first place.

For each vertex v in Q, the matched vertices set $S(v)$ is obtained in the previous step. The number of vertices in $S(v)$ is used to approximate how likely a partial match involving v can be matched during the matching process. Therefore, the query vertex v with the smallest $S(v)$ that is adjacent to some vertex in P_i will be chosen first.

For example, for vertices in query graph q_2 in Figure 1 (b), the upper vertex has one candidate vertex in the database graph in Figure 1 (a), while the bottom vertex has two. Thus, we will select the upper vertex first and put into P_1, as it has the least number of matching vertices. Since the bottom vertex is adjacent to the upper vertex and the only vertex left, it will be selected next to form P_2. The query vertex order determination algorithm is described in Algorithm 3.

After adding v into P_i, we need find matches for M_{i+1}, the set of matches of P_{i+1}. Assume query vertex v is the newly added vertex. For each $u \in S(v)$ ($S(v)$ is generated in the vertex match

Algorithm 3 *Vertex Matching Order*

Input: query graph q, database graph G.
Output: Vertex Matching Order of vertices in q, $orderQueue$.

Queue $orderQueue = \varnothing$
$V \leftarrow$ vertices in q
$orderQueue \leftarrow orderQueue + v$, v has the least number of matches among all vertices in q
$V \leftarrow V - v$
while V is not empty **do**
  $TempV \leftarrow \varnothing$
  for each vertex w in V **do**
    if w adjacent to at least one vertex in $orderQueue$ **then**
      $TempV \leftarrow TempV + w$
    end if
  end for
  $orderQueue \leftarrow orderQueue + v$, v has the least number of matches among all vertices in $TempV$
  $V \leftarrow V - v$
end while
return $orderQueue$

step) and a match $m \in M_i$, we check whether u and m can form a match for P_{i+1}. For every edge e in Q such that one end of e is v while the other end is a vertex in P_i, we verify whether there is a corresponding edge in G between u and corresponding matching vertices. If so, u and m form a match in M_{i+1}. Otherwise, u and m does not form a new match.

5.3 Processing Existence Query

The existence query processing procedure is similar to that of location queries with one significant difference: the query is processed in a depth-first manner. The goal of the existence query is either to (1) generate a match for Q or (2) determine that there does not exist a match for Q as efficient as possible. In the case that Q does not have a match in G, the most efficient way is to match these vertices that could not grow to a full match of Q. Thus, it is beneficial to first match these query vertices v with small $S(v)$ since small $S(v)$ indicates few matches involving v exist. By matching v first, it can reduce the time to determine that there is no match for Q. On the other hand, in the case that there exists a match of Q in G, the match should involve all vertices in Q. Therefore, any query vertex order will perform the same since all query vertices need to be matched. Based on these two cases, we choose the same query vertex growth order as that in the location query.

For the existence query, we also maintain a partial query pattern P_i as in the location query. Initially, P_1 contains one query vertex. **One** match m_1 of P_1 is obtained. (In the location queries, all matches of P_1 are obtained.) Next one query vertex is added to P_1 to obtain P_2. The query vertex insertion order is the same as in the location queries. It is possible that after adding a vertex to P_i, we could not find any match of P_{i+1}. In this case, a new match of P_i (m_i) would be generated based on m_{i-1} and we try to find a match of P_{i+1} based on the new m_i. The algorithm terminates when one of the following two conditions occur. (1) One match of Q is discovered. (2) It is determined that no match of Q exists.

In the case of no match of Q existing, all matches of P_1, P_2, $\ldots$, P_i have to be searched. (P_{i+1} is the partial query pattern that we could not find any match.) Therefore, the order of generating database matches is not important at all. On the other hand, if there exists a match of Q, our aim is to generate a partial match of P_i that could successfully grow to the complete match of Q. Since it is impossible to know which partial match can grow to the final complete match, we only can make some "guess". Let's assume that we have found a match for P_i and v is added to P_i to form P_{i+1}. Since we know the next vertex v' that will be added into P_{i+1} to form P_{i+2}, we "look-ahead" one step. We choose the match that might grow to the most possible matches for P_{i+2}. Thus, among all vertices in $S(v+1)$, the vertex u is chosen if u has the most adjacent vertices in $S(v+2)$. u is added to the current match for P_i to obtain a match for P_{i+1}. In this case, the resulting match for P_{i+1} has the highest probability to grow to most matches for P_{i+2}.

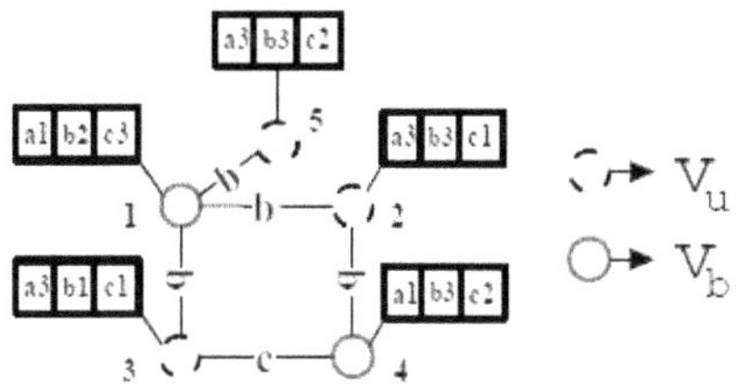

Figure 3: A Database Graph G_2

For example, for query graph q_2 in Figure 1 (b) and database graph G_2 in figure 3, we first match the query graph vertex v_b in the bottom, as it has fewer matches than the upper query graph vertex v_u. v_b has two matched vertices in the database graph, v_1 and v_4 (v_i is the database vertex with vertex ID i). We select v_1 over v_4 because v_1 is adjacent to three matches of v_u (v_2, v_3, v_5) while v_4 is adjacent to only two matches of v_u (v_2, v_3). The existence query processing algorithm is shown in Algorithm 4.

Algorithm 4 Query_Exist($q, G, orderQueue, S$)

Input: query graph q, database graph G, vertex matching order $orderQueue$ of q, candidate vertex match sets S
Output: Whether q is subgraph isomorphic to G

$v \leftarrow orderQueue.remove()$, $P \leftarrow P + v$
$n \leftarrow S(v).size()$
for $i = 0; i < n; ++i$ **do**
  remove v_i in $S(v)$ that has the most adjacent vertices in $S(v+1)$
  $matchesStack.push(v_i)$
  while !matchesStack.empty() **do**
    if orderQueue.size()==0 **then**
      return true
    end if
    $v \leftarrow orderQueue.remove()$
    $P \leftarrow P + v$
    $m \leftarrow matchesStack.top()$
    remove v_i in $S(v)$ that has the most adjacent vertices in $S(v+1)$
    $matchesStack.push(m + v_i)$
    if cannot find a v_i in $S(v)$ **then**
      $matchesStack.pop()$
      $P \leftarrow P - v$
    end if
  end while
end for
return false

6. EXPERIMENTAL RESULTS

The DELTA framework consists of several innovations. To fairly analyze these innovations, the experimental results consist of three parts: neighborhood label set containment computation, the location query process, and the existence query process. We will evaluate each innovation independently. To characterize the effects of the neighborhood index structure, three versions of DELTA indexing structures are implemented: DELTA-basic, DELTA-bloom, and DELTA-R. In the DELTA-basic method, the straightforward neighborhood containment computing method is used. With the DELTA-bloom approach, we treat $NL_G(u, k)$ as the union of all labels and a bloom filter as in [20] is constructed for $NL_G(u, k)$. The method of transforming vertex labels into a high dimension box is used in DELTA-R (DELTA with R-tree). All programs used in this section are implemented in C++ and all tests are run on a PC with the Intel Core2 CPU 2.6GHz and 4GB memory.

6.1 Experiments on Real Data Sets

One real data set is a protein interaction network of homo sapiens. Each vertex represents a protein with three labels which corresponds to the gene ontology terms of cellular component, molecular function, and biological process. Each edge represents that there is an interaction between the two proteins. There are 6410 vertices, 53844 edges, 1896 distinct labels and the average degree is 16.8. Four known different size of signal transduction pathways from the KEGG database [10] are used as the query graph Q. The pathways are from species other than homo sapiens, e.g., yeast, fly.

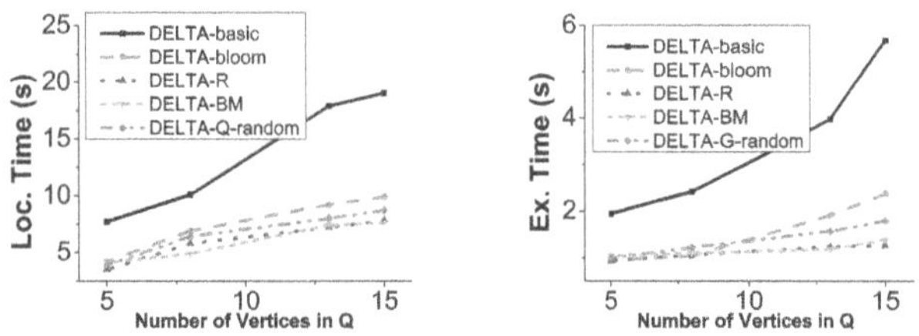

(a) Loc. Query (b) Exist. Query

Figure 4: Experiments on a real data set

It takes 26 second to build a 37MB R-Tree based index and 17 second to build a 6MB Bloom filter based index. Figures 4(a) and 4(b) show the location and existence query performance of different versions of DELTA. For all methods, the query time increases with the size of the query graph, while the query time of DELTA-R and DELTA-BM grow much slower than the alternatives. The gap between DELTA-BM and DELTA-bloom is more evident with the larger size of the query graph due to the false positives introduced by the bloom filter at the pruning step. It is interesting to observe that the query time of DELTA-BM and DELTA-R is very similar. There are three labels in the database graph and one specified label for each query vertex. In this case, the label set collision is not frequent, and thus the benefit of the bipartite match pruning is not significant. However, as shown with the synthetic data sets, when $gval/|L|$ ratio is larger, DELTA-BM would outperform DELTA-R. The query time of both DELTA-Q-random and DELTA-G-random is slightly higher than that of DELTA-R, showing that the designed vertex matching order can improve the query performance up to 20%.

Another biological network is also used. The network consists of 7496 vertices and 25408 edges. Each vertex represents a fly gene and is labeled with multiple proteins. An edge exists if there is a functional relationship between two endpoint genes.We observed the similar trends of each algorithm and thus do not show the figures due to the space limitation.

6.2 Experiments on Synthetic Data Sets

The synthetic database graphs are generated by the GenGraph_win tool [24] according to the following set of parameters: the number of vertices, the average degree, and the number of labels $gval$. The query graphs Q are also generated by the GenGraph_win tool according to three parameters: number of vertices, average degree, and the average number of specified labels. The default parameter values are shown in Table 1. We vary one parameter at a time. Biological graphs and system dependency graphs usually have between tens of thousands vertices and several million edges, which fall into these parameter value settings.

Table 1: Default Parameter Value

Parameter	Default Value
Num. of Vertices in G	100,000
Avg. Degree of G	10
$gval$	5
Num. of Vertices in Q	20
Avg. Degree of Q	5
Num. of Specified Labels in Q ($\|L\|$)	2

6.3 Index for Neighborhood Containment Computation

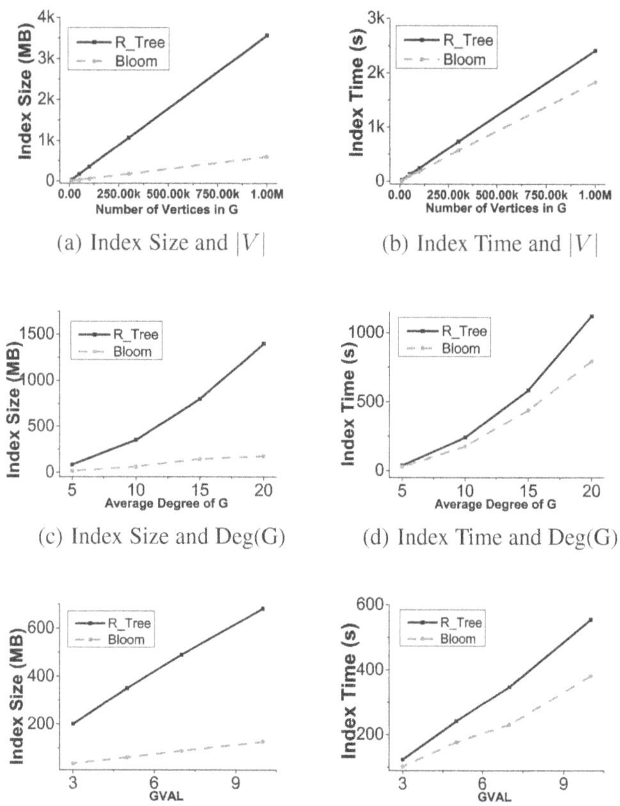

(a) Index Size and $|V|$ (b) Index Time and $|V|$

(c) Index Size and Deg(G) (d) Index Time and Deg(G)

(e) Index Size and $gval$ (f) Index Time and $gval$

Figure 5: Index comparison

First we show the index size and construction time with various parameters of the database graph in Figure 5. When the average degree is fixed, both the size and time of the R tree index and the bloom filter index grow linearly with respect to $|V|$ or $gval$, which is reflected in the first and third rows of subfigures, indicating these two indices scale well in terms of the size of the graphs and the label categories. The second row of subfigures shows that the costs of both indices grow exponentially with respect to the average degree of graphs. However, the index size and construction time is well within the tolerable range on a modern computer. The cost of the bloom filter index is consistently smaller (around 20% of size and 70% of construction time) than the cost of the R-tree based index. However, the index is only built once and our goal is to improve the query time, which is performed many times after the index is built.

Next, we show the query time with these different indexing structures. The location queries are chosen for this experiment since location queries are more widely used and it takes longer time to process.

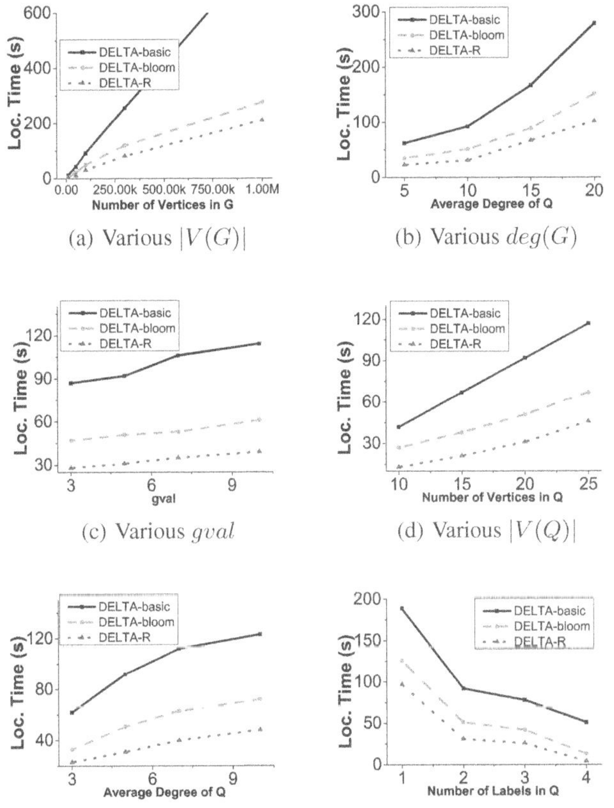

(a) Various $|V(G)|$ (b) Various $deg(G)$

(c) Various $gval$ (d) Various $|V(Q)|$

(e) Various $deg(Q)$ (f) Various $|L|$ in Q

Figure 6: Index Structure Query Time Comparison

The first parameter we vary is the number of vertices in G, ranging from $10K$ to $1M$ vertices. With the growth of the database graph size, the query time increases. DELTA-basic could not terminate within a reasonable amount of time when G is large. DELTA-R outperforms DELTA-bloom and the acceleration is more evident when the size of the database graph is large since the bloom filter may falsely report many vertex matches due to the union approach.

The second parameter is the average degree of G and the result is shown in Figure 6(b). Without any pruning technique, DELTA-basic grows exponentially. DELTA-R outperforms DELTA-bloom with a wide margin especially in denser graphs because more vertices are in the neighborhood, which increases the chance of false positives for the bloom filter based index.

In Figure 6(c), with various $gval$, the query time of all versions of DELTA does not vary significantly. This is due to the fact that the average number of specified labels in the query graph is fixed, thus the computation of identifying candidate matches does not change too much.

Next we vary parameters concerning the query graph. The fourth parameter is the number of vertices in Q. In Figure 6(d), the location query time of all methods increases linearly with the size of the query graph because when the size of the query graph increases, it needs to match more vertices.

In Figure 6(e), when the average degree of Q is varied, the location query time follows the same trend as in Figure 6(e), but the curves grow at a sub-linear pace because higher degree means more edges to match, where each one is in fact a constraint for a match. Although more edges need to be matched, with more constraints, the number of matches is reduced.

The last parameter is the average number of specified labels (L) of each vertex in the query graph. The query time is shown in Figure 6(f). With more labels specified, fewer candidate vertex matches can be retrieved and thus it takes less time to grow these vertex matches to graph matches. This leads to a smaller query time. From this set of experiments, it is clear that the R-tree method can achieve a much faster query time at a price of 30% larger index structure comparing to the bloom filter approach.

6.4 Bipartite Pruning

To evaluate the effects of the Bipartite pruning method, the Delta-R is compared with Delta-BM. Delta-BM is the same as Delta-R except that Delta-BM employs the bipartite pruning during the query processing time. As we shown above, the query time does not vary significantly with different $gval$ and $deg(Q)$ values. Thus, the query time with respect to these two parameters is not shown in the remainder of this section.

Figure 7 (a), (b) and (c) show that the processing time of DELTA-BM is around 10% less than that of DELTA-R. However, in Figure 7(d), when the number of average specified labels in a vertex in Q is 3 or larger, DELTA-BM takes a longer query time DELTA-R. This may be due to the fact that that with more labels in a query vertex, the possibility of label set collision becomes less frequent. Thus, the extra work on bipartite pruning may not be worthwhile.

6.5 Location Query

To demonstrate the effects of the query vertex insertion order, DELTA-Q-random is used as a baseline method, which employs a random query pattern growth order, i.e., with a pattern P_i, a vertex that is adjacent to any vertex in P_i is randomly selected to form P_{i+1}. The specified pattern growth order, i.e. choosing a vertex based on $S(a)$, can provide up to 15% improvement over the random order, which is reflected by the gap between DELTA-R and DELTA-Q-random in Figure 7. This demonstrates the benefits of the particular query pattern generation order in the DELTA scheme.

6.6 Existence Query

For the existence query, the baseline method is DELTA-G-random which is the same as DELTA-BM with one modification. When choosing a match for the partial query pattern P, the pattern grows in a breadth-first style and any vertex has the same probability to be chosen.

In Figure 8, both methods grow with respect to the corresponding parameters, but at a much slower pace comparing with the location query. In this type of query, our goal is to discover the first match

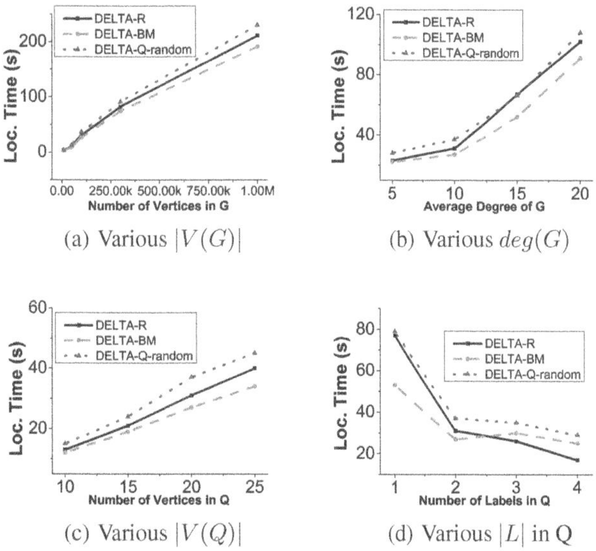

(a) Various $|V(G)|$ (b) Various $deg(G)$

(c) Various $|V(Q)|$ (d) Various $|L|$ in Q

Figure 7: Location query comparison

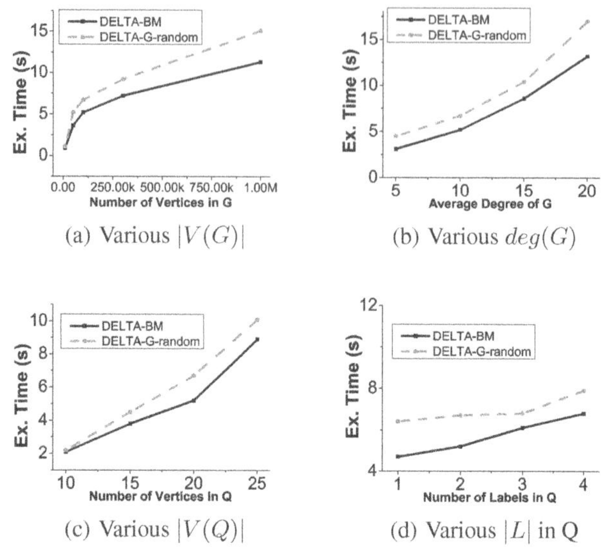

(a) Various $|V(G)|$ (b) Various $deg(G)$

(c) Various $|V(Q)|$ (d) Various $|L|$ in Q

Figure 8: Existence query comparison

as fast as possible. The size and density of the database graph do not affect the query performance as much as they do in the location query. The query time is approximately linear to the size of the query graph. Moreover, in the existence queries, the order is more important than the location query, and DELTA-BM is around 20% faster than DELTA-G-random, which demonstrates the benefits of match generation order.

7. CONCLUSION

Due to the prevalence of multi-labeled graphs and lack of algorithms for such graphs, we investigate the subgraph indexing and query processing methods for multi-labeled graphs. To adapt to the nature of multiple labels in a vertex, the vertex match pruning problem is transformed into a high dimension spatial query problem and the R-tree index is used to store and index the label sets on vertices. After introducing how to find candidate vertices, we provide detailed algorithms for processing existence queries and location queries. To the best of our knowledge, this is the first attempt to index multi-labeled graphs and process the location and existence queries on these graphs.

8. REFERENCES

[1] D. Abadi, A. Marcus, S. Madden, K. Hollenbach. Scalable Semantic Web Data Management Using Vertical Partitioning. *Proc. of VLDB*, 2007.
[2] J. Cheng, J. X. Yu, B. Ding, P. S. Yu, and H. Wang. Fast graph pattern matching. *Proc. of ICDE*, 2008.
[3] J. Cheng, Y. Ke, W. Ng, and A. Lu. FG-Index: Towards Verification-free Query Processing on Graph Databases. *Proc. of SIGMOD*, 2007.
[4] T. Corman, C. Leiserson, R. Rivest, and C. Stein. *Introduction to Algorithms*, McGraw-Hill, 1990.
[5] R. Giugno and D. Shasha, GraphGrep: A Fast and Universal Method for Querying Graphs. *Proc. of ICPR*, 2002.
[6] A. Guttman, R-Tree: A dynamic index structure for spatial searching. *Proc. of SIGMOD,* 1984.
[7] S. Horwitz, T. Reps, and D. Binkley. Interprocedural slicing using dependence graphs. *ACM Trans. Program. Lang. Syst.* 12, 1 (Jan. 1990), 26-60.
[8] H. He and A. K. Singh. Closure-Tree: An Index Structure for Graph Queries. *Proc. of ICDE*, 2006.
[9] H. He and A. K. Singh. Graphs-at-a-time: Query Language and Access Methods for Graph Databases, *Proc. of SIGMOD*, 2008.
[10] M. Kanehisa and S. Goto, KEGG: Kyoto encyclopedia of genes and genomes, *Nuc. Ac. Res*, vol 28, 27-30, 2000.
[11] M. Mitzenmacher, A brief history of generative models for power law and log normal distributions. *Proc. of ACCCC*, 2001.
[12] D. Shasha, J. Wang, and R. Giugno. Algorithmic and Applications of Tree and Graph Searching. *PODS*, 2002.
[13] B. Sun, R. Y. Chang, X. Chen, and A. Podgurski. Automated support for propagating bug fixes. *Proceedings of Software Reliability Engineering (ISSRE)*, 2008.
[14] Y. Tian and J. Patel. TALE: A Tool for Approximate Large Graph Matching, *Proc. of ICDE*, 2008.
[15] H. Tong, C. Faloutsos, B. Gallagher, and T. Eliassi-Rad. Fast best-effort pattern matching in large attributed graphs. *Proc. of KDD*, 2007.
[16] X. Yan, P. Yu, and J. Han. Graph Indexing, a Frequent Structure-based Approach. *Proc. of Sigmod*, 2004.
[17] S. Zhang, M. Hu, and J. Yang. Treepi: a Novel Graph Indexing Method. *Proc. of ICDE,* 2007.
[18] S. Zhang, S. Li, and J. Yang. GADDI: distance index based subgraph matching in biological networks. *Proc. of EDBT*, 2009.
[19] S. Zhang, S. Li, and J. Yang. SUMMA: subgraph matching in mass graphs. *Prof. of CIKM*, 2010.
[20] S. Zhang, J. Yang, and J. Wei. SAPPER: subgraph indexing and approximate matching in large graphs. *Prof. of VLDB*, 2010.
[21] P. Zhao, J. Han. On Graph Query Optimization in Large Networks. *Proc. of VLDB*, 2010.
[22] P. Zhao, J. X. Yu, and P. S. Yu. Graph indexing: Tree + delta $\geq$ graph. *Proc. of VLDB*, 2007.
[23] L. Zou, L. Chen, and M. T. Özsu, Distance-Join: Pattern Match Query in a Large Graph Database, *Proc. of VLDB*, 2009.
[24] gengraph_win. http://www.cs.sunysb.edu/ãlgorith/implement/viger/distrib/.

Skynets: Searching for Minimum Trees in Graphs with Incomparable Edge Weights *

Huiping Cao
hcao@cs.nmsu.edu
New Mexico State University
Las Cruces, NM 88003, USA

K. Selçuk Candan
candan@asu.edu
Arizona State University
Tempe, AZ 85283, USA

Maria Luisa Sapino
mlsapino@di.unito.it
Universita di Torino
Torino, Italy

ABSTRACT

Query processing over weighted data graphs often involves searching for a minimum weighted subgraph –a tree– which covers the nodes satisfying the given query criteria (such as a given set of keywords). Existing works often focus on graphs where the edges have scalar valued weights. In many applications, however, edge weights need to be represented as ranges (or *intervals*) of possible values. In this paper, we introduce the problem of *skynets*, for searching minimum weighted subgraphs, covering the nodes satisfying given query criteria, over interval-weighted graphs. The key challenge is that, unlike scalars which are often totally ordered, depending on the application specific semantics of the $\preceq$ operator, intervals may be partially ordered. Naturally, the need to maintain alternative, incomparable solutions can push the computational complexity of the problem (which is already high for the case with totally ordered scalar edge weights) even higher. In this paper, we first provide alternative definitions of the $\preceq$ operator for intervals and show that some of these lend themselves to efficient solutions. To tackle the complexity challenge in the remaining cases, we propose two optimization criteria that can be used to constrain the solution space. We also discuss how to extend existing approximation algorithms for Steiner trees to discover solutions to the skynet problem. For efficient calculation of the results, we introduce a novel *skyline union operator*. Experiments show that the proposed approach achieves significant gains in efficiency, while providing close to optimal results.

Categories and Subject Descriptors

H.3.3 [**Information Storage and Retrieval**]: Information Search and Retrieval: Search process.

General Terms

Algorithms, Performance.

Keywords

Graph search, skyline union, incomparable edge weights, interval weighted graph, minimum spanning tree

*This work is partially supported by an NSF Grant #1016921 "One Size Does Not Fit All: Empowering the User with User-Driven Integration", and NMSU Interdisciplinary Research Grant # 111721.

CIKM'11, October 24–28, 2011, Glasgow, Scotland, UK.

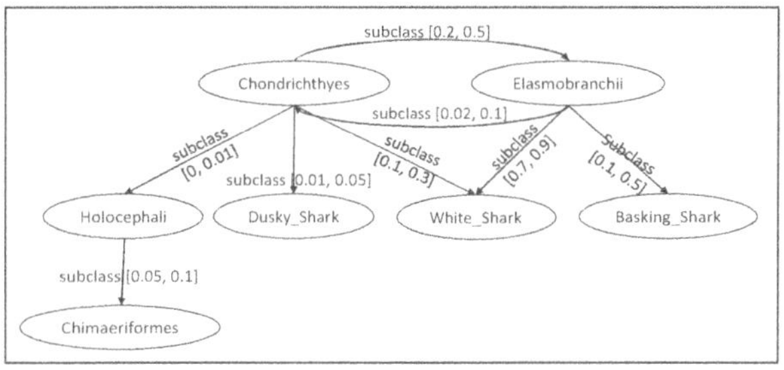

Figure 1: A sample knowledge base (integeration of two taxonomies) where utilities associated to each edge indicates the range of confidence associated to each assertion

1. INTRODUCTION

Graphs and networks are widely used in many applications. For example, the Web can be modeled as a directed graph by treating each page as a graph vertex (or node) and the hyper-links between pages as edges. A resource description framework (RDF) database, consisting of triples describing relationships between pairs of data objects, is often seen as a graph. Discover [13] views relational databases as graphs. Many systems, such as [12], treat XML documents as graphs. Some scientific knowledge management systems, such as [4], also represent integrated data as a graph.

In these and many other works, each node in the graph is associated with one or more data elements (e.g., tags or keywords) and each edge is given a weight, representing the application-specific desirability or *cost* of the edge. The ability to annotate statements in the database is especially important for applications which need to impose additional parameters, like validity, trust, or preference. In other applications, such as transportation networks (Figure 2(a), [7, 14, 20, 36]), weights may represent costs of the edges.

Query processing over graphs and networks has gained significant interest [2, 8, 9, 12, 16, 17, 22, 27]. In a graph database, given a query, the system's goal is often to return a subgraph – e.g. a *Steiner tree*– whose nodes collectively satisfy the query (e.g. cover all the query keywords) and whose total edge weight is minimum among all possible subgraphs satisfying the query.

We note that, despite the flurry of works tackling diverse (Web, relational, XML, RDF) data graphs, existing approaches to the problem are often limited to graphs where the edges have scalar valued weights. In many applications, however, the weights of the edges in the graph are not precisely known and, as in Figure 1, need to be represented as ranges (or *intervals*) – as opposed to scalar weights. Interval based computations and interval weighted graphs also commonly appear in various application domains [18] (including transportation networks, spatial databases (Figure 2(a) [31]).

Other data management applications that require *interval weighted* edges include Steiner searches over summarized graphs

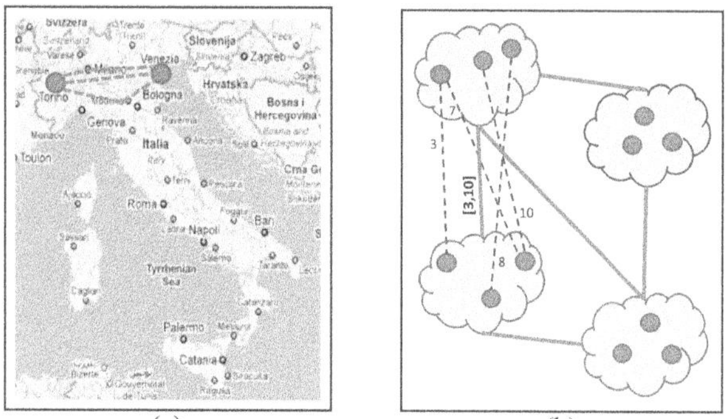

(a) (b)

Figure 2: (a) Expected driving time between two cities may be imprecise due to the weather and road conditions as well as the driving style and other driver choices; (b) in summarized/anonymized graphs, each summarized edge may represent multiple edges, with a range of weights

(where several nodes in the original data graph are grouped and collapsed into a single node, resulting in edges that cannot be represented with scalar edge weights – see Figure 2(b)) and searches over anonymized graphs [23] (where edge weights are anonymized using recoding techniques [32], which replace precise scalar values, with less precise value ranges or intervals).

1.1 Challenges and our Contributions

When the weights of the edges in the graph are represented using intervals –specifying a minimum and maximum value for each edge– standard operator semantics, that assume scalar edge weights, are not applicable: For example, the total weight of a subgraph with two edges with scalar weights, 6 and 7, is 13. On the other hand, computing the total weight of a subgraph with two edges with weights $[1.0, 3.0]$ and $[3.0, 3.5]$ requires an appropriate definition for the *interval summation*.

A more significant challenge in developing query processing algorithms for graphs with interval edge weights is that the *minimum weight* condition cannot always be evaluated in an *unambiguous* manner. For example, given two edges with totally-ordered scalar weights, it is trivial to unambiguously pick the edge with the smaller weight. On the other hand, picking the smaller weighted edge among two edges with interval weights, is not trivial. In fact, different preference, $\preceq$, semantics can give us different results. For example, if we use the average values of the intervals to compare two edge weights $[1.0, 5.0]$ and $[3.0, 4.0]$, the interval $[1.0, 5.0]$ can be said to be smaller than $[3.0, 4.0]$. However, if we require for $\preceq$ that both starting and ending points of one edge be smaller than or equal to the corresponding bounds of the other, these two intervals would be *incomparable*. Unfortunately, in cases where edge weights can be incomparable (i.e., are partially ordered), existing Steiner tree solutions are not applicable.

As we discuss in Section 3, many basic graph operations (such as selecting the minimum weighted subgraph among many candidates or recomputing the weight of a larger subgraph after two small subgraphs are combined) need to be redefined to accommodate non-singular subgraph weights. Moreover, these need to be implemented in ways that avoid significant increases in computational costs due to the potentially large numbers of alternative weights that may need to be considered.

When there are large numbers of incomparable objects, one way to reduce the number of results is to focus on the *skylines* [1, 3, 7, 14, 15, 20, 30] of the result sets instead of all possible results. In this paper, we introduce the *skynet* discovery problem: i.e., searching for minimum weighted sub-graphs, covering the nodes satisfying given query criteria, over graphs with partially ordered (more specifically, interval weighted) edge weights:

- We first define the *skynets* problem of searches on interval weighted graphs. We introduce and compare alternative preference and combination operators and provide alternative formulations of the optimization criterion.
- We discuss how to extend existing approximation algorithms for minimally weighted Steiner trees in the presence of partially ordered edge weights. We also theoretically establish the approximation ratio for the proposed extension.
- We develop a *skyline union operator* to reduce the computational cost of the search algorithms.

The paper is organized as follows: We formally define the metrics, optimization criteria, and our problem in Section 3. In Section 4, we present the *skyline union operator* used for limiting the computational cost of the graph algorithms we develop in the rest of the paper. Section 5 proposes an approximation algorithm to solve the problem and provides the corresponding error bound. Section 6 reports our experimental results over real datasets. Finally, Section 7 summarizes our work.

2. RELATED WORKS

In this section, we describe related works on searches on graphs and skyline query processing.

2.1 Applications of Steiner and Group Steiner Tree Searches

For data represented as a graph, where each vertex represents a data unit (e.g., a tuple in RDB, or a web page) and where edges represent connections between the data units, the search problem can often be formulated as follows: given a graph G and a query $Q = \{K_1, \cdots, K_m\}$ with m keywords, a query result over G is a minimum-weighted subgraph G' of G such that the vertices in G' collectively contain all the keywords in G.

[22] is one of the first papers focused on keyword searches over (web) graphs. Other works, such as DBXplorer, DISCOVER [13] and others [2, 9, 12, 17, 24, 27] focus on answering keyword queries on structured (such as relational) databases by returning results which collectively contain the query keywords and are connected (for example using foreign key constraints). It has been shown [22] that the search problem over weighted graphs can be formulated as an instance of Steiner or Group Steiner Tree (GST) problem. Since it is known [28] that both of these problems are NP-complete, existing algorithms are often heuristics or provide approximate solutions. [2, 17, 22] present memory-based techniques to perform graph search (i.e., the graph data are all in the memory). [22] introduced a heuristic algorithm to perform the query and discover information unit (IU). Initially, the algorithm treats all the vertex nodes covering any query keyword as a forest. Then, it expands this forest by linking subtrees using smaller cost edges. Later, the BANKS system proposed a backward expanding technique [2] and the bidirectional search strategy [17]. A second group of algorithms, including [12], leverage indexes to further improve the search efficiency. BLINKS presented by He et al. in [12], for example, utilizes a bi-level index to facilitate ranked top-k keyword searches.

2.2 Skylines, Skyline Joins, and Route Skylines

Given an ordering relation on multidimensional data, the *skyline* operation searches for a set of objects that are not dominated by other objects in the database [3]. Intuitively, the skyline is the set of maximal vectors in the space [21] and is also known as the *pareto frontier* (or pareto curve) on the vector space. As mentioned above, most existing skyline algorithms [3, 5, 21, 33] consider the case where the data elements within which the skyline set is searched are all available in advance. Recent works, such as [1, 15, 30], consider skyline joins where the skyline sets of the result of join queries are sought. In this paper, we are interested in finding Pareto optimal solutions to common graph problems, such as shortest paths, minimum spanning trees, and Steiner trees.

[7, 14, 20] and other consider various skyline problems with focus on road network applications; i.e., unlike our work, these works assume Euclidean constraints on the original graph. The ordering operator considered in [20] is equivalent to one of the ordering semantics we study in our work (the se_bef operator introduced in the next section). Unlike the more general approach presented in this paper, however, the approach proposed in [20] selects among the many candidates a dominating path based on a weighted combination of the attributes.

2.3 Multi-Constrained and Multi-Objective Graph Problems

In the literature, there are many works that recognize that the graph edges may represent more than one data dimension. For example, in a communication network, each edge may have both delay and jitter parameters. On a road network, the edge weights may represent distances as well as expected times to travel through. As a consequence, there has been a plethora of work addressing multi-constrained and multi-objective graph problems (see [10, 11, 34, 35] for samples and overview of works in the area). In this paper, we note that while an interval may also be seen as a bi-dimensional weight, there is a key difference from multi-constrained and multi-objective graph problems: since the ending value of an interval is always larger than or equal to the starting value, an interval cannot be seen as consisting of two separate parameters. Here, we focus on interval weights as opposed to generic bi-criteria problems.

3. PROBLEM DEFINITION

We introduce the problem of searches over graphs with interval-valued edge weights.

3.1 Intervals

Each interval $I = [i_\bot, i_\top]$ has a starting point $i_\bot \geq 0$ and an ending point $i_\top \geq i_\bot$. As a convention, in this paper, we use a capital letter (e.g., I, U, W) to represent an interval and use its corresponding non-capital letter with subscript '$_\bot$' and '$_\top$' to represent the starting and ending points of the interval.

3.2 "$\oplus$", "$\preceq$", "$\equiv$" Operators for Intervals

Many graph operations, including those involved in the computation of Steiner trees, assume that the edge weights are *commutative monoids*: A monoid is a set, $\mathbb{W}$, on which a binary operation $\circ$ is defined, such that (a) the set $\mathbb{W}$ is closed under $\circ$, (b) $\circ$ is associative, and (c) there exists an element $0 \in \mathbb{W}$, such that for all elements $w \in \mathbb{W}$, $w \circ 0 = 0 \circ w = w$. A monoid where $\circ$ is commutative is called a *commutative monoid* and each commutative monoid has an associated $\preceq$ such that $a \preceq b$ iff there exists positive c such that $a \circ c = b$. Scalars (integers, rational, real, and complex numbers) are all commutative monoids when the *addition* semantics is associated to $\circ$ operation.

Graph algorithms leverage the commutative monoid nature of the scalar edge weights: the $\circ$ operator is used to define the subgraph weight in terms of the weights of the constituents edges and $\preceq$ enables the comparison of different subgraphs (or sub-results) to choose the one that is more desirable. The associativity and the commutativity of these operators are leveraged to reduce the computational complexity of the underlying search problems.

To define search problems over interval-weighted graphs, we need counterparts of the "$+$" and "$\leq$" operators (commonly used for integers, rational, real, and complex numbers) . Thus, we first need to define interval-based counterparts, "$\oplus$" and "$\preceq$", of these two operators.

3.2.1 "$\oplus$" Interval Operator

While many definitions of the $\oplus$ operator are possible, the following definition for $\oplus$ is intuitive:

DEFINITION 3.1 (INTERVAL $\oplus$). *Given two intervals $U = [u_\bot, u_\top]$ and $W = [w_\bot, w_\top]$, the plus operator (denoted as $\oplus$) on them is defined as $U \oplus W = [u_\bot + w_\bot, u_\top + w_\top]$.*

$[0, 0]$ is the *zero* element under $\oplus$ and it is trivial to show that this operator is associative and commutative.

3.2.2 "$\preceq$" and "$\equiv$" Boolean Operators

The following are commonly used definitions for $\preceq$ in various application domains.

DEFINITION 3.2 (INTERVAL $\preceq$). *Let $U = [u_\bot, u_\top]$ and $W = [w_\bot, w_\top]$ be two intervals. We can define $\preceq$ as follows:*

- $\mathbf{U \preceq_{start} W}$: *$U$ starts before or simultaneously with W. i.e., $(U \preceq_{start} W) \longleftrightarrow (u_\bot \leq w_\bot)$.*
- $\mathbf{U \preceq_{end} W}$: *$U$ ends before or simultaneously with W. i.e., $(U \preceq_{end} W) \longleftrightarrow (u_\top \leq w_\top)$.*
- $\mathbf{U \preceq_{avg} W}$: *$U$'s mean is smaller than or equal to W's i.e., $(U \preceq_{avg} W) \longleftrightarrow (\frac{u_\bot + u_\top}{2} \leq \frac{w_\bot + w_\top}{2})$.*
- $\mathbf{U \preceq_{len} W}$: *$U$ is shorter than or equal to W. i.e., $(U \preceq_{len} W) \longleftrightarrow ((u_\top - u_\bot) \leq (w_\top - w_\bot))$.*
- $\mathbf{U \preceq_{bef} W}$: *$U$ ends before or at the same time as W starts. i.e., $(U \preceq_{bef} W) \longleftrightarrow (u_\top \leq w_\bot)$.*
- $\mathbf{U \preceq_{se\_bef} W}$: *$U$ starts before or simultaneously with W,* and *U ends before or simultaneously with W. i.e., $(U \preceq_{se\_bef} W) \longleftrightarrow ((u_\bot \leq w_\bot)$ and $(u_\top \leq w_\top))$.*

U and W are equivalent (i.e., $U \equiv W$) iff $U \preceq W$ and $W \preceq U$. If $U \preceq W$ and U is not equivalent to W, in this paper, we consider that U dominates W.

3.3 Minimal Interval(s)

The first four of the $\preceq$ semantics above lead to non-ambiguous selection of the minimal interval(s) in $\mathcal{I}$. This is, however, not the case for the latter two $\preceq$ semantics (i.e., $\preceq_{bef}$ and $\preceq_{se\_bef}$). For example, let $\mathcal{I} = \{[3, 7], [4, 6]\}$, the two intervals in this set are not comparable to each other based on either $\preceq_{bef}$ or $\preceq_{se\_bef}$. In fact $\preceq_{bef}$ and $\preceq_{se\_bef}$ define not a total order, but a partial order on the elements in $\mathcal{I}$. In the presence of such partially ordered intervals, we need an appropriate minimality criterion:

DEFINITION 3.3 (MINIMAL INTERVAL(S)). *Let $\mathcal{I}$ be a set of intervals and let $\preceq$ impose a partial order among the elements in $\mathcal{I}$. The interval $I \in \mathcal{I}$ is said to be* minimal *in $\mathcal{I}$ iff there exists no other interval $J \in \mathcal{I}$ such that $(J \not\equiv I)$ and $(J \preceq I)$.*

In other words, $I \in \mathcal{I}$ is *minimal* in $\mathcal{I}$ iff for all $J \in \mathcal{I}$, one of the following is true: $(I \equiv J)$, $(I \preceq J)$, or I and J are incomparable.

3.4 Skynets on Interval-Weighted Graphs

Let $G = \langle V, E, \phi \rangle$ be a graph where each edge, e, is associated with an interval-valued edge weight $\phi(e)$

DEFINITION 3.4 (WEIGHT OF A GRAPH). *We define the weight of a graph, $G = \langle V, E, \phi \rangle$, as*

$$\bigoplus_{e \in E} \phi(e) = [\sum_{e \in E} i_{e,\perp}, \sum_{e \in E} i_{e,\top}].$$

Here, $i_{e,\perp}$ and $i_{e,\top}$ refer to the starting and ending points of the interval on the edge e respectively.

Given this, we can define the general *skynet problem* over interval-weighted graphs as follows:

DEFINITION 3.5 (SKYNET PROBLEM). *Given an interval-weighted graph $G = \langle V, E, \phi \rangle$, operators "$\oplus$" and "$\preceq$" on intervals, and a search condition Θ, find subgraph(s) G_{res} of G such that (a) $\Theta(G_{res}) = true$ and (b) G_{res} is* minimal *among all the subgraphs of G that satisfy the query condition Θ.*

Note that, there can be several *minimal* solutions to the problem that have *different* (and incomparable) overall weights (this is a major difference from the traditional search problems, where all minimal solutions have the same weight). Traditionally, most graph problems (including the Steiner tree search problem, the shortest path problem, and the minimum spanning tree problem [6]) are all commonly formulated to seek for *only one* result among all minimal results. In this paper, we formulate two distinct search problems, eliminating redundant matches and maintaining a core subset of results in different ways: let M be the set of all minimal matches,

- the **search-for-one skynet** problem seeks for one sample result, $r \in M$; whereas
- the **search-for-ps skynet** (or the *search-for-pareto-set*) problem seeks for a maximal $R \subseteq M$ consisting of mutually-incomparable results; in other words, any minimal result, $m \in M$ and $m \notin R$, is equivalent to some $r \in R$.

4. SKYLINE UNION OPERATOR

A common aspect of the skynet problems we consider is that they require the ability to combine two sets, each containing a group of mutually incomparable intervals, in such a way that the resulting set consists of the Pareto optimal intervals of the union of the two sets. We refer to this as the *skyline union* ($\uplus$) operation:

DEFINITION 4.1 (SKYLINE UNION OPERATOR $\uplus$). *Given two sets of mutually incomparable intervals, $\mathcal{I}_1$ and $\mathcal{I}_2$, $\uplus$ generates another set $\mathcal{I} = \mathcal{I}_1 \uplus \mathcal{I}_2$ such that $\forall U \in \mathcal{I}$, (1) $U \in \mathcal{I}_1$ or $U \in \mathcal{I}_2$; and (2) $\forall U \in \mathcal{I}_1 \cup \mathcal{I}_2$, either $U \in \mathcal{I}$ or $\exists W \in \mathcal{I}$, $W \not\equiv U$ and $W \preceq U$.*

In other words, $\mathcal{I}$ contains all the intervals which are not dominated by any other interval in $\mathcal{I}_1$ or $\mathcal{I}_2$.

EXAMPLE 4.1. *Given $\mathcal{I}_1 = \{[3,5],[2,8]\}$, $\mathcal{I}_2 = \{[1,7],[4,6]\}$. When we consider the "$\preceq_{se\_bef}$" definition, $\mathcal{I}_1 \uplus_{se\_bef} \mathcal{I}_2 = \{[3,5],[1,7]\}$: $[1,7] \preceq_{se\_bef} [2,8]$, $[2,8]$ is not in $\mathcal{I}$ and, similarly, $[3,5] \preceq_{se\_bef} [4,6]$, $[4,6]$ is not in $\mathcal{I}$. When we consider the "$\preceq_{bef}$" definition, however, $\mathcal{I}_1 \uplus_{bef} \mathcal{I}_2 = \{[3,5],[2,8],[1,7],[4,6]\}$.*

In this section, we describe the interval-based skyline union operations for both $\preceq_{se\_bef}$ and $\preceq_{bef}$ partial order semantics.

SkylineUnion$_{se\_bef}$ $(\mathcal{I}_1, \mathcal{I}_2)$

1. Initially, all intervals in $\mathcal{I}_1$ and $\mathcal{I}_2$ are sorted in the ascending order of the starting points and $\mathcal{I}$ is set to $\emptyset$.
2. We sequentially get an interval $I[i_\perp, i_\top]$ (either from $\mathcal{I}_1$ or from $\mathcal{I}_2$) with the smallest starting point.
3. Let $\mathcal{I}_{\top min}$ be the smallest ending point for the intervals in $\mathcal{I}$. If the starting point $i_\perp$ of the newly seen interval I is larger than $\mathcal{I}_{\top min}$, it means the new interval is greater than at least *some* interval in $\mathcal{I}$. Accordingly, all the intervals after I would also be greater than some existing interval (based on the sorted nature), then the program terminates.
4. Otherwise,
   (a) If $i_\top < \mathcal{I}_{\top min}$, it means that interval I is incomparable with all the existing intervals in $\mathcal{I}$. Then, I should be put into $\mathcal{I}$.
   (b) On the other hand, if $i_\top \geq \mathcal{I}_{\top min}$, then $\exists I' \in \mathcal{I}$ dominating I, since $i_\top \geq i'_\top = \mathcal{I}_{\top min}$ and $i_\perp \geq i'_\perp$ (based on the process).
5. The program terminates either when there is no interval in $\mathcal{I}_1$ and $\mathcal{I}_2$, or the starting point $i_\perp$ of the newly seen interval I is larger than $\mathcal{I}_{\top min}$. In the later case, the new interval is greater than some existing interval in $\mathcal{I}$.

Figure 3: Skyline union ($\uplus_{se\_bef}$) for $\preceq_{se\_bef}$ ordering

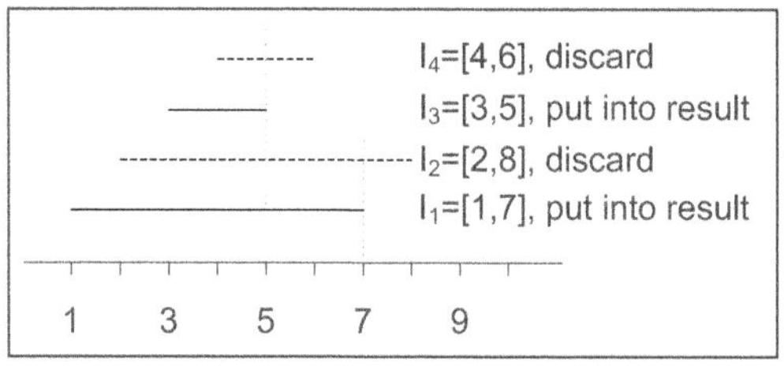

Figure 4: Sample execution scenario for $\uplus_{se\_bef}$

4.1 Skyline Union for the $\preceq_{se\_bef}$ Ordering

Given two interval sets $\mathcal{I}_1$ and $\mathcal{I}_2$, the skyline union operator algorithm for $\preceq_{se\_bef}$ works as follows. Initially, all intervals in $\mathcal{I}_1$ and $\mathcal{I}_2$ are sorted in the ascending order of their starting points. During the process, the algorithm maintains the smallest ending point $\mathcal{I}_{\top min}$ for the intervals in the solution set $\mathcal{I}$ to facilitate the calculation of incomparable intervals. In particular, for a newly seen interval I, only when (a) its starting point $i_\perp \geq \mathcal{I}_{\top min}$ and (b) its ending point $i_\top < \mathcal{I}_{\top min}$, which means that interval I is incomparable with all the existing intervals in $\mathcal{I}$, we can put I into $\mathcal{I}$. The pseudo-code is presented in Figure 3.

EXAMPLE 4.2. *Consider Figure 4 with four intervals:*

- *Initially, $\mathcal{I} = \emptyset$ and $\mathcal{I}_{\top min} = \infty$.*
- *First, the operator gets the interval with the smallest starting point, $[1,7]$, from $\mathcal{I}_1 \cup \mathcal{I}_2$. Then $\mathcal{I} = \{[1,7]\}$ and $\mathcal{I}_{\top min}$ is set to 7.*
- *The second interval we need to process is $[2,8]$. Since its ending point $8 > \mathcal{I}_{\top min} = 7$, it violates condition (b). Thus, it is not put into $\mathcal{I}$.*
- *The next interval we need to deal with is $[3,5]$. Its ending point $5 < \mathcal{I}_{\top min} = 7$, thus it is incomparable with the existing intervals. This new interval is put into $\mathcal{I}$. Now, $\mathcal{I} = \{[3,5],[1,7]\}$ and $\mathcal{I}_{\top min} = 5$.*
- *A similar process is applied to $[4,6]$, which is greater than one of the existing intervals, $[3,5]$, in I; thus $[4,6]$ is not put into $\mathcal{I}$.*
- *Finally, the skyline union result is $\mathcal{I} = \{[3,5],[1,7]\}$.*

The complexity of the algorithm is linear in the sizes of the two input sets (i.e., $O(|\mathcal{I}_1| + |\mathcal{I}_2|)$) assuming that the sets are initially sorted (as is the case in our scenario).

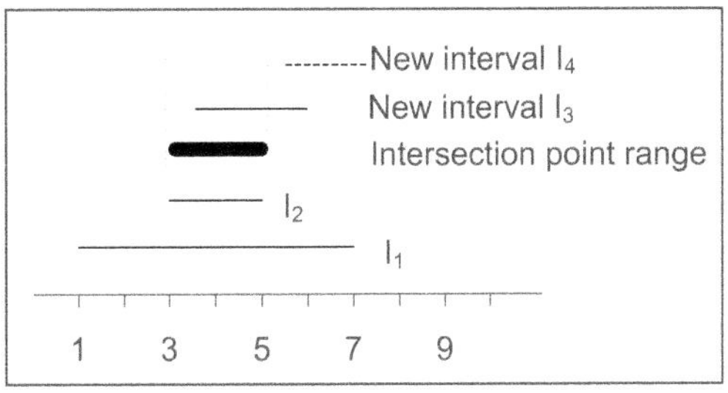

Figure 5: Illustration of the operation of the $\uplus_{bef}$ operator: after seeing I_1 and I_2, the range for the interval intersection is shown as the bold line $\mathcal{I}_\cap = [\mathcal{I}_\perp^\cap, \mathcal{I}_\top^\cap] = [3,5]$. (a) Any new coming interval with ending point not greater than 5 ($\mathcal{I}_\top^\cap$) – e.g. I_3 – will be in the union result; (b) any new interval with starting point greater than 5 – e.g., I_4 – is not put in the result. The algorithm stops once it sees a new interval with starting pointer larger than 5.

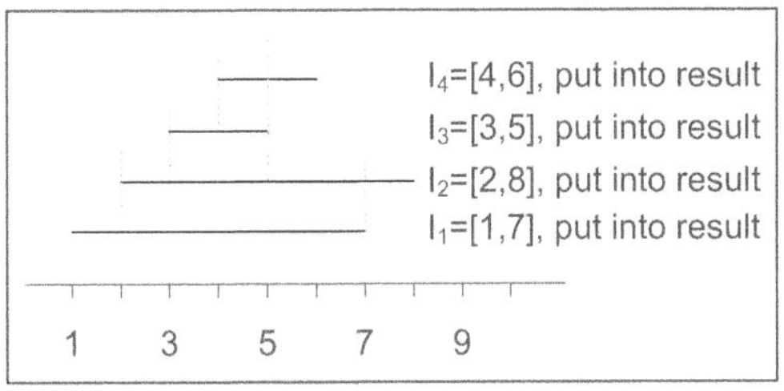

Figure 6: Sample execution scenario for $\uplus_{bef}$: the interval intersection gradually shrinks after seeing I_1, I_2 (shrinks to [2,7]), I_3 (shrinks to [3,5]), and I_4 (shrinks to [4,5]).

4.2 Skyline Union for the $\preceq_{bef}$ Ordering

For the $\preceq_{bef}$ ordering of the intervals, the skyline union operator needs to work slightly differently. Figure 5 illustrates the algorithm: As is the case for $\preceq_{se\_bef}$, initially, all intervals in $\mathcal{I}_1$ and $\mathcal{I}_2$ are sorted in ascending order of the starting points and $\mathcal{I}$ is set to $\emptyset$. Different from the algorithm for $\preceq_{se\_bef}$, however, this time we maintain an intersection point range $\mathcal{I}_\cap = [\mathcal{I}_\perp^\cap, \mathcal{I}_\top^\cap]$ for all intersected intervals in $\mathcal{I}$. If a new interval $I[i_\perp, i_\top]$ intersects with $\mathcal{I}_\cap$, it is incomparable with the intervals in $\mathcal{I}$. On the other hand, if (a) $i_\top < \mathcal{I}_\perp^\cap$ or (b) $i_\perp > \mathcal{I}_\top^\cap$, the new interval I is smaller or greater than some interval in $\mathcal{I}$. To make the computation easier, the operator first gets the intervals with smaller starting points, then unions the intervals with larger starting points. This way, $\mathcal{I}_\perp^\cap$ increases monotonically and $\mathcal{I}_\top^\cap$ decreases monotonically. Then, when the operator sees a new interval, it only needs to check condition (b). If the new interval's starting point $i_\perp$ is larger than the upper bound of the intersection $\mathcal{I}_\top^\cap$, then there must be some existing interval in I which is $\preceq_{bef}$ than this interval and, thus, we do not need to place the new interval in $\mathcal{I}$. At this point the algorithm stops.

EXAMPLE 4.3. *Figure 6 shows how $\uplus_{bef}$ computation works for $\mathcal{I}_1 = \{[2,8],[3,5]\}$ and $\mathcal{I}_2 = \{[1,7],[4,6]\}$ to obtain the result $\mathcal{I}_1 \uplus_s \mathcal{I}_2 = \{[3,5],[2,8],[1,7],[4,6]\}$.*

Again, assuming that the input sets are sorted, the complexity of this algorithm is $O(|\mathcal{I}_1| + |\mathcal{I}_2|)$.

5. STEINER TREE SKYNETS

In this section, we consider the computation of Steiner tree skynets, with incomparable edge weights.

DEFINITION 5.1 (STEINER TREE SKYNETS). *Given an undirected interval-weighted graph $G = \langle V, E, \phi\rangle$, operators "$\oplus$" and "$\preceq$" on intervals, and a set of query vertices $V_S \subseteq V$, find subgraph(s) G_{res} of G such that (a) G_{res} satisfies the Θ condition "$G_{res}.V$* covers *V_S" and (b) G_{res}* is minimal *among all graphs that cover V_S.*

The basic Steiner tree problem (on undirected graphs with scalar edge weights) is known to be NP-complete; thus, most non-trivial solutions are often heuristics or approximation algorithms [19, 29]. In [19], Kou et al. present Algorithm H, an approximate algorithm known to return trees with at most $2\times$ the weight of the optimal Steiner tree. While Algorithm H is **not** the best known approximate Steiner tree algorithm[1], with the tightest known bounds, it provides the appropriate structure[2] for us to explain the challenges that are faced in developing solutions for the problem of searching for minimal Steiner trees on graphs with incomparable weights:

Path Skynet Discovery: The Steiner tree algorithm first constructs a complete graph G' such that the weight of the edge between two nodes v_j and v_k in V' is the weight of the shortest path from v_j to v_k in V. In the presence of interval weights, there may exist multiple paths from v_j to v_k with incomparable weights. Thus, we need to identify "*path skynets*" in the graph.

Spanning Tree Skynet Discovery: Next, the algorithm identifies minimum spanning trees on the modified graph. When we are dealing with graphs with interval weighted edges, we need to be able to identify "*spanning tree skynets*" in the graph.

5.1 Path Skynets

Let us first consider the well known Dijkstra's shortest path algorithm [6] for scalar weighted graphs: The algorithm starts from a given source vertex and continuously updates the distance from the source vertex to the vertices in the graph (reachable from the source) by always picking the currently closest unconsidered vertex from a priority queue. For each vertex v in the graph, the algorithm maintains the *minimum* distance $minDist(v)$ from the source to v. In addition, in order to be able to reconstruct the shortest path, for each vertex v, the algorithm also maintains the previous vertex $prevVertex(v)$ which is currently on the shortest path from the source to v. In contrast, as Example 5.1 illustrates, in the presence of incomparable edge weights, it is not sufficient to maintain a single $minDist(v)$ for vertex, v.

EXAMPLE 5.1. *Let us consider the interval-weighted graph in Figure 7 to illustrate the skyline path discovery. Let v_0 be the source vertex and assume that we are using $\preceq_{se\_bef}$ comparison operator. From v_0 to v_1 there is one path with smallest interval [1,1]. From v_0 to v_2, there are two paths with incomparable intervals: (1) [2,3] for path $v_0 \rightarrow v_1 \rightarrow v_2$ and (2) [1,6] for path $v_0 \rightarrow v_2$. From v_0 to v_3, there are four paths. The first path is $v_0 \rightarrow v_3$ with interval [1,7]. The second path is $v_0 \rightarrow v_1 \rightarrow v_3$ with interval [4,6]. The third one is $v_0 \rightarrow v_1 \rightarrow v_2 \rightarrow v_3$ with intervals [3,5]. The fourth one is $v_0 \rightarrow v_2 \rightarrow v_3$ with interval [2,8]. But when we union the four intervals, [4,6] and [2,8] are in the result since $[3,5] \preceq_{se\_bef} [4,6]$ and $[1,7] \preceq_{se\_bef} [2,8]$. Figure 7(b) shows the minimal paths from v_0 to other vertices. For v_3, one path is from the source vertex v_0. The second is reached through v_2.*

Since there may be more than one (mutually-incomparable) minimal paths from the source to a vertex, we potentially need to maintain multiple minimal path weights for each vertex, v. In order to

[1]The problem is APX-complete, which means that arbitrarily good approximation ratios cannot be achieved using a polynomial time approximation scheme, unless P=NP. The other Steiner tree algorithms (e.g., relative greedy [37] and loss contracting algorithms [29]) provide similar upper- (~ 1.6) and lower- (~ 1.3) bounds.

[2]The relative greedy [37] and loss contracting algorithms [29] also have similar structures: they compute minimum spanning trees and Steiner trees over subsets of the input graph.

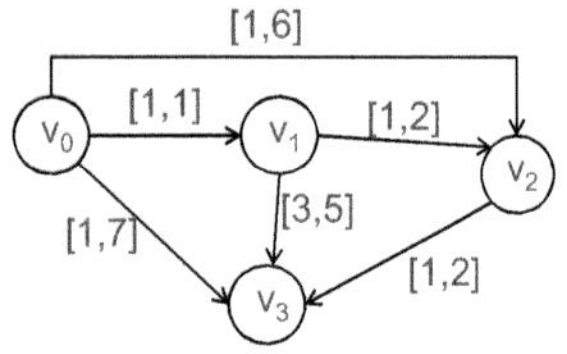

(a) Interval-weighted graph

Vertex	Incomparable intervals	path vertex
v_0	0: [0,0]	null
v_1	0: [1,1]	v_0
v_2	0: [2,3]	$v_0 \rightarrow v_1$
	1: [1,6]	v_0
v_3	0: [1,7]	v_0
	~~1: [4,6]~~	~~$v_0 \rightarrow v_1$~~
	2: [3,5]	$v_0 \rightarrow v_2$ (through v_1)
	~~3: [2,8]~~	~~$v_0 \rightarrow v_2$~~

(b) Path skynets from v_0

Figure 7: Example for skyline path discovery

SkynetPath_QuadrupleClustered (s, V)
/* s is the source vertex and V is the set of all vertices; */

1. Initialization
   (a) Let $quad_0 = \langle s, [0,0], null, null\rangle$
   (b) Insert $quad_0$ into a $\preceq$ lattice, PQ
   (c) Let $quadSet(s) = \{q_0\}$
   (d) For each vertex $v_i \in V - \{s\}$, let $quadSet(v_i) = \{\langle v_i, [\infty, \infty], null, null\rangle\}$
2. **While** ($PQ! = \emptyset$)
   (a) Let $minSet(PQ)$ be the set of minimal quadruples of lattice PQ
   (b) Let v be any vertex with a quadruple in $minSet(PQ)$
   (c) Let $quadSet$ be the maximal subset of $minSet(PQ)$ consisting of quadruples from v
   (d) Remove $quadSet$ from PQ
   (e) For each $e = v \rightarrow v'$
      i. $qSet' = \{\langle v', (int \oplus weight(e)), v, int\rangle \mid \langle v, int, *, *\rangle \in quadSet\}$
      ii. $quadSet(v') = quadSet(v') \uplus qSet'$
      iii. Update the lattice PQ based on the changes (additions and removals) in $quadSet(v')$

Figure 8: (Quadruple-clustered) Path skynets algorithm; at each iteration, the algorithm picks and operates on the entire maximal subset of quadruples from the selected vertex v

be able to trace these minimal paths back to the source, we also need to keep track of the corresponding previous vertex information for each path weight. Note that, unlike the basic case with scalar edge weights, since now each previous vertex may itself have several incomparable weights, for each minimum distance/previous vertex combination, $\langle minDist_i(v), prevVertex_i(v)\rangle$, we also need to maintain the relevant weight, $prevVertexDist_i(v)$ $(= minDist_j(prevVertex_i(v)))$, of the previous vertex from which $minDist_i(v)$ has been computed. Therefore, during the execution of the algorithm, for each vertex v, we need to maintain a set of quadruples of the form $\langle v, minDist_i(v), prevVertex_i(v), prevVertexDist_i(v)\rangle$.

Figure 8 provides the pseudo-code for path skynet computation: unlike the basic algorithm which considers nodes of the graph by picking them one at a time from a priority queue, this algorithm maintains a priority queue of quadruples, in the form of a lattice of the corresponding intervals. At all times, $minSet(PQ)$ is the set of minimal quadruples in the priority queue. As long as the priority queue of the quadruples is not empty, the algorithm dequeues a quadruple, $\langle v, int, *, *\rangle$ in $minSet(PQ)$ and relaxes the nodes reachable by the outgoing edges of v.

In the standard Dijkstra's algorithm, relaxing the weight of a vertex involves selecting the minimum among all possible (scalar) candidate weights. In the case of path skynets, however, we need to maintain the Pareto-optimal set of weights (i.e., a set of weights that are minimal and mutually incomparable) as discussed next:

5.1.1 Priority Queue and its Impact on Relaxation

The algorithm assumes that the $minSet(PQ)$ is available and uses this to reduce the overall cost of relaxations. We refer to this as the *quadruple-clustered processing:* Instead of considering dequeuing intervals one at a time, when a quadruple corresponding to a node, v, is picked from the priority queue, the algorithm considers the entire maximal subset of $minSet(PQ)$ consisting of quadruples from v. The algorithm relaxes the weights of the neighbors of v (using $\uplus$) with this maximal subset of quadruples. This reduces the number of times each node needs to be relaxed.

Note that due to the partially ordered nature of the intervals, we cannot implement the priority queue as a simple minheap; instead, this priority queue of partially ordered intervals is implemented in the form of a dynamically maintained lattice or Hasse diagram; the worst case maintenance cost of adding one interval to this lattice is $O(|\mathcal{I}|)$, where $\mathcal{I}$ is the set of intervals in the priority queue.

Alternatively, we could impose a total order on the intervals by breaking the incomparabilities: if two intervals are incomparable, we can declare the node with the smaller t_s (or smaller t_e when t_s is the same) as the smaller one. The intervals can then be indexed in a minheap based priority queue, which relies on the resulting total order: since, both in $\preceq_{bef}$ and in $\preceq_{se\_bef}$, an interval with the smallest t_s is either smaller than or incomparable to others with largest t_s, this order will ensure that the interval dequeued from the priority queue is always in the minimal set. This strategy, on the other hand, has the disadvantage that the $minSet(PQ)$ will not be available as a whole and consequently, it is not possible to select the maximal subset of $minSet(PQ)$ consisting of quadruples from a vertex v. When $minSet(PQ)$ is not available, the following priority management strategies are applicable:

- *Quadruple-at-a-time processing:* In this strategy, at each iteration, only one quadruple (the one most recently dequeued from the priority queue) is considered. Since the intervals are considered one at a time, this approach cannot leverage clustered processing of $\uplus$.
- *Node-as-a-whole processing:* Let v be the vertex corresponding to the dequeued quadruple. In this strategy, all quadruples of v (even those that are not in $minSet(PQ)$) are processed. Note that this strategy may give rise to intervals that may become obsolete in the future. Since repeatedly identifying and propagating "obsolescence" can be prohibitively expensive, we perform this as a post processing step, after the relaxation process finishes.
- *Node-clustered processing:* In this strategy, we continue dequeuing from the priority queue quadruples as long as they are from the same vertex; we stop dequeuing when a quadruple from a new vertex is met. The quadruples from the same vertex are then all processed in $\uplus$ together as a cluster. Note that the likelihood of finding a longer run of minimal vertices from the same vertex can be boosted by using the vertex id as an additional tie breaking criterion.

5.1.2 Cycle Management

In the standard Dijkstra's shortest path algorithm with scalar weights, each vertex is visited once, even in the presence of cy-

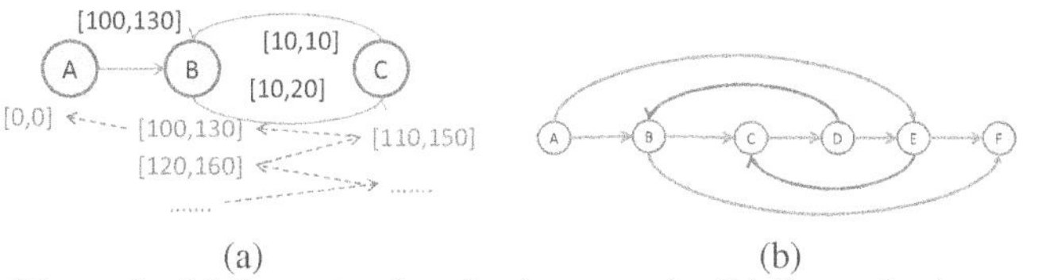

Figure 9: (a) Impacts of cycles in a graph; (b) the path $A \rightarrow E \rightarrow C \rightarrow D \rightarrow B \rightarrow F$ on this graph would require forward-backward-forward-backward-forward relaxation stages (red edges correspond to the "backward" edges)

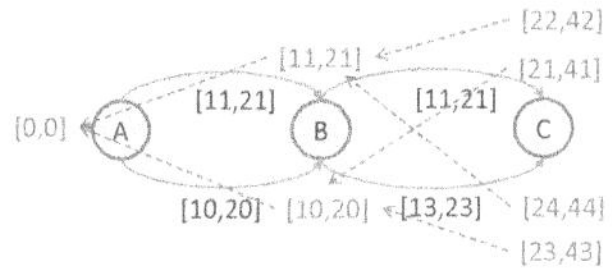

Figure 10: Exponential growth in the number of quadruples

cles (as long as cycles are not negative). As shown in Figure 9(a), however, during path skynet computation a given node may be visited multiple times for different incomparable paths and thus the paths that are discovered may stop being simple paths.

One way to avoid cycles in the identified paths is to "trace-back" the attached pointers at each relaxation step to ensure that there are no cycles. This, however, is likely to be extremely costly. In this paper, we consider two different mechanisms: In the *path signatures* based strategy, we associate a path signature to each quadruple: each path signature is used for quickly identifying the vertices that are on the path from the source to this quadruple.

In the *iterative topological sort* strategy, on the other hand, we eliminate cycles on the graph using a topological sort operation, which will label edges in the graph as "forward edges" and "backward edges". We can then perform shortest path computation in repeated forward and backward stages: Since the cycles are eliminated, in the forward stage (where only forward edges are used), there is no reason to check for cycles. The backward stage (where only backward edges are used) may introduce quadruples corresponding to cycles and these can be eliminated by post-processing after that stage. Note that, as shown in Figure 9(b), a path of length, l, may include up to $l/2$ alternating forward and backward edge pairs. Thus, this approach may require up to $|V'|/2$ iterations of the forward/backward stages until the list of quadruples stabilizes.

5.1.3 Complexity

The precise complexity of the algorithm depends on the specific priority queue and cycle management strategies selected. In the worst case, however, as shown in Figure 10 the number of quadruples maintained may grow exponentially with the length of the paths on the graph. In practice, however, since many of the weights associated to the same node will be comparable to each other, the minimal incomparable set that needs to be maintained tends to be much smaller. Indeed, as we see in Section 6, in practice, the complexity of this step is much closer to linear in the graph size. Therefore, in this paper, we do not consider any further heuristics to reduce the number of quadruples.

5.2 Spanning Tree Skynets

Once the necessary shortest path information is collected, in its second step, the Steiner tree H algorithm constructs a complete graph G' and finds its minimum spanning tree. However, in the presence of incomparable weights, each edge of the complete graph G' may be associated with a *set of incomparable weights*. Instead of treating each such edge independently, we design the minimum spanning tree skynet algorithm in a way that leverages the skyline union operator ($\uplus$) described in Section 4.

The well known Kruskal's minimum spanning tree algorithm [6] grows the minimum spanning tree by starting from individual vertices and incrementally combining partial spanning trees. The algorithm repeatedly picks the edge (v_i, v_j) with the minimum weight from a priority queue and, if no path exists between v_i and v_j in the existing forest of minimum spanning trees, this edge is used to combine the two partial spanning trees containing v_i and v_j. Naturally, in the presence of sets of incomparable weights the priority queue needs to be maintained differently.

5.2.1 Obtaining a Single Spanning Tree

If the user's goal is to find only one tree whose overall weight is smaller than or incomparable to all the others, then we can achieve this relatively cheaply: A min-heap based priority queue can maintain intervals; to achieve this we impose a total order on the intervals by breaking the incomparabilities: if two intervals are incomparable, we can declare the node with the smaller t_s (or smaller t_e when t_s is the same) as the smaller one. Note that, for each edge of G', in the priority queue, we need to maintain only one interval; i.e., the minimal interval, according to the total order, corresponding to that edge. Let the number of edges in G' be $|E'|$; then, this operation is of complexity $O(|E'| \cdot log|E'|)$.

5.2.2 Obtaining a Pareto Set

If we want to find a set of incomparable solutions, as before we first impose a total order on the intervals and sort the available intervals in the ascending order. Then, we maintain two cursors on this ordered interval list to control the exploration of the search space. The first cursor denotes the starting checking point of one candidate solution space. The second cursor plays the role of the priority query in this search space. Initially, the first cursor points to the first interval in the list. Once all the incomparable solutions containing the interval that the first cursor points to are found, this cursor moves forward to test another candidate solution. The second cursor retrieves intervals in order from the interval that the first cursor points to. When a tree is found or the second cursor reaches the end of the list, the search of this solution space finishes. When the first cursor gets to the end of the list, we have found all the incomparable trees. Let the length of the list (i.e., the total number of incomparable intervals considered) be L (which is exponential in the size of the graph G' in the worst case as discussed earlier); then, this operation is of complexity $O(L^2|E'|)$.

5.3 Obtaining the Steiner Tree Skynet

Given the spanning tree skynets, in the final step, we construct the sought after Steiner tree skynets. It has been shown that the trees returned by the algorithm with scalar edge weights have at most $2\times$ the weight of the optimal Steiner tree [19]. A similar result also holds for the version with incomparable edge weights:

THEOREM 5.1. *The proposed algorithm returns solutions to the Steiner tree skynet problem, such that $S_{appx} \leq 2 \cdot OPT$, where OPT is a Pareto-optimal solution. More specifically, let U be the interval weight of S_{appx}. Then, either (a) there exists a Pareto-optimal solution $OPT = [opt_\perp, opt_\top]$, such that $u_\perp \leq 2 \cdot opt_\perp$ and $u_\top \leq 2 \cdot opt_\top$, or (b) U is incomparable with $[2 \cdot opt'_\perp, 2 \cdot opt'_\top]$ for all Pareto-optimal solutions $OPT' = [opt'_\perp, opt'_\top]$.*

Proof Sketch: Let $G = (V, E, \phi)$ be an undirected graph with interval weights and let us assume that we are given a set, V_S, of Steiner points. Let T be a Steiner tree produced by our approximate algorithm and $weight(T) = [t_\perp, t_\top]$ be the total weight of this tree. Let OPT be an optimal Steiner tree with total weight $[opt_\perp, opt_\top]$. The proof follows the outline of the proof of Kou's algorithm [19]. First, let us consider an Eulerian graph G^* obtained from OPT by doubling each edge in OPT. Obviously,

G^* connects all the Steiner points. Second, consider a Euler tour of graph G^*. The weight of this Euler tour, g^*, is $weight(g^*) = 2 \cdot weight(OPT)$; i.e., $g'_\perp = 2 \cdot opt_\perp$ and $g'_\top = 2 \cdot opt_\top$. Next, we obtain a Hamiltonian cycle H on the Steiner vertices by traversing the Euler tour and short-cut previously discovered vertices. The construction of G^* ensures triangular inequality[3] of the edges of the graph and this guarantees that this Hamiltonian cycle's weight is no more than $2 \cdot weight(OPT)$. This Hamiltonian cycle H is also a spanning tree. Based on the process of the approximation algorithm, H either equals to T or H's weight is incomparable with T. Thus, $t_\perp \leq 2 \cdot opt_\perp$ and $t_\top \leq 2 \cdot opt_\top$.

Next, we experimentally show that, in practice, the observed approximation ratios for both $\preceq_{se\_bef}$ and $\preceq_{bef}$ are much better than $2\times$. Note that the Algorithm H does not lend itself into tighter bounds; as mentioned earlier, other Steiner tree algorithms also have lax bounds (e.g., relative greedy [37] and loss contracting algorithms [29] provide $\sim 1.6\times$ upper- and $\sim 1.3\times$ lower bounds).

The worst case complexity of approximate Steiner tree skynet discovery is exponential in the size of the graph since, as described earlier, the number of quadruples maintained may grow exponentially in the length of the paths embedded in the graph (see Figure 10). This is not surprising since the Steiner tree problem itself is APX-complete and the Steiner tree skynet problem is doubly exponential (firstly due to Steiner requirement and secondly due to the existence of incomparable intervals). While additional heuristics (such as the size of the intervals) can be used to prune the number of quadruples to polynomial in the graph size, we do not consider such heuristics in the paper because, as we see in the next section, in practice the growth in the execution time is much closer to linear in the graph size even without such heuristics.

6. EXPERIMENTS

In this section, we examine the effectiveness of the proposed skynet approach by comparing the optimal and the approximate solutions under different semantics of $\preceq$. We implemented the algorithms using Java with the JGraphT library (`jgrapht.sourceforge.net`). The experiments were run with 2.99 GHZ CPU and 2G memory on a Java virtual machine.

6.1 Data Sets

The graph topology used in our scalability experiments are generated using the DBLP dataset (`dblp.uni-trier.de/xml/`). First, as is common, we have removed the isolated entries from the graph using common data cleaning steps [12] to obtain a graph with $\sim 400K$ vertices and $\sim 600K$ edges. Then, to obtain interval edge weights (as in Figure 2(b)), we partitioned the graph using the METIS graph partitioning strategy [25]. We construct a reduced undirected graph by treating each partition as a single vertex and connecting these vertices if the corresponding partitions are connected with an edge in the original graph. We tested our algorithm over summarized graphs with various number of vertices: 100, $1K$, $2K$, $5K$, $10K$, and $20K$ (with corresponding approximate number of edges $7K$, $60K$, $80K$, $104K$, $130K$, $170K$). We considered three different interval weight distributions: *DBLP distance*, *uniform*, and *Gaussian* distributions – details about the distance calculation are omitted because of space limitation.

We have computed the optimal results by enumerating all possible edge combinations and maintaining the incomparable solutions (Steiner trees) in the result set. Note that the problem is doubly exponential (firstly due to Steiner requirement and secondly due to the existence of incomparable intervals). This leads to high time and

[3]We extended the definition of triangular inequality for incomparable edge weights; details are outside of the scope of this paper.

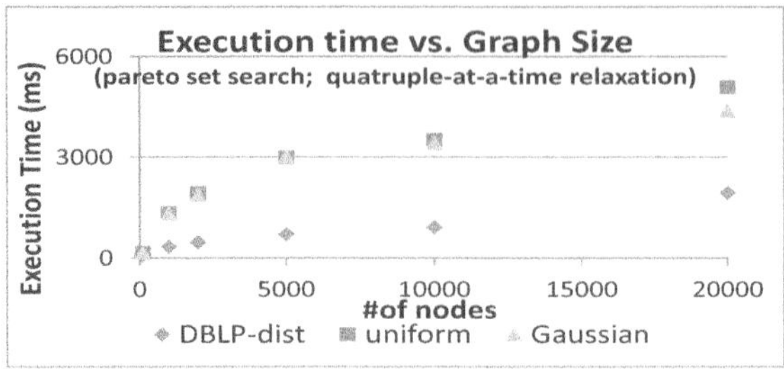

(a) Execution time vs. number of vertices

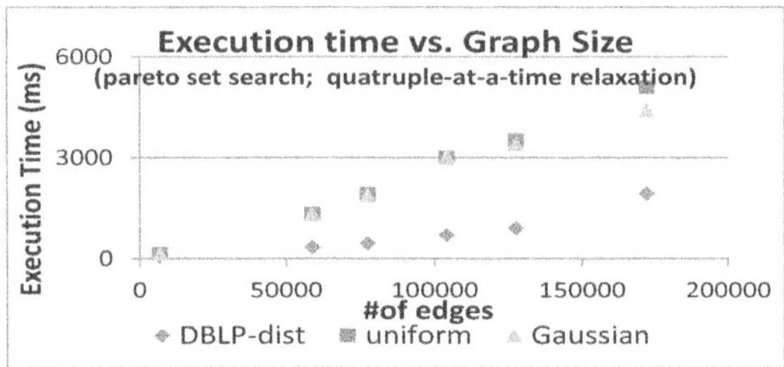

(b) Execution time vs. number of edges

Figure 11: Impact of the graph size on the execution time of the Pareto set search ($qvn = 3$)

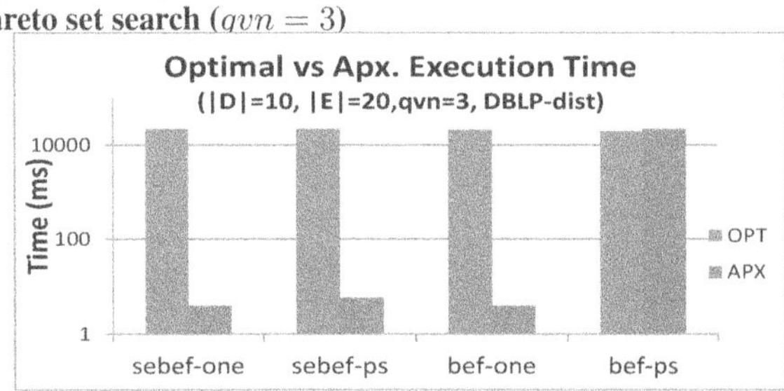

DBLP distance weights

Figure 12: Comparison of execution times for approximate and optimal solutions (quadruple-at-a-time strategy)

space complexities in $O(2^{|E|})$ and, using the available memory, an optimal algorithm that could give us the ground truth was feasible only for very small graphs (num of nodes$\sim$10, num of edges$\sim$20). Thus, in those experiments in which we need to compare the execution time or approximation effectiveness of the the proposed skynets directly to the optimal algorithm, we could only use relatively small graphs for which the execution of the optimal algorithm was feasible. However, we used larger graphs (num of nodes$\sim$20K, num of edges$\sim$200K) in scalability experiments which did not require comparison with the ground truth.

6.2 Discussions of the Results

In this subsection, we present experiments that relate the performance of the approximate Steiner tree skynets to optimal Steiner tree skynets and analyze the impact of various decision parameters on the proposed schemes. Here, $|D|$ refers to the number of vertices and $|E|$ refers to the number of edges in the graph; qvn is the number of query vertices. Unless specified otherwise values reported in the experiments are averaged over 20 different queries.

Efficiency. We first evaluate the scalability of the algorithm. Figure 11 analyzes the impact of the graph size on the execution cost of the Pareto set search problem. As Figure 11 shows the cost of Pareto set search is much better than the worst case estimations. The cost of the algorithm increases only slightly higher than linear with the number of edges. Note that a significant portion of the increase in the execution time is due to a parallel increase in the number of results in the resulting Pareto set.

Figure 12 compares the execution times for the approximation

Average # of trees in the pareto solutions		
Order semantics (edge weight dist.)	OPT	APX
sebef-search-ps (DBLP distance)	1	1.05
bef-search-ps (DBLP distance)	69.95	56.15

Table 1: Number of trees in the pareto solutions

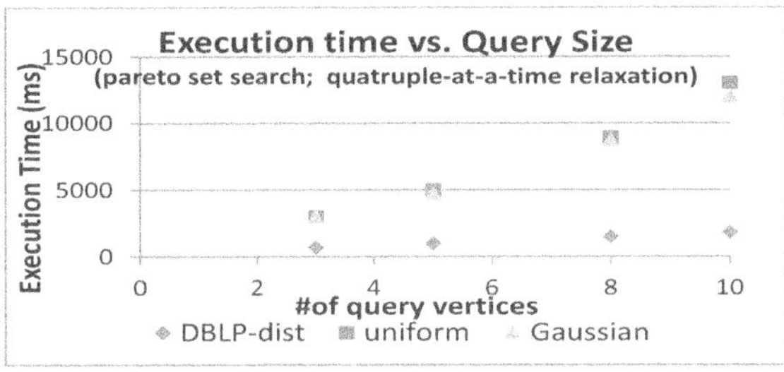

Figure 13: Impact of the query size on the Pareto set search (the reduced graph contains 5000 vertices)

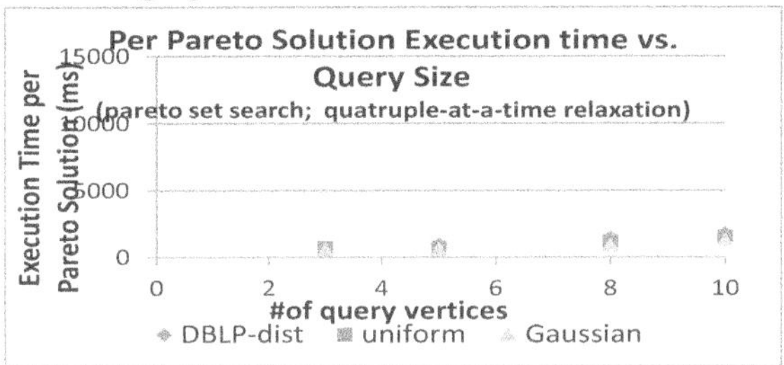

Figure 14: Impact of the query size on the Pareto set search (per Pareto-solution time, the reduced graph contains 5000 vertices)

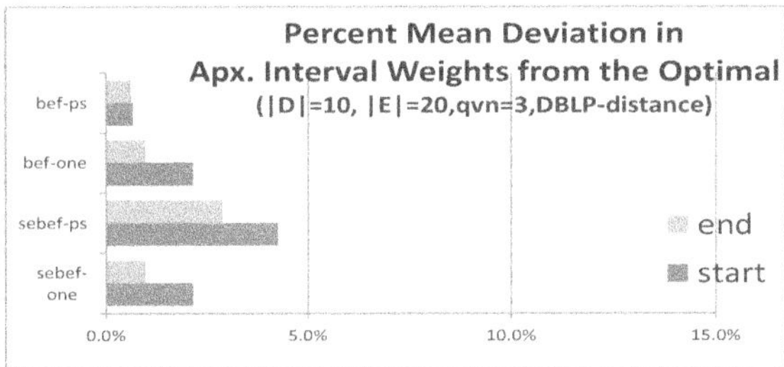

Figure 15: The mean deviations of the start and end times of the approximate Steiner tree weights from those of the optimal Steiner tree weights ($|D|$=10, $|E|$=20, qvn=3), DBLP-distance

and optimal approaches to skynet Steiner tree computation, under the DBLP distance weight distribution and the quadruple-at-a-time relaxation strategy. This figure shows that for most $\preceq$ semantics, the approximation approach works **several of orders faster** than the optimal computation. The only case where the approximation approach fails to provide an advantage is when the user is searching for the entire Pareto-optimal set under the DBLP-distance distribution. The reason for this is that, under this distribution all edge weights are of the form $[1,*]$ and this leads to a large Pareto optimal set, even under the approximation scheme as Table 1 shows. This does not occur for the other distributions, whose results are omitted because of space limitation.

Figure 13 considers the impact of the number of Steiner vertices on the Steiner tree skynet computation. As Figure 13 shows, the algorithm scales roughly linearly with the number of query vertices. Again, as the Figure 14 shows that the per Pareto-solution time scales even better than the full Pareto set search.

Effectiveness of the Approximation. We can see from Figure 15 that when using DBLP-distance weights, the search problem *search-for-one* using both comparison operators $\preceq_{se\_bef}$ and $\preceq_{bef}$, we are able to obtain a solution tree which is very close to the

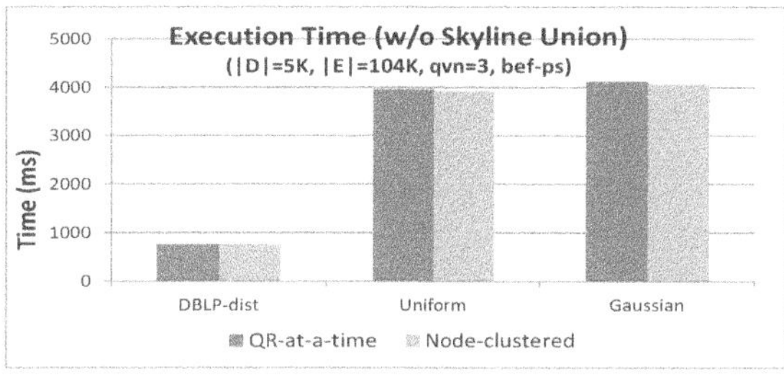

(a) Execution time

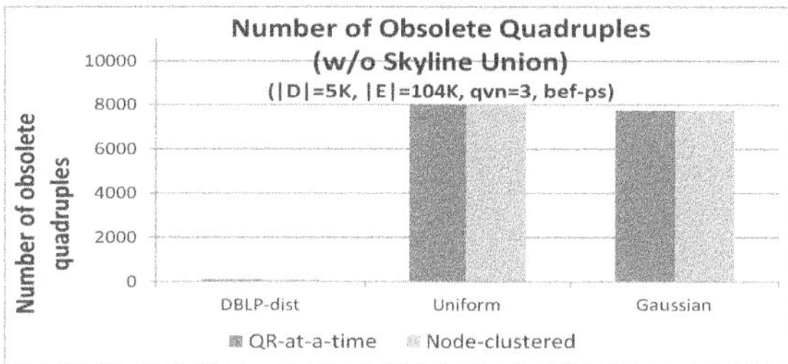

(b) Obsolete quadruples

Figure 16: Comparison of the impacts of different relaxation approaches on the Pareto set search for the $\preceq_{bef}$ ordering semantics ($|D|$=5K, $|E|$=104K, qvn=3)

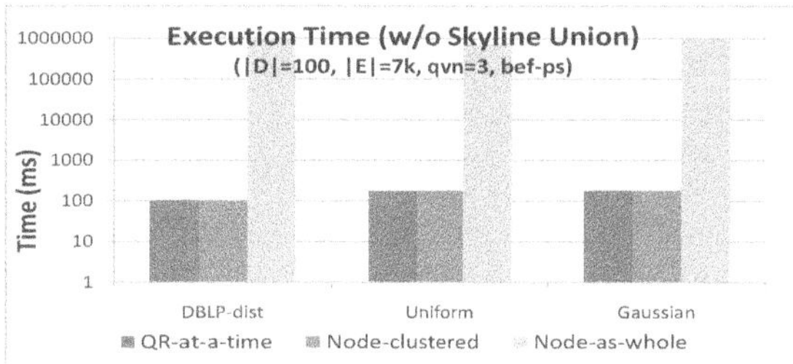

Execution time

Figure 17: Comparison of the impacts of different relaxation approaches on the Pareto set search for the $\preceq_{bef}$ ordering semantics ($|D|$=100, $|E|$=7K, qvn=3)

optimal solution (*OPT-sebef-search-one* and *OPT-bef-search-one*). Similarly, for *search-for-ps*, the solutions returned by our approach are very close to the optimal solutions. Similar results are also obtained for the other weight distributions. Table 1 provides a confirmation of the similarities between the approximation results and optimal results: the table shows that the Pareto sets located by the approximation are similar to the sizes of the optimal Pareto sets.

These results suggest that the $2\times$ approximation ratio is a very conservative worst case and the solutions we obtain in practice are much closer to the optimal solutions (on the average $< 10\%$ deviation in interval start and end times).

Impact of the Different Relaxation Approaches. Figure 16 compares the impact of two different relaxation approaches (quadruple-at-a-time and node-clustered) mentioned in Section 5.1.1. As Figure 16(a) shows, both schemes have execution times that are comparable to each other. Figure 16(b) confirms that this is because both schemes result in the similar numbers of obsolete quadruples. Figure 17 also reports the third relaxation approach, node-as-a-whole, for a smaller dataset $|D| = 100$. As the figure shows, node-as-a-whole strategy is much costlier than the other relaxation approaches.

Impact of the Skyline Union Operator. As Figure 18 shows, under most edge weight distributions and relaxation strategies, the skyline union operator ($\uplus$) provides $\sim 10-20\%$ reduction in execution times for the Pareto set search process.

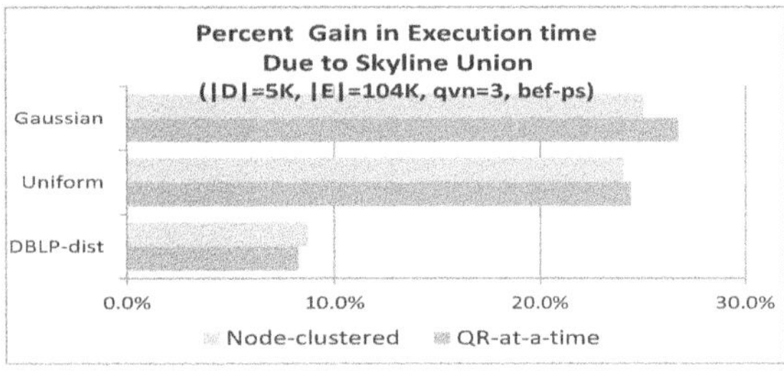

Figure 18: Impact of the skyline union (⊎) on the Pareto set search for the $\preceq_{bef}$ ordering semantics ($|D|$=5K, $|E|$=104K, qvn=3)

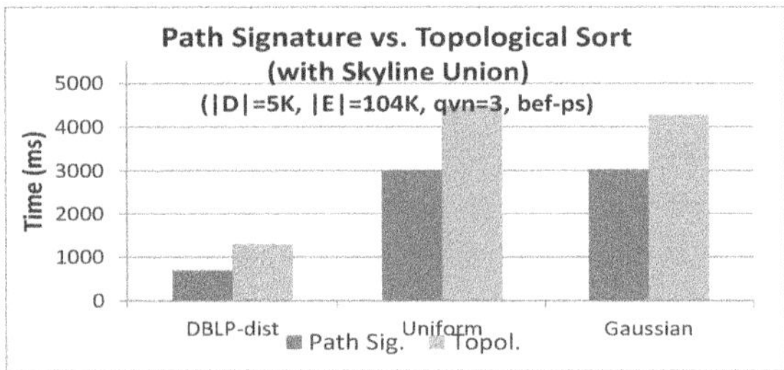

Figure 19: Comparison of the impacts of the two alternative cycle management techniques on the Pareto set search for the $\preceq_{bef}$ ordering semantics ($|D|$=5K, $|E|$=104K, qvn=3)

Impact of the Cycle Management Strategies. In Section 5.1.2, we have seen that there are two different strategies for cycle management: propagating path signatures to eliminate cycles in the identified paths and performing topological sort to limit the trace-back operations to the ends of the forward and backward relaxation stages. As Figure 19 shows, under different edge weight distributions, the path signature mechanism is faster; this is because the topological sort trades-off signature storage for more iterations.

7. CONCLUSIONS

In this paper, we introduced and studied the search problem on interval-weighted graphs that appear in various applications, including graph summarization, transportation and communication network, data (tree or graph) integration. In particular, we have formulated a general *skynet* problem of searches on graphs with partially ordered weights. We introduced alternative interval weight combination and comparison operators. We have also proposed alternative optimization criteria for the skynet search problem. We have then discussed how to extend existing Steiner tree search approximation algorithms to handle searches for *Steiner tree* skynets on graphs with incomparable edge weights. We have seen that computation of Steiner tree skynets also necessitate the definition and implementation of *path* and *spanning tree* skynets. We also presented a skyline union operator to efficiently process intervals when we try to find the incomparable solution trees to cover the query keywords. The experiment results have shown that the proposed approximation algorithm provides close to optimal results and shows excellent scalability against graph and query sizes. In fact, experiments show that the actual approximation factor is better than the analytic upper-bound. Unfortunately, the algorithm H used in this paper for Steiner tree construction does not lend itself into lower-bound computations. We note that there are other Steiner tree algorithms (such as relative greedy and loss contracting algorithms) with upper- ($\sim$1.6) and lower- ($\sim$1.3) bounds. Investigation of SkyNets based on these, for cases where tighter upper-bounds are needed, is our future work.

8. REFERENCES

[1] I. Bartolini, P. Ciaccia, and M. Patella. Salsa: computing the skyline without scanning the whole sky. *CIKM'06*, pp. 405–414, 2006.

[2] G. Bhalotia, A. Hulgeri, C. Nakhe, S. Chakrabarti, and S. Sudarshan. Keyword searching and browsing in databases using BANKS. *ICDE*, pp. 431–440, 2002.

[3] S. Borzsonyi, K. Stocker, D. Kossmann. The skyline operator. *ICDE 2001*.

[4] K. S.Candan, H. Cao, Y. Qi, M. L. Sapino System support for exploration and expert feedback in resolving conflicts during integration of metadata. *VLDB J.* 17(6): 1407-1444, 2008.

[5] Jan Chomicki, Parke Godfrey, Jarek Gryz, and Dongming Liang. Skyline with presorting. In *ICDE*, pages 717–719, 2003.

[6] T. H. Cormen, C. E. Leiserson, and R. L. Rivest. *Introduction to Algorithms*. MIT Press and McGraw-Hill, 2001.

[7] K. Deng, X. Zhou, and H. T. Shen. Multi-source skyline query processing in road networks. *ICDE'07*, 796–805, 2007.

[8] S. K. Dey, and H. Jamil. A hierarchical approach to reachability query answering in very large graph databases. In *CIKM'10*.

[9] K. Golenberg, B. Kimelfeld, and Y. Sagiv. Keyword proximity search in complex data graphs. In *SIGMOD'08*, pp. 927–940, 2008.

[10] A. T. Haghighat, K. Faez, M. Dehghan, A. Mowlaei and Y. Ghahremani. A genetic algorithm for Steiner tree optimization with multiple constraints using Prufer number. LNCS,Vol.2510/2002, pp. 272-280, 2002.

[11] P.Hansen. Bicriterion path problems. Lect. Notes Econ. Math. Syst., Vol.117, 1979.

[12] H. He, H. Wang, J. Yang, and P. S. Yu. BLINKS: ranked keyword searches on graphs. In *SIGMOD'07*, pp. 305–316, 2007

[13] V. Hristidis and Y. Papakonstantinou. DISCOVER: Keyword search in relational databases. In *VLDB*, pp. 670–681, 2002.

[14] X. Huang and C. Jensen. In-route skyline querying for location-based services. W2GIS 2004.

[15] W. Jin, M. Ester, Z. Hu, and J. Han. The multi-relational skyline operator. *ICDE'07*,pp. 1276–1280, 2007.

[16] R. Jin, H. Hong, H. Wang, N. Ruan, and Y. Xiang. Computing label-constraint reachability in graph databases. In SIGMOD'2010.

[17] V. Kacholia, S. Pandit, S. Chakrabarti, S. Sudarshan, R. Desai, and H. Karambelkar. Bidirectional expansion for keyword search on graph databases. In *VLDB*, pp. 505–516, 2005.

[18] R.B. Kearfott. Interval computations: Introduction, uses, and resources. *Euromath Bulletin*, vol. 2, pp. 95-112. European Mathematical Trust, 1996.

[19] L. Kou, G. Markowsky, and L. Berman. A fast algorithm for steiner trees. *Acta Informatica*, 15(2). pp.141–145, 1981.

[20] H.-P. Kriegel and M. Renz, and M. Schubert. Route skyline queries: A multi-preference path planning approach. In *ICDE*, pp. 261–272, 2010.

[21] H.T. Kung, F. Luccio, and F.P. Preparata. On finding the maxima of a set of vectors. *J.ACM*, 22(4). pp. 469–476, 1975.

[22] W.-S. Li, K. S. Candan, Q. Vu, and D. Agrawal. Retrieving and organizing web pages by "information unit". In *WWW*, pp. 230–244, 2001.

[23] L. Liu, J. Wang, J. Liu, and J. Zhang. Privacy preserving in social networks against sensitive edge disclosure. Technical Report CMIDA-HiPSCCS 006-08, Department of Computer Science, Univ. of Kentucky, 2008.

[24] Y. Luo, X. Lin, W. Wang, and X. Zhou. Spark: top-k keyword query in relational databases. In *SIGMOD'07*, pp. 115–126, 2007.

[25] METIS. http://glaros.dtc.umn.edu/gkhome/metis/metis/overview.

[26] S. Navlakha, R. Rastogi, and N. Shrivastava. Graph summarization with bounded error. In Proc. SIGMOD'08, pages 419–432, 2008.

[27] L. Qin, J. X. Yu, and L. Chang. Keyword search in databases: the power of rdbms. In Proc. *SIGMOD'09*, pp.681–694. 2009.

[28] G. Reich and P. Widmayer. Beyond steiner's problem: A VLSI oriented generalization. In *15th Int. Work. WG '89*, pages 196–210, 1989.

[29] G. Robins, A. Zelikovsky. Improved Steiner tree approximation in graphs. in *SODA'00*, pp.770–779, 2000.

[30] D. Sun, S. Wu, J. Li, and A. K. H. Tung. Skyline-join in distributed databases. In *ICDEW'08*, pp. 176-181, 2008.

[31] A.Sengupta, T.K Pal, Solving the Shortest Path Problem with Interval Arcs, Fuzzy Optimization and Decision Making, 5(1), 2006, pp. 71–89.

[32] L. Sweeney. Achieving k-anonymity privacy protection using generalization and suppression. *IJUFKS* 10(5), 2002.

[33] K. L. Tan, P. K. Eng, and B. C. Ooi. Efficient progressive skyline computation. In *VLDB'01*, pages 301–310, 2001.

[34] Z.Tarapata. Selected Multicriteria Shortest Path Problems: An Analysis of Complexity, Models and Adaptation of Standard Algorithms. Int. J. Appl. Math. Comput. Sci. 17, 2 June 2007.

[35] A. Warburton. Approximation of Pareto optima in multiple-objective, shortest-path problems. Operations Research. 35(1), pp. 70–79, 1987.

[36] S. Winter, M. Sester, O. Wolfson, and Glenn Geers. Towards a Computational Transportation Science. In *SIGMOD Record*, vol.39(3), 2010.

[37] A. Zelikovsky. Better approximation bounds for the network and Euclidean Steiner tree problems. Technical report CS-96-06, University of Virginia, 1996.

Fast Fully Dynamic Landmark-based Estimation of Shortest Path Distances in Very Large Graphs

Konstantin Tretyakov[*] [†]
University of Tartu
Estonia
kt@ut.ee

Abel Armas-Cervantes
University of Tartu
Estonia
abel.armas@ut.ee

Luciano García-Bañuelos
University of Tartu
Estonia
luciano.garcia@ut.ee

Jaak Vilo
University of Tartu
Estonia
jaak.vilo@ut.ee

Marlon Dumas
University of Tartu
Estonia
marlon.dumas@ut.ee

ABSTRACT

Computing the shortest path between a pair of vertices in a graph is a fundamental primitive in graph algorithmics. Classical exact methods for this problem do not scale up to contemporary, rapidly evolving social networks with hundreds of millions of users and billions of connections. A number of approximate methods have been proposed, including several landmark-based methods that have been shown to scale up to very large graphs with acceptable accuracy. This paper presents two improvements to existing landmark-based shortest path estimation methods. The first improvement relates to the use of shortest-path trees (SPTs). Together with appropriate short-cutting heuristics, the use of SPTs allows to achieve higher accuracy with acceptable time and memory overhead. Furthermore, SPTs can be maintained incrementally under edge insertions and deletions, which allows for a fully-dynamic algorithm. The second improvement is a new landmark selection strategy that seeks to maximize the coverage of all shortest paths by the selected landmarks. The improved method is evaluated on the DBLP, Orkut, Twitter and Skype social networks.

Categories and Subject Descriptors

E.1 [**Data**]: Data Structures—*Graphs and networks, Trees*; H.2.4 [**Database Management**]: Systems—*Query processing*

General Terms

Algorithms, Experimentation, Performance

[*]Corresponding author.

[†]All authors are also affiliated with Software Technology and Applications Competence Center (STACC), Estonia

Keywords

Graph Databases, Shortest Paths, Social Networks, Landmarks, Trees, Dynamic Updates

1. INTRODUCTION

Finding the shortest path between a given pair of vertices in a graph is a fundamental primitive in graph algorithmics. For example, in the context of social network analysis, this primitive is useful for *socially-sensitive* search [18, 20], whereby a user of a social network searches for an individual by name and expects to see the results ranked in the order of their shortest path distance to him. Similarly, a user may wish to know what chain of contacts allows him to reach another user in the network.

There exists a large body of methods to address this problem [21]. Existing methods can be broadly classified into exact and approximate. Exact methods, such as those based on Dijkstra's traversal, are prohibitively slow for performing online queries on graphs with hundreds of millions of vertices, which is a typical size for a contemporary social network. Among the approximate methods, a family of scalable algorithms for this problem are the so-called *landmark-based* (or *sketch-based*) approaches [4, 5, 7, 9, 18]. In this family of techniques, a fixed set of landmark nodes is selected and distances or actual shortest paths are precomputed from each vertex to some or all of the landmarks. Knowledge of the distances to the landmarks, together with the triangle inequality, typically allows one to compute approximate distance between any two vertices in $O(k)$ time, where k is the number of landmarks, and $O(kn)$ space, where n is the number of vertices in the network. Those estimates can then be used as-is, or exploited further as a component of a graph traversal or routing strategy in order to obtain an exact shortest path [7, 10].

Although landmark-based algorithms do not provide strong theoretical guarantees on approximation quality [11], they have been shown to perform well in practice, scaling up to graphs with millions or even billions of edges with acceptable accuracy and response times of under one second per query [5, 9, 16].

In this paper we describe two improvements to existing landmark-based estimation methods for undirected graphs.

These improvements allow us to achieve higher accuracy than existing methods with millisecond-execution times on a graph with over three billion edges.

The first improvement derives from the use of *shortest path trees (SPTs)* to maintain the paths between each landmark and every vertex in the graph. Based on this data structure, we present three novel strategies for computing an approximate shortest path between any pair of nodes. Moreover, the use of SPTs makes the proposed method suitable for continuously evolving graphs, since practically efficient algorithms exist for incremental SPT update [3, 6]. For completeness' sake we explicitly present a version of the incremental update algorithm from [6], simplified to unweighted graphs.

The second improvement relates to the selection of landmarks. Specifically, we propose a greedy approach to select those landmarks that provide the best coverage of all shortest paths in a random sample of vertex pairs.

We evaluate the proposed method on four large social network, the largest of them (Skype) consisting of circa 500 million users and 3 billion connections. The evaluation demonstrates improved precision of distance estimates gained by both the landmark selection technique and the use of SPTs.

The rest of the paper is structured as follows. Section 2 introduces the notation used to present the algorithms, which are themselves given in Section 3. Section 4 summarizes the experimental evaluation results. Finally, Section 5 discusses related work, while Section 6 provides concluding remarks.

2. BASIC DEFINITIONS

Let $G = (V, E)$ denote a graph with $n = |V|$ vertices and $m = |E|$ edges. For simplicity of exposition, we shall consider an undirected, unweighted graph, although our approach can be easily generalized to accommodate weighted directed graphs as well.

A *path* $\pi_{s,t}$ of length ℓ between two vertices $s, t \in V$ is defined as a sequence $\pi_{s,t} = (s, u_1, u_2, \dots, u_{\ell-1}, t)$, where $\{u_1, u_2, \dots, u_{\ell-1}\} \subseteq V$ and $\{(s, u_1), (u_1, u_2), \dots, (u_{\ell-1}, t)\} \subseteq E$. We denote the length ℓ of a path $\pi_{s,t}$ as $|\pi_{s,t}|$. The *concatenation* of two paths $\pi_{s,t} = (s, \dots, t)$ and $\pi_{t,v} = (t, \dots, v)$ is the combined path $\pi_{s,v} = \pi_{s,t} + \pi_{t,v} = (s, \dots, t, \dots, v)$.

The *distance* $d(s, t)$ between vertices s and t is defined as the length of the shortest path between s and t. The shortest path distance in a graph is a metric and satisfies the *triangle inequality*: for any $s, t, u \in V$

$$d(s,t) \leq d(s,u) + d(u,t)\,. \tag{1}$$

The upper bound becomes an equality iff there exists a shortest path $\pi_{s,t}$ which passes through u.

The *diameter* of a graph is the maximal length of a shortest path in the graph. In this work we rely on an important property of social networks – their diameter is small [19].

Centrality of a vertex is a general term used to refer to a number of metrics of importance of a vertex within a graph. *Betweenness centrality* corresponds to the mean proportion of shortest paths passing through a given vertex. *Closeness centrality* measures the average distance of a vertex to all other vertices in the graph. Computing centrality measures for all vertices exactly is typically hard (e.g., the best betweenness centrality algorithm so far requires $O(mn)$ time on unweighted graphs [2]), but can be approximated using random sampling [1].

Algorithm 1 LANDMARKS-BASIC

Require: Graph $G = (V, E)$, number of landmarks k.

procedure PRECOMPUTE
  $U \leftarrow$ SELECT-LANDMARKS(G,k) ▷ Algorithm 4
  for $u \in U$ **do**
    Do a BFS traversal starting from u.
    For each $v \in V$ store its distance from u as $d_u[v]$.
  end for
end procedure

function LANDMARKS-BASIC(s, t)
  $d_{\text{approx}} \leftarrow \min_{u \in U}(d_u[s] + d_u[t])$
  return d_{approx}
end function

3. ALGORITHM DESCRIPTION

3.1 Landmark-based distance estimation

As noted in Equation 1, if we fix a single landmark node u and precompute the distance $d(u, v)$ from this node to each other vertex v in the graph, we can get an upper bound approximation for the distance $d(s, t)$ between any two vertices s and t:

$$d^u_{\text{approx}}(s,t) = d(s,u) + d(u,t) \tag{2}$$

If we now select a set $U = \{u_1, u_2, \dots, u_k\}$ of k landmarks, a potentially better approximation can be computed:

$$d^U_{\text{approx}}(s,t) = \min_{u \in U} d^u_{\text{approx}}(s,t) \tag{3}$$

In principle, the triangle inequality also allows to compute a lower bound on the distance, but previous work [16] indicates that lower-bound estimates are not as accurate as the upper-bound ones.

In the following we refer to this algorithm as LANDMARKS-BASIC (Algorithm 1). For unweighted graph, the algorithm requires $O(km)$ time to precompute distances using k BFS traversals and $O(kn)$ space to store the distances. Each query is answered in $O(k)$ time. Note that this approach only allows us to compute an approximate distance, but does not provide a way to retrieve the path itself.

3.2 Improved landmark-based algorithms

3.2.1 Shortest path trees

The central contribution of this paper is the idea of maintaining an explicit shortest path tree (SPT) for each landmark, instead of simply storing the distances to landmarks as numbers. More precisely, let $p_u[v]$ be the next vertex on an arbitrarily chosen shortest path from a vertex v to a landmark u. We shall refer to $p_u[v]$ as the *parent link* of v in the SPT of u (Figure 1). Similarly to distances, parent links can be computed in a straightforward manner during a BFS traversal of the graph in $O(m)$ time per landmark.

The availability of parent links enables us to recover an exact shortest path from each vertex v to each landmark u by simply following the corresponding links. Consequently, it also allows to compute the shortest path distance $d(u, v)$ and thus directly apply the ideas of the LANDMARKS-BASIC algorithm, with the only difference that each distance computation now requires $O(D)$ steps, where D is the diameter of the graph. As the diameters of social network graphs tend

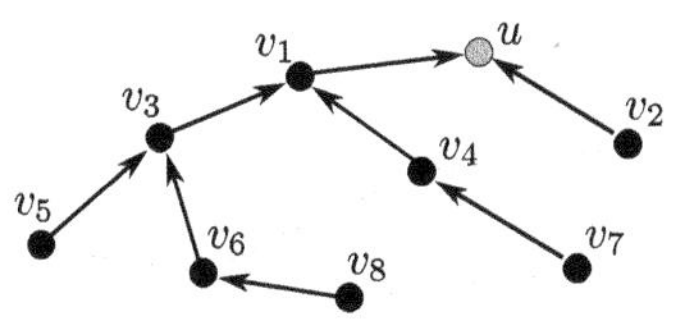

Figure 1: Shortest path tree for landmark u. Black arrows denote parent links. Dashed lines are graph edges that are not part of the tree.

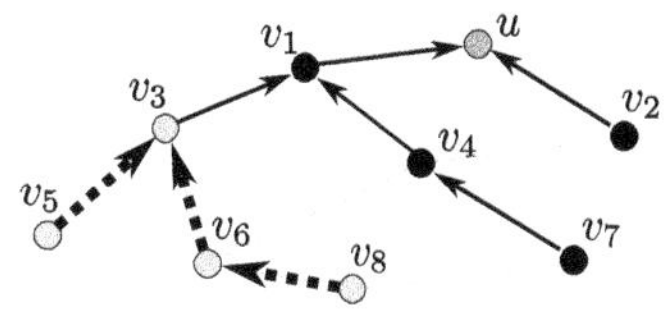

Figure 2: Lowest common ancestor technique. When approximating distance between v_5 and v_8 we use their lowest common ancestor v_3 instead of the landmark u as a reference.

to be small, the expected overhead of such a computation is minor.

Note that this approach allows to retrieve an actual path between any two vertices in addition to the distance approximation.

3.2.2 Lowest common ancestor method

Besides performing basic landmark-based approximation, the availability of the SPT allows us to significantly improve the upper bound estimates on distances for many vertex pairs. Consider the situation depicted in Figure 2 and suppose we wish to approximate the distance between v_5 and v_8. By applying the basic technique we obtain an upper bound estimate of $d(v_5, v_8) \leq d(v_5, u) + d(u, v_8) = 3 + 4 = 7$. Observe, however, that once we have the explicit shortest paths:

$$\pi_{v_5,u} = (v_5, v_3, v_1, u), \qquad \pi_{v_8,u} = (v_8, v_6, v_3, v_1, u),$$

we can note that both of them pass through v_3 and thus the estimate

$$d(v_5, v_8) \leq d(v_5, v_3) + d(v_3, v_8) = 1 + 2 = 3.$$

will result in a better upper bound. In general, whenever two shortest paths $\pi_{s,u}$ and $\pi_{t,u}$ have a common vertex $v \neq u$, we have

$$d(s,t) \leq d(s,v) + d(v,t) < d(s,u) + d(u,t), \tag{4}$$

and thus if we use v instead of u to approximate $d(s,t)$ we obtain a tighter bound. Naturally, it makes sense to select the vertex v providing the best such approximation. It can be easily seen that this vertex is the *lowest common ancestor (LCA)* of s and t in the SPT of u.

This observation provides the basis of our LCA approximation method (DISTANCE-LCA, Algorithm 2). By substituting this distance estimate into Equation (3), we obtain a new algorithm LANDMARKS-LCA with increased accuracy. Note that this algorithm can also be trivially extended to return the actual path.

One way to understand the extent of improvement is to note that the basic algorithm will provide exact estimates only for shortest paths that pass through the landmark vertex. In Figure 2 those are only the paths connecting v_2 with v_1 and v_3. The LCA algorithm, however, will provide exact answers for all shortest paths that lie along the SPT, and there will be typically considerably more of those.

3.2.3 Shortcutting

Denote the lowest common ancestor of s and t by v. The LCA algorithm approximates $\pi_{s,t}$ by a concatenation of $\pi_{s,v}$ with $\pi_{v,t}$. However, it may happen that a vertex $w \in \pi_{s,v}$ is connected directly by an edge with a vertex $w' \in \pi_{v,t}$. In this case, an even shorter approximation to $\pi_{s,t}$ can be obtained by concatenating the paths $\pi_{s,w}$, $\pi_{w,w'}$ and $\pi_{w',t}$. For example, in Figure 2, the edge (v_5, v_6) acts as a shortcut from π_{v_5,v_3} to π_{v_3,v_8}. If we account for this edge, we may further improve the LCA distance estimate to the true shortest path $d(v_5, v_8) = 2$.

In order to locate shortcuts we can simply examine all pairs of vertices in $\pi_{s,v} \times \pi_{t,v}$ and if some of them are connected by an edge, find the edge providing the best distance estimate. This can be done in $|\pi_{s,v}| \times |\pi_{t,v}|$, i.e., at most $O(D^2)$ steps. We refer to the resulting distance approximation method as DISTANCE-SC (Algorithm 2). By using this upper bound estimate in Equation (3) we obtain the landmark-based algorithm LANDMARKS-SC.

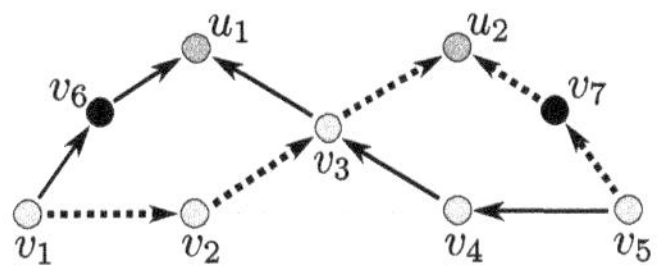

Figure 3: Landmark-BFS technique. Here, solid arrows belong to the SPT of u_1, and dotted arrows belong to the SPT of u_2.

3.2.4 Landmarks-BFS

The algorithms LANDMARKS-BASIC, LANDMARKS-LCA, and LANDMARKS-SC use each landmark for distance approximation independently of the other landmarks. This is not the best possible use of all available landmark data. Consider Figure 3, for example. When approximating distance between vertices v_1 and v_5, we would obtain a path of length 5 if we used the two landmarks independently. By combining the two subtrees we can find a better path of length 4. Finally, by taking other graph edges (i.e., "shortcuts") into account, we further improve the distance approximation to 3.

This suggests a very simple, yet powerful improvement over the previous approaches. In order to approximate distance between two vertices, collect all paths from those vertices to all landmarks, and perform a usual BFS (or, in the case of weighted graphs, Dijkstra) traversal on the subgraph, induced by the union of those paths. We refer to this algorithm as LANDMARKS-BFS (Algorithm 3).

For k landmarks, the size of the subgraph will be less than $2kD$. Consequently, the memory complexity of LANDMARKS-BFS is $O(kD)$ and the time complexity is at most $O(k^2 D^2)$.

3.3 Landmark selection techniques

Although landmarks can be selected uniformly at random, experiments of Potamias *et al.* [16] show that selecting land-

Algorithm 2 LCA-based upper bounding algorithms

Require: Graph $G = (V, E)$, a landmark $u \in V$, a parent link $p_u[v]$ precomputed for each $v \in V$.

function $\textsc{Path-To}_u(s,\pi)$
  Returns the path in the SPT p_u from the vertex s to the closest vertex q belonging to the path π
  Result $\leftarrow (s)$ ▷ Sequence of 1 element.
  while $s \notin \pi$ **do**
    $s \leftarrow p_u[s]$
    Append s to Result
  end while
  return Result   ▷ $(s, p_u[s], p_u[p_u[s]], \ldots, q), q \in \pi$
end function

function $\textsc{Distance-LCA}_u(s,t)$
  $\pi^{(1)} \leftarrow \textsc{Path-To}_u(s, (u))$
  $\pi^{(2)} \leftarrow \textsc{Path-To}_u(t, \pi^{(1)})$
  LCA $\leftarrow$ Last element of $\pi^{(2)}$
  $\pi^{(3)} \leftarrow \textsc{Path-To}_u(s, (\text{LCA}))$
  return $|\pi^{(2)}| + |\pi^{(3)}|$
end function

function $\textsc{Distance-SC}_u(s,t)$
  $\pi^{(1)} \leftarrow \textsc{Path-To}_u(s, (u))$
  $\pi^{(2)} \leftarrow \textsc{Path-To}_u(t, \pi^{(1)})$
  LCA $\leftarrow$ Last element of $\pi^{(2)}$
  $\pi^{(3)} \leftarrow \textsc{Path-To}_u(s, (\text{LCA}))$
  Best $\leftarrow |\pi^{(2)}| + |\pi^{(3)}|$
  for $(w, w') \in (\pi^{(2)} \times \pi^{(3)}) \cap E$ **do**
    Current $\leftarrow |\pi_{s,w}| + |\pi_{w,w'}| + |\pi_{w',t}|$
    Best $\leftarrow$ min(Current,Best)
  end for
  return Best
end function

marks with the highest *degree* or lowest *closeness centrality* typically ensures better distance estimates, whereas it is shown that the two methods provide similar accuracy. In our experiments we use the highest degree landmark selection method and compare it with the following one.

Best coverage. When a landmark u lies on the shortest path between s and t, its upper bound distance estimate is exact. We say that such a landmark *covers* the pair (s, t). Consequently, the most desirable set of landmarks would be the one that covers as many vertex pairs as possible. It can be shown that the task of finding the *optimal* landmark set (i.e., the one with the maximal coverage) is NP-hard [16]. Instead, we propose a simple greedy strategy based on sampling (Algorithm 4). We sample a set of M vertex pairs, and compute exact shortest path for each pair. As the first landmark we select the vertex that is present in most paths of the sample. We remove the paths covered by that first landmark from the sample and proceed to select the second landmark as the vertex, which covers most of the remaining paths, etc.

3.4 Incremental updates

If the graph is subject to intensive edge insertion and deletion, landmarks that have been computed originally become

Algorithm 3 Landmarks-BFS

Require: Graph $G = (V, E)$, a set of landmarks $U \subset V$, an SPT parent link $p_u[v]$ precomputed for each $u \in U, v \in V$.

function $\textsc{Landmarks-BFS}(s,t)$
  $S \leftarrow \emptyset$
  for $u \in U$ **do**
    $S \leftarrow S \cup \textsc{Path-To}_u(s, (u))$ ▷ (see Algorithm 2)
    $S \leftarrow S \cup \textsc{Path-To}_u(t, (u))$
  end for
  Let $G[S]$ be the subgraph of G induced by S.
  Apply BFS on $G[S]$ to find a path π from s to t.
  return $|\pi|$
end function

Algorithm 4 Select-Landmarks

Require: Graph $G = (V, E)$, number of landmarks k, sample size M.

function Highest-Degree
  For each $v \in V$ let $d[v] \leftarrow \textsc{Degree}(v)$.
  Sort V by $d[v]$.
  Let $v_{(i)}$ denote the vertex with i-th largest $d[v]$.
  return $\{v_{(1)}, v_{(2)}, \ldots, v_{(k)}\}$
end function

function Best-Coverage
  $P \leftarrow \emptyset$
  for $i \in \{1, \ldots, M\}$ **do**
    $(s_i, t_i) \leftarrow$ Random pair of vertices
    $p_i \leftarrow \textsc{ShortestPath}(s_i, t_i)$
    $P \leftarrow P \cup \{p_i\}$
  end for
  $V_P \leftarrow \cup_{p \in P}\, p$
  for $i \in \{1, \ldots, k\}$ **do**
    For each $v \in V_P$ let $c[v] \leftarrow |\{p \in P : v \in p\}|$
    $u_i \leftarrow \text{argmax}_{v \in V_P}\, c[v]$ ▷ Resolve ties arbitrarily
    $P \leftarrow P \setminus \{u_i\}$
  end for
  return $\{u_1, \ldots, u_k\}$
end function

outdated and the approximation performance deteriorates. Therefore, landmarks have to be maintained up to date. Although this can be achieved by means of daily or hourly full recomputation, such a solution is computationally expensive. Moreover, for certain applications, such as the abovementioned social search, it can be particularly important to maintain landmarks up to date at all times. Indeed, if the social search feature is relied upon by new users to establish their first list of contacts, it is important that adding a new contact would be immediately reflected in the consequent search orderings.

Fortunately, when landmarks are maintained in the form of shortest path trees, they can be updated incrementally to accommodate edge insertions or deletions. The procedures for maintaining SPTs under insertions and deletions are well-known [3, 6]. In the particular case of unweighted graphs with a small diameter, they are fairly straightforward.

As an informal example, consider the SPT presented on Figure 1. Suppose that an edge $\{u, v_8\}$ has just been inserted

Algorithm 5 INSERT-EDGE

Require: Graph $G = (V, E)$, a landmark $u \in V$, a parent link $p_u[v]$ precomputed for each $v \in V$.

```
function INSERT-EDGE_u(s,t)
    if DISTTO_u(s) > DISTTO_u(t) then
        (s,t) = (t,s)
    end if
    DistChanged ← FIFOQueue()
    UPDATEIFBETTERPARENT_u(s, t, DistChanged)
    while not DistChanged.empty() do
        s ← DistChanged.pop()
        for t ∈ Neighbors(s) do
            UPDATEIFBETTERPARENT_u(s, t, DistChanged)
        end for
    end while
end function

Helper routines

function DISTTO_u(s)
        Distance to u in the current SPT
        Note that we compute it in O(D) steps.
    d ← 0
    while p_u[s] ≠ u do
        s ← p_u[s]
        d ← d + 1
        if s == null then
            return ∞                    ▷ used in DELETE-EDGE
        end if
    end while
    return d
end function

function UPDATEIFBETTERPARENT_u(s,t,queue)
        Checks whether s is a better parent for t in the SPT.
        If so, updates p_u and pushes t to the queue.
    if (p_u[t] ≠ s)
        and (DISTTO_u(t) > DISTTO_u(s) + 1) then
        p_u[t] ← s
        queue.push(t)
    end if
end function
```

Algorithm 6 DELETE-EDGE

Require: Graph $G = (V, E)$, a landmark $u \in V$, a parent link $p_u[v]$ precomputed for each $v \in V$.

```
function DELETE-EDGE_u(s,t)
    if p_u[s] == t then
        (s,t) = (t,s)
    else if p_u[t] ≠ s then
        return                          ▷ SPT not affected
    end if
    prevDist ← DISTTO(t)
    p_u[t] ← null
    DistChanged ← PriorityQueue()
    PUSHIFDISTCHANGED_u(t, prevDist, DistChanged)
    while not DistChanged.empty() do
        t ← DistChanged.pop()
        Find the neighbor s of t
            with minimal DISTTO_u(s)
        p_u[t] ← s
    end while
end function

Helper routines

function PUSHIFDISTCHANGED_u(t, prevDist, pqueue)
        Checks whether there exists a new parent for t with
        which its DISTTO will stay unchanged.
        If so, updates p_u. Otherwise, pushes t to queue and
        descends into leaves.
    Find the neighbor s of t
        with minimal DISTTO_u(s)
    For all neighbors of t that are in the pqueue,
        and have their key >DISTTO_u(s)+2,
        update their key to DISTTO_u(s)+2.
    if DISTTO_u(s) == prevDist-1 then
        p_u[t] ← s
    else
        pqueue.push(t, key=DISTTO_u(s)+1)
        for v ∈ children of t in the SPT do
            p_u[v] ← null
            PUSHIFDISTCHANGED_u(v, prevDist+1, pqueue)
        end for
    end if
end function
```

into the graph. The SPT update algorithm would proceed as follows. Firstly, note that the newly added edge provides a shorter path from v_8 to the landmark than what was previously available. Therefore, the parent pointer of v_8 has to be changed to make use of the new edge: $p_u[v_8] := u$. Now that the path to the landmark from v_8 has improved, we have to recursively examine all neighbors of v_8 (i.e., v_6 and v_7) and check, whether switching their parent pointer to v_8 would improve their previously known path to the landmark. This is true both for v_6 and v_7, hence we set $p_u[v_6] := v_8$, $p_u[v_7] := v_8$. We repeat this again for all neighbors of v_6 and v_7. Having found no new path improvements, we complete the update.

The deletion of an edge involves two passes. Consider again Figure 1 and suppose the edge $\{v_1, v_3\}$ was deleted from the graph. In order to find a new path to the landmark (and a new parent pointer) for v_3, we first examine its neighbors (v_5 and v_6). Unfortunately, both of them relied on v_3 for reaching the landmark, hence they provide no immediate fix. We record v_3 temporarily in a priority queue, using the best available new path length (∞ so far) as the key. We then recursively descend to process the children of v_3 in the SPT. Vertex v_5 has no immediate fix and gets recorded in the priority queue with key ∞. Vertex v_6, however, can be connected to v_4, retaining a path to the landmark of length 3. Consequently, there is no need to process children of v_6. After reconnecting v_6 we must update the keys of its neighbors (v_3 and v_5) in the priority queue – the new potential path of length 4 is better than the previously recorded ∞. This completes the first pass. In the second pass we empty the priority queue, rebuilding the rest of the SPT.

We provide a more formal description of the update procedures in Algorithms 5 and 6, and refer the reader to [6] for detailed explanations.

In theory, a single update may trigger the SPT recomputation for the whole graph (e.g. deleting an edge that was a bridge between the landmark and all the other nodes). In practice, however, such situations are rare and, according to our experiments, the amortized time necessary to process a single update in a real Skype network is in the order of milliseconds (see Section 4.3).

4. EXPERIMENTAL EVALUATION

4.1 Datasets

We tested our approach on four real-world social network graphs, representing four different orders of magnitude in terms of network size.

- **DBLP.** The DBLP dataset contains bibliographic information of computer science publications [13]. Every vertex corresponds to an author. Two authors are connected by an edge if they have co-authored at least one publication. The snapshot from May 15, 2010 was used.
- **Orkut.** Orkut is a large social networking website. It is a graph, where each user corresponds to a vertex and each user-to-user connection is an edge. The snapshot of the Orkut network was published by Mislove *et al.* in 2007 [14].
- **Twitter.** Twitter is a microblogging site, which allows users to *follow* each other, thus forming a network. A snapshot of the Twitter network was published by Kwak *et al.* in 2010 [12]. Although originally the network is directed, in our experiments we ignore edge direction.
- **Skype.** Skype is a large social network for peer-to-peer communication. We say that two users are connected by an edge if they are in each other's contact list. A subset of the network comprising 454M users was obtained in February 2010.

The properties of these datasets are summarized in Table 1. The table shows the number of vertices $|V|$, number of edges $|E|$, average distance between vertices $\bar{d}$ (computed on a sample vertex pairs), approximate diameter Δ, fraction of vertices in the largest connected component $|S|/|V|$, and average time to perform a BFS traversal over the graph t_{BFS}.

Dataset	$\lvert V\rvert$	$\lvert E\rvert$	$\bar{d}$	Δ	$\lvert S\rvert/\lvert V\rvert$	t_{BFS}
DBLP	770K	2.6M	6.3	25	85%	345 ms
Orkut	3.1M	117M	5.7	10	100%	8 sec
Twitter	41.7M	1.2B	4.2	25	100%	9 min
Skype	454M	3.1B	6.7	60	85%	20 min

Table 1: Datasets.

4.2 Experimental setup

To evaluate the performance of our methods we first select a random sample of 500 vertex pairs from each graph and precompute the actual shortest path distance for every pair. We then apply the distance approximation techniques to those vertex pairs and measure their *Approximation error*, *Time*, and *Disk space*.

Approximation error is computed as $(\ell' - \ell)/\ell$, where ℓ' is the approximation and ℓ is the actual distance. *Time* refers to the average time required to compute a distance approximation for a pair of vertices. Finally, the *Disk space* corresponds to the amount of data stored for each landmark.

We run our measurements on a server with 32× Quad-core AMD Opteron 64bit 2.2GHz processors, 256G of RAM, accessing IBM DS 3400 FC SAN disk array, running Red Hat Enterprise Linux 5 operating system. We used C++ for algorithm implementation.

4.3 Results

4.3.1 Approximation Error

The approximation quality measurements are summarized in Figure 4 and Table 3. Observe that landmark selection strategy has a significant effect on approximation quality for the LANDMARKS-BASIC and the LANDMARKS-LCA algorithms. The use of shortcutting in the LANDMARKS-SC and LANDMARKS-BFS seems to reduce the importance of landmark selection. Indeed, in case of LANDMARKS-BFS randomly selected landmarks often outperform the more sophisticated techniques. Overall, the *best coverage* and *highest degree* techniques perform nearly equally well, and depending on the particular graph either one or the other should be preferred to achieve the best possible results.

Note that the use of the *LCA* approach reduces the error of the basic technique consistently by 10–50%, with further slight improvements obtained by shortcutting and BFS methods.

4.3.2 Query Time and Disk Usage

The disk usage in all the discussed methods is linear with respect to number of vertices, because we have to store a single value for each vertex-landmark pair. In the basic method this value is a distance and can be stored in a single byte, as distances in the studied social network graphs are small. When using SPTs, a vertex pointer needs to be stored for each vertex-landmark pair. For a graph as large as Skype, a 4-byte pointer is necessary. Consequently, the per-landmark disk space is 4 times greater when using SPTs than when storing distances only (see Table 2).

Dataset	Graph file	Landmark file	
		Basic	LCA/SC/LBFS
DBLP	27M	753K	3.0M
Orkut	918M	3.0M	12.0M
Twitter	9.3G	40M	160M
Skype	27G	433M	1.7G

Table 2: Disk usage.

Table 4 reports the average execution time per query. This is computed as the total time required process 500 random queries sequentially divided by 500. This also includes the time spent to load precomputed data from disk on-the-fly using Linux `mmap` facilities. We observe that the LCA and SC methods are 3-6 times slower than the basic algorithm, but the execution times still remain in the order of a few milliseconds even for the Skype graph. The Landmarks-BFS method can be considerably slower, especially so for the Twitter graph, due to the presence of nodes with very high degree in this network.

Dataset	Landmark selection	Method			
		Basic	LCA	SC	LBFS
DBLP	Random	0.46	0.07	0.04	0.02
	Highest Degree	0.11	0.05	0.03	0.03
	Best Coverage	0.07	0.04	0.03	0.02
Orkut	Random	0.50	0.13	0.08	0.04
	Highest Degree	0.14	0.12	0.10	0.07
	Best Coverage	0.13	0.11	0.08	0.05
Twitter	Random	0.53	0.07	0.02	0.02
	Highest Degree	0.06	0.05	0.03	0.03
	Best Coverage	0.07	0.06	0.03	0.02
Skype	Random	0.56	0.25	0.23	0.21
	Highest Degree	0.21	0.19	0.18	0.16
	Best Coverage	0.19	0.17	0.16	0.15

Table 3: Approximation error for different methods (using 100 landmarks).

Dataset	Method	No. of Landmarks		
		20	60	100
DBLP	Basic	0.03	0.09	0.14
	LCA	0.10	0.29	0.46
	SC	0.13	0.47	0.78
	LBFS	0.45	1.00	1.42
Orkut	Basic	0.08	0.11	0.39
	LCA	0.31	0.78	1.10
	SC	0.40	0.95	1.26
	LBFS	1.87	8.05	12.49
Twitter	Basic	0.15	0.49	0.84
	LCA	0.72	0.81	1.21
	SC	0.82	0.99	1.87
	LBFS	240	633	889
Skype	Basic	0.18	0.56	0.91
	LCA	1.06	2.43	3.69
	SC	1.22	2.92	4.85
	LBFS	5.10	13.24	16.25

Table 4: Query execution time averaged across 500 queries (in ms).

4.3.3 *Precomputation Time*

Precomputation time is comprised of two parts – landmark selection and the computation of SPTs (or distances, in the case of the basic method) for each landmark.

- **Landmark selection.** In the case of *random* landmark selection, the time is negligible. The *highest degree* method requires a single pass through the set of vertices of the graph, which is dominated by the time needed to read the graph data from disk. The most complex method is *best coverage*, which requires a sampling of pairs of vertices and the precomputations of their exact shortest paths (e.g. using BFS). Table 5 summarizes timing measurements obtained with a naïve sequential implementation (i.e. shortest paths were computed one after the other using BFS).
- **SPT computation per landmark.** The time needed to compute each landmark is equal to the time needed to perform a full BFS over the graph and is given in Table 1. For the DBLP graph each landmark can be computed in about 500ms, while for the Skype graph this time is approximately 20 minutes. Note that this operation can be trivially parallelized by assigning one thread per landmark.

Dataset	Highest degree	Best coverage
DBLP	140 ms	2 min
Orkut	2 s	15 min
Twitter	22 s	15 h
Skype	1 min	54 h

Table 5: Landmark selection timings.

4.3.4 *Incremental Updates*

We tested the performance of the incremental update procedures on our graphs by simulating a random sequence of 1000 edge modifications and using the landmark update procedures to maintain 100 landmarks up to date. Each edge modification was randomly chosen to be a deletion or an insertion of an edge between two random vertices. Table 6 presents the average time necessary to update one landmark.

	DBLP	Orkut	Twitter	Skype
Insertion	$1\mu s$	$10\mu s$	$10\mu s$	$30\mu s$
Deletion	$100\mu s$	2ms	12ms	11ms

Table 6: Average time to perform one update for one landmark.

5. RELATED WORK

The task of finding a shortest path between an arbitrary pair of vertices is known as a *point-to-point shortest path (PPSP)* problem. The naïve solution is to run the Dijkstra's traversal from the source to the destination vertex on every query. An improvement to this can be obtained by running a *bi-directional* search [15]. A further improvement is obtained by exploiting the A* search with landmark-based heuristics [7, 8, 10].

Sometimes it makes sense to precompute all pairwise distances. The corresponding algorithms are typically referred to as *all pairs shortest paths (APSP)*. Although a variety of elegant techniques have been proposed for this task, such as dynamic programming, path-forming and Boolean matrix multiplications, most known exact APSP algorithms are about $O(n^3)$ in time, with a few subcubic solutions for cer-

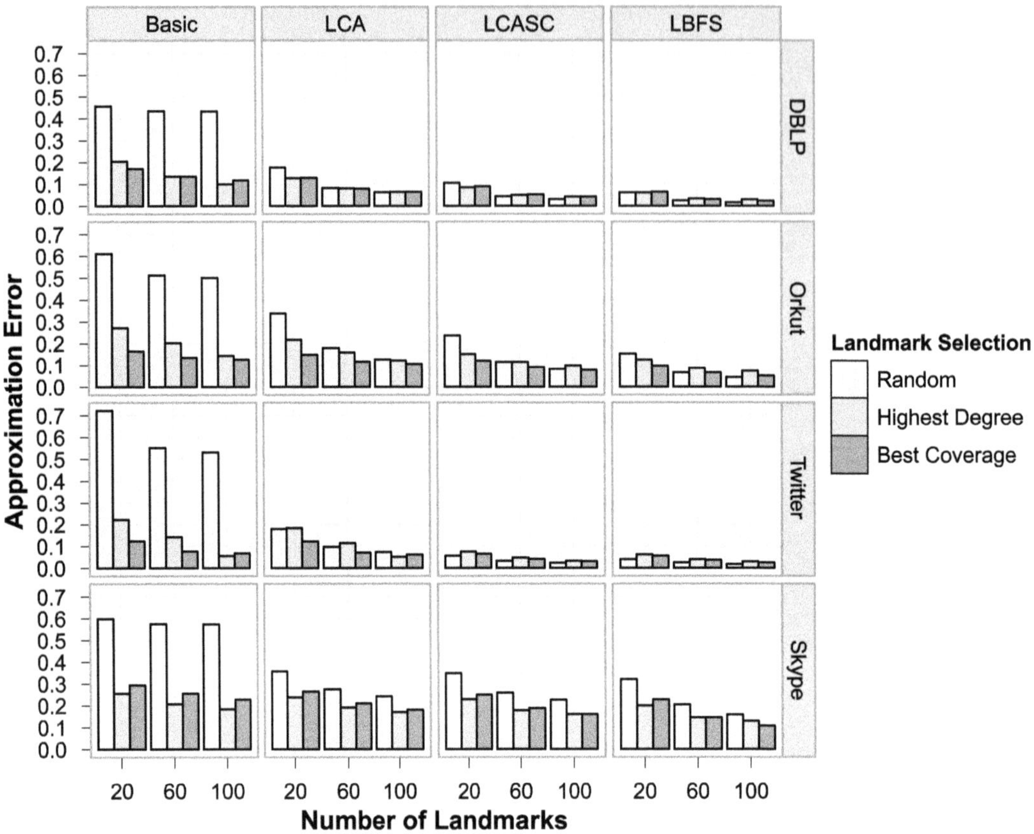

Figure 4: Approximation error results. The best accuracy is consistently obtained using *Landmarks-BFS* distance estimation method.

tain types of graphs [21]. This is not significantly better than simply performing a separate SSSP run for each vertex.

For many practical applications, finding out approximate distances between vertices can be sufficient. Careful indexing of the graph can provide a way to later provide approximate answers to arbitrary distance queries in constant or logarithmic time. Thorup and Zwick [17] coin the term *approximate distance oracles* for such algorithms. They present a method which requires $O(kn^{1+1/k})$ space and $O(kmn^{1/k})$ expected time for preprocessing and allows constant $O(k)$ query time. The idea of their method is to compute a sequence of nested sets of randomly picked landmarks. The closest landmark from each set is located and stored for each vertex together with the distance to it. A distance query $d(s,t)$ can then be answered by finding a landmark u which is one of the closest to both s and t and using the approximation given by Equation (2). The authors prove that their algorithm provides distance estimates which can be wrong up to a factor of $2k-1$.

An interesting analogy of our method to this algorithm can be observed. Indeed, let u be a single landmark. Consider the collection of nested sets $A_0 \subseteq A_1 \cdots \subseteq A_D$, where $A_i = \{v \in V\ ,\ d(u,v) \leq i\}$, and D is the diameter of the graph. Then the complete shortest path $\pi_{s,u}$ corresponds to the *bunch* concept from Thorup's algorithm, and the process of finding the LCA is similar to the distance estimation technique used in that paper. However, the strategy of selecting the nested sets A_i is completely different. Besides, the analogy does not hold as soon as more than one landmark is used in our algorithm.

In general, the idea of landmark-based estimation has been widely studied in previous works (see, e.g., [4, 5, 7, 9, 16, 18]). A closely related work is that of Potamias *et al.* [16], where the LANDMARKS-BASIC algorithm is evaluated under different landmark selection strategies. The major innovation of our work is the use of SPTs instead just keeping the distance from each landmark to every vertex.

The algorithms LANDMARKS-LCA, LANDMARKS-SC and LANDMARKS-BFS are also similar to those suggested by Gubichev *et al.* [9]. However, the algorithms in [9] use different sets of landmarks for each vertex and thus store complete shortest paths to each landmark at each vertex. This results in higher memory requirements ($O(Dkn)$ instead of $O(kn)$ for storing only a single pointer per vertex-landmark pair in our approach) and prevents the possibility of performing incremental updates. The execution times reported in [9] are considerably slower when compared to ours – more than 4 seconds on a graph with 10 times less edges and 100 times less vertices than the Skype graph.

An important aspect of landmark-based methods is the way landmarks are selected – a careful selection strategy can have a significant positive effect. Strategies, which rely on selecting landmarks with high *degree*, *betweenness*- and *closeness centrality* as well as ensuring proper *dispersion* of landmarks over the graph and its parts, have been suggested, with *highest degree* and *closeness centrality* being shown to typically yield highest accuracy in [16]. In our work, we proposed and evaluated an additional method that can compete with the *highest degree* approach, outperforming it slightly on some datasets. The combined effect of our improvements (*best coverage* landmark selection with LANDMARKS-BFS algorithm) for the large Skype network is a 40% smaller error.

6. CONCLUSION

This paper described and evaluated two improvements to existing approaches for landmark-based estimation of shortest paths. These improvements strike a tradeoff between accuracy, query execution time and disk usage for precomputed data. With respect to previous related work, we achieve notable accuracy improvements while maintaining the response time per query within a few milliseconds – even for a graph with billions of edges – and a space consumption comparable to previous state of the art methods. An exclusive property of the proposed methods is the support for dynamic updates.

Several extensions to the proposed method are possible.

Generalization to directed weighted graphs. We have presented the algorithms for the case of an undirected unweighted graph. The generalization to weighted graphs is obtained by replacing the BFS in the SPT precomputation phase and in the LANDMARK-BFS algorithm with a Dijkstra traversal. The generalization to directed graphs requires computing two shortest path trees for each landmark – the first one holding distances *to* the landmark, and the second one with distances *from* the landmark. The algorithms then need to be updated slightly to use both trees appropriately (e.g. lines 4 and 5 of Algorithm 3 will refer to two different trees rather than one).

Exact distance estimation. Being a distance approximation scheme, a landmark-based algorithm can be used as a heuristic in the (unidirectional or bidirectional) A* search, as described in [7, 10]. In particular, this ability to efficiently estimate exact shortest paths allows us to take larger samples for *best coverage* landmark selection. Note that due to the incremental update capabilities of our approach, the result is a fast fully-dynamic exact shortest path algorithm.

Evolutionary landmark selection. In the presented approach, all landmarks are selected *ex ante* and the selection of landmarks is never revised. A further improvement might be obtained by using information collected during the processing of queries in order to add or remove landmarks. Each time a query is answered, we can identify which vertices are used in the shortest path. Based on this information we could promote certain vertices, which lie on shortest paths frequently, to become landmarks, or we could drop landmarks that are infrequently used.

7. ACKNOWLEDGMENTS

The authors gratefully acknowledge the contributions of Andres Kütt and André Karpištšenko from Skype Technologies. This research is funded by the ERDF via the Estonian Software Technology and Applications Competence Center.

8. REFERENCES

[1] D. A. Bader, S. Kintali, K. Madduri, and M. Mihail. Approximating betweenness centrality. In *Proceedings of the 5th international conference on Algorithms and models for the web-graph*, WAW'07, pages 124–137, Berlin, Heidelberg, 2007. Springer-Verlag.

[2] U. Brandes. A faster algorithm for betweenness centrality, 2001.

[3] E. P. F. Chan and Y. Yang. Shortest path tree computation in dynamic graphs. *IEEE Trans. Comput.*, 58(4):541–557, 2009.

[4] L. J. Cowen and C. G. Wagner. Compact roundtrip routing in directed networks. *Journal of Algorithms*, 50(1):79 – 95, 2004.

[5] A. Das Sarma, S. Gollapudi, M. Najork, and R. Panigrahy. A sketch-based distance oracle for web-scale graphs. In *Proceedings of the third ACM international conference on Web search and data mining*, WSDM '10, pages 401–410, New York, NY, USA, 2010. ACM.

[6] D. Frigioni. Fully dynamic algorithms for maintaining shortest path trees, 2000.

[7] A. V. Goldberg and C. Harrelson. Computing the shortest path: A* search meets graph theory. In *Proc. 16th ACM-SIAM Symposium on Discrete Algorithms*, pages 156–165, 2005.

[8] A. V. Goldberg, H. Kaplan, and R. F. Werneck. Abstract reach for A*: Efficient point-to-point shortest path algorithms, 2006.

[9] A. Gubichev, S. J. Bedathur, S. Seufert, and G. Weikum. Fast and accurate estimation of shortest paths in large graphs. In *CIKM '10: Proceeding of the 19th ACM conference on Information and knowledge management*, pages 499–508. ACM, 2010.

[10] T. Ikeda, M.-Y. Hsu, H. Imai, S. Nishimura, H. Shimoura, T. Hashimoto, K. Tenmoku, and K. Mitoh. A fast algorithm for finding better routes by ai search techniques. In *Proc. Vehicle Navigation and Information Systems Conf.*, pages 291–296, 1994.

[11] J. Kleinberg, A. Slivkins, and T. Wexler. Triangulation and embedding using small sets of beacons. In *Proc. 45th Annual IEEE Symp. Foundations of Computer Science*, pages 444–453, 2004.

[12] H. Kwak, C. Lee, H. Park, and S. Moon. What is Twitter, a social network or a news media? In *WWW '10: Proceedings of the 19th international conference on World wide web*, pages 591–600, New York, NY, USA, 2010. ACM.

[13] M. Ley and P. Reuther. Maintaining an online bibliographical database: the problem of data quality. in egc, ser. revue des nouvelles technologies de l' information, vol. rnti-e-6. *Cépaduès Éditions*, 2006:5–10, 2006.

[14] A. Mislove, M. Marcon, K. P. Gummadi, P. Druschel, and B. Bhattacharjee. Measurement and Analysis of Online Social Networks. In *Proceedings of the 5th ACM/Usenix Internet Measurement Conference (IMC'07)*, San Diego, CA, October 2007.

[15] I. Pohl. Bi-directional search. In D. Meltzer, Bernard; Michie, editor, *Machine Intelligence*. Edinburgh University Press, 1971.

[16] M. Potamias, F. Bonchi, C. Castillo, and A. Gionis.

Fast shortest path distance estimation in large networks. In *CIKM '09: Proceeding of the 18th ACM conference on Information and knowledge management*, pages 867–876, New York, NY, USA, 2009. ACM.

[17] M. Thorup and U. Zwick. Approximate distance oracles. In *Proceedings of the thirty-third annual ACM symposium on Theory of computing*, STOC '01, pages 183–192, New York, NY, USA, 2001. ACM.

[18] M. V. Vieira, B. M. Fonseca, R. Damazio, P. B. Golgher, D. d. C. Reis, and B. Ribeiro-Neto. Efficient search ranking in social networks. In *Proceedings of the sixteenth ACM conference on Conference on information and knowledge management*, CIKM '07, pages 563–572, New York, NY, USA, 2007. ACM.

[19] D. J. Watts and S. H. Strogatz. Collective dynamics of 'small-world' networks. *Nature*, 393(6684):440–442, Jun 1998.

[20] X. Zhao, A. Sala, C. Wilson, H. Zheng, and B. Y. Zhao. Orion: shortest path estimation for large social graphs. In *Proceedings of the 3rd conference on Online social networks*, WOSN'10, pages 9–9, Berkeley, CA, USA, 2010. USENIX Association.

[21] U. Zwick. Exact and approximate distances in graphs – a survey. In *ESA '01: 9th Annual European Symposium on Algorithms*, pages 33–48. Springer, 2001.

CP-Index: On The Efficient Indexing of Large Graphs

Yan Xie
Department of Computer Science
University of Illinois at Chicago
Chicago, Illinois, USA
yxie@cs.uic.edu

Philip S. Yu
Department of Computer Science
University of Illinois at Chicago
Chicago, Illinois, USA
psyu@cs.uic.edu

ABSTRACT

Graph search, i.e., finding all graphs in a database D that contain the query graph q, is a classical primitive prevalent in various graph database applications. In the past, there has been an abundance of studies devoting to this topic; however, with the recent emergence of large information networks, it places new challenges to the research community.

Most of the traditional graph search schemes utilize the strategy of graph feature based indexing, whereas the index construction step that often involves frequent subgraph mining becomes a bottleneck for large graphs due to the high computational complexity. Although there have been several methods proposed to solve this mining bottleneck such as summarization of database graphs, the frequent subgraphs thus generated as indexing features are still unsatisfactory because the feature set is in general not only inadequate or deficient for the large graph scenario, but also with many redundant features. Furthermore, the large size of the graphs makes it too easy for a small feature to be contained in many of them, severely impacting its selectivity and pruning power. Motivated by all the above issues we identify, in this paper we propose a novel CP-Index (*Contact Preservation*) for efficient indexing of large graphs. To overcome the low selectivity issue, we reap further pruning opportunities by leveraging each feature's location information in the database graphs. Specifically, we look at how features are touching upon each other in the query, and check whether this contact pattern is preserved in the target graphs. Then, to tackle the deficiency and redundancy problems associated with features, new feature generation and selection methods such as *dual feature generation* and *size-increasing bootstrapping feature selection* are introduced to complete our design. Experiment results show that CP-Index is much more effective in indexing large graphs.

Categories and Subject Descriptors

H.3.1 [**Information Storage and Retrieval**]: Content Analysis and Indexing—*Indexing methods*

General Terms

Algorithms, Performance, Experimentation

Keywords

Graph database, Graph indexing, Graph querying

1. INTRODUCTION

In recent years, given the expressiveness of graph, we have seen an ever increasing usage of graphs in representing complicated structures and schemaless data, such as proteins, software flows, social networks, and the Web. In many graph-related database applications, a common and critical primitive is graph search, i.e., given a graph database $D = \{g_1, g_2, \ldots, g_n\}$ and a graph query q, find all graphs in D that contain q as a subgraph. Obviously, it is inefficient to perform graph search by checking subgraph containment between the query q and each of the database graphs $g_i \in D$, because subgraph isomorphism is NP-complete and it has to be executed for all n entries in the database D.

This is where the graph search index comes in with graph feature based indexing being the key idea [8, 25, 3, 23, 28, 20, 29, 26, 27]. To summarize, during off-line index construction, a set of indexing features are selected carefully. For each feature f, we build an index which points to those database entries that contain f. When an on-line query q is issued, a graph g_i in the database can be safely pruned without performing any subgraph isomorphism checking, if feature f is contained in q ($f \subseteq q$) but is not contained in g_i ($f \not\subseteq g_i$). Suppose a good set of features is indexed, the graph feature based scheme described above has been shown to result in a significant query processing speed-up.

However, nowadays more and more graph data come with a large size, and the need to perform search on such databases is urgently expected. For instance, a software system call graph describes the dependencies among various system call procedures in a software package, and one may want to determine which programs have been contaminated by viruses or security holes by performing a graph search. Unfortunately, as we encounter more real examples, traditional graph feature based indexing, originally designed for graphs with moderate size such as those representing chemical compounds, do not fit well in the large graph scenario.

To start with, generating an initial set of indexing features is a bottleneck for the case of large graphs. Historically, people have been using frequent subgraphs for indexing features which were shown to provide satisfactory performance. However, the time complexity of subgraph isomorphism, the core routine of any frequent subgraph mining algorithms, grows exponentially with the graph size. As shown in [9], all the representative graph indexing schemes are tested for databases of small graphs only. Though not aimed at indexing, there exist several studies to conduct mining on large graphs, e.g., the one using a summarization technique for frequent subgraph mining [1]. But even that, directly using frequent subgraphs thus mined will not lead to satisfactory indexing performance as will be shown in the experiments of Section 6, with the major reasons analyzed as follows.

The first obstacle we are facing is that the query processing in the large graph scenario may be less efficient. Consider the following example in Figure 1, given a query q that contains f_1 and f_2, any graph $g_i \in D$ not indexed by $f_j (j = 1, 2)$, i.e., $f_j \not\subseteq g_i$, can be safely pruned. However, as the database graph g_i becomes larger, more diverse internal structures are added. Consequently, it becomes more and more likely for any small size feature f_j to appear in g_i, limiting f_j's selectivity and generating much more candidates that require direct verification against q. The root cause behind this inefficiency is that, during query processing, different features, e.g., f_1 and f_2, are always treated separately. Looking at Figure 1, the only instance of f_1 in g_i is at its top-left corner, while the only instance of f_2 is at the bottom-right. Treating f_1 and f_2 separately leads to the conclusion that g_i is a candidate containing q since $f_1 \subseteq g_i$ and $f_2 \subseteq g_i$, and traditional graph feature based indexing inevitably breaks down here. But does that really mean no pruning opportunities? For the situation shown in Figure 1, we are sure that q is not a subgraph of g_i; otherwise, it would imply a non-disjoint pair of f_1 and f_2 appearing in g_i, and this is contradicting to what we observe. So, interestingly, if we consider f_1, f_2 in an interdependent context and remember the way they combine into the full query q, then it provides important hints as to whether g_i is a valid candidate containing q. Essentially, the relative positioning of features in g_i has to be exactly the same as that in q.

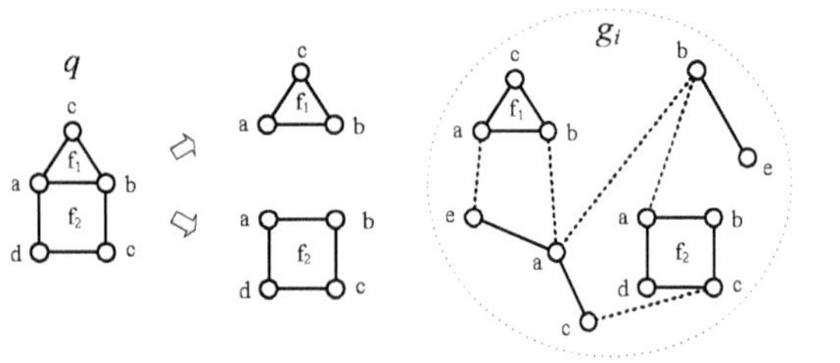

Figure 1: The Concept of Contact Preservation

Apart from the low selectivity issue above, another disadvantage of conventional methods is its inability to provide effective indexing features. There are two issues here: inadequacy and redundancy. When mining indexing features from large graphs, we want to set the support level somewhat high to curb the computational complexity. Because of the high support, this kind of features cannot prune much as they tend to be small and focus more on the commonalities between different graph instances. We need a mechanism to consider the potentially substantial differences among large graph instances. Meanwhile, given the large size of graphs, it is quite possible that we end up with an explosive set of frequent subgraphs that are quite similar to each other in terms of their indexing utilities. This introduces a huge amount of redundancy.

The key contributions of this paper are outlined next. We are the first to identify the three major issues associated with direct indexing using frequent patterns mined from large graphs (say using the summarization technique): low selectivity, inadequacy and redundancy. Towards the resolution of these issues, we propose a novel indexing scheme: CP-Index (**C**ontact **P**reservation Index), which consists of *contact preservation filtering*, *dual feature generation*, and *size-increasing bootstrapping feature selection* to tackle each of them, respectively. Our newly designed CP-Index framework is depicted in Figure 2.

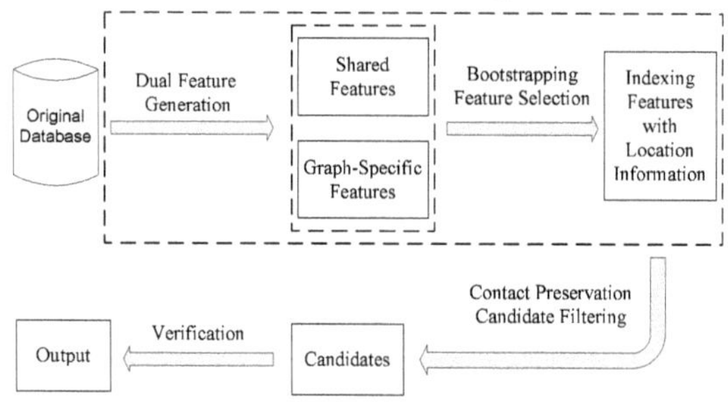

Figure 2: CP-Index Framework

The key concept behind our scheme is leveraging contact preservation among features for more effective indexing. Different from traditional schemes, we record every feature's locations of occurrences in the database graphs off-line and check their relative positioning during querying time to make sure that, if two features touch upon each other in a query (e.g., they share some vertices/edges in some particular way), then the same *contacts* are *preserved* in any true candidate graph in the database. In another word, these contacts work just like nails, which can correctly glue multiple features together and form a valid occurrence image of the query. Fortunately enough, with contact preservation, we alleviate the need to mine larger subgraph features in search for higher selectivity.

To account for the potentially large variabilities among graphs because of their big size, a new *dual feature generation* method is proposed to address the inadequacy issue. In addition to generating *shared features* common to the whole database, we decide to mine *graph-specific features* that are particular to one single graph because they offer better query indexing for individual database entries. Furthermore, regarding the potentially explosive size of the subgraph feature collection, we introduce a strategy called *size-increasing bootstrapping* to select an optimal subset for index construction, which directly uses the CP-Index query processing framework to decide whether it pays off to index an additional feature. Note that our size-increasing bootstrapping strategy is general enough to handle both shared and graph-specific features.

The rest of this paper is organized as follows. Preliminary concepts are reviewed in Section 2. Then the overall indexing and search framework utilizing contact preservation is outlined in Section 3. We focus on indexing feature generation and selection in Section 4, with Section 4.1 on dual feature generation and Section 4.2 on size-increasing bootstrapping. In Section 5 we discuss some practical aspects of implementing CP-Index, while Section 6 presents experimental results. Related work are listed in Section 7, and Section 8 concludes this study.

2. PRELIMINARIES

In this paper, we use the following notations: For a graph g, $V(g)$ is its vertex set, $E(g) \subseteq V(g) \times V(g)$ is its edge set, and l is a label function mapping a vertex or an edge to a label.

DEFINITION 1. *(Subgraph Isomorphism). For two labeled graphs g and g', a* subgraph isomorphism *is an injective function $f : V(g) \rightarrow V(g')$, s.t.,: first, $\forall v \in V(g), l(v) = l'(f(v))$; and second, $\forall(u,v) \in E(g), (f(u), f(v)) \in E(g')$ and $l(u,v) = l'(f(u), f(v))$, where l and l' are the labeling functions of g and g', respectively. Under these conditions, f is called an* embedding *of g in g'.*

DEFINITION 2. *(Subgraph and Supergraph). If there exists an embedding of g in g', then g is a* subgraph *of g', denoted by $g \subseteq g'$, and g' is a* supergraph *of g.*

DEFINITION 3 (GRAPH SEARCH PROBLEM). *Given a graph database $\mathcal{D} = \{g_1, \ldots, g_n\}$ and a graph query q, find all graphs g_i in $\mathcal{D}$, s.t., $q \subseteq g_i$.*

As can be seen, the problem definition is exactly identical to normal graph search tasks discussed in the past, except that the graphs we look at have much larger size, usually orders of magnitude larger than those targeted in previous studies, e.g., one typical dataset people used for testing is the graph structures of chemical compounds, which have around 20 vertices and 20-30 edges on average.

3. CONTACT PRESERVATION

As mentioned in the introduction, we propose utilizing the contact preservation property of features to test their compatibility with each other and explore further pruning opportunities, in an attempt to augment feature selectivity. This requires us to first pre-compute each feature's locations in the database graphs, so that its position relative to others can be quickly assessed during on-line query processing.

Given a feature f and a graph g_i in the database D, an embedding of f in g_i records one location where f exists in g_i. We can surely store every embedding of f in g_i before queries come in, but in order to keep things compact, we decide to *summarize* the full information as follows. Suppose f has t vertices, i.e., $V(f) = \{v_1, v_2, \ldots, v_t\}$; for each $v_k \in V(f)$, we store a list of vertices in g_i which v_k can be mapped to. Denote this list as $L_f^k(g_i) \subseteq V(g_i)$, where $1 \leq k \leq t = |V(f)|$, then for each vertex $u \in L_f^k(g_i)$, there must exist a subgraph isomorphism from f to g_i under which u is the image of $v_k \in V(f)$. In the following, we shall refer to $L_f^k(g_i)$ as the CP-Index of node v_k in g_i, the set $\{L_f^k(g_i) | v_k \in V(f),\ k = 1, 2, \ldots, t\}$ as the CP-Index of feature f in g_i. Similarly, when all graphs in D are considered, we will obtain the CP-Index of a node or a feature in the whole database.

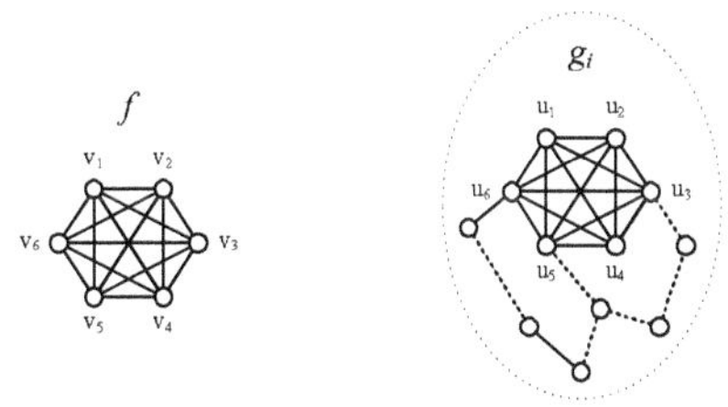

Figure 3: Constructing the CP-Index

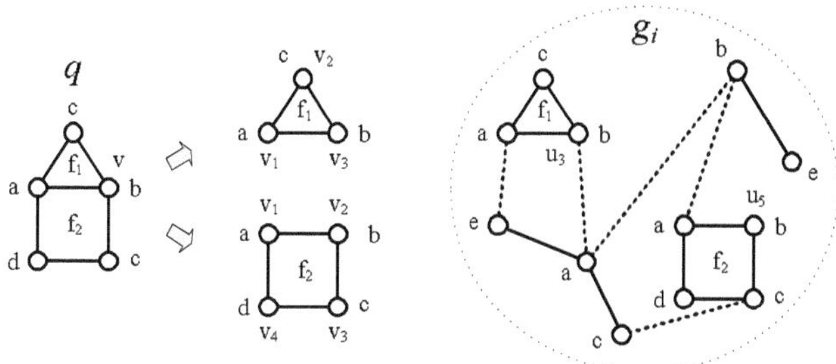

Figure 4: Query Processing in CP-Index

In Figure 3, feature f is a clique with 6 vertices, while database graph g_i happens to have a clique with the same size in it. All vertices in f and g_i have the same label. If we record all embeddings of f in g_i, there will be $6! = 720$ embeddings, and to store each of them, a list of 6 IDs is needed, e.g., $(u_2, u_5, u_6, u_3, u_1, u_4)$. In comparison, any of $v_1, v_2, \ldots, v_6$ has a CP-Index of

$$\{u_1, u_2, u_3, u_4, u_5, u_6\},$$

so in total the space saving of CP-Index is $\frac{720 \cdot 6}{6 \cdot 6} = 120$ fold.

Let us use an example to demonstrate how the CP-Index could help graph search query processing. Looking at Figure 4, which is redrawn based on Figure 1, if $f_1 \subseteq g_i$, $f_2 \subseteq g_i$, then the traditional graph feature based indexing paradigm cannot prune g_i based on the respective containment relationships between f_1 or f_2 and g_i. However, with CP-Index, we know that if the query q is contained by g_i, then the subgraph isomorphism that embeds q in g_i must map f_1's 3rd vertex and f_2's 2nd vertex to the same vertex u in g_i, i.e., $u \in L_{f_1}^3(g_i) \bigcap L_{f_2}^2(g_i) \neq \phi$, because they both correspond to $v \in V(q)$. The same holds for f_1's 1st vertex and f_2's 1st vertex. Based on this non-empty requirement, g_i can now be easily pruned. With f_1 only existing at the top-left corner of g_i and f_2 only existing at the bottom-right corner, the CP-Index of v_3 in f_1 is

$$L_{f_1}^3(g_i) = \{u_3\},$$

while the CP-Index of v_2 in f_2 is

$$L_{f_2}^2(g_i) = \{u_5\}.$$

The two intersect to ϕ. This clearly shows that no valid embedding of query q should exist in the target graph g_i.

Now we are ready to formally introduce our proposed CP-Index framework. It consists of three steps: index construction, search and verification, with enhanced capabilities compared to traditional schemes.

1. **Off-line index construction**: Generate and select a feature set F from the graph database D. For feature $f \in F$, let D_f be the set of graphs in D that contain f, we compute the CP-Index of f for each $g_i \in D_f$, which can be easily implemented as inverted vertex ID lists over $V(g_i)$.
2. **Search**: Test indexed features in F against the query q. It returns all features that are a subgraph of q, $F_q = \{f | f \in F, f \subseteq q\}$. Then we compute the candidate query answer set $C_q = \bigcap_{f \in F_q} D_f$. To make use of the CP-Indices, we consider F_q as a whole and check whether the contacts made among features in F_q are preserved in each of the candidates. This will further cut down C_q's size, just as what we saw in Figure 4.

3. **Verification**: Directly check subgraph isomorphism between query q and each graph g_i in the final candidate set C_q to see whether q is contained in g_i.

Before moving forward, let us spend a bit more time on each of the steps above. For index construction, we have assumed that a feature set F is already available, after which the CP-Index of each feature $f \in F$ are computed and stored. However, generating such an F is never a straightforward task. We will come back to this topic in Section 4 for a more detailed discussion.

To make the framework clear, we have intentionally omitted elaborated descriptions in the search step. As can be seen, the first phase of this step is identical to traditional feature based indexing, but since for each $f \in F$, we have further saved the CP-Index of f in g_i instead of simply a graph ID i that indicates f is a subgraph of g_i, more pruning possibilities exist. The whole procedure of leveraging CP-Indices during query processing is outlined below.

- After getting the set of features contained in q, we locate each $f \in F_q$ in the query, which results in a mapping between f's vertices and q's vertices.
- Considering all these mappings for all features $f \in F_q$, now for each of query q's vertices $v \in V(q)$, we have a set of vertices, each of them belongs to some feature $f \in F_q$ and has been mapped to v when we located f in the query , e.g., in Figure 4, for q's vertex v, we have f_1's v_3 and f_2's v_2 corresponding to it. These vertices all have their associated CP-Indices pointing to the list of nodes in a candidate graph g_i where they can appear. Let us intersect all CP-Indices, and the resulting vertex list should narrow down the possible nodes in g_i which v could be mapped to if q is embedded in g_i.
- After multiple intersections, the list mentioned above should have minimal length, and could sometimes be empty, e.g., in Figure 4, the CP-Index of v_3 in f_1 and the CP-Index of v_2 in f_2 intersect to ϕ, hinting that there is no single vertex in g_i which v in the query q can be mapped to. Thus, if there exists some $v \in V(q)$ such that the intersection result for v is empty after all aforementioned processing, then g_i is safely pruned from the candidate set C_q.

Alternatively, we may understand this pruning strategy as follows. Given a query q, we leverage the location information entailed in the CP-Indices of features in F_q to pinpoint q's location in the graph g_i. In a word, the contacts made among features in F_q must be fully preserved, as otherwise, they cannot combine into a full query graph q in g_i. This *contact preservation* property among features is checked by examining the compatibility of their associated CP-Indices. Now, every vertex $v \in V(q)$ works like a nail that glues multiple indexed features together: It nails down their relative positioning, which must be held intact as we try to embed q in g_i. This is why we could intersect relevant CP-Indices to narrow down the possibilities of mapping q's vertices to g_i's, and also prune g_i if the intersection result is empty.

Finally, verification works as a last resort by directly executing a subgraph isomorphism test when contact preservation based query processing still could not prune a candidate graph out of consideration. Hopefully, at the time of verification, the candidate set has been shrunk to a very small portion of the initial database. Note that, for any remaining candidate say g_i, the contact preservation property can only yield a non-empty subset of vertices for each node v in the query q, denoted as $V_{v\to}(g_i) \subseteq V(g_i)$, which points to all possible nodes in g_i which v can map to. We call $V_{v\to}(g_i)$ as v's *location list* in g_i. Interestingly, even though the location lists are not null, they still prune away lots of possibilities. In fact, now the subgraph isomorphism test routine could limit its scope by only mapping v to some vertex in $V_{v\to}(g_i)$, instead of trying all possible vertices in $V(g_i)$ without any guidance. In other words, the pruning we have achieved in the search step can to a large extent cut down the computation time that has to be spent in the verification step. Considering an extreme situation, if the set $V_{v\to}(g_i)$ for every $v \in V(q)$ contains one single vertex, then there is only one probable way to embed q in g_i by mapping each $v \in V(q)$ to that single vertex, and our verification procedure just needs to test this sole potential embedding and verify whether it is true or not.

4. FEATURE GENERATION AND SELECTION

As we pointed out in the introduction, using frequent subgraphs as indexing features on a database of large graphs is inflicted by the inadequacy and redundancy issues, even if summarization techniques could help reduce the time complexity to mine out an initial feature set. In this paper, we introduce two novel concepts to address these two problems in separate steps: 1) *dual feature generation*, which summarizes the database graphs and then mines both shared and graph-specific features to tackle the inadequacy issue, and 2) *size-increasing bootstrapping*, which treats the output of step 1 as an initial set, and then performs contact preservation based redundancy analysis to select an optimal subset for index construction. The details of both steps will be given in Section 4.1 and Section 4.2, respectively.

4.1 Dual Feature Generation

Given the big graph size, most frequent graph pattern mining algorithms would experience a hard time to produce results efficiently due to the high time complexity of subgraph isomorphism. To solve this dilemma, the authors of [1] proposed a way to summarize graphs in the database by randomly merging groups of nodes with identical labels and collapsing respective edges. With the graph summarization technique, it is feasible to obtain an initial frequent subgraph set F_0 in a given database with large graphs. However, unfortunately, using this initial set F_0 to build indexing for large graphs as in traditional graph feature based schemes will not lead to satisfactory indexing performance. One issue that might stem from it is that, we may have to set the minimum support threshold *min_sup* somewhat high as compared to the regular settings in previous works. Since small structures are very easy to be contained by a large graph, there would be too many patterns if the support threshold is low. Now, adjusting *min_sup* upwards definitely makes the mining much easier, but it also negatively influences the pruning power of obtained features, because they are contained in many entries of the database and thus not very selective. In Section 3, we proposed to leverage contact preservation properties and alleviate this issue by considering multiple features inter-dependently during query processing. Here, we further suggest another round of *graph-specific mining* to directly tackle the low selectivity problem.

As a large graph offers the opportunity to use its own subgraph features to improve pruning, graph-specific mining generates a feature set specific to a single graph g_i in the database D. Considering a g_i-specific feature, we simply compute and store its CP-Index for only one graph g_i. With the additional graph-specific indexing, this is referred to as the *dual feature generation* approach. Now, suppose we have a shared feature set F^D for the database and n graph-specific features sets F^{g_i} for each $g_i \in D$ (details about how F^D and F^{g_i}'s are determined will be given in Section 4.2), the search process of a query graph q proceeds as follows.

1. **Shared feature indexing.** With the index on shared features F^D, follow the search process described in Section 3 and obtain a candidate query answer set $C_q \subseteq D$.
2. **Graph-specific feature indexing.** For each remaining candidate $g_i \in C_q$, we have a non-empty location list $V_{v\rightarrow}(g_i)$ for every $v \in V(q)$ after phase 1. Now consider g_i-specific features F^{g_i} and determine the subset $F_q^{g_i}$ that are subgraphs of q. We use $F_q^{g_i}$ and their associated CP-Indices on g_i to further prune the location lists above by taking intersections, so that some list would finally drop to empty, letting us remove g_i from C_q.

As one could easily see, this query processing procedure is very similar to what we outlined in Section 3, except that it works in two phases and the pruning only happens for g_i (instead of the whole database) when doing g_i-specific feature indexing. Back to how graph-specific features should be mined in the first place, we still leverage graph summarization techniques, transform g_i to its summary s_i and mine the database $\{s_i\}$ with $min\_sup = 100\%$. Strictly speaking, we are only borrowing frequent pattern mining algorithms here to extract subgraphs of g_i for use as indexing features, because every subgraph of g_i would have a support of 100% in such a single-entry database. So, to avoid pattern explosion, we decide to only find patterns up to $maxL$ edges and terminate the mining process beyond. Meanwhile, one can also repeat the summarization-mining workflow for multiple rounds, i.e., transform g_i to $s_i^1, s_i^2, \dots$ and merge the result patterns obtained on $\{s_i^1\}, \{s_i^2\}, \dots$. Since summarization may cause pattern loss, i.e., a pattern in g_i might not necessarily be a pattern in s_i, it will be exponentially harder for a g_i-pattern to miss from the output of all mining rounds given that the merging/collapsing of nodes/edges during summarization is fully randomized. Consequently, patterns found on summarized graphs can go arbitrarily close to the true ones, which is desirable for indexing purposes. At last, when it is appropriate, either early termination after $maxL$ edges or repeated mining can also be applied in generating the shared feature set for indexing the whole database.

4.2 Feature Selection by Size-Increasing Bootstrapping

To make things compact, we do not want to keep everything output from step 1 in the index. Suppose the initial feature set is F_0, in this section, we are going to perform redundancy analysis and select a non-redundant set of features $F \subseteq F_0$ for CP-Index construction. The result set should preserve the utility of F_0 to the largest extent. Together with the query processing procedure discussed previously, this completes our indexing and search pipeline on large graphs.

As the name implies, if a feature f is *redundant* with regard to a feature set F, it means that most of its utility can be well substituted by those already in F. Referring to our query processing procedure, maintaining f in the index allows us to use f's CP-Index and directly point to the locations where f occurs in the database graphs. How can we not index f but still achieve almost the same benefit? For an on-line query q, feature f is only useful when $f \subseteq q$. Due to the chain effect, each $f' \in F, f' \subseteq f$ must be contained in q, as well, implying that f's subgraphs in the feature set F can also be used when searching q in the database. Now, a natural question to ask is, can the utility of f be substituted by the set $\{f'|f' \in F, f' \subseteq f\}$?

Keeping f out of the index, the impact is low if we can reconstruct f's CP-Index with little effort during on-line query processing. Note that, with an existing set of features F, we do not have to compute from scratch the locations where f can appear in a target graph, but rather with the help of CP-Indices maintained for $\{f'|f' \in F, f' \subseteq f\}$, which is exactly what we are going to do when searching f on the graph database D. So, interestingly, we could reuse the search framework proposed above to help decide an optimal set of features. This is referred to as the *size-increasing bootstrapping* approach of feature selection.

DEFINITION 4. *(Redundant Feature). Given a database D, an existing feature set F and another feature f, treat f as the query and perform a search of it in D, with F being the set of indexed features. Now, for each candidate graph g_i, we obtain a set of location lists for vertices in f by intersecting the CP-indices of features in F. Comparing with the true set of f's location lists in g_i (i.e., f's CP-Index), we say that f is* redundant *with regard to F on graph g_i, if these two sets are very similar to each other.*

There are many possibilities of defining the above similarity between location lists and aggregating the metric over all graphs in D, which is the reason why we did not want to stipulate a particular way in Definition 4. In this paper, we choose to use the following specification for redundancy. Referring back to the end of Section 3, we used $V_{v\rightarrow}(g_i), v \in V(f)$ to denote the location list of v in a target graph g_i. Multiplying the length of all location lists for f, we can model the search space of testing whether f is a subgraph of g_i as

$$\prod_{v \in V(f)} |V_{v\rightarrow}(g_i)|,$$

because a potential embedding of f in g_i may result from taking one vertex from each of the location lists and using them to comprise a full image of f. If this metric of search space size is further aggregated over the whole database D, we have

$$\text{Cost}(f) = \sum_{g_i \in D} \prod_{v \in V(f)} |V_{v\rightarrow}(g_i)|$$

to model the cost of searching f in D. Note that, if there exists some $v \in V(f)$ such that $V_{v\rightarrow}(g_i) = \phi$, i.e., the location list of v in g_i is empty after pruning, then the cost entry corresponding to g_i is 0, which is inline with our indexing framework because it means that CP-Index can directly remove g_i from the candidate set without checking further.

Obviously, the cost of searching a query in the database depends on the composition of available indices. So, we want to write $\text{Cost}(f)$ as $\text{Cost}_F(f)$ to signify that F is feature set that has been indexed. We now define the redundancy of a feature f with regard to F on database D as

$$R_D(f, F) = \frac{\text{Cost}_{F \bigcup f}(f)}{\text{Cost}_F(f)},$$

meaning that if the cost of searching f in D decreases a lot after f is integrated into the index, i.e., $\text{Cost}_{F \bigcup f}(f)$ and thus $R_D(f, F)$ is small, then the redundancy of f is low and it is worthwhile to index f in addition to F.

One might have already noticed that $\text{Cost}_{F \bigcup f}(f)$ cannot be larger than $\text{Cost}_F(f)$, and thus $R_D(f, F) \leq 1$. This is because, if the index includes f, then the pre-computed CP-Index associated with f would directly point to the true location lists of searching f in D, which cannot be shrunk any further. In comparison, $\text{Cost}_F(f)$ refers to a larger search space as we need to use features that are: 1) already indexed in F, and 2) contained by f, to deduct f's location lists. Finally, the ratio between $\text{Cost}_{F \bigcup f}(f)$ and $\text{Cost}_F(f)$ is a good measure of how redundant f is if one wants to merge it into the indexed feature set.

A formal description of the feature selection process is given in Algorithm 1, where we sequentially go through the set of available features and only retain those non-redundant ones. Note that, since calculating the redundancy of f with regard to F requires all features in F that are subgraphs of f, we want to follow a predetermined order in traversing F_0 so that subgraphs are always visited before supergraphs. This could be easily achieved by checking features that have a smaller number of edges first, because a feature with $e+1$ edges cannot be contained in a feature with e edges for sure.

As proposed in Section 4.1, in order to enhance index performances, apart from a set of features shared among all graphs in the database D, we want to pick some graph-specific features for each $g_i \in D$. Interestingly, Algorithm 1 is general enough to handle dual feature generation. The only difference is instead of starting from the empty set, we will use $F = F^D$ in line 1 of Algorithm 1, because graph-specific features are picked on top of shared features.

Algorithm 1 Size-Increasing Bootstrapping

Input: Graph database D, Initial feature set F_0,
The redundancy threshold r.
Output: A subset of selected features $F \subseteq F_0$.

Feature_Selection(D, F_0, r) {
1: $F = \phi$;
2: **for** each $f \in F_0$ **do**
3: Search f in D, obtain its location lists, with F indexed;
4: Calculate f's true location lists as well as $R_D(f, F)$;
5: **if** $R_D(f, F) < r$ **then**
6: $F = F \bigcup f$;
7: Integrate f and its true location lists (i.e., CP-Index);
8: **return** F;
}

5. PRACTICAL ASPECTS

5.1 Indexing Feature Tree

In this section, we want to describe how the CP-Index storage is organized. In fact, we could store all indexed features in a tree-like structure: If feature f_2 is a supergraph of feature f_1, then f_2 is linked under f_1 as one of its direct or indirect children, just as what Figure 5 depicts. With such an indexing feature tree T, the CP-Index of each feature f is stored at the node corresponding to f on T. Since many frequent subgraph mining algorithms, such as gSpan (which is the one we used for experiments), maintain a pattern tree during the mining process, it is often very easy to obtain an initial feature tree as the by-product of mining. After that, we can run Algorithm 1 to filter those redundant tree nodes, leading to the final indexing tree. Note that, since Algorithm 1 is based on size-increasing bootstrapping, one only needs to pass the initial tree level by level, so that smaller features are visited before larger ones.

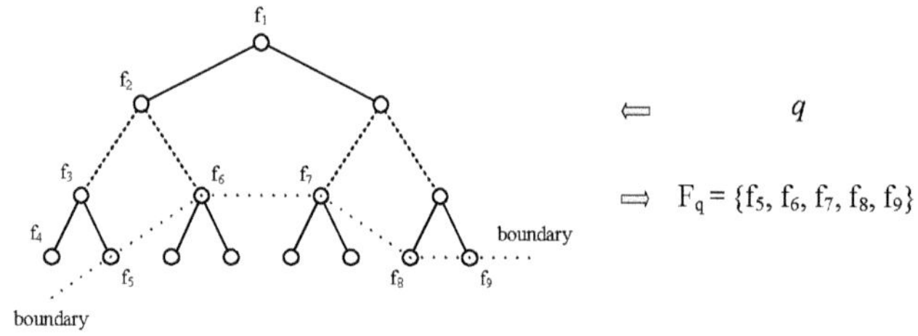

Figure 5: Indexing Feature Tree

Both shared and graph-specific features are stored and organized in the way mentioned above, and their respective indexing feature trees are treated similarly during query processing. When a query q comes, we do a post-order traversal (i.e., parent node is visited after its children) on the indexing feature tree T to obtain those largest features contained in q. As shown in Figure 5, we get a boundary in T where each node on it is a subgraph of q and all of their children are not. These boundary features comprise the set $F_q \subseteq F$ we use in the search step of Section 3's framework, whose CP-Indices would help us look for q in the database. There are several reasons for doing this here.

- We can stop traversing a feature f's direct or indirect parents in the tree, if f has already been found as a subgraph of q. This saves us much time in testing the containment relationship between indexed features in F and the query q. Also, with a smaller subset of features F_q working against q, the CP-Index intersection time and associated index operation costs would all be reduced.
- Larger features must have better selectivity, so for example, in Figure 5, if $f_4 \subseteq q$, then f_3 is contained in q and thus can be used for querying q, as well; however, f_4 should offer less graph candidates compared to f_3, which is a better indexing option.
- Having larger size, features may overlap to a larger degree in the query. This gives us better opportunity to leverage contact preservation properties for pruning.

5.2 Incremental Index Maintenance

Interestingly, our CP-Index framework also makes the index we construct a naturally incremental one. First, the deletion of a graph from the database is very easy to handle: Without additional efforts, we only need to retain the same set of shared features and their associated indices on the remaining graphs, together with respective graph-specific indices, and all future queries would be handled in exactly the same manner. On the other hand, when new graphs are inserted, we keep the same set of shared features and extend their indices to new graphs by computing corresponding CP-Indices on them; meanwhile, Algorithm 1 is executed to add graph-specific features for these new database entries, as well. Usually, the pattern distribution of new graphs is pretty similar to those existing ones since they belong to the same database, so it is expected that the shared feature set picked previously should continue to work well after insertions take place. Moreover, even if some of the new entries are significantly different, the graph-specific features selected for them can to a large extent compensate for the possible negative effect on query performance. This will keep the built index running efficiently for a long time before we need to decide a new shared feature set and reconstruct everything from scratch.

6. EMPIRICAL STUDIES

In this section, we will provide empirical evaluations of CP-Index. We have two kinds of databases with graphs of large size: a real program analysis database and a synthetic database. We note that there is no indexing algorithm dedicated to indexing a database with large-sized graphs because of the computational complexity involved. Consequently, for comparison purposes, we choose a baseline that follows the framework of traditional graph feature based indexing but conducts mining on summarized database graphs [1] to generate the indexing feature set. To be more specific, in the baseline algorithm, we first summarize each database graph for off-line feature selection and index construction, and then apply normal filtering and verification procedures [25] for online query processing. This method is referred to as direct indexing on summarized graphs (DI Summarization). All experiments are done on a Debian GNU/Linux server with two dual-core Xeon 3.0GHz CPUs and 16GB main memory, and the program is written in C++.

6.1 Results on Real Data

Program Analysis Data. Program dependence graphs appear in software-security applications that perform characteristic analysis of malicious programs [6]. In a dependence graph, vertices are different types of system calls and edges representing the dependency relationships among them. For example, an edge with label $y = f(x)$ between two vertices v_1 and v_2 means that the system call at v_1 assigns the variable x and the system call at v_2 uses the variable y whose value is derived from x.

Graph search is an important analytical task to perform on such system call graphs. It can reveal latent security holes if we search the database using a known malicious pattern. Our testing data has 238 graphs, with an average size of around 300 vertices and 600 edges. In addition, following what traditional schemes did, queries are randomly drawn from the database graphs as connected subgraphs. Note that, the size of the graphs here is 15-20 times larger than those in a typical chemical compound dataset that was used to test various traditional indexing methods. Also, with 238 graphs in the database, it might seem small at a first glance. In fact, this is to keep our experiment more manageable. Given the large size of graphs, many involved graph routines such as isomorphism checking would understandably be much slower; moreover, as we show later in the scalability analysis of Figure 10, CP-Index has a linearly scalable trend, which means that experiment results achieved on a smaller database is representative, as well.

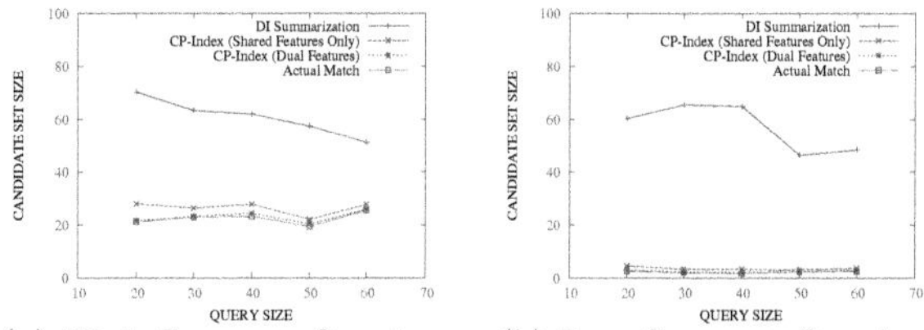

(a) High Support Queries (b) Low Support Queries

Figure 6: Performance on Query Sizes

We set parameters in our algorithm as follows. For mining, we summarize each graph to 20 vertices, i.e., the compression ratio is about $\frac{300}{20} = 15$, and min_sup is set to 50%. To avoid pattern explosion, we only mine features up to $maxL = 4$ edges, and later we shall have an experiment for the synthetic data (Figure 12(b)) to show how this parameter $maxL$ would impact actual indexing performance. Finally, the redundancy thresholds is $r = 0.5$.

Figure 6(a) and Figure 6(b) well demonstrate the usefulness of CP-Index. We generate five groups of queries, with query size ranging from 20 to 60 (in terms of number of edges), which is drawn on the x-axis. We then process all these queries, and report the average candidate answer set size for each of the groups on the y-axis. Since it represents the number of time-consuming subgraph verification tests that need to be executed, we have chosen to use the candidate set size for performance gauging. To set up an objective standard concerning the index pruning power, we also draw a line with label "Actual Match" in the figures, which displays the number of true answer graphs that really contain the input query. Since no index could/should prune away any true answer graph, the "Actual Match" line is a firm lowerbound for all indexing schemes.

We divide all queries into two categories: high support and low support. If a query has an "actual match" number that is greater than 5, then it belongs to the high support category. Figure 6(a) and Figure 6(b) display the candidate answer set size for high support and low support queries, respectively. As can be clearly seen, even with shared features only, CP-Index is already much better than DI Summarization; if we further use both types of features, then the candidate set achieved by CP-Index becomes nearly indistinguishable from the true answer set. This is regardless of whether the query is small or large and whether the query is frequent or not. It proves the comparative advantage of leveraging contact preservation properties and building CP-Indices, as the pruning power of DI Summarization methods severely degrades in the large graph scenario.

Figure 7 depicts the query performance in a different way, where x-axis is the true query answer set size, i.e., its support. Still, we could see a much better performance of CP-Index, lying very close to the theoretical optimum. The gap between CP-Index and DI Summarization narrows at the right end of the picture, mainly due to a constant increase of the "actual match" number, which is the best our CP-Index can possibly achieve.

Directly watching response time measured in seconds could be a more intuitive way to understand the query answering cost of searching on large graphs. So let us take a look at Figure 8, where the average query response time for each group of queries is drawn against its size. Note that, one

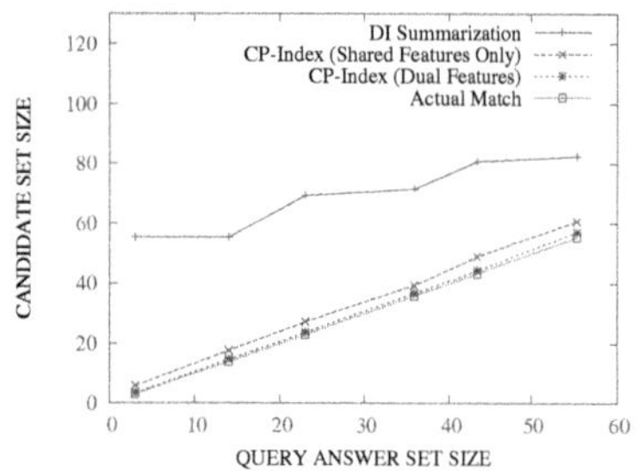

Figure 7: Performance on Query Support Levels

may think that the several hundred seconds on y-axis is a little too large; however, considering that at least for each of the "actual match" we still need to run an isomorphism test for verification, it does not sound a big surprise since one might need tens of seconds to verify a large, complex graph. As can be seen, with DI Summarization, queries will take much longer to complete. Also, the gap between shared features only and dual features is more prominent here than in Figures 6(a) and 6(b). For example, when the query size is 20, indexing graph-specific features reduces the response time from 270 seconds to 45 seconds. Considering that only 34% more space is needed (1182 shared features, 405 graph-specific features), we can see that dual feature generation is a very cost-effective way to promote index performance.

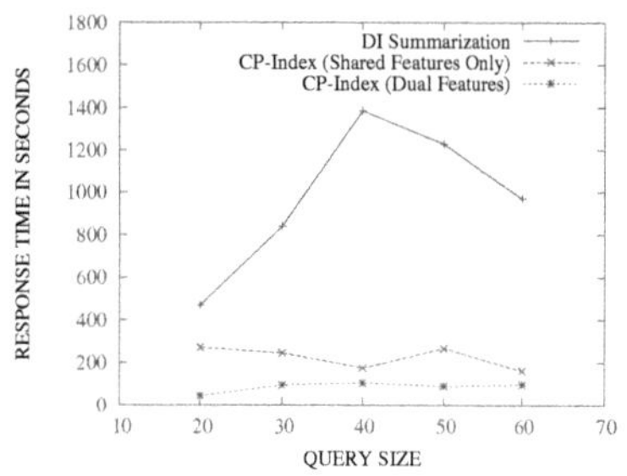

Figure 8: Response Time

Lastly, we focus on the sensitivity to redundancy threshold r used in our size-increasing bootstrapping and the result is depicted in Figure 9. Here we set the query size to be 20. Figure 9(a) illustrates the impact of r on the number of output index features. As expected, the number of features decreases monotonously while r becomes smaller. When r is 1, the output set is exactly the same as the one we could get by performing dual feature generation step without any selection. On the other hand, as showed in 9(b), the size of the candidate set after filtering gradually increases when r decreases. It is a natural trade-off between the performance and the cost. However, the result of CP-Index is very close to the true answer set anyway no matter how small r is. For example, when r decreases from 1 to 0.6, the feature set size reduces almost six folds from 18,653 to 2,745, but the candidate set size remains nearly the same.

6.2 More Results on Synthetic Data

Synthetic Generator Description. The synthetic graph generator follows a similar mechanism as the one used to generate itemset transactions, where we can set the number

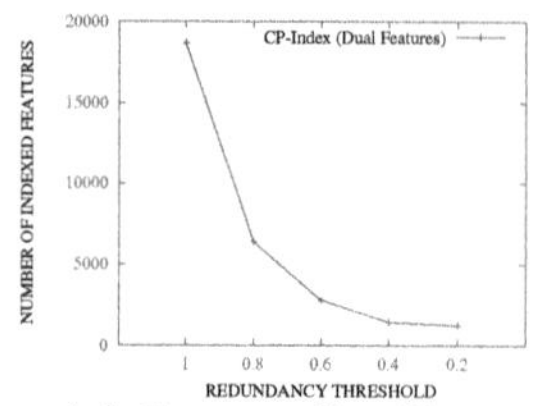

(a) Feature Set Size

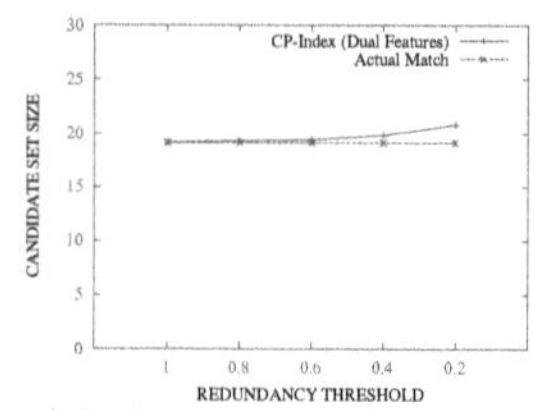

(b) Candidate Set Size

Figure 9: Sensitivity to Redundancy Threshold

of graphs (D), average size of graphs (T), number of seed patterns (L), average size of seed patterns (I) and number of distinct vertex/edge labels (V/E). To begin with, a set of L seed patterns are generated randomly, whose size is determined by a Poisson distribution with mean I; then, seeds are randomly selected and inserted into a graph one by one until the graph reaches its size, which is the realization of another Poisson variable with mean T. Due to lack of space, we refer interested readers to [15] for further details.

The synthetic dataset we take is D200T400L100I50V4E1, i.e, 200 transactions with 400 vertices on average, which are generated by 100 seed patterns of average size 50; the number of possible vertex/edge labels is set to 4/1. For scalability and index size tests in Figure 10 and Figure 11, we vary $|D|$, the number of graphs in the database, and generate multiple datasets D($|D|$)T400L100I50V4E1. Queries are generated similarly as in the real data case. Algorithm parameters: Each graph is summarized to 20 vertices, i.e., the compression ratio is $\frac{400}{20} = 20$; $min\_sup = 70\%$, which is a bit higher than that in the real data, because the synthetic data generator produces graphs based on a pool of seed patterns, thus tending to have higher similarities among database entries; maximum indexed feature length is $maxL = 5$; redundancy threshold is $r = 0.5$.

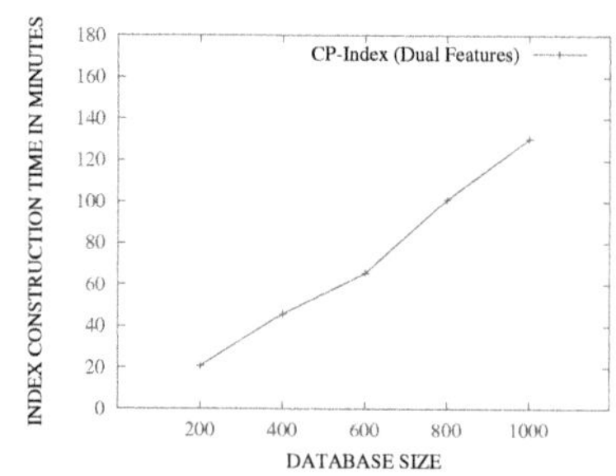

Figure 10: Index Construction Time

The scalability of CP-Index is shown in Figure 10. We vary the database size, i.e., the number of graphs inside, from 200, 400, ..., to 1,000, and measure the respective index construction time. As demonstrated, the implementation is highly efficient and our method is linearly scalable with regard to the data size. This is in strong contrast to state-of-the-art graph indexing methods. We tested gIndex, due to the mining bottleneck on large graphs, it cannot finish in one day.

Figure 11 displays the index size (in terms of number of features being indexed). The same experiment setting as testing scalability in Figure 10 is used: We vary the number of graphs from 200 to 1,000, and see how the index size responds. The observation is that the index size grows sublinearly, definitely a desirable property when dealing with a large graph database. Also, we could see that the gap between "Dual Features" and "Shared Features Only" is not very large, meaning that the addition of graph-specific features does not cost too much index space indeed.

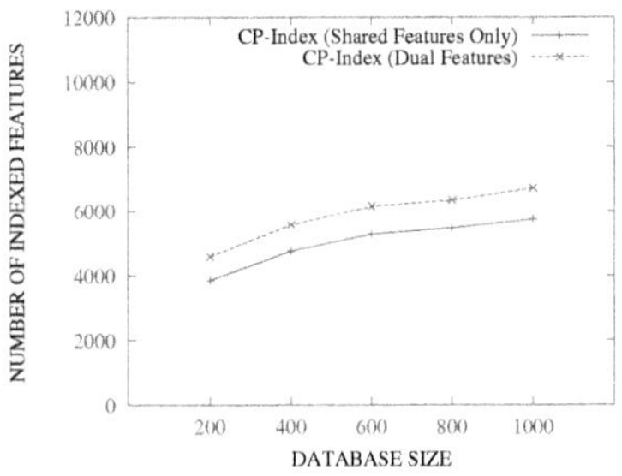

Figure 11: Index Size

Figure 12(a) shows the performance of CP-Index on synthetic data. Trends depicted here are quite similar to those in the corresponding Figure 7 of real data empirical studies. We also tested other datasets generated with different parameter settings and obtained similar results.

Fixing all other parameters, in Figure 12(b), we want to examine the impact of $maxL$, maximum indexed feature size, on the performance. Here, x-axis is $maxL$, y-axis is the candidate set size, and the queries we use have 40 edges. Both the "CP-Index" and "Di Summaraization" lines have a downward trend because the index pruning power increases when more features are considered. The "Actual Match" line is horizontal. Interestingly, the performance of CP-Index seems to have almost reached its peak at $maxL = 5$, as features with at most 5 edges have provided enough index coverage, without resorting to larger ones. Even at $maxL = 4$, CP-Index is already very close to "Actual Match", while "Di Summaraization" lags behind by a large gap. This suggests from yet another angle the stronger pruning power of CP-Index and contact preservation.

7. RELATED WORK

Graph search is a basic primitive in the management and analysis of complex structured data, which has stimulated much interest on indexing techniques from the research community. Most of the traditional graph indexing algorithms are graph feature based, as they follow the strategy of filter-and-verification. These methods achieved great success by exploiting different types of features and various verification strategies. GraphGrep [8] is the first work of this kind, which uses paths as indexing features. gIndex [25] makes a breakthrough by indexing frequent subgraphs of the database, offering much better selectivity than paths. gIndex defines a framework representative of many later methods that use graphs as features, and provides very good performance in many different situations, according to the empirical studies of [9]. Tree+Delta [28] only extracts tree fragments for indexing, since the cost of tree mining is much lower; in addition, it also generates on-demand a small delta of graph features during query processing to compensate for the limited pruning power of trees. Regarding verification strategies, FG-Index [3] introduces a verification-free concept, while

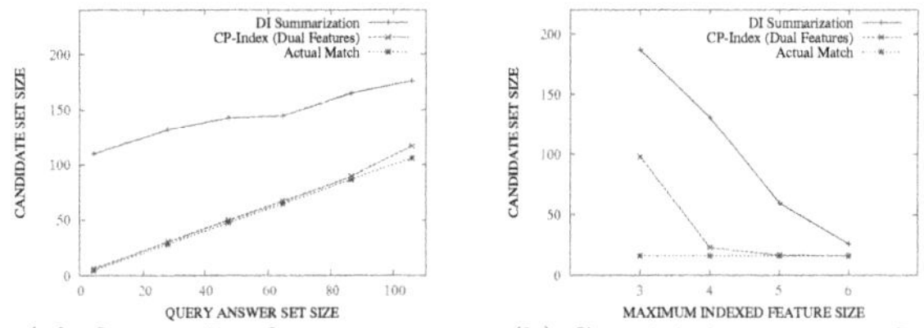

(a) Query Performance (b) Sensitivity to $maxL$

Figure 12: Experiments on Synthetic Dataset

SwiftIndex [20] proposes an encoding plan based on the frequencies of vertices/edges, etc. to improve the efficiency of subgraph isomorphism tests. Quite unfortunately, none of the methods here is suitable for the large graph scenario, because of the problems shared by all graph feature based indexing schemes as we mentioned in the introduction.

There are also graph indexing methods that are not filter-and-verification based. Williams et al. store all unique, induced subgraphs of the database graphs in a directed acyclic graph for query processing [23]. gCode [29] computes vertex signatures according to local information and adopts spectral graph coding to encode the topology of both database graphs and queries in a numerical space. Empirical studies of [9] show that the pruning of gCode is not very powerful for sparse datasets.

Compared to the easier setting that comprises a database of small-sized graphs, there has been much less research focusing on large graph search and indexing. Similar works mainly focus on indexing on a single large graph rather than a database with many large graphs. GraphQL [11] leverages neighborhood subgraphs and vertex profiles for global and local pruning, respectively. GADDI [26] defines NDS (neighboring discriminating substructure) distance for every neighboring vertex pair in the graph and based on that develops some inequality property for candidate elimination. Both GraphQL and GADDI uses a vertex-at-a-time mechanism when searching for a query in the graphs; essentially, this is like using single vertices as indexing features, which might not be very selective compared to the subgraph features deployed in CP-Index. Making a step forward in this respect, [27] proposes a path-at-a-time query processing strategy. The low mining cost and more manageable structures all make paths very desirable indexing features. However, as we already pointed out in this paper, feature selectivity is very important in the large graph scenario. Given their better selectivity, one might want to look at subgraph features if the mining and indexing complexity can be well controlled, just like what summarization techniques do in the construction of a compact and efficient CP-Index.

Frequent subgraph mining algorithms exist in abundance, including [15], [24], [12] that work on a graph transaction database and [16], [2] that work on a single large graph, followed by many others. There are also works such as [17] that focus on the extraction of patterns with specific structural characteristics. Chen et al. suggest summarizing graph instances before mining them [1], which is inline with what we do in this paper. Other strategies have also been proposed to reduce either the pattern space [10] or the data space [21] by picking delegates. They are orthogonal to graph summarization, and can be integrated together to further accelerate the mining process.

The idea of leveraging summaries to facilitate data processing on graphs is also not new. For example, it has been used in XML data [18] and computing approximate personalized PageRank [19], while [22] mines the dense sub components of a big network to compress and visualize its internal structures. Exploring the technique, these works inspired our design of a compact CP-Index, which nicely summarizes the features' location information in database graphs.

Quite a few studies, e.g. [4], have been dedicated to the acceleration of subgraph isomorphism testing, which can definitely help the verification step of CP-Index. Besides the containment queries discussed in this paper, there are works that try to handle other types of queries on graphs, e.g., keyword search [13], correlation search [14], reachability queries [5] and bounded graph simulation [7]. These are all of important use and greatly enhance the primitives available for graph database management.

8. CONCLUSIONS

As a basic primitive, graph search is critical for the success of many graph database management applications. With the recent emergence of large-scale data sources, e.g., biological networks, software programs, and social networks, in this paper, we reconsider the graph indexing problem within the context of large graphs. Given the large size of the target, traditional indexing techniques will break down, and still do not perform well even after advanced strategies such as summarization are utilized to mine frequent subgraphs as indexing features. We identify three challenging issues for the feature set thus selected: low selectivity, inadequacy and redundancy, and propose a new indexing technique, CP-Index, to overcome them. First, a new graph search framework is presented, which leverages the *contact preservation* properties we introduced to enhance the selectivity of small features that have been severely impacted in the large graph scenario. Then, we use this search framework and develop a *size increasing bootstrapping* scheme to decide the utilities of individual features and pick a non-redundant subset of them, resulting in a compact but rather optimized graph index. Accounting for the much bigger variabilities among different graphs due to their size, we devise a *dual feature generation* approach to address the inadequacy issue, where our index consists of not only a feature set shared among all database graphs, but also multiple graph-specific feature sets. Experiments on real and synthetic large graph datasets confirm the efficiency and effectiveness of our method.

9. ACKNOWLEDGMENTS

This work is supported in part by NSF through grants IIS 0905215, DBI-0960443, OISE-0968341 and OIA-0963278.

10. REFERENCES

[1] C. Chen, C. X. Lin, M. Fredrikson, M. Christodorescu, X. Yan, and J. Han. Mining graph patterns efficiently via randomized summaries. *PVLDB*, 2(1):742–753, 2009.

[2] J. Chen, W. Hsu, M.-L. Lee, and S.-K. Ng. Nemofinder: Dissecting genome-wide protein-protein interactions with meso-scale network motifs. In *KDD*, pages 106–115, 2006.

[3] J. Cheng, Y. Ke, W. Ng, and A. Lu. Fg-index: Towards verification-free query processing on graph databases. In *SIGMOD*, pages 857–872, 2007.

[4] J. Cheng, J. X. Yu, B. Ding, P. S. Yu, and H. Wang. Fast graph pattern matching. In *ICDE*, pages 913–922, 2008.

[5] J. Cheng, J. X. Yu, X. Lin, H. Wang, and P. S. Yu. Fast computing reachability labelings for large graphs with high compression rate. In *EDBT*, pages 193–204, 2008.

[6] M. Christodorescu, S. Jha, and C. Kruegel. Mining specifications of malicious behavior. In *ESEC/SIGSOFT FSE*, pages 5–14, 2007.

[7] W. Fan, J. Li, S. Ma, N. Tang, Y. Wu, and Y. Wu. Graph pattern matching: From intractable to polynomial time. *PVLDB*, 3(1):264–275, 2010.

[8] R. Giugno and D. Shasha. Graphgrep: A fast and universal method for querying graphs. In *ICPR (2)*, pages 112–115, 2002.

[9] W.-S. Han, J. Lee, M.-D. Pham, and J. X. Yu. iGraph: A framework for comparisons of disk-based graph indexing techniques. *PVLDB*, 3(1):449–459, 2010.

[10] M. A. Hasan, V. Chaoji, S. Salem, J. Besson, and M. J. Zaki. Origami: Mining representative orthogonal graph patterns. In *ICDM*, pages 153–162, 2007.

[11] H. He and A. K. Singh. Graphs-at-a-time: Query language and access methods for graph databases. In *SIGMOD*, pages 405–418, 2008.

[12] A. Inokuchi, T. Washio, and H. Motoda. Complete mining of frequent patterns from graphs: Mining graph data. *Machine Learning*, 50(3):321–354, 2003.

[13] V. Kacholia, S. Pandit, S. Chakrabarti, S. Sudarshan, R. Desai, and H. Karambelkar. Bidirectional expansion for keyword search on graph databases. In *VLDB*, pages 505–516, 2005.

[14] Y. Ke, J. Cheng, and W. Ng. Efficient correlation search from graph databases. *IEEE Transactions on Knowledge and Data Engineering*, 20(12):1601–1615, 2008.

[15] M. Kuramochi and G. Karypis. Frequent subgraph discovery. In *ICDM*, pages 313–320, 2001.

[16] M. Kuramochi and G. Karypis. Finding frequent patterns in a large sparse graph. *Data Mining and Knowledge Discovery*, 11(3):243–271, 2005.

[17] J. Pei, D. Jiang, and A. Zhang. On mining cross-graph quasi-cliques. In *KDD*, pages 228–238, 2005.

[18] N. Polyzotis and M. N. Garofalakis. Xsketch synopses for XML data graphs. *ACM Transactions on Database Systems*, 31(3):1014–1063, 2006.

[19] T. Sarlós, A. A. Benczúr, K. Csalogány, D. Fogaras, and B. Rácz. To randomize or not to randomize: Space optimal summaries for hyperlink analysis. In *WWW*, pages 297–306, 2006.

[20] H. Shang, Y. Zhang, X. Lin, and J. X. Yu. Taming verification hardness: An efficient algorithm for testing subgraph isomorphism. *PVLDB*, 1(1):364–375, 2008.

[21] H. Toivonen. Sampling large databases for association rules. In *VLDB*, pages 134–145, 1996.

[22] N. Wang, S. Parthasarathy, K.-L. Tan, and A. K. H. Tung. Csv: Visualizing and mining cohesive subgraphs. In *SIGMOD*, pages 445–458, 2008.

[23] D. W. Williams, J. Huan, and W. Wang. Graph database indexing using structured graph decomposition. In *ICDE*, pages 976–985, 2007.

[24] X. Yan and J. Han. gSpan: Graph-based substructure pattern mining. In *ICDM*, pages 721–724, 2002.

[25] X. Yan, P. S. Yu, and J. Han. Graph indexing: A frequent structure-based approach. In *SIGMOD*, pages 335–346, 2004.

[26] S. Zhang, S. Li, and J. Yang. Gaddi: Distance index based subgraph matching in biological networks. In *EDBT*, pages 192–203, 2009.

[27] P. Zhao and J. Han. On graph query optimization in large networks. *PVLDB*, 3(1):340–351, 2010.

[28] P. Zhao, J. X. Yu, and P. S. Yu. Graph indexing: Tree + delta >= graph. In *VLDB*, pages 938–949, 2007.

[29] L. Zou, L. Chen, J. X. Yu, and Y. Lu. A novel spectral coding in a large graph database. In *EDBT*, pages 181–192, 2008.

Learning to Target: What Works for Behavioral Targeting

Sandeep Pandey[◇§], Mohamed Aly[◇§], Abraham Bagherjeiran[*◇†], Andrew Hatch[◇§],
Peter Ciccolo[*‡], Adwait Ratnaparkhi[*♯], Martin Zinkevich[§]

§ Yahoo! Research, 4301 Great America Parkway, Santa Clara, CA 95054, USA
† ThinkersR.Us Inc., 1262 Socorro Avenue, Sunnyvale, CA 94089, USA
‡ Google Inc., 1600 Amphitheatre Pkwy, Mountain View, CA 94043, USA
♯ 33Across Inc., 440 N. Wolfe Road, Sunnyvale, CA 94085, USA

{spandey | aly}@yahoo-inc.com | abagher@thinkersr.us | aohatch@yahoo-inc.com |
ciccolo@google.com | adwait.ratnaparkhi@33across.com | maz@yahoo-inc.com

ABSTRACT

Understanding what interests and delights users is critical to effective behavioral targeting, especially in information-poor contexts. As users interact with content and advertising, their passive behavior can reveal their interests towards advertising. Two issues are critical for building effective targeting methods: what metric to optimize for and how to optimize. More specifically, we first attempt to understand what the learning objective should be for behavioral targeting so as to maximize advertiser's performance. While most popular advertising methods optimize for user clicks, as we will show, maximizing clicks does not necessarily imply maximizing purchase activities or transactions, called *conversions*, which directly translate to advertiser's revenue. In this work we focus on conversions which makes a more relevant metric but also the more challenging one. Second is the issue of how to represent and combine the plethora of user activities such as search queries, page views, ad clicks to perform the targeting. We investigate several sources of user activities as well as methods for inferring conversion likelihood given the activities. We also explore the role played by the temporal aspect of user activities for targeting, e.g., how recent activities compare to the old ones. Based on a rigorous offline empirical evaluation over 200 individual advertising campaigns, we arrive at what we believe are best practices for behavioral targeting. We deploy our approach over live user traffic to demonstrate its superiority over existing state-of-the-art targeting methods.

Categories and Subject Descriptors

H.4.m [**Information Systems**]: Miscellaneous

General Terms

Algorithms, Performance, Experimentation

Keywords

Behavioral targeting, user modeling, advertising

1. INTRODUCTION

Advertisers want to spend the smallest amount of money to get the largest increase in profit, irrespective of the form of advertising they are involved in such as newspapers, magazines, television (*offline advertising*), and internet *(online advertising*). However, online advertising provides advertisers with more immediate feedback (when users click on their ads and visit their web pages) and publishers have greater knowledge of their users (demographic information and past behavior). For example, suppose that you want to sell trucks. You could advertise during baseball games and football games on television, hoping that people watching the game want a truck. If you advertise online, you could put your truck advertisements next to sports stories on an online publisher's site. Also, you could have your advertisements appear in "Car and Driver" or on "Yahoo Autos" (where the content is related to the ad). But the more remarkable power of online advertising is that you could show an advertisement next to a sports page only for people who have recently visited Yahoo Autos. This is *behavioral targeting*.

The key behind behavioral targeting is that the advertisers can show ads only to users within a specific demographic of high value (such as people likely to buy a car) and combine that with a larger number of opportunities (places to show ads) per user. Moreover, as we gather more information about a user, we can provide them with a better experience in every future interaction.

In general, targeting methods match the users within a given context to an appropriate ad. The context of the user consists of the page the user is currently visiting, the time, and the user's historical online behavior. Three types of targeting methods are popular in the advertising industry: *property*, *user segment*, and *behavioral targeting*. Property targeting refers to placing ads on specific web pages where interested users will appear, such as showing online brokerage ads on financial related pages. Although this reaches users who visit these finance pages, it may miss users who

◇ The first four authors have contributed equally to the paper.
* Work done while at Yahoo!.

use some other web sites for their financial information. User segment targeting focuses on the gender and age of a user, and is only capable of targeting broad groups. Behavioral targeting involves using historical online information about the user to aid the publisher in showing them relevant ads wherever they appear. Whereas property targeting targets pages, and user segment targeting targets generic groups, behavioral targeting targets individuals.

Clearly, understanding user interests is critical to effective behavioral targeting. As users interact with content and advertising, their passive behavior can reveal their interests towards advertising. Exploiting this behavior at a large scale is the goal of behavioral targeting solutions. In this paper we frame the targeting problem as an optimization problem and describe a machine learning based approach for solving it. We tackle with two key issues in doing so. First, it is important to optimize behavioral targeting so that advertisers get most bang for their buck. Most existing work in behavioral targeting uses clicks on ads as a proxy of interest [4, 11, 14]. Clicks are used simply because they are available and other information is not available at a large scale. Recently, however, advertisers have been willing to share feedback at the level of individual users, telling publishers which of the users who saw the ad have actually purchased the product [1, 2, 3, 6, 12]. Since conversions are the ultimate goal of advertisers, we test whether models based on conversions or clicks better predict whether a conversion eventually occurs. In particular, we show that maximizing for clicks does not lead to maximizing for conversions, hence providing evidence for the necessity of developing models that are specifically optimized for conversions.

Conversions are so rare that developing models for them presents further challenges, which is the second issue we address in this paper. Rarity of conversions forces us to parsimoniously mine the user historical online behavior. Several questions are worth investigating here. For example, how should we represent and combine different user activities such as search queries, page views and ad clicks? Which activities are more indicative of user's interests, browsed pages or issued queries? Does more activity on a certain topic imply more chances of converting? How does the temporal aspect of user behavior (i.e., timestamps associated with the activities) relate to conversion likelihood?

Our main contributions in this paper are as follows:

- We provide insights into which types of user behavior and activities (e.g., page views, search logs, ad views/clicks, *etc.*) are informative. See Section 4.3.
- We give methods for how to translate user activities into features which work best for capturing ad-relevant information in user behavior. See Section 4.4.
- We show that although conversions are more rare, they can be more informative for targeting than clicks when available. Also, we describe how clicks can be used in conjunction with conversions to improve the targeting. See Section 5.
- We look into understanding the temporal aspect of user history and study how recency of a user activity and length of user history affect the targeting performance. See Section 6.
- We perform extensive experiments using data from more than 200 display advertising campaigns to arrive at what we believe are best practices for behavioral targeting. Lastly, we deploy our approach on live user traffic and compare its performance with conventional methods. See Section 7.

2. USER TARGETING

Advertisers are now spending increasingly larger fractions of their overall advertising budgets on online advertising. Effective online advertising is based on three key factors: the *context* in which the ad appears; the *audience* to whom the ad is targeted; and the *creative* that specifies the message being delivered via the ad. We focus on the audience for the purposes of this paper.

Next we present a generic framework for understanding audience targeting problems. Users are modeled as streams of *typed events*. The targeting system is modeled as a function defined over user histories. Within this framework the popular targeting methods such as property, user segments, and behavioral targeting are special cases.

2.1 User Modeling

We denote a user $u \in U$ as a process that emits a sequence of events $\langle e_1, \ldots, e_m \rangle$, where events $e_i \in E$ are defined as follows:

$$e = (t, T, p)$$

where t is the *timestamp*, T is the *type* of the event such as "search" or "page visit", and p is a *payload*. Examples of events include "issued a search query for shoes at 5PM" in which the type is "search query", the payload is "shoes" and the timestamp is 5PM.

Any targeting method can be abstracted as a function such that given a particular ad campaign a, the function outputs a binary decision as to whether or not to target the user. The function is defined as $g_a : U \rightarrow \{0, 1\}$ where for each user $u \in U$, whether the user should be targeted or not. As a targeting function, it cannot guarantee that the ad will be shown to the user. We can then abstract an ad server as a process that for a given a set of ads $a \in \mathcal{A}$, performs two main operations at each serving opportunity. First it determines the set of ads for which the user is said to qualify as follows:

$$Q(u; \mathcal{A}) = \{a \mid a \in \mathcal{A} \wedge g_a(u) = 1\}$$

where the function $Q : U \times \mathcal{A} \rightarrow 2^{\mathcal{A}}$ returns the set of ads which the user is allowed to see — qualify. Given this set of ads, the ad server then decides which one of these ads should actually be shown to the user, based on some set of business policies which are outside of the scope of this paper. Based on this description of an ad server, we see that the purpose of a targeting system is simply to target users prior to the actual ad serving.

2.2 Property Targeting

Property targeting is a simple, yet popular targeting mechanism. The advertiser specifies some set of pages P on which the ad should be shown. Users visiting those page are targeted with the corresponding ads. For example, an advertiser who sells cars could show ads on websites about cars.

This form of property targeting is completely independent of the user's history or state, instead it exploits exactly one feature — the page the user is visiting at this moment. The property targeting function is defined as follows:

$$g(u) = \begin{cases} 1 & u \text{ is visiting } p \in P \\ 0 & \text{otherwise} \end{cases}$$

where p is the current webpage. The effectiveness of this model assumes that there is a causal link between the page and the user's interest.

2.3 User Segment Targeting

Marketing research and practice has a long history of advertising based on user profiles or personas [10]. Users are grouped into homogeneous segments and different segments are targeted with appropriate ads. For example, a major beverage company conducts market research for its low-calorie carbonated beverage and determine that the drink would appeal to the following segments:

- "young adults": $g_{1,1} = age(u, (15, 25))$, $g_{1,2} = country(u, \text{USA})$
- "moms": $g_{2,1} = gender(u, F)$, $g_{2,2} = age(u, (25, 45))$, $g_{2,3} = country(u, \text{USA})$

Segments are defined as logical predicates such as $age(u, (15, 25))$ which is true if the age of user u is between 15 and 25 years. Common types of segments are *demographic*, *geographic*, and *psychographic* attributes [8].

In the above example, the advertiser would define the targeting function as follows:

$$g(u) = \begin{cases} 1 & u \in S \\ 0 & u \notin S \end{cases}$$

$$\text{where } S = \bigcup_{i=1}^{n} S_i = \bigcup_{i=1}^{n} \bigcap g_{i,j}$$

where $S_i$is the i^{th}segment and $g_{i,j}$ is the set of users who qualify for the j^{th}predicate of segment S_i.

Segment targeting is popular since it is easy to understand and implement and moreover provides advertisers transparency and control over the audience selected for targeting their ads. There are two main limitations. a) The advertiser must match the ad to the pre-existing segments. b) The segments may not be expressive enough to truly capture the audience of interest to the advertiser. For example in the "moms" segment, we are missing the important attribute $hasChildren(u)$, which is clearly a defining feature of the persona.

2.4 Behavioral Targeting

Behavioral targeting provides an approach to learn the targeting function from historical data [4, 14]. In general, behavioral targeting focuses on leveraging the past behavior of a user to predict their future behavior. Although behavioral targeting methods vary in terms of the set of features, the objective optimized, they can be generalized within our targeting framework. A behavioral targeting method B can be viewed as a process that learns a targeting function $g(u)$ from data about users and ads. Formally this can be described as function $B : \{U\}^m \rightarrow \mathcal{G}$ that maps a sample of m users from the set of all users U onto a specific space of targeting functions $\mathcal{G}$ such as linear classifiers trained on feature vectors constructed from user histories.

The predictive model can leverage a very rich set of user features and can be trained to directly optimize for the performance of the ad, e.g., CTR, conversion rate etc. More importantly, the framework of the behavioral targeting model is general enough to accommodate other information such as the current context – the webpage the user is visiting, membership in various user segments, and more recently social network data [11].

Continuing with the targeting example, online behavior could be used for targeting rather than simple segments.

- "young adults": heavy usage of messenger / social networking sites, searches for common school topics.
- "moms": searching for products related to children, reading parenting articles.

The focus of this paper is on behavioral targeting that goes beyond age and gender. By training our algorithm on actual data, we can move beyond simple ad targeting based on stereotypes (showing pickup trucks during baseball games) and towards a personalized experience that can benefit the user and the advertiser alike.

3. PROBLEM DESCRIPTION

In our setting, we are trying to improve various existing campaigns where the advertisers pay per conversion, called CPA campaigns. Each campaign has already been tuned manually with user segment targeting and property targeting. However, no behavioral targeting has been done. As noted in previous work [3], our objective with this system is to refine the targeting constraints using past behavior of the user. Through refinement we can improve the number of conversions per ad impression without greatly increasing the number of impressions, which increases the value of our inventory.[1]

Note that when making a decision about whether to target an impression based on user behavior, we cannot use any information from the day of the impression or any day afterward to impact the classification of the impression. As shown in Figure 1, we consider user history as a sequence of events relative to some *target time*, τ, at which time the user is being considered for targeting. We decompose the user's sequence of events around the target time τ as follows.

$$\begin{aligned} u(\tau) &= (E_F(\tau), E_T(\tau)) \\ \text{where } E_F &= \{e \mid e \in E \wedge t(e) < \tau\} \\ \text{and } E_T &= \{e \mid e \in E \wedge \tau \leq t(e) \leq \tau + \delta\} \end{aligned}$$

Here $E_F(\tau)$ denotes the events prior to the target time which we call the *feature window* and $E_T(\tau)$ denotes the events that occur between τ and $\tau + \delta$ (where δ is 1 day) which we call the *target window*.

Hence, when we model behavioral targeting as a machine learning task where each user history forms an example: a user is a positive example if it is credited to a conversion in the target window, a negative example otherwise.[2] Given training users $\{1, \ldots, m\}$ define $T = \langle (x^1, y^1), ..(x^m, y^m) \rangle \in (\mathbb{R}^n \times \{-1, +1\})^m$ to be the training data, where x^i is a feature vector constructed from the events of the user i in

[1]Although it is interesting to imagine relaxing these constraints, that is impossible to analyze offline.

[2]If several impressions are shown to a user and the user eventually converted, no more than one impression from that user is considered a positive example.

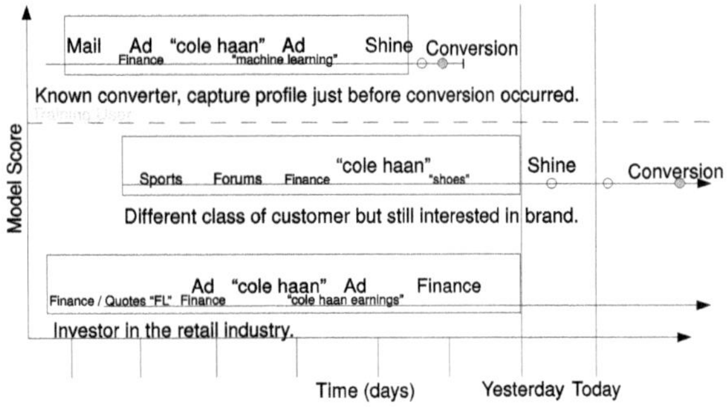

Figure 1: Targeting model is trained on user histories (rectangles) as they existed prior to the start of the conversion process (open circle) that led to the conversion (solid circle). For evaluation, all users are given the same target time (yesterday) and the ad server may choose to show ads at some point in the future to start the conversion process (open circle).

the feature window, $y^i = +1$ if the ith example is positive, and $y^i = -1$ otherwise. The test set is defined similarly.

The most significant difference between traditional targeting and this work is in exploiting the user profiles for maximizing conversions. Hence, in this paper we fix our learning algorithm to be a support vector machine [13] and focus on the issue of how to leverage user history efficiently. In particular, how to convert user profiles into feature vectors (e.g., representing different events as features, computing their weights, incorporating timestamps) and how to construct target labels (e.g., clicks, conversions). A user representation method consists of a function $\phi : U \rightarrow \mathbb{R}^n$, where $\mathbb{R}^n$ is the Euclidean space of dimension n. A target label function is defined as $\gamma : U \rightarrow \{-1, +1\}$. Given this, we extract an appropriate feature and target label set as $(x, y) = (\phi(u), \gamma(u))$. We then select a vector $w \in \mathbb{R}^n$ by solving the following optimization:

$$\arg\min_{w \in R^n} w^2 + C \sum_{i=1}^{m} L(w \cdot x^i),$$

where $L(\hat{y}, y) = \max(1 - \hat{y}y, 0)$ and C is a constant that controls the balance between regularization and minimizing the loss on the training set.

In this work, we investigate different user representation operators $\phi(u)$ and different target labeling functions $\gamma(u)$. These are summarized as follows:

- User representation function: convert events to features, compute feature weights, incorporate timestamps and history length.

- Target labeling function: clicks or conversions

4. USER REPRESENTATION

In this section we propose and empirically compare different feature extraction methods for behavioral targeting.

4.1 Data Setup

In our experiments we build targeting models for display advertising campaigns. We collected 4 weeks of data for 226 campaigns. Each campaign is treated as a separate targeting task. The first three weeks of data is used for training, while the last week is used for testing. Each example impression is preceded by at least 4 weeks of user events. In total, with some sampling of negative examples we have a total of approximately 40M examples in training and 80K of these examples are positive. This is a benchmark set that enables us to do rigorous offline experiments.

4.2 Baseline Method

In each of the experiments, we compare targeting methods in terms of the area under the ROC curve (AUC). The benchmark baseline consists of a simple application of the support vector machine classifier. Based on some simple experiments, we arrived at the following parameters. Because we have a large number of mostly irrelevant features, we choose a strong regularization parameter of $C \in [0.001, 0.05]$. Next, since we have an highly imbalanced class distribution, we choose a class weighting parameter of 10:1 cost for the positive and negative class, respectively. In order to have a single parameter configuration for all learning tasks, we sample the negative examples such that the class ratio is always satisfied. The empirical evaluation is based on this baseline. Unless otherwise specified, all metrics are measured as conversion-weighted average of AUC across all campaigns in the benchmark set.

4.3 Event Types

When collecting the user's historical online behavior, we consider both *active* and *passive* activities. Passive activities include viewing ads and visiting pages in which an action is not specifically required upon seeing the page. Active activities include issuing search queries and clicking ads in which users actually perform an action on the page. Browsing activity is somewhat active because the user took action to visit the page, but we argue that the activity is less than specifically typing a search query or clicking on an ad. We investigate which source of activity is stronger in predicting the user's propensity to convert on a set of advertisements.

The activities of the users are a sequence of events collected from server logs. Events are associated with both a timestamp and metadata. For example, an event could be a visit to a finance web page and the metadata associated with the event is the content of the page, which is logged separately and then joined with the event along with the anonymized identifier of the user and the time. We consider several different events, each with a corresponding feature extraction method.

- *Pages visited*: Website pages are clustered into several smaller subdirectories. Some features extracted are the id of the cluster and the category of the page from an existing hierarchical page categorizer.

- *Search queries*: Searches issued, clicks on search links, clicks on search advertising links. Some features extracted are the query category, the click information and the unigrams in the query (details later).

- *Graphical Ads*: Views and clicks on ads. Some features extracted are the ad category, the click information and the id of the ad (details later).

For all feature types, we use a common feature representation (i.e., weighting) operator $\phi : E^{\star} \rightarrow \mathbb{R}^n$ which we call relative frequency bag of events. The frequency of an event is defined as the number of days in which the user has performed the event. We consider events separately by type (e.g., page visits, search queries). For example we concentrate on page visits and denote by event p the "visit to any e-mail page" and other page view events by q and r. If the user had visited the pages p, q, and r in a sequence over four days as follows:

$$e = (p_1, p_1, p_2, q_2, r_3, q_4)$$

where each event p_i denotes the visit on page p on day i, then the frequency bag of events representation for page visits would be: $F_p(e) = (p:2, q:2, r:1)$ where we use the convention of $p:n$ to mean that the feature p has the value n in the feature vector. Here, the page p was visited 3 times but on just 2 distinct dates. The relative frequency representation normalizes within each feature type such that the final feature vector is defined as follows:

$$\phi(e) = \left(\frac{F_1(e)}{\|F_1(e)\|}, \ldots, \frac{F_n(e)}{\|F_n(e)\|} \right)$$

where n is the number of feature types such as page views, ad views, ad clicks, *etc.*

4.3.1 Browsing Activities

As users interact with a website they consume content either through direct action such as searching for information or casual browsing such as checking e-mail or reading news headlines. However, the particular stream of content consumed gives us some insight into the user' interest.

Rather than considering each individual URL, we group different URLs together and count visits on any of them. We considered 3 grouping methods: *site index*, *semantic categories*, and *server location*. The site index is based on the navigational pattern within the specific website. For example, if a user visits a page showing the profile of a company in the stock market, then the site index would be something like "stock_quotes" which is a sub-index of the main "finance" page. This reduces the set of URLs from millions into approximately 30,000. The benefit is a reduced space, but the main disadvantage is that we lose the granular information such as which stock quote the user is viewing. The semantic categories come from a manually annotated categorization system and map the pages into a taxonomy of roughly 1,000 nodes that describe the information on the page. In our example of a stock quote page, we consider the categories along the path in the taxonomy. If the category is "Finance / Stocks / Quotes", then we add the features "Finance", "Finance / Stocks", and "Finance / Stocks / Quotes" to the user's profile. With the rollup, the model should consider the hierarchical placement of the page even when the coverage is low at the leaf nodes. Finally, we reduce the space of pages even further to consider the international location of the user when he or she saw the page. For example, if the user is viewing a finance page in the US, then the feature would be "Page in US", however if user were to see the same page in Europe, then the page would be "Page in EU". This encoding of pages is at a high level of aggregation but can still tell us something about the user–language, location, etc.

Table 1 compares the improvement in average area under the ROC curve for the benchmark campaigns when considering the different browsing patterns. In the figure the user location information makes the baseline and has the least

	ΔAUC
User Location	0.0%
Only Categories	9.29%
Only Site IDs	11.92%
All Browsing Activity	15.53%

Table 1: Relative difference in performance relative to user location when adding more browsing activity.

	ΔAUC
Raw Ads	0.00%
Categorized Ads	0.01%
Raw + Categorized Ads	0.39%

Table 2: Relative difference with respect to baseline when adding more ad activities.

information , but we note that it is significantly better than random targeting despite being very coarse. The site index grouping performs very well as a single source of page visits, slightly better than the semantic categories. We think that the semantic categories can be too coarse as a 30:1 decrease in the number of features. Overall, however, adding all page browsing features is best, which indicates that the different aggregations bring some useful signal.

4.3.2 Ad Activities

When users visit pages, they typically interact with graphical ads either by clicking or simply viewing ads. Although ad clicks are clearly useful features in predicting ad activities, the ad views may also be useful. To see this, we consider the following example, an advertiser targets users who previously visited their home page and the ad is shown to these users anywhere they go (this is a common targeting method). If the only way that the users have seen this ad is by going to the advertiser's site in the past, we can infer that if the user saw the ad, he or she must have visited the advertiser's site regardless of whether we have the browsing history.

Like the browsing activity features, we consider multiple groups of ad features. Ads are placed on pages in prespecified positions such as on the left or right sides and in different sizes such as 300×250-pixel rectangles or tall vertical bars. Of course each ad is a different image and may be a static image, video, or flash. All of these features influence the click rate on the ad as well as the degree to which the user notices the ad. In order to capture all the factors that influence ad interest, we denote an ad by a triplet of: creative, position id, and targeting parameters. Each of these elements is denoted by a unique identifier. Like the browsing history, we consider both the clicks and views for ad triplets as well as clicks and views on semantic categories of ads.

Table 2 shows the relative improvement of adding categorized ads to raw ads. We see that there is not much difference in performance for ad triplets and categorized ad activities when treated separately. These results indicate that categorized ads do provide some signal in addition to just the raw ad activities.

4.3.3 Search History

Presumably the most direct user behavior is a search query because users have to manually type in the query. The po-

	ΔAUC
Raw Queries	0.00%
Categorized Queries	-0.29%
Raw + Categorized	0.13%

Table 3: Relative difference with respect to base when adding more query features.

	ΔAUC
User Location	0.00%
Only Browsing Activity	15.53%
Only Ads Activity	18.23%
Only Query Activity (*)	18.34%
Browsing + Ads + Query	18.23%

Table 4: Relative difference in feature types. For query activity (*), we note that the testing set is a subset of the larger set.

tential disadvantage to queries is that they are typically very short and are very ambiguous, containing misspellings, synonyms, different spacing etc. We consider three types of behavior for queries: simply issuing a query, clicking on a link, and clicking on a search ad on the results page for the query. We group all these activities together and evaluate whether they are predictive of conversions. We group queries together into semantic categories using a machine learned query categorizer. We consider both categorized and raw queries. For the raw queries, we split on white space to create unigrams.

Table 3 shows the relative improvement from adding categorized query features to raw queries. There is a performance decrease from considering only the categorized queries versus raw queries. This is interesting when we consider that there are only about 1,000 categories but millions of unique queries issued by the users. This suggests that the categorization of the queries may be noisy or incomplete. However, it seems that when available the categorized queries help in conjunction with the raw queries.

4.3.4 Discussion

We see that within each feature type, categorized features alone do not perform as well as the raw features. However, the best strategy seems to be to combine raw and categorized features. We now consider adding all the feature types together. Table 4 shows that, relative to user location, considering each feature type alone does very well. In addition, adding all feature types does very well. Of all the features we considered, ads and browsing activity appear to be the most informative.

In Table 4 we see that queries show the largest improvement in performance; however, we argue that this is misleading. To better understand the results, we consider the coverage of the different feature types. We define coverage as the proportion of users that have the feature defined over the set of all users. From our dataset we see that all users have some browsing activity, and nearly all users have some ad activity. However, a smaller proportion of users have search activity. And the fewest users have some ad click activity. This indicates that the most intuitively informative features: searches and ad clicks have the lowest coverage. Hence, although they are very informative and might have good performance when available, their overall impact is lower. Based on the coverage analysis, we see that even if browsing activity is less informative when users have ad click or query activities, when we consider the union of all activities, those which occur most frequently are preferred–especially in regularized learning algorithms.

Table 5 shows the relevant features from 3 example campaign models. These features support our hypothesis that the baseline approach of adding all features is better overall. In both the university model and the airline, we see that searches are relevant. In addition, these searches are very relevant to the subject of the ad such as air travel or airports. However in the home telecom model, we see that ads are the most relevant features. To see why ads are most relevant for home telecom versus the other campaigns is that for the telecom service there are no good search terms that indicate interest. Instead, the main customers are people who own homes or rent apartments. Viewing health-related ads and checking news and mail are activities common to homeowners — the events that describe the persona of the target audience.

4.4 Feature Representations

In Section 4.3, we use L_2 normalized frequency across each feature group (e.g., page visits and search queries) to define a baseline feature representation. In the following section, we discuss an alternative representation based on statistical measures of how predictive individual features are of conversion events.

4.4.1 Log-Likelihood Ratios (LLRs) as Features

We tried using a feature representation based on log-likelihood ratios (LLRs) of raw features occurring in conversion events. This approach is based on the campaign-dependent feature representation described in [7]. In this representation, ad campaign i extracts feature vectors of the form, $\psi_i\left(e^j\right) \equiv \left(\psi^j_{i,0},\ldots,\psi^j_{i,N}\right)^T$, where e^j is an input example. These features are derived from the corresponding baseline feature vector of Section 4.3: $\phi\left(e^j\right) \equiv \left(\phi^j_1,\ldots,\phi^j_N\right)^T$. If baseline feature ϕ^j_n exists in example e^j— that is, if it has a non-zero count — then feature $\psi^j_{i,n}$ is set equal to the log-likelihood ratio of ϕ_n occurring in a conversion event for ad campaign i. We use $c\,(a_i)$ to represent a conversion event on ad campaign i (conversely, $\bar{c}\,(a_i)$ represents a non-conversion event). Feature $\psi^j_{i,n}$ can now be expressed mathematically as follows:

$$\psi^j_{i,n} \equiv \mathbf{1}(\phi^j_n > 0)\cdot\log\frac{Pr\left(\phi_n > 0|c\,(a_i)\right)}{Pr\left(\phi_n > 0|\bar{c}\,(a_i)\right)} \quad \forall n \in \{1,\ldots,N\}. \tag{1}$$

We also define feature $\psi^j_{i,0}$ as

$$\psi^j_{i,0} \equiv \log\frac{Pr\left(c\,(a_i)\right)}{Pr\left(\bar{c}\,(a_i)\right)}. \tag{2}$$

It can be shown that if the baseline features are conditionally independent of one-another given $c\,(a_i)$, then the following is true [7]:

$$\sum_{n=0}^{N}\psi^j_{i,n} = \text{logit}\big(Pr\left(c\,(a_i)\,|\Phi_+\left(e^j\right)\right)\big),$$

where $\Phi_+\left(e^j\right)$ is defined as

$$\Phi_+\left(e^j\right) \equiv \left\{\mathbf{1}\left(\phi^j_1 > 0\right),\ldots,\mathbf{1}\left(\phi^j_N > 0\right)\right\}.$$

#	University Model	#	Low-Cost Airline	#	Home Telecom
5	Social Networking Search	1	Mail Page	1	Groups Page
2	Mail Pages	3	Generic Search Activity	4	News Ads/Page
7	Credit-Score Ads	4	Brand-relevant terms	6	Credit Ads
2	Search "university"	3	Credit-score ads	4	Car/Health Ad
4	financial aid searches	5	Search Results on Air Travel	1	Mail Page
		2	Search for Airports	3	Technology Ad

Table 5: Number of features in each type for three selected campaigns.

	ΔAUC
large campaigns	+2.25%
medium campaigns	-0.89%
small campaigns	-2.11%

Table 6: Gain in AUC for LLR-based feature representation relative to baseline.

Since summing over $\{\psi_{i,0}^{j}, \ldots, \psi_{i,N}^{j}\}$ yields the logit of $Pr\left(c\left(a_i\right)|\Phi_+\left(e^j\right)\right)$, it follows that if the $\Phi_+\left(e^j\right)$ features are conditionally independent of one-another given $c\left(a_i\right)$, then $\psi_i\left(e^j\right)$ is the globally optimal representation of $\Phi_+\left(e^j\right)$ (note, however, that this optimality depends on one's ability to exactly compute the LLRs in (1) and (2); this is often not possible in practice). One can further show that the following linear decision function is equivalent to a Naive Bayes classifier trained on $\Phi_+\left(e^j\right)$ if the weight vector w in the following expression is composed of all ones (i.e., $w = (1, \ldots, 1)^T$) :

$$\hat{y}_i\left(e^j\right) \equiv \begin{cases} 1 & w^T\psi_i\left(e^j\right) > 0 \\ -1 & otherwise \end{cases}$$

Here, $\hat{y}_i\left(e^j\right)$ represents the hypothesized class (1 or -1) of example e^j in ad campaign i. In our experiments, we estimated the probabilities in (1) and (2) empirically from the training data. We used the following count threshold when estimating probabilities: For all ϕ_n that appear in fewer than 5 conversion examples in ad campaign i, we set $\psi_{i,n}^{j} \leftarrow 0$ for all j.

Table 6 shows the AUC results for the LLR-based feature representation relative to the baseline. We divided our campaigns into three categories, large, medium and small. The large group contains the top one-third of the campaigns with the most number of conversions, while the small group contains the bottom one-third. These results show that the LLRs tend to outperform the baseline representation on large campaigns but not on small campaigns. One explanation for the reduced performance on small campaigns is that the probability estimates in Equation 1 tend to be noisy when only a small number of events are available. We believe that it may be possible to improve the performance of the LLR-based representation on all campaigns by using smoothed probability estimates when computing the LLRs. We leave this as future work.

5. RELATION BETWEEN CLICKS AND CONVERSIONS

As mentioned before, behavioral targeting can be optimized using a variety of metrics, e.g., number of ad impressions (CPI), clicks obtained (CPC), number of conversions made (CPA), revenue earned. While CPA (revenue) is the end goal, clicks (CPC) are often used for evaluation since they are easy to instrument and measure. In this section we study the relation between clicks and conversions.

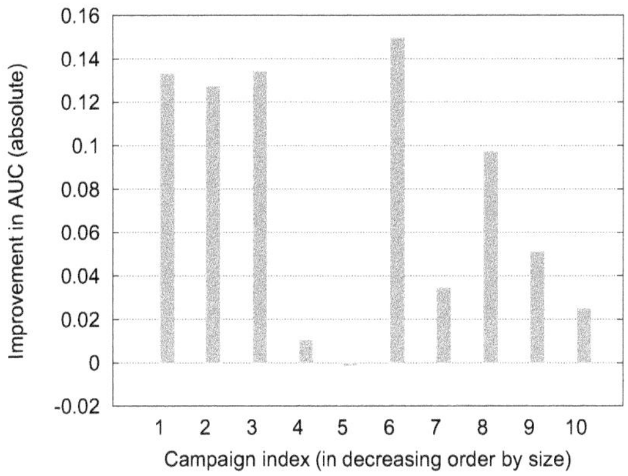

Figure 2: Improvement in prediction accuracy by using conversions for training instead of clicks. Testing is done using conversions in both cases.

5.1 Using Clicks in Place of Conversions

We start by performing the following experiment: use clicks to predict conversions and see how it compares to using conversions. In other words, in one case we train the model using clicks in the training set while in the other case the model is trained using conversion examples. Of course, the testset is labeled by conversions in both cases. As before we use support vector machines for training the models.

Clearly, using conversions for both training and testing is naturally superior. But if this hypothesis is true that clicks are "well aligned" with conversions, then using clicks for training should also perform comparable.

In Figure 2 we show the improvement in prediction accuracy achieved by using conversions for training, in comparison to using clicks for training, on 10 large campaigns. The y-axis is the difference between the performance of using conversions and using clicks (in terms of the area under the ROC curve for a campaign). Except on campaign index 4 and 5, on other campaigns using clicks performs significantly worse than using conversions. This implies that targeting users based on clicks does not necessarily mean maximizing for conversions.

5.2 Using clicks in Conjunction with Conversions

From the previous experiment we found that clicks and conversions are related but cannot be substituted for each other. In other words, for predicting conversions it is better

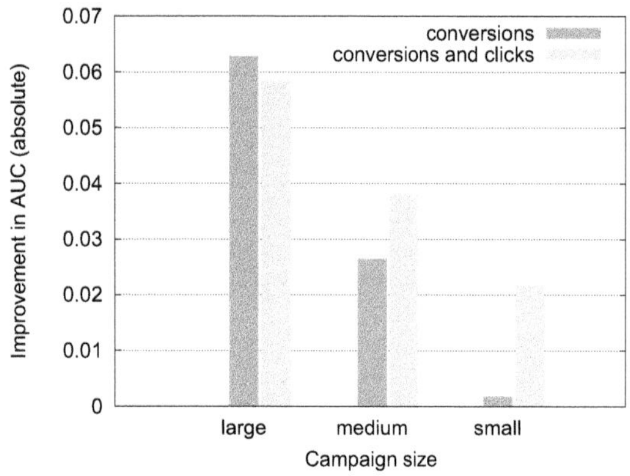

Figure 3: Improvement in prediction using clicks in conjunction with conversions.

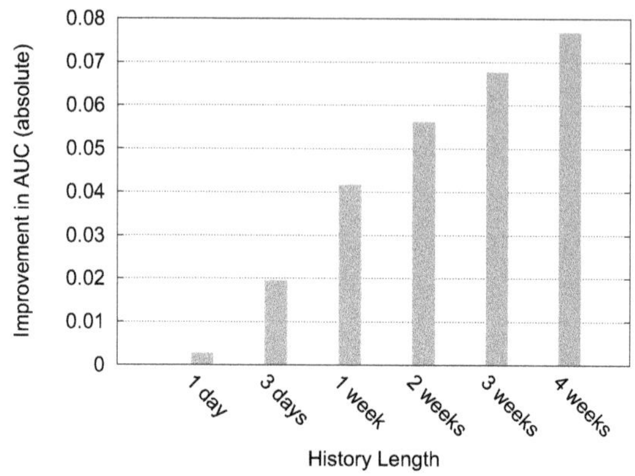

Figure 4: Effect of the length of user history.

to train the model using conversions. However, in a practical setting we often lack positive examples to train conversion models for two reasons: (a) clicks are known to be rare and conversions are even rarer, (b) due to business constraints, examples from different campaigns are not allowed to be mixed together. As a result, while we can afford to learn conversion models on large campaigns, for the medium and small campaigns we face great difficulty in doing so. Also, when the model is learned using a small number of positive examples, it often does not perform well on the testset.

To deal with this challenge, we tried a hybrid approach whereby we use clicks, which are much more abundant compare to conversions, in conjunction with conversions to train models. In particular, we treat those examples as positives which contained any of the two, a conversion(s) or a click(s). It makes sense because clicks hint of positive intent of the user. Hence, instead of grouping them with negative examples, perhaps we can generalize from them to identify other potentially interested users.

Next we compare the performance of the following two approaches: (a) label positive examples for training using conversions only and (b) using both clicks and conversions. The results are shown in Figure 3. We divided our campaigns as in Section 4.4 into three categories, large, medium and small. We treat the performance of the conversions-only approach on the small group as the baseline and show other performance numbers with respect to this baseline.

We notice that the performance of conversions-only approach worsens as we go from the large to the small group. This is expected because as the positive examples get rare, it becomes difficult to train models and perform well. We note that in the medium and small campaigns, by using clicks we can improve the performance significantly. This validates how clicks examples show positive intent of the user and when conversions are scarce, these examples can help in generalizing the model.

When there is abundant positive conversion data, like the campaigns in the large group, click examples do not help. In fact, they make the model slightly worse, which is in line with our observation from the previous section (Figure 2).

6. UNDERSTANDING THE TEMPORAL ASPECT OF USER HISTORY

In this section we focus on understanding the temporal aspect of user history. In particular, we investigate how far we should track back the user history before it stops paying off in terms of prediction performance. Also, we explore whether recent activities are more indicative of online purchases than the older ones.

6.1 Effect of History Length

In this experiment we study the effect of history length on prediction performance. More specifically, when history length is set to l days, we take into account the user history from $[\tau - l, \tau]$ period to make the prediction where τ is the target time. We treat the one day history length ($l = 1$) as the baseline and show other performance numbers with respect to this setting. The results are shown in Figure 4. We note that using the recent two weeks of user history performs significantly well. However, to our surprise, we note that we get a substantial improvement by extending the history from 2 weeks to 4 weeks.

These results show that a short recent history may not be enough for behavioral targeting. A reason behind this is that, broadly speaking, users make two kinds of conversions/online purchases on the web: (a) transactions which are quick and do not take much thought such as purchasing a movie ticket (**short-term conversions**) and (b) transactions which span a longer period of time such as car purchase or online education enrollment, and can often take several days/weeks for the user to make up her mind before making the purchase/conversion (**long-term conversions**). While short-term conversions can be made using a short history (of 1 or 2 weeks), in order to be able to predict long-term conversions, a longer history of user's activities is essential.

Longer history can also help with short-term conversions because more data allows better inferencing and refinement of user interests, e.g., within movie enthusiasts distinguish between those interested in horror versus romantic movies. As a result, longer history leads to better targeting of users, in general. However, beyond a certain history length the improvement obtained (in terms of revenue dollars) by extending history might surpass the cost of maintaining the systems storing the data. Hence, in a practical setting one might have to truncate the history beyond a certain length.

6.2 Effect of Recency

From the previous section we concluded that longer user history leads to better performance. In this experiment we

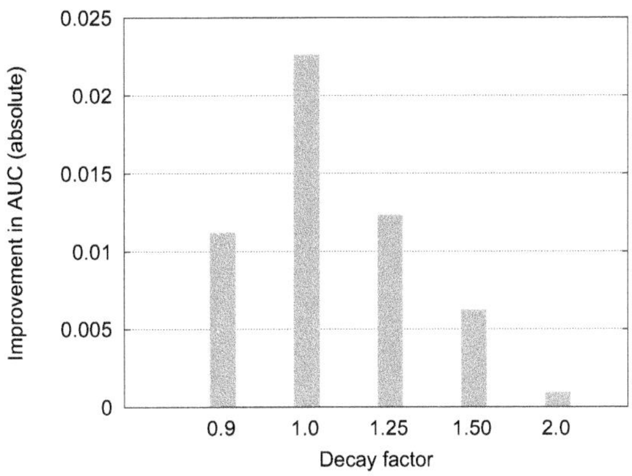

Figure 5: Effect of recency.

investigate whether by giving more weight to the recent activities in comparison to the older ones, we can further improve the performance.

As described before (Section 4.3), we set the weight of each feature in user profile based on the number of days on which the feature is present. Hence, we do not not distinguish between the features which occurred in recent days and those which had occurred earlier. For this experiment, to give more weights to recent features we set the weight of feature f to:

$$\sum_{t_i \in <f,u>} \alpha^{-(\tau - t_i)}$$

where τ is the target time (when the prediction is being made), α is the decay factor and (f, u) is the sequence of days on which feature f is present in the history of user u. When $\alpha = 1$ the above weighting approach reduces to uniform weighting. By setting α to a larger constant, we can give more weight to recent user activities in comparison to the older ones. (The weights are then normalized within each feature type, as before.)

In Figure 5 we show the effect of decay constant α on the prediction performance. (We treat $\alpha = 2$ as the baseline and report other performance numbers with respect to it.) For the sake of completeness, we also show $\alpha < 1$ which favors older features compare to the recent ones. It is clear that the best performance is achieved by uniform weighting (i.e., $\alpha = 1$). This is somewhat counter-intuitive since we expect recent activities to be a better indicator of user interests.

Given our experiments from Section 6.1, a possible explanation for this result can be that decay effectively shortens the user history. For example, when $\alpha = 2$ a feature that is 10 days old gets a weight of smaller than 10^{-3}, hence the history length is practically reduced to 10 days (or smaller). As a result, long-term conversions (explained earlier) become more difficult to predict. In other words, there is a trade-off between recency and history length. While the former might help in predicting short-term conversions, the latter is needed for long-term conversions.

To further validate this finding, we tried another approach for taking recency into account. For this experiment we divided the user history into multiple buckets based on time periods, e.g., activities from the last day are put into one bucket, activities from 2-7 days in the next bucket and so on. We labeled the features with the buckets they occurred in and let the SVM learn weights for different (feature, bucket)

	Δ Conversion Rate	Δ eCPA
Campaign 1	+80%	-37.55%
Campaign 2	+57.14%	-27.39%
Campaign 3	+264%	N/A
Campaign 4	+83%	N/A

Table 7: Gain in conversion rates and eCPA values over existing CTR-based targeting methods in live experiments.

pairs. Unlike the previous experiment where we were confined to exponential decay, this method allows us to automatically learn non-uniform weighting of features to account for recency.

However, similar to the decay experiment, we found that the results from this bucket experiment were worse than the uniform weighting approach.

7. COMPARISON WITH EXISTING TARGETING IN LIVE EXPERIMENTS

Driven by the good performance of our behavioral targeting approach in offline experiments, we tested the system on live traffic on a few ad campaigns on a major US advertising network. We trained our models using the practices described in the previous sections. We compared our models to those trained by an existing behavioral targeting system (as in [4]): (a) which targets users whose activities/interest in the advertiser's category is above a certain threshold, (b) the model optimizes for click-through rates.

For training/scoring the models we generated user profiles spanning 8 weeks of user history. We scored the models on a daily basis and the experiment was run live for three months. For each of the campaigns, each of the existing and new models received at least a total number of 1M impressions on a monthly basis.

Table 7 shows the overall performance of our models as compared to the original CTR-optimized behavioral targeting models. In terms of the conversion rate, i.e., the percentage of viewers that convert, we note that our models achieved significant improvements compared to the existing models (while keeping the same coverage). This demonstrates the ability of our models to target users with much higher tendency to convert than existing CTR-optimized models. Another important metric that we report is the Effective Cost Per Action (eCPA), used to measure the effectiveness of the inventory purchased by the advertiser. Effectively, the eCPA tells the advertiser what they would have to pay for each conversion. Our results show a considerable decrease in eCPA that our models achieved compared to the other models (we could not report eCPA values for campaign 3 and 4 for business reasons). This is considered as a major gain from the point of view of the advertisers, as this means that we are able to reach the audience desired for the campaign while decreasing the amount of impressions (i.e., retries) needed. Both these results demonstrate the effectiveness of our models in large-scale behavioral targeting.

8. RELATED WORK

In this work, we use behavioral targeting to improve the conversion rate. Targeting users who will convert is a difficult problem: often, the problem is divided into predicting clicks, and predicting the probability that the click will convert [6, 1, 12]. The advantage of this division relates to business logic: the publisher (such as Yahoo! or Google) has data about how likely users are to follow various paths towards clicks on advertisements on their site. On the other hand, advertisers have more information about the paths of users on their website. Therefore, there is a certain cleanliness with regards to data ownership.

On the other hand, paying for conversions has two effects. First of all, there is the maximum level of quality control of the traffic. Problems such as click fraud [5, 9, 15] do not arise. Second, when creating a conversion model, one is aware of the abundance of users who did not click. This plethora of negative data can really help: intuitively, knowing that someone was unlikely to click makes it quite possible that they are unlikely to convert.

In this paper we focused on building such conversion models. We compared our approach with existing behavioral targeting methods (such as [4, 14]) which optimize for click-through rates and showed how optimizing directly for conversions can lead to improved performance. Compared to previous work on conversion optimization [1, 2, 3, 6, 12], our work makes several new contributions: we look into understanding the effect of different user activities on prediction, give insights about the temporal aspect of user behavior (recency vs. long-term trends) and explore different variants (user representation and target label) through large offline and online experiments.

9. CONCLUSION

Determining which users are most likely to respond to a given advertisement is the primary goal of targeting. By using the user's historical online behavior, behavioral targeting can greatly improve in terms of performance and reach relative to hand-tuned segments. In training models for behavioral targeting, we are concerned with both what to predict and how to leverage user profiles. Our empirical analysis of over 200 advertising campaigns has yielded some useful best practices for targeting.

First, we compare whether training on clicks or conversions is best. Our results indicate that clicks often suffice but they are not always good proxies for conversions. By predicting directly for conversions, we can now improve the impact of targeting methods on ad campaigns. Most existing behavioral targeting systems are limited to clicks because it is the only data readily available. But, recently, advertisers have been willing to share individual responses to ads [3], facilitating such conversion-optimized models.

Second, of critical importance to behavioral targeting is the online behavior of the users. Although the behavior we can observe is only passive, we find there is considerable signal in the profile. We first consider the types of events: browsing, ads, or query activity. The results indicate that although query activity is quite useful, browsing activity is more valuable overall. Then given a set of selected user events, we consider a feature representation (LLRs) that encodes the correlation between feature and conversion. We found that using LLRs improves performance on large campaigns but not on small campaigns. Next we turn to the amount of user history to use for prediction. The results indicate that more data is better, but there is a point of diminishing returns of roughly 30 days which is primarily due to the changing nature of user interests and web sites. We next find that rather than explicitly incorporating temporality into the features, simply aggregating events performs well.

Lastly, based on extensive offline and online experiments, we validate our findings and have arrived at several best practices for behavioral targeting.

10. REFERENCES

[1] N. Archak, V. S. Mirrokni, and S. Muthukrishnan. Mining advertiser-specific user behavior using adfactors. In *Proceedings of the 19th International World Wide Web Conference*, 2010.

[2] A. Bagherjeiran, A. O. Hatch, and A. Ratnaparkhi. Ranking for the conversion funnel. In *Proceeding of the 33rd SIGIR conference on Research and development in information retrieval*, 2010.

[3] A. Bagherjeiran, A. O. Hatch, A. Ratnaparkhi, and R. Parekh. Large-scale customized models for advertisers. In *ICDM Workshops*, 2010.

[4] Y. Chen, D. Pavlov, and J. Canny. Large-scale behavioral targeting. In *Proceedings of the 15th SIGKDD International Conference on Knowledge Discovery and Data Mining*, 2009.

[5] I. Click Forensics. Click fraud index. `http://www.clickforensics.com/resources/click-fraud-index.html`, 2010.

[6] Google, Inc. Google analytics. `http://www.google.com/analytics`.

[7] A. Hatch, A. Bagherjeiran, and A. Ratnaparkhi. Clickable terms for contextual advertising. In *ADKDD*, 2010.

[8] I. Nielsen Company. Nielsen Claritas PRIZM. `http://en-us.nielsen.com/tab/product_families/nielsen_claritas/prizm`.

[9] Y. Peng, L. Zhang, M. Chang, and Y. Guan. An effective method for combating malicious scripts clickbots. In *Proceedings of the 14th European Symposium on Research in Computer Security*, 2009.

[10] B. J. Pine. Mass customizing products and services. *Strategy & Leadership*, 21(4):6 – 55, 1993.

[11] F. Provost, B. Dalessandro, R. Hook, X. Zhang, and A. Murray. Audience selection for on-line brand advertising: privacy-friendly social network targeting. In *Proceedings of the 15th SIGKDD international conference on Knowledge discovery and data mining*, 2009.

[12] B. Rey and A. Kannan. Conversion rate based bid adjustment for sponsored search auctions. In *Proceedings of the 19th International World Wide Web Conference*, 2010.

[13] X.-R. Wang, K.-W. Chang, C.-J. Hsieh, R.-E. Fan, G.-X. Yuan, H.-F. Yu, F.-L. Huang, and C.-J. Lin. Liblinear – a library for large linear classification. `http://www.csie.ntu.edu.tw/~cjlin/liblinear/`.

[14] J. Yan, N. Liu, G. Wang, W. Zhang, Y. Jiang, and Z. Chen. How much can behavioral targeting help online advertising? In *Proceedings of the 18th International Conference on World Wide Web*, 2009.

[15] L. Zhang and Y. Guan. Detecting click fraud in pay-per-click streams of online advertising networks. In *Proceedings of the 28th IEEE International Conference on Distributed Computing Systems*, 2008.

Large-Scale Behavioral Targeting with a Social Twist

Kun Liu
Yahoo! Labs
4301 Great America Pkwy
Santa Clara, CA 95054
kun@yahoo-inc.com

Lei Tang
Yahoo! Labs
4301 Great America Pkwy
Santa Clara, CA 95054
ltang@yahoo-inc.com

ABSTRACT

Behavioral targeting (BT) is a widely used technique for online advertising. It leverages information collected on an individual's web-browsing behavior, such as page views, search queries and ad clicks, to select the ads most relevant to user to display. With the proliferation of social networks, it is possible to relate the behavior of individuals and their social connections. Although the similarity among connected individuals are well established (*i.e.*, homophily), it is still not clear whether and how we can leverage the activities of one's friends for behavioral targeting; whether forecasts derived from such social information are more accurate than standard behavioral targeting models. In this paper, we strive to answer these questions by evaluating the predictive power of social data across 60 consumer domains on a large online network of over 180 million users in a period of two and a half months. To our best knowledge, this is the most comprehensive study of social data in the context of behavioral targeting on such an unprecedented scale. Our analysis offers interesting insights into the value of social data for developing the next generation of targeting services.

Categories and Subject Descriptors

H.2.8 [**DATABASE MANAGEMENT**]: Database applications—*Data mining*; J.4 [**SOCIAL AND BEHAVIORAL SCIENCES**]: Economics

General Terms

Algorithms, Experimentation

Keywords

advertising, social targeting, behavioral targeting, social-network analysis, large-scale data mining

1. INTRODUCTION

Behavioral targeting (BT) [4, 5, 25] is an online marketing service that infers the specific interests of consumers based on their online activities. By understanding factors such as the frequency of content consumed, the recency of user engagement, and interactions on the site, BT can aggregate large, yet granular audience to whom advertisers can deliver the most relevant messages. Industry research shows that behaviorally targeted ad spending will reach $4.4 billion by the end of 2012, nearly 25% of US display ad spending [10]. Almost all major online publishers such as Yahoo!, Microsoft and Google have enthusiastically embraced this business model.

Today, the advertising inventory of BT often comes in the form of some kind of demand-driven taxonomy, *e.g.*, *Finance/Loans* and *Life Stages/Parenting and Children*. For each category of interest, BT system builds a model that can derive a response score for each individual from his past online activities (*e.g.*, page views, search queries). The score indicates the likelihood that this user will respond to an ad in that category. The response can be ad clicks or conversions (*e.g.*, product purchases and account sign-ups).

Should the user appear online during a targeting time window, the ad-serving system will qualify this user (to show ads in that category to the user) if her score is above a certain threshold. The threshold is predetermined by domain experts in such a way that both a desired level of *response* (measured by the cumulative click-through-rate) and *reach* (measured by the volume of targeted ad impressions served or the number of qualified users) can be achieved. The revenue generated by BT is a function of both *response* and *reach*.

With the proliferation of social media and social-networking sites, it is now possible to relate the behavior of individuals and their social contacts. In fact, a few startup companies have begun to target consumers based on who they are connected to – generating a lot of buzz around a new advertising model called *social targeting*. If information from social networks can drive more accurate and effective advertising, it is desirable to devote more effort to developing new targeting technologies that combine both behavioral data and social signals. However, before we jump on this bandwagon of *social targeting*, it is important to answer the following fundamental questions:

- *Whether and how can we leverage one's friend activities for behavioral targeting?*
- *Whether forecasts derived from such social information are more accurate than standard behavioral targeting models?*

In this paper, we strive to answer the above questions by

CIKM'11, October 24–28, 2011, Glasgow, Scotland, UK.

evaluating the predictive power of social data on a large online network of over 180 million users in a period of two and a half months. We develop a wide array of supervised and unsupervised machine-learning approaches to incorporate social signals to standard BT models. We conduct extensive experiments to assess the effectiveness of these methods on users with different levels of online activities, and across over 60 consumer domains including *Technology*, *Retail*, *Entertainment*, *Finance*, *Travel*, *Life Stages*, *Automotive*, etc.

As the behavioral and social data are intrinsically in large scale (*e.g.*, tens of terabytes of data and hundreds of billions events in two months), we parallel all the machine-learning algorithms using Hadoop MapReduce framework. Specifically, we have designed and implemented a highly scalable end-to-end solution to conduct large-scale data analysis using Hadoop. Our solution handles the generation of behavioral and social features, model training, scoring, network propagation, and model evaluation in a very efficient and scalable fashion.

To the best of our knowledge, this is the most comprehensive large-scale social-network data analysis in the context of BT. Our study based on real-world applications offers interesting insights into the value of social data for developing the next generation of targeting products. Our findings offer a solid and quantitative guideline for both publishers and advertisers in decision making about social targeting versus behavioral targeting. Our algorithm implementations also serve as the building blocks for future researches in this domain.

Organization of the material: Section 2 reviews related work. Section 3 describes our behavioral and social data. Section 4 introduces BT baseline model and evaluation metrics. In Section 5 we develop a wide array of supervised and unsupervised approaches to evaluate the value of social data for BT. In Section 6 we briefly discuss how these different approaches are implemented on Hadoop using a unified framework. We conclude the paper in Section 7.

2. RELATED WORK

Friends are similar along a variety of dimensions is a long-observed empirical regularity, which sociologists called the *homophily* [16]. The study of this pattern is a recurring theme with increasing interests owing to the boom of online social networking services. Researchers from Microsoft [20] found that people who chat with each other using instant messaging are more likely to share similar personal characteristics (*e.g.*, age, location) and interests (*e.g.*, search topics). Engineers from Facebook [12] developed techniques to infer users' undeclared profiles (*e.g.*, age, gender, profession) from their friends so that advertisers can precisely target more consumers. Scientists from academia also developed models to evaluate the quality of algorithms that derive one's interests from their social contacts [17, 24]. However, most existing work is limited to the inference of "static" profiles such as age, gender, education. Understanding the role of homophily with respect to one's online behavior, and particularly in the context of behavioral targeting has been largely ignored.

The most relevant work to ours is by Bagherjeiran and Parekh [1]. The authors observed that online friends tend to see and click on similar display ads. They developed an ensemble classifier to combine both behavioral and social features to boost the probability that a user will click on an ad. We also evaluated this approach in our experiment (to be described later). We observed that the computational cost of this approach is prohibitively high, which makes it not very much practical in large-scale production systems. Further, our work differs from [1] in that we systematically studied a wide array of supervised and unsupervised data mining strategies to incorporate social data into traditional behavioral targeting. To our best knowledge, our work is the most comprehensive study of the value of social data in the context of behavioral targeting at an unparalleled scale.

Another seemingly relevant work is by Provost *et al.* [18]. The authors proposed to construct a quasi-social network that connects people who visit the same user-generated micro-content sites. Given a set of valued seed customers from advertisers, Provost *et al.* identified more users on the quasi-network who are in close proximity to the seed users for brand advertising. The "proximity" between two users is based on the similarity of the contents they have viewed. The idea, though called "social targeting", is closely related to traditional behavioral targeting because the network is derived from users' browsing activity (*i.e.*, page views).

There is another large body of work in the literature on network *influence modeling*, which is one of the fundamentals to viral marketing [13]. Although Watts [23] challenged the existing influence hypothesis and claimed that the so-called *influencers* in social networks were just accidental, viral marketing recently received increasing attention. Hill *et al.* [11] found that consumers who were linked to prior adopters adopt a telecommunication service at a rate 3-5 times higher than the control group. Bhatt *et al.* [3] also investigated how we might use network information to predict product adoptions. They observed strong signals of peer pressure, but very little evidences of influence from highly connected users. Furthermore, they found that the propagation of the adoption remains mostly local to the initial adopters and their close friends, echoing the discovery made by Bakshy *et al.* [2] that most information cascade in social networks are very shallow. We note that influence analysis is primarily interested in how information spreads over the network, whereas our focus is to understand the value of social data, and how we can leverage social data for behavioral targeting.

3. BEHAVIORAL AND SOCIAL DATA

The analysis and experiments in this paper are conducted on vast amounts of behavioral and social-network data from a large IT company in a period of two and a half month. In this section, we describe the data and its properties.

3.1 Data

Behavioral data: Behavioral data serves as the backbone of our study. It contains individuals' web-browsing behavior such as the pages they have visited or the searches they have made, all aggregated at the BT category level, *e.g., 10 page views in category "Retail" at time t*. For evaluation, we split the data into training and test sets. Figure 3 illustrates the generation of both training and test data. The **training data** is collected from a 10-week period of time (2010/08/23–2010/10/31), where the last 4 weeks (2010/10/4–2010/10/31) are used to generate the targets (*i.e.*, clicking on an ad or not). For each user u on each day t_{n+1} in the 4-week target window, we set the *target* to 1 if u clicked on an ad in the BT category being mod-

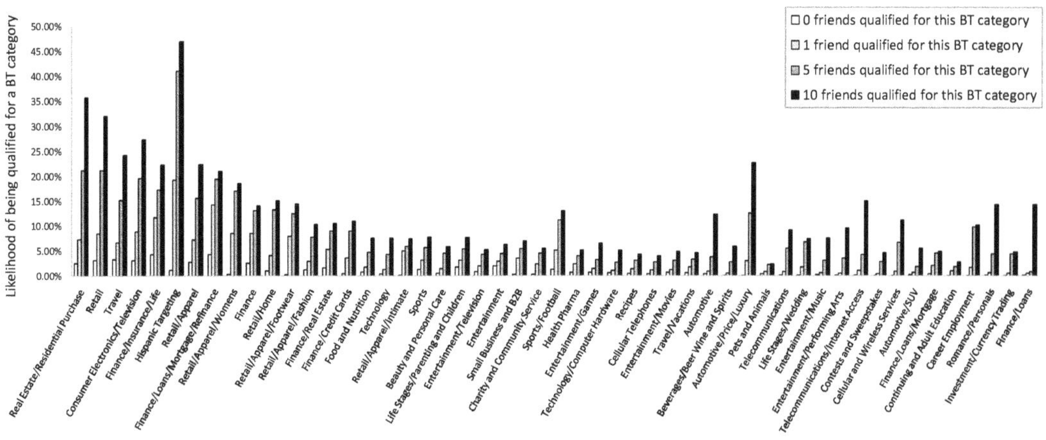

Figure 1: Likelihood of being qualified for a BT category as a function of having social contacts who are also qualified for the same category.

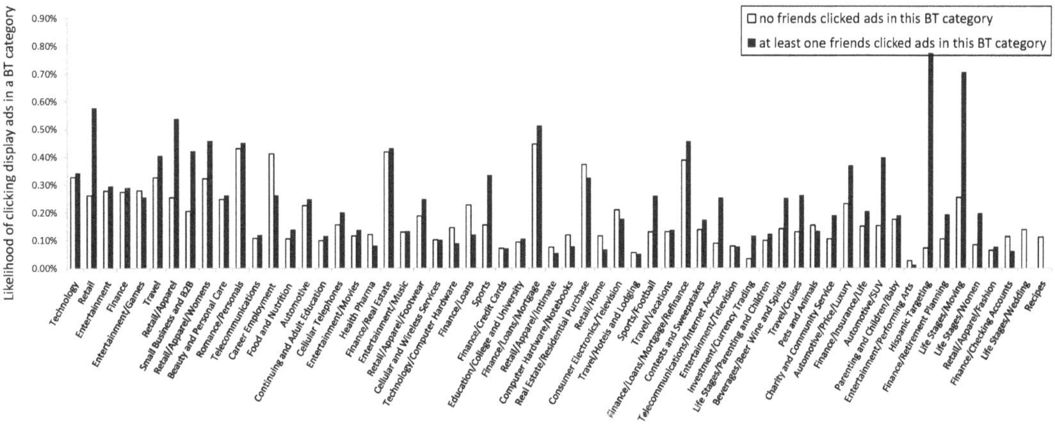

Figure 2: Likelihood of clicking on display advertisements in a BT category as a function of having social contacts who have done the same before.

eled, or 0 if u saw the ad but did not click on it. Next, we create the corresponding *behavioral features* from this user's activities in the preceding 6 weeks (details in Section 4.1). The **test data** is generated from a 7-week period of time (09/20/2010–2010/11/07), where the last 1 week (2010/11/01–2010/11/07) is used to form the targets. This process produces ***13 billion*** training and test examples and approximately ***7 terabyte*** data.

Social data: Our social graph is constructed from users in an Instant Messaging (IM) network operated by a large IT company. We remove singleton users and establish an edge between all pairs of users who mutually authenticate each other as buddies. The resulting network has over ***390 million nodes*** and ***5 billion edges***. Intersecting the behavioral data (training and test, respectively) with this communication network results in approximately ***180 million*** users, for whom we have a record of both their own behaviors as well any behaviors of their friends.

Remarks: We conduct our research in a privacy-friendly fashion. Specifically, we do not use any demographic or geographic information. The behavioral data is aggregated at category level, *e.g.*, 10 *page views in category "Travel/Cruise" at time t*. We do not use any granular user activities.

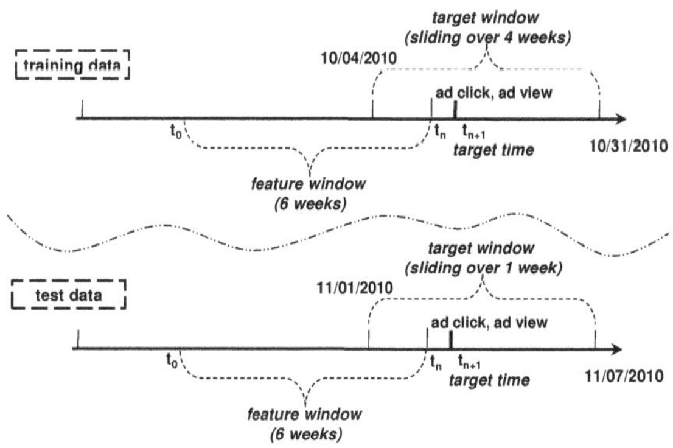

Figure 3: Generating training and test behavioral data.

3.2 Homophily

It is a long-observed empirical regularity that friends are similar on a variety of aspects – a pattern sociologists called *homophily*. As McPherson *et al.* write in their seminal review [16], "homophily limits people's social worlds in a way that has powerful implications for the information they receive, the attitude they form, and the interactions they experience." In other words, where there is *homophily*, one can in principle predict an individual's behavior based on the information from his or her social contacts. Thus, to assess the value of social data for behavioral targeting, we first attempt to answer the following question: *Can we observe the presence of homophily in our social data, and in particular, along certain dimensions related to behavioral targeting?* We answer this question by studying *BT qualifications* and *ad clicks*.

BT qualifications: Recall that a user is qualified for a BT category if her BT score derived from the corresponding model is above the serving threshold. The plot in Figure 1 shows that it is possible to infer one's BT qualifications from that of her friends. For almost all the 60 major BT categories we studied, users with more friends who are qualified for a certain category are more likely to be qualified for the same category. For example, among all consumers with 5 friends qualified for *Retail*, 21% are also qualified for *Retail*, 6 times higher than consumers with no friends qualified for *Retail*.

Ad clicks: Since a majority of online publishers adopt the pay-per-click model for their BT products, *i.e.*, advertisers pay publishers when their ads are clicked, we also study the homophily of *ad clicks* using our data. Specifically, we compute the likelihood that a user will click on the display ads in a BT category as a function of having friends who have done the same within the last few days. The results are illustrated in Figure 2. Similar to the trend we observed for *BT qualifications*, social data are in general informative for predicting ad clicks as well, though the effect varies considerably across different categories. For 42 of the 60 categories shown in the plot, users whose friends clicked on the ads before have markedly higher rates of clicking themselves, with increases ranging from 0.3% to over 977.0%.

Remarks: Goel and Goldstein [9] also investigated social homophily using data from off-line sales, sign-ups for an online service, and clicks on ten online banner ads. Our findings echo the observations made by them.

4. BEHAVIORAL TARGETING (BT)

In this section, we briefly introduce BT baseline model and evaluation metrics.

4.1 BT Baseline Model

The baseline model [5] takes users' browsing habits as input, and builds a classifier to predict the likelihood that a user is going to click on an ad in a certain BT category. The actual data-mining algorithm to learn the classifier is often not crucial. In fact, it is generally intractable to use algorithms of time complexity higher than linear in solving large-scale machine learning problems of industrial relevance [4]. Our previous experience shows that linear classifiers such as logistic regression, linear regression and support vector machines do not differ significantly in terms of prediction performance. In this paper, we use a customized version of LIBLINEAR [7] to train all models on Hadoop MapReduce platform.

On the other hand, how to construct features for training and scoring has a huge impact on large-scale production systems. As online users constantly change their behaviors by browsing different web pages and searching different subjects, it is generally impractical to continuously create new features and score hundreds of millions of users from scratch – after all, online systems often need to make ad serving decisions in near real time (in the order of millisecond). Next we introduce a simple linear-time method that can incrementally update behavioral features, allowing linear classifiers to incrementally update scores as well.

For each type of user activities $a \in \{$ *page view, search query, ad click, ...*$\}$ in the BT category being modeled, the baseline model computes two types of input features:

- ***intensity*** I_{a,t_n}: the cumulative count of activity a that the user has performed in the feature time window $[t_0, t_n]$.

$$I_{a,t_n} = \sum_{t=t_0}^{t_n} \alpha^{t_n - t} A_{a,t},$$

  where $A_{a,t}$ denotes number of times the user has activity a at time t, and $\alpha \in [0,1]$ is a decay factor used to diminish the importance of old events.

- ***recency*** R_{a,t_n}: the time elapsed since the user has performed activity a most recently.

$$R_{a,t_n} = \begin{cases} t_n - t_0, \text{ if } \nexists A_{a,t} > 0, t_0 \le t \le t_n; \\ t_n - \max\{t | A_{a,t} > 0, t_0 \le t \le t_n\}, \text{ otherwise.} \end{cases}$$

As the feature window moves from $[t_0, t_n]$ to $[t_0, t_{n+\delta}]$, it is easy to update features without having to re-process all the prior events:

$$I_{a,t_{n+\delta}} = \alpha^{t_{n+\delta}-t_n} I_{a,t_n} + \sum_{t=t_{n+1}}^{t_{n+\delta}} \alpha^{t_{n+\delta}-t} A_{a,t};$$

$$R_{a,t_{n+\delta}} = \begin{cases} t_{n+\delta} - t, \text{ if } \exists A_{a,t} > 0, t_{n+1} \le t \le t_{n+\delta}; \\ t_{n+\delta} - t_n + R_{a,t_n}, \text{ otherwise.} \end{cases}$$

The target of the model is a binary variable indicating a click on an ad in the category being modeled ($y = 1$), or not ($y = 0$). Although it is possible to use conversions such as product purchases as the target, in this paper we mainly focus on pay-per-click model, where advertisers pay the hosting service when the ad is clicked.

4.2 Evaluation Metrics

We build a BT model for each category c and measure its performance by two metrics: 1) the cumulative CTR of a collection of targeted users whose scores are above a certain serving threshold (or at a certain reach level); and 2) the area under the ROC curve [8].

The cumulative CTR at a certain serving threshold is denoted by $\text{CTR}_c^{\text{reach}}$ and illustrated in Figure 4. It is calculated as the total ad clicks received from users whose scores are above the threshold, divided by total ad impressions served to these users. To eliminate the potential variance across different models, we normalize $\text{CTR}_c^{\text{reach}}$ by the corresponding population CTR where the threshold is set to the minimum (rightmost value on x-axis). We denote this normalized metric by $\text{CTR\_Lift}_c^{\text{reach}}$:

$$\text{CTR\_Lift}_c^{\text{reach}} = \frac{\text{CTR}_c^{\text{reach}}}{\text{CTR}_c^{\text{population}}} - 1. \quad (1)$$

CTR lift provides a sneak peek of the model performance at certain reach levels. To have a global picture, we use the area under the ROC curve, denoted by AUC_c, to examine a

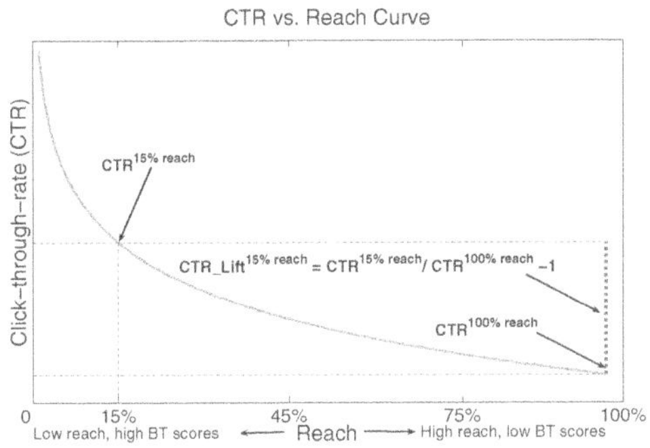

Figure 4: CTR vs. Reach curve. BT scores (sorted in descending order) and reach are along the same x-axis. The serving threshold is set to a value on x-axis where 15% users are qualified. The higher the serving threshold, the less the number of qualified users, and therefore the lower the reach.

model's discrimination power over the entire score distribution. The higher the AUC value, the better the model.

Since we build models for 60 major BT categories in one batch, and ads in different categories receive distinctive serving demands, we report average AUC_c and $\text{CTR\_Lift}_c^{\text{reach}}$, weighted by ad impressions served in each category.

$$\overline{\text{CTR\_Lift}}^{\text{reach}} = \frac{\sum_c \text{CTR\_Lift}_c^{\text{reach}} \cdot v_c}{\sum_c v_c}, \quad (2)$$

$$\overline{\text{AUC}} = \frac{\sum_c \text{AUC}_c \cdot v_c}{\sum_c v_c}, \quad (3)$$

where v_c is the ad impressions in category c. Weighting by ad impressions allows us to pay more attention to revenue-bearing categories which usually have a large amount of contracted impressions to deliver.

5. LEVERAGING SOCIAL DATA FOR BT

In this section, we develop various supervised and unsupervised methods to incorporate social signals into traditional BT. We evaluate the efficacy of these methods through extensive experiments on large-scale real-production data across 60 major consumer domains. Our results offer very interesting insights into the value of social data, allowing us to answer the questions raised before: *How can we leverage one's friends activities for behavioral targeting? Are forecasts derived from such social features more accurate than standard behavioral targeting models?*

5.1 Supervised Approach

5.1.1 BT with Social Features

Our preliminary study in Section 3.2 shows that connected users share similar behavioral patterns such as BT qualifications and ad clicks. Motivated by this finding, we propose to train BT models with additional social features extracted from the network. Specifically, we develop two types of social features: *neighborhood features* and *community features*.

Neighborhood features: These features provide simple statistics of one's social circle. The first set of neighborhood features includes: 1) the number of friends; 2) the number and percentage of *active* friends, where *active* means that the user has certain online activities (*e.g.* browsing pages,

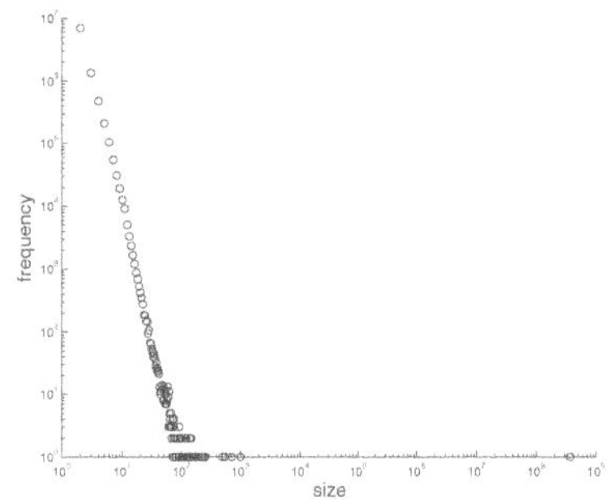

Figure 5: Distribution of the sizes of the connected components in our social network.

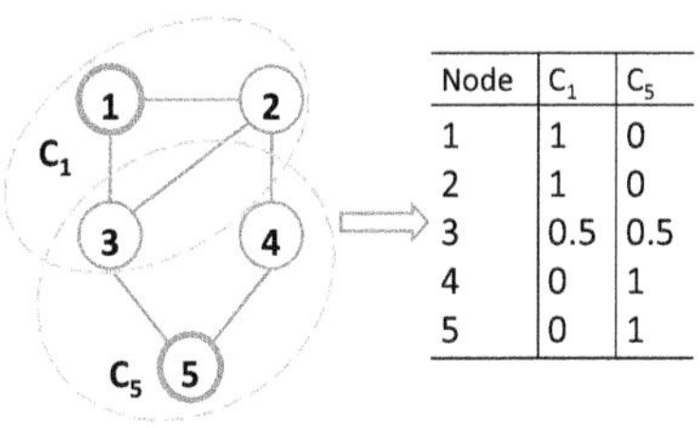

Figure 6: Example of creating community features. Node 1 and 5 are ad clickers, each forming a separate community C_1 and C_5.

clicking ads) in the feature time window; and 3) the number and percentage of ad clickers in one's neighborhood (recall that a user is likely to click the ad if her friends also clicked on the ad). We denote these features by **Neighbors1**.

Note that ad clicks are extremely rare events – the population CTRs on Automotive and Travel display ads are only about 0.15% and 0.08%, respectively according to a DoubleClick report in 2009 [6]. Thus, the volume of users that can benefit from friends' ad-clicking behavior are quite small. On the other hand, views of web pages and ads represent the most dominant patterns of online activities. Hence, we construct the second set of neighborhood features on top of **Neighbors1** by introducing the number and percentage of friends with page views and ad views in the same category being modeled. We denote these features by **Neighbors2** and **Neighbors1** $\subseteq$ **Neighbors2**. The absolute values of these features may vary drastically in practice (approximately follow a power-law distribution), we apply a logarithmic transformation to scale all quantities to a reasonable range.

Community features: The second approach is to extract latent traits based on network structure. One typical example is the *online community* where members inside the group have more inter-connections than with others outside. Recently, Tang and Liu [21, 22] utilized community membership as features to solve a network-based classification problem. The algorithm first identifies communities from the network, and then treats community memberships as latent features for classical supervised learning. They showed that this approach outperforms other collective-classification methods [19], especially in noisy social-media networks.

However, finding communities in a large-scale social network with 390 million nodes and 5 billion edges is not a trivial task. It is necessary to first understand the over-

	Method	$\Delta_{\overline{\text{AUC}}}$	$\Delta_{\overline{\text{CTR\_Lift}}^{\text{reach}}}$					
			5% reach	10% reach	20% reach	30% reach	40% reach	50% reach
1	**BT baseline**	0.00%	0.00%	0.00%	0.00%	0.00%	0.00%	0.00%
2	**Random targeting**	−24.25%	−100.00%	−100.00%	−100.00%	−100.00%	−100.00%	−100.00%
3	**Neighbors1**	−16.58%	−89.19%	−85.65%	−80.28%	−75.69%	−70.78%	−64.51%
4	**Neighbors2**	−13.34%	−87.19%	−82.27%	−72.90%	−63.85%	−54.18%	−44.81%
5	**Community**	−15.84%	−86.13%	−84.87%	−81.19%	−75.38%	−67.30%	−56.42%
6	**BT + Neighbors1**	+0.97%	−0.14%	+0.22%	+0.84%	+1.20%	+1.73%	+3.63%
7	**BT + Neighbors2**	+0.86%	+0.13%	+0.22%	+0.79%	+1.21%	+1.38%	+2.53%
8	**BT + Community**	+0.08%	−0.08%	−0.08%	+0.07%	+0.43%	+0.62%	+0.63%
9	**Ensemble**	+0.00%	−1.02%	−1.56%	−3.51%	−5.48%	−3.55%	−0.77%

Table 1: Performance improvement over BT baseline model, measured by the lift of view-weighted average AUC and CTR_Lift across all 60 BT categories on all users.

all network structure before delving into any specific algorithms. Figure 5 illustrates the distribution of the connected components in our network. There are more than 9 million connected components, among which the largest component alone covers 94.21% of nodes – a very typical power-law distribution. Standard community-detection algorithms such as matrix factorization and statistical inference, if not well tuned, are very likely to end up finding these connected components instead of real "latent features".

To tackle this challenge, we develop a simple notion of community as *a user and her 1-hop neighborhood*. Recall again that users with clickers in the neighborhood are more likely to click on ads, we only keep communities that are centered at an ad clicker. We treat each such community as a feature; if a user belongs to that community, the corresponding feature value is 1, and 0 otherwise. We further normalize each user's membership features so that they sum up to 1. We denote this type of feature by **Community**. Figure 6 illustrates an example of creating such features.

5.1.2 Ensemble BT with a Social Model

Another way of combining social and behavioral data is to build an ensemble classifier, which merges the outputs of behavioral model with social model to improve predictions. Mathematically, the output of an ensemble model S_e is calculated as

$$S_{\text{ensemble}} = \alpha \cdot S_{\text{behavioral}} + (1-\alpha) \cdot S_{\text{social}}, \quad (4)$$

where $\alpha \in [0, 1]$ is a weighting parameter.

A constant weight, say $\alpha = 0.5$, often leads to a poor performance based on our experience. In practice, α is learned through a third classifier that takes both $S_{\text{behavioral}}$ and S_{social} as inputs and the original targets as outputs. Bagherjeiran and Parekh [1] discussed this approach for online advertising in ICDM 2008 workshop. However, we would like point out that the computational cost of this approach is prohibitively high because it needs to train three models: behavioral model, social model, and the ensemble classifier, and score each user multiple times. Thus, this method does not scale very well to large production systems.

5.1.3 Experiments – All Users

We build a bunch of new BT models using the aforementioned social features and ensemble approach. We evaluate these models with respect to the baseline in terms of both $\overline{\text{AUC}}$ and $\overline{\text{CTR\_Lift}}^{\text{reach}}$ (see Section 4.2 for definitions). For illustration purpose, we report the relative improvement of these metrics as follows:

$$\Delta_{\overline{\text{AUC}}} = \left(\frac{\overline{\text{AUC}}_{\text{new}}}{\overline{\text{AUC}}_{\text{baseline}}} - 1\right) \times 100\%; \quad (5)$$

$$\Delta_{\overline{\text{CTR\_Lift}}^{\text{reach}}} = \left(\frac{\overline{\text{CTR\_Lift}}^{\text{reach}}_{\text{new}}}{\overline{\text{CTR\_Lift}}^{\text{reach}}_{\text{baseline}}} - 1\right) \times 100\%. \quad (6)$$

The *reach* takes a value of $5\%, 10\%, \ldots, 50\%$, meaning that ad serving thresholds are chosen for each model that top $5\%, 10\%, \ldots$ users are qualified for ad serving.

Results I: The experimental results are summarized in Table 1. A positive value in the cell means that the new model is performing better than the baseline, whereas a negative value indicates that the new model is worse. Line 1 is the baseline model compared with itself, therefore all entries are 0s. Line 2 is a random targeting model that randomly assigns scores to users, so its $\overline{\text{AUC}}_{\text{random}} = 0.5$ and $\overline{\text{CTR\_Lift}}^{\text{reach}}_{\text{random}} = 0\%$ at all reach levels. Line 3–5 are models built from social features alone. From Line 1–5 we have two interesting observations:

- Social features do carry certain informative signals because the models built from social features alone are still better than random targeting.
- BT baseline model substantially outperforms all other models trained from social features alone in terms of both AUC and CTR. In other words, individuals' own behavioral information is much more useful than their friends' in the context of BT.

Line 6–8 are models built from hybrid features that combine both behavioral and social data. We can observe that these models have higher AUC and CTR than baseline, though the improvement seems only marginal (we will elaborate more on this shortly). It is also worth noting that ensemble classifier surprisingly underperforms the BT baseline, possibly due to overfiting in the training phase. Considering its computational cost as well, we exclude it from the subsequent analysis.

5.1.4 Experiments – Type-0, Type-1, Type-2 Users

The experimental results in Table 1 show that models built from the combination of social and individual behavioral features outperform the baseline. But the actual gains

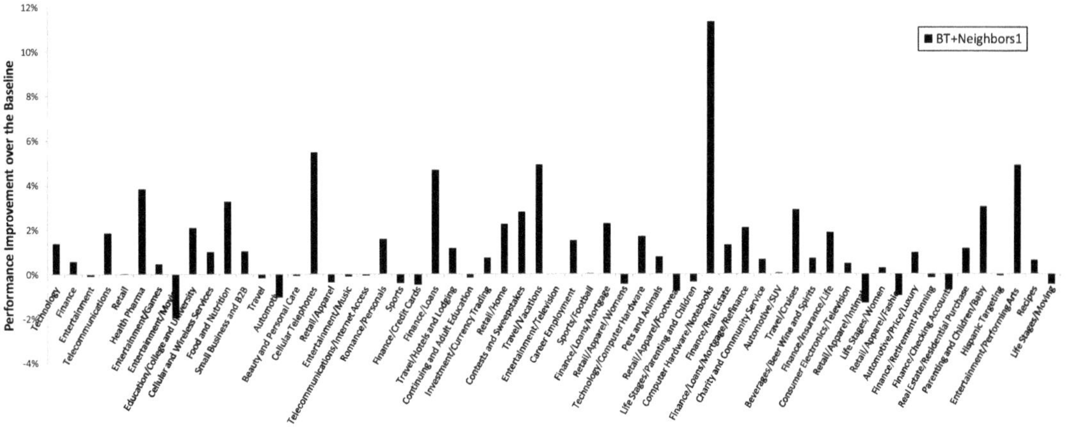

Figure 7: Category-level performance improvement, measured by the relative lift of AUC, *i.e.*, $(\mathbf{AUC}_c/\mathbf{AUC}_{\text{baseline}} - 1) \times 100\%$. Categories are sorted in descending order of ad impressions served in that category. The method is BT + Neighbors1.

on Line 6–9 seem rather marginal (less than 1% of $\Delta_{\overline{\text{AUC}}}$ and $\Delta_{\overline{\text{CTR\_Lift}}^{20\%\ \text{reach}}}$). Since the reported metrics are averaged over 60 BT categories, we conducted further analysis to examine the performance improvement of each individual category. In particular, we chose **BT+Neighbors1** method to study as it is one of the best performing methods. The category-level results are shown in Figure 7. We can see that the improvement is highly skewed, some category has as large as 11% boost and some others only less than 1%. So our next questions are: *why could this happen? When does social features help most?*

To answer these questions, we further partition our users into the following three groups:

- Type-0 users: for these users we do not have their behavioral information in the feature time window. It is possible that they are newly registered users; or they do not visit us recently; or they have online activities, but those activities are in a different category not being considered by the model.
- Type-1 users: for these users we only know what ads they have seen in the feature time window. Usually these are mail or messenger only users who do not browse other pages on our site, and their mail pages cannot be captured due to privacy policies. Note that what ads a user can see is often determined by a variety of targeting services including demographic and geographic targeting, search re-targeting, and other behavioral targeting products. Therefore, ad views are still indicative of users' characteristics and interests to certain extent.
- Type-2 users: these are the active users who have lots of online activities which can be utilized for modeling and scoring.

It is clear that the magnitude of behavioral signals vary significantly among these three types of users: Type-0 is the weakest, followed by Type-1, and Type-2 is the strongest.

In the following experiments, we choose the best performing models **BT + Neighbors1**, **BT + Neighbors2** and **BT + Community**, and evaluate their performance against each type of users, in an attempt to answer the questions we raised in this section.

Results II: The experimental results are illustrated in Figure 8. We can observe that

- Type-0 users benefit most from social features. New models improve by +4% with respect to this type of users, much higher than the improvement obtained from all users which is less than 1%. Similarly, for Type-1 users, we also observe a 2% lift. This result implies that social data is most useful for users without much behavioral information.
- On the other hand, the performance of new models decays when evaluated on Type-2 users. It indicates that when users have sufficient behavioral data to characterize themselves, social data can introduce redundancy, if not noise, to the model.

So how does these findings help us answer the questions raised at the beginning of this section? We further investigated categories with large performance improvement and found that they often have more Type-0 and Type-1 users. This is the case when social features are playing important roles. In addition, the findings also help us understand the pattern we observed in Line 6-8 of Table 1, that is, the performance improvement increases as the reach level increases. We found that when the reach is small, only those users with high BT scores are qualified, and most of them are among Type-2 users. Hence, we do not see much gain of performance. As the reach increases, more and more Type-0 and Type-1 users are qualified and targeted with ads, consequently, the value of social features starts to manifest.

5.2 Unsupervised Approach

In this section, we employ network-propagation methods [15, 26, 14, 27] to infer users' BT scores directly from their friends'. The motivation behind this approach is again the *homophily* property we observed in Section 3.2 – users in close proximity share similar behavioral patterns. One advantage of this approach is that we may only need to score a small set of active users and use them as the seeds of the

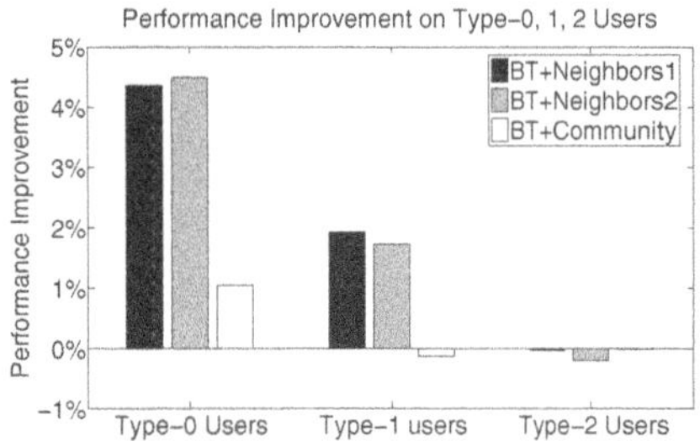

Figure 8: Performance improvement with respect to different types of users, measured by the lift of view-weighted average AUC across all BT 60 categories.

propagation, thus reducing the storage and computational cost of creating a large set of BT features for classification models. We test this idea using three network-propagation schemes as follows.

5.2.1 Methods

SCHEME 1. *Let $s^{(t)}(u)$ denote the score of user u after the t-th iteration, $N(u)$ be the set of users who are friends with u, $d(v)$ be the out-degree of user v (the number of friends of v), $|G|$ be the total number of users in the social network, and $0 < \alpha < 1$ a dumping factor. The first propagation is defined recursively as follows:*

$$s^{(t)}(u) = (1-\alpha) \sum_{v \in N(u)} \frac{s^{(t-1)}(v)}{d(v)} + \alpha \frac{1}{|G|}. \quad (7)$$

SCHEME 1 is essentially the PageRank algorithm [15]. PageRank is used to measure the quality of a web page based on the structure of the hyperlink graph. A page that receives "endorsements" from many other good quality pages in the form of hyperlinks tends to be of good quality too. The stationary state of this propagation depends on graph structure, but not on initial scores.

SCHEME 2. *Let $s^{(0)}(u)$ denote the initial BT score of user u according to the standard BT models, and $0 < \alpha < 1$ a weighting parameter. The second propagation is defined recursively as follows:*

$$s^{(t)}(u) = (1-\alpha) \sum_{v \in N(u)} \frac{s^{(t-1)}(v)}{d(v)} + \alpha s^{(0)}(u). \quad (8)$$

SCHEME 2 has its roots in semi-supervised learning [27]. The basic assumption there is *consistency*: data points close to each other, or on the same cluster or manifold are likely to have the same class labels. The propagation allows every data point to iteratively spread its label information (BT scores in our scenario) to its neighbors until a global state is achieved. During each iteration, each point receives the information from its neighbors, and also retains its initial information. The stationary state of this propagation depends on graph structure as well as the initial scores.

SCHEME 3. *The third propagation is defined recursively as follows:*

$$s^{(t)}(u) = (1-\alpha) \sum_{v \in N(u)} \frac{s^{(t-1)}(v)}{d(v)} + \alpha \frac{1}{|G|} + s^{(t-1)}(u). \quad (9)$$

SCHEME 3 is a variation of PageRank with the exception that a user's score computed in the previous iteration is carried over to the next iteration in computing her new score – a sort of *self-reinforcement*. This propagation is used in [26] to search experts on an author-citation network.

5.2.2 Experiments

Our study of supervised models in Section 5.1 have shown that 1) social features appreciably improve the prediction accuracy for users without much behavioral information (Type-0 and Type-1 users); indicating that these types of users benefit most from their active neighbors; and 2) social features are not quite informative for users with lots of activities (Type-2 user); meaning that for this type of users, baseline model is sufficiently trustworthy. Hence, to evaluate the effectiveness of network-propagation approaches, we hide BT scores (computed from BT baseline model) of Type-0 and Type-1 users (their scores are set to zeros), and initiate propagation from Type-2 users. After each round of propagation, we compute $\Delta_{\overline{AUC}}$ on Type-0 and Type-1 users respectively to evaluate the performance.

Results III: The experimental results are summarized in Figure 9. Unfortunately, we find that propagation in general does NOT increase prediction accuracy of baseline models on either Type-0 or Type-1 users. Since ad click is rare, it often requires vast amounts of data to train a classification model in order to optimize CTRs. Consequently, unsupervised approaches such as network propagation may not be able to capture this weak signal.

Nevertheless, we still have some interesting observations to point out. First, Type-0 users benefit from the first round of propagation with $\Delta_{\overline{AUC}}$ of 0.55% while Type-1 users do not; indicating again that when users do not have any behavior data, social information can provide valuable signals. Second, $\Delta_{\overline{AUC}}$ decays as propagation continues (hold true when the number of iterations $\gg 3$); showing that information from remote friends are noisy and not much useful. Third, the decay of $\Delta_{\overline{AUC}}$ from propagation SCHEME 3 is slower than other two approaches; implying that the *self-reinforcement* strategy adopted by SCHEME 3 may protect users' scores from being significantly skewed by their neighbors.

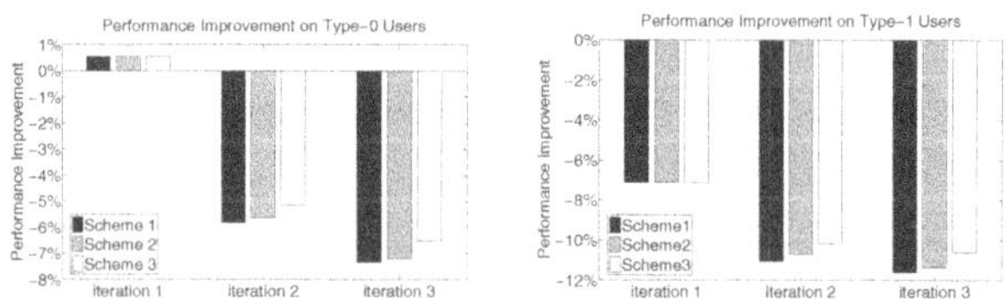

Figure 9: Performance of three network-propagation schemes, measured by the lift of view-weighted average AUC across all 60 BT categories with respect to Type-0 users (Left) and Type-1 users (Right), respectively.

Remarks: It is also possible to initiate propagation from past clickers who often have high BT scores. However, since CTRs are low and the degrees of most nodes are small, relatively few users are connected to any clickers at all. Thus, even though neighbors of clickers have relatively high CTRs, including them in an even moderately-sized set of individuals results in negligible improvement.

6. IMPLEMENTATIONS ON HADOOP

Another contribution we have made is that we designed and implemented a highly scalable end-to-end solution to conduct large-scale data analysis using Hadoop MapReduce framework. Our solution handles the generation of behavioral and social features, model training, scoring, network propagation, and model evaluation in a very efficient fashion. Due to space constraints, we only present a sketch of two major components: *social-feature generation* and *network propagation*. Although they serve different purposes with different specs, we can implement them on Hadoop using a unified framework as follows:

- **Preparation:** join each individual's personal information with her friend list. The output will be user id, the list of her friends' ids, and her personal information. This step is done only once at the very beginning.
- **Map Task:** for each user, emit her personal information to each of her friends. The personal information could be behavioral data (for neighborhood features), clicker data (for community features), or BT scores (for network propagation).
- **Reduce Task:** for each user, aggregate the information received from all her friends to produce social features or prediction scores.

The pseudo-code for *social-feature generation* and *network propagation* are presented in Algorithms 1 and 2.

Algorithm 1: Social-feature Generation

```
1  Mapper(key:uid, value:< adj, f_b >)
   /* adj : graph adjacency list associated with node uid;
      f_b : behavioral features associated with node uid;          */
2  begin
3      emit(uid, f_b)           /* pass along its own BT info for itself */
4      foreach neighbor ∈ adj do        /* pass info to neighbors */
5          if (FeatureType == Neighborhood) then
6              emit(neighbor, f_b)
7          else if (FeatureType == Community) then
8              if isAdClicker(uid) then  /* pass clicker info only */
9                  emit(neighbor, f_b)

10 Reducer(key:uid, value:[v_1, v_2, ...])
11 begin
12     Q_f ← φ                       /* a queue to store friends BT info */
13     foreach v ∈ [v_1, v_2, ...] do
14         if fromNeighbor(v) then enqueue v into Q_f ;
15         else if fromSelf(v) then f_b ← v
16     if (FeatureType == Neighborhood) then
17         f_s ← CreateNeighborhoodFeature(Q_f, v)
18     else if (FeatureType == Community) then
19         f_s ← CreateCommunityFeature(Q_f, v)
       /* the outputs serve as inputs to model training and scoring       */
20     emit(uid, <f_b, f_s>)
```

In Algorithm 1, a user passes her behavioral information to other users she is connected to (Line 4–9). Note that if we want to create **Community** features, only ad clickers will pass information to neighbors (Line 7–9). In the reducer, each user aggregates all information received from friends (Line 12–15) and invokes CreateNeighborhoodFeature and CreateCommunityFeature functions to construct **Neighborhood** and **Community** features, respectively (Line 16–19). The outputs of the reducer serve as inputs to the model training and the scoring components.

Algorithm 2: Network Propagation

```
1  Mapper(key:uid, value:< adj, s_0, s_t >)
   /* adj : graph adjacency list associated with node uid;
      s_0 : initial BT score;
      s_t : current BT score                                        */
2  begin
3      emit(uid, < adj, s_0, s_t >)    /* pass along graph structure */
4      s ← (1 − α) · s_t/|adj|         /* α is the dumping factor */
5      foreach neighbor ∈ adj do
6          emit(neighbor, s)           /* pass score to neighbors */

7  Reducer(key:uid, value:[v_1, v_2, ...])
8  begin
9      foreach v ∈ [v_1, v_2, ...] do
10         if isGraph(v) then /* input value contains graph info? */
11             adj ← v.adj; s_0 ← v.s_0; s_t ← v.s_t    /* get graph */
12         else
13             s ← s + v                         /* sum incoming scores */
14     if (Propagation == Scheme 1) then s_{t+1} ← s
15     else if (Propagation == Scheme 2) then s_{t+1} ← s + α · s_0
16     else if (Propagation == Scheme 3) then s_{t+1} ← s + s_t
       /* the outputs serve as input to the next MapReduce iteration    */
17     emit(uid, < adj, s_0, s_{t+1} >)
```

In Algorithm 2, the mapper computes for each user the scores need to be distributed to her neighbors (Line 4–6). In the reducer, each user sums up all score contributions from her neighbors and computes updated BT score (Line 12–16). Since it is impossible to maintain a global graph structure in memory, we need to pass along the graph from one iteration to the next. This is accomplished by emitting the adjacency list of each user keyed by the user id (Line 3), and this structure is written back out to disk in the reducer (Line 17). The outputs of the reducer have the same data structure as the inputs to the mapper, which can be used for the next round of MapReduce iteration.

7. CONCLUSIONS

In this paper, We developed a wide-array of supervised and unsupervised methods to leverage social data for BT. We conducted extensive experiments to assess the effectiveness of these methods on a large network of 180 million users, and across 60 consumer domains. To our best knowledge, this is the most comprehensive study of the value of social data for advertising. To conclude, we summarize our major findings here.

1) Social data alone do carry informative signals that can be utilized to compliment standard BT models. However, its value for targeting must be stated carefully as it is not always a *silver bullet*. In our study, categories with a strong homophily effect are more likely to benefit from social data, but the degree of improvement depends on the amount of behavioral information the targeted users have, and how strong the baseline is.

2) Among all the methods we have investigated, appending social features directly to standard BT features seems to be the most effective and scalable way to go.

Finally, we want to point out that this study explores only one aspect of utilizing social-network data for advertising. We mainly treat it as an additional information source, and try to understand its value in the context of BT. However, social networks can be employed in other forms such as improving user engagement with products, and identifying influencers to promote word-of-mouth marketing. All these problems merit further systematic and quantitative study.

8. REFERENCES

[1] A. Bagherjeiran and R. Parekh. Combining behavioral and social network data for online advertising. In *Proceedings of IEEE International Workshop on Data Mining for Design and Marketing (DMDM'08)*, pages 837–846, 2008.

[2] E. Bakshy, J. M. Hofman, W. A. Mason, and D. J. Watts. Everyone's an influencer: quantifying influence on twitter. In *Proceedings of the fourth ACM International Conference on Web Search and Data Mining (WSDM'11)*, pages 65–74, 2011.

[3] R. Bhatt, V. Chaoji, and R. Parekh. Predicting product adoption in large-scale social networks. In *Proceedings of the 19th ACM International Conference on Information and Knowledge Management (CIKM'10)*, pages 1039–1048, 2010.

[4] Y. Chen, D. Pavlov, and J. F. Canny. Large-scale behavioral targeting. In *Proceedings of the 15th ACM SIGKDD Conference on Knowledge Discovery and Data Mining (KDD'09)*, pages 209–218, 2009.

[5] C. Y. Chung, J. M. Koran, L.-J. Lin, and H. Yin. Model for generating user profiles in a behavioral targeting system. U.S. Patent 7809740, Issue date: October 5, 2010.

[6] DoubleClick. 2009 year-in-review benchmarks: A doubleclick report. http://www.google.com/doubleclick/pdfs/DoubleClick-07-2010-DoubleClick-Benchmarks-Report-2009-Year-in-Review-US.pdf, 2009.

[7] R.-E. Fan, K.-W. Chang, C.-J. Hsieh, X.-R. Wang, and C.-J. Lin. LIBLINEAR: A library for large linear classification. *Journal of Machine Learning Research*, 9:1871–1874, 2008.

[8] T. Fawcett. An introduction to ROC analysis. *Pattern recognition letters*, 27(8):861–874, 2006.

[9] S. Goel and D. G. Goldstein. Birds of a feather shop together. `http://messymatters.com/2010/09/01/birdshop/`, September 2010.

[10] D. Hallerman. Behavioral targeting: Marketing trends. `http://www.emarketer.com/Reports/All/Emarketer_2000487.aspx`, June 2008.

[11] S. Hill, F. Provost, and C. Volinsky. Network-based marketing: Identifying likely adopters via consumer networks. *Statistical Science*, 21(2):256–276, 2006.

[12] T. Kendall and D. Zhou. Leveraging information in a social network for inferential targeting of advertisements, April 2009. US Patent App. 12/419,958.

[13] J. Leskovec, L. Adamic, and B. Huberman. The dynamics of viral marketing. *ACM Transactions on the Web*, 1(1):5, 2007.

[14] S. A. Macskassy and F. Provost. Classification in networked data: A toolkit and a univariate case study. *Journal of Machine Learning Research*, 8:935–983, 2007.

[15] C. D. Manning, P. Raghavan, and H. Schütze. *Introduction to Information Retrieval*, chapter 21, page 464. Cambridge University Press, 2008.

[16] M. McPherson, L. Smith-Lovin, and J. M. Cook. Birds of a feather: Homophily in social networks. *Annual Review of Sociology*, 27:415–444, 2001.

[17] A. Mislove, B. Viswanath, K. P. Gummadi, and P. Druschel. You are who you know: inferring user profiles in online social networks. In *Proceedings of the 3rd ACM International Conference on Web Search and Data Mining (WSDM'10)*, pages 251–260, 2010.

[18] F. Provost, B. Dalessandro, R. Hook, X. Zhang, and A. Murray. Audience selection for on-line brand advertising: privacy-friendly social network targeting. In *Proceedings of the 15th ACM SIGKDD Conference on Knowledge Discovery and Data Mining (KDD'09)*, pages 707–716, 2009.

[19] P. Sen, G. Namata, M. Bilgic, L. Getoor, B. Galligher, and T. Eliassi-Rad. Collective classification in network data. *AI Magazine*, 29(3):93, 2008.

[20] P. Singla and M. Richardson. Yes, there is a correlation – from social networks to personal behavior on the web. In *Proceeding of the 17th International Conference on World Wide Web (WWW'08)*, pages 655–664, 2008.

[21] L. Tang and H. Liu. Relational learning via latent social dimensions. In *Proceedings of the 15th ACM SIGKDD International Conference on Knowledge Discovery and Data Mining (KDD'09)*, pages 817–826, 2009.

[22] L. Tang and H. Liu. Leveraging social media networks for classification. *Data Mining and Knowledge Discovery*, 23(3):447–478, 2011.

[23] D. Watts. Challenging the influentials hypothesis. *WOMMA Measuring Word of Mouth*, 3:201–211, 2007.

[24] Z. Wen and C.-Y. Lin. On the quality of inferring interests from social neighbors. In *Proceedings of the 16th ACM SIGKDD International Conference on Knowledge Discovery and Data Mining (KDD'10)*, pages 373–382, 2010.

[25] J. Yan, N. Liu, G. Wang, W. Zhang, Y. Jiang, and Z. Chen. How much can behavioral targeting help online advertising? In *Proceedings of the 18th International Conference on World Wide Web (WWW'09)*, pages 261–270, 2009.

[26] J. Zhang, J. Tang, and J. Li. Expert finding in a social network. In *Advances in Databases: Concepts, Systems and Applications*, volume 4443 of *Lecture Notes in Computer Science*, pages 1066–1069. Springer Berlin / Heidelberg, 2007.

[27] D. Zhou, O. Bousquet, T. N. Lal, J. Weston, and B. Schölkopf. Learning with local and global consistency. In *Advances in Neural Information Processing Systems*, volume 16, pages 321–328. MIT Press, 2004.

Evolving Social Search Based on Bookmarks and Status Messages from Social Networks

Bastian Karweg
Mobile Advertising GmbH
Karlsruhe, Germany
Karweg@mobile-advertising.com

Christian Hütter
Karlsruhe Institute of Technology
Karlsruhe, Germany
Christian.Huetter@kit.edu

Klemens Böhm
Karlsruhe Institute of Technology
Karlsruhe, Germany
Klemens.Boehm@kit.edu

ABSTRACT

Social search is a variant of information retrieval where a document or website is considered relevant if individuals from the searcher's social network have interacted with it. Our ranking metric *Social Relevance Score (SRS)* is based on two factors. First, the *engagement intensity* quantifies the effort a user has made during an interaction. Second, users can assign a *trust score* to each person from their social network, which is then refined using social network analysis. We have tested our hypotheses with our search engine www.social-search.com, which extends the existing social bookmarking platform folkd.com. Our search engine integrates information the folkd.com users share through the popular social networks Twitter and Facebook. With permission of 2,385 testers, we have connected to their social graphs to generate a large-scale real-world dataset. Over the course of a two-month field study, 468,889 individuals have generated 24,854,281 website recommendations. We have used those links to enhance their search results while measuring the impact on the search behavior. We have found that social results are available for most queries and usually lead to more satisfying results.

Categories and Subject Descriptors

H.3.3 [**Information Storage and Retrieval**]: Information Search and Retrieval – *Information filtering, Search process.*

General Terms

Algorithms, Performance, Design, Experimentation.

Keywords

Social Search, Social Networks, Social Graph, Search Engine, Status Messages, Friend Networks.

1. INTRODUCTION

1.1 Motivation

With the huge growth of information available on the internet, it is increasingly challenging to pick the 10 first results for a query. According to [14], combining classical approaches such as measuring the number of links that point to a website (e.g., PageRank) with complementary ranking criteria from the user's social network increases result quality significantly. Considering broad topics like "books" or unspecific queries like "restaurant", leveraging information about the searcher can lead to better results [10]. Consider the following use case:

Example 1: The pancake recipe

Jane is looking for a pancake recipe which one of her friends has recommended. Searching on Google for 'pancake recipe', she only has a slim chance of finding it. Using social search, Jane is more likely to get results that both contain the query and have been recommended, commented upon, bookmarked, or liked by her friends.

Research has proposed various approaches to social search, e.g., [2],[4],[6]-[9]. However, we are not aware of a systematical evaluation of how users interact with real data from their social networks. One of the authors runs a startup company that provides the social bookmarking platform folkd.com. This service has more than 1,500,000 users worldwide who share over 24,000,000 bookmarks. We leverage this massive user base to evaluate social search techniques that are promising in a real-world setting. More specifically, we examine the following questions: (a) Do users generate enough content such as bookmarks and status messages to serve as data base for an internet search engine? (b) How many friends does an average user need to obtain good search results tailored to him personally? (c) Do complementary ranking criteria from the user's social network actually improve search quality? – Studying these questions is difficult because one needs a very large number of users who grant access to their social networks. Furthermore, it is still an open issue how to carry out social search such that users get satisfying results on real-world data.

Folkd.com already comes with a full-text search engine that allows users to search through the bookmarks. We have extended this search engine to rank the result elements of a query according to their social relevance for the user. We refer to the metric that we use as *social relevance score* (SRS). It calculates the result ranking, individually for each user, based on two factors, which we call *engagement intensity* and *social trust*. The *engagement intensity* specifies how strongly a user has interacted with a result element using social services. For example, both clicking on a link and recommending a restaurant to a friend are interactions/engagements. However, the first one is weaker than the second one. The *social trust* determines how intense the relation of the user is to other individuals from his social network. This value is fine-tuned based on the reputation of the users in the network. Apparently, some users are more active than others, and not all individuals from the user's social network are equally trustworthy. One hypothesis, which we examine in this paper, is that the ranking improves as the searcher adds more friends, or his friends create more content over time.

CIKM'11, October 24–28, 2011, Glasgow, Scotland, UK.

Our social search engine www.social-search.com is operational since January 2011. Users of folkd.com may connect their accounts to Facebook and Twitter. These networks currently are popular to publish links and recommendations for friends through what is called "status messages". Being allowed to aggregate status messages of these users as well as their friends, we have conducted a field study that has run for 58 days and has had 2,385 participants. The participants had more than 460,000 friends, who have published 24,854,281 link recommendations during that time. After filtering for spam, empty and duplicate queries, we have been able to collect (with permission of the users) 2,098 sessions to analyze.

On average, each friend creates one new link recommendation per day. The number of search results available also depends on the social graph of the users, the activity of their friends, and the broadness of the search term. Given a network of 50 friends, the average user will get about one highly relevant social result for a random query. If he has as many as 300 friends, social search even delivers more than 5 social results on average. The results of our field study show that, using social-search.com with SRS ranking, users find a satisfying result about 2 to 3 positions earlier and with 0.25 clicks less than using plain folkd.com with a classic full text ranking. We conclude that ranking search results through social criteria can lead to great improvement in search quality.

2. RELATED WORK

According to [6], there are three types of social search: collective, collaborative, and friend-filtered. Collective search leverages the "wisdom of the crowds" [13] to assess the relevance of a website. Collaborative search is based on the "village paradigm" [2] where experts from the social network of the user answer search queries. Friend-filtered search offers personalized results based on recommendations from the user's social network. Our work adapts the friend-filtered approach. We assign users to different levels of trust based on their social relationship. The user may adjust these levels to control how much which friend is influencing his personal rankings.

Research has proposed various metrics for ranking social search results. *SBRank* [4] simply counts how many users have bookmarked an item. It focuses on collective social search and does not respect different engagement types or different trust levels. More closely related to this study are *SocialTrust-Ensemble* [12] and *FriendshipSimilarity* [1], which do incorporate friend recommendations. However, these measures lack the option of individual adjustments. In addition, both require the system to precalculate the results on a static data base. This renders their application difficult on systems whose content changes frequently, like social web services.

Next, according to the classification in [16], there are three types of queries: navigational, informational, and transactional. With navigational queries, the user already knows the destination he wants to reach, e.g., "CIKM 2011". Most queries are informational, where the user searches for a certain topic, but does not know the destination. Transactional queries always reveal the next intended action of the user, e.g., buying a certain product after searching for "cheap digital camera". We expect navigational queries to benefit the least from social search. In contrast, we hypothesize that transactional and informational queries in particular can capitalize on friend recommendations.

Some approaches to social search [7], [13] rely on tags used to represent a topic in a folksonomy. However, a single tag can hardly cover an entire topic and is more ambiguous than a contextual sentence [8]. Given the recent developments in social media, the usage of tags is on a decline [9]. People rather use status messages to describe a link. This contextual information serves as a personal recommendation and is more trustworthy than metadata provided by the content producers [4]. Further, [8] sees status messages as "good summaries" of the content and as a good approach to better understand why something has been recommended.

Our metrics to classify user relations have been inspired by [1] who have experimented with a similar value called *FriendshipStrength* and [12], who have proposed a probabilistic matrix-factorization framework to combine characteristics of user recommendations by his friends. Their metric did not include flexible trust levels, but tried to estimate the strength of a relation by deriving transitive relations (e.g., same interest in a certain topic). However, both have followed the assumption that "you trust recommendations of your close friends more than those of your casual acquaintances".

3. OVERVIEW

When social bookmarking services like folkd.com or digg.com started to implement friend connections and recommendations, users did not adapt it very well. They instead already had opted for the opposite, using bookmarking or sharing functionalities that social networks like Facebook or Twitter had implemented. The demand for a unified and easy access to this information grows steadily. With a massive amount of nearly 7,000 tweets[1] and 16,000 status messages[2] per second it is justified to assume that these messages contain a lot of relevant links that can improve search results. We leverage the user base of folkd.com to aggregate link recommendations from social networks. We have implemented the search engine www.social-search.com that takes these link recommendations into account.

3.1 Data Aggregation

Before discussing the search engine in detail, we describe what happens when a new user joins our platform. We have recruited participants by means of the well-known pyramid scheme: we have invited randomly selected users from folkd.com. They then announced their participation through their social network accounts, which in return lead to a chain reaction of more friends joining. This has worked very well, and the group of participants is still expanding even after the actual experiment has finished.

The first step when a user connects his folkd.com account with a social network is to aggregate the profile data from the account of the user and his network of friends. All of the platforms discussed above provide APIs for external developers. Our system parses the social content streams to determine if they contain a link reference to a web page. Aside from simple links, the Facebook API also provides references to other "objects" in the so-called social graph. For example, if somebody "likes" a band or a celebrity, the network creates a "fan" relation. We combine these relations and links into what we call an *interaction* or *user engagement*.

As a side note, we mention that there is a very common technique to shorten links that are posted using services like bit.ly or tinyurl.

[1]http://blog.Twitter.com/2011/01/celebrating-new-year-with-new-tweet.html

[2]http://www.Facebook.com/press/info.php?statistics

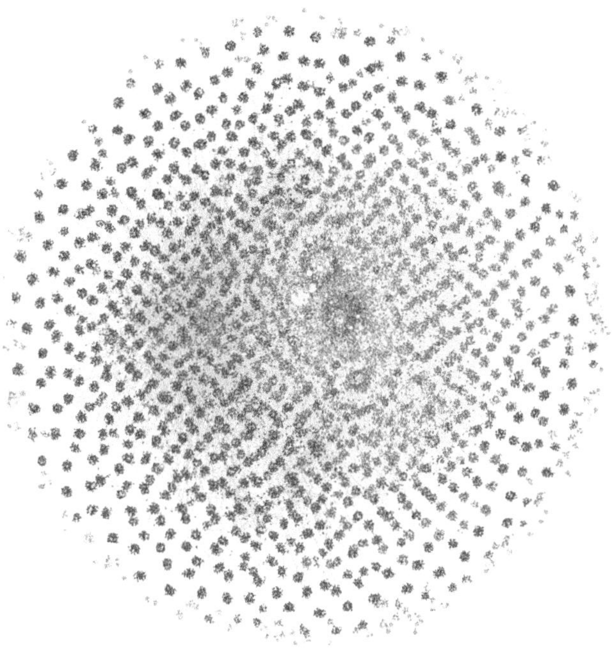

Figure 1. Visualization of User Relations in Test Dataset

It is necessary to expand those to prohibit the creation of duplicate documents. Our crawler fetches the meta tags of the web page, checks for dead links and sorts out spam.

In the third step, we replicate the user-to-user relations existing in the social networks. To give an idea of how the users are connect to each other we have visualized a selection of 40,000 users (nodes) and 65,000 friend relations (edges) in Figure 1. This sample consists of all participants of our field study (see Section 5) plus those users who could be reached by following one hop of inbound or outbound friendship relations. We only considered additional relations from those friends if they reached a user that has already been selected. The total number of users in Figure 1 is limited to 100,000 due to limitations of the visualization tool. Looking at the edges of the graph, the small circles of flower-shaped groups correspond to testers whose friends do not have any other inward connections to the graph. The visualization was generated by using Gephi [18]. The layout of the graph was produced using the OpenOrd algorithm. The network diameter here is 8 with an average degree of 2.8.

The size of the nodes is in line with their PageRank [5]. The layout algorithm tends to locate nodes with a higher degree more in the middle. An interesting effect shows when aligning the nodes according to their source: While some accounts already existed in folkd.com (orange in bottom right), others have been created when pulling data from Twitter (light top right) and Facebook (dark on the left). This results in clusters of people of the same group. Other individuals who are connected to multiple networks are located between these clusters. We also could observe that the connectivity in the Twitter network is higher. This is because it does not enforce a confirmation when creating a connection.

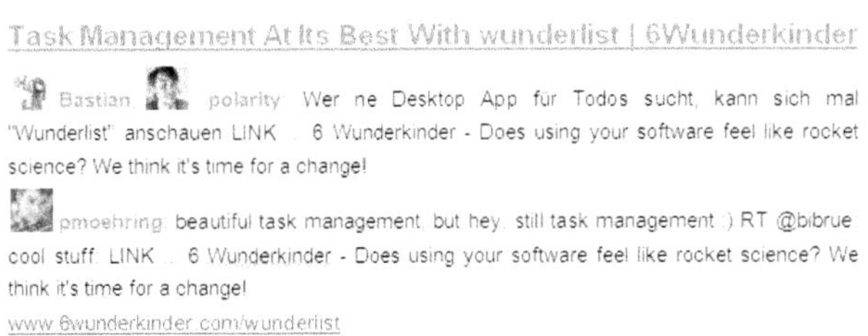

Figure 2. Example of a Social Search Result

A very important issue for us has been to respect privacy settings when including data from Facebook or Twitter. If a link was posted as public, we could use it freely. If it was posted to be only visible to friends, we have used this link for the social search of these friends, but not for other users. We refer to [19] for a discussion of more sophisticated privacy settings.

The total time for initializing and calculating the user's first individual social search result depends on the amount of data that has to be gathered. We set up a periodical re-crawl (every 15 minutes in the background) to fetch new or updated data for the user.

3.2 Social Search

Once the data is aggregated (which currently takes about 30 seconds), the user's first query is ready to be executed. The effect of our SRS metric is that results his friends have interacted with are pushed to the top. Figure 2 shows an example of a search result with our implementation. We point out that each entry also shows the name of the user (preferably a friend) who has engaged with the result item as well as the comment of that user.

The user is also able to refine the search to be more objective or more social. This adjustment allows for numerous applications: The most basic one is that users search for information that friends have recently mentioned, cf. *Example 1*. Another application is that a search for "YouTube" not only displays a link to the popular video site but also shows videos that friends have enjoyed most.

Interestingly, social search has also caused the inverse behavior: Testers started actively seeking out people to befriend who had served good recommendations around certain topics like photography, celebrities and others. Our approach of letting users arrange their friends into different trust levels supports this (see Section 4.1).

3.3 Technology

With our system all data is stored in a replicated, relational database. To support fast queries on the huge dataset we have indexed important tables using high-performance full text indexes built with SphinxSearch[3] in addition. The application itself is handling the search requests from the user as well as constantly updating the latest available social data by accessing the external social graph data through the APIs of Facebook and Twitter. As core programming language for this business logic PHP5 with a custom made MVC-framework was used. To calculate the individual user trust levels we needed to calculate different centrality measures on our user relations table, which we found to be most easily done by MATLAB. The presentation tier is a classic web-frontend application, running on top of an Apache2 web server executing simple HTML5 and AJAX components.

The size of the search index in our project has become approximately 0.5 gigabyte per one million documents indexed.

[3]http://www.sphinxsearch.com

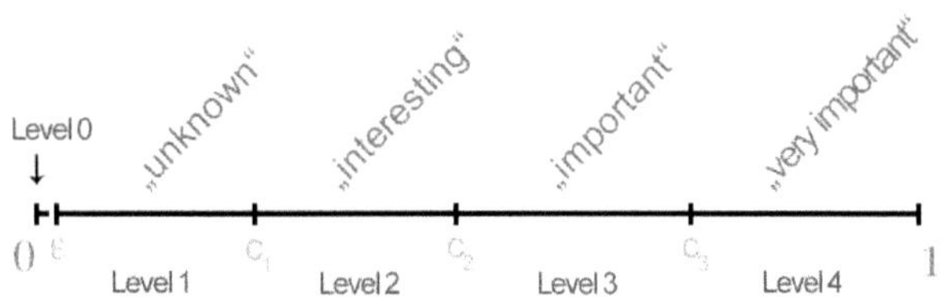

Figure 3. Different Trust Levels

But even with a fast and out-of-the box full text solution like SphinxSearch the high dynamics of internet and social media content is challenging for the system. The frequent (near real-time) document updates in particular are problematic. Indexing software is adding additional documents fast, but frequent updates of existing ones will slow down query times significantly. From a user point of view updates need to be fast. When a friend posts a new link, the user wants to be instantly able to find it, also if that specific links had also been posted by somebody else in the past. We have used parallel indexes in combination with a cached Delta Index to provide live updates as well as very fast querying.

3.4 Full Text Relevance

In the regular folkd.com system, users can search through bookmarks that users have added manually. The system ranks them by a full text search metric which is calculated upon the titles, descriptions and tags of the web paged recommended by the users. We combine two approaches when calculating the full text score: phrase ranking and statistical ranking. Phrase rank is based on the length of the longest common subsequence (LCS) of the search term and the documents, the statistical approach is a based on the probabilistic BM25 retrieval framework introduced by [17] which considers word frequencies.

For the implementation of folkd.com, we rely on the full text search engine SphinxSearch[4]. They state that, while in general better partial phrase matches are ranked higher, one can achieve better full text results by pushing perfect phrase matches to the top. Having tested different metrics on the folkd.com system, we have observed that, considering full text rankings, plain BM25 indeed performs better on single-word queries. However, the combination with the phrase proximity based ranking provides a better search quality overall than any statistical scheme alone.

4. RANKING THE SEARCH RESULTS

In our effort to improve the search experience for our users, we identify commonalities of existing approaches to social search, which we then combine into a new ranking metric called *Social Relevance Score* (SRS). We also say how we have combined the new ranking with classic full text ranking metrics.

4.1 Trust Score

Analyzing the dynamics in social networks, [3] and [6] have found similar usage patterns: Some users are very active, sharing a lot of information with their friends, whereas others just follow what is going on in their social circle. Some social networking services such as Facebook offer the possibility to arrange friends into groups. However, this grouping does not have any implication on how the service handles link recommendations of individuals from different groups. In the worst case, all links published by any friend are contained in one update stream. This causes the problem that the update stream tends to be dominated by few users. Consider the following scenario:

Example 2: Lost in the shuffle

Kate is interested in volleyball; therefore she is listed as a "fan" of various volleyball teams on Facebook. Most of the teams regularly publish their match scores. By searching for "volleyball", Kate could easily overlook the personal invitation of a friend to a volleyball event. By not being able to distinguish between different levels of trust, this recommendation by a close friend can easily get lost in the shuffle.

To address the issue discussed in Example 2, we propose to have five trust levels, which the system assigns to each friend. The user can then adjust these by hand. If a Person A recommends a link, and A is a friend of the searcher, then the trust level of A influences the personalized ranking of that link. The more important A is to the searcher (i.e., the higher his trust level), the higher the link will be ranked. If the trust between the two persons is zero (i.e., the lowest level), then the recommendation by A has no influence at all.

The *trust levels* follow the schema presented in Figure 3. Our search engine individually calculates the trust levels of all individuals based in their relationship to the user. The user can then adjust the trust level for each of his friends by hand. The 0-value is the lowest level used to block others intentionally. Level 1 is the default setting for unknown users. Level 2 is intended for contacts that are loose but interesting, e.g., organizations or celebrities the user is a fan of. Level 3 should be used for confirmed relationships like real friends on Facebook, LinkedIn, or Xing. Finally, one may promote special relations like close friends or family members to Level 4. Note that the assignment to a certain level is not reflexive and remains undisclosed to the user affected. There are various ways to calculate the borders c_i of each trust level i. We preferred an inverse logarithmic scale along the number of people who fall into those clusters.

The *trust score* $t_s(x)$ of user s for his friend x ranges between the lower and the upper bound of x's trust level $c_s(x)$. The system adjusts the trust score within this level according to the overall popularity $r(x)$ of x in the social network.

$$t_s(x) = c_s(x) + r(x)$$

That is, popular friends have more impact. This is because the popularity $r(x)$ puts their trust score within the bounds of the trust level assigned to them. To determine the popularity of each user, we calculate the PageRank [5] centrality measure on the graph consisting of the friend connections from the social network. We have chosen PageRank because it combines good accuracy with moderate computation complexity.

4.2 Engagement Intensity

In the time before web 2.0, user interactions were limited to the creation of links from one website to another one [4]. Nowadays, there are various online interaction possibilities. We propose the term *user engagement* as a generic term for these possibilities, standing for all cases where a URI identifies the recommending user and the object of interaction. In other words, whenever one can track User X (link to his user profile) having interacted with

[4] http://sphinxsearch.com/docs/current.html#weighting

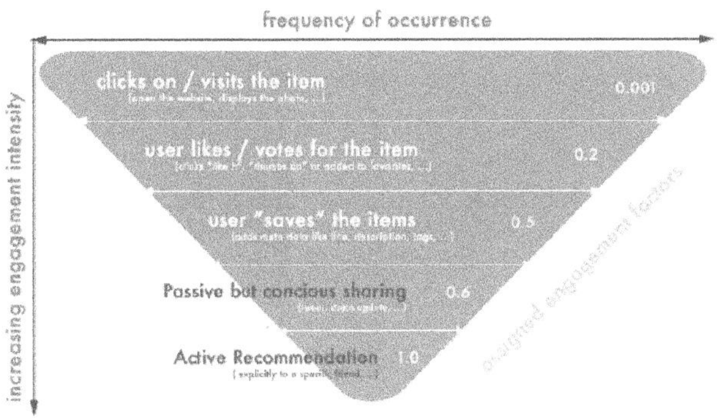

Figure 4. Different Levels of User Engagement

Object *Y* (link to their profile/homepage), we have a user engagement. Examples are restaurants reviews, recommending music and rating books or movies [8]. All these engagements express relevance, and a social search engine should consider them. Status messages on Facebook and Twitter have become widespread aggregators for those recommendations. This is because many services have integrated their interfaces.

Next, not all interactions are equally intense: The engagement factor should increase with the effort the user spends in order to engage in this specific way. For example, giving a "thumbs up" to a movie trailer is much easier than writing a review about a restaurant. This is why we have come up with the notion of *engagement intensity* $e_x(i)$, i.e., how much user x has engaged with document i. The scale ranges from 0 (neutral, no engagement) to 1 (strong engagement). Figure 4 shows the different levels of engagement.

Note that the range of the engagement-level values is continuous. This allows to reflect how often different engagements occur in relation to each other. For example for about every 200 visits, one vote has occurred. Spreading the levels relative to each other across the scale, the lowest level has a factor of 0.001, the second one of 0.2 etc. In case of several engagements of a user with a resource (e.g., he both clicks on it and rates it), the highest engagement factor counts.

4.3 Social Relevance

Our new *Social Relevance Score* (SRS) ranks the result elements of a query according to their social relevance for the user. The ranking considers how intense the interactions with the result items have been, and how much the searcher trusts the individuals recommending a link.

$$SRS_s(i) = \sum_{x \in E_i} \left(t_s(x) \cdot e_x(i)\right)$$

The SRS is calculated for each element i of the result set of a full text search (see Section 4.5). For each user x who has interacted with (i.e., recommended) a document i, we add up the product of the trust score $t_s(x)$ of searcher s in that user x and the engagement intensity $e_x(i)$.

Note that the engagement of several low-trust users can outweigh a recommendation of a close friend. Further, the popularity of the user interacting in the network influences his trust score. This means that users who are important to the social network gain more influence compared to others on the same trust level.

Figure 3 shows that we define the lower border of Level 1 by a value ε above zero. By setting the value of ε, we define how big the impact of an average unknown user on SRS should be. For example, a YouTube video with one million views can gain a high SRS value even if none of the friends of the user has seen it yet. Increasing ε boosts documents that are popular in general.

4.4 Combining SRS with Full Text Relevance

Considering the different types of search queries, it sometimes makes sense to deliver objective results, while sometimes the searcher is looking for results biased by recommendations from his social contacts. To address this issue the *combined social rank* (CSR) is composed of the classical full text relevance (FTR) of a document and the social relevance score (SRS). Parameter α serves a as weight:

$$CSR(i) = \propto \cdot SRS(i) + (1 - \propto) \cdot FTR(i)$$

Because it is difficult and sometimes impossible to automatically classify queries by type, we have made α adjustable by the user during the search, using a slider. Whenever the user wants more objective results or more socially biased ones, he can simply adjust the slider and repeat the search.

To save the necessity of computing an SRS value for all elements that contain a certain word, we first send each query to a full text search engine. We then only calculate SRS for the top 1,000 FTR results.

A search for the empty word "" turns off the full text relevance. This transforms social search into a plain recommender system of elements friends have interacted with in the past.

Search quality is boosted by the aggregation of user-generated content that relates to a given web page. The following example shows how three Twitter messages ("tweets") about a website can add valuable context data:

Example 3: Status messages
While bookmarks of a page are structured:

ID:	*#453567*
URL:	*http://www.flickr.com*
Title:	*Welcome to flickr - Photo Sharing*
Tags:	*photos, flickr, photography, photo, sharing, images*

Twitter and Facebook status messages embed a link into a contextual sentence:

@thomas56: "using flickr.com to store and share our family vacation photos"
@photographerX: "interested in my photography work? see my portfolio on flickr.com"
@Areporter: "I just uploaded fotos of today's train crash at grand central to flickr.com"

■

Example 3 illustrates the difference between placing a link into a natural context instead of performing a manual classification. This leads to broader contextual document and better search results: For example, different spellings like "fotos" and "photos" become searchable.

5. EVALUATION

To evaluate our social search engine in a real-world setting, we have conducted an extensive field study. We have formulated various hypotheses, referring to different aspects of our approach.

We then discuss the evaluation criteria we have used to test our hypotheses.

5.1 Hypotheses

Comparing the number of links bookmarked on folkd.com with the number of links posted to Facebook and Twitter, we notice an increasing dominance of sharing through social networks over classic methods of content exchange like shared bookmarks. We hypothesize that social networks already produce enough content to fuel an internet social search engine:

- **Hypothesis 1: Link recommendations**
  Status messages of social networks produce a significant number of link recommendations usable for social search.

Following the observations of [3], [4], and [13], the participation of users in social bookmarking services can be described using a power law distribution. That is, someone with a few active friends will benefit more from the service than someone who is connected to many people who are inactive. We expect that this observation also holds for the amount of link recommendations that are produced for social search.

- **Hypothesis 2: Social graph**
  The number of links available for social search depends on how active the friends of the user are.

A result of related work is that "a searcher can improve search by joining larger networks and having more friends" [11]. However, we are not aware of any study that provides concrete information on how many friends a user needs for social search to work. We hypothesize that there is a minimum degree of connectivity for social search to work.

- **Hypothesis 3: Search quality**
  There is a minimum number of friends the user needs to be connected to for social search to produce an adequate number of results.

From [2] we know that the more complex a query is, the longer its search term tends to be. For systems based on a full text search, we assume that increased complexity will lead a smaller result base to filter and re-rank according to social factors. The consequence will be fewer results of the social search.

- **Hypothesis 4: Query types**
  The number of results depends on the type (informational, navigational, and transactional) and length of the query.

Even when a user with a reasonable number of friends has submitted a suitable query, the most important question remains: Does data from social networks improve search quality? According to [11], results from social networks "provide richer and more reliable clues about the purposes and interests of the user". We therefore assume:

- **Hypothesis 5: Ranking improvement**
  The result ranking of classic full text search improves when combining it with the Social Relevance Score (SRS).

5.2 Evaluation Metrics

We now explain the metrics used to test our hypotheses. In classic search-engine architectures, the crawler clearly finds enough links on a website to follow. This is not necessarily true for status messages in social networks because their availability depends on the friends of the user. A first metric to test Hypotheses 1 and 2 is the correlation between the number of friends the user has and the number of links they produce in a given timeframe.

The classic measures of search quality are precision and recall [15]. For social search however, it is difficult to decide whether a document is relevant for a query. This is because relevance might be different for each user. So there is not only one reference set but many different ones. In addition, the high dynamics of the data set can cause the pool of documents noticeable by the individuals to change, i.e., when a user adds or removes friends from his network. A document is noticeable in social search if it contains the query term at least once (i.e., FTR > 0) and at the same time has an engagement of at least one of the user's friends (i.e., SRS > 0). To test Hypothesis 3, we count how many results social search generates compared to full text search. That is, we measure how the result set changes by incorporating user recommendations.

Another issue is the length and type of queries entered by a user (Hypothesis 4). To evaluate it, we have looked at the word count per query as well as at their type (informational, navigational, and transactional).

Finally, the metrics we have used to measure the improvement of the ranking (Hypothesis 5) are:

- the *RankingPosition* of an item that the user has clicked,
- the *ResultClickCount*, the number of results the user has clicked, as well as
- the *SearchTime*, the latency between the search and the first click on a result item.

We assume that by clicking on a specific result one expresses his interest in the information behind it. Consequently, if the user clicks on a higher result position (position 1 is the highest), this indicates a better ranking. A good search result also requires fewer clicks per query. Namely, the user has been able to find a suitable result with less effort. Finally, taking longer to decide which site to visit indicates that the result tends to be worse/less clear.

Letting the user adjust his search to be more objective or more biased by social engagements, we also have obtained good indications about when either ranking (SRS or FTR) could improve a certain result. Thus, we set the parameter α to be 0.5 initially. If the users repeat a search request with a higher α value, we conclude that social recommendations could improve the results shown. In what follows, we will also look at the adjustment of α in repeated searches.

6. Experimental Results

In this section, we describe the results of our field study.

6.1 Analyzing Data from Social Networks

Our field study has lasted for 58 days, from November 9, 2010, until January 5, 2011. Table 1 contains some descriptive statistics on the data collected during our field study.

Averaging over all testers, we have found that each user produced one link recommendation per day on average. This observation is independent of the number of friends and their level of activity. Multiplied by the average number of friends, each user receives $130 \cdot 30 \cdot 1 = 3{,}900$ new links a month. This probably is too little data to fuel a search engine. If we also include friends-of-friends, we get $130^2 \cdot 30 \cdot 1 = 507{,}000$ new links a month (not counting overlaps). This in turn appears to be a decent corpus size for a personalized social search engine.

Table 1. Social Stream Dataset

Number of testers	*2,385*	
Number of friends of testers	468,889	
Number of links crawled	24,854,281 = 428,522 / day	
Data by Social Network	Facebook	Twitter
Number of testers	1,651	1,164
	430 people using both networks	
Number of friends	217,010 (46.28%)	251,879 (53.72%)
AVG No. of friends per user	131.44 (± 281.80)	216.40 (± 410.25)
No. of links crawled	3,344,286	21,509,995
No. of links per user-stream	2,026 = 34.92/day	18,480=318.62/day
No. of links per user-friend	18.70 (± 175.07) = 0.33/day	102.61 (± 600.14) = 1.77/day

We also have tested for a correlation of the number of link recommendations a user receives and the number of friends he has. The data shows a strong positive correlation ($r = 0.58$, $p < 0.05$), which supports Hypothesis 2. In summary:

Result 1:

- Having more friends will provide more content for social search.
- On average, users get one new link recommendation per friend per day.
- To get a significant number of link recommendations from social networks, also friends-of-friends must be considered.

Somebody with fewer friends may have more results if he is connected to more active people (Hypothesis 2). To test this, we have analyzed the distribution of links shared through the networks Facebook and Twitter. Applying the Kolmogorov-Smirnov test shows that it actually is a power law distribution, returning estimated fit parameters of [$\alpha = 2.4100$, $x_{min} = 133$, $L = -2.8150e+04$, $p < 0.05$, $gof = 0.0178$] for Facebook and [$\alpha = 2.1600$, $x_{min} = 587$, $L = -6.4030e+04$, $p < 0.05$, $gof = 0.0314$] for Twitter users.

Moreover, the statistics reveal that the average number of links shared on Twitter is about twice the number on Facebook at the lower activity levels. In fact, we have found a lot of examples such as in Table 2 where a user had more results despite having fewer friends. This heavily depends on the search topic. If one chooses to befriend someone with great knowledge regarding a certain topic this would obviously benefit his queries in that field.

Table 2. Social Results comparison

Users:	*John243*	*Chris Rowlan*
# of friends	**79**	59
Number of social results for the query:		
„Winter"	67	**133**
„SEO"	21	**162**
„Pizza"	9	**13**
„Buy Car"	2	**7**
„Android App"	**3**	0

Result 2:

- The number of link recommendations available for a user depends on his choice of friends as well as their activity.

6.2 Social Search Queries

Hypothesis 3 states that there is a minimum number of friends the user needs for social search to produce an adequate number of results. To investigate this hypothesis, we have defined two

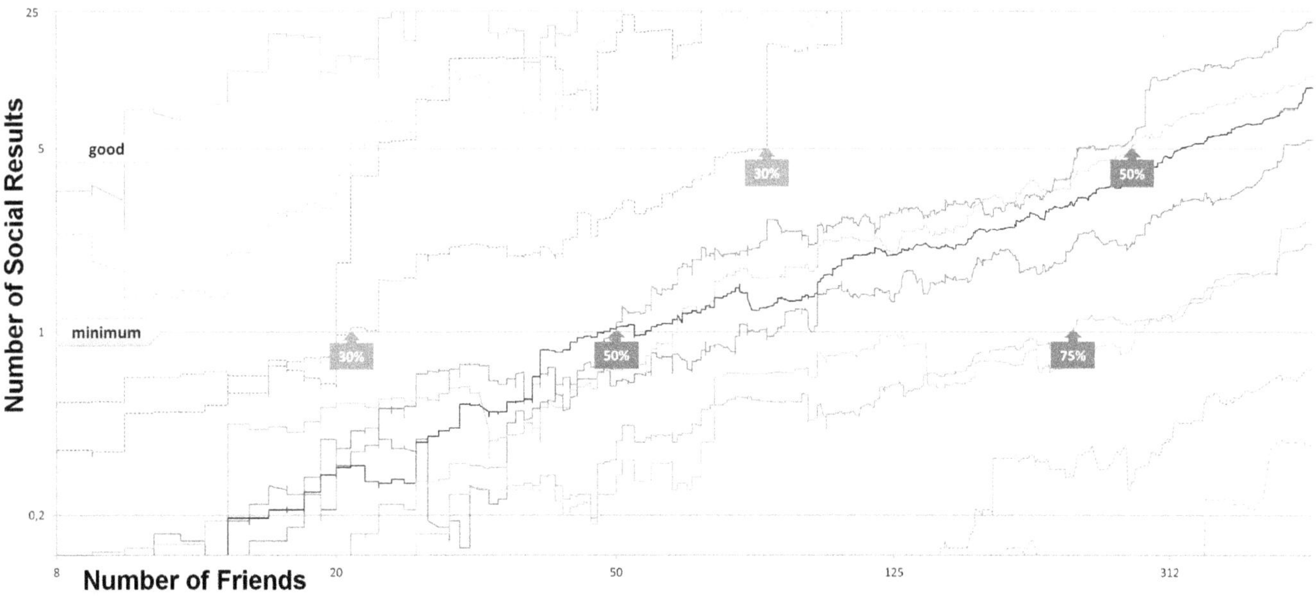

Figure 5. Social Result Count for one-word queries

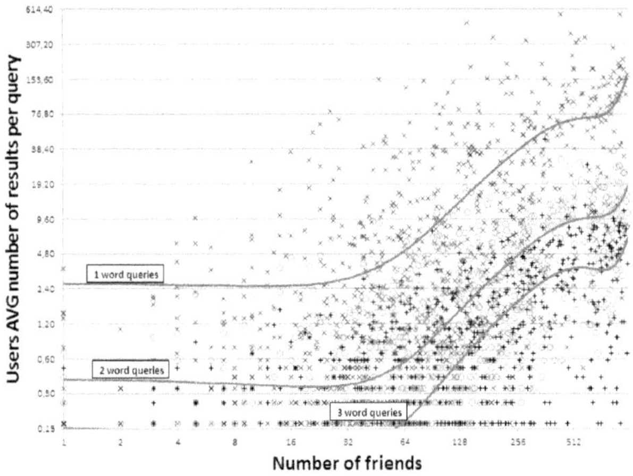

Figure 6. Results by Query Term Length

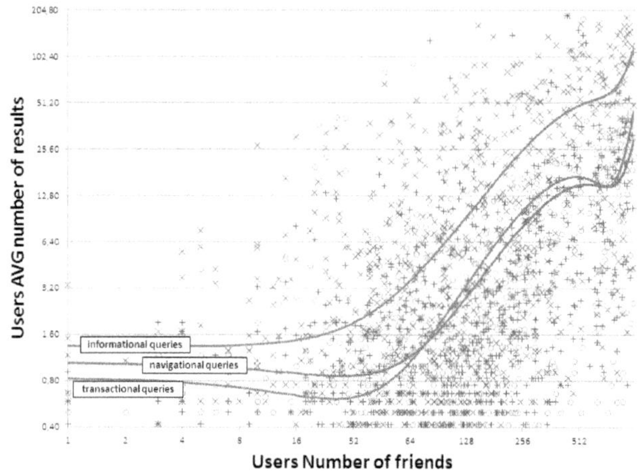

Figure 7. Results by Query Type

threshold values. An average of one social result per query will be the minimum. Below this value, social search does not work. An average of five social results (out of 10) in turn is good. This is because half of the results on the first page are recommended by friends.

From the search log, we have randomly selected 36 queries with a length of one to three words and have classified each one as informational, navigational, and transactional by hand. We then have executed these queries for the social graph of each of our 2,385 test users. Figure 5 represents each search query as a line. Our data shows that a user with 20 friends will touch the minimum (one result) for about 30% of all one-word queries. To check whether social search "works" on average queries, we define that at least 50% of the queries must return one social result or more. With this definition, a user needs about 50 friends for social search to work at a minimum level and about 300 friends to work well. That is, the longer and more complicated the queries become, the more friends someone needs to reach the minimum number of results.

Result 3:

- For every other query, the minimum threshold is reached with 50 friends and the optimum with 300 friends.
- For more complex queries, the thresholds are reached only in a quarter of all cases, even with 300 friends.
- The number of social search results strongly depends on the number and the degree of activity of friends.

Hypothesis 4 states that social results also depend on the length and type of the query. To evaluate this hypothesis, we have calculated the average result count for different query lengths. Figure 6 plots the average number of social results against the number of friends per user. We found that there tend to be fewer social results for longer queries.

Next, we look at the different query types. Figure 7 shows the average number of social results for different types. As expected, informational queries perform best and navigational ones worst. Surprisingly, transactional queries do not benefit from social search. In a second analysis, we observe that results of actual (logged) queries outperform the simulated queries executed for each user by a factor of almost two. This can be explained by the implicit knowledge of context of the user about topics in his environment: This means that the possibility for such queries to deliver results is higher than on random queries.

Result 4:

- Social search tends to work better on shorter queries.
- Social search works best on informational queries, while navigational and transactional ones are more difficult.
- In social search, the performance of real queries is significantly higher than that of random ones because the user already knows which result he can expect.

6.3 Search Behavior

Our final question is whether result ranking based on the Social Relevance Score (SRS) increases the search quality, compared to classic full text search (Hypothesis 5). To study this question, we have logged the search sessions of our test users (with their permission). We record how many results the user has clicked on, which position the selected result was at, and whether or not it has been a friend recommendation.

Table 3. Analysis of SRS Ranking Performance

Results (random sample)	*No. Search Sessions*	*Ranking Position*	*Result Click Count*	*Search Time*
Clicks on Social Results	117	2.92 (± 6.63)	1.14 (± 0.49)	13.56 sec (± 19,90)
Clicks on Full text Results	56	5.70 (± 8.26)	1.39 (± 8.26)	24.64 sec (± 84,14)
Difference	-	+2.78	+0.25	-11.08 sec
Confidence Level(T-test)	-	0.14 % (t = 2,93)	0.55% (t = 0,32)	6.19 % (t = 1,39)

For this analysis, we have examined a random sample of 173 of all search sessions recorded where users actually clicked results. Table 3 shows that, in these search sessions, most users decided to click social results. Further, users have deemed social results more relevant. Over all sessions, the *RankingPosition* of clicked results was 2.92 for social and 5.7 for full text searches. We have verified the statistical relevance of this data with a T-test.

The same holds for the number of clicks a searcher needs to reach a satisfying result. While the *ResultClickCount* is 1.39 for full text results, it is only 1.14 for social results. A T-test confirms that this difference is significant. While we could also observe a decrease in the time a user needs to decide which result to click, this result has not been significant.

Another approach to measure which results users prefer is to look at the alpha slider. This slider allowed users to adjust the search results to be more social or more objective. Its default value is 0.5. Most of the users (77.3%) have used the default setting. Of those who have adjusted their search, 60.79% have chosen to shift the slider towards "more social" results. The average value of the manually adjusted sliders has been 0.64 (towards social) with a standard deviation of 0.11. One could argue that the users are just curious about the new feature. This is not the case. We could verify this with a control group of students. We explicitly advised them to test different alpha settings and to only click on a link in the best result set. Therefore, we conclude that users indeed tend to find social results more compelling.

Result 5:

- When combining full text results with social relevance by SRS, users tend to find interesting results earlier (2-3 positions).
- Users are more satisfied with social search results: They need 0.25 clicks less to find a suitable item.
- When confronted with the option to adjust their search to be more social or more objective, 61% choose the first.

7. CONCLUSIONS & FUTURE WORK

7.1 Conclusions

In this paper, we have studied the question whether leveraging data from social networks, status messages in our case, improves search quality. We have analyzed existing approaches to social search and have identified the patterns of "user engagement" and "social trust". We combine these patterns into a ranking metric called *Social Relevance Score* (SRS). To evaluate this metric, we have implemented a working search engine www.social-search.com on top of the social bookmarking platform folkd.com.

During the course of our field study, over 2,300 people connected their folkd.com accounts with Twitter or Facebook. These users granted access to their social graphs and allowed us to crawl over 24 million links from their network of over 480,000 friends. We found that, on average, each friend creates one link recommendation per day. One should have more than 50 friends for friend-filtered social search to deliver significant improvements. The results of our field study show that social search results are more relevant: They decrease the time required for the search process and increase the user satisfaction.

7.2 Future Work

Some of our testers have participated in a survey after finishing the field study. Most of them have stated that the perceived value of receiving personal recommendations by friends is much higher than just getting "anonymous" results. Promoting more of these intangible values is interesting to improve the system in terms of user satisfaction.

In our implementation of social-search.com we have put much emphasis on minimizing the number of steps between accessing the site for the first time and getting to an individual search result. To improve this even further we will work on processing external user data more quickly. We are also thinking about a process to predict which recommendations a user might also like based upon sample data. By identification of key users, we might introduce information hubs, which can act as trusted entities for users who do not have many friends.

8. REFERENCES

[1] Schenkel, R., Crecelius, T., Kacimi, M., Michel, S., Neumann, T., Parreira, J. X., and Weikum, G. 2008. Efficient top-k querying over social-tagging networks. *SIGIR '08.*

[2] Horowitz, D. and Kamvar, S. D. 2010. The anatomy of a large-scale social search engine. *WWW '10.*

[3] Lerman, K. and Ghosh, R. 2010. Information contagion: an empirical study of the spread of news on digg and Twitter social networks. *ICWSM '10.*

[4] Yanbe, Y., Jatowt, A., Nakamura, S., and Tanaka, K. 2007. Can social bookmarking enhance search in the web? *JCDL '07.*

[5] Page, L., Brin, S., Motwani, R., and Winograd, T. 1999. The PageRank citation ranking: Bringing order to the Web. *Stanford InfoLab.*

[6] Evans, B. M. and Chi, E. H. 2008. Towards a Model of Understanding Social Search. *CSCW '08.*

[7] Heymann, P., Koutrika, G., and Garcia-Molina, H. 2008. Can social bookmarking improve web search? *WSDM '08.*

[8] Bao, S., Xue, G., Wu, X., Yu, Y., Fei, B., and Su, Z. 2007. Optimizing web search using social annotations. *WWW '07.*

[9] Rowlands, T., Hawking, D., and Sankaranarayana, R. 2010. New-web search with microblog annotations. *WWW '10.*

[10] Clements, M., de Vries, A. P., and Reinders, M. J. T. 2008. Optimizing single term queries using a personalized markov random walk over the social graph. *ESAIR.*

[11] Gou, L., Chen, H., Kim, J., Zhang, X., and Giles, C. L. 2010. SNDocRank: document ranking based on social networks. *WWW '10.*

[12] Ma, H., King, I., and Lyu, and M. R. 2009. Learning to recommend with social trust ensemble. *SIGIR '09.*

[13] Hotho, A., Jaschke, R., Schmitz, C., and Stumme, G. 2006. Information Retrieval in Folksonomies: Search and Ranking. *ESWC '06.*

[14] Mislove, A., Gummadi, K. P., and Druschel, P. 2006. Exploiting social networks for Internet search. *HotNets-V.*

[15] Cleverdon, C., Mills, J., and Keen, M. 1966. Factors Determining the performance of indexing Systems. Aslib Cranfield research project, Vol. 2.

[16] Jansen, B. J., Booth, D. L., and Spink, A. 2008. Determining the informational, navigational, and transactional intent of Web queries. *Information Processing and Management, 44.*

[17] Robertson, S. and Sparck Jones, K. 1976. Relevance weighting of search terms. *Journal of the American Society for Information Science, 27.*

[18] Bastian, M., Heymann, S., and Jacomy, M. 2009. Gephi: an open source software for exploring and manipulating networks. *ICWSM '09.*

[19] Truls A. Bjorklund, Götz M., and Gehrke J. 2010. Search in social networks with access control. *KEYS '10.*

Social Ranking for Spoken Web Search

Shrey Sahay, Nitendra Rajput
IBM India Research Lab
4, Block C, ISID Campus, Vasant Kunj
New Delhi, India
shrsahay,rnitendra@in.ibm.com

Niketan Pansare
Rice University
Houston
Texas, USA
np6@rice.edu

ABSTRACT

Spoken Web is an alternative Web for low-literacy users in the developing world. People can create audio content over phone and share on the Spoken Web. This enables easy creation of locally relevant content. Even on the World Wide Web in developed regions, the recent increase in traffic is due to the locally relevant content created on social networking sites. This paper argues that content search and ranking in the new scenario needs a re-look. The generic model of using in-links for ranking such content is not an appropriate measure of the content relevance in such a collaborative Web 2.0 world.

This paper aims to bring the social context in Spoken Web ranking. We formulate a relationship function between the query-creator and the content-creator and use this as one measure of the content relevance to the user. The relationship function uses the geographical location of the two people and their prior browsing preferences as parameters to determine the relationship between the two users. Further we also determine the trustability of the content based on the content creatorś acceptance measure by the social network. We use these two features in addition to the term-frequency—inverse-term-frequency match to rank the search results in context of the social network of the query-creator and provide a more specific and socially relevant result to the user.

Categories and Subject Descriptors

H.3.3 [**Information Search and Retrieval**]: Information Filtering; H.5.1 [**Multimedia Information Systems**]: Audio input/output; H.5.4 [**Hypertext/Hypermedia**]: Navigation

General Terms

Algorithms, Design, Experimentation, Human Factors

Keywords

developing regions, audio search, social network, content ranking

1. INTRODUCTION

"A squirrel dying in front of your house may be more relevant to your interests right now than people dying in Africa" [12].

Content search on the World Wide Web involves retrieval of documents that contain the query terms. With more than 20 billion pages now available on the Web [8], for any given query, there are usually a large number of documents that can contain the query terms. Therefore content ranking plays a critical role in determining the set of few most likely documents that can provide the user with the required content. Content ranking on the Web has been dominated by the in-links which use the link structure of the Web to determine the *importance* of the content [16]. The underlying assumption in such an approach is that the most relevant content will be referenced by a maximum number of web pages. The second factor that determines the *importance* of the content, which is somewhat related to page ranks, is the trust that people have on the site that hosts the content. As Web users gain understanding of the different sites, they tend to trust content from some sites more than from other sites. As an example, a news story on CNN may be trusted more as compared to the same news on a politician's blog.

However the Web has evolved significantly over the last couple of years, with the increase in user generated content [4]. Social groups now create a large amount of content that is usually relevant mostly across a a specific group of people. This paper contends that the interpretations of *important* content needs a relook in this Web 2.0 world. We focus on the content that is local to a particular group of users who know each other in real life. In such contexts, the real-world social structure of the relationships between people is likely to have an influence on the *importance* of the content that is created or consumed in the group. We claim that the relationship between the query-creator and the content-creator plays a significant role in the content relevance to the user, and therefore in the content ranking for such a community. Further, we establish that the trust on a particular content is also linked to the trust that the community has on the content-creator. We use these two features to introduce the concept of social ranking for content search.

1.1 Motivation

While there could be different data sets on the World wide Web to which these social concepts can be applied to rank the content, we specifically focus on users in the developing regions as the community to validate the claims presented above. Rural developing world represents 58% of the total world population and the Internet penetration in such regions is estimated to be below 2%. Low literacy and low Internet penetration, coupled with the increasing phone penetration in these geographies suggest that phone and voice could be better means of content creation and access. Low literacy forces these users to create and access such locally relevant content in audio rather than textual means.

The World Wide Telecom Web (or Spoken Web) [14, 13, 17] is a system that leverages the pervasiveness of mobile phones in developing countries and allows the creation, deployment and hosting of voice-driven applications called VoiceSites by any phone subscriber. It attempts to empower users by giving them the opportunity to become content creators and provides a mechanism for users to access information and content with affordable devices (just a regular telephone). Being a voice-driven system, it extends the access to ICTs (Information and Communication Technologies) to illiterate users. Many users in the developing world are now creating and accessing information through the Spoken Web platform. The content ranges from information about people and events in a village [1] to information about the crop prices in the market [2], to business information for the unorganized workforce in developing regions [13].

However, effectively searching through VoiceSites on a voice user interface for navigation and browsing poses significant challenges for Spoken Web. Searching and browsing problems are exacerbated by the audio modality of the content and interaction. Audio is a sequential interface and so presentation of the search results is a non-trivial translation from the visual Web world. As an example, even if the system returns 10 search results, each with 5 second of audio, it will take about one minute for the user to listen to all the search results. *Given the nuances of the audio interface, content ranking plays an even more critical role.*

The second motivation to perform social ranking for the Spoken Web is derived from the demographics of the users. The low-literate population in rural regions usually has very local information needs [1]. In most cases, the users have a real-world relationships with each other and have a concept of trusting specific people in the community. When a technology is introduced to such a population, its adoption is determined by how the social structure is folded in it. *The demographics of such users would therefore desire that content importance and trust be derived from the real-world social structure.*

2. SCOPE AND PAPER CONTRIBUTION

This paper introduces the concepts of using the social structure of the community to perform content ranking on the Spoken Web. We illustrate the high level approach of our solution using the Figure 1. The figure uses the analogy with the page ranks concept that is used in the world wide web. There are two main entities considered by the social ranking system. First is the query-creator and the second is the content-creator. The relationship between the query creator and the content creator is used to influence the ranking

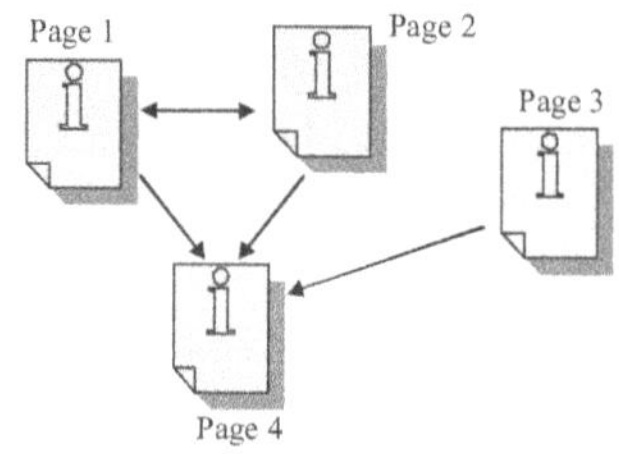

(a) Page rank

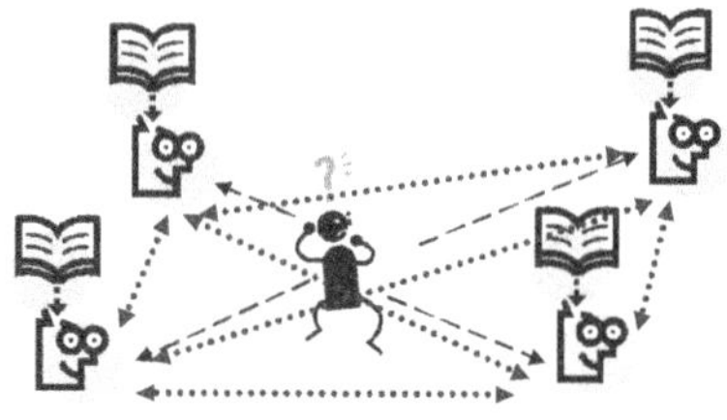

(b) Social rank

Figure 1: While the current web search uses (a) page ranks and exploits the link relationship across *content*, (b) the social rank uses the relationship across *people* who create and seek the content.

of the content with respect to the query. In this paper, this high-level concept is realized by specifically focusing on the Spoken Web content and users. This determines the scope of the concept and the context in which the work presented in this paper has been performed. Given this scope, following are the key contributions of this paper:

- We propose the concept of social ranking which utilizes the real-world relationship between a query-creator and a content-creator to for ranking content.
- We provide an algorithm to extract the similarity between users by mining their previous browsing patterns for the content on the Spoken Web.
- We provide an algorithm to determine the trust-level in the community for a particular content-creator.
- We provide an algorithm to rank content based on the above two features.
- We evaluate the correctness of the algorithm by performing a user study with users in the community.

The paper organization follows a standard structure of first presenting the related research in the field (Section 3). We then describe the data set and the users (Section 4) since we believe that the techniques can be better understood once the reader has an idea of the data and the user environment. Then we present the method used to determine the two key pieces that are used in ranking: similarity across users and social status of a the content creator (Section 5). We then provide a ranking algorithm that ranks the content using the above two features (Section 6). Finally we present the experiments (Section 7) that demonstrate that the social information that we derive from our algorithm correlates with what the users perceive on the field.

3. RELATED WORK

The problem presented in this paper and the approach have been motivated by some pioneering work in the area of spoken document retrieval, personalized search and semantic search areas. In this section, we present the key publications in these areas and highlight the differences from our work and the key findings that we have borrowed.

3.1 Audio Search and Browsing

Searching audio content is usually dependent on converting the audio to text using a speech recognizer and then performing the standard text based search. However the accuracy of speech recognizer is not very high for spontaneous conversational speech. Over the last five years, researchers have started to look at searching speech not through speech recognition, but by indexing speech at a subword level [5]. Such techniques are more robust to speech recognition errors since they consider multiple recognition hypothesis in the index [6].

Most systems for audio search use a visual query interface for accessing content indexed from audio. This is typical in call centers where supervisors wish to monitor offline content of the call center agents [15]. In such situations, the query interface is still visual and hence simple. In [18], the authors address this specific problem and suggest use of dichotic stream (one audio stream for one ear) to play back the search results. However this cannot be applied to a phone channel audio, which is not stereo. *What differentiates our problem is that the query interface and the content, both are in audio.*

3.2 Personalized Search and Ranking

Researchers have suggested approaches to personalize a search result for a particular user [7] or to a community [11] or for a specific domain [9]. The PROS system [7] uses information from the bookmarks of a particular user to determine the interest of the user with respect to his preferences in content and then users those terms to rank the content. On the other hand, authors in [11] use the interaction network between the agents and the end-users and exploit the personal relationship between them to weight the search results accordingly. community has on the agent who creates the content. Domain specific search techniques [9] benefit from the collective search queries within a particular domain and use this effective knowledge of the content preference of the community to improve the relevance of the search results within the domain. *While all of these techniques do provide more relevant results to a particular user, they do not exploit the real-world relationships between people to influence the search results.*

3.3 Semantic Search

Metadata has been the backbone for information retrieval in Digital Libraries [10]. Since it is difficult to process and extract semantics from images, metadata has been the key for image search systems [20]. Not surprisingly, the metadata based content management systems for mobiles have started to appear in the research community. The authors in [19] have used metadata to manage the images on a mobile. *Semantic search therefore is focused on understanding the content in a more intelligent fashion. On the other hand, the proposed social search has its strength on understanding the content creators in a more intelligent manner.*

4. DATA SETS AND USER ECOSYSTEM

The experiments were performed on the data set of a live VoiceSite which is used by people in the western state of india, Gujarat. There are 250 registered participants on this VoiceSite. Only registered users are allowed to create the content and listen to it. The users of this VoiceSite are grain farmers who need to deal with agricultural issues during the growth season and would deal with commercial entities only during the end of a season so their social network comprises mostly of farmers. The NGO broadcasts a 15 minute weekly radio program about best farming practices. Most farmers would listen to the radio program in a group and would later discuss on topics aired on the program. So the social network of the farmers already existed through the radio program. Before we started the pilot, farmers could directly call/write to the radio station staff and get answers to their queries. However, the aim of posting their questions and answering the questions posted by others on VoiceSite was to build a persistent knowledge base that could be later reused. A farmer can always go back to the archive at any time and access the data from the knowledge base from the VoiceSite. *This provided a perfect setting for testing the social ranking concept since the social structure of the farmers was strong and therefore the baseline real-world network was available for any comparative study.*

The data for performing the experiments is extracted by mining previous browsing patterns of the farmers from the Spoken Web log file. The log file captures all the user actions when a person is browsing the VoiceSite. The following actions were logged: calling, listening to a question, listening to an answer posted by an expert, listening to an answer posted by a user, recording a question, recording an answer, navigating to the top-level menu, and hanging up. After recording a question or an answer, the SW updates the log file with the total length of the audio recording. Such log files are input to the social ranking system.

A total of 4827 audio documents were considered for the experiment conducted in this paper. The information related to the content creators of these documents was available through the log file. Additional information was available in the form of structured data that consisted of the locatoin of the participants and their names and phone numbers. This was provided to us at the time of registration. Therefore the log file, the structured demographics and the audio documents formed the data on which the experimetns were conducted.

5. SOCIAL STRUCTURE EXTRACTION

With respect to Figure 1, this section is focused on determining the social structure based on the browsing logs of users in the community. More specifically, we are interested in determining (a) the relationship between the query creator and the content creator, and (b) the effective community trust level of the content creator. In order to use these factors for ranking in a search scenario, these relationships need to have a measurable value which can then be stored along with the content index. These are the main items that we present in this section.

Let $U = \{u_1, u_2, ..., u_N\}$ be the set of users in the community. We take a specific case of any two users in the set U, one of which is the query creator (denoted by u_q) and the other being the content creator (u_c). The relationship between these users is denoted by $R_{q,c}$. We calculate the relationship between all such ${}^{N}P_2$ possible user pairs in U. It is to be noted that this relationship is not commutative since a user u_i may consider another user u_j to be close, but the reverse may not be true. Further, each user in the set is assigned a trust level, T_c, which is then associated to every content that this user has created. In this section we formalize the relationship between two users in the set U. The calculations can be performed for any two users to derive the relationships between all the users in the set.

5.1 Relationship between Query Creator and Content Creator

We are interested in determining if a particular query creator user U_q considers the content of the content creator U_c as important or not. Our assumption is that if U_q has listened to the content created by U_c in the past, then he is perhaps an avid listener of U_c. Further, our algorithm also captures the fact that if the U_q and U_c have listened to similar content in the past, then the two users could be considered similar and therefore should have a closer relationship with each other. We define the distance between any two users in the community by using the above to assertions in Equation 1 below:

$$R_{q,c} = \lambda f_f\,(q, c) + (1 - \lambda) f_s\,(q, c) \qquad (1)$$

where , $0 > \lambda > 1$.

In Equation 1, the function f_f measures the importance that the user u_q places on any content that has been created by u_c. This is determined by finding the percentage of content that u_q has listened of u_c as a fraction of the total content listened by u_q.

$$f_f(q, c) = \frac{L_{c,q}}{\sum_{i=1}^{N} L_{i,q}} \qquad (2)$$

where $L_{c,q}$ is the total number of times that the user u_q has listened to content created by user u_c. The denominator determines the total number of times that the user u_q has listened to any content across all the users in the system. $L_{c,q}$ is computationally inexpensive as it involves counting (in the log file) the number of times that the user has listened to any content and then filtering the content that was created by u_c. f_f looks at the entire space of content listened by u_q and finds the fraction of it that was created by u_c. Being a fraction, f_f has a lower bound of 0 (which is when the u_q has *never* listened to content from u_c) and an upper bound of 1 (when u_q has listened *only* to content from u_c).

On purpose, the counting L does not remove duplication. For example if u_q had listened to a specific content more than once, that will be counted as many times. This ensures that f_f captures the additional interest in the user u_c if s/he listens to the same content multiple times.

In Equation 1, the function f_s aims to determine the similarity between the query creator u_q and the content creator u_c. While f_f measures how much u_q follows u_c, f_s measures how many common content do both u_q and u_c follow. This is calculated by finding the space of the content that is listened by both u_q and u_c and then determining the fraction of the content that is common to both. If F_q is the set of content that is listened by user u_q and F_c is the content that is listened by user u_c, then Equation 3 defines the function f_s as:

$$f_f(q, c) = \frac{\mid F_q \cap F_c \mid}{\mid F_q \cup F_c \mid} \qquad (3)$$

the larger will be the value of f_s. Unlike f_f, the function f_s is a commutative function so that $f_s(q, s) \equiv f_s(c, q)$. Thus this function is calculated only for ${}^{N}C_2$ value pairs in a community of N users. However f_s is computationally more complex than f_f since we need to determine the common elements across two sets, which has the complexity of the order of $O(N)$.

After formalizing the f_f and the f_s functions, the only unknown element in Equation 1 is the value of λ. It determines the relative weight that we give to the two functions and is derived empercically. The relationship between u_q and u_c is therefore established by calculating $R(q, c)$ and it takes into account the browsing similarity of the two users and the *relative importance* that u_q gives to u_c.

5.2 Measuring the Trust for Content Creator

For every content creator u_c in the community, we associate a trust factor T_c that determines the *importance* that any content of this creator should be provided. We calculate the value of T_c by determining how many times has the community as a whole listened to the content created by u_c. This fraction over the total listening space of the community provides the *listenability* of the content creator u_c.

$$T_c = \frac{\sum_{i=1}^{N} L_{c,i}}{\sum_{i=1}^{N}\sum_{j=1}^{N} L_{i,j}} \qquad (4)$$

It is important to determine the importance of a user from a community perspective, in addition to finding it from the query creator perspective. The reason for this is that even if the relationship of the query creator is not good with the content creator u_c, but if the community regards u_c's content important, then the search results for the query should also increase the ranking of the content created by u_c who is heavily regarded in the community.

6. SOCIAL RANKING FOR CONTENT SEARCH

In addition to the standard index that contains the information about the data, we also store the relationship information R for each content. Detailed information on the Spoken Web indexed data is provided in [3]. When a query is presented to the indexer, we identify the user as well. The query term along with the identity of the user is the input to our indexer. The query term is used to generate the list of audio documents that have an association with the query. This list is then ranked based on the two measures of relationship and trust to generate a final ranked list of search results. This section presents the ranking algorithm that uses the social measures that have been described in the previous section.

We begin by defining a social ranking S to a content c for a query q:

$$S = \gamma R_{q,c} + (1 - \gamma) T_c \qquad (5)$$

The constant γ determines the amount of personalization that we wish to factor in to the search results. A value of $\gamma = 0$ would result in completely ignoring the other users' perception of the content, while a value of $\gamma = 1$ will result in a completely community oriented view of the social ranking, ignoring any personal biases of the query creator.

6.1 Computing the Social Rank

The computation of the social rank takes the identity of the query creator and the content creator in account. If the query Q is created by u_q and the content that matches the query is set $C = \{c_1, c_2, ...c_M\}$ where each content is created by u_ci, then the social rank S_{ci} for each content in the set C can be computed as follows:

$$\begin{aligned} u_q &\leftarrow Q \\ C &\leftarrow Q \\ loop: & \\ u_{ci} &\leftarrow c_i \\ S_{ci} &\leftarrow \gamma R_{uq,ci} + (1-\gamma)T_{ci} \\ while\ i < M & \end{aligned}$$

The index stores the values of R and T along with the content. So once the relevant content set C that has the query terms is determined, there is an extra step of identifying the corresponding user who created this content. Once the content creator (referred to as u_{ci} in the above algorithm), the social rank computation is straightforward. The social rank is computed for all the documents that had the query term and then the order is sorted and the top few socially most relevant results can then be presented to the user in response to the query Q.

7. EXPERIMENTS

Section 5 propose that relationship R and trust T are effective measures to capture the social structure of the community that has the query creator and the content creator. However the intuition that these parameters are effective enough to determine the social structure needs to be verified. We conducted an experiment with 15 users of the system and evaluated if the algorithm scores have a correlation with what the users perceive of the social structure.

The experiment was conducted in three very different parts. The first part involved interviewing 15 the farmers and asking them questions that lead us to derive their social structure — within the context of the Spoken Web. We also had the demographics information of all the 250 users in terms of their location. The second part of the experiment was to use this demographic information in addition to the interview answers to determine the social structure in the real-world. This provided us the baseline of the social structure. The third part involved mining of 2 years of log data of the 15 query users and the 250 content users in the community to calculate the R and T scores for these 15 users.

7.1 Farmer Interviews and Demographics

We conducted a subjective study to determine the content preferences from 15 farmers. Their age ranged from 18 years to 49 years, with a mean of 33 years. They completed a mean of 11 years of formal education, wherein only one farmer was illiterate (though he was number literate and so could operate the basic phone features).

Following were the questions that we asked from these farmers:

1. Name the experts whose answers you value the most?
2. Which fellow farmers' questions you value the most?
3. Are you more interested in questions and answers pertaining to your region - your taluka (town) or not?
4. Name the people whose questions you listen carefully?

12 farmers provided specific names in response to the first question. Others did not remember the names. Except for 4 farmers, none other could suggest names of fellow farmers in response to question 2. Most people had problems associating names with content, that too when asked in a spontaneous interview. 10 farmers answered the third question in an affirmative – which means that they were more interested in the content that is relevant to their geography. 6 farmers could provide names with respect to the last question. The 250 registered users to the system were from 18 different districts, which in turn spanned 18 different talukas (towns). This span across these many districts ensured that we had sufficient variety in the social structure.

7.2 Correlation with the Relationship Scores

Figure 2 shows the R score for the 15 users with whom we had conducted the subjective interview. The lines against each user shows the R score calculated according to Equation 1. We plot the top 5 scores against each user and this range is shown by the line. The blue colored blobs show the R scores for the names of farmers who the subjects had spoken about in the interview.

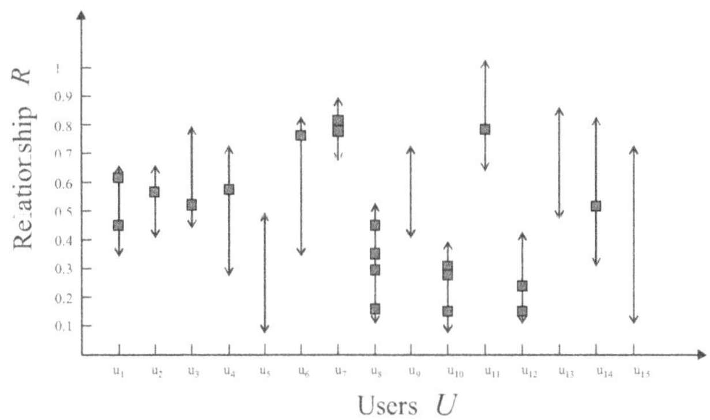

Figure 2: The R score plotted against what the farmers perceive as important people in the community.

In most cases, the top 5 results of the R score consists of the farmer names that were spoken. This suggests that the R score is able to determine with a high accuracy the content from the farmers which the subjects considered as *important*. Since some farmers did not speak out any names, there is no blob against their line. This was the case with u_5 and u_9. However u_{13} and u_{15} had spoken of the farmer names that they consider as important, but the R score for those was not in the top 5 list and so there is no blob against those names. These two cases can be considered as a failure of the R measure to determine the social importance.

7.3 Correlation with the Trust Scores

We calculated the community trust score T for each of the 250 farmers who are registered to the system. Figure 3 shows the T score plotted with the highest scored user being on the left, with others following towards right in the descending order of their T score. The T score for a large number of users is 0 since they never created any content and so on one ever listened to their content.

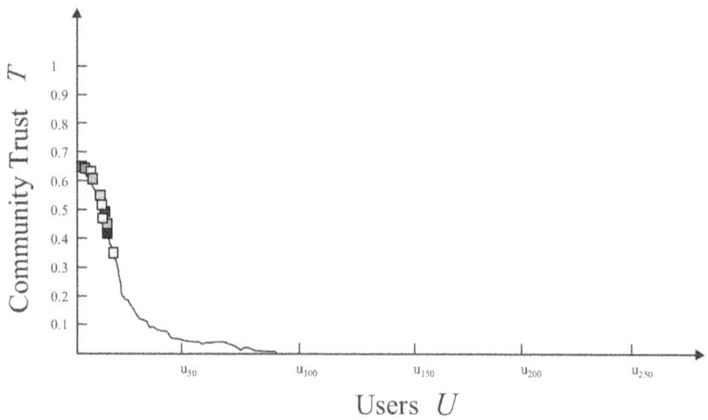

Figure 3: The T score for all the 250 registered users.

The circled entries show the 14 people whose names came up in the subjective interview with the 15 farmers. The fact that these 14 *trusted* people are in the top 10% percentile of the T value suggests that Equation 4 is able to determine the community trust to a considerable extent. *The fact that the R and T scores for farmers whose names appeared in the subjective interview establishes that the measures use to derive the social structure has merits.*

8. CONCLUSION AND FUTURE WORK

In this paper we introduced the concept of social ranking for the Spoken Web. It uses the real-world social structure and argues that the content that interests users is influenced by the relationship between the content seeker and the content creator. We then establish that it is possible to extract the social structure by mining the browsing history of a community of users. We present an algorithm to rank content based on this structure. The social ranking technique has been effectively applied to one particular instance of a Spoken Web community of 250 users that are a reasonable representation of of low-literacy users in developing countries.

Though we have developed the social ranking algorithm, its effectiveness in a search application needs to be tested extensively. Further, we will have to compare the social ranking technique with another standard baseline technique such as the page rank and derive relative improvements. However the initial results reported in the paper clearly establish the importance of the concepts of social ranking in the context of Spoken Web.

9. REFERENCES

[1] S. Agarwal, A. Kumar, A. A. Nanavati, and N. Rajput. Content Creation and Dissemination by-and-for Users in Rural Areas. In *ICTD*, April 2009.

[2] S. Agarwal, A. Kumar, A. A. Nanavati, and N. Rajput. Organizational, Social and Executional Implications in Delivering ICT Solutions: A Telecom Web Case-study. In *ICTD*, December 2010.

[3] J. Ajmera, A. Joshi, S. Mukherjee, N. Rajput, S. Sahay, M. Shrivastava, and K. Shrivastava. Two Stream Indexing for Spoken Web Search. In *WWW*, 2011.

[4] A. Bruns. *Blogs, Wikipedia, Second Life, and Beyond: From Production to Produsage* . Peter Lang Pub Inc, 2008.

[5] C. Chelba and A. Acero. Position specific posterior lattices for indexing speech. In *ACL*, 2005.

[6] T. K. Chia, K. C. Sim, H. Li, and H. T. Ng. A lattice-based approach to query-by-example spoken document retrieval. In *SIGIR*, 2008.

[7] P.-A. Chirita, D. Olmedilla, and W. Nejdl. Pros: A personalized ranking platform for web search. In *AH'04: Adaptive Hypermedia and Adaptive Web-Based Systems*, 2004.

[8] M. de Kunder. Daily Estimated Size of the World Wide Web. http://www.worldwidewebsize.com/, Last accessed on 20 May 2011.

[9] B. Geng, L. Yang, C. Xu, and X.-S. Hua. Ranking model adaptation for domain-specific search. In *CIKM*, 2009.

[10] B. Hughes and A. Kamat. A metadata search engine for digital language archives. *Digital Libraries Magazine*, 11(2), 2005.

[11] S. Kameshwaran, V. Pandit, S. Mehta, N. Viswanadham, and K. Dixit. Outcome aware ranking in interaction networks. In *CIKM*, 2010.

[12] D. Kirkpatrick. *The Facebook Effect: The Inside Story of the Company That Is Connecting the World.* Simon & Schuster, 2010.

[13] A. Kumar, N. Rajput, S. Agarwal, D. Chakraborty, and A. A. Nanavati. Organizing the Unorganized – Employing IT to Empower the Under-privileged. In *WWW*, April 2008.

[14] A. Kumar, N. Rajput, D. Chakraborty, S. Agarwal, and A. A. Nanavati. WWTW: A World Wide Telecom Web for Developing Regions. In *ACM SIGCOMM Workshop on NSDR*, Aug 2007.

[15] G. Mishne, D. Carmel, R. Hoory, A. Roytman, and A. Soffer. Automatic analysis of call-center conversations. In *CIKM*, 2005.

[16] L. Page, S. Brin, R. Motwani, and T. Winograd. The pagerank citation ranking: Bringing order to the web. *Technical Report, Stanford University Database Group*, 1998.

[17] N. Patel, D. Chittamuru, A. Jain, P. Dave, and T. S. Parikh. Avaaj Otalo - A Field Study of an Interactive Voice Forum for Small Farmers in Rural India. In *CHI*, April 2010.

[18] A. Ranjan, R. Balakrishnan, and M. Chignell. Searching in audio: the utility of transcripts, dichotic presentation, and time-compression. In *CHI*, 2006.

[19] R. Sarvas, E. Herrarte, A. Wilhelm, and M. Davis. Metadata creation system for mobile images. In *MobiSys*, 2004.

[20] K.-P. Yee, K. Swearingen, L. Li, and M. Hearst. Faceted metadata for image search and browsing. In *CHI*, 2003.

Effects of Search Success on Search Engine Re-Use

Victor Hu
Department of Statistics
Stanford University
Stanford, CA 94305
vhu@stanford.edu

Maria Stone and Jan Pedersen
Microsoft Bing
65 La Avenida
Mountain View, CA 94043
{mariast, jpederse}@microsoft.com

Ryen W. White
Microsoft Research
One Microsoft Way
Redmond, WA 98052
ryenw@microsoft.com

ABSTRACT
People's experiences when interacting with online services affects their decisions on re-use. Users of Web search engines are primarily focused on obtaining relevant information pertaining to their query. Search engines that fail to satisfy users' information needs may find their market share to be negatively affected. However, despite its importance to search providers, the relationship between search success and search engine re-use is poorly understood. In this paper, we present a longitudinal log-based study with a large cohort of search engine users that quantifies the relationship between success and re-use of search engines. We use time series analysis to define two groups of users: stationary and non-stationary. We find that recent changes in satisfaction rate do correlate moderately with changes in rate of return for stationary users. For non-stationary users, we find that satisfaction and rate of return change together and in the same direction. We also find that some effects are stronger for a smaller player on the market than for a clear market leader, but both are affected. This is the first study to explore these issues in the context of Web search, and our findings have implications for search providers seeking to better understand their users and improving their experience.

Categories and Subject Descriptors
H.3.3 [**Information Search and Retrieval**]: *search process.*

General Terms
Experimentation, Measurement.

Keywords
Search success, user satisfaction, longitudinal log analysis.

1. INTRODUCTION
Search success is the primary goal of information seeking. Satisfaction may be a critical determinant of continued use of search engines, or a range of other goods or services, over time [1][17]. Indeed, research on search engine switching behavior has shown that satisfaction is important in predicting switching [12][30]. Research on the success-reuse relationship is necessary to help search providers better understand factors affecting their usage and improve the search experience for their users, retain and grow their user base, and increase revenue from search advertising.

While it is commonly assumed that user satisfaction with a search engine will lead to more frequent returns to that engine, there have been no previous attempts to characterize and document this relationship. General literature on the relationship between customer satisfaction and market share finds that some relationship exists [1], but the relationship between satisfaction and rate of return was never studied for Web search specifically. There has been some research on modeling engine usage patterns over time [19][24][30][33]. This work has focused on modeling engine loyalty, or predicting switching events or encouraging the use of multiple search engines. However, research is needed on the relationship between search satisfaction and engine re-use.

In this paper, we analyze log data gathered from the toolbar of a large commercial search engine for a random sample of users over a period of six months. We estimated search satisfaction from result clicks over 30 seconds in duration [7][8], and compute satisfaction ratio for each user for each week for each search engine. We also compute the rate of return to a search engine (total number of searches conducted on each search engine by each user for each week). We first use time series analysis to define two groups of users: (i) *stationary users* whose rate of return and satisfaction ratios remain stable over the course of 25 week duration (the vast majority of users), and (ii) *non-stationary users*, users for whom probability distribution for both rate of return and satisfaction ratios change over the study duration (a small minority of users). We investigate the relationship between satisfaction ratios and return behavior for stationary users, and users whose satisfaction ratio and rate of return are both changing. We also compare success and re-use dynamics across the major and minor engines.

The remainder of this paper is structured as follows. Section 2 describes related work. Section 3 describes the study that we performed, and the results are presented in Section 4. These results and their implications are discussed in Section 5.

2. RELATED WORK
There are four areas of prior work that are most relevant for this investigation: (i) customer satisfaction and loyalty, (ii) online metrics to measure the quality of user experience, (iii) defining search success based on online signals, and (iv) characterizing and predicting short- and long-term search engine switching behavior.

Customer Satisfaction and Loyalty: There is a large body of work regarding product or brand switching and the relationship between satisfaction and loyalty (e.g., [23]). Although customer satisfaction is the predominant metric used by companies to detect and manage defections to competitors [1], more recent research has found that knowledge of competitors and attitudinal and demographic factors, among other influences, can also play an important role [24]. Research in these areas has also shown that complete satisfaction is significantly more important than just satisfaction, and even satisfied customers may still defect [17].

Online User Experience Metrics: Since the business community focuses on user return rather than user satisfaction [4], it is not surprising then that most commercially available Web analytics packages (e.g., [9][25]) do not include metrics related to user satisfaction. Rodden *et al.* [27] refer to traditional business analytics-driven metrics as PULSE metrics (page views, uptime, latency, seven day active users, and earnings). While these metrics

CIKM'11, October 24–28, 2011, Glasgow, Scotland, UK.

may tell us how well a product or service is doing, it does not facilitate any links between user success and business success. To address this shortcoming, Rodden *et al.* propose an alternative framework for user-centric metrics, called HEART (happiness, engagement, adoption, retention, and task success). This suite of metrics focuses instead on user happiness. The authors recommend a process by which specific goals for a product can be articulated and measured, but this approach still does not make the connection between measures of user satisfaction (e.g., task success) and measures of retention and engagement (e.g., number of visits a week per user).

Online experimentation is useful to evaluate new features or new ranking methodologies [21][28], but it is unclear what metrics should be used. It is not unusual for these experiments to observe an increase in one kind of metric (e.g., task success), but also observe no change or a decrease in other metrics such as engagement. It is important to investigate whether an increase in task success leads to increased usage, for what users and under what circumstances. That is the goal of the research that we present.

***Search Success in Online Experimentation*:** One significant obstacle to overcome in using online metrics is selecting a reliable measure of success using only online signals. Search success is subjective and frequently cannot be inferred from logs alone [11]. Many different sources of information need to be used to establish with certainty that a search was successful. Extensive literature exists on trying to derive indicators of task success or failure from online user behavior. In search, specifically, several fruitful approaches have been tried. One approach is to correlate behavior with either self-reported success [8] or labels of success provided by expert judges [7][15]. Early investigations correlated self-reported measures of search satisfaction with implicit signals, such as clicks and dwell time for clicks [8]. More recently, a sequence of user actions in a session was presented to an independent judge, who determined if a user was successful [15]. These labels can then be learned from online signals, such as click order, click dwell time, and click sequence. A similar methodology was employed to define user frustration [7]. One clear association that emerged from these early investigations is that longer clicks are more likely indicative of search success than shorter clicks.

***Search Engine Switching*:** Heath and White [16] developed models for predicting switching within search sessions. White and Dumais [18] used log analysis and a survey to characterize search engine switching behavior, and used query, session, and user features to predict engine switching. Guo *et al.* [13] used a browser plugin to capture people's motivations for engine switching. Their findings show that dissatisfaction was the most common rationale for switching. Mukhopadhyay *et al.* [24] found that dissatisfaction with search engine results had both short-term and long-term effects on search engine choice. Juan and Chang [19] looked at weekly search engine switching behavior as a predictor of market share. They found that user engagement, engine preferences, market share and number of search sessions are positively correlated.

The question left unanswered by Juan and Chang's study is what will drive engagement for a search engine. Many different factors impact the rate of user return—there are seasonality changes and sudden, unexpected disruptions in usage patterns due to users' history or events around them. With so few search engine choices, most users are settled in a stable pattern of usage and may have learned a seemingly optimal way to search, such that neither their satisfaction rates nor rate of return change significantly. A better understanding of the relationship between search success and rate of return can help search engines better understand users' decision making processes and help those engines more effectively tailor the services they offer and more accurately measure their impact.

We now present a novel methodology for detecting and describing the relationship between satisfaction and engine rate of return[1].

3. DATA AND METHODOLOGY

We describe the log data used to perform our longitudinal study, the methods used to estimate searcher satisfaction from those data, and the methods to study the satisfaction-return relationship.

3.1 Log Data

The data that we use in this analysis is the same as the data underlying prior work by White and Dumais [30]. We analyzed six months of interaction logs from September 2008 through February 2009 inclusive. The logs came from hundreds of thousands of consenting users through a widely-distributed browser toolbar. To remove variability caused by geographic and linguistic variation in search behavior, included entries were from the English speaking United States locale. From these logs we extracted *search sessions*. Every session began with a query issued to the Google, Yahoo!, or Microsoft Live Search Web search engines, and could contain further queries or Web page visits, including search engine result page (SERP) clicks and post SERP click navigation. A session ended if the user was idle for a period of more than 30 minutes. Similar criteria have been used previously to demarcate search sessions in search log data (e.g., [30]).

3.2 Estimating Searcher Satisfaction

Given the large number of searchers and search queries, we needed an automated way of estimating search satisfaction with search engine results. To do this, we use a searcher's dwell time on a clicked result as our primary indicator of satisfaction. Dwell time was computed as the difference between page load times in the logs of subsequent pages in a search session. This definition of search satisfaction is justified by prior findings that longer clicks are more likely to be successful clicks [7][8][21]. Search satisfaction in this study is defined as at least one click of 30 or more seconds following a query. The *satisfaction ratio* for each user for each week for each search engine is the ratio of the number of queries with search satisfaction and the total number of queries for that week, for that user, and for that engine. We also compute total number of queries issued on each engine by each user for each week as number of returns to the search engine. We refer to these query counts as the *return rate* in the rest of the paper.

3.3 Methodology

We focus on how the satisfaction with the engine itself impacts the rate of return to that engine. It is likely that satisfaction with a competitor may also be a factor in search engine usage, as well as many other external factors that may be near impossible for us to study remotely using search engine logging. We wanted to first examine satisfaction with the search engine itself and rate of return to that engine. Our overarching goal was to develop a methodology for understanding how a short-term behavioral marker (search satisfaction) impacts long-term return behavior.

As a first step, we performed time series analysis of both search satisfaction ratio and number of returns (number of searches a week) for all users over the nearly six-month duration of the study

[1] Note that for the purposes of our analysis we use search satisfaction as a proxy for search success in the remainder of this paper.

for each search engine. This was necessary to understand whether both or either of the variables changed systematically over the course of 25 week duration of the study. The data from all users of the major engine and all users of minor engine were included into the analysis. The minor and major engines were a subset selected from the three search engines present in our data (i.e., Google, Yahoo!, and Live Search). We computed summary indices of search satisfaction and rates of return for every user for every week in the logs. There were a total of 111,908 users of the major search engine who had non-zero number of returns and non-zero satisfaction rate for at least one of the 25 weeks included in this data analysis, and 95,969 users of the minor search engine who met the same standard. We also identified the two user groups—*stationary* and *non-stationary*—that are central to our study of the satisfaction-return relationship. Stationary users have unchanging search satisfaction ratio and number of returns processes; non-stationary users have both processes changing over the 25 weeks.

As a second step, we performed separate analyses on stationary and non-stationary users. Rate of return and satisfaction both constitute time series data. When both time series are stationary processes (that is, they are fluctuating but not changing over time around a fixed value), standard regression analysis is appropriate to understand whether the two series are related. However, when time series data are changing over time (non-stationary processes), regression analysis is not appropriate because the assumptions behind standard regression and correlation analysis are violated, and the expected value of the correlation coefficient under the null hypothesis is no longer zero [10]. We defined groups as follows:

Stationary users: We used a general linear model constructed with each week's data to understand if changes in satisfaction led to changes in rates of return. We computed a change in satisfaction ratio for each user for each week relative to the mean satisfaction ratio, obtained over the study duration. We also computed change in rate of return, both relative to the mean return rate for each user and relative to previous week's rate of return. The formulae that were used are presented in the analysis section later in the paper.

Non-stationary users: We performed co-integration analysis to understand if changes in satisfaction ratio and rate of return are related (co-occur in time-series) [6][10]. Co-integration analysis was created specifically to deal with spurious correlation when dealing with changing time series data. This analysis determines whether or not any linear combination of these two variables is stationary. Suppose $Y(t)$ is the number of return process, $X(t)$ is the satisfaction ratio process. A test for co-integration will first regress $Y(t)$ on $X(t)$ to get a coefficient ß. If ß is above zero, then there is a positive relationship between $X(t)$ and $Y(t)$. Once ß is determined for each user, co-integration will test whether $Y(t) - ß \cdot X(t)$ is stationary. That is, co-integration will test if the leftover residual error in the regression exhibits any trends (up or down). If the error does *not* exhibit a trend, then all change in $Y(t)$ is accounted for by change in $X(t)$. For users for whom this is true, we can assume that the success-reuse correlation is real.

4. RESULTS OF DATA ANALYSIS

4.1 Aggregate Data Description

To understand whether or not overall user satisfaction ratio and the rate of return were associated, we looked at some basic descriptive statistics for satisfaction ratio and number of returns. The correlation between average satisfaction ratio and average return rate for all users across the full 25-week period is moderate and positive for the minor search engine (r=0.39, p<0.001), and weak and positive for the major search engine (r=0.12, p<0.001). The very presence of such differences suggests that satisfaction and usage may relate differently depending on the search engine.

Table 1 summarizes our data set and aspects of the search activity of those who used the major and/or minor search engine.

Table 1. Summary statistics of the 25-week data set. Standard deviation values are parenthesized where appropriate.

Statistic	Major engine	Minor engine
Number of users	111,908	95,969
Percentage of all queries	80.8%	19.2%
Avg. return rate [queries]	78.1 (sd=23.2)	33.3 (sd=16.6)
Avg. satisfaction ratio	0.34 (sd=0.04)	0.26 (sd=0.03)

There is an imbalance between the major and minor engines in the fraction of all queries observed in our data. Users also issue more queries on average per week to the major engine, and interestingly for this study, users of the major engine appear to experience significantly higher levels of satisfaction than the minor engine. All differences between the major and minor search engine are statistically significant at $p < 0.01$ using independent measures t-tests.

4.2 Time Series Analysis

The first component of our analysis involved treating both return rate and satisfaction ratio as time series. Time series are a set of observations arranged in chronological order according to the time at which they occurred. The characteristic property of a time series is the fact that the data are not generated independently, their dispersion may vary in time, they may exhibit a trend, and/or they may have cyclic components [11]. Since our data match this description, statistical procedures supposing independent and identically distributed data cannot be used to analyze our data.

The first task in our time series analysis is establishing if either of the variables in question (satisfaction or return) exhibits a trend. We performed time series analysis for each of the time series involved—return rate for each of the two search engines and satisfaction ratio for each of the two engines. We did this for each user to determine what proportion of the users meet our definition of stationary users: that the distribution for a given user remains time invariant, suggesting that the joint probability distribution is stable with a time shift. The behavioral implication is that the data fluctuates around this user's mean, but does not change over time.

We used the Kwiatkowski–Phillips–Schmidt–Shin (KPSS) test [22], with the alpha for statistical significance testing set to 0.05, to determine whether our 25-week data was stationary. Table 2 reports the percentage of users who had significant trends in both variables (non-stationary users), the percentage of users with no significant trends in either (stationary users) or who had significant trend in only one variable (satisfaction or return). "SAT" is used in the table and elsewhere an abbreviation for satisfaction.

Table 2 shows that most of the users in our data set (around 70%), on both of the engines are stationary with no changes in the satisfaction ratio of the return rate in the course of our study. We assign those users whose success and re-use patterns remain time invariant for the duration of the study to our groups of *stationary* users (one group per engine). Those users with trends in satisfaction and returns over time (around 5% of users on both engines) form our groups of *non-stationary* users (one group per engine).

Table 2. Results of time series analysis.

Analysis Outcome	Major Engine	Minor Engine
Both SAT ratio and return rate stationary	70.1%	76.6%
Only return rate changes	16.2%	13.9%
Only SAT ratio changes	8.9%	5.8%
Both SAT ratio and return rate non-stationary	4.6%	4.8%

We now present a more detailed analysis of two of the four groups identified in this section: stationary and non-stationary users. These groups differ the most in terms of the satisfaction and return relationship, and are hence most likely to offer meaningful differences out of the possible pairwise comparisons of groups.

4.3 Analyzing Stationary Users

Stationary users are those for whom neither the rate of return nor satisfaction ratio change directionally over time. For these users, simple linear regression is appropriate to understand the relationship between satisfaction and return. Given that the mean satisfaction itself does not change and neither does rate of return for these users, correlation between these values over time is likely to be near zero. An interesting question about these users is whether slight changes in satisfaction from their respective means correlates with slight changes in return relative to their respective means, either this week or in previous weeks. Another question is whether or not this week's return changes relative to previous week's return in response to changes in satisfaction ratio.

We defined two response variables ($R1$, $R2$) for each user:

$$R1 = \frac{Current\ Week\ Num.Returns - Mean\ Num.Returns}{Mean\ Num.Returns}$$

$$R2 = \frac{Current\ Week\ Num.Returns - Previous\ Week\ Num.Returns}{Mean\ Num.Returns}$$

The response variables are variants of the normalized changing number of returns for each week. $R1$ lets us study changes in the current week relative to the mean, whereas $R2$ lets us study changes in the current week relative to the previous week.

To capture the satisfaction ratio at different times, allowing us to look for time lag effects where changes in satisfaction may not be immediately reflected in return, we defined three interest variables ($F1$, $F2$, and $F3$) using the normalized changing satisfaction ratio:

$$F1 = \frac{Current\ Week\ SAT\ ratio - Mean\ SAT\ ratio}{Mean\ SAT\ ratio}$$

$$F2 = \frac{Previous\ Week\ SAT\ ratio - Mean\ SAT\ ratio}{Mean\ SAT\ ratio}$$

$$F3 = \frac{SAT\ ratio\ Two\ Weeks\ Ago - Mean\ SAT\ ratio}{Mean\ SAT\ ratio}$$

To examine the effect of the features on the response variables, we use simple linear regression. $R1$ is a change in rate of return this week relative to mean rate of return for this user. The analysis for the major engine and the minor engine on the market are summarized in the Table 3. In the table, R^2 denotes the standard coefficient of determination in a standard regression model and ß denotes the coefficient in the regression equation. ß is positive when increases in satisfaction ratios are associated with increases in return rate (when ß is negative it means the opposite).

Table 3. Overall effect of SAT change on return change in stationary users relative to 25-week mean.

Engine	R^2 for $F1$	ß for $F1$	R^2 for $F2$	ß for $F2$
Major engine	0.23	0.49	>0.000	-0.001
Minor engine	0.26	0.40	>0.000	0.006

For $R1$, only $F1$ is significant, and neither $F2$ nor $F3$ have any effect for either the major search engine or the minor engine. That means that a positive relationship between current week's normalized satisfaction ratio and current week's normalized return exists, but normalized satisfaction ratio from the previous week (or earlier) has no impact on this week's normalized return rate. Table 3 does not include $F3$ because coefficient is virtually zero and p-value well exceeds α (meaning non-significant).

We also performed similar analysis related to the change in return rate relative to previous week's return ($R2$). This additional analysis tells us how normalized changes in rate of return from week to week respond to changes in satisfaction ratio. The findings are summarized in Table 4 in the same format as the $R1$ analysis.

Table 4. Overall effect of satisfaction change on return change in stationary users relative to previous week's return.

Engine	R^2 for $F1$	ß for $F1$	R^2 for $F2$	ß for $F2$
Major Engine	0.11	0.48	0.14	-0.53
Minor Engine	0.13	0.40	0.14	-0.41

As we can see in the table above, for the response variable $R2$, the effects of $F1$ and $F2$ are nearly opposite (as indicated by the different signs for), and once again $F3$ has no effect. For stationary users, the current week's increase in satisfaction ratio helps lift the return, and the previous week's increase in satisfaction ratio makes return rate drop (perhaps since it causes previous week's return to be higher), and their effects almost cancel each other out. Any changes in satisfaction rate prior to the previous week appear to have no effect. Essentially, we can take from this analysis that although the satisfaction ratio and rate of return fluctuate together, the effect of any fluctuations is very short-lived.

4.4 Analyzing Non-Stationary Users

Given that around 5% of users of each search engine were non-stationary, if satisfaction ratio and return rate both changed, to what extent did they change together and in the same direction?

Figure 1 illustrates average satisfaction ratios and average rates of return for co-integrated and not co-integrated non-stationary users. The charts illustrate clearer trends for co-integrated users, especially on the minor search engine, suggesting (at least visually) that the co-integration analysis is successfully identifying users with a clearer relationship between satisfaction and return. However, these plots of averages across all users are only a summary, and do not tell the full story, especially since the co-integration analysis was performed individually for each user.

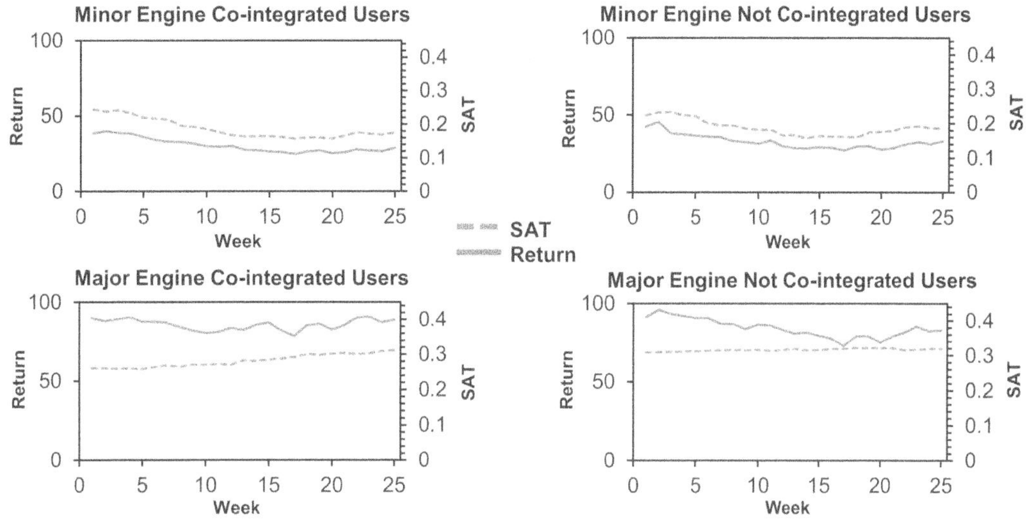

Figure 1. Average SAT and Return over Time for Co-integrated and Not Co-integrated users.

Table 5 shows the comparison between stationary users and non-stationary users for both search engines. The percentage in the left column is the fraction of users in each (user group, search engine) pair with a positive correlation between satisfaction and return. In the right column we show the percentage of users who were co-integrated, and for whom there may be a real relationship between satisfaction and return (per co-integration analysis).

Table 5. Results of regression analysis for all users and co-integration analysis for non-stationary users.

User Group and Search Engine	% of ß > 0 (positive correlations)	% of $Y(t) - ß \cdot X(t)$ (co-integrated users)
Non-stationary, minor engine	100.0%	70.6%
Non-stationary, major engine	100.0%	41.8%
Stationary, major engine	33.9%	n/a
Stationary, minor engine	74.6%	n/a

For non-stationary users, the relationship between satisfaction and return is uniformly positive. In contrast, stationary users do not react consistently to changes in satisfaction ratio over 25 weeks. For the minor search engine, 70.6% of the non-stationary processes show the pattern of co-integration. That means that for those users we can expect changes in rate of return and changes in satisfaction to co-occur. If we are tracing market share, and given that 4.8% of the users are changing their search behavior, we can be reasonably confident that 4.8% × 70.6% = 3.4% of all the users of the minor search engine will increase (or decrease) their long term rate of return as a result of increase (or decrease) in their satisfaction ratio. The result for major engine (the market winner) is a lot weaker. If roughly 4.6% of users are non-stationary, only 4.6% × 41.8% = 1.9% of that engine's users will increase (decrease) their long-term return rate as a result of increase (decrease) in success.

This analysis may be useful to carry out periodically to understand how many users of each search engine fall into the non-stationary category, and for how many of them the two variables are co-integrated. This underscores the opportunity that the minor engine has to gain more traffic by improving search satisfaction for its users. It also suggests that improving search satisfaction may not result in similar gains for the major search engine in the market.

5. IMPLICATIONS AND FUTURE WORK

We characterized the success-reuse relationship for two groups of users. We showed that changes in search satisfaction ratio and changes in rate of return are positively correlated when these two variables are relatively stable over time (as they are for the vast majority of *stationary* users, who comprise 70-75% of our all users) and when both variables change (as they are for a small minority of *non-stationary* users, totaling 5% of all users). For these non-stationary users, the satisfaction ratio and rate of return change in the same direction. For a sizeable proportion of the changing users, the change in satisfaction ratio variable completely accounts for the change in rate of return. This proportion is higher for the minor player on the market than for a market winner. This is a place where the minor engine could gain (or lose) more market share than the major engine.

One explanation for why a stronger relationship was observed for the minor player may be that the average satisfaction ratio for the minor player was much lower. It may very well be that once the minor market player improves search performance to be equivalent to the market winner, it will be harder to see movements in rates of return in response to changes in satisfaction.

An important limitation of the research presented is that we relied upon a single, rudimentary definition of search success, namely result clicks of at least 30 seconds in duration. Although this definition has been used extensively in related work, online signals can be noisy and this measure in particular not normalized relative to user expectation or query difficulty. More difficult queries may result in fewer satisfied clicks, but users may adjust their expectations for such queries. To make further progress, we need to better understand how to adjust on-line signals of satisfaction for different levels of query difficulty. The information retrieval community has already studied the automatic estimation of query difficulty that could be useful here (e.g., [12]).

One area for future work is to understand whether more and less restrictive automatic definitions of search satisfaction (e.g., search engine switching behavior) exhibit the same relationship with rates of return. Another, more laborious approach, may be to identify satisfaction by manually labeling clicked search results, rather than relying on a purely online definition. Specific metrics that take query difficulty into account already exist for relevance labels (such as *normalized discounted cumulative gain* [18]). Alternatively, we could deploy a browser plugin to gather satisfaction judgments from volunteers *in-situ* at session time, as has been used previously in similar scenarios in the search domain [8][13].

In this paper we demonstrate that satisfaction with a search engine can contribute to users' propensity to use and re-use its service. There are many factors that drive increases in market share and search volume that are not connected to satisfaction with search. These factors may include advertising campaigns, browser defaults and toolbars that alter the convenience and availability of the search engine services when and where users may need this service, etc. Although the analysis shows a correlation between satisfaction and engine re-use, it does not prove causation. Only through comprehensive experimentation can we offer a convincing demonstration of causality. Such experiments are not always possible, especially remotely at Web scale, and a notion of *statistical causality* [10] might have useful applications here.

Tracking rates of return and better understanding searchers' rationales is critically important for engine success. Reliable changes in rates of return are slow to accumulate and take a long time to track. Finding short-term surrogate measures that are associated with long term changes could be useful to rapidly estimate long-term implications of feature additions or ranking enhancements.

REFERENCES

[1] Anderson, E.W. and Sullivan, M.W. (1993). The antecedents and consequences of customer satisfaction for firms. *Marketing Science* 12: 125–143.

[2] Anderson, R.E. and Srinivasan, S.S. (2003). E-satisfaction and e-loyalty: a contingency framework. *Psychology and Marketing*, 20(3): 123–138.

[3] Bolton, R.N. (1998). A dynamic model of the duration of the customer's relationship with a continuous service provider: the role of satisfaction. *Marketing Science*, 17(1): 45–65.

[4] Burby, J.Y. and Atchson, S. (2007). *Actionable Web Analytics*. Wiley Publishing, Inc., Indianapolis, IN.

[5] Capraro, A.J., Broniarczyk, S., and Srivastava, R.K. (2003). Factors influencing the likelihood of customer defection: the role of consumer knowledge. *Journal of the Academy of Marketing Science*, 31(2): 164–175.

[6] Engle, R. F. and Granger, C.W.J. (1987). Co-integration and error correction: representation, estimation, and testing, *Econometrica*, 55: 251–276.

[7] Field, H., Allan, J., and Jones, R. (2010). Predicting searcher frustration. *Proc. SIGIR*, 34–41.

[8] Fox, S., Karnawat, K., Mydland, M., Dumais, S.T., and White, T. (2005). Evaluating implicit measures to improve the search experience. *ACM TOIS*, 23(2): 147–168.

[9] Google Analytics (http://www.google.com/analytics).

[10] Granger, C.W.J. (2003). The Nobel Prize Lecture. http://nobelprize.org/nobel_prizes/economics/laureates/2003/granger-lecture.html

[11] Grimes, C., Tang, D., and Russell, D.M. (2007). Query logs alone are not enough. *Proc. Query Log Analysis Workshop*.

[12] Guo, Q. White, R.W., Dumais, S., Wang, J. and Anderson, B. (2010). Predicting query performance using query, result, and user interaction features. *Proc. RIAO*.

[13] Guo, Q., White, R.W., Zhang, Y., Anderson, B., and Dumais, S.T. (2011). Why searchers switch: Understanding and predicting engine switching rationales. *Proc. SIGIR*, 335–344.

[14] Hamilton, J.D. (1994). *Time Series Analysis*. Princeton University Press, Princeton, NJ.

[15] Hassan, A., Jones, R., and Klinkner, K. (2010). Beyond DCG: user behavior as a predictor of a successful search. *Proc. WSDM*, 221–230.

[16] Heath, A.P. and White, R.W. (2008). Defection detection: predicting search engine switching. *Proc. WWW*, 1173–1174.

[17] Jones, W.E. and Sasser, T.O. (1995). Why satisfied customers defect. *Harvard Business Review* (November-December)

[18] Järvelin, K. and Kekäläinen, J. (2000). IR evaluation methods for retrieving highly relevant documents. *Proc. SIGIR*, 41–48.

[19] Juan, Y.F. and Chang, C.C. (2005). An analysis of search engine switching behavior using click streams. *Proc. WINE*, 806–815.

[20] Keaveney, S.M. and Parthasarathy, M. (2001). Customer switching behavior in online services: an exploratory study of the role of selected attitudinal, behavioral, and demographic factors. *Journal of the Academy of Marketing Science*, 29(4): 374–390.

[21] Kohavi, R., Henne, R.M., and Sommerfield, D. (2007). Practical guide to controlled experiments on the web: listen to your customers not to the hippo. *Proc. SIGKDD*, 259–267.

[22] D. Kwiatkowski, P. C. B. Phillips, P. Schmidt, and Y. Shin (1992): Testing the null hypothesis of stationarity against the alternative of a unit root. *Journal of Econometrics*, 54: 159–178.

[23] Mittal, B. and Lassar, W.M. (1998). Why do customers switch? the dynamics of satisfaction versus loyalty. *Journal of Services Marketing*, 12(3): 177–194.

[24] Mukhopadhyay, T., Rajan, U., and Telang, R. (2004). Competition between internet search engines. *Proc. Hawaii International Conference on System Sciences*.

[25] Omniture (http://www.omniture.com).

[26] *Pew Internet and American Life Project: Search Engine Users* (2005) (accessed December 2010)

[27] Rodden, K., Hutchinson, H., and Fu, X. (2010). Measuring the user experience on a large scale user-centric metrics for web applications. *Proc. SIGCHI*, 2395–2398.

[28] Tang, D., Agrawal, A., O'Brien, D, and Meyer, M. (2010). Overlapping experiment infrastructure: more better faster experiments. *Proc. SIGKDD*, 17–26.

[29] White, R.W. and Drucker, S.M. (2007). Investigating behavioral variability in Web search. *Proc. WWW*, 21–30.

[30] White, R.W. and Dumais, S.T. (2009). Characterizing and predicting search engine switching behavior. *Proc. CIKM*, 87–96.

[31] White, R.W., Kapoor, A., and Dumais, S.T. (2010). Modeling long-term search engine usage. *Proc. UMAP*, 28–39.

[32] White, R.W. and Morris, D. (2007). Investigating the querying and browsing behavior of advanced search engine users. *Proc. SIGIR*, 255–262.

[33] White, R.W., Richardson, M., Bilenko, M., and Heath, A.P. (2008). Enhancing web search by promoting multiple search engine use. *Proc. SIGIR*, 43–50.

Enriching Textbooks with Images

Rakesh Agrawal Sreenivas Gollapudi Anitha Kannan Krishnaram Kenthapadi
Search Labs, Microsoft Research
Mountain View, CA, USA
{rakesha, sreenig, ankannan, krisken}@microsoft.com

ABSTRACT

Textbooks have a direct bearing on the quality of education imparted to the students. Therefore, it is of paramount importance that the educational content of textbooks should provide rich learning experience to the students. Recent studies on understanding learning behavior suggest that the incorporation of digital visual material can greatly enhance learning. However, textbooks used in many developing regions are largely text-oriented and lack good visual material. We propose techniques for finding images from the web that are most relevant for augmenting a section of the textbook, while respecting the constraint that the same image is not repeated in different sections of the same chapter. We devise a rigorous formulation of the image assignment problem and present a polynomial time algorithm for solving the problem optimally. We also present two image mining algorithms that utilize orthogonal signals and hence obtain different sets of relevant images. Finally, we provide an ensembling algorithm for combining the assignments. To empirically evaluate our techniques, we use a corpus of high school textbooks in use in India. Our user study utilizing the Amazon Mechanical Turk platform indicates that the proposed techniques are able to obtain images that can help increase the understanding of the textbook material.

Categories and Subject Descriptors

H.3 [**Information Storage and Retrieval**]: Information Search and Retrieval

General Terms

Algorithms, Experimentation, Human Factors

Keywords

Education, Textbooks, Data Mining, Image Mining, Text Augmentation

1. INTRODUCTION

Education is the key for improving the economic well-being of people living in developing regions [1, 24]. While the problem of providing high-quality education is multi-faceted and complex [8, 50], textbooks have been shown to provide the most cost-effective means of improving the educational quality [11, 16, 26]. They are the primary conduits for delivering content knowledge to the students and the teachers base their lesson plans primarily on the material given in textbooks [18, 55]. Unfortunately, textbooks in many developing countries often suffer from the lack of clarity as well as the inadequacy of information provided [2, 44].

It has been shown that the linking of encyclopedic information to educational material can improve both the quality of the knowledge acquired and the time needed to obtain such knowledge [12]. In [4], a decision model has been proposed for diagnosing deficient sections of a textbook. In [5, 40, 41, 43], techniques have been proposed for finding articles from the web with which such sections should be augmented.

We extend prior work and propose techniques for augmenting textbooks with links to selective, highly relevant images. Our work has been instigated by the research in the learning literature showing that the use of visual materials enhances learning, not only by enabling retention of information but also by promoting comprehension and transfer [35, 39, 48]. Some researchers even suggest that visual materials should be given as much attention as text and not viewed as merely supporting the text [36].

The learning literature informs us that any supplementary material is most effective when it is presented in close proximity to the main material [9]. We therefore find images that are relevant to a particular section of the textbook. In order to avoid undue cognitive burden, we select only a small number of images that collectively best aid the understanding, shunning repetition of an image in different sections of the same chapter.

Our solution has three components:

1. *Image Assignment.* Given a set of candidate images and their relevance scores for every section of a chapter, this component assigns images to various sections in a way that maximizes the relevance score for the chapter while maintaining the constraints that no section has been assigned more than a certain maximum number of images and no image is used more than once in the chapter. We provide a polynomial time algorithm for implementing the optimizer.

2. *Image Mining.* This component comprises of algorithms that mine the web for images relevant to a particular section and provide a ranked list of top k images along with their relevance scores. It is preferable to have algorithms that make use of orthogonal signals in their search for images in order to have a broad selection of images to choose from. We provide two specific algorithms, namely AFFINITY and COMITY, which satisfy the above properties.

3. *Image Ensembling.* Since the relevance scores provided by different image mining algorithms will in general be incomparable, the assignment of images to different sections of a chapter needs to be performed separately for each algorithm. The image ensembling component aggregates the ranked lists of image assignments to produce the final result.

   While it is possible to use any rank aggregation algorithm, we wanted a voting scheme that considers all the elements of a ranked list and provides consensus ranking. The popular Borda's method fits the bill [52]. Ensembling is done sequentially within a chapter, starting from the first section. Top images selected for a section are eliminated from the pool of available images for the remaining sections. The image assignment is then rerun, followed by an ensembling for the next section.

In order to assess the usefulness of our proposal, we conducted a user study employing the Amazon Mechanical Turk platform [29]. The corpus used in this evaluation comprises of the high school textbooks published by the Indian National Council of Educational Research and Training (NCERT). We wanted to use a corpus from a developing country and settled on the NCERT books because of their ready availability online. However, our techniques are not country-dependent. We consider fourteen textbooks from grades IX to XII, covering eight subjects, seventy chapters, and over a thousand sections. The results of this study indicate that the proposed techniques are able to discover images that can help increase the understanding of the textbook material.

Scope of the paper. We present techniques for proposing images with which a section of a textbook can be augmented, but do not discuss specific mechanisms for integrating the augmentations into the textbook. Our techniques could be integrated into authoring tools for helping textbook authors decide what images to use when writing or revising a book. They can also be used for creating supplementary material that is distributed with the paper version of the books. Furthermore, there are ongoing efforts aimed at creating platforms and inexpensive devices for distributing books in a digital form (see, for example, the use of interactive DVDs as an educational platform [17], inexpensive e-book readers [3, 7], and mobile learning devices [31]). Our work fits quite naturally with these efforts.

Complementary approaches and issues that merit serious investigation, but are beyond the scope of this paper include: (a) refining and enhancing the results produced by our techniques using collaboration and crowdsourcing [2, 53], (b) implications for royalty sharing and intellectual property rights [14, 20], and (c) integration with other interventions for improving the learning outcomes [19, 45].

Organization of the paper. The rest of the paper is structured as follows. We discuss related work in §2. The particular algorithms used in our solution are described in §3. The results of experimental evaluation are presented in §4. We conclude with a summary and directions for future work in §5.

2. RELATED WORK

There has been research on translating short textual sentences to pictures [42]. The work in [10] uses semantic representation of the text to synthesize three-dimensional scenes from English text. Such translations work well only with descriptive sentences that can be effectively mapped to corresponding object models. Our focus is on finding a few representative images relevant for a section of a textbook, not on synthesizing scenes from sentences, which leads to different techniques.

The goal of research in story picturing is to find a set of pictures to describe a fragment of a text. In [32], key phrases are extracted from the text to retrieve matching images, which are then ranked by weighting image region similarity and phrase overlaps. In [59], the picturable key phrases are extracted from a given text; the picturability of a phrase is measured as the ratio of the frequencies under regular web vs. image search. Each picturable phrase is then associated with an image using image search coupled with computer vision and finally graphics is used to spatially arrange the images to represent the story. In [15], the meaning of images and their surrounding texts are represented jointly as probability distributions over a set of latent topics, which are then used to find pictures to illustrate a story. While close in spirit, the setting and the solution techniques in these works and ours are quite different.

The rich literature on image retrieval in response to key word queries is relevant for the image mining component of our work. Indeed, one of our mining algorithms (COMITY) issues queries to the commercial search engines as a subroutine. We refer the reader to [13] for a comprehensive survey of recent advances in image retrieval. While there is ground breaking research on retrieving images solely based on the content of the images, most image search engines work by indexing associated metadata and matching keyword queries with the stored metadata. The metadata may include a description of the image, the filename of the image, the anchor text pointing to the image, the queries that led to a click on the image, or the text adjacent to the image. The ImageCLEF competition, for example, uses an image repository consisting of Wikipedia images that have been tagged with the associated title and description of the image extracted from the Wikipedia page for the image [46].

Several web based applications (e.g. Flickr) provide facilities for any web user to tag pictures hosted on their websites with textual descriptions that can serve as metadata for the image. Lui von Ahn developed an interactive ESP game in which the players labeled images while playing the game [56]. There is rich body of image processing research on automatically linking text to image. The survey in [6] distinguishes the task of annotation from that of correspondence. The former attempts to predict the annotation of an entire image using all information present, whereas the latter attempts to associate particular words with particular image substructures. There is also work on extracting image regions containing text that can then be fed to an optical character recognition module [30, 38].

Related work also includes the proposal in [2] to create an education network to harness the collective efforts of educators, parents, and students to collaboratively enhance the quality of educational material. Some websites (e.g. Notemonk.con) allow students to download textbooks, ask questions on a topic, and annotate books for quick reference. Several institutions are making the videos of the course lectures available through Internet and there are websites (e.g. EducationPortal.com) that aggregate links to them. We view these crowdsourcing efforts as complementary approaches to improving the quality of textbooks.

3. SYSTEM DESIGN

We now describe the design of our system. We first present the image assignment component consisting of an optimization problem, followed by two algorithms for mining relevant images from the web, and finally the image ensembling component.

3.1 Image Assignment

Given a set of candidate images relevant to the various sections of a chapter and their relevance scores, the goal of the image assignment component is to allocate to each section the most relevant images, while respecting the constraints that each section is not augmented with too many images and that each image is used no more than once in a chapter. The rationale for these constraints is that an augmentation of a section with too many images will put undue cognitive burden on the reader while the repetition of an image across sections in the same chapter would be redundant for the reader.

First, a few notations. Let $I = \{1, 2, \ldots, n\}$ denote the set of images and $S = \{1, 2, \ldots, m\}$ denote the set of sections in a chapter. Let λ_{ij} denote the (non-negative) relevance score of image $i \in I$ for section $j \in S$ ($\lambda_{ij} = 0$ if the image i is not present in the candidate set of images for section j). Let K_j denote the maximum number of images that can be associated with section j. K_j could be either a fixed integer for all sections or a function of the length of the section j.

This problem admits a natural greedy algorithm. Sort the λ_{ij} values in decreasing order and go through them. At each step, the greedy algorithm picks the highest λ_{ij} value such that an image can still be assigned to section j (that is, less than K_j images have so far been assigned to j) and then assigns image i to section j. This process ends when either all sections have been assigned the maximum number of images or there are no more images to be assigned.

At a first glance, the greedy algorithm might seem optimal in terms of the sum of relevance scores of all assigned images. But the following counterexample shows that the optimal value can be substantially larger. Consider a chapter consisting of two sections and suppose that we want two images each for a section ($K_1 = K_2 = 2$). Represent by (i, λ) that image i's relevance score is λ. Let the top images and their relevance scores obtained by an image mining algorithm for various sections be as follows: $s_1 \leftarrow \langle(i_1, 1), (i_2, 1-\epsilon), (i_3, 1-3\epsilon)\rangle, s_2 \leftarrow \langle(i_2, 1-2\epsilon), (i_4, \epsilon), (i_5, \epsilon)\rangle$, where $\epsilon = 0.01$. Then the greedy assignment would be $s_1 \leftarrow \langle i_1, i_2\rangle, s_2 \leftarrow \langle i_4, i_5\rangle$ with a total score of $2 + \epsilon$. On the other hand, an optimal assignment is $s_1 \leftarrow \langle i_1, i_3\rangle, s_2 \leftarrow \langle i_2, i_4\rangle$ with a total score of $3 - 4\epsilon$.

Therefore, we instantiate the image assignment component as an optimization problem. We show that this optimization problem can be solved optimally in polynomial time and provide an efficient algorithm as part of the proof. The following is the statement of the optimization problem:

MAXRELEVANTIMAGEASSIGNMENT

$$\max \sum_{i \in I} \sum_{j \in S} x_{ij} \cdot \lambda_{ij} \quad (1)$$

s.t.

$$x_{ij} \in \{0, 1\} \ \forall i \in I \ \forall j \in S \quad (2)$$

$$\sum_{i \in I} x_{ij} \leq K_j \ \ \forall j \in S \quad (3)$$

$$\sum_{j \in S} x_{ij} \leq 1 \ \ \forall i \in I \quad (4)$$

Here, x_{ij} is an indicator variable that takes value 1 if image i is selected for section j and 0 otherwise. Eq. 2 captures this binary constraint. Eq. 3 ensures that the number of images assigned to a section is at most K_j. Eq. 4 enforces that each image is assigned to at most one section in a chapter. The optimization objective (Eq. 1) is the total relevance score for the chapter, defined as the sum over all sections of relevance scores of the images assigned to the section. Thus the goal of the optimization is to compute the binary variables x_{ij} such that the total relevance score for the chapter is maximized.

Algorithm 1 AFFINITY

Input: A textbook section j; Number of desired image results k; Number of desired closest articles from an authoritative external source t'; Number of desired concept phrases c.
Output: A list of top k image results from the authoritative source, along with value scores.

1: Obtain (up to) top c concept phrases from section j.
2: Obtain (up to) top t' closest articles from the authoritative external source, based on content similarity with section j.
3: Extract the set of images present in these t' articles, as well as the metadata associated with each image aggregated over all occurrences of the image.
4: For each image i, let n_{ij} := Number of articles in which image i appears, d_{ij} := Number of concept phrases contained in the metadata for image i, w_{ij} := Number of matching words from all concepts in the metadata for image i.
5: Assign the relevance score $\lambda_{ij} := n_{ij}^{w_1} \cdot d_{ij}^{w_2} \cdot w_{ij}^{w_3}$ for image i (w_1, w_2, w_3 determine the relative weight given to the three counts above).
6: Return top k images along with their λ_{ij} values.

THEOREM 3.1. MAXRELEVANTIMAGEASSIGNMENT *can be solved optimally in polynomial time.*

PROOF. The proof follows by showing an efficient reduction from MAXRELEVANTIMAGEASSIGNMENT to the MAXIMUM WEIGHTED BIPARTITE MATCHING problem [49], which admits an efficient polynomial time solution. Given an instance of MAXRELEVANTIMAGEASSIGNMENT, form a complete weighted bipartite graph $G = (V, E)$ as follows. Associate a node u_i with each image $i \in I$ and associate K_j nodes, $v_{j1}, v_{j2}, \ldots, v_{jK_j}$, with each section j. Create an edge between every image node and every section node copy. Weight of the edge (u_i, v_{jk}) is set to λ_{ij} for each $k \in \{1, 2, \ldots, K_j\}$, that is, each of the K_j edges joining an image i to the section j has the same weight, equal to the corresponding relevance score.

We observe that any feasible solution to MAXRELEVANTIMAGEASSIGNMENT corresponds to selecting a matching in G. Given a satisfying assignment of x_{ij}'s, we can obtain a matching in G by picking one of the K_j edges corresponding to any x_{ij} that is set to 1. Similarly, given any matching in G, there is a corresponding feasible solution. Further the objective of MAXRELEVANTIMAGEASSIGNMENT can be maximized by obtaining the maximum weight bipartite matching in G. As the MAXIMUM WEIGHTED BIPARTITE MATCHING problem can be solved optimally in $O(nm(n + m))$ time, it follows that MAXRELEVANTIMAGEASSIGNMENT can also be solved optimally in $O(nm(n + m))$ time. □

3.2 Image Mining

Here we give particulars of the AFFINITY and COMITY algorithms, the two algorithms used for obtaining the ranked list of top k images along with their relevance scores for a given section. Note that our system design admits various possible variants of these algorithms as well as additional image mining algorithms one could conceive.

Algorithm AFFINITY

The intuition behind this algorithm is the observation that the images included in an authoritative article relevant to a topic are often illustrative of the key concepts underlying the topic. We therefore find authoritative articles whose contents have high textual similarity with a given section of the book. We then extract images contained in these articles and use their relevance scores to find top k images for the section.

Algorithm 1 (AFFINITY) first obtains the key concept phrases present in a section as well as the closest authoritative articles from the web. Thus the key topics discussed in the section are available in the form of the concept phrases while the search space for images is refined to the set of articles with high document similarity to the section. The relevance score for an image is computed by analyzing the overlap between the concept phrases and the cumulative metadata associated with the various copies of the image present in the narrowed set of articles. The metadata for an image comprises of text adjacent to the image including caption and alternative text, filename of the image, anchor texts pointing to the image, and queries that led to clicks on the image. The scoring has desirable properties such as: (a) an image occurring in multiple articles gets a higher score, (b) an image whose metadata contains multiple concept phrases gets a higher score, and (c) an image whose metadata contains words from many concepts gets a higher score.

In the rest of this subsection, we provide implementation details of steps 1 and 2. If a textbook includes a back-of-the-book index [47], it can be used for obtaining concept phrases for a section. There is also rich literature on algorithmically extracting key phrases from a document that can inform the task of extracting key concepts from a section [33]. The current approaches primarily involve detection of the key phrases based on rules or statistical and learning methods. In the former, the structural properties of phrases form the basis for the rule generation. In the latter, the importance of a phrase is computed based on statistical properties (e.g., relative frequency, document frequency) of the phrase.

Our study of several textbooks from the developing regions revealed that they often do not include a back-of-the-book index, but the concept phrases typically consist of terminological noun phrases containing adjectives, nouns, and sometimes prepositions. It is uncommon for concepts to contain other parts of speech such as adverbs, conjunctions, or verbs. Following [34], we adopt the linguistic pattern A^*N^+, where A refers to an adjective and N a noun and use the algorithm from [5] to determine the top c concepts. Examples of concepts satisfying this pattern include "cumulative distribution function", "fiscal policy", and "electromagnetic radiation".

Early research on finding documents similar to a given document includes techniques based on relevance feedback [51], which were subsequently used to show similar results by some of the search engines [54]. Recent research includes the query by document work [58] that extracts key phrases and uses them as queries to search for similar documents (see also references therein). We index the corpus of authoritative articles using Lucene [25] and use its in-built scoring to retrieve the closest articles to a given textbook section.

Algorithm COMITY

One might think that one could simply use the text string of a section to query a commercial image search engine and obtain the relevant images. However, the current search engines do not perform well with long queries [28, 37]. Indeed, when we queried the search engines using even the first paragraph of a section, we got none or meaningless results. In one major stream of research on information retrieval with long queries, the focus is on selecting a subset of the query, while in another it is on weighting the terms of the query [57]. This body of research however is not designed to work for queries consisting of arbitrary textbook sections.

Algorithm 2 (COMITY) is based on using the key concepts present in a section to query the commercial image search engines. However, each concept phrase in isolation may not be representative of the section as a typical book section can discuss multiple concepts. Hence we form $\binom{c}{2} + \binom{c}{3}$ image search queries by combining two and three concept phrases each, in order to provide more context about the section. A relevant image for the section is likely to occur among the top results for many such queries. Thus, by aggregating the image result lists over all the combination queries, we end up boosting the relevance scores of very relevant images for the section. We further increase the coverage by obtaining and merging results across e different search engines. We treat each search engine as a blackbox [23, 28], that is, we have access to the ranking of results but do not have access to the internals of the search engine such as the score given to a document with respect to a query.

Aggregation across multiple lists is performed as follows. Each of (up to) t images in a result list is assigned a position-discounted score equal to $1/(p+\theta)$ where p denotes the position and θ is a smoothing parameter. For the same image occurring in multiple lists, the scores are added, weighted by a function f of the importance of the concept phrase present in the underlying query: $\lambda_{ij} := \sum_q f(\text{Importance scores of concept phrases used in } q) \times (1/(p(i,q,R(q))+\theta))$. Here the summation is over $e(\binom{c}{2} + \binom{c}{3})$ queries issued and $p(i,q,R(q))$ denotes the position of image i in the result list $R(q)$ for query q if i is present in $R(q)$ and ∞ otherwise. This choice is based on our empirical observation that an image occurring among the top results for multiple queries was more relevant to the section than an image that occurred among the top results for only one query.

Algorithm 2 COMITY

Input: A textbook section j; Number of desired image results k; Number of desired image search results per query t; Number of desired concept phrases c.

Output: A list of top k image results from web, along with relevance scores.

1: Obtain (up to) top c concept phrases from section j.
2: Form queries consisting of two and three concepts phrases each ($\binom{c}{2} + \binom{c}{3}$ queries in total).
3: Obtain (up to) top t image search results for each of the queries from e different search engines.
4: Aggregate over (potentially $e(\binom{c}{2} + \binom{c}{3})$) lists of images, to obtain λ_{ij} values for each image.
5: Return top k images along with their λ_{ij} values.

3.3 Image Ensembling

We next describe our ensembling algorithm for combining the different image assignments. Since the relevance scores computed by the image mining algorithms will be incomparable in general, we combine the results *after* the MAXRELEVANTIMAGEASSIGNMENT optimization has been performed independently for each algorithm. We use only the ordering returned by these algorithms and do rank aggregation without considering the magnitudes of the scores.

We employ Borda's method to merge l ranked lists corresponding to l different image mining algorithms. Borda's method tries to achieve a consensus ranking and satisfies certain desirable properties such as reversal symmetry [52]. It assigns a score corresponding to the positions in which an image appears within each ranked list of preferences, and the images are sorted by their total score.

However, a consequence of performing rank aggregation for each section independently is that the same image may appear more than once in a chapter. Consider a chapter consisting of two sections

Algorithm 3 ENSEMBLE

Input: Set of sections $S = \{1, 2, \ldots, m\}$ in a textbook chapter; Set of images $I = \{1, 2, \ldots, n\}$; Number of desired images K_j for each section $j \in S$; Scores assigned by l different image mining algorithms for each image $i \in I$; Orderings produced after the optimization for these l algorithms.
Output: A new assignment of images to sections.

1: Let $I_0 := I$ and $S_0 := S$. For each of l image mining algorithms, perform MAXRELEVANTIMAGEASSIGNMENT optimization over I and S to get an assignment of images for all sections in S.
2: **for** section $j = 1$ to m **do**
3: Merge l ranked lists (corresponding to l algorithms) for section j using Borda's method, and assign the top K_j images from the merged list to section j. Let A_j denote the set of assigned images.
4: Remove the assigned images from consideration for subsequent sections, that is, $I_j := I_{j-1} \setminus A_j$ and $S_j := S_{j-1} \setminus \{j\}$.
5: For each of l image mining algorithms, perform MAXRELEVANTIMAGEASSIGNMENT optimization over I_j as the set of images and S_j as the set of sections, and thereby obtain the new assignment of images for sections $j+1$ through m.

and suppose that we want two images for every section. Assume that the optimal assignments (ranked lists) corresponding to the two image mining algorithms are as follows. Alg_1(OPT): $s_1 \leftarrow \langle i_1, i_2 \rangle, s_2 \leftarrow \langle i_3, i_4 \rangle$ (that is, image i_1 has the highest relevance score and i_2 has the second highest score for section s_1 and similarly $\langle i_3, i_4 \rangle$ in that order are the top two images for section s_2), and Alg_2(OPT): $s_1 \leftarrow \langle i_3, i_4 \rangle, s_2 \leftarrow \langle i_1, i_2 \rangle$. Then the rank aggregation would give: $s_1 \leftarrow \langle i_1, i_3 \rangle, s_2 \leftarrow \langle i_1, i_3 \rangle$.

Algorithm 3 (ENSEMBLE) avoids this problem by taking advantage of the logical linear organization of sections within a chapter. It considers sections in a chapter sequentially from the first section to the last, ensembling at a section level, and then removing images selected for this section from the pool of available images for the remaining sections. Before moving to a subsequent section, it reruns the image assignment optimization for the remaining sections over the remaining images. Thus images discarded due to merging for a section are taken into account for consideration in subsequent sections as such images may be more relevant than any of the candidate images for a section.

Consider a chapter consisting of three sections and suppose that we want two images for every section. Assume that the images and their relevance scores for different sections found by the two image mining algorithms are as follows. Alg_1: $s_1 \leftarrow \langle (i_1, 1), (i_2, 0.9) \rangle$, $s_2 \leftarrow \langle (i_7, 0.7), (i_8, 0.6) \rangle, s_3 \leftarrow \langle (i_2, 0.5), (i_3, 0.4), (i_5, 0.3) \rangle$, and Alg_2: $s_1 \leftarrow \langle (i_3, 1), (i_4, 0.9) \rangle, s_2 \leftarrow \langle (i_7, 0.6), (i_8, 0.4) \rangle$, $s_3 \leftarrow \langle (i_4, 0.5), (i_1, 0.4), (i_6, 0.3) \rangle$. The optimal assignments would be: Alg_1(OPT): $s_1 \leftarrow \{i_1, i_2\}, s_2 \leftarrow \{i_7, i_8\}, s_3 \leftarrow \{i_3, i_5\}$, and Alg_2(OPT): $s_1 \leftarrow \{i_3, i_4\}, s_2 \leftarrow \{i_7, i_8\}$, $s_3 \leftarrow \{i_1, i_6\}$. The rank aggregation for the first section would give: $s_1 \leftarrow \{i_1, i_3\}$, thereby dropping i_2 from Alg_1 and i_4 from Alg_2 respectively. We note that i_2 is more relevant than current assignments for section s_3 under Alg_1 and similarly, i_4 is more relevant than current assignments for section s_3 under Alg_2. The benefit of rerunning the optimization is that such dropped images can be assigned to later sections (s_3 in our example). ENSEMBLE would result in the final assignment: $s_1 \leftarrow \{i_1, i_3\}, s_2 \leftarrow \{i_7, i_8\}, s_3 \leftarrow \{i_2, i_4\}$, which is more desirable than an assignment that excludes assigned images from later sections but does not rerun optimization ($s_3 \leftarrow \{i_5, i_6\}$).

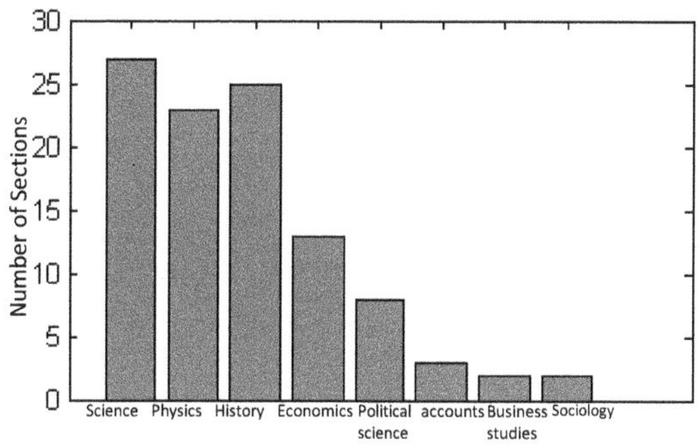

Figure 1: Subject-wise distribution of sections

4. EXPERIMENTS

The difficulty of evaluating a system like ours has been earlier experienced in works with similar goals (e.g. story picturing [32, 59], scene synthesis from text [10], translating sentences into pictorial representations [42]). We believe that defining standard benchmarks will greatly accelerate research into these topics and represents an interesting research opportunity. Meanwhile, we resort to conducting a user study to understand the performance of our proposal. Ideally, we would have liked to have high school students from India participate in this study. In the absence of the availability of this subject population to us, we use the Amazon Mechanical Turk platform, which is becoming increasingly mainstream for carrying out user studies [29].

4.1 Methodology

Data Sets

We wanted to evaluate our techniques on textbooks from a developing country. We chose a corpus of high school textbooks published by the National Council of Educational Research and Training, India because of the online availability of these books. We considered fourteen books from grades IX to XII, covering eight subjects: Accounting, Business Studies, Economics, History, Physics, Political Science, (General) Science, and Sociology. They covered seventy chapters and over a thousand sections. Out of these, we randomly selected 100 sections for the user study. This sample size keeps the cost of carrying out the study within a reasonable budget, and yet it is big enough for having meaningful results. Figure 1 shows the subject-wise distribution of sections.

For mining images, AFFINITY limits itself to finding similar Wikipedia articles and extracts images only from them. This constraint allows us to contain the crawling and image extraction effort. Similarly, when querying the search engines, COMITY uses the site restriction feature to obtain only Wikipedia images, which allows the behavior of the two image mining algorithms to be compared. It also reduces the determination of whether the two images are the same to comparing their Wikipedia URLs. We note that the Wikipedia articles are known to differ from the general web pages in characteristics such as the encyclopedic orientation and the style of writing [22], and restricting to Wikipedia reduces the available pool of relevant images to choose from. In spite of these handicaps, our techniques emerge as quite effective in the user study.

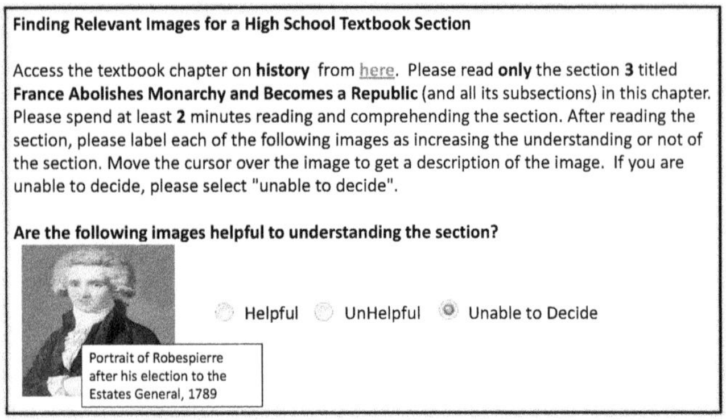

Figure 2: A sample Mechanical Turk HIT

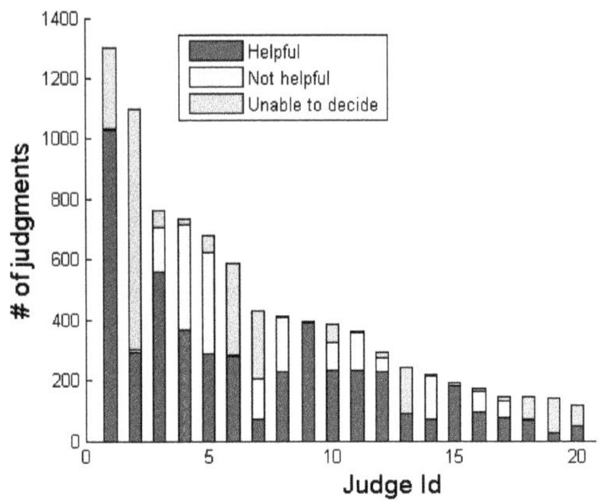

Figure 3: Distribution of judgments for top 20 judges who participated in the most number of HITs

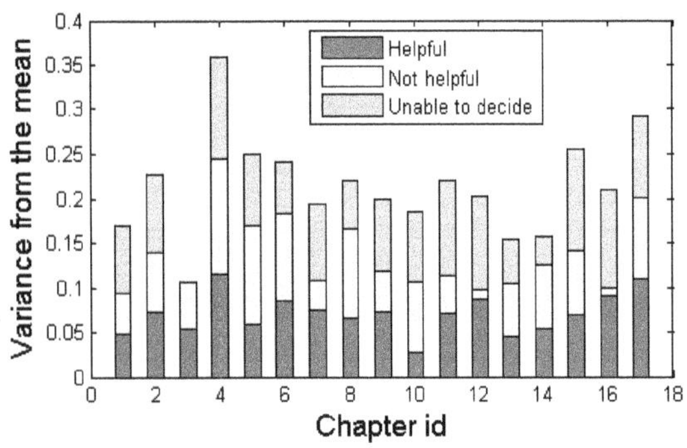

Figure 4: Variance from the mean for the three types of judgments for the Science books

Parameters

In the image mining component, we set the number of images per section parameter k to 5 and the number of desired concept phrases parameter c to 20. For COMITY, we set the number of desired image search results per query t to 10. We use two different search engines ($e = 2$): Google and Bing. We use $\theta = 10$ as the smoothing parameter and give equal importance to all the concepts. For AFFINITY, we obtain $t' = 10$ closest articles for every book section and set $w_1 = 1$, $w_2 = 1$, and $w_3 = 1/3$. During the image assignment, we set the maximum number of images that can be associated with any section to 5 (that is, $K_j = 5$ for all sections).

Judges

Each section along with the candidate images produced by AFFINITY, COMITY, and ENSEMBLE (five per algorithm) was provided to Mechanical Turk as a HIT (Human Intelligence Task). Images within a HIT were intermixed and randomly ordered. Fig. 2 illustrates a sample HIT. Each judge was asked to read the section (provided as a link in the HIT) and rate every image separately as helpful or unhelpful in understanding the material. We also provided the 'unable to decide' option. Images were also provided with the associated captions that the judge could use in making the decision.

We also specified the minimum time a judge was required to spend on a given HIT. This time was arrived at by considering the length of the section and the statistics on average reading speed [21, 27]. We rejected any HIT (and resubmitted it) where the time spent was less than the minimum. We found that different judges took varying amount of time on a particular section which is what we expected (and hoped).

Each HIT was judged by 7 judges. There were 58 judges who took part in the study. Fig. 3 shows the distribution of judgments in terms of helpful, unhelpful, and undecided for the top 20 judges. This figure shows that the distribution of judgments varied across the judges, which indicates the absence of impostor judges who repeatedly judged a HIT using multiple identities. The same figure also indicates that judges were not providing random judgments; otherwise the distribution would have been more uniform.

We also computed the three-dimensional normalized mean vector using all the available judgments for a given chapter. This vector captures the probability of each of the three types of judgments for the images shown for that chapter. Fig. 4 shows the averaged variance from the mean for chapters in the Science books (similar trends held for other subjects). Here the average was performed across all the judges. The deviation is not large, indicating the absence of outlier judges.

Helpfulness Index

We propose *helpfulness index* as the measure for understanding the effectiveness of an image augmentation system. Given the total number of images an image augmentation system can propose, the helpfulness index is defined to be the total number of images deemed helpful for understanding the corresponding section divided by the total number of images.

For an image to be considered helpful for understanding a section, we require that the majority of judges find it helpful. Although we have odd number of judges for every image, judges are allowed to vote 'unable to decide'. Thus, there may be a split vote on an image. We can therefore compute the majority in two different ways:

- *Conservative:* #Helpful > (#Helpful + #Unhelpful)/2,
- *Liberal:* #Helpful $\geq$ (#Helpful + #Unhelpful)/2.

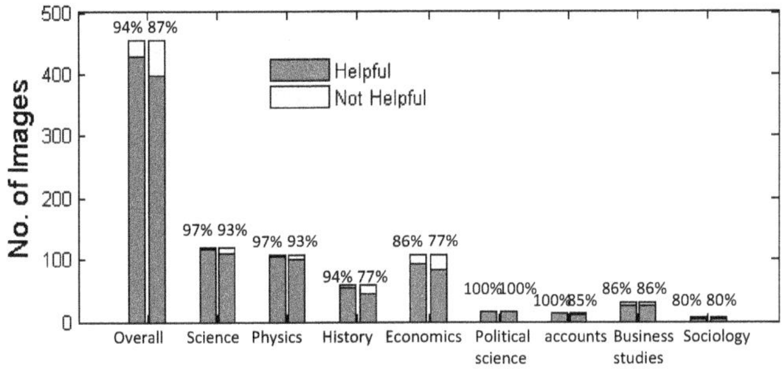

Figure 5: Performance of our system. The first bars correspond to the *Liberal* and the second to the *Conservative* definition of majority. The numbers above the bar give the corresponding helpfulness index.

Conservative requires that an image has a clear helpful majority. *Liberal* breaks ties in the favor of helpfulness. We can thus have two definitions of helpfulness index. By default, we use the *Conservative*.

Note that the helpfulness index is analogous to the notion of *precision* used in information retrieval. One could similarly define a measure analogous to *recall* in terms of the number of images for which a helpfulness decision could be made. This measure turns out to be 100% in our case as there was no image on which all judges were undecided.

4.2 Main Results

Fig. 5 shows the performance of our system, both at the aggregate level ("overall") as well as at the individual subject level. These results were produced by the ENSEMBLE algorithm.

The results are quite encouraging. We see that when we use *Conservative* definition of the majority of judgments, the judges considered 87% of the images assigned to various textbook sections to be helpful. This number increases to 94% under the *Liberal* definition. We can also see that the performance is maintained across all the subjects.

We also manually inspected the results. We discuss next some anecdotal examples.

Anecdotal Examples

Fig. 6(a) shows some examples where ENSEMBLE performed well. We show top five images produced by ENSEMBLE for three different sections from three different subjects. We can see that the images are quite relevant. We discuss the first example in more depth. This example shows the proposed augmentations for the section on how organisms create exact copies of themselves, appearing in the eighth chapter titled 'How do organisms reproduce' in the grade X Science book. This section discusses three main points: (1) due to evolution, organisms are similar in their blueprint; (2) DNA replicates to pass on genetic material; and (3) DNA copying during reproduction should be consistent so that the organism is well adjusted to its ecosystem. We observe that proposed images convey related information. The image on Phylogenetic tree captures the evolutionary relationships among biological species. The two images of DNA (chemical and physical structure) are illustrative of how the DNA can be easily replicated by breaking its double Helix structure. The section describes the consistency requirement of DNA copying using bacteria as the example organism. The images of RecBCD pathway in E. coli bacterium are complementary as it

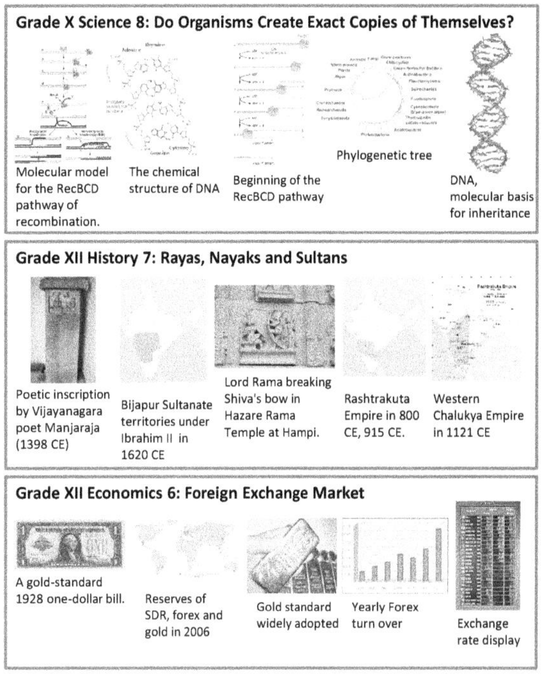

(a) Examples where ENSEMBLE performed well

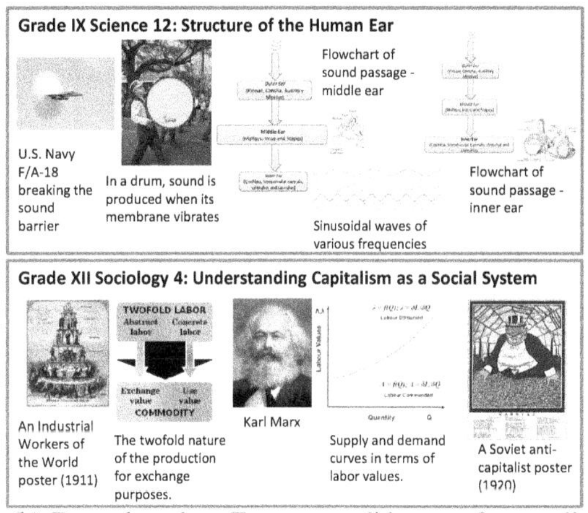

(b) Examples where ENSEMBLE did not perform well

Figure 6: Anecdotal examples

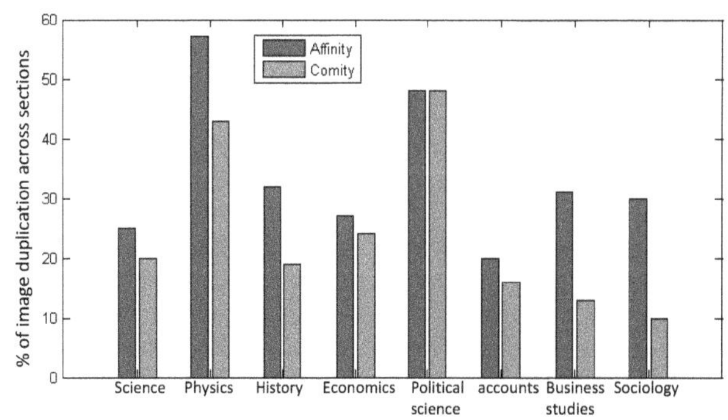

Figure 7: Chapter level duplication in images for AFFINITY and COMITY

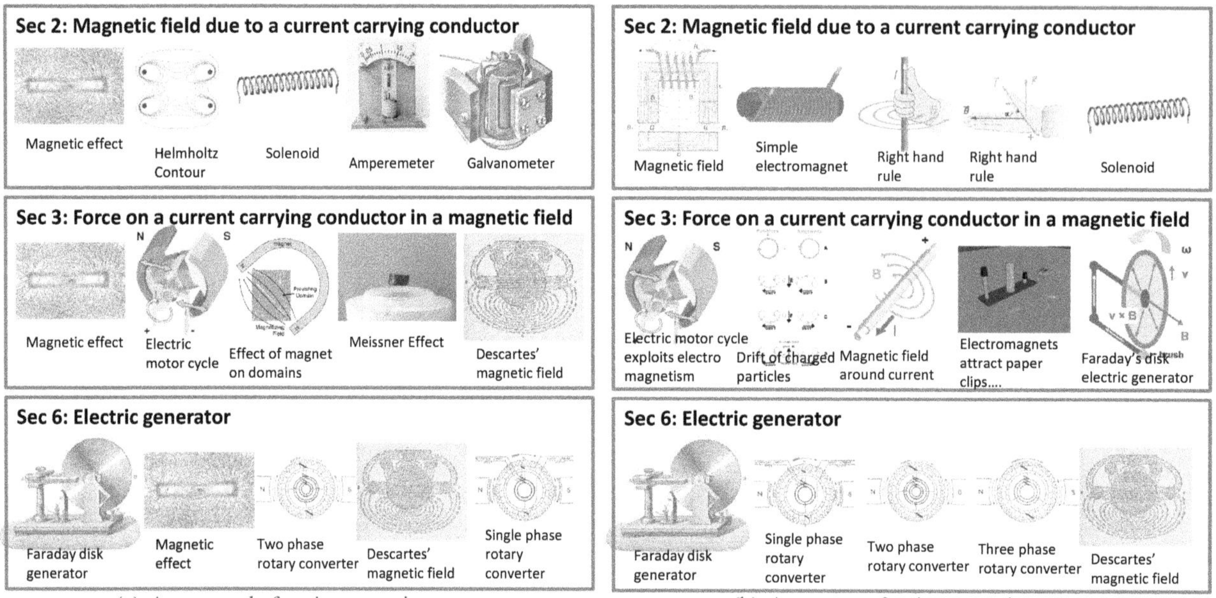

(a) AFFINITY before image assignment

(b) AFFINITY after image assignment

Figure 8: Effect of optimization: Comparison of top five images for three sections from the chapter titled 'Magnetic effects of electric current' in the grade X Science book

plays crucial role of initiating recombinational repair of potentially lethal double strand breaks in DNA.

Fig. 6(b) shows the cases that illustrate opportunity for further work. The first example is from a section in the twelfth chapter titled 'Sound' in the grade IX Science book. This section describes the structure of the human ear and how it enables conversion of pressure variations in air with audible frequencies into electric signals that travel to the brain via the auditory nerve. The last two images that depict the passage of sound through the middle and inner ears are obviously useful. The image illustrating the sinusoidal waves of various frequencies is also helpful. While the first two images are also relevant for the chapter as a whole, they are not particularly suited for this section. The reason these images were ranked high was that they have overlapping words; an important component of human ear is the thin membrane called the ear drum, which can be confused with a playing drum or membrane on it.

4.3 Virtue of the Image Assignment Optimization

The image mining algorithms retrieve images that can potentially repeat across multiple sections of the same chapter. In fact, as can be seen in Fig. 7, this duplication is quite high for both AFFINITY and COMITY. The duplication in this figure has been computed at the subject level by averaging the overlaps computed at the chapter level for all the chapters in that subject. The image assignment algorithm reorders the images and uses more of the available ordered set of images so that the images selected within a chapter are distinct.

We illustrate this point further with an example from the chapter on 'Magnetic effects of electric current' in the grade X Science book. Fig. 8a shows the top five images for three sections in this chapter proposed by AFFINITY before image assignment. Clearly, while all the sets of images shown are relevant to the chapter and can serve as illustrations for the corresponding sections, there is redundancy amongst them. Fig. 8b shows the top five images for the same sections, after applying the image assignment optimization.

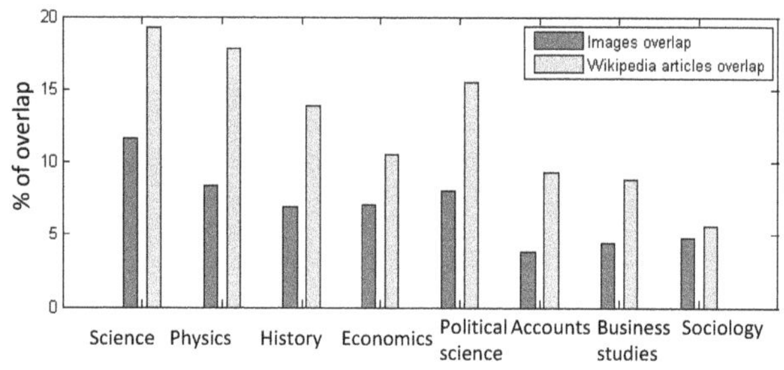

Figure 9: Overlap between AFFINITY and COMITY

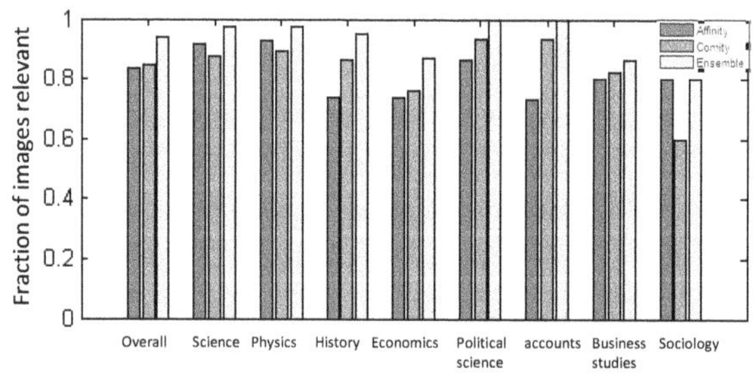

Figure 10: Comparison between AFFINITY, COMITY, and ENSEMBLE

Besides removing redundancy, the optimization also enabled selection of images more relevant to the sections. For instance, Section 2 on 'Magnetic field due to current carrying conductor' now includes images for the right hand rule, which is a guide to finding the direction of magnetic field around a current-carrying wire. Section 6 on 'Electric generator' now includes wiring schematic for each of (single, two, three) phase to rotary converter, which is a motor generator that leverages magnetic field to generate power.

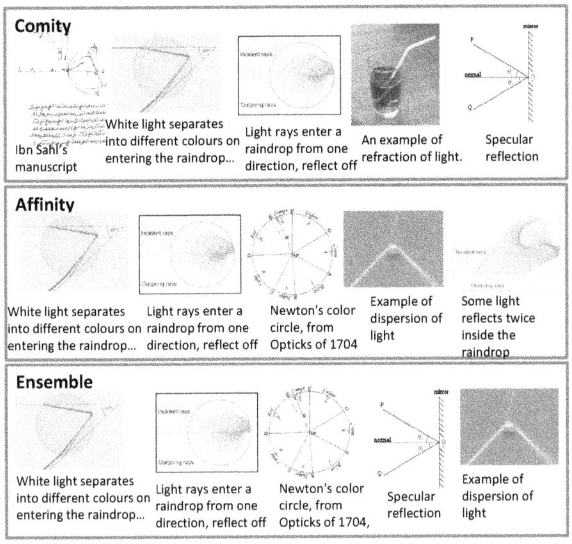

Figure 11: Illustration of the benefit of ENSEMBLE for the section on 'Dispersion of white light by a glass prism' in grade X Science textbook

4.4 Orthogonality of AFFINITY and COMITY

ENSEMBLE is best suited when the ensembled algorithms use largely non-overlapping signals. In order to understand the overlap between AFFINITY and COMITY, we compute two statistics: one using the overlap in the retrieved images and the other using the overlap in the articles from which these images are retrieved.

Fig. 9 provides the two statistics, subject-wise. The image overlap is computed by measuring the ratio of intersection to union in the top five images retrieved by the two algorithms. We compute overlap at the chapter level, and average it across all chapters for a subject. To compute article overlap, we pool the articles from which the top images for a particular chapter were retrieved for each algorithm. Then, we compute the ratio of intersection to union of these articles for every chapter. We can see that the overlap is small. These numbers are substantially lower when analyzed at the section level.

4.5 Benefit of Ensembling

Fig. 10 compares ENSEMBLE with AFFINITY and COMITY. We can see that ENSEMBLE consistently produces a larger fraction of the helpful images than either of the other two, thereby confirming the value of ensembling.

We use Fig. 11 to provide an illustration, using the results for a section from the chapter on 'Human eye and colourful world' in the grade X science book. This chapter describes the optical phenomena in nature, including rainbow formation and the splitting of white light and blue color of the sky. The section we discuss introduces the concept of dispersion and assumes that the students are already familiar with refraction. The ensembled results are clearly superior than the results of the other two algorithms.

5. CONCLUSIONS AND FUTURE WORK

We studied the feasibility of enriching textbooks with links to relevant images and presented a solution for this problem. The solution comprises of three components: a component for optimizing the assignment of images to different sections within a chapter on a per algorithm basis, another for mining images from the web using multiple algorithms, and finally a component for ensembling the results of the per algorithm assignments. We devised a rigorous formulation of the image assignment problem and gave a polynomial time algorithm for solving the problem optimally. We also presented two particular image mining algorithms that utilize orthogonal signals and hence obtain different sets of relevant images. Finally, we provided an ensembling algorithm for combining the assignments.

We conducted a user study employing a corpus of fourteen high school textbooks, published by the central body for education in India. We used the Amazon Mechanical Turk platform for this purpose. Seven judges each, coming from a population of 56 judges, judged the results produced by our implementation for a random sample of 100 textbook sections. The results demonstrate the promise of the proposed system: the judges conservatively considered 87% of the images assigned to various sections to be helpful for understanding the corresponding section and the performance was maintained across the subjects.

The directions for future work include investigating what new issues arise if the ideas from this paper were to be extended for enriching textbook material with other media types. Another important research direction is developing benchmarks for measuring the performance of these systems. Finally, it is worthwhile to examine synergies between algorithmic approaches such as the one presented in this paper and the collaborative approaches such as the one proposed in [2].

6. REFERENCES

[1] *Knowledge for Development: World Development Report 1998/99.* World Bank, 1998.

[2] Improving India's education system through information technology. *IBM*, 2005.

[3] A. Adams and J. van der Gaag. First step to literacy: Getting books in the hands of children. *The Brookings Institution*, January 2011.

[4] R. Agrawal, S. Gollapudi, A. Kannan, and K. Kenthapadi. Identifying enrichment candidates in textbooks. In *WWW*, 2011.

[5] R. Agrawal, S. Gollapudi, K. Kenthapadi, N. Srivastava, and R. Velu. Enriching textbooks through data mining. In *First Annual ACM Symposium on Computing for Development (ACM DEV)*, 2010.

[6] K. Barnard, P. Duygulu, D. Forsyth, N. de. Freitas, D. M. Blei, and M. I. Jordan. Matching words and pictures. In *Journal of Machine Learning Research*, volume 3, 2003.

[7] S. Boss. What's next: Curling up with e readers. *Stanford Social Innovation Review*, Winter 2011.

[8] J. P. G. Chimombo. Issues in basic education in developing countries: An exploration of policy options for improved delivery. *Journal of International Cooperation in Education*, 8(1), 2005.

[9] J. Coiro, M. Knobel, C. Lankshear, and D. Leu, editors. *Handbook of research on new literacies*. Lawrence Erlbaum, 2008.

[10] B. Coyne and R. Sproat. WordsEye: An automatic text-to-scene conversion system. In *SIGGRAPH*, 2001.

[11] M. Crossley and M. Murby. Textbook provision and the quality of the school curriculum in developing countries: Issues and policy options. *Comparative Education*, 30(2), 1994.

[12] A. Csomai and R. Mihalcea. Linking educational materials to encyclopedic knowledge. In *AIED*, 2007.

[13] R. Datta, D. Joshi, J. Li, and J. Z. Wang. Image retrieval: Ideas, influences, and trends of the new age. *ACM Computing Surveys*, 40, September 2008.

[14] L. Downes. *The laws of disruption: Harnessing the new forces that govern life and business in the digital age*. Basic Books, 2009.

[15] Y. Feng and M. Lapata. Topic models for image annotation and text illustration. In *HLT-NAACL*, 2010.

[16] B. Fuller. What school factors raise achievement in the third world? *Review of educational research*, 57(3), 1987.

[17] K. Gaikwad, G. Paruthi, and W. Thies. Interactive DVDs as a platform for education. In *ICTD*, 2010.

[18] J. Gillies and J. Quijada. Opportunity to learn: A high impact strategy for improving educational outcomes in developing countries. *USAID Educational Quality Improvement Program (EQUIP2)*, 2008.

[19] P. Glewwe, M. Kremer, and S. Moulin. Many children left behind? Textbooks and test scores in Kenya. *American Economic Journal: Applied Economics*, 1(1), 2009.

[20] R. Gorman and J. Ginsburg. *Copyright: Cases and materials*. Foundation Press, 2006.

[21] W. Grabe. Efficiency in reading – thirty fiver years later. In *Reading in a Foreign Language*, 2010.

[22] G. Grefenstette. Comparing the language used in Flickr, general web pages, Yahoo images and Wikipedia. In *LREC Workshop on Language Resources for Content-Based Image Retrieval (OntoImage)*, 2008.

[23] G. Guo, G. Xu, H. Li, and X. Cheng. A unified and discriminative model for query refinement. In *SIGIR*, 2008.

[24] E. A. Hanushek and L. Woessmann. The role of education quality for economic growth. *Policy Research Department Working Paper 4122, World Bank*, 2007.

[25] E. Hatcher and O. Gospodnetic. *Lucene in Action*. Manning, 2004.

[26] S. Heyneman, J. Farrell, and M. Sepulveda-Stuardo. Textbooks and achievement in developing countries: What we know. *Journal of Curriculum Studies*, 13(3), 1981.

[27] K. Holmqvist, J. Holsanova, M. Barthelson, and D. Lundqvist. Reading or Scanning? A study of newspaper and net paper reading. In J. R. Hyönä and H. Deubel, editors, *The mind's eye: Cognitive and applied aspects of eye movement research*. Elsevier Science, 2003.

[28] S. Huston and W. B. Croft. Evaluating verbose query processing techniques. In *SIGIR*, 2010.

[29] P. G. Ipeirotis. Analyzing the Amazon mechanical turk marketplace. *ACM Crossroads*, 17(2), 2010.

[30] A. Jain and B. Yu. Automatic text location in images and video frames. *Pattern recognition*, 31(12), 1998.

[31] A. Jawa, S. Datta, S. Nanda, V. Garg, V. Varma, S. Chande, and M. K. P. Venkata. Smeo: A platform for smart classrooms with enhanced information access and operations automation. In *10th International Conference on Next Generation Wired/Wireless Advanced Networking*, 2010.

[32] D. Joshi. The story picturing engine: Finding elite images to illustrate a story using mutual reinforcement. In *ACM SIGMM International Workshop on Multimedia Information Retrieval*, 2004.

[33] D. Jurafsky and J. Martin. *Speech and language processing*. Prentice Hall, 2008.

[34] J. S. Justeson and S. M. Katz. Technical terminology: Some linguistic properties and an algorithm for indentification in text. *Natural Language Engineering*, 1(1), 1995.

[35] P. Katsioloudis. *Identification of Quality Indicators of Visual-Based Learning Material in Technology Education Programs for Grades 7-12*. PhD thesis, North Carolina State University, 2007.

[36] E. Kuiper, M. Volman, and J. Terwel. The Web as an information resource in K-12 education: Strategies for supporting students in searching and processing information. *Review of Educational Research*, 75(3), 2005.

[37] G. Kumaran and V. R. Carvalho. Reducing long queries using query quality predictors. In *SIGIR*, 2009.

[38] R. Lienhart and A. Wernicke. Localizing and segmenting text in images and videos. *IEEE Transactions on Circuits and Systems for Video Technology*, 12(4), 2002.

[39] R. Mayer. *Multimedia Learning*. Cambridge University Press, 2001.

[40] O. Medelyan. *Human-competitive automatic topic indexing*. PhD thesis, The University of Waikato, 2009.

[41] R. Mihalcea and A. Csomai. Wikify!: Linking documents to encyclopedic knowledge. In *CIKM*, 2007.

[42] R. Mihalcea and C. W. Leong. Toward communicating simple sentences using pictorial representations. *Machine Translation*, 22(3), 2008.

[43] D. Milne. *Applying Wikipedia to Interactive Information Retrieval*. PhD thesis, University of Waikato, 2010.

[44] R. Mohammad and R. Kumari. Effective use of textbooks: A neglected aspect of education in Pakistan. *Journal of Education for International Development*, 3(1), 2007.

[45] J. Moulton. How do teachers use textbooks and other print materials: A review of the literature. *The Improving Educational Quality Project, South Africa*, 1994.

[46] H. Müller, P. Clough, T. Deselaers, and B. Caputo. *ImageCLEF: Experimental Evaluation in Visual Information Retrieval*. Springer, 2010.

[47] N. Mulvany. *Indexing books*. University of Chicago Press, 2005.

[48] S. Panjwani, L. Micallef, K. Fenech, and K. Toyama. Effects of integrating digital visual materials with textbook scans in the classroom. *International Journal of Education and Development using Information and Communication Technology*, 5(3), 2009.

[49] C. Papadimitriou and K. Steiglitz. *Combinatorial optimization: Algorithms and complexity*. Dover, 1998.

[50] A. Riddell. *Factors influencing educational quality and effectiveness in developing countries: A review of research*. Deutsche Gesellschaft fur Technische Zusammenarbeit (GTZ), Germany, 2008.

[51] J. Rocchio. Relevance feedback in information retrieval. In *The SMART Retrieval System – Experiments in Automatic Document Processing*, 1971.

[52] D. Saari. *Decisions and elections: Explaining the unexpected*. Cambridge University Press, 2001.

[53] B. W. Speck, T. R. Johnson, C. P. Dice, and L. B. Heaton. *Collaborative writing: An annotated bibliography*. Greenwood Press, 1999.

[54] A. Spink, B. Jansen, and H. Ozmultu. Use of query reformulation and relevance feedback by Excite users. In *Internet Research: Electronic Networking Applications and Policy*, 2000.

[55] M. Stein, C. Stuen, D. Carnine, and R. M. Long. Textbook evaluation and adoption. *Reading & Writing Quarterly*, 17(1), 2001.

[56] L. Von Ahn and L. Dabbish. Labeling images with a computer game. In *CHI*, 2004.

[57] X. Xue, S. Huston, and W. B. Croft. Improving verbose queries using subset distribution. In *CIKM*, 2010.

[58] Y. Yang, N. Bansal, W. Dakka, P. Ipeirotis, N. Koudas, and D. Papadias. Query by document. In *WSDM*, 2009.

[59] X. Zhu, A. B. Goldberg, M. Eldawy, C. R. Dyer, and B. Strock. A text-to-picture synthesis system for augmenting communication. In *AAAI*, 2007.

Exploring the Corporate Ecosystem with a Semi-Supervised Entity Graph

Hassan H. Malik
Thomson Reuters
New York, NY, USA
hassan.malik
@thomsonreuters.com

Ian MacGillivray
Thomson Reuters
New York, NY, USA
ian.macgillivray
@thomsonreuters.com

Måns Olof-Ors
Thomson Reuters
Baar, Switzerland
mans.olof-ors
@thomsonreuters.com

Siming Sun
Thomson Reuters
New York, NY, USA
siming.sun
@thomsonreuters.com

Shailesh Saroha
Thomson Reuters
New York, NY, USA
shailesh.saroha
@thomsonreuters.com

ABSTRACT

Investment decisions in the financial markets require careful analysis of information available from multiple data sources. In this paper, we present Atlas, a novel entity-based information analysis and content aggregation platform that uses heterogeneous data sources to construct and maintain the "ecosystem" around tangible and logical entities such as organizations, products, industries, geographies, commodities and macroeconomic indicators. Entities are represented as vertices in a directed graph, and edges are generated using entity co-occurrences in unstructured documents and supervised information from structured data sources. Significance scores for the edges are computed using a method that combines supervised, unsupervised and temporal factors into a single score.

Important entity attributes from the structured content and the entity neighborhood in the graph are automatically summarized as the entity "fingerprint". A highly interactive user interface provides exploratory access to the graph and supports common business use cases.

We present results of experiments performed on five years of news and broker research data, and show that Atlas is able to accurately identify important and interesting connections in real-world entities. We also demonstrate that Atlas entity fingerprints are particularly useful in entity similarity queries, with a quality that rivals existing human-maintained databases.

Categories and Subject Descriptors

E.1 [**DATA STRUCTUR S**]: Graphs and networks; H.4.2 [**Information S stems Applications**]: Decision support

General Terms

Algorithms, Design, Experimentation, Performance

CIKM'11, October 24–28, 2011, Glasgow, Scotland, UK.

1. INTRODUCTION AND MOTIVATION

Financial analysts and investors often rely on news stories, press releases and legal documents to make critical investment decisions. However, facts or events reported in a single document are rarely sufficient for an investor to make an informed decision. Therefore, investors must conduct additional research that typically involves browsing and searching multiple structured and unstructured databases. Since the windows of opportunity in financial markets are typically short, investors often face a difficult tradeoff between conducting thorough research and making timely decisions.

We observe that an interesting property of new documents is that they sometimes substantially increase the significance of existing documents. This is because significant new facts or events that are related to an entity tend to revive interest in older information about that entity. Often, this 'boost in information significance propagates to entities that may not even be mentioned in the new document. Due to this phenomenon, seemingly unrelated news stories may have substantial financial implications on real-life assets.

For example, the initial news alerts reporting the recent political unrest in Egypt merely reported the events. Since Egypt is one of the largest importers of wheat in the world, the unrest soon negatively impacted wheat prices in the international markets, which in turn may have impacted the financial standing of some of the commodity-based investment vehicles and private and publicly traded companies with significant exposure to wheat, in addition to companies with exposure to the country or the region in general. Again, existing databases (and news archives) are likely to contain all information needed to analyze possible implications of the unrest, but an average investor may not even be able to find all relevant information before the markets start responding to the events.

In this paper, we present Atlas, a novel entity-based information analysis and content aggregation platform that uses heterogeneous structured and unstructured data sources to construct and maintain the 'ecosystem around tangible and logical entities such as organizations, products, industries, geographies, commodities and macroeconomic indicators. Atlas uses a directed graph as the main data structure where entities are represented as vertices, and edges are generated using entity co-occurrences in unstructured documents and supervised information from structured data sources. To facilitate efficient access to underlying content and to allow for temporal analysis, vertices and edges store pointers to relevant unstructured and structured content and metadata.

Since each entity may be connected to a large number of other entities, Atlas computes significance scores for edges using a novel method that combines supervised, unsupervised and temporal factors into a single score. In addition, Atlas automatically summarizes important entity attributes from the structured content and the entity neighborhoods in the graph into entity 'fingerprints . As we show in Section 6.2.1, these fingerprints are particularly useful in entity similarity queries. Finally, a highly interactive user interface provides exploratory access to the graph and supports common business use cases.

The rest of this paper is organized as follows. We begin with a discussion of related work (Section 2) and provide an overview of Atlas system architecture (Section 3). We then describe the graph construction in detail (Section 4) providing information on the data sources used (Section 4.1), issues and challenges encountered (Section 4.2.1), the computation of significance scores for edges (Section 4.3), the generation of entity fingerprints (Section 4.4), and the characteristics of the generated graph (Section 4.5). Next, we provide an overview of the user interfaces (Section 5) and empirically evaluate the graph s performance (Section 6). We finally conclude and discuss ideas for future work (Section 7).

2. RELATED WORK

Our research relates to existing work in entity extraction and disambiguation, entity-relation graphs, news event tracking and news document chaining, standardized analysis and management of unstructured information, and cross-database visualization, along with other research areas in information retrieval, database management, knowledge management and machine learning. We discuss a few representative methods and systems here.

Entity extraction and disambiguation serves as the basic building block in our system. Earlier entity extraction systems were mostly rule-based [11, 24, 15] whereas statistical methods [28, 12, 10] gained more popularity in recent years. These methods convert the entity extraction task to a problem of decomposing the unstructured text, and then labeling various parts of the decomposition [25]. Common methods of decomposing unstructured text include splitting the unstructured text along a predefined set of delimiters or into word chunks using NLP-based methods. Statistical methods such as Hidden Markov Models [1, 3], Maximum-Entropy-based methods [4], and Conditional Random Fields [18] are popular for labeling the decomposed text. Since multiple extracted entities may represent the same physical entity (e.g., International Business Machines and IBM both represent the same company,) extracted entities must be disambiguated to avoid unnecessary duplication.

Bunescu and Pasca [6] used Wikipedia to train a disambiguation SVM kernel whereas Cucerzan [9] proposed a disambiguation process that focuses on maximizing the agreement between the document context, Wikipedia context, and the category tags associated with the candidate entities. In contrast, Hassell et al. [14] used an Ontology as background knowledge for entity disambiguation.

Entity-Relation (ER) graphs have been proposed to model entity relationships. Chakrabarti et al. [8] used ER graphs to represent personal information networks, where nodes represented entities such as organizations, people, places, events, projects etc and edges represented explicit or probabilistic relationships obtained by parsing unstructured text. A proximity-based query language supported queries on the graph. In follow-up work [7], they used a PageRank-like method to improve the query execution performance. Minkov and Cohen [22] also used ER graphs to model personal information, and used finite graph walks to induce a measure of entity similarity and to facilitate searching the graph.

News event tracking and finding connections between news stories is another active research area that is related to our work. Nallapati et al. [23] studied the problem of recognizing events and their dependencies in news stories. They generated a graph structure by discovering sub-clusters in news events and organizing them by their dependencies. In a similar approach, Mei and ChengXiang [21] discovered latent themes from text, constructed an evolution graph of themes and used HMMs to analyze the life cycle of these themes. Recently, Shahaf and Guestrin [27] studied the problem of finding coherent chains that connect a pair of news stories. They formalized the notion of story coherence as a linear program, and used a bipartite graph to measure the influence of a document on other documents. They also proposed methods to find and evaluate coherent chains.

Managing, analyzing and visualizing data from many structured and unstructured data sources is often challenging. Ferrucci and Lally [13] proposed a middleware that provides standardized interfaces to acquire, analyze and access unstructured data. Their framework supports document-level and collection-level analysis and enables semantic searches and standardized access to resulting metadata. Lieberman et al. [19] proposed a query-based approach to visualize and explore heterogenous biomedical databases. They modeled database records as nodes in an ER graph, and used edges to link related records. Keyword-based queries return an initial set of nodes, and the user is then able to explore the links to records from multiple databases in a unified way.

Existing entity centric content aggregation systems are either community maintained or use proprietary methods. Freebase[1] is a community maintained entity graph that contains information on about 20 million[2] unique entities. Entities are associated with one or more types, and may have additional properties: they are stored as nodes in a graph database and links represent relationships between entities. DBpedia [2] is another community effort that aims to extract structured information about entities from Wikipedia and make it accessible on the web. Various facts about entities, relationships to other sources, classifications in multiple concept hierarchies and data-level links to other web data sources are also maintained. The OKKAM [5] project aims to create a web-scalable entity name system to enable entity-centric information integration, and Quid[3] uses proprietary methods to map the world s technologies with a goal of helping businesses identify their next strategic opportunities.

Similarly to the community maintained systems, Atlas utilizes supervised information about entities and their relationships, where available. However, our work differs from

[1]http://www.freebase.com
[2]At the time of writing
[3]http://www.quid.com

these systems in that we do not wholly rely on supervised information to add entities to the graph, or to establish connections. Instead, we use any available entity extraction and resolution system to find entities in unstructured documents, establish entity connections based on co-occurrences in these documents, and apply a novel method to compute the significance of these connections. In addition, we may then use any available supervised information, entity-to-document mappings, and the entity s neighborhood in the graph to automatically summarize important attributes as an entity 'fingerprint, resulting in a significantly more scalable system.

3. SYSTEM ARCHITECTURE

The underlying data structure of the Atlas system is a complex directed graph, where each vertex represents an entity and each edge a connection between entities. The overall Atlas system, however, also includes the creation of this graph (Section 4) and a set of query interfaces that support a number of real-world use cases (Section 5). Here we introduce the terminology used in the rest of this paper and present the architecture of our system, along with tools and technologies used in various system components, and describe in more detail the fundamentals of the graph itself.

3.1 The Entity-Centric Model

The key component in the Atlas system is that of an entity. An entity in this model may be a tangible reality, such as a person or a commodity; or an intangible concept, such as inflation, or a war. Both vertices and edges have properties and references to relevant documents, and a single edge may represent multiple types of relationships between a source and a target vertex. The entity types used in the version of Atlas presented here are organizations, geographies, products, industries, commodities and macroeconomic indicators. Further entity types available in alternate versions of Atlas include people, technologies, facilities and media.

Entities may either be *validated* or *discovered*. *Validated* entities are mapped to a known entity from a human-maintained structured data source whereas *discovered* entities are solely obtained from unstructured data sources.

3.2 The Document-Powered Approach

The fundamental principle behind Atlas is that if two entities co-occur in a document, then a relationship between them is present. Two key caveats to this assumption must be fully understood in order to faithfully implement it: firstly, it must be understood that the simple appearance of a text string matching an entity in a document does not mean that the document is *about* that entity; secondly, we must realize that whilst, on a per-document basis, this is likely to result in false-positive relationships, that over the aggregate of millions of documents, these false positives will have a negligible impact on the usefulness of the Atlas graph, as they are likely to receive low significance scores (Section 4.3).

Thus, Atlas takes in a wide range of unstructured documents (Section 4.1) and the graph is built using the occurrences of entities in these documents as raw data, combined with any structured information that may also be available. The core of the resulting system therefore loosely relates to the semi-supervised learning paradigm.

3.3 Accessing the graph

The majority of queries to the Atlas graph specify one or more entities as a parameter along with additional information to fine tune the returned results. The queries are answered by analyzing (a) the query entities intrinsic properties (such as a person s birth-date or an organization s country of incorporation) (b) the query entities *fingerprint*, an abstraction of the entity s properties (Section 4.4) and (c) up to degree-2 neighbors of the query entities in the graph.

Atlas makes use of as many types of evidence as are available, but is able to provide meaningful answers when nothing more than the name of an entity and a set of documents in which the name appears are available. The more complete the data available, the more precise the answers returned are, but much may be inferred about an entity from its neighbors in the graph.

3.4 Implementation

The main programming language used in the development of the Atlas system is Java. The graph is loaded in memory as a runtime Java object, and persisted to the file system as a serialized Java object. All information needed to construct the graph from scratch is stored in a relational database. Due to the scale and complexity of the application, a number of open-source libraries were used in developing the system. Amongst there were: Apache Lucene and XML Beans, Jetty and VTD-XML.

The Atlas system is deployed as a set of services, accessed by Flash or HTML-based client applications (Section 5), or programmatically by a number of products and internal tools that master and update content for our organization. Requests and responses are sent using either standard HTTP, XML over HTTP, or batched using Google s Protocol Buffers[4]. Data partitioning is used to allow vertical and horizontal scalability, i.e., the graph is distributed between multiple nodes in a de-centralized peer network, each of which owns a subset of documents or entities. Protocol Buffers are used for inter-node communication to service user requests in the distributed graph (Figure 1).

4. GRAPH CONSTRUCTION

Atlas graph construction (Figure 2) begins by selecting suitable documents from all data sources (Section 4.1) and

[4]http://code.google.com/p/protobuf

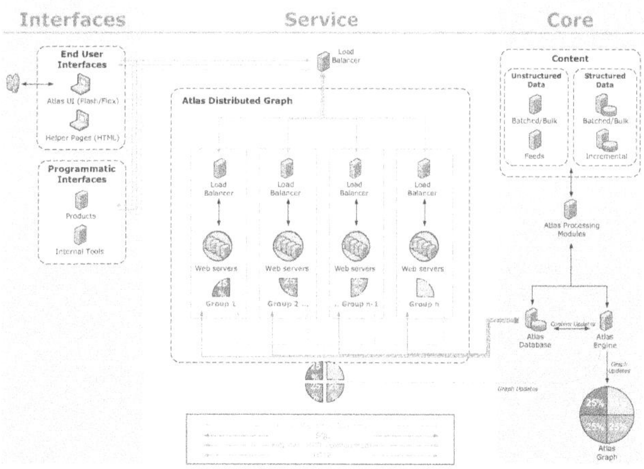

Figure 1: Distributed Implementation

preprocessing these documents (Section 4.1.1). The selected documents are then processed to extract entities and to resolve these against structured data sources (Section 4.2).

At this stage, links – which are in essence, the edges of the graph – between these resolved entities are created, and the significance of these links is established (Section 4.3). As a final step, an intrinsic representation of each entity that we call its *fingerprint* is then created (Section 4.4) using available supervised information, entity to document mappings, and the entity neighborhood in the newly established graph.

4.1 Data Sources and Preprocessing

3.8 million news stories from the Reuters News Service published between December 2005 and October 2010, and 110,000 broker research documents from a number of leading financial institutions from the same time period were used to build the graph evaluated in this paper. Multiple human-maintained, structured databases available within our organization or from on web were also used. The "Product Master" database was constructed from Freebase, and contains about 8,000 product names. The TRCS[5] database contained structured information relating to the news documents. For organizations, "Organization Authority" contains corporate, industrial and geographical information for public and private companies; "Business Sectors" maps companies to predefined industries; and "Competitors," contains a list of competitors for a small fraction of public companies.

4.1.1 *Pre-processing*

News is written in takes (incremental updates), each of which is published as soon as it is ready. To avoid duplication, and to allow the users to correlate all takes of a story, journalists use the same unique identifier for all takes of a story. However, there are cases where the same story is filed under multiple identifiers, causing duplications. Since these duplications may inflate the statistics, we use simple heuristics such as headline matches and cosine similarity within a time window to drop these duplicates.

In a separate problem, news and broker research documents are heavily sprinkled with boilerplate data — standard terms and phrases which often mention company names and can cause misleading connections to be formed. In our removal algorithm, we hash each period and/or newline-delimited sentence that occurs in the entire dataset, and eliminate those which occur more than a given number of standard deviations from the mean. One of the most common pieces of Boilerplate seen by Atlas is provided below:

"This information is provided by RNS The company news service from the London Stock Exchange"

After these steps, any documents which are mostly empty were removed. Further, any documents which mention more than a given number of entities n were also not considered when building our graphs, as for high values of n no examples were found where n / 2 (n-2) meaningful connections were actually present in the document. The value of n used in our experiments was empirically selected as 20.

[5]TRCS (Thomson Reuters Classification System) is a manually applied journalistic classification scheme, which was available to us for news documents, with tags such as OILG for a news story about Oil and Gas.

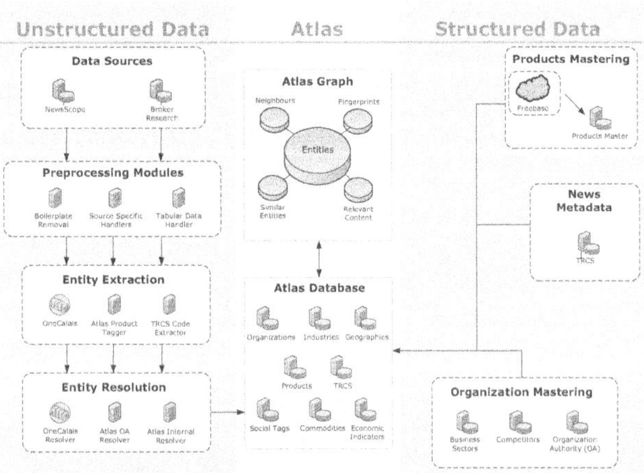

Figure 2: raph Construction

4.2 Entity Extraction and Resolution

Once pre-processing is complete, we aim to find the entities mentioned in each document, and where possible, resolve these mentions to a structured dictionary of known entities, forming the basis of the Atlas graph. As we discuss in the next section, attempting to deal with every instance of every entity type supported by Atlas that was mentioned in five years of news turned out to be a significant challenge.

Entity extraction was mostly dealt with through OneCalais, the enterprise version of OpenCalais[6] provided by ClearForest, a Thomson Reuters company. OneCalais uses NLP and machine learning techniques and has been commonly used by the research community [26, 17, 16]. Whilst Atlas contains additional features to extract entities that Calais currently has little support for, these are quite trivial in nature and focused mainly on basic string matching. The Calais platform also provides some degree of entity resolution against structured data, but in cases where it was unable to do so, the job of entity resolution fell to Atlas. Atlas entity resolution mechanisms included string similarity, aliases from user feedback and expert-supplied rules.

In addition to extracting entities from documents, OneCalais also provided a list of *social tags* associated with each document. Social tags are a new feature within OneCalais that provide automated classification based on an organic taxonomy derived from Wikipedia.

4.2.1 *General Resolution Issues & Challenges*

It was discovered that in our structured datasets, entities are often listed by unintuitive names, such as the full legal names of organizations. Large corporations may have many subsidiary companies, and structured data on the relationship between these subsidiaries was not always available. For example, Microsoft has at least 70 separate legally-recognized organizations worldwide. Where a parent-child chain was available in structured data, Atlas made use of it by counting each mention of a child as a mention of itself, and of every parent in the chain. A configurable parameter allows Atlas users to select the degree of desired granularity, i.e., from considering every legal entity to only considering top-level parent organizations. In cases where this information was not available in structured data, a number of heuristics were applied in an attempt to identify such relationships. Of particular utility was a list of legal suffixes for companies that was made available to us by domain experts.

[6]http://www.opencalais.com/

Entity extraction is not an exact science and a number of erroneous matches were returned by the OneCalais engine. Since our significance computation method tends to assign low scores to connections involving erroneous entities, these had little impact on aggregate results, but they became prominent when we developed user interfaces to display emerging or unusual relationships. Some common patterns that required special handling involves the journalistic style of listing companies in news, e.g. "Intel Samsung Toshiba join hands to halve chip size — Nikkei" was originally extracted as a company called Intel Samsung Toshiba.

Certain companies with short names containing common English words proved very difficult to accurately extract and resolve to. Examples include Business (a French publication) and General Corporation (an American realtor). Where non-English words were present in the dataset, these often provided entity resolution problems, a common issue being person names extracted as organizations.

A final common issue in entity resolution was that of distinguishing between mentions of a location, and mentions of that location s governing body: 'New York State, for example, is interchangeably used to refer to either the geographical area or the governing body of that area.

4.2.2 Media Companies

It is an unfortunate fact that those who report the news are often incidentally mentioned within it, despite having no connection to the story itself. Whilst our boilerplate removal algorithm was able to strip out the vast majority of inappropriate mentions of media companies, a significant number remained in free text. An example from our dataset is "...from Morgan Stanley told Reuters in an interview on Friday that." Whilst entity extraction and resolution was perfect in this example, it skewed Atlas results as no useful connection exists between Morgan Stanley and Reuters. Ratings agencies were also affected by this problem.

The current version of Atlas does not handle these situations well. In the future, we plan to incorporate NLP-based rules to handle common patterns that exhibit this problem, and also to utilize relevance scores returned by OneCalais.

4.2.3 Financial Institutions

It can be seen from a cursory examination of our data that large financial institutions truly have a sphere of influence that touches nearly every point of the corporate world. Whether providing funding, services or advice, or buying or selling products, genuine relationships seem to exist between any given large financial organization and tens of thousands of other companies. Whilst aggregate results again solve the issue of ranking a large financial s relationships, two problems emerge from this situation.

The first is that, for small companies with few mentions, a large financial may be seen not only as a relatively strong connection, but also as a similar entity (given that the two appear in the same documents with relatively high frequency and therefore acquire the same neighbor entities). The second is that it can become very difficult to statistically guess or use attributes about the large financial: whilst they may be based in a given geography for example, it may be that the companies they are advising are doing business in a completely different geography. The chained relationship which is therefore formed is not always true or meaningful, and can cause issues with a number of metrics.

4.2.4 Optimization

A final issue in dealing with large datasets was that of optimization. As an example, there were over 0.75 billion pairs of organizations for which the similarity scores needed to be calculated in the graph evaluated in this paper. Distributing the workload achieved only so much, and the use of vertical bitmaps to compare entities (e.g. based on document co-occurrence or possession of structured attributes) was a key factor in improving the performance of some of the algorithms used to generate the final graph.

4.3 Significance Scores

As we have discussed in Section 3.2, Atlas uses entity co-occurrences in unstructured documents as primary means to establish connections between entities. This approach indeed maximizes the recall, but results in a lot of noisy connections. We address this problem by assigning a significance score to each edge, where higher values indicate stronger connections. Since we use a directed graph, there are always two edges between each pair of connected entities, each of which is assigned a different significance score. This allows Atlas to model a common real-life situation where a given entity E_1 may be very significant for a connected entity E_2, but E_2 may not be equally significant for E_1. Consider, for example, two companies that compete in an area that represents the core business for one company but only a small fraction of the other company s business.

Figure 3 presents actual Atlas significance scores between Facebook and some of its neighbors. The scores indicate that Twitter is more significant for Facebook than Microsoft, and both are more significant than Apple. In contrast, Facebook is important for Microsoft but not equally significant: Microsoft is a major shareholder and investor in Facebook, but is also involved in a variety of other business areas. The relationship between Facebook and Google exhibits a similar behavior. By contrast, Facebook is the major threat to MySpace s core business, making the most significant connection in Figure 3 the MySpace —> Facebook edge; whereas MySpace s actions are now much less important to Facebook, which is clear from the fact that the connection in the opposite direction is of nearly $\frac{1}{3}$ the strength.

To compute the significance scores, we have considered a variety of strategies, and finally selected a few that capture different aspects of the relationship and produce superior results when combined (Section 6.1). Therefore, the Atlas significance scores are computed as a weighted average of multiple factors (where weights were empirically selected). The factors we have evaluated (Section 6.1) include:

a) **Interestingness:** Computed by considering the source and target entities as two variables, populating a 2x2 contingency-table with their frequencies from all available documents (as in Section 1 of [29]), and applying an interestingness measure on the contingency table. Originally proposed for finding interesting association rules, interestingness measures have been successfully used in many applications [20]. We evaluated all measures in Table 5 of [29], and selected "Mutual Information" based on its superior performance on our data (another measure "Added Value" was very close in terms of performance). We have omitted the interestingness measure comparison for the reason of space.

b) **Recent Interestingness:** Same as interestingness, but computed only using documents in a user-definable (fixed to 6 months in our experiments) recent period. This factor aims to boost emerging relationships.

c) **Validation:** A value of 1 if the relationship between source and target entities was validated by a human expert (in available structured data), 0 otherwise.

d) **Common Neighbors:** A percentage of the degree-1 neighbors of the source entity that also occur in the degree-1 neighborhood of the target entity.

e) **Industr O erlap:** A percentage of the industries in source entity s neighborhood that also occur in the degree-1 neighborhood of the target entity.

f) **eograph O erlap:** A percentage of the geographies in source entity s neighborhood that also occur in the degree-1 neighborhood of the target entity.

g) **Temporal Significance:** A comparison of the recent interestingness value, with an interestingness value computed from historic (non-recent) documents giving a value of 1 to the factor if the former increased by more than α, a value of 0 if the the recent interestingness decreased by more than α or a value of 0.5 otherwise, where α was fixed to 0.05. This factor rewards relationships that had gained strength in the recent time period, and penalizes relationships that had lost strength.

h) **lement of Surprise:** Using the same definitions of recent and historic documents as in the previous factor, this factor is assigned a value of 1 if the source entity s neighborhood contains any new industries or geographies in the recent period that did not occur in the historic period, and the target entity shares at-least one such industry or geography, 0 otherwise.

4.4 Entity Fingerprints

A primary business use-case from our organization for Atlas was the need to find companies that were *similar* to a given company, overlooking any geographical differences. Should such functionality be made available, a party with an interest in a successful catering company in Denmark would, for example, be able to find similar opportunities for investment in the emerging Chinese markets. Once geographical boundaries were crossed, it soon became obvious that two similar companies – in our example, companies that may be affected by the same commodities and laws and share similar types of neighbors – may never co-occur in documents, and would therefore never have an edge between them in the

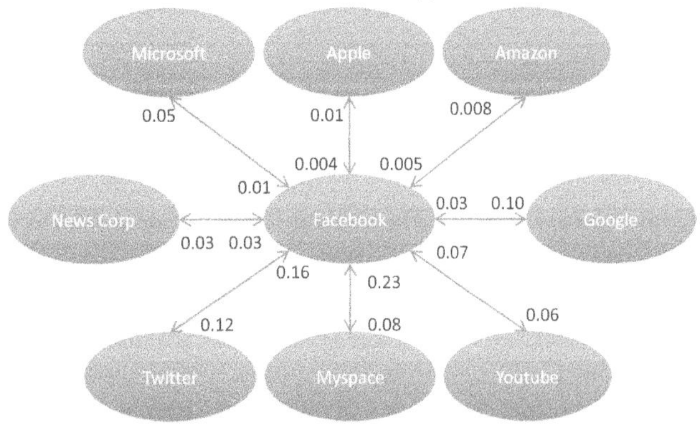

Figure 3: Atlas significance scores between Facebook and some of its neighbors

Atlas graph. However, the aggregate properties of each company s neighbors, and the other information we were able to infer about them from Atlas, allowed us to construct a *fingerprint*, an abstract representation of the company which could be compared to any other fingerprint in order to calculate a *similarity score* and support this use-case.

An entity s fingerprint is a multi-dimensional abstraction of the entity based on a number of its attributes. Once a fingerprint is obtained for an entity, it may then be compared to fingerprints of other entities to understand the similarities and differences that exist. Fingerprints may therefore also be used to generate feature vectors in classification and clustering tasks. In the version of the Atlas graph presented in this paper, fingerprints were calculated and used only for organizations, to support the business case described above.

The factors used to generate fingerprints were, in the majority, related to the neighborhood of a given organization: the entities of a given type to which it was related and temporal aspects of these (e.g. one attribute was 'emerging neighbors , thus fingerprints can represent a point-in-time view of an entity). Structured information about the organizations, such as the country they are incorporated in and the industries they are known to operate in, were also incorporated into the fingerprints. Finally, we have used entity to document relationships to add the top-k classification codes (i.e., TRCS codes) and top-k social tags (i.e., Wikipedia article titles related to a document, as determined by OneCalais) for each company to the fingerprint. This was achieved by sorting each TRCS code or Social Tag with respect to the number of documents that contained the target company and were also assigned with the TRCS code or Social Tag, and selecting k most frequent results.

Each company s fingerprint therefore includes the following attribute groups: industry hierarchy; geography hierarchy; related industries; related geographies; related macroeconomic indicators; related commodities; related TRCS codes; related social tags; and related entities (in two groupings — those that are emerging and those that are stable).

A feature vector is created for each attribute group, and a similarity score between two fingerprints is computed as a weighted linear combination of the cosine similarity scores of group feature vectors, where weights were empirically selected by domain experts. This score represents how alike two companies are, rather than simply how connected they are in the graph.

4.5 Characteristics of the final graph

Presented in Table 1 are the number of distinct entities (nodes) – a total of 85,163 – found in the graph. Between these, 13.3 million connections (edges) were found, with each node having an average of 156 connections (std. dev. 886). On a single server with 32 CPU cores and 128GB of RAM, the graph took a little over 9 hours to build, and included the creation of data-stores such that the vast majority of queries were comfortably sub-second.

The concept of validation is important in a number of calculations in the Atlas system, and in displaying information back to end users. Furthermore, in the case of organizations, non-validated nodes were almost always entity extraction or entity resolution errors. In use-cases that reward surprise, such as those looking for emerging trends or uncommon connections, these caused a significant issue.

An organization is said to be validated if it is present in

Type	Count	% Validated
Organization	44,117	95%
Geography	37,902	3%
Product	2,762	19%
Industry	189	100%
Commodity	130	100%
Macroeconomic	63	100%
Total	85,163	52%

Table 1: Distinct ntities in the raph

a database containing all public, and a good number of private, companies. This database is maintained and updated by a large team of analysts and researchers and powers some of our company s largest commercial products. It took the Atlas team hundreds of man-hours to reach 95 validation level for organizations, and this work led to improvements to both the internal database and the OneCalais core engine.

Geographies were also validated against an internal database, but in this case the 3 validation figure isn t quite as damning. Whilst a significant number (nearly 60) of geographies in the graph are invalid, these occur infrequently and do not affect many of the primary use-cases of Atlas. The remaining number are simply small or hyper-localized geographies not meriting a place in the database used, but extracted nonetheless by the OneCalais engine.

Products were validated against a database compiled specifically for this project from the open-source repository Freebase. Those that are not validated were returned from the OneCalais entity extraction module and appear to be valid, in the majority, although no formal evaluation of this has yet been performed.

5. THE USER INTERFACES

In order to effectively explore a complex graph with tens of thousands of nodes and millions of edges, a set of novel user interfaces were designed and developed. The focus was to deliver specific business use-cases which would directly benefit the customers of Atlas. A select few rich user interfaces were developed in Adobe Flex & Flash with a larger number of HTML "helper pages" made available for those who wished to drill deeper into the raw data. Examples of these include the ability to look up a filtered list of any entity s connections, together with supporting documents; the ability to view a side-by-side overlap of the characteristics of two similar entities; or the ability to provide manual feedback for future resolution (e.g. that 'MSFT should be resolved to 'Microsoft where no other evidence is available).

5.1 Find Similar

The Find Similar view in Atlas (Figure 4) makes use of the fingerprint (see Section 4.4) of an organization. For any given company, the Find Similar view shows a list of the most similar companies along with their fingerprints in a given time range, and highlights the reasons for the match.

Other useful information returned includes an overview of the fingerprint for all companies returned, and a graph showing how each resulting company has trended with the query company over a recent period, with document links.

6. EMPIRICAL EVALUATION

The output of machine learning and information retrieval systems is typically evaluated against human-labeled gold data, using standard objective metrics such as precision and recall. There are an unknown number of useful 'questions that could be asked of a system like Atlas, and many of these have very subjective and constantly-changing answers, making it extremely difficult to obtain and maintain labeled data for evaluation. Even for well-defined tasks (e.g., retrieving top-K neighbors for a given entity), a comprehensive evaluation was resource-prohibitive because of the number of entities available in the system.

Therefore, we have evaluated Atlas by selecting representative samples of entities; obtaining Atlas output for two common tasks; and having domain experts review and grade the output. The next two sections present the results of these experiments. We also present a subjective comparison of Atlas output against existing systems and analyze the fingerprint overlap between two entities.

6.1 Significance Scores

Fifty companies were randomly selected for evaluation from the Justmeans Global 1000 Sustainable Performance Leaders list[7], twenty-five from the top 500 and twenty-five from companies ranked between positions 500 and 1000. For each of these companies, the most significant fifty connections in Atlas were manually evaluated, with human experts identifying each result as either a genuine real-world connection; as a connection with no meaningful foundation in the real-world; or as a duplicate connection (including a duplicate of the source company).

6.1.1 Significance Factors

A number of significance factors were discussed in Section 4.3, but each of these was found to incorrectly skew the results when presented with certain classes of entity, or types of source information. A weighted approach, was therefore taken, and its precision evaluated relative to each individual factor. A precision of 100 would be achieved where a significance factor s top-K connections were all valid, non-duplicate connections, where K is the total number of valid, non-duplicate connections that exist for the given source company. The graphs in Figure 5 present the results of this experiment, with the y-axis representing precision and the x-axis enumerating each of the fifty source companies considered, sorted in decreasing order of weighted significance precision.

[7] http://www.justmeans.com/top-global-1000-companies

Figure 4: The Find Similar View

Metric	Average Precision
Weighted Significance	58.69%
Recent Interestingness	55.57%
Temporal Significance	54.08%
Interestingness	52.4%
Validation	50.49%
Common Neighbours	20.6%
Geography Overlap	17.43%
Industry Overlap	14.83%
Element of Surprise	8.06%

Table 2: A erage Performance of Significance Factors

Whilst individual factors occasionally achieve higher precision than the final weighted significance, the average performance of the latter was found to consistently outperform any individual factor (see Table 2).

6.1.2 *Top Neighbors*

In the previous section, we have evaluated various significance factors and concluded that our weighted significance score outperforms individual factors. We now evaluate its usefulness in a real scenario. A major business use-case for our organization was that of being able to identify the important commodities for any given geography — currently a manual and error-prone task. Twenty countries of varying size were selected for evaluation, and their top-ten commodity neighbors in Atlas were evaluated by a domain expert.

In Figure 6 we present the results of this evaluation, sorted in the increasing order of the number of documents that contained each country in our dataset. We note that without any thresholding on the Atlas results, the system was still able to achieve 76 precision, and also that the majority of false-positives found were located towards the lower ends of Atlas ranking lists. A significant exception here was Israel s most significant commodity, Nuclear Power: an unfortunate example of entity resolution gone awry: the supporting documents were referring to nuclear weapons.

6.2 Fingerprint Factors

6.2.1 *Similarity*

It is difficult to find ground truth against which to evaluate the lists of most similar companies produced by Atlas for a given entity. *Similarity* is a vague and subjective term, and often closely coupled with the context in which a user is searching. Here, the Atlas system is compared against two well-known and well-used datasets, Reuters Knowledge

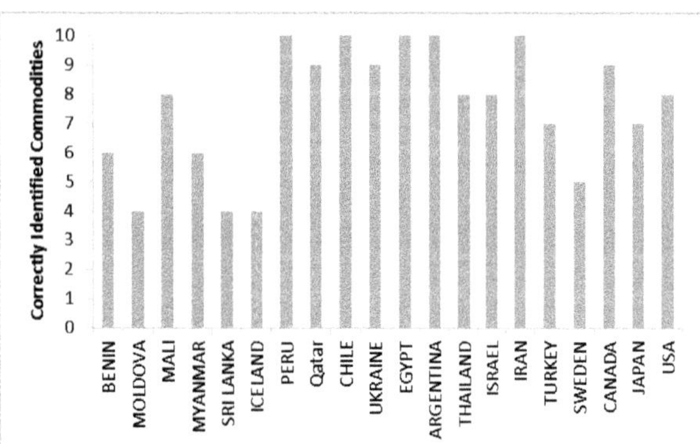

Figure 6: Top Commodit Neighbors for Countries

Company	Atlas	Google	Reuters
	Atlas Top Ten		
General Mills	1	0	0
Keebler Foods	2	0	0
Ralcorp Holding Inc	3	9	0
Green Mountain Coffee	4	0	0
Tate Limited	5	0	0
J&J Snack Foods Corp	6	7	0
Campbell Soup Company	7	3	3
J.M. Smucker Company	8	0	0
Koninklijke Wessanen Nv	9	0	0
Premier Foods	10	0	0
	Google Top Ten		
Tasty Baking Company	0	1	0
Kellogg Company	16	2	0
Grupo Bimbo S.A.B.	20	4	2
Sara Lee Corp	12	5	1
Vitafort Intl. Corp	0	6	0
Treehouse Foods Inc	14	8	0
Snyder S Lance Inc	17	10	0

Table 3: Similar Companies for Flowers Foods Inc

and Google Finance s Related Companies. Reuters Knowledge provides a manually-maintained list of similar companies generated by analysts from company publications and releases. Google, like Atlas, uses an algorithmic approach.

The "most recent quarter" option was selected in Google Finance, and a three-month time period selected in Atlas. Reuters Knowledge offers no time-sensitive options, and may list between 0 and 30 similar companies. Google offers only the top-ten most similar companies (and in the majority of cases seen, returns 10 companies), whereas we have access to the entire list for Atlas, which, without thresholding, often contains in excess of 30 results. The company we selected for detailed evaluation, based on the belief that it represents some of the key positive and negative features of Atlas in evaluating similar companies compared to Google Finance and Reuters Knowledge, is Flowers Foods Inc, a company based in the USA that markets a range of top-selling consumer brand packaged foods. Table 3 shows the top similar results for Flowers Foods in each dataset.

The first point to note is that entity resolution is ever an issue when dealing with organizations. Whilst Keebler Foods and Keebler Holding are indeed separate legal entities, for the vast majority of use-cases, the distinction is not a useful one. Further, it is not rare for companies to merge or be acquired, and the multiple processes by which this may occur may also lead to confusion in a system.

Whilst both Atlas and Google were able to nearly flawlessly[8] extract companies with very similar business offerings as Flowers Foods Inc, their ranking differed. Only three of the Atlas top 10 were found in the Google top 10, all the Google top 10 except Vitafort were found within Atlas top 20. The only clear pattern was that Atlas seemed to favor similarity based on product offerings (core business), whereas Google favored companies based in the same country – the USA – with the exception of Grupo Bimbo S.A.B., based in Mexico (with a significant American presence).

Over a sample of 25 companies from various industries and geographies, 87 of Google top 10 similar companies appeared in Atlas top 20, and 34 of Atlas top 10 similar companies appear in Google s top 10.

Reuters Knowledge returned a mere three similar companies for Flowers Foods, all of which were also identified by

[8]Vitafort being the exception, it appears to be an erroneous match from Google Finance: Vitafort is wholly involved in entertainment intellectual property.

Figure 5: Weighted Significance compared to indi idual significance factors

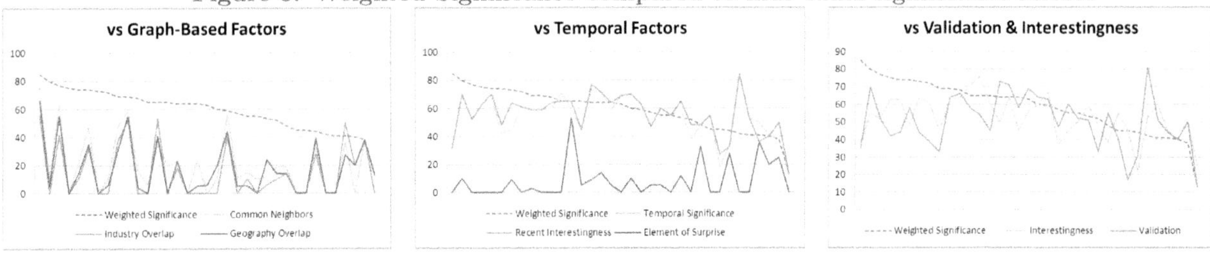

both Atlas and Google. There was a strong correlation here between the top companies in Google and the top companies in Reuters Knowledge, whereas Atlas ranked the three companies from Reuters in positions 12, 20 and 7 respectively — suggesting that Atlas ranking methodology may differ to that used in current products. Of the 25 sample companies, Flowers Foods was found to be one of the worst examples of Atlas rankings corresponding with Reuters Knowledge. When querying on Toll Brothers, Inc, for example, Reuters Knowledge provided five results which Atlas ranked in positions 3,9,5,1 and 2 respectively. For a larger company, Google, Reuters Knowledge provided seven results, which Atlas ranked in positions 1,2,10,19,14,4 and 6 respectively.

We stress once again that Atlas is not intended to reproduce the results of either Google Finance or Reuters Knowledge, but find that correlation with these two well-used tools, together with expert opinions provided to us, show the utility of Atlas-generated similar companies.

6.2.2 *Overlap*

In addition to using entity fingerprints to compute similarity, it may often be useful to understand in detail the overlap between two entities. Take, for example, YouTube (now owned by Google) and Facebook. These are both prominent Web companies, which shows in the overlapping attributes they have. However, their differences may also be easily seen at a glance using the companies fingerprints (Table 4), in which a score of −1 implies an attribute owned only by YouTube, and a score of 1 an attribute owned only by Facebook. A score of 0 implies a perfect overlap.

$$Overlap(a,b) = \begin{cases} \frac{b}{a} - 1 & a \geq b \\ 1 - \frac{a}{b} & a < b \end{cases} \quad (1)$$

In this example, we can see that the Atlas graph correctly provides a strong bias towards YouTube in considering the geography attribute "San Mateo ," YouTube s home county. Despite having no presence in San Mateo, Facebook is somewhat linked to it by documents mentioning both YouTube (with San Mateo as a corollary) and Facebook, a common problem in evaluating similarity for two entities that are connected in the graph. An extraction error resulting from the suffix -ville has led to the popular Facebook social game "Farmville" being identified as a geography, and this is therefore understandably considered related only to Facebook: it will provide negative evidence in computing a similarity score between these two companies.

In the Social Tags attribute type, "World Wide Web" is correctly a strongly shared connection, providing positive evidence towards similarity, whereas "Video Hosting" for YouTube and "Social Network Service" for Facebook exemplify the core differences between these two companies activities on the Web.

Geographies	
San Mateo	−0.81
Farmville	1
Social Tags	
World Wide Web	0.07
Video Hosting	−1
Social Network Service	1
Recent Organizations	
Viacom Inc	−0.77
Twitter	0.42

Table 4: Fingerprint o erlap for YouTube and Facebook

In the Recent Organizations attribute type, Viacom Inc was an attribute most related to YouTube, and Twitter an attribute biased somewhat towards Facebook. Viacom offers many video services, and has a natural relationship with YouTube, but also made offers to buy Facebook on multiple occasions. Twitter competes with Facebook for the real-time microblogging market: although it is mentioned in many news stories alongside YouTube, the relationship is often incidental. The final bi-directional similarity score between YouTube and Facebook given was 56 , and each of these companies was top of the others most similar list. Facebook s second most similar company (51) was LinkedIn, which offers professional social networking; YouTube s second most similar company (49) was its parent, Google.

7. CONCLUSIONS AND FUTURE WORK

In this paper, we presented Atlas, an entity-centric information analysis, content aggregation, and visualization platform that uses all available structured and unstructured content to automatically model the ecosystem around entities. Atlas uses a novel method to compute the significance of entity connections, and automatically summarizes key entity attributes into a fingerprint. The results of our objective and subjective evaluation indicate that our significance computation method is able to reward important and interesting connections, and the fingerprints are useful in finding similar companies, an important use case in our domain.

In the future, we plan to work on automatically identifying relationship types for entity connections, incorporating Web and markets fundamental data in graph generation, and improving entity resolution for geographies and products.

8. REFERENCES

[1] E. Agichtein and V. Ganti. Mining reference tables for automatic text segmentation. In *Proceedings of the tenth ACM SIGKDD international conference on Knowledge discovery and data mining*, KDD 04, pages 20–29, New York, NY, USA, 2004. ACM.

[2] C. Bizer, J. Lehmann, G. Kobilarov, S. Auer, C. Becker, R. Cyganiak, and S. Hellmann. Dbpedia - a crystallization point for the web of data. *Web Semantics: Science, Services and Agents on the World Wide Web*, 7(3):154 – 165, 2009. The Web of Data.

[3] V. R. Borkar, K. Deshmukh, and S. Sarawagi. Automatic text segmentation for extracting structured records. In *International Conference on Management of Data*, 2001.

[4] A. Borthwick, J. Sterling, E. Agichtein, and R. Grishman. Exploiting diverse knowledge sources via maximum entropy in named entity recognition. In *Proceedings of the 6th workshop in very large corpora*

[5] P. Bouquet, H. Stoermer, C. Niederee, and A. Maña. Entity name system: The back-bone of an open and scalable web of data. In *Proceedings of the 2008 IEEE International Conference on Semantic Computing*

[6] R. C. Bunescu and M. Pasca. Using encyclopedic knowledge for named entity disambiguation. In *EACL*. The Association for Computer Linguistics, 2006.

[7] S. Chakrabarti. Dynamic personalized pagerank in entity-relation graphs. In *Proceedings of the 16th international conference on World Wide Web*, WWW 07, pages 571–580, New York, NY, USA, 2007. ACM.

[8] S. Chakrabarti, J. Mirchandani, and A. Nandi. Spin: searching personal information networks. In *Proceedings of the 28th annual international ACM SIGIR conference on Research and development in information retrieval*, SIGIR 05, pages 674–674, New York, NY, USA, 2005. ACM.

[9] S. Cucerzan. Large-scale named entity disambiguation based on wikipedia data. In *In Proc. 2007 Joint Conference on EMNLP and CNLL*, 2007.

[10] A. Culotta, T. Kristjansson, A. Mccallum, and P. Viola. Abstract corrective feedback and persistent learning for information extraction. *Artificial Intelligence*, 170, October 2006.

[11] H. Cunningham, D. Maynard, K. Bontcheva, and V. Tablan. GATE: A framework and graphical development environment for robust NLP tools and applications. In *Proceedings of the 40th Anniversary Meeting of the Association for Computational Linguistics*, 2002.

[12] T. G. Dietterich. Machine learning for sequential data: A review. In *Structural, Syntactic, and Statistical Pattern Recognition*. Springer-Verlag, 2002.

[13] D. Ferrucci and A. Lally. Uima: an architectural approach to unstructured information processing in the corporate research environment. *Nat. Lang. Eng.*, 10:327–348, September 2004.

[14] J. Hassell, B. Aleman-Meza, and I. Arpinar. Ontology-driven automatic entity disambiguation in unstructured text. In *The Semantic Web - ISWC 2006*, volume 4273 of *Lecture Notes in Computer Science*, pages 44–57. Springer, 2006.

[15] J. R. Hobbs, J. Bear, D. Israel, and M. Tyson. Fastus: A finite-state processor for information extraction from real-world text. pages 1172–1178, 1993.

[16] F. Hopfgartner and J. Jose. Semantic user modelling for personal news video retrieval. In S. Boll, Q. Tian, L. Zhang, Z. Zhang, and Y.-P. Chen, editors, *Advances in Multimedia Modeling*, volume 5916 of *Lecture Notes in Computer Science*, pages 336–346. Springer Berlin / Heidelberg, 2010.

[17] F. Iacobelli, L. Birnbaum, and K. J. Hammond. Tell me more, not just "more of the same". In *Proceedings of the 15th international conference on Intelligent user interfaces*, IUI 10, New York, NY, USA, 2010. ACM.

[18] J. D. Lafferty, A. McCallum, and F. C. N. Pereira. Conditional random fields: Probabilistic models for segmenting and labeling sequence data. In *ICML'01*, pages 282–289, 2001.

[19] M. D. Lieberman, S. Taheri, w. Guo, F. Mirrashed, I. Yahav, A. Aris, and B. Shneiderman. Visual exploration across biomedical databases. *IEEE ACM Trans. Comput. Biol. Bioinformatics*, March 2011.

[20] H. H. Malik, J. R. Kender, D. Fradkin, and F. Moerchen. Hierarchical document clustering using local patterns. *Data Min. Knowl. Discov.*, 21:153–185, July 2010.

[21] Q. Mei and C. Zhai. Discovering evolutionary theme patterns from text: an exploration of temporal text mining. In *In Proceedings of KDD ï£¡05*, pages 198–207. ACM Press, 2005.

[22] E. Minkov and W. W. Cohen. Improving graph-walk-based similarity with reranking: Case studies for personal information management. *ACM Trans. Inf. Syst.*, 29:4:1–4:52, December 2010.

[23] R. Nallapati, A. Feng, F. Peng, and J. Allan. Event threading within news topics. In *Proceedings of the thirteenth ACM international conference on Information and knowledge management*, CIKM 04, pages 446–453, New York, NY, USA, 2004. ACM.

[24] E. Riloff. Automatically constructing a dictionary for information extraction tasks. In *Proceedings of the eleventh national conference on Artificial intelligence*, AAAI 93, pages 811–816. AAAI Press, 1993.

[25] S. Sarawagi. Information extraction. *Found. Trends databases*, 1:261–377, March 2008.

[26] S. Sen, N. Stojanovic, and R. Lin. A graphical editor for complex event pattern generation. In *Proceedings of the Third ACM International Conference on Distributed Event-Based Systems*, DEBS 09, New York, NY, USA, 2009. ACM.

[27] D. Shahaf and C. Guestrin. Connecting the dots between news articles. In *Proceedings of the 16th ACM SIGKDD international conference on Knowledge discovery and data mining*, KDD 10, New York, NY, USA, 2010. ACM.

[28] K. Takeuchi and N. Collier. Use of support vector machines in extended named entity recognition. pages 119–125, 2002.

[29] P.-N. Tan, V. Kumar, and J. Srivastava. Selecting the right interestingness measure for association patterns. In *Proceedings of the eighth ACM SIGKDD international conference on Knowledge discovery and data mining*, KDD 02, New York, NY, USA, 2002. ACM.

Generating Links to Background Knowledge: A Case Study Using Narrative Radiology Reports

Jiyin He
Centrum Wiskunde en Informatica
Science Park 123, 1098XG
Amsterdam, the Netherlands
J.He@cwi.nl

Maarten de Rijke
University of Amsterdam
Science Park 904, 1098XH
Amsterdam, the Netherlands
derijke@uva.nl

Merlijn Sevenster
Philips Research
High Tech Campus 34,5656AA
Eindhoven, the Netherlands
merlijn.sevenster@philips.com

Rob van Ommering
Philips Research
High Tech Campus 34,5656AA
Eindhoven, the Netherlands
rob.van.ommering@philips.com

Yuechen Qian
Philips Research
345 Scarborough Road
Briarcliff Manor, NY 10510, USA
yuechen.qian@philips.com

ABSTRACT

Automatically annotating texts with background information has recently received much attention. We conduct a case study in automatically generating links from narrative radiology reports to Wikipedia. Such links help users understand the medical terminology and thereby increase the value of the reports.

Direct applications of existing automatic link generation systems trained on Wikipedia to our radiology data do not yield satisfactory results. Our analysis reveals that medical phrases are often syntactically regular but semantically complicated, e.g., containing multiple concepts or concepts with multiple modifiers. The latter property is the main reason for the failure of existing systems. Based on this observation, we propose an automatic link generation approach that takes into account these properties. We use a sequential labeling approach with syntactic features for anchor text identification in order to exploit syntactic regularities in medical terminology. We combine this with a sub-anchor based approach to target finding, which is aimed at coping with the complex semantic structure of medical phrases. Empirical results show that the proposed system effectively improves the performance over existing systems.

Categories and Subject Descriptors

H.3 [**Information Storage and Retrieval**]: H.3.3 Information Search and Retrieval; H.3.4 Systems and Software; H.4 [**Information Systems Applications**]: H.4.2 Types of Systems

General Terms

Experimentation, Algorithms

Keywords

Automatic link generation, Wikipedia, radiology reports

1. INTRODUCTION

Hypertext links are useful because they offer users a way of getting to pertinent information when they are not aware of that information or when they simply do not know enough about the topic at hand to be able to explicitly ask for it. Many types of links exist, e.g., categorical links (such as the navigation of a website), links to related items (such as linking events in news along a timeline), links to "similar items" (in book reviews, or in online shopping environments), etc. In this paper we focus on explanatory links; that is, the target of a link provides definitions or background information for the source of the link. We study the problem of automatically generating this type of link with Wikipedia: Given a piece of text, identify terms or phrases whose meaning is important for understanding the text and link them to Wikipedia pages for explanations or background information.

Automatic link generation with Wikipedia has received much attention in recent years [9, 20, 28, 29, 31]. Most of the studies are interested in solving a generic problem (e.g., developing an automatic link generation approach using Wikipedia as training material [29, 31]), or applying link generation techniques in general domains that cover diverse topics, (e.g., news, blogs, web, etc. [5, 9, 20, 28]). We consider a scenario in the radiology domain where we aim to link medical phrases found in radiology reports, which are typically anatomy or diagnosis terms, to corresponding Wikipedia concepts.

A radiology report gives a narrative account of the radiologist's findings, diagnoses and recommendations for followup actions. Radiology reports are the principal means of communication between radiologists and referring clinicians such as surgeons and general practitioners. The structure of radiology reports may vary over institutes but generally consists of several sections, including patient history, image protocols, findings and conclusions. Depending on the complexity of the cases, reports may have varied lengths, e.g., more than 40 lines of text for a complicated case.

Linking medical phrases to Wikipedia is a typical application of generating explanatory links and is useful in various realistic scenarios. For example, while reading a medical report, the patients concerned are usually not familiar with its medical terminology. By automatically identifying medical terms and explaining them through a link to a knowledge resource that is accessible and understandable by non-experts, the reports become more valuable for non-experts, thereby improving expert-patient communication. In Figure 1 we show an excerpt from a radiology report, with medical terms requiring explanation highlighted, together with a snippet from a Wikipedia page describing one of the highlighted medical terms.

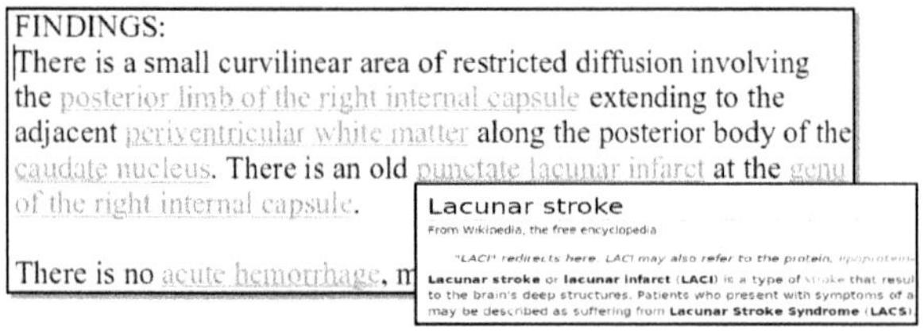

Figure 1: An example of linking medical phrases in radiology report to Wikipedia.

There exist many medical knowledge source; Wikipedia turns out to be a competitive resource for the purpose of providing explanatory background material to laymen, for the following reasons. (i) Quantity: Wikipedia densely covers the medical domain; it contains medical lemmas from multiple medical thesauri and ontologies, such as International Statistical Classification of Diseases and Related Health Problems (ICD-9, ICD-10), Medical Subject Headings (MeSH), and Gray's Anatomy, etc. (ii) Quality: although written collaboratively by Internet volunteers, the quality of Wikipedia articles is guaranteed by the Wikipedia content criterion "verifiability," that is, material in a Wikipedia page should be verifiable against a reliable source; errors in the content are often spotted quickly and corrected by collaborative editors [39]. (iii) Accessibility: Wikipedia is a free online resource. All users can access its content without registering or creating an account. (iv) Readability: the content of Wikipedia is usually written at non-expert level.

Given the above scenario and motivation, we seek answers to the following research questions through empirical method:

RQ1 Can state-of-the-art automatic link generation systems, which are in principle domain independent, be effectively applied to annotating radiology reports? If not, how do links in radiology reports differ from links in a general domain, e.g., Wikipedia links?

RQ2 How can we exploit these differences to effectively annotate radiology reports with links to Wikipedia, and how does the resulting approach compare to domain-independent link generation systems that are state of the art in the field?

We evaluate two state-of-the-art systems, the Wikify! system [29] and the Wikipedia Miner system [31], on a test collection of radiology reports that have been manually annotated by domain experts with links to Wikipedia concepts; see Section 3 for details about the test collection. Neither system yields satisfactory results on our test collection. Two properties of medical phrases are key. First, they are often syntactically regular: they are mostly noun phrases with one or more modifiers (e.g., adjectives). Second, while syntactically regular, medical phrases often have a complicated semantic structure, due to the presence of multiple modifiers as well as conjunctions of concepts within a single phrase. The latter property is the major reason for the failure of both systems, as Wikipedia concepts are often relatively simple, e.g., consist of a single concept or concepts without modifiers. We propose an automatic link generation approach that takes these properties into account. We use a sequential labeling approach with syntactic features to identify anchor texts, i.e., medical phrases, in order to exploit syntactic regularities in medical terminology. We then combine this with a sub-anchor based approach to target finding, which is aimed at coping with the complex semantic structure of medical phrases. The proposed system is shown to effectively improve over the two state-of-the-art systems.

Our contribution is two-fold. First, our study shows that automatically generating links to Wikipedia for reports in the radiology domain requires non-trivial adaptations to the existing domain-independent linking systems; our analyses contribute to the understanding of the state-of-the-art linking systems as well as the problems that are specific to the radiology domain. Second, we propose a link generation approach that takes into account these domain-specific properties, which is shown to be able to effectively link medical concepts from radiology reports to Wikipedia concepts.

Section 2 below discusses related work. In Section 3, we introduce our notation and evaluation setup, including a test collection developed for evaluating automatic link generation for radiology data. In Section 4 we evaluate and analyze the performance of the two state-of-the-art link generation systems on this test collection. Based on our analysis, we introduce our proposed approach in Section 5. In Section 6 we evaluate it and include a comparison to the two state-of-the-art systems, followed by a further analysis and discussion in Section 7. Section 8 concludes the paper.

2. RELATED WORK

Automatic link generation with Wikipedia. Automatically generating hypertext links has a long history, going back nearly two decades. Early publications include [1, 3, 10, 14]. Later commercial approaches have met with limited success [32]. In the context of Wikipedia, renewed interest in automatic link generation emerged. A relatively early paper on the topic is [11], where the problem of discovering missing hypertext links in Wikipedia is addressed. The method proposed consists of two steps: first, clustering highly similar pages around a given page, and then identifying candidate links from those similar pages that might be missing on the given page. The main innovation is in the algorithm that is used for identifying similar pages and not so much in the link detection. Meanwhile, the task of disambiguating links to Wikipedia has received special attention as part of semantically oriented tasks such as named entity normalization. Cucerzan [9] uses automatically generated links to Wikipedia to disambiguate named entities in news corpora. Generalizing Cucerzan [9]'s work to user generated content with additional heuristics, Jijkoun et al. [20] focus on the named entity normalization task on blogs and comments. Recently, Meij et al. [28] study the problem in the scenario of semantic query suggestions, where each query is linked to a list of concepts from DBpedia, ranked by their relevance to the query.

In 2007, INEX, the INitiative for the Evaluation of XML retrieval, launched the Link-the-Wiki (LTW) track; the goal is to automatically generate links among Wikipedia pages as well as between Wikipedia and other another encyclopedia collection [13, 19]. Within the LTW track, various heuristics as well as retrieval-based methods have been proposed [13, 19]. One important issue discovered is that there exist many trivial links in Wikipedia, such as year, country, etc., which are actively rejected by human assessors [18]. Our case study is partly motivated by this finding, as the disagreement between human assessors and the existing Wikipedia links can be amplified when we switch to a specific domain such as the radiology domain where the language usage is expected to be very different from that in a general domain.

The work that is closest to ours has been presented in [29] and [31]. The Wikify! system [29] identifies the anchor texts from a given text based on term statistics derived from Wikipedia links. Further, the authors experimented with both knowledge-based and machine learning-based approaches for identifying the corresponding Wikipedia concepts for recognized anchor texts. Milne and Witten [31] tackled the problem with machine learning techniques; contextual information in the source text was used to determine the best related Wikipedia concepts, which in turn also served as features for anchor text detection. Their approach greatly improved the performance in terms of precision and recall over [29]. We will discuss further details of the two systems in Section 4 and analyze their performance on the task of generating links from radiology reports to Wikipedia concepts.

Information extraction and encoding for narrative radiology reports. A number of information extraction systems have been developed that focus on narrative medical reports of the kind that we are interested in. The Special Purpose Radiology Understanding System (SPRUS) [16] is an early system that extracts and encodes findings and interpretations from chest radiology reports. The authors experiment with syntactic extensions of SPRUS, reporting a 81% recognition rate in small scale experiments (10 reports) [17]. The MetaMap tool [2] extracts medical phrases from free text and maps them to the vocabulary of the Unified Medical Language System (UMLS) ontology. The Medical Language Extraction and Encoding System (MedLEE) [12] is a rule-based natural language processing system that extracts clinical information from radiology reports and encodes it using a controlled vocabulary. It reports 70% recall and 87% precision scores on identifying four diseases from a set of 230 radiology reports.

The automatic link generation task bears considerable similarity to automatically extracting concepts from free text: both revolve around recognition of medical phrases and mapping the phrases found to a controlled space. However, in the case of automatic link generation the elements in the controlled space are complex and lengthy (e.g., the contents of a Wikipedia page), whereas they tend to be simple and short in the case of ontologies (e.g., the synonymous labels of an ontology concept).

Unlike the systems mentioned above, our approach will be strictly based on machine learning techniques. While we choose Wikipedia as our target collection for the reasons mentioned in Section 1, our approach is sufficiently flexible to allow for extensions with hand crafted rules or expert knowledge in the form of features as well as to be adapted for generating links to other collections.

3. PRELIMINARIES

In this section, we introduce our notation and describe the experimental setup that we use to answer the two research questions introduced in Section 1.

Terminology and notation. Let $T = \{t_i\}_i$ be the set of *source texts*, e.g., our corpus of radiology reports. Let $W = \{d_i\}_i$ be the set of Wikipedia concepts, where each concept is represented by a Wikipedia page. We split the link generation task in three subtasks:

1. *Anchor detection* (AD): Given a source text t with ngrams $NG^t = \{ng_i\}_i$, extract a set of *anchors* $A^t \subseteq NG^t$, that is, phrases that we want to link to a Wikipedia page.
2. *Target candidate identification* (TCI): Given an anchor $a \in A^t$, select a set C^a of candidate *targets*, that is, the set that contains the Wikipedia page to which a is linked. The set C^a can be the entire Wikipedia collection W, but it is often more efficient to consider a subset of W.
3. *Target detection* (TD): Given a set of candidates C^a, select a target $w \in C^a$ to which a linked.

A link generation system maps each source text t to a set of L pairs (a, w), i.e., the links it establishes between anchors a in t and Wikipedia pages w. In the literature, the notion of *target finding* is used to refer to the combined TCI and TD task; for ease of exposition we split the target finding task in two.

We use the functions $AD(\cdot)$, $TCI(\cdot)$ and $TD(\cdot)$ to refer to the above components. For instance, AD is a function that maps t to a subset of NG^t, and TD maps the set $\{C^a : a \in AD(t)\}$ to $\{(a, w) : a \in AD(t), w \in C^a\}$.

Collection of radiology reports. Our collection of radiology reports consists of 860 anonymized neuroradiology reports, obtained from a US-based radiology institute, written in the 2001–2008 time frame. The reports were obtained by querying the institute's picture archiving and communication system for neoplasm cases in the optic nerve region.

The collection was annotated by three annotators, all with a background in medical informatics. The anchor texts are phrases referring to body locations, findings and diagnoses. In total, 29,256 links, i.e., anchor–Wikipedia page pairs, are extracted from the 860 reports, which can be resolved to 6,440 unique links. The set was created as follows.

The corpus was divided in three subsets; each subset was assigned to an annotator. Each annotator manually selected anchor texts in all reports assigned to him. For each anchor, the annotators use Wikipedia's search engine to search for the most appropriate page. If an anchor text does not have a directly matching Wikipedia page, a more general concept that reasonably covers the topic was sought. If no such page was found, no target was assigned. Thus every anchor was assigned at most one Wikipedia page.

The annotations of the three annotators were merged by concatenating their lists of anchor–target pairs. In case two annotators assigned different target pages to the same anchor (which happened in less than 5% of the anchors), disagreements were discussed among annotators and one annotator manually corrected this by picking the best target page. Then, the selections in the reports were updated on the basis of the concatenated list of anchor–target page pairs ensuring that two occurrences of the same phrase, possibly in different reports, are assigned the same Wikipedia page, if any. Note that this indicates that our anchor texts are not ambiguous within the test collection. This is a strong assumption in a general domain as well as in the medical domain. For instance, in the medical domain, "ventricle" is ambiguous as it may refer to a space in the heart as well as an area in the brain. In our corpus, however, it turned out to be a weak assumption as all reports are on the topic of neuroradiology and no ambiguous phrases were encountered during the annotation process.

Wikipedia collection. For annotation, the online version of Wikipedia during 2008 was used. For system development, we use the INEX 2009 Wikipedia collection [36] as our target collection. It is a snapshot of the October 8, 2008 dump of the English Wikipedia articles, with a total of 2,666,190 articles.

Note that the content of the Wikipedia collection may change over time. In order to resolve possible differences between different versions of Wikipedia, we map all the resulting urls to the online version. This is the same for both the state-of-the-art systems discussed in Section 4 and our proposed approach discussed in Section 5. Around 8% of the target urls in the annotation have a redirection at the time we evaluated the systems.

Evaluation setup. We evaluate an automatic link generation systems' performance in terms of precision, recall and F-measure. We evaluate the systems' performance on each radiology report, and show their overall performance, i.e., the averaged performance over all reports. Further, we use a paired t-test for significance testing. The symbol $^{\blacktriangle}$ ($^{\blacktriangledown}$) indicates a significant increase (decrease) with p-value < 0.01; and a $^{\triangle}$ ($^{\triangledown}$) indicates a significant increase (decrease) with p-value < 0.05.

4. A SOLVED PROBLEM?

In order to answer the first research question, RQ1, we evaluate and analyze the performance of two state-of-the-art systems, i.e., Wikify! [29] and Wikipedia Miner [31] in automatically generating links from radiology reports to explanatory Wikipedia concepts. We start with a brief introduction of the two systems and specify our implementation.

4.1 Two state-of-the-art systems

Wikify!. The workflow of Wikify! [29] is summarized in Algorithm 1 using the notations introduced in Section 3. For detecting

Algorithm 1 Wikify!

```
Input: t
L = ∅
for a ∈ AD(t) do
    C^a = TCI(a, W)
    w = TD(a, C^a)
    L ← L ∪ {(a, w)}
end for
return L
```

anchor texts from NG^t, i.e., $AD(\cdot)$, Wikify! ranks $ng \in NG^t$ according to a score and uses the top τ ranked ng's as anchor texts for t. Mihalcea and Csomai [29] experimented with several scores, including tf.idf, χ^2 and a *keyphraseness* score, which turns out to be the most effective score among the three. The keyphraseness score is defined as follows.

$$keyphraseness(ng) = \frac{|A_{ng}|}{|W_{ng}|}, \quad (1)$$

where $|W_{ng}|$ is the number of Wikipedia pages that mention the ngram ng and $|A_{ng}|$ is the number of Wikipedia pages where ng occurs as anchor text.

Wikify! collects C^a for a given anchor a via existing links in Wikipedia. Whenever a is used as an anchor text in Wikipedia, the page it links to is added to the set of candidate targets C^a.

To identify the target page w from C^a for a given a, two approaches were proposed [29]. The first one is knowledge based and picks out the candidate target page w that maximizes the score calculated by the Lesk algorithm [24], i.e., the word overlap between the candidate page w and the context of a in t. The second is a machine learning-based approach. For each a, a classifier is trained to classify whether it links to a candidate target page.

We re-implemented the Wikify! system as described in [29]. For anchor detection, following [29], we set the threshold τ to 6% of the length of the source text. For target finding, we implement both the knowledge based approach and the machine learning based approach. A combination of the two approaches was evaluated in [29], but no consistent improvement was found in terms of precision, recall and F-measure, therefore we decide to leave it out.

Wikipedia Miner. The workflow of Wikipedia Miner [31] is summarized in Algorithm 2. Unlike Wikify!, Wikipedia Miner performs $TCI(\cdot)$ and $TD(\cdot)$ on ngrams instead of identified anchors.

Algorithm 2 Wikipedia Miner

```
Input: t
L = ∅, L_tmp = ∅
for ng ∈ NG^t do
    C^ng = TCI(ng, W)
    w = TD(C^ng, ng)
    L_tmp ← L_tmp ∪ {(ng, w)}
end for
for (ng, w) ∈ L_tmp do
    if ng ∈ AD(t) then
        L ← L ∪ {(ng, w)}
    end if
end for
return L
```

To collect target candidates C^{ng}, Wikipedia Miner uses existing Wikipedia links. To improve efficiency, a threshold is used to filter out candidate pages that have very low chance of being linked to a given ng based on inspecting existing Wikipedia links. Wikipedia Miner trains a classifier for target detection. For details of the features as well as the combination of features employed in the system, we refer to [31]. Wikipedia Miner does not have an explicit anchor detection phase, instead, anchor detection is achieved by filtering the set of pairs from L_{tmp}. A classifier is trained over instances consisting of ngram-target pairs. Various features are used to train the classifier, including the keyphraseness score proposed in [29] and features reflecting the relatedness between source text and candidate target page.

For evaluation, we use the online Wikipedia Miner server,[1] which is provided by the authors, with default parameter settings. The server was accessed remotely and used as a black box.

4.2 Evaluation of the two systems

Results. Table 1 shows the evaluation results in three aspects: anchor detection, target finding and overall system performance. Here, target finding is evaluated over the anchor texts that are correctly identified by each system.

Table 1: Results of the two systems, Wikify! and Wikipedia Miner(WM) on the test collection of radiology reports, in terms of precision (P), recall (R) and F-measure (F).

System	Anchor detection			Target finding			Overall		
	P	R	F	P	R	F	P	R	F
Wikify! (Lesk)	0.35	0.16	0.22	0.40	0.40	0.40	0.14	0.07	0.09
Wikify! (ML)	0.35	0.16	0.22	0.69	0.69	0.69	0.25	0.12	0.16
WM	0.35	0.36	0.36	0.84	0.84	0.84	0.29	0.30	0.30

We see that for both systems, the overall performance is far from their performance on the data from general domain as reported in [29] and [31].[2] Further, both systems show a relatively reasonable performance of target finding on correctly identified anchor texts compared to the reported scores achieved in the general domain. This observation indicates that the major bottleneck of the systems' performance occurs in anchor detection. Given this observation, below we conduct an analysis of the anchor texts aiming at finding the answer to the question: how do links in radiology

[1] `http://wikipedia-miner.sourceforge.net`

[2] Milne and Witten [31] report a precision/recall of 0.73/0.74 on overall system performance; Mihalcea and Csomai [29] do not report overall system performance, but an upper bound is estimated to be 0.53/0.55 in terms of precision/recall [31].

Table 2: The number of annotated anchor texts/sub-anchors in radiology reports covered by Wikipedia anchor texts.

Evaluation type	Occur. in WP links	coverage (%)
exact match	923	14.3
partial match	1,038	16.1
sub-exact match	5,257	81.6

reports differ from links in a general domain, i.e., Wikipedia links? What causes the failure of the state-of-the-art systems?

An analysis of radiology anchor texts. Upon closer inspection of the anchors in the test collection, we have the following observations. Medical phrases often have a regular syntactic structure. For example, 70% of our annotated anchor texts are noun phrases, where 38% are single-word nouns and 32% are nouns with one or more modifiers (e.g., adjectives). Such regularity can provide useful features for recognizing these medical phrases in the reports.

Furthermore, Wikipedia anchors are generally shorter and less complex than radiology anchors. The average length of the annotated anchor texts in radiology reports is 3.29 words, while the average length of the title of their corresponding targets in Wikipedia is 1.98 words. Often the presence of multiple modifiers as well as conjunctions within a single medical phrase results in a complex semantic structure. For example, the phrase "acute cerebral and cerebellar infarction" contains two concepts "cerebellar infarction" and "acute cerebral infarction," where "cerebellar" and "cerebral" are synonyms. When linking this phrase to Wikipedia, one needs to identify the main concept it represents prior to searching for a target page in Wikipedia. Thus, there is a structural mismatch between the Wikipedia anchors and the anchors in the radiology reports.

In order to quantify the above mentioned difference between radiology anchor texts and Wikipedia anchors, in Table 2 we list a set of statistics about the coverage of Wikipedia anchor texts over the annotated anchor texts found in our test collection. Let A^W be all the anchor texts found in Wikipedia. We evaluate the coverage on three aspects:

exact match the number of annotated anchor texts occurring in A^W;

partial match the number of annotated anchor texts occurring in A^W, including the cases when an annotated anchor text is a substring of a Wikipedia anchor; e.g., the phrase "arachnoid" partially matches the Wikipedia anchor "arachnoid mater".

sub-exact match the number of annotated anchor texts containing at least one sub word sequence that occurs in A^W. For example, "left internal capsule" sub-exact matches the Wikipedia anchor "interal capsule".

Relatively few (<20%) annotated anchor texts occur (fully or as as a substring of the anchor texts) in A^W. However, over 80% of the annotated anchor texts do contain one or more sub-word sequences that occur in A^W. That is, most of the annotated anchor texts contain one or more Wikipedia concepts.

Now let us look at what these statistics mean for the system performance. For anchor detection, both state-of-the-art systems rely heavily on the Wikipedia anchor texts. The keyphraseness score is used as the only score for identifying anchor texts in the Wikify! system, and used as an important feature for Wikipedia Miner. However, from Eq. 1, we can see that an anchor text only receives a non-zero score if it occurs in A^W. Given the low coverage of the annotated anchor texts in A^W, it is not surprising that the keyphraseness score is not effective, as around 85% of the annotated anchor texts would receive a 0 score.

For target detection, both systems retrieve candidate target pages via Wikipedia links. The difference between the systems can be explained as follows. Recall that Wikify! finds its candidate target pages with respect to an identified anchor text, whereas Wikipedia Miner selects its candidate target pages from the set of all ngrams extracted from a report. The approach employed by Wikify! suffers from the same problem as in anchor detection: low coverage of Wikipedia anchor texts over annotated anchor texts in our test collection. In the case of Wikipedia Miner, since all possible ngrams in a report are considered, the whole pool of candidate target pages at the report level cover a majority of the annotated target pages for that report, which leads to a much improved performance compared to that of Wikify!.

In summary, the main reason that the state-of-the art systems do not yield a satisfactory performance in generating links from radiology data is caused by the structural mismatch between the radiology anchors and the Wikipedia anchors and the fact that both systems rely on existing Wikipedia links. Based on this observation, we now introduce our proposed approach aimed at tackling these problems.

5. LINK GENERATION REVISITED

How can we exploit the unique properties of radiology reports identified above? In order to exploit the regularity of the syntactic structure of medical phrases in the radiology reports, we treat the anchor detection problem as a sequential labeling problem. Sequential labeling is an effective approach in part-of-speech tagging as well as terminology recognition, including terminology from the biomedical domain [7, 21, 23, 27, 37, 38, 40]; it has been shown to be able to effectively capture the regularity in language usage. In addition, unlike the two state-of-the-art link generation systems, we learn the pattern of anchor texts from radiology data instead of Wikipedia. Wikipedia anchors are restricted to single concepts, while the radiology anchors can contain one or more concepts, or concepts with multiple modifiers, therefore Wikipedia anchors may not provide effective training material for sequential labeling to determine the boundaries of anchors in radiology reports.

Note that even though we expect that the sequential labeling approach can be useful in determining anchor text boundaries, the structural mismatch between Wikipedia anchors and radiology anchors remains for the target finding stage. To cope with the complex semantic structure of medical anchor texts, we propose a *sub-anchor-based* approach to retrieving candidate targets and to formulate features for target detection. By retrieving target candidates with respect to sub word sequence of an anchor text, referred to as *sub-anchors*, we collect candidate pages that are potentially relevant to different related concepts contained in the anchor text. During the target detection phase, we aggregate features extracted at sub-anchor level to anchor level. The feature of a single sub-anchor text is weighted by its relevance to the original anchor, as measured by its similarity to the original anchor text.

The proposed system is called LiRa, after Linking Radiology reports. Its workflow is the same as that of the Wikify! system, as illustrated in Algorithm 1. That is, it follows the following steps: anchor detection, target candidate identification and target detection. In the rest of this section, we first describe our approaches to the three components (Section 5.1-5.3), followed by the training and configuration details of the proposed system in Section 5.4.

5.1 Anchor detection

We define the sequential labeling task for anchor detection as follows. Given a text document, identify anchor texts by annotating each of the words in the text with one of the following labels: begin of anchor (BOA), in anchor (IA), end of anchor (EOA), outside anchor (OA), and single word anchor (SWA). SWA defines a single word anchor; BOA-(IA)-EOA defines an anchor with multiple words. Within this framework, we use a conditional random fields (CRF) model [22], which has shown state-of-the-art performance in solving sequential labeling problems [27, 37].

Let $WS = w_1, \ldots, w_n$ be an observed word sequence of length n, and $SS = s_1, \ldots, s_n$ a sequence of states where s_i corresponds to the label assigned to the word w_i. Following Settles [37], we use linear-chain CRFs, which define the conditional probability of the state sequence given the observed word sequence as

$$p(SS|WS) = \frac{1}{Z(WS)}\exp \sum_i^n \sum_k^m \lambda_k f_k(s_{i-1}, s_i, w_i, i), \quad (2)$$

where $Z(WS)$ is a normalization factor over all state sequences, $f_k(\cdot)$ is a feature function and λ_k is a learnt weight for feature $f_k(\cdot)$. The feature function describes a feature corresponding to the position i of the input sequence, states at position i and $i-1$, and word at position i.

The goal of the learning procedure is to find feature weights λ that maximize the log-likelihood of the training data:

$$LL = \sum_i \log p(s_i|w_i) - \sum_k \frac{\lambda_k^2}{2\sigma^2}. \quad (3)$$

The second term in Eq. 3 is a spherical Gaussian weight prior [6] used to penalize the log-likelihood term to avoid over-fitting.

In the literature various types of features have been explored, particularly syntactic features such as part-of-speech (POS) tags and orthographical features such as the combination of digits and letters [37, 40]. This is due to the fact that biomedical terminology, such as gene and protein names, often displays syntactic regularities as well as uncommon word spellings. Here, we expect that our medical phrases share the same properties as the biomedical terminology. Following the literature, we explored a number of features, including the word itself, its POS tag, its syntactic chunk tag, orthographical features as well as bigram and trigram features. Preliminary experiments show that three features, namely the word itself, its POS tag and syntactic chunk tag, are the most effective features. Adding other features does not result in significant improvement to the system's performance. Therefore in the rest of the paper we focus on these three basic features.

5.2 Target candidate identification

For an identified anchor text a, we retrieve Wikipedia pages related to the sub word sequences contained in a, i.e., sub-anchors, so as to collect candidate target pages with respect to different concepts related to the original anchor text.

Given a, we decompose it into the set of all sub-sequences $S_a = \{s_i\}_i$, while keeping the original order of the words within the identified anchor text. For example, for the anchor text "white matter disease", we have a set of sub-sequences {"white", "matter", "disease", "white matter", "matter disease", "white disease", "white matter disease"}.

In addition, there exist redirect pages in Wikipedia, which provide synonyms or morphological variations for a concept. For example, the concept "acoustic schwannoma" is redirected to "vestibular schwannoma." While decomposing an identified anchor text, we add its redirects to the set of sub-anchors. Further, in order to reduce the morphological variance of terms and phrases, we preprocess the radiology reports and the Wikipedia collection using the Porter stemmer [35]. In order to avoid adding trivial phrases, we filter out sequences that consist entirely of function words.

For each sub-anchor s, we retrieve a set of candidate target pages $C^s = \{c_i\}_i$, ranked in descending order of their *target probability*. Let $L_{s,c} = \{l(a,d) | a = s, d = c, d \in W\}$ denote all pairs of links found between s and c in Wikipedia links, that is, links between target page s and all occurrences of s as anchor texts. The target probability is calculated as

$$p(c_i|s) = \frac{|L_{s,c_i}|}{\sum_{j=1}^{n} |L_{s,c_j}|}, \quad (4)$$

where $n = |C^s|$ and $|\cdot|$ is the number of elements in a set. In other words, the target probability indicates how likely an anchor text is linked to a candidate page. An underlying assumption is that, the more an anchor text is linked with a candidate page in the existing Wikipedia links, the more likely it is that the anchor and the target page are closely related.

When examining the occurrence of sub-anchor s in existing Wikipedia links, we consider partial matches of phrases. That is, if all terms in s appear ordered within a Wikipedia anchor text, it is considered to be an occurrence.

We collect the top-K Wikipedia pages in terms of their target probability scores for each sub-anchor and use the union of all the collected pages from each sub-anchor as the candidate target pages for the anchor. While not all sub-anchor texts are semantically related to the original anchor texts, nor are they necessarily meaningful phrases, we leave the task of identifying (among all retrieved candidate target pages) the target page that is most relevant to the original anchor text, to the target detection component.

5.3 Target detection

We use a machine learning based approach to identify the target page d^* for a given anchor text a. Specifically, we train a classifier over the *anchor–candidate target* pairs (a, c), which are labeled as "link" or "non-link". We extract the following three type of features to train the classifier: (i) title matching, (ii) target probability, and (iii) language model log-likelihood ratio. The first two features are calculated at the sub-anchor level, and the third feature is calculated for a candidate target page; see below.

Title matching. One important feature of Wikipedia is that the title of each Wikipedia page represents the concept explained by the page. A match between an anchor text and the title of a Wikipedia page is therefore a strong indication that the content of the page is about the concept represented by the anchor text. The title matching score reflects the degree of matching between the anchor text and the title of c.

We consider the title matching scores for each of the sub-anchors. For a sub-anchor s of anchor a, and a candidate target page c, the title matching score is defined as follows:

$$tm(s,c) = f_{tm}(s,c)\frac{len(s)}{len(a)}, \quad (5)$$

where

$$f_{tm}(s,c) = \begin{cases} 1 & \text{if } s \text{ equals title of } c \\ 0 & \text{otherwise.} \end{cases}$$

and $len(\cdot)$ is number of words in a word sequence. The longer the sub-anchor, the more similar the sub-anchor is to the original anchor text, and therefore we have a higher degree of matching between the anchor text and the title of c. That is, a higher degree of word overlapping between the anchor text and the title of $ctar$.

Target probability. The target probability is the probability that a Wikipedia page will be selected as target page, given the anchor text, as defined in Eq. 4. It is pre-computed during the candidate retrieval procedure and calculated for each sub-anchor s.

Since the target probability is calculated at the sub-anchor level, we need to aggregate those scores for the original anchor texts.

Note that in the case of title matching, no explicit aggregation is needed, since for a given candidate target page, it can only match one of its sub-anchors. In the case of candidate target probability, we aggregate the features extracted from the sub-anchors into three features. For an anchor a and its sub-anchors S_a of a candidate target page c we define:

$$\max_{tp}(c) = \max_{s \in S} p(c|s);$$
$$\min_{tp}(c) = \min_{s \in S} p(c|s);$$
$$\mathrm{wsum}_{tp}(c) = \textstyle\sum_{s \in S_a} \frac{len(s)}{len(a)} p(c|s).$$

Language-model log-likelihood ratio (LM-LLR). We use the LM-LLR as a feature to measure the extent to which a candidate target page is about radiology. It will help us to discriminate between e.g., the Wikipedia page about the journal *Brain* and the page about the body part that we are interested in.

Language models are statistical models that capture the statistical regularities in generating a language, often used to estimate the probability of a text being relevant to certain topic in the context of information retrieval [34]. Here we consider two language models. The first, θ_R, models the language used in the radiology reports, which we refer to as the *radiology model*, and the second, θ_W, models the language used in Wikipedia pages on topics in a general domain, which we refer to as *Wikipedia model*.

Each model defines a probability mechanism, which can be explained as follows. Assuming the two models sample terms from the radiology collection and the Wikipedia collection that follow a multinomial distribution, using a maximum likelihood estimation, the probability that a certain term t is selected given a collection C can be estimated as the relative frequency of the term in the collection, i.e., $p(t|\theta_C) = \frac{count(t \in C)}{|C|}$. Now, given a piece of text with n terms, $T = \{t_i\}_{i=1}^{n}$, the two models repeatedly sample n times, assuming independence between successive events. The probability that T is generated by the radiology model can be defined as

$$p(t_1, t_2, \ldots, t_n|\theta_R) = \textstyle\prod_{i=1}^{n} p(t_i|\theta_R), \quad (6)$$

while the probability that T is generated by the Wikipedia model is

$$p(t_1, t_2, \ldots, t_n|\theta_W) = \textstyle\prod_{i=1}^{n} p(t_i|\theta_W). \quad (7)$$

Given the above language models, we use the log-likelihood ratio (LLR) [26], a widely used model-comparison metric, to decide which model is more likely to have generated T:

$$\begin{aligned} \textit{LM-LLR}(T) &= \log\left(\frac{p(T|\theta_R)}{p(T|\theta_W)}\right) \\ &= \textstyle\sum_{i=1}^{n} \log p(t_i|\theta_R) - \sum_{i=1}^{n} \log p(t_i|\theta_W). \end{aligned} \quad (8)$$

To avoid zero probabilities, which come up if terms in T do not occur in the radiology reports or in Wikipedia, we use Laplacian smoothing [25]. That is, we assume that each word has been seen at least once. The LM-LLR score indicates which of the two models θ_R and θ_W is most likely to have generated T. A score larger than 0 indicates T is more likely to be generated by the radiology language model, hence more likely to be relevant to the anchor text identified from a radiology report.

In summary, we list the final features we use to train a classifier for identifying a target page from a set of candidate targets: (i) Title matching between a and c; (ii) Maximum target probability $\max_{tp}$; (iii) Minimum target probability $\min_{tp}$; (iv) Weighted sum of target probability wsum_{tp}; (v) Language model log-likelihood ratio of c.

5.4 Training and configuration

We specify the training procedure and the configuration of LiRa with respect to the three components described above.

Anchor detection. For anchor detection, we use the CRFsuite [33] implementation of CRFs with default parameter settings. A POS tagging and chunking tool TagChunk[3] is used to create the POS and chunk features. For training and evaluating the anchor detection performance, we use 3-fold cross-validation.

Target candidate identification. At the target candidate identification stage, we rank Wikipedia pages in descending order of target probability scores and select the top K candidate target pages. Heuristically, we set K to 10.

Target detection. We calculate the LM-LLR feature using the first 100 words of each candidate target page, for two reasons. First, the first paragraph of a Wikipedia page is usually the summary of the content of that page which covers the most important content of that page. Second, by using a constant number of words from each candidate target page, we eliminate the effect that the total number of words in the page has on the LM-LLR score. This makes the LM-LLR scores comparable across different Wikipedia pages.

Following [31], we experimented with three classifiers: Naive Bayes (NB), SVM [8], and Random Forest (RF) [4],[4] using the Weka implementations [15]. After preliminary experiments, we found that RF significantly outperforms the other two classifiers, in terms of efficiency and effectiveness. Therefore, all of LiRa's results reported below are based on RF. Further, with respect to the five features introduced in previous sections, we find in a preliminary feature selection experiment that all features are important to the classifier, removing any causes a decrease in performance.

Along with the predicted labels, the classifiers also provide a prediction confidence score. After classification, we execute a post-processing procedure. For anchor texts whose candidate target pages are all classified as "non-link," we select the candidate target with the lowest prediction confidence for being a "non-link." For anchor texts that have multiple candidate target pages labeled "link," we choose the one with the highest prediction confidence.

Again, we use 3-fold cross-validation for training and evaluating the classifiers.

6. EVALUATION

In this section, we show the evaluation results and compare the performance of the three link generation systems.[5]

6.1 Anchor detection

Table 3 lists the results of anchor detection for the three systems considered. We observe that LiRa outperforms both Wikipedia Miner and Wikify! in anchor detection in terms of all three evaluation metrics, i.e., precision, recall and F-measure. This suggests that the sequential labeling-CRF approach trained on radiology data is more effective than the approaches employed by Wikify! and Wikipedia Miner, which learn the patterns of anchor texts solely from existing Wikipedia links.

[3] `http://www.umiacs.umd.edu/~hal/TagChunk/`

[4] We use Random Forest, an ensemble decision tree classifier, instead of C4.5.

[5] In all the tables listed in this Section, boldface indicates the best performance across systems. For significance testing we use the same setting as described in Section 3. All runs are compared against LiRa.

Table 3: **Results on anchor detection.**

System	precision	recall	F-measure
LiRa	**0.90**	**0.80**	**0.85**
Wikipedia Miner	0.35▼	0.36▼	0.36▼
Wikify!	0.35▼	0.16▼	0.22▼

6.2 Target finding

In order to compare the target finding performance of the systems, we need to run the target finding components of each system on the same set of anchor texts. Consequently, we cannot simply evaluate each system on the set of anchors it finds in the anchor detection phase, as it is bound to differ from the set of anchors found by the other two systems. We consider two sets of anchor texts for evaluation. The first contains the annotated anchors from the test collection. However, since we run Wikipedia Miner as a black box, we cannot instruct it to generate a Wikipedia page for a given anchor. Therefore we only use this set to compare our system against Wikify!. The second set contains the anchor texts identified by Wikify! or by Wikipedia Miner. That is, we run LiRa on the anchor texts identified by Wikify! (Wikipedia Miner), and compare the target finding performance of LiRa against that of Wikify! (Wikipedia Miner, respectively) on the same set of anchor texts.

Table 4 shows the target finding performance of LiRa and Wikify! on the annotated anchors from the test collection. Table 5 (Table 6, respectively) shows the performance of LiRa and Wikify! (Wikipedia Miner, respectively) on the annotated anchor texts that are correctly identified by Wikify! (Wikipedia Miner).

In Table 4 and 5 we see that the target finding performance of LiRa is better than that of Wikify!.

Further, in Table 6 we see that LiRa also outperforms Wikipedia Miner on the target finding task, on the anchor texts found by the latter. The difference in performance between LiRa and Wikipedia Miner is smaller than the difference between LiRa and Wikify!.

Table 4: Comparing the performance of LiRa and Wikify! on target finding. The target finding algorithms are run on the annotated anchor texts found in the ground truth.

System	precision	recall	F-measure
LiRa	**0.68**	**0.68**	**0.68**
Wikify! (Lesk)	0.13▼	0.13▼	0.13▼
Wikify! (ML)	0.26▼	0.26▼	0.26▼

Table 5: Comparing the performance of LiRa and Wikify! on target finding. The target finding algorithms are run on the anchor texts identified by Wikify!.

System	precision	recall	F-measure
LiRa	**0.80**	**0.80**	**0.80**
Wikify! (Lesk)	0.40▼	0.40▼	0.40▼
Wikify! (ML)	0.69▼	0.69▼	0.69▼

Table 6: Comparing the performance of LiRa and Wikipedia Miner on target finding. The target finding algorithms are run on the anchor texts identified by Wikipedia Miner.

System	precision	recall	F-measure
LiRa	**0.89**	**0.89**	**0.89**
Wikipedia Miner	0.84▼	0.84▼	0.84▼

6.3 Overall performance

In Table 7 we show the overall performance of the three systems, i.e., the performance on the combined anchor detection and target finding task. We see that LiRa dramatically outperforms the state-of-the-art systems in terms of overall performance. This is no surprise as we have seen above that it also outperforms the other systems on the core subtasks, anchor detection and target finding.

Table 7: Overall system performance.

System	precision	recall	F-measure
LiRa(LL)	**0.65**	**0.58**	**0.61**
Wikipedia Miner	0.29▼	0.30▼	0.30▼
Wikify! (Lesk)	0.14▼	0.07▼	0.09▼
Wikfy! (ML)	0.25▼	0.12▼	0.16▼

Further, Table 4 can be seen as an "oracle run" of the overall system performance of Wikify! and LiRa, under the assumption that the systems' anchor detection modules are flawless, since we evaluate them on the anchors from the test collection as if the systems' found these anchors themselves. Again, we see that LiRa outperforms Wikify!. However, the performance of LiRa is far from perfect.

7. DISCUSSION AND ANALYSIS

In the previous section, we compared our approach to the state-of-the-art. LiRa consistently outperforms Wikify! and Wikipedia Miner on all aspects of the link generation task. Earlier findings in Section 4 help us understand the difference in performance.

For anchor detection, LiRa exploits the regularity of the syntactic structure of the annotated anchor texts in the radiology reports by using syntactic features within a sequential labeling approach. The sequential labeling approach captures this regularity, and is therefore more effective for anchor detection.

Further, even though all three systems retrieve candidate target pages on the basis of existing Wikipedia links, their performance differs considerably on target detection. Recall that Wikify! selects candidate target pages on the basis of identified anchor texts. It becomes clear that the marginal overlap between the Wikipedia and radiology anchors also hampers Wikify!'s target detection approach. The sub-anchor matches used by LiRa allow it to retrieve not only candidate pages that are relevant to the anchor text itself, but also pages that are relevant to related concepts, which improves the target detection performance. Recall that Wikipedia Miner uses yet another strategy to deal with the overlap between Wikipedia and radiology anchors: all possible ngrams in a radiology report that match Wikipedia anchor texts are considered, which results in a set of candidate target pages that cover the majority of the annotated target pages for that report. We saw that Wikipedia Miner's target finding performance is comparable to that of LiRa's.

Do linking systems perform differently with respect to different anchors? Are there anchors more difficult than others in terms of being correctly recognized and linked to a target page? While anchor texts can "differ" in many aspects, we decide to focus on one specific aspect: their frequency. In the test collection, we observe that some anchor texts occur more often than others. Specifically, in Figure 2, we rank the annotated anchor texts in decreasing order of their frequency and then plot their frequency against their ranks on a log scale. We see that the anchor text frequencies exhibit the typical properties of Zipf's law [30]. That is, a distribution consisting of a few anchors with high frequencies and a long tail of anchors with low frequencies. In addition, Table 8 lists the most frequent and least frequent anchors in our test collection. We see that

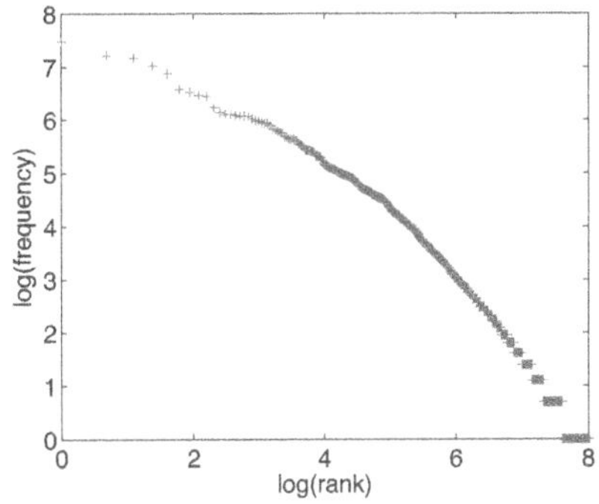

Figure 2: Distribution of anchor frequency. Anchors are ranked according to their frequency of occurrence in the radiology reports. The X-axis shows the logarithm of the ranks of anchors, and the Y-axis shows the logarithm of the frequency of the anchor at that rank.

frequent anchors tend to refer to an "easier" concept than the infrequent ones, i.e., with which (non-medical) users are more likely to be familiar. For instance, it is reasonable to assume that more users require background information about "xanthogranulomas" than on "brain" if such a term appears in a radiology report. Intuitively, frequent phrases are likely to refer to general concepts in the radiology reports while infrequent ones are likely to be used to describe a specific medical condition. Further, we expect that general concepts are more likely to occur in Wikipedia and therefore link generation is likely to be relatively easier for frequent phrases than for infrequent ones.

Table 8: The five most frequent and five least frequent anchor texts in the test collection.

Top 5	Bottom 5
mass	vestibular nerves
brain	Virchow-Robin space
meningioma	Warthin's tumor
frontal	Wegner's granulomatosis
white matter	xanthogranulomas

Based on the above observations and assumptions, we conduct a further analysis aimed at finding out whether and how anchor text frequencies have an impact on the performance of linking systems.

Table 9: Segmentation of anchor texts based on their frequencies in the test collection.

	1	2	3	4	5	6
Freq. range	>100	51–100	11–50	6–10	2–5	1
# of anchors	116	108	527	482	1,399	2,149
Avg. freq.	271.1	70.1	20.7	6.5	2.6	1

We divide the radiology anchors into different segments based on their frequencies, as listed in Table 9. We evaluate the performance of the three systems on anchor detection and overall link generation for the different segments. The performance of each system on segment seg is measured using the *recall* function.

$$recall(seg) = \frac{n_{seg}}{|seg|} \tag{9}$$

where n_{seg} is the number of anchor texts in seg that are correctly recognized in the case of anchor detection, or whose target pages are correctly identified in the case of target finding.

We show the systems' performance of anchor detection in Figure 3(a) and that of target finding in Figure 3(b). Since we do not

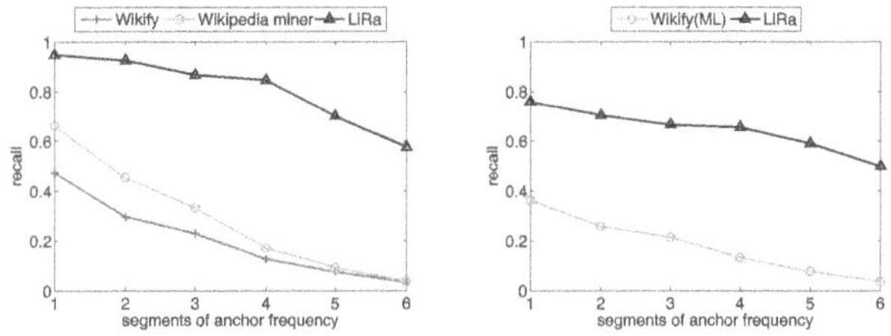

(a) (b)

Figure 3: Systems' performance differentiated by anchor texts' frequency. Anchors are ranked according to their frequency of occurrence in the radiology reports. X-axes show the ranks of anchors; Y-axes show the systems' scores on the r most frequent anchors, see Eq. 9. Figure 3(a) shows the anchor detection rate; Figure 3(b) shows the automatic link generation rate.

have access to the intermediate results of the Wikipedia Miner system as discussed in Section 6, we only show the performance of Wikify! (machine learning version) and LiRa on target finding.

Both anchor detection and target finding show a general trend: the more frequent the anchor texts, the better the systems' performance. Further, we see that LiRa shows more robust performance compared to other systems with respect to infrequent anchor texts.

We conclude that anchor frequency has an impact on the performance of link generation systems in both anchor detection and target finding. Our results indicate that the link generation systems considered achieve better performance on frequent anchor texts than on infrequent anchor texts.

8. CONCLUSION

We conclude the paper by summarizing answers to the research questions raised in Section 1 and discuss directions for future work.

With respect to RQ1, we find that existing link generation systems trained on general domain corpora do not provide a satisfactory solution to linking radiology reports. The major problem is that medical phrases typically have a more complex semantic structure than Wikipedia concepts.

With respect to RQ2, we used a sequential labeling based approach with syntactic features to anchor detection in order to exploit the syntactic regularity present among medical phrases. We then used a sub-anchor based approach to target finding, in order to resolve the complexity in the semantic structure of medical phrases. Our proposed approach was shown to be effective as evaluated on our test collection.

Further, we found that automatic link generation systems tend to achieve better performance in recognizing and finding targets on frequent anchor texts than on anchor texts with a low frequency. In order to achieve robust performance, it is therefore important that a system is effective when dealing with low frequency anchor texts.

A number of directions are left to be explored in the future. These include linking (from radiology reports) to other resources, such as the MedLink encyclopedia. Next, the techniques can be used to provide background information for terminology-rich documents in other domains, ranging from, say biology to zoology. A third line of generalization concerns a slightly different problem to what we have been considering so far, viz. linking textual documents to suitable ontologies, using Wikipedia as a pivot.

Acknowledgements

This research was supported by the EU's ICT Policy Support Programme as part of the Competitiveness and Innovation Framework

Programme, CIP ICT-PSP under grant agreement nr 250430, the Fish4Knowledge project and the PROMISE Network of Excellence, funded and co-funded by the 7th Framework Programme of the European Commission, grant agreement nr 257024 and nr 258191, respectively, the Netherlands Organisation for Scientific Research (NWO) under project nrs 612.061.814, 612.061.815, 640.004.802, 380-70-011, the Center for Creation, Content and Technology (CCCT), the Hyperlocal Service Platform project funded by the Service Innovation & ICT program, the WAHSP project funded by the CLARIN-nl program, and under COMMIT project Infiniti.

9. REFERENCES

[1] J. Allan. *Automatic hypertext construction.* PhD thesis, Cornell University, 1995.

[2] A. R. Aronson and F.-M. Lang. An overview of metamap: historical perspective and recent advances. *JAMIA*, 17:229–236, 2010.

[3] W. Bluestein. *Hypertext versions of journal articles: Computer aided linking and realistic human evaluation.* PhD thesis, University of Western Ontario, 1999.

[4] L. Breiman. Random forest. *Machine Learning*, 45(1):5–32, 2001.

[5] M. Bron, B. Huurnink, and M. de Rijke. Linking archives using document enrichment and term selection. In *TPDL 2011*, 2011.

[6] S. F. Chen and R. Rosenfeld. A gaussian prior for smoothing maximum entropy models. Technical report, Carnegie Mellon University, 1999.

[7] N. Collier, C. Nobata, and J.-i. Tsujii. Extracting the names of genes and gene products with a hidden markov model. In *COLING '00*, pages 201–207, Morristown, NJ, USA, 2000.

[8] C. Cortes and V. Vapnik. Support-vector networks. *Machine Learning*, 20:273–297, 1995.

[9] S. Cucerzan. Large-scale named entity disambiguation based on Wikipedia data. In *EMNLP '07*, pages 708–716, 2007.

[10] D. Ellis, J. Furner, and P. Willett. On the creation of hypertext links in full-text documents: Measurement of retrieval effectiveness. *J. Am. Soc. Inform. Sci.*, 47(4):287–300, 1996.

[11] S. Fissaha Adafre and M. de Rijke. Discovering missing links in Wikipedia. In *LinkKDD-2005*, 2005.

[12] C. Friedman, P. Alderson, J. Austin, J. Cimino, and S. Johnson. A general natrual language text processor for clinical radiology. *J. Am. Med. Inform. Assoc.*, 1(2):161–174, 1994.

[13] S. Geva, J. Kamps, and A. Trotman, editors. *INEX' 08*, 2009.

[14] S. Green. Building newspaper links in newspaper articles using semantic similarity. In *NLDB '97*, pages 178–190, 1997.

[15] M. Hall, E. Frank, G. Holmes, B. Pfahringer, P. Reutemann, and I. H. Witten. The WEKA data mining software: an update. *SIGKDD Expl. Newsl.*, 11:10–18, 2009.

[16] P. Haug, D. Ranum, and P. Frederick. Computerized extraction of coded findings from free-text radiologic reports. *Radiology*, 174(2):543–548, 1990.

[17] P. Haug, S. Koehler, L. M. Lau, P. Wang, R. Rocha, and S. Huff. A natural language understanding system combining syntactic and semantic techniques. In *Ann. Symp. Comp. Appl. in Medical Care*, pages 247–151, 1994.

[18] W. C. Huang, A. Trotman, and S. Geva. The importance of manual assessment in link discovery. In *SIGIR '09*, pages 698–699, New York, NY, USA, 2009.

[19] W. C. Huang, S. Geva, and A. Trotman. Overview of the INEX 2009 link the wiki track. In *INEX '09*, 2010.

[20] V. Jijkoun, M. A. Khalid, M. Marx, and M. de Rijke. Named entity normalization in user generated content. In *AND '08*, pages 23–30, New York, NY, USA, 2008. ACM.

[21] J. Kazama, T. Makino, Y. Ohta, and J. Tsujii. Tuning support vector machines for biomedical named entity recognition. In *ACL 2002 workshop on Natural language processing in the biomedical domain*, volume 3, pages 1–8, 2002.

[22] J. D. Lafferty, A. McCallum, and F. C. N. Pereira. Conditional random fields: Probabilistic models for segmenting and labeling sequence data. In *ICML '01*, pages 282–289, 2001.

[23] K.-J. Lee, Y.-S. Hwang, and H.-C. Rim. Two-phase biomedical ne recognition based on SVMs. In *ACL 2003 workshop on Natural language processing in biomedicine*, volume 13, pages 33–40, Morristown, NJ, USA, 2003.

[24] M. Lesk. Automatic sense disambiguation using machine readable dictionaries: how to tell a pine cone from an ice cream cone. In *SIGDOC '86*, pages 24–26, 1986.

[25] G. Lidstone. Note on the general case of the Bayes-Laplace formula for inductive or a posteriori probabilities. *Transactions of the Faculty of Actuaries*, 8:182–192, 1920.

[26] C. D. Manning and H. Schutze. *Foundations of Statistical Natural Language Processing.* MIT Press, 1999.

[27] R. McDonald and F. Pereira. Identifying gene and protein mentions in text using conditional random fields. *BMC Bioinformatics*, S6, 2005.

[28] E. Meij, M. Bron, L. Hollink, B. Huurnink, and M. de Rijke. Learning semantic query suggestions. In *ISWC'09*, pages 424–440, 2009.

[29] R. Mihalcea and A. Csomai. Wikify!: linking documents to encyclopedic knowledge. In *CIKM '07*, pages 233–242, 2007.

[30] G. A. Miller and E. B. Newman. Tests of a statistical explanation of the rank-frequency relation for words in written english. *American Journal of Psychology*, 71:209–218, 1958.

[31] D. Milne and I. H. Witten. Learning to link with wikipedia. In *CIKM '08*, pages 509–518, New York, NY, USA, 2008.

[32] W. Mossberg. New Windows XP feature can re-edit others' sites. *The Wall Street Journal*, 2001.

[33] N. Okazaki. CRFsuite: a fast implementation of conditional random fields (CRFs), 2007. URL `http://www.chokkan.org/software/crfsuite/`.

[34] J. M. Ponte and W. B. Croft. A language modeling approach to information retrieval. In *SIGIR '98*, pages 275–281, 1998.

[35] M. Porter. An algorithm for suffix stripping. *Program*, 14(3): 130–137, 1980.

[36] R. Schenkel, F. Suchanek, and G. Kasneci. YAWN: A semantically annotated Wikipedia XML corpus. In *BTW2007: Datenbanksysteme in Business, Technologie und Web*, 2007.

[37] B. Settles. Biomedical named entity recognition using conditional random fields and rich feature sets. In *JNLPBA '04*, pages 104–107, 2004.

[38] K. Takeuchi and N. Collier. Bio-medical entity extraction using support vector machines. *Artificial Intelligence in Medicine*, 33(2):125–137, 2005.

[39] F. B. Viégas, M. Wattenberg, and K. Dave. Studying cooperation and conflict between authors with history flow visualizations. In *CHI '04*, pages 575–582, 2004.

[40] G. Zhou, J. Zhang, J. Su, D. Shen, and C. Tan. Recognizing names in biomedical texts: A machine learning approach. *Bioinformatics*, 20:1178–1190, 2004.

Information Extraction from Pathology Reports in a Hospital Setting

David Martinez
NICTA & University of Melbourne
Dept. of Computer Science and Software Engineering, University of Melbourne
3010, Australia
david.martinez@nicta.com.au

Yue Li
NICTA & University of Melbourne
Dept. of Computer Science and Software Engineering, University of Melbourne
Victoria 3010, Australia
yolandali.nz@gmail.com

ABSTRACT

As more health data becomes available, information extraction aims to make an impact on the workflows of hospitals and care centers. One of the targeted areas is the management of pathology reports, which are employed for cancer diagnosis and staging. In this work we integrate text mining tools in the workflow of the Royal Melbourne Hospital, to extract information from pathology reports with minimal expert intervention. Our framework relies on coarse-grained annotation (at document level), making it highly portable. Our evaluation shows that the kind of language used in these reports makes it feasible to extract information with high precision and recall, by means of state-of-the-art classification methods, and feature engineering.

Categories and Subject Descriptors

J.3 [**Computer Applications**]: Life and Medical Sciences

General Terms

Algorithms

1. INTRODUCTION

As new technologies for health care are implemented, hospitals have to efficiently manage large amounts of data for each patient in their care. Pathology reports are one of those sensitive pieces of data, used to record information about cells and tissues of a patient. These reports are employed for cancer diagnosis and staging (describing the extent of cancer within the body), and to help to determine the treatment options. Having extensive and precise pathology reports would allow us to perform optimal clinical planning, offer treatments based on the best evidence, and identify the major prognostic factors across different populations. However, the current situation makes the implementation of this kind of analysis unfeasible, because of the lack of a structured and connected network of pathology reports.

One of the major stumbling blocks for the better management of this information is that pathology reports are created in natural language, and this makes it difficult to obtain the structured knowledge required for high-level analysis. Only in some cases the information is converted into structured format, and even then, we face the problems of different standards, data entry errors, and incomplete entries [7]. For this reason, the Australian National Cancer Data Strategy has identified the collection of population-based structured data as a fundamental strategical problem[1].

This scenario is promising for text mining research, because tools that can perform well in this space are likely to make an impact in the way health information is stored and used. The main challenges for developing these kinds of tools are the need of expert domain knowledge (by means of hand-coded rules or manual annotation), and the portability to different subdomains. However a recent systematic literature review has shown limitations of existing text mining tools for the biomedical domain, which tend to be context-dependent and not readily portable [10].

In this paper we try to overcome the portability limitations of text mining tools by automatically learning from the data generated in the workflow of the Royal Melbourne Hospital, with minimal expert intervention. Our framework relies on coarse-grained annotation, Machine Learning (ML), feature engineering, and error analysis in order to extract information for a set of categories in cancer pathology reports. Our feature set includes lemmatisation, different lexical databases (*SNOMED* and *UMLS*), and negation detection. We evaluate our performance using a reference corpus, and compare with other state-of-the-art results when possible. Differently to previous work in this area, we do not rely on domain experts for fine-grained annotation of examples or rules.

Our empirical evaluation will give us insight to build a classification framework for cancer pathology, and for the best methods to implement a practical system for the hospital. Our aim is to integrate a recommendation system in the hospital workflow, where the main features in the text will be highlighted, and where practitioners will accept or correct the system's suggestions. This will make the management of pathology reports easier, and it will help to avoid data input errors, which can have serious consequences in this domain. Another advantage of this approach is that the interactions of the users will be saved, and used to improve the underlying models. In order for this system to be of practical use, we first need to evaluate the quality of predictions over a sample of real data, and this is our goal in this paper.

Text mining from pathology reports has unique characteristics,

CIKM'11, October 24–28, 2011, Glasgow, Scotland, UK.

[1] http://www.canceraustralia.gov.au/cancer-data/cancer-data-improve-cancer-survival

due to the very specific terminology, and the short and semantically-dense content. These can be advantages for text mining, but there are few references in the literature to this domain, because of the lack of pathology reports freely available for research. Pathology reports contain sensitive material, and even after de-identification it is not easy to make them widely available. We obtained a test collection through our collaboration with the Royal Melbourne Hospital, and one of our goals is to provide insight into the type of text that can be found in this domain, and the type of features that contribute to automatic approaches. We expect our contribution to be useful for the implementation of tools for hospitals, and also to new datasets that are being made public, such as the repository of de-identified clinical reports available for research from the University of Pittsburgh NLP group (BLULab)[2]. These clinical records include 2,877 surgical pathology reports, which will be very valuable for researcher in the area. The whole collection of 101,711 clinical reports will be used in the upcoming TREC-MED 2011 challenge [3], which shows the growing interest on this area.

2. BACKGROUND

Our domain of application is colorectal cancer, and we study pathology reports from the Royal Melbourne Hospital. In the current hospital workflow, these reports are written in natural language, and then manually converted into standard forms to represent the structured knowledge. This is a complex task, involving heterogeneous classes with a large set of possible values, both numeric and nominal. It requires clinicians to carefully read each report searching for the relevant information. We will analyse the contribution of text mining to this process, requiring minimal expert intervention to build our classifiers.

The core information contained in pathology reports refers to the staging and location of the cancer, and we will build classifiers to predict 6 categories that represent these factors, which are shown in Table 1. These categories can be seen as 6 multiclass problems, where the goal is to identify a unique goldstandard label.

Staging information has been the target of previous work in the literature, and this will allow us to compare our performance to other approaches. Early work on lung cancer staging was conducted by [8] using Support Vector Machines. Their initial experiments showed the difficulty of the primary tumour stage detection (T), with a top accuracy of 64%. In a follow-up paper they explored richer annotation, and a combination of ML and rule-based post-processing [7]. They performed fine-grained annotation of stage details for each sentence in order to build their system, and they observed improvements over a coarse-grained (document-level) multiclass classifier. However, the authors explain that the annotation cost is high, and the performance for "Stage T" was still low (65% accuracy). In their latest work [9] rely heavily on the *SNOMED* (Systematized Nomenclature of Medicine - Clinical Terms)[4] concepts and relationships to identify the relevant entities. They argue that this approach is more portable than fine-grained annotation, although there is a loss in accuracy with respect to their best ML approach, and it requires involvement from the experts. They report accuracies of 78% for ML, and 73% for rules.

Another relevant work in this area was conducted by [3], where the authors defined an extensive knowledge model for pathology reports. Their model was linked to hand-built inference rules to process unseen data. They reported high performance over 9 target classes for a hand-annotated 300-report dataset. This system

[2]http://nlp.dbmi.pitt.edu/report_repository.html

[3]http://groups.google.com/group/trec-med

[4]http://www.nlm.nih.gov/research/umls/Snomed/snomed_main.html

Category	Description	Type
Tumour site	Location of Tumour	Nominal
Nodes examined	Number of nodes analysed	Numeric
Nodes positive	Number of nodes found positive	Numeric
Staging T	Primary tumour staging	Nominal
Staging N	Regional lymph nodes staging	Nominal
Staging ACPS	Australian clinico-pathological stage	Nominal

Table 1: Categories and description.

seeks to build a representation of the domain by relying on human experts, and its portability to a different dataset or class-set could be problematic. The classes they evaluate on are not present in our dataset.

3. EXPERIMENTAL SETTING

3.1 Dataset

For our analysis we rely on a corpus of 217 de-identified clinical records from the Royal Melbourne Hospital. These records were first written in natural language, and then structured information concerning 36 fields of interest was introduced to the Colorectal Cancer Database of the hospital, by means of a standarised form. The written records tend to be brief, usually covering a single page, and semantically dense. Each report contains three sections describing different parts of the intervention: macroscopic description, microscopic description, and diagnosis. All sections contain relevant information for the database.

The annotation we have is coarse-grained (at document level), and we do not know which parts of the document contain the relevant information for each class of interest. However, in some cases we can parse the text and identify the target labels to find the exact surface representation. For instance, if the target class is "Nodes examined", and the goldstandard value is "9"; then we can search for the strings "9" and "nine" and create a fine-grained training instance. This approach will be noisy, because there may be other uses of the number in the document that do not refer to the target class, and therefore we manually correct the outcomes. We used this method to build sentence-annotated data for numeric classes and non-zero values only, while for nominal classes we rely on the document-level annotation.

3.2 Target classes

The selection of 6 target classes was made according to their importance for determining the staging and location of the cancer. The first category we analyse is "Tumour site", which refers to the location of the tumour. Our dataset contains 11 different locations, such as "Rectosigmoid", "Caecum", etc. There is a balanced distribution of records for this class, with the most frequent location having 40 instances, and the less frequent having 6 records[5].

The next target categories are "Nodes examined" and "Nodes positive", which are numeric categories that contain information about the number of lymph nodes studied and found positive respectively. These classes, and especially "Nodes positive" represent a crucial part of the knowledge contained in the report.

The last three categories refer to the staging of the tumour with regards to the TNM cancer staging system. This protocol describes the extent of cancer in a patient's body, and it has been studied previously in the text mining literature (cf. Section 2). The first staging category is staging T, which refers to the primary tumour staging, and we can see its values and document frequencies at the

[5]Here we calculate the distribution for the 203 instances we use in cross-validation, and not for the held-out data (cf. Section 3.5).

Staging T							
Code	0	IS	1	2	3	4	X
Frequency	8	0	15	22	127	20	8
Staging N							
Code	0	1	2	X			
Frequency	113	46	27	14			
Staging ACPS							
Code	A	B	C	O	X	Y	
Frequency	30	73	38	0	0	6	

Table 2: Values and frequencies for staging categories. See http://en.wikipedia.org/wiki/TNM_staging_system and [4] for a full description of the codes.

Feature type	Features
BOW	*No, evidence, of, metastatic, tumour, is, seen in, any, of, 11, lymph, nodes, NUMBER*
Lemma	*No, evidence, of, metastatic, tumour, be, see in, any, of, 11, lymph, node, NUMBER*
UMLS	C0332120:Evidence, C0027627:Tumor (metastatic) C0205397:Seen, C0024204:lymph nodes
SNOMED	Tumor (metastatic)
ConcNeg	Tumor (metastatic)

Table 3: Feature representation for *"No evidence of metastatic tumour is seen in any of 11 lymph nodes"*; features separated by ",".

top of Table 2. This category has a strong bias for code "3", and this will affect classifier performance.

The next main staging category, "Staging N", describes regional lymph nodes that are involved, and its codes and frequencies are given in Table 2, with a strong bias towards the "0" value. The last piece of information of the TNM system is "Staging M", which refers to distant metastases. This category is not well represented in our dataset, with a strong bias towards the negative label, and few textual clues to identify it. We decided to leave this category from the analysis for this work, and instead we work on "Staging ACPS", which is the Australian Clinico-Pathological Staging system [4]; the possible values for this class (and their frequencies) are shown at the bottom of Table 2. We can see that the main 4 labels are well represented in the data.

3.3 Knowledge sources and feature representation

In order to better represent the document for information extraction, we rely on diverse tools and knowledge sources that will allow us to test different aspects of the text. We will introduce each feature type in turn, and as an example we show in Table 3 the feature representation for the sentence *"No evidence of metastatic tumour is seen in any of 11 lymph nodes"* from our corpus.

The most basic representation we apply is the widely-used bag-of-words (*BOW*), which treats each token in the document as a separate feature, without including information about the relationships and ordering of the tokens. We extract this feature by tokenising the text with an in-house tokeniser based on regular expressions to separate words, numbers, and punctuation. We also use regular expressions to convert the textual mentions of numbers into their numeric representation. Finally, we include the binary feature "NUMBER" to indicate whether there is a numeric reference in the text. We do not rely on stopwords.

We also analyse the use of lemmas instead of *BOW*, and for that we rely on the GENIA tagger [11], which provides information about lemmatisation, part-of-speech, entities, and phrase chunking. For our experiments we only rely on lemma information, since the entities belong to a different domain.

For semantic features we employ the Metathesaurus from the *Unified Medical Language System* (*UMLS*) [6], which provides a set of ontologies for the biomedical domain with semantic relationships between terms (e.g. synonyms and hypernyms). We use this resource by parsing each sentence in the document with the MetaMap analyser [1] (version 2009), and default parameters. As a result we obtain concept identifiers, which map the text into the ontological concepts. This allows us to identify connections between different word forms of the same concept (e.g. "disease" and "disorder").

The concepts in the Metathesaurus originate from terminologies used in different areas[6], and due to the diversity of this database, we also explored using a subset that comprises a medical terminology: *SNOMED* [7]. In this case we also rely on MetaMap to extract the concepts, but we filter out those that are not present in *SNOMED*.

Finally, we also identify phrases that are negated in the text, and for that we rely on the tool Negex [2], which indicates whether a clinical condition has been negated by relying on regular expressions in context. We use this tool both over *UMLS* and *SNOMED* outputs, and the negated concepts are marked accordingly in the feature representations; we refer to this feature as "ConcNeg". For combining different feature sets we simply join their representations into a single vector.

3.4 Method

Our classification methods will be initially based on ML and feature selection, with a second phase for difficult categories, where we will perform error analysis and identify salient features manually. Another goal of the second step is to provide insight on the cost-benefit of performing fine-grained annotation and of building manual rules for classification.

We develop two types of models, depending on the target category. For nominal classes we define a straightforward document classification problem, where the features are extracted from the full document for classification. On the other hand, for the numeric classes we apply a two-step process, and for that we rely on the sentence annotation that we build semi-automatically (as explained in Section 3.1). The reason for this is that numeric values are easier to manually-annotate than the nominal classes at sentence level, and the information is usually given at a single sentence in the document, without repetition.

We define the process for numeric classes as follows. The first step is to build sentence classifiers for each class, by using the sentence-level annotations. Note that only numbers different to zero are detected, and the zero label is assigned only in cases where the sentence classifiers fail to identify any number. After the model identifies the positive sentences, the numeric values are extracted, and the number closest to the median of the class (in training data) is assigned. In the cases where no positive sentences are identified the number zero is assigned.

Each of our models is tested with a suite of classifiers provided by the Weka toolkit [12]. We chose a set of classifiers that has been widely used in the text mining literature in order to compare their performances over our dataset: Naive Bayes (*Naive Bayes*), Support Vector Machines (*SVM*), and AdaBoost (*AdaBoost*). We use the default parameter settings of Weka (version 3-6-2) for each of the classifiers. As underlying classifier for *AdaBoost* we rely on simple Decision Stumps (one-level decision trees).

We also explore the contribution of feature selection to the classification performance. We apply a correlation-based feature subset selection method, which considers the individual predictive ability

[6]http://www.nlm.nih.gov/pubs/factsheets/umlsmeta.html
[7]http://www.nlm.nih.gov/research/umls/Snomed/snomed_main.html

Features	MC	Naive Bayes	SVM	AdaBoost
BOW	19.7	40.4	38.4	34.0
BOW (FS)	19.7	54.2	44.8	34.0
Lemma	19.7	39.9	37.4	34.0
Lemma (FS)	19.7	51.7	43.8	34.0
BOW and *UMLS*	19.7	40.9	36.5	34.0
BOW and *UMLS* (FS)	19.7	56.7	52.2	34.0
BOW, *UMLS* and ConcNeg	19.7	39.4	36.5	32.0
BOW, *UMLS* and ConcNeg (FS)	19.7	55.7	50.2	32.0
SNOMED and *UMLS*	19.7	40.9	36.0	34.0
SNOMED and *UMLS* (FS)	19.7	**58.1**	53.7	34.0
SNOMED, *UMLS* and ConcNeg	19.7	39.9	35.5	32.0
SNOMED, *UMLS* and ConcNeg (FS)	19.7	55.7	50.2	32.0

Table 4: Machine Learning performances for the "Tumour Site" category (F-score). The best result is given in bold.

Features	MC	Naive Bayes	SVM	AdaBoost
BOW	7.4	68.4	68.4	67.6
BOW (FS)	7.4	33.6	22.2	25.9
Lemma	7.4	67.1	68.2	63.4
Lemma (FS)	7.4	34.9	20.4	24.2
BOW and *UMLS*	7.4	63.7	**70.1**	68.0
BOW and *UMLS* (FS)	7.4	33.1	21.7	25.9
BOW, *UMLS* and ConcNeg	7.4	64.3	68.6	57.0
BOW, *UMLS* and ConcNeg (FS)	7.4	23.6	13.2	11.3
SNOMED and *UMLS*	7.4	62.6	69.1	68.0
SNOMED and *UMLS* (FS)	7.4	33.2	25.3	27.3
SNOMED, *UMLS* and ConcNeg	7.4	64.7	68.6	59.1
SNOMED, *UMLS* and ConcNeg (FS)	7.4	20.7	13.1	11.4

Table 5: Machine Learning performances for the "Nodes Examined" category (F-score). The best result is given in bold.

of each feature and the redundancy of each subset [5]. We relied on Weka's implementation of this technique, and used Best-First search, with a cache-size of one element, and 5 levels of backtracking.

3.5 Evaluation

In order to evaluate the different models and classifiers we report F-score, which is the harmonic mean of precision and recall. We apply balanced F-score in all experiments, giving equal weight to precision and recall, and we micro-average the results over the different class values. 10-fold cross-validation is used in all our ML experiments. We kept 14 random records from the full collection of 217 as held-out data, in order to separately evaluate the performance of manually-built rules; therefore the cross-validation experiments are performed over the remaining 203 instances. As baseline we rely on the Majority Class (*MC*) classifier, which assigns the most frequent class from training data to all test instances. In case of ties the value is chosen randomly among those tied.

4. RESULTS

4.1 Tumour site

The first target category is "Tumour site", and the results of the different ML systems and feature sets are given in Table 4, with and without feature selection. We can see that the best performance only reaches 58.1% F-score, which seems insufficient for an application, even if it is well above the *MC* baseline. Regarding the different systems, the best results are obtained when using *Naive Bayes*, and when applying *BOW*, *UMLS*, and feature selection.

We analysed the causes of the low performance, and found that this class would be difficult even for non-expert human annotators, because the target values are rarely explicitly written in the text. We searched for the goldstandard label in the reports, and this only retrieved 45% of matches, and in particular, for the value "Hepatic flexure" there is only a single mention in the 10 reports that are annotated as such. We studied the top features chosen in the feature selection approach, by measuring their entropy and frequency. This showed that only a few of the target labels had features with low entropy and high frequency, and this makes it difficult to classifiers to generalise. All top features were of type *BOW*.

For this category, we have to conclude that we are not able to deploy a practical extraction system with the current data. However, we can provide aids to the manual process at the hospital, where top features are highlighted, and the top predictions are presented.

4.2 Nodes

We evaluate in this section both the the number of nodes that have been examined, and the number of nodes found positive. We start with the examined nodes, and present the result of ML approaches in Table 5. We can see that the *MC* baseline is very low in this case (7.4%), and ML approaches produce F-scores around the 70% mark, which could be useful for the implementation of a prediction system at the hospital. In this case the best approach is *SVM*, with *BOW* and *UMLS*.

Our next step was to perform error analysis over our best classifier to find the main causes of error. We observed that our binary sentence classifier was biased towards the negative class, and therefore the recall for identifying positive sentences was low. However, the major problem was that when the target sentence was correctly identified, in most cases both "nodes examined" and "nodes positive" were provided in the same sentence (e.g. *2 out of 9 nodes were found positive*), and our simple strategy of using the median was not good enough to identify the right number.

In order to implement a practical system for the hospital, we then manually analysed the top features selected by the correlation-based feature subset selection method, and identified that features "lymph", "tumour", and "metastatic" had a strong correlation with the positive class. We focused in the top feature, and our manual analysis of the sentences allowed us to observe a frequent pattern in the way "nodes examined" was given in the text. We devised two simple rules to apply this knowledge for improved performance:

- if the "lymph" word is found in the sentence, select highest number (maximum 50)
- if the "lymph" word is found, and "further <NUMBER>" or "other <NUMBER>" patterns are found, add # to current count

This simple approach achieved high performance (93.8% F-score), which would be very useful for a practical system. However, there is risk of overfitting the data, and we rely on the 14 held-out instances for validation of the rule-based approach. We achieve an F-score of 85.7%, which shows that this method could be useful for the implementation of a practical system. The rules could be applied directly to make predictions, and this approach could be used to collect more data from clinicians, who will validate or reject the recommendation.

The next target category is "nodes positive". The results of our ML systems are given in Table 6. In this case the *MC* baseline is high (64% F-score), because most records found zero positive nodes, but the ML approaches are able to improve this number to reach 80% F-score (using *SVM* with lemmas). We then perform error analysis to observe the ways this type of information is given in the reports. The problems are similar to those observed for "nodes examined", with low recall and difficulty extracting the right number from the target sentence. We find that in most cases the number of positive nodes is given together with the examined nodes, and we define the following rule to identify the number of positive nodes:

- if the "lymph" word is found in the sentence, and two numbers (smaller than 51) occur, then select the smallest number

Features	*MC*	*Naive Bayes*	*SVM*	*AdaBoost*
BOW	64.0	62.3	77.4	67.5
BOW (FS)	64.0	68.0	68.0	67.8
Lemma	64.0	57.8	**80.1**	74.1
Lemma (FS)	64.0	72.0	71.1	69.7
BOW and *UMLS*	64.0	53.7	76.1	67.5
BOW and *UMLS* (FS)	64.0	68.5	68.0	68.3
BOW, *UMLS* and ConcNeg	64.0	57.6	77.8	69.1
BOW, *UMLS* and ConcNeg (FS)	64.0	72.2	69.3	68.8
SNOMED and *UMLS*	64.0	55.3	77.1	67.5
SNOMED and *UMLS* (FS)	64.0	73.8	68.8	68.3
SNOMED, *UMLS* and ConcNeg	64.0	57.8	78.8	69.1
SNOMED, *UMLS* and ConcNeg (FS)	64.0	71.7	69.3	68.8

Table 6: Machine Learning performances for the "Nodes Positive" category (F-score). The best result is given in bold.

Features	*MC*	*Naive Bayes*	*SVM*	*AdaBoost*
BOW	62.6	62.1	67.5	63.1
BOW (FS)	62.6	80.8	71.9	63.1
Lemma	62.6	63.1	67.5	61.6
Lemma (FS)	62.6	77.8	75.4	61.6
BOW and *UMLS*	62.6	62.6	66.0	61.6
BOW and *UMLS* (FS)	62.6	79.8	75.9	61.6
BOW, *UMLS* and ConcNeg	62.6	63.1	64.5	60.6
BOW, *UMLS* and ConcNeg (FS)	62.6	**82.3**	73.9	60.6
SNOMED and *UMLS*	62.6	63.1	65.5	61.6
SNOMED and *UMLS* (FS)	62.6	81.3	75.9	61.6
SNOMED, *UMLS* and ConcNeg	62.6	62.6	64.5	60.6
SNOMED, *UMLS* and ConcNeg (FS)	62.6	80.8	72.9	60.6

Table 7: Machine Learning performances for the "Staging T" category (F-score). The best result is given in bold.

In this case there is another improvement over the ML system, with an F-score of 85.2%. We also test this rule over the held-out data, and again obtain an F-score of 85.7%. However, in this case rules may not be necessary for "Nodes Positive", since the ML system performs above 80% F-score, and there is less risk of overfitting.

4.3 Staging

We start this section by predicting the category "Staging T", which refers to the progression of the primary tumour. The results of the different ML approaches are given in Table 7. We can see that the results of *Naive Bayes* with feature selection reach a promising 80% F-score (with *BOW*, *UMLS*, and ConcNeg), which compares positively with the state of the art. Recent work on the detection of "Staging T" over 710 reports of lung cancer patients presents accuracies of 73% using a rule-based approach [8], and 78% using Machine Learning [9].

The next staging category is "Staging N", which refers to the staging of regional nodes. In this case we do not apply the document classifier directly, but we rely on the predictions from "Nodes positive" to infer the label of "Staging N" using deterministic rules (e.g. if "Nodes Positive" is between 1 and 3, then assign code 1; cf. Table 2). Our first step is to rely on the outputs of the ML classifiers to apply the rules, and the results are shown in Table 8. We can see that the best F-score is 73.2%, which is above the baseline, but with a high error rate. The best approach is *SVM* with lemmas.

Apart from the ML predictions, we can also rely on the rule-based system to obtain values of positive nodes, and then use the meta-rules on top of these. We show the results of this approach in Table 9, together with the results of applying rules on top of "Nodes Positive" goldstandard results. We do this in order to illustrate that the application of the rules does not give us 100% F-score, but 91.1% instead. The main reason for this is the presence of the code "X", which is indistinguishable from "0" in our approach. However, the error analysis also allowed us to discover two mismatches in the annotation. In one of the cases the text in the

Features	*MC*	*Naive Bayes*	*SVM*	*AdaBoost*
BOW	57.1	56.4	72.0	64.0
BOW (FS)	57.1	60.2	61.7	61.6
Lemma	57.1	53.4	**73.2**	68.5
Lemma (FS)	57.1	63.3	63.0	63.0
BOW and *UMLS*	57.1	57.1	57.1	57.1
BOW and *UMLS* (FS)	57.1	60.7	61.7	62.1
BOW, *UMLS* and ConcNeg	57.1	57.1	57.1	57.1
BOW, *UMLS* and ConcNeg (FS)	57.1	66.2	63.4	62.6
SNOMED and *UMLS*	57.1	57.1	57.1	57.1
SNOMED and *UMLS* (FS)	57.1	66.0	62.2	62.1
SNOMED, *UMLS* and ConcNeg	57.1	57.1	57.1	57.1
SNOMED, *UMLS* and ConcNeg (FS)	57.1	65.7	63.4	62.6

Table 8: Machine Learning performances for the "Staging N" category (F-score). The best result is given in bold.

Base classifier ("nodes positive")	F-score
Rule-based	81.3
Goldstandard	**91.1**

Table 9: Performances for the "Staging N" category (F-score) using rules over "nodes positive". The best result is given in bold.

pathology report is incomplete, and the information that one positive node was detected cannot be found; the other mismatch occurs when the text clearly specifies that two nodes were found positive, but this information is not recorded in the form. These examples illustrate that text mining techniques can be helpful to identify inconsistencies in the way the information is recorded.

Thus, as illustrated in Table 9, the performance of our rule-based classifier is 81.1% F-score. Regarding the state of the art, previous work on "Staging N" has reported accuracies of 87% for a rule-based approach [8], and 82% for Machine Learning [9]. Similarly, we obtain our best results when using rules, which could indicate that we need more data for the ML system to be practical. At an initial stage, the rule-based approach seems more promising for "Staging N" and the underlying "Nodes Positive".

Finally, we present the results for "Staging ACPS", which is the Australian Clinico-Pathological Staging system. The results for our ML systems are given in Table 10. We can see that the best results achieve 74.9% F-score, and are obtained with *Naive Bayes* and feature selection; using *UMLS* in two different configurations (lemmas and *SNOMED*). We performed error analysis, and observed that frequently the label codes are used explicitly in the text, although they can be confused with section headings. This analysis also allowed us to see that for 4 instances the annotations were not correct, and manual input errors were made[8]. We expect that the implementation of a recommendation system will help to avoid these kinds of errors in the future.

5. DISCUSSION

The six categories that we have studied behave differently, and we present a summary of the best results per category in Table 11, where we show the results of the *MC* baseline, ML methods, and rules. Note that we classify "Staging N" as numeric, because the underlying classifier that we use is based on the numeric prediction of "Nodes positive". The results show that all categories are able to clearly improve over the *MC* baseline, which indicates that they are able to learn useful clues from the text.

Looking first at the classification techniques, we can see that nominal classifiers benefit from the *Naive Bayes* model with feature selection and rich features, while the best approach for all numeric classes is *SVM* with basic features. The main reason for this is the short representation (sentence-level) used by numeric classifiers, which requires robust models such as *SVM*. Regarding *AdaBoost*,

[8]The figures in the result tables refer to the corrected goldstandard.

Features	*MC*	*Naive Bayes*	*SVM*	*AdaBoost*
BOW	36.0	43.8	48.3	49.3
BOW (FS)	36.0	71.9	59.1	49.3
Lemma	36.0	42.9	48.8	35.5
Lemma (FS)	36.0	66.5	59.6	35.5
BOW and *UMLS*	36.0	42.4	51.2	49.3
BOW and *UMLS* (FS)	36.0	**74.9**	62.1	49.3
BOW, *UMLS* and ConcNeg	36.0	50.7	56.2	48.3
BOW, *UMLS* and ConcNeg (FS)	36.0	69.5	65.0	48.3
SNOMED and *UMLS*	36.0	42.9	51.2	49.3
SNOMED and *UMLS* (FS)	36.0	**74.9**	61.1	49.3
SNOMED, *UMLS* and ConcNeg	36.0	50.2	56.2	48.3
SNOMED, *UMLS* and ConcNeg (FS)	36.0	69.0	66.0	48.3

Table 10: Machine Learning performances for the "Staging ACPS" category (F-score). The best result is given in bold.

the small dataset seems to be a strong limitation to build a robust meta-learner, and it performs poorly.

With regards to the feature sets and resources, we can see that all types of features contribute to one or other task. Nominal classes are clearly the most benefited from rich features, and *UMLS* is the most robust feature type. *SNOMED* is helpful for "Tumour site" and "Staging ACPS", while negation contributes to the best performance for "Staging T".

On the different categories, we observe that the main staging categories perform in the state of the art using ML, and that "Staging N" can boost its F-score by using rules to predict "Nodes Positive". It is promising that all 6 categories perform above the *MC* baseline; 4 out of 6 categories perform above 80% F-score; and "Staging ACPS" performs at 74.9%, which suggests that a practical recommendation system could be implemented using our framework.

Finally, our experiments have also allowed us to identify 6 manual errors in the manual collection of the data, which is a considerable amount for such a sensitive and small dataset. A recommendation tool could be useful to prevent these errors, by highlighting the relevant textual features used by the classifier; it could also be used to process already collected data, and double-check disagreements between the classifiers and the human input to identify errors.

6. CONCLUSIONS

We have implemented and evaluated a framework to identify relevant categories from pathology reports written in natural language. Our results indicate that we are able to predict the labels of 5 of the 6 multiclass problems with F-scores above 74.9%, and above 85% for two of the categories. We also observed that simple feature representations (*BOW* and lemmas) have clear limitations for some target categories, and richer semantic resources are needed for improved performance. Also for classifiers there were big differences in performance depending on the task; *Naive Bayes* with rich features and feature selection was more effective for nominal classes (document classification), while *SVM* with basic features performed better for numeric classes (sentence classification).

Our work also illustrates that this domain is well suited for text mining, even with minimal expert input. The performance for all categories is well above the *MC* baseline, and this is an indication that our classifiers are able to learn useful information from the textual clues. The main reason for the good performance seems to be the type of language used in the texts. In contrast to other domains, such as medical literature, these reports are written economically, using highly repetitive and structured language, and our classifiers are able to build models that show good performance.

For future work our plan is to integrate our prediction system to make recommendations into the Royal Melbourne Hospital workflow. Apart from off-line performance, we will evaluate the impact

Type	Category	*MC*	Rules	ML	Class.	Features
Nom	Tumour site	19.7		58.1	NB	*SNOMED* and *UMLS* (FS)
	Staging T	62.6		82.3	NB	*BOW*, *UMLS* and ConcNeg (FS)
	Staging ACPS	36.0		74.9	NB	(*BOW* | *SNOMED*) & *UMLS* (FS)
Num	Nodes Exam.	7.4	93.8	70.1	*SVM*	*BOW* & *UMLS*
	Nodes Positive	64.0	85.2	80.1	*SVM*	Lemma
	Staging N	57.1	81.3	73.2	*SVM*	Lemma

Table 11: Summary of best F-scores per category and method, together with the feature combinations.

that the usage of our tool produces in a real setting, both in terms of efficiency and efficacy to avoid human errors.

7. ACKNOWLEDGMENTS

NICTA is funded by the Australian Government as represented by the Department of Broadband, Communications and the Digital Economy and the Australian Research Council through the ICT Centre of Excellence program. We would like to thank Henry Gasko and his colleagues at the Royal Melbourne Hospital for providing pathology reports for our research.

8. REFERENCES

[1] A. R. Aronson. Effective mapping of biomedical text to the UMLS Metathesaurus: the MetaMap program. In *AMIA Annual Symposium Proceedings*, pages 17–21, Washington DC, 2001.

[2] W. W. Chapman, W. Bridewellb, P. Hanburya, G. F. Cooperb, and B. G. Buchananb. A simple algorithm for identifying negated findings and diseases in discharge summaries. *Journal of Biomedical Informatics*, 34(5):301–310, October 2001.

[3] A. Coden, G. Savova, I. Sominsky, M. Tanenblatt, J. Masanz, K. Schuler, J. Cooper, W. Guan, and P. C. de Groen. Automatically extracting cancer disease characteristics from pathology reports into a disease knowledge representation model. *Journal of Biomedical Informatics*, 42:937–949, 2009.

[4] N. C. Davis and R. C. Newland. Terminology and classification of colorectal adenocarcinoma: The australian clinico-pathological staging system. *Australian and New Zealand Journal of Surgery*, 53(3):211–221, 1983.

[5] M. Hall. *Correlation-based Feature Subset Selection for Machine Learning*. PhD thesis, Department of Computer Science, University of Waikato, New Zealand, 1999.

[6] D. A. Lindberg. The unified medical language system. *Method of Information in Medicine*, 32(4):281–291, 1993.

[7] I. A. McCowan, D. C. Moore, A. N. Nguyen, R. V. Bowman, B. E. Clarke, E. E. Duhig, and M.-J. Fry. Collection of cancer stage data by classifying free-text medical reports. *Journal of the American Medical Informatics Association (JAMIA)*, 14:736–745, 2007.

[8] A. Nguyen, D. Moore, I. McCowan, and M.-J. Courage. Multi-class classification of cancer stages from free-text histology reports using support vector machines. *Proceedings of the IEEE Engineering in Medicine and Biology Society Conference*, 2007:5140–5143, 2007.

[9] A. N. Nguyen, M. J. Lawley, D. P. Hansen, R. V. Bowman, B. E. Clarke, E. E. Duhig, and S. Colquist. Symbolic rule-based classification of lung cancer stages from free-text pathology reports. *Journal of the American Medical Informatics Association (JAMIA)*, 17:440–445, 2010.

[10] M. H. Stanfill, M. Williams, S. H. Fenton, R. A. Jenders, and W. R. Hersh. A systematic literature review of automated clinical coding and classification systems. *J Am Med Inform Assoc*, 17(6):646–651, Nov 2010.

[11] Y. Tsuruoka, Y. Tateishi, J.-D. Kim, T. Ohta, J. McNaught, S. Ananiadou, and J. Tsujii. Developing a robust part-of-speech tagger for biomedical text. In *Advances in Informatics – 10th Panhellenic Conference on Informatics*, pages 382–392, Volas, Greece, 2005.

[12] I. H. Witten and E. Frank. *Data Mining: Practical machine learning tools and techniques*. Morgan Kaufmann, San Francisco, USA, 2005.

Extract Knowledge from Semi-structured Websites for Search Task Simplification

Yingqin Gu[1], Jun Yan[2], Hongyan Liu[3], Jun He[1†], Lei Ji[2], Ning Liu[2], Zheng Chen[2]

[1]Key Labs of Data Engineering and Knowledge Engineering, Ministry of Education, China
School of Information, Renmin University of China, {guyingqin, hejun}@ruc.edu.cn

[2]Microsoft Research Asia, Beijing, China, {junyan, leiji, ningl, zhengc}@microsoft.com

[3]Department of Management Science and Engineering, Tsinghua University, hyliu@tsinghua.edu.cn

ABSTRACT

Simplifying the key tasks of search engine users by directly retrieving to them structured knowledge according to their queries is attracting much attention from both industry and academia. A bottleneck of this challenging problem is how to extract the structured knowledge from the noisy and complex Web scale websites automatically. In this paper, we propose an unsupervised automatic wrapper induction algorithm, named as Scalable Knowledge Extractor from webSites (*SKES*). SKES induces the wrapper in a divide and conquer mode, i.e., it divides the general wrapper into several sub-wrappers to learn from the data independently. Moreover, through employing techniques such as tag path representation of Web pages, SKES is verified to be efficient and noise-tolerant by the experimental results. Furthermore, based on our automatically extracted knowledge, we also built a prototype to serve structured knowledge to end users for simplifying their key search tasks. Very positive feedbacks were received on the prototype.

Categories and Subject Descriptors

H.3.m [**Information Storage and Retrieval**]: Miscellaneous – *Data Extraction, Template Induction, Search*; H.3.5 [**Information Storage and Retrieval**]: Online Information Services – *Commercial services, Web-based services*

General Terms

Algorithms, Performance, Experimentation.

Keywords

Search task simplification, structured knowledge extraction, semi-structured Web sites, auto wrapper induction.

1. INTRODUCTION

User search task simplification is recognized as one important problem for search engine companies to improve users' search experiences. However, among various state-of-the-art search engines, many users with knowledge seeking tasks are still enduring from complex query-click-browsing procedures. Directly returning the structured knowledge to user queries instead of requiring them click a long list of Web pages is regarded as an effective approach for user search task simplification. As shown in Figure 1, in Bing [1] search engine, it directly triggers the side by side comparison table between athletes to users whose queries have the intent to compare them. In this paper, we define the table formatted structured information, which could complete the search tasks of end users, as *knowledge* for user search task simplification.

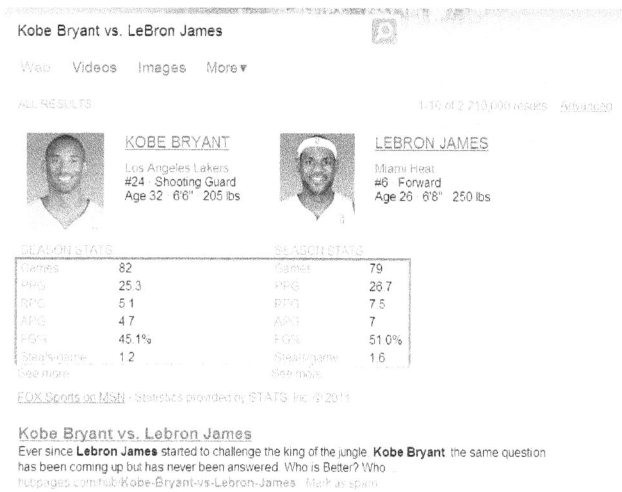

Figure 1. An example of search task simplification in Bing.

To directly return the structured knowledge for simplifying user tasks, there are two major challenges. The first challenge is how to construct the large scale structured knowledge base, by which the search tasks of end users can be satisfied. The second challenge is how to understand the intent of user search queries for triggering the structured knowledge. In this paper, we adopt a simple solution for user query intent understanding and mainly discuss how to construct the large scale knowledge base automatically for user search task simplification.

It is a challenging task to extract the structured knowledge from the semi-structured and unstructured Web automatically. Notice the fact that the structured data on the Web generally cannot be

†Corresponding author.

[1] http://www.bing.com/

accessed directly since it is always encoded and displayed as semi-structured or unstructured HTML pages. The major challenge is thus known as how to develop an effective and efficient auto wrapper induction algorithm for automatic knowledge extraction. Different research efforts have been tried for this wrapper induction problem. Among these efforts, structured data extraction from a set of detail pages, each of which displays detailed information of an entity, is recognized as a very effective way [6, 1]. However, existing algorithms still have limitations in real application such as their inability to handle noisy situations and low efficiency in Web-scale data. Motivated by this observation, in this paper we develop a scalable and noise-tolerant knowledge extraction algorithm, which is named as SKES, from detail pages.

We propose a top-down template induction method which divides the general template induction problem into several sub-templates' induction problems and conquers them separately. By further employing the tag path [9] representation of input pages, our method is much more efficient than existing methods. The noisy situation is handled by introducing a support threshold so that the underlying templates in noise pages will not be generated due to insufficient support. Experimental results show that we can achieve the knowledge extraction precision as high as 97% with high efficiency and a certain portion of noise pages can be tolerated. We also implement a prototype system for search task simplification and very positive feedbacks are collected by user study.

The rest of this paper is organized as follows. In Section 2, we introduce the related works of Web Information Extraction. In Section 3, we introduce our algorithm SKES in detail. In Section 4, we show the experimental results to verify the effectiveness and efficiency of our proposed solution in terms of structured knowledge extraction. In addition, we use the real user study to verify the user task simplification feature based on the extracted structured knowledge. Finally, Section 5 gives the conclusions and our future work.

2. RELATED WORK

The key challenge of our work is much related to the field of Web Information Extraction (WIE). WIE aims to extract information with a specific structure (e.g. ontology) from the World Wide Web. Different research efforts have tried to extract information from different perspectives. Considering the data type, they could be generally classified into two categories, which are unstructured data and semi-structured data respectively. Different techniques have been applied, such as the NLP and pattern learning in unstructured data [3, 7, 2], wrapper induction and table extraction in semi-structured data [5, 10, 4]. Our work belongs to the latter category, i.e. structured data extraction from semi-structured HTML pages.

Structured data extraction from detail pages are deemed as an effective way as detail pages contain much information. Detail pages in a Website are usually machine-generated from backend databases by using an underlying template. Therefore, the task of structured data extraction from detail pages is to induce the underlying template (wrapper) automatically and use this template to extract structured data. RoadRunner [6] and EXALG [1] are two methods that are fully automatic and are much related to our work. RoadRunner develops a novel matching technique to compare HTML pages of the same format and generate a template based on their similarities and differences. It relies on a greedy approach that starts from one page as an initial template and compare other pages one by one to induce more general template. EXALG is an improved data extraction method which handles all pages' tokens at the same time. It detects the underlying template by two techniques: *differentiating roles of tokens* and *equivalence classes*. A template will be generated from equivalence classes by further filtering those with insufficient support and size. As it detects template in the unit of tokens and filter template with insufficient, templates that consist of few tokens are filtered and unable to be detected by EXALG.

Based on several sites' experimental results, RoadRunner and EXALG work well in pure detail pages. However, the above two methods fail to handle noisy situations. RoadRunner generates template by comparing pages one by one and will generate incorrect template from noisy detail pages. EXALG also neglects the noisy situation as its support threshold is to filter template parts which occur rarely instead of the noise pages. In addition, they are not efficient enough in Web scale data. The match algorithm in RoadRunner has exponential time complexity with respect to the length of input page. EXALG has a polynomial time complexity which is still not efficient enough due to its complex techniques.

Compared to the two methods, our algorithm employs a divide and conquer manner which divides the general template induction problem into several sub-templates' induction problems and conquers them separately, which makes our algorithm much more efficient. In addition, we use tag path representation of HTML pages, which can reduce the number of tags dramatically and differentiate roles of tags naturally. A support threshold is also introduced to handle noisy situations so that the underlying templates in noise pages will not be generated due to insufficient support.

3. METHODOLOGY

The key of structured data extraction from detail pages is to induce a good template (schema) of these pages, since the induced template can be used to automatically extract corresponding data fields encoded in HTML pages. However, the problem of inducing a good (unambiguous) template is complicated due to the existence of missing data fields. It has been proved as a NP-complete problem [8]. Due to this limitation, we make some reasonable assumptions to make our method useful and scalable. SKES consists of three steps: (1) template induction, (2) structured data extraction, and (3) post-processing extracted data.

3.1 Template Induction

To induce templates in a more scalable manner, we employ two techniques: (1) using tag paths to represent the original HTML pages, and (2) inducing templates in a top-down manner, which is inspired by the divide-and-conquer strategy. The first technique is a powerful presentation of HTML pages and reduces the number of tags in pages dramatically. The second technique is based on the observation that templates and data fields can be differentiated more easily if a more specific section can be identified. Then the general idea is to induce a template with some confident wrappers first, which splits the general template into several sections, and induce more specific templates in each section respectively.

3.1.1 Page Representation

Each node in a HTML Dom tree (tag tree) can be identified by following a path from the root to the node. Such a path is a *tag path* [9]. For each HTML page, we identify those text nodes (i.e. nodes containing text information) and store their tag paths and corresponding texts. These tag paths and texts are used to represent the original page. An example is shown in Figure 2 and Figure 3, where Figure 2 is a sampled HTML code and Figure 3 is our representation.

We represent HTML pages in this way because of two reasons. First is that representation in tag paths is very powerful. It naturally differentiates roles of tags in different tag paths, i.e. tags of same name in different tag paths can be differentiated due to the tag path representation. The second reason of our representation is that by only considering text nodes' tag paths and texts, the scale of the number of tags will reduce dramatically.

```
Page 1
01:  <html><body>
02:  <a>
03:     Archipelago 1.14
04:  </a>
05:  <dl>
06:     <dt>Price:</dt>
07:        <div>$2.99</div>
08:     <dt>Last updated:</dt>
09:        <div>09/26/2010</div>
10:  </dl>
11:  <a>
12:     Recommendations
13:  </a>
14:  <ul>
15:     <li>Par 72 Golf</li>
16:     <li>Mathpac 5.6</li>
17:     <li>FourNumGuess 1.0.6</li>
18:  </ul>
19:  </html></body>
```

Figure 2. Sampled HTML code of one detail page.

```
Page 1
01: <html><body><a>                 Archipelago 1.14
02: <html><body><dl><dt>            Price:
03: <html><body><dl><dt><div>       $2.99
04: <html><body><dl><dt>            Last updated:
05: <html><body><dl><dt><div>       09/26/2010
06: <html><body><a>                 Recommendations
07: <html><body><ul><li>            Par 72 Golf
08: <html><body><ul><li>            Mathpac 5.6
09: <html><body><ul><li>            FourNumGuess 1.0.6
```

Figure 3. Our representation of the detail page.

3.1.2 Top-Down Template Induction

Since inducing a good template is NP-complete, based on observation on real Websites pages we make two assumptions for scalable template inductions. The first is that across pages of same format, the invariant parts are deemed as template, and the variant parts are deemed as encoded data fields. The second assumption is that different data fields (including templates) are displayed in the same order in one site. That is, if data field A displays in precede of data field B in one page, B should never display in precede of A in other pages.

As we construct extracted data into a table format and it is hard to organize data with complex structures, templates of very complex structures are not induced in SKES. We only extract three kinds of data fields: (a) data fields in a single slot, (b) data fields displayed in a list pattern, and (c) data fields across multiple slots (called data section). Each data field will be organized in a column of the extracted table.

Based on the assumptions and this simplification, we start to (1) identify several data sections to construct a general template (called root template) first. Then (2) in each data section, we furthermore identify more specific data fields and data sections to generate a more specific template. Step 2 will reapply on the new generated template until no more templates can be generated.

Before describing our approach in detail, we first give some formal definitions:

Definition 1 (tag path): A *tag path* (tp) is a path from the root node to a text node in the DOM tree.

Definition 2 (tag path text): A *tag path text* (tpt) is a text node's *tag path* and the text carried by this node.

Definition 3 (occurrence vector): An *occurrence vector* of a tag path (or a tag path text) is an integer vector V_{tp} (V_{tpt}) = $[f_1, f_2, \ldots, f_n]$, where n is the number of input detail pages, and f_i is the occurrence frequency of tp (tpt) in page i.

Definition 4 (occurrence positions): An *occurrence positions* of a tag path (or a tag path text) is a vector PS_{tp} (PS_{tpt}) = $[p_1, p_2, \ldots, p_n]$, where n is the number of input pages, and p_i is a set of line number where tp (tpt) occurs in page i.

Definition 5 (equivalence class): An *equivalence class* (es) is a set of tag paths whose occurrence vectors have same elements in m pages, where m/n is larger than a user defined support threshold s. Notice that a single tag path can be an equivalence class.

Based on the above definitions, we now introduce our top-down template induction method, which generates a more specific template in each iteration. First we identify several general data sections to construct root template by detecting from tag path texts, their corresponding occurrence vectors and occurrence positions (shown in Algorithm 1).

Algorithm 1 InduceRootTemplate

Input: A set of input HTML pages D_n, a support threshold s
Output: Induced root template *RT*.
Steps:

```
Convert D_n into pages of tag path representation DP_n
Go through DP_n, and get all distinct tag path texts TPT,
  occurrence vectors V_TPT and occurrence positions PS_TPT
Initialize RT to be empty.
for each tag path text tpt in TPT do
  get occurrence vector V_tpt for tpt from V_TPT
  if support(V_tpt) >= s*n then
    add tpt to RT
  end if
end for
Identify "Data Section" between tag path texts
return RT
```

The support threshold s is a ratio which is set for handling noisy situations. (It is set to 0.9 in experiments.) Tag path texts whose supports are above this threshold will be added to the root template. Algorithm 1 takes this threshold and a set of input

HTML pages as input to generate root template RT. Algorithm gives more detail steps for root template induction.

Given an induced root template, the problem of template induction problem is divided into sub templates' induction in each data section of the template. For each data section, we further detect patterns of tag paths to identify more data fields and generate more specific template. Specifically, three kinds of data fields are detected: (a) data fields in a single slot, (b) data fields displayed in a list pattern, and (c) other data sections. A data field of the first kind can be identified after a tag path which occurs exactly once in most pages or in certain portions of pages. It is marked as "#value#" or "#optional value#" respectively. A data field of the second kind can be identified after an equivalence class which occurs one or more times, and among which no more other tag path exists (not nest structure) in most pages. It is marked as "#list#". Then more specific data sections are able to be detected since data fields of the first two kinds which have been identified split the original data section into several data sections. Then these data sections will be processed in the next iteration. Algorithm 2 gives more detailed steps for specific template induction.

Algorithm 2 InduceSpecificTemplate

Input: Root template RT, a set of input pages DP_n, a threshold s
Output: A specific template ST.
Steps:

Go through DP_n, get all distinct tag paths TP, occurrence vectors V_{TP} and occurrence positions PS_{TP}
Initialize $ST = RT$, template T to be empty.
while $T \,!= ST$
  $T = ST$
  for each *Data Section* in T **do**
    get TP_d, V_{TPd}, PS_{TPd} from TP, V_{TP}, PS_{TP}
    Initialize SubTemplate T_s to be empty
    for each tp in TP_d **do**
      get V_{tp} from V_{TPd}, PS_{tp} from PS_{TPd}
      Template Line tl = check(tp, V_{tp}, PS_{tp}, s)
      Add tl to T_s
    end for
    sort T_s
    insert T_s to ST
  end for
  Go through PS_{TP}, add flag "Data Section" into ST
end while
return ST

3.2 Structured Data Extraction

Given the induced template, it is straightforward to extract structured data from pages represented by tag paths. We apply the template on each page to get several data fields and construct all results into a table format. We can summarize all the related information of one site in a table where each row is an entity in a detail page and each column is an attribute. Thus each cell in the table will be the attribute value of the entity in corresponding row. The number of the table's columns is determined by the number of data fields in template.

For those columns containing data fields of the first kind, they can be stored directly in a database since they are single values of various attributes. As for data fields of the second kind, currently we regard them as multi-valued attributes and store a list of attribute values in one cell of the table where each value is separated by a particular delimiter. Then it is straightforward to normalize the table for more convenient storage and retrieval. For each data section in the final template, we store them in a column as an attribute. This is reasonable as a Web site may encode a long data field across multiple text nodes (e.g. data field of attribute "description").

3.3 Post-Processing Extracted Data

We post-process the extracted data because of two reasons. First is that in template induction we only consider the template among text nodes. That is, template within a text node will be neglected by our method. For example, if two data fields "1.10" and "Game" in an underlying data base are encoded into a text node "Price: $1.10 Category: Game" in the page, our method will identify such text as a data field which is incorrect. This step aims to split such column in the structured data into several columns by common tags and remove common template in the prefix or suffix. The second reason is that the extracted data may rely on manually attribute labeling if automatic labeling method (which usually depends on a set of training data) is not available. The fewer the columns in the extracted data, the less labor consuming for manually labeling. Therefore, this step also aims to filter some unrelated columns.

To detect template in each text node, we identify common tokens in each column of extracted data. If common tokens exist in a column, they will help us split the column or filter these tokens if they are common prefix or suffix. In addition, we also detect a common delimiter (e.g. ':') in each column. If such a delimiter exists, it will be used to separate the attribute and value. The column will be split to several columns which are organized by their attribute name

Notice that our method may extract some varying templates as data fields because of the failure of assumption 1 (mentioned in Section 3). We filter such columns by a heuristic rule that a column will be removed if there is only one distinct data field in this column. Also we will filter those columns that contain only a small number of data fields (fewer than 5% of the input pages). For those noise pages in the input collection, there will be no data field or very few data fields in their corresponding rows. We also filter such very sparse rows.

4. EXPERIMENTAL RESULTS

4.1 Experimental Setup

We have crawled thousands of data intensive Websites of 3 domains (which are Mobile application, Movie and Restaurant) from Bing's indexed pages to extract structured knowledge. For experimental evaluation, we choose 30 Websites of them. We compare the efficiency of our approach with that of RoadRunner, whose implementation in Java is available on the Web[2].

All the experiments are performed on an AMD Opteron 254 computer with a 2.8GHz CPU and 16G of RAM. Our algorithm is implemented in C#, which utilizes Html Agility Pack[3] to build HTML DOM tree for each page. For all detail pages in each Website, we run our algorithm to get structured data in a table format. After that, we manually label attributes of each column to build knowledge base. To compare with the algorithm of RoadRunner, which is not scalable on such large data, we sample

[2] http://www.dia.uniroma3.it/db/roadRunner/

[3] http://htmlagilitypack.codeplex.com/

hundreds of pages in each Website. On these sampled pages, both algorithms are run in the exactly same procedure and platform.

4.2 Effectiveness Evaluation

Table 1. Performance of SKES on some Websites

Website	Precision	Recall
www.imdb.com	99.13%	81.21%
www.zap2it.com	99.44%	87.59%
www.moviefone.com	98.62%	81.06%
www.allmovie.com	99.82%	53.32%
movies.msn.com	95.59%	45.45%
movies.yahoo.com	100%	84.72%
www.fandango.com	97.36%	81.56%
www.movies.com	96.47%	74.38%
www.amctheatres.com	95.87%	65.98%
www.mrqe.com	98.12%	73.84%
www.androidzoom.con	96.73%	78.92%
www.apple.com	97.64%	82.54%
www.brothersoft.com	99.13%	90.91%
iphoneapplicationlist.com	96.86%	85.54%
www.cyrket.com	95.31%	72.68%
www.pocketgear.com	96.14%	76.35%
www.mobiletopsoft.com	95.15%	64.34%
appworld.blackberry.com	98.68%	68.48%
www.freewarepocketpc.net	97.25%	74.59%
www.pocketpc-freeware.net	99.36%	80.14%
www.allmenus.com	98.45%	82.36%
www.menuism.com	99.02%	72.31%
www.restaurantrow.com	97.35%	82.41%
www.city-data.com	96.45%	70.63%
www.cityguide.com	95.18%	71.49%
www.opentable.com	97.53%	76.14%
www.agoda.com	96.58%	81.39%
www.insiderpages.com	97.35%	64.28%
www.tripadvisor.com	98.24%	63.57%
www.yellowbot.com	96.54%	78.17%
Average	97.51%	74.88%

We use precision and recall as primary metrics to evaluate the effectiveness of SKES. Since our datasets are very large, to generate a complete ground truth is very hard. Thus, we randomly choose 100 pages from each Website and manually label all data fields in these pages by 6 invited editors as ground truth. To evaluate the precision of our approach, they label the extracted results of the sampled pages in each Website to get true positives and false positives. True positives are the set of data fields correctly extracted by our approach, and false positives are the set of data fields extracted incorrectly. Then the precision and recall for each Website can be calculated. Experimental results of our approach are shown in Table 1. As is shown in Table 1, our approach achieves very high precision and good recall on most Websites.

4.3 Efficiency Evaluation

We generate six datasets from each Website by random sampling, which contains 40, 80, 120, 160, 200, and 240 detail pages respectively. Table 2 shows the experimental result of our approach and RoadRunner, which has been averaged on the 30 Websites. We can see that the runtime of our approach increases linearly with respect to the number of pages, while the runtime of RoadRunner increases sharply. The author of RoadRunner reported in their work [6] that the AND-OR tree used in RoadRunner has in the worst case exponential size due to the need to explore different alternatives for each mismatch. Although some techniques have been proposed to lower the complexity, it seems that the algorithm is still very time consuming in dealing with real pages. While our algorithm uses a divide-and-conquer strategy, which shows very high efficiency.

The runtime of SKES is mainly affected by two aspects: the number of pages and the average number of tag path texts in a page. Since the variance of the number of tag path texts is not very big in different Websites, here we evaluate the runtime of our approach in pages with different scales. SKES is applied on over 10 thousand high traffic Websites indexed by Bing to verify its efficiency. The runtimes of our approach in each Website are recorded, some of which are shown in Figure 4. As the figure shows, the runtime of SKES is generally linear with respect to the number of pages. For clusters containing hundreds of thousands pages, our approach can finish in hours.

Table 2. Comparison of Efficiency

Number of Pages	Runtime of RoadRunner	Runtime of SKES
40	20"	3"
80	4'54"	7"
120	24'25"	9"
160	1h1'48"	12"
200	2h47'49"	15"
240	4h52'17"	16"

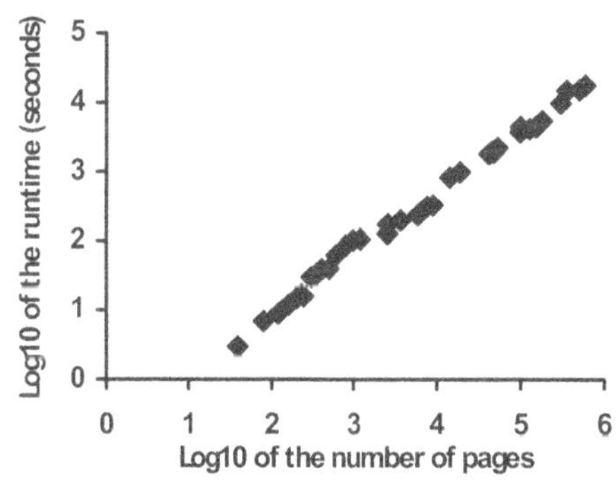

Figure 4. Runtime of SKES in pages with various scales.

4.4 Noise-Tolerance Evaluation

Table 3. Performance in noisy situations

Percent of Noises	Precision	Recall
0%	97.51%	74.40%
2%	97.68%	73.32%
4%	96.98%	73.16%
6%	96.79%	72.21%
8%	97.54%	69.35%
10%	97.63%	61.13%

In this section we evaluate the performance of our approach in noisy situation. By adding irrelevant pages (e.g. index pages, list pages) into the original detail pages dataset in a Website, we generate 5 more clusters which contain 2%, 4%, 6%, 8% and 10% noise pages respectively. Our approach is run on the 5 clusters, the performance of which is shown in Table 3. As is shown in Table 3, the performance of our approach only has a light degradation when the percent of noise pages is less than 8%. It demonstrates that our approach can tolerant a certain portion of noise pages.

4.5 Performance of Search Simplification

We also implement a prototype system for user search task simplification (shown in Figure 5) that utilizes the knowledge base extracted by SKES. Since the problem of how to identify the intent of user queries and trigger related structured knowledge to users is also very difficult, in this system we employ a naive keyword based method. That is, if user queries contain words that equal to data fields in our knowledge base, we just select and return structured knowledge of entities that satisfy all the keywords. If there is no satisfied entity, a traditional page list from Bing API[4] will be returned. Notice that it is only a prototype system currently. Understanding more complex queries correctly is our future work.

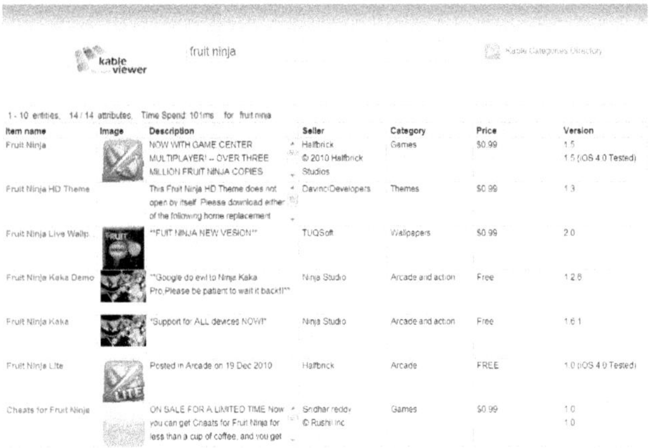

Figure 5. An example of returned structured knowledge by our prototype system.

Table 4. Average rating of some questionnaire items

Question	Rating
Is the Demo helpful for knowledge seeking?	4.36
The Demo usually returns correct table?	4.16
A number of queries can trigger the Demo to return structured table?	3.87
You need not browse any pages to seek knowledge?	3.53
Is the user interface of the Demo acceptable?	4.06
Can you save a lot of time by using this Demo?	4.10

We designed a questionnaire and distributed it to 15 users who used this prototype system for a week to get their feedback and subjective evaluation of our system. In the questionnaire, we asked users some general information about the prototype system. Several interesting items are listed in Table 4. These questions were answered on a scale of 5 with 5 = strongly agree and 1 = strongly disagree. As is shown in Table 4, users generally satisfied the prototype system and admitted that it was helpful for them to seek knowledge.

[4] http://www.bing.com/developers

5. CONCLUSIONS

The paper presents an algorithm SKES to automatically extract structured knowledge from semi-structured Websites for search task simplification. By employing techniques such as top-down template induction algorithm and tag path representation, SKES is shown to be quite efficient and noise-tolerant in real Websites. After running our algorithm on thousands of related sites, a large structured knowledge base of high quality is built on three domains. We also develop a prototype system to simplify user search task by using the built knowledge base. User study shows that it really helps users for knowledge seeking.

6. ACKNOWLEDGEMENT

The work was supported by MSRA Funding with No. FY11-RES-OPP-058.

7. REFERENCES

[1] ARASU, A. AND GARCIA-MOLINA, H. 2003. Extracting structured data from web pages. In *SIGMOD Conference*. 337–348.

[2] BANKO, M., CAFARELLA, M. J., SODERLAND, S., BROADHEAD, M., AND ETZIONI, O. 2007. Open information extraction from the web. In *IJCAI*. 2670–2676.

[3] BRIN, S. 1998. Extracting patterns and relations from the world wide web. In *WebDB*. 172–183.

[4] CAFARELLA, M. J., HALEVY, A. Y., ZHANG, Y., WANG, D. Z., AND 0002, E. W. 2008. Uncovering the relational web. In *WebDB*.

[5] COHEN, W. W., HURST, M., AND JENSEN, L. S. 2002. A flexible learning system for wrapping tables and lists in html documents. In *Proceedings of the 11th international conference on World Wide Web*. WWW '02. ACM, New York, NY, USA, 232–241.

[6] CRESCENZI, V., MECCA, G., AND MERIALDO, P. 2001. Roadrunner: Towards automatic data extraction from large web sites. In *VLDB*. 109–118.

[7] ETZIONI, O., CAFARELLA, M. J., DOWNEY, D., POPESCU, A.-M., SHAKED, T., SODERLAND, S., WELD, D. S., AND YATES, A. 2005. Unsupervised named-entity extraction from the web: An experimental study. *Artif. Intell. 165*, 1, 91–134.

[8] YANG, G., RAMAKRISHNAN, I. V., AND KIFER, M. 2003. On the complexity of schema inference from web pages in the presence of nullable data attributes. In *Proceedings of the twelfth international conference on Information and knowledge management*. CIKM '03. ACM, New York, NY, USA, 224–231.

[9] ZHAO, H., MENG, W., WU, Z., RAGHAVAN, V., AND YU, C. T. 2005. Fully automatic wrapper generation for search engines. In In *Proceedings of the 14th international conference on World Wide Web* (WWW2005). 66–75.

[10] ZHAO, S. AND BETZ, J. 2007. Corroborate and learn facts from the web. In *proceddding of the 13th ACM SIGKDD conference on Knowledge Discovery and Data Mining (KDD2007)*. 995–1003.

Privacy Protected Knowledge Management in Services with Emphasis on Quality Data

Debapriyo Majumdar Rose Catherine Shajith Ikbal Karthik Visweswariah
{debapriyo, rosecatherinek, shajmoha, v-karthik}@in.ibm.com
IBM Research, Bangalore, India

ABSTRACT

Improving productivity of practitioners through effective knowledge management and delivering high quality service in Application Management Services (AMS) domain, are key focus areas for all IT services organizations. One source of historical knowledge in AMS is the large amount of resolved problem ticket data which are often confidential, immensely valuable, but majority of it is of very bad quality.

In this paper we present a knowledge management tool that detects the quality of information present in problem tickets and enables effective knowledge search in tickets by prioritizing quality data in the search ranking. The tool facilitates leveraging of knowledge across different AMS accounts, while preserving data privacy, by masking client confidential information. It also extracts several relevant entities contained in the noisy unstructured text entered in the tickets and presents them to the users. We present several experimental evaluations and a pilot study conducted with an AMS account which show that our tool is effective and leads to substantial improvement in productivity of the practitioners.

Categories and Subject Descriptors

H.3.3 [**Information storage and retrieval**]: Information search and retrieval

General Terms

Design, Experimentation, Security, Management

Keywords

Ticket Search, Measuring Quality, Sharing Knowledge

1. INTRODUCTION

Application Management Services (AMS) form a major chunk of the services business. In an AMS scenario, a services organization manages a set of applications for a client organization, by involving a dedicated set of practitioners, who are trained in the domain of the application, solving issues raised by clients about that application. These issues and their resolution details are entered into a system, commonly referred to as a *ticketing tool*. Some of the popular enterprise ticketing tools are TSRM[1], SAP Solution Manager[2] and Remedy[3].

Delivering top quality service is of at most importance to any services organization, to distinguish themselves and excel in the field. This business problem has two dimensions – first is to reduce the time taken to solve tickets, and the second is to determine the optimal team structure.

Most ticketing tools do provide a search functionality on tickets, but they fail miserably in a large fraction of cases, because it is observed that, most of the times, the resolution field of the solved tickets are incomplete, very badly written or simply had no technical details. For example, a resolution statement: "Directly guided her through fixing the issue over a phone call", doesn't help a practitioner trying to solve a similar issue later.

Another commonly reported issue while searching in the ticket repository is that, a significant fraction of tickets have noisy content in the resolution field, leading to irrelevant tickets getting ranked higher. This noisy data is usually due to copy-pasting emails that were exchanged between the practitioner and the client in the process of solving the ticket. The final resolution steps are therefore cluttered with a lot of non-technical content.

Practitioners do search on the web for solutions to tickets. Apart from using web search engines such as Google, Bing, Yahoo, etc., they also search in domain specific repositories or discussion forums. For example, SDN[4] is a discussion forum for SAP domain issues. However, public repositories on the web can help only in solving general problems, not account specific ones. So, building a knowledge management tool for confidential data is very important in Services.

In this paper, we describe a knowledge management tool, hereafter referred to as KM Tool, which enables top quality service delivery in Application Management Services business. The key aspects of our tool are:

(1) Estimating the quality of resolution information in

CIKM'11, October 24–28, 2011, Glasgow, Scotland, UK.
Copyright 2011 ACM 978-1-4503-0717-8/11/10 ...$10.00.

[1]www.ibm.com/software/tivoli/products/service-request-mgr
[2]http://www.sap.com/platform/netweaver/components/solutionmanager/index.epx
[3]http://www.bmc.com/products/product-listing/53035210-143801-2527.html
[4]http://www.sdn.sap.com

tickets, and incorporating such information in the search algorithm to improve the ranking of the tickets so that, the useful results are ranked at the top, and

(2) Leveraging knowledge across accounts, while preserving data privacy, by masking client confidential information.

We also present results of piloting the tool with an AMS account. The results show a substantial improvement in productivity and efficiency of the practitioners, demonstrating the effectiveness of our tool. We also present results of evaluation of a few selected sub-components to illustrate their usefulness in the overall tool.

The rest of this paper is organized as follows. Section 2 discusses the prior research that is relevant to our work. In Section 3 we discuss our method on searching in ticket data with emphasis on data quality, and in Section 4 we describe how we ensure privacy protection in knowledge sharing between accounts. In Section 5 we provide some details on the architecture and components of our tool. The experiments and the pilot study that we conducted using our tool are discussed in Section 6. Finally, Section 7 discusses our conclusions and future directions of work.

2. RELATED WORK

Knowledge management to improve the efficiency of service delivery has been addressed previously by Lenchner et al [14], but in the domain of server management, where they integrate different data sources and facilitate search using eSearch [6], but do not aim to de-prioritize results that are useless, possibly because the average quality of the data is good in that domain. Most ticket management tools also come with some knowledge management features. For example, Tivoli Service Request Manager (TSRM) offers searching of the ticket database, but their ranking is based on exact text match and number of hits. In the scenario where majority of the data has non-informative content, such a system is not likely to provide an effective search.

Classification constitutes an important component of knowledge management systems. Support Vector Machine (SVM) [12] and MaxEnt [16] are examples of commonly used classifiers for text data. A major challenge in classifying ticket data is dealing with noise. Past work in the classifying noisy text include [4, 24] for web data and [11] for call transcripts. Extracting useful information by classifying parts of a document were discussed in [23] and [17]. Detecting spam was studied in [3] and [25].

A key distinguishing aspect of our tool is that it facilitates leveraging of knowledge across different AMS accounts. This is achieved by masking confidential information in the data, to preserve privacy. Approaches to hide identities and preserve sensitive information was studied in [2, 8, 9, 13, 22], but in other different contexts like data mining and publishing, and in speech data.

Automatically creating structure out of the heterogeneous text data contained in problem tickets, has been studied previously. [23] focuses on classifying each sentence to a pre-defined information type, while [21] discusses methods to identify the discourse structure in ticket data. However, both of them do not have an end-to-end system where the usefulness of this structuring can be demonstrated. [15] proposed a system called TroubleMiner, which clusters tickets into a hierarchy such that frequently occurring problems are closer to the top, to help network operators in maintenance activities. [10] suggested that correlating an incoming ticket with Configuration Items (CI) stored in a Configuration Management Database can help quicken the resolution of the ticket. Here, the focus is to identify the CIs, and not to identify resolution information from similar tickets.

There is quite some research done in the area of trouble ticket routing, like the papers [18, 19, 20]. Here, the focus is to automatically decide on an expert or a resolving group that can resolve the ticket quickly, but taking into account, multiple other factors like number of unresolved tickets in the system, tickets that are already assigned to that group and service level agreements.

3. DATA QUALITY-AWARE SEARCH

The important aspects of our knowledge search tool that distinguish it from other similar systems are: (a) its ability to extract useful parts of a ticket and (b) incorporating this information to provide an effecting ranking technique.

3.1 Detecting useful parts in tickets

A ticket contains sentences that provide useful information and those that are not useful as technical information. Observing the contents of different tickets, it becomes clear that sentences that belong to the later category can be characterized by a particular set of words, usage etc. For example, salutations, email headers etc. use a set of words that enable humans to identify that they do not give technical details on how to solve a problem. So, we categorize the sentences into two categories, namely `Non-Technical (N)` and `Technical (T)`. Technical sentences can be of three major sub-categories: `Problem Description (P)` – sentences that specify the details about the issue being reported, `Root Cause (R)` – sentences that discuss the cause of the problem, and `Solution (S)` – sentences that describe how it was solved.

We frame the detection of the useful parts of a ticket as a classification problem at sentence level. A classifier was trained on manually labeled data to classify sentences of tickets to one of `P`, `S`, `R` and `N` categories. But as experiments show in Section 6.1, classifying to `R` and `S` categories achieved negligible accuracies, mostly owing to the small fraction of such examples in the training data and ambiguities between the classes `R` and `S`.

Hence, we simplified the approach and focused on the two-class classification problem – for each sentence, determine if it has technical content (class `T`) or not (class `N`). Results of experiments conducted for `T-N` classification, as discussed in Section 6.1 show that, it is possible to obtain reasonable accuracy for this task.

3.2 Ranking with quality scores

Determining the set of sentences of a ticket that contain technical information is then used to compute the quality score for that ticket. For each ticket t, we pre-compute the quality score as:

$$qual(t) = \min(\frac{n_T}{c}, 1) \times w + \frac{n_T}{n} \times (1 - w)$$

where n_T is the total number of words in sentences classified as T, n is the total number of words in the resolution description of t and the constant c is a tuned parameter (set as 40 in our experiments) which is regarded as the minimum number of words present in all sentences classified as `T`. Essentially the first part of the formula becomes close to (or equal to) 1 if the number of words in technical sentences of the resolution of a ticket is close to (respectively equal to or more than) the ideal number, and the second part computes the fraction of length of the technical part in the text. The parameter w is tuned (set to 0.75) to compute the weighted average of the two parts for the overall quality score.

For our system, the keywords of a query are expected to describe the problem. So, we boost the weight of the problem description and problem details fields for the search to be performed by Lucene. We retrieve up to top 1000 results with score from the Lucene engine. However, since the problem statement in many of these tickets may match the query but the resolution statement may be useless or incomplete, we re-rank them. For the final ranking, the similarity between a query q and a ticket t is computed as a weighted average, with equal weights, of the text-similarity score between q and t returned by the search engine and the pre-computed quality score of t.

4. PRIVACY PROTECTED SEARCH

Our tool enables privacy protected technical knowledge sharing across different accounts. Protection of the client-specific confidential information in the ticket text is achieved through data sanitization, i.e., detection and masking of the instances of entities in the text that contain sensitive information or can disclose the identity of the customer.

4.1 Sanitization of client sensitive data

A few entities that could potentially violate the privacy and thus should be masked in the ticket data include company name, product name, location, person name, telephone number, email address, and web address. Sanitization of these entities in our tool is achieved through a combination of dictionary look-up and regular expression matching. The above entities are divided into sub-entities such as proper names and number strings. Then all possible variants of these sub-entities are specified in a dictionary to further build the complex entities in order to detect their instances in the ticket text through regular expression match. The tool also provides an option to mask entities and patterns that are specific to the accounts and not covered in the above specified general list. The account administrators can specify such patterns by simple regular expressions.

Furthermore, the tool removes some account specific jargon to prevent practitioners belonging a different account from speculating about the identity of the account of the sanitized ticket. For example, the date of creation of a ticket could be referred to as `Date into OCF MH` in the original ticket. In the sanitized version, this would simply be referred to as `CREATED ON`.

4.2 Knowledge sharing with customizable privacy settings

Using the masking techniques described in the previous section, the sanitizer module creates a sanitized version corresponding to each ticket. The sanitized version contains the same technical information as the original ticket, except for some confidential data, which is masked. This data is usually not important for specifying the resolution for a technical problem.

In our system, the administrator for an account can set the data privacy setting for their tickets by choosing one of the following three options: (1) Strict – only users from the same account can view the data. (2) Knowledge sharing with sanitization – users from the same account search and view the data in original form; other users are restricted to search and view the data in sanitized form. This scenario is illustrated in Figure 1. (3) Unprotected: the data is shared to all users without sanitization.

Figure 1: Creation of sanitized data and access control in search

Among these, the second option is recommended as it protects the sensitive information of the client's data but also enables knowledge sharing across teams leading to improvement in efficiency.

5. THE SYSTEM

In this section we describe the architecture and details on how our system is built. Figure 2 shows a high level architecture of the tool. The input data goes through a mapping and sanitization module and get stored inside a database, which also stores all user information, configuration details and domain specific semantics. The ticket data to be made available for search is stored inside a Lucene index. The search engine, including other modules that are used online at query time, interact with both the database and the index, to support various functionalities of the system.

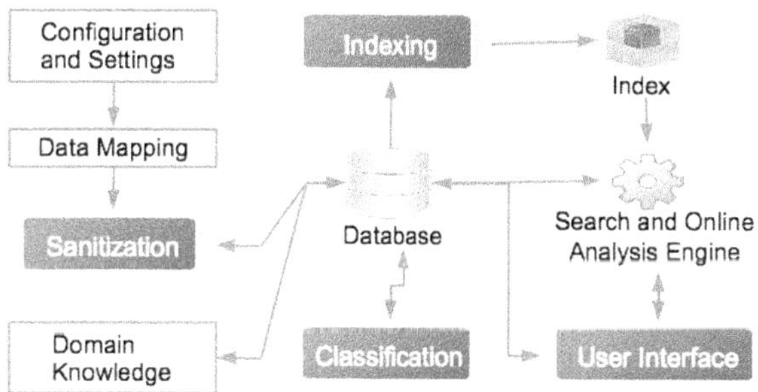

Figure 2: System Architecture of the KM Tool

5.1 Importing data

The solved tickets that are input to the tool come from various ticketing tools. All tickets, before being passed to the backend pre-processing stages, are first converted to a standard format using pluggable adapter modules written specifically for the input source type. The tool supports two types of import mechanisms:

(1) Offline import via Excel files: Most ticketing tools support exporting ticket data into excel files. Account administrators export ticket data into excel files and use a UI to upload these files to our tool. These are converted to a standard format using an excel adaptor module and then passed to the backend pre-processor.

(2) Automated import from ticketing tools: In this scenario, our tool directly connects to the ticketing tool and pulls new solved tickets. In the current implementation, our

tool can import data from Tivoli Service Request Manager (TSRM), a widely used ticket management product available in market today.

New ticket sources can be easily supported by plugging in appropriate adapter modules, that can convert the input source data into the standard format used by the tool.

5.2 Batch processing in the backend

Once the tickets are converted to the standard format, they are passed through a *processor* module. The tasks of this module are to compute the *quality score*, as described in Section 3.2 and to derive some structured fields by extracting domain specific entities and classification of tickets according to their issue type. With derived attributes, it is possible to facilitate efficient drill-down through facets in our tool for accurate retrieval.

Classification of issue types: Problems being addressed in tickets can typically be categorized into a set of broader issue categories. Thus categorizing the tickets according to the problem being addressed and assigning the issue category label as structured attribute to the ticket would help in grouping together the tickets of similar categories within the tool. In our tool, we extract the issue category of the tickets using a version of regularized linear classifier that has behavior similar to the SVM [26], trained using a training set that is manually marked with issue class labels.

Extraction of domain specific entities: Ticket data typically includes information about the process area and the department of its origin. In addition, in case of problem tickets related to a specific product or module, the description includes mentions of the module, product, program, and version. We use manually written rule based annotators to extract the presence of the above mentioned entities. Use of these entities as structured attributes can facilitate an efficient grouping and retrieval of the historical problem tickets related to a particular module, product, and version.

Sanitization: The processed tickets are then passed to the Sanitizer module which creates a sanitized version for each input ticket. The sanitized version has the client confidential information masked out, as described in Section 4. The sanitized tickets, along with the original tickets are then written to the backend database of the tool.

Indexing: An Indexer module picks up the new tickets and adds them incrementally to an index. The present implementation of the tool uses Lucene [1], which is a commonly used open source Java text search engine library for creating full text indexes for efficient searching and retrieval.

5.3 The user interface

The main user interface of our tool used by the practitioners is shown in Figure 3. The user enters her search query in the search box, which also supports interactive query suggestion using the method presented in [5]. The search engine ranks the results and shows, on the right side, the relevance of each result t to the query q, along three dimensions, namely the *text match* or the text similarity score between t and q, the quality score of t and the overall score, as described in Section 3.2.

The facets in the left side of the page help the user to zoom into the results using structured fields. Some of these facets are present in the tickets as structured fields, while some are derived. The tool also supports synonym based query expansion. A dictionary of synonyms specific to the domain are provided by experts and loaded in the tool. These are shown as synonym suggestions that the user can then choose to add to her list of keywords.

Apart from the main search interface, there are several role-based user interfaces for several other system related features, such as for managing users, tracking usage, uploading and managing ticket data.

Class	#examples	κ	Precision	Recall	F-measure
P	240	0.73	0.84	0.84	0.84
S	33	0.63	0.5	0.16	0.25
R	24	0.85	0.42	0.18	0.25
N	477	0.63	0.85	0.92	0.88

Table 1: Label distribution in PRSN and classification accuracy using SVM

6. EXPERIMENTS AND ANALYSIS

We conducted several experiments to assess the effectiveness of our data quality detection and search ranking. We also conducted a controlled user study to measure the benefits of using our tool. Since the data used for these experiments contain client confidential information from several clients, details about the data have been provided only at a macroscopic level. The number of tickets present in our system at the time of these experiments were about 200,000.

6.1 Detecting useful parts of tickets

For extracting useful parts of the ticket as detailed in Section 3.1 we consider each sentence in the ticket to be one of `P`, `R`, `S` or `N`. Around 800 sentences from 220 tickets were manually tagged by a volunteer, which will henceforth be referred to as the PRSN dataset, the distribution of which is given in Table 1. As can be seen from the table, more than 60% of the sentences were tagged as junk, which motivates the requirement of detecting useful parts of the ticket and separating it from the junk. From the above 800 sentences, 200 sentences were randomly chosen and tagged by a second volunteer to calculate the inter-annotator agreement. Kappa statistic for these two manual tagging is also given in Table 1. The Cohen's Kappa coefficient [7] is a statistical measure of inter-annotator agreement. Lower the Kappa value, lower the chances of being able to train a statistical classifier that can give good classification accuracy.

Table 1 gives the accuracy measures obtained using SVM. Other algorithms like Decision Tree and Naive Bayes were also used for classification, but the accuracy numbers remained similar or were lower than that of SVM. From the table, it is clear that accuracy values for `R` and `S` are very low, owing to the small number of examples available in the training set. Hence, in the next experiment, `P`, `R` and `S` labels were merged to their parent class – `T`, as discussed in Section 3.1. This merging gives the TN dataset. Classification accuracies on TN at a label level and weighted averages are given in Table 2. Now, the individual class accuracies have significantly improved and this is the classifier that is used in the ranking experiments described in the next section.

6.2 Ranking of tickets

To evaluate the effectiveness of our ranking algorithm based on the combined score of text match and resolution

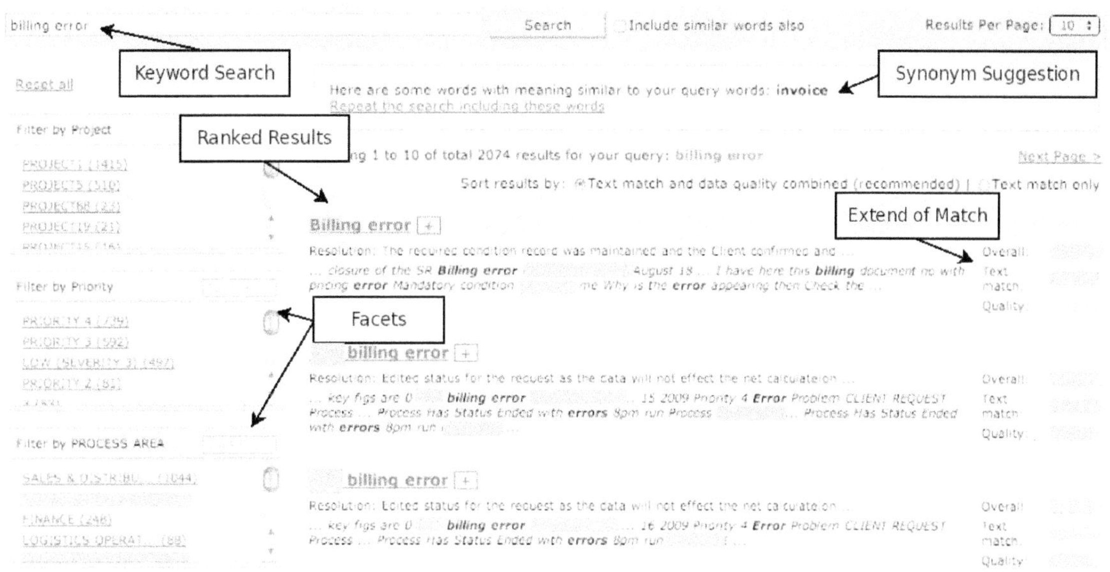

Figure 3: Screenshot of KM Tool Search UI (confidential data masked out) TODO

Label	Precision	Recall	F-measure
T	0.825	0.747	0.784
N	0.851	0.901	0.876
Weighted Avg	0.841	0.842	0.841

Table 2: Classification Accuracy on TN using SVM

	prec@5	prec@10	ndcg@5	ndcg@10
TXT	0.41	0.37	0.40	0.38
TXT + RES	0.63	0.56	0.62	0.57

Table 3: Effectiveness of the ranking

score, we performed a manual evaluation of our system with some domain experts. With the help of the domain experts we created 15 search queries and let the experts evaluate each of the top 10 results as relevant or non-relevant in two versions of the system, one which ranked the results using only content match (TXT) and another which ranked the results with a combination of content match and resolution scored (TXT+RES). We computed the precision at top 5 and 10 results, and the normalized discriminative cumulative gain (ndcg) at top 5 and 10 results for both the methods.

As we see in Table 3 our TXT+RES method improves over the baseline TXT method by more than 50% consistently in all measures. Although our evaluation set of 15 queries is rather small (as we could not perform such a thorough evaluation on a larger set of queries due to unavailability of experts), the improvement is very significant. It can be said that our method improves the effectiveness of the system by a considerable amount.

6.3 User study and business benefit

In this section, we present the results of user studies done with three accounts. The first two evaluations were guided user studies where our team met with a team of members engaged in solving problem tickets for an account, picked

Type of ticket	A	B	C
Baseline turnaround time (hours)	40	3.7	1
Improvement on average	29%	24%	Not significant
Number of tickets per month	28	5	205

Table 4: Benefit measurement of our tool

n tickets randomly from the open tickets at that time, and performed search in our tool together with the practitioners. For each query, if any of the first four results had adequate information about how the open problem in hand could be solved, that search was considered a success; otherwise it is marked as a failure. In one of these studies, our tool reported 4 successes out of 6 trials and in the second study, 6 out of 10 tickets could be solved leveraging knowledge from top results found by our tool. Although the number of trials we could perform was rather small, each one took some time due to the complexity of the tickets in this domain.

A more systematic and longer pilot was performed with a team of 30 practitioners in an account for a duration of two months. Before starting the pilot, their baseline performances were measured for three types of problem tickets of varying degree of difficulty, measured by the average turnaround times for each type. The same measurement was taken during the time the team used our tool.

As given in Table 4, the results of this pilot showed that, for tickets that take a long time in general, our tool helped in reducing the turnaround time significantly. For the easier type of problem tickets, the turnaround time did not reduce from the original one hour, as we expect that those tickets were not complicated enough to leverage previous knowledge. The account also reported that for new practitioners, the tool was particularly helpful.

7. CONCLUSION AND FUTURE WORK

In this paper, we presented several real challenges of knowledge management in the application management industry and presented an effective system to overcome those challenges. We also presented a method for automatically detecting quality of resolution information in ticket data and showed by our experiments that using the quality score in ranking tickets improve the effectiveness of knowledge search significantly, in fact turns an unusable system to an effective one. Our system consists of several advanced features such as faceted search, ticket classification, and entity detection to derive structure out of unstructured data and present those as facets while searching tickets. Finally, we show by a user study and a pilot, that our system increases the productivity of the users significantly.

Most of the novel components of our system were built while working with the users and understanding their requirements, and some of the features provide us scope for improvement and direction for further research. Systematic evaluation and improvement of our method for detecting quality of resolution information in ticket data is a future research direction on its own. It can also be investigated if such methods apply to other types of data consisting of problems and solutions such as technical forums and mailing lists and if quality detection enhances retrieval in those domains. Also, the classification of tickets into categories for such very noisy data, if possible with minimal training, is another very important research problem which is of huge interest for the industry, to manage risks and resources.

8. REFERENCES

[1] Apache Lucene. http://lucene.apache.org, 2009.

[2] C. C. Agarwal and P. S. Yu. Privacy-preserving data mining: Models and algorithms. *Springer*, 2008.

[3] I. Androutsopoulos, J. Koutsias, K. V. Chandrinos, and C. D. Spyropoulos. An experimental comparison of naive bayesian and keyword-based anti-spam filtering with personal e-mail messages. In *Proc. SIGIR*, 2000.

[4] T. Baldwin, D. Martinez, and R. B. Penman. Automatic thread classification for linux user forum information access. In *Proc. of the 12th Australasian Document Computing Symposium*, 2007.

[5] S. Bhatia, D. Majumdar, and P. Mitra. Query suggestions in the absence of query logs. In *SIGIR*, pages 795–804. ACM, 2011.

[6] D. Carmel, M. Shtalhaim, and A. Soffer. eresponder: Electronic question responder. In *CoopIS*, 2000.

[7] J. Cohen. A coefficient of agreement for nominal scales. *Educational and Psychological Measurement*, 20, 1960.

[8] T. Dalenius. Finding a needle in a haystack - or identifying anonymous census record. *Journal of Official Statistics*, 1986.

[9] B. C. M. Fung, K. Wang, R. Chen, and P. S. Yu. Privacy-preserving data publishing: A survey of recent developments. *ACM Computing Survey*, June 2010.

[10] R. Gupta, K. Hima Prasad, and M. Mohania. Information integration techniques to automate incident management. In *IEEE Network Operations and Management Symposium*, 2008.

[11] P. Haffner, G. Tur, and J. Wright. Optimizing svms for complex call classification. In *Proc. of ICASSP*, 2003.

[12] T. Joachims. Making large-scale support vector machine learning practical. In *Advances in Kernel Methods: Support Vector Machines*. MIT Press, 1998.

[13] B. L., B.-S. K., P. A., and A. H. The gene trustee: A universal identification system that ensures privacy and confidentiality for human genetic databases. *Journal of Law and Medicine*, 10, 2003.

[14] J. Lenchner, D. Rosu, N. F. Velasquez, S. Guo, K. Christiance, D. DeFelice, P. M. Deshpande, K. Kummamuru, N. Kraus, L. Z. Luan, D. Majumdar, M. McLaughlin, S. Ofek-Koifman, D. P, C. Perng, H. Roitman, C. Ward, and J. Young. A service delivery platform for server management services. *IBM Journal of Research and Development*, 53(6), 2009.

[15] A. Medem, M.-I. Akodjenou, and R. Teixeira. Troubleminer: Mining network trouble tickets. In *IFIP/IEEE International Symposium on Integrated Network Management-Workshops*, 2009.

[16] K. Nigam, J. Lafferty, and A. McCallum. Using maximum entropy for text classification. In *Proc. IJCAI-9 9 Workshop on Machine Learning for Information Filtering*, 1999.

[17] P. Raghavan, R. Catherine, S. Ikbal, N. Kambhatla, and D. Majumdar. Extracting problem and resolution information from online discussion forums. In *Proc. of International Conference on Management of Data (COMAD'10)*, 2010.

[18] Q. Shao, Y. Chen, S. Tao, X. Yan, and N. Anerousis. Easyticket: a ticket routing recommendation engine for enterprise problem resolution. *Proc. VLDB*, 2008.

[19] Q. Shao, Y. Chen, S. Tao, X. Yan, and N. Anerousis. Efficient ticket routing by resolution sequence mining. In *Proc. KDD*, 2008.

[20] P. Sun, S. Tao, X. Yan, N. Anerousis, and Y. Chen. Content-aware resolution sequence mining for ticket routing. In *Business Process Management*, volume 6336 of *Lecture Notes in Computer Science*. Springer Berlin / Heidelberg, 2010.

[21] S. Symonenko, S. Rowe, and E. D. Liddy. Illuminating trouble tickets with sublanguage theory. In *Proc. HLT/ NAACL, Companion Volume: Short Papers*, NAACL-Short '06, 2006.

[22] M. Tang, D. Hakkani-Tur, and G. Tur. Preserving privacy in spoken language databases. In *Proc. of the International Workshop on Privacy and Security Issues in Data Mining, ECML/PKDD*, 2004.

[23] X. Wei, A. Sailer, R. Mahindru, and G. Kar. Automatic structuring of it problem ticket data for enhanced problem resolution. In *10th IFIP/IEEE International Symposium on Integrated Network Management*, 2007.

[24] L. Yi, B. Liu, and X. Li. Eliminating noisy information in web pages for data mining. In *Proc. ACM SIGKDD*, 2003.

[25] L. Zhang, J. Zhu, and T. Yao. An evaluation of statistical spam filtering techniques. *ACM Transactions on Asian Language Information Processing (TALIP)*, 3, December 2004.

[26] T. Zhang. On the dual formulation of regularized linear systems. *Machine Learning*, 46, 2002.

Author Index

www.ingramcontent.com/pod-product-compliance
Ingram Content Group UK Ltd.
Pitfield, Milton Keynes, MK11 3LW, UK
UKHW051454290926
15471UKWH00008B/1199

9 781450 313551